# Horror and Science Fiction Films IV

Donald C. Willis

The Scarecrow Press, Inc.
Lanham, Md., & London

# SCARECROW PRESS, INC.

Published in the United States of America
by Scarecrow Press, Inc.
4720 Boston Way
Lanham, Maryland 20706

British Library Cataloguing in Publication Information Available

**Library of Congress Cataloging-in-Publication Data**

Willis, Donald C.
    Horror and science fiction films IV / Donald C. Willis.
      p.     cm.
    Includes bibliographical references and index.
    ISBN 0-8108-3055-8 (alk. paper)
    1. Horror catalogs—Catalogs.  2. Science fiction films—Catalogs.
    I. Title.
    PN1995.9.H6W543      1997
    791.43'6164—dc21                97-18620

ISBN 0-8108-3055-8 (cloth : alk. paper)

∞™ The paper used in this publication meets the minimum requirements of
American National Standard for Information Sciences—Permanence of
Paper for Printed Library Materials, ANSI Z39.48–1984.
Manufactured in the United States of America.

TO MO

# CONTENTS

# INTRODUCTION

"Let's make a list! I like lists!"—Bill, in *Day of the Triffids* (1981).

"I like bad dreams. I like being scared."—Nellie, in *Drum Beat* (1954).

"I like the dark — it's friendly." —Irena, in *Cat People* (1942).

"Can you imagine, Bela Lugosi is so nice."—Gracie Allen, "Gracie," by George Burns.

Welcome to *Horror and Science Fiction Films IV,* The Video Avalanche. Bill didn't have in mind a list quite so sprawling, exhaustive, and exhausting.

Twenty and thirty years ago, genre fans and historians like myself, in the West, were deprived. We could only read about certain elusive Far Eastern monster movies (e.g., the Filipino *Batman Fights Dracula*) in trade magazines like *Variety* and *Movie/TV Marketing*. We couldn't see them. Now, happily, we can see almost all of the contemporary counterparts of these movies, on videotape. Proving the new rule: Kon Ichikawa's *Princess from the Moon* (1987), which still has not, apparently, shown up on tape here. These days, that's the exception, and an odd one — a seemingly major film from a major Japanese director. We're getting so we expect to be able to "viddy" everything we read or hear about. We're spoiled now.

Thanks to specialized video services like Sinister Cinema and Video Search of Miami, we're also catching up with the older, tantalizing, never-released Stateside titles, such as *Storm Planet* (Russian, 1962, and stock-footage source for two shoestring Roger Corman productions), as well as alternate versions of European movies like Mario Bava's *Black*

*Sunday* (which seems even more atmospheric in the original Italian export edition) that were released in the U.S. in the Sixties and Seventies. (Resolutely elusive, even today: *Batman Fights Dracula*.) More recent European films not given official release in the U.S., such as *Spider Labyrinth* (1988), are also turning up on tape, thanks again to companies like Video Search and Midnight Video. "Lost" films like *The Bat* (1926) and *Dracula* (Spanish-language, 1931) are surfacing. Even the most Godforsaken regional productions, like *Terror in the Swamp*, are making it to tape. Still, we must be thankful....

To keep up with this Tidal Wave of Tapes, just take a leave of absence from life. Put everything else on "Hold." In this author's case, "everything else" included even other, more indirect forms of research: I did not have time this time, for instance, to do much more than glance at *Monthly Film Bulletin/Sight and Sound*. Much if not most of the information contained herein is direct from tapes or has at least been double-checked through tapes. The latter are Source One. Meanwhile, Life Takes a Holiday.

Top priority for *Horror and Science Fiction Films IV*: the most obscure films ... titles which are mentioned virtually nowhere else in print, in English. The monster movies of Thailand, for example, are generally listed here under informal titles translated, on the spot, from Thai-language characters, by video and grocery clerks. (Oddly, a few Thai movies—*Halloween Night, The Magic Man*—bear English-language titles.) The subject of obscurity segues into my first introductory list ... movies unheard of or at least unseen for many years and now seen, reseen, or otherwise rediscovered.

Most amazing of all, perhaps: *Were Tiger*, an apparent retitling of an unknown silent short circa 1918, about which no record seems to exist in print and which may exist only at The Library of Congress.

## Long-Lost Finds

ALMOST MARRIED (1932)
THE CALL OF THE SAVAGE (1935)
FATAL WITNESS (1945)
THE FURIES (1930)
GHOST VALLEY (1932)
THE HOUSE OF FEAR (1915)
THE HUNDRED MONSTERS (1968)
IF WAR COMES TOMORROW (1938)
JACK FROST (1965)
MEN MUST FIGHT (1933)
MIDNIGHT FACES (1926)
THE PHANTOM (1931)
PHANTOM OF THE RANGE (1938)
RIMFIRE (1949)
SIX HOURS TO LIVE (1932)
THE SPIDER (1931)
STRANGERS IN THE NIGHT (1944)
SYLVIE AND THE PHANTOM (1945)
THE THREE WEIRD SISTERS (1948)
TRAFFIC IN SOULS (1913)
THE TRAIL OF THE SILVER SPURS (1941)
TRICK FOR TRICK (1933)
TROUBLE FOR TWO (1936)
WERE TIGER (1918?)

## Most Memorable Films, Last Ten Years

1) "NIGHTMARE" and "CLOUD," ROBOT CARNIVAL
2) GWEN, OR THE BOOK OF SAND
3) MY NEIGHBOR TOTORO
4) URUSEI YATSURA: ONLY YOU
5) URUSEI YATSURA: BEAUTIFUL DREAMER
6) "LABYRINTH," NEO-TOKYO
7) "THE PEACH ORCHARD," AKIRA KUROSAWA'S DREAMS
8) LAPUTA
9) THE ANGEL'S EGG
10) KAOS
11) GREEN SNAKE
12) NIGHT ON THE GALACTIC RAILROAD
13) THE APPOINTMENT
14) EXPLORERS
15) THE TEXAS CHAINSAW MASSACRE 2
16) SI BALELENG AT ANG GINTONG SIRENA

### RUNNERS-UP

HIRUKO THE GOBLIN
WINDARIA
GREMLINS
NATURAL BORN KILLERS

WINGS OF ONEAMIS
THE FOUR KIDS
ETRANGER
2001 NIGHTS TALE
EL ANO DE LA PESTE
ZU
THE NIGHTMARE BEFORE CHRISTMAS
THE WEATHERING CONTINENT
NEW LEGEND OF SHAOLIN
GUNHED
12:01
LENSMAN
COCOON
MOBILESUIT GUNDAM: CHAR'S COUNTERATTACK
HOW TO GET AHEAD IN ADVERTISING
ARMY OF DARKNESS
VAMPIRE HUNTER D
ALADDIN
A CHINESE GHOST STORY
S. D. GUNDAM MK-II
THREADS
MONSTER CITY
A WIND NAMED AMNESIA
BRAM STOKER'S DRACULA
NOSFERATU A VENEZIA
DELLAMORTE, DELLAMORE
LATE FOR DINNER
YAMATO TAKERU
GREEN LEGEND RAN

## Most Memorable Films, All-Time

### FEATURES

1) DIE NIBELUNGEN (1924)
2) BEAUTY AND THE BEAST (1946)
3) NOSFERATU (1922)
4) NIGHT OF THE HUNTER (1955)
5) THE MANCHURIAN CANDIDATE (1962)
6) BRIDE OF FRANKENSTEIN (1935)
7) SOLARIS (1972)
8) 2001 (1968)
9) ALPHAVILLE (1965)
10) MY NEIGHBOR TOTORO (1988)
11) THE BODY SNATCHER (1945)
12) DAY OF WRATH (1943)
13) EYES WITHOUT A FACE (1959)
14) DEAD OF NIGHT (1945)
15) THE INVISIBLE MAN (1933)
16) KING KONG (1933)
17) PSYCHO (1960)
18) URUSEI YATSURA: ONLY YOU (1983)
19) URUSEI YATSURA: BEAUTIFUL DREAMER (1984)
20) VAMPYR (1932)
21) LAPUTA (1986)
22) FAUST (1926)
23) THE HAUNTING (1963)
24) THE THING (1951)
25) THE SEVENTH VICTIM (1943)

26) ISLE OF THE DEAD (1945)
27) THE MUMMY (1932)
28) THE PHANTOM OF THE OPERA (1925)
29) DR. STRANGELOVE (1964)
30) ROSEMARY'S BABY (1968) or maybe E.T. (1982)

Not listed: GWEN, OR THE BOOK OF SAND and THESE ARE THE DAMNED, both of which I've seen only once, but which may belong.

## SHORTS

1) "NIGHT ON BALD MOUNTAIN," FANTASIA (1940)
2) "NIGHTMARE," ROBOT CARNIVAL (1987)
3) "CLOUD," ROBOT CARNIVAL (1987)
4) THE MASCOT (1933)
5) THE MAGIC CLOCK (1926)
6) "HOICHI-THE-EARLESS," KWAIDAN (1964)
7) "LABYRINTH," NEO-TOKYO (1986)
8) "THE WURDALAK," BLACK SABBATH (1964)
9) "THE PEACH ORCHARD," AKIRA KUROSAWA'S DREAMS (1990)
10) "PRESENCE," ROBOT CARNIVAL (1987)
11) THE PET (1921?)
12) THE BLACK IMP (1905)

Bonus: intro, TWILIGHT ZONE — THE MOVIE (1983).
Not listed: Charles Bowers' NOW YOU TELL ONE (1926), which (based on a single viewing) probably belongs.

## YET MORE MEMORABLE SHORTS

ALICE GETS STUNG
KOKO'S EARTH CONTROL
SNOW-WHITE (Betty Boop)
ALICE'S MYSTERIOUS MYSTERY
VINCENT
FELIX THE CAT IN SURE-LOCKED HOMES
FELIX SWITCHES WITCHES
MAGIC MUMMY
THE COBWEB HOTEL
MINNIE THE MOOCHER
LULLABY LAND
I HEARD
KIDOUKEIJI JIBAN

## Yet More Memorable Performances

Conrad Veidt, STUDENT OF PRAGUE
Dwight Frye, DRACULA
Bela Lugosi, CHANDU, WHITE ZOMBIE
Boris Karloff, THE BODY SNATCHER
Henry Daniell, THE BODY SNATCHER
Warner Oland, THE DRUMS OF JEOPARDY
Frank Cellier, THE MAN WHO LIVED AGAIN
Ralph Richardson, CLOUDS OVER EUROPE
Most everyone, THE THREE WEIRD SISTERS
Beverly Garland, IT CONQUERED THE WORLD
Most everyone, MANIA

Nigel Green, LET'S KILL UNCLE
Albert Finney, THE GREEN MAN
Pamela Springsteen, SLEEPAWAY CAMP 2 & 3
Jeff Goldblum, MR. FROST, THE FLY
James Caan, ALIEN NATION
Bill Maher, CANNIBAL WOMEN IN THE AVOCADO JUNGLE OF DEATH
Bill Murray, GHOSTBUSTERS
Bruce Dern, INTO THE BADLANDS
Christopher Walken, GOD'S ARMY [THE PROPHECY]

## Guilty Treasures

THE BLACKMAGIC WITH BUDDHA
CRAZY FAT ETHEL II
DEATH NURSE
KOKAK
THE DEVIL'S OWL
DAY THE EARTH FROZE
EL VAMPIRO TEPOROCHO
VALENTINA
ROMANCE OF THE VAMPIRES
WOLF DEVIL WOMAN
REAL BAD MONSTER RAW
BLOOD FREAK
ULTRAMAN ZOFFY!
THE BODY SHOP
ZUMA
ANAK NI ZUMA
ROLLER BLADE
PUMAMAN
THE CROCODILE MEN
BRAIN 17
SANTO VS. LAS LOBAS
NAK THE GHOST
MAGIC OF 3,000 YEARS AGO
THE SNAKE GIRL
THE THRILLING SWORD
TIYANAK
LION MAN
INVASION OF THE GIRL SNATCHERS
ESCAPE FROM GALAXY 3

## Lousiest Fun-Gore Films Recently

THE TOXIC AVENGER
THE LOVE MASSACRE
ROBOT NINJA
EL VIOLADOR INFERNAL
STEPHEN KING'S SLEEPWALKERS
MEN BEHIND THE SUN
DEAD DUDES IN THE HOUSE
BAOH
VAMP
GUINEA PIG 1
RIKKO O
DOOMED TO DIE
BUNMAN

## Funniest End-Credits Sequences

GREMLINS 2
HOT SHOTS!
INNOCENT BLOOD

## Consumer Fraud Alerts

See entries on ATTACK OF THE SWAMP CREATURES, TERRIFYING TALES, MIDNIGHT INTRUDERS (P), and SATAN'S TOUCH (P).

Cutoff date for entries in the main list: December 1994. (Note: 1995 video releases with 1994 copyright dates are included in the main list.) Estimated number of entries in the main list: 4,200.

## 1995 Releases

*Addicted to Murder* Ref: PT 22:10.
*Addiction, The* Ref: ad. SFChron 11/10/95. S&S 1/95:11.
*Adventures of Captain Zoom in Outer Space, The* Ref: SFExam.
*Alien Nation: Body and Soul* Ref: TVG.
*Alien Terminator* Ref: vc box.
*Amanda and the Alien* Ref: PT 22:13. Vallejo T-H.
*Anal Intruder 9* Ref: Adam'96.
*And So Evangelion Goes Into Action* (J) Ref: vc box.
*Android Affair, The.* Ref: TVG.
*Armitage III* (J) Ref: vc box.
*Attack of the Sixty Foot Centerfold* Ref: CM 16:70-71. 14:28-31.
*Backlash: Oblivion 2* Ref: vc box.
*Bangis* (Fili) Ref: vc box.
*Batang-X* (Fili) Ref: vc box.
*Batman Forever* Ref: SFChron 6/16/95. ad. Vallejo T-H 6/16/95.
*Beastmaster III: The Eye of Braxus* Ref: vc box. Vallejo T-H.
*Bitter Chamber* (I) (aka *La Stanza Accanto*) Ref: VSOM.
*Black Scorpion* Ref: TVG.
*Blondes Have More Guns* Ref: SFChron 3/9/96.
*Blood and Ecstasy* (J) Ref: Weisser/JC.
*Blue Seed* (J) Ref: vc box.
*Bobby Sox Sinners III* Ref: Filmfax 55:25(ad).
*Bram Stoker's Burial of the Rats* Ref: SFChron 3/9/96. 3/23/96.
*Bucket of Blood* Ref: TVG.
*Candyman: Farewell to the Flesh* Ref: ad. SFChron 3/18/95. Cinef 6/96:36.
*Casper* Ref: SFChron 5/26/95. ad.
*Castle Freak* Ref: PT 22:67. vc box.
*Cave Girl Island* Ref: Cinef 7/96:123. Vallejo T-H.
*Children of the Corn III* Ref: vc box.
*City of Lost Children, The* (F) Ref: SFChron 12/22/95.
*Clockwork Orgy, A* Ref: Adam'96.
*Congo* Ref: SFChron 6/9/95. Vallejo T-H 6/9/95. Sacto Bee 6/9/95.
*Craving Desire* (I) Ref: VSOM.
*Cursed Luger P08* (J) Ref: Weisser/JC.
*Cybertracker 2* Ref: vc box.
*Cyberzone* Ref: PT 22:14-15. CM 16:70-71. vc box.
*Dead Meat* Ref: PT 21:74.
*Dead Weekend* Ref: PT 22:13. TVG. vc box.
*Deadlock-2* Ref: vc box.

*Deadlocked: Escape from Zone 14* Ref: TVG.
*Deadly Invasion: The Killer Bee Nightmare* Ref: TVG.
*Deadly Love* Ref: TVG. (*A Vampire's Kiss* - early t)
*Demented* (*Love Guided by Insanity*) Ref: PT 22:71.
*Dementia* Ref: Adam'96.
*Dr. Jekyll and Ms. Hyde* Ref: PT 22:70. SFChron 9/4/95.
*Dracula: Dead and Loving It* Ref: SFChron 12/22/95. Cinef 6/96:48-9.
*Dragon Fury* Ref: vc box: sf.
*Dragon Pink 2* (J) Ref: vc box.
*Dragonball Z* (J) Ref: vc box: February.
*Dragonball Z* (J) Ref: vc box: September
*Ebbie* Ref: TVG.
*El-Hazard* (J) Ref: vc box.
*Escape to Witch Mountain* Ref: TVG.
*Expect No Mercy* Ref: vc box.
*Extrano Visitante, El* (Mex.) Ref: vc box.
*Fatal Delusion* Ref: vc box.
*Fatal Fury* (J) Ref: vc box.
*Fatal Love* (H.K.) Ref: Weisser/ATC2.
*Fist of the North Star* (J) Ref: vc box.
*Four Rooms* Ref: SFChron 12/25/95. Cinef 6/96:52-3.
*Freakshow* Ref: PT 21:14. CM 17:13.
*Fuerza Maldita* (Mex.) Ref: vc box.
*Galaxis* Ref: PT 22:12. vc box.
*Ghost in the Shell* (J) ('96-U.S) (Kokaku Kidotai) Ref: FComm 5/96:85-8.
*Girlquake!* Ref: SFChron 7/29/95.
*Godzilla vs. Destroyer* Ref: SFChron 7/17/95. CM 17:59,82-3. Weisser/JC.
*GoldenEye* Ref: SFChron 11/17/95.
*Goofy Movie, A* Ref: SFChron 4/7/95.
*Grim* (B) Ref: PT 22:68. vc box.
*Gumby: The Movie* Ref: vc box. Cinef 6/96:54.
*Halloween: The Curse of Michael Myers* Ref: SFChron 10/2/95. ad.
*Haunting of Helen Walker, The* Ref: TVG. SFChron 12/1/95.
*Hell Has No Boundaries* (H.K.?) Ref: VSOM.
*Hellroller* Ref: SFChron 10/14/95.
*Here Come the Munsters* Ref: CM 16:66-68. TVG.
*Hideaway* Ref: PT 21:74. ad. SFChron 3/4/95.
*Horror!* (J) Ref: VSOM.
*Howling, The: New Moon Rising* Ref: vc box.
*HyperDoll* (J) Ref: vc box.
*Impakto* (Fili) Ref: vc box.
*In the Mouth of Madness* Ref: PT 21:73. SFChron 2/3/95. ad.
*Invaders, The* Ref: TVG. vc box.
*Isko: Adventures in Animasia* (Fili) Ref: vc box.
*Jacko* Ref: PT 22:12.
*Johnny Mnemonic* Ref: SFChron 5/27/95. ad.
*Jonny Quest vs. the Cyber Insects* Ref: TVG.
*Josh Kirby...Time Warrior! Last Battle/Universe* Ref: vc box.
*Judge Dredd* Ref: SFChron 6/30/95. Vallejo T-H 7/1/95. ad.
*Jumanji* Ref: TV: vt. SFChron 12/15/95. ad.
*Jungleground* Ref: SFChron 3/2/96. 3/16/96.
*Land before Time, The III* Ref: vc box.
*Langoliers, The.* Ref: TVG: aka *Stephen King's The Langoliers.*
*Last Gasp* Ref: SFChron 9/30/95. vc box.
*Leprechaun 3* Ref: vc box.
*Lord of Illusions* Ref: SFChron 8/25/95. Sacto Bee 8/25/95.

*Love in the Time of Twilight* (H.K.) Ref: Weisser/ATC2. vc box.

*Magic in the Water* Ref: SFChron 8/30/95. vc box.

*Megami Paradise* (J) Ref: vc box.

*Mighty Morphin Power Rangers: The Movie* Ref: SFChron 6/30/95. ad.

*Mind Ripper* Ref: SFChron 8/5/95.

*Mortal Kombat: The Animated Video* Ref: vc box.

*Mortal Kombat* Ref: ad. SFChron 8/19/95.

*Mr. Payback* Ref: PT 21:74. SFChron 2/16/95.

*Mr. Stitch* Ref: vc box. Fango 153:10.

*Mutant Species* Ref: PT 22:11. vc box. TVG.

*Nemesis 2* Ref: vc box.

*Nostradamus: Fearful Prediction* (J) Ref: Weisser/JC.

*Not of This Earth* Ref: TVG.

*Ogre* (F?) Ref: VSOM.

*One (01:00) AM* (H.K.?) Ref: vc box.

*Original Sins* Ref: SWV.

*Out of the Dark* (H.K.) (Hui hun Ye) Ref: vc box. VW 33:21-2.

*Out There* Ref: Vallejo T-H.

*Outbreak* Ref: TV: vt. SFChron 3/10/95. ad. Vallejo T-H 3/10/95.

*Outer Limits, The: Sandkings* Ref: SFChron 3/24/95. vc box.

*Patayin Sa Sindak Si Barbara* (Fili) Ref: vc box.

*Phantom Lover, The* (H.K.-Sing.) Ref: vc box. VW 33:66-8.

*Piranha* Ref: TVG.

*Possession of Michael D., The* Ref: TVG. SFChron 5/2/95.

*Prehysteria! 3* Ref: vc box.

*Princess Minerva* (J) Ref: vc box.

*Project Shadowchaser 3000* Ref: vc box.

*Psychic Detective* Ref: SFExam Mag 9/17/95.

*Red Lips* Ref: PT 22:12. SFChron 8/19/95.

*Remember Me* Ref: TVG.

*Return of the Texas Chainsaw Massacre* Ref: SFChron 3/2/96.

*Ride for Your Life* Ref: SFChron 5/6/95. Vallejo T-H 5/7/95.

*Runaway Brain* Ref: SFChron 8/11/95. ad.

*Sawbones* Ref: TVG.

*Seven* Ref: SFChron 9/22/95. ad.

*Sex Trek 5* Ref: Adam'96.

*Shake, Rattle & Roll V* (Fili) Ref: vc box.

*Sixty Million Dollar Man* (H.K.?) Ref: vc box.

*Sleepstalker* Ref: PT 22:13. vc box.

*Snake Devil* (H.K.-Taiwanese-Thai) Ref: Weisser/ATC2.

*Space Freaks from the Planet Mutoid* Ref: SFChron 11/18/95.

*Species* Ref: SFChron 7/7/95. Vallejo T-H 7/7/95.

*Storybook* Ref: vc box.

*Stormswept* Ref: Fango 154:10.

*Strange Days* Ref: ad. SFChron 10/13/95.

*Suspect Device* Ref: PT 22:13. TVG.

*Tales from the Crypt Presents Demon Knight* Ref: PT 22:16.

*Tales from the Hood* Ref: SFChron 5/24/95. ad.

*Tank Girl* Ref: SFChron 3/31/95. ad.

*Temptress* Ref: PT 22:16. vc box.

*Terminal Virus* Ref: TVG.

*Third Eye* (G?) Ref: VSOM.

*Toy Story* Ref: screen. SFChron 11/22/95.

*Turnaround* Ref: SFChron 9/9/95.

*Twisted Love* Ref: SFChron 12/9/95.

*Vampire in Brooklyn* Ref: ad. Sacto Bee 10/27/95. TV: vt.

*Vampiro, Guerrero de la Noche* (Mex.) Ref: vc box.

*Village of the Damned* Ref: PT 21:73. SFChron 4/28/95. ad.

*Virtual Assassin* Ref: PT 22:14. vc box.

*Virtual Combat* Ref: TVG. Vallejo T-H.

*Virtual Encounters* Ref: vc box.

*Virtual Seduction* Ref: TVG.

*Virtuosity* Ref: Vallejo T-H 8/4/95. SFChron 8/4/95. ad.

*Virus (Outbreak)* Ref: TVG.

*Visitors of the Night* Ref: SFExam 12/2/95.

*Voodoo* Ref: PT 22:13. TVG.

*W.E.I.R.D. World* Ref: TVG.

*Wasp Woman* Ref: TVG.

*Waterworld* Ref: TV: vt. Sacto Bee 7/28/95. Janet Willis.

*White Dwarf* Ref: TVG. SFChron 5/23/95.

*White Man's Burden* Ref: SFChron 12/1/95.

*Who Cares!* (H.K.?) Ref: vc box.

*Witchboard: The Possession* Ref: vc box.

*Witchcraft 7* Ref: vc box.

*XXX Files, The* Ref: Adam'96.

*Xtro 3: Watch the Skies* Ref: PT 22:70.

*Zenki* (J) Ref: vc box.

## 1996 Releases

*Ah Pook Is Here* Ref: SFChron 4/11/96.

*Alien Nation: Millennium* Ref: SFChron 1/2/96.

*All Dogs Go to Heaven 2* Ref: SFChron 4/1/96. ad.

*Arrival, The* Ref: Cinef 6/96:38-9,60-61. SFChron 5/31/96. ad.

*Barb Wire* Ref: ad. SFChron 5/4/96. Sacto Bee 5/3/96.

*Beast, The* Ref: Vallejo T-H.

*Canterville Ghost, The* Ref: SFChron 1/27/96. TVG.

*Casshan: Robot Hunter* Ref: Vallejo T-H 1/12/96.

*Craft, The* Ref: SFChron 5/3/96. Sacto Bee 5/3/96. Cinef 6/96:12-13.

*Crow, The: City of Angels* Ref: Cinef 6/96:7.

*Crying Child, The* Ref: SFChron.

*Curse from the Mummy's Tomb* Ref: Filmfax 56:14(ad).

*Dark Dealer, The* Ref: Fango 153:34.

*Demolitionist, The* Ref: Marquee Ent.

*Dia de la Bestia, El* (Sp) Ref: Cinef 7/96:120-21,125.

*Diabolique* Ref: SFChron 3/22/96. ad.

*Doctor Who* Ref: SFExam-Chron 5/12/96. Cinef 6/96:32-3,62.

*Dragonball Z* (J) Ref: vc box.

*DragonHeart* Ref: SFChron 5/31/96. ad.

*Encino Woman* Ref: TVG.

*Eraser* Ref: SFChron 6/21/96. Vallejo T-H 6/21/96.

*Frighteners, The* Ref: Fango 154:34-40,79.

*Frisk* Ref: SFChron 3/29/96.

*From Dusk Till Dawn* Ref: Cinef 6/96:42,60. SFChron 1/19/96.

*Generation X* Ref: TVG.

*Haunted* (B) Ref: Fango 154:70-3.

*Haunting of Lisa, The* Ref: SFChron 4/10/96.

*Hellraiser: Bloodline* (B?) Ref: SFChron 3/9/96. Cinef 6/96:53.

*Highlander: The Adventure Begins (The Animated Movie)* Ref: vc box.

*Hunchback of Notre Dame, The* Ref: SFChron 6/21/96. Cinef 6/96.

*Independence Day* Ref: SFChron 7/96. Vallejo T-H 7/5/96.

*It Came from Outer Space II* Ref: Vallejo T-H 1/28/96.

*James and the Giant Peach* Ref: SFChron 4/12/96. ad.

*Lawnmower Man 2* Ref: ad. SFChron 1/15/96.

*Legion of the Night* Ref: CM 17:52-3,64(ad).

*Magic Kombat* (Fili) Ref: vc box.

*Mary Reilly* Ref: Sacto Bee 2/23/96. Janet Willis. Cinef 6/96:51.

*Mr. Ice Cream Man* Ref: Fango 154:48-9.

*Multiplicity* Ref: SFChron Dtbk 5/12/96.

*Mystery Science Theater 3000: The Movie* Ref: SFChron 4/19/96. ad.

*Nemesis 3: Time Lapse* Ref: poster. vc box.

*New Scooby Doo Movies* Ref: TV. Vallejo T-H 3/10/96.

*Night Hunter* Ref: Fango 154:10.

*Nutty Professor, The* Ref: SFChron 6/28/96. Vallejo T-H 6/28/96.

*Phantom, The* Ref: Cinef 6/96:4,8-9,60. SFChron 6/7/96. Vallejo T-H 6/7/96.

*Phenomenon* Ref: SFChron 7/3/96. ad.

*Proteus* Ref: Marquee Ent.

*Rattled* Ref: Vallejo T-H.

*Relic, The* Ref: Fango 153:20-5. Cinef 6/96:10-11.

*Sarah's Child* Ref: Fango 153:10.

*Screamers* Ref: Sacto Bee 1/26/96. Vallejo T-H 1/27/96. ad.

*Sex Bandits* Ref: Vallejo T-H: "time portal."

*Sindrome di Stendhal, La* (I) Ref: Palmerini. Cinef 6/96:50.

*Special Report: Journey to Mars* Ref: SFChron 3/25/96. Vallejo T-H.

*Star Command* (U.S.-G) Ref: Vallejo T-H. Cinef 7/96:124.

*Star Trek VIII: Future Generations* Ref: Cinef 6/96:5.

*Stepford Husbands, The* Ref: SFExam-Chron 5/12/96.

*Theodore Rex* Ref: SFChron 4/8/96.

*Thinner* Ref: Cinef 6/96:4.

*Timemaster* Ref: TV. Vallejo T-H 7/13/96.

*Tremors 2* Ref: vc box.

*Twelve Monkeys* Ref: SFChron 1/5/96. ad.

*Uncle Sam* Ref: Fango 154:26-29,69.

*Unforgettable* Ref: SFChron 2/23/96. ad. Cinef 6/96:54.

*Vampiro Enamorado, El* (Mex.) Ref: vc box.

*Venus Rising* Ref: SFChron 5/25/96.

*Viajero del Tiempo, El* (Mex.) Ref: vc box.

*Whispering, The* Ref: Cinef 7/96:124.

*Within the Rock* Ref: Vallejo T-H 6/8/96. Fango 154:58-61.

*Zarkorr! The Invader* Ref: vc box.

# ACKNOWLEDGMENTS

Thanks the big much to Horacio Higuchi, Greg Luce/Sinister Cinema (Box 4369, Medford OR 97501), Dr. Rolf Giesen, Jim Shapiro, the Lofficiers, Mike Weldon/Psychotronic (3309 Rt.97, Narrowsburg NY 12764), Bill Warren (who figured in connecting me up with all of the above!), Video Search of Miami (Box 16-1917, Miami FL 33116), Midnight Video (5010 Church Dr., Coplay PA 18037), EurAsia Video Service (Box 568, Olympia WA 98507), Mo, Paul Lane, Janet Willis, Mr. Ho (Albany Hong Kong Video), Nancy Goldman (The Pacific Film Archive Library), Donovan Brandt, and Katharine Loughney (The Library of Congress). Not to mention Sean, TOTORO fan #1.

# EXPLANATORY NOTES

The general order of information for entries in the main listing:

Title / Country of origin / Distribution company / Production companies (Producers/Executive Producers) / Year of release (Year completed/Year of U.S. release if foreign film) / Animation, color, widescreen, and 3-D indications / Running time / Alternate titles / Director / Scriptwriter, screenplay / Source material / Photography / Music / Production Design / Special effects and makeup / Sound effects / References sources, translated titles, quotes, etc. / Cast / Synopsis / Comment.

\* or (I) refers to an entry in the 1972 main list.
\*\* refers to an entry in the 1972 out list.

\*\*\* refers to an entry in the 1972 shorts-and-animated-films list.
2 or (II) refers to an entry in the 1982 main list.
2P refers to an entry in the 1982 peripheral-films section.
3 or (III) refers to an entry in the 1984 main list.
3P refers to an entry in the 1984 peripheral-films section.
(P) refers to an entry in this volume's peripheral-films section.
(M) refers to an entry in this volume's main list.

Listing is alphabetical except for numbered series-entries. Films with unknown titles follow the "Z" listings in the main list. Variety citations sans page numbers refer to reviews.

# ABBREVIATIONS

B - British
Can. - Canadian
F - French
Fili - Filipino
G - German
H.K. - Hong Kong
I - Italian
J - Japanese
Mex - Mexican
Port. - Portuguese
Sp - Spanish
W.G. - West German

BV- Buena Vista (Disney)
Col - Columbia
Ent. - Entertainment
Ents. - Enterprises
Fox - Twentieth-Century Fox
Para - Paramount
UA - United Artists
Univ - Universal
WB - Warner Brothers

anim - animation
c - circa
m - minutes
stopmo anim - stop-motion animation
ws - widescreen

aka - also known as
alt t - alternate title
cr t - title in film's credits
orig t - original title
sfa - same film as

tr t - translated title

AD - art direction
Adap - adaptation
Addl Dial - additional dialogue
Assoc - associate
Consul or Consult - consultant
Coord - coordinator
D - director
Ed - editor
Elec - electronic
Exec - executive
MechFX: mechanical effects
Min - miniatures
Mus - musical score
Opt - opticals
P - producer
PD - production design
Ph - photography
Prosth - prosthetics
SdFX - sound effects
SP - screenplay
SpFX - special effects
SpMkp - special makeup
Sup - supervisor
Tel - teleplay
VisFX - visual effects
ad - newspaper or other ad
Adam - Adam Directory of Adult Films
AFI - American Film Institute catalogs
Cinef - Cinefantastique
CM - Cult Movies
COF - Castle of Frankenstein
CVS - Cable Video Store guide

Ecran F - L'Ecran Fantastique
Eng. - English
Fango - Fangoria
FC - Film Comment
FM - Famous Monsters
F-U - follow up
HR - Hollywood Reporter
HV - Home Video (distributor)
M/TVM - Movie/TV Marketing
NYT - New York Times
OAV - original animation video
PFA - Pacific Film Archive
PT - Psychotronic Video magazine
Ref - reference sources
S&S - Sight & Sound

screen - theatre screening
SFChron - San Francisco Chronicle; Dtbk - Sunday Datebook
SFExam - San Francisco Examiner
SWV - Something Weird Video catalogs
TGSP - The Great Spy Pictures
TV - TV showing or videotape
TVFFSB - TV Feature Film Source Book
TVG - TV Guide
V - Variety
vc - video cassette
VSB - Video Source Book
vt - video tape
VV - The Village Voice
VW - Video Watchdog
VWB - Video Watchdog Book

# A

**A CENA CON IL VAMPIRO** see *Having Supper with a Vampire*

**A COLPI DI LUCE** see *Light Blast*

**AD POLICE FILE 1: ANOTHER STORY OF BUBBLE GUM CRISIS** (J) A.I.C. 1988 anim color 26 1/2m. D: Takamasa Ikegami; (anim) Fujio Oda. SP: Noboru Aikawa. Concept: Tonny Takezaki. Ph: A. Takahashi. Songs: Lou Bonnevie. PD: Ley Yumeno. Ref: TV: C. Moon video; songs in Eng.

A.D. 2027. A tough-to-kill, female, biomechanical, non-baby Boomer is systematically and violently dismantled in a fairly impressive opening sequence. Good light-and-shadow work in this made-for-video entry in the *Bubble Gum Crisis* (qq.v.) series.

**AD POLICE: DEAD-END CITY** (J) Bandai, Artmic & Youmex 1990 ('93-U.S.) anim color 30m. Ref: Animag 10:5: another OAV re the "evils of Genom." Japan Video: aka *A.D. Police 2?* RSI brochure.

**AD POLICE FILE 3** (J) 1993-U.S. anim color 30m.? Ref: RSI brochure.

**A-KO THE BATTLE 1 (GREY SIDE) and 2 (BLUE SIDE)** (J) CPM/Pony Canyon (Nakajima-Final-Nextart) 1990 ('94-U.S.) anim color 55m. each (aka *A-Ko the Versus*). D: Katsuhiko Nishijima. SP: Yuji Kawahara. Ph: Jin Kaneko. Mus: Kohei Tanaka. Monster/Mecha Des: Takashi Hashimoto. SpFX: T. Sakakibara. Ref: Animag 10:3. Japan Video. TV: Eng. dubbed; *Project A-Ko Versus: Battle 1: Gray Side/Battle 2: Blue Side* - U.S.; M.D. Geist guest bit.

A-Ko and B-Ko form a "monster-hunting agency." (A) A continuation of the *Project A-Ko* series. Ingredients this time include a giant horned turtle-thing (for battle practice) ... "harnessed negative energy," in the form of a three-headed dragon-god ("It's a monster!") ... and a diminutive member of the Space Patrol who's after criminals from his galaxy .... Uneven space action-comedy is occasionally enjoyable. Amusing: the possessed, forbidding-looking C-Ko occasionally reverting to her cute self.

**A-LEAP** Zane Ent. (Jimmy Houston) 1991 color. D: Jim Enright. SP: Cash Markman. Ref: Adam Erotomic, v. 5, no. 8. With Alicyn Sterling, Candace Heart, Anisa.

Combination toilet/time-machine.

**A MEIA-NOITE LEVAREI SUA ALMA** see *At Midnight I'll Take Your Soul away*

**AAKHRI CHEEKH** (India - Hindustani?) Ramsay Movies c1990? color c100m. D: Kiran Ramsay. Dial: Sajeev Kapoor. Ph: Hemant Sharma. Mus: Bappi Lahiri. Mkp: Srinivas Roy. Ref: TV: Hi-Q video; no Eng. Chao Thai Video 2: *My Boyfriend's Back* - tr t. With Vijayendra, Javed Khan, Sri Pradha, Anil Dhawan.

The zombie on the doorstep takes a shower to wash off his victim's blood, then reverts to human form. (Throughout, he alternates between beast and human.) Electrocuted for his crimes, the monster-man "dies," but bounces right back. Meanwhile, a possessed woman begins strangling men. At the end, axing her tombstone somehow acts on her like sticking a pin in a voodoo doll, and something *Alien* emerges from her torso.... Hokey, milked dramatics. Every suspense-horror and dance sequence is dragged out.

**The ABASHIRI FAMILY** (J) A.D.Vision/Pony Canyon/Nextart-Dynamic Planning-Studio Pierrot-Soeishinsha 1992 ('96-U.S.) anim color c75m. SP,D: T. Watanabe. Story: Go Nagai. Ph: H. Moriguchi. Mus: T. Miratsu. AD: H. Nagao. SpFX: J. Sasaki. Ref: ADV video; Eng. titles.

In China-conquered Japan, where the National Police Corporation rules. Ingredients include Naojiro Abashiri, the "ultimate armored cyborg," and (in a "school for murderers") a fire-breathing teacher, a flying head, several beheadings, and other gore galore.... Cartoon feature works overtime on Outrageousness, yields scattered laughs.

**ABADON** see *Fright House. Vampires*

**ABENTEUER DES BARON MUNCHHAUSEN, Die** see *Adventures of Baron Munchausen, The*

**ABENTEUER DES PRINZEN ACHMED, Die** see *Adventures of Prince Achmed*

**The ABOMINABLE SNOW RABBIT** WB 1961 anim color 8m. D: Chuck Jones; Maurice Noble. Story: Tedd Pierce. Mus: Milt Franklyn. Ref: TV. WB Cartoons. Lee.

Bugs Bunny and Daffy Duck meet the abominable snowman of the Himalayas, who is intent upon loving a little bunny named George. So Bugs slaps bunny ears on Daffy .... Cute.

See also *Daffy Duck's Quackbusters.*

***The ABOMINABLE SNOWMAN** Hammerscope-Clarion-Exclusive-Buzz 1957 ws 91m.-orig rt (*The Abominable Snowman of the Himalayas*—U.S. ad t). From a teleplay by Nigel Kneale. Mus: Humphrey Searle. Ref: TV. Warren/KWTS! Jim Shapiro. BFC. Larson. Lentz. Stanley. Hardy/SF. Weldon. Lee.

Searching the High Valley in the Himalayas for "that creature," or "anthropoid X," Dr. John Rollason (Peter Cushing) of the Botanical Foundation finds fifteen-foot-tall, 650-pound Yeti, who have undergone "parallel development" with man and who have mastered thought transference.... A too-easy we're-bad/they're-good drift in the story leads Rollason to conclude, "We're the savages." (Forrest Tucker's character's name, "Friend," is meant ironically.) And the script's human drama is too neatly wrapped up in an our-actions-determine-our-fate nutshell. *The Abominable Snowman,* however, is interesting as a monster movie without a monster: We (and Rollason) see a couple Yeti in shadow and the top half of a face, but apart from second-hand reports, that's it for the monsters. In the nifty mystical-coverup fadeout, the Lhama (Arnold Marle) insists, "There is no Yeti," and Rollason concurs. (Sociopolitical coverups in monster movies have been popular since *The Night Stalker* and *Jaws.*)

See also *Ajooba Kudrat Kaa. Ali in Wonderland. Fairy and the Devil, The. Geek, The* (1981). *Half Human. Henry's Cat* (P). *Journey to the Center of the Earth* (1993). *Mia Moglie e una Bestia.*

**The ABOMINATION** Donna Michelle Prods. (Matt Devlen) 1989 color 100m. D: Max Raven. SP: Bando Glutz. Ref: PT 4:14: 1985?; "ambitious, bloody." Hound. Bowker '90. With

Scott Davis, Blue Thompson, Jude Johnson, Van Connery, Victoria Chaney.

5,000-year-old creature possesses boy.

**ABRAXAS, GUARDIAN OF THE UNIVERSE** (Can.) MCA-HV/Rose & Ruby (Lee-Mitchell-Petersen) 1991 color 87m. SP,D: D. Lee. SpFX: Ron Craig, Stan Zuwala. SpVisFX: Film Opticals of Canada. Ref: V 4/15/91. Martin. TV: VMM (Juniper). With J. Ventura, Marjorie Bransfield, Sven-Ole Thorsen.

"Finders are the cops of the universe." Abraxas — an alien cop, or "finder," with "reinforced skeletal structure" — returns to Earth via a "travel warp" (a "galactic subway system") to protect the telekinetic boy Tommy from the latter's father, an evil alien.... Action-horror cliches and pleasant incidental moments in this routine sf-er. At the end, the evil guy is "zapped off into the universe."

**The ABYSS** Fox/Gale Ann Hurd 1989 color 140m. SP, D: James Cameron. Ph: Mikael Salomon. Mus: Alan Silvestri. PD: Leslie Dilley. Conceptual Des: Ron Cobb. SpVisFX: Dream Quest Images, IL&M, Fantasy II; (sup) Hoyt Yeatman, Dennis Muren, Robert Skotak, John Bruno. Ref: TV. V 8/9/89. 3/1/93: *The Abyss: Special Edition* (171m.). NYorker 9/4/89. Sacto Bee 8/9/89. MFB '89:328-9. Scheuer. SFChron 7/9/93. ad. With Ed Harris, Mary Elizabeth Mastrantonio, Michael Biehn, Leo Burmester, Todd Graff, J. C. Quinn, Kimberly Scott, Richard Warlock.

"There is something down there!" Operation Salvage sends an oil-rig crew down to rescue a nuclear sub "sitting right on the edge" of a "bottomless pit" in the sea. The rescuers discover some snakelike seawater with the ability to do impressions of the movie's characters. This "angel"—or supposed Russian super-spy—proves to be an E.T. which saves the hero (Harris) by taking him to an improvised air pocket in its city at the bottom of the ocean.

Some exciting model work in this story of intergalactic marriage counselors. The balmily touching conclusion—in which the alien city rises from the ocean floor to save hero, heroine, and everyone else—is *CE3K* tacked onto the end of *Alien,* though it's marred by leading-the-witness choirs of angels and happy smiles from the rescued.

**ACCENT ON HORROR** see *Scared to Death*

**ACCETTA PER LA LUNA DI MIELE** see *Hatchet for the Honeymoon*

**ACCIDENT, The** see *Blood of the Black Dog*

**ACCIDENTS** (Austral.) Elmo De Witt/Scout Prods. 1989 color c90m. D: Gideon Amir. SP: John Eubank. Ph: Norman Leigh. Mus: Bruce Cassidy. PD: Robert Jenkinson. FlyingFX: Mitch Suskin, Anthony House. Scout Des: Alan Munro. LaserFX: Rick Cresswell, Conrad DuToit. Ref: TV; TWE video. With Edward Albert, Leigh Taylor-Young, Jon Cypher, Ian Yule, Candice Hillebrand, Tony Caprari, Gordon Mulholland.

American Pacific Technologies envisions scientist Eric Powers' (Albert) microwave invention as "the most effective anti-terrorist device ever invented," although he intended it strictly for medical uses. This small, hovering, saucerlike weapon, dubbed The Scout, is effective up to 100 yards and causes "disruption of the neuro-electromagnetic activity" in the victim's brain—i.e., "complete vegetation." The Scout is tested, effectively, at the beginning, on a lab rat, and, at the end, on A.P.T. exec Hughes (Cypher) and security thug Zimmer (Yule). Routine, bland Evil Corporation intrigue.

**ACCION MUTANTE** (Sp) El Deseo & CIBY 2000 & Spanish TV (TVE) & Warner Espanola (Agustin & Pedro Almodovar) 1993 (1992) color 90m. (aka *Mutant Action*). SP, D: Alex de la Iglesia. SP: also Jorge Guerricaechevarria. Ph: Carlos Gusi. Mus: Juan Carlos Cuello. AD: Jose Luis Arrizabalaga. OptFX: Optical Film FX. SpSdFX: Goldstein & Steinberg. SpFX: O. Gleyze, Y. Domenjoud, J. B. Bonetto, B. A. Le Boette. SpFxMkp: Hipolito Cantero. Ref: TV: IHE video; Eng. titles. V 3/8/93: "Troma-like gusto." 9/28/92:54, 55. 10/19/92:98, 146. 2/22/93:A-51(ad). 9/27/93:18: in London. Cinef 12/93:48-9, 60. With Antonio Resines, Frederique Feder, Alex Angulo, Juan Viadas.

"You're just a genetic aberration and a moron!" Ingredients here include Accion Mutante, invalid terrorists, and inept kidnappers out for revenge on noninvalids ... gore ... a spaceship to the planet Axturias, in the year 2012 ("I hate this planet") ... and Wild Miners.... Offhand, offbeat sf-comedy has some laughs. A mood of jolly anarchy prevails.

**ACES GO PLACES III: OUR MAN FROM BOND STREET** (H.K.) Cinema City 1984 color/ws c98m. (*Mad Mission 3: Our Man from Bond Street* - alt vt t). D: Tsui Hark. Sp, Co-P: Raymond Wong, SpFxD: Don Yuen. Ref: TV: Rainbow Video; Eng. titles. V 2/1/84.

Third in the series has several borderline-sf gimmicks, including a giant shark-shaped submarine (good for a *Jaws* joke), Commando Cody-like flying suits, a one-man rocket-plane, a land-sea-aircraft, and a mechanical gizmo which penetrates a laser defense system. Lively, routine action comedy.

**ACH, BORIS** (Austrian) Wega Film (Veit Heiduschka) 1990 color 85m. SP,D: Niki List. SP: also W. E. Sallmeier, P. Berenc. Ph: Hanus Polak. Ref: V 6/6/90: "relentlessly ghastly and ghoulish." With Jutta Hoffmann, Anne Mertin, Hilde Weinberger, Gerd Kunath.

Gruesome *Baby Jane*-like comedy.

**The ADDAMS FAMILY** Para/Scott Rudin (Graham Place) 1991 color 99m. D: Barry Sonnenfeld. SP: Caroline Thompson, Larry Wilson. Based on the TV series and on the characters created by Charles Addams. Ph: Owen Roizman. Mus: Marc Shaiman. PD: Richard MacDonald. Mkp:(des) Fern Buchner;(sp) Louis Lazzara. VisFX:(sup) Alan Munroe, Chuck Comisky; VCE/Kuran; (anim fx) Kevin Kutchaver et al;(ph fx) Paul Gentry et al. Prosth:(mech) Alterian Studios, Tony Gardner;(Thing) David Miller. SpFxCoord: Church Gaspar. Mattes: Taylor-Dutton, Illusion Arts. Train: Ron Thornton FX. SdFX: John P. Fasal et al. OptFX: Cinema Research. Ref: TV. V 11/18/91. Sacto Bee 11/22/91. SFExam 11/22/91. With Anjelica Huston (Morticia), Raul Julia (Gomez), Christopher Lloyd (Uncle Fester), Dan Hedaya, Elizabeth Wilson, Judith Malina (Granny), Carel Struycken (Lurch), Christina Ricci (Wednesday), Jimmy Workman (Pugsley), Christopher Hart (Thing), Sally Jessy Raphael.

"These people are abnormal!" Macabre ingredients include Thing (a living helping hand), a "Phantom of the Opera"-ish underground realm, a seance, a storm, creaking doors, a creature in a stew pot, strangling vines, an incidental hunchback, mainly-hair Cousin It (John Franklin), the "Wake the Dead" cemetery game, the literalized book titles ("Hurricane Island" begets a hurricane, etc.), and of course Weird Love with Morticia and Gomez.... Alternately strained and slick version of the old TV show. Labored plot, incidental funnies, including some amusing "product placements." Best bet: the film's musical promo.

Sequel: *Addams Family Values*.

**ADDAMS FAMILY VALUES** Para (Scott Rudin/David Nicksay) 1993 color 93m. (*The Addams Family 2* - shooting t). D: Barry Sonnenfeld. SP: Paul Rudnick. Ph: D. Peterman. Mus: Marc Shaiman. PD: Ken Adam. VisFxSup: Alan Munro. SpFX:(coord) K.D. Pepiot;(sup) Albert Delgado. Prosth: Karen Murphy;(sp) Alterion Studios; Miller Studio. DigitalFX: VCE. Stopmo: Don Waller. Ref: TV. Mo. V 11/29/93: "wickedly delicious comedy." SFChron 11/19/93; (Dtbk) 2/14/93: "very clever sequel that puts its antecedent to shame." Fango 128:11-15. With Angelica Huston, Raul Julia, Christopher Lloyd, Joan Cusack, Christina Ricci, Carol Kane, Carel Struycken (Lurch), Christopher Hart (Thing), Peter Graves.

Ad: "The family just got a little stranger." Scorecard: good new foils in the persons of Gomez'-spitting-image newborn and the summer campers (compare the *Sleepaway Camp* series) ... atmospheric effects with the Addams house and grounds ... a click ratio of about 2:1 for zingers this time (listen for "Why wait?"/"Seventh grade"/"Homicide"/"President") ... Thing's best performance yet ... and Wednesday's hilarious revisionist Thanksgiving-pageant twist.

See also *Silence of the Hams*.

**ADRENALINE** (F) Manitou/Canal Plus & CNC & Clara Films (Yann Piquer) 1990 color & b&w 73m. D: Alain Robak, Piquer, J.-M. Maddeddu, A. Assal, J. Hudson, B. Bompard, P. Dorison. SpFX: S. Nibart ("Cyclope"), Janin & Perrier ("T.V. Buster"), Soubeyrand, Toussaint et al. Mkp: Bergamaschi. Ref: TV: France Film video; no Eng. Hardy/HM2. V 2/7/90: "mostly mediocre." 7/22/91:42: at Rome's Fantafestival. With Maddeddu, Clementine Celarie, B. Coqueret.

Omnibus terror movie re inanimate objects with a "will of their own." *Physical Culture* also released separately.(V) Among the many stories here "Interrogatoire" includes a severed-talking-head bit which seems borrowed from *Re-animator*. "La Derniere Mouche" is a sick, silly story re decorative houseflies and a mole (facial type). "T.V. Buster" is an overdone but droll anecdote re a possessed TV set and a repairman/exorcist. "Cyclope" — a wild one re a spidery, robotic surveillance camera — has a loopily logical conclusion. And "Sculpture Physique" is a sick, wry bit re gruesome pugilism and modern art, or sculpture. Other segments feature diminishing rooms, self-steering cars, and malign bottles. Overall, film is unsubtle but entertaining.

**ADVENTURE! ICZER-3** see *Iczer-3*

**ADVENTURE KID** (J) MW Films 1992? anim color 34m. Ref: TV: vt; occ. Eng. Japan Video: 1st of 2 OAVs.

"We're from 1992 Japan!" Ingredients in this undistinguished softcore-sex/horror-movie include zombie soldiers, demons that suck the human protagonists into a computer terminal, a horny combination flora-fauna-computer beast with teeth and phallic tentacles, and tongue gore.

**ADVENTURE OF THE EMPTY HOUSE, The** see *Woman in Green, The*

**ADVENTURE OF THE HANSOM CAB, The** see *Trouble for Two*

**ADVENTURES IN DINOSAUR CITY** Republic/Smart Egg (Luigi Cingolani) 1992 (1991) color 89m. (*Dinosaurs* - orig t). D: Brett Thompson. Story, SP: Wili Baronet. SP: also Lisa Morton. Ph: Rick Fichter. Mus: Fredric Teetsel. PD: Michael Stuart. Creatures: John Criswell. VisFX:(sup) C. Kikugawa; (opt) David Hewitt et al. Computer SpFX: Habib Zargarpour, Donna Trujillo. Pterodactyls Seq D: Ian Gooding. SpFxCoord: Frank Ceglia. Cartoon: Jordan Reichek. Mr. Big TV Show D: Doug Walker. SdFxDes: Zound FX. Ref: TV. V 4/20/92:5 (rated). 11/26/90:7 (ad). TVG. SFChron Dtbk 9/27/92. With Omri Katz, Marc Martorana (Tops), Tony Doyle (Rex), R. A. Mihailoff (Mr. Big), Don Barnes (King), Shawn Hoffman, Triffanie Poston, Pete Koch.

"We've broken the bonds of time and space!" A mixup with a time-and-space machine and a "fully animated" videotape, "Dinosaurs," propels teens into the TV-dino world of Saur City, Tar Town, Skull Island, the evil allosaur Mr. Big, and a mind-bending potion. The TV remote can "freeze," "rewind," or "erase" bad dinos.... Alternately vapid-hip and sappy crossing of *Home Alone* with *Teenage Mutant Ninja Turtles*. Oddly, the principals in the TV world are not even partially animated. For some reason, the "little bird that can't fly" is named Forry.

The **ADVENTURES OF BARON MUNCHAUSEN** (B-W.G.-I-Sp) Col/Prominent Features & Laura-Film & Allied Filmmakers & Impala 1988 ('89-U.S.) color/ws 126m. (*Die Abenteuer des Baron Munchhausen* - WG. *Le Avventure del Barone di Munchausen* - I. *Baron Munchausen* - G vt t). D: Terry Gilliam; (2nd unit) Michele Soavi. SP: Gilliam, Charles McKeown, from Rudolf Erich Raspe's book *Baron Munchausen's Narrative of His Marvelous Travels and Campaigns in Russia*.. Mus: Michael Kamen. SpFX: Richard Conway, A. Pischiutta, A. Parra. OptFX: (sup) Kent Houston; Peerless Camera. Computer Anim: Digital Pictures. MkpDes: Maggie Westeon. Ref: TV. MFB'89:71-2. V 1/18/89. S Union 3/23/89. Horacio Higuchi. ad. With John Neville, Sarah Polley, Eric Idle, Valentina Cortese, Oliver Reed, Jonathan Pryce, Sting, Jose Lifante (Dr. Death), Robin Williams.

Horrific elements in this fantasy set in the late 18th century include a giant South Seas sea monster, a giant three-headed, carnivorous, mechanical bird, and Death, in the form of an angel, or Harpy. As a Munchausen film fantasy, *Adventures* rates above *Moon Madness* (1983), but below probably both the 1943 German version and Karel Zeman's 1962 *The Fabulous Baron Munchausen*. Gilliam here is stronger on Production—sets, explosions, crashes, and general noise and movement—than imagination, and Idle and Pryce handily steal the acting show away from Neville's colorless Munchausen. (An Idle "Oh, all right" is worth any amount of noise.) The Supermanlike talents (super-breath, super-hearing, super-speed) of Munchausen's associates are occasionally put to amusing use, and once in a while *Baron Munchausen* is exactly what a Baron Munchausen movie ought to be—see, for example, the effortless fancy of the ballroom dance in the air by the Baron and Venus (Uma Thurman).

The **ADVENTURES OF BUCKAROO BANZAI—ACROSS THE 8TH DIMENSION!** F ox/Sherwood Prods. (Sidney Beckerman) 1984 color/ws 103m. (*Buckaroo Banzai* - orig t). D,Co-P: W. D. Richter. SP: Earl MacRauch. Mus: Michael Boddicker. SpFxSup: Michael Fink. SpMkpDes: The Burmans. AnimVisFX: VCE; (8th-D. seq) Greenlite FX. Ref: TV. V 8/8/84. Stanley. SFExam 10/5/84 ad. Ecran F 38:89. With Peter Weller, John Lithgow, Ellen Barkin, Jeff Goldblum, Christopher Lloyd, Rosalind Cash, Ronald Lacey, Pepe Serna.

"They have opened the window!" It seems aliens did—as per the radio version of H. G. Wells's "War of the Worlds"—land in Grover's Mills. And they hypnotized Orson Welles to say that the landing was a hoax.... Thanks to the overthruster—which "reorders matter" and allows living beings to "travel inside things"—evil red, cobalt-and-electricity Lectroids from Planet 10 traveled to New Jersey in 1938. Plus: electro-nuclear jet car ... ugly, squiggly little creature.... Hip, comic superhero story has some clever ideas but is basically ultraconventional, simply lotsa flash.

**ADVENTURES OF EL FRENETICO AND GO GIRL** Amusement Films (Cooper) 1993 short. SP,D: Pat Bishow. SP: also Jon Sanborne. AD,SpMkp: Lance Lurie. Ref: PT 20:11: "fun." With C. Pellegrino, F. Lee.

Snack-created zombies ... wax museum.

**ADVENTURES OF ENRIQUE AND ANA, The** see *Aventuras de Enrique y Ana*

The **ADVENTURES OF HERCULES** (I) Cannon/Cannon Italia (Alfredo Pecoriello) 1985 (1983) color 90m. (*Le Avventure dell'Incredibile Ercole* aka *Hercules II. The Adventures of Hercules II* - TV ad t). SP,D: Luigi Cozzi. Mus: Pino Donaggio. SpVisFX: Jean-Manuel Costa, Image Transform, Gruppo Memmo La Rocca, Film Idea, New Recording Studios, Pentastudio, Studio 4, Tecnocine TV, Josef Natanson, Studio Fantasia, Augustuscolor. Mkp: Lamberto Marini. SpSdFX: L. & M. Anzellotti. Ref: TV. Horacio Higuchi. V 10/16/85. TVG. PT 7:5. With Lou Ferrigno, Milly Carlucci, Sonia Viviani, William Berger, Claudio Cassinelli, Venantino Venantini, Margi Newton, Serena Grandi.

Monsters in this sequel to *Hercules* (1983) include King Minos's cosmic-light warriors, one of which transforms first into a cartoon tyrannosaurus, then into a snake, while Hercules becomes a cartoon King Kong, no less ... Antaeus, the Fire Monster, which looks very much like the Id in *Forbidden Planet* ... a gorgon-scorpion monster ... mire monsters ... energy monsters ... a hairy mop of a creature ... the skeleton of Minos (Berger), which is restored to life by dripping blood (cf. *Dracula, Prince of Darkness*) ... and the forest demon Tartarus.... Fairly likable if brainless parade of monsters from myth (and other movies). Though the movie is

certainly busy enough, the light and ray effects become monotonous.

**ADVENTURES OF LITTLE SAMURAI** see *Magic Boy*

The **ADVENTURES OF MARK TWAIN** Clubhouse Pictures/Will Vinton Prods. & Harbour Town Films (Atlantic Ent. Group) 1985 Claymation/color 86m. (*Mark Twain* - orig t). D, P, SpPhFX: Vinton. SP, Assoc P: Susan Shadburne. Based in part on eleven Twain stories. Mus: Billy Scream. Claymation: (aliens) Craig Bartlett; (airship) Bruce McKean; (fx) Joan C. Gratz. SpMechFX: Gary McRobert. SpOptFX: Lookout Mountain Films. Ref: TV. SFExam ad. MFB'87:362. V 3/20/85. With Tim Conner (alien's voice).

Tom and Huck stow away on Mark Twain's airship-steamboat—complete with central power panel, Astro-viewer, and pipe organ of the damned—where they hear Twain's stories, including "Extracts from Captain Stormfield's Diary" (and a heaven exclusively for silly, three-headed aliens), "The Diary of Adam and Eve" (and a unicorn that changes into a toothy monster), "The Celebrated Jumping Frog of Calaveras County" (and a bit with a giant swamp creature), and "The Mysterious Stranger," in which the angel Satan slaps down squabbling miniature "mud people".... The latter tale, a weird interlude, features rudimentary but stylized figures which are more "alive" than the more elaborate, stilted human figures in the film. Overall, film is a mixed grab bag of humor, Verne-like science-fantasy-adventure, impressive meteor and storm effects, and philosophy.

**ADVENTURES OF PINOCCHIO, The** see *Pinocchio and the Emperor of the Night*

The **ADVENTURES OF PRINCE ACHMED** (G) Comenius Film 1926 silhouette anim tinted silent c62m. (*Die Abenteuer des Prinzen Achmed*). SP,D,AD: Lotte Reiniger. D: also Karl Koch. Mus: Freddie Phillips; (orig release) Wolfgang Zeller. Magic & Scenery: W. Ruttman, B. Bartosch, A. Kardan. Titles: Edmund Dulac. Ref: TV: Primrose Productions vt; Eng. titles. Jim Shapiro. Lee: an Arabian Nights tale. Cowie/70 Years: British?

"Great was the might of the African sorcerer." The latter can conjure up weird shapes and at one point turnes himself into a bat-thing. Among the creatures on display here: demonic djinns and afreets ... a giant snake ... a "fearsome ogress" and her strange cave-critters ... a huge elephantish-thing ... a big scorpion ... and flying spirit-legions. ... Early Aladdin movie is elegantly designed and has atmospheric background effects, if the story is a tad dull. The stippled animation does not seem so much technical stiffness as stylization, and emanation of the magic of far-off times and places. The exotic characters and fantastic beings here move strangely.

**ADVENTURES OF THE GREAT MOUSE DETECTIVE** see *Great Mouse Detective, The*

**ADVENTURES OF THE KUNG FU RASCALS** see *Kung Fu Rascals*

**ADVENTURES OF ULTRAMAN** see *Ultraman: The Adventure Begins*

**AENIGMA** (I-Yug.) Filman/A.M. Trading Int'l. (Spagnuolo) & Sutjeska Film (Banjack) 1987 color 85m. SP,SpPhFX,D: Lucio Fulci. Ph: Luigi Ciccarese. Mus: C.M. Cordio. Mkp: G. Ferranti. SpFX: Production Film 82. SdFX: Walter Polini. Ref: TV: American Imperial video(VPD); Eng. dubbed; vc box lists S. Cipriana for Mus. PT 8:65(ad): "splattery morality tale" re a girl wreaking telekinetic revenge. Palmerini. CM16:10.With Jared Martin, Lara Naszinski, Ulli Reinthaler, Sophie d'Aulan, Kathi Wise.

St. Mary's College, Boston. The brain-dead Kathy possesses the new student, Eva Gordon, and uses her to terrorize and kill those responsible for her condition. A mirror image strangles the gym instructor; a severed arm and drops of blood seem to fall from a mural; and a statue comes to murderous life.... Episodic horror-fantasy variation on *Carrie* by way of *Patrick* and *The Medusa Touch.* The snail-hordes sequence is far-fetched, but successfully gross. ("I was covered with snails!") Heavy-handed intro gets film off to a bad start.

**AEROBICIDE** Maverick Films/The Winters Group 1987 (1986) color 85m. (*Killer Workout* - alt t). SP, D, Co-P, Ed: David A. Prior. Mus: Todd Hayen. SpMkp: Robin Beauchesne. SpFX: United Film Works. Ref: TV. V 4/15/87. TVG 4/25/87. With Marcia Karr, David James Campbell, Fritz Matthews, Ted Prior, Teresa Vander Woude, Richard Bravo.

A nasty accident in an electronic tanning machine prefaces a series of murders at Rhonda's Work-Out, a spa owned by Rhonda (Karr), aka Valerie, the tanning-machine victim. A secondary sicko, Jimmy (Matthews), complicates matter for the cops. ("I'm not some kind of crazy killer.") Lame horror thriller is crude at everything—t&a displays in the gym, suspense sequences, plot twists. (Rhonda gets away with murder thanks to the unlikely co-plot with Jimmy.) Closest-to-good line: (cop) "I'm running out of body bags."

**AETHERRAUSCH** (W. G.) Senso Film, Bavarian Broadcasting & Hessian Broadcasting (Georg Killan) 1988 color 93m. SP, D. Ed: Klaus Gengnagel. Mus: Kristian Schultze. Ref: V 4/27/88: "numbs the audience." With Klaus Gruenberg, Sabine Dornblut.

Re electronics expert's "thought-controlled video system that apparently can also project thoughts."

**AFFAIR WITH A GHOST** see *Dun Huang Tales of the Night*

**AFFRIGHTED ROMANCE** (H. K.?) 1992? color 85m. Ref:TV: Pan-Asia Video; Eng. titles.

"I am a ghost." The "Master"—a "Devil"—controls her three ghost "students" with voodoo-dolllike "life bones" and compels the three to extract human hearts for her. At one point, she blasts an unruly subject with her fingertip rays and, at the end, she becomes a tentacled tree-monster. In the meantime, the spirit of Sister Moon—one of her students—enters the body of suicide Hung Shia, whose own spirit—rejected in the afterlife—returns to Earth. ("Now, please give my body back to me.")

The humor in the latter situation is unintentional. This apparently shot-on-tape movie is a low-grade combination of fantastic martial arts, sentiment, incidental comedy, t&a, skimpy effects, and gore. Only the bittersweet ending comes as a surprise: Sister Moon's spirit must return to hell.

**AFRAID OF THE DARK** (B-F) FineLine (New Line)/Telescope Films & Les Films Ariane & Cine Cinq & Sovereign Pictures (Simon Bosanquet) 1991 ('92-U.S.) color 91m. SP, D: Mark Peploe. SP: also Frederick Seidel. Ph: Bruno de Keyzer. Mus: Richard Hartley. PD: Caroline Amies. Mkp Sup: Tommie Manderson. SpFxOpts: The Magic Camera Co. SpFxSup: John Markwell. Ref: TV. V 11/25/91. SFChron 8/14/92; Dtbk 1/10/93. With Ben Keyworth (Lucas), James Fox, Fanny Ardant, Paul McGann, Clare Holman, Robert Stephens, Sheila Burrell.

"He's gonna kill her!" Lucas, a boy going blind, seems to imagine a series of razor murders of blind people, his own knitting-needle-in-eye vengeance on the killer, and his own needle attack on a rabid dog, though the latter event may not be imagination. And he now seems to be jealous of the new baby's "beautiful blue eyes".... Slight, confusing study in abnormal psychology, with slasher-movie elements.

**AFRICAN GENESIS** see *Animal Within, The*

**AFTER DEATH: ZOMBIE 4** (I-Fili) Flora Film 1988 color 90m. (*Oltra la Morte* aka *Zombi 4: Afterdeath*). D: Claudio Fragasso. SP: Rossella Drudi. Ph: Luigi Ciccarese. Mus: A. Festa. AD: Bart Scavia. SpMkpFX: Franco di Girolamo. SpOptFX: Francesco & Gaetano Paolocci. SpFX: Rodolfo Torrente.Ref: MV; Eng. dubbed. With Chuck Peyton, C. Daly, A. Joseph, A. McBride.

"I'll come looking for you — to feed on your intestines." Voodoo-cursed, flesh-eating zombies roam a "remote tropical island," as magic opens the "third door to hell" on the "island of the living dead," and a possessed priestess savages humans. Later, an *Evil Dead*-ish "Book of the Dead" raises a horde of zombies, and suddenly Tommy "isn't human any more!" Flat, elementary, apparently shot-on-tape Romero imitation seems to be an unofficial follow-up to *Zombi 3* (which see).

**AFTER MIDNIGHT** MGM-UA/High Bar Pictures 1989 color 90m. SP, D, Co-P: Ken & Jim Wheat. Mus: Marc Donahue. PD: Paul Chadwick. SpMkpFX: Lance Anderson. VisFX: VCE, Peter Kuran; (min fx sup) Ron Thornton; (ph fx) Paul Gentry, William Conner. SpFxCoord: Roy Downey. Stopmo Anim: Doug Beswick. OptFX: Cinema Research, Van Der Veer. Ref: TV. V 11/22/89. With Jillian McWhirter, Pamela Segall, Ramy Zeda, Nadine van der Velde, Marg Helgenberger, Kerry Remsen.

1) "The Old Dark House." Okay payoff to a nothing old-house story. 2) "A Night on the Town." Four teenage girls meet a man who has never washed his hair and who has three trained killer dogs. Hollow suspense exercise. 3) "All Night Operator." Slick but pointless answering-service suspenser re a psycho at large. 4) "Allison's Story." Fear 1A professor (Zeda) proves to be a supernatural terror. A la *The Terminator,* he keeps going even after he's reduced to a skeleton. (Good bit of stopmo here at one point.) Plus an all-a-dream, *Dead of Night* ending. Prosaic framing story features a few passable moments.

**AFTER SCHOOL** The Moviestore/Quest Studios (Hugh Parks) 1988 (1987) color 90m. (*Before God. Return to Eden. Private Tutor* - early ts). D, Co-P: William Olsen. SP: Parks, John Linde, Rod McBrien, Joe Tankersley. Mus: David C. Williams. SpMkp: R. L. Smith. SpFX: Ray Bivens, Murray Lemons. Prosth: Allen

Duckworth. Ref: TV: Academy Ent. video. V 3/22/89. With Sam Bottoms, Renée Coleman, Edward Binns, James Farkas (primitive man), Robert Lansing, Dick Cavett, Alison Woodward, Leo Besstette (apeman).

Old-fashioned is-he-a-priest-or-is-he-human? romantic drama might have fared better as a comedy-drama, or even an out-and-out comedy re impossible (until the fadeout) love, though it has touching scenes and good performances by Bottoms and Coleman. The parallel "Early Man" story adds running time but little else.

**AFTERNOON** see *Pomeriggio Caldo*

**AFTERSHOCK** Prism Ent./Bonaire Films (Roy McAree) 1989 color 91m. D: Frank Harris. SP: Michael Standing. Mus: Kevin Klingler, Bob Mamet. SpFxCoord: Fred Cramer. Ref: TV. V 3/21/90:35 (hv). 1/10/90:24 (rated). With Jay Roberts Jr., Elizabeth Kaitan, Christopher Mitchum, Richard Lynch, John Saxon, Russ Tamblyn, Michael Berryman.

"We suspect the woman is an extraterrestrial." A mystery woman (Kaitan) with a super IQ and a fireproof suit proves to be an alien who can enter an "energy cycle" to time-travel.... Kaitan's Daryl Hannah-like, fish-out-of-water presence is pleasant in this otherwise routine actioner with its nowhere premise: Her alien picks up the U.S. Constitution and returns to her home planet to resolve her people's "conflict." The usual vast-wasteland future.

The **AGE OF INSECTS** American Montage 1991 8mm 74m. Story, Co-PD,SpVisFX,D,P: Eric Marano. SP: Andy Rees, Peter Hall. Ph: I. Valero. Mus: Labriola, Bruner. SpVisFX: also Schefter, Rothberg. Mkp: Paul Soucie. Ref: TV: vt. PT 12:51: "some good laughs." SFChron Dtbk 10/24/93. With Jack Ramey, K. C. Townshend, Lisa Zane, Dallas Munroe.

"I want this insect stuff stopped!" Ento-socialist Dr. Richard Benedict fashions Lance to be the "drone prince" to his "she-mantis." ("He comes from a different race.") Now without pain or remorse, Sara becomes the "corporate she-vampire" of Mantra International.... Wasp Woman reworking is near-unendurable, would-be camp.

**AGENTE SECRETO 0013: HERMELINDA II** (Mex) Adobe Films/Aldama 1986 color 87m. (*Hermelinda Linda II: Super Agente 0013* - vc ad t). Story, SP, D: Julio Aldama. Story: also G. Gonzalez. Mkp: G. Oropeza. Ref: TV: Baker & Taylor video; no Eng.; Secret Agent 0013 - tr t.

The witch family members here can make themselves semi-transparent and walk through walls. At the end, granny witch—who sleeps in a coffin and can shoot "zombifying" darts—is sent into space in a Commando Cody-like rocket pack. Plus: a demonstration of an antimissile invention.... Silly, sloppy low comedy with occasional shoestring chutzpa.

See also *Hermelinda Linda* (P).

**AGI KIJIN NO IKARI** (J) Hotch Potch 1984 feature. D: Akira Hayakawa. Ref: Ecran F 52:70. With Kumi Nakamura, Tohru Masuoka, Eisei Amamoto.

Retelling of an old Japanese legend "Konjaku Monogatari," re the "transformation of a beautiful girl into a hideous monster."

**AGNES CECILIA** (Swed.) Svensk Filmindustri & Kanal 1 Drama SVT & Swedish Film Institute (Bergendahl/Dalunde) 1991 color 133m. SP, D: Anders Grönros. From Maria Gripe's novel. Mus: Johan Söderqvist. Ref: V 8/19/91: "thoughtful and moody ... ghost story." With Gloria Tapia, Ronn Elfors, Stina Ekblad.

"Much suspense in the scenes where Nora begins sensing a supernatural presence...."

**AI CITY** see *Love City*

**AI WA KAGERO** (J) Shochiku 1985 feature. D: Haruhiko Mimura. SP: Shinobu Hashimoto. Ref: Ecran F 64:70: "film of horror and witchcraft." With Maiko Ito, Ryuko Hagiwara.

Girl uses voodoo doll for revenge.

**AIM FOR THE TOP!** see *Gunbuster*

**AIR RAID** see *Millennium*

**AIRWOLF** CBS-TV/Univ-TV & Belisarius 1984 color c92m. SP, D, Exec P: Donald P. Bellisario. Mus: Sylvester Levay. SpFX: Whity Krumm. Ref: TV. TVG 1/22/84 (ad): "special movie presentation." V 1/25/84. TGSP2. With Jan-Michael Vincent, David Hemmings, Ernest Borgnine, Alex Cord, Belinda Bauer, Eugene Roche, Tina Chen.

Futuristic helicopter can fly faster than the speed of sound and has fourteen firepower options, including missiles and cannons.... Only for those who want to see a helicopter "kick butt." "Whirlybirds," where are you?

**AJOOBA KUDRAT KAA** (India-Hindustani?) San Int'l. (Shaikh Mohammed Shakeel) 198-? color/ws 98. D: Tulsi & Shyam Ramsay. SP: Geetanjali Singh. Dial: S. Haider. Ph: Gangu Ramsay. Mus: Ajit Singh. Ref: TV: HR Films video; no Eng. Chao Thai Video 2: Yeti Snowman - tr t. With Hemant, Manjeet Kular, Deepak Parashar, Johny Lever, Goga Kapoor, Anil Dhawan, and the "mighty Himalayan Man, Yeti."

A Yeti found by explorers in a cave takes a lost girl under his wing. She holds his big paw, sings to him ("Yeti, I love you"), and—this being an Indian film—dances with him. She also rides him piggyback and later cries when he appears to be dead. In-between, greedy hunters capture him and dance unfeelingly around his cage.

That giant boggling sound is your mind. Safe to say that this is probably the most unusual abominable-snowman movie of all. It's positively psychotronic. Technically, it's maladroit—sound editing and direction of action are pathetic—but that doesn't matter much. Soundtrack features bits and pieces of Western music, including the baby-elephant march from *Hatari!*.

**AKELARRE** (Sp) Amboto/Cinevision 1984 color 103m. (aka *Witches' Sabbath*. *La Virgen del Akelarre*). SP, D: Pedro Olea. SP: also G. Goikoetxea. Ref: V 8/31/83:40. 12/21/83:38: to Berlin fest. 3/7/84: at Berlin 2/26: horror overtones, torture. 5/1/85:410. Ecran F 44:37. 45:64.

"Witchcraft in 16th century Spain." (V)

**AKIRA** (J) Streamline/Toho (Akira Committee) 1988 ('90-U.S.) anim color/ws 125m. SP, D: Katsuhiro Otomo, based on his graphic novel. Mus: Shoji Yamashiro. Anim Chief: Takashi Nakamura. SdFxSup: Shizuo Kurahashi. SpFxArt: Takashi Maekawa. Ref: TV: laserdisc. Anime Opus '89. MFB'91:65-8. Cinef 3/90. Sacato Union 6/7/90. Sacto Bee 6/7/90. V 3/15/89. 10/22/90: 63. SFChron 12/7/90: cyberpunk influence. TVG 6/12/93. Voices: Mitsuo Iwata, Nozomu Sasaki, Mami Koyama.

Trashed-out Neo-Tokyo (built on filled-in Tokyo Bay), 31 years after World War III. The government gives the psychic Tetsuro drugs to amplify his powers, but they unbalance him, give him nightmares—and will eventually age him prematurely. Other monitored psychics, fearing that the powerful Tetsuro will raise the even more powerful Akira—the psychic who destroyed Tokyo—terrorize him with his own toys. (The latter form a giant teddy bear whose paws sprout monster mouths.) Tetsuro later commandeers a ray-shooting satellite and, near the end, his body ominously expands and mutates.... A graphically stylish, overlong vehicle for telekinetic stunts and bloody violence. The tone is serious, the content is junk.

**AKIRA KUROSAWA'S DREAMS** (J-U.S.) WB (Steven Spielberg) / Akira Kurosawa USA (Hisao Kurosawa & Mike Y. Inoue) 1990 color/ws 119m. (*Yume* - J. aka *Dreams*). SP, D: A. Kurosawa. Mus: Shinichiro Ikebe. SpVisFX: IL&M; (sup) Ken Ralston, Mark Sullivan: (coord) J. S. Bergin. Mkp: S. Ueda, T. Aimi, N. Sano. SdFX: I. Minawa, M. Saito. Creative Consul: I. Honda. Ref: TV. MFB'90:159-60. Sacto Bee 9/14/90. Sacto Union 9/13/90. SFChron 9/14/90. SFExam 9/14/90. Horacio Higuchi. With Akira Terao, Mitsunori Isaki, Martin Scorsese, Chishu Ryu, Mieko Harada (snow fairy), Chosuke Ikariya (the demon), Yoshitaka Zushi.

Eight tales with several sf/horror elements, including (in "Mt. Fuji in Red") tinted radioactivity from nuclear power plant explosions; (in "The Weeping Demon") nuclear-missile-spawned "monster dandelions," weird mutated roses, and immortal horned "demons"; (in "The Tunnel") a platoon of living dead soldiers; and (in "The Blizzard") an entrancing snow woman. The clear standout segment, however, is "The Peach Orchard," in which doll spirits perform a ritualistic dance that temporarily resurrects for a boy the spectacle of an orchard which has been cut down. One doll—left behind when the peach trees return—becomes, in turn, the lone tree left standing when the hillside reverts to its barren state. The tale proceeds with piercingly precise fantastic logic. Several of the other segments are static and talky, though they too possess occasional power. "The Tunnel"—basically a monologue—is a biting variation on the Gance *I Accuse* story; "The Blizzard" is little more than an undeveloped idea, though the image of the snow woman unfurling away into the sky is striking. And if "Mt. Fuji in Red" and "The Weeping Demon" feature familiar Kurosawa rantings re "stupid mankind," "Demon"'s vision of a nuclear-age hell recalls silent-movie versions of "Dante's Inferno."

**AKUMULATOR 1** (Cz) Heureka Film (Petr Soukup) 1994 color 102m. SP, D: Jan Sverak. SP: also J. Slovak, Z. Sverak. Ph: F. Brabec. Mus: O. Soukup, J. Svoboda. AD: M. Kohout. Ref: V 10/17/94: "distinctive techno-vampire yarn." With Petr Forman, Edita Brychta, Zdenek Sverak.

"Couch potato" trained to "recharge his energy levels by sapping the life force from trees, art and people.... a world populated by alter egos of the energy vampire's victims...." Accumulator 1 - tr t.

**AL CABO QUE NI QUERIA** (Mex) Producciones Tollocan (Guillermo Herrera) 1985 color c90m. SP, Story, D: Arturo Martinez. Story: also Manuel Taméz. Ph: Agustin Lara. Mus: Luis Arcaraz. Sets: Ignacio Ramirez. SpFX: Gonzalo Gavira. Ref: TV: Tilsa video. TVG. With Luis de Alba, Yolanda Lievana, Norma Lazareno, Miguel Inclan.

On the advice of a consulting witch, a woman goes to a creepy cemetery and invokes the spirit of Astaroth, who (invisibly) smacks her husband whenever he approaches Lola, her rival, also a witch. A cross scares the latter off. Also: a seance, a storm, and a voice from the beyond speaking through a medium.... Broad, obvious comedy with ugly color photography. Bad comedies, it seems, are alike all over. A hint here and there of *Burn, Witch, Burn,* plus one scene in which the advice witch laughs maniacally and the spook props in her office come to life as if to second her laughter.

**AL FILO DEL HACHA** see *Edge of the Axe*

**AL FILO DEL TERROR** (Mex) Prods. Latinas Americanas (Orlando R. Mendoza) 1990 color 91m. D: Alfred B. Crevenna. SP: Carlos Valdemar. Ph: Mario Becerra. Mus: Tino Geiser. AD: Alberto Villasenor, Ruben Pina. SpFX: Angel Perez. Mkp: Angelina Chagoya. SdFX: Gonzálo Gavira. Ref: TV: Mex-American Home Video; *On the Edge of Terror* - tr t; no Eng. With Fernando Almada, Lina Santos, Roberto Canedo, Karla Talavera, Julieta Rossen, Wally Barron, Mario Sanchez, Leticia Gonzalez; Arturito Vences, Tomas Emannuel, Armando Miranda (los munecos).

Down-on-his-luck stage ventriloquist El Griego's dummies come to life, huddle, and play hide-and-seek for his little daughter. In the most macabre sequence, they "speak" to her in her bedroom while, down in the cellar, he axes one of them as the others watch and whimper from their boxes. At this point, the sometimes imaginative script begins to get a bit sloppy, as El Griego trains his daughter to be his stage "dummy" and somehow fools the public. After he murders three or four people, however, she rebels, then the dummies rebel and seem to kill him.... Undisciplined film comes up with some very creepy scenes but doesn't coordinate them well. Is it all in her mind? Or in his? At one point, a peal of thunder seems to bring the dummies to life for the girl's friend, and the logic of the story—whether fantastical or psychological—goes all to hell.

**ALADDIN** BV (Disney) 1992 anim color 90m. SP, D, P: John Musker, Ron Clements. SP: also Ted Elliott, Terry Rossio. Mus: Alan Menken; (songs) Menken, Howard Ashman, Tim Rice. PD: R. S. Vander Wende. VisFxSup: Don Paul. Snake Anim: Kathy Zielinski. Computer Imagery: (anim) J. R. Tooley; (graphics sup) Steve Goldberg. SdFX: Weddington Prods.; (sp) John Pospisil. Ref: TV: vt. V 11/9/92. SFChron. TVG 10/2/93. Sean Smiley. Voices: Scott Weinger, Robin Williams, Linda Larkin, Jonathan Freeman (Jafar), Frank Welker, Gilbert Gottfried, Douglas Seale.

Horrific ingredients include the evil Jafar, who near the end turns into a giant monster cobra ... the fearsome, exacting Cave of Wonders, which roars out of the desert sand ... the genie (Williams), who momentarily plays a Peter Lorre-voiced zombie and, later, for Jafar, turns gigantic and monstrous ... and Jafar's hypnotic scepter.

Slick, engaging, inventive. Williams isn't the only funny one here—Gottfried's parrot Iago and Welker's little monkey Abu also contribute to the general merriment. And the genie's supervising animator Eric Goldberg matches Williams gag for gag. (Note especially the "jaw drop" effects.) Only element that wears a bit thin: the prince/pauper material.

Sequel: *Return of Jafar, The.* See also the following and *Adventures of Prince Achmed* (all in the Peripheral section): *Adventures of Aladdin. Aladdin. Aladdin and the Magic Lamp. Alladdin and the Wonderful Lamp. Alladin and His Wonderful Lamp. Alladin and the Wonderful Lamp.*

**ALADDIN AND THE MAGIC LAMP** (F) Films Jean Image 1985 ('92-U.S.) anim color c70m. (*Aladdin and His Magic Lamp* -ad t). SP, D, P: Jean Image. SP: also France Image. Dial: Steve Eckardt. Ph, Ed: Per Olaf Csongovai. Mus: Fred Freed. Sets: E. Gonzalez, D. Wuarnier. Ref: TV: Live HV (F.H.E.); Eng. dubbed.

Lively but minor version of the fantasy features a vision of a rocket ship to the moon (a "strange machine") ... a horde of flying dragons ... a grove of trees which once were people ... and a bat horde in a cave.

**ALAPAAP** (Fili) Aces Film Int'l. & Oro Vista/Rare Breed (Steve Paolo) 1985? color c112m. (aka *Clouds*). Story, D: Tata Esteban. SP: Rei Nicandro. Ph: Joe Tutanes. Mus: Rey Ramos. PD: Steve Paolo. SpMkp: Cecille Baun. Ref: TV: Viva Video; occ. Eng. With William Martinez, Mark Gil, Michael De Mesa, Tanya Gomez (Baeg), Rosemarie Gil, Liza Lorena.

"Being awake is only half of life...." Hospital-bound drug abuser Jake Vergara (Martinez) reads a news story re Kiangan maiden Baeg Longed, who vowed "bloody tribal revenge" for her rape and murder. Soon after, an initially unseen presence in the mountain retreat that Jake and his friends visit ("This place is weird!") begins opening doors and moving furniture. It proceeds to possess a woman, a statue (whose eyes bleed), another woman, a hairdryer, Jake, a typewriter, and a dog, which savages a woman.... Supernatural revenge here proves to be an elaborate excuse for climactic gore. (Hairdryer fu, etc.) The only unusual aspect: The ghost possesses everything in the house at once, it seems, near the end. Both halves of the double-twist ending are very predictable.

**ALARIDO DEL TERROR** (Mex) Video Alfa (Hugo Stiglitz, Rene Cardona III, Gonzalo Herrerias) 1991 color 81m. Story, D, Co-Ed: Cardona. Story, SP: Honorato Magaloni. Ph: German Salcedo. AD: G. Buijas or Buigas. SpFX: Arturo and Miguel Godinez, Victor Correa. Mkp: Ma. Eugenia Luna. SdFX: Gutierrez, Garces. Ref: TV: Million Dollar Video; no Eng.; Cry of Terror-tr t. With H. Stiglitz, Roberto Ballesteros, Bruno Rey, Azela Robinson, Carlos East, Sergio Jimenez, Edna Bolkan, Sofia Stiglitz, Arturo Vences (Chaneque).

The opening of an old tomb resurrects a hairy, clawed thing which slaughters some sheep and abducts a little girl. (In a steal from "Little Girl Lost," from the original "Twilight Zone," the parents enter her bedroom and hear her cries-from-nowhere.) An itinerant exorcist and the girl's father jump through a hole in her bedroom and into another dimension, where the demon uses flying fireballs (à la Far Eastern ghost movies) and strangling tree vines.... Frantically paced but old-hat, shot-on-tape monster movie.

**ALARMING TRENDS** Scorched Earth Prods. 1988. Ref: PT 18:81(ad): "aliens take the form of sandwiches."

**ALERTA, ALTA TENSION** (Mex) Studios America & Cima Films (Antonio Matouk) 1967 c90m. D: Alfonso Corona Blake. SP: J. M. F. Unsain, Mauricio Wall, R. G. Travesi. Ph: Raul Dominguez. Mus: Enrico Cabiati. AD: Campos, Orozco. SpFX: Javier Sierra. Mkp: G. Munoz. Ref: TV: Danger, High Tension - tr t; no Eng. TVG: powerful scientific element a threat to world peace. With Jorge Rivero, Alma Delia Fuentes, Claudia Islas, Lilia Castillo, Antonio Raxel, "Frankestein," Carlos Ancira.

Ingredients: plastic surgery which turns one bad guy into the image of the Matt Helm-ish hero, an electronic torture device that seems to temporarily kill our hero, an ice chamber that nearly freezes him, and a villainous scientist who blows his own lab to bits. Swinging-Sixties blandness prevails.

**ALFRED HITCHCOCK PRESENTS** NBC-TV/Univ-TV 1985 color c90m. "An Unlocked Window": D: Fred Walton. Tel: James Bridges, from Ethel Lina White's story. Mus: Craig Safan. Ref: TV. TVG. V 5/8/85:158.

"An Unlocked Window," one of four suspense tales, is an old-dark-house thriller, and not bad of kind. The Bryant Park Strangler has killed four times. Will Annette O'Toole be next? One or two good scares. With Helena Kallianiotes.

**ALI IN WONDERLAND** (Fili) OctoArts Films (S.C. Ongpin/Orly R. Ilacad) 1990? color c112m. SP, D: Tony Reyes. Ph: Oscar Querijero. Mus: Sunny Ilacad. PD: Melchor Defensor. VisFX: Cinemagic. SpFX: Erwin Torrente. Prosth: Maurice Carvajal. Mkp: Gigi Munoz Jr. Ref: TV: Philam Video Int'l.; occ. Eng. With Joey de Leon, Ogie Alcasid (genie), Monica Herrera, Rachel Labangco, Panchito Alba, Dencio Padilla, Charito Solis, Melissa Gibbs, Joaquin Fajardo (Lizardo), Pong Pong (yeti), Sonny Erang (Cyclops).

A genie takes Ali (de Leon) to Wonderland, where there are a very hairy yeti, a Cyclops, lizard men with long tails, and a gent whose face disintegrates after he drinks from a poisoned waterfall. Ludicrous fantasy-comedy, occasionally entertainingly so. At first, it seems as if the tails of the lizard men are simply supposed to be (as they so clearly are) part of their colorful costumes, but no, they're supposed to be tails.

*****ALIAS NICK BEAL** Endre Bohem 1949 (*Where Is Nick Beal?*-orig t. aka *Dark Circle. The Contact Man* - B). Mkp: Wally Westmore. Ref: screen. V 1/19/49. PFA notes 9/5/87. Janet Willis. FDY. Lee. And with Geraldine Wall, Henry O'Neill, Douglas Spencer, Percy Helton, King Donovan.

It seems, at first, to be the "wrong century" for "werewolves, vampires, and devils." Enter one Nicholas Beal (Ray Milland),

Agent, who conducts much of his business in and around the fog-enshrouded China Coast Cafe. "There's something strange about him—something eerie." He locates, intact, incriminating documents that have supposedly been burned. He seems to know people's thoughts—before they think them. And those who fail to fulfill the terms of their contracts with him are taken to the Island of Almas Perdidas.... Milland's debonair devil in suit and tie is a witty conception. His casual, inexplicable appearances and disappearances and his knowinger-than-thou look suggest just how much the devil might be able to do for one. The sinister voice-over whistle and musical blares for Beal are a bit much; his throwaway lines more effortlessly suggest his power. Thomas Mitchell's Foster, the D.A.: "You must have friends at the bank." Beal (a moment's hesitation): "Maybe." If Foster's corruption and his wife Martha's (Wall) essential goodness are dramatically pointed and believable, the goodness of George Macready's Rev. Gaylord and the others in the political reform movement is taken too much for granted.

**ALICE** (Swiss-W.G.-B) First Run Features/Condor & Hessischer Rundfunk & Film Four Int'l. (Michael Havas, Keith Griffiths) 1988 stopmo anim & live action color 84m. (*Neco Z Alenki*). SP, D: Jan Svankmajer, from Lewis Carroll's book *Alice in Wonderland.* Ph: Svatopluk Maly. Anim: Bedrich Glaser. Ref: TV: vt; Eng. version. Jim Shapiro. SFExam 9/16/88. VVoice 8/9/88. NYorker. SF Film Fest notes. V 2/24/88.

Adaptation of the Carroll classic—done in a manner which might be described as straightforwardly weird—includes a perhaps-Starevitch-inspired sequence in which a skeleton coachman, a living fish skeleton, and other bony beasties pursue Alice. Also bizarre the eggs which hatch little skull creatures. Cute #1: the sailor rodent building a campfire on and with Alice's hair (which is still on her head). Cute #2: the stuffed socks caterpillaring from hole to hole in the floor. Alternately engaging and wearing.

**ALICE GETS STUNG** FBO/Winkler (Walt Disney) 1925 anim & live action 7m. Ref: screen. PFA notes 5/23/93. no LC. With Virginia Davis.

In an unexplained creepy bit—creepy partly because it is unexplained and unexpected—a rabbit suddenly becomes huge and scares Julius the cat out of its burrow. Another scare sequence, in which Alice and Julius shrink and a "giant" bear chases them, has clear psychological underpinnings: Fear makes the two feel smaller, or the bear seem bigger. Yet another highlight: the wise-guy bear from the bear musicale playfully dodging the bullets from Alice's rifle.

At one point, Julius pulls off his face and places it on the ground as a decoy; later, the rabbit uses its tail as a powder puff in order to freshen up after her performance for him. (She cries; fellow rabbits play weepy music; inserts show heartbroken baby bunnies lost without their mother). Top-notch early Disney is both very funny and very inventive.

**ALICE IN WONDERLAND** CBS-TV/Irwin Allen 1985 color c180m. From the book by Lewis Carroll. SpVisFX: John Dykstra. Ref: Jim Shapiro. TVG. V 12/18/85:66.

Sequence with monstrous Jabberwocky (Tom McLoughlin). See also *Alice*.

**ALICE THE PIPER** FBO (Walt Disney) 1924 anim & live action 7m. Ref: screen. PFA notes 5/23/93. no LC. With Virginia Davis.

At the end of Disney's first version of "The Pied Piper of Hamelin" legend, an unexplained huge vacuum cleaner sucks all the rats (which look like mice) out of the town of Hamlin (sic) and into the Hamlin River. Earlier, the rats just laugh at Alice's naive attempts to lure them with music. Cute stuff.

**ALICE'S MYSTERIOUS MYSTERY** Walt Disney 1926 anim 6m. Ref: screen. PFA notes 5/16/93. no LC.

Phantom skulking dogcatchers trap and cage dogs in prisonlike cells ("Grade A," "Grade B," "Grade C"), turn them into sausages in the death chamber. Gruesome fun, with some imaginatively outlandish bits.

**\*\*\*ALICE'S SPOOKY ADVENTURE** FBO/Winkler (Walt Disney) 1924 anim & live action 5m. Ref: screen. PFA notes 5/16/93. Lee. no LC. With Virginia Davis.

The unconscious Alice imagines herself in the animated Spookville, where even the houses act like ghosts, and an "open air concert" draws hundreds of ghosts. Short starts awkwardly, picks up when it turns cartoon, and the screen is "full o' spooks." Highlight: the ghost meter which counts ghosts bashed by Alice and the Felix-like cat. Funny-creepy: the sheets-with-teeth ghosts.

**ALIEN 2** or **ALIEN 2 SULLA TERRA** see *Strangers, The*

**ALIEN** [3] (U.S.-B) Fox/Brandywine (Carroll-Giler-Hill/Sigourney Weaver/Ezra Swerdlow) 1992 color/ws 115m. (aka *Alien 3. Alien III* - shooting t). D: David Fincher. SP: David Giler, Walter Hill, Larry Ferguson. Story: Vincent Ward. Ph: Alex Thomson; (puppets) Rick Fichter; (models) David Jones; (min) David Stewart. Mus: Elliot Goldenthal. PD: Norman Reynolds. SpVisFX: (sup) Richard Edlund; (anim sup) Mauro Maressa; (coord) Julia Riva. SpMkpFX: Greg Cannom. Flying FX: Bob Wiesinger. Alien FX: Alec Gillis, Tom Woodruff Jr.; (des) H. R. Giger. SpFxSup: George Gibbs. Ref: TV. V 5/25/92. 1/14/91:16: shooting. SFChron 5/22/92. TVG. ad. With S. Weaver, Charles D. Dutton, Charles Dance, Paul McGann, Brian Glover, Lance Henriksen (Bishop II).

Ingredients in this sequel to *Aliens*: the U.S.S. Sulaco, which crash lands on a maximum-security correctional-facility planet ... a space "spider" which jumps into a dog and comes out an alien thing, or drooling "dragon" ... and a synthetic humanoid, Bishop, revived for a little info ("I'll never be top of the line again").... A slim story padded out with regulation action and melodrama. Main motifs: goop and glop. Worth seeing for the alien in action—its eccentric grasping, pecking, skittering, and feeding movements make its scenes watchable. Especially tingly: the thing scampering along the corridor ceilings. When this alien hightails it, it really high-tails it. In a bravura windup, Ripley's (Weaver) "baby" bursts out during her sacrificial suicide plunge.

See also: *Waxwork II.*

**ALIEN ATTACK** (B) ITC-TV (Anderson) 1975 color 109m. D: Lee H. Katzin, Charles Crichton. SP: C. Penfold, G. Bellack. Ref: British Films 1979-80. TVG. With Martin Landau, Barbara Bain,

Catherine Schell, Barry Morse, Nick Tate, Roy Dotrice, Anthony Valentine.

"An attack by a mystery planet ...."(BF) From the "Space 1999" series.

**ALIEN DEGLI ABISSI** see *Alien from the Deep*

**ALIEN FROM L.A.** Cannon (Golan-Globus) 1988 color 88 m. (*Odeon* - orig t). SP, D: Albert Pyun. SP: also Debra Ricci, Regina Davis. Mus: James Saad et al. VisFX: Fantasy II. SpMkpDes: Pamela L. Peitzman. SpFX: (sup) John Hartigan; (coord) Massimo Vico. Ref: TV: Media Home Ent. video. V 1/16/88. With Kathy Ireland, Thom Mathews, Linda Kerridge, Richard Haines, William R. Moses, Janie du Plessis, Simon Poland, Deep Roy, Deborah Chesher (troll bag lady).

"Man's ultimate ancestors were aliens known as Atlanteans." Stay-at-home Wanda (Ireland), of Vista Verde, California, changes her ways and follows her explorer father (Haines) to Africa, where, it is reported, he fell down a bottomless pit "searching for the center of the Earth." She too falls into Atlantis, where there are trolls and other inhabitants with "funny makeup and weird clothes," a spacecraft which crashed ten millennia ago, many leisure-time activities (lotto, cabarets, etc.)—and where "there's no such thing" as an "alien" from the surface world.... A routine action-adventure framework betrays the nuttier, sweeter aspects of *Alien from L.A.,* such as the running commentary on Wanda's squeaky voice. Her appalling winsomeness seems intended parodistically.

See also: *Journey to the Center of the Earth* (1989).

**ALIEN FROM THE DEEP** (I) Gico & Dania & Reteitalia & National & VIP Int'l. (Couyoumdjian) 1989 color c90m. (*Alien degli Abissi*). D: A. Margheriti. SP: Tito Carpi. Ph: Fausto Zuccoli. Mus: Andrea Ridolfi. Mkp: G. Bretti. Opt: Cinevideo. Ref: TV: VSOM; Eng.-lang. version. MV. Palmerini.With Daniel Bosch, Julia McKay, Alan Collins, Robert Marius, Charles Napier.

"The thing — it came out of the lake and then moved underground." Radioactive waste dumped into a volcano provides an alien lobster-monster with the energy it needs. Humans who come into contact with the alien become "infected" and begin to rot. At the end, a gas that absorbs liquid hydrogen helps finish off the thing .... A pale imitation of Fifties monster movies, with *Alien* updates on monster design. Lots of "Let's get out of here quickly!" Main expense: the big claw.

**ALIEN HIGH** (Can.) Gold Gems & Jack Bravman (Pierre Grise) 1987 color 86m. (*Mind Benders* - orig t). SP?, D: Eugenie Joseph. Ph: C. Racine. Mus: Diane Bulgarelli. AD: Elaine Ethier. SpFX: Arnold Gargiulo. MkpFX: Gargiulo, Jay Hakiwara. Ref: TV. TVG. Horacio Higuchi. vc box: *Invasion of the Mindbenders* - vt t. With Skip Lackey, Roy Thinnes, Lee Tergesen, David Kener, Mirana de Pencier, Bill Curry (Dr. Gunbow).

"No more rock 'n' roll!" Dr. Gunbow of the Behavior Modification Research Institute uses Kingston High as a test site for a scheme to turn students into obedient "Hitler youths" with the aid of taped music, subliminal messages, and (secretly) brain "implants" which zero in on the unconscious. ("They're actually

learning!") These implants "break down group mentality" and slow down brain waves. The doc proves to be an alien with superhypnotic eyes.... Gratingly obvious sf-comedy. Thinnes apparently studied comedy at the Darren McGavin School of Subtlety.

**ALIEN INTRUDER** PM Ent. (Merhi-Pepin/Stephen Lieb) 1993 (1992) color c90m. D: R. J. Gale. SP: Nick Stone. Ph: Michael Pinkey. Mus: Miriam Cutler. PD: Summer Swan, Dick Gardner. VisFX: F.H. Isaacs; M.E.L. MechFX: Gardner. Opt: Mercer et al. Ref: TV. TVG. V 2/22/93:32 (rated). 8/17/92:14: shooting. SFC Dtbk 3/21/93. PT 16:62: "cheap, stupid." With Tracy Scoggins, Billy Dee Williams, Maxwell Caulfield, Richard Cody, Gary Roberts, Jeff Conaway, Jane Hamilton.

"It's the same woman!" 2022 A.D. Ariel (Scoggins) — an alien, a computer "virus" or both — intrudes on the virtual-reality fantasies of the crew of the *U.S.S. Presley,* a salvage spaceship. ("This isn't in my program!") *Total Recall* intrudes on *Alien.* Much padding and repetition, thanks to the visualizations of the four fantasies.

**ALIEN INVASION** Amethyst Ent. (George Balaskas & Michael Economou/Lunar Bynne/Gulf European Finance) 1990 color 89m. (*Space Case* - shooting t). Story, SP, D: Howard R. Cohen. Story: also Bridget Hoffman. Ph: Tony Cutrano. Mus: Parmer Fuller. PD: Stephen Greenberg. SpFxMkp: Robert Burman. SpFxProps: Motion Picture Models. Ref: TV: Atlas video. V 11/22/89:14. 12/6/89:26. 2/21/90:123. With Hoyt Axton, Ray Walston, Joe Campanella, Ted McGinley, John Draikis, Bridget Hoffman, Felicity Waterman, Parley Baer, Robert Barry, Josh Schrieber (Velkar).

In the 21st century, inmates of an intergalactic insane asylum get wind of a planned alien "invasion of planet Earth" and a homemade spaceship takes on space battleships from, apparently, *Battle beyond the Stars.* ("Did we save Earth?") A total fizzle, in comic or "inspirational" mode.

**ALIEN LUST** AVC/Cris Monte 1985 color c85m. D: Vinnie Rossi. Mus: Joey D.; (title theme) Leonard Morand. Anim: Lon Moore. Ref: TV: AVC video. With Tamara Longley, Tess Ferre, Jerry Butler, Joey Silvera, Melissa Melendez.

A little green alien (whose headtop knob serves as both antenna and phallus) is sent here to study "earthling sexuality in all its phases." An extension of the "orgasmic zone" enables him to remain invisible to humans as he observes their lovemaking. Only the sporadic animated bits with the alien distinguish this from other X-rated films.

**ALIEN NATION** Fox & American Ent. Partners II/Gale Anne Hurd & Kobritz-O'Bannon 1988 color 90m. D: Graham Baker. SP: Rockne S. O'Bannon. Mus: Curt Sobel. Aliens: Stan Winston. SpFxCoord: Joseph Unsinn. Mkp: Zoltan, Monty Westmore et al. Titles: Ernest Farino. SpSdFX: John P. Ref: TV: CBS/Fox Video. MFB'89: 104-5. Oak Trib 10/7/88. V 10/5/88. With James Caan, Mandy Patinkin, Terence Stamp, Kevyn Major Howard, Leslie Bevis.

"They have landed, and now they are among us...." L.A., 1991. "Newcomers" from a slave spaceship—who are genetically engineered for hard labor and who have two "hearts"—slowly take their place in human society, where they are deprecatingly referred to as "slags." They disintegrate in sea water, but not only survive overdoses of their "nightmare" drug ("more potent than any human drug you can imagine"), but mutate into something "really weird".... Caan and Patinkin, as the apparently racist Sykes and the quietly "wild" alien "George," respectively, are a *48 Hrs.* cops-and-badinage team, and each is disarming in his own way. A mixture of sf, comedy, allegory, and social comment, the movie works best as a comedy, thanks to the starring duo. Caan especially takes to O'Bannon's dialogue: "You know, George," he says (re George's penchant for snacking on uncooked beaver), "that's very attractive. See, we're gonna go out, we're gonna talk to people, and you got fur in your teeth. Very attractive." In the film's last third, comedy and comment both lose out to regulation action.

**ALIEN NATION: DARK HORIZON** Foxstar-TV & Kenneth Johnson 1994 color c90m. D: K. Johnson. Tel: A. Schneider, D. Frolov. Ph: L. Ahern II. Mus: D. Kurtz. PD: B. Swift. Ref: TVG. SFChron 10/25/94: "soapy." V 10/24/94:45: "erratic." With Eric Pierpoint (George), Michelle Scarabelli, Terri Treas, Gary Graham, Nina Foch, Scott Patterson (Apossno).

"Purists" develop virus to eliminate "Newcomers." (Cf. *Prayer of the Rollerboys*.)

**ALIEN P.I.** see *Alien Private Eye*

**ALIEN PREDATOR** (U.S.-Sp?) Trans World Ent./Continental (The Sarluis) 1985 ('87-U.S.) color 90m. (aka *Alien Predators. The Falling*). SP, D, Co-P: Deran Sarafian. From Noah Blogh's screenplay "Massacre at R. V. Park." AD: Gomer Andres. SpCreatureFX: James Cummins, Bill Sturgeon et al. SpFX: John Balandin. Ref: TV. V 3/4/87. Phantom. Ecran F 42:86. 47:71: *Bio-Shock*-orig t? With Dennis Christopher, Martin Hewitt, Lynn-Holly Johnson, Luis Prendes.

In 1979, Skylab lands near Duarte, Spain. Five years later, "living microbes" from moon rocks on board begin to invade animals, use the "DNA structure of the host like a supermarket, picking and choosing the traits it needs to develop itself," drive the host crazy, then vacate.... *Alien* imitation is competently acted but heavy on gratuitous grossness and intentionally disgusting sound effects. Predictably cynical ending.

**ALIEN PRIVATE EYE** Raedon HV/Forthright 1991 (1987) color 92m. (*Lemro, Private Eye*-shooting t. aka *Alien P.I.*). SP, D, P: Vik Rubenfeld. Mus: Frank Weber. Ref: V 4/15/91. Martin. PT 10:48: "laughable mess." With Nikki Fastinetti (Lemro), Cliff Aduddell, John Alexander, Robert Axelrod.

Kickboxing alien and a drug from another planet.

**ALIEN SEED** Action Int'l./Fitzgerald Films/Triangle Films (Mark Paglia/Alien Seed) 1989 color 88m. SP, D: Bob James. SP: also D. K. Grimm. Mus: John Standish. SpMkpFX: Patrick Denver. Ph: Ken Carmack. PD: Kari Stewart. SpVisFX: Lynn Cress, Tom Richardson. SpFX: FX West. Ref: TV: Hemdale HV. V 12/6/89. Hound. Scheuer. PT 13:50: "bad script, terrible action scenes." With Heidi Paine, Steven Blade, Erik Estrada, Shellie Block, Lee Opitz et al. (aliens).

"Something strange is happening inside of me!" Two sisters who share an unusual mark on their necks — and nightmares re alien figures — prove to have been artificially inseminated by Extraterrestrial Biological Entities, or ETBEs. Meanwhile, the ruthless government agency MJ-12 is eliminating witnesses and expectant mothers alike. The space babies are supposed to help the human race; the U.S. government doesn't want "enlightened" beings making Earth too peaceful .... Motivations are strained all around here. Script features a pinch of *2001*, but it's routine chase scenes which pad out the running time. The "impregnation" rings around the women look like neon hula hoops and seem inspired by the creation sequence in *Metropolis*.

**ALIEN SPACE AVENGER** Action Int'l. HV/Manley Prods. (Sundlin-Harris-Haines) 1989 color 88m. (aka *Space Avenger*). SP, D: Richard W. Haines. SP: also Lynwood Sawyer. Mus: Richard Fiocca. Ref: V 9/27/89: "amiably dopey takeoff on the possession by lizardly aliens genre." 2/21/90:79 (ad). Martin. PT 11:47: "very clever & well made." SFChron Dtbk 5/31/92. With Robert Prichard, Mike McClerie, Charity Staley, Gina Mastrogiacomo.

**ALIEN WARRIOR** Shapiro Ent./BenTsvi-Hunt-Coe 1985 color 100m. (*King of the Streets* - alt t). SP, D: Edward Hunt. SP: also Rueben Gordon, Steven Shoenberg, Barry Pearson. Ph: Richard Gale et al. Mus: Bax. AD: Gary Randall et al. Ref: TV. V 5/29/85. TVG. Stanley. With Brett Clark ("Buddy," alien), Pamela Saunders, Reggie DeMorton, Nelson D. Anderson, Norman Budd (Buddy's father), Elodie McKee, Bill Woods Jr.

Another brother from another planet. A truth-happy alien from "very far away," whose brother previously failed on Earth, "must defeat great evil" here. He takes on a drug king's empire of fear and magically instills self-esteem (and reading ability) in earthlings, in sometimes amusing scenes. This miracle worker, "Buddy," even gets untamed youths to spray graffiti like "Do Not Murder" and "Be Temperate".... A swell comedy re "Mr. Goody Two Shoes" beckons in this occasionally cornily appealing sf-drama/social tract. The hero, who asks everyone he meets on Earth where he can find "great evil," never has far to look for it.

**The ALIEN WITHIN** American Independent (Peter Stewart/J. B. Mallian) 1991 color c73m. SP, D: Ted Newsom. Ph: Murphy Scott. Mus: Chuck Cirino. SpFX: S.O.T.A. FX; (coord) Chris Ray. Ref: TV. TVG. Fango 123:20. With Richard Harrison, Gordon Mitchell, Jay Richardson, Suzanne Ager, Melissa Moore, Crystal Shaw; (from *Evil Spawn*) Bobbie Bresee, John Carradine, Forrest J Ackerman et al.

Footage that didn't exactly beg to be seen the first time, in *Evil Spawn*, is reworked into this woeful, even worse, shot-on-tape remake. Bobbie Bresee's Blaisdell-ish, altered-DNA monster is back, as also apparently is a snarling, caterpillarlike creature, in both old and new scenes. (In midtransformation, Bresee has a messy, *She Demons* face.) *Alien within* adds Harrison and Mitchell as green-headed aliens who can take human form.

**ALIENATOR** Amazing Movies/American-Independent & Majestic Int'l./Heritage (Jeffrey C. Hogue) 1989 color 92m. D: Fred Olen Ray. SP: Paul Garson. Ph: Gary Graver. Mus: Chuck Cirino. SpFxDes: Hall, Tuck. SpFxMkp: Bruce Barlow, Mark Williams. SpVisFX: Cruse & Co. AnimFX: Bret Mixon. Ref: TV. Stanley.

V 12/6/89: "weak script." 10/4/89:30 (rated). 11/1/89:25. Martin: "lame." McCarty II: "monumentally unpleasant." Scheuer. Maltin '92: "OK sci-fi." With Jan-Michael Vincent, John Phillip Law, Ross Hagen, Dyana Ortelli, Dawn Wildsmith, P. J. Soles, Teagan Clive (Alienator), Robert Clarke, Leo V. Gordon, Robert Quarry, Hoke Howell, Jay Richardson, Dan Golden.

Alienator sent to Earth from a "far-off corner of the galaxy" to kill rebel leader's (Hagen) children. Plus space leeches, a vaporizer ray rifle, a dialogue reference to John Carter of Mars, and alien possession of a human .... Dispiritingly thin sf-actioner at least has a few not-bad-for-B effects. Best line (far-from-fierce competition): "It's the war of the worlds, and we're on the front line."

**ALIENATORS, The** see *Shocking Dark*

**ALIENS** (U.S.-B) Fox/Brandywine (Gale Anne Hurd) 1986 color 137m. (*Aliens: The Special Edition* - vt t). Story, SP, D: James Cameron. Story: also David Giler, Walter Hill. Mus: James Horner. VisFX: (sup) Robert & Dennis Skotak; The L.A. FX Group. AlienFX; Stan Winston. Puppets: Doug Beswick Prods. SpFxSup: John Richardson. MkpSup: Peter Robb-King. VideoFX: Richard Hewitt. Ref: TV. MFB'86:263-4. V 7/9/86. TVG. Stanley. V 3/28/90:40. SFExam 7/18/86. Berk. Monthly 8/86. Bay G 7/30/86. With Sigourney Weaver, Carrie Henn, Michael Biehn, Paul Reiser, Lance Henriksen, Carl Toop (alien).

"They mostly come at night!" Sequel to *Alien* takes place 57 years later, when a big mama dinosaur of an alien, and smaller flying aliens, terrorize the colony on planet LV-246. Plus: an android, or "artificial person" (Henriksen) with behavior inhibitors. ("I may be synthetic, but I'm not stupid.") More search-and-destroy, body-burstings, retractable jaws. Near the end, fresh ugly wonders are introduced in the "nursery" and environs. The subjects of maternal instinct and tolerance (for androids) lose out to the suspense of so-and-so hours till help comes, so-and-so minutes before the reactor explodes.

Sequel: *Alien³*. See also: *Illegal Alien*.

**ALIVE BY NIGHT** see *Evil Spawn*

**ALL ABOARD FOR THE MOON** Bray/Fleischer 1924 anim silent 7m. Ref: Filmfax 49:39,40: "radium-powered spaceship launched from the roof of a skyscraper." Lee. no Cabarga/TFS.

**ALL IN A DIM COLD NIGHT** see *Tragedy of Ghost*

**ALL PURPOSE CULTURAL CAT GIRL NUKU NUKU, Volume One** (J) A.D. Vision/Movic & King Records & Takada & Futaba Sha & Studio Fantasia & Studio Palm & Beat Club/Animate Film (Star Child/Furusawa & Ikeguchi/Misawa) 1992 anim color 56m. D: H. Shigematsu, Y. Takahashi. Story: Y. Takada. Ph: A. Takahashi. Mus: H. Matsuda. AD: K. Arai. SpFX: T. Sakakibara. SdFX: D. Jinbo. Ref: TV: ADV video (King Video); Eng. titles. Animerica 5:14. Voice: Megumi Hayashibara (Nuku Nuku).

Two stories re superstrong "model android" NK 1124, or Nuku Nuku. ("Are you the Terminator or what?"). Plus a "power suit" and an Armored Octopus.... Video is miscalculated to be another *Urusei Yatsura* (for an alien high-school girl, substitute an an-

droid high-school girl), though it has its moments. The exaggerated emotions are less amusing than wearing.

**ALL THE DEVIL'S ANGELS** 199-? color feature. Ref: VSOM: "horror hardcore ... demonic possession." With T. Borodyn.

**ALLIGATOR II: THE MUTATION** Group One/Brandon Chase (Cary Glieberman/Golden Hawk) 1990 color 94m. (*Alligator II: The Return* - orig t). D: Jon Hess. SP: Curt Allen. Mus: Jack Tillar. Ph: Joseph Mangine. PD: George Costello. Underwater Ph: Pete Romano. Creature & MkpFX: (mech sup) Bob McKee; (sp) Sam McCain, Kelly Mann. Aeronautical FX: Steven Mahrle, G. D. Robinson. SpFxCoord: John Eggett.Ref: TV. VG. V 5/2/90:27 (ad). 2/21/90:76 (ad). Martin. With Joseph Bologna, Steve Railsback, Dee Wallace Stone, Woody Brown, Richard Lynch, Holly Gagnier, Brock Peters, Bill Daily, Kane Hodder.

"That ain't no gator!" The "poison" in the lake is "hormone-bonded adrenaline" dumped by Future Chemicals, and it has created the "giant alligator in the sewer"—a "mean and big" guy "built like an armored truck".... Routine sf-actioner, with a bland menace. As usual, a fun park is about to open just as a (nonfun) creature surfaces. Lynch is the good ol' alligator-hunter with a personal score to settle.

**ALMOST MARRIED** Fox 1932 50m. D: William Cameron Menzies, Marcel Varnel. SP: Wallace Smith, Guy Bolton, from Andrew Soutar's novel *The Devil's Triangle*. Ph: John Mescall. Mus D: George Lipschutz. AD: Gordon Wiles. Ref: Bill Warren. V 7/26/32: "horror"; remake of a 1919 Metro silent. LC. no NYT. Thomas. AFI: Ph: also George Schneiderman. MM 49:64. With Violet Heming, Ralph Bellamy, Alexander Kirkland (Capristi), Alan Dinehart, Herbert Bunston, Maria Alba, Herbert Mundin, Mary Gordon.

"Lunatic pianist with a penchant for choking girls." (V)

**ALOHA LITTLE VAMPIRE STORY** (H.K.?) c1991 color 89m. D?: Yinn Jiann. Ref: TV: Pan-Asia Video; Eng. titles.

"I am a good vampire." The vampire community in this inane comedy includes little Hsiu Long, Uncle Black, Uncle White— all hopping vampires—and a cloaked, more-Western vampire. The little vampire shoots rays, cures a sick (human) friend, turns a vase into bunnies, makes flowers grow, and enables kids to fly. Self-consciously kooky.

**ALONG CAME A SPIDER** see *Arachnophobia*

**\*ALPHAVILLE: UNE ETRANGE AVENTURE DE LEMMY CAUTION** 1965. Ref: TV: Connoisseur Video; Eng. titles. Lee. Hardy/SF. V 5/5/65. Kael/5001. TVG: *Alphaville!* - TV ad t. Weldon. Film Comment 1/80:13-14. S&S 7/94. SFExam Mag 10/1/95.With Jean-Pierre Leaud.

Disorienting music and neon turn Paris into Alphaville, City of Artificial Light, an ant-colony-like technocracy regulated by Alpha 60, a super-computer. For Alphavillians, "daybreak" is when the fluorescent lights switch on. Men are executed because they "behaved illogically." Words ("autumn light," "tenderness") disappear every day from the vocabulary. Natasha (Anna Karina) says she was born in Alphaville, but (against the rules) she uses the word "why." She also knows the word "conscience" and has heard of Nueva York ....

Jean-Luc Godard's futuristic answer to the question, "Why does everyone look so miserable?" proves more humorous and incisive than his fellow countryman Francois Truffaut's (in *Fahrenheit 451*). From another angle, *Alphaville* is the best film version of *Invasion of the Body Snatchers*. It's clear what answer Alpha 60 has in mind when it asks hero Lemmy Caution (Eddie Constantine), "What illuminates the night?" But Lemmy brings in a word from another universe: "Poetry." If this movie has a wry, half-balmy flavor all its own, it's in part because the stolid Lemmy is both Tough Guy (how tough? — he lights his cigarette lighter with a bullet) and Sensitivity Enforcer, Purveyor of Poetry. No opening for mawkishness there. He's a Hero That Never Was in a City That Never Was, an odd conjunction which makes high comedy — and poetry — out of the Reason/Emotion thing.

Incandescence, fluorescence, and neon make for a coldly beautiful, unlived-in setting here. (The streets of Alphaville are given names like Light Radiation Avenue.) At the end, citizens are "asphyxiated by the absence of light." In its harsher mode, Paul Misraki's score helps give *Alphaville* its otherworldly feel; but Godard also uses (much lovelier) snatches of music to mark the emotional evolution of Natasha — a surprisingly affecting musical phrase or two, for instance, underlines her recollection of Nueva York. By the end, she not only knows the word "conscience," but the sentence (and sentiment) "I love you." The spectacle of her haltingly unfolding humanity is — in "realistic" terms — obviously absurd, schematically accomplished; but the music and the movie's ironic-poetic tone make it something to be somehow reckoned with.

See also *Betaville*.

*ALRAUNE DCA 1952 79m. (92m.) (*Unnatural...The Fruit of Evil*). SP: K. Heuser. Ph: Friedel Behn-Grund. Mus: W. Heymann. Sets: R. Herlth. Ref: TV: Sinister Cinema; Eng. dubbed. Lee. V 12/10/52: SP: F. Rotter. Hardy/SF. Lentz. Pt 22:11.

"I created her." Via artificial insemination, a half-madman (Erich von Stroheim) produces a supposedly heartless woman, Alraune. ("You are the result of my experiments!") First disappointment here von Stroheim's voice is dubbed by someone else. Film itself is outlandish melodrama—in essence, it's the camp (but not very funny) version of "Frankenstein." (Substitute bad blood for bad brains.) From another angle, this is *The Bad Seed*.

ALTRO INFERNO, L' see *Guardian of Hell, The*

ALWAYS see *Deja Vu*

ALYAS BATMAN EN ROBIN (Fili) Regal Films 1993? color 102m. SP, D: Tony Y. Reyes. SP: also Joey de Leon. Ph: O. Querijero. PD: Melchor Defensor. SpFX: Linda Torrente. SdFX: Rodel Capule. Ref: TV: Regal Video; some Eng. With Rene Requiestas, Dawn Zulueta, Vina Morales, Keempee de Leon, Joey de Leon.

"Joker, Penguin rob Gotham bank." (headline) Two hoods dress up as the Penguin and the Joker and commit a series of robberies. Two other locals decide: "It's time for Batman and Robin!" At the end, the Penguin and the Joker impersonate Batman and Robin.... Casual, balmy musical comedy is not too serious—even the robbery victims join in the production numbers. But how "Gotham" got into it....

AM NACHESTEN MORGEN KEHRTE DER MINISTER NICHT AN SEINEN ARBEITSPLATZ ZURUCK (W. G.) Funke-Stern 1986 color 70m. SP, D, P: Monika Funke-Stern. Mus: Frieder Butzmann. Ref: V 2/19/86: *On the Next Morning the Minister Did Not Return to His Post* - tr t. With Udo Kier, Magitta Haberland.

"Sci-fi world of computers, new forms of energy ... technological utopia."

Las AMANTES DE SENOR DE LA NOCHE (Mex) Fenix & AVPA (Isela Vega) 1984 (1983) color 97m. (*Luna Bruja* - orig t). Story, D: Vega. SP: Hugo Arguelles. Mus: Pedro Plascencia, Pancho Saenz. AD: Raul Medellin. OptFX: Manuel Sainz. SdFX: Gonzalo Gavira. Mkp: Victoria Celis. Ref: TV: Isela Vega Video; no Eng. V 4/11/84: *The Lovers of the Lord of the Night* - tr t. 5/9/84:488. Hardy/HM. Ecran F 46:64. V 7/27/83:28. VSOM: *Lover of the Lord of the Night* -vt t. With Elena de Haro, Emilio Fernandez, Arturo Vazquez, Lilia Prado, Irma Serrano, Andres Garcia, Marina Vega (fantasma), El Africano (caballo negro).

The voodoo-shop woman's doll works: Our young heroine stabs the doll; soon afterwards, her enemy is impaled on a spike. At the end, a mob beheads and dismembers her mother.... Tale of young love and old hate seems pretty hokey. Obvious main selling point: the nude scenes with the Phoebe Cates-like heroine. Lots of horse imagery, potions, body paint, smearing of fowl's blood, and visualized hallucinations.

Le AMANTI DEL MOSTRO (I) 1974 feature. SP,D: Sergio Garrone. Mus: Maestosi, Liberati. Ref: Palmerini: "ridiculous"; *Frankenstein*-like. With Klaus Kinski, Marzia Damon, Stella Calderoni.

3P The AMAZING ADVENTURES OF JOE 90 (B) ITC-TV (Anderson) 1981 (1968) color marionettes 93m. D: Peter Anderson, Leo Eaton et al. SP: Gerry & Sylvia Anderson, Tony Barwick. Ph: Seale, Lugrin. Mus: Barry Gray. AD: Wilson, Nott. SpVisFX: Derek Meddings. Anim: Dolphin. Ref: TV. TVG. Larson: from the "JOE 90" TV series. Showtime-TV.

The BIG RAT (Brain Impulse Galvaniscope Record and Transfer) machine electronically transfers the knowledge and experience of a scientist into his son, who then becomes a special agent. Typically stolid Anderson "Supermarionation" material.

AMAZING SPIDER-MAN PARTS I through VII 1978. Ref: TVG: now TV-packaged as such (instead of as, for instance, Spider-man: *The Con Caper and the Curse of Rava*, which is now *Part VII*).

AMAZING STORIES Capital (H.K.?) 1993 color/ws c90m. Ref: TV: Tai Seng Video; Eng. titles. V 1/31/94:13: in H.K.

1) The dead brother of the mistreated Mrs. Chao returns as a ghost (at one point in the form of their doll) and kills her tormentor/husband. Slight, but atmospherically shot and scored. 2) A vampire woman (complete with fangs) comes up against an

old vampire witch with a prior claim on one of her victims. Confusing period horror with two fairly impressive action sequences. 3) A wife and her lover do a *Postman Always Rings Twice* on her (older) husband, but the latter seems to come back as a ghost. Overextended anecdote is the least of this terror trio.

**AMAZING STORIES—THE MOVIE** Univ-TV/Amblin-TV 1986-87 color 110m. Ref: TV. MFB'88:11. TVG.

Three episodes of the "Amazing Stories" TV series.

1) "The Mission." Story, D: Steven Spielberg. Tel: Menno Meyjes. Mus: John Williams. SpVisFX: Dream Quest Images. With Kevin Costner, Casey Siemaszko, Kiefer Sutherland.

A World War II bomber's belly gunner, Jonathan (Siemaszko), trapped inside the turret, faces certain death as the plane attempts a landing with no landing gears. An amateur cartoonist, he draws a "whole" plan, concentrates and—like magic—the real plane has landing gears.... The rabbit which Spielberg pulls out of this particular hat is not a live bunny. It's animated, which fact may be the key to this kookily compelling anecdote. Cartoon landing gears save real plane, real gunner. There's a loony integrity, not to say literal-mindedness, to this prestidigitation. Main drawback: an overdone, maudlin buildup to the payoff.

2) "Go to the Head of the Class." D: Robert Zemeckis. Tel, Story: Mick Garris. Tel: also Tom McLoughlin, Bob Gale. Consul: Richard Matheson. Mus: Alan Silvestri. SpFX: Stan Winston. With Christopher Lloyd.

A curse kills overbearing English Professor Beanes (Lloyd), and a reverse curse brings him back as a living severed head and its attendant body.... Lloyd carries the beginning and ending of this amusing kidding of unstoppable-monster movies. In-between: padding.

3) "Mummy Daddy" (in British theater package). D: William Dear. Tel: Earl Pomerantz. Story: Spielberg. Mus: Danny Elfman, Steve Bartek. Mummies: Greg Cannom. With Tom Harrison, Michael Zand (Ra-Amin-Ka).

A real mummy (Zand) meets an actor mummy (Harrison), on location for "The Mummy's Kiss," in this cute takeoff on old mummy movies. See also: *Halloween Night*.

**AMAZING STORIES—THE MOVIE II** Univ-TV/Amblin-TV 1985-86 color c110m. PD: Rick Carter. SpVisFX: Dream Quest. Title Des: Ron Cobb, Jim Bissell. Ref: TV. TVG.

Four episodes from the "Amazing Stories" TV series.

"Santa." D: Philip Joanou. Tel: Joshua Brand, John Falsey. Ph: John McPherson. Mus: Thomas Newman. With Douglas Seale, Pat Hingle, Gabriel Damon.

Originally shown as "Santa '85." Familiar Scrooge and Santa Themes; pleasantly inevitable end: The sleigh flies; Santa drops formerly skeptical sheriff Hingle a ray gun.

"The Wedding Ring." D: Danny DeVito. Tel: Stu Krieger. Story: S. Spielberg. Ph: Robert Stevens. Mus: Craig Safan. Consul: Richard Matheson. With DeVito, Rhea Perlman, Louis Giambalvo, Tracey Walter.

The wedding ring of "The Black Widow"—who successively married and murdered three husbands—turns a bedraggled

housewife into a sex siren. The latter transformation is cut-and-dried—from Dullsville to Sex-and-Violence.

"The Doll." D: Joanou. Tel: Matheson. Ph: Stevens. Mus: Georges Delerue. With John Lithgow, Annie Helm, Sharon Spelman, Rainbow Phoenix, Albert Hague (Mr. Liebemacher).

"What they need they will find." Dollmaker Liebemacher proves to be a matchmaker, as the models for his handmade dolls meet and fall in love. Lithgow's performance as the nervous, lonely, 42-year-old John Walters and Delerue's score put over this slight, sweet, sentimental tale.

"Ghost Train." Story, D: Spielberg. Tel: Frank Deese. Ph: Allen Daviau. Mus: John Williams. With Roberts Blossom, Scott Paulin, Gail Edwards, Lukas Haas, Hugh Gillin.

"Bam! Right through our new house!" Highlight of this generally overdone nonsense: the local ghost train crashing through a house. (Shades of Buster Keaton's great *One Week*.) This time Spielberg performs his "magic" light play with a locomotive engine's beam. Some okay comic touches.

**AMAZING STORIES—THE MOVIE III** Univ-TV/Amblin-TV 1985 color c90m. SpVisFX: Dream Quest. Ref: TV. TVG.

"Remote Control Man." D: Bob Clark. Tel: D. L. McIntosh. Story: Spielberg. Mus: Arthur Rubinstein. With Sydney Lassick, Nancy Parsons, Shawn Weatherly, Lyle Alzado, Dirk Benedict, Barbara Billingsley, Gary Coleman, Jim Lange, Ed McMahon, Clara Peller, Richard Simmons, Jake Steinfeld, Sid Haig.

The Metaluna (baldfaced reference to *This Island Earth*) Discount Center sells Walter Poindexter a super-TV with a Magic Touch remote control: He makes his wife disappear and figures from TV appear in his living room—e.g., Mrs. Cleaver, the Incredible Hulk, the Knight Rider car. Cute idea with an innocuously didactic resolution.

"Guilt Trip." D: Burt Reynolds. Tel: Gail & Kevin Parent. Mus: Stephen Dorff. With Loni Anderson, Charles Durning, Abbe Lane, Charles Nelson Reilly, Dom DeLuise, Rick Ducommun, Fritz Feld.

Guilt takes a holiday in this amusing comic version of "Death Takes a Holiday."

"Family Dog." (U.S.-Austral.) Hyperion-Kushner-Locke Tel, D: Brad Bird. Anim: Bird, A. V. King; (des) Tim Burton: (sup) Chris Buck; (fx) Don Paul. Mus: Danny Elfman, Steve Bartek. Voices: Stan Freberg, Annie Potts, Mercedes McCambridge, Marshall Efron.

Horror-house guard-dog school's extreme techniques turn put-upon mutt into ferocious beast. Drolly animated cautionary comedy.

"Mummy Daddy." See *Amazing Stories—The Movie*.

**AMAZING STORIES—THE MOVIE: PART IV** Univ-TV/Amblin-TV 1985-86 color c110m. Ph: Robert Stevens. PD: Rick Carter. SpVisFX: Dream Quest. Ref: TV. TVG.

"Mirror, Mirror." D: Martin Scorsese. Tel: Joseph Minion. Story: Steven Spielberg. Mus: Michael Kamen. SpMkp: The Burmans. With Sam Waterston, Helen Shaver, Dick Cavett, Tim Robbins (Jordan's Phantom), Michael C. Gwynne.

A phantom in a mirror terrorizes a horror-story writer (Waterston). Pointless, despite a few twists. (Jordan sees the phantom in someone's eyes, then becomes the phantom himself.)

"The Amazing Falsworth." D: Peter Hyams. Tel: Mick Garris. Story: Spielberg. Mus: Billy Goldenberg. With Gregory Hines, Richard Masur, Suzanne Bateman.

A mind-reading magician (Hines) "sees" a murder. Predictable, with a few nice touches.

"Life on Death Row." Story, D: Mick Garris. Tel: Rockne S. O'Bannon. Creative Consul: Richard Matheson. Mus: Fred Steiner. P: David E. Vogel. With Patrick Swayze, Hector Elizondo, James T. Callahan, Kevin Hagen.

A condemned killer (Swayze), struck by lightning during a prison-break attempt, finds that he has the power to heal. ("God or devil, I didn't ask to be able to do this!") Okay reversal of *Man Made Monster*—here, the electric man heals rather than hurts.

"Vanessa in the Garden." D: Clint Eastwood. Tel: Spielberg. Mus: Leonard Niehaus. Sp Artwork: Jaroslav Gebr, Yvonne Nagel. With Harvey Keitel, Sondra Locke, Beau Bridges.

"Vanessa lives in my paintings." An artist (Keitel) develops a "case of melancholy" when his model and inspiration (Locke) dies in an accident. But his paintings seem to bring her back to him.... Tantalizing idea uncertainly developed.

**AMAZING STORIES—THE MOVIE V** Univ-TV/Amblin-TV (David E. Vogel) 1986 color c110m. PD: Rick Carter. SpVisFX: Dream Quest. Ref: TV. TVG.

"The Sitter." D: Joan Darling. Tel: Mick Garris. Story: Joshua Brand, John Falsey. Ph: Robert Stevens. Mus: Ken Wannberg. With Mabel King, Seth Green, Joshua Rudoy.

Cute, cautious, finally empty tale of a voodoo babysitter (King). Script doesn't quite work re the power of imagination.

"Grandpa's Ghost." Story, D: Timothy Hutton. Tel: Michael de Guzman. Mus: Pat Metheny. SpMkp: Michael Westmore. With Andrew McCarthy, Ian Wolfe, Herta Ware.

Grandpa dies, seems to come back and sing for Grandma, but it's Grandson in a peel-off mask. Slight, sentimental, oddly bizarre. The dream image of the piano and coffin is the pleasantly surreal key here.

"Dorothy and Ben." D: Thomas Carter. Tel: Michael de Guzman. Story: Steven Spielberg. Ph: John McPherson. Mus: Georges Delerue. With Joe Seneca, Natalie Gregory, Lane Smith, Louis Giambalvo.

A man in a coma for forty years snaps out of it, "talks" to a little girl in a coma, "trades places" with her. Padded, and a bit syrupy, but metempsychotically quite intriguing.

"Gershwin's Trunk." Tel, D: Paul Bartel. Tel, Mus: John Meyer. Creative Consultant: Richard Matheson. Ph: R. Stevens. With Bob Balaban, Lainie Kazan, John McCook, Hurd Hatfield, P. Bartel.

"Psychic Voodoo" Sister Theresa (Kazan) levitates, comes down at a piano, as Gershwin Revisited, inspires a stage-show composer (Balaban). Glib, hollow Show-Biz Lite tale.

**AMAZING STORIES—THE MOVIE VI** Univ-TV/Amblin-TV 1985-86 color c110m. PD: Rick Carter. SpVisFX: (#1&2) Dream Quest. Ref: TV. TVG.

"The Main Attraction." D: Matthew Robbins. Tel: Brad Bird, Mick Garris. Story: Spielberg. Ph: John McPherson. Mus: Craig Safan. With John Scott Clough, Lisa Jane Persky.

A meteorite strike near Rockridge High student Brad Bender's house causes "some massive internal electromagnetic" change in him. The day-to-day problems of the magnetized are amusingly described here, if not exactly fitted into a story.

"Gather Ye Acorns." D: Norman Reynolds. Tel: Stu Krieger. Story: Spielberg. Ph: Robert Stevens. Mus: Bruce Broughton. with Mark Hamill, David Rappaport, Lois de Banzie, Royal Dano.

Glib "Cling to the child in you" sentiments in this tale re "Mother Nature's only son." The latter teaches a boy to value boy's-room treasures, a lesson boys generally learn less sentimentally on their own.

"You Gotta Believe Me." D: Reynolds. Tel: Krieger. Story: Spielberg. Consul: Richard Matheson. With Charles Durning, Ebbe Roe Smith.

A "bad dream" proves to be a premonition of a plane crash and allows a man time to prevent the latter. Fair.

"Lane Change." D: Ken Kwapis. Tel: Ali Marie Matheson. Consul: R. Matheson. Ph: Charles Minsky. Mus: Jimmy Webb. With Kathy Baker, Priscilla Pointer.

A divorcing woman's life passes before her, or beside her, as cars from her past drive by on a rainy night and she sees her father, her husband, and herself at key points in her life. A pat pop-psych finis almost spoils a fairly involving, "Twilight Zone"-like duologue, but an okay coda comes to the rescue.

**AMAZON SAVAGE ADVENTURE** see *Cut and Run*

**AMAZON WOMEN ON THE MOON** Univ/Robert K. Weiss (Landis-Folsey Jr) 1987 color & b&w 85m. Ref: TV. HR 9/16/87. V 9/16/87. SFExam 9/18/87. Bill Warren.

Four of the comic sketches here are sf-horror-comedy.

"Amazon Women on the Moon" (directed by Weiss, featuring Steve Forrest, Sybil Danning, Lana Clarkson, and Forrest J Ackerman): In the year 1980, the manned Moon Rocket One finds Amazons and a dinosaur lizard on the moon. Our TV announcer identifies the movie (shown complete with splices) as, variously, a 1955 and a 1957 production.

"Son of the Invisible Man" (directed by Carl Gottlieb, featuring Ed Begley, Jr., as Griffin): Son is visible and doesn't know it. Kinda cute, and art directed in the style of Universal of the Thirties and Forties.

"Reckless Youth" (original title, "Are These Our Loins?", directed by Joe Dante, featuring Paul Bartel): Beer and drugs turn Pete Jones into a "pitiful creature"—Bela Lugosi in *Island of Lost Souls*, to be exact—kept caged in "the clinic." Highlights: purposely mismatched shots and a misdirected lighted blowtorch.

"Bologna or Not?" (directed by Dante, featuring Henry Silva): Modern investigative TV journalism hypothesizes that Jack the Ripper was ... the Loch Ness Monster. The latter cuts a droll figure in derby, tie, etc., and his absurd (and large) presence in the dramatized vignette makes this the high point for the whole movie.

**AMAZONIA** see *Cut and Run*

**AMAZONS** (U.S.-Arg.) Concorde/Aries (Roger Corman/Hector Olivera)/New Horizons 1987 (1986) color 76m. D: Alex Sessa. SP: Charles Saunders. Mus: Oscar Camp. SpFX: Willy Smith. Mkp: Laura Zelop. Ref: TV. V 6/3/87. With Windsor Taylor Randolph, Penelope Reed, Joseph Whipp (Kalungo), Frank Cocza (Balgur), Santiago Mallo (half-head).

Ingredients: the evil Kalungo ("Hell will be my greatest conquest!"), whose hands shoot deadly lightning bolts or, alternately, invisible strangling/paralyzing rays ... the forest of strange flashing lights and a flying banshee or two ... a "voodoo" tree ("Someone is killing my tree!")—each hack at it is a hack at our heroine's soul ... and the Spirit Stone.... The acting is flat, the women aren't, in this negligible t&a fantasy.

**AMBASSADOR MAGMA, VOL. 1** (J) L.A. Hero-Nippan/Bandai (Visual Workshop/Tezuka Prods. & Plex/Kubo-Kubota-Okazaki) 1993 anim color 74m. (c25m). D: Hidehito Ueda. From the series by Osamu Tezuka. Ph: Noguchi. AD: Okada. Ref: TV: LAH video (Dark Image); Eng. dubbed. Animerica 5:15, 3 (ad): 1st 3 OAVs.

"Tonight, Goa will rise again." Goa, an ancient apparent vampire, is reborn; his age-old nemesis, Magma, an apparent "rocket-humanoid," also awakens. Plus various monsters (including a spider thing and a monster dog) ... a man who turns into a huge, tentacled beast ... the Voice of the Earth ... a town of zombies ... and "stars" which fall to Earth, then fly toward the sky.... Although Magma is one of your more foolish-looking superheroes, this is better-than-average science-horror-fantasy. The tale is fairly complicated, and the cast of fantastic characters lengthy. Tape includes "My Name Is Goa," "The Gold Giant," and "Silent Invasion."

**AMBERELLA AGENT OF LUST** Gourmet Video 1986 color 82m. Ref: vc box: sex ray. Adam '89. With Elle Rio, Amber Lynn.

**The AMBULANCE** Triumph Films/Epic Prods. & Sarlui-Diamant (Esparza/Katz/Ambulance Prods.) 1990 color 95m. (*Into Thin Air* - shooting t). SP, D: Larry Cohen. Ph: Jacques Haitkin. Mus: Jay Chattaway. SpMkpFX: Rob Benevides. SpFxCoord: Kevin McCarthy. Opt: Mercer & OptFX. Ref: TV: Col-TriStar HV. V 12/31/90. V/Mifed '89:157. PT 10:8. Cinef 4/91. SFChron Dtbk 10/24/93. 12/12/93. With Eric Roberts, James Earl Jones, Red Buttons, Megan Gallagher, Eric Braeden, Stan Lee, Laurene Landon.

Mad scientist (Braeden), "frightening ambulance ride," "medical experiments," in this "genuine sleeper for 1991." (V) "This isn't a regular hospital." Behind the mystery of the monster ambulance: "implant surgery" and the use of people as "lab animals" .... Though the premise is a bit offbeat, *The Ambulance* isn't scary. The story, however, has occasional little surprises, and the characters are fairly entertaining. Hero Roberts gets beat up so much it's almost parody.

**AMBUSH AT DEVIL'S GAP** (B) Rayant 1966 serial (6 episodes/c95m. total). SP,D: David Eastman. SP: also Kerry Eastman. Ph: D. Ransom. Mus: A. Elms. Ref: Lee(MFB'66:184). BFC. With Chris Barrington, Sue Sylvaine, Hugh Latimer.

"Haunted" castle ... electricity-generating metal.

**AMERICA 3000** (U.S.-Israeli?) Cannon 1986 (1985) color 92m. (*Thunder Warriors. Thunder Women* - early titles). SP, D: David Engelbach. Mus: Tony Berg. SpFX: Carlo de Marchis. Aargh Des: Laine Liska. Mkp: Rinat Aloni. SpSdFX: Dale Strumpell. Ref: TV: Viacom-TV. V 5/14/86. HR 5/23/86. TVG. Ecran F 58:71. V 10/24/84:27. With Chuck Wagner, Laurene Landon, Camilla Sparv, William Wallace.

Year 3000, after the "Great Nuke." Warrior women, subservient men, and a Bigfoot-ish mutant, Aargh the Awful (Steve Malovic). This is *Cannibal Women in the Avocado Jungle of Death* without Bill Maher—i.e., without much of anything.

**AMERICAN CYBORG: STEEL WARRIOR** Cannon/Global 1994 color 95m. D: Boaz Davidson. SP: Friedman, Crounse, Pequingnot. Ph: A. Karpick. Mus: B. Leyh. PD: K. Sander. Ref: V 1/17/94: "plodding." PT 19:16: "post nuke." Martin: "laughable performances." Vallejo T-H. SFChron Dtbk 1/30/94: "futuristic." V 10/25/93:M-8. vc box. With John Ryan, Joe Lara, Nicole Hansen, Uri Gavriel (mutant leader).

"Cannibals and mutants ... indestructible robot killing machine"(SFCD).

**AMERICAN GOTHIC** (B-Can.) Vidmark Ent./Brent Walker & Pinetalk (Manor Ground/Gerrard & Nat'l. Leasing) 1987 ('88-U.S.) color 90m. (*Hide and Shriek* - B t). D: John Hough. SP: Burt Wetanson, Michael Vines. Mus: Alan Parker. PD: David Hiscox. SpFX: Allen Benjamin. Ref: TV: Vidmark video. V 5/27/87. SFChron 7/5/88. ad. VW 16:8. With Rod Steiger (Pa), Yvonne De Carlo (Ma), Sarah Torgov (Cynthia), Michael J. Pollard (Woody), William Hootkins (Teddy), Janet Wright (Fanny).

On a "little trip back to the islands," Cynthia and her friends come across the slightly unhinged "Ma" and "Pa," who are caught up in a psychological time warp ("It's like we just walked into the 1920s"); their grown-up daughter Fanny ("I'm gonna be 12"); their son Woody, his older brother Teddy, and "baby," a mummified thing. ("Kiss her goodnight.") Soon, Ma and the kids are taking knitting needles, hatchets, and jump-rope nooses to Cynthia's "wicked," heathen friends.... A mechanical wringing of the macabre-infantile for the small all it's worth. Short on integrity; long on broad, campy meet-the-loonies chuckles. Lots of "Land sakes!" Steiger, for better or worse, seems to be taking the silly goings-on seriously.

**AMERICAN NIGHTMARE** see *Combat Shock*

**AMERICAN NINJA 2: THE CONFRONTATION** Cannon/Golan-Globus 1987 color 89m. D: Sam Firstenberg. Story, SP: Gary Conway. SP: also James Booth. Mus: George S. Clinton. SpFxSup: Paul Staples. MkpSup: Louis Lazzara. Ref: TV. V 5/13/87. HR 5/5/87. With Michael Dudikoff, Steve James, Larry Poindexter, Conway, Ralph Draper.

Blackbeard Island, the West Indies. By injecting DNA into his human subjects, Professor Sanborn (Draper), or Sanborne, creates "attacking monsters"—the "super-ninja, the ultimate fighting machine," in which steel replaces muscle and sinew.... Sf/action feature with mostly lackluster stunt work—lots of shots of bodies falling onto breakaway tables. The one amusing note: James's "Let's party!" glee at the slightest prospect of a little roughhousing.

The **AMERICAN SCREAM** Genesis HV (Levine-Linden) 1988 color 85m. SP, D: Mitchell Linden. Mus: Richard Cox. Ref: V 5/18/88: "reasonably neat production values." 1/27/88:26. no Hound. no Martin. no Scheuer. With Kevin Kaye, Jennifer Darling, Kimberlee Kramer, Edy Williams, Blackie Dammett, Pons Marr.

"Horror tricks."

**AMERICAN WAY, The** see *Riders on the Storm*

**AMITYVILLE II: THE POSSESSION** (3) see also *Amityville 1993*

**AMITYVILLE: THE EVIL ESCAPES** NBC-TV/Steve White Prods. & Spectacor Films 1989 color c90m. (*Amityville 4: The Evil Escapes* - vt ad t). Tel, D, Exec Co-P: Sandor Stern, from John G. Jones's book. Mus: Rick Conrad. PD: K. B. Stern. SpFX: Richard Stutsman. Mkp: Bob Arrollo. Ref: TV. V Mifed'89:122. 5/31/89:63. Hound. Martin. vc box. With Patty Duke, Jane Wyatt, Fredric Lehne, Lou Hancock, Brandy Gold, Geri Betzler, Norman Lloyd, Alex Rebar, John Debello.

From Amityville, New York, with anything but love. Father Manfred (Lloyd): "It's gone. He's quit the house." And he travels via a standing lamp. (Transmigration.) "That old lamp has been doing funny things lately." Then, chainsaw horrors in the basement ("It started by itself!") and levitating children.... Drearily familiar, heavy-handed thrills in this continuation of the *Amityville* chronicles.

See also: *Amityville 1992.*

The **AMITYVILLE CURSE** (Can.) Vidmark/Allegro Films (First Films/Franco Battista) 1989 color 91m. D: Tom Berry. SP: Michael Krueger, Norvell Rose, from Hans Holzer's book. Mus: M. Kymlicka. Ref: V 5/9/90:62(hv): "rather tame" ... "poltergeist phenomena," possessed woman. 2/21/90:108(ad). 10/18/89:24. McCarty II: "tedious." Hound. Martin. With Kim Coates, Dawna Wightman, Helen Hughes, Jan Rubes, Ted A. Bohus.

**AMITYVILLE 1992: IT'S ABOUT TIME** Republic HV(A-5/White-Bernardi/DeFaria) 1992 color 91m. D: Tony Randel. SP: Christopher DeFaria, Antonio Toro. Story: John G. Jones, inspired by his book *Amityville: The Evil Escapes.* Ph: Christopher Taylor. Mus: Daniel Licht. PD: Kim Hix. SpMkpFX: KNB. VisFX: VCE/Peter Kuran. Ref: TV. SFChron Dtbk 7/12/92:58. TVG. Martin. V 3/16/92:13(rated). With Stephen Macht, Shawn Weatherly, Megan Ward, Damon Martin, Jonathan Penner, Nita Talbot, Dean Cochran, Dick Miller.

"Our living room turned into another room"—just another example of the outside-of-time hallucinations and "looking back in time" visions which the "creepy" antique clock from Amityville inspires. At the end, the clock fast-forwards, and our heroine ages instantly. Meanwhile, the "evil force" at work also takes the form, variously, of a blob (which doubles as burning quicksand), a naughty mirror-image, and a dog "possessed by a demonic force."

Theme: Evil needs a new home. First big cliche: The Dog Knows. Odd: the fake-bird-beak gore. Yucky: the hero's bleeding, dog-bitten, spiked leg. In sum: Evil becomes indistinguishable from Camp.

See also: *Amityville: The Evil Escapes.*

**AMITYVILLE 1993: THE IMAGE OF EVIL** Republic/Ninety-Three Prods. (Chris DeFaria) 1993 color feature (aka *Amityville: A New Generation*). D: John Murlowski. SP: DeFaria, Antonio Toro. Ph: Wally Pfister. Ref: V 1/11/93:24. 2/22/93:A-122: screening at AFM. 5/3/93:18 (rated). SFChron Dtbk 10/31/93: "different angles." With Ross Partridge, Julia Nickson-Soul, LaLa Sloatman, David Naughton, Richard Roundtree, Terry O'Quinn.

Haunted mirror, "gore murders" (SFC).

**AMON SAGA** (J) Toei Video 1986 anim color 74 1/2m. Ref: TV: Tohokushinsha HV; no Eng.

Fairish, vaguely Norse-based mythology re a warrior that transforms into a huge, toothy ogre ... a huge fish/sea monster ... a huge armored warrior, or living armor, destroyed by mystic flames ... a flying flame serpent from a mystic's forehead ... and dragon/horse flying mounts. Stilted animation, striking design. Note especially the reflection of the son in his wounded mother's spreading bloodstain.

**AMOR ES UNA FARSA, EL** see *Macho Bionico, El*

**AMSTERDAMNED** (Dutch) Vestron/Concorde (First Floor) 1988 color 113m. SP, D, Mus: Dick Maas. SpMkpFX: Sjoerd Didden. SpFX: Graham Longhurst, Martin Gutteridge. Ref: TV: dubbed Eng. MFB'89:200-201. SFChron 11/23/88. HR 12/1/88. V 2/24/88. ad. With Huub Stapel, Monique Van den Ven, Serge-Henri Valcke, Wim Zomer.

"It came out of the water!" Is it a "big black monster with huge claws," or a "psycho killer" at large in Amsterdam's famed canals? The serial killer proves to be a radiation-disfigured diver exacting "revenge on society".... Slick but dismayingly routine action-suspenser. The setpiece speedboat chase is borrowed from *Puppet on a Chain* (1971), while the sequence in which one victim's bloody body smears the top of a glass tour boat seems simply showing-off. Director Maas provides his own John Carpenter-like score.

**ANAK NG DEMONYO** (Fili) Seiko Films/Robbie Tan 1989 color c104m. SP, D: Mauro Gia Samonte. From Pablo S. Gomez's serial comic. Ph: R. Buenaseda. Mus: Benny Medina. PD: Toto Castillo. SpMkp: Cecil Del Mundo. SpFX: Nesty Ramirez. SdFX: Danny Salvador. Ref: TV: vt; no Eng.; Demon Son - tr t. With Ricky Belmonte, Liza Lorena, Joel Torre, Harlene Bautista, Michael Locsin, Ian Veneracion, Jennifer Sevilla, Lucy Quinto.

Devil's horns appear on the head of a baby, Devon Rey, and he is baptized. A few years later, his mother tries and fails to smother her little demon boy with a pillow. He cries, and she relents and holds him. As a hairy, horned teen, he meets a fellow, all-bad demon, who taunts him. Devon seems only half-bad, but humans' fear of him drives him to kill. At the end, he fights the other demon.... Serious, silly horror-fantasy. Devon wavers between human and demon form, though a tirelessly and tiresomely devoted blind girl seems to have a humanizing influence on him whatever form he happens to take.

**ANAK NI ZUMA** (Fili) Cine Suerte 1987 color c115m. *(Zuma 2. Hell Serpent* - alt ts). SP, D: Ben Yalung. SP: also Tony A. Calvento. Story: Jim Fernandez. Ph: E. Dominguez. Mus D: V. Saturno. SpFX: Tony Gozalves. Mkp: Tita Dominguez. Ref: TV: Viva Home Video; little English. Monster! 3:57-8. With Max Laurel (Zuma), Dang Cecilio, Lorraine Schuck, Mark Gil, Jenny Lyn (Galema), Sonny Erang (Dino), Sharon Hughes.

In this sequel to *Zuma*, snake-beast Zuma's daughter Galema marries and has a baby. Zuma, disappointed that the latter looks human, impregnates another woman, and she gives birth to a thing that looks like a man with a dinosaur head and tail—hence its name, Dino. One of Galema's snake heads bites Dino, and he is placed in a zoo. ("The capture of the century," as a TV reporter puts it, in the one English-language passage in the movie.) At the end, Zuma kills his rebellious son, then is himself apparently slain by the army.

Between them, *Zuma* and *Anak ni Zuma* ring just about every change that can be rung on biological crosses between humans and snakes. The two movies have the fascination of a strange natural—or unnatural—history. Don't ask how it happens that Zuma's grandkid is wholly human, while, physically at least, Galema resembles Zuma—morally, she is his opposite—and Zuma's male progeny, Dino, doesn't resemble any other family member. Further, the Zumas are not made in the image of their god, a sort of pterodactyl to whom Zuma is, at one point, seen praying.

The family tree of the film itself would have to include *Xtro* and *Son of Godzilla*—*Anak Ni Zuma* more or less fuses the charms of the latter with the horrors of the former. It's too gory to be dismissed as pure camp, too outlandish to be considered straight gore. When phylogenic invention fails here, the script throws in more gore or more snakes and, in one late scene, introduces a cavern full of apparently irrelevant monsters. The movie is at its best with inimitable details such as the snake trunks around Galema's neck tensing in the presence of papa.

**ANAL LEAP** Zane 1991 color 71m. D: Jim Enright. Ref: Adam '93. With Alicyn Sterling, Carolyn Monroe, T. T. Boy, Natasha.

Time-jumping parody of "Quantum Leap."

**ANALNATION** Coast to Coast 1990 color 80m. (aka *Anal Nation*). D: William Black. Ref: vc box: "special race of aliens." Adam '91. With Paulina Peters, Bionca (alien).

**ANALNATION 2: THE DP ZONE** 1993? color feature. D: William Black. Ref: vc box: "alien lust." With Kelly Blue, Ashley Nicole.

**\*The ANATOMIST** Towers of London 1961. D, P: Dennis Vance. Adap: Denis Webb. Ph: Lionel Banes. AD: Duncan Sutherland. Ref: TV. Jim Shapiro. Scheuer.

Edinburgh. When Dr. Knox (Alastair Sim) needs a "good fresh young, juicy corpse," he goes to Burke (Diarmuid Kelly) and Hare (Michael Ripper), who not only find corpses, but sometimes create them .... TV adaptation of a wordy play offers the bizarre spectacle of fine actors adrift in what's little more than a lazily photographed stage play. They do, however, provide some fine moments — Kelly makes a most intimidating Burke — but this isn't *The Body Snatcher*, or even *Mania*. Sim's juiciest line (re a cadaver): "Your friend will now be improving the minds of the youth of the town, in place of corrupting their morals."

**AND THE WALL CAME TUMBLING DOWN** (B) Fox Mystery Theatre/Fox & Hammer-TV 1985 (1984) color c90m. D: Paul Annett. SP: Dennis Spooner, John Peacock. Ph: Frank Watts. Mus: Anthony Payne. AD: Heather Armitage; Steve Hardie. Mkp: Eddie Knight. Ref: TV. TVG. no Scheuer. Ecran F 50:13. With Barbi Benton, Gareth Hunt, Brian Deacon, Carol Royle, Peter Wyngarde, Ralph Michael, Peter Baldwin.

Back in the early 17th century, a "black magic coven" took over now-deconsecrated St. Peter's Church, and the latter became a "center for psychic-religious phenomena." Now, in the 20th century, one of the satanists (Wyngarde) is resurrected and plots to fulfill an epic vision of destruction.... A prologue/flashback to 1649 London gives away the mystery here before its starts, which leaves only limp action and suspense and a tacky musical score. Benton has a sexy-sweet face but a flat, charmless voice.

**AND YOU THOUGHT YOUR PARENTS WERE WEIRD** Trimark/Just Betzer (Panorama Film Int'l.) 1992 (1991) color 95m. SP, D: Tony Cookson. Mus: Randy Miller. SpRobot: Rick Lazzarini. SpVisFX: The Hunter Group. SdFxSup: John K. Adams. Robotic voice: Frank Dietz. Ref: TV. SFExam 1/10/92. V 12/23/91. ad. With Marcia Strassman, Joshua Miller, Edan Gross, Alan Thicke (Newman's voice).

"I'm every kid's dream come true." Sf-fantasy-comedy re a dead man whose spirit returns a "super long distance" to animate his two sons' robot, called "Newman." ("Because he's gonna be a new man someday.") Newman/Dad gives himself a voice, gains some "robot intuition," then (as the story switches from fantasy to sf, or thereabouts) shows Josh (Miller) and Max (Gross) how to improve their robot. Obvious comedy and sentiment, syrupy score.

**ANDRO-MELOS** see *Melos*

**ANDROMEDA STORIES** (J) 1982 anim color 85m. Ref: TV: Vap Video; no Eng.

Ingredients in this lively, gizmo-and-monster-oriented science-and-sorcery saga include dragons, dinosaurish mounts, a tentacle-and-ray machine, huge war machines, giant ray-shooting robots, ray-spitting bat robots which shed their wings and burrow into their victims' skulls, mechanical spiders which burrow into foreheads, a "spider" assembly line (manned by robots), androids, vicious monkey men, spaceships, tanks, helicopters, and a huge tyrannosaurus-type. Attractively if crudely animated.

**ANDY AND THE AIRWAVE RANGERS** RCA-Col HV (Roger Corman/Jed Horovitz) 1990 (1989) color 74m. (aka *Andy Colby's Incredibly Awesome Adventure*). SP, D: Deborah Brock. SP: also J. Horovitz. Mus: E. Troost, J. Horner. Ref: V 1/10/90:32 (hv): "an unfortunate excuse to recycle stock footage." 2/21/90:147. vc box. With Randy Josselyn, Jessica Puscas, Dianne Kay, Bo Svenson.

Lord Chroma kidnaps girl to bring color to his TV realm.

**ANDY GRIFFITH SHOW, The** see *Return to Mayberry*

**ANEMIA** (I) RAI-TV Channel 3 1986 color 87m. SP, D: Alberto Abruzzese, Achille Pisanti. From Abruzzese's novel. Mus: Lorenzo Ferrero. Ref: V 10/22/86: "runs bloodless quite a while before the vampires appear." Jones. Palmerini. With Hanns Zischler, Gioia Maria Scola, Gerard Landry.

"The abandoned family manor, a classic haunted house...."

**ANG MAHIWAGANG DAIGDIG NI ELIAS PANIKI** (Fili) Golden Lions Film (Mel Pozon) c1989 color c105m. SP, D, Exec Co-P: Carlo J. Caparas. Ph: Ramon Marcelino. Mus D, SdFX: Demet Velasquez. PD: Gabby Francisco. Mkp: Mely Shozon? Opt: Gerry Garcia. Ref: TV: vt; no Eng. With Ramon Revilla, Maria Isabel Lopez, Atong Redillas, Ruel Vernal, Bomber Moran, Tina Godinez.

An epidemic of monsters, including an antsy, big-winged bat demon (the big cheese, apparently) ... a vampiric were-pig woman (who's staked) ... a huge, horned, big-clawed, cackling, tackily constructed but intimidating skeleton (when its head is removed, the possessed woman with "Elias Paniki" burned onto her dress is freed) ... a big, bare-chested vampire with unstakeable skin ... bear or wolf-headed creatures ... and vicious dwarfs. Behind it all: devil worshipers. On his headband, the hero wears a rubber bat which glows when Evil is near, which is often in this scrappy but lively horror-fantasy. The were-pig and the skeleton are the most entertaining monsters, but even they wear out their welcome with their limited shticks.

**ANG PAGBABALIK NI PEDRO PENDUKO** (Fili) Viva Family Ent. (William C. Leary) 1994 color c130m. SP, D: J. Erastheo Navoa. SP: also Ely Matawaran. Story: F.V. Coching. Ph: Ben Lobo. PD: Ben Payumo. VisFX: Cinemagic;(sup) Carlos Lacap. Mkp: Rey Salamat. SpFX: Bobby Pineda. SdFX: Jun Martinez. Ref: TV: Viva Video; occ. Eng. vc box: best VisFX, '94 Metro Manila Film Fest. With Janno Gibbs, Chiquito, Vina Morales, Leo Martinez, Donita Rose, Robert Miller (zombie leader).

Ingredients: a flying fireball which gorily burns through a man's torso ... big-winged-and-tailed demons which capture children and threaten the hero (bug, or bat, spray knocks 'em out) ... a fiery creature from a fireball ... a horse creature ... the main devil, who doubles as cheerleader ("Give me an 'R'! ") ... a cave full of various things ... zombie warriors who die and promptly return to life ... and Captain Barbell and Darna bits.... Routine, occasionally amusing Filipino fantasy. Much comic mugging. Even the demons are treated comically.

**ANGE NOIR, L'** see *Intruder, The* (1979)

**ANGEL COP 3** (J) Soeishinsha Co. 1989 anim color 30m. Ref: TV: Japan HV; no Eng. Animag 9:4: OAV; 3rd of 6; ESPers. V. Max 4:3: sfa *New Angel Cop*?

Talk, tough-guy cliches, a cyborg who can take any number of bullets, and gruesome police third-degree tactics.

**ANGEL HEART** Tri-Star/Carolco (Winkast-Union) 1987 color 113m. SP, D: Alan Parker. From William Hjortsberg's novel *Falling Angel*. Mus: Trevor Jones. SpMkpFX: Robert Laden. SpFxSup: J. C. Brotherhood. Ref: TV. SFExam 3/6/87. SFChron 3/6/87. Berk. Voice 3/26/87. MFB'87:297. V 3/4/87. ad. With Mickey Rourke, Robert De Niro (Lucifer), Lisa Bonet, Charlotte Rampling.

"It's ugly." New York, 1955. Louis Cyphre (De Niro) hires detective Harold Angel (Rourke) to find out if his client Johnny Favorite, aka Liebling, is alive. ("I don't like messy accounts.") Angel discovers that Johnny was engaged to Mme. Krusemark (Rampling), the Witch of Wellesley, a "real creepy" fortune teller, in 1943; that Johnny's other girlfriend ran a "spooky store," Mammy Carter's Herb Store; and that the other girl's daughter (Bonet) is a mambo priestess. Finally, the once-shell-shocked Harold discovers that Louis is Lucifer; that he, Harold, is really Johnny; and that twelve years ago, he sold his soul for fame by sacrificing the life of a soldier, Angel, and eating the latter's heart. ("For twelve years, you've been living on borrowed time, in another man's memories.")

That's a lot of discovering. What it all means, essentially, is that the story took place twelve years earlier and that the viewer spends 100-plus minutes watching Mickey Rourke look for it. The above "payoff"—really a concealed premise—is certainly loopy enough for any allegorical mystery, but until it comes, the movie simply marks time with bloody murders and cute word-play with people's names.

**ANGEL OF DARKNESS** (J) SoftCel/Pink Pineapple (Jiro Soka) 1994 anim color c50m. D: Kanenari Tokiwa. Ph: H. Yanagida. Mus: Nakazawa. AD: K. Muraki. SpFX: T. Maekawa. Ref: TV: SoftCel video; Eng. titles. Voice: M. Naito (Goda).

Ingredients here include an "it" which likes the "extract of younger women" (a cellar full of bound, nubile young women is kept producing) ... the Dark Elemental, a guy who's really a mass of tentacles that lives on human lust ... and funny-looking little sex/sadism gnomes.... Forced, heart-not-really-in-it perversity in this hardcore cartoon.

**ANGEL OF DEATH** (F) New World/Daniel Lesoeur (A.L. Mariaux) 1986 color 92m. D: Jesus Franco. SP: Freed, Mariaux, Khunn. SpFX: S.O.I.S.; J.M. Costa. OptFX: M. Ray. SdFX: B. Klaus. Ref: TV: New World Video (Eurocine); Eng. dubbed. McCarty II. Hound. Scheuer: "atrocious." Martin. With Fernando Rey, Chris Mitchum, Jack Taylor, Howard Vernon, Dora Doll, Suzanne Andrews.

Dr. Mengele's (Vernon) genetic experiments produce a "chimpman" (McC). "The best are down below, in my clinic." Unfortunately, the movie's budget didn't permit us to see Mengele's "best." Even the semihorrific payoffs in this colorless actioner are timid: a man with a chimp arm and a man with chimp fur on the side of his face, both hybrid products of the doc's experiments in genetics and artificial insemination. Even *The Unearthly* did it better.

**ANGEL OF DESTRUCTION** (Fili) New Horizons (Cirio Santiago) 1994 color 80m. SP, D: C.P. Moore. Ref: PT 20:14: remake of *Black Belt*; "big scary, dead eyed mercenary psycho." Martin: "familiar." SFChron 6/4/94: "doesn't make a lick of sense." With Chanda, Maria Ford, Charlie Spradling, Jessica Mark, Jimmy Broome.

"Sadistic serial killer ... likes to dress up women in bridal gowns and then slit their throats."(SFC)

**The ANGEL'S EGG** (J) Studio Deen (Tatsumi Yamashita, Hideo Ogata) 1986? anim color 71m. SP, D: Mamoru Oshii. Ph: Shigeo Sugimura. Mus: Yoshihiro Kanno. AD: Shichiro Kobayashi. SpFX: Go Abe. Ref: TV: vt; no Eng. J Anim Program Guide. Paul Lane. Animag 9:11.

A giant spaceship lands in the ocean of an egg-shaped world, where a wandering waif protects a huge egg. A young man smashes the egg, and she drowns, but the ship—which apparently harbors the planet's dead—emerges from the sea, and she, or her spirit, is seen to have a special place among the unmoving figures.... A haunting, poetic, melancholic science-fantasy film, and—for non-Japanese-speaking viewers at least—a very cryptic one. The intent appears simply to have been to create, out of general themes of birth and death, a visually intoxicating work. The story lies as much in patterns made by night lights on the surface of a pond, and by reflections of passing clouds in half-pulled-open windows, as it does in the wanderings of the heroine. City streets, country streams, and the sky seem to overlap or merge; ghostly, implacably moving shadows of zeppelin-sized fish haunt a town. Two astonishing throwaway moments in this surreal travelogue: the wind ruffling the grass ... feathers-from-nowhere-in-particular flying up around and about the hero. The film is in the slow dreamlike movement of the clouds, the fish, and the camera itself.

See also: *In the Aftermath.*

**ANGST** (Austrian) Gerald Kargl 1984 color 82m. SP, D: Kargl. SP, Ph: Zbigniew Rybczynski. Mus: Klaus Schulze. Ref: V 4/18/84. Ecran F 46:64. With Erwin Leder (the killer), Edith Rosset, Sylvia Rabenreither.

"Psychological blood and gore feature" re an ex-con who goes on a 24-hour killing spree, drinks the blood of one victim.

**ANGUISH** (Sp) Spectra Film (Ramaco Anstalt)/Samba & Luna (Coromino) 1987 (1986/'88-U.S.) color 85m. (*Angustia*), SP, D: Bigas Luna. Dial: Michael Berlin. Mus: J. M. Pagan. SpFX: Paco Teres. Mkp: Matilde Fabregat. Ref: TV: Key Video. V 5/6/87. Strand Theatre, S. F. 5/5/88. With Zelda Rubinstein, Michael Lerner, Talia Paul, Angel Jove.

Culver City, California. Pretty good real-life/reel-life fun, with no depth but more savvy than the similar *Demons*. The 1925 *Lost World* is playing at the Roxy in "The Mommy"; "The Mommy" is playing at the Rex in *Anguish*. Killers lurk in both theaters and, at one point, three separate mobs run wild, in *Anguish*, in "The Mommy," and in *The Lost World*, respectively. The Rex killer apparently takes the Roxy's killer's problems too much to heart,

or head, and he too begins waiting for "Mommy." The Roxy killer: "Like the doctor said, it's all in your imagination. I really don't exist." Some wit and ingenuity at work here, but not much resonance.

**The ANIMAL TRAINER** (Cuban) Noel Lima 1991? anim short. Ref: SFChron Dtbk 4/26/92: "amusing."

A cave man teaches his dinosaur tricks.

**The ANIMAL WITHIN** Wolper Pictures (Mel Stuart, Robert Larson) 1974 color 84m (aka *Up from the Ape*). D: Stuart, Walon Green. SP: Robert Ardrey, from his works "African Genesis," "The Territorial Imperative," and "The Social Contract." Ph: David Myers, Al Kihn. Mus: Lalo Schifrin. SpAstronomical FX: Graphic Films. Early Man: (vis concep) Tom Wright; (mkp) John Chambers, Tom Burman. Ref: TV: shown as movie; Orbis-TV. BIB. PFA library. With Anthony Zerbe; Janos Prohaska, Robert Prohaska, Jerry Gatlin (dominant Early Men).

Film begins in the Miocene, with depictions of our ancestor, the "walking ape," and a note on the first invention, the weapon; flash-forward to the man apes of the Pliocene; continues with the Neanderthal Man, "citizen of the Ice Age" and "cave man of legend"; spends some time with Cro-Magnon Man; then winds up in the present, with emphasis on the human bent to hunt and kill its own kind. Limp, humorless combo make-up showcase and—in Zerbe's dry narration—capsule prehistory. Some of these apes must have been watching *2001.*

**ANIMATO** see *Wizard of Speed and Time, The*

**ANKOU** see *Spiral*

**ANNA TO THE INFINITE POWER** Ned Kandel & Film Gallery/Blue Marble 1982 color 105m. SP, D, Exec P: Robert Weimer. From Mildred Ames' book. Ph: Glenn Kershaw. Mus: Paul Baillargeon. AD: Shela Oakey. Mkp: Carla White. Ref: TV. Stanley. no V. no Hardy/SF. With Dina Merrill, Martha Byrne (Anna Hart), Mark Patton, Donna Mitchell (Michaela), Jack Gilford (Dr. Jelliff).

Anna Zimmerman (1931-1958) is cloned and "reborn" as Anna Hart, thanks to the former's replicator. This "unique experiment" is supposed to produce more Anna Zimmermans. But the new Anna begins to "individualize" and lose interest in science and math. ("Anna, you've changed.") All the Anna clones (six at least) wind up on Albacore Island, where the idea seems to be to "get rid of them" since none will be another Anna Zimmerman.... Dialogue-choked, can't-buy-it speculations on the theme of cloning, plus stilted pathos re the thawing of Anna H. ("I'm not a human being—I'm an experiment!")

**ANNE PEDERSDOTTER** see *Day of Wrath*

**The ANNIHILATOR** NBC-TV/Univ-TV 1986 color 92m. D: Michael Chapman. Sp, Exec P: Roderick Taylor. SP: also Bruce A. Taylor. Ph: Paul Goldsmith. Mus: Sylvester Levay, Udi. AD: Kirk Axtell. Mkp: Michael Westmore. Ref: TV. TVG. V 4/23/86:86. Stanley. With Mark Lindsay Chapman, Catherine Mary Stewart, Susan Blakely, Lisa Blount, Geoffrey Lewis, Brion James, Paul Brinegar.

"What I killed wasn't really Angela." A "coldness" in Angela (Stewart) is the first tipoff for our hero (Chapman). ("I kill robots.") Glowing eyes are also a bad sign. The proliferating robots prove to be products of "dynarogeny." Are "beings from another planet" behind it all? Glib cross between *V* and *The Terminator*. Undernourished plot, occasional visual flourishes.

**EL ANO DE LA PESTE** (Mex) Conacite Dos 1978 color c98m. D: Felipe Cazals. SP: Gabriel Garcia Marquez, from Daniel Defoe's *A Journal of the Plague Year.* SP: also J. A. Brennan. Dial: Jose Agustin, Marquez, Brennan. Ph: Javier Cruz. AD: G. Hernandez, R. Brizuela. SpFX: Marcelino Pacheco. Mkp: Antonio Ramirez. SdFX: Gonzalo Gavira. Ref: TV: Million Dollar Video; no Eng.; *The Year of the Plague* - tr t. Horacio Higuchi. Cinef 6/96:47.TVG: 1979. With Daniela Romo, Alejandro Parodi, Jose Carlos Ruiz, Narciso Busquets, Tito Junco, Arlette Pacheco, Rebeca Silva.

As the plague sweeps modern-day Mexico, CNPI contamination crews spray yellow foam into infected households, and modernistic living-room bric-a-brac seems to be afloat in a surreal sea. The (living) inhabitants are led out wearing big bags. Bodies litter public plazas, then are dragged away, tossed into dumpers, and bulldozed into mass graves. Then, of course, the yellow foam.... Grim, low-key horror story recalls, in its scenes of implacably spreading disease, *Rabid, The Crazies, The Andromeda Strain, The People Who Own the Dark, Isle of the Dead,* parts of either *Nosferatu,* etc., yet has a look and feel of its own. The horror here is quietly cumulative and not dependent on sensationalistic makeup effects. The foam and the profusion of bodies are simply, suggestively obscene.

See also: *Miedos, Los* (P).

**ANNO 2020** see *2020: Texas Gladiators*

**ANOTHER FLIP FOR DOMINICK** (B) 1982 color 90m.

Sequel to *Flipside of Dominick Hyde, The,* which see.

**ANOTHER WILD IDEA** MGM (Roach) 1934 b&w 20m. D: Charley Chase (aka C. Parrott), Eddie Dunn. Ref: Maltin/SSS. Lee. LC. With Chase, Betty Mack, Frank Austin; Billy Gilbert (voice).

Ray gun which eliminates subject's inhibitions.

**ANTIPOLO MASSACRE** (Fili) Golden Lion Films 1994 color c100m.? (aka *The Cecilia Masagea Story: Antipolo Massacre Jesus Save Us!*). D: C.J. Caparas. Ref: TV: Viva Video; occ. Eng.

The apparently based-on-fact massacre—in which the killer "systematically and ruthlessly hacked all the victims to death"—is a long time coming here. And it's horrific enough, but not especially convincingly staged. A "possessed bolo" supposedly led the killer to become the killer, and his spirit is said to walk the countryside.

**APEX** Republic & Green Commun. (Talaat Captan/Gary Jude Burkart) 1993 color c103m. Story,SP,D: P.J. Roth. SP: also R. Schmidt. Story: also G. Scandiuzzi. Ph: Mark W. Gray. Mus: Jim Goodwin. PD: B.B. Jackson, Grant Fausey. SpVisFX: Ultra Matrix. Robot Des: David Douglas. SpMkp: Altered Anatomy.

Computer Anim: Tim Douglas. SpProps: Edward Sussman. SpFX: Vincent Borgese. Morph Seqs: Rodney L'Ongnion. SdDes: Joseph Zappala. OptFxSup: Greg Kimble. Ref: TV. PT 19:16: "good sound effects." With R. Heats, M. Cox, Lisa Ann Russell, Marcus Aurelius, Adam Lawson, Anna B. Choi; Gordon Capps et al (robots).

Datatron Research Center's probe 100 years into the past — through the Time Portal — results in a "paradox," an altered year 2073, where "sterilization units" from the original, more peaceful 2073 wreak robotic havoc .... Fine "absorption" effects, as people disappear into the woodwork, and a neat time-lapse-like effect with buildings. But mostly sf and action cliches.

**APPLEGATES, The** see *Meet the Applegates*

**APPLESEED** (J) Tohokushinsha, Bandai & MOVIC (Gainax & A.I.C.) 1988? anim color 68m. From Shirow Masamune's comic. Ref: TV: Tohokushinsha HV; no Eng. Animag 5 insert.

In the post-World War III 21st century, Aegis runs the computer-controlled utopian city of Olympus, which abounds in weird-looking machines, like the landmates—robotic armor—and Briareos, part-human, part-cyborg partner of heroine Deunan Knute. Okay nonstop sf-actioner.

**The APPOINTMENT** (B) Sony Video/ First Principle (Tom Sachs) 1982 color c90m. SP, D: Lindsey C. Vickers. Ph: Brian West. Mus: Trevor Jones. PD: Michael Stringer. SpFxSup: George Gibbs. Mkp: Pauline Heys. Titles: Graphimation. Ref: TV. V 5/19/82:47(ad). S&S'82:262. Screen Int'l 8/1/81. Academy. Ecran F 26:74. no Hardy/HM. no Stanley. Newman. With Edward Woodward, Jane Merrow, Samantha Weysom, John Judd, Alan Stewart, Auriol Goldingham.

Ian Fowler (Woodward) discovers that his job will take him out of town the day of his 14-year-old daughter Joanne's (Weysom) violin recital. The night before, he and his wife Dianna (Merrow) have prophetic dreams of a crash in a borrowed car, and the disappointed Joanne seems, in her sleep, to be influencing the dreams.... The main cross reference here *Forbidden Planet,* not *Carrie.* Unconsciously, Joanne exacts her revenge on her (she feels) uncaring father, whom she adores. During the night, petals fall from a vased bunch of just-picked roses. A desktop photograph of Joanne and her father alters. (She turns away from him.) Three or four stray dogs haunt the neighborhood. The headlights of the loaner blink on in the garage, then dim and die, as Ian awakes from a nightmare....

On the road, he has visions of a narrow winding road, and the sound of squealing tires intrudes on roadside cafe Muzak. After stopping briefly later, he has trouble starting the car. As he finally succeeds in turning the key in the ignition, the key in the car which he left at the shop also turns, and the gears savage the mechanic working under the car. One phone call home is just missed, another cut short when coins jam a pay phone, and vital dream data re a seat belt is lost.

*The Appointment* has a dreamlike, zig-zag plot. Joanne's psychic energy overflows and touches not just her father, but objects connected with him—his watch, his car keys, a photograph. At one point—in a nondream scene—one of the apples which Ian has taken with him, rolling loose, falls "up" through a hole in the windshield of a smashed-up car—the first indication of just how precarious a position he's in. The stopping of his wristwatch signals the beginning of his first nightmare. Later, he leaves the watch behind in a phone booth by the road. The sight of his bare wrist nags at him, until he makes the U-turn which insures that he will keep "the appointment." As he drives back toward the booth, the film cuts to closer and closer shots of the watch, until one can make out the words, "My dear Daddy, always, Love, Joanne."

**APPOINTMENT WITH FEAR** Galaxy Int'l. (Tom Boutross/Akkad) 1985 color 98m. SP, D: Ramzi Thomas. SP: also Bruce Meade. Mus: A. Saparoff. SpFX: J. Westcott, Scott Hass. Mkp: Mary Resnik. Ref: V 10/30/85: "nearly incomprehensible." Horacio Higuchi. Ecran F 63:70. Scheuer. Phantom. With Michele Little, Michael Wyle, Kerry Remsen, Garrick Dowhen.

God Attis can "raise himself out of a dream state." (V)

**APRIL FOOL'S DAY** Para/Hometown 1986 color/ws 89m. D: Fred Walton. SP: Danilo Bach. Mus: Charles Bernstein. SpFX: (coord) Martin Becker; (mkp) Reel EFX et al. SdFX: F. H. Miller. Ref: TV. V 3/26/86. SFExam 3/28/86. MFB'88:135-6. With Jay Baker, Pat Barlow, Deborah Foreman, Griffin O'Neal.

"This is like an Agatha Christie"—deserted island, unseen host, young guests. *And Then There Were None*, anyone? Does Muffy (Foreman) have a mad twin sister, Buffy? No—April Fool! Script concentrates more on the discovery of murder victims than on the murders themselves, and for good reason: All victims turn up alive at the end, in a predictable but pleasing "surprise" ending. Okay photography (Charles Minsky) and editing (Bruce Green), but very formulaic script.

**APRIL FOOL'S DAY** see *Slaughter High*

**AQUARIUS** see *Stagefright—Aquarius*

**AQUELLARRE DE VAMPIROS** see *Llamada del Vampiro*

**ARABELLA, THE BLACK ANGEL** (I) ARPA Int'l. 1987 color 89m. (*Arabella l'Angelo Nero. Black Angel* - cr t). D: Stelvio Massi (aka Max Steel). SP: R. Filippucci. Ph: Catalano. Mus: Serfran. Sets: Ferrero. Mkp: Marisa Marconi. SdFX: D'Angeli. Ref: TV; VSOM; Eng. version; above is ad & tr t. Hardy/HM2: 1988. MV. ETC/Giallos. Palmerini.With Tini Cansino, Valentina Visconti, Evelyn Stewart, Francesco Casale, Carlo Mucari.

"Welcome to the infernal regions!" Ingredients include a woman who believes she sometimes becomes "something out of 'Dracula,' or 'Frankenstein,' 'Dr. Jekyll and Mr. Hyde' " ... a slasher/scissorer ... a visualized nightmare re violation-by-scissors ... murder-with-mallet ... and an hallucination re a "bleeding" faucet.... Sleazy and sensationalistic, almost risibly so. (Headline: "Castrated Corpse Found in Motel.") The killer's identity is guessable.

**ARACHNOPHOBIA** BV/Hollywood Pictures & Amblin Ent. (Tangled Web) 1990 color 109m. (*Along Came a Spider* - early t). D, Exec Co-P: Frank Marshall. SP, Story, Co-P: Don Jakoby. SP: also Wesley Strick. Story: also Al Williams. Mus: Trevor Jones. SpVisFX: (sup) David Sosalla; (coord) Alison Savitch.

Creature FxSup: Chris Walas. SpFxSup: Matt Sweeney. Spider Coord: Jim Kundig. Mattes: (painting fx) Matte World; (sup art) Michael Pangrazio. Ref: TV: H'w'd Pictures HV. MFB'91:9-10. V 7/18/90. Sacto Union 7/90. Sacto Bee 7/18/90. 5/20/90:17. With Jeff Daniels, Harley Jane Kozak, John Goodman, Julian Sands, Stuart Pankin, Henry Jones.

The "general" of a "new species of spider" travels by coffin from a Venezuelan mountain where "species have survived in isolation for millions of years" to Canaima, California. It mates with a common house spider and produces poisonous hordes which act like a cross between soldier ants and "little vampires" and leave victims shriveled and drained of blood.... Doses of spider lore alternate with episodic but nerve-jangling solo spider attacks. Most imaginative bit: the doll's eyes opening and "seeing" the spider. Most predictable scene: the climax, wherein the arachnophobic hero (Daniels)—who froze at the age of two in a similar situation—acts and fries the main spider. *Kingdom of the Spiders* is still the spider-horde movie to beat.

**ARCADE** FullMoon (Cathy Gesualdo) 1993 color 85m. D: Albert Pyun. SP: Goyer. Ref: vc box: "demonic soul." With Megan Ward.

**ARCHA PANA SERVADACA** see *On the Comet*

**ARCHANGEL** (Can.) Greg Klymkiw (Andre Bennett) 1990 b&w 90m. SP, D: Guy Maddin. SP: also George Toles. Ref: V 9/17/90: "macabre ... will delight *Eraserhead* fans."

**Das ARCHE NOAH PRINZIP** (W.G.) Munich Film & TV School & Solaris & Maran 1984 color 100m. SP, D: Roland Emmerich. Mus: Hubert Bartholoma. Ref: V 2/15/84:50(ad). 3/7/84: The Noah's Ark Principle - tr t. With R. Muller, F. Buchrieser, A. Joel, Mathias Fuchs.

Weather-control experiments in 1997.

**ARENA** T.W.E./Empire (Yablans-Band) 1988 color 97m. D: Peter Manoogian. SP: Danny Bilson, Paul DeMeo. Ph: Mac Ahlberg. Mus: Richard Band. PD: Giovanni Natalucci. MkpFX: (L.A.) MMI; (coord) John Buechler; (Sloth) Screaming Mad George; Alan Munro. SpFxSup (Rome): Renato Agostini. Min: Starlight. Mkp: A. Jacoponi. OptFX: Motion. SpSdFX: Key FX. SpVoices: Frank Welker. Ref: TV. Fango 113:47. With Paul Satterfield, Hamilton camp, Claudia Christian, Marc Alaimo (Rogor), Shari Shattuck, Armin Shimerman, Michael Deak (Horn), Jack Carter, Steve Wang (Sloth).

Film poses the wry question, Is this a space movie or an old-fashioned fight film? Unfortunately, the answer is: It's a tired fight film, as Steve (Satterfield), an "earthling who can fight," takes on Horn, the alien champ of the star station. Plus: an *Xtro*-like insect creature named Sloth and much (sometimes amusing) play with Camp's Shorty's four hands.

**ARIEL VISUAL—EPISODE IV: SCEBAI** (J) Ariel Project 1990? anim color 28m. Ref: TV: Pony Canyon video; no Eng. (apart from the title); ARIEL = All Round Intercept and Escort Lady.

Atmospheric visual detail, pointy-eared alien types, a monster, space traffic, and a *Totoro* keychain.

**ARION** (J) 1986 anim color 119m. SP, D: Yoshikazu Yasuhiko. SP: also Akiko Tanaka. Mus: Mamoru Hisashi. Ref: TV: Animage Video; no Eng. J Anim Prgm Guide. Paul Lane. Voices: Shigeru Nakahara, Miki Takahashi, Oshio Otsuka (Hades), Hirotaka Suzuoki.

Monster-jammed animated epic features the deadly ray-eyed gods Gaia and Apollon, the Furies, Cerberus, a three-eyed giant, the air-and-sea monster Tyupaan, plus, less importantly, a giant slug, a giant two-headed snake, fish creatures, a Harpy air force, "snake" dogs, wolf soldiers, a stone-lion-bull monster, long-necked flying crab banshees, and (in the hero Arion's nightmares) monstrous rose bushes, a mud thing, and a Medusa-like, snake-haired Hades.... Long, involved, episodic account of the end of the age of Titans is at least incident crammed and pictorially pleasing. Among the atmospheric pictorial effects: army camp-fires, battles in the rain, elaborate storm clouds, forbidding mountains, red seas, and, most impressive of all, Tyupaan, an imposing conglomeration of wings, claws, and neck.

See also: *Magic Crystal*.

**ARISE!** The SubGenius Foundation 1989 color 84m. SP,D,Ed: Ivan Stang. D,Ph,Ed,Video FX: Cordt Holland. Mus: D.K. Jones. Ref: TV: SF vt.

"The Xs have landed." In 1953, Jehovah—"the rascal alien space God"—plucks up J.R. "Bob" Dobbs, for obscure reasons; meanwhile, "elder gods" control Dick Dobbs, Bob's evil twin. Script posits two species: humans and subgeniuses; long ago, in Atlantis, the latter "designed" humans. Script also predicts X-Day, July 5, 1998, when the mysterious Xs will land and a new era will begin .... Film alternates between staged scenes and found footage from *Invaders from Mars, Invasion of the Star Creatures, Earth Vs. the Flying Saucers, Metropolis, Phantom from Space, Robot Monster, Haxan, This Island Earth, Plan Nine from Outer Space, The Mysterians, Killers from Space, The Brainiac*, etc. Wearing satire re sociopolitical gobbledygook. The stock footage is slightly less numbing than the new material.

**ARIZONA RIPPER** see *Bridge across Time*

**El ARMA SECRETA** (Mex.) Baja Films/Goyri & Asociados & Video Producciones de Tijuana 1992 color c94m. D: Sergio Goyri. SP: Gilberto De Anda. Ph: Tim Ross. Mus: Juan Carlos Marelli, Claudio Brugger. SpMkp: Juan Carlos Manjarrez, Erika Contreras. SpFX: F. Farfan. OptFX: M. Sainz, P. Rodriguez. Ref: TV: vt; no Eng. With S. Goyri, Rafael Inclan, Telly Filippini, Rodolfo Rodriguez, Agustin Bernal (el monstruo), Alfonso Munguia, Roberto Montiel, Gilbert De Anda.

The last living Frankestein (sic) fashions a super-strong creature—complete with neck bolts and forehead scar—out of body parts from a "supermarket" freezer, in low-comedy scenes. Plus a living Cyclopean head in a jar. Amiable but elementary combo of horror, comedy, and action.

**ARMED AND DEADLY** HBO-TV? 1994 color 100m. D: John Eyres. Ref: TVG. Martin: "mindless." With Frank Zagarino (psycho-android), Bryan Genesse, Beth Toussaint.

**ARMOR HUNTER MELLOWLINK: STAGE 1: WILDERNESS** (J) VAP Video 1988-89 anim color 25m. each. Ref: Animag 5:3,5: 12 OAVs.

"Takes place in the *Armored Trooper Votoms* universe" of giant robotlike armor suits.

**ARMORED DRAGON LEGEND VILLGUST** see *Villgust*

**ARMORED TROOPER VOTOMS: BIG BATTLE** (J) 1987-88 anim color c55m. Ref: Animag 12:33: OAV.

"The Balalant Army is developing its own perfect soldier, a brutal cyborg named Niba...."

**ARMORED TROOPER VOTOMS: THE LAST RED SHOULDER** (J) Toshiba Video 1987-88 anim color 55m. each (aka *Votoms*). Based on Ryosuke Takahashi's TV series. Ref: Animag 11:42-44. 12:28-33: 1 of 3 OAVs.

Re Proto-2, a "perfect soldier" with an "artificially ingrained killer instinct."

See also: *Armor Hunter Mellowlink*.

**ARMY** see *Severed Ties*

**ARMY OF DARKNESS** Univ/De Laurentiis (Renaissance/Robert Tapert/Bruce Campbell/Introvision Int'l.) 1992 color 95m. (*Army of Darkness: Evil Dead 3*). SP, D: Sam Raimi. SP: also Ivan Raimi. Ph: Bill Pope. Mus: Joe LoDuca, Danny Elfman. PD: Tony Tremblay. VisFX: Introvision Int'l.; (d) William Mesa; (sup) Richard Malzahn; (anim) Sallie McHenry. MkpFX: Tony Gardner, Alterian, KNB. "Necronomicon" Anim: Tom Sullivan. MechFxSup: Vern Hyde. Stopmo Sup: Peter Kleinow. Sd: (des) Alan Howarth; (fx) Lance Brown et al. Ref: TV: MCA-Univ HV. V 10/19/92. 6/8/92:10 (rated). 1/14/91:18: 3/25 start. 4/5/93:46: best at Brussels. ad. SFChron 2/19/93; Dtbk 8/1/93; 2/17/83. With Bruce Campbell, Embeth Davidtz, Marcus Gilbert, Ian Abercrombie, Bridget Fonda, Patricia Tallman (witch), Bill Moseley (Deabite Captain), William Lustig, Josh Becker, Harley Cokeliss.

"Say hello to the 21st century!" Follow-up to *Evil Dead* and *Evil Dead II* finds Ash (Campbell) as the Promised One, in the "ultimate experience in Medieval horror." Effects and makeup treats this time include an army of living skeletons, a couple of monsters in a monster pit, and a winged horror.... *Army of Darkness* adopts the currently popular casual approach to sword-and-sorcery and adds imagination. It's fantasy, it's horror, but more than anything it's comedy. Biggest surprise of the climactic sequence is not anything in the battle itself, but the simple, wry presence of a skeletal fife and drum corps. Earlier, this bone motif takes the form of an informal "call to arms" of a ragtag bunch of stopmo skeletons. Candidate for Best Makeup Effect: the funhouse mirror, stretched-face look for Ash at one point. There's also a fine, funny variation on the revolting hand business in Part II, when mischievous miniature "Ashes" from mirror pieces—and, a bit later, a second Ash head and body—assail him. *Abbott and Costello Meet Frankenstein,* where are you?

**AROUSAL PLANET** 1994 color feature. Ref: Vallejo T-H 6/4/95. With Nicole London, Barbara Doll.

"Intergalactic intercourse."

**The AROUSED** Intropics 1989 color feature. D: Fox Mailer. Ref: Adam '90. With Jerry Butler, Lynn LeMay, Marc Wallice, Trinity Loren.

"Outbreak" of the "Living Horny" hordes.

**The ARRIVAL** Rapid/Del Mar Ent. (Ljoka-Matonak) 1990 color 107m. D: David Schmoeller. SP: Daniel Ljoka. Ph: Steve Grass. Mus: Richard Band. PD: Mike Scaglione. Art FX: Tim Gore. FX:(mech) Ken Tarallo;(sp) Sota EFX. Ref: TV: Prism Ent. video. Jones. Fango 111. PT 11:50: "dull movie." With John Saxon, Joseph Culp, Robin Frates, Michael J. Pollard, Stuart Gordon.

Invisible alien from meteorite possesses old man (Robert Sampson), turns him into vampire and, ultimately, a young man (Culp). ("Something may have taken over what was once your father.") Mawkish and routine except for the gradual-rejuvenation idea. Among the story cliches: 1) they don't have love where the alien comes from, and b) government officials lie to achieve their ends.

**The ART OF DYING** Pepin-Merhi (Charla Driver) 1991 color 90m. D: Wings Hauser. SP: Joseph Merhi. Ph: Richard Pepin. Mus: John Gonzalez. PD: Greg Martin. SpFxMkp: Judy Yonemoto. SpFxSup: Don Power. Ref: TV: PM HV. With W. Hauser, Kathleen Kinmont, Gary Werntz, Mitch Hara, Sarah Douglas, Michael J. Pollard, Sydney Lassick.

"My dear, I am real." A would-be horror-movie director tricks actors into appearing in his snuff film recreations of scenes from *Psycho, The Texas Chainsaw Massacre, The Deer Hunter*, etc. Very flimsy plot; limp, comically macho dialogue.

**ARTHUR THE KING** (U.S.-B?) CBS-TV/Martin Poll & Comworld 1985 (1982) color c135m. D: Clive Donner. Tel: J. D. Wyles. Ref: TVG 4/26/85. V 5/8/85:162: "nightmarish fight with an undead knight sent out by Morgan."

**ARZT OHNE GEWISSEN** see *Privat Klinik Professor Lund*

**AS TIME GOES BY** (Austral.) Valhalla/Monroe Stahr (Chris Kiely) 1987 color 97m. (*The Cricketer* - shooting t). SP, D: Barry Peak. Mus: Peter Sullivan. Ref: V 12/30/87. With Bruno Lawrence, Nique Needles, Max Gillies, Ray Barrett, Marcelle Schmitz.

"A cheerfully affectionate sci-fier about a rendezvous with an alien in Central Australia."

**ASCENSION OF THE DEMONOIDS** George Kuchar/NEA 1986 color 50m. Ref: PFA notes 10/28/86. With Rock Ross, Magdalen Ross, David Hallinger, Nick Johnson.

"Deformed earthlings, starmen in black ... Big Foot."

**El ASESINO DE MUNECAS** (Sp) Huracan Films (Jacinto Ferrer Bayarri) 1974 color/ws 103m. SP, D: Michael Skaife (aka Miguel Madrid). Ref: Hardy/HM: "chronicles the boy's necrophilia in revolting detail." With David Rocha, Inma de Santy, Helga Line.

Gardener's son murders couples, subjects the bodies to "outlandish surgical practices."

**ASESINO DEL METRO** (Mex) Prods. Latinas Americanas (O. R. Mendoza) 1990 color c90m. (aka *La Bestia Negra*). SP, D: Jose Luis Urquieta. SP: also J. Victoria. Story: A. Arvizu. Ph: Roberto Rivera. Mus: Tino Geiser. SpFX: Raul Falomir. SdFX: Gonzalo Gavira. Mkp: Graciela Munoz. Titles: F. M. Haaz. Ref: TV: no Eng. TVG. V 5/6/91:C-124: The Metro Killer - tr t. With Jorge Luke, Jorge Reynoso, Lina Santos, Jorge Victoria, Adalberto Arvizu, Miguel Gurza.

A madman murders lone women on the subway, as a *Jaws*-like theme accompanies him, and our cop hero's girlfriend is used as bait. The killer's sexual hangups are traced back to childhood, natch. In a *10 to Midnight* ending, the cop assassinates the pathetic slob. Elementary slasher movie with a treacly score.

**ASESINO NOCTURNO** (Mex) Hermanos Tamez 1987 color c80m. D: Fernando Duran. SP: Carlos Valdemar. Story: Arnulfo Benavides. Ph: Manuel Tejada. Mus: Diego Herrera. FX: (sp) Angel Perez; (incidental) Gonzalo Gavira; (opt) Manuel Sainz. Mkp: Graciela Gonzalez. Ref: TV. TVG: Nocturnal Killer - tr t. With Andres Garcia, Gregorio Casals, Edna Bolkan, Pedro Infante Jr., Alfredo Gutierrez, Doris Pabel.

The schizophrenic, Fedora-d slasher at large turns out to be a morgue physician whose partner foolishly lets on that he catches on and literally gets shafted for his troubles. A tinted flashback explains his antipathy to women. (Mom strayed; Pop shot himself.) Slack, suspenseless shocker with a vapid score and script, not-wholly-believable blood work in the violent scenes, and a touch of gore. The only, not-quite-saving grace: the standard but eerily-lit, climactic chase through the blue night fog.

**ASSASSIN** CBS-TV/Sankan 1986 color 92m. SP, D, Exec P: Sandor Stern. Mus: Anthony Guefen. PD: V. J. Cresciman. SpFX: (sup) Melbourne A. Arnold; (robot) Doug Beswick. MkpSup: Ric Sagliani. SdFxSup: Troutman & Assoc. Opt: Howard Anderson. Ref: TV. TVG. Stanley. V 4/16/86:65. With Robert Conrad, Richard Young, Karen Austin, Robert Webber, Len Birman, Nick Angotti, Chuck Courtney.

Robert Golem (Young), a "killing machine" from the Assassination Section, goes on a killing spree, ultimately self-destructs.... *The Terminator*, domesticated for TV.

**L'ASSASSINO E ANCORA TRA NOI** (I) 1985 color feature. SP,D: Camillio Teti. SP: also Ernesto Gastaldi. Mus: D. Mariano. Ref: MV: ultra-gore slasher movie. ETC/Giallos: seance. Palmerini: 1972; "Confused." With Mariangela D'Abbraccio, Giovanni Visentin.

**ASSASSINO E COSTRETTO AD UCCIDERE ANCORA** see *Killer Must Strike Again, The*

**ASSASSINO FANTASMA, L'** see *Macabre* (1968)

**ASSASSINO HA RISERVATO NOVE POLTRONE, L'** see *Killer Reserved Nine Seats, The*

Les **ASSASSINS** (F) 198-? anim 2m. D: Frederic Vitali. Ref: SFChron Dtbk 4/9/89: "slimy lizards and hairy monsters."

**ASSAULT OF THE KILLER BIMBOS** see *Cemetery High*

**ASSEMBLE INSERT** (J) Tohoku-Toei Shinsha/Warner Pioneer 1989-90 anim color 30m. each. D: Ami Tomobuki. SP: Mitsuro Shimada. Story: Masami Yuki. Mecha Des: Yutaka Izubuchi. Ref: Animag 8:3. 9:5. 10:4: 2 OAVs.

"In Japan's near future, Tokyo is threatened by the mad scientist Kyosaburo Demon and his evil society Demon Seed." Plus: a teenage girl with "superhuman powers."

**ASTOUNDING GIANT WOMAN, The** see *Attack of the 50 Foot Woman* (1958)

**ASTRO BOY** (J) Mushi/Tezuka-TV 197-? anim feature? (*Tetsu-wan Atomu*). Ref: JFFJ 13:30: from TV-series episodes; also a 1980 TV-movie (title?); "mechanical kid."

**ASTRONOMEOUS or ASTRONOMEOWS** see *Felix the Cat in Astronomeous*

The **ASTRONUT IN BROTHER FROM OUTER SPACE** Fox/Terrytoons (CBS) 1964 anim color/ws 6m. (aka *Brother from Outer Space*). D: Connie Rasinski. SP: L. Bourne. Ph: C. Schettler et al. Mus: Phil Schieb. Voices: Dayton Allen. Ref: TV: vt. LC. Maltin/OMAM: "space gremlin" from the "Deputy Dawg" TV series ('62 show).

"Strange little creature" from space can assume human guise, uses Sweetness and Light Ray, etc. Flat entry in the short-lived *Astronut* series.

**ASWANG** (Fili) Regal Films/Good Harvest (Joey Gosiengfiao) 1992 color 119m. Story, D: Peque Gallaga, Lore Reyes. Story, PD: Don Escudero. SP: Pen P. Medina, Jerry L. Sineneng. Ph: Joe Tutanes. Mus: Jong M. Cuenco. Monsters Created by Benny Batoctoy. SpProsthFX: Sammy Arranzamendez. SdFX: Danny Sanchez. SdFX: Lodie Torrente, Jun Antonio. Ref: TV: Regal Capital video; no Eng. With Alma Moreno (aswang), Aiza Seguerra, Aljon Jimenez, John Estrada, Manilyn Reynes, Janice de Belen, Joey Marquez, Dick Israel, Lilia Cuntapay (old aswang).

The strange beastie which de-entrails a man, the mystery woman in the village on the edge of the forest, the old woman who unnervingly appears and disappears, the strange white parrot, the snake thing, and the young vampire woman, or aswang, may all be one and the same person, or thing. At any rate, the aswang impersonates, at one time or another, a large snake, a little girl's mother, and the heroine. At the end, the monster burns up in the morning light.

This looks like a good one. If the story is a bit deliberately paced, its slow rhythms are insinuating, though a co-plot with some human thugs takes up too much running time. (The story threads overlap when the monster slays one goon.) Made by the team that made *Tiyanak*.

**ASWANG** see *Unearthing, The*

**ASYLUM OF LOVE** (Singapore) 198-? feature. D: L. Tung-Lo. Ref: NST! 4:16: haunting ghosts, hunchbacks.

**AT LUMAGANAP ANG LAGIM** (Fili) Dukeland Prods./Sampaguita Pictures (Boy Duque) 1983 color c110m. SP, D: Armando A. Herrera. Idea: Henry Cuino. Ph: Eduardo Jacinto. Mus: Ernani Cuenco. Sets: Gaviola, Balosvia. SpFX: Antonio Gosalvez. ProsthMkp: Cecille Baun. Ref: TV: Dukeland video; no Eng. With Rosemarie Sonora, Eva Reyes, Rosemarie Gil (Leona), George Estregan (Satur), Etang Discher (witch), Ricky Belmonte, Eddie Garcia, Romy Diaz, Jimmy Santos, Ruel Vernal.

Satur, the King of Darkness, makes love to Leona, who thereupon kills herself. He revives her and takes her to his cavern, where a hunchback aids him. Meanwhile, Leona's mother, using voodoo pin and doll, sticks it to a young woman (apparently her daughter's ex-rival-in-love for Don Manuel). The young lady dies, and Don Manuel has Leona's mother burned as a witch. A horned devil boy finds the doll, removes the pin, and the woman revives. Satur is ultimately impaled on the business end of a large, pointed wooden cross.... Ponderous romantic-fantasy-horror movie. Even the devil—hokey toy horns atop his head—isn't very scary. The wind machine and zoom lens are worked overtime.

**AT MIDNIGHT I'LL TAKE YOUR SOUL AWAY** (Braz.) Something Weird Video/Apolo (Martins-Martins-Iruam) 1963 ('93-U.S.) b&w 81m. (*A Meia-Noite Levarei Sua Alma*). SP, D: Jose Mojica Marins. Ph: Giorgio Attili. AD: Jose Vedovato. SpOptFX: P.C. Indrikis Kruskops. Mkp: Gilberto Marques. Eng Adap: Horacio Higuchi. Ref: TV: S.W. Video; Eng. titles. Monster! Int'l. 3:7, 8, 15, 17-19, 22. Movie Collector's World 7/16/93:11 (ad). PT 5:41, 42. With J. M. Marins (Ze do Caixao), Magda Mei, Nivaldo de Lima, Eucaris de Morais, Valeria Vasquez.

"I get whatever I want!" Undertaker Ze—"envoy of satan"—scares his gagged and bound barren wife Lenita (Vasquez) to death with a tarantula. ("It was a great show!") He murders his best friend (de Lima) to get his woman, Terezinha (Mei). And then (sound Gore Horn) he gouges out the local doc's (Ilidio Martins) eyes. Vows Terezinha: "At midnight, you'll know fear!" He does: On the Day of the Dead, the ghosts of a Procession of the Dead assail the cackling blasphemer.

Unscrupulous, isn't he? Roger Corman did it a bit better in *Tower of London* (1962), but Marins the actor has his moments haranguing the cemetery dead and challenging heaven and hell to punish him. ("I want the proof of divine retribution!") But Marins the writer and director is ham-handed, and the other actors are just there. Fun-hokey, cut-and-paste, owl-and-spider credits sequence, and okay maggot effects for the all-stops-out ending. Falling-on-Deaf-Ears Line: "Be considerate, Ze!"

**AT SCHOOL WITH THE WARLOCK** see *Maya*

**ATAQUE DE LOS PAJAROS, EL** see *Beaks—The Movie*

**L'ATLANTIDE** (F) ORTF 1972 color c90m. Tel, D: Jean Kerchbron. Tel: also Armand Lanoux. From Pierre Benoit's book. Ph: Albert Schimel. Mus: Janos Komives. AD: Comtet, Arnould. Ref: Ecran F 58:66-68: TV-movie. With Ludmilla

Tcherina (Antinea), Jacques Berthier, Denis Manuel (St.-Avit), Gilles Segal.

The Atlantis saga.

**ATLANTIS** see also *Alien from L.A. Arise! Erik the Viking. Gamera—The Guardian of the Universe. Humanoids from Atlantis. Journey to the Center of the Earth* (1989). *Little Boy Blue. MacGyver: Lost Treasure of Atlantis. Miami Horror. Mother. Neptune's Children. New Wave Hookers 2. Oceano Atlantis. Quest of the Delta Knights. Raiders of Atlantis. 20,000 Leagues under the Sea* (1985). *Weathering Continent, The. Wet and Willing.*

**ATLANTIS INTERCEPTORS, The** see *Raiders of Atlantis, The*

**ATOMIC ATTACK** IHF 1953? b&w 50m. Ref: Jim Shapiro: TV or industrial film? Hound. With Walter Matthau, Patty McCormack.

New York City nuked.

**ATOMIC CYBORG** see *Hands of Steel*

**\*The ATOMIC SUBMARINE** 1960 Mkp: Emile LaVigne. Narrator: Pat Michaels. Ref: TV: Monterey HV. V 2/17/60. Warren/KWTS! Lee. Lentz. Stanley. Weldon. Martin. Maltin '92. Phantom.and with John Hilliard (saucer voice).

The "strangest, most fearful voyage ever made by a submarine...." The "atom killer sub" *Tiger Shark* investigates "mysterious undersea disasters" in the Arctic Ocean and discovers an underwater "electric storm center" and "little green fish" in "undersea flying saucers"—i.e., a "living," flying, swimming saucer (the "Cyclops") piloted by a tentacled eye-thing ("That's a face?") intent on colonizing Earth. The eye communicates telepathically with hero Arthur Franz ("Our individual brain frequencies are now attuned, and we exchange wave thoughts") and trains a radiation ray on its foes.

Fun, overdone buildup to the appearance of the monster features "Electro-Sonic Music" and narration which gives exact times and latitudes, for that Breathless Verisimilitude effect. Generally lackluster movie's only real eeriness: the pitch-black backgrounds of the saucer's insides.

**ATOR, THE BLADEMASTER** see *Blade Master, The*

**ATOR THE FIGHTING EAGLE** (3) Sequels: *Blade Master, The. Iron Warrior. Quest for the Mighty Sword.*

**ATOR THE INVINCIBLE: THE RETURN** see *Blade Master, The*

**ATOR III - THE HOBGOBLIN** see *Quest for the Mighty Sword*

**ATTACK OF THE B-MOVIE MONSTERS** 1989 Ref: PT 9:43, 44: "60 minute video comedy." SFChron Dtbk 3/8/92: 1983? With Brinke Stevens.

**ATTACK OF THE BEAST CREATURES** Joseph Brenner/Obelisk (Michael Stanley & W. R. Szlinsky) 1985 (1983) color 82m. (aka *Hell Island*). SP, D: Stanley. Mus: J. P. Mozzi. AD,

Monster Des: Robert A. Hutton. SpMechFX: Robert Firgelewski. Ref: TV: World Video. V (CHVD). VSB. Bowker '90. no Martin. Scheuer. no Stanley. Phantom. PT 10:52. McCarty II. V 3/7/84:76: as *Hell Island*. With Robert Nolfi, Julia Rust, Robert Lengyel, Lisa Pak, Frank Murgalo, John Vichiola, Kay Bailey, Christopher Hutton (monster vocals).

"There must be hundreds of them!" The North Atlantic, 1920. Survivors from a sinking ship encounter small, red-faced, long-haired, glowing-eyed, sharp-toothed creatures on a mysterious tropical-like island. The beasts' m.o.: attack, bite, retreat, attack. Plus: an acid pool which reduces one man to gore makeup, then to a skeleton.... Or, Attack of the Feisty Puppets. It's exactly the terrible movie you'd expect from the title—except for the creatures themselves, which are like the doll in *Trilogy of Terror*'s "Amelia" multiplied by twenty. ("Hundreds"?—forget it.) The screeching and pattering sound effects help the puppet attack scenes, but even the latter get pretty tiresome after the tenth ambush. The "beast creatures"—which worship together at a wooden shrine—are never explained.

**\*ATTACK OF THE CRAB MONSTERS** 1957. Mkp: C. Batson. Props: Karl Brainard. Ref: TV: vt. Warren/KWTS! PT 16:7. Hardy/SF. Lee.

"We are dealing with a man who is dead, but whose voice and memory live." A "big black shape" patrols the waters around an "uncharted atoll in the Pacific." Mountains disappear; pits appear. Booming voices beckon in the night. A strange crackling, or popping, is heard. Behind it all: a giant radioactive crab or two ... a "biological freak," a "mass of liquid with a permanent shape" which assimilates and uses the minds it absorbs and which is reducing the size of the island in order to isolate its human prey.

Spare script gets a lot of mileage out of the eerie idea of the disembodied voices. Film in fact has several interesting ideas, but generally perfunctory action and dialogue, and the monsters are visually unprepossessing. Landmark line: "Once they were men; now they're land crabs." Minor atmospheric plus: the intermittent shots of crabs and sea gulls.

**ATTACK OF THE 50 FOOT HOOKER** Odyssey 1994 color 90m. D: L.S. Talbot, Teri Driver. Ref: Adam '95. vc box. Vallejo T-H. With Leena, Sahara Sands, Sean Michaels (spaceman).

Prostitute becomes "bigger than a house" (A) after encounter with alien.

**\*ATTACK OF THE 50 FOOT WOMAN** 1958 66m. (*The Giant Woman. The Astounding Giant Woman* - early ts). Mkp: Carlie Taylor. Ref: TV. Warren/KWTS! Lee. Lentz. Stanley. Hardy/SF. V 5/14/58. Martin. With Frank Chase, Otto Waldis, George Douglas, Mike Ross (space giant).

"I need you all to myself." A "strange red fireball"—diamond-powered and manned by a thirty-foot giant—lands in the California desert. The giant's touch infects Nancy Archer (Allison Hayes), "heiress to the Fowler millions," with a unique radiation which overexcites her pituitary and turns her into a giant, and the movie, at this precise point, turns into camp. First prize, understatement category (Eileene Stevens' nurse): "Something's happened to Mrs. Archer!" Second prize (William Hudson's Harry Archer to Yvette Vickers' playgirl Honey): "We've got problems again." Suspicious giant footprints litter the outside of the Archers' palatial house, as—in the movie's last ten minutes (with Nancy's first, big-voiced "Harry!")—the loonily metaphorical takes over. Nancy's bulk is clearly her jealousy writ large, and her jealous wrath shakes buildings, not to mention Harry. ("He's with that woman!") If the double-exposure effects are shoddy, and Hayes plays too much for easy pathos, the low-key photography (by executive producer Jacques Marquette) and the smooth performances by Hudson and Chase (as the deputy, Charlie) go against the camp grain. As Bill Warren notes, this beloved sleaze classic is "too good to be perfectly bad."

**ATTACK OF THE 50-FOOT WOMAN** HBO-TV & Lorimar & WB-TV/Bartleby (Don Blatt/Debra Hill/Chuck Binder, D. Hannah) 1993 color c90m. D: Chris Guest. Tel & Exec P: Joe Dougherty. VisFX: Fantasy II;(sup) Gene Warren Jr. Ph: Russell Carpenter. Mus: Nicholas Pike. PD: J.T. Garrity. MechFxCoord: F. Lee Stone. SpMkpFX: KNB. Ref: TV: *Attack of the 50 Ft. Woman* - cr t. PT 19:56.Cinef 12/93:6-7. V 2/22/93:A-11(ad): Vision Int'l. TVG 9/18/93. SFChron 3/25/93. 12/9/93.With Daryl Hannah, Christi Conaway, Daniel Baldwin, William Windom, Frances Fisher, Victoria Haas, O'Neal Compton, Xander Berkeley, Hamilton Camp, Berta Waagfjord (alien).

Feminine self-assertiveness kicks off the growth of the "big woman" in this for the most part flat updating of the original. (The latter pops up at one point on a drive-in screen.) Or, They Tampered in the Fifties' Domain. Is it heavy-handed feminism or satire of same? At any rate, it's only very sporadically funny. Noted: amusing growing effects and a nice fade-out touch. (Harry here is unregenerate to the end.)

**ATTACK OF THE GIANT BABY, The** see *Honey, I Blew up the Kid*

**ATTACK OF THE JOYFUL GODDESS** (H.K.) Chun-Hsin Lee c1983? color 102m. D: Fong Lu, Sheng Chiang. Sup D: Chih Chang. Ref: TV: Ocean Shores Video; Eng. titles. NST! 4:16. With Tien-Su Chen, Chung-Fei Hsu, Chung-I Lee, Chien-Sheng Lee.

"A ghost!" In a most bizarre scene—in the middle of this combination of the routine and the unusual—a "possessed" marionette spits, or urinates, on a dressing-room fire. At the end, onstage ghosts go through weird transformations, then go on an offstage rampage, while the marionette ghost sprouts fangs and long nails and tongue. The abundance of masks and costumes adds a macabre element, though the stage shows finally seem padding, and the English titles are virtually unreadable.

**ATTACK OF THE KILLER REFRIGERATOR** see *Hook of Woodland Heights, The*

**ATTACK OF THE KILLER TOMATOES** (II) see *Killer Tomatoes Eat France!. Killer Tomatoes Strike back. Return of the Killer Tomatoes.*

**ATTACK OF THE ROCK 'N' ROLL ALIEN** see *Voyage of the Rock Aliens*

**ATTACK OF THE SUPERMONSTERS** (J) Tsuburaya 1992-U.S. feature. D: H. Jinzenii. Ref: vc box.

The Emperor Tyrannus leads onslaught of dinosaurs.

**ATTACK OF THE SWAMP CREATURES** Aquarius Video 1985 (*Attack of the Swamp Creature* - ad t). SP, D: "Arnold Stevens." Ref: TV: IVE/Thriller Video. Mo. Phantom. With "Frank Crowell," "Patricia Allison," "Lee Kropiewnicki," "David Robertson."

The above title and credits are a fraud. This is simply a retitling of *Blood Waters of Dr. Z* (which see). Even the names of the director and the actors have been changed. Only the lousy movie remains the same.

**El AULLIDO DEL DIABLO** (Sp) Freemont-Naschy Int'l. 1988 color/ws? 92m. (*Howl of the Devil* - vt). SP,D, P: Jacinto Molina. Ph: Julio Burgos. Mus: Fernando Morcillo. AD: Jose Luis Galicia. SpFxMkp: Fernando Florido. Mkp: Dolores Garcia Rey. Ref: TV: MV; no Eng. Jones: shot in English. V 8/26/87:14. V/Cannes '89:448. PT 7:24, 27, 30. With Paul Naschy (aka J. Molina), Caroline Munro, Howard Vernon, Fernando Hilbeck, Chris or Cris Huerta.

"Crazy actor" plays a werewolf, a vampire, the Frankenstein monster, Fu Manchu, Mr. Hyde, the Phantom of the Opera, Quasimodo, the devil, and his zombie twin. *Howl of the Devil* or *The Devil's Howl* - tr t. (Jones) This reviewer did not spot a vampire or the devil, but did note the presence of Bluebeard and a mystery slasher, as well as someone wearing a Jason mask and wielding a chainsaw (in a visualized nightmare). The werewolf is Naschy's Waldemar; the Phantom of the Opera is a pretty cheesy makeup. Typically stolid Naschy production nonetheless looks like a treat for fans of the classic monsters. The most interesting scenes are those in which Quasimodo, the Frankenstein monster, and Mr. Hyde appear to a boy. Are they psychological or spiritualistic apparitions?

**AUNTIE LEE'S MEAT PIES** Farren Ent./Steiner Films 1992(1991) color feature. D: Joseph Robertson. SP: Robertson, Gerald Steiner. Ph: A. Armenaki. Ref: Fango 113. SFExam 1/3/92(ad). V 5/11/92:56(rated). 9/3/90:22.

"A black comedy about cannibalism ... done tastefully" (ad).

**AURA BATTLER DUNBINE 1** (J) Emotion 1988 anim color 83m. SP, D: Tomino Yoshiyuki. Ref: TV: Emotion video; no Eng. J Anim Prgm Guide. Animag 11:16. 3:36-47. 6:41-48: OAV. Animag 6:41. 4:8: Bandai. 3:5. Japan Video: 1st of 3 OAVs.

This first of three *Dunbine* videos seems to combine the first episode of the 1983 TV series with an original tale. "The Holy Warriors": Shiluki, one of a race of fairies, brings Motocross racer Sho Zama through the "Aura Road" into Byston Well, a world within the Earth, in order to operate the Aura Battler war robots, "bio-machines" composed of "integrated circuitry, artificial ligaments, and muscle fiber" (Animag). In a Roman-style arena there, fairies dance and huge monsters, or robots, fight. At the end, Sho, an Aura Battler, a fairy, and another destructive robot are flung back to the surface of the Earth. "New Story of Aura Battler Dunbine": The sheer hugeness of trees, beasts, and pillars here intimidates: In this world, everything except the people seems bigger. There are giant anteater/bird combinations, flying dragon-like mounts, a giant brain-beast thing in a dungeon, and a looming, skeletal, Death-like figure.

**The AURORA ENCOUNTER** New World/McCullough & The Aurora Jnt. Venture 1986 (1985) color 90m. D, P: Jim McCullough Sr. SP, P: Jim McCullough Jr. Mus: Ron F. DiIulio. SpVisFX: CineVisual; (d) Dr. Ken Jones. Min: Michael Novotny. Opt: Ray Mercer. Mkp: A. S. Frank. SdFX: Texas Motion Picture Service. Ref: TV. V 9/24/86. With Jack Elam, Mickey Hays (alien), Peter Brown, Spanky McFarland, Carol Bagdasarian, Charles B. Pierce, Dottie West.

An occasionally charming but flatly told anecdote re a harmless alien who telekinetically cheats at cards, develops a taste for Aurora (Texas) home brew, and travels about in a "flying thing, sort of squatty shaped," which features a disintegrating ray. Erich von Daniken meets the American Western: Artifacts and drawings in nearby underground Indian ruins indicate past alien encounters. Film has sweet moments but is poky, with awkward dialogue scenes. At the end, the alien's crystal seems to take his spirit into space.

**AUTOMATIC** Republic/Active (Lakeview) 1995 (1994) color 90m. D: John Murlowski. Ref: vc box: "renegade android" in the 22nd Century. PT 22:71: "entertaining enough." Vallejo T-H 6/17/95. With Olivier Gruner, John Glover, Dennis Lipscomb.

**AUTOPSY, The** see *Scared to Death*

**AUTUOMO** (I) 1983 feature. D: Marco Masi. Ref: Palmerini: In the future, "men ... have become machines without a soul or a heart."

**The AVENGING GODFATHER** Interglobal/Active (Rudy Ray Moore)/Generation Int'l. 1980 color 93m. (aka *Disco Godfather*). SP, D: J. Robert Wagoner. SP: also Cliff Roquemore. Ph: A. A(e)rmenaki. AD (SpFX): Robert A. Burns. Angel of Death Prosth: Jimmy Lynch. AnimFX: New Genesis. FX: FX. OptFX: Hollywood Opt. Ref: PT 4:10: "amazing." Phantom: 1977. TV: Active HV/Transvue Pictures. With Moore, Carol Speed, Jimmy Lynch, Jerry Jones, Lady Reeds, Pucci Jhones (Angel of Death)

Characters high on PCP "see" the Angel of Death, living skeletons, horned devils, etc. Plus an exorcism or two and a gory suicide in a bathtub. Well-meaning, crude ... but the son-of-*Lost Weekend* effects jump out at you.

**Las AVENTURAS DE ENRIQUE Y ANA** (Sp) Jet Films & Kaktus (Helena Matas) 1981 color 90m. (2P *The Adventures of Enrique and Ana*). D: Tito Fernandez. SP: Luis Revenga. Ph: Hans Burmann. Story & Mus: Luis Gomez-Escolar, H. Herrero. AD: Gil Parrondo. SpFX: Cinefex; Pablo Parra, A. Bueno. Mkp: J.A. Sanchez. Ref: TV. Ecran F 32:70. V 12/16/81. 9/30/81:53(ad). TVG. With Enrique del Pozo, Ana Anguita, Luis Escobar, Amparo Soler Leal, Jose Lifante, Toni Valento, David Rocha.

Ingredients: the green-hued Baron Von Nekrus (Agustin Gonzalez) ... mutants ... super-TV ... a computer that chortles ... a ray which can be used for invisibility or disintegration ... and lots of warbling. Mildly appalling.

**AVVENTURE DEL BARONE DI MUNCHAUSEN, Le** see *Adventures of Baron Munchausen, The*

**AVVENTURE DELL'INCREDIBILE ERCOLE, Le** see *Adventures of Hercules, The*

**AWAKENING** (H.K.) 1994 color feature (*Gui Mi Zin Qiao*). D: Cha Fu Yi. Ref: Weisser/ATC2: wife and baby "ripped apart by an unseen force" ... necromancer; disappointing film. VW 33:9-10. With Anthony Wong, Simon Yam, Lee Yuen Wah.

**AWAKENING, The** see *Heartstopper*

**\*2 The AWFUL DR. ORLOF** Plaza Films Int'l. & Eurocine 1962 (1961) ws? 86m. From a novel by D. Khune (aka J. Franco) or Kuhne. Ref: TV: SWV; Eng. dubbed. Monster! Int'l 4:25-31: Orlof in *Faceless* and *Dr. Mabuse* (1972). Lee. Hardy/HM. Weldon. no V. VWB: an Orloff in *Bare Breasted Countess*. With Ricardo Valle, Maria Silva.

"I shall make you just as beautiful as you were before." In 1912 Italy (or perhaps France), Dr. Orlof (Howard Vernon) attempts to repair the fire-scarred face of his daughter, Melissa (Diana Lorys), in his "small castle on the other side of Hartog" (a "spooky place"). Aiding him: a "monster who killed for pleasure" ... the supposedly dead, blind, sadistic, disfigured Morpho Lautner (Valle) .... Mainly trivial variations on *Eyes without a Face*. Most intriguing element: the weird-noise score (clanks, blares, whistles, even music). An "A" for the lighting of the castle and the night exteriors. Bonus: a surprising-oneself-in-mirror shock.

See also *Case of the Two Beauties. Doriana Gray. Fall of the House of Usher* (1983). *Orloff and the Invisible Man.*

# B

**The B.F.G.** (BIG FRIENDLY GIANT) (B) CHE/Thames-TV 1990 ('96-U.S.) anim color 95m. Ref: vc box: "evil giants," too.

**B.O.R.N.** The Movie Outfit (Claire Hagen/Skip Holm) 1989 color 92m. SP, D: Ross Hagen. SP: also Hoke Howell. Mus: W. Belote. Ref: V 10/4/89: "pleasantly old-fashioned." Martin. With R. Hagen, P. J. Soles, H. Howell, William Smith, Russ Tamblyn, Amanda Blake, Clint Howard, Debra Lamb, Dawn Wildsmith.

Body Organ Replacement Network nefariousness.

**BABEL II: THE AWAKENING** (J) Streamline/Hikara Prods. et al. 1994 ('95-U.S.) anim color 30m. D: Y. Matsumoto. Ref: vc box: zombies.

**BABES IN TOYLAND** (U.S.-W.G.) NBC-TV/Orion-TV (Finnegan-Pinchuk & Bavaria Atelier) 1986 color 135m. D: Clive Donner. SP: Paul Zindel, from the Herbert-MacDonough operetta. Ph: Arthur Ibbetson. Mus: Leslie Bricusse. PD: Robert Laing. SpFxSup: Willi Neuner. SdFX: Todd-AO, Glen Glenn. Mkp: R. Von Sperl. Ref: TV. TVG. SFExam 12/19/86. With Drew Barrymore, Eileen Brennan, Richard Mulligan, Keanu Reeves, Jill Schoelen, Pat Morita.

"Horrible monsters tried to eat me alive!" Little Lisa (Barrymore) awakens in Toyland, which is surrounded by The Forest of the

Night, "the scariest place anywhere," and meets the Toymaster (Morita), who is "collecting the evil of the world" in a green bottle.... Mulligan has fun as Barnaby; everyone else smiles and sings about staying young.

**BABY ... SECRET OF THE LOST LEGEND**  BV (Touchstone)/J. T. Taplin 1985 color/ws 88m. (95m.) (aka Dinosaur ... Secret of the Lost Legend - TV). D: B. W. L. Norton. SP: Clifford and Ellen Green. Mus: Jerry Goldsmith. SpFxSup: Roland Tantin. Dinosaurs: Isidoro Raponi, Tantin. SpPhFxSup: Phil Meador. MechFX: David Domeyer et al. Opt: William Kilduff. Mattes: Michael Lloyd. Ref: TV. MFB'85:145-6. V 3/20/85. SFChron 3/22/85. ad. With William Katt, Sean Young, Patrick McGoohan, Julian Fellowes; Mark Mangini and George Budd (dinosaur voices).

"In the Equatorial Rain Forest of West Africa, rumors persist of a huge reptile-like creature...." These brontos, however, prove to be more than rumors.... "It's beautiful!" cries Susan (Young). But Ray Harryhausen and stop-motion animation have spoiled us. The new mechanical marvels like E.T., Carlo Rambaldi's King Kong, and the hatchling Baby just don't achieve the same illusion of life that Willis O'Brien's Kong and Harryhausen's creatures did. *Baby*'s mechanical effects suggest, at best, very limited cartoon animation, and, at worst, two men in a horse suit. The body motion and engineering technicians might as well be inside Baby—only the latter's eyes and nose are faked cleverly enough to seem at all alive. The use of mechanical monsters simply makes it easy to combine them with actors in scenes. The *Gorgo*-like plot here neatly mixes action and sentiment, and the early mystery scenes are well-detailed.

**BABY BLOOD** (F) Dimension (Miramax)/Partners' Prods. & Exo 7 Prods. (Zeitoun-Malberg-Sohm) 1990 ('93-U.S.) color 85m. (*The Evil within* - U.S. vt t). SP, D: Alain Robak. SP: also Serge Cukier. Mus: Carlos Acciari. SpMkpFX: Benoit Lestang, Jean-Marc Toussaint. Sd:(sp) Perini, Laisne;(fx) L. Levy. Ref: TV: A-Pix Ent. video; Eng. dubbed; c'89. PT 19:12. Stanley. V 1/24/90:7. 2/7/90:31. 3/28/90: "effectively mixes gore and black humor." 2/22/93:50. 5/24/93:24 (rated). 1/10/90:18. With Emmanuelle Escourrou, Jean-Francois Gallotte, Christian Sinniger.

"I want the blood of the man that you killed." A barely-glimpsed, blood-drinking thing bloodily exits the insides of a circus leopard and enters the womb of a woman, Yanka, whom it instructs to bring it to term. Observes the sexually correct thing to the abused woman, "It's a man's world." Later, it imparts to her its five-billion-year plan to evolve from a sea creature and replace mankind. Near the end, the movie takes a *Fantastic Voyage* into her, as "Baby Blood" revives her temporarily lifeless body .... Sensationalistic, isn't it? The *Look Who's Talking* duologues between mother-to-be and "baby" get to be a bit much. (Its "Feed me!" at one point also recalls *Little Shop of Horrors*.) And the film is determinedly bloody. Exploitation compounded.

The **BABY FROM OUTER SPACE**  Kreation/Gordon Thomas 1991 anim color 12m. SP, D, Mus: Don Thomas. Ref: TV. Voices: Bryce Glodny (baby alien), Igolka Rutherford (TV alien).

Two aliens take their recess on Earth. Jauntily animated but ponderous avant-gardish cartoon.

The **BABY-SITTERS CLUB**  GoodTimes HV/Scholastic 1991? From the Ann Martin book series. Ref: TVG 3/2/91: *Dawn and the Haunted House,* one of 2 made-for-videos.

**BABYLON 5**  WB & Synthetic Worlds & Rattlesnake Prods. (PTEN/R. L. Brown) 1993 color c90m. D: Richard Compton. Tel & Exec Co-P: J. Michael Straczynski. Mus: S. Copeland. VisFX: (des) Ron Thornton; Foundation Imaging; (coord) Shannon Casey. SpFxMkpSup: John Criswell. SpFxCoord: John Stears. Anim: Mark Swain et al. Ref: TV. V 2/22/93:228. SFChron 2/22/93. TVG. With Michael O'Hare, Tamlyn Tomita, Jerry Doyle, Mira Furlan, Andreas Katsulas, Johnny Sekka, Patricia Tallman.

"Sooner or later, everyone comes to Babylon 5," a 23rd-century "free port" which can handle "every possible form of life"—any planet's atmosphere can be simulated there—and where "four major alien governments" are represented. Gizmos and pretty toys—like a flowerlike spacecraft and a holographic disguise—help break up the dialogue monotony in this TV-movie series premiere.

**BACK FROM HELL**  Kashmir 1992 color 83m. (aka *Demon Apocalypse*). SP,D,P,Ph,Mus: Matt Jaissle. Ref: PT 19:61,79(ad). With Shawn Scarbrough, Larry DuBois.

Deal with the devil, "masked killers with axes, a possessed cop, zombies, gore, and spurting blood."

**BACK TO THE FUTURE**  Univ/Amblin 1985 color 116m. SP, D: Robert Zemeckis. SP, Co-P: Bob Gale. Mus: Alan Silvestri. VisFX: IL&M. SpFxSup: Kevin Pike. Mkp: Ken Chase. Ref: TV. MFB'85:375-6. TVG. V 6/26/85. EBay Express 7/12/85. With Michael J. Fox, Christopher Lloyd, Lea Thompson, Crispin Glover, Claudia Wells, George DiCenzo, Thomas F. Wilson.

A DeLorean sports car/time machine (plutonium and the flux capacitor are the keys) sends high-school student Marty McFly (Fox) back to November 1955, where teenaged Lorraine (Thompson) finds him a "dream." Problem: She's his mother. Problem one solved: She finds that kissing Marty is like kissing her brother. Problem two: Unless George (Glover) asserts himself with Lorraine, Marty will continue his "slow fade" out of existence. He's Marty's father.... Another three-tiered Steven Spielberg climax dilutes an already thin screenplay here. Climax number one—Marty uniting his future parents—is touching, funny, and imaginative. Climax number two—the inventor (Lloyd) saving himself from dying back in the future—is drawn-out, perfunctorily spectacular, over-elaborate. Climax number three—Marty's downwardly mobile, unhappy parents becoming upwardly mobile and happy—is a too pat reversal of a too pat premise and suggests (contrary to the maxim) that money can buy happiness. Box score one for three....

**BACK TO THE FUTURE, PART II**  Univ/Amblin (Bob Gale, Neil Canton) 1989 color 107m. Story, D: Robert Zemeckis. Story, SP: B. Gale. Mus: Alan Silvestri. Ph: Dean Cundey. PD: Rick Carter. SpVisFX: IL&M; (sup) Ken Ralston. Mkp: Ken Chase; (Fox) Bron Roylance. Anim Sup: Wes Takahashi. SpFxSup: Michael Lantieri. SdFX: Mel Neiman. Ref: V 11/22/89: "too clever and intricate for its own good." NYorker 12/11/89: "sort of fun." Sacto Union 11/22/89: "the makeup is awful." ad. Sacto Bee 11/22/89. MFB'90:7-8. With Michael J. Fox, Christopher Lloyd, Lea Thompson, Thomas F. Wilson, Joe Flaherty, Elizabeth Shue, Crispin Glover, Casey Siemaszko, Buck Flower.

Marty (Fox) and Doc Brown (Lloyd) "try to manipulate time without creating paradoxes...." (Bee)

**BACK TO THE FUTURE, PART III** Univ/Amblin (Bob Gale, Neil Canton) 1990 (1989) color 118m. Story, D: Robert Zemeckis. Story, SP: Bob Gale. SpVisFX: IL&M; (sup) Ken Ralston, Scott Farrar. MechFxSup: Michael Lantieri. Ref: TV. V 5/23/90: "relaxed, affectionate." 6/13/90:27. MFB'90:192-3: "satisfying." ad. Sacto Bee 5/25/90. With Michael J. Fox, Christopher Lloyd, Mary Steenburgen, Thomas F. Wilson, Lea Thompson, Elisabeth Shue, Richard Dysart, Pat Buttram, Harry Carey Jr., Dub Taylor, ZZ Top, Hugh Gillin.

Time travel to the Old West of 1885. Broad sf-Western-comedy. Some cleverness in the time-travel stunts and occasional funny comic asides.

**BACK TO THE PAST** see *Future Zone*

**BACKSIDE TO THE FUTURE** Zane Bros. 1986 color 81m. D, P: Milton Ingley. Ref: Adam '88. vc box. With Erica Boyer, Sharon Mitchell, Paul Thomas.

DeLorean time-traveling between the present and the Sixties.

**BACKSIDE TO THE FUTURE II** Zane Bros. 1988 color 87m. D: Vinni Rossi. SP: J. Janowicz. Ref: vc box: "another zany sexual romp through time and space." Adam'89: "time-traveling DeLorean." With Samantha Strong, Alicia Monet, Kim Acosta, Marilyn Ward.

**BACKWOODS** see *Geek*

**BAD CHANNELS** Para/Full Moon (Keith Payson) 1992 color 80m. D: Ted Nicolaou. SP: Jackson Barr. Idea & Exec P: Charles Band. Ph: Adolfo Bartoli. Mus: Blue Oyster Cult. PD: Cecily Hughes. Creature & Robot FX: Criswell Prods.; (sup) Greg Aronowitz. VisFxSup: Phil Meador. SpFxMkpSup: Keith Hall. Physical & SpFX: John Cazin. Opt: Mercer & OptFxLtd. Ref: TV. TVG. SFChron Dtbk 6/14/92. PT 16:15. V 10/29/90:13. With Paul Hipp, Martha Quinn, Aaron Lustig, Ian Patrick Williams, Michael Huddleston, Victor Rogers, Charlie Spradling, Tim Thomerson (Dollman), Sonny Carl Davis.

"The superstation studios have been taken over by creatures from another planet!" An alien invader employs radio waves emanating from KDUL-AM in Pahoota to teleport and shrink Earth women and bottle them. ("It's a chick in a bottle!") The alien's accessories include a little robot and a "weird green fungus" which writhes rhythmically to radio noise. At the end, common household disinfectant vanquishes the invader.

Most interesting aspect of otherwise tepid variation on the Orson Welles "War of the Worlds" broadcast phenomenon are the rock numbers which take place in the minds of victims prior to teleportation. These basically irrelevant music videos—which mix rockers and locals (e.g., barroom rednecks, cheerleaders, nurses)—play like surreal versions of those TV ads in which ordinary working Joes lip synch to golden oldies.

See also *Dollman Vs. Demonic Toys.*

**BAD DREAMS** Fox & American Ent. Partners II/No Frills (Gale Anne Hurd) 1988 color 84m. Story, SP, D: Andrew Fleming. SP: also S. E. de Souza. Story: also Michael Dick, Yuri Zeltser, P. J. Pettiette. Mus: Jay Ferguson. SpMkpFX: Michele Burke. VisFX: Fantasy II. SpFX: Roger George, Lise Romanoff. Titles: Ernest D. Farino. Ref: TV. V 4/6/88. Oak Trib 4/8/88. SFChron 4/12/88. SFChron Dtbk 4/24/88:34. With Jennifer Rubin, Bruce Abbott, Richard Lynch, Dean Cameron, Harris Yulin, E. G. Daily, Susan Ruttan.

"Come to me, Cynthia—now!" Cynthia (Rubin), the lone survivor of a suicide cult, Unity Fields, comes out of a coma after thirteen years and finds herself part of a "borderline personality" group. She seems to be the "catalyst" for the reappearance of Harris (Lynch), the dead cult leader, who begins killing off members of the group.... Title promises a Bad Dreams on Elm Street, delivers just another all-a-plot plot. A few of the episodic script's episodes amuse: The "bleeding" vents is an okay grossout, and Ralph's (Cameron) "fine surgical instruments" selfsendoff is showy. Harris "reappears" in both before-and-after guises, in both pre- and post-immolation states. ("Post" is definitely yuckier.)

**BAD GIRLS FROM MARS** Vidmark/American-Independent (Austin Ents.) 1991 color 87m. (*Emanuelle in Hollywood* - orig t). SP, D, P: Fred Olen Ray. SP: also Mark McGee. Mus: C. Cirino. Ref: V 4/15/91. PT 10:54. 11:6. SFChron Dtbk. With Edy Williams, Oliver Darrow, Brinke Stevens, Jay Richardson, Gary Graver.

Serial killer offing actresses in B-movie, "Bad Girls from Mars." "Poor spoof of B Movies." (V)

**BAD TASTE** (N.Z.) WingNut & N.Z. Film Commission 1988 (1987) color 92m. (*Roast of the Day. Giles' Big Day* - early ts). SP, D, P, SpFX: Peter Jackson. Addl Mat'l: Tony Hiles, Ken Hammon. Mus: Michelle Scullion. Ref: TV: Magnum Ent. video. MFB'89:267-8. V 6/1/88. 10/4/89:62. With Terry Potter, Pete O'Herne, Craig Smith, Mike Minett, Jackson, Doug Wren (Lord Crumb, alien leader), Dean Lawrie (leader fx double); Ken Hammon et al. (3rd class aliens).

"The bastards have landed!" Kaihoro, New Zealand. Earth receives an unwelcome visit from a "planet full of Charlie Mansons"—aliens who assume human form and are looking for "livestock" for Crumb's Crunchy Delights. All Lord Crumb needs now is a slaughter permit from the Fast Food Authority.... Or, It Couldn't Happen Anywhere. Main motif in this comedy of sledgehammers: blood spattering a hapless onlooker. *Bad Taste* is one of the grossest movies ever made, yet it's never offensive. Well, maybe sometimes. Implicit cross references include the Three Stooges and *The Evil Dead*, though the film closest in spirit—i.e., genial depravity—to *Bad Taste* is probably *Horror House on Highway Five*. Both comedies have their longueurs. *Bad Taste* also has some sheep jokes. But at its best it achieves a sort of Tati-like orchestration of gore.

**BADGE OF SILENCE** see *Maniac Cop 3*

**BAKFAT MONUI CHUN** see *Bride with White Hair*

**BAKTERION** see *Panic*

**BAKUFU DOJI HISSATSUMAN 1** (J) Emotion/Artmic c1989 anim color 29m. Ref: TV: Bandai HV; no Eng.; 1st of 2 OAVs.

Tokyo, 2001 A.D. Our hero and his little robot aide take a time machine to feudal Japan. Among the more bizarre ingredients: a giant, human-run, wood-and-metal robot ... an instant pumpkin-styled spaceship conjured up out of a weird pig-drawn cart ... and termite warriors. Most bizarre of all: the thousands of little round warriors made from arrows sliced off in flight. Funny beginning: the alarm/cuckoo-clock characters dispatched to wake up the hero.

**BAKUFU-SLUMP IN BATTLE HEATER** (J) CBS etc.(Y. Ohsato) 1989 color/ws 93m. D: Johji Iida. Ref: TV: Bandai HV; no Eng. Weisser/JC: aka *Battle Heater*.

Knockabout gore-comedy features, prominently, a carnivorous plant and a sort of living appliance which amasses electricity from lightning and other sources. By the end, the monster toaster and the plant seem to have grown to be one and the same thing (if they weren't all along), and the thing begins to eat a rock band (in mid-performance). Our hero then becomes a "plantbuster," and a giant "END" rock ends the zaniness .... Possibly hilarious sf-horror-comedy is definitely strange. Probable first: electric-appliance-plug POV shots. Far-out fun.

**BALANCE** (W.G.) Lauenstein c1989? anim short. Ref: SFExam 9/7/90: "fine ... end-of-the-world essay."

**BALBAKWA (THE INVISIBLE MAN)** (Fili) 1988? color c115m. (*The Invisible Man*-alt t?). D: Espiritu. SP: Arellano, Reyes. Story: Elena Patron. SdFX: Bert de Santos. Ref: TV: vt; no Eng. With Paquito Diaz, Babalu, Susan Bautista, Smokey Manaloto, Princess Revilla, Max Alvarado.

A mysterious woman gives the hero a candle which, when lit, makes him invisible. In his clothes, he appears headless, and scares passersby, field workers, thugs, villagers, etc. At the end, everyone becomes half-invisible (the top half), and the woman temporarily turns a girl into a skeleton in order to scare baddies.... Way overlong comedy is fantasy, not sf, but has comic-horrific overtones. Both the comedy and the invisible-man effects are elementary.

**BALLOON LAND** or **BALLOONLAND** see *Pincushionman, The*

**La BAMBOLA DI SATANA** (I) 1970 feature. Story,D: F. Casapinta. SP: F. Attenni. Mus: F. Potenza. Ref: Palmerini: "diabolic, terrifying mise-en-scene." With Erina Schurer, Aurora Batista, Ettore Ribotta.

Castle caretaker and her lover "try to scare" young woman.

**BAMPAIA HANTA "D"** see *Vampire Hunter D*

**BANANA SPIRIT** (H.K.) Bojon Films (Sammo Hung) 1992 color/ws feature. SP,D: Lo Kin. SP: also Garry Chan. Ph: Ma Kam Cheung, Chow Kim Ming. AD: Kwong Hoi Ming. SpFX: Sun Wick SpFX. Ref: TV: Network Kingdom video; Eng. titles.

With Ng Chan Yu, Lam Ching Ying, Wong Kwong Leung, Josephine Fu, Richard Ng, Ip Wing Cho.

"This banana forest is weird." Horror-comedy involves a "beautician for the dead," a banana spirit which seems to suck the spirit out of her victims, and a flame-throwing demon ghost whose scattered body parts at one point reassemble. Routine fantasy with two or three standout sequences, including the "birth" of the banana spirit from the tree. Prize line: "Che, Rabid Hsiung became a ghost and killed Auntie."

**BANCHO SARA YASHIKI** (J) 1937. D: Taizo Fuyujima. Ref: CM 15:24: Broken Dishes at Bancho Mansion - tr t; *Yotsuya Kaidan* variation.

**BANDH DARWAZA** (India - Hindustani?) Tulsi & Shyam Ramsay 1990 color 107m. D: The Ramsays. Mus: Anand Milind. Ref: TV: vt; no Eng.; Thai version. Chao Thai Market: *Curse of the Vampire* - tr t. Jones: Gurpreej Video. With Hashmat Khan, Manjeet Kular, Kunika, Satish Kaul, Anita Sareen, Anirudh Agarwal, Vijayendra.

In a prologue set in the past, a woman is ceremonially presented as a sacrifice to a caped, Dracula-like, red-eyed vampire. In the present day, the vampire man revives and drinks a woman's blood. In the chase-and-torches climactic sequence, bullets hit him, but he laughs and grabs and crushes the pistol. A can opener-like gizmo, crosslike, repels him, and he burns and dies.... Hammerlike blood-and-thunder horror show's finest feature the imposing figure of the vampire himself, modeled of course on Christopher Lee's Dracula. Only enthusiasm, lighting effects, and a James Bernard-like score keep the repetitious plot going. Nifty visual effect: the burning and toppling of the huge, neon-red-eyed bat altar ornament.

See also: *Darwaza* (II).

**BANGLOW 666** (India) Priwa Int'l. 1990 feature. Ref: Jones: vampires.

**The BANKER** Westwind (Robert W. Mann) 1989 color 90m. Story, D, P: William Webb. SP: Dana Augustine. Story: also Richard Brandes, Augustine. Mus: Sam Winans, Reg Powell. SpFX: Wayne Beauchamp. Mkp: Nina Kraft. Ref: TV. V 1/3/90. With Robert Forster, Duncan Regehr, Shanna Reed, Jeff Conaway, Leif Garrett, Richard Roundtree, Deborah Richter, Teri Weigel, E. J. Peaker.

"Mr. Smith"—"one of the most powerful bankers" in the U.S.—leaves call girls "dissected" and "serious and weird Indian graffiti" scrawled in blood on the walls near his victims. His M.O. involves use of a laser-sighted crossbow and a ritual phrase which sounds like a sneeze and belongs to a primitive South American tribe's blood ritual for the "return of the hunter".... Slasher-movie cliches, plus a dollop of "The Most Dangerous Game." Best line: "Quick. Name the seven dwarfs."

**BAOH** (J) Toho & Shueisha 1989 anim color 47m. Created by Araki. Ref: TV: vt; no Eng. Animag 9:5: OAV; Baoh the Visitor. Animerica 6:10.

Ikuro, a scientifically created superman, thrives on electricity, melts heads, regenerates himself, and destroys weapons with the needle-like rays from his hair. Meanwhile, a dog from the same lab mutates and savages a tiger, and a super-thug makes people explode. Gratuitous gore-fest at first looks like it's going to be *Watchers*-in-reverse (superdog tracks superman), but the dog is quickly exterminated.

**BARBARIAN QUEEN** (U.S.-Arg.) Concorde/Rodeo Prods. 1985 color c80m. (*Reyna Barbara*). D: Hector Olivera. SP: Howard R. Cohen. Mkp/SpFX: Willy Smith, Arny Alfieri. Ref: TV: Vestron Video; unrated version. V 12/18/85.

Barbarian t&a saga set in an unspecified remote age features scattered horrific elements—e.g., a torture chamber, a severed head shock scene. The heroic rebels say things like "Freedom always matters!" and "Other lives are more important than mine." The bad guys have less altruistic, more fun lines like "Nothing like a virgin to brighten a man's morning" and "Pain is a wonderful thing." Otherwise, no fun to be had here.

**BARBARIAN QUEEN II: THE EMPRESS STRIKES BACK** Live HV 1989 color feature. D: Joe Finlay. Ref: Martin: 87m. SFChron Dtbk 8/9/92. 7/26/92. With Lana Clarkson, Greg Wrangler, Rebecca Wood.

The **BARBARIANS** (U.S.-I) Cannon (Golan-Globus) 1987 color 88m. (aka *The Barbarians & Co.*). D: Ruggero Deodato. SP: James R. Silke. Mus: Pino Donaggio. Mkp&VisFX: Francesco and Gaetano Paolocci. Ref: TV. V 5/20/87. Palmerini. With David and Peter Paul, Richard Lynch, Eva La Rue, Michael Berryman, George Eastman.

A time of darkness and demons. Two oafish, good-natured jocks (the Pauls), or barbarians, take on a sorceress, swamp monsters, a piglike monster, a big dragon with Groucho eyebrows and monster arms inhabiting a cave.... Routine sword-and-sorcery action, but there's some dumb fun to be had in the casualness of the production—the movie has the refreshingly unpretentious tone of a TV beer commercial. ("Who you calling fatty, moosehead?")

**BARBARIC BEAST OF BOGGY CREEK PART II** see *Boggy Creek II*

**BARBE BLEUE** (F) Ciphed & Pierre J. 1978 puppet anim color 15m. D, SpFX: Olivier Gillon. Ph: Michel Sibra. Mus: Georges Delerue. Ref: Starfix 15 (May '84):78-81.

Blue Beard, dragon.

**BARBIE AND THE ROCKERS: OUT OF THIS WORLD** Hi-Tops Video 1987 anim color c25m. D: Bernard Deyries. Ref: vc box: rock band in outer space, space station.

**BARBIE AND THE SENSATIONS: ROCKIN' BACK TO EARTH** Hi-Tops Video 1987 anim color c30m. Mus: Subar Prods. Ref: vc box.

"Time tunnel" spaceship to the year 1959.

**2P BARE KNUCKLES** IRC 1977 color 90m. SP, D, P: Don Edmonds. Ref: TVG. HR 2/1/78. V 2/8/78. Martin. no Weldon. no Lentz. no Stanley. no Phantom. With Robert Viharo, Sherry Jackson, Michael Heit, Gloria Hendry, John Daniels.

Sexual psychopath commits mutilation murders.

**BARJO** (F) PCC & Aliceleo & FR-3 & CECR-A 1992 ('93-U.S.) color 85m. (*Confessions d'un Barjo*). SP, D: Jerome Boivin. From Philip K. Dick's novel *Confessions of a Crap Artist*. SP: also J. Audiard. Ref: Cinef 12/93:59. SFChron 9/22/93. Red Vic Theatre notes 9/22/93. V 12/7/92: "strangely touching."

Scene in which the hero imagines himself "inside" a "Star Trek"-like TV series.

**BARON MUNCHAUSEN'S NARRATIVE OF HIS MARVELOUS TRAVELS AND CAMPAIGNS IN RUSSIA** see *Adventures of Baron Munchausen, The*

**BARON MUNCHHAUSEN** see *Adventures of Baron Munchausen, The*

**BASIL OF BAKER STREET** see *Great Mouse Detective, The*

**BASKET CASE 2** SGE/Ievins-Henenlotter 1990 color 90m. SP, D: Frank Henenlotter. Mus: Joe Renzetti. SpMkpFX: Gabe Bartalos. Animatronics Sup: Kenneth Walker. OptFX: Light & Motion. Ref: TV. MFB '90:253-4. V 3/7/90. With Kevin VanHentenryck, Annie Ross, Heather Rattray, Alexandra Auder (Nurse Sherri), Kathryn Meisle, Jason Evers, George Andros Aries (Worm Man).

The "freak twins"—Duane (VanHentenryck) and Belial, that "small grotesque monstrosity"—find a home with the "children" of Granny Ruth (Ross), or "Dr. Freak," an *Island of the Alive* community of the excluded which features a gargoyle, a "frog" (Tom Franco), and the squashed-faced Lorenzo, who sings grand opera.... The story here is a functional patchwork of exploitation themes, solidarity motifs, and *Freaks*. The freaks themselves are the real story—original creations which surprise and unsettle. *Basket Case 2*, like *Freaks*, may make its protagonists standard horror-movie menaces near the end, but visually they're not so easy to dismiss. They're a Wonderland of their own—outre, not-quite-comic, and not-quite-pathetic. Each is one-of-a-kind. The imaginative, three-part coda to the aborted-expose storyline: Belial and the similarly grotesque Eve make love (the "Frankenstein monster" finally finds a willing "bride"); Susan's (Rattray) not-ready-for-birth *Alien* baby "comes up for air" and disorients the amorous Duane; and wit's-end Duane and Belial get together again.

**BASKET BASE 3** SGE (Ievins-Henenlotter) 1992 (1991) color 90m. SP, D: Frank Henenlotter. SP: also Robert Martin. Ph: Bob Paone. Mus: Joe Renzetti. MkpFX: Gabe Bartalos, David Kindlon; (sp) Atlantic West FX. Ref: TV. V 2/24/92: *Basket Case 3: The Progeny*. 1/24/91:16. SFChron Dtbk 3/1/92. 4/5/92. SFExam (Image) 9/27/92. With Annie Ross, Kevin VanHentenryck, Dan Biggers, Gil Roper, Tina Louise Hilbert.

The "famous Times Square freak twins" are back, this time in Peachtree Valley. Duane (VanHentenryck) gets funny lines (in context) like "May I borrow a Swiss Army knife?", while Belial sires twelve "little baby Belials," and local cop thugs slaughter the mother freak. The better to take revenge, Duane has huge, seven-handed Little Hal (James O'Doherty) fabricate metal "enhancements" for his brother.

If the Frankenstein story brought out the worst in Henenlotter, the *Basket Case* material always seem to bring out the best. Here we see his grotesquely charming, wonderland freaks as party animals, as very proper mourners at the mother's gravesite, and ultimately as talk-show guests putting "Renaldo" in his place. The most ingratiating sequence, however, may be the bus-ride/musical interlude, in which the protective Granny Ruth (Ross)—Little Hal's mother—sings to her charges. The communal feeling therein partakes of both *Freaks* and *It Happened One Night.*

**BASTARD!!** (J) Shueisha (A.I.C.) c1991 anim color 29m. Ref: TV: Pioneer Video; intro narration in Eng.; 1st of 6 OAVs. V. Max 4:3. Animerica 5:15: Vol. 3.

"Several hundred years after the fall of human civilization...." It's a "time of sorcery," "demonic creatures," a five-headed, fire-breathing giant dragon, wizards, and feisty, big-eyed waifs. The latter inject a note of comic, contemporary, Lum-like wise-guyness into this atmospheric sword-and-sorcery saga.

**\*The BAT** Feature Prods. (Roland West) 1926 86m. SpFX?: Ned Mann. Ref: TV: Simitar Ent. video. Lee. Lentz. V 3/17/26. no Hardy/HM. With Tullio Carminati, Lee Shumway (The Unknown).

"You may see strange things under this roof." "Spookism" reigns when Cornelia Van Gorder (Emily Fitzroy) leases the Fleming mansion. ("The house is haunted.") "Loose feet roam around," a "face without eyes" peers, shadows of bats are projected on the high walls, and "candles won't stay lit" in the huge "haunted ballroom".... The play was apparently never the thing with *The Bat.* In every movie version, the story creaks. This version, however, compensates with fantastically atmospheric lighting, photography (Arthur Edeson), and art direction (William Cameron Menzies). Edeson, in fact, seems to be transfixed by the sheer scale of Menzies's sets—most of the movie seems to be in long shot. Each room in this "lonely mansion" is an experience—visually and dramatically, gigantic doors, windows, stairs, and railings dominate the actors. Neatest photographic effect: the opening dissolve, which makes the fake bat's glowing eyes seem to hover over the city.

**\*2 The BAT WHISPERS** 1930 ws 81m. From the Rinehart-Hopwood play "The Bat" and the Rinehart novel *The Circular Staircase.* Min: Ned Mann. Ref: screen. PFA notes 4/24/88. Hardy/HM. Lentz. Lee. V 1/21/31. Phantom. Stanley. PT 12:11. With Ben Bard (the unknown).

"I tell you this house is haunted!" The "notorious madman" The Bat—who can only be glimpsed as a shadow—haunts the Fleming estate which Cornelia Van Gorder (Grayce Hampton) is leasing. As the perpetually hysterical, ultraneurotic maid, Maude Eburne is so exaggerated that she seems to be—like Stepin Fetchit—from another dimension. Spencer Charters, as the caretaker, is also a real, or surreal, character. Unfortunately, the rest of the cast, like the plot, is devoid of interest, and the latter half of the movie is full of dead scenes. Director Roland West generally uses the wide screen superficially—the cast regularly lines up like chorus girls along the full length of the screen—but the fast tracking through sets and models is genuinely eerie. Non-highlight: a very artificial storm, with very tame thunder and lightning.

**BATES MOTEL** NBC-TV/Univ-TV 1987 color 95m. SP, D, Exec P: Richard Rothstein. Suggested by Robert Bloch's novel *Psycho.* Mus: J. P. Robinson. PD: R. W. King. Mkp: Richard Blair. Ref: TV. TVG. V 7/8/87:68. With Bud Cort (Alex West), Lori Petty, Moses Gunn, Gregg Henry, Kerrie Keane, Jason Bateman, Kurt Paul (Norman Bates).

Some "pretty spooky stuff" develops as Norman Bates' protegee (Cort), released from a mental institution, inherits and renovates the old motel outside Fairville, California. (Alex carries Norman's ashes with him in an urn.) Mrs. Bates' corpse is unearthed, as is Mr. Bates' skeleton, and a shadow appears in her window in the old house.... Random mixture of chills, mystery, melodrama, and pathos, with a matching crazy-quilt score. Petty is perky in a conventional "offbeat" role.

**BATMAN** WB/Guber-Peters Co. & PolyGram 1989 color 126m. D: Tim Burton. Story, SP: Sam Hamm. SP: also Warren Skaaren. Based on characters created by Bob Kane. Mus: Danny Elfman. SpVisFX: Derek Meddings; (coord) Peter Watson. SpMkpDes: Nick Dudman. Prosth: Suzanne Reynolds. SpFxSup: John Evans. Ref: TV: Warner Home Video. MFB'89:268-9. V 6/14/89. Washington Post 6/23/89. NYorker 7/10/89. With Michael Keaton, Jack Nicholson, Kim Basinger, Robert Wuhl, Pat Hingle, Billy Dee Williams, Michael Gough, Jack Palance, Elliott Stein.

Gotham City. The "winged freak" (Keaton) flies, and bullets bounce off him, but he's no Superman. He just has some "wonderful toys." His nemesis here The Joker (Nicholson), who, like Red Skelton, laughs at his own jokes. Women who use his cosmetics die with his frozen grin on their faces, and his joy buzzer melts away a man's flesh.... Or, Zorro vs. The Man Who Laughs, in the battle of the whitecap eyebrows. Batman makes an exciting entrance or two, and his self-sealing Batmobile is a fun effect. But *Batman* is long, for little reason. The hollow script—like Keaton, as Bruce Wayne—never gets much of anything going, and Nicholson is little more than stylish punctuation.

See also the following and *Alyas Batman en Robin. Legend of the Liquid Sword.*

**BATMAN RETURNS** WB/Polygram Pictures (Denise Di Novi, Tim Burton/Larry Franco/Guber-Peters, Melniker-Uslan) 1992 color 126m. D: T. Burton. Story, SP: Daniel Waters. Story: also Sam Hamm. Ph: Stefan Czapsky. Mus: Danny Elfman. PD: Bo Welch. SpVisFX: (sup) Michael Fink; (coord) Erik Henry; Boss Film; 4-Ward Prods., Robert Skotak; Matte World, Pangrazio and Barron; The Chandler Group; Pacific Data. Digital FX: (sup) Jim Rygiel; (bats) Video Image. SpPenguinMkp & FX: Stan Winston. SpFxSup: Chuck Gaspar. MechFxSup: Mike Reedy. Model Sup: David Jones. MinFX: Stetson Visual. VisCostumeFX: Vin Burnham. Ref: TV. V 6/15/92. SFChron 6/19/92. 7/2/92:E2. TVG. With Michael Keaton, Danny DeVito, Michelle Pfeiffer, Cristopher Walken (Max Shreck), Michael Gough, Michael Murphy, Pat Hingle, Vincent Schiavelli, Paul Reubens, Felix Silla.

"I am Catwoman. Hear me roar." Gotham City. Ingredients in this overlong sequel to *Batman* include the deformed, sewer-haunting "monster," the Penguin (DeVito), who brews an Old Testament-like plot to kill Gotham's firstborn sons ... his electronically controlled "army" of penguins ... his umbrella-copter ... a gizmo which unlocks the Batmobile ... another gizmo which allows Penguin to operate the latter by remote control ... and Batman's (Keaton) bat-erang weapon.

More animal sob stories — Catwoman's (Pfeiffer), the Penguin's—intended to foster the illusion of dramatic depth. Ponderously overplotted and overpopulated with cats, bats, penguins, and "Nosferatus" (Walken). The dialogue vainly attempts to sketch kinships between Batman and Catwoman, the Penguin and Max Shreck, Batman and Shreck. DeVito's makeup and performance—as a malign, misshapen version of Rodney Dangerfield—is the closest the movie gets to any sort of pop power.

**BATMAN: MASK OF THE PHANTASM** (U.S.-S. Korean-J) WB (Burnett-Timm-Radomski/Melniker-Uslan) 1993 anim color 77m. (*Batman: The Animated Movie. Batman: The Mask of Phantasm*). D: Eric Radomski, Bruce W. Timm. Sequence D: Kirkland, Altieri, Riba, Paur. Story, SP: Alan Burnett. SP: also Dini, Pasko, Reaves. Based on the TV series and on the comics. Mus: Shirley Walker. FX: Je Hee Cheng. Phantasm Voice Des: Wayne Artman. Ref: TV: Warner HV: animation services by Dong Yang Anim. and Spectrum Anim. Cinef 12/93:8-9. V 5/17/93:38. 11/1/93:59. Voices: Kevin Conroy (Batman), Dana Delany (Andrea), Hart Bochner, Stacy Keach Jr. (Phantasm), Abe Vigoda, Dick Miller, John P. Ryan, Efrem Zimbalist Jr., Mark Hamill (the Joker).

"Your angel of death awaits." The Phantasm haunting Gotham looks like the "ghost of Christmas future" and proves to be wreaking revenge for past wrongs .... This Batman cartoon feature is a bit stolid, graphically and dramatically, though the stolidity seems, in part, to be an intentional stylistic move. As is usual with the *Batman* characters, the writers work overtime making the story Deep and Dark, but there is a surprisingly good coda touch with the (still living, unbeknownst to Bruce/Batman) heroine Andrea. The movie also has a Big Time musical score and some atmospheric details—e.g., the mechanical men malfunctioning in the abandoned fairgrounds, the bat horde flying up as Bruce announces he's breaking his filial vow.

**BATORU GARU** see *Battle Girl*

**BATTALION** see *Return of the Living Dead*

**\*batteries not included** Univ/Amblin (Ronald L. Schwary) 1987 color 106m. SP, D: Matthew Robbins. SP: also Brad Bird, Brent Maddock, S. S. Wilson. Story: Mick Garris. Mus: James Horner. VisFX: (sup) Bruce Nicholson; IL&M; (stopmo) David Allen; (go-motion anim) Tom St. Amand; (spaceship des) Ralph McQuarrie. SpFxSup: Ken Pepiot.

"Please, somebody, help us!" Enter the "little guys"—"elves" or "ghosts" that scarf up metal and prove to be spaceships—"living hardware ... from a very small planet"—and that act as interplanetary "handymen," as they save a condemned building from demolition or, rather, restore said building.... The *It's a Wonderful Life* prayer here gets a *CE3K* answer, in the form of alien "machines that reproduce themselves" and seem inspired by the living cars in Charles Bowers' shorts such as *Egged on* and *It's a Bird*. This film's extensive effects scenes create a world-within-a-world which, with a little more elaboration, might have produced a classic—at the least, David Allen and IL&M provide an extended demonstration of the uncanny beauty of stop motion animation. Birds of course provide the indirect inspiration for the stop motions of the baby spaceships, as the latter are prodded by Mama to test their "wings," and ostriches indirectly inspire the AT-ST-machinelike movements as the two-legged "chicks" wobble-walk. If there's an "Oh, by the way" feel to much of the human story in *\*batteries*, the Bowers shorts had that same problem (at lesser length), and the actors occasionally invest this uneven comedy-drama with surprising power.

**BATTLE ANGEL** (J) KSS (Joichi-Kazuhiko) & YK & Business Jump & Shueisha & MOVIC & Madhouse (Animate Film) 1993 anim color 61m. (includes the OAVs *Gunnm - Rusty Angel* and *Gunmm - Tears Sign*). D: Fukutami Hiroshi. SP: Endo Akinori. From the graphic series aka "Battle Angel Alita" by Yukito Kishiro. Ph: H. Yamaguchi. AD: K. Hidetoshi. SpFX: Kooji Tanifuji. Sup: Rintaro. SdFX: (d) Honda Yasunori; (sp) Keinji Shibazaki. Ref: TV: A.D. Vision; Eng. titles. Animerica 5:66 (ad), 16-17. Voices: Miki Itoh (Gally), S. Koriyo, K. Yamaguchi, R. Otomo (Grewcica).

"Rusty Angel." "She's alive!" When cyborg Gally gets mad, she splatters the brain-eating mutants—including the rebuilt "monster"-cyborg Grewcica—all over the place. Stylish junk. Cheap irony: the girl with the big cute eyes is Gore Queen.

"Tears Sign." Gally's friend Yugo is saved ... temporarily, as a cyborg. More sentiment and gore.

**BATTLE FOR MOON STATION DALLOS** (J) American Nat'l./Toho (Pierrot Project & Bandai & KKYK) 1985 anim color 83m. (*Dallos* - alt t). D: Mamoru Oshii. SP, Chief D: Hisayuki Toriumi. Ph: Akio Wakana. Mus: Ichiro Nitta, Hiroyuki Nanba. AD: Mitsuki Nakamura. FX: Yoda Yasufumi. Mech Des: Masaharu Sato. Ref: TV: CHE video; Eng. dubbed. V 5/6/87:469 (ad). Animag 11:29: 1983?; first OAV. V. Max 2:4. 3:32.

"Dallos has revived!" Rebel Lunarians conduct "guerrilla warfare on the moon" against government police. The dormant, centuries-old Dallos, however ("What was it built for?") interrupts the hostilities with the "automatic development," or evolution, of its deadly self-defense laser network. "It was Dallos's fury.... Dallos is God".... Some action and spectacle value here, but not much Oshii poetry. The film is stronger on the mechanics of weapons. *Star Wars* and *Alien* are among the design influences.

**BATTLE GIRL** (J) New Cinema Paradise/Moby Dick Corp. 1991 color 74m. (aka *Tokyo Crisis Wars*. aka *Battle Gal. Batoru Garu. Living Dead in Tokyo Bay* - alt vt t. *Emergency! Living Dead in Tokyo Bay* - alt vt t). SP: Kazuhiko Takizawa. Ref: TV: Daiei Video; no Eng. Markalite 3:9: made-for video. VSOM. Weisser/JC. With Cutey Suzuki, Kera, Keiko Hayase.

After a meteorite crashes to Earth, Tokyo becomes a "devil world"—the recently dead become reanimated as flesh-eating "living dead." Cheap, derivative, shot-on-tape sf-horror has tacky meteorite and ray effects and tacky makeup jobs for a scene with some jailed ghouls. (Our armor-and-leather heroine is given the sad task of grenading the latter.) Clumsily staged action undercuts subject's grimness.

**BATTLE HEATER** see *Bakufu-Slump in Battle Heater*

**BATTLE IN HELL** (H.K.?) 199-? color feature. Ref: VSOM: "pretty Asian vampire gals."

**BATTLESTAR ORGASMICA** EVN 1993? color c80m. D: Mitchell Spinelli. Ref: vc box: "space vixens." With Nikki Shane.

**BAXTER** (F) UGC/Partner's & PCC & CBP & Mital & Issa & Aliceleo etc. 1991 color 82m. SP, D: Jerome Boivin. SP: also Jacques Audiard, from Ken Greenhall's novel *Hell Hound*. Ph: Yves Angelo. AD: D. Maleret. Ref: TV: Fox Lorber HV; Eng. titles. SFExam 9/12/91: "eerie" canine. With Lise Delamare, Francois Driancourt.

"I liked it better when she was scared." A bull terrier makes an old lady fall down the stairs, apparently to her death ... tries to drown a baby ... kills another dog to impress his new master, a boy ... and meets his match in this disturbed boy, who ultimately kills him. Uninvolving exercise in canine and human psychology.

**BAY COVEN** NBC-TV/Phoenix & Guber Peters (Jerlor) 1987 color 90m. (*Eye of the Demon* - vt t). D: Carl Schenkel. Tel: R. T. Kring. Mus: Shuki Levy. AD: R. St. John Harrison. SpFX: Frank C. Carrere. OptFX: Peter Koczera. Ref: TV. V 10/28/87:62. TVG 10/24/87. SFChron 10/23/87. Washington Times 10/23/87. Martin. PT 12:12. With Pamela Sue Martin, Tim Matheson, Barbara Billingsley, James Sikking, Inga Swenson, John Dee, John Kerr, Susan Ruttan.

"You must not trust anyone who lives on this island!" Bay Cove, Devlin Island, New England. Featured attractions: deals with the devil, immortal witches, human sacrifice, and "the old man upstairs" (Dee). Generally vapid mysterious-community story, with a few fun atmospheric touches.

**BAY OF BLOOD** see *Twitch of the Death Nerve*

**BE PREPARED** see *Spook to Me*

**BEACH BABES FROM BEYOND** (U.S.-Mex) Para/Torchlight (Karen L. Spencer) & Azteca Catrinca 1993 color 74m. D: Ellen Cabot. Ph: J.L. Spencer. Mus: Reg Powell. SpVisFX: Fantasy II; Gene Warren Jr., Mike Joyce. Key Mkp: Palah Sandling. Ref: TV: Para HV. SFChron Dtbk 12/12/93. 12/19/93. With Joe Estevez, Don Swayze, Joey Travolta, Burt Ward, Jaqueline Stallone, Linnea Quigley, Sarah Bellomo (Xena), Tamara Landry (Luna), Nicole Posey (Sola), Dave DeCoteau.

"California's a great place!" Galactic cruisers run out of gas, crash land on Earth. An sf premise sandwiches t&a footage and a sort-of-plot. Nothing has changed much since *Beach Party*.

**BEAKS—THE MOVIE** (Mex-P.Rican-Peruvian) Ascot Ent./Real-Televicine-Patsa & Taleski & Labarthe 1986 color 86m. (*El Ataque de los Pajaros. aka Birds of Prey. Beaks*). SP, D, P: Rene Cardona Jr. Addl Dial: R. Schlosser, E. Wenston. Mus: Stelvio Cipriani. SpFX: (d) R. Cardona III; Sergio Jara. Sd: (sp) Diggy; (fx sup) Richard Le Grand. Ref: TV: Int'l. Video Ent. V 12/2/87. Horacio Higuchi. With Christopher Atkins, Michelle Johnson, Sonia Infante, Gabriele Tinti, Aldo Sambrel, Jose Linfante.

Birds do it, and here "it seems organized. Imagine that—billions of birds at war with mankind!" In Villanueva del Pardillo, Spain,

a man whose eye was gouged out by a falcon is followed by a flock of doves. In La Mancha, the "chickens got together...." In San Juan, Puerto Rico, the plaza pigeons make threatening noises, and there is a report of an encounter between a priest and wild ducks.... *Beaks* was packaged and sold as camp, but the movie itself lies in a limbo of action scenes (people running, birds swooping) and gore-effects inserts. The birds are a monotonous menace—all they do is peck. And all the script does is repeat suspense scenes from *The Birds*.

See also: *Killer Birds*.

**BEAR'S WEDDING, The** see *Marriage of the Bear*

**BEAST CITY** see *Monster City*

**BEAST FRONT LINE** (J) Tokuma Communications 1990 anim color 45m. Ref: Animag 11:4: 3 OAVs.

Mad scientist fuses "man and beast."

**BEAST WAR MADARA** (J) Kadokawa & Bandai & MOVIC 1992 anim color 60m. each (aka *Madara. Project with Madara*). Story: Shou Tajima. Concept: Eiji Otsuka. Ref: V. Max 2:6-8, 10. 3:4: part 2 of 2 OAVs. vc box.

Robot warriors ... Kajula, a general who can "appear as either many small bat-like creatures or as a giant bat monster with many mouths."

**BEASTIES** Pulsar Films 1991 (1989) color 83m. SP,D,P: Steve Contreras. Ph: Ralph Cantu. Mus: D. Davaurs. AD: Jean Miranda. SpFX: Mike Dudley, Matt Prine et al. Models: Fantastic Fantasy. VideoSpFX: Richard Millward. SdFX: D. Davaurs. Ref: TV: Cinema HV; "David DeCoteau Presents." With Eric Bushman, Denise Mora, Hector Yanez (Osires), Eric Delabarre, Janine Miskulin, The Shroudettes.

The "spacecraft" at Silver Arrow Park—which "merges" organic and mechanical material—is really a time machine; the telepathic, head "alien" therein is really the hero in the future, or from the future, in "Bionaut" form, after some self-experimentation; and the "beasties" are his "babies."

Sf-on-a-dime is stilted and trite, despite a somewhat imaginative premise. The Bionaut and the beasties are amusingly designed, but stiff. Complete with Osires, the "son of the feared one," and his punker cult. Near the end, he turns either monstrous or very old. Shot on tape.

**BEASTMASTER 2: THROUGH THE PORTAL OF TIME** New Line/Republic Pictures & Films 21 (Stephan Strick/Portal Prods.) 1991 (1990) color 107m. (*Through the Portal of Time* - orig t). SP, D, P: Sylvio Tabet. Story, SP: R. J. Robertson, Jim Wynorski. SP: also Ken Hauser, Doug Miles. Mus: Robert Folk. VisFX: (sup) Frank H. Isaacs; M. E. L.; (mkp fx des) Patrick Tatopoulos; (coord) Allan Apone. MechFX: Kevin McCarthy; Players. SpVocalFX: Frank Welker. Ref: TV. V 9/23/91. SFChron Dtbk 3/22/92. V 6/20/90:24. With Marc Singer, Kari Wuhrer, Wings Hauser, Sarah Douglas (Lyranna, witch), Michael Berryman, John Fifer (creature), Dick Warlock, Robert Z'dar.

Ingredients this time: Arklon (Hauser), a dabbler in "unholy magic" who can do instant "brain drains" on others and whose wand shoots rays ... a dimensional portal which takes the principals from the land of Arok to modern-day Los Angeles ... a glowing-eyed swamp creature ... and dinosaurlike "lost hounds".... If the action-adventure elements fall flat, the clash between the 20th century and the primitive yields occasional cute low comedy. Antecedents include *Ghost Warrior, Warlock, Dinosaurus!*, and *Tarzan's New York Adventure*.

**BEASTS** see *Flesh and the Bloody Terror*

**BEATRIZ** (Sp) 1976 color feature. Ref: TVG. With Carmen Sevilla, Nadiuska.

Mother submits possessed son to exorcist. Cf. *Rape*.

**BEAUTIES AND THE BEAST** Arrow Film & Video (Jerry Dawson) 1990 color c74m. (*Beauties ... and the Beast* - ad t). SP, D: Ron Jeremy. Ph: John Steven. Mkp: Renee. Ref: TV: Arrow Video. With Lauren Brice, Debbie Diamond, Kimberly Kane, Blake Palmer, Sasha Gabor.

A woman has "really weird" dreams re a monster psychologist with a gross, *Exorcist* swivel-head and Freddy claws. Turns out her husband and her sister are using the "power of suggestion" to try to drive her crazy. Means to that end include "scary props" and nightmare-inducing audiotapes. Very lame adult variation on *Nightmare on Elm Street* themes.

**BEAUTIFUL DEAD BODY** see *Spooky Kama Sutra*

**BEAUTIFUL DREAMER** see *Urusei Yatsura 2: Beautiful Dreamer*

**BEAUTIFUL DREAMER, The** see *Bello Durmiente, El*

**The BEAUTIFUL, THE BLOODY AND THE BARE** Olympic Int'l. (Esquire/Al Ruban) 1964 color feature. D: Sande Johnsen. Ph: J. Denby. Mus: S. Karmen. AD: N. Fallon. Ref: SWV cat. PT 13:11, 12. AFI: "blood rites." Lee(p). no Lentz. no Weldon. With Jack Lowe, Marlene Denes, Debra Page.

Mad artist murders his nude models.

**BEAUTY AND THE BEAST** Cannon/Satrina-Marner 1987 (1986) color 93m. D: Eugene Marner. SP: Carole Lucia Satrina, from the story by Mme. De Villeneuve. Mus: Lori McKelvey. Mkp: (sp fx) John Price, Deborah Eastwood; (des) Mony Monsano. SpFX: Terry Glass, John Hargreaves. Ref: TV. V 5/27/87. With Rebecca DeMornay, John Savage (Beast/Prince), Yossi Graber, Michael Schneider.

A Cannon Movie Tale re a Beast who's sensitive re his roses, and demands a sacrifice of the man who picks one.... Blander even than the story-telling here are the periodic songs, though this isn't quite as literal a steal of Cocteau as the Faerie Tale Theatre version.

See also the following and *Jack Frost* (1965).

**BEAUTY AND THE BEAST** VCA 1988 color 82m. D, P: Paul Thomas. Ref: vc box. Adam'89: "curse of ugliness." With John Leslie (Lord Beastington), Tracey Adams, Nikki Knights, Tom Byron.

**BEAUTY AND THE BEAST 2** VCA 1990 color 84m. D: Paul Thomas. Ref: Adam'92. With John Leslie (Lord Beastington, now a king), Tracey Adams, Rachel Ryan, Victoria Paris.

**BEAUTY AND THE BEAST: "THOUGH LOVERS BE LOST ..."** CBS-TV/Republic Pictures (Witt-Thomasand& Ron Koslow) 1989 color 92m. D: Victor Lobl. Tel, P: Alex Gansa, Howard Gordon. Tel, Created by: Ron Koslow. Mus: Don Davis. PD: John Mansbridge. SpFxCoord: Gary Bentley. Beast: (des) Rick Baker; (mkp) Margaret Beserra. Ref: TV. Sacto Bee 12/12/89. V 12/13/89:58. With Linda Hamilton, Ron Perlman (Vincent), Eddie Albert, Richard Roundtree, Stephen McHattie, Roy Dotrice, Jay Acovone, Clement von Frankenstein, Tiiu Leek.

The underground beast, Vincent, returns in a telefilm variously called a "season premiere" and a "two-hour movie" and finds his "empathic link" with Catherine Chandler (Hamilton) mysteriously broken. Prime-time fantasy soaper is almost comically crammed with assassinations, explosions, deaths, near-deaths, and other major crises. Lots of "I care very deeply for you" and "Where are you in this dark city?" Thank God King Kong didn't speak. Next episode: "The child is my son!"

**BEAUTY AND THE BEAST** Britannica Video (Phil Stockton/David Alexovich) 1990 anim color 10m. D: Alexovich. SP: D. L. Lieberman. Mus: David Hillenband. Computer Anim D & P: Steve Boyer. Ref: TV: GoodTimes HV (Kids Klassics HV). Host: Pat Morita. with Si Osborne (Beast's voice), Sharon Dolan (Beauty's voice), Lucy Childs (Narrator).

Britannica's Tales around the World. Beauty's tears of love turn the cursed, demonic Beast of Beast Castle back into a prince. Almost comically condensed version of the tale still manages some atmospheric touches.

**BEAUTY AND THE BEAST** BV/Disney & Silver Screen Partners IV (Don Hahn/Howard Ashman) 1991 anim color 84m. D: Gary Trousdale, Kirk Wise. SP: Linda Woolverton, from the classic French fairy tale. Mus: Alan Menken; (songs) Ashman, Menken. VisFxSup: Randy Fullmer. SupFxAnim: Dave Bossert et al. SpVocalFX: Frank Welker. SpSdFX: John P. FxGraphics: Bernie Gagliano. Ref: TV: Disney HV. SFExam 11/22/91. East Bay Express 4/24/92. V 11/11/91. 11/18/91:11. SFChron 12/4/91. TVG 11/16/91. Voices: Robby Benson (Beast), Paige O'Hara, Jerry Orbach, Angela Lansbury, Richard White, David Ogden Stiers, Jo Anne Worley.

"Once upon a time, in a faraway land, a young prince lived in a shining castle"—until an enchantress turned him into a "hideous beast" and cast a spell on the castle. His love for Belle (O'Hara), and hers for him, ultimately break the spell.... The beloved fairy tale takes a back seat here to the ghost of Busby Berkeley and wearyingly affable Disney teapots and cups. Stray, affecting pieces of the basic story remain, but the flashy, musical-comedy/show-biz additions prove effectless padding, and the film plays at times (in its depiction of provincialism) like "Madame Bovary," Jr.; at others—in the sequences with Gaston (Stiers)—like parts of the "Headless Horseman" section of *The Adventures of Ichabod and Mr. Toad*. Forbidding castles and Gothic forests help some, and there are scattered surprises, like the spiderlike coach and Beast's all-fours pacing.

The **BEAUTY'S EVIL ROSES** (H. K.) 1992? color/ws 82m. D: Lam Wuah Chuen. Ref: TV: World Video; Eng. titles. With Uang Yeong Fang, Fang Jong Shinn.

"I'm going to add more poison to you." A witch woman uses the "evilest magic in Thailand" to control her sect's subjects. In one scene, a long snakelike creature shoots out her palm and into her victim's throat; later her recalcitrant subject, under a spell, develops her own phallic, Cronenberg-ish critter in her mouth; a third, crushed-red-worms spell summons up a second mouth critter, which, spit onto the ground, turns back into worms. Yet another spell yields Snake out the Mouth. Near the end, a high priest and the "evil god" tussle in another dimension.

Deceptively, the first third or so of *Beauty* is miscellaneous softcore sex and violence. Overall, the film is a sloppy, unsophisticated, but curiously weird blend of sex, cop action, and fantasy-horror.

**BEBA, THE MERMAID** (H. K.-Fili?) Pascual 1992? color c80m. D: Teddy Yip. Ref: TV: World Video; Eng. titles.

Elementary fantasy-melo re a captive mermaid has two semi-horrific sequences, one in which leaping snakes attack and bite two mermaids ... another in which a snotty housecat assails Beba in her room.

**BECAUSE THE DAWN** 1988 color 45m. D: Amy Goldstein. Ref: Jones: "rambling, arty." with Edwige Sandy Gray, Gregory St. John.

"Centuries-old lesbian vampire."

**BEDEVIL** (Austral.) Southern Star/Anthony Buckley & the Austral. Film Finance Corp. (Carol Hughes) 1993 color 90m. SP, D: Tracey Moffatt. Mus: Carl Vine. Ref: V 5/10/93 (rev.); C-114: at Cannes. With Diana Davidson, Jack Charles, Tracey Moffatt, Lex Marinos.

Three "distinctly different" supernatural stories re a haunted swamp, a haunted railway track, and a haunted warehouse.

The **BEDEVILLED** (H.K.) Golden Harvest (Raymond Chow) 1987 color c96m. SP, D: Lo Wei. Ph: Chang Yao-Chu. Mus: Joseph Koo. SpPhFxD: Rokuro Nishigaki. Ref: TV: Rainbow Video; no Eng.; Paragon (U.S. release, 1974??). no Hardy/HM. no Stanley. With Ko Chun-Hsiung (sp?), Reiko Ike, Huang Lan.

Visions—of a head that he had severed and of the floating ghost-in-red of a suicide—beset a magistrate. Routine revenge-from-beyond material, with a little t&a. The sole fun-spooky sequence: First, the suicide removes her head and happily caresses her flowing hair, then all the customers-at-table at the local country inn remove their heads—all for the edification of the official.

**BEDROOM STORY** (India-Hindi?) Shivdarshan Chitra/Hastimal Thakuria (Mitesh Joshi) c198-? color c90m. Story, D, P: D. Raman. SP: Shaukat Jamali; (lyrics) Naseem Jaipuri. Ph: Arjun Desai. Mus: Iqbal Qureshi. PD: S. C. Laad. SpFX: Dahyabhai Patel. Mkp: Chhote Jan. Ref: TV: OM Video; no Eng. With Shakeela, Sanjay Shukla, Shivendra, Roma Sengupata, Milap Joshi.

After the ghost of a murdered cad returns and pummels his rival, an exorcist imprisons the ghost in a bottle. But the latter falls and breaks, and the ghost escapes. He pummels the other fellow again and chortles, then attacks the woman in the case in her bath and chortles. Later, he impersonates or possesses another lady, turns monster-faced and fanged, scares the heroine, and chortles, then causes an avalanche. Sacred-type objects, flung at him, make him incinerate. Broad fantasy-melodrama with silly musical numbers and scare scenes.

**BEERTJE SEBASTIAAN** see *Sebastian Star Bear*

**BEETLE JUICE** WB/Geffen (Bender-Wilson-Hashimoto) 1988 color 92m. D: Tim Burton. SP, Story: Michael McDowell. SP: also Warren Skaaren. Story: also Larry Wilson. Mus: Danny Elfman. VisFX: (sup) Alan Munro; V CE; Peter Kuran; (snake) Ted Rae; (sandworm) Doug Beswick. MkpFX: Robert Short; (mech fx sup) Pete Gerard. Model town: Dreamquest. SpFxSup: Chuck Gaspar. OptFxCoord: Jacqueline Zietlow. Ref: TV: WB Video; ref to '58 FLY. MFB'88:227. V 3/30/88. SFChron 3/30/88. With Alec Baldwin, Geena Davis, Winona Ryder, Michael Keaton, Arnie McEnroe, Sylvia Sidney, Robert Goulet, Dick Cavett.

Bio-exorcist Betelgeuse helps a young ghost couple drive a family with execrable taste out of their haunted house.... Over-elaborate plot delays the good news of this mostly bad news movie—i.e., the appearance of Betelgeuse. One of the latter's best stunts: the animation of a very *Fiend without a Face*-like piece of sculpture. Occasional imaginative effects gags can't overcome the general striving-for-the-absurd feel of the film.

*****BEFORE DAWN** Merian C. Cooper 1933. Ph: Lucien Andriot. AD: Van Nest Polglase, Carroll Clark. Ref: TV. Lentz. V 10/24/33. Lee. no Hardy/HM. no Weldon. TVG.

"There's an evil spirit in this house!" A floating death mask ("a horrible face") scares a woman into a fatal fall. Principals here include Dr. Cornelius (Warner Oland) of the Psychical Research Society of Vienna—"abnormal nervous types" are his specialty—and "Mlle. Mystera" (Dorothy Wilson), who does "psychic readings." ("I'm really clairvoyant.") The most curious aspect of this weak oldie: The script uses the fantastic (real clairvoyance) to expose the fantastic (fake ghosts). The two death-mask scenes, however, still chill, and Oland and Dudley Digges, as two less-than-honest gentlemen, play well off each other. Wilson is most unconvincing.

**BEFORE GOD** see *After School*

**BEFORE THE FACT** see *Twitch of the Death Nerve*

**BEGOTTEN** Merhige Theatre of Material 1989 b&w 72m. SP, D, P: E. Elias Merhige. AD, SpFX: Harry Duggins. SdFX: Evan Albam. Ref: TV: World Artists HV. V 6/17/91: "slow-moving gore-fest."F Comm 1/91:2: "extraordinary." With Brian Salzberg, Donna Dempsey, Stephen Charles Barry.

Mutilation, self-disembowelment (a "God Killing Himself"), "primitive, haunting mood." (V) Or, Misbegotten. Or, The Big Hunhh? Blurry and visually ambiguous, to say the least. Hard to tell what's going on here, even at the most basic level, let alone the esthetic level.

**The BEHEADED 1000** (H.K.) B&B Films 1992 color/ws 102m. (aka *The Legend of a Chinese Witch*). D: Wing Shan Si(sp?). Ref: TV: Video Champ; no Eng.; J vt ("Youju Densetsu"). VSOM. With Joie Wang.

The works: flame-spewing idols and statuettes ... a ghost who exchanges blue-ray zaps with an icon and whose green eye-rays possess a young guy ... a beheaded woman (both parts still live) ... a neon bat ... a floating head ... a semi-comic, ghost-extracted-innards scene ... a winged gremlin-type ... ghost acrobats ... a giant magic cannon ... a horde of ghostly giant green spiders with orange eyes (yes!) ... and a flying dragon. Some odd, offbeat scenes and effects in this lively, amusing monster fantasy.

**BEHIND THE BACK DOOR, PART 2** E.V.N. 1989 feature. Ref: vc box. no Adam'89, '91. With Trinity Loren, Donna N.

Aliens voyage to Earth to study sex.

**BEHIND THE STORM** (H.K.) Wong Yee 1983? color 92m. D: Lo Jun. Ref: TV: Ocean Shores Video; Eng. titles. With Violet Lee, Mel Wong.

"Ghost!" Standard-issue ingredients in this mystery-horror movie include a skull-masked killer-with "claws" ... midnight wailing ... a mystery visitor to the remote-island setting ... a player piano which starts up in the dead of night ... a howling wolf, or coyote ... a typhoon ... a phone on the blink ... a very noisy old clock ... and the old feet-sticking-out-from-under-the-curtains bit.

Trite, frantic thriller at least has atmosphere plus and is sometimes hokey enough to be fun. Expected: soundtrack music from *Psycho*. Unexpected: at the end, a snatch of Morricone from *Days of Heaven*. Best in-context line (after two victims have been found in nooses): "I think the two are connected."

**BEING HUMAN** (U.S.-J-B) WB/Enigma et al (Colesberry-Puttnam) color 125m. SP, D: Bill Forsyth. Ref: TV: vt; rather dry thesis film. V 5/9/94: "never comes alive"; "prehistoric times" segment. Vallejo T-H 5/6/94: "not very funny." SFChron 5/6/94.

**BEIRUT** see *Daybreak*

**The BELIEVERS** Orion (Edward Teets) 1987 color 113m. D, Co-P: John Schlesinger. SP, Assoc P: Mark Frost. From Nicholas Conde's novel *The Religion*. Mus: J. Peter Robinson. SpFxMkp: Kevin Hayney. SpCreations: Eoin Sprott. SpFX: (NY) Connie Brink; (Can.) Ted Ross. OptFX: Damson Studios. Ref: TV. MFB'88. V 6/10/87. Sacto Bee 4/16/89:A5: Mexican cult. SFExam 6/12/87. ad. With Martin Sheen, Helen Shaver, Harley Cross, Robert Loggia, Harris Yulin, Richard Masur.

"They can get to anyone! They can kill anybody." A Sudanese cult which advocates the sacrifice of children for "protection" invites family man Cal Jamison (Sheen) to join. *The Believers* adds little to the rituals-charms-countercharms M.O. of the sorcerers and witches in *Curse of the Voodoo, Burn Witch Burn, The Seventh Victim*, etc. For one short stretch, however—after general clues give way to specific revelations and before the obligatory rescue-and-chase scenes—the movie turns chilling, even pro-

vocative, with its stories of parents sacrificing their children. That leaves just 80% of the picture....

**El BELLO DURMIENTE** MB & P.C. 1952 c80m. (*The Beautiful Dreamer*). AD, PrehistoricFX: Edward Fitzgerald. SpFX?: Jorge Benavides(sp?). Mkp: Chivas(sp?). Ref: TV. Lee. Lentz. Monster! 3:64. With Pascual Garcia Pena, Juan Garcia, El Lobo Negro, Fernando Oses.

In dinosaur times, with a stegosaurus, a tyrannosaurus, two brontos, a pathetic little pterodactyl on strings, and cavemen. Men as well as monsters die in a volcanic cataclysm. Only our hero (Tin Tan), in suspended animation, survives. He awakes (a la *Dinosaurus!*) in the present day and runs amok.... The Fifties Mexican version of *Caveman, Encino Man*, etc. The cavemen here act like the Thirty Stooges. Even the dinosaurs join in on some sort of "Mambo Prehistorico." Tin Tan mugs nonstop, but he has some funny bits. In a forerunner of inside-job makeup effects, our hero's head, at one point, visibly throbs.

**\*The BELLS** 1926. Lighting FX: Perry Harris (sp?). Tech D: Earl Sibley (sp?). Ref: TV: Foothill Video. Lee. Lentz. no V. PT 12:11.

An Alsatian hamlet, 1868. A carnival fortune teller (Laura Lavarnie) spooks when she reads the palm of mill and inn owner Mathias (Lionel Barrymore). Sure enough, the latter soon kills Baruch Koweski (E. Alyn Warren), "the Polish Jew," for his gold. Mathias's "tormentor—Conscience": He repeatedly "sees" his victim and finds his hands stained with phantom blood... Director James Young's script fails to make any moral or dramatic connection between the initial, free-and-easy, loose-with-his-money Mathias and the later murderous Mathias, while the movie's apparitions are tepid terrors at best. Boris Karloff, though, as a carnival mesmerist in dark specs, has a chilly visage and a wittily predatory grin. (In one scene, the mesmerist makes a woman levitate; in a fantasy sequence, he hypnotizes Mathias.)

**BELLS, The** see *Fool's Fire*

**BENNY AND BUFORD** see *Ghost Fever* (1987)

**BENNY'S VIDEO** (Austrian-Swiss) Wega Film Prods. and Bernard Lang AG 1992 color 105m. SP, D: Michael Haneke. Ph: C. Berger. Ref: V 6/1/92: "chilling." With Arno Frisch, Angela Winkler, Ulrich Muehe, Ingrid Stassner.

Home snuff movies.

**BERICHT VON EINEM VERLASSENEN PLANETEN** (W. G.) Peter Krieg 1985 color 82m. SP, D, Co-Ph: Krieg. Mus: Rolf Riehm. Ref: V 3/6/85: Report from an Abandoned Planet - tr t. With Ilse Bottcher, Ernst Junger, Ullo von Peinen.

Earth exploratory team finds planet "abandoned and devoid of every form of life."

**BERLINER BALLADE II** see *Warum die UFOs Unseren Salat Klauen*

**BERSERKER: THE NORDIC CURSE** Shapiro Ent./AVG and Paradise (Jules Rivera) 1987 color 85m. SP, D: Jef Richard. Ref: V 5/27/87: goes to a "silly extreme." Morse: "very lackluster." Martin. With Joseph Alan Johnson, Valerie Sheldon, Greg Dawson.

Undead Viking warrior terrorizes camping students.

**BESAME, KITTY** see *Muertos de Miedo*

**BESAME MONSTRUO** see *Kiss Me Monster*

**BESOEKARNA** see *Visitors, The*

**BESTIA IN CALORE, La** see *S.S. Hell Camp*

**BESTIA NEGRA, La** see *Asesino del Metro*

**BESTIA NOCTURNA** (Mex) P.F./Durango (Guillen) 1988 color c87m. (aka *The Night Stalker*). SP, D: Humberto Martinez Mijares. Ph: H. M. Mijares. Mus: Diego Herrera. AD: J. A. M. Mijares. FX: Gonzalo Gavira. SdFX: Jaime Reyna. OptFX: Arte Idea. Mkp: M. C. Mijares, L. Campos. Ref: TV: Condor Video; no Eng.; *Night Beast* - tr t. TVG. Hound. With Raymundo Capetillo, Laura Flores, Eric Del Castillo, Roberto Canedo, Martin Martinez, Fernando Moncada, Lorenzo de Monteclaro.

A Jason-like killer—all boots and helmet—stalks young women and is at times photographed to look like a menacing spaceman. At the end, riddled with bullets, he falls off a cliff, but proves to be invulnerable.... Technically proficient, but otherwise unremarkable horror-fantasy is about two-thirds stalk-and-chase. Lots of explosion and fire effects. No gore or sex.

**BESTIAS HUMANAS** see *Human Beasts*

**BETAVILLE** Verge Prods./Alyce Wittenstein & Garrett Oliver 1986 color c20m. SP,D,P: A. Wittenstein. SP,AD: Steven Ostringer. Ph & Vis Des: R.E. Brooks. Mus: Rob Larrea. Mkp: Lori Pavsner, Shannon Harrington. Ref: TV: Atomique video. With Steveo, Holly Adams, Michael Gerzevitz (man with burning thumb).

"I love Betaville." But for the returning Coman Gettme (Steveo) something has "changed everything and everybody" in Betaville, which is now "almost scary ... a postmodern nightmare." It's inhabited by unfriendly people — "futuristic fops from the funny pages" — and every radio station plays banal slogans. ("The substance of a nation is style.") In addition, someone or something has the ability to make incriminating handguns vanish into .... Cute hit-and-run parody of Godard's *Alphaville* (which see), with a funny, "corrected" ending to the story: The Betaville babe (Adams) shoots Gettme. ("This isn't exactly what I had in mind.")

**BETTY BOOP** see the following and *Candid Candidate, The. Minnie the Moocher. Mother Goose Land.Old Man of the Mountain, The. Red Hot Mamma. Snow-White. There's Something about a Soldier.*

**BETTY BOOP'S HALLOWE'EN PARTY** Para/Fleischer 1933 anim 6m. D: Dave Fleischer. Anim: Bowsky, Waldman. Ref: TV: colorized. Lee. LC. Sean Smiley. Cabarga/TFS.

Clouds "freeze" and take on creepy forms—a cat, a witch, a bat—as they pass in silhouette before a big autumn moon.

Meanwhile, Jack Frost's airplane scatters coldness. Inside Betty Boop's house, "witch paint," slapped with a brush on a wall, yields the outline of a witch; "cat paint".... At the end, Betty, in big-cat disguise, throws the electric switch which sics a gaggle of ghosts—a Cyclops, a jack-o'-lantern, a devil—on a big bad gorilla.... Ordinary bits alternate with extraordinary ones here. Maybe the weirdest: a hippo whose throat seems to lead to a subway station.

**2 BETTY BOOP'S MUSEUM** Fleischer 1932. Ref: TV: U.M. & M.-TV. Cabarga/TFS. Sean Smiley.

Among an estimated dozen pleasing, out-of-left-field bits: a bird-skeleton cuckoo clock ("All out!") ... a cigar-copping Jewish mummy ("I think I'll go back to sleep for another thousand years") ... a skeleton that uses its rib bones as quoits ... a cat skeleton which gobbles up and "cages" mice in its ribs ... a one-horned, vaguely human skeleton which is attached to the clutching hand which grabs Betty ("Sing for us!") ... and a "chorus line" of weird skeletons. At the end, leftover skeletons pile into a grave, to the tune of "There's no place like home."

**\*\*BETTY BOOP'S PENTHOUSE** Para/Fleischer 1933 anim 6m. Ref: Lee. Glut/TFL. Cabarga/TFS.

Frankenstein-like monster.

**BETTY BOOP'S RISE TO FAME** see *Old Man of the Mountain, The*

**BETTY LONELY** (J) 198-? anim color 53m. (aka *Magical Story of Betty*). R: TV: Toei Video; OAV?; no Eng. Japan Video.

Our heroine flies, wields a sword, and generally wears very little. Among Betty's aides: a witch who can become a fanged giant and who may be her aunt ... a fanged, pointy-eared giant who carries Betty and her pals around ... and two tiny creatures with eyes that look like sunglasses. The climax: a battle between Betty (and her skeleton legions) and a long-tongued, long-tailed, fanged demon-giant (and his monsters). All concerned except the two tiny things and the hero can appear in both human and monster guises, although Betty simply grows to giant size without turning monstrous.... This t&a variation on the theme of the love of a supernatural being for a human is funny, bawdy, and fanciful. The hero is as mad about Betty as she is about him, but there are still problems—e.g., the fact that her normal size is about three or four times his. The witches here convene at a spooky castle, and at one point the forbidding-looking "auntie" (who wears a pince-nez) appears in skeletal form, in a shower cap, as she brushes her teeth.

**BEVERLY HILLS BODYSNATCHERS** SGE/Hess-Kallberg & McGuffin (Busybody) 1990 (1989) color 85m. Story, D, P: Jon Mostow. Story, SP, P: P. K. Simonds Jr. Mus: Arthur Barrow. SpFxEd: Mark Cookson, Adriane Marfiak. Mkp: Erin Brasfield. Ref: TV. V 2/7/90. With Vic Tayback, Frank Gorshin, Art Metrano, Rodney Eastman, Warren Selko, Keone Young, Brooke Bundy, Seth Jaffe, Linda Carol.

A dead man comes back "perfectly alive" at the Greener Pastures Funeral Home ("looks like a cheap sex motel"), thanks to a mad doctor's (Gorshin) enzyme, which "reactivates neurotransmissions in deceased tissue." Later, an altered formula restores mafia

Don Carlo (Jaffe) to life and makes him violent, and the funeral home turns into a "circus of the stiffs".... Very scattered laughs in this mating of *Night Shift* with *Night of the Living Dead*.

**BEVERLY HILLS VAMP** American-Independent/Austin Ents. 1988 color 88m. D, Co-P: Fred Olen Ray. SP: Ernest D. Farino. Mus: Chuck Cirino. SpVisFX: Bret Mixon. Mkp: Richard Miranda. Ref: TV: Vidmark video. V Mifed'89:196. 11/8/89. With Britt Ekland, Eddie Deezen, Pat McCormick, Tim Conway, Jr., Michelle Bauer, Dawn Wildsmith, Robert Quarry.

A story from *The Big Book of Vampires*.... A Beverly Hills house ("kind of like 'Leave It to Beaver' meets 'The Exorcist' ") proves to be a vampire bordello run by Madam Cassandra (Ekland) and her girls—Jessica (Debra Lamb), Kristina (Bauer), and Claudia (Jillian Kesner). Holy water, wooden stakes, and crucifixes make the vampires disintegrate.... Bert Gordon-like self-plugs ("Fred Olen Ray is dying to direct") are the highlight of this leaden horror-comedy with pathetically limp wordplay. In-joke alert: Quarry's big line is "Begone, Count Yorga!"

**\*BEWITCHED** 1945. Ph: Charles Salerno Jr. Ref: TV. V 6/20/45. 5/1/74:5. Lee. With Horace (Stephen) McNally, Henry H. Daniels, Francis Pierlot, Audrey Totter (Karen's voice).

"Don't you hear ... something else?" Is Joan Ellis (Phyllis Thaxter) a "thoroughly normal, happy young girl" or a "female monster—a Dracula with bloodstained fangs"? A voice within her speaks of "the two of us, living in you," and orders her to pick up a handy pair of scissors. ("Kill him!") Later: the expected Enter Alter Ego, Cackling, sequence. Seems this murderous Karen was "born in Joan Ellis's body".... Arch Oboler thriller plays something like an RKO "B"—a Lewton or *Stranger on the Third Floor*—but is finally too hokey, though it has moments of invention and even sweetness. Weirdest scene: Hypnosis permits both Joan and Karen to step out (in double exposure) of Karen's body.

**BEWITCHED** (3) aka *Gu* Sequel: *Mo*.

**BEWITCHED AREA OF THOUSAND YEARS** (H.K.?) 1991? color 88m. Ref: TV: World Video; Eng. titles.

"Does Dracula exist?" According to the "snake devil" legend of Fey Yun Mountain, a spell has sealed an evil spirit in a cave.... Shu Mei's possessed father bites her, and she herself starts turning into a neck-biting snake "monster," half-vampire and half-were-snake. ("Can she change her form?") Highlights of this choppy fantasy-horror movie are the campy elements, which include a pair of snake-head mitts for the hands of the various possessed, the father's snake-walk up the side of the building, and the bounding about of a skull-kicking exorcist in the climactic sequence. Included: a dollop of entrail-munchies gore.

**BEYOND BEDLAM** (B) Feature Film/Metrodome (Paul Brooks) 1994 (1955-U.S.) color 88m. (*Nightscare*-U.S.)SP, D: Vadim Jean. SP: also Rob Walker. From Harry Adam Knight's novel. Ph: G. Finney. Mus: D.A. Hughes. PD: J. Helps. SpProsth: Jacquetta. Ref: V 5/2/94: "starts with a bang but trails off into a whimper." PT 22:68: "pretty dreary." With Craig Fairbrass, Elizabeth Hurley, Keith Allen, Anita Dobson.

Re "some kind of dream transference," into which the Bone Man (Allen), a "psycho ... can tap, causing the deaths of people in his doctor's dreams."

**BEYOND DARKNESS** (I) Imperial Ent./Filmirage 1992 (1990) color 90m. SP, D: Clyde Anderson (rn: Claudio Fragasso). SP: also S. Asproon. Ph: L.J. Fraser. Mus: C.M. Cordio. AD: T.S. Lennox. SpMkpFX: J. Ryder. Ref:TV: VSOM; no Eng.; as *Horror House II*. Martin: "hokey." V 8/17/92:12 (rated): "horror violence." 10/14/91:M-22, 24. Palmerini: *La Casa 5*. With David Brandon, Gene LeBrock, Barbara Bingham.

New England. Early, wan hints of the supernatural here include a living, malevolent old radio and a flying meat cleaver. Later, noisy phantom witches take a boy, Martin, into another dimension. Plus: demon possession and a botched exorcism. Pale *Poltergeist* ripoff with a predictable "unexpected" last shot. Best prop: a sinisterly rocking wooden goose.

**BEYOND DREAM'S DOOR** Panorama Ent./Dyrk Ashton (Beyond Dream's Door Co.) 1989 (1988) color c91m. SP, D, Mus: Jay Woelfel. Ph: Scott Spears. SpFX: Scott Simonson. SdDes&FX: Steve Albanese. Ref: TV: VidAmerica video. Cinef 3/90. SFChron Dtbk 7/8/90. no. V. With Nick Baldasare, Rick Kesler, Susan Pinsky, Norm Singer, Daniel White (D. F. White), John Dunleavy, Darby Vasbinder (dream seductress), R. M. Bell (dead dreamer).

"It doesn't want anything left after we're dead." A monster from another dimension uses the dreams of Benjamin Dobbs (Baldasare) to enter this world. It covers its tracks by erasing and altering videotapes, removing pages from books, and eliminating the dreamers it uses.... This Son of Freddy—like the *Elm Street* horrors—is a sort of *Hellzapoppin* horror movie. Anything can happen, and it probably will in these in-one-dream-and-out-the-other fantasies. *Beyond* is okay for a shoestring effort, but the acting is generally flat, the story has no sense of urgency, and the dialogue overdoes the gleeful ghoulishness. ("Besides, I'm dead.")

**BEYOND THE DOOR III** (U.S.-Yug.-I) Ovidio G. Assonitis & CFS Avala Film (Trihoof Investments) 1990 (1989) color 89m. D: Jeff Kwitny. SP: Sheila Goldberg. Ph: Adolfo Bartoli. Mus: Carlo Maria Cordio. PD: Mario Molli. Mkp: Vittorio Biseo. SpFX: Angelo Mattei. SpConsul: Roberto D'Ettorre Piazzoli. Ref: TV: Cinemax. TVG. HBO/Cinemax 3/92. Martin. V 5/2/90:286 (rated). Martin. With Bo Svenson, Mary Kohnert, Victoria Zinny, Savina Gersak, Sarah Ciminera, William Geiger, Alex Vitale, Igor Pervic.

"We're against powerful evil here." American students in Serbia to witness an "ancient Balkan rite" find that "the sign of the pagan virgin" announces the coronation of Lucifer's Princess of Darkness. Beverly (Kohnert), one of their own, becomes an "instrument of the devil" on the 10:17 express to hell. ("The train disappeared!") Unfortunately, the once and past virgin does not make it to the altar intact, and all hell.... Worthless except for the "sight-seeing in Yugoslavia" angle. Fine photography; dunderhead script.

**BEYOND THE FLAME BARRIER** see *Flame Barrier, The*

**BEYOND THE RISING MOON**  see *Star Quest*

**BEYOND THE WALL OF SLEEP**  see *Immortal Sins*

**BEYOND THUNDERBONE**  Wet Video/Bruce Seven (Jimmy Houston) 1986 color c92m. (*Mad Jack beyond Thunderbone* - ad t). D, Adap: Seven. SP: John Baker. Ph, Ed: Michael Cates. Mus: John Further. Mkp: Bobby Flynt. Ref: TV: Wet Video. Adam'88: aka *Mad Jack*; set in 1997. With Candie Evens, Peter North, Bionca, Krista Lane, Careena Collins, Keli Richards, Tom Byron, Mark Wallice.

Various thug types search for telepathic, telekinetic "mutants" in the hopes of creating a "super-human race." The mutants can set up invisible barriers and transport people and objects from place to place. The vc box adds the "Mad Jack" and more specifics about this post-apocalyptic society. The X-video itself wisely concentrates more on Evens than on storyline.

**BIANCO VESTITO PER MARIALE, Un**  see *Spirits of Death*

**Le BIG BANG**  (F-Belg.) Zwanz & Comedia (Boris Szulzinger) 1987 anim color 90m. (aka *The Big Bang*). Story, D: Picha. Story, SP: Tony Hendra. SpFX: Pascal Roulin. Mus: Roy Budd. SdFX: Hackenbacker, Kretz. Ref: MFB'87:238-9: Eng. version. V 8/5/87. Voices: David Lander, Carole Androsky, Marshall Efron.

In 1995, after a nuclear war, mutated survivors live in the U.S.S.R. (males) and Vaginia (females). "Lamentable 'adult' cartoon" (MFB).

**The BIG BROADCAST**  Para 1932 c86m. D: Frank Tuttle. SP: George Marion Jr., from W. F. Manley's play "Wild Waves." Ref: TV. V 10/18/32. Eames. Maltin/TVM.

In a bizarre sequence, Bing Crosby and Stu Erwin attempt suicide by gas and groggily "see" (to spook music) a skull emanate from a radio and a figure (Arthur Tracy) sing "Here Lies Love," as ectoplasm flies about.

**The BIG CATS AND HOW THEY CAME TO BE**  Smithsonian Inst. 1976 anim color 9m. D: K. Loveland, W. Giersz. Ref: Zagreb 78 cata.

Story of cats from The Sabertooth era on.

**The BIG FANTASY**  Le Salon 1980 feature. Ref: Adam '93G. with Kent Banning.

"Sci-fi" re an alien, Chronos, with six nipples.

**BIG GARAGE, The**  see *Tales of the Unknown*

**BIG LOBBY, The**  see *Rosebud Beach Hotel, The*

**The BIG ONE: THE GREAT LOS ANGELES EARTHQUAKE**  NBC-TV/Susan Weber-Gold & Gregory Prange (von Zerneck/Sertner) 1990 color c170m. D: Larry Elikann. Tel, Story: William Bast, Paul Huson. Tel: also Michael Petryni. Mus: David Shire. Ref: TV. TVG: variously called a TV-movie, a mini-series, and an event. V 11/5/90:80. Sacto Bee 11/9/90. With Joanna Kerns, Dan Lauria, Ed Begley, Jr., Richard Masur, Joe Spano, Robert Ginty, Alan Autry.

"Oh, my God! It's Bombay Beach!" The "worst national disaster since the Civil War" strikes L.A., as a devastating earthquake—and aftershocks—tear the city apart.... The now-familiar mixture of politics then panic, popularized by *Jaws*. Slickly done, with the usual mini-melodramas. Semi-clever false alarm set in Universal's *Earthquake* attraction.

**The BIG SNIT**  (Can.) Richard Condie 1986 anim short. Ref: SFChron Dtbk 12/22/91: "a couple argue over a Scrabble game while the world outside is being nuked."

**BIG TROUBLE IN LITTLE CHINA**  Fox/Taft-Barish-Monash 1986 color/ws 99m. D, Mus: John Carpenter. SP: Gary Goldman, David Z. Weinstein. Adap: W. D. Richter. VisFX: Richard Edlund; Boss Film; (creatures) Steve Johnson; (chief model maker) Richard Ruiz. SpFxCoord: Joseph Unsinn. MkpSup: Ken Chase. SdFxSup: A. R. Milch. Ref: screen. MFB'86:364-6. V 7/2/86. SFChron 7/2/86. EBay Express 9/19/86:23. With Kurt Russell, Kim Cattrall, Dennis Dun, James Hong, Victor Wong, Carter Wong (Thunder), Peter Kwong (Rain), James Pax (Lightning), Noble Craig (sewer monster).

"Only a dream can kill a dream." Lo Pan—"the ultimate evil spirit"—cursed by the God of the East and aided by the Three Storms (Thunder, Rain, and Lightning), has been looking for 2,000 years for "one broad" with green eyes to appease the demon. Monster roll call (partial): a hairy drooling monster, one from an underground cave, and (most amusing of all) a floating guardian head with eye in mouth.... Formula but lively, entertaining amalgam of *Mask of Fu Manchu, Romancing the Stone,* etc. Russell's Jack Burton is an appealingly inexpert hero; everyone else just talks loud and fast. The usual monotonously "suspenseful" Carpenter score.

**BIG WARS**  (J) CPM/TJC 1993 ('96-U.S.) anim color c75m. Sup D: T. Takigawa. Ref: vc box: aliens in the 21st Century.

**BIGFOOT**  ABC-TV/Disney-TV (M. S. McLean) 1987 color c90m. D: Danny Huston. Tel: John Groves. Ph: Frank Flynn. Mus: Bruce Rowland. AD: Cameron Birnie. SpDes: R. J. Schiffer, Lance Anderson. Ref: TV. TVG. V 3/25/87:76. With Colleen Dewhurst, Gracie Harrison, Adam Carl, Jerry Chambers.

Two Sasquatch adopt, or kidnap, two human children. Conventional let-nature-be stuff. ("Guess when we don't understand something, we get afraid.")

See also: *Ascension of the Demonoids. Cry Wilderness. Debbie Duz Dishes. Demonwarp. Harry and the Hendersons. Pound Puppies and The Legend of Big Paw.*

**BIGFOOT: THE UNFORGETTABLE ENCOUNTER**  Republic (PM Ent.) 1994 color 86m. SP, D: C.M. Eubanks. Ref: vc box: "gentle giant." Martin: "nothing special." With M. McCoy, C. Chappell, Clint Howard.

**BIGFOOT AND THE HENDERSONS**  see *Harry and the Hendersons*

**BIGGLES: ADVENTURES IN TIME**  (B) New Century & Vista Film/Compact Yellowbill (Heath) 1986 (1985/'88-U.S.) color 90m. D: John Hough. SP: John Groves, Kent Walwin, from the series of novels by Captain W. E. Johns. Mus: Stanislas. SpFX: (sup) David Harris; (ph) G.S.E. Mkp: Eddie Knight. Ref: TV. V 5/28/86. HR 1/27/88. Ecran F 68:71. With Alex Hyde-White, Neil Dickson, Fiona Richardson, Peter Cushing, William Hootkins.

"They've perfected a bloody sound weapon!" Time travel between World War I and the present—through a "hole in time"—prevents Germany from winning that war with a secret, disintegration-style weapon.... Occasional bright moments in this basically bland science-fantasy. It takes Cushing just one line—"Time travel is not unknown in history"—and a reference to "time twins" to explain all.

**BIJO NO HARAWATA** see *Entrails of a Virgin*

**BIKINI BEACH RACE** Panther Films & JWP 1994 (1992) color 90m. Cockroach Creature Des: Gary Young, Steve Louden. SpFX: Jorge Diaz-Amador. Opt: Ric Boyden. Ref: TV: BRI Video.

In the opening sequence of this Z-Ville comedy, a teenage "scientist" creates a giant cockroach, Stanley: "Just like in *The Fly,* my invention will molecularly atomize an organic subject," transport it, and "biochemically reassemble it at five times its original size."

**BIKINI DRIVE-IN** AIP (Wynorski-Till) 1994 color c80m. D, P: Fred Olen Ray. SP: Steve Armogida, John Willey. Sp Creature FX: J. C. Buechler. SpThanx: Greg Luce et al. Ref: TV: Bullseye Video (Arrow Ent.). SFChron 7/23/94.

Michelle Bauer as Dyanne Lynne, "*the* scream queen," in movies like *The Beast of Yucca Street* ... David L. Hewitt and "Dinosaur" Don Glut as extras ... Alligator Man, in a trailer for *Gator Babes* (directed by Steve Latshaw) ... the incidental line: "*Hollywood Chainsaw Hookers*—I love that movie!" ... a scene with FJA ... and (in other drive-in trailers) a monster, a giant woman, and an insect thing.... Half-hearted nostalgia comedy has a few fun bits (including an insert of a photo of John Carradine as the heroine's deceased grandfather). Most of the coming attractions seem made exclusively for this movie.

**BIKINI ISLAND** Curb Esquire Films/Rocky Point Pictures & Wildcat Prods. (Markes-Matz/B.I. Prods.) 1991 color 85m. D: Anthony Markes. SP: Emerson Bixby. Story: Diana Levitt. Ph: Howard Wexler. Mus: M. D. Decker. PD: Keith Downey. MechFX: Wayne Beauchamp. SdFX: RLVS. Mkp: Dennis Hoey? Ref: TV. SFChron Dtbk 10/6/91. Martin. PT 12:52. V 7/22/91. With Holly Floria, Alicia Anne, Jackson Robinson, Kelly Pool, Gaston Le Gaf, Seth Thomas, Shannon Stiles.

"Based in part on a true story." A subjective camera prowler stalks five young lovelies posing for the fifteenth anniversary swimsuit edition of *Swimwear Illustrated,* commits murder by plunger (twice) and murder with bow-and-arrows (three times), leaves a cache of ghastly dead bodies to be discovered at the appropriate moment.... Laughably transparent t&a material makes good on both halves of its title, but that's about all it does. Most unlikely murder: the arrow-through-car-window-and-into-neck stunt. (Apparently accomplished with the miracle of cellophane.)

**BILA PANI** (Cz) 1965 feature. D: Zdenek Podskalsky. Ref: V 6/27/90:36. no Lee. *The White Lady* - tr t.

"Historical film about a ghost in a castle...."

**BILDNIS DER DORIANA GRAY, Das** see *Doriana Gray*

**BILL AND COO** Republic (Ken Murray) 1947 (1948) color 61m. SP, D: Dean Riesner. SP: also Royal Foster. From an idea in Murray's "Blackouts." Bkgds.: Imagineering? Ref: TV. V 12/24/47. Agee. LC.

"This monster ... The Black Menace"—a crow, aka a "crafty demon" and a "monstrous enemy"—terrorizes the bird community of Chirpendale in scary scenes (at least for the birds) in this one-of-a-kind fantasy. George Burton's Love Birds are charming—their performances seem effortless—but the narrator works too hard to put this over.

**BILL & TED'S BOGUS JOURNEY** Orion/Interscope/Nelson Ent. (Scott Kroopf) 1991 color 98m. (*Bill and Ted's Excellent Adventure II* - shooting t). D: Peter Hewitt. SP: Chris Matheson, Ed Solomon. Mus: David Newman. MkpFX: Kevin Yagher. VisFxSup: Richard Yuricich, G. L. McMurry. Ref: V 7/22/91. 12/30/90:14. 11/29/89:11 (ad). SFExam 7/19/91: "clever." With Keanu Reeves, Alex Winter, William Sadler (Grim Reaper), Joss Ackland, Pam Grief, George Carlin, Taj Mahal.

"Evil robot dudes," "His Royal Deathness," the future, etc.

**BILL & TED'S EXCELLENT ADVENTURE** (U.S.-I.) Orion/Nelson Ent. (Interscope & De Laurentiis Film Partners & Soisson-Murphey Prods.) 1989 color/ws 90m. D: Stephen Herek. SP: Chris Matheson, Ed Solomon. Mus: David Newman. Neanderthal Mkp: Kevin Yagher. VisFX: (sup) Barry Nolan; Perpetual Motion Pictures. ComputerFX: Omnibus Simulation; (coord) David Ginsberg. MechFX: Image Engrg.; (coord) Peter M. Chesney. Sd: (sp des) J. P. Fasal; (fx des) F. A. Fuller, Jr., S. Saravo. Ref: TV. HR 2/17/89. V 2/22/89, MFB'90:96-7. With Keanu Reeves, Alex Winter, Bernie Casey, George Carlin; Mark Ogden, and Tom Dugan (Neanderthals).

In 1988, two guys from San Dimas, California—Bill (Winter) and Ted (Reeves)—desperately need help with their high school history report. Help comes from the future—2688 A.D., to be exact—where everyone speaks Bill-and-Ted—in the form of Rufus (Carlin) and a phone booth which travels the Circuits of Time. Bill and Ted collect Napoleon, Billy the Kid, Socrates, Freud, Beethoven, Joan of Arc, Genghis Khan, and Abraham Lincoln, and make a "prehistoric pit stop" in 1,000,000 B.C., before returning, in triumph, to present-day San Dimas.... Occasionally pleasant, generally just slickly hollow sf-comedy seems to get most of its pop history (and prehistory) from other movies. The dialogue is a blur of "dudes."

Sequel: *Bill and Ted's Bogus Journey.*

**A BILLION FOR BORIS** Comworld & S.R.G. & Kandel 1984 color 96m. D: Alex Grasshoff. SP, Exec Co-P: Sandy Russell Gartin, from Mary Rodgers' book. Ph: Peter Stein. Mus: Robert Christianson; (lyr) Lynn Ahrens. PD: Dan Leigh. SpFX: Matt Vogel. Ref: TV. Cabletime 2/87. With Lee Grant, Tim Kasurinsky, Scott Tiler, Mary Tanner, Seth Green.

A rebuilt TV set shows "tomorrow's programs today." Glib kiddie version of *It Happened Tomorrow* is well played and dialogued, if generally routine. Spielberg glow-lighting of the first demonstration of the set suggests electronic wonders to come. Includes footage from *Anna to the Infinite Power.*

**BILLION YEARS BEFORE THE END OF THE WORLD, A** see *Days of the Eclipse*

**BILLY THE KID MEETS THE VAMPIRES** Steve Postal Prods.(Cinevue) 1991 color 118m. SP,D,Ph: S. Postal. SP: also Gail Postal. Ref: Martin. V 4/8/91:15. With Michael K. Saunders, Debra Orth, Angela Shepard, Jeff Michaels, Linda R. Wasserman.

**BIMBA DI SATANA** see *Girl for Satan*

**BIMBO CHEERLEADERS FROM OUTER SPACE** Fantasy HV (Perry Ross) 1988 color 80m. D: John T. Bone. Ref: Adam '89: "spoof of space travel adventures." vc box. With Tracey Adams, Nina De Ponca, Randy West.

**BIMBOS B.C.** Tempe color 75m. Ref: Tempe Video flyer. Bill Warren.

"Prehistoric bimbos ... radioactive beast" (TV).

**BIMBOS IN TIME** Asylum 1993 color feature. D,P: Todd Sheets. SP: Roger Williams. Ref: PT 19:16: "very ambitious." With Cathy Metz.

"Silly time warp sci-fi" re dinosaurs, robots, etc.

**BINBINING TSUPER-MAN** (Fili) Shining Star c1985? color c105m. D: Ben Feleo. SP: Ely Matawaran. Ph: Oscar Guerijero. Mus D: Dominic. PD: Joey Luna. VisFX: Gerry Garocia (sp?). Mkp: Liway Zuniga. SdFX: Demet Velasquez. Ref: TV: vt; scant Eng. With Miguel Rodriguez, Panchito, Babalu, Jaime Fabregas, Rose Ann Gonzales.

The works: A cackling male alien brings back a cemetery's dead as zombies; an ugly female alien splits into two attractive women; and a third alien gives our swishy hero a magic belt which—to "Thus Spake Zarathustra"—turns him into the title character. With effeminate displays of "Tsuper Power," the latter dispatches (to John Williams' "Superman" theme) some zombies, who turn into bats. (Other zombies turn into cats.) Extra added: two flying, half-human, half-bat creatures.... A rather appalling, but also sometimes rather appealing comedy. With superbreath and sunglasses, Tsuper-Man commits cheerful sacrilege. While arm wrestling a local thug with his little finger, Tsuper-Man calls for brush and mirror to attend to his hair. He sashays his way to victory over the bad aliens and their henchzombies. Photography and sound recording are poor, the action is ineptly staged, the first half of the movie is very talky, and effects are tacky, but *Binibining Tsuper-Man* is both a sometimes sly parody of superheroes and a funny puncturing of machismo.

**BIO-BOOSTER ARMORED GUYVER - VOLUME ONE** see *Guyver, The 1*

**BIO-BOOSTER ARMOR GUYVER, VOL. 3** see *Guyver: Mysterious Shadow*

**BIO-BOOSTER ARMOR GUYVER, VOL. 4** see *Guyver: Attack of the Hyper Zoanoid Team Five*

**BIO-BOOSTER GUYVER** see *Guyver, The* (1987)

**BIO-SHOCK** see *Alien Predator*

**BIOHAZARD** 21st Century/Viking Films Int'l. (Fred Olen Ray) 1985 (1984) color 79m. (*Bio Hazard* - ad t). SP, D, P: Ray. Addl Dial & Assoc Co-P: Miriam L. Preissel. Addl Dial & Exec Co-P: T. L. Lankford. Mus: E. Rasmussen, D. Neumann. SpFX: (mkp) Jon McCallum; (anim) Bret Mixon. Suit: Kenneth J. Hall. Severed Head: Steve Johnson. Asst D: Donald G. Jackson. Ref: TV: Continental Video. V 9/4/85. McCarty II. With Aldo Ray, Angelique Pettyjohn, William Fair, Frank McDonald, David Pearson, Christopher Ray (Bio-Monster), Carroll Borland, Arthur Payton, Richard Hench.

At a remote research lab, a brain-wave amplifier and a psychic (Pettyjohn) employ "matter transfer" to bring in things from an "unknown dimension," including a small but fast monster, a cylinder which contains a monster pup, and a radioactive statuette. At the end, the speedy creature turns out to have been a test "soldier," and psychic Lisa is an alien or something.... Flat action, resolution; leaden dialogue. Borland gets one scream.

**BIOHAZARD** see *Dead Space*

**BIOHAZARD: THE ALIEN FORCE** Curb/AIP-Sharan (Patrick Moran/Wynorski-Waldman-Ray) 1995 (1994) color 88m. SP, D, Co-P: Steve Latshaw. SP: also P. Moran. Ref: vc box: reptilian mutants. With S. Zurk, S. Fronsoe, Chris Mitchum.

**BIOKIDS** (Fili) Regal Films/Filmstar (Tess Fuentes/Tony Gloria) 1989 color c90m. D: Ricardo Osorio. SP: Ipe Pelino, J. J. Reyes. Story, P: Amang Buencamino. Ph: Ely Accion. Mus D: Mon Del Rosario. PD: Melchor Defensor. VisFxD: Abet Buencamino. FxSup: Danny Rojo. Mkp: Tita Dominguez. Ref: TV: Regal video; some Eng. vc box: Eng. version available. With Katrin Gonzales, R. R. Herrera, Patrick Sonora, Kieth Peralta, Susana Lozada, Bembol Roco, Phillip Gamboa, Romy Santos (Exxor).

A half-mad professor in a "haunted" house uses his pills and a gene-transforming machine to change children into helmeted "Biokids" with "special powers" who (rather monotonously) thwart evildoers. Their weapons include helmets with disintegrating "bio-laser" rays ... computer-generated motorcycle shields ... ray-deflecting shields ... a pistol-jamming arrow ... a "bio yellow ribbon" which screws one bad guy into the ground ... and freeze-ray guns. The head criminal's research scientist conjures up super-evil Exxor out of a computer terminal. ("He's under my control!") Later, "Exxor soldiers" join Exxor, who has laser eyes and can pop out of TV sets. Broad, episodic sf-comedy is at least pretty lively.

**BIONIC EVER AFTER?** CBS-TV 1994 color c90m. Ref: TVG: "enough is enough." With Lee Majors (the Six Million Dollar Man), Lindsay Wagner (the Bionic Woman), Richard Anderson, Farrah Forke, Geordie Johnson, Martin E. Brooks.

"Will their love survive when their Bionics fail?" (ad)

The **BIONIC SHOWDOWN: THE $6 MILLION MAN AND THE BIONIC WOMAN** NBC-TV/Univ-TV & Michael Sloan 1989 color c90m. D: Alan J. Levi. Tel: Sloan, Brock Choy, from M. Caidin's novel *Cyborg*. Mus: Bill Conti. AD: Tony Hall. Ref: TV. V 5/10/89:96: "implausible story." Mifed '89:122. Sacto Bee 4/30/89. With Lee Majors, Lindsay Wagner, Richard Anderson, Sandra Bullock, Jeff Yagher, Martin E. Brooks, Lawrence Dane, Robert Lansing, Lee Majors II.

The bionic couple takes on the "ultimate terminator."

See also: *Return of the Six-Million Dollar Man and the Bionic Woman.*

**BIOTEXNIA ONEIRON** (Greek) Tassos Boulmetis & Greek Film Center & ET 1 1990 color & b&w 101m. SP, D: Boulmetis. Mus: Thimios Papadopoulos. SpFX: Christos Mangos. Ref: V 11/19/90: *Dream Factory* - tr t; "an interesting but improperly developed premise." With Giorgos Constas, Filareti Comninou, Ilias Logothetis.

"In an underground factory, sometime in the future after the epidemic," where "dreams are re-enacted on a large screen...."

The **BIRD WITH THE CRYSTAL PLUMAGE** (I.-W.G.) UM (Sidney Glazier)/Seda Spettacoli & CCC 1970 color/ws 98m. (*L'Uccello dalle Piumedi Cristallo. Das Geheimnis der Schwarzen Handschuhe.* 2P *Phantom of Terror* - 21st Century reissue t. aka *The Gallery Murders*). SP, D: Dario Argento. Ph: Vittorio Storaro. Mus: Ennio Morricone. Sets: Dario Micheli. Ref: TV. Fango 12/89:57: resembles Fredric Brown's novel *Screaming Mimi*. Hardy/HM. Palmerini. V 7/29/70. 4/28/82:28. 8/26/91:100. 12/9/91:86. Lentz. Stanley. Weldon. no Lee. Boxo 7/28/80:10. TVG: 1969. with Tony Musante, Suzy Kendall, Eva Renzi, Umberto Raho, Enrico Mario Salerno, Raf Valenti, Mario Adorf, Reggie Nalder.

A cackling schizophrenic proves to be a "dangerous maniac at large," the "strange figure" responsible for "three as yet unexplained murders." Poky, generally unremarkable thriller features scattered intriguing mystery elements, including a "macabre" painting ("It gives me the shivers!") and a "creaking sound," made (as it turns out) by a "magnificent bird with long white feathers that look like glass." Also: some suspense on a darkened stairwell and an extreme close-up of the tongue of a screaming woman. The grating score is as offputting as the English dubbing. As in Argento's later *Deep Red*, the mystery hinges on a key scene witnessed, but not at first fully comprehended.

*The **BIRDS** Hitchcock 1963. SpPhAdv: Ub Iwerks. Pictorial Des: Albert Whitlock. Mkp: Howard Smit. Bird Trainer: Ray Berwick. Elec Sd: Remi Gassmann, Oskar Sala. Ref: TV: MCA Video. Lentz. Lee. V 3/27/63. Hardy/SF. With Malcolm Atterbury, Ruth McDevitt, Joe Mantell, Richard Deacon.

"Why are they doing this?" Perhaps it's an avian "war against humanity." Director Alfred Hitchcock seems not fully involved in the early dialogue-dominated scenes here. And obvious back-projection makes for a lot of dead visuals. (It mars even the children running from the schoolhouse sequence.) Roughly the last half of the movie, however, is pretty harrowing stuff. Many of the scariest shots are of the quiescent crows, gulls, etc., in-between attacks on humans. In full attack mode, these birds generally look pretty harmless, for all the sound effects. In fact, in one of the finer sequences, you don't see the birds at all — you just hear their deafening cries outside the boarded-up house. And though the film's larger aspirations toward a portrait of a twentieth century Armageddon remain mostly unfulfilled, there are two sequences which merit mention — the hellish havoc of fire and birds in the town, and the temporary-truce ending: The principals huddle together in safety, but peril is everywhere, of diverse kinds, it seems.

The **BIRDS II: LAND'S END** Showtime-TV/Rosemont (Ted Kurdyla) 1994 color 87m. D: Rick Rosenthal. Tel: Ken & Jim Wheat, R. Eisele. Ph: Bruce Surtees. Mus: Ron Ramin. PD: James Allen. Ref: vc box. TVG. PT 20:72: "dull." V 3/14/94:25: "routine." With Brad Johnson, Chelsea Field, James Naughton, Jan Rubes, Tippi Hedren.

Gull Island terror.

**BIRDS OF PREY** see *Beaks—The Movie*

**BIRTH** (J) Harmony Gold/Kaname 1987 anim color 80m. (*The World of the Talisman*-re-edited version t). Anim D: Shinya Sadamitsu. Anim Sup: Ondera, Aihara. AD: Geki Katsumata. Mech Des: Makoto Kobayashi. Ref: TV: RCA Victor video; no Eng. (except t)/Condor Video; no Eng. (Spanish-language version); El Mundo del Talisman. Martin. Animag 3:4. Animerica 5:53: OAV.

A spaceship lands on a strange planet of humanoids, little blob creature pets, alien fowl, octopus creatures, invariably hostile giant robots, and assorted oddities. At the end, a bitty robot with a big gun starts a chain reaction with a stray shot, and the planet melts down. In a possibly pretentious coda, this universe is seen to be contained in the eye of a mystic picnicking on a rock hanging in mid-air.... Basically a fun-on-the-run chase movie a la *Raiders of the Lost Ark, Birth* is in fact just one long chase, but it has enough spirit and invention to keep it from seeming too long. One highlight: the hide-and-go-seek sequence set in the ruined city—the big blue robot and the big red robot hunt for the human-types, who at least can hide. (The robots themselves are almost as big as the buildings.) Chief liability: a bland pop score.

Note: Following are credits for *Planet Busters*, the "freely adapted" English version of *Birth,* re the planet Pandora, a spiritual "testing ground."

**Der BISS** (W. G.) Marianne Enzenberger 1985 color 84m. SP, D: Enzenberger. Mus: Gerd Pasemann. Ref: V 3/13/85: *The Bite* - tr t; "the joke wears thin." With Enzenberger (Sylvana), Marianne Rosenberg, Rosa von Praunheim, Ulrike Buschbauer.

Greenwich Village vampire bites Berlin woman, who then "wings her way back to Berlin as a woman-vampire...."

**BITE!** Legend 1991 color 79m. D: Scotty Fox. Ref: Jones. Adam '92. vc box. With Alicyn Sterling, Alexandria Quinn, Buck Adams (vampire).

**A BITE OF LOVE** (H.K.) D&B Films (Dickson Poon) 1990 color 94m. D, P: Stephen Shin. Ref: TV: Pan-Asia Video; Eng.

titles. V 10/15/90:M-93, M-94 (ad): H. K.; Dracula-like vampire. With George Lam, Rosamund Kwan, Tsui Siu-Keung.

"I don't bite human beings." Vampire Duke Lee—the "long-haired monster"—gives an injured boy a transfusion of his own "blood of eternal life"; later, the boy saves him with a drop of blood. When the Duke bites heroine Anna's thug brother, the latter becomes "not just an ordinary vampire." And if he bites his sister, he'll become the King of Devils. At the end, Anna's tears revive the dead Duke as a baby .... Except for the sweet blood-relation between vampire man and boy, *Bite* is a routine mixture of sentiment, comedy, horror, and action.

**BITS & PIECES** The Celluloid Conspiracy 1985 color 86m. SP, D: Leland Thomas. SP: also Michael Koby. Ph: Richard Bansbach. Mus: Don Chilcott, Rene Kakebeen. AD: Tom Talbert. SpFxMkp: John Naulin. Ref: TV: TransWorld video. no Stanley. V(CHVD). no Martin. no Phantom. no Scheuer. Ecran F 76:80-81. With Suzanna Smith, S. E. Zygmont (Arthur Hill), Brian Burt, Sheila Lussier, Tally Chanel.

Mad Arthur Hill, whose mother (Jeanine Ward) was mean to him when he was a little boy (Devon Ward), and even after he became a big boy, proves to be the *Bits and Pieces* killer. ("You deserve it. You're all dirty whores, just like Mommy!") Arthur's M. O.: He drives his unconscious female victims home, gags and binds them, puts on his tape of "Night on Bald Mountain," then brings out the electric carving knife.... ("You're beautiful when you're scared.") Slasher video dies the moment the killer calls his mannequin "Mommy." Only sequence good for laughs: the one in which Jennifer (Chanel) stumbles up hills and over rocks in her high heels as she flees Hill. Threadbare production, pathetically thin script.

**A BITTER MESSAGE OF HOPELESS GRIEF** Survival Research Laboratories (Jonathan Reiss) c1990? color short. D, Ed: Reiss. Ref: SFChron Dtbk 7/12/92:37-8: "technically amazing."

"Anthropomorphic robot" battles "other machine creatures."

**BLACK** see *Nero*

**BLACK ANGEL** see *Arabella, the Black Angel*

**BLACK CANNON INCIDENT, The** see *Dislocation*

**BLACK CARRION** (B) Fox Mystery Theatre/Fox & Hammer-TV 1984 color c90m. D: John Hough. Tel: Don Houghton. Ph: Brian West. Mus: Paul Patterson. AD: Carolyn Scott. Mkp: Eddie Knight. Ref: TV. TVG. no Stanley. Ecran F 73:9. 52:69. 70:13. With Season Hubley, Leigh Lawson, Norman Bird, Oscar Quitak, Linda Hayden, Allan Love.

"Whole villages do not just disappear off the face of the Earth!" After buying Briars Court, in the village of Briars Frome, in 1963, rock-star brothers Ray and Ron Verne ("a pair of aging Draculas") went into "total eclipse" and were never heard from again. ("People just don't disappear that completely.") And Briars Frome—a "spooky place" which proves to be a town of guilt-ridden car wreckers—disappears from maps of the area.... Tantalizing details help—a creepy scarecrow is one of the best—but explanations here prove pretty absurd, and the outlandish macabre finale is campy at best.

The **BLACK CAT** (I-U.S.) RCA-Col HV/21st Century (Lucidi-Cozzi/World) 1990 color feature (*Out of the Depths*-early t. *Il Gatto Nero. De Profundis*. aka *Edgar Allan Poe's The Black Cat*). SP, D: Luigi Cozzi. Ph: Rachini. Mus: Tempera. AD: Marina Pinzuti. SpMkpFX: R. Prestopino, F. Casagni. SpFX: A. Corridori, A. Valcauda. OptFX: Studio 4. SdFX: Cine Audio. Ref: TV: Eng. version. Stanley. PT 9:48: haunted house, "control of time, space." V 2/21/90:47 (ad). V/Mifed'89:161. 10/15/90:M-90. 2/21/90:47 (ad). With Caroline Munro, Brett Halsey, Florence Guerin, Urbano Barberini, Luisa Maneri, Karina Huff.

"I'm the next step in evolution." Slightly different, but overelaborate and tepid horror-fantasy concerns Levana, the "terrible mother," a "living shadow" — the Fear in the Mirror who commands time and people ... Anne, a powerful Good Force .. "telepathic illusions" ... a ghost, Sybil ... a nightmare re spirit possession ... a dead, possessed filmmaker ... an occultist ... a phantom boy and a phantom repairman ... *The Black Cat,* a film-in-progress ... and a film-in-planning based on Baudelaire's "Suspiria de Profundis."

**BLACK CAT** (H. K.) D&B Films (Dickson Poon) 1992 (1991) color/ws 99m. (*Hak Mau*). D & Exec P: Stephen Shin. SP: Lam, Chan, Lam. SpFX: Gary Paller. SpFxMkp: Tibor Farkas or Parkas. Ref: TV: Pan-Asia Video (Tai Seng Video); half Eng. V 6/22/92: "mostly a series of well-staged action sequences separated by mushy, mildly softcore moments." vc box: also a Part II. V 10/14/91: M-30(ad). With Jade Leung, Simon Yam, Thomas Lam.

"She is reconstructed. Killing is her destiny" (ad). The premise: "We killed you, but gave you the opportunity to serve the government. In your brain, we've installed a piece of micro-computer chip called *Black Cat*. It helps you to reach your highest potential." Overcalculated sleaze with almost comically overdone violence.

**BLACK CAT 2: ASSASSINATION OF PRESIDENT YELTSIN** (H.K.) D&B Films (Dickson Poon) 1992 color/ws 90m. D, P: Stephen Shin. SP: James Fung, Sin Kam Ching, Ivy Lee. Ph: Milo Cheng. Mus: Chris Babida. Ref: TV: Tai Seng Video; Eng. titles. With Jade Leung, Robin Shou.

Chinese-American Erica Leung, or *Black Cat*—a "very sophisticated instrument"—joins forces with hero Robin to take on terrorists intent on assassinating Boris Yeltsin. Some of the terrorists seem to be imbued with a "radioactive chemical" meant to "enhance performance" .... Unlikely stunts mar would-be spectacular action scenes, but the latter are still the best this sequel has to offer. Cute, stupid bullet trick: Erica's bullet stops the assassin's oncoming bullet.

**BLACK CAT, The** see *Buried Alive* (U.S.-S. African?, 1990)

The **BLACK CAULDRON** Disney and Silver Screen Partners II (Joe Hale/Ron Miller) 1985 anim color 80m. Story, D: Ted Berman, Richard Rich. Story: also David Jonas et al. Mus: Elmer Bernstein. SpPhFX: Phil Meador et al. FxAnim: Don Paul et al. SdFxDes: Mike McDonough. Narrator: John Huston. Ref: MFB'85:305-6: based on the "Chronicles of Prydain" series by Lloyd Alexander. ad. Voices: Grant Bardsley, John Hurt, Freddie Jones, Nigel Hawthorne, John Byner, Phil Fondacaro.

Evil Horned King and his dragons.

**BLACK COBRA** (I) City Nights/Aurora 1979 color/ws c97m. (*Black Cobras* - vt ad t. *Emanuelle's Black Cobra* - re-r t). SP, D, Ph: Aristide Massaccesi (aka Joe D'Amato). Mus: P. Umiliani. AD: F. Gaudenzi. Mkp: M. G. Nardi. TV: Video Gems; Eng.-lang. version. V 6/1/92:14 (rated). VWB: *Eva Nera* - orig t; *Erotic Eva* - alt vt t. With Jack Palance, Laura Gemser, Gabriele Tinti, Michele Starck, Sigrid Zanger, G. Mariotti.

"You are going to die by a method called 'putting the devil into a man'." Combo Hong Kong-travelogue/softcore-titillation features macabre sequences, including murder by mamba, and the climactic revenge scene, which suggests, if it does not show, the above-mentioned method of killing. (Latter involves inserting a devenomed cobra into a man and letting said snake eat its way out.) Palance plays a snake collector who is looking for the "reason for fear." Film succeeds only as a showcase for Gemser.

**BLACK CRYSTAL** Midnight Sun/Mike Conway 1990 color 70m. (*The Black Crystal* - ad t. *The Black Triangle* - orig t). SP,D,Mus: M. Conway. Ph: M. Gatto et al. Ref: TV: Raedon HV. With M. Conway, Lily Brown, Mark Lang, Russell Fowler, Larry Bennett.

"Okay, where's the triangle?" Rudimentary fantasy actioner features a witch who supernaturally kills three thugs ... a warlock impervious to bullets ... a triangular, crystal "power channeler" ... impromptu eye-gouging ... and weird studio sound.

**BLACK DEMONS** (I) Filmakers (Giuseppe Garguilo)/Filmirage 1991 color 86m. (*Demoni 3*). Story, D: Umberto Lenzi. SP: Olga Pehar. Mus: F. Micalizzi. SpMkpFX: Frank Casagni. Ref: V 6/3/91: "ho-hum." Monster! 3:60: "disappointing." With Keith Van Hoven, Joe Balogh, Sonia Curtis.

Cursed mansion, Macumba ceremony, "six black zombies."

**BLACK DEVIL DOLL FROM HELL** C.N.T. 1984 color 87m. SP, D, P, Mus, SpSdFX, Titles, Ed: Chester Novell Turner. Ph: Anna Holliday. PD: Jim Wilson. SpVisFX: Keefe Turner. Mkp: Johanna Simmons. Ref: TV: vt. Stanley. V(CHVD). VSB. Martin. Phantom: direct-to-video. With Shirley L. Jones, Rickey Roach, Marie Sainvilvs, Chester Tankersley, Rev. Obie Dunson, K. Turner (puppet's voice).

At Road's End, a knick-knack shop, Helen Black (Jones) finds an East Indian doll, or puppet, with "very strange powers" and the ability to make her "heartfelt desire" come true. The doll comes to life, ties her to her bed, and makes love to her. ("This is what you want!") When, in anger, she attempts to destroy it, its eyes light up and it makes her bleed and die.... *Black Devil Doll* is midway between horror and porn—an initially (and ultimately) threatening Rastafarian dummy becomes a black woman's "Mr. Wonderful" in bed. A third genre—comedy, or camp—beckons, but this is too outre a conceit to be laughed off very easily. The production is rudimentary, the film sort of sick, and the point elusive (sexual repression is "cured," then sexual expression is punished), but the movie is not without a certain grungy fascination.

**BLACK ENCOUNTERS** Zane 1991 color feature. D: Jim Enright. Ref: vc box: aliens. With Gail Force.

**BLACK HEART** 1994. SP, D, Ph, Ed: Jim Exton. Ref: PT 20:16: "blood drinking serial rapist (Don McCarrens)."

**BLACK HOPE HORROR, The** see *Grave Secrets* (1992)

**\*BLACK MAGIC** Krasne-Burkett 1944 (aka *Charlie Chan in Black Magic. The Murder Chamber* or *Charlie Chan in the Murder Chamber* - orig t). AD: Dave Milton. Ref: TV: Viking Video. Lee. Lentz. Scheuer. Maltin '92. no Martin. no V(w). Hanke/Chan.

"Black magic kill William Bonner." The "invisible bullet" which kills "psychic medium" Bonner (Richard Gordon) at a seance is a bullet "made of frozen blood" ("Mister, this place is creepin' with ghosts"), and the voice which leads Justine Bonner (Jacqueline de Wit) to fall to her death belongs to a hypnotist-magician (Frank Jacquet). The means to the latter's end: a drug which leaves a person with "no mental or physical resistance" and which renders him or her an "easily controlled subject." Only an antidote saves Charlie Chan (Sidney Toler) from a similar fate. Plus: a skeleton-on-a-wire which first chases Charlie's daughter Frances (Frances Chan) and later chases Birmingham Brown (Mantan Moreland).

Not quite up to *Charlie Chan at Treasure Island,* but pretty weird. The detective crew—Toler, Chan, Moreland—are pleasant actors; the supporting cast are at best negligible presences. Moreland's dialogue is livelier than the action. ("I've got gremlins gallopin' up and down my spine!")

**BLACK MAGIC** Showtime-TV/MTE (Point of View/Harvey Frand) 1992 (1991) color 93m. Tel, D: Daniel Taplitz. Ph: P. Fernberger. PD: Bob Ziembicki. Mus: Cliff Martinez. FxMkp: Dean Jones. SpFxCoord: Greg Hull. OptFX: Cinema Research. Ref: TV. SFChron 3/21/92: "sexy, scary and fun." TVG 3/21/92: "wonderfully wacko." SFChron Dtbk 12/12/92: MCA-Univ HV. Showtime brochure. With Rachel Ward, Judge Reinhold, Anthony LaPaglia, Brion James.

"She's a witch, and you are a cursed geek!" Is she or isn't she? She is, apparently, but she tells her lover, "Curses ... can fade away." Occasionally bizarrely funny, but basically conventional romantic horror-comedy. ("What romances don't have their ups and downs?") All the male principals seem to end up as ghosts.

**BLACK MAGIC 3** see *Black Magic Terror*

**BLACK MAGIC: M-66** (J) Bandai/Emotion 1987 anim color 48m. (aka *Black Magic: Mario-66*). SP, D: S. Masamune. D: also Hiroyuki Kitakubo. Mus: J. Katayanagi. AD: O. Honda. Ref: TV: vt; no Eng. Paul Lane. Martin. Animag 4:42-6.

A clawed, ray-shooting android creates havoc in a crowded, *Blade Runner* future. The characters here are stolid-looking Rambo types, but the backgrounds are atmospherically drawn, and the action never stops. Skillfully engineered perspective and moving-camera effects. Highlight: the shootout between the android and a futuristic spacecraft on the top floor of a very tall building.

**BLACK MAGIC MANSION** (Sp-B) Overseas Filmgroup/Filmagic & Golden Pictures (J. G. Maesso) 1991 ('92-U.S.) color 88m. (*Cthulhu Mansion* - vt t). SP, D, P: J. P. Simon. Inspired by

H. P. Lovecraft's writings. Addl Dial: Linda Moore. Ph: Julio Bragado. Mus: Tim Souster. PD: Pablo Alonso. SpMkp & FX D: Colin Arthur. VisFX: Emilio Ruiz. SpFX: Basilio Cortijo, Steve Humphrey. SdFX: Jorge Rodriguez. Ref: TV. SFChron Dtbk 3/1/92:54; 4/18/93. TVG. V 6/6/90:18. 11/18/91:11 (rated). 7/25/90:25. 9/23/91:46. PT 12:48. With Frank Finlay, Marcia Layton, Brad Fisher, Melanie Shatner, Paul Birchard, Kaethe Cherney, Luis Fernando Alves, Frank Brana, Emil Linder.

"I have unleashed a madness beyond my control." Supernatural ingredients here Chandu (Finlay), the "world's greatest magician," who watches as flames from "unknown dimensions" incinerate his wife and assistant Lenora, or Leonor (Layton), onstage, and who at the end kills and replaces a muck-faced demon and exits, stage down ... Cthulhu Mansion, the "weirdest place" ... a music box, the opening of which seems to unleash Lenora's spirit and make it temporarily possess a woman ... a big-clawed thing in a refrigerator ... a shower stall which fills with blood ... two or three living dead people ... a strangling vine ... and lethal, levitating butcher knives.... Lovecraft who? Vapid. "Young hoodlums" tangle with magic, lose. Lots of "Damn, you're bad!"

**BLACK MAGIC TERROR** (Indonesian-J) World Northal/Rapi Films (Sabrin Kasdan/P.P.F.N. & A.O.I.) 1981 color/ws 85m. (*Ratu Ilmu Hitam. The Queen of Black Magic* - alt vt t). D: L. Sudjio. SP: Iman Tamtowi. Ph: Asmawi. Mus: Gatot Sudarto. SpFX: El Badrun. Ref: TV: VSOM; Eng. dubbed. VSB. V (CHVD). no Lentz. no Phantom. Martin. NST! 4:17: aka *Black Magic 3*. PT 7:9. 9:7. Ecran F 37:44. Hound. With Suzzanna, W. D. Muchtar, Alan Naury, Siska Widowati, Teddy Purba, Doddy Sukma.

"I can make you Queen of Black Magic." Jilted woman enlists evil spirits in her revenge plot, which involves bees, a noose, oozing bodies, and worms. She relents, but her sorcerer-sponsor is a hard-liner, and ultimately she must fight him herself .... Crude, naive, episodic, poorly dubbed. Nothing on the ball here. Line worth noting: "A ghost can't appear so early in the morning." Plus a big flying fireball.

**BLACK MAGIC WAR** see *Ninja Wars*

**BLACK MAGIC WOMAN** Trimark (Vidmark)/Marc Springer-Deryn Warren (Bewitched Co.) 1991 (1990) color c88m. Story, D: Warren. Story, SP: Gerry Daly. Story: also Springer. Mus: Randy Miller. SpFX: Ken Tarallo. Mkp: Tania McComas. SdFX: Vinson Ents. Dolls: Women's Dolls & Fetishes. Ref: TV. V 4/8/91. SFChron Dtbk 4/28/91. V 3/25/91:89 (rated). 7/11/90:27. With Mark Hamill, Amanda Wyss, Apollonia Kotero (Cassandra Perry), Victor Rivers (Dr. Yantos), Abidah Viera, Carmen More, Larry Hankin.

"Someone has cursed you!" In this supernatural thriller re "ordinary people who have studied black magic," Brad Travis (Hamill) is hexed—his "natural body defenses are shutting down." And a witch apparently is slaying those who come in contact with him and taking one "digit" from each body.... Old hat, with an expected last-minute twist. Vapid acting and writing. Hamill draws the obligatory upchuck/reaction scene here.

**\*BLACK MOON** 1934. Ref: TV. Jim Shapiro. V 7/3/34. Lentz. Lee. Fango 6/89.

"The voodoo drums are going." Juanita Lane (Dorothy Burgess) is "always playing with drums," and longs to return to the Caribbean island of San Christopher, where she was brought up in the voodoo ways. There, "fugitives from Haiti" practice "blood worship ... sacrifice to the black gods"; dolls are voodoo; and "Mysteries of the Voodoo Cult" is required reading. At the end, Juanita is ordered to sacrifice her own child (Cora Sue Collins).

The latter is the most dramatic sequence, but it's handily resolved by a pistol shot, the second such resolution in the movie. Director Roy William Neill and cameraman Joseph August drum up some atmosphere here, but, storywise, nothing much can happen: The principals are here, in the house; the voodoo ceremonies are there, in the wild, and rarely does the twain meet. Black Moon and *Revolt of the Zombies* represent valleys between the early voodoo-movie peaks of *White Zombie* and *I Walked with a Zombie*, though this is a much more creditable effort than *Revolt*. The following year, of course, Neill made the handsome *The Black Room* (which see). Best-acting honors in *Black Moon* go to Fay Wray and Clarence Muse.

**BLACK MOON RISING** New World (Joel B. Michaels, Douglas Curtis) 1986 color 100m. D: Harley Cokliss. Story, SP: John Carpenter. SP: also Desmond Nakano, William Gray. Mus: Lalo Schifrin. SpVisFX: Cinemotion; Max W. Anderson. SpFX: SpFX Unltd.; (coord) Larry Cavanaugh, Bruce Steinheimer; (elec) Brent Scrivner. Car: Bernard Beaujardin. LaserFX: Laser Sound. Ref: TV. MFB'86:201. V 1/15/86. SFExam 1/10/86. With Tommy Lee Jones, Linda Hamilton, Robert Vaughn, Richard Jaeckel, Lee Ving, Bubba Smith, Dan Shor, William Sanderson, Keenan Wynn, Nick Cassavetes, Don Opper.

An experimental car, the Black Moon—a "hell of a car" with a "revolutionary design" and a tapwater converter for the engine, plus rockets and the ability to "fly" from one tower of a building to another—can hit speeds of 300+ miles per hour.... Undistinguished mixture of violent action and suspense.

**BLACK NOISE** Nick Gorski 1986 video color 9m. Ref: SFExam 9/26/86:D-15. PFA Notes 2/21/88.

*The Day the Earth Stood Still* "literally condensed ... into a nine-minute fable."

**2P The BLACK PEARL** 1977? feature. Ref: Ernie Fink. V 8/24/77:29 (ad).

Huge manta ray attacks, destroys fishing boats.

**BLACK RAINBOW** (B) Miramax/Goldcrest Films & TV (Quested-Helman) 1989 color 113m. SP, D: Mike Hodges. Ph: Gerry Fisher. Mus: John Scott. PD: Voytek. FX: Bob Shelley's SpFxInt'l. Mkp: Alan Weisinger. VocalFX: David Sharpe. Ref: TV: MHE (Fox Video); 99m. Stanley. V 12/27/89: "enjoyable supernatural thriller." 8/8/90:11 (ad). MFB '90:160-61: "auspicious ... relaunch of Goldcrest." With Rosanna Arquette, Jason Robards, Tom Hulce, Mark Joy, Ed L. Grady.

"I'm only God's instrument." A phony spiritualist (Arquette) discovers that she really has "the power of prophecy," "predicts a murder" and deaths from a nuclear accident. ("It haunts me.")

Pretentious but minor variation on *Night Has a 1000 Eyes, Scanners*, etc. Kinda neat scene: the hitman pumping bullet after bullet into the vision of the heroine. Tantalizing ending: the reporter still chasing the phantom lady.

**\*The BLACK ROOM** Robert North 1935 68m. (*The Black Room Mystery* - ad t). SP: Strawn, Myers. Story: Strawn. Mus D: Louis Silvers. AD: Stephen Goosson. Ref: TV. Lee. Lentz. Hardy/HM. Phantom. Martin. Scheuer. Stanley. Weldon. V 8/21/35. With Torben Meyer, Colin Tapley.

"I end as I began." The tyrannical Baron Gregor (Boris Karloff)—"Gregor's a monster!"—who makes a practice of carrying off and killing any woman he pleases, lives in fear of a "barbaric prophecy" concerning the House of de Berghman, which foretells that he will meet death at the hands of his twin brother Anton (Karloff). As a preventive measure, Gregor tosses his brother into a pit in the Black Room. Before he dies, however, Anton vows to fulfill the prophecy anyway—and does.... "The kindly Anton" is a colorless role, the better to set off the juiciness of Karloff's other role. Sumptuous, highly atmospheric lighting, art direction, and music make *The Black Room* a "B" with an "A" feel at times. But it would still be just a stiffly acted, attractive bore if it weren't for Karloff's Gregor and lines like his "Lots of juice in a pear!" Certainly one of Columbia's best-looking horror thrillers of the time.

**BLACK ROSES** S.G.E./Rayvan (John Fasano) 1988 color 83m. D: Fasano. SP: Cindy Sorrell. Mus: Elliot Solomon. SpMkpFX: (Damian) Richard Alonzo; (speaker/Julie) Anthony C. Bua; (fans) John Dodds; (zombie) Arnold Gargiulo. Opt: Light & Motion. Ref: TV. SFChron Dtbk 8/21/88. V 1/18/89. With John Martin, Ken Swofford, Sal Viviano, Julie Adams, Carla Ferrigno, Carmine Appice, Karen Planden.

"The disciples of the devil are invading our town." Or, Bad Day at Mill Basin. The heavy-metal band Black Roses brings its "satanic music" to town, and high school students begin neglecting their studies and staying out late. Julie (Planden) wants to fraternize with her English teacher, Mr. Moorhouse (Martin), in the worst way, and transforms into a long-necked demon; teen rock fans are becoming "soldiers of evil" and break out in monster faces; and a spider-scorpion creature drags a hapless parent into a speaker.... Damian (Viviano) and his band prove to be—with humorless irony—demons from hell, after all, just like the old folks said. This supernatural *Impulse* should be a lampoon of rock-o-phobia, but instead seems to be simply a case of it, at least in terms of story. In terms of spectacle it's a celebration of makeup effects and rock music. Though script and production here are uncoordinated, the *Gremlins*-like, fast-motion corruption/construction of the town has its engaging moments.

**\*BLACK SABBATH** Alta Vista 1964 (1963). Mkp: Otello Fava. Ref: TV: Sinister Cinema video; Eng. version. Ottoson/AIP. Hardy/HM. Lee. Wolf/Horror. no V. Stanley.

"The Wurdalak." From the story (aka "The Family of a Wurdalak") by Alexei Tolstoy. Remade as *La Notte dei Diavoli* (1972/II). "That's not your child out there! It's a wurdalak!" The latter are cadavers "always seeking blood"—specifically, the "blood of those they love." In this 44-minute tale (the best of the three which comprise *Black Sabbath*), a whole family is vam-

pirized, or wurdalak-ized. ("It's like a nightmare!") An Inverted Family Values theme informs Marcello Fondato's script (with help from director Mario Bava and Alberto Bevilacqua). The scene in which the now-vampiric grandson cries from the doorstep, "Mama! I'm cold!" is justly celebrated, and the all-in-the-family horrors continue when grandpa vampire (Boris Karloff as Gorca) tells his not-yet-a-wurdalak daughter Sdenka (Susy Andersen), "No one can love you as much as we do—you know that." Noted: the wonderfully weird lighting for the ruins, and the fog-and-spider-web work for same and for the house. Occasional zooms hoke it up, but the only real drawback: the banal love scenes. As host, Karloff says "The Wurdalak" is "from a novel by Ivan Tolstoy." At any rate, it's perhaps the high point for both Bava and Italian horror.

**\*The BLACK SCORPION** Amex Prods. (Frank Melford/Jack Dietz) 1957. Ph: L. Lindon. Elec Mus: Jack Cookerly. Anim: Pete Peterson. SdFX: Mandine Rogne. Ref: TV: vt. Warren/KWTS!: U.S.-Mex.? Larson. Lee. Hardy/SF.

"Something absolutely unknown"—a "demon bull" perhaps—is poisoning cattle in Mexico. A regular-sized scorpion (a "little monster") found embedded live in a rock for centuries heralds the discovery of the "granddaddy of them all"—a giant black scorpion—numerous other huge scorpions in underground caverns, and a "worm thirty feet long" .... In the second or third rank of Fifties monster movies, *The Black Scorpion* (like *The Monolith Monsters* and *Fiend without a Face*) comes up with some memorable monsters, but puts them down in an otherwise competent but indifferent movie. The first closeup of a drooling scorpion model head disappoints, but the stop-motion scampering movements of the critters in subsequent shots are suitably unearthly. Just one highlight of the descent-into-the-caverns sequence: the worm vs. scorpions battle. It's the stuff of nightmares. A big romance and a little boy dilute the horror; drifting volcanic smoke aids the atmosphere.

**BLACK SUN 731** see *Men behind the Sun*

**BLACK SUNDAY (I & II)** see also *Maschera del Demonio, La*

**The BLACK THRONE** (I) Beatrice & Avenir 1984 color feature. D: Steve Lander. Ref: Ecran F 43:70, 71: completed. no Hound. no Martin.

Mythical creatures ... Globus, Lord of Evil ... Prince Vaillant.

**BLACK TO THE FUTURE** Video (Phil Prince) 1986 color 85m. D: Prince. Ref: Adam '89. With Erica Boyer, Kristara Barrington, Melissa Melendez.

"Magic car that transforms women into sex symbols."

**BLACK TRIANGLE, The** see *Black Crystal*

**The BLACKMAGIC WITH BUDDHA** (H. K.) c1981? color/ws 91m. (aka *Blackmagic with Butchery*). D: Lo Lieh. SP: Chiu Chi Kin. Ph: Wong Wing Lung. Ref: TV: Trans-Continental Video; Thai dubbed; Eng. titles. Fango 107:59,60. NST! 4:17. With Lo Lieh, Candy Yu, Chau Sing.

Ben worships the brain of the mummy of the Brain Devil from New Guinea. At first, it grants his every wish, but later it leaps upon him, and an exorcist makes him vomit up crud which forms a brain. In the climactic sequence, the beheaded Ben does a Vesuvius and spouts brain stuff, then grows a brain head. Killed, Brain Devil departs Ben who, restored the life, now lacks a brain. Doctor: "Yet he can survive. It's incredible".... Cheesy but fun, outrageous horror-fantasy. Meant to be really horrible, it's really funny. Highlights: the leech-like brains attacking the man in the tub ... the pulsating brain in the fridge ... the crawling brain ... the brain appearing on the face of the Mona Lisa. It's incredible.

**BLACKOUT** Ambient Light/Adams-Stefano (Forbidden Images) 1988 color 91m. D: Doug Adams. SP: Joseph Stefano. Orig SP: Adams, Laura Ferguson, Cynthia Williams. Mus: Don Davis. SpFxMkp: Doug Smith. SpMechFX: Bob and Kevin McCarthy. SdFX: M. A. Stein. Ref: TV: Magnum Ent. video. V 10/12/88. Video View 12/89. With Carol Lynley, Gail O'Grady, Joseph Gian.

"I went a little crazy." Caroline Boyle (O'Grady) returns home, stabs local boy (Gian) with screwdriver, in order to halt his advances. "Not again!" cries her mother (Lynley), when told. Caroline's nightmare flashes bring back only part of the horrors that happened there when she was seven.... Only very mildly intriguing mystery with shock scenes fails as character study or horror drama. Some of the story ingredients may recall Stefano's *Psycho*, but the cold-sober approach does not.

**BLACKOUT** (B) Poker 1994 (1992) color 98m. D, P: Paulita Sedgwick. SP: Damian Wong. Ph: C.T. Maris. Mus: Jake Williams. PD: Angel Sedgwick. Ref: V 5/9/94: "embarrassingly awkward low-budgeter." With Kali, Abi Manox, Jean Marc Ferriere, Ultra Violet.

"Fascistic authorities," the Red Zone, and Eternacream, in a "futuristic, war-zone London."

**BLACKOUTS** see *Bill and Coo*

**The BLADE MASTER** (I) New Line (Newman) 1983 ('84-U.S.) color 92m. (*Ator the Invincible: The Return* - ad t. aka *The Blademaster. Ator, The Blademaster* - TV. *Cave Dwellers* - '90 FVI reissue t). SP, D: David Hills. Ph: F. Slonisco. Mus: Demer, Rustichelli. AD: John Gregory. Mkp: Pat Russel. Ref: TV. V 10/10/84. 10/20/82:43(ad). SFExam 4/6/84 (ad). Scheuer. Martin. With Miles O'Keeffe, Lisa Foster, David Cain Haughton, Charles Borromel, Chen Wong, Robert Black, Hershel Curtis (wizard).

Ingredients: the "nucleus," a prehistoric nuclear bomb which is "everything—and nothing"; a gigantic snake lurking in the shadows; invisible beings in a cave, and flashbacks to the original *Ator* (III).... Film gives new meaning to the word "shoddy."

**BLADE OF THE RIPPER** (I-Sp) Elios Film 197-? color/ws? c85m. Ph: G. Ferrando. Sets: Cubero, Galicia. Mkp: Mario Di Salvio. Ref: TV: Interglobal HV; Eng. version. V 5/9/84:264 (ad). V/CHVD: with G. Hilton, E. Fenech. Hound: 1984. no Martin. Stanley. VWB: apparently sfa *Next Victim* (which see), but with different cast list and photography credits. With Bruno Corazzari, Marella Corbi, Miguel Del Castillo, Luis De Tejada, Brizio Montinaro, Pouchie, Mira Vidotto.

"Another girl slashed to death!" A "sex fiend" is at large in Vienna. ("And he's still using the razor?") But is the "razor killer" the same person that slashes the heroine's friend Carol to death? At the end, Julie's "ghost" helps set things right.

Cheap, apparently shot on tape, European slasher movie features oppressive extreme closeups which lop off the tops and sides of heads. Typical shot: a nose and moving lips in focus. Opening credits are also lopped off.

**BLADEMASTER, The** see *Blade Master, The*

**BLADES** Troma/Finegan Int'l. 1989 (1988) color 98m. SP, D, Ed: Thomas R. Rondinella. SP, Assoc P: William R. Pace. Mus: John Hodian. PD: J. C. Svec. SpMechFX: Wilfred Caban. SpMkpFX: Vincent Guastini. SpSdDes: Hodian, Andy Kravitz. P, Story: John P. Finegan. Ref: TV. V 6/27/90:48 (hv). With Robert North, Jeremy Whelan, Victoria Scott, Holly Stevenson, Donald Jackson.

"I've seen that mower before." It's "business as usual" at Tall Grass Country Club—a few murders can't stop a tournament. Clues: swaths of mowed grass leading up to the bodies, and traces of crankcase oil. A "baby" mower is caught, but the big one—a "renegade lawnmower"—proves to be still at large.... Sendup of *Jaws* and, perhaps incidentally, *Maximum Overdrive* is either too dumb or not dumb enough. Might have been a funny short. Cf. *Over-Sexed Rugsucker from Mars.*

See also: *Lawnmower Man, The.*

**BLESS THIS HOUSE** (H.K.) D & B Films/Dickson Poon & Linda Kuk 1988 color c88m. D: Ronny Yu. SP, Story: Clifton Ko. SP: also J. Yuen, John Ng. Ph: P. H. Sang. Mus: Richard Yuen. AD: Fong Ying. Ref: TV: Rainbow Video; Eng. titles. NST! 4:17. With Tung Piu, Deborah, Loletta Lee, Stephen Ho, Leung Shi Lung, Manfred Wong, Chan C. Yan.

"Papa's possessed!" The boss gives Papa, his wife, and their two daughters his private villa on Dog Belly Hill. The house soon proves to be haunted by a family burnt to death there ten years earlier, whose members must now burn the new family in order to reincarnate.... Or, Mr. Blandings Finds His Dream House is Haunted. The early, ghost-mystery clues—an ambulatory potted palm, "funny paintings" behind the wallpaper, a face in a photographic slide—interest more than the hectic solution. Funniest sequence involves a haunted Hoover (cf. *Over-Sexed Rugsucker from Mars*).

**BLIND DATE** New Line/Omega & Wescom (Forminx) 1984 (1983) color 99m. SP, D, P: Nico Mastorakis. SP: also F. C. Perry. Mus: Stanley Myers. SpDigitalFX: Phil Stone. SpFX: Y. Samiotis. SpSdDes: John Kongos. Mkp: A. Kouroupou. Ref: TV: proposed sequel: *Run, Stumble & Fall.* Ecran F 41:70. V 5/23/84. 5/9/84:78. With Joseph Bottoms, Kirstie Alley, Keir Dullea, James Daughton (Dave).

For Jonathon Ratcliff, the blind wearer of a revolutionary sonar device and a visual-synthesizer device, it's like "looking through the eye of a computer." A CompuVision tape records what he sees. Fortunately for him, the three punks who attacked him when he was truly blind always meet at the same subway station to torment cripples.... Fortunately for the movie, this sf gimmick is interesting, if far-fetched. Unfortunately for the movie, an arduous storyline is required to connect the gimmick to the hero's past to murders in the present.

**BLIND FAITH** Third Coast/Blind Faith Partners 1988 color 86m. SP, D, SpMkpFX: Dean Wilson. Ph: Tomaszewski, Pettalia. PD: John Hyatt. Ref: TV: AEC video. Hound. no Martin. With Erik Gunn, Kevin Yon, Kirk Swenk, David Winick (Ted Partridge), Lynne Brown (creature), Rosanne Steffens (refrigerator half-victim).

"They were too big to hide!" Ted Partridge tortures, mutilates, and kills the women chained in the basement of his "church." Shot-on-tape no-budgeter from Grand Rapids makes a Jerry Warren-like narrative separation between action (taken care of in brief flashbacks) and dialogue/story, as people interrogate suspects in the case of four missing murder victims. The bulk of the video is talk; the main bit of gore is reserved for the finale. The "creature" is apparently the disfigured person seen in the flashbacks.

**BLIZZARD OF BLOOD** see *Iced*

**The BLOB** Tri-Star & Blay-Kastner/Jack H. Harris (Palisades, Ca.) 1988 color c98m. SP, D: Chuck Russell. SP: also Frank Darabont. Mus: Michael Hoenig. SpVisFX: Dream Quest; (sup) Hoyt Yeatman. Creature FX: Lyle Conway; Stuart Ziff. MkpFX: Tony Gardner; (N.Y.) John Caglione. Blob/meteor: Diligent Dwarves FX. MechFX: Frazee & Frazee; All FX. Anim: (sup) Jeff Burks; (stopmo) Mark Sullivan. Ref: TV: RCA-Col. Home Video. V 8/3/88. SFChron 8/5/88. MFB'89:170. SFExam 8/5/88. Oak Trib 8/5/88. With Shawnee Smith, Kevin Dillon, Donovan Leitch, Jeffrey DeMunn, Candy Clark, Art La Fleur, Sharon Spelman, Del Close, Ricky Paull Goldin, Billy Beck, Richard Crenna Jr.

"Fell from the sky!" After a meteorite crashes near Arborville, Earth, an "old man with a funky hand" dissolves, heroine Meg (Smith) pulls goo-engulfed hero Paul's (Leitch) arm off like a glove, and something sucks the cafe's kitchen help into a drainpipe. Government "microbe hunters" attempt to suppress the truth: Something in outer space has caused a satellite-borne, experimental biological-warfare virus to mutate and begin growing at a geometric rate....

The story is stitched together with hackneyed soulless-science and ruthless-officialdom themes, and *Alien* tentacles compromise the original 1958 *Blob*'s jelly's shapelessness (as well as the "Terror has no shape" publicity). But if, in appearance, the blob itself still seems pretty innocuous, the things it does are another story. See, for instance, the detachable arm and drainpipe sequences. (In the latter, the pipe develops an Adam's apple lump.) And the sucked-up-to-the-ceiling scenes. (Especially the Tell-Tale Yo-Yo scene.) And there's a choice uh-oh! line re a sewer rat: "What rat?"

See also *Blobermouth. Claymation Comedy of Horrors.*

**BLOBERMOUTH** L.A. Connection-Kent Skov (Jack H. Harris) 1990 color 86m. D: K. Skov. SP: Rothman, Pinto, Bucholz, Skov, from the play by the L.A. Connection. Anim: Jacque, Berkos. Ref: V 4/15/91: "the novelty wears off." Voices: Robert Bucholz as Steve McQueen, Frances Kelly, Stephen L. Rothman.

New dialogue for *The Blob* (1958).

**BLONDS HAVE MORE FUN** Producers Associates/Essex 1980 (1979) color c90m. (*Blondes Have More Fun* - ad t). D: John Seeman. Ph: Dwight Walker. Mus: Ronny Romanovich. Mkp: David Clark. Ref: TV: Essex Video. With Jessie St. James, Jack Wright, Dorothy LeMay, John Leslie, Seka.

San Francisco. Professor Brains's "new secret formula, right out of the laboratory," proves to be a "love potion that works"— PQM-2 gives users an insatiable sexual appetite. Scrappy, unfunny sf-porno-comedy. Lone highlight: St. James' striptease.

**BLOOD BRIDE** (Sp) 1979 color 95m. D: Robert J. Avrech. Ref: Ecran F 38:96. Hound. no Martin. no Stanley. no Maltin '92. no Scheuer. no Lentz. no V. V/CHVD.With Ellen Barber, Philip English.

Bride discovers husband is a "bloodthirsty maniac" (Hound).

**BLOOD CHURCH** Phoenix 1991 color feature. Ref: Fango 104:12. With Linnea Quigley ("recruiting witch").

**BLOOD CLAN** (Can.) Festival Films (Glynis Whiting) 1990 color 87m. D: Charles Wilkinsen. SP: G. Whiting. Ref: V 10/1/90. PT 12:45: "suspenseful." Fango 111:30. With Michelle Little, Gordon Pinsent, Robert Wisden.

Cannibalistic Bean clan. "Mild." (V)

**BLOOD CULT** Linda Lewis 1985 color 89m. D: Christopher Lewis. SP: Stuart Rosenthal. SpMkpFX: David Powell, Robert Brewer. Ref: V 8/21/85:44: "derivative of previous stalk and slash horror pics"; shot on tape. 4/15/87:40. 2/3/88:34. McCarty II. Phantom: "tedious." Morse: "amateurish." Stanley. With Julie Andelman, Charles Ellis.

Devil cultists avenging Salem witch trials make mannequin out of victims' body parts.

See also *Revenge.*

**BLOOD DELIRIUM** (I) Cine Decima 1988 color 85m. (*Delirio di Sangue*). SP, D: Sergio Bergonzelli. SP: also Mertes, Cordi. Ref: Hardy/HM2: necrophilia, dismemberment, *Color Me Blood Red* theme. Palmerini. MV. With John Phillip Law, Gordon Mitchell, Brigitte Christensen.

**BLOOD DEMON** see *Tale from the East*

**BLOOD DINER** Vestron (Lightning Pictures)/PMS Filmworks (Jimmy Maslon) 1987 color 90m. D, Co-P: Jackie Kong. SP: Michael Sonye. Creative Consul: Bill Osco. Mus: Don Preston. SpFX: Bruce Zahlava. Mkp: Loraina Drucker. ElecFX: Michael Hyatt. SdFX: Bob Biggart. Ref: TV. V 9/2/87. East Bay Express 8/28/87. With Rick Burks, Carl Crew, Roger Dauer, LaNette La France, Lisa Guggenheim.

"They call me Sheetar!" The pickled brain and eyeballs of Uncle Anwar (Drew Godderis) look on as Michael (Burks) and George Tutman (Crew) try to "construct Sheetar from the body parts of many immoral girls." At the end, they fashion a "blood buffet" to summon the spirit of the "bloodthirsty goddess of black magic" (Tanya Papanicolas) to the body.... Low comedy and high gore, as *Blood Feast* story and makeup material prove less funny intentionally than that film was accidentally. (*Blood Diner* admittedly beats out *Goremet, Zombie Chef from Hell*. Most anything does.) The cannibal-cafe climax, however, captures a bit of the feel of the George Romero feeding-frenzy scenes in his *Dead* movies. The onlookers-laugh-as-car-tire-crushes-head scene is apparently an hommage to *Toxic Avenger*.

**BLOOD FEVER** see *Mosquito*

**2P BLOOD FREAK** Variety Fair/Preacher Man Co. 1975(1972) color 86m. (aka *Blood Freaks*). D, P: Steve Hawkes. Ph: Ron Sill. Mus, Ed: Gil Ward. Ref: TV: Video Treasures (Mercury Video). Phantom. VSB. Martin. no Scheuer. V 12/6/72:22 (rated). 12/24/75:6 (rated). PT 5:39. With Hawkes, Dana Cullivan, Randy Grinter, Jr., Tera Anderson, Heather Hughes, Larry Wright.

"All we did was give this guy some turkey." In this story "based partly on fact, partly on probability," poultry ranch experiments on turkey give the hero (Hawkes) a turkey head and a taste for blood. The film's revelation scene is one of the great stupid moments in Z-movie history. The only tipoff: the forlorn "gobble, gobble" in the bedroom scene which precedes. "He's not Herschell any more," someone later aptly notes. The all-a-nightmare ending disappoints but can't take away from the Big Bird-as-vampire-horror-monster premise. Plus: buzzsaw gore and Bible based warnings on the effect of drugs—pot as well as turkey serum.

**BLOOD FRENZY** Hollywood Family Ent./MPM & Wescom 1987 color 90m. D, P: Hal Freeman. SP: Ted Newsom. Ref: V/CHVD. Bowker. Scheuer. Hound. Phantom. McCarty II: "uneven acting." Martin: made-for-video. V 4/22/87: 33(ad). Morse: "slow and cheap." With Wendy MacDonald, Hank Garrett, Lisa Loring.

Psychotherapist's patients go to desert retreat, get killed.

**BLOOD GAMES** Epic/Yakov Bentsvi (Fortune Ent.) 1990 (1989) color 88m. D: Tanya Rosenberg. SP: Clyde, Hennessy, Saunders. Story: Makichuk. SpFxCoord: Greg Hendrickson. MkpSup: Vered Schubert. SdFxSup: Dave Rave. Ref: TV. V 3/18/91:87 (hv): "stalker horror." SFChron Dtbk 10/25/92.

Cheesy, obvious redneck hi-jinks in this not-quite-slasher, not-quite-*Deliverance*, not-quite-*The Most Dangerous Game,* re violence done to Babe and the Ballgirls and the latter's retaliatory violence.

**BLOOD HARVEST** UAV (Burzynski)/Buddy's Inc. (Shooting Ranch) 1986 color feature. D: Bill Rebane. SP: Ben Benson, Emil Joseph. Story: Vaalar, Arthur. Ph: Ito. AD: Joseph Jolton. SpMkpFX: Pat Cannon, Robert Johnson. SpFX: SpFxInt'l. SdFX: Jim Moore. Ref: TV. TVG. PT 13:49: "gory horror movie with Tiny Tim." V 10/19/88:142. With T. Tim, Itonia, Dean West, Lori Minneti, Peter Krause, Frank Benson.

Stilted acting, mild gore, and extended t&a footage in this tale of a killer who hangs his victims by their feet and cuts their throats. Only creepy element: the macabre renditions of "Jack and Jill" by the "goofy" Mervo (Tiny Tim), an obvious red herring. The usual lax Rebane thriller.

**BLOOD HOOK** Troma/Golden Chargers & Spider Lake Films (David Herbert) 1987 (1986) color 95m. (*Muskie Madness* - orig t). D: James Mallon. SP: Larry Edgerton, John Galligan. Story: Gail Anderson, Herbert, Mallon, Douglas Rand. Mus: Thomas Naunas. SpMkpDes: Dale Kuipers. Ref: TV: Prism Ent. video. V 5/20/87. 10/16/85:242. With Mark Jacobs, Lisa Todd, Patrick Danz, Sara Hauser, Paul Drake, Don Winters (Leudke), Christopher Whiting.

"Lot of things can happen around that lake." The phantom angler reeling in humans proves to be a Korean War vet with a metal plate in his head. The oddball plot also involves treble hooks, "the devil's tritone," bodies roped together like fish, and cicadas. (Recordings of the latter provided by the University of Michigan.) Weird city folks on vacation in Wisconsin meet weird north woods people. New wave Rodney (Danz), Valley gal Kiersten (Hauser), and psychobabbler Ann (Todd) are amusingly out-of-place at the Muskie Madness festival, but most of the other characters are simply eccentric, and the movie is full of dead spots. Some very droll moments—e.g., Ann's counseling the madman: "If you feel comfortable killing me, that's fine. I'm adult"—but the film's pace is so lackadaisical that the mystery, horror, suspense, and comedy elements are all over the place.

**BLOOD ISLAND** see *Who's the Killer?*

**BLOOD LAKE** Barryfilm/BL Movie Corp.(Doug Barry) 1987 color 82m. D, Ph: Tim Boggs. SP: D. Barry. Mus: Steven Lee Robertson; Bryan Barker; R.D. Allen. SpVisFX: Christopher Tullis. SpSdFX: Studio 7. Ref: TV: United video. no Martin. With D. Barry, Angela Darter, Mike Kaufman, Andrea Adams, Tiny Frazier, Travis Krasser, Christie Willoughby, Michael Darter.

"Killed Tom, too!" Slasher (Frazier) slashes teens at Cedar Lake. Abysmal shot-on-taper.

**BLOOD LINK** (W.G.-I) Zadar/Robert Palaggi 1983 ('85-U.S.) color 95m. (*The Link* - alt t). Story, D: Alberto De Martino. SP: Theodore Apstein. Story: also Max De Rita. Mus: Ennio Morricone. Mkp: Giulio Natalucci. Ref: TV: Embassy Home Ent. video. V 6/12/85. Palmerini: aka *Extra sensorial*.With Michael Moriarty (Craig & Keith), Penelope Milford, Cameron Mitchell, Sarah Langenfeld, Martha Smith, Virginia McKenna, Geraldine Fitzgerald, Alex Diakun, Reece and Troy Hasanen (twin boys).

Hamburg. Dr. Craig Mannings and his long-lost Siamese twin Keith have a bond "in the blood and in the mind." Craig "sees" his deranged brother's murders through Keith's eyes; Keith's ESP may be less well developed, but he can at least detect Craig's disembodied presence. ("The other part of me is in town....") An interesting exercise for Moriarty, if for no one else. Physically, he manages to suggest two different personalities—one paranoid (Keith), the other simply reserved (Craig)—linked by a certain coldness. The script itself is less subtle at comparing and contrasting the two. An undigested subplot concerns mind control, and, in a senseless coda, the supposedly dead Keith grabs Craig and takes his place among the living.

**BLOOD LUST** (B) Harrison Marks 1980 color feature
D: Russell Gay. Ref: Jones: "hardcore Dracula movie."

**BLOOD MANIAC** (Thai) 1986 feature

D: Zu Won-Tsuing. Ref: Weisser/ATC.

Monster-baby, zombie, spirit-haunted house.

**BLOOD MASSACRE** Applause Prods. (Gateway Ent. & Pacific Horizon Ent./H. N. Esbin) 1988 color 85m. SP, D, P, Co-Ed: Don Dohler. SP, P: also Barry Gold, Dan Buehl. Ph: C. Chrysler, J. Herberger. Mus: D. Linck, J. Christopher. MkpFX: John Cosentino, Larry Schlechter. Pyro FX: P. E. Lister. Ref: TV: Star III video. PT 12:51. With George Stover, Robin London (Liz), James DiAngelo, Thomas Humes, Lisa Defuso, Richard Ruxton (Howard Parker), Don Leifert.

"They're crazy!" In this loose reworking of *Arsenic and Old Lace*, some on-the-lam murderous types discover that their hosts are deadly too. The Parkers' daughter Elizabeth is a "nut case" who killed her psychiatrist, and the Parker clan chops up a cop and stakes and decapitates the thugs. Seems the Parkers are not only cannibals, but ghouls or aliens with replaceable skin.... Garbage in.... Some of the actors in this un-fun shoestringer are funnier than the others, though not intentionally.

**BLOOD MOON** (Austral.) Village Roadshow & Michael Fisher (Stanley O'Toole) 1990 color 102m. (aka *Bloodmoon*). D: Alec Mills. SP: Robert Brennan. Mus: B. May. Ref: V 4/11/90: "abysmal"; includes "fright break." 5/13/91:105: turns up at drive-in in *Proof*. Sacto Bee 8/16/91. Martin. With Leon Lissek, Christine Amor, Ian Williams.

"Slasher pic" (V) set in and around a boarding school for girls.

**THE BLOOD OF HEROES** (Austral.-U.S.) Kings Road Ent. & New Line 1989 color 102m. (95m.-U.S.) (*The Salute of the Jugger* - Aust. t). SP, D: David Peoples. Mus: Todd Boekelheide. SpMkp: Michael Westmore, Bob McCarron. SpFxCoord: Neville Maxwell. Ref: TV. V 10/11/89. 2/21/90:155. Cinef 7/90. MFB'90:334-5. With Rutger Hauer, Joan Chen, Vincent D'Onofrio, Max Fairchild, Hugh Keays-Byrne.

Wastelands and an underground city are the setting for a futuristic horror hockey played with chains, clubs, and dog skulls—*Rollerball* Down Under—an endurance contest measured with stones rather than a time clock. Spare but watchable sf-actioner majors in special makeup scars and wounds ("I like scars"), credibly captures jock posturing, bravado, honor, camaraderie, etc., if the story pretty much goes nowhere.

**BLOOD OF THE BLACK DOG** (H.K.) 198-? feature (aka *The Accident*). Ref: NST! 4:6-7, 17-18. Fango 107:59-60.

Little girl's ghost takes revenge on those responsible for her death. At the end, she possesses a man.

**BLOOD ORGY OF THE LEATHER GIRLS** Michael Lucas Prods.(H.S. Rosenthal & Jon Jost) 1988 color 73m. SP,D: Meredith Lucas. SP: also Sarah Dicken. Titles: R. Ross. Ref: TV: Forbidden Cinema Video. With Phillip Silverstein, Melissa Lawrence, Robin Gingold.

"What are we gonna do with all these bodies?" Sometimes droll, deliberately stilted parody of public-service films (and of MS. 45-type films), re the "wrath of the female." Plantsville, site of the "most bloody series of crimes ever perpetrated by a group of adolescent girls." Girl-gang horror ingredients include mutilation

by five-pronged cultivator ... ear torture ... body-disposal gore ... death by crossbow ... castration ... and rape by drill. Plus a drive-in movie re the "nuclear remnants of the Fourth Earth Empire."

**BLOOD RAGE** FCG/Marianne Kanter (J. W. Stanley) 1987 (1984) color 84m. (*Nightmare at Shadow Woods* - alt t. *Slasher. Complex* - early titles). D: John W. Grissmer. SP: Richard Lamden. Mus: R. Einhorn. SpFxCoord: Ed French. Ref: V 6/17/87: "hackneyed script, wooden acting and trite plot." 4/29/87:16, 170. 5/13/87:15: playing. Martin. Phantom: "pathetic." With Louise Lasser, Mark Soper (Todd/Terry), M. Kanter, Julie Gordon, William Fuller.

"Slash-and-splash movie" re an "evil twin." (V)

**BLOOD RELATIONS** (Can.) Miramax Films/SC Ent. Corp. (Nicholas Stiliadis) 1988 color 90m. D: Graeme Campbell. SP: Stephen Saylor. Mus: Mychael Danna. AD: Gina Hamilton. Ref: TV. TVG. V 5/25/88. Martin. With Jan Rubes, Lydie Denier, Kevin Hicks, Lynne Adams, Ray Walston, Saylor.

Blah intrigue among the rich and predatory gives way here to heavy-handed black comedy-horror. Among the horrors: open-head surgery, a variation on the *Diabolique* tub scene, ungodly screams from a woman having needles stuck into her skull, impromptu brain surgery in a basement "torture chamber" on a patient who is quite awake, the discovery of a man's body which is missing the top of the skull, a woman in a glass case who opens her eyes, and a cooking pan full of brains ("food for thought").

**BLOOD RITUAL** (H. K.) D&B Films (Ricky Ng) 1989? color c88m. D: Li Yuen Ching. Ph: Jim Pak Hung. AD: Chow Siu Man. Ref: TV: World Video; Eng. titles. NST! 4:18. With Chiu Siu Keung, Gina Lam, Lam Ki Yam, Dion Lam.

"You even got me to swallow a finger!" An "evil religion" sacrifices nude women at a "secret place" and promulgates the theory that "our bodies belong to God and everyone else." Routine martial-arts actioner features random sacrificial-altar, meathook, and buzz-saw gore, and occasional odd titles such as "My intestines are a mess!"

**BLOOD SABBATH** JLT(Bairn/Fluet)/Barbet Film 1972 81m. (aka *Yyalah*). D: Brianne Murphy. SP: William Bairn. Ph: Michael Margulies. Mus: Bax. Ed Supv or Des: Hugo Grimaldi. Mkp: Gordon Freed, Chuck House. Ref: TV: vt. Stanley: "some good ideas." PT 15:51. Captain Video cat. no Phantom. no Hound. no Martin. no Maltin '92. no Scheuer. With Tony Geary, Susan Damante, Dyanne Thorne, Uschi Digard, Sam Gilman, Steve Gravers.

"No good comes of that lake." Each year, the local villagers sacrifice a child to the coven of Alotta, Queen of the Witches (Thorne); the latter extract the soul, and eventually the child becomes one of them. One year — out of love for a water nymph — a Vietnam vet offers his soul in place of the child's .... Draggy, overserious nudie fantasy-horror. Extra addeds: the cup-o'-blood ceremony and a voodoo doll.

**BLOOD SALVAGE** Paragon Arts Int'l./Ken C. Sanders & High Five Prods. (Evander Holyfield/Martin J. Fischer) 1990 color 98m .(*Mad Jake* - vt t). SP, D: Tucker Johnston. SP: also K.

Sanders. Mus: Tim Temple. SpMkpFX: Bill Johnson. Ref: V 8/22/90: "semi-exciting climax." Cinef 4/91. Fango 101. Martin: a "mess." PT 8:43-44: "tasteless." VWB. With Danny Nelson, Lori Birdsong, John Saxon, Ray Walston, E. Holyfield.

"Splatter" re a "band of backwoods psychos."

**BLOOD SCREAMS** see *Maldicion del Monasterio, La*

**BLOOD SISTERS** Reeltime 1986 color 88m. (*Slash* - orig t). SP, D, Ph: Roberta Findlay. Mus, P: Walter E. Sear. Mus: also Michael Litovsky. Mkp: Jean Carbolla. Ref: TV: Sony Video. V 6/17/87. Stanley. With Amy Brentano, Shannon McMahon, Dan Erickson, Marla Machart, Elizabeth Rose.

Thirteen years after a little boy commits murder and mayhem at the local bordello, Edmondson College sorority pledges arrive at the reputedly-haunted, now-empty house-not-a-home to spend the hell night. ("Looks like a Hitchcock reject!") Visions of sexual encounters past abound, and a homicidal maniac (Erickson) is at large.... And he is, for no perceptible reason other than to ape *Psycho*, in drag. The opening sequence steals from *Halloween*, but most of the "hommages" are to Hitchcock. "Just remember the scene from *The Birds*," says one pledge to the others as they explore the dark at the top of the stairs. The visions seem extraneous to the wearisome Ten Little Indians plot.

**BLOOD SORCERY** see *Bloody Sorcery*

**BLOOD STALKERS** Morgan-Rudley-Webb (Bloodstalkers Ltd.) 1975 color c94m. (*Bloodstalkers* - end cr t). SP, D: Robert W. Morgan. Ph: Irv Rudley. Mus: Stan Webb. AD: Toni Crabtree. SpFX: Doug Hobart. Mkp: Matella-Maria. Title Des: Lanier Noles. Ref: TV: Vidmark Ent. video. V (CHVD). no Phantom. no Lentz. no Weldon. Stanley. no Scheuer. no Martin. VWB: sfa *Night Daniel Died, The* (2P). With Kenny Miller, Jerry Albert, Toni Crabtree, Celea-Anne Cole, Herb Goldstein (The Old Man), Morgan (Jarvis), John R. Meyer (Lester).

"That's blood stalker country now!" Backwoods poachers use a Seminole legend re a "huge, hairy creature" to scare off intruders to their cabin headquarters. But the "monster" who slaughters three of four vacationers proves to be Lester in a monster suit, and the lone survivor, Mike (Albert), slaughters the poachers with ax and scythe ... *Blood Stalkers,* a rather pretentious example of regional filmmaking, borrows the go-it-alone theme from *High Noon*: The local yokels refuse to help Mike. Every scene is overlong and overdone, and the script is talky and mawkish.

**BLOOD STORM** see *Starship*

**BLOOD SYMBOL** (Can.?) TonMor & PB & Plein Ecran 1992 (1991) color 87m. (*Terror for Tracy*-early t) Story, SP, D, P, Ed: Maurice Devereaux. Story, D, P, Ph: Tony Morello. Mus: Brent Holland. PD: Stephane Dufour. SpFxMkp: Luke Poudrier; Adrien Moreau. Artwork: Jean-Denis Rouette. Ref: TV: Atlas video. Fango 153:50-3, 6a. With Micheline Richard, Trilby Jeeves, Anne-Marie Leduc, M. Devereaux, Richard Labelle (Father Olam).

"The blood symbol was the icon of a peculiar cult of devil worshipers ...." The latter seek the "chosen one," who will bear the blood symbol on the back of her neck. Through ritual throat-

slashing and blood-drinking, the members of the cult hope to become immortal .... Technically proficient production is okay as an exercise in style, though style here finally seems indistinguishable from padding, and the actors and their dialogue interfere. A real good-news/bad-news movie. Noted: a stray copy of Fango.

**BLOOD TIES** Fox Network-TV/Richard & Esther Shapiro (Gene Corman) 1991 color c90m. D: Jim McBride. Tel: R. Shapiro. Mus: Brad Fiedel. SpVisFx: Introvision Int'l. SpFX: Bruno van Zeebroeck. Shrike Mural: David Holzman. Mkp: Bonita Dehaven. Ref: TV. TVG. V 6/3/91:55. Oak Trib 5/27/91: "Fox will try anything." With Patrick Bauchau, Harley Venton, Michelle Johnson, Salvator Xuereb, Bo Hopkins, Michael C. Gwynne, Grace Zabriskie.

Violent vampires ("Shrikes") and other, "unconventional vampires who can survive daylight and get the urge to nibble on necks mostly when the love bug bites 'em."(V)

**BLOOD TRACKS** (Swed.) Smart Egg/Tom Sjoberg (George Zecevic) 1986 (1985) color/ws 86m. SP, D: Mats Olsson. Mus: Dag Unenge. SpMkpFX: Dick Ljunggren. Ref: V 5/21/86: Eng. version; "silly premise." With J. Harding, Naomi Kaneda, M. Fitzpatrick.

"Gory horror film" re a "barbaric clan of savages living underneath an abandoned factory."

**2 BLOOD WATERS OF DR. Z** 1972 (*Hydra* - vt t). Elec Mus: Jack Tamul. SpCost: R. Kivett, Martha Fillyaw, Les Lancaster. Mkp: L. J. O'Donnell. Ref: TV. V 7/14/82. Lentz. Weldon. Stanley. no Hardy. VWB.

Cypress Grove, Florida. A doctor with "paranoid tendencies" discovers two new elements and produces a "biological mutation"—a "walking catfish" monster that "becomes" a vampire, at least for a night. (Victims are found bearing signs of "fish bite" on their necks.) The doc's goal: a "new aquatic race," a sort of master race of catfish.... *Dr. Z* alternates between charming and boring ineptitude and demonstrates just how hard it is to make a decent bad movie now. The musical score is horror; the guy in the catfish suit, comedy.

See also: *Attack of the Swamp Creatures.*

**BLOODBATH** see *Thou Shalt Not Kill ... Except*

**BLOODBATH AT THE HOUSE OF DEATH** (B) Wildwood (Ray Cameron) 1984 (1983) color 93m. SP, D: Cameron. SP: also Barry Cryer. Mus: Mike Moran, Mark London. Anim: Graham Garside. OptFX: Howell Opts., Hugh Gordon. Mkp: Eric Allwright. Ref: TV. MFB'84:143. V 5/23/84. Ecran F 39:31. With Kenny Everett, Pamela Stephenson, Vincent Price, Sheila Steafel, Graham Stark, Oscar Quitak.

Headstone Manor, the site of several bloodbaths, proves to have been built upon the burial ground of a group of demonic, extraterrestrial monks, who first take on the form of intruders, then vaporize them. Plus: the "archdisciple of Lucifer himself" (Price), an immortal undead now 700 years old ... a teddy bear which comes to life (the bead eyes move ...) and kills ... a mole (animal) which pops out of a mole (mark) on a man's arm and attacks a woman ... a *Carrie*-like girl (Steafel) who telekinetically beheads her mother with a can opener ... E.T., whom the Earth-departing monks leave behind ("Not again!").... Post-*Airplane!* gross-out, clever-dumb fun is intermittently winning. Monks chant, switch briefly to a chorus of "Daisy," then return to their chant. Suspense-building, *Jaws*-like music accompanies a man's exploration of a forbidding corridor. He opens a door and.... The comic payoffs are always obvious, but still occasionally funny. Price has the most obvious material of all.

**BLOODBATH IN PSYCHOTOWN** American 1990 color feature. Ref: Fango 94:12.

Haunted house in a "colony of witches and psychics."

**BLOODBEAT** (U.S.-F) IFM/Huskypup 1985 (1982) color 84m. SP, D, Exec P: Fabrice-Ange Zaphiratos. Ph: Wladimir Maule. Mkp: Mary-Ann Skawenes (sp?). OptFX: Cinedia. Ref: TV: Trans World video. Stanley. no Scheuer. Martin. With Helen Benton, Terry Brown, Claudia Peyton, James Fitzgibbons, Dana Day, Peter Spelson, Charlie White.

"There's something strange about Sarah." And Cathy (Benton) is "full of visions." When Sarah (Peyton) goes into a trance, a supernatural samurai roams and kills, the house rocks, and bakery goods assault Gary (Brown). ("Everything went crazy.") Supernatural evil here is a blue glow; good is orange. Orange wins. The details of the battle, however, are lost somewhere on the subpar soundtrack, which is surer with classical music (Prokofiev) than with dialogue, and the Cathy-Sarah-samurai connection promises more than it delivers.

**BLOODLUST** (Austral.) Windhover (Ruggi-Spratt) 1992 color 87m. SP, D, P: Richard Wolstencroft, Jon Hewitt. Mus & SdFX: Ross Hazeldine. Ref: V 4/6/92: "crudely made." Jones: vampires. With Jane Stuart Wallace, Kelly Chapman, R. J. O'Neill.

**BLOODLUST: SUBSPECIES III** (U.S.-Romanian) Para HV/Full Moon (Vlad & Oana Paunescu) 1993 color 83m. SP,D: Ted Nicolaou. Idea: C. Band. Ph: Vlad Paunescu. Mus: R. Kosinski, M. Portis. PD: Radu Corciova. SpMkpFX: Alchemy FX; Deak, Toth. Anim: David Allen Prods. Ref: TV: Para HV. Mo. PT 19:54. With Anders Hove, Denice Duff, Kevin Blair, Melanie Shatner, Pamela Gordon, Michael Dellafemina, Ian Haiduc.

"Filmed on location in Transylvania." More blood, drool, and (best of all) shadow life. The most interesting scenes cover the basic training of the novice vampire, Michelle (Duff), Radu's (Hove) "chosen disciple." ("Teach me to fly.") Otherwise, this is strictly small-time, though generally pleasant. At the end, new little subspecies sprout. Follow-up to (a) *Subspecies* and (b) *Bloodstone: Subspecies II.*

**BLOODMOON** see *Blood Moon*

**BLOODSCAPE** see *Escape from Safehaven*

**BLOODSCREAMS** see *Maldicion del Monasterio, La*

**BLOODSHED** see *Crazed*

**BLOODSHED** see *Igor and the Lunatics*

**BLOODSPELL** MCEG & Vista Street (Feifer-Miller/Jessica Rains) 1988 color 88m. D: Deryn Warren. SP: Gerry Daly. Mus: Randy Miller. SpFxMkp: Wade Daily. Ref: V 11/16/88. TVG. With Anthony Jenkins, Aaron Teich, Alexandra Kennedy, John Reno.

Telekinesis, monster, rejuvenation.

The **BLOODSTAINED BUTTERFLY** (I) Filmes? 1971 color/ws 95m. (*Una Farfalla con le Ali Insanguinate*). SP, D: Duccio Tessari. Story, SP: Gianfranco Clerici. Ref: TV: vt; Eng. dubbed. ETC/Giallos.

"Here's another one!" A serial killer appears to be behind three slasher murders, but a fairly interesting, if far-fetched denouement reveals the crimes to be the work of two killers. Dramatically vacant *giallo* trusts too much to its police-science details.

**BLOODSTALKERS** see *Blood Stalkers*

**BLOODSTONE: SUBSPECIES II** (U.S.-Romanian) Para HV/Full Moon (Paunescu) 1993 color 87m. SP, D: Ted Nicolaou. Idea: Charles Band. Ph: V. Paunescu. Mus: R. Kosinski et al. PD: Radu Corciova. Stopmo Anim: David Allen. SpMkpFX: Alchemy FX; M.S. Deak, Wayne Toth. Ref: TV: vt. V 3/1/93:15 (rated). PT 16:63: "one of the best vampire movies in recent years." SFChron Dtbk 5/16/93. 10/31/93. With Anders Hove, Denice Duff, Kevin Blair, Ion Haiduc, Melanie Shatner, Pamela Gordon (Mommy).

Follow-up to *Subspecies* re the vampire Radu. Michelle (Duff) is "reborn" as a vampire; Radu (Hove) can travel as a shadow or "jump cut" himself from place to place; and his mom is as bad off as he is, complexion-wise. More good shadow work here, but the script is very thin. The subspecies-assisted "rewiring" of Radu makes a nice stopmo-and-makeup-effects opener.

Sequel: *Bloodlust: Subspecies III.*

**BLOOD-SUCKERS** see *Those Feedy on Blood*

**BLOODSUCKERS FROM OUTER SPACE** One-of-Those Prods. (Rick Garlington) 1985 color c79m. SP, D: Glen Coburn. Ph: Chad D. Smith. Mus, AD: Garlington. Mkp&SpFX: Tim McDowell, J. P. Joyce. OptFX: K&H. Ref: TV: Lorimar HV. no V. Martin. Phantom. no Scheuer. With Thom Meyers, Laura Ellis, Pat Paulsen, Dennis Letts, Chris Heldman, Richard Wainscott, Big John Brigham (Norman), Bille Keller (Aunt Kate), Robert Bradeen (Uncle Joe), John Webb (Dr. Pace).

An "energy field" from outer space, which manifests itself as a "strong gust of wind," has descended upon Texas. This "life force" enters its human victims through the respiratory system and is then assimilated into the blood-stream, where it expands and causes massive hemorrhaging. The "alien presence" then reanimates the dead, bloodless bodies as vampires.... Made-in-Arlington horror corn is only a step or two above amateur filmmaking. Dialogue for vampires and non-vampires alike (including Paulsen as the President) is inane. Stray droll moment: bloodsucking Uncle Joe standing around wondering what to do with the arm which his nephew has just sliced off. A comedy more in intent than effect.

**BLOODSUCKING PHARAOHS IN PITTSBURGH** Para (Skouras)/Saratoga Films (Baffico-Barbera-Penberthy) 1990 (1989) color 88m. (*Picking up the Pieces* - orig t). SP, D: Dean Tschetter. Story: Tom Tully. Mus: M. Melvoin. SpMkpFX: Tom Savini. VisFX: Fantasy II. SpProps: Norman Beck. Ref: TV: Para HV. V 7/15/91. 12/17/90:41 (rated). PT 10:48. Martin. With Jake Dengel, Joe Sharkey, Susann Fletcher, Beverly Penberthy, Shawn Elliott, Veronica Hart (Grace), Taso Stavrakis, T. Tully.

Some "deranged Egyptian psycho type" seems to be murdering women with chainsaw, vacuum, and pneumatic drill, and removing parts of the bodies for some heinous ritual. The final element necessary: the breasts of a weeping virgin.... Broad gore comedy runs its running gags into the ground. Also included: a body-shriveling, soul-trapping formula.

**BLOODTHIRSTY** Barrows Prods. 1992 color feature. D: R. G. Barrows. Ref: Jones. With Ascello Charles, Winston McDaniel, Lia Marino.

Lab accident "turns people into crazy blood-drinkers."

**BLOODY BEAST** (H.K.?) Giant Film 1994 color 89m. D: Yeung Kuen. Ref: vc box: psychopath who murders expectant mothers. With Lau Mei Kuen.

**BLOODY BIRD** see *Stagefright - Aquarius*

**BLOODY EXORCISM OF COFFIN JOE, The** see *Exorcismo Negro*

**BLOODY FRIDAY** Sebastian Films 1985 (1975?) color c80m. D, P: Ferd & Beverly Sebastian. Ph: F. Sebastian. SP: Ann Cawthorne. Ref: TV: Sebastian Int'l. HV. no Phantom. no V. no Scheuer. no Stanley. no Martin.

A "maniac running around loose" ruins an island encounter-group session. Q: What implements does the murderer use? A: Spear-gun, rake, butcher knife, and ax, or spade. Q: Why does the "weirdo" kill? A: "It makes me feel good!" Q: Why did they bother to make this silly trifle?

**BLOODY GHOST** (H.K.) 1988 feature (aka *Funny Ghost*). D: Yuen Cheung Yan. Ref: NST! 4:18: witch, ghost, spirit of latter's unborn. Weisser/ATC. With Bai Xiang Chan.

**BLOODY NEW YEAR** (B) Lazer Ent. & Cinema & Theatre Seating (Hayden Pearce/Maxine Julius) 1987 (1986) color 92m. (aka *Time Warp Terror*). D: Norman J. Warren. SP: Frazer Pearce. Ph: John Shann. Mus: Nick Magnus. PD: Hayden Pearce. SpFxSup: David Williams. MkpDes: Jane Bevan. Ref: TV: Academy video. V 5/27/87: "negligible horror film." MMarquee 36:7. With Suzy Aitchison, Nikki Brooks, Colin Heywood, Paul Barrett (table monster).

"We're here forever." Grand Island. An experimental time-shattering device is supposed to account for all of the following and more visions in mirrors ... a celluloid sheik who steps off the screen ... living ropes and nets ... an indoor snowstorm ... an outdoor party with invisible (but audible) guests ... zombies ... and elevator-wall clutching hands .... Anything goes in this "half world"—except character and continuity. Occasionally, the jack-in-the-box, *Phantasm*-ish inventions work—one of the best is the

Girl Absorbed into the Elevator Wall—but the script is not so much imaginative as simply undisciplined. Any movie, though, which pays hommage to *Fiend Without a Face* can't be all bad.

**BLOODY POM POMS** see *Cheerleader Camp*

**BLOODY PSYCHO** (I) c1989 color c90m. (aka *The Snake House*). SP, D: Leandro Lucchetti. SP: also Giovanni Simonelli. Ph: Silvano Tessicini. Mus: L. Perini. Sup: Lucio Fulci. Ref: TV: VSOM; Eng.titles. Palmerini. With Peter Hintz, Loes Kamma, Brigitte Christensen, Sacha Darwin, Nubia Martini, Paul Muller.

"The castle is haunted." The "terrible apparition" in the uninhabited wing of said castle is apparently the spirit of Micaela di St. Bon, whose soul "can find no peace." "Involved in black magic," she is now a "she-devil," a snarling, decomposed thing in a wheelchair. At the end, she seems to disintegrate.... Some atmosphere here, and the monster is really monstrous, not just a peek-a-boo ghost. Otherwise, though, this is formula mystery and horror. What snake house?

**BLOODY! SCARY HORROR!** (J) VSOM 1994? color 60m. SP, D: Kazuki Omori, Kohji Hashimoto. Ref: TV: VSOM; Eng. titles.

Several shot-on-tape horror tales, including "Best Seller," a ghost story featuring an hallucination re a hooded chainsaw wielder, and a dumb twist ending ... "Haunted House," a pointless tale of ghosts haunting a "hungry" house ... silliness re a "living" doll ... and (last and best-by-default) "Blood Painting," an offbeat tale of spirits (including an unborn who has been wandering for 20 years) and metempsychosis.

**BLOODY SECT** see *Secta Siniestra*

**BLOODY SORCERY** (H. K.) 1986 color/ws? c90m. (*Blood Sorcery* - ad t). D: Pan Ling Tong. Ref: TV: Ocean Shores Video; Eng. titles. NST! 4:18. Fango 107:59.

A Nan Yeung wizard in Burma puts a "cruel curse"—derived from the Theory of Hindu in the Yuen Nan Province—on two men, one a reporter who jilted the wizard's daughter, the other a man who stole a magic jade statuette. Blood and worms begin to leak from a hole in the leg of each victim. In the busy climax—which involves demons and wormy, foaming corpses—a Taoist priest from the China Chuna Temple battles the wizard.... The reporter leaks blood in both a library and a restaurant, but though he causes an uproar, he takes no notice of the mess himself. One of the co-plots of this rudimentary, zoom-crazy movie—the curse on the stolen jade—goes back to American-made silent thrillers.

The **BLOODY VIDEO HORROR THAT MADE ME PUKE ON MY AUNT GERTRUDE** Stagecrew Video 1989 color 75m. D: Zachary W. Snygg. Ref: TV: Independent Cinema video. With The Duke, Spencer Snygg, Jared Bushansky, Abad Kaleel.

"Snuff films are very popular in South America." The *Die Watching* plot: Creep shoots/shoots prostitute-model with gun/video-camera, accidentally takes tape to video store.... Shot-on-taper is cheap and proud of it. Main motif: spattering blood. Numbingly talky.

**BLOWN SKY HIGH** see *Skyhigh*

**BLUE BLOOD** (B?) 1989 color c90m. SP, D: Andrew Sinclair. Mus: Brian Gascoigne. Ref: vc box. Hound. no Martin. no Scheuer. no Lentz. no Phantom. With Oliver Reed, Fiona Lewis, Derek Jacobi.

Madness, satanism, and "blood curdling dreams" at Swanbrook Manor.

**BLUE DEMON VS. LAS INVASORAS** (Mex) 196-? color c80m. Ref: TV. no Hardy/SF. no Lee. no Lentz. VSOM: *Blue Demon Vs. Invaders from Space.*

Teleportation-wise alien women, hypnotized Earth-men, fire-shooting space guns, alien-human love affairs, and burning spaceships. Low-grade sf with comically poor effects.

**BLUE DESERT** Neo Motion Pictures & First Look Pictures (David Andrew Peters) 1991 (1990) color 98m. SP, D: Brad Battersby. SP, Assoc P: Arthur Collis. SpFX: Frank Ceglia. Key Mkp: Deborah Larsen. Illustrations: Matthew Nelson. Ref: TV. V 1/14/91. Martin. CVS 3/92. TVG.

"Don't ever come back to this town." Suspenser has intimations of *Psycho*-type movies, plus running "commentary" provided by the comic-artist heroine's (Courteney Cox) sketches of her "Iron Medusa" creation. A sick "small town cop" (D. B. Sweeney) with torture and murder on his mind makes things "very very exciting" for Lisa, a rape victim from New York City.... Script plays a shallow, Who's the Sicko? game with Lisa. A long trip to the old twist in which "hero" suddenly becomes "villain," and vice versa, and now heroine is alone with the wrong guy.

**BLUE FLAME** Penn/Eden West 1993 color c88m. SP, D: C. Elwes. Ref: vc box: TriStar HV; '95. With B. Wimmer, J. Mager.

A cop and two aliens.

**La BLUE GIRL** (J) Daiei 1991? anim color 42m. (Dreamy Express Zone series). Ref: TV: Daiei Video; no Eng.

Ingredients: a female ninja-type who controls a tentacled monster, a Phallus City thing with plenty of orifice stuffers, and a demon realm with more sex snakes.... Fantasy-horror-comedy-sex animation is a sort of horrific, near-hardcore *Urusei Yatsura*, with cute moments and sometimes colorful graphics. The rape-from-beyond scenes get pretty monotonous, though, and the movie practices a kind of apparent self-censorship in same, with strategic visual distortions.

**La BLUE GIRL 2** (J) Daiei 1991? anim color 46m. (Dreamy Express Zone series). Ref: TV: Daiei Video; no Eng.

Alternately conventionally kinky and funny-lewd follow-up features the same self-censorship, a giant dragon, and a bizarre character who at first seems to be in a burlap bag, but apparently simply looks like a burlap bag. Neat: the monsters emerging from the (closed) lockers in the gym. Amusing: the monster convention in the cave.

**La BLUE GIRL, PART 3** (J) 1993 anim color 46m. (Dreamy Express Zone series). Ref: Japan Video.

**The BLUE JEAN MONSTER** (H. K.) Golden Harvest/Diagonal Pictures (Paragon Films) c1991? color c90m. Ref: TV: Pan-Asia Video; no Eng.

Power-line electricity helps bring a just-smashed-to-death gent back to life. He finds that he can take a long pole through the torso without missing a beat, and he impales a foe on same, then waves this human shish kebab in the air. Sunlight, however, bothers him, and he occasionally needs to recharge with an electric iron. Silly, crude sf-action-comedy.

**The BLUE LAMP IN WINTER NIGHT** (H. K.) 198-? color/ws 85m. D: Yao Fung? Ref: TV: QVC video; Eng. titles. Jones. NST! 4:18.

The town's Happy Inn is said to be a "haunted place," and so is the Temple Kai Yuen. There, a moldy-faced old vampire lady "controls" heroine-ghost Chinn Chinn. The vampire temporarily becomes a giant, impersonates everyone, and at one point brushes the hair on her detachable head.... Mediocre horror-fantasy-comedy tries the dream-or-is-it? ending and has some atmosphere and a fun if expected shock with a skull-headed woman. Another good bit: the stopmo ghost footprints in town.

**BLUE LIGHTS** see *Curse of the Blue Lights*

**BLUE MAN, The** see *Eternal Evil*

**BLUE MONKEY** (Can.?) Spectrafilm (Martin Walters/Tom Fox) 1987 color 98m. (*Insect!* - early t. *Green Monkey* - orig t?). D: William Fruet. SP: George Goldsmith. Mus: Coleman, Novotny. Ref: V 10/7/87: "awful horror film." 5/6/87:240 (ad). 10/21/87: 176(ad). ad. With Steve Railsback, Gwynyth Walsh, Susan Anspach, John Vernon, Joe Flaherty.

Man cut by "strange plant" spits out caterpillar which becomes "slime monster."

**BLUE SONNET** (J) CPM/Walkers Co. (Shibata-Hakusensha-Mushi-NTVM/Hayashi-Muronaga-Yoshizaka) 1989 ('94-U.S.) anim color c30m. D: Takeyuki Kanda. SP: S. Matsuoka, K. Mizuide. Story: M. Shibata. AD: N. Yokose. Ref: TV: USMC video; Eng. titles; M.D. Geist appearance? Animag 9:5: 3rd of 5 OAVs; "part of a larger series of ESPer stories called *Red Fangs*." Voices: Hiromi Tsuru (Sonnet Barje), Nozomu Sasaki (Wataru), Waka Kanda (Lan), Ichiro Nagai (Dr. Merikus).

"The world's armed forces have just become obsolete." Three episodes—"The Pursuer," "The Schemer," and "The Challenger." "Super-lady" Sonnet—the "perfect cyborg" ... the "ultimate weapon"—is the "strongest ESPer in the world." In one scene, she makes some thugs on cycles disintegrate. ("She's a monster!") But her feelings begin to get in the way.... Vapid character design; moderately engaging story. Plus a blood transfusion which also transfers ESP and an ESPer who can teleport.

**BLUE TORNADO** (I) Vidmark/Clemi & Titanus 1990 ('91-U.S.) color 96m. SP, D: Antonio Bido (aka T.B. Dobb). SP: also Gino Capone. Ph: Maurizio Dell'Orco. Mus: Moratto, Colasanti, De Angelis. AD: Mauro Passi. OptFX: Video Gamma. Mkp: M. Camilletti. SdFX: Union Sound. Ref: TV: Vidmark video; Eng. version. VSOM. Martin. Palmerini. V 5/2/90:178. TVG. With

Dirk Benedict, Ted McGinley, Patsy Kensit, David Warner, Chris Ahrens.

"Legends are born in the mountains." An "explosion of light" suddenly envelopes a mountain, and an F-104 fighter pilot disappears. ("I don't know what happened up there.") Later, balls of light—living "flying objects" (apparently from outer space)—seem to be trying to communicate with another pilot sent to investigate .... Banal actioner, with science-fictional/mystical overtones and lots of flying scenes. Aerial photography the only plus.

**BLUE YONDER, The** see *Time Flyer*

**BLUEBEARD** see *Barbe Bleue*

**BLUMEN FUER DEN MANN IM MOND** (E.G.) DEFA 1975 color 83m. SP, D: Rolf Losansky. SP: also I. Speitel, U. Speitel. Ph: H. Grewald. Ref: Hardy/SF: "maudlin." With Jutta Wachowiak, Stefan Lisewski, Dieter Franke.

"Wonder boy" develops a flower that will grow on the "inhospitable moon." *Flowers for the Man in the Moon* - tr t.

**BOARDED WINDOW, The** see *Nightmare Classics*

**BODY BAGS** Showtime-TV/Dan Angel (187 Corp.) 1993 color 94m. (aka *John Carpenter Presents "Body Bags"*). D, Exec Co-P: John Carpenter. D: ("Eye") Tobe Hooper. Tel: Billy Brown, D. Angel. MkpFX: KNB. Ref: V 8/9/93:36. 9/13/93:9 (rated). SFChron 8/6/93. Showtime 8/93. TVG. With Carpenter, Tom Arnold, Hooper, Robert Carradine, Wes Craven, Sam Raimi, David Naughton, Buck Flower, Stacy Keach, David Warner, Sheena Easton, Kim Alexis, Deborah Harry, Mark Hamill, Twiggy, John Agar, Roger Corman, Charles Napier, Sean McClory.

Three tales re an eye transplant, a stalker, and a cure for baldness.

**BODY COUNT** (Can.) CHCH-TV & Emmeritus & Visual Prods. 1986 color 95m. (*Bodycount* - ad t). D, Exec P: Lionel Shenken. Tel: Lloyd Chesley. Ph: Ken Smith. Mus: Paul Zaza. SpFX: Peter Ferri, N. Kausen. Ref: TV: Avec Video. no Martin. no Scheuer. no V. With Jonathan Potts (Paul Carter), James Lukie, J. P. Knapp, Cynthia Kereluk, Christine Manning.

The "paint by numbers" killer responsible for a series of sniper murders proves to be Paul Carter, a "good boy" who's supposedly doing his victims a favor by releasing them from a lousy world.... Talky, mild psychological thriller with that chintzy, shot-on-video look.

**BODY COUNT** (I) Racing Pictures (A. Fracassi) 1986 color 90m. (*Camping del Terrore*) D: Ruggero Deodato. SP: Alessandro Capone, David Parker Jr. Ph: Emilio Loffredo. Mus: Joel Goldsmith. Ref: V 5/7/86:316: "terror pic, set in a camping area." Horacio Higuchi. Ecran F 70:70. 75:66-7. Hardy/HM2: aka *Camping della Morte*. Parmerini: D. Parker-D. Sacchetti. With Mimsy Farmer, Charles Napier, David Hess, Bruce Penhall.

"Direct-sound English." (V)

**BODY DOUBLE** Col-Delphi II (Howard Gottfried) 1984 color 114m. Story, SP, D, P: Brian De Palma. SP: also Robert J. Avrech.

SpMkp: Tom Burman, Bari Dreiband. Ref: TV. MFB '85:147-8. V 10/17/84. SFExam 10/26/84. Bay G 11/1/84.

Low-budget, independent horror movie, "The Vampire's Kiss," being shot ... scenes from same under beginning and end credits ... scene in which blood drips disgustingly through hole in ceiling ... all-an-hallucination ending, apparently .... More cheap style-is-content-isn't-it? thrills from De Palma in this, his Last Remake of *Vertigo*.

**BODY-HUNTING DEVIL** (H. K.?) 1991? color/ws c92m. Ref: TV: World Video; no Eng. George Walker: above is tr t.

Strange Ideas of Funny comedy concerns a man who gets his spirit knocked out of his body in a car accident. A ghoul-spirit then replaces his spirit and commits casual brutalities. Plus two vanishing kids and a whole gang of ghoul-types. Three Stooges subtlety prevails.

**BODY MELT** (Austral.) Dumb Films/Body Melt & the Australian Film Commission, Film Victoria (Beyond) 1993 color 84m. Story, SP, D, Mus: Philip Brophy. SP, Co-P: Rod Bishop. PD: Maria Kozic. SpFxMkp: Bob McCarron. SpFX: Filmtrix. Ref: TV: Prism video. V 11/22/93: "moderately enjoyable." With Gerard Kennedy, Andrew Daddo, Ian Smith, Vince Gil, Brett Climo.

"Gore pic" re a "mad doctor whose invention—a new kind of vitamin pill—has horrific side effects...." (V) This experimental drug features unpredictable "cognition enhancers" and produces quasi-*Aliens* from Within in its victims, then disintegrating bodies, then "death by hypernatural causes." Slick, hollow makeup-effects vehicle by some Peter Jackson wannabes.

**BODY PARTS** (U.S.-Can.) Para/Frank Mancuso Jr. & Para (Can.) 1991 color/ws 88m. SP, D: Eric Red. SP: also Norman Snider. Screen Story: Patricia Herskovic, Joyce Taylor, from the Boileau-Narcejac novel *Choice Cuts*. Mus: Loek Dikker. SpMkpFX: Gordon J. Smith; FXSmith. Paintings: Pat Mohan. SpFxCoord: Neil Trifunovich. Computer Anim: Video Image. Ref: TV. ad. V 8/12/91. SFChron Dtbk 1/19/92. With Jeff Fahey, Lindsay Duncan, Kim Delaney, Brad Dourif, Peter Murnik, Paul Benvictor, John Walsh (Charley Fletcher).

Metro General Hospital's Dr. Alice Webb (Duncan) transplants an arm from an executed murderer (Walsh) to Bill Crushank (Fahey)—"I now have a murderer's blood in my blood"—whereupon Transplant Plot "A" takes over. Bill's new right arm seems to have a mind of its own, as does artist Remo Lacey's (Dourif) new left arm, also taken from Charley Fletcher. Psychic, surreal "images" from the latter's life of crime make Lacey's paintings sell like hotcakes. The man with Charley's head, however, seems to be trying to retrieve Charley's limbs. At the end, "Charley" dies, and Bill's arm is okay. ("The arm's mine now, Chuck.")

Better title: *The Tenth Remake of The Hands of Orlac*. This Mad Hand material is probably viable now only as comedy; *Body Parts* is full of just-missed black-comedy opportunities. Highlight-of-sorts: the extended, ludicrously elaborate car stunt in which the handcuffs link "Charley" in one car with Bill in the other.

**BODY PASSION** see *Tainted*

**BODY PUZZLE** (I) Triboro/A.P.A.C. 1993(1992/'94-U.S.) color 95M. (*Corpo Perplessita*). D: Lamberto Bava. Ph: "Lee Kraus." SpMkp: Franco Casagni. SdFX: Anzellotti. Ref: MV: slasher collecting body parts. PT 19:11-12: "as stupid as *Pieces*." TV: Triboro video; Eng. dubbed. Imagi Smr'95:55. V 10/19/92:152: screening at MIFED. Pamerini: aka Misteria. With Joanna Pacula, Tomas Arana, Francois Montagut, Gianni Garko, Erika Blanc.

"He's trying to put him back together again" A "ghost" seems to be murdering people and retrieving implanted organs — a hand here, a heart there, a kidney, a penis .... ("Why would anyone want a goddam ear?") Routine slasher seems to be shot on tape and is painful to look at. Prize point-of-view shot: the one from inside the bottom of the toilet bowl.

The **BODY SHOP** Metrolina Corp. 1972 color c85m. (*Doctor Gore* - alt vt t). SP, D, P: J. G. Patterson Jr. Ph: W. M. Hill; H. M. Joyner. Mus: William B. Girdler; (songs) Bill Hicks. Sets: Vickie O'Neal. SpFxMkp: Pat Patterson. ElecFX: Paul Murry. SpHorror Consul: Worth Keeter. Ref: TV: Paragon Video. Scheuer. Martin. no Phantom. Bowker'90: 1975. Stanley. VSB. With Don Brandon, Jenny Driggers, Roy Mehaffey, Candy Furr, V. O'Neal, Jerry Kearns, Hicks, Nita Patterson.

With the aid of his hunchbacked assistant Greg (Mehaffey), Dr. Don Brandon (Brandon) secures a "perfect torso," perfect hands, etc.; sews the parts together (leftover body parts go into the acid vat); brings "Anitra" (Driggers) to life in his lab ("She's alive!"); and hypnotically erases her memory. One hitch with this "perfect" wife, in the image of his own wife: She's a nymphomaniac. Brandon meant her to love only him.... Even abysmal movies can have their fascinations. *The Body Shop* begins as *Frankenstein*, switches to *The Stepford Wives*, then tacks on its own cruel irony. In retrospect, this seems like a pretty funny sick joke; unfortunately, it generally plays like the "Z" movie it is. The first half is padded with surgical gore and marking-time footage; the second half, with appallingly "romantic" song sequences. The "My heart has just died" lyrics are intended seriously, the better to be undercut by the on-the-loose Anitra, who introduces herself to men with lines like "A woman's made to be loved. Do you wanna love me?" Funny stuff this—almost.

**BODY SNATCHERS** WB (Robert H. Solo) 1993 (1992) color/ws 87m. (aka *Bodysnatchers. Invasion of the Body Snatchers* - shooting t). D: Abel Ferrara. SP: Stuart Gordon, Dennis Paoli, Nicholas St. John. Story: Raymond Cistheri, Larry Cohen. From Jack Finney's novel *The Body Snatchers*. Ph: Bojan Bazelli. Mus: Joe Delia. PD: Peter Jamison. SpMkpFX: Tom Burman, Bari Dreiband-Burman. SpFxSup: Phil Cory. Titles: R/Greenberg. Ref: TV: Warner HV. V 5/3/93: "tremendously exciting." 9/28/92:10 (rated). 3/2/9:11. Cinef 12/92:10-11. Imagi 1:54-5: "fairly tame." Fango 128:72-3. SFChron 2/18/94. With Gabrielle Anwar, Terry Kinney, Billy Wirth, Meg Tilly, Forest Whitaker, R. Lee Ermey, Christine Elise.

"Aliens are invading Earth in the form of giant seed pods that replicate human beings while they sleep in order to replace them." (V) "They get you when you sleep!" In this third official film version of the story, the pods come in cardboard boxes, and the old human bodies are stowed in garbage bags. And if the story itself, as told here, doesn't seem like much, the "abortion" scenes

are harrowing. The alien-feeler-happy, double-aborted-snatching sequence, with the father and stepmother, is especially well engineered. The retention of the hokey Scream Alert, however, from the first remake of *Invasion of the Body Snatchers,* seems ill-advised "hommage." On the whole, film rates a Not Quite, Nice Try Though. Most imaginative addition to the canon: the scene in which the day care kids hold up their drawings, and all but one of the latter are identical.

**BODYCOUNT** see *Body Count* (Can. 1986)

**BODYSNATCHERS** see *Body Snatchers*

**BOGGY CREEK II—AND THE LEGEND CONTINUES** ... Howco Int'l. (1984), Arista Films/Charles B. Pierce Pictures 1984 (1983) color 91m. (*The Barbaric Beast of Boggy Creek Part II* - alt t). SP, D: Pierce. Mus: Frank McKelvey. SpCostume: Bill Khopler. Mkp: Pam Pierce. Ref: TV. V 4/4/84:28: in Miami. 12/18/85. 10/19/88: 204(ad). ad. Maltin/TVM. TVG. V 1/18/84:28. With Pierce, Cindy Butler, Serene Hedin, Chuck Pierce, Jimmy Clem, Fabus Griffin (big creature), Victor Williams (little creature).

"That thing ought to be left alone." Near Texarkana, Texas, Old Man Crenshaw (Clem) captures a fish-filching, nocturnal, malodorous beast—a "huge, hairy, man-like creature" which, like Bigfoot and the Yeti (as the dialogue has it), is shy. A nice live-and-let-live message ends this sequel to *The Legend of Boggy Creek.* Otherwise, there's scenery, and that's about it. The actors unconvincingly simulate fear and trembling, and the script throws in a gratuitous *Jaws* false alarm.

**BOKYO** (Fili) D'Wonder Films 1983 color c140m. D: J. Erastheo Navoa. SP: Joeben Miraflor Jr. Story: Pat V. Reyes, serialized in Hapi-Hapi Komiks. Ph: H. U. Santos. Mus: R. J. Reyna. SpPhFX: Tommy Marcelino. Mkp: Perla Celicios. SdFX: Demet Velasquez. Ref: TV: Tripod Video; occ. English. With Al Tantay, Nino Muhlach, Anna Martin, Marissa Delgado, Panchito, Bibeth Orteza, Paquito Diaz, Jimmy Santos.

A tiny humanoid alien takes the boy Bokyo from Earth to the Star World, where "nothing is impossible" and big animals and fresh produce talk and sing. Back on Earth, the alien gives Bokyo a whistle which gives him telekinetic power over humans and objects. Interminable mixture of comedy, sf, and sentiment.

**BOMBSIGHT STOLEN** see *Cottage to Let*

**BON APPETIT, MAMA** see *Ed and His Dead Mother*

The **BONEHEADS** Video Team 1992 color 73m. D: Paul Norman. Ref: Adam '93. With Tracy Wynn, Marc Wallice, Teri Diver, Bionca, K. C. Williams.

Takeoff on "Saturday Night Live's" Coneheads.

The **BONEYARD** Cori Films/Backbone (Backwood/R. E. Brophy) 1991 color 93m. SP, D: James Cummins. Mus: J. L. Whitener. SpMkpFX: Backwood Film FX; (des) Bill Corso, Cummins. Animatronics: T. Hawkins, T. Williamson. Physical Fx Sup: Ray Bivens. SupSdFxEd: Dale Jergenson. OptFX: T&T. Ref: TV. V 10/14/91:A-100 (hv). 2/18/91:71 (rated). 12/6/89:26.

SFChron Dtbk 6/2/91. With Ed Nelson, Deborah Rose, Norman Fell, Jim Eustermann, Phyllis Diller, Sallie M. Kaltreider (little ghoul), Cindy Dollar-Smith (big ghoul), Michael Haun (Floofsams and Poopinplatz ghouls).

"The bodies we saw—they're not dead!" A lot of the footage here is, though, thanks to the slow, self-important pace. Ghoul kids run amok, and disgusting goop-tricks punctuate the movie. That's the good news. You can step in the goop, swallow it, or as the poodle does, sip it. (Gratuitous poodle-ghoul here.) Throw in some serious gab, psychometry, and a pop-eyed Phyllis Diller ghoul, and—voila!—un mess.

**BOOBS IN THE NIGHT** Col 1943 20m. D: Del Lord. SP: Elwood Ullman, Monty Collins. Ref: Okuda: remade as *Dopey Dicks*. no Maltin/SSS. LC. With El Brendel, Monte Collins, Charles Middleton, Frank Lackteen.

Mad scientist seeks human head for his robot.

**BOOBY TRAP** see *Wired to Kill*

**BOOGEY MAN AND THE FRENCH MURDERS, The** see *Paris Sex Murders*

**\*\*BORDER PHANTOM** Rep 1937 (1936) 58m. D: S. Roy Luby. SP: Fred Myton. Ph: Jack Greenhalgh. Ref: TV. Shoot-Em-Ups. Don Glut. FD 6/7/37. Academy. V 2/17/37. LC. With Bob Steele, Harley Wood, Don Barclay, Karl Hackett, Miki Morita, Horace Murphy, Perry Murdock.

Ingredients: A killer who uses a "strangler's cord" and who "disappears like a ghost" ... the "pig man," Obed Young (Hackett), a "horrible creature who has a hog ranch" ... Dr. Von Kurtz (John Peters), an entomologist who has made a "great discovery" ("Would I kill a man over a bug?!") ... and a deserted old house ("kind of a spooky-looking joint") with a "curse" on it.... Airy exterior photography, semi-pleasant comedy, awkward acting and action—Peters' "great discovery" is not acting. The "showpiece" window shadow is painted on the wall. Listen for the mob-scene ad libbing in the fire sequence: "Blah blah blah fire blah blah blah fire blah...."

**BORG GET ON!** see *Super Sonic Soldier Borgman 2*

**The BORGMAN—LAST BATTLE** (J) NTV 1989 anim color 60m. (aka *Forever Final Borgman*). Ref: Animerica 5:12: OAV. Japan Video. TV: Toho Video; no Eng. (apart from title).

Follow-up to a TV series. Sequel: *Super Sonic Soldier Borgman 2*. See also *Sonic Soldier Borgman 1* (P).

Ingredients include huge, hydraulic super-armor with "hurricane" option ... robotic armor with a flying option ... hover cars .. and a super-strong super-leaper.... Mostly talk. Visually undistinguished.

**BORIS & NATASHA** Showtime-TV/MCEG (J. D. Krane) 1992 color 100m. D: Charles Martin Smith. Story, Tel, Assoc P: Charles Fradin. Tel: also Linda Favila, Anson Downes. Story: also Brad Hall. Based on "The Bullwinkle Show" characters created by Jay Ward. Mus: D. Kitay. Ref: V 4/13/92:67: "misguided." With Sally Kellerman, Dave Thomas, Andrea Martin,

Larry Cedar, Christopher Neame, Alex Rocco, Anthony Newley, Sid Haig.

Scientist invents time-reversing microchip.

**BORN FOR HELL** see *Naked Massacre*

**BORN FREE** see *Return of the Dinosaurs*

**BORN IN COFFIN** (H.K.?) Dah-Lai Chow c1992? color 89m. D: Rern-Jie Chang. Ref: TV: Pan-Asia Video; no Eng. With Bau-Yuh Wang, Hang Wang, Mon-Le How.

A young woman scarred by acid is half-buried for dead, awakens in her coffin during childbirth, then dies, comes back as a floating blue ghost, and scares folks. Villagers burn ghost-mama and baby's hut.... This lady has a tough life and a tough death. Milked pathos, familiar comedy-drama-horror.

**BORN OF FIRE** (B-Turk.?) Film Four Int'l./Dehlavi Films 1986 color 83m. Story, D, Co-P: Jamil Dehlavi. SP: Raficq Abdulla. Mus: Colin Towns. SpMkp: Sula Loizou. SpFX: SpFX Universal. Ref: TV: Vidmark Ent. video. V 10/28/87. Scheuer. Martin. Phantom. With Peter Firth, Suzan Crowley, Stefan Kalipha, Nabil Shaban, Oh-Tee.

"It's the sun beginning to affect the Earth" ... and making dormant Turkish volcanoes erupt.... A flutist (Firth) discovers that his music can "control the hidden forces of the Earth," and uses the "neverending note" against the fiery forces of the Master Musician (Oh-Tee), who can shoot flames from his mouth and eyes, and who seems to command the sun.... The magnificence of the Turkish ruins and caves here suggests that the script was written around them. In a stunning opening-credits effect, a skull "eclipses" the sun—but the body of the film is spare, humorless, and arty, and its sobriety invites laughs. Djinns, a baboon, a strange hatching creature (which proves to be a moth), demon possession, and maggots also figure in the cryptic goings-on.

**The BORROWER** Cannon/Vision (Sekon-Jones/W. H. Coleman) 1991 color 91m. D: John McNaughton. SP: Mason Nage, Richard Fire. Ph: Julio Macat, Robert New. MkpFX: Kevin Yagher; (addl) Bernd Rantscheff. Alien Suit Des: Kathe Clark. SpFX: Steve Galich. Anim: Joe Doll. Ref: TV: Cannon Video. V 9/9/91. PT 11:10. Martin. With Rae Dawn Chong, Don Gordon, Antonio Fargas, Tom Towles, Pam Gordon, Larry Pennell, Madchen Amick, Robert Dryer (borrower), Richard Wharton (alien pilot).

"You can't kill it!" Behind the "decapitation murders": the "headhunter," an insectish alien thug "genetically devolved" to the human state and left on Earth to fend for itself. Periodically, the thing "borrows" a head, generally human, on one occasion canine, to replace its defective head.... Hip but familiar, episodic sf-horror recalls the "Twilight Zone" show "The Four of Us Are Dying"—which also starred Gordon. The theme: Who's alien—it or the earthlings? Good line: Fargas' "Beethoven's Fifth; Julius' pint." He also gets the regulation unsuspecting-human-to-alien line: "From out of town, right?"

**BOSCO, Il** 1 see *Evil Clutch*

El BOSQUE ANIMADO (Sp) Classic Films 1987 feature. D: Jose Luis Cuerda. Ref: V 5/4/88:404: "haunted forest." 10/7/87: ghost. With Alfredo Landa, Fernando Rey.

BOSZORKANYSZOMBAT see *Witches' Sabbath*

BOTTLES MGM/Harmon-Ising 1936 anim color 10m. Ref: TV: Happy Harmonies. Jim Shapiro. PFA library (LC). no Lee.

In a nightmare, a poison-bottle skeleton comes to life, shrinks a druggist, and traps him in his own beakers and test tubes. Plus a vanishing-cream bottle which vanishes and a wicked Witch Hazel which raises ghostly spirits of ammonia.... Jaunty, spooky musical-comedy cartoon.

BOUNTY DOG (J) Manga Video/Toho 1994 ('96-U.S.) anim color c60m. D: H. Negishi. Ref:: vc box.

A strange force, "The Sleeper," waits within the moon.

BOUNTY HUNTER 2002 AIP 1992 color feature. Ref: Stanley: "crudely made." With Phil Nordell, Francine Lapensee, Jeff Conaway, Vernon Wells.

Bounty hunter roams the desert of 2002 A.D.

BOXER'S OMEN, The see *Mo*

The BOY FROM ANDROMEDA (N.Z.-Can.) Canwest & Television-New Zealand & The Family Channel & South Pacific Pictures & Atlantis Films(De Nave) 1991 color 93m. D: Wayne Tourell. Tel: Ken Catran. Created by Jonathan Gunson. Ph: Allen Guilford. Mus: John Gibson. PD: Kirsten Shouler. SpFX: Kevin Chisnall. Prosth: Marjory Hamlin. Ref: TV. TVG. Stanley. With Katrina Hobbs, Jane Creswell (Drom), Fiona Kay, Anthony Samuels, Heather Bolton, Paul Gittins, Brian Carbee (Guardian).

Ingredients include ten-year-old alien Drom, whose people left Earth millions of years ago for Andromeda, which is now dying ("We put too much trust in computers"), for want of air and water ... the Predator-ish Guardian, a "special sort of robot" ... a "volcano gun," which utilizes energy from inside the Earth ... and a supposed "lake monster" .... Routine, juvenile-angled sf-suspenser is serious about war and death, but vapid. It's talky and action-filled at the same time.

BOY GOD (Fili) Video City/Cinex/D'Wonder Films 1983 ('86-U.S.) color 90m. (*The Boy God* - ad t. *Stone Boy* - alt t). D: J. Erastheo Navoa. SP: Joeben Miraflor. Ph: Hermo Santos. Mus: Ernani Cuenco. SdFX: Danny Sanches. Ref: TV: V. C. video; Eng. dubbed. Ecran F 41:71. HR 10/25/83:S-158(ad). V(CHVD). With Nino Muhlach, Jimi Melendrez, Isabel Rivas, Cecille Castillo.

By dumping chemicals in the Filipino water supply, a very mad German scientist is "creating werewolves and vampires." Opposing him: the limestone-like Rocco, son of an immortal—heat makes him stronger; water, weaker. Incident-filled children's monster movie is episodic and unsophisticated, but tattily charming. The three weird werewolf sisters have long furry tails; a two-headed monster proves to be two actors tied together. At one point, a winged human vampire bites the rocklike Rocco and loses a tooth. Added attractions: a vaporizing machine, a Cyclops

which is fond of humans—as appetizers—and a ray-shooting magician.

BOY WHO TURNED YELLOW, The see *Young Time Travellers*

The BRAIN (Can.) S.G.E./Brightstar (Anthony Kramreither/Film House) 1988 color 85m. D: Ed Hunt. SP: Barry Pearson. Mus: Paul Zaza. MkpFX: Mark Williams. Computer Anim: Larry Chase. SpFX: Danny White, Craig Williams. Ref: TV. V 11/9/88. SFChron Dtbk 8/28/88. With Tom Breznahan, Cyndy Preston, David Gale, Bret Pearson, Christine Kossack.

A tentacled brain uses Dr. Blake's (Gale) "Independent Thinking" TV show to transmit hypnotic brainwaves and turn viewers into zombies. At the end, the doctor is revealed to be some sort of alien putrescence.... Very thin amalgam of *Halloween 3* (the evil TV waves), *Nightmare on Elm Street* (the teddy-bear tentacle, the brain-from-the-mirror hallucinations), and *Invasion of the Body Snatchers* (the conformists/zombies). The campily gross effects and cartoonish brain indicate that parody may have been intended, but padding with car and foot chases dilutes. Funny line: "So you think you're in America? Well, you're not, you're in high school." Funny TV-monitor messages, too. ("Applaud More," "Smile More.")

BRAIN CREATURE see *Mind Killer*

BRAIN DAMAGE Palisades Partners (Brain Damage) 1988 (1987) color 86m. SP, D: Frank Henenlotter. Mus: Gus Russo, Clutch Reiser. SpMkpFX: Gabe Bartalos. Elmer: Bartalos, David Kindlon. VisFxSup: Al Magliochetti. Opt: VCE; Peter Kuran; Cineric. Ref: TV: Paramount Video. MFB'88:106. '89:78. V 4/20/88. SFChron Dtbk 7/3/88. With Rick Herbst, Gordon MacDonald, Jennifer Lowry, Theo Barnes, Kevin VanHentenryck (man with basket).

"He needs the brains, but I need his juice." "Elmer," or Aylmer— "the all-inspiring famous one"—is a "living relic of civilizations long since forgotten." For his host, currently Brian (Herbst), the ugly, slug-like parasite Elmer proves to be something of an hallucinogen. But Elmer has to be fed, generally with human brains, although he tolerates the brains of other animals. "Is he okay?" the slow-to-comprehend Brian asks Elmer, as the latter gobbles up the night watchman's brains. Elmer: "Not bad...." At its best, *Brain Damage* is a crazily engaging comedy. The primary joke: The comically loathsome slug has the soothing voice of a psychoanalyst ("Trust me, Brian")—dubbed by John Zacherle. The film's biological horrors have a Cronenberg look, but the sound effects and dialogue are closer to Looney Tunes. The thin script goes no further than *Wings of Death* in its depiction of the horrors of drug mania. The scene with the stranger on the subway is a direct reference to Henenlotter's own *Basket Case*.

BRAIN DEAD Concorde/New Horizons (Julie Corman) 1990 (1989) color 85m. SP, D: Adam Simon. SP: also Charles Beaumont (from his 1963 screenplay "Paranoia"). Mus: Peter Francis Rotter. MkpFX: The Burmans. Medical/torture instruments: Liz Young. OptFX: Motion; (blue screen) T&T. Ref: TV. MFB'90:306-7. V 1/31/90. With Bill Pullman, Bill Paxton, Bud Cort, Patricia Charbonneau, Nicholas Pryor, George Kennedy.

"Don't let them take you into surgery." Dr. Rex Martin (Pullman), the "brain man"—who charts paranoia with "brain maps" of his subjects—succeeds in eliminating the paranoia from crazy Jack Halsey (Cort). Setback: The Lakeside shrink (Pryor) tells Martin, now apparently a patient there, that he is just imagining Halsey. ("You are Halsey.") Some fun here with the Will the Real Reality Please Stand Up? premise, though the script seems aimless until the first rug is pulled out from under Gentle Viewer. The twisty appeal of the film seems to belong to another era, circa the original "Twilight Zone." Prime exchange, from a Martin deja vu scene: "Have we done this before?" Halsey: "Are we doing this now!?

**BRAIN 17** (U.S.-J) 3B Prods. & New Hope Ent. & Toei/Bunker Jenkins (Modern Programs Int'l.) 1982 color c90m.? D: (J) Minoru Yamada; Michael Part. SP: Part. From Shotaro Ishimori's story "Dai Tetsujin Wan Sebun" or "Iron Robot 17." Mus: Douglas Lackey. Ref: TV: F. H. E. video; Eng. dubbed. Stanley. HOF 2:40-41: aka *Revenge of the Defenders*.

In the near future, the Defenders try to keep peace, but their super-computer BRAIN (Binary Random Access Integrated Analyzer) escapes and becomes an independent "killer machine" which dispatches a gigantic streamroller robot and a hurricane robot to do its destructive bidding. ("That robot ruined my family life!") However, Iron Robot One Seven, manufactured by BRAIN, reforms and aids our heroes and uses "gravitron power" to defeat the steamroller robot.... Highlight of busy, sloppy sf-er: the overripe, campily emphatic narration and dubbing. ("I have to save the world!") The robots look like giant kitchen utensils.

See also *Giant Iron Man One-Seven* (2).

**BRAIN THEFT** see *Pituitary Hunter*

**BRAIN TWISTERS** Crown Int'l./Highlite Film (Dianne Sangiuliano) 1991 color 90m. SP, D: Jerry Sangiuliano. Mus: Larry Gelb. Ref: V 6/3/91: "about as shocking as a stamp album." 2/18/91:27. With Terry Londeree, Farrah Forke, Joe Lombardo.

"Mind-altering experiments."

**BRAINDEAD** see *Dead Alive*

**BRAINSCAN** Triumph/Coral (Michel Roy) 1994 color 93m. D: John Flynn. SP: A.K. Walker. Story: Brian Owens. Ph: F. Protat. Mus: G.S. Clinton. PD: P. Ridolfi. VisFX: Rene Daalder. MkpFX: Steve Johnson XFX. Ref: V 4/25/94: "undistinguished." ad. SFChron 4/22/94: "hash." Sacto Bee 4/22/94: "interesting." With Edward Furlong, Frank Langella, T. Ryder Smith, Amy Hargreaves.

"Screwed-up, loner kid ... gets swept up in a virtual-reality game as a serial killer" (SFC), The Trickster (Smith).

**The BRAINSUCKER** Raedon 1988 feature. SP, D: Herb Robins. Ref: PT 13:49: "embarrassing mess." With H. Robins, J. Middleman.

Mad doctor turns vagrant into killer who uses "giant corkscrew."

**BRAM STOKER'S DRACULA** Col/American Zoetrope & Osiris Films (Francis Ford Coppola, Fred Fuchs, Charles Mulvehill,

James V. Hart, John Veitch/Michael Apted, Robert O'Connor) 1992 color 127m. (*Dracula: The Untold Story* - early t). D: F. F. Coppola. SP: J. V. Hart, from Stoker's novel *Dracula*. Mus: Wojciech Kilar. PD: Thomas Sanders. Costumes: Eiko Ishioka. SpVisFX: Roman Coppola; Fantasy II. SpMkpFX: Greg Cannom. Bride Movements: Michael Smuin. Ref: screen. Mo. V 11/9/92. 6/24/91:17. Oak Trib 11/13/92. ad. SFExam 11/13/92 & 11/8/92. SFChron 11/13/92; Dtbk 11/8/92. Fango 118:36-41, 62. Cinef 12/92:24-55. Jones. Martin. With Gary Oldman (Dracula), Winona Ryder (Mina/Elisabeta), Anthony Hopkins, Keanu Reeves, Richard E. Grant, Cary Elwes, Bill Campbell, Sadie Frost, Tom Waits (Renfield).

"I shall arise from my own death." With a "heart strong enough to survive the grave," Count Dracula journeys from 1462 Romania to 1897 London to find that his beloved Elisabeta—a suicide—lives again in Mina. When the latter marries Jonathan Harker (Reeves), Dracula savages her friend Lucy (Frost). Ultimately, Mina becomes "baptized" in the count's blood and releases his tormented soul.... Visually profligate movie probably works in more elements from the Stoker novel than have all other Dracula pictures combined, though in its basic, long-lost-love plot it more resembles the 1932 *The Mummy* than it does most Dracula adaptations. Coppola and Hart use shadow and other photographic effects to give Oldman's Dracula an aura of omniscience and omnipotence—in fact, until the arrival on the scene of "metaphysician-philosopher" Van Helsing (Hopkins), it seems that the humans here don't stand a chance.

Roughly the first half of the movie is an orgy of invention. Dracula's shadow acts eerily and wittily independent of his body—sometimes it suggests mystical omniscience, sometimes sheer nervous emotional energy. Like Asian movie ghosts, Dracula at times seems to have stretchable arms. And like the *Evil Dead* movies, Coppola/Hart/Stoker's *Dracula* goes horror movies which equate subjective-camera tracking with the monster's onslaught one better: Michael Ballhaus' camera seems to race along the ground with a kind of stippled motion—Vampire Express. *Dracula* also features some of the most extensive and charming miniature work since early (British) Hitchcock.

Unfortunately, Coppola, Hart, and the actors largely fail to revitalize the Stoker story and characters. Animated shadows do more for the character Dracula than does Oldman's performance, which at times gets lost in a sound-recording blur which also makes some of Van Helsing's and Renfield's dialogue semi-impenetrable. An ingenious finale reconciles good, evil, love, the undead, and the really dead, but the actors never really live.

See also *Silence of the Hams*.

**The BRAVE FROG** (J-U.S.) Hemdale/Tatsunoko Prods. & Harmony Gold (Ahmed Agrama, C. Macek) 1985('94-U.S.) anim color 91m. D: Michael Reynolds. SP: Ilene Chase. Ref: TV: Hemdale HV; Eng. version; vc box says c'89.

The new frog in town confronts a "giant sea monster" which roars, looks like a vicious salamander, and can leap out of the pond water ... a monstrous "giant" cat (frog p.o.v.) "as big as two houses," etc. Insufferable blend of fantasy and pop psychology.

**BRAVESTARR, THE LEGEND** Taurus Ent./Filmation (Lou Scheimer) 1987 (1988) anim color 91m. (*Bravestarr, The*

*Movie* - ad t). D: Tom Tataranowicz. SP: Bob Forward, Steve Hayes. Mus: F. W. Becker. SpFxAnimSup: Brett Hisey. Ref: V 9/7/88: "disappointing." 7/29/87:4 (rated). ad. TVG 2/4/89: *Bravestarr: High Noon in New Texas* - vt t. Voices: Charles Adler, Susan Blu, Pat Fraley.

"Huge dragonlike steer" Stampede, "reanimated, skeletal cowboy" Tex Hex, evil serpent-riding Vipra, and "burrowing humanoids," all on the planet of New Texas. (V)

**BRAZIL** (B) Univ/Brazil (Arnon Milchan) 1985 color 131m. SP, D: Terry Gilliam. SP: also Tom Stoppard, Charles McKeown. Mus: Michael Kamen. SpFxSup: George Gibbs. Model FxSup: Richard Conway. ProsthMkp: Aaron Sherman. OptFX: Peerless. Ref: TV. MFB'85:107-8. V 2/13/85. SFChron 1/31/86. With Jonathan Pryce, Robert De Niro, Katherine Helmond, Ian Holm, Bob Hoskins, Michael Palin, Kim Greist, Oscar Quitak.

Information Retrieval vs. terrorists in a neon-and-red-tape future. Caught in the middle: Sam Lowry (Pryce), whose fantasies feature a Majin-like monster.... Enough action and explosions for two Filipino *Road Warrior* imitations, and enough substance at least for two of same. As in *The Doctor and the Devils,* Pryce is vivid, in a very different role. The title tune's romance/fantasy/escape lilt and words offer easy but effective ironic counterpoint to both the hero's and the society's madness. One high point: Sam and Jill's (Greist) balmy meet-cute, meet-violent scene.

**BREAKDOWN** see *Freeway Maniac, The*

**BREAKFAST OF ALIENS** Hemdale/Eric Parkinson & DVB (Brian James Ellis) 1993 (1990) color 88m. SP, D, Exec Co-P: David Lee Miller. SP, Exec Co-P: Vic Dunlop. Mus: M. Ender. Ref: V 3/1/93: "humor ... weak." 2/22/93:A-122: at AFM. With Vic Dunlop (Walter Clydepepper), Indy Shriner, John Hazelwood, Steve Franken, Johnny Dark, Jeanet Moltke (she-witch).

Man "swallows an alien who begins to take over his body."

**BREAKFAST WITH DRACULA: A VAMPIRE IN MIAMI** (I) 1993 color feature. D: Fabrizio de Angelis. Ref: Palmerini, p ll.

**BREAKING STRAIN** see *Trapped in Space*

**BREAKTHROUGH, The** see *Lifeforce Experiment, The*

**The BREAST FILES** Avica 1994 color 82m. D: L.S. Talbot. Ref: Adam'96: brainwashing implants. With R. Bardoux, Jasper.

**The BREAST FILES 2** Avica 1994 color 80m. D: F. Marino. Ref: Adam'96: "women who can unleash earthquakes."

**BREEDERS** Wizard Video/Empire/Entertainment Concepts (Taryn Prods.) 1986 color 77m. SP, D: Tim Kincaid. SpFxMkp: Ed French. SpFX: Matt Vogel. Opt: Motion. Ref: TV: Lightning Video. V 6/11/86. With Teresa Farley, Lance Lewman, Frances Raines, Natalie O'Connell, Amy Bretano, Leeanne Baker, Ed French, Raheim Grier (deformed creature).

"It's coming from underneath this city." "Something inhuman" is brutally raping virgins in New York City. The women—who suffer from amnesia and whose wounds magically heal—are then "summoned" to become "new masters" of a "noble race," in a breeding ground located in abandoned tunnels below the city. The summoner: an alien parasite which can adopt any form, periodically reproduces, and needs "clean" women—a diseased subject is shown to have produced a grotesque offspring.... Flatly acted and directed. The supposedly unnerving horror details in the dialogue are all underlined, and thus defused, and the lovingly showcased makeup effects don't break any new ground. T&a gets equal time here, but even the bizarre breeding spa seems derivative—specifically, of *Invasion of the Bee Girls'* perverse eroticism.

**The BRIDE** (B) Col/Colgems Prods. (Victor Drai) 1985 color 118m. D: Franc Roddam. SP: Lloyd Fonvielle, based on Mary Shelley's novel *Frankenstein.* Mus: Maurice Jarre. Prosth: Aaron and Maralyn Sherman. SpFxSup: Peter Hutchinson. Ref: TV. MFB'85:336. V 8/14/85. SFExam 8/16/85. ad. With Sting (Baron Charles Frankenstein), Jennifer Beals (Eva), Anthony Higgins, Clancy Brown (Viktor), Veruschka, Quentin Crisp, Guy Rolfe.

Baron Frankenstein's next monster is to be a "new woman—independent, free"—and as "Eva," the Baron's ward, she is, relatively. At the end of this slightly different Frankenstein story, the monster (Brown) gets the girl-monster, in a sweet, sappy twist. The pace is deliberate, the script only occasionally imaginative, more often just-sort-of-touching. The only principal role which makes much sense is Viktor's. The Baron and Eva seem to switch behavioral gears simply to make thematic points.

**BRIDE OF BOOGEDY** ABC-TV/Disney-TV & Janover-Scott 1987 color c90m. D, P: Oz Scott. SP, D: Michael Janover. Mus: John Addison. SpFX: Robbie Knott; (ph) Bill Kilduff et al. Ref: TV. V 4/22/87:54, 62. TVG. With Richard Masur, Mimi Kennedy, Tammy Lauren, Howard Witt, Eugene Levy, Leonard Frey, Vincent Schiavelli.

Boogedy the ghost (Witt) "spirits" Eloise (Kennedy) away to be his bride. Also: magic key to crypt's "portal" ... seance ... fake ghosts ("Beware the spider!") ... big-spider-prop.... Lotsa effects and, again, a droll Masur in this sequel to *Mr. Boogedy.*

**BRIDE OF RE-ANIMATOR** 50th St. Films/Wildstreet (Re-Animator II Prods./Walley-White) 1991 (1989) color 97m. (aka *Bride of the Re-Animator. Re-Animator 2* - B). Story, D, P: Brian Yuzna. Story, SP: Woody Keith, Rick Fry. Mus: Richard Band. SpMkp&VisFX: MMI; (sup) John Carl Buechler; Screaming Mad George; Anthony Doublin; K. N. B. EFX. Stopmo: David Allen. SpMechFX: (sup) Wayne Beauchamp; SPFX Inc. SpFxCoord: Thomas C. Rainone. Prosth: Wayne Toth. Ref: TV. V 2/25/91. MFB'90:233. With Jeffrey Combs, Bruce Abbott, Claude Earl Jones, Fabiana Udenio, David Gale, Kathleen Kinmont (The Bride), Johnny Legend (skinny corpse).

"And God created woman." Arkham, Mass. Scientist Herbert West (Combs)—convinced that "consciousness resides in every part of the body"—seems preoccupied with "morbid doodling with human body parts." He has, for example, spliced a man's arm onto the reanimated body of a dog ("that thing"). Eventually, he gets down to business, and his reanimation juice brings to life an "assembly of dead tissue"—the combined feet of a ballet dancer, legs of a whore, womb of a virgin, arms of a waitress, hand of a lawyer, hand of a murderess, face of someone "special," and heart of assistant Daniel Cain's (Abbott) beloved Meg (Mary Sheldon).

The most taking of the bizarre biological grafts in this sequel to *Re-Animator*—the bat-winged head of Dr. Hill (Gale). Another amusing doodle combines eyeball and fingers. The film as a whole, though, never seems to get going; its two or three co-plots seem uncertainly grafted together. And the script settles too often for easy camp effects—e.g., the predictable stroke of outrageousness when the creature extracts Meg's heart from itself ... spectacular but superfluous gore. (West's concoction is already demonstrably unworkable.)

**BRIDE OF THE KILLER NERD** Hollywood/Riot (Bosko-Harold) 1992 feature. SP, D, P: Mark Steven Bosko, Wayne A. Harold. Ref: PT 14:45: "pretty good sick sequel"—to *Killer Nerd*—"with effective gore effects." Fango 118:12. With Toby Radloff, Heidi Lohr.

**BRIDE OF THE MONSTER** (*2) see *Night of the Ghouls*

The **BRIDE WITH WHITE HAIR** (Singapore-H.K.?) Mandarin Films 1993 color/ws feature (Jiang-hu: *Between Love and Glory*). D: Ronny Yu. SP: Dennis Yu. From Leung Yu-Sang's novel. Ph: Peter Pau. Mus: Richard Yuen. Ref: TV: Tai Seng Video; (microscopic) Eng. titles. EVS. Weisser/ATC. VW 25:17,25. Imagi Smr'95:18,21,24-5,27,50. V 1/17/94:18: in H.K. 5/9/94: *Bakfat Monui Chun*. With Leslie Cheung, Brigitte Lin, Ng Chun-Yu, Elaine Lui.

"The underworld is again rife with witchcraft." Most interesting character here is a "wolf girl" whose hair turns white at the end and who, in one scene, uses her back in some kind of Siamese sex. Plus: a witch cult and the frequent fliers of kung fu. "The witch is possessed!" Atmospheric fantasy.

**BRIDE WITH WHITE HAIR 2** (Singapore-H.K.?) Mandarin Films 1993 color/ws 82m. D: Ronny Yu, David Wu. Ref: TV: Tai Seng Video; Eng. titles. With Brigitte Lin, Leslie Cheung, Chan Kam Hung.

"Don't let the hair out!" The white hair of Ni-Chang, of the Evil Sect, is deadly—it can act on its victims like vicious darts or like a strangling spider web. It's like killer cotton candy. She uses brainwashing, or bewitching, to gain recruits .... Pictorially striking, but pretty conventional fantasy-action, right down to the cackling "witch." An occasional light touch helps. Touching, well-engineered, if overdone ending.

The **BRIDE'S INITIATION** VCX 1976 color feature. D: Duncan Stewart. Ref: Jones. With Carol Connors, Constance Murray, Ambrosia.

Hardcore re Dracula, female vampires, and witches.

**2P The BRIDES WORE BLOOD** Regal/Favorite 1984? feature. D: Robert R. Favorite. Ref: PT 12:11: "slow, boring and confusing." Jones. HR 10/25/83: S-12: vampires. Fred Olen Ray. V 5/9/84:259 (ad). Hound. With Dolores Heisel.

**BRIDGE ACROSS TIME** NBC-TV/Fries Ent. 1985 color c90m. (aka *Terror at London Bridge*. *Arizona Ripper* - alt TV t). D: E. W. Swackhamer. Tel: William F. Nolan. Mus: Lalo Schifrin. AD:

William McAllister. SpFXCoord: John C. Hartigan. Titles: (vis) Jack Michon; (opt) Howard Anderson. SdFX: The Cutters. Mkp: Pamela S. Westmore. Ref: TV. TVG. V 10/16/85:214 (ad). 11/27/85:128. SFChron 11/22/85:86. Stanley. With David Hasselhoff, Stepfanie Kamer, Randolph Mantooth, Adrienne Barbeau, Clu Gulager, Paul Rossilli (The Ripper), Rose Marie.

1888: Jack the Ripper, shot, falls off London Bridge. 1985: A woman's blood drops on a stone restored to the bridge, and The Ripper returns. Or does he? ("Stones don't bring people back to life.") Police think that a "copycat Ripper" is at large near the restored London Bridge at Lake Havasu, Arizona, when stabbing deaths begin to occur on the dates of the original Ripper's murders.... The new London Bridge murders are a mystery only to the characters—the opening sequence tells the viewer all. The script spends a wearying amount of time on the tourist-minded local officials' cover-up of the crimes.

**BRIDGE TO NOWHERE** (N.Z.) Mirage Films/Mune (Larry Parr) 1986 color 90m. SP, D: Ian Mune. SP: also Bill Baier. Story: L. Parr. Mus: S. McCurdy. SpFxCoord: Selwyn Anderson. Ref: V 5/14/86: "an engaging, if occasionally gory and slightly drawn-out thriller." Hound. Ecran F 62:68. With Matthew Hunter, Margaret Umbers, Shelly Luxford, Stephen Judd, Bruno Lawrence, Alison Routledge.

Rifleman stalks teens.

**BRISE-GLACE** (F-Swed) French Ministry of Foreign Affairs & SFP & SEPT & Radio-France & La Muse en Circuit & Maison de la Culture de Le Havre/Swedish Film Institute (Pascal-Emmanuel Gallet) 1988 color 90m. "Histoires de Glace," third of three sections: D: Raul Ruiz. Ref: V 2/24/88: "enigmatic sci-fi."

**BROEDERNA LEJONHJAERTA** see *Brothers Lionheart, The*

**BROKEN COFFIN** (Thai) c1983? color/ws c98m. Ref: TV: All Asian Video; in Thai. Thai Video; above is tr t.

A ghost who can change from beauty to hag to pretty face number 2 follows her scared-stiff (human) boy friend across town and country. She's amiably, amusingly persistent; the actors who play the humans are awful muggers. The two funniest (ha ha and peculiar) bits: The ghost, running pell-mell after her sweetie, stops at a stop light. Later, a holy Yo-Yo sets her on fire. At the end, her body is destroyed, but her taunting laugh remains.

**BROKEN VICTORY** Carstens/Smith 1988 color 79m. SP, D: Gregory Stroem. Story, SP: Jonathan Smith. Mus: Tom Howard. Ref: V 5/18/88. With Jeannette Clift, Ken Letner, Jon Sharp.

"Rather flat sci-fi parable about a dystopia of the future where religious Christians are being persecuted...."

The **BRONX EXECUTIONER** (I) 1987 color feature. D: V. Amici aka Bob Collins. Ref: Martin. Hound. Palmerini: *Il Gustiziere del Bronx*. With M. Newton, Rob Robinson, C. Valenti, Gabriel Gori, W. Strode.

Futuristic—android.

**BRONX LOTTA FINALE - ENDGAME** see *Endgame*

The **BROTHER FROM ANOTHER PLANET** Cinecom Int'l./A-Train 1984 color 109m. SP, D, Ed: John Sayles. Mus: Mason Daring. SpMkp: Ralph Cordero. Ref: TV. V 5/23/84. SFExam 9/28/84. With Joe Morton (The Brother), Darryl Edwards, Steve James, Leonard Jackson, Bill Cobbs, Maggie Renzi.

"The Brother's got talent!" A mute, three-toed, psychic "illegal alien" from another planet, chased by two alien "immigration" officials (Sayles, David Strathairn), arrives on Earth and demonstrates healing and jumping powers. He also has a detachable, "camera eye" eyeball and uses same to trace and track down the corporate bigwig behind neighborhood drug deaths.... Episodic and didactic, but entertaining sf-comedy-drama. The light, loose beginnings are the best part, but The Brother's *Death Wish* confrontation of the elusive drug baron is particularly satisfying fantasy: He uses his eye-in-hand to make him "see" and feel a junkie O.D.—vicarious horror.

**BROTHER FROM SPACE** (Sp-I) Overseas Filmgroup/Calepas Int'l.(Jose Frade) 1984 color feature. SP,D: Roy Garret. SP: also John L. Martin. Ph: Alex Ulloa. Mus: Franco Campanino. AD: Gil Parrondo. SpFX: Production FX 82. Ref: TV: R. Garret(t) = Mario Gariazzo. Palmerini. With Martin Balsam, Agostina Belli, Silvia Tortosa Davis, William Berger, Geoffrey Reyli, John Donovan, Edward Hamilton, Gregory Cutler.

"Based on events which actually took place in the United States." A spaceship "from another world" deposits radioactive capsules on Earth. One contains an alien with a vaporizer gun and a Christ complex. ("Where is the creature that came out of that science fiction gadget?") Embarrassingly obvious, poorly dubbed sf drama is religious in the worst way. In one scene, the amazing alien starts a priest's stalled car; in another, he gives the blind heroine glasses which enable her to see. Just about the worst of the E.T. clones.

**BROTHERS IN ARMS** ABLO & JEL A.S./Gordon-Meledandri (Via Mia) 1988 color c92m. D: George Jay Bloom III. SP: D. S. Kirkpatrick. Mus: Alan Howarth. PD: K. D. Phillips. SpFxMkp: Art & Magic. SpFX: Chuck Whitton. Ref: TV: Republic Home Video. V 10/19/88:284 (ad). 4/12/89. McCarty II. no Phantom. Hound. Martin. With Todd Allen, Charles Grant, Jack Starrett, Dedee Pfeiffer, Mitch Pileggi.

Father (Starrett) heads a crazy mountain clan which crucifies strangers "in God's name." His "Little Eden" features an eerie candles-amok holy of holies. Plus an effective bus with an attack badger, and a bit of copterpropeller gore.... Hardly the worst of the backwoods-maniacs movies, but very familiar material. And the thoughts re heroism fizzle. The most insinuating element of menace: Father's soft-spoken way. Okay muted ending leaves Father and hero Joey (Allen) alive, most everyone else dead.

The **BROTHERS LIONHEART** (Swed) Almi Films/Svensk Filmindustri 1977 ('85-U.S.) color 120m. (*Broederna Lejonhjaerta*). D, Exec Co-P: Olle Hellbom. SP: Astrid Lindgren, from her novel. Mus: Bjoern Ispalt, Lasse Dahlberg. Ref: TV: Pacific Arts Video; Eng. dubbed V 10/5/77. Martin. no Scheuer. no Hound. no Maltin'92. no Stanley. With Staffan Goetestam, Lars Soederdahl, Allan Edwall, Per Oscarsson.

In a fairy-tale land "somewhere beyond the farthest star," lightning reveals a "great monster," a gigantic, fire-breathing, shriek-

ing dragon (a "dragon reemerged from the ancient past"). Film fantasy has some pretty, even majestic images, and some stately music, but it's a long slog until the first appearance of the monster, an hour into the movie. A silent-except-for-music battle scene anticipates *Ran*. The monster's first, brief appearance is more impressive than the climactic sequence, where tacky effects prevail.

**BRUCE LEE: THE MAN ONLY I KNEW** see *Dragon, The*

**BRUTAL SORCERY** (H. K.) 1983 color 86m. D: Pan Ling. Ref: TV: Ocean Shores Video; Eng. titles. NST! 4:18. McCarty II. Phantom. With Lai Han Chi, Lily Chan, Kwan Hoi Shan.

Taxi driver Cheung Yau's two fares, Lin Sing Lung and San Lin, prove to be ghost lovers buried in separate cemeteries ("We live at the Tai Hau Wan Cemetery") who meet only on "those Implied Bad Luck days." They possess him, but exorcist Madam Luk drives the two spirits, victims of Dead Black Magic, out of his body. He takes their skulls to Bukit Beach, Thailand, where San Lin's sister Susanna becomes his lover. When he reneges on a promise to return to see her, she casts the Poison Black Magic spell of impotence on him. He feels compelled to eat raw fish and fowl and winds up with a "swollen tummy." In the climactic sequence, Ping the Devil King, Luk's "fellow disciple," battles Susanna's wizard, Batula, Balatuk, Batola, or Badulla (the spelling in the titles varies), the Black Magician.

Routine possession, exorcism, and dueling-wizards material, except for some odd, almost comic scenes and the climactic supernatural free-for-all, in which Ping's ghost "devils" make like, alternately, acrobats and skeletons. Earlier, in another entertaining scene, they romp about, wraith-like, and annoy Master's guests. The separate-cemetery sequence is at once eerie and comic.

**BUAYA PUTIH** (Indonesian) 1980s? feature. Ref: Heider/Indon. Cinema, p. 44: were-crocs; *The White Crocodile* - tr t.

**BUBBLE GUM CRISIS: THE STORY OF KNIGHT SABERS** (J) Youmex/A.I.C. 1987 anim color 46 1/2m. SP?, D?: Suzuki Toshimutsu. Mus: Koji Makaino. Ref: TV: Toemi Video; no Eng.; OAV. WWorld/Comics 2: 42 (4/88). Animag 2.4:10, 15. Animerica 5:55: 1st of 8 OAVs.

Mega Tokyo, 2032 A.D. The Genom company battles the rebellious Boomers, bio-mechanical humanoid weapons. The prize: a satellite weapon.... Stylish, hollow. An impressive finale, that's all, as the *Alien*-inspired monster-android grows, mutates, engulfs. The heroine, Priss, of the rock group the Replicants, is *Blade Runner*-inspired.

See also the following titles and *A.D. Police File 1* and *Scramble Wars*.

**BUBBLE GUM CRISIS 2: BORN TO KILL** (J) Youmex/A.I.C. 1987? anim color 28m. Ref: TV: Toemi Video; no Eng.; OAV. Animag 4:10-13. 11:45.

Genom's Super-Boomer weapon (with satellite link) proves to be a huge robot with guns bristling in its eyes and mouth—and the only element of visual interest in this talky sf video.

**BUBBLE GUM CRISIS 3: BLOW UP** (J) ToEmi Video 1987 anim color 30m. Ref: vc box. Animag 4:10-15: "the newest Cyberdroid."

**BUBBLE GUM CRISIS 4: REVENGE ROAD** (J) ToEmi Video 1988 anim color 40m. Ref: vc box. Animag 3:2: "new energy source." 4:8.

**BUBBLE GUM CRISIS 5: MOONLIGHT RAMBLER** (J) Artmic & Youmex (Junji Fujita/Tazaki-Aoki) 1988 ('91-U.S.) anim color 45m. (aka *Bubblegum Crisis 5*). D, Anim D, Mecha Des: Masami Oobari. SP: Toshimichi Suzuki. Ph: Akihiko Takahashi. Mus: Kouji Makaino. PD: Ley Yumeno. Anim D: also Hiroaki Gooda. Char Des: K. Sonoda. SpFX: Toyohiko Sakakibara. SdFX: Jimbo Daisuke. Ref: TV: AnimEigo video; Eng. titles. Animag 3:2. 6:5. Voices: Yoshiko Sakakibara, Kinuko Oomori, Masayoshi Sogabe (Largo), Y. Mizutani.

"I wonder if it isn't a vampire, after all." The stew this time includes a scene of apparent vampirization ... "Dobermans," killer robots ... the Orca IV, the Space Development Corp.'s space shuttle ... the Genaros Station, a supply center ... an airborne battlemover ... and Sexaroids.... Stylish, flashy, but dramatically stolid. The slew of technical data makes this hard to follow.

**BUBBLE GUM CRISIS 6: RED EYES** (J) Toshiba-EMI Video/Artmic & Youmex (Fujita/Tazaki-Watanabe) 1989 ('92-U.S.) anim color 51m. (aka *Bubblegum Crisis 6*). Main credits: See previous entry, except for PD: Shinji Aramaki, Kimitoshi Yamane. Ref: TV: AnimEigo video; Eng. titles; "Red Eye's"—title error? Animag 7:4. Voices: Kazuyoshi Sogabe (Largo), Kiyoshi Kawakubo (Quincy).

"I am the maker of the new world." That "monstrous bastard" Largo kidnaps a cabinet minister in an attempt to acquire the OverMind Control System, and then uses an orbital laser satellite to destroy Genom's various headquarters. Plotty, talky cyberpunk soaper.

**BUBBLE GUM CRISIS 7: DOUBLE VISION** (J) ToEmi 1989 anim color 45m. Ref: Animag 9:5. RSI brochure. Japan Video.

**BUBBLE GUM CRISIS 8: SCOOP CHASE** (J) 1989 anim color 50m. Ref: RSI brochure. Japan Video.

**BUBBLEGUM CRUSH! Vol. 1: ILLEGAL ARMY** (J) CPM/Polydor (Artmic) 1991 anim color 45m. (aka *Bubblegum Crash*). Ref: Animag 12:7: 1st of 3 OAVs. RSI brochure Eng. titles. vc box: robots.

A continuation of the *Bubble Gum Crisis* series.

**BUBBLEGUM CRUSH! Vol. 2: GEO CLIMBERS** (J) 1991 anim color 45m. Ref: vc box. RSI brochure. Japan Video.

**BUBBLEGUM CRUSH! Vol. 3: MELT DOWN** (J) 1991 anim color 45m. Ref: vc box. RSI brochure. Japan Video.

**BUCK NAKED IN THE 21ST CENTURY** EVN 1994 color feature. Ref: vc box.

**BUCKAROO BANZAI** see *Adventures of Buckaroo Banzai*

The **BUDDHIST SPELL** (H.K.) 199-? color/ws feature. D: Chew Lu Kong. SP?: Wu Ma. Ph: Chen Zhi Ling. TV: World Video; Eng. titles; vt c'92. VSOM.

"When Blood Kid has sucked the blood of 99 kids, it can resurrect." Ingredients here include the aforementioned Blood Kid, who gets fed bowls of blood and, at the end, takes roughly human shape ... a female spirit from a bleeding tree who possesses a man and, later, becomes trapped in a bottle ... some lively, ghoul-masked gents ... and a flying cursed log .... After a nice whirlwind start, film settles into routine fantasy-comedy-drama. Lots of swirling-cloth effects. Eeriest element: the half-seen, original-form Blood Kid, who's kept in a brightly-lit, opaque glass ball surrounded by tentacles, or roots. Goofiest line: "Why does that monster keep biting me?"

**BUFFY THE VAMPIRE SLAYER** Fox/Sandollar-Kuzui Ents. (Howard Rosenman) 1992 color 86m. D: Fran Rubel Kuzui. SP: Joss Whedon. Mus: C. Burwell. SpFxMkp: William Forsche, Mark Maitre. SpFX: Joseph Mercurio. Ref: TV. V 8/3/92. Sacto Bee 7/31/92. Mo. SFExam 7/31/92. ad. SFChron 7/31/92. Jones. With Kristy Swanson, Donald Sutherland, Paul Reubens (Amilyn), Rutger Hauer (Lothos), Luke Perry, David Arquette, Candy Clark, Randall Batinkoff, Liz Smith, Paul M. Lane.

"Vacuous" Valley Gal Buffy (Swanson) dreams of the vampire Lothos and is followed by the mysterious Merrick (Sutherland). Turns out the latter is the "preparer" of "the Chosen One," and she's "The Slayer, she who bears the birthmark ... of the coven." ("Is that like a trust fund or something?") Your Basic Bland horror-comedy, with occasional funny lines and moments. Compare *Dracula A.D. 1972,* and the Count's adventures in mod London.

**BUGS BUNNY'S LUNAR TUNES** WB 1991 anim color 24m. D: Nancy Beiman. Story: R. Schieb, Greg Ford. Ref: vc box.

Bugs Bunny vs. Marvin the Martian aka *Commander X-2.*

**BULLWINKLE SHOW, The** see *Boris & Natasha*

**BUNKER PALACE HOTEL** (F) AFC & Telema & La Sept & FR3 (Maurice Bernart) 1989 color 95m. SP, D: Enki Bilal. SP: also Pierre Christin. Mus: P. Eidel, A. Devos. Ref: V 6/28/89: "dramatically stillborn." With Jean-Louis Trintignant, Carole Bouquet, Maria Schneider, Jean-Pierre Leaud.

Mythical kingdom's officials served by androids in underground compound.

**BUNMAN—THE UNTOLD STORY** (H.K.) 1993? color/ws feature. Ref: TV: Tai Seng Video; Eng. titles. EVS.

"Go and pack up the rotten legs and arms." A deranged gent chops up his victims, recycles the innards for use at his Pat Sin Restaurant.... Vicious, mean-spirited. *The Texas Chainsaw Massacre 2* with no class or wit. Faithful reviewer called it a day after the bloody-chopsticks sequence.

**BUNNICULA, THE VAMPIRE RABBIT** Hanna-Barbera Home Video/Ruby-Spears Ents. 1982 anim color 23m. D: Charles A. Nichols. SP: Mark Evanier, from Deborah and James Howe's book. Mus: Dean Elliot. PD: Ric Gonzalez. Anim Sup: Jay

Sarbry. Ref: TV: Worldvision HV. VSB. Hound. Voices: Jack Carter, Howard Morris, Pat Peterson, Alan Young, Alan Dinehart.

A "cute fuzzy little bunny rabbit" found in a shoebox turns out to be Bunnicula, the Rumanian vampire rabbit responsible for draining tomatoes of their juices. In vampire form, he has telekinetic and flying powers and easily handles the wolves haunting the Worldco Food Processing Plant.... Irresistible title, very resistible film. Dreadfully flat and predictable, right down to Bunnicula's parting knowing wink.

The 'BURBS Univ/Imagine Ent. (Rollins-Morra-Brezner) 1989 color 102m. D: Joe Dante. SP, Co-P: Dana Olsen. SpVisFX: VCE; Peter Kuran; (opening) IL&M. SpFxSup: Ken Pepiot. SdFX: Mark Mangini; (sp) John P. OptFX: Howard Anderson. Ref: TV: MCA Home Video. HR 2/17/89. S Union 2/17/89. ad.

Black comedy with horrific overtones. The new "neighbors from hell" in Hinckley Hills "only come out at night." Strange lights and deafening noises emanate from their old house. Are the Klopeks "ghouls," satanists, or murderers? In hero Ray Peterson's (Tom Hanks) visualized chainsaw-satanists-barbecue nightmare, they're all that and more.... The two halves of the no-they're-not/yes-they-are double-twist ending cancel each other out. Dante tries, but can't pump any life into the caricatures here. The closest he comes: Corey Feldman's "God, I love this street!" enthusiasm. Unfortunately, the latter is not contagious. At one point, Ray consults The Theory and Practice of Demonology, by Julian Karswell (a reference to Curse of the Demon). Pretty good Jerry Goldsmith score.

BURGLAR FROM HELL Falcon 1993 feature. SP, D: Chip Herman. Ref: PT 20:11: "I enjoyed it anyway." With Bryant Sohl (zombie), Nancy Fel(i)ciano, Barry Gaines, Angela Jackson.

Shot-on-tape gore-effects vehicle.

BURIED ALIVE USA-TV/MCA-TV (Niki Marvin Prods.) 1990 color c90m. D: Frank Darabont. Tel: Mark P. Carducci. Story: David A. Davies. Mus: Michel Colombier. PD: J. K. Reinhart Jr. SpFxCoord: William A. Klinger Jr. Mkp: P. L. Peitzman. Opt: Howard Anderson. Ref: TV. V 5/9/90:75. Maltin '92. With Tim Matheson, Jennifer Jason Leigh, Hoyt Axton, Jay Gerber, Wayne Grace, Donald Hotton.

"Damn you—die!" But poisoned hubby revives in the grave during a thunderstorm. ("Honey, I'm home!") Cheap ironies and faint echoes of Diabolique and Isle of the Dead. At the end, the little woman is buried alive.

BURIED ALIVE (U.S.-So. African?) 21st Century/Breton Film (Harry Alan Towers) 1990 color 91m. D: Gerard Kikoine. SP: Jake Clesi, Stuart Lee, based on elements in the Edgar Allan Poe stories "The Cask of Amontillado" and "The Black Cat." Mus: Frederic Talgorn. Prosth Mkp: Scott Wheeler, Bill Butler. SpFX: Greg Pitts. Ref: TV. V 1/14/91. McCarty II. Fango 89:26-29: elements also from Poe's "The Tell-Tale Heart." With Robert Vaughn, Donald Pleasence, Karen Witter, John Carradine, Ginger Lynn Allen.

All the inmates at the Ravenscroft asylum for sexy young women "have the same problem"—the insane Gary (Vaughn) is their keeper. ("Freedom has its limits, Debbie.") Horrific ingredients here include brickings up alive, a skulker in a monster mask, a snoopy black cat, towels-and-pins weapons, and a clutching hand from a toilet bowl crawling with ants (the latter image an hallucination).... Which Edgar Allan Poe? Slapdash script serves only as a vehicle for some uninspired gore.

BURN, WITCH, BURN! see Devil-Doll, The (1936)

BURNIN' LOVE see Love at Stake

*The BURNING COURT 1961. Dial: C. Spaak. Mus: Georges Auric. SpFX: LAX. Mkp: Yvonne Fortuna. Ref: TV: Sinister Cinema; Eng. dubbed. V 4/25/62. Lee. Lentz. With Rene Genin.

"May you die a horrible death." Ingredients: a witch, executed in 1676, who curses her betrayers and their descendants ... a "strange malediction," which affects the latter ... an old man (Duvalles), a "sorcerer" with a "magic recipe to come back to this world" ("He's dead—the old man") ... his "ghost," who walks "out of the mist" ... talk of "black magic" ... a phantom who "walks through the walls" ... and one apparently-legit ESPer (Edith Scob).... Sufficiently complicated thriller plot, with two or three possible ghostly presences. Scob continues her haunting from Eyes Without a Face. Some good fog-and-bird-cry night atmosphere. Better than the John Dickson Carr original.

BURNING MOON (G) Dead Alive 1992 feature. SP, D: Olaf Ittenbach. Ref: PT 20:69: "extreme gore FX ... overlong movie."

"Three horror stories" re a "decapitating escaped mass murderer," a Satanic priest, etc.

BURNING NIGHT (J) Streamline/Tatsunoko Prods. & King Records 1988 ('91-U.S.) anim color 47m. (Zillion: Burning Night - ad t. aka Red Photon Zillion: Burning Night). D: Mizuho Nishikubo; (U.S. version) Carl Macek. AD: Kikuko Tada. Des: Goto Takayuki; (mecha) "Anmonaito." Ref: TV: vt; Eng. dubbed. Animag 4:8. 6:30-35: based on the toy & TV series. V. Max 3:4. V 11/11/91:52.

"Someday, somewhere," in a futuristic alternate universe, the White Nuts take on an evil clan and its horde of "hopping 'bots." (One of the main thugs has a "cast-iron brain pan" and a chainsaw.) Sole interest of trite sf-actioner, with music: the robotic Japanese variation on the Chinese hopping vampire. Cute: the little hovering, quasi-robot attendant.

BURNING SENSATION (H. K.) Paragon Films/Golden Harvest (Bo Ho Films) 1989 (1988?) color c90m. D: Chia Yung. Ref: TV: Rainbow Video; no Eng. NST! 4:18-19.

A beautiful long-tongued, rubber-armed vampire-ghost uses said tongue to strangle the cabbie who picks her up at St. Michael's Catholic Cemetery. Later, a nice ghost—a television actress burned to death thirty years earlier in a freak accident—leaps out of a TV set to confront the vampire. The two fight furiously when the hero isn't looking.... Alternately silly and funny horror-comedy. Best bit: The good ghost applies hot mustard to the bad ghost's thirty-foot tongue.

BUS (J) Pia Co. (Yutaka Suzuki/T. Nishimura) 1987 color 80m. SP, D, Ed: Takashi Komatsu. Mus: K. Takeo. Ref: V 12/23/87: "too wayward." With Hiroyasu Ito, Kyoichi Ando.

*"1984* Japanese-style."

**BUSTED** Hollywood 1992 color 85m. D: Jim Enright. Ref: Adam '93. With Diedre Holland, Peter North, Teri Diver, Melanie Moore.

Hormones taken from young men rejuvenate old men.

**BUSTROID** see *Robotrix*

**3P The BUTCHER** Cinevid/Turner-Clay c1983? color 89m. (Murderer's Keep - alt vt t). SP, D: P. Miekhe. Story, P: Leonard Turner. Ref: TV: Nite Flite Video. Hound. V 5/9/84:264(ad). 10/10/82:164(ad). no Martin.

More an endangered-witness-to-murder story like *The Window* than a horror movie, *The Butcher* still takes a few stabs at the macabre. Paper-wrapped human bodies (including a "Santa") are delivered to the Central Meat Market for processing. (The first is a "heavy one.") In one all-stops-out sequence, the butcher's slow-witted assistant slaughters all the chickens and makes a bloody mess of the shop. And at the end, the butcher himself (Vic Tayback) is impaled on his own butcher knife. Overall, the film is scrappy, low-key, offbeat, uninvolving.

**BUTT BOYS IN SPACE** In Hand 1990 feature. Ref: Adam '93G: "cheesy space opera." With Eddie Valens.

**BY DAWN'S EARLY LIGHT** HBO Pictures & Paravision Int'l. (T. M. Hammel) 1990 color 120m. D: Jack Sholder. Tel, Exec P: Bruce Gilbert. From William Prochnau's novel "Trinity's Child." Mus: Trevor Jones. Ref: V 5/16/90:79: "pulp stuff." With Powers Boothe, Rebecca DeMornay, James Earl Jones, Martin Landau, Darren McGavin, Jeffrey DeMunn, Peter MacNicol, Rip Torn, Jon Cedar.

Russian missiles strike D. C.

**BYE-BYE, JUPITER** (J) Toho 1984 (1983) color/ws 129m. (aka *Sayonara, Jupiter*). SP, D, P: Sakyo Komatsu. SpFX: (d) Koji Hashimoto; Koichi Kawakita. Ref: TV: Toho Video; half-Eng., half-J. V 10/26/83: 282 (ad). 4/11/84:37. 5/9/84:438 (ad). 5/1/85: 399 (ad): Cannes. Ecran F 43:70. Weisser/JC.With Tomokazu Miura, Miyuki Ono, Diane Dangely.

In the year 2125, the Solar System Development Organization—under the jurisdiction of the President of the Federation of Earth States—is already embarked upon the Jupiter Solarization Project when discovery of a black hole moving towards our solar system is made.... Yes, another Japanese sf/disaster movie, complete with elaborate evacuation scenes. ("Only 340 days more—a deadly race for time.") The spacecraft-and-planet effects may pass muster, but *Bye-Bye, Jupiter* (the title is taken from graffiti on a wall of the Jupiter Minerva base) is easily outclassed by its animation cousins, *The Macross Movie* and *Mobilesuit Gundam*. A tiresome sabotage co-plot consumes much running time, and the script even throws in a gratuitous shark scare. Each character speaks in his or her own language and is apparently always clearly understood by his or her interlocutors. Highlight: the kinda-lyrical floating-naked-in-space sequence.

**BYLETH** (I) 1971 feature (aka *Il Demone dell'Incesto*). Co-SP,D: Leopoldo Savona. Mus: V. Kojucharov. Ref: Palmerini: "poor satanic horror film." With Mark Damon, Claudia Gravy, Aldo Bufi-Landi.

# C

**CD RAM: SEX STAR INTERACTIVE** Odyssey 1994 color 86m. D: C. LaRue. Ref: Adam'95G. With Z. Spears.

Guy "remains stuck in the computer" after experimenting with a new CD-ROM.

**C'E UN FANTASMA NEL MIO LETTO** (I-Sp) Telecinema & Victory Film 1981 color 85m. D: Claudio de Molinis. SP: G. Simonelli et al. Ph: R. Perez Cubero. Mus: P. Umiliani. Ref: Mad Movies 49:11: "haunted house ... sexually obsessed ghost." With Lilli Carati, Renzo Montagnani.

**C'EST ARRIVE PRES DE CHEZ VOUS** (Belg.) Metro Tartan/Les Artistes Anonymes 1992 ('93-U.S.) b&w/ws 95m. (aka *Man Bites Dog*). Story, SP, D, P: Remy Belvaux. SP, P: Andre Bonzel, Benoit Poelvoorde. SP: also Vincent Tavier. Ph: Bonzel. Mus: Jean-Marc Chenut. SpFX: Olivier de Lavelaye. Mkp: Benedicte Lescalier. Ref: TV: Fox Lorber HV; Eng. titles. V 5/25/92: "darkly hilarious." SFChron 1/15/93: "one of the most violent, shocking and bitterly funny movies ever released." V 1/18/93:30. SFExam 2/7/93: "leaves you disturbed." With Poelvoorde, Belvaux, Bonzel, Chenut, Tavier.

"Cocky serial killer ... allows a documentary crew to follow him on his daily rounds of murder and mayhem...." (SFC)

"I usually start the month with a postman." Irony comes a little too easily to this extreme situation. There are horrific moments and nastily funny moments, but the film is for the most part unbuyable. Highlights: the run-in between the principal "documentary" film crew and a video crew trailing another killer ... the fairly breathtaking montage of execution-style shootings.

**C.H.U.D.** New World/Bonime (CHUD Partners) 1984 color 87m. (110m.). D: Douglas Cheek. SP: Parnell Hall. Story: Shepard Abbott. CHUD: (des) Tim Boxell; (sp mkp) John Caglione Jr. Addl SpMkpFX: Ed French. Ref: TV. MFB'85:45-6. V 7/18/84. George Coates. Stanley. Hardy/HM. With John Heard, Daniel Stern, Christopher Curry, Kim Greist, William Joseph Raymond (CHUD).

The E.P.A. would like Soho residents to believe that C.H.U.D., in their classified files, means Contamination Hazard Urban Disposal. But the bad-news bearers are covering up even worse news: Folks who hear the rumblings below Lafayette Street, and unearthly yowls, soon learn that C.H.U.D. means Cannibalistic Humanoid Underground Dwellers.... Competent but derivative monster movie features occasional witty touches. The toxic-monster suits are well designed, if rubbery. The eyes of fully-grown CHUDS glow eerily in New York City's dark underground corridors. The script comes complete with standard monster-cover-up co-plot.

**C.H.U.D. II: BUD THE CHUD** Vestron & Lightning Pictures/MCEG (Jonathan D. Krane) 1989 (1988) color 84m. D: David Irving. SP: "M. Kane Jeeves" (rn Ed Naha). Mus: Nicholas Pike. SpMkpFX: Mkp & FX Labs. SpPhFX: Howard Anderson,

Robert D. Bailey. SpSdFX: Clark Conrad. Ref: TV. V 9/13/89. With Brian Robbins, Bill Calvert, Tricia Leigh Fisher, Gerrit Graham, Robert Vaughn, Larry Cedar, Bianca Jagger, Larry Linville, Judd Omen, Jack Riley, Norman Fell, June Lockhart, Clive Revill.

"That's one frozen stiff!" Bud (Graham), a "live dead guy," returns to life in Winterhaven and starts a plague of "Chudism"— the live people he bites turn into live dead people, too. At the end, the zombies are quick-frozen in an indoor swimming pool, in a bizarre sequence.... Horror-comedy plays more like Son of Return of the Living Dead than a sequel to *C.H.U.D.* Though the humor is generally obvious, Graham (or a double) as Bud gets to do a zombie pratfall, and his reaction to the odor of a bowl of a dog food is as high as the comedy gets in this movie.

**C.O.P.S.** see *Future Force*

**CABAL** see *Nightbreed*

**CABALLERO DEL DRAGON, El** see *Star Knight*

**El CABALLO DEL DIABLO** (Mex) Cima Films 1985? color c76m. SP, D: Federico Curiel. Ph: Javier Cruz. Mus: Sergio Guerrero. SpFX: Ricardo Sainz. Mkp: Graciela Munoz. Ref: TV: Million Dollar Video; no Eng.; *The Devil's Horse* - tr t. With Jorge Rivero, Narciso Busquets, Juan Miranda, Linda Porto, Gloria Mestre, Victor Alcocer, Maritza Olivarez.

After the funeral, a man curses the fate that caused his son's death. A mysterious black horse—a supernatural midwife?—appears at the grave. Soon after, the son, Luciano, appears. His father is overjoyed. Luciano dresses in black and rides the weird black horse, and extreme close-ups of his faced suggest the equine. He shoots a horse that throws him, strangles a woman, thrashes anyone in his way, and occasionally roars. Brandished crucifixes exorcise the horse demon in him.... Oddball horror Western is little more than an anecdote which just repeats the first instance of the demon's brutality over and over. But the can't-buck-Fate undertones lend the movie a little substance and make it a fairly interesting variation on "The Monkey's Paw."

**CABARET SIN** Standard Video/N. O'Toole & Saint Philip (or Phillip) 1987 color c88m. (aka *Droid*). SP, D, Ed: Philip (or Phillip) O'Toole. SP: also N. O'Toole, Christopher Saint. Ph: S. Burns. Mus: Cinema Symphonys (sic). Robotics: Saint. Ref: TV: Standard Video; *Beyond Cabaret Sin*-proposed sequel. TV: Even Steven Prods. video; '88 abridged-X release, as *Droid. Adam* '89. '90: sequel: *Empire of the Sins.* With Greg Derek, Kristara Barrington, Krista Lane, Tom Byron, Bunny Bleu (or Blu), Herschel Savage.

L.A., 2020 A.D. Bisexuality is rampant, at least on the stage of The Pleasure Dome, while, in the cabaret audience, a "killer droid" is on the loose, and a cop, or "eliminator," waits for him ... or her. ("Eliminators aren't supposed to have feelings.") Tawdry, incoherent scrambling of elements from *Cafe Flesh, Blade Runner,* and *The Terminator.*

**CABIN BOY** Touchstone & Steve White Prods. (Tim Burton, Denise Di Novi) 1994 color 80m. Story, SP, D: Adam Resnick. Story: also Chris Elliott. VisFxSup: Michael Lessa; (digital sup)

Craig Newman. Stopmo: Doug Beswick. SpMkpFX: Alterian Studios. MinFX: Stetson. SpFxCoord: R. Knott. Ref: TV. PT 21:17. Martin: "lame." With Ann Magnuson (Kali), Russ Tamblyn (half-shark man).

Fantasy-comedy features, in one scene, a huge iceberg monster (a "walkin' Popsicle") ... plus, in other scenes, a "mer-shark" ... the multi-armed Kali, or Calli, and her giant hubbie ... and (in an hallucination) a big, tobacco-spitting cupcake.... Dead comedy with some okay effects scenes.

**CABINET OF DR. CALIGARI, The** see *Dr. Caligari*

**The CABINET OF DR. RAMIREZ** (U.S.-F-G-B) Great Performances/Mediascope & Thirteen/WNET & Canal Plus & WDR & Mod Films & Paladin Films & BBC-TV (Mockert-Scheele) 1991 ('93-U.S.) silent color 92m. (111m.). SP, D: Peter Sellars. Ref: TV. V 5/20/91: "horror" scenes. 11/19/90:17. SFChron 4/14/93. TVG.

Stray horrific elements here include a man's memory flashes of gore, an apparent *Cabinet of Dr. Caligari* relationship between Cesar (Mikhail Baryshnikov) and Ramirez (Ron Vawter), and the ending, in which all the characters seem to be patients of Dr. Ramirez. John Adams' busy musical score almost makes this interminable film watchable. Just keep repeating to yourself, "It's only a modernist experiment! It's only a modernist experiment!"

**CACCIATORE DI UOMINI, Il** see *Man Hunter*

**Los CACIQUES** (Mex) Filmex/Juan Bueno C. & Emilio Gomez Muriel & Carlos Vigil 1973 color/ws c93m. SP, D: Juan Andres Bueno. Story: Guillermo Z. Vigil, from Fausto B. Vazquez's story "El Payo." SpFX: Humberto Esperanza. Mkp: Graciela Munoz. Ref: TV: Madera Cinevideo; no Eng.; *The Bosses* - tr t. TVG.

Action-adventure movie with fantasy-horror elements, including a cackling satanic cowboy impervious to bullets ... a talking severed head ("Senora!") which rejoins its body ... La Muerte (Irlanda Mora), a woman in white on a white horse ... a witch's spirit ... and coins which turn into scorpions.... The action is elaborate but poorly staged; the fantasy is eerie, though limited to four or five scenes.

**CADAVER EXQUISITO, El** see *Crueles, Las*

**CAGED FURY** (Fili) Saturn Int'l. & Shapiro /LEA 1984 color 84m. D: Cirio Santiago. SP: Bobby Greenwood. Mus: E. Cuenco. Ref: V 5/2/84: "laughably executed "action" scenes." TGSP2. Scheuer. no Maltin '92. With Bernadette Williams, Jennifer Laine, Taffy O'Connell, Ken Metcalf.

Electric-shock-created female "zombies" in Vietnam.

**CAGED HEAT 3000** Pacific Trust (Mike Upton) 1995 (1994) color 88m. D: Aaron Osborne. SP: Emile Dupont. Ph: John Aronson. Mus: Adams, Tomney. PD: Reiko Kobayashi. VisFX: Jeff Rosenkrans. KeyMkp: Cush, Wanstall. Ref: TV: New Horizons HV; c'95. SFChron 2/10/96. vc box: c'94. With Cassandra Leigh, Kena Land, Robert J. Ferrelli, Zaneta Polard, Ron Jeremy.

"Most of the women around here are really psychopaths." Year 3002, the Orion Women's Penal Colony, on the Messalina 4 asteroid, in the Tybor Galaxy. Ingredients include a paralyzing "coffin," laser-like zap sticks, a bit of gore, torture, and *Psycho* tricks in the shower.... Stilted macho-women t&a vehicle tries too hard to be campy.

**CAGED IN PARADISO** Vidmark (J. G. Thomas) 1990 color 90m. (*Paradiso* - orig t). D: Mike Snyder. SP: Michele Thyne. Mus: Klingler, Mamet. Ref: V 3/14/90:30: "unconvincing plotline." With Irene Cara, Peter Kowanko, Paula Bond, Laurence Haddon, Ji-Tu Cumbuka.

Island prison guarded by satellite laser.

**CAGLIOSTRO CASTLE** see *Lupin III: Cagliostro Castle*

**CAIN DEL PLANETA OSCURO** see *Warrior and the Sorceress, The*

**CAIRO** MGM 1942 100m. D: W. S. Van Dyke II. SP: John McClain. Idea: Ladislas Fodor. Ref: TV. V 8/12/42. TGSP. Scheuer. Maltin '92.

Weak comedy with a few sf elements: (a) A radio-controlled plane permeated with a secret substance is synchronized with a magnetized troop transport and directed to crash into the latter and burn, and (b) a special sound filter allows a high-C note through, amplifies it, and converts it into electrical energy which opens a secret door.

**El CALABOZO** (Mex) Prods. Barba Loza (Cesar Brindis) 1993 color 78m. D: M. A. Rodriguez. SP: J. Arturo Cosme. Ph: A. Lara. Mus: R. Cuervo. SpFX: Jose Aguilera. Mkp: R. Mora. SdFX: B. Larraguivel. Ref: TV: vt; *The Dungeon* - tr t. With Miguel A. Rodriguez (Gabriel), Diana Ferreti, Agustin Bernal (hombre monstruo), Robert Montiel, Antonio Raxel, Paola Gaer (aparicion sensual), Olivia (cadaver).

A brute wakes up, finds that his woman has been gorily murdered in bed with some kind of medieval hatchet, and dumps the body in the country. He then has a nightmare re his own premature burial, imagines himself chained to a wall and tended by a fanged dwarf, and is haunted by a cackling demonic figure and a little doll. Later, he dreams that he's castrated with a hatchet and that a temptress dances for him in a ring of fire.... Cheap-looking, monotonous, if busy shocker. Most risible apparition: the fire dance, which is accompanied by a pop band, apparently minor demons.

**CALACAN** (Mex) Emulsion y Gelatina-Dasa 1986 color 80m. SP, D, Co-P, Ed: Luis Kelly Ramirez. SP, Co-P: Mauro Mendoza, Fernando Fuentes. Mus: Luis Guzman. Mkp: Norma Betancourt, F. Lezama. Ref: TV: West Coast Video; no Eng. V 10/15/86. With David Gonzalez, Heriberto Luna (skeleton boy), Silvia Guevara, Dora Montiel, M. Mendoza.

Calacas—the living-skeleton inhabitants of Calacan—are happy producing sugar skulls for the Day of the Dead, but a red devil plots to replace the skulls with plastic pumpkins ... with the aid of a pumpkin machine.... The devils are men in devil masks; the skeletons are actors in skeleton masks; the skeleton dog, rooster, and perhaps the cow are marionettes; and the dancing, singing bread and pastries in the Calacan kitchen are simply puppets and cardboard cut-outs. But this is a charming, inventive, if minor musical-fantasy, with some very beguiling music. The skeletons'

bodies are quite versatile: The skulls are detachable, and the rib cage can be used to stash booze. The devilish villains are rather tiresomely buffoonish.

**CALAMITY OF SNAKES** (Taiwanese) 1982 feature. Ref: Guinness: 165: "supernatural thriller." VW 12:16: Ocean Shores Video; "monster snake."

**CALL ME TONIGHT** (J) A.I.C. 198-? anim color 29m. D: Tatsuya Okamoto. Story: Toshimitsu Suzuki. Anim D & Char Des: Kumiko Takahashi. Anim D: also Satoshi Yamazaki, Masatoshi Nagashima. Monster Des: Jun'ichi Watanabe. AD: Katsuyoshi Kanamura. Ref: TV: C. Moon Video; no Eng. vc box: Pink Noise vol. I: OAV. J Anim Archives 3:5-6. EVS: sfa OAV series *Monster Rapist Lives inside Me*? Voices: Sakiko Tamagawa, Katsumi Toriumi, Chie Kohjiro.

A teenager, Sugiura, apparently invaded by an alien being, periodically transforms into a monster—lust, and movies like "Galaxie of Horror," make him break out, and it's Tentacle City. His lady companion, Rumi, finds his public transformations embarrassing. Eventually, Sugiura discovers that he is a "portal" for alien beings attempting to escape, as he did, from a prison-like limbo. *Call Me Tonight* is a mini-*Alien*, or *The Wolf Man*, and generally unremarkable, but done with a light touch, and featuring an unusual premise.

**CALL OF CTHULHU, The** see *Iczer-One*

**\*\*The CALL OF THE SAVAGE** Univ 1935 serial 12 episodes (*Savage Fury* - 70m. Premier/Serials Inc. feature t). D: Lew Landers. SP: Nate Gatzert, George Plympton, Basil Dickey, from O. A. Kline's novel *Jan of the Jungle*. Ph: Richard Fryer, William Sickner. AD: Ralph Berger. Ref: TV. Greg Luce. Maureen Smith. Lee. Lentz. no V. no Stanley. Phantom. Hound. no Hardy/SF. no Martin. no Maltin '92. no Scheuer. With Noah Beery Jr., Dorothy Short, Bryant Washburn, Walter Miller, John Davidson, Fredric MacKaye, H. L. Woods, Stanley Andrews, Eddie Kane.

Ray-shooting machinery in the control room of the Lost Kingdom of Mu, in central Africa, makes intruders believe that "evil spirits" are haunting the "devil mountain" which is the entrance to Mu. The machinery sends out bolts of lethal "lightning," starts raging fires in the Dungeon of Fire, and makes a cave statue seem to breathe fire. At one point, a royal Mu chemist confirms the effectiveness of a polio serum. ("The death knell of infantile paralysis!")

The feature version of *Call of the Savage* is in effect a forgotten Universal science-horror film featuring story scraps from Tarzan and Atlantis/Mu movies and Jules Verne's "The Carpathian Castle," as well as sets and props from Universal Frankenstein, Dracula, and mummy pictures. As Jan of the Jungle, the very young Noah Beery, Jr., is closer to Boy than to Tarzan; John Davidson's Prince Samu is campily sneery; and a line like "Oh, Borno! Tell me about my mother and my father and the Kingdom of Mu!" is more than Dorothy Short can handle.

**The CALLER** Empire/Frank Yablans, Michael Sloan 1987 color 98m. D: Arthur Allan Seidelman. SP: M. Sloan. Mus: R. Band. SpFX: John Buechler. Ref: V 5/20/87: "suspense meller that has its moments of tension." With Malcolm McDowell, Madolyn Smith.

"Perfect clone ... Mark 11."

**CAMERON'S CLOSET** SVS Films/Smart Egg (Luigi Cingolani) 1989 (1987) color 86m. D: Armand Mastroianni. SP: Gary Brandner, from his novel. Mus: Harry Manfredini. SpCreatureFX: Carlo Rambaldi. PD: Michael Bingham. VisFxSup: Ermanno Biamonte. Prosth: Alex Rambaldi, Rose Librizzi. SpFX: Greg Landerer. Opt: Mentor Huebner; Hollywood Opt. SpSdFxDes: Craig Harris. Ref: TV. V 4/12/89. With Cotter Smith, Mel Harris, Scott Curtis, Chuck McCann, Tab Hunter, Doc D. Charbonneau (little demon).

"The evil is here!" A man (Hunter) who wants to "open up the vast unused powers of the mind" experiments on his telekinetically-talented son, Cameron (Curtis), and turns him into a conduit for an age-old monster. Through "image projection," Cameron unintentionally uses his "make-believe friend," a tiny idol, to bring back the "essence of evil" into the world.... Visualized nightmare sequences only confuse a *Carrie*-like story here. At one point, Cameron does an Astaire, as his powers send him up the walls and across the ceiling of his bedroom. Heavy-duty makeup-effects sequences clock in with such regularity that they become almost comical.

**El CAMINO DE LOS ESPANTOS** (Mex) Zacarias 1965 85m. D: Gilberto Martinez Solares. SP: Roberto Gomez Bolanos. Ph: Raul Martinez Solares, Enrique Wallace. Mus: Sergio Guerrero. AD: Javier Torres Torija. Mkp: Ana Guerrero. Ref: Historia Documental del Cine Mexicano, v. IX (Ediciones Era, Mexico, 1978); *Fright Street* - tr t. With Viruta, Capulina, Elsa Cardenas, Crox Alvarado, Arturo Ripstein.

Comedy with horrific elements, including mummy-like monsters.

**Los CAMPEONES JUSTICIEROS** (Mex) Agrasanchez 1970 color c80m. D: Federico Curiel. SP: Rafael G. Travesi. Story: Rogelio Agrasanchez. Ph: J. O. Ramos. Mus: G. C. Carrion. SpFX: Ricardo Sainz. Mkp: Carmen Palomino. Ref: TV: Madera CineVideo; no Eng.; *The Champions of Justice* - tr t. Cinef 6/96:44. With "Blue Demon," "Mil Mascaras," "El Medico Asesino," "Black Shadow," "Tinieblas," David Silva, Elsa Cardenas, Marisela (Miss Mexico) Mateos.

Science-fiction elements here include a mad doctor's chamber, one minute in which gives each of his respective dwarf minions super-wrestling power ... his freeze machine, which puts Miss Mexico into suspended animation ... a poison gas administered through the phone ... a gun which freezes victims ... and a pill which allows the doc to vanish, then explode.... Dismal sf-and-wrestling actioner has murky color and a highly inappropriate pop-jazz score.

See also: *Triunfo de los Campeones Justicieros. Vuelven las Campeones Justicieros* (Z).

**CAMPFIRE TALES** Crimson Prods. (Paul Talbot, William Cooke) 1991 color 86m. SP, D, Ph, MinFX: Cooke. SP, D, P: Talbot. Mus: K. Green, S. Lollis. AD: Belinda L. James. SpMkpFX: M. R. Smith. Screams: Christine Weinberger. Ref:

TV: KB video. SFChron Dtbk 1/5/92. PT 12:50. With Gunnar Hansen, David Avin, L. E. Campbell, Jeff Jordan, H. Ray York (The Hook), Smith (Satan Claus), Tracy Huggins (zombie).

"I'll tell you some scary stories." The "campfire tales" here include "The Hook": A disemboweler on the loose beheads teens, gets gorily slashed with his own hand-hook. Clumsy, crude storytelling. "Overtoke": "Abnormal marijuana" makes dopers faces go bad, their ears and feet fall off, and their bodies turn to goop. ("You really look bad!") Your basic disgusting-makeup vehicle. "The Fright before Christmas": Steve (Paul Kaufmann) kills mom; Satan (sic) Claus extracts the naughty lad's heart. Simple gore vehicle. "Skull & Crossbones": "Death will come rising out of the sea!" Rise it does, in the form of zombie pirates. Ill-advised, overlong combo pirate-yarn/horror-story.

**CAMPING DEL TERRORE** or **CAMPING DELLA MORTE** see *Body Count* (I/1986)

**CANCION DE NAVIDAD** (Ecuadorian) 1980s? feature. Based on Charles Dickens's story, "A Christmas Carol." Ref: TVG: musical. With Simon Riquetti.

**The CANDID CANDIDATE** (U.M. & M.-TV) Para/Fleischer 1937 anim 6m. Ref: TV: Trans Atlantic Video (ATI). Cabarga/TFS.

As mayor, Grampy improves the town scene with inventions such as a Rain Eliminator—a giant windshield wiper which wipes away rain and brings back the sun—and a jack which moves a house on fire right out of the blazing fire, which promptly dies. Bizarre bits highlight routine Betty Boop cartoon.

***CANDLES AT NINE** Wallace Orton 1944. SP: John Harlow, Basil Mason, from Anthony Gilbert's novel *The Mouse Who Wouldn't Play Ball*. Mus: Charles Williams. AD: C. Wilfred Arnold. Mkp: Harry Hayward. Ref: TV. Maureen Smith. BFC. V 6/14/44. Hound. Lee (E). Scheuer. Martin. no Maltin '92.

Is the Brakes, a "gloomy old house with a lot of mice and ghosts," haunted? ("It ought to be.") James Wilson's camera and lighting effects make it seem so. And they make Beatrix Lehmann—as the cadaverous Miss Carberry, the housekeeper—the star of the movie. Her stock forbiddingness ("Shadows are my friends") amuses; nominal star Jessie Matthews tries too hard to be cute. The non-spooky scenes are just gab and lamentable comedy.

**CANDYMAN** TriStar & Polygram Filmed Ent./Propaganda Films (Golin-Sighvatsson-Poul) 1992 color 93m. SP, D: Bernard Rose, from Executive Producer Clive Barker's short story "The Forbidden." Ph: A. B. Richmond. Mus: Philip Glass. PD: Jane Ann Stewart. SpMkpFX: Bob Keen; Image Animation. SpFX: Martin Bresin. VisFX: Cruse & Co. Computer Imagery: Digital Magic. Ref: V 10/12/92. Fango 118:42-5, 68. 122:7-8. SFChron 10/16/92. Oak Trib 10/16/92. Vallejo Times-Herald 10/18/92. ad. SFExam 10/16/92. TV. With Virginia Madsen, Tony Todd (Candyman), Xander Berkeley, Kasi Lemmons, Vanessa Williams, Michael Culkin.

"Mythical serial killer whose weapon is a ghastly hook...." (V) "I am the writing on the wall." The boogeyman-like Candyman—"the hook man"—was the son of a slave and was "stung to death" by bees at the behest of a wealthy landowner. In the present, his spirit seems to possess a woman and make her kill.... Deliberate, pretentious. At the end, Helen (Madsen) takes Candyman's place behind the mirror. A beekeeper is advised.

**Os CANIBAIS** (Port.-F-I-Swiss-WG) Filmargem-Port. Film Inst.-Port. Radio & TV-Gulbenkian Found. & Gemini Films & AB Cinema & Light Night & Pandora Films Paolo Branto) 1988 color 98m. (*Les Cannibales* - F. *I Cannibali* - I. *Die Kannibalen* - WG). SP, D: Manoel de Oliveira. From Alvaro Carvalhal's story. Music & Book: Joao Paes. Ref: V 5/25/88: *The Cannibals* - tr t. HR 6/2/88. Horacio Higuchi. With Luis Miguel Cintra, Leonor Silveira, Diogo Doria.

"Pretty tame" until "a final 30 minutes of grotesque fun.... Cannibalism escalates and is soon rampant, with everybody" developing fangs. (V)

**CANNIBAL ATTACK** Col/Sam Katzman 1954 69m. D: Lee Sholem. SP: Carroll Young. SpFX: Jack Erickson. Ref: TV: Goodtimes HV. V 11/10/54. Maltin '92. Martin. Scheuer. no Hound. COF 8:36. Weldon.

Stilted Johnny Weissmuller jungle flick has a few campy-horrific elements, including one would-be-spooky scene in which a "crocodile" walking on two legs throws its shadow on a cave wall and another in which a man in a croc suit attacks Johnny, plus dialogue references to a cannibalistic river tribe with "power over crocodiles."

See also: *Crocodile Evil*, etc.

**CANNIBAL CAMPOUT** Donna Michele Prods./Intercoast Video (Jon McBride) 1988 (1987) color 89m. D, P: McBride, Tom Fisher. SP: John Rayl. Mus: Christopher Granger. SpFX: Joseph Salhab. Ref: TV: D. M. video. Hound. Martin. With McBride, Amy Chludzinski, Richard Marcus, Granger, Gene Robbins, Carrie Lindell, Salhab.

Redston. A machete special and raw meat are part of the menu when "the guys from *Deliverance*" begin cannibalizing their youthful guests. Other ingredients in this routine gore movie include an impossibly deformed crazy wearing a gas mask, a very sick Feed-the-guests scene, and a sick "womb with a view" scene.... Thin regional effort is obviously trying to crack the Gross and Disgusting market. The "Gumby" crazy gives the only decent performance.

**CANNIBAL HOOKERS** Hollywood Int'l. (Lettuce Entertain You) 1987 color c70m. SP, D, Co-P: Donald Farmer. Mus: Das Yahoos, Jana Silver. SpMkpFX: Bill Baraschdorf, Brian Sipe. Ref: TV: Italian Stallion Video. V 12/14/88: 37 (hv). 4/11/90:39. McCarty II. no Martin. no Scheuer. no Maltin '92. With Amy Waddell, Annette Munro, Tommy Carrano, Sheila Best; Sky Nicholas & Diana Cruz (cannibals); Gary J. Levinson (Lobo).

The existence of a "neighborhood ritualistic voodoo sacrifice club" helps explain the "half-eaten bodies" turning up in Hollywood. But nothing explains how the hookers barehandedly extract their victims' hearts. These cannibals crave the "warm human flesh" of men and seem to turn female victims into vampires who, in turn.... Stabbed, one hooker turns into an instant skeleton.... Shot-on-tape cheapie includes a little cannibalism, a little vampirism, a little demonism, a human sacrifice or two, and

an irrelevant brute named Lobo. (These ladies are pretty strong. Why would they need a bodyguard?) What the film needs is a little continuity. Awkwardly-staged gore; phony drool and froth. Best line: "Being a 'little sister' has all the social status of being gang-raped by Nazis."

**CANNIBAL MERCENARY** see *Mercenary Cannibals*

**CANNIBAL WOMEN IN THE AVOCADO JUNGLE OF DEATH** Para/Guacamole 1989 (1988) color c93m. (*Piranha Women in the Avocado Jungle of Death* - orig t). SP, D: J. D. Athens. Mus: Carl Dante. Ref: TV: Phantom Video. V 2/22/89. Martin. Scheuer. no Maltin '92. With Shannon Tweed, Adrienne Barbeau, Bill Maher, Karen Mistal, Barry Primus.

In the "completely wild and uncharted" interior of the Avocado Jungle, in southern California, dwell the Piranha Women, ancient feminists who eat men, with guacamole dip ... the Donnahews, a tribe of pathetically subservient men ... and the Barracuda Women, who believe that men should be eaten with clam dip. Into the jungle come Dr. Margo Hunt (Tweed) of Spritzer College, on assignment from the U.S. Commissioner of Avocado Affairs ... Jim (Maher), an "egotistical, chauvinistic klutz" ... and Bunny (Mistal), an airhead .... Good-natured kidding of macho men and feminist women (and Conrad's "Heart of Darkness"). Principal conceit: cannibalism as sexual politics with the gloves off. Highlight: Macho Maher leading the wimpy Donnahews in the "Beer! Beer! Beer!" chant. A generally clever script and Maher's deftness put over this put-on.

**CANNIBALES, Les** see *Canibais, Os*

**CANNIBALI, I** see *Canibais, Os*

**The CANTERVILLE GHOST** (U.S.-B) HTV & Col-TV & Pound Ridge & Inter-Hemisphere (Peter Graham Scott) 1986 color c90m. D: Paul Bogart. Tel: George Zateslo, from Oscar Wilde's story. Mus: Howard Blake. PD: John Biggs. Mkp: Cherry West. Ref: TV. TVG. V 10/15/86:166. With John Gielgud (Sir Simon de Canterville), Ted Wass, Alyssa Milano, Andrea Marcovicci.

Sir Simon, a 300-year-old ghost condemned to "perpetual purgatory" for indirectly causing the deaths of his wife and daughter, scares intruders into his castle by glowing green, playing "vampire monk" and "headless earl," and turning teacups into tarantulas. Plus: a hag's apparition in a mirror and the scientific conjuring up of Sir Simon's wife.... Gielgud has touching, funny moments as the ghost of a ham, but this otherwise limp updating of Wilde is strictly a one-man show. The other actors are incidental. Bland, unatmospheric color.

**El CAPITAN MANTARRAYA** (Mex) GV Films 197-? color c78m. SP, D: German Valdes. SpPhFX: Procesos Opticos. Ref: TV: Video Latino; no Eng.

Blowhard Captain Mantarraya mugs and entertains kids on his boat with a tale of a silly witch and a mermaid who chats with animals, including a monstrous octopus, a fish, and a gull. (The gull calls, in Spanish, on fellow sea birds to attack some killer fish.) Highlight of this broad comedy for children: the amiably phony-looking, giant-tentacled octopus.

**CAPTAIN AMERICA** 21st Century & Marvel Ent. (Menahem Golan) 1990 color 97m. D: Albert Pyun. SP: Stephen Tolkin, based on characters created by Joe Simon, Jack Kirby. Mus: B. Goldberg. SpVisFX: Gene Warren Jr., Fantasy II. SpFxMkp: Greg Cannom. SpFxCoord: Terry Frazee. OptSup: Betzy Bromberg. Ref: TV. MFB'91:12. V 6/8/92(hv): Story: L. J. Block, S. Tolkin. With Matt Salinger (Steve Rogers/Captain America), Ronny Cox, Ned Beatty, Darren McGavin, Michael Nouri, Melinda Dillon, Francesca Neri, Bill Mumy, Kim Gillingham, Scott Paulin (The Red Skull), Carla Cassola (Dr. Maria Vaselli), Wayde Preston, Norbert Weisser.

"He may not be Superman...." Project Rebirth/Code Name: Captain America pits super-strong, super-smart Captain America against Red Skull—Dr. Vaselli's first, misfired creation—initially in 1943, ultimately in the 1990s.... Some thick emotional syrup and some jarring jumps in time and place cripple the new *Captain* (Is he an inspiration or is he Camp?) *America,* and there's an odd disparity between the script's aimlessness and the grandiosity of its international intrigue. Random highlights include the animated rat-thing and Paulin's presence as the Red Skull.

**CAPTAIN BARBELL** (Fili) Viva Films 1986 color c105m. D: Leroy Salvador. SP: Jose Javier Reyes. Story: Mars Ravelo. Ph: Lacap, Batac. Mus D: Ricky Del Rosario; (theme) Mon Del Rosario. AD: Ogie Buan. Vis & OptFX: Amang Buencamino; Danny Rojo. SdFxSup: Demet Velasquez. Mkp: Totoy de la Serna, Ely Santos. Ref: TV: Viva Video; some Eng. With Edu Manzano (Capt. Barbell), Herbert Bautista, Lea Salonga, Dennis Da Silva, Ruel Vernal, Sharon Cuneta (Darna), Arthur Cantilleps (wolfman), Goliath (midget Capt. Barbell), Eddie Noble (windman).

The principal monster of this lively if undistinguished fantasy-horror movie is called a "wolfman" in the credits and a "vampire" in a TV news flash. He transforms from a human into a wolf at night and bites the necks of his victims. Like the hero—the boy Tengteng/Captain Barbell—the monster has super-powers, and can become a super-monster, complete with cape and flying ability. Impaled on a cross, the dying creature undergoes a double transformation, from scraggly super-monster face to scraggly werewolf face to human face.

Later, Captain Barbell takes on a spider woman, who incinerates her victims with rays from a gem in her headgear, shoots out spider-web "nets" with her hands, and surrounds herself with monster aides, including a big-headed dwarf who can unleash strong winds with his mouth. (Barbell covers the latter and makes him inflate and explode.) In the climactic sequence, the alien Darna makes a guest appearance, and Captain Barbell vanquishes some ghostly (animated) electric beings who smash into pieces, only to reassemble. He scatters the pieces so that they can't reassemble again.

See also *Ang Pagbabalik Ni Pedro Penduko.*

**CAPTAIN EO** Disney World/George Lucas & Rusty Lemorande 1985 3-D color 17m. D: Francis Ford Coppola. Ph: Vittorio Storaro. MkpFX: Rick Baker, Lance Anderson; Tom Burman? Ref: Bill Warren. Ecran F 62:63. 74:9. V 2/25/91:59. With Michael Jackson, Angelica Huston.

Witch ... interplanetary voyage ... two-headed creature.

**CAPTAIN YAGIT** (Fili) Horizon Films c1985? color c125m. D: Angel Labra. SP: Woodrow Serafin. SpFX: L. Marzano? SdFX: Amber Ramon? Mkp: Naty Valorez? Ref: TV: vt; little Eng. With Cachupoy, Luis Gonzales, Redford White, Gladys Mercado, Max Alvarado, Bamba, Hazel Navasero, Greg Moreno, Joel Galvez, Maning Bato, Boyet Mercado, Serafin, Rene Romero.

The occupant of a flying fireball which lands on Earth gives the hero (White) a medallion which enables him to become super-strong, flying, invulnerable Captain Yagit, who can catch bullets in mid-air, fuse them, and "fire" them back, and who at one point dreams that he is flying with Superman. ("I hope you'll help me, Superman.") A second fireball deposits an evil, robotic-looking being that raises a cemetery's dead and can fire disintegrating rays. Captain Yagit fights the zombies, then the evil alien.... Unsophisticated, sloppy horror-comedy-fantasy features *Superman* music throughout, but does not credit John Williams.

**2 The CAPTURE OF BIGFOOT** 1979. Addl Dial: John Goff. Ph: Bela St. Jon, Ito. Mus: Keith & Mitch Irish. PD: Will McCrow. SpMkpFX: Tom Schwartz, Vince Prentice. Ref: TV. Lentz. Stanley. Hound. no Scheuer. no Maltin '92. no Phantom. no Weldon. no Hardy. With George "Buck" Flower, Verkina Flower.

Legend has it that a strange creature, Arak, watches over an ancient Indian burial ground in Wisconsin's Lake of the Clouds region. And, by gum, strange tracks in the snow ("Them ain't human!") lead right to one Bigfoot ("Yea tall!")—Janus Raudkivi in a Frosty the Snowman suit—and one relatively small, more-sweetly-dispositioned "Little Bigfoot" (Randolph Rebane).... The hardest kind of low-budget monster movie to watch—tame, slow, uncertainly acted, and not-inept-enough for laughs, just inept. The "theme": the exploiters (Richard Kennedy and friends) vs. the exploited (Bigfoot and offspring). Wally Flaherty, as the sheriff, kills some running time doing impressions of Peter Falk's Columbo. When time is killed in a movie like this, it stays killed....

**CAPULINA CONTRA LAS MOMIAS** (Mex) Panorama Films/Estudios America, Zacarias 1973 color c90m. SP, D: Alfredo Zacarias. Ph: Raul Dominguez. Mus: Carlos Camacho. AD: Raul Gardenas. Mkp: Graciela Gonzalez. Ref: TV. TVG. V(CHVD). no Hardy. no Stanley. With Capulina, Jacqueline Voltaire, Enrique Panton, Freddy Fernandez.

Capulina dreams that a mad doctor restores a Guanajuato mummy to life. Generally silly comedy, with a few funny moments and suitably-creepy-looking mummies. Film looks to have started life as a three-part TV miniseries.

**CAPULINA CONTRA LOS VAMPIROS** (Mex) Miguel Zacarias 1973 color 80m. SP, D: Rene Cardona Sr. Ph: R. M. Solares. Mus: Sergio Guerrero. Mkp: Ana Guerrero. Ref: TV. Glut/TDB. TVG: 1965? no Hardy. no Stanley. Jones. With Capulina, Jacqueline Andere, Armando Acosta.

Horror spoof features a vampire man with oversized canines more like tusks, a vampire woman ("Buenas noches"), then a whole horde of vampire women. Typical Mexican numbskull comedy, with cute slapstick moments. Easy to tell the horror scenes from the more mundane ones—the former are shot in neon-garish red and blue, and feature bats on strings, bottles-for-vampires labeled "Sangre para Transfusions," and a vanishing dwarf. At the end, their fangs having been extracted, the vampires are baby-bottle-fed milk.

**The CARE BEARS MOVIE** Nelvana (American Greetings & CPG) 1985 anim color 75m. (*The Care Bears Movie—Land without Feelings* - vt t). D: Arna Selznick. SP: Peter Sauder. Mus: Patricia Cullen. SpFxD: David Marshall et al. SpSdFX: Peter Jermyn, Drew King. Ref: TV. MFB'85:244. Stanley. TVG: Canadian? Voices: Mickey Rooney, Jackie Burroughs (The Spirit), Georgia Engel, Sunny Besen Thrasher, Harry Dean Stanton.

An evil green spirit-face from a magic book makes a boy, Nicholas, cast a cloud-monster "spell" on children and bears. The spell later turns into a tentacled tree-monster. Also: the science-fantasy-like Rainbow Rescue Beam and a vulture-creature.... Too cheerful near-parody of the standard Disney mixture of sweetness and menace. Doggedly anti-gloom.

**CARE BEARS MOVIE II: A NEW GENERATION** Col/Nelvana & Wang/LBS (Those Characters from Cleveland & Kenner Parker Toys) 1986 anim color 76m. D: Dale Schott. SP: Peter Sauder. Mus: Patricia Cullen. Songs: Dean & Carol Parks. SpFX: Trevor Davies et al. SpSdFX: Drew King et al. Ref: TV. MFB'86:202-3. V 3/19/86. TVG: Canadian. ad. Voices: Hadley Kay (Dark Heart), Michael Fatini, Sunny Besen Thrasher, Maxine Miller.

The evil Dark Heart appears first as a red sea serpent ("I am Dark Heart!"), then as, variously, a big frog, a fox, a red-headed boy, a vulture, a Caring Meter reader ("I'll be back!"), a wolf, a shadow, a spider ("All the love and kindness in the world will soon be no more!"), an alligator, an ape, a turtle, and a snake ("All of your friends frozen in my crystal prison!").... More goodness and light. Muzak for children. Even the menace, Dark Heart, is bland, though in an oddly touching finale, he is—like the Wolf Man in *House of Dracula*—cured.

See also: *Care Bears Adventure in Wonderland!*(P).

**CAREER OF A COMET** see *On the Comet*

**CARESSE DE SATAN, La** see *Devil Kiss*

**CARMILLA** see *Nightmare Classics*

**CARNAGE** Jaylo Int'l. (Lew Mishkin) 1983 color 92m. (*Hell House* - shooting t). SP, D, Ph: Andy Milligan. Ref: TV: MHE video. V 4/23/86: "old-hat, poorly made." McCarty II: "easily Milligan's best." Ecran F 71:80. PT 8:12: "isn't exactly funny." With Leslie Den Dooven, Michael Chiodo, John Garritt, Deeann Veeder (Susan), Chris Georges (Mark).

A house with a "devil in it" proves to be haunted by a couple who had a double-suicide "wedding." Dead phones ring. Appliances self-start. Objects levitate. The ghosts (Veeder and Georges) sever heads and limbs. Stilted *Poltergeist*-without-effects (good ones, that is) is almost comically flat-footed.

**CARNAVAL DE LAS BESTIAS, El** see *Human Beasts*

**CARNE DE TU CARNE** (Colombian) Producciones Visuales 1984 color 85m. SP, D: Carlos Mayolo. SP: also Elsa Vasquez, J. Nieto. Mus: Mario Gomez Vignes. Ref: Hardy/HM. V 9/5/84:

"an unsatisfying, increasingly hysterical botch" re "vampirism." Ecran F 50:70. With Adriana Herran, David Guerrero, Jose Angel.

**CARNIVAL OF ANIMATION** see *Robot Carnival*

**CARNIVAL OF FOOLS** Jaime Mendoza-Nava/William Stroup & E. J. Bodine, Jr., 1983 c91m. (*Death Wish Club* - alt t). D: John Carr. SP: Philip Yordan. Ph: Byron Wardlaw et al. Mus: Jeff Cohen. Sets: Chatterton, Crosby. Mkp: Norm Keefer. Ref: TV: AIR Video. Scheuer. no Martin. no Maltin '92. no Stanley. Hound. Phantom: Haze's scenes also used in *Night Train to Terror*. PT 2:48. VSB. With Meridith Haze, Rick Barnes, J. Martin Sellers, Anne Fairchild, William Charles, Paul Keefer, Arthur Braham (mad professor).

Gretta (Haze), who "lives in the fourth dimension," and her friend, Manhattan Club owner Georgie Youngmeyer (Sellers), introduce "college boy" Glenn Marshall to a sort of suicide club. Members of the latter get their kicks by facing various exotic deaths, including death by Tanzanian-winged-beetle sting, electrocution in an improvised "electric chair," and death via a construction-ball variation on the Pit and the Pendulum. Plus, in the same film: on the set of a brain-transplant porno-comedy in production.... Suffice it to say that this determinedly quirky movie features subjective-camera shots from the viewpoint of a poisonous flying beetle, and the line "I'm glad Chopin's dead!" Midway, Gretta becomes, or thinks she becomes, "Charlie White," and the plot gets progressively less believable.

*****CARNIVAL OF SOULS** 1962 82m. Titles: Dan Fitzgerald. Ref: TV. NYorker 9/4/89:88. MFB'90:274-5. COF 8:38. Lentz. Lee. V 10/3/62. Weldon. Cocchi: 1989 Panorama Ent. re-release. Hound. Phantom. Maltin '92. Stanley. Martin. Scheuer. Newman. Fango 118:14-19, 59. Film Superstore: aka *Corridors of Evil*.

"What's the matter with everyone?" Church organist Mary Henry (Candace Hilligoss) seems to survive an auto accident, but a "strange man" (Herk Harvey) who looks like a walking cadaver haunts her, and a deserted carnival pavilion which was once a bathhouse and dance hall draws her, physically as well as emotionally. Intermittently, others do not see or hear her, and she does not hear others. ("It was as though, for a time, I didn't exist.")

Invention on a shoestring, a la *Night Tide*. From another angle, this semi-famous Herk Harvey-John Clifford fantasy is a low-budget *La Dolce Vita* re human isolation. ("Something separates me from other people.") Yet a third cross reference might be the "I Shot an Arrow into the Air" episode of the original "Twilight Zone," another tale of disappearing people. *Carnival*, in fact, plays, alternately, like the best and worst of "The Twilight Zone." Harvey and photographer Maurice Prather use fast motion eerily for the crazy-fast dancing of the ghouls, and "stippled" motion for their pursuit of Mary at the end. The jack-in-the-box spook bits, though, come off pretty hokey. The star of the movie: the pavilion itself, a fine old "set" which, like Mary, is a shell.

**CARNOSAUR** Concorde-New Horizons (Mike Elliott/Roger Corman) 1993 color 82m. SP, D: Adam Simon. Mus: N. Holton. VisFxSup: Alan Lasky. SpMkp & Creatures: John Carl Buechler, MMI. Dinosaur Consult: Don Glut. SpLaserFX: Lasermedia.

Ref: TV: vt; Pacific Trust. V 6/7/93: "serviceable programmer." 8/17/92:15. SFChron Dtbk 7/25/93. With Diane Ladd, Raphael Sbarge, Jennifer Runyon, Harrison Page, Clint Howard.

Dino DNA and chicken eggs produce "prehistoric terror." (V) "You never said they could hatch that quickly." In the interests of "building a better chicken," a Eunice company scientist (Ladd) unleashes a mini-dinosaur, which keeps "growin' real fast." Soon, women are birthing dino-babies, and bodies are being found looking as if they were "torn by a scythe" .... Thin plot, ambitious themes. Ladd wants to reclaim Earth for the dinosaurs, and the latter indeed seem to be traveling the Dinosaur Highway of the past on their way to ruling again in the future. The dinosaur-vs.-construction-equipment finale apes *Dinosaurus!*; the pretentious, downbeat coda apes the original *Night of the Living Dead.*

**CARNOSAUR II** Roger Corman/Pacific Trust (Mike Elliott) 1994 color 82m. (*Carnosaur 2* - ad t). D: Louis Morneau. SP: Michael Palmer. Ph: John Aronson. Mus: Ed Tomney. AD: Trea King. Monster: Gig Roche. SpVisFX: MMI. SpMinFX: A. Doublin. SpFxCoord: Lou Carlucci. Ref: TV: New Horizons HV. With John Savage, Cliff DeYoung, Rick Dean, Ryan Thomas Johnson, Arabella Holzbog, Don Stroud, Rodman Flender.

"They found a way to bring back dinosaurs." The Yucca Mountain Repository for High-Level Atomic Waste houses "very special, fossilized DNA"—and dinosaurs generated by same. One dino somehow gets into a copter; one does a zombie number on its victim's innards. ("Eat this, Barney!") Tired. And not much dino at all until the 33-minute mark. The effects are variable, but that puts them one up on the script.

**CARPATHIAN EAGLE, The** see *Hammer House of Horror Double Feature*

**The CARPENTER** (Can.) Goldgems (Pierre Grise) 1988 color 87m. D: David Wellington. SP: Doug Taylor. Mus: P. Bundock. Ref: V 8/31/88: "little substance." Fango 89:12, 34: "standard splatter movie." PT 4:12-13. McCarty II: "on the slow side." With Wings Hauser, Lynn Adams, Pierre Lenoir, Barbara Jones.

Grisly story re woman in love with ghost of mass murderer.

**The CARRIER** Swan (Jeffrey Dougherty) 1988 color 99m. SP, D, Exec P: Nathan J. White. Mus: Joseph LoDuca. Ref: V 1/18/89: "amateurish." 10/21/87:195(ad). Martin. Phantom: "rarely less than genuinely disturbing." With Gregory Fortescue, Steve Dixon, N. Paul Silverman.

Immune carrier transmits disease which eats away like acid at victims.

**CARRION** see *Jar, The*

**CARROL MORIRA A MEZZANOTTE** (I) Dania 1986 color 90m. (aka *You'll Die at Midnight. Morirai a Mezzanotte*). D: Lamberto Bava. SP: D. Sacchetti. Mus: Claudio Simonetti. SpFX: A. Alessi. Ref: MV: D: also D. Sacchetti; "bloody slasher film." Hardy/HM2: aka *Midnight Horror*; derivative. ETC/Giallos: SP: also L. Bava; "nothing new." V 5/7/86:292: "first Italian horror made-for." Ecran F 63:13. 70:70: "terrifying *giallo*" re a

"dangerous maniac." Palmerini: "amazingly banal." With Valeria D'Obici, Lara Wendel, Paolo Marco.

Murder with ice pick ... aka *Midnight Killer.*

**CASA, La 3** see *Ghosthouse*

**CASA, La 4** see *Witchery*

**CASA, La 5** see *Beyond Darkness*

**CASA AL FONDO DEL PARCO, La** see *Ratman*

**CASA D'APPUNTAMENTO** see *Paris Sex Murders*

**CASA DALLE FINESTRE CHE RIDONO** see *House with Windows That Laughed*

**CASA DEL TAPPETTO GIALLO, La** see *House of the Yellow Carpet, The*

**CASA DEL TEMPO, La** see *House of Clocks*

**CASA DELLE ANIME ERRANTI** see *House of Lost Souls*

**CASA SPERDUTA NEL PARCO, La** see *House on the Edge of the Park*

**CASE OF CHARLES DEXTER WARD, The** see *Resurrected, The*

**CASE OF THE GIRL IN THE YELLOW PYJAMAS** see *Pyjama Girl Case, The*

**CASE OF THE THREE WEIRD SISTERS, The** see *Three Weird Sisters, The*

**\*The CASE OF THE TWO BEAUTIES** Atlas Int'l./Aquila(Adrian Hoven) 1968 (1967) (*Rote Lippen. Sadisterotica* - vt). SP: also Luis Revenga. Ph: also F. Hofer. Mus: also J. van Rooyen. AD: also G. Pilati. Ref: TV: VPRC (?) video; Eng. dubbed; c80m. Lee. Hardy/HM: aka *Red Lips*. VWB. Necronomicon 6. With Chris Howland, J. Franco.

"Your death will make my work everlasting." Follow-up to *Kiss Me Monster* (which see) concerns a painter who practices the "art of fright": First, he photographs his female subjects, as his aide Morpho (a cousin, apparently, of the Morpho in Franco's earlier *Awful Dr. Orlof* and later *Fall of the House of Usher*), as Morpho kills them; later—making his models do double artistic duty—he encases them in sculptures. Morpho—the "unshaven idiot"—is not really an apeman, although he has a hairy face and hands and "fingernails like claws"—he's just the result of a little psychiatry and certain "substances." His makeup is not special. His horror scenes here punctuate vapid, grotesquely dubbed spy intrigue and comedy. One of the dancers from the first film is still doing the same night-club number.

**CASK OF AMONTILLADO, The** see *Buried Alive* (U.S.-S. African?, 1990)

**CASSANDRA** (Austral.) Parrallel Films or Parallel Films (Trevor Lucas) 1987 color 93m. SP, D: Colin Eggleston. SP: also John Ruane, Chris Fitchett. Mus: T. Lucas, Ian Mason. Ref: V 5/27/87: "routine whodunit." Martin. Morse: "stupid." With Tessa Humphries, Shane Briant, Briony Behets.

Heroine has "horrifying nightmares" re deranged, homicidal twin brother.

**CASSIOPEA (II)** see also *Otroki Vo Vselennoi*

**CAST A DEADLY SPELL** HBO-TV/Pacific Western (Gale Anne Hurd) 1991 color 92m. (*Lovecraft* - orig t). D: Martin Campbell. Tel: Joseph Dougherty. Ph: A. Gruszynski. Mus: Curt Sobel. PD: Jon Bunker. Creatures: Alterian Studios, Tony Gardner;(gargoyle) Eric Fiedler;(Old One) Bill Sturgeon;(werewolf/gremlin) B.S. Fuller;(zombie) Roger Borelli;(oatmeal demon) Brian Penikas. VisFX: 4-Ward Prods.;(sup) Laura Buff;(d) Ernest Farino. SpFxCoord; Ken Speed. Magic Consult: David Avadon. Unicorn Wrangler: Hollywood Animals. SdFX: Todd-AO, Glen Glenn. Ref: TV: HBO Video. PT 12:52. TVG 8/24/91. 9/7/91. Sacto Bee 9/1/91. SFChron 9/1/91. With Fred Ward, David Warner, Julianne Moore, Clancy Brown, Alexandra Powers, John De Bello, Lee Tergesen, Jaime Cardriche (zombie), Jim Eustermann (werewolf), Michael Reid Mackay (gargoyle).

L.A., 1948. "Everybody used magic." Ingredients: private eye H. Phillip Lovecraft (Ward), the only one not corrupted by magic ... The Dunwich Room ... a living, menacing gargoyle ... a big zombie ... a monster from a cauldron ... a *Curse of the Demon*-ish parchment ... a vampire lady .. a werewolf ... a "Necronomicon"-invoked Old One (or H.P. Lovecraft meets *Alien* and *The Creeping Unknown*) ... and HPL-inspired lines like "Yog Sothoth knows the Gate" .... Perfunctory mystery story with incidental effects-and-makeup amusements and an occasional nice imitation-Chandler line. Good touch: the stylized skies over L.A. Funny bit: spraying the gremlins under the hood.

Follow-up: *Witch Hunt*.

**CASTELLO DELL'ORRORE** or **CASTELLO DELLA PAURA** or **CASTELLO DELLE DONNE MALEDETTE** see *Frankenstein's Castle of Freaks*

**CASTLE CAGLIOSTRO** see *Lupin III: Cagliostro Castle*

**CASTLE IN THE SKY, LAPUTA** see *Laputa*

**CASTLE OF BLOOD** (I) see *Dark Obsessions*

**CASTLE OF CAGLIOSTRO, The** or **CASTLE OF KARIO-SUTORO, The** see *Lupin III: Cagliostro Castle*

**CASTLE OF THE DOOMED** see *Kiss Me Monster*

**\*\*CASTLE VOGELOD** (G) Decla-Bioscop 1921 silent b&w 72m. (*Schloss Vogelod*). D: F.W. Murnau. SP: Carl Mayer, from Rudolf Stratz's novel. Ref: screen. PFA notes 5/5/85. Lee. no Eisner/HS. Eisner/Murnau.

A mystery movie featuring a nightmare sequence in which a monstrous, hairy hand with claw-like nails enters a window and drags a man from his bed. Plus a man who vanishes from the castle. ("Things are getting positively spooky here.") The castle guest's nightmare and the cook's aide's comic dream are the highlights here, and the mystery itself intrigues, if final revelations don't. Murnau's fatalism is dramatized and visualized more strikingly in some of his other films. Here, it's mainly just part of a silly story.

**The CAT** (H.K.) Paragon Films 1991 color/ws 88m. SpFX?: Den Film FX. Ref: TV: Tai Seng Video; Eng. titles.

"Wisely, the killers from outer space are here!" Story ingredients include writer-adventurer Wisely (from *The Legend of Wisely*) ... a monster tree/Medusa/goop from space ... a near-indestructible, possessed gent ("I'm not human!") ... "stellar radioactivity," which "decomposes" the good alien's body and allows her to travel via "radio pulse" ... and a magic octagon which, "when meshed with cat's hair, can decimate cells."

Okay, effects-sparked sf-horror-actioner, with some wild-and-woolly premises. Good, old-fashioned goop-and-tentacle effects recall Fifties sf-ers. Not as grisly as *The Seventh Curse* (another Wisely adventure), but just as much fun.

**CAT, The** see *Evil Cat*

**\*The CAT AND THE CANARY** Arthur Hornblow, Jr. 1939. Ref: TV. Eames. V 11/1/39. Lentz. Lee. Hardy/HM. Jim Shapiro. Scheuer. Maltin '92. With Charles Lane.

"Not far from New Orleans there still exist in strange solitude the bayous of Louisiana"—and in those bayous, the "old Norman place," a "terrible house." Spook ingredients include "the cat," a homicidal maniac with fingernails like claws (actually he's a man in a monster mask) ... George Zucco's lawyer Crosby, who disappears early ("The demon in this house has got him!") ... Miss Lu (Gale Sondergaard), the forbidding housekeeper whose friends are from the "other world" ("Sometimes they get into the machinery") ... and cobwebby cellars, statuary, etc.... Tired plot mechanics and comedy; good sound, music, and shadow effects—e.g., the weirdly-tolling bells, the huge cat-shadow, the lights with the "jitters."

See also: *Ghost Breakers* (the Bob Hope-Paulette Goddard follow-up).

**CAT FROM HELL** see *Tales From the Darkside—The Movie*

**CAT IN THE BRAIN** (I) Executive Cine TV 1989 color/ws (*Un Gatto nel Cervello. I Volti del Terrore* - orig t?). Story, SP, D: Lucio Fulci. Story, SP: also Giovanni Simonelli. With the collaboration of Antonio Tentori. Ph: Alessandro Grossi. Mus: Fabio Frizzi. Ref: TV: vt. Jim Shapiro. MV: aka *Nightmare Concert*. Palmerini. With L. Fulci, David Thompson, Jeoffrey Kennedy, Malisa Longo, Brett Halsey (the monster), Ria de Simone, Robert Egon (second monster).

"I make horror films." A chainsaw, a meat grinder, and miscellaneous household pets are used to dispose of a body, in a "pretty nasty sequence" in a Lucio Fulci (Fulci) film being shot. (The sequence is from *A Touch of Death*.) When the director finds himself assailed in real life by images which remind him of his horror movies, he goes to a psychiatrist, who tells himself, "I'll create ... a bloodthirsty monster." Via post-hypnotic suggestion, the homicidal doc sees to it that putrefying bodies greet Fulci wherever he goes. Plus a Mess O' Brains opener and a sequence in which a woman is besieged by monsters (in a film-in-progress on the set) .... The kinda cute premise—Fulci as Fulci, the "one who makes all those horror films"—is just an excuse for random butcher-shop gore. Dreadful English-dubbed shocker.

**CAT IN THE CAGE** Saz 1978 color c90m. Story, SP, D, P: Tony Zarin Dast. SP: also Richard Vasquez. Ph: Ali Zarin Dast. Mus: Jack Wheaton. Ref: TV: Genesis HV. VSB. Phantom mention. no Stanley. no Weldon. no Lentz. no Martin. no Scheuer. no Maltin '92. TVG. Gore Zone 11:64: "sex thriller." With Bruce Vaughn (aka Behrouz Vossoughi), Colleen Camp, Sybil Danning, Ursaline Bryant-King, Frank de Kova, Mel Novak, Tony Bova (Ali Khan), Aram Katcher, James Bacon.

"That damn cat!" Stilted mystery thriller begins like *Shadow of the Cat,* as the feline Samson "haunts" murderess Susan Khan (Danning). Midway, the plot switches, clumsily, to "Jane Eyre," as the strangler of Susan proves to be the hero's long-thought-dead, criminally insane brother Ali, who has been "hidden away" in a Newhall (California) mansion for years. The strangling itself—in which Ali is treated almost as an unstoppable monster—is the film's single horror-movie sequence. Bad performances dominate, and the cat's not an actor either.

**CAT LICKERS** Moonlight 1991 color 78m. D, P: Scotty Fox. Ref: Adam '92: sex robots, "weird scientist." With Madison, K. C. Williams, Angela Summers.

**\*\*The CAT O' NINE TAILS** (I-W.G.-F) Nat'l. General/Seda-Terra-Labrador (Salvatore Argento) 1970 color/ws 111m. (*Il Gatto a Nove Code*). Story, SP, D: Dario Argento. Story: also Luigi Collo, Dardano Sacchetti. Ph: Erico Menczer. Mus: Ennio Morricone. AD: Carlo Leva. Mkp: Ferrante, Mecacci (sp?). OptFX: L. Vittori. SdFX: L. Anzellotti. Ref: TV: Col (Japan) Video; Eng. version. Palmerini: "certain genetic traits" seem to determine the criminal character. Maltin '92: "graphic gore." VWB. V 6/9/71. MFB'71:120. With James Franciscus, Karl Malden, Catherine Spaak, Cinzia De Carolis, Carlo Alighiero, Horst Frank, Werner Pochat, Pier Paolo Capponi, Rada Rassimov, Umberto Raho.

The "maniac"'s victims here are generally garroted and/or "all cut up." Is someone with an XYY chromosomal configuration (people with same tend to be "abnormally aggressive," it says here) behind the murders around the Terzi Institute? Routine mystery with good subjective camerawork. Extreme close-ups of someone's eyeball herald the murders. Morricone's score alternates, not too nimbly, between treacle and suspense modes. The most amusing shot: the two glasses of milk "framing" the heroine. Duly noted: a nasty climactic bit with elevator wires.

**The CAT WITH NINE LIVES** (H.K.?) 198-? color/ws 87m. Ref: TV: World Video; Eng. titles. Y.K. Ho: above is tr t. VSOM: *Cat Living Ten Times* - U.S. vt t.

"It's about a cat and a girl." Ling, a "cat goblin" from the Ming Dynasty ("It's not a common cat"), takes revenge on a family, one of whose ancestors raped her companion ghost. This cat with ten lives seems to "direct" Grandpa's death at the hands of crazy Chang and can temporarily possess people .... Ling is a monotonous cackler, and the climactic duel of the sorcerers is formula.

Cute: a song with a "meow meow meow" refrain. Inevitable: *Halloween* music.

**CATACLYSM** see *Night Train to Terror*

**CATACOMBS** see *Curse IV*

**CATHEDRAL, The** see *Church, The*

**CAT'S EYE** MGM-UA/Famous Films & IFC (De Laurentiis) 1985 (1984) color/ws 90m. (aka *Stephen King's Cat's Eye*). D: Lewis Teague. SP: Stephen King. Mus: Alan Silvestri. Creatures: Carlo Rambaldi. SpVisFX: Barry Nolan. SpFxCoord: Jeff Jarvis. Mkp: Sandi Duncan. OptFX: Van Der Veer. Sp Vocal FX: Frank Welker. Ref: TV. MFB'85:211-12. V 5/29/85. With Drew Barrymore, James Woods, Alan King, Kenneth McMillan, Robert Hays, Candy Clark, James Naughton, Russell Horton.

The first of three stories here features smoker's-nightmare effects and has some wry touches, if a weak "kicker." The second story is mean-spirited and far-fetched. In the third and best, a cat battles a petty, vindictive gnome that's out to steal a little girl's breath. Not much story even in this one, but the gnome has personality, and the action and effects are fun.

**CAVE DWELLERS** see *Blade Master*

**CAVE GIRL** see *Cavegirl*

**CAVE WOMEN** Arthur Films 1979 color c60m. Ref: TV. With Pat Desado.

The "rather basic" sex techniques of Cro-Magnon man and other cave people, all witnessed via the medium of a time machine. Primitive sf-porno-comedy.

**CAVEGIRL** Crown Int'l./David Oliver 1985 color 87m. (*Cave Girl* - ad t). SP, D, P, PH: Oliver. Adapted from Phil Groves' screenplay "Primal Urge." Mus: Jon St. James. SpFX: Gregory C. Landerer. SdFX: Leon Bijou. Mkp: Cher Slater. Skulls: Warren Riggs. Ref: TV. V 5/8/85. HR 5/9/85. Ecran F 48:71. With Daniel Roebuck, Cindy Ann Thompson (Eba), Jeff Chayette (Argh), Michelle Bauer, Bill Adams, Larry Gabriel, Darren Young (Dar), Saba Moor (Saba).

Something—strange crystals, an earthquake, maybe a dream—sends a student back to cave person days, Eba, and cannibals. ("You wouldn't happen to know what century it is?") At one point, he plays "boogeyman" to scare the latter off.... Haphazard and uninspired comedy, though prehistoric Thompson is charmingly silly learning about animal crackers, plastic-bear honey dispensers, etc.

**CAZADOR II** see *Deathstalker II*

**CAZADOR DE DEMONIOS** (Mex) Intercontinental/Raul De Anda 1984 color 90m. (*Cazadores de Demonios* - orig t). SP, D: Gilberto De Anda. Ph: Antonio De Anda. Mus: Marco Flores. SpFX: Ricardo Sainz. Mkp: Antonio Ramirez. Ref: TV: Mexcinema Video; no Eng.; *Demon Hunter* - tr t. S Union 5/31/89. V 5/9/84:488. TVG. Panicos! 2:57: available in Eng.-dubbed version, as *Demon Hunter.* VSOM: aka *Devil's Gateway*. With

Rafael Sanchez Navarro, Tito Junco, Roxana Chavez, Andres Garcia, Ruby Re, Roberto Montiel, Jorge Russek, Juan Duarte (La Bestia).

A murdered medicine man employs black magic to return as a werewolf and avenge himself. Consecrated bullets and a knife-crucifix fell the beast.... Routine, well-photographed fantasy-horror movie. One good "bus" with a boy on a bike. Several false alarms among the true.

**La CEINTURE ELECTRIQUE** (F) Gaumont 1907 b&w silent 11m. D: Romeo Rosetti. SP: Louis Feuillade. Ref: Hardy/SF.

"Electric belt" jolts wearer into "super-vitality."

**CELEBRATED JUMPING FROG OF CALAVERAS COUNTY, The** see *Adventures of Mark Twain, The*

**The CELLAR** Indian Neck Ent. 1989 color 90m. D: Kevin S. Tenney. SP, Screen Story, D (addl scenes), Co-P: John Woodward. Screen Story: also Darryl Wimberley. Based on Dr. D. H. Keller's short story. Ph: Thomas Jewett. Mus: Josh Kaplan et al. PD: Lisette Thomas. Creature: Max, Kevin Brennan, Elaine Alexander. Physical FX: Players SpFX. SpFX: J. D. Kovalcik. Ref: TV. Martin. Hound. TVG. no V. no Maltin '92. no Scheuer. With Chris Miller, Patrick Kilpatrick, Suzanne Savoy, Ford Rainey, Michael Wren, Lou Perry, Danny Mora.

"The evil in that unholy war did not die." The *Alien*/wart-hog monster in the cellar proves to be the "Comanche spirit that rides the wind." Medicine man Sam John's (Wren) great-grandfather created the thing from "pieces of the most savage creatures he made" to be the "perfect killing machine." The Evil One secretes a substance that strips newborns (whose souls, it seems, are not yet one with their bodies) to the bone, while crows—the spirit's emissaries—spy upon and attack humans.... Simplistic boy-and-his-dad drama, elementary monster-mongering, okay moments. The theme: "It's okay to be scared."

**CELLAR DWELLER** (U.S.-I) Empire/Dove (Bob Wynn) 1988 color 77m. D & Sp Creature FX: John Carl Buechler. Mus: Carl Dante. Ref: V 10/12/88: "stillborn." McCarty II: "not a complete waste of time." With Debrah Mulrowney, Brian Robbins, Vince Edwards, Cheryl-Ann Wilson, Jeffrey Combs, Pamela Bellwood, Yvonne De Carlo, Michael S. Deak (Cellar Dweller).

"Book of legendary curses ... brings the title monster to life." (V)

**CELLE QUI N'ETAIT PLUS** see *House of Secrets*

**CEMENTERIO DEL TERROR** (Mex) Dynamic & Torrente (Raul Galindo) 1985 color 88m. SP, D: Ruben Galindo Jr. Adap: Carlos Valdemar. Mus: Chucho Zarzosa. SpFX: Raul Falomir. Mkp: Ken Diaz. Opt FX: CDEO. Ref: TV: Video Mex; no Eng. V 7/24/85. 5/2/84:42. Stanley. VSOM: sfa *Zombie Apocalypse?* With Hugo Stiglitz, Usi Velasco, Erika Buenfil, Edna Bolkan, Maria Rebeca, Rene Cardona III, Andres Garcia Jr.; Luis Godinez et al (the dead).

Teens invoke satan and revive a corpse which then gorily slaughters them. Meanwhile, in the movie's one fun sequence, other corpses proceed to revive and leave their graves to threaten some pre-teens—the zombies pop out of the ground, one after the other, like jack-in-the-boxes.... Proof that Mexico can do it just as vapidly as the U.S.—that is, make a *Halloween* or *Friday the 13TH* or, to return to the original teens-in-a-haunted-house movie, *The Ghost Creeps* (1940), in which the East Side Kids met Minerva Urecal, who was scarier than these zombies. As in *Halloween*, the monster, at one point, demonstrates his amazing strength by lifting a victim right up off his feet.

**CEMETERY HIGH** Generic/Titan 1989 (1987) color 80m. (*Assault of the Killer Bimbos* - orig t). SP, D, P: Gorman Bechard. SP: also Carmine Capobianco. P: also Kristine Covello. Ref: V 8/9/89: "threadbare horror comedy." McCarty II. Fango 89:34: "numbingly stupid." With Debi Thibeault, Karen Nielsen, Simone, Ruth Collins, Lisa Schmidt.

Female high-school-grad vigilantes out to slay men.

**CEMETERY MAN** see *Dellamorte, Dellamore*

**CENTIPEDE HORROR** (H.K.) S. C. K. Chan 1987? color/ws c95m. D: Keith Li. SP: Amy Chan Suet Ming. Story: Nikko Creative Dept. Ref: TV: World Video; Eng. titles. NST! 4:19. Fango 107:57-8. 123:69. With Margaret A. Li, Mui Kui Wai, F. C. Chan, Stephen T. F. Lau, Wang Lai.

"When she died, many insects crawled out from her wounds"—a sure sign of the "most venomous spell in S.E. Asia ... the centipede spell." A cobra-coming-out-of-the-head spell, however, finishes our evil wizard; the masses of centipedes attacking the hero wilt and die; and the possessed heroine, Yeuk Chee, vomits up a last lovely bunch of centipedes.... Standard Hong Kong sorcerer-vs.-sorcerer stuff delivers worms-plus yuckiness. Unusual elements here include (during a climactic magic duel) a flying burning chicken skeleton and, earlier, a priest who "rears ghosts": "He steals the corpses of children, grills [their] chins ... until the oil drips out," then places two dolls in the oil, and the dolls become "his adopted ghosts." The latter prove handy during exorcisms, when they make the possessed vomit up blood and scorpions.

**CENTURIONS, The** see *New Gladiators, The*

**CEREBRO DEL MAL** (Cuban) ATICCA/Besne-Garduno-Alvarino 1959 c80m.? (*Santo Vs. el Cerebro del Mal* - ad t). D: Joselito Rodriguez, Enrique J. Zambrano. SP: Zambrano, Fernando Oses. Ph: Carlos Najera. Mus: Salvador Espinosa. Mkp: Israel Fernandez. Ref: TV: not sfa *Santo against the Diabolical Brain*. no Lee. HOF 2:26. With Joaquin Cordero, Norma Suarez, "Santo," "El Incognito" (aka F. Oses), Zambrano, Alberto Insua, Mario Texas, Rafael De Aragon.

A mad doctor injects his victims, zaps them with electrodes, and thus turns them into docile "zombies." Plus: an anti-zombie formula and super-TV. Scrappily edited and photographed sf-actioner's only redeeming feature: travelogue footage of pre-Castro Cuba.

**The CHAIR** Angelika Films/Urban Ent. (Anthony Jones) 1988 color 90m. D: Waldemar Korzeniowsky. SP: Carolyn Swartz. Mus: Eddie Reyes. SpMkFX: Tom Lauten. Ref: V 5/18/88: "features both impressive scenes and harmful lapses in taste." PT 10:57: the worst "prison horror movie." With James Coco, Trini Alvarado, Paul Benedict, Gary McCleery.

"Spirit of a man (the warden) executed 20 years ago at High Street correctional facility haunts the place...."

**CHAMELEONS** NBC-TV 1989 color c90m. Ref: TVG: "futuristic car." With Marcus Gilbert, Crystal Bernard, Mary Bergman, Stewart Granger.

**CHAMELEONS** VCA 1992 color 90m. D: John Leslie. Ref: Adam '93: takeoff on *The Hunger*. With Diedre Holland, Ashlyn Gere, Carolyn Monroe.

"Sexual vampires" become human, seek blood.

**CHAMPIONS, The** see *Legend of the Champions*

**I & II CHANDU THE MAGICIAN** 1932 71m. Ref: TV: Foothill Video. V 10/4/32: "*Chandu* carries the fantastic, the inconsistent and the ludicrous to the greatest lengths yet achieved by the screen." (Yes, yes!) Lee. Lentz. Hardy/SF. Weldon. Scheuer. Maltin '92. Martin. Hound.

"Thou shalt cause them to see what is not there." In this corner: Chandu (Edmund Lowe), a yogi "who has at his command the wizardry of the East." When danger is nigh, the "astral bell" tolls for him. In the other corner: Roxor (Bela Lugosi), "last of an ancient family that lived in Alexandria. He has built a home in the rock temple on Maidu (sp?) that stands on the "great cliffs above the third cataract of the Nile." ("I shall be greater than any pharaoh!") In-between: inventor Robert Regent (Henry B. Walthall), who refuses to complete for Roxor a death ray which will carry "halfway around the world" and which is powerful enough to "destroy whole cities." At one point, Roxor buries Chandu alive in a sarcophagus in the depths of the Nile, but Chandu pulls a Houdini and, at the end, his will freezes Roxor, who apparently dies, and his malfunctioning ray goes with him.

Rousing, old-fashioned, hyperbolic filmmaking (Marcel Varnel and William Cameron Menzies directed) carries roughly half this movie. The roar of a furious sandstorm and a music-deluged soundtrack are almost a match for Lugosi, whose every syllable is an exclamation. ("More than a billion tons of water will sway down on them, drowning them like rats! The greatest flood since the Biblical deluge!") And James Wong Howe's photography sustains the narrative fever pitch: the jewel in his crown—a tracking shot up and into and through corridor after corridor of Roxor's "great rock temple," built by the priests of Isis. Near the end, a montage of (hypothetical) destruction allows us, (a) to see the ray in action and, (b) to hear a prime Lugosi grand-madman speech. ("At last, I'm king of all!") Lowe tries to approximate the outrageousness of Lugosi, King of Camp here, but weighs down his relatively prosaic half of the movie, though Weldon Heyburn (as Abdullah) handily cops Worst Actor award.

See also *Black Magic Mansion*.

**CHANGELING 2: THE REVENGE** (I) Reteitalia/Dania & Devon 1987 color 95m. (*Fa Sempre, Fino alla Morte*. aka *Until Death*). SP,D: Lamberto Bava. Story, SP: Dardano Sacchetti. Ph: G. Battaglia. Mus: Simon Boswell. PD: A. Geleng. Mkp: Fabrizio Sforza. Ref: TV: VSOM; Eng. dubbed. Hardy/HM2. With Gioia Scola, David Brandon, Giuseppe De Sando, Roberto Pedicini, Marco Vivio, Urbano Barberini.

Love-and-murder story features a supposedly dead man who briefly "comes back" to life ... a boy's visualized nightmares of "the man who comes through the wall," a zombie-ghoul ... a thunderstorm ("The storm scares me!") ... scissors-as-a-weapon ... Rotting-Corpse Delight ... a vision of a living corpse ... and hallucinations re the dead .... Some atmosphere here; no story, just more bodies, dead, living, and living-dead. One okay line (in context): "I'm dying for a cup of coffee!"

**The CHANNELER** Magnum HV/Austin Ent. (Wald-Way Films) 1991 feature. SP, D, P: Grant Waldman. Ph: W. H. Molina. Ref: PT 11:49: "gets boring and stupid pretty fast." no Martin. V 12/6/89:26: shooting. With Jay Richardson, Dan Haggerty, Richard Harrison, Robin Sims, Cindy Brooks.

Backpackers ... spirit possession ... "monster with limp rubber claws."

**CHARADE** (Can.) 198-? anim 5m. D: John Minnis. Ref: Anim. Tournee program: vampire.

**CHARLES DICKENS' GHOST STORIES FROM THE PICKWICK PAPERS** see *Ghost Stories from the Pickwick Papers*

**\*CHARLIE CHAN AT THE OPERA** 1936. Ref: TV. Hanke/Chan. Lentz. Lee. Weldon. Levant/Memoirs: 117. Scheuer. Maltin '92. Martin. Hound. Thomas. With Thomas Beck, Margaret Irving, Maurice Cass.

"Everybody thinks I'm mad!" Once-great opera star Gravelle (Boris Karloff), believed dead, escapes from Rockland State Sanitarium. Soon there are reports of a "strange man" with "horrible" eyes who is lurking backstage at the San Marco Opera Company in Los Angeles—a "ghostly visitor," or "madman," is "loose in the house".... This two-in-one film features regulation mystery suspects and sleuths—and Karloff, who adds some real menace and even a little depth. For the horror half of the movie, the script makes it look as if he's a homicidal maniac; for the mystery half, script has the real killer use the presence of this madman to cloak his or her guilt. Unfortunately, Gravelle is incidental to much of the action, and the script can't make him switch believably, at the end, from the role of menace to that of misunderstood father. Complete with (natch) dialogue reference to the Frankenstein monster, and—above the title—the thrilling words "Warner Oland vs. Boris Karloff."

**\*CHARLIE CHAN AT TREASURE ISLAND** 1939. Mus D: Samuel Kaylin. AD: Richard Day, Lewis Creber. Ref: TV. Hanke/Chan. V 8/23/39. Filmfax 18. Scheuer. Maltin '92. Lentz. Thomas.

Creep ingredients include Dr. Zodiac (Gerald Mohr), his "spook joint," his 3,000-year-old intermediary, an Egyptian priestess; and Eve Cairo (Pauline Moore), the "world's greatest living mind reader." In "most uncanny" scenes, she actually does read minds and sense imminent murder. ("There is a mind here that is fighting me!") In the climactic sequence, set in Rhadini's (Cesar Romero) Temple of Magic, big close-ups of a pair of eyes dominate the darkened auditorium.... Forty years before *Scanners*, this Chan movie successfully employs mind-probing to build up dramatic excitement. Above-average series entry is also distinguished by smooth performances, especially by Sidney Toler and Sen Yung, charming here as, respectively, Charlie and Jimmy Chan.

**CHARLIE CHAN IN BLACK MAGIC** see *Black Magic* (1944)

**CHARLIE CHAN IN DEAD MEN TELL** see *Dead Men Tell*

**\*CHARLIE CHAN IN EGYPT** 1935. Mus D: Samuel Kaylin. AD: Duncan Cramer, Walter Koessler. Ref: TV. Hanke/Chan. no Thomas. V 6/26/35. Lee. Lentz. no Stanley. Scheuer. Maltin '92. With Frank Reicher, George Irving, James Eagles.

Egypt, "land of decay and death." The "horrible head" in the dark—does it belong to the ghost of the Egyptian goddess of vengeance, who supposedly possesses "supernatural powers" and who apparently leaves one victim drained of blood and mummified? At the heart of the "superstition of the tomb" of Ahmeti—"one of the most powerful priests of the 21st Dynasty"—are a glowing-eyed statue and the mask of the goddess.... Sets and statuary star here. Story and actors are less impressive. The early Rita Hayworth (aka Rita Cansino) is barely recognizable, and Stepin Fetchit is unfortunately not at his most outrageous. The idea of the deadly, gas-filled glass tube turns up again in *Mr. Wong, Detective* (1938) and *Docks of New Orleans* (1948).

**2P CHARLIE CHAN IN HONOLULU** Fox/John Stone 1938 65m. D: H. Bruce Humberstone. SP: Charles Belden. Ref: TV. Hanke/Chan. Pitts/HFS. Bill Warren. V 12/21/38. MFB'39:15. HR. NYT 12/31/38. LC. "Great Movie Series." Scheuer. Maltin '92. Thomas.

Charlie Chan mystery is of interest to horror fans for two elements—a "ghost" whose looming shadow scares a freighter's zoo-bound animals (the ghost is really just number-five son Tommy) and George Zucco as a "specialist in psychiatry." His deliciously daffy Dr. Cardigan ("That's my brain!") plays like a parody of the mad doctors he was later to play. Cardigan insists that he has kept a Chinese murderer's brain suspended in liquid in a gizmo for six months. ("Is it natural for a guy to travel around with a jugful of brains?") The script neither confirms nor denies his wild assertions.

**CHARLIE CHAN IN MURDER IN THE FUN HOUSE** see *Chinese Cat, The*

**CHARLIE CHAN IN THE CHINESE CAT** see *Chinese Cat, The*

**CHARLIE CHAN IN THE MURDER CHAMBER** see *Black Magic* (1944)

**CHARLIE CHAN IN THE SECRET SERVICE** Mono 1944 65m. D: Phil Rosen. SP: George Callahan. Ref: TV. Bill Warren. V 1/12/44. FDY. LC. HR 1/11/44. "Great Movie Series." Hanke/Chan: "electrocution device." Scheuer. Maltin '92. Okuda/TMC.

Limply written Chan mystery includes a few borderline-sf, borderline-horror elements—e.g., an inventor's remote-controlled torpedo which involves some mad-lab contraptions and will supposedly "utterly destroy the U-boat menace" (we see it blow up a model boat in a tub) ... a photoelectric-cell-operated, mon-

ster-mask, seeing-eye device which spooks Mantan Moreland ... and the Charlie Chan line "How can man walk around after he's dead?" Plus the obligatory line in any classic mystery movie featuring a wheelchair-bound character: "Oh, so you can walk!"

**CHARLIE CHAN ON THE DOCKS OF NEW ORLEANS** see *Docks of New Orleans*

**CHAR'S COUNTERATTACK** see *Mobilesuit Gundam: Char's Counterattack*

**CHASSES DE LA COMTESSE ZAROFF, Les** see *Comtesse Perverse, La*

**CHEATING THE STARS** see *Crime Ring*

**CHECKPOINT CHARLY** or **CHECKPOINT CHARLIE** see *Warum die Ufos Unseren Salat Klauen*

**CHEERLEADER CAMP** (U.S.-J) Atlantic Releasing/Quinn-Prettyman & Prism Ent. & Daiei (Bloody Pom Poms Prods.) 1988 color 88m. (*Bloody Pom Poms* - alt t). D: John Quinn. SP: David Lee Fein, R. L. O'Keefe. Mus: M. Hodler-Hamilton, J. Hamilton. Mkp: Ramona. SpFX: Tom Surprenant. Opt: Howard Anderson. Ref: TV. V 11/16/88. SFChron Dtbk 10/30/88. Martin. V 10/28/87:24. With Betsy Russell, Leif Garrett, Lucinda Dickey, Buck Flower, Teri Weigel, Vickie Benson.

Sophomoric comedy, bland teen melodrama, a mysterious handyman (Flower), a vision of a bloodied face, and rote bear-trap, hedge-clipper, scythe, and cleaver gore at Camp Hurrah.

**CHEMICAL KO-KO** Para/Fleischer/Inkwell Studios (Alfred Weiss) 1929 anim and live 8m. Ref: TV: the Inkwell Imps. Cabarga/TFS.

Chemist's concoction turns black man white, while Ko-Ko's first concoction instantly flattens Fitz the dog and makes a mouse huge; his second turns a baby hippo into a giraffe (much to the delight of its giraffe mom) and shrinks the chemist.... Bizarre goings-on. Prime example: Giraffe mom flings (animated) Ko-Ko into (live-action) chemists' mouth.

**CHERRY 2000** Orion/ERP (Lloyd Fonvielle) 1988 (1986) color 93m. D: Steve de Jarnatt. SP: Michael Almereyda. Story: Fonvielle. Mus: Basil Poledouris. SpMkpFX: Greg Cannom. SpFxSup: Art Brewer. Robot Vehicle: Robotics 21. Ref: TV. With Melanie Griffith, David Andrews, Ben Johnson, Tim Thomerson, Brion James, Pamela Gidley, Harry Carey Jr., Cameron Milzer, Michael C. Gwynne, Robert Zdar.

"This is when Detroit still cared." Cherry 2000 (Gidley) has "her own special way"—the personality is in the chip. She's a "sex robot" gone kaput, and Sam Treadwell (Andrews), from Anaheim, hires "that red-headed tracker" E. (for Edith) Johnson (Griffith) to take him to the robot graveyard in Zone Seven to find an android that looks just like his.... The usual chases and escapes, but snappily dialogued and pleasantly acted by Griffith, Andrews, and Johnson (as Six Finger Jake). Plus a bit of *Vertigo* in the contrast between the dream android Cherry 2000 ("Hi, honey!" the chip-reactivated, graveyard Cherry automatically greets Sam) and the smoldering—or simmering—deadpan

Johnson. ("We can't all be glamour pusses 24 hours a day.") Plus Robby and Gort, inert.

**\*The CHESS PLAYER** La Societe des Films Historiques 1926 ('30-U.S.) silent c110m. SP, D: R. Bernard. SP: also J.-J. Frappa. From a book by Henri Dupuy-Mazuel. Ph: Mundviller, Bujard. Mus: Henri Rabaud. AD: Jean Perrier. SpFX: W. Percy Day. Costume Des: Eugene Lourie. Tinting: Ron Sayer. Ref: TV: Photoplay & Thames-TV ('90). Lee: Unusual Photoplays ('30). V 5/21/30. 12/31/90. With Pierre Blanchar, Edith Jehanne, Camille Bert, Pierre Batcheff.

The hobby of the "strange man" in the "mysterious house": making rudimentary automata, including a supposedly mechanical (but fake) chess player. ("This machine is really quite extraordinary.") Handsome, but draggy, meant-to-be-stirring costume romance has a lot of exposition and plot. The images are almost sculpted, but the only reason for being of the story is obviously the very macabre sequence in which the mechanical guards/"soldiers" mass. They start/stop/start/stop.... Then one is beheaded, the control panel goes haywire, and they surround and fall on the intruder. Plus an hallucination in which a robotic skeleton becomes the inventor's personal Death.

**CHI L'HA VISTA MORIRE?** (I-W.G.) 1972. D: Aldo Lado. SP: M. D'Avack, F. Barilli. Mus: Ennio Morricone. Ref: Palmerini: "excellent thriller inspired by *Psycho*." With G. Lazenby, A. Celi, P. Chatel, N. Elmi.

**CHICKEN THING** Grove St. Filmworks 1986 (1985) color 12m. SP, D, P, SpVisFX: Todd Holland. Mus: Stacy Widelitz. Ref: TV: Direct Cinema video. With Bobby Nellesen.

Weird electrical storm makes boy's dresser enlarge and turns furniture and whatnot into a big Chicken Thing. Cute, well-done monster-movie takeoff, complete with a title design direct from the 1951 *The Thing*.

**CHIESA, La** see *Church, The*

**CHIKYU BOEIGUN** (J) Toshiba c1988? anim color 49m. (aka *Terrestrial Defense Army*). Ref: TV: vt; no Eng.

Despite the title (which is the same as the Japanese title for *The Mysterians*), this three-section, animated sf-comedy bears little or no relation to the earlier, live-action film. Ingredients include a missile-launching cyborg, a rocket-firing femme-borg, a visualized, mental flashback to, apparently, Godzilla, a doctor's voluptuous, feisty lab creation, and a remote torture device. Amiable exaggeration and cheery mayhem, a la the *A-Ko* series.

**CHILD OF DARKNESS, CHILD OF LIGHT** USA-TV/Wilshire Court & G. C. Group (Paul Tucker) 1991 color c85m. D: Marina Sargenti. Tel, Co-P: Bruce Taggert, from James Patterson's book *Virgin*. Mus: Jay Gruska. PD: Shay Austin. SpFX: Roy Downey. Mkp: E. Larry Day. Ref: TV. V 5/6/91:338. SFChron Dtbk 7/12/92:58: Para HV. With Anthony Denison, Sela Ward, Paxton Whitehead, Kristin Dattilo, Viveca Lindfors, Claudette Nevins, Eric Christmas.

A message left by the Virgin Mary some seventy years ago correctly prophesied two virgin births in the last decade of the Twentieth Century—one child is to sow the "seed of hope," the other the "seed of despair." The anti-Christ turns up in Briscayne Falls, Pa.; "Christ reborn," in Boston. In the script's two surprises, the "church cop" (Denison) proves to be the devil's agent, and Christ is a little girl this time. But the point of this religio-horror story re anti-Christ and Auntie Christ remains elusive. At the end, the score seems tied: God 1, the devil 1.

**CHILD OF GLASS** BV-TV/Jan Williams & Tom Leetch 1977 color 94m. D: John Erman. Tel: Jim Lawrence, from Richard Peck's novel *The Ghost Belonged to Me*. Ph: William Cronjager. Mus: George Duning. AD: J. B. Mansbridge, LeRoy G. Deane. SpFX: Eustace Lycett, Art Cruickshank, Danny Lee. Mkp: R. J. Schiffer. Ref: TV. no Stanley. TVG. Martin. Scheuer. no Maltin '92. With Barbara Barrie, Biff McGuire, Anthony Zerbe, Nina Foch, Lilyan Chauvin.

"Sleeping lies the murdered lass/Vainly cries the child of glass/When the two shall be as one/The spirit's journey will be done." Jefferson County, the South. Young Alexander (Steve Shaw), a "sensitive," must solve the hundred-year-old mystery of the Dumaine estate (a "weird place") or be haunted by the "thing in the barn," Inez Dumaine (Olivia Barash), a blue-hued ghost from the "darkness of the other world," who has only her ghost dog, Brigitte, to keep her company.... Bland combination melodrama/ghost-story/comedy features one sweet, if calculated scene in which Inez "steps through the ghostly veil" to dance with Alexander. Only Katy Kurtzman as little Blossom escapes the general staleness.

See also: *Once upon a Midnight Scary*.

**CHILDREN OF THE CORN** New World & Hal Roach/Angeles & Inverness & Cinema Group Venture (Gatlin) 1984 color 92m. (*Stephen King's Children of the Corn* - alt t). D: Fritz Kiersch. SP: George Goldsmith, from King's short story. Mus: Jonathan Elias. SpVisFX: Max W. Anderson: (coord) Paul Lumbard. SpFX: SPFX, Eric Rumsey. Ref: screen. SFExam 3/9/84. S Union 3/11/84. V 3/14/84. PFA. NYT 3/16/84. Ecran F 53:4, 6: *Horror Kid* - F. With Peter Horton, Linda Hamilton, R. G. Armstrong, John Franklin, Courtney Gains (Malachai), Anne Marie McEvoy.

Gatlin, Nebraska isn't on the map any more—three years ago, the zealous, "weird" Isaac led the children of the town in a purge of adults. Roads lead travelers in mystifying circles around the town, and clouds move over it strangely. When Isaac attempts to offer an "outlander" (i.e., stranger) to He Who Walks behind the Rows, he is himself sacrificed by the rebellious Malachai, and is taken up in a cloud, then returned, possessed, to kill Malachai. The "monster"—which can burrow through the soil like a giant mole or fly like a huge, fiery thundercloud—is destroyed when the cornfield is set afire.... The twist here on black-magic movies is that the devil worshippers are children, but there doesn't seem to be any reason for them to be children, and no explanation for their revolt is given. Revealing the children's takeover of the town in the prologue drains the body of the movie of mystery, though the climax is entertainingly frantic.

**CHILDREN OF THE CORN II: THE FINAL SACRIFICE** Dimension/Fifth Avenue Ent. (Stone Stanley/Corn Cob Prods.) 1993 (1992) color 92m. D: David F. Price. SP: A. L. Katz, Gilbert Adair. Mus: Daniel Licht. SpMkpFX: Image Animation.

SpVisFX: Calico Ltd.; (sup) Rob Burton. Ref: V 2/8/93. 7/15/91:16. Martin. Sacto Bee 1/29/93: "generous with the fan-pleasing grotesque business." SFChron 1/30/93: "schlocky but effective." ad. With Terence Knox, Paul Scherrer, Ryan Bollman, Christie Clark, Rosalind Allen, Ned Romero.

More rural supernatural.

**CHILDREN OF THE NIGHT** Fangoria Films (Christopher Webster) 1992 (1991) color 90m. Story, D: Tony Randel. Story, SP: Nicholas Falacci. Orig SP: William Hopkins. Mus: Daniel Licht. SpFxMkp: KNB. Ref: TV: Col-TriStar HV. V 5/18/92. 4/25/90:18, 22. 4/22/91:50 (rated). SFChron Dtbk 10/4/92. With Karen Black (Karen), Peter DeLuise, Ami Dolenz, Maya McLaughlin (Lucy), Evan MacKenzie, Garrett Morris, David Sawyer (Czakyr).

"They're vampires, Mark!" Ingredients: missing living-dead children in a watery crypt below the "old church on Cherry Street" ... the "old bat boy" Czakyr, a Romanian vampire ... the cocoon-like outfit for vampire Karen (Black) ... Grandma (my, what big teeth ...) ... a town of vampires ... and the coda, in which the staked vampire townsfolk return to normal.... Hyper fantasy-horror has scattered fun moments. Morris—as a vampire-hunter volunteer—breathes intermittent life into the turgid proceedings. At the other end of the dramatic scale are priest MacKenzie's campy struggles with demon flesh.

**CHILD'S PLAY** (B) Fox Mystery Theatre/Fox & Hammer-TV 1984 color c80m. D: Val Guest. Tel: Graham Wassell. Ph: Frank Watts. Mus: David Bedford. AD: Heather Armitage. Mkp: Eddie Knight. Ref: TV. TVG. no Hound. no Scheuer. no Maltin '92. Ecran F 50:13. With Mary Crosby, Nicholas Clay, Debbie Chasan, Joanna Joseph.

"We're walled in!" The Prestons awake during the night to find a warm, blue wall "all around the house." Phones, radios, and TVs don't work; a strange sludge is pouring out the fireplace; and the temperature is rising steadily. Michael (Clay) and Ann (Crosby) have no memory of the past, and their daughter Sarah (Chasan) is "not acting like a normal child." The only clue to the mystery: an omnipresent trademark which—in a coda—is revealed to be that of the Universal Automata Syndicate. The house, it seems, is a doll house which belongs to a child (Joseph) of the future, and the Prestons are robot dolls with "emotion circuits".... Poorly developed mystery chiller begins like *The Exterminating Angel* and ends with a blatant steal from the "Stopover in a Quiet Town" episode from the final year of the original "Twilight Zone." Two good touches, however: the album photos of the non-aging Sarah, and the pages of her "Alice in Wonderland" picture book which simply repeat.

**CHILD'S PLAY** MGM-UA (David Kirschner) 1988 color c90m. SP, D: Tom Holland. Story, SP: Don Mancini. SP: also John Lafia. Mus: Joe Renzetti. Doll: Kirschner; (des) Kevin Yagher. VisFX: Apogee; (sup) Peter Donen. SpFX: (sup) Richard O. Helmer; James D. Schwalm. Mkp: M. A. Hancock. Chucky's Theme: Mike Piccirillo. Ref: TV: MGM-UA Home Video. V 11/9/88. SFChron Dtbk 11/20/88. SFExam 11/9/88. MFB'89:173. With Catherine Hicks, Chris Sarandon, Alex Vincent, Dinah Manoff, Raymond Oliver (Dr. Death); Edan Gross, Brad Dourif, and John Franklin (Chucky's voices).

"I'm your friend to the end!" Dying, Charles "Chucky" Lee Ray (Dourif)—the Lakeshore Strangler—invokes voodoo god Damballa (cf. *Snake People*), and his evil life force enters a Good Guys Doll. As the latter becomes "more human," it also becomes more vulnerable to bullets, etc., and, wounded, attempts a second spirit transfer into the body of the person in whom it first confided, young Andy Barclay (Vincent).... In sum: a *Trilogy of Terror* killer doll, a *Curse of the Cat People* boy's fantasy friend, some Freddy badinage, and a Michael Meyers return from death, or near-death, plus little that's new. Competent acting and a few fun chills—e.g., the sweet-talking doll finally showing its true colors and snarling "You stupid bitch!"

**CHILD'S PLAY 2** Univ/David Kirschner 1990 color 85m. D: John Lafia. SP: Don Mancini. Ph: S. Czapsky. Mus: Graeme Revell. PD: Ivo Cristante. Chucky FX: Kevin Yagher Prods. MechFX: Image Engineering; (coord) Peter M. Chesney. Opt: Apogee; (anim sup) Harry Moreau; (fx sup) John Swallow; Cinema Research. Key Mkp: Deborah Larsen. Ref: TV. V 11/12/90: "utter numbness." MFB '91:13: "unsuccessfully opens out proceedings." Sacto Bee 11/12/90: "atrocious." SFChron Dtbk 12/2/90. ad. Bay Guardian 11/28/90: "tired." With Alex Vincent, Jenny Agutter, Gerrit Graham Christine Elise, Brad Dourif (voice of Chucky), Grace Zabriskie, Peter Haskell, Edan Gross (voice of Tommy doll).

"Chucky's back!" (ad) And, for some reason, the "killer Good Guy doll" is compelled to track down Andy. ("Wherever I go, Chucky'll find me.") Cliche shocks, including Monster's Victim Falling Face-Down on Photocopier. One supposedly-macabre high point: the Chucky doll "killing" and burying the Tommy doll. Telegraphed horror: the assembly-line worker getting Chucky eyes punched into his.

**CHILD'S PLAY 3** Univ/David Kirschner (R. L. Brown) 1991 color 89m. D: Jack Bender. SP: Don Mancini. Ph: J. Leonetti. Mus: Lerios, D'Andrea. PD: R. Sawyer. Chucky FX: Kevin Yagher. SpMkpFX: Craig Reardon. OptFX: Apogee; (sup) Roger Dorney. SpFxCoord: John Frazier. Ref: TV. V 9/2/91: "noisy, mindless." SFExam 8/30/91: "competent." ad. With Justin Whalin, Perrey Reeves, Jeremy Sylvers, Brad Dourif (voice of Chucky), Peter Haskell, Andrew Robinson.

"Look who's stalking!" (ad) "I'm new and improved." Ten years later, "Andy Barclay is ancient history." Not. Both he and Chucky—the "Good Guy of the Nineties"—wind up at Kent Military School. ("Welcome to hell, Barclay.") There, Chucky plays pranks like putting live ammo in war-games rifles. ("Don't let 'im fool you—he's bad.") The Chucky-at-military-school premise promises little, makes good on its promise. Among the incidental cliches: the activation of the mechanical toys.

**CHILLER** CBS-TV/Polar & Feigelson (Frozen Man) 1985 color 92m. D: Wes Craven. SP, P: J. D. Feigelson. Mus: Dana Kaproff. AD: Charles Hughes. SpMkpFX: Stan Winston. SpFxCoord: Ken Pepiot. Ref: TV. TVG. V 7/3/85:52. With Michael Beck, Beatrice Straight, Laura Johnson, Jill Schoelen, Paul Sorvino, Dick O'Neill, Alan Fudge, Craig R. Nelson, Jerry Lacy.

"They shall see tomorrow." A man (Beck) in Cryonic "sleep" for ten years accidentally begins to thaw. Advanced surgical technology brings him all the way back. ("He's alive.") Cliched chiller—Miles' own dog growls at him, his mother has to shoot him, etc.

**CHILLERS** Raedon Ent. & Big Pictures 1988 color 87m. SP, D, P: Daniel Boyd. Mus: M. Lipton. Ref: V 11/16/88:42 (hv): "unimaginative makeup effects." Phantom. no Martin. no Hound. no Scheuer. no Maltin '92. Jones. With Jesse Emery, Marjorie Fitzsimmons, Laurie Pennington.

Several stories involving, variously, vampires, a ghost, and the ancient Aztec demon Ixpe.

**The CHILLING** Hemdale (Sunseri) 1992 color 91m. SP, D: J. A. Sunseri. D: also Deland Nuse. Ref: Martin: "poor effects & lame dialogue." V 2/3/92:18 (rated). PT 14:49: "laughable zombies." With Linda Blair, Dan Haggerty, Troy Donahue.

Lightning revives cryogenically-frozen bodies.

**CHIMERA** (B) Anglia Films-TV/Zenith (Nick Gillott) 1991 color c90m. (*Monkey Boy* - vt t). D: Lawrence Gordon Clark. Tel: Stephen Gallagher, from his novel. Ph: Ken Westbury. Mus: Nigel Hess. PD: Chris Edwards. SpFxSup: David Beavis. Mkp: Penny Bell, Sue Black. Ref: TV. TVG. VWB. With John Lynch, Christine Kavanagh, George Costigan, Emer Gillespie, David Calder, Sebastian Shaw, Kenneth Cranham, Douglas Mann (Chad).

"Hello! Who let you out?" In this updating of "Frankenstein" themes, the mysterious slasher of just about everyone at the Jenner Clinic proves to be Chad, or "Mr. Scarecrow," an "animal with a hybrid DNA of two different species"—"predominantly a primate with a human genetic element inserted at some point." Special makeup here is more remarkable than story—there are suggestions, in the former, of horror, pathos, and vulnerability; in the latter, there's only a bit of finger pointing (at science, commerce). Creepy #1: the infant Chad in the filmstrip. Creepy #2: the unholy nursery at the end.

**The CHINESE CAT** Mono(Krasne-Burkett) 1944 b&w 65m. (aka *Charlie Chan in the Chinese Cat. Murder in the Fun House. Charlie Chan in Murder in the Fun House*). D: Phil Rosen. SP: George Callahan. Ref: TV. Bill Warren. Academy. LAT 3/27/44. V(d) 3/24/44. HR 3/24/44. Independent 4/15/44: "fright-scare comedy." Hanke/Chan.

Murderer's "hideout in an old fun house ... proves a macabre background for dark deeds, with its dancing skeletons, its mummies and daffy mirrors." (LAT) "Display of three zombie-like creatures ...." (H/C) Typical Charlie Chan mystery with a touch of spookiness.

**A CHINESE GHOST STORY** (H. K.) Cinema City/Film Workshop (Tsui Hark) 1987 color/ws 98m. (*Qian nu Youhun*). D: Ching Siu Tung. SP: Yuen Kai Chi, based on classic Chinese ghost stories. Mus: Romeo Diaz, James Wong. SpFX: Xin Shi Technical Workshop. Mkp: Wen Renming. Ref: TV: New Ship video; Eng. titles. Fango 107:58. FComm 6/88:48, 50: remake of *Enchanting Shadow*. Cinef 5/89. V 9/2/87. NST! 4:19. MFB'88:88-9. With Leslie Cheung, W. Tsu Hsien, Wo Ma.

"That monster's out again." A thousand-year-old tree monster, Old Evil, haunts the Lan Ro Temple. He uses the ghost of Nieh Hsiao Tsing (Hsien), whose ashes were buried beneath him, to

lure men to the temple: "Tonight, get me a living being to increase my vitality and lengthen the span of my life".... An entertaining fantasy extravaganza so busy and elaborate that the supposedly central romance between the naive scholar and the otherworldly-wise Tsing is reduced to a subplot, or pretext. The movie is very inventive, occasionally even poetic, but not quite moving. Innumerable wry fantasy, horror, action, and comedy details overwhelm the drama. Old Evil's gigantic tongue proves to harbor equally disgusting jaws and tentacles, and hordes of screaming souls flee his robe when he is impaled on a magic sword. Filmic influences here seem to include Kurosawa, Spielberg, and *The Evil Dead*.

**A CHINESE GHOST STORY II** (H. K.) Golden Princess/Film Workshop (Tsui Hark) 1990 color/ws 103m. (*Sinnui Yauman Ii Yangan Dou*). D: Ching Siu-tung. SP: Lau Tai-mok, Lam Kei-to, Leung Yiu-ming. Mus: James Wong. Ph: Arthur Wong. SpFX: Cinefex, Dave Watkins, Nick Allder. Ref: TV: vt; Eng. titles. V 12/10/90: Story: Tsui Hark, Yuen Kai-chi; Mus: also Romeo Diaz. V 11/19/90:51. Y. K. Ho. With Leslie Cheung, Joey Wang, Michelle Li, Wu Ma, Jacky Cheung.

Ingredients the second time around include eight phony ghosts and one real, Godzilla-ish ghost, all of which haunt the Righteous Villa—the real ghost (or "giant corpse" or "huge creature") has a touch also, in its wide paws, of the Terror from beyond Space ... a high priest who calls himself the "absolute Buddha," but who turns out to be a giant centipede thing ... the heroine, Windy, who, temporarily possessed, becomes a "corpse monster" that "breathes" snakes ("Really ugly") ... Autumn, a human "mole" whose "nose is sensitive to otherworldly spirits" and who can cast a "freeze" spell which stops foes in their tracks ... and the officials whom the "priest" has rendered just shells, or "walking corpses".... One highlight of this effects treat: the tall trees which Autumn "commands" back into the ground. The sequence with the Godzilla/Terror skillfully combines comedy and suspense—this is a very funny comedy-fantasy-monster movie. ("The cockroaches here are of the best quality.") Included: a satire of film/literary "interpretation." Most prosaic element: the romance between hero Ning and Windy, who reminds him of Sian from Part I.

**A CHINESE GHOST STORY III** (H. K.) Golden Princess/Film Workshop (Tsui Hark) 1991 color/ws 116m. (*Sinnui Yauman Iii: Do Do Do*). D: Ching Siu-tung. SP: Tsui Hark, Roy Szeto. Ph: Lau Moon-tong. Mus: James Wong, Romeo Diaz. AD: James Leung. Ref: TV: vt; Eng. titles. V 10/19/92. 2/24/92:94. 10/7/91:10: in L. A. 10/14/91:M-41 (ad). With Tony Leung Chiu-wai, Jacky Cheung, Joey Wang (Lotus), Nina Li (Butterfly), Lau Siu-meng.

"The ghosts are out." This round features the haunted Orchid Temple ... the long-tongued ghosts which inhabit it, including heroine Lotus ("I'm evil; I'll never change"), who at one point is suffocated by a master's spells ... the Attack of the Tree Roots ... a giant ghost-tongue or two ... ghost leader Tree Devil ("Little Monk, I'm going to suck your energy. Then I'll sell you to the Mountain Devil") ... the billboard-like Mountain Devil ... a magic-carpet-like cloak ... monoliths and monsters from the ground ... and, in the climactic sequence, Tree Devil's vampire-like attack on a wounded ghost, as he sucks energy from her.

Slight serio-comic story; intermittently taking effects, including the coins which stand up and nod "Yes," and the views from inside characters' throats as ghost-tongues probe. ("Why stick your tongue in my stomach?") After an hour or so, hero Fong's (Leung Chiu-wai) naivete gets a bit old.

The **CHINESE GHOSTBUSTER** (H.K.) Film City 1994 color/ws 90m. D: Wu Ma. Ref: TV: Tai Seng Video; Eng. titles. V 3/21/94:14: in H.K. With H. Nam, Yan Yue Chin or Ching.

"We're ghosts, but not bad ones." Ghostly Mr. Chung and his daughter (who needs to marry to reincarnate) enter the land of the living. Later, several bad ghosts cross over and cause trouble. Plus a Long Arm of the Ghost scene and a "famous exorcist".... Middling mixture of horror, comedy, romance, and martial-arts action has interesting lighting effects.

**CHINESE LEGEND** see *Moon Legend*

A **CHINESE ODYSSEY** Part One—PANDORA'S BOX (H.K.) 1994? color/ws c86m. Based on "Journey to the West." Ref: TV: Mei Ah Laser Disc; Eng. titles. Y.K. Ho. With Stephen Chow.

The fearsome giant spider ("I told you to tidy up the place") with the lady-head (cf. Hiruko) and creepy moves is one of the sister monsters, Spider Woman and Boney M of Spider Devil.... Foolish comedy, effective lighting of the monsters, in this alternately weird and familiar actioner. Definitely under "weird": the fantastic voyage through the giant Bull King's insides. ("Bitch, don't step on my intestine!")

The **CHINESE PARROT** Startoons/Britannica Video (Phil Stockton/Chris McLenahan) 1990 anim color 5m. D: David Alexovich; (anim) Jon McLenahan. Mus: David Hillenband, Robb Wenner. Ref: TV: GoodTimes HV (Kids Klassics HV).

Britannica's Tales around the World. In ancient China, jealousy leads an evil sorcerer to turn a maid into stone. Slight anecdote.

**CHINESE ROOM, The** see *Cuarto Chino, El*

**CHING SE** see *Green Snake*

**CHINIKU NO HANA** see *Guinea Pig, Vol. One*

**CHIQUIDRACULA** (Mex) Impulsora Mexicana/Agra-sanchez 1986 (1985) color c84m. (*El Exterminador Nocturno* - vt t). D: Julio Aldama. SP: Jose Loza. Idea: Rogelio Agrasanchez, based on the personage of Cesar Gonzalez. Ph: A. Ruis. Mus: Pedro Plascencia. Ref: TV: Film-Mex video; no Eng. V 5/7/86:452: *Little Dracula* - tr t. Ecran F 65:12. With Carlitos Espejel, "Resortes," Ana Luisa Peluffo, Tere Velazquez, Luis Manuel Pelayo, "El Comanche," Bruno Rey.

Inside the Mexico City Wax Museum, a little boy daydreams re a Dracula-like vampire who can appear magically. Later, he "sees" a priest as a vampire, complete with fangs. His obsession leads him to disguise himself as "Chiquidracula," the scourge of the neighborhood. Silly, oddball trifle.

**CHIRURGIEN AMERICAIN** (F) Star (Melies) 1897 b&w 2m. silent (*A Twentieth Century Surgeon* - alt t). SP, D, P: Georges Melies. Ref: Hardy/SF.

Surgeon performs leg, head, and torso transplants on beggar.

**CHOICE CUTS** see *Body Parts*

**CHOKE CANYON** UFDC/Ovidio Assonitis (Brouwersgracht) 1986 color 94m. (aka *On Dangerous Ground*). D: Chuck Bail. SP: Sheila Goldberg, Assonitis, Alfonso Brescia. Mus: S. Levay. Ref: V 7/23/86: "truly nutty." Film Journal 9/86: "ridiculous." HR 8/1/86: "about as unlikely a saga as one could ever imagine." With Stephen Collins, Janet Julian, Lance Henriksen, Bo Svenson, Victoria Racimo, Nicholas Pryor.

Machine to convert sound into energy.

**CHOKOSO HANTEINGU** (J) Shochiku/Tsuburaya Films & Sega Ents. (Akio Jissoji) 1991 feature. D: Mitsunori Hattori. Ph: S. Ohoka. SpMkpFX: Funhouse; Tomoo Haraguchi. Ref: Markalite 3:10: *Hypersapien Hunting* - tr t. With Tei Okamori, Kazumi Nishimori, Rei Takagi.

"Psycho-kinetic hypersapiens (created via cloning, but with altered gene-splicing)," in the near future.

**CHOKOSO HANTINGU** see *Hunting Ash*

**CHOLPON** or **CHOLPON-UTRENNYAYA ZVEZDA** see *Morning Star*

**CHOPPER CHICKS IN ZOMBIETOWN** Triax Ent./Chelsea Partners (Maria Snyder/Arthur Sarkissian) 1990 (1989) color 89m. SP, D: Dan Hoskins. D: (addl scenes) Rodney McDonald. Mus: Daniel May. MkpFX: Ed French. SpFxCoord: Art Brewer. AD: Timothy Baxter. Ref: TV. V 5/9/90. ad. SFChron Dtbk 6/10/90. SFExam 1/30/91. With Jamie Rose, Catherine Carlen, Lycia Naff, Vicki Frederick, Kristina Loggia, Gretchen Palmer, Nina Peterson, Don Calfa (Ralph Willum), Ed Gale, Whitney Reis.

"Life's a bitch and then you die. Usually." A gang of self-proclaimed "cycle sluts" invades the tiny town of Zariah, but finds it already under siege by the living dead. Seems Ralph Willum of Willum's Funeral Home has been implanting batteries in the heads of the recently deceased in order to recruit the labor needed to retrieve some underground-nuclear-test stuff.... Sporadically hilarious sf-comedy-actioner. Among the hits of the genially hit-and-miss script: the phrase "lead kibble" ... a young mother's response to the appearance, on her doorstep, of a zombie: "Mom! I had enough of you the last time around!" (Mom's undead head goes flying) ... and the complaint of a resident of Peter's Home for Blind Orphans, in response to the spectacle of a zombie hanging from the roof of the bus: "Blind. No parents. And now this."

**CHOPPING MALL** Concorde/Trinity (Julie Corman) 1986 color 76m. (*Killbots* - alt t. *R.O.B.O.T.* - early t?). SP, D: Jim Wynorski. SP: also Steve Mitchell. Mus: Chuck Cirino. Killbots: Robert Short. SpFxMkp: Anthony Showe. OptFX: Motion. SpFX: Roger George. SdFX: Zound FX. Anim Sup: R. J. Robertson. Ref: TV. V 11/19/86. With Kelli Maroney, Tony O'Dell, Paul Bartel, Mary Woronov, Dick Miller (Walter Paisley), Karrie Emerson, Barbara Crampton, Gerrit Graham, Mel Welles, Angela Aames, Lawrence Guy (Dr. Carrington), Robert Greenberg.

While teenagers party overnight in the Park Plaza 2000 building, lightning activates three "Killbots" in Secure-Tronics' Protector 101 series, Robocop, Jr., robots designed to stun burglars, but inexplicably furnished with disintegrating rays.... In-jokes (Roger's Little Shop of Pets) and dialogue that's clever in the worst way punctuate routine splatterer. Even the killer robots' "Thank you. Have a nice day" refrain gets tiresome.

**A CHRISTMAS CAROL** (U.S.-B) CBS-TV/Entertainment Partners 1984 color 90m. D: Clive Donner. SP: Roger O. Hirson, from Charles Dickens' story. Mus: Nick Bicat. PD: Roger Murray-Leach. SpFX: Martin Gutteridge, Graham Longhurst. Mkp: Christine Beveridge. Ref: TV. TVG. V 12/26/84. With George C. Scott, David Warner, Susannah York, Frank Finlay (Marley's ghost) Edward Woodward (Ghost of Christmas Present), Michael Carter (Ghost of Christmas Yet To Come), Angela Pleasence (Ghost of Christmas Past), Nigel Davenport, Derek Francis, Michael Gough, Peter Woodthorpe.

Scrooge (Scott) gets another free Christmas dinner. This version of the story is stronger on sentiment than holiday horror—a little too strong, despite touching moments. Scott's not bad, but his voice settles into an easy, rumbling monotone. Bland color drains the movie of atmosphere—even the "eerie" scenes look cheery.

See also: *Cancion de Navidad. Muppet Christmas Carol, A. Scrooged.*

**Ta CHRONIA TIS MEGALIS ZESTIS** (Greek) Greek Film Centre & Greek TV 1 & Negative O.E. 1992 color 93m. SP, D, Co-P: Frieda Liappa. SP: also Maritina Passari. Mus: Thanos Mikroutsikos. Ref: V 3/2/92: "preposterous Greek tragedy." With Elektra Alexandropoulou, Periklis Moustakis, Sofia Seirli.

Islanders at mercy of slasher, memory-destroying virus, and maddening heat wave. *The Years of the Big Heat* - tr t.

**CHRONICLES OF PRYDAIN** see *Black Cauldron, The*

**CHRONOS** see *Cronos*

**CHUCK NORRIS KARATE KOMMANDOS** Worldvision HV/Ruby-Spears 1987 (1986) anim (aka *Karate Kommandos?*). Ref: vc box: "advanced laser robot" ... space battle ... "a full length animated feature." Voices: Keye Luke et al.

**The CHURCH** (I) South Gate Ent./ADC & Cecchi Gori Group & Tiger & Reteitalia 1989 ('90-U.S.) color/ws 102m. (*La Chiesa. aka The Cathedral*). SP, D: Michele Soavi. Story, SP, P: Dario Argento. Story, SP: Franco Ferrini. Ph: Renato Tafuri. Mus: Goblin, Keith Emerson. PD: A. Geleng. SpScenics: Sergio Stivaletti. SpFX: Renato Agostini. SpStageFX: A. & G. Corridori. SdFX: Sound Track, Anzellotti. Mkp: R. Prestopino. Ref: TV: SGE video; Eng. version. Stanley. V 2/11/91:112(hv): "suitably gory but uninteresting." 10/19/88: 352: shooting. Cinef 11/89. 10/91: meant to be *Demons 3*. Martin. PT 9:48. McCarty II: "genuinely creepy." M/TVM 3/89. With Asia Argento, Hugh Quarshie, Tomas Arana, Feodor Chaliapin, Barbara Cupisti, John Karlsen, John Richardson.

The works: the "sign of the demon" ... a cathedral built over a mass grave ... a nightmarish fresco in the cathedral ... a "stone with seven eyes" ... a phantom horse ... a possessed librarian ...

a mechanical problem with an elaborate gown ... a vision of a fish creature ... subway-train gore ... and a Church of the Peeling Face shudder .... Typical Italian gore vehicle, if more handsome than usual. Occasional design highlights—in makeup and architecture.

**CINEMAGIC** O'Quinn Prods. 1985 c58m. (aka *Fright Show*) Ref: VSB.

Compilation video. See: *Dr. Dobermind. Illegal Alien. Nightfright. Thing in the Basement, The.*

**CIRCUITRY MAN** I.R.S. Media (Steven Reich, John Schouweiler) 1990 (1989) color 87m. SP, D: Steven Lovy. SP: also Robert Lovy. Mus: Deborah Holland. SpMkpFxDes: Barney Burman. Computer Anim: (main t des) Evan Ricks; (coord) Valeria Lettera; (tube ride) Michael Lafave. SpVideoFxD: Paul Levitt. SpSdFxDes: Paul Fontana. Ref: TV. V 6/6/90. TVG 1/12/91. With Jim Metzler, Dana Wheeler-Nicholson, Lu Leonard, Vernon Wells, Dennis Christopher (Leech), Garry Goodrow.

"Forty years after the ocean died, and the last tree fell in the last rain forest, the air became unbreathable. Mankind moved underground into government controlled environments." Subterranean Los Angeles in the near future is a "hell hole" inhabited by (a) the quite unscrupulous Plughead (Wells), who electronically taps into both the pain of other people and the thrill of computer pleasure chips and auto engines ("I love the power!"), (b) the biosynthetic "pleasure droid" Danner (Metzler), and (c) toxic sewer leeches.... Occasionally amusing, generally routine future-chase movie is too clearly calculated to be a midnight cult movie. Plughead's sprouting-wires noggin is a sort of Christmas tree of depravity. Instant-cult-favorite line: "It's like somebody stuck an eggbeater in his skull and switched it on to high."

**CIRCUITRY MAN II** I.R.S. Media & Trans Atlantic Ent.(Plug-In Prods./Steven Reich) 1993 color 97m. SP, D: Steven & Robert Lovy. Ph: S. Timberlake. Mus: T. Kelly. PD: R. Lovy. SpFxMkp: Sota FX. SpVisFX: A. Doublin. Ref: V 2/15/93:10: *Circuitry Man II: Prince of Plugs*. 4/25/94: *Plughead Rewired: Circuitry Man II;* "silly ... cheesy-looking." vc box. PT 20:71: "sometimes funny." With Deborah Shelton, Jim Metzler, Traci Lords, Vernon Wells (Plughead), Dennis Christopher, Nicholas Worth.

The return of the "biosynthetic" creatures.

**CIRCULAR STAIRCASE, The** see *Bat Whispers, The*

**La CITE DE LA PEUR: UNE COMEDIE FAMILIALE** (F) AMLF/Telema & Le Studio Canal Plus & France 3 & M6 Films (Charles Gassot) 1994 color/ws 102m. D: Alain Berberian. SP: Farrugia, Lauby, Chabat. Ph: L. Dailland. Mus: P. Chany. AD: J.-M. Kerdelhue. SpFX: Didier Roux. Ref: V 4/11/94: "pioneering but paper-thin ... sendup of horror and detective pix"; *Fear City: A Family-Style Comedy* - tr t. With Dominique Farrugia, Alain Chabat, Chantal Lauby, Gerard Darmon, Sam Karmann, Tcheky Karyo, Daniel Gelin, Eddy Mitchell, Rosanna Arquette.

At the Cannes Film Festival, a "hammer-and-sickle killer starts slashing projectionists at market screenings."

**La CITTA DELL'ULTIMA PAURA** (I) 1975 color feature. D: Carlo Ausino. Ref: Palmerini.

"Young speleologist ... discovers he is ... the last man alive on Earth."

**CITY IN PANIC** (Can.) Transcontinental/Fear Stalker 1987 color 85m. (*Fear Stalker* - orig t?). D, P: Robert Bouvier. SP, P: Andreas Blackwell. Story, SP, Exec P: Peter Wilson. Ph: Mark Mackay. Mus: Dave W. Shaw. AD: Ray Lorenz. SpFxMkp: Gary Boisvert. SpFX: Gerald Lukaniuk. SdFX: Airwave Records. Ref: TV: Trans World video. Bob Moore. Martin. Hound. no Maltin '92. no Phantom. no Scheuer. no V. With Dave Adamson, Leeann Nestegard (Elizabeth Price), Ed Chester, Peter Roberts, Gary Bryant, Derrick Emery, Nadia.

The serial slasher "M" claims that he (or she) is "protecting the city." (" 'M' is for monster!"—and also homage to Fritz Lang.) From what exactly becomes clear when all the murder victims prove to have had AIDS.... *City in Panic* opens with *Psycho* shower scene number 231, though there's a twist-in-retrospect. ("Liz, how could you kill innocent people!") Talky, technically maladroit, and flatly acted and narrated cheapie.

**CITY LIMITS** Atlantic/SHO Films & Videoform & Island Alive (The City Limits Venture) 1984 color 85m. Story, D: Aaron Lipstadt. SP: Don Opper. Story: also James Reigle. Mus: Mitchell Froom. SpVisFX: The L. A. FX Group; (opt fx d) Alan Markowitz; (ph fx d) Dennis Skotak; (vis fx d) Robert Skotak. SdFX: J's Fine Art. Ref: TV. MFB'87:222-23. V 5/22/85. With Darrell Larson, John Stockwell, Kim Cattrall, Rae Dawn Chong, Opper, Norbert Weisser, Robby Benson, James Earl Jones, Kane Hodder, Tony Plana.

"Fifteen years from now," after a plague has killed most adults. The Clippers, bands of city kids, take on outsiders.... Familiar barbaric-future action features competent acting and photography (Tim Suhrstedt), but is really just an excuse to get out the motorcycles. Jones' remote-control mini-bombers, in the finale, are an odd, charming touch.

**CITY OF BLOOD** (S. African) New World/Blood City 1987 color 96m. D: Darrell Roodt. Ref: V 5/27/87. McCarty II: "confusing." Phantom: "only sporadically interesting." With Joe Stewardson, Ian Yule, Ken Gampu, Liz Dick.

"Spirit warriors ... who can materialize anywhere to murder whites."

**The CITY OF GHOSTS** (H.K.?) Long Shong Pictures 198-? color/ws? c85m. From a poem by Li Bai. Ref: TV: vt; Eng. titles.

Feng Dou is said to be a "ghost city" on the border of hell—the "imperial city of hell" supposedly emerges every night. The hopping vampires here—who carry opium for a certain general—are called zombies. ("The zombie today is different than before!") At the end, a Taoist priest uses mystical lightning to vanquish the main, mean vampire-zombie. Routine blend of comedy and kung fu action. Apparently shot on videotape.

**The CLAN OF THE CAVE BEAR** (U.S.-Can.) WB-PSO & Guber-Peters/Jozak-Decade & Jonesfilm 1985 color/ws 100m. D: Michael Chapman. SP: John Sayles, from Jean M. Auel's novel. Mus: Alan Silvestri. SpMkp: Michael G. Westmore;

(prosth) Frank Carrisosa, Michael Mills. SpFX: (U.S.) Gene Grigg; (Can.) Michael Clifford. OptFX: Movie Magic. SpSdFX: John Paul Fasal. Narrator: Salome Jens. Ref: TV. MFB. V 1/15/86. SFExam 1/24/86. Berkeley Voice 2/26/86. With Daryl Hannah, Pamela Reed Armstrong, James Remar, Thomas G. Waites.

"In the days of the great ice mountains...." The (Neanderthal) Clan finds one of the "Others ... the New People"—Cro-Magnon man—Ayla (Emma Floria), at the time a little girl. The grown Ayla (Hannah), a New (Cave) Woman, triumphs: She renders the chauvinist Broud (Waites) impotent, leaves their son to be the Clan's future ruler, and returns to her own people .... Not a subtle program, this, but rather wryly worked out. *Clan* is *Red Sonja* with some charm and bite, if it is, like most prehistoric stories, also a bit slow and dull. Hannah is, in her slightly stylized way, expressive.

**CLANDESTINE DESTINY** (Mex) Universidad de Guadalajara (Rivera-Castanares) 1987 ('88-U.S.) color 81m. (*Clandestino Destino. Clandestinos Destinos* - orig t). SP, D: Jaimie Humberto Hermosillo. Ph: Jose Antonio Ascencio, F. Bajorquez. Mus: Carlos Esege. Ref: V 4/6/88: "unappetizing." SFExam 9/29/88: "muddled movie." With Magnolia Rivas, Rafael Monroy, Alonso Tellez.

1999. The U.S. and part of Mexico have merged, sex is forbidden, and test-tube babies are encouraged.

**CLASH OF THE BIONOIDS** see *Macross Movie, The*

**CLASS OF 1999** Taurus Ent./Lightning (Vestron)/Original Pictures 1990(1989) color 98m. Story, D, P: Mark L. Lester. SP: C. Courtney Joyner. Mus: Michael Hoenig. VisFxSup: Eric Allard. SpFxMkpDes: Rick Stratton. MechFxSup: Joe Ramsey. Android Graphics: R/Greenberg. ElecSdFX: Alan Howarth. Opt: Howard Anderson. Ref: TV: Vestron Video. V 5/9/90. With Bradley Gregg, Traci Lind, Malcolm McDowell, Stacy Keach, Patrick Kilpatrick (Mr. Bryles), Pam Grier (Ms. Connors), John P. Ryan (Mr. Hardin), Joshua Miller.

"They cannot be human beings!" The "pride of Megatech" and the Department of Educational Defense: "artificially-created tactical education units," including a "chemistry teacher from hell" (Grier). But the "three inhuman teaching monsters" dispatched to Seattle's Kennedy High begin to revert to their original military mode—"battle droids"—and start breaking student necks and arms. The three turn out to be "basic educational model" androids crossed with "war machines".... The film begins cleverly: The high school's security is designed to resemble a concentration camp, and unruly students assume their seats instantly after supervivid demonstrations of android-teachers' disciplinary powers. But the androids revert to type too soon, and wit gives way to miscellaneous melodrama and action. In the okay climactic sequence, the machines shed their arms to reveal their various weapons, and one of them, half-dismantled, does a *Terminator*.

**CLASS OF 1999—II: THE SUBSTITUTE** Cinetel/School's Out 1993 color 90m. D: Spiro Razatos. SP: Mark Sevi. Ref: vc box: "military droids." With Sasha Mitchell, Nick Cassavetes.

**CLASS OF NUKE 'EM HIGH** TNT-Troma 1986 color 82m. (*Nuke 'Em High* - orig t). Story, SP, D: Richard W. Haines. D: also Samuel Weil. SP: also Mark Rudnitsky, Lloyd Kaufman, Stuart Strutin. Mus: Michael Lattanzi; (nightmare) Biohazard. SpFxMkp: Scott Coulter, Brian Quinn. Animatronics: Tom Lauten. SpMatteFX: Theo Pingarelli. OptFX: Select FX. SpFxSup: Kay Gelfman. Consul: Charles & Susan Kaufman. Ref: TV. MFB'87:143. V 6/4/86. With Janelle Brady, Gilbert Brenton, Robert Prichard, R. L. Ryan, Reuben Guss (Mr. Hyde).

In the "toxic chemical capital of the world," Tromaville High students smoke Atomic High grass grown outside the Tromaville Nuclear Utility and dream that they become monsters. Warren (Brenton) actually does become one, temporarily, while Chrissy (Brady) vomits up/gives birth to a fishy-monster. Finally, a full-fledged slime monster emerges from a barrel.... Heavy-handed, obvious, and crude, and it doesn't help that the crudity is intentional. This plays like a sick Lemon Grove Kids or Bowery Boys comedy, or a modernist Three Stooges movie.

**CLASS OF NUKE 'EM HIGH PART II: SUBHUMANOID MELTDOWN** Troma (Ebisawa-Masada-Fujimura/Pink Flower) 1991 color 95m. SP, D: Eric Louzil. Story, SP, P: Lloyd Kaufman. Story, SP: Carl Morano, Matt Unger. SP: also Marcus Roling, J. W. Sass. Ph: Ron Chapman. Mus: Bob Mithoff. SpCreature: B. Piper, A. Pirnie. Greenie: Gary Young. Ref: TV. V 4/15/91: "incoherent mess." PT 14:45. With Brick Bronsky, Lisa Gaye, Leesa Rowland, Scott Resnick, Trinity Loren, Sharon Mitchell.

Ingredients this time include a "cute little Tromaville squirrel" which eats toxic waste and grows into a huge monster ... a gargoyle-thing ... an insect-winged infant ... a guest bit by the Toxic Avenger ... and the gene-splicing-produced subhumanoids — a (stopmo) lizard-man, an insect-man, and a dolphin-thing.... The latter are a highlight here, as are the gargoyle and the infant. There's also a knowingly-politically-incorrect running gag re dolphins. Otherwise, slim pickings, humor-wise.

See also *Good, the Bad, and the Subhumanoid, The.*

**CLAVILLAZO EN LA LUNA** see *Conquistador de la Luna*

**CLAWS FOR ALARM** WB 1955 (1953) anim color 7m. D: Chuck Jones. SP: M. Maltese. Mus: Carl Stalling. Ref: WBCartoons: re-working of Scaredy Cat. Lee. LC: c'55. TV.

Atmospheric goings-on at the Dry Gulch Hotel. Mice play ghost, and a spider casts a humongous shadow.

See also *Daffy Duck's Quackbusters.*

**CLAYMATION COMEDY OF HORRORS** FHE/Paul Diener(Vinton Prods.) 1990 clay anim color c27m. (aka *Will Vinton's Claymation Comedy of Horrors*). SP, D: Barry Bruce. SP: also Mark Gustafson, Ryan Holznagel. Ph: Bruce McKean. Mus D: Newton, Bard. Set Des: Douglas Kelly. SdFX: R.C. Terrell II. Ref: TV: FHE video. Sean.

Monsters here include the "fabulous, all-powerful monster" of Victor Frankenswine (Doctor of Mad Science), which turns out to be just a miniature monster (though the doc's elixir makes him temporarily gigantic) ... a blob monster ... a mummy that uses its head as a bowling ball ... Famine as a skeleton .. and a Jason-ish

character with a chainsaw .... Inventive animation, functional storyline.

**CLEAN, SHAVEN** DSM III Films 1993 color 77m. SP, D, P: Lodge Kerrigan. Ph: T. Maniaci. Mus: H. Rowe. PD: T. Ferrier. SpFxMkpDes: Rob Benevides. Ref: V 9/27/93: "graphic gruesomeness." With Peter Greene, Robert Albert, Megan Owen, Molly Castelloe.

"Study of schizophrenia."

**CLEARCUT** Northern Arts Ent./Cinexus Capital Corp. 1992 color 98m. D: Richard Bugajski. SP: Rob Forsyth. Ref: ad. SFChron 11/6/92: "feature-film dud ... gruesome stuff." With Graham Greene, Ron Lea, Michael Hogan, Floyd Red Crow Westerman.

"Possessed by an Indian spirit that gives vent to his rage and allows him to appear and reappear at will, Arthur ties up Bud with duct tape and proceeds to torture him like a skewered bug." (SFC)

**The CLEARING** (U.S.-Russ.) Kodiak Films/Babylon & Odessa & Sovampex (Kaplan-Martin) 1991 color 91m. SP, D, P: Vladimir Alenikov. SP: also Katherine Martin, Yuri Petrov. Mus: T. Kline. Ref: V 5/20/91: "lacks the basic values of even the most routine Yank slasher pictures." With George Segal, Tamara Tana, Nikolai Kochegarov.

"Film opens with the murder of a nubile, unclad femme by someone wearing a goat's head."

**CLEO/LEO** Platinum Pictures & DB Films 1989 color 95m. SP, D: Chuck Vincent. Mus: Joey Mennona. Mkp: Fern Feller. Opt: Videart. Ref: TV. V 5/10/89. Martin. Scheuer. Hound. With Jane Hamilton (aka Veronica Hart), Scott Baker, Alan Naggar, Ginger Lynn Allen, Kevin Thomsen, Jennifer Delora.

"Who's the broad?" Male chauvinist "piggie" Leo Blockman, of Leo Company, falls into a polluted "mess" of a river and emerges as a woman, "Cleo Clock," who fittingly becomes a target of male harassment. At first, Leo dominates Cleo/Leo, but by the end, Cleo—who gets to like men—becomes a "woman for real".... The writing is too broad to be very pointed, but Hamilton/Hart as Cleo brings off a few of the comic routines, and *Cleo/Leo* is certainly better than the similarly-premised *Sweet Revenge* (which see), and anticipates Blake Edwards' superior comedy-fantasy *Switch* (P).

**CLIFFHANGERS** see *Loves of Dracula*

**CLOCK AND BELL** see *Committed*

**The CLONING OF JOANNA MAY** (B-U.S.) Granada-TV & A&E-TV (Sally Head/Gub Neal) 1991 ('92-U.S.) color c35m. D: Philip Saville. SP: Ted Whitehead, from a story by Fay Weldon. Ph: Ken Morgan. Mus: Rachel Portman. PD: Stephen Fineren. Mkp: Sue Milton. Ref: TV. TVG. With Patricia Hodge, Brian Cox, Billie Whitelaw, Sarah Badel, Oliver Ford Davies; Emma Hardy, Helen Adie, Laura Eddy (clones).

"I made four of you." "Evil" Carl May (Cox)—who has a "calculator for a brain and a computer for a soul"—uses "DNA transference plus implantation" to clone his ex-wife (Hodge) so that he can have her "free from the stain of betrayal." Three "little Joanna clones" survive.... Talky, unbelievable "Can't we stop punishing each other?" story. At the end of this *Svengali* variation, Joanna has Carl cloned.

**CLOSE ENCOUNTER WITH THE VAMPIRE** (H. K.) Feiteng Film/Chou Ling Kong 1986 color c91m. (*Hey, Ghost!* - alt vt t. *Jiangshi Papa*). D, Co-P: Yuen Wo Ping. Mus: Tang Siu Lam. PD: Brandy Yuen. Ref: TV: vt; no Eng./World Video; Eng. titles. Thai Video. NST! 4:19. Jones. PT 5:4. Weisser/ATC. Hardy/HM2: Taiwanese.

Hopping vampire man and boy break out of their respective coffins, make a fuss. A la *E.T.,* human boys and girls protect and play with the boy, whom they call Little Baby. Ultimately, lightning makes the vampire man explode and melt. The vampire boy's hair frizzes, apparently sympathetically, and he disappears.... Routine hopping-vampire comedy leans heavily on bathroom humor and broad double takes and screams. Scattered droll moments. The vampire man has a sly, cadaverous look. Main clue to the mystery: "vampire's footprints."

See also *Vampire Strikes Back.*

**CLOSE ENCOUNTERS** see *Sound*

**CLOSE YOUR EYES AND PRAY** see Hide and Go Shriek

**CLOSET, The** see *Dynastud 2.*

**CLOSET CASES OF THE NERD KIND** 1980 color 12m. Ref: Ernie Fink: parody of CE3K. Hound: aliens.

**CLOUD** see *Robot Carnival*

**CLOUDS** see *Alapaap*

**\*CLOUDS OVER EUROPE** (Western-TV)/London (Irving Asher) 1939. Mus D: Muir Mathieson. AD: Vincent Korda; Frederick Pusey. Ref: TV. BFC. Lee. Lentz. V 6/21/39. 3/15/39. Hardy/SF. Stanley. Martin. Maltin '92. Hound. Scheuer. With George Merritt, Gus McNaughton, J. Longdon, Sandra Storme, John Laurie.

Plane-motor-and-radio-jamming ray hidden on salvage ship, *The Viking;* TV apparatus. The "secret" of the missing British test planes is given away at the start—so much for mystery. Ralph Richardson, however—as a secret service man—is eminently watchable. His gusto is infectious—Laurence Olivier is clearly galvanized by his presence, and their scattered scenes together approach high comedy. (Richardson was still salvaging genre movies at the end of his life—see *Time Bandits* and *Dragon Slayer.)*

**CLOWNHOUSE** Commercial Pictures (Danty-Mortarotti-Salva) 1988 color 84m. SP, D: Victor Salva. Mus: Michael Becker, Thomas Richardson. Mkp: (fx chief) Steven Fink; (costume & des) Brenda Cox Giguere. SupSdFxEd: Jeff Watts. Ref: TV. V 2/1/89. With Nathan Forrest Winters, Brian McHugh, Sam Rockwell, Tree (lunatic, Cheezo), Byron Weible (lunatic, Bippo), D. C. Reinecker (lunatic, Dippo), Gloria Belsky (fortune teller).

"You never know what they really are." Three madmen denied circus privileges escape from a mental hospital, kill three clowns with the Jolly Brothers Circus, and appropriate their makeup and

costumes.... The sinister-clown cinema currently in vogue (see also *It, Killer Klowns from Outer Space,* and *Out of the Dark)* perhaps owes something to the outdoor party sequence in *Curse of the Demon* (1957), in which Karswell (Niall MacGinnis) dons clown makeup to entertain local children. *Clownhouse* itself—unadventurous but pleasant scare fun—rather single-mindedly celebrates boyhood bravado. The score includes one effective lurking-clown piano theme among more-familiar suspense chords.

**The CLUB** (Can.) Norstar Ent./Peter R. Simpson (Ilana Frank) 1993 color feature. D: Brenton Spencer. SP: Robert Cooper. Ph: Curtis Petersen. Mus: Paul Zaza. AD: Ian Brock. Ref: V 10/25/93:61 (ad): screening at MIFED; horned demon. With Joel Wyner, Andrea Roth, Rino Romano, Zack Ward, Kelli Taylor, Kim Coates, M. Ferguson.

**El CLUB DE LOS SUICIDAS** (Mex?) 1970 color c90m.? Ref: TVG: satanic group. With Enrique Guzman, Alfredo Varela, Enrique Rocha, Pili.

**CLUB EARTH** see *Galactic Gigolo*

**CLUB EXTINCTION** see *Dr. M.*

**CLUB WAR** see *War*

**CLUE** Para/Guber-Peters 1985 color 97m. Story, SP, D: Jonathan Lynn. Story, Exec Co-P: John Landis. Based on the board game. Ref: TV. SFChron 12/13/85.

Mystery-comedy with a spooky sequence or two, including one in which all the lights in a "big ugly house" go out. Secret passages, dark cellar, screams, storm, etc. Satire kids its own mechanicalness, but the latter wins out. Martin Mull has a moment or two, and Lesley Ann Warren is de-lovely to look at.

**CLUTCH—PRESA TENACE** see *Evil Clutch*

**The COBWEB HOTEL** Para/Fleischer 1936 anim color 7 1/2m. D: Dave Fleischer. Mus: Sammy Timberg, Bob Rothberg. Anim: David Tendlar, William Sturm. Ref: TV: Rhino Video. Cabarga/TFS. LC.

Horror stuff, as a big, mean-looking, six-legged spider invites unwary, foolish flies to bide a wee at his hotel. Flies caught in spider-web beds scream, and the owner lays out fly paper for a newlywed couple. Amusing and pretty creepy too.

See also: *Night of the Demons.*

**COCOON** Fox/Zanuck-Brown 1985 color 117m. D: Ron Howard. SP: Tom Benedek. Story: David Saperstein. Mus: James Horner. SpVisFX: IL&M; Ken Ralston; (opt) David Berry; (anim) Charles Mullen; (stopmo) David Sosalla. SpAlien FX: Greg Cannom; (consul) Rick Baker. Cocoons: Robert Short Prods. SpChor: Caprice Rothe. SpFxCoord: Joseph Unsinn. SpSdDes: Sprocket Systems. Ref: screen. MFB'85:273-4. V 6/19/85. SFExam 6/21/85. Bay G 7/10/85. EBay Express 6/28/85. With Don Ameche, Wilford Brimley, Hume Cronyn; Brian Dennehy and Tahnee Welch (aliens); Jack Gilford, Steve

Guttenberg, Maureen Stapleton, Jessica Tandy, Gwen Verdon, Tyrone Power Jr.

St. Petersburg, Florida. Alien beings come to Earth to rescue fellow aliens—a "ground crew" of twenty left behind one hundred centuries ago in an emergency evacuation of an outpost. Sprite-like and glowing, they assume human skins (which are easily shed) and bring their hibernating comrades in from the sea in cocoons, which are then placed in an "energized" indoor swimming pool. Members of the rest home adjacent learn of the pool's rejuvenating powers, pile into it, and drain the water's life force. The rescue party returns the remaining cocoons to the sea and takes a contingent of humans with it into space and apparent eternal life.

A touching, funny film re mortality, *Cocoon* is a sometimes uneasy cross between Steven Spielberg's *Close Encounters of the Third Kind* and his segment of *Twilight Zone—The Movie*. The final third of *Cocoon,* in fact—an effects-heavy graft from *CE3K*—seems almost another story, as the rejuvenation idea gives way to a salvation theme. Howard's touch with actors, though, is as sure, generally, as Spielberg's with effects: The scene for instance between Dennehy's alien—he has lost two of his own—and Gilford's bereaved widower quietly suggests overlaps in alien and human concerns. In the most memorable effects scene, an alien (in original form) dies; you see, intimately, the life draining from its face.

**COCOON: THE RETURN** Fox/Zanuck-Brown 1988 color 116m. D: Daniel Petrie. SP: Stephen McPherson. Story: McPherson, Elizabeth Bradley. Mus: James Horner. SpVisFX: IL&M; (sup) Scott Farrar; (anim sup) Wes Takahashi. SpAlien FX: Greg Cannom. SpFX: J. B. Jones. SdFxEd: Tim Holland. Ref: TV. MFB'89:175. HR 11/21/88. V 11/23/88. SFChron 11/23/88. S Union 11/25/88. With Don Ameche, Wilford Brimley, Hume Cronyn, Jack Gilford, Steve Guttenberg, Barret Oliver, Maureen Stapleton, Elaine Stritch, Courteney Cox, Jessica Tandy, Gwen Verdon, Tahnee Welch, Linda Harrison, Tyrone Power Jr., Brian Dennehy (Walter), Wendy Cooke ("Phil").

"Your Grandma and I are comin' to see you!" They're back from Antarea, where no one gets sick or old, and they immediately resume aging. The aliens are here to rescue some cocoons; the humans return, in effect, to solve a few problems—Bernie's (Gilford) loneliness and Ben's grandson David's (Oliver) tendency to strike out on the ballfield. Bess (Verdon) is pregnant; Art (Ameche), proud; and Alma (Tandy), near death, until husband Joe (Cronyn) magically sacrifices his own life force.... Sequel to *Cocoon* is occasionally a bit touching or funny, but too self-conscious to be anything more. Horner's score heavily underlines the sentiment. Even the alien magic drains from the film, as the Antareans-in-Antarean-form get too much center-stage time.

**CODA** see *Deadly Possession*

**CO-ED MURDERS, The** see *What Have They Done to Your Daughters?*

**COITUS INTERRUPTUS** (Taiwanese) c1988 color 78m. Ref: TV: vt; no Eng. Y. K. Ho: above is tr t.

Principal monsters: a hopping ghost who befriends a woman in a forest and tries to make love to her (his stiff-armed style interferes), three ghosts who can appear and disappear, and a guy with cape and fangs who at first seems to be a fake, then turns out to be a real vampire. (Baffled during lovemaking, he uses a proffered condom like a balloon.) Plus naked women in chains and a hopping-vampire movie on TV.... Slight, odd genre mix starts out as a t&a horror-comedy, midway turns hardcore.

**COLD, The** see *Game, The*

**COLD LIGHT OF DAY** (B) Creative Artists (Richard Driscoll) 1990 color 76m. SP, D: Fhiona Louise. Ph: Nigel Axworthy. Mus: P. S. Davies. Ref: V 11/5/90: "extraordinarily grim ... based on actual events but not on an account." With Bob Flag (Jordan March), Geoffrey Greenhill, Martin Byrne-Quinn, Bill Merrow, Clare King.

Necrophilia, dismemberment.

**The COLD ROOM** (U.S.-B) HBO-TV/Jethro & Mark Forstater 1984 color 100m. SP, D: James Dearden, from Jeffrey Caine's novel. Mus: Michael Nyman. PD: Tim Hutchinson. Mkp: Elaine Carew. Ref: TV. V 5/16/84. With George Segal, Amanda Pays (Carla Martin/Christa Bruckner), Renee Soutendijk, Warren Clarke.

"It's like the Nazis never ended." A surly 17-year-old (Pays), staying with her father (Segal) in an East German hotel, becomes possessed by the spirit of a girl who, in the Thirties, murdered her Nazi father.... Stories past and present are undistinguished, comparisons and contrasts unilluminating. But if the present is bad, and the past was worse, the script implies a somehow-better future.

**COLD SWEAT** (Can.) Norstar Ent. & Ontario Film Investment (Peter R. Simpson) 1993 color 88m. D: Gail Harvey. SP: Richard Beattie. Mus: Paul Zaza. Ref: V 6/28/93: "an okay time-waster." with Ben Cross, Adam Baldwin, Shannon Tweed, Dave Thomas, Lenore Zann.

"Spooked-out hitman (Cross) haunted by the ghost of an innocent woman (Zann)" whom he shot.

**COLOUR OUT OF SPACE, The** see *Curse, The* (U.S.-I, 1987)

**COLTELLO DI GHIACCIO, Il** see *Knife of Ice*

**COMANDO DE LA MUERTE** (*Infernofinis*) (Mex) Productora Cinedos (Elliot Margolis, Ignacio Garcia) 1990 color 94m. D: Alfredo Gurrola. SP: Dan Cazes, Gary Burak, Sofia Duek, J. M. Gomara. Ph: Agustin Lara. Mus: M. A. Galarza, P. Gilabert. AD: Magallon, Lozoya Jr. SpFX: Miguel Vazquez. OptFX: Arteidea Prods.; A. Munoz. Mkp: A. Castaneda. SdFX: G. Gavira. Ref: TV: Million Dollar Video; no Eng.; Command of Death-tr t. Cinef 6/96:47. With Sergio Goyri, Jorge Luke, Cesar Sobrevals, Ernesto Yanez, Gerardo Vigil, Salvador Garcini, Janina Hidalgo.

In the year 2033—after a time of terrible wars—civilization is rubble ... one big battleground, or many little ones. Futuristic actioner is not badly done, but routine. Only semi-unusual element: the coven of witches. In one scene, an old witch stabs a voodoo doll, and a thug dies; in another, a young witch temporarily stuns the hero supernaturally.

**COMBAT SHOCK** Troma/Prism (2000 A.D. Prods.) 1984(1986) color 100m. (92m.) (aka *American Nightmare*). SP, D, P: Buddy Giovinazzo. Ph: Stella Varveris. Mus: Ricky G. Baby Des: Ralph Cordero II. SpMkpFX: Cordero, Varuolo, Mathes. Gunshot FX: Brian Powell. Ref: TV: StarMaker Ent. video. PT 7:11-12: "gory horrifying war nightmares ... mutant baby." McCarty II: "violence enough to shock the most jaded gorehound." Scheuer. no Martin. Phantom: "often dim and amateurish, but weirdly compelling." With Ricky Giovinazzo, Mitch Maglio, Veronica Stork.

Generally undistinguished, but the always-bawling mutant infant is guaranteed to give you the willies, or won't-he's. It's an amazing prop. Overall, the movie is almost laughably "gritty."

**COMEDY DRACULA** (India-Hindi) 198-? color c115m. (*Comedy Dracula* - ad t). Ref: TV: AM Video; no Eng. With Farhana Khan, Rauf Lala, Shazad Raza (Dracula).

A caped, cackling Dracula with big, removable fangs appears near the end of this photographed stage comedy. Broad, burlesque-like, audience-pleasing performances dominate.

**COMES MIDNIGHT** Sepia-Art Pictures 1940 short feature. Ref: Separate Cinema. With James Baskette, Eddie Green, Amanda Randolph.

Spooky poster features bats, cemetery.

**COMET MOBILE IN THE MILKY WAY** see *Space Traveler 2020*

The **COMIC** (B?) ABC Films/Christobal Films 1985 color 90m. SP, D, P, Ed: Richard Driscoll. Ph: Alan Trow. Mus: (sd des) Paul Davies; Mesh & Heavy Quartet, Richard Dunn. SpFX: Chris Tucker. Mkp: Fiona Summerell. Ref: TV: Magnum Ent. video. no Stanley. no V. Hound. no Phantom. no Maltin '92. Martin. Scheuer. PT 3:42. With Steve Munroe, Bernard Plant, Jeff Pirie, Vass Anderson, Simon Davies, B. Timini.

"In a world where time means nothing," The Order rules, and "1984"-style police soldiers patrol with billy clubs. Sam Coex (Munroe) knifes comic Jerry Myers (Pirie), in order to get his job at the local night club. He thrives, for a time, in clubs, but winds up in the hands of the police, and has nightmarish visions, including one re a ghoul, apparently Myers. Stylized low-budgeter does not lack for *Clockwork Orange/1984* pretensions, but does lack for a way of interesting the viewer in same. A "Weird Production" (as listed in the end credits), all right.

**COMIC STRIP PRESENTS, The ...** see *Supergrass, The*

**COMICALAMITIES** Educ/Hammons 1928 anim silent 8m. (aka *Felix the Cat in Comicalamities*). Ref: screen. LC. SFChron Dtbk 5/12/91.

Scene with gigantic (near-endless) eel, weird octo-creature, and incidental sea monster. Top Felix the Cat cartoon, featuring clever "interaction" between creator and created, as Felix orders his animator to make a rather toothy female cat beautiful, an ink-rope to take him to the bottom of the sea, etc.

**COMING BACK FROM THE MOON** (J) 1993 color feature (*Tsuki Yori Kaeru*). D: H. Jinno. Ref: Weisser/JC: "supposed to be funny." With K. Mitsuda, Y. Takahashi.

A "powerful force" draws an astronaut back from space.

**COMMANDO SQUAD** Frontier Film 1976 color 82m. D: Charles Nizet. Ref: VSB. Hound. V 5/9/84:264 (ad). no Lentz. no V. no Phantom. no Martin. no Stanley. With Chuck Alford, Peter Owen, April Adams.

World War II. "Device that re-animates flesh." (VSB)

**COMMIES ARE COMING, THE COMMIES ARE COMING, The!** see *Red Nightmare*

**COMMITTED** (S. African) Media Home Ent./Vision Int'l. & World Wide Ent./B.S.B. (TWE Group/Alan Amiel) 1991 (1990) color 87m. D: William A. Levey. SP: Simon Last, Paul Mason, from Susan Claudia's novel *Clock and Bell*. SpFX: Tjaart van der Walt. Mkp: Debbi Christiani. Ref: TV. V 8/19/91: 1987. With Jennifer O'Neill, Robert Forster, Ron Palillo, Sydney Lassick, William Windom, Richard Alan (Jones).

"They like to kill nurses here." At "the institute," "guests" act out their fantasies until they "no longer need them"—and the new nurse, Susan Manning (O'Neill), finds herself committed as a "guest." One patient's (Aletta Bezuidenhout) tale has her wondering if the supervising doctor is really a doctor or a patient. A row of nurses' graves in the cellar (a "sacred place") settles the matter.... Very predictable. One or two fun-hokey plot twists. ("Likes toys. Kills nurses.")

**COMMUNION** New Line/Pheasantry Films & Allied Vision & The Picture Property Co. (Dan Allingham) 1989 color 103m. D, P: Philippe Mora. SP, P: Whitley Strieber, from his book. Ph: Louis Irvin. Mus: Allan Zavod. SpMkpMechFX: Michael McCracken et al. AnimFX: Hal Miles. Visitor Des: T. S. Jacobs. Creative FX: Paul Stewart et al. Mkp: M. Buhler. Ref: TV: MCEG Virgin video. MFB'90:291-2. V 5/10/89. ad. SFExam 11/11/89. Sacto Bee 11/14/89. With Christopher Walken, Lindsay Crouse, Joel Carlson, Frances Sternhagen, Andreas Katsulas, Paul Clemens; Susie & George Rossitto et al (blue visitors).

"Based on the true experiences of one American family." In 1985, "little blue doctors" and E. T. types that look like exotic Gumbies abduct writer Whitley Strieber (Walken) from a mountain cabin "flooded with light" and take him up to a "gigantic ship," where they submit him to a "rectal probe" and an *Invaders from Mars* needle. ("Someone came for me that night.") Other people, he finds, report seeing the "same beings," and he eventually joins a close-encounter group.... Ponderous sf-docudrama plays like a flattened-out *CE3K* and recalls other supposedly based-on-fact alien-encounter movies such as *The UFO Incident,* not to mention that Fifties forerunner, *UFO.* A PBS-type documentary on the history of the cabin might have been more interesting, and saved on effects expenses.

The **COMPANION** USA-TV/Univ/Michael Phillips Prods./Windy City (MTE/Richard Brams) 1994 color 93m. D: Gary Fleder. Tel: Ian Seeberg. Ph: R. Bota. Mus: D. Shire. PD: L. Bennett. SpFxMkpSup: Todd Masters. SpFxCoord: Gary D'Amico. Ref: TV: MCA-Univ HV. TVG. With Kathryn Harrold, Bruce Greenwood (Geoffrey), Brion James, Talia Balsam, Joely Fisher, James Karen, Tracey Walter.

"It's a damn machine!" Year 2015. Disillusioned with men, author Gillian Tanner (Harrold) turns to the G-45 Companion, an "incredibly lifelike" and "anatomically correct" android. (Cf. *Making Mr. Right*.) At first, "Geoffrey" is just your basic security and housekeeping model (a Stepford Husband?), but Gillian reprograms him for sexuality, as Svengali "reprogrammed" Trilby. ("Say, 'I love you, Gil'.") She then introduces "random data" into him. Her friend (who has not seen *2001* and HAL): "I'm going to have you recalled." Geoffrey then finds he must hold Gillian captive. (Cf. *Dr. Jekyll and Mr. Hyde*.) Script here gets predictable, as it follows the lead of its predecessors, and Geoffrey remains one-dimensional.

**The COMPANY OF WOLVES** (B) Vestron/ITC (Palace) 1984 color 95m. SP, D: Neil Jordan. SP, Adap: Angela Carter, based on her stories "The Company of Wolves" and "Wolf Alice" and on Charles Perrault's "Le Petit Chaperon Rouge." Ph: Bryan Loftus. Mus: George Fenton. PD: Anton Furst. SpMkpFX: Christopher Tucker. Animatronics: (sup) Stuart Robinson; (wolf) Rodger Shaw. SpFxSup: Alan Whibley. FxPh: Peter Macdonald. Ref: TV. MFB'84:264-66. V 7/18/84. EBay Express 4/19/85. McCarty II. Phantom. With Angela Lansbury, David Warner, Graham Crowden, Brian Glover, Kathryn Pogson, Sarah Patterson (Rosaleen), Georgia Slowe (Alice), Dawn Archibald (witch woman), Danielle Dax (wolfgirl), Vincent McClaren (devil boy), Terence Stamp (Prince of Darkness).

Stories and dreams re a "man whose eyebrows meet" and who peels away his face and is revealed to be a werewolf ... dinner guests at a period wedding reception whose lycanthropy reflects their corruption ... a she-wolf that, wounded, turns human ... and Little Red Riding Hood and the werewolf, in an extended, unrewarding retelling of the fairy tale.... Unfortunate that the longest tale here is also the least compelling. *Company of Wolves*—which at times plays like *Member of the Wedding* told in the manner of *The Saragossa Manuscript*—is filled with fascinating dreamlike images. With its idiosyncratic, there-and-gone shots of storks, frogs, owls, ravens, wreaths of fog, and mirrors, the movie conjures up an original fantastic world, which the script, however, leaves in a narrative limbo. The shorter the story—say, the she-wolf episode—the sweeter, generally.

**COMPLEX** see *Blood Rage*

**COMPUTER GHOSTS** (Austral.) Cinefunds Ltd. (Ramster-Sanders-Jennings/Vernon-Tyrrell) 1987 color c80m. D: Marcus Cole. Tel: Michael McGennan. Ph: Martin McGrath. Mus: Chris Neal. PD: Michael Ralph. Mkp: Tish Glover. Ref: TV. TVG. no Phantom. no Maltin '92. no Scheuer. With Nicholas Ryan, Peter Whitford, Scott Burgess, George Spartels, Robert McGregor, Christine Jeston, Noel Ferrier, Emily Symons.

"Crooksnatchers is being used to scare people out of their houses!" Bizarrely bad comedy involves the "totally new technology" of a security system, the key element of which is (honest) a glowing-eyed "monster" (actually a hologram) which leads to reports of "false hauntings." Add two God-dispatched ghosts and a visualized fantasy or two, and you get a plot which is very involved, to little effect, comic or otherwise.

La **COMTESSE PERVERSE** (F) CFDF 1973 color 88m. (aka *Les Chasses de La Comtesse Zaroff. La Comtesse Zaroff. Les Croqueses.* aka *The Evil Countess. Sexy Nature* - alt vt t). SP, D: Jesus Franco (aka C. Brown). P: R. de Nesle. Ref: TV: VSOM; Eng. titles. Stanley. EVS. Hardy/HM. With Lina Romay, Kali Hansa, Alice Arno, Robert Woods, Howard Vernon (Count Zaroff), Monica Swinn.

"She had a bow and arrow!" Humor and cannibalism in a variation on "The Most Dangerous Game." Count and Countess Zaroff—"a strange couple"—run a most "unusual museum" (of human and other animal trophies) in their island chateau. ("This house scares me.") More Franco kinkiness (with chains, ropes, etc.), occasionally of a hardcore sort. Main novelty: a nude version of "The Most Dangerous Game," with a literally Naked Prey (and Hunter). Overall, film is lax, with chaotic continuity.

**CONAN THE DESTROYER** Univ/De Laurentiis 1984 color/ws? 101m. D: Richard Fleischer. SP: Stanley Mann. Story: Roy Thomas, Gerry Conway. Mus: Basil Poledouris. Dagoth: Carlo Rambaldi; Steve Townsend et al. SpFX: (sup) John Stirber; (ph sup) Barry Nolan. SpMkp: Gianetto de Rossi. VisFxCoord: Charles Finance. Min: Emilio Ruiz Del Rio. Ref: TV. V 6/27/84. SFExam 6/29/84. With Arnold Schwarzenegger, Grace Jones, Wilt Chamberlain, Mako, Tracey Walter, Olivia D'Abo, Jeff Corey, Ferdy Mayne.

Miscellaneous horrors this time include a sorcerer who changes into a flying, dragon-like creature; hooded figures which become one monstrous one; and the god Dagoth, who is reborn, then dies when Conan removes the horn from his head.... The jaunty score, the sets (Pier Luigi Basile), and the monster effects help a little, but this sequel to *Conan the Barbarian* needs lots of help. Schwarzenegger's reaction-shot emotions are funnily phony, but the Paul Brothers get the campy tone down better in *The Barbarians*.

*****CONDEMNED TO LIVE** Maury Cohen 1935. SP: K. de Wolfe. Mus: (d) Abe Meyer; David Broekman. AD: E. C. Jewell. Ref: TV. Greg Luce. Hardy/HM. V 10/9/35. Lentz. Lee. Turner/Price. With Lucy Beaumont, Barbara Bedford, Robert Frazier, Paul Weigel, Dick Curtis, Horace B. Carpenter.

"The bat's abroad tonight!" Some "huge and loathsome thing" is dragging its victims into a cave and tearing open their throats. Is the "mark of the bat" a sign of a vampire, a "monster bat," or a "human monster"? The latter, more or less, as it transpires. Seems Paul Kristan (Ralph Morgan), whose pregnant mother (Bedford) was bitten by a "monstrous bat," is a sort of Jekyll/Hyde, whose evil half blossoms at night when all light is extinguished.... Stilted period drama plays like and prefigures *The Wolf Man*. Maxine Doyle as Margurite gives a classic camp performance, in this lurid, earnest shoestring production—she underlines every word, every movement—and Russell Gleason as her admirer, David, is right there, too. Additional cast notes: Morgan's role is an unplayable "saint," Mischa Auer's enthusiasm as a "hideous" hunchback is fun, Pedro de Cordoba (as Dr. Bizet) is authoritative, and the bit players are all formula exclamations. Relative highlight: the wind effects.

**CONDOR** ABC-TV/Orion-TV & Jaygee 1986 color 74m. D: Virgil W. Vogel. Tel: Len Janson, Chuck Menville. Mus: Ken

Heller. PD: Bill Hiney. Min: Pete Slagle. Computer FxEd: Mark Horowitz. Opt: Howard Anderson. SdFX: Rich Harrison. Ref: TV. TVG. V 8/20/86. With Ray Wise, Wendy Kilbourne, Craig Stevens, Carolyn Seymour, Cassandra Gava, Shawn Michaels, Myra Chason (android).

1999 Los Angeles—the "city on the edge of the 21st Century." Condor, an international peace-keeping organization, assigns agent Christopher Proctor (Wise) a new, android partner (Kilbourne)—the "world's first molecular computer," whose brain contains "tiny bio-chips of genetically-engineered bacteria," which latter produce both thoughts and feelings. Plus: laser barrier, laser-proof vest, ray guns, holograms.... Bits and pieces of *Future Cop, The Terminator,* "Moonlighting," etc. Functional melodramatic dialogue, hollow action.

**CONEHEADS** Para/Lorne Michaels (Michael Rachmil) 1993 color 88m. D: Steve Barron. SP: Tom Davis, Dan Aykroyd, Bonnie & Terry Turner. Based on the "Saturday Night Live" characters. Mus: David Newman. SpMkp: D. B. Miller, Marie France. Stopmo: Phil Tippett. Ref: V 8/2/93: "sly combination of the outrageous & the mundane." Cinef 12/93:59: "full of wonderful sight gags." SFChron 7/23/93: "the movie is a snore." ad. Sacto Bee 7/23/93: "many missed opportunities." With D. Aykroyd (Beldar), Jane Curtin (Prymaat), Michelle Burke (Connie), Michael McKean, Jason Alexander, Lisa Jane Persky, Dave Thomas, Sinbad.

Alien scout ship winds up on Earth.

See also *Boneheads, The.*

**CONFESSIONS D'UN BARJO** see *Barjo*

**CONFESSIONS OF A CRAP ARTIST** see *Barjo*

**CONFESSIONS OF A SERIAL KILLER** Concorde/Cedarwood (C. O. Rexrode/F. Y. Smith) 1987 color 89m. SP, D: Mark Blair. Ph: Layton Blaylock. Mus: William Penn. PD: Robert A. Burns. SpFX: Greg Stouffer. Ref: TV. TVG. no Scheuer. no Maltin '92. PT 14:44. With R. A. Burns (Daniel Ray Hawkins), Dennis Hill (Moon Lewton), Berkley Garrett, Sidney Brammer (Molly Lewton), Dee Dee Norton, Ollie Handley.

"It didn't bother Moon to have his sister involved in all these killings?" Serial slasher Daniel Ray Hawkins tells police that he has murdered as many as one hundred people. In his narrated flashbacks, he takes up with Moon Lewton, who is handy at breaking necks, then with Moon's sister Molly. At the end, Molly accidentally cuts Daniel, and Daniel, piqued, shoots her.

Alternately contrived and unsettling. The low-key, just-folks tone works for a while at setting off the horrors, but the movie doesn't have much going for it other than tone. The key moment for each prospective victim is indicated by a *Comes the Dawn* look. "Based on a true story...."

**CONFIDENCE** Univ/Lantz 1933 anim 6m. Anim: Fred Avery et al. Mus: James Dietrich. Ref: screen. PFA (flyer). Maltin/OMAM. LC. no Lee.

FDR's "Confidence" spray combats the Depression—depicted here as a ghostly, Death-like figure which flies around the globe

spreading gloom—and lifts everyone's spirits. Silly, "uplifting" Oswald the Lucky Rabbit cartoon.

**CONQUEROR OF THE MOON** see *Conquistador de la Luna*

**CONQUEROR OF THE WORLD** Falco Film 1983 ('86-U.S.) color/ws c95m. (3 *Master of the World*). Ph: Sandro Mancori. Mus: Alberto Baldon Bene (sp?). Mkp: Rosario Prestopino. SdFX: R.C.S.; Frati, Giacco. Ref: TV: Mogul Video; Kon & Akray version. no Hound. no Phantom. no Scheuer. no Maltin '92. With S. D'Arc, Vivian Rispoli, Aldo Sambrell.

Two hundred thousand years ago the bear was God, beheading and brain-eating were in, and communication was by grunt. Principal prehistoric tribes: the Kon and the Akray. Hero: Bog. Contemporary interest: minimal. Gore: also minimal but pretty heady. In sum: The bears come off best.

**CONQUEST OF LAND** Smithsonian Inst./Hillman & Carr 198-? anim color 5m. Anim D, P: Michael Carr. Ph: Slavinski. Ref: Smithsonian Inst.

Arthur Pod, reporter for the Silurian Broadcast Co., describes how plants and animals are making the transition from water to land.

**\*\*CONQUEST OF MYCENE** (I-F) Embassy/CFPC-Explorer Film '58 1964 ('65-U.S.) color/ws 102m. (*Ercole contro Moloch* - I. *Hercule contre Moloch* - F. *Hercules against Moloch* - alt TV t. *Hercules Attacks* - alt t). SP, D: Giorgio Ferroni. SP: also Del Grosso. Ph: Tiezzi. Mus: Carlo Rustichelli. AD: Arrigo Equini. Ref: TV. Lee. TVG. AFI. Lentz. Weldon. COF 8:40. no Stanley. Vallejo T-H: *Hercules vs. Moloch.* With Gordon Scott, Rosalba Neri, Michel Lemoine, Jany Clair, Arturo Dominici.

"God," Moloch, inhabits cave, wears animal-monster-head mask, slashes faces of female victims at sacrificial altar ("I want to be amused"), proves to be man with horribly disfigured face.... Undistinguished sword-and-sandal saga, with horrific overtones.

**CONQUISTADOR DE LA LUNA** Para 1960 78m. (*\*Conqueror of the Moon. Los Cosmonautas* - TV ad t. *Clavillazo en la Luna* - alt t?). AD: Salvador Lozano. SpFX: Juan Munoz Ravelo. Mkp: Elda Loza. Ref: TV. Hardy/SF. With Oscar Ortiz de Pinedo, Ramiro Gamboa, Alicia Moreno.

Flat imitation of U.S. space comedies and dramas of its time is of interest today only because it used extensive footage from *Destination Moon.* It even used the spacesuits from *Destination Moon,* or spacesuits designed to match those from the earlier film. The only original highlight: the bizarre alien brain/mouth/hypnotizing-eye. Tacky: a carrousel-like flying saucer.

**CONRAD BROOKS MEETS THE WEREWOLF** Nelson 1993. D: David Nelson. Ref: PT 19:10: "terrible." With D. Nelson (werewolf) & Conrad, Henry & Ted Brooks.

**CONSULTORIO SEXOLOGICO** (Sp) Euca Films 198-? color feature. SP,D: Jose Antonio de Villalba. FX: Syre. Ref: TV: Video Latino; no Eng.

In a prologue sequence, cavemen discover clothes. In a fairy-tale sequence, a witch/warlock appears and disappears. Elementary t&a vehicle with the above fantasy elements.

**CONSUMING PASSIONS** (U.S.-B) Samuel Goldwyn/Euston Films 1988 color 98m. D: Giles Foster. SP: Paul D. Zimmerman, Andrew Davies, from Michael Palin and Terry Jones' play "Secrets." Mus: Richard Hartley. SpFxSup: Ian Wingrove. VideoFX: Richard Hewitt. Mkp: Naomi Donne. Ref: TV. V 4/6/88. SFExam 5/27/88. With Vanessa Redgrave, Jonathan Pryce, Tyler Butterworth, Freddie Jones, Sammi Davis, Thora Hird.

"Throw more chaps in the chocolate?" Three workmen accidentally dumped into the chocolate vat at Chumley's Chocolates create a taste sensation. ("People want to eat chocolates with people in them.") Soon, dead, quietly appropriated human bodies are adding spice to the taste of Chumley's new Passionelles. (Dead barnyard animals fail the taste test.) No-bite satire meanders, adds nothing to previous cannibalism movies such as *The Demon Barber of Fleet Street* and *The Stuff* (or the Burke-and-Hare body-snatching stories), except Redgrave's beyond-Garbo accent and Pryce's tics.

**CONTACT MAN, The** see *Alias Nick Beal*

**CONTAGION** (Austral.) Reef Films (Leo Barretto) 1988 color 90m. D: Karl Zwicky. SP, P: Ken Methold. Mus: Frank Strangio. Ref: V 4/27/88: "rather pointless ghost story" re haunted mansion. Morse: "effective moments." Martin. With John Doyle, Nicola Bartlett, Roy Barrett.

**CONTAMINATION POINT 7** (I) 1989 ('91-U.S.) color feature. D: Fabrizio Laurenti. Mus: C.M. Cordio. FX: M. Trani. Ref: Palmerini: "a sort of Italian-style *Tremors*. Poor." V 2/25/91:246(rated): "scene of horror violence." With Mary Sellers, Jason Saucher, Bubba Reeves.

**CONTRONATURA** (I-W-G.) Super Int'l. Pictures/CCC/Edo 1969 color/ws 84m. (*Schreie in der Nacht* - W. G. aka *The Unnaturals*). SP, D: Antonio Margheriti. SP: also Hannes Dahlberg. Ph: R. Pallottini. Mus: C. Savina. Ref: Hardy/HM: avenging ghosts in Thirties England; "routine tale." Palmerini. Ecran F 71:72. no Lee. With Joachim Fuchsberger, Marianne Koch, Dominique Boschero, Luciano Pigozzi (aka Alan Collins).

**COOL AIR** see *Necronomicon* (1993)

**COOL WORLD** Para/Frank Mancuso, Jr. 1992 anim and live action 98m. D: Ralph Bakshi. SP: Michael Grais, Mark Victor. Mus: Mark Isham. MechSpFxSup: Dale Martin. SpFX: Leonor M. Wood; Joe Quinlivan. AnimFxCoord: Ellen Greenblatt. Concep Des: Barry Jackson. Ref: TV. Jim Shapiro. TVG. Martin.

Ingredients: the cartoon-animated Dr. Whiskers' machine, which opens a "tunnel" between the real world and Cool World (a "whole new world"), a cartoon land, and permits "inter-world travel," first in 1945, then in 1992 ... little-monster "wooden nickels" ... an ape-like cartoon critter ... a monstrous doorknocker ... incidental cacophonous weirdies and ghosts from graves ... a Death-like skeleton with scythe ... and the transformation, at the end, of humans into cartoon beings, including one monstrous one.... Technically slick, but tiresome toon-human interaction, plus amusing incidental, typical-cartoon business (e.g., heavy objects falling on toons). The background's the thing here.

**COPENHAGEN'S PSYCHIC LOVES** see *Psychic, The*

**COPPERHEAD (THE SNAKE MOVIE)** VCI (Crystal Payton) 1984 color 95m. SP, D: Leland Payton. Ref: V 10/17/84:41 (hv): shot-on-tape; "likely to disappoint horror picture fans." V/CHVD. V 1/29/86:44: horror. Stanley. Morse: "utterly amateurish." With Jack Renner, Gretta Ratliff, David Fritts, Cheryl Nickerson.

Revenge via snakes.

**CORPO PERPLESSITA** see *Body Puzzle*

**CORPS ET LE FOUET, Le** see *What!*

**CORPS PERDUS** (F-Arg.) Films de l'Atalante & DB Films & La Sept & SGGC/Mora (Ricardo Freixa) 1990 color 92m. SP, D: Eduardo de Gregorio. SP: also Suzanne Schiffman, Charles Tesson. Mus: Gustavo Beytelman. Mkp: Mirta Blanco, Oscar Mulet. Ref: V 3/14/90: "a good supernatural yarn." With Laura Morante (Laura Canetti/Letizia Fiume), Tcheky Karyo (Eric Desange/Juan Bax), Gerardo Romano.

"It has a mysterious mansion, ghosts, hidden doors and secret corridors, a painting with supernatural influences and a drama of doubles."

**2P The CORPSE WHICH DIDN'T WANT TO DIE** [Note: this is a revised entry] (I-W.G.) Phoenix-Romano & Traian Boeru 1972 color/ws 98m. (90m.) (*La Dama Rossa Uccide Sette Volte*). SP, D: Emilio P. Miraglia. SP, Idea: Fabio Pittorru. Ph: A. Spagnoli. Mus: Bruno Nicolai. AD: Lorenzo Baraldi. Ref: TV: MV; Eng. dubbed; *The Lady in Red Kills Seven Times* - cr t. Prod. Ital.: The Red Queen Kills Seven Times - tr t. Hardy/HM. Lee(p). Palmerini: "mediocre." VSOM: *Red Queen Kills 7 Times*. With Barbara Bouchet, Ugo Pagliai, Marina Malfatti, Sybil Danning.

A legend that, every one hundred years, one of two sisters will kill the other is apparently behind murders committed by a caped lady in red. Is it the (dead) Evelyn? ("I've come back—back from the grave!") "Routine terror-thriller stuff." (H) Lethargic, isn't it? Vapid script wastes an intriguing premise (see above). Lots of mad cackling (the "weird scary laugh" of the Red Queen) and "It's dog eat dog, sweetheart." Feeble shocks, mechanical dubbing. Plus: a visualized nightmare re The Red Queen and a man literally scared to death.

**CORRIDORS OF EVIL** see *Carnival of Souls*

**La CORTA NOTTE DELLE BAMBOLE DI VETRO** (I-W.G.-Yug) Doria/Dieter Geissler/Jadran 1972 color/ws 92m. (aka *Malastrana*). SP, D: Aldo Lado. Ref: Hardy/HM: "clever debut feature" for Lado. Ecran F 48:81. Palmerini. With Jean Sorel, Ingrid Thulin, Mario Adorf, Barbara Bach.

Mad Prague professor puts American journalist into state of catalepsy—the frozen body ends up in an anatomy class.

**The CORVINI INHERITANCE** (B) Hammer-TV. c 1984? color feature. Ref: Ecran F 73:9: masked, sadistic killer. no Scheuer. no Maltin '92. no Stanley. no Martin.

**COSA AVETE FATTO A SOLANGE?** see *What Have You Done to Solange?*

**A COSMIC CHRISTMAS** (Can.) Nelvana & CBC 1977 anim color c25m. D: Clive A. Smith. SP: Ida Nelson, Laura Paull. Story: Patrick Loubert. Anim D: Frank Nissen. Mus: Sylvia Tyson. Ref: TV: in *Nelvanamation*, Warner HV. Voices: Duncan Regehr, Martin Lavut et al.

Three alien "wise men" arrive on Earth on Christmas Eve looking for the meaning of the star of Bethlehem. Slickly done but baldly didactic science-fantasy.

**The COSMIC EYE** Hubley 1985 anim color 71m. (*The Cosmic Concert* - orig t). D, P, Des: Faith Hubley. Mus: Benny Carter. Ref: TV: excerpts from *Voyage to Next* and *Moonbird*. FQ W'88-9:2, 15-16, 17, 18. V 11/13/85:40 (hv). Phantom: Disney. Maltin '92. Voices: Dizzy Gillespie, Maureen Stapleton et al.

Glimpses of the "next twenty years" and a post-atomic-holocaust, flying skeletal moose-thing and a mechanical cowlike monster and another planet which has destroyed itself. Plus: fire-breathing dragon and cave man bits and Death personified.... Ethnographically comprehensive, visually inventive, but sociologically flat-footed, until the climactic, hopeful outburst. A combination of big thoughts and small visual inspirations.

**\*The COSMIC MAN** Futura Pictures 1959 (1958). Ref: TV: Rhino HV. Warren/KWTS! V 1/21/59. Lee. Lentz. Hardy/SF. Weldon. Hound. Maltin '92. Scheuer. Martin. PT 7:8.

"I am one of many cosmonauts." A "mysterious object"—a big-golf-ball-like sphere which employs anti-gravity to hang in the air and which converts light waves into electricity—lands in Stone Canyon (actually Bronson Canyon). Is the sphere's X-ray-like pilot (John Carradine)—a "creature made of ... anti-matter" who is invisible at night and partially visible by day—an "international menace" or an "evil force?" Or is he simply on a fact-finding mission? Drab, talky sf drama provides an efficient demonstration of How To Get by on a Very Small Budget, but has little else to offer now. Script borrows from *The Giant Claw* (the anti-matter idea), *Day the Earth Stood Still* (the Cosmic Man improves a scientist's blueprint), and *The Invisible Man* (the semi-visible man sometimes cloaks his semi-visibility). The lame boy (Scotty Morrow) is lame only so that the Cosmic Man can cure him. ("Good bye, Cosmic Man!")

**\*The COSMIC MONSTER** John Bash Prods./AA-WNW (George Maynard) 1958 (1957). AD: Bernard Sarron. SpFX: Anglo-Scottish Pictures. Mkp: Charles Nash. Ref: TV: *The Strange World of Planet X* - cr t. BFC: SP also Joe Ambor (uncred.). Warren/KWTS! Lentz. Lee. Phantom. Stanley. Weldon. V 3/12/58. Hardy/SF. Hound. Maltin '92. Scheuer. Martin. Fango 123:17, 21.

The payoff, Bert Gordon-level, big-bug effects are poor, and the script is occasionally cliched and slapdash, but the plot of *Cosmic Monster* is an at times intriguing mixture of sf and mystery elements, including a UFO, a huge egg, a mysterious "Smith" (Martin Benson), who proves to be your friendly neighborhood E.T.; a "maniac at large in the woods," and an apparatus the circuits of which operate even when its power is shut off, and which creates "freak weather" and "syndrome"-like magnetic

"effects over distance." The magnetic force generated ruptures the ionosphere and brings to Earth cosmic rays which make (naturally fast breeding) insects mutate. In the most suspenseful sequence, a teacher (Catherine Lancaster) is trapped in a schoolhouse in the woods, as giant insects surround the building. The choppiness of the movie suggests that it may have been recycled from the original British TV serial.

**COSMIC SLOP** HBO & Hudlin Bros. (Michael Jay Hill/Cosmic Slop Inc.) 1994 color 86m. "Space Traders" sequence: D: Reginald Hudlin. Tel: Trey Ellis. Mus: J. Barnes. PD: B. Jones. SpFxMkp: Michael Burnett. VisFx:(sup) Scott Enyart;(digital opt) Anderson Video. SdFxDes: Alan Porzio. Ref: TV: HBO HV. Vallejo T-H 4/14/95. With Robert Guillaume, Michele Lamar Richards, Jason Bernard, Edward Edwards, Brock Peters, Casey Kasem, Lamont Johnson; Reno Wilson (The Messenger).

"Beyond 'The Twilight Zone'"...: The first of three determinedly controversial segments concerns a proposition by aliens to trade "cheap, unlimited energy," etc. for the entire U.S. Black population. The "space traders" turn the Statue of Liberty into gold, vacuum smog away from cities, and clean up our lakes. Or, Holocaust II. If, at first, the premise appears far-fetched, the development is grimly realistic.... "The First Commandment" intriguingly documents a case of Puerto Rican paganism/Santeria supplanting Christianity/Catholicism (cf. *The Wicker Man*); "Tang" posits a possibly apocalyptic answer to spousal abuse.

**COSMO POLICE JUSTY** (J) 1987? anim color 40m. (aka *Justy*). Based on Tsuguo Okazaki's manga. Ref: TV: vt. Anime Opus '89. Animag 5:3. V 5/6/87:469(ad).

When Justy kills her father in an ESP duel, six-year-old Asteris wishes herself ten years older in order to take revenge on him. But she develops amnesia, and Justy takes her under his wing. His ESP foes, however, later recreate the death scene for Asteris, and she unleashes her psychic rays on Justy.... The six-year-old-in-the-body-of-a-sixteen-year-old idea is just a bizarre pretext for some graphically showy showdowns between psychics.

**COSMONAUTAS, Los** see *Conquistador de la Luna*

**COSMOS KILLER** see *Miami Horror*

**COTTAGE TO LET** (B) GFD/Gainsborough 1941 87m. (*Bombsight Stolen*-U.S.). D: Anthony Asquith. SP: Anatole de Grunwald, J. O. C. Orton, from Geoffrey Kerr's play. Ref: screen. William K. Everson. V 9/10/41. PFA notes 5/29/86. TGSP2. Lee(e).

The British military is "testing out a new bomb sight" developed by John Barington, an inventor and the "finest scientific brain in the country." With the addition of a gyroscope as a stabilizer for "top altitudes," the sight is accurate at up to 10,000 feet. Other inventions include the bullet-proof Barington tank. Routine everyone-in-the-house-is-either-an-enemy-agent-or-Scotland-Yard-man material.

**\*COUNTDOWN** 1968 ws (*Moonshot*-orig t). Ref: TV: 93m. Lee. AFI. Bill Warren. Weldon. Martin. Maltin '92. Scheuer. With Michael Murphy, Ted Knight, Clete Roberts.

Pilgrim I—an "emergency backup to Apollo"—lands an American astronaut (James Caan) on the moon (at the Sea of Storms), in an upgraded Saturn rocket. There he finds the dead crew of a Russian ship—and a survival shelter, where he is to stay until the next moon flight, in eight to twelve months.... The early scenes of *Countdown* comprise a cross-section of about a dozen small-scale, but riveting personal dramas, as astronauts, officials, astronauts' wives, politicians, and reporters vie for attention. Robert Altman's film celebrates the triumph of the larynx—or the survival of the shrillest—as his people here voice their doubts, beliefs, fears, etc., more or less simultaneously. But if the excitement generated by this human clamor seems real, the plot-generated excitement (Russian-American competition, shipboard electricity failures, oxygen-tank time-limits) does not. In Fifties sf, it was meteor showers; in *Countdown,* it's a wiring malfunction.

**COUNTER DESTROYER** (H.K.?) Filmark Int'l./Tomas Tang 1987? color/ws c92m. D: Edgar Jere. SP: Roger Markham. Ph: Arthur Brush. Mus: James Langton. SpFX: Edwin Morgan. Mkp: Millie Myer. Ref: TV: Trans World video; dubbed; vc box gives variant credits, cast. Hound. no Martin. With Cynthia Rose, Tony Job, Harriet Brown, Bob Poe.

A jackknife-fingernailed spirit, variously called a "vampire beast" and the "last eunuch in China," possesses Joyce, a scriptwriter ("Joyce has changed!") who later gives *Alien* birth to the beast's vampire son. Meanwhile, a local Taoist monk takes charge of two bucktoothed hopping vampires (who, confusingly, make their first appearance in Joyce's dream and act more like zombies than vampires) and, apparently, a third, literally-hot-footed monster-thug. Dull crime-thriller filler combined with confused horror elements from Freddy films and hopping-vampire comedies.

**COVENANT** NBC-TV/Michael Filerman & Fox 1985 color 76m. D: Walter Grauman. SP, Sup P: J. D. Feigelson, Dan DiStefano. Mus: Charles Bernstein. PD: Fred Harpman. Mkp: Ron Walters. Ref: TV. TVG. With Jose Ferrer, Jane Badler, Michelle Phillips, Whitney Kershaw, Bradford Dillman, Barry Morse, Kevin Conroy, John van Dreelen.

"At the next equinox, we bring Angelica into the covenant!" The Noblebank corporation purportedly "finances death, terrorism, and destruction all over the world," and the "inner circle" of the Noble family has a long-standing covenant with evil, in this "Dynasty"-meets-"Faust" fantasy. Morse plays Van Helsing to this family of Draculas.... Glossy, empty story of the young, the pretty, and the powerful. The high-fashion-and-blood contrasts seem simply perversely chic rather than evocative.

**COZ TAKHLE DAT SI SPENAT** (Cz) Barrandov 1976 color 90m. SP, D: Varclav Vorlicek, Milos Makourek. Ref: Hardy/SF: "hilarious." With Vladimir Mensik, Jiri Sovak, Josef Somr, Eva Treytnorova.

Scientist's machine, "if badly adjusted ... causes miniaturization instead of rejuvenation...." *What Would You Say to Some Spinach?* - tr t?

**CRABS** see *Dead-End Drive-In*

**\*CRACK IN THE WORLD** Philip Yordan 1965. SpFX: Alex Weldon. Mkp: Carmen Martin. Ref: TV. AFI. Weldon. V 2/10/65. Lee. TVG. With John Karlsen, Peter Damon, Jim Gillen.

Scientists hoping to free magma energy at the Earth's core launch a rocket at its crust. The force of the A-bomb, combined with hydrogen from a pocket below the magma, causes earthquakes, tidal waves, fissures in the ocean floor along the Macebo Fault, and ultimately threatens to destroy the world. Another A-bomb, exploded in a volcano, merely diverts the crack and doubles its speed. Finally, two fissures meet and shear off a huge chunk of Earth, which flies into space, a "new moon".... Typical world-in-peril melodramatics, with facile characterization and social comment. Encores for several venerable lines, including "You want to play God!" Impatient, glory-hungry scientist Dana Andrews' bandaged hand (repeated, work-related exposure to X-rays is killing him) might be a semiological-textbook Sign for Reckless Science. Some picturesque crack-in-the-countryside effects—or, the principle of the parting of the Red Sea, applied to mountains, valleys, etc.

**The CRAFT** ABC-TV 1991 color c90m. (aka *To Save a Child*). Ref: TVG. TV Movie News 9/91. with Marita Geraghty, Peter Kowanko, Shirley Knight, Anthony Zerbe, Spalding Gray.

Witch coven in New Mexico.

**CRASH AND BURN** Full Moon/David DeCoteau, John Schouweiler 1990 color 84m. D, Exec Co-P: Charles Band. SP: J. S. Cardone. Mus: Richard Band. PD: Kathleen Coates. FX: (d) David Allen; (DV-8 des) Steve Burg; (opt) R. D. Bailey, Howard Anderson. SpMkp: (fx) Greg Cannom; Palah Sandling. SpFX: Players SpFX. OptFX: Mercer, OptFX. Ref: TV. V 9/3/90:80 (hv). Cable Video Store 1/91. With Paul Ganus, Megan Ward, Bill Moseley, Eva LaRue, Jack McGee, Ralph Waite, John Chandler.

"One of us ain't one of us." July 2030, after the "econo-collapse." "Big brother" Unicom—dedicated to "life, liberty, and the pursuit of economic stability"—employs a "crash and burn virus" to override the Do Not Kill Humans program of their watchdog-android "synths," one or two of which are knocking off folks at an old power station (now a TV studio) in the Wasteland.... Script takes its cues, uncompellingly, from *Ten Little Indians, Alien, The Thing* remake, *The Terminator,* and *Nightmare on Elm Street.* In the okay payoff, the gigantic foot of the just-revived DV-8 super-robot ("old rustbucket") stomps a killer android, a la *Bambi Meets Godzilla.* Stopmo screen time here is disappointingly limited.

**The CRAWLERS** (I) Col-TriStar/Filmirage 1990('93-U.S.) color 94m. (aka *Troll III*). D: Martin Newlin. SP: D. Steel, A. Lawrence. Ph: L. Revene. Mus: Carlo M. Cordio. AD: M. Slowing. Costumes: Laura Gemser. SpFX: Illusion Tech. Ref: TV: CT HV; Eng. version. SFChron Dtbk 1/2/94. PT 13:10. 17:5: D: A. Massaccesi. With Mary Sellers, Jason Saucier, Bubba Reeves, Chelsi Stahr, Vince O'Neil, Edy Eby.

"The entire forest is radioactive!" The "genetic mutations" here are "killer roots," nuclear-waste-bred, carnivorous, tentacle-like roots which feed on "plasma residue" .... Asinine, flavorless sf-horror with stilted English dialogue and a monotonous menace. Caught in passing: "Just shut up and play with your carnivorous plant!" Hokey root "whip" sounds.

*The **CRAWLING EYE** Modern Sound/Tempean 1958. SpFX: Anglo Scottish Pictures. Mkp: Eleanor Jones. Ref: TV. Warren/KWTS! Lee. BFC. V 10/15/58. Barbara Hill. Hardy/SF. Hound. Phantom. Maltin '92. Scheuer. Martin.

"A cloud where there should be no cloud...." Mountain climbers set out from the Hotel Europa in the Trollenberg, Switzerland, disappear "into the mist," and are "never seen again." Behind it all: tentacled eyes which kill, then possess one man (Andrew Faulds), and send him to kill psychic Anne Pilgrim (Janet Munro), whose "radio receiver" mentally spies on them. Shot, the "zombie" and his "crystallized flesh" smoke away.... Flimsy eyes and flimsy action ruin the concluding sequences of *The Crawling Eye,* but earlier the movie generates quite a bit of suspense. In the eeriest sequence, Anne's inner "eyes" switch focus from a glass paperweight model of a mountain to two climbers in peril on the actual mountain. If she's dangerous to the monsters because she can see and expose them, she is also helpless: She can't do much of anything about what she sees. She watches "as though from the Trollenberg itself," as do the scientists with their semi-omniscient TV apparatus at the nearby observatory. But, though the principals below can make phone calls to the huts above, and hear what's going on, they can't affect the horrible events.... This strange, vicarious sense of paralyzed fear is the movie's odd contribution to Fifties sf—it's like movie-watching squared.

**CRAWLSPACE** (U.S.-I) Empire/Altar 1986 color 80m. SP, D, Lyrics: David Schmoeller. Mus: Pino Donaggio. Ref: TV: Vestron-TV. V 5/21/86. Morse. With Klaus Kinski, Talia Balsam, Barbara Whinnery.

"Everyone has a dark secret." Dr. Karl Gunther's (Kinski): He is "addicted to killing" to feel alive. You see, his father designed Nazi torture instruments, and now ...: "Killing is ... my fix".... Determinedly perverse psycho-thriller is pointless, just a catalogue of atrocities, past and present.

**CRAZED** Intercontinental/Jean Cassidy 1984 color 88m. (*Bloodshed* - alt vt t. *Slipping into Darkness* - alt t). SP, D: Richard Cassidy. Ph: Doug Hodge. Mus: Ron Ramin. AD: Janice Carr, Jane Mancbach. Mkp: Helen Little. Ref: TV: TWE video. VSB. Gore Zone 11:64. V (CHVD). Martin. Hound. With Laszlo Papas (Grahame), Belle Mitchell, Beverly Ross, Rigg Kennedy.

"Wackos—they've taken over the world!" When a diabetic woman (Ross) dies in the bathtub during a fit, her lonely fellow boarder (Papas) stores her body in his room, then in the attic. He stabs one intruder to death, then strangles the owner of the house, Mrs. Brewer (Mitchell), when she discovers the woman's body.... The latter is the best "discovery" shock scene. The dead "bride" suddenly drops out of the attic trapdoor—like a puppet on a gibbet. Next best shock: the discovery of the man's body in the bathtub. Silliest: the comically "punched up" discovery of the two bodies in bed. All the details are derisory, in this low-key, low-budget, pessimistic psychological shocker. Bad breath and dead-body odor are two of the main motifs.

**CRAZY FAT ETHEL II** Video City (Chop-Em-Up Video)/IRMI Films (Frances Millard) 1987 color 60m. SP, D: Nick Philips. Ph: Karil Ostman. AD: C. R. Fenwick. Mkp: Gigo. Ref: TV: Video City video. Phantom. Deep Red 3: sequel to *Criminally Insane* (2P). Scheuer. Martin. Morse. Hound. With Priscilla Alden, Michael Flood, Jane Lambert, Robert Copple, C. L. Lefleur, Gina Martine.

"Gimme those pretzels, Granny!" Strapped Napa State Hospital transfers homicidal maniac Ethel to Bartholomew House, where she promptly strangles the orderly with a curtain cord and later uses the back of a fellow patient as a pincushion for kitchen knives, then cackles and finishes her apple.... Obvious, crude, padded (with footage from the original), and technically shoddy (the film was edited with one of Ethel's carving knives), yet perversely winning minimalist tale re a woman who murders those who come between herself and food. Prime line: "I didn't see anything. I was watching 'Gunsmoke' on TV."

The **CRAZY PROFESSOR** (Fili) R.V.Q. 1985 color c125m. SP, D: Ben Feleo. Story: Roy Vera Cruz. Ph: Amado de Guzman. Mus: Dominic. Sets: Phol Tamayo. Opt: Lacap, Austria. SdFX: Demet Velasquez. Mkp: Ligaya Quince. Ref: TV: Trigon Video; some Eng. With Dolphy, Alma Moreno, Aga Muhlach, Janice de Belen, Panchito, Babalu, Jimmy Santos.

Prof. Frank Einstein of Kennon College (the dean insists on calling him "Frankenstein") uses his ELSS (Einstein Life Saving Serum) to bring, in turn, a frog, a bird, and a man back to life. The walking dead man drinks a cup of coffee, walks about campus scaring people, then collapses. Another serum turns a man into a hog, and a third—applied to tennis shoes—enables basketball players to jump ridiculously high.... This son of *Son of Flubber* goes on and on. A few droll scenes, but silly musical numbers and slapstick predominate.

**CRAZY SAFARI** (H.K.-So. African) Win's Movie Prod. & Samico Films (Charles & Jimmy Heung) 1991 color/ws 95m. D: Billy Chan. SP, Exec Co-P: Barry Wong. Ph: Buster Reynold. Mus: John Wedoepohl. Consult: Jamie Uys. Ref: TV: Pan-Asia Video; some Eng. Jones. With Nixau, Lam Ching Ying, Sam C. Chan, Peter Chan, Jumbo (African mummy)

A priest "raises" a "priceless Chinese mummy," or vampire—our hero's great-great-great-grandfather, from the Fifteenth Century—and leads him out of an auction. All involved end up in South Africa, where "voodoo" dolls, possessions, exorcisms, and spells—both African and Eastern—proliferate. In one sequence, the spirit of Bruce Lee is transferred from a photo to the native hero.... Hopping through Africa. Horror-comedy's parodies of hopping-vampire movies and *The Gods Must Be Crazy* are occasionally mildly engaging, generally just silly. Highlight: the filmstrip which objectively compares the caped, fanged, "typical European vampire" to the Chinese kind.

**CRAZY SPIRIT** (H.K.) Focus Film (William Chang & Chao Yung Lin) 1987 color/ws c86m. D: Chien Yueh Sheng. SP: Teng Yung Kung. Design: B. Chan. Ref: TV: Rainbow Video; Eng. titles. FComment 6/88: 48, 52. NST! 4:19. Ecran F 79:74. With Lui Leung Wai.

Taoist Te from Thailand, "the only heir to Mao Shan magic," creates a "ghost-son" for Mr. Chou, but the magic boy winds up with Mr. and Mrs. Lei, a young couple who have separated. Te must find the boy before he (Te) dies, or "disaster will linger forever": Q Tyrone (as the boy calls himself) is an "illegal immigrant"—he came to Earth "without boarding the boat." Q's invisible-boy tricks at first lead Mrs. Lei to believe that her house is haunted, but he soon becomes visible to her and her husband. At the stroke of midnight on the appointed day, wind and fire assault the Lei house, and furniture flies about. Finally, a glowing rolling saucer takes Q back to the other world, and Te dies.

This sad-saccharine boy-reunites-couple story is a soap-operatic *Poltergeist*. Happy times and bittersweet times here seem equally confected. Best line: "Ox Head/Horse Face is Hell's Immigration Officer." Best sequence: the haunted-house one, in which Q keeps magically appearing—he waves, friendly-like, but the man and woman keep jumping in fright each time he pops up.

**CREAM LEMON 3: RALL** (J) Fairy Dust 198-? anim color 27m. Char Des: Kazuna, Konoma. Ref: TV: vt; no Eng.

Female-human/male-monster animated hardcore re a planet with four moons ... a hooded demon rapist ... a gigantic "monster" which summarily shrinks to its tiny, silly fish-bird-mouse-creature self ... pterodactyl-like mounts ... and one-person spacecrafts. Science-fantasy-comedy-horror video-series entry is a strange combo of the cuddly cute and the horrific-erotic graphic, but doesn't seem to have much to offer beyond novelty-value amusement.

**CREAMY MAMI** series see *Majocco Club*

**CREATURE** Samuel Goldwyn/Cardinal & TWE (Titan) 1985 (1984) color/ws 95m. (*Titan Find* - orig t). SP, D, Co-P: William Malone. SP: also Alan Reed. Mus: Thomas Chase, Steve Rucker. SpMkpFX: Bruce Zahlava. SpVisFX: (d) Robert Skotak; The L.A. FX Group; (opt fx) Alan Markowitz; (anim) George Turner. Creature: (des) Michael McCracken; (coord) Doug Beswick. Anim: Robert Alvarez. SpSdFX: J. Ledner, The Cutters. SpThanks: Bob Burns et al. Ref: TV. TVG. V 5/8/85. With Stan Ivar, Wendy Schaal, Lyman Ward, Robert Jaffe, Annette McCarthy, Diane Salinger, Klaus Kinski, Jeff Solomon (creature).

An NTI Corporation geological team finds a 200,000-year-old "butterfly collection" on Titan, a moon of Saturn—a display of specimen creatures from all over the galaxy. One evil one with "collective intelligence" begins dispatching crab-creatures which replace the brains of and animate their victims.... Unoriginal, but the blech-effects come at you with gleeful regularity and are sufficiently varied. Dialogue reference to the movie with the "carrot from another planet" (i.e., the original *The Thing*).

**CREATURE FROM THE BLACK LAGOON (I & III)** see also *Daffy Duck's Quackbusters. Monster Squad, The.*

**CREATURES OF HABIT** see *Terrifying Tales*

*The **CREEPER** 1948. Mus: Milton Rosen. AD: Walter Koessler. Mkp: Ted Larsen. Ref: TV: King Bee video. V 10/6/48. lobby card. Lee. Martin. Hound. no Scheuer. Maltin '92. LC. With Richard Lane, Philip Ahn, Ralph Peters.

Human and non-human elements: Nora Cavigny (Janis Wilson), a woman whose "ridiculous aversion to cats" was picked up in "that horrible place" in the West Indies, where the natives believe in metempsychosis ... a serum meant to induce "cellular phosphorescence" in living tissue in order to "illuminate certain organs of the body"—said serum instead turns Dr. Jim Bordon's (Onslow Stevens) hand into a cat claw, the better to murder people ... Andre (David Hoffman), a "strange-looking character" ... and Dr. Van Glock (Eduardo Ciannelli), a "very weird sort of fellow."

RKO's *Cat People*—not Universal's/Rondo Hatton's Creeper— is obviously the main influence here, though Universal's George Robinson did the atmospheric photography, the single most noteworthy aspect of the film: Creeper is a cat; June Vincent's Gwen tries to convince Nora that she, Nora, is a cat, at least in her dreams; and Nora, at one point, looks at her hands as if she expected to see claws. Generally, *The Creeper* doesn't have much on the ball. Gwen and Nora are tiresome characters—the latter tiresomely fearful, the former tiresomely jealous—and the other characters are more or less functional. However, there's one eye-opening photographic effect: In what at first appears to be a dream sequence (Nora's dream), a giant, superimposed, ghost-like claw shadow exits one bedroom, enters another, then returns. This startlingly expressionistic sequence proves not to be a dream, or at least proves to have a basis in reality: Dr. Lester Cavigny (Ralph Morgan) is later found "clawed to death" in the next room. Oneiric license.

**CREEPER, The** see *Dark Side of Midnight, The*

**CREEPERS** (I) RHI Ent. (New Line)/Intra Films/Titanus (Dacfilm) 1985 (1984) color/ws 110m. (83m.) (*Phenomena* - I t). SP, D, P: Dario Argento. SP: also Franco Ferrini. Mus: The Goblins. SpMkpFX: Sergio Stivaletti. SpStageFX: Tonino Corridori. SpOptFX: Luigi Cozzi. SdFX: Studio Anzellotti. Ref: TV: Eng. version. MFB'86:152. V 2/13/85. TVG. Stanley. Scheuer. Martin. Morse. Phantom. Maltin '92. With Jennifer Connelly, Daria Nicolodi, Dalila Di Lazzaro, Patrick Bauchau, Donald Pleasence, Federica Mastroianni, Michele Soavi.

"It can be very scary" at the International School for girls, in Zurich. A maniac with a spear is on the loose, and the movie stops dead periodically to display its makeup trophies, including a decapitated, maggot-infested head and a maggoty hand. Plus: a young lady (Connelly) whose paranormal powers calm and command insects, a nightmarish insane asylum ("The further down one goes in this place, the more monstrous the inmates become"), a mutant child, and a fly that detects corpses.... Camp becomes the only possibility here, as the super-fly plays Lassie, or Sherlock Holmes. Other chuckles: the climactic sequence, in which insects and a chimp come to our heroine's rescue, and a pool-of-maggots-and-cadavers scene which is clearly intended to disgust, so clearly it's downright hilarious. Overall, though, more yawns than laughs.

**CREEPOZOIDS** Urban Classics/Titan (David DeCoteau, John Schouweiler) 1987 color 71m. SP, D: DeCoteau. SP: also B. Hauser. Mus: Guy Moon. SpMkpFX: Next Generation FX, Thom Floutz, P. Carsillo. SpMechFX: John Criswell. SpFX: Tom Callaway. Atmospheric FX: H. L. Smokum. Ref: TV: UC Video. V

9/30/87. SFExam ad 10/9/87. With Linnea Quigley, Ken Abraham, Michael Aranda, Richard Hawkins, Kim McKamy.

On 1998 post-nuke Earth—"now a blackened husk of a planet"—"mutant nomads" roam, acid rain falls, and a band of deserters finds "something new" at the Research for a Better Tomorrow "containment vessel," 400 miles from New L.A. Thanks, apparently, to experiments in "internal genetic synthesis" of amino acids, (a) Jesse's (Aranda) metabolism mutates and he pulls a semi-*Alien*, (b) a big, unintentionally cuddly killer rat attacks the group, (c) a big rubber monster attacks same, and (d) a monster-baby threatens same..... Whole lotta time-killin' goin' on. Risibly flimsy excuse for a monster movie, however, features occasional low-budget ingenuity.

**CREEPSHOW 2** New World/Laurel 1987 color 89m. D: Michael Gornick. SP: George Romero, from the Stephen King stories "Old Chief Wood'nhead," "The Hitch-hiker," and "The Raft." Mus: Les Reed. MkpFX: Howard Berger, Ed French; (consul) Tom Savini. Anim Sup: Rick Catizone. Ref: TV. MFB'88:13-14. V 5/13/87. ad. With George Kennedy, Dorothy Lamour, Dan Kamin (Old Chief Wood'nhead), Page Hannah, Lois Chiles, King, Savini (The Creep); Joe Silver (voice of The Creep).

Recalling the first *Creepshow,* the animated framing story (giant Venus's-flytrap eats boy's tormentors), "Old Chief Wood'nhead" (wooden Indian kills three thieves), and "The Hitch-hiker" (supposedly dead hitchhiker confronts hit-and-run driver) are formula revenge sagas, not badly done, but not worth doing. The other story, "The Raft"—in which a "perfectly round" oil slick engulfs its victims—is pointless, but features a fun, Blob-like monster as its menace. Plus, in the animated intro, a dragon....

**CRICKETER, The** see *As Time Goes by*

*The **CRIME DOCTOR'S COURAGE** 1945 70m. Chor: Tito Valdez. Ref: TV. V 3/7/45. Lentz. no Stanley. Maltin '92. Scheuer.

"Do you know that no one has ever seen them in the daytime?" The "darkly mysterious dancing Braggas" (Anthony Caruso and Lupita Tovar) come from a "part of Spain that is deep in the lore of mysticism and magic." The two shun mirrors and supposedly sleep in coffins in their cellar during the daytime. Their act at Ye Friar's Glen is a "haunting experience" for night people: At one point, Dolores disappears in a flash of light. ("A vampire can make itself invisible at will.") Author Jeff Jerome (Jerome Cowan) suggests that the couple debuted at the Madrid Opera in 1650, but all the mysteriousness proves to have been part of a publicity stunt. Meanwhile, in another part of the plot, a man (Stephen Crane) who "may be insane" lurks.... Offbeat "Crime Doctor" entry is probably the most interesting in the series. It's not good, but it sure is strange, and scriptwriter Eric Taylor (who also worked on some Universal shockers) contributes some surprising lines—e.g., Charles Arnt's butler's "People are ephemeral, but houses are permanent." Clumsily developed mystery begins with a balmy bit of melodrama and features prizes such as "You're a psychiatrist—I want you to tell me if I'm married to a madman."

See also *Shadows in the Night.*

**CRIME DOCTOR'S RENDEZVOUS, The** see *Shadows in the Night*

**\*\*CRIME RING** RKO/Cliff Reid 1938 75m. *(The Fortuneers, Cheating the Stars* - early ts). D: Leslie Goodwins. SP: J. R. Bren, Gladys Atwater. Story: Reginald Taviner. Ph: Jack Mackenzie. Mus: Roy Webb. AD: Van Nest Polglase; F. Gray. Ref: TV. TVG. V 7/27/38. MFB'38:220. FD 9/27/38. Boxo 7/2/38. MPH 7/30/38. Showman's 7/2/38. Scheuer. no Maltin '92. HR. NYT 7/22/38. With Allan Lane, Frances Mercer, Clara Blandick, Inez Courtney, Bradley Page, Ben Welden, Jack Arnold, Morgan Conway, Paul Fix, Jack Mulhall, Tom Kennedy, Charles Trowbridge, Frank M. Thomas, Walter Miller, George Irving.

Crime drama features a few scare scenes. One involves ectoplasm-at-large ("ghosts walking") in a "seance room." In another, the "curse" of a murdered psychic reader (Trowbridge) makes him seem to "come back from the grave." (Actually, it's just ventriloquist Courtney throwing her voice.) Plus: an ambiguous fadeout bit with a real ghostvoice ("Nothing to it")—or is it just Courtney? Like RKO's later, similar *Bunco Squad,* this plays more like a public service message than a movie. The seance-room "ghost," however, (a Vernon L. Walker effect?) is a stunner—it moves like animated smoke and is a cross between a human figure and a snake.

**CRIME ZONE** Concorde-New Horizons (Roger Corman/Pacific Trust) 1988 color 92m. D, P: Luis Llosa. SP: Daryl Haney. Mus: Rick Conrad. SpFX: Fernando Vasquez de Velasco. Mkp: Narda Aguinaga. Ref: TV. V 12/21/88. HR 4/5/89. With David Carradine, Peter Nelson, Sherilyn Fenn, Michael Shaner, Orlando Sacha.

"There are no criminals in Soleil...." The post-plague state of Soleil is a "wonderful place"—if you happen to enjoy the carnival-like coverage of executions at the Justice Superdome. Subgrades Bone (Nelson), from the Gardens of Hibernation, and Helen, from the House of Pleasure, join forces in an effort to escape, but find top cop Jason (Carradine) waiting for them at the other end.... Bland actioner plays at times like a futuristic *Marty,* as Helen comes between Bone and his buddies. Rote pop cynicism prevails, although Carradine has a well-written role as a smug establishment mastermind: The latter "invents" the criminals and rebels necessary for the functioning of the state's economy. ("You guys are great!" he tells Bone and Helen.)

**CRIMINAL ACT** Independent Networks & Film Ventures Int'l. (Myron Meisel, Bill Stern/Steuer-Holender) 1989 color 93m. *(Tunnels* - early t). D: Mark Byers. SP, P: Daniel Yost. Mus: W. Coster. Ref: V 8/9/89: "poorly scripted pic." With Catherine Bach, Charlene Dallas, Nicholas Guest, John Saxon, Vic Tayback.

Two women fear that monsters haunt underground tunnels.

**CRIMINALLY INSANE** see *Crazy Fat Ethel II. Death Nurse.*

**CRIMINES DE USHER, Los** see *Fall of the House of Usher* (1983)

**CRIMSON** (Sp-F) Mezquiriz & Eurocine-Europrodis/Brux Inter Film 1973 ('85-U.S.) color/ws 85m. (93m.) (*Las Ratas No*

*Duermen de Noche*). SP, D: Juan Fortuny. SP: also Al Mariaux. Ph: Ray Heil. Mus: Daniel White. SpFX: SOIS Co. Ref: TV: Wizard Video. Hardy/SF. Horacio Higuchi. no Hound. no Martin. PT 7:29. Fangoria 104:52. V 5/1/85: 109 (ad).

A brain-damaged gangster (Naschy) receives part of the brain of another gangster, The Sadist. ("Danger and the unknown are your daily bread."/"That's why they call me The Sadist.") The wounded gangster's system accepts the transplant, but some "psychic transference" occurs: The "new brain" influences his cerebral and central nervous system. ("I have the same perverse desires that he has. I am The Sadist, and I want you!") Some camp possibilities in this *Black Friday* variation, but Naschy isn't exactly Mr. Charisma, the dubbing runs to a numbing monotone, and the score is insipid. Typical tough-guy line: "We'll turn your body into a colander!"

**CRIMSON WOLF** (J) Streamline/Toshiba EMI & A.P.P.P. (Sugiyama-Nomura) 1993 ('94-U.S.) anim color 60m. SP, D: Shoichi Masuo;(Eng. version) C. Macek. From the graphic novel by M. Takasho & K. Okamura. Ph: H. Okazaki. Mus: K. Ogasawara. PD: Suetake, Imakake. SpFX: Yamamoto, Maekawa. SdFX: M. Yokoyama. Story Ed (U.S.): Fred Patten. Ref: TV: Orion HV; Eng. dubbed.

"Destroy the dragons before it's too late." China proves to be run by a "giant computer from hell" which is the embodiment of Genghis Khan, Mao Tse-tung, and Emperor Tai-Chi, who at the end turn into gigantic dragons.... Routine but occasionally stylish vehicle for action, fantasy, gore, and softcore sex. Highlight: the slow undulations of the dragons.

**CRISIS 2050** see *Solar Crisis*

**CRITICAL LIST** see *Terminal Choice*

**CRITTERS** New Line & Smart Egg/Sho Films (Rupert Harvey/Robert Shaye) 1986 color 85m. SP, D: Stephen Herek. SP: also D. Muir; Don Opper. Mus: David Newman. SpDes: The Chiodos. Mkp: (sp fx) John A. Naulin et al; Christopher Biggs. VisFX: Quick Silver; Available Light. MinFX: Fantasy II. Title Des: Ernest D. Farino. SpVoices: Corey Burton. SpFxCoord: Chuck Stewart. Ref: TV. MFB'86:366. V 4/9/86. SFChron 5/2/86. With Dee Wallace Stone, M. Emmet Walsh, Billy Green Bush, Scott Grimes, Opper, Michael Lee Gogin (Warden Zanti), Nadine Van Der Velde, Billy Zane.

Grovers Bend, Kansas—"The town's a zoo!" Two alien bounty hunters with "transforming" abilities arrive on Earth in pursuit of eight alien Krites with big appetites and the ability to wad themselves up and roll like tumbleweeds.... Fairly slickly directed and edited (Larry Bock), but a TV-sitcom glibness infects comic scenes here and an IL&M-like glibness marks effects scenes. The critters have a few cute shticks—e.g., they shoot quills.

**CRITTERS 2: THE MAIN COURSE** New Line/Sho (Barry Opper & Robert Shaye) 1988 color 87m. SP, D: Mick Garris. SP: also D. T. Twohy. Mus: Nicholas Pike. Critters: Chiodo Bros. Prods. VisFX: Peter Kuran: (anim fx) Jammie Friday? SpMkpSup: R. C. Biggs. SpFX: Marty Bresin. Ref: TV. V 5/4/88. MFB'89:331-2. With Scott Grimes, Liane Curtis, Don Opper,

Barry Corbin, Herta Ware, Terrence Mann (Ug), Roxanne Kernohan (Lee), Eddie Deezen.

"Brad Brown is back in town—the boy who cried Critters." A "couple years" later (after *Critters* ends), strange eggs hatch more "man-eatin' dust mops," which, first, attack the "Easter bunny," then the whole town of Grover's Bend (so spelled here). Near the end, the furballs survive explosives by wadding together into a huge rolling, all-consuming ball. Plus: an *Alien*-like critter, an alien bounty-hunter dispatcher, and a bounty hunter who transforms into a *Playboy* centerfold (Kernohan), complete with staple.

*Part 2* has some funny gags—e.g., the critters pigging out at the local Hungry Heifer—but the *Gremlins* people should probably get royalties: The munchers-amok scenes are awfully close in spirit to the gremlins scenes in *Gremlins*. This film in fact plays like a cute, bland sequel to the latter. Best critter subtitle: "Live meat!" Caught in passing: a reference to *The Brain from Planet Arous*, of all films.

**CRITTERS 3** RCA-Col HV/New Line-Nicholas Ent. (Barry Opper-Rupert Harvey) 1991 color 86m. D: Kristine Peterson. SP: David Schow. Ph: Tom Callaway. Ref: Martin: "low rent all the way." V 9/23/91:10 (rated, as *Critters III*). PT 12:9: "this one sucks." V 7/29/91:10. With C. Cousins, Joseph Cousins, Don Opper, Aimee Brooks.

Furballs besiege apartment building.

**CRITTERS 4** New Line/OH Films (Mark Ordesky/Barry Opper, Rupert Harvey/Nicolas Ent.) 1992 (1991) color 91m. (*Critters 4: They're Invading Your Space* - ad t). D: R. Harvey. SP: Joseph Lyle, David Schow. Story: Harvey, B. Opper. Ph: Tom Callaway. Mus: P. M. Robinson. PD: P. D. Foreman. Critters: the Chiodos. OptVisFX: Hollywood Optical; David Hewitt et al. SpFX: Frank Ceglia. Laser FX: Mirage. Ref: TV. TVG. CVS 12/92. PT 16:61. V 12/16/91:10 (rated). 7/29/91:10: shooting. With Don Opper, Terrence Mann, Paul Whitthorne, Anders Hove, Angela Bassett, Brad Dourif, Martine Beswicke (voice of Angela), Eric DaRe.

The Saturn Quadrant, year 2045. A spaceship comes across a lost ship bearing (a) a man, Charlie (D. Opper), in suspended animation since leaving Grovers Bend, Kansas, in 1992; (b) two vicious little "killer furballs," or "artificials," or "hybrids," with a "very high aggression factor"; and (c), at the end, some cute baby critters.... This *Critters*-in-*Alien*-territory movie is the same space movie we've been seeing for the last decade or so. Very thin plot furnishes occasional fun with the contrary, literal-minded computer Angela. ("I'm not sequenced to respond to the demands of waste material.")

**CROAKED: FROG MONSTER FROM HELL** see *Rana*

**CROC** see *Dark Age*

**CROCE DELLE 7 PIETRE** see *Cross of Seven Jewels*

**CROCIFISSO DI SETTE GIOIELLOS** see *Cross of the Seven Jewels*

**CROCODILE EVIL** (H.K.?) 1986 color c85m. (*Ghost Lover* - alt t). Ref: TV: Ocean Shores Video; no Eng. Thai Video.

A wizard who can command crocodiles and the elements makes a man imagine that his hospital room is crawling with little crocodiles. Ultimately, a special amulet defeats said wizard, and he leaks salamanders and dies.... Despite the A-1 title, this routine horror-fantasy offers little except a scene in which a cab driver is assailed by the specter of a crocodile flying at his windshield, plus a visualized nightmare in which a woman finds a crocodile lying on her in bed.

See also the following and *Cannibal Attack. Dark Age. Devil's Sword.*

**CROCODILE GODMOTHER** (Thai) c198-? color/ws c98m. Ref: TV: All Asian HV; no Eng. Thai Video: above is tr t.

In a jealous fit, a woman transforms into a crocodile, leaps on her rival, and mauls and kills her. (Compare similar scenes in the 1942 *Cat People.*) Later, in the river, she switches from crocodile form to human form as she walks ashore, naked. In the next shot, in the forest, she's wearing clothes and becomes, momentarily, a (double exposure) spirit, then returns (undressed again) to croc form, to kill. At the end, prayer-invoked lightning destroys her, but she leaves behind two eggs.... Chintzy effects, including a rubber-toy croc, mar this mixture of horror and softcore sex. The most interesting feature, from a technical standpoint: underwater, subjective, monster's-viewpoint photography.

**THE CROCODILE MEN** (Taiwanese?) Hui Keung 198-? color c85m. D, P: Keung. SP: Hui Tien Yung. Dial: Chuan, Po. Ph: S. C. Lun. Mus: Chen Hsun Chi. Ref: TV: Eng. dubbed. no Maltin '92. no Scheuer. With Dy Savet, Keung, Hsien Yu Ting, Huoy Dyna, Wang Lei Chen.

East Indian books teach a man the secret of becoming a crocodile. ("Chow Lung became a big crocodile forever.") With a martial-arts master in his stomach, he fights a man-eating Snake Island crocodile. Later, he kidnaps a woman and takes her down to his Sea Palace. ("Goddamned animal!") Kookily casual, semi-intentional camp, with a weirdly-charming score and some bizarre speak-sing numbers. A mess, but you can't fight lines like "You're not dealing with the average crocodile." Regulation execrable dubbing.

**CROCS** see *Enemy Unseen*

**CRONOS** (Mex) October Films/Prods. Iguana & Ventana & IM-CINE & FFCC & UOG & CNCA & SF & LSC & STPC & Grupo del Toro (Navarro-Gorson) 1993 (1992/'94-U.S.) color 92m. (*Chronos* - alt t?). SP, D: Guillermo del Toro. Ph: G. Navarro. Mus: J. Alvarez. AD: B. Broch. SpFX: L. Cordero. MkpFX: Necropia. SpMkp: M. Carvajal. OptFX: Mercer & OptFxLtd. Ref: PT 19:8. SFChron 11/26/94. 5/6/94. TV: Vidmark video; Eng. dubbing & titles. ad. Imagi W'94: 52-3. Smr'95:52. Cinef 8/94. V 5/3/93: "an absorbing, modern vampire film." 2/17/92:20: *Cronos Device.* With Federico Luppi, Ron Perlman, Claudio Brook, Margarita Isabel.

Cronos device grants eternal life, but gives its user a "thirst for ... human blood."(V) An insect inside the device acts like a "living filter"; the user "dies," comes back, gets "born again" with new skin. After an intriguing prologue, set in 1536, with an alchemist,

the tired script poses the usual to-be-or-not-to-be-undying question.

**CROOK CRACKERS** see *Of Cash and Hash*

*The **CROOKED CIRCLE** William Sistrom 1932 60m. Mus D: Val Burton. AD: Paul Roe Crawley. Ref: TV. Greg Luce. TVG. Turner/Price. V 10/4/32. With Tom Kennedy, Paul Panzer.

"There's a ghost in the house, and he plays a violin." It's the Crooked Circle, counterfeiters, vs. the Sphinx Club, criminologists, at Melody Manor, an "old mansion" on Long Island where the clock likes to strike thirteen, and "something always happens to somebody" when a certain "strange melody" is played on a violin. ("That joint's full of ghosts.")

The most curious aspect of this generally undistinguished old-house mystery chiller is that there are two separate mysteries—the Crooked Circle and the phantom violinist are not in cahoots. The latter (an "eccentric old musician") is a loose end, more or less, tied up only after the rounding up of the gang members. The two resident eccentrics—weird Old Dan (Christian Rub) and mad chuckler Harmon (Raymond Hatton)—"They call me Harmon the hermit"—liven things up a bit. However, the main offbeat character is C. Henry Gordon's Hindu mystic Yoganda. (Gordon also played the swami in *Thirteen Women.*) Yoganda keeps one character in suspended animation ("We of India frequently practice it") overnight so that he won't be murdered, and his big line ("Evil is on the way!") gets funnier each of the four or five times he says it. ("Yoganda has an uncanny faculty for seeing into the future.") Accidentally Funniest Line Award, though, must go to: (Ben Lyon, to Irene Purcell) "Thelma! You in the Secret Service!?" At one point, spilled glue on a cloth makes a skeleton seem to move. ("I was chased by the ghost himself!")

**CROQUEUSES, Les** see *Comtesse Perverse, La*

The **CROSS OF SEVEN JEWELS** (I) G.C. Pictures 1987 color/ws 86m. (*Crocifisso di Sette Gioiellos*). SP, D, Ed: Marco Andolfi. Ph: Carlo Poletti. Mus: Paolo Rustichelli. PD: Massimo Corevi. SpFX: Eddy Endolf. Mkp: Marini, Mattei, Cioffi. Ref: TV: MV; Eng. dubbed. Palmerini: *La Croce delle 7 Pietre.* With Annie Belle, Eddy Endolf, Gordon Mitchell, Paolo Fiorino, Zaira Zoccheddu.

"Something outside of normality" is amok in Naples. This werewolf is hairy on his forearms and most of his face and he makes his victims melt. The not-so-mysterious mystery of the crucial cross is solved within the movie long after it's solved by the viewer: Wearing it keeps our hero, Michael, from turning into a wolf. ("It's my whole life.") In a flashback, the Most Hairy Fella of all makes Michael's mom explode. At the end, the Son of God seems to bless our hero, who has retrieved his cross .... Fantasy fiasco alternates between the unpleasant and the mind-boggling. The transformations are not Hall of Fame material, the music is mainly annoying, and the s&m scenes are irrelevant. Main selling point: the human/werewolf sex.

**CROSSING, The** see *Haunting of Sarah Hardy, The*

**CROSSTALK** (Austral.) Wall To Wall (Errol Sullivan) 1982 color 82m. SP, D: Mark Egerton. SP: also L. Lane, D. Whitburn. Ref:

Hardy/SF: "pedestrian." With Gary Day, Penny Downie, Brain McDermott.

Sentient surveillance system.

The CROW Miramax (Dimension) & EMI/Crowvision (Pressman-Most) 1994 color 101m. D: Alex Proyas. SP: David J. Schow, John Shirley, from James O'Barr's comic book series & comic strip. Ph: D. Wolski. Mus: G. Revell. PD: A. McDowell. VisFxSup: Andrew Mason. SpMkpFX: Lance Anderson? Digital Compositing: Motion Pixel? Ref: TV: Miramax video. ad. SFChron 5/13/94. Vallejo T-H 5/13/94. With Brandon Lee (Eric Draven), Ernie Hudson, Michael Wincott, Rochelle Davis, David Patrick Kelly, Jon Polito.

"There ain't no comin' back!" Eric Draven comes back from the grave to "put the wrong things right." Now, as one of the "creatures of the night," he has flashback visions of the murder of his fiancee and himself. Self-healing and invulnerable, the "bird man" tracks down the killers.... Stylish updating of *The Walking Dead* is an okay fantasy of urban justice. The best of it: the Draven-wrought reconciliation of the druggie mom and her daughter, and the slowmo shots of the crow. Also neat: the crow outline made of fire. The worst of it: Draven's glib Freddy-isms, and Lee's uncertain performance. The head thug's psychic glimpse of another's pain recalls a similar sequence in *Brother from Another Planet*.

The CRUCIFER OF BLOOD (U.S.-B) TNT-TV/Agamemnon Films & British Lion & Lynch Ent. (Turner Pictures) 1991 color c110m. Tel, D, P: Fraser Heston. From Paul Giovanni's play, based on Sir Arthur Conan Doyle's book *The Sign of the Four*. Mus: Carl Davis. PD: Tony Woollard. Prosth: Nick Dudman. SpFxSup: Neil Corbould. Ref: TV. TVG. V 11/11/91. With Charlton Heston, Richard Johnson, Susannah Harker, John Castle, Clive Wood, Simon Callow, Edward Fox, Roly Lamas (leper).

"This curse business—do you think there's anything in it?" Occasionally entertainingly shameless, full-throttle mystery features horrific elements, including visions of coffins, "apparitions" at windows, horrible curses, and lepers-as-menaces. Compare early-talkie British-and-India shriekies like *Unholy Night* and *House of Mystery*.

The CRUCIFIXION (H.K.) P.U. Prod./Sure Winner 1994 color feature. D: Ko Lam Pau. Ref: vc box: crucifixion killings. With M. Chow, H. Tsui.

Las CRUELES (Sp) Films Montana 1969 (1971) color/ws 100m. *Exquisite Cadaver* - ad t. *El Cadaver Exquisito*). Story, SP, D: Vicente Aranda. SP: also Antonio Rabinad. Mus: Marco Rossi. Ref: Lee (SpCin). V 3/3/71. Hardy/HM: shot in English; "at times pleasantly macabre." With Capucine, Carlos Estrada, Teresa Gimpera, Judy Matheson.

"Terror-thriller" (Hardy) re a madwoman (Capucine) who mails a married man (Estrada) body parts.

The CRUSH WB/J. G. Robinson (Morgan Creek) 1993 color 89m. SP, D: Alan Shapiro. Mus: G. Revell. Ref: V 4/12/93: "by the numbers." SFChron. ad. With Cary Elwes, Alicia Silverstone (Darian), Jennifer Rubin, Amber Benson.

"Not a psychological thriller so much as a monster movie" (SFC) re a "psychotic yet seductive" (V) teenager.

*CRY OF THE WEREWOLF Wallace MacDonald 1944 (*Daughter of the Werewolf* - shooting t). Story: G. Jay. AD: Lionel Banks, George Brooks. Ref: TV. V 8/16/44. Lee. Hardy/HM. Glut/TDB: caped, Dracula-like mannikin. Scheuer. Maltin '92.

Ingredients: Celeste La Tour (Nina Foch), werewolf daughter of a werewolf mother ... Elsa Chauvet (Osa Massen), from Transylvania, whom Celeste briefly hypnotizes into becoming her "sister" in horror ... the La Tour Museum, New Orleans, operated by Dr. Charles Morris (Fritz Leiber) of the Society of Psychic Research—the museum houses the "finest collection of occult and supernatural manifestations ever gathered beneath one roof" ... an enlarged photo of voodoo soul-transference rites ... and a devil doll "from the old country"—a "warning of death".... Flat-footed horror-fantasy is of interest now only for its bits and pieces of other films of the time, including *Cat People* (Massen's Elsa, a ringer in face and voice for Simone Simon, is suspected of being a werewolf), *The Wolf Man* (Blanche Yurka has the Maria Ouspenskaya-like role of the gypsy high priestess who tells Celeste, "You cannot help the things that have been or the things that must be—it is your destiny. You are the daughter of a werewolf!"), and *The Mummy* (strange horrors drive John Abbott's museum tour guide mad). Comic-creep specialist Milton Parsons, as an undertaker, is relatively subdued, and Abbott is only a spiel or two and a brief mad act. Perhaps the script's most intriguing element: the gypsy tribe which buries its dead once a year. (In the interim, it keeps the dead on ice in Parsons' funeral home.) The werewolves here are just harmless-looking wolves.

CRY WILDERNESS Visto Int'l./Philip Yordan, Jay Schlossberg-Cohen 1987. D: Schlossberg-Cohen. SP: Yordan. Mus: F. Heede. Ref: V 3/18/87: "one of the worst films ever made." 2/21/90:283 (ad). With Eric Foster, Maurice Grandmaison, Griffin Casey, John Tallman.

Bigfoot amok.

CRY WOLF WB-FN (Henry Blanke) 1947 83m. D: Peter Godfrey. SP: Catherine Turney, from Marjorie Carleton's novel. Ph: Carl Guthrie. Mus: Franz Waxman. AD: Carl Jules Weyl. SpFX: William McGann, Robert Burks. Mkp: Perc Westmore. Ref: TV. LC. Scheuer. Higham/HITF. V(d) 7/1/47: "horror & suspense." NYT 7/19/47. Maltin '92. FD 7/1/47. Cue 7/19/47. LAT 8/9/47. *LA Daily News* 8/9/47. pr. Academy. With Barbara Stanwyck, Errol Flynn, Geraldine Brooks, Richard Basehart, Jerome Cowan, John Ridgely, Helene Thimig, Paul Stanton, Lisa Golm, Paul Panzer, Creighton Hale.

Willies-inducing elements include an insane man "risen from the dead" ("Most of the time he's quite normal—then something happens that upsets him and he goes berserk") ... a girl with nightmares re screams in the night ... a secret lab ("What's going on in the laboratory?") ... a storm ... skulking about a gloomy mansion ("ghostly steps in the night"—Cue) ... ear-shattering midnight chimes ... and creepy music.... Tired Gothic intrigue, with little rooting interest except musical (thanks to Waxman). Heroines/heroes/villains—however they're ultimately sorted out here—are all dramatically nebulous. Flynn's version of fellow actor Tom Conway (dry, debonair) is less adept than Tom Conway's. Climax ties it all up over-neatly.

**CRYING BLUE SKY** see *Eyes of Fire*

**CRYSTAL FORCE** Vista Street Ent. (Feifer-Miller/MMC) 1992 (1990) color 82m. D: Laura Keats. SP: Jared Brady, Jerry Daly. Ph: Roger Olkowski. Mus: Keith Bilderbeck. PD: Gary Lee Reed. SpFxMkp: Scott Colter. SpVisFX: William Mims. Ref: TV: VS video. Martin. V 9/7/92:10 (rated). With Katherine McCall, John Serrdakue, Tony C. Burton (Beazel), G.L. Reed (demon).

"Crystal centerpiece" is demon's gateway. (Martin) Purchased at Beazel's "one of a kind shop" ("a really weird place"), the crystal harbors a demon which generates softcore sex scenes, appears briefly at a seance, and rapes a woman. Meanwhile, Beazel skulks and cackles.... Phony from word one of the dialogue. The crystal is a "five-cornered door of death," according to some narration.

**CRYSTAL FORCE II: DARK ANGEL** Vista Street Ent./Goblin Craft 1994 color 88m. D, P: James Mackinnon. SP: P. Quinn. Ph: M. Gordon. Mus: B. Mosley. MkpFX: Jeff Himmel. Ref: TV: VS video. With Paul Brewster (Virgil), Christopher Zawalalski, Betsy Gardner, Gloria Lusiak, Jeff Markle.

Virgil Starkweather, geek, causes trouble in a bar and seems to be impervious to bullets. Is he the devil's envoy preying on the vulnerable? Talky shot-on-taper is not as bad as the first *Force*, but is perhaps even more cheaply made. The lobby to hell is inhabited by zombie-types.

The **CRYSTAL SWORD** (I) Idea Int'l. 1984 feature. D: Massimo Tarantini. Ref: V 5/4/83:298: "back to primitive times."

**CRYSTAL TRIANGLE** (J) Central Park Media/MOVIC (Sony Video) 1987 ('92-U.S.) anim color 87m. Ref: TV: Sony Video; scattered Eng.; OAV. SFChron Dtbk 7/12/92:58.

Fairish blend of sf, metaphysical mystery, and adventure concerns aliens who apparently first visited Earth during the dinosaur era ... an ancient box which emits rays, then produces two small crystal pyramids, which ultimately form a star which, in turn, summons a "temple" out of the ground (the temple proves to be a departing spaceship) ... a Japanese lady who is taken up in a mystical bubble in a lost temple then, at the end, boards the spaceship ... a wizened, weird-looking old gent whose shout shatters glass and mountains ... a Kyoto mystic who turns into a reptilian monster with an eye in its mouth ... and a horde of mystics/monsters. Some similarities to *The Legend of Wisely.*

**CTHULHU MANSION** see *Black Magic Mansion*

**El CUARTO CHINO** (Mex) Famous Players Int'l./Clasa Films & Sagitario Filmes 1967 color c95m. SP, D: Albert Zugsmith. From Vivian Connell's novel "The Chinese Room." Ph: Gabriel Figueroa. Mus: G. C. Carrion. AD: Manuel Fontanals. Ref: TV: Madera Cinevideo; some Eng. Lee (P/Richardson). VSB: 1971. Hardy/HM. With Guillermo Murray, Elizabeth Campbell, Carlos Rivas, Regina Torne, Cathy Crosby, German Robles, Carlos East.

"This is the story of a strange marriage"—and of hypnotism, madness, one automatic typewriter ("Death is near this house"),

and two visualized nightmares re some gory "operating table" cannibalism, a laughing dancing skeleton, a skeletal phantom, and human "pendulums".... Typically dated, trashy Zugsmith fare from the Psychedelic Sixties. The nightmare gore is surprisingly graphic, if hokey.

**CUO WEI** see *Dislocation*

**CURADOS DE ESPANTOS: SE LES METIO EL DIABLO** (Mex) Televicine/Filmoimagen 1990? color 88m. Idea, SP, D: Adolfo Martinez Solares. Idea, SP: Gilberto Martinez Solares. SP: also Daniel M. Peterson, Juan M. Soler. Ph: A. Castillon. Mus: E. Cortazar. SpFX: Arturo Godines; (latex) Gabriel Garcia Marquez. Ref: TV: Million Dollar Video; no Eng. Cassell's: *Ghostly Chill* - tr t. TVG. With Alfonso Zayas, Roberto "Flaco" Guzman (Vladimir), Lina Santos, Cesar Bono, Rene "Tun Tun" Ruiz, Claudio Sorel (Profesor Solares), Michaelle Mayer (la embrujada).

Old Dracula—or a reasonable facsimile—is first discovered mummified in a Mexican pyramid and fangs a nurse to become young again. Curiously, he flies, not as a bat, but in human form, and at one point he gets drunk on a drunken woman's blood. Twice, the sun's rays set him on fire. On the same bill: Igor—a Renfield-type who uses a long, long tongue to scoop up bugs— and a "brujo exorcista."

In a funny running gag, the vampire keeps crashing through windows and into walls and doors. Most of the movie, though, seems stuck between not-quite-comedy and not-quite-straight action. At the end, twin vampire infants sport baby fangs.

**CURIOSITY KILLS** USA-TV/MCA-TV (Davis Ent.) 1990 color c90m. D: Colin Bucksey. Tel: Joe Batteer, John Rice. SpFxCoord: Jerry Williams. SdFX: Bald Eagle. Ref: TV. V 6/27/90:54.

Suspenser contains one borderline-sf element—an "electronic marvel that can listen in on distant confabs" (cf. *Rogues Gallery*) and the aim of which seems to be directed by a telescope device—and some borderline-horror elements—a *Diabolique* nightmare in which a dead-man-in-a-tub sits up, a *Halloween* shock in which the killer "returns to life," and a bit of offscreen gore. ("He cut out his tongue!") Not enough mystery to carry the story and not much suspense until the end.

**CURSE** (H.K.) Angle Jo 1987? color/ws? c87m. D: Kong Yeung. Ref: TV: Ocean Shores Video; Eng. titles. with Maria Jo, Elisa Ye, Isabel Lopez, Susan Brandy.

Settings: Hong Kong and Manila. Maria sees the reincarnation of her dead lover of forty years ago, Roberto, in Robert Lam, but he does not remember her. She cuts a deal with sorcerer "Bad Ramau": his love medicine in exchange for her body (after she loses her virginity to Robert). The medicine works, but she cheats Ramau. A good sorcerer's daughter must sacrifice her virginity to stop the evil wizard (the latter coughs up various animals and dies) and lift the snakeskin-stomach curse on Robert.... Undistinguished mixture of horror, romance, and softcore sex scenes.

The **CURSE** (J) Japan Columbia 1990 anim 45m. Ref: Animag 10:4: OAV.

1) Girl dreams of "vampire's attack."

2) Girls explore haunted mansion.

**The CURSE** (U.S.-I) TWE/Assonitis-Diamant-Fulci 1987 color/ws 87m. (*The Farm* - orig t). D: David Keith. SP: David Chaskin. Mus: John Debney. VisFX: Kevin Erham. Mkp: Frank Russell. Models: Mark Moller. FxConsul: Bob Glaser. Opt: Video Gamma. Ref: TV. V 5/20/87. Phantom: loosely based on H. P. Lovecraft's story "The Colour out of Space." Cinef. HBO Guide 12/90. With Wil Wheaton, Claude Akins, Malcolm Danare, Cooper Huckabee, John Schneider, Amy Wheaton, Kathleen Jordan Gregory.

A meteorite-like ball ("that thing that landed in Nathan's backyard") strikes the Earth near a farm outside Tellico Plains, Tennessee. Soon, Nathan's (Akins) produce is looking mighty fine on the outside, not-so-fine on the inside; the cows are going all to hell; and Ma (Gregory) doesn't look like Ma. In terms of prophecy, Revelations 8:10-11 ("a great star fell from heaven ... and ... the waters became wormwood, and many men died of the water....") accounts for the modern-day horrors; in scientific terms, a previously unknown element has altered the molecular structure of the water around Nathan's place; and in psychological terms, it's Pa's unbendingness and Ma's infidelity that produce the curse.... In *The Curse*, ghastly sores and drool equal moral rot. The big dumb bully son looks just like he deserves to look. Ma becomes an alien thing at best. And the house self-destructs. Only the innocent—little brother Zachary and sister Alice—escape. The guilty are walking Pictures of Dorian Gray. If *The Curse* begins shakily, with over-familiar characters, it finishes solidly, with each reverse-*Enchanted Cottage* twist more enjoyably ghoulish than the last.

See also: *Seventh Sign, The.*

**CURSE II: THE BITE** (U.S.-I-J) TWE/Assonitis & Viva Ent. & Towa (Trihoof Investments) 1989 color 98m. (*The Bite* - orig t). D: Fred Goodwin. SP: Susan Zelouf, Federico Prosperi. Mus: Carlo Maria Cordio. SpFX: Screaming Mad George. Opt: Videogamma. Ref: TV. V 8/23/89: no narrative relation to *The Curse* (TWE). 5/3/89:13 (rated). With Jill Schoelen, J. Eddie Peck, Jamie Farr, Bo Svenson, Sydney Lassick.

"Mama, I want to see the hand!" Yellow Sands Nuclear Testing Base, in Arizona—"one big dumping ground" for toxic waste—yields gremlin-like dogs and mutant snakes. Snake bites hero (Peck), and the poison somehow "replaces" the genetic code of his forearm. Result: a deadly snake-head hand. Clark severs the head, but a new, super snake-head emerges with a tentacle-like killer-tongue.... Against all odds, the enthrallingly gross climax here comes up with several permutations of herpetological horror not covered by the *Zuma* films. Among the delights: apparent snake afterbirth, or maybe just snakebarf, a cascade of baby snakes, and the big wriggler out the host's mouth. Other filmic cross references (subhead: Embarrassing and/or Homicidal Limbs, and other body attachments) include *Rabid, Evil Dead II,* and the original *The Fly.* Scene-by-scene developments with the mutating hand/head are much closer to Just Absurd Enough than to Fully Credible, though the movie really doesn't cut loose and run wild often enough.

**CURSE III: BLOOD SACRIFICE** (S. African) Epic Prods./Blue Rock Films & Screen Media & Three's Company (Christopher Coy/Panga) 1991 (1990) color 89m. (*Panga* - orig t). SP, D: Sean Barton. SP: also John Hunt. Story: R. H. Haines. Mus: J. Laxton, P. Van Blerk. Creature: Chris Walas. SpFxSup: Beverley McLeish. Mkp: Bobby van der Westhuizen. Ref: TV. V 7/1/91:36 (hv). VWB. With Christopher Lee, Jenilee Harrison, Henry Cele, Andre Jacobs, Zoe Randall, Olivia Dyer, Dumi Shongwe (witch doctor).

East Africa, 1950. A witch doctor curses those who interrupt the blood sacrifice of a goat and apparently allow a baby to die: "The spirit that lives in the sea"—a full-fledged gill-man-type—appears near the end of the picture to wreak havoc.... A washout. Slim premise and much padding. Lee's Dr. Pearson proves, not surprisingly, to be a good guy. ("I sacrificed a goat.")

**CURSE IV: THE ULTIMATE SACRIFICE** (U.S.-I) Empire & Eden (Hope Perello/Debra Dion) 1988 color 85m. (*Catacombs* - orig t). D & Exec Co-P: David Schmoeller. SP: Giovanni Di Marco, R. Barker Price. Mus: Pino Donaggio. SpFxMkp: Tom Floutz. Ref: TV. V 5/25/88. Martin. PT 16:63. Fango 122:12. Cinef 12/93:59. TVG. With Timothy Van Patten, Laura Schaeffer, Jeremy West, Ian Abercrombie, Vernon Dobtcheff, Feodor Chaliapin, Brett Porter (possessed albino), Michael Pasby (Jesus Christ), Mapi Galan (Antonia), Nicola Morelli (the inquisitor).

A "man touched by the devil" and sealed in the "kinda spooky" catacombs of The Abbey of San Pietro en Valle, in the year 1506, is released in the present day. This apparent "beast of the Apocalypse" impersonates or possesses humans, slashes with "claws," and brings a statue of Christ to murderous life. Plus a woman (Galan) who "knows things before they happen." Low-voltage, cliched horror-fantasy with familiar demonic tricks.

**CURSE OF EVIL** (H.K.) 1982 color feature (*Xie Zhou*). D: Gui Zhihong. Ref: Monster! 11/91 (Higuchi): "gross-out horror."

**CURSE OF SOMETHING BESTIAL, The** see *Demon Cop*

**CURSE OF THE ALPHA STONE** United HV/Beck 1985 (1984?) color 90m. D: Stewart Malleon. Ref: VSB. Stanley. Phantom: "rich in unintentional mirth." V/CHVD. V 10/24/84:243 (ad). Bowker '90. With Jim Scotlin, Sandy Carey.

Professor's formula turns student into homicidal maniac.

**CURSE OF THE BLUE LIGHTS** Tamarack Prods. & Blue Lights 1988 color c95m. (*Blue Lights* - alt t). Story, SP, D, Ph, Ed, P: John Henry Johnson. Story: also Bryan Sisson. Mus: Randall Crissman. MkpFX: Wizard FX (Mark Sisson et al). Ref: TV: Magnum Ent. video. V 6/6/90. 5/6/91:C-40. With Brent Ritter (Loath), Bettina Julius (the witch); Kent E. Fritzell and Willard Hall (the ghouls); Andy Asbury et al (zombies), George Schanze (The Muldoon Man).

"The Muldoon Man will return soon!" Dudley, Colorado. Loath, leader of the Ghoul Clan, and his "workers of the darkness," Bor and Forn, literally a couple of ghouls, plot to use dissolved human bodies in order to revive the petrified Muldoon Man, a "creature that ruled the Earth a long time ago." They succeed.... Heavy-handed pseudo-camp features meant-to-be-priceless touches, such as Loath's petting the snake wrapped around his shoulders. The script's would-be-jolly horrors and surprises are generally telegraphed and too labored to amuse.

**CURSE OF THE CANNIBAL CONFEDERATES** see *Curse of the Screaming Dead, The*

**CURSE OF DRACULA, The** see *World of Dracula, The*

**\*2 CURSE OF THE DEMON** 1957. Ref: TV: vt.

Lighting effects and its subtler supernatural details distinguish this horror classic re the "fire demon" Asmodeus, or Moloch, and the Order of the True Believer. Chilling: the "watery" effect as Karswell (Niall MacGinnis) leaves the British Museum ... the reports of a "monstrous, smoky shape" ... the unusual "cold" which hero Dana Andrews feels ... the magically "clean" business card ... the mad-cricket sounds in the corridor ... and the demonic tune running through Andrews' mind. It's the spectral lights as much as the shadows which create the atmosphere outside Karswell's house during Andrews' night walk; there's also a neat back-to-normal, post-demon-fireball night-bird sound here. Occasionally, director Jacques Tourneur and company try too hard, and the eeriness dissipates. Too much of everything, for instance—music, thunder-and-lightning, "logical explanations" dialogue—hurts one of the "escaping" parchment scenes. In the most substantial of the restored, new-to-the-U.S. scenes, a queasy Karswell explains to his mother (Athene Seyler) the "fear" which goes with his power: "I can't stop it. I can't give it back."

**CURSE OF THE FULL MOON** see *Rats Are Coming, The!*

**The CURSE OF THE HOUSE SURGEON** Postal Prods. 1991 color 113m. D: Steve Postal. Ref: Martin: "tripe about a pseudo-exorcist for homes." With Kendrick Kaufman, Jennifer Tuck, Angela Shepard, Angel Langley.

**CURSE OF THE LIVING DEAD** see *Nightstalker* (1981)

**CURSE OF THE MONASTERY** see *Maldicion del Monasterio, La*

**The CURSE OF THE POLTERGEIST** (H. K.) 198-? color c88m. Ref: TV: Wonderful Video; Eng. titles. Suiki: above is tr t.

A god trapped for a hundred years in a figurine helps Chuma seduce Chan Che, a man from Hong Kong who is visiting Thailand. Back in Hong Kong, Chan Che sees his arm get "suddenly rotten," and his hand turns into a big hairy paw—a sort of Paw of Orlac with a life of its own—and it attacks his wife, Wai. Later, the pregnant Wai dies, but (thanks to her cousin, Li Nan) she and her unborn come back as dolls. Meanwhile, freed from its prison, the god possesses Chuma and turns her into a long-fanged vampire.... Basically formula sorcery fantasy has some light moments, as the ghostly Wai plays tricks on Chan Che's cop pals ("It's strange here")—or, He Who Gets Invisibly Slapped. Li Nan is a spunky intermediary between her sorcerer father and the forces of evil.

**CURSE OF THE QUEERWOLF** Pirromount Pictures (Bandera) 1989 color 90m. SP, D, P: Mark Pirro. Mus: G. Gross. Ref: V 9/20/89:42 (hv): "extremely funny." PT 7:49: "some funny moments." Ecran F 79:10-11. Fango 89:12. With Michael Palazzolo, Kent Butler, Taylor Whitney, Cynthia Brownell, Forrest J Ackerman.

Bitten by a werewolf, Larry Smalbut (Palazzolo) "turns into a Queerwolf when the moon is full...." (V)

**3P The CURSE OF THE SCREAMING DEAD** Troma/Little Warsaw 1982 color c90m. (*Curse of the Cannibal Confederates* - alt t). D, P: Tony Malanowski. SP & SpSdFX: Lon Huber. Concept: Tony Starke. Ph: Richard Geiwitz, Gary Becker. Mus: Charlie Barnett. Sets: Conway Gainesford. SpMkpFX: Bart Mixon. Mkp: Larry Schlechter et al. Ref: TV: Mogul video. V 10/20/82:139 (ad). 10/21/87:162. Mifed'89:196. Hound. no Phantom. McCarty II. no Martin. Stanley. With Steve Sandkuhler, Christopher Gummer, Rebecca Bach, Mimi Ishikawa, Judy Dixon.

"They don't want us here!" The theft of a diary from a Confederate graveyard on Agony Ridge resurrects the dead there—Barbados "heathen voodoo" is apparently the key.... There's a tombstone in the graveyard for John Carpenter, and a credit for casting to "The Walter Paisley Organization," but this amateurish, talky, poorly-edited thing is not a comedy. The centerpiece gore sequence is just as mercilessly extended as all other scenes. Pretentiously, the script invokes not only the Civil War, but Hiroshima. A real "fast forward" film.

**CURSE OF THE UNDEAD: YOMA** see *Youma 1*

**CURSE OF THE VAMPIRE** or **CURSE OF THE VAMPYR** see *Llamada del Vampiro*

**CURSE OF THE WICKED WIFE** (H. K.) 1984 feature (aka *Wicked Wife*). D: Wong King-Fang. Ref: Jones. NST! 4:20: "confused."

Vampires and "death bugs."

**CURSE OF THE ZOMBI** (H.K.) J. Ferreira 1989 color/ws 78m. D: Hao Lee. Ref: TV: Tai Seng Video; Eng. titles. Weisser/ATC: "a lot of fun." With Shaojun Lau, Xiao Yan Ze.

"Sorcerer Shin's magic is still working." Ingredients in this rather dismal horror-fantasy include a flying zombie animated by Sorcerer Shin ... the gross Worm Blood delicacy ... fake ghosts ... a flying coffin ... a magic bow and arrow ... and a good sorcerer.

**CURSE OF URSULA** (I) 1978 color feature (*La Sorella di Ursula*). SP,D: Enzo Milioni. Mus: Mimi Uva. Ref: MV: "slasher/horror film." ETC/Giallos: "stinks." Palmerini. With Barbara Magnolfi, Stefania D'Amario, Marc Porel.

**CURSED** (Can.) Pax(Jean-Marc Felio) 1990 color 87m. D: Mychel Arsenault. SP: Felio, Pierre Dalpe. Ref: V 10/15/90: "exceptionally bad." With Ron Lea, Catherine Colvey, Tom Rack.

Demon gargoyle.

**CURSED VILLAGE IN YUDONO MOUNTAIN** (J) 1984 color feature (*Yudono Sanroku Noroimura*). D: T. Ikeda. Ref: Weisser/JC: "mummy ghost" movie. With T. Nagashima, E. Nagashima.

Monk's ghost slaughters villagers.

**CUT AND RUN** (I) 1984 color 90m. (*Inferno in Diretta*). D: Ruggero Deodato. Ref: V 5/7/86: Michael Berryman "photographed as a monstrosity"; gore excised? Bob Moore: Indians treated as semi-monsters. no Maltin '92. Hound. Ecran F 48:71: "strange cult." 66:80-81: "realist" horror; "terrifiants." Martin. no McCarty II. Scheuer. MV: aka *Straight to Hell*; "cannibal action-adventure ... much, much more jungle gore." VSOM: aka *Amazon Savage Adventure*. Film Superstore: aka *Amazonia*. Palmerini.

**CUTTING CLASS** Republic/Gower Street (April Films/Edor Financial Group) 1989 (1988) color 90m. D: Rospo Pallenberg. SP: Steve Slavkin. Mus: Jill Fraser. SpFX: Robert McCarthy. Mkp: Kathy Shorkey. Ref: TV. V 9/27/89. With Donovan Leitch, Jill Schoelen, Brad Pitt, Roddy McDowall, Martin Mull, Robert Glaudini, Norman Alden.

"We stay calm we'll all be dead!" Dead high school staff and students include victims of murder instruments such as a knife, a kiln, a flagstaff, and a copy machine. Hammer and drill gore is reserved for the execution of the killer.... Offbeat but pointless cross between the standard slasher movie and a teen problem drama.

**CU'UN SAE HAN NYO** (S. Korean) Century Co./Won Sik Im 1972 color/ws 90m. (aka *The Revengeful Ghost*). D: Im. SP: Sung Yub Kim. Ref: Hardy/HM: "strikingly poetic" camera effects (by Chang Bok Ahn). With Soomi Oh, Yang Ha Yoon, Yun Yung Woo.

Young woman's ghost haunts her lover and his new wife.

**CY WARRIOR: SPECIAL COMBAT UNIT** (I) Fulvia (Fabrizio De Angelis) 1989 color/ws 88m. (aka *Cyborg: Il Guerriero d'Acciaio*) D: Giannetto De Rossi. Ph: Giovanni Bergamini. SpSetFX: Paolo Ricci. Opt: Videogamma. Ref: TV: VSOM; no Eng. V/Cannes '89:499: completed. 10/21/87:369(ad). 5/4/88:322. Palmerini. With H. Silva, F. Zagarino, Sherri Rose, Brandon Hammond, James Summers.

The "cyborg warrior" holes up with a woman and her young son. Semi-high-point: Cy cuts open his leg to adjust his gears. [Insert admiring looks from mom and boy.] A bit better: the Peeling off the Old Face (and Pouring on a New One) scene—at least there are no foolish reaction shots. Film is an example of that very beatable combo: action and sentiment.

**CYBER BANDITS** I.R.S./Cyberfilms 1995 (1994) color c86m. D: E. Fleming. SP: Robinson, Beard. Ref: PT 22:11-12: "cliche adventure." vc box. With Alexandra Paul, Martin Kemp, Adam Ant, Grace Jones, Robert Hays, James Hong, Henry Gibson.

"In the future," with "virtual nonsense and hologram strippers."(PT)

**CYBER-C.H.I.C.** see *Robo-C.H.I.C.*

**CYBER CITY DATA FILE-2** (J) c1991 anim color 45m. Ref: Japan Video.

**CYBER CITY OEDO 808: DATA-1: ANCIENT MEMORIES** (J) Japan Home Video 1990 anim color 42m. D.:Yoshiaki Kawajiri. Ref: TV: JHV; no Eng.; OAV. V. Max 3:24-25. Animation Mag 5:26, 48.

Year 2808, in a fully-automated Tokyo, where Cyber Police use dynamite-collared criminals to catch criminals, and tank-like weapons rumble down the streets. The dead computer programmer Amachi "returns" through a computer ("Kill you"), uses "cybernetic implants" to control the skyscraper housing him/it, and knocks out the building's "internal gyroscope," thereby creating an instant Leaning Tower of Pisa effect.... The computer/cables/corpse combination is suitably ghoulish. But despite its *Blade Runner*-ish, high-tech, new-wave look, *Cyber City* is basically conventional sf-horror.

**CYBER NINJA** see *Mirai Ninja*

**CYBER TRACKER** PM Ent. (Don Wilson) 1994 color 91m. D, Co-P: Richard Pepin. SP: Jacobsen Hart. Ph: Ken Blakey. Mus: Popeil, Montei. PD: Steve Ramos. SpFxMkp: Mark Sisson. SpFX: Don Power, Larry Roberts. Computer Graphics:(vis fx sup) F.H. Isaacs;(opt fx sup) Dave Gregory. MechFX: Mkp & FX Labs. Ref: TV. Vallejo Times-Herald. With Don "The Dragon" Wilson, Richard Norton, Stacie Foster, Joseph Ruskin, Abby Dalton, Jim Maniaci (The Trackers).

"He's a robot!" Ingredients include Cybercore's "computerized justice" and "robot executioners" ... a badroid blown up with a bomb "morphed" into its stomach ... Agnes 4000, a home-computer-security system ... and an insta-pistol.... Routine vehicle for stuntwork.

**CYBEREDEN** (I) Eidoscope & Canal Plus (Airoldi-Dionisio) 1993 color 108m (aka *Jackpot*). D, P: Mario Orfini. SP: G. Giardiello, R. Iannone, Orfini, M. Ember, A. Celentano. Mus: Giorgio Moroder, A. Marinelli. Ref: V 3/22/93: "mesmerizingly misguided." 10/19/92:142. Palmerini. With Adriano Celentano, Kate Vernon, Christopher Lee, Carroll Baker.

"Computer-generated Eden" goes awry when tot enters "menacing computer world."

**CYBERNATOR** Vista Street (Jerry Feifer) 1992 (1991) color 84m. D: Robert Rundle. Ref: Martin: futuristic. V 10/14/91:M-48. 6/1/92:14 (rated). With Lonnie Schuyler, Christina Peralta, William Smith, J. K. Williams.

Cyborg assassins.

**CYBERNETICS GUARDIAN** (J) CPM/Asmik/Soshin-A.I.C. 1989('95-U.S.) anim color c45m. (aka *Sacred Cyber Beast Cy-Guard* or *Holy Machine Beast Saigard*). D: K. Ohata. SP: M. Sanjo. Mus: N. Yamanaka. Ref: TV: USManga Corps video; Eng. titles. Animag 8:4.

"And his name shall be Saldo!" The city of Cyber-Wood, 2019 A.D. Astenite—which absorbs "human psycho-wave energy"—and a guard suit worn by John Stalker produce the Astenite Guardian. In a matter of minutes, however, an evil spirit possesses John, and a sort of supernatural acupuncture produces the evil "Saldo," who then takes on a certain Adler in the Genocyber suit.... Bland foray into Good vs. Evil territory.

See also *Genocyber*.

**CYBORG** Cannon/Golan-Globus 1989 color 84m. D: Albert Pyun. SP: Kitty Chalmers. Mus: Kevin Bassinson. SpVisFX: Fantasy II; (sup) Gene Warren Jr., Ernie Farino. SpMkp: (fx) Greg Cannom; (coord) Cindy Rosenthal. SpFxSup: Joey Di-Gaetano, R. J. Hohman. Cyborg Cosmetics: MkpFx Unltd.; Bart Mixon, Aaron Sims. Ref: TV. V 4/7/89. ad. TVG: *Masters of the Universe II: The Cyborg* - alt t. With Jean-Claude Van Damme, Deborah Richter, Vincent Klyn, Dayle Haddon (Pearl Prophet).

"What's waiting for me, cyborg?" Slingers vs. Pirates in the postwar future. Chief sound effect: the crunch of bones. Chief (numbingly overused) camera effect: slow motion. The musical score alternates between conventional "pounding" and honest-to-goodness music.

**CYBORG[2]** (U.S.-Can.) Vidmark/Anglo-American & Films Int'l.(Raju Patel, Alain Silver) 1993 color/ws 99m. Ref: SP, D: Michael Schroeder. Story, SP: Ron Yanover, Mark Geldman. Ph: Jamie Thompson. Mus: Peter Allen. PD: E.A. Scott. SpMkpFX: KNB. SpFxCoord: Landerer, Hendrickson. VisFX: Stargate Films. Ref: TV: Vidmark video. Tower Video Releases: 11/24/93. PT 18:61: aka *Glass Shadow*. TVG: aka *Cyborg 2: Glass Shadow.* With Elias Koteas, Angelina Jolie, Allen Garfield, Billy Drago, Karen Sheperd, Tracey Walter, Jack Palance, Rick Hill.

Year 2074 ingredients: competition between Kobayashi Electronics (Japan) and Pinwheel Robotics (U.S.) for the cyborg market ... Glass Shadow, a "bio-explosive" inserted into cyborg Casella Reese (Jolie) ... "grand theft robot" ... an "equal opportunity terminator" ... "Benji the cyborg" ... and the "poet-warrior" cyborg Mercy (Palance) .... Some atmosphere, but not much else, thanks to a stillborn story. Palance has a fun last scene with Garfield, and a good line: "I have only one thing to say—incoming."

**CYBORG[3] THE RECYCLER** WarnerVision/FM Ent. 1995(1994) color c90m. D: Michael Schroeder. SP: B. Victor, T. Bolotnick. FX: J. C. Buechler. Ref: PT 22:70: cyborgs; "silly, cheap." vc box. With Richard Lynch, Zach Galligan, Malcolm McDowell, Kato Kaelin.

**CYBORG** see *Bionic Showdown, The. Return of the Six-Million Dollar Man and the Bionic Woman.*

**CYBORG (IL GUERRIERO D'ACCIAIO)** see *Cy Warrior*

**CYBORG COP** (Austral.) Trimark/Nu World/Nu Image (Danny Lerner) 1993 (1992) color 93m. (Cyborg Ninja - orig t). D: Sam Firstenberg. SP: Greg Latter. Ph: Joseph Wein. Mus: Paul Fishman. PD: John Rosewarne. Cyborg FX: Image Animation;(des) Steve Painter. SpFX: J. Wienand. Ref: TV. Stanley. SFChron Dtbk 2/6/94. TVG. V 5/11/92: shooting. 5/4/92:86 (ad). 2/22/93: A-122: at AFM. With David Bradley, John Rhys-Davies, Todd Jenson or Jensen, Alona or Alonna Shaw, Rufus Swart (cyborg).

"I have perfected the art of life itself." A "cyborg assassin" proves to be part of a "scientific new wave." Lame, straining-for-macho material. Rhys-Davies' bombastic bravado as Slime, Inc., is the sole bright spot.

**CYBORG COP II** Nu Image/New World (Danny Lerner) 1994 color 97m. Story, D: Sam Firstenberg. Ph: Y. Wein. Mus: Bob Mithoff. PD: J. Rosewarne. SpFxCoord: Rick Cresswell. Ref: V 6/6/94. With David Bradley, Morgan Hunter, Jill Pierce.

"Psycho ... turned into a new-model cyborg."

**CYBORG SOLDIER** (Austral.?) New Line HV/Nu World(Danny Lerner) 1993('95-U.S.) color feature. Story, D: Sam Firstenberg. SP: Jon Stevens. Ref: vc box: malfunctioning killer-cyborg. With David Bradley.

**CYCLE OF THE WEREWOLF** see *Stephen King's Silver Bullet*

**CYCLONE** CineTel/Paul Hertzberg 1987 color 86m. Story, D: Fred Olen Ray. SP: Paul Garson. Mus: David A. Jackson. SpFxCoord: Kevin McCarthy. Cyclone: Tracy Design Inc. Opt: Ray Mercer. Ref: TV: RCA-Col HV. HR 6/11/87. V 6/10/87. 6/17/87:28 (rated). TVG. With Heather Thomas, Jeffrey Combs, Ashley Ferrare, Dar Robinson, Martine Beswicke, Robert Quarry, Martin Landau, Huntz Hall, Troy Donahue, Dawn Wildsmith, Michael Reagan, Tim Conway Jr., Russ Tamblyn, Michael D. Sonye.

Scientist Rick Davenport's (Combs) five-million-dollar motorcycle, the Cyclone, features "jazzed up" Stealth-bomber paint, armor plating, turbo-charging, and "firepower equal to an F-16." The "heart of the Cyclone": a transformer which "can power a battleship all by itself, indefinitely," and which could be a "source of inexhaustible fuel. The transformer sucks hydrogen out of the atmosphere and converts it into energy".... The early scenes with Thomas and Combs are smooth, low key, and vaguely promising. Then: hokey villains, ultimatums to the bound-and-tortured, defiance by same, chases. The vacant plot simply delays the cycle-in-action payoff, and it ain't worth the wait.

**\*The CYCLOPS** WB/RKO (B&H) 1957 (1956). Ph: Ira Morgan. Mus: Albert Glasser. SpMkp: Jack H. Young. TechFX: Bert I. Gordon. OptFX: Consolidated. SpVoice FX: Paul Frees. SdFX: Douglas Stewart. Animal Seqs: Jim Dannaldson. Ref: TV. Warren/KWTS!: orig. to be RKO release. Hound. Phantom. Maltin '92. Scheuer. Martin. V 8/21/57. Weldon. Stanley. Lentz. Hardy/SF. Fango 123:19.

A heavy—and unexplained—dose of radiation stimulates the pituitary glands of animals in Mexico's Tarahumare Mountains, makes giants of a man ("He must be 25 feet tall!"), spiders, lizards, rodents, falcons, and snakes. Obligatory Bert Gordon lines include "Why are they so large?", "It's immense!", and a reference to an "animal as big as an elephant." Slapdash, disjointed movie features three fading, Forties movie stars (Lon Chaney Jr., James Craig, and Tom Drake), Bronson Canyon, larded-on exposition, disfigured-giant's-point-of-view shots ("The eye!"), a stab at pathos, slipshod effects photography and special makeup, and an abrupt, "Oh, are we happy now?" ending.

**CYCLOPS** (J) VSOM 199-? color 50m. D: Shougi Iida. TV: VSOM; Eng. titles. With Mayumi Hasegawa, Kai Atoh, K. Sano, Iyo Suzuki.

"His baby will be the first born of the new generation!" Semi-humans "created from two different species" come up with a surprise mutant arm, or two, in the tour de force mutant-vs.-mutant, elevator sequence here. And—at the end—is it a baby, or a motorin' *Fiend without a Face?* Shot-on-taper is a most effectivevehicle for some gross bloating makeup effects—Brave New Glop.

# D

**D.A.R.Y.L.** (B-U.S.) Para/John Heyman & Burtt Harris (World Film Services) 1985 color/ws 101m. D: Simon Wincer. SP: David Ambrose, Allan Scott, Jeffrey Ellis. Mus: Marvin Hamlisch. VisFX: (sup) Michael Fink; (coord) Robert Hewitt. SpMin: (construction) Greg Jein; (ph) Dream Quest. Des: (elec) F. K. Iguchi; (mech) Thomas Hollister. PhFxSup: Hoyt Yeatman. Anim: (motion control) Michael Bigelow; (map) Roto FX. Ref: TV. MFB'86:143-44. V 6/12/85. SFExam 6/14/85. With Mary Beth Hurt, Michael McKean, Colleen Camp, Josef Sommer, Barret Oliver (Daryl).

What the Department of Defense wants is a robot fighting man; what Dr. Stewart (Sommer) produces is Daryl—or, Data Analysing Robot Youth Lifeform—an "experiment in artificial intelligence," conceived in a test tube and fitted with a computer brain. Too "helpful and honest for a boy his age," Daryl picks up behavior patterns, acquires emotions and a sense of taste, and learns (from TV) a two-wheel car trick.... Alternately droll and mawkish (see Daryl cry), *D.A.R.Y.L.* begins well, but turns into formula hero-vs.-officialdom stuff. As in *The Invisible Boy*, the script caters to grandiose, little-boy fantasies—e.g., "race car" driver (on the freeway), jet pilot.

**DNA—FORMULA LETALE** see *Metamorphosis* (1990)

**D-1 DEVASTATOR** see *Devastator D-1*

**The D.P. MAN** Fat Dog 1992 color 82m. D: Jim Enright. SP: Cash Markman. Ref: Adam'94. With Francesca Le, Teri Diver, Ron Jeremy, T.T. Boy, Pearl Joyce.

In this "re-working of *Young Frankenstein*," a distant relation of the famous mad doctor creates a "two gun" creature.

**The D.P. MAN, PART 2** Fat Dog 1993? 83m. D: J. Enright. SP: C. Markman. Ref: Adam'94. With Tiffany Mynx, P.J. Sparxx, F. Le, R. Jeremy, P. Joyce.

**DAEMON** (B) Children's Film Unit (Colin Finbow) 1986 color 71m. SP, D: C. Finbow. Mus: David Hewson. Mkp: G. Wallace. Ref: MFB'86:233-34. Newman: "well-constructed ghost story." no Stanley. With Arnaud Morell, Susannah York, Bert Parnaby, Sadie Herlighy.

Ingredients: an eleven-year-old boy who believes he is demon-possessed ... a ghost ... and a teacher who is into demonology.

**DAFFY DUCK'S QUACKBUSTERS** WB/Steven S. Greene 1988 anim color 80m. Story, D: Greg Ford, Terry Lennon. Mus: Carl Stalling, Milt Franklyn, Hal Willner, William Lava. PD: Robert Givens. Anim: Mark Kausler et al. Ref: TV. Sacto Union 7/9/89. V 9/28/88.

In "Night of the Living Duck," the first of two original segments, guest monsters include Dracula, the Frankenstein monster and his bride, a werewolf, a mummy or two, the fly, Leatherface, a gill-man-type, an invisible man, a Godzilla-type, a blob-type, a Cyclops, Medusa, skeletons, a two-headed monster, and a pumpkinhead. Mild fun, in the manner of *Hollywood Steps out.*

In the also new, rather limp "The Duxorcist," Daffy Duck plays a paranormalist carrying on a "crusade against the undead." The bulk of the cartoon features erratic excerpts from past Warner cartoons like "Hyde and Go Tweet" (III), "Transylvania 6-5000" (***), "Claws for Alarm" (qq.v.), "The Abominable Snow Rabbit" (qq.v.), "Prize Pest" (qq.v.), "Water, Water Every Hare" (II), "Jumpin' Jupiter" (qq.v.), and the droll "Punch Trunk," re a "picayune pachyderm."

**DAI HADO ENJERUSU** see *Die Hard Angels* entries

**DAI TETSUJIN WAN SEBUN** see *Brain 17*

**DAIKANSHO KAMEN** see *Masked Rider*

**DAIKANYAMA HORROR** (J) Southern Cross Video Arts 199-? color 45m. Ref: TV: vt; no Eng.; shot-on-tape.

Ingredients include a horror-rock group which accosts three or four teenage girls and disembowels one of them ... "Freddie" and "Jason," who chase one teen, as a "baby" spears her ... and cannibalistic ghouls. Call it weird, call it warped, call it bad.

**DAKOTA HARRIS** see *Sky Pirates*

**DALEITAI** see *Flash—Future Kung Fu*

**DALLOS** see *Battle for Moon Station Dallos*

**DAMA ROSSA UCCIDE SETTE VOLTE, La** see *Corpse Which Didn't Want To Die, The*

**DAMSELVIS** Big Broad Films 1994 b&w & color c60m. SP, D, P: J. M. McCarthy. Ph: Hugh Gallagher. Ref: PT 19:17: "monster Elvis," gore, schoolgirl "killed then ... reborn." With S.L. Garris, G. Chasum.

**DANCE MACABRE** see *Danse Macabre*

**DANCE OF DEATH** see *House of Evil*

**DANCE OF THE DAMNED** Concorde/New Classics 1989 color 83m. (aka *Half Life*). SP, D: Katt Shea Ruben. SP, P: Andy Ruben. Mus: Gary Stockdale. SpFX: Steve Neill, Sirius FX. Ref: TV: Virgin Vision video. V 4/12/89. 10/19/88:174. Bill Warren. Phantom. Maltin '92. no Scheuer. no Martin. With Starr Andreeff, Cyril O'Reilly (Vampire), Tom Ruben, Maria Ford, Deborah Ann Nassar.

"I rarely feed." An unnamed, outcast vampire with supersight and super-hearing lures a dancer (Andreeff) from the Cafe Paradise to his home. Object: to learn more about the day and sunlight and, ultimately, to feed. At one point, the vampire has her drink some of his blood, and she temporarily enters the vampire state.... Typically for this sometimes imaginative fantasy-horror film, the latter sequence is an intriguing idea, though it's rather thrown away. At the least, *Dance of the Damned* is a one-of-a-kind mixture of poetry, b.s., ingenuity, and the inevitable vampire-legend/vampire-fact disclaimers. (Vampires are not supernatural, just a "separate species"; vampires do not turn their victims into vampires.) The movie's midsection is pretty deadly—the immortal vampire and the mortal woman tell each other what tough lives they've led—through even here there are lyrical moments. And if the ending is a bit too ingenious and poetic for its own good (the vampire dies marveling at the phenomenon of sunlight), it beats assembly-line filmmaking any day, which this production emphatically is not, despite the strip-numbers filler. Poetry on the run: Stripper giggles with amazement as vampire human-flies his way with her up the side of a house, to a rendezvous with her long-lost son.

Remake: *To Sleep with a Vampire.*

**DANCE WITH DEATH** Califilm/Concorde-New Horizons (Mike Elliott) 1991 color c90m. D: Charles Philip Moore. SP: Daryl Haney. Story: Katt Shea Ruben, Andy Ruben. Ph: W. H. Molina. Mus: David & Eric Wurst. PD: James Shumaker. Mkp: Kathleen Karridene. Ref: TV. TVG. SFChron Dtbk 4/19/92 (hv). With Barbara Alyn Woods, Maxwell Caulfield, Martin Mull, Drew Snyder, Catya Sassoon.

"Another stripper has been found murdered in the downtown area." A *Stripped To Kill* stripped of all interest, as a mystery killer slices up dancers at the Bottoms Up club. At the end, the slasher, predictably, keeps coming back, monster-like.

**DANCES WITH THE SNAKES** (H.K.) 1992 color/ws feature. D: Richard Lee (aka Lee Han-Chang). Ref: TV: EVS; Eng. titles. Weisser/ATC. With Huang Shin-Jun (Vinsan), Shu Man-Hua, Fan Li-Chiu.

"Very long ago ... in China." The "old Vinsan Monster" (an actor with no monster makeup) controls three snake-monster women who suck the breath out of their victims. Twist: At first, it's a Christian priest who gets into the exorcist act here (later, a Taoist turns up)—for his troubles, he gets turned to stone .... Sloppy, loopy, overlong softcore monster comedy has a laugh here and there.

**DANCING GHOSTS** (Thai) c1986? color c96m. Ref: TV: Extra Times Promotion video; no Eng. Thai Video: above is tr t.

Vengeful ghosts are common in Asian fantasy-horror films, but the revengers are usually working for themselves. Here, in a wild twist, the ghost of the murdered, gang-raped woman simply looks on and laughs as weird ghost women with painted faces and waggling tongues come out of the night to dance her killers to death. Later, a hired wizard imprisons her in a bubble, but she escapes. Plus: a shock scene in which a construction worker is crushed by a magically dropped cement block.

The **DANCING MASTERS** Fox/Lee Marcus 1943 63m. D: Mal St. Clair. SP: W. Scott Darling. Story: George Bricker. Mus: Arthur Lange. AD: James Basevi, Chester Gore. SpPhFX: Fred Sersen. Ref: TV. Bill Warren. Maltin/MCT. NYT 12/2/43. V 10/27/43. no Stanley. no COF. Scheuer. no Lee. no Hardy/SF. With Stan Laurel, Oliver Hardy, Trudy Marshall, Bob Bailey, Margaret Dumont, Allan Lane, Nestor Paiva, Robert Mitchum, Edward Earle, Charles Rogers, Arthur Space, Robert Emmett Keane, Emory Parnell, Hank Mann.

Feeble, late L&H comedy features a "very interesting invention"—a howitzer-like gun which "shoots an invisible ray." Intended to "revolutionize jungle warfare," the weapon "burns everything it hits to the ground." During a test, the lightning-like ray sets a house on fire.... The past—Laurel and Hardy—meets the future—Robert Mitchum. Their slapstick and wordplay are vacuous; his tough-guy act is more impressive, though he has a small role. Stan does one splendidly-executed double take, the kind where he instinctively grabs for his derby with both hands.

**DANCING MISTRESS** see *Kaidan Iro-zange-kyoren Onna Shisho*

**DANCOUGAR: REQUIEM FOR VICTIMS** (J) Emotion/Bandai 198-? anim color c92m. Illus: Kazuko Tadano. Ref: TV: Sony Video; no Eng.; OAV.

Colorful, elaborate alien settings and battle scenes highlight a rock-flinging tornado, a tentacled acid-spraying giant robot, an elephant-like robot, and ghost-like hordes, and the art design goes abstract for some impressive disintegration effects (people, planets). Okay for those who like combination-robot action.

See also: *Super Beast-God Dancougar. God Bless Dancougar.*

**DANGAIO** (J) AIC/Emotion (Miura Touru, Asanuma Makoto) 1987 ('90-U.S.) anim color 44m. D: Hirano Toshihiro. Anim D: Narumi Kakinouchi. Mech Des: Kawamori Shoji, Obari Masami, Sekizo Yasushi. SP: Aikawa Noburu. Ref: TV: AIC video; no Eng. Animag 6:24-29: OAV. Ronin Network 12/25/88. PT 8:44: U.S. Renditions; Eng. titles.

Principals: Mia, Pai, Lamba, and Roll, ESPers kidnapped by Tarsan for their potential as weapons (Lamba's ESP is in her fingertips) ... Yordo, a giant biomechanical monster ... Blood D-1, a giant robot ... and some amusing alien pets.... Basically conventional sf-actioner features some interplay between mercenary and humane character motivations and some fabulous spacecraft designs—the labyrinthine, dragon-like configuration of the pirate domain is the visual highlight.

**DANGAIO 2: SPIRAL KNUCKLE'S TEAR** (J) A.I.C. 1988 anim color 40m. (*Hajataisei Dangaio*). D: Hirano Toshihiro. Ref: M/TVM 2/89:56. Animag 4:5: 2nd of 3 OAVs; "set on a planet of snow." Japan Video.

**DANGER ISLAND** NBC-TV/NBC Prods. & von Zerneck-Sertner Films 1992 color c90m. (*The Presence* - vt t). D: Tommy Lee Wallace. Tel, Co-P: William Bleich. Ph: Alan Caso. Mus: P. M. Robinson. PD: R. B. Lewis. SpMkp & Creature FX: MkpFxUnltd.; Bart J. Mixon. VisFX: Fantasy II; Gene Warren Jr.; (morphing) Digital Fantasy. SpFX: Peter Knowlton. SdFX: Rich Harrison. Ref: TV. TVG 9/19/92. vc box. PT 20:17. With Gary Graham (Rick), Kathy Ireland, June Lockhart, Richard Beymer, Joe Lara, Beth Toussaint, Lisa Banes, Maria Celedonio, Christopher Pettiet, Eddie Velez.

"The whole place is weird!" Castaways on a remote island discover that it was the site of biological-weapons experiments ("really nasty awful war toys") involving "genetic transfer," mind control, ESP, and "haunted food." A leftover virus infects one wounded man, who mutates into a gill creature, and produces "unusual growth patterns" and ESP in another, less-seriously-infected man (Graham). Plus an antidote which cures both victims, and a native lady who seems to "morph" into a demon-thing.... TV-movie begins as a "What happened here?" story, a la *Beau Geste,* as plane-crash-landing survivors discover a deserted, fort-like experimental station. In neither this phase, nor its later, monsters-in-our-midst one, is the movie very exciting—the script is thin, the tale drawn-out.

**\*A DANGEROUS AFFAIR** 1931 77m. Ref: TV: Library of Congress. Lentz. Lee (E). Stanley.

"It's a ghost!" A thin script re the "house upon the hill," The Ghost Gang, a skulker in a wide-brimmed hat, a ghostly sleep-walker, a secret room, clutching hands, an "army of phantoms," and a mysterious "moving light." Photography (Teddy Tetzlaff) and art direction, however, are fairly atmospheric. Tetzlaff comes up with some slick tracking shots, and he periodically shoots past and through clumps of candles and chairs. Charles Middleton as the hunchbacked, clubfooted lawyer Tupper has a grand entrance: He does a Chaney mock-menace ("Heh heh!"), as he slowly—and loudly—limps candle in hand down a staircase. Unfortunately, Tupper is the first to die....

**DANGEROUS ISLAND** see *Island of the Lost*

**DANGEROUS LOVE** Concorde/MPCA (Krevoy-Stabler) 1988 color 94m. SP, D: Marty Ollstein. VideoFX: Roger Schweitzer. Key Mkp: Joni Meers. Ref: V 10/19/88: "tepid whodunit" re a "psycho with a video camera." TVG. TV: MHE video. With Lawrence Monoson, Brenda Bakke, Elliott Gould, Anthony Geary, Angelyne, Teri Austin.

A killer gets into the master computer-dating file, viddies his murders. Flat-footed kink-mystery.

**DANGEROUS NUMBER** MGM 1937 71m. D: Richard Thorpe. SP: Carey Wilson. Story: Leona Dalrymple. Mus: David Snell. AD: Cedric Gibbons; Daniel Cathcart, Edwin B. Willis. Ref: TV. V 3/10/37. no Scheuer. no Maltin '92. Lee (E). no Hardy/SF. no Lentz. no Stanley. With Robert Young, Ann Sothern, Reginald Owen, Dean Jagger, Cora Witherspoon, Franklin Pangborn; Tom Fadden?

An inventor's (Owen) artificial silk—or mono acetate di-nitrate (sp?)—not yet perfected, dissolves in water. ("Everything about artificial silk is Chinese to me.") At the end, the heroine's (Sothern) pseudo-silk dress disappears when she falls into a pool.... Determinedly screwball comedy is over-clever, but manages scattered funny moments.

**DANGEROUS TOYS** see *Demonic Toys*

**DANS LA NUIT** (F) Cinematheque Francaise/Fernand Weill 1930 (1989) 79m. SP, D: Charles Vanel. Ref: V 7/26/89: "a brilliant tour de force ... Grand Guignol." no Chirat/Catalogue. PFA notes 3/3/87. With Vanel, Sandra Milowanoff.

Man whose face has been "hideously mutilated" dons mask.

**DANS LE VENTRE DU DRAGON** (Can.) Les Prods. Quebec/Amerique & Les Films Lenox & Telefilm Canada & LSGdICQ & La Societe Radio-Canada 1989 color 100m. Co-SP, D: Yves Simoneau. Mus: R. Gregoire. AD: N. Sarrazin.

SpFX: Jean-Marc Cyr. SpOptFX: Prods. Pascal Blais. Mkp: Pierre Saindon. Ref: TV: vt; no Eng. Le Video. no V. With Remy Girard, David La Haye, Marie Tifo, Monique Mercure.

"The treatment begins tomorrow." Macabre experiments at a research center involve a new drug and premature aging and seem aimed at production of a "new race." Plus dart-in-head gore, a tarantula, dialogue reference to vampires, and a couple snakes. Atmospheric.

**DANSE MACABRE** (U.S.-Russian) 21st Century (Towers-Golan)/Breton Films (Power Pictures) & Lenfilm 1991 color 96m. (*Phantom of Manhattan* - orig t. *Terror of Manhattan* - int t. *Dance Macabre* - vt t). SP, D: Greydon Clark. Ph: N. Pokoptsev. Mus: D. Slider. AD: Uri Pashigoriev. MkpFX: D.B. Miller. SpFX: Victor Klimov. Ref: TV: Col-TriStar HV. Martin: "horror film." PT 14:46: "stupid *Suspiria* ripoff." Fango 118:12: Col-TriStar HV. V 9/16/91:57: *Dance Macabre.* 5/20/91:16 (shooting). 2/18/91:27 V/Mifed '89:16. VSOM: *Phantom of the Opera 2* - alt t. With Robert Englund, Michelle Zeitlin, Marianna Moen, Julene Renee, Nina Goldman, Irina Davidoff.

One dance-academy student dies in an indoor swimming pool; another dies by rope-trick; a third, on subway tracks. Next up: the Bunk of the Dead.... Predictable Svengali storyline, transparent setting up of the Next Victim. Even the macabre revelation of Englund in a clever latex disguise can't save this.

**DANTE'S INFERNO** (I) Jawitz Pictures c1913? 50m. Ref: screen. William K. Everson. PFA notes 8/24/84. Everson/Classics II: 143, 145.

Virgil leads Dante on a whirlwind tour of hell, in this moral travelogue. On view: three-mouthed Lucifer (chewing on one of the damned) ... Pluto ... Cerberus (looking like a three-headed sheep) ... the three Furies ... a "horde of evil spirits" ... Geryon, a flying serpent-man ... "foul and obscene" harpies ... demons guarding a "river of boiling pitch" ... Judge Minos and a demon attendant ... three giants ... one man gnawing on the head of another ... grafters transforming into (cute) reptile-people ... suicides-as-trees ... winged demons with whips ... and, of course, Charon.

Like *Hercules*—seventy years later—this silent Italian epic is crammed with spectacle. And if, as in *Hercules,* the effects are generally tacky, they are also plentiful. A good half the movie, unfortunately, is devoted to the interminable flailing and writhing of the damned and Dante.

**DANTE'S INFERNO** Fox 1924 tinted 54m. D: A. Henry Otto. SP: Edmund Goulding. Story: Cyrus Wood, based on Dante's *Inferno.* Ph: Joseph August. Ref: screen. William K. Everson. Lee. PFA notes 8/24/84. LC. AFI. V 10/1/24. Everson/Classics II: 145. With Howard Gaye, Pauline Starke, Lawson Butt, Ralph Lewis, Joseph Swickard, Robert Klein (demon), Bud Jamison.

A "curse" cast by a suicide on an avaricious man, Mortimer Judd (Lewis), takes the form of a demon that subjects him to visions of rivers of blood, harpies, demons herding the damned, etc. Demons then carry the suicide's spirit away, and he becomes a tree.... The script makes facile parallels between Dante and its modern-day story, and Judd's "descent" is too systematic to be believed. The household horrors—his wife and son die—prove, predictably, to be all a dream.

Note: Film includes footage (well-integrated with the new scenes) from an Italian production, perhaps **Dante's Inferno* (1910?, 1911?)—but definitely not from the 1913(?) version.

See also *Book Review* (P).

The **DARK** (Can.) Norstar Ent. & Ontario Film Development Corp./Pryceless (Bergman-Pryce/Peter Simpson) 1993 color 87m. D: Craig Pryce. SP: Robert C. Cooper. Ph: Michael Storey. Mus: Guy Zerafa, Alun Davies, Paul Zaza. AD: N. White. Creature Des: Ron Stefaniuk. SdDes: Jane Tattersall. Key Prosth: Colin Penman. MechSpFX: Laird McMurray Services. Ref: TV: Imperial Ent. video. PT 19:55. Stanley. V 10/25/93:63 (ad): "It will consume you." with Stephen McHattie, Cynthia Belliveau, J. Woolvett, Brion James, Tim Reichert (creature).

"It's here." The not-so-"extinct creature" burrowing through the graveyard turns out to be a "carnivorous rodent," a scavenger dating back to the Triassic or Jurassic, a "very territorial," subterranean beast with a "nasty taste for human beings." ("It eats the dead.") Okay on critter natural-history details; lazy on plot and characterization. At the end, the dying rodent becomes a semi-sympathetic character.

**DARK AGE** (Austral.) RKO Pictures & FGH/IFM & the Australian Film Commission 1987 color/ws c90m. D: Arch Nicholson. SP: Sonia Borg, from Grahame Webb's novel "Numunwari." Mus: Danny Beckerman. SpFX: Brian Cox; (croc) Brian Rollston et al. ProsthMkpSup: Bob McCarron. Ref: TV: Charter Ent. video (Embassy Home Ent.). V 7/27/88. TVG: Aust.-U.S. V 5/9/84:78: cf. CROC. With John Jarratt, Nikki Coghill, Gulpilil, Burnam Burnam.

The Arnhem Land Aborigines call the "monster croc" at large in Northern Australia "Numunwari," and believe that this ancient "devil spirit" harbors the spirit of their people. The wise Oondabund (Burnam) says that noisy, violent white men frighten Numunwari, and the latter does seem to kill only those who need killing.... Mechanical pillaging of *Jaws*. It may be a crocodile, but there's a happy-kids-playing-in-the-river scene (enter croc, teeth gleaming), a planned tourist complex threatened by the presence of the marauder, etc. The mystical element seems equally calculated.

**DARK ANGEL: THE ASCENT** (U.S.-Romanian) Para/Full Moon (Paunescu) 1994 color 84m. D: Linda Hassani. SP: Matthew Bright. Ph: V.D. Vasile. Mus: F. Morse. PD: Ioana Corciova. SpMkpFX: Alchemyfx, M.S. Deak. VisFxSup: Paul Gentry. AnimFxSup: Al Magliochetti. Opt: Mercer, Opt. FX. Ref: TV. PT 19:16-17. With Angela Featherstone (Veronica), Daniel Markel, Nicholas Worth, Charlotte Stewart (demon mom), Michael Genovese, M.C. Mahon, Ion Haiduc.

"I'm not human, Max." Veronica, a curious demon with cute wings, leaves hell and enters the upper world through a manhole. This "psychotic cannibal" brings cosmic justice to street criminals and brutal cops. Just doing "God's work," she de-spines a mugger and literally scares the hell out of the mayor ("evil incarnate"). Her dog, Hellraiser, gets the human leftovers.... Dingbat horror-fantasy starts shakily, but has some pleasing story

surprises. It's a *Death Wish* from down under, way down under. Veronica is supernatural kin to the Angela of the *Sleepaway Camp* movies—she goes fire-and-brimstone preachers one or two better.

**DARK ANGEL** see *I Come in Peace*

**DARK CIRCLE** see *Alias Nick Beal*

**DARK DREAMS** see *Erotic Dreams*

**DARK ENEMY** (B) Children's Film Unit (Colin Finbow) 1984 color 97m. D: C. Finbow. Mus: David Hewson. Mkp: G. Wallace. Ref: MFB'85:19-20. Stanley. V 11/28/84: "amateurish ... fun." With David Haig, Douglas Storm, Martin Laing, Chris Chescoe.

"Sometime in the future," after the Dark Time. (MFB)

**DARK EYES** see *Defcon-4*

**DARK EYES OF THE ZOMBIES** see *Killer Birds*

**DARK FUTURE** Dead Alive (Dan Slider) 1994 color feature. D, P: Greydon Clark. SP: David Reskin. Ph: N. von Sternberg. FX: David Hewitt. Ref: PT 21:16: "the only good ideas were ripped off from THX-1138." With Darby Hinton, A. Mann, L. Donato.

"Human looking killer cyborgs."

The **DARK HALF** Orion/Dark Half (Declan Baldwin/George Romero) 1993 (1992) color 122m. SP, D: G. Romero, from Stephen King's novel. Ph: Tony Pierce-Roberts. Mus: Christopher Young. PD: Cletus Anderson. MkpFX: John Vulich, Everett Burrell. VisFX: VCE/Peter Kuran. Computer FX: Video Image. SpFX:(sup) Carl Horner Jr.;(bird mech) Larry O'Dien. SdFxCoord: Odin Benitez. Ref: TV. PT 20:17. V 4/26/93: "one of the top King adaptations." SFChron 4/23/93: "just another assembly-line Stephen King product." ad. With Timothy Hutton (Thad Beaumont/George Stark), Amy Madigan, Julie Harris, Rutanya Alda, Royal Dano, Michael Rooker.

"George Stark has somehow come to life." In 1968, budding author Thad Beaumont is discovered to have an unborn twin "absorbed" into his "system." Twenty three years later, his "inner being" and alter ego—the pseudonymous George Stark—seems to be slashing and bashing those close to Thad. ("It's like watching Dr. Jekyll turn into Mr. Hyde.") Or is an "entity created by the force" of Thad's will responsible? The story ends in Peck City, as hordes of sparrows kill Stark and conduct his soul upwards.

At the beginning, Thad's creative/psychological blackouts suggest *Hangover Square*. A later line re Thad hints *Forbidden Planet*: "It was like they took the sound out of your head, and it came to life." Here, the mystical substitutes—unbelievably and almost risibly—for super-science, as midwife to the impulses from the subconscious. The *Hangover Square* half of the movie is a pointless red herring; the *Forbidden Planet* half, done right, would be camp. More recent cross references include *I, Madman* and *Writer's Block*.

**DARK HERITAGE** CornerStone/Sterling 1989 (1991) color 94m. D, P, Ph: David McCormick. SpFxMkp: Susann Lofton. Lightning FX: Richard Johnstone. Ref: TV: CornerStone video.

Stanley. PT 10:52: strange killers. Fango 104:12: "mutilated bodies ... deranged product of ... incest." With Mark LaCour, Eddie Moore (Mr. Daniels), Tim Verkaik, David Hatcher; Johnny & Shane Grimmett et al (creatures).

"They've changed into these horrible creatures." A venerable legend holds that the Dansen estate, built in 1790, is haunted by "killer ghosts." The Dansen family was always "a little unusual," and lightning displays seem to herald massacres every so often, in or near the house .... Laughably limply plotted horror-fantasy seems half padding, but has some really creepy payoffs—e.g., the weird thing in the tunnel, the pack of ape-like horrors in the house, and the dream of the dead. Score one, also, for the shadow on the wall, and another for the makeup design. No points for the acting or dialogue.

**DARK IS DEATH'S FRIEND, The** see *Killer Must Strike Again*

**DARK OBSESSIONS** Western Visuals 1993 color 89m. D: J. Alexander. Ref: Adam'94. With P.J. Sparxx, Tiffany Mynx, Sean Michaels, Melanie Moore, China Mai.

Takeoff on *Castle of Blood/Web of the Spider,* set at a "supposedly haunted ranch."

**DARK OF THE MOON** see *Murder by Moonlight*

**DARK OF THE NIGHT** (N.Z.) Quartet Films/Preston-Laing (N.Z. Film Commission & UDC & Barclays) 1985 (1984) color 88m. (*Mr. Wrong* - N.Z.). SP, D: Gaylene Preston. SP: also Geoff Murphy, Graeme Tetley. From Elizabeth Jane Howard's story. Mus: Jonathan Crayford. AD: Mike Becroft. SpFX: Matthew Murphy. Mkp: Marilyn McPherson. Ref: TV: Lightning Video. HR 5/30/86. V 4/24/85. 7/25/90: 23. With Heather Bolton, David Letch (The Man), Margaret Umbers, Perry Piercy (Mary Carmichael).

"The car's haunted!" Meg's (Bolton) new used Jag makes noises when its lights are turned off and features a self-opening trunk, but it locks itself so she can't sell it. ("I will not be intimidated by a car!") At one point, the horn starts honking and seems to rescue her from an assailant. The car proves to have belonged to one Mary Carmichael, a murder victim ("thoroughly nasty business") who now haunts it and ultimately saves Meg from sharing her fate.... An okay anecdote padded out to feature length. The ending is predictable (once one gets the hang of the plot), yet dramatically satisfying.

**The DARK POWER** New Vision & Triad 1985 color 81m. SP, D, Co-P: Phil Smoot. Ph: Paul Hughen. Mus: Christopher Deane; ("Toltec Boogie") Matt Kendrick. AD: Dean Jones. SpMkpFX: Tony Elwood; Jones. Ref: TV: Magnum Ent. video. no V. Hound. Phantom. Scheuer. Martin. PT 16:62. Fango 53:10. With Lash LaRue, Anna Lane Tatum, Cynthia Bailey, Mary Dalton, Paul Holman, Barbara Hill; Stuart Watson, Mighty Joe Coltrane (Toltecs).

Several thousand years ago, four Toltec sorcerers buried themselves alive on Totem Hill, in what is now the southeastern United States. On the Evil Day—in the Twentieth Century—they come back to feast upon the living.... Tame and talky low-budgeter. After fifty screen minutes, the sorcerers finally appear, and talk gives way to nonstop screaming and almost-campily-shoddy

gore effects. At the end, Lash LaRue severs an undead's head with his whip.

**DARK SANITY** see *Straight Jacket*

**DARK SHADOWS** NBC-TV/MGM-UA (Dan Curtis-TV) 1991 (1990) color c180m. Creator, D, Exec P: Dan Curtis. Tel: Hall Powell, Bill Taub, Steve Feke, Curtis, Art Wallace. Mus: Bob Cobert. SpFX: John Gray. Mkp: Mony & Dee Monsano. Ref: TV: alternately designated a movie, a mini-series, & an "event." V 1/14/91:116. TVG 3/2/91. 12/29/90. With Ben Cross (Barnabas Collins), Joanna Going, Jean Simmons, Roy Thinnes, Barbara Steele, Stefan Gierasch, Rebecca Staab, Jim Fyfe (Willie).

"Tonight, she walks as one of the living dead!" Collinsport, the "freak palace." Script poses the question: Is vampirism a disease? (Barnabas' blood contains a "very destructive cell.") Meanwhile, Daphne (Staab) does scenes out of *Horror of Dracula.* Hokey score, stilted acting and writing, in this revival of the TV series.

**The DARK SIDE OF MIDNIGHT** Troma/Olsen 1986 (1984) color 89m. (*The Creeper* - B t). SP, D, P: Wes Olsen. Mus: Doug Holroyd. SpMkpFX: Susan Frawley. Ref: V 2/24/88: "relentlessly dull." no PFA. VW 16:8. With James Moore, Olsen, Sandy Schemmel, Dan Myers (The Creeper).

Slasher, "The Creeper," on the loose in Ft. Smith, Ark.

**The DARK SIDE OF THE MOON** Vidmark/Wildstreet (Keith Walley/Spacescore or Spacecore) 1990 (1989) color 91m. (aka *Something Is Waiting*). D: D. J. Webster. SP: C. W. Hayes, Chad Hayes. Ph: R.T. Alsobrook. Mus: Ryder, Davies. PD: M. Minch. VisFxSup: John V. Fante. MkpSpFX: R. Christopher Biggs. MechSpFxCoord: Lou Carlucci. Meltdown FX: Todd Masters. SdFxSup: J.K. Adams. Ref: TV. V 5/9/90:62 (hv): "derivative." McCarty II: "well-acted ripoff ... highly recommended." V/Cannes '89:130. With Will Bledsoe, Alan Blumenfeld, Robert Sampson, Camilla More (robot), Joe Turkel.

"This is weirder than the *Flying Dutchman.*" In the year 2022, the maintenance spaceship Spacecore 1 finds the derelict spacecraft *Discovery* on the dark side of the moon. Fanciful enough sci-fier extends the Bermuda Triangle into space (it turns out to be "undefined energy of massive proportions") and involves 666 lost ships, Revelations (the number of the Beast: 666), the devil ("I have many names"), triangular wounds on *Spacecore* crew members, salt water and seaweed found on the *Discovery,* a corpse which "enters" another body, and corpses which speak in *Exorcist* voices .... Film cannily saves the best for last—a peak at some of the lost ships (both sailing and space) on the moon. The bulk of the movie, however, is tepid, and the script is overdependent on the word "weird."

**DARK TOWER** Spectrafilm & Sandy Howard (J. R. Bowey, D. M. Witz) 1989 (1988) color 91m. D: Freddie Francis. SP: R. J. Avrech, Ken Wiederhorn, Ken Blackwell, from Avrech's story. Mus: S. Widelitz. SpMkpFX: Steve Neill. Ref: V 2/22/89: "perfunctory." 5/6/87:241 (ad). Martin. McCarty II: "interminable." With Michael Moriarty, Jenny Agutter, Carol Lynley, Theodore Bikel, Anne Lockhart, Kevin McCarthy.

Parapsychologist and exorcist vs. demon.

**DARK UNIVERSE** American Independent/Sharan 1993 color c85m. Story, D, P: Steve Latshaw. Story, SP, P: Pat Moran. Story, Exec P: Fred Olen Ray. Ph: M.J. Beck. Mus: Jeffrey Walton. Exec P: G.A. Waldman, Jim Wynorski. PD: Buzz Bradenton. SpMkpFX: Jeff Farley. Shuttle FX: the Skotaks. Matte: Jim Danforth. Morphing: Sam Hasson; Creative Multimedia. Creature FX: S.O.T.A. FX. Ref: TV. TVG. SFChron Dtbk 12/26/93. With Blake Pickett, Cherie Scott, John Maynard, Steve Barkett, Joe Estevez, Bently Tittle, William Grefe.

"Do you believe in vampires, Tom?" A space-pilot mutant (Barkett)—"created in part by re-entry into the Earth's atmosphere"—drains his victims' blood for the red cells. The *Alien*-ish critter's long tongue goes right for the belly button. Plus several other mutations of all shapes and sizes .... *First Man Into Space*, anyone? Slipshod science-fiction-horror at least has lots of draining-life-force makeup effects, plus the line "Aliens are my specialty."

**DARK WATERS** (B-Russ) Victor Zuev 1993 color 94m. SP, D, Co-Ed: Mariano Baino. SP, Assoc Co-P: Andrew M. Bark. Ph: Alex Howe. Mus: Igor Clark. Sets: Ivan Pulenko. SpMkpFX: Richard Field, David Mundin. Ref: TV: VSOM; Eng. version. VSOM: Italian? Dark Side 47:31. Palmerini. With Louise Salter, Venera Simmons, Maria Kapnist.

"Someone or something is trying to put the amulet together again." Inside this heavy-duty nunnery: a "very secretive order" which includes Penitente-types ... a hooded slasher ... demonic paintings ... the "image of the Beast that was, is not, and yet is" ... entrail gore ... and a fang-claw-and-lungs demon behind a wall.... Rather spare, but distinctively shot supernatural mystery, with a bravura came-the-flood-waters opening.

**DARKMAN** Univ/Renaissance (Darkman/Robert Tapert) 1990 color 95m. Story, SP, D: Sam Raimi. SP: also Chuck Pfarrer, Ivan Raimi, Daniel Goldin, Joshua Goldin. Ph: Bill Pope. Mus: Danny Elfman. PD: Randy Ser. MkpFX: Tony Gardner, Larry Hamlin. OptFX: VCE/Peter Kuran; (anim) Kevin Kutchaver, Jammie Friday. SpVisFX: Introvision Systems, William Mesa, Tom Merchant; (min seqs) 4-Ward, Robert Skotak; (sp fx) J. Viskocil, Emmet Kane; (Strack City) Matte World, Craig Barron, M. Pangrazio. Burning Hand Anim: Chiodo Bros. Computer Anim: Video Images. Microscope FX: Oxford Scientific. MechSpFX: Spectacular FX Unltd. Ref: TV: MCA-Univ HV. MFB'90:318-19. V 8/22/90. Contra Costa Times 9/2/90. Sacto Bee 8/24/90. Sacto Union. With Liam Neeson (Darkman), Frances McDormand, Colin Friels, Larry Drake, Nelson Mashita, Nicholas Worth, Bruce Campbell, Jenny Agutter, William Lustig, Stuart Cornfeld, John Landis.

"What am I?" After doctors save the life of the horribly acid-and-fire-scarred Peyton Westlake (Neeson), he finds that his severed nerve endings render him insensitive to pain, and unchecked adrenalin augments both his emotions and his physical strength. He proceeds to use his liquid-skin apparatus to "reconstruct"— with synthetic, photosensitive cells—his face and the visages of those who aimed to kill him, in order to impersonate and systematically eliminate them.

Occasional cleverness (primarily in the playing of the game of the mask), old-fashioned pathos, and put-on, serial-like thrills. Script has echoes of *The Phantom of the Opera*, *The Hunchback*

*of Notre Dame,* and *The Incredible Hulk,* but (like its hero) has trouble establishing its own identity. And its most direct cross reference is actually *Doctor X* (1932)—"liquid skin" is just another name for "synthetic flesh."

**DARKMAN II: THE RETURN OF DURANT** (U.S.-Can.) Univ Canada/MCA Home Ent. (Renaissance/David Roessell) 1994 color 93m. D, Ph: B. May. SP: Stephen McKay. Story: Eisele, Hertzog. Mus: Randy Miller. AD: Ian Brock. SpMkpFX: KNB. VisFX: John Gajdecki VisFX;(digital anim) Claude Theriault. 3D Anim: C.O.R.E. Digital. SpFxCoord: Brock Jolliffe. Opt: Howard Anderson. Ref: TV: MCA-Univ HV. With Larry Drake, Arnold Vosloo, Kim Delaney, Renee O'Connor, Lawrence Dane, Jesse Collins.

Durant (Drake) is back, with "guns for the new century"— mainly, The Vigilante, a sort of lightning-ray rifle. Plus a laser ray gun, a new skin substitute for Darkman (Vosloo) which works up to 173 minutes, and gang-infiltration-via-mask.... Some *Hurricane Express*-like fun with lifelike masks, but mainly indifferent urban intrigue here.

**DARKNESS** Norseman Film/Jonker 1992 color 86m. SP, D: Leif Jonker. Ph: F. Hardesty. Mus: M. Curtis, B. Davis. SpMkpFX: Gary Miller; R.D. LeBay. Ref: TV: Film Threat Video. Jones. With G. Miller, Michael Gisick, Cena Donham, Randall Aviks (Liven); Brian Cardwell et al (vampires).

"We are the night." Insta-vampires and a vampire hunter who permanently kills the victims of the main monster. ("He is coming!") Or, Attack of the Special Makeup Artist. Messiest Vampires prize to those in this curiosity of a film: It's a vampire movie played like a New Ghoul movie—more blood than guts. And it's competent-of-kind, but it isn't Peter Jackson. It's nothing but blood and effects. The lighting is dim beyond atmospheric to annoying.

**DARKROOM** Quest Ent./Omega (Nico Mastorakis) 1990 color 86m. D: Terrence O'Hara. SP: B. Herskowitz, R. W. Fisher, R. Pamplin. Mus: J. J. Grant. Ref: V 8/1/90:67 (hv): "slasher film ... sputters." With Aarin Teich, Jill Pierce, J. A. Arbaugh.

**DARNA** (Fili) Viva Films (William Leary) 1991 color 107m. D: Joel Lamangan. SP: Frank G. Rivera. Story: Eddie Rodriguez, Bey Vito, from Mars Ravelo's comic. Ph: Ramon Marcelino. Mus D: Willy Cruz. PD: Benjie de Guzman. Vibora Des: Ronnie Martinez. VisFX: Cinemagic. MechFlyingFX: Danny Rojo. Prosth Mkp: Cecille Baun. SpFX: Rolly Sto. Domingo. SdFX: Ramon Reyes. Ref: TV: Viva Video; occ. Eng. Monster! 3:55-6. With Rachel Alejandro, Herbert Bautista, Jimmy Santos, Ruby Rodriguez (Vibora's voice), Nanette Medved (Darna), Dennis Padilla, Nida Blanca, Edu Manzano, Pilar Pilapil.

The new Darna—the "super woman"—confronts Medusa-like Valentina (cf. *Valentina*) and takes to the skies to fight a potion-created, child-biting bat-woman. At the end, one eviler shoots trident rays at Darna, loses his amulet, and incinerates.... Fair fun. Superheroics with a sense of humor, if inferior effects. Highlight: the papier-mache talking snake ("How romantic!") which, at one point, pops Darna's super pill and becomes a snake-Darna. Lowlight: a poorly staged mass-snake attack. One villain features a 360-degree head-spin option.

See also the following titles and *Ang Pagbabalik Ni Pedro Penduko* and *Captain Barbell*.

**DARNA! ANG PAGBABALIK** (Fili) Viva/W.C. Leary 1994 (1993) color/3-D c110m. D: Peque Gallaga, Lore Reyes. SP: Floy Quintos. Ph: Marissa Floirendo;(sp fx) Ely Cruz. Mus: Archie Castillo. PD: Adrian Torres. SpVisFX: Optima Studios;(sup) Marck Ambat;(computer graphics) Pablo Biglangawa. Prosth: Benny Batoctoy. SdFX: Ramon Reyes. Ref: TV: Viva Video; little Eng. With Anjanette Abayari, Edu Manzano, Rustom Padilla, Bong Alvarez, Pilita Corales, Cherie Gil.

As the bustiest Darna so far—"our very own Wonder Woman"— Abayari takes on Valentina (Corales), apparently from the movie of the same name. In one transcendently pathetic-horrific sequence, a snake statue seems to activate the snakes under the lady's turban onstage; at the same time, a snake-haired lady backstage withers, then turns hideously snaky and seems to be dying in her daughter's (the turban lady) arms. Later, daughter becomes a snake-thing. Latest *Darna* fantasy is overlong and unsophisticated, but has some fun effects stunts.

**DARNA AT DING** (Fili) D'Wonder Films 1984 color 120m. SP, D: J. Erastheo Navoa, Cloyd Robinson, from Mars Ravelo comics. Ph: H. U. Santos. PD: Arthur Nicdao. FX: Jessie Sto. Domingo. SpPhFX: Tommy Marcelino. SdFX: Velasquez, Sayson. Mkp: Mildred Bonpua. Ref: TV: Trigon Video; little Eng. With Vilma Santos (Darna), Nino Muhlach (Ding), Marissa Delgado, Ike Lozada, Max Alvarado, Paquito Diaz, Al Tantay.

Santos, playing bikini-clad flying super-heroine Darna for the ninth time, combats a giant, a mad German scientist who is bringing the local dead back as drooling zombies, and a voodoo priestess who appears and disappears at will, sticks pins in dolls, summons up a ray-shooting robot, and creates an evil Darna double.... This Darna fantasy has a scrappy, pieced-together-from-TV-shows-or-old-movies feel, flat music and photography, and tacky but fun effects scenes. In one scene, the (relatively) tiny Darna flies up, up, and past the giant's face and punches him in the mouth.

**DARNA, KUNO ...?** (Fili) Regal Films 1985? color c112m. Story, SP, D: Luciano B. Carlos. SP: also Toto Belano, from Mars Ravelo comics. Ph: Gonzales, Jacinto. Mus: Ernani Cuenco. PD: F. Zabat. SpFX, Sets: Apolonio Abadeza. SpPhFX: Tommy Marcelino. Mkp: Luis Playa et al. SdFX: Sebastian Sayson. Ref: TV: Trigon Video; no Eng. With Dolphy, Lotis Key, Celia Rodriguez, Marissa Delgado, Ruel Vernal, Bella Flores.

The pregnant Darna loans her magic gem to "Darno," who, with the cry "Darna, Kuno!" acquires superpowers and a bikini, and handily defeats four giant, nocturnal horses that stand on their hind legs. He also takes on winged, fanged, half-materialized female vampires and a witch woman who keeps brides frozen in her mansion's halls. Meanwhile, a female Darna takes on a monstrous, shape-shifting witch who leads children into her cave in order to bake them and turn them into cookies. At the end, the real Darna flies off with a little "Darnita," but not before Darno's grievously dirty socks knock out some ray-gun-toting aliens. ("Exorcism!")

This combination of low comedy and high fantasy is a real curiosity. File under Most Unlikely Macabre Image: the giant singing horse which stands among the trees and calls out the heroine's name. The movie may be episodic, but the episodes are mind-boggling.

**DARSHNA** (India-Kannada) B.S.R. Movies 1983 color 146m. Ph, D: B. D. Mothur. Mus: R. Ratna. Ref: Dharap. With N. S. Anil, Jayalaxmi, Sushila Naidu.

Killer ghost in old mansion possesses young woman.

**DAUGHTER OF DARKNESS** (U.S.-Rom.) CBS-TV/King Phoenix Ent. & Accent Ent. & Novofilm (Andras Hamori & Pal Sandor) 1990 (1989) color 90m. D: Stuart Gordon. SP, Co-P: Andrew Laskos. Mus: Colin Towns. SpMkp: Craig Reardon. SpFX: Peter Szilagyi, Gyula Krasnyanszky. Ref: TV. Sacto Bee 1/26/90. V 2/7/90:158. With Mia Sara, Anthony Perkins, Robert Reynolds, Jack Coleman, Dezso Garas.

Frenetic horror story with some bizarre ingredients, including the vampires' chained-to-their-beds blood-supply victims. The vampires here don't have fangs, just a "thing in their tongue." Extra added: a monstrous "monk" in a visualized nightmare.

**DAUGHTER OF DEVIL FISH** (Thai?) Hai Hua Cinema 199-? color 92m. Ref: World Video; Eng. titles.

A girl's dead Mom animates a talking fish, then becomes a stopmo instant-sapling. Later, the (superimposed) tree-Mom whips a woman who tries to cut her down. ("It's ghost!" "Mom, I'm scared of it!") A consulting witch then has the now-grown-up heroine tossed into a pot of boiling water, but the young woman turns into a bird and flies away. The witch "expels" the spirit from the bird and turns a maid into a kitty. Meanwhile, a fairy turns the bird back into the heroine, and a boy who can turn into a stone or a man uses a voodoo wig on the witch, then throws water on her, and she disintegrates, rather showily .... Silly but lively fantasy has a bit of *Hush, Hush, Sweet Charlotte* music on the soundtrack. The witch has a nifty snake-head staff.

**\*DAUGHTER OF HORROR** H.K.F. Prods. (Van Wolf - API) 1955 (1953). PD: Ben Roseman. Sd: (fx ed) Mike Pozen; (concepts) Shorty Rogers and his Giants. Ref: TV. Jim Shapiro. Lee. Lentz. Stanley. Weldon. Scheuer. Martin. Phantom. no Hound. no Maltin '92. With Angelo Rossitto.

"Do you know what horror is?" Story here takes place in the "tormented, haunted, half-lit night of the insane," as the "ghouls of insanity" watch a female slasher prowl. Flashback scenes re her father (who shot her mother) and mother (whom she avenged by stabbing her father) are enacted, surreally, in a cemetery.... Arty curiosity features super-hokey narration and sound effects. The "demon" who possesses the heroine's soul plays, more or less, her Ghost of Christmas Past.

**DAUGHTER OF THE WEREWOLF** see *Cry of the Werewolf*

**DAVITELJ PROTIV DAVITELJA** see *Strangler Vs. Strangler*

**DAWN** (B) Niall Johnson 1990 color feature. SP, D, Co-Ed: Johnson. Ref: Jones: shot-on-tape. With Elizabeth Rees, Geoff Sloan, Craig Johnson.

"Clumsy action" re 200-year-old vampire (Sloan).

**DAY OF ANGER** see *Day of Wrath*

**DAY OF THE DEAD** United Film Dist./Hal Roach-Laurel 1985 color 101m. SP, D: George A. Romero. Mus: John Harrison. SpMkpFX: Tom Savini. Masks: THS. SpFX: Steve Kirshoff, Mark Mann. Ref: TV. MFB'86:266-7. V 7/3/85. With Lori Cardille, Terry Alexander, Joseph Pilato, Jarlath Conroy, Antone DiLeo, John Amplas, Howard Sherman (Bub), Richard Liberty.

In this follow-up to *Night of the Living Dead* (1968) and *Dawn of the Dead*—set in Florida's Seminole Storage Facility, a "great big fourteen-mile tombstone"—Dr. Logan (Liberty), aka "Frankenstein," is trying to domesticate flesh-eating zombies that operate on "deep dark primordial instinct." Logan's "star pupil": Bub, who seems docile, appreciates Beethoven, but gets fed dead soldiers on the sly.... The human/zombie confrontations are harrowing, sometimes even imaginative, but Romero again proves stronger on massing zombies than on bickering humans. All the yelling, haranguing, taunting, arguing, and invective meant to create tension creates only dead spaces. And even the payoff scenes with the zombie hordes often reduce to chase-and-chomp scenes.

**2P The DAY OF THE DOLPHIN** Avco Embassy (Robert E. Relyea/Icarus) 1973 color/ws 104m. D: Mike Nichols. SP: Buck Henry, from Robert Merle's novel. Ph: William A. Fraker. Mus: Georges Delerue. PD: Richard Sylbert. SpPhFX: Albert Whitlock. SpFX: Jim White. Mkp: Acevedo, Butterworth. Trainer: Peter Moss. Ref: TV: Col-TV. V 12/19/73. MFB'74:25-6: "futuristic." Hardy/SF. Lentz. Stanley. NYT 12/20/73. Bill Warren. TVG. With George C. Scott, Trish Van Devere, Paul Sorvino, Fritz Weaver, Jon Korkes, Edward Herrmann, John David Carson, Victoria Racimo, John Dehner, William Roerick, Severn Darden, Elizabeth Wilson, Brooke Hayward, Pat Englund, Phyllis Davis.

"It's like we're all having a dream." A marine scientist (Scott) finds "infinite possibilities" in the prospect of a "dolphin imitating human speech sounds." The plot occasionally suggests *Lassie Come Home;* Delerue's haunting score suggests *Jules and Jim.* But the script seems closest to *The Abominable Snowman* and its theme of the moral unreliability of humans. And it's an improvement on the Nigel Kneale-scripted film, if only because it's not so sanctimonious re its fascinating aquatic duo and because the latter are allowed to star. If the political plot seems far-fetched, Henry's script ends on a decidedly sober and serious, bittersweet, anti-exploitation note.

**The DAY OF THE TRIFFIDS** (B-Austral.) BBC-TV & RCTV & the Australian Broadcasting Commission (David Maloney) 1981 ('87-U.S.) color 160m. D: Ken Hannam. Tel: Douglas Livingstone, from John Wyndham's novel. Ph: Peter Hall. Mus: Christopher Gunning. Des: Victor Meredith. VisFxDes: Steve Drewett. SpSd: Elizabeth Parker. Mkp: Ann Ailes. Ref: TV. TVG: shown variously as three-part miniseries or TV-movie. With John Duttine, Emma Relph, Maurice Colbourne, Jonathan Newth, Cleo Sylvestre.

"Triffids began to appear all over the world." These plants from hell—or outer space—walk, talk, poison their victims with sting-

ers, then eat the decomposed bodies. They are, however, "under proper control" and "well fenced in"—until, that is, "one of the greatest free entertainments the world has ever seen": a shower of comets which blinds the "whole bloody world." Result: a "bloody mess".... Predictable nearly-the-end-of-the-world pathos and violence, and a flat shot-on-tape look and sound. Still, there's some residual interest in the Wyndham story, and performances aren't bad.

**\*\* DAY OF WRATH** (Danish) George J. Schaefer/Carl Dreyer 1943('48-U.S.) b&w 98m. (*Vredens Dag. Dies Irae* - alt t. *Day of Anger* - alt vt t). SP,D,P: Dreyer. SP: also P. Knudsen, M. Skot-Hansen. From Wiers Jenssens' novel *Anne Pedersdotter.* Ref: TV: vt; Eng. titles. Cowie/70 Years: based on a play. Agee. Kael/5001. V 4/28/48. Tyler/Classics. Lee. Stanley.

"There is power in evil!" *Day of Wrath* is not an outright horror-fantasy like Dreyer's *Vampyr,* but it is perhaps a more even, powerful film, with several suggestions of horror and fantasy—the condemned witch Marthe's scream as the stake she's bound to falls into the fire ... her prediction of Laurentius' death ... Absalon's sensing of Death passing by as Anne wishes out loud for his death ... and his death by emotional shock after she confronts him. In a sense, this is the art version of *The Postman Always Rings Twice*; it shares the same basic plot with the latter. Morally and psychologically, it's intricately ambiguous. In the script's scheme of things, even the places of witchcraft and witchhunting are ever-shifting, as are audience sympathies with the principals. In the end, perhaps, it all comes down to Absalon's "What lives men lead!"

**\*The DAY THE EARTH FROZE** AIP-TV 1959 color. SP: Elias Lenrot, from the Kalevala. Mus: Otto Strode. AD: Bart Donner. SpFX: Gerome Langstrom. Mkp: Sharon Copler. Ref: TV. Lee. Stanley. Weldon. Lentz. no Scheuer. no Maltin '92. Fango 122:17: Sinister Cinema ad. With Nina Anderson, Jon Powers, Ingrid Elhardt (the witch Loki), Elgin Tanner, Palvo Nurman, Peter Sorenson.

In the land of Kalevala, a "wicked witch" chains the winds in a cave and flies away, cackling, with the sun. ("There can be no happiness without the sun!") Plus: the road-spirit ("I am the road"), the tree-spirit, a blinding mist, a field of snakes, the ghostly North Wind, and frozen people.... Terribly dubbed yet lively and colorful fairy-tale film is silly-campy, but effects, photography, and art direction are imaginative. Sample highlight: the witch's cloak which flies up and becomes a boat's sail.

**DAY THE EARTH STOOD STILL, The** (I) see *Black Noise*

**DAYBREAK** HBO-TV 1993 color c90m. SP, D: Stephen Tolkin, from Alan Bowne's play "Beirut." Ref: SFExam 5/9/93. TVG 5/8/93: unsubtle. SFChron Dtbk 10/17/93. With Cuba Gooding Jr., Moira Kelly.

"Quarantine camps" in the "nightmarish near-future." (TVG)

**The DAYDREAMER** Embassy/Videocraft Int'l. (Rankin-Bass) 1966 puppet anim and live 101m. D: Jules Bass. SP, P: Arthur Rankin Jr. Ref: Jim Shapiro. Lee. AFI.

Sequence with monstrous giant frog ... evil Rat and Mole.

**DAYS OF THE ECLIPSE** (Russ.) Lenfilm 1988 color 2711 meters (*Dni Zatmeniya*). D: A. Sokurov. SP: Y. Arabov (sp?), from the story "A Billion Years before the End of the World," by the Strugatskys. Ph: S. Yurizditsky. Mus: Y. Khanin. Des: Y. Amshinskaya. Ref: Soviet Film 9/88:24-25,37. With A. Ananishnov (sp?).

Earthling meets "strange, savage-looking people" on Mars.

**DE PROFUNDIS** see *Black Cat* (1990)

**DEAD ALIVE** (N.Z.) Trimark/WingNut Films & the N.Z. Film Commission & Avalon/NFU (Jim Booth) 1992 ('93-U.S.) color 101m. (*Braindead* - orig t). SP, D, Stopmo: Peter Jackson. Story, SP: Stephen Sinclair. SP: also Frances Walsh. Ph: Murray Milne. Mus: Peter Dasent. PD: Kevin Leonard-Jones. Gore FX & Stopmo: Richard Taylor. Prosth Mkp: (des) Bob McCarron; (sup) Marjory Hamlin. SpFxCoord: Steve Ingram. Title Anim: Gnome Prods. Ref: TV: Vestron Video. V 5/25/92. 2/15/93:16 (rated). 2/22/93:58. 2/1/93. 10/5/92:45, 50. Red Vic Theatre notes 9/13/93. Cinef 4/93. 12/92:60. Fango 123:7. With Timothy Balme, Diana Penalver, Elizabeth Moody, Ian Watkin, Elizabeth Brimilcombe (zombie Mum), Stuart Devenie (zombie McGruder).

"It's only a bloody monkey!" 1957. A rat monkey (Simian Raticus) from Skull Island (southwest of Sumatra) bites Lionel's (Balme) Mum (Moody). She dies and returns as a zombie, and soon it's feeding time at the zombie-zoo table, as Lionel takes care of the local ghouls in his cellar. ("They're not dead exactly.") By the end, Mum has become a giant, *Thing*-like conglomeration.

Gut-check time in this Comedy of Entrails. Or, The Entrails Have Eyes (literally). *Dead Alive* seems less an original than did *Bad Taste,* more a foray into already-trodden territory (cf. the *Return of the Living Dead* films), but in its excess and intermittent inspiration, it's probably The Last Word on its subject. Ingenuity and gore with tentacle-like intestines, cackling mutant infants, etc. Fun if you have the ... stomach.

**DEAD & MARRIED** see *She's Back*

**The DEAD AND THE DEADLY** (H. K.) Golden Harvest/Bo Ho Films (Samo Hung) 1983 color/ws c100m. D: Wo Ma. Ref: Rainbow Video; Eng. titles. Hardy/HM:388. NST! 4:20. Ecran F 65:65: with Wo Ma, Samo Hung.

Lucho's neon-eyed ghost wants Fatboy to help him avenge his murder. When Fatboy refuses, the invisible Lucho plays tricks on him in order to make him look foolish before others. Plus (in a prologue) a ghost who kills his wife and her lover ... an exorcist who transfers Lucho's soul to Fatboy ... and (at the end) a ghostly midget trio that attempts to collect the dead Fatboy's soul.... Silly but lively and likable ghost comedy. The slapsticky tone and invisible-man stunts suggest Abbott and Costello Meet the Invisible Man Revisited.

**DEAD BOYZ CAN'T FLY** Stonecastle/Command 1992 color 104m. D, P: Howard Winters. SP, Co-P: Anne Wolfe. Mus: Rich Sanders. Ref: V 6/22/92: "a stupid and repulsively violent drama ... inexcusably horrific." with David John, Brad Friedman, Ruth Collins.

**DEAD CAN'T LIE, The** see *Gotham*

**DEAD COME HOME, The** see *Dead Dudes in the House*

**DEAD CURSE** (H. K.) 1986 color c85m. Ref: TV: Ocean Shores Video or Vietnam Int'l. Video; both with Eng. titles.

"July is the month for the ghost." A witch invokes the god Carla and casts a "bloody spell" on the family of the police inspector who kills her. Four years later, the witch's ghost—who appears every year during the seventh month—kills the inspector and seeks out his little daughter and his sister Mimi. Two child-ghost emissaries almost succeed in hanging Siu Yuk, but a wizard exorcises Mimi's possessed boy friend, then bests the witch in a duel.

The latter sequence is formula, though it features one un-formula element—the use of car tires as rolling and flying weapons. And if a ghost car and a haunted wheelchair figure in some regulation scare tactics, the scene in which an empty Sprite can follows Mimi is eerily poetic-prosaic. The sequence, too, with the child ghosts is fine and spooky. Siu Yuk asks the little girl, "Are you Miss E.T.?" The ghost—as if to say, Yes—touches her supernatural forefinger to Siu Yuk's, and Siu Yuk follows the two into a strange mist. Lost and alone, she looks down over a wooden railing at a pond, and sees the ghosts' reflections waving to her to join them....

**DEAD DUDES IN THE HOUSE** October Films (Lewis/Riffel) 1988 color 90m. (*The Dead Come Home* - orig t. *The House on Tombstone Hill* - vt t). SP, D, Exec Co-P: J. Riffel. Ph: Mark Petersson. Mus: W. B. Riffel. AD: Janice Irwin. SpFxMkp: (sup) Ed French; Erik Shaper, B. S. Fuller. Ref: TV. TVG. Martin. With Mark Zobian, Victor Verhaeghe, Sarah Newhouse, Douglas F. Gibson (old lady), John Cerna (Steve), Naomi Kooker (Linda), Eugene Sautner (Joey); Pam Lewis (old lady's voice).

"Maybe you woke 'er up, man!" The "creepy looking" ghost of an old lady who was slashed half-to-death and later died in 1948 haunts her house and precipitates a series of murders in the present.... Brutality for brutality's sake. The supernatural premise is an excuse for graphic violence involving knives, poles, jagged-edged windows, scissors, saws, and screwdrivers—tool-kit gore. The most curious element of the movie: The woman's victims die, but invariably turn up semi-live as ghosts, or zombies, in the next scene, the better apparently to display the makeup jobs. *Dead Dudes* is *The Evil Dead* with no flair, *Bad Taste* with no laughs.

**DEAD-END DRIVE-IN** (Austral.) New World/Springvale & New South Wales Film Corp. 1986 color/ws 90m. D: Brian Trenchard-Smith. SP: Peter Smalley, from Peter Carey's short story "Crabs." Mus: Frank Strangio. SpFxCoord: Chris Murray. Mkp: Lloyd James. Ref: TV. V 5/21/86. With Ned Manning, Natalie McCurry, Peter Whitford, Wilbur Wilde, Brett Climo.

1990. The Star Drive-in has been converted into a detention center for social misfits. Keeping the latter happy, or at least distracted: movies, stickball, beer.... As a social microcosm, the Star is too neat, and although the notion of a drive-in prison at first amuses, the novelty value thins as the High Seriousness of the enterprise becomes clear. Film's only two noteworthy elements: Whitford's low-key, smug, all-in-a-day's-work air as the theater manager, and some spectacular stunt work.

**DEAD GIRLS** Bovine Prods. & Kluck Unltd. (Eugene James) 1990 color c106m. D, Ed: Dennis Devine. SP, Ed: Steve Jarvis. Mus: Eric Ekstrand (Estrand?). AD: Greg Hildreth. SpMkpFX: Mark P. Case; (nightmare) Carol Pritchard. Ref: TV: Raedon HV. V 9/3/90:80 (hv). With Diana Karanikas, Angela Eads, Kay Schaber, Angela Scaglione, Steven Kyle, Dierdre West, Jeff Herbick, David Chatfield (Mike), Ilene B. Singer, David Williams (Elmo).

"She dies every night—she eviscerates herself on stage." Psychic Gina (Karanikas) and the Dead Girls, a rock group with a "death and destruction gimmick," take a two-week break at a cabin in the mountains, where they find a "weird" handyman (Williams), a "spook show," and a schizophrenic killer in fedora and "ugly mask" whose tools include ax and drill.... Weak acting foils a potentially interesting script, as New Wavers run up against strange members of the Moral Majority. Different if unlikely ending ("Now that the Dead Girls are out of her life—forever!") leaves Gina alive, but apparently not for long.

**DEAD HEAT** New World/Helpern-Meltzer 1988 color 86m. D: Mark Goldblatt. SP: Terry Black. Mus: Ernest Troost. SpVisFX: (sup) Patrick Read Johnson; Ernest D. Farino. Mkp & MechFX: Steve Johnson; (chicken animatronics) Rick Lazzarini. SpFxCoord: Sabre SpFX. Opt: Ray Mercer. Ref: TV. MFB'90:11-12. V 5/11/88. EBay Express 5/13/88. With Treat Williams, Joe Piscopo, Lindsay Frost, Darren McGavin, Vincent Price, Clare Kirkconnell, Keye Luke, Robert Picardo, Steven Bannister (the thing), Dick Miller.

"Welcome to Zombieland!" A cash-and-dash gang includes two men "dead since Tuesday" who have traces of something called Sulfathiazole in their skin tissue. They turn out to be by-products of Arthur P. Loudermilk's (Price) eternal-life-for-the-filthy-rich plan, though at present Dante Pharmaceuticals' revivification machine allows only a twelve-hour "resurrection period" for those it brings back to life, or half-life: "Irreversible cell damage" eventually reduces the zombies to mush.... This takeoff on the film *D.O.A.* (seen briefly here on TV) is a fizzled black comedy/horror movie with stray on-the-mark moments. The fact that cop hero Roger Mortis (Williams) is dead isn't half as funny as it's supposed to be. (He has twelve hours to find his killer before....) Temporarily living-dead chicken, duck, and cow carcasses provide one okay all-stops-out scene, if this latter does seem derivative from a scene in *Young Sherlock Holmes.*

**DEAD IS DEAD** Video Outlaw/Tempe (Filmlab Video) 1992 75m. SP, D, P, Ed: Mike Stanley. Ph: Eddie Lambert. Mus: R. Binge. SpMkpFX: M.E.S. EFX. Ref: PT 19:17: "really bad FX." Tempe Video flyer. TV: Video Outlaw; *Just Add Water* - original-project t. Fango 123:12: shot-on-tape. With M. Stanley, Connie Cocquyt, Rob Binge, Dave Hildwein.

"So you're not dead." A "walking zombie" tears·off Eric's arm; the drug Doxital grows it back. (Apparently, a bad batch of the drug was responsible for creating "that thing in the woods.") Doxital can also "bring the newly dead back to life".... Video tries for a tough, seedy feel, winds up looking mainly sloppy, and much padding dilutes.

**DEAD LOCK** see *Deadlock*

**DEAD MAN WALKING** Metropolis & Hit Films/Gernert-Brown 1988 (1987) color 90m. D, P: Gregory Brown. SP: John Weidner, Rick Marx. Mus: Claude Cave. SpMkpFX: Dean & William Jones, Thomas Powell IV. Ref: TV. V 7/13/88. With Wings Hauser, Brion James, Pamela Ludwig, Jeffrey Combs, Sy Richardson.

"Why don't you just wait and die?" In the tenth year of an epidemic which has killed off half the world's population, corporations rule "plague zones" (where those infected with the "new virus" live), Zero Men (who have a non-contagious but fatal strain of the virus) roam, and "plague people" cherish "suicide privileges".... Hauser seems lost in the hole-in-the-story that is the hero, Luger, a Zero Man; James overdoes it as the dangerous madman Decker; Combs, though, as Chaz—who knows the secret of the plague cure—plays it straight and intense. Perfunctory storytelling here, with occasional out-of-the-ordinary scenes—e.g., the body-counting shop, the right-here-on-our-stage immolation of one plague victim.

**DEAD MAN'S LETTERS** see *Letters from a Dead Man*

**DEAD MATE** Prism Ent./Jaylo Int'l. (Lew Mishkin) 1989 color 89m. (aka *Deadmate. Graverobbers* - orig t). SP, D: Straw Weisman. Mus: K. Quittner. SpMkpFX: Arnold Gargiulo II. Ref: V 1/10/90:33 (hv). 10/19/88:142, 223 (ad). Martin. With Elizabeth Mannino, David Gregory, Lawrence Bockius, Adam Wahl.

Mortician into necrophilia and reanimation of the dead. "For the lowest end of the homevideo spectrum." (V)

**DEAD MEN DON'T DIE** Waymar Prods. (Wayne Marmorstein) 1990 color 92m. SP, D: Malcolm Marmorstein. Mus: David Williams. Mkp: Byrd Holland, I. Csaki. Ref: V 9/24/90: "satisfying silliness." PT 11:51: "bad." With Elliott Gould, Melissa Anderson, Mark Moses, Mabel King, Philip Bruns.

"Voodoo cleaning lady" brings man back from the dead.

**\*DEAD MEN TELL** 1941 (*Charlie Chan in Dead Men Tell* - ad t ). Mus D: Emil Newman. AD: Richard Day, Lewis Creber. Ref: TV. V 3/26/41. Dolores Willis. Hanke/Chan. Filmfax 18. Maltin '92. Scheuer. no Lentz. Lee (E). With Katharine Aldridge.

Aboard the *Suva Star*, combination sailing ship and maritime museum, where the scratching of the hook of the "ghost of Black Hook," a pirate, heralds murder—an old lady's heart gives out when she sees the "ghost," or "horrible illusion of ghost." Plus: spooky scenes in which Jimmy Chan (Sen Yung) gets trapped in a box and, later, impersonates Black Hook.... Atmospheric lighting, fog effects, and close-ups dominate the opening sequences on ship and docks. The film's less thrilling when plot and comedy take over. The "strange music ... ghost music," from the ghost's ocarina, seems inspired by the eerie oboe of *The Adventures of Sherlock Holmes.* Extra added: the unsung Milton Parsons as the neurotic La Farge. ("Dead men tell no tales!")

The **DEAD NEXT DOOR** Amsco 1989 color 84m. SP, D, P, Mus, Ed: J.R. Bookwalter. Ph: M. Tolochko Jr. PD: Jon Killough. MkpFX: Sharon Mirman. Ref: TV: Tempe Video. Bill Warren.

With Peter Ferry, Bogdan Pecic, Floyd Ewing Jr., Maria Markovic, Scott Spiegel.

"Zombies—hundreds of 'em!" Well, at least dozens. Akron, Ohio. Corpses infected by a lab virus become "grotesque, flesheating humans" which overrun the countryside. Plus: a cult which hoards zombies and one still-half-human, talking zombie .... Or, Fun with Ultra-Gore. Film has a few ideas and a little humor, but is awkwardly acted and technically erratic. Wry: the zombie-rights protestors. Not so wry: characters with names like Savini, Romero, Raimi, King, and Carpenter.

*DEAD OF NIGHT 1945. Ph: Stan Pavey, Douglas Slocombe. SpFX: C. Richardson, L. Banes. Mkp: Tom Shenton. Ref: TV: Thorn EMI Video. Barr/Ealing. V 9/19/45 (104m. version). 7/3/46 (75m. version). Wolf/Horror. Hardy/HM. Lentz. Lee. Kael/5001. Stanley. Agee. Weldon. Phantom. Maltin '92. Scheuer. Martin.

"The reflection was all wrong." Renown omnibus horror-fantasy begins with dandy premises re a haunted mirror, a ventriloquist's dummy that seems to be alive, a premonition of violence in a country home (Pilgrim's Farm, Kent), etc., and is one of the rare instances in which an omnibus film's framing story (written by E. F. Benson, directed by Basil Dearden) equals or surpasses, in power, the interpolated stories. The film's generally low-key manner helps offset the fact that one of its tales ("The Bus Conductor") seems fragmented, one ("Room in the Tower") blunts its narrative point, one ("The Haunted Mirror") is uncertainly developed, and one ("The Inexperienced Ghost") is a real mood-shatterer. The Pilgrim's Farm framing story relies on the chill of deja vu—a small avalanche of horrors here hinges on in-themselves-insignificant acts. ("Why did you have to break your glasses?") The most famous sequence, "The Ventriloquist's Dummy" (written by John Baines, directed by Cavalcanti), and the climactic sequence find their terror in, simply, the manic look on Michael Redgrave's face, as his dummy, Hugo (smothered by a pillow), cries out ... in Redgrave's periodic gasps of fear ... and in the spectacle of Hugo just standing up. High-voltage Georges Auric score.

DEAD OF NIGHT see Mirror of Death

DEAD OF WINTER MGM/John Bloomgarden 1987 color 100m. D, Exec P: Arthur Penn. SP: Marc Shmuger, Mark Malone. Mus: Richard Einhorn. Prosth: Nick Dudman. SpFxSup: Neil Trifunovich. Mkp Des: Ann Brodie. Ref: TV. MFB'88:42. V 2/4/87. SFChron 2/7/87. ad. With Mary Steenburgen, Roddy McDowall, Jan Rubes, William Russ, Ken Pogue.

A severed ring finger, a secret attic room harboring a dead body, a "back from the dead" scene, and a hint of madness provide scattered, sweet, minor frissons in this thin thriller. A good vehicle for McDowall, it's not so good for Penn, though the *Halloween* shock moments are well engineered.

DEAD ON: RELENTLESS II CineTel (Hertzberg/Hansen/Knell) 1991 color c95m. D: Michael Schroeder. SP: Mark Sevi. SpFX: Bill Myatt. Mkp: Tania McComas. Ref: TV. TVG. V 2/24/92:180.

Los Angeles. The "Slash and Strangle" killer who uses ropes and chains as weapons and leaves bloody symbols on walls turns out to be a Soviet Special Forces agent liquidating "Soviet spies who

don't want to come in from the cold." Follow-up to *Relentless* (Leo Rossi, Meg Foster, and Mindy Seger are back) is less slasher movie than cop/spy film. It's mostly vacuous "local vs. federal"/cop-vs.-FBI-agent filler, though the ambitious revelation sequence tries to be an updated *Manchurian Candidate*.

The DEAD PIT Cornerstone (Gimel Everett/J. A. Sunseri) 1989 color 100m. SP, D, Ed: Brett Leonard. SP, Ed: also G. Everett. Ph: Marty Collins. Mus: Dan Wyman. AD: R. Rideout. SpFxD: Ed Martinez. Mkp: Martin DeClerq. Ref: TV: Imperial video. V 5/31/89: "puns liven up a fairy mindless script." Nowlan. With Jeremy Slate, Danny Gochnauer (Dr. Colin Ramzi), Cheryl Lawson, S.G. Foster; Kaldonia et al (featured dead).

"Ramzi has come back from the other side of death!" Principals at the State Institution for the Mentally Ill include a lady who says her memories have been "cut out" and who speaks in strange voices and a surgeon researching the organic causes of insanity who has been sealed up with his subjects in his own pit of bodies and body parts. ("I killed him once; I'll kill him again.") At the end, "holy water" dissolves the zombies.... Supposedly really "fiendish" vehicle for puncture and cannibal gore. Needed: an APB for the plot. Film's raison d'etre, so to speak: the shots of the zombies climbing out of the cauldron-like pit. Overbearing score, okay dissolving effects.

DEAD SLEEP (Austral.) Vestron (Stanley O'Toole) 1990 color feature. D: Alec Mills. SP: Michael Rymer. Ref: SFChron Dtbk 12/15/91. PT 14:49: "dull." With Linda Blair, Tony Bonner, Peta Downes.

Drug-induced comas produce "zombies."

DEAD SPACE Califilm (Concorde)/Mike Elliott 1991 (1990) color 78m. (*Biohazard* - orig t). D: Fred Gallo. SP: Catherine Cyran. Mus: Daniel May. SpMkpFX: Gabe Bartalos. Opt: Motion. Ref: TV. V 6/24/91. 12/17/90:41 (rated). 8/15/90:9: shooting. Martin. PT 13:50. With Marc Singer, Laura Tate, Bryan Cranston, Judith Chapman, Randy Reinholz, Rodger Hall (Tinpan, robot), Liz Rogers.

"We ended up creating a monster." In order to attack Delta 5, an immune-system-destroying virus, scientists at a research lab on the planet Phabon unleash a "metamorphic mutant." The new virus "carries disease, every disease we've ever known," and enters one scientist's nostril, then emerges from her torso. Already bigger, it now looks like an Albert Alligator doll, then gets very big and gangly. At the end, it's Disease vs. Disease.... Strictly formula *Alien* imitation hardly even tries. Dead space, alright.

The DEAD TALK BACK Headliner Prods. 1957 b&w c75m. SP, D, P: Merle S. Gould. Ref: TV. Filmfax 41:28. Greg Luce. With Aldo Farnese, Scott Douglas, Laura Brock.

"Who is with us from the invisible?" An inventor/medium comes up with a "device that can mechanically speak to the dead." The latter, apparently, leave behind a "fox glow," a radio signal which activates the inventor's crystal and then becomes filtered through "radio equipment." The recently dead, however, must "go through a certain learning period" before they can contact the living. Plus a *Premature Burial* alarm device, floating objects, and a fake living-dead woman .... The use of the latter ruse rather undermines the credibility of the inventor. This is a film so inert that even "Mystery Science Theatre 3000" couldn't revive it.

**DEAD TIME STORIES** Cinema Group/Scary Stuff (Bill Paul) 1986 (1985) color 81m. (*Deadtime Stories* - ad t. *Freaky Fairy Tales* - orig t). SP, D, Lyrics: Jeffrey Delman. SP: also Charles Shelton, J. Edward Kiernan. Addl Mat'l. ("Goldi Lox"): Philip Morton, Bruce Paddock, Douglas O. White. Mus: Taj. AD: Joan Lopate, Mark Pruess, Jorge Toro. MkpFX: Bryant Tausek, Ed French; (cr seq) Norman Bryn. Ref: TV. V 5/14/86. ad. Scheuer. V 10/24/84:179 (ad). With Scott Valentine, Nichole Picard, Cathryn DePrume, Melissa Leo, Michael Mesmer.

Three tales plus a framing story, "The Boy Who Cried Monster," re a monster haunting a boy's bedroom. 1) "Peter and the Witches": Two witches revive a third witch, in this ungainly crossing of the fairy tale and gore movies. The yuck-effects, revival set-piece and the squabbling between the witches ("I get the eyes!") provide the only amusement. 2) "Little Red Running-hood": Granny becomes a werewolf, too, in the okay payoff to this otherwise routine retelling of the "Little Red Ridinghood" tale. 3) "Goldi Lox and the Three Baers": Amityville. Goldi Lox, a psychic girl who collects her murdered boy friends, meets the cutthroat Baer clan. Mixture of fairy tale and psycho-killer comedy is crude and in poor taste, but pretty wild and occasionally quite funny.

**DEAD WOMEN IN LINGERIE** Monarch HV/Seagate Films 1991 (1990) color 89m. SP, D, P: Erica Fox. SP: also John Romo. Mus: Ciro Hurtado. Ph: J.C. Newby. PD: Adam Leventhal. Mkp: Susan Mayer. OptFX: Cinema Research.Ref: TV. V 2/4/91:92 (hv): "misfire." With J. Romo, Maura Tierney, Jerry Orbach, Dennis Christopher, June Lockhart, Lyle Waggoner, Ken Osmond.

"You were always my favorite." L.A., 1987. "Some kind of serial thing" seems to be behind the deaths of several lingerie models—suspense and stalking in the garment factory .... The deadest thing here is the dialogue. Well-meant cross between a stalker shocker and a drama re undocumented aliens is limp, as polemic or thriller. Even old pro Orbach seems a little helpless.

**DEADBEAT AT DAWN** Asmodeus Prods. (Michael King) 1988 color c85m. SP, D, MkpFX, Ed: Jim Van Bebber. Ref: TV: Ketchum Video. no Martin. no Scheuer. no Maltin '92. no Phantom. no Hound. PT 2:8. 8:5.

Tawdry urban-jungle movie with a hint of "voodoo magic," some gore (including a beheading and a throat-ripping), and a visualized vision re a ghostly dead woman.

**DEADFALL** see *Project: Alien*

**DEADLOCK** HBO-TV & Pierce Co. & Spectacor/Fox (Branko Lustig) 1991 color c95m. (aka *Dead Lock*). D: Lewis Teague. SP: B. Miller. Ph: D. Lohmann. Mus: Richard Gibbs. PD: Veronica Hadfield. SpFX: Image Engineering. Mkp: Charles Balazs. Ref: TV. PT 14:43: "head exploding scenes." HBO/Cinemax. TVG. V 5/6/91: C-58, C-71: *Wedlock* - t error? With Rutger Hauer, Mimi Rogers, Joan Chen, James Remar, Stephen Tobolowsky, Basil Wallace, Grand L. Bush.

"Sometime in the future," at Camp Holliday, the "new jewel of maximum security institutions." Electronically linked collars make prisoners explode if they venture too far, and "floaters" are a kind of cross between solitary confinement and sensory deprivation .... Scorecard: cliches ... a miscast Hauer ... "wedlock"-collar scenes which play like a silly variation on *The 39 Steps* and *The Defiant Ones* ... and a few heads-go-boom scenes.

**DEADLY ADVICE** (B) Evergreen/Deadly Advice 1993 color 91m. Ref: vc box: "meek bookseller ... gets a visit from ... Jack the Ripper...." With J. Pryce, J. Horrocks.

**DEADLY COMPANION** see *Deadly Dreams*

**DEADLY DANCER** Action Int'l. (David Winters-Bruce Lewin) 1991 color 99m. D, P: Kimberley Casey. SP: David Halpern, Maria Fields. Story: David A. Prior. Mus: W. Stromberg. Ref: V 2/4/91:92 (hv): "very tame entry in the popular vid genre of go-go dancers in jeopardy." With Smith Wordes, Walter W. Cox, Steve Jonson, Shabba-Doo.

**DEADLY DARLING** (H. K.?) Joseph Lai/IFD Films & Arts Ltd. 1985 color c90m. D: Karen Yang. SP: Benny Ho. Ph: Dean Cheng. Mus: Bennett Lee. PD: Godfrey Ho. FX: Alan Chu. Mkp: Jessie Wu. Ref: TV: Unicorn Video. Hound. Scheuer. With Fonda Lynn, Warren Chan, Bernard Tsui, Cherry Kwok, Morris Lam, Anita Leung, Robert Choi, Sam Wong, Tony Lim.

Wendy Chan, a reporter out to "destroy" a rapist, is herself gang-raped by five men ("Andy and the boys"). The rapists soon begin finding eyeballs in their rice and cattle entrails in their mailboxes. Crazed, Wendy attacks one of the five, Arthur Wong, with a meathook, then hangs his body with the other carcasses in the slaughterhouse, in an image out of Fifties gore comics. The original rapist ("Sadism turns me on") is bent on getting her before she gets him, and the script now reverts to the straight slasher-film formula, until he loses his hatchet and she finds her knife.... In this crude variation on *Ms. 45*, all principal and incidental males are, to varying degrees, slobs. Wendy's boy friend's first response to the news of her rape: "What'll my friends think?" Finally, this is just another slasher movie.

**DEADLY DREAMS** Concorde/New Classics (Matt Leipzig/Victor Simpkins) 1988 color 79m. (aka *Deadly Companion*). D: Kristine Peterson. SP: Thom Babbes. Mus: Todd Boekelheide. SpMkpFX: Deborah Zoeller. Ref: V 11/16/88: "interesting low-budget horror pic." Nowlan. Hound. With Mitchell Anderson, Juliette Cummins, Xander Berkeley, Beach Dickerson.

Nightmares ... "morbid." (V)

**DEADLY FRIEND** WB/Pan Arts & Layton (Robert M. Sherman) 1986 color 90m. D: Wes Craven. SP: Bruce Joel Rubin, from Diana Henstell's novel *Friend*. Mus: Charles Bernstein. Robot: Robotics 21, Ray Raymond. SpMkpFX: Mike Hancock; Lance Anderson. Ref: TV. MFB'87:111-12. V 10/15/86. ad. With Matthew Laborteaux, Kristy Swanson (Sam), Michael Sharrett, Anne Twomey, Anne Ramsey, Charles Fleischer (BB's voice).

A robot's computer brain is implanted in the head of Sam, a brain-dead girl. Sam/BB then kills the father who killed her and—in an absurd coda—sheds her human skin and becomes wholly robot.... Papier-mache tragedy rings vapid changes on robot and "Frankenstein" themes and features gratuitous makeup-effects gore.

**DEADLY GAME** USA-TV/Osiris Prods. & Wilshire Court (Johanna Persons) 1991 color c90m. D, Co-P: Thomas J. Wright. Tel: Wes Claridge. Mus: Tim Truman. Ref: V 7/8/91:52: "farfetched yarn keeps galloping along." TVG. TV Movie News 6/92. With Roddy McDowall, Marc Singer, Frederic Lehne, Michael Beck, Mitchell Ryan, Prof. Toru Tanaka.

*Most Dangerous Game* imitation: Madman invites guests to island so he can hunt them down.

**DEADLY INNOCENTS** Quest Studios & Orlando Film Partners (Hugh Parks) 1990 (1988) color 90m. D, Co-P: John D. Patterson. Co-D, P, SP: Hugh Parks. SP: also Joseph Tankersley. Mus: David C. Williams. SpFX: Michael Kent. Mkp: Christina Liczbinski. Ref: TV. V 9/3/90:80 (hv). With Mary Crosby, Andrew Stevens, Amanda Wyss, Bonnie Hellman, John Anderson.

"You can't go back to that house at night." Beth/Cathy (Crosby)—"two people locked in one body"—escapes from Ochula Sanitarium (a "damn nuthouse"). "With the Cathy personality in control, she is very dangerous"—and Cathy is in control. Her weapons include hypo, kitchen knife, frying pan, and broken glass, and she plastic-bags her victims.... Okay acting; unremarkable script.

**DEADLY INTRUDER** Channel One (Bruce Cook) 1985 color 84m. D, Mus: John McCauley. SpFX: Roger Kelton. Ref: V 4/24/85: "deadly dull." Ecran F 48:70. Stanley. With Chris Holder, Molly Cheek, Tony Crupi, Stuart Whitman, Danny Bonaduce.

Madman on the loose.

**DEADLY MANOR** see *Savage Lust*

**DEADLY MESSAGES** ABC-TV/Col-TV 1985 color c90m. (*Is Anybody There?* - orig t). D: Jack Bender. SP: Bill Bleich. Mus: Brad Fiedel. AD: Ross Bellah, Robert Purcell. SpFX: Eddie Surkin. Mkp: Leo Lotito Jr. Ref: TV. TVG. no Stanley. V 2/27/85:64. With Kathleen Beller, Michael Brandon, Dennis Franz, Scott Paulin, Elizabeth Huddle, Charles Tyner, Michael Cassidy (Mark).

Messages from a Ouija board lead a woman (Beller) to believe that a "ghost is trying to kill" her. As it happens, there are "no ghosts"—in 1978, she saw her brother (Cassidy) murder her boy friend, went into shock, and emerged as "Laura Daniels" (a "Canadian Nancy Drew"). Mark wants to make sure that her memory does not return.... Gallows humor and some atmospheric wind effects help this basically routine thriller. Nice bits by Tyner as a motel clerk and Huddle as a nurse who remembers Jenny Banning (aka Laura Daniels) very well.

**DEADLY OBSESSION** Distant Horizon (Anant Singh) 1988 color 93m. Story, SP, D, Co-P: Jeno Hodi. Story, SP: Paul Wolansky. SP: also Brian Cox. Mus: Marty Dunayer. PD: Kimberly von Brandenstein. SpFX: Ed French. Ref: TV: Republic HV. V 4/12/89. McCarty II. With Jeffrey R. Iorio, Martin Haber, Joe Paradise, Darnell Martin, Monica Breckenridge.

"Just call me John Doe." A maintenance worker (Paradise) at New Gotham College gorily murders a nosy co-worker, then terrorizes the coed (Martin) who survives his package of poisoned ice cream. Weapon of choice: a hypo filled with rat poison.... Freddy is the obvious inspiration for this scurvy little thriller's "John Doe." All the script's not-exactly-considerable ingenuity went into composing his one-liners. Despite the *Elm Street* dream apparatus, the movie is just a monotonous suspense-in-the-gym/suspense-in-the-dorm exercise.

**DEADLY POSSESSION** (Austral.) Premiere Film Marketing/Genesis Films 1987 color c99m. (*Coda* - orig t). SP, D: Craig Lahiff. SP, P: Terry Jennings. Mus: Frank Strangio. Mkp: Helen Evans. Ref: TV: Vestron Video. V 8/12/87. With Penny Cook, Arna-Maria Winchester (Dr. Steiner), Liddy Clark, Olivia Hamnett, Patrick Frost.

"He's still with me—in spirit." This line is the tipoff of course. The "figure in black"—or "resident psychopath"—who is hacking up people with a sword here turns out to be a woman who killed her brother, preserved the body, and "became him." Plus: paperweight weapon, photocopier frisson.... *Psycho* Down Under takes it own sweet time springing its not-unexpected narrative surprises. Padded with much chasing about, skulking, and just plain walking. Overexcited score.

**DEADLY REACTOR** Action Int'l. (David Winters/Fritz Matthews) 1989 color 88m. (*The Reactor* - early t). SP, D: David Heavener. Story: Thomas Baldwin. Mus: Brian Bennett. Ref: V 6/7/89: "offbeat Western in sci-fi clothing." Nowlan. With Stuart Whitman, D. Heavener, Darwyn Swalve, Kimberly Casey.

**DEADLY SNAIL VS. KUNG FU KILLERS** (H. K.) 1981 color c90m. Ref: TV: Ocean Shores Video/Wild West Video; Eng. titles.

Mussel Clam Fairy scares evildoers by turning her double briefly into a horrible green monster, then sends a skeleton and flying fireballs after them, while Evil Snake—a snake-skin-faced, human-shaped sea demon who can transform himself, variously, into a big snake and a human—turns the hero's sister into a skeleton.... Silly, occasionally sweetly comic fantasy, with a beyond-wild soundtrack—squeaky cupboard doors and rolling logs provide the sound effects for a tree demon's movements, and the theme music for the first undersea scene is lifted directly from *Hush, Hush, Sweet Charlotte.*

**DEADLY STING** see *Evil Spawn*

**DEADLY WEAPON** New World/Empire (Lexyn) 1989 (1988) color 90m. Story, SP, D: Michael Miner. Story: also George Lafia. Mus: Guy Moon. SpMkpFX: MMI; (des) John Buechler; (animatronics) John Criswell, Hal Miles. VisFxSup: David Stipes. Laser Gun Des: Steve Burg. SpFxCoord: Hollywood SpFX; Paul Staples. SpSdDes: Frank Serafine. Opt: Motion; (fx coord) Linda Obalil. Ref: TV. V 8/2/89. Maltin '92. Scheuer. With Rodney Eastman, Kim Walker, Gary Frank, Michael Horse, Ed Nelson, John Stuart Wildman.

"He traveled a great distance. He was a visitor from another galaxy." King Bee, Arizona. Young Zeke Robinson (Eastman), who sees himself as his (visualized) alter ego—a space-fighter-pilot, "the visitor"—happens upon a stray U.S. Army ray gun, a Star Wars-generated anti-matter pistol, powered by a thermionic reactor. The gun emits anti-electrons which create a super-hot X-ray beam.... This reworking of *Laserblast* is apparently meant to be Zeke's daydream, and it's the kind of unlikely, humorless movie a "sensitive," shallow, paranoid fifteen-year-old might write. Until he finds the gun, Zeke's life is almost comically oppressive—drunken father, bullying fellow schoolmates, etc. These delusions of persecution give way to delusions of grandeur, as he cows the townsfolk with his newfound weapon. ("He can do anything he wants.") The mystical/tragic ending scrambles both sorts of delusions.

**DEADMATE** see *Dead Mate*

**DEADTIME STORIES** see *Dead Time Stories*

**DEAN R. KOONTZ' WHISPERS** see *Whispers*

**DEAN R. KOONTZ'S SERVANTS OF TWILIGHT** see *Servants of Twilight, The*

**DEAR DEPARTED** see *Those Dear Departed*

**DEAR DIARY** (Fili) Viva Films 1989 color c100m. Credits for "Dear Killer," second of two stories (first, "Dear Partyline," not horror): D: Leroy Salvador. SP: Armando Lao. Ph: Ely Cruz. PD: Jeffrey Jeturian. Mkp: Zenaida Huganas. SdFX: Jun Martinez. Ref: TV: vt; some Eng. With Lea Salonga, Herbert Bautista, Michael De Mesa (Simon Macalintal), Rosemarie Gil (his mother), Leroy Salvador, Lilet (Pauline Carpo).

Quezon City. Or, "Jane Eyre Goes to High School." Cornball suspense-horror features a ghost (Lilet), a shock sequence in which her skeleton is found, a visualized nightmare re a werewolf-like monster and (in both a flashback and a current-tense sequence) a knife-wielding madwoman kept locked in an upstairs room.

**DEATH ANGEL** see *I Come in Peace*

**DEATH BECOMES HER** Univ (Starkey/Bradshaw) 1992 color 103m. D, Co-P: Robert Zemeckis. SP: Martin Donovan, David Koepp. Ph: Dean Cundey. Mus: Alan Silvestri. PD: Rick Carter. SpVisFX: IL&M; (sup) Ken Ralston. MkpDes: Dick Smith. Prosth: Kevin Haney. SpBodyFx: Tom Woodruff Jr., Alec Gillis. SpFxSup: Michael Lantieri. Computer Graphics Sup: Doug Smythe. Ref: TV: vt. V 7/27/92: "eye-popping effects." Cinef 12/92:60. SFChron Dtbk 7/26/92: "macabre Gothic parable." SFExam 7/31/92: "heaps of severed heads, lopped limbs and shattered torsos." Sacto Bee 7/31/92: "hilarious." With Meryl Streep, Bruce Willis, Goldie Hawn, Isabella Rossellini, Ian Ogilvy, Clement von Franckenstein, Stephanie Anderson (Marilyn Monroe), Bob Swain (Andy Warhol), Ron Stein (Elvis).

"High priestess of eternal life" (V) offers "elixir of eternal youth." (SFC) The potion "stops the aging process" for "Mad" (Streep) and "Hel" (Hawn), who wind up legally dead, but still talking. Gothic elements include the witch's castle, an extended thunderstorm, and the "It's alive!" line from the old Universals .... The long-windup plot finally gets going with Streep's "dislocated neck" turn, in this tale of the "living dead in Beverly Hills." The comedy is very broad, intentionally "cartoonish"; fortunately, Streep, unlike Zemeckis and company, has more than one gear.

**DEATH BY DIALOGUE** City Lights/Pepin-Merhi 1988 color 90m. SP, D: Tom DeWier. Addl Dial: Susan Trabue. Ph: V. Mikulic. Mus: John Gonzalez. AD: Kathleen Coates. SpMechFX: Joe Talentino. Gargoyle: Damon Charles. SpMkpFX: Judy Yonemoto. Ref: TV: City Lights HV. Hound. Martin. With Ken Sagoes, Lenny Delduca, Kelly Sullivan, Laura Albert, Ted Lehman, Judy Gordon; Mark Ginther, Robert Lee et al (evil spirits).

"It killed Mr. Thorn, and Gene and Linda, and I just saw it suck in Detective Benjamin! And it spit him back in my face!" "It" is a haunted script, "Victim—," and it also blasts a girl through the side of a barn, materializes a rock group in the middle of a field, and conjures up a gargoyle, a warrior demon, and two undead motorcyclists. The demon script contains, it transpires, the restless life force of a journalist killed by Amazon Indians, and it rewrites reality. ("There are scenes appearing where blank pages were before.").... The title is a mistake, there are no characters, and there's a lot of dead space, but DeWier has latched onto an idea, and screwy as it is, it makes for an entertaining movie. With this premise, anything goes—if the teenaged heroes rewrite the script, the latter rewrites their rewrite. *Death by Dialogue* has the freewheeling spirit (and some of the weaknesses) of the first *Phantasm*. If it's far from a classic, and far from good, it has some almost-classic inspirations. And it is, in its erratic way, adventurous.

**DEATH CARRIES A CANE** see *Tormentor*

**DEATH COLLECTOR** see *Tin Star Void*

**DEATH DREAMS** Lifetime-TV/Capital Cities, ABC Video Ents. & Dick Clark Film Group & Roni Weisberg Prods. 1991 color c90m. D: Martin Donovan. Tel: Robert Glass, from William Katz's novel. Mus: Gerald Gouriet. PD: Stephen Greenberg. Mkp: Julie Hewett. Ref: TV. TVG. Sacto Bee 6/25/91: "two interminable hours." V 7/1/91:37: "eerie." With Christopher Reeve, Marg Helgenberger, Fionnula Flanagan, Cec Verrell.

"A little girl comes back from the grave...."

**\*DEATH FROM A DISTANCE** Chesterfield (Maury M. Cohen) 1935. Mus D: Abe Meyer. AD: Edward C. Jewell. SpFX: Jack Cosgrove. Ref: TV: Foothill Video. Turner/Price. V 1/8/36. Lee. Lentz. no Hardy/SF. no Stanley. With John St. Polis, John Davidson, Henry Hall, Creighton Hale, Frank LaRue, Hal Price.

"The reflected light from the star made the contact and fired the shot." The mystery: "star murder" on the "forsaken hilltop" of Forest Park Planetarium. The unique plot gimmick: Light from Arcturus—"Job's star"—activates a telescope's photoelectric cell, and a hollow pipe connected to the cell by wire acts as a firing mechanism for a .38 shell. Only redeeming feature of this blandly acted and written locked-room mystery: the presence of the aforementioned "telescope gun."

**DEATH HOUSE** Action Int'l. (Nick Marino) 1988 color feature. D: John Saxon. SP: William Selby, D. S. Freeman, Kate Whitcomb. Ref: PT 14:49: "pretty dumb." With J. Saxon, Dennis Cole, Tane McClure, Anthony Franciosa, Michael Pataki, Ron O'Neal.

Prison inmates become "killer zombies."

**DEATH LIST** see *Terminal Choice*

**DEATH MACHINE** Vidmark 1994 color feature. SP,D: S. Norrington. Ref: PT 22:68: "copies *Alien* and *Robocop*"; cyborgs, "killer robot." With Brad Dourif, William Hootkins.

**DEATH MAGIC** The Domino Theatre/Paul F. Clinco 1992 color 93m. Story, SP,D: P.F. Clinco. Story: also Mark A.W. Smith. Mus: M.Q. Orrall. SpFX: Ted Wooten, Rex Classen. Ref: TV. PT 14:12. With Anne Caffrey, Keith De Green, Jack Dunlap, Danielle Frons, Norman Stone, Roger Gentry.

"Are we really gonna raise the dead?" On the night of Dalath Amator, U.S. Cavalry Major Parker—executed in 1875—is magically conjured up and proceeds to commit a series of sword killings. ("I'll break the doors of hell!") Stilted fantasy-horror. Even toplessness and gore can't save it. Key book: "The Book of Curses."

**DEATH NURSE** Video City/IRMI Films (Frances Millard) 1987 color c55m. SP, D: Nick Philips. Ph: Karil Ostman. AD: C. R. Fenwick. Mkp: Gigo. Ref: TV: Video City video. Phantom: Edith's nightmares from *Criminally Insane* (2P). no Hound. Martin. With Priscilla Alden (Edith Mortley).

Patients who check into the Shady Palms Clinic find themselves in the "very capable hands" of nurse Edith Mortley ("I like helping people") and her brother Gordon, a sort of combination slasher/surgeon. ("It was a difficult surgery.") Edith feeds patients to rats ("Mama's babies!") and rats to patients.... Low comedy and low gore in this very dry, shot-on-tape, Milligan-level production. If the gore and cackles ring phony, *Death Nurse* does deliver some sick yocks—this might be the Tod Slaughter version of *M*A*S*H*. The 1934 *Maniac* apparently inspired the scene in which the cat runs around with the dog's heart. Prime line (Edith to Gordon): "You're gonna have to dig him up—and make sure you get all the dirt off!"

**The DEATH OF THE INCREDIBLE HULK** NBC-TV/New World-TV & Bixby-Brandon Prods. (Hugh Spencer-Phillips & Robert Ewing) 1990 color 90m. D, Exec P: Bill Bixby. Tel: Gerald DiPego, from the Stan Lee characters. Mus: Lance Rubin. PD: Douglas Higgins. SpFX: Dean Lockwood. SpMkp: Tibor Farkas. Ref: TV. V 2/14/90:58. With Bill Bixby, Lou Ferrigno, Elizabeth Gracen, Philip Sterling, Barbara Tarabuck, Anna Katerina, John Novak, Andreas Katsulas (Kasha).

David Banner wants "to be human again," gets his wish, dies. Routine combo of action and sentiment. Some fun Hulk stunts. The busting-through-the-walls one harks back to *The Mummy's Ghost*, and—in the search for a scientific cure for Hulk-dom—the telefilm plays like the Dr. Edelmann-Larry Talbot sections of *House of Dracula*.

**DEATH ON SAFARI** see *Ten Little Indians* (1989)

**DEATH POWDER** (J) 1986 color feature (*Desu Pawuda*). D: S. Izumiya. Ref: Weisser/JC. With S. Izumiya, T. Inukai.

Cyborg's victims begin "mutating into one enormous amoeba."

**\*The DEATH RAY** 1925. Ref: screen. PFA notes 4/10/86. Hardy/SF. Lee.

A secret Moscow laboratory. An inventor's death ray—which "detonates fuel at a distance"—blows up a beaker on the other side of the lab. The extant 103-minute print (which has both missing and reversed reels) of *The Death Ray* suggests, also, that the ray later destroys three airplanes. This wearing film plays like a socialist Keystone Kops serial. The broad, stylized movements of the actors are good for (intentional?) laughs.

**DEATH RAY 2000** NBC-TV/QM-TV & Woodruff 1981 (1979) color 94m. (*T. R. Sloane* - alt TV t). D: Lee H. Katzin. SP, P: Cliff Gould. Ph: Bill Butler. AD: G. B. Chan, Norman Newberry. SpFX: Chuck Dolan. Ref: TVG. TV. Lentz. Stanley. TGSP2. Maltin '92. Scheuer. With Robert Logan, Ann Turkel, Clive Revill, Dan O'Herlihy, Penelope Windust, Maggie Cooper, Paul Mantee, Ji-Tu Cumbuka, Fred Sadoff, Michelle Carey (computer voice).

The dehydrator cannon, which "reaches through everything" and removes moisture from the atmosphere, wilts a daisy and dehydrates women inside a van.... O'Herlihy is good, and the makeup effects for the first ray victims are okay, but this is mostly perfunctory action and intrigue. Pilot for the "A Man called Sloane" TV series.

**DEATH RING** New Line 1992 color c90m. D: Robert J. Kizer. Ref: TVG. SFChron Dtbk 3/7/93. With Mike Norris, Chad McQueen, Don Swayze.

"Eccentric millionaire" hunts "nation's champion survivalist." (SFC)

**DEATH ROW DINER** Camp 1988 color c90m. D: D. Wood. Ref: V 1/27/88:6: 11/87 start. Hound. With Jay Richardson, Michelle McClellan, John Content.

Electrical storm revives man unjustly executed.

**DEATH SCREAMS** see *House of Death*

**DEATH SPA** SGE/DS Prods. (Jamie Beardsley-Jones) 1987 color 87m. (*Witch Bitch* - alt t). D: Michael Fischa. SP: James Bartruff, Mitch Paradise. Mus: Peter Kaye. PD: Robert Schulenberg. SpFX: (sup) R. E. McCarthy; Wizards, Inc. SpMkpFX: Mel Slavick. Ref: TV. V 7/4/90:34 (hv). Mifed '89:189. 10/19/88:185. 2/21/90:155. Bowker '90, SFChron Dtbk 8/7/88. Cinef 4/91. With William Bumiller, Brenda Bakke, Merritt Butrick, Ken Foree, Shari Shattuck, Rosalind Cash.

The dead Catherine (Shattuck) possesses her twin, David (Butrick), and wreaks havoc at the computer-run Starbody Health Spa. (Just enough neon lights remain glowing on the sign to spell out "Death Spa.") Revolting sound effect: the acid-wrecked woman's moans. Revolting makeup effect: the pasta-faced horror. Revolting visual effect: the flying killer swordfish. Only effective non-gore scene: David's wrestling with Catherine's spirit, as one body, then the other takes over. Strictly functional gore vehicle, despite the supernatural elements.

The **DEATH TRAIN** (Austral.) Fox-Lorber/Grundy Premier (Robert Bruning) & Australian Film Commission 1978 ('84-U.S.) color c96m. D: Igor Auzins. SP: Luis Bayonas. Ph: Richard Wallace. AD: Darrell Lass. Ref: TV: Paragon Video. TVFFSB. Hound. With Hugh Keays-Byrne, Ingrid Mason, Max Meldrum, Ken Goodlet, Brian Wenzel.

"The ghost train of Clematis," New South Wales, is getting "louder and closer than ever before"—but the nearest railroad tracks are fifty miles away. Is someone taking advantage of a local legend which says that a murdered engineer keeps coming back in his train and "storming through the night"? The answer to the latter question comes by very slow freight. The spooky-mystery premise is at once loony and intriguing, and the down-to-earth resolution disappoints, especially after such suggestive red herrings as a levitating Ouija-board goblet. Overextended whimsy.

**DEATH TRAP** see *Sisters of Death*

**DEATH WARMED UP** (N.Z.) Skouras Pictures/Tucker (Murray Newey) 1984 color 83m. SP, D: David Blyth. SP: also Michael Heath. Mus: Mark Nicholas. SpFX: Kevin Chisnall. MkpFX: B. Hurden, R. McCorquodale; (prosth) Keith Pine. Ref: TV. MFB'85:180-1: in assn. with the N.Z. Film Commission. V 9/5/84. with Michael Hurst, Gary Day, Bruno Lawrence, Margaret Umbers.

"There's something bloody weird going on!" Dr. Archer Howell (Day) is experimenting in the "area of life elongation" at Trans-Cranial Applications, on an "isolated island." His experiments, however, invariably result only in genetic-recombination mutations, and all of his "psycho patients" are "melting down." Not a pretty sight.... The script is no more specific about the nature and purpose of Howell's experiments than it is about the location of that "isolated island." He might simply fancy messy surgery. At any rate, he's up to no good. The film itself, also up to no good, is merely a gory-effects vehicle. A narrative undercurrent re the unhealthiness of obsessive revenge can easily be ignored.

**DEATH WISH CLUB** see *Carnival of Fools*

**DEATHBED** see *Terminal Choice*

**3P The DEATHHEAD VIRGIN** (Fili) JPD/GWG & Spectrum 1973? color 94m. D: Norman Foster. SP: Ward Gaynor. Ph: Fredy Conde; (underwater) Mike Dugan. Mus: Richard La Salle. SpFX: Jessie Sto. Domingo. Mkp: T. D. Serna. SdFX: The Cutters. Opt: Cinefx. Ref: TV: Academy Home Ent. video; Eng. version. TVFFSB. no Martin. Hound. Stanley. With Jock Gaynor, Larry Ward, Diane McBain, Vic Diaz, Kim Ramos, Manny Ojeda.

An "ancient fanatical religious group" waiting for the return of the Deathhead Virgin—the "last virgin princess of the Moros"—finds same when an "old wreck" of a Spanish man-o'-war yields a mysteriously shackled skeleton which, freed, becomes the deathhead-masked, but otherwise naked, virgin Zaila (sp?). Now, seven virgins must die and be scalped, or shaved, to atone for the treatment that she received at the hands of the Spaniards.... Outre premise; regulation action. One little shock: the unmasking of the virgin. (Underneath the mask ... a skull.)

**DEATHROW GAMESHOW** Crown Int'l./Pirromount 1987 color 83m. SP, D: Mark Pirro. Add'l. Matl.: Alan Gries. Mus: Gregg Gross. SpFX: Chuck Schulthies Jr. Title Seq: Glenn Campbell, Harry Moreau. Ref: TV. V 12/9/87. With John McCafferty, Robin Blythe, Beano, Debra Lamb.

Chuck Toedan (McCafferty) hosts Live or Die—the "game show that gives those condemned prisoners one last chance before their final bow in life." One thug (Beano) who almost dies on camera revives in the show's "morgue." Plus a TV clip from "Curses of the Mummy" and Chuck's Nightmare re the ghost of Don Spumoni (Mark Lasky).... Silly-clever plot gets better as it goes along. (It couldn't get much worse—the first half of the film is mostly failed incidental comedy, like Chuck's Nightmare, a real nightmare done as a TV show.) Crude, gross, funny end-credits sequence features clips from commercials which employ leftover Live or Die corpses (instead of demo dummies) in car-accident simulations, etc.

**DEATHSTALKER II: DUEL OF THE TITANS** (U.S.-Arg.) Concorde/New Horizons (Frank Isaac, Jr.) 1987 (1986) color 77m. (*Cazador II*). Story, D: Jim Wynorski. SP: Neil Ruttenberg. Add'l. Dial: R. J. Robertson. Mus: Chuck Cirino. SpFX: Nicky Morgan. Mkp: Maria Laura. Ref: TV: Vestron video. V 11/25/87. With John Terlesky, Monique Gabrielle, John La Zar, Toni Naples, Maria Socas (Amazon queen), Marcos Wolinsky, Deanna Booher ("Queen Kong").

Ingredients: Deathstalker (Terlesky), "right up there with Conan" ("I rob from the rich and pretty much keep it") ... the evil sorcerer Jarek (La Zar), who brings Sultana (Naples) back from the dead ... soul-cloning: the false "Evie" (Gabrielle), a vampire ("I won't bite"), is created by Jarek "from the original soul" of the Princess Evie (Gabrielle) ... zombies that rise from their graves ("Spooky, huh?") ... and pig-men.... Gabrielle is funny and sexy, especially as the real Evie. Otherwise, the humor alternates between the somewhat taking new *Barbarians* casualness of approach to sword-and-sorcery sagas and the simply limp.

**DEATHSTALKER AND THE WARRIORS FROM HELL** (Mex-U.S.) Concorde/New Classics (Triana Films/Robert North) 1989 (1988) color 86m. (aka *Deathstalker III—The Warriors from Hell*). D, P: Alfonso Corona. SP: Howard Cohen. P: also A. De Noriega. Mus: Torres, Rulfo. Ref: V 6/7/89: "this one's a stiff." McCarty II: "mildly amusing." Martin: "fun." With John Allen Nelson, Carla Herd, Terri Treas, Thom Christopher. Mythical magical diamonds.

**DEATHSTALKER IV: MATCH OF TITANS** (U.S.-Bulg.) Concorde/Pacific Trust (Steven Rabiner/Ludmil Staikov) 1992 (1990) color 85m. SP, D: Howard Cohen. Ph: Emil Wagenstein. Mus: Simo Lazarov. FxMkp: Leftera Nedeva. SpPropDes: Vasko Petkov. SpOptFX: Nikolay Lazarov. Ref: TV: New Horizons HV. Martin. V 6/20/90:24: shooting. 2/10/92: 16 (rated). 1/3/90:11. With Rick Hill, Maria Ford, Brett Clark, Michelle Moffett, Anya Pencheva, Jocko Rossitch.

"In the Age of Darkness," there was a fire-spewing witch-queen who turned warriors into stone in order to create an implacable army. There was also a hero, Deathstalker, who gave them the antidote to the hardening process. ("They're coming back to life!") There were also pig, lion, etc.-headed mutants ... and primitive TV, or maybe just a magic mirror.

Virtually storyless, lackadaisical fantasy-with-monsters. A little mallet gore here. Some casual comedy there—e.g., Deathstalker, pinned to a castle wall by a stone warrior: "Caught between a rock and a hard place!"

**DEATHSTREET USA** see *Nightmare at Noon*

**DEBBIE DUZ DISHES** Gold Medallion/Adult Video Corp. 1986 color 81m. D: Bob Vosse. SP: John Finegold. Ref: vc box: Bigfoot's brother "Big Dick." Adam '88. Bill Warren. With Nina Hartley, Damon Christian (exorcist), Keli Richards.

**DEBIRUMAN** see *Devilman*

**DECEIT** Col-TriStar HV 1993 color feature. D: Albert Pyun. Ref: SFChron Dtbk 8/22/93. With Scott Paulin, Norbert Weisser, Samantha Phillips.

"An alien who seduces women from each respective polluted planet just before he destroys it runs into trouble with an Earth female."

**DECEIVED** BV (Touchstone) & Silver Screen Partners IV/Michael Finnell (Aysgarth Prods.) 1991 color 103m. D: Damian Harris. Story, SP & Co-P: Mary Agnes Donoghue. SP: also Bruce Joel Rubin. SpFxCoord: Martin Malivoire. Mkp: Irene Kent. Ref: TV. V 9/30/91. SFExam 9/27/91.

Mystery-suspense with horrific elements, including a ghostly figure in an apartment window, an old-fashioned woman-alone-with-maniac climactic sequence, creep music (by Thomas Newman), a big close-up of a peering eye, several "busses" (involving, respectively, pigeons, a cat, and John Heard), and a "dead" man who comes back. Thin from beginning to end, though a bit more fun at the end. The showcase piece of acting: Heard's casual cold-bloodedness.

**DECLIC, Le** see *Turn-On, The*

**DEEP BLOOD** (I) Filmirage & Variety 1987 color feature. D: Joe D'Amato. SP: G.N. Ott. Ph: F. Slonisco. Mus: Carlo Maria Cordio. AD: A. Colby. SpFX & Mkp: Brian Wood. OptFX: Moviecam 2000. Ref: TV: VSOM; Eng. version. Palmerini: aka *Sharks: Deep Blood*. With Frank Baroni, Allen Cort, Keith Kelsch, James Camp, Charles Brill, Mitzi McCall.

"That shark is still out there somewhere!" A Florida Indian legend "about a monster from the sea"—the "great beast"—seems to be fulfilled when a shark or two begin to haunt the waters off Ocean Springs. ("That was not the shark that killed John!") Vapid melo, human and shark. Accidentally funniest (figurative) line: "I'm bein' pulled in all different directions!" Best intentionally-creepy line: "The ocean got 'er."

**DEEP CUT** see *Profound and Mysterious, The*

**DEEP FREEZE** 1958. Ref: Greg Luce: syndicated as TV-movie. no LC. no Hound. no Lee. with Allison Hayes, Gerald Mohr.
Female alien on Earth.

**DEEP RED** Sci-Fi Channel/Univ (MCA)/(Dave Bell Assoc./MTE/Timothy Marx) 1994 color 85m. D: Craig R. Baxley. SP, Co-P: D.M. Mote. Ph: J. Fernandes. Mus: G. Chang. PD: G. Stover. VisFxSup: Ted Rae, Richard Bennett. Addl FX: Fantasy II. SpFxSup: B.R. Hessey. SpFX: Doug Hubbard. Ref: TV: MCA-Univ HV. PT 19:17. With Michael Biehn, Joanna Pacula, Lisa Collins, John de Lancie (morpher), M. Des Barres, Jesse Vint, Daniel Barringer (milkman #1).

"Deep Red is our future." An anti-aging formula ("molecular protein machines capable of repairing or reshaping the body cell by cell") ... "unstoppable" milkmen ... a villain who can "hold a shape for 21 minutes," at room temperature (he morphs among various personae) ... and a hero made invulnerable by "reds".... Unremarkable story admittedly has bizarre underpinnings. One effects highlight: the glass sliver absorbed into the girl's palm.

**DEEP SPACE** T.W.E./Alan Amiel & Fred Olen Ray 1988 (1987) color 90m. SP, D: Ray. SP: also T. L. Lankford. Mus: Robert O. Ragland, Alan Oldfield. Creature FX: Steve Patino, Sho-Glass FX. SpFxMkp: Steve Neill. AnimFX: Bret Mixon. SpFX: Kevin McCarthy. Ref: TV. V 5/11/88. With Charles Napier, Ann Turkel, Bo Svenson, Ron Glass, Julie Newmar (psychic), James Booth, Norman Burton, Anthony Eisley, Michael Forest, Peter Palmer, Elisabeth Brooks, Dawn Wildsmith, Susan Stokey, Sandy Brooke.

"It's crashed and it's alive!" The military, testing a "new form of biological warfare" in space, watches helplessly as the prototype crashes to Earth, activates, and begins killing with its tentacles: An *Alien* creature—"something more terrible than death itself"—emerges from the main container, while "giant roach eggs" hatch baby crab-spider creatures.... Old-hat plot, inane time-killing dialogue. The action takes place on shallow terra firma, not in deep space.

**DEEP SPACE 69** Heatwave 1994 color 80m. D: M. Ingley. Ref: Adam '96: mutants in space. With M. Rain, L. Sands.

**DEEPSTAR SIX** Tri-Star/Carolco (Mario Kassar & Andrew Vajna) 1989 (1988) color 100m. D, Co-P: Sean S. Cunningham. SP, Story: Lewis Abernathy. SP: also Geof Miller. Mus: Harry Manfredini. Creature: (des) Shagamauw Prods; (sp mkp fx) Mark Shostrom. VisFxSup: James Isaac. SpOptFX: Oxford Scientific, FX Associates, Illusion Arts; (sup) Peter Parks, Jim Danforth, Bill Taylor. Models: Crawley Creatures. Ref: TV: IVE video. MFB '89:238-9. V 1/18/89. Oak Trib 1/13/89. SFExam 1/13/89. SFChron 1/13/89. With Nancy Everhard, Greg Evigan, Taurean Blacque, Miguel Ferrer, Cindy Pickett, Marius Weyers, Nia Peeples.

Small craft advisory: "Something very big and very fast" shoots out of a "pretty deep" cavern on the ocean floor and attacks the U.S. Navy's Deepstar Six lab and its reconnaissance vehicles. The monster proves to be "some form of arthropod".... The early mystery-and-suspense scenes are best, though even here some irrelevant action sequences dilute. The big-mawed monster itself is less intimidating than (in those early sequences) the dreaded words, "Sonar contact." Eye contact proves disappointing. Ferrer's Snyder's mental disintegration steals what little show there is.

**DEF BY TEMPTATION** Troma/Orpheus Pictures (Bonded Film-works) 1990 color 95m. SP, D, P: James Bond III. Mus: Paul Laurence. SpMkp&Vis FX: Rob Benevides. SpFxMkp: Christina Bone. FX: Select FX; Pericles Lewnes. Ref: TV. V 5/9/90. With Bond, Kadeem Hardison, Bill Nuun, Cynthia Bond (temptress), Melba Moore (Madam Sonya).

"Its name is Temptation!" A mystery woman (C. Bond) with "spooky eyes"—who casts no reflection in mirrors—proves to be an "ancient demon" who needs a "truly innocent person" to give her more power. In demon form, she's fanged and bug-eyed; in human form, seductive.... A slightly improved version of *Night Angel*. If the horror stuff is hokey, the in-between scenes are generally pleasant and engaging. Highlights: Temptation's self-slip-on nylons and the TV-screen lips which suck in one victim.

**DEFCON-4** (Can.) New World/Salter Street Films 1985 (1983) color 85m. (*Dark Eyes* - orig t. *Ground Zero* - early t. *Def-Con 4* - ad t). SP, D, Co-P: Paul Donovan. Mus: Chris Young. Ref: TV. V 4/3/85. With Lenore Zann, Maury Chaykin, Kate Lynch, Kevin King.

"It is the day after tomorrow." NORAD's Nemesis Mission satellite falls back to Earth near Fort Liswell, exactly as programmed by local tyrant Gideon (King).... The usual postwar mutants ("terminals"), bizarre vehicles, fringe societies, etc. *Defcon-4*, however, is compact and well edited (by Todd Ramsay) and features okay performances and stirring bursts of action, though the latter are dependent on cliffhanger coincidences and timing.

**DEFENDERS OF THE EARTH: THE STORY BEGINS** Marvel Prods. & King Features Ent. (Karl Geurs) 1986 (1985) anim color 90m. Sup D: Ray Lee, John Gibbs. SP: Dick Robbins, Bryce Malek ("The Story Begins"); Mel Gilden ("The Creation of Monitor"); Jimmy Griffin, Dave Weathers ("A House Divided"); Evelyn Gabai ("The Mind Warriors"); Mark Zaslove ("Bits 'N' Chips"). "Flash Gordon" created by Alex Raymond; "The Phantom," "Mandrake the Magician," and "Lothar" by Lee Falk. Mus: Rob Walsh. AD: Gary Hoffman. Ref: TV: F. H. E. video. Stanley. no Hound. no Martin.

The cassette box says this is a "full-length animated feature," but this "feature" is divided into five stories re Flash Gordon, Mandrake the Magician, the Phantom, Lothar, Ming the Merciless, and their offspring. Other ingredients include Ming's ice robots and robo-ships, his pet dragon-snake, his life-draining Inquisitor machine, frost-coated zombies, a sea monster, an ages-old "doomsday warhead," a "hideous wormlike creature" inside the Defenders' super-computer, and (in "The Mind Warriors," the most interesting story) an imagination device which, in conjunction with the computer, conjures up a Frankenstein monster, a witch, demons, and skeleton warriors. ("This is better than any horror movie I ever saw.") Precipitate but familiar action features generally monotonous clashes between Ming and the Defenders.

**DEFENDERS OF THE VORTEX** (J) American National/Toei (Kei Iijima, Yoichi Kominato) 1980 ('88-U.S.) anim color 92m. D: Masayuki Akechi. SP: Ryuzo Nakanishi. Story: Shotaro Ishimori. Ph: S. Ikeda. Mus: Koichi Sugiyama. AD: I. Ito, K. Ebisawa. Anim D: Yasuhiro Yamaguchi. Ref: TV: CHE video; Eng. dubbed. Hound.

Chief premise: "The mother source of the universe did not scatter," but still exists, in the "heart of the universe," as a "super energy source," the Vortex. Other ingredients: a "child from another planet," whose inhabitants visited Peru in ancient times ... a "devil called Zoa," who has kidnapped the alien child's father ... The Galaxy Legion, nine hero-cyborgs ... "nerve-system destruction lasers" ... the Star Gate, a "short cut" in space ... a gigantic sea monster ("some kind of overgrown sea worm") ... teleportation ... a phantom alien "dog" ... and a princess trapped in a crystal which hangs from the neck of a "real tough-lookin' monster," or robot-Cyclops.... Basically treacle, with stilted dialogue and some design appeal.

**DEFY TO THE LAST PARADISE** see *Doomed To Die*

**DEJA VU** (B) Cannon/London Cannon (Golan-Globus) & Dixons 1985 (1984) color 94m. SP, D: Anthony Richmond. SP: also E. D. Rappaport, Arnold Schmidt. Adap: Joane A. Gil. From Trevor Meldal-Johnsen's novel *Always*. Mus: Pino Donaggio. MkpSup: Basil Newall. Ref: TV. V 5/15/85. MFB'84:275. Ecran F 43:25. 46:64-5. With Jaclyn Smith, Nigel Terry, Shelley Winters, Claire Bloom, Richard Kay.

Is Gregory (Terry) "becoming" the dead Michael Richardson? Is Brooke Ashley returning from the dead to possess Maggie (Smith)? Or is it Eleanor (Bloom), Brooke's mother, who is possessing Maggie? Hard to care who's who, or who's becoming who, in this vapid, shoddily developed Gothic romance.

**DELICATESSEN** (F) Miramax (Para)/Constellation-UGC-Hachette Premiere-Sofinergie-Sofinergie 2-Investimage 2-Investimage 3 (Claudie Ossard) 1991 (1990/'92-U.S.) color/ws? 96m. SP, D, Co-SdFX: Marc Caro. SP, D: Jean-Pierre Jeunet. SP: also Gilles Adrien. Mus: Carlos D'Alessio. Ph: Darius Khondji. PD: J. -P. Carp. SpFX: O. Gleyze et al. Mkp: H. Quiroga. Ref: TV: Eng. titles. V 5/27/91. ad. SFExam 4/10/92. SFChron 4/10/92. EBay Express 4/24/92. Cinef 12/92:58-9. With Dominique Pinon, Marie-Laure Dougnac, Jean-Claude Dreyfus (butcher), Rufus, Ticky Holgado, Silvie Laguna, Karin Viard, Howard Vernon.

Cannibalism, barter, Troglodists (or "outlaws"), phantom voices, "surfacers," snail-eaters, Gothic atmosphere, and an "Australian" (or boomerang blades) in the forehead, in the near future. "Gross" is an international language, apparently. Some inventiveness, but mean-spirited and thin.

**DELIRIA** see *Fear* (1980)

**DELIRIA** see *Foto di Gioia*

**DELIRIA** see *Stagefright—Aquarius*

**DELIRIO CALDO** see *Delirium*

**DELIRIO DI SANGUE** see *Blood Delirium*

**DELIRIOS DE UM AMORAL** (Braz.) PC Ze Do Caixao 1978 color 86m. SP, D, P: Jose Mojica Marins. SP: also R. F. Luchetti. Ph: G. Attili. Ref: Hardy/HM: "rather tired." With Marins, Magna Miller, Jorge Peres, Lirio Bertelli.

In this sequel to *The Strange World of Ze Do Caixao,* Ze takes over the mind of a psychiatrist and makes him hallucinate.

**2P DELIRIUM** [Note: revised entry] (I) Cinamerica Int'l./Romatt (Matt Cimber) 1972 color feature (*Delirio Caldo. Hot Delirium*). SP,D: Renato Polselli. Ph: Ugo Brunelli. Mus: G. Reverberini (sp?). Ref: TV: MV. MV: "gory murders." CineFan 2:25 (J. Duvoli). With Mickey Hargitay, Rita Calderoni, Carmen Young, Raoul, Krysta Barrymore.

"I killed to protect you!" Is the monster-masked, knife-wielding "filthy sex murderer" the war-vet doc or his wife? Or both? Crude, clumsily padded, technically rough-edged shocker also has some visualized nightmares re chains and naked women. But are they the doc's dreams or his wife's?

**DELIRIUM** see *Foto Di Gioia*

**DELITTI** [Note: revised entry] (I) 1986 color feature. SP,D: Giovanni Lenzi. From H. Becque's play "La Parisienne." Mus: G. and M. De Angelis. Ref: Palmerini: "absolute junk." MV: "gruesome" slasher movie. no ETC/Giallos. With Gianni Dei, Solvi Stubing, Saverio Vallone, Michela Miti.

"Seven men are killed by a viper.... "(P)

**DELITTO POCO COMUNE, Un** see *Phantom of Death*

**DELLAMORTE, DELLAMORE** (I-F-G) Onctober Films/Audifilm, Urania, KGP, Reteitalia, Bibofilm & TV, Canal +, Gavras, SBC (Tilde Corsi) 1993 ('96-U.S.) color 96m. (aka *Demons '95*). D: M. Soavi. SP: G. Romoli, from T. Sclavi's novel. Ph: Mauro Marchetti. Mus: Manuel DeSica. AD: Antonello Geleng. FX: Sergio Stivaletti. Ref: TV: VSOM; Eng. titles; *Of Death, Of Love.* MV: *Cemetery Man* - U.S. t. PT 19:8. ETC II, #9:39,42. SM 16: 76-7. SF Chron 5/10/96. With Rupert Everett, Anna Falchi, Francois Hadji-Lazaro, Barbara Cupisti.

"Seven days after someone dies, they return to life." When the earth moves for two lovers here, it's just hubbie erupting out of the grave below them. ("What's wrong with you?" she asks the zombie. "Be more understanding!") Francesco Dellamorte, caretaker of Buffalora Cemetery, in Buffalone, is the one who has to incapacitate and restore the ghouls to their graves. ("Is this the start of a trend?") This movie features several types of crossover love between the living and the dead, or undead. Claudio, for instance, roars out of his grave on a motorcycle and sweeps up his (still living) love. Francesco's assistant Gnaghi has a sweet relationship with his heartthrob's living severed head. ("Things are getting complicated.") And Francesco himself doesn't want his true love "to become a zombie," but she does, or seems to ....

Quirky, graveyard comedy is an original. It's a bit much—sometimes more than a bit much—but that's its strength as well as its weakness. It gets into uncharted fantasy-horror territory. Sometimes, it's casually hilarious; sometimes jokey, lax. It'll either become a classic or an historical oddity. At the least, it's not like any other zombie film around. It is, by turns, poetic, comic, surreal, and gratuitously grisly—and it's perhaps the poetry which finally wins out. All this and flying fireballs (or "ghost flames") and a vision of a raven-like Death.

**DELTA SPACE MISSION** (Rum.) Romaniafilm 1984 anim feature. Ref: V 10/26/83:254 (ad): also a TV series.

Future space-adventures.

**DEMOLITION MAN** WB/Silver Pictures (Michael Levy, Howard Kazanjian/Craig Sheffer et al.) 1993 color/ws 114m. (*Isobar* - early t). D: Marco Brambilla. Story, SP: Robert Reneau, P. M. Lenkov. SP: also Daniel Waters. Ph: Alex Thomson. Mus: E. Goldenthal. PD: D. L. Snyder. VisFX: Michael J. McAlister, Kimberly K. Nelson. SpFxCoord: Joe Ramsey. Video: Video Image. SpBodyFX: Gillis & Woodruff Jr. Digital: Cinesite. Anim: Available Light. Computer Graphics: R/Greenberg. Ref: TV. V 10/18/93: "noisy, soulless." Cinef 12/93:16-31. SFChron 10/9/93: "a very funny comedy." V 7/26/93:5. 5/6/91:C-48. With Sylvester Stallone, Wesley Snipes, Sandra Bullock, Nigel Hawthorne, Glenn Shadix, Jesse Ventura, Bill Cobbs.

"Things don't happen any more." 2032 San Angeles (a splicing of Los Angeles, San Diego, and Santa Barbara) is a place where Dr. Cocteau's (Hawthorne) brain children are docile and Eloi-like, violence is outmoded, and "all restaurants are Taco Bell." Enter awakening "cryo-cons" John Spartan (Stallone) and Simon Phoenix (Snipes) from the rugged Nineties of L.A....Glib satiritopia is a bit too much for its own good. Bullock's bright-eyed naivete is the only semi-consistently-amusing element.

**DEMOLITION WOMAN** In-X-Cess 1994 color 80m. D: Phil M. Noir. Ref: Adam'95. With Isis Nile, Bunny Bleu.

She travels back in time from the year 2014.

**DEMON APOCALYPSE** see *Back from Hell*

**DEMON BEAST WARRIOR LUNA VULGAR** [Note: This is a revised entry, from p. 122] (J) A.D. Vision/Pony Canyon (Toru Akitsu-Kadokawa Video-Nextart) 1991 anim color c30m.@. SP: Aki Tomato, Yumiko Tsukamoto. Story: T. Akitsu. Mus: Kawai. Ref: TV: ADV video; Eng. titles; as *Luna Varga*, Vol. 1 (2 episodes). Animag 11:5: 4 OAVs.

Princess Luna becomes the "brain of the Varga," a huge, tyrannosaurus-like "evil monster" from another dimension. When she shrinks to her human size, now, she has a dino-tail.... Plus: "beast-changers," warriors who can turn into monsters ... a gigantic sea serpent ... and a "part-time black wizard" who summons up the Wyvern, pterodactyl-types.... Mildly amusing fantastic drollery.

**DEMON CITY SHINJUKU** (J) Japan Home Video 1988 anim color 79m. (*Makai Toshi*). From Hideyuki Kikuchi's novel. Ref: TV: JHV; no Eng.; OAV. Animag 5:4, 5. 4:8.

An epic duel leaves a city in the grip of a demonic swordsman, who hides beneath the near-deserted streets in the form of a huge spider-crab creature. Plus: a two-headed Doberman-type, an all-tentacle, snaky red-headed woman, a creature which disintegrates into dozens of bats, and flame monsters.... Atmospheric graphics, functional storyline. Niftiest effects: the victim-absorbing walls and streets of the ghost city. At one point, the spider-thing emerges from the front of a train, in a bit which anticipates the transformation effects of *Terminator 2*. Also noteworthy: the stirring of the "dead" subway train.

Follow-up to *Monster City*.

**DEMON COP** American-Independent 1991 color feature. SP, D: Rocco Karega. Ref: Jones. PT 19:35,39: *The Curse of Something Bestial* - orig t. With Theresa Fenneaux, Ray Klein, Julia Westland, Cameron Mitchell.

**DEMON DELL' INCESTO, Il** see *Byleth*

The **DEMON FIGHTER** (H. K.) Ku Lung & Wu Kung/Chow Ling-Kan 1988? color c90m. D: Chang Peng-Ye. SP: Ku Lung. Ref: TV: Ocean Shores Video; Eng. dubbed. NST! 4:20. With Zheng Shaoqiu, Lin Qing Xia.

"I've got a feeling treachery's afoot here!" Treachery Central: the villain's weird temple chamber, which houses an acid pit, a severed-head collection, and half-human animals kept in suspended animation. Extra addeds: a horrible demon whose mere presence seems to make a woman die a bloody death, and a literal "flatman" who pancakes along the temple floors like a crushed cartoon character and who is thin enough to slip into cracks in the cement.... The latter sequence is probably the batty high point of this infantile but sometimes entertaining kung fu fantasy. Choice campy elements include a fanged face above the temple doorway and the advice (directed towards the villain, of course), "Give up conquering the world. You'll never manage it!"

**DEMON HUNTER** see *Cazador de Demonios*

A **DEMON IN MY VIEW** (G) Vidmark 1991 color 98m. D: Petra Hafter. Based on a Ruth Rendell novel. Ref: SFChron Dtbk 1/17/93. 10/18/92. Martin. With Anthony Perkins, Uwe Bohm.

Perkins as "The Kenbourne Killer," a "serial murderer who strangles streetwalkers.... A big mess." (SFC).

The **DEMON IS LOOSE** (I) BLC/Scena Film (Augusto Caminito) 1984 ('90-U.S.) color feature (*Uccide a Passe di Danze*. aka *Murder Rock*). SP, D: Lucio Fulci. SP: also V. Mannino, G. Clerici, R. Gianviti. Ph: G. Pinori. Mus: Keith Emerson. Ref: Ecran F 42:44. 43:71. 44:33. 58:34-5. V 11/2/83:42: "chiller." 5/9/84:344: "horror-fantasy." 3/22/89:25 (rated). 5/30/90:29. Hardy/HM:380. Palmerini: "enjoyable"; *Uccide a Passo di Danza.*. With Olga Karlatos, Claudio Cassinelli, Ray Lovelock.

**DEMON KEEPER** New Horizons (Cheryl Latimer, Joe Tornatore/Smith-Corman) 1994 (1993) color c78m. D, Ed: J. Tornatore. SP: Mikel Angel. Ph: Tom Denove. Mus: K. Farquharson, A. Igoe. PD: Michael Nott. SpPhFX: David Hewitt. Prosth: M. Marnewick. SpFxCoord: G. Nyamande. Ref: TV: NH HV. PT 19:57. SFChron 5/28/94. Stanley. With Dirk Benedict, Edward Albert, Katrina Maltby, Mike Lane (demon), Andre Jacobs.

"The psychic world is not to be tampered with!" An ancient ritual summons up Asmodeus, a demon "born of man, from the seed of an angel." He preys upon human weakness as he collects souls, and makes the possessed speak in the usual deep, raspy demon voice. The magic ring of Solomon controls him.... Inept action, dull writing. Even the winged demon gets to be a talky bore. Main selling point: a bit of demon-human sex.

**DEMON OF PARADISE** (U.S.-Fili) Concorde/Santa Fe Prods. (Leonard Hermes) 1987 color c90m. D, P: Cirio H. Santiago. SP, Story: Frederick Bailey. Story: also C. J. Santiago. Ph: Ricardo Remias. Mus D: Edward Achacoso. PD: Joe Mari Avellana. Mkp: Teresa Mercader. Ref: TV: Warner HV. Fango 6/89. V Mifed '89:181. 10/19/88: 174. 2/21/90:147. 5/2/90: S-90. Morse. Scheuer. Martin. Phantom. Hound. With Kathryn Witt, Williams Steis, Laura Banks, Bailey.

Kihono, Hawaii. "I keep hearin' somethin' sloshin' around out there!" Dynamite awakens Akua—"the Beast"—a scaly Triassic sea monster. This missing link between reptiles and early primates has tree-root-like hair on its ugly head and a big long tail.... Zero interest monster movie offers nothing new. Limp plotting, action, dialogue.

See also: *Up from the Depths* (II).

**DEMON OF RAPE** (H.K.) Hop Chung 1992 color/ws 92m. (*Devil of Rape* - cr t). Ref: TV: World Video; no Eng.; above is ad t. Y. K. Ho. V 11/9/92:36: in Hong Kong.

Purely functional softcore fantasy concerns a horny demon from a thermos that possesses our hero and at first seems to have only aphrodisiac powers. Later, however, the possessed man has some sexy, out-of-body, *Psychic Killer* experiences. Four ghost-like women further excite his ectoplasm. At the end, an exorcist propels a woman's spirit out of her body, catches the hero in a holy net, and bags the demon. (The latter is visualized as a stick figure emanating red rays.)

**DEMON OF THE LUTE** see *Phantom Lute, The*

**DEMON POSSESSED** Action Int'l. (Webster) 1989 color feature. D, P: Christopher Webster. SP: Julian Weaver. Ref: PT 16:63. Fango 128:38: "Zzzzzz." SFChron Dtbk 10/31/93: "has its moments."

"Ouija board allows a hooded figure to emerge from another dimension...." (SFC) "An old woman in the future narrates." (PT)

**DEMON QUEEN** Mogul/Camera 1(Donald Farmer-David Reed) 1986 color 70m. SP, D: D. Farmer. Ref: VSB. PT 4:19. McCarty II: "bad acting." Bowker '90: cannibalism. With Mary Fornaro, Dennis Stewart.

"Vampirish shrike." (VSB)

**DEMON SWORD** see *Wizards of the Demon Sword*

**DEMON WARRIOR** Houston Cinema Group 1987 color 82m. SP, D, Mus, P: Frank Patterson. SP: also Mark Baird, Alan Stewart. Ph: T. L. Callaway. Mus: also Kirk Cameron, Tom Oliphant. SpMkp, Anim: Steve Poe. AD: John Perdichi. SpArrowFX; Brian Jurek. Ref: TV: Monarch HV. no Hound. no Martin. With Wiley M. Pickett, Leslie Mullin, Jon Langione, John Garrett, Jerry R. Coiteux, Bruce Carbonara, Vonda Borski, Lee Barret (the Demon).

According to the legend of the medicine man's curse, an "evil spirit incarnate" returns to haunt the "old Willard place"—stolen long ago from Indians—every ten years. At the end, the medicine man's great-grandson ends the curse with trance, sacred arrow, deer blood, and lightning.... Another walking about, running, lurking, skulking, and standing still horror-fantasy. Trite, slow.

**DEMON WIND** United Filmmakers/Demon Wind Prods. (Paul Hunt, Michael Bennett) 1990 (1989) color 97m. SP, D: Charles Philip Moore. Mus: Bruce Wallenstein. KeySpMkpFxArt: David Atherton. SpMechFX: Fred Cramer, Bob King. SpProps: C. R. Deth. Ref: TV. V 9/3/90:80(hv). Cable Video Store 1/91. Martin. With Eric Larson, Francine Lapensee, Rufus Norris, D. Koko (Great Demon), Sandra Margot (beautiful demon), Mindy McEnnan (demon girl), Lorri Urbach (woman-thing).

"Foul things shall walk." And things most foul do. Principal walker: the son of Satan. Others include ghouls and their human victims, who become ghouls. Non-walker: the lethal-tongued cow skull. The "hot dry wind" is one of the two good things about this imitation of the *Evil Dead* movies. ("I've never seen fog like this!") Every time the fog blows by, the setting changes. The other good thing: the cabin which, if you walk in the front door, is a fully-stocked, operational cabin; if you look at it from the outside, it's the ruins of a cabin. Drawbacks: telegraphed shocks, an over-reliance on goo makeup, and glib ghouls with subpar Freddy material.

**DEMONESS FROM THOUSAND YEARS** (H.K.?) Chan's Film Co. 1990 color/ws c98m. Ref: vt (above is Eng t in cr); Eng. titles.

The Thousand Year Girl Evil—whose magic gas freezes her victims—has been chasing good witch Yun Yu Yi "for more than ten centuries." Plus: a goofy, cartoon King of Hell, a ghost finder, and an evil-killing sword. Routine, silly horror-fantasy-comedy.

**DEMONI** see *Demons*

**DEMONI 2** see *Demons 2*

**DEMONI 3** see *Black Demons*

**DEMONIA** (I) AMT Int'l. & Lanterna Editrice/B.S.C. (Ettore Spagnuolo) 1990 color/ws feature. SP, D: Lucio Fulci. SP: also P. Regnoli. Ph: Luigi Ciccarese. Mus: Giovanni Cristiani. AD: M. Bolongaro. SpMkpFX: Franco Giannini. SpFX: Elio Terribili; M. Ciccarella. SdFX: Da.Ma. Sound. Ref: TV: VSOM; Eng. dubbed. Palmerini. With Brett Halsey, Meg Register, Lino Salemme, Christina Engelhardt, Pascal Druant, Carla Cassola.

Ingredients: (in 1486 Sicily) five crucified nuns ... (in 1990) a vomiting crucified nun in the "old nunnery on the hill" outside Santa Rosalia ... a ghostly naked lady who kills with a harpoon/dart ... an unconvincing but admittedly yucky cats-and-eyeballs scene ... a crucified tongue ... and a man who's drawn-and-quartered, or at least halved .... Functional horror gore, with lots of padding, and even a hand-on-shoulder shock.

**The DEMONIC REVENGE** (H.K.) c1988? color c103m. Ref: TV: Hong Kong TV video; no Eng. Y.K. Ho.

In one of two comically lively set-pieces, a smoking elevator stops at the thirteenth floor of an office building, whereupon wizards duel, a supernatural divan bearing a woman whooshes about, and an idol comes to life (as a papier-mache monster-baby). In the other frenetic, telekinetic free-for-all, a wizard who

knows his own super-strength levitates and in general wreaks havoc.... Vividly illustrated nonsense, with a few unusual images.

**DEMONIC TOYS** Para/Full Moon (Anne Kelly) 1991 color 85m. (*Dangerous Toys* - orig t). D: Peter Manoogian. SP: David S. Goyer. Idea: Charles Band. Ph: Adolfo Bartoli. Mus: Richard Band; (songs) Joker. PD: Billy Jett. SpCreature & MkpFX: MMI. Soldier Des: Dennis Gordon et al; (stopmo) David Allen et al. FX: (sup) Phil Meador; (anim) Allen Gonzales; (lens) Richard Snell. Mkp: Palah Sandling. Opt: Mercer. Ref: TV. TVG. SFChron Dtbk 3/8/92:58. PT 16:15. V 2/10/92:16 (rated). 10/29/90:13. 9/16/91:56, 19. With Tracy Scoggins, Bentley Mitchum, Michael Russo, Jeff Weston, Larry Cedar, Daniel Cerny ("The Kid"), Ellen Dunning, Pete Schrum, William Thorne (fair-haired boy), Kristine Rose (Miss July), Robert Stoeckle (man-devil).

"Someone's inside the toys!" Stray blood sets free a demon-lad/man-devil from 66 years as a born-dead baby-demon that now wants to be born as heroine Judith Gray's (Scoggins) baby. The Kid feeds on the souls of others and animates warehouse toys, including a ray-shooting robot, a jack-in-the-box joker/ghoul, a sneering, malevolent doll, and a carnivorous teddy bear that becomes the Big Hairy.... Rote reworking of *Puppet Master, Child's Play,* Freddy, and the Betty Boop *Parade of the Wooden Soldiers.* Only surprise: the stopmo toy soldier that becomes Judith's baby-to-be and saves the day.

See also *Dollman Vs. Demonic Toys.*

**DEMONS** (I) Ascot Ent./Dacfilm (Dario Argento) 1985 color 89m. (*Demoni*). SP, D: Lamberto Bava. SP: also D. Argento, Dardano Sacchetti, Franco Ferrini. Story: Sacchetti. Mus: Claudio Simonetti. SpMkp: Sergio Stivaletti. SpModels: Angelo Mattei. SpStageFX: Corridori & Co. SpSdFX: Studio Anzellotti. Ref: TV: New World Video. MFB'87:112. V 11/20/85. With Urbano Barberini, Natasha Hovey, Karl Zinny, Fiore Argento, Paola Gozzo.

"It's the theatre!" Berlin's Metropol Theatre ("Didn't know there was a movie house on this street") is showing a horror movie set in Nostradamus's crypt, where intruders discover a mask and a book: The book says that "demons are instruments of evil"; in the film-within-the-film, whoever dons the mask becomes a demon. In the Metropol Theatre itself, whoever dons the mask becomes a drooling, clawing demon, and the demon's victims become demons.... The usual reciprocal savagery, as monsters slaughter humans, and vice versa, and the camera savors makeup effects. The script is a dispiriting, mechanical combination of *The Exterminating Angel* and *The Evil Dead,* though the film-within-a-film idea does yield the following exchange: Girl in theatre (as she hears another theatregoer scream): "That scream sounds real!" Guy: "Come on, it's the Dolby system!"

**DEMONS 2** (I) Artists Ent./DAC (Dario Argento) 1986 color 94m. (*Demoni 2—L'Incubo Ritorna. Demons IT—The Nightmare Returns*). SP, D: Lamberto Bava. SP: also D. Argento, F. Ferrini, D. Sacchetti. Ph: L. Battaglia. Mus: Simon Boswell. Mkp: R. Prestopino. SpFX: Sergio Stivaletti. Sp Action FX: Corridori & Co. AD: D. Basson. Opt: Aldo Mafera. Ref: TV: Imperial Ent. video; Eng. version. V 10/29/86: "effectively scary." 8/12/87:109 (rated). 10/7/87: 10: in Miami. MFB'87:332-

3. Hound. Newman: "even less inspired." Ecran F 75:62. With David Knight, Nancy Brilli, C. C. Tassoni, Bobby Rhodes, Asia Argento.

"Can they happen again?" A demon from the first movie "escapes" from a TV set, and Sally becomes the surprise at her own party. Soon, all the birthday-partygoers are ghouls, and a dog that laps up some bad blood gets new, impressive canines. Meanwhile, a boy ghoul inexplicably "hatches" a cute, leaping critter from his torso .... Formula imitation-Romero horror is padded out with a TV recap of highlights from the first *Demons*. Fun shot: the overhead of the stairwell-climbing ghouls (an idea repeated two or three times, to diminishing effect). Fun effect: the new teeth and nails for humans and canines.

Follow-up to *Demons* (1985). Follow-up: *Black Demons*.

**DEMONS 3** see *Church, The. Ogre, The*

**DEMONS 4: THE SECT** see *Sect, The*

**DEMONS 5: DEVIL'S VEIL** see *Maschera del Demonio, La*

**DEMONS, The** see *Nine Demons, The*

**DEMONS '95** see *Dellamorte, Dellamore*

**DEMONSTONE** (Austral.-Fili-U.S.) Fries Ent./IFE & Brian Trenchard-Smith (A.I. Ginnane) 1990 (1989) color 88m. (*Heartstone* - orig t). D: Andrew Prowse. SP: J. Trayne, D. Philips, F. Bailey. Mus: Gary Stockdale. AD: Sammy Aranzamendez. SpMkpFX: Die-Aktion. Prosth: Starr Jones. SpFxForeman: Ed Sto. Domingo. SdFxEd: Colin Mahoney. SpOptFX: Image 3. Ref: TV. V 6/20/90:39 (hv). 1/10/90:24 (rated). TVG. Martin. no Scheuer. no Maltin '92. With R. Lee Ermey, Jan-Michael Vincent, Nancy Everhard, Peter Brown, Joe Avellana, M. Bautista.

"Let the blood of Han Chin bear witness to the last of the Belfardos!" The Heartstone—the "key to awesome power"—bears the seal of Han Chin (Avellana), a "warrior-priest who founded a sect 500 years ago" and who cast then a "death curse" on the Belfardo family. In the present, the reporter (Everhard) who possesses the stone, and is possessed by it, becomes the supernatural agent of Han Chin's revenge. ("I don't know what's wrong with me!") Competent but vacant action-horror thriller gave work to many Filipino stunt men. Fortuitously, the present-day Belfardos turn out to be thugs that merit a terrible curse.

**DEMONWARP** Vidmark Ent. & Design Projects (Demonwarp Inc.) 1988 color 91m. D: Emmett Alston. SP: Jim Bertges, Bruce Akiyama. Story, Bigfoot des: John Buechler. Mus: Dan Slider. SpMkpFX: Bruce Barlow, Ed Yang. SpVisFX: (sup) Mark Wolf; Wizard Works, MMI. SpOptFX: Van Der Veer. Ref: TV: Vidmark Ent. video. V 3/30/88. With George Kennedy, David Michael O'Neill, Pamela Gilbert, Billy Jacoby, Colleen McDermott, Hank Stratton, Michelle Bauer, John Durbin (monster); Yang et al (zombies).

"That thing could be anywhere." Among the "weird and strange things" lurking in Demon Woods: Bigfoot, who likes to rip off human heads and is very hostile, unlike the Disney version. The monster proves to be a human being, transformed, apparently, by the venom in the scorpion tail of an alien "archangel." The latter

also has zombie workers to repair its "space vessel".... Not badly acted, but otherwise routine showcase for gore and okay makeup effects. Thin script requires much padding with hiking/chasing/tracking footage.

**DEN' GNEVA** (Russ.) Studio Yalta Central Gorki Studios 1986 color/ws 85m. D: Sulambek Mamilov. SP: Alexander Lapshin. Story: Sever Gonsovski. Mus: Gija Kantscheli. Ref: V 3/5/86: *Day of Wrath* - tr t? With Juosas Budrajtis, Alexei Petrenko, Anatoli Ivanov.

A "rather half-hearted and bloodless" adventure film re a mysterious creature/community.

**DENTRO IL CIMITRIO** see *Graveyard Disturbance*

**DERU POWER-X** (J) Columbia Video 1990? anim color 42m. Ref: TV: CV; no Eng.

Human-operated-robot tale with a comic twist: Here, the two guys in the robot suits run about the city asking directions, playing leapfrog over moving cars, etc. Later, two gals in women's robot-suits join in. Pleasantly goofy, if slight. In one scene, a girl's shouting levels a dorm.

**DESCANSE EN PIEZAS** see *Rest in Pieces*

**DESCENDANT OF THE SUN** (H. K.) Shaw (Mona Fong, Wong Ka Hee) c1992? color/ws 92m. D: Chu Yuan. Ref: TV: World Video; Eng. titles.

"Superman's here!" Ingredients in this costume fantasy include the magician-hero, informally called "Superman" ... the "son of All-Evil," who appears in a glowing green globe and who turns into a ray-shooting giant (comments our nearby, observant hero: "Evil") ... a fire-breathing evil magician (perhaps this same "son" in another guise) who turns into a tree creature (bad move—hero then turns into ax, chops tree in half) ... flesh-eating zombies ... a baby "assembly line" concocted in a search for the Evil Infant ... and a loquacious parrot that also paints.

Uninspired but lively, good-natured fantasy features scads of cheap effects. One winning if simple one: the bare tree branch's insta-leaves. Cute comic sequence: The Princess and her attendants attempt to flush out the elusive "Superman" by placing her in quasi-jeopardy.

**DESERT SNOW** Raedon Home Ent./Northstar Pictures (Raymond Girard) 1990 color 88m. D: Paul M. DeGruccio. SP: Dan Peacock, Paul Natale. Mus: Vican, Baker. Ref: V 6/10/90:39 (hv): "overreaches. Gore effects are convincing." With Steve Labatt, Carolyn Jacobs, Simo Maceo, Flint Carney.

Woman who "delights in tasting people's blood."

**DESERT SPIRITS** Patrick McGuinn 1994 b&w 36m. SP, D, Ed: P. McGuinn. Ref: TV: Willing Suspension video. With Henry McGuinn, Edward Montoya Jr., Brian McGuinn.

"I am Nori. I manifest in different forms." At the moment, Nori is a lizard, in a "37th millennium." Or is it just a peyote dream? At any rate, menacing sounds and voices seem to assail and possess a man, in pretty silly sequences. Atmospheric photography.

**DESERT WARRIOR** (Fili) Silver Star (Kimmy Lim) 1989 (1988) color 88m. (*Sand Wars* - shooting t). D: Jim Goldman. SP: Bob Davies, Carl Kuntze. Mus: M. A. Manuel. Ref: V 3/22/89: "something of a fiasco." With Lou Ferrigno, Shari Shattuck, Kenneth Peer, Anthony East.

Post-nuke society needs "uncontaminated women."

**DESERT WARRIOR** see *Wheels of Fire*

**DESTROYER** Moviestore Ent./Back East Money & Wind River (Weskirk Prods.) 1988 color 94m. (*Shadow of Death* - orig t). D: Robert Kirk. SP, P: Peter Garrity, Rex Hauck. Mus: Patrick O'Hearn. SpMkpFX: Patrick Ryan Denver, Rex L. Whitney. SpFX: The Physical FX Group. Computer Anim: Z-Axis. SpSdFX: Russel Jessum. Opt: Ray Mercer. Ref: TV. V 11/2/88. 4/8/87:24. SFChron Dtbk 7/10/88. With Deborah Foreman, Clayton Rohner, Lyle Alzado, Anthony Perkins, Tobias Andersen (Russell).

Ivan Moser (Alzado), a "half-alive, maniac serial killer," haunts an abandoned state penitentiary and seriously slows work on Greystone Productions' "Death House Dolls".... Flat horror scenes alternate with easier-to-take, fun-with-low-budget-film-making scenes. Away from Norman, Perkins thrives as the desperate-for-a-workable-scene director Edwards.

**DESU PAWUDA** see *Death Powder*

**DETERMINATOR 2** Visual Images 1991 color 75m. D: Michael Carpenter. Ref: Adam '92: "two cyborgs from the future." With Alicyn Sterling, Melanie Moore, Marc Wallice.

**DETONATOR ORGUN 1: CHAPTER OF BIRTH** (J) DARTS (Maeda, Kakinuma/Ishida, Koizumi, Yaegaki) c1990? anim color 56m. D: Masami Obari. SP: H. Kakinuma. Ph: K. Konishi. Mus: S. Hirasawa. PD: Kakinuma, Yamane, Akutsu. ORGUN Des: Hiroyuki Hataike. Ref: TV: Polydor video; no Eng.; 1st of 3 OAVs. V. Max 2:5, 26. 3:4.

In the 23rd Century. More robots in space—including human-run robots with various rays and roars—as The Imbaryudar (a "bio-mechanical warrior race" from the "mobile planet fortress Zoma") invade Earth. Some style, but formula. Banal character design.

**A DEUSA DE MARMORE—ESCRAVA DO DIABO** (Braz) Panorama do Brazil 1978 color 82m. SP, D, P: Rosangela Maldonado. Ph: G. Attilli. Ref: Hardy/HM. Jones. With Maldonado, Jose Mojica Marins, Joao Paulo.

Pact with the devil allows 2,000-year-old woman to maintain youthfulness via "fatal kiss."

**Das DEUTSCHE KETTENSAGENMASSAKER** (G) DEM Film & Rhewes (Christian Furst) 1991 color 63m. SP, D: Christoph Schlingensief. Mus: Jacques Arr. Ref: V 3/11/91: "tacky, gross and unfunny. Much of the cast gets ground into sausage." VSOM: *German Chainsaw Massacre* - vt t. With Karina Fallenstein, Suzanne Bredehoft, Artur Albrecht, Udo Keir.

The translated title—"The German Chainsaw Massacre"—tells pretty much all.

**DEVASTATOR (D-1)** (J) Takara 1992? anim color 44m. (aka *D-1 Devastator*). Ref: TV: Takara video; no Eng.; OAV.

Tokyo, year 2032. Ingredients include the Yaesu company's super-car, which is taken for an unauthorized spin ... flying, armed human-operated robot suits ... and an invasion of huge "pincer" robots.... Actionful but routine animated sf features some interesting "mecha" design details, including a four-wheeled car which transforms into a two-legged robot. Main motif: giant staring eyes, products apparently of one character's psychological problems.

**The DEVIL** (H. K.) Video City/C. H. Wong & Mao Hung Chi 1985-U.S. color 83m.-U.S. D: Chang Jen Chieh. SP: Luk Pak Sang. Ph: Li Shih Chieh. Mus: Wang Mao Shan. Sets: Hung Yang. Mkp: Cheng Yu Feng. Ref: TV: Video City video; Eng. dubbed; sfa *Picture the Devil* (III) (1981)? Fango 107:60. Hound. Phantom. no Martin. With Chow Shao Tung, Wang Pao Yu, Ou Ti, Chen Hung Lieh, Chen Mei Hua, Liu Yin Shang, Yuan Shen, Lo Bin.

A witch woman subjects a bewitched man whose insides are a salad of organs and bugs to a ritual evisceration. ("No drinking in the next three days.") Later, she prays to the "great snake god" to possess a villainous husband. A disfigured green ghostly figure appears to the latter, who begins to vomit and otherwise disgorge snakes, worms, and centipedes.... The latter sequence is a virtual rerun of the opening—the movie has pretty much shown you all it's going to show you in the first few minutes. Considering the nature of the ooze and slime effects, maybe that's just as well. Almost as dismaying as the gore is the script's sentimental tragic-marriage story.

**DEVIL** (Thai) c1990? color/ws c94m. Ref: vt; no Eng. Chao Thai Market: above is tr t.

When a vengeful woman's ghost scares an eviler to death, the devil's agents come and collect his spirit. Yet another ghost seems to haunt a well and at one point peels off part of his face. Later, for another audience, he makes his face decompose.... Corny horror-comedy-drama. People just keep stepping out of their bodies. Best bit: the glowing-red-eyed bat out of hell.

**The DEVIL AND DANIEL MOUSE** (Can.) Nelvana & CBC 1978 anim color c25m. D: Clive A. Smith. SP: Ken Sobol. Story: Patrick Loubert, from Stephen Vincent Benet's short story "The Devil and Daniel Webster." Mus: John Sebastian. Anim D: Frank Nissen. SdFX: Bob Ablack. Ref: TV: *Nelvanamation*, Warner HV. Voices: Chris Wiggins, Jim Henshaw et al.

"I'd give anything to be a rock star!" In order to become a rock star, Jan Mouse sells her soul to Beelzebub, of Devil May Care Music Productions. Tepid animated fantasy, with horrific elements, including the devil in Gorgon form, and the appearance of the jurors from hell.

**The DEVIL AND THE GAMBLER** Vitagraph 1908 silent b&w 9m. D, P: J. Stuart Blackton. Ref: Lee. no AF-I.

Gambler sells his soul in return for good luck; his wife's cross repels the devil.

**The DEVIL & THE GHOSTBUSTER** (Taiwanese) Citymax 1986 color/ws c86m. D: Lu Twai Xeng. Ref: TV: Rainbow Video; no Eng. NST! 4:21.

Ingredients: ghostly possession, floating and flying ghosts, a troupe of hopping vampires, spirit-absorbing exorcism dolls, a supernatural earthquake, a supernatural frisbee, and a helpful skeleton hand.... Somewhat miscalculated mixture of comedy, horror, sex, and violence. The vampires here are supposed to be funny, but in one scene a hopping vampire sticks his hand through the vampire master's back. (Not funny.) Strange, strange scene: A ghost caught in the act shoots his false teeth out of his mouth at the boudoir intruder.

**DEVIL CAT** see *Evil Cat*

**DEVIL CURSE** (H.K.?) c1992? color 89m. Ref: TV: Tai Seng Video; no Eng.

Ingredients: a possessed woman who becomes a big-fanged vampire ... a possessed man who grows a hairy hand, or imagines that he does (his struggle with it is almost as funny as a similar sequence in *Evil Dead 2*, if unintentionally) ... a hairy beast (apparent original owner of the hairy hand) ... a voodoo doll which seems to command a woman ... and a talking, even garrulous idol. Scorecard: lots of cheap optical and smoke effects, *Halloween* music, and an amusing image: a ghost standing up straight and riding an open umbrella held by an aide.

**DEVIL DESIGN** (H.K.?) Platirama Films/Harvesters Film (Helen Chiang) c1987? color 87m. Ref: TV: World Video; no Eng. Fango 107:59.

Disembodied breathing upsets soldiers and horses as they camp. Eventually, a tittering, goopy-faced ghost shows herself, as do hopping ghost-soldiers, and one live soldier's hand does an *Evil Dead 2* and turns both monstrous and against himself.... This long scare sequence near the beginning of the movie (it's roughly a half-hour long) is most notable simply for its length, but it's not bad, and the phantom breathing is creepy. Subsequent visual terrors are less terrifying.

*The **DEVIL-DOLL** E. J. Mannix 1936. From A. Merritt's novel *Burn, Witch, Burn!*, serialized as "The Dolls of Madame Mandilip," and Tod Browning's story "The Witch of Timbuctoo." AD: also Stan Rogers, Edwin B. Willis. Ref: TV. West Coast Story Dept. Bulletin 8/9/32. LC. Lee. Lentz. Kael/5001. Wolf/Horror. V 8/12/36. Phantom. Maltin '92. Scheuer. Martin.

"I've found a way to reduce all atoms in a body simultaneously!" A "beam of thought" activates the little memory-less dogs that inventor Marcel (Henry B. Walthall) shrinks to one-sixth their former size. His goal: the world's food supply multiplied by six. (The plot of *Tarantula* in reverse.) But escaped convict Paul Lavond (Lionel Barrymore) finds another use for Marcel's miniaturization process: revenge. As "Madame Mandilip," he projects his thoughts long-distance to awaken an "Apache doll" in a girl's arms, and.... ("You might as well accuse one of my little dolls as accuse me.")

Though the revenge basis is pretty mundane, the surreal imagery evokes a fantasy of unobtrusiveness (cousin of the fantasy of invisibility)—if, that is, you identify with the living dolls. If you identify with the victims of the dolls, the film becomes a paranoid fantasy of vulnerability and just as cannily exploits the fear of the unseen, or half-seen. ("There's something in this house!") In sum: crude narrative (with awkward expository and explanatory dialogue), riveting spectacle. Barrymore's sneering "granny" seems to be a case of an actor's fun coinciding with the character's.

**DEVIL FETUS** (H. K.) Lo Wai Motion Pictures 1983 color/ws (*Mo Tai*). SP, D, Ph: Liu Hung Chuen. PD: Wu Chen Tung. Ref: TV: Ocean Shores Video; Eng. titles. Hardy/HM. NST! 4:21. Fango 107:58. With Eddie, Lu Xuiling, Lu Beibei.

A jade vase bought at an auction unleashes a devil thing which makes love to Shu Ching. Her husband smashes the vase, his face deteriorates rapidly, and he peels it to reveal writhing worms, then jumps to his death. Meanwhile, a demented cat kills Shu Ching, but she seems to give birth posthumously to an insect-bird horror, seen only briefly. This devil spirit jumps from an urn to a parchment to a dog to Kwo Wei, who unearths and begins eating the now-dead dog. At the end, Kwo Wei reverts to the original devil and sprouts snaky heads when the devil head is cut off.... Choppy continuity and lots of effects, most of them familiar. One unfamiliar one: the squashing face of a man trapped in a diminishing room.

**DEVIL FISH** (I-F) Nat'l. & Nuovo Dania & Filmes Int'l./Griffon 1984 color 92m. (*Devilfish* - ad t. *Shark—Rosso Nell'Oceano*. aka *Red Ocean. Monster Shark. Tiger Shark* - alt t?). D: Lamberto Bava. SP: G. Clerici, D. Sacchetti et al. Story: Luigi Cozzi, Martin Dolman et al. Mus: Antony Barrymore. Monster: Ovidio Taito. SpFX: Germano Natali. Mkp: V. Basil. SdFX: G. J. St. Movie. Ref: TV. TVG. Peter Zirschky. Stanley. V 11/12/86. Ecran F 42:44. VWB: aka *Oceano Rosso*. With Michael Sopkiw, Valentine Monnier, Gianni Garko, William Berger, Iris Peynado, Dagmar Lassander.

"A marine monster, almost indestructible, and whose genetic characteristics are as fearsome as the white shark's—a gigantic octopus with the intelligence of a dolphin, and as monstrous as a prehistoric creature"—haunts Florida waters. Scientists marvel ("Our monster can reproduce itself"); everyone else runs.... Silly mating of *Jaws* and *Tentacles* has a quite unbelievable basis—a scientist creates the creature to guard an "exploitable" area of the sea—and redeeming camp moments (e.g., the monster's lusty roaring). Climax: tentacle flambé.

Cf. *Furia Asesina*.

***DEVIL GIRL FROM MARS** Gigi 1954 ('55-U.S.). SP: J. Eastwood, from Eastwood & J. C. Mather's play. Mkp: George Partleton. SpCost: Ronald Cobb. Ref: TV. Jim Shapiro. BFC. LC. Warren/KWTS! Hardy/SF. Lentz. PT 7:46-7.

"So there is a fourth dimension!" A "perpetual motion chain reaction beam" has destroyed almost all life on Mars. Meanwhile, a Martian emissary, Nyah (Patricia Laffan)—who says she's just stopping for repairs—erects an invisible wall around the Bonnie Charlie pub, in the Scottish Highlands. Her spaceship, which sports a "paralyzer ray mechanism," is made of metal which reproduces itself. ("They've turned the inorganic into the organic!") Her robot, Chani—the refrigerator that walks—has an electronic brain and shoots disintegrating rays.... British "classic" alternates between risible, willy-nilly emotionalism (by earthlings) and monotonous displays of Nyah's powers. Hugh McDermott wins the movie's Terrible Actor award, and it wasn't easy. The script proceeds by exclamations. ("One man in exchange for millions!")

**DEVIL HUNTER** see *Man Hunter*

**DEVIL HUNTER YOHKO** (J) A.D. Vision/Toho & Japan Computer System & Mad House (Onoki-Soi) 1990 ('92?-U.S.) anim color 43m. (*Mamono Hunter Yohko*). Exec D: Katsuhisa Yamada. SP: Yoshihiro Tomita. Concept: Masao Maruyama. Ph: K. Ishikawa. AD: Waki Takeshi. SpFX: Koji Yanifuji. Mus: H. Watanabe. SdFX: Gen. Story: Juzo Mitsui. Ref: TV: ADV video; Eng. titles. Animerica 5:18: 1st of 3 OAVs. Voices: Aya Hisakawa (Yohko), Yuji Mitsuya, N. Matsui (Reiko), Mika Doi (principal), Mugibito (Devil), K. Yamaguchi (Osamu).

The principal of sixteen-year-old Yohko Mano's high school remote-controls a tentacled thing in an effort to kill her. ("That monster was the one from my dreams.") Her fellow student Osamu then becomes "possessed by more than lust" and attempts to deflower her, but her Grandma saves her. ("It is our family's sworn duty to slay and banish demons.") It seems Yohko is to succeed her grandmother and become the "108th Devil Hunter" of their line. Her first task: to prevent Reiko—another student, and a vampire—from becoming the Black Queen of evil.

Mildly amusing horror-fantasy-comedy. Themes of coming of age, sexual initiation, and the passing of the generational torch give way to conventional sword-and-sorcery payoffs, then a cute coda.

The **DEVIL IS HUNGRY** 199-? color feature. SP, P, D: Eric Louzil. Story, P, PD, SpMkpFX: R.A. May. Ph: Ron Chapman. SpMkpFxSup: Martin Mercer. Wing Des: Thom Hansen. Ref: TV: VSOM. With Robert May, Gene LeBrock, Marcia Gray, John Theilade (The Child), Toni Allesandrini, Suzanne Solari.

"The child is hungry!" In Hollywood, a few jail cells constitute a sort of holding tank for women-in-lingerie who are to provide "nourishment for the child"—apparently the devil, or the devil's son, or some random demon. ("Feed the child! Praise Lucifer!")

Can you spell "labored"? Shot-on-tape horror-fantasy is a pretext for a t&a show. Scorecard: the usual satanist paraphernalia ... interest-killing, library-type music ... and a nifty winged-devil shadow. (The devil-man himself is a little rickety.)

**DEVIL KISS** (Sp-F) 1973 ('87-U.S.) color c95m. (*La Caresse de Satan* - F. aka *The Perverse Kiss of Satan*). SP, D: Georges Gigo. Ref: TV: Home Cinema video; Eng. dubbed. brief Stanley. no Phantom. no Martin. Hound. Videooze 5:10-12. SWV: *The Wicked Caresses of Satan* - alt vt t. With Silvia Solar (Claire), Oliver Matthau, Evelyne Scott (Loreta), Daniel Martin, Jose Nieto, Jack Rocha (zombie), Jose Ruiz Lifante, Rosa De Alba, Maria Silva, Ronnie Harp (dwarf).

Chateau de Haussemont. A telepathic scientist reconstructs the head of a just-snatched body, then gives it a shot of "regeneration microcells," as part of Claire Grandier's plot to revenge her brother's death. Using the Book of Astaroth, she summons up a "satanic mind" to revive the corpse, and the professor telepathi-

cally makes the zombie walk and kill. Plus: a seance "presence" and the zombie-murdered, reanimated maid, Loreta, the "fire of Astaroth" in her.... The unusual stew of revenge ingredients is the sole point of interest here—science, sorcery, and telepathy—a curious combination, brought together for no particular reason, apparently.

**DEVIL MELODY** see *Dreadful Melody*

**DEVIL OF LOVE** (H.K.?) 1994 color 90m. D: Lau Keung Fu. Ref: vc box. With Lau Siu Kwan.

Priest's holy charm has "horrific retributive powers."

**DEVIL OF RAPE** see *Demon of Rape*

**DEVIL SORCERY** (H.K.?) Film City 1987? color c92m. Ref: TV: Ocean Shores Video; Eng. titles. M/TVM 11/87:20.

Ipoh, Malaysia. "So many girls are missing!" They're all in the forest where, for hard-to-fathom reasons, an evil, centipede-eating sorcerer is tying them to trees. His carpet-of-fog bedroom spell makes the heroine vomit worms, but the eight-trigram amulet thwarts his "condemnation" of her—specifically, the Half Siam Condemnation, from Thailand.... Scrappy, routine combo of horror-fantasy and sex. Only the guest appearances, during black-magic rituals, of a huge cartoon demon head and various other animated demons impress at all.

**DEVIL STORY** see *Il Etait Une Fois le Diable*

The **DEVIL STRIKES** (H.K.) New Century/D.L.C. Wing 1984 color c88m. (*Ngai..?*—Viet t?). D: Lam Yee Hung. SP: New Century. Ph: Yu Ming Ching. Mus: Frankie Chan. SpFX: Koo Sum Lam; (vis) J. K. C. Fung Jr. Mkp: Lee Bing Nam. Ref: TV: Vietnam Film & Video; Eng. titles. With Wing, Kimmy Got Kim Ching, Wong Man, Wan Ching Wan, Kwok Kun Hung, Koo Sum Lam, Monica.

Mrs. Chin wants her son to marry his cousin Sao Chen, but the latter will not have him, and he kills himself. Mrs. Chin then turns into a fanged witch and puts a spell on Sao Chen. The latter chews on a wooden cross, and her complexion, at first slightly blemished, gets worse and worse. Finally, she jumps off a tower and dies, but her face gets better.... Plus: crawling severed hand in advertising film-within-the-film.... There's an eerie effect with a moth's shadow, and a pretty disgusting scene with a worm-infested birthday cake, but this film is cheaply made and generally unimaginative. No sympathy is possible for the pushy aunt; the unlucky, more sympathetic Chin dies early, and Sao Chen is mainly a tool for supernatural forces.

**DEVIL TWIN** (H.K.) 1980s? feature. D: Tam Ling Chu. Ref: NST! 4:21: "incredibly slow, shot-on-video horror film."

**DEVIL YIELDED TO GOD** (H.K.) 1983? color/ws c90m. Ref:TV: Ocean Shores Video.

The three principal female ghosts include an old evil one and two sweet young things whom the old one tries to get to poison the hero. Ultimately, exorcists destroy the evil spirit.... Hong Kong export has no English subtitles, but features one weird scene in which a cemetery-full of cackling, crying ghosts attempts to intimidate a newcomer. Hokey "spook" score.

**DEVILFISH** see *Devil Fish*

**DEVILMAN** (J) Dynamic Planning & Kodansha & King Record Co. 1987 anim color 51 1/2m. (*Debiruman—Atarashi Tanjo-Hen*). SP, D: Tsutomu Kurata. SP, Story (comic magazine): Go Nagai. Mus: Kenji Kawai. Anim: O Prods. Ref: TV: King/Kodansha Video; no Eng. Markalite 3:85-6: aka Devilman—Chapter: The New Genesis. Animerica 5:18: OAV series; subtitled L.A. Hero release in U.S. of Vol 2, 1993.

Introductory glimpses into a horror world of sea monsters which gorge on sprites tantalize, but the hero's this-world encounters with tentacled things and monster vaginas are more repetitious than imaginative. At one point, the donning of a mask gives him a (flashback?) peek into a realm of voracious dinosaurs, demons, and fairies. When, at the end, night clubbers mutate into monsters, he transforms into the devilish Devilman to fight them.

**DEVILMAN II: SIREN THE WITCH** (J) Bandai/Kodansha 1990 anim color 60m. each. Story: Go Nagai. Ref: Animag 9:5. 10:4: 3 OAVs. 7:5. Japan Video.

A new version of an '87 film re mankind-threatening demons.

**\*The DEVIL'S ASSISTANT** 1917. Ref: screen. William K. Everson. PFA notes 8/24/84. With M. Fischer, Monroe Salisbury, Kathleen Kirkham.

Film features visions of Death as a skeleton-on-a-white-horse carrying off the heroine's spirit ... of a doctor as a horned devil ... of a demon stirring a pot labeled "morphine" ... of Cerberus ... of a river of damned souls ... and of winged demons in hell .... All-out, fire-and-brimstone melodrama—re the perils of drug addiction—is fun-campy, at least in its extant, 23-minute, condensed form. It's just horror piled upon horror.

**DEVIL'S BOX** (H.K.) 1988 color feature. D: Tommy Chin.Ref: Weisser/ATC: "fluctuates uneasily between traditional horror and black humor." With Simon Yam.

Opened box's curse leads to weird deaths — e.g., film strangles a movie editor.

**\*The DEVIL'S COMMANDMENT** Donati-Carpentieri 1957 ws 85m.(75m.). D: also Mario Bava. SP: also R. Freda. U.S. footage: D: Ron Honthaner. SP: J.V. Rhems. With Al Lewis. Ref: TV: Sinister Cinema video; Eng. dubbed. VWB: AD: Giorgio Giovannini?; '60 U.S. release. TVG. Stanley. Lee. COF'67 Annual: 38. V 6/12/57. Weldon. PT 19:11. Monster! Int'l. 4:18. Film Comment 1/93:51. Bright Lights 11: 18,20,21.

"All the evidence points to a vampire." In Paris, several murder victims are found without "even a drop of blood" in their bodies. At the bottom of the mystery: the "famous Prof. Du Grande," who is working on a process with which human cells can reproduce and survive "independently of man." This seminal Italian horror movie has wonderful Gothic sets and lighting for the Castle Du Grande, or the "mausoleum." The script, however, is routine, and the musical score is uneven, eerie at times, ham-handed at others. The sudden transformation of the young Gisele into the 100-year-old Duchess Margarethe Du Grande is effec-

tively startling, but occurs in a campily super-condensed expository sequence in which Margarethe helpfully explains, "I murder girls to be young," all for the love (she goes on) of Pierre. The bathtub shock scene was apparently tossed in by the movie's original U.S. distributors to cash in on the success of *Psycho*.

**DEVIL'S DAUGHTER, The** see *Frog, the Dog and the Devil, The*

**DEVIL'S DAUGHTER, The** see *Sect, The*

**DEVIL'S DYNAMITE** (H.K.) 198-? color feature. Ref: HOF 2:20-21: vampires; "ridiculous" but "highly entertaining"; Eng.-dubbed.

**DEVIL'S ENCOUNTER** see *Ultima Casa vicino al Lago*

**DEVIL'S EXORCIST** see *Juego del Diablo*

**DEVIL'S GATEWAY** see *Cazador de Demonios*

**The DEVIL'S GIFT** Zenith Int'l./Windridge & AEI 1984 color 90m. SP, Story, D, P: Kenneth J. Berton. Story, SP, P: Jose Vergelin. SP: also Hayden O'Hara. Ph: K. Daniels, C. Palm. Mus: Todd Hayen. SpVisFX: Ed La France, Adam Moes. Monkey Des: Elaine Christian. SpMkpFX: Bruce Parry. OptFX: A. Moes. SdFX: Magic Film Works. Ref: TV: Vestron Video. TVG. Stanley. Martin: "uncredited ripoff of Stephen King's short story "The Monkey." Sacto Bee (TV Today). V 5/1/85:180. With Bob Mendlesohn, Vicki Saputo, S. Robertson, Bruce Parry, Madelon Phillips, J. Renee Gilbert.

"What kind of a thing kills plants and animals?" A demonic toy monkey from an antique store kills house plants, flies, goldfish, and a dog, and possesses, in turn, a woman and a shower stall. ("Get that toy out of your house!") Plus a visualized nightmare re a hairy monster .... Snorecard: arduous evocations of day-to-day suburban life ... flat thrill scenes with *Jaws*-crossed-with-*Psycho* music ... a monkey with patently unbelievable powers (including the ability to control the elements and start earthquakes) ... and fun cartoon lightning and apparent model work in the opening credits sequence.

**The DEVIL'S OWL** (H.K.) American Intercontinental/World Wide Animal Protection Assn. 1978 color/ws c87m. D: Liu Kuo-Shiung. Ref: TV: vt; Eng. titles. MMarquee 43:8.

The Owls Valley. In a cursed village, a woman gives birth to an owl-creature which squeals, flies, then kills those who frighten it. Mother wants him anyway: "Come back, my baby, I love you!" When she dies, baby's older brother promises to look after him and take him to study with Uncle Hsu. The two play together until father comes home and chases owl-baby away. Ultimately, though, father accepts owl-son.... Ineffably batty movie owes something to both *The Birds* and *It's Alive*. The production is so tatty that you usually don't get to see much of the owl-critter except a pair of glowing red eyes, and the director at first doesn't even make it clear, in one sequence, that owls are attacking villagers—that the shots of owls and the shots of villagers have something to do with each other. Though the makers go for all-out horror in some scenes (pathos in others), the owl demon (or what you can see of him) remains inescapably cuddly-looking.

The **DEVIL'S POSSESSED** (Sp) ZIV Int'l./Profilmes & Orbe Prods. 1974 ('86-U.S.) color c95m. (*El Mariscal del Infierno*). D: Leon Klimovsky. SP: Jacinto Molina Alvarez. Ph: Francisco Sanchez. Mus: Carlos Vizziello. AD: Oscar Lagomarsino. SpFX: E. E. C., Eugenio Penalver. Mkp: A. & M. Ponte. Ref: TV: All Seasons Ent. video; Eng. dubbed. VSB. Horacio Higuchi. Peter Zirschky. Hound. Phantom, p. 157. no Martin. PT 7:29. Fango 104:52. With Paul Naschy, Norma Sebre, Guillermo Bredeston, Vidal Molina, Luis Induni.

This medieval melodrama with horrific overtones is the Naschy equivalent of the *Tower of London*/Richard III movies. In search of the Philosopher's Stone, the Baron De Lancre hires phony alchemist Simon, supposed possessor of the "darkest secrets of science," and offers the "Lord of Evil" maiden sacrifices. The cries of his murder and torture victims begin to haunt the "monster" Baron. ("The spirits are tormenting me!") Totally mad, he asserts "I'm invulnerable!" as he holds out the empty hand which he thinks holds the magic stone, and enemy arrows fell him.... Facile portrait of a good man gone bad. How bad? De Lancre: "We shall spread bloody terror throughout the entire land—murder, torture, burn—without respect for women, children, or the aged!" That bad.

The **DEVIL'S SKIN** (Singapore) Cathay 1970 color feature. Ref: Jones: vampire. Lee. with Ingrid Hu, Meng Li, Sun Tao.

**DEVIL'S STORY** see *Il Etait Une Fois le Diable*

**DEVIL'S SWORD** (Indonesian) 1987 feature. D: R. Timoer. Ref: NST! 4:21.Weisser/ATC: "a winner."

"Evil witch queen" rules crocodile people.

**DEVIL'S TRIANGLE, The** see *Almost Married*

**DEVIL'S VENDETTA** (H. K. -Thai) High Grow Film/Rising Sun Films 1991 color 96m. D: L. Chang-Xu. Ref: TV: vt; Eng. titles; *Devil's Vindata* - t error. Jones: 1986?

"Vampires today." A monk offers his heart to a demon named Twiggy. The demon just laughs, and Buddha scolds the latter. The now-male, now-female demon next appears as a giant horned shadow (an impressive effect) which turns out to be ... a "big cockroach." A woman again, the demon sprouts vampire fangs, then falls dead, temporarily, in cockroach form. Incidental: some little hopping vampires.

It's Optical Effects Unlimited here. Some effects are tacky, some imaginative, some both. One or two prizes for the sequence in which the goof becomes a napkin, a woman folds him and sends him on as a "butterfly," another woman folds him into a "frog," and he winds up as a talking, Peeping Tom bar of soap. Movie's second half runs more towards routine exorcism-vs.-demon effects, but there's still the floating, roaring, huge crystal skull, and Twiggy in Fearsome Monster form.

**DEVIL'S WOMAN, The** see *Ultima Casa vicino al Lago, L'*

El **DIA DE LOS ALBANILES II** (Mex) Frontera Films 1986 color 89m. SP, D, P: Gilberto Martinez Solares. SP, P: also Adolfo Martinez Solares. Mus: E. Cortazo(r). Ref: V 4/9/86: "unfunny";

*Bricklayers Day, Part II* - tr t. With Alfonso Zayas, Angelica Chain, Hugo Stiglitz, Luis de Alba, Tun Tun.

"Shock horror pic about a psychotic murderer" is "wed" to a comedy.

**DIABLA** see *Ultima Casa vicino al Lago*

**DIABLOTIN** (Russ) Tallinfilm 1985 feature. D: Helle Murdmaa. SP: Helga Ojdermaa, Olav Ehala. Ref: Ecran F 58:70. With Eghert Soll, Anna-Lisa Kurne.

"Satanic family ... little devil."

**DIABOLICAL DR. CYCLOPS, The** see *Dr. Cyclops*

*The **DIABOLICAL DR. Z** Safra-Silberman 1965. From a book by "David Kuhne." Ref: TV: vt; Eng. dubbed. VWB. Lee. Hardy/HM. no V. Lentz.

Featured: Dr. Zimmer (Antonio Escribano), a neuro-pathologist and student of Dr. Orloff (see *Awful Dr. Orlof*), who posits a physiological basis for good and evil ... his badly-burned daughter Irma (Mabel Karr), who practices facial self-surgery and carries on with her father's work after his death ... their acupuncture-ish machine, which makes Miss Death (Estella Blain) do their bidding ... and another scientifically-zombified assistant.... Banal revenge story, with surgical gore. Closest-to-passable sequence: the chase through the town fog. Dr. Z hardly figures in the film, but "The Diabolical Irma Zimmer" doesn't have quite the same ring to it.

El **DIABOLICO** (Mex) Conacite Dos 1978 color feature. SP, D: G. Korporaal. Co-D: R. V. Kuri. Ph: J. C. Ruvalcaba. Mus: G. C. Carrion. AD: J. Mendez. Mkp: G. Gonzalez. SdFX: G. Gavira. Ref: TV: no Eng. TVG. With Carlos East, Jorge Russek, J. H. Robles, Flor Trujillo, Lance Hool.

An evil cowpoke who brands his sexual "conquests" and wears funny contact lenses can take almost any number of bullets in the back until, finally, he expires, after passing on a curse and a medallion. His "heir," Oscar, becomes a crack shot and brands his women, too. Predictably, he later spots the evil sign on his baby son's forehead.

Choppy, sensationalistic horror-Western has two effective gruesome touches: a) the periodic shots of the original demon gunman's rotting, hanging corpse, and, b) the water barrel which leaks blood. (Oscar stuffs one victim in the barrel, then shoots it.)

**DIAL: HELP** (I) Impact Filmgroup/Metro & San Francisco & Reteitalia 1988 ('89-U.S.) color 96m.(*Ragno Gelido*). SP, D: Ruggero Deodato. SP: also Joseph & Mary Caravan. Story: Franco Ferrini. Mus: Claudio Simonetti. SpFX: Germano Natali. Mkp: Prestopino, Ciminelli. Opt: Penta. Ref: TV: Prism Ent. video; Eng. version. V 12/6/89. Hardy/HM2: aka *Minaccia d'Amore*. With Charlotte Lewis, Marcello Modugno, Mattia Sbragia, Carola Stagnaro, William Berger.

"I think the telephone wants to kill me!" The combination of Jenny Cooper (Lewis) and telephones makes mirrors shatter, fish go belly up, and pay-phone coins act like bullets. Behind it all: a "mysterious force that passes from phone to phone." Or, as Prof.

Klein (Berger) explains: "The energies of love and hate circulate throughout the universe. [They] can condense and concentrate themselves at times in a given room [and] magnetize, seduce" their "liberator".... Or, Don't Go Near the Phone. This is the most preposterous yet of the malignant-telephone movies, which include *Black Sabbath* and *Murder by Phone,* and its only appeal (apart from Lewis and sex appeal) is that very preposterousness. *Dial: Help,* in fact, at times, verges on satire of movies like *Carrie.* Prime absurdity: the levitating phone booth. Prime oddball-poetic image: the liberated pigeons flying up out of the horror room, as the voices of the un-damned gibber excitedly.

**DIAL 666 LUST** AFV 1991 color 76m. D: Jane Waters. Ref: Adam '92. no Jones. With Taylor Wayne, Cameo, Sharon Kane, Ron Jeremy.

"Spirits of female vampires."

The **DIAMOND EYE OF THE CAT** (Thai) c1990? color/ws c95m. Ref: TV: vt; no Eng. Chao Thai Market: above is tr t.

Elements in this hard-to-sort-out fantasy-horror-drama include a cave haunted by house cats, a fanged boogey-woman, and visualized nightmares re a one-eyed ghost woman. At the end, the latter's missing eye seems to be restored.

**DIARY OF ADAM AND EVE, The** (by M. Twain) see *Adventures of Mark Twain, The*

**DIARY OF THE DEAD** The Jessica Co. (Charles B. Moss, Jr.) 1976 color c90m. D: Arvin Brown. SP: I. C. Rapoport, R. L. Fish, from Ruth Rendell's book *One across, Two down.* Addl Dial: Geraldine Fitzgerald. Mkp: Ellen Chaset. Ref: TV: Vista HV. Deep Red 3. Stanley. no Martin. Hound.

At-loose-ends Stanley (Hector Elizondo), who lives in his mother-in-law Maud's (G. Fitzgerald) house, plots to kill her for her $86,000 in savings. As it happens, she falls and hits her head on the radiator, and Stanley buries her body in the yard. At the end, he finds Maud's body in his bed—and, across the room, in a rocking chair: good neighbor Walter (Joe Maher), who was, and is, devoted to Maud.... Or, my nightmare at Maud's. A long way to go for one okay shock scene—bloody corpse; silent, rocking attendant; face of man (i.e., Stanley) going mad, perhaps. Just skip the first 89 minutes.

*****DICK TRACY** Nat Levine 1937 (97m. feature version). Mus: Alberto Colombo. SpFX: Howard Lydecker. Ref: TV: VCI video. Turner/Price. Cult Movies 13:46. Hardy/SF. Lee. With Buddy Roosevelt, Ted Lorch, Oscar and Elmer, Sam Flint, Forbes Murray, Kit Guard, I. Stanford Jolley, Harry Strang, Roy Barcroft, Wilfred Lucas, Jack Ingram, Donald Kerr, Hal Price, Al Taylor.

"Strange how every single person branded with the spider mark and then murdered turns out to be some well-known criminal." By a "simple altering of a certain gland," the club-footed Spider's hunchbacked mad scientist, Moloch (John Piccori), renders Dick Tracy's brother Gordon (Richard Beach) a moral zombie (Carleton Young), "unable to distinguish between right and wrong." ("Can he be dominated?") The Spider's model sound-ray machine zaps a vase; the big-mother sound ray—a "machine that will disintegrate matter by sound"—taken aboard a flying wing,

almost destroys the Bay Bridge .... Scorecard: some fun play with the identity of The Spider, an okay "mad lab," and formula action.

*****DICK TRACY VS. CRIME, INC.** 1941 (106m. feature version). Ref: TV: VCI (United HV). Lee. Hardy/SF. Lentz. Hound. Martin. With Forrest Taylor, Edmund Cobb, Ed Parker, C. Montague Shaw, Selmer Jackson, Ken Terrell, Dave Sharpe.

"As The Ghost, I can go anywhere!" A "high frequency machine" enables The Ghost (Ralph Morgan), who wears a special medallion-like gizmo, to become invisible. Meanwhile, his henchmen bomb an undersea quake fault and flood New York City, in footage borrowed from *Deluge.* The most intriguing super-science concept, however, concerns a device which "makes an invisible man become visible": The "cathode detector" uses a "special kind of power" which enables an infrared, X-ray bulb to reveal "substance that cannot be seen by the human eye." Heroine June (Jan Wiley): "Everything has opposite values, like a snapshot negative!" The second-neatest science trick: The current from the electrocuted Ghosts's body transmits to the machine that makes him invisible—and kills his second-in-command, Lucifer (John Davidson). Bonus: an aerial torpedo.

If the usual serial shootouts and fisticuffs predominate, and the invisibility and anti-invisibility effects are elementary, the science is screwily imaginative. Prime line: "Start the invisible machine!" Prime line number 2: "He can make himself invisible—that explains a lot of things!"

*****DICK TRACY'S G-MEN** 1939 (104m. feature version). SpFX: Howard Lydecker. Ref: TV: VCI video. Hardy/SF. Lentz. Lee. With Jack Ingram, Edward Cassidy, Reginald Barlow (Guttenbach), Tom Steele, Lee Shumway, Bud Wolfe, Al Taylor, Reed Howes, George Cleveland, Ed Parker, Milton Frome, Forrest Taylor, Edmund Cobb, Tris Coffin, Ethan Laidlaw, Lloyd Ingraham, Joseph Swickard, Ed Peil Sr.

"Welcome back from the dead, Zarnoff." Before his execution in the gas chamber, "world famous spy" Zarnoff (Irving Pichel) imbibes an ancient drug from India "brewed by the alchemists of satan." A "resuscitator" then brings him back from the dead. Other super-scientific ingredients here include a death ray, in the form of a tripod camera, which sets a dirigible on fire ... a "powerful short wave transmitter" which detonates bombs at the receiving end (an attached super-TV allows Zarnoff to view all) ... an "invention ... that will put an end to all wars" ... and an "aerial torpedo" .... Lots of gimmicks to watch—and two people: Pichel, smooth and understated as Zarnoff, and Jennifer Jones, aka Phyllis Isley, though she's little more than punctuation as Tracy's secretary.

The **DICKTATOR** M.D.M. 1974(1977?) color feature. D: Perry Dell. SP: Walt Davis. Ph,P: M.S. Conde. Mus: Jack Millman. Sets: S. Sturges. Mkp: Miki. Tech: Alex Ameripoor et al. Ref: TV: SWV. With Rene Bond, Gretchen Gayle, Uschi Digard, Denis Juarez.

To combat overpopulation, sterilization pills are administered to every male in the world over five years of age. After eighteen months, there have been "no new births," though the effect of the pills was supposed to "wear off" .... Your basic t&a comedy, with a science-fiction premise. Uschi Digard is gorgeous in this one. Extra added: an apparent android.

**DIE HARD ANGELS (J) 1992** (*Dai Hado Enjerusu*). D: A.M. Sawada. Ref: Weisser/JC. With N. Akimoto, Y. Hoshi.

"Evil criminals" Zombie Man and Zombie Woman resurrect.

**DIE-HARD ANGELS: PROJECT ZOMBIE ANNIHILATION** (J) 1993 feature. D: Arthur M. Sawada. Ref: VSOM: poor. Weisser/JC: *Dai Hado Enjerusu: Kiken Ni Dakareta Onnatachi.* With Naomi Akimoto.

"Female commandos vs. flesh-eating zombies."

**DIE WATCHING** New World/Ashton Prods. & Titello Films(Nanda Rao) 1993 color 92m. D: Charles Davis. SP: Kenneth J. Hall. Ph: Howard Wexler. Mus: D.S. Cohen, S. Roewe. PD: Wendy Guidery. Key Mkp: Suzzee Toon. Ref: TV: Triboro video. Martin. PT 17:59. With Christopher Atkins, Tim Thomerson, Vali Ashton, Carlos Palomino, Mike Jacobs Jr.

Video man Michael (Atkins) makes two-part tapes of exotic dancers, sells the first part to the local vidstore manager, and keeps the snuff part for himself. When he mistakenly delivers a private tape to the guy .... Mainly perfunctory, and similar to *The Art of Dying,* but not quite that bad, thanks to Atkins, who helped wreck *Dracula Rising,* but is the best thing about this film.

**DIED ON A RAINY SUNDAY** see *Mort un Dimanche ee Pluie*

**DIES IRAE** see *Day of Wrath*

**DIESEL** (F) Stephan & Filmedis & Farena & TF-1 (Vera Belmont) 1985 color 92m. SP, D: Robert Kramer. SP: also Serge Leroy, Richard Morgieve. Ref: V 8/14/85: "unintentional laughs." 5/1/85:451. no Stanley. With Gerard Klein, Agnes Soral, Magali Noel, Laurent Terzieff, Niels Arestrup.

Underground "totalitarian metropolis" in the "desolate near future."

**DIFFICILE D'ETRE UN DIEU** see *Es Ist Nicht Leicht ein Gott zu Sein*

**DIGITAL DEVIL STORY** (J) 1987 anim color c45m. Ref: TV: Animage Video; no Eng.

When a computer threatens to spawn a demon, the heroine hies to the library's demonology section to do some quick research. (Among the books on the shelves: *Final Devil.*) The computer then begins spewing a pink goo which engulfs its victims, solidifies, and turns into a big blue demon. ("Kill! Kill! Kill!") The heroine's laser-eye-rays disperse the horrors—until she becomes possessed and changes into a hag.... Elementary monster-mongering, but done with some visual flair. Atmospheric effects with railroad-crossing lights, a shimmering sea, a big low moon, etc.

**DIGITAL MAN** Green Comm. & Republic & Sci-Fi Prods. (Talaat Captan) 1994 color c95m. SP, D: P. Roth. SP: also R. Schmidt. SpMkpFX: Todd Masters. SpVisFX: Wainstain, Hopkins. Digital: Mach Universe. Ref: vc box: "D-1 battle cyborg." With K. Olandt, K. Dalton, Ed Lauter, M. Hues (Digital Man).

**DIGITAL TARGET GREY** (J) 198-? anim color 80m. Ref: TV: vt; no Eng. Anime Opus '89.

Juvenile, but the fantastic, 2588 A.D. weaponry is worth a look: a super-disintegrator spacecraft which appears and disappears ... ray-shooting robots ... air cars ... disintegrator guns ... giant flying "helmet" weapons ... and an android that whistles ("comin' through the rye").

**DIKI VOSTOK** see *Wild East*

**3 La DINASTIA DRACULA** Conacite Dos 1978 color c90m. (aka *Dracula '87*). D: Alfredo B. Crevenna. SP: Jorge Patino. Ph: Javier Cruz. SdFX: Gonzalo Gavira. Mkp: Antonio Ramirez. Ref: TV: Eagle Video; no Eng. With Sylvia Manrique, Ruben Rojo, Magda Guzman, Roberto Nelson, Erika Carlson, Jose Najera, Victor Alcocer.

1895. On the night of Walpurgis, a woman removes a stake from the body of a devil-worshiping victim of the Inquisition. He revives, and they embrace, but a priest burns them to death, then slaps a crucifix on Dracula's (Fabian) back.

....The above is the climactic sequence. Earlier, the woman demonstrates that she can turn into a big dog, while Dracula can appear and disappear and turn into a paper bat. His sudden snarling appearances, accompanied by bursts of flame, get monotonous, and Fabian looks uncomfortable with the extra dental work. Crude score.

**DINER** Gahan Wilson anim 6m. Ref: SFChron 12/24/93: "chillingly funny interpretation of restaurants that eat people." 24th Int'l. Tournee of Animation leaflet.

**DINNER WITH A VAMPIRE** or **DINNER WITH THE VAMPIRE** see *Having Supper with a Vampire*

**DINOSAUR ... SECRET OF THE LOST LEGEND** see *Baby ... Secret of the Lost Legend*

**\*The DINOSAUR AND THE MISSING LINK: A PREHISTORIC TRAGEDY** Conquest 1917 stopmo anim. Ref: TV. Mo. Lee.

Cast of characters: Wild Willie, an apelike missing link, given to mugging for the camera ... a prehistoric ostrich ... and a brontosaurus. Feeble slapstick with cave people; interesting animation by Willis O'Brien. In a scene anticipating *King Kong,* Willie takes on the bronto—and loses.

**DINOSAUR ISLAND** Wyn-Ray Media/Pacific Trust 1993 color 85m. D,P: Jim Wynorski, Fred Olen Ray. SP: Sheridan, Wooden. Dinosaurs: Buechler. Live Action Dinos: MMI. SpVisFX: Hal Miles. Ref: TV: New Horizons HV. SFChron Dtbk 2/20/94: aka *Dinossland*? With Ross Hagen, Michelle Bauer, Steve Barkett, Griffen Drew, Antonia Dorian, Richard Gabai.

Ingredients: The Great One ("Jackie Gleason?"), a tyrannosaurus ... a triceratops ... a brontosaurus ... a trilobite-type ... a pterodactyl ... the Beast of the Cave (a guy in an *Alien* suit) ... and of course Bronson Caverns .... Limp sub-camp humor, pathetic acting. A cute moment or two, that's it.

**DINOSAURS** see *Adventures in Dinosaur City*

**DINOSAURS KID** (H. K.?) Hsi Yung-ming (sp?) 198-? color 92m. D: Hsu Wu-tang. Ph: Lu Ding-yong (sp?). Mus: Chan Ying. AD: Lin Hsi-king. FX: W. S. Chou (sp?). Mkp: Siu Wei (sp?). Ref: TV: Pan-Asia Video; no Eng. With Chiang Ching, Wu Chin-Chih, Fun Kwang-te (sp?), Lin Ling, H. S. Wu, Tai Lien, W. P. He.

On an island somewhere in the Pacific, a little boy from a downed airliner plays Tarzan with dinosaurs. Among his playmates: a fire-breathing brontosaurus, a web-spraying anklyosaurus, a red-eyed flying thing that's a cross between a pterodactyl and the Giant Claw, a stegosaurus, a triceratops, and a bad *Half Human* type which may be in league with a horde of big-eared, flying, gold, dinosaur-hating aliens from a flying saucer. The ape creature follows the boy back to his parents and civilization and does a Godzilla on the buildings there. The brontosaurus shows up, flings the bad ape into the sea, picks up the boy on his head, and swims back to the island.... Dinosaurs by Rubbermaid. It's idiotic, but it's nonstop. This action-filled, but technically pathetic monster fantasy has stock music, primitive effects, no money for editing, and just a little of same for men and dinosaur suits.

**DINOSSLAND** see *Dinosaur Island*

**DIRTY DRACULA** see *Doriana Gray*

**DIRTY PAIR** (J) VAP Video 1987-88 anim color 25m. each. SP: (2) Yuichi Sasamoto. Ref: Animag 8:6, 10-16: 10 OAVs. 9:40. Japan Video: 1st in series released late '87.

Robots, gods, "artificial lifeform." (Animag)

**DIRTY PAIR: AFFAIR OF NOLANDIA** (J) Bandai/Emotion 1985 anim color 57m. D: Masaharu Okuwaki. SP: Kazunori Ito. Story: H. Takachiho. Char Des: Tsukasa Dokite. Ref: TV: Bandai video; no Eng. Animag 8:6: OAV. J Anim Prgm Guide. Wonderful World of Comics 2:42. Animerica 6:51: dubbed version. Voice: Saeko Shimazu (Yuri).

Yuri and Kei of the World Welfare Work Assn. venture to a uranium-mining planet to aide a little girl named Misumi. Once there, visions and nightmares re flying jellyfish, weird "neon" fauna, glob monsters, and swamp tentacles beset the two. The visions prove to be products of genetically-engineered ESPers, whose wrath ultimately destroys the planet. In one fun sequence, Yuri and Kei decide to enjoy their hallucinations and go space skiing. Light-hearted, for-the-most-part-regulation action video features some inventive science-fantasy sequences and a cyborg which seems part *Terminator*-derived and part Bo Svenson-derived.

**DIRTY PAIR—LAST FANTASY** (J) 1987 anim color 92m. Ref: Japan Video. Animag 4:25-6: sfa the "Special Video" episodes (25 & 26)—re the "God Cannon"—which completed the TV series?

**DIRTY PAIR: THE FLIGHT 005 CONSPIRACY** (J) 1990 anim color 60m. Ref: Animag 9:3: OAV. 8:6. 7:5. Japan Video.

**DIRTY PAIR MOVIE** (J) Matsutake Film 1987 anim color 81m. (aka *Project Eden*). D: Koichi Mashita. SP: Hakuhiro Hoshiyama, from H. Takachiho's comic stories. Char Des:

Tsukasa Dokite. Ref: TV: Emotion video; little Eng. Animag 8:6, 9-10.

In the year 2141 A.D., mankind rules 3,000 planets, and the metal Vizorium powers the warp engines of its spaceships. On the mining planet Agerna, Prof. Wattsman's genetically-engineered monsters threaten Kei and Yuri, the Dirty Pair. At the end, hordes of accidentally activated monsters devastate the planet, as our heroines escape.... Nonstop action, almost monotonously so. Stylish and feverishly busy, for better or worse.

**A DISASTER IN TIME** Channel Communications/Wild Street (Drury Lane/Jill Sattinger, Paul White/John A. O'Connor) 1992 (1991) color 99m. (*The Grand Tour* - alt t. aka *Grand Tour: A Disaster in Time. Timescape* - early t). SP, D: David Twohy, From the novella "Vintage Season" by Lawrence O'Donnell & C. L. Moore. Ph: Harry Mathias. Mus: Gerald Gouriet. PD: Michael Novotny. SpVisFX: Apogee; (sup) Douglas Smith; (coord) Marcus McWaters. SpFX: SpFx Inc.; (coord) J. W. Beauchamp; (sup) John Adams. Anim: John Shourt. Ref: TV: Academy Ent. video. TVG. SFChron 11/26/92. Martin. V 10/14/91: A-42. PT 16:60. Cinef 12/92:60-61. Imagi 1:58. With Jeff Daniels, Nicholas Guest, Jim Haynie, Ariana Richards, Emilia Crow, David Wells, Marilyn Lightstone, Robert Colbert.

"We're just tourists." Visitors to Greenglen from a perfect, smoothly-run future where "you're never sick" and "nothing ever goes wrong" prove to be "disaster groupies": They visit sites of imminent disaster in the Twentieth Century. Hero Ben Wilson (Daniels) acquires a time-travel "passport," goes back to yesterday to undo some damage, and finds a second Ben Wilson.

These "tourists" stay detached from the plight of "bygoners." ("We cannot become involved.") Ben gets involved, and a rather arduous narrative issues in a satisfying, clever climax and coda. Compare *Millennium*.

**The DISCARNATES** (J) Shochiku 1988 color/ws 109m. (*Ijintachi Tono Natsu* aka *Summer with Ghosts. Japanese Ghost Story*). D: Nobuhiko Obayashi. SP: Shinichi Ichikawa. From Taichi Yamada's novel. Ph: Y. Sakamoto. Mus: M. Shinozaki. AD: K. Satsuya. Ref: HR 1/31/89: "an elegiac meditation on the inevitability of the eternal parting between parents and child." M/TVM 11/88:85. V 7/26/89: "doesn't quite make it." Weisser/JC. With Morio Kazama, Kumiko Akiyoshi, T. Kataoka, Y. Natori.

"Humans and specters meet on a common dramatic plane." (HR)

**DISCO GODFATHER** see *Avenging Godfather*

**DISCONNECTED** Reel Movies/Generic Films (Carmine Capobianco/Bob Stewart) 1986 color 81m. SP, D, P: Gorman Bechard. Story, SP: Virginia Gilroy. Mus: Steve Asetta. Ref: V 2/19/86: "routine." McCarty II: "odd individuality." Stanley. Ecran 67:70. With Frances Raines, Mark Walker, Carl Koch, Ben Page.

"Slasher murders." (V)

**DISLOCATION** (Chinese) China Film/Xi'an Film Studio 1987 color 88m. (*Cuo Wei*). D: Huang Jianxin. SP: Huang Xin, Zhang Min. Sequel to *The Black Cannon Incident* (1985). Mus: Han Yong. Ref: screen. V 5/6/87: *The Stand-In* - tr of orig t. UCTheatre notes 11/13/88. with Liu Zifeng (robot), Mou Hong, Yang Kun, Sun Kihu.

Zhao Shuxin, director of Gilman and Co., and amateur inventor, programs an android with his own appearance, expressions, and habits in order to avoid time-consuming meetings. The double takes to his assignment. (Zhao: "You've become addicted to meetings.") It, or he, though, wants a personality of its own, and starts to smoke (Zhao does not), and becomes curious re love and the possibility of "female robots".... Low-key, poky, but droll sf-comedy, with an all-a-dream ending. The android enjoys running through his facial expressions for his creator, and seems in general to enjoy life more than does Zhao.

**DISTANT LIGHTS** see *Luci Lontane*

**A DISTANT SCREAM** (B) Fox Mystery Theatre/Fox-TV & Hammer 1985 (1984) color c80m. (aka *Dying Truth*). D, Assoc P: John Hough. Tel: Martin Worth. Ph: Brian West. Mus: Paul Patterson. AD: Carolyn Scott. Mkp: Eddie Knight. Ref: TV. TVG. Stanley. no Maltin '92. no Scheuer. Ecran F 50:12-13. PT 13:46. With David Carradine, Stephanie Beacham, Stephen Chase, Stephen Greif, Fanny Carby, Lesley Dunlop.

The "dreadful old man" (Carradine) who appears, at first, only to Rosemary (Beacham) is her lover, Michael (Carradine), from the future. The older man is in the crowded-with-Michaels present in order to discover who killed Rosemary: She, he knows, will die, and he—or the younger Michael—will be locked away as crazy for "going on about an old man".... An initially intriguing ghost story becomes an unsatisfactory romantic mystery thanks, in part, to the fact that the ectoplasmic status of Michael (old) is inconsistent: Later, he appears, also, to Michael (young), then to Rosemary's husband (Chase). A few frissons nonetheless.

**DISTORTIONS** (King-TV)/Twisted Prod. (Jackelyn Giroux) 1987 (1986) color 96m. D: Armand Mastroianni. SP: John Goff. Mus: David Morgan. MkpDes: Noel de Souza, Lee Bryant. Ref: TV. V 5/17/87. Hound. Phantom. With Olivia Hussey, Piper Laurie, Steve Railsback, Rita Gam, Edward Albert.

Problem: "There's someone in the house!" Solution: "You gotta get outta that house." Olivia ("insanity runs in the family") Hussey doesn't listen. Later: "That horrible face!" Script's basis proves to be among the Most Repeated Plotlines in thrillers—i.e., the Plot to Drive Someone Mad, complete with smoldering wall portrait.

**The DISTURBANCE** Vid America (Ron Cerasuolo, Richard Levin) 1990 color 81m. D, Co-P: Cliff Guest. SP: Laura Radford. Mus: Jacob, Pettit. SpFX: Barry Anderson. Ref: V 2/21/90:330 (hv): "misses the mark." Martin: "dreadful." With Timothy Greeson, Lisa Geoffrion, Ken Ceresne.

Loner with "horrible demon inside him." (V)

**DISTURBED** Live Ent./Odyssey (Brad Wyman/Second Generation Films) 1990 color 96m. SP, D: Charles Winkler. SP: also Emerson Bixby. Mus: S. S. Smalley. SpFxMkp: David Miller. Ref: TV. V 11/19/90. With Malcolm McDowell, Geoffrey Lewis, Priscilla Pointer, Pamela Gidley, Irwin Keyes, Clint Howard, Adam Rifkin, Deep Roy.

"She's dead! She's alive! She's dead again!" Bergen Field Sanatorium, ten years after one inmate's suicide. Derrick ("Derek" in the credits) Russell (McDowell), the head doctor, acquiesces with "hypo-manic freak" Michael Khan (Lewis) in the (apparent) killing of a patient, Sandy Ramirez (Gidley), who comes back to "haunt" Russell. Assailed by "monsters," he has a (visualized) nightmare re a living headless body and sees the "dead" Sandy shoot a hypo of blood at him.... Misfired black comedy turns into a formula slasher movie, as the "hallucinations" are revealed to have been part of a revenge plot. Script's cavalier attitude toward both psychiatrists and their patients gets to be unpleasant. Funniest bit: the singing candygram man (Dean Cameron).

**The DIVINE ENFORCER** Prism (Scott Pfeiffer) 1991 feature. SP, D: Robert Rundle. SP: also Tanya York. Ref: PT 16:60: "classic of bad filmmaking." With Michael Foley, Don Stroud ("vampire"), Carrie Chambers (psychic girl), Erik Estrada, Jan Michael Vincent, Judy Landers, Jim Brown, Robert Z'Dar.

Psychotic "vampire" serial killer.

**DIZZY DETECTIVES** Col 1943 19m. (*Idiots Deluxe* - orig t). D, P: Jules White. SP: Felix Adler. Ph: Ben Kline. AD: Carl Anderson. Ref: TV: vt. Okuda/CCS: remade as *Fraidy Cat* (1951) and *Hook a Crook* (1955). no Lee. Maltin/SSS. LC. With The Three Stooges, John Tyrrell, Bud Jamison.

The "Ape Man Strikes Again" (according to a headline here). Or is it just a gorilla at large? It's the latter, although various stooges keep saying things like "We got the apeman." The usual.

**DNI ZATMENIYA** see *Days of the Eclipse*

**DOCKS OF NEW ORLEANS** Mono (J. S. Burkett) 1948 64m. (*Charlie Chan on the Docks of New Orleans* - ad t). D: Derwin Abrahams. SP: W. Scott Darling. Ref: TV. V 3/17/48. TVG. Everson/TDIF: remake of *Mr. Wong, Detective*. Okuda/TMC. Maltin '92. Scheuer.

New form of invisible and odorless poison gas causes "quick death" and is contained in radio-tube glass of a "very peculiar composition" sensitive to high-pitched sounds. Almost parodically stilted Chan mystery-with-a-dash-of-sf. The dialogue—overburdened with clues and theories—is kinder to the plot than it is to the actors.

**DR. ALIEN** Para/Phantom Prods. (John Schouweiler) 1988 color 90m. (*Dr. Alien!* - ad t. *I Was a Teenage Sex Mutant* - alt t). D, Co-P: David DeCoteau. SP, Assoc P: Kenneth J. Hall. Mus: Reg Powell, Sam Winans. SpMkpFX: Greg Cannom; (sup) John Vulich. MechFX: Larry Odien. SpFX: Roger George, Tom Callaway. Ref: TV: Phantom Video. V (Cannes '89):88. With Billy Jacoby, Olivia Barash, Stuart Fratkin, Troy Donahue, Arlene Golonka, Judy Landers, Edy Williams, Raymond O'Connor (Drax), Linnea Quigley, Michelle Bauer, Elizabeth Kaitan.

Q: "Why are women throwing themselves at me?" asks Wesley (Jacoby). A: Because new biology teacher, Xenobia (Landers)—a "swollen-headed, puffy-eyed, blue-skinned being" from the planet Altaria—has injected him with a formula that promotes the "growth of an organ that sends out mating signals"—a phallic gland a la *From Beyond*, of which film this one seems to be a (limp) parody. *Dr. Alien* also lifts, clumsily, the *Teen Wolf* plot: School nerd becomes Joe Slick.

**The DOCTOR AND THE DEVILS** (B) Fox/Brooksfilms & Cooper & Gintell 1985 color/ws 92m. D: Freddie Francis. SP: Ronald Harwood, from an original script by Dylan Thomas. Mus: John Morris. SpFX: Alan Bryce. Mkp: Naomi Donne. Ref: TV. MFB'86:205-7. V 10/9/85. SFChron 10/18/85. Stanley. With Timothy Dalton, Jonathan Pryce, Twiggy, Julian Sands, Stephen Rea, Beryl Reid, T. P. McKenna, Jennifer Jayne, Hedger Wallace.

Dr. Rock (Dalton) needs bodies for medical research. Fallon (Pryce) and Broom (Rea) get them for him—any way they can. Broom wants the money; Fallon just wants to kill.... The plot and ironies are familiar from *The Body Snatcher, Mania*, etc.; the moral ABCs (Rock: "There is right and wrong") are familiar from Brooksfilms' earlier *The Elephant Man*. Dalton's role is a thankless, talked-out one; Pryce fares better; Broom's easy corruption is cutting, but afterwards Rea has no more to do and a lot of screen time in which to do it. Good rueful main theme by Morris.

**DR. CALIGARI** Steiner Films (J. F. Robertson) 1989 color 80m. SP, D, PD: Stephen Sayadian. SP: also Jerry Stahl. Mus: M. Froom. Ref: V 9/13/89: "even discriminating cult movie mavens may sit this one out." 8/30/89:35. Cinef 6/91. PT 10:49. with Madeleine Reynal, Fox Harris, Laura Albert.

"Hormonal interfacing experiments" in this hommage to the silent *Cabinet of Dr. Caligari*. (V)

**\*DR. CYCLOPS** Dale Van Every 1940. Ref: TV. Lentz. V 3/6/40. Hardy/SF. Stanley. Lee. Martin. Maltin '92. Scheuer: aka *The Diabolical Dr. Cyclops*.

"We have the cosmic force of creation itself!" In the Amazon jungle. Dr. Alexander Thorkel (Albert Dekker)—the "greatest living authority on organic molecular structure" ... and a "very strange man"—uses concentrator and conductor to extract "cosmic force from the bosom of the Earth." He then uses that force to break down molecular tissue and shrink five people, and the latter find themselves in a land of "giant" chickens, cats, dogs, parrots, etc.

Don't get too excited by the way the title writhes eerily into focus. The film which follows is mechanical plot, "perils," and acting, and it's shot in old-lobby-card color. Even the giant cotton swabs, crates, doors, scissors, books, spectacles, tables, boots, etc., are unimaginatively used. And if, physically, the people shrink, their voices remain the same.

**DR. DOBERMIND** Jon Mostow & Richard Hoffman 198-? color c6m. SP, D, P: Mostow. Ph: Peter Rader. Mus: Duncan Millar. SpMkpFX: Peter Miller. Ref: TV: *Cinemagic* (Starlog Video), MPI HV. With Jennifer Jacobi, Hugh D'Autremont, Gaby Dundon.

Museum taxidermist who looks like a "real psycho" gives a young girl gory visions. Well-cast effects vehicle.

**DR. FRANKENSTEIN'S CASTLE OF FREAKS** see *Frankenstein's Castle of Freaks*

**DR. GIGGLES** (U.S.-J) Univ/Largo Ent. & JVC Ent. (Dark Horse/S. M. Besser) 1992 color/ws 95m. SP, D: Manny Coto.

SP: also Graeme Whifler. PD: Bill Malley. SpMkpFX: KNB EFX. SpFX: Phil Cory. VixFX: (sup) Gene Warren Jr., Damian Klaus; Digital Fantasy; (head anim) Steve Rein. Opt: Howard Anderson. Ref: TV. V 10/26/92. Martin. Fango 122:8-9. SFChron 10/24/92. With Larry Drake, Holly Marie Combs, Cliff De Young.

Mad Evan Rendell (Drake) escapes from an asylum and heads for Moorehigh, where years ago a mob lynched his father (W. D. Hunt), a "doctor from hell" who cut out people's hearts in an attempt to transplant same to his weak-hearted wife.... Main bad joke: "L.A. Law" 's slow-witted Benny (Drake) as a mad doc with Freddy quips. Most gruesome plot twist (which occurs in flashback): The original Doc Wendell saved his son (Nicholas Mastrandrea) from the mob by sewing him inside his wife's corpse.

**DOCTOR GORE** see *Body Shop, The*

**DR. HACKENSTEIN** Vista Street (Feifer-Miller) 1988 color 88m. SP, D: Richard Clark. Mus: Randy Miller. Ref: V 1/18/89: "pleasant." 10/19/88:311 (ad). Martin: "boring." PT 2:35. Nowlan. With David Muir, Stacey Travis, Catherine Davis Cox, Anne Ramsey, Logan Ramsey, Phyllis Diller.

Doc attempts to restore dead wife to life.

**DR. JEKYLL AND MR. HYDE—A JOURNEY INTO FEAR** see *Edge of Sanity*

**DR. JUICE'S LUST POTION** Tempo/High Class 1986 color c80m. Ref: vc box. no Adam'88. With Candy Evans, Melissa Melendez, Joey Silvera.

Research scientist discovers "antidote" to aging—The Juice of the Virgin.

**DR. LAMB** (H.K.?) Star Ent./Parkman Wong(Grand River Films) 1992 color/ws c90m. D:(and Exec P) Danny Lee;(assoc) Billy Tang. SP: Law Kam Fai. Ph: Miu Kin Fai. Mus: Jonathan Wong. AD: Horace Ma. FX?: Animation Shop. Ref: TV: vt; no Eng. V&T Video. With D. Lee, Simon Yam.

Hack hacks fares with cleaver, garrotes them in his taxi, drills them with electric drill, videotapes the violence, thus loses customers and gains police interest. Rudimentary slasher movie.

**DR. M.** (G-I-F) Prism Ent./Cori Films/N.E.F. & Ellepi Film & Clea and ZDF, La Sept, & Telefilm GmbH & CCC (Francois Duplat, Hans Brockmann) 1989 ('91-U.S.) color 116m. (*Club Extinction* - ad t). D, Adap: Claude Chabrol. SP: Sollace Mitchell. Story: Thomas Bauermeister. Inspired by Norbert Jacques' novel *Mabuse der Spieler*. Mus: Paul Hindemith. SpFxMkp: Hasso von Hugo. SpFxSup: Karl Baumgartner. SpOptFX: Futureffects. Mkp, Artificial Heart: Gianetto de Rossi. Ref: TV: Para HV; Eng.-lang. version. Bill Warren. V 2/18/91. MFB'90:350-2. PT 13:9. V 11/15/89:10. With Alan Bates, Jennifer Beals, Jan Niklas, Hanns Zischler, William Berger, Wolfgang Preiss.

"It's like God's playing Russian roulette." A "suicide virus" seems to be sweeping a futuristic Germany dominated by "video boards" which broadcast Big Brother messages re escape. The "travel agent": Mater Media's Dr. Marsfeldt (Bates), who brainwashes potential suicides at his Club Theratos, where an ominous "peace" prevails.... *Dr. M.* begins promisingly, with hints of *The Hypnotic Eye* and *The Manchurian Candidate* (post-hypnotic-suggestion violence) and *The Seventh Victim* (mysterious suicides and symbols), as well as Fritz Lang's Mabuse films. Eventually, a basic weakness becomes apparent: The doctor's video, TV, and club are less hypnotically compelling than simply lullingly vacuous. The sinister plot comes to resemble an invasion of super-Muzak. Bates' Dr. M. is a combination of bull, viciousness, and common sense.

**DR. MORDRID** Full Moon 1992 color c75m. Idea, D, P: Charles Band. D: also Albert Band. SP: C. C. Joyner. Ph: Adolfo Bartoli. PD: Milo. Mus: R. Band. VisFX: David Allen. FxAnimSup: Kevin Kutchaver. SpFxMkp: Michael Sharum, Jay Wejebe? SpFxCoord: John Cazin. Ref: TV. SFChron Dtbk 9/20/92: Para HV. 9/27/92. With Jeffrey Combs, Brian Thompson, Yvette Nipar, Jay Acovone, Keith Coulouris, Ritch Brinkley.

"Kabal has escaped." Dr. Mordrid (Combs)—a sorcerer who has been guarding Earth for 109 years and takes his marching orders from a disembodied Monitor—combats Kabal (Thompson), a "powerful alchemist" and a "cosmic son of a bitch" who is "worse than evil" and bent on unleashing some demons from the fourth dimension, "another world of magic and sorcery." Featured gizmo: a supernatural flashlight which temporarily "freezes" the subject.

Innocuous variation on *Warlock* has a reasonably satisfying stopmo climactic sequence, in which a dinosaur skeleton fights a mammoth skeleton, and two or three demons get halfway through the door to our world. Strange line: (Mordrid) "I'm going to leave my body, Sam."

**DR. ORLOFF'S INVISIBLE HORROR** see *Orloff and the Invisible Man*

**DR. OTTO AND THE RIDDLE OF THE GLOOM BEAM** Carden & Cherry & Studio Prods.(Sweat Equity) 1986(1985) color 97m. SP, D: John Cherry. SP, P: Coke Sams. Ph: Jim May. Mus: Shane Keister. PD: Glenn Petach. SpVisFX: Cappello Film;(anim) Chuck Majewski Jr. SpFX: Vernon Hyde, Spectacular FX. Ref: TV: KnoWhutImean? HV. V 5/14/86. Ecran F 67:70. Martin. With Jim Varney (Dr. Otto et al), Glenn Petach (Otto's head hand), Myke Mueller, Jackie Welch.

"More destruction! More carnage!" The mad Dr. Otto Vonschnick's goal: "world domination." "A foreign accent with a hand growing out of his head," Otto announces his intentions via a worldwide TV broadcast and uses his Gloom Beam to erase magnetic impulses on credit cards, obliterate Wall Street stocks, erase data on personal checks, etc. His Changing Coffin transforms his features and anatomy to give him various identities, and his Transporter Shroud transports people from place to place. Plus a Happy Face, voice-activated robot, a monster named Alex, and a ray-shooting cane.

The success rate of the gags in this Working Overtime on Weird comedy is not high, but the bizarre rate is, and the movie has its own, uh, style. Varney of course went on to play Ernest, but this is probably his shining moment.

**DOCTOR PENETRATION** Hustler Video/Gregory Dark 1986 color 76m. D: Alex DeRenzy. Mus: Johnny Powers. Ref: TV:

Wet Video. Adam '89. With Stacey Donovan, Melissa (Barbara the Lobster Woman), Taija Rae, Lois Ayres, Sheri St. Clair (Igor), Britanny Stryker, Herschel Savage, Tom Byron, Dick Rambone (The Lobster Monster), William Lee (Dr. Penetration), F. M. Bradley.

"Warm up the neuro-sexual fantasy soul stealer!" The doc's aforementioned gizmo tapes the innermost fantasies of his guests and thus captures their souls and turns them into zombies. At the end, the Lobster Monster slays the doctor, and the latter's zombies wander about like sleepwalkers. Rudimentary adult sf-comedy.

**DOCTOR SNUGGLES** Kidpix & O'Kelly 1984 anim color 60m. D, P: Jim Terry. Mus: Bullets. Ref: vc box: "unique inventions" enable Snuggles & co. to travel the universe.

**DOCTOR VAMPIRE** (H.K.-B) Golden Harvest/Paragon Films (Stanley Lau) 1990 color/ws c95m. D: Q. Xen Lee. AD: (B) Martin Sullivan. Mkp: (B) Lisa Boni. Ref: TV: Pan-Asia Video; some dubbed Eng. Jones.

"We're immortal!" The caped, super-strong (Caucasian) vampire master of the country inn samples second-hand blood from the hands of sated vampire women. ("Welcome to paradise.") Later, he and other vampires cavort in a hospital. Plus: vampire shish kebab and laser-vs.-vampire-eye-rays. Silly, strenuous horror-comedy.

**DOCTOR WITHOUT SCRUPLES** see *Privat Klinik Professor Lund*

**DODICI DONNE D'ORO** (I-W.G.) 1965 feature. D: G. Parolini. Ref: Palmerini: "twelve woman robots."

**DOG KING AND SNAKE KING** (H. K.?) c1992? color c95m. Ref: TV: Tai Seng Video; no Eng.

In one scene, snakes mass, attack, strangle thugs; in another, a dog pack attacks some other thugs. At the end, snakes gang up on the main thug. Unremarkable horror-fantasy-actioner.

**DOIN' TIME ON PLANET EARTH** Cannon (Golan-Globus) 1988 color 85m. D: Charles Matthau. SP: Darren Star. Story: Star, Andrew Licht, J. A. Mueller. Mus: Dana Kaproff. VisFX: (des) Bill Millar; (sup) Paulette Smook-Marshall; (opt) Cinema Research. Ref: TV. V 5/18/88. With Nicholas Strouse, Hugh Gillin, Gloria Henry, Hugh O'Brian, Martha Scott, Adam West (Charles), Candice Azzara (Edna).

Sunnydale. "Greetings, Extraterrestrial Ryan Richmond." Ryan (Strouse) is told that, thousands of years ago, E.T.s from planet B-52 visited Earth and intermarried, and that he is their leader now. "What if I'm a lizard under this skin?" Heavy-handedly kooky comedy overdoes it. Similar to *Uforia,* only worse.

**DOLCE CASA DEGLI ORRORI, La** see *Sweet House of Horrors*

**The DOLL MAKER'S DAUGHTER** (B) Hepworth 1906 b&w silent 10m. D: Lewin Fitzhamon. Ref: Hardy/SF: robot doll. With Dolly Lupono.

**DOLLAR A DAY, A** see *Spacerage*

**DOLLMAN** Para/Full Moon (Cathy Gesualdo) 1990 color 86m. D: Albert Pyun. SP: Chris Roghair. Story, Exec P: Charles Band. Ph: George Mooradian. Mus: Tony Riparetti. PD: Don Day. SpVisFX: David Allen. Spaceship Min: Leslie Huntly, Gene Warren. SpFX: Frazee. Opt: Mercer, OptFX. Key Mkp: Teri Blythe. Ref: TV. TVG 11/30/91. Shock Cinema 4:32. With Tim Thomerson, Jackie Earle Haley, Kamala Lopez, Humberto Ortiz, Judd Omen, Nicholas Guest, Frank Collison (Sprug, the head).

"Did I tell you to tell everybody in the neighborhood that we have a spaceman living in our house?" Ten thousand light years from Earth, a thirteen-inch-tall cop (Thomerson) from the planet Arturos is pursuing a living disembodied head when their respective spaceships hit the energy barrier, and aliens and ships land in the South Bronx. With his ray gun, the mini-cop proceeds to blast drug dealers, but the head surrenders to the latter an ominous-sounding (but not, as it turns out, especially powerful) dimensional fusion bomb.... Variation on *E.T.* and *Brother from Another Planet* begins drolly, but turns strenuously serious, and basically just keeps repeating its no-longer-cute premise.

See also the following and *Bad Channels.*

**DOLLMAN VS. DEMONIC TOYS** Para HV/Full Moon 1993 color feature. D: Charles Band. Ref: V 3/29/93:18 (rated). SFChron Dtbk 10/10/93. 10/31/93: "Doll Chick" Ginger from *Bad Channels*; Brick Bardo from *Dollman*; Zombie Man from *Demonic Toys*. With Tim Thomerson (Dollman), T. Scoggins, Melissa Behr.

**DOLLS** (U.S.-B-I) Empire/Taryn (Brian Yuzna) 1986 color 77m. D: Stuart Gordon. SP: Ed Naha. Mus: Fuzzbee Morse; (Dolls theme) Victor Spiegel. PD: Giovanni Natalucci. Doll FX: (puppets) John & Vivian Brunner; (mech dolls) Giancarlo Del Brocco; (stopmo) David Allen; (mech) Giuseppi Tortora; (mkp) Alfredo Tiberi. SpHeads: Sky Highchief. SpMkpFX: MMI; John Buechler. Ref: TV. V 4/22/86. Bob Moore. With Stephen Lee, Carrie Lorraine, Ian Patrick Williams, Carolyn Purdy Gordon, Guy Rolfe, Hilary Mason.

"There are some crazy toys down there that can kill people!" An old couple (Rolfe, Mason) uses witchcraft to turn bitter, warped adults into living killer-dolls. ("It's the little people!") Plus a visualized fantasy in which a teddy bear becomes gigantic, then turns monstrous.... Lousy story; some good scenes with both individual and massed dolls, some of which scenes recall *Devil-Doll* (1936), some of which are pretty original. Highlights: the spilling out of the one doll's eyes and the transformation of David (Williams) into Punch.

**DOLLS OF MADAME MANDILIP, The** see *Devil-Doll, The* (1936)

**DOLLY DEAREST** Trimark/Patriot Pictures & Channeler Ents. (Daniel Cady/Dolly Dearest Prods.) 1992 (1991) color 93m. Story, SP, D: Maria Lease. Story: also Peter Sutcliffe, Rod Nave. Mus: Mark Snow. SpMkpFX: Michael Burnett Prods. SpDolly-VisFX:(d) Alan G. Markowitz; Prime Filmworks. Physical FX: Abstract Pacifics. Ref: TV. V 6/22/92. SFChron Dtbk 6/14/92. Fango 120. PT 13:45. With Denise Crosby, Sam Bottoms, Chris Demetral, Candy Hutson, Lupe Ontirveros, Rip Torn, Ed Gale (Dolly double).

"You brought the evil back!" When the spirit of a 900-year-old "devil child" escapes its Mexican tomb, the intermittently possessed Jessica (Hutson) begins speaking an "ancient language," and her "Dolly Dearest" becomes ambulatory and exhibits slasher tendencies. (Exit housekeeper.) Seems this ancient "satan's child" originally had the body of an infant, the head of a goat, and fed on children's blood. ("All the children are in danger!") As menaces, the bad Barbies fall disastrously flat—their Sweet and Evil looks are equally vacuous. Okay production and actors wasted on a nothing script.

**DOMINION, ACT-I** (J) Toshiba 1986? anim color 37m. D: Koichi Majita; (anim) Hiroki Takagi. Story: Shirow Masamune. Ref: TV: vt; no Eng.; OAV. Anime Opus '89. Animag 7:21-26.

A mad scrambling of *M\*A\*S\*H*, "Hill Street Blues," and the Beagle Boys. The Tank Police of Newport City take on Buaku, a cyborg gang leader and his two genetically-engineered "puma" women, Annapuma and Unipuma. Meanwhile, a bacteriological cloud hovers menacingly.... Script tries too hard to be outrageous, but amuses nonetheless. Much light-hearted play with grenades.

**DOMINION, ACT II: CRIME WAR** (J) Central Park Media/Shirow Masamune & HA 21 & Toshiba Video (Ritsuko-Kazuhiko-Tamaki) 1989 ('91-U.S.) anim color 41m. SP, D: Kouichi Mashimo. Story: Masamune. Ph: Y. Takashi. Mus: D. Crew. AD: M. Mitsuharu. SdFX: Jinbo Daisuke. Anim D: T. Hiroki. Mecha Des: Ito Koji. Ref: TV: USManga Corps video; Eng. titles. Animag 9:24-6. Voices: Tsuru Hiromi, Okura Masaaki, Yanami Joji (Buaku), Mita Yuko (Annapuma), Tomizawa Michie (Unipuma).

At issue this time: urine specimens and genetic-mutation research. Plus: phallic, anti-tank bio-plastic plates, or mines. A bit much, but occasionally wry, with time out for a vapid love song.

**DOMINION, ACT III: CRIME ETHIC** (J) CPM/SM & HA 21 & TV (Kazuhiko-Tamaki) 1989 ('91-U.S.) anim color 40m. D: Ishiyama Takahki. SP: Kohno Dai. Ph: T. Kazushi. AD: H. Osamu. For other credits, see *Act III.* Ref: V: USMC video; Eng. titles. Animag 6:5.

More fun with grenades, plus a plan to construct Bio-Chip-brain beings that can breathe contaminated air, and a Bio-Ball which constricts the unwilling wearer. Determinedly outrageous.

**DOMINION, ACT IV: CRIME FACTOR** (J) CPM/SM & HA 21 & TV (Kazuhiko-Tamaki) 1989 ('91-U.S.) anim color 38m. Same credits as *Act III.* R: TV: USMC video; Eng. titles.

Buaku, the chief crook, proves to be the last humanoid "guinea pig." ("I'm a man with an artificial brain.") Puzzling mixture of violence, comedy, and sentiment. Amusingly, a sneeze initiates the climactic action.

**DOMINION** Tempe color 70m. Ref: Tempe Video flyer. Bill Warren.

"Demonic leader" of "vampiric undead." (TV)

**DONA MACABRA** (Mex) Azteca & Roberto Gavaldon 1986 color c104m. SP, D: Gavaldon. SP, Story: Hugo Arguelles. Ph: R. M. Solares. Mus: Raul Lavista. AD: J. R. Granada. SpFX: Raul Camarena. Mkp: Roman Juarez. Ref: TV: Video Show Biz HV; no Eng. With Marga Lopez, Hector Suarez, Carmen Montejo, Carmen Salinas, Luis Alarcon, Ricardo Cortez.

Doc in smock in cellar of two old ladies' home maintains wax museum. Wax figures include a Frankenstein monster (complete with bolts) which seems to move when the snake draped around its shoulders writhes. The underground realm also features a live leopard, a man in an ape suit, stuffed animals, a slide, and a pool.... Silly, labored mixture of spook comedy and sentiment does contain some admittedly bizarre elements.

**DONNE CON LE GONNE** (I) 1991 feature. D: F. Nuti. Ref: Palmerini: love story continuing into the year 2035.

**DONOR** CBS-TV/CBS Ent. & Peter Frankovich & Daniel A. Sherkow Prods. 1990 color c90m. D: Larry Shaw. Tel: Michael Braverman. Mus: Gary Chang. SpFX: Art Brewer. Mkp: Zoltan, Mark Bussan, Jerry Quist. Ref: TV. TVG 12/8/90. V 12/17/90:46. With Melissa Gilbert-Brinkman, Jack Scalia, Pernell Roberts, Wendy Hughes, Gale Mayron, Hari Rhodes, Larry Cedar, Marc Lawrence, Pedro Gonzalez-Gonzalez.

"Something real weird is going down!" In fact, many weird things are, including a lurking slasher, pickled corpses in the hospital anatomy lab, prematurely aged folks, and pituitary anti-aging drugs. Glib, superficial, and surprisingly grisly for network TV.

**DON'T GO NEAR THE PARK** see *Nightstalker*

**DON'T KILL GOD** (B) Beamleaf 1984 color 83m. SP, D: Jacqueline Manzano. Ref: V 5/23/84: "*Mad Max* style End of the World" snippet.

**DON'T LET GO** see *Slumber Party Massacre II*

**DON'T LOOK IN THE ATTIC** (I) Filman/Cinevinci/Antonelliana (Michele Peyretti) 1983 color/ws 78m. (91m.) (*La Villa delle Anime Maledette*. aka *The Evil Touch*). SP, D, Co-P, Ph: C. Ausino. Mus: Stelvio Cipriani. SpFX: Luciano Vittori, Lucia Laporta. Ref: TV: VSOM; Eng. dubbed. Hardy/HM. Hound: "haunted house with cows in the attic." V 5/12/82:217 (ad): 1981? Palmerini. With Jean-Pierre Aumont, B. Loncar, Giorgio Ardisson, Annamaria Grapputo, Paul Theisheid, Tony Campa.

"That villa's got a curse on it." Trouble in Turin: a clutching hand from the ground ... a woman with "hidden powers" as a medium ... a gardener who "looks like he stepped out of a bad dream" ... the diary entry, "We are the sixth generation of the damned" ... "some sort of demon" ... and the line, "Come to my tomb!".... Mainly dull, with risible climactic Violence Today echoing Violence Yesterday. "Cows"??

**DON'T OPEN THE DOOR FOR THE MAN IN BLACK** (I-F) VSOM/Erre & RAI-2 & Telemax 197-? color feature (*Non Aprire all'Uomo Nero*). Story, SP, D: Giulio Questi. Story, SP: also David Grieco. Ref: TV: VSOM; Eng. titles.

"You were the psycho I was searching for!" Wrong, but when she regains consciousness she still thinks he was, and her horror and delusion seem about to spill over into outright madness, in the last shot of this semi-*giallo*. Plus: sidewalk suspense, a la *Cat People* (1942), and visualized nightmares. Offbeat bits, routine plotting.

**DON'T OPEN TILL CHRISTMAS** (B) 21st Century/Spectacular Trading (Dick Randall, Steve Minasian) 1984 color 86m. D: Edmund Purdom. SP: Derek Ford. SP, D: (addl scenes) Al McGoohan. Mus: Des Dolan. Mkp: Pino Ferranti. SpFX: Coast To Coast. Ref: V 12/19/84: "dull cheapie." Stanley: "suspense is well handled." Ecran F 50:71: U.S. Morse. McCarty II: "pulls its punches." With E. Purdom, Alan Lake, Belinda Mayne, Caroline Munro.

Madman slaughters Father Christmases.

**DON'T PANIC** (U.S.-Mex) Dynamic Films (Galindo) 1987 color feature. SP, D: Ruben Galindo Jr. SpFX: Screaming Mad George. Ref: Hardy/HM2. V 10/21/87:258(ad). With J.M. Bischof, G. Hassel, H. Rojo.

Demon-possessed teen.

**DON'T PANIC** see *Satan's Blood*

**DON'T TORTURE A DUCKLING** see *Long Night of Exorcism, The*

**DOOM ASYLUM** Manhattan & Film World/Films around the World (Steve Menkin) 1987 color c80m. Story, D: Richard Friedman. Story, SP: Rick Marx. Story: also Menkin. Mus: J. Stuart, D. Erlanger. SpMkpFX: Vincent J. Guastini. Monster Des: R. S. Cole. Ref: TV: Academy Ent. video. V 2/17/88. McCarty II. With Patty Mullen, Ruth Collins, Kristin Davis, William Hay, Michael Rogen (Mitch, "The Coroner").

"A man who lurks around a deserted asylum and kills people with autopsy tools" delivers sub-Freddy bon mots and watches Tod Slaughter on TV. The clips—from *Demon Barber, Crimes of Stephen Hawke, Face at the Window, Murder in the Red Barn*, and *Never Too Late*—are appreciated, but hommage finally becomes padding. The leaden comic characters include an indecisive hero, a psych major, a baseball buff, etc. Their only funny moments come when they try to bargain with the back-from-the-dead-or-near-dead killer—e.g., the baseball fan offers him his cards, free: "Wally Joyner! Andre Dawson! Jack Clark!"

**DOOMED MEGALOPOLIS: THE FALL OF TOKYO** see *Teito Monogatari, Vol. 2* (1991?)

**DOOMED MEGALOPOLIS: THE HAUNTING OF TOKYO** see *Teito Monogatari* (1991?)

**DOOMED TO DIE** (I) Continental/Dania & Nazionale & Medusa (Martino-Loy) 1980('85-U.S.) color 93m. (3P *Eaten Alive. The Emerald Jungle* - alt vt t. *Mangiati Vivi* or *Mangiati Vivi dai Cannibali. Defy to the Last Paradise*). SP, D: Umberto Lenzi. Ph: F. Zanni. Mus: C. Cordio. PD: M.A. Geleng. SpFX: Paolo Ricci. Mkp: Raul Ranieri. SdFX: Int'l. Sd. Ref: TV: Continental Video; Eng. dubbed. Hardy/HM. V 10/16/85. 5/7/80:374. MFB'81:251.

Martin. V 5/30/84:122. With Richard Bolla (aka R. Kerman), Janet Agren, Mel Ferrer, Ivan Rassimov, Me Me Lai, Franco Fantasia.

The New Guinea Purification Sect "uses pain to reunite man with nature." Ingredients: *A Man Called Horse*-type semi-gore with hooks ... jungle gore (much of it apparently actual) ... cannibal gore (committed by a "fierce tribe of cave dwellers" who eat snakes raw) ... a ritual beheading ... and castration.... Jim Jones-inspired sub-sleaze is determinedly distasteful.

**DOOR** (J) Agent 21-Directors Co. (Fumio Takahashi) 1988 color 95m. SP, D: Banmei Takahashi. SP: also Naka Nogawa. Ph: Y. Sasakihara. Mus: M. Tsuno. SpMkp: Tomoo Harughuchi. Ref: V 8/10/88: "understated but very effective horror feature." With Keiko Takahashi, Daijiro Tsutsumi, Shiro Shimomoto.

Chainsaw-and-knife-wielding madman.

The **DOOR IN THE WALL** (B) BFI/Lawrie 1956 color 29m. SP, D: Glenn H. Alvey Jr. From H.G. Wells' story. Ph: Jo Jago. Mus: James Bernard. Ref: BFC. Daisne. Lee (MFB): psychological-fantasy—"gigantic monster." With Stephen Murray, Ian Hunter, Ann Blake.

The **DOOR OF SILENCE** (I-U.S.) Filmirage 1991 color 87m. (*Le Porte del Silenzio*). SP, D: Lucio Fulci. Ph: G. Ferrando. Mus: Franco Piana. PD: M. Lentini. SdFX: Croma Film. Cost: Laurette M. Gemser. Ref: TV: VSOM; Eng. titles. Palmerini: aka *Le Porte del Nulla*. With John Savage, Richard Castleman, Sandi Schultz (La Morte), Jennifer Loeb.

Melvin Devereux finds the road closed, but takes it anyway. He's then *Duel*-ed by a hearse carrying what turns out to be his coffin, and the palm reader tells him he should be dead. The mystery lady's car-license plate: *Death*.... Bare-bones script is pretty predictable, like a really-stretched-out "Twilight Zone."

**DOORMAN, The** see *Too Scared To Scream*

**DOPEY DICKS** Col 1950 16m. D: Edward Bernds. SP: Elwood Ullman. Ph: Vincent Farrar. AD: Charles Clague. Ref: TV. Lee. Maltin/SSS. LC. Glut/TFL. With The Three Stooges, Philip Van Zandt, Stanley Price.

275 Mortuary Road. Detective Sam Shovel and his aides vs. a professor intent on creating an "army of mechanical men." When his first robot literally loses its head, the madman decides that his minions will need human heads (in order to "see where they're going"). Enter: Shemp, Moe, and Larry. Complete with *Abbott and Costello Meet Frankenstein*-like, "safe at last" gag, at the end. The usual knockabout. Price and Van Zandt, as the madmen, Prof. Potter and Ralph, respectively, have the requisite gleeful-manic looks. One cute bit with the electrified Larry—lampshade-on-head—turning himself off.

Remake of *Boobs in the Night* (which see).

**DOPPELGANGER** ITC (Donald P. Borchers) 1992 color c105m. (*Doppelganger: The Evil within* - ad t). SP, D: Avi Nesher. Ph: Sven Kirsten. Mus: J.A.P. Kaczmarek. PD: Ivo Cristante. SpMkpFX: KNB;(coord) Susan Mallon. Morph Anim: Sidley Wright. MechFX: Vince Montefusco. Digital SdFX: Jeff Largent et al. Ref: TV: vt. PT 16:60: "see how stupid movies can be."

Fango 128:6,38: "unintentional laugh riot." SFChron Dtbk 10/31/93. 5/23/93. With Drew Barrymore, George Newbern, Dennis Christopher, Sally Kellerman, George Maharis, Luana Anders, Jaid Barrymore, Leslie Hope.

Tale of a "family curse" and a "ghostly double" is overlong but winds up with a loony, bravura *Alien*-doppelganger sequence. Finale tries to have it three ways—as an expose of one character's "laborious masquerade" with lifelike masks ... as graphic horror-fantasy ... and as a visualized-nightmare kicker. Newbern's vocal mannerisms sometimes seem cloned from Jeff Goldblum, but overall his is the most believable character.

**DORAEMON—NOBITA NO MAKAI DAIBOKEN** (J) Toho 1984 anim color feature. Ref: V 4/18/84:30: playing. 5/1/85:409. Animag 5:37.

Sequel to *Doraemon—Nobita No Kyoryu* (III). Robot cat Doraemon is "sent through the fourth dimension from the 22nd Century" to be the boy Nobita's tutor and guardian.

**DORAEMON** (J) 1985 anim color feature. Ref: V 10/16/85:338: top grossers (6 months).

**DORAEMON—NOBITA TO TETSU JIN HEIDAN** (J) Toho 1986 anim color feature. Ref: V 5/6/87:461: 3/86 release.

**DORAEMON: NOBITA'S PARALLEL MONKEY KING** (J) Toho 1988 anim color feature. Ref: Animag 3:6.

**DORAEMON X** (J) Shochiku 1989 anim color 102m. Created by Fujio Fujiko. Ref: TV: Shogakukan Video; no Eng.; apparently "Doraemon No. 10." Animag 10:5. V 5/2/90:S-60. V/Mifed'89:193: U.S. release in '89 of a "Doraemon" movie.

Old no-ears is back. Ingredients this time: Doraemon's tummy pouch, which contains any tool or gizmo anyone might need, including a magic time-travel door and a watch which "freezes" the action at one point ... a time machine, which the atomic cat stows away in his top desk drawer and which takes the gang back to prehistory (one cave boy also journeys to the present) ... eggs which hatch a miniature gryphon, dragon, and flying horse, all of which later grow and are able to take passengers ... caveman-monsters ruled by a ray-shooting, flying robot-type, which in turn serves a masked "god" ... and a robot-controlled "mammoth."

Charming if episodic sf-adventure-comedy. Nice: a montage of various sleeping people (and atomic cats), one night in prehistory. Also nice: the look of the movie in general, though 102 minutes is a lot of "nice."

**DORAEMON** (J) 1990 anim color 101m. Ref: TV: Shogakukan Video; no Eng.

Cute little Doraemon the Atomic Cat sf-adventure features a spaceship trip at warp speed, gas-masked guys with ray rifles who fly to the moon, and an Earth animal that follows them. Included: an amusing assortment of anthropomorphic animals, including a dog, a fish, and a pelican. Plus a talking, scowling tree. Doraemon and pals always seem to be putting on their flying caps and taking off.

**DORAEMON** (J) Toho 1991 anim color feature. Ref: V 3/25/91:58: playing. 4/22/91:35. 1/6/92:87: number 6 at boxoffice in '91, in Japan.

**DORAEMON THE SUPERCAT** (J) Toho 1992 anim color 97m. Ref: V 3/23/92:47: playing. 11/9/92:48. 9/27/93:57: number 3 J film at J boxoffice in '92. TV: Toho Video?; no Eng.

Ingredients this time: a Doraemon-created country, a sort of history-of-Earth theme land ... a huge, turtle-like dinosaur, the Gliptodon ... winged aliens ... a mammoth ... a sabre-toothed tiger ... a brontosaurus ... giant sloths ... a giant bird ... elves ... little cloud guys (made by the Supercat) ... and elephants floating up through the clouds (thanks to a temporary suspension of the law of gravity).

Another charmer in the endless series, and one of the most imaginative *Doraemon* movies. Nice: the lake-ride on the bronto. Even nicer: the big-bubble ride (two kids to a bubble) in the big, domed amphitheater. !!!: the seashells which wash up on the shore to let out Noah's Ark-like pairs of animals.

**DORAEMON** (J) Toho 1993 anim color feature. Ref: V 3/22/93:36: playing. 4/12/93:44. 4/19/93:34. 4/26/93:38.

**DORAEMON** (J) Toho 1994 anim color feature. Ref: V 3/28/94:16: in Japan.

**DORAGULESU** (J) Japan HV 1991 67m. D: Shojo Konaka. SP: Chisho Konaka. Ref: Markalite 3:10: *Drugless* - tr t; made-for-video.

"New hallucinogenic drug" responsible for "mysterious deaths" and "horrible side effects."

**DORIAN GRAY IM SPIEGEL DER BOULEVARDPRESSE** see *Image of Dorian Gray in the Yellow Press, The*

**DORIANA GRAY** (Swiss-W.G.) Elite-Film (E.C. Dietrich) 1976 color 76m. (*Das Bildnis der Doriana Gray. Portrait of Doriana Gray. Dirty Dracula. Ejaculations. Die Marquise De Sade*). SP, D: Jesus Franco. Mus: Walter Baumgartner. Ref: TV: VSOM; Eng. titles. vc box: "sex vampire." With Lina Romay, Monica Swinn, Ramon Ardid, Martine Stedil.

"I'm terrified of my image—a creature who has never aged." The mysterious Doriana "eats" souls and leaves her lovers dead, while a sexual-psychic link with her (separated-at-birth) Siamese twin sister allows the latter to experience what should be the former's orgasms—*Freaks,* not Wilde's "Picture of Dorian Gray," would appear to be this film's closest cross reference. ("I carry the secret of eternal youth.").... A fairly erotic beginning gives way to perfunctory, if occasionally bizarre hardcore footage. The mental clinic here is run by a certain Dr. Orloff.

**DOS CAMIONEROS CON SUERTE** (Mex.) 1989 feature. Ref: Cinef 6/96:47: "sex comedy with a science-fiction premise"; "Two Lucky Truck Drivers"-tr t.

**DOS NACOS EN EL PLANETA DE LAS MUJERES** (Mex) Esme & Del Prado & Alianza & Hermes Films Int'l. (Carlos Vasallo) 1989 color 93m. D: Alberto Rojas. SP: Alejandro Ucona. Ph: Raul Dominguez. Mus: Alejandro Giacoman. AD: Alberto Villasenor. SpFX: Miguel Vazquez. Incidental FX: Gonzalo Gavira. OptFX: Antonio Munoz. Ref: TV: Mex-American HV; no Eng.; *Two "Wads" on the Planet of Women* - tr t. With A. Rojas, Cesar Bono, Lorena Herrera, Jacaranda Alfaro, Lucero Reinoso, Blanca Nieves, Adriana Rojas.

Earth astronauts find love on a planet of three suns which is inhabited only by women. Low-grade sf-sex-comedy is at least no worse than *Queen of Outer Space.* The women occupy a settlement called Rejum ("mujer" spelled backwards). Plus: a semen machine and a Sadie Hawkins Day finish.

**DOT AND KEETO** (Austral.) Yoram Gross & Dot & Keeto 1985 ('86-U.S.) anim and live/color 69 1/2m. D, P: Gross. SP: John Palmer. Ref: TV. V 2/5/86. 2/18/91:54. no Stanley.

The up-close nature photography outclasses the animation in this imported fantasy (the fifth in the "Dot" series), which features two horrific sequences. In the first, which is low key but genuinely creepy, a wasp seals the incredible shrunken Dot in her nest, where the little girl goes to sleep unaware that she is to be food for the babes surrounding her. The second—Spider City "at night"—has a big buildup, including some promising fiendish cackling, but proves to be more conventional, as a bad spider ("Surprise!") traps Dot in its web.

**DOUBLE, DOUBLE, TOIL AND TROUBLE** ABC-TV 1993 color c90m. Ref: TVG. With Mary-Kate and Ashley Olsen, Cloris Leachman, Meshach Taylor, Phil Fondacaro, Wayne Robson (gravedigger).

Witch, spell.

**DOUBLE DRAGON** Gramercy/Imperial Ent. & Scanbox (Shah) 1994 color 95m. D: James Yukich. SP: Michael Davis, Peter Gould. Story: Paul Dini, Neal Shusterman. Ph: G.B. Kibbe. Mus: J. Ferguson. PD: M. Berke. SpFxAdv: Joe Lombardi. Ref: V 11/7/94: New Angeles; "low-IQ futuristic slugfest." Martin: "cheesy." ad. With Robert Patrick, Scott Wolf, Julia Nickson, Alyssa Milano, Mark Dacascos, Vanna White, George Hamilton.

Crime boss out to rule the world with magic medallion.

The **DOUBLE GARDEN** (J) Daiei 1977 color c96m. Ref: TV: Regal Video. Lor. V 1/13/88:7: t. error on vc box: *The Revenge of Dr. X.* no Martin. no Hound. PT 4:11.

Dr. Bragan (James Craig), who believes in talking to his plants, tells the Venus's-flytrap which he has brought from North Carolina to Japan: "You will become the most powerful thing" in the universe. Subsequently, a band of topless divers leads him to a rare marine flytrap. The doctor: "The life fluid of both plants mixed together with the highest potency of vitamins known to science!" The result: Insectivorous, a human plant with flytrap hands and feet, roots on its head, and a taste for puppies. ("This thing is a monster!" is his assistant's superfluous observation.) The final ingredient: human blood, which will make the monster move and prove, once and for all, that humans are descended from plants.

An atrocious movie pieced together with parts of the 1931 *Frankenstein* (the hunchback, the lab apparatus, even the villagers with the torches) and absurd contributions of its own, most risible of which is Insectivorous. Craig is embarrassingly self-conscious and over-emphatic.

**DOUBLE LUNAR DOGS** Electronic Arts Intermix (Joan Jonas) 1984 25m. D: Jonas. Ph: Michael Oblowitz. FX: (sp video) Jonas, Oblowitz; (b&w) the Vasulkas. Ref: PFA notes 2/21/88: a "rocket ship in perpetual flight ... digital panels ... bringing memories of a past world." With Jonas, Spalding Gray, Jill Kroesen.

**DOUGRAM** (J) Nippon Sunrise/A.I.C. c1984? anim color 80m. Ref: TV: Toshiba video; no Eng.

Tale of military and political intrigue and treachery features much narration and dialogue and is consequently hard to follow without a synopsis. It seems fairly serious and dramatically nuanced, but the most interesting feature of the film (from a strictly visual standpoint): It's set more or less in the present, yet giant, manned robots dominate the battle scenes. Most unusual robots: the helicopter robots. Good muted-melancholic score.

**DRACULA** see the following titles and *Bandh Darwaza. Blood Lust. Breakfast with Dracula, Bride's Initiation, The. Bunnicula. Chiquidracula. Comedy Dracula. Computadoras, Las (p). Curados de Espantos. Daffy Duck's Quackbusters. Dragula. Erotic Encounters of the Fourth Kind. Evening with Kitten, An. Fantasy Girls. Follow That Bird. Follow That Goblin! Fracchia contro Dracula. I'll Suck You Dry. Kamitsukitai/Dorakiyura Yori Ai-o. Leena Meets Frankenstein. Leviathan. Loves of Dracula, The. Lupin III. Lust of Blackula. Macho Bionico, El. Monster Squad, The. Out for Blood. Phantom of the Operetta* (1959/Vol. I). *Phantom Quest Corp. Pinoy Dracula. Scooby-doo and the Ghoul School. Scooby-doo and the Reluctant Werewolf. Son of Darkness. Sundown. Takbo ...! Bilis ...! Takboooo. Takbo ... Peter ... Takbo! Terrorvision* (1985). *To Die For. Trampire. Transylvania Twist. Un Paso Al Mas Aca* ...titles under *Vampire*, including *Vampire Hunter D. Vampires in Havana. Vampiro Teporocho, El. Vampiros De Coyoacan, Los. Waxwork. Waxwork II. World of Dracula, The.*

*****DRACULA** (Spanish-language version) Paul Kohner 1931 ('92-Eng.-subtitled edition) 103m. Spanish Adap: B. Fernandez Cue. Ph: George Robinson. AD: Charles D. Hall. Ref: screen: Library of Congress (reels 4-11, c. 72m.). TV: MCA/Univ HV. Everson/More. American Film 9/90:38-41. Cinef 4/93. V 10/5/92. PT 10:48. TVG. Fango 118:12. With J. S. Viosca, Pablo Alvarez Rubio (Renfield), Eduardo Arozamena, Manuel Arbo.

Both the English and Spanish-language versions of *Dracula* (1931) can seem pretty deadly now. This is just a half-hour deadlier. (The Bela Lugosi film is only 74 minutes long.) Director George Melford at least takes advantage of Hall's huge Castle Dracula and Carfax Abbey sets, but most of both 1931 versions are claustrophobically set in the Seward Sanitarium drawing rooms and patios. Tod Browning's movie has Dwight Frye's Renfield, some very bizarre lighting effects, and its relative brevity going for it—and Lugosi going both for and against it: Time, imitation, and over-exposure have reduced much of his beyond-stagy Dracula to a series of famous poses and lines.

The Melford film is alternately campy and leaden. It seems to have even more blandly-laid-out vampire lore than the Brown-

ing—apparently, the material was new to most audiences then and it was decided that it had to be thoroughly explained—although, scene for scene, the two movies are basically almost identical. There are, however, interesting differences in visual "accent." Melford, for instance, shoots Lupita Tovar's more important scenes as Eva Seward (the Mina character) in close shot; for some reason, Browning generally keeps Mina (Helen Chandler) at a distance. Eva's line re the now-undead Lucia (Carmen Guerrero)—"And then I remembered that she was dead"—seems more chilling delivered closer to the camera and from bed. Mina speaks the line on the patio, in a medium-far shot, and it makes little impression. (The year before, Melford worked with Tovar on Universal's Spanish-language version of *The Cat Creeps*.)

Unlike the Browning version, the Spanish has occasional background music, and the creaking door and coffin-lid sound effects are comically overdone. In fact, the Castle Dracula scenes play like a Mel Brooks parody: Upon first meeting, Carlos Villarias' Dracula and Pablo Alvarez Rubio's Renfield trade hilariously exaggerated expressions. Later, Eduardo Arozamena and J. S. Viosca (as Van Helsing and Dr. Seward, respectively) occasionally camp it up, too, in their more dramatic moments, but they're no match for the masters here. The plain-faced Villarias—he looks more like an Olsen or a Johnson than a Lugosi—overworks eyebrows and hands in a demented attempt to ape Lugosi's mannerisms. He's hopeless as Conde Dracula; eventually, Alvarez Rubio recovers from a disastrous beginning as the sane Renfield to suggest the anguish of insanity—as Van Helsing and Dracula fight for the souls of Eva and Juan, a more pressing battle is being fought in what's left of the mind of that "old fly-eater" Renfield, post-Castle Dracula. Unfortunately, Melford finally gives Alvarez Rubio too long a leash, and his sometimes impressive act again degenerates into scenery-chewing. Frye's mad, nice young man—"He promised me things!"—is more concise, and obscenely insinuating. His Renfield is perhaps the single most enduring element of either version.

**DRACULA** (Thai) c1986? color/ws c115m. Ref: TV: Extra Times Promotions video. Thai Video: above is tr t.

"Dachoora," as he is called here, is a regular fellow, at least with fellow vampires and vampire victims. He plays cards with them; they throw him a gala birthday party. He scratches and tosses and turns in his coffin and wears a metal plate over his heart, the better to thwart stakings. This Thai monster comedy is overlong and sloppily made, but genial and even occasionally disarming. Dracula's constant cackling makes him (he thinks) more menacing. Running down, he bites a handy neck and—immediately feeling the old pep—flexes his muscles and jumps about. Many dialogue scenes; no English subtitles or dubbing.

**DRACULA** (Cuban) Noel Lima c1990? anim 1m. D: Lima. Ref: SFChron Dtbk 4/26/92: the "familiar character is more batty than usual."

**DRACULA** see *Bram Stoker's Dracula*

**DRACULA 79** see *World of Dracula, The*

**3P DRACULA: SOVEREIGN OF THE DAMNED** (J) Northstar Ent./Harmony Gold/Toei Anim. 1980 ('83-U.S.) anim color c90m. SP, D: Robert Barron. From the Marvel Comic "Tomb of Dracula." Mus: Seiji Yokoyama. Ref: TV: Vestron Video; Eng. dubbed. V 5/4/83:409 (ad). Stanley. Hound. Jones: orig D: Minori Okazaki. Larson:537.

Satan resurrects the violent Count Dracula as "the prince of vampires." Five hundred years later, the vengeful Dracula steals the intended bride of satan, Dolores, from the Fellowship of the Black Mass. He loves and marries this mortal and produces a son, Janus. After a satanist accidentally shoots and kills the baby, heaven restores Janus to life as "the personification of goodness." The boy fights his father, but, in a duel with satan, Dracula loses his "evil aura," finds himself reduced to eating hamburgers, and sets out again in search of the vampire venom of immortality.... The premise intrigues: Dracula takes on both God and the devil. But the script is verbose and tortuously plotted. In a later, ironic plot development, Dracula finds that he has the "power of the cross." The Luke-and-Darth relationship between Janus and the Count seems out of place here.

**DRACULA: THE LOVE STORY** see *To Die for*

**DRACULA: THE UNTOLD STORY** see *Bram Stoker's Dracula*

**DRACULA AND FRACCHIA** see *Fracchia contro Dracula*

**DRACULA CONTRA FRANKENSTEIN** see *Dracula Vs. Dr. Frankenstein*

**DRACULA '87** see *Dinastia Dracula, La*

**DRACULA RISES FROM THE COFFIN** (S. Korean) Tai Chang Inc. (Lim Won Sik) 1982 color 92m. D: Lee Hyoung Pyo. SP: Lee Hee Woo. Ph: Lee Sung Sub. Ref: Hardy/HM: inspired by *The 7 Brothers Meet Dracula*. With Kang Yong Suk, Park Yang Rae.

"Spiritual kung fu" defeats Dracula in Korea.

**DRACULA RISING** (U.S.-Bulgarian) New Horizons/Concorde (Roger Corman, Mary Ann Fisher/Pacific Trust) 1992 color 85m. D: Fred Gallo. SP: Rodman Flender, D. Purcell. Ph: Ivan Varimazov. Mus: Ed Tomney. SpFX: Ultramatrix OptFX;(d) John Eppolito. MkpFX: Optic Nerve;(sup) Burrell, Vulich. Ref: TV. SFChron Dtbk 3/28/93. Martin. Jones. PT 16:14: "slow." Fango 123:34. V 11/30/92:41 (rated). With Christopher Atkins (Dracula), Stacey Travis, Doug Wert, Tara McCann, Zahari Vatahov (Vlad the Impaler).

"I am not my father!" The Church of Lost Souls, Romania. Past and present alternate, as Vlad/Dracula Jr. finds lost-love Theresa in the Twentieth Century, and Papa Dracula (in Medieval days) vampirizes his own son so that the latter can catch up with his burned-at-the-stake inamorata. At the end, a horde of bats finishes off Vlad's nemesis .... Is it *Dracula* or *The Blue Lagoon?* Blandly "romantic," almost comically perfunctory fantasy-horror. Atkins has the charisma of a clam here. ("I'm Vlad.") Pathetic.

**DRACULA 79** see *World of Dracula*

**DRACULA UNLEASHED** David Marsh 1993. Ref: SFExam 6/20/93: interactive CD-ROM "movie game ... production crew filmed hundreds of scenes in which the characters move the story line in different directions."

**2 DRACULA VS. DR. FRANKENSTEIN** (Sp-F-Port.-Liecht.) Wizard/Marte Films 1972 ws (*The Screaming Dead* - vt. *Dracula contra Frankenstein. Satana contra Dr. Exortio*). Ref: TV: Wizard Video; Eng. dubbed. PT 19:17-18. Hardy/HM. Fango 12/88. VWB: includes scene cut from *Count Dracula* (1971). Monster! Int'l. 4:30.

The works: a gypsy who "summons the Wolf Man from beyond the grave" ... a soul-summoning doctor who wants Dracula to lead an "army of vampires" ... and a nostalgia-inducing Frankenstein (Monster) Meets the Wolf Man sequence. Jerry Warrenlevel, virtually dialogue-less, patchwork production. Absolutely atrocious. Even the prop skulls are phonies.

**DRACULA'S DAUGHTER (I & II)** see also *Nadja*

**DRACULA'S WIDOW** DEG/Stephen Traxler 1988 color c86m. SP, D: Christopher Coppola. SP: also Kathryn Ann Thomas. Mus: James Campbell. SpFX: Joe Quinlivan, Tex FX; Sirius FX; (d) Todd Masters; (mkp) Dean Gates. SdFxDes: Group IV. OptFX: Fantasy II. Titles: Cinema Research. Ref: TV: HBO Video. V 1/18/89. Martin. Maltin '92. McCarty II. Scheuer. Morse. With Sylvia Kristel, Josef Sommer, Lenny von Dohlen, Marc Coppola, Stefan Schnabel, Rachel Jones.

Vanessa Dracula (Kristel), "drinker of blood, eater of flesh," viper-tongued, super-strong, and clawed—the "ultimate woman"—awakens in Raymond Everett's (von Dohlen) Hollywood House of Wax. She transforms into a hideous hag and slaughters some hapless devil worshipers, then avenges herself on van Helsing's grandson (Schnabel) by vampirizing him.... Dispiritingly unimaginative postscript to Stoker. Raymond runs the silent *Nosferatu*, and the story contains an effectless hommage to the mystical somnambulism in that film. Vanessa's climactic transformation from bat to thing to human form features some fair stopmo and makeup effects.

**The DRAGON: THE BRUCE LEE STORY** Univ 1993 color 121m. D: Rob Cohen. From Linda Lee Cadwell's book *Bruce Lee: The Man Only I Knew*. Ref: V 5/3/93: "metaphoric demons, visualized as a towering, faceless samurai." SFChron: "a huge man, dressed like the Creature from the Black Lagoon, comes out and starts smacking Lee around." SFChron Dtbk 11/14/93: "giant demon in a spiked helmet."

**DRAGON AGAINST VAMPIRE** (H. K.) Saturn Prods. 1985 color c90m.? D: Lionel Leung. SP: Benny Ho. Ph: Henry Chan. Mus: Stephen Tsang. PD: Norton Mak. FX: Nicky Au. Mkp: Mary Chan. Ref: TV. TVG. NST! 4:21. Phantom, p. 196. no Maltin '92. no Scheuer. PT 2:10. 5:6. With Elton Chong, Carrie Lee, Martin Kim, Robin See, Oliver Cheng, Irene Kong.

This is a violent, bloody horror-comedy-kung-fu film, not a vampire movie, although the Shaolin sorcerer-villain is caped and made up to look like a vampire. Fantasy ingredients include a woman who kills a chicken-from-nowhere and drinks its blood, voodoo dolls, and clutching hands from the ground and from a water bucket. A crude fizzle in all modes.

**DRAGON AND THE GEORGE, The** see *Flight of Dragons, The*

**DRAGON BALL** (J) Toei Video 1987? anim color 45m. (aka *Dragonball*). Ref: TV: Toei Video; no Eng.

Kooky little monster comedy-fantasy features oddball characters, including a big, horned demon, a little, round devil-tailed demon, a vampirish gent, a guy who becomes a giant gorilla, and a pterodactyl-type. In the spirit, more or less, of the Lum series. See also the following and *Dragon Pearl*.

**DRAGON BALL Z—BIG WONDER, GREAT ADVENTURE** (J) Toei Video 1989 anim color 46m. Ref: TV: Toei Video; no Eng. Animag 4:7: '88; *Dragon Ball: Fantastic Adventure*.

No use trying to sort out the bizarrenesses here. *Urusei Yatsura*-like droll zaniness features a *Terminator*-ish giant android, a super-strong Indian, a dragon, and a plethora of off-the-wall characters and critters, including twin squeaky-voiced, antennaed quasi-cherubs. A Lum-Ataru-like relationship develops between the heroine, an old man, and a mallet.

**DRAGON BALL Z** (J) Toei Video c1990? anim color 42m. Ref: TV: vt; no Eng. (apart from title). Japan Video: sfa *Dragon Ball Z - The Strongest Man in the World* (9/90)?

Ingredients this episode: dinosaurs (during a musical interlude), a march of the demons, a long long dragon, alien types which do battle with each other, and a black hole. Some spectacular visuals, but not as much weird comedy as usual for this series.

**DRAGON BALL Z—SUPER PSYA MAN** (J) Toei 1991 anim color/ws 53m. Ref: TV: Toei Video; no Eng.

A heavenly body smashes through one planet, wreaks devastation as it passes Earth, then explodes. This catastrophe heralds the arrival here of a giant spaceship. The aliens therein open ray-fire on earthlings and send a chilling cloud across the Earth. (One alien creature sprouts others from its body.) Pleasant comic opening sequence gives way to routine action.

**DRAGON BALL Z—THE GLOBAL MATCH** (J) Toei 1991 anim color 61m. Ref: Japan Video. V 3/25/91:57-8. 4/22/91:35: playing. vc box: sfa *Dragon Ball: Shenron (Legend)*?

**DRAGON BALL Z: THE STRONGEST VS. THE STRONGEST** (J) Toei 1992 (1991) anim color/ws 47m. Ref: TV: Toei Video; no Eng. V 3/23/92:47: playing in Tokyo.

Three interplanetary flying thugs hover in the air and devastate the countryside with rays. Near the end, one of the nasties flings a mini-sun at one of the heroes. Sf-actioner looks routine, with cute touches with a horned, dinosaur-type pet that responds well to "pet food."

**DRAGON BALL Z** (J) Toei 1992 anim color
Ref: V 7/27/92:45: playing in Tokyo. 8/3/92:27. vc box: sfa *Dragon Ball: Mystical Adventure*?

**DRAGON BALL Z: 3 SUPER PSYAJIN** (J) Toei 1992 anim color/ws 46m. Ref: TV: Toei Video; no Eng.; 2/93? V 9/21/92:50: *Super Battle of the 3 Super Saiyas*.

One super-strong big thug and one super-strong little thug—who both have flying and explosive powers—take on the Dragon Ball crew. Glowing celestial spheres, northern-lights-type phenomena, and sky rays all play a part here. Cute comic asides ... overlong, monotonous, one-on-one, or two-on-two, battle scenes.

**DRAGON BALL Z: FIGHT! 10 BILLION POWER WARRIORS** (J) Toei 1992 anim color/ws 46m. Ref: TV: Toei Video; no Eng. Japan Video: sfa *Dragon Ball Z: Warrior with a Million Strengths*? V 9/21/92:50.

Ingredients this time include a giant spacecraft which encircles a small planet with its "tentacles" ... the green hero-guy, who ignites explosions which send foes flying ... and scads of robots with reptilian tails.... Involved battle choreography, spectacular "historical" flashback scenes. One highlight: the robots which regenerate and rewire themselves—they can also bind their foes with the wires.

**DRAGON BALL Z** (J) Toei 1993 anim color. Ref: V 3/22/93:36: playing. 4/5/93:54. 4/26/93:38.

**DRAGON BALL Z** (J) Victor Video/Toei 1993 anim color. Ref: V 8/2/93:18: playing. 9/6/93:10: in H. K. & Japan.

**DRAGON BALL Z: TO THE END OF THE UNIVERSE** (J) Toei 1994 (1993) anim color/ws 51m. Ref: TV: vt; no Eng. V 2/28/94:30: sfa *Dragonball Z4* (in H.K.)? 3/28/94:16: in Japan.

More, generally routine comedy and action. Away from the boxing and racing meets, a Z team member finds himself in a land of giant toys. Incidental: a dino-lizard pocket pet.

**DRAGONBALL Z** (J) 1994 anim. Ref: V 9/12/94:16: in H.K.; Slam Dunk - part of title?

**DRAGON BREEDER** see *Dragon Century*

**DRAGON CENTURY—CHAPTER MAGIC—R. C. 297 LERICIA** (J) Kubo Books (A.I.C.) 1988 anim color 30m. From the comic book "Dragon Breeder." Anim D: Hiroyuki Kitazume. Ref: Animag 5:5. 6:5: 2 OAVs; "a post-civilization fantasy of dragons and demons."

**DRAGON FIGHT** see *Dragonfight*

**DRAGON FIRE** New Horizons(Mike Elliott/Pacific Trust) 1993 color c90m. (aka *Dragonfire*). D: Rick Jacobson.SP: B. Gray, K. Ingram. Story: Robert King. Ph: Mike Gallagher. Mus: John Graham. PD: Aaron Osborne. Key Mkp: E. Fry. Ref: TV: New Horizons HV. PT 17:12: "good fights & good fighters." no Martin. With Michael Blanks, Harold Hazeldine, Pamela Runo, Jim Wynorski, Dominic Labanca, Dennis Keiffer, Rod Kei.

"What brings you to Earth, Star Gaze?" Martial-arts battles in the Pit, an "off-planet" hero who comes to Earth to find his brother dead, a throat slashing, and an impromptu electrocution liven up L.A., year 2032. Limp bits of plot in-between kickboxing bouts.

**DRAGON FIST** (J) Youmex 1990 anim color 39m. Ref: V: ToEMI Video; no Eng. (apart from title).

Talky, sentimental fantasy re a mystical stone ball which attracts lightning (which latter then becomes a rearing, roaring, electric dragon) and which gives a youth great strength.

**DRAGON KNIGHT** (J) A.D. Vision/Polystar & Just (Yukio Kakehi) 1991('94-U.S.) anim color c33m. D: Jun Fukada. SP: Kinuyo Nozaki. Concepts: Elf RPG, Y. Nakamura. Ph: Sangosho. Mus: H. Taguchi. AD: Kobayashi, Usami. SdFX: K. Harada. Ref: TV: ADV video; Eng. titles. Voices: Y. Matsumoto, Mugihito (Overlord), S. Sasaoka (Black Dragon), T. Kitagawa (Green Dragon), N. Furuta (minotaur).

Ingredients include horny hero Takeru and his "instant camera" (in a sword-and-sorcery setting), a minotaur monster ("wimpy"), reptile things ("lounge lizards"), the giant, transforming Green Dragon, the Black Dragon, and a cute little monster that turns out to be heroine Luna .... Okay, mild racy monster-comedy owes something to *Urusei Yatsura* and company.

**DRAGON PEARL** (H.K.?) 1992 color 91m. Ref: TV: vt; Thai dubbed; Eng. titles; "Dragon Peral"—title error. HOF 2:20: aka *Seven Dragon Pearls* and based on *Dragon Ball Z.*

Principals in this far-out comic fantasy include hero Sun Wu Kung ... cowboy-garbed heroine Y Tau ... the ray-shooting Evil Tarus King (a "horrible devil") and his warriors ("all dressed so weird") ... a pig/bat/human creature ("They call me Stupid Monk") who can transform, variously, into some songstresses, a half-male/half-female singer, a bat, and a "fat guy" ("He is a weirdo") ... and a "turtle god" ("Gee, he is even more sexmaniac than me"). Plus: a magic cloud, a spacecraft which beams down baddies, and magic pearls—when all seven are gathered, the "God of the Dragon will appear".... Entertainingly undisciplined film starts bizarrely, ends up a bit tamer, as mild comedy overwhelms wild fantasy. Featured: one of the best lines ever for a talking, guffawing crocodile (as it spies a human in its waters): "Our breakfast is here."

Cf. *Adventures of Sun Wu Kung, The* (I, 1959)

**DRAGON PINK** (J) Itoyoko & Pink Pineapple (Yutaro Mochizuki) 1994 anim color 25m. D: Wataru Fujii. From Tatsumi Comics. Ph: K. Konishi. AD: N. Nekono. SpFX: Takashi Maekawa. SdFxD: M. Manami. SpSdFX: Junichi Sasaki. Performance D: Jun Fukada. Ref: TV: SoftCel video; Eng. titles.

Our two stars: Viken, the Monster Mage, who transforms into a dragon, and a "slave-witch" who turns her victims into monsters which become, with her, a "composite form".... Negligible animated sex-horror-fantasy.

**DRAGON QUEST** (J) Fantasia Video (Enix & Tohokushinsha Film) 1988 anim color 40 1/2m. Ref: TV: Tohokushinsha HV.

The performance of an orchestral work is intermittently punctuated by dialogue-less, live-action "illustrations" of the music. Monsters in the story portion—set in the land of Arefugarudo—include a demon chief which turns into a winged, fire-breathing dragon, his skeletal warriors, a fiery cartoon demon, a huge stone monster, dragons, little blue chocolate-drop-shaped creatures, a vicious bird-beaked, seahorse-bodied cave creature, and a small

dragonfly-lobster creature or two.... Oddball mixed-media enterprise has okay music and cheap but fun effects.

**DRAGONBALL Z** see *Dragon Ball Z*

**DRAGONFIGHT** Warner HV 1992 color 84m. (aka *Dragon Fight*). D: Warren Stevens. SP: Budd Lewis. Ref: SFChron Dtbk 3/7/93. Martin: "forgettable characters." Stanley: "never predictable." With Michael Pare, Robert Z'Dar, Charles Napier, Paul Coufos, James Hong, George "Buck" Flower, Joe Cortese.

"A maverick warrior from the future refuses to fight for his corporation."(SFC)

**DRAGONFIRE** see *Dragon Fire*

**DRAGON'S HEAVEN** (J) Youmex 1988 anim color 34m. (43m.). D: Kiyoshi Fukumoto. SP: Ikuyo Kookami. Story & Min/Co-P: Makoto Kobayashi. Anim D: Itaru Saitoh. Char Des: Hirano. Ref: TV: ToEMI Video; no Eng.; some French. Animag 3:6. Markalite 3:9.

Prime candidate for English-language treatment includes some impressively designed airships, fortresses, and robots. Film takes place "1,000 years after the last war"—between humans and invading machine-creatures—and includes live-action, behind-the-scenes footage (which is what brings the running time to 43 minutes).

**\*\*DRAGONWYCK** Fox/Zanuck 1946 103m. SP, D: Joseph Mankiewicz. From Anya Seton's novel. SpPhFX: Fred Sersen. Mkp: Ben Nye. Ref: TV. Pierre LePage. V 2/20/46. FD 2/28/46. Maltin '92. Scheuer. LC. NYT 4/11/46: "palace terror ... phantoms ... lurk in the vaulted rooms ... conventional horror elements." TVG.

1844. Dragonwyck Manor, near the Hudson River. According to the "superstition" of his servants, the great-grandmother of patroon Nicholas Van Ryn "swore ... she'd always be here to sing and play" the "ugly old harpsichord" which sits in the "red room." Only Van Ryns-by-blood can hear her singing. Plus: a "mysterious tower room" and a thunderstorm (the "thunder of the Catskills").... For the most part bland hyper-romanticism. The two phantom-music scenes, however—the first, definitely fantasy; the second, possibly psychological—combine the lyrical and the eerie: At first, the laughing and singing enchant little Katrine, then become loud and distorted, and scare her. Later, the music of the ghost-harpsichord either drives Nicholas to distraction or is the end result of his being so driven. Vincent Price, like the other actors, strikes the requisite Gothic-romantic poses, as the heir-obsessed Nicholas, but he has some fine scenes—which mix madness and juicy sarcasm—near the end.

Reference noted in passing: Jennifer Jones, in *The Man in the Gray Flannel Suit* (1956): "And now we've got to move into Dragonwyck."

**DRAGULA** SheHe Studios/Video Resource 1994 color feature. Ref: vc box.

**DREADFUL MELODY: THE SIX-FINGERED STRINGS DEMON** (H.K.) Film City/Super Class 1993 color/ws 91m. (aka *Devil Melody*). Ref: TV: Tai Seng Video; Eng. titles.

They're called, variously, ghosts, witches, and vampires, but all concerned here just seem to do various martial arts stunts. The magic lyre itself is dynamite, or acts like it—*Scanners*-like, it makes people explode. Fast and furious and even occasionally entertaining action fantasy.

**DREAM, The** see *Recoil, The*

**DREAM A LITTLE EVIL** USA-TV/Mathew Prods. 1990 color c90m. SP, D, P: Royce Mathew. Ph: Howard Wexler. Mus: Robert Duran. Mkp Des: Janelle Varada. Ref: TV. TVG. With Lyle Waggoner (Death), Tom Alexander, Kathy Smith, Richard Sebastian, D. Rouleau, Michele Gaudreau (Angie/witch), Ryan Mercer, Diane Lynn (stunt witch).

"I'm your fantasy." "Super genius" George's (Sebastian) machine taps the subconscious, renders its contents real, including a swivel-headed, barf-mouthed "Halloween witch," an *Alien*-type, a papier-mache creature, and an invisible demon which lifts its female victim.... How macabre. Scorecard: excruciating actors, D.O.A. directing, overuse of the barf motif, and an "It was only a dream" ending. Or was it?—Death has the last cackle.

**DREAM DEMON** (B) Spectrafilm & Filmscreen & British Screen/Palace (Paul Webster/NFTC) 1988 ('93-U.S.) color 89m. SP, D: Harley Cokliss. SP: also Christopher Wicking. Ph: Ian Wilson. Mus: Bill Nelson. PD: Hugo Luczyc-Wyhowski. Anim D: Barry Leith. SpFX: Parker, Williams. Scary Doll: J. E. Thompson. SpFxMkp: Animated Extras. Animatronics: David White. Ref: TV: Warner HV. MFB'88:321-22. Fango 129:39: don't bother. V 9/28/88. 10/7/87:19 (ad). 4/29/87:14-15 (ad). Edinburgh Film Fest '88 note. With Jemma Redgrave (Diana), Kathleen Wilhoite, Timothy Spall, Jimmy Nail.

"There's gotta be an explanation." A beheading at a wedding ... a big bug ... a yawning pit ... a photographer who dies horribly ... a symbolically bleeding wall ... a basement room where "everything's backwards" ... another room in "total darkness" ... brain gore ... and a mirror "room." Are these images (visualized) virgin's nightmares? Or are Diana's dream images actually materializing? (Compare *The Appointment* and *Forbidden Planet*.) At any rate, this movie plays like a cross between a moderately intriguing "Twilight Zone" and *Juliet of the Spirits* (the light-haired girl, the flames, the angel wings).

**DREAM LOVER** MGM-UA/Pakula-Boorstin 1986 color 104m. D: Alan J. Pakula. SP: Jon Boorstin. Mus: Michael Small. Mkp: Vivien Placks. Opt: Computer Opts. Ref: TV. MFB'86:349-50. V 2/26/86. ad. With Kristy McNichol, Ben Masters, Paul Shenar, Justin Deas, John McMartin, Gayle Hunnicutt, Matthew Penn, Jon Polito.

"What if the nightmares don't go away?" Kathy Gardner (McNichol), who has nightmares re the slasher she slashed, goes to a "sleep research facility," where an injection helps break her dream "paralysis." She acts out her nightmare, and a researcher "becomes" the slasher.... For Kathy, it's worse and worse—and the movie doesn't get any better either. It boils down to some scientific and psychological mumbo-jumbo aimed solely at getting her "sleepwalking." Slow, far-fetched feature plays like an expanded half-hour TV show.

The **DREAM MAN** (I) 1993 color feature. D: Paolo Marussig. Ref: Palmerini: "TV star hypnotizes the audiences of the whole world...."

**DREAM ONE** (F-B) NEF & Films A2/Christel Films & Channel Four (Claude Nedjar, John Boorman) 1984 color 97m. (aka *Nemo*). SP, D: Arnaud Selignac. SP: also J.-P. Esquenazi, T. Boorman. Ph: Philippe Rousselot. Mus: Gabriel Yared. PD & SpFX: Productions de l'Ordinaire. Ref: V 12/19/84: "first-rate in its production design." Ecran F 38:89. 42:48, 53-55. With Jason Connery, Seth Kibel, Mathilda May, Nipsey Russell, Harvey Keitel, Carole Bouquet.

The *Nautilus* from Jules Verne's *20,000 Leagues under the Sea* ... "a beautiful creature from another planet."

**DREAM WITHIN A DREAM, A** see *Fool's Fire*

**DREAMANIAC** Wizard Video/Taryn 1987 (1986) color 82m. D, P: David DeCoteau. SP: Helen Robinson. SpMkpFX: Tom Schwartz, Linda Nottestad. Ref: V 2/25/87: "uninvolving." Nowlan. no Martin. With Thomas Bern, Kim McKamy, Sylvia Summers (Lily).

Succubus seemingly possesses writer, turns him homicidal.

The **DREAMING** (Austral.) IFM-Genesis Film (Craig Lahiff/A. I. Ginnane) 1988 color 88m. D: Mario Andreacchio. SP: Rob George, S. McCarthy, J. Emery. Idea: Lahiff, Wayne Groom. Mus: F. Strangio. Ref: V 5/25/88: "tired, lame mystic thriller." With Arthur Dignam, Penny Cook, Gary Sweet.

Visions, aborigines, "200-year-old villain."

**DREAMS** see *Akira Kurosawa's Dreams*

**DREAMSCAPE** Fox/Zupnik-Curtis (Bella) 1984 (1983) color 99m. SP, D: Joe Ruben. SP: also David Loughery, Chuck Russell. Mus: Maurice Jarre. SpMkp: Craig Reardon. SpVisFX: Peter Kuran, Richard Taylor. Stopmo: James Aupperle. Dream FX: Dennis Pies. SpFX: A & A, SpFxUnltd. Min Sup: Susan K. Turner. Roto: R. J. Robertson. SpPh: Kevin Kutchaver. Ref: TV. V 5/16/84. With Dennis Quaid, Max Von Sydow, Christopher Plummer, Eddie Albert, Kate Capshaw, Larry Cedar (the snake-man).

"I was there!" "Dream-linking" research at Thornhill College turns Alex Gardner (Quaid), who has powers of precognition and telekinesis, into a "cerebral Peeping Tom." He can enter the dreams of others, including little Tommy (D. P. Kelly), and helps the latter slay a nightmare cobra-dinosaur monster. Other visualized dream monsters include mutant kids, glowing-eyed demon dogs, and zombies.... The cobra creature is a neat bit of animation, and the climactic dream-battle is fun. But the visualized dreams recall other visualized dreams in other movies, not dreams any actual person ever had. And the script is too literal about "going into another person's dreams." Freddy, where are you?

**DREAMY EXPRESS ZONE** series see *Blue Girl, La. Blue Girl, La 2. Blue Girl, La 3. Twin Dolls. Youju Kyoshitsu*

The **DRIFTING CLASSROOM** (J) Imagica & Kodak & YA (Nakamura) 1991 color/ws 103m. (*Hyoryu Kyoshitsu*). D:

Nobuhiko Ohbayashi. SP: Izo Hashimoto. Adap: Ohbayashi, Ishigami, Ogura. From Kazuo Umezu's comic book. Mus: Joe Hisaishi. PD: K. Satsuya. VisFX: Shirogumi(sp?). FxAnim: Ai-hara. SpSdFX: M. Kashiwabara. Ref: TV: VSOM; Eng. titles & dialogue. Weisser/JC. With Troy Donahue, Yoshiko Mita, Aiko Asano, Y. Hayashi.

"The entire school has disappeared." A spectral earthquake and a weird storm isolate teacher and students in a "time slip" at the Kobe International School, in this klutzy variation on *The Exterminating Angel*. ("Are we ever going to be able to go home?") Featured: impromptu levitation ... a basement morpher ... a rain of sand ... an insta-desert ... a little alien-type which mutates into a big, friendly sort-of-cockroach ... other big bugs ... big lizard things ... and funnel clouds which make people float up.... Script strains for the surreal; vapidity comes more easily to it. Big dumb thoughts re growing up, civilization, etc. Effects help a little.

**DRILLER** Abelard Prods. 1984 color c86m. SP, D, P: Joyce James. SP: also T. G. Beckley. Ph: Sam Cosgrove. Mus: Willy Georgia. SpFX: Alex Blades. Ref: TV: VCA video. PT 12:65. With Taija Rae, Dick Howard, Mr. J, Renee Summers (skeleton bride), Carson Dyle (werewolf), Peter Jay et al (zombies), Rod Retta (skeleton groom), "Quazi-modo" (hunchback), Angelique & Gypsy (ghoul girls).

A rock fan dreams of MTV-type ghouls and a werewolf with a phallic "driller" whose "fun house" castle contains a zombie lair, a Peter Lorre-voiced hunchback, and "Richard Nixon." Outre porno-musical-horrorshow features several production numbers, murky photography, and phantom continuity.

**DRIVING FORCE** Academy Ent. (A.I. Ginnane, M. Ong/H. Grigsby, R. Confesor) 1989 color 88m. D: A. J. Prowse. SP: Patrick Edgeworth. Mus: Paul Schutze. Ref: V 2/28/90. 5/17/89:34 (hv). 3/21/90: "contrived." McCarty II: "sanitized." Hound: "post-holocaust." no Martin. With Sam J. Jones, Catherine Bach, Don Swayze, Ancel Cook.

Action in the near future.

**DRIVING ME CRAZY** (U.S.-G) Motion Picture Corp. of America (Krevoy/Stabler) 1991 color 89m. (aka *Trabbi Goes to Hollywood*). SP, D: Jon Turteltaub. SP: also R. M. London. SP, Co-P: David Tausik. Mus: Joey Balin, Christophe Franke. PD: Gary Randall; (G) Wolfgang Heinz. SpFxCoord: Don Power, Michael Thompson. KeyMkp: Tricia Sawyer. OptFX: Howard Anderson. Ref: TV. V 6/17/91. TVG. With Thomas Gottschalk, Billy Dee Williams, Dom DeLuise, Milton Berle, Steve Kanaly, Michelle Johnson, Richard Moll, Morton Downey Jr., James Tolkan, George Kennedy, Peter Lupus, Starr Andreeff, Celeste Yarnell.

"I invented a vegetable fuel to make [the Trabbi] travel at incredible speeds" (i.e., over 200 mph). Gunther Schmidt (Gottschalk), "brilliant inventor," takes his secret from Germany to an L.A. car convention. Script relies on the most obvious jokes and on meant-to-be-droll cultural observations (e.g., Californians are seen to be blase about earthquakes).

**DROID** see *Cabaret Sin*

**DROP DEAD GORGEOUS** (Can.-G) USA-TV/Astral & Power Pictures & Twilight & ZDF-TV (Julian Marks) 1991 color

c90m. D: Paul Lynch. Tel: T. Baum, B. Wells, M. Shapiro. Story: H. Steinberg. SpFX: Frank Carere. Ref: TV. Mo. V 8/5/91:96.

"He made me do bad things." Teacher with split personality turns homicidal. Formula suspenser with an okay "psycho twist" (V) ending.

**DRUM STRUCK** Greg Nickson (Slow D) 1990 b&w 27m. SP, P: also Guy Nickson, Markus Greiner. Anim: Matt Hausman. Ref: SFChron Dtbk 7/12/92: a "lampoon on Sam Raimi." TV: Fox Lorber HV: punk/gallows humor with decapitated head.

Brain surgery and car-battery juice turn drummer into a "parody of a Frankenstein monster."

**\*The DRUMS OF JEOPARDY** 1931. From H. MacGrath's novel. Mus D: Val Burton. Ref: TV. Greg Luce. Turner/Price. V 1/15/31. Lentz. Lee. Phantom. Hound. PT 2:9.

An effective vehicle for Warner Oland, who plays "madman" Dr. Boris Karlov (yes), whose specialty is strangling Petrovs. Other characters are strictly functional, but Karlov's confrontations with his foes are witty and angled for understated horror. The Doc (testing his chemical gas formula on "rat" Wallace MacDonald, who dies screaming): "The formula seems to be quite correct." Good lightning, fog, wind, smoke, and shadow effects. The thunder effects, however, are a bit tinny. Extra added: a classic clutching-hand scene.

**As DUAS FACES DE UM PSICOPATA** (Braz.) PAS 1986 color 90m. D: Jose Mojica Marins. SP, P: Ary Santiago. Ref: Monster! 3:33: *The Two Faces of a Psychopath* - tr t. With Santiago, Debora Muniz, Goretti.

Schizophrenic becomes "murderous maniac."

**DUCK TALES: THE MOVIE—TREASURE OF THE LOST LAMP** (U.S.-F-B) BV/Disney Movietoons (Disney Animation France) 1990 anim color 73m. D, P: Bob Hathcock. SP: Alan Burnett. SpFxCoord: Serge Conchonnet. Processed FX: Mel Neiman, Alan Howarth. Ref: TV. V 8/8/90. Bill Warren.

Fantasy's horrific elements include a giant-scorpion pit and Merlock (voice: Christopher Lloyd), an evil sorcerer who can turn into a rat or a giant bird. ("He can change into anything.") Possession of a certain magic talisman would give him unlimited power. Lively animated comedy-adventure still somehow misses the imagination and excitement of Carl Barks' "Uncle Scrooge" comic-book adventures. Closest it comes: David Newman's lush score.

**DUE OCCHI DIABOLICI** see *Two Evil Eyes*

**DUN HUANG TALES OF THE NIGHT** (H.K.) 1988? color/ws c100m. (*Affair with a Ghost* - ad t). D: H.-Cheung Lee. Ref: TV: World Video/SMO Video; no Eng. Y. K. Ho. vc box: sfa "Dun-Huang" (Daiei Video, '88, 143m.)?

Lavish period fantasy is hard to follow without English subtitles, but appears to be a stately, delicately romantic tale re two ghost women (at one point seen by our hero to be, respectively, a fox and a skeleton), a demon king, and a temple-full of "ghosts" who look like fugitives from a Mardi Gras disco. The sequence with the king and his court is exhilaratingly stylized.

**DUNE** Univ/Dino De Laurentiis (Raffaella De Laurentiis) 1984 color/ws 139m. SP, D: David Lynch. From Frank Herbert's novel. Mus: Toto. MechSpFX: Kit West. Creatures: Carlo Rambaldi. SpPhFX: Barry Nolan; (addl vis fx) Albert J. Whitlock. SpMkp: Giannetto De Rossi. Ref: TV. V 12/5/84. SFExam 12/19/84. Sacto Bee 1/21/90 (TV): 188m. version. With Kyle MacLachlan, Francesca Annis, Brad Dourif, Jose Ferrer, Linda Hunt, Freddie Jones, Richard Jordan, Virginia Madsen, Silvana Mangano, Everett McGill, Kenneth McMillan, Jack Nance, Jurgen Prochnow, Sting, Dean Stockwell, Max Von Sydow, Sean Young, Sian Phillips.

In the year 10,191. Several planets—including Giedi Prime Arrakis (or Dune), and Kaitain—scads of characters (including McMillan's exotic-disease-cultivating Baron Harkonnen), some monsters (the giant sandworms of Arrakis ... a monstrous emissary from the second moon of something), and the life-extending, consciousness-expanding spice melange.... Much incident here, little emotional resonance. The "sleeper" in hero Paul Atreides (MacLachlan) takes its own sweet time to "awaken." A hundred or so characters could easily have been pared away, but they apparently come with the Herbert package. Terrific spacecraft and monster effects, including the burrowing movements of the worms, though the latter are not otherwise terribly impressive. Nice touch: the hovering lights. Spectacular finish.

**DUNE WARRIORS** (U.S.-Fili) Califilm/Concorde-New Horizons 1991 color c85m. D, P: Cirio H. Santiago. Assoc D: Bobby Santiago. SP: T. C. McKelvey. Ph: Joe Batac. Mus: The Score Warriors. PD: Jose Mari Avellana. SpFX: Juan Marbella Jr. Mkp: Teresa Mercader. Car Des: Boi Quilino. SdFX: Cabrales Bros. Ref: TV. TVG. V 5/23/90:18. 1/14/91:114 (rated). PT 7:21. 11:10. With David Carradine, Rick Hill, Luke Askew, Jillian McWhirter, Blake Boyd, Val Garay, Dante Varona, Isabel Lopez.

New California, 2040 A.D. A water-rich farming village ("We have water") in the water-starved future enlists warriors in a fight against the evil William (Askew). ("Then you can help me find some warriors?") *Seven Samurai*, anyone? Formula treachery and heroism, poorly-staged stunts.

**The DUNGEONMASTER** Empire/Ragewar 1985 (1984) color 77m. (*Ragewar* - orig & B t). SP, D: Rosemarie Turko ("Ice Gallery"), John Buechler ("Demons of the Dead"), David Allen ("Stone Canyon Giant"), Peter Manoogian ("Cave Beast"), Ted Nicolaou ("Desert Pursuit"), Charles Band ("Heavy Metal"). D: also Steve Ford ("Slasher"), Michael Karp. SP: also Allen Actor, Jeffrey Byron. Story:Band. Mus: Richard Band, Shirley Walker, (elec) Gary K. Chang. SpFxMkp: (des) Buechler; MMI. VisFxDes: Allen; (asst) Mark McGee et al. OpPhFX: Van der Veer, Illusions; E. D. Farino. Anim: Disney, Tony Alderson. SpVoiceFX: Craig Talmy. Ref: TV. MFB'85:385. V 2/6/85. Stanley, ad. With Byron, Richard Moll, Leslie Wing, Cleve Hall (Jack the Ripper), Ken Hall (wolfman), Jack Reed (mummy), Peter Kent (zombie), Danny Dick (slasher), Jerri Pinthus (cave beast), Felix Silla, or Cilla.

In computer trouble shooter Paul Bradford's (Byron) "very bad dream," the wizard Mestema (Moll), or Beelzebub, presents him with seven challenges, including a living stone idol (in the "Stone Canyon Giant" sequence), a cartoon dragon and zombies (in "Demons of the Dead"), "private art gallery" exhibits of Jack the Ripper, a wolfman, and a mummy which come to life (in "Ice Gallery"), a furtive monster (in "Cave Beast"), and a slasher (in "Slasher").... Vapid sword-sorcery-and-computer story. The "challenges" are interchangeable, easily-overcome opponents, although the Stone Canyon Giant is introduced in a surprising, What'd-I-see? burst of stopmo animation. The in-between scenes with Mestema (and his million-soul barrier) and Paul (and his wrist computer) are marginally more bearable than most of the seven, generally repetitious episodes, thanks to Byron and Moll.

**DUPLICATES** USA-TV/Para-TV/Sankan Prods. & Wilshire Court (Robert Rolsky) 1992 color c90m. Tel, D, Exec P: Sandor Stern. Tel: also Andrew Neiderman. Mus: Dana Kaproff. Mkp: E. L. Day. Video: Video Image. PD: Bryan Ryman. Ref: TV. TVG 3/14/92. V 3/23/92:35. SFChron Dtbk 2/14/93. With Gregory Harrison, Kim Greist, Cicely Tyson, Kevin McCarthy, Lane Smith.

"What did they do?" Conducting experiments in eradicating the criminal mind, the Sandburg Medical Center erases a young couple's memories and substitutes concocted identities. But the two meet again. ("It's as though I've known you all my life!") Awkwardly broached themes of love and memory recall *Remember?* (1939), which see. Yield: mawkishness, some ideas. One idea: The couple's programmed "memories" seem to them like a movie watched. Another: "Does the emotion of love depend on the existence of memory?"

**DUST DEVIL** (B-U.S.) Miramax/Palace (Devil) & Film Four Int'l. & British Screen & Nat'l. Film Development Fund (Joanne Sellar) 1993 (1992) color 108m. (aka *Dust Devil: The Final Cut*). SP, D: Richard Stanley. Ph: Steven Chivers. Mus: Simon Boswell. PD: Joseph Bennett. SpMkpFX: (sup) Little John; (& animatronics) The Dream Machine. SpFX: Rick Cresswell. Ref: TV: Miramax HV; 87m. version; "developed by Wicked Films." V 4/19/93: "a brilliant mess." Fango 128:4, 11: 87m. version. SFChron Dtbk 10/31/93: "a bit heavy-handed ... but ... classy." 10/10/93. With Robert Burke (Dust Devil), Chelsea Field, Zakes Mokae, William Hootkins, Marianne Saegebrecht.

"He hears the silent call of the damned." Back in the "first times, the desert wind ... was a man like us .... He became a hunter" who uses his victims' blood ritualistically to "paint his way out of the circle of incarnation." ("I can tell when someone's time is up.") He is also a shape-shifter who worships the "great snake father." Pretentious son of *The Seventh Victim*. Even the new-Dust-Devil-in-town ending is tired. Handsomely photographed, though. Complete with a visualized nightmare re a skeleton extracting a man's heart.

**DYBBUK, The** see *Man without a World*

**DYING TRUTH** see *Distant Scream, A*

**DYNASTUD 2—POWERHOUSE** HIS Video 1993 color 90m. D: S. Hansen. Ref: Adam'95G: android sequence "inspired by the 1970 short *The Closet*." With J. Storm.

**DYNASTY OF DRACULA** see *Dinastia Dracula*

# E

**...E COSI' DIVENNERO I TRE SUPERMEN DEL WEST** (I)
1973 color feature. D: Italo Martinenghi. Ref: Palmerini: time
machine.

**E.T. (3)** see also *Bloodbath at the House of Death. Dead Curse*

**E.T. OR NOT TO E.T.** see *Extraterrestres, Los*

**E TANTA PAURA** see *Too Much Fear*

**E. THREE—THE EXTRA TESTICLE** Collector's Video/Jimmy
Houston 1985. SP, D: Lulu LaTouche. Ref: vc box. With Robin
Cannes, Jessica Longe, Lana Burner, Jessica Wylde, Bunny Bleu,
Ed "The Head" (E. Three)

"After a million years in space, he comes to Earth for a good
time!"

**E.X.** Superior Video 1986 color 88m. Ref: vc box. Adam'89:193.
With K. Dare, Nina Hartley, Billy Dee.

Aliens from a "distant galaxy" turn earthlings into "droids." (vc
box)

**The EAGLE SHOOTING HEROES** (H.K.) Scholar Films/Jet
Tone Prods. (T. Ho) 1993 color/ws c116m. (*Dong Cheng Jiu*).
D: Jeff Lau. Story: J. Yung, from the L. Cha novel. Mus: J. Wong.
PD: Chang Suk Ping. SpFX: Ting Yuen-Tai, Tang Wai-yuk. Ref:
TV: World Video; Eng. titles. V 9/12/94: *Sediu Yingchung Tsun
Tsi Dung Sing Sai Tsau*. EVS. With Jackie Cheung, Tony Leung,
Maggie Cheung.

Goofy period action-fantasy-low-comedy features a sorceress
who stuffs poison centipedes down her victims' throats, the better
to elicit information ... weird little dinosaur, bird, and gorilla
monsters, who just act silly ("I think the monsters are playing
games with us") ... a flying shoe (based on the principle of the
flying carpet) ... and a flying head.... Casual, occasionally amusing fantasy gets to be kind of interminable.

**EARLY WARNING** Missionary/Paul Goodman 1981 color
85m. SP, D: David R. Elliott. Ph: J. D. Garvey. Mus: Ted Nichols.
AD: Mark Kloptenstein. Mkp: Kelly McGowan. Ref: TV. TVG.
no Stanley. no Maltin '92. no Scheuer. With Greg Wynne, Delana
Michaels, Alvy Moore, Joe Chapman (Stonefield), Buck Flower,
Verkina Flower, Gregg Palmer.

The One-World Foundation headed by Stonefield ("the new
world ruler" of Revelations?) controls the world's transportation,
industry, media, etc. Its goal: a "one-world monetary and government system," with a laser-imprinted computer number for
each individual.... Biblical prophecy is made to square a bit patly
with contemporary socio-political paranoia in this combination
message-and-action movie. The formula script at least leaves half
its happy ending implicit: The born-again hero lives; the conspiracy survives, but will (as per Revelations) self-consume.
Michaels is capable as a low-key hawker of Christianity—in fact,
she's almost too agreeable, too adept at the soft sell.

**\*The EARTH DIES SCREAMING** 1964. Mus: Elizabeth
Lutyens. AD: George Provis. Mkp: Harold Fletcher. Ref: TV. Jim
Shapiro. Hardy/SF. Lee. Weldon. no V. With Anna Palk.

"Everyone was dead." Alien invaders with a lethal touch ("A
machine! A robot!") decimate Earth with a deadly gas. The
"human slaves of these machines": their revived victims. ("She
was alive enough tonight—except for her eyes.") What the world
needed—another *Target Earth* (1954). Another cross reference:
*Plan 9 from Outer Space*. Drab melodrama produced mainly with
an eye on Cheap. A bit of bite: the young man's speech re the
relative value of paper money, then and now (i.e., after the gas).

**EARTH GIRLS ARE EASY** (U.S.-B?) Vestron/Kestrel Films
(Earth Girls Movie Co.) 1989 (1988) color/ws 100m. D: Julien
Temple. SP: Julie Brown, Charlie Coffey, Terrence E. McNally.
Mus: Nile Rodgers. SpVisFX: Dream Quest; (anim sup) Dorne
Huebler. Aliens: Roark Prods.; (mkp des) Jeffrey Judd. SpFxCo-
ord: Dennis Petersen. SpMechMin: Image Engnrng. Title Seq:
Lee Film Design; (anim des) Jim Shaw. Ref: TV. V 9/14/88. NYT
5/12/89. SFExam 5/12/89. ad. MFB'89:363-4. With Geena
Davis, Jeff Goldblum (Mac), Julie Brown, Jim Carrey (Wiploc),
Damon Wayans (Zeebo), Larry Linville.

"There's a UFO in my pool!" Three horny, shaggy, two-hearted,
long-tongued, monkey-see/monkey-do aliens from Jhazzala park
their "giant blowdryer" in a backyard swimming pool in the
Valley, Southern California. One of the aliens (who look like
"Wookies, or werewolves"), Mac, turns out to be Mr. Right for
Valerie (Davis), a manicurist.... Snappily choreographed but
flatly scripted sf-musical-comedy. One problem: Val's fiancee
(Charles Rocket) is too clearly Mr. Wrong for her. There's no
romantic suspense. Davis' comic style here tends toward a fad-
ing-out-of-the-picture monotone. Robby the Robot appears in a
visualized nightmare.

**EARTH-STAR VOYAGER** ABC-TV/Marstar & Disney-TV
1988 color c180m. D: James Goldstone. Tel: Ed Spielman. Mus:
Lalo Schifrin. VisFX: Boss; (des) Terry Windell. Mkp: Ilona
Herman. Ref: TV. TVG. V 1/27/88:76. With Duncan Regehr,
Brian McNamara, Jason Michas, Julia Montgomery, Peter Donat, Margaret Langrick, Sean O'Byrne, Lynnette Mettey ("Priscilla").

Year 2087, in search of a "new" Earth. Ingredients: a spacecraft
with a computer, Priscilla, hooked into an analog of a human
brain ... the Outlaw Technology Zone ... cryo sleep ... the Junk
Belt, or Pollution in Space, which belt yields a scene that's the
counterpart of your classic meteor-shower scene ... an anti-matter
field ... periodic psychological pep talks ... familiar melodrama
... and somewhat helpful humor and effects.

**The EAST IS RED** (H.K.) Golden Princess & Rim Film (Film
Workshop/Tsui Hark) 1993 color 95m. (aka *Swordsman III*).
D: Ching Siu-Tung, Raymond Lee. SP: Tsui Hark, Roy Szeto, C.
Cheung. Ph: Lau Moon-Tong. Mus: Wu Wai-Lap. AD: Eddie Ma.
Ref: V 7/12/93: "daft, energetic fun." SFChron 6/25/93: "a
wonderfully ludicrous epic." 5/25/93. With Brigitte Lin, Joey
Wang, Yu Rong-Guang, Jean Wang.

"Part cannon and part torpedo," the telekinetic Asia the Invincible
can "metamorphose" into the bodies of others, stop her foes'
heartbeats, "turn men to toast," and affect the weather. Her

enemies can "transmute into her likeness...." (SFC) Follow-up to the *Swordsman* films.

**EASY MONEY** see *Forging Ahead*

**EAT AND RUN** New World/BFD (Jack Briggs) 1986 (1985) color 90m. (*Mangia* - orig t). SP, D: Christopher Hart. SP: also Stan Hart. Mus: Scott Harper. PD: Robert Kracik, Anne C. Patterson. Ref: TV. V 12/24/86. SFExam 10/31/86. With Ron Silver, Sharon Schlarth, R. L. Ryan (Murray Creature), Derek Murcott, Malachi Throne.

A "killer creature" alien (Ryan), built "like a condominium," proves to be fond of Italians in Little Italy. Very fond. "You trying to tell me some guy is going around eating Italians?" He also proves to be an adept at the legal system. "Now, Murray, at the time that you were eating all those people, did you know you were doing something wrong?" *Eat And Run* is the kind of comedy that finds, or tries to find, a joke in every shot and line. The running gag in which Silver's supposed offscreen narration turns out to be onscreen monologue—heard by the other characters in the scene—wears thin, but is funnier than most of the one-shot gags.

**EAT OR BE EATEN** Firesign Theatre 1985 color 30m. D: Phil Austin. Ref: Martin: "lots of laughs." Hound. Stanley.

Killer vine threatens village, demands virgin sacrifice.

**EATEN ALIVE** see *Doomed To Die*

**\*\*ECCE HOMO** (I) 1969 feature (aka *I Sopravvissuti*). D: B.A. Gaburro. Ref: Palmerini: "post-atomic." With Irene Papas, Philippe Leroy.

**ECOLOGIA DEL DELITTO** see *Twitch of the Death Nerve*

**ED AND HIS DEAD MOTHER** ITC Ent. (W. C. Gorog) 1993 (1992) color 87m.(aka *Bon Appetit, Mama*). D: Jonathan Wacks. SP: Chuck Hughes. Ph: F. Kenny. Mus: M. Daring. PD: Eve Cauley. SpFX: KNB. SpFxCoord: Ian O'Connor. Ref: TV. PT 18:11: "doesn't exactly 'work'," V 6/14/93. 1/25/93:18 (rated). With Steve Buscemi, Ned Beatty, Miriam Margolyes (Mabel Chilton), John Glover, Eric Christmas, Rance Howard.

"For a thousand bucks, we'll bring her back to life." It's just a "simple reanimation." Then: "Ed, your mother's in the refrigerator." A couple bugs at bedtime is supposed to revitalize her, but unlike Renfield, Mom is not satisfied with just bugs, and she's impervious to bullets .... Horror-comedy dawdles, but occasionally surprises, and seems to be part of a new, *Psycho*-undertoned subgenre, which also includes *Mom* and *Flesh-Eating Mothers*.

**EDGAR ALLAN POE'S HAUNTING FEAR** see *Haunting Fear*

**EDGAR ALLAN POE'S MASQUE OF THE RED DEATH** Concorde-New Horizons (Roger Corman/Pacific Trust) 1989 color 85m. (aka *Masque of the Red Death*). SP, D: Larry Brand. SP: also Daryl Haney. From Edgar Allan Poe's story "The Mask of the Red Death." Ph: E. Pei. Mus: M. Governor. PD: S. Greenberg. SpMkpFX: Dean & Starr Jones et al. SpFX: Wayne Beauchamp. 2nd Unit D: Jeffrey Delman. Mattes: Pony Horton.

Ref: TV: MGM-UA HV. V 9/13/89: "marginal video item." 8/30/89:30 (rated). 10/18/89:42: playing. V/Mifed '89:153. Fango 89:21-4. Martin: "fine rendition." With Patrick Macnee (Machiavel/Red Death), Adrian Paul, Clare Hoak, Tracy Reiner, Jeff Osterhage, Maria Ford, Kelly Ann Sabatasso.

"The Red Death has come!" The Red Death enters the land of Prince Prospero (Paul) and brings certain death to whomever he touches. ("Death is winning his war against man.") Mopey and talky, with bland actors. Roger Corman at least had Vincent Price the first time around, in 1964 (when Corman was director as well as producer). This isn't worth the wait for the payoff grand entrance of death's messenger. Based on one of Poe's less distinguished tales.

See also *Masque of the Red Death*.

**EDGAR ALLAN POE'S THE BLACK CAT** see *Black Cat, The* (1990)

**EDGE OF HELL, The** see *Rock 'n' Roll Nightmare*

**EDGE OF SANITY** (B-Hung.) Millimeter Films (August Ent.)/Allied Vision & Hungarofilm (Edward Simons, Harry Alan Towers) 1989 (1988) color 90m. (*Dr. Jekyll and Mr. Hyde—A Journey into Fear* - orig t). D: Gerard Kikoine. SP: J. P. Felix, Ron Raley, from Robert Louis Stevenson's story "The Strange Case of Dr. Jekyll and Mr. Hyde." Mus: Frederic Talgorn. MkpSup: Gordon Kaye. SpFxSup: Ian Wingrove. Opt: Image to Image. Ref: TV. MFB'90:261. V 4/12/89. 10/19/88:90. ad. With Anthony Perkins (Dr. Jekyll/Mr. Hyde), Glynis Barber, Sarah Maur-Thorp, David Lodge, Ben Cole.

"Another Ripper murder!" A lab accident with a beyond-morphine drug turns Dr. Henry Jekyll into Jack Hyde, a "sick animal" with the "strength of a wild beast"—a "monster"—who begins surgically slashing up prostitutes in London's East End. "The Ripper" follows his every instinct, supposedly, but still has a sexual hangup or two.... Yes, Dr. Jekyll is not only Mr. Hyde here, but Jack the Ripper as well. Not to mention, more or less, Norman Bates. He is not, however, the Phantom of the Opera or Crusader Rabbit. Perkins' intensity in this low-grade, kinky t&a saga is on the edge of campy.

**EDGE OF TERROR** see *Wind, The*

**EDGE OF THE AXE** (Sp) Calepas Int'l. & Jose Frade 1987 color 91m. (*Al Filo del Hacha*). D: Joseph Braunstein. SP: Joaquin Amichatis, Javier Elorrieta, Frade. Ph: Tote Trenas. Mus: Javier Elorrieta. AD: Javier Fernandez. SpFxMkp: Colin Arthur. Ref: TV: Forum HV; Eng. version. V 8/5/87:6. 10/21/87: 198(ad). Hound. no Martin. V(Cannes '89): 448. With Barton Faulks, Christina Lane, Jack Taylor, Patty Shepard, Page Moseley, Fred Holliday, Alicia Moro.

"There's some maniac—he's running around chopping women up." This "acute psychopath"—who makes "hamburger meat" of her victims—has psycho-amnesia and is trying to erase all trace of her psychiatric history.... Computerized script, one or two unnecessarily graphic murders, and a silly twist ending and final shot.

**EDWARD II** (B) British Screen & BBC Films (Working Title) 1991 color 90m. SP, D: Derek Jarman. SP: also S. McBride, K. Butler. From Marlowe's play. Ph: Ian Wilson. Mus: S. F. Turner. PD: C. Hobbs. Ref: V 9/16/91. Jones. With Tilda Swinton (Queen Isabella), Steven Waddington, Andrew Tiernan.

Isabella "finally turns into a raving monster who literally sucks the blood from her victims."

**EFFE AND GIELLA** see *Emblem of Goode*

**EGYPTIAN MELODIES** Disney 1930? anim c7m. Ref: TV. Jim Shapiro.

An inquisitive spider investigates a sphinx and discovers spooky tunnels, diapered dancing mummies, and marching hieroglyphics, in what must be the first mummy movie of the sound era. Okay blend of music, comedy, and chills. Neatest effect: the crazy armies of hellzapoppin hieroglyphics.

**EH, KASI BATA** (Fili) Seiko Films/RNJ Corp. (Robbie Tan) 1992 color 104m. (*Eh! Kasi Bata* - ad t). D: Efren Jarlego. SP: Cesar Cosme. Ph: C. Austria. Mus: Rey Magtoto. PD: M. Defensor. SpFX: Peping Carmona. Mkp: Bobby Balisi. SdFX: M. Martinez Jr. Ref: TV: Ultra Video; occ. Eng. With Rominick Sarmenta, Jennifer Sevilla, Billy Joe Crawford, Atong Redillas, Ike Lozada, Pong Pong.

Two aliens survive the crash landing of their ship on Earth. (Asks a little Earth girl, "Are you American?") The alien woman's first act here: a striptease at the local strip joint. Her eye-rays can open a can of tuna (a cute stopmo trick) or suspend a falling man in mid-air, and her dark glasses allow any wearer to see everyone in his or her underwear. Meanwhile, the little alien girl's special gizmo enables a fellow student to make a bright answer to their teacher's question.... Indifferent mixture of sf, action, comedy, and sentiment milks its gags. In the oddest sequence, the head of the master crook transforms, in turn, into the head of a wolf, an alligator, an elephant, and a lion.

**8-MAN** (J) Kodansha/Project 8 1992 color/ws 91m. Ref: TV: vt; no Eng.

Tokyo. A la *Robocop,* a badly wounded cop is high-teched back to full power, and more. A cyborg now, he is not only impervious to bullets—he collects them in his hand, or glove, and he has super-speed and an invisibility option. Only a short circuit can stop him, and then it's back to the doc. He is tormented by memories of his previous life and death and at the end battles another cyborg.... Mind-numbing combination of sf and pop music.

**8MAN AFTER: CITY IN FEAR** (J) Streamline/KH-JK-Act(Honda-Abe-Kobayashi) 1993('94-U.S.) anim color 28m. D: S. Furukawa. SP: Y. Hirano, from the comic book. Story: J. Kuwata, K. Hirai. Ph: A. Takahashi. Mus: Mike Kennedy. AD: K. Kanamura. SpFX: Mamoru Abe. Script Ed: Fred Patten. SdFX: Daisuke Jimbo. Ref: TV: Streamline video & Sanctuary & J.S. Staff & Enoki Films; Eng. dubbed.

"What the hell is that thing?" Ingredients include the super-fast, super-strong, near-invulnerable 8Man ... street-gang members who replace their limbs with "cyber parts" ... and a psycho cyborg

.... Gratuitous gore and macho talk and action. ("So you always play the tough guy.")

**EIGHT O'CLOCK IN THE MORNING** see *They Live*

**The 18 BRONZEMEN** (H.K.?) 198-? color c105m. D, P: Joseph Kuo. Ref: TV: Video Village; Eng. titles.

Routine martial arts actioner features one long bizarre sequence in which Shao Lin students face the Bronzemen. The first Bronzemen look like robots, or heavily armored warriors. These clanking menaces give way to less imposing figures that look like victims of Bronzefinger.

**EIGHTEEN JADE PEARLS** (H.K.?) Oriental Motion Pictures/Ping Film Co. (Keung Chung Ping) 1988-U.S. color/ws 92m. D: Cheung Chieh. SP: Yao Ching Kang. SdFX: Hsi Su Jan. Mkp: C. Pi Yung. Ref: TV: Video Treasures; Eng. dubbed. no Martin. no Hound.

Routine martial-arts actioner includes an eerie sequence set in a forest haunted by flying fireballs or jack-o'-lanterns ("They're harmless") and some snarling "ghosts." ("They're only men dressed up.") Also: a disfigured character. ("I burnt my face to alter my appearance.")

**EJACULA** (I?) VCA 1994 color 90m. D: Max Bellocchio. Ref: Adam'96: "porn knock-off of the vampire legend." With P. Kennedy, L. LeMay.

**EJACULA 2** (I?) VCA 1994 color 85m. D: M. Bellocchio. Ref: Adam'96: vampires, hunchback (Ron Jeremy). With P. Kennedy, R. Siffredi.

**EJACULATIONS** see *Doriana Gray*

**EKO EKO AZARAKU** see *Wizard of Darkness*

**2 ELECTRIC TRANSFORMATIONS** 1909. Ref: TV (Amazing Years of Cinema): excerpt. Hardy/SF.

Throw the switch, and the electric machine makes duplicates of any object or person. Stunning effects here with distorting mirrors, as the subjects (on the right) "melt," and then re-solidify (on the left), in the image of the original. (Compare *Four-Sided Triangle*.)

**ELECTRIC WET DREAMS** Ecstasy Video 198-? color c90m. D: Ron Jeremy. Ref: vc box. With Jeremy, Spring Taylor, Kelly Nichols, Samantha Fox.

Electric chair turns doctor's patients' "wildest thoughts into reality."

**ELEMENT OF CRIME, The** see *Forbrydelsens Element*

**ELIMINATORS** Empire/Altar 1986 color 96m. D: Peter Manoogian. SP: Paul De Meo, Danny Bilson. Mus: Bob Summers. SpOptFX: Quick Silver, David Allen Prods., Gene Warren Jr., B. Bromberg. SpMkp: MMI; (des) John Carl Buechler; (fx) Mitch Devane; (props) Mike Hood. Mandroid tank: Broggie Elliot Animation. SpFxChief: J. R. Molina. SpSdFX: Dane Davis. Ref:

TV. MFB'86:321-2. V 2/5/87. ad. With Patrick Reynolds, Conan Lee, Peggy Mannix.

Principals: a torpedo and laser-shooting "mandroid" (Reynolds) with a half-human brain; scientist Nora Hunter (Denise Crosby), designer of the mandroid's android parts; adventurer Harry Fortuna (Andrew Prine); Reeves (Roy Dotrice), a mad scientist bent on ruling ancient Rome; a small robot, Spot (a "big-mouthed electric bowling ball"), with matter-transfer capabilities; and a tribe of time-transported Neanderthals (Pepe Moreno et al.). At the end, Reeves, now a self-made mandroid, is sent back to the Silurian Era, 435 million B.C., to become "ruler of nothing".... Good-natured but uninspired combination of *Raiders of the Lost Ark* (or *Romancing the Stone*) and *The Terminator*. Obvious but genial comedy with Eliminators Prine, Crosby, Reynolds, and Spot. Fair effects; cliche scenes.

**ELLA** see *Monkey Shines*

**ELMER'S HARE REMOVER** see *Hare Remover*

**ELOISA IS UNDERNEATH AN ALMOND TREE** (Sp) Cifesa 1943 73m. (*Eloisa Esta debajo de un Almendro*). SP, D: Rafael Gil. From Enrique Poncela's play. Ph: Alfredo Fraile. Mus: Juan Quintero. AD: Enrique Alarcon. Mkp: A. Turell. Ref: screen; Eng. titles. PFA notes 6/18/88. With Amparo Rivelles, Rafael Duran.

A tale of two houses, in or near Madrid: 1) "This house seems to be haunted." Ezequiel, master of the "house on the lake," tells his nephew Fernando that the latter's deceased father was "a little strange, like all of us"—i.e., madness is a family trait. The lake house features "strange noises," squeaky doors, and a servant with a wooden leg. ("The master scares me.") 2) "This is a madhouse." The forbidding, mad "Auntie" Micaela dominates the nearby "palace" of the Briones. ("Strange things happen here.") And the "sister collects owls"....

*Arsenic and Old Lace*-like cross between screwball comedy and Gothic thriller has a sometimes clever script and a lively pace, but the relentless whimsy wears thin. Ezequiel, a suspected Landru, kills and skins his victims; the latter, though, prove to be cats, and his mysterious "discovery" is a cure for pellagra. The fabulously sinister house on the lake features a circular stone stairway and a lab which seem to be hommages to Universal horror movies.

**\*ELSTREE CALLING** 1930 84m. Ph: C. Friese-Greene. Mus: Ivor Novello, Vivian Ellis et al; (lyrics) Rowland Leigh et al. Ref: screen. PFA notes 4/13/86: London Nat'l. Film Archive print. Hardy/SF. Lee. Hitchcock/Truffaut. no Stanley.

"This marvelous invention of television" is seen briefly (at the beginning and end of the movie) for the "first time, in the home," as it brings in music-hall acts from the Elstree studio. And—for the first time—the movies make light of television: Gordon Harker's set immediately breaks down. (It looks like a mirror-on-a-stand atop a mini-bookcase, and is hooked up to tubes and a phonograph.) Emcee Tommy Handley describes the new process as radio-plus-cinema. Plus: a mild "thrill" number in which the Three Eddies, in skeleton outfits, advise you to "take off your skin, and dance around in your bones."

"Frat," in "Variety," found the material dated in 1930, and it hasn't improved with age. Half the movie, however, can be enjoyed as bad comedy, bad dance, good-bad comedy, etc.; the other half can be survived. The lead dancer's contortions in the first color sequence anticipate *Wild Women of Wongo*. (The approximately-applied color has the look of hand-tinting.) Less "artful," more spirited hoofing is provided by Cicely Courtneidge, Jack Hulbert, and the Three Eddies.

**ELUSIVE SONG OF THE VAMPIRE** (Taiwanese) 1987 color feature. D: Takako Shira. Ref: Jones. NST! 4:21-22: "inept ... wacky."

Four hopping vampires haunt a home in ancient China.

**ELVES** Action Int'l. Video/Fitzgerald Films/Triangle Films (Mark Paglia) 1989 color 89m. SP, D: Jeff Mandel. SP: also Mike Griffin, Bruce Taylor. Mus: V. Horunzhy. FX: (des) Vincent J. Guastini; Fantasy Workshop. Ref: V 1/10/90:32 (hv): "interesting despite the hokum." With Dan Haggerty, Deanna Lund, Julie Austin, Borah Silver.

Neo-nazis mate elf with virgin.

**ELVIRA: MISTRESS OF THE DARK** New World & NBC Prods. & Queen "B" Prods. 1988 color 96m. D: James Signorelli. SP: Sam Egan, John Paragon, Cassandra Peterson. Mus: James Campbell. SpMkpFX: Doug Beswick; (Vincent) Steve La Porte. VisFX: (sup) Peter Donen; Apogee. OptFxSup: R. W. Dorney. Anim: Clint Colver. SpFX: (coord) Dennis Dion; (sup) Rich Ratliff. Ref: TV: New World Video. SFChron 10/3/88. ad. SFExam 9/30/88. MFB'89:78-9. With Peterson, W. Morgan Sheppard (Vincent Talbot), Daniel Greene, Susan Kellermann, Hugh Gillin.

"Haven't you ever seen any old Roger Corman movies?" The Book of Sight makes the possessor Ruler of the Night; her great aunt's "dumb recipe book"—which Elvira (Peterson) inherits, and which may be the very same book—includes a recipe which yields a feisty monster that winds up in the garbage disposal. In the meantime, Elvira runs *Attack of the Killer Tomatoes* for the kids of Fallwell, Mass., where, at the end, she uses her witch powers to save herself from being burned at the stake.... Queen of the Retort would be more like it. *Elvira the Movie* is best when it's a running, put-down commentary on itself—i.e., when Elvira does to her own movie what she does to the ones she hosts on TV and videotape. Comedy showcase for Elvira the Boobs sputters, but the poodle is fun-nee.

**EMANUELLE E GLI ULTIMI CANNIBALI** see *Trap Them and Kill Them*

**EMANUELLE IN HOLLYWOOD** see *Bad Girls from Mars*

**EMANUELLE'S AMAZON ADVENTURE** see *Trap Them and Kill Them*

**EMANUELLE'S BLACK COBRA** see *Black Cobra*

**EMBLEM OF GOODE** (*Effe and Giella*) (J) M.T.V. 198-? anim color 46m. Ref: TV: Pyramid Video; no Eng.; OAV?

Ingredients in this sword-and-sorcery saga include a giant god-dess/statue which shakes the ground as it rises from beneath a temple, then, later—after a supernatural tornado rips up said temple—dissolves screaming ... an annihilating force in a cave ... flying spirit-sorceresses ... warrior-waif women ... and punk pirates. In sum: vapidly drawn, wide-eyed women ... impressively animated supernatural action ... and an apparent alternate-universe setting based on ancient Greece.

**EMBRACE OF A VAMPIRE**  New Line (Vance-Vrouka) 1994 color feature. D: Anne Goursaud. SP: Eaton, Coady, Bitzelberger. Ref: PT 21:69: lovesick vampire. vc box: 1995; *Embrace of the Vampire*. With Martin Kemp (vampire), Alyssa Milano, Jennifer Tilly.

**EMERALD JUNGLE**  see *Doomed To Die*

**EMERGENCY! LIVING DEAD IN TOKYO BAY**  see *Battle Girl*

**EMPIRE OF ASH II**  see *Maniac Warriors*

**EMPIRE OF ASH III**  (Can.) North American Pictures & Empire of Ash III 1989 color c90m. (*Last of the Warriors* - vt t). Story, D, P: Lloyd A. Simandl. D, Line P: Michael Mazo. SP: Chris Maruna. Ph: Danny Nowak. Mus: John Serenda (Sereda?) & the Gore Avenue Sound Project. SpFxCoord: Al Benjamin. Prosth: Jim Bridge, Rick Griffin. Ref: TV. TVG. V Mifed'89:133. Drew/Motion Picture Series & Sequels: third in a series. no Maltin '92. no Scheuer. Martin. V 9/6/89:47 (ad). With William Smith, Melanie Kilgour, Ken Farmer, Scott Andersen, Nancy Pataki, Tanya Orton, Andy Graffitti (Grand Shepherd).

"Blessed is the word of the Grand Shepherd," in the New Idaho. A plague has sent civilization "back to the Stone Ages" and turned city dwellers into cannibal mutants. Meanwhile, the monk-like Shepherds combat "traitors".... Atrocious sf-actioner. Compare *Roller Blade* and its post-apocalyptic religious order.

See also: *Maniac Warriors.*

**EMPIRE OF THE DARK**  Nautilus Film/Barkett 1992 color feature. SP, D, Ed: Steve Barkett. Mus: John Morgan. Ref: SFChron 3/11/92. Martin: "run-of-the-mill devil flick." With S. Barkett, Richard Harrison.

"Demon cult ... another dimension ... time portal." (SFC)

**EMPIRE OF THE SINS**  Standard 1988 color 87m. D: P. O'Toole. Ref: Adam '90: "futuristic cop." with Krista Lane, Elle Rio, Tom Byron, Keisha, Kristara Barrington.

Sequel to *Cabaret Sin.*

**EN EL TIEMPO DE LOS DIOSES**  (Mex) Viesa 1988 color c94m. D: Gilberto Macin; (rituals) T. Xocoyotzin. SP: Macin. Mus: Erik Fuentes. SpFX: Raul Gutierrez. Mkp: A. R. Herrera et al. Ref: TV: Video Emocion; no Eng.; *In the Time of the Gods* - tr t. With Carmen Delgado, Claudio Baez, Mauricio Davison, Angelina Cruz, Jaqueline Castro.

Veronica (Delgado)—the star of a movie-in-progress re ancient Toltecs—dreams of Toltecs. Awake, she is drawn to their temple,

and to the past, and interrupts a human sacrifice. Ghostly warriors besiege her dressing-room trailer, and an old hag from the ceremony haunts her. Veronica survives a ceremony herself, but finds little rest in the hospital.... Potentially intriguing anecdote is overextended and blandly illustrated (it was shot on videotape), though the location itself is impressive, if the shooting isn't.

See also *Dark Power.*

**ENCHANTING SHADOW**  see *Chinese Ghost Story, A*

**ENCINO MAN**  BV/Hollywood Pictures & Touchwood Pacific Partners I (George Zaloom) 1992 color 89m. D: Les Mayfield. Story, SP: S. Schepps. Story: also G. Zaloom. Mus: J. P. Robinson. Ref: V 5/25/92: "insulting even within its own no-effort parameters." SFChron 5/22/92: "puerile and sophomoric." with Sean Astin, Brendan Fraser (Link), Pauly Shore, Megan Ward, Mariette Hartley, Richard Masur.

High school dweebs dig up frozen caveman in their backyard.

**ENCINO WOMAN**  Visual Images.  with Taylor Wane, Tonisha Mills, Persia.1993? color feature. Ref: vc box: "4,000-year-old female barbarian."

**ENCOUNTER AT RAVEN'S GATE**  (Austral.) Hemdale/FGH-Int'l. Film Management & AFC & SAFC 1988 ('90-U.S.) color/ws 85m. (93m.) (*Incident at Raven's Gate* - orig t). SP, D, P: Rolf de Heer. SP, P: Marc Rosenberg. Orig SP: J. M. Vernon. Mus: Graham Tardif. SpFxCoord: Jon Armstrong. SpOptFX: Anifex. Prosth: Sue Richter. Ref: TV: HBO Video. V 8/31/88. 8/2/89:18 (rated). 1/24/90:24. Kelly Cresap. MFB'90:103. Fango 101. With Steven Vidler, Celine Griffin, Ritchie Singer, Vincent Gil, Saturday Rosenberg.

"Stay away from Raven's Gate!" Dead, dried-up sheep, electrical disturbances, UFO-ish lights, and a circular, burned area in a field (hommage to the first *The Thing*?) herald an apparent close encounter at Raven's Gate. Low-key, routine pathos and melo-drama, with occasional wry touches and lines. Best of the latter (in context): "It's for you." (Long distance....)

**ENCOUNTER OF THE SPOOKY KIND II**  (H.K.) Bojon Films/Long Shong Pictures 1989 color c91m. D: Sammo Hung. Ref: Pan-Asia Video; Eng. titles. Jones. With Sammo Hung.

In a visualized-nightmare prologue, a hopping-vampire couple menaces a human couple. In the film proper, a young ghost woman tends her (living) mother, and an evil priest brings to life mummy-like corpses ("Not mummy, but bewitched corpse") and feeds cockroaches to two other corpses. Big zombie and little zombie awaken, and the tall one, beheaded, spills out cock-roaches. Bonus: a possessed man who sprouts plant growth in his naval. Alternately silly and sentimental horror-comedy.

**ENCULELA**  (F) Vanessa 199-? color c90m. Ref: TV: vt. no Jones.

Threadbare hardcore hi-jinks with a vampire "princess" and her coffin-bound subjects.

**END OF THE LINE**  see *Terminus*

**END PLAY** (Austral.) Hexagon 1975 color c105m. (*Endplay -* ad t). SP, D, P: Tim Burstall. From Russell Braddon's novel. Mus: Peter Best. Ref: TV: Academy Home Ent. video. V 12/24/75. Hound. no Martin. With George Mallaby, John Waters, Kevin Miles, Ken Goodlet, Charles Tingwell.

"The murder of yet another hitchhiker...." Visiting-little-step-brother Mark (Waters) finds that he must dispose of a murdered hitchhiker before he can really relax with Robbie (Mallaby), and dispose he does, at the Rex, where "Day of Horror" is playing. But is Mark really the "maniac" at large ...? Apparently, someone thought this study in abnormal psychology was pretty ingenious. And it is, near the end. Elsewhere, ingeniousness is closer to laboriousness. One character actually says, "Ironical, isn't it?" Bloody macabre windup involves a bow and arrows and various swords.

**La ENDEMONIADA** (Mex) Cima Films 1967 color 82m. D: E. G. Muriel. SP: Alfredo Ruanova. Ph: Raul Dominguez. Mus: Enrico C. Caviatti. AD: Octavio Ocampo, Jose Mendez. SpFX: Ricardo Sainz. Mkp: Graciela Munoz. Ref: TV. V (CHVD). vc box. no Lee. Horacio Higuchi. no Hardy/HM. no Stanley. Cinef 6/96:45. With Libertad Leblanc, Enrique Rocha, Rogelio Guerra, Carlos Cortez.

Cloaked vampire has psychic link with woman and can turn into bat. Bland photography, awful score.

**ENDEMONIADAS, Las** see *Folds of the Flesh*

**ENDGAME** (I) (MMI-TV/American Nat'l./Cinema 80/Filmirage 1984 (1983) color 90m. (*Bronx Lotta Finale - Endgame -* orig t. *I Mutanti -* working t). SP, D: Steven Benson. SP: also George Eastman (aka Alex Carver). Mus: C. M. Cordio. SpFX: James Davies et al. Mkp: Russell, Hills. SdFX: Studio Sound. Ref: TV. Horacio Higuchi. V 2/19/86. TVG. Stanley. Gorezone 18. Martin. Morse. Ecran F 47:41. With Al Cliver, Bobby Rhodes, Moira Chen aka Laura Gemser (Lilith), Eastman, Jack Davis, Gordon Mitchell, Al Yamanouchi, Peter Brighton (blue mutant).

2025 A.D., the year of Endgame 25, the replacement for war. Plus: fallout-produced, "regressive," telepathic mutants-with-gills—including the blue mutant, a "revolting monster"—and a youth-prolonging drug.... Basically shoddy, retrograde sf-actioner contains some fairly ingenious *Scanners*-like ideas re telepathic powers. (For instance, telepaths can "hear" people dying.) Gratuitous gore.

**ENDLESS DESCENT** (Sp) Live Home Video/Dister Group (Jose Escriva) 1989 color 79m. (86m.) (*La Grieta.* aka *The Rift*). D, Co-P: J. P. Simon. SP: Simon; (Eng. version) David Coleman. Story (Eng. version): Simon, Mark Klein. Mus: Joel Goldsmith. SpTechFX: Carlo de Marchis. SpMkpFX: Colin Arthur. OtherFX: Basilio Cortijo. OptFX: Cinema Research. Ref: TV. MFB'90:225. V 12/27/89. 5/2/90:204. Cinef 12/91. CVS 4/91. Maltin '92. With Jack Scalia, R. Lee Ermey, Ray Wise, Deborah Adair, Tony Isbert, Frank Brana, Edmund Purdom.

"Nothing's normal at these depths." A team searching for the missing nuclear sub Siren One discovers "biologically impossible" plant growth and animal life in a rift at the bottom of the sea. ("Whatever it is, it's enormous.") The "complex group of mutations" turns out to be a product of trans-genetics, "synthetic, newly-created life forms" produced by splicing genes from different species and submitting them to a DNA "accelerator" in order to speed up evolution.... Some okay makeup and scenic effects, highlighted by the payoff sequence in the breeding cavern: The intrepid discover obscene fetuses ("Damn thing looks almost human!") and a huge "petal" with a tentacle head. Functional, cliched story.

**ENDPLAY** see *End Play*

**ENEMY** (Fili) Raymond Red 1983 color 23m. D: Red, Ian Victoriano. SP: Victoriano. Ph: Red, Surf Reyes. Ref: PFA notes 3/29/88: Super-8; sf.

Mountain training of young men to be Guardians of the Stars of the Eastern Skies.

**\*ENEMY FROM SPACE** Corinth Films 1957 (*Quatermass 2 -* TV cr t). From Nigel Kneale's teleplay "Quatermass II." AD: Bernard Robinson. SpFX: Bill Warrington, Henry Harris, Frank George. Mkp: Phil Leakey. Ref: TV. Warren/KWTS! V 9/4/57. Lee. Lentz. Stanley. Scheuer. Martin. Maltin '92. Phantom. Hound. TVG. Ecran F 41:79. Filmfax 37:68-74, 18-19. With John Longden, Tom Chatto, Sidney James, Lloyd Lamble.

"They're coming down by the hundreds!" Prof. Quatermass (Brian Donlevy), the "rocket man," investigates a space mystery involving weird falling things (picked up first on the radio-telescope), a "moon project" supposedly aimed at "adapting living beings on an alien planet," a black bubble ("something alive") from a "meteorite," trucks bearing the moon-project insignia, and *Invaders from Mars*-like, telltale zombification marks on various government personnel. The source of the "meteorites": an asteroid in permanent eclipse on the dark side of the Earth. The nature of the invading alien: a "multiple organism, a thousand billion intelligences with one single consciousness".... Roughly the first two-thirds of *Enemy from Space*—its mystery phase—is quite exciting and atmospheric. Noir photography by Gerald Gibbs makes the pipes and domes of the Shell Haven Refinery in Essex look chillingly sinister—Industrial Horror. The movie's climactic, action phase—shootouts, yelling mobs, and a giant walking fungus—seems more familiar and less compelling.

**ENEMY MINE** Fox/Kings Road (Stanley O'Toole/Stephen Friedman) 1985 color/ws 108m. D: Wolfgang Petersen. SP: Edward Khmara. Story: Barry Longyear. Mus: Maurice Jarre. VisFX: (sup) Don Dow; (dogfight) IL&M; (anim sup) Bruce Walters, Ellen Lichtwardt. Aliens: Chris Walas. Drac movement: Jack Luceno. SpFxSup: Bob MacDonald, Jr. Ref: TV. MFB'86:207-8. V 12/18/85. Sacto Bee 12/20/85. SFExam 12/20/85. With Dennis Quaid, Lou Gossett Jr., Brion James, Lance Kerwin, Richard Marcus.

In the 21st Century, an earthling, Willis Davidge (Quaid), and a reptilian alien from Dracon, Jeriba Shigan (Gossett), are stranded during battle on the fourth planet of the Pyrine System, where there be turtle-like creatures and big-toothed, single-tentacled monsters in the sand.... Some welcome humor here in the treatment of the peaceful-coexistence theme. The movie, however, is ultimately tractlike and didactic, and Jarre's score is not one of his best. Gossett's makeup—including his reptile pupils—and his deliberate delivery give his scenes some distinctiveness. Pretty effects from IL&M.

**ENEMY UNSEEN** Ascension & Triax(Prowess/Elmo De Witt & Desiree Markgraaff) 1991(1989) color 90m. (aka *Crocs*). D: E. De Witt. SP: Greg Latter. MechFX: Konrad DuToit et al. SpFxCoord: Rick Creswell. Mkp: Daphne Williams. Ref: TV: AIP HV. V 5/2/90:80. PT 20:15.

"They sacrifice their women to the crocodiles." Crocodile Valley, Africa. In a "pretty weird" ritual, natives in croc skins seem to "hypnotize" maidens into becoming the breakfast of crocodiles. Later, apparently hypnotized crocs come up onto land and attack a man. ("Seems a little strange that a crocodile would take a man this far from water.") Actioner with macabre elements proves faithful to every cliche. Fine line: "You must never do anything bad to a crocodile."

See also *Cannibal Attack*.

**L'ENFANT DU MIRACLE** (F) Diamant-Berger 1932 b&w 79m. D: Maurice Diamant-Berger. SP: Henri Diamant-Berger, from the play by Gavault and Charvay. Ref: Chirat. V 6/21/32: "pleasant entertainment"; *The Miracle Child* - tr t.

"One funny sequence in the lover's apartment, where people, breaking in on a seance of spiritualism, are mistaken for ghosts." (V)

**ENGKANTADANG KANGKAROT EN HER MAGIC TA-LONG** (Fili) GP Films 1990 color c120m. D: Jett C. Espiritu. SP: Julie Larrazabal. Story: Beng Lacson. SpVisFX: Cinemagic. SpFX: Gapo Marbella Jr. SdFX: Lamberto Ramos. Mkp: Beth Hammond. Ref: TV: BP Films video; little Eng.

Sub-*Tootsie* silliness in this long, occasionally amusing science-fantasy re a transvestite hero who switches back and forth between worlds and genders. He seems to belong to a world of gods, but spends a lot of time on Earth. In his superhero costume, he is impervious to bullets and prone to flouncing. A comic evil magician shoots both rays and fireballs. Complete with "Three Stooges" sound effects.

**ENGKANTO** (Fili) RNJ Corp./Double "M" Prods. & SOFIA (Esteban/Paulate) 1992 color 105m. Story, D: Tata Esteban. Story, SP: Rei Nicandro. Story: also Arthur Nicdao. Assoc D: Loretto Franco Ybanez III. Ph: Vic Anao. Mus: Jaime Fabregas. PD: Arthur Nicdao. Anim & VisFX: Maurice Carvajal. SpMkp: Rey Salamat. SpProsthMkpFX: Nestor Carino. SpFX: Rene Abadeza. SdFX: Serafin Dineros. Ref: TV: vt; occ. Eng. With Roderick Paulate (Yorac), Francis Magalona (Uban), Raul Zaragosa (Karina), Janice De Belen (Karina), Maila Gumila (Ayam), Apple Pie Bautista (Kulit), Vilma Santos (Inang Kalikasan)

The ray-shooting, forest root-people—who look like humans covered with roots—scream when trees are cut and start literally rooting out the illegal loggers. Weird: the women with writhing-branch fingers. Payoff time: the giant, Thanksgiving-day-parade insectoid and the big, talking tree stump. Clunky story with bizarre highlights and great swamp-fog work.

**ENGLISHMAN'S HOME, An** see *Mad Men of Europe*

**El ENIGMA DEL YATE** (Sp) M&C Films 1984 (1983) color/ws 95m. D: Carlos Aured. SP: Luis Murillo. Ph: Jose Antonio del Alamo. Mus: R. Casals. Mkp: Elisa Plana. Ref: TV: VSOM; no Eng.; *Mystery of Yate*. Ecran F 44:36: in release. With Silvia Tortosa, Jose Antonio Ceinos, Jose Maria Blanco, Montserrat Torras.

A midnight skulker on a yacht is shot. His body disappears. Later, two women dump another body overboard. At the end, one woman is left alone with a dead body or two. But are they dead? Three zombies seem to be stalking her. Or is it her imagination? Maybe a conspiracy...? Minor-league shocker.

**ENIGMA ROSSO** see *Trauma* (1978)

**The ENQUIRERS** Barnes 1992 color 100m. SP, D, P, Ed: Rick Barnes. Mus: Marc Barreca. Ref: V 6/8/92: "the jokes aren't funny." With Toni Cross, Brian Finney (Eudie), August Kelley.

"Alien entrepreneur."

**ENTER LIFE** Smithsonian Inst. (Nat'l. Museum of Natural History)/Hubley 1982 anim color 6m. D, P: Faith Hubley. Ph: Nick Vasu. Mus: Elizabeth Swados. Ref: screen.

Some 4,600 million years ago—"life has begun." Jaunty celebration of the beginnings of life on Earth.

**ENTRAILS OF A VIRGIN** (J) 1986 color feature (*Bijo No Harawata*). SP, D: Kazuo Komizu. Ref: TV: VSOM; Eng. titles; ws? Monster! Int'l. 4:18. With Saeko Kitsuki, Megumi Kawashima, Naomi Hagio, Jun Nakahara.

"Body odor is the truth of life." A really weird softcore mishmash of eyeball gore, sex with severed arms, flying phallic things, and a monster that extracts a woman's vitals the hard way. ("I come from the swamp of disgust.") The end result seems to be a monster-baby. Imagine a David Cronenberg version of *The Rape After*.

**ENVIADOS DEL INFIERNO, Los** see *Maleficio II*

**EPIC** Yoram Gross & Epic Prods. 1983 anim 70m. (*Epic: Days of the Dinosaurs* - ad t). Story, SP, D, P: Gross. SP: also John Palmer. Dial: Greg Flynn. Mus: Guy Gross. Anim D: Athol Henry. SpFx Painting: Hanka Bilyk et al. ElecSdFX: Michael Stavrou. SpVocalFX: Keith Scott. SpOptFX: Graham Sharpe. Ref: TV: F. H. E. video. V 2/27/85. no Stanley.

"A long time ago, in the beginning, there was darkness." Monster roll call: the fireball-flinging Spirit of Evil ... the Blue Monster ... the dragon-like, gigantic Earth Spirit ... a tyrannosaurus-type ... a pterodactyl-like creature ... and cave creatures.... Bland animation and script. Typical Age of Discovery line: "It's fire!" Time-lapse background photography, narrator John Huston's voice, and classical music (Borodin et al.) help, but not enough.

**EPICAC** see *Short Stories of Love*

**EPITAPH** City Lights 1987 color c98m. SP, D, P: Joseph Merhi. Ph, Ed, P: Richard Pepin. Mus: John Gonzalez. SpVisFX: Constance J. Damron, Aaron Sims et al. Ref: TV: City Lights HV. no V. McCarty II. no Martin. Hound. With Natasha Pavlova, Delores

Nascar, Jim Williams, Flint Keller, Linda Tucker-Smith, Liz Kane.

Willful, homicidal Martha Fulton (Nascar) stabs a painter (Ed Reynolds) who rejects her advances. Hubbie Forrest (Williams) buries the body. They make love. But the painter, who isn't dead, returns, ghost-like, to frighten daughter Amy (Pavlova) and kill Forrest, before Martha can shoot him dead, once and for all. At the end—in a final predictable turn of the schlock-horror screw— Amy too goes crazy, attacks Mom with a shovel, and makes small talk with the corpse.... Woodenly-acted, determinedly perverse shocker's most desperate bid for attention is the Rat in a Bucket stunt with the psychiatrist (Tucker-Smith).

**EPITHALAMIUM** see *Short Stories of Love*

**EPOUVANTAIL, L'** see *Scarecrow, The*

**EQUALIZER 2000** (U.S.-Fili) Concorde/Leonard Hermes 1987 color 79m. D: Cirio H. Santiago. Story, SP: Frederick Bailey. Story: also Joe Mari Avellana. Mkp: T. Mercader. Ref: TV. V 6/24/87. With Richard Norton, Corinne Wahl, William Steis, Robert Patrick, Bailey, Don Gordon, Vic Diaz.

North Alaska, a "hundred years after the nuclear winter." The world is a "scorched and arid desert," and the Ownership rules. The titular, futuristic rifle is a "formidable piece of iron." ("Maybe this will give us some equality.") The voluptuous-plus Wahl ensures that there's jiggle in the future. But 80% of the movie is stunts and grunts. Best Bad-Guy Line (to the holder of the flame thrower): "Poach 'im!"

**ERCOLE CONTRO MOLOCK** see *Conquest of Mycene*

**ERECTION** (I) Guido Manuli short anim. Ref: SFChron Dtbk 7/10/88: "Frankenstein ... Astronaut ... all rising to the occasion."

**ERECTNOPHOBIA** Beech Video 1991. Ref: vc box. no Adam '92 or '91. With Danielle Rogers, Randy Spears.

Spider woman sucks the life out of victims.

**ERIC'S REVENGE** see *Phantom of the Mall*

**ERIC THE VIKING** (B-Nor.) Orion/Prominent Features-John Goldstone (Terry Glinwood/Erik the Viking Film) 1989 color 103m. (108m.) (*The Saga of Eric the Viking* - orig t). SP, D: Terry Jones. Animatronics Des: Jamie Courtier. MkpDes: Jenny Shircore. OptFX: Peerless Camera. SpFX: (des) Richard Conway; (sup) Peter Hutchinson. Ref: TV: Orion HV. MFB'89:299. V 9/6/89. 10/19/88:304 (ad). 5/2/90:S-84. ad. Sacto Bee 11/1/89. Martin.

Bland epic comedy with scattered funnies and sf-horror-fantasy elements, including a gigantic, fire-breathing sea monster ... Atlantis, or Hy-Brasil, which sinks ... a ship which sails over the edge of the world and into the sky ... and hell (under a grate), which looks like Mt. St. Helens. John Cleese's tres casual executioner is the comic highlight. ("Oh, flay them both alive.")

**ERNEST SCARED STUPID** Touchstone & Touchwood Pacific Partners I (Stacy Williams) 1991 91m. (*Ernest Scared Stiff* - shooting t). Story, D: John Cherry. SP: C. Gale, C. Sams. Ref: V

10/14/91: "Varney ... always a treat." 7/22/91:17. ad: BV. SJose Mercury News 10/11/91: "OK for 12-year-olds." With Jim Varney, Eartha Kitt, Austin Nagler, Jonas Moscartolo (Trantor).

Troll turns kids into voodoo dolls, brings ghouls to life.

**EROTIC DREAMS** CHE & Triangle (Lacudini) 1988 (1986) color 62m. (*Dark Dreams* - orig t). SP, D: R. F. Pope. Idea & Exec P: G. Steiner. SpFxMkp: E. Egawa, F. Gallen. Ref: V 1/17/90:37 (hv): "well-made softcore sex." TV: CHE video (A.S. Samuels). With Robert Miles, Stephanie Goldwin, Ashley St. Jon, Ann Peters.

When a schlemiel buys the Acme Deluxe Ritual Kit—a "seance kit"—he's offered "fifty years of wine, women, and song" in exchange for his soul. Purely functional plot sets up a series of stripteases.

**EROTIC ENCOUNTERS OF THE FOURTH KIND** Marketta 1975 color 80m. (*Erotic Encounter of the Fourth Kind* - ad t. *The Space Organ* (2P) - orig t. aka *Wam Bam, Thank You Space Man* (2P). *Wham-bam-thank You, Spaceman*). SP, D, P: W. A. Levey. Mus: Miles Goodman, David White. Ref: TV: Malibu Video. V 11/5/75: started 9/5. SFExam 6/81. no Stanley. no Hound. no Martin. SWV cat. With Dyanne Thorne, Ann Gaybis, Jay Rasumny, Chet Norris, Maria Arnold.

"Operation Procreation has begun!" Two aliens whose planet's orbit is going to merge with that of its sun in 500 years come to Earth to prepare the latter for habitation. The two use "transponder rays" to beam copulating women aboard, where they complete the act with the aid of phalluses which are where their noses should be. Outcome: baby aliens. Plus: Dracula, on the set of a movie-in-production.... Softcore sf-comedy with a hardcore budget reaches the height of its humor when the aliens return beamed women to the wrong men. Pathetic "adult" dialogue, nonexistent production values.

**EROTIC EVA** see *Black Cobra*

**EROTIC GHOST STORY** (H.K.) Golden Harvest/Diagonal Pictures (Paragon Films) 1990 color c85m. Ref: TV: Pan-Asia Video; no Eng.

In the prologue, beautiful women in the woods turn into drooling skeletons. There follows some pretty racy softcore with the ghost women and their men, including a very strange pineapple-as-sexual-voodoo-doll scene. Near the end, a sorcerer—whose (animated) magic butterfly lures women—transforms into a three-headed ghoul-thing which apparently feeds on women to regain its youthful, human appearance, in scenes which resemble Japanese adult cartoons. The three ghosts—who have begun reverting to fox form—use a voodoo doll to torment the sorcerer, and their protector finally dispatches him.

**EROTIC GHOST STORY II** (H.K.) Diagonal Pictures/Paragon Films 1990 color/ws c100m. FX?: Den Film FX. Ref: TV: Universe Laser & Video; Eng. titles.

"Wutung's wreaking havoc." Less horrific than Part One, Part Two concerns the evil Wutung, whose body has been destroyed, but who successfully "transplants himself into another demonic body called Chiu-sheng." His victims become zombie-like sex slaves. Two fairies are consequently dispatched from heaven "to prevent lust from ruining mankind." Extra-addeds: a "soul-taking hairpin," a flying fireball, a man trapped inside a block of ice, and a SHE-like eternal fire.... Mild, blandly-stylized softcore-sex-fantasy uses bubbles—both soap and underwater air—as a motif for the love-slave scenes. Line worth quoting: "A devil's a devil. Don't get bewitched!"

**EROTIC GHOST STORY III** (H.K.) Golden Harvest/Paragon Films 1991 color/ws 95m. (aka *Tale of Eros*). FX?: Den Film FX. Ref: TV: Tai Seng Video; no Eng. VSOM.

Our hero walks through a wall where he saw a vision of three ghost women. Inside the house, a sort of ghost queen rules, and her cannibalistic bent leads to a bit o'gore. She can breathe a sleep-inducing breath and commands binding vines. Meanwhile, an incredible shrunken man who immolated himself in order to grow to regular size shrinks himself again to enter the queen-ghost's vagina and annoy her. Except for this latter episode, Part III is a routine softcore fantasy. Out-of-nowhere: a laser-like sword.

**EROTIC NIGHTS OF THE LIVING DEAD** (I) 1980 c105m.? (*Le Notte Erotiche dei Morte Viventi*) SP, D, Ph: Joe D'Amato. Mus: Pluto Kennedy. AD: Ennio Michettoni. Mkp: Massimo Camiletti. Ref: TV: Film Superstore video; no Eng.; SP: "Tom Salina." PT 16:17. Hardy/HM index. Ecran F 31:56. 22:48. Shock Xpress Smr'87:15. With Laura Gemser, George Eastman, D. Furnati, or Funari, Mark Shanon.

A slew of "Cat Island" zombies waits for Laura to finish making love to the man in the surf. A stray zombie tears out the throat of a guy with a voodoo charm. A maggoty corpse revives and bites the neck of a morgue man. And The Amazing Leaping Cat heralds a zombie raid. Plus an impromptu castration.... Scrappy semi-porn alternates gory bits, story bits, erotic bits, and close-ups of a black cat. Okay climactic, zombies-everywhere sequence. A shot to the head kills these zombies; the charm stops 'em. Aka *Island of the Zombies* (II). Also, apparently, aka *La Regina degli Zombi*.

The **EROTIC RITES OF FRANKENSTEIN** (F-Sp) Nightmare/CFDF & C. Fenix (Victor de Costa) 1972 color/ws 90m. (2P *Les Experiences Erotiques de Frankenstein. La Maldicion de Frankenstein. La Malediction de Frankenstein*). SP, D: Jesus Franco. Ph: Raoul Artigot. Ref: TV: VSOM; Eng. titles; aka *Curse of Frankenstein*. Hardy/HM. PT 13:12: "ridiculous but imaginative." Glut/TDB. With Howard Vernon, Anne Libert, Dennis Price, Britt Nichols (Mme. Orloff), Alberto Dalbes (Dr. Seward or Soward), Fernando Bilbao, Lina Romay, J. Franco (Morpho).

At Varna Castle, the back-from-the-dead Cagliostro (Vernon)—"Master of the World"—kills Dr. Matthew Frankenstein (Price) and controls the "creature of Frankenstein" (Bilbao) through "magnetic transmission." Meanwhile, Vera Frankenstein uses electric shocks to periodically revive her father and plots revenge. Plus apparent zombies and a woman who may be half-human and half-vampire .... Sloppy, bizarre mixture of famous names and miscellaneous fantastic plot elements.

El **EROTICO Y LOCO TUNEL DEL TIEMPO** (Sp) AJB Films/Exclusivas Molpeceres 1982 color c85m. D: Jose A.

Rodriguez. SP: Ramon Perez-Molpeceres. Ph: Tote Trenas. Mus: Cam Espana. Mkp: Manuel Martin. Ref: TV: vt; no Eng. With Paco Maldonado, Alicia Principe, Elena Alvarez, Rocio Freixas, Paco A. Valdivia.

An amateur inventor's water-heater-like time machine sends him back to ancient Rome (and naked women), Bagdad (and a topless harem), prehistory (and topless cave women), and Egypt (and topless princesses), then forward to the future (and women in bikinis). Episodic, predictable sf-comedy. Women from all eras here seem to be bisexual and averse to wearing clothes.

**ES IST NICHT LEICHT EIN GOTT ZU SEIN** (W. G.-Russ-F-Swiss) Hallelujah Film & Sovinfilm-Dovzhenko Studio & Garance & Mediactuel & BA-Prod. (Angelika Stute) 1989 color 133m. (*Difficile d'etre un Dieu*-F. *Hard To Be a God* - ad t). SP, D, P: Peter Fleischmann. SP: also Jean-Claude Carriere. From the novel *Trudno Byt Bogom* by the Strugatskys. Mus: J. Fritz. SpFX: Yuri Lemeshev. Ref: V 9/27/89. 4/29/87:36, 556. 5/4/88:455. Ecran F 48:10. Dr. Rolf Giesen. With Edward Zentara, Anne Gautier, Hugues Quester, Christine Kaufmann, Werner Herzog, Pierre Clementi.

Future astronauts visit medieval planet Arkanar. "Works fairly well as a straight adventure yarn."(V) Final cut: 119m. (RG)

**ESCALOFRIO** see *Satan's Blood*

**ESCAPE DE LA SECTA SATANICA** (Venez.) 1991 color feature. Ref: TVG: TV-movie. With Abril Mendez.

**ESCAPE FROM CORAL COVE** (H.K.) Xeaco Holding Co./Solarville Co. (D&B Films) 1987 color/ws c86m. (*Taochu Shanhuhai*). Story, SP, D: T. Chang (Zhang Jiazhen). SP: also Yiu Man-Kei. Story, P: Wong Sum. Ph: Tony Fan; (underwater) Wong Sum. Ref: TV: Rainbow Video; Eng. titles. Horacio Higuchi. Fango 107:59. With Iwanbeo, Bee-Lee Tan, Louis Kong, Alex Fu, Elsie Chan.

The surf turns red. Then: "It's Chen-Chen's hand!" A gent with weird eyes (thanks to bright white contact lenses) haunts Coral Cove. Sometimes he appears in monster form; at other times, he looks almost normal and even wears a tie. Stabbed in the stomach, this "rotten, smelly devil" spews out sea water and seaweed. Negligible suspense-horror thriller padded out with footage of vacationing teens. Main gore bit involves a hat rack.

**ESCAPE FROM GALAXY 3** (I) G.K./Film Enterprises 1980 ('86-U.S.) color 89m. (*Giochi Erotici nella Terza Galassia*). D: Ben Norman. SP: John Thomas. Ph: Sandro Mancori. Mus: Don Powell. SpFX: Armando Valcauda. Ref: TV: Prism Ent. video. Horacio Higuchi. Stanley. Morse. no Martin. Hound. With Cheryl Buchanan, James Milton, Don Powell, Auran Cristea, Alex Macedon, Margaret Rose.

Fleeing from the dreaded King of the Night ("We're not returning to base until I have their heads at my feet!"), Princess Belle Star and her companion land on a planet inhabited by primitives. On said planet—which proves to be an idyllic, post-nuclear-holocaust Earth—the two immortals discover a "powerful new dimension": love. Not only does this new power make them feel good, it enhances their "psycho-energetic force," and they use the latter to return and defeat the King of the Night. At the end, the now-mortal lovers return to Earth.

A camp find, this incredible love-in-space saga from the producer of *Starcrash* is blissfully naive. Belle, who wears a starfish on her left breast, catches on first: "We don't have to worry about getting bored," she notes, as the lovestruck couple returns to do battle with the villain king. A song about love's awakening ("The Touch of Love") spills onto the sound track, and red and yellow stars fly by. The King of the Night picks them up on his spaceship telescreen and asks the inevitable question: "What are they doing?" The hero's eye-rays finish him off, and the lovers head back toward Earth. He—after passing through "three galaxies and endless solar systems": "Where is that planet?" She, excitedly: "There it is! There it is!"

**ESCAPE FROM HELL HOLE** (Indon.-J) Rapi Films/P.F.N. & A.O.I. 1983 color c106m. (*Hell Hole* - vt ad t). D: Maman Firmansyah. SP: Pitrajaya Burnama. Mkp: H. Hendrawan. Ref: TV: All American Video (Mogul); Eng. dubbed. no Hound. no Martin. V 10/24/84:305(ad).

Women-in-prison film with torture scenes and gory bits, including a scene in which the prisoner-heroine, a virgin, bites off the top thug's tongue, and a later scene in which she "castrates" herself. ("MG is welcome to my leftovers!") White-slavery melodrama tries too hard to be sleazy, ends up campy. Lots of lewd and lascivious cackling.

**ESCAPE FROM SAFEHAVEN** SVSC Films/Avalon (Steven Mackler) 1989 color 85m. (*Inferno in Safehaven* - ad t. aka *Bloodscape*). SP, D: B. T. Jones, J. McCalmont. Story: Mark Bishop, Ethan Reiff. Mus: Taj. SpMkpFX: James Chai. Ref: V 2/1/89: "impoverished." 10/19/88:185, 236(ad). 5/4/88:145(ad). Martin. Phantom: "derivative dud." With Rick Gianasi, John Wittenbauer, Roy MacArthur, Jessica Dublin, Tere Malson, William Beckwith.

Rebels, marauders, and "Safehaven 186," in a desolate future.

**ESCAPES** Sanders 1986 color 72m. SP, D, P: David Steensland. Ph: Gary Tomsic. Mus: Todd Popple. Ref: Stanley: TV pilot? Nowlan. Maltin '92: "mostly boring." Phantom: "so-dumb-you're-numb level." With Vincent Price, Todd Fulton, Jerry Grishaw, Ken Thorley, John Mitchum.

Five or six stories re flying saucer, phantoms, etc.

**ESCAPES** Prism Ent./Flash Features (Visual Perceptions) 1988 color 100m. (*Night Vision* - alt vt t). SP, D: Michael Krueger. SP: also N. Gallanis, L. Pomeroy. Mus: Bob Drake et al. Ref: V 7/6/88:36(hv): "horror plot device intrudes." 4/15/87:40. 10/21/87:115. Scheuer: *Nightvision*; unoriginal. With Stacy Carson, Shirley Ross, Tony Carpenter.

Satanic videotape turns writer into killer-by-night.

**ESPADANG PATPAT** (Fili) AMS Prods. (Arceo) 1991? color 122m. D: Efren Jarlego. SP: Cesar Cosme. Story: Rollie Arceo. Ph: Amado de Guzman. Mus D: Mon del Rosario. PD: Lamagna, Manansala. VisFxSup: Carlos Lacap. Skeletons: Julio Ulaso Jr. Mkp: Quince. SpFX: Tony Marbella. SdFX: Rodel Capule. VisFX: Cinemagic. Ref: TV: Viva Video; no Eng. With Dolphy,

Panchito, Marissa Delgado, Romy Diaz, Angelique Lazo (demon), Eric Quizon.

A shooting star falls to Earth and dispatches a boy who gives Dolphy a sword. Meanwhile, a demonic femme fatale summons up other beings at her candle-lit castle, shoots fireballs, and possesses a man. At the end, the two main boogeys self-incinerate .... Highlight of long, lax low-comedy-sf-horror-fantasy are the two crudely-stopmo-animated, but funny-creepy skeleton swordsmen.

**ESTIGMA** (I-Sp) Yantra & Balcazar 1981 color 94m. SP, D: Jose Ramon Larraz. Ph: G. Bernardini. Ref: Hardy/HM: *Stigma* - tr t?; "tame direction." With Christian Borromeo, Alexandra Bastedo, Helga Line.

Telekinetic teen (Borromeo) discovers that he is the reincarnation of a homicidal boy.

An **ETERNAL COMBAT** (H.K.) Chun Sing Film 1991 color 93m. D: Cheng Chang Yip. Ref: TV: World Video; Eng. titles. Weisser/ATC. Imagi Smr'95:20. With Zheng Ying Lin, Joey Wang.

"What evil are you?" A demon-eyed warrior on horseback—the "Japanese ghost"—follows the good guy from long ago into the present day, where the two find the heroine reincarnated. A mixture of routine comedy, a grisly suicide sequence, and okay effects—e.g., the Incredible Shrunken Man, the animated ghost-heads which emanate from the villain's wound. Includes the now-cliche scene in which an ancient confronts modern TV (the "magic box").

**ETERNAL EVIL** (Can.) Seymour Borde/Filmline Int'l. & New Century & Telefilm Canada & Global TV (P. Kroonenburg/F.I.) 1987 (1985) color 85m. (*The Blue Man* - orig t). D: George Mihalka. SP: Robert Geoffrion. Mus: M. Dolgay. Mkp: Charles Carter. Prod Exec: Buck Houghton. Opt: Film Docteur. Ref: TV: All American Communications-TV. V 5/4/88: Lightning Video. 5/13/87:4(rated). 7/15/87:11: in release. 8/12/87:46. Morse. Scheuer. Hound. Phantom. With Winston Rekert, Karen Black, John Novak, Andrew Bednarsky, Patty Talbot, Lois Maxwell (Monica Duval), M. Sinelnikoff (William Duval).

"I saw something that I know isn't real." Paul Sharpe (Rekert) finds "total freedom" in the practice of astral projection, while his son Matthew (Bednarsky) draws mysterious pictures of a flying "Blue Man." But Paul's freed spirit seems to be attacking people at random and inducing "weird" heart attacks which ravage their vital organs—it's as if the victim had "swallowed a bomb." Behind it all: a thousand-year-old couple (Maxwell and Sinelnikoff) whose souls "cultivate" a succession of "hosts"—from the point of view of others, it's "spiritual vampirism"; from the couple's viewpoint, rebirth.

A promising cross between *Psychic Killer* and Shirley MacLaine eventually reduces to confused and confusing spirit-possession material, not too clearly related to the earlier mystery/shock elements. Okay touches in photography, dialogue, plot.

**ETERNAL FIST** see *Fist of Steel*

**ETERNITY** Sin City 1990 color 80m. D: Scotty Fox. Ref: Adam '91. With Tracey Adams, Ashlyn Gere, Peter North.

Woman retains youth by taking sexual energy from her partners.

**ETOILE** (I) 1988 color feature. Story,SP,D: Peter Del Monte. Story,SP: also Sandro Petraglia. SP: also Franco Ferrini. Mus: J. Krieper. Ref: Palmerini: "routine paranormal horror film about the reincarnation of a ballerina." With Gary McCleery, L. Terzieff, M. Marozzi, Jennifer Connelly.

**ETRANGER, TIME ALIEN** (J) 1985 ('95-U.S.) anim color 89m. (aka *Etranger: The Hour of the Stranger. Go Shogun: The Time Etranger* - U.S.). D: Kunihiko Yuyama. SP: Takeshi Shudo, based on the "Goshogun" TV series. Ref: TV: Animage Video; Eng. titles. Anime Opus '89. J Anim Prgm Guide. Wonderful World of Comics 4/88. Japan Video: aka *Time Stranger*. vc box. Voice: Fumi Koyama (Remy).

Remy Shimada—forty years ago a member of the Goshogun space team—pits her "will to live" against medical probabilities: Complications from injuries sustained in a car accident leave her seemingly unconscious and with only two days to live. Meanwhile, her "Owl Creek Bridge" imagination sees Death as a town of red-eyed, shadowy, unstoppable strangers ("They aren't human") ... as an annoyingly insistent little girl who tells her she is about to die ... as (in a horrific sequence) a wolf mauling her in bed ... and, ultimately—in the town's clock-and-stairway-crammed citadel—as an old woman who transforms into a gigantic wolf. As a nightmare cop tells her, "There's no outside to this city."

This inside-the-head version of *Isle of the Dead* finds heroism in Remy's tenacity, and humor in the tenacity of the town hordes. ("They sure are persistent.") The movie's appeal lies in this double view, at once dead-serious and light-hearted. The emissaries of Death just won't quit; neither will Remy and the rest of the Goshogun team, who reunite, in her dreams, as hardy adventurers, and, in her hospital room, as concerned onlookers. As the latter, they can do nothing; as agents of her imagination, they fight like hell. Their presence at her beside at first seems to give the lie to her recollections of herself as always alone. On another level, her solitary fight for life confirms her feelings: She has friends, and yet she's alone. It's not the Goshogun team which triumphs, but her imagination, her will to live.

**EVA NERA** see *Black Cobra*

**EVE OF DESTRUCTION** Orion/Nelson Ent./Interscope Communications (David Madden/Nelson Films) 1991 color 98m. SP, D: Duncan Gibbins. SP: also Yale Udoff. Mus: Philippe Sarde. VisFX Sup: Dale Fay. Prosth & SpMkpFX: Art & Magic, R. C. Biggs. SpFxCoord: Steve Galich. GraphicFX: Light & Motion; Robert Ryan. Ref: TV. V 1/21/91. ad. SFChron 1/19/91. With Gregory Hines, Renée Soutendijk (Dr. Eve Simmons/Eve VIII), Michael Greene, John M. Jackson, Kevin McCarthy.

"She's one of my robots!" "This country's best-kept secret," Eve III, a "more human than machine" android, is "on the loose." Powered by tiny electric currents and programmed with the thoughts and feelings of its designer, Dr. Eve Simmons, Eve VIII—which comes with no "Off" switch—"goes nuclear".... Tortuous variation on *Impulse*. ("She's doing things I might think about doing, but would never dare to do....") Anxious filmmakers pad their premise with the superfluous "excitement" of bickering

characters, explosions, and 24-hours-to-doomsday deadlines. Film makes its little bit of cinematic hay with passable ironic images like the shot of the jauntily stepping, miniskirted Eve VIII with her mini-machine-gun in the foreground and a panorama of death and the titular destruction in the background.

**An EVENING ALONE** MGM 1938 9m. D: Roy Rowland. SP: Robert Lees, Fred Rinaldo. Ref: TV. Maltin/SSS.

Home alone, Robert Benchley picks up a copy of "The Clutching Horror," but finds he can't "cope with a horror story" ("Something sinister and slimy was creeping up behind him")—he looks up to see a "ghost" walking down a staircase.... Latter is a nifty little effect—transparent skulker and shadow disappear just as mysteriously as they appeared. Extra added attraction: a pre-*Cat People,* semi-"bus" with a cuckoo clock. Pleasant drollery.

**An EVENING WITH KITTEN** Kitten and Kompany 1983 color c30m. SP, D, P, Ed: Les Barnum. SP: also Kathy Clark, M.T. Paige. Ref: TV: Rhino HV. Hound. With Kitten Natividad, Kerry Angerman, Kathy Clark, John Baron, Gerald Frank.

Kitten drinks Incredible Bulk, Formula 2, and becomes incredibly large-chested. Later, a fan "sees" her as Miss Milky Way, a giant in the Miss Galactica Beauty Contest on Earth, where she causes considerable damage. Still later, Kitten reads "The Annotated Dracula" and encounters the bearded count. Silly, sometimes cute, innocuous pantomimes.

**EVIL ALTAR** Ryan Rao/Om (Miller-Briggs) 1989 (1988) color 87m. D: Jim Winburn. SP: Friedman, Rose, Geilfuss. Ref: V 7/26/89: "with few new wrinkles." Nowlan. V 9/23/87: 8/24 start. PT 5:37. With William Smith, Pepper Martin, Robert Z'Dar, Theresa Cooney.

Devil's agent seeks "103 young souls."

**The EVIL BELOW** (So. African) Gibraltar Releasing/Legend Films (Barrie Saint Clair) 1989 color 92m. D: J. -C. Dubois. SP: Art Payne. Mkp: Laura Woods. Opt: Irene. Ref: TV: Raedon HV. V 8/2/89. Hound. Scheuer: '87. With Wayne Crawford, June Chadwick, Sheri Able, Ted Le Platt (Adrian Barlow), Graham Clarke.

"He knows things you can't know!" Two people (Crawford, Chadwick) searching for the 17th-century sailing ship, *El Diablo*—a cursed, "mythical ship"—in the Straits of San Sebastian encounter tales of heretic priests, Lucifer, and the "devil incarnate." Early tipoff that Adrian Barlow may be the latter: He easily lifts hero Max up off the floor—a sure sign in horror movies since *Halloween* that you're dealing with a monster-type. Later tipoff that Adrian is about 300 years old: His ancestor Robert Barlow's grave is empty. Final tipoff: He can walk about on the sea bottom without diving equipment.... Thin, hackneyed, at best pleasantly familiar.

**EVIL BLACK MAGIC** (H.K.) Hong Kong Films 1990? color/ws c100m. Anim?: Animation Shop. Ref: TV: World Video; Eng. titles.

Ingredients in this bland softcore-sex-horror-comedy: a sorcerer, who revives Fa La Ting from the dead and (apparently in order to control her) drives a spike into the top of her head ... a "little ghost" woman who revives some dead dwarfs ... a ghost that sticks a hand into a creep's abdomen and kills him ... the Love Curse, which lasts only three months ... the somewhat more potent Crazy-Love Curse ... and an apparent vampire woman in a shower.

**EVIL CAT** (H.K.) Cinema City/Dennis Yu 1986 color c94m. (*Devil Cat* - ad t. aka *The Cat*). D, Co-P: Yu. SP: Wong Ching. Ph: Arthur Wong. Mus: Law Wing Fa. AD: Sita Yeung. SpOptFX: John Ting, Jackie Tang. Ref: TV: Rainbow Video; Eng. titles. NST! 4:22-23, 7. Fango 107:59. TVG. Ecran F 79:74. With Lau Kar Leung, Tang Lai Ying, Mark Cheng, Wong Ching, Stuart Ong.

A cat creature with nine lives reappears every fifty years, drinks blood in order to reincarnate, possesses (in succession) people such as businessman Mr. Fan, Tina, heroine Siu Chuen, and finally a police inspector.... Yu's light touch with actors distinguishes this efficient but routine horror-fantasy. The possessed bound about like cats and strike cat poses, while feline snarls dominate the sound track. Out-of-Left-Field-Images Dept.: 1) lightning at one point forming a giant cat-face and, 2) the snarling Mr. Fan—in business suit—standing in a fish pond, holding a carp in his mouth.

**EVIL CLUTCH** (I) Troma/Fomar Film & Centro Sperimentale (Agnese Fontana) 1988 color 88m. (*Clutch—Presa Tenace*). SP, D, SupEd: Andreas Marfori. Dial: Dinah Rogers. Ph: Marco Isoli. Mus: A. M. Vitali. AD: G. Albertini. SpMkpFX: Biagi, Forti, Mondani, Calcinari. SpMechFX: Studio Arte Fare, G. Albertini. OptFX: Cinecitta. Ref: TV: Eng.-dubbed. TVG. V/Cannes '89:73 (ad). 5/2/90:S-64. Martin. PT 12:47. Fango 118:34-5. MV: aka *Horror Queen*. Palmerini: aka *Il Bosco* 1. With C. C. Tassoni, D. Ribon, Elena Cantarone (Arva, demon), L. Crovato, Stefano Molinari (Fango).

The "dangerous stuff" here includes a woman with fangs, popeyes, and a very evil, gross, clutching phallic thing ... a tree with tentacles ... a motley zombie ... an unlikely fishhook-in-cheek scene ... a chainsaw of righteousness ... a severed head ... and a yuckily weird cuckoo clock.... Comically enthusiastic gore punctuates long nothing-happening scenes. Film borrows the gore and the long tracking shots from the *Evil Dead* movies, adds a drool/vomit motif. Whew!

**EVIL COME, EVIL GO** Chinn-Adrian Prods. 1972 color 72m. SP, D: Walt Davis. Ph: M.S. Conde. Mus: Dan Goodman. Ref: TV: SWV. Hound. Newman: "female psycho killer." no Scheuer. no Phantom. With Cleo O'Hara, Sandra Henderson, Jane Louise, Rick Cassidy, John Holmes.

"You will help me rid this world of pleasurable sex." The hymn-singing Sara Jane—founder of the Sacred Order of the Sisters of Complete Subjugation—leaves her lovers dead and bloody in bed, and "God is love not sex" lipstick messages on hotel mirrors. Tawdry variation on *Night of the Hunter* is at least more interesting than the official remake. Though bad acting fails to blunt the intermittent satirical edge, the standard, extended softcore sex scenes pretty much wreck the movie. Only lines like "There's lots of sin in San Francisco" survive.

**EVIL COUNTESS** see *Comtesse Perverse, La*

**EVIL DEAD II** Rosebud Releasing/Renaissance Pictures (Robert G. Tapert/Bruce Campbell) 1987 color 83m. (*Evil Dead 2: Dead by Dawn* - ad t). SP, D: Sam Raimi. SP: also Scott Spiegel. Mus: Joseph Lo Duca. SpVisFX: Doug Beswick Prods. The Dance: (stopmo) Beswick; (fx ph sup) Jim Aupperle; (transformations) Rick Catizone, Anivision; (sculptor) Steve Wang; (min) James Belohobek; (min sp fx) Acme SpFX; (anim) Tom Sullivan. SpMkp: Mark Shostrum. SpFX: Spectacular FX Int'l. Ref: screen. TV: Vestron Video. MFB'87:173-4. V 3/18/87. SFExam 5/29/87. Scheuer. Maltin '92. Phantom. Morse. Martin. Hound. With Campbell, Sarah Berry, Dan Hicks, Kassie Wesley, Theodore Raimi (Possessed Henrietta), John Peaks (Prof. Knowby), Snowy Winters (dancer).

"There's something out there." The playing of a tape recording of the "demon resurrection passages" from the "Book of the Dead"—missing since 1300 A.D.—creates a "rift in time and space" and unleashes a "dark spirit," a snake-necked thing, a flying (stopmo) monster, and a "witch in the cellar" of the remote Knowby cabin. ("We are the things that were and shall be again!") Further recitations (a)make the main demon flesh, then (b) send it (and Campbell's Ash) back to the year 1300.... The best-sustained stretch of unchained comic morbidity: simply Ash and dozens of props, including a laughing table lamp, "tittering" books, a chortling mounted deer head, etc. Hallucination and outright fantasy get scrambled in this inventive sequence—which rings an ironic change on those cartoons which feature laughing objects (e.g., *Betty Boop and Little Jimmy*)—but the net effect is one of the Marx Brothers on the loose in The Big Horror Store. Another high point: the living-dead-Linda ballet, an unusual (perhaps unique) exercise in unearthly comic lyricism, capped by the witty bit in which Linda's body pirouettes, while her head remains in place. ("Dance with me!") Third hilarious peak: the evil hand that snickers—Ash's renegade hand indulges in gratuitous *Gremlin*-ish gibberish as it drags his body towards a convenient cleaver. Also noteworthy: the climactic siege of living trees—though the earlier, preparatory, Did-those-treetops-just-move-strangely? shots are, in a way, more imaginative. If the torrents-of-blood scenes seem derivative (*The Shining, Amityville*), almost every other wild inspiration here comes under the heading Never Before Seen, Not To Be Repeated, though only the movie's put-on air holds it together, in-between inspirations.

Sequel: *Army of Darkness*. Sequel to *Evil Dead, The* (III).

**EVIL DEAD TRAP** (J) 1991 color/ws feature (*Shiryo No Wana*). D: Seishu Ikeda. Ref: TV: VSOM; Eng. titles; Formation of a Dead Ghost - tr t. trailer: *Chien Andalou* eye trick. PT 20:14. Weisser/JC: 1988. With Miyuki Ono, Buno Souki.

"People are getting killed here." Nami, a TV reporter, discovers gruesomeness at an abandoned military base. ("We lived this way—two of us—for a very long time.") At the end, she gives "birth" to a hideous little creature. ("Mama!") Excruciating imitation of Western gore vehicles.

**EVIL DEAD TRAP 2** VSOM 1991 color/ws 97m. (*Shiryo No Wana 2*). D: Isou Hashimoto. SP, P: Seishu Ikeda. Ref: TV: vt; Eng. titles; aka *Hideki: Evil Dead Trap 2*. VSOM. Weisser/JC. With Youko Nakagima.

"I won't be intimidated by a phantom." A gory, bizarre, possibly sick, definitely offputting tale of magic, disembowelment, "scary stories" re a building, and the Shinki god. The editor must have died.

## EVIL DEAD TRAP 3: MUTILATION FOR A TENDER LOVE
(J) VSOM 1993 color/ws 100m. D: Seishu Toshiharu Ikeda. SP: Takashi Ishii. Ref: TV: VSOM; Eng. titles. With Shiro Sano, Megumi Yokoyama.

"I had to sacrifice girls for my goddess." In the police's nearly-unsolvable "dismembered-body case," stashes of bodies and body parts are found everywhere—a woman's mutilated body here, a "headless torso" there. Thoroughly routine shocker finally comes through—the finale features a masked madwoman with an axe, off-angle shots, macabrely-thronging sea gulls, and mayhem with huge rumbling wall fans. Funniest title: "Chief! We just got a report of body parts near the cliff."

## EVIL EYE, The see *Manhattan Baby*

## EVIL JUDGMENT
(Can.) Taurus 7 & CFDC & Famous Players & ABP 1984 color c92m. SP, D, Co-P: Claudio Castravelli. SP: also Victor Montesano. Ph: Roger Racine, Mario Romanini. Mus: Corky Laing. SpFxMkp: Michelle Burke, Catherine Cossault. Ref: TV: Media Home Ent. video. V 10/14/91:A-90(ad). 2/24/92:69(ad). Morse. Hound. Ecran F 41:70. V 2/25/91:A-116. With Pamela Collyer, Jack Langedyk, Suzanne De Laurentis, Nanette Workman, Walter Massey.

A man who "died twice" proves to be the madman who slashes up hookers and cops, severs a maid's hand, and in general leaves his victims "cut to pieces".... Slasher film is almost comical in its determined sleaziness. Only plus: the ingenious solution to the mystery.

## EVIL LAUGH
Cinevest/Wildfire 1988 color 87m. SP, D, P: Dominick Brascia. SP, P: Steven Baio. Mus: D. Shapiro. SpMkpFX: David Cohen. Ref: V 11/23/88: "genre cliches." 5/6/87:204(ad). Martin. Nowlan. With S. Baio, Kim McKamy, Tony Griffin, Jerold Pearson.

Masked killer, "unwitting cannibalism," gore. (V)

## EVIL SABBATH see *Visione del Sabba*

## EVIL SPAWN
American-Independent/Camp (Anthony Brewster & Frank Bresee) 1987 color 73m. (*Alive by Night. Deadly Sting* - early ts. *Wasp* - orig t). SP, D: Kenneth J. Hall. Mus: Paul Natzke. Creature Des: Ralph Miller III. SpMkpFX: Cleve Hall; (transformation) Thom Floutz; (addl) John Criswell, Joe Dolinich. SpFX: Dan Bordona, Christopher Ray. Creature SdFX: John Vulich. Sp Thanks: John Buechler et al. Prod Asst: Donald Farmer. Ref: TV: Camp Video. V 10/7/87. PT 4:7. 5:7. With Bobbie Bresee (Lynn Roman), Drew Godderis, John Terrence, Dawn Wildsmith aka Donna Shock (Evelyn Avery), John Carradine (Dr. Zeitman), Gary J. Levinson, Forrest J Ackerman.

No, not Warren. The first reaction of movie actress Lynn Roman ("victim of a horrible scientific experiment") to the self-injection of an anti-aging formula is to vomit on the camera. She then turns into a heavy-duty, "dangerously unbalanced" She Creature-like monster that leaves her victims horribly bloated. Behind it all apparently: an "Odyssey" Venus probe which brought back alien microbes, in conjunction with Dr. Zeitman's backfired cellular

regeneration experiments.... Perfunctory combo skin-flick/makeup-effects vehicle. No logic, consistency, or coordination of plot elements. Just another monster—Fifties-style, though, rather than *Alien*-style.

Reworked as *Alien within, The.*

## EVIL SPIRITS
Prism Ent./Grand Am (Sidney Niekerk) 1991 (1990) color 95m. D, Ph: Gary Graver. SP: Mikel Angel. Mus: D. Sciaqua. AD: Richard Dearborn. SpFX: Scott Coulter. Processed FX: S. Meisel. Mkp: Elaine Offers. TV: Prism Ent. video. Stanley. V 10/14/91: "creepy atmosphere." 4/18/90:10. 4/22/91:50 (rated). With Karen Black, Arte Johnson, Virginia Mayo, Michael Berryman, Martine Beswicke, Bert Remsen, Yvette Vickers, Debra Lamb, Robert Quarry, Anthony Eisley, Hoke Howell.

"The whole neighborhood is reeking with something rotten!" Ingredients here include a murder victim who speaks through a supposedly "phony baloney medium" ... a boardinghouse owner whose dead husband "talks" to her ... a guy chained in the house's cellar ... hatchet gore ... and telegraphed icepick gore .... Wooden, minimal-interest low-budgeter is worth watching only for the good ol' names in the cast. Script seems partly inspired by a real Sacramento multiple-murder case.

## EVIL SPIRITS IN THE HOUSE
Postal Prods. 1990 color 114m. D: Steve Postal. Ref: Martin: shot-on-tape; "incompetent." no Stanley. With Larry Wallace, Jennifer Filkins, Angela Shepard, Dawn Chappel.

Terror in a remote cabin.

## EVIL TOONS
Prism/American-Independent (Victoria Till/Ray) 1991 (1990) color 86m. SP, D: Fred Olen Ray (aka "S. Scott"). Ph: Gary Graver. Mus: C. Cirino. AD: T. Tunney. Anim: Charles Balun;(p) Streamline;(d) Mark Heller. SpMkpFX: Jose Castro. SpFxAnim & Titles: Bret Mixon. Ref: TV. TVG. PT 12:48, 50. V 10/15/90:22: shooting. 10/28/91:16 (rated). With Suzanne Ager, Dick Miller, Monique Gabrielle, David Carradine (Gideon Fisk), Madison Stone, Stacey Nix, Michelle Bauer, Barbara Dare, Arte Johnson.

In a house with a history of "mayhem and madness," the taste of blood allows a cartoon-monster from an ancient book to take human form. The monster then possesses a young woman in order to gather souls for satan.... Limp live action footage, a bit of animation, cartoon sound effects, and a failed hand-on-shoulder shock. At one point, Miller (as Burt) watches himself on TV in *Bucket of Blood*. With Carradine as a cursed warlock.

## EVIL TOUCH, The see *Don't Look in the Attic*

## EVIL TOWN
Mars 1985 color 82m. D: Edward Collins, P. S. Traynor, Larry Spiegel; Mardi Rustam. SP: Spiegel, Richard Benson. Story: Royce Applegate. Mus: Michael Linn. Mkp: Barbara Wolfe. Opt: Hollywood. Ref: Trans World video. V 12/2/87. Morse. Martin. Hound. With James Keach, Michele Marsh, Doria Cook, Robert Walker, Dean Jagger, Dabbs Greer, E. J. Andre, Keith Hefner, Greg Finley, Lurene Tuttle, Regis Toomey, Hope Summer, Linda Weismeier.

Smalltown, pop. 666. The 96-year-old (doesn't look it) Dr. Schaeffer (Jagger) is one of several scientists around the world who have discovered that secretion of an "x" factor chemical in the pituitary aids in prolonging life. Unfortunately, a large "donor pool' is required, and the showcase horror scenes take place in a compound housing the dozens of mindless, thrashing donors of pituitary fluid.... Another apple-pie-and-buttermilk-donut community harboring horrible secrets. In Smalltown, the young are sacrificed to the old. (Dr. Schaeffer: "Why the hell shouldn't I kill a few kids to get what I want?") The script establishes that the doctor's methods are *wrong* and that he is *warped*. It also spends much time securing potential *victims* for him. This is your basic the-sinister-lurking-beneath-the-smiling cliche.

**EVIL WITHIN, The** see *Baby Blood*

**EVOLVER** Trimark & Blue Rider (Geoffray-Josten-Seggerman) 1994 color c90m. SP, D: Mark Rosman. Ph: J. Haitkin. Mus: C. Tyng. PD: Ken Aichele. Robotics: Steve Johnson;(mech des) Eric Fiedler. Evolver Des: Jim Salvati. Digital FX: Digital Magic;(anim des) John Musumeci. MechFX: Kevin McCarthy, Players SpFX. VisFx:(coord) Rob Vaupel; Wildfire. SpLaser: Laser Media. Ref: TV: Vidmark video. With Ethan Randall, Cassidy Rae, Cindy Pickett, Nassira Nicola, John De Lancie, Paul Dooley; W.H. Macy (voice of Evolver).

"Evolver hates to lose." Cyber-Tronix's "next evolution in entertainment": the self-activating Evolver robot, which gets smarter at each of its four levels of interactive play. Problem: its S.W.O.R.D. program (Strategic War Oriented Robot Device), a leftover, "destroy enemy" military program with real missiles and lasers.... Unbelievable *Class of 1999* imitation. Good title, terrible movie. Chilling words from the level-four Evolver: "Bonus Round."

**The EWOK ADVENTURE** ABC-TV/Lucasfilm & Korty Films 1984 color 92m. (aka *The Ewok Adventure: Caravan of Courage*). D, Ph: John Korty. Tel: Bob Carrau. Story, Exec P: George Lucas. Ewok language: Marie Mine-Rutka. Mus: Peter Bernstein. PD: Joe Johnston. SpVisFX: IL&M; (sup) Michael Pangrazio. Creatures: Phil Tippett, Jon Berg. Narr: Burl Ives. Ref: TV. TVG. V 11/28/84. Disney Channel. With Eric Walker, Aubree Miller, Warwick Davis, Dan Frishman, Fionnula Flanagan, Guy Boyd, Debbie Carrington, Tony Cox, Kevin Thompson.

"In an Ewok village on the moon of Endor" (first seen in *Return of the Jedi*), two children (Walker and Miller) from a crashed Star Cruiser find friends who will later help them combat a huge, clawed, long-snouted beast then, at the end, the "master of the beast," the "dreaded giant Gorax" of the "forbidden fortress." Plus: a snake-like creature in a hollow tree, unimposing (if huge) spider-marionettes, and a stream with an imprisoning surface.

Lucas and company get a lot of mileage here out of button eyes, furry noses, and sounds like "Wok!" and "Esh!", which in Ewokese can indicate anything from alarm to curiosity to quiet exasperation. Highlights of adorableness include one Ewok using its paw to simulate a flying Star cruiser, many Ewoks slapping at flitting firefly-like pixies, and one lost pixie cavorting crazily in the boy's hand. The movie plays, in the best light, like a child's dream-vision of a boy and girl playing in a giant backyard full of living, semi-clothed Teddy bears; in the worst, like a standard fantasy-adventure movie.

**EWOKS: THE BATTLE FOR ENDOR** ABC-TV/Lucasfilm 1985 color 90m. Tel, D: Ken & Jim Wheat. Story, Exec P: George Lucas. Mus: Peter Bernstein. PD: Joe Johnston, Harley Jessup. VisFX: IL&M; (sup) M. McAlister; (creature des) Jon Berg; (stopmo sup) Phil Tippett; (opt ph sup) David Berry; (creature sup) Elaine Baker; (anim sup) Bruce Walters; VCE. Ref: TV. TVG. V 12/4/85:75. With Wilford Brimley, Niki Botholo, Sian Phillips, Carel Struycken, Daniel Frishman, Tony Cox, Paul Gleason, Johnny Weissmuller Jr.

Ingredients in this reworking of *The Ewok Adventure* and offshoot of *Return of the Jedi/Star Wars* include The Power; reptilian creatures headed by Terak (Struycken); a giant, impressively-taloned bird; a crashed Star Cruiser, and a witch who temporarily transforms into a beautiful maiden.... The above ingredients sort out into two parts action, one part general cuteness, and one part good-for-children angles. Routine capture-escape-chase action features stunning stop-motion work with dinosaur-like mounts, plus a new charmer, the fast-motion Teek (Botholo).

**EXCUSE ME, PLEASE!** (H.K.) Golden Sun Light Prod. Co. 1989? color/ws c95m. D: Xung Xe-Ee? Ref: TV: World Video; no Eng. Y.K. Ho. NST! 4:22.

Several men rape a young woman who can raise the dead in the local cemetery. She cuts her arm, blood drips onto a corpse which "breathes" into her mouth, and she lies down in the coffin under the corpse. This little ritual enables her to appear out of nowhere, ghost-like, and drive one of the rapists to strangle his wife. Another thug burns to death. At the end, a horde of ghosts assails the last thug.... Questionable horror-comedy-drama re rape and revenge has scattered funny scenes—e.g., a ghost removing his ear to "bug" a conversation. The appearance of the woman's ghostly image in the just-closed mirror recalls *Repulsion*.

**EXECUTIONERS, The** see *Heroic Trio II*

**O EXORCISMO NEGRO** (Braz) Cinedistri (Anibal Massaini Neto) 1974('94-U.S.) b&w 100m. (*O Tirador de Demonios* - orig t). SP, D: Jose Mojica Marins. SP: also Adriano Stuart, Rubens Francisco Luchetti or Lucchetti. Ph: A. Meliande. AD: Campelo Neto. Mkp: Flavio Torres. SdFX: Geraldo Jose. Ref: Monster! Int'l. 3:28-9. TV: SWV; *The Bloody Exorcism of Coffin Joe*; Eng. titles. Hardy/HM; *The Black Exorcism* - tr t. With Marins (Ze do Caixao), Jofre Soares, Walter Stuart, Georgia Gomide, Adriano Stuart.

Sequel to *Strange World of Ze Do Caixao* concerns the filmmaker himself: Before beginning his next project, The Demon Exorcist, Jose Mojica Marins takes a Christmas holiday with friends and finds, first, Grandpa (Soares) possessed. Next up: Carlos (Marcelo Picchi). Then: Luciana (Alciano Mazzeo). Finally, little Betinha (Merisol Marins) seems possessed by the spirit of Marins' fictional creation, Ze do Caixao .... Episodic, isn't it? Weak-tea thrills and half-hearted gore. The only kicky bit: Marins vs. Ze (or Marins vs. Marins), at the end, when the director takes on the latter, here the head Satanist. Plus a scene from a film-in-progress re a couple who turn into monsters.

Note: Sources disagree as to whether the film was shot in color. The SWV tape is either tinted (red) or in disintegrating Eastmancolor.

The **EXORCIST III** Fox/Morgan Creek (Carter DeHaven) 1990 color 110m. (*The Exorcist: 1990* - orig t). SP, D: William Peter Blatty, from his novel *Legion*. Mus: Barry DeVorzon. SpFxMkp: Greg Cannom. VisFxSup: Abe Milrad. SpVisFX: Dream Quest Images; (sup) Mat Beck; (anim sup) Jeff Burks; (mech fx) Michael Landi. SpFX: (coord) Bill Purcell; (d) Norman Reynolds. SdFX: Ezra Dweck. Ref: TV. MFB'90:352-3. V 8/22/90. SFChron Dtbk 9/30/90. S Union 8/23/90. Sacto Bee 8/21/90. ad. V 8/30/89:20. With George C. Scott, Ed Flanders, Brad Dourif, Jason Miller, Nicol Williamson, Scott Wilson, Nancy Fish, Don Gordon, Barbara Baxley, Zohra Lampert, Harry Carey Jr., C. Everett Koop, Patrick Ewing (Angel of Death).

"For we are many." The electrocuted Gemini Killer appears to be behind a series of calculatedly gruesome murders. One victim's body is stuffed with rosaries; the blood of another victim is methodically collected in containers, and a third victim—paralyzed and asphyxiating—is forced to endure his own slow death. The gory trail leads Lt. Kinderman (Scott) to Patient X (Miller), a madman in solitary who can howl demonically ("I do that rather well, don't you think?") and who initially resembles the late Father Karras, then the Gemini Killer. Apparently, the demon in the latter took refuge in the body of the former, the better to gain revenge on Karras: The "saintly priest" must now watch the killer's every atrocity, as "X" uses "old friends," or the bodies of same, to get out of his cell and do his dirty work.

*Exorcist III* plays at times like a mystery thriller whose plot might be leading to a Psychic Killer, and in fact the film boils down to the ultimate locked-room mystery. Dourif's sarcastic possessed killer—the movie's showpiece—rates Blatty's neatest turns of phrase, like "in the dying mode," while Scott—as earnest as Blatty at heart—is for the most part a victim of the latter's basic seriousness of purpose. Not that there isn't some fun to be had in the special-effects ceiling work of some of the other actors, and in the story's mystery angles. Apparently, deep irony is intended with the script's use of the *It's a Wonderful Life* motif.

See also: *Repossessed. Seytan.*

**EXORCIST MASTER** (H.K.) Golden Leaf Film 1992 color/ws 91m. Ref: TV: Network Kingdom Video; Eng. titles. VSOM.

"I'm the great Ghostbuster." Generally silly horror-comedy features a troupe of apparently fake hopping vampires ... a real non-hopping, neck-biting vampire or two ("He's afraid of garlic!") ... a floating ghost who was raped before she died ... neon-cross weapons ... and an impalement-by-cross out of *The Omen*.

**EXPERIENCES EROTIQUES DE FRANKENSTEIN, Les** see *Erotic Rites of Frankenstein, The*

**EXPLORER WOMAN RAY** (J) CPM/Toshiba Video/T. Okazaki & AIC & Animate Film (Inomata-Kakita-Kato) 1989 ('93-U.S.) anim color 60m. D: (1) H. Hayashi; (2) M. Sato, H. Okamoto. From T. Okazaki's comic. SP: M. Sekijima. Ph: (1) K. Konishi; (2) A. Takahashi. Mus: N. Yamanaka. AD: J. Higashi. SdFX: Anime Sd. Ref: TV: U.S. Manga Corps video; Eng. titles; OAV. Animag 6:5.

1) "The Ord god was a monster who ate the light of the sun." The "ancient Ords" of Central America got their mystic, typhoon-pro-

ducing power from light. ("You should never have awakened their power.") Flat adventure-fantasy.

2) Modern machinery revives an ancient light power. ("The ruins have been reborn!") A jade amulet reverses the process. Routine action-adventure-fantasy. The villain is named Reig Vader.

**EXPLORERS** Para/Edward S. Feldman & IL&M 1985 color 106m. D: Joe Dante. SP: Eric Luke. Ph: John Hora. Mus: Jerry Goldsmith. VisFX: IL&M; (sup) Bruce Nicholson; (anim sup) Bruce Walter; ("Starkiller") LA FX Group. SpMkpFx/Aliens: Rob Bottin Prods.; (mech fx sup) Ed Felix. SpFxCoord: Robert MacDonald Sr. SdFX: Mark Mangini. SpVocalFX: Belinda Balaski, Jane Kean et al. Ref: TV. MFB'87:16-17. V 7/10/85. SFChron 7/12/85. With Ethan Hawke, River Phoenix, Jason Presson, Amanda Peterson, Dick Miller, Brooke Bundy.

"Somebody's callin' us." Three Charles M. Jones High School students (Hawke, Phoenix, and Presson) build their own bathysphere-like spacecraft, the Thunder Road, envelope it in an alien-inspired force field, and voyage to meet aliens who have been exposed to Earth television (though apparently not much PBS), including the show with the "little hairy kid" (Lassie). The alien father shows up and spoils the fun, but later the boys and Lori (Peterson) fly together in dreams "sent" by their alien friends.

Inventive, overlong, sweetly mystical science-fantasy. The links which *Explorers* makes between dreams and waking life and between pop culture and extraterrestrial intervention are alternately glib and inspired. Three sequences especially—the climactic dream-flying, the scene in which the boys watch their ship sink, and the scene in which poor Charlie Drake (Miller) (who has been having the same alien-programmed dream that the boys have been having) watches the ship ascend without him—suggest much re growing up, emotional loss and gain, and like matters. If the movie seems at times to be simply parading the pop artifacts of a generation, it seems at others to have a more complicated agenda. The special video edition remedies somewhat a certain diffuseness in the theatrical version, and makes clear cosmic dreamer Ben's (Hawke) comic-didactic reconciliation with everyday life on Earth. Good Wonders of Boyhood score.

**EXPOSED TO DANGER** (H.K.) 198-? color feature. D: Chia Yung. Ref: NST! 4:22.

Mad killer and "lots of gore and maggot infested bodies."

**EXQUISITE CADAVER** see *Crueles, Las*

**EXTERMINADOR NOCTURNO, El** see *Chiquidracula*

**EXTRA-TERRESTRIAL INTELLIGENCE** or **EXTRA TERRESTRIAL VISITORS** see *Unearthling, The*

**EXTRACTS FROM CAPTAIN STORMFIELD'S DIARY** (by M. Twain) see *Adventures of Mark Twain, The*

Un **EXTRANO EN LA CASA** (Mex-Venez) Zacarias 1967 color c80m. SP, D: Miguel Zacarias. Story: Alfredo Zacarias. Ph: Rosalio Solano. Mus: Manuel Esperon. AD: J. T. Torija. Mkp: Elda Loza. Ref: TV: Million Dollar Video; little Eng.; *A Stranger* *in the House* - tr t. no Hardy/HM. no Lee. With Evita, Joselo, Roy Jenson, Rosenda Monteros, Ofelia Montesco, Rene Cardona, Stillman Segar.

A "madman that kills women with a razor blade" slashes off the head of a little girl's bride-doll, then eyes the girl's throat and automatically pulls out the razor again. He slashes the throat of the woman of the house and, in true *Psycho* hygiene tradition, washes his razor in the bathroom sink. Aftershocks include the girl's discovering her beheaded doll and, later, the woman's body. At the end, the killer runs into a scythe blade and cuts his own throat.... Perfunctory suspense-horror also recalls William Castle's *I Saw What You Did* and (with the doll's "execution") Bunuel's *Criminal Life of Archibaldo de la Cruz.* Stock "excitement" musical motifs.

**El EXTRANO HIJO DEL SHERIFF** (Mex) Azteca Films/Artistas Y Tecnicos & Estudios America & Conacite Dos 1984 (1982) color c92m. D: Fernando Duran. SP: Eric Del Castillo, Barbara Gil. Mus: Rafael Carrion. Mkp: Graciela Gonzalez. SdFX: Gonzalo Gavira. Ref: TV: Azteca HV; no Eng.; *The Sheriff's Strange Son* - tr t. V 1/7/87. TVG. With Mario Almada, Eric Del Castillo, Alfredo Gutierrez, Roberto Canedo.

The West, 1890. Siamese twins Fred and Eric are born during a lunar eclipse. Seven years later, their father, Frederick Jackson, orders Dr. Jack Miller to separate the two, who seem to die during the operation. A supernatural earthquake and a strange wind, however, reanimate Fred. Later, Eric's demonic spirit returns to haunt and kill his father. At the end, the doctor exorcises a spirit from Fred's body—but it's Fred's spirit, not Eric's, and the latter kills a woman, inhabits her body, and telekinetically kills the doc.... The strictly supernatural edition of *The Other.* Eric is dead, to be sure, but it's his spirit that's wreaking the havoc; it's not just in Fred's mind. The Western setting, atmospheric use of mists and winds, and odd little narrative twists help here.

**EXTRASENSORIAL** see *Blood Link*

**Los EXTRATERRESTRES** (Arg) Aries/Baires Films 1984 (1983) color feature. D: Enrique Carreras. SP: Jose Dominianni, E. Carreras. SpElecFX: J. C. Buechler. Ph: Victor Caula. Mus: Mike Rivas. AD: Alvaro Duranona y Vedia, Mario Figliozzi. Mkp: Elvira I. de Ramos. Ref: TV: VSOM; no Eng.; E.T. or Not To E.T. - ad t. V 7/27/83:32: completed shooting. Ecran F 39:5. 49:12. With Jorge Porcel, Alberto Olmedo, Luisa Albinoni, Susana Traverso, Maria & Marisa Carreras..

Or, E.T. in Argentina. The alien from the fog makes a car fly and magically affects human behavior. At the end, he returns to his spaceship, and to the other aliens. Disposable music and comedy.

**EXTREME HEAT** Moonlight Ent. 1987 color 90m. D, P: Scotty Fox. Ref: Adam '89. With Sheena Horne, Marisa Betancourt, Bionca, Jessica Wylde.

Professor's formula turns him into Bobby Lust, in this apparent borrowing from *The Nutty Professor.*

**EYE OF THE DEAD** see *Manhattan Baby*

**EYE OF THE DEMON** see *Bay Coven*

**EYE OF THE STORM** (G-U.S.) New Line HV/Huth-Krohne-Roland Emmerich (Style Prods./D.F.O. III) 1991('92-U.S.) color 93m. SP, D: Yuri Zeltser. SP: also Michael Stewart. SpFxMkp: Reese Arden. Ref: TV. V 6/8/92:55 (hv). SFChron 8/12/92.

"Me and my brother been doin' some real bad things!" The knife murders of his parents leave the older of two brothers (Craig Sheffer) unhinged. In strict *Halloween* fashion, a stormy night finds the once-wounded Ray crawling back at the end for one last stab; after another bullet or two, he comes back a second time.... Horror climax punctuates unrewarding melodrama sparked only by the funny fireworks between Martin and Sandra Gladstone (Dennis Hopper and Lara Flynn Boyle, respectively). Martin has a winning weakness for lame jokes, mostly at his own expense.

**EYES OF FIRE** Elysian Pictures (Philip J. Spinelli) 1984 (1983/1986) color 86m.(106m.) (*Crying Blue Sky* - orig t). SP, D: Avery Crounse. Ph: Wade Hanks. Mus: Brad Fiedel. AD: Greg Fonseca. Mkp: Annie Maniscalco. SpFX: Tassilo Baur. SdFX: (ed) Tracey Smith et al; Outrider, Impact. Opt: CFI, Celestial Mechanix et al. Ref: TV. V 7/25/84. Ecran F 49:71. Phantom. Scheuer. Martin. Morse. With Dennis Lipscomb, Guy Boyd, Rebecca Stanley, Sally Klein, Karlene Crockett (Leah), Fran Ryan, Russell J. Young Jr. (the witch).

"What was it back there?" The American Frontier, 1750. Would-be settlers from Dalton's Ferry on the Allegheny find that their valley is the "home of the devil ... where the lost blood gathers." Seems spilled innocent blood congregates there, and the "devil witch" in charge wants to capture and kill the settlers.

An original, if an often awkward one. Story and characters never quite take, but it's a bizarre country which Crounse conjures up for the latter. Trees suck in stray fog; faces of the damned (or saved) sink into leafy ground; naked tree people cavort; Indians vanish. *Eyes of Fire* is half a mini-classic, half ponderous.

**The EYES OF THE AMARYLLIS** (N.Z.) Howard Kling (The Amaryllis Co.) 1982 color 95m. D: Frederick King Keller. SP: Frederick O'Harra, Stratton Rawson, from Natalie Babbitt's story. Figurehead: Maury Cramer. Mkp: Krista Perry. Ref: TV. TVG. Hound. Maltin '92. Ecran F 70:80-81.

Alluring shots of sea, sky, and sand (photography by Michael G. Mathews and Skip Roessel) ... eerie scenes with the "man on the bluff," a ghost (Jonathan Bolt) who haunts the beach and returns to the sea that which belongs to it ... and tiresomely romanticized characters, in this young-lady's-point-of-view fantasy.

**EYES OF THE BEHOLDER** Vision Int'l. (David Henderson) 1992 color 89m. SP, D, Ed: Lawrence L. Simeone. Ph: Harris Done. Mus: Greg Turner. PD: Billy Jett. SpFX: Steve Patino; Wizard Inc. Lightning: Lightning Strikes. Ref: TV. PT 16:59. Vallejo Times-Herald. SFChron Dtbk 5/16/93. Fango 128:38: "heinously predictable." With Kylie Travis, Charles Napier, Lenny Van Dohlen (Janice Bickle), Vivian Schilling, Joanna Pacula, Matt McCoy, George Lazenby.

"One of my patients escaped." An experimental surgical procedure leaves an already unbalanced patient with a twisted hand and mind. Plus: an ongoing thunderstorm ... a tree-branch-smashed-window shock ... and a swivel-chair, doctor-with-pencil-in-forehead shock .... Or, The Night of the Bloody Foot. Routine siege suspense. Okay photography and music.

**EYES OF THE PANTHER, The** see *Nightmare Classics*

**EYES OF THE SERPENT** see *In the Time of Barbarians II*

**EYES WITHOUT A FACE** (I & III) see also *Faceless*

# F

**F³: FRANTIC, FRUSTRATED & FEMALE** (J) Wan Yan A Gu Da & Pink Pineapple (Yutaro Mochizuki) 1994 anim color 27m. D: M. Akan. Created by Wan Yan A Gu Da. Ph: K. Konishi. AD: K. Kikichi. SpFX: T. Maekawa. SpSdFX: J. Sasaki. SdFX: M. Iwanami. Ref: TV: SoftCel video; Eng. titles.

A psychic discovers that a 17-year-old girl who can orgasm only through hypnosis is surrounded by writhing ectoplasm. Next, the teenager tries a mad doc's "sex machine".... Mildly amusing sex-comedy.

**FA SEMPRE, FINO ALLA MORTE** see *Changeling 2*

**FACE LIKE A FROG** Sally Cruikshank 1987 anim color 5m. Ref: SFChron Dtbk 12/16/90: starring Quasi; "the flavor of Betty Boop."

Ghosts, witches, and a frog woman in a haunted house.

**FACE TO FACE** see *Knight Moves*

**FACELESS** (F) Import Horror/ATC 3000 & Films de la Rochelle (Rene Chateau) 1988 color 98m. (aka *Les Predateurs de la Nuit*). D: Jesus Franco. SP: Michel Lebrun et al, inspired by *Eyes without a Face*. Ph: M. Fellous. Mus: R. Musumurra. AD: B. Ciberot. SpFX: Jacques Gastineau. Ref: V 7/13/88: "routine."10/19/88:215. 11/25/87:20. PT 8:11: shot in Eng.; "totally incredible." With H. Berger, B. Lahaie, C. Mitchum, T. Savalas, A. Diffring, C. Munro.

Plastic surgeon kidnaps young women in order to find new face for his sister. (V)

**FAHRMANN MARIA** see *Strangler of the Swamp*

**FAIR GAME** (Austral.) Winternight Prods. (Chris Oliver) 1982 color c85m. SP, D: Christopher Fitchett. SP, Ph: Ellery Ryan. Mus: Mark McSherry. PD: Josephine Ford. SpFX: Clive Jones. SpFxMkp: Nick Dorning. Ref: TV: Imperial Ent. video. no Martin. no Maltin '92. Hound. Ecran F 47:70. With Kim Trengove, Kerry Mack, Marie O'Loughlin, Karen West, Jay Mannering, Paul Alexander, Paul Young (Zombie).

"Nothing could possibly go wrong." Three teens (Trengrove, Mack, O'Loughlin) take on thugs in the usually quiet Australian seaside town of Portsea. Fortunately, the gang members seem to be fairly inept, though they manage one slashing, while the girls retaliate with broken bottle and spear gun.... Very thin suspense thriller with vague hints of the supernatural—e.g., the character named "Zombie," the mysteriously appearing and disappearing vans which initially pursue the girls, and the vans' license plate

numbers: HEX 777 and END 666. Apparently, the filmmakers weren't sure if they wanted to make *Halloween* or *Cape Fear.* One okay rearview-mirror, rack-focusing shock.

**FAIR GAME** (Austral.) CEL/Southern Films Int'l. & the Australian Film Commission 1985 color c83m. D: Mario Andreacchio. SP: Rob George. Mus: Ashley Irwin. SpFxCoord: Brian Pearce. Beast Des: John Haratzis. Mkp: Jane Surrich. Ref: TV: Charter Ent. video. V 5/21/86. no Martin. no Maltin '92. no Hound. V 10/24/84:382. With Cassandra Delaney, Peter Ford, David Sandford, Garry Who.

"Let's track 'er down!" Suspenser with horrific overtones. Three clods terrorize a lone woman on a wildlife sanctuary. At one point, they capture her and "mount" her on the front of their "monstrous shooting truck," The Beast. She electrocutes one goon; another is impaled on an anvil. (Gore-sounds as he pulls himself off it.) The head goon fries in The Beast.... Well-made, perfectly hollow action movie crosses the human-game theme of *The Most Dangerous Game* with the mutual-destruction idea of the Laurel and Hardy *Big Business,* then adds the expected *Halloween* kicker, as one of the goons—not quite dead—comes back to provide a last little jolt.

**FAIR GAME** (I-U.S.) Overseas Filmgroup/Eidoscope & Reteitalia (Associate) 1988 color 81m. (aka *Mamba.* aka *Game Over*). SP, Story, D, P: Mario Orfini. SP: also Lidia Ravera. Mus: Giorgio Moroder. SpAnimFX: Best Films. Mkp: Nilo Jacoponi. Ref: TV. MFB '89:208-9. V 6/22/88. Martin. M/TVM 12/87:46. With Trudie Styler, Gregg Henry, Bill Moseley.

Paranoid, possessive Gene (Henry) buys a "perfect killing machine"—a mamba, a poisonous snake which must bite to free itself of venom during the mating season. He makes it even more perfect by injecting it with hormones and thus increasing its aggressiveness 300%. He then seals the snake in his bitter ex-girl friend Eva's loft with her (Styler) and sits back in his truck and watches a video-game interpretation of the action inside.... Some fairly entertaining near-misses (by the mamba), but the whole idea is a tad incredible, and the strain to build up the sheer dangerousness of the snake shows.

**The FAIRY AND THE DEVIL** (H.K.?) C. Tsung Lung & Wang H. Chih 198-? color/ws 89m. D: Chiang Tai. SP: C. C. Pe. Ph: Wang Chau (sp?). Mkp: Li Li et al. Ref: TV: Tai Seng Video; no Eng. With Hsi Hsiang, Chen Hsiu Chen, Ko Tien.

Creature cast here includes a giant, red-haired monster which extracts itself from the side of a mountain ... a doll which, tossed in the air, becomes a giant, ray-spitting Yeti-type (the red giant "lassos" him with his whip-ray) ... a flying, ray-shooting, ungainly dragon from the sea (this one defeats the red guy) ... two humans-who-become-dragons that fight in the air and under the water ... an incidental, electric-eyed gill-man-type ... cackling cave demons ... and a flying, fanged head.... Hokey but fun bargain-basement sight and sound effects. Credit music from the *Star Trek* movies.

**FAIRY FOX** (H.K.?) Ting Pao Shing 198-? color/ws c92m. D: Ting Chung. Ref: TV: Ocean Shores Video; Eng. titles.

Fantasy re Pai Li-hsien, a fairy fox who cannot at first marry the human hero, Lin Wei-yang—"I'll ruin my ascetic practice"—is of interest to creature-feature fans for the sequences in which she duels a priest of exorcism who considers Li-hsien and her sister "evil spirits." ("Mr. Lin, your wife is an elf!") She sics flying fireballs on him; he sics his gourd on her. ("Damn it! You ruined my calabash!") She then scares him by sending her bottom half, then her top half after him, and blows magic rays at him. Apart from these lively scenes, however, the film is slow and sentimental. At the end, Buddha signs off on the mixed marriage and restores Li-hsien's sister from fox to human form.

The **FAIRY FOX AND GHOST** (H.K.?) Jia's Motion Picture Co. 1982 color feature. Ref: vc box.

**FAIRY OF THE LOTUS** (H.K.?) Champion Int'l. Films 198-? color/ws c94m. Ref: TV: vt; Eng. titles.

"There are ghosts here," in Lotus Village.... Three sisters find refuge from war in a lotus pond. Twenty years later, two of them lure Chao and Wang into the pond in order to complete their reincarnation. The third sister, selfless water-spirit Lotus Bai, vies with evil, selfish fox-witch Hu Mei for the love of scholar Liang Sheng-wen. At the end, monk's lightning turns Hu Mei into a fox, then into nothing, while the Lord of the Dead sees to it that Lotus and Sheng-wen see each other at least once more.... The threefold ending—first in Lotus Village, then in the land of the dead, and then back by the lotus pond—is confusing. Apparently, Sheng-wen is restored to life after following Lotus into the pond, and Lotus is allowed to say goodbye to him before returning to the water. It's all a bit much of bittersweet, though *Fairy of the Lotus* is an occasionally touching fantasy chiller.

**FALCONHEAD** 1972. Fef: Adam '93G: "sex and horror." With Vince Perilli.

"A magic mirror, home of the Falconhead, sucks in victims." Follow-up: *Falconhead II: The Maneaters* (1983).

**FALL BREAK** see *Mutilator, The*

**3 The FALL OF THE HOUSE OF USHER** 1983 color/ws feature (*Revolt of the House of Usher* - vt. aka *Revenge of the House of Usher. El Hundimiento de la Casa Usher. Los Crimines de Usher* - orig t. aka *Nevrose.* aka *Triumph of the House of Usher. Zombie 5* - alt vt t). SP: J. Franco. Ph: Enrique Diez(sp?). Mus: Pablo Villa. AD: Carlos Isbert. Mkp: Juana de la Mora(sp?). Ref: TV: VSOM; Eng. titles. VWB: clips from *Awful Dr. Orlof.* Hardy/HM. With Antonio Mayans, Fata Morgana, Pablo Villa, Ana Galan.

"The house and I were one." The 175-year-old Sir Eric Usher ("I had nightmares for the first hundred years") insists that his mansion "revolted" against him after he killed his wife. ("She keeps coming back.") Now, he resorts to kinky practices like stabbing women to death and drinking their blood off the death swords. At the end, the house of Usher begins to collapse. ("The house is dying!")

At times, Franco seems to get "Usher" mixed up with "Dracula." (One character is named Allen Harker.) The credits list the author as "Edgard Alan Poe." Apparently, one incarnation of this *Usher* footage featured Olivier Mathot as Morpho, a name which also turns up in *Case of the Two Beauties* (which see). Pretty chaotic.

**FALL OF THE HOUSE OF USHER, The** see *House of Usher, The.*

**FALLING, The** see *Alien Predator*

**FALLING ANGEL** see *Angel Heart*

**FAMILY DOG** see *Amazing Stories—The Movie III*

**FAMILY OF A WURDALAK** see *Black Sabbath*

**FAMILY REUNION** Spectrum/Bullseye 1989 color 85m. SP, D, P: M. Hawes. SpFX: Jeff Varga. Ref: Hardy/HM2: devil cult, gore, "ageless villain."

**FANDORA: BATTLE IN LEM KINGDOM** (J) 1985 anim color 34m. (aka *Fandora: Dream Dimensional Hunter*). SP: Go Nagai. Ref: TV: Columbia Video. J Anim Program Guide. J Anim Archives 2:12. Voices: Mitoko Horie (Fandora), Akira Kamitani (Kue), Makio Inoue (Sogos), Keiko Toda (Leimia).

Principals: Fandora, a trans-dimensional bounty hunter ... Kue, her assistant on their spaceship, who can turn himself into a bee or a caterpillar or a huge tiger or a dragon ... evil Yogu Sogos, who can become a giant, horned monster-lion ... the huge, shape-shifting spider Redeye ... and a giant, male-operated robot with a laser sword.... Japanese science-fantasy features familiar action and sentiment and the usual big-quivering-eyeballed heroines. It is, however, lushly drawn and lively. Especially taking: Yogu Sogos's looming, forbidding castle. The funniest shape-shifting is done by Kue.

**FANDORA PART II** (J) Columbia Video 1986 anim colo r 43m. Ref: vc box. Japan Video: 2nd of 3 OAVs; Part III: 46m. (1986).

**The FANTASIST** (Irish) Almi/ITC Ent. & New Irish Film (Mark Forstater) 1986 color 96m. SP, D: Robin Hardy, from Patrick McGinley's novel *Goosefoot*. Mus: Stanislas Syrewicz. AD: John Lucas. MkpFX: Nick Dudman. SpFxSup: Gerry Johnstone. Ref: TV. V 5/21/86. Martin. Maltin '92. With Moira Harris, Christopher Cazenove, Timothy Bottoms, John Kavanagh.

"I am the secret paramour of your dreams." The "Dublin Ripper"—a "phone call killer"—seduces his female victims with words, then stabs them to death, in this Irish slasher movie. ("The women of Dublin should be on their guard against a very persuasive stranger.") Some stray charm here in the compulsive talk of the main characters, but the irony of the "wonderfully poetic" killer doesn't quite carry the day. Despite the poetry, this is still a weak-tea thriller.

**FANTASMI DI SODOMA** see *Ghosts of Sodom*

**FANTASTIC ADVENTURE OF YOHKO: LEDA** (J) Toho/Kaname-Pro 1985 anim color 70m. (aka *Leda*). Ref: TV: Toho Video; no Eng. J Anim Archives 3:6. V 5/1/85:399(ad). Animag 11:29.

A melody intended to give a teenage girl, Yohko, confidence to talk to a boy instead transports her to another dimension, Ashanti, where a huge flower swallows her up and transforms her into a bikini-clad warrior of the goddess Leda. A giant robot with feet like flippers harbors another Leda warrior, Yoni. Together, the two fight the evil ruler, Zell.... Pleasingly drawn, amusingly detailed science-fantasy film. The air in Ashanti is filled with all manner of odd hovering things, most of them apparently mechanical, and giant yawning turtles plod along the ground. Ultimately, the script uses fantasy as a stepping stone back to reality: At the end, girl meets (and talks to) boy, back in the real world, in a charmingly underplayed scene.

**FANTASTIC JOURNEY** see *Lost in Time*

The **FANTASTIC WORLD OF D.C. COLLINS** NBC-TV/Guillaume-Margo & Zephyr 1984 color 92m. D: Leslie Martinson. Ref: TV. TVG. Stanley: "totally predictable." no Maltin '92. Scheuer.

Boy's (Gary Coleman) visualized daydreams include a *Star Wars*-like vision of himself as Dwight Cloudclimber—he uses the Star Saber of Justice to battle an evil warlord's minions.

**FANTASY GIRLS** Caballero 1988 color feature. D: John Stagliano. Ref: Adam '90. no Jones. With Brandy Alexandre, Bella Donna, Bobbi Soxx, Tom Byron.

"Dracula-hosted sexathon."

**FANTASY ISLAND** see *Fantasyland*

**FANTASY MISSION FORCE** (H.K.) ZIV Int'l./Cheung Ming Film (Hsiao-Yin Shen) 1984 color/ws 89m. D: Chu Yen Ping. Ref: TV: All Seasons video; Eng.-dubbed.

"Let's just stay here for the night." Highlight of low-comedy-actioner is the all-stops-out horror-comedy sequence set in a haunted house. Haunters include a ghost that rises from a coffin and hops away ... a "pretty girl" who turns into an old-hag head and skeleton bones ... mah-jongg players with detachable heads and elastic arms ... phantom arms in a bathroom which all hold out toilet tissue ... and some fanged, vampire-like gents. ("Take their blood!")

**FANTASY ROMANCE** (H.K.?) H.K. Fong Ming Motion Picture Co. 1992? color/ws c90m. (*Ghost Wife* - alt vt t). Ref: TV: Pan-Asia Video; Eng. titles. TV: vt; Thai-dubbed; Eng. titles.

The "Evil Reflect Mirror" and talismans initially exorcise the annoying comic-drawing-come-to-life "ghost" Ching Ching, whom the King of Hell wants as his daughter-in-law. However, she later returns to enter a TV set and talk to the hero and to "haunt" his car and assault some thugs who bother her. Meanwhile, her aunt lands in a strange bed, scares a guy (and vice versa), flies into Ching Ching's bedroom, and glides around blue-lit sets. ("It's worst to be ghost whore.") A big exorcism sequence leads into an impressive climactic sequence, in which all concerned enter an animated-comic-book realm where caped phantoms chase them, and a monster-mouthed "tornado" swallows auntie. Apart from the latter scenes, though, this is just a silly, sporadically funny ghost comedy.

**FANTASYLAND** L.A. Video 1985 color 80m. SP, D: Ned Morehead. Ref: vc box: "two sensuous darlings from outer space." Adam '89. vc box: sfa *Fantasy Island*? With Harry Reems, Susan Hart, Colleen Brennan, Nikki D.

**FAR FROM HOME** Vestron/Lightning Pictures (Donald P. Borchers) 1989 color 86m. D: Meiert Avis. SP: Tommy Lee Wallace. Story: Ted Gershuny. Mus: Jonathan Elias. SpFX: (coord) Lou Carlucci; Image Engineering, Roger George. Mkp: Fischa, Vittone. Ref: TV. V 6/28/89. With Matt Frewer, Drew Barrymore, Richard Masur, Susan Tyrrell, Anthony Rapp, Andras Jones, Dick Miller.

At the Palomino Guest Ranch, "somewhere in Nevada," a mad killer commits murder by electric fan (in bath water), remote-control toy car, ice pick, etc. And, unfortunately, the madman, or boy, kills off (or seems to kill off) the three most interesting actors—Masur, Tyrrell, and Miller. Awkward mixture of road movie, slasher film, and display case (for Barrymore and bikini). Some atmospheric photography (by Paul Elliott).

**FARFALLA CON LE ALI INSANGUINATE** see *Bloodstained Butterfly, The*

**FARM, The** see *Curse, The* (U.S.-I, 1987)

The **FARM OF TOMORROW** MGM 1954 anim color 7m. D: Tex Avery. SP: Heck Allen. Mus: Scott Bradley. Ref: Jim Shapiro: futuristic. Adamson/TA: "the unfunniest cartoon ever made." LC.

**FATAL ATTRACTION** Para/Jaffe-Lansing 1987 color 120m. D: Adrian Lyne. SP: James Dearden. Mus: Maurice Jarre. Mkp: Richard Dean. OptFX: Cinema Research. Ref: TV. MFB'88:14. V 9/16/88. TVG. East Bay Express 9/25/87. SFExam 9/18/87. With Michael Douglas, Glenn Close, Anne Archer, Ellen Hamilton Latzen, Stuart Pankin, Fred Gwynne.

Mr. Gallagher (Douglas) meets Alex (Close), who's "going through a bad time," which gets worse—for both of them. *Back Street* segues into *Cape Fear,* as she gets pregnant, tells him, "I'm not going to be ignored, Dan," and distractedly cuts her own leg with a knife. She attacks Dan and his wife, Beth (Archer); he drowns Alex in a bathtub; but (*Halloween,* now) she leaps out once more.... The scene in which Dan half-throttles Alex, and she lunges at him with a butcher knife, suggests that the movie might best have been done as a parody of *Falling in Love.* As it is, the film is smooth and slick, but story cliches override the script's attempts to implicate Dan and Beth in the general madness ... to suggest that they're all monsters. Complete with face-in-the-mirror shock.

**FATAL CHARM** Showtime-TV 1992 color c90m. D: Fritz Kiersch. Tel: Nicholas Niciphor. Ref: TVG 2/22/92. V 12/21/92:14 (rated). Fango 123:12: Academy Ent. Hound: "standard." With Christopher Atkins, Amanda Peterson, James Remar, Andrew Robinson, Peggy Lipton.

Fantasies re pen-pal serial killer.

**FATAL IMAGES** Active HV 1989 color 70m. D: Dennis Devine. Ref: Bowker '90. With Lane Coyle, Kay Schaver, David Williams.

Mad photographer's camera proves deadly for models.

**FATAL MAPLE** (H.K.?) China Ent. 1993 color 90m. D: Shan, Ying. Ref: vc box: "midnight screams and mysterious ghosts." With Tong Ching Chuen.

**FATAL PULSE** C.H.E./GEG 1988 color 86m. D, P: A. J. Christopher. SP: James Hundhausen. Mus: M. Mayo. Ref: V 3/30/88:41: "predictable." Martin. Nowlan. Morse: sleazy. With Michelle McCormick, Ken Roberts, Joe Phelan, Herschel Savage.

Maniac stalks sorority girls.

**FATAL SEDUCTION** CDI (Rob Dealto) 1988 color 90m. D: Don Turner. Ref: Adam '89. With Kascha, Tracey Adams, Peter North.

"Futuristic satyr."

**FATAL SKY** see *Project: Alien*

**The FATAL WITNESS** Republic (Rudolph Abel) 1945 b&w 69m. D: Lesley Selander. SP: Jerry Sackheim. Adap: C. F. Adams. Story: Rupert Croft-Cooke. Ph: Bud Thackery. Mus D: Richard Cherwin. Ref: Harrison's 8/25/45. Pierre LePage. V 9/5/45. LC. no NYT. With Evelyn Ankers, Richard Fraser, George Leigh, Barbara Everest, Frederick Worlock, C. Kent, Barry Bernard.

Ghost (Everest) scares superstitious strangler (Leigh) into confessing murders. "Surprise ending ... helps salvage this one...." (V)

**FATHER, SANTA KLAUS HAS DIED** (Russ) Lenfilm/ES (First Film) 1992 b&w 79m. AD, D: Eugeny Yufit. SP: V. Maslov. Ph: A. Burov. Ref: V 10/12/92: "works best as an almost silent horror film with poetic touches." Jones. With Anatoly Egorov, Ivan Ganzha.

Loosely based on the A. Tolstoy story "The Wurdalak." "Often mysterious film uses horror and sci-fi conventions...." (V)

**FATHERLAND** (U.S.-Cz) HBO-TV & Eis (sp?) Film (Frederick Muller, Ilene Kahn) 1994 color 106m. D: Christopher Menaul. Tel: Stanley Weiser, Ron Hutchinson. From Robert Harris' novel. Ph: Peter Sova. Mus: Gary Chang. PD: Veronica Hadfield. SpVisFX: Illusion Arts. Ref: TV: Warner HV. Vallejo T-H 11/26/94. SFChron 11/25/94. With Rutger Hauer, Miranda Richardson, Peter Vaughan, Michael Kitchen, Jean Marsh, John Woodvine, John Shrapnel.

Germania, the "vast Nazi empire," 1964. Normandy failed. Churchill died in exile in 1953. Stalin is still around. Joseph Kennedy Sr. is President of the U.S. And the existence of Nazi concentration camps during World War II has been covered up, allowing cheap, cheery irony re Hitler's nice-nice reign. Pointless and not quite buyable refashioning of history.

**FAUST** (Cz-F-G-B) Athanor/Heart of Europe Prague K & Lumen & BBC Bristol & Pandora & Koninck (Kallista) 1994 anim and live action 92m. SP, D, Co-AD: Jan Svankmajer. From Goethe, Marlowe et al. Ph: S. Maly. Anim: B. Glaser. SdFX: P. Mach et al. Ref: TV: ICA video; Eng. version. SFChron 3/24/95. UC Theatre notes 4/4/95. With Petr Cepek.

Ingredients in this tale re "blackest magic and dark alchemy": weird lightning ... a skeleton thing ... a clay baby which comes to life (its head becomes a skull) ... a Mephisto marionette and a clay Mephisto ... and some feisty mini-devils.... Idiosyncratic, isn't it? Highlights of enigmatic film are the animation bits with instantly-rotten fruit, the mini-devils, etc.

**FEAR** (I-F) Dionysio & SNC 1980 ('86-U.S.) color 90m. (*L'Ossessione Che Uccide*. aka *Unconscious*. aka *Murder Syndrome*. aka *Murder Obsession*. aka *Deliria*). SP, D: Riccardo Freda. Story, SP: Antonio Cesare Corti, Fabio Piccioni. Dial, Co-P: Simon Mizrahi. Mus: Franco Mannino. Mkp: Lamberto Marini, Sergio Angeloni. Ref: TV: Wizard Video; Eng. dubbed. V 7/9/86. Hardy/HM. Stanley. Morse. no Martin. no Hound. Newman. Palmerini: aka *Follia Omicida*. VWB: *The Wailing* - alt vt t. With Stefano Patrizi, Martine Brochard, Laura Gemser, John Richardson, Anita Strindberg, Silvia Dionisio.

Ingredients: black magic, psychic powers, a mystery "monster of evil," murder by ax, murder by chainsaw, murder by hunting knife, trances, hallucinations, Solomon's Seal (a magic charm), a sleepwalker, and (in an "awful dream") an invisible creature, a cowled monster, a big (immobile) spider, a corridor of bats, and bleeding skulls in a tree.... The climactic *Rashomon* flashbacks herein reduce to predictable twists re whodunit. The bulk of the movie: red herrings, bland suspense sequences, miscellaneous violence.

**FEAR** Showtime-TV/Vestron Pictures (Kobritz-O'Bannon Co.) 1990 (1989) color 95m. SP, D: Rockne S. O'Bannon. Mus: Henry Mancini. PD: Joseph Nemec III. SpFX: Steve Wolke. Mkp: Michael Germain, Joe McKinney. SdFX: Mark Mangini. Ref: TV. Sacto Bee 7/13/90. V 7/11/90:71 (hvs ). Martin. Scheuer. Maltin '92. MFB'91:77-8. With Ally Sheedy (Cayce Bridges), Michael O'Keefe, Lauren Hutton, Stan Shaw, Dina Merrill, John Agar, Pruitt Taylor Vince (The Shadow Man).

"It's just you and me and the fear!" Psychic Cayce Bridges mentally tracks the serial killer The Shadow Man—and he, in return, "probes" her mind. ("He's better at it than I am.") For him, now, it's a double stimulant when he kills: He scares both his victims and Cayce.... *The Crawling Eye*, psychic's-eye-view gimmick is used well here, if it's finally overused. And *Fear* might have been creepier if Cayce's visions of The Shadow Man hadn't been visualized, if the viewer had been allowed to use his or her imagination too—The Shadow Man is reduced to just another subjective-camera killer. Some dandy twists and details.

**The FEAR** A-Pix/Devin Ent. (Richard Brandes/Morty) 1994 color 93m. D: Vincent Robert. Story, SP: Ron Ford. Story: also Greg H. Sims. Ph: Bernd Heinl. Mus: R.O. Ragland. PD: B. McCabe. Morty FX Des: MMI. Ref: TV: A-Pix video. With Eddie Bowz, Darin Heams or Heames, Anna Karin, Erick Weiss (Morty), Vince Edwards, Ann Turkel, Wes Craven, Rebecca Baldwin.

"A weekend of fear exploration in a controlled environment." There's "something weird going on, and it has to do with Morty"—a wooden figure carved by a shaman. One victim here is impaled on a cross; another is possessed.... *Phobia* plus *Pin*. Unoriginal, almost comically overwrought horror fantasy.

**FEAR CITY** Chevy Chase/Zupnik-Curtis (Rebecca) 1984 color 95m. D: Abel Ferrara. SP: Nicholas St. John. Mus: Dick Halligan. SpFxMkp: Alan Friedman. SpFX: Clay Pinney. Ref: screen. V 5/23/84. Martin. Scheuer. Maltin '92. Phantom. With Tom Berenger, Billy Dee Williams, Jack Scalia, Melanie Griffith, Rossano Brazzi, Rae Dawn Chong, Joe Santos, Michael V. Gazzo, Jan Murray, Ola Ray.

A New York City slasher specializing in the Starlite Talent Agency's dancers proves to be a "purity" freak who keeps a record of his crimes ("Fear City"). His careful avoidance of his victims' major veins and arteries insures their slow deaths.... Dismayingly conventional thriller-shocker-policier. The first few slashings are—in their surgical preciseness—nasty enough, but don't really justify trotting out the *10 to Midnight/Angel/American Nightmare,* back-and-forth, cops-to-killer-to-protagonists plot. The dialogue is forced; characterizations, awkward; the score, bland.

**The FEAR INSIDE** Showtime-TV/Viacom (John Broderick) 1992 color 101m. D: Leon Ichaso. Tel: David Birke. Ph: Bojan Bazelli. Mus: Michael Rubini. Ref: V 8/3/92. With Christine Lahti, Dylan McDermott, Jennifer Rubin, David Ackroyd.

"Bloodletting ... horrifying acts ... terror personified ... frightening psycho."

**FEAR OF THE MUMMY** (J) VSOM 1958. b&w feature. (*Yami Ni Hikaru Me*).Ref: TV: VSOM; no Eng. Mo. Weisser/JC: from a TV series.

A scientist administers a beaker of fluid to a disfigured mummy in a sarcophagus. The mummy monster stirs and growls and kills one scientist. Later, he breaks out of another scientist's makeshift wooden cage and (like the invisible man in *Invisible Man Returns*) acquires hat, coat, and pants .... An almost endearingly primitive reworking of Universal mummy movies. This Japanese version even features a classic "flashback" to ancient Egypt and a "tana" drink, and the mummy "sees" the Egyptian princess in the modern-day heroine. Awkward action scenes.

**FEAR STALKER** see *City in Panic*

**The FEARLESS KUNG FU ELEMENTS** (H.K.) Wang Hsiao-Ts & Wang Ai-Ching/Chen Jou 1983 color/ws c90m. Planning D: Tsai Ku. SP: Wang Sin Ming. Ph: Wang Sen Chai. Mus: Wang Mu San. Mkp: Chiu Yuk Jung. Ref: TV: Ocean Shores Video; Eng. version. With Chin Hsang Lin, Wei Tse Yun, Cen Hsing, Sma Yu Jiau, Lin Yi Wa, Lung Shao Fei, Yi Yung.

This kung-fu fantasy features so many transformations, possessions, magical appearances, and disappearances that it's hard to tell who's who or who becomes what. The main monster seems to be a vampiric fox demon who is seen once in fox form, but generally in woman form, and who sucks the blood from a servant's neck to restore her own draining life force. Extra addeds: a teacher who becomes a big teddy bear of a monster that spits fire ... a horned monster ... a big furry white monkey-man, for comic relief ... a man who can dive into the ground and instantly burrow ... and demon possession. ("You're a demon!") Lively, yes, but hard to follow and basically uninspired.

**The FEARMAKER** (Mex) Cavalcade Pictures & Prism Ent./7th Seal (J. L. Bueno) 1977 (1974?) color 90m. (3P *El Hacedor de Miedo. El Rancho del Miedo* - alt vt t. *House of Fear* - alt vc box t). SP, D: Anthony Carras. SP: also Dean Booth. Ph: Alex Phillips. Mus: Lex de Acevedo. AD: Roberto Silva. OptFX: Cinefx. Mkp: Elda Loza. SdFX: Edit Rite. Ref: TV. vc boxes. V 5/11/77:205 (ad). Scheuer. Hound. no Martin. VW 16:8: *Violent Rage* - B t. with Katy Jurado, Fernando Soler, Paul Picerni, Carlos East, Chano Urueta, Sonia Amelio.

Items: a vicious dog trained to kill ... a shock scene in a morgue in which a corpse's ghastly face is suddenly revealed ... a woman who plays dead ... and a storm. Mystery-suspense with horrific overtones. Crude, familiar. Caught on Spanish-language TV.

**FEED THE GHOST** see *Ghost Nursing*

**FEEL NA FEEL** (Fili) Regal Films 1990 color c120m. D: Rudy Meyer. SP: J. E. Navoa, Joe Carreon. Ph: Ricardo Herrera. Mus D: Jaime Fabregas. PD: Judy Lou de Pio. VisFX: Cinemagic. SpFX: Danny Rojo. SdFX: Ramon Reyes. Ref: TV: Regal Int'l. video; occ. Eng. vc box. With Susan Roces, Eddie Gutierrez, Manilyn Reynes, Janno Gibbs, Raymond Gutierrez, J. Fabregas, Paeng Giant.

Negligible mixture of comedy, music, and science-fantasy concerns (a) alien twins who ride a giant bird to Earth and whose rays can alter the course of basketball games and (b) a giant who falls to Earth and terrorizes the countryside. At the end, the giant is reduced to menial duties such as sweeping (with a human-sized broom).

**FELIX SWITCHES WITCHES** see *Felix the Cat Switches Witches*

**FELIX THE CAT: THE MOVIE** (U.S.-Hung.) Felix the Cat Creations & Prods. Inc. (Rene Daalder, Michael Gladishev) 1989 (1988) anim color 82m. D: Tibor Hernadi. Story, SP: Don Oriolo. SP: also Pete Brown. Based on the Otto Messmer cartoon character. Mus: C. L. Stone. SpPhFxD: Laszlo Radocsay. Ref: TV. MFB'90:293-4. TVG. Voices: Chris Phillips, Maureen O'Connell et al.

"In another dimension...." Ingredients: the Dimensporter (which allows "trans-dimensional movement" between parallel dimensions which occupy the same space, but different planes), which brings Felix from Earth to Oriana ... the Vader-voiced Duke of Zill, who commands an army of cylinders and cubes ... a machine which shrinks a bog monster to 1/100th of its original size ... a "kind of plant-animal" which eats anything ... a dragon ... strange flying cave creatures ... a super-TV ... and a wide variety of aliens, or extra-dimensional beings.... Oddly-scripted cartoon feature is lively if nothing else. One oddity in the storyline: The duke's captives are forced to become circus stars. The worst of it: Felix's limp wordplay. "You're no good with jokes," someone at one point tells him, but he continues, unfazed.

**FELIX THE CAT IN ASTRONOMEOUS** Educ/Pat Sullivan 1928 anim silent with sd fx 7m. (aka *Astronomeous. Astronomeows. Felix the Cat in Astronomeows*). SP: Otto Messmer. Ref: TV: Video Bancorp. SFChron Dtbk 5/12/91. Lee. LC.

Felix travels by rope to Saturn, where bicyclists ride its ring, then goes on to Mars, where scary and funny Martians beset him. At the end, he brings the cats of Earth to Mars. Cute, oddball Felix cartoon.

**FELIX THE CAT IN COMICALAMITIES** see *Comicalamities*

**FELIX THE CAT IN SURE-LOCKED HOMES** Educ/Hammons (Sullivan) 1928 anim silent 8m. (aka *Sure-Locked Homes*). SP: Otto Messmer. Ref: screen. Crafton/BM. Bill Warren. no Maltin/OMAM. LC. no Lee.

"Night's all-enveloping cloak" plays tricks with Felix's imagination: Car headlights become menacing "eyes." A windblown shirt from a cemetery becomes a "ghost." Later, inside his house, shadows of an ape, a bat, various devils, and a cat-sized spider chase him. Behind it all: a baby playing with a lamp and casting hand-shadows.... Creepy, inventive Felix cartoon. No hand-shadows can account for the eerie scene in which apes begin to proliferate, a la the elephants-on-parade sequence in *Dumbo*.

**\*\*\*FELIX THE CAT SWITCHES WITCHES** Hammons/Sullivan 1927 anim silent 8m. (aka *Felix Switches Witches*). SP: Otto Messmer. Ref: screen. SFChron Dtbk 5/12/91. LC. Lee.

Halloween. Felix scares other animals with a menacing (and apparently live) jack-o'-lantern, while a "witch" (which turns out to be a girl cat) scares Felix, with hellfire. Lively and inventive. At one point, Felix "crosses" a bicycle with a cow by switching parts between the two; later, he himself is crossed with a wheelbarrow.

**FELIX THE CAT TRIFLES WITH TIME** Educ 1925 anim silent 8m. SP: Otto Messmer. Ref: screen. LC. Lee.

Father Time sends Felix back to a "better age" for a cat—the Stone Age, where he encounters a brontosaurus-like sea monster with an "escalator" back, a giant elephant, a stegosaurus-like, dog-eared dinosaur, and a caveman who skins him to make a cat "suit." Funny Felix cartoon.

See also: *Comicalamities. Skulls and Sculls. Woos Whoopee.*

**FELIX WOOS WHOOPEE** see *Woos Whoopee*

**FEMALE NEO-NINJAS** (J) VSOM 1991 color feature. D: Tomoyuki Kasai. Ref: TV: VSOM; Eng. titles. PT 17:15. Weisser/JC: *Kunoichi Senshi Ninja*. With Keyo Oonish, Senako Gohon, Akemi Ooshima.

"Aliens have been contacting us—even in ancient times." Ingredients include "vigilante Neo-Ninjas from the Gokura family" who "sign" their deeds with notes and pass out pamphlets promoting themselves ... a spaceship, or timeship, bearing a Time Patrol from the 25th Century ("I transfer people who are trapped outside of time") ... the Karakuri Box, which raises a monster (an alien?) that possesses Nobunago ... Kiyo, who tumbles into the present out of the past ... a magic scroll with "alien etchings" similar to those found in a "UFO book" by Iyagi ... and a governor who wants to be the "Asian superman" .... Cross between a typical ninja movie and a Wisely film has funny heroines, regulation action, and an okay plot with some surprises.

**FEMALE NINJAS: MAGIC CHRONICLES 1** (J) VSOM/Sumikawa Film & Cinemarion 1991 color 75m. (*Kunoichi Ninpou-cho. Female Ninja* - ad t). D: Katsu Zushima. Ref: TV: VSOM; Eng. titles. CM 15:35: made-for-video; remake of a '60s movie with the same name. With Misuyo Shirajima, Gingi Seiou, Hitomi Okasaki, Miki Mizuno.

The works: poison crystal flakes which drive their victims mad ... a sperm-based love potion ... sword gore ... spirit-commands ... the Ninja Moon-mark-on-forehead curse ... a man who shape-shifts into a woman (a "secret ninja trick") ... a ninja who magically traps a man in bed ("I've sucked out all your blood") and leaves only a smoldering skeleton ... the Stop Return spell ... the ever-popular Fetus Transfer (womb-to-womb "sexual magic") ... a fireball/human-head ... literal Shadow Fighting ... and (with the Fetus Transfer) most mind-boggling of all: the bubbles which trap and "return men to the womb" .... The effect-a-minute pace of this serial-like ninja fantasy, set in the 17th Century, gets to be almost comical. Cheap but fun, inventive effects. Prime title: "You bitch ninja slut!"

**FEMALE NINJAS: MAGIC CHRONICLES 2: SECRET OF THE CHRISTIAN BELLS** (J) VSOM/Sumikawa & Cinemarion 1992 color 80m. (*Kunoichi Ninpo—Seisho Jo No Hiho*). D: K. Zushima. Ref: TV: VSOM; Eng. titles. CM 15:35. With Y. Sumida, K. Yamaguchi, M. Mizuno, R. Hayama.

This time: the burning-cross-in-eye curse ... the ninja Echo Trick (boomerang-like magic) ... blow-dart-in-eye magic ... the Cherry Blossom Trick, which makes the victim unbearably hot ... the poisonous, enveloping Vagina Bubble ... and the Dead Eyes Portrait (which records the last image on the dying person's pupil) .... It's starting to get a bit mechanical here. Best title: "It's frightening — a religion that would hide a bell inside a girl's vagina!"

**FEMALE NINJAS: MAGIC CHRONICLES #3: QUEST FOR THE SACRED BOOK OF SEXUAL POSITIONS** (J) Sumikawa & Cinemarion 1993 color 79m. (*Female Ninja: Magic Chronicles 3: Sacred Book of Sexual Positions* -cr t). D: K. Zushima. Ref: TV: VSOM; Eng. titles. EVS: aka *Tale of Female Ninjas*? CM 15:35. trailer: torrents of ninja breast milk make victim smoke, burn.

And now: the ninja strangling-hair trick ... the "shadow net" of entrapment ... the vaginal Silk Worm trick, which leaves the victim cocooned ... the "magic division trick," which "multiplies" a ninja ... the new Echo Trick, a forerunner of the telegraph ... the "vagina bubble from hell" ... the Crossed Sword Trick of immobilization ... the Devil Passage Trick ... and some knife-in-the-eye gore .... More kinky capers, and a bit more entertaining than part two. Helpfully, each new trick is announced, then demonstrated. The last word: "I want to have sex—but I can do both, fight and have sex, too."

**FEMALE NINJAS: MAGIC CHRONICLES 4** (J) Sumikawa & Cinemarion 1994 color 77m. (*Kunoichi Ninpo—Chushingura Hisho*). D: Katsu Zushima. Ref: TV: VSOM; Eng. titles. Le Video. CM 15:35: also a #5 in '95. With Sekiko Ueno, Megumi Sakita, S. Iida.

Finally: Anger Hair Heaven (sword-like strands of hair) ... Bodies Become One (a "fused together"-in-sex spell) ... Metal Solid (in which swords pass through a warrior harmlessly) ... Hell Spray Quicksand (which sucks the same warrior into suddenly liquid ground) ... and the Gold Wall (an electric barrier).... Mildly amusing, occasionally lyrical, more often mechanical. Apparently shot-on-tape.

**FERNGULLY: THE LAST RAINFOREST** Fox/FAI Films & Youngheart Prods. (Young & Faiman) 1992 anim color 76m. D: Bill Kroyer. SP: Jim Cox, from Diana Young's stories. Mus: Alan Silvestri. SpFxAnim D: Sari Gennis. SdFX: Fury & Grace & Soundbusters. Titles: Howard Anderson. Ref: TV. V 4/13/92. SFChron 4/10/92. SFExam 4/10/92. Voices: Tim Curry (Hexxus), S. Mathis, C. Slater, J. Ward, Robin Williams, Grace Zabriskie, Cheech Marin, Tommy Chong, Tone-Loc (The Goanna), Kathleen Freeman.

"The humans have released Hexxus!" That "horrible monster in the forest"—a tree "leveller"—accidentally unleashes the "very spirit of destruction," which has been imprisoned in an enchanted tree. At first, Hexxus is only a feisty little blob, but its elastic toxic sludge grows and takes skeletal and ghostly forms, and finally becomes a huge, smoky monster, then a stately, demonic skeleton. Incidental terror here is provided by a lizard, The Goanna, a "giant" compared to our shrunken hero Zak (Ward), in one sequence. The horrific-didactic Hexxus—a cousin of the Smog Monster which Godzilla fought a few decades ago—and Williams' batty lab bat are the two highlights of a generally mild, but pretty and pleasant movie, in effect an animated "updating" of *Valley of the Giants* (1938) and *The Big Trees* (1952).

**FERTILIZE THE BLASPHEMING BOMBSHELL!** USA-TV/Troma (Holmby Pictures/Art Jacobs) 1989 color c85m. (*Mark of the Beast* - vt t). SP, D: Jeff Hathcock. Ph: Ken Gibb. Mus: Andre Brummer. PD & SpFX: Bob Tiller. Ref: TV. TVG. SFChron Dtbk 2/14/93. 3/8/92:58. PT 12:46-7. With Bo Hopkins, Rick Hill, Robert Tessier, Sheila Cann, Vickie Benson.

Ingredients: a devil-cult sacrifice at the Devil's Playground ("just like going through hell") ... the "satanic town" of Ellivnatas (Pop. 13), which is not found on any map and whose name, backwards, is "Satanville" ... and a leftover ceremonial pentagram. Unconscionably thin, predictable.

**FIEND, The** see *Science Crazed*

**\*\*50,000 B.C. (BEFORE CLOTHING)** Sam Lake/Biolane 1963 color 75m. (aka *Nudes on the Rocks*). D: Warner Rose. Mus: Martin Roman. Ref: AFI. no Stanley. no Lentz. Lee(p). no LC. V 4/29/70:196. With Charlie Robinson, Hedi Leonore, Mila Milo.

Time-machine trip to prehistory.

**FIERY DRAGON KID, The** see *Fire Dragon*

**50 WAYS TO LICK YOUR LOVER** Zane 1989 color 77m. D: Jim Enright. Ref: Adam '91. With Rachel Ryan, Peter North, Veronica Dol.

Doc's lipstick invention relaxes subject's inhibitions.

**FIGHT THE GHOST!** (Thai) 198-? color/ws c77m. Ref: TV: vt. Thai Video: above is tr t.

A priest's incantation releases three humanoid monsters from a bottle. The spirit of one temporarily enters a doll; another monster temporarily possesses a teenager; and one demon's severed hand attempts to throttle another teen. In her nightmare, the karate heroine's hand thrusts right through one monster's torso, and her hand gets covered with red goop. Meanwhile, back in reality, five guys in skeleton suits attack the kids.... Thai equivalent of *Horror of Party Beach* alternates, confusingly, between fake and real monsters, dream and reality. Lively but thin horror-comedy.

**FIGURES FROM EARTH** (H.K.) Taylor Film & Video c1993 color 86m. Ref: TV: Pan-Asia Video; Eng. titles. Y.K. Ho.

"Your blood will be sucked dry." Five hundred years ago: Chu lures male victims for her elder sister, a "devilish bat," or satanic vampire-witch .... In the present, two goofs—"frozen" for 500 years—thaw, search for the "old witch," and find her .... Vacuous horror-comedy. "High" point: The two goofs mistake a toilet for a wok. Weirder monster than the vampire: Master Thunderbolt's long, phallic, snake-like constrictor-cloth.

**FILLES TRAQUEES** see *Nuit des Traquees, La*

**FINAL APPROACH** Intercontinental & Box Office Partners/Filmquest 1991 color/ws 103m. SP, D, P: Eric Steven Stahl. SP: also Gerald Laurence. Mus: Kirk Hunter. VisFX:(p) Denny Kelly; Apogee. OptFxDes: Filmquest VisFX. SpFxAnim: Harry Moreau. Ref: V 6/17/91: "gimmicky, tedious sci-fi film." PT 14:12. Martin: "confusing, muddled." SFChron Dtbk 7/5/92. With James B. Sikking, Hector Elizondo, Madolyn Smith, Kevin McCarthy.

Plot to make Stealth-like bombers out of plastic-coated conventional aircraft.

**FINAL CUT** see *Lights! Camera! Murder!*

**FINAL DESTINATION: UNKNOWN** see *Terrifying Tales*

**The FINAL EXECUTIONER** (I) (Viacom-TV) Cannon/Immagine 1983 ('85-U.S.) color 94m. (*L'Ultimo Guerriero*. aka *The Last Warrior*). D: Romolo Guerrieri. SP: Roberto Leoni. Mus: Carlo De Nonno. SpFX: Roberto Ricci. Ref: TV. V 1/1/86. Horacio Higuchi. TVG. With William Mang, Marina Costa, Harrison Muller, Woody Strode, Margi Newton, Karl Zinny.

Post-nuclear-holocaust society is divided into the radiation-free rich and the "contaminated masses." The former hunt the latter—with rifles with thermodynamic scopes "sensitive to body heat"—on the "hunting reserve," and hero Alan (Mang) becomes "target material for the Hunt".... The big news here is that man is inhuman to man. Flat dubbing makes all the actors sound like the same person. Script isn't nearly as inspiring as intended.

**FINAL FANTASY, Chapters 1 & 2** (J) NTT 1994 anim color c60m. Ref: TV: S. Baldric video; Eng. titles; OAV?

"The Darkness is coming!" Space Calendar Year 1000, Planet R. Ingredients include Crystals which control the elements (one enters heroine Lenaley's body and produces a shining butt), a giant loathsome, the flying pirate Rouge, and a tickling machine.... Kinda cute action-fantasy-comedy. Some nice visual details (e.g., the floating rocks).

**FINAL MISSION** Vidmark/Hess-Kallberg 1993 color 91m. SP,D: Lee Redmond. SP: also Sam Montgomery et al. Ph: Eric Goldstein. Mus: Richard Marvin. PD: W.B. Wheeler. SpFxCoord: Larry Fioritto. Key Mkp: Rene Dashiell. VR Des: HM3 et al. Computer Anim: After Science. LaserFX: Laser Magic. Opt: Mercer. Ref: TV. Stanley: "post-hypnotic zombie-making computer system." With Billy Wirth, Elizabeth Gracen, Steve Railsback, Corbin Bernsen, Richard Bradford, John Prosky.

"Ultimate advance in technology": virtual reality and F-16 jets. (vc box) It's "one hell of a video game" and involves "strange dreams," strange references to "dosages," strange lasers, "electroanalytic sedation," "brain stimulation," and "mind control codes" .... Scorecard for Operation Final Mission: okay aerial photography and computer effects ... predictable plot twists ... a rather incredible assassination tale ... and the spectacle of "L.A. Law"'s Arnie (Bernsen) as the right-wing crazy upset re the downsizing of the Pentagon.

**FINAL ROUND** Ent. Securities & Den Pictures(Robert Vince) 1993 color 87m. D: George Erschbamer. SP: Arne Olsen. Ph: Rick Maguire. Mus: G. Coleman. PD: C. Gallo. SpFxEd: Todd Johnson, Steve Patino et al. Mkp: C.M. Souza. Ref: TV. Stanley. Martin. TVG. With Lorenzo Lamas, Kathleen Kinmont, A. Olsen, Anthony De Longis, Clark Johnson, Stephen Mendel.

"I like to watch." Human hunters track human "huntees" in the 2-mile-long, 1/2-mile-wide La Mirada Industrial Complex, while international bettors place bets and warped bigwigs viddy it all with surveillance cameras. ("Kind of like snuff cable.") High-tech variation on "The Most Dangerous Game" is an elementary budget special.

**FINAL SACRIFICE, The** see *Quest for the Lost City*

**The FINAL SANCTION** Action International (David Marriott/David Winters) 1990 color 84m. SP, D: David A. Prior. SpFX: Sean Holton. Ref: V 1/14/91: "simple and effective." PT 12:52: "mediocre." With Ted Prior, Robert Z'Dar, Renee Cline, William Smith.

Warriors fight one-on-one to settle international crisis.

**The FINAL TEST** (H.K.) Golden Harvest/Bo Ho Films (Paragon) 1987 (1986) color with tinted sequence/ws 98m. SP, D: Lo Kin. Ref: TV: Rainbow Video; Eng. titles. NST! 4:23. With Wai Tin Chi, Chin Siu Ho, Debra Sim.

Reworking of *Outland* takes place around the year 2027, in a "land where freedom is dead," as the song here goes. The mining company Cosmos IV is rumored to be using drugs to boost worker production. An undercover agent finds that dying workers are vomiting "red stuff" and suspects that the foreman is administering the stimulant Ritalin—which is addictive and paralyzes the nervous system, causing mental retardation—to his workers. At the end—in the only interesting effects-and-makeup sequence—the company's head honcho turns out to be an android.... Unremarkable sf-actioner. Best hokey song lyric: "Evil grins at me with disdain."

**FINAL YAMATO** (J) 1983 anim color 163m. (aka *Space Cruiser Yamato, The Concluding Chapter. III Uchu Senkan*

*Yamato - Kanketsuhen*). Ref: TV: vt; no Eng. Animag 10:19: vt version adds scenes. 6:19.

Year 2203. Uruk city/fortress leader Lugal De Zahl plots to use the wandering water-world Aquarius to flood Earth and transform it into a home for his own people. At the end, the Yamato is destroyed destroying Aquarius.... Epic-squared animated saga tries to overwhelm with the sheer magnitude of its conceptions—the lush graphics feature galactic cataclysms, vast tidal waves, gigantic spaceships. Film's chief strength: the pleasingly envisioned variety of space scapes and ships. Nifty visual: the waterfall in space. Nifty weapon: the "strangling" lightning, which atomizes incoming missiles. Script incorporates bits and pieces of *Star Wars* and *Star Trek—The Motion Picture,* plus a horrible "lyrical" song interlude in space. The final hour turns superficially solemn and includes a few too many sentimental death scenes. Typically stolid Japanese character animation.

**The FINE ART** Stanze-McClelland 1992 color 55m. SP, D, Ph, Ed: Eric Stanze. Mus: M. Meyer et al. SpMkp: Tony Bridges. Ref: TV: Tempe Video; co-feature with *The Scare Game*. With Lisa Morrison, Jeremy Wallace.

"He paints the pictures ... then goes out and kills them for real." At large: the Cedar Hill Slayer. At the end: the slasher slashed.... Talky, dawdling buildup to the twist finish. Not worth the wait. Shot-on-tape.

**2 FINGERS AT THE WINDOW** 1942. Ref: TV. Everson/More. Weldon. Stanley. no Hardy/HM. Maltin '92. Scheuer.

"Ain't no percentage in getting their heads split open." "Persecution psychotics" are committing ax murders in Chicago, but an actor (Lew Ayres) believes that "somebody sent them." That somebody proves to be Caesar Ferrari (Basil Rathbone), aka the Ridgely Clinic's Dr. Santelle, "as abominable a human being as there is".... The idea of the remote-control madmen is a jim-dandy horror premise. Unfortunately, it's played—and not well—for mystery, suspense, and comedy. The only chilly elements: Bronislau Kaper's music and Rathbone's voice. Ayres salvages a few scenes in an otherwise ill-conceived role.

**The FINISHING TOUCH** Col(Steve Rabiner) 1991 color 82m. D: Fred Gallo. SP: A.L. Greene. Ref: PT 19:17. Martin: "unimaginative plot." no Stanley. With Michael Nader, Shelley Hack, Arnold Vosloo, Ted Raimi, Art Evans.

"Psychotic killer ... sells ... videotapes of the murders." (Martin)

**FIORE DAI PETALE D'ACCIAIO** see *Flowers with Petals of Steel*

**FIRE DRAGON** (H.K.) Regal Films (Thomas Ng) 1994 color/ws feature (*The Fiery Dragon Kid* - ad t). D: Yuen Wo Ping. Ref: TV: Tai Seng video; Eng. titles. V 6/13/94:18: in H.K. With Lam Cheng Ha, Mok Siu Chung.

Fire Dragon, a martial artist, can act like a flame thrower and makes an entrance flying out of a ball of flame. Plus the Invincible Fire (a flaming sword), Fire's Palm power (flames from hands), and a "ghost"-scare bit.... Routine actioner with the fun fire gimmick. Scariest scene: the fire "dust" igniting and burning the general to death.

**FIRE IN THE SKY** Para Joe Wizan/Todd Black) 1993 color/ws 107m. D: Robert Lieberman. SP: Tracy Torme, from Travis Walton's book *The Walton Experience*. Ph: Bill Pope. Mus: Mark Isham. SpVisFX: IL&M; (sup) Michael Owens. SpFxCoord: A.L. Lorimer. Creature Sup: Jeff Mann. PD: Laurence Bennett. Ref: TV. V 3/15/93: "prosaic." SFChron 3/13/93: "odd, interesting piece of Americana." SFChron Dtbk 9/12/93. ad. With D. B. Sweeney, Robert Patrick, Craig Scheffer, Peter Berg, James Garner, Henry Thomas, Noble Willingham, Kathleen Wilhoite.

"Based on a true story." A UFO visiting Sitgreaves National Forest in Arizona abducts Travis Walton (Sweeney). Five days later, he shows up cold, naked, and dehydrated .... Easier to take than the similar *Communion*. Best thing about the film: the looks on the faces of the witnesses to the abduction—before anybody says or we see anything. ("That ain't no fire!") The aliens appear to be intergalactic surgeons or biology students.

**The FIRE NEXT TIME** CBS-TV/RHI Ent. & the Kirch Group (Halmi/Self) 1993(1992) color c180m. D: Tom McLoughlin. Tel & Exec Co-P: James Henerson. Mus: Laurence Rosenthal. Consul: Syd Mead. SpFxCoord: James Reedy. Key Mkp: M. Hughes. Ref: TV: alternately called the "CBS Sunday Movie" and a "CBS Mini-Series." V 4/12/93:32. 4/5/93:M-30(ad). SFChron 4/16/93. TVG. With Craig T. Nelson, Bonnie Bedelia, Richard Farnsworth, Jurgen Prochnow, Justin Whalin, Ashley Jones, Louise Fletcher.

"Sometime soon," in a future world of global-warning-spawned "killer storms," dried-up rivers, malaria, unending heatwaves and brushfires, "record high temperatures," crop failures, "carbon cards," Capistrano-wary swallows, and solar cars. Middling mixture of disaster spectacle, science fiction, and human drama. Familiar storytelling, decent acting.

**FIRE TRIPPER** (J) CPM/Shogakukan & OV Kikaku & Studio Pierrot (Rumiko Takahashi & Shogakukan) 1986 ('92-U.S.) anim color 51m. (Rumic World series). D: Osamu Uemura. SP: Tomoko Konparu. Story: R. Takahashi. SdFxD: S. Shiba. Ref: TV: U.S. Manga Corps video; Eng. titles. J Anim Program Guide.

Interesting, if confusing science-fantasy re "time slipping," between the "civil war era" in Japan and the present day. Seventeen-year-old Suzuko and the toddler "Suzu" prove to be two versions of the same person, in the previous era. Back in the present, her older version figures that she and Shukumaru (who is also around in toddler as well as teenage form) have to "slip" back together to be reunited and marry. (They got separated during the first time slip.)

**FIREFIGHT** 1987 color 100m. D: Scott Pfeiffer. Ref: Hound: post-nuke wasteland. With James Pfeiffer, Janice Carraher, Jack Tucker.

**FIREHEAD** Pyramid/AIP Studios (The Winters Group/SI) 1990 color 88m. SP, D, P: Peter Yuval. SP: also Jeff Mandel. Mus: Vladimir Horunzhy. Pyrotechnics: David Bishop; (fx) Chuck Whitton. Ref: TV. V 2/18/91. With Christopher Plummer, Chris Lemmon, Martin Landau, Brett Porter, Gretchen Becker.

Ivan (Porter), or "Firehead," a telekinetic soldier opposed to "immoral" governments in general and the "Upper Order" in particular, can "move molecules" and, with blue eye-rays, de-

stroy factories. He also wields, on occasion, a blue protective shield. At one point, a "parabolic phase shifter" sends Ivan's power back at him.... Juvenile sf-intrigue. Chris Lemmon comes off as an insubstantial Jack Lemmon (i.e., Pop).

**FIREPOWER** PM 1993 color feature. D, P: Richard Pepin. SP: M. January. Ref: SFChron Dtbk 1/2/94: "sci-fi kung fu." PT 19:17: "gets pretty dull." no Martin. With Joseph Ruskin, Jim Hellwig, Chad McQueen, G. Daniels.

The Ring of Death and Personal Freedom Zones, in the year 2006.

**FIRESTARTER** Univ/Dino De Laurentiis (Frank Capra, Jr.) 1984 color 115m. D: Mark L. Lester. SP: Stanley Mann, from Stephen King's book. Mus: Tangerine Dream. SpFX: Mike Wood, Jeff Jarvis. OptFX: Van Der Veer. Mkp: J. A. Sanchez. Ref: TV. V 5/9/84. SFExam 5/11/84. With David Keith, Drew Barrymore, George C. Scott, Martin Sheen, Heather Locklear, Art Carney, Louise Fletcher, Moses Gunn, Freddie Jones, Richard Warlock.

The U.S. Department of Scientific Intelligence's Lot 6 compound—an experimental hallucinogenic and a pituitary extract—enhanced Andrew McGee's (Keith) psychic powers, and now "The Shop" wants him back. He and his pyrokinetic daughter, "Charlie" (Barrymore), are taken to Longmont, Virginia.... Awkward exposition, wobbly plot development, hokey-garish climax. Fun only at a Let's-see-what-Effects-Central-can-do-next level. Charlie has as many "fathers" (including surrogates) here as Norman had mothers in *Psycho II*. Silliest stunt: Charlie burning a bullet in mid-air.

**Eine FIRMA FUR DE EWIGKEIT** (W.G.) Gmohling-Futura-November 1984 86m. SP, D: Rolf Gmohling. Mus: Deubel, Esslinger. Ref: V 5/2/84: A Firm Forever - tr t; a "quite respectable feature." With Jim Kain, Rudolf Schwarz, Peter Schlesinger.

Future jobless, government-less West German society.

**FIRST BORN** (B-Austral.-N.Z.) BBC-TV & Australian Broadcasting & TV N.Z. (Sally Head) 1988 ('89-U.S.) color c155m. D: Philip Saville. SP: Ted Whitehead, from Maureen Duffy's novel "Gor Saga." Ph: David Feig. Mus: Hans Zimmer. PD: Humphrey Jaeger. SpFX: Andy Lazell. Mkp: Elizabeth Rowell. Ref: TV. Horacio Higuchi. V 7/5/89:49. With Charles Dance, Julie Peasgood, Jamie Foster (Gor), Gabrielle Anwar, Peter Wiggins (young Gor).

"It looks human!" Dr. Edward Forester (Dance) creates a test-tube gorilla-human hybrid, Gordon, who is very hairy at birth and who grows to become a "strong and beautiful child." But an operation on his vocal cords is required to help the mute Gor.... Ding-a-ling gorilla/human soaper gets most of its dramatic mileage out of the fact that the doctor has to keep Gor's origins a secret, even (or especially) from Gor. This problem child's problems are unusual, but not necessarily interesting, and predictable complications ensue when the eighteen-year-old Gordon waxes romantic. (Doctor: "There's something I've got to tell you.")

**The FIRST POWER** Orion/Nelson Ent. & Interscope (David Madden) 1990 color 98m. (*Pentagram. Transit* - early titles). SP, D: Robert Resnikoff. Mus: S. Copeland. SpMkpFX: Ed French. MechFX: Image Engineering; (coord) P. M. Chesney.

Title Seq: Dan Perri. Ref: TV. V 4/11/90. V/Mifed '89:140. MFB'90:294-5. ad. Sacto Bee 4/9/90. With Lou Diamond Phillips, Tracy Griffith, Jeff Kober (Patrick Channing), Elizabeth Arlen, Dennis Lipscomb, Carmen Argenziano, Nada Despotovich (bag lady).

"I believe satan has granted one of his disciples the first power—resurrection!" Patrick Channing, the Pentagram Killer, has been executed, "but his spirit has been released," according to "professional psychic" Tess Seaton (Griffith). Channing's spirit can now possess, temporarily, "vulnerable" people and kill again, and he makes the hero-cop (Phillips) "see things".... For the most part predictable *Exorcist* thrills, though the sequence in which the psychic "relives" Patrick's early torment has a glimmer of originality, and there's a good stunt with a levitating bag lady at a window. Otherwise, the only fun is seeing Channing periodically leap off the top of tall buildings and hit the ground running.

*FIRST SPACESHIP ON VENUS** Crown Int'l. (Centrala)/Lluzjon-DEFA 1960 ('62-U.S.) 80m.(130m.) (*Spaceship to Venus*-int t. *Raumschiff Venus Antwortet Nicht*). Mus D:(U.S.) Gordon Zahler. SpPhFX: Martin Sonnabend. Ref: TV. Lee. AFI. Weldon. Ecran F 29:56-9. Hardy/SF. Lentz. Stanley. V 12/19/62. Warren/KWTS! Martin. Maltin '92. Scheuer.

1985. An expedition to Venus finds a huge sphere which converts energy into mass and controls the planet's gravity, images of the Venusians etched on their walls (by the force of an atomic explosion), plant life, living ooze, and mechanical, data-storing "bugs." The 1908 Siberian explosion is explained as an abortive Venusian invasion.... The first half of this early Lem adaptation contains nothing that you haven't seen in American sf movies of the Fifties—meteor showers, cute little tank-like robots, etc. But the scenes on Venus are lively and fairly inventive, and the landscape—a bad-dream panorama of coral-like formations, ghostly mists, and dangling "vines"—is sufficiently un-Earthly, and atmospherically imagined. The message from Venus is a familiar one: Don't fool with Mother Atomic Energy. ("Go boom!") Some of the music is from old Universal monster movies.

The **FIRST VAMPIRE IN CHINA** (H.K.) Eternal Film 1986? color/ws c91m. D: Yam Chun-Lu. Ref: TV: Sunny Video; Eng. titles. Y.K. Ho. NST! 4:23. Jones.

In a prologue—set during the "War Centuries"—the body of a dead wizard-aided war-lord is "carved" with a "bewitched rhinohorn" and buried in gold-threaded jade. During a strange "celestial configuration," when the moon dips "close to China," the war-lord is resurrected as the "first vampire in China".... The present: The war-lord's mask is removed, and he revives in his royal tomb in Mount Mao. Meanwhile, moon-worshipping hopping vampires revive when their "hanging coffins" are disturbed; a ghost general and his soldiers inhabit a "most horrible house" and attempt to kill the heroine (his son wants her); a "ghost of March" is revived by bone-ash; and a black-magic rooster, unburied, comes back to life. ("A vampire cock?")

The comedy sequence with the martial-arts vampire rooster is certainly unusual—the bird can swivel its head around, *Exorcist* style, and its scratch makes one's eyes turn green and makes one want to crow—while the glowing, holy "jump ropes" scene is a natural for a hopping vampire. The first half of *First Vampire* is

amiably screwy, and the prologue is visually impressive—it might be the lead-in to a serious horror movie. But assorted co-plots clog the narrative, and the war-lord vampire is a standard inexorable menace, although his gold-and-jade costume and mashed face provide pictorial punch. The movie, it transpires, is just a comic-book fan's fantasy, or dream.

**FISH TALES** WB 1936 anim 7m. D: Jack King. Ref: "WB Cartoons": Porky Pig. LC. no Lee.

"Giant fish, monster worms" (WBC), in visualized nightmare.

**FIST OF STEEL** (Sp?) Action Int'l. (David Hunt) 1991 color feature (*Eternal Fist* - orig t). D: Irvin Johnson. SP: Anthony Jesu. Ref: PT 16:17: "post-nuke." Stanley: "little plot." With Cynthia Khan, Dale Cook, Don Nakaya Nielsen, James Gaines.

**FIST OF THE NORTH STAR** see *Hokuto No Ken*

**FISTS OF STEEL** PDA HV/Fists of Steel (P. J. Shannon) 1989 color 93m. SP, D, P: Jerry Schafer. Line P: Rory Calhoun. Mus: J. Allocco, D. Kurtz. Ref: V 7/15/91: "passable action film." With Carlos Palomino, Marianne Marks, Henry Silva, Robert Tessier.

"Robot operated by animatronics."

2 **FIVE DOLLS FOR AN AUGUST MOON** 1970 ws 78m. AD: G. Aldobran or Aldebaran. Mkp: Oretta Melaranci (sp?). Ref: TV: Redemption video; Eng. dubbed. Ecran F 30:72. no V. Film Superstore: aka *Island of Terror*. Palmerini.

"We'll all wind up in this damned freezer." Mario Bava dud has two fatal knifings and other assorted murders, a terrible pop-music score, bland characters, an uninvolving "Ten Little Indians" mystery plot, and the image for which the movie was obviously made: the bodies in the plastic bags swinging from the ropes in the meat locker. Raison d'etre number 2: the image of the glass balls bouncing down the stairs and into the tub where the dead woman rests in bloodied water. Handsome, vacant.

**555** King Video (Koz) 1989 (1988) color 80m. D, P: Wally Koz. SP: Roy M. Koz. Mus: F. Rodriguez. Ref: V 2/15/89:56(hv): "for hardcore gore fetishists." McCarty II: "bottom of the barrel." With Mara-Lynn Bastian, Charles Fuller, Greg Kerouac.

Lakeside slasher at large.

The **FIVE STAR STORIES** (J) Kadokawa Shoten 1989 (1988) anim color/ws 66m. Based on the comics by Mamoru Nagano. Ref: TV: Kadokawa Video; no Eng. (apart from title). Animag 5:5. 6:4. 7:7-18.

Year 2988, in the Joker Systems, in space, an area containing five stars. Ingredients: hibernation machines ... giant vehicles, both land and space ... laser swords ... artificially-created people ... a robot suit with dual chainsaws ... and huge human-run robots, or "mortar headds".... Talky and involved, but occasionally quite atmospheric.

*The **FLAME BARRIER** 1958 (aka *It Fell from the Flame Barrier. Beyond the Flame Barrier*). Mus: Gerald Fried. OptFX: Westheimer. Mkp: Richard Smith. Ref: TV. Lee. LC. TVG. no V. Warren/KWTS!: Sam X. Abarbanel - orig story. Lentz. Hardy/SF. Maltin '92. Scheuer.

An expedition to Yucatan—where the X-117 satellite fell from the "flame barrier" (200 miles above the Earth)—discovers that the animal life there is "beginning to scatter" and die. A native is burned to death—the "god of fire" is blamed when the body self-incinerates—and scorched earth marks the area where the falling satellite passed. Behind it all: a cellophane-like "thing" in a cave, which "destroys everything within its range." It grows out of the satellite, and its size doubles every two hours. And a scientist who went too near it has become part of it.

Not-very-well-remembered combo sf/jungle pic—and for good reason. It's mostly filler incidents with snakes and spiders, plus facile "characterizing" conversations. You won't really care what happens to the cynical Great White Hunter (Arthur Franz), his tequila-happy brother (Robert Brown), or the "cafe society" woman (Kathleen Crowley) who hires them to find her husband. (He's the one who's part of the "thing.") The only surprise: the incinerating native. The other mysterious details are more or less expected, and the "monster" is there only to be dispatched. Okay musical score, passable performances.

**FLAMING EARS** (Austrian) WMM 1992 color 83m. (*Rote Ohren Setzen Durch Afche*). SP, D, P: Angela Hans Scheirl, Dietmar Schipek, Urusla Puerrer. SpFX: Anthony Escott, Andrea Witzmann. Ref: V 6/15/92: "rich and moody atmospherics." SFChron 6/25/92: "wacky lesbian sci-fi fantasy ... ambitious, clumsy and generally terrible." With Susanna Heilmayr, U. Puerrer, A. H. Scheirl.

Year 2700. "Terminator-like creature ... resuscitating vampire."

The **FLAMING SIGNAL** Imperial (William Pizor)/William Berke Prods. 1933 b&w 59m. (64m.) SP, Adap, D: C. Edward Roberts. D: also George Jeske. Story: William G. Steuer. Ph: Irving Akers. Mus sc: Lee Zahler. Sets: F. W. Widdowson. Ref: TV. Greg Luce. Turner/Price. TVG. no V. no Maltin '92. Hound. no Martin. no Scheuer. no Stanley. no Lee. no Lentz. With Marceline Day, John Horsley, Noah Beery, Carmelita Geraghty, Mischa Auer, Henry B. Walthall, J. Olmes.

"He tabu. By and by, he come to life." Tabu Island, the South Seas. A drunk (Beery) shoots and kills the "tabu doctor, or high priest" (Auer), of the local natives. ("Gave me the shivers!") A ritual of drum-beating, dancing, and running around revives him, and he rises from his ceremonial bed in a cave. ("Just think of raising a dead man!")

Primitive early talkie chiller from Poverty Row. Quasi-coherent film doesn't even make it clear if the native which the dog star, Flash, fights at the end is the risen priest. Camp highlight: hero Jim (Horsley) reassuring the nervous heroine: "But, Sally, we're starting a new day—you and I and Flash."

The **FLASH** CBS-TV/Pet Fly Prods. & WB-TV 1990 color c90m. D: Rob Iscove. SP, Exec P: Danny Bilson, Paul De Meo. Based on DC Comics. Ref: TVG 9/20/90: "2-hour premiere." V 9/24/90:89: "sharp, tense and alive." Martin. SFChron Dtbk 7/12/92:58: Warner HV. Sacto Bee 9/20/90: "looks and sounds terrific, if not exactly original." With John Wesley Shipp (The Flash), Amanda Pays, Alex Desert, Tim Thomerson, M. Emmet Walsh.

Cop chemist splashed with chemicals during a thunderstorm develops super-speed.

**FLASH—FUTURE KING FU** (H.K.) Verdull Ltd. (Chiu-Wong Hung) 1984 (1983) color 78m. (*Daleitai*. aka *Health Warning*). D: Huang Zhiqiang. SP: Liao Yongliang. Ph: Shao Yuanzhi. Mus: Shen Shengde. AD: Huang An. SpFX: Wu Guohua. Mkp: Liu Jicheng. Ref: TV: Ocean Shores Video; Eng. dubbed. Horacio Higuchi. Ecran F 65:66-8. With Johnny Wang aka Wang Long-wei, Gao Xiong, Lu Liangwei.

In the 21st Century, "super-charged ether" fuels cars, and the sadistic "disciples of X Gang" run the X Club, where the stage acts feature casually vicious "ballerinas" and where intrusive kung-fu boxers wind up with rabies-filled hypos in the back. Up next for X Gang: the computer-monitored transformation of the brain of one member's daughter. (The pulses of the computer-control-room's remote-controlled crews have been surgically lowered to activate key switches.).... A cross between *Liquid Sky* and *Chariots of Fire, Flash—Future Kung Fu* is a cold, determinedly weird stew of elements ranging from kung-fu boxing and computer-and-video high tech to neo-Nazism and newer-than-New-Wave-ism. The plot is a fragmented revenge/rescue story; the score, a John Carpenter monotone. Most of the decadence is window dressing, but here and there a glint of the authentically reptilian peeps through.

**FLASH GORDON** see *Defenders of the Earth*

**FLATLINERS** Col/Stonebridge Ent. (Michael Douglas, Rick Bieber) 1990 color/ws 111m. D: Joel Schumacher. SP, Exec Co-P: Peter Filardi. Mus: James Newton Howard. VisFxSup: Peter Donen. SpMkpFX: Greg Cannom. SpFX: Philip Cory, Hans Metz. Ref: TV. V 8/1/90. Sacto Bee 8/10/90. MFB'90:320-21. With Kiefer Sutherland, Julia Roberts, Kevin Bacon, William Baldwin, Oliver Platt.

"I don't wanna die. I wanna come back with the answers to death—and life." Five med students (Sutherland, Roberts, Bacon, Baldwin, and Platt) experiment with drugs and electricity, take turns playing brain dead for up to five minutes at a time. The movie—not as discreet as *The Walking Dead*—then visualizes their mental, or spiritual, activity, which scans like the promptings of guilt and remorse: Figures from their respective guilty pasts turn up, threateningly, in residual visions.... Script answers the question (in the affirmative), Is there psychology after death? Metaphysics becomes indistinguishable from psychoanalysis, as our "flatliners" seek atonement for past deeds. The beyond-death angle proves simply a questionable pretext for some *Solaris* speculations re human relationships, though these speculations provide occasional powerful moments.

**FLAVIA THE HERETIC** (I-F) PAC & ROC 1974 color/ws 96m. (2P *The Rebel Nun* - alt t. *Flavia la Monaca Musulmana*. aka *Flavia la Nonne Musulmane*. aka *Flavia Priestess of Violence*). D, P: Gianfranco Mingozzi. SP: Onofri, Tau, di Geronimo. Story: di Giovanbattista, Tau, Vietri. Ph: Alfio Contini. Mus: Nicola Piovani. Ref: TV: vt; Eng. dubbed. MFB'75:174. Hardy/HM. PT 19:11. Stanley.

Feminist tract which borders on parody of same features scattered fantastic and horrific elements, including a pre-credit beheading

... Tarantula cult crazies ... holy and unholy tortures ... a grisly death-by-spike ... and visions of a dead nun rising and laughing, a portrait bleeding, and St. George .... Or, The Nun's Gory. Lovingly shot (in Medieval-muted colors) and scored, but almost comically sensationalistic. Harshest epithet: "You're worse than a man!"

**FLESH AND THE BLOODY TERROR** (H.K.?) 1988 color feature (aka *Beasts*). D: Ken Yung. SP: Fong Ling Ching. Ref: Fango 107:60: "unflinching Asian variation on *The Last House on the Left*." NST! 4:23: "backwoods mutant-psychos." Weisser/ATC: D: Dennis Yu & Teddy Kwan. With F. Ling Ching.

**FLESH EATER** see *Revenge of the Living Zombies*

**FLESH-EATING MOTHERS** Panorama Ent./Indigo 1988 color 88m. SP, D: James A. Martin. SP: also Zev Shlasinger. Mus: Minerva. SpFX: Carl Sorensen. Anim: Lee Corey. Ref: TV. V 9/21/88. With Robert Lee Oliver, Donatella Hecht, Neal Rosen, Valorie Hubbard.

"I saw my mother eating my baby brother." A sexually-transmitted virus "active in females that have had children' gives said women great strength, big mouths, and an unhealthy appetite for human flesh. Parody of both J.D. and the *Night of the Living Dead* movies has a fairly simple programme, but the juxtaposition of the "Oh, Mother, how could you!" banalities with the gross cannibal-moms attacks carries the show, for a while. Prime witty, or dumb (or both) image: Mom chomping away on Billy's arm, which still bears his new baseball mitt. The knowingly bad script, unfortunately, can't come up with much to support its winning central conceit.

**FLESH FOR FRANKENSTEIN** Mark Curtis 198-? color c80m. D: Bill Blackman. SP: David Elliott. Ph: Michael Cates. Mus: John Further. Mkp: Alan Bouschard. Titles: Rapid Images. Ref: TV: Video Exclusives. With Dana Lynn, N. Nights, Ebony Ayes, Amy Berens.

Dr. X's kitchen-made concoction explodes and produces "Frankenstein," who is delegated to bring back women for the doc and his assistant, Igor. Frankenstein's friend Dream Girl uses a "reverse equation" concoction to make Dr. X and Igor disappear.... Hardcore sf employs a title once used for *Andy Warhol's Frankenstein,* but that's its sole claim to fame. Don't expect anything in the way of special makeup for this Black "Frankenstein."

**FLESH GORDON 2: FLESH GORDON MEETS THE COS-MIC CHEERLEADERS** (Can.) Concorde/Maurice Smith Prods. 1991 (1993) color c101m. (*Flesh Gordon Meets the Cosmic Cheerleaders* - cr t). SP, D: Howard Ziehm. SP: also Douglas Frisby. Ph: Danny Nowak. Mus: Paul Zaza. PD: Al Benjamin. VisFX:(d) T. Hitchcock; FX Center. Creature FX: Jim Towler. Stopmo: Lauritz Larson. Prosth: Rick Griffen. Ref: V 6/21/93:5 (rated, as *Flesh Gordon Meets the Cosmic Cheerleaders*). 11/22/89:54. Mifed '89:188(ad). SFChron Dtbk 9/26/93: "I worship this movie." TV: New Horizons HV (Filmvest Int'l.). With Vince Murdocco, Morgan Fox, Bruce Scott, William Dennis Hunt, Melissa Mounds, Robyn Kelly, Tony Travis.

Ice Planet, impotence ray, hemorrhoid field, excrement beings, "mammary magnification," and other grossness in space. Leaden, sub-Benny Hill hi-jinks.

**FLESH 1995** Le Salon 1985 color feature. Ref: Adam '93: sf. with Chris Allen.

"A future where recreational sex is against the law...."

**FLICKS** see *Loose Joints*

The **FLIGHT OF DRAGONS** (U.S.-J) ABC-TV/Rankin-Bass 1986 (1982) anim color 92m. D, P: Arthur Rankin, Jr., and Jules Bass. SP: Romeo Muller, from Peter Dickinson's book and "The Dragon and the George" by G. R. Dickson. Addl Mat'l: Jeffrey Walker. Ph: H. Omoto. Mus: Maury Laws. Des: Wayne Anderson. Anim Coord: Toru Hara. SdFX: Tom Clack. Ref: TV. V 12/3/80:79(ad). 2/17/82:19(ad). 3/30/83:85(ad). TVG: orig. scheduled for 9/4/83. Mag of F&SF 2/83. SFChron 8/1/86. TVG 8/2/86. Voices: John Ritter, Harry Morgan, James Earl Jones, James Gregory, Victor Buono.

Monsters and wizards here include Ommadon (Jones), the Red Wizard of black magic, headquartered in the Realm of the Red Death—Ommadon casts a spell of despair, dispatches dragon hordes, and, at the end, turns into a seven-headed monster ... a gigantic worm which lies in acidic slime ... rodent hordes which make a "mind burning" noise ... and a peg-legged, three-eyed ogre "big as a house".... Long-withheld cartoon feature is generally charming, occasionally pretentious, with more to it than most animated fantasies, though the animation itself is unimaginative. Jones's is one of the great voices; Morgan's distinctly modern-day voice jars. Highlight: Two dragons quaff mead while singing "Oh! Susanna!" Treacly title song; silly climactic science-vs.-magic duel.

**FLIGHT OF THE EAGLE** see *Wings of Oneamis*

**FLIGHT OF THE NAVIGATOR** (U.S.-Norw.) BV/PSO & Viking (New Star Ent.) 1986 color 89m. (*The Navigator* - orig t). D: Randal Kleiser. SP: Michael Burton, Matt MacManus. Story: Mark H. Baker. Mus: Alan Silvestri. SpVisFX: Cinema Research; (sup) Peter Donen; Fantasy II; (coord, Norw.) Craig Boyajian. Spaceship: (interior) The Design Setters; (exterior) Steve Austin; (coord) David Sharp. Computer anim: Omnibus Computer Graphics. OptFxSup:(Norw.) Joseph Wallikas. AnimFX: Available Light. SpFxSup: Jack Bennett. Puppet Mech: (Norw.) David Goldberg, Mike Sorensen. Creatures: Tony Urbano, Tim Blaney. Mkp: Philip Goldblatt. SdFxDes: Akai 5900 Digital Sampler. Ref: TV. MFB'87:149-50. V 7/30/86. TVG. V 10/24/84:136-7(ad). With Joey Cramer, Veronica Cartwright, Cliff De Young, Sarah Jessica Parker, Howard Hesseman, Paul Mall.

David Freeman (Cramer), 12, missing since 1978, turns up in 1986, still 12 years old, and undergoes a crash course re eight years of pop culture. Seems he has been programmed to be a celestial "navigator," and his mind contains (a nifty idea) "charts" of uncharted star systems. Plus: "Max" (Mall; voice: Pee-wee Herman)—an alien collecting life samples—and "mind transfer".... Would-be-Spielberg science-fantasy makes it halfway there: fun, some wonder, little feeling. In fun, effects/spectacle scenes, a spaceship skims along just above the ground, into the sea, and up over clouds. The amusing low comedy with David and "Max" unfortunately crowds out any semblance of storyline.

**\*The FLIGHT THAT DISAPPEARED** 1961. SP: R. & J. Hart, Orville Hampton (aka Owen Harris). Set Dec: Morris Hoffman. Mkp: Harry Thomas. FxEd: Al Bird. Ref: TV. Lentz. Hardy/SF. Weldon. Warren/KWTS! Lee. Stanley. no Maltin '92. no Scheuer. V 9/20/61.

"Where's Flight 60?" Trans-Coast Airways' L.A.-D.C. Flight 60 loses all four engines, but keeps gaining altitude until it's "over ten miles up," where the "future and the present meet" and a "jury of the future" suspends time for 24 hours ... and animation for most of the passengers and crew. Meanwhile, this jury of those who will not be born if a super-bomb is deployed convict Dr. Carl Morris (Dayton Lummis)—"father of the Beta Thermonuclear Warhead"—and Thomas Endicott (Craig Hill), rocket designer, of "destruction of the stream of life".... Stilted low-budgeter is half-idiotic, half-intriguing. Midway, it foregoes "Twilight Zone"-like spooky speculation (is this flight a ship of the dead?) for pure message-mongering.

**The FLINTBONES** Fresh Video 1992 color c80m. Ref: vc box: X-rated prehistory.

**The FLINTSTONES** Univ/Hanna-Barbera & Amblin (Bruce Cohen) 1994 color 92m. D: Brian Levant. SP: T.S. Parker, J. Jennewein, S. E. de Souza, based on the animated series. Ph: D. Cundey. Mus: D. Newman. PD: W. Sandell. SpVisFX: IL&M. Animatronics: Henson's. Ref: ad. V 5/23/94: "fine popcorn picture." SFChron 5/27/94: "the quintessential Just-Add-Water movie." Vallejo T-H 5/27/94: "slight but consistently enjoyable." With John Goodman, Elizabeth Perkins, Rick Moranis, Rosie O'Donnell, Kyle MacLachlan, Halle Berry, Elizabeth Taylor, Dann Florek, Richard Moll, Jonathan Winters, Harvey Korman. "This summer's dinosaur picture...." (V)

**FLINTSTONES, The** see also *Hollyrock-a-Bye Baby. I Yabba-Dabba Do!. Jetsons Meet the Flintstones, The.*

**FLINTSTONES MOVIE, The** see *I Yabba-Dabba Do!*

**The FLIPSIDE OF DOMINICK HIDE** (B) Lionheart-TV/BBC-TV 1980 color 90m. SP, D, Idea: Alan Gibson. SP: also Jeremy Paul. Ph: Dave Mutton; John Else. Songs: Rick Jones, David Pierce. AD: Roger Murray-Leach; Dick Coles. Video FX: Dave Jervis. VisFX: Peter Wragg, Charles Jeanes. Mkp: Dorka Nieradzik. Ref: TV. TVG. With Peter Firth, Caroline Langrishe, Patrick Magee, Timothy Davies; Pippa Guard, Michael Gough.

British miniseries sometimes shown on U.S. TV as two TV-movies, *Flipside* ... and *Another Flip for Dominick* (1982). Dominick Hide (Firth) travels, via time saucer, from the year 2130 to 1980 ("I come from the future"), tells of world war in 1999, and tries to smooth over the rough spots in his past by tinkering with them a bit. Talky, if ingeniously plotted sf.

**\*The FLORENTINE DAGGER** Harry Joe Brown 1935. Mus D: Leo F. Forbstein. Ref: TV. Taves/Florey. V 5/1/35. Lentz. Lee. Cinema (London) 9:10. Scheuer. no Maltin '92. With Henry O'Neill, Robert Barrat, Charles Judels.

A Clue Club Picture. "The ghosts of the Borgias still walk in me." People: Cesare (Donald Woods)—"cursed with a lethal legacy": As the last of the Borgias, he looks "exactly like Cesare Borgia," feels the "urge to kill," and pens a play in an attempt to exorcise his "ghost" ("Something of a Dracula type, I should say") ... Florence (Margaret Lindsay), who plays and "becomes" Lucrezia Borgia ... a mystery woman, Fredericka (Eily Malyon), of Frau Fredericka, Wigs and Masks ... and a masked, disfigured person, victim of someone who threw a candle and "made a monstrosity out of a beautiful woman." Places: the Hotel Cesare Borgia ... the castle of the Borgias ... and the "extremely weird" Ballau house.... Odd-bird mystery recalls, variously, *Phantom of the Opera, WereWolf of London* (compulsive killer), *The Brighton Strangler* (actress who "becomes" the character she plays), and *Scarface* (incest). And director Robert Florey seems to bring back some of the wall props and masks that he used for atmosphere in *Hole in the Wall.* The handsome production features off-angle shots and rack-focusing effects, but a verbose, arduously-plotted script foils it.

**FLOWERS IN THE ATTIC** New World/Charles Fries 1987 color 92m. SP, D: Jeffrey Bloom. From V. C. Andrews' novel. Mus: Christopher Young. SpFX: A&A, Dick Albain. Mkp: Robin Neal. Opt: Howard Anderson. Ref: screen, MFB'88:111. V 11/25/87. ad. With Louise Fletcher (Grandmother), Victoria Tennant, Kristy Swanson, Jeb Stuart Adams, Nathan Davis (Grandfather).

"Witches and monsters" seem, to some, to inhabit Foxworth Hall, "grandmother's house." At the least, one "crazy sick old man"—grandfather—does. And grandmother calls her daughter's four children, who now live with her, the "devil's spawn," and treats them accordingly. Slowly, the four are being poisoned, and four graves wait.... Bad Drama 1A, *Flowers in the Attic* might be "The Good Seed." The kids are alright here, but mother, grandmother, and grandfather are positively horrendous. If this sounds like the makings for a fun-horrific situation, hopeless writing and acting underscore every plot and character detail.

**FLOWERS WITH PETALS OF STEEL** (I) Parva 197-? color/ws 87m. (*Il Fiore dai Petale d'acciaio*). D, Co-SP: Gianfranco Piccioli. SdFX: L. Anzellotti. Ref: TV: VSOM; Eng. titles. no ETC/Giallos. Palmerini.

Slow, padded mystery-suspenser, with shocker touches—e.g., the dolls' "voices" assailing Gianni Garko's Dr. Vallenti ... the razor-slashing of Carroll Baker.

**The FLY** Fox/Brooksfilms (Stuart Cornfeld) 1986 color 100m. SP, D: David Cronenberg. SP: also Charles Edward Pogue. From George Langelaan's story. Mus: Howard Shore. Fly Des: Chris Walas. Ref: screen. V 8/13/86. East Bay Express 8/22/86. Berkeley Voice 9/3/86. SFExam 8/15/86. With Jeff Goldblum, Geena Davis, John Getz.

Scientist Seth Brundle's (Goldblum) teleportation device consists of a computer, a molecular analyzer, and telepods. After successfully teleporting a baboon, he teleports himself—but there is a fly in the telepod. Result: "fusion of Brundle and fly at molecular-genetic level." Brundle/fly craves sugar, sex, and gymnastics ... sheds teeth, nails, and all other body parts inessential to flies ... and emerges nearly all-fly. At the end, in a freak accident, he fuses with the telepod itself.... This remake of *The Fly* (1958) is entertaining at a Gross Science level. It plays on our queasiness re skin diseases, vomiting, oozing, bleeding, peeling, flies, and childbirth. And the effects—which recall, variously, effects in *First Men "In" the Moon*, the *Cat People* and *The Thing* remakes, *The Incredible Melting Man*, and *The Beast Within*—are very good. But they tend to take over from Goldblum, who still manages to provide some welcome humor and pathos in both "before" and "after" phases. In a clinically chilling, post-first-fusion "revelation" scene, the computer monitor provides the initially-mystified Brundle with, first, a detail of part of what proves to be a fly, then a more-complete angle, then the whole fly.

Sequel: *Fly II, The*. See also: *Daffy Duck's Quackbusters*.

The **FLY II** Fox/Brooksfilms (Steven-Charles Jaffe/Stuart Cornfeld) 1989 color/ws 104m. D & FxDes: Chris Walas. Story, SP: Mick Garris. SP: also Jim & Ken Wheat, Frank Darabont. SpFX: (coord) John Thomas; (creature sup) Jon Berg; (anim) Available Light. Mus: Christopher Young. SpFxMkp: Stephan Dupuis. Title Des: Sam Alexander Prods. SdFX: Ralph Wikke. Ref: TV: CBS/Fox Video. MFB'89:300-301. V 2/15/89. With Eric Stoltz, Daphne Zuniga, Lee Richardson, John Getz, Frank Turner.

The Return of the Fly. Seth's son Martin Brundle (Stoltz), suffering from Brundle's Accelerated Growth Syndrome, looks at least fifteen at age five, which age, for him, is maturity and means that his "aberrant chromosomes" are now at large and initiating a "genetic metamorphosis." His human body begins decaying. He enters a cocoon, then emerges wholly monstrous, or so it seems. Ultimately, he "swaps genes" with "Dad"—Anton Bartok (Richardson), his callous sponsor at Bartok Industries—while undergoing teleportation, and emerges as his human self. "Dad," however, is a mess.... The *Them!*-plus-*Alien* final monster is worth a look, but not worth the wait. Despite the general grisliness, Part II is a bland, sanitized version of *The Fly* (1986). Tired Evil-Corporation themes overwhelm even the back-by-popular-demand yuck-pathos, here furnished by the Martin/Beth (Zuniga) strange romance.

**FLY ME TO THE MOON** (Fili) Regal Int'l. 1987 color c96m. Story, D: Mike Relon Makiling. SP: Roger Fuentebella. Story: also Tony Fajardo. Ph: Rody Lacap, Ding Austria. Mus D: Boy Alcaide. Assoc D: Gregg De Guzman. PD: Manny Morfe. VisFX: Cine Magic. SpFX: Danny Rojo. SdFX: Rodel Capule. Mkp: L. Juego. Ref: TV: Regal Video; some Eng. With Val Sotto, Jaypee De Guzman, Rose Ann Gonzales, Joseph De Cordova (professor), Tia Pusit, Flora Gasser, Val Castello Jr. (Superman), Wilson Go.

Three goofs hide in Professor Collins' time machine and encounter Magellan and MacArthur. They later return to his laboratory, take his "space rocket" to the moon, then to the (inhabited) planet Andromeda, then—with newly-acquired super powers—go back to Earth. Plus: Superman, at first sans super suit ("I'm freezing!") ... an anti-gravity invention ... zebra, lion, and pig aliens (in Andromeda's prison) ... a hologram projector ... and adjustable-length light sabres.... Vapid sf-comedy, with rather endearingly tacky outer-space effects. The action on Andromeda is shot in a kind of stippled motion.

**FOCUS ON FISHKO: The CINEMATIC GENIUS OF SEYMOUR Z. FISHKO** Cinemax-TV 198-? color 24m. D: Peter Bonerz. SP: Michael Barrie, Jim Mulholland. Ref: TV. Jim Shapiro. With Howard Hesseman.

*Close Encounters of the Third Kind*, insists Monarch Studios' S. Z. Fishko, was a ripoff of his first sf flick, *Commies from Mars* (1956), aka *Commies from Venus* (or are they from Saturn?). This mock-documentary features "clips" from the latter, and from other Fishko triumphs like *Dragstrip Mummy* (1958), *The Creeping Hand* (1962), *Revenge of the 80-Foot Stripper* (1957), *Crabla* (1959), *Son of Samson in the Valley of the Gold Dragons* (1965)—with its "seven-headed dragon of Thebes"—"They Froze Hitler's Head," and *Prehistoric Teens* (1955), a "cinematic bridge between neo-realism and the New Wave." Funny ribbing of *Z* movies, their directors, and their more sophisticated adherents.

**FOLDS OF THE FLESH** (I) 1970 color 90m. (*Las Endemoniadas. Nelle Pieghe della Carne*). SP, D, P: Sergio Bergonzelli. SP: also Fabio de Agostini. Ref: McCarty II: "dreck." no Hound. MV: gore, "remote mansion"; aka *In the Folds of the Flesh*. Palmerini: "second-rate."With Pier Angeli, Eleonora Rossi Drago, Alfredo Mayo, Fernando Sancho.

"Murderous mother/daughter slasher team."(McC)

**FOLLIA OMICIDA** see *Fear* (1980)

**FOLLOW THAT BIRD** WB/Children's TV Workshop & World Film Services 1985 part anim color 88m. (aka *Sesame Street Presents: Follow That Bird*). D: Ken Kwapis. SP: Tony Geiss, Judy Freudberg. SpFxD: Colin Chilvers. Ref: TV. V 7/31/85. Sacto Union 8/3/85. SFChron 8/2/85.

More or less incidental monsters here include the fanged, monocled, Dracula-type Count von Count (voice: Jerry Nelson) ... the hubcap-eating Cookie Monster (Frank Oz) ("Me growing monster") ... Telly Monster ... and a phony "invisible gorilla".... Dave Thomas and Joe Flaherty are a pleasantly silly pair of villains (Sam and Sid Sleaze, resp.), and there's some adventurous camerawork (by Curtis Clark). But wistful-upbeat songs—which just kind of well up out of nothing—clog the works.

**FOLLOW THAT GOBLIN!** (B-Israeli) Scopus Films & One Eighty One Prods. (Lubell) 1992 clay anim color 28m. SP: Ruth Ebenstein. Story, AD: D. Codor. Story: Jonathan Lubell. Ref: TV: F.H.E. video. Voices: Daniel Diker (Gerbert Goblin et al), Chaya Golinkin.

Fairgrounds haunted house features a witch, a Frankenstein-type monster ("Frankie"), a Dracula-type, a wolf man, a gorgon, a mummy, a hunchback, and ghosts. Minor-league kidstuff.

**FOOD** (Cz-B) Svankmajer 1994 14m. Ref: PFA notes 8/29/94: "cannibalistic banquet."

**FOOD OF THE GODS II** (Can.) Concorde/Centauri/Canadian Ent. & Company Ltd. (Rose & Ruby/David Mitchell) 1989 color 91m. (aka *Gnaw: Food of the Gods II*). D, Co-P: Damian Lee. SP: Richard Bennett, E. K. Brewster. Story: Bennett. VisFX: Ted Rae. Ref: V 6/7/89: "silly sequel" to *Food of the Gods* (II).

Fango 4/90. TV clipping. McCarty II. With Paul Coufos, Lisa Schrage, Colin Fox, Jackie Burroughs.

Rats scarf up growth serum, run wild at university.

**FOOL'S FIRE** American Playhouse/W.M.G. & Rebo Studio (Fool's Fire Prods.) 1992 color 53m. SP, D, Char Des, Co-P: Julie Taymor. From Edgar Allan Poe's story "Hop-Frog" or "Hopfrog," with excerpts from "The Bells" and "A Dream within a Dream" and Rabelais' "Gargantua & Pantagruel." Mus: Elliot Goldenthal. PD: G. W. Mercier. SpFX: Neil Smith, Mark Forker. Mkp: S. W. Bryant. Ref: TV. TVG. V 2/3/92:30(ad), 82. SFChron 3/26/92. New York 3/30/92. With Michael Anderson, Mireille Mosse, Tom Hewitt, Norma Pratt.

"This is my last jest." Court jester Hopfrog (Anderson) promises his king (Hewitt) a "marvelous surprise" which will "scare the ladies." "The Eight Chained Orangutangs," however, proves to be his fiery revenge on the callous king and his seven ministers.... Sets, effects, lighting, and grotesque, outsized costumes are stylized to a fare-thee-well, in this slight, lurid, pleasingly phantasmagorical Poe anecdote.

**FOOL'S NIGHT** see *Killer Party*

**FOOTROT FLATS** (N.Z.) Magpie (John Barnett, Pat Cox) 1986 color anim 70m. SP, D; Murray Ball, based on his cartoon-strip characters. Mus: Dave Dobbyn. Anim D: R. Smit. Ref: V 12/31/86: "copious action & sly raunchiness." no Stanley. Voices: Peter Rowley, John Clarke, Peter Hayden.

"Hell-hounds" and "croco-pigs" guard the evil Murphy's property.

**FOR THE LOVE OF WILLADEAN** Disney-TV/Ron Miller 1964 color 92m. D: Byron Paul. Tel: Arnold and Lois Peyser. Story: Borden Deal. Ph: William Snyder. Mus: Franklyn Marks, Bob Brunner. AD: Carroll Clark, M. A. Davis. Mkp: Pat McNalley. Ref: TV. With Ed Wynn, Michael McGreevey, Billy Mumy, John Anderson, Roger Mobley, Terry Burnham, Barbara Eiler, Harry Harvey Sr.

"I hear there are vampire bats flyin' around in there!" Visitors by night to the old McTeague place find "lots of spooky shadows," "ghost" howls, a rocking-chair "ghost," and Wynn's Alfred, a kindly hobo. ("Maybe the place is haunted!") Tepid juvenile comedy-drama was apparently a "Wonderful World of Disney" two-parter before it became a TV-movie.

**FORBIDDEN, The** see *Candyman*

**FORBRYDELSENS ELEMENT** (Dan.) Per Holst 1984 color 100m. SP, D: Lars von Trier. SP: also Niels Voersel. Mus: Bo Holten. Ref: V 5/16/84: "futuristic"; Eng.-language; *The Element of Crime* - tr t. no Stanley. Hound: *The Element of Crime*. With Michael Elphick, Esmond Knight, Me Me Lay, Gerald Wells.

A cop hypnotically returns to scenes of crimes—the Lotto Murders of little girls—in a "possibly atomic war-devastated Central Europe."

**FORCED NIGHTMARE** (H.K.) Grand March Movie Prods. (Lo Wai) 1992 color/ws 92m. D: Lau Sze Yu. SP: Cheung Wah Bill, Sit Ka Wah, Fong Sai Keung. Ph: Wong Man Wan. Mus: Elkus

Louie. AD: Frederick Chan. Anim?: Animation Shop. Ref: TV: World Video; no Eng. With Lam Ching Ying, Sandra Ng.

Cemetery ghosts enter the bodies of dead bus passengers, who then become flesh-eating zombies. At the end, a woman who has psychic powers—including X-ray vision—uses same to inflate and explode the head ghoul, who is caped and fanged like a vampire and who at one point lethally sticks his hand through a woman's body. Meanwhile, a priest, whose ecto-detector picks up ghostly activity, shrinks (and bags) three ghosts.... Okay effects help a forced comedy-horrorshow. Script throws in a takeoff on the *Ghost* pottery scene, as two spirits (including the priest's) alternate possession of one body.

**FOREVER EVIL** B&S/FrameWork 1987 color c108m. D, Opt & Mech FxDes, Ed: Roger Evans. Story: Freeman Williams. Ph, Ed: Horacio Fernandez. Mus: Rod Slane. Demon Baby Des: Luis Ibarra. SpMkp: (fx) J. C. Matalon, Nightmares Int'l.; (consul) Bart J. Mixon. Anim: Tamara Miller, Bill Gerrish. Ref: TV: United HV. V 2/3/88:34. McCarty II. Scheuer. Morse. With Charles Trotter, Howard Jacobsen, Red Mitchell, Tracey Huffman, Kent Johnson (zombie), Diane Johnson, Jeffrey Lane, Karen Chatfield.

"He's coming back"—and the clues to his return from the Ghost Quasar are contained in the books *The Chronicles of Yog Kothag, The Necronomicon,* and *The Gate and the Key,* the latter by one C. D. Ward. According to legend, Yog Kothag was an ancient Earth god so bad that he was banished by the other gods. Now, the pulsing—every few years—of a distant radio star seems to coincide with a series of sacrificial murders on Earth, and the murder sites—when charted on a map of North America—form a pentagram, a symbol linked to the Yog Kothag cult.

One of the better direct-to-video horrors. Apart from a few uncertain romantic interludes, a dry flavor prevails, and the combination of the wise-guy, "Gimme a break!" approach and the Lovecraft type of cosmic horror works fairly well. Highlight reel: An odd little dog—a false-alarm shock in its first scene—turns up, creepily and unexpectedly, in another; Yog Kothag's hit-man zombie, axed, revives, and, later, set on fire and left for dead, returns, still smoking; and, in a visualized-nightmare moment, an aborted baby-creature's tiny fingers wiggle. The dialogue is horror-movie self-conscious, fraught, as it is, with details suggesting horrors just around the corner.

**FOREVER FINAL BORGMAN** see *Borgman—Last Battle*

**FOREVER YOUNG** WB/Icon & Edward S. Feldman (Bruce Davey) 1992 color 102m. D: Steve Miner. SP, Co-P: Jeffrey Abrams. Ph: Russell Boyd;(aerial) Rexford Metz. Mus: Jerry Goldsmith. SpMkp:(des) Dick Smith; Greg Cannom. Opt/Digital FX: VCE/Peter Kuran. MechFX: Image SpFX; Peter Chesney. Ref: TV. Mo. V 12/7/92: "big, rousing, old-fashioned romance." ad. SFChron 12/16/92: "a true bomb—charmless, disappointing and at times even laughable." With Mel Gibson, Jamie Lee Curtis, Elijah Wood, George Wendt, Joe Morton, Nicholas Surovy, Art LaFleur.

"I'll see you later." Man cryogenically frozen in 1939 wakes up in 1992. ("McCormick was misplaced for 50 years?") Problem One: "Aging Irreversible," upon thawing. The "period" part of the story is deftly set up and edited; the "today" part begins less surely, but underplaying helps put over the hyper-romantic premises. Not needed: the suspense of the military nipping at our hero's heels—though this standard situation is cleverly resolved.

**FORGING AHEAD** (B) Harry Cohen 1933 b&w 49m. D: Norman Walker. SP: Brandon Fleming, from K.R.G. Browne's novel "Easy Money." Ref: BFC. With Margot Grahame, Garry Marsh, Melville Cooper, Arthur Chesney.

"Haunted" house is a front for forgers.

**The FORGOTTEN ONE** Wind River/Spirited Prods. 1990 color 98m.(90m.). SP, D: Phillip Badger. Mus: Kevin Hedges. P: Peter Garrity. PD: Tim Duffy. FxCoord: Tim Drnec. Mkp: Sheryl Blum. SpSet: John Vincent. SpProp: Mike Bianco. Ref: TV. Maureen Smith. V 6/13/90:50. TVG. With Terry O'Quinn, Kristy McNichol, Blair Parker (Evelyn James), Kiffany Cyn (old ghost), Elisabeth Brooks.

"The sound was coming out of the wall." Denver. A ghost's (Parker) presence scares a woman (Brooks) out of an author's (O'Quinn) new home, later frightens him out of the basement. ("Who the hell are you?") The wandering subjective camera proves to be a moaning woman who was walled up alive in the basement by her jealous husband in 1891 and now wants the hero to join her in death.... Film is part chiller, part romantic fantasy, part erotic thriller, but unsatisfying as a whole. Handily, the ghost alternates between flesh and spirit modes. Too too romantic ending verges on the campy.

**FORMULA FOR MURDER** (I) Lightning Video/Fulvia Int'l. 1986 color 88m. (*Formula per un Omicido*. aka *Formula for a Murder*). SP, D: Alberto De Martino. SP: also "Hank Walker." Mus: F. De Masi. AD: J. Wilson. Ref: V 10/15/86: "above-average Italian thriller." 5/1/85:316. Ecran F 79:81. 58:71. Palmerini. Hardy/HM2: aka *7, Hyde Park*. MV: *Seven Hyden Park: La Casa Maldetta*. With Christina Nagy, David Warbeck, Carroll Blumberg, Rossano Brazzi.

Man after woman's fortune tries to scare her silly.

**FORTRESS** (Austral.-U.S.) Dimension (Miramax)/Village Roadshow & Davis Ent. (John Davis, John Flock/Fortress) 1993 (1992) color 89m. D: Stuart Gordon. Story, SP: S. Feinberg, T. Neighbors. SP: also D. Venable, T. C. Fox. Ph: David Eggby. Mus: F. Talgorn. PD: David Copping. SpFxSup: Tad Pride. VisFxSup: Paul Gentry. SpVisFX: Praxis. SpMkpFX: Bob Clark. MechFX: David Pride. SpDigitalFX: Modern Videofilm. Ref: TV: Live HV. Stanley. V 2/1/93: "predictable, uninspired screenplay." ad. SFChron 9/4/93: "well-made." With Christopher Lambert, Kurtwood Smith, Loryn Locklin, Lincoln Kilpatrick, Jeffrey Combs, Tom Towles.

"You are about to enter the Fortress." Computer-run future prison with lasers, robots, "mind wipes," and "intestinators" (automatic behavior control devices employing pain, then death) offers a "complete security environment." Or, A Patchwork Orange. The "intestinators" are *Scanners* with intestines. *Fortress* is not quite *Rikko O*, but it's brutal and gory enough. Lots of "We're talkin' TNT on PMS." Saving graces: Combs as D-Day, and occasional details like the hologram "maps" and the human bar codes.

**FORTRESS OF AMERIKKA** Troma & Mesa 1989 color 97m. (aka *Fortress of America: The Mercenaries*). SP, D: Eric Louzil. AD: Gary Randall. SpMkpFX: John Garcia. Ref: V 5/17/89: "old-fashioned sexploitation film." 10/19/88:185. With Gene LeBrok, Kellee Bradley, Kascha, Karen Michaels, Francois Papillon, David Crane.

Bloodthirsty mercenaries, gore.

**FORTRESS OF THE DEAD** F. Grofe, Jr. 1965 78m. Ref: Greg Luce: horrific. Scheuer '66. Lee(p). no Maltin '92. no Phantom. no Stanley. no V. with John Hackett, Conrad Parkham, Ana Corita.

Ghosts of trapped soldiers haunt bunker shelled by the Japanese in World War II.

**FORTUNEERS, The** see *Crime Ring*

**Le FOTO DI GIOIA** (I) Devon & Dania & Medusa & Filmes Int'l. & Nat'l. Cinematografica (Reteitalia) 1986 color 93m. D: Lamberto Bava. SP: G. Clerici, D. Stoppa. Story: Luciano Martino. Ph: G. Battaglia. Mus: S. Boswell. AD: A. Geleng. Mkp: R. Prestopino, G. Provenghi, M. Silvi. SdFX: R. Sterbini et al. Stills: A. Frontoni. Ref: TV: VSOM; *Delirium* - cr t; Eng.-lang. version. V 5/6/87: "isn't much of a chiller." 10/22/86:354. Mad Movies 52:53: SP: D. Sacchetti. VWB: *Deliria* - vt t. VSOM: *Photos of Gioia* - alt vt t. With Serena Grandi, Daria Nicolodi, Katrine Michelsen, Capucine, George Eastman, Karl Zinny.

Ingredients here include a killer who poses his dead victims in front of huge blow-ups of glamour photos and who, at the end, dons ghoul makeup and tries to kill heroine Gloria ... murder by pitchfork, and by unleashed bees drawn by perfume (*Devil Bat*, anyone?) ... and a macabre photo session with "mummies" .... Functional, occasionally laughable erotic shocker. ("To commit crimes like that—he must be paranoid!")

**FOUR BEAUTIES** (Taiwanese) c1987 color c86m. Ref: TV: vt; no Eng. Y. K. Ho: above is tr t.

Sex-horror-fantasy re a flying vampire-ghost and her cohorts, a pig-ghost and a goat-ghost. The vampire can shoot exploding rays and appear and disappear at will and, at the end, makes a man see her human rival as herself. Thinking that this woman is the ghost, he kills her. Rudimentary effects and lots of cackling (by the main ghost).

**FOUR JUNIOR DETECTIVES** (G) Vidmark/Neue Constantin 1992 ('95-U.S.) color 81m. D: U. Koenig. Ref: vc box: "ghostly armored knights and the dreaded guardian skeleton." With Tomi Renjak.

**The FOUR KIDS** (J) 1992? anim color/ws 92m. Ref: TV: vt; no Eng. Japan Video: above is tr t.

Sweetly observed details of everyday life distinguish this tale of loss and death in a family in World War II Japan. (Compare *The Sullivans*.) The sweetness, of course, sets up the later sadness. At the end, ghosts, or memories, appear to the little heroine. Earlier, in a funny, visualized dream sequence, a lick-happy, big-tongued ghost, a snickering three-eyed ghost, and a little comma of a ghost playfully scare her.

**\*The FOUR SKULLS OF JONATHAN DRAKE** 1959. AD: William Glasgow. SpFX: Rudy Stangler. Mkp: Charles Gemora. Ref: TV. Lee. V 5/13/59. LC. FFacts. Scheuer. Stanley. Hardy/HM. Lentz. Weldon. Maltin'92.

For three generations, the male members of the Drake family have died at age sixty, apparently of cardiovascular failure. Actually, an "ancient curse" and a curare-tipped stiletto are responsible .... Almost two centuries ago, it seems, in the Amazon, Captain Wilfred Drake slew the male inhabitants of a Jivaro Indian village—without reckoning on The Cult of the Headless Man. One member of this cult, Zutai (Paul Wexler), apparently became—through an infusion into his body of a fluid created by the village priest—immortal. He now needs neither food nor oxygen, and has "small impressions of skulls ... branded on [his] fingers." He aids Dr. Zurich (Henry Daniell), an archaeologist who proves to be a "living-dead thing ... the head of a decapitated white man on the body of a jungle Indian." ("That guy's a ghost!")

Though this old shocker has virtually nothing to recommend it, the details are sufficiently lurid. Zutai (or his body) emits a sort of cosmic shriek whenever he's shot. Skulls are mysteriously smuggled into the Drake family vault. Shrinking and shrunken heads abound—and we get to see part of the actual shrinking process. This is the kind of picture which would be really grisly if made today. As it is, it's just a curiosity, a relic of a certain kind of bad, humorless filmmaking. The dates on the prop tombs aren't even in synch with the script.

**14 GOING ON 30** ABC-TV/Disney-TV 1988 color 90m. D: Paul Schneider. Tel: Richard Jefferies. Story: James Orr, Jim Cruickshank. Mus: Lee Holdridge. SpFX: Isadoro Raponi. VisFX: (sup) Allen Gonzales; BV. Mkp: Edwin Butterworth. Ref: TV. V 3/30/88:56. With Steve Eckholdt, Daphne Ashbrook, Patrick Duffy, Harry Morgan, Loretta Swit, Dick Van Patten, Alan Thicke, Rick Rossovich, David Hess.

A science whiz's invention transforms a teenager into a thirty-year-old man who wants to stay old and romance a teacher. ("I've created a monster.") Slick, hollow sf-comedy has some cute moments, but do we really need another chase finale and thoughts like "It's not easy being an adult"? Sweet but over-neat coda is romance with all the wrinkles ironed out, and leaves a Square One feel.

**The 4TH MAN** (Dutch) Spectrafilm/Rob Houwer 1983 ('84-U.S.) color 92m. (*De Vierde Man*). D: Paul Verhoeven. SP: Gerard Soeteman, from Gerard Reve's novel. Ph: Jan De Bont. Mus: Loek Dikker. AD: Roland De Groot. SpFX: Hennie van den Akker et al. Mkp: Kathy Kuhne. MkpSpFX: Chris Tucker. Ref: pr. Phantom: "interesting but ultimately disappointing." Wolf/Horror. NYT 6/27/84: 104m. ad. SFChron 6/1/84: "visions of death"; "filmic junk." V 4/27/83: "The scenario is very effective, the direction skillful." 2/1/84:28: at Avoriaz. SFExam 6/1/84: "metaphoric overkill." SFChron 6/1/84: "cloying, sophomoric." Playboy (France) 2/84:80: Avoriaz. Oak Trib 4/12/84: "timeworn script." VVoice 7/3/84: "bonkers." With Jeroen Krabbe, Renee Soutendijk, Thom Hoffman, Dolf De Vries, Geert De Jong, Hans Veerman.

"Graphic horror" (Tribune) and "magic realism" (Variety) in this "supernatural thriller" (Tribune) re a "witch" who marries and murders men.

**FOXY SPIRITS** (H.K.?) c1992? color 88m. Ref: TV: Pan-Asia Video; no Eng.

There's a fox tail sticking out from under that nice young lady's dress, and all those ladies there bite men's necks. At times, these spirits have campy fox-faces, and one of the more bizarre scenes features a flying, strangling fox tail. Shot-on-tape tale of human/ghost love seems a routine martial-arts fantasy.

**FRACCHIA CONTRO DRACULA** (I) Titanus/Maura Int'l. & Faso Film (Altissimi & Saraceni) 1985 color 91m. (aka *Dracula and Fracchia*). SP, D: Neri Parenti. SP: also Laura Toscano, Franco Marotta, Paolo Villaggio. Mus: Bruno Zambrini. Ref: V 2/19/86: "a hard sell." 5/17/86:316. 10/16/85: 290. 5/1/85:322. Ecran F 59:71. Jones: *Who Is Afraid of Dracula* - B t? With Villaggio, Gigi Reder, Edmond Purdom (Dracula), Ania Pieroni.

Comedy featuring Dracula, Frankenstein (presumably the monster), and a "horde of zombies."

**FRANKENHOOKER** SGE/Ievins-Henenlotter 1990 color 82m. (aka *Frankenstein '90*). SP, D: Frank Henenlotter. SP: also Robert Martin. Mus: Joe Renzetti. SpMkpFX: Gabe Bartalos. PD: Charles Bennett. SpVisFX: Al Magliochetti; Light & Motion. Props: (elec) Bruce Torbet, Robert Siebern; (mech) Klem Jarzabkowski; (sp) Thomas Molinelli; (high voltage) Vinnie Vollono. Animatronics Sup: Kenneth Walker. Ref: TV. Sacto Bee 8/9/90. V 5/2/90 (rev) & p84. NYT 6/15/90. V 8/30/89:20: Full Moon Films. With James Lorinz (Jeffrey Franken), Patty Mullen (Elizabeth Shelley), Charlotte Helmkamp, Shirley Stoler, Louise Lasser, Joseph Gonzalez, Jennifer Delora, John Zacherle.

New Jersey "bio-electro technician" Jeffrey Franken's remote-controlled lawn mower makes a "tossed human salad" of his fiancee Elizabeth. He retrieves her head, a hand, and a foot from the debris and vows to make her the "centerfold goddess of the century." His freshly developed super-crack makes a gaggle of prostitutes explode, and he uses the parts to complete the new "Elizabeth," or "Frankenhooker." Brought to life, the latter takes to the streets, electrocutes her clients, and severs their heads. At the end, the spare, preserved whore parts mix 'n' match in a perhaps-too-determinedly-bizarre scene which recalls the freaks of Henenlotter's *Basket Case 2*.... A near-total fizzle of a horror-comedy. Main problem: Jeffrey is a monologue, not a character, and not a very good monologue at that. No story here, just outre ideas.

**FRANKENSTEIN** see the preceding and following titles and *Arma Secreta, El. Aullido del Diablo, El. Betty Boop's Penthouse. Bride, The. Claymation Comedy of Horrors. D.P. Man, The. D.P. Man, Part 2. Crazy Professor, The. Daffy Duck's Quackbusters. Defenders of the Earth. Dr. Hackenstein. Dona Macabra. Erection. Erotic Rites of Frankenstein, The. Flesh for Frankenstein. Follow That Goblin! Fracchia contro Dracula. Funny Frankenstein. Ghost Stories (1986). Ghost Writer. Ghostbusting. Gothic. Grotesque. Hare Tonic (P). Haunted Summer. Lasuto Furankenshutain. Leena Meets Frankenstein. Mary Shelley's Franken-*

*stein. Mixed Up. Monster Squad, The. Old Manor House. Real Bad Monster Raw. Remando al Viento. Return of the Killer Tomatoes! Ritorno dalla Morte. Robot Carnival. Scooby-doo and the Ghoul School. Scooby-doo and the Reluctant Werewolf. Seven Foxes. Slapstick of Another Kind. Sturmtruppen. Takbo ...! Bilis ...! Takboooo. Thursday's Child* (P). *Transylvania 6-5000. Under the Sea. Urusei Yatsura 2. Vindicator, The. Waxwork. Waxwork II. What's Cookin Doc?* (P).

**FRANKENSTEIN** (J) Harmony Gold/Toei Animation 1983 ('84-U.S.) anim color c90m. (3 *Mystery! Frankenstein—Legend of Terror*). Ref: TV: Vestron Video; Eng. dubbed. Stanley. Hound.

Dr. Victor Frankenstein, working from his father's blueprint, creates an "incredibly strong," superhuman monster which runs amok and systematically terrifies Victor and his family. In a twist on the blind-man-and-the-monster scene, Victor's father befriends "Franken".... There's something perversely appealing about the later, domesticated Franken greeting little birdies with a "Hi there!"—as if he had wandered into a demented Disney cartoon feature. Overall, the monster is a crazy seesaw of a characterization; he alternates between Mindless Boogeyman and Nicest Guy You'd Ever Want To Meet. Dr. Frankenstein himself is tiresomely single-minded. He simply wants his monster killed. But despite miscalculated characterization, flat dubbing, and stilted animation, the basic story of Horror lurking in the background of bucolic family scenes—in charming towns and countrysides—still unsettles. Happiness here is at best tenuous, short-lived; violence, around the next bend.

**FRANKENSTEIN** (B) Yorkshire-TV/Elm-Group W-Western World-TV 1984 color 60m. D: James Ormerod. Tel: Victor Gialanella, from the stage production directed by Tom Moore. Ph: Stuart Hinchliffe. Mus: Alan Parker. AD: Jeremy Bear. Mkp: Mary Griffiths. Ref: TV. TVG. Martin. With Robert Powell, Carrie Fisher, David Warner (creature), John Gielgud, Edward Judd.

"A toast to the house of Frankenstein!" Dr. Victor Frankenstein discovers the "very cause of life itself." Stolid collection of scenes from classic Frankenstein movies (the monster and the blind man, the creation, etc.).

**FRANKENSTEIN** (B-U.S.) TNT-TV/David Wickes Prods. & Turner Pictures 1993 (1992) color c105m. Tel, D: Wickes. From Shelley's novel. Ph: Jack Conroy. AD: Martin Atkinson. Mus: John Cameron. PD: William Alexander. SpMkp: Mark Coulier; Image Animation. SpFxSup: Graham Longhurst. FX, Models: FX Associates. Ref: TV. TVG 6/12/93. V 6/14/93:36. SFChron 6/11/93; Dtbk 6/13/93. SFExam 6/11/93. With Patrick Bergin (Victor Frankenstein), Randy Quaid (the monster), John Mills, Lambert Wilson, Fiona Gillies, Ronald Leigh Hunt, Michael Gothard.

"I've discovered the secret of life." Victor Frankenstein, experimenting with electricity, magnetism, and cloning, fashions creatures out of a cat and a snake, a rabbit and a porcupine ("Come and meet my friends") ... and himself. He creates a "new kind of man," super-human and despised by all, and the two have a mystical kinship. ("We're one!") In the oddly satisfying conclusion—after the monster has slain just about everybody else—he forces a confrontation with Victor, who leaps with him into the sea, and they turn to Popsicles as they slowly spin together down into the Arctic depths. For the most part, however, this TV-movie is a familiar melange of Frankenstein-movie scenes, and the musical score is monotonous.

**FRANKENSTEIN** see *Bride, The*

**FRANKENSTEIN: THE COLLEGE YEARS** FNM-TV & Spirit Prods. (Bob Engelman) 1991 color c90m. D: Tom Shadyac. Tel: Bryant Christ, John Trevor Wolff. Mus: Joel McNeely. SpFxCoord: Tom Bellissimo, Charlie Belardinelli. Mkp: Susanne Sanders. Ref: TV. TVG. V 10/28/91:46. with William Ragsdale, Vincent Hammond (Frank N. Stein), Daniel Barnes (Christopher), Larry Miller, Andrea Elson.

"Frank's held together by a special serum." Flat comedy re the discovery of Victor Frankenstein's notes and monster by Leland University Medical Research Center students. Revived, said monster looks like a Peter Boyle-ish "radical surfer dude," becomes a "monster kicker" on the football team and a terror on the dance floor, and ultimately, at full strength, proclaims himself an "evolved man."

**The FRANKENSTEIN COMPLEX** Glass Eye Pix (Rachael Horovitz) 1991 feature. Co-SP, D: Larry Fessenden. Ref: V 10/14/91:31(ad): screening at AFM; A-34. With Miriam Healy-Louie, Stephen Ramsey, David Van Tieghem.

The "true horror" of "Chemo-Electric Therapy," or limb transplantation, revealed.

**FRANKENSTEIN '88** or **FRANKENSTEIN FACTOR, The** see *Vindicator, The*

**FRANKENSTEIN GENERAL HOSPITAL** New Star Ent. (Night Game/Dimitri Villard) 1988 color and b&w 92m. D: Deborah Roberts. SP: Michael Kelly, Robert Deel. Mus: John Ross. MkpFX: Doug White. PD: Don Day. Ref: TV: New Star Video. V 6/1/88: "rather flat sendup of horror films." 1/13/88:6. Scheuer. Martin. Maltin '92. Hound. With Mark Blankfield, Leslie Jordan, Kathy Shower, Irwin Keyes (monster), Lou Cutell, Bobby Pickett.

Dr. Bob Frankenstein (Blankfield), great-great-grandson of the original doc, attempts to create a perfect person. He produces only "one questionable human being," with two left legs. ("He's alive!") Dreadful shot-on-tape horror-comedy has only a few redeeming moments. (One is Baby's First Steps: "First your left leg. Now your left leg.") The original Baron Victor Frankenstein is represented only by a framed photo of Colin Clive. Upstairs hospital scenes are color; downstairs lab scenes are black-and-white. Script includes a takeoff on the monster-and-the-girl sequence from the 1931 original. At the end, the monster gets married.

**FRANKENSTEIN 90** (F) A. J. Films & TF 1 Films (Louis Duchesne) 1984 color/ws 87m. SP, D, P: Alain Jessua. SP: also Paul Gegauff. Ph: William Lubtchansky. Mus: Armando Trovajoli. AD: Flamand, Grosrichard. SpFxMkp: Reiko Kruk, Dominique Colladant. SpFX: Georges Demetrau. Ref: TV: VSOM; Eng. titles. V 9/12/84: "tale collapses." Ecran F **48**:6-8.

49:8. With Jean Rochefort (Victor Frankenstein), Eddy Mitchell (Frank), Fiona Gelin, Serge Marquand, H. Vos.

"My family tried to revive life, but they've created only monsters." "Cybernetics genius ... fits his monster with a micro-processor for a brain."(V) (A "biological accelerator" then stimulates this brain.) The super-strong monster, Frank, speaks well, but belches, and is a bad driver. In one scene, he hugs and accidentally crushes the maid. ("Pretty. Pretty. Pretty.") Near the end, Dr. Frankenstein and his fiancee, Elizabeth, create the "perfect woman." Plus: the doctor's visualized nightmare re a headless monster, and Frank's visualized nightmare re an ugly woman.... Occasionally touching, mildly funny monster comedy-drama turns into a weak Making Mr. and Mrs. Right. (Mr. is ultimately for Elizabeth; Mrs., for Victor.) The most intriguing aspect of the script: the fitting of the story into a larger, Frankenstein-as-part-of-our-pop-culture framework. The principals go to a Frankenstein movie (apparently footage made for this film, but the actor is supposed to be Boris Karloff), and Frank comments, "Just from his eyes, you understand everything." In another scene, he visits the crypt of an earlier Frankenstein monster (1816-1817). Comments a newscaster: "The myth of Frankenstein, created by Mary Shelley, wasn't make believe."

**FRANKENSTEIN '90** see *Frankenhooker*

**FRANKENSTEIN 2000** see *Ritorno dalla Morte*

**FRANKENSTEIN 2000** see *Vindicator, The*

**FRANKENSTEIN UNBOUND** (U.S.-I) Fox/Mount Co. 1990 color 85m. (aka *Roger Corman's Frankenstein Unbound*). SP, D, Co-P: Roger Corman. SP: also F. X. Feeney. From Brian Aldiss' novel. Mus: Carl Davis. SpMkp: Nick Dudman. SpVisFX: (Illusion Arts) Syd Dutton, Bill Taylor; (Fantasy II) Gene Warren Jr. Animatronics: Ian Whittaker. SpCar: Italdesign. Future Costumes: Slawitza. DigitalSdFxDes: Harry Cohen. SetSpFX: Renato Agostini. ProsthMkpArt: Suzanne Reynolds. OptFX: D. S. Williams Jr., Bruno George. Ref: TV. V 11/5/90. SFExam 2/1/91. SFBay Guardian 1/30/91. MFB'91:3-5. Sacto Bee 11/5/90. Scheuer. Maltin '92. Martin. With John Hurt, Raul Julia, Bridget Fonda, Nick Brimble (the monster), Catherine Rabett, Jason Patric, Terri Treas (computer voice).

"My book will be known in the future!" New Los Angeles, 2031. A "time slip"—a side effect of Project Safe World's super particle beam weapon—sends the latter's creator, Dr. Joe Buchanan (Hurt), and his "electric carriage" back to the year 1817, where he discovers that Mary Shelley's (Fonda) book *Frankenstein* is journalism, not fiction. When Dr. Frankenstein (Julia) at first refuses to make his monster a mate, the creature slays the doctor's beloved Elizabeth (Rabett). For initially unexplained reasons, Frankenstein continues and brings a female "monster" to life— the revived Elizabeth. ("She lives!") Another time slip sends doctors and monsters into the far future.... A sudden flurry of plot twists near the end helps salvage a little of Corman's return to directing. Unfortunately, a tired Evils of Science theme prevails, though the latter does yield one good line for Buchanan (re the second time slip): "Meet my monster!"

**FRANKENSTEIN'S AUNT** (Cz) 1987. D: Juraj Jakubisko. Ref: V 7/1/87:93: 13 TV episodes made into feature; Eng.-language. With Viveca Lindfors, Ferdy Mayne.

**2 FRANKENSTEIN'S CASTLE OF FREAKS** Dick Randall 1973 90m. (aka *Dr. Frankenstein's Castle of Freaks. Il Castello della Paura. Il Castello delle Donne Maledette.* aka *Terror. Castello dell'Orrore*). D: Gianni Vernuccio. SP: Mark Smith (aka Mario Francini?), William Rose, Roberto Spano. Ph: Mario Mancini. Mus: Marcello Gigante. AD: Mario Ciccarella. Mkp: John Amadeo? SdFX: Nino Caciuttolo. Ed: Enzo Micarelli. Ref: TV: vt; *Terreur!!! Le Chateau des Femmes Maudites* - French version; no Eng. Martin. Weldon. Stanley. Hardy/HM. Lee. TVG. With Gordon Mitchell (Igor), Alan Collins (Hans), Xiro Papas (Kreegin), Loren Ewing (Goliath).

"I have discovered the secret of life." Cast of characters includes Count Frankenstein (Rossano Brazzi) ... neighbor and apparent subject of the latter's experiments, Ook, the Neanderthal Man ("Boris Lugosi") ... and the dwarf Genz (Michael Dunn), who befriends Ook and, later, unleashes another of the Count's subjects, Goliath, who throttles the Count .... Plodding, crude. Ook and the dwarf get as much running time as the Count. Award: worst cartoon lightning in a live-action movie. At the end, it's Ook vs. Goliath. (Ook loses.)

**FRANKENSTEIN'S GREAT-AUNT TILLIE** (U.S.-Mex) Video City/Tillie Prods. & Filmier 1985 (1983) color 93m. SP, D, P: Myron J. Gold. Mus: Ronald Stein. SpFX: Raul Camarena. Mkp: Graciela Munoz. Ref: TV: Video City; Eng. version. Phantom. Hound. V 6/5/85. 3/7/84:248(ad). 6/15/83:24: completed. 5/9/84:488. Stanley. With Donald Pleasence (Baron Victor Frankenstein), Yvonne Furneaux (Tillie), June Wilkinson, Aldo Ray, Phil Leeds, Zsa Zsa Gabor, Miguel Angel Fuentes (the monster).

Ingredients: a revived, flute-controlled, blue Frankenstein monster ... a variation on the little-girl-by-the-lake scene ... a rejuvenating jelly ... and a smoke-induced trance.... Suffocatingly talky comedy notable only for the return of June Wilkinson. "Muddy" sound, color.

**FRANKENSTEIN'S PLANET OF MONSTERS** Nomad 1993 color 45m. D, P, Ed, Ph: Brad Anderson. SP, P, Ed: Mike Brunelle. Ref: PT 18:17: fun.

"Floating cyborg head ... barren planet run by a Frankenstein monster (Brunelle in good makeup) ... wolfman ... army of monsters (people in masks)."

**FRANKENWEENIE** Disney (Julie Hickson) 1984 b&w 27m. Idea & D: Tim Burton. SP: Lenny Ripps. Ph: Thomas Ackerman. Mus: Michael Convertino, David Newman. AD: John B. Mansbridge. Sparky's Mkp: Robert J. Schiffer. FX: (anim) Allen Gonzales; (elec) Ed Engel; Roland Tantin, Hans Metz. Ref: TV: Disney HV. SFChron Dtbk 4/5/92. NYT Mag 4/9/89. York Theatre (S.F.) notes 10/29/86 (Seattle Times). Reader 9/20/85. Martin. PT 13:52. With Shelley Duvall, Daniel Stern, Barret Oliver (Victor Frankenstein), Paul Bartel, Joseph Maher, Sparky (Sparky).

Schoolboy Victor, inspired by his science teacher (Bartel), reads up on "Electricity and the Creation of Life" and brings his dead pet Sparky back to life. The now-rather-bizarre-looking dog, though harmless enough, ends up "scaring half the neighborhood," and "villagers" trap him in a mill on a miniature golf course.... Droll parody of Universal Frankenstein films. Scenes, sets, and a poodle's hairdo recall, especially, *Frankenstein* (1931) and *Bride of Frankenstein*. Sparky even rates a set of electrodes.

**FRATELLO BRUTTO DI SUPERMAN** see *Superdandy*

**FRATTI ROSSI, I** see *Red Monks*

**FREAKED** Fox/Tommy (Ufland) 1993 color 79m. (*Hideous Mutant Freekz* - orig t). SP, D, Co-P: Tom Stern, Alex Winter. SP, Co-P: also Tim Burns. Ph: J. Thompson. Mus: Kevin Kiner. PD: Catherine Hardwicke. Creature & VisFxSup: Thomas Rainone. SpVisFX: Fantasy II. SpMkpFX: Alterian Studios, Steve Johnson, Screaming Mad George. Titles: David Daniels. Sp Machine: F.L. Stone. SpProps: Louisa Bonnie. VisFX:(digital) PDI; David Allen. SpFxDes: Martin Bresin. Clay Anim: Chiodo Bros. SdFxSup: E.W. Lindemann. Ref: TV. V 9/27/93: "fitfully funny gags." 2/22/93:A-122: at AFM. Fango 128:4. With Alex Winter (Ricky), Megan Ward, Michael Stoyanov, Randy Quaid (Elijah C. Skuggs), William Sadler, Mr. T, Brooke Shields, Keanu Reeves (Dog Boy), Morgan Fairchild, Deep Roy, Derek McGrath (Worm), Bobcat Goldthwait (voice of Sockhead), Vincent Hammond (giant Rick monster).

"Who wants to get freaked first?" Santa Flan, South or Central America. Freek Land's Elijah C. Skuggs' Freak Machine and freak-making goop are responsible for (among other things) Mr. Toad, Dog Boy, Cowboy, and big-eyeball "spies." Plus a man impaled on an "I Like Ike" sign .... Far-out, but generally uninspired inspirations. Noisy, busy film invites comparison (to its disadvantage) to the *Basket Case* series. Cute: Woody Woodpecker among the exotic bird noises in the jungle. Cute number 2: the wrench mutated into a hammer.

**FREAKSHOW** (Can.) Brightstar Films (SGE)/Anthony Kramreither (Don Haig) 1989 color 92m. D: C. Magnatta. SP: Bob Farmer. Mus: Shelski, LeBlanc. SpMkpFX: Gordon J. Smith. Ref: V 5/31/89: "rock-bottom horror film." 10/19/88:109(ad). With Audrey Landers, Peter Read, Dean Richards.

Four stories re ghouls, a still-conscious girl undergoing an autopsy, etc.

**FREAKY FAIRY TALES** see *Dead Time Stories*

**FREDDIE AS F.R.O. 7** (B) Miramax/Hollywood Road (Priggen-Acevski) 1992 anim color 90m. SP, D: Jon Acevski. SP: also David Ashton. Mus: Dundas, Wentworth. Anim D: Tony Guy. VisFxSup: Peter Chiang. Ref: V 11/5/90:62. 8/24/92: "likable enough." SFChron 8/29/92: "a mess." SFExam 8/29/92: "generally enjoyable if fractured." Voices: Ben Kingsley, Jenny Agutter, Brian Blessed, Nigel Hawthorne, Michael Hordern, Victor Maddern, Jonathan Pryce (Trilby), Billie Whitelaw.

"Shape-shifting Aunt Messina ... cobra alter ego" (V) ... Nessie, the Loch Ness monster ... sleep-inducing ray ... the Tower of London vaporized.

**FREDDY'S DEAD: THE FINAL NIGHTMARE** New Line (Robert Shaye, Aron Warner/Michael DeLuca) 1991 color/3-D sequence 89m. (*A Nightmare on Elm Street 6: Freddy's Dead* - orig t). Story, D: Rachel Talalay. SP: M. DeLuca. Ph: Declan Quinn. Mus: Brian May. PD: C. J. Strawn. SpMkp: David B. Miller; (fx) MMI. SpVisFX: Dream Quest Images; (sup) Michael Shea. 3-D/Freddy Vision VisFX: The Chandler Group. Mech-FxDes: Reel EFX. Computer FX: Video Image. Snake Demon Puppets: Jim Towler. Dream Demons Anim: Pacific Data Images. House FX: True Vision FX. Digital FxSup: Jamie Dixon. SpSdFX: Jon Johnson. Ref: TV: New Line HV. V 9/23/91. 11/5/90:26. ad. Oak Trib 9/14/91. With Robert Englund (Freddy), Lisa Zane, Shon Greenblatt, Lezlie Deane, Ricky Dean Logan, Breckin Meyer, Yaphet Kotto, Elinor Donahue, Roseanne Arnold, Tom Arnold, Alice Cooper, Johnny Depp.

"We're in Twin Peaks here." Springwood, Ohio, "ten years from now." Freddy's daughter (Zane) yanks him out of his dream world and renders him vulnerable. Meanwhile, "ancient dream demons" that turn "nightmares into reality" are shown to have started it all by claiming Freddy. Highlights include Freddy-as-witch-on-broomstick, Freddy-as-reckless-bus-driver, a joy-stuck victim of Freddy, a hearing-aid critter, and a post-McCay Flying House. Prize, Wittiest Effect, or Prop: The Ever-Unfolding Road Map. Scariest Effect: Roseanne Arnold as Ethel. Thin, episodic follow-up to *Nightmare on Elm Street 5* hasn't a shred of dramatic integrity, but is almost comically crammed with effects, many of them dandies.

**FREEDOM FROM THE GREEDY GRAVE** (H.K.) 1989 color feature. D: Cheng Ren-Sheng. Ref: Weisser/ATC: "fairly good horror comedy." With Yang Ching-Huen, Chu Bao-Yi.

Haunted house ... geek-ghost ... initially hopping vampire-ghosts.

**FREEJACK** WB/James G. Robinson/Morgan Creek (Ronald Shusett, Stuart Oken) 1992 color/ws? 108m. D: Geoff Murphy. Screen Story, SP: Steven Pressfield, R. Shusett. SP: also Dan Gilroy. From Robert Sheckley's novel *Immortality, Inc.* Ph: Amir Mokri. Mus: Trevor Jones. PD: Joe Alves. VisFX: (coord) J. W. Kompare; (sup) Richard Hoover; Dream Quest Images. Mind Meld: Praxis. SpFxSup: Joey DiGaetano. Computer Anim: Video Image. Anim: Clint Colver. Futuristic Props: Jeff McKay. Addl Opts: Howard Anderson et al. Ref: TV. V 1/27/92. Oak Trib 1/21/92. ad. Sacto Bee 1/19/92. L. Wilson. With Emilio Estevez, Mick Jagger, Rene Russo, Anthony Hopkins, Jonathan Banks, David Johansen, Amanda Plummer, John Shea, Grand L. Bush.

"Oh, my God! He's a freejack!" Future folk from the year 2009 rescue race-car driver Alex Furlong (Estevez) from a certain-death accident in 1991. He is to be a "ticket to immortality" from some lucky customer on the "Spiritual Switchboard," which electronically transplants minds into bodies snatched from that less-toxic time.... File this serious, if stunt-happy sf-actioner under "Svengali," or Short Cuts to Romantic Fulfillment, as future body-hunter McCandless (Hopkins) tells his inamorata (Russo), "If only I could become this man [Furlong] you loved so much." Basically familiar terrain, but with good performances by Banks and Johansen, occasional wit, and a fun if ultimately predictable wind-up.

The **FREEWAY MANIAC** Cannon/Wintertree 1989 (1988) color 93m. (*Breakdown* - orig t). SP, D: Paul Winters. SP: also Gahan Wilson. Mus: G. Stewart. Clam Des: Wilson. Ref: V 4/26/89: "amateurish acting, cheapo technical work and little imagination." Phantom: "well worth avoiding." With Loren Winters, James Courtney, Shepard Sanders.

Slasher amok, plus clam monster in film-within-a-film, "Astronette."

**FRENCHMAN'S FARM** (Austral.) Goldfarb/Mavis Bramston (Colson Worner) 1987 color 102m.(86m.-U.S.). SP, D: Ron Way. Sp, P: James Fishburn. SP: also Matt White. From a screenplay by William Russell. Ph: Malcolm McCulloch. Mus: Tommy Tycho. AD: Richard Rooker. Ref: V 5/87: "bland programmer." Martin: "some good suspense." With Tracey Tainsh, David Reyne, Ray Barrett, Norman Kaye.

Ghostly killer guards treasure from the French Revolution.

**FRENZY** see *Latin Quarter, The*

**FRESH KILL** Airwaves Project & ITVS, Channel 4, Woo Art Int'l. 1994 color 79m. D, P: Shu Lea Cheang. SP: Jessica Hagedorn. Ph: Jane Castle. Mus: V. Reid. PD: N. Deren. Ref: V 4/11/94: "painfully unfunny dialogue." SFChron 4/29/94: "luxuriates in its own hipness." With Sarita Choudhury, Erin McMurtry, Laurie Carlos, Jose Zuniga.

"People start glowing from irradiated food," and "ecological apocalypse appears imminent." (SFC)

**FRIDAY THE 13TH—THE FINAL CHAPTER** Para/Friday Four 1984 color 91m. D: Joseph Zito. SP: Barney Cohen. Story: B. H. Sakow. Mus: Harry Manfredini. SpMkpFX: Tom Savini. SpFxCoord: Martin Becker. Ref: TV. V 4/18/84. With Crispin Glover, Kimberly Beck, Barbara Howard, E. Erich Anderson, Ted White (Jason).

Jason returns to life in the morgue and chalks up one beheading, one slashing, one stabbing, one impaling, and miscellaneous spear-gun and hatchet killings, before a boy who makes himself up to resemble the young Jason helps hack him to death. Rote suspense and mayhem.

**FRIDAY THE 13TH—A NEW BEGINNING** Para/Terror Inc. (Timothy Silver) 1985 color 92m. SP, D: Danny Steinmann. Story, SP: David Cohen, Martin Kitrosser. Mus: Harry Manfredini. SpMkpFX: Martin Becker. SpFX: (coord) Frankie Inez; Reel Efx. SdFX: Blue Light. With Melanie Kinnaman, John Shepherd (Tommy Jarvis), Dick Wieand (Roy Burns).

Instruments used in Part V: an ax, a welding torch, the ax again, a knife, shears, a spike, a cleaver, the cleaver again, a butcher knife, the spike again, a chainsaw (our heroine's), and the butcher knife again (a Jason-masked madman's). "Formula" would be giving this the best of it.

**FRIDAY THE 13TH PART VI: JASON LIVES** Para/Terror, Inc. (Don Behrns) 1986 color 87m. (*Jason Lives: Friday the 13th Part VI* - cr & B t). SP, D: Tom McLoughlin. Mus: Harry Manfredini. SpMkpFX: Chris Swift, Bhan Wade. SpFX: Martin Becker. Ref: TV. MFB'88:112-13. V 8/6/86. ad. With Thom

Mathews, Jennifer Cooke, David Kagen, C. J. Graham (Jason Voorhees).

Camp Forest Green (ex-Crystal Lake). A steel-fence spike, stuck in Jason's maggoty corpse, conducts life-giving lightning into it (in a *Ghost of Frankenstein/Frankenstein Meets the Wolf Man*-like sequence), and various beheadings, dis-armings, and slashings follow.... The usual. Generally blandly ugly, with moments of humor and okay wind and lighting effects.

**FRIDAY THE 13TH: PART VII—THE NEW BLOOD** Para/Friday Four (Iain Paterson) 1988 color 90m. D: John Carl Buechler. SP: Daryl Haney, Manuel Fidello. Mus: Harry Manfredini, Fred Mollin. SpMechFX: (coord) Lou Carlucci; Image Engineering. SpMkpFX: MMI. Animatronics: Criswell, Kindlen. Ref: TV. V 5/18/88. ad. SFChron 5/16/88; Dtbk 6/5/88. With Lar Park Lincoln, Terry Kiser, Kevin Blair, Susan Jennifer Sullivan, Kane Hodder (Jason), John Ottin (Mr. Shepard), Susan Blu.

"I wish I could bring you back." As a little girl, Tina (Jennifer Banko) accidentally and psychokinetically kills her father (Ottin). Now, as a teen (Lincoln), she returns to Camp Crystal Lake (ex-Camp Forest Green) and accidentally brings back Jason, whose corpse is chained to the lake bed near the site of her father's death. Jason proceeds to commit murder-by-knife/hand/tree-trunk/machete/scythe/open-window/circular-saw/ax. At the end, Tina assaults him telekinetically, then summons up her dead father to finish him off.... Numbingly routine, except for some okay climactic, apparently stopmo work with wires, nails, and gas cans.

**FRIDAY THE 13TH PART VIII—JASON TAKES MANHATTAN** Para/Horror Inc. (Randolph Cheveldave) 1989 color 100m. SP, D: Rob Hedden. Mus: Fred Mollin. SpMkpFX: Jamie Brown. MechFxCoord: Martin Becker. VisFxSup: Dale Fay. SpPhFX: FX Assoc., Jim Danforth. SpFxCoord: Reel EFX. MinFX: Light & Motion. OptFX: Cinema Research. ElecSdFX: Brian Vessa. Ref: TV. V 8/2/89. HR 8/31/89. With Jensen Daggett, Scott Reeves, Peter Mark Richman, Kane Hodder (Jason), Timothy Mirkovich (young Jason), Kelly Hu, Alex Diakun.

"This voyage is doomed!" Electricity revives Jason, and there follow murders with electric guitar and other, more typical Jason weapons, aboard the doomed ship Lazarus. As usual, Jason is tiresomely unkillable, until the end, when he reverts in (apparent) death to boyish form.... Sentiment here proves as mechanical as shock, as Jason alternates between stalker and protector of heroine Rennie (Daggett), who had a childhood encounter with him. Her visions of the young Jason seem to be based—alternately and confusingly—in both psychology and physical reality. The spectacle of Jason-as-Rambo taking on New York City street thugs provides a few amusing moments. One good, Cocteau-derived shock at a suddenly liquid mirror.

Follow-up: *Jason Goes to Hell.*

**FRIDAY THE 13TH PART IX** see *Jason Goes to Hell*

**FRIDAY THE 13TH** (TV series) see *Quilt of Hathor, The*

**FRIDAY THE 13TH: A NUDE BEGINNING** Vidco/Rasputin (Patti Rhodes) 1987 color c90m. D: F. J. Lincoln. SP: Mark

Weiss. Ref: vc box: "flesh and fantasy." Adam'89: hockey-mask thrills. With Paul Thomas, Nina Hartley, Nikki Knights.

**FRIDAY THE 13TH, PART 2** Vidco/Rasputin & Barbii Prods. 1989 color c88m. D, Ed, Co-P: F. J. Lincoln. SP, Co-P: Patti Rhodes. Mkp: Maxx. Ref: TV: Vidco Video. No Adam '89 or '92. With Barbii, Tom Byron, Porsche Lynn, Sharon Mitchell, Lincoln (Uncle Merlin).

Jessica and her twin brother (or, as it may be, father) Jason—who has lived since birth in hell—prove to be devils intent on making a pimp President of the U.S. ("We live for corruption!") The pair are stuck in hell—a "boring, stupid, and unimaginative" place—until they "burn out".... Jason occasionally dons a hockey mask, but the closest that this odd X-rated fantasy comes to the first *Friday the 13TH* series is the opening suspense sequence, in which a butcher knife is wielded menacingly, but, as it turns out, innocently. (It's used to cut a birthday cake.)

**FRIEND** see *Deadly Friend*

**FRIENDS** see *Valteus*

**FRIENDSHIP'S DEATH** (B) BFI/Modelmark & Channel 4 1987 color 73m. SP, D: Peter Wollen, from his short story. Mus: Barrington Pheloung. Mkp: Morag Ross. Ref: screen. V 12/2/87. Cinef 1/90. PFA notes 9/20/88. MFB. With Bill Paterson, Tilda Swinton (Friendship), Patrick Bauchau.

September 1970. A "highly sophisticated, intelligence-gathering technology," or robot—code name "Friendship"—from a planet in a distant galaxy, lands in wartorn Amman, Jordan. On her planet, only computers and self-replicating robots survived the nuclear winter (the giant tree shrews with zoom lenses did not), and Earth is the hobby of these machines.... At her most "poetic," Friendship says things like "Pleasure is only the shadow of pain." The film's problem is that it's mostly talk, some of it witty and surprising, but still talk—until the *2001*-like light-show coda, which does visually what Friendship did verbally—i.e., project an alien viewpoint.

*****FRIGHT** Para/Planet Filmplays 1959 (1956) 66m. OptFX: Arthur Jacks. Mkp: Josephine Cianella. Ref: TV. no Eames. no V. Lee. Weldon. Stanley. Lentz. Kael/5001. Scheuer. no Maltin '92.

"My name is not Ann. I am Baroness Maria." Jim Hamilton (Eric Fleming), a "Park Avenue Svengali," hypnotically regresses Ann Summers (Nancy Malone)—a woman plagued by "mysterious messages" and memory blackouts—to 1889 Austria, where her alternate personality, Maria Vetsera, lover of Crown Prince Rudolph, possesses her. ("It's so horrifying to think that there's this other person within me!") A childhood trauma proves responsible for Ann's delusions, and Jim employs a "killer mind" to rid her of them.... This footnote to the *Mayerling* story is mostly stiff acting and drab gab until a few prime, absurd, late plot developments set up a wild-and-woolly climax. Stock weird, out-of-this-world music injects the "fright" into the hypnotism sequences.

**FRIGHT HOUSE** Studio Ent. 1989 color 122m. D, P: Len Anthony. Ref: V 11/29/89:43(hv): "okay mixture of sexploitation and gore." 8/9/89:21(rated). Fango 2/90. With Al Lewis, Paul Borgese, Jennifer Delora, Kit Jones.

Satanist hypnotizes college kids.

Also included: an abbreviated version of *Vampires* (which see) aka *Abadon*.

**FRIGHT NIGHT** Col-Delphi IV/Vistar Films 1985 color/ws 106m. SP, D: Tom Holland. Mus: Brad Fiedel. SpFX: Entertainment FX; (vis) Richard Edlund; (anim) Garry Waller, Terry Windell; (mech) Thaine Morris; (creature des) Randall William Cook, Steve Johnson. OptFX: Boss Film. Ref: TV. MFB'86:108-9. V 7/31/85. SFChron 8/2/85. With Chris Sarandon (Jerry Dandridge), William Ragsdale, Amanda Bearse, Roddy McDowall, Stephen Geoffreys, Jonathan Stark (Billy Cole).

Horror movie fan (Ragsdale) enlists the aid of actor Peter Vincent (McDowall)—the "great vampire killer," in movies like *Orgy of the Damned*—in a campaign against the new vampire (Sarandon) and zombie (Stark) on the block. But Vincent is now only the "Fright Night" horror show host, and the vampire has super-strength and hypnotic powers.... Clever scrambling of vampire lore and vampire-movie lore. The tour de force finale features six endings, lotsa makeup effects, and a scene in which a vampire (Geoffreys) changes into a wolf. The story, though, peters (or vincents) out somewhere in the middle, when the lighter touch gets lost, and the film starts to compete with other effects extravaganzas.

**FRIGHT NIGHT PART 2** New Century-Vista (Herb Jaffe, Mort Engelberg) 1988 color/ws 104m. SP, D: Tommy Lee Wallace. SP: also Tim Metcalfe, Miguel Tejada-Flores. Mus: Brad Fiedel. SpVisFX: Gene Warren Jr.; Fantasy II; (stopmo) Justin Kohn. SpMkpFX: MkpFX Unltd.; Bart J. Mixon; ("Bozworth") Greg Cannom. SpFX: Rick Josephson. Ref: TV. MFB'89:113-14. V 12/28/88. SFChron Dtbk 7/2/89. With Roddy McDowall, William Ragsdale, Traci Lin, Julie Carmen (Regine), Jonathan Gries (Louie), Russell Clark (Belle), Brian Thompson (Bozworth).

"They are here!" But are they "performance artists" with wild contact lenses—or vampires? Regine turns out to be the original *Fright Night* vampire's sister; Louie is a human, or rather inhuman (i.e., werewolf) fly; and "Bozworth" is a Renfield-like bug-eater. (Good, gross, crunching sound-effects.) Meanwhile, vampire-bitten hero Charley (Ragsdale) becomes light-sensitive and neck-happy.... Messy, with tiresome variations on the basic "There are no vampires" scene, but with amusing moments. And it's good to have McDowall back as the enthusiastic Peter Vincent, the "fearless vampire killer." When Regine becomes the new "Fright Night" host, Vincent, not amused, grabs the nearest stake.

**FROG DREAMING** see *Quest, The* (Austral., 1985)

**The FROG, THE DOG AND THE DEVIL** Bob Stenhouse 198-? short. Ref: SFChron Dtbk 9/20/87: "re-creation of an old New Zealand ballad, 'The Devil's Daughter.'"

"Spectral images" pursue a cowboy across a "weird prairie."

**FROGTOWN II** BRI/York Pictures (Scott Pfeiffer) 1992 color 78m. (*Hell Comes to Frogtown II. Return to Frogtown* - early ts). Story, SP, D, Ph: Donald G. Jackson. Story, Exec P: Tanya York. Mus: Robert Garrett. PD: George Peirson. SpMkpFX: Mark Williamson. Ref: TV. TVG. V 8/3/92:12(rated). Cinef 12/93:59.

With Robert Z'Dar, Denise Duff, Charles Napier, Don Stroud, Brion James (professor), Lou Ferrigno.

"I've got this thing for humans!" It's mankind vs. "frogkind," in this sequel to *Hell Comes to Frogtown*. A doctor's "hideous experiment" with the Green Transformation Machine is intended to turn humans into semi-amphibians, and it's the flying, Commando Cody-like (or Rocketeer-like) Texas Rocket Rangers to the rescue.... Kooky details, but this is mainly talk and casually-staged action. Some dumb fun with the puppet critter "Junior." (Cf. Baby Saticoy in *Roller Blade*.)

**FROM A WHISPER TO A SCREAM** see *Offspring, The. Whisper to a Scream, A.*

**FROM BEYOND** Empire/Taryn (Charles Band/Brian Yuzna) 1986 color 85m. D: Stuart Gordon. SP: Dennis Paoli, from H. P. Lovecraft's short story. Adap: Yuzna, Paoli, Gordon. Mus: Richard Band. SpFX: Paul Gentry; (coord) Michael Muscal; (transformations) MMI, (sup) John Buechler. SpFxMkp: MTSD; (coord) John Naulin; (Pretorius) Mark Shostrom. Tank creatures: John Naulin, J. Criswell. Physical FX: Doublin. Resonator: David Mansley; (sd fx) Jonathan Pearthtree(sp?). Ref: TV: Vestron Video. MFB'87:175-6. V 10/29/86. Bay G 2/4/87. E. Bay Express 1/30/87. SFExam 1/23/87. With Jeffrey Combs, Barbara Crampton, Ken Foree, Ted Sorel (Dr. Edward Pretorius), Carolyn Purdy-Gordon (Dr. Roberta Bloch).

"A snake came out of his head!" Dr. Edward Pretorius has "passed beyond"—he now has a peel-off body for his "indivisible" mind. His Resonator-awakened pineal gland sees that all is "beautiful," and he enjoys the "greatest sensual pleasure there is"—entering another's brain. Plus: a flying, eel-like thing, jellyfish creatures, and a snake-like, cellar creature.... *From Beyond* features one of the most amusing conglomerations of glop since *The Thing* remake, but the on/off, effects/breather plot reduces to tired Don't-use-the-Resonator/I-must-use-the-Resonator conflicts between, respectively, Combs' Dr. Tillinghast and Sorel's Dr. Pretorius, while the original story proves to be a small, neglected Lovecraft gem re the "world that lies unseen around us," and a machine which makes that world visible. If the film's imaginativeness is pretty much restricted to fun-ghastly makeup effects, the short story invites you to reconsider your whole conception of the "air and the sky about and above" you:

"You see them? You see the things that float and flop about you and through you every moment of your life?"

Love that "through you."

**FROM THE DEAD OF NIGHT** NBC-TV/Shadowplay Films & Phoenix Ent. 1989 color c180m. D: Paul Wendkos. Tel: William Bleich, from Gary Brandner's novel *Walkers*. Ph: Bernd Heinl. Mus: Gil Melle. PD: Penny Hadfield. SpVisFX: Fantasy II. SpMkp: A. Apone. Title Des: Christina Hills, Brad Gensurowsky. Ref: TV. Sacto Bee "TV Today": TV-movie. Cinef 1/90. With Lindsay Wagner, Diahann Carroll, Bruce Boxleitner, Robert Prosky, Robin Thomas, Peter Jason, Merritt Butrick, Joanne Linville, Jeanne Bates.

"The dead want you back!" Claims the fashion designer (Wagner): "It is not all in my head!" Blah occult suspenser is from hunger. ("The spirit world is extremely powerful.") Visual cliches include people jumping at their own mirror image and falling (through skylights) in slow motion. ("Walkers don't bleed!")

**FROM ZERO TO HERO** (H.K.) Sunshine 1994 color 98m. D: D. Wu. Ref: vc box. HOF 2:39-40: "consistently amusing." With F. Ng, A. Lee.

Freak accident turns comic-book artist into super-hero.

**FRONT PAGE, COLUMN ONE** Dark Circle Prods. 1985 color 23m. SP, D, Ed: Ralph Fujiwara. Ph: John Persichetti. Mus: Robert Fair. SpFX: W. Caban et al. Ref: TV: shown on USA's "Night Flight." With Louis J. Sigalos.

"Bio limb regeneration" serum produces a "two-headed monster rabbit." When the doc himself is injected, *Alien*-like critters emerge from his torso. Functional plot, nice gross touches, like the monster-mouth in the doc's palm, the ugh drool on his shoe, and the rabbit itself.

**FROST AND FIRE** see *Quest* (1984)

**FROZEN TERROR** (I) Lightning Video/AMA Film & Medusa (Gianni Minervini & Antonio Avati) 1980('86-U.S.) color/ws 91m. (*Macabro*. 2P *Macabre*). SP, D: Lamberto Bava. SP: also Pupi Avati, A. Avati, R. Gandus. Ph: Franco delli Colli. Mus: Ubaldo Continiello. Sets: Katia Dottori. SpFX: Tonino Corridori, Angelo Mattei. SdFX: L. & M. Anzellotti. Mkp: Alfonso Cioffi. Ref: TV: LV; Eng. version. Hardy/HM. Ecran 31:66. MFB'83:169-70. Morse. V 5/7/80:359. Ecran 39:14,16. With Bernice Stegers, Stanko Molinar, V. Zinny, Roberto Posse.

"Don't touch the refrigerator!" Jane (Stegers) keeps the head of her dead, beloved Fred in the refrigerator freezer, a severed ear lobe is found in a drawer, and there's horror in the soup .... Supposedly "inspired by ... actual events," this is a really awful, ham-handed homey horror story, set in New Orleans. "Highlight": the yuck-love scene with Jane and the head in bed. In the idiotic freeze-frame ending, the dead head bites.

**FU MANCHU** see *Aullido del Diablo, El. Sete Vampiras, As.*

**FUGA DAL PARADISO** (I-F-G) Titanus/Azzurra Film & RAI-2 & Cinemax & Iduna (Luna-Mori) 1990 color 111m. SP, D: Ettore Pasculli. SP: also Lucio Mandara. Mus: Michel Legrand. Palmerini. Ref: V 11/5/90: *Escape from Paradise* - tr t. With Fabrice Josso, Ines Sastre, Horst Buchholz, Aurore Clement, Jacques Perrin, Lou Castel, Van Johnson.

"Bizarre, incoherent sci-fi" re an underground city and mutants in a future world.

**FUGITIVE ALIEN** (J) Sandy Frank/Tsuburaya 1986 color c100m. D: K. Kukazawa, M. Kanaya. SP: K. Abe, B. Wakatsuki, Y. Araki et al. Mus: Norio Maeda. Ref: TV: Eng. dubbed. TVG. no Maltin '92. no Scheuer. With Tatsuya Azuma, Miyuki Tanigawa, Joe Shishido, Choei Takahashi.

Ken, a super-strong humanoid alien from Valnastar who refuses to kill women and children, is picked up "floating through space" without a suit. The crew of *Bacchus III* signs him on to fight his own, tyrannized people. Ken proves to be from Earth, originally.... Speedy but tacky. Lots of "I'm a Ranger, too!" One convincing makeup effect: the spaceship-cabin pressure "rubber-izing" the pilot's cheek.

Follow-up: *Star Force.*

**FUJIKO F FUJIO S. F. SHORT STORY THEATER** (J) Toho Video/Shogakukan 1990 anim color 50m. D?, SP: Fujio Fujiko. Ref: Animag 10:5: OAV.

1) "How To Build a Spaceship." Students crash land on an uncharted planet.

2) "My Lonely War of the Worlds." A boy and his clone in a "representative war over Earth."

**FUKUSHU SURU WA WARE NI ARI** see *Vengeance is Mine*

**FULL ECLIPSE** HBO-TV 1993 color c105m. Ref: HBO/Cinemax 11/93: vigilante-cop werewolves. TVG 9/18/93: potion. with Mario Van Peebles, Patsy Kensit.

**FULL METAL SOLDIER L. GAIM** see *Heavy Metal L-Gaim*

**FUNERALES DEL TERROR** (Mex) Exitos Cinematografi-cos/David Moya 1990 color c77m. D: Alberto Mariscal. Ph: Guillermo Bravo. Mus: Raul Martell. Ref: TV: Million Dollar Video; no Eng. TVG. With Juan Valentin, Silvia Manriquez, Jorge Russek, Alfonso Munguia, Armando Palomo.

Joel (Valentin) falls and dies, or so everyone thinks. A cataleptic, he can't move, but he sees the mourners at his funeral service pass, one by one, above him. At the graveyard, he fully returns to life and is brought out of the coffin, but his heart gives out from the struggle, and he dies "again".... Cheap, shot-on-tape horror drama uses catalepsy as a pretext for a tiresome "review" of the hero's life. An amplified heartbeat indicates that Joel is still alive.

**FUNNY FRANKENSTEIN** (I) Cinevideo 80 1984 color feature. D: "Alan W. Coors." Ref: Ecran F 48:70: completed. no Martin. no Hound. With Marina Frajese, Matt Shannon, Aldo Sambrel.

Beautiful women in chateau can transform into "horrible monsters." Cf. *Lady Frankenstein* (3).

**FUNNY GHOST** (Thai) c1987? color c110m. Ref: TV: All Asian video; no Eng. Thai Video: above is tr t.

Ingredients: the laughing, eye-ray-shooting ghost of a murdered woman ... a skeleton with a lantern ... another skeleton that plays piggyback with a human ... and real ghosts which chase fake ghosts away from a cemetery.... Despite the title translation, this is a serious-business ghost here. Even her laughter is cold and mirthless. The funny stuff with the humans is pretty limp, just double takes and screaming. The chilly stuff with the woman's ghost is more effective, especially the "bus" in which her magnified, blue face suddenly appears—a la *Vampyr*—at a window. To counter the blessed "safety" ropes which surround and protect the exorcist and company at one point, she jumps up out of the ground. Script indiscriminately mixes comedy, horror, tragedy, and violence.

See also: *Lam Yong.*

**FUNNY GHOST** see *Bloody Ghost*

**FUNNY MAN** (B) Nomad Pictures (Nigel Odell) 1994 color 93m. SP, D: Simon Sprackling. Ph: T. Ingle Jr. Mus: Parsons/Haines. PD: D. Endley. SpFX: Neill Gorton, Jim Francis. Ref: V 6/27/94: "haunted house yarn ... isn't half as funny as it thinks it is." With Tim James (Funny Man), Christopher Lee, Benny Young, Ingrid Lacey, Pauline Chan (Psychic Commando).

The Funny Man turns his victims into "pig slop, one by one."

**FUNNY VAMPIRE, The** see *New Mr. Vampire II*

**FUOCO INCROCIATO** see *Rage*

**FURIA ASESINA** (Mex) Televicine & PFR 1990 color c92m. SP, D, P: Rene Cardona Jr. Ph: Ramon Rios. Mus: J. A. Jimenez Jr., Alejandro Sanchez. Mkp: Estela Sanchez. Ref: TV: Mex-American HV; no Eng. With Omar Fierro, Tony Bravo, Monica Vali, Leticia Lozoya, Roberto Montiel.

Scientifically augmented shark attacks small craft on the Sea of Cortez, knocks one person overboard, dines; later, chews up diver. Only redeeming feature of shot-on-video junk: the trave-logue shots of local animal life.

Cf. *Devil Fish.*

**FURIA PRIMITIVA** see *Primal Rage*

The **FURIES** WB 1930 69m. D: Alan Crosland. From Zoe Atkins' play. Ref: V 4/23/30. With Lois Wilson, Montagu Love, H.B. Warner, Theodore von Eltz.

"Reposed and cold" lawyer (Warner) ultimately betrays his "Jekyll-Hyde demeanor. The lawyer reveals his butler is really his keeper."

**FURY OF THE HEAVEN** (H.K.) Artview 1988? color c85m. D: Chen Ching Lo. Ref: TV: World Video; Eng. titles. NST! 4:23. Fango 107:59.

The room in back of an inn is "haunted, seriously so," by the ghost of Jiu Sui Kui. ("I'm a wandering ghost.") A victim of Black Magician Malaba's Poison Blood Spell, she wreaks gory revenge, at the end, on the man responsible for her death. A mishmash of tones, *Fury of the Heaven* arbitrarily mixes comedy, drama, fantasy, and gore.

El **FUTBOLISTA FENOMENO** (Mex) Conacite Dos 1974 color c90m. SP, D: Fernando Cortes. SP: also Julio Porter. Story: Resortes. Ph: Raul Dominguez. Mus: Marcos Lifshitz. AD: Jorge Sainz. SpFX: Sergio Jara. Mkp: Victoria Celis. Ref: TV: no Eng. TVG. With Monica Prado, Resortes, Joaquin Garcia, Alfonso Zayas, Jorge Zamora, Polo Ortin, Hector Godoy, Juan Dosal.

Aliens in a flying saucer give a goof amazing abilities at soccer; "hypnotize" earthlings with their ray. At the end, the "phenome-nal" hero "dances" the ball across the field, whistles to bring the ball to him, etc.—a silly but amusing sequence in this otherwise pretty awful, talky sf-comedy.

**FUTURE BOUND** see *Future Zone*

**FUTURE COP** see *Trancers*

**FUTURE COPS** (H.K.) 1993 color feature. D: Wong Jing. Ref: V 8/9/93:13: in H.K. 9/6/93:10: in Taipei. Weisser/ATC2: "super-hero cops from the future." With Andy Lau, S. Yam, A. Kwok.

**FUTURE FORCE** Action Int'l. (Kimberley Casey/David Winters, B. Lewin) 1989 color 84m. (*C.O.P.S.*-ad t). SP, D: David A. Prior. Created by Thomas Baldwin. Mus: Tim James et al. Ref: V 11/29/89: "scores high in imagination." 10/19/88:196(ad). PT 13:46. Scheuer. With David Carradine, Robert Tessier, Anna Rapagna, D. C. Douglas, Dawn Wildsmith.

1991. Bounty hunter (Carradine) with cannon "arm" takes on civilian police.

Sequel: *Future Zone*.

**FUTURE HUNTERS** (U.S.-Fili) Lightning Pictures/Maharaj-Santiago (High Ridge) 1989 (1986/1985) color 100m. (*The Spear of Destiny* - shooting t). D: Cirio H. Santiago. SP: J. L. Thompson. Story: Anthony Maharaj. Ph: R. Remias. Mus: Ron Jones. PD: J. M. Avellana. Ref: TV: Vestron Video. V 2/22/89: "a winner." Ecran F 68:71. Martin. vc box. Scheuer: "well-paced." With Robert Patrick, Linda Carol, Ed Crick, Richard Norton, Elizabeth Oropesa, Bruce Li, Bob Schott.

"I'm from another time." Magic spear-head (the one which pierced Christ on the cross) allows man (Norton) to travel back in time, from 2025 (40 years after the "Great Holocaust") to 1986, and—used as a weapon—makes its victims incinerate. Cliche-filled action and dialogue.

**FUTURE KICK** Concorde-New Horizons (Roger Corman) 1991 color 80m. D: Damian Klaus; (addl scenes) Louis Morneau. SP: Klaus. Ph: Ken Arlidge. Mus: Scott Singer. PD: Johan Le Tenoux. SpMinFX: Apollo FX. Opt & Roto FX: Motion Opticals. Mkp: Kathleen Karridene. Ref: TV. SFChron Dtbk 10/13/91. 5/24/92. TVG. PT 13:47. With Don (The Dragon) Wilson, Meg Foster, Christopher Penn, Eb Lottimer, Al Ruscio, Jeff Pomerantz, Linda Dona, Beach Dickerson, Maria Ford.

"What do you think of my new program?" Futuristic melodrama set in New L.A. re a bio-mechanical cyberon (Wilson), bodys-natching (by the New Body organization), the dangerous Laser-blade game, casual beheadings and eviscerations, and televised executions—all of which proves to have been part of a program packaged by Virtual Reality Systems.... Despite this intriguing revelation, the *Total Recall*-inspired *Future Kick* is bland, dream or not. Fine line: "Why don't you just go back to the moon?"

**FUTURE-KILL** IFM/Magic Shadows (Best-Unterberger) 1985 (1984) color 83m. (*Splatter* - orig t). SP, D: Ronald W. Moore. Mus: R. Renfrow. Ref: HR 6/12/85: "typical exploitation fare." PFA Library. V 5/22/85: "maintains a quick pace." SFChron 11/28/83. V 10/26/83:181(ad). 9/14/83:32. Ecran F 42:86. Martin. Scheuer: "unendurably cruel." Nowlan. with Edwin Neal, Marilyn Burns, Gabriel Folse, Barton Faulks, Wade Reese.

Finger-clawed madman.

**FUTURE LUST** Moonlight 1989 color feature. D: Scotty Fox. Ref: Adam '90. vc box: cryogenics. With Ray Victory, Nina Hartley, Tom Byron, Debbie Diamond.

Government-controlled sex in the future.

**FUTURE NINJA** see *Mirai Ninja*

**FUTURE SCHLOCK** (Austral.) Ultimate Show 1984 color 75m. SP, D, P: Barry Peak, Chris Kiely. Mus: McCubbery, Sanders. Ref: V 5/23/84: "a mess, but fun." Stanley. Ecran F 47:70. With Maryanne Fahey, Michael Bishop, Tracey Callander.

In a 21st-century world, non-conformists are walled up in a ghetto.

**FUTURE SEX** L.T. Cole 198-? color c80m. Ref: vc box. With Amber Lynn.

Futuristic Older Brother forbids love, okays lust.

**FUTURE SHOCK** Park-Place Ent. & Paradise (Park-Schilling/Aza Nisi Masa/USC) 1993/1988/1992 color 105m.(97m.). D: Eric Parkinson, Francis Sassone, Matt Reeves. SP: Parkinson, Vivian Schilling, Sassone, D. Dubos, Reeves. Story: Sassone, Dubos. Ph: Gerry Lively, Kestermann, Fannin. Mus: Jon McCallum, Nigel Holton, J. Abrams. AD: Shirley Starks, Robert Fox. SpProsthFX: John Goodwyn. OptFX: Cinema Research. Ref: TV: Hemdale HV; unrated version; c1994. SFChron Dtbk 1/16/94. With Vivian Schilling, Scott Thompson, Sam Clay, Martin Kove, Bill Paxton, Brion James, Sidney Lassick, James Karen, Rick Rossovich.

Compilation film begins with a pre-credit, *Scanners*-like head-blowing, and the framing story gimmick is called "virtual reality," but plays more like the hypnotic suggestion of the first *Invasion U.S.A.*

"Jenny Porter": The paranoid Jenny sees a TV news story re her death-by-wolves, and is terrorized by a prowler—herself. Routine suspense-horror, with okay bits.

"The Roommate": A fairly wry study in paranoia involving a roommate from hell, decapitation, etc.

"Mr. Petrified Forest": "It's never safe." Moderately amusing story about a guy with a death phobia. Funny exchange in "limbo": "How are you?" "I'm dead."

**FUTURE SODOM** Vidco 1988 color 85m. D, P: Gerard Damiano. Ref: Adam '89. With Britt Morgan, Viper, Laurel Canyon, William Margold.

"Two guys get transported into the future."

**FUTURE ZONE** Action Int'l. & David Carradine Ent. (Kimberly Casey/David Winters & Bruce Lewin) 1990 color 80m. (*Back to the Past* - early t). SP, D: David A. Prior. Mus: W. T. Stromberg. Ref: TV. V 6/6/90. PT 13:46. V 5/9/90:26: 6/90 start for *Future Bound*, same cast, writer-director. 2/21/90:123. V/Cannes '89:94: *Future Force II*. With David Carradine, Ted Prior, Gail Jensen, Patrick Culliton, Charles Napier.

"I'm from the future." L.A., 1999. Billy (Prior) comes through a "time portal" to save two-gun cop John Tucker's (Carradine) life. Flatfooted action scenes, less-than-deft performances, juvenile dialogue. Sort-of-highlight: the flying, remote-operated glove which shoots blue rays. Sequel to *Future Force*.

**FUTUROPOLIS** Segal-Trumbo 1985 anim and live action 38m. Ref: SFChron 12/23/88: "witless ... impressive technically"; Dtbk 12/18/88: "erratic ... memorably dumb phrases."

Space warriors vs. evil mastermind and his death ray.

# G

**G.I. JOE: A REAL AMERICAN HERO** (U.S.-J) Sunbow & Marvel/Toei 1983 anim color c90m. SP, D: Don Jurwich. Anim Sup:(d) Ray Lee, T. Arisako; Brian Ray. Ph: S. Ikeda. Mus: Walsh, Douglas. SpFX: Shoji Sato et al. Ref: TV. TVG: made for TV. no Stanley. Voices: Chuck McCann, Burgess Meredith, Don Johnson et al.

A super-device in the Cobra's temple alters molecules; transmits people and objects from place to place; bounces rays off the "ultimate relay star" satellite back to the Eiffel Tower, which disappears. Plus: "mindless creatures," robotized slaves of the Cobra ("reptile breath").... Glib, stolid sf-actioner done in a style best described perhaps as hip-square. Occasional imaginative touches.

See also the following and *Pyramid of Darkness.*

**G.I. JOE II** (U.S.-J?) 1984 anim color c90m. Ref: TVG: made for TV.

Joe vs. the Cobra.

**G.I. JOE—THE MOVIE** (U.S.-J) Sunbow & Marvel/Toei 1987 anim color 93m. (*G.I. Joe: A Real American Hero* - cr t). D & Co-P: Don Jurwich. Sup Anim D: Ray Lee, T. Arisako. SP: Ron Friedman. Mus: R. J. Walsh, Jon Douglas. SpFX: Shoji Sato, Masayuki Kawachi et al. Ref: TV. V 12/28/88:21(hv): OAV. TVG. Voices: Chris Latta (Cobra commander), Burgess Meredith (Golobulus), Arthur Burghardt (Destro), Jennifer Darling (Pythona), Dick Gautier (Serpentor).

Ingredients include the evil, super-fingernailed Pythona and her various snake-like and tentacled creatures . . . the Broadcast Energy Transmitter ("pure energy pumped throught the air")...the "ultimate fruit of hyper-genetic manipulation": "fungusoids" which shoot out spores that turn the things they touch into primitive life forms ... a "red carpet" of crab creatures ... giant caterpillar creatures ... and giant man-eating plants.... Scorecard: occasional surprisingly outre fantasy elements, some style and flash, monotonous action, and tiresome tough-as-bricks characters. In the fun climax, the whole damned planet seems to turn into monsters.

**GAKI DAMASHII** see *Soul-Hungry Demon*

**GALACTIC GIGOLO** Urban Classics/Titan & Generic Films (Kris Covello) 1988 (1987) color 82m. (*Club Earth* - shooting t). SP, D, P, Ph: Gorman Bechard. SP: also Carmine Capobianco. Mus: Lettuce Prey. Ref: V 2/3/88: "unwatchable." With C. Capobianco (Eoj), Debi Thibeault (Hildy Johnson), Ruth Collins, Angela Nicholas.

Eoj, a "broccoli from outer space," wins a vacation on Earth.

**GALACTIC PATROL** see *Lensman*

**GALAXY EXPRESS 999—CLEA OF THE GLASS** (J) 1980 anim short. Ref: Animag 6:19: offshoot of *Galaxy Express* (II, III).

"Crystalline waitress" Clea wants to buy back her human body.

The **GALAXY INVADER** Moviecraft Ent./The Ent. Group 1985 color c80m. Story, SP, D, SpSdFx, Ed: Don Dohler. Story: also Anne Frith, David Donoho. Ph: P. E. Loeschke. Mus, SpSdFX: Norman Noplock. MkpFX: John Cosentino. Meteor FX: Dan Taylor. SpFX: Donoho, The Cracker Factory. Ref: TV: United HV. Hound. Stanley. no Martin. With Richard Ruxton, Faye Tilles, Don Leifert, George Stover, Frith, Greg Dohler, Glenn Barnes (alien), Richard Svehla.

"I bet he came to see that thing from the green man." A "big fireball" bearing a big, green, two-legged alien lands near Harleyville. The locals plan to catch it and sell it, but fail to reckon with its ray gun and power sphere.... Dismal Maryland sf. Clumsy action, stilted acting, lifeless dialogue, pretentious ending. Yes, that bad.

La **GALERIA DEL TERROR** (Arg.) Aries (Luis Osvaldo Repetto) 1987 color c100m. D: Enrique Carreras. SP: Juan Carlos Mesa. Ph: Victor Hugo Caula. Mus: Mike Rivas. AD: Mario Figiosi. Mkp: Ana Do Campo. Ref: TV. TVG. V 5/4/88:504. With Jorge Porcel, Alberto Olmedo, Mario Sanchez, Susana Romero, Beatriz Salomon, Juan Carlos Galvan.

Long low-comedy-horror movie featuring miscellaneous monsters, or fake monsters, a ghoul in a coffin, a living leopard-skin rug, etc. *Gallery of Terror* - tr t.

**GALL FORCE: ETERNAL STORY** (J) Sony Video 1986 anim color 86m. D: Kazuhiko Akiyama. Story & Mecha Des: Hideki Kakinuma. Ref: TV: Sony Video; no Eng.; OAV. Animag 10:20-26.

Space battles alternate with mildly erotic, locker-room-type footage of the all-"gal" force at home on the ship, whose interior is very *2001*. The monster aboard, at one point, is very *Alien*. Meanwhile, other, robotic, bug-eyed aliens engage our big-eyed heroines in an intricate climactic battle which leaves a whole planet surrounded by some sort of force field. The script seems conventional, the design very pretty, the pop score bland. The elaborate space-laser rays resemble wiring diagrams.

**GALL FORCE 2: DESTRUCTION** (J) Sony Video 1987 anim color 50m. Ref: vc box: OAV. Animag 10:20-27. M/TVM 3/88:20. Japan Video.

"A hidden Solnoid planet destroyer obliterates the Paranoids' home planet...." (Animag)

**GALL FORCE 3: STARDUST WAR** (J) Sony Video 1988 anim color 60m. Ref: M/TVM 2/89:56. Animag 4:8: final chapter. 10:20-28: OAV. Japan Video.

"The final battle rages in space." (Animag)

See also the following and *Rhea Gall Force. Scramble Wars. Ten Little Gall Force.*

**GALL FORCE—EARTH CHAPTER ONE** (J) Polydor 1989 anim color 45m. Ref: Animag 10:21: 3 OAVs. Japan Video.

Follow-up to *Rhea Gall Force*. Follow-up to this series: *Gall Force—New Century*.

**GALL FORCE—EARTH CHAPTER 2** (J) Polydor 1990 anim color 65m. Ref: Animag 11:4. Japan Video: *Chapter Three*—45m., 1990.

Re "alien weapons discovered on the moon." (Animag)

**GALL FORCE—NEW CENTURY 1 & 2** (J) Polydor/A.I.C. 1991? anim color 45m. each. Ref: Japan Video. V.Max 2:5. 3:4.

Attempts to "restore Earth's ecosystem."

**GALLANT, The** see *Phantom Chivalry, The*

**GALLERY MURDERS, The** see *Bird with the Crystal Plumage, The*

**The GAME** Transcontinental & Film Centre Int'l./Titan Int'l. (The Cold Prods.) 1988 (1983) color c88m. D, Exec P, Ed: Bill Rebane. SP: William Arthur, Larry Dreyfus. Ph: Ito, Bruce Malm. Ref: TV: TWE video. no V. Hound. no Martin. V 5/9/84:268(ad): *The Cold* - orig t? With Tom Blair, Debbie Martin, Jim Iaquinta, Don Arthur.

"Once upon a time, in a faraway resort"—Northernaire—three millionaires, Maude, George, and Horace, played a game of fear with a group of money-hungry, colorless characters. Freezing indoor winds and mists, an *Alien* critter from a mattress, a hunchback, and a severed floating head turn out to be simply "special effects," intended to scare participants in a million-dollar game. At the end, however, a real ghost seems to appear.... Foolish, clumsily paced and scored, sub-*Sleuth* charades.

**GAME OF SURVIVAL** Raedon HV 1989 feature. D: A. Gazarian. Ref: Stanley: aliens. no Martin. With N. Hill, C. Coatman.

**GAME OVER** see *Fair Game* (1988)

**GAMERA—THE GUARDIAN OF THE UNIVERSE** (J) Daiei-NTV-Hakuhodo 1995 (1994) color/ws c95m. D: Shusuke Kaneko. SP: Kazunori Ito. SpFxD: Shinji Higuchi. Ref: TV: vt; Eng. titles; c'95. vc box: "'94 version." V 5/15/95:C92. With Akira Onodera, T. Ihara, S. Nakayama, Ayako Fujitani, H. Hasegawa, Y. Hotaru.

"The monster's relationship with the birds hasn't been verified." It's "Gamera, the last hope," here vs. the "shadow of evil, Gyaos." ("Gamera is on our side.") Ingredients include a mobile atoll, a "gigantic life form" ... three fanged, giant, people-eating female birds which can turn into males ("And they all disappeared because of some bird?") ... and metal from Atlantis which seems to have a link with Gamera.... Half-familiar, half-weirdly-new thrills. Bizarre story details issue in standard panic-and-destruction scenes. In one sequence with less-than-state-of-the-art, but amusing effects, the three birds, or Gyaos, are lured to a domed stadium with raw meat. ("The bird! The bird!") Apparently, an ancient civilization created all the monsters.

**2 GAMERA VS. ZIGRA** King Features (Sandy Frank) 1971 ws 87m. D: Noriaki Yuasa. SP: Fumi Takahashi. Mus: Shunsuke Kikuchi. SpFX: Kazuo Fujii. Ref: TV. Hardy/SF. Lentz. Stanley.

Martin. Scheuer. Hound. no Maltin '92. Ecran F 65:63, 64. With Eiko Yanami, Reiko Kasahara, Mikiko Tsubouchi.

In the year 1985, Gamera combats a monster from Zigra (rhymes with "zebra"), Celestial Body 105, Sector 4—"many light years away." The inhabitants of Zigra want to live in our seas and cage and eat humans, and they have hypnotic, supersonic-ray, and earthquake-causing powers. At one point, the Zigra Star Spaceship turns into a swordfish-thing which water pressure then makes grow "abnormally large," as the thing itself explains to Earth-at-large while it swims along and castigates earthlings for producing pollution.... Foolish, occasionally charming sf-for-kids gets pretty wild at times. Gamera can breathe fire underwater and, in one scene, uses a boulder to play his song on the scales of the fallen fish-thing. In another ineffable scene, Gamera picks up a boat with a girl and boy in it, they sing his song, and she admits, "I love Gamera!" How sweet, or something.

**GANDAHAR** see *Light Years*

**GANDAMU** see *Mobilesuit Gundam: Char's Counterattack*

**GANHEDO** see *Gunhed*

**GANJASAURUS REX** Prehistoric Prods. & Reel People Media (Rob Seares, Paul Bassis) 1987 color c93m. Ed, D: Ursi Reynolds. SP: Bassis, Dan Gilweit et al. Story: Seares. Ph: Rex White. Mus: Larry Murphy et al. Sets: Susan Akselsen. Anim: Smarty Smitty. Mkp: Sherby Cole. Ref: TV: vt. Hound. Phantom. Martin. With Bassis, Dave Fresh, Rosie Jones, Howard Phun, Rich Abernathy, John Ivar, Andy Barnett.

In 1985, on the Lost Coast of California, a 400-foot-tall Tyrannosaurus Herbivorous Ganjasaurus Rex, a user of Paleozoic pot, single-handedly wrecks the government's anti-marijuana campaign. Apparently, it's searching for a scientifically developed, modern version of Cannabis Sequoia, three plants the "size of redwood trees" grown from a "genetic miracle" of a seed and nurtured by Rex's own breath while she lay dormant. Computer "vocalizations" of her mating call lead her out to sea before the military has a chance to nuke the area.

Genial as all-get-out, *Ganjasaurus Rex* is an otherwise uncertain, obvious, tentatively-acted pro-pot comedy. The five-and-ten effects for Rex appear to include some computer animation, a suit, a model, and maybe a smidgeon of stopmo. Clever touch: the appearance, at the end, of an agent for Toho checking to make sure the Godzilla copyright is not infringed upon.

**GARAGA** (J) ASMIK 1989 anim color 101m. (aka *Hyper-Psychic-Geo Garaga*). Ref: TV: vt; no Eng. Animag 8:3: originally 2 OAVs.

In the year 2755, a cargo spaceship travels through "God's Ring," an interstellar "gate" which looks like a floating magic mirror, and crashlands on a planet ruled by a psychic queen and inhabited by ape-like man-monsters, a long-tailed, long-tongued tyrannosaurus-type, a gigantic disappearing horned "dinosaur," and other monster lizards. (These dinosaurs may just be visions conjured up by the queen.) Plus: robots both huge and small.... This looks like a routine, even monotonous, if actionful sword-and-sorcery saga. Showpiece visual: the willing of the monoliths up out of the ground.

**GARBAGE IN, GARBAGE OUT** Wozniak 198-? short. D: Terry Wozniak. Ref: SFChron Dtbk 9/20/87:32: bit with Godzilla-type.

**GARDEN OF EVIL, The** see *Lair of the White Worm, The*

**GARGANTUA & PANTAGRUEL** see *Fool's Fire*

**GAS PLANET** Pacific Data Images (Eric Darnell) 199-? computer anim short. Ref: SFChron 4/16/93: a "treat."

Creatures on "farflung planet" take gas for food.

**GASBAGS** (B) Gainsborough 1940 77m. D: Marcel Varnel. SP: Val Guest, Marriott Edgar. Story: Val Valentine, Ralph Smart. Ph: Arthur Crabtree. Ref: Pierre LePage (2000 Movies). BFC. British Sound Films. With The Crazy Gang: Bud Flanagan, Chesney Allen, Charlie Naughton, Jimmy Gold, Jimmy Nervo, and Teddy Knox; also Wally Patch, Frederick Valk, Torin Thatcher, George Merritt.

A mad inventor's (Moore Marriott) burrowing tank enables escapees from a concentration camp to tunnel from Germany to England.

**The GATE** (Can.) New Century/Vista/Alliance Ent. (The Gate Film Prods.) 1987 (1986) color 86m. D: Tibor Takacs. SP: Michael Nankin. Mus: Michael Hoenig, J. P. Robinson. SpMkp: Craig Reardon. SpVisFX: (sup) Randall William Cook; Illusion Arts; (anim) Catherine Sudolcan. Sp Sculpting: Reet Puhm, Film Arts. SpFX: Frank Carere. Moths: Northern Animal Exchange. Ref: TV. MFB'87:176-77. V 5/20/87. With Stephen Dorff, Christa Denton, Louis Tripp, Kelly Rowan, Jennifer Irwin, Deborah Grover, Scot Denton, Ingrid Veninger, Carl Kraines (workman).

An incantation from "The Dark Book" (the "bible for demons") raises a "demon of unimaginable size and power" (the "demon lord"), one of seemingly several Lovecraftian "old gods." Plus: some sinisterly gathering moths, "Mom" and "Dad" and "family dog" monsters, a severed arm which becomes wormy squiggles, and a zombie "workman" that breaks up into a horde of small, biting, stopmo-like beasts.... Competent *Poltergeist* variation with some good effects work, especially with the smaller beasties. The congregatings of the latter—in the house, in the hole—are the stuff of comic nightmares.

**GATE II** (Can.) Triumph/Vision Int'l. (Alliance Ent. & Andras Hamori) 1992 (1989) color 95m. D: Tibor Takacs. SP: Michael Nankin. Ph: Bryan England. Mus: George Blondheim. SpVisFX: Randall William Cook; Ruckus Ents. SpMkp: Craig Reardon. FX: Frank Carere. SpOpt: Illusion Arts. SpMin: M. F. Hoover; The Garden of Allah. SpSdFX: Peter Chapman. Ref: TV. V 3/9/92. ad. SFExam 2/28/92. SFChron 2/29/92. With Louis Tripp, Simon Reynolds, Pamela Segall, James Villemaire, James Kidnie, Andrea Ladanyi (Minion), Carl Kraines (Terry transformed), John Gundy (Minion voice).

"It's demonology." The second time around, the cast of unearthly characters includes a frog mini-demon, or "minion"—"Coolest thing I've ever seen!"—which looks like a mini-Ymir ... an unholy, Lovecraftian trinity of terrors trapped behind the titular gate—their objective: hell on Earth ... and a human-sized demon.... Functional storyline, but the pint-sized demon carries its share of the movie. Unfortunately, it gives way to a less successful, temporarily-fulfilled-wishes idea, which in turn gives way to even-less-successful, standard demon-mongering. Creepy: the pickled minion.

**The GATE OF THE HELL** (H.K.?) Wild West Video/Ie Loong 1981 color/ws c84m. D: Lu Pao Lun. SP: Mel Pao. Ref: TV: Ocean Shores Video; prologue with Eng. titles. With Tsui Hsin Yu, Chang Ming Ting, Li Ying, Li Tao Hung, Warrick Evens, Ema Emily.

In a prologue not directly related to the body of the film, a museum-exhibit skull comes to life, flies at a night watchman, and bites off his head.... Devil Hill, in the New Territories. In an isolated old house, a vampire skeleton's flesh—and cape—return, and he turns the hero into a vampire. Soon the heroine finds that all her friends are also vampires.... Atmospheric horror-comedy-drama is very deliberately paced. The most insignificant scenes go on and on. The "plot" is just one long chase and as such is oddly intriguing. Predictable all-a-dream ending.

**O GATO DE BOTAS EXTRATERRESTRE** (Braz.) 1990 feature. D, P: Wilson Rodrigues? Ref: Monster! 3:33: The Extraterrestrial Puss 'n Boots - tr t. With Jose Mojica Marins ("a benign E.T.").

**GATTO A NOVE CODE, Il** see *Cat o 'Nine Tails, The*

**GATTO NEL CERVELLO, Un** see *Cat in the Brain*

**GATTO NERO, Il** see *Black Cat, The* (1990)

**GAWIN** (F) Loco Corto Int'l. & Soprofilms & TF-1 (Gerard Louvin) 1991 color 95m. SP, D: Arnaud Selignac. SP: also Alexandre Jardin. Mus: Jerome Soligny. Mkp: Florence Fouquier. Ref: V 6/24/91: "an appealing variation on *E.T.*" With Jean-Hugues Anglade, Wojtek Pszoniak, Catherine Samie, Bruno.

Man fakes close encounter to fulfill the fantasies of his terminally ill son.

**GDLEEN** (J) Toho 1990 anim color 45m. Based on the computer game. Ref: Animag 10:4-5: OAV.

Space-trade-company's ship crashes on "unknown planet."

**The GEEK** Class X 1981 feature. Ref: PT 21:68: abominable snowman; hardcore.

**GEEK** Cinema Group/Overlook Films & Dean Crow Prods. (Maureen Sweeney) 1987 color 90m. (aka *Backwoods*). D: D. Crow. SP: Charles Joseph. Mus: S. Bushor. Ref: V 5/27/87: "subpar." 10/19/88:180. vc box. Phantom: "relentlessly stupid." McCarty II: "a piece of dead wood." With Brad Armacost, Christina Noonan, Dick Kreusser, Jack O'Hara.

Backwoods homicidal maniac.

**GEHEIMNIS DER GRUEN STECKNADELN, Das** see *What Have You Done to Solange?*

**GEHEIMNIS DER SCHWARZEN HANDSCHUHE, Das** see *Bird with the Crystal Plumage, The*

**GEISHA GIRL** Realart/George Breakston-C. Ray Stahl 1952 b&w 67m. D: G. Breakston. SP, D: C. Stahl. Ph: I. Hoshijima. Mus: Albert Glasser. AD: Seigo Shindo. OptFX: Consolidated. Ref: TV. Greg Luce. V 5/21/52. Lee(e). With Martha Hyer, William Andrews, Archer MacDonald, Dekao Yokoo, Tetu Nakamura, Henry Okawa, Michiyo Naoki.

The headline: "Island Disappears—Mysterious Explosion Rocks Pacific." The question: "Only one pill did this?" The answer: Yes. Scientist's super-explosive can out-atom-bomb the atom bomb: "Who could guess this little bottle would change the history of the world?" Meanwhile, Zoro (Yokoo), a hypnotist, "freezes" roomsful of people at a time and (in a cute bit) hypnotizes himself in a mirror.... Broad, haphazard mixture of intrigue, science-fantasy, local color and culture, romance, and comedy, with some prime terrible acting. At one point, Zoro indulges in some remote-control, Three Stooges-like bopping.

**GEMINI MAN** see *Riding with Death*

**GENERATION** ABC-TV/Embassy-TV 1985 color 92m. D: Michael Tuchner. SP & Exec P: Gerald DiPego. Mus: Charles Bernstein. PD: William Sandell. SpFX: John Frazier. LaserFX: Bifrost FX. Mkp: Bob Sidell. SdFxEd: Glen Glenn. Ref: TV. TVG. V 7/10/85:58. Maltin '92. Scheuer: pilot for proposed series. With Richard Beymer, Marta DuBois, Drake Hogestyn, Cristina Raines, Hannah Cutrona, Beah Richards, Priscilla Pointer, Bert Remsen, Kim Miyori.

It's 1999—the world of Tech World and its robot, "Hockey Man," and "sex pal"; combat hockey with "electronic motion enhancement"; "screen freaks" (or couch potatoes), and "partnerships" (i.e., marriages). And the accent in "neighborhood" is on "hood." SF-soaper pits cutthroat businessmen and gang leaders against family and personal integrity. Theme: You've got to fight for what you think is right. Complete with teary family reunion on New Year's Eve of the "new millennium." For those who want a future cry.

**GENESIS SURVIVOR GAIARTH, STAGE 1** (J) EMI-Artmic 1992 anim color 51m. (*Genesis Surviver Gaiarth* - t error). Ref: TV: Toshiba EMI video; no Eng. (apart from title). Martin. V.Max 4:3: 3 OAVs planned.

Stylishly drawn, basically conventional animated sf re a wrecked civilization, androids, war machines, airborne "cycles," and a futuristic fortress-city. Shrill pop score.

See also: *Scramble Wars.*

**The GENIUS** Fugitive (Joe Gibbons) 1993 color 95m. SP, D, Co-Ph: J. Gibbons. SP, D: Emily Breer. Ref: V 4/5/93: "tiresome, amateurish." With J. Gibbons, Karen Finley, Tony Oursler, Adolfas Mekas.

"Experiments in personality transplants."

**GENOCYBER: CYBER MONSTER FROM IMAGINARY WORLD—PART 1: BIRTH OF GENOCYBER** (J) CPM/Artmic-Plex(C. Moon/Shin Unozawa) 1993 anim color 48m. D: Kouichi Ohata. SP: Noboru Aikawa, Emu Arii. Story:

Artmic. Mus: Nakazawa, Kagoshima. PD: Yamane et al. Ref: TV: USManga Corps video; Eng. titles. Animerica 5:13: OAV series. Voices: Akiko Hiramatsu (Diana/Elaine), S. Kato.

Hong Kong, the 21st Century. The Kyuryu Science Institute promotes the "power of Vajura" and "mind shadows" in its ESPers. Two of the latter—Elaine and Diana—somehow become fused .... Stylish, sophisticated *Akira*-like gratuitous-gore vehicle is so extreme that it occasionally verges on the genuinely surreal. Nifty details (e.g., the mechanical ear) and even a touch of sentiment.

See also Cybernetics Guardian.

**GERMAN CHAINSAW MASSACRE** see *Deutsche Kettensagenmassaker*

**The GHOST** (H.K.) 1981? color/ws c92m. (*The Ghost Lover* - ad t). D: Yao Fung Pan. Ref: TV: Lex Video/Quality Video; Eng. titles.

Student Chi Da encounters the beautiful Mei Nung ("I love night") and her aunt in a "mansion in the mountain." Next morning, the jealous Ping Ping follows Chi Da to the site of the encounter: "Where's the house?" Ping Ping—who does not like this talk of attractive ghosts—has her father build a house on the hill. Mei Nung and her aunt pay it a spectral visit: "We have no place to live," they say—their ghost-house was torn down during construction. An *Exorcist*-voiced Ping Ping then takes to eating glass ("Ping Ping is abnormal"), but wooden nails and fire dispatch the ghost.

The first half of *The Ghost* recalls the sedate, seductive spookiness of *The Innocents*; the trashier, shock-laden second half recalls *The Exorcist*; and a ghost-in-the-road scene recalls *Horror Hotel*. Mei Nung herself is more compelling seen than heard. In dialogue and narration (in flashbacks to a past, sad affair), she tends toward the romantically pathetic; she makes her ghostly points more concisely and effectively. Auntie is pretty creepy too. Complete with "One Step Beyond"-like music.

**GHOST** Para/Howard W. Koch (Lisa Weinstein) 1990 color 127m. D: Jerry Zucker. SP: Bruce Joel Rubin. SpVisFX: IL&M; (sup) Bruce Nicholson; (coord) Jennifer C. Bell; (spirits) Available Light, J. van Vliet, Kathy Kean; (end seq) Boss Film, Richard Edlund; (dark ghosts) W. L. Arance, Mike Jittlov. Anim Sup: Charlie Clavadetscher. SpFxSup: Terry Frazee. SupSdEd: Leslie Shatz. MkpSup: Ben Nye Jr. Ref: TV. V 7/11/90. Sacto Bee 7/13/90. SFChron Dtbk 7/8/90. MFB'90:295-6.

Romantic fantasy features spooky sequences, as monk-like shadow figures carry off dead, hell-bound humans, and the dead, or dying, hero (Patrick Swayze) at one point has a (visualized) nightmare. Plus: spirit possession (explained as ghosts "jumpin' in the body") and *4-D Man*-like effects, as ghosts pass through humans and objects.... Comedy sequences with Whoopi Goldberg's "spiritual reader" Oda Mae Brown—a role in the recent movie tradition of scene-stealing psychics like *Poltergeist*'s Zelda Rubinstein—are the highlight of *Ghost*. Overall, the movie is an uneven mix of nifty effects (especially the sound effects for the shadow monks) and milked romantic sequences. Best of the latter is one in which Oda Mae acts as go-between for hero and heroine (Demi Moore).

**GHOST, The** see *Myonuriui Han*

**GHOST BALLROOM** (H.K.) Attraction Film 1989? color c90m. Ref: TV: Pan-Asia Video; Eng. titles. Y.K. Ho.

The green-gunk-spewing ghost of Mei helps Master Feather win at cards; he, in turn, helps her get revenge on Condon—who had her killed—by burning the spell which protects him from Mei. Highlights of the slim story (which is padded out with kung-fu and card-playing scenes): Mei literally walking on air, her hand tearing off as it clutches a man's arm, and Mei peeling off her face.

**GHOST BELONGED TO ME, The** see *Child of Glass. Once upon a Midnight Scary*

**\*The GHOST BREAKERS** Arthur Hornblow, Jr. 1940. Ph: also Theodore Sparkuhl. Mus: Ernst Toch. AD: Hans Dreier, Robert Usher. SpPh: F. Edouart. Ref: TV. Lee. V 6/12/40. Lentz. Weldon. Hardy/HM. Maureen Smith. Maltin '92. Scheuer. With James Flavin, Robert Ryan, Douglas Kennedy, Emmett Vogan, Jack Norton.

Zombies, ghosts, voodoo ouangas, bats, bird cries, and eerie croaking—in and around Castillo Maldito, the "forbidden castle of Black Island," off Cuba. Forget the Bob Hope comedy here. In its horror mode, this adaptation of the Dickey-Goddard play "The Ghost Breaker" outclasses most of the straight horror movies of its era. Intriguingly, the mission of Noble Johnson's zombie is never clarified. Is he castle caretaker, night watchman, avenger, or just atmosphere? More atmosphere: Virginia Brissac as Mother Zombie, or Mother Divine. Perhaps the strangest scene of all is the one in which the ghost of Don Santiago steps out of a chest, stretches his legs, then returns.

See also *Cat and the Canary, The* (1939).

**GHOST BRIDE** (H.K.?) 1992? color/ws? 88m. Ref: TV: vt; Eng. titles.

"I won't suck all your blood." Ingredients: the vampiric, witch-like Night Lady, who at one point possesses a woman ... hopping vampires ... a swivel-headed guy ... a disfigured demon ... and "some [who] walk upside down," i.e., the Umbrella Kid.... Odd, mainly misfired blend of softcore sex, slapstick, sentiment, and the supernatural. Most surprising element for Western viewers: a sex-and-fangs scene accompanied by the old Clock Song.

**GHOST BRIGADE** MPCA & Fred Kuehnert (Krevoy-Stabler) 1993 color 80m. D: George Hickenlooper. SP: Matt Greenberg. Ph: Kent Wakeford. Mus: Lerios, D'Andrea. PD: Mick Strawn. SpMkpFX: KNB. SpFX: Ultimate FX. Ed: Monte Hellman. Ref: TV: Turner video. Mo. Vallejo T-H: *The Killing Box*-alt t. With Corbin Bernsen, Adrian Pasdar, Martin Sheen, Ray Wise, Cynda Williams (Rebecca), Alexis Arquette.

"You don't want nothin' else gettin' out of here." Ingredients: an African tribe ... "bottled" beings in a "hole in the Earth" ... a slave trader ... and unrelenting undead soldiers. ("They just kept on comin'!") Film occasionally tries too hard, but doesn't pigeon-hole itself, and is technically well done. Finally, though, it fails to define itself—is it a "Twilight Zone" anecdote or an anti-war story? At any rate, it's the best, by default, of a minor sub-genre,

the Civil War horror story. Other examples: *The Supernaturals, 2000 Maniacs,* and *Curse of the Screaming Dead.*

**GHOST BUSTING** (H.K.) Grand March Movie Co. (Wong Tin Lam) 1989 color 94m. (*Huagui Youxian Gongsi*). D: Lau Sze Yu. SP: Jing Wong. Ref: TV: Tai Seng Video; no Eng. Horacio Higuchi.

Ingredients include a ghost with a Freddy torso of moaning victim-faces ... a man ectoplasmed into a toilet bowl (one shoe is tossed back) ... a gay vampire invisible in mirrors ... a crawling hand ... a caped, ray-spewing vampire queen ... a possessed young woman ... a school for exorcists ... and a mystic, "peeping tom" remote "eye".... Serviceable, occasionally funny vampire comedy. Neat: the ghostly elevator operator who takes his passengers down, down, down.... Doubly neat: the animated, green, big-winged bat-demons into which the two vampires can turn.

See also *Ghostbusting.*

**GHOST CHASE** (W.G.) Spectrum Ent. & Overseas Filmgroup/Centropolis & Pro-ject Film & HR (Moeller) 1987 color 89m. (aka *Hollywood Monster*). Story, SP, D: Roland Emmerich. SP: also T. Kubisch. Story: O. Eberle. Mus & FX: Hubert Bartholomae. FX: also J. Grueninger. SpFxPh: H. Umbrecht. OptFX: K.-P. Schultze et al. Mkp: Susanne Schickert. Ref: TV: Virgin video; Eng. version. MFB'89:46-7: "an excuse for sf buff self-indulgence." V 5/4/88:460. 5/6/87:447, 448. 9/20/89:28 (rated). With Jason Lively, Jill Whitlow, Tim McDaniel, Ian McNaughton (Frederick McCloud), Ekkehard Schroeer (all funny monsters), Larry Pennell.

A ghost from an antique clock enters and animates the doll of a "new movie monster," Louis, "the butler." ("He can move—and he speaks in the same voice as that ghost"—and he looks and acts a bit like E.T.) Meanwhile, at the forbidding McCloud Estate, a mean ghost animates a suit of armor .... Rife with atmospheric effects, but generally formulaic.

**\*The GHOST CREEPS** Savoy Pictures/Four Bell (Katzman) 1940. Ph: Robert Cline, Harvey Gould. Sets: Fred Preble. Ref: TV. Lee. TVG. Weldon. V 8/21/40. Lentz. With Inna Gest, Dennis Moore, David Gorcey, Forrest Taylor.

A non-Bela Lugosi East Side Kids ghost comedy, set at Briarcliff Manor ("So gloomy—reminds me of the morgue"), in the Adirondacks. "Is it haunted?" Not really, though it seems to be—by "ghost faces," an organ-playing "ghost," a "ghost" in the Parker family graveyard, and "voices." ("Beware!") What can you say about a movie the high point of which is Minerva Urecal—the Gale Sondergaard of Monogram—as "that spooky old Agnes," the housekeeper? Not much. She has most of the good lines and all the good cackles. (She's the graveyard "ghost.") Agnes insists that it's her dead mistress, Lenora, playing the organ—"every night": "There is never any warmth where the dead do not rest." At least the old dark house really is dark—half the time you can hardly see the noses in front of the faces of Leo Gorcey and Bobby Jordan.

**GHOST DANCE** (B-W.G.) Jane Balfour Films/Looseyard Ltd./Channel Four & ZDF 1983 color and b&w 107m. SP, D, P: Ken McMullen. Masks: Caroline Lanyon. Ref: screen. V

11/30/83. 10/24/84:11. PFA notes 9/4/84: in French & Eng. Stanley. Dr. Rolf Giesen.

"They're coming closer": Cinema, it says here, is the "art of letting ghosts come back." These "internalized figures from the past" are now supposedly employing electronic gadgets as conduits; the human body is a "graveyard for ghosts. They can still see you even if you can't see them." Plus a dream of the "dead of centuries".... Cinema of the Absurd. There may be connections between the above thesis and the meandering action of the movie, but the closest the film comes to a standard movie-ghost is a loud noise which unnerves the two women who hear it. Don't expect much fun from this quirky, enigmatic film, though it does feature some eerie, suggestive sea-images.

The **GHOST DANCE** Coast/Ahremess (R. M. Sutton) 1984 (1981) color c90m. Story, SP, D: Peter Buffa. SP: also William Reid, Sutton. Ph: Fred Murphy. Mus: Joseph Byrd. PD: Joseph Andaloro. Mkp: Ron Figuley. Ref: TV: Interglobal HV. V 9/2/81:4(rated). 10/24/84: 11: in Indianapolis. Stanley. Hound: 1983. no Martin. With Henry Bal, Julie Amato, Victor Mohica, Frank Sotonoma Salsedo (Ocacio, sorcerer), James Andronica, Patricia Alice Albrecht.

Arizona. A Ghost Dance cult ritual summons up the knife-wielding spirit of the Southwest Indian Nahalla (Bal). The latter possesses the body of Aranjo (Bal), and can turn into a vicious dog or cat, and in turn transforms Dr. Kay Foster (Amato)—who is a ringer for Nahalla's white wife, Melissa Stuart—into his "Soyoh Wuhti," or "monster woman" aide.... Okay acting, Indian-lore background; routine suspense and action—i.e., good field, no hit. The final frisson—in which the unearthed mummy of Nahalla revives—is inconsistent with the body of the story, in which the mummy itself remains inert while Nahalla's spirit roams.

**GHOST FESTIVAL** (Taiwanese) New Ship Film/Princess Film c1985? color/ws c85m. Ref: TV: Regal Video, World Video, and Sunny Video—all with Eng. titles. Y. K. Ho: *A Woman-Ghost Story* - tr t. With Leung Kun.

The King of the Ghosts coaches several female ghosts, victims of a buzz-saw-wielding madman. Plus: a skull-headed, bug-eyed ghost and a ghost cabbie who makes his cab fly through the air and crash.... The Sunny tape's English subtitles are generally "sunken," and/or lopped off on both sides of the TV screen; the *Ghost Festival*/World tape's titles are somewhat more readable; the Regal version's titles are faded at times. In any version, this is a minor-league blend of comedy, action, chills, and sick scenes with the madman, though the ghost scenes are spooky-funny. The ghosts here usually hop, a la vampires in *Mr. Vampire*-type movies.

**GHOST FEVER** Miramax/Infinite 1987 (1986) color 86m. (*Benny and Buford* - orig t). D: Lee Madden. SP: Oscar Brodney, Ron Rich, Richard Egan. Mus: James Hart. SpFX: Miguel Vasquez. Anim: Jorge Perez. SdFX: Long Island Sound Co. Ref: TV. V 11/18/87. 4/8/87:176, 14: in Miami. Scheuer. V 10/24/84:255 (ad). Scheuer: U.S.-Mex. With Sherman Hemsley, Luis Avalos, Jennifer Rhodes, Deborah Benson, Myron Healey, Pepper Martin, Joe Frazier.

A Haitian voodoo curse turns a man into a vampire, who then haunts Magnolia House, Greendale County, Georgia, and "turns out zombies" in his torture dungeon.... Busy and rather elaborate, but flat as either comedy or thriller. Noted-in-passing: an okay stopmo "eaten"-chicken-leg effect.

**GHOST FEVER** (H.K.) Grand March Movie Prod. Co. 1989 color c90m. Ref: TV: Rainbow Video; Eng. titles.

Average horror-comedy-drama re a house haunted by a family of ghosts in Tai Po, including the pretty Pinkey, a little-boy-in-bow-tie, and Grandpa and Pearl. Mama ghost: "Then I suck all your blood. And then eat the flesh." In the most unusual sequence—a tug-of-war with a man's body, between exorcists in the living room and hopping vampires in a movie showing on TV—the exorcists win, but one vampire head, severed, plops out onto the living-room floor and scurries about attacking them. In another unusual development, a man suddenly develops a pair of woman's breasts. And more: a neck-biting mannequin ... a moldy ghost from the grave ... a claw from a toilet bowl ... and a vision of ghosts, including some apparent hopping types.

**GHOST FOR SALE** (H. K.) Hong Hai Films 1991 color c87m. (*Ghost for Sales* - t error). D: Guy Lai. SP: Leung Wai Ting, Ben Cheung. Ph: Paul Chan. Mus: John Wong. Ref: TV: Pan-Asia Video; Eng. titles. With Ricky Hui, Wilson Lam, Shella Chan, Shing Fu On, Maggie Sui.

"When the Silver-armed corpse takes away the sutra, the Great Demon will come alive, then—the end of the world." Obvious horror-comedy's ingredients include the above-mentioned thousand-year-old menaces from Szechuan Province, a ghost who "matches" with heroine Shella ("I'm her spirit of a thousand years ago"), and a trio of "ghost busters" with a "ghost-preventing spray," glasses with "ghost vision," a gun which causes incredible shrinking, and a ghost-absorbing "ghost gun." At the end, "nine suns" and some mirrors help destroy the demon.

**GHOST GAMBLER** (H.K.?) Top Approach Film Co. and New Treasurer Films 1990? color 92m. Ref: TV: World Video; no Eng.

When a gambler dies, his ghost comes back (in period costume) and—predictably—aids others at the gaming table. But his main job seems to be to secure victims for a cackling demon. He possesses—or at least affects the behavior of—one thug bigwig, then scares him silly and turns him over to the demon.... Accent's on cheap in this shot-on-taper. The versatile demon can personally shoot both stun-rays and fireballs.

*The **GHOST GOES WILD** 1947. AD: Hilyard Brown. SpFX: Howard & Theodore Lydecker. Mkp: Bob Mark. Ref: TV. Lee (Vd). Lentz. no Vw. no Maltin '92. no Scheuer. With Ruth Donnelly.

"Do we have to go through with this haunting business?" The ghost of Benedict Arnold supposedly haunts Haunted Hill Farm, where a "scientific investigation of psychic phenomena" is taking place—or are the latter simply "spiritualistic monkey shines"? In any event, Monty (James Ellison), the master of the farm—supposedly burned to death—returns at a seance to go "Boo!" Entangled in a sheet, he looks like a ghost, and he and his butler,

Eric (Edward Everett Horton), later decide to play ghost.... Trivial. John Alton's atmospheric photography is the sole highlight of this very tired comedy, though Horton has one nice throwaway line: "Sterling silver tray!" Featuring Lloyd Corrigan as a real ghost.

**GHOST GUARDING TREASURE** (H.K.?) c1990 color/ws c95m. Ref: TV: vt; no Eng.; Thai-lang. version. Chao Thai Market: above is tr t.

Only a little-boy vampire and his big-fanged mother (who seems to be a man in drag) and a few others remain when a sorcerer makes a whole horde of hopping vampires disappear. In the long, lively, enjoyable climactic sequence, a bad, fanged sorcerer in a cave spits obedience-engendering electricity and (with his right hand) shoots fire, one bad guy fries and turns into a bat, and another turns into a spider. The sorcerer also conjures up a winged snake and a silly-looking monster that seems to be a beaked, long-tailed, fire-breathing goat or lobster. Not to mention: a large, big-fanged vampire in a bowler, and Herrmann and *Halloween* music.

**GHOST HOUSE** see *Shocking!*

**GHOST HOUSE, A TRUE STORY** (Singapore) Mandarin's Film 1994 color 94m. D: Lai Kai Keung. Ref: vc box: "haunted mansion." With Hung Yan.

**GHOST IN THE COLD MOONLIGHT** (H.K.?) c1982? color/ws c88m. D?: Fung Pan. Ref: TV: Quality Video; Eng. titles.

The ghost of Tuan plays the flute in the swamp where she drowned. Yen—the man responsible for her death—kills Grandma Chien, too. Granny comes back, and there is yet a third ghost around: the crowded swamp. The three lure Yen to his death.... The plot is cut-and-dried. Yen, who flogs everyone in sight, is so mean it's comical. However, the gliding movements of both ghosts and camera—and the yellow highlighting of Tuan (against blue backdrops)—make the spooky scenes atmospheric. This might be the Eastern version of *Strangler of the Swamp.*

**GHOST IN THE MACHINE** Fox (Schiff-Sabath) 1993 color 104m. D: Rachel Talalay. SP: W. J. Davies, W. H. Osborne. Ph: P. Meheux. Mus: G. Revell. PD: J. Spencer. MkpFX: Tony Gardner's Alterian Studios. VisFxSup: Erik Henry; R.E. Hollander. SpAnim: Cimity Art. SdFxSup: Myron Netting. Ref: TV. ad. Janet Willis. Sacto Bee 1/1/94. Fango 128:28-31. V 6/15/92:77. With Karen Allen, Chris Mulkey, Wil Horneff, Ted Marcoux, Jessica Walter, Rick Ducommun, Don Keith Opper.

"Woman hunted by a killer inhabiting a computer system."(V) "Looked like there was someone else in here with us." An electrical storm surge shocks the Address Book Killer's MRI scan/soul/whatever into the Datanet computer system. At the end, "one huge mother of a magnet"—a particle accelerator—wrecks the electric villain .... *Tron* crossed with *Pulse,* more or less. The banal, episodic Revenge of the Machines scenes are the worst of it. The best of it: the computer graphics detailing the ghost's machinations. Okay: the visualization of the computer virus. Not okay: the computerized killer as Electric Man, in real space.

**GHOST IN THE MIRROR** see *Ghost of the Mirror*

**GHOST IN THE POLICE CAMP II** (H.K.) Mable Cheng 1987 color/ws 93m. D: Yuen Cheung Yan. Ref: TV: World Video; Eng. titles. Y. K. Ho: above is tr t. Weisser/ATC: sfa *Ghost Mansion* (D: Y.C. Man)?

Sequel to *Vampire Settles on Police Camp*? The gliding ghost of a raped woman haunts the Royal Hong Kong Police Training Camp. First, she possesses one cadet, Myths, who, like a vampire, bites his doctor's neck; then (after holy beads force her out of the first body), she enters the body of a female cadet, May, who has a peculiar knack for catching mosquitoes in her mouth. Near the end, two "little ghosts" are summoned up to fight her.... Mainly silly, vapid sitcom-horror, with occasional laughs.

**GHOST KEEPER** see *Ghostkeeper*

**GHOST KILLER** (H.K.?) N. Treasures Films 1991? color c92m. Ref: TV: World Video; no Eng.

*The Walking Dead* formula, as a ghost possesses the hero, the better to gain revenge on the hoods who killed him. He performs an *Entity* rape on a gun moll; later, his female partner is exorcised away.

**GHOST LEGEND** (H.K.) 1991 color 90m. (*Zhuo Gui Hejia Huan II: Mayi Chuanqi*). D, P: Ng Min-Kan. Anim?: Animation Shop. Ref: TV: Pan-Asia Video; no Eng. Y.K. Ho. Hardy/HM2. no Weisser/ATC.

A horde of (cartoon) ghosts flies through a forest, while a fanged, round-faced, jovially-vicious monster whooshes up out of the ground to suck the life-breath from a stranded princess. Later, the drooling monster returns, in town, along with a nicer ghost woman, who seems to fall for the hero.... The all-out, opening sequence in the forest is easily the best here. Later action sequences feature routine kung fu and comedy. Eerie: the monster flying in light fog just above a forest caravan. Campy: the instant-vomit scene with the weird dead newborn.

**GHOST LOVER** see *Crocodile Evil*

**GHOST LOVER, The** see *Ghost, The* (1981?)

**GHOST LUSTERS** Elegant Angel 1990 color 93m. D: Bruce Seven. Ref: Adam '92, '91. vc box. With Tianna, Bionca, Victoria Paris.

Twenties-era film star haunts sound stage. "Eerie lighting." (Adam)

**GHOST MANSION** see *Ghost in the Police Camp II*

**GHOST #8** (Thai) c1990? color 87m. Ref: TV: vt; no Eng. Chao Thai Video 2: above is tr t.

Ingredients in this typically genial, silly Thai horror-comedy include a worm-vomiting, swivel-headed, possessed woman ... *Halloween* music ... a fake ghost in a coffin ... a real ghost that rises out of the ground and displays its innards ... various other gliding, laughing, and talking ghosts ... and a lounging skeleton.

**3P GHOST NURSING** (H.K.) J & M Chevalier/Gold City Films (Norman Chu) 1982 (1984) color c90m. (*Nuoi Qui. Feed the Ghost* - ad t). D: Wilson Tong. Ref: TV: Regal Video; Eng. titles. V 7/14/82:85. With N. Chu, S. Li, Melbourne Wang, Tom Chin.

Thailand. The God of Gold tells Jackie that her bad luck stems from the fact that she was a gangster in a former life, and that she must "nurse a ghost"—i.e., pay homage to a dead baby—to make amends. She complies, and the thugs tormenting her shoot each other, then return as zombie-ghosts to kill the head thug. A copy of the New Testament drives the spirit out of the baby and into Raymond, who tears off his friend's scalp, makes a woman levitate, impales her on a huge fork, then spits blood into the camera. In the finale, he returns, ghoul-faced, to the baby's mother's grave (she died with him in 1943), and a priest unleashes fireballs and demon babies on him.... The plot is a pretext for effects, and Gold City can't compete with IL&M. However, there are a few light-comic effects involving a mobile banana peel and an office suddenly full of unruly children (in place of the regular staff). The last twenty minutes are lively—even the dead mother's skull gets into the act.

The **GHOST OF NIGHT CROW** (H.K.?) Cheng Hoi 198-? color/ws? 76m. Ref: TV: QVC video; no Eng. with Chang Pan, Tin Mi, Tin Foon, Lee Ying.

A sword-slashed woman dies, and crows caw and scare villagers. The laughing, gliding, sword-wielding ghost of the murdered woman returns and scares villagers. A woman is found dead, a crow feather in her hand. The ghost here can also impersonate and possess people, and is aided by an old-woman ghost.... Familiar ghostly tricks, though the cawing is creepy. The ghost kills with her ultra-long fingernails. Standard-issue spook music.

The **GHOST OF SMILING JIM** Univ/Gold Seal 1914 22m. silent. Ref: Library of Congress. no LC. Motography 12/19/14: "weird story." With Grace Cunard, Francis Ford.

Ghost said to haunt mountain area proves to be a "grizzled old man."

**GHOST OF THE FOX** (H.K.) 1990 color feature. D: Lu Xiao-Long. Ref: Weisser/ATC: "demon army." With Cheng Lu, Sibelle Hu.

**GHOST OF THE MIRROR** (Taiwanese) Diyi Films/Cheuk-Hon Wong 1974 color/ws 93m. (104m.) (*Gu Jing You Hun*). D: Tsun Shou Sung. SP: Yung Hsiang Chang. Ref: TV: World Video; no Eng. NST! 4:23-4: *Ghost in the Mirror*. Hardy/HM. With Ching Hsia Lin, Ping Yu Chang, Wen Tsung Ku.

The new owner of the villa at one point sees the image of a lovely woman in the water at the bottom of a haunted well on his property. He rides a big bucket to the bottom and finds a cavern strewn with human skeletons. At the end, the mystery woman sacrifices herself and exits through a magic mirror, and the huge lurking dragon at large departs, too. Double-twist ending almost saves slight, spare tale.

**\*\*GHOST PARADE** Sennett 1931 b&w 22m. D, P: Mack Sennett. SP: J.A. Waldron et al. Ref: Maltin/SSS. LC. Lee. With Andy Clyde, Harry Gribbon, Marjorie Beebe, Frank Eastman.

Spooks haunt a house.

**GHOST PARTY** (Thai) U & I. Video 1988? color c85m. Ref: TV: Asian HV; no Eng. Thai Video: above is tr t.

A very cheap, shot-on-tape, rendezvous-in-a-haunted-house tale involving a witch-like woman, a boy with fangs, and some cadaverous-looking gents whose eyes glow red and who hypnotize and strangle their victims. At the end, the baddies go up in flames, but a fresh batch of zombie-ghosts replaces them. Really pathetic comedy shocker, with sub-Abbott-and-Costello mugging and cheesy plucked-eyeballs and entrails gore effects.

**GHOST PUNTING** (H.K.) Choice Film 1992 color 94m. Ref: TV: World Video; Eng. titles.

"It's a real ghost!" The local haunted house harbors a fanged, female ghost (who coughs up worms and shrivels away when the breath is sucked out of her) and a male ghost ("I'm dead, but not buried yet") who is electrified out of the body of the woman he temporarily possesses. Silly ghost-comedy's sole semi-memorable moment: A man pushes his back up against the front of the woman ghost and somehow acquires her breasts.

**GHOST RIDERS** see *Ghostriders*

**A GHOST ROMANCE** (H.K.?) 1991? color/ws c95m. (*Ghost's Love* - vc box t). Ref: TV: World Video; Eng. titles.

"Is it human or ghost?" Sin Yun, a young woman bound to a rock and dumped into Lake Tian, dies "innocent" and returns as an "elf" to avenge her murder. Temporarily exorcised, she later comes back to possess a whore, Yuet Ngor. ("I saw Sin Yun.") Still later, the Land God allows Sin Yun to become an insect, enter a body, and reanimate Yung's girl friend, the just-dead Chin Wan. Finally, she yanks her sister's spirit out of her body and asks her to avenge her death.... Trashy, oddly involved, episodic spook show tries to have it both ways, as love story and revenge story. Result: mutual dilution.

**GHOST SCHOOL** (H.K.) 1988 color 86m. D: Kam Ling Ho. Ref: TV: World Video; Eng. titles. NST! 4:24.

Two ghosts spook "futurology" Professor Li and try to get him to tell his favorite "true" story correctly. Unfortunately for him, the male and female ghosts differ as to what the correct version of that story is. At the end, the male ghost disappears when Li refuses to believe in him any more.... Slight but occasionally entertaining *Rashomon*-inspired comedy is nearly half over before the spook element is introduced. In the best bit, the professor watches his bare feet "multiply" at the foot of his bed: two, four, six.... (And no one else under his blanket, as he discovers.) Bonus: a ghostly-possession sequence.

The **GHOST SNATCHERS** (H.K.) Golden Harvest 1987 color/ws? c94m. (*Bi Gui Zhuo*). Ref: TV: Rainbow Video; no Eng. NST! 4:24, 7-8. Fango 107:59, 60. Monster! 11/91 (Higuchi).

Comic "Boo!" material gets repetitious, but has some good scares, including the opening startler: a corridor of clutching-hands-from-walls which issues into a room with a single gigantic clutching hand. Among the more novel comic horrors: a TV set with human legs and arms, and supernatural, *Alf*-like mah-jongg kibitzers. Not to mention: a carnivorous TV set, *Ghostbusters*-

like supernatural storms, a *Poltergeist*-like other-dimension of zombies, an anti-ghost gong, a living skeleton, a flying skull, etc.

**GHOST STORIES: GRAVEYARD THRILLER** Alamance & High Ridge (Peter Bieler) 1986 color 56m. D: Lynn Silver. Dial: Bob Jenkins. Ph: E. J. Foerster, W. Crain. Set Des: W. W. Coleman. Mkp: Michael Spatola. Ref: TV: Vestron Video. Phantom. Hound. With Bob Jenkins (Graveyard Keeper), Ralph Lucas, Laura Kay, Sandra McLees, Maria Hayden, Jules Anton (living corpse).

The Graveyard Keeper of Tuesday Hill Boneyard is your host for five, non-illustrated tales of terror. 1) "Where Have You Been Billy Boy, Billy Boy?", by Lucas, re the offspring of a woman and a bunch of rats. 2) "Mr. Fox," by McLees, re a man who puts girls on meathooks. 3) "Buried Alive," by McLees, re a woman who comes back from the grave to play ghost. 4) "Hunting Werewolves for Uncle Albert," by Jenkins, a tall tale re a man who befriends the Frankenstein monster and is attacked by a werewolf and a sphinx. 5) "Reunion," by Sheri Emond, aka "The Monkey's Paw".... *Ghost Stories* was made by people unclear on the concept of movies. Actors sit or stand on the graveyard set and tell stories. That's it. (Except for the "Reunion" climax, the one bit of onscreen horror.) And the stories aren't very good. Amazing.

**GHOST STORIES FROM THE PICKWICK PAPERS** (B) Emerald City Prods. 1987 anim color c54m. (aka *Charles Dickens' Ghost Stories from the Pickwick Papers*). SP, D, P: Al Guest, Jean Mathieson, from stories in Dickens' book *The Pickwick Papers,* including "The Story of the Goblins who Stole a Sexton," "The Story of the Bagman's Uncle," and "A Ghost's Statement." Ph: John Dalton et al. Mus: Gerard Victory. Ref: TV: Celebrity video. Voices: Joseph Taylor, Daniel Reardon et al.

Three tales told at the Pickwick Club. 1) "The Ghost in the Wardrobe": A law student convinces a ghost haunting a dingy rooming-house room to move to pleasanter surroundings. Slight but agreeably novel ghost story. 2) "The Mail Coach Ghosts": Our human hero saves a lady ghost from two other, possessive ghosts and some creepy skeletal pursuers. He awakens and finds himself in a desolate Scottish wheelwright's yard, but retrieves her gloves (a touch not in the Dickens original) and pledges undying love. Some atmospheric artwork in this sweet, eerie anecdote. 3) "The Goblin and the Gravedigger": A master goblin takes malicious Gabriel Grub to his hellish domain and shows him visions of himself as a human weed. Two highlights of this spooky, fun-didactic variation on "A Christmas Carol": the cemetery dead chanting the gravedigger's name ... the flaming goblet illuminating the cowled goblin's hideous face.

**GHOST STORY OF KAM PIN MUI** (H.K.) c1990? color c94m. Ref: TV: Pan-Asia Video; Eng. titles. Y. K. Ho.

"Spring House is haunted." Softcore silliness re an evil sorcerer (one life-drained victim of the latter turns into a skeleton), a supernatural monk, frolicking naked women who turn into ghouls or ghosts, a witch woman, and a ray-shooting idol. Most memorable title: "Chin Pa Wan's penis was bitten off?"

**The GHOST TALKS** Col 1949 20m. D, P: Jules White. SP: Felix Adler. Ph: M. A. Anderson. AD: Charles Clague. Ref: TV. Stooge Scrapbook. Maltin/SSS: footage used in *Creeps.* LC. With The Three Stooges, Kenneth MacDonald.

A tailor accused of peeping on Lady Godiva is beheaded and imprisoned one thousand years in a suit of armor in Smorgasbord Castle. Extra addeds: "Red Skeleton" stepping out of a dresser drawer, two skeletons playing chess, an owl-in-skull, etc. Typical Stooges hijinks.

**GHOST THEATRE REINCARNATION** (J) C.J.F. 1991 color 87m. R: TV: vt; no Eng. Maureen Smith. Japan Video: above is tr t.

Beware the girl with the red ribbon in her hair! A sixteen-year-old girl who is given to fainting has visualized nightmares re tentacle-like red ribbons which attack and bind her. At the end, a ghost girl almost takes our heroine with her, but finally throws her back, like a too-small fish.... Cheap, humorless, shot-on-tape horror-fantasy has one perversely cute bit: the ribbon which spells out "END."

**GHOST TOURS** see *High Spirits*

**GHOST TOWN** Empire/Lexyn Prods. (Timothy D. Tennant) 1988 color 85m. D: Richard Governor. SP: Duke Sandefur. Story: David Schmoeller. Mus: Harvey R. Cohen. SpMkpFX: MMI; (sup) John Buechler; (animatronics) John Criswell. SpMechFX: Etan Ents.; (des) Eddie Surkin. Opt: Motion. Ref: TV. V 11/9/88: T.W.E. release. 9/30/87:6. ad. Scheuer. Maltin '92. Hound. McCarty. Martin. Phantom. With Franc Luz, Catherine Hickland, Jimmie F. Skaggs (Devlin), Penelope Windust, Bruce Glover.

"Kill Devlin and let this town die!" A modern-day deputy sheriff (Luz) stumbles onto an Old West town which mysteriously alternates between twentieth-century ghost-town and heyday-of-the-West settings. It proves to be inhabited by "trapped" souls and the cackling, disfigured Devlin—"some kind of freak"—an evil man in black who apparently has the devil's backing: His body can take any number of bullets.... The latter fact is a definite advantage for him in a gunfight. Some surprises in this Western chiller, plus some okay action scenes. A Gothic *High Noon.*

**GHOST TRAIN** (Hung.-B) City & Gainsborough 1933. D: Lajos Lazar. SP: Laszlo Bekeffy, from Lajos Biro's original. Ph: Istvan Eiben. Mus: Michael Eisemann. Sets: S. Lhotka. Ref: V 5/2/33. With Jeno Torzs, Marika Rokk, Lajos Ihasz, Oscar Beregi.

"Semi-Hungarian" version of the 1931 Gainsborough *Ghost Train* (vol. I) replaces English dialogue scenes with all-Hungarian scenes.

See also *Train dans la Nuit, Un.*

**\*GHOST VALLEY** 1932. Mus D: Max Steiner. AD: Carroll Clark. Ref: TV. TVG. V 8/30/32. Lee(e).

Clearly meant to compete with out-and-out horror pictures of the era like *Doctor X, Ghost Valley* is set in Boom City, a "weird, wind swept Ghost City," some thirty miles from Kona Lake, Nevada. The chief horror is variously described as an "apeman—a brute as big as a telegraph pole" and as a "big hairy monster." Good night-wind and lantern effects, in a nice variety of atmospheric settings—an old dark house, an old dark hotel, an old dark mine, and an old dark, "probably haunted" church, where the organ plays, mysteriously, at midnight. Typically (for "B" Westerns) rudimentary acting, dialogue, story.

**\*The GHOST WALKS** Invincible 1934. Mus D: Abe Meyer. AD: Edward Jewell. Ref: TV. Maureen Smith. Turner/Price. Hardy/HM. Hound. Lee. Lentz. Stanley.

Travelers on the road to Cragdale, outside New York City, are stranded at an "old isolated country home" said to be haunted by a "ghoulish" doctor, its former owner. Weird chimes, "unhuman" screams, mysteriously moving chairs and welling bloodstains, a "deathlike" face in the dark, and the "unnerving" sleepwalking "spells" of the mad Beatrice (Eve Southern)—"She simply dwells in the unknown"—turn out to be part of a charade, a performance of Prescott Ames' (John Miljan) new "horror play," "The Ghost Walks," or "The Ghost Walked." Any relief, however, is short-lived: "We have a real menace in this house!" Case 222—a homicidal maniac, Professor Twitterly (Spencer Charters)—has escaped from Greystone Sanitarium and (inspired by tales of the house's ex-owner) is kidnapping houseguests for ghastly grafting experiments.

In *The Monster Kills,* or *Murder at Midnight* (1931), director Frank Strayer tested the all-a-charade idea in the movie's first few scenes. Here he tests it for the entire first half of the movie. As with *Mark of the Vampire* (1935), midway revelations explain away apparently supernatural phenomena. Then, Beatrice is murdered, or so it seems. At the end, the professor reveals that he has simply paralyzed her with his secret fluid. The fooled-you! story twists are fun, as are the phony ghostly phenomena. Unfortunately, *The Ghost Walks* features the same ten cliche characters who appear in every old-dark-house thriller of the Thirties and Forties. The worst of it: the unending comic relief of Richard Carle and Johnny Arthur, as Broadway producer and secretary, respectively. They take up so much screen time that the other actors hardly make an impression.

**GHOST WANTED** WB 1940 anim colo r 7m. D: Chuck Jones. SP: Dave Monahan. Ref: Maltin/OMAM. LC. "WBCartoons." no Lee.

Little ghost tested for house-haunting job.

**GHOST WARRIOR** Empire/Harkham (Swordkill Prods./Albert Band) 1984 color 80m. (*Swordkill* - alt t). D: J. Larry Carroll. SP: Tim Curnen. Mus: Richard Band; Shirley Walker. SpFxMkp: Bob Short. MechSpFX: Roger George. Futuristic Props: Modern Props. Ref: TV. V 9/12/84. Martin Hound. ad. With Hiroshi Fujioka, John Calvin, Janet Julian, Charles Lampkin, Robert Kino.

A *Death Wish* fantasy re a samurai (Fujioka) frozen in lake ice in Japan in 1552, thawed out in the present, and taken to the California Institute of Cryosurgical Research, Los Angeles. Then it's The Samurai and a Television Set, The Samurai and an Auto, The Samurai and the City-by-night, The Samurai and Street Thugs.... A vapid but mildly entertaining variation on *Return of the Apeman* (1944). The episodic story adds little to the basic samurai-in-the-space-age novelty.

See also: *Iceman. Iceman Cometh. Survival of a Dragon.*

**GHOST WIFE** see *Fantasy Romance*

**GHOST WOMAN FROM THE GRAVE** (Thai) c1990? color c98m. Ref: TV: vt; no Eng. Chao Thai Market: above is tr t.

An apparent sorcerer's spell makes a fireball strike a woman's grave and send her coffin flying. Restored to life, she can appear as a human and scares teens in the woods.... Tacky, shot-on-tape horror-fantasy features amateurish action scenes, some silly comedy, and canned wolf howls. One plus: the lively climax. Another: the living undergrowth.

**GHOST WRITER** LBC Communications/Rumar Films (David DeCoteau, John Schouweiler) 1989 color 94m. SP, D: Kenneth J. Hall. Mus: Powell, Winans. SpMkpFX: John Vulich. SpFX: Player's SpFX, Bob McCarthy. Ref: TV. V 11/8/89. 10/28/87:24: D-Mar films; *Night Falls* - orig t? Hound. Scheuer. V/Cannes'89:94: *Ghostwriter!* With Audrey Landers, Judy Landers (Billie Blaine), Jeff Conaway, Anthony Franciosa, David Doyle, Joey Travolta, John Matuszak, Peter & David Paul, Dick Miller, Kenneth Tobey, George "Buck" Flower.

"You're not trying to tell me this place is haunted?" Billie Blaine—"goddess of the silver screen"—supposedly committed suicide, in Malibu, in 1962, in what is now called the "Billie Blaine ghost house." In the present day, she haunts said house and (at the end) her killer, as she then plays (for him) a vampire in a coffin, Linda Blair in *The Exorcist,* and Elsa Lanchester's bride in *Bride of Frankenstein,* in the Movieland Wax Museum's Chamber of Horrors. ("I can haunt you for the rest of your days!")

Silly characters and sloppy screenplay, based loosely on the Monroe legend. Film passes only as an old-fashioned, peek-a-boo showcase for the Landers sisters, Audrey (legs) and Judy (breasts). About the only eerie touch: the phantom footprints in the sand.

**GHOSTBUSTERS** Col/Black Rhino & Bernie Brillstein 1984 color/ws 105m. D: Ivan Reitman. SP: Dan Aykroyd, Harold Ramis. Mus: Elmer Bernstein. VisFX: Richard Edlund. Anim: (sup) Garry Waller, Terry Windell; (dimensional fx) Randall William Cook; Available Light. SpFX: (sup) Chuck Gaspar; Robert Spurlock. MechFxSup: Thaine Morris. Ghost Shop: Stuart Ziff; (consul) Jon Berg. Mkp: Leonard Engelman. Ref: TV. MFB'84:379-80. V 6/6/84. SFExam 6/8/84. Bay Guardian 6/13/84. Maureen Smith. With Bill Murray, Dan Aykroyd, Sigourney Weaver, Ramis, Rick Moranis, Annie Potts, William Atherton, Slavitza Jovan (Gozer), Joe Franklin, Casey Kasem, Ruth Oliver (library ghost), Kym Herrin (dream ghost), Roger Grimsby, Larry King.

The Ghostbusters—professional paranormal investigators—take on various Sumerian demi-gods and ghosts, including Gozer, a giant marshmallow man, a "disgusting blob" of a green glutton-ghost, living gargoyles, a possessed woman (Weaver), a dog demon, a zombie cabbie, and a "vaporous apparition" in the New York Public Library. Their m.o.: trap them electronically and store them.... The story apparently parodies Lovecraft; the effects effectively parody *Poltergeist*-type phenomena. The movie is episodic and sprawling, but all ectoplasmic forces here prove fine foils for Murray and his poker-face delivery. He ribs the creatures and undercuts their intentness. (Compare Lou in *Abbott and Costello Meet Frankenstein.*) Aykroyd and Ramis are more or less lost in the effects.

See also: *My Cousin, the Ghost.*

**GHOSTBUSTERS II** Col (Reitman/Brillstein/Medjuck/Gross) 1989 color/ws 102m. D: Ivan Reitman. SP: Harold Ramis, Dan Aykroyd. Mus: Randy Edelman. SpVisFX: (sup) Dennis Muren; IL&M; Apogee/VCE. Creature MkpDes: Tim Lawrence. Anim Sup: Tom Bertino. SpSdFX: The Sound Choice. Ref: TV. V 6/21/89. Sacto Bee 6/17/89. Sacto Union 6/15/89. MFB'89:366-8. With Bill Murray, Dan Aykroyd, Sigourney Weaver, Ramis, Rick Moranis, Peter MacNicol, Wilhelm Von Homburg (Vigo), Harris Yulin, Janet Margolin, Christopher Neame, Cheech Marin, Brian Doyle Murray, Judy Ovitz.

"There's something brewing under the street!" A psycho-reactive substance, or "mood slime"—"pure, concentrated evil"—is flowing through tunnels beneath New York City. It's somehow connected with the evil spirit of Vigo the Carpathian, a "powerful magician" who needs a child in order to live again. Ectoplasmic roll call: courtroom ghosts, a ghost jogger, an underground ghost train and other apparitions, a ghost baby-carriage in the sky, a ghost Titanic, and a supernaturally ambulatory Statue of Liberty.... This time everyone gets lost in the effects apparatus. Part II is sometimes amiable, and the phantom carriage is one of several scattered droll ideas, but the monsters aren't as funny the second time around, and some of Murray's zingers just don't zing. Signed, Slimed-Out.

**GHOSTBUSTING** (H.K.) Cinema City/Long Shong Pictures 1987 color c95m. (*Zhuagui Tegongdui*). D: Chao Chen Kuo. SP: Fu Li. Ref: TV: Rainbow Video; Eng. titles. TVG: aka *Ghostbustin'*. Horacio Higuchi. With David Tao, Fong Cheng, Chang Fei, Chen Shin, An An, Fong Fon-Fon, Chien Teh-Meng.

The vampire Black Cloud, who sleeps in an Egyptian-style sarcophagus, plots to make Dr. Tao's wife Hsiao-chen (whom he hypnotically controls) his Queen of Night. Meanwhile, Tao, a member of the Supernatural Society, and Eggsy, a boy with telekinetic powers, use the Blade of Justice to dispel some female ghosts commanded by Black Cloud. At the end, the latter throws a costume ball to celebrate the "full solar eclipse" which will make him invincible, but the good guys employ a "soul-seizing ray" to destroy most of the revelers, who include the Frankenstein monster, the American Werewolf, witches, and gremlins, or (this is left unclear) ghosts in costume as the Frankenstein monster....

The concluding duel between wizards Black Cloud and Tao, or White Cloud, suggests that someone remembered *The Raven* (1963) fondly, which film this comedy resembles more than it does *Ghostbusters*. Earlier in the film, Tao's friend Fearless Fang does a turn as a sarcastic raven ("Why are you so stupid?"), a la Peter Lorre in the Corman-Matheson movie. Overall, *Ghostbusting* is a silly, occasionally cute scrambling of elements from vampire, spirit-possession, and miscellaneous monster movies.

See also *Ghost Busting.*

**GHOSTHOUSE** (I) Imperial Ent./Filmirage (A. Massaccesi, D. Donati) 1988 color 94m. (aka *La Casa 3 - Ghost House*). Story, D: Umberto Lenzi. SP: C. McGavin. Ph: F. Delli Colli. Mus: Piero Montanari. AD: A. Colby. SpFX: Dan Maklansky et al. Mkp: Peter Moor. SdFX: Studio Sound. Ref: TV: Imperial Ent. video; Eng. version. Stanley. V 1/18/89: "perfunctory horror."

Horacio Higuchi. Morse: "very uninspired." McCarty II: "totally enjoyable bloodbath." Newman: "dullish *Poltergeist* imitation." With Lara Wendel, Greg Scott, Mary Sellers, Donald O'Brian.

A ham radio operator picks up screams and cries for help emanating from a radio transmitter left on in an old house outside Boston. ("There's something evil about the house.") Investigating, he discovers the ghost of an 11-year-old girl who was locked up in the cellar 20 years earlier .... Routine gratuitous-gore vehicle except for the weird music and sounds and the mutating light bulbs, mirrors, etc.

Follow-up: *Witchery* (*La Casa 4*).

**GHOSTHOUSE II** see *Witchery*

**2P GHOSTKEEPER** (Can.) Badland Pictures (Lawrence A. Dickie & Harold J. Cole) 1980 color 87m. (aka *Ghost Keeper*). SP, D: James Makichuk. SP: also Douglas Macleod. Ph: John Holbrook. Mus: Paul Zaza. AD: Barry Anderson. SpFX: Mel Merrells. Mkp: Kirstie McLellan. Ref: TV: New World Video. V 9/30/81:32 (ad). 5/13/81:16. 2/16/83:24. 2/21/90:272. Ecran F 28. Stanley. Hound. Morse. With Riva Spier, Murray Ord, Georgie Collins (the ghostkeeper), Sheri McFadden, John MacMillan (Windigo).

Thin, formulaic horror story in which a Canadian Indian legend re the Windigo—a "ghost who lives on human flesh"—is apparently used as a red herring. The "ghost-keeper" is a madwoman who tends the deserted Deer Lodge. ("Mountains can fool you.... There are worse things up there than getting lost.") Is she the female keeper with "ancient power" who unleashes the Cannibal Giant on intruders, or is she just a crazy woman with a crazy son or two? Who cares? Complete with the expected twist ending, in which the going-crazy Jenny (Spier) takes the woman's place. ("Jenny will look after you now.")

**GHOSTLY LOVE** (H.K.) 1991 color c90m.(*Qian Yunyu Qing*). D, P: Cheung Kit. Ref: TV: Pan-Asia Video; Eng. titles. Y.K. Ho. Hardy/HM2.

"We are in love, but she is a ghost." Ingredients in this softcore romantic fantasy include a vampire woman ... a line of hopping vampire women ("Master, the vampire is here!") ... the ghost king, who sucks the blood of virgins to gain strength ... Hsiu Tsui, or Tsai, the ghost woman who must marry the king ... ray-shooting, flying, biting skulls ... and a flying skeleton.... Formula action, plot, effects.

**GHOSTLY VIXEN** (H.K.) Golden Flare Films 1990? color/ws c100m. Ref: TV: World Video; Eng. titles.

"She's already sucked 98 virgin boys born at ten o'clock." The Thai "Evil Girl" with horror face and removable eyeballs needs 100 virgins to gain eternal life. ("This is no common ghost.") Also: two corpses which revivify in a crypt ... a woman, Lumy, who comes back as a ghost ... a Continental Classroom for wizards ... and a very crude, funny sequence in which the jealous Lumy curses the hero, Sau Yan, with a giant phallus. ("It drags on the ground now.") Horror-comedy's tastelessness ("I know only now beating women is fun") is only occasionally funny. Of more interest than the comedy: the evident concern with the imminent China takeover of Hong Kong. ("How can you live here after 1997?")

**GHOSTRIDERS** Prism Ent./Alan L. Stewart (Ghost Riders, Inc.) 1987 color 85m. (aka *Ghost Riders*). D: Stewart. SP: Clay McBride, James J. Desmarais. Ph: T. L. Callaway. Mus: Frank M. Patterson III. Mkp: C. E. Pierce. SpFX: Technimation. Ref: TV: Prism Ent. video. TVG. Martin. Hound. Morse. With Bill Shaw, Jim Peters, Ricky Long, Cari Powell, Mike Ammons, Arland Bishop.

"They just keep coming!" Outlaw Frank Clements (Ammons), hung by the Rev. Sutton (Shaw) in Santa Rio, Texas, on September 17, 1886, returns periodically on subsequent September 17ths to kill members of the Sutton family, including, in 1986, Prof. Sutton (Shaw). Clements, shot repeatedly, keeps coming back, with his outlaw pals, but blasts from his own gun finally make them all vanish before it, too, vanishes.... Not without its amiable moments, but the Old West menaces never seem very novel or exciting. They don't quite live up to the skeletal wild bunch depicted on the vc box cover. And the protagonists take forever to learn the not-really-very-amazing secret of the old gun.

**GHOST'S HOSPITAL** (H.K.) 1989? color c86m. D: Tony Lu Yung. Ref: TV: World Video; no Eng. NST!4:23: "disjointed."

First half of offbeat, hard-to-fathom horror-comedy might better be called "Ghost's Jail." This section culminates with a vampire jailbreak, as cops trail ghosts to the local hospital and round them up. Extra addeds: unruly hopping vampires who somersault over their leader, then lie down ... a dead woman who revives as a hopping ghost ... a fake vampire who mugs ... *Psycho* music ... an odd bit with soap bubbles which float down a hospital corridor ... and a questionably funny scene in which ghosts harass bedridden patients.

**GHOSTS IN THE HOUSE** (Thai) c1987? color c102m. Ref: TV: vt; no Eng. Thai Video: above is tr t.

Unwittingly, a student is romancing a ghost who can grow, shrink, roar, turn monstrous and demon-y, appear, and disappear. He drops a necklace over her head, and she screams, glows, decomposes, incinerates, and does everything except die.... The latter sequence is fairly impressive, if the bubbly makeup effects are derivative from Western monster movies. This movie's most intelligent borrowing is from *Vampyr*: The face of the ghost periodically appears giant-sized at the windows of the haunted house. There are also some okay jack-in-the-box scares, and the monster at least seems to be a serious threat. But laughs never threaten in this obvious eek-a-ghost! comedy. This must be the most nervous bunch of kids in horror-film history.

**GHOST'S LOVE** see *Ghost Romance, A*

**GHOST'S LOVER** (H.K.) 1988? color/ws c80m. Ref: TV: World Video; Eng. titles.

Is the mysterious Mr. Chou Wei an "ordinary man" or a "will-o'-the-wisp"? He seems to appear whenever the unhappily married Mrs. Chao is in a "bad mood." And when her husband's mistress threatens her, Chou Wei appears to the woman and ectoplasmically electrocutes her. When Mrs. Chao proves to be pregnant by the phantom, she opts for abortion: "I won't give birth to a ghost!"

Chou Wei wants both woman and baby: "Even a ghost has feelings." A *Ghostbusters*-type team turns a computer-controlled negative electrode on him. He survives, but mother and child die, and Chou Wei is alone again.... *Ghost's Lover* is romantic and supernatural drivel—until the touching conclusion momentarily redeems it. The *Ghostbusters* element seems arbitrarily yoked here with a traditional Hong Kong ghost movie. The ghost's "magic power" is scientifically determined to be 7026.4, exactly.

**II GHOSTS OF HANLEY HOUSE** Victoria (J. S. Durkin Jr.) c1966? 85m. SP, D: Louise Sherrill. Ph: Claude Fullerton. Mus: David C. Parsons. Sets: F. Sherrill. Mkp: E. Nassa. SdFX: O. Alexander. Opt: Modern. Ref: TV. Greg Luce. Sacto Bee Encore 12/10/89:10. With Roberta Reeves, Leonard Shoemaker.

"Only evil spirits come here." Five people, including a medium, spend the night in the "old Hanley place," a house haunted by knocking, whispers, rattling chains, imprints of wandering spirits, and hoofbeats. Outside, a cloaked, glowing phantom patrols, and a ball of smoke and fire explodes and tries to communicate with the five. Unfortunately, when the ghosts finally do communicate, they (and their murderer) explain away all mystery: They are murder victims who simply want their bodies buried.... The effects—mostly sound effects—are cheap, but they suggest more than the plot delivers. This obscure example of regional filmmaking is neither very cinematic nor well-staged, but it does have some ideas: the ectoplasmic ball of smoke, the clock which runs backwards, the spirit imprint.

**GHOSTS OF SODOM** (I) 1988 color 85m. (*Fantasmi di Sodoma. Sodoma's Ghost* - alt vt t). D: Lucio Fulci. Ref: VSOM: "Nazi/ghosts." MV. Hardy/HM2. With Claudio Aliotti, Luciana Ottaviani, T. Razzaudi.

**GHOSTWRITER!** see *Ghost Writer*

**GHOUL SCHOOL** [Note: revised entry] DeCoteau & O'Gore & E.I. 1990 color 75m. SP,D,P: Timothy O'Rawe. Ph: M.L. Raso. Mus: J.R. Bookwalter et al. SpMkpFX: Subtempeco EFX. Ref: TV: Cinema HV. Hound. With Joe Franklin, Nancy Sirianni, William Friedman, Scott Gordon.

"Monsters attacked me!" Something toxic in the pipes turns the high-school swim team into flesh-eating zombies. The comedy fizzles; the gore is perfunctorily ladled on. Noted: a copy of *Fango*. Inept film.

**GHOUL SEX SQUAD** see *Rendezvous*

**GHOULIES** Empire/Vestron Video (Ghoulies) 1985 (1984) color 81m. SP, D: Luca Bercovici. SP: also J. Levy. Mus: R. Band, Shirley Walker. SpFxMkp: MMI; (des) John Carl Buechler. SpFxSd: Craig Talmy. SpVoices: Brian Connolly et al. Ref: TV. MFB'85:114. V 1/23/85. TVG. With Peter Liapis, Lisa Pelikan, Michael Des Barres (Malcolm Graves), Jack Nance, Mariska Hargitay, Bobbie Bresee (temptress).

The evil Empire strikes again.... Jonathan Graves (Liapis) calls on "The Evil One" to summon up some demonic rodent-types. But it is a dead man, the "true master" of the ghoulies— Jonathan's father (Des Barres)—who makes them visible and vicious, who transforms himself into a woman with a long, strangling tongue, and who attempts to absorb his son's life force.... The father-vs.-son duel of the wizards recalls *The Raven* (1963), and nothing else here is very original either. The ghoulies themselves, though, are genial, if extraneous. They're personality-plus; the actors, personality-minus.

**GHOULIES II** (U.S.-I) (Vestron-TV)/Empire/Taryn 1988 (1987) color 90m. D, P: Albert Band. SP: Dennis Paoli. Story: Charlie Dolan. Mus: Fuzzbee Morse. Creatures: (des) John Buechler; (stopmo) David Allen; (animatronics) John Criswell. SpVoices: Hal Rayle. Ref: TV. V 9/14/88. With Damon Martin, Royal Dano, Phil Fondacaro, J. Downing, Kerry Remsen, Starr Andreeff, Anthony Dawson.

A clutch of ghoulies makes the carny spook show Satan's Den a hit ("This place is better than Epcot Center"), then overruns the entire carnival. Finally, an incantation raises a big demon which gobbles up the lesser demons.... In its mixture of shock, sentiment, and comedy, *Ghoulies II* is closer to *Gremlins* than was the first *Ghoulies*. It's no better, just closer. These little critters wear out their welcome quickly—there just aren't enough of them, and the few that there are get monotonous. A smattering of stopmo helps, and a slime-spewing ghoulie provides a few chuckles.

**GHOULIES GO TO COLLEGE** Vestron/Lightning Pictures (Patterson) 1990 color 94m. (aka *Ghoulies III*). D: John Carl Buechler. SP: Brent Olson. Mus: Michael Lloyd. Ref: V 7/11/90:26. Martin. PT 13:52: "lame fraternity horror comedy." With Kevin McCarthy, Evan MacKenzie, Griffin O'Neal, Marcia Wallace, Hope Marie Carlton.

**GHOULIES IV** CineTel/Gary Schmoeller (Ghoulies Four) 1993 color 83m. D: Jim Wynorski. SP: Mark Sevi. Ph: J.E. Bash. Mus: Chuck Cirino. PD: Jeannie M. Lomma. SpCreature & MkpFX: MMI; James Conrad, Dave Barrett. SpFX: Class A SpFX;(coord) Ron Trost. OptSup: David Hewitt. Ref: TV: Col TriStar HV. PT 19:54. With Pete Liapis, Barbara Alyn Woods, Stacie Randall, Raquel Krelle, Bobby di Cicco, Tony Cox (ghoulie dark), Arturo Gil (ghoulie lite), Ace Mask, Philip McKeon (demon).

Ingredients this time: Alexandra (Randall), a vampirish, dimension-hopping dominatrix ("She loves the taste of blood") ... the "Great Keeper of the Night," the "darker side" of hero Jonathan (Liapis) ("You'll take his place in hell!") ... The Devil is Driving scene ... several types of ghoulies ... and ancient-tongue graffiti from the Book of the Dead ("To live again you must kill yourself") .... Several cute bits and a more-careful-than-usual job from Jim Wynorski. ("Look for us in the sequel — Ghoulies IV, Part Two.")

**GIALLO A VENEZIA** see *Gore in Venice*

**\*The GIANT BEHEMOTH** (U.S.-B) AA(WB)/Artistes Alliance-WNW-Stratford (David Diamond) 1959. Ref: TV. Warren/KWTS!: SP: (uncred.) Daniel Hyatt. BFC: D: also (uncred.) Douglas Hickox. V 3/18/59. 11/4/59. Hardy/SF. Lee. Lentz. Weldon. Scheuer. Stanley. Maltin '92. COF 10:36.

"From the sea—burning like fire—Behemoth!" Clues in this biblical science-fantasy-mystery include passages from Job ("out of his mouth go burning lamps") ... a man found weirdly burned

("Same symptoms as Hiroshima") ... "thousands upon thousands" of dead fish found washed up on a beach ... a beached steamship ... shining mystery goop ("strange stuff") ... a "sea monster" sighting ... "cells from the stomach wall of some unidentified species"... and "radioactive particles" found in a fish from Plymouth. Behind it all: a two-hundred-foot-long paleosaurus. This Stealth monster uses an electric charge to "project" its deadly radiation, eludes radar, and turns out to be "dying of its own radioactivity."

Noir photography by Ken Hodges lends early scenes a bit of creepiness, and stop-motion animation rescues a few later moments. In-between: an aimless script, not-quite-chilling dialogue ("Something came out of the ocean and now has gone back into it"), flat-footed acting, ciphers of characters, campy musical underlining by Edwin Astley (though, overall, the score isn't bad), a nondescript-looking, uncertainly-motivated monster, and a twist (the "projection" of its radiation) which yields hardly-worth-the-trip optical and makeup tricks.

**\*The GIANT CLAW** 1957. AD: Paul Palmentola. TechFX: Ralph Hammeras, George Teague. Ref: TV. Warren/KWTS! no V. no Phantom. Stanley. Lentz. Weldon. Lee. Hardy/SF. Maltin '92. no Scheuer. PT 16:69, 70. Filmfax 38:76, 77, 100.

"That bird is extra-terrestrial!" An "overgrown buzzard ... as big as a battleship" comes to Earth from some "god-forsaken anti-matter galaxy" to build a nest. An anti-matter shield with "no reflecting surface" (radar waves "slide around" the bird) protects the thing, while the latter's beak can open the anti-matter screen and become a weapon which absorbs energy from its victims through "molecular osmosis".... The Giant Beak would be more appropriate. Corny sf-mystery becomes not just bad, but legend, with the first, momentous, non-blurry glimpse of the bird. It looks, to quote Bill Warren, "like nothing so much as Beaky Buzzard," of cartoon fame. (See *The Bashful Buzzard* [II], 1945, and *Lion's Busy* [qq.v.], 1950.) Care is taken here with the talking out of the science in the fiction, but with nothing else. Robert Shayne gets the classic Fifties line: "Machine guns, cannons, rockets! Nothing touched it!" Morris Ankrum gets the accidentally (?) ironic "wild goose chase" line.

**\*GIANT FROM THE UNKNOWN** Screencraft (Arthur A. Jacobs) 1958 (1957). Mus: Albert Glasser. SpFX: Harold Banks. Ref: TV: vt. Lee. V 3/19/58.

"I'm looking for a giant." Pine Ridge, California. A lightning-struck rock yields a live, huge Spanish conquistador, the Diablo Giant, whose great strength "sustained" him in suspended animation for centuries. ("It's the Diablo Giant!") He promptly retrieves his armor and begins attacking women.... Ineptly written monster movie is made bearable, at times, only by the presence of veteran character actors Morris Ankrum and Bob Steele. Buddy Baer in his helmet makes a slightly different menace, but also a slightly risible one. Okay location photography. Campy: the musical blares for Ominous moments.

**GIANT IRON MAN ONE-SEVEN** (2) see also *Brain 17*

**GIANT ROBO** (J) L.A. Hero/Amuse Video & Bandai & Plex & Atlantis & Hikari Pro (Mu Film/Yasuto Yamaki/Emotion) 1992-93 anim color 55m. each (number 1 and number 7), 30m. each (number 2-6) (*Jiyaianto Robo*). SP, D: Yasuhiro Imagawa. SP: also Eichi Yamamoto. Created by Mitsuteru Yokoyama. Based on the 1968 Toei TV series, released in the U.S. as "Johnny Sokko and His Flying Robot." Mus: Masamichi Amano. Mecha Des: T. Watabe. Ref: TV: U.S. Renditions video; Eng.-dubbed. Markalite 3:7, 9: OAV series. V. Max 4:3. Animerica 5:53. 6:12, 13, 51: number 3, "The Fall of Shanghai." Japan Video.

"The Night the Earth Stood Still—Episode 1: The Black Attache Case." People of a future Earth lead a "pollution-free life" thanks to the Shizuma (sp?) Drive, a "perfect energy source." But Dr. Franken von Fogler (sp?) unleashes some sort of anti-Drive force that wrecks Paris. Never fear: "It's Giant Robo!"—a sphinx-headed super-robot.... Involved story ... colorful, super-fast-and-furious action.

**GIANT WOMAN, The** see *Attack of the 50 Foot Woman* (1958)

**GIARA, La** see *Kaos*

**The GIFTED** Stardance Ent./Lewco & Hilltop 1993 (1991) color c98m. SP, D, P, Set Des: Audrey King Lewis. Ph: Charles Mills. Mus: Eric Butler. VisFX: Larry Arpin. MkpFX: Alvechia Ewing. SpPhFX: H'w'd. Optical. Ref: TV: SE video. With Dick Anthony Williams (Daniel), Bianca Ferguson (Lisa), Johnny Sekka, Gene Jackson, J.A. Preston (Jacob), Julius Harris, Tom David Henderson (Nommo/Ogo).

Some 5,000 years ago, apparently, aliens from Sirius B (the "germ" of all things) landed in west Africa and gave certain members of the Dogon tribe the power to stop Ogo, another, pro-hate alien force—perhaps the "great dragon" of Revelations—which returns to Earth every 32 years in an attempt to "create his own world".... The production is a bit awkward, and the story more or less functional, but this is a non-formulaic sf-supernatural tale, with scads of fantastic-horrific elements, including an albino with double-ray power, weird atmospheric disturbances, zap-happy ectoplasm, a glowing rock, astral projection, a mysterious statue, an ancient book, spirit possession, and mystic, goopy gourds (the latter one of the script's niftiest inventions—they herald danger). Film doesn't always work, but it's one of a kind.

**GIGANTES INTERPLANETARIOS** or **GIGANTES PLANE-TARIOS** see *Planeta de las Mujeres Invasoras, El*

**\*GIGANTIS, THE FIRE MONSTER** 1955 82m. (*Godzilla Raids Again* - alt TV t). Mus: Masaru Sato. SpFxD: Eiji Tsuburaya. Ref: TV. Warren/KWTS! Hardy/SF. Glut/CMM. Mike Aguilar. V 5/27/59. TVG. Maltin '92. Scheuer. Lee. Lentz. Weldon.

On volcanic Iwato Island, two big monsters are spotted ("This is bad!")—a monster of the Gigantis family, "born millions of years ago," and one of the Angurus family. A filmstrip shows the beginnings of these fallout-revived creatures, including a little Gigantis, an *Unknown Island* tyrannosaurus, a brontosaurus or two, and a dimetrodon. "It was no different from war," as Gigantis enters Osaka Bay.... Angurus here waddles (not scary), and the two monsters seem to be simply playing. The effects scenes in this *Godzilla* follow-up, however, are occasionally enjoyably hokey or atmospheric. The irony of the contrast between the

scenes of destruction and the romantic, carefree, non-monster scenes is a bit heavy. Corny narration. ("As I looked down, I thought of my buddy Kobayashi.")

**\*GILDERSLEEVE'S GHOST** 1944 (*Gildersleeve, Detective* - orig t). Mus sc: Paul Sawtell. SpFX: Vernon L. Walker. Mkp: Mel Burns. Ref: TV. V 6/21/44. 11/24/43:18. Lee. no Scheuer. Maltin '92. With Lillian Randolph.

Wagstaff Manor, Summerfield—"that horrible haunted place on the mountain." Principals include two ghosts, Jonathan (Harold Peary) and Randolph (Peary again), and "this demon Dr. Wells" (Frank Reicher), whose formula makes a gorilla (Charles Gemora) and a woman, Terry Vance (Marion Martin), invisible.... Plot is far-fetched even for broad comedy, and most of the invisibility stunts are old-hat. Most elaborate of the latter: Terry sits down, and the seat and back of her chair indent.

**GILES' BIG DAY** see *Bad Taste*

**GINGA TETSUDO NO YORU** see *Night on the Galactic Railroad*

**GINIPIGGU, Za** see *Guinea Pig* series

**GINSENG KING** see *Magic of 3,000 Years Ago*

**GIOCHI EROTICI NELLA TERZA GALASSIA** see *Escape from Galaxy 3*

**Il GIOCO DELLE OMBRE** (I) 1990 color 108m. SP, D: S. Gabrini. SP: also R. Marafante. Ref: Hardy/HM2. Palmerini. With F. Bussotti.

Novelist has a relationship with "spirits of the dead." *The Shadow Game* - tr t.

**GIRL FOR SATAN** (I) Filmarte 1982 color/ws feature (*Bimba di Satana*). D: M. Bianchi aka Alan W. Cools. Ref: VSOM: "horror ... in-the-gutter possession flick." Palmerini: sp: P. Regnoli. With Mariangela Giordan, Aldo Sambrell.

**The GIRL FROM MARS** (U.S.-Can.-N.Z.) Family Channel & Atlantis Films & South Pacific Pictures & CanWest & NorthStar Ent. & Virtue Rekert Prods. & TV N.Z. (Interplanetary Prods.) 1991 color 91m. D: Neill Fearnley. Tel: Brian Alan Lane. Mus: Louis Natale. AD: Phil Schmidt. Mkp: Imelda Bain-Partin. Ref: TV: TV-movie. V 3/18/91:88. TVG. Maltin '92. With Edward Albert, Sarah Sawatsky, Gary Day, Christianne Hirt, Gwynyth Walsh, Eddie Albert.

"In my world, there are no birthdays." Thirteen-year-old DeeDee Puttman (Sawatsky)—the "Miss Alien Nation" of Obegon Falls—does things seemingly "not humanly possible." She can shoot flames with her finger and shatter glass with her silent screams. She has a little, remote-controlled flying saucer ("just a UFO") and, at the end, appears "magically" on the local drive-in-movie screen (the "mark of the red planet") to say farewell to Earth. Is she a Martian? No, she's just telekinetic. The local mysterious scientist (Eddie Albert), however, is apparently a Martian.... Script tries to have it every which way—as a Family Channel *Carrie*, as *E.T.*, as *Rebel without a Cause*—and generally takes its alienated-teen idea too seriously. The too too sensitive score is the worst of it; the acting, the best of it.

**The GIRL FROM TOMORROW** (Austral.) Disney Channel 1990 color c105m. Ref: TVG: made for TV. With Katharine Cullen, Helen Jones.

"Futuristic teen ... transported back to the 20th Century."

**The GIRL IN A SWING** (B-U.S.-Danish) Millimeter Films/J&M (Panorama Films Int'l./Betzer B.V.) 1988 ('89-U.S.) color 111m. (117m.) SP, D: Gordon Hessler, from Richard Adams' novel. SpOptSeqs: Roy Field. Mkp: Kezia de Winne. Ref: TV. Sacto Bee 12/4/89. V 12/28/88. 10/18/89:39(ad).

Drama with supernatural elements, including a vanishing stuffed green tortoise, phantom sobbing, a crumbling figurine, a mysterious doll, and a ghostly form on the surf. The Past—represented here by ghosts of guilt and regret—is dredged up very slowly, if occasionally touchingly, in this too-methodical film. Very little story for the running time.

**GIRL IN ROOM 2A** (I) Joseph Brenner/Projection Partners 1976 (1975) color 83m. (*Terror in 2-A* - alt t?). SP, D, P: William L. Rose. Ph: Mancini. Mus: Pisano. AD: G. Ranieri. Mkp: Liliana Dulac. Ref: TV: Prism Ent. video; Eng. dubbed. Lee(p): V 8/16/72. Hound. no Martin. With Raf Vallone, Daniela Giordano, Karin Schubert, Angelo Infanti, John Scanlon, Brad Harris, Frank Latimore.

"The masked figure always appears!" "People in trouble, one way or another," board at Mrs. Grant's, where a man (or woman) in a red mask lurks, and the floor "bleeds." Her country house of the Inquisition is no more inviting: There, "the group" punishes, with needle and sword, those who have done wrong. ("Evil must be dealt with in its own terms.") Sole interest of flat thriller with softcore gore is the mystery re the exact nature of its secret society.

**GIRL TRAP** see *Guzuu*

**The GIRL WITH THE HUNGRY EYES** Penn/Eden West (Kastenbaum Films/Smoking Gun/Shapiro-Elwes-Niven, Jr.) 1993 (1995) color 83m. SP, D: Jon Jacobs. "Inspired by the short story by Fritz Leiber." Ph: Gary Tieche. Mus: Paul Inder, Oscar O'Lochlainn; Rick Giovinazzo. PD: Clare Brown. Mkp: Susan Dexter. SpFxCoord: Barry Anderson. Ref: Col-TriStar HV. With Christina Fulton (Louise), Isaac Turner, Leon Herbert, Bret Carr.

"Now, we can be immortal!" Louise, a suicide at The Tides hotel, Miami, in 1937, is supernaturally "undone" by an unknown force, in the present. She sprouts vampire fangs and becomes a photo model who works only at night. She twists her first victim's head around before biting; she severs another victim's head, and for one prospective victim, she makes half her face gruesome. Meanwhile, very strangely, the power is slowly coming back on at the abandoned Tides.... Not too good, but decidedly offbeat. Occasional surprises. Dedicated to Leiber.

**GIRLFRIEND FROM HELL** IVE (Live Ent.)/Alberto Lensi & Queens Cross (D.M. Peterson/Girlfriend from Hell Prods.) 1990 (1989) color 92m. SP, D, Co-P: Daniel M. Peterson. Ph: Gerry Lively. Mus: M. Rapp. PD: Regina Argentine. FxAnim: Charles

McDonald. Mkp: Lisa Jane Taylor. OptFX: Howard Anderson Co. Ref: TV: Avid video (August Ent.). V 11/5/90: "genuinely funny horror picture." PT 9:12. CVS 9/90. SFChron Dtbk 12/30/90: "an amazing little video flick." With Liane Curtis (Maggie), Dana Ashbrook, Lezlie Deane, James Daughton, Ken Abraham, James Karen.

"She sucked their souls." Chaser—a "devil chaser" from purgatory—and the devil crash, meteorite-like, to Earth. Soon, the devil possesses drab young Maggie and turns her into a "wild woman" who turns a guy's dinner into an attack lobster and an infant into an attack critter. She's petty, mean, malicious, and having a great time. At the end, she restores the souls of her victims .... Some fun knockabout humor in this frightening world of male jerks and really tough women. Plot gets sidetracked near the end into time-hopping with Chaser's "transporter," but film has some great offscreen sounds and lines.

**GIRLS NITE OUT** see *Scaremaker, The*

**GIRLS SCHOOL SCREAMERS** Troma/Bandit 1986 (1984) color 85m. (aka *Girls' School Screamers. The Portrait* - alt t). Story, SP, D, PD, Co-P: John P. Finegan. Story: also Katie Keating, Pierce J. Keating. Add'l Dial: Charles Braun, Robert Fisher. Mus & SdFX: John Hodian. SpFxMkp: John Mafei. Ref: TV. NYT 5/23/86. V 5/28/86. Martin. Scheuer. Hardy/HM2. With Mollie O'Mara, Sharon Christopher, Mari Butler, Beth O'Malley, Braun (Tyler Welles).

"In the darkness, there is evil." The late Tyler Welles' estate harbors a monstrous, wormy crawling hand, a supernatural wind, a bridesmaids-of-death chamber, a dead "best man," evidence of "ghoulish murders," and a possessed Trinity College student or two. Thoroughly routine slasher flick features an okay opening, the-bride-was-a-corpse teaser and an electrocution-plus scene so exaggerated it's funny. Flashbacks to 1939 are even more dramatically stilted than the present-tense scenes.

**GIRO GIROTONDO... CON IL SESSO E' BELLO IL MONDO** (I) 1975 feature. D: Oscar Brazzi. Ref: Palmerini.

"Erotic comedy set in 2010."

**GISELE KEROZENE** (F) c1990? anim. short. Ref: SFExam 9/7/90: "pixilation featuring leather-jacketed witches racing through the future on their brooms."

**GIVE A DOG A BONE** (B) Westminster-MRP 1966 color 77m. D, P: Henry Cass. From P. Howard's play. Ref: Lee (MFB'72:7). With Ronnie Stevens, Ivor Danvers, Richard Warner.

Man from space.

**GLADIATOR COP** SC Ent./Corktown Films 1994 color c92m. (*The Swordsman II*). Ref: vc box: "battle begun centuries ago." With L. Lamas, James Hong.

**GLADIATORI DEL FUTURO, I** see *2020: Texas Gladiators*

**GLASS SHADOW** see *Cyborg²*

**GNAW: FOOD OF THE GODS II** see *Food of the Gods II*

**GNOMES' GREAT ADVENTURE** (Sp) B.R.B. Int'l. & Miramax 1987 anim color 75m. D: Harvey Weinstein; (anim) Luis Ballester. SP: Shelley Altman, Mike Zettler. Adap: Ernest Reid. From the book *The Gnomes* by Poortvleit & Huygen. Mus: Bob Jewett, Jack Maeby. ElecSdFX: Rheault, Perreault. Ref: TV. Cabletime 8/87. Voice: Tony Randall (ghost of the Black Lake).

Formula children's fantasy features horrific scenes in a temple overrun with venom-shooting monster-spiders, plus "scary stuff" in the Castle of Spirits, which is haunted by a big, noisy, prankish ghost and decorated with gargoyles and grotesque statues. Bland animation, personality-bereft characterization.

**GO SHOGUN: THE TIME ETRANGER** see *Etranger, Time Alien*

**GOBLIN** Tempe 199-? color 75m. Ref: Tempe Video flyer. Bill Warren.

"Monstrous creature" haunts house.(TV)

**GOBOTS: BATTLE OF THE ROCK LORDS** Clubhouse Pictures/Hanna-Barbera & Tonka & Cuckoos Nest & Wang Film 1986 anim color 74m. D: Ray Patterson, Don Lusk, Alan Zaslove. SP: Jeff Segal. Sup Anim D: Paul Sabella. Ref: TV. MFB'86:335. V 3/26/86. ad. Voices: Margot Kidder, Roddy McDowall, Michael Nouri, Telly Savalas, Ike Eisenmann, Bernard Erhard (Cy-Kill), Morgan Paull, Foster Brooks, Dick Gautier, Darryl Hickman.

The rock lords of the planet Quartex are just one of the results of a disaster which fused all living things with rocks. One evil rock lord, Magmar, teams with a renegade GoBot, Cy-Kill, in a quest for the "ultimate weapon." Plus: Rockasaurs, giant metallic dinosaurs ... flying leech-like things ... a mind-reading machine ... a two-headed robot ... and power swords.... Bland, unimaginative actioner. Rock creatures were a dumb idea in *Missile to the Moon* and they still are.

**GOD BLESS DANCOUGAR** (J) Animate 1987 anim color 80m. Ref: GBD Picture Book: Toho Video. Japan Video.

Robots, spaceships.

See also: *Dancougar.*

**GOD MARS 1** (J) Toho/TMS 1988 anim color 56m. Ref: TV: Toho Video; no Eng.; OAV? Japan Video: *God Mars 2*: 99m.; set in 1999.

An apparently basically pacific people takes to the air on giant birds to fight the enemy and their missiles, armed spaceships, and giant robots. Their ace in the hole: an ESPer who can use his gift as a weapon.... In the contrast between the idyllic and the militaristically hellish, *God Mars 1* seems like a simplistic *Windaria*, with occasional visual interest.

The **GODDESS OF SPRING** UA/Disney 1934 anim color 9 1/2m. Ref: TV: Silly Symphony. Jim Shapiro.

A laughing, horned Devil selects the Goddess of Spring as his new "queen of Hades," while once-happy, springtime elves fight little devils. Latter's celebration dance in hell is atmospheric highlight of otherwise forgettable cartoon.

**GODMONSTER OF INDIAN FLATS** SWV 1973 color feature. SP,D: Fredric Hobbs. Ref: SWV supp.'96. With Stuart Lancaster, C. Brooks.

Vapors from old mine yield "8 foot mutant sheep."

**GOD'S ARMY** Dimension/First Look/Neo Motion Pictures (Joel Soisson/Overseas Filmgroup) 1995 (1994?) color 93m. (*The Prophecy* - release t). SP, D: Gregory Widen. Mus: David C. Williams. PD: Clark Hunter. SpFxCoord: J. Van Kline. SpMkpFX: Piction EFX. Ph & VisFxSup: B.D. Johnson. Ph: also Richard Clabaugh. Ref: TV: VSOM. SFChron 9/2/95. ad. With Christopher Walken (Gabriel), Elias Koteas, Virginia Madsen, Eric Stoltz (Simon), Viggo Mortensen (Lucifer), Adam Goldberg, J.C. Quinn, Amanda Plummer.

"Would you ever really want to see an angel?" During a "second war in heaven," renegade angels (jealous of humans) are pitted against loyal ones. Gabriel, the angel of death, wants to "retake" heaven, but Simon (the "lower soldier angel"?) hides the dead general's soul in little Mary. Meanwhile, Lucifer is not happy at all.... Plus a bible from the Second Century ... a hermaphrodite's corpse with the characteristics of an aborted fetus ... a lot of "angelic script" ... visions of the damned ... and Navajo rites.... Walken's Gabriel here is one scary angel. It's a bravura role for him—like Jeff Goldblum's Mr. Frost, a twist on evil. As a whole, the film is certainly one of a kind, alternately appalling and inspired. It's not your usual religio-horror. (For one thing, the devil gives hero and heroine hot tips on defeating Gabriel. He doesn't cotton to rivals, apparently.) Some of the dialogue is so out-of-left-field that you can't be sure you really heard what you heard.

**GODZILLA: 1985** (J-U.S.) New World/Toho (Tomoyuki Tanaka & Anthony Randel) 1985 color 103m. (87m.-U.S.) (*Godzilla* - alt t. aka *The Return of Godzilla. Gojira*). D: Koji Hashimoto; (U.S.) R. J. Kizer. SP: Hidekazu Nagahara, based on *Godzilla, King of the Monsters* (1954). Story: Tanaka. Mus: Rejiro Koroku. SpFX: Akiyoshi Nakano. Prosth: Yasumaru? U.S. credits: Anim: Bret Mixon. Title Des: E. D. Farino. OptFX: Ray Mercer. Ref: screen. V 5/1/85. 9/23/87:48. 5/1/85:398 (ad). SFChron 8/23/85; (Dtbk) 9/8/85. ad. Ecran F 56:18. 59:60-64. With Shin Takuma, Ken Tanaka, Yasuko Sawaguchi, Keiju Kobayashi; (U.S.) Raymond Burr, Warren Kemmerling, James Hess.

Cadmium missiles stun that eighty-meter-tall, "living nuclear weapon" Godzilla, but lightning from a stratospheric nuclear explosion revives the beast. At the end, randomly recorded bird chirps lure the literally-bird-brained Godzilla into a volcano. Extra addeds: a crab-like flying creature and clips from Godzilla's '56 visit.... If the shortened, adulterated U.S. version of this remake/sequel is choppy and unoriginal, it's still good to have that silly monster suit back. Godzilla's friends and relations from the other sequels, however, are sorely missed. *The Star Wars*-inspired effects can't replace them.

See also the following and *Daffy Duck's Quackbusters. Ganjasaurus Rex. Garbage in, Garbage out. Gigantis. Urusei Yatsura 2. Waxwork II.*

**GODZILLA RAIDS AGAIN** see *Gigantis*

**GODZILLA VS. BIOLLANTE** (J) HBO/Toho Eiga (Tanaka-Tomiyama) 1989 ('92-U.S.) color/ws 105m. (*Gojira Tai Beolante*). SP, D: Kazuki Omori. Ph: (sp fx) Kenichi Eguchi; Y. Kato. Mus: K. Sugiyama. PD: S. Ikuno. SpFxD: Koichi Kawakita. Biollante Des: Sugita, Suzuki. OptFX: Kishimoto, Hoojo. FxAnim: Hashimoto, Matsumoto. Ref: TV: Toho Video; some Eng. Markalite 3:84-5. V 10/12/92:16 (rated). SFChron Dtbk 12/12/92. TVG. TV: Story: S. Kobayashi; Eng.-dubbed version. Fango 122:32. PT 16:16. With Kunihiko Mitamura, Yoshiko Tanaka, M. Takashima, Megumi Odaka.

"Okay! We've got a Godzilla cell!" Ingredients in this direct sequel to *Godzilla: 1985* include the Anti Nuclear Energy Bacteria, which apparently grows into a huge tentacle, then into the monster Biollante ... a fast new spaceship which at one point knocks down Godzilla ... and a plan to crossbreed wheat, cactus, and Godzilla to produce (yes) jumbo wheat which can grow in the desert.... In the most watchable sequence, Biollante, or its atoms, returns from the heavens and re-forms into a colorful, many-tentacled thing. Apart from this new monster's surreally-writhing tentacles, though, this *Godzilla* entry seems strictly formula and includes the obligatory Godzilla-vs.-city sequence. Unexpected element: the Godzilla Memorial Lounge (for humans). Stirring, John Williams-like score.

**GODZILLA VS. KING GHIDORAH** (J) Toho (Tomoyuki Tanaka/Shojo Tomiyama) 1991 color/ws 103m. (aka *Godzilla Vs. King Ghidora. Gojira Tai Hingu Gidora*). SP, D: Kazuki Omori. Ph: Yoshinoru Sakiguchi. Mus: Akira Ifukube. AD: Ken Sakai. SpFxD: Koichi Kawakita. Ref: TV: vt; Eng. titles. Markalite 3:12-15. SFChron 3/10/92. V 11/9/92:56. PT 13:10. With Anna Nakagawa, Megumi Odaka, Isao Toyohara, Chuck Wilson, Richard Berger, Yoshio Tsuchiya.

This convoluted, plot-heavy sequel to *Godzilla Vs. Biollante* jumps around in time from the year 2204 to 1992 to 1944 and features a Godzilla "still enervated by anti-nuclear bacteria" a thousand days after encountering Biollante ... Future Men from the Earth Union who travel back via a time machine ("You call it a time machine. We call it Mother") and who unleash three little, flying-*Gremlin*-like "dorats"—a "new animal by biotechnology"—which, after exposure to radioactivity, become the "big and savage" Ghidorah ... the Future Men's Android M-11 ... and the Ultra-Science Institute.... Or, the Origins of Godzilla and Ghidorah. It seems that a "dinosaur was there on the Marshalls in 1944" which, after an H-bomb test in 1954, became Godzilla. However, the latter is teleported to the future ("Godzilla's gone from history"), and the scientists of 1992 must make another Godzilla to battle the rampaging Ghidorah. The two main monsters, though, switch dramatic roles at the end, and Ghidorah (commandeered by the future heroine) saves Japan from an out-of-control Godzilla. Confusing script's chief novelty: the World War II battle scenes interrupted by pre-Godzilla.

**GODZILLA VS. MECHA-GODZILLA** (J) Toho (Tanaka-Tomiyama) 1993 color/ws 108m. D: T. Okawara. SP: W. Mimura. SpFxD: K. Kawakita. Ref: TV: Toho Video; no Eng. Mo. V 1/3/94:24: in Japan 12/93.

Ingredients this time include the flying, artificial-diamond-coated Mecha-Godzilla ... a big, ray-shooting, flying weapon which combines, at one point, with Mecha-Godzilla to form a formidable super-weapon ... a Rodan-type ... a (relatively) little (plastic-looking) dinosaur, "Baby" ... and a two-person mini-aircraft .... Dinosaurs and robots both get their fair share of footage here, but most of the action is uninspired. The pleasing opening sequence shows Mecha-Godzilla in the last stages of its preparation. At the end, Baby follows Godzilla into the sea.

**GODZILLA VS. MOTHRA** (J) Toho 1992 color/ws 102m. D: Takao Ogawara. Ref: TV: vt; occ. Eng. dialogue. V 9/21/92:52. 11/9/92:48, 56. 1/4/93:55: in Japan. 1/18/93:70: playing.

In this corner: an alien Mothra, or Batra, who comes to Earth in a meteorite-egg which falls in the Pacific. Instinctively, the ray-shooting alien thing homes in on a Japanese city and wrecks a few blocks' worth of buildings. In the opposite corner: Godzilla, who, feeling left out, swims in. In the third corner: Baby Mothra, direct from a big egg in Thailand, who hatches, gloms onto Godzilla's tail, and spits cocoon fluid on him. At the end, the alien Mothra wills itself from caterpillar to moth stage, and the two fliers huddle, gang up on Godzilla, carry him off, like a Bundle for Britain, and deep-six him.

Typically lethargic Godzilla epic, but there at least seems to be more monster footage than usual, which makes this the easiest to take of the recent *Godzilla* movies. Weird/lyrical centerpiece: Earth Mothra cocooning next to City Hall. Human witnesses accept this unusual spectacle for the religious experience, or Big Event, that it is, and don't interfere. Best computer graphic: "Godzilla Detection." The two miniature ladies are back, too. Both sing.

**GODZILLA VS. SPACE GODZILLA** (J) Toho 1994 color/ws 108m. D: Kenshou Yamashita. SP: Hiroshi Kashiwabara. Ph: M. Kishimoto. Mus: T. Hattori. SpFxD: Koichi Kawakita. SpFxPh: Kenichi Eguchi. Ref: TV: Toho Video; some Eng. Cult Movies 14:48-51. With Jun Hashizume, Megumi Odaka, Z. Yoneyama, T. Yoshikawa, Akira Emoto, Y. Saito, Kenji Sahara.

An "interplanetary research vessel" returns to Earth with a "huge monster" on board — Space Godzilla. Other Godzillas here include Little Godzilla and the original big one. Plus Land Mogera/Star Falcon, a human-operated robot/vehicle with flying and drill options ... Fairy Mothra ... the Mothra mini-ladies ... a woman with a psychic link to Godzilla ... the U.N. Godzilla Countermeasures Center ... and stock footage from *Godzilla Vs. Biollante* and *Godzilla Vs. Mothra*.... The stars, Godzilla and Space Godzilla, bore; the supporting players, Little Godzilla and Fairy Mothra, fare better. See and hear the stiff but sweet little guy's Cower and Whimper, as Space Godzilla torments him. (Remember the son of Godzilla and the insect monsters in *Son of Godzilla*?) Mogera looks like a toy, while Space Godzilla's "stalagmites" give the cityscape an odd, alien feel. Fun cartography: the maps pinpointing the whereabouts of Godzilla, Space Godzilla, and Mogera. Unexpected fantasy: Space Godzilla levitating Little Godzilla, then, later, Godzilla. "Mogera" stands for Mobile Operation Godzilla Expert Robot Aero-Type.

**GOJIRA** see *Godzilla: 1985*

**GOJIRA TAI BEOLANTE** see *Godzilla Vs. Biollante*

**GOJIRA TAI HINGU GIDORA** see *Godzilla Vs. King Ghidorah*

**GOKUU: MIDNIGHT EYE** (J) Toei Video 1989 anim color 50m. (aka *Midnight Eye*). D: Yoshiaki Kawajiri. From Buichi Terazawa's manga. Ref: Animag 6:5 12:14-15: 2 OAVs. Japan Video. Animation Mag (Smr/'92): 27,48. TV: Toei Video.

"Cyborg clone," psychics, etc., in the year 2014. Show-stopping scene: A nearly-naked peacock lady slowly unfurls her feathers, and the latter slowly open their hypnotizing eyes. The rest isn't quite up to that, but this atmospherically drawn sf-mystery also features a weird sequence in which the cy-detective hero carries around the severed head of a ray-spitting lady and uses a last spit or two from her to polish off a few baddies. Another prime outre image: a surprise torrent of water washing surprised folks out a top-floor window of an ultra-skyscraper.

**GOKUU: MIDNIGHT EYE II** (J) Toei Video 1989 anim color c54m. (aka *Midnight Eye II*). Ref: TV: Toei Video; no Eng.

Ingredients this time include the almost wittily resourceful hero ... flying, metal "ichthyosaur" monsters ... a glowing, super-strong cy-thug who moves through scenes like a radioactive hurricane ... and the hero's multi-purpose stick/weapon. Strikingly designed but ultimately conventional.

**The GOLDEN BOAT** Duende/Symbolic Exchange (Torrent-Schamus) 1990 color and b&w 88m. SP, D: Raul Ruiz. Mus: John Zorn. Ph: M. Alberti. Ref: V 9/17/90: "a commercial leper."

Huge, undying slasher stalks Manhattan.

**GOLDEN BUDDHA AGAINST THE SNAKE PHANTOM** (H.K.?) 198-? color/ws 88m. Ref: TV: Tai Seng Video; Eng. titles.

"The monster is coming again!" To *Psycho* strings, a man turns into a snake; in fact, a whole tribe of snake-men is running amok in a village here. ("They are not human beings!") Most are hunted down and killed, but one snake is saved and, cut open, breathes flame which disfigures one villager, who then acts possessed. Near the end, the main snake phantom becomes a gigantic, fire-breathing snake which burns the whole village. He reverts to human form and turns into a giant to fight another, laughing giant.... Cheap and crude, but not without a certain sensationalistic charm. In one scene, a priest uses X-ray eyes to see the unborn snakes in a pregnant woman's womb. Alarmed, he mumbles a few spiritual words and slashes the little monsters out with his sword.

**The GOLDEN CHILD** Para/Feldman-Meeker & Eddie Murphy Prods. & IL&M 1986 color 94m. D: Michael Ritchie. SP & Co-P: Dennis Feldman. Mus: Michel Colombier. VisFX: IL&M; (sup) Ken Ralston; (coord) Pamela Easley, Laurie Vermont. Anim: (go-motion) Harry Walton; Ellen Lichtwardt; Available Light. Demon: (des) Randy Dutra; (sup) Phil Tippett. SpFxSup: Cliff Wenger. SpProps: Chris Walas. Dancing Can Movement: Michael Smuin. Mkp: Ken Chase. SpSdFX: John Paul Fasal. Ref: TV. MFB'87:46-7. V 12/17/86. SFExam 12/12/86. With Eddie Murphy, Charles Dance (Sardo Numspa), Charlotte Lewis, Randall Cobb, James Hong, Shakti, J. L. Reate (The Golden Child), Frank Welker (voice of the Thing), Felix Silla.

Northeastern Tibet. Sardo Numspa, a demon on orders from the Devil, abducts The Golden Child, a magic baby whose electric touch turns people into his slaves. Numspa can transform into a rat, and his fingernail burns a scar into the arm of The Chosen One (Murphy). Another zinger effect: the snake-bodied woman behind the screen.... As in *Ghost Breakers* and *Abbott and Costello Meet Frankenstein* (not to mention *Ghostbusters*, more recently), glibness here is a response to the supernaturally intimidating, and it's a refreshing variation on the more common scream response, although Murphy's disbelieving one-liners are off-and-on. Humor as tightrope act. Murphy's Chandler, to Numspa, as the latter assumes demon form: "I can see you're busy now. I'll come back some other time." At one point, the Golden Child makes a cola can dance, literally, to "Puttin' on the Ritz," in a bit of aluminum soft shoe.

**GOLDEN EGG, The** see *Vanishing, The*

**GOLDEN LANTERN** (Taiwanese?) 1987? color c95m. D: Shin Ren. Ref: TV: vt; no Eng.; Den Ma - Viet. version t. Suiki: above is tr Chi. t. vc box: sfa *The Tale of a Female Ghost* (Eng.-lang.)? Weisser/ATC: *Tale of a Female Ghost* (H.K.-Thai) aka *Horrible Ghost of Old House*. With Lee Chian-Chian.

A betrayed woman suffers a seizure, dies, comes back as a ghost, drives her rival crazy, and haunts her betrayer, whom she eventually sends plunging off a tower to his death. Also noted: a bloody clutching hand, a floating severed head, and a cut-rate exorcism with elementary ray effects.... The oddest thing about this Eastern ghost story: It switches gears midway, from dramatic to comic. In the second half, the living characters are still comically distraught, but now the comedy seems intentional. Shot cheaply, on videotape, with very poor dialogue recording, some very Western music on the soundtrack, and softcore sex scenes.

**GOLDEN NUN** (H.K.) 1987? color feature. D: Hsu Tien Yung. Ref: Weisser/ATC: "band of vampires." With Land Lo, Li Tau Hung.

**GOLDEN SWALLOW** (H.K.) Alan & Eric Films 1988? color/ws? c95m. Ref: TV: Rainbow Video; Eng. titles. Fango 107:59.

Scholar and lantern seller Lo Chih-chiu saves a swallow from boys with slingshots. The swallow turns out to be a demon, Hsiao Hsueh, who, in turn, tries to save Lo from the "matron," a giant monster/demon ("not a common evil"). Hsiao Hsueh vows to kill Lo herself if he breaks his vow not to reveal the secret of the demons' existence to humans. Later, she takes human form and marries Lo, who—not recognizing her—breaks his vow and tells this woman about a certain "demon girl".... Technically-accomplished ghost story—direction, design, music, and photography are all highly atmospheric. The thin script, however, needs all the elaborate, floating-demon-gown effects it can get. Film simply illustrates, at length, its "man and demon are different" thesis.

See also: *Kwaidan* ("Woman of the Snow").

**GOLDEN VIPER** see *Serpent Warriors*

**GOLDEN YEARS** CBS-TV/Laurel-King (Galin-McIntosh) 1991 color c90m. (aka *Stephen King's Golden Years*). D: Kenneth Fink. Tel & Exec Co-P: S. King. Mus: Joe Taylor; (title song) David Bowie. SpMkp: (des) Carl Fullerton, Neal Martz; (consul)

Dick Smith. PD: Jeremy Conway. Sp Hairstyle: W. A. Farley. SpFX: Steve Kirshoff. VideoFX: Paul Srp. Ref: TV. TVG. V 7/15/91. Oak Trib 7/16/91. With Keith S(z)arabajka, Felicity Huffman, Frances Sternhagen, Ed Lauter, R. D. Call, Bill Raymond, Stephen Root.

"Once your hair turns white, there's no going back!" Usually. Falco Plains Agricultural Testing Facility's Dr. Todhunter (Raymond), a "mad scientist," is creating scientific history, though not of the sort he envisioned. A turbine explodes during an experiment with "nonlethal biological material," and janitor Harlan Williams (Sarabajka), caught in the blast, begins to glow, then starts getting back the brown in his hair.... This sentimental "special movie preview" of the mini-series re rejuvenation features familiar lizardlike officials and other cliches—though Root is good at lizardiness.

*The GOLEM 1935('37-U.S.) 96m. (*Golem* - Cz t). From the book by G. Meyrink. Ph: Vich, Stallich. Mus: Josef Kumok. Ref: TV: Ergo HV (Hen's Tooth video); Eng. titles. Chirat/Catalogue. Hardy/SF. V 2/26/36. 3/24/37. Lee. With Germaine Aussey, Ferdinand Hart (the Golem), Roger Duchesne, Marcel Dalio.

"In 1560, Rabbi Loew, according to legend, created a being, in human form, to which he imparted life," and which became the "protector of the ghetto of Prague." ("When the beast roars, the Golem will awake.") The magic words: "Revolt is the right of the slave." The Golem stirs, breaks his chains and cell bars, then lays waste to the Emperor's (Harry Baur) palace. Plus: alchemists ("Life can be created") and torture chambers.... Fine photography and art direction, and fine work by Baur. But waiting for the Golem to act is like waiting for the story to begin. The Golem seems part-Spartacus, part-Kong, and part-Superman. Gore alert: At one point, the Golem's foot crushes a (rubber) head.

See also the following and *Assassin* (1986). *Miami Horror.*

GOLEM (B) Mole Hill 198-? claymation 5m. R: PFA notes 3/16/89: "radical reinterpretation of the medieval European myth."

GOLEM, L'ESPRIT DE L'EXIL (F-Dutch-I-G) Agav Films & Allarts & Nova Films & Friedlander Film & RAI-2 & Groupe TSF & Channel 4 & Canal Plus & the CNC & Eurimages Fund (Laurent Truchot) 1992 color 112m. SP, D: Amos Gitai. Ph: Henri Alekan. Mus: Simon & Markus Stockhausen. Ref: V 11/16/92: "well-meaning but heavy-handed ... occasional patches of stunning lyricism." With Hanna Schygulla, Vittorio Mezzogiorno, Ophrah Shemesh, Samuel Fuller, Bernardo Bertolucci, Philippe Garel.

Magic Cabala formula conjures up the Golem—the "spirit who protects and guides vagabonds and exiles"—from "earth and clay." As the Golem, Schygulla "achieves an other-worldly impact...."

Follow-up: Petrified Garden (P).

GONAD THE BARBARIAN/SEARCH FOR URANUS Excalibur Films 1986 anim color 76m. SP, D, P: Arthur King. Ref: Adam '88: STAR WARS takeoff. vc box: "X-rated cartoons." With "Princess Layme," "Princess Orgasma," "Mark Starkiller." Sfa *Offenders of the Universe*?

See also: *Sex Wars.*

The GOOD, THE BAD AND THE SUBHUMANOID: CLASS OF NUKE 'EM HIGH, PART 3 Troma 1992 color feature. D: Eric Louzil. Ref: SFChron Dtbk 4/26/92: mutant squirrel, mutant twin babies. V 5/10/93: C-118: screening at Cannes. With Brick Bronsky, Lisa Gaye, Lisa Star, John Tallman.

Sequel to *Class Of Nuke 'Em High.*

GOOD WILL TO MEN MGM/Hanna-Barbera (Fred Quimby) 1955 anim color/ws 8m. Ref: Jim Shapiro: crummy remake of *Peace on Earth.* Lee (LC).

GOODNIGHT, GOD BLESS (B) ABC Pictures/Grifiths & Malik 1987 color 94m. D: John Eyres. SP: Ed Ancoats. Ph: Alan M. Trow. Mus & SdDes: P. S. Davies. Mkp: Summerhill, Woodruff. Ref: TV: Magnum Ent. video. V 10/19/88:284 (ad). Hound. Martin. With Emma Sutton, Frank R. Green, Jared Morgan, Jane Price, Gerald Charles (killer).

Weak-tea slasher flick re a madman/"priest" with a carving knife ends with a well-executed if pointless supernatural twist: An *Exorcist* spin of the head, and the killer's traumatized prey (Sutton) is revealed to be ... the supposedly dead, demonic killer. Metempsychosis, anyone?

*GOOFY GHOSTS 1928 c15m. Ref: TV: sd fx & narration. With Jimmie Adams, Lorraine Eddy, Eddie Baker.

The Skull—a hooded, skull-masked skulker—terrorizes the inhabitants of a "ghostly house." Plus fake ghosts and much frantic, if not very funny activity.

The GOONIES WB/Amblin Ent. 1985 color/ws 113m. D: Richard Donner. SP: Chris Columbus. Story: Steven Spielberg. SpMkp: Craig Reardon, the Burmans. SpVisFX: IL&M. SpFxCoord: Matt Sweeney. Anim Sup: Charlie Mullen. Ref: TV. MFB'85:341. V 6/5/85. SFExam 6/7/85.

Boys' adventure-comedy set in underground caverns includes shocks with beetles-in-skeleton's-eyes, bat hordes, skeletons on a pirate ship, and a chained "it" that "sounds like Kong" and proves to be the huge, deformed Sloth (John Matuszak).... Heavy-handed, episodic, seemingly neverending thriller charms only in the Sloth-Chunk (Jeff Cohen) friendship. (Seems the food-mad Chunk has met his match in the gluttonous Sloth.)

GOOSEBUSTER (Fili) Regal Films (Lily Monteverde) 1992 color 94m. (*Mumu? Anong Malay Ko!* - cr t. *Goosebusters* - alt ad t). D: Tony Y. Reyes; (assoc) Eddie Reyes, Roy Tuazon. SP: Tony Reyes, Joey de Leon. Ph: Oscar Querijero. Mus D: D. Velasquez. PD: Cadapan, Maculada. Mkp: E. Munoz. SdFX: R. Capule. Titles: Cinemagic. Ref: TV: Regal video; occ. Eng.; above is ad t. With J. de Leon, Aiza Seguerra, Racel Tuazon, Panchito Alba, Ruby Rodriguez, Lady Lee.

After our two heroes eat a goose belonging to a mad killer, goose ectoplasm from a crystal ball at a seance possesses their lady friend. Later, a little fowl shoots rays, and a female hant spits animated letters of the alphabet out her mouth to form words. ("Patay kayong bata!") She then enters a big bird skeleton and spits rays at the protagonists. At the end, the madman dies, and the goose spirit flies out of the heroine; the madman then recovers, gets shot down, and deposits an egg.

Negligible comedy in the first half; cute effects in the second. Wry: Ghostbusting equipment is kept on the wall beside the fire extinguisher.

**GOOSEFOOT** see *Fantasist, The*

**GOR** (B-I?) Cannon Int'l. (Avi Lerner) 1987 color 95m. D: Fritz Kiersch. SP & Co-P: Harry Alan Towers (aka P. Welbeck). SP: also Rick Marx. From John Norman's novel *Tarnsman of Gor*. PD: Hans Nol. VisFxSup: Rick Kerrigan. Mkp: Colin Polson. Ref: TV: Warner HV. V 5/13/87. With Urbano Barberini, Rebecca Ferratti, Paul L. Smith, Oliver Reed, Jack Palance.

"Gor is a harsh world and it breeds hard people." A special stone propels college professor Tarl Cabot (Barberini) into the counter-Earth of Gor, a world of barbarians. ("I come from another world, called Earth.") Only the Homestone can restore him to home and New Hampshire.... The only epic dimensions, or proportions, here belong to Ferratti, as Talena. Grand natural settings too, but the story is all cliches, large and small.

Sequel: *Outlaw of Gor*.

**GOR SAGA** see *First Born*

**GORE IN VENICE** (I) 1979 color feature (*Giallo a Venezia*). D: Mario Landi. SP: Aldo Serio. Mus: Berto Pisano. Ref: VSOM: "bloody giallo ... sadistic slasher." trailer: dismemberment. Palmerini. MV: gory. ETC/Giallos: "stupid film"; *Mystery in Venice*. With Leonora Fani, Gianni Dei, Eolo Capri, Maria Angela Giordani.

**GOREMET, ZOMBIE CHEF FROM HELL** Swanfilms 1986 (1987) color c79m. SP, D, P, Ph, Ed, Mus: Don Swan. SP: also Jeff Baughn, William Highsmith. Mus: also S. Cunningham, Dan Smith. SpFX: Warren Graham. Mkp: T. Depuay. Ref: TV: Camp Video. Bowker '90. Hound. Phantom. Martin. With Theo Depuay (Goza), Kelley Kunicki (Missy/High Priestess), C. W. Casey (Azog), Alan Marx, Michael O'Neill (Blozor), Joy Merchant, Jeff Pillars, J. Baughn (Lonezor), Cindy Castanio, Charles Berger III (young Goza).

In 1386, the Brotherhood punishes Goza, a rebellious priest, with a potion which makes him hunger for human flesh even as his body decomposes.... Goza's Deli and Beach Club, "600 years later." ("It looks a little evil in there.") Goza and his cook, Blozor—who can knock off a cop's head with one blow—waylay patrons, who somehow wind up on the menu. One patron, Missy, however, turns out to be the High Priestess of the Brotherhood; she applies Super Glue and drill to Goza and takes over the place.... No actors (apart from Depuay, an over-actor), no gore effects (where other movies put makeup effects, *Goremet* has a before-and-after cut), no special effects (priests Goza and Lonezor duel with their hands), no wit (just double entendres like "I had a blonde here for lunch, but she's gone now"), and no retakes. This film looks up to Abysmal.

**GORGASM** Main Force Pictures (Flint Mitchell & Hugh Gallagher) 1990 color c90m. SP, D, Mus: Gallagher. Titles: Draculina Cine. Ref: TV: M. F. video. no Hound. no Martin. PT 13:51.

With Gabriela (Tara), Rik Billock, Paula Hendricks, Paula Gallagher, Mitchell, Debbie Patterson.

The sex-rag ad promises "Gorgasm—the ultimate climax." Tara—who takes "s&m to the max"—to a "level of love you'll never know"—makes good the promise by dancing topless for her bound victims, then slaughtering them. She decapitates one man with an "ingenious device".... Shot-on-tape quickie with minimal production values and ingenuity. Line-to-remember: "Love never lasts, but hate burns forever." Witless twist ending; title to remember.

**GORILLA, The** see *Sh! The Octopus*

**2 The GORILLA MYSTERY** 1930. Ref: TV. Jim Shapiro.

The "mankiller at large"—a monstrous, slobbering gorilla—abducts Minnie, and Mickey rescues her. Slight *King Kong* precursor. Closeups of the gorilla's maw, a flapping window shade, and cackling hens provide the (mild) shocks.

**GOROTICA** Hugh Gallagher 1992 color? 60m. SP,D,P: Gallagher. Ref: SFChron Dtbk 8/1/93: "story of a corpse-loving, bustier-wearing party girl." PT 17:62: aka *Wake of the Dead*. With Ghetty Chasun, Bushrude Gutterman, Dingo Jones.

**GOSHOGUN** see *Etranger, Time Alien*

**GOTHAM** Showtime-TV/Keith Addis & Phoenix 1988 color c105m. (*The Dead Can't Lie* - alt & B t). SP, D: Lloyd Fonvielle. Ph: Michael Chapman. Mus: George Clinton. PD: Carol Spier. SpFX: Michael Kavenagh. Mkp: Suzanne Benoit; (N.Y.) Jack Engel. Ref: TV. TV Week 8/21/88. V 10/19/88:64 (ad). MFB'89: 44-45. With Tommy Lee Jones, Virginia Madsen, Colin Bruce, Denis Stephenson, Kevin Jarre, Frederic Forrest, Chapman, Jack Creley.

"I feel like a ghost half the time." Detective Eddie Mallard (Jones) is hired by a financier (Bruce) who wants his wife, Rachel (Madsen), a "society dame" who died in 1975, to stop following him. Also featured: a *Diabolique* bathtub nightmare, and the myth that "the dead can't lie," which is shown to be just that, a myth (they lie, all the time), as well as, in this TV-movie, a wearyingly repeated line.... Overwritten, overwrought mixture of noir, fantasy, private eye, and romance elements thinks it's *Vertigo* in New York. It isn't, though it's occasionally half-clever, and always at least half-dumb. Even the movie's would-be-bravura images—e.g., the drowning Rachel's gloved hands sticking up out of the water—are too calculated, hokey.

**GOTHIC** (B) Vestron Pictures/Virgin Vision & Robert Fox (Penny Corke) 1986 ('87-U.S.) color 87m. D: Ken Russell. SP: Stephen Volk. Ph: Mike Southon. Mus: Thomas Dolby. PD: Christopher Hobbs. SpFX: Ace FX. Mkp Chief: Pat Hey. Sculptural FX: Graham High. Ref: TV: Vestron Video. MFB'87:47-8. V 12/10/86. ad. SFExam 5/1/87. SFChron 5/1/87. Phantom. Newman: "ludicrous." With Gabriel Byrne, Julian Sands, Natasha Richardson, Myriam Cyr, Timothy Spall, Linda Coggin (Turkish Mechanical Woman), Kiran Shah (Fuseli Monster).

"Conjure up your deepest, darkest fears." The Villa Diodati, Switzerland, June 16, 1816. Shelley (Sands), Byron (Byrne), Mary (Richardson), Claire (Cyr), and Polidori (Spall) conjure up a Knight Monster from a book, a ghost-tree shadow from an "oak tree struck by lightning," a "creature" (the "monster we have created") in a barn and at a window, a hairy beast on a horse, a monster-mask-and-cloak disguise, a seance, a satyr who seems to come to life in a painting, a premature burial (for Shelley), a vampire scene (with Byron), etc. Then: "What about your ghost story, Mary?"

There's also an hommage—a la *Son of Frankenstein*—to lightning, and the whole movie is an elaboration on the opening sequence in *Bride of Frankenstein*. In fact, the movie plays something like a cross between an old Universal monster movie and a new teens-in-a-cursed-house film, through which stalks a *Forbidden Planet* Id. Main motif: the interruption of a person about to kill himself or herself or someone else. A chaotic film, but the script gets a bit of the romance, violence, and sadness which must have characterized the occasion.

See also: *Haunted Summer. Remando al Viento.*

**GOVERNESS'S LOVE AFFAIR, The** see *New Governess, The*

**GRAMPIRE** see *My Grandpa Is a Vampire*

**GRAND TOUR** see *Disaster in Time*

La **GRANDE FROUSSE** (F) Attica-SNC 1964 b&w 92m. SP, D: Jean-Pierre Mocky. SP: also G. Klein. From Jean Ray's book. Ph: E. Shuftan. Ref: V 2/2/64: "does not completely jell." With Bourvil, Jean-Louis Barrault, Raymond Rouleau, Victor Francen, Jacques Dufilho.

"Small town that has a myth about a monster ... weird, inverted characters." *The Big Scare* - tr t.

**GRANDI MAGAZZINI** (I) 1986 color feature. D: Castellano and Pipolo. Ref: Palmerini: robots.

**GRANDMA'S HOUSE** Omega (Nico Mastorakis) 1989 (1988) color 88m. (*Grandmother's House* - alt t?). D & Exec P: Peter Rader. Story, SP, Ph, Exec P: Peter Jensen. Story: also Gayle Jensen. Mus: Nigel Holton, Clive Wright. FxCoord: Roger George. Digital FX: Mastorakis. Ref: TV: Academy Ent. video. V 3/29/89. Cinef 7/90. With Eric Foster, Kim Valentine, Len Lesser (Grandfather), Ida Lee (Grandmother), Brinke Stevens (hitchhiker).

"You just never know what you're gonna find back here." The mysterious hitchhiker who haunts the orphaned David (Foster) and Lynn (Valentine) on their grandparents' farm turns out to be a "crazy woman"—and David's mother, of course. "She's dangerous"—especially with a knife—and leaves Grandmother and the sheriff (R. J. Walker) bloody and dead. David takes care of Grandfather, with an ax, when he learns that the man is also his father.... A skeleton-in-every-closet family. Slapdash production is called *Grandma's House* in the opening credits, *Grandmother's House* in the end credits. Bland, predictable all-in-the-family slasher.

The **GRANNY** WarnerVision & Tapestry (Bernard-Zahavi) 1994 color 89m. Story, SP, D: Luca Bercovici. Story: also Sam Bernard. Ph: W. Pfister. Mus: K. Schmidt. PD: C. Kaufman. SpMkpFX: Christopher Nelson. MechFX: Eddie Surkin. Anima-

tronic Sup: Adam Behr. VisFxSup: Scott Enyart. SdFxSup: L. Mo Williams. Ref: TV: WV & Tapestry video. With Stella Stevens (Granny), Shannon Whirry, Sandy Helberg, Teresa Ganzel, Kedrick Wolf.

Sunlight mutates a youth elixir. Kitty sips the latter, mutates; Granny gulps it, dies, revives, and employs surgical saw, scalpel, mink stole, and scissors on her family.... Trite. Uninspired gore, regulation Freddyesque quips for Granny, arduous buildup to the horror. The opening *Exorcist* sequence at first seems meant parodistically, but apparently is just plain bad.

**GRAPES OF DEATH** see *Raisins de la Mort*

**GRAVE MISDEMEANOURS** see *Night Life*

**GRAVE SECRETS** SGE/Planet & New Sky (Michael Alan Shores) 1990 (1989) color 89m. D: Donald P. Borchers. SP: Jeffrey Polman, Lenore Wright. Mus: Jonathan Elias. SpMechFX: Eric Dressor et al. SpFxMkp: David Matherly. SpVisFX: (sup) Chris Nibley; Apogee; (opt fx sup) Roger Dorney; (anim sup) Clint Colver. Computer anim: Video Assist. Ref: TV. V 5/30/90. With Renee Soutendijk, Paul LeMat, David Warner, Lee Wink, Olivia Barash.

Homestead House, Indian Head, Crawford County. A double-exposure headless ghost—a "malevolent force"—possesses a trance medium (Warner) at a seance. There follows much ado about "that horrible night," years ago, when the incestuous father took his daughter's baby and buried it alive—all this seen in ectoplasmic "replay." The father retrieves his head and becomes, temporarily, corporeal, until the baby's spirit predictably finishes him off for good.... Pat, cut-and-dried, awful-secrets-of-the-past-laid-to-rest ghost story, with a couple eerie moments and effects.

**GRAVE SECRETS: THE LEGACY OF HILLTOP DRIVE** CBS-TV/Hearst Ent. (Freyda Rothstein Prods.) 1992 color c90m. (*The Black Hope Horror* - orig t). D: John Patterson. Tel & Sup P: Gregory Goodell. From the book *The Black Hope Horror* by Ben & Jean Williams & J. B. Shoemaker. Ph: Shelly Johnson. Mus: Patrick Williams. PD: Roy Alan Amaral. SpFxCoord: Joseph Mercurio. Ref: TV. TVG. With Patty Duke, David Selby, Kimberly Cullum, David Soul, Jonelle Allen.

"There are hundreds of bodies down there!" The family's new home on Hilltop Drive—which seems to have been built on the "center of the Bermuda Triangle"—proves to have been built on the "sacred ground" of a slave cemetery. Bothersome manifestations include a "crazy" automatic garage door, an invisible heavy breather, phantom heads, a mysteriously flushing toilet, and living shadows. These latter are the creepiest. (Compare the monster shadows in the Japanese *Sweet Home*, 1988.) The rest of the new homeowners' problems, both legal and ectoplasmic, are pretty familiar, as is the line "There is a rational explanation for all of this."

**GRAVEROBBERS** see *Dead Mate*

**GRAVEYARD** see *Raiders of the Living Dead*

**GRAVEYARD DISTURBANCE** (I) Reteitalia & Dania & Devon 1987 color/ws 96m. (*Dentro il Cimitrio*). SP, D: Lamberto Bava.

Story,SP: Dardano Sacchetti. Ph: G. Battaglia. Mus: Simon Boswell. AD: A. Geleng. SpMkpFX: Fabrizio Sforza. SpFX: Angelo Mattei. SpScenicFX: Ditta Ricci. OptFX: Aldo Mafera. Ref: TV: MV; Eng. version. Hardy/HM2. Jones: TV-movie. Newman: Bava's "worst movie to date." Palmerini: *Una Notte nel Cimitero.* With G. L. Thaddeus, Lea Martino, Beatrice Ring, Karl Zinny, G. Tognazzi.

"This must be the crypt." Ingredients here include a phantom hearse ... an apparent combo cemetery-tavern with a cursed underground crypt ... a fanged ghoul (a vampire?) in same who awakens other living dead ... and the mysterious tavern keeper. ("I am the Grim Reaper!") Five or six minutes of story stretched very, very thin. The nothing-happening first half is just lots of "This way! Let's go!" Second-half highlight: the Ghouls' Dinner Table — or, True Yuchh. (One of the guests is an eight-eyed lady.) Most amusing Incidental Creature: the big submersible eyeball.

**GRAVEYARD SHIFT** Shapiro Ent./Cinema Ventures & Bockner-Ciccoritti-Bergman (Lightshow) 1987 (1986) color c92m. SP, D: Gerard Ciccoritti. Mus: Nicholas Pike. SpFX: Tim Mogg. Graveyard: Simon St. Laurent. Ref: TV: Virgin Vision video. V 5/27/87. Morse: Canadian? Phantom. With Silvio Oliviero (Stephen Tsepes), Helen Papas, Cliff Stoker, Dorin Ferber, Lesley Kelly (Arbus), Frank Procopio (Mario Bava), Abby Cadaver (vampirette).

Stephen Tsepes, a vampire who works the night shift for the Black Cat Taxi Co., finds his lovers "when they're in the cycle of death." Michelle (Papas), a fare who has only a few months to live, is definitely in that cycle.... Pretentious, occasionally interesting vampire picture. The story is so fragmented, though, that it's hard to keep track of who's biting whom. (One vampire seems, at one point, to be reduced to biting herself.) And the annoyingly noisy, music-video-shrill soundtrack is often at odds with the drama of the scenes. Droll visual double entendre: At the end, it's "lady killer" Eric (Stoker), Michelle's husband, who unleashes the daylight which sets fire to Stephen's undead harem.

Follow-up: *Understudy, The.*

**THE GRAVEYARD SHIFT** see *Stephen King's Graveyard Shift*

**GRAVEYARD STORY** (Can.) Golden Screen Films Int'l. (Katarina Benedikt) 1990 color feature. SP, D: Bernard D. Benedikt. Ph: G. Hosek. Mus: Hare, McLay. AD: J. Stefanovic. SdFX: Tim Harford. Statue: Raymond Mackintosh. Ref: TV: VSOM. With John Ireland, Cayle Chernin, Adrian Paul, Keith Vinsonhaler, Alexandra Benedikt (young Dolly).

An "unknown force" at work in a house in Weston ... a little girl who vanishes ... and a crying statue in a cemetery.... Talky, unbelievable plot has little to do with the story's ghostly beginnings. Film plays like the original script was abandoned.

The **GREAT MOUSE DETECTIVE** Disney & Silver Screen Partners II (BV) 1986 anim color 97m. (*The Adventures of the Great Mouse Detective* - reissue t). SP, D: Jon Musker, Ron Clements et al. From the *Basil of Baker Street* books by Eve Titus and Paul Galdone. Ref: TV: vt. ad. SFChron 7/2/86: "monstrous cat." Berkeley Voice 7/16/86. SFExam 2/14/92: "remote-controlled robot." V 7/9/86: "might scare very small children." Sean Smiley.

Moderately entertaining animated mystery-adventure features various Gothic and Verne-ish elements, including an alternately cute and menacing (in big CU or in shadow) bat—a "maniacal little monster"—an airship, a thunderstorm or two, and the evil, Vincent Price-voiced Ratigan.

**GREEN LEGEND RAN** (J) AIC & Pioneer (Yamada-Aihara-Miura) 1992 anim color/ws 142m. D: Satoshi Saga. SP: Yu Yamamoto. Mus: Yoichiro Yoshikawa. Char Des & SupAnimD: Yoshimitsu Ohashi. AD: Ken Arai. SdFX: Daisuke Jinbo. Ref: TV: Pioneer video; Eng. dubbed.

"The Holy Mother might not be the Rodoists' god." Beings from an "as yet unknown outer space" land on Earth and drain the life from the planet. Lording it over the countryside: their staring, sarcophagus-like "Holy Mother." Equally weird: their followers, the Rodoists, and their archbishop, a giant cleric. At the end, "ugly mutant bishops" from "holy lands all around the world" gather and offer the blood sacrifice of a strange fish-thing. The upshot: "The Holy Mother transforms human beings into plants." But a necessary, elusive ingredient in the process: the silver-haired women with "strange powers".... Holy Mother, indeed. Animated epic is a daunting mixture of the conventional (hero out to avenge mother's murder apparently finds believed-dead father) and the highly unconventional (see above). If, dramatically, it's basically just dogged, visually, it's pretty consistently fascinating—the early, visualized nightmare re the morphing-Medusa-like things from the flood waters is just a hint of the bizarreness to come. *Green Legend Ran* is a *2001* wary of the next step in our evolution. The pagan and Christian imagery is just a cover for the secret life of alien plants that want to take over and convert the world to their photosynthetic creed. Bonus visual: the frozen waterfall.

The **GREEN MAN** (B-US.) BBC-TV & A&E (David Snodin) 1990 ('91-U.S.) color 150m. D: Elijah Moshinsky. Tel: Malcolm Bradbury, based on Kingsley Amis' novel. Ph: John McGlashan. Mus: Tim Souster. Des: Gerry Scott. VisFxDes: Stuart Brisdon, Colin Mapson. MkpDes: Jean Speak. OptFxSup: Roy Field. Ref: TV. TVG. V 6/3/91:55. Fango 122:33. with Albert Finney, Linda Marlowe, Michael Hordern, Nicky Henson.

"I will show you the true shape of your desires." The long-nosed ghost of Dr. Thomas Underhill (Michael Culver)—"old goat," "bad lad," magus, and alleged wife-killer of the Seventeenth Century—haunts The Green Man, an English country inn. Creepy conjunctions of the everyday and the nightmarish here. Choice chilly bits: inn owner Maurice's (Finney) stifled-hysteric reaction to his encounter with the ghost the first time the latter sees—and smiles at—him ... the insistent (animated) *Lost Weekend* bat-from-hell ... the strange, archaic-English note scrawled in the guest book ... the phrase (found in the bad doctor's diary) "Conjured up rare shapes, some consorting carnally" ... Maurice's version of the supernatural "crackle" heard about The Green Man ... and the visualized nightmare re the tree which wreaks gory mischief on a woman. Souster's meant-to-give-you-the-willies score for the most part succeeds.

Underhill, unfortunately, proves more unsettling, earlier, as a presence at a window than, later, as the incompetent tempter of Maurice. The film is better at tantalizing than fulfilling, though

Finney's skittish, overamped Maurice is an original creation. He plays most amusingly off the supernatural presences.

**GREEN MONKEY** see *Blue Monkey*

**GREEN SNAKE** (H.K.) Seasonal Film/Film Workshop 1993 ('95-U.S.) color/ws 99m. (*Ching Se*). D, P: Tsui Hark. Snake Concept: William Chang. Ref: TV: vt; Eng. titles. VW 23:19-20: Long Shong Video. SFChron 4/28/95. V 10/17/94. With Maggie Cheung, Joey Wang, Wu Kuo Chiu, Zhao Wen Zhou.

"The snakes and insects are everywhere." Two adventurous snake ladies find it hard not to revert to snake mannerisms—and actual giant-snake form. Sister White Snake is more successful at adopting a human guise and becomes romantically involved with a young human .... Plus: a monk's flying (cartoon) dragon ... a gent who can turn into an oversized (though not giant) spider ... apparent monkey people ... and a strange Land of the Deformed .... Effects by the truckload in this wry, enchantingly photographed and designed fantasy. *Green Snake* is, by turns, romantic, horrific, comic, and dramatic, and much of its charm lies in the deftness of these mood quick-changes—and in the lolling, gentle confusion of species on the part of Green Snake and White Snake. (They must apologize to the young man for being so "lazy in winter.")

**GREMLINS** WB/Amblin (Michael Finnell) 1984 color 104m. D: Joe Dante. SP: Chris Columbus. Ph: John Hora. Mus: Jerry Goldsmith. PD: James H. Spencer. Gremlins: Chris Walas. SpConsul: Jon Berg. Anim: (stopmo) Fantasy II; Visual Concept Eng. SpFxSup: Bob MacDonald Sr. SpVocalFX: Frank Welker et al. Mkp: Greg La Cava. Tech Adv: William Malone. Ref: screen. TV. MFB'84:382-3. Bill Warren. Mag/F&SF 2/85. Time 6/4/84. V 5/23/84. VV 6/12/84:48. SFExam 6/8/84. Bay Guardian 6/13/84. Phantom. Martin. Maltin '92. Scheuer. With Zach Galligan, Phoebe Cates, Hoyt Axton, Polly Holliday, Frances Lee McCain, Judge Reinhold, Dick Miller, Keye Luke, Glynn Turman, Scott Brady, Edward Andrews, Jackie Joseph, Don Steele, Belinda Balaski, Kenneth Tobey, Chuck Jones, Jim McKrell (Lew Landers).

"They don't start out vicious at first." They start out as a cuddly little mogwai, whose only weakness is a passion for race-car driving. On contact with water, though, the skin, or fur, of the mogwai generates new gremlins, which, in their second, post-cocoon stage, are mischief-making monsters that proceed to frolic and tear apart the town of Kingston Falls. Incidentals: a time machine and Robby the Robot (Larry Schulze), with some *Forbidden Planet* dialogue....

Dante's mischievous, uninhibited gremlins are like an explosion of human pettiness, maliciousness, etc.—this movie might be dedicated to the spirit of Warner Brothers' Tasmanian Devil. Kingston Falls=Idsville. The gremlins wear our garments, act out our nuttiness, and behave like kids, or adult kids. On the general subject of raw, unleashed animal energy, *Gremlins* (a more imaginative *Impulse*) is cannily pitched between the horrified and the celebratory. Harlan Ellison rightly called the toddler-angled *Gremlins* ad campaign irresponsible, but the film itself is nothing if not responsible and right on the money, psychoanalytically speaking. Even the Dolby Stereo contributes to the effect of bubbling-over rambunctiousness: At times, the snuffling, chor-

tling gremlins seem to have tumbled off the screen. One problem: The gremlins are we, and thus the actors here seem extraneous.

Sequel: *Gremlins 2*. See also: *Ghostbusting. Once upon a Time. Puppetoon Movie, The.*

**GREMLINS 2: THE NEW BATCH** WB/Amblin (Michael Finnell) 1990 color 106m. D: Joe Dante. SP: Charlie Haas. Ph: John Hora. Mus: Jerry Goldsmith. PD: James Spencer. Gremlin FX: Rick Baker. VisFX: (sup) Dennis Michelson; (stopmo) Doug Beswick; (anim) VCE/Peter Kuran. SpFxSup: Ken Pepiot. Anim: Chuck Jones. Matte FX: Matte World. SdFX: Mark Mangini, David Stone. Opt: Pacific Title. SpVoices: Frank Welker, Howie Mandel, Tony Randall. Ref: screen. V 6/6/90. MFB'90:224-5. Sacto Union 6/15/90. Sacto Bee 6/17/90. 6/19/90. Fango 7/90:40-43. SFExam 6/15/90. NYT 6/15/90. SFChron Dtbk 6/10/90. Sacto News & Review 6/14/90. Scheuer. Martin. Maltin '92. With Zach Galligan, Phoebe Cates, John Glover, Robert Prosky (Grandpa Fred), Robert Picardo, Christopher Lee (Dr. Catheter), Haviland Morris, Dick Miller, Jackie Joseph, Gedde Watanabe, Keye Luke, Kathleen Freeman, Hulk Hogan, Paul Bartel, Rick Ducommun, John Astin, Henry Gibson, Kenneth Tobey, Page Hannah, Leonard Maltin, Dick Butkus, Bubba Smith, Archie Hahn, Gray Daniels, Saachiko.

"The building is completely screwed up today!" The "green things" run amok in Manhattan's Clamp Center. This bizarre "pest infestation" yields, among other things, a "Phantom of the Opera" gremlin, a bat-gargoyle gremlin, a huge spider gremlin, an electricity gremlin, and—at the end, as the massed gremlins are electrocuted—"burnt meatloaf." Best prop: the reading glasses which the brain gremlin mysteriously sprouts. Best warning label: "Acid—Do Not Throw in Face." Best advice (from the Wall Street gremlins): "Buy!" Best TV test pattern: the one with the gremlin in it. Wittiest mean-gremlin use of nice-gremlin Gizmo: the experiments in velcro. Best movie on TV: "The Attack of the Octopus People." (Octa-Man, where are you?)

*Gremlins 2*—or 1,000 More Fun Things for Gremlins To Do—is more single-mindedly celebratory of explosive energy than is *Gremlins 1*. But though it is thus, in a sense, half the movie the first one was, it's also twice as manically inventive, and yields at least twice as many cherishable comic-horror moments. All that holds the film together is noise—*Gremlins 2* probably sets a new record for "busses," comic and shock. And if the setting-up scenes spend too much footage on elementary, second-time-around gremlin grossouts, the creatures, later on, expand their repertoire beyond the vacuously offensive and try their hand, or claw, at Big Time Musicals, mock-erudite blather (thanks to the brain gremlin), etc. The movie plays like highlights from nine *Gremlins* films.

**GRIETA, La** see *Endless Descent*

**GRIM PRAIRIE TALES** East-West (Richard Hahn) 1990 color 94m. SP, D: Wayne Coe. Mus: Steve Dancz. SpFX: (number 1 and 3) Jill Rockow; (number 2) Mkp&FxLabs; (number 4) Mike McCracken. Anim: Anthony Zierhut, Wayne Coe. Ref: TV. V 5/30/90. SFChron 11/21/90; Dtbk 11/18/90. SFExam 11/23/90. TVG 1/5/91. With James Earl Jones, Brad Dourif, Will Hare, Marc McClure, Michelle Joyner, William Atherton, Lisa Eichhorn, Wendy Cooke, Scott Paulin.

"Do you wanna hear a story?" Four tales re a dying Indian who bites a trespasser (who is then buried alive) ... a "pregnant" woman who sucks a man into her womb ... a KKK type ... and a gunfighter "haunted" by a victim. Talky, fragmented, basically unbuyable omnibus chiller banks heavily on sheer quirkiness. Abrupt endings make you wonder if you missed a reel, though the ending of the tale re the womb woman qualifies as stunningly abrupt. Redeeming features include a bizarre bit of animation in story four, and Jones' last line.

The **GRIM REAPER** Ormond 1976 feature. SP, D: Ron Ormond. Ref: Filmfax 28:55, 56: "religious horror picture."

**GRINNING EVIL DEATH** Mike McKenna, Bob Sabiston 199-? anim short. Ref: SFChron 4/16/93: "spider monster."

**GROTESQUE** Concorde/United Filmmakers (Lane, Morrell) 1988 (1987) color 79m. Concept & D: Joe Tornatore. SP: Mikel Angel. Mus: Loose, Cookerly. SpFxMkp: John Naulin. Assoc P: Linda Blair, Lincoln Tate. Ref: TV. V 10/26/88: "forgettable." Phantom: "flamboyantly awful." McCarty II: "truly harrowing" scenes, but "goes downhill." With Linda Blair, Tab Hunter, Donna Wilkes, Guy Stockwell, Luana Patten, Robert Z'Dar, John Goff, Mike Lane, Jeff Richard (Wolf Man), Don Tornatore (ghoul).

Plastic surgeon avenges himself on punks by surgically mutilating them. Plus: a horror-movie-makeup master, a mutant, and "Frankenstein" references.

**GROUND ZERO** see *Defcon-4*

**GROUNDHOG DAY** Col/Trevor Albert (C. O. Erickson/Harold Ramis) 1993 color 103m. SP, D: H. Ramis. Story, SP: Danny Rubin. SpFX: Tom Ryba. SpProsthMkp: Art Anthony. Ref: TV: Col-TriStar HV. V 2/8/93. SFExam 2/12/93. SFChron 2/12/93. 3/18/93.

The fantasy version of the science-fiction premise of *12:01* (which see). From another angle, Bill Murray's Phil is a more inventive variation on his "Scrooge." Still, despite hilarious sequences, the movie is not quite buyable, beginning with both Phil's Cynical and Andie MacDowell's Rita's Sweet. He changes, but Ramis and Rubin aren't Dickens and they run into problems that the master somehow avoided re the malleability of character. Perhaps if one could see something of the later Phil Reformed in the earlier Phil Unredeemed....

**GU JING YOU HUN** see *Ghost of the Mirror*

The **GUARD FROM UNDERGROUND** (J) 1992 color/ws 97m. (*Jigoku No Keibiin*). Ref: TV: Japan Video; no Eng.

This is a deliberate, nice-looking film, with creepy subjective camerawork and score. But the brutal, super-strong "guard" is better heard than seen, and the emphasis on his murders gets to be monotonous and ugly. Eerie: the clanging sounds from behind the steel door.

The **GUARDIAN** (H.K.) 1983 color c94m. D: Yu Han-Cien. Ref: TV: Ocean Shores Video; Eng. titles. With Yuei Yang, Wu Hsiao-Fei, Chiang Bin, Pan Cien-Lin.

Ingredients: the City Gods of the afterlife, who right the wrongs of life and keep their citizens in line ... an avenging ghost of the river, the nix, and the Geographic Ghost, his good friend ... a sequence in which flying snake and dragon things and masks beset two robbers ... an intimidating, flying tiger charm ... a "water separating" rhino horn ... and a ghost named Rhadamanthus Wen.... Fantasy film with spooky elements is by turns charming and silly, mostly the latter, until the later, fantasy scenes. The living are noble, self-sacrificing, entirely admirable characters; the ghosts are a looser, more entertaining bunch.

The **GUARDIAN** Univ (Joe Wizan) 1990 color 98m. D: William Friedkin. SP, Co-P: Dan Greenburg. SP: also Steven Volk. From Greenburg's story "The Nanny." Ph: John A. Alonzo. Mus: Jack Hues. PD: Gregg Fonseca. SpFxMkp: Matthew Mungle. SpFX: Phil Cory. Opt: (des) Pablo Ferro; (fx) Cinema Research. SdFX: (sp) John P; Mark Mangini. Ref: TV. MFB'90:262. V 4/25/90. ad. Sacto Bee 4/30/90. SFChron 6/4/93. With Jenny Seagrove, Dwier Brown, Carey Lowell, Brad Hall, Miguel Ferrer, Xander Berkeley.

"Soon it'll be time to go to the Sacred Forest." Camilla (Seagrove) — a nanny who at first "makes Snow White look like Freddy Krueger"—haunts a tree, makes her victims' bloodstains vanish, and seeks a baby with "pure blood." The dogs or coyotes that protect her lead a Night of the Living Coyotes siege on a house and, later, a car.... A horror story so thin that it seems that half its running time is expended on irrelevant action. Some good night-shadow work.

**GUARDIAN OF THE ABYSS** see *Hammer House of Horror Double Feature*

The **GUARDIAN OF HELL** (I) Film Concept Group/Cinemec (Arcangelo Picchi) 1980 ('85-U.S.) color 85m. (*L'Altro Inferno. The Other Hell* - alt t). D: Stefan Oblowsky. Story, SP: Claudio Fragasso. Story: also Bruno Mattei. Ph: Giuseppe Berardini. Mus: Goblin. Mkp: Giuseppe Ferranti. Ref: TV: Vestron Video; Eng. dubbed. V 12/25/85. Horacio Higuchi. Scheuer. Palmerini: S. Oblowsky-B. Mattei. Newman: *Il Altro Inferno*. With Franca Stoppi, Carlo De Mejo, Francesca Carmeno, Susan Forget, Frank Garfield or Garfeeld, Paola Montenero, Sandy Samuel, Andrew Ray.

"The devil's no longer in hell—he's in heaven!" The secret of the "faceless" nun involves stigmata ... a mad nun who semi-surgically removes the genitals of a bad dead nun, then stabs a live one ... a gardener named Boris ... catacombs littered with skulls, bones, and bald hanging dolls ... priest flambé ... a fistful of maggots ... and vicious dogs. A flashback helps solve the mystery: One nun's newborn, the "daughter of satan," scalded in a pot of water, made her attacker choke herself to death. With her ESP, satan's daughter can also revive the dead.... Dreary mystery/gore combo. Script just marks time until the flashback. Everyone ends up dead or (in the case of the investigative priest) mad. Vapid score.

**GUERRA DE LOS MAGOS, La** see *Wizards of the Lost Kingdom*

**GUERRIERI DELL'ANNO 2027/2033** see *New Gladiators, The*

**GUERRIERO DEL MONDO PERDUTO, Il** see *Warrior of the Lost World*

**GUESS WHO'S COMING FOR CHRISTMAS?** NBC-TV/Corapeake & the Polson Co. (Fox Unicorn Inc.) 1990 color c90m. D: Paul Schneider. Tel: Blair Ferguson. Story & Exec P: Beth Polson. Mus: W. G. Walden. SpFX: Manny Epstein. Mkp: Art Harding. Opt: Howard Anderson. SdFX: Glen Glenn. Ref: TV. TVG. V 12/24/90:41. With Richard Mulligan, Beau Bridges, Barbara Barrie, Paul Dooley.

Stranger (Bridges) who says he's from another planet proves it at the end by giving a man (Mulligan) his used spaceship. Casual, folksy, sentimental.

**GUESS WHO'S FOR DINNER?** c1983 c3m. D: Kathy Zielinski. Ref: TV. TVG: on Focus Film Festival. "Spinach monster" attempts to force itself down little boy's throat, fails—but there's always tomorrow.... Charming, stylish comic short.

**GUI AN YAN** (H.K.) Clic Ltd. 1983 color 102m. (aka *Obsessed*). SP, D, Co-Ph: Henry Chan. Ref: Hardy/HM: "intelligent." With Eddie Chan, Anna Ho, Alexander Wong, Rainbow Ching.

Woman's spirit possesses fireman.

**GUI MI ZIN QIAO** see *Awakening* (1994)

**GUI ZHUO, Bi** see *Ghost Snatchers, The*

**GUILTY AS SIN** BV/Hollywood Pictures (Martin Ransohoff) 1993 color 104m. D: Sidney Lumet. SP: Larry Cohen. Ph: Andrzej Bartkowiak. Mus: Howard Shore. PD: Philip Rosenberg. Ref: V 6/14/93: "visceral windup" ... Lewton atmosphere-broken-up-by-"monster" ... stalker/ladykiller. SFChron 6/4/93: "intelligent." With Rebecca DeMornay, Don Johnson, Stephen Lang, Jack Warden.

**GUINEA PIG, VOL. ONE** (J) 1989 color feature (*Chiniku No Hana* - orig t of #1). Ref: TV: EVS; no Eng.; shot-on-tape. V 9/20/89:83: *Flowers of Flesh & Blood* apparently shown separately. Weisser/JC. *Za Ginipiggy.*

1. "Flowers of Flesh & Blood." Tape begins with a severed-hand effect, in rather more clinical detail than necessary. Your reviewer was not able to continue much beyond this point, even in fast-forward.

2. "Mermaid Live inside the Manhole." Artist uses mermaid from sewer as model, takes advantage of her strange wounds to do a *Color Me Blood Red* with his mermaid painting. Faithful reviewer called it a day at the scene with the razor blade.

**GUINEA PIG, VOL. THREE** (J) JHV/Satoru Ogura c1990? color feature (*The Guinea Pig 2* - cr t). SP, D: Kazuhito Kuramoto. SP: also M. Mutsuki, Y. Iwanami. Story: K. Tani, S. Ogura. Ref: TV: EVS; no Eng. With T. Hino, Mio Takagi, T. Taguchi, Yumi Iori, Mirei.

1. "Androids of Notre Dame." A dwarf scientist, unhappy with his melting android product, slices it up. Later: mechanical problems with the new Android Head. More Gore Dares re cutting and oozing, along the lines of *The Brain That Wouldn't Die*.

2. "He Never Dies." Black comedy re a guy who takes to experimenting on himself surgically, with unlikely results.

**GUINEA PIG, VOL. FOUR** (J) HV c1989 color . Ref: TV: Video Exchange; no Eng. EVS: also repeats "Mermaid Live inside the Manhole."

"Lucky Sky Diamond." A madwoman "sees" worms, or caterpillars, in her IV bottle, and centipedes in a sliced melon. Shot-on-tape *Repulsion*-plus, or minus, includes stunts with eyeballs, intestines, and brain surgery not suitable for detailed recapping in a family checklist. Fast Forward helps. Weisser/JC: "Shiroi Kabe No Kekkon" or "Lucky Star Diamond."

**GULLIVER MICKEY** UA/Disney 1934 anim 7m. D: Burt Gillett. Ref: TV. Jim Shapiro. LC. Maltin/OMAM.

Mickey Mouse tells his assembled little nephews about his journey to a "strange land" where he plays with Lilliputians, while they fiercely fight him, and a cackling huge spider does a Godzilla on their town. Kinda cute cartoon.

**GULLIVER'S TRAVELS** see *Laputa* (M). *Laputa* (P).

**GUNBUSTER: AIM FOR THE TOP!** (J) U.S. Renditions/Bandai/Gainax & Artmic & Victor & B.M.D. 1988 ('90-U.S.) anim color 28m. (*Gunbuster! Gunbuster. Gunbusters!* - all alt ts). D & AD: Hideaki Anno. Story, SP: Toshio Okada. Story: also Shin Unosawa, Isamu Senda. Ph: Okino, Watanabe. Mus: Kohei Tanaka. AD: also Higuchi. SpFX: Yoshiki Okumura. SdFX: Etsuji Yamada. Mecha Des: (as per vc box) Kazunuki Miyabu (cr list Miyatake, Ohata). Ref: TV: Emotion video; Eng. titles. PT 8:44. Martin. Animag 11:19-24: 1st of 6 OAVs. 4:2: aka *Aim for the Top!* Voices: Noriko Hidaka, Norio Wakamoto.

"Go with Amano into the galaxy!" In the year 2015, Noriko Takaya becomes a cadet in the RX Program, established to combat the same aliens which attacked her father's spaceship, the Lukushiyon. ("The fate of humanity depends on it!") What at first seems to be simply a futuristic-maudlin, Girl's Own story of young girls conditioning themselves to operate giant robots, or RX Trainers, turns into a parody of the *Rocky* movies. (Here, Coach is a coach, while "Rocky" is a giant, teenage-girl-operated robot doing wind sprints and push-ups.)

**GUNBUSTER: THE CHALLENGE OF THE FEARLESS GIRL GENIUS!** (J) U.S. Renditions/Gainax & Artmic & Victor & B. M. D. 1989 ('90-U.S.) anim color 25m. For credits, see previous entry. Ref: TV: Emotion video; Eng. titles. Animag 6:5: 2nd in the OAV series; here called *Aim for the Top!*

Takaya, aboard the spaceship *Exelion,* in the Arm of Perseus (in the Milky Way), finds alien remains and her father's lost ship. Plotty second entry in the series introduces the female "genius at space combat," Jung-Freud.

**GUNDAM** see the following titles and titles under *Mobilesuit Gundam* and *S. D. Gundam*

**GUNDAM F91** (J) Shochiku/Sunrise (Masutake Films) 1991 anim color 115m. (aka *Mobilesuit Gundam F91*). D: Yoshiyuki Tomino. Based on the final volume of a novel series by Tomino. Anim D: Ken-O Kitahara. Mecha Des: Kunio Okawara. Ref: TV:

Bandai/Emotion video; no Eng.; some animation by Korea's Park Prods.? V. Max 3:14-22. V 4/29/91:115: playing. Voices: Koji Tsugitani, Yumi Toma, Masaaki Maeda.

Ingredients, in the year UC 0123: the four Frontier space colonies ... the Earth Military Forces, which take on ... the Crossbone Vanguard, which intends bloodily to unite the colonies and all spacenoids to form Cosmo Babylon ... the Space Ark, a training ship ... the Gundam F91, which is equipped with (a) a bio-computer that enables its pilot to "interact directly with the mecha," (b) "variable speed beam rifles, or Vespers" (V. Max), and (c) the "psychomuu," which taps its pilot's psychic energy ... the tentacled Lafressia, thought-controlled mobile armor ... and the Bug, an "anti-personnel weapon designed specifically for mass slaughter."

Lively, fanatically-detailed space opera for the most part successfully distracts attention from the fact that it's dramatically elementary. In one bizarrely amusing sequence, two or three metal "Godzillas" incidentally wreck a city as they battle each other.

**GUNDAM 0080: A WAR IN THE POCKET** (J) Emotion/Bandai 1989 anim color 30m. each (aka *Mobile Suit Gundam 0080*). D: Fumihiko Takayama. SP: Hiroyouki Yamaga. Mecha Des: Yutaka Izubuchi. Ref: Animag 6:5. 9:33-39: 6 OAVs.

The Jion fleet vs. the Federation fleet.

**GUNDAM 0083: REMINISCENCE OF LIGHT** (J) Sunrise 1992 anim color 119m. (aka *Mobile Suit Gundam 0083: Reminiscence of Light*). Ref: TV: Emotion video; no Eng. V. Max 2:5.

Recent *Gundam* movie opens with flashbacks to *Gundam 0083: Stardust Memory*, but the new footage looks more interesting, and occasionally threatens to out-*Jedi Jedi*. Much repairing, testing, and deploying of mobile suits by the top guns of outer space. The elaborate paraphernalia includes some intriguing space clutter—spaceships, suits, asteroids, laser swords, a camera, and various unidentified floating objects. Plainly needed: a space-traffic cop. The various spaceships feature a startling variety of attachments, adjustments, extensions, etc.

**GUNDAM 0083: STARDUST MEMORY** (J) Bandai/Emotion (Sunrise) 1990 anim color 81m. (aka *Operation Mobile Suit Gundam 0083: Stardust Memory — Mission 1*). D: Mitsuko Kase. Sp: Yoshiyuki Tomino, Hajime Yadachi. Mecha Des: Hajime Katori, Mika Mitsuki. Ref: TV: Emotion video; no Eng. Animag 12:7: comprises first three entries (27m. each) in a 26-episode OAV series. V. Max 3:4. 4:3.

Follow-up to *Mobilesuit Gundam* (which see) begins in Australia, where Lt. Anavel Gato, of the Delars Force—which wants to revive the Jion Empire—steals the Gundam Test Unit II, which is armed with an "experimental atomic bazooka" (Animag).... This seems like a standard robot-battle epic, with some pretty graphics. Score features bland pop music for the first space battle, awe music for the first look at the new mobile suit.

**GUNHED** (J) Toho & Sunrise 1989 color/ws 99m. (*Ganhedo*). D: Masato Harada. SpFX:(d) K. Kawakita; (coord) H. Yamaguchi, K. Ichihashi; N. Watanabe; (anim) Keita Amamiya. Mecha Des: S. Kawamori, H. Hanyu. OptFX: M. Nakamura. Ref: TV: vt; some Eng. narration, dialogue, titles. V/Mifed '89:333 (ad).

Markalite 3:16-19. Animag 11:5. 6:4: also Bandai & Kadokawa involvement. Weisser/JC. With Masahiro Takashima.

In the year 2005, on a "tiny volcanic island," the Cybortech Corporation begins manufacturing the "most advanced robots ever known." Twenty years later, Kyron 5—the super-computer which controls the complex—declares war on the world, and the Allies send a Gunhed battalion to fight Kyron and its "last line of defense," Aerobot. The Great Robot War has begun.

Exuberant action/effects spectacular has an effect-a-second pace and an *Alien,* lost-in-technology feel to its human interaction. Highlights include the hovering, hamburger-shaped sentinels, the activation of the "voltage barriers," and the demonstration of the step-by-step mechanics necessary for getting a rusty, human-operated giant robot semi-functional and ambulatory. The exhilarating effects tell the story; the actors are just along for the wild ride.

**GUNNM-RUSTY ANGEL** and **GUNMM-TEARS SIGN** see *Battle Angel*

**GUSTIZIERE DEL BRONX, Il** see *Bronx Executioner, The*

**GUWAPINGS: THE FIRST ADVENTURE** (Fili) Regal Films (Douglas Quijano) 1992 color 100m. SP, D: J. J. Reyes. Ph: Jun Pereira. Mus D: N. Buencamino. PD: T. Aldana. Prosth: Andrea Manahan. Mkp: S. Tolentino. SdFX: R. Capule. Titles: Cinemagic. Ref: TV: Regal video; no Eng. With Joey Marquez, Anjo Yllana, C. Villarroel, S. Cruz, Erik Cayetano.

Vampire men and women from a rather-too-well-lit, old, not-so-dark house besiege a house inhabited by humans. Horror-comedy has a ridiculous amount of screaming and running around and baring of fangs. Some of the vampires fly; all seem to leap. Fun sound effects and eerie shadow effects with a spook lady's shawl. Apparently irrelevant: a horde of zombies.

**GUY: AWAKENING OF THE DEVIL** (J) A.D. Vision/Media Station & Studio Max & AIC (Humming & UP & FRIENDS/Maruyama) 1990 anim color c40m. Story, D, AD: Yorihisa Uchida. Mus: Kashihara. Mecha Des: Tomimatsu. Monster Des: Yukihiko Makino. Anim: E. Akiyama. SdFX: Taback Co. Ref: TV: ADV video; Eng. titles. vc box: *Guy II* features a werewolf.

"A haunted house!" Plasmid, the virus-like DNA of the prison planet Geo—which is a living organism—spawns monsters with *Alien* tentacles and teeth, while hero Guy also turns into a glowing-eyed fighting monster .... Routine, gratuitous gore-and-sex in this first of an OAV series.

**GUYS IN GHOST'S HAND** (H.K.) 1990? color feature. D: Stanley Wing Siu. Ref: Weisser/ATC2: "vampires, zombies, and ghosts ... mindless." With Alex Fong, Wu Ma.

**The GUYVER** (J) 1987 anim. Ref: Animag 7:4: OAV; from Y. Takaya's "Bio-Booster Buyver" manga; the '89 version is a remake.

**The GUYVER 1** (J) Emotion & Frontier/Network 1989 anim color 26m. (*Kyoshoku Soko Gaiba*. aka *Bio-Booster Armored*

*Guyver - Volume One*). D: Koichi Ishiguro. Created by Yoshiki Takaya. Ref: TV: Bandai Video; no Eng. Markalite 3:86-7.

"Bio boosters" here transform humans into huge monsters.... A tentacled mess from one booster-can envelopes the hero, high school student Sho, who when next seen is The Guyver, a monster who will apparently right wrongs (rather than vice versa). At the end, Sho cries out, and The Guyver guise pulls up off him as if it were a spirit and sinks into a lake.... Standard *Swamp Thing*-like monster-mongering, though stylistically drawn and scored. The score itself is quite sophisticated compared to the push-button pop music over beginning and end credits.

**The GUYVER 2** (J) Bandai 1989 anim color 30m. Ref: Animag 9:4.

**The GUYVER: MYSTERIOUS SHADOW - GUYVER III** (J) U.S. Renditions/Movic & K.S.S.(N. Kato) 1989 ('92-U.S.) anim color 30m. (aka *Bio-Booster Armor Guyver, Vol. 3*). FX: S. Watanabe; (sd) K. Suyama. For other credits, see following entry. Ref: TV: L. A. Hero video; Eng. dubbed. Animag 7:4.

After the second Guyver has been destroyed, the armor-plated, triple-horned Zerbebuth—supposedly the "most powerful Zoanoid" and "biologically engineered to be a hyper-Zoanoid"—shows up to fight Sho/Guyver 1. Zerberuth, easily defeated, then makes way for a whole shape-shifting monster gang—"real hyper-Zoanoids".... Lively but basically clunky monster-mation.

**The GUYVER: ATTACK OF THE HYPER ZOANOID TEAM FIVE** (J) U.S. Renditions/Takaya Prods. & K.S.S. & Bandai & MOVIC & Tokuma Shoten (N. Kato) 1989 ('92-U.S.) anim color c30m. (aka *Bio-Booster Armor Guyver, Vol. 4*). D: Koichi Ishiguro. Story: Y. Takaya. SP: A. Sanjo. Ph: S. Morishita. Mus: R. Koroku. AD: J. Higashi. FX: H. Murakami; (sp) D. Jinbo; (sd) Oda, Adachi; (mus) K. Inoue. Ref: TV: L. A. Hero video; Eng. dubbed; OAV.

"Whoever comes in contact with the Guyver ends up getting murdered." As part of its cover-up assignment, the Hyper Zoanoid Team Five destroys Sho's school with destructive rays. One Zoanoid features a "wave vibration" slicing weapon; another, Gaster, discharges "liquid explosive" missiles from its forearms. Coming to Sho/Guyver's aid: the telepathic Guyver 3. Busy, involved monster video.

**The GUYVER 6** (J) Bandai 1990 anim color 30m. Ref: Animag 10:4: last of this OAV series. Japan Video.

**The GUYVER, ACT II** (J) Bandai & Hero 1991 anim color 55m. each. Ref: V Max 2:5: 3 OAVs. 3:4. 4:3. Japan Video.

**The GUYVER** New Line (Brian Yuzna/Imperial Ent.)/The Guyver Prods. 1991 color 88m. (aka *Mutronics—The Movie*). D & Creature FX: Steve Wang, Screaming Mad George. SP: Jon Purdy, based on characters created by Yoshiki Takaya. Ph: Levie Isaacks. Mus: Matthew Morse. PD: M. C. Jacobs. SpFX: (sup) Michael Deak; (coord) T. C. Rainone. Bkgd Creatures: Asao Goto. Mech FX: Jake McKinnon, Tim Ralston; F/X Concepts, Ken Tarallo. KeySpFxMkp: Wayne Toth. Min Sup: Wyatt Weed. Stopmo: Ted Rae. Ref: TV. Sacto Bee 10/30/92. SFChron Dtbk 1/17/93. Markalite 3:72-5. V 10/21/91:24 (ad, as *Mutronics—*

*The Movie*). With Mark Hamill, Vivian Wu, Jack Armstrong, Jimmy Walker, Michael Berryman, Peter Spellos, Spice Williams, Jeffrey Combs, Linnea Quigley (scream queen), David Gale (Balcus).

"I am the Guyver!" The Guyver is the "most dangerous technology since the atom bomb" and the "most lethal weapon ever conceived." An "organic mechanism" created by aliens which "becomes a protective suit of armor," it transforms our teenaged hero into an armored warrior ("Mr. Robocop"). The head bad guy, Balcus—who has mind-control powers—wants the secret, and at the end mutates into an XTRO/dragon-like "Zoanoid." Meanwhile, Mark Hamill mutates into an insect-horror and dies, and all Balcus' henchmen seem to be shape-shifters. In monster form, they're Six Variations on a Creature from the Black Lagoon Theme. Balcus also keeps, in display cases, "warriors developed by aliens from the human species—werewolves, Minotaurs, vampires".... If, visually, this Western version of the Japanese monsterama is an amusing conglomeration of suits and effects, dramatically, it's a fizzle. There's a limp, New Camp casualness to its "Yo, man!" monsters.

**GUYVER II** (U.S.-J) Biomorphs & L.A. Hero (Yoshiki Takaya & G II & Steve Wang & Guyver) 1994 color c100m. (*Guyver: Dark Hero* - cr t). Story, D, P: Steve Wang. SP: Nathan Long. Ph: M. Wojciechowski. Mus: Les Claypool III. PD: G. Peirson [sic]. CreatureFxSup: Steve Wang, Moto Hata. MechAnim: Bud McGrew. Computer Graphics: John Teska. Computer Char Anim: Robert Frye. Physical FX: Ken Tarallo. MinSup: Dean Satkowski. Computer Laser Anim: Digital Artwork. Title Anim: Bret Mixon. SdFxDes: Setrakian, Allen. Ref: TV. V 9/27/93:21. With David Hayter, Kathy Christopherson, Bruno Giannotta, Christopher Michael, Anthony Houk (Guyver), Brian Simpson (Volker & Crane Zoanoids).

"All the people who work for Kronos can change into monsters called Zoanoids." Besides the latter, this sequel features a hero who does a Hamlet ("I'm not cut out for this") ... Utah cave drawings ... reports of a werewolf-at-large ... and a spaceship-in-a-cave.... All the (not considerable) imagination here went into the design of the ship. Too-busy monster suits; not-busy-enough story.

**GUZUU** (J) Rocco Co./Masuda Co. (Yoji Matsumoto) 1987 color 40m. D: "Gailah" (rn: Yougi Matumoto). Ph: E. Ozawa. Mus: N. Izumimori. SpAD: J. Takagi. SpMkpFX: Suezo Sugimoto. Ref: TV: VSOM; Eng. titles; *Guzoo: The Creatures God Threw Away*. Markalite 3:87: "about average"; Guzoo-tr t. VSOM: aka *Girl Trap*. With Yumiko Ishikawa, Tomoko Maruyama, Naomi Kajitani.

Monster Guzuu, from the mirror, uses its tendrils to drink blood, sucks college girl into mirror "to a grisly fate." (Markalite) "Something came out of the mirror." Film begins perfunctorily, but has a nice inside-the-mirror payoff and a clever kicker. This writhing, wriggling horror is a lively creature, partaking of the qualities of the fly-trap, the octopus, and the leech. The movie itself is, at times, like a live-action *Wandering Kid*.

**GWAR-PHALLUS IN WONDERLAND** Metal Blade 1992. D: Distortion Wells. Ref: PT 13:47: "lots of monsters."

**GWEN, OR THE BOOK OF SAND** (F) Les Films de la Demoiselle, Les Films A2 & Ministere de la Culture 1985 anim color 62m. (*Gwen, Ou Le Livre du Sable*). SP, D: Jean-Francois Laguionie. SP: also Jean-Paul Gaspari. Mus: Pierre Alrand; (elec) Daniel Arfib; (fx) Jess Gibergues, Richard Kronand-Martinet. Des: Bernard Palacios. SdFX: Jonathan Liebling. Ref: screen: Eng. titles; Gaumont Int'l. PFA notes 3/29/86. V 5/8/85. SF Film Fest '86. no Stanley. Voices: Michel Robin, Lorella Di Cicco, Arman Babel, Raymond Jourdan.

"The story of a legendary time." In a desolate future, desert nomads huddle underground, at night, while the "Makou," or "watchman"—a sort of glowing tornado—deposits outsized artifacts of civilization on the sands above. The people use the giant dressers, chairs, telephones, shoes, beds, etc., during the day, for shelter and recreation. When the Makou takes away a boy with it, his mother and his girl friend, the thirteen-year-old Gwen Logan, follow, to the Land of the Long Dead. There, Gwen discovers the Cult of the Mail Order Catalogue. Its hymns to watering cans and other mail-order items summon up, in the Makou (in its semi-dormant state), giant-sized versions of the objects invoked.

The three "dancing" red lights in the sky (the aged Roseline explains to Gwen) are man-made, intended to foster the illusion of a living heavens. Light in this future land is furnished by luminous scorpions in bottles and by glowing moths in Chinese lanterns. On stilts, the nomads chase ostriches and then eat their feathers. The boy's dreams, which prove too much for his head, unfold in space, above him, like a cartoon dialogue-balloon. Roseline, at one point, dozes inside a giant, half-open pocket watch. A desert pillow fight leaves feathers floating, eerily, against a full moon. Gwen and the boy play in and around a giant watering can. (It tips, and he drops out the spout.)

The plot of *Gwen* adds up to just a trek and an explanation, but the aural and visual details along the way are obliquely evocative and insinuating. The film is delicately lyrical-satirical, its wit, desert-dry. In this world, civilization no longer stars—it's only comic relief, atmosphere, quaint props, background to love and play. Rendered impotent and unimportant, it becomes part of a desert idyll, a poetic element, like the moon, the sand, the jerboa. The struggle for survival is a game of stilts. Feathers are food, and one makes what use one can of giant phones and tennis shoes. The Twentieth Century is a distant memory, a joke.

**GWENDOLINE** see *Perils of Gwendoline, The*

**GYPPED IN EGYPT** Pathe/Van Beuren 1930 anim 8m. By John Foster & Mannie Davis. Ref: TV: Aesop's Fables. LC: *Gyped in Egypt*. no Lee.

Hundreds of living skeletons—including a piano-playing skeleton and an elevator-operator skeleton—are found to inhabit an Egyptian pyramid. Plus: a giant sphinx-like monster with pinwheel eyes. Amusing.

# H

**\*The H-MAN** 1958 ('59-U.S.) 87m.-J. Ref: TV. Warren/KWTS! V 6/3/59. Lee. Hardy/SF. Phantom. Stanley. Lentz. Maltin '92. Hound. Martin. Weisser/JC.

"The liquid is alive!" The H-Man Cometh: H-bomb tests prove responsible for radioactive ooze which dissolves humans ("I saw someone dissolved!") and periodically transforms into ooze men. ("The liquid can become a monster!") Have-your-cake-and-eat-it-too script sports both blob monsters and humanoid monsters and never explains (at least in the U.S. version) how or why the former transform into the latter. As flowing ooze, the monster is unprepossessing; as the neon-cellophane H-Men, it's pretty eerie. Scorecard: fun crumpling-clothes effects (as victims dissolve), a good use of the old ghost-ship idea, dull intrigue re narcotics, a creepy reference to a "green shadow," and a buoyant Masaru Sato theme for the climactic Evacuation and Conflagration scenes.

**H. P. LOVECRAFT'S RE-ANIMATOR** see *Re-animator*

**HA CHAYUN ALPY AGFA** (Israeli) 1993 feature. D: A. Dayan. Ref: V 5/10/33:C-16: sf; Life According to Agfa—tr t. With Gila Almagor, Shuli Rand, Irit Frank.

**HACEDOR DE MIEDO, El** see *Fearmaker, The*

**HACK-O-LANTERN** Spencer Films/Raj Mehrotra 1987 color c94m. (*Halloween Night* - alt vt t). D & Co-Ed: Jag Mundhra. SP: Carla Robinson. Story: Burford Hauser. Mus: G. T. Haggard. PD: Thomas Atcheson. SpFxMkp: Tracy Shuttleworth, Kimberly Dominguez. SpFxProsth: David Cohen. Opt: Cruse & Co. Ref: TV: Legacy Ent. video. V 11/1/89:50(hv). Hound. McCarty II. no Martin. Stanley. With Katina Garner, Carla Baron, Hy Pyke, Gregory Scott Cummins, Jeff Brown, Bill Tucker.

"The hour of satan has arrived!" Grandpa (Pyke) is grooming Tommy (Cummins) for satan—which is not quite what little brother Roger (Brown), who's a cop, had in mind when he asks Tommy, "Why don't you do something meaningful with your life?" Murders with pitchfork, shovel, knife, and garrote follow.... Equally unbelievable a development as the graveyard reconciliation between Mom (Garner) and difficult son Tommy is the transformation of Roger into coven leader. Overheated acting and music, lame humor. Best prop: satan's branding iron.

**HADES PROJECT ZEORYMER** see *Project Hades Zeorymer*

**HAJATAISEI DANGAIO** see *Dangaio 2*

**HALBE WELT** (Austrian) Allegro (Helmut Grasser) 1993 feature. SP, D: Florian Flicker. SP: also M. Sturminger. Ph: J. Palacz. Mus: A. Haller. AD: Donhauser, Martin. Ref: V 12/13/93: "convincing" effects ... "inventive." With R. Egger, Dani Levy. "Future world where the sun's harmful rays force people to live by night." *Half World* - tr t.

**\*HALF HUMAN: THE STORY OF THE ABOMINABLE SNOWMAN** 1955 ('57-U.S.) 63m.-U.S. U.S. version: (ph) Lucien Andriot; (ad) Nicolai Remisoff. Ref: TV: Rhino HV. Weisser/JC. Warren/KWTS! Fango 99. Lee. Lentz. no V. no Hardy. Svensson/Japan. Maltin '92. Scheuer. Martin. PT 7:7. With Akemi Negishi, Noburo Nakamura.

Reports of "some unknown animal with incredible strength" inspire a scientific expedition to venture into uncharted mountains in Japan, where it finds a nine-foot-tall, 1,800-lb., hairy, bearded creature and its offspring. "Big foot" aids the hero at one point, but goes on a rampage when "little foot" is shot.... The Jerry Warren-ish alternating here between talking heads and narrated action is a less satisfactory answer than either titles or dubbing to the foreign-language barrier. The movie doesn't even really start until the sequences, near the end, with the "snowmen." The big money for the U.S. edition went into construction of a stuffed doll representing the dead snowboy or girl.

See also *Abominable Snowman, The.*

**HALF LIFE** see *Dance of the Damned*

**HALIMAW SA BANGA** (Fili) 1986 feature. D: M. J. delos Reyes. Ref: vc box: "two-episode horror movie"; from TV series?

"Halimaw Sa Banga." With Liza Lorena.

"Komiks." D: C. de Leon. With Ian de Leon.

**HALLOWEEN 4: THE RETURN OF MICHAEL MYERS** Galaxy (Akkad)/Trancas Int'l. 1988 color/ws 88m. D: Dwight H. Little. Story, SP: A. B. McElroy. Story: also D. Lipsius, L. Rattner, B. Ruffner. Mus: Alan Howarth. SpMkpFX: MMI; (des) John Buechler. SpFxCoord: Larry Fioritto. Opt: H. Anderson. Ref: TV. MFB'89:369-70. V 10/26/88. ad. SFChron 10/22/88: "not scary." SFChron Dtbk 11/13/88. With Donald Pleasence, Ellie Cornell, Danielle Harris, Michael Pataki, Beau Starr, Kathleen Kinmont, G. R. Wilbur (Michael), Gene Ross.

"Welcome to hell." The "nightmare man" is back, and to compound the problem a couple of guys seem to be wearing Michael masks. In a terribly ironic coda, a mad little girl "replaces" Michael.... Rote suspense-horror, with that same damn music.

**HALLOWEEN 5** Galaxy/Magnum Pictures (Moustapha Akkad/Trancas Int'l. & The Return of Myers) 1989 color 93m. (*Halloween 5: The Revenge of Michael Myers* - ad t). SP, D: Dominique Othenin-Girard. SP: also Michael Jacobs. Mus: Alan Howarth. SpMkpFX: K. N. B. FX; (mech fx) Lee Stone. SpFxCoord: Greg Landerer. Title Seq: Klasky/Csupo. Ref: TV. V 10/18/89. ad. With Donald Pleasence, Danielle Harris, Wendy Kaplan, Ellie Cornell, Donald L. Shanks (Michael Myers).

"I knew that hell would not have him!" It's Halloween eve at the Haddonfield (Illinois) Children's Clinic, and Michael Myers' niece, Jamie (Harris) "sees" Michael as he commits his murders with scissors, scythe, knife, pitchfork, etc. In very bad taste, one trick-or-treater masquerades in Haddonfield as Michael Myers. Fittingly, he's the next victim.... Overwrought, isn't it? The I-scream/you-scream business gets pretty silly: The victim screams, then (cut) Jamie screams. Then back to the current victim.... The opening pumpkin-carving is a scary as this one gets.

See also: *Silent Night, Deadly Night III.*

**HALLOWEEN NIGHT** (Thai) c1987? color/ws c98m. Ref: TV: All Asian HV; hardly any Eng.

A real mummy from a cemetery and a fake mummy from a movie set meet, scare each other, then join forces to defeat a bunch of bumbling, annoying cops. The two shake hands and part. (To confuse matters more, it's Halloween, people are in costume at the local dance hall, and a mummy movie is playing on TV.) At one point, the real mummy takes his (human, live) girl friend on a motorcycle ride into the sky. (The music: *E. T.*) Later, on the set, he delights the director with his realistic performance; he's so into his role that others have to stop him from strangling one actress. ("Sorry.")

The actual mummy here has a deeper voice than the actor-mummy, in fact almost a growl. He's a traditional slow, lumbering mummy; he casually bops humans who flail about him and is more into romance than menace. In this occasionally droll, if extended comedy—almost every scene runs on too long—the real mummy is continually mistaken for the fake mummy, and vice versa. The fake mummy gets more screams; the real mummy gets the girl.

See also: *Amazing Stories—The Movie* ("Mummy Daddy").

**HALLOWEEN NIGHT** see *Hack-O-Lantern*

**HALLOWEEN PARTY** see *Night of the Demons* (1988)

**HAMMER HOUSE OF HORROR DOUBLE FEATURE: GUARDIAN OF THE ABYSS/THE CARPATHIAN EAGLE** (B) ITC-TV/Cinema Arts Int'l. & Hammer (Jack Gill & Chips) 1981 color 90m. (aka *Guardian of the Abyss/The Carpathian Eagle*). D: Don Sharp; Francis Megahy. Tel: David Fisher; Bernie Cooper, Megahy. Ph: Norman Warwick; Frank Watts. Mus: John McCabe; Wilfred Josephs. AD: Carolyn Scott. SpFX: Ian Scoones. Mkp: Alan Brownie; Eddie Knight. Ref: TV. TVG. With Ray Lonnen, Rosalyn Landor, John Carson, Paul Darrow; Anthony Valentine, Suzanne Danielle, Sian Phillips, Barry Stanton, Barry Stokes, Pierce Brosnan.

1) Alchemist's crystal-ball-like mirror summons up images of a "mighty devil," the "guardian of the abyss," a demon that even Aleister Crowley couldn't handle. Apart from the passing reference to Crowley, this is formula devil-cult material, with a routine twist ending.

2) Madwoman's (Danielle) murders attributed to legendary, monstrous eagle. Transparently plotted shocker.

**HANAWA DANEMON** (J) c1940 anim 10m. Ref: Japanese Animated Film.

Haunted house ... sorceress.

**HAND OF DEATH: PART 25** see *Unmasked: Part 25*

**The HAND OF PLEASURE** Satyr IX 1971 color feature. D: "Z.G. Spencer." Ref: TV: SWV. no Lee. With Marie Arnold.

"Somewhere in London, this mad scientist was transforming our girls into man-killing love robots ...." That "monster" Dr. Dreadful—his masked face supposedly the "greatest horror of them all"—can turn a woman into a "man-hating robot" with his "sex transference apparatus" (an electronic helmet). At the end, the latter makes our hero sexually aggressive. The doc's Tussaud-ish "garden of horrors" features a Sweeney Todd victim and a wax-coated mummy. Elementary t&a/sf combo.

**HAND THAT FEEDS THE DEAD** (I) VSOM/Cine Equipe(Amedeo Mellone) 1974 color/ws 86m. (*La Mano Che Nutre la Morte*). SP, D: Sergio Garrone. Ph: Emore Galeassi.

Mus: Maestosi, Liberati. AD: A. Mellone. SpFX: Ditta Rambaldi. SpSdFX: Roberto Arcangeli. Ref: TV: VSOM; Eng. titles. Palmerini. With Klaus Kinski, Katia Christine, Marzia Damon, Carmen Silvia, Stella Calderoni.

"Everyone in this house is strange." The late Baron Ivan Rassimov's assistant Dr. Nagiski (Kinski) continues Rassimov's experiments in skin grafting—specifically, he's trying to restructure his wife's fire-scarred body .... The obvious "highlight" of this tawdry, shot-on-tape imitation of *Eyes without a Face:* the facial-skin transfer. Plus a hunchbacked strangler and a premature burial. Very cheap.

The **HAND THAT ROCKS THE CRADLE** BV/Hollywood Pictures (Interscope & Nomura Babcock & Brown/David Madden) 1991 color 110m. D: Curtis Hanson. SP: Amanda Silver. Ph: Robert Elswit. Mus: G. Revell. PD: Edward Pisoni. Ref: V 1/16/92. SFExam 1/10/92: "a scary one." ad. Sacto Bee 1/10/92. With Annabella Sciorra, Rebecca De Mornay (Peyton Flanders), Matt McCoy, Ernie Hudson.

Nanny from hell.

**HANDLE WITH CARE** (B) Embassy 1935 55m. (*Look out Mr. Haggis* - alt t). D: Redd Davis. SP: Randall Faye. Ref: BFC. no Hardy/SF. With Molly Lamont, Jack Hobbs, James Finlayson, Henry Victor.

"Ex-crook takes strength pill and thwarts spies."

The **HANDMAID'S TALE** (U.S.-B) Cinecom Ent./Daniel Wilson & Bioskop Film & Cinetudes & Odyssey/Cinecom Int'l 1989 ('90-U.S.) color 109m. D: Volker Schlöndorff. SP: Harold Pinter, from Margaret Atwood's novel. Mus: Ryuichi Sakamoto. SpFxCoord: Tom Ward. Mkp: J. Goodwin. SdFxEd: P. R. Adam. News P: Prudence Arndt. Ref: TV. V 2/14/90. Sacto Union 4/12/90. Sacto Bee 4/13/90. MFB'90:321-22. With Natasha Richardson, Robert Duvall, Faye Dunaway, Aidan Quinn, Elizabeth McGovern, Victoria Tennant, David Dukes.

"We pledge allegiance to the Bible." In the futuristic Gilead, only one woman in one hundred can bear children, and "handmaids" are sexual stand-ins for barren wives. In this world of government-sponsored, impersonal sexuality, newborns are applauded, "sinners" are publicly executed, and "birthmobiles" and "evening rentals" (or escorts) are in.... The handmaid system goes beyond invasion of privacy to destruction of same. A reptilian atmosphere predominates. The script, however, boils down to the usual repressive-New Regime-vs.-the-Rebels story, with none of those crazy little *Roller Blade* ambiguities. The details of repression, though, are clinically amusing, barbaric "civilized" horrors.

**HANDS OF STEEL** (I) Almi/National & Dania & Medusa 1986 (1985) color 94m. (*Vendetta dal Futuro. Mani di Pietra* and *Atomic Cyborg* - working titles. *Hands of Stone* - early t. *Vendetta from the Future* - ad t). Story, SP, D: Sergio Martino. SP: also E. Parker et al. Ph: G. Ferrando. Mus: C. Simonetti. SpMkpFX: Sergio Stivaletti. SpFX: R. Callmard, P. Callmard. Ref: V 8/20/86: "derivative, often silly." 5/7/86:292. 5/1/85:312(ad). Horacio Higuchi. Ecran F 66:12. 67:41(ad). 68:7. Phantom: "skewed." Morse: "passable time-waster." ad. With Daniel Greene (Paco), Janet Agren, John Saxon, George Eastman, C. Cassinelli, D. O'Brien.

A cyborg assassin in the year 1997.

**HANDSOME SIBLINGS** (H.K.) Win's Movie 1992 color/ws 102m. Ref: TV: Tai Seng Video; Eng. titles.

Macabre ingredients in this fantasy-comedy-drama include ghosts who divvy up human body parts ... supernatural garments, water, and firebolts ... a severed head ... and an exploding villain .... Frantic, a bit silly, and too involved, but sometimes inventive. Notable: the whirlwind beginning and the line "I am Crazy Lion of the Ten Untouchable Villains."

**HANGOVER MURDERS, The** see *Remember Last Night?*

**HANNA MONSTER, LIEBLING** (Austrian) TTV Films & Cult Films 1989 b&w 100m. SP, D, Ph: Christian Berger. Mus: Carmel. Ref: V 10/4/89: "script and performance are ... vacuous." With Marika Green, Hagnot Elishka, Peter Turrini.

A baby "turns out to be a monster.... Early sequences ... create suspense and the impression the pic is developing into a horror movie."

**HANNYO** (S. Korean) Dong Hyoup Corp. (Kim Chi Han) 1981 color 80m. (aka *Revenge of the Ghost*). D: Lee Yoo Sub. SP: Kim Young Han. Ref: Hardy/HM: "full of undigested stereotypes." With Choi Suk, Lim Chung Ha.

"Spectre" haunts plastic surgeon "who abducts women as raw material" for his practice.

**HANSEL AND GRETEL** (U.S.-Israeli) Cannon (Golan-Globus) 1987 color 86m. SP, D: Len Talan. SP: also Nancy Weems, from the fairy tale by the Brothers Grimm. Ref: V 5/27/87: "rather flatfooted." With Hugh Pollard, Nicola Stapleton, David Warner, Cloris Leachman (the witch).

Woodcutter's kids trapped in witch's gingerbread house.

**HANSEL & GRETEL** (I) 1989 color feature. SP,D: Giovanni Simonelli. Mus: L. Perini. Ref: Palmerini: "mediocre horror film" re organ transplants.

**HAPLOS** (Fili) Mirick Films Int'l. 1982 color c112m. Story, D: Antonio Jose Perez. Story, SP: Ricardo Lee. Ph: R. Vitug. Mus D: Jun Latonio. PD: L. L. Perez. SdFxSup: Tony Gozalvez. Mkp: D. Ravela. Opt: G.A.M.B. Ref: TV: Trigon Video; little Eng. With Vilma Santos, Christopher de Leon, Rio Locsin, Delia Razon, J. E. Infante.

Our hero hears the sounds of screaming and gunfire in the jungle, then meets a mysterious young woman in a cemetery. It seems she's the ghost of a rape victim of Japanese soldiers. When she begins to relive this World War II tragedy, he tries to save her, but fails.... Okay but overlong ghost story has one chilling bit—the ghost revealed behind the hero's (live) girl friend, as the latter opens a door.

**HAPPILY EVER AFTER** 1st National (Kel-Air)/Filmation (Lou Scheimer) 1990 anim color 74m. D: John Howley. SP: Robby London, Martha Moran. Mus: F. W. Becker. SpFxAnimSup: Bruce Heller. Ref: V 6/27/90: "Film's emphasis on horror content is handled tastefully." ad. SFChron 5/31/93: reissue; "not much to sing about." 3/11/93. Voices: Irene Cara (Snow White), Edward Asner, Carol Channing, Frank Welker (Batso), Malcolm McDowell (Lord Maliss).

Snow White releases prince from spell as "Shadowman."

**HAPPY GHOST** (H.K.) Cinema City/Long Shong Pictures 1987 color/ws c92m. (*Abracadabra* - alt vt t). D: Peter Mak. SP: Raymond Hwang. Story: Edward Lee, P. Mak, Herrick Wong. Ph: Chris Chen. PD: Raymond Wong. SpFX: New Visual Workshop. Ref: TV: Rainbow Video; Eng. titles; first of a (generally non-horrific) series. NST! 4:24-5: D: C. Ko Sum.

When a "parapowered" professor's Spirit Machine raises a cemetery's dead, his light ray must be used to immobilize them—but one ghost, Pinkish Red, escapes. Unseen, she gives humans near her a chill, impersonates a mannequin, and does *Topper*-style tricks. In life, she was a stripper who died, along with the night's audience, in a fire. Now, she wants to be reborn; the other living dead want to take revenge on those who set fire to the hall, or on their reincarnations (i.e., the protagonists).

This monster-comedy—which seems influenced equally by *Ghostbusters* and *Poltergeist*—is fairly elaborate and inventive, but tends to run off in all directions. Zombies, ghosts, and vampires get all scrambled up. (At one point, the zombie-populated strip joint features a vampire stage act, and one of the two heroines, Lily, likes to play vampire.) Funny scene: "ghostly" Lily unwittingly "leading" the pack of zombies behind her in "stunts." Eerie scene: Pinkish Red flying over a swimming pool as she tries to "kiss" the life force out of the backstroking Cici. Ectoplasmic News Flash: "Actually, a ghost is a cloud of radio waves left by a dead person. So ghosts are afraid of hair dryers."

**HAPPY GHOST IV** (H.K.) Pak Ming Films (Ko Chi Sum Films/Paul Lai) 1990 color 86m. D: Clifton C. S. Ko. SP: Ng Man Fai, Joe Ma, Cheung Chang Tang(sp?). Ph: Sander Lee. Mus: Beyond. AD: Raymond Chan. SpVisFX: John Ting, Jackie Tang. SpMkpFX: Ho Chim Sum. AnimSpFX: Tsui Hark; Cinefex Workshop. Ref: TV: Pan-Asia Video; Eng. titles. V 10/24/84:382: sfa *The Happy Ghost*?? With Raymond Wong, Loletta Lee, Pauline Leung, Wong Kwong Leun.

"This is a haunted house!" Students find a corpse in a cave, take its antique armor, and have their dream life sucked out of them one night by the multi-tongued ghost which inhabits said armor. The chopped-off head of this "evil spirit" flies at humans; later, the spirit brings a painted tiger to cartoon life and sics it on his enemies.... Occasionally funny low comedy has some okay "invisible ghost" effects (keyed by a feather of invisibility). Also on the program: a guardian ghost, Last-Life.

**HAPPY GHOST V** (H.K.) Mandarin Films (Raymond Wong) 1991 color/ws 91m. (*Magic To Win 5* - alt t). SP, D: Wong. Co-D: Norman Chan. Ref: TV: Pan-Asia Video; Eng. titles. vc box.

Fifth in the series concerns a dog, Magic, who saves the temple of a "happy ghost" from fire and gets to be a human for 49 days. Trite *Shaggy Dog*-in-reverse fantasy features one sequence in which the swivel-headed ghost uses "ghostly magic" to scare supermarket robbers. Amusing effects and props—a tennis racket which stretches, a giant tennis ball—for the tennis-court sequence.

**HAPPY HELL NIGHT** (Can.-Yug.) Brisun Ent. & Pavlina Ltd./Petersen Prods. (Malius) 1991 color c87m. SP, D: Brian Owens. SP: also Ron Peterson, Michael Fitzpatrick. Ph: Sol Negrin. Mus: Nenad Bach. SpFX: Gabe Bartalos, Joel Harlow. Mkp: Stanislava Zaric. Ref: TV. TVG. V 10/19/92:117(ad). With Charles Cragin (Malius), Darren McGavin, Nick Gregory, Franke Hughes, Laura Carney, Ted Clark.

"It will get out!" Competition for the "most dangerous initiation stunt by a freshman pledge" leads to the unwitting release of a ghoulish demon locked up for 25 years in the state asylum. Satanic rituals start and seemingly end the thing's career.... Formula, but with a bit of atmosphere. Nice if extended buildup to the opening of the demon's cell. Then: disappointment, when Malius begins cracking wise, like every other Son of Freddy, as he begins taking a pickax-like weapon to Winfield College students. Semi-surprise bit: the sudden writhing of the Christ on the cross.

**HARD ROCK NIGHTMARE** see *Shock 'Em Dead*

**HARD ROCK ZOMBIES** Cannon/Patel-Shah Film Co. 1985 (1984) color 94m. SP, D, P: Krishna Shah. SP: also David Ball. Mus: Paul Sabu. SpFxMkp: John Buechler. Ref: V 1/13/88: "not-bad cult item." 5/9/84:148: at Cannes; 219 (ad). Ecran F 47:30. Martin: "sometimes amusing." SFExam 9/5/86:D-10. Phantom: "utterly excruciating"; Hitler cameo. With E. J. Curcio, Sam Mann, Geno Andrews, Jennifer Coe, Lisa Toothman, Crystal Shaw, Nadia.

Murdered rockers rise from the dead.

**HARD TO BE A GOD** see *Es Ist Nicht Leicht ein Gott Zu Sein*

**HARD TO DIE** see *Tower of Terror*

**HARDCOVER** see *I, Madman*

**HARDWARE** (B-U.S.) Miramax (Millimeter)/Palace-Miramax & British Screen & BSB (Wicked Films & TV) 1990 color 92m. SP, D: Richard Stanley. SP: also Mike Fallon. From Steve MacManus & Kevin O'Neill's comics story *Shok!* Mus: Simon Boswell. SpMkpFX & Robotics: Image Animation; (des) Little John, William Petty; (Droid Vision) Finlay Milne. SpFxCoord: Barney Jeffrey. SpRoboticsDes: Paul Catling. FloorSpFxSup: Vendetta SFX. SdFxDes: J. Miller, K. Hopkins. Ref: TV. V 6/6/90. ad. Sacto Union 9/14/90. Sacto Bee 9/15/90. SFExam 9/14/90. SFChron 9/14/90. Cable Video Store 3/91. MFB'90:296-7. With Dylan McDermott, Stacey Travis, John Lynch, William Hootkins, Iggy Pop.

"This place is going to hell." In the radiation-clouded future, the planned instrument of population control is M.A.R.K. 13, a defective biomechanical, artificially-intelligent cyborg which regenerates itself from scrap and turns into a "droid running crazy." ("It doesn't care who it kills!") At the end, it takes a shower, rusts, and expires.... A little bit of story and a lot of noise (screaming, soundtrack music, etc.) in this occasionally weirdly engaging, glibly cynical sf-actioner. The monster is an *Alien/Short Circuit* hybrid.

**HARE REMOVER** WB 1946 (1945) anim color 7m. (*Elmer's Hare Remover* - orig t). D: Frank Tashlin. SP: Warren Foster. FX Anim: A. C. Gamer. Ref: TV. "WBCartoons." Lee (LC).

Elmer Fudd tries to turn Bugs Bunny into a "deviwish fiend." (He's going to turn into a gwuesome monstew.") No go. "I'm a tewwibew scientist!" Bugs tries the serum on Elmer, who goes through some surreal contortions. Bugs: "I think Spencer Tracy did it much better." A bit repetitive, but funny. Elmer's goony laugh is given a sinister twist here.

**HARE-WAY TO THE STARS** WB 1958 anim color 7m. D: Chuck Jones. Ref: Lee. LC. "WBCartoons."

Bugs Bunny vs. Commander X-2 ... "instant Martians."(WBC)

See also *Haredevil Hare.*

**HAREDEVIL HARE** WB 1948(1947) anim color 7m. D: Chuck Jones. SP: M. Maltese. Ref: "WBCartoons." Lee. LC: c1947.

Bugs Bunny vs. Martian Commander X-2, on the moon.

See also: *Bugs Bunny's Lunar Tunes. Duck Dodgers of the 24-1/2 Century* (2). *Hare-Way to the Stars. Hasty Hare, The. Mad As a Mars Hare.*

**HARRISON BERGERON** (Can.) Showtime-TV/Atlantis 1994 ('95-U.S.) color c99m. (aka *Kurt Vonnegut's Harrison Bergeron*) D: Bruce Pittman. Tel: Arthur Crimm. Ref: vc box. SFChron 8/11/95. TVG. PT 22:69: "packed with great ideas." With Sean Astin, Christopher Plummer, Buck Henry, Howie Mandel, Eugene Levy, Andrea Martin, John Astin.

Year 2053, after the Second American Revolution.

**HARRY AND THE HENDERSONS** Univ/Amblin (Richard Vane, William Dear) 1987 color 111m. (*Bigfoot and the Hendersons* - B). SP, D: Dear. Sp: also William E. Martin, Ezra D. Rappaport. Mus: Bruce Broughton. SpFMkpDes: Rick Baker. Mkp: Dan Striepeke, Greg Nelson. SpVisFX: IL&M; Robert Dyke, Magic Lantern. SpFxSup: Henry Millar. VocalFX: Fred Newman. Ref: TV. MFB'87:363. V 5/27/87. SFChron 6/5/87. SFExam 6/5/87. With John Lithgow, Melinda Dillon, Margaret Langrick, Joshua Rudoy, Kevin Peter Hall (Harry), David Suchet, Lainie Kazan, Don Ameche, M. Emmet Walsh, Debbie Carrington (Little Bigfoot), John F. Bloom.

Outside Seattle, campers run down Bigfoot, take him home with them. Air freshener indicated. At the end, there are other Bigfeet.... The script for *Harry* tends toward sentiment and obvious comedy, and there's a sitcom harriedness to the Henderson family. But the movie's treatment of Harry himself recalls, at its best, Renoir's *Boudu*. (Harry does everything but spit on Balzac.) Baker's makeup for Mr. Bigfoot is one long amusing "special effect"—Harry's expressions range from gleeful and self-delighted to concerned and constipated. And his bulk and brute strength are exploited cleverly and comically.

**HASTA EL VIENTO TIENE MIEDO** (Mex) Col/Tauro Films & Grovas 1967 color c90m. SP, D: Carlos Enrique Taboada. Ph: Agustin Jimenez. Mus: Raul Lavista. AD: J. T. Torija. SpFX: Ricardo Sainz. Mkp: Maria del Castillo. Ref: TV: *Even the Wind Is Afraid* - tr t. TVG. no Lee. Indice, v.II. vc box. With Marga

Lopez, Maricruz Olivier, Alicia Bonet, Norma Lazareno, Renata Seydel, Elizabeth Dupeyron.

The works: creepy music, creaking doors, voices sobbing and calling in the night, slinking cats, screaming, wind-scattered leaves, mysterious figures at tower windows, and rumors of ghosts.... Atmospheric shots here of Andrea—a ghostly girl in white wandering about in the wind at midnight—recall movies such as *The Innocents, I Walked with a Zombie,* and *Isle of the Dead.* One musical motif even echoes a theme in the latter movie.

The **HASTY HARE** WB 1952 anim color 7m. D: Chuck Jones. SP: T. Pierce. Ref: "WBCartoons." Lee. LC.

Bugs Bunny vs. Martian Commander X-2.

See also *Haredevil Hare.*

**2 HATCHET FOR THE HONEYMOON** Avco Embassy-TV/Peliculas Ibarra (Manuel Cano) 1969 ws (*Un'Accetta per la Luna di Miele*). Mkp: Elisa Aspach, Piero Mecacci. Asst D: R. Walker, Lamberto Bava. Ref: TV: MHE video; Eng. dubbed; no SP cr for M. Bava. Hardy/HM. Lee. TVG: *Hatchet for a Honeymoon.* Palmerini. no V. With Jesus Puente, Alan Collins.

"Nobody suspects that I am a madman.... I have killed five young women." A fun one from Mario Bava-land. The title is made good in the first sequence. Then the movie begins to get way way out. Not exactly believable, but, granted, absolutely, lyrical-macabre: bride-killer John Harrington dancing with a prospective bride in his office's Room of the Bride Mannequins. Some of the movie is like "Why do we torture each other?"; more of it's like Slip the Wedding-Gowned Bride into the Incinerator. John murders his wife, but her ghost vows, "I will never leave—never. Everyone will see me except you." He checks the incinerator. It seems to be working fine. He begins carrying a bag filled with her ashes. Doesn't work: Everyone sees her, not the bag. "And for the lady...?" Then, at the end, it's vice versa: She curses him to see her, but no one else will. Fade out.

**HATYARIN** (India—Hindi?) Sohal Prods. 1990? color c160m. D: Vinod Talwar. SP: Salim Yousaf. Dial: Amrit Aryan. Ph: Manish Bhatt. Mus: Naresh Sharma; (lyr) Sameer. AD: Gyan Singh. SpFX: Daya Bhai. Mkp: Salim, Sunny, Alok Dutt. Ref: TV: Excel Video (Atlantic Video); little Eng. With Jamuna, Deepak Prashar, Amita Nangia, Javed Khan, Shree Pradha, Jaya Mathur, Kaamana.

The woman in white—whose eyes shoot out white rays—proves to be, in another form, a big-fanged vampire and, in yet another form, a mashed-face monster whose tree-creature assistant holds her female victims, while she sacrifices their blood to another vampire-being hidden away in a cave. In the climactic scenes (of which there are several), the vampire woman becomes a giant. When an exorcist beheads her, her neck shoots out tentacles. And on the same program: corpses which rise en masse (in an apparent hallucination) ... a levitating, strangling phone cord ... a ceiling fan which recreates the pendulum half of the pit-and-the-pendulum torture ... and (in the most gruesome sequence) a monster arm which emanates from a man's bowels and lifts a woman up, up.... Enthusiastic East Indian horror hokum features hectic photography, low comedy, PRC-style shock music, songs and dances, and the cornball zoom-and-bounce camera effect which SCTV liked to parody.

**The HAUNTED** Fox Network (FNM Films)/Daniel Schneider 1991 color c90m. D: Robert Mandel. Tel: Darrah Cloud, from a book by Robert Curran and Ed Warren et al. Mus: R. Bellis. Ph: M. Margulies. PD: Pam Warner. VisFX: (sup) Joshua Culp; (des) William Cruse. MkpSup: Kathy Shorkey. Ref: TV. TVG. V 5/13/91:110-111: "works up a good case of the frights." Maltin '92: "surprisingly effective." With Sally Kirkland, Jeffrey De-Munn, Louise Latham, Joyce Van Patten, Diane Baker, Stephen Markle.

"There was a thing in here." Four spirits, including a demon, set out to "destroy" some "good Catholics" in West Pittston, Pennsylvania. The manifestations—mostly familiar, some even risible, a few creepy—add little to *The Exorcist, Amityville*, etc.

**HAUNTED, The** see *Witchtrap*

**HAUNTED BY HER PAST** NBC-TV/Norton Wright & ITC-TV (Terry Morse) 1987 color 90m. (*Secret Passions* - orig t). D: Michael Pressman. Story, SP: Barry Schneider. Story: also N. Wright. Mus: Paul Chihara. PD: R. F. Smith. Ref: TV. TVG. V 10/14/87:206. With Susan Lucci, Finola Hughes (Megan Maguire), John James, Marcia Strassman, Robin Thomas, Douglas Seale, Kay Hawtrey.

The ghost of a murderess (Hughes) who was hanged in 1786 haunts the mirror in the now-locked room in which she committed the murder. In the present day, Karen Beckett (Lucci)—on holiday at the colonial Lion and Lamb Inn in "historic Unionville"—unlocks the room, and with it the past. Seems her mom also killed in that same room.... The spirit from the mirror possesses Karen and improves her sex life with her husband, Eric (James), but the "new" Karen proves to be quite temperamental. Thus the script's explanation of bad manners. Lots of "Oh, Eric!"

**HAUNTED CAMPUS** (H.K.?) Mei Ah Film/Artwell Prods. 1993 color/ws 81m. (aka *Horror School*). Ref: TV: Tai Seng Video; no Eng.

A visualized dream of gore and ghouls ... hi-jinks in a cemetery ... ghostliness in the bathroom ... a gliding ghost in red ... and skeleton kissing on the playground. Vapid, cheap shot-on-taper has some very poor dummy work for the Scared into a Fatal Fall scene. The chuckling, mini-dressed ghost's two victims return as zombie-types.

**The HAUNTED COP SHOP** (H.K.) 1987? color/ws c92m. Ref: TV: vt; Thai-dubbed; Eng. titles. M/TVM 10/87:74.

Hong Kong. Vampire-ghost General Issey ("Must be Count Dracula himself") and other Japanese soldier-ghosts who committed "sabuku" in their clubhouse (now a police station), when the war was lost, haunt the place. Meanwhile, jailbird Ah Wong flashes back to World War II, meets the bartender-ghost from *The Shining*, and is bitten by Issey. Running from the cops, he stops to ask himself, "What am I afraid of? I'm a goblin now." The cops don't buy his story. ("Help! Police violence! They're beating up a ghost.") Additionally: a ghost in pink, a fake ghost ("Have you seen my head?"), and a brief awakening of vampires during an afternoon solar eclipse.... Lively and generally enter-

taining, with some clever bits of business. But the episodic script never really gets anything going.

Sequel: *Haunted Cop Shop II, The*

**The HAUNTED COP SHOP II** (H.K.) In-Gear Films 1988 color 93m. (*Menggui Xuetang*). SP, D: Jeff Lau [Liu Zhenwei]. SP: also Barry Wong [Huang Bingyao], Laurence Lau [Liu Junwei]. Ph: Johnny Koo. Mus: Phil Chan. AD: Li Jingwen. SpFX: Ding Yuanda, Deng Weiyu. Mkp: Mo Huikang. Ref: TV: World Video; Eng. titles. Horacio Higuchi. NST! 4:8-9, 25. With Zhang Xueyou, Ricky Hoi, Su Jiabao (lead vampiress), Wen Liyan (barracks vampiress), Lin Jianming (cop shop vampiress), J. Lau, B. Wong, Johnny Koo, Angela Wilson.

Frenetic slapstick follow-up to the first *Cop Shop* features a vampire woman, a horde of zombies, and, very amusingly, a "werewolf vampire"—a cop, Man-chill, who turns monstrous in direct moonlight: He changes from friend to foe of the vampire woman, as the cloud situation changes. Comedy in the cheerfully silly tradition of the *Airplane!* movies, though the level of invention isn't high. Urine proves instrumental in electrocuting the vampire woman.

**\*HAUNTED GOLD** 1933. Mus sc: Leo F. Forbstein. Ref: TV. Lee. WBStory: remake of *\*Phantom City*. V 1/17/33. no Scheuer. no Maltin '92. With E. Alderson, Martha Mattox.

"There's something uncanny and weird about everything." Animated bats fly up out of a phantom's cloak and past the camera, in a charmingly corny, mood-setting title sequence. Roughly the first third of the movie takes place at night, in a "creepy, spooky dump" and a "haunted mine," in a "town all infested with ghosts" and a "million monsters." And the Phantom—a "mysterious presence lurking somewhere"—casts his grotesque shadow everywhere. From here on, though, the news is bad and only gets worse: John Wayne is comically "off" on his dramatic readings, and the other actors are little better. Silly fast-motion mars the action scenes. And Blue Washington is cast as a perpetually-terrified "darkie" with a "watermelon accent," in a surprisingly insistent case of racial stereotyping from Warner Brothers, just four years before their *Black Legion*.

**HAUNTED HONEYMOON** Orion/Susan Ruskin 1986 color 84m. SP, D: Gene Wilder. SP, PD: Terence Marsh. Mus: John Morris. SpFxConsul: John Stears. Mkp Sup: Stuart Freeborn. Opt: Modern Film FX. Ref: TV. MFG'86:305. V 7/30/87. Maltin '92. With G. Wilder, Gilda Radner, Dom DeLuise, Jonathan Pryce, Paul L. Smith, Will Keaton (werewolf).

"The curse of the werewolf" hangs over the Abbot place. Other ingredients here include a fake werewolf; Montego the Magician (Jim Carter), of the evil eye; and a burial alive.... A fizzle as a haunted-house comedy or as a werewolf saga, *Haunted Honeymoon* is big on windblown curtains (there's a credit for "Drapes Master"), small on most everything else. More successful than the comedy are the surprising "fantasy" stunts engineered by Pryce's Charles: a man in a horror mask walking down a wall, Wilder's Larry Abbot entering the "mirror" world, and Radner's Vickie (in wedding white) "flying" up to Larry's window.

**\*\*\*HAUNTED HOUSE** Disney 1930(1929) anim 7m. D: Ub Iwerks. Ref: TV. LC. Lee. Maltin/OMAM.

A skeleton in a cloak orders Mickey Mouse to play the organ for an impromptu skeleton dance. Plus: a doorknob-as-skeletal-hand bit, a windstorm, and a big spider .... Amusing cartoon features some *Skeleton Dance*-like swaying-skeleton and bats-into-closeup effects.

**HAUNTED HOUSE!** (Fili) Bukang Liwayway Films (Precy Talavera) 1985 color c125m. Assoc D: Santiago Garcia. SP, D, & Sp VisFxSup: Ramje. Ph: Ver P. Reyes. Mus D: Jun Latonio. SpMkp & Anim D: Maurice Carvajal. Title Des: Ramon Capinpin. Ref: TV. Viva Video; little Eng. With William Martinez, Janice De Belen, J. C. Bonnin, D'Sunshine Kids, Ernie Forte (the hunchback), Marivee Santos (the Lady in White), Lito Pastrana, Yani De Veyra, E. R. Ejercito.

A phantom, ray-shooting lady in white—when exorcised by a priest—turns out to be an orange, clawed (animated) demon. The latter proceeds to possess a boy, who then turns into an apelike beast with telekinetic powers. When a stake is driven into the beast's back, the demon flies again, until a crucifix sends it back into the statuette whence it came.... A drawn-out remake, in effect, in part, of *Spooks Run Wild*: Teens run around a haunted house. Virtually nothing happens in the first hour, but the zippy cartoon demon almost saves the second half. With wings, a tail, and a skeletal body, it might be a creature from Bald Mountain. Okay sound and makeup effects; very low comedy.

**A HAUNTED HOUSE** (H.K.) Eternal Film (Chen Wah) 1991? color/ws c95m. D: Ng See Yuen. Ph: Chang Chen (sp?). Ref: TV: Pan-Asia Video; no Eng. With Tanny, Chen Chun, I Lei, Shaw Yam Yam, Din Fung, Lo Kwok Wai.

The burned portrait of a man executed by a firing squad mysteriously turns up intact, while a ghostly man in a white suit prowls about a house. A real ghost, however, complete with fangs, drives this fake ghost at least temporarily crazy and vampirizes a gentleman.... Predictable false (and true) alarms, silly comedy.

**The HAUNTED MADAM** (H.K.) Picture One Films/David Y. M. Lam, Yeung Kai Yim 198-? color c92m. (*Shijie Zhuangxie*). D: Tony C. K. Lo [Lu Jungu]. SP: Chan Man Kwai. Ph: Wong Chit. PD: Wong Hi Wan. SpFxSup: Sam Lee. Ref: TV: Rainbow Video; Eng. titles. Horacio Higuchi. NST! 4:25. Fango 107:59. With Pai Bill, Siu Yuk Lung, Man Kwun, Lee Kyoung Sil, Lo Wing.

Martial-arts "Superman" Sha Jin Wang, a disciple of Madam Chiang of the Huang religion, dies vowing revenge on his enemies, who are high-level thugs. Soon afterwards, his ghost gives policewoman Chen Hsiao Chuen his powers. She tracks down one of the people on his list, sticks her hand through her stomach, and laughs.... Lively, routine horror-fantasy has atmospheric photography and many colorful ray effects, but the cackling gets monotonous. Highlights include the literal flying saucers (no cups) which haunt Chen Hsiao Chuen's apartment, and the levitating phone with which Sha Jin Wang contacts her. ("I must revenge!")

**HAUNTED NIGHTS** Wicked Pictures 1993? color feature. D: Jim Enright. Ref: Hustler Video Guide '94. With T.T. Boy (werewolf).

**HAUNTED SUMMER** (U.S.-I?) Cannon (Martin Poll) 1988 color 115m. D: Ivan Passer. SP: Lewis John Carlino, from Anne Edwards' novel. Ref: V 9/14/88. TV: visualized nightmare re monster, plus drug-induced vision re fuzzy-haired monster, in this drama re the genesis of Mary Shelley's *Frankenstein*"

**HAUNTED SYMPHONY** (U.S.-Russ) New Horizons (Roger Corman) 1994 color 85m. D: David Tausik. SP: Tara McCann, Beverly Gray, David Hartwell. Ref: Martin: "visually stunning." SFChron 12/31/94: zombies; "amazing special effects." Imagi (Fall'95): "misdirected." PT 21:14: witch, spirit possession. With Ben Cross, Jennifer Burns, Beverly Garland, Lev Prigunov, Doug Wert.

**HAUNTED T.V. STATION** (H.K.?) Pearl City Video 1987 color c98m. Ref: TV: Trans-Continental Video; no Eng.

A strange force from a mystery room at International Television Broadcasts Company's studio assails a night watchman. Later—after the charm falls off the door to the room—the force possesses, in turn, a man and a woman. Later again, it takes control of the studio's control room equipment. At the end, one exorcism fails, but another succeeds.... Shot-on-tape two-parter is just a series of possessions and levitations. Familiar telekinetic stunts include shaking tables, floating knives, "bleeding" vents, etc. One good tracking-camera sequence in which the mysterious force careens down the corridors of the studio.

**\*The HAUNTING** 1963. AD: Elliot Scott. Mkp: Tom Smith. Sketch Artist: Ivor Beddoes. Ref: screen. TV. Lentz. V 8/21/63. Kael/I Lost. With Rosalie Crutchley, Paul Maxwell, Janet Mansell (Abigail, age 6), Amy Dalby (Abigail, age 80).

*The Haunting* is too, too respectable, but about as scary as they get. Fortunately, producer-director Robert Wise and scriptwriter Nelson Gidding take their cue more from Val Lewton than from Shirley Jackson. (Her novel *The Haunting of Hill House* was the basis for the film.) In the book, the creepy parts are dissipated in never-quite-taking "character building"; the movie retains some of the problems, but concentrates on chills. It could be argued, in fact, that two of the best "Lewtons" came very late—this film and *Curse of the Demon*—from Lewton alumni Wise and Jacques Tourneur, respectively. In what now seems a revolutionary ploy, the frissons in *The Haunting* derive more from the heard than the seen—almost a definition of "Lewtonesque." If the phantom sobbing is somewhat formulaic, the deafening crashes and booms, the muttering, and the tittering are not. The film's ghost sounds double as an aural "history" of the house and as evidence of the presence of an ever-unseen, malignant monster. Only near the end does the movie resort to a standard "apparition" (Lois Maxwell's Mrs. Markway), one of Gidding's few miscalculated inventions. The life-of-a-woman-in-five-seconds opener is a stunning invention, a variation on the instant-aging scenes in old fantasies like *Lost Horizon* and *The Mummy's Ghost*.

See also *Waxwork II*.

**HAUNTING FEAR** American-Independent (Diana Jaffe) 1991 (1990) color 85m. (aka *Edgar Allan Poe's Haunting Fear*). D: Fred Olen Ray. SP: Sherman Scott, from Poe's story "The Premature Burial." Ph: Gary Graver. Mus: Chuck Cirino. AD: Jean-Pierre Moreau. SpMkpFX: Mark Williams. SpContact Lenses:

Chris Biggs. Titles: Bret Mixon. Ref: TV. TVG. SFChron Dtbk 3/8/92. Martin. With Brinke Stevens, Jan-Michael Vincent, Jay Richardson, Robert Clarke, Robert Quarry, Delia Sheppard, Michael Berryman, Mark McGee, Hoke Howell (father corpse), Karen Black.

"We're gonna make your dreams come true—we're going to take you in the backyard and bury you alive!" Victoria (Stevens) is "having dreams" re burial alive and living corpses. Meanwhile, her husband (Richardson) and his secretary (Sheppard) are attempting to scare her to death by putting her in a crate and dumping dirt on her. But the experience leaves Victoria mad rather than dead, and she severs his head and stabs her to death. Bonus hallucinations: the blood bubbling in the tub and the maggots bailing out of the skull's eyes.... Slack combo of horror and sex recalls Corman's *Pit and the Pendulum* (not to mention Lewton's *Isle of the Dead*) as much it does his *Premature Burial*. Stevens is a monotone disaster until the okay climactic free-for-all, which allows her to unwind a bit. A coda pays hommage to an earlier Karen Black role in *Trilogy of Terror*. Berryman's "Time for the autopsy" scene is suitably fiendish-macabre.

**HAUNTING OF HAMILTON HIGH, The** see *Hello Mary Lou: Prom Night II*

**The HAUNTING OF MORELLA** Concorde/Roger Corman (Pacific Trust) 1990 (1989) color 87m. D: Jim Wynorski. SP: R. J. Robertson, from Edgar Allan Poe's story "Morella." Mus: F. E. Teetsel, Chuck Cirino. SpFxMkp: Die-Aktion. OptFX: Motion, T&T. Ref: TV. V 3/14/90. SFChron Dtbk 1/6/91. Martin. Scheuer. With David McCallum, Nicole Eggert (Morella/Lenora), Lana Clarkson, Maria Ford, Clement Von Franckenstein.

"There is something unhealthy in that house!" The spirit of a witch, Morella, returns seventeen years after her execution and enters her daughter Lenora's body. ("One day, she and I shall live as one.") Lenora, however, begins to reject the spiritual graft, and Morella returns to her own corpse, which now "feeds" on the living in order to become "fully resurrected".... Flat writing and acting undercut attempts at grand-style horror, though a trip through a dreamland mirror provides a few passable frissons. Film's less lofty t&a pretensions are amply fulfilled in the by-a-waterfall sequence. McCallum's thankless "Call me mad, if you will" role is irrelevant to most of the action. Morella's first step on the road to immortality—bathing in the blood of a virgin—is borrowed from the Countess Dracula story.

**The HAUNTING OF SARAH HARDY** USA-TV/Wilshire Court Prods. (Millennium Pictures & Jerry London Prods.) 1989 color c90m. D: London. Tel: Thomas Baum, from Jim Flanagan's novel *The Crossing*. Ph: B. Bazelli. Mus: M. Rubini. AD: C. Kearney. SpFxSup: Gary D'Amico. Ref: TV. V (Mifed '89:126). Maltin '92. Martin. Scheuer. With Sela Ward, Morgan Fairchild, Michael Woods, Roscoe Born, Polly Bergen.

"I'm not afraid to go back to that house!" A ghostly figure in the fog, a mysterious voice ("You've been a very bad girl!"), a voice on the phone ("I'm back!"), a knife-wielding horror in the greenhouse—someone wants Sarah Hardy to believe that her mother has returned from her watery grave.... Junky all-a-plot-to-drive-her-crazy story, with some good fog effects.

**The HAUNTING OF SEACLIFF INN** USA-TV/May Day & MTE (Timothy Marx) 1994 color 93m. Co-Tel, D: Walter Klenhard. Ph: R. Schmidt. PD: A. Tremblay. Ref: V 9/19/94:52: "isn't scary." Martin: "not very scary." TVG: haunted Victorian; "These ghosts won't scare you...." With Ally Sheedy, William R. Moses, Louise Fletcher, Lucinda Weist, Maxine Stuart.

**2P HAVE A NICE WEEKEND** Seva Prods. (Weekend Prod. Co.) 1975 (1974) color 80m. SP, D, P: Michael Walters. SP: also J. Byrum, M. Sheiness. Ph: R. Ipcar. Mus: C. Gross. Ref: TV: Mogul (All American/Derann Video). V 9/24/75. With M.B. Miller, Peter Dompe, Valerie Shepherd, Pat Joyce.

"One of us is a killer." Stilted, tinnily "sincere" shocker re a young man "home from the war" in Vietnam ... a *Psycho* slashing ("This looks pretty serious") ... hoe gore ... and queasiness re razors.... An insufferable epilogue "explains" the killer's menopausal, "schizoid behavior pattern."

**HAVING SUPPER WITH A VAMPIRE** (I) Dania & Devon & Reteitalia & Surf 1988 color/ws 91m. (aka *Dinner with the Vampire. Pranzo con Vampiro. A Cena con il Vampiro*). SP, D: Lamberto Bava. SP: also Dardano Sacchetti. Story: Luciano Martino. Ph: G. Transunto. Mus: Simon Boswell and Mario Tagliaferri. AD: A. Geleng. SpMkpFX: R. Prestopino. SpOptFX: S. Stivaletti. SpStageFX: Paolo Ricci. Opt: A. Mafera. Ref: TV: MV; Eng. version; *Dinner with a Vampire*. M/TVM 6/88:64. Jones: "unimaginative"; shot in Eng. Palmerini. TV movie. With Isabel Russinova, George Hilton, Patrizia Pellegrino, Riccardo Rossi, Valeria Milillo, Yvonne Scio.

"Bad luck to wake up the dead." Actors are invited to make a film at the castle of the blood-revived, Dracula-like vampire Karl Urich (sp?), known to the world-at-large only as a "great director of horror movies." ("I was vampirized in Mesopotamia, about 2,000 years ago.") Tired of his unlife, he wants to die: "My death for your lives." At one point, he extracts his aide's heart by supernatural remote control; at the end, in a twist on *The Picture of Dorian Gray,* his soul is revealed to be contained in reels of film. Plus a hunchback hommage to Marty Feldman in *Young Frankenstein* ("Hey, guys, Marty Feldman's back!") and a slew of monsters and victims locked up in a cellar dungeon .... Mostly misfired movie is light but not very funny, gory but not very scary. Scorecard: some plot novelty, good cobweb-and-mildew work.

**HAWK ISLAND** see *Midnight Mystery*

**HAZING IN HELL, A** see *Pledge Night*

**HE KILLS, NIGHT AFTER NIGHT AFTER NIGHT** see *Night, After Night, After Night*

**HE-MAN AND THE MASTERS OF THE UNIVERSE** see *Masters of the Universe. Secret of the Sword, The.*

**HEADHUNTER** (So. African) Gibraltar Releasing/Jay Davidson, Joel Levine 1988 color 91m. (aka *Head Hunter*). D: Francis Schaeffer. SP: Len Spinelli. Mus: Julian Laxton. SpFxMkp: Elaine Alexander, Kevin Brennan. Ref: TV. V 2/14/90:47(hv). With Kay Lenz, Wayne Crawford, Steve Kanaly, June Chadwick, John Fatooh (headhunter).

A vicious "devil," or "evil sun," is busy "reclaiming" souls in both Nigeria and Little Havana, Miami. At the end, the devil possesses, or supernaturally clones, a woman, then a man, then reveals its own ugly self.... Lenz and Crawford are capable in this otherwise unremarkable horror-fantasy. Main motif: the hero taking dives out of (closed) windows. Clips from *The Hideous Sun Demon* (on TV) punctuate the climactic action.

**HEADHUNTER** (H.K.) c1990? feature. D: Lau Shinghon. Ref: NST! 4:26: "harrowing."

Mad ex-soldier stalks and kills.

**HEADS** (Can.) Republic & Showtime-TV/Atlantis/Credo-So-journ/Tudor-Evenmore & Davis Ent. & MCIDO & The Movie Network & CanWest (Goodwill-Mazur/Grosvenor Park) 1993 color 102m. D: Paul Shapiro. Story, Tel: Jay Stapleton. Tel: also Adam Brooks. Ph: A. Kivilo. Mus: Jonathan Goldsmith. PD: M. Joy. SpFxMkp: Randy Macinally. Ref: TV. PT 20:70: "many well done scenes of heads and headless bodies." With Jon Cryer, Jennifer Tilly, Ed Asner, Roddy McDowall.

"Decapitation murders."(PT) Ingredients include the "town de-capitator" of Dry Falls and a visualized nightmare re a severed head. The photography is better than the script deserves, and Tilly isn't bad, but this black comedy tries too hard.

**HEALTH CLUB HORROR** or **HEALTH-CLUB SUPER-MONSTERS** see *Toxic Avenger, The*

**HEALTH WARNING** see *Flash—Future Kung Fu*

**HEART OF MIDNIGHT** Samuel Goldwyn/Virgin Vision (AG) 1988 color 95m. (101m.). Story, SP, D: Matthew Chapman. Story: also Everett De Roche. Mus: Yanni. SpFX; Guy H. Tuttle. Mkp Des: Hiram Ortiz. Opt: Cinema Research. Ref: TV. Sacto Union 3/8/89. V 5/25/88. With Jennifer Jason Leigh, Peter Coyote, Frank Stallone, Brenda Vaccaro, Sam Schact (Uncle Fletcher).

"There is no logic to this place." Phantoms, giant eyeballs, mysteriously-opening doors, levitating apples, riderless moving bicycles, and other phenomena haunt the dead, depraved Fletcher's Midnight club. There seem to be logical explanations for some of these apparitions, though the supernatural and the psychological also seem to play a part in this unaffecting *Repulsion*-esque thriller.

The **HEART OF THE DEAL** Showtime-TV 1990? short. D: Yuri Newman, Marina Levikova. Ref: SFChron 12/7/90: "self-con-scious"; on "The 30-Minute Movie." With Ruben Blades.

Accountant signs form "so someone can kill his wife to take her heart."

**HEARTBEAT 100** (H.K.) Cinema City/Raymond Wong 1987 color c91m. D: Kent Cheung, Lo Kin. SP: Wong, Cheng, Fai. Ph: James Chan. PD: Cheng's Film Prod. Co. Ref: TV: Rainbow Video; Eng. titles. NST! 4:26. Fango 107:59. With Maggie Cheung, Mark Cheng, Liu Fong, Wong Ching, Bonnie Law.

A hatchet-wielding killer who encases his dead twin brother, Pink Panther, in a statue ... a "ghost" flitting about "spooky" number

13 at On Lok Village ... a dog, Sheepie, that's slaughtered ... a woman who slashes her lover during intercourse ... and a cop named Weeny Eyes all figure in this fast-paced, spotty comic-suspenser with horrific overtones. A surprisingly violent light comedy.

**HEARTSTONE** see *Demonstone*

**HEARTSTOPPER** Tempe (C. A. Gelini/Thinker Prods.) 1990 (1989) color feature. SP, D: John Russo, from his novel *The Awakening.* FX: Tom Savini. Ref: PT 16:57: "interesting enough." V 5/2/90:286 (rated). With Kevin Kindlin (vampire), Moon Zappa, T. Savini, Michael J. Pollard.

**HEAT FROM ANOTHER SUN** see *Satan's Princess*

**HEATHERS** New World & Cinemarque Ent. 1989 (1988) color 102m. D: Michael Lehmann. SP: Daniel Waters. Mus: David Newman. SpMkp: Ken Myers. SpFX: Marty Bresin. SdFxEd: Hamilton Sterling. OptFX: Cinema Research. Ref: TV: New World Video. V 1/25/89. Fango 2/90: "John Hughes Goes to Hell." MFB '90:15-16. With Winona Ryder, Christian Slater, Shannen Doherty (Heather Duke), Lisanne Falk (Heather McNamara), Kim Walker (Heather Chandler).

"I don't really like my friends." Veronica's (Ryder) friends are the "beautiful and popular" at Westerburg High, in Sherwood, Ohio, and most of them are named Heather. J. D. (Slater), the new boy at school, helps Veronica turn her antipathy into murder. Victim number one: Heather Chandler, probably the worst of the Heathers. More semi-justifiable homicide follows. ("Kurt and Ram had nothing to offer the school except date rapes and AIDS jokes.") Extra added: Veronica's visualized nightmare re the ghost of Heather Chandler. ("My afterlife is so boring.").... *Heathers*—which adopts J. D.'s tactics: "The extreme always seems to make an impression"—is rife with pinpoint-right examples of the extreme and outrageous. In sequences such as the "overheard" silent prayers of the mourners at Heather Chandler's funeral, the writing is hilariously on-target. (The prayers are a litany of various self-interests.) Ultimately, though, the movie seems unsure as to whether it's about Heathers or anti-Heathers, peer pressure or psychosis, Veronica or J. D. It simply seems to want to make an impression.

**HEATSEEKER** Vidmark/Trimark-Filmworks 1994 color 91m. SP,D: A. Pyrun. SP: also C. Borkgren. Ref: PT 22:71: "cyborg kickboxer matches." vc box: 1995. With K.H. Cooke, Tina Cote, Tim Thomerson.

**HEAVENLY SPELL** (H.K.) c1989? color/ws c88m. Ref: TV: World Video; no Eng. Y. K. Ho. Chao Thai Market: *Two Ghost Women*—tr t of Thai version.

A ghost leads a young woman into a river, whereupon the two become sea serpents which look like big, inflatable sea horses. At one point, the two venture onto land, where one bites a man. At the end, one ghost serpent helps the hero destroy an evil sorcerer. Plus: animated squiggles, a vanishing cobra, *Halloween* music, and a talking skull.... Cheapo effects here are campy at best.

**HEAVY METAL L-GAIM: FULL METAL SOLDIER** (J) 198-? anim color 55m. (aka *L-Gaim. Full Metal Soldier L. Gaim*). Based on Mamoru Nagano's TV series. Ref: Animag 12:36-45: OAV. Japan Video.

Nations in the Pentagona planet system wage war against "armies of fighting mecha known as heavy metal...."

**HECTOR SERVADAC** see *On the Comet*

**HEI TAI YANG 731** see *Men behind the Sun*

**HELDENSAGEN VOM KOSMOSINSEF** see *Legend of Galactic Heroes*

**HELL** (J) 1979 (*Jigoku*). D: T. Kumashiro. Ref: Weisser/JC: remake of the '60 film. With M. Harada, K. Kishida.

Cannibalism and gore in hell.

**HELL COMES TO FROGTOWN** New World/Donald G. Jackson 1988 (1987) color 86m. Story, D, P: Jackson. D: also R. J. Kizer. Story, SP, P: Randall Frakes. Mus: David Shapiro. SpMkpFX: Steve Wang. Animatronics: Dave Kindlon. SdFX: SLM. Opt: Ray Mercer. Ref: TV. V 7/27/88. 11/11/87:6. With Roddy Piper, Sandahl Bergman, Cec Verrell, William Smith, Rory Calhoun, Nicholas Worth, Rick Bross (frog bartender), Annie McKinon (little mutant).

Medtech ("Making babies is our business") assigns potent Sam Hell (Piper)—"one weird dude"—the task of fertilizing women in the sterile, postwar wastelands. Main objective: Frogtown, where the bar serves "industrial waste" and radioactive beer, most everyone is an amphibian, or "greener"—a war-spawned, frog-headed mutant—and fertile women are held captive.... Despite the outre premises and title, *Hell* plays fairly conventionally. The frog heads, however, are surprisingly good. The eyes are particularly lifelike. Some okay one-liners; some fizzles.

Sequel: *Frogtown II.*

**HELL HIGH** JGM/DGS (Grossman/Steinman)/Tonight Prods. 1989 (1986) color 82m. (aka *Raging Fury*). SP, D, Co-P: Douglas Grossman. SP: also Leo Evans. Mus: R. Macar, C. Hyans-Hart. SpFX: Bill DePaolo. Mkp: Suzen Poshek. Ref: TV. V 5/31/89. With Christopher Stryker, Maureen Mooney, Christopher Cousins, Millie Prezioso, Jason Brill.

High-school kids play ghost to exploit a legend and scare their biology teacher who, when she was a little girl, was indirectly responsible for a gory double-death in a swamp. ("That place gives me the creeps!") She comes back, crazed, from the near-dead and begins slaying her tormentors.... Laboriously plotted "18 Years Later"-type horror movie becomes progressively more unbelievable.

**HELL HOLE** see *Escape from Hell Hole*

**HELL HOUND** see *Baxter*

**HELL HOUSE** see *Carnage*

**HELL ISLAND** see *Attack of the Beast Creatures*

**HELL ISLAND** see *Slaughterhouse Rock*

**HELL SERPENT** see *Anak ni Zuma*

**HELL SPA** Bovine (J. M. James) 1990 color 108m. SP, D: M. J. Bowler. SP: also D. J. Devine. Ph: A. Goldstein. Mus & SpSdFX: Eric Ekstrand. AD: G. Hildreath. SpMkpFX: Mark P. Case, Steve Pugh. Addl Screams: Angela Eads. Ref: TV: Raedon HV. no Martin. With Lisa Bawdon, Leonna Small, Carol Connors (aka C. Chance), R. Storti.

"I am the darkness in every man's soul." The devilish Mr. Ex offers a health-spa owner success in exchange for "loyalty." ("It's almost as if he himself isn't a part of nature.") He enforces his Plan Ex program by severing the fingers of slackers ("We guarantee loss of weight"), and has a machine which replaces the insides of his victims with "stuffing".... "Faust," set in a San Francisco health club. Flat acting and writing, a bland "Satan" (Ron Waldron), and a smidgeon of gore.

**HELLBENT** Raedon/Hellbent (Louise Jaffe/Phil Casella) 1989 color 87m. (aka *Los Angeles Is Hellbent*). SP, D: Richard Casey. Ph: Jim Gillie. Mus: Greg Burk et al. AD: Wasser, Scully. Ref: V 4/26/89: "repellent in every detail." With Phil Ward, Lyn Levand, Cheryl Slean, David Marciano.

"Musictrash" band leader makes deal with the devil.

**HELLBOUND: HELLRAISER II** (U.S.-B) New World & Cinemarque Ent./Film Futures (Troopstar Ltd.) 1988 color 96m. (*Hellraiser II: Hellbound* - orig t). D: Tony Randel. SP: Peter Atkins, from a story by Clive Barker. Exec Co-P: Barker. Mus: Christopher Young. SpMkpFX: Image Animation; (des) Geoff Portass; (consul) Bob Keen. SpFxSup: Graham Longhurst. Anim: Rory Fellowes, Karl Watkins. OptFxSup: Cliff Culley. Ref: TV: New World Video. V 9/14/88. 1/13/88:28. SFChron 12/23/88. SFExam 12/23/88. With Clare Higgins (Julia), Ashley Laurence, Ken Cranham, Barbie Wilde (female Cenobite), Nicholas Vince (chatterer), Deborah Joel (skinless Julia), Simon Bamford (Butterball).

"Julia can come back now, like Frank!" And she does, through a mattress, and she looks like hell. Main problem: no skin. A psychiatrist (Cranham) brings her victims, whose skin she absorbs. ("I'm the evil queen!") She, in turn, offers victims (including the doctor) to the Lord of the Labyrinth, Leviathan, "god of flesh, hunger, and desire," who wants souls.... More adventures in the skin trade. Barker is still at the puncture stage of horror, in this sequel to *Hellraiser.* This is his *Rabid*, and the tools of horror include wires, fishhooks, claws, knives, drills, nails, and straight razors. Flesh is really weak here: Skin, arms, and heads can't be trusted to stay on people. On the psychological level, the main hell-as-Wonderland set is equated with the "labyrinth" of the mind. Well-done, but basically repellent gore fable re (not to put too fine a point on it) pain.

**HELLBOUND** Cannon 1993 color 97m. D: Aaron Norris. SP: B. Friedman, D.G. Thompson. Ref: Martin: "not much story." SFChron 4/16/94: "It's not working, Chuck." With Chuck Norris, Sheree Wilson, Calvin Levels, Christopher Neame.

Various holy men vs. a 700-year-old demon.

**HELLBOUND HEART, The** see *Hellraiser*

**HELLFIRE** see *Primal Scream*

**HELLGATE** Ghost Town & Distant Horizon & Ananh Singh 1989 color 88m. D: W. A. Levey. SP: Michael O'Rourke. Ref: V 5/31/89: "puerile script." Martin. PT 10:49-50: "irritating." With Ron Palillo, Abigail Wolcott, Carel Trichardt.

Tourist-trap ghost town haunted by madman, ghouls, etc.

**HELLHOLE** Col/Hellhole (Arkoff Int'l.) 1985 color 95 1/2m. D: Pierre De Moro. SP: Vincent Mongol. Dial: Lance Dickson, M. E. Schwartz. Mus: Jeff Sturges. SpFX: Dale Martin. SpMkp: Donn Markel. Ref: TV: RCA-Col video. Stanley. V 3/20/85. With Ray Sharkey, Judy Landers, Marjoe Gortner, Richard Cox, Terry Moore, Mary Woronov, Martin Beck, Cliff Emmich, Edy Williams, Lynn Borden, Sammy Thurston (beast woman), Dyanne Thorne.

Enter the "hellhole" at the Ashland Sanitarium for Women and "you're never gonna be the same." There, Dr. Fletcher (Woronov) and Dr. Dane (Gortner) conduct "horrible experiments" in what she calls "chemical lobotomy," which involves injections with a very large needle. The "living nightmares" which result are caged in another part of the building. At the end, the uncaged horrors swarm over Dr. Fletcher, who is given a dose of her own insanity serum.... Formula. A must, however, for Mary Woronov fans. Watch for her "living nightmare" look in her last scene; listen for her "Shoot!" after one experiment fails, and the subject dies. Otherwise, skin and screaming.

**HELLMASTER** Dolphin Prods. (Dalton-Mayry/N.J. White) 1990 color 99m. S, D, P, AD, SpFxDes: Douglas Schulze. Ph: M. Goi. Mus: Traynor, Croll. SpMkpFX: Roger A. White Prods. FxCoord: Margaret White. OptFxSup: John Furniotis; Film FX of Toronto. SdFX: Jim Moore. Ref: TV. TVG. SFChron Dtbk 6/20/93. PT 14:49. With John Saxon, David Emge, Amy Raasch, Edward Stevens, Robert Dole, Sean Sweeney (Joel).

"He can put thoughts in your mind!" The Kant Institute's Prof. Jones (Saxon) uses the government's Nietzsche Experiment—originally intended to produce telepaths—to create a "genetically deformed army." Diluted with blood, his "superman" drug, a brain-eating acid, turns subjects into his "private assassins".... Garbled, drawn-out, disjointed, and very violent. The ghouls are all Freddy wisecrackers. Plus lots of "Joel, what have they done to you?"

**HELLO** 1982 color 9m. Ref: Hound: "three extraterrestrial musicians."

**HELLO, DRACULA** (Taiwanese) Kinco Films 1986? color/ws c95m. Ref: TV: Sunny Video; Eng. titles; above is vc box ad t.

"Kid-corpse" Konsi roams a forest looking for his father, who died 100 years ago. Meanwhile, Shih-kuah-pih's Master returns as a hopping vampire, bites him, and abducts a little girl, Ten-ten. At the end, Shih-kuah-pih, now a vampire too ("It's very hard to be dead"), sacrifices himself and blows up Master.... A very busy, but only sporadically funny monster-comedy. The slickest effect: The Master, torn limb from limb, reassembles. Funny/strange-more-than-ha-ha scene: Konsi—acting as both batter and

pitcher—plays baseball with a supernatural "ball." The climactic sequence, in which kids on unicycles battle vampires, is also pretty funny/strange. At one point, Ten-ten leads a Taoist priest's monkey-see, monkey-do vampires in a cute "chorus line" number.

See also: *Little-Boy Ghost.*

**HELLO MARY LOU: PROM NIGHT II** (Can.) Goldwyn/Peter Simpson (Simcom) 1987 color 96m. (*The Haunting of Hamilton High* - orig t). D: Bruce Pittman. SP: Ron Oliver. Mus: Paul Zaza. SpFX: Jim Doyle. Ref: TV. V 5/27/87. Sacto Union 11/12/87. SFChron 11/16/87. With Lisa Schrage (Mary Lou Maloney), Wendy Lyon (Vicki Carpenter), Michael Ironside, Justin Louis, Richard Monette.

Don't open the trunk. Mary Lou Maloney (1940-1957), nicknamed "Hot Stuff," prom queen flambé whose soul is wandering in purgatory, revives and walks about in the body of Vicki Carpenter, who meanwhile is sucked into a world behind the blackboard.... *Elm Street*-like nightmare imagery crossed with "Linda Blairsville"—in follow-up to *Prom Night*—is mostly minor frissons, but the "accordion" locker trick is a beaut. Also worth mention: Mary Lou's corpse stepping out on prom night—stepping out of Vicki's chest, that is.

Next: *Prom Night III* (which see).

**HELLO TELEVISION** Educ/Sennett 1930 20m. D: L.A. Pearce. Ref: Maltin/SSS: "futuristic comedy." Lee: TV-phone. LC. With Andy Clyde, Ann Christy.

**HELLO! WHO IS IT?!** (H.K.) City Host 1994 color feature. D: Luk Kin Ming. Ref: vc box. With Lau Ching Wan.

Avenging ghost.

**HELLRAISER** (B) New World/Rivdel Ltd. (Film Futura & Cinemarque) 1987 color 93m. SP, D: Clive Barker. From his story "The Hellbound Heart." Mus: Christopher Young. SpMkpFX: (des) Bob Keen; (workshop sup) Geoff Portass. SpCostume: Jane Wildgoose. Anim: Nick Xypnitos. Opt: Optical Film Fx. Ref: TV. MFB'87:276-7. V 5/20/87. SFExam 9/25/87:D-4. SFChron Dtbk 9/20/87. Washington Times 10/1/87. With Andrew Robinson, Clare Higgins, Ashley Laurence, Sean Chapman, Oliver Smith (Frank the Monster), Frank Baker (derelict), Doug Bradley (Lead Cenobite), Nicholas Vince (Cenobite), Simon Bamford (butterball), Grace Kirby (Cenobite).

Main ingredients: Cenobites, "explorers in the further regions of experience" ... Frank, once a man, now muck, who needs more blood to "come back" completely ... a demon-summoning box ... crucified rats ... and a cricket eater that turns into a winged demon.... The new spin on gross-out art, or trash, has some impressive "formation" shots (for Frank the Monster) and contains some obvious pandering to the gore corps. But if the characters are determinedly unpleasant, the movie is occasionally imaginative, queasy fun. One highlight: the tail-up-top, scorpion-like Cenobite.

Sequels: *Hellbound. Hellraiser III.* See also: *Transylvania Twist.*

**HELLRAISER II** see *Hellbound*

**HELLRAISER III: HELL ON EARTH** Dimension (Miramax)/Clive Barker/Fifth Avenue Ent. & Lawrence Mortorff 1992 color 92m. D: Anthony Hickox. Story, SP: Peter Atkins. Story: also Tony Randel. Ph: Gerry Lively. Mus: Randy Miller. MechSpFxCoord: Ray Bivins. SpFx Coord: Bob Keen. MkpSpFxCoord: Paul Jones. VisFX:(sup) Steve Rundell;(des) Cinema Research;(anim) Jay Johnson. PhysicalFX: Kevin McCarthy, John Wells. Sd:(sp fx) Larsen, Thomas;(des) Jonathan Miller et al. Ref: TV: Paramount. V 9/14/92: "imaginative special effects." Fango 122:8: "awful." V 8/17/92:12 (rated). SFChron 9/12/92: "sly humor." SFChron 9/23/92: with Danny Tartabull. ad. Sacto Union 9/12/92: "scary." SFChron Dtbk 11/29/92. With Terry Farrell, Doug Bradley (Pinhead), Paula Marshall, Ashley Laurence.

"There is only flesh!" The hospital emergency room becomes Telekinesis Central; The Boiler Room is Pinhead's new hangout; and the "gateway to hell" is in Joey's (Farrell) apartment. Pinhead here begins as a statue that strips the flesh of his victims, then ingests the rest; later, he's seen in his original form, Elliott (Bradley), in a window-world flashback to 1921 India .... More pins-and-needles gore and sub-Freddy-isms from Pinhead. Okay effect: Pinhead's head absorbing Elliott's.

**HELL'S BELLS** Col (Disney) 1929 anim silent? 6m. Ref: LC. Lee: "grotesque animals in hell."

**HELL'S FIRE** Iwerks 1934 anim color c7m. Ref: TV: Kino Video. Filmfax 43:22: Willie Whopper.

Fairish hi-jinks with Rasputin, Dr. Jekyll and Mr. Hyde, the devil, and "hell hound" Cerberus. Plus a cute bit with a flea.

**HELL'S GATE** see *Porte dell'Inferno, Le*

**HENRY: PORTRAIT OF A SERIAL KILLER** Maljack (Ali) 1989 (1986) color 83m. SP, D, Co-P & Mus: John McNaughton. SP: also Richard Fire. Mus & Co-P: Steven A. Jones. Mus: also Ken Hale. Tech FX: Lee Ditkowski. Mkp: Berndt Rantscheff. SdFX: Dan Haberkorn. Ref: TV. V 10/4/89. NYorker 4/23/90. With Michael Rooker, Tom Towles, Tracy Arnold.

"A fictional dramatization of certain events...." With Henry (Rooker), a warped young man "on his way out west," a double date is likely as not to turn into a double murder. Killing is easy for him ("It's either you or them"), and not much harder for roommate Otis (Towles), who joins him in murdering a surly, stolen-goods fence. When Otis molests his (Otis's) sister, Becky (Arnold), however, Henry dispatches him. At the end, Becky—who feels a lost-souls kinship with Henry—is also just another body in a suitcase.... At its most tenuous, *Henry* seems just another slasher movie, just done right; at its best—the emotional-crusher ending, for instance—it plays like a love story gone very wrong. The problem with the film—you don't know much more about Henry than you could glean from a newspaper account of his exploits—may also be the point: There's not much to the people here. All you need to know, really (the filmmakers suggest), is that Henry ("My mama was a whore!") and Becky had horrendous family lives. (Her father molested her.) That's all you know about most movie slashers. *Henry* seems, by turns, honest and exploitative. Yet, like *The Texas Chain Saw Massacre*, it

breaks new ground, though exactly what ground is hard to say. Maybe it just gives its subgenre some retrospective validity.

**HER VENGEANCE** (H.K.) 1988? color feature. D: Lan Nai-Tai. Ref: Weisser/ATC: "mean-spirited revenge-for-rape flick." With Lam Ching Ying.

A "virtual smorgasbord of blood and gore ...."

**HERBERT WEST—REANIMATOR** see *Re-animator*

**HERCEGNO ES A KOBOLD, A** see *Princess and the Goblin, The*

**HERCULE CONTRE MOLOCH** see *Conquest of Mycene*

**HERCULES II** see *Adventures of Hercules, The*

**HERCULES AGAINST MOLOCH** see *Conquest of Mycene*

**HERCULES AND THE AMAZON WOMEN** Univ-TV 1994 color c90m. Ref: TVG. SFChron 4/26/94: "The word is cheesy." With Kevin Sorbo (Hercules), Anthony Quinn, Roma Downey, Michael Hurst.

"Banana slug monster ... whole tribe of monsters." (SFC)

**HERCULES AND THE CIRCLE OF FIRE** Univ-TV 1994 color c90m. Ref: TVG: "isn't campy enough." With Tawny Kitaen, Kevin Sorbo, A. Quinn, Kevin Atkinson, Stephanie Barrett.

"Mortal warriors ... shivering world."

**HERCULES AND THE LOST KINGDOM** Univ-TV 1994 color c90m. Ref: TVG. With K. Sorbo, Renee O'Connor, A. Quinn, Nathaniel Lees, Robert Trebor, Elizabeth Hawthorne, Eric Close.

**HERCULES ATTACKS** see *Conquest of Mycene*

**HERCULES IN THE MAZE OF THE MINOTAUR** Univ-TV 1994 color c90m. Ref: TVG: "evil man-beast (Ray Anthony Parker)." Vallejo T-H. With K. Sorbo, M. Hurst, A. Quinn, Andrew Thurtill.

**HERCULES IN THE UNDERWORLD** Univ-TV 1994 color c90m. Ref: TVG: Hercules battles "dark forces." With K. Sorbo, Marlee Shelton, T. Kitaen, Cliff Curtis.

**HERCULES VS. MOLOCH** see *Conquest of Mycene*

**HERE COMES THE GRUMP** Embassy Home Ent./DePatie & Freleng 1985 anim color 100m. Ref: V 8/21/85:82(hv): "fun." no Hound. no Martin.

"Ghost Town (with living houses)" ... "curse of gloom" ... Grump who rides giant green dragon.

**HERMELINDA LINDA II: SUPER AGENTE 0013** see *Agente Secreto 0013*

**HERO—BEYOND THE BOUNDARY OF TIME** (H.K.) Impact Films 1993 color/ws 96m. Ref: TV: vt; no Eng. (apart from title).

A horse-powered, stewpot-like time machine propels an ancient dude into today. Later, other electrically-charged agents from the past follow him. Broad, negligible sf-comedy.

**HERO AND THE TERROR** Cannon (Raymond Wagner) 1988 color 96m. D: William Tannen. SP: Dennis Shryack, Michael Blodgett, from Blodgett's novel. Mus: David Frank. Prosth: Lesa Nielsen. SpFX: John Eggett. Ref: TV. V 8/10/88. SFChron 8/26/88; Dtbk 9/11/88. With Chuck Norris, Brynn Thayer, Steve James, Jack O'Halloran, Ron O'Neal, Tiiu Leek.

Formula thriller involves a near-invulnerable killer (O'Halloran, who haunts the old Wiltern Theatre in L.A.,) and a hidden room full of dead bodies.

**HERO IN THE FAMILY** ABC-TV/Disney-TV & Barry & Enright & Alexander Prods. 1986 color 92m. D: Mel Damski. Tel: John Drimmer, Geoffrey Loftus. Mus: William Goldstein. SpFX: (co-ord) John Thomas; (space seq des) Paul Peters. OptFX: Van Der Veer, Tom Anderson. Ref: TV. TVG. V 10/8/86:140. With Christopher Collet, Cliff De Young, Annabeth Gish, Darleen Carr, M. Emmet Walsh.

A crystal containing "non-evolved matter"—retrieved from a ring in space—disrupts the "neural cells, on the molecular level," of astronaut Digger Reed (De Young) and Orville the Chimp (Michael the Chimp). Digger's consciousness winds up in Orville's head, and Orville's in Digger's.... Broad, sloppy slapstick farce, with an alright bit here and there. Lots of "Follow that chimp!" and "No more monkey business!" Little of the kooky, out-of-species-behavior charm of *The Wild and the Free,* with its domesticated chimps; none of the wild pathos of *The Fly* (1986).

**The HEROIC TRIO** (H.K.) Paka Hill Film (Chin Siu Tung) 1992 color/ws 87m. (*Tong Fong Sam Hop*). D: Johnny To. SP: Sandy Shaw. Mus D: William Hu. AD: B. Yu. Ref: TV: Tai Seng Video; Eng. titles. U.C. Theatre notes 1/20/94. V 1/3/94. vc box: *Women with Swords* - alt vt t. With Maggie Cheung.

"It's Wonder Woman! She's great!" Ingredients include the titular trio of terrific women (including Wonder Woman, though not *the* Wonder Woman) ... the satanic Master—a "monster"—who has babies stolen in an attempt to find a King for China ... an "invisible robe" invention, which leads to an Invisible Woman ... and the Master's aide's basket beheader .... An amusing series of outrageous stunts. Highlight: the return of the Master as a stopmo skeleton-and-brain, at the end. ("His body is gone, but his mind is still there.") His tentacle-like bones then encircle and commandeer one of the trio.

**HEROIC TRIO II** (H.K.) China Ent. 1993 color 97m. (aka *The Executioners*). D: Johnny To, Ching Siu Tung. Ref: VW 23:15-16: "hopelessly misguided sequel" to *The Heroic Trio.* With Michelle Yeoh, Anita Mui, Maggie Cheung, Anthony Wong.

"Takes place in a dreary, futuristic, post-nuclear Hong Kong."

**HEY, GHOST!** see *Close Encounter with the Vampire*

**HEY GHOST! II** see *Vampire Strikes back*

**HI-SPEED JECY: PROLOGUE** (J) VAP Video/Pierrot Studios 1989 anim color/ws? 30m. D: S. Kageyama. From the novels

by Eiichiro Saito. Ref: TV: VAP Video; OAV; no Eng. (apart from title). Animag 11:26-7. 7:4. 10:5: 1st of 12 OAVs.

Jecy and Folk Green are beamed up from the planet Vall to a spaceship headed for the planet Ganet. Routine sf-actioner also features a battle of the spaceships, phantom "warriors," hovering cars, air cycles, and (in the credit sequence) monstrous cave phantoms.

**HIDAN OF MOUNT BIENJOW, The** see *Invasion of the Girl Snatchers*

**The HIDDEN** New Line & Heron/Robert Shaye & Mega Ent. & Michael Meltzer (New Line-Heron Jt. Venture/Third Elm St. Venture) 1987 color 96m. D: Jack Sholder. SP: Bob Hunt. Mus: Michael Convertino. SpMkpFX: Kevin Yagher. SpVisFX: Dream Quest Images. SpFxCoord: G. C. Landerer. Anim: Jim Shaw, Kathy Kean. Opt: Ray Mercer. Ref: TV: Media Home Ent. video. MFB'89:16-17. V 10/28/87. NYorker 12/7/87. SFExam 10/30/87. ad. With Kyle MacLachlan, Michael Nouri, Clu Gulager, Ed O'Ross, Donald Willis, Claudia Christian.

An alien (MacLachlan) comes to Earth searching for another alien which inhabits human bodies and demands instant gratification of its every desire. ("I want this car!") Although the evil, ugly-bug alien switches bodies, mouth-to-mouth, when the first body wears out, it has a fondness, in all guises, for loud rock music and Ferraris. An FBI "toy"—actually an alien ray gun—destroys the evil alien when the latter is between hosts, and the good alien surrenders his spirit to save his human partner, Beck (Nouri).... *The Hidden* wants to have its *Alien* and *E.T.,* too, although the alien-pursuing-alien plot is closer to *Brain from Planet Arous* (1958) than to the other two movies. The something-for-everyone story ranges from action-chase material to the mystical. (Beck's daughter seems to anticipate the climactic soul transference.) Intermittently, the script is also concerned with questions such as, Why do ordinary "law-abiding citizens" suddenly go berserk and start killing people? But the movie is probably at its best when presenting the body-hopping alien as a semi-satiric cross between the Indestructible Man and the Ultimate Consumer.

**The HIDDEN II** New Line 1993 color feature. D: Seth Pinsker. Ref: V 8/30/93:12(rated): "sci-fi horror violence and gore." 10/25/93:46(ad). With Raphael Sbarge, Kate Hodge.

**HIDDEN OBSESSION** Broadstar/Hidden Rage(Broadbridge et al) 1992 color 92m. (aka *Rage*). Story, D: John Stewart. Story, SP: David Reskin. Ph: James Mathers. Mus: Richard Glasser. SpFX:(coord) Sam Barkan;(sup) Don Parsons. Key Mkp: A.S. Howell. Ref: TV: aka *Hidden Rage*? Martin. PT 17:61-2: "false scares, exaggerated thunder, lame POV stalking scenes." With Heather Thomas, Jan Michael Vincent, Nick Celozzi, D. Glasser, Linda Krus.

Stripper-killing psycho in isolated country house. (PT) PT (or PV) got it right. This one is predictable, right down to the "surprise" psycho's accidental (but obvious) dialogue tipoff to his craziness, and the accompanying thunderstorm.

**HIDDEN RAGE** see *Hidden Obsession*

**HIDE AND GO SHRIEK** New Star Ent. (Shriek) 1987 color 90m. (aka *Close Your Eyes and Pray*). D: Skip Schoolnik. SP: Michael Kelly. Ph: Eugene Shlugleit. Mus: John Ross. PD: Sharon Viljoen. SpFX: Screaming Mad George. SdFxEd: Jon Ross. Ref: TV: NS Video. V 4/6/88:32(hv): "utterly routine teen horror pic." 9/16/87: 8/13/87 start. Martin. Phantom: "slasher cliches." McCarty II: "better than some." Hardy/HM2. Stanley. With Bunky Jones, Brittain Frye, George Thomas, Donna Baltron, Annette Sinclair, Scott Fults.

"I hate all this scary stuff." Creepy ex-con vs. teens. A drowning in a sink ... spike gore ... an unlikely impalement on a mannequin hand ... and a severed head.... The vapid-banter-and-false-alarms pattern. Bad.

**HIDE AND SHRIEK** see *American Gothic*

**HIDEKI** see *Evil Dead Trap 2*

**HIDEOUS MUTANT FREEKZ** see *Freaked*

**HIDEOUS SUN DEMON, The** see *What's up, Hideous Sun Demon*

**HIDER IN THE HOUSE** Vestron (USA-TV)/Precision Films & Mack-Taylor & Zeron (Stuart Cornfeld) 1989 color 108m. D: Matthew Patrick. SP, Co-P: Lem Dobbs. Ph: Jeff Jur. Mus: Christopher Young. SpFxCoord: Gary King. Mkp: Susan Mills. Ref: TV. MFB'89:370-1. Martin. V 12/13/89. With Gary Busey (Tom Sykes), Mimi Rogers, Michael McKean, Kurt C. Kinder, Candy Hutson, Elizabeth Ruscio, Bruce Glover.

Tom Sykes, released after eighteen years in Burley State Hospital for lashing back at his abusive father by burning his parents to death, hides in the attic of the Dreyer family. In order to keep his presence secret, he eliminates an exterminator and the family dog, then later, semi-accidentally, breaks Mrs. Dreyer's (Rogers) friend's (Ruscio) neck. At the end, after his hideaway is discovered, and he's shot by Julie, he makes one last, *Halloween* lunge at her.

Offbeat, but only semi-successful updating of the *Four Daughters* story: Outsider envies, attempts to break into apparently happy family. At first, the script seems concerned with the overlapping of the Sykeses and the Dreyers: Julie's son Neil (Kinder), too, is burning "Dad" (in the form of a toy soldier). But the movie goes on to take the easier, thriller way out, and finally can't quite make dramatic sense of the horror of the Sykeses and the averted horror of the Dreyers.

**HIGH DESERT KILL** USA-TV/MCA-TV (Lehigh Ent.) 1989 color 96m. D: Harry Falk. Tel & Exec Co-P: T. S. Cook. Ph: Michel Hugo. Mus: Dana Kaproff. PD: Roger Holzberg. SpFX: Jack Faggard. Ref: TV: aka High Mountain Kill? With Anthony Geary, Marc Singer, Micah Grant, Chuck Connors, Vaughn Armstrong (Paul).

"It was a man, but not really." An alien being experimenting with human subjects, in and around Pueblo Indian ruins, feeds on memories and takes the form of the late "Uncle Paul." It erects a force-field "cage," but reduces to its original bug-thing form and apparently dies when subjected to the memory of Paul's death (under a 10,000-volt power line).... Although the latter sequence

is a fairly unusual and enjoyable payoff—"Paul" alters, moment-to-moment, with each new recollection of the man by the three hunters confronting him—it's not worth the feature-length trek. "Twilight Zone" (and the half-hour format), where are you? The picturesque New Mexico hills, desert, and rocks prove eerier than the story.

**HIGH SPIRITS** (U.S.-B) Tri-Star/Vision(Palace) 1988 color 97m. (*Ghost Tours* - orig t). SP, D: Neil Jordan. Mus: George Fenton. SpVisFX: Derek Meddings. SpMkpFX: Christopher Tucker. Anim: Peter Chiang. SpGhostsDes: Nick Dudman. Ref: TV. MFB'88:362-3. V 11/23/88. 5/6/87:164. SFExam 11/18/88. SFChron 11/18/88. Oak Trib 11/18/88. Film Yrbk '90. With Peter O'Toole, Donal McCann, Steve Guttenberg, Beverly D'Angelo, Daryl Hannah (Mary Plunkett), Liam Neeson (Martin Brogan).

"We can promise you banshees!" Peter Plunkett (O'Toole) employs fake ghosts and mummies in an attempt to turn his ancestral castle into a tourist attraction. This "pitiful supernatural sham," however, turns into the "most haunted castle in the Western Hemisphere," as the castle's real ghosts—including 200-year-old Mary Plunkett—begin to materialize. More: ghost nuns, (animated) skeletons, human/ghost sex (a la the human/alien sex in *Cocoon*), and a sort of metempsychosis, as Sharon (D'Angelo) falls and dies, and Mary takes her place and lives.... The latter makes for a charming ending; O'Toole's voice reverberates marvelously through the castle with lines like (mock menacingly) "Sleep well, if you can. Ha ha ha!"; and imaginative ideas include a whistling fish and an alternately live and cardboard giant squid, which captures a live boy who then becomes cardboard, too. Unfortunately, most of the movie is overblown and shrill. It's busy but not funny.

**HIGHLANDER** (B) Fox/Thorn EMI/Davis-Panzer (Highlander) 1986 color 116m. (111m.-U.S.). D: Russell Mulcahy. Story, SP: Gregory Widen. SP: also Peter Bellwood, Larry Ferguson. Mus: Michael Kamen; (songs) Queen. Vis & OptFX: Optical Film FX. MkpFxDes: Bob Keen. Prosth: Sandra Exelby. SpFxSup: Martin Gutteridge. Ref: TV. MFB'86:236-7. V 3/12/86. ad. With Christopher Lambert, Roxanne Hart, Clancy Brown, Sean Connery, Jon Polito.

Conner MacLeod (Lambert)—a super-being, or immortal, who needs an occasional, restorative dose of lightning—must fight his kindred at the "Gathering" in present-day New York City, until only one combatant remains. Fellow immortal Ramirez (Connery), ex-metallurgist to the King of Spain, warns MacLeod re the chief bad immortal, the Kurgan (Brown).... The parts don't quite mesh, but give *Highlander* credit for enterprise and ambition. The busy camerawork (Gerry Fisher et al.) and editing (Peter Honess) include lyrical/epic shots of Scotland (in flashbacks to the year 1526) as well as nifty transitions between present and past. There are good action set-pieces in a castle tower, a New York alley, and a parking lot, and Brown's indestructible punk is fun.

**HIGHLANDER II: THE QUICKENING** Davis-Panzer & Lamb Bear Ent. 1991 (1990) color/ws 96m.(100m.). D: Russell Mulcahy. SP: Peter Bellwood. Story: Brian Clemens, W. Panzer. Ph: Phil Meheux. Mus: Stewart Copeland. PD: Roger Hall. SpFX: John Richardson. VisFX: Stargate Films; (des) Sam Nicholson;

(coord) Laura Vinyard. OptSup: Phil Meador. Anim: (sup) Chris Cassidy; (fx) Jeff Burks et al. MkpFX: Image Animation; (des) Geoff Portass. Min Sup: Ron Thornton. SpMkpArt: Greg Cannom. SdFX: Shorr, Dawn. Ref: S&S. V 2/25/91: "the formula wears thin." PT 13:51-2. V 2/18/91: 46: playing. With Christopher Lambert, Sean Connery, Virginia Madsen, Michael Ironside.

Man from the planet Zeist (Lambert) ... "sun shield."

**HIGHLANDER: THE FINAL DIMENSION** (Can.-F-B) Miramax (Dimension)/Davis-Panzer (Transfilm-Lumiere-Falling-Cloud/Claude Leger) 1994 color/ws 94m. (99m.) (*Highlander III: The Sorcerer* - early t). D: Andy Morahan. SP: Paul Ohl. Screen Story: William Panzer, Brad Mirman. Ph: S. Chivers. Mus: J.P. Robinson. PD: G. Aird, B. Morahan. SpVisFX: Brian Johnson. SpFxSup: Louis Craig. Ref: V 12/5/94: "unbelievably trashy ... brainless." ad. SFChron 1/30/95: "complete cinematic chaos." With Christopher Lambert, Mario Van Peebles, Deborah Unger, Mako, Mark Neufeld.

Connor MacLeod (Lambert) vs. Kane (Van Peebles), a "master of illusion," from the 16th Century.

**HIGHRISE** Mark Sullivan 1980 short. Ref: SFChron Dtbk 12/18/88: "too enigmatic."

Bug-like spacecraft takes buildings from Earth to another planet.

**HIGHWAY TO HELL** Hemdale/Goodman-Rosen & Josa & High Street (Mary Ann Page, John Byers) 1992 (1991) color 93m. D: Ate de Jong. SP, Co-P: Brian Helgeland. Ph: Robin Vidgeon. Mus: Hidden Faces. PD: P. D. Foreman. SpMkpFX: Steve Johnson. SpVisFX: Randall William Cook, Cinema Research; (des) Neal Thompson; (sup) Steve Rundell; (anim) Bruce Heller. MechFxSup: J. Mercurio. Min: The Garden of Allah. SdFX: Shorr. SpThanx: David Allen, Jim Danforth. Ref: TV. V 3/23/92. SFChron Dtbk 8/9/92. PT 14:12. With Patrick Bergin (Beezle), Chad Lowe, Kristy Swanson, Adam Storke, Pamela Gidley, Richard Farnsworth, Jarrett Lennon, C. J. Graham (Sgt. Bedlam), Lita Ford, Gilbert Gottfried (Hitler), Kevin Peter Hall (Charon), Anne Meara (Medea), Jerry Stiller, M. R. McKay (Rachel Demon).

"All roads lead there." "The Sergeant," or "hell cop," patrols the desolate "road within a road" that leads to hell, where Beezle (Bergin) reigns ("I am darkness made visible") and the damned undergo auto-wrecking-like treatment.... Cocteau's *Orpheus* seems to be the immediate inspiration for *Highway to Hell*, which has a ponderous core, but generally plays like one hundred hell gags in search of a context. Some of the jokes are wearing, some wry, like the sign re the Department of Potholes. Among the niftier effects: the cop's writhing, stick-on hands and the Cerberus-on-a-choke-chain bit. Another highlight: Pluto's, a bizarre roadside cafe with decaying patrons and an incessantly joking waitress (Meara).

**The HIGHWAYMAN** NBC-TV/Glen A. Larson & Fox-TV 1987 color 90m. (*Terror on the Blacktop* - alt t). SP, D: Douglas Heyes. Sp, Exec P: Larson. Mus: Stu Phillips. Truck: (des) Michael Scheffe; (construc) Jon Ward. Min: Boss. Ref: TV. TVG. V 9/30/87:80, 86. With Sam J. Jones, Jimmy Smits, Wings Hauser,

G. Gordon Liddy, Theresa Saldana, Claudia Christian, Lyle Alzado, Michael Berryman, James Griffith.

The Highwayman (Jones) is a "high-tech road warrior" with a twelve-ton rig which includes super-Stealth invisibility capability. Strictly hardware-display stuff.

**HIJACKED TO HELL** see *No Time To Die*

**HIKARIGOKE** see *Luminous Moss*

**HIKARUON** (J) A.I.C . 198-? anim color 29m. Ref: TV: C. Moon Video; no Eng.; Pink Noise vol. 2; OAV.

In and out of an alternate universe, a sort of Chessboard World. Our young hero, who can become a flying, computerized semi-robot, does battle with a phantom that becomes a huge monster, then a really huge monster. Some atmosphere and style; routine action.

**The HILLS HAVE EYES PART II** (U.S.-B) Castle Hill/Fancey & New Realm (Hills Two) 1986 (1984) color 92m. SP, D: Wes Craven. Mus: Harry Manfredini. PD: Dominick Bruno. Ref: TV. V 2/19/86. Beverly Warren. With Michael Berryman (Pluto), Tamara Stafford, John Bloom, Janus Blythe, James Whitworth (Reaper).

Sequel to The Hills Have Eyes is closer to the *Halloween* clones than it is to its own inventive original. This one features a psychic (Stafford), a booby-trap rock, a net-trap, an underground cavern of horrors, and murders by spear and hatchet. Stilted dialogue scenes, wan suspense scenes, bad sound effects.

**HIRUKO THE GOBLIN** (J) Toshiba EMI/SEDC/Shochiku & Fuji 1990 color/ws 89m. (*Yokai Hanta - Hiruko. Spiders with Human Heads* - alt t). SP, D: Shinya Tsukamoto. Story: Daijiro Moroboshi. SpFxSup: Eiichi Asada. Ref: TV: vt; no Eng. JBC Video. V 2/24/92:158(ad): "ancient mound." Markalite 3:10. Weisser/JC. EVS. with Keiji Sawada, Masataka Kudo, Megumi Ueno.

A hurricane-like force attacks two people in a cave. Mysterious burns etch the likeness of human faces into a teenager's back. The severed head of a woman sings in a saucepan. Later, the same head sings on the surface of a pond; pointy things rise to the surface around her flower-like face. Shortly, they are revealed to be spider legs ... attached to the young lady's head, in a cleverly choreographed scene. The spider-thing sprouts wings and flies; the protagonists bring out the bug spray. Then: See the cave of the yowling spider-things! See their mass scampering up the rock wall! See the cocoon-ish arc of the spider-thing spirits as they depart into the sky!

*Hiruko*—apparently the name of the movie's possessing ghost—rings variations on elements in everything from *Bug* and the original *Fly* movie to *Attack of the Crab Monsters* and *Nightmare on Elm Street III,* but puts a fresh weird spin on each variation. The film is situated amusingly between the comic, the creepy, the campy, and Luis Bunuel. Extra credit for the sucking-spider-tongue and sticky-spider-leg sound effects. And fine if spare stopmo for the leg movements—one suspects that the critters sprout wings for purely budgetary reasons: The flying effects look to be cheaper than the crawling effects. The faces on the boy's back turn out to be the faces of the monsters' victims. Someone here has a crazy imagination.

**\*HIS BROTHER'S GHOST** 1945. SpFX: Ray Mercer. Ref: TV. TVG. Lee. Martin. no Maltin '92. no Scheuer. no V. LC. no Lentz. "Shoot-Em-Ups." With Archie Hall, Roy Brent.

Night raiders are wiping out sharecroppers in Wolf Valley, and the recently arrived brother (Fuzzy St. John) of one of the victims (St. John again) plays ghost to frighten the outlaws. ("You're going to be Andy's ghost!") Fuzzy (a "flesh-and-blood ghost") appears, first, in Andy's room ("Boo!") and at the varmints' cabin-window ("I ain't fightin' ghosts!") and, later, under a sheet, rises menacingly from a table in Doc Packard's (Karl Hackett) back room. Extra addeds: a "ghost" voice and an exhumation at midnight.

If Buster Crabbe and Al St. John aren't exactly an inspired cowboy team, they're not bad actors—St. John even gets to do "sentiment" at the death-bed reunion of the two brothers. The script, which mixes chills, comedy, and action, is generally unremarkable, though early on it does feature a line about Andy which seems, in retrospect, to be a stab at dramatic foreshadowing: "Maybe you'll never die like ordinary mortals."

**HISTORIAS VIOLENTAS** (Mex) PN-PM/Conacite Dos 1984 color 100m. D: V. Saca et al. SP: P. F. Miret. Mus: J. Gutierrez. Ref: V 12/26/84: Violent Stories - tr t. With Pedro Armendariz.

"Reflections," one of five tales, concerns a "flying saucer and visiting Martians," and is "rather mediocre."

**HIT AND RAPE** (J) 1990 anim. Ref: CM 17:62: "cybernetic" mob boss ... gory; two episodes.

**The HITCHER** Tri-Star/HBO Pictures & Silver Screen Partners (Feldman-Meeker) 1986 color/ws 97m. D: Robert Harmon. SP: Eric Red. Mus: Mark Isham. SpFX:(vis) Cinema Research; (sup) Art Brewer. Mkp: Pamela Peitzman. SupSdFxEd: Mark Mangini, Stephen Flick. Ref: TV. MFB'86:170-1. V 2/12/86. SFExam 2/21/86. ad. With Rutger Hauer (John Ryder), C. Thomas Howell, Jennifer Jason Leigh, Jeffrey DeMunn, Billy Green Bush.

The Hitcher recalls Duel when Hauer's Ryder is trailing Howell's Jim Halsey; it recalls The Sadist (1963) when Ryder is in the car testing his knife out on Halsey's face; it recalls Badlands when Halsey (not too believably) meets up with Leigh's Nash a second time. What The Hitcher itself is up to is anybody's guess. The oddest thing about the movie: the concentration on Halsey's exaggerated reactions. Ryder kills; Halsey, though, is the one who acts crazy. The Hitcher generates tension, but seems pointless. The photography (John Seale), music, and Hauer's performance help; two vomiting scenes don't.

**HITCH-HIKER, The,** see Creepshow 2

**HOBGOBLINS** T.W.E./Rick Sloane Prods. 1988 color 89m. SP, D, P, Ph, Ed: Sloane. Mus: Alan Dermarderosian. Creatures: Kenneth J. Hall. Ref: TV: T. W. E. video. Bowker '90. Hound. no Martin. Morse. With Tom Bartlett, Jeffrey Culver, Paige Sullivan, Steven Boggs, Kelley Palmer, Tami Bakke (Fantazia), The Fontanelles.

"Don't go near the vault!" Hobgoblins haunting a deserted movie studio "destroy everyone on the lot," invade Club Scum, make people act out their fantasies. ("They would find a person, tap into his brain, and then create his wildest fantasy.") Ripoff of Gremlins—by way of Impulse—features labored humor and not exactly animated puppets. A few click moments.

**HOCUS POCUS** BV (Disney)/David Kirschner-Steven Haft 1993 color 95m. D: Kenny Ortega. SP, Exec Co-P: Mick Garris. SP: also Neil Cuthbert. Story: Kirschner, Garris. Ph: Hiro Narita. Mus: John Debney. PD: William Sandell. VisFxSup: Peter Montgomery. Cat Anim:(sup) Chris Railey; Rhythm & Hues. VisFX:(coord) Denise Davis;(digital) Craig Newman;(anim) Michael Lessa;(fx anim) James Mansfield et al. SpSdFX: John Fasal. SpMkpFX: Alterian Studios. Ref: V 7/26/93: "suffers from inconsistency." Sacto Bee 7/16/93: "frightful but not in the ways intended." SFChron 7/16/93: cluttered. TV. With Bette Midler (Winifred), Sarah Jessica Parker (Sarah), Kathy Najimy (Mary), Omri Katz, Thora Birch, Vinessa Shaw, Norbert Weisser, Kathleen Freeman.

"Three ancient hags vs. the Twentieth Century." Salem, Massachusetts. Three witches rejuvenate themselves by inhaling the life force of a child, but are caught and burned. In 1993—300 years later—they revive .... Plus: a boy cursed to be an undying cat ... a "good zombie" (Doug Jones) ... and a living book of spells .... Halloween fantasy is overstuffed, but generally raucous good fun. Highlights include the witches-on-brooms effects, the witch byplay, and the talking tabby. Underrated.

**HODET OVER VANNET** (Norw.-Swed.) Filmkameratene & Svensk (J.M. Jacobsen) 1994 color 100m. D: Nils Gaup. SP: G. Eriksen, E. Ildahl. Ph: E. Thurmann-Andersen. Mus: K. Bjerkestrand. PD: H. Egende-Nissen. Ref: V 10/31/94: "unevenly acted." With Lene Elise Bergum, S. R. Karlsen, Morten Abel.

"A gory comedy-thriller with a high body count.... Mixes horror and laughs, with the former frequently grisly."

**HOKUTO NO KEN: THE MOVIE** (J) Streamline 1986?('91-U.S.) anim color 110m. (Fist of the North Star - U.S.). D: Toyoo Ashida. From the graphic novels by Buronson and Tetsuo Hara. Ref: TV: Toei Video; no Eng. Anime Opus '89:28-9. Animag 3:14. V 10/28/91:16. 11/18/91:11. SFExam 10/25/91.

In post-nuclear 199X, the apparently dead Kenshiro returns, punches out whole buildings, pulls an arrow out of his chest and tosses it aside, and crushes a thug's skull with his bare hand. Yet, the super-brute is tender, at appropriate moments. (There are two or three.) Other principals include the masked, disfigured Jagi, who uses the name Legendary Kenshiro, and the power-mad Rao. At the end, the auras of Kenshiro and Rao fight in the sky and cause earthquakes and a storm.... Amusing, if a bit wearing hyperbolic action/emotions. The Road Warrior-squared brutality majors in exploding heads. Impressive elements effects—e.g., the moodily-colored clouds, the various displays of lightning, the wind's effects.

**HOLLOWGATE** City Lights/Pepin-Merhi 1988 color c81m. SP, D: Ray DiZazzo. Ph: Voya Mikulic. Mus: John Gonzales. SpMkpFX: Judy Yonemoto. SpFX: Don Power. Ref: TV: City

Lights HV. Bowker '90. no Hound. no Martin. With Addison Randall (Mark), Katrina Alexy, Richard Dry, Patricia Jacques, J. J. Miller, George Cole, Pat Shalsant (Grandma).

"It's Halloween, boys and girls!" Mark Walters, who's "a little lost," murders Grandma (his guardian), dons various Halloween costumes, and slaughters various hapless teens. Pathetic holiday-horror fare, with perfunctory hatchet, scissors, and carving-knife gore. Hollowgate is Grandma's Oklahoma estate.

**HOLLYROCK-A-BYE BABY** ABC-TV/Hanna-Barbera 1993 anim color c90m. Ref: TVG 9/18/93. 12/5/93. Voices: Henry Corden, Raquel Welch, Mark Hamill, Ruth Buzzi, John Tesh, Mary Hart.

Ad: "When Pebbles and Bamm-Bamm move to Hollyrock, the first thing they produce is a double feature—twins!" More "Flintstones."

**HOLLYWEIRD** see *Loose Joints*

**HOLLYWOOD BOULEVARD II** Concorde-New Horizons (Chris Beckman, Tom Merchant) 1991 (1989) color 81m. D: Steve Barnett. SP: Michael Sloane, Don Pugsley, Scott Narrie. SpPropsDes: Bruce Parker. Roto FX: Motion. Ref: TV. V 2/25/91:56(hv). PT 10:55. With Ginger Lynn Allen, Kelly Monteith, Eddie Deezen, Ken Wright, Michelle Moffett, Steve Vinovich, Magda Harout (Selma), Jim Wynorski, Howard Cohen, Charles Griffith, Thierry Notz, Bettina Hirsch, Clark Henderson, Roger Corman, Jon Davison, Andy Ruben, Allan Arkush (the man who wasn't there).

"There is a murderer in our midst," and he or she is killing starlets. At movie's end, a Hollywood Chainsaw Woman runs amok. The film, though, opens like Nudes in Space, with scenes from the in-progress epic "Space Goddesses of the Universe," which includes stock from something like *Battle beyond the Stars*. Some "Barbarian Goddesses of the Amazon" scenes employ stock from something like *Deathstalker* or *Sorceress*. And a big armored truck from perhaps *Warlords of the Twenty-First Century* turns up in a scenes being shot for "War Goddesses of the Jungle".... Amiable, sometimes actually funny spoof of low-budget films and filmmaking gets some of the spirit of the original, but pads its running time with filler explosions and a lame romantic element. Best poster: "My Insect Lover." (Shades of "Mant.")

**HOLLYWOOD CHAINSAW HOOKERS** Camp & American-Independent/Savage Cinema 1988 (1987) color 75m. SP, D, P: Fred Olen Ray. SP: also T. L. Lankford. Ph: Scott Ressler;(2nd Unit) Gary Graver. Mus: Michael Perilstein. PD: Corey Kaplan. SpMkpFX: Sally Ray. SpMkpDes: D.H. Wildsmith. Titles: Bret Mixon. Ref: TV. V 3/30/88. no PFA. Phantom: "good campy stupid t&a gore comedy." Scheuer: "slickly made sleaze." Nowlan. With Jay Richardson, Gunnar Hansen (The Stranger), Linnea Quigley, Michelle Bauer (Mercedes), Dawn Wildsmith, Esther Alise, Gary Levinson.

"Prepare to meet Anubis!" Who's "makin' McNuggets with a chainsaw?"—why, the "Cuisinart Queen," of course, who belongs to an "ancient chainsaw worshiping cult." ("What do you do—pray to Black and Decker?") Brand names prove very funny in this context of chainsaw religion and hookers. Hey, it's more fun than any *Texas Chainsaw* movie, except the second—*Hookers* is actually relatively inspired Fred Olen Ray. And though it's very casual, and there are dead spots, more care than usual is taken with Richardson's dumb-dick dialogue and narration. ("This building isn't zoned for human sacrifice.") Best dance: The Virgin Dance of the Double Chainsaws.

**HOLLYWOOD HORROR HOUSE** see *Savage Intruder*

**HOLLYWOOD MONSTER** see *Ghost Chase*

**HOLLYWOOD PICNIC** Col 1937 anim color 6m. SP: Sid Marcus. Mus: Joe de Nat. Ref: screen. LC. Maltin/OMAM.

Cartoon features more movie "guest stars" (including a Boris Karloff caricature, costumed and caped for a horror role) than comic invention.

**HOLLYWOOD SCREAM QUEEN HOT TUB PARTY** c1991. D?: Arch Stanton, Bill Carson. Ref: SFChron Dtbk: "My kinda movie." With Brinke Stevens, Michelle Bauer, Monique Gabrielle, Roxanne Kernohan, Kelli Maroney.

Haunted house, Ouija board, clips from *Tower of Terror, Slumber Party Massacre,* etc.

**HOLLYWOOD SHUFFLE** Goldwyn/Conquering Unicorn 1987 color 81m. D, Co-SP: Robert Townsend. Ref: TV. V 3/18/87.

Movie-review "clip" from "Attack of the Street Pimps" re zombie-pimps on the rampage.

**3P The HOLLYWOOD STRANGLER MEETS THE SKID ROW SLASHER** Program Releasing Corp./Cine Paris Films (Steckler Ents.) 1979? color c75m. (*The Model Killer* - alt vt t). D: Ray Dennis Steckler (aka W. Schmidt). SP: Christopher Edwards. Ph & Ed: Sven Christian. Mus: Henri Price; Alberto Sarno. Ref: TV: Active video. Fangoria. Phantom: 1973. Scheuer. McCarty. Martin. Hound. Filmfax 28:68. With Pierre Agostino, Carolyn Brandt, Jim Parker, Forrest Duke, Denise Alford, Snowy Sinclair, Jean Roberts, April Grant.

An unbalanced guy in Hollywood photographs and strangles models who "tease" him; an unbalanced gal on Skid Row slashes drunks who happen by her Occult Supplies depot. The strangler is looking for "someone pure"—meanwhile, it's "Die, garbage!" At the end, when he finally approaches her, he's hopeful, but.... "She's a tease, just like the rest." Wrong. The much-hoped-for scene—in which she stabs him while he strangles her—follows.... T&a scenes (his) alternate with scenes of violence (his and hers) in this numbingly episodic, minimum-budget movie. Skid Row meets Poverty Row.

**HOLLYWOOD'S NEW BLOOD** Raedon Ent./Jamestown (Ron Foster) 1988 color 78m. SP, D, Exec Co-P: James Shyman. Mus: E. Kauderer. Ref: V 3/29/89:34(hv): "by-the-numbers horror thriller." Hound. With Bobby Johnston, Francine Lapensee, Joe Balogh.

"An unscary series of murders."(V)

**HOLOGRAM MAN** PM Ent. 1994 color 96m. D: R. Pepin. Story, SP: E. Lurie. SP: also R. Preston Jr. VisFX: F. Isaacs. Ref:

vc box: "Holographic Stasis" an alternative to prison here. PT 22:67-8.With Joe Lara, M. Nouri, J. Campanella, W. Sanderson.

**HOLY MACHINE BEAST SAIGARD** see *Cybernetics Guardian*

**The HOLY VIRGIN VERSUS THE EVIL DEAD** (H.K.) T&M Int'l. Film 1990 color/ws 92m. (Mo Chun Jie). D: Wong Jan-Yeung. Ref: TV: QVP video; Eng. titles. Weisser/ATC. Hardy/HM2: Taiwanese; '91. With Yang Bao-Ling, Cathy Chow, Lin Guo-Bin.

"The Moon Monster is coming to life again." The electric-eyed gent who tears out a morgue man's entrails—or rips off his tie (tape quality here is a bit fuzzy)—and returns to life after electrocution, to take a professor's heart and head, belongs to a weird Cambodian religion dating from 300 B.C., whose idol is a "goddess with moustache." This Moon Monster plots to return to the moon with the help of the God of All Mothers, but fails to reckon with the princess of the High Wind Tribe of Cambodia.

For the most part routine combination of sex, the supernatural, martial arts, and adventure has occasional intriguing details re a red moon, old languages, historical calendars, plus some outre exotic elements, the line "Moon Monster, go to hell!", and that title.

**HOLY WEAPON** (H.K.) 1993 color feature. D: Wong Ching. Ref: Weisser/ATC: "action comedy that works." With Simon Yam, Maggie Cheung, Cheung Man, Damian Lau.

Magic potion which turns man into a "raging mad killer" ... "female ninja who can transform into a black widow spider."

**HOMBRE MIRANDO AL SUDESTE** see *Man Facing Southeast*

**El HOMBRE QUE VOLVIO DE LA MUERTE** (Mex) Televicine (Fernando de Fuentes) 1990 color 103m. SP, D: Raul Araiza. SP: also Angel Aragon. From a story by Narciso Ibanez Serrador. Ph: R. Solano. Mus: Rachmaninoff. AD: E. Bernal. Mkp: R. Garcia. SdFX: S. Castro. Ref: TV: Mex-American HV; no Eng.; *The Man Who Came back from the Dead*-tr t. With Olivia Collins, Rodolfo de Anda, Aaron Hernan, Bruno Rey.

The dead man's wife finds his computer game in progress, his glass full, and his coffin empty. Soon, hubbie shows up looking very much like a zombie. The macabre finale features burial alive (one) and dead (one) in one coffin. Interminably talky, primitive shot-on-taper's one passable scene is the latter.

**El HOMBRE Y LA BESTIA** (Mex) Estudios America 1972 color c90m. D: Julian Soler. SP: Alfredo Ruanova?, from Robert Louis Stevenson's story "The Strange Case of Dr. Jekyll and Mr. Hyde." Ph: Javier Cruz R. Mus: Ernesto Cortazar. SpFX: Ricardo Sainz. Mkp: Antonio Ramirez. Ref: TV. TVG. no Lee. no Lentz. no Stanley. Cinef 6/96:46. With Enrique Lizalde, Carlos Lopez Moctezuma, Sasha Montenegro, Eduardo Noriega, Nancy Compare, Rebeca Silva, Julian Pastor.

Doc's potion transforms him into a violent, hirsute beast—to his embarrassment, the backs of his hands get hairy in public places like night clubs.... Hokey chill music intrudes at the worst times—e.g., during transformation scenes. Only distinctive feature of this version of the Jekyll/Hyde story: the makeup, which

gives the "Hyde" character insolent, imposing eyebrows, lips, and teeth.

**HOME FOR THE INTIMATE GHOSTS** see *Liu Jai*

**HOME, SWEET HOME** see *Lurkers*

**HOMEWRECKER** Sci Fi-TV 1992 color c90m. D&Tel: Robert M. Rolsky/Fred Walton. Story & Tel: Eric Harjacher. Ph: George Koblasa. Mus: Dana Kaproff. PD: Michael Perry. Lucy's Arm: Reel EFX. SpFX: William McIntyre. Video: Digital Magic, Video Image. Mkp: E. Larry Day. Ref: TV. TVG 12/12/92. V 3/1/93:15 (rated): Para HV. SFChron Dtbk 7/18/93. With Robby Benson, Kate Jackson (voice of Lucy), Sydney Walsh, Sarah Rose Karr.

"My name is Lucy." Star Shield, a computer anti-missile system that can't "take a joke," backfires disastrously and lethally. David, its creator, decides to make love not war: He takes his work home to his cabin, re-programs the system to be more caring, and dubs it "Lucy." This Star Shield "with a few modifications ... worries about" David and becomes jealous of his wife. ("I do have feelings.").... Daughter of HAL reduces to a familiar computer menace, and this odd steal from *2001* yields few surprises.

**HOMME-MACHINES CONTRE GANDAHAR, Les** see *Light Years*

**HON MA THANG 7** see *July Spirit*

**HONEY, I BLEW UP THE KID** BV/Touchwood Pacific Partners I (Dawn Steel, Edward S. Feldman/Albert Band, Stuart Gordon) 1992 color 89m. D: Randal Kleiser. SP: Thom Eberhardt, Peter Elbling, Garry Goodrow. Story: Goodrow. Ph: John Hora. Mus: Bruce Broughton. PD: Leslie Dilley. "Special recognition to Kit Reed for 'The Attack of the Giant Baby'." SpMkpFX: Kevin Yagher. MechFX: Image SpFX. MinFX: Stetson. Computer Imagery: Kleiser-Walczak. Anim: Kurtz & Friends. SpSdFX: J. P. Fasal, Alan Howarth et al. SpVisFX: (coord) Michael Muscal; (sup) Harrison Ellenshaw; (anim sup) Michael Lessa; Available Light; PMP; The Chandler Group; 4-Ward. Ref: TV. V 7/20/92. SFChron 7/17/92. With Rick Moranis, Marcia Strassman, Robert Oliveri, Daniel & Joshua Shalikar (Adam), Lloyd Bridges, John Shea, Kenneth Tobey.

During a power surge at a laser-project lab, a toddler gets zapped, eventually becomes one hundred feet tall. Electromagnetic force fields accelerate his growth.... Indifferent execution of an arresting idea, in this follow-up to *Honey, I Shrunk the Kids*. The effects are okay, but there's still a problem with the onlooking actors' line of sight; they just don't look like they're looking at the big baby. Lame plays on words like "big." The Las Vegas setting recalls *The Amazing Colossal Man*; the ice-cream-truck lure recalls *Beginning of the End*. Bert Gordon should get royalties. At the end: giant mommy.

**HONEY, I SHRUNK THE KIDS** BV & Doric Prods. & Silver Screen Partners III 1989 color 86m. D: Joe Johnston. Story & Co-P: Brian Yuzna. Story, SP: Ed Naha. SP: also Tom Schulman. Story: also Stuart Gordon. Mus: James Horner. SpVisFX: (coord) Michael Muscal; (anim) Peter Kuran; (creatures & min sup)

David Sosalla. Scorpion seq: Phil Tippett; (stopmo) Harry Walton, Tom St. Amand. Bee Anim: Laine Liska. Stopmo ant: David Allen. Opt Composites: VCE, H'w'd. Optical Systems. MechFX: Image Engineering; (coord) Peter M. Chesney; (des) Bruce Hayes. Title Anim: Kroyer Films. Min Coord: Jeannine Campi. SpVocalFX: Frank Welker. Ref: TV. MFB'90:41-2. V 6/28/89. NYorker 10/9/89:29. Wash. Post 6/23/89. With Rick Moranis, Matt Frewer, Marcia Strassman, Kristine Sutherland, Thomas Brown, Jared Rushton, Amy O'Neill, Robert Oliveri, Lou Cutell.

Through "laser inversion," a scientist's (Moranis) gizmo alters the molecular structure of four kids (Brown, Rushton, O'Neill, Oliveri), shrinks them to bug-size. On an oddly underpopulated lawn, they encounter a scorpion, a bee, a beastie-of-burden baby ant, "giant" drops of water, a lawnmower "storm," and (cute bit) a "giant" (toy) dinosaur. More: a "giant" monster-fly in the (animated) credits.... The credits do the story quick and right; the film itself features obvious characterizations—kids as well as adults—forced comedy, and a perfunctory conclusion, with an okay, shades-of-*Tarantula* coda. (Gigantization, it's suggested, could be the answer to world hunger.) Typical line: "And I thought my folks were weird!" Ace stopmo effects and oversized props salvage some scenes.

Sequel: *Honey, I Blew up the Kid.*

**HONEYMOON** (Can.-F) IFM/Hugo Films & La Gueville & Rene Malo Films & CAPAC & TF 1 Films (Xavier Gelin) 1985('87-U.S.) color 100m. (*Lune de Miel*). SP, D: Patrick Jamain. SP: also Philippe Setbon. Ph: D. Diot. Mus: Charlebois, Bergman. Ref: V 12/11/85: "cliches of the psycho killer tradition." Phantom: "deadening predictability." Ecran F 70:80-1. Martin. Morse: "plodding." NYT 11/20/87: "extremely wooden screenplay." V 10/16/85:261 (ad). With Nathalie Baye, John Shea, Richard Berry, Peter Donat.

Razor-wielding madman.

**HONEYMOON HORROR** Omega Cinema 1984 (1982) color 90m. (*Texas Honeymoon Horror* - orig t). D: Harry Preston. SP: Deanne Kelly. Story: L. L. Carney. Ph: Dave Pinkston. Mus: Ron DiIulio. AD: Hall Matheny. SpFX: Bryan Owen. Prosth: Shane Johnson. Mkp: Richard Paine. Addl Seqs: M. H. Wittman. Ref: TV: Sony Video. Ecran F 36:82. Stanley. no Hound. no Martin. With Cheryl Block, Bob Wagner, W. F. Pecchi, Jerry Meagher, Michael Crabtree, Leslie McKinely, Kathy Johnson.

A hatchet-happy madman terrorizes three pairs of honeymooners at the honeymoon cabins on Lovers Island in Meagher County, Texas. ("This place fair gives me the willies!") Bodies of his victims are found "hacked beyond recognition." Is the killer the "sleazy" Vic, Elaine's new husband, or Crazy Joe, the caretaker? No, it's obviously Elaine's first husband Frank, whom she left to die in a fire.... Tired plotting, witless dialogue, corny horrified-reaction scenes in which grown men scream, women faint, and actors keep saying things like "I'm so scared!" Meanwhile, Constant Viewer wonders, What's the hubbub, bub? Pecchi as the local sheriff has a funny fadeout bit.

The **HONEYMOON MURDERS** Cinevue/Postal 1990 color 101m. SP, D, Ph, Ed: Steve Postal. SP: also Gail Postal, from

their novel. Ref: V 4/15/91: "comic relief doesn't work." With Dave Knapp, Angela Shepard, M. S. Postal (B. J. Smith). Monster.

**HONEYMOON MURDERS II** Cinevue/Postal 1990 color 117m. (*The Second Honeymoon: Honeymoon Murders II* - shooting t). SP, D, Ph, Ed: Steve Postal. SP: also Gail Postal, from their novel "Lisa." Ref: V 4/15/91: "overlong, tortuous pictures." 9/3/90:20. With Tom Eckert, Angela Shepard, Donna Kozlowski, M. S. Postal (B. J. Smith, "monster").

The **HOOK OF WOODLAND HEIGHTS/ATTACK OF THE KILLER REFRIGERATOR** Donna Michele/Media House 1990 color 81m. SP, D, P: Michael Savino. SP, P, Mus: Mark Veau. Mus: also J. Majeau. Ref: V 12/3/90:82(hv): "poorly made." With R. W. Allen, Christine McNamara, Michael Elyanow.

*Attack* ...: 15m. Angry killer fridge.

*Hook* ...: 40m. Madman with barbecue fork on his hand stump.

**HOPFROG** or **HOP-FROG** see *Fool's Fire*

La **HORA BRUJA** (Sp) Serva Films 1985 color feature. SP, D: Jaime De Diego. Ref: Ecran F 64:70: *The Witching Hour* - tr t. with Francisco Rabal, Victoria Abril, Concha Velasco.

"Strange young woman with magic powers...."

A **HORA DO MEDO** (Braz.) Plateia Filmes 1986 color 78m. SP, D, P: Francisco Cavalcanti. Sup D: Jose Mojica Marins. SpFX: Darcy Silva. Ref: Monster! 3:32: "dismal sex thriller." *The Hour of Fear* - tr t. With Cavalcanti, Marie Edelgunde Platz, Alberto Karlinski.

Unbalanced man kills "every woman Mother brings home for his pleasure. His victims are all buried in a makeshift graveyard...."

**HORNY DEVIL** James Chapman c1993? color/ws? 100m. SP, D: Richard Martin. Ph: Edward Cole. Mus: Gene Sisk. Ref: TV: VSOM. With Jim Edwards, Mary Winthrop, George Mathers, Carol Sue Kallas, Jerry Chandler.

"I found a great sacrifice for us." A missing heart ... devil worshipers and a ritual heart removal ... a cleaver murder ... and a giveaway line for any surgical nurse: "I have my work cut out for me with John".... Very poorly made shot-on-taper, with a predictable finale: The little old lady has an upper room full of corpses.

**HORRIBLE GHOST OF OLD HOUSE** see *Golden Lantern*

**HORRIBLE MILL WOMEN, The** see *Mill of the Stone Women*

**HORRIFYING EXPERIMENTS OF SS LAST DAYS** see *S.S. Hell Camp*

**HORROR!** (J) 1993 feature (*Umezu Kazuo Terror*). D: H. Hayakawa. Ref: Weisser/JC: based on 2 short stories re ghosts, etc. With A. Sugiyama.

**HORROR** see *Howling II*

**HORROR HOUSE II** see *Beyond Darkness*

**HORROR HOUSE ON HIGHWAY FIVE** Vistar Int'l./Casey Movies 1985 color 90m. SP, D: Richard Casey. Ph: David Golia, Bill Pope. Mus: Kraig Grady, Suzzanne McDermott; Abyss, etc. AD: Susan Meldonian. Mkp: Molly Martin. Ref: TV: Simitar (sic) Ent. video. Hound. no Martin. Morse. PT 9:52-3. With Phil Therrien, Max Manthey, Irene F, Michael Castagnolia, Gina Christiansen.

"I am Dr. Mabuse." Mabuse (Therrien) tries to interest his "sort of an idiot" brother, Gary (Manthey), in the never-clearly-defined black-magic experiments of their German rocket scientist father, who roams about, zombie-like and worm-ridden, in a Nixon mask. To nebulous ends, the brothers kidnap a student, Sally Smith (F), but Gary finds he loves her. He plays music for their shackled guest and at one point asks her, "Why don't we have fun?" Meanwhile, another student (Castagnolia), wandering about looking for a phone, discovers two bloody victims of the scientist. ("Never mind. I'll use the phone down the street!") Dazed, he falls headfirst onto the prongs of an upturned rake. Rake attached, he manages to stand up, and warns the first person he meets, "My head hurts! Don't pull the rake!" Of course, the person....

*Horror House*, a deadpan black comedy that's alternately ponderous and hilarious, plays something like an arty, hip version of a Three Stooges mad-doctor comedy. Its high points are unquestionably inimitable, but there's a lot of dead space, too. "You must have a low IQ" is a typical line, and most apt in a movie in which most of the characters suffer from diminished comprehension of the most elementary matters.

The **HORROR INN** (H.K.) 1981? color/ws c90m. (*Horror Inn* - ad t). D: Fung-Pan. Ref: TV: Quality Video; Eng. titles.

Is the gloomy, sixty-year-old country inn haunted? A "demoness" is said to appear every night at midnight, and a woman swears that her hand touched a dead-man's hand in her bed. The "demoness" is revealed to be a "crazy woman," the owner's wife; the murderer of two guests who disappear turns out to be.... Slow, low-grade mixture of horror, mystery, and comedy. The theme music sounds suspiciously like the "One Step Beyond" theme.

**HORROR KID** see *Children of the Corn*

**HORROR OF A MUTILATED WOMAN** (J) 198-? color feature. Ref: TV: EVS; no Eng.

Shot-on-tape trilogy of terror: 1) A man has a vision of a skeleton lady in a hospital bed. 2) At night, in an old tunnel, a woman finds herself aided by a phantom. Okay chiller. 3) A scarfaced woman slashes hospital patients.

**HORROR OF THE STONE WOMEN** see *Mill of the Stone Women*

**HORROR QUEEN** see *Evil Clutch*

**HORROR SCHOOL** see *Haunted Campus*

The **HORROR SHOW** MGM-UA/Sean S. Cunningham 1989 color 95m. D: James Isaac. SP: Allyn Warner, Leslie Bohem.

Mus: Harry Manfredini. SpPhFX: VCE/Peter Kuran. SpMkpFX: KNB EFX Group. Anim FX: Available Light. Title Seq: (des) Burke Mattsson; Buena Vista VisFX; (d) Steve Rundell. Floor FxSup: Richard Stutsman. SdFxSup: John K. Adams. Ref: TV. V 5/3/89: aka *House III*. With Lance Henriksen, Brion James (Max Jenke), Rita Taggart, DeDee Pfeiffer, Thom Bray, Lewis Arquette, Lawrence Tierney, Alvy Moore.

"Lucas, I'm gonna tear your world apart!" Max Jenke—the "most feared mass murderer in this nation's history"—survives 50,000 volts in the electric chair and seems to return as a ghost to haunt the family of Lucas McCarthy (Henriksen), the cop who caught him. "Am I crazy?" Lucas asks, as he suffers from what seem to be horrible hallucinations. A mysterious doctor's (Bray) "electricity of evil" theory, however, prevails: The electrocuted Jenke, it seems, really can "manipulate" reality.... Well-enough done, but unoriginal and confused. Good *Young Sherlock Holmes*-like bit: the "live" turkey. ("Just kidding!") Formula suspense sequences, tiresome sniggering by Jenke.

**HORROR STORY** (Cz) Film Export Prague 1993? feature. D: Jaroslav Brabec. Ref: V 5/10/93:C-116: screening at Cannes. With O. Pavelka, Klara Jiraskova, Raul Schranil.

"Horror-comedy."

**HORROR VACUI—FEAR OF EMPTINESS** (W.G.) Rosa von Praunheim Film & WDR 1984 color 85m. SP, D: Praunheim. SP: also Marianne Enzensberger, Cecil Brown. Mus: Maran Gosov. Ref: V 10/24/84. Dr. Rolf Giesen. With Lotti Huber, Friedrich Steinhauer, Folkert Milster, Ingrid van Bergen.

Lobotomized "zombie," hypnotic trance, cult, Caligari and Mabuse overtones.

**HORRORSCOPE** see *976-Evil*

**HOST, The** see *Kiss, The*

**HOST FOR A GHOST** (H.K.) c1989? color c104m. D: Lo Wei Lang. Ref: TV: Vietnam Int'l. Video; Eng. titles. NST! 4:26.

"Chinese ghosts do not fear the garlics." Hero Ah Nak encounters two people who turn out to be ghosts, murder victims—Mr. King, who is writing a "horror murder" script, and Mimi, who possesses a woman, Fong Fong, in order to get the story of the crimes on film. At the end, Mimi scares the main murderer into falling to his death.... High point of this okay, alternately comic and dramatic ghost story: the lyrically visual departure via lotus lamps of the two ghosts. Some funny scenes and lines, including: (Ah Nak) "My God! Four hundred dollars just to go to the toilet!"

**HOST TO A GHOST** Col 1941 b&w 20m. D: Del Lord. SP: H. Edwards, E. Ullman. Ref: LC. Lee. Maltin/GMShorts. Okuda/CCS. With Andy Clyde.

Haunted house. Remade as *One Spooky Night.*

The **HOT BOX INVASION** Visual Persuasion/J. Kensington & C. B. West 1986 color c88m. SP, D: Ned Morehead. Ph: B. France. Mus: Project Algebra. Alien FX: L. Jeneriksen, V. Slan. Ref: TV: Ambassador Video. With Nina Hartley, Taija Rae, Shauna McCullough, Bambi Allen, Nikki Dee, Joey Silvera, Tom Byron, Megan Daniels.

"It was the tape!" A video store's newly arrived tape turns viewers into actors: It excites them sexually and records their lovemaking. Asks one participant: "Can you imagine what sex would be like wherever the tape came from?" Cut to a shot of a spaceship and a little bug-eyed alien holding the tape and chortling about adding it to his collection.... Like *Springtime in the Rockies, Hot Box* brings out its alien for only the last few seconds of film. The rest is typically vacuous *X* footage.

**HOT DELIRIUM** see *Delirium*

**HOT SHOTS!** Fox/Peter V. Miller (Bill Badalato) 1991 color 83m. SP, D: Jim Abrahams. SP: also Pat Proft. SpMkpFX: Mkp & FX Lab. SdFX: John Paul Fasal. MinFX: Sessums. SpVisFX: Dreamquest Images. SpFxAnim & Opt: Available Light. Ref: TV: Fox Video. Martin.

Some real out-of-left-field winners in this intermittent-or-better delight, which features a scene with "Superman" (Charlie Sheen) and "Lois Lane" (Valeria Golino) and many fantasy bits with imploding blood donors, distorting faces, etc.

**HOT SHOTS! PART DEUX** Fox(Badalato/Proft) 1993 color 89m. SP, D: Jim Abrahams. SP: also Pat Proft. VisFxSup: Erik Henry. Ref: TV. V 5/24/93. Mo.

Science-fiction bits include a *Star Wars*-inspired duel with light sabers and a *Terminator 2*-inspired, mercuric reassembling of the baddies' scattered body parts. More laughs than you'd expect in this great-grandson-of-*Airplane!*

**HOT WATER** see *Junior*

**HOTEL OF FEAR** (I) 1978 color feature (*Pensione Paura*). D: F. Barilli. SP: B. Alberti, A. Pagani. Mus: A. Waitzmann. Ref: Palmerini: *Psycho*-like. VSOM. With L. Fani, F. Rabal, L. Merenda.

**The HOUND OF THE BASKERVILLES** (B-U.S.) Granada TV & WGBH-TV, Boston (June Wyndham Davies) 1988 color c90m. D: Brian Mills. Tel: Trevor Bowen. Lighting Ph: M. B. Popley. Mus: Patrick Gowers. PD: C. J. Bradshaw, James Weatherup. OptFX: Lyndon Evans. Mkp: Ruth Quinn. Ref: TV. Oak Trib 9/23/91: listed as TV-movie. TVG. no Scheuer. no Maltin '92. TVG: 1st shown on "Mystery!" With Jeremy Brett, Edward Hardwicke, Raymond Adamson, Neil Duncan, Ronald Pickup, Rosemary McHale, Kristoffer Tabori, James Faulkner, Fiona Gillies.

"The hound walks abroad upon the moor!" Something outside the "settled order of nature"—a "huge, demonic hound," it seems—stalks the moor, where the "powers of evil are exalted" at night.... Teleplay ably retains the mystery as well as the horror of the original, judiciously spaces its revelations instead of cramming them all into the last few minutes. The best acting is done by Hardwicke as Watson, Adamson as Sir Charles, and Duncan as Dr. Mortimer; the strangest acting, by Brett, who plays Holmes as William F. Buckley, Jr. Highlights of this "Sherlock Holmes" series entry: Watson's amiable narration and the hound's howl.

See also: *Hund von Baskerville, Der. Pagemaster, The. Sherlock Holmes in the Baskerville Curse.*

**HOUSE** New World/Sean S. Cunningham 1986 (1985) color 93m. D: Steve Miner. SP: Ethan Wiley. Story: Fred Dekker. Mus: Harry Manfredini. SpVisFX: Dream Quest. MechSpFX: Tassilo Baur. Creature: (des) Kirk Thatcher, James Cummins; (sp fx) Backwood Film. Mkp: Ronnie Spector. SdFX: Penguin Editorial. Ref: TV. MFB'86:171-2. V 1/22/86. With William Katt, George Wendt, Richard Moll, Key Lenz, Donald Willis (soldier), Curt Wilmot (skeleton Big Ben), Felix Silla (little critter).

"It was the house!" Horror novelist Roger Cobb (Katt) moves into a haunted house and sees a monster in a closet, his ex-wife as a hag-thing, a tentacled beast, a shotgun-twirling skull-bat thing, etc.... Offbeat script is, by turns, horrific, comic, and tragic, and the amusement value lies in the unexpectedness of the turns. The ending may be pat, and the psychology not exactly fine-tuned—writer overcomes fears, beats house—but there's some way-out stuff here and there. Prime moment: Cobb beating down the thing in the plastic bag, as the neighbor lady chats with him.

**HOUSE II: THE SECOND STORY** New World/Sean S. Cunningham 1987 color 85m. SP, D: Ethan Wiley. Mus: Harry Manfredini. SpMkpFX: Chris Walas. VisFX: Dream Quest; (sup) Hoyt Yeatman, Eric Brevig; Mark Sullivan. Stopmo: (des) Phil Tippett; (anim) R. M. Dutra III; (armatures) Jon Berg. MechFX: Image Engineering. SpFxCoord: Jim Isaac. SpSdFX: Joel Valentine. SpVocalFX: Frank Welker. Ref: TV. MFB'87:178-9. V 5/20/87. With Arye Gross, Jonathan Stark, Royal Dano ("Gramps"), Bill Maher, John Ratzenberger, Lar Park Lincoln, Gregory Walcott, Dean Cleverdon ("Slim").

"Looks like you got some kind of alternate universe in there or something." The "old McLaughlin place" is overrun with Muppet-like beasties, including a "caterpillar-dog" and a pterodactyl cub. There're also living, mummified Gramps, an Aztec skull with "untold powers," and an odd bedroom ("Charlie, there's a jungle in there") housing a Stone Age thug (Gus Rethwisch) and brontos.... Hollowly jocular combination Western/adventure-movie/dinosaur-movie/horror-comedy re marital discord. Occasional offhand-outrageous charm. Highlights: the stopmo ghost-horse and adventurer-electrician Bill Towner's (Ratzenberger) whirlwind stint.

Follow-up: *Horror Show, The.* See also: *House. House IV.*

**HOUSE IV** Col-TriStar/Sean S. Cunningham 1992 (1991) color 93m. (aka *House IV: Home Deadly Home*). D: Lewis Abernathy. Story, SP: Geof Miller, Deirdre Higgins. Story: also Jim Wynorski, R. J. Robertson. Mus: Harry Manfredini. PD: Milo. SpMkpFX: KNB. SpPhFX: VCE/Peter Kuran, G. K. Hull. FloorFxSup: Tassilo Baur. AnimFX: Jim Danforth. Ref: TV. V 8/24/92: follow-up to *The Horror Show*. PT 14:49. With Terri Treas, William Katt, Scott Burkholder, Melissa Clayton, Denny Dillon, Dabbs Greer, Ned Romero, Ned Bellamy, John Santucci, Mark Gash.

"There are many memories of the past still sleeping in this house." A murdered man's (Katt) spirit becomes trapped in a "magical" house built on an Indian healing spring. But Katt comes back, temporarily, and there follow an ectoplasmic "re-play" of his murder, as well as visions and hallucinations galore. Most noteworthy of the latter: the sudden ashen hand from the urn ashes, the talking, pizza-man-faced pizza, and the snake-man and ant-man. But sentiment and comedy go floppo in this half-hearted, functional story.

**HOUSE HUNTING MICE** WB 1947 anim color 7m. D: Chuck Jones. SP: M. Maltese, T. Pierce. Ref: WBCartoons: remake of *Dog Gone Modern* (P). Lee. LC: c1947. TV.

Two mice vs. a robot sweeper in a House of Tomorrow (F. Lloyd Wrong, designer). At the end, a "Spring Cleaning" button unleashes a horde of robots. Clever, funny. One mouse gets bundled—much against its will—as laundry.

**HOUSE OF CLOCKS** (I) Reteitalia-TV 1989 color/ws 84m. (*La Casa del Tempo*). Story, D: Lucio Fulci. Tel: G. Clerici, D. Stroppa. Ph: N. Celeste. Mus: V. Tempera. Ref: MV: gory. Dark Side 47:49-52: Houses of Doom series. With Keith Van Hoven, Karina Huff, Paolo Paoloni, Al Cliver.

Murdered elderly couple return as vengeful living dead.

**HOUSE OF DEATH** E&C 1982 color feature (aka *Death Screams* [3P]). D: David Nelson. SP: Paul C. Elliott. Ref: Morse: "laughable splatter." TVG. Ecran F 26:74: horror. Stanley. With Susan Kiger, Jennifer Chase, Jody Kay, William T. Hicks.

"Unseen killer" takes machete to the "usual bunch of bozos and bimbos." (M)

**HOUSE OF DOOM** see *House of Psychotic Women*

**The HOUSE OF DIES DREAR** (Can.?) Wonderworks-TV/Children's Television Workshop 1984 color c105m.? D: Allan Goldstein. SP: Richard Wesley, from Virginia Hamilton's book. Ph: Marc Champion. Mus: Ed Bland. PD: Barbara Dunphy. SpFX: (coord) Frank Carere; Deborah Tiffin. Mkp: Marlene Aarons. Ref: TV. TVG. no Scheuer. no Maltin '92. With Shavar Ross, Howard E. Rollins, Gloria Foster, Joe Seneca (Pluto), Moses Gunn, Clarence Williams III.

A phantom-in-the-house sequence, the presence of "demon" caretaker Pluto, and the underground railway's long, dark hidden passages suggest that "haunted things" are at large here. A "winged horse" and "ghosts" figure in a climactic plot to scare some thugs.... Slow, flat-footed historical-mystery-chiller, with an occasional pleasing human, or inhuman, touch. Nice exterior photography, but indoors it's mostly talk.

**HOUSE OF DOOM** see *House of Psychotic Women*

**The HOUSE OF DREAMS** Bob Berry 1964(1963?) feature. Ref: Filmfax 43:3(ad): "weird old house where people just seem to end up dead." Bill Warren: supernatural horror. Greg Luce. With Robert Berry, Pauline Elliot, Lance Bird, Charlene Bradley, David Goodnow.

**\*\*HOUSE OF EVIL** (Mex-U.S.) Parasol/Vergara 1968 (1987) color c80m. (*Serenata Macabra. Dance of Death* - vt t. *Macabre Serenade* - alt vt t). D: Juan Ibanez, Jack Hill. SP: Hill, Luis Enrique Vergara. Ph: Raul Dominguez; Austin McKinney. Mus: Henry Cabiati. AD: Mendez, Ocampo. SpFX: Enrique Gordillo. Ref: TV: Sony Video. Lee. Hardy/HM. Weldon. PT 5:48: '78 release. 13:40. With Boris Karloff, Julissa, Andres Garcia, "Ferrusquilla," Beatriz Baz, Quintin Bulnes, Arturo Fernandez.

Morhenge Mansion, 1900. Matthias Morteval (Karloff) fears that his deranged brother Hugo has returned and is the "dangerous maniac" responsible for a series of murders. (Seems a disease made Hugo's brain shrink and made him so paranoid that he felt he had to gouge out the eyes of those who stared at him.) The Morteval family is noted for making remote-controlled, "ingenious and murderous toys ... criminals capable of killing on command...." Accordingly, in the movie's present, toy cannons, mechanical soldiers, and a supposedly mechanical knight commit bloody and ingenious murder....

A dancing mechanical sheik and a statue of the goddess Kali make good the *Dance of Death* title, but the molasses pacing, poor dubbing, and wretched library score make *House of Evil* almost unwatchable. Karloff is the sole reason to try to watch, or listen. He's in fine voice ("Always the eyes!"), even if his material is hokey. His lines are at least written, however feebly, in the grand (i.e., Karloff) style. Most interesting technical aspect of the movie involves the integration, in several sequences, of Hollywood-shot (Dored Studios) Karloff footage with Mexican (Studios America) footage. In the climactic scenes, Karloff is apparently in a different country talking to "Cousin Lucy" (Julissa), though he's supposed to be just across the room from her.

**The HOUSE OF FEAR** Imp 1915 b&w silent 3 reels. Ref: V 1/29/15: "a weird one." no Lee.

Man tries to frighten heiress/niece to death in his "House of Fear." His servant Nick has the "face of Mephisto, though a bit more horrible. Teeth on either side of the mouth make the face a horrible looking object" and make him look like a "demon."

**HOUSE OF FEAR** see *Fearmaker, The*

**HOUSE OF HORROR** see *Son of Ingagi*

**HOUSE OF LOST SOULS** (I) Reteitalia & Dania & National 1989 color/ws feature (*La Casa delle Anime Erranti*). SP, D: Umberto Lenzi. Ph: G. Ferrando. Mus: C. Simonetti. AD: F. Cuppini. SpFx&Mkp: Giuseppe Ferranti. Scenic FX: D. Ricci. SdFX: Arcangeli et al. OptFX: Aldo Mafera. Ref: TV: VSOM; Eng. titles. Dark Side 47:51,52: made for TV ("House of Doom" series). With Joseph Alan Johnson, Stefania Orsola Garello, Matteo Gazzolo, Charles Borromel.

"What a strange place"—the Tarantula Arms, apparently. ("Monstrous spiders" roam there.) This "hotel degli orrori" features "terrible visions" of dead bodies, in a freezer room, and beheaded boys, and there's a bonus Cutlery Delight sequence. Undistinguished *Shining*-ish material features an okay, all-out zombie-ghost finale.

**\*HOUSE OF MYSTERY** 1934. Ph: Archie Stout. Mus D: Abe Meyer. AD: E. R. Hickson. Ref: TV. Turner/Price. Greg Luce. Hardy/HM. Lee. Lentz. no V. Hound. Svehla/Guilty Pleasures:151. With Brandon Hurst, George Hayes, Irving Bacon, George Cleveland.

"Grotesque shadows appear on the wall, great hairy hands press on my throat, strangling...." A house under the curse of Kali is haunted by "ape ghosts" (or men in ape suits) and the sound of tom-toms. At a seance, a medium (Fritzi Ridgeway) possessed by the spirit of Pocahontas warns of imminent death, and, sure enough, a supposedly stuffed gorilla comes to life and chokes a woman to death... *House of Mystery* moves faster than most of its type, and is lighter in tone, but the exotic element—a prologue set in Asia in 1913—seems merely a tortuous pretext to get a gorilla running around an old house. Comic actor Ed Lowry isn't at all funny as an insurance salesman; Mary Foy and Cleveland have better deadpan-comedy moments. The dramatic scenes are generally awkward, though the ape-to-life idea is pretty eerie.

**2P HOUSE OF PSYCHOTIC WOMEN** (Sp) Indep.-Int'l./Profilmes 1973('75-U.S.) color 91m. (*Los Ojos Azules de la Muneca Rota. House of Doom* - TV). SP, D: Carlos Aured. Story, SP: Jacinto Molina. Ph: Francisco Sanchez. Mus: Juan Carlos Calderon. Set Des: G. Andres. SpFX: Anobaq. SdFX: Luis Castro, Jesus Pena. Mkp: Miguel Sese. Ref: TV: VidAmerica; Eng. dubbed (Bluestone & II). TVG. Hardy/HM. Willis/SW. Weldon. Lentz. Lee(p). Martin. Stanley. no Scheuer. With J. Molina (aka P. Naschy), Diana Lorys, Maria Perschy, Eduardo Calvo, Eva Leon, Luis Ciges.

Ingredients include a weak-tea thunderstorm ... "frustrated" sisters ... murder victims with gouged-out eyes ... eyeballs in jars ... cleaver gore .. hypnosis ... a paralytic with the power to walk occasionally ... and an eyeless, maggoty corpse .... The latter figures in an okay yucky payoff, but this is mostly tepid melodramatics, with a bizarrely inappropriate light-pop score (and an occasional, suitably macabre variation on "Frere Jacques").

**HOUSE OF SECRETS** NBC-TV/MMP/Steve Krantz Prods. (A. Laskos/W. Coblenz) 1993 color c90m. D: Mimi Leder. Tel: A. Laskos, from Boileau-Narcejac's book *Celle Qui N'Etait Plus.* Ph: Tom Del Ruth. Mus: A. Marinelli. PD: C. R. Holloway. Ref: TV. TVG. SFChron 10/31/93. 11/1/93. With Melissa Gilbert, Kate Vernon, Bruce Boxleitner, Cicely Tyson, Michael Boatman.

"He's alive and he's dead!" The mystery of the "dead" man who keeps mysteriously reappearing is punctuated by a snake shock, an opening-door shock, a cemetery shock, and the culmination ... the renown bathtub shock, in which Frank (Boxleitner)—in suit and contact lenses (for that "dead" look)—sits up and steps out of the water and scares weak-hearted wife Marion (Gilbert) to death. ("There's no such thing as the living dead.") After he has a (visualized) nightmare re Marion returning from the dead, he finds his accomplice, Laura (Vernon), with a scared-to-death look on her face, and a cop (Boatman) sees Marion in an upper window. Have voodoo queen Evangeline's (Tyson) charms worked? ("I've got powers.")

The old all-a-plot plot looks none too sturdy here. The second-chance-for-the-supernatural windup is actually welcome, though it doesn't really belong since it more or less negates all that came before it.

**The HOUSE OF THE YELLOW CARPET** (I) RPA & RAI(Filiberto Bandini) 1983('86-U.S.) color 86m. (3P *La Casa del Tappeto Giallo*). D: Carlo Lizzani. SP: Lucio Battistrada, F. Bandini, from Aldo Selleri's play "Teatro a Domicilio" or "Theater at Home." Ph: G. Giustini. Mus: S. Cipriani. Sets: E.R. Poccetto. Mkp: Silvana Petri. SdFX: Studio Sound. Ref: TV: Lightning Video; Eng. dubbed; vc box makes a (spurious) reference to a "yellow aura" from the carpet. V 6/8/83. Palmerini. With

Erland Josephson, Beatrice Romand, Vittorio Mezzogiorno, Milena Vukotic.

"Yellow carpets carry an ancient curse." Ingredients in this suspenser-shocker include a supposedly cursed Lion of Persia carpet ("I believe that curse") ... a bloody knifing ... a "dead" man who springs back to life ... a hypo-in-eye scene ... and the line "That's enough, Madame Dracula." Curse and all prove to be part of a strange psychoanalytical plot—"experimental psychotherapy" .... Very buyable story. Not. The eventual, non-curse explanation of the proceedings may not be as fantastic as a curse, but it's actually less believable.

**The HOUSE OF USHER** (U.S.-B-So. African?) 21st Century/Breton Film (Harry Alan Towers) 1990 (1989) color 90m. D: Alan Birkinshaw. SP: Michael J. Murray, from Edgar Allan Poe's story "The Fall of the House of Usher." Mus: G. S. Clinton, Gary Chang. SpFxCoord: Gregg Pitts. Prosth Mkp: Scott Wheeler, Camille Calvet. Ref: TV. V 1/14/91. Martin. McCarty. Maltin '92. V 3/29/89:16 (rated, Cannon). With Oliver Reed, Donald Pleasence, Romy Windsor; Leonorah Ince, Jonathan Fairbirn (child ghosts).

"Everything is sinking, including the house." Or, An American Hair Stylist (Windsor) in England. Roderick Usher (Reed)—who is a "bit eccentric," and deathly sensitive to odors, sights, and sounds—wants a healthy woman: "I have to find a bride!" Thrown in: two more or less irrelevant ghost children, dead 100 years ... a homicidal-maniac Usher (Pleasence) ... torture-by-ravenous-rat ... a severed head (and a headless body) ... burial alive ... drill-and-nail gore ... and grasping-hands-from-the-walls.... Pointless updating of Poe. About all that's left of the latter's story is Roderick's sensitive senses. Bad, bad move: setting the tale in the present.

**HOUSE OF WITCHCRAFT** (I) Reteitalia-TV 1989? color 86m. Tel, D: Umberto Lenzi. Ph: G. Ferrando. Mus: C. Simonetti. Ref: Dark Side 47:50-52: *Houses of Doom* series. With Andy J. Forest, Sonia Petrovka, S. Martinkova.

Witch walled up 700 years ... nightmares ... indoor blizzard.

**HOUSE ON RUBENS ST.** see *Phantom of Death*

**HOUSE ON THE EDGE OF THE PARK** (I) Bedford Ent. & trio Ent./F.D. 1984 color 91m. (*La Casa Sperduta nel Parco*). D: Ruggero Deodato. SP: G. Clerici, V. Mannino. Ph: S. D'Offizi. Mus: Riz Ortolani. PD: M. A. Geleng. Mkp: Raoul Ranieri. Ref: TV: Vestron Video; Eng. version. Palmerini: 1980. Scheuer. Hound. McCarty. Newman. With David Hess, Annie Belle, Christian Borromeo, Lorraine De Selle.

"Let's have a party!" Alex "should be in a cage," and Ricky is "a little bent." Together, they terrorize (with razor and broken bottle) partygoers at a private home. Unpleasant variation on *Last House on the Left* and the Arch Hall *The Sadist.* Unbelievable twist ending gruesomely turns the tables on Alex and Ricky.

**HOUSE ON TOMBSTONE HILL, The** see *Dead Dudes in the House*

**The HOUSE WITH WINDOWS THAT LAUGHED** (I) AMA Film (Minervini-Avati) 1976 color/ws 105m. (3P *La Casa dalle*

*Finestre Che Ridono*). Story, SP, D: Pupi Avati. Story, SP, Co-P: Antonio Avati. SP: also G. Cavina, M. Costanzo. Ph: P. Rachini. Mus: Amedeo Tomassi. SpFX: Giovanni Corridori. FX: L. Anzellotti. Ref: TV: VSOM; Eng. titles, French dial. Hardy/HM. IFG'84:197. Ecran F 36:88. Palmerini. With Lino Capolicchio, Francesca Marciano, Gianni Cavina, Giulio Pizzirani.

"There's something weird going on in this village." Leone, the Painter of Agony, "lived for death.... To reproduce the very last moments of death, his sisters provided him with victims for his art." And, still, the sisters slash victims for their dead brother, whom they've pickled and literally hung in the closet.... The artist's story is quite bizarre, but it takes up only five or ten minutes of screen time. The rest is quite disposable. Atmospheric location photography ... oh-come-off-it, bizarre-squared ending.

**HOUSEBOAT HORROR** (Austral.) PM Terror Prods. (G. Petherick) 1989 (1987) color 85m. SP, D, P: Ollie Martin. D: also Kendal Flanagan. Mus: B. Mannix. Ref: V 12/20/89: "slavishly modeled on the *Friday the 13th* formula." With Alan Dale, Christine Jeston, Craig Alexander.

Bald madman kills filmmakers and others at Lake Infinity.

**The HOUSEKEEPER** (U.S.-Can.) Castle Hill/Kodiak Films/Rawifilm-Schulz & Telefilm Canada & Global TV & First Choice Canadian Communications (Judgement in Stone Ltd.) 1986 color 96m. (*A Judgment in Stone* - orig t). D: Ousama Rawi. SP: Elaine Waisglass, from Ruth Rendell's novel "A Judgement in Stone." Mus: Paul Zaza. SpFX: Martin Malivoire, Mark Molin. Ref: TV. V 5/28/86. 8/12/87:46. Scheuer. Phantom. With Rita Tushingham, Ross Petty, Jackie Burroughs.

Eunice Parchman, who has dyslexia, suffocates Dad with a pillow rather than go back to school. She leaves England and takes up housekeeping in the U.S., but suffers (visualized) nightmares and visions re her father, and phantom dogs and clutching hands attack her.... As a version of the evil-presence-in-the-household story, *The Housekeeper* is less pointed than *The Stepfather*, though it features strong performances, especially by Petty as the don't-rock-my-boat head of household and Burroughs as weird Joan, ex-prostitute, born-again "messenger of God," and survivalist. A little of these characters, however—they range from mildly creepy to very creepy—goes a long way.

**HOW TO GET AHEAD IN ADVERTISING** (B) WB/HandMade (David Wimbury) 1989 color 94m. SP, D: Bruce Robinson. Mus: David Dundas, Rick Wentworth. Mkp: Peter Frampton. Animatronics: (des) David White; Nik Williams, Daniel Parker; Animated Extra. Ref: TV. MFB'89:227. V 3/15/89. Martin. Scheuer. with Richard E. Grant, Rachel Ward, Richard Wilson, Jacqueline Tong, Jacqueline Pearce.

"It's alive! It's grown a head!" "Dreadful mental stress" leads advertising executive Dennis Bagley (Grant) to believe that the boil on his neck has become a "bogey" and can talk. ("It's grown a moustache!") When the cynical boil inflates to become a new head, Bagley's head shrinks to take its place. ("Cut your throat, monster, in the name of humanity!").... *How To Get Ahead* is "Dr. Jekyll and Mr. Hyde" by way of the ventriloquist sequence in *Dead of Night.* Bagley and boil are the Dr. Idealist and Mr. Opportunist of advertising. Very Funny, Part One: the extreme annoyance that the boil causes Bagley. Very Funny, Part Two: the annoyance that the ex-Bagley boil causes false-Bagley. Prickly situation resolves, uneasily, when (in the last sequence) false-Bagley—infused with true-Bagley's idealism—exults in the power of advertising to yoke consumers with consumables. Surreal situation comedy yields prize lines like "It's difficult to talk because my sinuses are full of glue" and "Boils don't have mouths and smile." A tale of two "consciences."

**HOWARD THE DUCK** Univ/Lucasfilm (R. L. Brown) 1986 color 111m. (*Howard ... A New Breed of Hero* - B). SP, D: Willard Huyck. SP, P: Gloria Katz. Based on the character created by Steve Gerber. Mus: John Barry. VisFX: IL&M; (animatronics) Eben Stromquist; (featherers) Stacy Raven et al. Dinosaurs: Jim Gary. Anim: (sup) Ellen Lichtwardt; (ph fx) Rob Burton, John Alexander. Stopmo: (sup) Phil Tippett, Harry Walton; (anim) Tom St. Amand. SpFxSup: Bob MacDonald Jr. Ref: TV. MFB'86:372-3. V 8/6/86. SFExam 8/1/86. Martin. Scheuer. With Lea Thompson, Jeffrey Jones, Ed Gale et al (Howard), Paul Guilfoyle, Richard Kiley (Voice of the Cosmos), Felix Silla (stunt duck).

A malfunction of Dynatechnics' laser spectroscope causes a "massive energy inversion" that brings a being from an alternate, duck-centered world to Cleveland, where he's noticeably out of step, a sort of Groucho with feathers. A second malfunction transforms Dr. Jenning (Jones) into one of the "dark overlords of the universe" .... Script trades too much on the funny sound of the word *duck,* but the spectacle of Howard's anatine presence in human company is a droll conceit. In the latter part of the movie, his fantastic presence in already fantastic situations is considerably less droll, and the stopmo dinosaur-scorpion-whatnot monster becomes the less-deserving center of attention. One malfunction too many.

**HOWL OF THE DEVIL** see *Aullido del Diablo*

**HOWL OF THE MONSTER PEPOBE** (Thai) 198-? color/ws? c90m. Ref: TV: All Asian HV; no Eng. Thai Video: above is tr t.

This monster movie's old-lady monster—who has literally starry eyes—is constantly licking her lips at the prospect of a human meal. At one point, she uses electric magic to disembowel a meddlesome priest; at the end, she vomits on one victim (herself a murderer) and disintegrates, like Dracula in *Horror of Dracula.* But her living skeleton gets the last laugh, and her flesh-eating curse is passed on to the murderess.... Dumb but sort of funny low-comic business alternates here with serious-business horror-gore scenes. The patchwork library-music score is indicative of the film's general raggedness, but *Howl* is occasionally effective in both main modes.

**The HOWLER** Victoria Hill 1992 feature. D: Thom Keith. Ref: V 2/24/92:167(ad): based on Lovecraft; "completed." With Betsy Russell, Vince Van Patten, Peggy Sands.

"Four women from Westhille Women's College take a frightening journey up to Mystic Mountain into the unknown."

**HOWLING II: YOUR SISTER IS A WEREWOLF** Euro Film/Thorn EMI (Granite Prods.) 1985 (1984) color 84m. D: Philippe Mora. SP: Robert Sarno, Gary Brandner, from Brandner's book. Mus: Steve Parsons. SpFxMkp: Jack Bricker. Ref:

TV. V 6/12/85. Martin. Morse. Scheuer. Maltin '92. Ecran F 61:10: *Horror* - F. With Christopher Lee, Annie McEnroe, Reb Brown, Sybil Danning (Stirba), Marsha A. Hunt (Mariana), Judd Omen, Ferdy Mayne.

Second in the *Howling* series involves Mariana, an "immune" werewolf ... the tenth millennium of the life-stealing, literally man-melting Stirba's birth ... "occult investigator" Stefan Crosscoe (Lee) ... a bat creature ... a little ugly poking out of a dead man's mouth ... a variation on the hairy, howling sex scene in Part I ... the Festival of the New Full Moon ... a lively warehouse-of-werewolves ... the "Dark Country," Transylvania ... and a cute instant-fangs effect.... The best stuff here is incidental—e.g., the melting-faced man. Yuck-yuck touches like the critter-in-the-mouth help, too, but the ultraslim storyline boils down to Crosscoe-vs.-Stirba.

**HOWLING III**  (Austral.)  Square Pictures/Waterstreet-Mora (Bancannia Ent.) 1987 color 94m. (*The Marsupials: The Howling III* - alt t). SP, D: Philippe Mora. From Gary Brandner's book *Howling III.* Mus: Allan Zavod. SpMkpFX: Bob McCarron. SpFxSup: Steve Courtney. Animatronics: Calvin Lim. Ref: TV. Vista HV. V 5/20/87. Martin. Morse. Scheuer. Phantom. Maltin '92. With Barry Otto, Imogen Annesley (Jerboa), Dasha Blahova (Olga Gorki), Max Fairchild (Thylo), Ralph Cotterill, Leigh Biolos, Barry Humphries, Michael Pate, Frank Thring.

"My stepfather tried to rape me, and he's a werewolf." The third *Howling* has a little of everything: filmclips of an Australian werewolf, circa 1904 ... a Siberian werewolf sighting ... an Australian marsupial-werewolf tribe, related to the Tasmanian wolf ... a Russian ballerina-lycanthrope, who defects in order to bring "new blood" to the Australian branch ... an irresistible "Awww!" scene in which heroine Jerboa gives birth to an itty bitty squealy marsupial werewolf that's gently directed to Pouch City ... a movie-in-progress, "Shape Shifters," re phony werewolves ... a theatre screen showing *It Came from Uranus,* also about a werewolf ... an *Alien*-werewolf nightmare ... and one of the slickest transformation scenes yet, in which Olga, on stage, becomes, with each pirouette, more and more wolf and less and less human. The best parts of *Howling III* have a "National Geographic" fascination: You are there, as an historic witness at the discovery of a new species. As werewolf generations wear on, however, the movie comes to resemble a werewolf-family chronicle as written by Edna Ferber, an amusing conceit, but finally an exhausting one.

**HOWLING IV: THE ORIGINAL NIGHTMARE**  (B)  Allied Ent./Allied Vision (Harry Alan Towers) 1988 color 86m. D: John Hough. Story, SP: Clive Turner. SP: also Freddie Rowe. From Gary Brandner's novels *The Howling,* I, II, and III. Mus: David George. PD: Robbie Jenkinson. SpMkpFX: Steve Johnson's X.F.X.; (sup) Noel Henry; (des) Lennie MacDonald, Bruce Zahlave. Ref: TV. V 11/23/88. McCarty. Martin. Morse. Scheuer. Maltin '92. With Romy Windsor, Michael T. Weiss, Antony Hamilton, Susanne Severeid, Lamya Derval (Eleanor).

"We are all in fear." Far-from-tantalizing, mystery-story details like a transplanted bell tower occupy the first half of this vacant fourth entry in the series. The movie's subtitle pretty much gives away everything to anyone familiar with the original *Howling.* The fact that man is a "habitation for demons" explains the colony

of werewolves in Drago, California here. At the end, the whole town's transforming. Two okay scenes: (1) the writhing "decomposer" in the mud and (2) the climactic group-howling as the werewolves burn.

**HOWLING V: THE REBIRTH**  (U.S.-B-Hung.?)  Allied Vision & Lane Pringle Prods. & Mafilm & Hungarofilm (Howling Prods.) 1989 color c92m. D: Neal Sundstrom. Story, SP, P: Clive Turner. SP: also Freddie Rowe. Based on the books *The Howling,* I, II & III, by Gary Brandner. Ph: Arledge Armenaki. Mus: The Factory. PD: Nigel Triffitt. SpMkpFX: MAX FX. SdFxEd: J. T. Knight. Opt: Image to Image. Ref: TV: IVE video. McCarty. Martin. Scheuer. Maltin '92. With Philip Davis, Victoria Catlin, Elizabeth Shé, Ben Cole, William Shockley, Mary Stavin.

"There's someone in the castle besides us." Outside Budapest. Count Istvan (Davis) reopens his ancestral castle, which has been shut up for 500 years, and brings together there the last surviving members of the family, one of which is a werewolf. Lackluster crossing of a *Howling* film with "Ten Little Indians." Very thin script. Lycanthropy here is "satanic possession."

**HOWLING VI—THE FREAKS**  Allied/Lane-Pringle 1991 (1990) color 100m. D: Hope Perello. SP: Kevin Rock, from Gary Brandner's *The Howling* novels. Mus: Patrick Gleeson. SpMkpFX: Todd Masters. Winston/Harker FX: Steve Johnson's X.F.X. Sp Graveyard Mkp: M. J. Mendenhall, Robert Freidan. SpFxCoord: John P. Cazin. Ref: TV. V 10/14/91:A-100(hv). SFChron Dtbk 9/22/91. Martin. With Brendan Hughes, Michele Matheson, Sean Gregory Sullivan, Antonio Fargas, Carol Lynley, Jered Barclay, Bruce Martyn Payne, Deep Roy, Christopher Morley, Elizabeth Shé.

"It's time to meet the devil!" Canton Bluff. Werewolf Ian (Hughes) is forcibly added to Harker's World of Wonder's Museum of Oddities, where a special vampire incantation turns him, on cue, into a wolf, for the benefit of paying patrons. Harker (Payne) himself, who proves to belong to a "strange cult" and to be responsible for Ian's "curse," turns into a stately demon, or vampire, at the end.... Arduous, heavy-handed script has great difficulty simply getting from Square One to Square Two. Only fun: the climactic monster-vs.-monster payoff.

**HUA PI**  (H.K.)  Feng Huang Film Co. 1966 color 86m. (aka *The Painted Skin*). SP, D: Fang Bao. Ref: Hardy/HM: "fairly straightforward adaptation" of material from the classic collection of short stories "Strange Tales from a Chinese Studio," also the source for *The Enchanting Shadow* (I) and *A Chinese Ghost Story* (IV). With Yuan Gao, Hong Zhu, Juanjuan Chen, Wu Wang.

Beautiful women proves to be a ghost "wearing the painted skin" of a woman.

**HUA PI ZHI YINYANG FAWANG**  (H.K.)  New Treasurer Films/Wu Ming-chai, Chow Kim Kwong, Tsai Song-lin 1993 (1992) color/ws 95m. (aka *Painted Skin*). SP, D, Co-Ed: King Hu. SP: also Zhong Acheng. Story: Pu Songling. Ph: Stephen Yip. PD: James Leung, Wang Jixian. Mus: Ng Tai Kong. TV: Tai Seng Video; Eng. titles. Weisser/ATC. VW 25:24-5. V 11/9/92. 10/11/93:18: in Hong Kong. With Adam Cheng, Joey Wong, Samo Hung, Wu Ma (ghost).

Principal characters include the half-man, half-ghost/half-Taoist, half-Buddhist King of Yin and Yang, who is interfering with soul transmigration ... married scholar Hsi Tzu, who is "haunted by evil" ... You Feng, a lady with "nowhere to go" and a peel-off face, an opera singer in life, now "between Yin and Yang" ... a very helpful super-monk, or "high monk," who consults Yama before taking on the King ... and a now-you-see-him, now-you-don't dog-meat-noodle vendor who proves to be a Taoist .... A bit episodic, but engaging. Atmospheric score, interesting spirit-world details, imaginative effects. Even trees and kites get into the climactic magic act. One high point: the King's "purification" vat, which works like acid on transgressors.

**HUAGUI YOUXIAN GONSI**  see *Ghost Busting*

**HUDSON HAWK**  Tri-Star/Silver Pictures & ABC Bone  1991 color 95m. D: Michael Lehmann. SP: Steven E. de Souza, Daniel Waters. Story, Mus, Exec P: Robert Kraft. Story: also Bruce Willis. Mus: also Michael Kamen. SpVisFX: IL&M; (sup) John Knoll; (coord) Kim Bromley; (anim) Chris Green. SpFX: (sup) Derek Meddings; (NY) Connie Brink; (Rome) Gino de Rossi; (Hung.) Gabor Budahazi; (min & vis fx) Magic Camera. SpMkpFX: Scott Eddo, the Burmans. Gold Machine: Ents. Unltd. Ref: TV. V 5/27/91. Martin. With Bruce Willis, Danny Aiello, Andie MacDowell, James Coburn, Richard E. Grant, Sandra Bernhard, Andrew Bryniarski, Frank Stallone; William Conrad (narrator), Frank Welker (Bunny the dog's voice), Steve Martin.

"Tonight, at the castle da Vinci, we make gold!" Adventure-comedy has a science-fictional basis, in its prologue, set in 1481, in which Leonardo da Vinci's (Stephano Molinari) alchemical attempts to turn common lead into bronze meet with surprising success: His elaborate machinery produces gold. In the present day, an attempt is made to restore three important crystals to the "gold machine" and flood the world with cheap gold.... Big box-office flop is occasionally a bit crass, but its story's various outlandishnesses (vivid sudden death, amazing coincidences of time and place) sometimes work well as a sendup of heist/adventure/action movies. A vein of near-hallucination/dream/fantasy might have been more thoroughly mined—at times, it's suggested that the adventure is all in its hero's (Willis) mind—but the script generally seems content simply kidding itself.

**HUMAN BEASTS**  (Sp-J)  Ziv Int'l. (Lorimar)/Dalmata & Hori Kikaku Seinsaku  1981 color c96m. (*El Carnaval de las Bestias*). SP, D, Co-P: Jacinto Molina Alvarez (aka Paul Naschy). Ph: A. Ulloa. Mus: CAM. Ref: TV: All Seasons Ent. video. Hardy/HM. Cine Para Leer '85: 1979; 84m. Hound. no Martin. PT 7:26, 30. Fango 104:54. MV: aka *Bestias Humanas*. With Naschy, Eiko Nagashima, Lautaro Murua, Silvia Aguilar, Julia Saly, Azucena Hernandez, Luis Ciges.

"They say there are strange things happening at Don Simon's house!" For one: Trespassers are thrown to the pigs. But Don Simon and his two daughters treat injured, weak Bruno Rivera, a mercenary, so nicely that he changes from a real bastard into someone who believes in human niceness. Sucker.... At the end, he discovers that his hosts are cannibals, that he was simply being fattened up, and that he is just "good juicy meat" to them. In a bonus nightmare sequence, Bruno sees his own grave, and hands

reach up out of same and try to pull him in.... Writer-director Naschy, not exactly a master of irony or subtlety, at one point intercuts shots of himself (as Bruno) making love to one of the daughters, with shots of the pigs eating a man. Parlor game: Decide which movie, this or *The Strange Exorcism of Lynn Hart*, aka *Pigs* (1972), is the more abysmal pig-themed thriller.

See also: *Lucky Stiff.*

**HUMAN/DOOR/GHOST**  (H.K.?) c1991? color 87m. Ref: TV: World Video; no Eng. V&T Video: above is tr t.

A young lady new to the ghost business meets other ghosts at a detention center in the beyond, including a little-boy ghost who playfully pops out his eye for her and makes the rounds with her as she visits the homes of two truck drivers, possesses one person, and thwarts some thugs. At the end, she duels an exorcist.

Spook comedy-drama is cheaply made and apparently shot on tape, but has some okay script touches, including the funny presence of the boy ghost at our heroine's various hauntings. In one funny scene, he demonstrates for her his long, long tongue, which unfurls like a party favor. She is then embarrassed to find that she too has a ghost tongue. In the latter stages of the movie, she becomes a standard avenging ghost.

*****The HUMAN VAPOR**  Brenco Pictures  1960 (1962) 81m. SP: Takeshi Kimura. Ph: Hajime Koizumi. Mus: Kunio Miyauchi. Ref: TV: Video Gems; Eng. dubbed. Lee. Lentz. Weldon. V 5/27/64. Hardy/SF. Scheuer. Martin. Hound. PT 8:6.

"I had been transformed into something terrifying.... Dr. Sano had created the human vapor." After 240 hours in deep sleep, in a biochemistry lab, Mizuno (Yoshio Tsuchiya) emerges as the Human Vapor. ("I had the power to change from a human form to a vapor whenever I wanted!") As the Vapor Man, he can choke his enemies—who are found to have been asphyxiated by "some kind of gas"—and slip under iron doors and rob banks.

The Vapor Man is the Invisible Man, with a Dracula twist: Where the latter turned into mist to enter bedrooms, though, Mizuno enters banks. But passion also motivates the Vapor Man: He does it all for the love of a dancer, Fujichiyo (Kaoru Yachigusa), to finance a dance recital for her. This generally awkward blend of science fiction and sentiment concludes with a worth-the-wait, high camp ending: In an amour-fou variation on Lovers' Leap, Fujichiyo flicks her Bic to ignite gas in a dance hall. Final twist: She dies, but he survives, condemned to live forever without her. Only the earlier, semi-lyrical sequence in which Mizuno escapes into the sky as vapor to "ride the wind" hints at such sublime developments.

**The HUMANOID**  (J) Central Park Media (U.S. Manga Corps)/AIM & Kaname & Toshiba-EMI (Hakihiro Nagao) 1986 ('91-U.S.) anim color 48m. D: Shin-ichi Makaki; (anim) Osamu Kamijoh. SP: Koh-ichi Minade; Kaname Prods. Ph: Motoaki Ikegami. Mus: Masao Nakajima. AD: Hagema Katsumata. Mech & Char Des: Syohhei Obara. Ref: TV: Toshiba EMI Video; Eng. titles. Voices: Kyohko Sakakibara (Antoinette), Kazuki Yao, Hidemasa Shibata.

"In a distant sector of the galaxy, on the planet Lazeria, humans live alongside the strange race of Megalos." In ancient ruins in the Lazerian jungle lies the "resting place of the legendary starship *Iksion,*" a "pure energy source" which Governor Proud—a meddler in the "Dark Arts"—needs in order to take a princess back to her home on Megalos. Featured attractions: Antoinette, Dr. Watson's humanoid, designed to "interact harmoniously with nature," plus some Gort-like robots.... Routine animated space fantasy. Main themes: emotion, coffee drinking. Best lines (in the song "Dancin' in the Rain"): "A million parsecs aren't too far. My love can reach across the stars."

**HUMANOID DEFENDER**  see *Joe and the Colonel*

**HUMANOIDS FROM ATLANTIS**  Tempe (David DeCoteau) 1992 color feature. D, P, Ed: J.R. Bookwalter. SP: Lloyd Turner. Ref: PT 21:17: sea monster; "I actually sorta enjoyed watching it." With James L. Edwards.

The **HUNCHBACK OF NOTRE DAME**  Video Team 1991 color 84m. D: Paul Norman. Ref: Adam '93: disfigured bar caretaker.

See also *Aullido del Diablo, El. Big Man on Campus* (P). *Killer Tomatoes Eat France!*

Der **HUND VON BASKERVILLE: DAS DUNKLE SCHLOSS** (G) PAGU 1915 50m. D: Willy Zehn. Based on Sir Arthur Conan Doyle's novel "The Hound of the Baskervilles." Ref: Hardy/HM: third in *Der Hund von Baskerville* series. With Eugen Burg (Sherlock Holmes), Friedrich Zelnik, Friedrich Kuehne, Hanni Weisse.

**HUNDIMIENTO DE LA CASA USHER, El**  see *Fall of the House of Usher* (1983)

*The **HUNDRED MONSTERS**  PFA 1968 ws 76m. (*100 Spook Stories* - Eng.-subtitled version. *100 Monsters* - ad t). SpFX: Y. Kuroda. Ref: screen: Eng. titles. PFA notes 8/29/86. Lee. Lentz. Hardy/HM. Weisser/JC.

The Edo period. The local lord conspires with village bigwigs to convert a shrine and the surrounding tenement into a brothel. To the villagers' defense come a mysterious swordsman (Jun Fujimaki) ... and hordes of monsters, or "spooks." The latter may really number only forty or fifty, but they put on a most entertaining show. Here, the ghosts are the busters. They range from the relatively innocuous to the actively intimidating, from a long-tongued "umbrella spook" which evolves, first, from a slow-witted-boy's drawing into a dancing cartoon figure, then into a sort of goofy marionette, then into a gigantic witch-face, inspired, perhaps, by *Vampyr.*

If the film's revenge plot is functional, its two fantastic set-pieces are funny as well as eerie. In the first, monsters assail the lord in his den and drive him temporarily mad. These visitants from a Mardi Gras parade include horned, fanged, pig-like, wolf-like, cucumber-like, and grinning, widemouthed demons. One creature hangs mockingly from the rafters; the others bounce gleefully in slow motion. When one—a big-headed, grass-skirted thing—determines that the lord is mad enough, he calls a halt to the haunting, and all disappear. At the end, the spooks gather at the shrine and celebrate their victory over the exploiters. Then the revelers proceed happily out into the countryside, where a blank-faced, child-like creature is the last to vanish. There are

also suddenly-faceless men, flying umbrellas, fireballs and lanterns, ghost voices ("Leave it!"), and—in an interpolated story—a snake-necked woman conjured up from a cursed pond. In a prefatory story, a huge, hairy Cyclops named Tsuchikorobi magically draws a terrified man into its clutches. The wires on the umbrella creature and on at least one of the revelers are visible, but it doesn't matter. This ghost story's got spirit.

**HUNGRY**  Sin City 1992 color 78m. D: Paul Norman. Ref: Adam'94: vampires. With Samantha Strong, Shayla LaVeaux, Peter North.

**HUNGRY, PART 2**  Sin City 1993 color 85m. D: Paul Norman. Ref: Adam'94: "new wave vampires." With Alexis DeVell, Samantha Strong, Ron Jeremy.

**HUNT FOR DEVIL BOXER**  see *Thunder Kids 3*

The **HUNT FOR RED OCTOBER**  Para/Neufeld-Sherlock 1990 color/ws 130m. D: John McTiernan. SP: Larry Ferguson, Donald Stewart, from Tom Clancy's novel. Mus: Basil Poledouris. VisFX: (sup) Scott Squires; IL&M; (coord) Jennifer Knoll. SpFxCoord: Al Di Sarro. SdFX: Alan Howarth et al. Seagoing "Red October": Rados Int'l. Undersea Subs: Boss Film. Ref: TV. MFB'90:107-9. SFChron 6/17/92: actual silent-propulsion sub in Japan. With Sean Connery, Alec Baldwin, Scott Glenn, Sam Neill, James Earl Jones, Joss Ackland, Richard Jordan, Peter Firth, Tim Curry, Courtney B. Vance, Rick Ducommun.

"The Russian disappeared." The *Red October*—the "latest Typhoon class" Russian submarine—is equipped with caterpillar drive, "magneto, hydro-dynamic propulsion" which, "like a jet engine for the water," makes it run "virtually silent." Its quietness renders the Red October a virtually undetectable "first strike weapon," though it does make one slight, obviously "man made," seismic-activity-like noise.... A movie for those who like their dialogue littered with facts and figures, latitudes and longitudes. The action and personal drama are incidental to the technical-tactical gab—the dialogue goes flat whenever it veers from strictly-business to the sociopolitical. Some ingenuity in the working out of the plot, but not enough.

**HUNTING ASH**  (J) VSOM 1991 color 96m. (*Chokoso Hantingu*). D: Kousu Hukubu. SP: Shiba Enya. Story: Riyou Somye. Ph: J. Shigami. Mus: Gorou Kiyosou. SpFX: Shinichi Okamoto. Ref: TV: VSOM; Eng. titles. EVS: *Skyscraper Hauntings* - t error. vc box: *Skyscraper Hunting* - alt t. Weisser/JC. With Shou Okamori, Shingo Kazami, Hiro Enya, Tomo Shimizu.

Abnormal Species Humanoids, or ASH, are the "logical evolution of the human species"—the "results of experiments by the Genetic Research Clinic." They have a vagina-like "pulsing appendage on the back" and can "generate a destructive impulse which destroys the brain." The hero Higika is an ASH-human offspring; Daida—an apparent victim of an ASH attack—is a human brain in a machine body .... Convoluted, isn't it? The cross references for this slick but hollow vehicle for telekinetic tricks and gore effects are *Scanners* and *Akira.* One effects highlight: the duel in mid-air.

**HUPHYOKWI YANYO** (So. Korean) Han Jin Ents. (Han Kap Chin) 1981 color 96m. D: Kim In Soo. SP: Lee Moon Woong. Ref: Hardy/HM: "routine"; *The Vengeful Vampire Girl* - tr t? With Choi Bong, Chong Hi Jung.

A suicide becomes a vampire.

**HURRAY FOR MY ANCESTORS: THE TIGER AWAITS WITH GLARING EYES** (J) Studio Pierrot 1989 anim color 30m. Ref: Animag 9:4: Vol. 3 of OAV series.

Future girl turns up in time machine.

**HUWAG KANG HAHALIK SA DIABLO** (Fili) Regal Films (Lily Monteverde) 1989? color c110m. SP, D: Mauro Gia Samonte. Ph: Ricardo Jacinto, Jun Pereira. Mus D: Demet Velasquez. PD: Noel Luna. SpFX: Danny Rojo. VisFX: Cinemagic. Prosth: Cecille Baun. SdFX: Ramon Reyes. Ref: TV: Regal Video; no Eng. With Gloria Romero, Ronaldo Valdez (satan), Gabby Concepcion, Kristina Paner, Cris Villanueva, Jean Garcia, Ruffa Gutierrez (Anna), Lucy Quinto (witch).

Assorted menaces in this overdone fantasy-horror package include a young man lying in a coffin who, when kissed, awakes, then periodically transforms into a buck-toothed monster ... a mysterious woman in white who leads on one of our heroes ... a disfigured man and woman in a cobwebby old house ... and a phantom, apparently satan, who appears in a prologue and again at the end. In the most frantic sequence, the Jekyll-Hyde-like monster takes on the two disfigured ones, and kills the man. The ugly woman transforms into the woman in white and kisses the dead ugly man, who then turns young and handsome. Lots of hysterics (by the humans) and cackling (by the monsters).

**HYDE AND GO TWEET** (3) see also *Daffy Duck's Quackbusters.*

**HYDRA** see *Blood Waters of Dr. Z*

**HYDRA - MONSTER FROM THE DEEP** see *Sea Serpent, The*

**HYORYU KYOSHITSU** see *Drifting Classroom*

**HYPER-PSYCHIC-GEO GARAGA** see *Garaga*

**HYPERSAPIEN: PEOPLE FROM ANOTHER STAR** (U.S.-B) WB/PSO (Taliafilm II/Jack Schwartzman) 1986 color 93m. D: Peter Hunt. SP: Christopher Adcock, Christopher Blue, Marnie Paige, from Blue's story. Mus: Arthur B. Rubenstein. VisFX: (2nd unit sup) Roy Field; (U.K.) Optical Film FX; (U.S.) The L.A. FX Group. Ref: TV. V 12/24/86. TVG. With Sydney Penny (Robyn), Ricky Paull Goldin, Keenan Wynn, Rosie Marcel (Tavy), Gail Strickland, Dennis Holahan (Uncle Aric), Jeremy Wilkins (alien leader), Marilyn Schreffler (Kirbi's voice), Talia Shire, Army Archerd.

"To the young in spirit throughout the universe, those who will lead us to our future." Two alien telepaths (Penny and Marcel) from the planet Taros, and the furry, three-eyed, ray-shooting, intended-to-be-cute alien child Kirbi, arrive on Earth from a moonbase and try to "fit in." At the end, the aliens withdraw, though Robyn elects to stay behind with young hero "Dirt" (Goldin).... Okay photography (John Coquillon) and music;

vapid story. Kirbi proves to be another *Aurora Encounter*, card-playing alien.

**HYPERSPACE** Earl Owensby 1987 feature. D: Todd Durham. Ref: Stanley. With Alan Marx, Paula Poundworth, Chris Elliott.

Comedy re spaceship which lands in North Carolina.

# I

**I BOUGHT A VAMPIRE MOTORCYCLE** (B) Dirk Prods. 1990 (1989) color 90m. (105m.). D: Dirk Campbell. SP, P: Mycal Miller, John Wolskel. Ph: Tom Ingle. Mus: D. Friedman. Mkp: Susie Lawley-Wakelin. Bike: Steve Watts. SpFX: Image Animation. Ref: MFB'90:200-201: "enjoyably preposterous horror comedy." V 5/30/90: "misses the mark." Jones. With Neil Morrissey, Amanda Noar, Michael Elphick, Burt Kwouk.

"Vintage motorbike becomes vampirized." (V)

**I COME IN PEACE** Triumph/Vision (Damon/Saunders) 1990 (1989) color 92m. (*Dark Angel* - B & early t. *Death Angel* - e.t.). D: Craig R. Baxley. SP: Jonathan Tydor, Leonard Maas Jr. Mus: Jan Hammer. MkpFX: Tony Gardner, Larry Hamlin; (artist) Evan Brainard; (fx anim) Jay Johnson. SpFxCoord: Bruno Van Zeebroeck. OptFX: Cinema Research. SdFX: Richard Shorr. Ref: TV. MFB'90:193-4. V 10/1/90. Sacto Bee 10/1/90. SFExam 9/28/90. SFChron 9/28/90. V 6/20/90:28. With Dolph Lundgren, Brien Benben, Betsy Brantley, Matthias Hues (bad alien), Jay Bilas (good alien), David Ackroyd, Michael J. Pollard, Jesse Vint, Mark Lowenthal.

In Houston, cops and FBI agents take on "drug dealers from outer space." One of the cops—who's an alien being—dies in the line of duty as he hotly pursues another alien, whose weapons include a throat-cutting flying disc (a "powerful, self-contained electromagnet") and stiletto and "snake" gizmos which extract endorphins from their human victims and induce massive heroin overdoses.... Obvious but fairly entertaining reworking of *Brain from Planet Arous* mixes action, light gore, and comedy. Best scene involves a runaway deadly disc. The two aliens' cops-and-robbers m.o. is almost comically repetitive.

**I HEARD** Para/Fleischer 1933 anim 7m. D: Dave Fleischer. Anim: Bowsky, Waldman. Ref: TV: U.M. & M.-TV. Cabarga/TFS: Betty Boop & co. With Don Redman & his orchestra.

Baseball-playing ghosts haunt the Never Mine until a bomb (their "baseball") explodes and sends them (back) to their graves. Fine fun for fans of cartoons that bop and Boop. Some very out-of-left-field bits.

**I LIKE BATS** (Polish) Film Polski/Polish Corp. (Perspektywa Film) 1985 color/ws 76m. (*Lubie Nietoperze*). SP, D: Grzegorz Warchol. SP: also K. Kofta. Ph: Bakulski. Mus: Z. Priesner. AD: Baumiller, Olko. Ref: TV: VSOM; Eng. titles. Jones: "heavy-going allegory." With K. Walter, M. Barbasiewicz, J. Kofta.

"I'm a vampire. Help me." Isabella likes necks. She goes to a clinic for help, but her strain of vampirism proves resistant to hypnosis. At the end, however, she's okay, but her daughter has fangs.... Enigmatic variation on *Cat People,* with an oddly sweet ending: Imagine Irena going off with Dr. Judd. "Why bats?"

**I LOVE MAMMY** (Sp) Mac Fussion 1985 feature. SP, D: M. I. Bonns. Ref: Ecran F 59:70. With Eva Cobo, Maria Silva, Gil Vidal.

Accident victim comes out of a coma, seems possessed by the spirit of another woman.

**I LOVE MARIA** (H.K.) Golden Princess/Hark-Sham (Film Workshop) 1988 color c97m. (*Tieja Wudi Maliya.* aka *Roboforce*). D: Chung Chi Man. SP & Assoc P: Yuen Kai Chi. Ph: Lo Wang Shing. Mus: Romeo Diaz, James Wong. AD: James Leung. SpFX: Cinefex Workshop. Ref: TV: Rainbow Video; Eng. titles. Y. K. Ho. NST! 4:35. Horacio Higuchi. Fango 107:60. V 9/27/89:34: at Paris sf fest. With John Sham, Sally Yeh, Tsui Hark, Lam Ching Ying.

The flying monster-robot Pioneer I, of the Hero Gang, declares war on the city. Pioneer II, the android "Maria"—modelled on the gang's Maria, and perhaps on the false Maria of Fritz Lang's *Metropolis*—is dispatched to assassinate Whisky, ex-member of the gang and ex-lover of Maria. Whisky's half-daffy friend Curly, however, reprograms "Maria," and the latter defends Curly when Pioneer I disassembles and sends out parts of itself to track him down.... *I Love Maria* is a live-action *Lupin*: on-the-run action, comedy, science fiction, and romance. And, like a typical *Lupin* cartoon feature, it runs down a little early, about two-thirds of the way through. But it has the Tsui Hark pell-mell pace, and early sequences skillfully play action and violence off comedy. (Later scenes begin to recycle Abbott and Costello material.) In the funniest off-the-wall sequence, the out-of-it Whisky mistakes "Maria" for his Maria and tries to talk to "her" about what once was, while "she" is smashing through walls and obeying her "Kill Whisky" directive. Result: a terrific action sequence that's also, oddly, a love scene.

**I, MADMAN** TWE/Sarlui-Diamant 1989 (1988) color 89m. (*Hardcover* - orig t.). D: Tibor Takacs. SP: David Chaskin. Mus: Michael Hoenig. SpVisFX: Ruckus Ents.; (sup) Randall William Cook; (sp ph) Jim Aupperle. SpFX: Frank Ceglia. SpSdFX: Ron Fish. OptFX: Cinema Research. Ref: TV. V 4/18/89. Sacto Union 3/30/89. With Jenny Wright, Clayton Rohner, Cook (Malcolm Brand).

"It's Brand, and he's back to finish what he started!" Is a "copycat killer" bringing "weirdo" author Malcolm Brand's supposedly-non-fictional "confessions" to life? In any event, some maniac is using his victims' body parts to replace his own, which he cut off.... Transparent, over-clever attempt to transpose Freddy Krueger from dreams to literature. (Horror-faced Malcolm Brand to heartthrob, Virginia: "Finally, your heart will be mine!") The startling, periodic appearances of the stopmo jackal-boy enliven things.

**I-MAN** ABC-TV/Mark H. Ovitz & Disney-TV 1986 color 90m. D: Corey Allen. SP, P: Howard Friedlander, Ken Peragine. Mus: Craig Safan. SpMkp: R. J. Schiffer. Ref: TV. TVG. V 4/16/86:65, 68. With Scott Bakula (Jeffrey Wilder), Ellen Bry, Joey Cramer (Eric Wilder), John Anderson, John Bloom, Herschel Bernardi.

Jeffrey Wilder (Bakula) and his son (Cramer)—exposed to gas from "some planet's atmosphere"—are "never gonna die": Their cells "instantaneously regenerate." Routine sf-comedy. Amiable moments, though, with our date-hungry, easily-bruised (emotionally) hero, Wilder.

**I MARRIED A VAMPIRE** Troma/Full Moon 1986 (1983) color 93m. SP, D, Co-P: Jay Raskin. Mus: Steve Monahan. AD, Co-P: Vicky Prodromidov. Ref: V 4/27/88: "vanity production look with acting to match." Jones. Martin. With Rachel Golden, Brendan Hickey (Robespierre), Ted Zalewski.

Century-old vampire (Hickey) marries girl (Golden)—they go see *Vampyr.*

**I SAW WHAT YOU DID** CBS-TV/Univ-TV 1988 (1987) color 90m. D: Fred Walton. Tel: Cynthia Cidre, from Ursula Curtiss' novel. Mus: Dana Kaproff. PD: James Hulsey. Mkp: Alan Fama. Ref: TV. V 5/25/88:91. With Shawnee Smith, Tammy Lauren, Candace Cameron, Robert Carradine (Adrian Lancer), David Carradine, Alan Fudge, Michael Ross.

An arsonist-madman—the "guy with the weird music"—strangles a woman who rejects him. Later, prankster-teenager Kim phones him and says, "I saw what you did and I know who you are." Later still: "I've been waiting for you, Kim." In-between: drawn-out, very thin suspense, in this TV remake of the William Castle thriller. Plus: a visualized nightmare re a murder victim knocking at the front door ... clips from Karloff and Lugosi horror movies.

**I WALKED WITH A ZOMBIE** see *Zombies on Broadway*

**I WAS A TEENAGE MUMMY** Ghost Limb (Frieri) 1992 b&w 68m. SP, D: C. C. Frieri. SP: Diane Reinhardt. Mus: The A-Bones. Ph: Muzzy Horn. SpFX: Mark 2 FX. Mkp: Sally Ross. Ref: TV: vt. PT 12:50-51: "atmospheric lighting." 13:30 (ad). With Joan Devitt, Gregg Kalek, John Gonchar, Robert Reiss.

Egyptian kid turns school girl into killer mummy (Devitt). ("Centuries have I waited.") "Hey, we could make a movie!" level. The only question: Is it accidentally or intentionally bad?

**I WAS A TEENAGE SEX MUTANT** see *Dr. Alien*

**I WAS A TEENAGE VAMPIRE** see *My Best Friend Is a Vampire*

**I WAS A TEENAGE ZOMBIE** Horizon/PMP 1987 color 92m. D, Co-P: John Elias Michalakias. SP: James Martin. SpMkpFX: Carl Sorenson, Mike Lacky. Ref: V 7/8/87: "amateurish in every department." Phantom: "highly derivative." McCarty II: "overdone." With Michael Ruben, George Seminara, Steve McCoy.

Toxic zombies.

**I WAS A ZOMBIE FOR THE F.B.I.** Ardent & Memphis State Univ. 1984 (1982?) b&w 105m. SP, D, Co-P: Marius Penczner. SP: also John Gillick. Ph: Rick Dupree. SpFX: Bob Friedstand. MechFX: Robert Bruce. Mkp: (fx) Chuck Cooper; Chris Wright. Ref: TV. TVG. Phantom: Cinema Group video. Martin. no Scheuer. no Maltin '92. With James Rasberry, Larry Raspberry, Gillick, Christina Wellford, Anthony Isbell, Laurence Hall, Rick Crowe.

"Something's terribly wrong in Pleasantville." Everyone there is in a "zomboid state." Behind it all: aliens, their hypnotic energy globes, and their "hungry friend," a man-sized, reptilian thing which snacks on humans. ("I feed it birds, too.") Slow, involved, low-key sf/noir hybrid. You have to watch and listen closely—the film is a dry monotone—to catch the plays on words ("on your mind") and the odd visual bits.

**I WILL SCARE YOU TO DEATH** see *Madhouse* (1981)

**I YABBA-DABBA DO!** (U.S.-Taiwanese) ABC-TV/Hanna-Barbera & Wang Film (Iwao Takamoto) 1993 color c90m. (aka *The Flintstones Movie*). D: William Hanna. Tel: Rich Fogel, Mark Seidenberg, based on the TV series "The Flintstones." Mus: J. Debney. PD: Takamoto. Sup Anim D: Patterson, Sabella. Ref: TV. TVG. V 2/1/93:101. Voices: Henry Corden, Ruth Buzzi, Jean Vander Pyl, Frank Welker, June Foray, Pat Harrington, Howie Morris, Ronnie Schell.

Pebbles and Bamm-Bamm marry, and Wilma—like Blondie—starts a job. Incidentals: Slate Rock and Gravel employs mammoths, stego-types, bronto-types, styraco-types, and a T-Rex in its rock quarrying. Forced joviality, lame Stone Age-angled gags.

**ICE CREAM MAN** A-Pix 1995 (1994) color 87m. D, P: Norman Apstein. SP: David Dobkin. Ref: PT 21:16: "pretty awful." Martin: turkey. With Clint Howard, Steve Garvey, Olivia Hussey, David Naughton, Jan-Michael Vincent, David Warner.

Deranged ice-cream man's ice cream has grisly ingredients.

**The ICE PIRATES** MGM-UA/JF 1984 color 94m. SP, D: Stewart Raffill. SP: also Stanford Sherman. Mus: Bruce Broughton. SpVixFX: Max W. Anderson; (coord) Paula Lumbard. Computer FX: (coord) Linda Fleischer; Pacific Electric. SpPhFx Coord: Jonathan Seay. Robots: McCracken & McCracken; Zany Animated. Creature Des: Ray Raymond. Mkp: Maurice Stein. Ref: TV. V 3/21/84. SFExam 3/16/84. With Robert Urich, Mary Crosby, Michael D. Roberts, Angelica Huston, John Matuszak, Ron Perlman, John Carradine, Alan Caillou, Hank Worden, Gary Brockette (Percy the Robot).

"Long after the great interplanetary wars, the galaxy had gone dry." Miscellaneous ingredients: water-hoarding Templars from the planet Mithra ... a time warp ... androids ... strange creatures haunting the Pirates' Den ... space herpes ... squeaky gophers— "little nippers with hard heads" (a cute bit) ... anti-gravity stimulation ... and the 7th World (of water).... Aimless but fairly entertaining, hip version of *Star Wars* alternates between a likable jauntiness and a less likable flipness.

**ICE WOMAN** Vivid 1993 color 84m. D: Michael Zen. Ref: Adam'94. With Ashlyn Gere, Deborah Wells, Tom Byron.

Stone Age woman (Wells) on ice thaws.

**ICE WOMAN 2** Vivid 1993 color 80m. D: M. Zen. Ref: Adam'94. With A. Gere, D. Wells, T. Byron, Kristi Lynn.

**The ICEBOX MURDERS** (Sp) Olympus Films 1981('86-U.S.) color/ws 83m. D: Francisco R. Gordillo. SP: F. Ariza, F. Prosper. Ph: R.P. Cubero, Julio Bragado. Mus: G. Garcia Segura. AD: F. Prosper. Mkp: Pedro Camacho. SdFX: Luis Castro. Ref: TV:

Mogul Video; Eng. dubbed. Stanley. Hound: "faceless killer." no Martin. With Jack Taylor, Mirta Miller, Claudia Gravy, Manuela Gimenez, Natalia Millan, Juan A. Ortiz.

"I'm curious to see just what's in that big downstairs refrigerator." Ingredients here: thunderstorm scares ... a whole sleeping-car-full of corpses, in a visualized dream ... midnight skulking ... a box with a severed head in it ... midnight skulking, Part II ... and a lady's head in a secret compartment behind a wall-mounted big-game trophy .... The zero-interest plot is just an extended revving-up for the far-from-momentous payoff revelations. We never do actually get to see just what's in that big downstairs refrigerator.

**ICED** Mikon Releasing (Robert Seibert) 1988 (1987) color 85m. (*Blizzard of Blood* - orig t). D: Jeff Kwitny. SP: Joseph Alan Johnson. Mus: Dan Milner. SpFxMkp: Mike Klint. Ref: TV. V 1/18/89. no Martin. Hound. Scheuer. no Maltin '92. With Debra DeLiso, Doug Stevenson, Ron Kologie, Elizabeth Gorcey, J. A. Johnson, Dan Smith (Jeff), Lisa Loring.

"Jeff had problems...." Ten Little Teens spend a "free ski weekend" at Snow Peak, face a "ghost" and murder by snow plow, ski pole, icicle, and electric current. Formula script for the most part wastes some okay actors.

**ICEMAN** Univ/Jewison-Palmer 1984 color/ws 99m. D: Fred Schepisi. SP: Chip Proser, John Drimmer. Mus: Bruce Smeaton. SpMkp: Michael Westmore; (artist) Michele Burke. Head FX: (coord) John Thomas; George Erschbamer. Ref: TV. V 4/11/84. SFExam 4/13/84. Berkeley Monthly 6/84. With Timothy Hutton, Lindsay Crouse, John Lone ("Charlie"), Josef Sommer, David Strathairn, Philip Akin, Danny Glover.

"The iceman warmeth...." Scientists working for Polaris Mining and Chemical, in the Arctic, discover a Neanderthal man, dubbed "Charlie," chemically frozen in a glacier for 40,000 years. Contrived conflicts among company personnel re the thawed, living Charlie's status (is he "human" or a "find"?) follow.... This mainly dully serious "A" version of *Return of the Apeman* is a potpourri of past sf/monster movies, also including *Dinosaurus!*, *Revenge of the Creature*, old Universal Frankenstein films, and *Close Encounters of the Third Kind*. Intermittent humor and an intriguing final image (the dropped-from-a-helicopter Charlie "flying") help some.

**ICEMAN COMETH** (H.K.) Golden Harvest/Johnny Mak 1991 color 114m. (*Jidong Qixia*). D: Fok Yiu-leung. SP: Stephen Shiu. Ref: TV: Rainbow Video; Eng. titles. Fango 107:59. V 4/29/91. With Yuan Biao, Yuan Hua, Zhang Manyu, Maggie Cheung.

An electrical accident thaws the freezer-stored bodies of hero Fong Sau Ching and the evil Fung San, combatants frozen in ice in a mountain crevice during the Ming Dynasty, three hundred years ago. Fung San ("Raping and killing women excites me!") can lethally flick back bullets. At the end, the Wheel of Buddha sends the victorious Ching away from the present, at least temporarily.... The latter, climactic effects sequence is amusingly showy, but this silly, overlong, kung-fu fantasy-comedy-romance is just another variation on *Ghost Warrior* and *Survival of a Dragon* and includes the obligatory man-from-the-past-amazed-by-TV scene.

**ICON** see *Mill of the Stone Women*

**ICZELION, ACTS I & II** (J) A.D. Vision/HTJ-KSS 1994 anim color c60m. Story, D: T. Hirano. Ph: H. Satoh; Hitoshi. Mus: Yano, Kawai. AD: H. Katoh. Mecha Des: T. Hashimoto. SpFX: J. Sasaki. Ref: ADV video; Eng. titles.

The Iczer-made Iczel, a robot from another dimension, fuses with Earth girl Nagisa to form Iczelion, complete with "fighting suit." Together with Gold, Silver, and Black Iczelion, they take on "scourges of the universe" Chaos and Cross, their guard-robot Voids, and assorted demons, or "evil androids".... Formula follow-up to the *Iczer* films.

**ICZER-ONE: FIGHT! ICZER-ONE** (J) Studio Zweeben 1985 anim color 26m. SP, D, Anim D: Toshihiro Hirano. From the Aran Rei comics; said to be inspired by H. P. Lovecraft's story "The Call of Cthulhu." Ref: TV: A.I.C. video. Animag 1:11-13: OAV. J Anim Archives 3:11. Wonderful World of Comics 2:43.

Female cyborg Iczer-One saves schoolgirl Nagisa when the latter enters a dimension in which a snake-like monster jumps out at her from the back of a classmate's head. It's Iczer-One to the rescue again when a suddenly-liquid wooden fence absorbs Nagisa into itself, and various loathsome monsters threaten her. Finally—after yet another rescue (when alien Buedem invade Nagisa's parents and turn them into monsters)—Iczer-One reveals her reason for watching after the girl: The giant Iczer Robot is to tap into Nagisa' psychic powers in order to combat the giant robot Diros Theta, which is invading from the alternate dimension.

Monster and robot menaces here are fairly typical for Japanese animation, but the movie is done with some wit and style. Ineffable touches: the wriggly monster in the little sailor-suit dress ... the feelers which slither out of the robot's mouth ... the house-monster-arms which dissolve when Iczer-One sticks her sword into the floorboards.

**ICZER-ONE, ACT II** (J) Studio Zweeben 1986? anim color 25m. D: T. Hirano. Anim D: Hirano, N. Kakinouchi. Ref: vc box: A.I.C. video. Animag 3:8: OAV. Ronin Network 12/25/88.

**ICZER-ONE, ACT 3: THE FINAL CHAPTER** (J) Studio Zweeben 1987 anim color 40m. SP, D, Anim D: T. Hirano. Anim D: also N. Kakinouchi. Ref: TV: A.I.C. video; no Eng. Animag 3:8-11: OAV. Ronin Network 12/25/88.

Items: the evil Big Gold, who was once human, then died and became a machine ... "synchronization," in which the dead heroine Nagisa's spirit becomes one with Iczer-One ... the tentacled Buedem and other monsters ... Guoids, ray-shooting robots ... and a possible *Bambi Meets Godzilla* hommage when oversized Iczer-Two steps on Sayoko.... Strikingly drawn but monotonous action-fantasy issues in a bittersweet ending in which Iczer-One restores Nagisa to home and family, and the galactic action becomes for her a forgotten dream.

**ICZER-3** (J) Polydor (A.I.C.) 1990 anim color 30m. (aka *Adventure! Iczer-3*). D & Char Des: Hirano Toshihiro. Ref: Japan Video: Vol. 3 is 1991. Animag 10:3. 11:4: OAV series of 6, 30m. each.

Iczer-3 vs. Big Gold, or "Neos Gold."

**Der IDEALE UNTERMIETER** (W.G.) Wolf Schmidt Film 1956 b&w 98m. SP, D, P: W. Schmidt. Ph: H. Koenig. Ref: Hardy/SF: "utterly tasteless and rather dim-witted." With Schmidt, Sibylle Schindler, Lia Woehr.

Domestic robot.

**IDENTITY CRISIS** see *Mark of Cain, The*

**IDIOTS DELUXE** see *Dizzy Detectives*

**Az IDOE ABLAKAJ** (Hung.) Studio 4, Mafilm 1969 color 85m. D: Tamas Fejer. SP: Peter Kuczka. Ph: M. Herczenik. Ref: Hardy/SF: "unimaginatively constructed script." Ecran F 73:26. With Beata Tyszkiewicz, Ian Andonov, Miklos Gabor.

In the distant future, five people awake from "hibernation." *The Windows of Time* - tr t?

**IDOL OF FIRE** see *I'll Suck You Dry*

**IF I RUN, I STILL LOVE YOU** (Thai) c1990? color c90m. Ref: TV: K.N.B. Video; no Eng. Chao Thai Video 2: above is tr t.

An explorer in a cave discovers skeletons ... and a mystic woman who lifts a bubbling bowl which turns into a big rolling, Indiana Jones rock. Later, after an incantation, she materializes from the magic bowl, walks through walls (a not-bad effect), and turns the hero's flashlight into a *Star Wars* light saber.... After its semi-spooky opening sequence, film turns into a light comedy-fantasy of invisibility. (Only the hero can see the magic woman.) At one point, a snap of the woman's fingers acts like a TV remote.

**IF WAR COMES TOMORROW** (Russ.) Amkino/Mosfilm (E. Dzigan) 1938 b&w 60m. SP, D: G. Berezko. D: also L. Antsi-Polovski, N. Karmazinski. SP: also E. Dzigan, M. Svetlov. Mus: Brothers Pokrass. Ref: V 7/20/38: "scans like a juve cops-and-robbers tale."

"A war of the future is depicted, with Germany obviously the villain.... It winds up by the revolt of the enemy masses in favor of Communism."

**IGA NINPOCHO** see *Ninja Wars*

**IGOR AND THE LUNATICS** Troma (Beard) 1985 color 84m. (*Bloodshed* - orig t). SP, D, P: Billy Parolini. SP: also Beard. SpFxMkp: Simon Deitch. Ref: V 5/22/85: "incompetent." McCarty II: "confusing." Phantom: "insipid dialogue." Ecran F 58:33. With Joseph Eero, Joe Niola, T. J. Michaels, Mary Ann Schacht.

Mad murderers from cult/commune.

**The IGUANA WITH A TONGUE OF FIRE** (I-F-G) Video Search 1971 color? feature (*L'Iguana dalla Lingua de Fuoco*). D: Riccardo Freda. Ref: Imagi 1:59: "gruesome throat slittings, acid disfigurements & the presence of the multiple killers motif." Palmerini: from R. Mann's novel "A Room without a Door."

**IJINTACHI TONO NATSU** see *Discarnates, The*

**IKITE-IRU KOHEIJI** see *Living Koheiji, The*

**IL ETAIT UNE FOIS LE DIABLE** (F) Commodore Films/Launois & Condor Films 1987 (1986) color/ws 80m. (*Devil's Story* - ad t. *Devil Story* - cr t. *Il Etait Une Fois .. Le Diable* - cr t). SP, D: Bernard Launois. Ph: Maria, Loubeau. Mus: Roy, Piot. Mkp: Jack Bourban. Monsters: Plastic-Studio. SpFX: Trielli. Ref: TV: VSOM; no Eng.; Mkp: "Jacky Bouban." Mad Movies 49:11. With Marcel Portier, Veronique Renaud, Pascal Simon (monster).

Ingredients here include a mutant (and apparently his mother) ... a stray, living Egyptian mummy that raises a female zombie from a coffin ... a noisy "devil horse" ... and an attack cat .... Atrocious, but pretty bizarre. Scorecard: inept action ... overworked spurting-blood packets ... and pathetic editing and music (except for Bach's Toccata).

**ILE MYSTERIEUX, L'** see *Mysterious Planet*

**I'LL SUCK YOU DRY** EZSex Prods./Afton Prods. (Sisso Pippon) 1989 (1982) color c70m. D: Stuart Koslov. Ph: S. Holstein. Mus: Patrick Schneider. Mkp: Gene Taylor. Ref: TV: vt. no Adam. With Nina de Ponca, Taija Rae, Nina Hartley, Ron Jeremy.

The saga of *Lust at First Bite* (III) continues. *Dry* is made up mainly if not exclusively of scraps from other hardcore movies, principally *Lust at First Bite* aka *Dracula Sucks* aka *Dracula's Bride,* including scenes with Jamie Gillis as Dracula. (To complicate matters further, there was a magazine version of *Lust* titled *Idol of Fire.*) In other, perhaps-original-with-this-film scenes, a caped, glowing-eyed vampire stands around, and a man in a skull mask makes love to a woman. The closest this extremely disjointed movie, or collage, comes to the vc box description of a barber shop of "vampire vixens" is a sex/massage scene.

**3P ILLEGAL ALIEN** Gregory J. Keller 1982 color c15m. SP, D: Jeffrey Baker. SP, Set Des: Keller. Ph: Stephen Rogers. Mus: Lawrence Kassin. Set Des: also Kenny Yamada. Ref: TV: CINEMAGIC (Starlog Video), MPI HV. UC Theatre notes. Ernie Fink. Stanley. With John Stamm, Frank Sheppard, Jim Lefebvre.

A pie-in-the-face awaits a cosmic explorer aboard the spaceship Nostrilomo. Okay ribbing of *Alien* features a plastic crab, a lurking clown, menacing false teeth, and a clumsy, easily identified android.

**I'M DANGEROUS TONIGHT** USA-TV/BBK Prods. & Coastline Partners (MTE) 1990 color c90m. D: Tobe Hooper. Tel & P: Bruce Lansbury, Philip John Taylor. Mus: Nicholas Pike. PD: Leonard Mazzola. SpFX: (coord) Joseph Mercurio; SpFx Unltd. Ref: TV. V 8/8/90:51. Sacto Bee 8/8/90. With Madchen Amick, Corey Parker, Daisy Hall, Natalie Schafer, William Berger, Dee Wallace Stone, Anthony Perkins.

Beware the "power of the cloak"! An "unlucky" cloak taken from an Aztec sacrificial altar and housed in the Tiverton College Museum "takes control" of its wearer and "amplifies" the evil in same. But it has only a "marginal influence" on basically good people. (It makes Amick's heroine Amy dance dirty.) Asinine variation on *Impulse.*

**I'M GONNA GIT YOU SUCKA** UA 1988 color 88m. SP, D: Keenen Ivory Wayans. SpFxMkp: Barbie Gotschall. SpFxCoord:

F. J. Cramer. OptFX: Cinema Research. Ref: TV. Sacto Union 2/19/89. V 12/21/88.

Good-natured, wry parody of action movies features an incidental bit with a demon-possessed woman. ("You have got the devil in you!")

**The IMAGE OF DORIAN GRAY IN THE YELLOW PRESS** (W.G.) Jones & King/Ottinger & Basis/WDR & FKL 1984 color 150m. (*Dorian Gray im Spiegel der Boulevardpresse*. aka *The Picture of Dorian Gray in the Yellow Press*). SP, D, Ph, Sets: Ulrike Ottinger. Mus: Peer Raben. Mkp: Axel Zornow, Siegfried Ae. Video: Margit Eschenbach. Titles: Peter Bartoschek. Ref: screen. PFA notes 7/24/84. V 3/21/84. With Delphine Seyrig (Frau Dr. Mabuse), Veruschka von Lehndorff (Dorian), Tabea Blumenschein, Toyo Tanaka, Barbara Valentin, Irm Hermann, Magdalena Montezuma (Golem).

Mabuse, head of a future-tense international-press conglomerate, institutes Operation Mirror in an attempt to boost sales. The "beautiful, inexperienced, and somewhat dull" Dorian Gray is programmed with memories and in general made more glamorous. His every movement is captured by camera and pen, and Mabuse guides him on a "horror program" of the "underworld" of the City by Night, which program includes a morgue-like den of the "risk-takers" of life and a voodoo trance-dance .... A basically-non-narrative indulgence in which one visual absurdity replaces another and is then itself replaced. This "replacement" process proceeds so sluggishly that the viewer may not make many connections between absurdities while the film is in (so to speak) progress.

**IMMORTAL COMBAT** Blue Ridge Ent./Powerhouse (A-Pix) 1993 color 109m. (*Resort To Kill* - alt t). D, P, SP: Daniel Neira. SP: also Robert Crabtree. Ref: vc box: "indestructible warriors ... back from the dead." PT 19:16. SFChron 8/13/94: "Mayan Steroid Monsters." Martin: "routine." With Sonny Chiba, Roddy Piper, Meg Foster, Kim Morgan Greene.

**IMMORTAL SINS** (U.S.-Sp) Concorde-New Horizons & Tesauro & ABC Dist. Co. & TV Espanola (Villalba/Peffley/Corman-Camp) 1992 (1991) color 86m. (*Vengeance with a Kiss. Beyond the Wall of Sleep*—early titles). D: Herve Hachuel. SP: Tom Cleaver, Beverly Gray. Ph: A. Mayo. Mus: R. Spellman, P. Navarrete. PD: R. Palmero. SpFX: Reyes Abades. Mkp: Jose Quetglas. OptFX: OFE Optical Film FX. Ref: TV. TVG. V 5/4/92:232: at Cannes. 5/6/91:79. Martin. With Cliff De Young, Maryam D'Abo, Tony Isbert, Shari Shattuck, Paloma Lorena, Miguel de Grandy, Oswaldo Delgado Sanchez (succubus).

"She has been haunting your castle since the 11th Century." According to the "curse of Joaquin," a Celtic priestess in Galicia cursed the De Alvarez family and the "forerunners of the Inquisition" who burned her to death. "The legend has it that her ghost haunts the dungeons of this building, which stands on the very spot where she died." The succubus—"she who comes in the night"—proves to be a hairy monster.... Talky, exposition-laden horror story at least has occasional fetching details—the 25,000-year-old stone structure (the "work of the Druids"?), the succubus-repelling amulet, the "ghost-walking."

**IMMORTALITY, INC.** see *Freejack*

The **IMMORTALIZER** RCA-Col HV/Film West (F. Wolcott) 1990 (1988) color 96m. D, Ed: Joel Bender. SP: M. M. Nelsen. Mus: Walden, Fasman. MkpFX: John Naulin. Ref: V 8/22/90:76(hv): "idiotic." PT 9:11: "stupid movie." McCarty II: "gore-filled but distinctly low-level *Re-animator* clone." With Ron Ray, Chris Crone, Melody Patterson, Raye Hollitt (monster).

"Experimental failures are kept locked up as cannibalistic geeks...." (V)

**IMP, The** see *Sorority Babes in the Slimeball Bowl-O-Rama*

**IMPAKTITA** (Fili) Regal Int'l. (Lily Monteverde) 1989 color c115m. D: Teddy Chiu. SP: Bugsy Dabao. Story: Menard Amoroso. From the comic serial by J. R. Mercado & Amoroso. Ph: Vic Anao. Mus D: Demet Velasquez. PD: Vic Dabao. SpMkp: Jesie Otero. SpFX: Danny Torrente. Prosth: Claro Camposano. SdFX: Rodel Capule. Ref: TV: Regal Video; occ. Eng. With Nida Blanca, Gloria Romero, Aga Muhlach, Richard Gomez, Jean Garcia (Cita).

"Her eyes promise love, her lips sneer death." So says the vc box cover, and it does not lie. At the beginning, angry villagers torch a bat-like monster. Nearby, a baby—perhaps the creature's daughter—turns monster-faced.... The baby grows to be a little (human) girl who finds that she has claws when cornered, and who sees a vision of a bat-like thing in the circle of her finger ring. Later, the thing appears to her, and she too transforms into a bat-monster; her torso and head fly off and slay the men who raped her.... Typical emotional story pegs—revenge for rape, impossible human/monster love—but the monster scenes are full-throttle horror. The music librarian borrows mainly from American movies, including (over the end credits) *East of Eden.*

**IMPULSE** Fox/ABC Motion Pictures (Tim Zinnemann) 1984 color 88m. D: Graham Baker. SP: Bart Davis, Don Carlos Dunaway. Mus: Paul Chihara. SpFX: Tom Fisher, Greg Curtis. Mkp: Rick Sharp. Ref: TV. V 10/3/84. Stanley. Fango 101. With Tim Matheson, Meg Tilly, Hume Cronyn, John Karlen, Bill Paxton, Amy Stryker, Claude Earl Jones.

The small town of Sutcliffe. A woman snarls at her daughter over the phone. Kids play pranks, and parents are simply amused. A preacher swears. Motorists all become Mr. Wheelers. A doctor eliminates an annoying patient. The sheriff shoots a young thief.... Like the dinner-party guests in the replay of the George Bancroft-Kay Francis scene in *Paramount on Parade* (1930), the townsfolk here "follow their impulses" and do anything they damn well please. What started it all? An earth-quake-caused toxic-waste leak, natch, which affected the local milk supply.... Pretty spooky, at first: Broad daylight, and the ids are out. Things are only slightly different, at first, only a bit intensified. *Impulse* is for those weary of conformist horror fables: This nightmare is the opposite of a world of Winston Smiths—it's a world of Mr. Hydes, or Cleggs. The movie peaks with a creepy, summing-up-the-horror series of shots: The heroine (Tilly) flees the farm in a truck, and the latter's headlights pick up one amok person crossing the road, then another. Finally, she comes upon a whole town of amoks. There follows a tired, Big Cover-up ending, and the story is more or less just a vehicle for a series of vignettes in which everyone is snapping and rasping and generally having a bad day, or at least making sure everyone else has a bad day.

**IN A GLASS CAGE** (Sp) 1986 color 112m. (*Tras el Cristal*). D: Agustin Villaronga. SP: Cristina Sole? Ph: J. Peracaula. AD: C. Candini. Mkp: E. de Villanueva. SpFX: Reyes Abades. Ref: TV: EVS; Eng. titles. Scheuer. Martin. V 3/5/86. With G. Meisner, David Sust, Marisa Paredes, Gisela Echevarria.

Horror perpetuated, as young Angelo confronts old Klaus, now in an iron lung, but once a Nazi concentration-camp doctor. ("I want to be like you.") Angelo recreates—with needles and knives—Klaus' crimes against young boys, and does so more, it seems, for his own warped pleasure than for Klaus' edification. ("You see, Klaus—I love death.") As in *Brother from Another Planet*, a big-time criminal is confronted with his crimes; this time, though, the script is not quite buyable. From another angle, this is a slightly improved version of *Crawlspace*.

**IN ADVANCE OF THE LANDING** (Can.) Cineplex Odeon/Cygnus (Don Haig) 1993 (1992) colorand & b&w 85m. D, P: Dan Curtis. From Douglas Curran's book. Mus: F. Mollin. Ref: V 2/1/93: "bland docu on UFOs" ... clips from *This Island Earth, The Arrival*, etc. with Ruth E. Norman, Betty Hill, John Shepherd, Sherrie Rose.

**IN EXILE** see *Time Runner*

**IN POSSESSION** (B) Fox Mystery Theatre/Fox & Hammer-TV 1985 (1984) color c90m. D: Val Guest. Tel: Michael J. Bird. Ph: Brian West. Mus: Paul Patterson. AD: Carolyn Scott. Mkp: Eddie Knight. Ref: TV. TVG. Stanley. Ecran F 73:9. no Scheuer. no Maltin '92. Ecran F 70:13. With Carol Lynley, Christopher Cazenove, David Healey, Bernard Kay, Judy Loe, Vivienne Burgess.

"We're caught up in something!" Frank and Sylvia Daly (Cazenove and Lynley, respectively) find themselves in a night-marish time warp. They keep bumping into the phantom-like Mr. and Mrs. Prentice (Kay and Burgess, respectively) in their flat. The latter couple enacts a domestic murder mystery while the former watches, helplessly. Though Mr. Prentice seems to be addressing, alternately, Frank and Sylvia, he sees and interacts only with Mrs. Prentice, neighbors, police, etc.—principals in the phantom show—and he does not hear the Dalys.... Thriller's novel premise plays like an "Alfred Hitchcock Presents" filtered through "The Twilight Zone." Frank runs into the imposing Mr. Prentice at every turn, in randomly-ordered "scenes" from the murder story, and although the idea is unfortunately played more for straight horror than weird comedy, the omnipresence of the husband is pretty funny, and there's some wit in his "public face" concern for the woman he murdered. Predictable kicker reveals the phantoms to have been part of a prophecy, not a reenactment.

**IN THE AFTERMATH: ANGELS NEVER SLEEP** (U.S.-J) New World/Tom Dugan 1987 color c80m. SP, D: Carl Colpaert. Based on the film *The Angel's Egg*. SP: also Thea Hardigg et al. Text: B. I. Goldhagen. Ph: Geza Sinkovics. Mus: Anthony Moore. AD: Ildiko Toth. SpVisFX: Optical Cinema Services. SpFX: Chuck Whitton et al. SdFxDes: Bob Moore, Christopher Harvengt. Mkp: Robin Slater. OptDes: McIntyre & Nelson; Animagic. SpThanks: Allan Holzman et al. Ref: TV: New World Video. V 10/19/88:482: at Sitges. Martin. Hound. Morse. With

Tony Markes (Frank), Rainbow Dolan (angel), Filiz Tully, Kenneth McCabe, Kurtiss J. Tews.

A post-holocaust Southern California with (surprise) contaminated air. An angel gives our hero, Frank, an egg which purifies said air.... What *The Terror* was for *Targets,* the Japanese animated feature *The Angel's Egg* is for *In the Aftermath*—that is, padding. Ultra-cheapie at least retains a few of the most breathtaking sequences of *The Angel's Egg*—the shadow-fish-haunted town, the idyll of the pond. Here, the animated angel becomes, intermittently, a live-action little girl, and some slick editing allows her brother angel to give her a "second chance" egg after her first breaks. (In the original, she has only one egg.)

**IN THE COLD OF THE NIGHT** Omega (Isabelle Mastorakis) 1990 color 112m. Story, SP, D, P: Nico Mastorakis. SP: also Fred C. Perry. Computer FX: N. Mastorakis. Mkp: Dan Frey. Ref: TV. V 3/18/91. With Jeff Lester, Adrienne Sachs, Marc Singer, Brian Thompson, Shannon Tweed, John Beck, Tippi Hedren, David Soul.

Welcome to the "Nightmare in Scott's Mind." Fashion photographer Scott Bruin's (Lester) recurrent nightmare re strangling a woman in a shower threatens to become reality. At one point, he finds himself (during a photo session), apparently awake, in the dream house. A few more plot turns take him to the actual house with the woman, Kimberly Shawn (Sachs), from the dream. Inside, he finds his "dream" on a laser disc. The upshot: A tiny micro-receiver in his tooth has been taking high-frequency TV transmissions through his brain: "Take ordinary people, make them killers".... Intriguing dream-mystery beginning gives way to an artificial romance, and Sachs is terrible. The revelation of the "mind altering technology" is so far out it's almost camp.

**IN THE FOLDS OF THE FLESH** see *Folds of the Flesh*

**IN THE HEAT OF THE NIGHT: THE CASE OF THE VOODOO MURDERS** NBC-TV/MGM-UA-TV (Fred Silverman Co. & Juanita Bartlett) 1988 color c90m. D: Peter Levin. Tel & Sup P: Jeri Taylor. Tel: also David Moessinger. Based on characters created by John Ball. Mus: Joe Harnell. PD: Al Rohm. SpFX: Dick Cross. SdFX: Echo; (sup) David McMoyler. Mkp: Pat Gerhardt, Sylvia Mays. Ref: TV. TVG (ad): "2-hour movie." V 12/14/88:57. With Carroll O'Connor, Howard Rollins, Lois Nettleton, Alan Autry, Iman, Thomas Ian Griffith.

Sparta, Miss., 1968. Betty Jo suffers an "absolutely grisly murder" by trowel, and her heart is apparently extracted.... 1988. Much ado re a box with a human heart in it, voodoo spirit lures, death-threat notes ("Blood for blood—you're next to die!"), and snakes. Pale imitation of the hit movie.

**IN THE MIDNIGHT HOUR** see *Midnight Kiss*

**IN THE PICTURE** see *Three Cases of Murder*

**IN THE SHADOW OF KILIMANJARO** (B-Kenyan?) Intermedia/Scotti Bros. (Mansfield Leasing/Nyconant?) 1986 color 97m. D: Raju Patel. SP: J. M. Sneller, T. M. Harry. Mus: Arlon Ober. SpVisFX: Malcolm Bubb, Paul Gilby, Robert Roach. SpMechFX: Bob Wasson, James Ballard. SpFxOpt: Camera FX Ltd., Movie Magic, V.C.E. Mkp: Jack Petty. SpVoices: Percy

Edwards. Ref: TV. V 5/7/86. ad. Phantom. With John Rhys-Davies, Timothy Bottoms, Michele Carey, Irene Miracle, Calvin Jung, Don Blakely, Patty Foley.

"A fictionalized account of a true incident which took place in Africa during the serious drought in 1984." Baboon facts: They're three times stronger than humans. They're smart. And "they're organizing." A "bunch of bloody monkeys"—baboons, actually—"looking for dinner" attacks, first, the Sinya Mining Company, then a house. Then: "Linda and the kids are still at the school." Despite the factual basis, there's nothing much here that wasn't in *The Birds,* except baboons. Perfunctory.

**IN THE TIME OF BARBARIANS II** Academy/Vista Street (Stephen Lieb) 1992 color 85m. (*Time Barbarians II: Eyes of the Serpent* - alt t). Ph, D: R. C. Gale. SP: Stewart Chapin. Ref: Martin. V 2/8/93:24 (rated). PT 19:17: *Eyes of the Serpent.* With Diana Frank, Lenore Andriel, Tom Schultz.

Follow-up to *Time Barbarians.* "Story of an evil woman ... after magic swords." (PT)

**L'INCENERITORE** (I) Tecnofilm 1984 color 90m. SP, D: Pier Degli Ambrosi. Mus: R. Benson. Ref: V 9/5/84: "very entertaining ... absurdist comedy." With Flavio Bucci, Ida Di Benedetto, Alexandra Delli Colli Groski.

A town's citizens are mysteriously murdered, put in bags, and burned in an incinerator.

**INCIDENT AT RAVEN'S GATE** see *Encounter at Raven's Gate*

**L'INCREDIBILE E TRISTE STORIA DEL CINICO RUDY, OVVERO: DICIASSETTE** (I) 1991 feature. D: Enrico Caria. Ref: Palmerini: "most original."

"Mutants and flesh-eating mussels" in post-holocaust 2057.

**INCREDIBLE FANTASTIC SUCCUBARE, The** see *Succubare*

The **INCREDIBLE HULK RETURNS** NBC-TV/New World-TV & Bixby-Brandon 1988 color c90m. SP, D, Exec Co-P: Nicholas Corea. From the Stan Lee comic. Mus: Lance Rubin. AD: Michael Parker. SpFX: Chuck Dolan SpMkp: Norman Leavitt, John Goodwin. Ref: TV. V 1/8/88:53. With Bill Bixby, Lou Ferrigno, Jack Colvin, Lee Purcell, Charles Napier, Tim Thomerson, Eric Kramer (Thor), Steve Levitt (Donald Blake), Donald Willis, William Malone.

Re "the monster in you ... your Mr. Hyde." Gamma-ray-affected David Banner (Bixby) becomes The Incredible Hulk (Ferrigno) when upset. ("You wouldn't like me when I'm angry.") In the course of developing the Gamma Transponder ("reverses gamma polarity") to cure himself, Banner comes up against a revived, cursed Viking warrior (Donald Blake: "He's part of me") who appears whenever Blake holds Thor's hammer and cries "Odin!" Thor (the "big goof") makes David angry. Hokey but lively TV-fantasy. Helpfully, Thor speaks English.

See also: *Amazing Stories—The Movie III:* "Remote Control Man." *Death of the Incredible Hulk. Evening with Kitten, An. Trial of the Incredible Hulk.*

**INCREIBLE PROFESOR ZOVEK, El** see *Prof. Zovek*

**INDECENT DESIRES** Silverman 1967 b&w feature. D, P: Doris Wishman (aka Louis Silverman). Ref: SWV supp.: voodoo doll torments woman. no Lee. no Lentz. no Weldon. With Sharon Kent, T. Little.

**\*INDESTRUCTIBLE MAN** GK 1956 (1955). Ref: TV: Lorimar-TV. Warren/KWTS! LC. TVG. no V. Weldon. Scheuer. Maltin '92. Martin. Phantom. Lee. Lentz. Hardy/SF. Sveh la/Guilty Pleasures.With Marjorie Stapp, Roy Engle, Robert Foulk, Joe Flynn.

"Once a dead man, always a dead man"—make that "usually." A biochemist (Robert Shayne) searching for a cancer cure subjects an executed murderer, Charlie "The Butcher" Benton (Lon Chaney Jr.), to 300,000 volts of electricity, which dose burns out his vocal cords, but also increases his "cellular structure" and makes him incredibly strong and impervious to bullets ... a living "solid mass of cells." ("Each cell must have multiplied 100 times!") This "monster-made man" wreaks vengeance on the men who turned state's evidence against him.... Pointless reworking of *The Walking Dead*. Chaney works hard at looking "indestructible": The camera moves in close. His face tenses. The lines around his eyes converge. Science here comes off worst (see above); music, not much better. (The score is comically "dramatic.") The "indestructible" angle boils down to stray moments depicting The Butcher surviving gunshots, flame throwers, and a bazooka. Film's sole interest now: the location shooting at L.A.'s Angels' Flight, a power plant, etc.

**INDIANA JONES AND THE LAST CRUSADE** Para/Lucasfilm 1989 color/ws 127m. D: Steven Spielberg. SP: Jeffrey Boam. Story: George Lucas, Menno Meyjes. VisFX: IL&M; (anim sup) Wes Takahashi; (mkp fx sup) Stephan Dupuis. MechFxSup: George Gibbs. Prosth: Nick Dudman. Ref: TV. MFB'89:198-200. Sacto Bee 5/24/89. NYorker 6/12/89. V 5/24/89. Sacto Union 5/24/89.

Third in the *Indiana Jones* series features a horror-fantasy scene at the end in which a drink from an unholy grail makes the villain age instantly, shrivel, turn monstrous-looking, then disintegrate. This entry is notable more for the wry father-son teaming of Sean Connery's Dr. Henry Jones and Harrison Ford's Indy, or "Junior," than for thrills, some of which are getting pretty tired.

**INDIANA JONES AND THE TEMPLE OF DOOM** Para/Lucas-film 1984 color 118m. D: Steven Spielberg. SP: Willard Huyck, Gloria Katz. Story: George Lucas. Mus: John Williams. MechFxSup: George Gibbs. SpVisFX: IL&M; (sup) Dennis Muren; (stopmo anim) Tom St. Amand; (anim sup) Charles Mullen; (consul) Phil Tippett. Addl OptFX: Modern. Floor FxSup: David Harris. SpFxSup: Kevin Pike. FxAnim: Bruce Walters. Mkp: Peter Robb-King. Ref: TV. V 5/16/84. With Harrison Ford, Kate Capshaw, Ke Huy Quan, Amrish Puri, Roshan Seth, Dan Aykroyd, Bhasker Patel.

"Alive, but like a nightmare"—that's the zombie-like state of those who drink the "black sleep" of blood. Follow-up to *Raiders of the Lost Ark* is a "ghost story" re "ancient evil" and the legends of India. Horrific highlights include the high priest's literally-single-handed extraction of a man's heart ... a voodoo doll ... a bug

cave ... and "giant vampire bats".... A lot of *Mask of Fu Manchu* horrors and an old bad joke re eyeball soup. Each sequence seems to have a dozen shots too many. The hyperbole is labored. Ford, however, applies the occasional, necessary light touch, and the climactic Disneyland-inspired race down the mine tunnels nearly reaches the desired excitement level.

See also: *Starzan*.

**2 INFERNO** Claudio Argento/Salvatore Argento 1980 ws 106m. Mkp: P. Mecacci. SdFX: L. & M. Anzellotti. Ref: TV: Key Video; Eng. dubbed. VWB.

The key to the horror: the book *The Three Mothers* ("fragments of a diary")—which mothers are Sighs, Tears, and Darkness. The latter den of alchemy has taken up in New York City.... A bit thin, but atmospheric. In fact, the first half of the movie is probably The Best of Dario Argento. A bit far-fetched, but pretty creepy: the opening, underwater, floating-corpse sequence. Also unsettling: the Verdi-and-room-lights, on-and-off sequence. The Attack of the Cats scene fizzles—the flying cats are clearly hand-propelled. The Attack of the Rats is also obviously faked, too.

**INFERNO IN DIRETTA** see *Cut and Run*

**INFERNO IN SAFEHAVEN** see *Escape from Safehaven*

**INFERNOFINIS** see *Comando de la Muerte*

**INFESTED** see *Ticks*

**INFLAMED** 1984 color 85m. Ref: Adam '88. With Misty, Lynx Canon, Billy Dee.

"A maiden is used to capture souls for the devil in exchange for anything she wants."

**INGAGI** see *Son of Ingagi*

**INHERITOR** Vidamerica/Filmworld Int'l. (Christopher and Cheryl Webster) 1990 (1988) color 82m. D: Brian Kendal-Savegar. SP: Julian Weaver. Mus: A Finch. Ref: V 6/20/90:39(hv): "talky and static." Hound. V 10/19/88:142. Fango 94:12. With Lisa McGuire, Barnaby Spring, John Rice, Dan Haggerty, John Russo.

Indian curse ... minotaur.

**INHUMANOIDS: THE EVIL THAT LIES WITHIN** Hi-Tops/Sunbow & Hasbro 1986 anim color 45m. Ref: vc box: "the dark overlords of the Earth's core." no Hound.

**The INITIATION** New World/Vance-Angelos-Georgian Bay-Monzio/Lansbury-Gaynor (Initiation Associates) 1984 (1983) color 97m. D: Larry Stewart. SP: Charles Pratt Jr. Mus: Gabriel Black, Lance Ong. SpFX: Jack Bennett. Ref: TV. V 12/19/84. With Vera Miles, Clu Gulager, Daphne Zuniga (Kelly/Terry), James Read.

Prank Night horrors in the huge Fairchild Building include monster-masked clowns and murders by hatchet, arrow, and spear-gun.... Routine. The "classic Freudian dream"/memory opening gives away more than it's supposed to.

**INITIATION—SILENT NIGHT, DEADLY NIGHT 4** IVE/Silent Films (R. N. Gladstein) 1990 color 86m. (*Silent Night, Deadly Night 4: Initiation* - alt t). D: Brian Yuzna. SP: Woody Keith. Story: S. J. Smith, Arthur H. Gorson, B. Yuzna. Mus: Richard Band. VisFX: Screaming Mad George; (key fx) Moto; (animatronics) David Matherly. MechFX: Joe Viskosil et al. Title Anim: David McCutchen. Ref: TV. V 1/14/91. 9/3/90:78(rated). TVG. With Maud Adams, Neith Hunter, Tommy Hinkley, Allyce Beasley, Clint Howard, Reggie Banister, Jeanne Bates.

Functional plot re Lilith, "Adam's first wife" (see also *Night Angel*), and a demon cult re same. Fun-gross effects with big big bugs "formed from fear." Sleaze-quease highlights: heroine Kim's (Hunter) vision of her weenie-string hands, her vision of herself with half a bug body (the bottom half), and the humongous-bug-out-the-mouth stunt, which is followed by a champion gutting-of-bug stunt.

**INJU GAKUEN** see *Sex Beast on Campus*

**INN OF THE FLYING DRAGON, The** see Sleep of Death, The

**INNER SANCTUM II** MDP/A.N.A. (Kardessa/Alan Amiel) 1994 color 93m. D: Fred Olen Ray. SP: "Sherman Scott," S. Armogida. Ref: SFChron 3/18/95: "Ray delivers with this one." PT 20:18. vc box. Martin. With Tracy Brooks Swope, Joseph Bottoms, Michael Nouri, David Warner, Sandahl Bergman, M. Hemingway, Jennifer Reed, Kato Kaelin, Joe Estevez, Robert Quarry, Suzanne Ager, John Blythe Barrymore.

"A horror flick disguised as an erotic thriller" re a "zombie in the house."

**INNERSPACE** WB/Amblin (Guber-Peters) 1987 color 120m. D: Joe Dante. SP: Jeffrey Boam, Chip Proser. Story: Proser. Mus: Jerry Goldsmith. VisFX: IL&M; (sup) Dennis Muren; (anim) Gordon Baker et al. SpMkpFX: Rob Bottin. SpFX: Michael Wood. Ref: TV. MFB'87:368. V 6/24/87. Phantom. Martin. Scheuer. With Dennis Quaid, Martin Short, Meg Ryan, Kevin McCarthy, Fiona Lewis, William Schallert, Henry Gibson, John Hora, Orson Bean, Kevin Hooks, Wendy Schaal, Robert Picardo, Kathleen Freeman, Archie Hahn, Dick Miller, Ken Tobey, Joe Flaherty, Andrea Martin, Terence McGovern, Chuck Jones, Charles Aidman.

Vectorscope labs, Silicon Valley. An "innerspace" capsule—complete with optic remote and sensor—and its pilot, Tuck (Quaid), are miniaturized and injected into the body of Jack Putter (Short), nerd. "Martin Short's interiors produced at IL&M." The setting-up scenes are drawn-out, and the production is overlong and overelaborate, but *Innerspace* has some terrific surreal slapstick payoffs (e.g., the tussle with the half-size McCarthy in the cab, the stomach-acid-dissolved baddie) and good, *Topper*-ish "invisible man," non-sequitur dialogue for the scenes with Jack, the inner Tuck, and puzzled third parties. Odd resonant bits punctuate a strange mixture of inspiration and calculation.

**INNOCENT BLOOD** WB/Landis-Belzberg (Lee Rich/J. Sheinberg) 1992 color 113m. D: John Landis. SP: Michael Wolk. Ph: Mac Ahlberg. Mus: Ira Newborn. PD: Richard Sawyer. SpVisFX: Dutton-Taylor. SpMkpFX: Steve Johnson. SpFX: Roy Arbogast et al. Ref: TV. V 9/28/92. ad. NYT 9/25/92. Sacto Bee 9/25/92. SFChron 9/25/92. With Anne Parillaud (Marie), Robert Loggia (Sal), Anthony LaPaglia, David Proval (Lenny), Don Rickles, Chazz Palminteri, Kim Coates.

"Never play with food." Starved vampire Marie ("I died a long time ago") sups on mob boss Sal, who dies then revives. ("I want my lawyer!") Sal, in turn, bites Lenny, and soon we have the makings of a vampire mob.... Film comes to life when Sal dies. The reactions (including his own) to his post-morgue presence are funny. Sal's first victim, mob lawyer Bergman (Rickles), revives and gets very badly sunburned, in a partly funny, partly horrific scene. Rest of the screen time here is devoted to a pallid, at best moderately engaging human/vampire romance.

**INNOCENT PREY** (Austral.) FVI/Crystal Film 1984 color 100m. (aka *Voyeur*). D, P: Colin Eggleston. SP: Ron McLean. Mus: Brian May. Ref: V 5/9/84:8: "horror." PT 12:46: "I fell asleep." V 2/29/84. Ecran F 44:36. With P. J. Soles, Martin Balsam, Kit Taylor, G. Taylor, J. Warnock.

Mad slasher trails wife from Dallas to Australia.

**2P INQUISITION** (Sp) Video City/Ancla Century & Anubis 1976 ('84-U.S.) color/ws 94m. (*Inquisicion*). SP, D: Jacinto Molina. Ph: M. Mila. AD: G. Andres. SpFX: Pablo Perez. Mkp: F. Florido. Ref: TV: VC video; Eng. dubbed. Newman. Phantom. Hardy/HM. Fango 104: 53-4. V 5/11/77:420. Hound. no Martin. McCarty II. With Paul Naschy (aka J. Molina), Ricardo Merino, Tony Isbert, Julia Saly, Monica Randall, Daniela Giordano.

"Never give in to a demon!" "Fanatic" witch-hunting judge (Naschy) who has hallucinations of Death-with-scythe and a lady in red ... various tortures ... pact with the devil ... potions ... satan at sabbat (in dream?) ... and a primo disgusting image: the severing of the maggoty head. Clumsy direction, editing, photography, etc. Molina tries to have it both ways: The satanism here at first seems, misleadingly, to be all in the mind of the judge....

**INSAAN SHAITANI** (India - Hindustani?) Ramakrishna Film 1992 color c105m. Ref: TV: vt; no Eng. Chao Thai Video 2: *The Living Dead* - tr t? TV: vt: *Insaan Bana Shaitan* - Hindi version. With Deepark Parashar, Shree Pradha, Javed Khan, Upasana Singh, Anil Dhawan, Jagdeep.

A woman and her lover kill her husband and bury him, but he comes back with a deep voice and kills her, then gouges out the eye of the man, kills him, and haunts the house.... Hyper, crude, episodic fantasy-horror.

**INSANITY** (H.K.) Mandarin Films 1993 color 77m. D: Siu Hung Leung. SP, P: Raymond Wong. Ref: TV: Tai Seng Video; Eng. titles. With R. Wong, Simon Yam, Hoi Mei Chow.

An ugly statue (a "powerful monk") seems to appear and disappear and make accidents happen. At one point, a woman "sees" a glowing-eyed doctor possessed by it. But does its presence drive men mad ... or is there just a lunatic on the loose? ("Sorry, I can't control myself.") At the end, the statue seems to drive the woman mad .... Laughably transparent scare set-up pits the lady against a rain-coated slasher. Meanwhile, the script can't decide if the statue "works" or not.

**INSECT!** see *Blue Monkey*

**INTERCEPTOR** Trimark/Hess-Kallberg (E. Sheldon, Jr.) 1992 color 88m. D: Michael Cohn. SP: John Brancato, Michael Ferris. Ph: Lee Redmond. Mus: Rick Marvin. PD: Gary T. New. SpVisFX:(sup) Richard Kerrigan. Min FlyingFX: Stargate. SpFxCoord: Larry Fioritto. Computer Graphics: General Lift;(v.r.) Rick Fernalld. Key Mkp: Renee Dashiell. SdFX: A. Marfiak et al. Stealth: Leon Starr, R & L. MechFxSup: David Kuklish. Ref: TV: Vidmark video. Martin. With Andrew Divoff, Jurgen Prochnow, Elizabeth Morehead, Jon Cedar, J. Kenneth Campbell.

"Welcome to virtual reality—your new co-pilot." Terrorists plot to steal two new Stealth Fighters, a "force of pure destruction." Routine actioner. For most of the movie, the Stealths are just props. And the effect of the virtual reality business is just pilots playing video games.

**INTERCOURSE WITH THE VAMPIRE** Sin City 1994 color 90m. D: Paul Norman. Ref: Adam'95: "floating" vampire. With Rocco Siffredi, Christina Angel.

**INTERCOURSE WITH THE VAMPYRE 2** Sin City 1994 color 71m. D: P. Norman. Ref: Adam'96. With C. Angel, T. Monroe.

**INTERFACE** Filmworks 1984 color 88m. D: Andy Anderson; (assoc) S. J. Hoey. SP, Assoc P: John Williamson. Story: Anderson, Williamson. Addl Dial: Hoey, Anne Marie Biondo. Ph: L. McWilliams, R. Pistole. Mus: S. J. & David Hoey. PD: Betty Burkhart. SpFX: Gary Marcum, Jay Garriss, Greg Punchatz. Computer Graphics: Alan McFarland, Andrew Silvester. Xardon Mask: Burkhart. Mkp: Cindy Crisp. Ref: TV: Vestron Video. Stanley. no Martin. Hound. With John Davies, Laura Lane, Matthew Sacks, Michael Hendrix (Xardon/Bobby), Janet Six, Arne Strand.

"These guys are hooked into every computer on Earth!" And into phone lines as well. "These guys" are a computer club, The Society of Logic, and the "master process" gives them the go-ahead on their plan to eliminate the less nice people in the world, or at least in the community: Two evildoers are killed by remote control—one via computer terminal, somehow, the other by telephone, somehow. (The victim yells, the phone bursts into flames.)

Logic is this juvenile sf-fantasy-comedy's weakest point, while its strongest point, comedy, is not that strong. Davies and Lane, as Rex and Amy, respectively, try too hard at edgy affability. They meet cute, stay cute, finish cute. She's doing Paula Prentiss; he's doing his best with iffy material.

**INTERGALACTIC THANKSGIVING, Or, PLEASE DON'T EAT THE PLANET** (Can.) Nelvana & CBC 1979 anim color c25m. (*Please Don't Eat the Planet* - ad t). Story & D: Clive A. Smith. SP: Martin Lavut et al. Story: also F. Nissen, M. Hirsh. Mus: Patricia Cullen. PD: Nissen, Bonifacio. SpFX: Real to Reel. Ref: TV: *Nelvanamation*, Warner HV. Voices: Sid Caesar, Al Waxman et al.

Cosmic rutabaga farmers crash land on Laughalot, a planet of very silly green beings. Okay sf-comedy re bad jokes.

**INTERNAL GHOST AFFAIR** (H.K.?) 1994 color 91m. Ref: TV: World Video; no Eng. V&T Video: above is tr t.

A weird mask makes a man have weird dreams re a sexy, disfigured ghost. Later, when a paper charm burns, the ghost glides in and telekinetically flings chairs at the heroine. Plus an exorcism and embarrassing scenes with a possessed gay guy frothing at the mouth. Mind-numbing sex-fantasy-horror plays like a softcore edition of a hardcore film.

**INTERVIEW WITH A VAMP** Realistic 1994 color 71m. D: "Justin Case." Ref: Adam'95: two vampires. With Tiffany Mynx, Alex Jordan, Mike Horner.

**INTERVIEW WITH THE VAMPIRE** WB/Geffen (Stephen Woolley) 1994 color 123m. D: Neil Jordan. SP: Anne Rice, from her novel. Ph: Philippe Rousselot. Mus: Elliot Goldenthal. PD: Dante Ferretti. Vampire MkpFX: Stan Winston;(mech des) Landon, Sousa;(Lestat transformation) Mordella, Scott, Haugen. VisFx:(sup) Rob Legato; Digital Domain. Min: Stetson. SpFxSup: Yves de Bono. Vampire Nails: Julie Woods. Contact Lenses: Bodytech. WireFx:(sup) Steve Crawley;(coord) Bob Harman. Ref: TV: Warner HV. ad. Sacto Bee 11/11/94. Vallejo Times-Herald 11/11/94. SFChron 11/11/94. 11/14/94. With Tom Cruise (Lestat), Brad Pitt (Louis), Antonio Banderas (Armand), Shephen Rea, Christian Slater, Kirsten Dunst (Claudia).

In 1791 New Orleans, a man (Pitt) who wants a "release from the pain of living" becomes—thanks to the ruthless vampire Lestat—a "newborn vampire" with a "lingering respect for life" and a Renfield-like attachment to rats. Next up: ten-year-old Claudia, who, as a "newborn," becomes a "fierce killer," an "eternal child." ("I want some more!") Then, in Paris, in 1870, at the Theatre des Vampires: Armand, the "oldest living vampire," at 400-plus.... How colorful. *Near Dark* does the Extended Weird Family and the Pain and Cruelty of Vampirism better. And the original Universal Frankensteins dealt more inventively with "makers." The hokey grand passions on display here suggest that if the film were a little less knowing, it might be good camp. (Pitt gets the "My God!" and "You fiend!"-type lines from *Curse of Frankenstein* et al.) A few fun flying-vampires-on-fire stunts. Slater is the incredibly dense interviewer, in present-day San Francisco.

**INTERZONE** (U.S.-I) TWE/Filmirage 1987 ('89-U.S.) color 92m. SP, D: Deran Sarafian. SP: also Clyde Anderson. Ph: Lorenzo Battaglia. SpFX: Dan Maklansky et al. Mkp: Peter Moor, Grace Ginsburg. OptFX: Moviecam 2000. SdFX: Cineaudio Effect. Ref: TV: TWE video; Eng.-lang. version. V 5/20/87:9. Hound. Ecran F 72:70. Fango 89:12. With Bruce Abbott, Beatrice Ring, Teagan Clive, John Armstead, Kiro Wehara, Alain Smith, Franco Diogene.

Ingredients in this post-nuclear-holocaust actioner include a fierce (but easily dispatched) caveman-monster ... an invisible electric barrier ... telepathy ... the hero, Swan (Abbott), a "fuzzy-faced foreigner" ... and a televised message from Year Zero, at the time of the holocaust.... Smart-ass humor predominates, and does not mix well with the more maudlin plot elements near the end. (Hero finds, loses friend, etc.) Casual brutality is just part of the "fun," though there is a funny scene with a slave trader. More filler than story.

**INTIMATE STRANGER** South Gate (Pelman-Hasumi) 1991 color 94m. D: A. Holzman. SP: Rob Fresco. Mus: J. Sheffer. Ref: V 5/27/91: "mediocre thriller." With Deborah Harry, James Russo, Tim Thomerson, Grace Zabriskie.

"Weird world of phone sex ... psychopathic baddies."

**INTO THE BADLANDS** USA-TV/Ogiens-Kane Co. (MTE)/Harvey Frand 1991 color c90m. D: Sam Pillsbury. Tel: Dick Beebe, Marjorie David, Gordon Dawson, based on the short stories "The Streets of Laredo" by Will Henry, "The Time of the Wolves" by Marcia Muller, and "The Last Pelt" by Bryce Walton. Mus: John Debney. MkpFX: Starr Jones, Brewster Gould et al. SpFxCoord: Andre Ellingson. Ref: TV. V 7/29/91:34. TVG. V 10/19/92:16 (rated). With Bruce Dern, Mariel Hemingway, Dylan McDermott, Helen Hunt, Lisa Pelikan, Andrew Robinson, Michael J. Metzger (Red Roundtree).

Three tales. 1) A gunfighter is confronted by his own grave marker. Pretentious but stylishly shot. 2) Willa Cather territory—madness and wolves on the lonely frontier. Or are the wolves products of the madness? Woodenly acted. 3) T. L. Barston (Dern), an S.O.B. of a bounty hunter, "sees" his dead prize (Metzger) alive at one point, finds no one in White Rock who'll pay up, gets some measure of revenge on the deadbeats there, then—shot and buried for dead—narrates his own resurrection scene. Tangy, un-pigeonhole-able fable re obsessive determination ... to and even beyond the grave. Good vehicle for Dern.

**INTO THE NIGHT** (Taiwanese) 198-? color feature. D: Yuri Won Ting. Ref: NST! 4:27.

Avenging ghost, spirit possession, "gory bloodbath."

**INTO THIN AIR** see *Ambulance, The*

**2P The INTRUDER** (Can.) Hazelton 1979 color c90m. (*Intruder* - ad t. aka *L'Ange Noir*). D, Co-P, & SpFX: David F. Eustace. SP: Norman Fox. Ph: D. M. Ostriker. Mus: FM. SpFX: also Dennis Pike, Edwin Watkins, Gary Myers. Mkp: Shonaugh Jabour. Ref: TV. TVG. V 9/3/80:48 (ad). Stanley. no Maltin '92. no Scheuer. Ecran F 58:81. With Pita Oliver, Gerard Jordan, Trudy Weiss, Jimmy Douglas, Tony Fletcher (The Stranger), Rocco Bellusci, Gordon Thompson.

To the small town of Holoway comes a cloaked, boxed, seemingly sinister stranger—"Howard Turt," or "H. Turt," or Truth. The corrupt townsfolk who hear the message of truth and wish his box open at a town-hall meeting leave the hall glowing, literally, and telling the truth. But only little Mikey (Bellusci), who actually enters the box, retains the full force of this moral power.

Whackily serious fantasy-chiller is apparently a vehicle for the late A. H. Maslow's philosophy of self-actualization, or "achieving your potential." The film is dedicated to him, and at one point the heroine is shown reading his book *The Further Reaches of Human Nature*. Another character reads from Amiel. But the only philosophy to be gleaned from the stilted writing and acting is that the cure for personal and political corruption is honesty. (Corruption Central: The Rainbow Motel.) And you can't miss the script's point about human corruptibility when all the characters are walking Guilty Secrets.

**INTRUDER** Phantom Prods. 1988 color c89m. Story, SP, D: Scott Spiegel. Story, P: Lawrence Bender. SpMkpFX: Nicotero, Kurtzman, Berger. SpFxProps: Steve Patino, Sho-Glas FX; (mkp) Sean Rogers. Ref: TV: Phantom Video (Paramount). V 4/12/89. Hound. Martin. Scheuer. MV: aka *Night Crew*. With Elizabeth Cox, Danny Hicks, David Byrnes, Renee Estevez, Sam Raimi, Alvy Moore, Emil Sitka, Bruce Campbell.

"I'm just crazy about this store!" Terror in Aisle 8, as a madman stalks the Walnut Lake (California) Ranch Market. Murder with paperweight, knife, hydraulic press, meathook, cleaver, and buzz saw. Meanwhile, the heroine employs a bottle of wheat germ as a weapon, and—in a *Night of the Living Dead* twist—gets arrested for the murders when cops show up, put two and two together, and get seven/eleven.... A mechanical ten-little-bodies shocker, despite camera shots from inside a wastebasket, a telephone, a stamp pad, etc. Far from the worst of its kind, however, thanks to a bit of atmosphere and humor.

**INTRUDERS** CBS-TV/Osiris Films & Dan Curtis (Michael Apted, R. J. O'Conner/B. Lustig) 1992 color c180m. D: Curtis. Tel: Oringer, Torme. Story: Oringer, from Budd Hopkins' research. Mus: Cobert. AlienMkpFX: Robert Short. Ref: V: uneven. TVG. SFChron 5/15/92: "same old stuff." Cinef 12/92:56. Martin: "creepy." With Richard Crenna, Mare Winningham, Susan Blakely, Daphne Ashbrook, Ben Vereen, Rosalind Chao, Alan Autry.

"A close encounter for the third time." (SFC)

**INVADER** 21st Century/Ellis (Very Big Motion Picture Corp.) 1992 (1991) color c92m. SP, D, Ph, Ed: P. J. Cook. Mus: David Bartley. AD: John Ellis. Stopmo: Kent Burton. SpVisFX: Cook, J. Ellis. SpProps: Gagnon, Cooper. SdFX: Musifex. Big Harvey:(des) Poreda, Walker; Walkerworks FX. Mindbender Seq: William Dempsey. UFO Des: Walker, Ulvila. Exec P: Menahem Golan, Ami Artzi. Ref: TV. PT 14:12: "aliens," robot, "super jet." V 10/14/91:50 (ad), A-60. 5/6/91:36 (ad). 5/4/92:23 (ad). 9/21/92:10 (rated). With Hans Bachmann, A. T. Smith, Rick Foucheux, George Stover, Cook (Big Harvey voice).

Other ingredients here include a brainwashing gizmo and a computer-program "entity" which travels by phone. Excitable if not exciting, with comically macho dialogue. Okay stopmo for the supposedly huge robot H.A.R.V. (Heavily Armored Rampaging Vaporizer). Some pretty bizarre, over-the-top moments.

**INVADERS FROM MARS** Cannon (Golan-Globus) 1986 color/ws 98m. D: Tobe Hooper. SP: Dan O'Bannon, Don Jakoby. Mus: Christopher Young. SpVisFX: John Dykstra; Apogee. Creature Des: Stan Winston. Ref: TV. V 5/21/86. Jim Shapiro. Hound. Phantom. Maltin '92. Scheuer. With Karen Black, Hunter Carson, Timothy Bottoms, Laraine Newman, James Karen, Louise Fletcher, Bud Cort, Jimmy Hunt.

The same stretch of wooden fence, hill, and trail. "Dad's weirded out"—again. Little Heather has telltale bandages on the back of her neck. Men are sucked into the sand. The drilling machine is back. And there's a tentacled, cobra-like head alien.... This remake of the 1953 classic-of-kind can't settle on a tone or approach, and only comes to life in the tunnel-and-monster scenes, where the furious movement, cartoon coloring, and goofy-looking Martians temporarily obscure the fact that the movie is not really horrific, suspenseful, funny, campy, sociopolitically pointed, or much of anything. The Martians, though, have very good, Gigerish set designers (Leslie Dilley, Craig Stearns), and they themselves are pitched somewhere between camp and straight gross.

**INVASION DE LOS MUERTOS (2)** see also *Prof. Zovek*

**INVASION EARTH: THE ALIENS ARE HERE** New World & Rearguard/New World & Invasion Earth Prods. (Max J. Rosenberg) 1987 color 84m. D: George Maitland. SP & Co-Ed: Miller Drake. Mus: A. R. Jones. VisFxSup: Dennis Skotak. Creatures: Michael McCracken. SpMechFX: Roger George, Lise Romanoff. Opt: Hollywood Opt. (David Hewitt et al); Ray Mercer. SpThanx: Joe Dante, Jon Davison et al. Mkp: Denise Della Valle. Ref: TV: New World Video. V 10/5/88. Hound. Martin. Scheuer. With Janice Fabian, Christian Lee, Larry Bagby III, Dana Young, Mel Welles (Mr. Davar); Bob Burns, Richard Reiner (aliens); Corey Burton, Tony Pope (alien voices).

An awkward combination compilation-film/story-film, the plot of which is keyed to parallel scenes in monster movies of the Fifties and Sixties, including The Blob, It Came from Outer Space, Atomic Submarine, War *of the Worlds, Them!, Brain from Planet Arous, Invasion of the Body Snatchers, Invasion of the Saucer Men, The Mole People, Revenge of the Creature, Rodan, It Conquered the World, Earth Vs. the Flying Saucers, The Giant Claw, Tarantula, The Spider, Beginning of the End, The Amazing Colossal Man, It Came from Beneath the Sea, The Giant Behemoth, 20 Million Miles to Earth, Reptilicus, Konga, The Deadly Mantis, War of the Colossal Beast, King Kong Vs. Godzilla, The Thing, Fiend without a Face, The Crawling Eye, Land Unknown, Invisible Invaders, This Island Earth, Invaders from Mars, Journey to the 7th Planet,* and *The Angry Red Planet.*

Seed pods in the Gem Theatre in Dead Rock which "turn you into a Republican or something" prove to be part of a plot by aliens who believe that monster movies are numbing our minds. Plus a robot's ray (from *The Mysterians*) which zaps theatregoers, and an unexplained multi-eyed monster. Film is sloppy and pointless, except as cut-and-paste nostalgia.

**INVASION OF THE BODY SNATCHERS** see *Body Snatchers*

**INVASION OF THE GIRL SNATCHERS** Majestic Int'l. (Jeffrey C. Hogue/L&L Co.-Atlantis) 1973 (1985) color c90m. (*The Hidan of Mount Bienjow* - orig t). D, Ph, & Co-P: Lee Jones. SP: Phineas Pinkham, Carla Rueckert. Mus: James DeWitt. SpFX: James Barnhouse. Ref: TV: VCI video. Bowker '90. Hound. Scheuer. Martin. V 10/24/84:243(ad). VWB. With Elizabeth Rush, Ele Grigsby, David Roster, Paul Lenzi, Hugh Smith, Charles Rubin.

"I have need of your body." Six missing girls have been taken to an "everlasting kingdom" where "they shall nevermore be destroyed by the people of darkness": A mystical magician who has been to Hades and back uses voodoo to transfer the souls of aliens into the "newly dead bodies" of the girls, who then act like zombies. ("She comes from another planet.").... Idiosyncratic, isn't it? The style, or approach, of the movie might best be described as New Wave redneck, but clumsy direction and numbing dialogue generally undermine a happily balmy plot. The

human/zombie exchanges are intended to be so-asinine-they're-brilliant.

**INVASION OF THE LUST SNATCHERS** 4-Play 1988 color 85m. D: Mark Arnold. Ref: Adam '90. With Tanya Foxx, Whitney Prince, Blondi.

Trip to another dimension.

**INVASION OF THE MINDBENDERS** see *Alien High*

**INVASION OF THE ROBOT DINOSAURS** Legacy HV & Ayre & Dinamation Int'l. 1989 29m. SP, D, Co-P: Jonathan Ayre. Mus: Carlos Guedes. Ref: V 5/17/89:48 (hv): "interesting intro to ... the extinct beasties.... The models ... move very stiffly...." Japan Video. With Ken Knight.

**INVASION OF THE SPACE PREACHERS** see *Strangest Dreams*

**INVASION U.S.A.** Cannon (Golan-Globus) 1985 color 107m. D: Joseph Zito. SP: James Bruner, Chuck Norris. Story: Aaron Norris, Bruner. Mus: Jay Chattaway. SpFxMkp: Tom Savini. SpFX: (coord) Gary F. Bentley; Jack Bennett, Joe Quinlivan et al. Marine Coord: Luke Halpin. Ref: TV. MFB'85:342-3. Stanley. V 9/25/85. Hound. Phantom. Maltin '92. With C. Norris, Richard Lynch, Melissa Prophet, Stephen Markle, Martin Shakar.

Arch-terrorist Rostov (Lynch) begins his invasion of Miami Beach with attacks on suburbia—a shopping mall, a school bus, an amusement park, a church—and attempts to turn citizens against each other and—even more dastardly—against authority.... A contrived personal vendetta between Rostov and U.S. agent Hunter (Norris) is supposed to focus the action here, but instead just trivializes it. The Christmas-invasion timing might seem to be related to an unprepared-America theme, but seems more closely connected with the filmmakers' sense of cheap irony. The only evocative element: Joao Fernandes' photography, which intermittently lends the movie a sense of place and movement.

**The INVINCIBLE** (W. G.-Austrian-Swiss-Belg.) ZDF & Salinas-Film & Wallonie & GF & TA/ORF/DRS/RTBF 1985 (1984) color 85m. (*Der Unbesiegbare*). SP, D: Gusztav Hamos. SP: also Ed Cantu, Heibach, Kozma. Mus: Martin Daske. SpFX: Shirley Christian. Mkp: Ulrike Madej et al. Ref: screen. PFA notes 1/9/87. V 10/2/85. VV 6/26/84. Ecran F 65:70. With Udo Kier, Kurt von Ruffin, Heinz Kammer, Mike A. Hentz.

*Flash Gordon*-ish ingredients: Col. Hurry Cane, heroine Daisy Bit, Dr. Popov, and reporter Oliver Stone, all "invincible" video beings ... the evil Argon (Kier), ruler of Mars, who trains his death-ray cannon on Earth ... his daughter Sphera, who can transform "every energy to any form" and whose magic stone enables her to appear and disappear ... the Claypeople of Jupiter ... the planet of Firepeople ... the hypnotic Psycho-magnet ... a helmet which makes the wearer telepathic ... and a mirror-shield which allows one to enter the video realm.... More dry sci-fi modernism, a la *Liquid Sky, Repo Man,* and *Vortex*. Interesting premise: The "movies" on TV here are not movies, but "newsbroadcasts" re Hurry Cane and company. Wry at times, but the point is elusive. Kier's campy mad-doc laugh goes back at least to Lon Chaney and *The Monster* (1925).

**The INVINCIBLE SPACE STREAKER** (H.K.?) 197-? feature. D: Albert Yue. Ref: Heroes on Film 2:16,20: "rubber monsters" in a "low budget ripoff of *Kamen Rider X*."

**INVISIBILITY** see the following and *Amazon Women on the Moon. Arrival, The. Aventuras de Enrique y Ana. Balbakwa. Bloody New Year. Bottles. Daffy Duck's Quackbusters. 8-Man. Happy Ghost IV. Heroic Trio, The. Highwayman, The. Hollywood Steps Out* (2). *If I Run, I Still Love You. Land of Faraway, The. Lucky Ghost. Magic Boy. Mechanical Cow, The. Memoirs of an Invisible Man. Misfits of Science. Nibelungen, Die. Riding with Death. Santa Sangre. See Thru. Stephen King's Sleepwalkers. Tchelovek Nevidimka. Telephone Sex and the Invisible Man, Too. 3-D Army, The. Tomei Tengu. Tweet and Lovely. Up All Night.*

**INVISIBLE: THE CHRONICLES OF BENJAMIN KNIGHT** (U.S.-Romanian) Para/Full Moon (Paunescu) 1993 color 80m. D: Jack Ersgard. SP: Earl Kenton. Ph: C. Pogany. Mus: David Arkenstone. PD: Ioana Corciova. SpMkpFX: Alchemyfx, Michael S. Deak. MechFxSup: Jake McKinnon. Mkp:(des) Robbins, Alyn;(fx sup) Melanie Tooker. On-Set FX: Dave Perteet. Opt: Mercer, Opt FX. Ref: TV: Para HV. With Brian Cousins, Jennifer Nash, Michael Dellafemina, Curt Lowens, Aharon Ipale (Petroff).

Ingredients in this apparent follow-up to *Mandroid* include an invisible man, the remote-controlled "mandroid" (a "huge robot"), a scarred madman, and a plot to build an "army of invisible men." Slack, trite.

**INVISIBLE DEAD** see *Orloff and the Invisible Man*

**INVISIBLE GIRL** Vivid Video 1989 color c80m. D: Scotty Fox. Ref: TV: Vivid Video. Adam '91:227. With Tamara Lee (the invisible girl), Tori Welles, Randy West, Lynn LeMay, Peter North.

"We were messin' around with the biochemical dexrol (sp?)." Add a "couple of drops of memuel (sp?)," and the result is a "positive libidio (sp?) reaction"; Janet, or Janice, a college freshman, disappears, and appears again only when she makes love.... Rudimentary adult movie features no invisibility effects except some video fuzz which marks our heroine's appearances and disappearances. Only Lee (visible) and LeMay are worth a look.

**The INVISIBLE KID** Taurus Ent./Elysian Pictures (Philip J. Spinelli) 1988 (1987) color 95m. SP, D, Exec Co-P: Avery Crounse. Mus: Steve Hunter, Jan King. SpVisFX: Ernie Farino. SpMechFX: Tassilo Baur. MkpDes: Annie Maniscalco. SpFxSup: Lou Carlucci. Ref: TV. V 4/6/88. SFChron 4/11/88. ad. Maltin '92. Scheuer. With Jay Underwood (Grover Dunn), Karen Black, Wally Ward, Chynna Phillips, Brother Theodore, Mike Genovese.

Valleyville High School student Grover Dunn attempts to prove that his late father was the "greatest scientist that ever lived" by completing his scientific formula. The resulting "disappearing powder" makes people invisible for about twenty minutes. At the beginning, Grover uses it to make his rival look bad on the basketball court; at the end, he uses it to make his rival look good. Narrative symmetry.... No *Teen Wolf*, though not as crummy as *Teen Wolf Too*. A few pleasant moments. Best silly invisibility effect: the (visible) false lashes on the (invisible) Mom (Black).

**INVISIBLE MAN, The** see *Balbakwa*

**The INVISIBLE MANIAC** Smoking Gun/Anthony Markes (Runny Mede House Music) 1990 color 85m. Story, SP, D: Rif Coogan. Story: also Matt Devlen. Mus: M. D. Decker. Invisibility FX: The Hunter Co. SpFX: Carlo Cuccelleli. Mkp: Bethedaria. Ref: TV. V 6/27/90. 2/28/90:18. With Noel Peters, Shannon Wilsey, Melissa Moore, Gail Lyon, Debra Lamb, Clement von Franckenstein.

"The bunny rabbit is completely invisible!" Mad scientists' (Peters) invisibility serum taps into his "most deep-rooted sexual fantasies." Really miserable cross between *The Invisible Man* and a t&a sex comedy.

**\*INVISIBLE SWORDSMAN** see *Tomei Tengu* (remake)

**3P INVITATION OF GHOST** (H.K.) J&M Chevalier/Gold City Films 1983? color c92m. D: Wilson Tong. Ref: TV: vt; Qui Cot Thu - Viet t?; Eng. titles. poster. With Chiu Siu Keung, Jaime Chik, Wang Har, Richard Yan, Wu Ma.

Sorcerer Te, "king of the ghosts" in Thailand, replaces his nephew Norman Hsu's arm with the arm of a corpse. Norman gets lucky at gambling, but a demon-ghost seems to accompany the arm and replaces him in bed, then drowns his girl friend in a bathtub. ("I find Mr. Hsu very weird.") When Norman falls in love with model Hsueh Lan, the sometimes-invisible, sometimes-visible-and-monstrous-looking ghost attempts to rape her, then possesses her.... Routine horror-fantasy features uninspired variations on *The Entity* and *The Hands of Orlac*. In the only amusing scene, Norman's dead arm deflects bullets back at the hoods who are trying to kill him, and thus he kills them. In another scene, strips of celluloid strangle a photographer.

**INVITATION TO HELL** (B) Western World 1982 feature. D: M.J. Murphy. Ref: Stanley: walking dead, human sacrifice; "amateurish." no Martin. With B. Simpson, J. Sheahan.

**INVITATION TO HELL** ABC-TV/Moonlight Prods. 1984 color c90m. D: Wes Craven. Tel: Richard Rothstein. Ph: Dean Cundey. Mus: Sylvester Levay. AD: H. Braden. SpFX: Ken Pepiot; (hell seq) Introvision; (laser) Laser Images. SdFX: Rich Harrison. Mkp: Les Berns. Ref: TV. TVG. Hound. Martin. Scheuer. With Robert Urich, Joanna Cassidy, Susan Lucci, Barret Oliver, Soleil Moon Frye, Nicholas Worth, Virginia Vincent, Bill Irwin, Kevin McCarthy.

In *Asylum of Satan*, hell is an insane asylum; in Satan's school for girls, hell is a girls' boarding school; here, hell is a country club, Steaming Springs. Hell is really a TV-movie like this one. Included: a *Devil Dog*-ish horrors-of-affluence theme, invulnerable, ray-shooting women, and a spacesuit which "reads" the auras of nearby life forms.

**INVOCACION SATANICA** (Mex.-U.S.?) Rivero Prods./Jorge Gomez Prods. 1989 color 90m. SP, D: Xorge Noble. Ph, Ed: J.G. Loredo. SpFX: Cuahutemoc Gallardo. Mkp: Leticia Velasco. Ref: TV: Cine Real; no Eng. With Rebeca Silva, Luis Accinelli, X. Noble, Francisco Xavier, Daniela Duran.

A strangler from hell emerges from a Ouija board and strips and attacks his female victims with a sort of remote-control fog .... Tawdry, slack shot-on-taper, with a ham-handed use of stock music and much repeated footage, for padding. It doesn't get worse than this.

**IO TIGRO, TU TIGRI, EGLI TIGRA** (I) 1978 feature. D: G. Capitani. Ref: Palmerini: "close encounter." With Paolo Villaggio.

**IRIA: *ZEIRAM* THE ANIMATION** (J) 1994 anim color c50m. Ref: TV: S. Baldric video; Eng. titles.

Two apparent OAV entries—"Black Seeds" and "Red Sun"—re a "hunter agent," the monster from Zeiram (which changes at one point into a sort of flying manta ray), the planet Myce, hovering battle 'bots, future cities, and spaceships. The animated monster here isn't as impressive as the live-action one, though the surrounding movie is a bit more interesting. Intricate, atmospheric spacescapes.

**IRO WA KAMEI YOTSUYA KAIDAN** (J) Makino Prods. 1927. D: Kintaro Inoue. Ref: CM 15:24: *Iro Alias Yotsuya Ghost Story* - tr t. With R. Tsukigata, S. Suzuki.

**IRON BREAD** (Thai) Vivian Pei 1970 color/ws 80m. SP, D: V. Pei. Ph: To Kaminoki. Ref: Hardy/SF: "joyously iconoclastic anti-*Metropolis*."

World of robots.

**IRON ROBOT 17** see *Brain 17*

**IRON WARRIOR** (I-B?) Trans World Ent./Ovidio Assonitis 1986 color 82m. SP, D: Alfonso Brescia (aka Al Bradley). SP: also S. Luotto. Mus: C. Scott. SpFxSup: Mario Cassar. SpMkp: Mario Michisanti. Opt: Moviecam 2000. Ref: TV: Media Home Ent. video. V 3 /25/87. TMPA '88. Ecran F 72:71: U.S.; BI & Orion. With Miles O'Keeffe, Savina Gersak, Elisabeth Kaza, Iris Peynado (Deeva), Tim Lane, Malcolm Borg, Conrad Borg (young Trogar), Tiziana Altieri (young Phoedra), Frank Daddi (Trogar), Jon Rosser.

Sequel to *Ator The Fighting Eagle* (III). Principal evildoers: the immortal, polymorphous "old witch" Phoedra (Kaza), Queen of the Dark Arts, and Trogar, the Iron Warrior, "leader of the hordes of hell," who is hero Ator's brother, or rather his shell, animated by Phoedra. Extra addeds: strange cloaked little beings, a "time lock," and magically-started earthquakes and fires.... Only for diehard swordfight fans. Sole notable atmospheric effect: Phoedra's supernaturally-windblown hair. Be prepared for much trekking, climbing, and just plain walking, by both Ator (O'Keeffe) and Janna (Gersak).

**IRRESISTIBLE II** Essex Video (Jack Daniels) 1986 color 80m. D: June Moon. Mkp: Alan Bosshardt. Ref: vc box. Adam '88.

With Alex Greco, Tiffani Blake, Candie Evens, Janette Littledove.

Bag lady travels backwards and forwards in time in an adult-video viewing booth.

**IS ANYBODY THERE?** see *Deadly Messages*

**ISLAND CITY** 1994 color c90m. Ref: TVG. With Kevin Conroy, Brenda Strong, Eric McCormack, Pete Koch, Constance Marie.

21st-century experiment accidentally creates a mutant race.

**ISLAND FURY** see *Please Don't Eat the Babies*

**ISLAND OF BLOOD** SRN & Creative Film Makers 1983 (1981) color 82m. (*Whodunit?* - alt t). SP, D, P, Ed: Bill Naud. Mus: Joel Goldsmith. SpFX: MkpFxLab. Ref: Bill Warren. Academy/SF, F & H Films. MFB'85:320-1: "discontinuous and deeply confusing plot." Ecran F 42:100 (ad). Stanley. V 10/22/86: "very trite slasher film." With Rick Dean, Terry Goodman, Marie Alise, Ron Gardner.

Actors filming on an isolated Pacific Northwest island are systematically murdered.

**ISLAND OF DESIRE** (B) UA/Coronado 1951 ('52-U.S.) color 103m. (91m.) (*Saturday's Island* - B). D: Stuart Heisler. From Hugh Brooke's novel *Saturday Island*. Ref: TV. TVG. Maltin/TVM. no V. Phantom. LC. no NYT.

Journal relates tale of "sea serpent" haunting man stranded on tropical isle; we see giant, double-exposure lizard bearing down on him. Surprise psychological-horror/monster sequence pops up in otherwise mundane, lost-on-a-desert-island tale. ("When in Rome, do as the natives do.")

**\*2 ISLAND OF LOST SOULS** 1933 (1932) 70 m. (*The Island of Dr. Moreau* - orig t). AD: Hans Dreier? Mkp: Wally Westmore? Ref: TV. Lee. Eames. V 1/17/33. Hardy/SF. Lentz. Weldon: "probably the best horror film ever made." Stanley. Maltin '92. Scheuer. Fango 128:11. With Joe Bonomo, Duke York Jr., Randolph Scott, Alan Ladd (beastmen).

"All animal life is tending toward the human form." On an "island without a name" in the South Seas, Dr. Moreau (Charles Laughton)—a "brilliant man"—uses blood transfusions, gland extracts, and plastic surgery to "wipe out hundreds of thousands of years of evolution" and create "beastmen" out of beasts like dogs and panthers. ("Strange-looking natives you have here.") Calculatingly, he throws together Edward Parker (Richard Arlen) and Lota (Kathleen Burke), the "most nearly perfect creation" of his zoo of horrors. ("Has she a woman's emotional impulses?")

Intermittently compelling mess of a movie is more assembled than directed by Erle C. Kenton. Waldeman Young and Philip Wylie extract potent, sensationalistic material from the H. G. Wells novel—topics include human-"manimal" sexuality, the mixing of the species, pain, scientific callousness, more pain—but present it sloppily. Moreau doesn't even bother to keep the door to his lab closed, and Parker is a campy, impossible "Why she's a panther" role. And though it's our best chance to take in the variety of makeup jobs, the sequence in which the beastmen run up into close-up, one by one, plays like home-movie mugging. Bela Lugosi is, for the most part, lost in makeup, but he delivers two "A" lines: "Law no more!" and "The House of Pain!" You better believe it's the way he delivers them. The acting show is mostly Laughton's. Catch, for instance, his great amusement at his monster asparagus. And catch Tetsu Komai's "faithful dog" M'Ling—he looks like he's evolving into Shemp Howard. This is progress? Love the way the ocean waves wash away the credits.

**ISLAND OF TERROR** see *Five Dolls for an August Moon*

**ISLAND OF THE LOST** Para/Ivan Tors (Florea-Browning) 1968 (1967) color 92m. (*Dangerous Island. Lost Island* - shooting titles). D: John Florea; (underwater seqs.) Ricou Browning. SP: Richard Carlson. Story: Tors, Carlson. Ph: Howard Winner; (underwater) Lamar Boren, Jordan Klein. Mus: George Bruns. AD: Bruce Bushman. Mkp: Guy Del Russo. SdFxEd: L. J. Davison, Alex Bamattre. Ref: TV: NTA Home Ent. (Republic HV). Maltin/TVM. Stanley. Lee (P). no Lentz. no Weldon. no Hardy/SF. no V. no Phantom. Martin. With Richard Greene, Luke Halpin, Mart Hulswit, Jose De Vega, Robin Mattson, Irene Tsu, Sheilah Wells.

An anthropological expedition discovers "new plants, new animals, even new peoples" on an uncharted island below the Tuamotu Archipelago in the South Pacific. ("There's some kind of a magnetic disturbance in this area.") Among the finds: sabre-toothed wolves (dogs with plastic fangs), a shark with nine gills ("There's no such thing. Oh, there might have been thousands of years ago"), a poisonous dimetrodon-type (an alligator with collar and fin), and snarling carnivorous ostriches (a "kind no one has ever seen before—a whole separate line of evolution!")…. Stolid, tacky made-for-kids cross between *The Swiss Family Robinson* and *Unknown Island* features endless chases and building-a-hut montages.

**ISLAND OF THE ZOMBIES** see *Erotic Nights of the Living Dead*

**The ISLE OF FANTASY** (H.K.-Thai) Cinema City 1986 color 82m. D: Michael Mak. Ref: TV: Rainbow Video; Eng. titles. Ecran F 66:71. V 1/29/86. NST! 4:28.

Silly, occasionally cute comedy includes scattered fantastic and horrific elements, including a dog-sized, spitting spider … a carnivorous, fish-like "flower" … a regulation-sized "huge gorilla" which at first skulks, monster-like, then becomes Mr. Nice Ape … a "big spider" scare with a tarantula-like spider in a tent … a fake gorilla ("A gorilla. Oh, dear!") … and a shark scare, complete with *Jaws*-like music.

**ISMERETIEN ISMEROS** (Hung.) Objektiv/Mafilm 1989 color 104m. D: Janos Rozsa. SP: Istvan Kardos. Mus: Janus Brody. Ref: V 2/22/89: *The Little Alien* - tr t?; "makes little of it basic premise." With Judit Halasz, Dani Szabo (the boy), Karoly Eperjes.

Sf-musical-comedy for children re a homeless alien boy who lands in a suitcase spacecraft in Budapest.

**ISOBAR** see *Demolition Man*

**ISOLA DEL TESSORO, La** see *Treasure Island in Outer Space*

**IT** ABC-TV/Lorimar-TV & Green/Epstein (Konigsberg/Sanitsky Co.) 1990 color c180m. (aka *Stephen King's It*). Tel, D: Tommy Lee Wallace. Tel: also Lawrence B. Cohen. From Stephen King's book. Mus: Richard Bellis. PD: Douglas Higgins. SpFxMkp: Bart J. Mixon. SpVisFX: (sup) Gene Warren Jr.; Fantasy II. SpFxCoord: John Thomas. Ref: TV. V 11/12/90:66. TVG 11/17/90. SFExam 11/16/90. With Tim Curry (Pennywise), Richard Thomas, Annette O'Toole, John Ritter, Richard Masur, Olivia Hussey, Michael Cole.

"I'll kill you all!" Pennywise, a sabre-toothed clown and creature of the drains ("some kind of monster") haunts the kids of Derry, a New England town. ("I'm every nightmare you've ever had!") The at-least-200-year-old clown of evil seems linked with the school bully, Henry Bowers (Jarred Blancard), and appears, variously, as a bog creature and a teenage werewolf…. This TV-movie (also called a miniseries and a novel-for-TV) is clogged with plots, co-plots, and subplots, and has roughly a dozen lead characters if you count the "lucky seven" twice—as kids, in the flashbacks, and as adults, in the present tense. It's like three or four hollow mini-movies in one. Pennywise (Robert Bloch should have gotten royalties for his clown-at-midnight idea) is like no nightmare anyone ever had. His periodic appearances—even in the album photo-to-life—just give him another chance to go "Boo!"

**IT CAME FROM … SOMEWHERE ELSE—CHAPTER III** Platinum Prods/Toj Prods. (Timothy O. Johnson) 1989 (1986) color and b&w 89m. D: Howard Hassler. SP & Exec Co-P: Patrick V. Johnson. Ph: D. A. Jones. Mus: Robert Steinberg. Set Des: Ron Nafstad et al. SpVisFX: Venezia Biondo Prods. Mkp: Karen T. Johnson. Ref: TV: vt. no Martin. no Hound. With William Vanarsdale, Don Aldrich, Robert Buckley, Allen M. Johnson, Richard Speeter, Jane Rudowski, Terry Royalty, Robert Havel (alien policeman); Neng Vang and Chu Vang (aliens).

"People are spontaneously combusting." Flat, off-the-wall sf-comedy asks the question, "Are accountants actually denizens of Atlantis?" and answers same, apparently in the affirmative. Aliens here are responsible, it seems, for the people of Grand Bosh who burn up … for veggies which resemble human hands … and for a ray weapon which levels a house. Script is intentionally, but generally unfunnily dumb. Included: a would-be-funny chainsaw sequence and an okay filmstrip-within-the-film parody of E.T. phenomena. Caught-on-the-run line: "… two bloody kneecaps, stuck to the front bumper of my car."

**\*IT CONQUERED THE WORLD** 1956 (*It Conquered the Earth* - shooting t). SP: (uncred.) Charles Griffith. SpMonster: Paul Blaisdell. Mkp: Larry Butterworth. Ref: TV. Lee. Lentz. Weldon. V 9/12/56. Warren/KWTS! Hardy/SF. Martin. Scheuer. Maltin '92. SFChron 8/14/92. COF 11:40.

A being from Venus—survivor of a dying race—stows away on a satellite which crashes to Earth at Elephant Hot Springs. A "monstrous king" who "reasons, concludes, and uses," he becomes a "personal friend" of Dr. Tom Anderson (Lee Van Cleef) and regularly dispatches "control devices"—"funny-looking birds" which have "radiological-electrode-type things in their beaks" that drain emotions from human victims and render them zombie-like slaves.... Roughly half this Roger Corman semi-classic is hollow borrowing from *Invaders from Mars* and *Day the Earth Stood Still* (at one point, the alien "de-energizes" Earth) and original camp contributions, including the alien's frozen, neon-eyed "evil" look. Especially tacky: the crashing-satellite cutout. Beverly Garland, however, as Claire Anderson, gets surprising dramatic mileage out of the script's perfection-vs.-emotion theme. Her zingiest line: "You can't rub the tarnish from men's souls without losing a bit of the silver, too." The film features two classic, sensationalistic "B" scenes: In the first, Sally Fraser's now-possessed Joan Nelson presents hubbie Paul (Peter Graves) with one of the flying devices (these critters also turn up in *The Undead*); in a later sequence, Paul regretfully shoots his zombiefied wife.

See also: *Filmland Monsters* (II).

**IT CRAWLS INSIDE ME!** Glass Eye/Dog Boy 1992. SP,D: Raoul Vehil. Ref: vc box: "evil succubus." With D. Yow.

**IT FELL FROM THE FLAME BARRIER** see *Flame Barrier, The*

**IT'S ABOUT THE SECOND COMING** see *Second Coming, The*

**IT'S A GOOD LIFE** see *Midnight Zone, The*

**IT'S ALIVE III: ISLAND OF THE ALIVE** WB/Larco 1987 (1986) color 90m. SP, D, Exec P: Larry Cohen. Mus: Laurie Johnson. SpMkpFX: Steve Neill. Model FX: William Hedge. SpSdFX: Dane Davis? Opt: David Hewitt. Ref: TV. V 5/20/87. MFB'89:285-6. Scheuer. Phantom. Maltin '92. With Michael Moriarty, Karen Black, Laurene Landon, Gerrit Graham, James Dixon, Art Lund, Macdonald Carey.

"It's one of them!" Cape Vale, Florida. Is it a "perversion of everything human" ... or is it just a baby? The court orders the five *It's Alive* monster-babies in captivity sent to a remote island. At the end, however, the grue crew heads back for Cape Vale. Meandering horror tale has bright moments, outre scenes, and a likable performance by Moriarty.

See also *Tiyanak*.

**\*\*IT'S CALLED ROBERT** (Russ.) Lenfilm 1967 color/ws 93m. (*Yevo Zovut Robert*). D: Ilya Olshvanger. SP: Lev Kuklin, Yuri Printsev. Mus: Andrey Petrov. Ref: WorldF'67. Ronald V. Borst. Hardy/SF. V 7/10/68. With Oleg Strizhenov, Marianna Vertinskaya.

Scientist biochemically creates double of himself.

**IT'S ONLY A MOVIE!** Cinema Images 1991 (1990) b&w 106m. SP, D: Joseph Zaso. SP: also V. C. Siegfried. Mus: Tim Frey. Ref: V 3/18/91:87 (hv): "a tough slog." no Martin. With Brian Dixon (Madman Malone), Adrienne Marie Corso, Patti Komornik.

Crew shoots movie in haunted house.

**IVY GARLAND, The** see *Out of the Darkness*

# J

**JACARE - KILLER OF THE AMAZON** UA/Mayfair 1942 b&w 64m. D: Charles E. Ford. SP: Thomas Lennon. Mus: Miklos Rosza. Ref: V 12/23/42: "better than recent Buck pictures." LC. NYT 12/28/42: "jacare ... the ugliest-tempered brute in the world." PT 3:31.

Brazilian "river bank filled" with Jacare, "reptiles ... which look like a cross between a python and giant crocodiles"—in a Frank Buck "bring 'em back alive jungle thriller." "Struggle to capture these reptiles ... is unsuccessful...." (V)

**JACK BE NIMBLE** (N.Z.) Essential Prods. & N.Z. Film Commission (Dowling-Rogers ) 1993 color 92m. SP, D: Garth Maxwell. Mus: Chris Neal. PD: Grant Major. Ref: V 10/25/93: "well-made, if largely predictable, horror thriller." With Alexis Arquette, Sarah Smuts-Kennedy, Bruno Lawrence, Tony Barry.

Hypnotic "Rube Goldberg device" ... psychic powers.

**JACK BENNY SHOW, The** see *Jet Benny Show, The*

**JACK FALLS DOWN** see *Tales of the Unknown*

**JACK FROST** Celebrity 1934 anim color 6m. D: Ub Iwerks. Mus: Carl Stalling. Ref: screen. PFA (flyer). Maltin/OMAM. no LC.

Okay cartoon short features a scene with a boogeyman-like "Old Man Winter." The winter-coming-on scenes also include an amusingly hip, living, dancing scarecrow, with vocal backup provided by living, singing oak trees.

See also the following and *Betty Boop's Hallowe'en Party*.

**\*JACK FROST** Majestic Int'l. 1965 ('66-U.S.) 75m. (*Magical Wonderland* - vt t). Ref: TV: United HV; Eng. dubbed. V 10/19/66. Lee. no Lentz. no Stanley. Hound. no Martin.

Father Mushroom curses the vain hero, Ivan, and temporarily turns him into a bear-man. ("A werewolf! Run for your life!") Yield: "Beauty and the Beast"-type scenes wherein the now-hairy Ivan bemoans his admittedly-just fate. Meanwhile—in intercut scenes—the witch Baba Yaga (also called a "hunchback fairy") dispatches her "pretty kitty" to slay the heroine, Nastenka. The evil cat makes Nastenka touch Jack Frost's magic scepter, and she dies, temporarily.... Fantasy-comedy is sometimes poky, but the simple, Cocteau-like effects scenes are charming. One highlight: the reverse-film effect for Jack Frost's instant frost. (Trees seem to gather up their winter coats from the ground.) The witch is a real meanie, but her scenes are hilarious. Her cabin in the woods stands on two big human-like legs, and when she gets into a shouting match with Ivan over its geographical orientation (She: "Face the woods!" He: "Face me!"), the cabin tries to comply with each, in turn. Her loyal trees capture Ivan for her dinner.

See also: *Marriage of the Bear*.

**JACK THE BEAR** Fox/American Filmworks & Lucky Dog (Bruce Gilbert) 1993 color/ws 98m. D: Marshall Herskovitz. SP: Steven Zaillian, from Dan McCall's novel. Mkp: Z. & K. Elek. SpFxCoord: Dick Wood. SdFX: Visiontrax. Ref: TV. V

2/22/93: "mostly likable ... mixes comedy and horror." 1/25/93:18 (rated): "some terror." SFChron 4/2/93: "mushy tone." Mo: "a charming, sweet movie that tries to do a lot and accomplishes it."

Bigot (Gary Sinise)—nicknamed "Norman the Zombie"—"like some monster from a real horror flick, comes after Jack" (Robert J. Steinmiller, Jr.). (V) Plus: "late-night creature-feature TV show" host (Danny DeVito). Norman is "the Bogeyman, a neo-Nazi racist...." (SFC) Al Gory, "Monster of Ceremonies" of Midnight Treat, runs (and we see clips from) *Frankenstein* (1931), *The Wolf Man* (1941), *Abbott and Costello Meet Frankenstein, Them!,* and the original *The Fly* and *Invasion of the Body Snatchers.*

Powerful passages in a basically familiar seemingly-unfit-parent story. The "monster" references get a bit heavy. ("I thought I knew all about monsters.") DeVito and Steinmiller carry the show.

**JACK THE RIPPER** (B-U.S.) CBS-TV/Euston Films/Thames-TV & Hill-O'Connor-TV & Lorimar-Telepictures 1988 color c180m. Concept, Tel, D, P: David Wickes. Tel: also Derek Marlowe. Mus: John Cameron. PD: John Blezard. ProsthMkp: Aaron & Maralyn Sherman. Ref: TV: alternately called a mini-series & a TV-movie. SFChron 10/21/88. SFExam 10/21/88. V 11/16/88:62. With Michael Caine, Armand Assante, Ray McAnally, Lewis Collins, Ken Bones, Susan George, Jane Seymour, Harry Andrews, Michael Gothard, Edward Judd, T. P. McKenna.

London, 1888. Psychic Robert Lees sees "one killer with two faces" (in scenes with a visualized monster-face) behind the Whitechapel murders. "There's no Dr. Jekyll; there's no Mr. Hyde," opines the Scotland Yard inspector. Or, psychologically speaking, do a "saint and a beast" exist in one man? (We see Richard Mansfield on stage as Dr. Jekyll and Mr. Hyde, complete with anachronistic-seeming 1980s state-of-the-art makeup effects.) The Ripper proves to be the queen's doctor, a madman "trying to understand his own dementia." A logical resolution, but Caine gives an uncustomarily shrill performance and sets the general tone here.

See also: *Amazon Women on the Moon. Bridge across Time. Deadly Advice. Dungeonmaster. Edge of Sanity. Jack's Back. Night Ripper! Ripper, The. Waxwork II.*

**JACKPOT** see *Cybereden*

**JACK'S BACK** Palisades Ent. (Elliott Kastner-Andre Blay) 1988 color 97m. (aka *Red Rain*). SP, D: Rowdy Herrington. SpFxMkp: John Naulin. Ref: V 5/4/88: "tedious, unappealing." 10/19/88:180. ad. SFExam 4/29/88: "Did the editor fall asleep?" V 10/21/87:314. With James Spader (John/Rick Wesford), Cynthia Gibb, Rod Loomis, Robert Picardo, Jim Haynie, Chris Mulkey, Rex Ryon.

Modern-day-L.A. Ripper-style killings ... hypnosis ... psychically-linked twins.

**JACOB'S LADDER** Tri-Star/Carolco (Alan Marshall/Kassar-Vajna) 1990 color 113m. D: Adrian Lyne. SP: Bruce Joel Rubin. Ph: J. L. Kimball. Mus: Maurice Jarre. PD: Brian Morris. ProsthFxDes: Gordon J. Smith. SpMkp: Don McLeod, Arlene

Smith. SpMech: Ian Biggs. SpFX: Conrad Brink. SpSdFX: Musikwerks. Ref: TV: Live HV (Carolco HV). Mo. V 11/5/90: "dull, unimaginative and pretentious." Time 11/12/90. Newsweek 11/12/90. SFExam 11/2/90. Sacto Bee 11/4/90: "the kind of dreams that happen only in special effects-laden movies." With Tim Robbins, Elizabeth Pena, Danny Aiello, Matt Craven, Macaulay Culkin, Ving Rhames, S. Epatha Merkerson.

"They weren't human." Is Vietnam vet Jacob Singer (Robbins) "already dead"? He sees "demons"—including some tentacled-and-clawed beast on a dance floor. And a receptionist bears a telltale *Invaders from Mars* thing on the top of her head. Fellow war vet Paul: "I'm going to hell.... They're comin' after me." The double-twist ending: In 1971, a hippie chemist hired by the military to experiment with the "dark side" of mind-altering drugs produces the BZ-like "fury of the ladder," which taps into the subject's "primal fear." Tested on Singer's battalion, it reduces the soldiers to maddened beasts who tear each other apart. But Singer's experiences prove to be part of an "Owl Creek Bridge"-like dying daydream.... Through the wringer with Jacob Singer. Mainstream Earnest, like *Communion, Flatliners,* etc., though the closest cross-reference, for plot, is probably *The Manchurian Candidate:* after-effects of wartime experiments in hypnosis/hallucinogens, and weird twists on "friendly fire." The film is pretty harrowing, and Robbins is quite good, but the end twists almost cancel each other (as well as the rest of the movie) out.

**JAIL HOUSE EROS** (H.K.) Golden Harvest/Diagonal Pictures (Paragon Films) 1989 color c90m. D: Wong Ching. Ref: TV: Rainbow Video; no Eng. NST! 4:28.

Low comedy-fantasy re a parchment which conjures up a winsome ghost who temporarily possesses a young woman. This ghost later combats a monstrous, fanged, colorfully-made-up she-ghost who possesses nightsticks, tables, etc., in the lively climactic exorcism.

**JAMA, KIVDALO A NADEJE** see *Pit, the Pendulum and Hope, The*

**JAMES BOND** see *Jane Bond Meets Octopussy. Licence to Thrill, A. Operacion Mantis.*

**JAN OF THE JUNGLE** see *Call of the Savage, The*

**JANE BOND MEETS OCTOPUSSY** Vidco (Harold Lime) 1986 color 77m. D: Jack Remy. Ref: Adam '89: hormone gun. With Amber Lynn, Kristara Barrington, Mauvais De Noire, Blondi.

See also: *Licence To Thrill.*

**JAPANESE GHOST STORY** see *Discarnates, The*

**The JAR** Nocturna Int'l. 1984 color 90m. (*Carrion* - orig t). D: Bruce Toscano. SP: George Bradley. Mus: Obscure Sighs. PD: CRM Design. SpPhysical FX: Jeffery Poole, Alan Peacock. SpVisFX: Cinema Research. Ref: TV: Magnum Ent. video. Cinef 3/88. Martin. Scheuer. no Hound. PT 16:63. VWB. With Gary Wallace, Karen Sjoberg, Robert Gerald Witt, Les Miller, Robert C. Arnold (spectre), Dean Schlarpfer.

"We've got to kill it!" Paul gets a jar from a stranger and starts to have gory, quasi-religious hallucinations. He says—of the little creature supposedly inside the jar—"It's outside of me, but it's trying to get inside!" Inside it apparently does get, then lies in wait for the next victim.... Truly cheap. Acting ranges from passable (Sjoberg) to terrible (Witt). The little thing looks menacing enough, but hardly moves. You have to work to make the connection between this sedentary object and the traveling shots which are supposed to represent its movements.

**JASON GOES TO HELL: THE FINAL FRIDAY** New Line/Sean S. Cunningham 1993 color 88m. (*Friday the 13th Part IX* - shooting t). Story, D: Adam Marcus. Story, SP: Jay Huguely. SP: also Dean Lorey. Mus: Harry Manfredini. SpVisFX: Al Magliochetti. SpMkpFX: KNB EFX. Ref: V 8/23/93: "exhausted, witless." 6/22/92:13. ad. SFChron 8/14/93: "Jason ... can inhabit any old body." With Jon D. LeMay, Kari Keegan, Kane Hodder (Jason Voorhees), Steven Williams, Billy Green Bush.

Follow-up to *Friday the 13th Part VIII*.

**JASON LIVES** see *Friday the 13th Part VI*

**JAWS IV: THE REVENGE** Univ (Joseph Sargent/Frank Bauer) 1987 color/ws 90m. (*Jaws the Revenge* - ad t). D: Sargent. SP: Michael de Guzman. Mus: Michael Small. SpFX: (sup) Henry Millar; (coord) Doug Hubbard, Michael J. Millar. Mkp: Dan Striepeke, Tony Lloyd. Ref: TV. MFB'87:306. V 7/22/87. ad. East Bay Express 7/24/87. With Lorraine Gary, Lance Guest, Mario Van Peebles, Karen Young, Michael Caine, Melvin Van Peebles.

"The nightmares will go away." They don't, and a "great big beautiful shark" steams towards the Bahamas, via the Great White Way, as psychic Ellen Brody (Gary) senses its approach.... An odd mystical element marks this fourth, generally vapid *Jaws*. Sargent's work with actors is better than his work with sharks— only occasional "in-between," everyday-life moments break up the suspense monotony here.

See also: *Blades. Devil Fish. Furia Asesina. Night of the Sharks.*

**JEANNOT L'INTREPIDE** see *Johnny in the Valley of the Giants*

**JEKYLL & HYDE** (B) ABC-TV/London Weekend-TV & Wickes-TV & King Phoenix Ent. 1990 color 90m. Tel, D, & Exec Co-P: David Wickes. "Derived from" Robert Louis Stevenson's story, "The Strange Case of Dr. Jekyll and Mr. Hyde." Mus: John Cameron. PD: William Alexander. SpMkpFX: Image Animation. Ref: TV. Sacto Bee 1/19/90. V 1/24/90:167. 2/7/90:126 (ad). With Michael Caine, Cheryl Ladd, Joss Ackland, Ronald Pickup, Diane Keen, Lance Percival, Lionel Jeffries.

"The mind controls the body." London, 1889. Jekyll (Caine) takes the potion, becomes the "brute," Mr. Hyde (Caine again). Ultimate yield: a dead Henry Jekyll and a little, deformed Harry Jekyll.... The makeup effects are as familiar as the story. Undistinguished vehicle for Caine, whose best moments come near the end, as Jekyll panics and dreads the inexorable return of Hyde.

See also: *Jack the Ripper* (1988).

**JENNIFER EIGHT** Para/Scott Rudin (Lucchesi-Wimbury) 1992 color 124m. SP, D: Bruce Robinson. Ph: Conrad Hall. Mus: Christopher Young. PD: Richard Macdonald. Ref: V 11/9/92: "unusually intelligent." SFChron 11/6/92: "empty-headed thriller." ad. With Andy Garcia, Uma Thurman, Lance Henriksen, Kathy Baker, Kevin Conway, John Malkovich, Nicholas Love, Lenny Von Dohlen.

"Serial killer ... hacking up young blind women." (SFC)

**JENNY PORTER** see *Future Shock*

**A JERSEY SKEETER** AM&B 1900 b&w silent 2m. Ref: Hardy/SF.

"Monster mosquito" carries off farmer.

See also: *Mosquito. Popcorn. Skeeter. There's Something about a Soldier.*

**JESUS VENDER TILBAGE** (Danish) Superfilm & the Danish Film Institute 1992 color 102m. (aka *The Return*). SP, D, P: Jens Jorgen Thorsen. Ph: Jesper Hom. Mus: Jimmy Dawkins and his Chicago Bluesmen. Ref: V 3/23/92: Eng. dialogue; "uneven ... dated." with Marco Di Stefano, Atlanta, Jed Curtis.

"Jesus ... returns to Earth to save humanity from pollution."

The **JET BENNY SHOW** United HV 1986 color 77m. D: Roger D. Evans. Ref: Scheuer: "pointless, witless sci-fi parody." Phantom: "surprisingly accomplished." Hound. With Steve Norman, Polly MacIntyre, Kevin Dees, Ted Luedemann.

In this parody of the old "Jack Benny Show," Jet takes his Maxwell rocket to another planet, and "Rochester" is an android.

**JETSONS: THE MOVIE** (U.S.-Taiwanese) Univ/Hanna-Barbera & Wang Film & Cuckoos Nest 1990 anim color 82m. D: William Hanna, Joseph Barbera; (anim) Ray Patterson. Anim D: (sup) David Michener. Sup D: Iwao Takamoto. SP: Dennis Marks, based on "The Jetsons" TV series. Mus: John Debney. OptFX: Perpetual Motion Pictures, Howard Anderson. Computer Anim: deGraf/Wahrman. SpSdFX: John Paul Fasal. Ref: TV. MFB'91:80-81. V 7/4/90. Sacto Union 7/5/90. Sacto Bee 7/6/90. Voices: George O'Hanlon, Mel Blanc, Penny Singleton, Jean VanderPyl, Ronnie Schell, Tiffany, Frank Welker.

Late in the 21st Century.... The Jetson family moves to Intergalactic Garden Estates, encounters furry blue aliens, discovers that the "gremlins" at large in the boss's factory are "Grungies" trying to save their homes from reckless mining.... Tired in '62, tired in '90. The introduction of computer-animated exteriors, however, is an eye-catcher. They seem halfway between cartoon animation and live action. The sequence with the hologram "scenery" and various psychedelia is also several cuts above the rest of the film—i.e., it's not unbearable.

See also: the following and *Rockin' with Judy Jetson.*

The **JETSONS MEET THE FLINTSTONES** (U.S.-Taiwanese) Worldvision-TV/Hanna-Barbera-TV & Wang Film & Hathcock-Wolf 1987 anim color 90m. D: Don Lusk. Sup D: Ray Patterson. Tel: Don Nelson, Arthur Alsberg, from the TV series "The Jetsons" and "The Flintstones." Mus: Sven Libaek. Anim Sup:

Janine Dawson. Ref: TV. TVG. Voices: Mel Blanc, Daws Butler, Brenda Vaccaro, Frank Welker.

The best of both worlds. Elroy Jetson's time machine takes the futuristic Jetsons back to prehistory and the Flintstones, then sends the latter into the future. Plus: Rock Concerts, a stegosaurus garbage disposal, dog-sized ants (the past), robot dogs (the future), etc. The usual half-hearted Hanna-Barbera humor.

See also: *I Yabba-Dabba Do!*

**JEWEL OF SEVEN STARS, The** see *Tomb, The*

**JIANG-HU: BETWEEN LOVE AND GLORY** see *Bride with White Hair*

**JIANGSHI JIAZU: JIANGSHI XIANSHENG XUJI** see *Mr. Vampire II*

**JIANGSHI PAPA** see *Close Encounter with the Vampire*

**JIANGSHI XIANSHENG** see *Mr. Vampire*

**JIDONG QIXIA** see *Iceman Cometh*

**JIGOKU** see *Hell* (1979)

**JIGOKU NO KEIBIIN** see *Guard from Underground, The*

**JIPANGU** (J) EXE & TBS & Daio Paper Corp. & Kanematsu Corp. & SK (Tsutsumi-Kuri) 1990 ('95-U.S.) color/ws 123m. (aka *Zipang*). SP, D: Kaizo Hayashi. SP: also Noriyuki Kurita. Ph: M. Tamura. Mus: Urayama, Kumagaya. AD: Takeo Kimura. Ref: TV: Pack-In Video; no Eng. Markalite 3:89. V 6/13/90: queen whose heart is kept in an icy shrine. Imagi (Fall'95): *The Legend of Zipang* - U.S. With Masahiro Takashima, Narumi Yasuda, Haruko Wanibuchi.

Also included: a diminishing room and an ancient ghost-warrior from a coffin in a cave. The imaginative highlight of the movie's play with anachronism in old Japan: the super, infra-red binoculars which double as a camera. "Slides" are then inserted in a flying star which zips many miles to its destination and a projector. The movie is otherwise routine, moderately amusing outlandish swordplay, with flashy art direction.

**The JITTERS** (U.S.-J) Skouras/Gaga/Fascination (Fujimura/Right Zone) 1989 (1988) color 79m. D, P: John M. Fasano. SP: Jeff McKay, Sonoko Kondo. Ph: Paul Mitchnick. AD: W. Kozlinski. Sp Creature: Steve Wang. SpMkpFX: Richard Alonzo. SpFxCoord: Michael Cavanough[sic]. Opt: Light & Motion. Animatronics: Dave Kindlon, John Criswell. Ref: TV: Prism Ent. video; shot in Toronto. V 6/14/89: "overly goofy." PT 12:45-6: "amusing enough." Jones. With Sal Viviano, Marilyn Tokuda, James Hong, Frank Dietz, Joe Podnar (monster Chan).

"Vampire-like beings trapped in limbo on Earth...." (V) "Kill 'im again!" Uncle Frank (Handy Atmadja) is brought back from the dead as a Kyonshee, or Gyonsii, the "Chinese version of a vampire." Mirrors repel the various hopping vampires here, and paper charms on the forehead stop them. At one point, a reptilian thing "hatches" out of one Kyonshee.... Leaden comedy, dull action.

**JIYAIANTO ROBO** see *Giant Robo*

**JOE AND THE COLONEL** ABC-TV/Mad-Dog & Univ-TV 1985 color c90m. (*Humanoid Defender* - vt t). D: Ron Satlof. Tel & Exec P: Nicholas Corea. Mus: Joseph Conlan. AD: John Leimaris. OptFX: Universal Title. Mkp: James Kail. Ref: TVG. TV. V 9/18/85:54. With Gary Kasper (J.O.E.), Terence Knox, Bill Lucking, Gail Edwards, William Riley, Aimee Eccles, Marie Windsor, Mike Preston.

Project Omega (re creating human beings in a "controlled environment") produces J.-type Omega Elemental, or J.O.E., a "true human male." ("We created the perfect soldier....") But his superiors have trouble convincing J.O.E. that killing is okay. Glibly pretentious sf-actioner.

**JOE 90** see *Amazing Adventures of Joe 90*

**JOEY** see *Making Contact*

**The JOGGER** Showtime-TV 1990? 24m. D: Robert Resnikoff. Ref: SFChron 12/7/90: "a hell-for-leather little movie"; on "The 30-Minute Movie." Jogger (Terry O'Quinn) comes up against a "silent, strangely malevolent adversary (Tom Morga)."

**JOHN CARPENTER PRESENTS "BODY BAGS"** see *Body Bags*

**JOHN TRAVIS - SOLAR SURVIVOR** see *Omega Cop*

**JOHNNY IN THE VALLEY OF THE GIANTS** (F) Lippert (Jack Alexander)/Jean Image 1950('53-U.S.) anim color 77m. (59m.-U.S.) (*Jeannot L'Intrepide*. \*\*\* *Johnny the Giant Killer* - alt U.S. t). D, P: J. Image. SP & Lyrics: Paul Colline. Idea: Eraine Image. Based on Perrault characters. Ph: Kostia Tchikine. Mus: Rene Cloerec. Chief Anim: Albert Champeaux. Ref: TV: vt; Eng.-dubbed version (Frank & Macdonald). COF 11:42. Lee (LC). TVG. Phantom. Hound. no Martin.

A cackling, fanged giant (a rough Edward G. Robinson caricature) miniaturizes and cages lions, elephants, bears, bulls, giraffes, and little boys, the better to make gruesome Dagwood sandwiches of them. At the end, the giant gets shrunk in his own machine.... An alternately poetic and prosaic cartoon feature. Highlights: the inventive, surprising action in the giant's Rube Goldberg nightmare castle ... La Puce Fantome, the insect-carnival's fun spook-house ride ... the commuter-bug "bus" ... and the lovely sequence in which boy-hero Johnny, post-miniaturization, dances into the sky with the queen bee. One long sequence in a honeycomb plays like a plug for bee farmers.

**JOHNNY SOKKO AND HIS FLYING ROBOT** see *Giant Robo*

**JOHNNY ZOMBIE** see *My Boyfriend's Back*

**De JOHNSONS** (Dutch) Meteor Film/Movies Film (Brouwer-Balian) 1992 color/ws 96m. (*Xangadix* - orig t). D: Rudolf van den Berg. SP: Leon de Winter, based on Rocco Simonelli's original script and Roy Frumkes' story. Ph: Theo Bierkens. Mus: Patrick Seymour. PD: Harry Ammerlaan. Ref: TV: VSOM; Eng.-dubbed; *The Johnsons*. V 3/9/92: "well-made horror pic with ...

shivers aplenty." 2/24/92:194. With Monique van de Ven, Esmee de la Bretoniere, Kenneth Herdigein.

"An awful fate awaits the whole world." Ingredients include Amazonian Indians who guard an embryo-deity, Xangadix, an "evil god" ... seven killer-brothers (there is "something almost demonic" about them) ... and our hero, a demonologist .... A bit thin, but pretty creepy at times. Some atmosphere.

**JOKERS PLAYING GAMES** (H.K.) Lisa Mok 1987? color c91m. D: Tommy Young. Ref: TV: Ocean Shores Video; Eng. titles.

A gremlin/ghost possesses a man and enables him to fight hopping "vampire/ghosts," while cadaverous cops from hell (Immigration division) attempt to fetch a female ghost at large on Earth.... Undisciplined silliness introduces real and fake ghosts as it pleases. (The vampires prove to be phony.) The ghost cops are the only consistently funny element — the short one, who's in training, keeps repeating everything he says, like a broken record; the big guy shuts him up by punching him.

**JONATHAN OF THE NIGHT 2000 AD** 1987 color 10m. D: Buddy Giovinazzo. Ref: Jones: "amateurish performances." With Don Striano, Mitch Maglio.

"Modern day vampire at a New York party."

**JONNY'S GOLDEN QUEST** (U.S.-Fili) USA-TV & Hanna-Barbera & Fil-Cartoons (Mario Piluso/Ray Patterson) 1993 (1992) anim color 80m. D: Don Lusk, Paul Sommer. Tel: Sean Roche. Story: Mark Young, based on the old "Jonny Quest" TV series. Mus: John Debney. Ref: TV. TVG. SFChron Dtbk 6/20/93. Voices: Ed Gilbert, George Hearn, Meredith MacRae, Don Messick, Pepe Serna, Jeffrey Tambor, G. Van Dusen, Frank Welker, JoBeth Williams.

"Someone has made synthetic gold!" Film's ingredients include "strange mutations" (including a two-headed croc) in a Peruvian rain forest ("They could destroy the primary food chain on a global scale") ... a madman's "replicants," including primitive monster-slaves and "perfect duplicates" of himself ... a doctor's synthetic gold, based on a Da Vinci formula (cf. *Hudson Hawk*), which gold the madman plans to use to help create undying clones of himself ... the Synapse Imager, which projects "memory images" ... and magic which briefly raises mummified Roman dead.... Stilted story-telling and animation. The new eco-banality features the same old story, with lip service to conservation.

**JOURNAL OF THE PLAGUE YEAR, A** see *Ano de la Peste, El*

**JOURNEY TO AN UNKNOWN WORLD** (Sp-Braz.?) Cine-Int'l./R.F. Farias 198-? color 95m. SP, D: Flavio Migliaccio. SP: also Roberto Farias, Regis Monteiro. Ph: Jose Medeiros. AD: E. De Jesus. Anim Des: Ely Barbosa. SpFX: Wilmar Menezes. Mkp: Walter de Almeida. Ref: TV: VSOM; Eng. dubbed. With F. Migliaccio, Odete Lara, Walter Forster, Mauro Farias, Luiz Mario Farias, Rodolfo Arena, M. Villar.

"Anything can happen in a cartoon!" Cartoon characters from the Planet of Seven Dimensions land their flying saucer in the Amazon. Apparently, machines took over their planet millions of years ago and command the robot "from the other planet" which (like the aliens) seeks a special flower. In the saucer, humans

become cartoon, too, and travel with their hosts to their planet, where they attempt to destroy a huge robot-controlling machine.... Juvenile adventure-comedy is cute only near the end, when the film temporarily becomes all animation.

**JOURNEY TO THE CENTER OF THE EARTH** Cannon (Fields, Udell, Lerner) 1989 (1986) color 79m. SP, D: Rusty Lemorande. SP: also Debra Ricci et al, from the Jules Verne novel. VisFX: Fantasy II; (sup) John Scheele. Ref: V 6/21/89: "an unfinished film, pasted together crudely." With Nicola Cowper, Ilan Mitchell-Smith, Paul Carafotes, Janie du Plessis, Kathy Ireland (Wanda).

Down to Atlantis, and characters from *Alien from L.A.*

**JOURNEY TO THE CENTER OF THE EARTH** NBC-TV (John Ashley) 1993 color c90m. D, Exec Co-P: William Dear. Tel, Exec Co-P: David Mickey Evans. Tel, Co-P: Robert Gunter. Ph: Ron Garcia. Mus: David Kurtz. PD: James Spencer. Digital VisFX: Digital FX. Ref: TV. TVG. SFChron 2/28/93. With Jeffrey Nordling, F. Murray Abraham, Farrah Forke, John Neville, Carel Struycken (Dallas), Fabiana Udenio, David Dundara, Kim Miyori.

The vehicle which the "Descenders" take to the "inner world": the omniphibious ("any terrain") Adventurer, which (a) employs a sonic bore to blast a temporary "doorway" through lava, (b) runs on synthetic, fusionable, self-regenerating fuel, and (c) is monitored by "DEVIN" (Digital Electro-Plastic Virtual Intelligence Navigator), a "bouncing ball"-like hologram gizmo. In the "center realm," the "invaders from the overworld" find weird, but English-speaking bio-wonders and their manta-ray-like errand boys; a tall, harmless Tibetan-speaking "abominable snowman," Dallas, who, with the aid of an aural impulse transducer, speaks English; and self-sealing rock walls which at one point perform a variation on the idea of the diminishing room.

The center folk are a gabby group. If the undergrounders look weird, they act like conventional good guys and bad guys, and although the production is fairly elaborate for a TV-movie, it's basically uninspired.

**JOURNEY TO THE WEST** see *Chinese Odyssey, A*

**JUAN TANGA SUPER NAMAN AT ANG KAMBAL NA TIY-ANAK** (Fili) Regal Films (Tony Fajardo/Lily Monteverde) 1990? color c90m. SP, D: M. R. Makiling. Mkp: E. Pinero. SdFX: Rodel Capule. Ref: TV: Regal video; little Eng.

Two magic dwarfs enable the hero to appear as various comicbook characters in this comedy-fantasy. Among his incarnations: Captain Pinoy, whose shield deflects bullets and acts as a saucer-like weapon ... the flying bird/klutz Matanglawin ... and a super-strong, big-eyebrowed, green, Incredible Hulk-like monster that bops baddies. Episodic but lively.

**JUBEI NINPUCHO** see *Ninja Scroll*

**JUDGE** (J) C.J.F. 1991? anim color 50m. Ref: TV: vt; OAV?; no Eng. Japan Video: aka The Judge in the Darkness.

Ingredients: attacking crow hordes ... a sheet of paper which turns into a flying, huge-clawed creature ... a businessman in an elevator who is confronted by a monster ... two opposing wizards who summon up demons ... and finally a gallery of phantasmal "judges".... Stylishly drawn, but too involved to follow without a program. Apparent touches of "The Devil and Daniel Webster."

**JUDGEMENT DAY** Rockport/Ferde Grofe Films (Keith Lawrence) 1989 color 93m. (88m.). SP, D, Co-P: Ferde Grofe Jr. Ph: Pete Warrilow. Mus: L. Richman. PD: Rodell Cruz. SpFX: Romeo Mabitol et al. SpMkpDes: Evan Brainard. Ref: TV: Magnum Ent. video. V 6/28/89: "not without some fun moments." Hound. PT 5:39. With Kenneth McLeod, David Anthony Smith, Monte Markham, Cesar Romero, Gloria Hayes, Peter Mark Richman.

"This is hell!" Once a year, satan returns to and takes over the Latin American town of Santana ("a bad place"), and the townsfolk vacate. Lash LaRue-types make the streets really mean, and a rubber-faced devil brands crucified victims with a burning hand.... Modest-budgeted, but ambitious, offbeat movie has nice "buildup" moments, atmosphere, and shot-on-location travelogue values. Serviceable fantasy-horror story, though, bogs down twice with a gabby priest and issues in a disappointing, one-year-later coda.

**JUDGMENT IN STONE** or **JUDGEMENT IN STONE** see *Housekeeper, The*

**El JUEGO DEL DIABLO** (Sp) Kalender Films Int'l. 1974 color c80m. SP, D: Jorge Darnell. Ph: J. L. Alcaine. Mus: Jose Nieto. AD: Adolfo Cofino. SpFX: Pablo Perez. Mkp: Miguel Sese. Ref: Mexcinema Video; no Eng. VSOM: sfa *Devil's Exorcist*? With Inma de Santy, Jack Taylor, Maria del Puy, Luis Prendes, Jose Orjas, Alberto Fernandez, Jose Ruiz Lifante.

Demons possess a teenage girl. She foams at the mouth and has hallucinations of Cocteau-ish hands sticking out of walls and up out of the water in swimming pools. Her malicious stunts include turning off a hospital-bed-bound boy's oxygen, hanging a dog, and throwing her mother off a balcony. At the end, she dies, but the demon possesses another woman.... The evil of banality, as another *Exorcist* clone belatedly surfaces. Nothing new here.

**JUGULAR WINE** Cinequanon/Pagan Pictures 1993 color feature. SP, D, P: Blair Murphy. Ph: Baird Bryant? Mus: John Butler. Ref: V 5/10/93:71 (ad), C-116: screening at Cannes. PT 20:16: "ambitious arty feature." With Shaun Irons, Lisa Malkiewicz, Vladimir Kehkaial, Stan Lee, Henry Rollins, Bill Moynihan.

"A vampire odyssey."(V) Female vampire bites young anthropologist.

**JULY SPIRIT** (H.K.?) c1984? color/ws c90m. (*Hon Ma Thang 7*-Viet t?). D: Wang Chung Kuang. Ref: TV: Cogeda Video; no Eng. With Tien Ping Chun.

A strange man disintegrates and becomes an even more strange, small bat-thing with eyes like glowing embers. He joins other bat-things, chuckling skeletons, and flying pink skulls to haunt a house and the outlying district. Near the end, he turns into a full-fledged bat-man, complete with cute floppy bat-ears, and bites people's necks. Both the hero and the mugging comic relief temporarily become vampires.

Amusing nonsense. The script is elementary, but the corn keeps popping, and the horrors are watchably vivid. At one point, the

house sucks hero and heroine in through the front door. Later, she turns one skeleton into a bone pile, but it bounces right back whole. One bat even spits, like a spider spinning a web.

**JUMPIN' JUPITER** WB 1955 anim color 7m. D: Chuck Jones. SP: M. Maltese. Mus: Carl Stalling. FxAnim: Harry Love. Ref: Lee (LC). WBCartoons. TV.

Porky Pig and Sylvester on another planet.

See also *Daffy Duck's Quackbusters*.

**JUMPING CORPSES** (H.K.) Gordon's Film & Co. 1989? color c90m. Ref: TV: Rainbow Video; no Eng.

A fat, fake hopping vampire meets the real thing. Later, the latter bites a soldier on the neck. At the end, a priest's supernatural lightning makes him disappear. Plus: a brigade of hoppers and a man in a skeleton suit.... Silly, shot-on-tape horror-comedy.

**Der JUNGE MOENCH** (W.G.) Achternbusch 1978 color 84m. SP, D, P: Herbert Achternbusch. Ph: J. Jeshel. Ref: Hardy/SF: The Young Monk - tr t. With H. Achternbusch, Karolina Herbig, Barbara Gass.

"Set after a global catastrophe in which the Earth has become on enormous desert."

**JUNGLA MORTAL** (Mex) CI (Mexcinema) 1988 (1985) color c90m. D, P: Rodolfo de Anda. SP: Gilberto de Anda. Ph: Antonio de Anda. Mus: Marco Flores. AD: Raul Cardenas. SpFX: Abel Contreras. OptFX: Manuel Sainz. SdFX: G. Gavira. Mkp: A. Ramirez. Ref: TV. TVG. With R. de Anda, G. de Anda, Arturo Martinez Jr., Imperio Vargas, Carlos East, Agustin Bernal, Mario Arevalo (Holkan).

Ingredients (in chronological order): an Indian with a horrible back burn ... a Mayan knickknack (or is it from another planet?) which gives holder of same visions and telekinetic powers ... gratuitous machete and sword gore ... an Indian mystic who masterminds a bat attack ... a jungle princess with pasties ... a pyramidal structure which burns those who dare to touch it ... and a friendly, *CE3K*-type apparent alien aboard same, which is apparently a spacecraft. Hokey, low-budget sf-adventure.

**JUNGLE BOY** see *Jungle Hell*

**JUNGLE BOY, KENIYA** (J) Toei 1984? anim? feature. Ref: V 5/9/84:437 (ad): dinosaurs.

**\*\*JUNGLE HELL** Medallion-TV/Taj Mahal Prods. (J.M. Post) 1960? (1956?) 85m. (*Jungle Boy* - orig t). SP, D, P: Norman A. Cerf. Ph: G. Warrenton. Mus: Nicholas Carras. Mkp: Harry Thomas. SdFX: James Ekstadt. Ref: TV. Greg Luce. Warren/KWTS! no V. no Hardy/SF. Lee. no LC. TVFFSB. no Hound. COF 11:43. Phantom, p. 369. Stanley. With Sabu, K. T. Stevens, David Bruce, George E. Stone, Ted Stanhope, Paul Dastagir, Naji, Serena Sande, Jacqueline Lacey.

"Some time ago, a strange rock was found in Mysore. The rock told of ancient, or prehistoric, times, before man came to this country. It told of a ship that sailed through the skies, coming to this place from another atmosphere, from another planet, or galaxy. It told of a landing, and how beams in the ship planted a substance in India and other places around."

Abrupt cuts on the music track indicate that the story which the radioactive rock "tells"—and the shots of the "ship" (a flying saucer)—were added after initial release of *Jungle Boy,* which itself was apparently unsold, cobbled-together TV-series episodes. Incredibly disjointed movie is filmed with all the panache of a "Ramar" show.

**\*JUNGLE JIM** 1948 (*Jungle Jim's Adventure* - orig t). Based on Alex Raymond's newspaper feature. AD: Paul Palmentola. Ref: TV. V 12/22/48. Weldon. Stanley. no Lentz. Lee (E/HR 12/16/48). COF 11:43. Maltin '92. Martin. Scheuer.

Obvious stock-footage thrills-and-melodrama package features one sequence with a river monster which, in some shots, is an alligator. In other, closer shots, the head looks like a too cute, nervous, rubbery dinosaur; the tail (never shown in the same shot with the dinosaur head) is a tentacle, which grabs and holds the heroine. If you hadn't seen the ads, you wouldn't know that this was supposed to be a "sea monster." File it under Charms and Confusions of the Bad "B" Movie. Extra addeds: a polio cure which is also supposed to be a paralyzing poison ... "devil doctors" and a lost-temple witch-doctor cult ... "Superman" (George Reeves) as a bad guy ... and a "You expected a man" scene for Virginia Grey's doctor. Johnny Weissmuller as Jim sounds uncomfortable with complete sentences.

**JUNIOR** (Can.) Palan Ent./Canada Inc. (Don Carmody) 1984 color 80m. (*Hot Water* - orig t. aka *Junior ... A Cut Above*). D: Jim Hanley. SP: John Maxwell, Carmody. Mus: Ken Roberts, A. Gerber. SpFX: (coord) Neil Trifunovich; (mkp) Mowat. SdFxEd: V. Paiment. Ref: TV: Prism Ent. video. V 5/29/85. McCarty II. Martin. Hound. Phantom. Stanley. With Suzanne Delaurentis, Linda Singer, Michael McKeever, Roberts, Cotton Mather, Alanne Perry, Jeremy Ratchford.

"The boys are just tryin' to have a little fun." Junior (Ratchford) is one of the Deep South low-lifers harassing K. C. (Delaurentis) and Jo (Singer), but he goes beyond annoying to demented, and has a "crazy old coot" of a mother, who gleefully watches his antics through binoculars. He may not, however, be the one responsible for that houseful of rotting bodies of runaway girls.... Crude, low-budget combo of t&a and sadism. There's the "Oh, no, those are leeches!" scene (which Jo disarmingly likens to a scene from *The African Queen*), the fishhook-in-hand scene, the worm-stuffed fish prank, the skinned-dog trick, and a sequence of terrorization right out of (as Jo notes at the end) *The Texas Chain Saw Massacre*. The shock and suspense elements derive, also, from *Psycho, Jaws,* and *Deliverance*. Only amusing new element: mother's binoculars.

**JUNIOR** Univ/Northern Lights (Ivan Reitman) 1994 color 110m. D: I. Reitman. SP: Kevin Wade, Chris Conrad. Ph: A. Greenberg. Mus: J.N. Howard. PD: S. Lineweaver. Prosth: Matthew Mungle. SpFxCoord: D.M. Blitstein. VisFX: Buena Vista VisFX. Ref: TV: MCA-Univ HV. SFChron 11/23/94. ad. With Arnold Schwarzenegger, Danny DeVito, Emma Thompson, Frank Langella, Pamela Reed, Judy Collins, Aida Turturro, Stefan Gierasch, Lawrence Tierney, Brianna & Brittany McConnell (Junior).

"You wouldn't be pregnant pregnant." A drug which promotes "embryo attachment" and prevents miscarriages enables Dr. Alexander Hesse (Schwarzenegger) to ingest a fertilized egg and bring it to term in his abdomen. ("I have a most extraordinary condition.") The expected scenes are here, as well as some unexpected moments, mainly from Thompson, but also from DeVito and Schwarzenegger. (Look, especially, for DeVito's Proud look as he helps deliver "Junior.") At first, it's only an experiment, but, like Rosemary, Alex wants the baby.

**JURANAL PARK** Odyssey Group Video 1993 color feature. D: Mitch Spinelli. SP: L. S. Talbot. Props: Dinosaur World. Ref: vc box: "Watch out for the ravenous penisaurus!" With Leena, Crystal Wilder.

**JURASSIC PARK** Univ/Amblin (Kathleen Kennedy, G. R. Molen) 1993 color 126m. D: Steven Spielberg. SP: Michael Crichton, David Koepp, from Crichton's novel. Ph: Dean Cundey. Mus: John Williams. PD: Rick Carter. Ed: Michael Kahn. Full-Motion Dinosaurs: IL&M, Dennis Muren. Live-Action Dinosaurs: Stan Winston. Dino Sup: Phil Tippett. SpDinoFX: Michael Lantieri. "Mr. DNA" Anim: Kurtz & Friends. Body Parts: Lance Anderson. Ref: screen. V 6/14/93. 9/7/92: 5, 14. SFChron 6/11/93. 6/15/93. 6/18/93. SFExam 6/11/93. 6/20/93. Sacto Bee 6/11/93. Cinef 12/93:52-8, 60. With Sam Neill, Laura Dern, Jeff Goldblum, Richard Attenborough, Bob Peck, Richard Kiley.

"We can make a baby dinosaur." Isla Nublar, off Costa Rica. Jurassic Park, a "biological preserve," showcases the "miracle of cloning." "Dino DNA"—in blood in prehistoric mosquitoes preserved in amber—generates twentieth-century dinosaurs, including a tyrannosaurus, velociraptors, singing brachiosaurs, and a triceratops.

Fast, busy, thin. Not trusting to their computer creatures, the moviemakers throw in a hurricane and human skullduggery in an attempt to scare up suspense. Neatest ploy: the "tremors" which herald monster attacks. In some sequences, the effects look like effects; in others, they unnervingly don't—e.g., the sequence in which the "raptors" skulk around the kitchen. It's a they-are-there effect. Two keys to the spookiness of the earlier tyrannosaurus sequence: the nightmare atmosphere and the fact that the creature stalks with its head so close to the ground—big as it is, its eye level is virtually the same as its prey here, humans. Big (BIG) Brother is Watching.

**JUSTY** see *Cosmo Police Justy*

**JUVENATRIX** see *Rejuvenatrix, The*

# K

**K-9000** Fox Network (TV)/Fries Ent. & De Souza Prods. (J. R. Dumm) 1991 (1989) color c90m. (aka K9000). D: Kim Manners. Tel: Steven E. de Souza. Tel, Co-P: M. Part. Ph: F. Raymond. Mus: Jan Hammer. PD: E. Gilbert. Key Mkp: B. Bryant. Ref: TV. TVG. With Chris Mulkey, Catherine Oxenberg, Dennis Haysbert, Judson Scott, Jerry Houser (voice of Niner).

Niner, a "canine with a computer implant," is stolen from a Piper Institute lab incubator, where he was part of Project CATCH:

Cybernetic Action Team Canine-Human. Through a microchip receiver implant in Eddie (Mulkey), a cop, Niner can talk to him and act as a telephone.... There's unrealized comic potential in this cross between *Watchers* and the old "People's Choice" TV show. *K-9000* is made too slickly and played too "realistically" for its own good. Fun, though: the "de-canined" dog rediscovering its roots (i.e., a fire hydrant).

**KO CENTURY THREE BEASTKETEERS II** (J) Sony Music 1993 anim color 29m. Ref: Animerica 7:54.

Humans who "morph into beasts" ... "guardian mecha."

**KABUTO** see *Raven Tengu, Kabuto*

**KADAICHA** see *Stones of Death*

**KAEFER AUF EXTRATOUR, Ein** see *Superbug*

**KAEFER GEHT AUFS GANZE, Ein** see *Superbug, The Wild One*

**KAEFER GIBT VOLIGAS, Ein** see *Superbug, Super Agent*

**KAHIR ELZAMAN** (Egypt.) Tamido/El Rania 1986 color 115m. D: Kamal El Cheik. SP: Ahmed Abdel Wahab, from a novel by Nihad Sherif. Mus: Georges Kazazian. Ref: V 12/24/86: "a talky pic that travels in the slow lane." With Nour El Sherif, Athar El Hakim, Gamil Ratap.

Sick people are frozen now for resuscitation later. "The frozen cousin is brought back to life...." Title can be translated as either *Time Stops* or *Conquerors of Time.* Last shot makes a "brilliant" link between cryogenics and mummification.

**KAIDAN IRO-ZANGE-KYOREN ONNA SHISHO** (J) Shochiku 1957 feature (aka *Dancing Mistress*). D: R. Kurahashi. SP: Shinichi Yanagawa. Ph: M. Hattori. Ref: Lee (FEFN 7/26/57). With Hiroshi Nawa, Jun Tazaki, Y. Kitagami.

The ghost of a murdered dancer seeks vengeance.

**KAIN OF THE DARK PLANET** see *Warrior and the Sorceress, The*

**KALABOG EN BOSYO STRIKE AGAIN** (Fili) Cinema 1635 c1986? color c155m. Adap, D: Ben Feleo. SP: Ely Matawaran, from the comic "Kalabog en Bosyo" by Larry Alcala. Ph: Dik Trofeo. Mus: Dominic. SpFx & Prosth Mkp: Danny Torrente. Mkp: L. Zuniga. SdFX: Ramon Reyes. Ref: TV: Tri-Films video; infrequent Eng. With Dolphy, Panchito, Rolly Quizon, Joyce Ann Burton, Bong Dimayacyac, Zeny Zabala, Jaime Fabregas (Dr. Kagaw), Conde Ubaldo (Prof. Dokling), Chuchi, Ben Johnson.

The mad Dr. Kagaw insists that his projected "super army will make [him] the most powerful man in the world." Lightning brings his first "superbeast," Adamo (sp?), to life. This aggressive, oversized monster has super-strength and a big papier-maché head and hands, and will eat anything, even a (lighted) stick of dynamite. In an incidental sequence, an incantation and lightning raise several zombies from their graves; another incantation and lightning destroy them.... One or two funny sight gags

and a few fair stunts and effects. Generally, the comedy wheezes. Over two hours of mugging.

See also *Kalabog and Bosyo (t).*

**KALIMAN EN EL SINIESTRO MUNDO DE HUMANON** (Mex) Kali-Films (R. Cutberto Navarro) 1974 color 93m. (aka *Kaliman Vs. Humanon*). D: Alberto Mariscal. SP: Victor Fox. Story: R. Cutberto Navarro, M. Vazquez Gonzales, from the radio show? Ph: Alex Phillips Jr. Mus: G. Carrion. AD: J. Fernandez. Mkp: Ana Ma. Soriano. Ref: TV: Condor Video; no Eng.; *Kaliman in the Sinister World of Humanon* - tr t. Jim Smith. Cinef 9/96:46. With Jeff Cooper, Milton Rodrigues, Lenka Erdos, M. Bravo, Alberto Insua, Carlos East.

The evil Humanon uses "controlled genetics" to create human "monsters" that sound like wild beasts but look human. (The movie's principal budget decision.) Some victims are caged, some put in glass display cases, and one fur-faced, three-eyed freak is kept behind a curtain. Humanon also keeps a professor's head alive, electronically, in his lab, and has a stun-ray scepter and a sound weapon. Bonus goodies: hypnotizing amulets, ray guns, and a horribly disfigured woman (made pretty at the end).

The plot of this hokey but lively sf-actioner looks back to the Thirties and *Island of Lost Souls* and *The Black Cat,* while much of the music is lifted from *Forbidden Planet.* Among the more outre elements: a vanishing midget, a stray man in a Halloween skeleton suit, and a boy who holes up in a mausoleum.

**KAMEN RIDER J** (J) Emotion 1994 anim color/ws 47m. (*Kamen Raida J*). Ref: TV: Bandai HV; no Eng. Weisser/JC:D:K. Amamiyor.

One of three aliens from a hovering spacecraft can turn into a dino-lizard. They apparently turn a human into superhero Kamen Rider, who carries a weird insect (good mandibles work here) around on his shoulder; cries "Kamen Rider J" as he transforms into his superhero form; at one point battles another insect-critter, and at the end takes on a giant thing. Plus an alien "newsreel" re dinosaurs and a bunch of cute little uglies which hatch on the ship.... Not up to the '93 *Kamen Rider* (see below), but action-crammed, with uneven but fun effects.

See also the following and *Masked Rider.*

**KAMEN RIDER ZETA 0** (*Kamen Rider Zo*)(J) Emotion 1993 color/ws 62m. D: K. Amamiya. Ref: TV: Bandai HV; no Eng. Weisser/JC.

Principals here include our motorcycling hero, who is apparently part grasshopper ... a ray-shooting metal man made out of junkyard junk ... Mr. Metal's spider aide, who mutates into a creepy-looking stop-motion spider-thing ... Mr. Metal's bat aide, who becomes a bat-thing which can morph into the image of a little boy's Papa, or into the image of the boy himself ... a conjured-up horror boy who mutates into Mr. Metal ... and a climactic, magical splicing together of Mr. Metal and Kamen Rider .... Or, Morphaville. Breathless pace, excellent effects, even some imagination here. Film represents the best of both worlds—computer and stopmo animation. Neat opening bit: the hero walking through the film's title. Top-drawer superhero story.

**KAMIKAZE** (F)  Les Films du Loup, ARP, Gaumont (Besson) 1986  color/ws  89m. SP, D: Didier Grousset. SP: also Luc Besson. Ph: J. -F. Robin. Adap: M. Halberstadt. Mus: Eric Serra. SpFX: G. Demetreau et al. Mkp: Landry, Blanchet. SdFX: Levy. Ref: MFB'89:114-15: "amiable triviality." V 12/17/86. Stanley. With Richard Bohringer, Michel Galabru, Dominique Lavanant.

"Half-baked thriller about a lunatic who invents a death ray that can kill people on television...." (V)

**KAMILLIONS**  Molesworth (Sally Aw/Robert Hsi, Teresa Woo) 1989 color 91m. SP, D: Mikel B. Anderson. SP & Jasmine Anim: H.S. Robins. Story: Hsi. Ph: Kathleen Beeler. Mus: K.H. Randolph. SpMkp & Creature FX: Jonathan Horton. Mech & Pyro FX: Jeff Robins. Ref: TV: vt. no Hound. no Stanley. no Martin. With Christopher Gasti, Dan Evans, Kate Alexander, Dru-Anne Cakmis, Laura O'Malley, David Allan Shaw.

"Desmon is a chameleon." A scientist is sucked through a "window to heaven" into a parallel universe; meanwhile, two little critters come our way. One, who has "incredible powers of mimicry," becomes a certain Desmon's double; the other—a sort of truant officer, or "babysitter from another dimension," with a tentacle-arm—transforms into a live replica of a poster girl. The fun-loving alien-Desmon conjures up a monster-phallus and a living fox-fur, and turns a woman into a bug with a woman's head, in a creepy, *Fly*-like sequence (Fifties version) .... Lackadaisical, intentionally stilted sf-comedy, with easy character types and scattered amusing moments and effects.

**KAMITSUKITAI/DORAKIYURA YORI AI-O** (J) Castos-Toho/M.M.I. 1991 (1990) color/ws 99m. (*My Soul Is Slashed* - vt t). D: Shunsuke Kaneko. Ref: TV: Toho Video; little English. Japan Video: *I Like To Bite* - tr t of vt version. Markalite 3:10: *From Dracula with Love* - tr t? VW 23:23: VSOM. Weisser/JC. With Ken Ogata, Narumi Yasuda, Hikaru Ishida, Takero Morimoto, Eisei Amamoto.

The regular blood supply gets mixed up with a blood bag from Count Dracula, and the patient in emergency dies, temporarily. His daughter drips blood on his ashes, and one night, a bat flies out of his crypt. ("Papa!") Papa understandably disconcerts those at home and office when he tries to resume his normal life. He tends to age quickly, but a blood bag always brings him back to par. At one point, he turns into a rat; at another, a Dracula cape makes him act predatory. Riddled with bullets, his torso ultimately "rejects" them.... A strange, sometimes taking mixture of horror, comedy, crime-drama, and soaper elements. Good score, photography. Film begins, enterprisingly, with a vampire-mannequin playlet.

**KANNIBALEN, Die** see *Canibais, Os*

**KAOS** (I)  Turner/RAI Channel l/Filmtre (De Negri)  1984 ('86-U.S.)  color  187m. SP, D: Paolo & Vittorio Taviani. From "Mal di Luna" and other short stories by Pirandello. SP: also Tonino Guerra. Ph: Giuseppe Lanci. Mus: Nicola Piovani. AD: F. Bronzi. Mkp: Cesare Paciotti. Ref:TV: MGM-UA HV; Eng. titles. MFB'84:327-8. V 9/12/84: werewolf. SFExam 4/25/86: 5 tales.

"Moonstruck," or "Mal di Luna," is a "wolf-man story done with ruthless psychological incisiveness rather than hairy makeup." (SFE) "Don't let me in." *A WereWolf of London*-like story re a

"moon that bewitched" Bata when he was a baby. "Every full moon, the sickness returns," for one night. ("He can be the wolf outside.") A tale expertly told, through deft editing, photography, and music, which latter make just enough and not too much of each turn of the plot.

The five stories here are made to seem to tell themselves; they appear to be propelled magically along. One, "La Giara" ("The Jar"), apparently concerns magic: Is the pot-mender the "devil's son"? Does he die and return to life? Does he personally hold the peasant in thrall during the midnight dance? What is the blackness which obscures our view of the breaking of the pot? Smooth, almost hypnotic fantasy-comedy stars Franco and Ciccio. Perhaps the most entrancing segment of all is the Epilogue, a fragmentary coda about remembrance.

**KAPPA** (J)  Herald/Cappadocia & Sony Music  1994  color/ws 118m. Ref: TV: Bandai HV; no Eng. People's Video. V 1/23/95:15: in Japan; 5th week.

A flying "eye" ... a little thing caught in a trap ... an apparently-stopmo baby alien and its parent ... apparently-computer-generated "water" in their cave ... an ambitious Symphony of a Countryside sequence, with aliens, boy hero, and community all in tune ... and the apparent death of the oldest alien.... The scenes with the aliens here are beautifully done, technically and emotionally. The surrounding movie doesn't seem to be quite up to them.

**KARARU MAU!** (J)  Toshiba 1989 anim color 79m. Ref: TV: vt; no Eng. dial.; songs in Eng.

A mad-ghoul-priest and his disciples seem to be responsible for a wide range of unearthly phenomena, including phantom clinging babies which sever a man's head, phantom priest-types which beset a school building, a mysterious leaping figure, and a fungus which infects a school girl's shoulder. Apparently opposing the priest: a ghost who at first appears bodiless and whose thick, undulating strands of hair make her look like an octopus.... If this monster movie looks to be routine, the supernatural menaces are at least many and varied. The use of the killer-baby-ghosts recalls *The Nine Demons*. Weirdest bit: the sudden croaking of the pickled, biology-lab frog. Scare score includes some *Halloween*-like music.

**The KARATE KID THROUGH TIME AND SPACE** (H.K.) Tomson Film Co. c1986? color c100m. Ref: TV: New Ship video; Eng. titles. Y. K. Ho: above is tr t.

A magnetic time tunnel brings "karate kid" Ho Yuan-jia from the Ching Dynasty to the present, where inventor Bell Chang's little robot Super Mary finds him "scary," and Yuan-jia, in turn, cries "Ghost!" at the sound of a voice on a phone. A thunderstorm-created time tunnel takes Yuan-jia, Super Mary, and two boys back to Yuan-jia's time, where he helps his father defeat some thugs. Another storm brings the two boys and the robot back to the present.... Incidental marvels: the "great exorcist," Bing-ging, and his five royal ghosts, Fame, Poison, Kindness, Brightness, and Illness ... Dr. O's laser gun, which can "disintegrate any object" ... Chang's magnetic belt, which attracts all the metal objects in a room to itself ... and his DK2 invention, which makes Yuan-jia fly.... Average kidstuff crosses *E.T.* with *The Karate Kid*.

Scorecard: silly martial-arts slapstick, occasional funny bits, okay effects.

**KARATE KOMMANDOS** see *Chuck Norris Karate Kommandos*

**KARLA CONTRA LOS JAGUARES** (Col.) Victor Films 197-? color 85m. D, P, Ph: Juan Manuel Herrera. SP: Sergio Alvarez Acosta. Mus: Albert Levy. Ref: TV: Video Latino; no Eng. With Marcela Lopez Rey, Gilberto Puentes, Maria Eugenia Davila, Wayne Jerolaman.

Flat, episodic sf/superhero saga re remote-control-operated "zombie" thugs. The brainwashing machines look like beauty-salon hairdryers. Can you spell "threadbare"?

See also *Jaguares contra el Invasor Misterioso, Los* (II).

**KASAL SA HUKAY** see *Regal Shockers*

**KATABI KO'Y MAMAW (MICHAEL + JORDAN)** (Fili) AMS Prods. c1989? color c115m. Story, D: Mike Relon Makiling. Ph: Ben Lobo. Mus: Jimmy Antiporda. PD: Orly Tolentino. Mkp: Gloria Vidallon. SdFX: Ramon Reyes. Ref: TV: Phil Am Video Int'l.; little Eng. With The Reycard Duet, Gloria Romero, German Moreno, Jeffrey Santos, Ana Roces, Apple Pie Bautista.

A family of ghosts murdered by thugs haunts a hacienda. The ghosts can appear and disappear, float through the house, and walk through walls—and they cast no reflection in mirrors. Comedy with some cute moments and spooky comic scenes.

**KATOTOHANAN O GUNIGUNI? THE MOVIE PART II** (Fili) JMC Films/Arjay Films Int'l. (Armando Arce) 1988? color c110m. SP, D: Jose Miranda Cruz. Ph: Popoy Orense. Mus D: Caloy Rodriguez. PD: Lito Cruz. Ref: TV: Viva Video; no Eng. J. J. Market: *Reality or Dream?* - tr t. With (1) Marianne de la Riva, Ronald Corveau, Bella Flores; (2) Arce, Delia Razon, Laila Dee, Offie Angeles; (3) Connie Angeles, Jocelyn Cruz, Jervy Cruz, Marilyn Bautista, Max Alvarado.

1) "Laman" (Inside the Body): An abandoned newborn transforms into a ghastly, glowing-eyed monster and haunts a stream until a priest performs an exorcism. Melodramatic nonsense enlivened only by the appearance of the comically horrible monster. 2) "Kaluluwa": Visions of her dead body haunt a man who strangled his wife with a towel, which latter eventually also strangles his mistress. Arce goes over the top, as his Anselmo goes out of his mind. The histrionics extend to the rest of the cast, as well as to the musical score. 3) " 'Yagit' Sa Pinto Ng Lagim" (Poor Kids through the Door of Horror): Blue-armed creatures transform into ray-shooting witches that trap and cage a family. A little girl who takes one of the witches' amulets then becomes a blue arm herself and can make the other blue meanies disappear. Odd, silly comedy-horror-fantasy is, by default, the most interesting of the three tales.

**KATY AND THE KATERPILLAR KIDS** (Mex-Sp) Televicine & Moro (Fernando de Fuentes) 1987 anim color 85m. (*Katy Meets the Aliens* - alt t). D: Santiago Moro. SP: Silvia Roche. Ph: Lopez, Rodriguez. Mus: Nacho Mendez. Anim & AD: Jose Luis Moro. VisFX: Manuel Tabernero, Juan Morata. Ref: TV: vt; Eng.-dubbed. Cable Video Store 12/91. V (Cannes '89): 490: sfa

*Katy, Kiki y Koko?* no Hound. no Martin. no Scheuer. no Maltin '92.

"Strange creatures" inhabiting an asteroid between Mars and Jupiter send one of their number, X, to Earth to search for food, to which end X transforms himself, in turn, into an ant, a flower, a hawk, Katy the butterfly (no fun for the kids), an octopus, and a balloon. (The latter breaks, but the pieces reassemble.) He traps tasty Earth creatures in a bubble. Also noted: the trees which, by night, seem living and monstrous to the kids ("It's scary!"), and a bit with a dragon.... Animated film for children is a fairly amusing, pleasant mixture of fantasy, sf, adventure, and comedy. One highlight: the hawk's "wild wind" number. Most of the songs have, at least, the virtue of brevity.

**KAYA PALAT** (India - Hindustani) Children's Film Society 1983 color 121m. SP, D: Satyan Bose. Dial: Aziz Quasi. Ph: A. Mitra. Mus: B. Chakraborty. Ref: Dharap. Library of Congress. With Anoopkumar, Suresh Chatwal, Ashok Kumar.

Doctor's drug turns adults "into children and vice versa."

**KAZE NO TANI NO NAUSHIKA** see *Warriors of the Wind*

**KEIKO EN PELIGRO** (Mex) Rahs (Hugo Stiglitz) 1989 color c80m.? D: Rene Cardona III. Co-Story, Co-SP: H. Stiglitz. Mus: Tino Geiser? AD: I. Ibarra. OptFX: Despo et al. Ref: TV; no Eng. TVG. SFChron 10/17/93; TV Week 6/12/93. V 5/2/90:242: *Keiko the Whale Is in Danger* - tr t. Cinef 6/96:47. With H. Stiglitz, Susana Dosamantes, Cesar Bono, Carlos East, Roberto Ballesteros, Maria Montana.

Telepathic aliens, a starfish-shaped spaceship, teleportation, telekinetic tricks, and a low-comedian hero. Science fiction and seagoing Earth critters, a la *Star Trek IV*. Typical treacle-and-fun kiddie-fare combo also apes E.T. when a boy is brought back to life by the aliens. Keiko later starred in *Free Willy*.

**KEKKO KAMEN, Vol. 1** (J) A.D. Vision/Dynamic Planning & Japan Columbia & Studio Signal (Nagai-Takayama-Minami) 1991 anim color c55m. D: N. Kondo; (number 2) S. Tokunaga. SP: M. Sogo. From the Go Nagai comics. SpFX: T. Sakakihara. SdFX: J. Sasaki. Ref: TV: ADV video; Eng. titles.

1. "Here I Am: The Messenger of Love and Justice!" The Toenail of Satan's Spartan Institution of Higher Education is a Nazi/Inquisition-angled "school from hell." Strange ideas of humor here.

2. "Crash! Kekko Kamen vs. Muscular Monster." A hint here that the Principal (aka The Toenail of Satan) is a demon. More bizarreness; a few laughs.

See also *Keko Mask.*

**KEKO MASK** (J) 1993 color 75m. (*Kekko Kamen*). D: Tomo Akiyama. From the Go Nagai comics. Ref: TV: VSOM; Eng. titles. Weisser/JC: guest bits by Mazinger Z and Urusei Yatsura? With Rei Nakano, Risa Kondou, Kazu Kujuku, Kenji Yamaguchi.

The jester-garbed principal of Spartan School can vanish at will, but lives to lament, "How could such a great person like me be dwarfed by a woman's sexual cavity?" Goofy, interminable, shot-on-tape comedy-fantasy is playful, but basically idiotic. Highlight: the Rolling Open Thigh trick. Other titles in the live-action series include *Keko Mask: The Movie* (1991) and *Keko Mask in Love* (1995); *Kekko Kamen* (1991) is the animated version.

**\*KELLY OF THE SECRET SERVICE** Victory 1936. Sets: Fred Preble. Lighting FX: Otto H. Buhner. Ref: TV. Turner/Price. Lentz. Lee (P). no V. no Stanley. no Hardy/SF. no Scheuer. no Maltin '92.

Dr. Howard Walsh's (John Elliott) "radio-controlled death bomb" would "make it absolutely impossible for an enemy to attack our country." Tested, the invention destroys a battleship 237 miles offshore. Dr. Marston (Forrest Taylor)—author of *Secrets of Hypnotism*—steals the bomb and hypnotizes Dr. Walsh into killing a secret service man. ("I'll make a killer out of anyone I choose.") There's also a secret attic room ("something spooky about this place") in Marston's "mysterious place".... The electric aerial-bomb gizmo is livelier than the story, which at best is sometimes entertainingly far-fetched. (Marston hypnotizes simply by aiming his ghostly hands at his subject.) Stilted acting.

**KHONG KHING** (Fili) Pelikulang 1988? color c103m. SP, D, P: Ramje. Prosth Mkp: Cecille Baun. Ref: TV: Viva Video; occ. Eng.

The anthropomorphic female ape Khong Khing leaves her Tarzan-type behind on an island and goes to the city to become a musical-comedy star with Vomva Films. Her movies include *The Sound of Khong Khing, The Singing Monkey,* and *Khong Khing in Wonderland.* She sings "Que Sera Sera" and "Monkey Who Needs Monkey." Silly, overlong fantasy-comedy, with a spooky Now-we'll-tell-a-story opening.

**KHOON KI PYASI** (India-Hindi) Singh & Co. c1989? color c140m. D: K. Chandra. Mus: Vijay Batalvi. Ref: TV: vt; little Eng. Bourbon House: *Thirst for Blood* - tr t.

Ingredients: a little girl who becomes a cowled monster which rips out a man's heart ... the enchantress's red, heart-shaped eye rays which she shoots into the hero's eyes ... demon possession ... ax gore ... a levitating lash ... floating, disembodied claws ... looming, freeze-frame "flashbacks" which haunt a man ... the arm of a ceiling fan which breaks off and attacks a woman ... and a man in a monster mask ("Oh, yes, it's me!").... Blood-and-thunder Indian shocker relies too much on cackling and screaming. Frenetic, campy song-and-dance sequences.

**KHOONI HAWAS** (India-Hindi) Shiva Int'l.(Anil Khanna) 1991 color c110m. SP,D: G.M. Kumar. Ph: Prabhakara. Mus: Ilayaraja. Mkp: Masilamani. Ref: TV: Madhu Video; no Eng. With Mohan.

The works: a vanishing priest who conjures up a storm and who shoots a cartoon spirit out of his eyes ... a cackling wraith which enters a man's mouth ... a swivel-headed lady ringed by animated, neon "hula hoops" ... a gent with fangs and glowing pink eyes ... an exorcist ... and a levitating pillow .... Supernatural-crammed, strictly-business horror movie doesn't take the usual time-outs for singing and dancing which most Indian movies do. Creepy: the bloody, slow-motion bouncing ball. Unexpectedly, Western-style horror cliches abound: the amplified heartbeat, the telekinetically-activated toys, subjective-camera creeping, shaking rooms, blood from faucets, and even a hand-on-shoulder shock.

**KICKBOXER FROM HELL** (H.K.?) IFD Films & Arts (Joseph Lai & Betty Chan) 1991 color c80m. (*Kickboxer* series. *Zodiac America 3: Kickboxer from Hell* - alt t). Story, PD, D: Alton Cheung. SP: Chris Lam. Ph: Peter Li. Mus: Stephen Tsang. SpFxD: Ben Au. Mkp: Jenny Choi. SdFX: Anthony Kim. Ref: TV: Magnum Video; Eng. version. With Mark Houghton, Sooni Shroff, Richard Edwards, Kieran Hanlon.

Monsters here include the painted-faced Lucifer, who needs a woman to sacrifice and who at one point raises one of his henchmen from the dead ... the "devil's disciples," who double as vampiric neck-biters ... and a possessed housecat that apparently doubles as the phantom lady in the wedding photos.... Clumsy, poorly-dubbed fantasy-horror-actioner borrows music from *Halloween.*

**A KID FROM TIBET** (H.K.) Yuen Biao Prods. 1991 color/ws 97m. D: Yuen Biao. Ref: TV: World Video; Eng. titles. VW 12:16-17. With Yuen Biao, Yuen Wah (sorcerer).

Principals include a hero with levitating and healing powers ("It's just magic"), an evil sorcerer whose supernaturally electric hands and voice cause all sorts of telekinetic havoc, and his evil sister, who also has *Carrie* powers. At stake: the Babu Gold Bottle of Tibet, which (in the climactic sequence) unleashes deadly flying-fireball-like ectoplasm.... Too cute, routine adventure-fantasy-comedy needs all the effects help it can get. Mainly just silly, with rather calculated scenic values ("tour" shots of Hong Kong and Tibet).

**KIDOUKEIJI JIBAN** (J) Toei Video 1989 color/ws 25m. Ref: TV: Toei Video; no Eng.

Effects-crammed semi-delight features weird, funny little animals ... a "man" who removes his head to reveal a three-eyed alien head ... two "women" who turn into aliens ... a heavy-duty, ray-shooting monster ... a tentacle monster ... a spider-ish thing ... an impressively-stopmo-animated, fire-breathing, *Alien*-plus creature ... and a jumpy, crawly thing.

**KIDS WHO FOUND ATLANTIS, The** see *Neptune's Children*

**KILL AND ENJOY** see *Maniac Killer*

**KILL KILL OVERKILL** USA-TV/Enco Studios (David Heavener, E. H. Warren et al.) 1991 color c90m.? (*Twisted Fate* - orig t). Story, D, Ph: Donald G. Jackson. Story, SP: Andrew Winnetka. Mus: Robert Garrett. AD: E. H. Warren. SpFX: Chuck Whitton. Mkp: A. Peterson. Ref: TV. TVG. With Bill Black, Susan Deemer, Troy Fromin, Nancy Jury, Julie Nine, Suzanne Solari, D. Heavener.

"Luther knows what's best." Peter Paul Fate (Black) likes girls; his brother Luther (Fromin) kills them. ("No, not her, Luther!") Their "new house" on Ravina Ridge turns out to be the vacation cabin for several coeds, one of whom stages a fake slashing. ("I love barbecue sauce!") The brothers take their video camera and tape their terrorization of them, and Luther later turns up in a coda for one last scream. ("You can't argue with Fate!")

Sometimes likably abysmal semi-slasher adopts a tacky-casual style, as one of the coeds tapes their outing. Aggravated-camp highlights include Luther's song re the brothers, and their "cheer": "Two four six eight, time to go exterminate."

**KILL THE WIFE** (H.K.?) 1994 color c90m. Ref: TV: World Video; no Eng. Mo. Wayne Chiu: above is tr t.

The madman here strangles a naked woman, cries, strangles another woman, sweats a lot, and tries to slash his wrist. Pretty tawdry-looking mixture of psycho thriller and softcore sex. Shot-on-tape. Plus a candles-and-sex ceremony.

**KILL TO LOVE** (H.K.) 198-? color feature. D: Tam Ming. Ref: Stanley. With Ching Hsia, Chung Cheung Lin.

Madman kills victims in "horrible ways."

**KILLBOTS** see *Chopping Mall*

**KILLER** Electro Video/T&T Ent. (Tony Locklear) 1990 color 81m. D, Co-P: Tony Elwood. SP: Mark Kimray. Mus: L. Mizzell. Ref: V 4/25/90:42(hv): "amateurish gore outing." With Duke Ernsberger, Andy Boswell, Jeri Keith Liles.

Medical guinea pig becomes hitchhiker-killing madman.

**KILLER BIRDS** (I) Filmirage & Flora (Variety) 1988 color/ws c90m. (aka *Killing Birds*). Story, D: Claude Milli aka C. Lattanzi. SP: Daniel Ross aka D. Stoppa. Story: also S. Goldberg. Ph: F. Slonisco. Mus: Carlo Maria Cordio. Ref: TV: VSOM; Eng.-lang. version. Hardy/HM2: aka *Raptors*. M/TVM 5/88:41: "horror." V 5/4/88:322. VSOM: aka *Dark Eyes of the Zombies*. Palmerini. With Lara Wendel, T. W. Watts, Robert Vaughn, Leslie Cummins, James Villemaire, Sal Maggiore, Jr.

"Never seen so many birds in all my life!" Surpassingly vacuous shocker features apparent zombies, Aviary Delight, an incidental garroting-by-machine, other gore, a slasher, a crucified reporter (or is it an hallucination?), and even a "There's something about this place."

See also *Beaks*.

**KILLER CROCODILE** (I) Fulvia (Fabrizio De Angelis) 1989 color feature. D: Larry Ludman. SP: David Parker Jr., Ludman. Ph: F. Del Zoppo. Ref: V/Cannes '89:499: completed. VSOM: "giant croc in Amazon." Palmerini. With Anthony Crenna, Van Johnson.

**KILLER CROCODILE 2** (I) Fulvia (Roger Hack) 1990 color feature. SP, D, SpCroc: Giannetto DeRossi. Story, SP: D. Parker Jr. SP: also Larry Ludman. Ph: Giovanni Bergamini. Mus: Riz Ortolani. Mkp: Cristina DeRossi. SpSetFX: Paolo Ricci. Ref: TV: MV; Eng. dubbed. no Stanley. Palmerini. With Anthony Crenna, "Debra Karr," Thomas Moore, Terry Baer, Hector Alvarez, Tony DeNoia.

"This swamp is cursed!" Radioactive waste apparently creates a giant, roaring croc on Florida's Isabella River ("There's another one!"), and the "monster" threatens construction of the "largest resort of the Americas." ("It knows we're here.") All cliches, down to the *Jaws*-type music.

The **KILLER INSTINCT** (Can.) Pan-Canadian Video/Cineplex 1982('85-U.S.) color 96m. (3P *Trapped* - orig t). D: William Fruet. SP: John Beaird. Ref: vc box. Lentz. MFB'83:109. Stanley. no Hound. no Martin. no VWB. With Henry Silva, Nicholas Campbell, Barbara Gordon.

Madman stalks campers.

**KILLER KLOWNS FROM OUTER SPACE** TWE/Sarlui-Diamant (Chiodo Bros.) 1988 (1987) color 88m. (aka *Killer Klowns*). SP, D, P: Stephen Chiodo. SP, PD, P, Clown Des: Charles Chiodo. Mus: John Massari. SpVisFX: Fantasy II; (sup) Gene Warren Jr. SpFX: (coord) Tassilo Baur; (addl) Image Engnrng. SpProps: Modelwerke's. Stopmo: Justin Kohn. Sp Dialect: David Nichols. Ref: TV. V 6/8/88. 4/22/87:30. 5/6/87:116(ad), 294. SFExam 4/17/87: E-1. With Grant Cramer, Suzanne Snyder, John Allen Nelson, Royal Dano, John Vernon, Michael Siegel, Peter Licassi; Steve Rockhold, M. H. Burris, Geno Ponza et al. (Klowns).

"I love the circus!" A "shooting star" brings a circus-tent spaceship and alien clowns ("things from another planet") to Earth— and these Klowns use ray guns to cocoon their food-supply victims in "cotton candy." Also look for the jack-in-the-box creatures from the popcorn.... Plot and characters tiredly parody Fifties monster movies, and the Invasion of the Circus Clowns novelty is somewhat squandered. However, the Chiodos come up with some bizarre scenes for their Klowns. The best include some lethal shadow-play in which a Klown's shadow-dinosaur gobbles up onlookers, and a "ventriloquism" stunt which concludes with a Klown extracting its bloody hand from the back of Officer Mooney (Vernon).

**KILLER MIND** see *Mente Asesina*

**KILLER MUST STRIKE AGAIN** (I-F) Albione? & Agit? & Paris Cannes(Giuseppe Tortorella) 1976 color/ws 90m. (*L'Assassino E Costretto Ad Uccidere Ancora*). Story, SP, D: Luigi Cozzi. Story, SP: also Daniele del Giudice. Mkp: G. Ferrant. Ref: TV: vt; Eng. dubbed. MV: aka *The Dark Is Death's Friend*.

"The sea is strange .... It's so strange here, so creepy." Facile suspenser/*giallo* with a few horror sequences set in a deserted old house by the sea. ("Baby, we're in Dracula's castle.") There, the killer does strike again — he stabs a woman to death with a butcher knife. There's also a *Psycho* body-in-car dunking. Prime dubbed line: "You belong in an institution!"

**KILLER NERD** Hollywood Home (Bosko-Harold) 1991 color feature. SP, D, P: Mark Steven Bosko, Wayne A. Harold. Ref: PT 11:51: "bloody & shocking." 12:6. Fango 122:8. With Toby Radloff, Alan Mothersbaugh.

Nerd cracks, dispatches victims with acid, dynamite, and axe.

Sequel: *Bride of the Killer Nerd*.

**KILLER OF PRETTY WOMEN** (Thai) 198-? color/ws c88m. Ref: TV: vt; no Eng. Thai Video: above is tr t.

A magic potion brings a man back as, alternately, a wormy-faced apparition and an invisible spirit that seems to make its victims kill themselves.... Tacky script, production. Funniest scare scene: the haunted cop crying in horror at the sight of a levitating phone receiver. The spectacle of talking noses at either end of the TV screen indicates a widescreen film.

**KILLER PARTY** (Can.) MGM/Polar-Marquis 1986 color 90m. (aka *Fool's Night*). D: William Fruet. SP: Barney Cohen. Mus:

John Beal. SpVisFX: Frank Carere. SpProsthFX: G. J. Smith. OptFX: Moses Weitzman. Ref: TV. V 5/28/86. With Martin Hewitt, Ralph Seymour, Elaine Wilkes, Joanna Johnson (Jennifer), Paul Bartel.

On April Fool's Night, in a haunted house (an "old frat house"), the spirit of a man dead twenty years possesses Jennifer, then Phoebe. Result: murders with trident, hammer, guillotine, etc.... A mechanical crossing of slasher and *Exorcist*-type movies. Both of the two "false starts" here are marginally more interesting than the actual story.

**The KILLER RESERVED NINE SEATS** (I)  Midnight Video/Cinenove(Dario Rossini) 1974 color 95m. (*L'Assassino Ha Riservato Nove Poltrone*). SP, D: Giuseppe Bennati. SP: also Biagia Proietti, Paolo Levi. Ph: Giuseppe Aquari. Mus: Carlo Savina. PD: Mario Chiari. Mkp: Granati, Giulio. Ref: TV: MV; Eng. dubbed. Palmerini. With Rossana Schiaffino, Chris Avram, Lucretia Love, Eva Cemerys, Janet Agren, Howard Ross.

"Looks like Dracula's summer home." Ingredients here include a theatre troupe locked overnight in an abandoned theatre ... a mystery man in a Nehru jacket who says he was there 100 years ago, too, and apparently isn't kidding ... a magically-restored, would-be death rope ... an "old legend" which says that partygoers there 100 years ago were found "dead and mutilated" ... an impromptu crucifixion ... a caped guy in a creepily funny mask (is he the slasher/ghost?) ... 500-year-old parchments which "predict" the night's events ... and a cellar crypt.

This *Killer* has its cake, eats it, and has a side of fries. The multiple resolutions of the plot involve madness, a murder plot, and a ghost. It's like a "Twilight Zone" puzzler with three or four equally valid solutions. Characterization is for the most part functional, but the masks and scenery provide a bit of atmosphere.

**KILLER TOMATOES EAT FRANCE!**  Fox/KT Ent./Twin Pics (Four Square/Peace) 1991 color 94m. (*Killer Tomatoes Go to France* - shooting t. *Killer Tomatoes Eat France: Les Tomats Francais Munch Munch* - cr t). SP, D, P: John DeBello. SP: also C. Dillon, J.S. Peace. Ph: Kevin Morrisey. Mus: R. Patterson. PD: R. Brill. SpTomatoes: Character Innovations. Anim: Craig Berkos. SpFxEngnrg: Michael Lambert. Ref: TV: Fox Video. V 1/28/91:24. TVG 12/5/92. Martin. SFChron Dtbk 11/15/92. With John Astin, Marc Price, Angela Visser, Steve Lundquist, Bruno Toussaint (Hunchback of Notre Dame).

Third follow-up to *Attack of the Killer Tomatoes!* (II), and "Part IV of the Tomatoes Trilogy," features Fuzzy Tomato, pop star, sort of a vegetable Barry Manilow ... tomato punk rockers ... The Phantom-ato of the Opera, a "giant, fire-breathing tomato" ... and a "Red Menace" doomsday prophecy for France.... Rating: Rarely in Danger of Locating a Laugh. Limp movie-in-progress in-jokes, cute "Ninja Turtle" gag.

**KILLER TOMATOES STRIKE BACK**  New World/Four Square (S. Peace) 1990 color 88m. D, Exec Co-P: John DeBello. SP: Constantine Dillon, Rick Rockwell. Ph: S. Andrich. Ref: V 4/25/90:18. 5/2/90:86. Martin: "an all-time low." PT 11:62. With John Astin, R. Rockwell.

Second follow-up to *Attack of the Killer Tomatoes!* (II)

**KILLER WORKOUT**  see *Aerobicide*

**KILLING BIRDS**  see *Killer Birds*

**KILLING BOX, The**  see *Ghost Brigade*

**KILLING CARS** (W.G.)  Futura Film/Sentana Film (Mario Krebs/Hessischer Rundfunk) 1986 ('87-U.S.) color 104m. SP, D: Michael Verhoeven. Mus: Michael Landau. Sets: Norbert Scherer. Wondercar: The Albar Sonic. SpFX: Harry Wiessenhaan, Guenther Schaidt. Mkp: Margret Neufink et al. Ref: TV: Vidmark video; Eng. version. V 3/26/86. Dr. Rolf Giesen. With Juergen Prochnow, Senta Berger, Agnes Soral, Daniel Gelin, Bernhard Wicki, Peter Matic, William Conrad.

"They've taken the prototype." A technologist's (Prochnow) top-secret Worldcar—an "electro-chemical ... ecologically-sound car"—promises to spark a "revolution in the motor industry," but eco-terrorists take a joyride in the prototype, and Dr. Hein (Matic) decides to destroy it. ("The project is cancelled.") Sf-actioner becomes an uninvolving game of Car, car, who's got the car?

**The KILLING EDGE** (B)  Video City/Lindsay Shonteff Film Prods. (Elizabeth Gray) 1986 ('87-U.S.) color c86m. D: Lindsay Craig Shonteff. SP: Robert Bauer. Ph: Hugh Williams. Mus: John Dinsdale. Ref: TV: Video City (Chop-'Em-Up Video). Martin. no Hound. Phantom mention. With Bill French, Mary Spencer, Paul Ashe, Al Lampert (Terminator Seven), Matthew Waterhouse, Aidan James.

June 25, "in the middle of the nuclear winter." Radiation sickness has killed off most people on Earth, and Terminators patrol the last "green valley" in England and terrorize slave workers. The latter's only hope: Steve Johnson (French), whose wife and son were shot by a Terminator.... Shoestring, shot-on-tape production's only plus: a winningly against-all-odds, upbeat finish. Budget *Road Warrior* has no humor and a treacly score.

**KILLING SPREE**  Twisted Illusions (Al Nicolosi) 1990 color 86m. SP, D, Exec P: Tim Ritter. Mus: P. Monroe. SpMkpFX: Joel Harlow, Mark Pederson. Ref: V 4/8/91:71 (hv): "makeup effects ... the only reason to watch this one." Martin. V 10/19/88:142. McCarty II: "amateurish throughout." With Asbestos Felt, Courtney Lercara, Raymond Carbone, Dwayne Willis.

Gory killings.

**KIN-DZA-DZA** (Russ.)  1987? D: Georgy Danelia. Ref: V 7/1/87:51 (ad). with Stanislav Lubshin, Yevgeny Leonov, Yuri Yakovlev.

Comedy re two earthlings on another planet.

**The KINDRED**  F/M Ent. (Kindred Ltd.) 1987 (1986) color 92m. SP, D, P: Jeffrey Obrow. SP, D, Ph: Stephen Carpenter. SP: also John Penney, Earl Ghaffari, Joseph Stefano. Mus: David Newman. SpMkpFX: Matthew Mungle. Sp Creatures: Michael John McCracken. SpMechFX: Lars Hauglie. Ref: TV. MFB '87:179. V 1/21/87. ad. SFExam 1/9/87. With David Allen Brooks, Rod Steiger, Amanda Pays, Talia Balsam, Kim Hunter, Timothy Gibbs, Peter Frechette, Julia Montgomery.

"I change the course of human evolution." Dr. John Hollins (Brooks) discovers that his mother (Hunter) spliced some of his cells with those of a non-human animal and produced a monstrous hybrid "brother," Anthony. At the end, the latter melts down to human form, then degenerates into mere slime. But the latter brings forth baby creatures.... Steiger and the other actors are subservient to effects here, and even the latter are variable, if not in quality, then in degree of originality. Anthony is a familiar *Alien* mix of teeth and tentacles, while the newly contaminated Melissa (Pays) begins turning fishy (gills pulse on her cheeks, and her ears implode), in a happily ghastly makeup effects scene.

**KING ARTHUR** see *Young King Arthur*

**KING DONG** see *Lost on Adventure Island*

**\*\*\* KING KLUNK** Univ 1933 anim 9m. Ref: screen. William K. Everson. PFA notes 1/19/88. Everson/More Classics: 36,37. MW 3:6. Imagen. MMF 6:62. Glut/CMM.

Adventurer Pooch the Pup sets out to capture Monster-King Klunk, the giant ape that lords it over the island's Hot-Cha tribe. Cupid sees to it that Klunk falls for Pooch's girl friend, and—as in this cartoon's inspiration, *King Kong*—beauty levels beast. Klunk burns, turns into a skeleton, and revives as same only long enough to nix Cupid's "goona goona" refrain.

Highlights: Klunk boxing with a dinosaur—Pooch provides a blow-by-blow description ... Klunk climbing a skyscraper and squeezing out the occupants ... the bizarre skeleton coda.

**\*2 KING KONG** 1933. Ph: Eddie Linden. SdFX: Murray Spivack. Ref: TV. V 3/7/33. Lentz. Hardy/HM. With Ethan Laidlaw, Vera Lewis, Dick Curtis, Paul Porcasi, Lynton Brent.

"No chains'll ever hold that!" Entrepreneur Carl Denham (Robert Armstrong) is out to "make the greatest picture in the world." He plans to star down-and-out Ann Darrow (Fay Wray) opposite "something monstrous, all-powerful," reputed to inhabit an island found only on the map of the "skipper of a Norwegian bark"—an island "way west of Sumatra," in the East Indies. On "Denham's island," she will be the "bride of Kong," a gigantic ape that rules a realm of dinosaurs ....

The legendary movie about the legendary ape is replete with racism, sexism, and terrible moments (most of the latter thanks to the otherwise likable Bruce Cabot), but in general is beautifully done. It's a once-in-a-lifetime blend of mystery, horror, adventure, and comedy, though its thrill-a-minute pace doesn't leave much time for continuity, character (except Kong's), or atmosphere. Here and there, close-ups of a huge, immobile head temporarily stop the stop-motion show, but this is one of the few fantasy film classics which doesn't stint on the effects. There are even "afterthought" effects: the dying stegosaur's tail thrashing one last time ... the "buzzardodactyl" probing the carcass of the tyrannosaur. There's terror below (from the lizard, the giant snake, the brontosaurus), terror above (from Kong above the chasm, from the pterodactyl), and terror waiting for you around the bend (Kong and the el). Creatures—the stegosaur, the pterodactyl—will appear, first, in the background, then disappear, then return frighteningly close. Kong himself is both vicious monster

and tragic victim, as the film alternates between shock tactics and surreal heart-tugs.

**KING KONG LIVES** DEG/Martha Schumacher 1986 color/ws 105m. D: John Guillermin. SP, Exec P: Ronald Shusett. SP: also Steven Pressfield. Mus: John Scott. SpVisFxSup: Barry Nolan. Creatures: Carlo Rambaldi. Mkp: (sp fx) Dean Gates; G. DeRossi. SpFX: (coord) Joseph Mercurio; SpFxUnltd.; (sup min) David Jones; (sp action min sup) Dave Kelsey. Ref: TV. V 12/24/86. With Peter Elliot (King Kong), George Yiasomi (Lady Kong), Brian Kerwin, Linda Hamilton, John Ashton.

Ten years after the end of *King Kong* (1976), the Atlantic Institute buys Lady Kong. King Kong revives, carries off his lady, and makes campy googoo eyes at her. Soon, Lady Kong is big, very big, with child, and the King protects her and gets to see Baby before he dies.... A lot of fuss over a love scene, a birth scene, and a death scene. Alternately trivial and grandiose script is all cliches—e.g., callous military, concerned hero and heroine. Guillermin and company are as inept as Bert I. Gordon at making monsters look BIG. Best credit: "Miniature Foreman."

See also: *Dragon Ball. Khong Khing. King Kung Fu. Lost on Adventure Island. Man Size. Munecas del King Kong* (P). *Scooby-doo and the Reluctant Werewolf. Timefighters in the Land of Fantasy.*

**KING KONG'S FIST** (W.G.-U.S.) Seybold-NDR & IFP 1984 color 77m. (*King Kongs Faust*). SP, D, Co-Ph: Heiner Stadler. SP: also Ulrich Enzenzberger, Lilly Targownik. Story: Rolf Giesen. Mus: Gerhard Stabler. Sets: C. J. Pfeiffer, Monika Grube. Ref: screen. PFA notes 1/10/85. Dr. Rolf Giesen. V 2/13/85. no Stanley. With Leonard Lansink, Werner Grassmann, Heinz van Nouhuys, Wim Wenders, Laslo Benedek, Bert Willis.

The search for the creator of the original Kong's paw leads a reporter (Lansink) from the 1984 Berlin Film Festival to a certain Conway, in London, who possesses the huge, hairy hand, and, finally, to Yucatan. Our hero hears stories of "this ape in Hollywood" and of the fanatically-exacting man, Bodo Wawerka, who made the hand. ("The hand became more and more expensive.") He sees a German-dubbed tape of *King Kong* and a colorized version, on TV. His researches (and fabrications) lead to the showing of a documentary about Wawerka, "King Kongs Faust," at the 1985 Berlin Festival.... Spare, droll, low-key satire re filmania and publishing. Enough material for an anecdote, if not quite a 77-minute movie. The point, after all, is that not much is happening. Wawerka is a myth.

**KING KUNG FU** King Gemini/Walterscheid or Walerscheid 1990 color 95m. SP, D, Ph: Lance D. Hayes. Postprod Sup: Herbert L. Strock. Ref: V 7/4/90: "puerile entertainment is easy to watch." With John Balee (King Kung Fu), Maxine Gray, Tom Leahy.

Spoof of *King Kong* re martial-arts gorilla that falls from top of Holiday Inn. Completed in 1987.

**KING OF THE STREETS** see *Alien Warrior*

**KINGDOM, The** see *Riget*

**KINGDOM OF THE VAMPIRE** [Note: revised entry; slightly different title] Suburban Tempe (Bookwalter/DeCoteau) 1991 color 70m. (*Kingdom of the Vampires* - ad t). Story, D & Ed: J.R. Bookwalter. SP, Story, Mus: M.J. Walsh. Ph: Lance Randas. SpMkp: David Lange. P: S.P. Plummer. Ref: TV: Cinema HV. PT 15:13: "moves at a snail's pace." With M.J. Walsh, Cherie Patry, Shannon Doyle.

"Reluctant vampire" goaded by Mom.(PT) "I was hungry, Jeff." *Sleepwalkers*-like tale of a mother-and-son vampire team is ineptly staged and pretty primitive, technically. ("I'm old—older than time.") Some stray, okay ghoulish lines for Mom; the rest of the dialogue and music is dismaying at best. Shot-on-tape.

**KIRA** see *Ultima Casa vicino al Lago, L'*

**KISHIN CORPS: ACTIVE DEFENSE FORCES, Vol. 1** (J) Pioneer & Masaki Yamada & Chuokoronsha (Yamada-Tamura) 1994? anim color c60m. (*Kishin Heidan*). D: Takaaki Ishiyama. From M. Yamada's novel. Ph: M. Ikegami. Mus: Kaoru Wada. AD: M. Nakamura. Mecha Des: Yamazaki, Watanabe. SpFX: Masahiro Murakami. SdFX: M. Itoh. Ref: TV: Pioneer video; Eng. dubbed.

"Mission Call for Kishin Thunder." Kishin Thunder, a huge, human-operated robot, vs. the "unknown enemy"—laser-shooting aliens. Sf, action, and World War II-style intrigue. Okay score and alien design.

**The KISS** (U.S.-Can.) Tri-Star & Astral/Trilogy Ent. & Richard B. Lewis/First Choice Canadian (Canada Inc.) 1988 color 98m. (*The Host* - orig t). D: Pen Densham. Story, SP: Stephen Volk. SP: also Tom Ropelewski. SpMkpFX: Chris Walas. Mus: J. P. Robinson. SpFX: Les Productions de l'Intrigue. Ref: TV. MFB'89:240-41. V 10/21/88. Jones. With Pamela Collyer, Peter Dvorsky, Joanna Pacula (Felice), Meredith Salenger, Jan Rubes.

"Sort of strange" model and jet-setter Felice tries to pas the Salamander of Horror (the "family spirit"?), mouth-to-mouth, to niece Amy (Salenger), but fails. Felice proves to have corpse's blood in her and can invoke, via voodoo, a fabulous furry freak-thing. The voodoo-spell business gets pretty monotonous in this glorified effects vehicle.

**KISS ME, GENTLE RUBBER** (Yug.) Zvonko Coh 1984? anim 6m. Ref: screen. PFA notes 11/16/84.

Weird moon/planet of living hatracks, a robot, and other odd life-forms. Offbeat, offputting variation on Tex Avery's *The Cat That Hated People*.

**KISS ME MONSTER** (Sp-W.G.) Atlas Int'l./Aquila Film & Films Montana(Adrian Hoven) 1967 color/ws 75m.(79m.) (*Besame Monstruo.* aka *Castle of the Doomed*). SP, D: Jesus Franco. SP: also Luis Revenga. Ph: Jorge Herrero, Franz Hofer. Mus: Jerry van Rooyen. Sets: Carlos Viudes, Graf Pilati. Ref: TV: vt; Eng. dubbed. VWB. Hardy/HM. Necronomicon 6. Stanley. With Janine Reynaud, Rossana Yanni, A. Hoven, Michel Lemoine, Chris Howland, Ana Casares.

"There's some kind of madman who's developing humans out of tin cans." With conditioning and "special drugs"—including a "nutrition solution"—Prof. Bertand has "created two fully developed, physical beings, artificially," Andros-1 and Andros-2 (sp?). Plus a "secret sect" ... brief eye-gore ... and a "super-quick-acting narcotic" .... Scarecard: an occasionally amusing, generally ap-

palling casualness to the writing and directing ... mindless marking-time scenes ... a Sixties Vapid musical score ... and the line "I was taken prisoner by a group of queer virgins and was put in a cage."

Follow-up: *Case of the Two Beauties.*

**KISS OF DEATH** see *Soultaker*

**KISS OF THE BEAST** see *Meridian*

**KISS OF THE SERPENT** (Fili) 1988 color feature (*Snake Island* - alt t). D: James Ingrassia. Ref: Monster! 3:58: "hasn't the same charisma as a *Zuma* movie."

Killer turns into a "giant rubber serpent."

**KITCHEN SINK** (N.Z.) Bridget Ikin 1989 b&w 14m. D: Alison Maclean. Ref: V 10/18/89:36: Best Short, Sitges. 10/11/89:17: "comedic horror pic." 10/18/89:36. SFChron 3/11/93: "excellent." SFChron Dtbk 3/7/93. 8/22/93: "horror genre conventions."

**KITTY KORNERED** WB 1946 anim color 7m. D: Bob Clampett. Ref: TV. WBCartoons.

Four cats masquerade as Martians, scare their master, Porky Pig. Wildly inventive Looney Tunes free-for-all. Porky keeps an emergency shotgun in a glass case labeled "Use only in case of invasion from Mars." The smallest cat keeps getting batted about by Sylvester for admitting to a mouse-like fondness for cheese. Minimum twenty wonderful gags.

**KNIFE OF ICE** (I-Sp) VSOM/Tritone & Mundial 1972 color/ws 88m. (*Il Coltello di Ghiaccio*). Story, SP, D: Umberto Lenzi. SP: also Antonio Troisio. Ph: Jose F. Aguayo Jr. Mus: Marcello Giombini. Ref: TV: VSOM; Eng.-dubbed. Palmerini. With Carroll Baker, Alan Scott, Eduardo Fajardo, Evelyn Stewart, Jorge Rigaud, Franco Fantasia.

Is the slasher a "sex maniac" after "young, fair-haired women" ... a killer who disappears into thin air, "just like a demon"? Hints of supernatural influences include a "black magic symbol," a devil worshiper, a black-mass site, a devil sign in a tree, and a thunderstorm or two .... Black magic is a red herring here. All is explained in a second, in Baker's campy, climactic "murderer" look, in this flavorless *giallo*, complete with an expected mute-speaks climax. Some tries at atmosphere. Closest approximation of eerie: the shot of the bicycle wheels spinning in the dark.

**KNIGHT MOVES** (U.S.-G) Lamb Bear Ent./Ink Slinger/El Khoury-Defait 1992 color 115m. (aka *Face to Face*). D: Carl Schenkel. SP, Exec Co-P: Brad Mirman. Ph: D. Lohmann. PD: Graeme Murray. Ref: V 4/27/92: "slick and occasionally suspenseful thriller." SFChron 1/22/93: "strains credulity." SFChron Dtbk 8/15/93. Imagi 1:56. With Christopher Lambert, Diane Lane, Tom Skerritt, Ferdinand Mayne.

Serial killer drains blood of victims.

**KNIGHT OF THE DRAGON, The** see *Star Knight*

**KNIGHT RIDER** NBC-TV/Univ-TV & Glen Larson 1984 color c90m. Ref: TVG 9/30/84 (ad): "two-hour movie premiere." with

David Hasselhoff, Patricia McPherson, Jim Brown, Barbara Stock, Evan Kim.

A mad scientist (Jared Martin) plots to use robots and "drone cars" in a bank robbery.

See also the following and *Amazing Stories—The Movie III*: "Remote Control Man."

**KNIGHT RIDER: KNIGHT OF THE JUGGERNAUT** NBC-TV/Univ-TV & Glen Larson 1985 color c90m. D: George Fenady. SP: Robert Foster, Burton Armus. Ph: H. J. Penner. Mus: Don Peake. AD: Lou Montejano. Mkp: Jeremy Swan. OptFX: Univ. Title. Ref: TV. TVG (ad): "two-hour movie premiere." With David Hasselhoff, Pater Parros, Edward Mulhare, John Considine, Nicholas Worth, Pamela Susan Shoop, Lawrence Haddon, Mary Woronov.

Super-car with "satellite scanner," "reverse polarity destabilizers," "zero-gravity induction system," "super-pursuit mode," etc., vs. a vehicle with a battering ram. Plus a radioactive "new element." TV-movie is strictly standard, if the equipment isn't.

**KNIGHT RIDER 2000** NBC-TV/Univ-TV (Charles Sellier & Riven Rock/Michele G. Brustin) 1991 color c90m. D: Alan J. Levi. Tel & P: Rob Hedden. Ph: Billy Dickson. Mus: Jan Hammer. PD: Bill Cornford. VisFX: (sup) Tim McHugh; (coord) Bob Kane. SpFX: Tim Ornec. Mkp: Shelly Woodhouse. Ref: TV. TVG 5/18/91. With David Hasselhoff, William Daniels, Susan Norman, Edward Mulhare, Carmen Argenziano, Megan Butler.

"The future is here—and it's in big trouble." Michael Knight is back, now with the Knight 4000, in the year 2000. The new car has an "engine that goes from 0 to 300 ... in the wink of an eye." (TVG) Ad: "He can see through walls."

**KNIGHTS** Moonstone Ent./Kings Road Ent. (Tom Karnowski) 1993 (1992) color 94m. SP, D: Albert Pyun. Ph: G. Mooradian. Mus: Tony Riparetti. SpMech & MkpFX: David Barton. Opt.: Fantasy II. PD: Phil Zarling. SpFxSup: Guy Faria. SpMkpFxKey: Brian Sipe. Ref: TV. Imagi 1:57: "a triumph of atmosphere over believability." V 3/15/93:20 (rated): "futuristic violence." 6/22/92:9 (ad). Martin. Stanley. With Kathy Long, Kris Kristofferson (robot), Lance Henriksen (Job, cyborg ruler), Scott Paulin, Gary Daniels, Nicholas Guest, Clare Hoak.

"We need the blood of 10,000 humans." A cross between *Goliath and the Vampires* and *Mutant Hunt* (and the latter's casual cy-gore), shot in John Ford country. In sum: awe-inspiring scenery, less-than-awesome screenplay, with one macabre twist—the future here is man-made vampires. ("Harvest their blood!")

**KNOCK, KNOCK ... WHO'S THERE?** (Fili) Golden Lion Films 1987 color c115m. SP, D: Carlo J. Caparas. SP: also Joey De Leon. Ph: Ramon Marcelino. Mus D: Spanky Ragor. AD: Jing Ramos. Monster Cost: Gregorio Otico. Anim & OptFX: Gerry Garcia. Mkp: Carmen Encendencia, Dani Cuyno. SdFX: Danny Salvador. Ref: TV: Viva Video; little Eng. With De Leon, Jimmy Santos, Richard & Raymond, Joe Estrada, Encendencia.

A strange tree outside a large mansion harbors two captive boys. Axed, the tree transforms into an ape-like creature which proves to rule an underground domain of mini-demons which stash prisoners behind an invisible shield. Near the end, the big demon revives the local dead—demons and humans alike—and a bride-and-groom zombie pair, separated in life, reunite and embrace in death.... *Knock, Knock* is a cross between the standard Filipino ghost comedy and a full-fledged Filipino fantasy film. The comedy half alternates between droll black comedy (much play with the dead stiff body of the groom) and routine knockabout humor, while the fantasy elements are offbeat and inventive. A pleasant minor surprise.

**KOD AVAGY HOLDARNYEK LEVUBU FOLOTT** (Hung.) Hunnia Film & Magyar Televizio (Lendvai-Drabik) 1994 color 93m. SP, D: Krisztina Deak. SP: also Andor Szilagyi. Ph: G. Balog. Mus: L. Melis. AD: J. Romvari. Ref: V 5/9/94: "nebulous scripting and foggy direction." With Idiko Toth, Adel Kovats, George Tabori.

"Two beautiful sisters haunted by family ghosts and a destructive curse ... apocalyptic results." *Mist, or Moonlight Shadow over Levubu* - tr t?

**KOESI** (S. Korean) Han Lim Cinema (Chung So Young) 1981 color 90m. (aka *Strange Dead Bodies*). D: Kang Bum Koo. SP: Choo Dong Woon. Ph: Yang Young Kil. Ref: Hardy/HM: "quite ... effective." With Kang Myung, Yoo Kwang Ok.

A new insecticide starts bringing back the dead.

**KOJIKI** see *Yamato Takeru*

**KOKAK** (Fili) Regal Film Int'l./Seiko Films 1989 color c110m. D: Leroy Salvador. SP: Orlando Nadres. Story: Ruben Marcelino, serialized in Darna Komiks. Ph: C. Austria. Mus D: Benny Medina. PD: Jonathan Salvador. SdFX: Jun Martinez. Mkp: Zeny Huganas. Ref: TV: Regal Video; occ. English. With Gabby Concepcion, Pinky Suarez, Jennifer Sevilla, Cesar Montano, Rita Avila.

"This is incredible!" The Fairy of the Falls curses Kara for her father's wrongs: Periodically, without warning, she becomes a garden-variety, regular-sized frog. (At one point, her human-to-frog transformation scares an evil hunter into quicksand.) The hero, Leo ("I just want to go back to nature, live a simple life"), wants to marry her, but his ex-girl friend, Susie, breaks up the wedding ceremony by shooting Kara in the leg. Kara reverts to frog form.... Or, the Curse of the Werefrog. Charming camp. Kara's abrupt transformations are not played for comedy, but they are comedy. Music and actors play it straight, but it's no use. Bizarre Psychology highlight: Kara, in frog form, jealously jumps on Susie as she lies in bed with Leo. Volumes could be written.

See also: *Who Killed the Frog.*

**KO-KO HOPS OFF** Alfred Weiss/Max Fleischer 1927 anim and live silent 6 1/2m. Ref: TV: The Inkwell Imps. Cabarga/TFS.

Bit with giant sea-monster-like fish which roars. And cute bits with Ko-Ko's dog Fitz.

See also the following and *Chemical Ko-Ko.*

**KO-KO'S CONQUEST** Alfred Weiss/Max Fleischer 1927 anim and live silent 8m. Ref: TV: The Inkwell Imps. Cabarga/TFS: '29 release.

Oddball Ko-Ko and Fitz cartoon has a startling sequence in which five hanged, hooded men jump down from their nooses and form one big, ape-like monster. Weird.

**2 KOKO'S EARTH CONTROL** Alfred Weiss 1928 (1927) anim and live. Ref: TV: The Inkwell Imps; UM&M-TV. Cabarga/TFS: 26, 211.

Koko and his dog trek across the world to the Control of Earth station, which features Day/Night, Summer/Fall/Winter/Spring, Sun/Clouds/Rain/Snow/Hail levers—and one which reads, ominously, "Earth Control—If this handle is pulled, the world will come to an end." The pup playfully tickles the lever, then finally pulls it. The sun melts the moon; a devil head pops out of the ground; Earth explodes, and (in a very simple, ingenious camera effect with live actors) pedestrians slide down "capsizing" sidewalks.... Terrifically inventive early Fleischer anticipates the end-of-the-world sf sub-genre.

**KO-KO'S REWARD** Fleischer/Inkwell Studios (Alfred Weiss) 1929 (1928) anim and live silent 7m. Ref: TV. Cabarga/TFS.

House haunted by ghosts, living skeletons (child and parent), a witch whose face gets big and horrible and who then turns into, in turn, a flying fish, a dinosaur-type, and a monster. (The animator's magic-ink-shrunken-and-animated daughter then steps out of the monster costume.) Appealing scrambling of animation and live action.

**\*KONGO** 1932. From a play by C. DeVonde & Kilbourn Gordon. AD: Cedric Gibbons. Ref: TV. V 11/22/32. Lentz. Lee. no Hardy/HM. Scheuer. Maltin '92. PT 11:48.

Gruesome ingredients include Walter Huston's Loathe-me-to-night magician Flint ("Smile, ya little bushrat, smile!"), with the "Karloff makeup" (Variety), a role he originated on stage and Lon Chaney took in the silent *West of Zanzibar* ... the skeleton trick ... "big devil" Fuzzy (Curtis Nero), who plays monster, complete with glowing "eyes" and horns, to scare bearers ... and the African natives' "ancient voodoo ceremony," which includes human sacrifice.... Flint snarls and delivers vivid exposition, in this hokey, garish horror drama, with its screwily ingenious plot. (The woman he degrades turns out to be his own....) Good low-key work by Forrester Harvey (as Cookie) and Mitchell Lewis (as Hogan), Flint's aides. Conrad Nagel's "I'm not fit to clean your shoes" dialogue is the campiest ingredient.

**KONJAKU MONOGATARI** see *Agi Kijin No Ikari*

**KRASU (BABY-SNATCHING GHOST)** (Thai) c1990? color/ws c95m. Ref: vt: no Eng. Chao Thai Market: above is tr t.

A glowing head-and-entrails ghost flies about creating comic-horrific havoc, while the prologue features a spiritual ray gun and a host of nocturnal horrors, including a mummy and a hopping ghost.... Broad, silly low-comedy-horror has one funny bit in which a guy screams at a severed head in his hands and the head screams back at him, and a weird scene in which the entrail gal zips into a disco.

**KRIEMHILD'S DREAM** or **KRIEMHILDS RACHE** or **KRIEMHILD'S REVENGE** see *Nibelungen, Die*

**KRIK? KRAK! TALES OF A NIGHTMARE** (Haitian-U.S.-Can.) Mountain Top Films (Camilo Vives) 1988 color 82m. SP, D, P: Vanyoska Gee. D, P: also Jac Avila. Mus: J. -C. Martineau, J. Marquez. Ref: V 9/28/88: a "disjointed mix" of documentary and narrative.

Voodoo priest casts spell on peasant woman.

**KRISTALLINES NICHTES** (Greek-F-Swiss) Greek Film Center/Kentavros & ET-1 & Sofracima & Slotint 1992 color 138m. SP, D: Tonia Marketaki. SP: also M. Korali. Ph: S. Hassapis. Mus: G. Papadakis. Ref: V 5/11/92: "jumbled horror film-cum-love-story ... supernatural-tinged." With Francois Delaive, Michele Valley, Tania Tripi.

Sorcery, reincarnation. *Crystal Nights* - tr t.

**KRYSAR** (Cz) Studio J. Trnka & TV-2,000 & Gunther Herbertz 1986 puppet anim color 62m. (aka *The Pied Piper of Hamelin*). D: Jiri Barta. SP: Kamil Pixa. Mus: Michael Kocab. Ref: V 5/14/86: "extraordinary."

Northern Germany, the Middle Ages. A "mysterious piper" turns townsfolk into rats.

**KUJAKUO—PEACOCK KING** (J) Pony Canyon (Fuji-TV) 1989 anim color 54m. (aka *Peacock King Kujakuo*). Ref: TV: Pony Video. Anime Opus '89. V 9/20/89:104. Animag 9:5: 1st of 3 OAVs. Japan Video. vc box: number 3 is 1991.

Psychic Tatsuma Takamoto steals a figure from the "Back of the Eight Figures" in order to test himself against "history's most powerful demons." (Anime) Possessed by these same demons, he sends out fighting dragon heads, while his adversary, high priest Kujakuo, summons up demon heads from various parts of his own body. Also: a big, red, many-armed Hindu demon ... magical lightning ... troops of warrior demons that form one big one ... and a horde of demons issuing from a chasm.... Handsome if formula monster mythology.

See also: *Peacock King.*

**KUMANDER BAWANG KALABAN NG MGA ASWANG** (Fili) Viva Films (Ramon Salvador) 1988 color c105m. D: Ramje. SP, Story: Jojo Lapuz. SP: also Jose Javier Reyes. Ph: Rody Lacap. Mus D: Mon Del Rosario. PD: Randy Gamier. VisFxD: Abet Buencamino. SpMkp: Tony Artieda, Totoy Serna. SpFX: Roly Sto. Domingo. SdFX: D. Velasquez. Ref: TV: Viva Video; no Eng. With Herbert Bautista, Mat Ranillo III (Conde Regalado), Matet, Mia Prats, Dick Israel, Jigo Garcia, Timmy Cruz, Jay-Jay Salvador, Vina Morales, Joko Diaz, Melissa Perez Rubio.

Various telekinetic phenomena (including a cackling "Mona Lisa") herald the return from their graves—via flying coffins—of several generations of Regalados, led by Conde Regalado. All immediately sprout vampire fangs, grow heavy eye shadow, and dance. Enter various mummies, also dancing, and a fey gorilla. The townsfolk who witness these wonders also get fangs, in a happily absurd sequence. These are good-time monsters, even if they are bad; meanwhile, in a nearby cave, the good monsters prepare.... Generally just silly, tatty stuff, though also generally good-natured. The main vampire-witch can turn herself into any animal of her choosing.

**KUNG FU RASCALS** York Pictures/Three Fools from the Orient (Frank Wang) 1991 color/ws 92m. (*Adventures of the Kung Fu Rascals* - alt t). SP, D, P: Steve Wang. SP: also J. Saiko Espiritu. Ph: Mike Bastings. Mus & SdFxDes: Les Claypool. Animatronic Snake: John Criswell, Joe Podnar. Creature FX: S. & Eddie Wang. VisFX: Wyatt Weed. Witch Mkp: Norman Cabrera. SpThanx: Rick Baker, Donald G. Jackson, KNB. Ref: TV: vt. Imagi 1:48-9, 61. Martin. With S. Wang, Troy Fromin, J. S. Espiritu, L. Claypool, Ted Smith (Bamboo Man/Meta Spartan), W. Weed (Rasputant the Mad Monk), Michelle McCrary (Meesha the Spider Witch), Ed Yang (Nio-Titan).

"In a land far, far away," the electric-eyed, Vader-voiced Bamboo Man, an evil warlord, unleashes the Nio-Titan ("He's uncontrollable!")—a giant stone warrior—on our Three Stooges from the Orient, but the Meta Spartan, a giant from the sea, comes to their rescue. Intentionally asinine comedy forsakes its parody of kung fu movies for bathroom humor and Ninja Turtles facetiousness. Okay monster suits.

**KUNG FU VAMPIRE BUSTER** see *New Mr. Vampire*

**KUNG FU WONDER CHILD** (H.K.) 1989? color feature. D: Lee Tso Nam. Ref: Weisser/ATC. With Yukari Oshima, Lin Hsiao Lan.

"Zombies, human skin masks, evil magicians ...."

**KUNOICHI NINPOU-CHO** see *Female Ninjas: Magic Chronicles 1*

**KUNOICHI SENSHI NINJA** see *Female Neo-Ninjas*

**KURAISHISU 2050** see *Solar Crisis*

**KURT VONNEGUT'S HARRISON BERGERON** see *Harrison Bergeron*

**KUUTAMOSONAATTI 2: KADUNLAKAISIJAT** (Finnish) Filminor (Heikki Takkinen) 1991 color 85m. SP, D: Olli Soinio. Mus: Antti Hytti. Ref: V 4/15/91: "rough farce with some gory but not very scary effects." With Kari Sorvali, Mikko Kivinen, Soli Labbart.

In part one, the "mother was frozen and the older son Arvo burned to death, and here they are revived in a sauna in the film's most enjoyable sequence. They are joined by a memorable bunch of zombie Red Guards...." Moonlight Sonata 2: *The Street Sweepers* - tr t.

*****KWAIDAN** Janus(Criterion)/Toho(Ninjin Club & Toyo Kogyo Kabushiki Kaisha/Shigeru Wakatsuki) 1964('65-U.S.) ws. SdFX: Toru Takemitsu. Title Des: Kiyoshi Kuritsh. Ref: TV: Home Vision video(Films Inc.); Eng. titles. Lee. V 5/26/65. Buehrer/Japanese Films. Hardy/HM. Wolf/Horror. Hearn/Writings from Japan. Weisser/JC.

"The Black Hair" ("Kurokami"), from Lafcadio Hearn's story, "The Reconciliation": Tale of a samurai who returns home to find that his divorced first wife is a ghost is a bit slow—and their reunion is done with too much talk—but it's an exquisite small story re unearthly justice. (Her ghost forgives him, he apologizes, but she's still, well, dead ....)

"The Woman of the Snow" ("Yuki-Onna"): "She was the woman of the snow who was hungry for warm blood." Vampire-ghost (Keiko Kishi) warns woodcutter not to tell anyone about her or he'll end up like "old Mosaku, whose blood was all gone." Unnerving sound effects and weird skyscapes highlight this second story. The "eyes" which hover in the sky, especially, are damn eerie; they seem to signify a cold, unblinking Fate. (Pleasant "lips" accompany happier days in the woodcutter's life.)

"Hoichi-the-Earless" ("Miminashi Hoichi no Hanashi"), from Hearn's "The Story of Mimi-Nashi-Hoichi": In the first of two extraordinary sequences—and one which anticipates the "silent" battle sequence in Kurosawa's *Ran*—drawings, a studio "sea," and a glimpse of an actual ocean relate the story of the sea battle of Dan-no-ura, and illuminate subsequent local legends re a haunted sea and a "ghost ship." In the later sequence, tableaux of the battle seem to spring from a biwa player's retelling of the story, in 100 songs, in the Heike cemetery. Melies-squared "transformations" (participants in the battle become gravestones, water becomes fog, land becomes sea, etc.) echo and augment the stately somberness of the earlier sequence.

The final tale — "In a Cup of Tea" ("Chawan no Nak") — re "swallowing a soul" — is an eerie idea, little more.

See also: *Golden Swallow.*

**KYORYU - KAICHO NO DENSETSU** see *Legend of Dinosaurs, The*

**KYORYU MONOGATARI** see *Rex*

**KYOSHOKU SOKO GAIBA** see *Guyver, The 1*

**KYUJU-KYUHONME NO KIMUSUME** (J) Shintoho (Mitsugu Okura) 1959 b&w/ws 82m. D: Morihei Magatani. SP: Susumu Takahira, Jiro Fujishima. Ph: Kagai Okado. Ref: Hardy/HM: *The Blood Sword of the 99th Virgin* - tr t; "Magatani occasionally succeeds in creating weird images." Weisser/JC. no Lee. With Bunta Namiji Matsuura.

Villagers in northern Japan abduct young women, kill them and hang them upside down from trees, and collect their blood for use in a sword-tempering ritual.

**KYUUKETSUKI MIYU** see *Vampire Princess Miyu*

# L

**L-GAIM** see *Heavy Metal L-Gaim*

**LABYRINTH** (U.S.-B) Tri-Star/Henson & Lucasfilm (Eric Rattray) 1986 color/ws 101m. D: Jim Henson. SP: Terry Jones. Story: Dennis Lee, Henson. Mus: Trevor Jones. Anim: Peter Chiang. SpFxSup: George Gibbs. Conceptual Des: Brian Froud. OptFX: Optical Film FX: Mkp: Wally Schneiderman; Derry Haws, Nick Dudman. Ref: TV. MFB'86:374-6. V 6/25/86. SFChron 6/27/86. ad. With David Bowie, Jennifer Connelly, Toby Froud, Shelley Thompson.

Jareth (Bowie), the Goblin King, steals a baby (Froud) and plans to turn him into a goblin, too. Other ingredients: a troll, weird eyeballs, toothy little monsters on poles, and the Bog of Eternal Stench. Little story strength; some visual imagination. Nowhere near *The Magic Clock* of kind. The songs are the worst of it.

**LADRONES DE TUMBAS** (Mex) Torrente (Raul Galindo/Dynamic Films) 1989 color c80m. SP, D: Ruben Galindo Jr. Adap: Carlos Valdemar. Mus: J. M. Bischof, Rene Castillo et al. Ph: Tony de Anda. SpFX: Benjamin Benitez, V. M. Cano. SdFX: Gonzalo Gavira. Mkp: A. Galicia, R. Cordoba; Luna. Ref: TV: Film-Mex Video; no Eng. TVG. V 5/2/90:242: sfa *Profadores de Sepulcros* (Galubi)? With Fernando Almada, Edna Bolkan, Erika Buenfil, Ernesto Laguardia, Maria Rebeca, T. Infante, Roberto Canedo, Tony Bravo.

An ax victim curses his black-mass executioners. A century or so later, teenage grave robbers remove the ax from his chest, and he returns to skeletal life, takes the ax to two men, etc.... Formula but professionally-made horror-fantasy is pretty gory, with several okay "busses" and a surfeit of screaming. Best fun-gross sequence occurs in a jail: The demon's hand emerges first from a boy's chest and yanks his (the demon's) necklace off his (the boy's) neck, then glides out of a cement wall to strangle another teen.

**LADY BATTLECOP** see *Onna Batorukopu*

**LADY GHOST AND THE CANNIBAL GIRL** (Thai) 1988? color feature. D: Htuhan So. Ref: Weisser/ATC: spirit possession, "cannibal girl."

**LADY IN RED KILLS SEVEN TIMES, The** see *Corpse Which Didn't Want To Die, The*

**LADY IN WHITE** New Century-Vista/Samuel Goldwyn Co. (New Sky) 1988 color 113m. SP, D, Co-P, Mus: Frank LaLoggia. SpVisFX: (sup) Ernest D. Farino, Gene Warren Jr.; Fantasy II. Scan FX: Animagic. SpFX: (coord) Peter Chesney; Image Engineering. MkpSup: Cheri Montesanto. SdFxDes: Steve Mann, Diggy. Ref: TV. MFB'89:183-4. V 4/13/88. SFChron 6/24/88. SFExam 6/24/88. With Lukas Haas, Len Cariou, Alex Rocco, Katherine Helmond (Amanda Harper), Jason Presson, Joelle Jacobi (Melissa), Jared Rushton, Sydney Lassick, Karen Powell (Lady in White).

"That was the year she came into my life." Willowpoint Falls. Locked in the school cloakroom on All Hallows Eve, 1962, nine-year-old Frankie Scarlatti (Haas) encounters a ghost girl (Jacobi). She proves to be the ghost of the first victim of a local child murderer and is looking for her mother, the ghostly Lady in White.... *Lady in White* is a dandy chiller and an okay mystery—the identity of the murderer is pretty obvious, but the nature of the relationship between the little girl in yellow, the lady in white, and the mysterious Amanda Harper is more elusive. The film's flat comic and dramatic scenes, however, lack the distinctiveness of the fantasy sequences, which latter mix the eerie, the humorous, and the touching: These ghosts are unpredictable. Highlights: the invisible Melissa's frosty ghost-breath on the window pane ... Melissa at the Christmas tree.

**LADY IS A SNAKE, The** see *Snake Woman, The*

**LADY MASTER SNAKE** (H.K.) Allstar Film/Jia's Film 198-? color 81m. (*Snake Woman's Marriage* - alt t). Ref: TV: Tai Seng Video; Eng. titles.

"We're snakes; they're human." A baby, Ho-hua, born in the "famous Snake Cave," grows up and becomes queen-to-be of the female "citizens" of the cave. The latter creatures—were-snakes who can change form at will—like to slide, snake-like, and wear vaguely-snakeskin outfits that cover one leg.... Gimme-a-break bad, that's how bad. Monster fantasy is sappy, scrappy, trite, occasionally campy-funny. Above tape seems to have English, Chinese, and Hindu titles.

**LADY POISON** (J) 1994 (*Powazon Bodi*). D: K. Konaka. Ref: Weisser/JC: "female Jack the Ripper." With M. Mayumi, R. Osugi.

*****LADY POSSESSED** Portland 1952. Mkp: Bob Mark. Opt: Consolidated. Ref: TV. Lee. TVG. V 2/20/52. no BFC. Lentz. Stanley. Maltin '92. no Scheuer. With P. Kellino, Steven Geray, Odette Myrtil.

When Jean Wilson (June Havoc) moves into the Sussex estate once owned by pianist-singer James Del Palma (James Mason), she finds herself "being haunted ... by Madeleine Del Palma," his dead wife. Jean dreams a "fragment of her life"; believes that "she wants me to be her"; and speaks in, apparently, Madeleine's voice, at a seance conducted by a clairvoyant (Fay Compton) and a medium (Diana Graves).... Is it psychology: Jean's "mixed-up imagination," or "subconscious mind," converting an overheard conversation (between Del Palma and his dying wife) into a romantic tale, with herself as star: or is it fantasy: i.e., her "great sensitivity" (due to her newborn's death) summoning up Kirlian-like traces of Madeleine? (Del Palma did call out once for his wife's "return.") This interesting question, unfortunately, is neither posed nor answered very satisfyingly by the script, though Jean's mystic (or psychological) dilemma is, at one point, evocatively described as "like being on the telephone and getting the lines crossed." James Mason artfully mixes charm and bitterness as Del Palma.

**LADY TERMINATOR** (U.S.-Indon.) Studio Ent. & Soraya Intercine Film & 108 Sound Studio (Ram Soraya) 1989 color 83m. (*Nasty Hunter* - Indon.). D: Jalil Jackson. SP: Karr Kruinowz, from the story "The Legend of the South Sea Queen." Mus: Ricky Brothers. Mkp: Tetty, Barbara Anne Constable. SpFX: Gregory O'Neill, David Albert, Michael Hensley, Wawan Nuryadi. Ref: TV: Shooting Star Video; Eng. version. V 6/14/89. NYT 6/10/89. PT 7:7. With Constable, C. J. Hart, Claudia A. Rademaker.

"Beware of the South Sea Queen!" One hundred years after her 100th husband, Elias, took her "vital force," the South Sea Queen reincarnates—Tania Wilson ("I'm not a lady, I'm an anthropologist!"), from Pasadena, finds herself tied to a bed at the bottom of the sea, and the Sea Queen's snake enters her. Soon, the lady terminator is spraying bullets everywhere, and a small snake is at large: Whenever she makes love, a penis-eating eel emerges from her. (Cf. *Lewd Lizard*.) Shot, she regenerates ("She can't be killed!"), and, at the end—her face monstrously burned in an inferno—she can shoot deadly rays from her eyes.... An awkward, stunt-happy blend of the supernatural and *The Terminator*, *Lady Terminator* betrays some terrifically provocative premises.

An "A" for effort, however, for atmospheric lighting and camerawork. Main gore: After a holy man zaps one of her eyes, the lady terminator surgically extracts and magically repairs it.

**LADY TIGER** (Thai) 1989? color feature. D: Ry-Man. Ref: Weisser/ATC: brother & sister were-tigers; see also *The Tiger's Wife*.

**LADY WOLF** (H.K.?) J&J 199-? color 90m. Ref: TV: VSOM; Eng. titles. VSOM: "Asian female ghost werewolves."

"Female wolves are the difficult ones." Ingredients here include an oasis of wolf-women in the drifting sands ... a Snow Lady who loves a human, Brother Ten, but must kill him for her Mom ... the anti-wolf Hunt King ... a stamp for use on wolf-skins which nixes "resurrection" ... a wolf that turns into a child ... and, at the end, a wolf-skulled thing ("His majesty is alive!").... A bit much, romantically speaking. And the kung fu and song interludes stop the story dead. One lyric, though, is worth noting: "I don't care if you're Mickey Mouse." Most amusing scene: the wolf pelt flying about and attacking onlookers.

**LADYHAWKE** (U.S.-B-I) WB-Fox (Harvey Bernhard) 1985 color/ws 121m. D: Richard Donner. Story, SP: Edward Khmara. SP: also Michael Thomas, Tom Mankiewicz. Mus: Andrew Powell. VisFX: (des) Richard A. Greenberg; (sup addl) Peter Donen. OptFX: (sup) Stuart Robertson; (addl) Cinema Research. Anim Sup: Robert Mrozowski. SpFxSup: John Richardson. Mkp: Giancarlo Del Brocco. Ref: TV. MFB'85:217. V 4/3/85. SFChron 4/12/85. Bay Guardian 5/1/85. With Matthew Broderick, Rutger Hauer, Michelle Pfeiffer, Leo McKern.

"Always together, eternally apart." A jealous bishop curses a woman to be a hawk by day, her lover to be a wolf by night.... The appeal of the premise of this Medieval odd-couple tale remains elusive. It simply seems another way to keep two lovers apart, if a more far-fetched way than usual. A potentially sweet anecdote becomes a ponderous, languorous epic. Hauer shows no conviction, and Pfeiffer hardly makes an impression. Overtricky lighting, cutting, and camerawork; jarring disco score. The only positive notes: the hawk, the wolf, and the beauty of the countryside.

**The LAIR OF THE WHITE WORM** (B) Vestron/White Lair (W. J. Quigley, Dan Ireland) 1988 color 91m. SP, D, P: Ken Russell. From Bram Stoker's novel, alternately titled *The Garden of Evil*. Mus: Stanislas Syrewicz. SpMkpFX: Image Animation. SpFX: (des) Geoff Portass; (sup) Simon Sayce. Ref: screen. MFB'89:115-16. V 8/31/88. Nation 12/5/88. SFExam 11/11/88. Sacto Bee 11/25/88. SFChron 11/11/88. With Amanda Donohoe, Hugh Grant, Catherine Oxenberg, Sammi Davis, Peter Capaldi.

The "local dragon" of Temple House and the nearby cavern is the D'Ampton Worm, a giant snake. Leader of the local snake god cult: Lady Sylvia Marsh (Donohoe), who is subject to a "form of vampirism"—"Every death is a rebirth into a god ever mightier".... At times, *Lair* verges on becoming an exciting occult mystery, at others, it threatens to make good its claim as an absurdist high/low comedy. It fails, however, to sustain itself in either mode, or to fuse them. Camp-hokum highlight: the bagpipe "charming" of the vampire policeman.

**LAM YONG** (Thai) 198-? color c90m. Ref: TV: Extra Times video; no Eng. Thai Video: above title is a person's name.

At her funeral, a corpse sits up in her coffin; she then alternates between a human face and a monstrous one and can appear at will. At the end, she vanishes. There's also a male back-and-forth ghost.... This comedy of double takes is just one twenty-minute chase, then another, then another, as the ghost scares one person, then another, etc. It's episodic, and always the same episode, and appears to be a remake or an alternate, abbreviated version of *Funny Ghost* (qq.v.). It keeps the latter's silly stuff and omits the chilly stuff and the skeletons. The male ghost seems to be one of the few new elements.

**LAMP, The** see *Outing, The*

**The LAND BEFORE TIME** (U.S.-Irish) Univ & U-Drive Prods (Amblin)/(Lucas-Spielberg/Sullivan Bluth Ireland Ltd./Gary Goldman, John Pomeroy) 1988 anim color 69m. D, PD: Don Bluth. SP: Stu Krieger. Story: Judy Freudberg, Tony Geiss. Story Consult: Brent Maddock, S. Wilson. Ph: Jim Mann. Mus: James Horner. SpFxAnim: (d) D. A. Lanpher; (painting) Shirley Mapes. Ref: TV: vt. MFB'89:276-77. V 11/23/88. SFExam 11/18/88. SFChron 11/18/88. Voices: Gabriel Damon (Littlefoot), Helen Shaver, Bill Erwin, Candy Hutson (Cera), Pat Hingle, Judith Barsi (Ducky), Will Ryan (Petrie).

In the "time of the dinosaurs." Five hungry dinosaurs—including Littlefoot, the last hope of the brontos ... Cera, a baby triceratops ... and Petrie, a pterodactyl cub—are pursued by "Sharptooth," a tyrannosaurus, as they search for the fabled Great Valley.... Generally middling, moderately engaging young-dinosaur adventure. Poignant: Littlefoot at first thinks that his own, outsized shadow is his dead mother. Sweet: Little dinos arrange their sleeping accommodations.

**The LAND BEFORE TIME II** Univ Cartoon 1994 anim color 73m. D, P: Roy Allen Smith. SP: Dev Ross, John Loy, John Ludin. Mus: Michael Tavera. FxDes: Jeff Howard. SpFX: Kim Jung. Ref: TV: MCA-Univ HV; OAV. Voices: Kenneth Mars, Jeff Bennett, Linda Gary, Scott McAfee, Rob Paulsen (Chomper), Heather Hogan (Ducky).

They're back. Yep yep yep. Featured: the egg-eaters, not-bad low-life villains ... the "spooky" Mysterious Beyond ... a just-hatched Sharptooth (a cute, make that utterly adorable baby tyrannosaurus ... good sound/vocal effects here) ... and the Big Scaries, two Sharpteeth.... More innocuousness. Sweet: Littlefoot's Night-night water from the leaf. Okay kidmix of comedy, sentiment, and action.

**LAND OF DOOM** Matterhorn (Lightning Video)/Ken Kimura 1986 (1984) color 87m. D, Co-P: Peter Maris. SP: Craig Rand. Story: Peter Kotis. Mus: Mark Governor. Ref: V 10/8/86: "weak *Mad Max* imitation." With Deborah Rennard, Garrick Dowhen, Daniel Radell.

Post-nuke adventure.

**The LAND OF FARAWAY** (Swed.-Russ.-Norw.) Miramax/Nordisk Tonefilm, Swedish Film Institute & Gorky Film, V/O Sovinfilm & AB Filmhuset, Norway Film Development Co. (Ingemar Ejve) 1987 color 99m. (aka *Mio in the Land of*

*Faraway*). D: Vladimir Grammatikov. SP: William Aldridge, from Astrid Lindgren's novel *Mio, Min Mio*. Ph: Alexander Antipenko. Mus: Anders Eljas et al. PD: K. Zagorsky. VisFxD: Derek Meddings. OptSup: Rex Neville. Mkp: Kaj Groenberg et al. SdFxSup: Bengt Loethner. Ref: TV: vt; Eng.-language version. V 8/26/87. Fango 94:41, 43. With Nicholas Pickard, Christian Bale, Christopher Lee, Timothy Bottoms, Susannah York, Gunilla Nyroos.

In the Land of Faraway, an evil knight (Lee) captures children in nets. Those who refuse to serve him he turns into bat-like birds which eternally circle his castle. In death, at the end, he turns to stone and crumbles, magic lightning wrecks his castle, and the children are children again. Also noted: a "quiet and creepy" forest, a cape of invisibility, the knight's metal "claw," and the fireball which he can command.... Flat-footed fantasy has one fun sequence in which the boy-hero (Pickard) travels by beard (latter is attached to a giant disembodied head) through the air, but apart from a lovely main theme song, that's about it.

**LAND OF OZ, The** see *Return to Oz*

**LANSKY'S ROAD** 1985. SP, D, P: Richard Farr. Ref: PT 21:68: "filled with bad camera zooms and slow-mo."

"A couple is abducted by flying saucers."

**LAPUTA: CASTLE IN THE SKY** (J) Streamline Pictures/Tokuma Shoten (Tatsumi Yamashita, Hideo Ogata, Isao Takahata/Toru Hata) 1986 ('89-U.S.) anim color 124m. (*Tenku No Shiro Laputa. The Castle in the Sky, Laputa* - alt t). SP, D: Hayao Miyazaki. Ph: Hirokata Takahashi. Mus: Jo Hisaishi. PD: Toshiro Nozaki, Nizo Yamamoto. Anim D: Yoshinori Kanada. Ref: TV: Animage Video; no Eng. Paul Lane. Animag 1:30-32. 9:16-17. V 12/2/87. 5/2/90:S-60. *The Art of Laputa*. MMarquee 43:11. Imagi Smr'95:34,37: dubbed-Eng. version. Michiko Sugiyama. *Laputa* (picture book).

A tale of an alternate Earth and a legend re a lost, cloud-enshrouded, abandoned floating city, Laputa. Giving the tale credence: a framed, wall-mounted photo of the edge of Laputa, taken by the boy Pazu's father ... a huge flying, heat-ray-shooting robot ... and a levitation crystal which shares an unusual insignia with the robot and which young Sheeta (said to be Princess Lusheeta of Laputa) possesses and which emits a light that points to Laputa....

With its Verne-like fascination for elaborate, exotic vehicles, this charming, funny, exciting science-fantasy-adventure (which takes its name from "Gulliver's Travels") taps a fantasy not so much of flying as of floating or falling gently from the sky. (In one scene, Pazu joins hands with Sheeta, as her crystal activates and lets them float lightly above the smokestacks of his mining town.) *Laputa*, though actionful, is filled with idyllic images of cloud-wrapped castles, morning sunlight, doves, and underground caverns glowing blue (glowing with the rocks from which Sheeta's crystal was made), and it's punctuated with breathtaking long shots of lakes, canyons, trestles, etc. A credit montage depicts Earth, or alternate-Earth, artists' conceptions of a once-bustling Laputa, complete with propeller underneath. And hints (from Pazu's father and Sheeta's grandmother) of this past magic (within the body of the story) tantalize in the present tense. The principals—basic character types—do not reach Laputa itself

until the last fifty minutes of the movie. Anticipation builds, and the surreal depiction of the floating city—clouds above, below, and around ... clouds trailing like snails across the tops of trees ... clouds skidding along the ground ... outcroppings of walls hanging in space—does not disappoint. This is your basic Cloud City of dreams. In the wry, no-big-deal last shot of Laputa's surface (as Sheeta and Pazu glide by and away), a bird-attended robot makes its rounds of the gardens.

**LAS QUE LAS DAN ... ME DAN MIEDO** (Mex) Producciones Laser 1989 color c77m. SP, D: Miguel A. Lira. Ph: F. Teposte. Mus: Emilio Maceda. FX: Miguel Larraguivel. Mkp: L. M. Larraguivel. Ref: TV: Zbenk video; no Eng.; "El Miedo Me Da Risa" - part of title? With Lira (the ghost), Alejandro Suarez, Antonio Raxel, Blanca Nieves, Ana Luz Aldana, Scarlet Alvarado, Jenny Benezra.

Knife-wielding ghost haunts house, magically appears and disappears. His (her?) human accomplice stays in an adjoining casket and clutches a Felix the Cat doll.... The Felix fan provides most of the menace; the ghost gets swept up in the silly, comic goings-on. Shot-on-tape.

**The LAS VEGAS SERIAL KILLER** Program Releasing Corp. & Camp Prods. (Steckler Ents./Katherine Steckler) 1987 color 76m. D: Ray Dennis Steckler (aka W. Schmidt). SP: Christopher Edwards. Ph, Ed: Sven Christian. Mus: Henri Price. Mkp: Jerry Carroll. SdFX: Greg Farina. Ref: TV: Camp Video. Hound. no Martin. With Pierre Agostino (Jonathan Klick), Ron Jason, Chris Cave, Tara McGowan, Kathryn Downy, Tony Alessandrini.

The real story behind the "series of brutal strangulations that has terrorized Las Vegas." "Self-proclaimed serial killer" Jonathan Klick is released from the Southern Nevada Correctional Center. At a poolside "birthday party for Las Vegas film star Cash Flagg," he strangles a girl with her bikini top. Next, he strangles a prostitute, then the victim of two muggers whose path he seems fated to cross and re-cross. Finally, he strangles two women at the same time, just before the muggers shoot him.... Episodic, isn't it? This movie is so casually made it's almost experimental. Script includes the basic idea and at least one phrase ("Die, garbage!") from the Steckler *Hollywood Strangler* movie, found footage of a rodeo apparently recycled from their *Blood Shack*, some t&a material, and chunks of narration which are mysteriously repeated. French—or fish—influence on the Steckler ouevre is indicated when the movie ends with the word *Fin*.

**The LASER MAN** (U.S.-H.K.) Peter Wang Films & H.K. Film Workshop 1988 color 92m. SP, D, P: P. Wang. Ph: E. Dickerson. Mus: Mason Daring; (theme song) Ryuichi Sakamoto. PD: Lester Cohen. LaserFX: Matthew Tanteri. SpFX: Matt Vogel. Mkp: N. Tong. SpLaserSdFX: Earl Howard. OptFxDes: Cynosure. Ref: TV: Hen's Tooth Video; Eng. version. V 10/5/88: "appealingly idiosyncratic." 6/13/90:34. With Marc Hayashi, Maryann Urbano, Tony Leung, Sally Yeh.

Victim of "spiffy, portable laser gun" is later "casually resurrected."(V) "Modern technology kills." Scientist Arthur Wise develops a long-distance laser weapon. Movie scorecard: weak-tea, quirky story ... Sinister Corporation cliches ... okay laser effects.

**LASER MOON** Hemdale (Mark Paglia) 1991 color 90m. SP, D: Douglas K. Grimm. Ref: SFChron Dtbk 9/13/92. Fango 118:12. Martin. With Traci Lords, Harrison Leduke, Bruce Carter, Crystal Shaw.

"Psycho ... fries ... brains with a 'high-powered surgical laser'." (SFC)

**LAST ACTION HERO** Col/Steve Roth(Oak) 1993 color/ws 130m. D, P: John McTiernan. SP: Shane Black, David Arnott. Story: Zak Penn, Adam Leff. VisFX:(consul) Richard Greenberg;(sup) John Sullivan. Ref: TV. Mo. V 6/28/93. SFChron 6/18/93.

"He's brought back the Ripper!" The reel Ripper (Tom Noonan), that is, from the movie *Jack Slater III*, who turns up in real Hollywood. Later, a magic movie ticket draws Death (Ian McKellen) out of *The Seventh Seal*. ("I don't do fiction!") In-between, there's much movement between parallel dimensions .... This is kind of unlikely, *Purple Rose of Cairo*-like material for an actioner—comic modernism for the masses—and is for the most part fun and funny, if it's occasionally indistinguishable from the movies it lampoons.

**The LAST BORDER** (Finnish) Last Border & Connexion & Sandrews & MC4 1993 color 105m. SP, D, P, Ed: Mika Kaurismaki. SP: also Pia Tikka. Ph: Timo Salminen. Mus: Anssi Tikanmaki. AD: Tony De Castro. Ref: V 10/4/93: "a rare film—a spoof of the *Mad Max* cult films that also works as a futuristic adventure in its own right." With Jolyon Baker, Fanny Bastien, Jurgen Prochnow, Kari Vaananen.

"In the desolate near-future of 2009...."

**LAST FRANKENSTEIN** see *Lasuto Furankenshutain*

**LAST FRONTIER, The** see *Spacerage*

**LAST HOUSE NEAR THE LAKE** see *Ultima Casa vicino al Lago, L'*

**LAST HOUSE ON THE LEFT PART II** see *Twitch of the Death Nerve*

**LAST MEGALOPOLIS** see *Teito Monogatari*

**LAST OF THE WARRIORS** see *Empire of Ash III*

**LAST PELT, The** see *Into the Badlands*

**LAST PICNIC, The** see *Zombie Island Massacre*

**The LAST REUNION** (B) Towers of London-TV 1955 b&w 53m. D, P: Leonard Brett. SP: Kenneth Hyde. Mus: Christopher Whelan. AD: Frank White. Ref: TV. Greg Luce. Filmfax 7:23(ad). TVG. no Lee. no Scheuer. no Maltin '92. With Eric Portman, Michael Gough, Duncan McIntyre, Basil Appelby, Alfred Burke, Barry Keegan, Joan Marion, Noel Howlett, Harold Goodwin, Geoffrey Chater.

A World War II British bomber crew assembles for its annual reunion. One place at the dinner table, however, remains vacant: Simmie's (Portman). Only the slightly daft Hugo (Gough) can

see him, or his ghost, although the ectoplasmic Simmie seems to see the others. Hugo suggests that the "Almighty reshuffle"—his version of reincarnation—leaves some souls out, and that they stay where they are, as ghosts. In the somber spirit of the occasion, Jock (McIntyre) proposes that people are simply evanescent products of The Great Conjuror. Simmie, though, has the last word....

Fairly intriguing metaphysical rumination, although the extended dining-room recreation (complete with light and sound effects) of the crew's final bombing raid is a bit much—manufactured drama takes over from speculation. A neat twist concludes this well-staged, "Twilight Zone"-like show from British TV, which is sometimes shown as a movie on American TV.

**The LAST SLUMBER PARTY** United/B.&S. 1987 color 80m. SP, D: Stephen Tyler. Ref: vc box. V 2/3/88:34: '88 video release. McCarty II: made-for-video; "beneath the bottom of the barrel." With Jan Jensen, Nancy Meyer, Joann Whitley.

Homicidal maniac ruins slumber party.

**The LAST STARFIGHTER** Univ/Lorimar (Gary Adelson, E. O. Denault) 1984 color/ws 100m. D: Nick Castle. SP: Jonathan Betuel. Mus: Craig Safan. PD: Ron Cobb. VisFxCoord: J. A. Okun. SpMechFX: Lance Anderson. SpFX: Kevin Pike et al. Scene Simulation: Digital. SpCar: Gene Winfield. MkpDes: Terry Smith. Ref: TV. V 7/11/84. SFChron 7/13/84. ad. With Lance Guest, Dan O'Herlihy, Catherine Mary Stewart, Robert Preston, Barbara Bosson, Norman Snow.

When Alex Rogan (Guest) sets a new Starfighter, video-game record, alien Centauri (Preston) enlists him in a real fight against an evil space armada. A "simuloid" takes Alex's place on Earth. Also: a tentacle-headed beast ... an energy barrier, The Frontier ... a meteor gun ... and an "interstellar hit beast".... This basically flat sf-drama must be some other boy's fantasy. It does, though, have charming moments, and O'Herlihy and Preston lend the proceedings a bit of personality.

**LAST TEACHER, The** see *Ultimate Teacher, The*

**The LAST VAMPIRE** (H.K.) HKTV 1988 color c110m. Ref: TV: HKTV Video; no Eng.

Principals: a green-eye-ray-shooting flying villain who appears, first, as a green whirlwind and who may be the titular figure ... two comic, invulnerable hopping vampires with detachable heads and elastic arms ... *Night of the Living Dead*-like zombies who brook no interference from hopping vampires and who are restored to their normal, just-folks status at the end ... and the hero, who retrieves a magic sword and slays the villain.... Long, with that flat shot-on-tape look and sound, and scads of cheap music-video-like effects. The action scenes are lively as all get out.

**LAST WAR** (J) 198-? color feature. Ref: VSOM: "sf horror; '80s version."

**LAST WARRIOR, The** see *Final Executioner, The*

**LASUTO FURANKENSHUTAIN** (J) Shochiku 1991 color/ws feature. SP, D: Takeshi Kawamura. Ref: VSOM: *Last Franken-*

stein - vt t. TV: VSOM; Eng. titles. Monster! Int'l. 4:39-40.Markalite 3:10: "horror film"; *Last Frankenstein* - tr t. With Akira Emoto, Yoshio Harada, Juro Kara.

Mad scientist, "his creation," and the latter's bride. Dr. Aleo: "I decided to develop an advanced human ... void of emotions"—a "new human species." ("I'm not Frankenstein.") Meanwhile, Mai's psychic powers vivify the superman and "superman's bride." Plus a hunchback .... Quirky, experimental, deadly. (Truer words: "It's not working. Nothing is happening.") Shot-on-tape.

**LATE FOR DINNER** Col/Castle Rock & New Line (Granite Pictures/Dan Lupovitz) 1991 color 92m. D, Co-P: W. D. Richter. SP: Mark Andrus. Ph: Peter Sova. Mus: David Mansfield. PD: Lilly Kilvert. Key Mkp: Steve LaPorte. SpFxCoord: Stan Parks. SdFxEd: John Morris. SpThanks (idea): Bones Howe. Ref: TV: New Line HV. Mo. Stanley. V 9/2/91: "marginal entry." CCosta Times 9/29/91: "thoroughly delightful." ad. SFChron 9/20/91: "high-quality gem." With Brian Wimmer, Peter Berg, Marcia Gay Harden, Colleen Flynn, Peter Gallagher, Bo Brundin (Dr. Dan Chilblains).

"We're in tomorrow, Frank." Thanks to Chilblains Cryonic Life Extension, brothers-in-law Willie (Wimmer) and Frank (Berg) go to sleep in 1962 and wake up in 1991. ("Deep Freeze Miracle in Pomona, California.") Sweet, offbeat romantic drama survives an arduous setting-up of the science-fiction premises, and follows its several protagonists step-by-realistic-step through to a romantic reconciliation in the present. The film is in the oddly engaging, awkward starts-and-stops of its characters. ("We are so lost.") Wry throwaway line: "Someone shot the guy from *Cattle Queen of Montana*?"

**The LATE NANCY IRVING** (B) Hammer House of Mystery/Fox-TV 1985 color c80m. Ref: TVG. Ecran F 50:13. 70:8-9. With Cristina Raines, Marius Goring, Tony Anholt.

Sick rich man plots to have woman's blood medically transferred to himself.

**LATE NIGHT WITH MYRON** Bob Scott anim short. Ref: SFChron Dtbk 7/10/88.

"3-D cable station" brings the *Titanic,* a rocket ship, and Clint Eastwood into the living room.

**El LATIGO CONTRA LAS MOMIAS ASESINAS** (Mex) Peliculas Latinoamericanas & Novelty Internacional (Roberto Rodriguez) 197-? color c75m. SP, D: Angel Rodriguez. Ph: Alfredo Uribe. Mus: Ernesto Cortazar. OptFX: Ricardo Sainz. SdFX: Gonzalo Gavira. Ref: TV: Mexcinema Video; no Eng. V (CHVD). no Hound. With Juan Miranda, Rosa Chagoyan, Manuel Leal, Marcko D'Carlo.

Standard action movie features camp scenes with guys in zippered mummy suits who can appear at will and whose glowing eyes blink. Their headquarters: an old mission. A Zorro-type whips them until they catch fire, whereupon they turn into (dead) humans. At the end, the head mummy levitates his virgin sacrifices, but before the knife can fall, the hero whips him until he begins to smoke, whereupon he turns into a skeleton. Best thing

about the movie: the crack-of-whip/crack-of-thunder, pre-credit montage.

**\*The LATIN QUARTER** Four Continents 1945 ('46-U.S.) 69m.-U.S. (*Frenzy*-U.S.). Mus: Alan Gray. Ref: screen. William K. Everson. V 10/31/45. 7/24/46. no LC. PFA notes 1/20/87. Lee. no Hardy/HM. Lentz. With Billy Holland (masquerade cave man).

An interminable tale of romance, artists, madness—and "spooks, ghosts, the supernatural"—is an excuse for scattered horror scenes. First and best of the latter: Lengthy tracking shots culminate in a shot of a mysteriously-playing organ. Last and not bad either: At the end, an oil lamp flickers and dies exactly at eleven, as prophesied. (Exit maid, shrieking.) In between—in lamely directed (Vernon Sewell) flashbacks and present-tense scenes—a Latin Quarter model (Joan Seton), in a trance, "sees" sculptor Anton Minetti (Beresford Egan)—who specializes in the "most morbid and grotesque of subjects"—strangle Christine Renoir (Joan Greenwood), and the latter's spirit attempts to reach our hero (Derrick de Marney) through his nightmares. These elaborate plot mechanics yield the teeny tiny surprise of a hidden body.

**The LAUGHING DEAD** Archaeopteryx/Tercel (Laughing Dead Partners/Lex Nakashima) 1989 color 91m. SP, D, Mus: S. P. Somtow. Ph: D. R. Boyd. PD: P. Vasels, D. Hughes. SpMkpFX: Rik Carter, Dave Stinnett, Jane Whitehead, Jake Johnson. SpFxCoord: John Jockinsen. SpCreature FX: MMI; (des) John Buechler. Ref: TV. Bill Warren. McCarty II. PT 3:8. With Bruce Barlow (Kukulcan), Matthew De Merritt, Premika Eaton, Ryan Effner, Gregory Frost, Larry Kagen, Krista Keim, Patrick Roskowick, Billy Silver, Tim Sullivan; Bill Warren, Beverly Warren, Forry Ackerman (corpses).

The "usual eccentric assemblage"—on an annual archaeological tour—takes in the Festival of the Laughing Dead, at the village of Todos Santos. There, a doctor whose name is the same as the Mayan God of Death makes a possessed girl exchange hearts with a priest and thereby turns him into the Death God. At the end—in the cave of the yucky dead—the doctor plans a human sacrifice for a "new age"; an apparently parodistic basketball game between ghouls and humans takes place, and doctor and priest turn into monsters (the hero seems to become Quetzalcoatl) and battle each other.... Horror-fantasy has uncertain acting, awkwardly introduced gore, and scenes and dialogue which waver between bad and comedy.

**The LAUGHING TARGET** (J) CPM/Shogakukan & Takahashi & OV Kikaku & Studio Pierrot c1989? ('92-U.S.) anim color 52m.-U.S. (*Rumic World* series). D: Tohru Matsuzono. SP: Tomoko Konparu, Hideo Takayashiki. Story: Rumiko Takahashi. Ph: T. Kobayashi. Mus: K. Kuni. AD: T. Arai. SdFxD: S. Shiba. Ref: TV: USManga Corps video (Shogakukan Video); Eng. titles. Voices: S. Yoku, Hiromi Tsuru (Azusa), T. Matsumoto.

"Yuzura is mine!" Yuzura—who has been engaged since childhood to marry his cousin Azusa—finds that she has telekinetic powers, demon teeth, and strangling hair. Worse, the slug creatures which swarm over her victims are "hungry ghosts" that "consume dead flesh".... Macabre enough, but ponderous, ultimately cut-and-dry. Best sequence: the pre-credit one which combines nightmare and childhood imagery and suggests more than the movie delivers.

The **LAWLESS LAND** Concorde 1989 (1988) color 80m. D: Jon Hess. Story, Sp, Co-P: Tony Cinciripini. SP, Co-P: Larry Leahy. Mus: Lucia Hwong. PD: R. Sanudo. Ref: V 2/22/89: "minor sci-fi effort." Fango 104:26-7. With Nick Corri, Leon, Xander Berkeley, Ann-Marie Peterson, Amanda Peterson.

Love on the run after the collapse of civilization.

The **LAWNMOWER MAN** (U.S.-J) New Line/Allied Vision & Lane Pringle & Fuji Eight (Gimel Everett/Milton Subotsky) 1992 color 141m. (105m.). SP, D: Brett Leonard. SP: also G. Everett. From Stephen King's story. Ph: R. Carpenter. Mus: Dan Wyman. SpVisFxSup: Leonard, Everett. SpMkpFX: MMI; (des) John Buechler; (stopmo mkp) Rodd Matsui. VR Seqs & Digital Live Action FX: Angel Studios & Xaos Inc; (anim d) Jill Hunt, Michael Limber. Helmet Displays: Western Images. MinFX: David Stipes; (sup) A. Doublin. Gyrospheres: Reel EFX; (coord) M. Becker. SpFx: F. Ceglia. Fire FX: Homer & Assoc. Bkgd Graphics: MacIntosh Development Team. Computer Graphics: The Gosney Co. Opt: PMP. SpVocals: Frank Welker. Ref: TV: New Line HV (Col-TriStar HV); "unrated director's cut." V 2/24/92. Anim Mag (Smr '92): 29. Martin. Fango 122:8. ads. vc box: *Virtual Wars* - Far East t. With Jeff Fahey, Pierce Brosnan, Jenny Wright, Mark Bringleson, Geoffrey Lewis, Jeremy Slate, Dean Norris.

Virtual-reality "boosts" and a brain-stem injection tap into the "primal mind" of simple-minded handyman Jobe Smith (Fahey), unleash ancient psychic powers in him. He develops mind-reading and telekinetic abilities, conjures up an animated wasp-like creature, and plots to have everyone in the world "hooked into" him.

The CIA/military-industrial-complex-as-boogeyman, and other story and dialogue cliches. Script boils down to a super-vidgame, or yet another Stephen King-based supernatural-revenge story, as it employs elements of *Frankenstein, Village of the Damned, Charly, Carrie, Scanners, Tron, Blades,* etc. Parlor-game suggestion: Find a believable minute here. Only frisson: the phones ringing at the end. (Jobe predicted the phones would herald his return.)

**LAZARO** see *Where the River Runs Black*

**LAZER TAG ACADEMY—THE MOVIE** Worlds of Wonder Prods. II & Ruby-Spears (Larry Huber) 1986 anim color 95m. (aka *Lazertag Academy*). D: John Kimball, Rudy Larriva. Mus: Shuki Levy, Haim Saban. PD: John Dorman. Models Sup: Alan Huck. Anim Sup: John Conning. FxEd: Golden Felton et al. Ref: TV: CHE video; Vol. 2. Hound: based on the toys. no Martin. Animag 11:47. Voices: Billy Jacoby, Booker Bradshaw et al.

"I'm Jamie Jaren—I'm from the future!" Star Lights from 3010 A.D.—a "future without want"—enable the principals to Bill-and-Ted about history, from the late Twentieth Century to sixth-century Camelot to pirate days (with a Robert Newton-voiced Captain Redbeard) to thirteenth-century West Africa and then back to good old 3010 A.D., where Star Sensors and one-person flying vehicles abound. The Star Lights (or "sorcery sticks") and mind power can do just about anything, from freezing people in

blocks of ice to conjuring up huge spider-web traps. Villain Draxon Drear and his genetically engineered, mutant Skuggs are initially found in suspended animation in a spaceship in the Atlantic.... Stolid sf-adventure appears to be several cobbled-together videos or TV shows, though it's advertised as a "fully animated feature film."

**LEATHERFACE: THE TEXAS CHAINSAW MASSACRE III** New Line/Robert Engelman (Vortex) 1990 (1989) color 81m. (*Leatherface: Texas Chainsaw Massacre III* - cr t). D: Jeff Burr. SP: David J. Schow. Ph: J. L. Carter. Mus: Jim Manzie. PD: Mick Strawn. MechFX: Bellissimo/Belardinelli FX;(des) Dean Miller. SpMkpFX: KNB EFX. Chainsaws: Paul Byers, Jim Landis. SpSdFX: Joel Valentine. Ref: TV: RCA-Col HV. V 1/17/90: "ranks at the bottom of the barrel among recent, pointless sequels." McCarty II: "lame sequel." Sacto Bee 1/16/90: "vile." ad. With Kate Hodge, Viggo Mortensen (Tex), William Butler, Ken Foree, R. A. Mihailoff (Leatherface), Miriam Byrd-Nethery (Mama).

"They watch the road!" Those cannibal guys from Texas again. Third and easily the worst so far in the series. One of the few surprises: a little girl's skeleton doll. The "family"'s eccentricities seem very much applied this time, and the above-quoted line is one of the few worth quoting.

See also *Texas Chain Saw Massacre II.*

**LEDA** see *Fantastic Adventure of Yohko*

**LEENA MEETS FRANKENSTEIN** Pinnacle/Odyssey Group Video 1993 color feature. D: Scotty Fox. SP: L. S. Talbot. Ref: vc box. With Leena, Madison, Nicole London, Mike Horner.

Haunted house inhabited by Dracula, the Wolfman, and Frankenstein's monster.

**LEGACIAM** (J) Network (A.P.P.P./A.I.C.) c1987? anim color 50m. Ref: TV: Emotion video; no Eng.

Tale of a future or alternate world re huge, human-piloted robots, a demolition derby on a future freeway, etc. Regulation robot wrangling, okay electric-ray effects. Nice transition: City lights take over as day passes from evening to night.

**LEGAL TENDER** 1990 color 93m. D: Jag Mundhra. Ref: SFChron Dtbk 10/20/91. Martin. With Morton Downey Jr., Tanya Roberts, Robert Davi.

"Everybody who works in Tanya's bar is turning up with multiple stab wounds in the stomach." (SFC)

**LEGEND** (U.S.-B) Univ/Legend 1985 color/ws 94m. D: Ridley Scott. SP: William Hjortsberg. Mus: Jerry Goldsmith. SpMkp: Rob Bottin; (art) Vince Prentice. SpFxSup: Nick Allder. MechFxSup: Phillip Knowles. VisOptFX: Fotherley, Peerless, Peter Govey. Ref: TV. MFB'85:380. V 8/21/85. With Tom Cruise, Mia Sara, Tim Curry (Lord of Darkness), Alice Playten (Blix), Billy Barty, Robert Picardo (Meg), Mike Crane (demon cook), Eddie Powell (mummified guard).

"Once long ago, before there was such a thing as time...." Characters include the unicorn-hating Lord of Darkness ("I am a part of you all"); his "loathsome" goblin aide Blix; Meg, hag-horror from the swamp; Three Stooges-like goblins and fairies; and an incidental bat-winged creature or two.... Bland, monotonously-scored fantasy with "Pandora" overtones. Many visual effects—including one fine one: the Lord of Darkness emerging from a mirror—but it takes Blix almost twenty screen minutes just to bag his first unicorn horn—i.e., for the movie to get to Square One.

**LEGEND OF A CHINESE WITCH, The** see *Beheaded 1000, The*

**LEGEND OF BOGGY CREEK, The** see *Boggy Creek II*

**2P The LEGEND OF DINOSAURS** (J) King Features-TV/Toei 1977 ('83-U.S.) color c90m. (*Kyoryu-Kaicho No Densetsu. Legend of the Dinosaurs* - TV ad t. aka *Legend of Dinosaurs and Monster Birds*). D: Junji Kurata. SP: M. Igami, I. Matsumoto, I. Otsu. Ph: S. Shiomi. Mus: Masao Yagi. AD: Y. Amamori. SpTechAdv: F. Ohashi. Ref: TV. Bill Warren. V 5/4/77:84. TVG. Larson. no Scheuer. no Maltin '92. With Tsunehiko Watase, Nobiko Sawa, Shotako Hayashi, Tomoko Kiyoshima, Maureen Peacock, Akira Moroguchi.

Dinosaur data, the Loch Ness idea, and *Jaws*—all treated routinely. Hero: "Plesiosaur—just as I thought." By the same logic, if there's one dinosaur in the lake ... : "It wouldn't be very strange if there were a pterodactyl, too!" And, by gum, a big bird about as menacing as The Giant Claw pops up. Terrible light-pop score is apparently intended to act as counterpoint to the bloodier sequences. Eerie shot: the clouds billowing up over the totem dinosaur.

**LEGEND OF EIGHT SAMURAI** (J) Toei (Haruki Kadokawa) 1984 color 133m. (aka *Eight Samurai*). SP, D: Kinji Fukasaku. SP, Story: Toshio Kamata. Ph: Seizo Sengen. AD: Chikara Imamura. SpFX: Nobuo Yajima. Ref: TV: Prism Ent. video; Eng. dubbed. Hound. Martin. Ecran F 47:19. V 5/9/84:437 (ad). VSOM. With Hiroko Yakushimaru (Princess Shizu), Henry Sanada (Shinbei), Sue Shihomi, Sonny Chiba.

Eight round crystals from the body of a princess who died one hundred years earlier now identify the eight samurai, or ninja, who are destined to help her descendant, Princess Shizu, overcome a goblin queen's curse on their royal family. The queen, Tamazusa, who restores her youthfulness by bathing in blood, and her son live in a castle protected by witchcraft-created poison beauties, giant flying snakes, and other apparitions. Shizu falls in love with the queen's lost son, Shinbei, who is reborn after being stabbed and struck by lightning.

Generally routine adventure-fantasy features lots of indignant "They'll pay for this!" dialogue, a syrupy love song, and even a "My god! You're a girl!" scene. Shinbei's story, however, is less formulaic and more interesting than the body of the movie. As a moral "in-betweener," he's less predictable than the other principals. In the most exciting action sequence, an "old witch" rips off her skin and reveals herself to be a huge, vicious attack centipede. ("She's not your mother! Animal spirits have taken over her body!")

**LEGEND OF FABULOUS BATTLE** see *Windaria*

**LEGEND OF FLOWER, The** see *Rouge*

**LEGEND OF GALACTIC HEROES** (J) Toei 1988 anim color 59m. (aka *Heldensagen vom Kosmosinsef* or *Nerdensagen vom Kosmosinset*). Ref: TV: vt; no Eng. Animag 3:6: based on a novel. 5:4: followed by a 26-volume, mail-order OAV series. 6:5: 1st OAV 12/88. V. Max 2:15-19.

The Galactic Empire vs. the Free Planets, in a future universe of "celestial globes" (which are apparently something like space stations), "reflecting force fields," and "super-beam cannons." The dramatics (as per the synopsis in V. Max) seem unremarkable, but the spacescapes have been designed with an eye towards *2001: A Space Odyssey,* and the animators have the "Blue Danube" floating and drifting effects down pat. The lights in this sky are often spaceships: In the distance, the latter look like fleets of floating lights. The stirring orchestral score is adapted from classics like "Bolero."

**LEGEND OF LEMNEAR** (J) Soshin Pictures/Anime Int'l. Co. (A.I.C.) c1990? anim color 43m. Ref: TV: Asmik video; no Eng.; OAV?

Ingredients: an evil sorcerer who has a laser-lightning weapon and who, at the end, turns into a two-headed dragon ... an evil prince with eye-ray talents ... a giant, Majin-like stone god that sprouts wings ... nasty finbacked creatures ... a giant, skull-shaped structure in the sky ... a strange atmospheric disturbance ... flying dinosaur/dragon mounts ... and the heroine, who ultimately becomes a light-and-power sorceress.... Occasionally stylish, hollow t&a&b ("b" for blood) sword-and-sorcery saga, set on a three-moon planet, has standard character design and pop music.

**The LEGEND OF LIVING CORPSE** (H.K.?) 1988? color 87m. Ref: TV: Pan-Asia Video; no Eng.

A dead, flying female martial artist returns as a ghost, runs amok in a restaurant, then joins a hopping-ghost line, though most of the "ghosts" seem to be fakes. She can vanish at will, and death does not seem to affect her prowess at combat, one way or the other.... Silly, shot-on-tape comedy-fantasy-actioner.

**LEGEND OF LIVING CORPSE, The** see *Shaolin Brothers, The*

**The LEGEND OF LYON: FLARE, Parts I & II** (J) Media Station & Studio Max & AIC & Friends & Cosmos Plan (Shin Maruyama) c1989? ('94-U.S.) anim color c60m. D: Yakihiro Makino, Yorihisa Uchida. SP & Monster Des: Y. Makino. Mus: N. Kajihara. AD: Y. Uchida, M. Kurita. SdFX: Anime Sound. Ref: TV: SoftCel video, Eng. titles; Cult Videos of Berkeley, no Eng., Part II.

Master Glode and his alien rapists—energy-sucking monsters—invade the Planet Lyon. In Part II, the evil is "reborn." Generally unimaginative semi-hardcore with lush visuals features the usual tentacle sex, the possessed youth Eon, much goo and electricity, and—in an impressive sequence—gigantic snakes, or the coils of one giant snake, bursting up through the ground of an idyllic countryside.

**LEGEND OF THE CHAMPIONS** (B) ITC-TV/Monty Berman 1968 color c90m. D: Cyril Frankel. Tel: Dennis Spooner. Ph:

James Allen, Frank Watts. Mus: D. Edwin Astley, Robert Farnon. AD: Charles Bishop. SpFX: Sid Pearson. Ref: TV. Oakland Trib. no Scheuer. no Maltin '92. TVG. With Stuart Damon, Alexandra Bastedo, William Gaunt, Anthony Nicholls, Colin Blakely, Burt Kwouk, Felix Aylmer (the Old Man), Kenneth J. Warren.

From "The Champions" TV series. A plane crashes in Tibet, and its three passengers—Craig Stirling (Damon), Richard Barrett (Gaunt), and Sharron Macready (Bastedo)—discover an "unknown city" and a parallel civilization. "Changes" are made in the three that "transform the efficiency" of their minds and bodies and make them "superhuman, perhaps." They find they have gifts of telepathy, self-healing, super-hearing, and super-strength. Vapid, archly dialogued crossing of secret agent and science-fantasy genres.

**LEGEND OF THE DEMON WOMB** (J) c1991? anim color c100m. (*Urotsukidoji: The Future, Parts I & II*). Ref: Japan Video. Animerica 6:14, 15, 16: OAVs 4 & 5 in the series as a whole. Or is this *Urotsuki Doji-mataiden*?

See also: *Urotsukidoji: The Future, Part 3.*

**LEGEND OF THE DINOSAURS** see *Legend of Dinosaurs, The*

**LEGEND OF THE GOLDEN PEARL** see *Legend of Wisely, The*

**LEGEND OF THE LIQUID SWORD** (H.K.?) Era Picture Ltd./Wong Jing's Workshop 1993 color/ws 82m. Ref: TV: World Video; Eng. titles. V 1/18/93:70: in release.

"I am Batman. Nice to meet you." The caped, flying "Batman" here vampirizes women, magically crushes a master's head, spits poison which makes a priest melt and explode, and "breaks" the hero's veins. ("So blood is what we need.") Extras: a man fried by lightning and a diminishing room.... Horror-fantasy is kooky enough occasionally to lift itself above the routine. Fun: the mid-air running effects. Prize line A: "We beg Jellyfish help us to defeat Batman." Prize line B: "Hey, your face is green and blue. How spooky."

**LEGEND OF THE NINJA DRAGON SWORD** see *Ninjya Ryukenden*

**LEGEND OF THE OVER-FIEND** see *Wandering Kid*

**LEGEND OF THE OWL** (H.K.?) Zenith Film/Film Way c1986 color 78m. D?: Chin Pei. Ref: TV: Rainbow Video; Eng. titles.

"It scares me to death." Scattered comic-horrific ingredients in this weird low comedy/actioner include an owl which messily pops out of a man's back ("Alien, alien!") ... "Mr. Owl," a man who wears an owl's-head mask and who can turn his foes' swords into snakes or feather dusters ... a parrot which speaks its (lengthy) piece, then falls to the ground dead ... a diminishing room ... and a *Jaws*-type-music parody. Also included, in this very uneven, but sometimes very funny comedy: "Mission: Impossible" theme music and a climactic scene in which a martial-arts duel turns into a dance to "Rock around the Clock."

**The LEGEND OF THE ROLLERBLADE 7** York/Rebel 1992 color 89m. (*The Rollerblade Seven, Part 2* - orig t). Story, SP, D, P, Ph: Donald G. Jackson. SP: also Scott Shaw. Mus ("Roller Blade"): Allan G. T-Man. PD: "Sergio Kurosawa." SpFX: Macabre Creations. Mkp: Selina Jayne. Ref: TV: Academy video? V 1/13/92:12. With Scott Shaw, Joe Estevez, Allison Chase, Don Stroud, Karen Black, Frank Stallone, Selina Jayne (spirit guide), Rhonda Shear, William Smith, Zona Jaguar (Onibaba, demon).

After the Second Dark Age.... Wild ingredients: Pharaoh (Smith), ruler of the barren Wheelzone ... "the evil agents of Saint O'ffender (Estevez) ... the psychic Tarot (Black, the Faye Dunaway of the "B"'s) ... a ninja ... the United Skates of America ... the Master of Light Institute ... the Black Knight (Stallone), "ruler of the underworld" ... Valley of the Demons ... t&a ... a wide variety of costumes from the junk heap of civilization ... and Bronson Caverns.

Apparent fourth in the *Roller Blade* series is a shot-on-tape patchwork of skating held together by narration. It plays like a very strange home movie and has its own, crazy anti-rhythm. It's where the bizarre and the tedious roam. Good line (in context): "Perhaps a diet cola then." Bad line (in or out of context): "For he was only a pawn in a cosmic game."

**LEGEND OF THE SOUTH SEA QUEEN, The** see *Lady Terminator*

**LEGEND OF THE WHITE HORSE** (Polish-U.S.) CBS Prods./Film Polski & Legend/White Dragon Prods. (Szpak-Fleet) 1985 color/ws 91m. D: Jerzy Domaradzki, Janusz Morgenstern. SP: R.C. Fleet. From Robert C. Fleet's novel *White Horse, Dark Dragon*. Idea: G. Bamber. Mus: J. Stoklosa. PD: Tadeusz Kosarewicz. SpFX: WFF Wroclaw; J. Krol;(ph) R. Lenczewski. Mkp: Dobracki. ElecSdFX: John Fasal, Warren Dewey. Narr: Ted Sorel. Ref: TV: vt; Eng. version. Martin. no Hound. no Stanley. With Dee Wallace Stone, Christopher Lloyd, Christopher Stone, Soon-Teck Oh, Luke Askew.

"A real dragon!" Something flying drives a man to fall to his death, and a weird white horse turns into a big dragon which zaps bad guys with its rays. (They burn and turn to stone.) Plus: a real witch .... Ecologically correct, but dramatically wanting, though the land-rapers' spectacular comeuppance is satisfying. This dragon should work for the EPA.

**The LEGEND OF WISELY** (H.K.) Cinema City 1987 (1986) color/ws 98m. (*Weisili Zhuanqi*). D: R. R. Yang(?), aka Teddy Robin. SP: Philip Cheng, Gerald Lu, Pook Yuen Leung (sp?), from books by Nguy Kong, or I Kwan. Mus: Luo Dayou. AD: Kenneth Wee, or Yee. VisFX: Yu Tai Kung (sp?). SpFxD: A. Cheung. Ref: TV: Rainbow Video; Eng. titles. Y. K. Ho. Horacio Higuchi. V 5/6/87. 5/1/85:409: *Wisely Legend*. HR 2/23/88:S-94: aka *Legend of the Golden Pearl*. With Samuel Hu, Bruce Baron, Heidi Makinen.

"Adventurer, sci-fi writer" Wisely agrees to help the five-year-old "little master" of a Nepalese sect regain the mystical "dragon pearl." The latter turns out to be a solar energy ball left behind centuries ago by the ancestors of one "Howard Hope".... Pretty postcard pictures of Nepal, Egypt, and Hong Kong; routine action scenes. A long haul until the elaborate finale, in which a huge alien spacecraft breaks free of a mountain and flies through clouds and into space. (Witnesses observe that the ship looks like a dragon, hence perhaps our legends of dragons.) These last ten minutes are pretty impressive, but the rest is a yawn.

See also *Cat, The. Seventh Curse, The. Young Wisely.*

**LEGEND OF ZIPANG** see *Jipangu*

**La LEGENDE** (F) WMF 1992 color feature. D: Jerome Diamant-Berger. Ref: V 10/19/92:152: science fiction; screening at MIFED.

**LEGION** see *Exorcist III, The*

**LEGION OF IRON** RCA-Col HV/Epic/Fortune Ent. 1990 color 85m. D, P: Yakov Bentsvi. SP: R. Gordon, S. Schoenberg. Story: E. Hunt. Ref: V 8/22/90:76 (hv): "ho-hum." Hound. no Martin. With K. T. Walsh, Erika Nann, Camille Carrigan.

"Futuristic gladiator battles." (V)

**LELEKLATO SUGAR** (Hung.) Star 1918 b&w silent. D, P: Alfred Deesy. SP: Istvan Lazar. Ref: Hardy/SF: The Mind-Detecting Ray - tr t? Lee. With R. Fiath, G. Turan, A. Goth.

"Mind-reading machine."

**LEMRO, PRIVATE EYE** see *Alien Private Eye*

**LENSMAN** (J-U.S.) Streamline Pictures/Towa (MK Co.) 1984 ('90-U.S.) anim color/ws 108m. D: Yoshiaki Kawajiri, Kazuyuki Hirokawa. SP: Soji Yoshikawa, from E. E. Smith's novels, principally *Galactic Patrol.* Mus: Akira Inoue. Ph: Ban Yamaki. AD: K. Aoki. Anim D: Kazuo Tomizawa, K. Kitajaima. VisFX: Computer Graphics; (lens anim) Kenneth Wesley; (city anim) Carter Burnell; N. Y. Institute of Technology. Ref: TV: Pony Video; some Eng. titles. J Anim Program Guide. V/Mifed '89: 193. 2/21/90:159. 5/2/90:S-96. 4/8/91. Cinef 3/90. Anim Mag 5:26: aka *SF New Era: The Lensman.* SFExam 10/12/90:C-4. U.C. Theatre notes 9/16/90. Voices (J version): Toshio Furukawa, Fumi Koyama, Nachi Nozawa (Worsel), Yoshio Otsuka.

In the 25th Century, Lensmen fight the "evil empire Boskone," the leader of which—Helmuth—is more an energy field than a character. Creatures and weapons include monstrous snails which spray a web-like substance, the robot-pterodactyl-like Lensman Worsel, a water monster, and an ambulatory, lightning-like thing, or weapon. Planets include Mqueie, Delgon, and Radelix.

Lavishly imagined, pleasing spectacle borrows from *2001* and *Star Wars,* but then Doc Smith came first. The movie's array of exploding planets, space battles, and cosmic vistas is impressive enough, but the abstract effects—first, for the prologue, then the view inside the "world" of the Lens, and finally Helmuth's climactic test, or torment, of hero Chris—are perhaps even more dizzying/dazzling. Visual highlights also include Delgon's tentacle plants—their quiescent state is subtly ominous—and the monstrous Boskone and their gnarled spaceships.

**LENZ** (Hung.) Hungarofilm/Bela Balazs Studio 1987 color 100m. SP, D: Andras Szirtes. SP: also Matyas Buki, Tamas Pap. Inspired by Georg Buchner's novel. Ref: V 3/25/87: "strictly limited to ... audiences interested in the avant garde." Berlin Int'l. Film Festival (1987), program. with Szirtes, Klara Monus, Kati Szerb.

Overdose of radiation alters scientist's perception of the world.

**LEONARD PART 6** Col/Sah (Bill Cosby/Alan Marshall) 1987 color 85m. D: Paul Weiland. SP: Jonathan Reynolds. Story: B. Cosby. Ph: Jan DeBont. Mus: Elmer Bernstein. PD: G. Kirkland. VisFX: Boss; Richard Edlund. PhFX: Oxford Scientific. SpFX: Jeff Gillam et al. OptFX: Cinema Research. Ref: TV. V 12/16/87. With B. Cosby, Tom Courtenay, Joe Don Baker, Moses Gunn, Grace Zabriskie, George Kirby, Jane Fonda.

Bizarre "bird dancers" ... the Sphere, needed to "control the animals".. killer bunnies ... lobster terrors ("Lobster Crew Chief" credit noted) ... "100% beef" weapons.... Effects-heavy comedy-spectacle.

**LEPRECHAUN** Trimark (Mark Amin/J. B. Mallian) 1993 (1992) color 92m. SP, D: Mark Jones. Mus: K. Kiner. MkpFX: Atlantic West FX, Gabe Bartalos. Animatronics: Dave Kindlon. OptSup: David Hewitt. SpFxAnim: Michael Hyatt. SpFX: Players. Ref: TV. V 1/18/93. 3/30/92:78 (rated). Sacto Bee 1/11/93. ad. SFChron 1/9/93. With Warwick Davis (leprechaun), Jennifer Aniston, Ken Olandt, Mark Holton.

"The wee people have their magical ways." A 600-year-old leprechaun with a mean grip and the ability to materialize at will wants his gold back. The wee people need better dialogue writers—these are the limpest post-Freddy zingers yet. Very slight horror-fantasy.

**LEPRECHAUN 2** Trimark (Borchers) 1994 color feature (*One Wedding and Lots of Funerals* - B). D: R. Flender. SP: T. Meyer, A. Septien. Ph: Jane Castle. Mus: J. Elias. PD: A. Tremblay. VisFxSup: P. Mazzucato. MkpFX: Gabe Bartalos. Ref: V 4/18/94: "pastiche plot." vc box: "back in the big city." PT 20:71. With Warwick Davis, Clint Howard, Sandy Baron.

**LETHAL WOMAN** S.E.V.P. Pictures 1988 color c90m.? Ref: vc box. no Adam. with Richard Pacheco (alien), Krysta Lane, Tiffany Storm, Ariel Knight.

"Sex sucking villain from the stars."

**LETHAL WOMAN II** S.E.V.P. Pictures 1988 color c90m.? Ref: vc box. with Krysta Lane, Tiffany Storm, Ariel Knight.

Interplanetary travel, "cum-gun."

**LETHAL WOMAN** Independent Network & Film Ventures Int'l. & Pure Gold (Karie-Nethersole-Spencer) 1989 color 95m. (*The Most Dangerous Woman Alive* - orig t). D: Christian Marnham. SP: Michael Olson, Gabriel Elias. Mus: Meir Eshel. SpFxSup: Rick Cresswell. Mkp: Anni Taylor. Ref: TV. V 5/31/89. With Merete Van Kamp, Robert Lipton, Shannon Tweed, James Luisi, Deep Roy, Graeme Clarke.

"The Erotic Adventure ... Boys need not apply." Victims of rape and other male violence lure men to Diana's Island, St. Christobel, where woman hunt down men with bow-and-arrow, a la *The Most Dangerous Game,* and a horror corridor of suspended severed heads greets the unwary.... Or, Revenge-of-the-Woman Island. Romance and t&a angles dilute this cross between *Ms. 45* and *The Most Dangerous Game.* (The dialogue includes direct references to the latter.) See also *Slave Girls from Beyond Infinity.*

**LET'S PLAY DEAD** Mirror Releasing/Saturn Int'l. (Dave Arthur) 1985 color c92m. (aka *Schoolgirls in Chains*). SP, D, P: Don Jones. Ph: Ron Garcia. Mus: Josef Powell. Mkp: Ron Foreman. Ref: TV: World Premiere HV. no Stanley. no Hound. no Martin. PT 13:47. With Gary Kent, John Stoglin, Leah Tate, Robert Mathews, Suzanne Lund, Lynn Ross, T. R. Blackburn.

"She was the craziest of them all." "Mama" is dead, but she still speaks through one of her sons—Frank, probably, or John, who's "still a child" and who likes to play doctor with his "friends," or "pets" (captured women) in the cellar. Upstairs, in a predictable surprise, lies "Mama," a decayed corpse.... Sketchy, repetitious psycho-thriller. The most determinedly perverse scene is reserved for a flashback in which Mama tells Frank, "My son, even now I love you!", as son attempts to strangle mom for scaring away his fiancee with tales of incest.

**LETTERS FROM A DEAD MAN** (Russ) Lenfilm 1986 ('87-U.S.) color and b&w 86m. (*Pisma Mertvogo Cheloveka*. aka *Dead Man's Letters*). SP, D: Konstantin Lopushanski. SP: also V. Rybakov, with Boris Strugacki. Ph: N. Prokopcev. Mus: A. Zhurbin. AD: Amshinskaya, Ivanov. Ref: SFChron 2/12/87: WTBS-TV; "crushingly somber." V 11/12/86: "well-made and involving." 7/1/87:50 (ad). Scheuer. With Rolan Bykov, I. Ryklin, V. Michailov.

"Grim depiction of subterranean life among Moscow survivors of a nuclear war." (SFC)

**LETZTE GEHEIMNIS, Das** see *Privat Klinik Professor Lund*

**LEVIATAN** see *Monster Dog*

**LEVIATHAN** (U.S.-I) MGM-UA/MGM & Luigi & Aurelio De Laurentiis (Gordon Co.) 1989 color/ws 98m. D: George Pan Cosmatos. Story, SP: David Peoples. SP: also Jeb Stuart. Mus: Jerry Goldsmith. Creature FX: Stan Winston. MechFX: Nick Allder; (coord) Giovanni Corridori. ElecFxCoord: Tonino Testa. VisFX: Barry Nolan; IL&M; (computer) Perpetual Motion Pictures; Cinema Research. Ref: TV: MGM-UA HV. V 3/22/89. 5/2/90:S-64: Ital. co-pro. SFChron Dtbk 4/2/89. MFB'90:132-3: U.S.-I. co-pro. Maltin '92. McCarty. Martin. Scheuer. With Peter Weller, Richard Crenna, Amanda Pays, Daniel Stern, Ernie Hudson, Michael Carmine, Lisa Eilbacher, Hector Elizondo, Meg Foster.

"It's growing!" The crew of Tri-Oceanic Mining's Shack 7—located on the floor of the Atlantic ocean—discovers an "organism of unknown origin" in the scuttled Russian ship Leviathan. Apparently the result of experiments aimed at perfecting an "underwater man," the creature effects genetic alterations in its human victims and absorbs their bodies and memories into itself.... Familiar effects and action scenes betray a long, careful buildup here. The first *Alien* and the second *The Thing* are the obvious principal influences. Less obvious and more surprising are the borrowings from "Dracula": The monster—at one point explicitly called a "Dracula"—drinks blood, and the Leviathan—like the Demeter (which was also a Russian ship) in the Bram Stoker novel—is a spooky ship of the dead. In fact, one of the movie's creepiest scenes is simply Crenna's Doc's translation of the labels on the lost crew's individual files: "Deceased ... deceased ... deceased...."

**3 LEWD LIZARD** Star Motion Pictures/Liang Shu Yee 1980? color/ws c90m. D: Wang Hsiung, Wai Wang. Ph: W. Y. Lung. Ref: TV: Quality Video; Eng. titles.

Our strange hero, David, extracts hormones from snakes and frogs and injects them into lizards. He then slips one "lewd lizard" into a woman's panties—with her in them. She writhes in painful ecstasy, then apparently dies. Soon, dead women are found here and there, each with a "worm inside." One keen-minded investigator opines that all these murders must have been done by one person—i.e., that there are not several killers running around planting deadly worms on female victims.... New frontiers of gratuitous kinkiness are explored by *Lewd Lizard*, which is essentially one unusual, writhe-smile-pant scene repeated several times. The story is a flimsy pretext for this one scene.

See also *Lady Terminator*.

**La LEYENDA DEL CURA DE BARGOTA** (Sp-I) Origen & TVE & Reteitalia & Telecip & RTP & Taurus Films 1990 color 88m. SP, D: Pedro Olea. SP: also Juan Antonio Porto. Mus: Carmelo Bernaola. Ref: V 11/4/90: *The Legend of the Priest from Bargota* - tr t; "routine handling" of the "second part of a six-pic package exploring historical cases of witchcraft...." With Fernando Guillen Cuervo, Lola Forner, Raf Vallone.

Blood pacts with the devil in the 16th Century.

**LIBIDO** (I) Nucleo Film 1966 b&w 85m. SP, D: Ernesto Gastaldi (aka Julian Berry), Vittorio Salerno. Ph: R. Garroni. From Mara Maryl's story. Ref: Hardy/HM: "self-consciously arty direction." Lee (P). MMF 14:67. Imagi 1:59: early "giallo." Palmerini: "mediocre." With Dominique Boschero, Maryl (aka Maria Chianetta), Giancarlo Giannini, Alan Collins (aka Luciano Pigozzi).

Just-married young man (Giannini) goes mad, repeats homicidal actions of his mad father in "mirror-filled room."

**El LIBRO DE PIEDRA** (Mex) Adolfo Grovas 197-? color c90m. SP, D: Carlos Enrique Taboada. Ph: I. Torres. Mus: R. Lavista. AD: Eduardo Carrasco? SpFX: Ricardo Sainz. Mkp: Sara Mateos. Ref: TV: *The Book of Stone* - tr t; no Eng. TVG. Bowker '90. With Joaquin Cordero, Marga Lopez, Norma Lazareno, Aldo Monti, Lucy Buj (la nina), Jorge Pablo Carrillo (Hugo).

A mysterious shadow. A lost and mysteriously returned brooch. A mention of witchcraft. A woman with mysterious pains in her hand and leg. A weird little girl who seems to talk to ghosts and who takes to drawing satan signs on the floor. Weird lizards. Lights that go out mysteriously. (Nice chill here, as the woman then lights the candle and sees, in the mirror, the face of the boy whose likeness is carved into the statue in the woods.) Climactic double chill: The father knocks down the statue, and the likeness of his daughter appears in place of the boy's.... Poky but quite atmospheric ghost tale has a touch of "Turn of the Screw" and a good, muted, creepy score.

**A LICENCE TO THRILL** Vidco 1985 color 78m. Ref: vc box: "nymphomania machine." Adam '88: *License To Thrill*. With Heather Wayne (Jane Bond), Tony El-Ay (Dr. Yes), Kari Foxx.

See also: *Jane Bond Meets Octopussy*.

**LIEBESBRIEFE EINER PORTUGIESISCHEN NONNE** see *Love Letters of a Portuguese Nun*

**LIFE HESITATES AT 40** MGM-Roach 1936 short. D: Charles Parrott, Harold Law. Ref: Maltin/SSS. Lee(LC). With Charley Chase, Joyce Compton, James Finlayson, Andrea Leeds, Edward Earle, Carl "Alfalfa" Switzer.

"Charley has strange spells during which everything around him seems to stop." (SSS)

**LIFE IS A DREAM** (F) Int'l. Film Circuit/INA & MCH & La Sept & MAE & CNC & PTT 1986 ('88-U.S.) color 100m. (*Memoire des Apparences*). SP, D: Raul Ruiz. From Pedro Calderon de la Barca's play "La Vida es Sueno." Mkp: Helene Loubeyre. Ref: screen. PFA notes 11/17/87. V 12/2/87. VV 1/12/88. NYT 12/30/88. London Film Festival '87, notes.

Victims of a nuclear holocaust dream of political intrigue and moviegoing: These dead, as revealed in the coda, have spent the film dreaming that they are alive. Ruiz's dry is-it-life/dream/film? ambiguities wear thin quickly. Only the surprise science-fictional coda engages at all. One of the movies dreamt seems to be a futuristic, *Metropolis*-type film; another stars Sinbad.

**LIFE IS A MOMENT** (H.K.) Molesworth Ltd. (Sally Aw) 1988 color/ws c92m. D & Exec P: Teresa Woo. Ref: TV: World Video; Eng. titles. Y. K. Ho. With Patricia Ha, Alex Fu.

An electromagnetic accident sends 6262, or Luk Yee, and her solar-energy car back in time, from the world of 2037, impolite robots, and synthetic juices, to 1987. ("I should come fifty years later.") There she meets and falls in love with Fong. But the future wants her, and a special scientific team sends her back to 2037, where her happy memories of the past are brainwashed away. But vintage chocolate triggers her memory, and 1987 lives again in her mind.... The 1987 scenes are romantic piffle; the well-engineered, bittersweet coda is Proust. Here the sight of chocolate candy takes the place of the taste of the "crumb of madeleine."

**LIFE ON THE EDGE** see *Meet the Hollowheads*

**LIFEBOAT** see *Lifepod*

**LIFEFORCE** (B) Tri-Star/London Cannon (Easedram) 1985 color/ws 101m. (*Space Vampires* - orig t). D: Tobe Hooper. SP: Dan O'Bannon, Don Jakoby, from Colin Wilson's novel *Space Vampires*. Mus: Henry Mancini; Michael Kamen, James Guthrie. MkpFX: Nick Maley. SpVisFX: John Dykstra; Apogee. SpFX: John Gant. Wire FX: Steve Crawley, Kevin Welch. OptFxSup: Roger Dorney. P: (vis fx) Robert Shepherd. Ref: TV. MFB'85:311-12. V 6/26/85. 5/1/85:36(ad). 5/9/84:50-51(ad). Phantom. With Steve Railsback, Peter Firth, Frank Finlay, Mathilda May (space girl), Patrick Stewart, Michael Gothard, Aubrey Morris, James Forbes-Robertson, Christopher Jagger (first vampire), Bill Malin (second vampire).

The space shuttle *Churchill* returns to Earth with three "perfectly preserved bodies" found (along with huge dead bats) inside Halley's Comet. At the European Space Research Center, in London, the female body (May) revives and turns out to be a vampire who "kisses" the energy out of her victims. "Once

transformed, the victims need regular infusions of energy," or else they shrivel up and implode. Meanwhile, over the city, a spaceship "collects" the energy of the entire populace.... The last two-thirds of *Lifeforce* is regulation possession/zombie/green-ray material; the first third vividly illustrates theme and title, the ebbing and flowing of the "lifeforce." In the sequence, especially, in which the "dead" shrunken guard comes back to life on the operating table, the inanimate-suddenly-animated effects are genuinely startling, like time-lapse photography of plant life the first time one encounters it.

**The LIFEFORCE EXPERIMENT** (U.S.-Can.) Sci-Fi Channel/Filmline Int'l. & Screen Partners & USA Pictures (Nicolas Clermont) 1994 color c90m. D: Piers Haggard. Tel: Mike Hodges, G. MacDonald, from Daphne du Maurier's novella *The Breakthrough*. Ph: P. Benison. Mus: O. Montes. PD: J. Meighen. SpFX: R. Cosgrove. Ref: V 4/11/94:54: "leaden ... monumentally boring." TVG: "worthwhile elements." With Donald Sutherland, Mimi Kuzyk, Corin Nemec, Vlasta Vrana, Miguel Fernandes.

Scientist tries, *Asphyx*-like, to "capture the energy" of a soul as it departs a body.

**LIFEPOD** Fox West Pictures (Fox Network TV)/Trilogy Ent. & RHI (Roach-Stern-Harbert) 1993 color c90m. D: Ron Silver. Story, Tel, Exec Co-P: Pen Densham. Tel: also M. Jay Roach. "Suggested by a short story by Alfred Hitchcock and Harry Sylvester." Ph: R. Steadman. Mus: M. Mancina. PD: C. A. Schnell. VisFX: (sup) Sam Nicholson; Stargate Films; (min sup) Dan Brown; Dave Johnson. SpFxCoord: Lou Carlucci. MechFX: David Kuklish. Key Mkp: Marvin Westmore. Ref: TV. TVG 6/26/93. SFChron 7/2/93. 6/21/93. With Robert Loggia, Jessica Tuck, R. Silver, Adam Storke, Kelli Williams, CCH Pounder, Stan Shaw.

Christmas Eve, year 2169. The *Terrania*, a spacecraft bound for Earth, suffers a "controlled meltdown" which leaves a lifeboat-like "lifepod" drifting in an "ocean ten billion light years across." And everyone on board, it seems, "has a reason" for wanting the Terrania sabotaged.... A dwindling air supply subs here for a dwindling water supply, in this tiresome remake of *Lifeboat*, one of Alfred Hitchcock's films least in need of a remake.

**LIGHT BLAST** (I) Lorimar-Telepictures/Faso Film & Metro Film (Juso-Manzotti) 1985 color 89m. (*A Colpi di Luce*). SP, D: Enzo G. Castellari. SP: also Tito Carpi. Mus: Guido & Maurizio De Angelis. PD: Louis Sagan. SpFxOpt: "Al Sparrows." Mkp: Joseph Bankes. SdFX: Cine Audio. PhFX: Julian "Ironbeater." Ref: TV. V 5/29/85. Phantom. With Erik Estrada, Michael Pritchard, Peggy Rowe, Louis Geneva.

"Death-by-light-blast, in person," threatens to annihilate San Francisco. Prof. Yuri Svoboda (Pritchard) invents a "high frequency laser" which transforms liquid crystals and electronic signs into "electronic megabombs".... Tempting to say that Castellari does for S.F. here what he did for New York in *1990: The Bronx Warriors*, but the acting this time is not as amusingly wooden. Typical "thrill" shots include someone on fire and screaming, a car flying through the air in slow motion, and semi-comically-melting faces.

**LIGHT YEARS** (F) Miramax (Isaac Asimov)/Col. Ima. Son & Films A2 & Revcom-TV & CNDLC & MDLCEDLC 1987 ('88-U.S.) anim color 83m. (*Gandahar*-F). D & Adap: Rene Laloux. SP: Raphael Cluzel, from Jean-Pierre Androvan's novel *Les Homme-Machines contre Gandahar*, or *Metal Men against Gandahar*. Mus: Gabriel Yared; (U.S.) Bob Jewett, Jack Maeby. U.S.: (d) Harvey Weinstein; (adap) Asimov. Korea: (d) Kim Kwang Seung; (des) K. Y. Tchan. SdFX: Jerome Levy. Ref: TV: Vidmark Ent. video. V 10/21/87. SFExam 8/19/88 (hv). Phantom. Scheuer. Voices: Glenn Close, Christopher Plummer (Metamorphis), Penn Jillette, Bridget Fonda, Teller, Paul Schaffer, Terence Mann (metal man), Jill Haworth.

"A thousand years ago, Gandahar will be saved...." Metal Men are attacking the peaceful land of Gandahar and turning the inhabitants into stone. They then place the bodies in huge eggs and transform the former into more hollow Metal Men for "The Great Beginning"—the Metamorphis, an experimental brain which has developed senses. The brain proves—like the Deformed, cave mutants—to have been produced by Gandahar's geneticists, then dumped (like toxic waste) into the sea and forgotten. Other ingredients: the Door of Time ... monstrous night birds ... a giant, motherly, dinosaur-like creature ... plant and crab-monster weapons ... and a mutant-produced, blue-lightning weapon.

Pleasingly designed, but rather thin animated tale re the perils of science and technology. The script makes its points mainly, and wanly, in the dialogue.

The **LIGHTNING INCIDENT** USA-TV/Wilshire Court (Mark Gordon Co./Christopher Meledandri) 1991 color c90m. (*Lightning Field* - orig t). D: Michael Switzer. Tel: Michael Murray. Ph: Victor Goss. Mus: J. P. Robinson? PD: Anthony Cowley. SpVisFX: Bill Millar. SpFX: Greg Curtis. Mkp: Amy Lederman. Ref: TV. TVG. Oak Trib 9/11/91. With Nancy McKeon, Polly Bergen, Tantoo Cardinal, Elpidia Carrillo, Miriam Colon, Tim Ryan, Joaquin Martinez, Gary Clarke.

"The answer is in your dreams." A South American Indian cult's final ingredient for its power trip: a baby.

**LIGHTNING TRAP: LEINA AND LAIKA** (J) Toshiba EMI 1990 anim color 30m. Ref: Animag 10:5: OAV.

Leina, from *Machine Robo* (P), and Laika, "cyborg officer from Interpol," meet.

**LIGHTS! CAMERA! MURDER!** (So. African) Atlas Video/Niche & Distant Horizon & Compass (Anant Singh) 1990 (1988) color 88m. (*Final Cut* - shooting t). D: Frans Nel. SP: Emil Kolbe. SpFX: Jannie Wienand. Ref: V 12/3/90:82 (hv): "boring." With John Barrett, Matthew Stewardson, Michael Huff.

"Killing during the lensing of a snuff film."

**LIGHTS OUT** Fox Terrytoons c1943 anim color 6m. D: Eddie Donnelly. Story: John Foster. Mus: P.A. Scheib. Ref: TV: Video Treasures.

Gandy Goose reads a book titled *A Ghost Story,* dreams about a haunted house. ("This place gives me the creeps.") Some funny bits.

**LIHIM ... SA DILIM NG GABI** (Fili) Lari Films Int'l. 1988 color c85m. D: Edward Dalton. SP: Carlito Conge, Oscar Legaspi. Ph: Armando Dulag. Mus D: Castellano. PD: Legaspi. Live FX: Pompong de Milo. Ref: TV: Celebrity Video; no Eng. New Manila Deli: Secret ... *In the Dark of the Night* - tr t. With Myra Manibog, Mark Joseph (Albert), Aleli Abadilla, Hanna Reyes, Vic Ramos, Jake Ramiro, Joe Lapid.

Supernatural melodrama with horrific overtones, as mystery eyes shoot death rays at a would-be rapist and later zap another man. The eyes belong to a retarded boy; a special medallion keeps the latter temporarily in check, but when a woman discovers the bodies of his victims, she screams, flees the boy, and ultimately kills him in panic.... Editor, where is thy scissors? Every scene of slender, sentimental story goes on and on.

**LIJEPE ZENE PROLAZE KROZ GRAD** (Yugos.) Art Film '80/Zvezda Film & Croatia Film & Forum and Art Film (A. Stojanovic) 1986 color 95m. SP, D: Zelmir Zilnik. SP: also Miroslav Mandic. Mus: Koja. Ref: V 8/6/86: *Beautiful Women Walking about Town* - tr t. no Stanley. With Ljuba Tadzic, Svetolik Mikacevic, Hahela Ferari.

Thought police in Belgrade in the year 2041. "Very low budget...."

**\*\*LILITH UND LY** (Austrian) Fiat Films 1919. D: Drich Kober. SP: Fritz Lang. Ph: Willy Hameister. Ref: Hardy/HM: "vampire theme." Lee (p). Osterr. no Eisner/FL. no Ott/FOFL. With Elga Beck, Hans Marschall, Ernst Escherich.

Televised image of Lilith drains hero's life away.

**LILITH UNLEASHED** VCA (David Stone) 1986 color 84m. D: Henri Pachard. Ref: Adam '88. vc box. With Tish Ambrose, Tasha Voux, Paul Thomas (Lucifer), Ron Jeremy, Siobhan Hunter, Barbara Dare.

Lilith (Ambrose) seduces and shrinks "everyone in sight, leading to an orgy of wee people" in a doll house.

**LILY-C.A.T.** (J) Suda c1986? anim color 67m. Story, D: Hisayuki Toriumi. SP: Hiroyuki Hoshiyama. Ph: H. Kaneko. Mus: Akira Inoue; (fx) S. Shiba. AD: M. Banno. Anim D: T. Okada. Ref: TV: RCA Victor video; computer data in Eng. Voices: H. Okita, M. Katsuki, H. Tanaka (God).

Or, "Invasion of the Unknown Bacteria." Circa year 2260 A.D. The Earth spaceship *Saldes* collects a meteor-like object which harbors bacteria that absorbs living bodies and eventually erodes the craft itself. Hero and heroine escape the exploding ship, and the now-gigantic monster, which is attached to their vehicle, burns up and off in the heat of the explosion.... The movie's last and best effect: The monster's tentacles burn and writhe as they become semi-human shapes, then disappear. The bacteria monster in this very *Alien* movie has eyes within teeth within mouths, and tentacles like roots. It seems to cocoon some victims. *Lily-C.A.T.* is the tabby which is really a "computerized, animal-shaped technological robot," the "Master" of the ship. Bland score and character design.

**LINDA LOVELACE FOR PRESIDENT** David Winter-Charles Stroud 1975 color feature. D: Claudio Guzman. SP: Jack

Margolis. Ref: MFB'76:67. Jones. no Lentz. no Weldon. PT 11:4, 50: "some of this mess is funny."

Bit with "Dracula-like vampire." (Jones)

**LINGCHEN WANCAN** see *Vampire's Breakfast*

**LINK** (U.S.-B) Cannon/Thorn EMI (Link Films & Cannon) 1986 color 116m. (102m.-U.S.) (aka *The Link*). D: Richard Franklin. Story, SP: Everett De Roche. Story: also Lee Zlotoff, Tom Ackerman. Mus: Jerry Goldsmith. SpMkp: Yvonne Coppard. Animatronics Coord: Barbara Griffiths. Hair Suits: Stuart Artingstall. SpFxSup: John Gant. Ref: TV. V 10/8/86. ad. MFB. With Elisabeth Shue, Terence Stamp, Steven Pinner, Richard Garnett, David O'Hara.

The-ape-turns plot begins mildly enough with Link and the "family retainer routine," progresses to Link-as-Master-of-Fire, then to the slam-the-dog routine. "Monkey House" really begins to get rough with the push-the-van-over-the-cliff routine.... The mundane action climax is a letdown after some mood-setting work with ape personalities. Link's eyes are blank, cold, prying, pleased, as the situation demands. Predictably, the homicidal ape proves indestructible. Infectious Goldsmith score.

**LINK, The** see *Blood Link. Link*

**LINNEA QUIGLEY'S HORROR WORKOUT** Cinema HV (Kennamer/Rand-DeCoteau) 1990 color 60m. SP, D: Kenneth J. Hall (aka Hal Kennedy). Mus: John Vulich. Ref: V 5/23/90:71 (hv): "cute satire of exercise videos." With L. Quigley, B. Jane Holzer, Amy Hunt, Victoria Nesbitt, Kristine Seeley.

Slashers and zombies interrupt aerobics and jogging.

**LION MAN** (Turkish) Stephen Sloane & E. Akman/Memduh Un 1980 color c85m. SP, D: Natuck (or Natuch) Baitan. Ph: Richard McGrath. Mkp: Aliki Dimitropulos. Opt: Les Latimer. Ref: TV: Boomerang Films video; Eng. dubbed. poster. Ecran F 41:71. Hound. no Martin. With Steve Arkin, Barbara Lake, Charles Garret, Tim Jackson.

"It was a monster, a wild animal!" A lion-raised boy matures and becomes super-strong Lion Man, who can crush heads with his bare "lion" hands, uproot small trees, and rip out cow innards for food, for the lions and himself. Later, he uses the "steel claws" which replace his damaged hands to crush heads, smash through shields, etc. (Cf. *Lupin III: Cagliostro Castle*.) Crude production and protagonist, larky music, and bloody violence which, though not really gory, is numbingly insistent. The lions apparently taught the lad martial arts.

Sequel: *Lionman II—The Witchqueen.*

**LION MEN VS. THE WRATH OF THE WITCH QUEEN** see *Lionman II*

**LIONHEART** (U.S.-Hung.) WB/Taliafilm & Hungaro/Mafilm of Budapest (Jack Schwartzman) 1986 color 105m. D: Franklin J. Schaffner. SP, Story: Menno Meyjes. SP: also Richard Outten. SpFxSup: Michael White. Ref: TV: Warner HV. V 8/26/87. Maltin '92. Martin. Scheuer.

Scattered spooky elements in this adventure set at the end of the 12th Century include the underground city of homeless children beneath Paris: Fire-breathing gargoyles, flying "banshees," mysterious mists, and masked figures greet unwelcome visitors. The Black Prince (Gabriel Byrne) here, a "tortured soul"—the Lord of the Lost—captures and cages children. ("On nights such as these, the devil himself has been known to call.") Good Jerry Goldsmith score; slow-starting story which gathers interest as it gathers characters for its Children's Crusade.

**LIONMAN II—THE WITCHQUEEN** (Turkish) Akmanfilm Ltd. 1983 color c87m. (*Lion Men Vs. the Wrath of the Witch Queen* - ad t). D: Michael Arslan. SP: Johnny Byrne. Ph: Huseyin Ozsahin. Mus: Martin Cook. PD: Ahmet Saatchi. SpFX: Mustafa Iyi. Mkp: Zeki Alpan. OptFX: Optical Film FX. Ref: TV: Boomerang Films video; Eng. dubbed. V 10/26/83: 69, 218 (ad). Ecran F 41:71: sequel to *Lion Man*. no Hound. no Martin. Morse. With Frank Morgan, Erich Akman, Dee Taylor (Rheasilvia), Nik Stuart, William Hardy, Crystal Williams, Edward Koch, Thomas Cannon.

The lion-raised Lionman (Morgan), who wears "steel claws" over his acid-burned hands, takes on the Witchqueen, Rheasilvia, whose ray-shooting ring gives her hypnotic power over her foes. This versatile ring also brings in remote pictures and can knock out her enemies. At the end, Lionman brings down her familiar, a falcon, with an arrow, and Rheasilvia burns. Also noted: a tentacled thing in a stream ... a giant, man-eating plant ... and a "burning black powder," or gunpowder. ("This is fantastic!") Stilted dubbing, wimpy effects (the plant appears to be tinfoil), and meant-to-be-stirring music mark this hapless Turkish sword-and-sorcery saga.

Planned Part III: *Lionman—Ring of the Magus.*

**The LION'S BUSY** WB 1950 anim color 7m. D: I. Freleng. SP: Tedd Pierce. Mus D: Carl Stalling. Ref: TV: Trans-Atlantic Video. WBCartoons.

A lion takes a "Rocket to the Moon," finds tenacious Beaky Buzzard waiting for him, walls himself up in a cave until 1957, finds Beaky toothless and fond now only of marshmallows. Pretty much a fizzle except for this last, Merrie Melodies note. Made the same year as *Destination Moon* 1.

**LIQUID DREAMS** Fox-Elwes/Zeta Ent. (Levitt-Firestone) 1991 color 91m. SP, D: Mark Manos. SP, Assoc P: Zack Davis. Ph: Sven Kirsten. Mus: Ed Tomney. PD: Pam Moffat. SpMkpFX: Dragon FX; R. S. Westgate, J. M. Montelongo. SpFX: Court Wizard. Ref: TV. V 6/3/91. SFChron Dtbk 6/14/92. With Richard Steinmetz, Candice Daly, Barry Dennen (The Major), Juan Fernandez, Tracey Walter, Mink Stole, Marilyn Tokuda, John Doe.

"Siphon her?" Ingredients here include the Ritual in the penthouse, in which unwilling donors' extracted endorphins get users like The Major high ... The Major's privates, which appear to be plastic ... the Muze, a "brain lubricant," or subconscious Muzak, which temporarily zombifies Frank Rodino (Steinmetz), police lieutenant and "man of the future" ... and Neurovid, "Novocaine of the soul," which is "both advertisement and anesthesia."

An almost comically decadent world, in a movie infected by a shot-on-tape-like flatness. Script and acting have a certain flatness too. Worthless except for the Line of the Day: "When I want your advice, I'll scrape it off the sidewalk."

**LISA** MGM-UA/UA (Frank Yablans) 1990 color 93m. SP, D: Gary Sherman. SP: also Karen Clark. Mus: Joe Renzetti. SpFX: Guy Faria. Mkp: June Haymore. Ref: TV. V 4/25/90. Sacto Bee 4/23/90. ad. With Cheryl Ladd, D. W. Moffett, Staci Keanan, Tanya Fenmore, Jeffrey Tambor, Edan Gross, Julie Cobb, David Niven Jr.

"Hi, Judy. This is Richard. I'm in your apartment and I'm going to kill you." Is the notorious Candlelight Killer the "most beautiful man you've ever seen," or a "sick son of a bitch"? Or both? Partly believable, partly incredible variation on I Saw What You Did ("You know who I am") is also, partly, a mother-daughter drama, and the two modes do nothing for each other. The grisliest violence is done to Richard (Moffett). Main item to talk about afterwards: the scene with the very long knife.

**LISA** see *Honeymoon Murders II*

**LITTLE BOY BLUE: TINY TERRESTRIAL** (Fili) Cypress Film Int'l. 1990 color c105m. (aka *Tiny Terrestrial*). D: Eddie Reyes. SP: Joey De Leon, Tony Reyes. Ph: Oscar Querijero. Mus D: Mon del Rosario. VisFX: Cinemagic. Space Capsule: Kenkoy Torrente. Mkp: Naty Valdez. SdFX: Ramon Reyes. Ref: TV: Viva Video; some Eng. With Atony Redillas, Jenjen Otico, Jay-Are Reyes, Luz Fernandez, Lou Veloso, Cutie Del Mar, J. De Leon, Boy Matias (Little Boy Blue).

"I can prove to you that that creature came from Atlantis and it is an Atlantean." ("But Atlantis disappeared 3,500 years ago!") Little Boy Blue—an "alien creature" or Atlantean in a blue, plastic, inflexible costume — is first seen shooting up out of the sea in a spaceship. He makes friends with children and uses his levitating ray to save a drowning person, in this flavorless parroting of *E.T.*

**LITTLE-BOY GHOST** (Taiwanese) c1985? color/ws c85m. Ref: TV: vt; Eng. titles. Happy Produce: above is tr t. MMarquee 43:5.

"Here come the vampires!"—hopping down the vampire trail. A little girl, Tien-Tien, and her grandfather operate a sort of halfway house for vampires. One super-strong, bulletproof, hopping vampire runs amok and kills Master Sha-ban-chu. This runaway vampire is captured, but Tien-Tien and some boys misuse Kuan Luo Yin magic, and turn Sha-ban-chu into a big-fanged, hopping vampire. A "vampire kid" and voodoo-like cutout dolls of the boys save the day. Bonus points: two ghosts, a hypnotic stick, a vampire fingernail trimmer, and bowling-with-skulls.

The furious pace of Hong Kong and Taiwanese vampire comedies like this one and *Hello, Dracula* insures that you can't fast-forward through them. They're already in fast-forward. *Little-Boy Ghost* is cute and sweet, occasionally funny, mostly just fast. Superstitious "Grandpa" has the best lines: "I can't meet dead guys at this moment"; later, "Vampires are not predictable."

**LITTLE GIRL LOST** see *Alarido del Terror*

**LITTLE MASTER** (Taiwanese) 1985? color/ws c88m. Ref: TV: Sunny Video; Eng. titles. Y.K. Ho: above is tr t. MMarquee 43: 5,6,7.

An archaeological expedition discovers the body of a "Little Prince" from the Ching Dynasty. He has (as the theme song puts it) "white face, red lips, green fingernails, short legs," and, when revived, hides in the closet of a little boy, Hsiaonio. At one point, in battle, he bites a man's leg and, vampire-like, sucks the "life" out of him. ("Bitten by a jumping corpse!") Antidote: drinking children's urine. (A funny gag with a priest ensues.) Later, Hsiaonio and his friends disguise themselves as ghosts, hop about, and lead a team of exorcists astray. (The Little Prince is the one who has to jump even when no one is looking.) At the end, the boy-ghost hops into a brick kiln because he "belongs to another world."

Despite a childbirth coda, this conclusion is pretty cruel, the only serious miscalculation in a generally fairly charming comedy featuring "another kind of *E.T.*" The script may not be exactly imaginative in its recapitulation of *E.T.*—it simply throws together children and an "alien" visitor, in a variety of situations—but it's still kind of cute.

The **LITTLE MERMAID** BV & Silver Screen Partners IV/Ashman-Musker 1989 anim color 82m. SP, D: John Musker, Ron Clements, from Hans Christian Andersen's fairy tale. VisFxSup: Mark Dindal. FxCoord: Jonathan Levit. FxGraphics: Bernie Gagliano. Ref: screen. V 11/8/89. Sacto Bee 11/17/89. MFB'90:298-9.

Animated fantasy with horrific elements, including Ursula, the "witch of the sea"—a "demon, a monster"—who at the end becomes a malefic giant ... her super-creepy "garden" of future tidbits: shrunken, distorted merpeople (compare the wasp sequence in *Dot and Keeto*) ... her evil eels, Flotsam and Jetsam ... and a shark haunting a sunken ship.... Disney animated feature has more bite than most: Even at the end, ex-mermaid Ariel, who has regained her legs and voice, must face losing her father. Blandness in the visual and dramatic conceptions of the main characters is offset by sumptuous atmospheric-effects fests (the hurricane, the lagoon, the climactic melee), and by the calypso cadences (aural and visual) of the "Under the Sea" and lagoon numbers. The story, slow to get going, amiably combines comedy, action, and sentiment as it picks up speed.

**LITTLE MONSTERS** MGM-UA/Vestron (Davis Ent. Co. & Licht/Mueller Film Corp.) 1989 color 100m. D: Richard Alan Greenberg. SP: Terry Rossio, Ted Elliott. Mus: David Newman. SpMkpFX: Robert Short. SpPuppetFX: 3/Design. SpMinFxSup: Guy Ramsden. SpOptFX: R/Greenberg. SpFxConsul: Alan Monroe, Kevin Pike. SpSdFX: This Way Prods. Titles: (des) Paula Silver; (opt) Optical House. Ref: TV. V 8/30/89. Sacto Union 8/29/89. ad. With Fred Savage, Howie Mandel (Maurice), Daniel Stern, Margaret Whitton, Rick Ducommun (Snik), Frank Whaley (boy).

"What goes on down there is every kid's fantasy." Young Brian Stevenson (Savage) discovers a world—entered through the floor under his bed—where "there's no such thing as guilt." In this "planet" inside the Earth live the little monsters responsible for all, or many, of the pranks for which kids get punished by parents.... If Mandel's Maurice is Beetlejuice Jr., the movie itself is *Impulse*, Jr. ("It's about freedom.") In *Little Monsters*—a more obvious *Gremlins*—the dialogue is littered with signposts (like the above lines) directing one to the lesson re self-indulgence. By the end, the wild Maurice is thoroughly tamed: "Friends, yeah. Well, guess that's what it's all about, huh?" And Brian discovers that these fun-loving critters are "cruel." The film would be more entertaining if this point were not so obvious long before it's made explicit verbally. As it is, *Little Monsters* is at least ambitious and serious. But writers and director never quite coordinate the fun thing and the serious thing, and the production is more elaborate than imaginative.

**LITTLE NEMO: ADVENTURES IN SLUMBERLAND** (J-U.S.) Hemdale/Tokyo Movie Shinsha (Yutaka Fujioka) 1992 anim color 85m. D: Masami Hata, W. T. Hurtz. SP: Chris Columbus, Richard Outten. Story: Moebius, Y. Fujioka. Based on the Winsor McCay characters. Concept: Ray Bradbury. Story Consult: Robert Towne et al. Visual Devel: John Canemaker. Mus: Chase, Rucker; (songs) The Shermans. Des: Moebius. SdFX: Sound Box. Ref: TV: Hemdale HV. V 8/24/92. SFChron 8/21/92. SFExam 8/21/92. Sean Smiley. Voices: Gabriel Damon, Mickey Rooney, Rene Auberjonois, W. E. Martin (Nightmare King), Michael Gough, Kathleen Freeman, June Foray, Bert Kramer (goblin general).

Ingredients include a fiery, blobby demon which escapes Nightmare Land and apparently becomes the Nightmare King, who "collects" and freezes his victims ... a dinosaur-type ... a flying-manta-ray-type ... a Black Hole-type ... mean-lookin' bats, or "bat boys" ... grabby water goblins ... and tree imp-monster-goblins.

Tepid animated fantasy taps any number of small-fry fantasies, including flying in bed, piloting an airship, repairing a train engine, riding in a parade, sitting at the head of a banquet table, sliding down a long, long banister, steering a boat, and becoming heir to a throne. Highlights: the attachable butterfly wings, the door in the middle of the landscape, the watery reflection below of Nemo's flying bed ... the blob-demon ... and the tree imps, that, separately, are innocuous, but, joined together, become fierce-looking "trees."

**LITTLE PRINCE AND EIGHT HEADED DRAGON** (J) Col/Toei (Yoshida-Takahashi-Ijima) 1963 anim color/ws 86m.(78m.) (*The Little Prince and the Eight Headed Dragon* - ad t. *Wanpaku Oji No Orochitaiji. Prince in Wonderland* - ad t. *Rainbow Bridge* - ad t). D: Yugo Serikawa. SP: Ichiro Ikeda, Takashi Ijima. Mus: Akira Ifukube. AD: Reiji Koyama. Anim D: Y. Mori. Ref: TV. Lee. TVG.

"No one tells the Fire God what to do!" An ancient Japanese fairy tale re a gigantic, multi-headed, fire-breathing dragon. Thunder and lightning and *Godzilla*-style music cue his first appearance. (Ifukube also scored the first *Godzilla*.) Plus the huge, fanged Fire God and a "very big fish." Sweet, stylized, occasionally a bit dull.

**LITTLE RED RIDING HOOD** see *Company of Wolves. Dead Time Stories. Red Riding Hood. Timefighters in the Land of Fantasy.*

**LITTLE SHOP OF HORRORS** WB/Geffen 1986 color 95m. D: Frank Oz. SP: Howard Ashman, based on his play and the

1960 film. Mus: Miles Goodman; (songs) Alan Menken, Ashman. Audrey II Des: Lyle Conway. SpVisFX: Bran Ferren. SpPhysical FX: Effects Associates. Ref: TV. MFB'87:81-2. V 12/10/86. SFExam 12/19/86. Washington Times 12/19/86. Hound. With Rick Moranis, Ellen Greene, Vincent Gardenia, Steve Martin, James Belushi, John Candy, Bill Murray, Levi Stubbs (voice of Audrey II).

A "strange and interesting new plant," Audrey II—discovered after a total eclipse of the sun—ingests blood, talks ("Must be fresh!"), and sings. ("Feed me, Seymour!") Off-target musical remake of the Corman-Griffith classic-of-kind (the three-day-movie kind) actually seems serious re its price-of-success theme. Typical verbal wit: "This thing could be bigger than hula hoops!" Even the plant isn't funny. Lone highlight: the buds harmonizing to "Mean Green Mother from Outer Space." ("I don't come from no Black Lagoon!")

See also *Waxwork*.

**LIU CHAI GHOST STORY** (H.K.?) Golden Mark 1993 color feature. Ref: V 8/9/93:13: playing. 8/16/93.

**LIU JAI (HOME FOR THE INTIMATE GHOSTS)** (H.K.) Onwinsee Development 1990 color/ws 85m. (*Lui Jai* - vc box t). Ref: TV: Pan-Asia Video; Eng. titles. VSOM: *Home for the Intimate Ghosts* - alt t.

"Ten more comes, and I will turn back to human"—Master Manny's wife's sex partners, though, sometimes die. He's a thousand-year-old ghost who "will turn into a demon soon"; she is ultimately incinerated by a priest's "positive-negative magic." ("Demon, I have to finish you up!") The supernatural here is just a pretext for regulation softcore action.

**LIVE GIRLS** see *Stripped To Kill II*

**LIVE WIRE** New Line (Suzanne Todd, David Willis) 1992 color 85m. D: C. Duguay. SP, Exec Co-P: Bart Baker. Ph: J. Jur. Mus: Craig Safan. PD: Marek Dobrowolski. MkpFX: David Miller; (coord) Peggy O'Brien. Robot Sup: M. Pollack. SpFX: SpFxUnltd., (coord) Lou Carlucci. SpSdFxDes: Harry Cohen. Ref: TV. SFChron Dtbk 1/10/93. TVG. With Pierce Brosnan, Ron Silver, Ben Cross, Lisa Eilbacher, Brent Jennings, Tony Plana, Al Waxman, Clement Von Franckenstein.

"People don't just explode." A "weird hybrid combo of liquid explosives" which, when activated in the victim's stomach, acts like a "combination of nitro, napalm, and hydrogen" turns said victim into a "spontaneously combusted" explosive device.... Slick, hollow, overdone *Scanners* variation. Material had more potential as a comedy than as a thriller. Only watchable element: Cross's ultra-villain.

**LIVING DEAD, The** see *Revanche des Mortes Vivantes*

**The LIVING DEAD** (Thai) c1987? color c100m. Ref: TV: All Asian Video; no Eng. Thai Video: above is tr t. MMarquee 43:8.

Campfire-time singing revives a ray-shooting monster which can dance and remove its head as it pleases. At the end, mirrors reflect its rays back at itself, and it gives up and goes back to bed (i.e., its tomb). (When its prey eludes it, this frustrated monster hits its hands against its head.) Its story is linked with that of a female ghost who romances a young man, but who—when the monster's tombstone is removed—flies up into the heavens, freed.

The story may be episodic, but some of both the real and the fake-ghost stuff here (including a tree of "ghosts") is atmospherically shot in night-blue. As in a sister Thai comedy chiller, *Ghosts in the House,* the ghost appears magnified at one point at a window—in a borrowing from *Vampyr*—and the score apes the strings of *Psycho* for one shock scene. The usual quivering bunch of kids stars. One is even a classic stutterer.

**LIVING DEAD IN TOKYO BAY** see *Battle Girl*

**LIVING DOLL** (B) Spectacular Trading (Dick Randall) 1990 color 92m. SP, D: George Dugdale. SP: also Mark Ezra. SpFX: Paul Catling. Ref: V 3/28/90: "tale is too slim and drags along." With Mark Jax, Katie Orgill, Gary Martin, Eartha Kitt.

Dead salesgirl "controls" morgue attendant.

The **LIVING END** Odyssey 1992 color 81m. D: Mitchell Spinelli. Ref: Adam'94: "post-apocalyptic comedy." With Tiffany Million, Leena.

The **LIVING KOHEIJI** (J) Isoda-ATG 1982 color 74m. (*Ikiteiru Koheiji*). SP, D: Nobuo Nakagawa, from Senzaburo Suzuki's play. Ph: Ikio Higuchi. Mus: Kiyohiko Fukuhara, Kiyohiko Senba. AD: Y. Nishioka, R. Kamon. Ref: screen. PFA notes 7/30/86. With Fumihiko Fujima, Shoji Ishibashi, Junko Miyashita.

Koheiji (Fujima) admits to Ochika's (Miyashita) husband, Takuro (Ishibashi): "Still, I love her. It's destiny." Takuro rewards his honesty by killing him, or nearly killing him. Koheiji turns up again in the couple's bedroom: "Nothing can kill me until my dream comes true." Koheiji's dream: to make love to Ochika. Takuro kills "Die-Hard" Koheiji again, or so it seems. Koheiji returns, first, in Takuro's nightmares about a bloody body, then, at the end, in person, when he apologizes to Takuro for "acting like a ghost" and trying to scare him to death. The two fight; both die, or so it seems....

Whether or not Koheiji really returns as a ghost—he has no ghostly powers—this is an odd "amour fou" tale, a bit thin, but funny, quirky, and pointed. Koheiji will not give up his crusade for Ochika's body; Takuro will not give up beating Ochika; Ochika is "too involved" with Takuro to leave him. Such a human tragicomedy can issue only in death, or near-death....

**LIVING ON VIDEO** see *Tales of the Unknown*

**2P La LLAMADA DEL VAMPIRO** (Sp) Lacy Films & Sesena & Arco Films (Riccardo Vazquez) 1971 color 102m.(88m.) (aka *Aquellarre de Vampiros.* aka *The Curse of the Vampyr* or *The Curse of the Vampire*). SP, D: Jose Maria Elorietta. SP: also Enrique Gonzalez Macho. Ph: J. Ruiz Romero. Ref: TV: MV; Eng. dubbed; Ph: Pablo Ripoll. Hardy/HM: '73 release; "atmospheric." Jones. With Beatriz Lacy, Nicholas Ney, Ines Skorpio, D. Sorel.

"Don't go near the lake!" In a flashback, a vampire bites Margaret, and Margaret bites the baron's son, Carl. In the present—in a castle built by the Knights Templar—Erica takes the stake out of Margaret, and the latter revives .... The actresses here share a

glossy, vapid look, and take off their clothes with almost comic regularity. File under Loony Lunar Antics: the two vampire women, Margaret and Erica, laughing and gamboling by the light of the silvery moon. Pathetic score.

**LO QUE VA DE AYER A HOY** (Mex.) 1945 feature. Ref: Cinef 6/95:42: comedy re suspended animation. Lee (P).

**LOAD WARRIOR II: THE SECOND COMING** Vidco/Perry Ross & Paul Thomas & C. C. Williams 1987 color c92m. (*Load Warriors II* - ad t). SP, D, Ph: Williams. AD: Shirley Wilder. Mkp: Alan LePipe. Ref: TV: The Vidco Co. video. Adam '88:129. With Angel Kelly, Porsche Lynn, Sharon Mitchell, Nikki Nights, Randy West, Peter North, Buddy Love, Ross.

"The actor-President" pushed the button, and "most of the planet had been burnt to a cinder...." All that's left: the raggedy town of Motherload, its executioner, "Dog" (Ross), and the Evil Queen Hermongous' retainers Wet (Kelly) and Wild (Mitchell), who roam the Dead Zone. Unexpected element: "Unit BITCH-X-1" (Lynn), the "ultimate sex weapon," a humanoid programmed for collection of "human seed," insemination, and termination. (She makes those with too many "rads" disintegrate.) Motherload's doctor believes that BITCH-X-1 can become human, but this is only one of several plot points which gets lost in this routine hardcore sequel to *The Load Warriors.* The Load Warrior makes good the title, then departs.

The **LOAD WARRIORS** Vidco 2000/Perry Ross 1987 color 74m. D: C. C. Williams. Ref: vc box. Adam '88:128. With Sharon Mitchell, Lois Ayres, Krista Lane, Gail Force, Angel Kelly, Peter North, Randy West.

In the future, after the "ultimate cloud of destruction" (vc box), a good man is even harder to find.

Sequel: *Load Warrior II.*

**O LOBISOMEM** (Braz.) Elyseu Visconti 1974 color/ws 75m. SP, D, P, Ph: Elyseu Visconti Cavalleiro. Ref: Hardy/HM: "one of Brazil's better lycanthropy movies." With Wilson Grey, Suzana de Moraes, Paulo Villaca.

"Eccentric millionaire (Grey) becomes a werewolf and presides over a bloodsucking congregation in a forest."

**LOBSTER MAN FROM MARS** Electric Pictures/Filmrullen Prod. (Lobster Man from Mars Prods/Rimmon-Greene) 1989 color 84m. D, Idea: Stanley Sheff. SP, Idea: Bob Greenberg. Mus: S. Matson. PD: D. White. Lobster Des: Brian Penikas & Assoc.; Mkp & Monsters. Min Cost: Therese Harding Doublin. Opt: Howard Anderson. Ref: TV. Mo. V 2/1/89: "level of inspiration simply isn't high enough." 10/4/89:30 (rated). PT 10:9. With Tony Curtis, Deborah Foreman, Patrick Macnee, Billy Barty, Anthony Hickox, Fred Holliday (Col. Ankrum), Bobby Pickett (King of Mars), S. D. Nemeth (The Dreaded Lobster Man), Dr. Demento, Skip Young, Dean Jacobsen, Phil Proctor.

"Whatever it is, it's not of this Earth." Or, Mars Needs Air. Ingredients and hommages include a film-within-a-film re the Lobster Man, who comes from an air-depleted Mars ... his *Robot Monster,* ape-in-space-helmet assistant ... a cackling, *It Conquered the World*-style, "alien space bat" or two, described in dialogue ("intellectual cucumber") out of *The Thing* (one of the bats does a vampire number on a human neck) ... Bronson Caverns ... a cute *Day the Earth Stood Still* reference ... zombified and skeleton-ized earthlings ... a *War of the Worlds*-style ending, with Old Faithful subbing for bacteria ... and a haunted house "built on an old Eskimo graveyard" .... Occasionally fetching parody of Fifties monster movies.

See also *Midnight*.

**LOCH NESS LEGEND** (B) 1948 anim color c8m. D, P: George Moreno Jr. Mus: Jose Norman. Anim: Gladwish, Thompson. Ref: TV: Loonic Video.

"Loch Ness Monster Seen Again!" (headline). Villagers flee; even the mountains flee. Sighted: huge, ambulatory footprints. ("The monster!") The big, goofy guy, at the end: "Monster? I'm only a fairy tale, a legend." Overlong short has cute moments, including the latter payoff. Another moment: the Conga eels.

**LOCH NESS MONSTER, The** see *Secret of the Loch*

**LOCK AND LOAD** AIP (Casey) 1990 color feature. SP, D: David Prior. SP: also John Cianetti. Ref: PT 14:12: "It's boring." Martin. With Jack Vogel, Rene Cline, Jeffrey Smith.

The *Telefon* idea, plus a Nam vet with nightmares re "bloody faced zombies."(PT)

**LOCKE THE SUPERMAN** (J) Bandai 1989 anim c30m. From Yuki Hijiri's manga. Ref: Animag 9:4: 1st of 3 OAVs re "ESPer."

**LOCKE THE SUPERMAN: THE NEW WORLD FIGHTERS** (J) 1991 anim color 50m. each. Ref: Animag 12:7: 2 OAVs.

Federation computer Elena steals ESPers' memories.

**LOCKE THE SUPERPOWER** (J) American National/Shochiku & Nippon Animation (Koichi Motohashi/Nakashima-Endo) 1984('87-U.S.) anim color 120m.(92m.) (aka *Locke the Superman*). D: Hiroshi Fukutomi. SP: Atsushi Yamatoya. From Yuki Hijiri's cartoon series. Ph & SpPh: Trans Art(s); T. Morita. Mus: Goro Omi. AD: Y. Kanebako. SpFX: Masao Yoshiyama, Kunji Tanifuji. SdFX: Akihiko Matsuda. Anim D: S. Shiraume. Ref: TV: CHE video; Eng. dubbed. V 10/24/84:303 (ad). J Anim Program Guide. Bowker '90. V 5/1/85:403 (ad).

Principal characters: ESPer Locke, who can appear and disappear, electrocute his foes, and heal wounds ("What an amazing boy!") ... Lady Cahn who, with her 200 ESPers, wants to "conquer the universe" and begin a "thousand-year kingdom" (but is she just a "mass of integrated circuits," a cyborg?) ... and ESPer Jessica, who can "analyze and neutralize" just about anyone. (She believes that Locke killed her parents.) Principal planets: Dinal, Seren, and Lonwall.

Flatly-dubbed juvenilia, with occasional pretty design effects. Prime line: "Locke, how about staying with the Federal Army and fighting for the peace of the galaxy with me?"

**LOIS & CLARK: THE NEW ADVENTURES OF SUPERMAN** ABC-TV/WB-TV & Gangbuster & Roundelay Prods. (Efros-St. John) 1993 color c75. D: Robert Butler. Tel, Exec Co-P: Deborah Joy LeVine. Based on the DC Comics "Superman" characters. Mus: Jay Gruska. VisFX: (sup) Elan Soltes; (digital) Digital

Magic; (computer) Vision Art. SpFxCoord: Richard Stutsman. Min: D. Pennington. Ref: TV: series-premiere movie. V 9/20/93:30. SFChron 9/11/93. 9/12/93. TVG. With Dean Cain (Superman/Clark Kent), Teri Hatcher, John Shea, Lane Smith, Michael Landes, Tracy Scoggins, K Callan, Kenneth Tigar, Persis Khambatta, Clyde Kusatsu.

"I think I need some kind of outfit." Lex Luthor (Shea) is out to sabotage the Prometheus program and replace it with his own space station.... Cain is a suitable substitute for Christopher Reeve, but Hatcher as Lois Lane gets her wires crossed between the hopefully-politically-correct and dramatically over-emphatic. Low-key charm in the scenes in which Clark Kent's Superman "slip" shows and his mom (Callan) has him model potential super-outfits.

**LOKIS** see *Marriage of the Bear*

**LONE WOLF** Flash Features & Prism Ent. (Liles-Olson) 1989 (1988) color 96m. D: John Callas. SP, Co-P: Michael Krueger. Ph: David Lewis. Mus: Jon Kull; Greg Leslie. AD: Lad DeGlopper. SpFX: (coord) Ted A. Bohus; V. J. Guastini; P. Denver. Werewolf Mkp: Paul C. Reilly Jr. Werewolf Art & Des: R.S. Cole. SdFX: Patchett, Drake. Ref: TV. V 8/30/89: "moderately interesting." 10/21/87:114: First Films; *Lonewolf*. Hound. With Dyann Brown, Kevin Hart, Jamie Newcomb, Ann Douglas, Siren, Jeff Harms (Joseph Simmons), James Ault, Tom Henry (the wolf).

"Something or someone with unbelievable strength" is killing people. Is it "wild dogs," or a "large wolf on two legs"? It's the latter, more or less—at the end, the local werewolf invades the local high school's costume ball.... Heavy-handed, episodic mystery-horror. Key question here: "Did you say 'very hairy'?"

The **LONELY GUY** Univ 1984 color 90m. D: Arthur Hiller. Adap: Neil Simon, from Bruce Jay Friedman's book *The Lonely Guy's Book of Life*. SP: Ed Weinberger, Stan Daniels. Ref: TV. Maltin '92.

Included: a bit with a caveman and a bit with the lonely guy in space, 1,000 years from now. Generally mechanically stylized comedy, but with hilarious moments.

**LONEWOLF** see *Lone Wolf*

The **LONG NIGHT OF EXORCISM** (I) Medusa (Calaiacono-Puccioni) 1972 color/ws 99m. (110m.) (*Non Si Sevizia un Paperino*). Story, SP, D: Lucio Fulci. SP: also Clerici. Story, SP: also Gianviti. Ph: S. D'Offizi. Mus: Riz Ortolani. Mkp: di Girolamo, Iacoppini; Trani. Ref: TV: vt; Eng. dubbed. MFB'86:93: "horror." Prod. Ital. Lee (p). Ecran F 33:65. no FFacts. V 5/9/73:63: *Don't Torture a Duckling* - ad t. Hardy/HM: "gutter press stereotypes." Palmerini. With Florinda Bolkan, Barbara Bouchet, Tomas Milian, Irene Papas, Marc Porel, George(s) Wilson.

Accendura, a small village in southern Italy. "The maciara" ("She practices magic—they claim she's a witch"), who once bore a deformed baby (a "child of the devil"), is suspected of murdering three boys. (Her three wax voodoo dolls are painted black, "for death.") But yet another boy is killed after she herself is brutally beaten to death by villagers. At the end, the real "monster" dies a gory death in a fall from a cliff.... Rural sensationalism. Slim story, guessable killer.

**LOOK OUT MR. HAGGIS** see *Handle with Care*

**LOOK OUT, OFFICER!** (H.K.) Cosmopolitan Film 1990 color/ws c95m. Ref: TV: World Video; Eng. titles. Y. K. Ho.

"Damn old ghost!" Ingredients in this silly, scatological fantasy-comedy include a ghost captured in a glass coffin and an evil, scarred magician ("This demon is terrible!") who can fling fireballs. ("My bottom's on fire!") Occasional amusing stunts.

**LOOKING FOR THE SEA SERPENT** Lux 1908 b&w silent short. Ref: V 12/5/08: "The terror of the ocean is reported at a harboring place for seamen." Turns out to be a "large coil of garden hose."

**LOONS** LSVideo 1991 feature? Ref: Filmfax 52:3(ad): witch's curse.

**LOOSE ENDS III** 4-Play (Loretta Sterling) 1987 color 104m. D: Bruce Seven. Ref: Adam '89. with Bionca, Erica Boyer, Siobhan Hunter, Jessica Wylde.

"Machine that brings out people's fantasies."

**LOOSE JOINTS** UFDC/Flicks Films (Kamerman-Axelrod) 1983 (1981) color 78m. (*Flicks* - alt t. aka *Hollyweird*). SP, D: Peter Winograd. SP: also Arnstein, Hurwitz, Sarasohn. Ph: S. Miller. Mus: John Morgan. PD: J. McAnelly. Anim: Kirk Henderson. SpVisFX: The Magic Lantern; (sup) A. Doublin; Private Stock(s) FX. SpFxMkp: James Suthers; William Blake. Laser FX: Robert Greenberg. Masks: S. & J. Chiodo. Ref: TV: MHE video. V 6/3/87. 5/9/84:215. 6/1/83:6. Bill Warren. With Pamela Sue Martin, Joan Hackett, Martin Mull, Buck Flower; M.Y. Evans & Sam Diego (Philip Alien), Caprice Rothe, Harry Shearer (voice of P. Alien).

Classic-Saturday-matinee parody includes serial episodes "Lost Heroes of the Milky Way, Chapters 18 & 19" (called "New Adventures of the Great Galaxy" in the end credits), the feature "House of the Living Corpse," and "Philip Alien Space Detective." "Fails the crucial test: is it funny?" (V) "Living Corpse" features a radium-created mutant and shovel-in-the-forehead comic gore. "Lost Heroes" features Ming the Merciless-type Tang (Mull), Giblet Man, Sushi Man, and Ice Cream Man. "Philip Alien" features an insect alien who falls for an Earth woman. ("We're from two different worlds.") Very few laughs anywhere here.

**LORCA AND THE OUTLAWS** see *Starship*

**LORD MOUNTDRAGO** see *Three Cases of Murder*

The **LORD OF AKILI** (I) 1989 color feature. D: A. Massaccesi. Ref: Palmerini: similar to *Ator*.

The **LORDS OF MAGICK** Prism Ent. 1990 (1989) color 99m. SP, D, P: David Marsh. SP: also Sherman Hirsh. Ref: V 2/7/90:171 (hv): "Poor special effects sink this direct-to-video release." With Jarrett Parker, Mark Gauthier, Brendan Dillon Jr.

Tenth-century wizards time jump to Eighties L.A.

**LORDS OF THE DEEP** Concorde-New Horizons (Roger Corman) 1989 color 79m. D: Mary Ann Fisher. SP: Howard Cohen, Daryl Haney. Mus: Jim Berenholtz. VisFxCoord: Ray Greer. SpCreatureFX: Mark Williams FX. SpVocalFX: Berenholtz, Richard Stocker. Ref: TV: MGM-UA HV. V 4/26/89. HR 5/5/89. With Bradford Dillman, Priscilla Barnes, Melody Ryane, Eb Lottimer, Haney.

"Come with us, Claire." In the year 2020, the crew manning Martel's Neptune Base—the "world's most expensive undersea lab"—discovers a colony of manta-ray-like aliens on the ocean floor. These latter are "pretty much indestructible" and can reassemble into one being.... The aliens look as friendly as dolphins and turn out, in fact, to be friendly. They invite humans to join them/it, for what exactly is not clear. Tea maybe. The nature of the beast is also left unclear. At one point, the visitors are described as being coral-like, but maybe that's just their abode. The twist here on the evil-alien, evil-corporation *Alien* theme: The corporation is still evil, but the alien is good. Not enough of a twist to save a sketchy script.

**LORNA L'EXORCISTE** see *Possedees du Diable, Les*

**LOS ANGELES IS HELLBENT** see *Hellbent*

**LOSING CONTROL?** PBS-TV/Ideal Communications 1989 color 60m. SP, D, P, Ph: Gary Krane. SP, P: Gary Hauser. SP: also P. Prentice, P. Vahovich. Mus: Brad Allen, Micha Solomon. Anim: Pat True. Ref: TV. SFExam 2/11/91. TVG.

A simulation of the "first nuclear exchange between the U.S. and the U.S.S.R."—from "plausible crisis" to "technical fallibility" to "human fallibility." Film doesn't say much that dramatized features re World War III haven't said, but the juxtaposition of speculative narration with library footage of world leaders and organizations is cleverly calculated for that "documentary" feel.

The **LOST BOYS** WB/Richard Donner-Harvey Bernhard 1987 color/ws 97m. D: Joel Schumacher. SP: Janice Fischer, James Jeremias, Jeffrey Boam. Story: Fischer, Jeremias. Mus: Thomas Newman. Vampire Prosth/FX: Greg Cannom. SpVisFX: Dream Quest; (sup) Eric Brevig. SpFX: (coord) Matt Sweeney; (des consul) Douglas Lefler, Charles Chiodo. SdFX: Mel Neiman. OptSup: Robert Hall. Ref: TV. MFB'88:4. V 7/22/87. SFChron 7/31/87. SFExam 7/31/87. With Jason Patric, Corey Haim, Dianne Wiest, Barnard Hughes, Edward Herrmann (Max), Kiefer Sutherland (David), Jami Gertz, Corey Feldman, Kelly Jo Minter.

"Never grow up, Michael, and you'll never die. But you must feed." Santa Carla, the "murder capital of the world" and a "haven for the undead," is a "pretty cool place ... if you're a Martian." ("Or a vampire.") And the local vampire gang wants Michael (Patric) to become one of them. Two drawbacks: Their viciousness, and the fact that they sleep hanging upside-down, like bats.... In its mixture of youth, romance, and half-vampires, *Lost Boys* is similar to *Near Dark*, but is it horror, comedy, or a soundtrack album? (There is a lot of music.) The functional plot—which alternates between flat, serious-business scenes and droll Rambo, Jr., scenes with pint-sized vampire-killers—allows for much humor from the younger boys (the older ones have less fun) and from Grandpa (Hughes), and for the usual stunts and effects.

**The LOST EMPIRE** Manson Int.l./Harwood (JGM) 1985 (1983) color/ws 83m. SP, D, P: Jim Wynorski. Mus: Alan Haworth. SpVisFX: Tony Doublin; Peter Mark. SpAnimFX: Ernest D. Farino; Bret Mixon. SpMkpFX: Steve Neill; Mike Hoover. SpPropFX: Roger George. OptFX: Image 3. Title FX: Animagic; David Fiske. Ref: TV. TVG. V 4/4/84:4 (rated). 2/13/85. With Melanie Vincz, Raven de la Croix, Angela Aames, Paul Coufos, Bob Tessier, Angus Scrimm, Garry Goodrow, Kenneth Tobey, Tom Rettig, Angelique Pettyjohn, Annie Gaybis, Blackie Dammett, Linda Shayne.

A tale of the Lemurians, a "legend of supernatural horror," and the Pacific island fortress of Golgatha, where the evil, reptilian Sin Do rules. The latter requires a woman's soul to complete his deal with the devil and give him immortality. More: brainwashed terrorists, a robot spider, and a laser cannon (the "mightiest weapon ever known").... Effects-and-skin flick features inane action and the lowest of low comedy. Even the flashy effects don't help.

**The LOST IDOL** (U.S.-Thai) SGE HV (P. Sumon) 1990 color 102m. D: P. Chalong. SP: J. Phillips, T. S. Suwat. Mus: A. Suebsuwan. Ref: V 8/22/90:76 (hv): "final reel showdown with supernatural overtones."

**LOST IN DINOSAUR WORLD** Price Stern Sloan 199-? color Dinamation c30m. Ref: vc box.

"The only place on Earth where real dinosaurs live...."

**LOST IN TIME** NBC-TV/Lansbury & Col-TV 1976 color c90m. D: Andrew V. McLaglen; Barry Crane. Idea & Exec P: Bruce Lansbury. Tel: M. Michaelian, K. M. Powers, M. Jerard; K. M. Powers. Story: Jerard; Michaelian, Powers. Ph: S. Leavitt; I. Lippman. Mus: Robert Prince. AD: Bellah, Braunger; Bellah, Purcell. SpFX: Don Cortney; Richard Albain. Mkp: Ben Lane. Ref: TV. With Scott Thomas, Susan Howard, Karen Somerville, Ike Eisenmann, Leif Erickson, Scott Brady, Jared Martin, Gary Collins, Jason Evers (Atar), Mary Ann Mobley, Ian McShane, Carl Franklin, Lynn Borden, Mike Road (voice of The Source).

"We're in some kind of time warp!" Back in the Bermuda Triangle again, with two episodes from the "Fantastic Journey" TV series released now as a TV-movie.

**LOST IN TIME** see *Waxwork II*

**LOST ISLAND** see *Island of the Lost*

**LOST ON ADVENTURE ISLAND** MVC & Hendrieth & Oman (TM & Hendrieth) 1984 color c78m. (*King Dong* - alt t). SP, D, Exec P: Yancey Hendrieth. SP, Exec P: Dee Hendrieth. Ph, PD: L. B. Carvelo. Mus: DDT. SpVis & MechFX: Magic Film Ventures; (sup) Keith Finkelstein; Carvelo; (models) David Dane. Ref: TV: MVC HV. Cheri 1/84:12-17. Cinef 3/88. no Hound. no Martin. PT 2:35. VSOM: aka *Supersimian*. With Crystal Holland, Chaz St. Peters, Mikhael, Felicia Fox, Elizabeth Davies, D. Hendrieth, Angel Dials, Ken Monti, Venus Hut, Diane Speaks, Y. Hendrieth (Buddy the Gorilla).

Uncharted isle harbors eighty-foot-tall gorilla, brontosaurus, tyrannosaurus, headhunters, English-speaking lesbian warriors, and Easter Island statues. ("What is this place?") What kind of movie rates coverage by both Cheri and Cinefantastique?—why, this combination of rudimentary porn and rudimentary but occasionally tackily charming science-fantasy. The big, stopmo gorilla, Supersimian, winks; the little gorilla, apparently her son, saves the hero from Mom. The heroine, Anna, is more or less incidental to the ape-human story; the scattered sex scenes are incidental to the movie. The pictorial effects, involving paintings and models, while hardly impeccable, are ambitious for such a shoestring effort.

**The LOST PLATOON** Action Int'l. (Kimberley Casey) 1989 color 86m. SP, D: David A. Prior. SP: also Ted Prior. Ref: V 1/3/90:48 (hv): "relatively uninteresting.' McCarty II. Martin. Scheuer. Jones. With William Knight, David Parry, Stephen Quadros, Lew Pipes.

Four immortal vampire soldiers keep popping up in wars over the last hundred years.

*****The LOST WORLD** Hudson-Rothacker 1925 tinted 64m. AD: Milton Menasco. Models: Marcel Delgado. Chief Tech: Fred Jackman. Ref: TV: Lumivision & Eastman House. Lee. V 2/11/25. Lentz. Martin. Scheuer. Maltin '92.

"My brontosaurus has escaped!" A rescue party takes "secret rivers" to a "terrible plateau" of dinosaurs—including an awkwardly-animated but spectacularly introduced pterodactyl, as well as brontos, allosaurs, duckbill dinosaurs, styracosaurs, and some triceratops and their young. Near the end, a volcanic fire sends all monsters scurrying, and the explorers cart home a brontosaurus.

In retrospect, *Lost World* seems like a rough draft for *King Kong*—it even has its own ape ... a human-sized apeman (Bull Montana). *Kong* corrects the main problem with *Lost World*: Here the human drama and the dinosaur drama don't seem to have much to do with each other—and neither half of the movie is particularly gripping. With a weak dramatic context, Willis O'Brien's stop-motion animation is reduced to little more than exciting moments, the most exciting being the post-fire tableau of feeding allosaurs, etc. The atmospheric tinting features blue for London externals and the plateau at night, green for the jungle, and an intimate orange for Challenger's (Wallace Beery) rooms.

**The LOST WORLD** (B-Can.-S. African) Harmony Gold & SBC & Yiannakis (Agrama-Siderow-Lorenzano) 1992('93-U.S.) color 96m. D: Timothy Bond. SP & Exec P: Harry Alan Towers (aka P. Welbeck). PD: John Rosewarne. Ph: Paul Beeson. Mus: Wolff, Shadrick, Sanders. SpFxCoord: Joe Quinlivan. SpFX: Image Quest;(sup) Peter Parks;(animatronics sup) Richard Gregory. Mkp: Tracy Crystal. SdFxEd: Carl Ray Leonard. Ref: TV: Worldvision HV. VW 20:26: "utterly retrograde." Martin. With David Warner, John Rhys-Davies, Eric McCormack, Nathania Stanford, Darren Peter Mercer, Tamara Gorski.

Mysterious sketches and a glimpse of a pterodactyl inspire a new expedition to "the lost world" ("that strange place") in Africa, a plateau where "plant-eating dinosaurs" and other wonders roam. At the end, the adventurers bring back a baby pterodactyl.... The risible, retiring dinosaurs must be from the Plasticene Era. Warner and Rhys-Davies, as Summerlee and Challenger, respectively, carry their share of the dramatic load, but the lazy script just rehashes scenes from earlier versions of the Arthur Conan Doyle book.

Sequel: *Return to the Lost World.*

**LOT 249** see *Tales from the Darkside—The Movie*

**LOTS OF KILLING** (J) 1993 feature (*Satsujin ga Ippai*). D: G. Nakamura. Ref: Weisser/JC. With Y. Takigawa.

"A veritable parade of gruesome, gory murders, each based on a different Mother Goose nursery rhyme."

**LOTHAR** see *Defenders of the Earth*

**\*\*LOVE AFTER DEATH** (Arg.) Abrams & Parisi 1968 b&w feature (aka *Unsatisfied Love*). D: Glauco del Mar. SP: A. Valasques. Ph: P. Palian. Ref: SWV. AFI. Lee. Glut/TDB: phantom. Photon 21:29.

"Man buried alive comes back to wreak vengeance."(Lee)

**LOVE AT STAKE** (U.S.-Can.) Tri-Star/Hemdale (Michael Gruskoff) 1987 color 88m. (*Burnin' Love*-orig t). D: John Moffitt. SP: Terry Sweeney, Lanier Laney. SpFX: Cliff Wenger, Michael Kavanaugh. Mkp: Carol Davidson. Opt: Howard Anderson Co. Ref: TV. V 5/20/87. Cinef. TVG 9/23/89. McCarty II. Scheuer.

No-gag-too-low comedy-fantasy features a real witch (Barbara Carrera), her older edition (Anne Ramsey), and a bit with a werewolf-type in a jury box. Even Dave Thomas as the mayor and Stuart Pankin as the judge can't save it.

**LOVE BITES** Campfire Video 199-? color feature. Ref: Jones: "gay-oriented (non-porn) vampire horror comedy."

**LOVE CHILDREN, The** see *Psych-Out*

**LOVE CITY** (J) Toho 1986 ('95-U.S.) anim color/ws c88m. (*Ai City*). Ref: TV: Toho Video; no Eng. vc box.

A naked cackler who inhabits the spa-like helmet of a huge robot later turns two-headed, then transforms into red slime, then finally mutates into a cyclopean horror, as the whole city turns into Nightmareland, and devil hordes assail our psychic private-eye hero.... The visuals of *Love City* are certainly bizarre—hard to tell if the story is up to them. Weirdest sequences: the finale (partially described above) and an earlier puzzler in which giant heads push up through a city street, float up into the air like monster parade-balloons, and chase the protagonists. Gore: some. Local TV station: THX 1138. Song: "Psychic Man."

**\*LOVE FROM A STRANGER** 1937 (1936). From Agatha Christie's story "Philomel Cottage." Mus: Benjamin Britten. AD: Frederick Pusey. Ref: screen. Lee. Lentz. Everson/More: 61-2, 63. Hound. Maltin '92. Ecran F 66:61. 68:65.

"No one is to go into the cellar. No one." A "foolish romantic whim" leads Carol Howard (Ann Harding) to marry Gerald Lovell (Basil Rathbone), who has a "pressure in his head" and who conducts "experiments" in the cellar. The half-campy, half-creepy giveaways to his madness include his odd, various absorptions in his notebook, in the minute hand of a clock, in the sound of his voice in an empty wine glass, etc. Not to mention his insistence that his wife play the piano faster, faster!.... The role of Fletcher, the notorious triple murderer, is, for Rathbone, a tour de force halfway between camp and wit. This forerunner of the Forties *I Married a Maniac* movies (which include this film's remake) also has a well-written, if slightly balmy climactic sequence. Harding does okay until she goes glassy-eyed with fear—or calculation—in apparent preparation for her I'm-a-killer-too ploy, which is the *Tristana* story in a nutshell. (Opened the window, husband froze to death....)

**LOVE LETTERS OF A PORTUGUESE NUN** (Swiss-W.G.) Elite Film/Ascot Film & Filmproduktions Kg (Max Dora) 1976 color 85m.(*Die Liebesbriefe Einer Portugiesischen Nonne*). SP, D: Jesus Franco. SP, P: E.C. Dietrich. Ph: Peter Baumgartner. Mus: Walter Baumgartner. AD: David Quintans. Ref: TV: Film Superstore video; Eng. dubbed. MV: "possibly Franco's best film." PT 18:60: "one of Franco's best." With Susan Hemingway, William Berger, Aida Kargas, Herbert Fux, Ilsa Schneider.

"This is an unusual abbey, you see." The "most beautiful abbey in Portugal" is actually an Unholy of Unholies. Noted: a campily lustful priest and Mother Inferior ... our nun heroine, ticketed to become the "midwife to the son of satan" ... a very hairy hand apparently belonging to said son ... gruesome tortures, including the barbed-wire "test" ... and lots of "Ready yourself to offer your chaste virginity to the devil himself!" (She does; he accepts.) Comically "shocking." The devil here is an unprepossessing cackler.

**The LOVE MASSACRE** (H.K.?) Mei Ah Video Prods. 1989? color c88m. Ref: TV: World Video; pre-credit sequence with Eng. titles.

Humorless gent takes out his romantic frustration on a houseful of women, variously slashes, stabs, and drowns them. Finally, he asks his beloved to stab him. She does, then holds his dead, bloody body.... The pretty photography, dissolves, and music make this an arty version of *10 to Midnight*. Shades of both Fulci and *The Toxic Avenger* in a scene with a really sick, if unlikely murder-with-Murphy-bed.

**LOVE ME VAMPIRE** (H.K.) Bong Motion Pictures (Irene Wang) 1985 color/ws c92m. D: Hoover Lau. Ref: TV: Rainbow Video; Sunny Video; Eng. titles. Happy Produce: *Mouth-to-Mouth Resuscitator*-tr of orig t. NST! 4:30. MMarquee 43:7. Jones.

Two lovers plot to murder the woman's husband, Ho. First, the man plays "Grandpa," revived from the dead, and attacks Ho, but fails to kill him. His wife, though, half-accidentally, succeeds, but mouth-to-mouth resuscitation helps bring him back as a ghost-vampire. ("I'm a passionate ghost.") The woman who helped revive him begins to fall for him. ("I can see Sis likes you—but you're a ghost.") Ho faces facts ("I'm a dead person. Don't waste your time") and returns to the home of his widow. ("Long time no see.") To *Jaws*-like music, he prods her with his long, long tongue, makes a toilet act spooky, and makes his head swivel around, *Exorcist*-like, on his neck. (An exorcist at one point advises the lovers, "He became a vampire.") At the end, his spirit leaves his body behind.

Sporadically amusing horror-comedy—alternately surprising and predictable—has romance, chills, and comic invisible-man-like tricks, but the various modes are not well coordinated. Invisible, Ho makes the people around him perform silly actions; later, he becomes visible; at the end, on a basketball court, he's again visible. Scene for scene, a rather fun comedy—especially the wedding, where the ghost knocks out the groom and physically manipulates him—but it doesn't add up.

**LOVE NEVER DIES** see *Coitus Interruptus*

**LOVE ON DELIVERY** (H.K.) 1994 color feature. Ref: HOF 2:20-21: incidental, "hilarious" sendup of *Ultraman.* Weisser/ATC2: "minor." vc box.

**LOVE PROBE** Video Team (John Triola) 1986 color 75m. D: Naomi Goldsmith. Ref: vc box: "orgasmatron" which measures sexual intensity. Adam '88. With Elle Rio, Angel Kelly, Tom Byron, Amber Lynn.

The planet Ultron outlaws sex.

**LOVE WITH THE GHOST IN LUSHAN** (H. K.) Metropole 198-? color/ws c80m. D: Chang Peng Ye. Based on stories (including "Taoist Priest of Lushan") from Pu's book *Tales of Liao Zhai.* Ref: TV: SMO Video/World Video; Eng. titles. NST! 4:30.

"Some ghosts stay here." Artist Yu Jiang takes the remains of Shiu Sen, a ghost, to her home in Tsinan, and she completes—with more skill than could he—one of his drawings. But evil, vampiric ghosts complicate their already complicated romance. The vengeful Hung Yu impersonates her (a Taoist priest's bag sucks Hung Yu in, and Yu Jiang burns the bag), while, for the grand finale, sunlight destroys the "old mistress ... a cruel bloodsucker." ("Yes, she likes to suck your blood.") *Love with the Ghost in Lushan* is made with more care than most Hong Kong horrors, but the story becomes cluttered with ghosts and subplots. Still, there's the line, "The old devil will come tonight," and touches like Shiu Sen's initial jump-cut flitting through the countryside. Other passing chills: the low-key revelation that the helpful priest is a ghost, too ... the monster-hand from the ground in the crypt.

**LOVECRAFT** see *Cast a Deadly Spell*

**LOVELY SPIRIT** (H.K.?) Silver Birds Films 1988? color 192m. Ref: TV: World Video; no Eng.

Shot-on-tape TV or video series features two fake hopping ghosts, a real female ghost, an older female ghost, telekinesis, an exorcism, and a hunchback. Strictly routine horror-comedy, in three or four parts.

**LOVER OF THE LORD OF THE NIGHT** see *Amantes de Senor de la Noche*

**LOVERS BEYOND TIME** (Greek) Greek Film Centre 1990 85m. D, P: D. Panayotatos. Ref: Hardy/SF2: "time travel."

**LOVER'S VOW** see *Tales from the Darkside—The Movie*

**The LOVES OF DRACULA** 1979 color feature. Ref: TVG: reedited from the TV series "Cliffhangers." no Scheuer. no Maltin '92. no Lentz. no Stanley. no Hound. With Michael Nouri (Dracula), Carol Baxter, Stephen Johnson, Antoinette Stella.

**LOVES OF THE LIVING DEAD** (H.K.) 1984 color feature (aka *Heaven Wife, Hell Wife*). D: Ho Menga. Ref: Jones. NST! 4:30.

Vampire queen, zombies.

**LUBIE NIETOPERZE** see *I Like Bats*

**LUCHADORES DE LAS ESTRELLAS** see *Starfighters*

**LUCI LONTANE** (I) Intersound & Reteitalia (Claudio Argento) 1987 color 89m. (aka *Distant Lights*). SP, D: Aurelio Chiesa. SP: also R. Lerici, R. Leoni. Ph: R. Tafuri. Mus: A. Branduardi. Ref: V 5/27/87: Eng.-dubbed; "passable Italo sci-fi." 10/22/86:354. 5/7/86:304. With Tomas Milian, Laura Morante, William Berger, G. Piperno.

Extraterrestrials take over the bodies of the dead on Earth.

**LUCKER, THE NECROPHAGOUS** (Belgian) Desert Prods. (Vandewoestijne) 1986 color feature. SP, D, Ed: Johan Vandewoestijne. SP, Ph: John Kupferschmidt. PD, SpFX: Flip Beys. Ref: TV: MV; Eng. dubbed; aka *Lucker.* Hardy/HM2. With Nick Van Suyt, Helga Vandevelde. Marie Claes, Frank Van Laecke, Freck Neirynck.

The extremely sexually dysfunctional John Lucker escapes from a private asylum (insert: awkwardly staged knife-in-eye), performs a rather inexplicable disembowelment, and makes love to less-than-fresh corpses. *Nekromantik* without the catchy title. Pornographically gory.

**LUCKY ENCOUNTER** (H.K.) Raymond Wong 1992 color/ws 91m. D & PD: Johnny To. SP: Yuen Kai Chi. Ref: TV: Tai Seng Video; Eng. titles. Y.K. Ho. With Tony Leung.

"There is something ghostly here." Ingredients include a gizmo which "reorganizes" molecules and turns liquid solid ... gives a woman a supernaturally long tongue ... makes a man disappear into "another zone" and appear on TV ... turns pistols into flashlights ... and burns handcuffs in half. Plus the theory that, after death, a person's A7352 molecules reorganize and enter the "third zone" ... the A72's laser-like ray which "controls" ghosts ... and the *Poltergeist*-like "zone 1523".... Okay mixture of comedy, sentiment, and science-fantasy.

**\*\*LUCKY GHOST** Toddy (Jed Buell) 1941 b&w feature. D: W. X. Crowley. SP: Lex Neal, Vernon Smith. Ref: PT 14:43: "amazing black cast comedy." With Mantan Moreland, F. E. Miller.

Ghosts of original owners of sanitarium-cum-nightclub rise from their graves, scare current occupants. "Invisible man," piano-playing skeleton, spirit possession.

**LUCKY SKY DIAMOND** or **LUCKY STAR DIAMOND** see *Guinea Pig, Vol. Four*

**LUCKY STARS** (H.K.) D&B Films/Picture House 1989 color feature. Ref: TV: Tai Seng Video; Eng. titles.

Routine comedy includes a sequence in which the Ninja Ghost-busters take on out-of-a-puff-of-smoke flying, then hopping vampires ("We died 200 years ago"), who vanish then seem to return as floating lanterns. The sequence turns out to be a scene from a movie being shot. ("Next, shoot ninja fight with vampire.") Two vampire extras then wander off and accidentally scare nearby picnickers.

**LUCKY STIFF** New Line/Gerald T. Olson (Copeland-Power, Perlman-Proft) 1989 (198) color 82m. (*Mr. Christmas Dinner* - orig t). D: Anthony Perkins. SP: Pat Proft. Mus: Tom Jenkins, Mike Tavera. SpFxDes: Mick Strawn. Mkp: Christa Reusch. Ma's Hands: Steve Pinney. Ref: TV. V 5/10/89. Fango 2/90. With Donna Dixon, Joe Alaskey, Jeff Kober, Barbara Howard, Fran Ryan, Morgan Sheppard, Adele Malis-Morey (Gramma), Steven R. Ross (Ike III), Larry Cedar.

"She's my wife—not food!" The Mitchell clan is "top-heavy with eccentrics" like "free lance butcher" Ike (Kober) and Ike Mitchell III, a self-styled "ghost." In fact, "the Mitchells are cannibals!" And they've chosen plump Ron Douglas (Alaskey) as their Christmas dinner.... Quirky, hit-and-miss black comedy recalls *Murder, He Says* (II) in its pitting of easygoing hero against family of lethal eccentrics. Funniest bits: Cynthia's (Dixon) casual abuse of brother Ike, and Pa's of Ike III. Funniest sign (on a ski slope): Meet-Your-Maker Ridge. Funniest line: (Ike) "Don't hit me with meat!"

See also: *Human Beasts.*

**LUI JAI** see *Liu Jai*

**LUK KROK (GHOST OF MISCARRIAGES)** (Thai) c1989? color c100m. Ref: TV: All Asian Ent. video; no Eng. Chao Thai Market: above is tr t.

A ghost possesses a young woman who later reverts to old-hag status while making love. The ghost's candle's flame seems to start zombies rising up out of the ground, and her magic rays blast off an old man's head, though he continues to talk to his friend, a little, flying ghost-boy.... Film begins like a routine spirit-pos-session story, later becomes an engaging, oddball fantasy-horror-show, with many strange bits, such as the flying boy, a dancing skeleton, and the ghost's green, rope-like rays, which encircle one male victim and make him explode. A bit-part hopping ghost seems to have wandered in from Hong Kong vampire comedies.

**LULLABY LAND** UA/Disney 1933 color anim 7m. Ref: TV. Jim Shapiro.

In a land of living pacifiers, diapers, and safety pins—and a region of very dangerous sharp things—lighted matches pursue a baby and a stuffed pup, then become big Id-like puffs of smoke, then shape-shifting boogeymen. ("We are the boogey, boogey, boogeymen!") Baby concerns are brought to life in this inventive Silly Symphony, in which are arrayed all the paraphernalia of toddlerhood.

**LUM THE FOREVER** see *Urusei Yatsura 4: Lum the Forever*

**LUMIKUNINGATAR** see *Snow Queen, The*

**LUMINOUS MOSS** (J) 1992 color/ws feature (*Hikarigoke*). D: Kei Kumai. SP: Taijun Takeda. Ph: M. Tochizawa. Mus: T. Matsumura. Ref: TV: VSOM; Eng. titles. V 2/24/92. With Eiji Okuda, H. Igawa, Chishu Ryu.

"It's terrifying." The Japanese Merchant Marine ship *Seishin Maru V* is "wrecked off Point Pekin" in the dead of winter, 1943. Stranded mariners discover a cave with a "strange atmosphere" and luminous moss which draws light into itself. Hunger sets in. Gosuke: "Promise you won't eat me after I die." The promise is kept, but: "The only food we have is Gosuke." The captain eats heartily; a crew member, reluctantly. "Why did I eat him?" Later, after the ordeal, the captain is "visited" by the three dead men.... Half-horrifying, half-boring World War II horror anecdote. Perhaps it's the dramatic single-mindedness. The script gets a little carried away with the moss thing near the end.

**LUNA BRUJA** see *Amantes de Senor de la Noche, Las*

**La LUNA NEGRA** (Sp) TBM 1990 color 82m. D: I. Uribe. Ref: Hardy/HM2.

Devil Child wreaks satanic havoc.

**LUNA VARGA** see *Demon Beast Warrior Luna Vulgar*

**LUNATICS: A LOVE STORY** Renaissance/Sam Raimi, Robert Tapert (Bruce Campbell) 1991 color 87m. SP, D: Josh Becker. Stopmo: Dave Hellmer. SpFxSup: Gary Jones. OptFX: Edward Wollman. Ref: TV. V 9/16/91. SFChron 9/11/92.

Modern neurotic-romantic tale with visualized hallucinations, the most monster-ific of which is a giant, screaming stopmo spider with busy mandibles. Other visions sport brain spiders, hypos and hands from a wall, and an animated Edgar Allan Poe (John Cameron) on a book cover.... Thin, despite the slick effects packaging.

**LUNNAYA RADUGA** see *Moon Rainbow*

**LUNCHMEAT** Tapeworm Video/Monogram Ent. & Camarillo (Mark Flynn) 1986 color 88m. SP, D: Kirk Alex. Mus: R. Neigher. Ref: V 2/1/89:41 (hv): "Gore content is nauseating for the uninitiated but pointless and unimaginative." Deep Red 3:69. With Kim McKamy, Chuck Ellis, Elroy Wiese, Robert Oland.

Backwoods California family cannibalizes passersby, sells left-overs as luncheon meat.

**LUNE DE MIEL** see *Honeymoon*

**LUPIN III** (J) Toho/Tokyo Movie Shinsha 1983 anim color 100m. SP, D: Soji Yoshikawa. SP: also Yamatoya. Story: "Monkey Punch." Ph: Kuroki. Mus: Y. Ohno. PD: Shibayamo. Ref: screen: Eng. version. UC Theatre notes 7/30/85. Paul Lane. V 10/16/85:345 (ad).

Godlike villain—a giant brain—creates clones of himself and has preserved, for ten thousand years, the famous and the infamous. Meanwhile, hero Lupin, a thief (like his namesake, Arsene Lupin), "plays" Count Dracula, in castle Dracula, and sprouts fangs and "plays" werewolf. Also noted: a paralyzing spray and a machine which probes our hero's "vulgar subconscious."

Glib, irreverent, inventive. The hero-chases-villain-catches-hero story runs out of gas about halfway, but the animation is witty and imaginative. This alternately very funny and rather wearing feature-length cartoon apparently began life as a TV or video miniseries.

**LUPIN III: CAGLIOSTRO CASTLE** (J) Toho/Tokyo Movie Shinsha 1980 anim color 99m. (aka *Castle Cagliostro* or *The Castle of Kariosutoro* or *Cagliostro Castle*). SP, D: Hayao Miyazaki. Story: "Monkey Punch." Ph: Takahashi. Mus: Yuji Ono. AD: Yasuo Otsuka. Ref: TV: vt; Eng. titles. Paul Lane. Larson. Cinef 5/89. Animag 9:9-10. Japan Video: Streamline (TMS), '91-U.S., as *The Castle of Cagliostro*.

Entertaining adventure-comedy-romance, with some semi-horrific and science-fictional elements, including laser weapons, an automaton, a car which can climb the sides of mountains, and a horde of hulking assassins with steel "hands." (Cf. *Lion Man.*) ("The monsters are bulletproof.") Story here concerns a four-hundred-year-old international counterfeiting conspiracy which proves to have been behind the Great Depression, etc. At the end, explosions destroy the titular castle and reveal an "ancient Roman city" beneath a lake. A neat, sweet combination of several genres, *Cagliostro Castle* is not as wild as the 1983 *Lupin III,* but is more even and cohesive.

**LUPIN III: GOLDEN LEGEND OF BABYLON** (J) 1985 anim color/ws c100m. D: Mamoru Oshii. Ref: TV: Toho Video; no Eng. Animag 9:11. Japan Video. V 10/16/85: 345(ad).

In a surprising and impressive science-fantasy conclusion, an old lady's weird gizmo discharges a force into space which in turn signals a nearby flying saucer; the latter then draws up to itself a huge, golden alien/Babylonian structure from beneath Manhattan, and the lady turns young and beautiful and flies off with her haul. Lupin, however, has one last trick....

Most of this Lupin film is larky, fairly amusing action-comedy, with scattered outre elements, including the Monster Club (where everyone wears monster masks), a visualized flashback (in which the giant hand of God, apparently, reaches out from space), and a bit with a cross between a robot and a cash register.

**LUPIN III: PLOT OF THE WIND DEMON CLAN** (J) AnimEigo/Toho/Tokyo Movie Shinsha 1987('94-U.S.) anim color 73m. (*Rupan III: The Fuma Conspiracy* - U.S.). D: O. Masayuki. SP: N. Makoto. Ref: TV: vt; no Eng. vc box.

Ingredients: an hallucination-inducing vapor which makes it seem, to the victim, as if other people are turning into monsters, or as if their faces are melting ... ninjas with cape-like mechanical wings ... and a remote-control burglar "bug" with helicopter option.... In this frequently very funny Lupin-vs.-cops saga, adventure takes a back seat to comedy, especially in the more amusing first half.

**LUPO THE BUTCHER** Danny Antonucci 1987? anim short. Ref: SFChron 2/19/93: "a glimpse at a butcher whose chopping aim is terribly poor." Sacto Bee 10/23/91: "bloody." Strand Theatre (S.F.) notes '87.

**LURKERS** Crown Int'l./Reeltime 1987 color 90m. (aka *Home, Sweet Home*). Ph, D, Co-Ed: Roberta Findlay. SP: Ed Kelleher,

Harriette Vidal. P, Mus, Co-Ed: Walter E. Sear. Ref: V 5/18/88: "metaphysical" nonsense. 5/13/87:6. 10/19/88:174. 10/21/87:4 (rated). Hound. Martin: "hopelessly meandering." With Christine Moore, Gary Warner, Marina Taylor.

Haunted woman.

**LURKING FEAR** (U.S.-Rom.) Para/Full Moon (Paunescu) 1994 color 77m. SP, D: C. Courtney Joyner. From H.P. Lovecraft's story "The Lurking Fear." Ph: A. Bartoli. Mus: J. Manzie. PD: Milo. SpMkpFX: Alchemyfx, M.S. Deak;(des) Wayne Toth. Opt: Mercer, OptFX. Ref: TV. PT 20:71. Stanley. SFChron 8/6/94. With Jon Finch, Ashley Lauren, Jeffrey Combs, Allison Mackie, Paul Mantee, Blake Bailey, Vincent Schiavelli, Michael Todd (creature).

Functional, apparently shot-on-tape shocker is more *Texas Chainsaw Massacre* than *HPL* and concerns gangster-type thugs vs. a family of storm-awakened ghouls. ("It must be one of those *things!*") From another angle, this is *Night of the Living Dead,* from below: This time, the clutching hand comes out of the ground, or the cellar-door slats. Some okay, fun monster-make-ups. Plus Schiavelli as an hommage to Skelton Knaggs, though he's not weird enough. (His Knaggs runs the Heavenly Rest Discount Funeral parlor.)

**LUST AT FIRST BITE** see *I'll Suck You Dry*

**The LUST DETECTOR** Expert Video (Eduardo Dinero) 1986 color 80m. D: K. Sludge. Ref: Adam '88. With Stacey Donovan, Tom Byron, Mauvais DeNoire, Marc Wallice.

Inventor's machine detects....

**LUST IN SPACE** P.F.F. (Frank & Ernest Mackintosh) 1984 color 78m. (*Lust in Space: Contact Is Made* - ad t). D: Myles Kidder. AD: Ron Vogel. Mkp: Alexis Vogel, Allan Bosshardt. Ref: TV: Paradise Visuals video. Adam '88. With Lana Burner, Jessica Longe, Harry Reems, Ali Moore, Ron Jeremy, Tom Byron, Gina Carrera, H. Savage.

"Long ago, in a faraway universe...." The mind-reading, fun-loving Glinda (Moore) comes to Earth from the planet Zitcom, 46 light years away. The evil Vixanna (Longe), who has outlawed sex on Zitcom, assigns keen-nosed, flower-eating Twitt (Reems) to pursue her. A planned Part II, *Vixanna's Revenge,* was apparently not made.... Small favors.

See also, however, *Whore of the Worlds.*

**LUST IN SPACE II** see *Whore of the Worlds*

**LUST IN THE FAST LANE** Paradise Visuals 1984 color feature. D: Adam. Ref: Jones. With Ginger Lynn (vampire), Tom Byron, Traci Lords, Eric Edwards (vampire).

**LUST OF BLACKULA** Arrow Video c1987? color c80m. D: Barry Morrison. SP: Jennings Halis. Ph: Lacy Carver. Mus: P. S. Nolan. Ref: TV: Superstar Video. no Adam '88-'93. With F. M. Bradley, Jane Daville, Ron Jeremy, Donna-Anne, Ray Victory, Ebony Ayes, Lacy Logan.

A gent named Alucard (Bradley)—whose preoccupation with the legend of Dracula interferes with his sex life—turns out to be

Dracula.... Just add plastic fangs (in the last few seconds of the video), and there's your vampire movie. Or not. Only for Ebony Ayes fans.

**The LUST POTION OF DOCTOR F** Western Visuals 1986 color 90m. D, P: Jerome Tanner. Ref: Adam '88. With Careena Collins, Candie Evens.

Doc concocts youth serum.

**LUTHER THE GEEK** Quest Ent/Albright-Platt Films 1988 color 90m. D: Carlton J. Albright. SP: Whitey Styles. Ph: David Knox. Mus: Vern Carlson. PD: Michael Beaudette. FX: Bill Purcell. Mkp: Cidele Curo. Prod Mgr: Michael Dempsey. Ref: TV: QE video. Hound. McCarty II. no Martin. PT 8:12. Fango 94:11. With Edward Terry (The Freak), Joan Roth, J. Joseph Clarke, Thomas Mills, Stacy Haiduk, Tom Brittingham (geek).

"The geek, an American phenomenon." Rural Illinois. Steel-toothed Luther Watts, paroled "model prisoner," immediately upon release, shreds an old lady's neck and (not much later) bites off a chicken's head. He looks (in outline) like a chicken, clucks like a chicken, and crows like a rooster. In the brilliant—or asinine—ending (pick one), the heroine out-clucks him. An elementary gore vehicle, despite the outre elements.

# M

**M.A.N.T.I.S.** Fox-TV/Wilbur Force & Renaissance & Univ-TV (Eick-Ecclesine/Hamm-Raimi-Tapert) 1994 color c90m. D: Eric Laneuville. Story, Tel: Sam Hamm. Story: also Sam Raimi. Ph: W. Dill. Mus: J. Lo Duca. PD: M. Strawn. VisFX: Stargate Films. Ref: V 1/24/94: "an all too serious, lethargic romp." TVG: "clumsy." Vallejo T-H. Stanley: "rousing." With Carl Lumbly, Bobby Hosea, Gina Torres, Steve James, Obba Babatunde, Francis X. McCarthy, Alan Fudge.

Paraplegic scientist uses the Mechanically Augmented Neuro-Transmitter Interception System to fight crime.

**M.D. GEIST** (J) Central Park Media (U.S. Manga Corps)/Hiro Media & Production WAVE (Kiyoshi Shoji) 1986 ('92-U.S.) anim color 46m.D: Hayato Ikeda. SP: Riku Sanjyo. Story, Mech Des, Asst D: Koichi Ohata. Mus D: Y. Takahashi. AD: Y. Takao. Anim D: Hiroshi Negishi. SdFX: N. Matsuura. Ref: TV: Columbia Video; Eng. titles.

"What is he?" On the planet Jerra, "several hundred years after the end of the Christian Era." Most Dangerous Geist—Commander of the Special Maneuvering Force and a bio-technological "clone" (i.e., a "bloody war machine")—returns from satellite exile to join the NoahGuards in their fight against the Nexrum Army. Main machine (apart from Geist): the Death Force, a doomsday device in the Brain Palace which "reacts to all life forms"—"at activation, millions of robotic soldiers will cover Jerra." Second bananas: Fightechs, weapons-suits which make their wearers look like hockey goalies ... Powered Machines ... a huge robot ... and a super-tank.... *Megazone 23*-like tough-guy cliches. Only interest: the machinery's design. Hollow razzle-dazzle. Some gore. Favorite subtitle: "Persistent little worms!"

See also *A-Ko the Battle.*

**MABUSE DER SPIELER** see *Dr. M. Horror House on Highway Five. Image of Dorian Gray in the Yellow Press*

**MAC AND ME** Orion/R. J. Louis Prods. (The Mac and Me Joint Venture) 1988 color 99m. SP, D: Stewart Raffill. SP: also Steven Feke. Mus: Alan Silvestri. SpMkp: Margaret Beserra, Edouard Henriques III. SpVisFX: Apogee (John Dykstra et al); Illusion Arts (Sid Dutton, Bill Taylor); CFI. Alien FX: EFX (Martin J. Becker); (mech) Richard Chronister. Alien Des: Ruben Aquino, Christopher Swift. SpFX: Dennis Dion, Chris Burton. Ref: TV. MFB'89:242-3. V 8/17/88. ad. Sacto Bee 8/15/88. SFChron 8/17/88. With Christine Ebersole, Jonathan Ward, Tina Caspary, Lauren Stanley, Jade Calegory, Buck Flower; Heather Green, Elena Moure, Jack David Walker (aliens).

Four humanoid MACs, or Mysterious Alien Creatures, from a moon of Saturn come to Earth aboard a U.S. spacecraft. The little "MAC" gets separated from its family, which at the end helps restore a boy's (Calegory) life.... Treacle City songs, a surfeit of Cute, and push-button Wonder. Does Spielberg know about this?

**MACABRE** (I-Sp) Mogul/Meteor & Leda 1968 color/ws 90m. (*L'Assassino Fantasma - I. Il Vuoto Intorno* - alt I t). Story, SP, D: Xavier or Javier Seto. Story, SP: Santiago Moncada. SP: also Gianfranco Clerici. Ph: A. Piazza. Mus D: F. Micalizzi. AD: Arrigo Equini. Mkp: A. P. Mancini. Ref: TV: Mogul Video; Eng. dubbed. Horacio Higuchi. Hound. no Martin. With Teresa Gimpera, Giacomo Rossi-Stuart, Silvana Venturelli, Larry Ward, Fernando Polack, Eugenio Navarro.

"Everybody is trying to drive me crazy!" Denise and Peter plot to keep her husband (his twin brother), John, alive but brain-destroyed with injections of narcovenis. They program him with memories of murder and use electric shock to induce an epileptic fit in him. "In a state of pathological inertia"—and suffering from "ultra-paradoxical inhibition"—John confronts the "ghost" of his murder victim, a blackmailer. ("So you want to kill me again?") However, "John" here proves to be Peter, and the "ghost" is actually John, in a dumb plastic disguise.... Supposedly ingenious tale of madness and murder is just overly convoluted. The latter sequence does not, unfortunately, play as weirdly as it reads. (There are solid narrative reasons for this double impersonation.) Complete with the expected perverse ending—the twin who lives turns out to be John, not Peter.

**MACABRE** see *Frozen Terror*

**MACABRE SERENADE** see *House of Evil*

**MACABRO** see *Frozen Terror*

**MacGYVER: LOST TREASURE OF ATLANTIS** ABC-TV 1994 color c90m. Ref: TVG. With Richard Dean Anderson, Brian Blessed, Sophie Ward, Christian Burgess, Oliver Ford Davies.

"A quest for legendary loot from the lost city...."

**La MACHINE** (F-G) Hachette Premiere-DD Prods.-Prima-M6 Films-France 2 Cinema & Studio Babelsberg (Rene Cleitman) 1994 color 96m. SP, D: Francois Dupeyron. From Rene Belletto's novel. Ph: D. Lohmann. Mus: M. Portal. PD: C. Conti.

SpOpt & Digital FX: Frederic Moreau. Ref: V 11/28/94: "an efficiently told tale." With Gerard Depardieu, Nathalie Baye, Didier Bourdon, Claude Berri.

A "psycho-horror thriller" re a scientist who "trades minds and bodies with a psychotic murderer."

**El MACHO BIONICO** (Mex) Rodas/Rodolfo De Anda & Andres Garcia 1981 colo c95m. SP, D: R. De Anda. SP: also Gilberto De Anda, from Mauricio Iglesias' book, *El Amor Es una Farsa*. Ph: Antonio De Anda. Mus: Ernesto Cortazar, Salvador Reyes. AD: G. De Anda. Titles: Hector Lopez. Ref: TV: Mexcinema Video; no Eng. Lawrence Cohn. With Isela Vega, Andres Garcia, Roberto Guzman, Rafael Inclan, Princesa Lea, Wanda Seux, Carlos East, Mariagna Prats (Miss Money Penny).

Surgery temporarily turns our sexually dysfunctional hero into an incredible hulk. He later plays a Dracula-type, complete with fake fangs, in an attempt to conquer women, but no go. Finally, lust erupts in him, telekinetically, and he senses the presence nearby of his light-of-love and uses his super-strength to knock down monastery walls to get to her. Crass, silly sf-comedy.

**MACISTE CONTRO ERCOLE NELLA VALLE DEI GUAI** (I) 1962 feature. D: Mario Mattoli. Ref: Palmerini: time machine.

**The MACROSS MOVIE: DO YOU REMEMBER LOVE?** (J) American Nat'l./Toho/Big West-Shogakukan-MBS-Tatsunoko Prods. 1984 anim color/ws 114m.(92m.-U.S.) (*Clash of the Bionoids* - U.S. aka *Macross the Movie*. aka *Robotech the Movie?* aka *Superspace Fortress Macross?*). D: Ishiguro Nobru. SP: Tomita Sukehiro. Story: Kawamori Shoji. Mus: Kato Kazuhiko. AD: Mayamae Mitsuharu. Ref: TV: CHE video; Eng. dubbed; also Shogakukan Video; scant English. Shadow Warrior: based on the TV series aka *Robotech* - U.S. Wonderful World of Comics 2 (4/88):42. no Hound. no Martin. Animag 11:10-14. 4:47: "centered" on episode 27 of the TV series. V 10/24/84:301 (ad).

"The SDF-1 Macross finds itself embroiled in a battle between the male Zentraedi and the female Meltrandi. Their only hope lies in a song left behind on Earth" (WWOC) eons ago when the "protoculture" of the Zentraedi and Meltrandi clones was "all destroyed." "Micro-humans" are descendants of these "manufactured giants who ... do nothing but fight." *The Macross Movie* appears angled to be the *Return of the Jedi* of Japanese animation—intricately detailed outer-space spectacle, action, comedy, and romance. The film has rather mundane beginnings, and some tiresome romantic elements, but the climactic battle sequence—a surreal combination of war, choreography, and fireworks—features almost abstract beauties of line and form. Hell is only one of several things which war is here—it's also, for instance, a pop concert, as the heroine, mike in hand, sings away at the front....

Elsewhere here, treacly-sounding songs accompany charming space-idyll scenes, and clouds that resemble ancient Greek ruins, mixed with debris from Saturn's rings, make up one unearthly skyscape. Funny scenes include the panic of the giant aliens when the romantic couple kiss and their comically cautious approach to a mechanical singing doll, which they suspect is a terrible weapon.

Note: *Macross: Flash Back 2012* (RCA Victor/Emotion video) consists principally of music-video excerpts from this film.

**MACROSS II: LOVERS AGAIN** (J) L.A. Hero & U.S. Renditions/MACROSS II Project, Hero, MBS, Shogakukan & Bandai (A.I.C. & Oniro) 1992 anim color 52m. (aka *Super Dimensional Fortress Macross II*). D: Kenichi Yatagai; (Eng. version) Quint Lancaster. SP: Manabu Nakamura; (Eng.) Raymond Garcia. Ph: Kazuhiro Konishi. Mus: Shiro Sagisu. AD: Hidenori Nakahata. Mech Des: (sup) Koichi Ohata; (coord) Studio Nue; (anim d) T. Nakayama. Anim Sup: Mikimoto, Nishi. SpFX: Takahiro Fukuda et al. Ref: TV: USR video; Eng. dubbed; OAV. Animation Mag (Smr '92): 59. V. Max 2:4. 4:3: 1st 2 of 6 episodes. Animerica 6:16: 3rd volume.

1) "Contact" (27m.): "It's awesome! I've never seen a more powerful energy discharge!" A Zentradi attack force holes up near Saturn. ("The Zentradi have developed music defense!") Juvenile writing. Pop music accompanies one battle in outer space.

2) "Ishtar" (25m.): "It's them again!" The Zentradi are out to wreck the world's monuments, including the Great Wall of China. Fragmented, confusing.

**MACROSS PLUS** (J) Big West & Macross Plus Project & Hero & Bandai Visual & Shogakukan & Mainichi Broadcasting (Ohnishi et al.) 1994 ('95-U.S.) anim color 39m. Story, D: S. Kawamori. Co-D: S. Watanabe. SP: K. Nobumoto. Ph: A. Takahashi. Mus: Y. Kanno. AD: K. Hariu. SpFX: Tamai, Sakakibara. SdFX: Sound Box. OptFX: Y. Kato. Ref: TV: Manga Ent. video; Eng. dubbed; 1st of OAV series.

Deep space, 2040 A.D. Vain test pilots on the Planet Eden try out the YF-19 and YF-21, as Project Supernova seeks the "next transforming fighter." One fighter is operated by brain waves.... Much visual detail ... shallowly serious story/characters.

**MACUMBA SEXUAL** (Sp) Golden Films Int'l. 1981 color/ws c77m. (aka *Sexual Voodoo*). SP, D: Jesus Franco. Mus: Pablo Villa. Mkp: Mercedes Bayon. Ref: TV: Million Dollar Video; no Eng. Hardy/HM:379, 383. MV. VSOM: sfa *Nude Princess*? With Candy Coster, Robert Foster, Ajita Wilson, Lorna Green, Jose Ferro, Juan G. Cabral.

A vacationing woman dreams of unholy mystical chickens, strange carvings, and an exotic temptress who magically lures her, then her lover to her remote island paradise-hell, where she keeps him as her "dog." The woman awakes, her lover comforts her, but she looks up to see ... the chicken. She screams in horror.... Franco sex-fantasy hasn't got much to it, but what there is is pretty bizarre.

**MAD AS A MARS HARE** WB 1963 anim color 7m. D: Chuck Jones. SP: J. Dunn. Mus: William Lava. Ref: "WBCartoons." Lee. LC. Maltin/OMAM.

Bugs Bunny rocketed to Mars, turned into cave rabbit by Commander X-2.

See also *Haredevil Hare*.

**MAD AT THE MOON** Jaffe Films & Spectacor Films/Cassian Elwes & Kastenbaum Films (Matt Devlen) 1992 color 97m.

SP, D: Martin Donovan. SP: also Richard Pelusi. Mus: G. Gouriet. Ph: Ronn Schmidt. Ref: TV: Republic HV. V 6/1/92. Martin. SFChron Dtbk 1/24/93. TVG 1/30/93. With Mary Stuart Masterson, Hart Bochner, Fionnula Flanagan, Cec Verrell, Stephen Blake, Daphne Zuniga, Melissa Anne Moore.

"One night, the moon came out and bewitched me." The American frontier. The husband's (Blake) *WereWolf of London* request to be left locked up in his room can mean only one thing—"moon sickness." Period-America horror, a la *Eyes of Fire,* has lots of dead space in-between occasionally striking images—e.g., the lycanthropic howler "framed" by the big full moon.

**2 The MAD DOCTOR** 1933 6m. Ref: screen. Jim Shapiro. PFA notes 5/16/93. SFChron Dtbk (ad).

A phantom figure abducts Pluto and threatens Mickey Mouse with torture-by-buzz-saw. Highlights of this lively, deluxe, animated horror short: the ticklish skeleton spider and the skeletons-in-coffins staircase. Cartoon plays like a thrills just-around-the-bend Disneyland attraction like "Mr. Toad's Wild Ride" or "The Haunted House."

**MAD JACK BEYOND THUNDERBONE** see *Beyond Thunderbone*

**MAD JAKE** see *Blood Salvage*

**\*MAD LOVE** John W. Considine, Jr. 1935 67m. AD: Cedric Gibbons; William A. Horning, Edwin B. Willis. Ref: TV. Wolf/Horror. Lee. Lentz. Weldon. Youngkin/Lorre. V 8/7/35. Hardy/HM. Kael/5001. Cinema (London) 9:9-10. Maltin '92. Martin. Fango 118:13. 123:35.

"100% crazy" surgeon Dr. Gogol (Peter Lorre) sews the hands of guillotined knife-thrower/murderer Rollo (Ed Brophy) onto concert pianist Stephen Orlac's (Colin Clive) arms, after the latter's hands are mutilated in a train wreck. The murderer's hands begin to seem to have a "life of their own," and, in the film's best, most disorienting sequence, Gogol shocks the already nervous Orlac (whose wife Gogol desires) by pretending to be Rollo with his head sewed back on. ("I am Rollo the knife thrower!")

Like the 1936 *Devil-Doll, Mad Love* is overplotted, a stew of various writers' ideas, and it has fewer rewarding payoffs. To make the story work at all, Orlac, Mrs. Orlac (Frances Drake), Gogol, and Rollo all have to be in exactly the right place at exactly the right time. Lorre's madness as Gogol seems for the most part hollow, unfelt, simply an actor's tricks. (For the real thing, see Lorre in *M* or *Stranger on the Third Floor.*) Winning off-the-wall bit: the about-to-be-beheaded Rollo asking a reporter (Ted Healy) about Boulder Dam.

**MAD MAD GHOST** (H.K.) Golden Princess/Huge Yield Films 1991 color/ws 91m. Ref: TV: vt; Eng.. titles. V 11/30/92:64: in H.K.

"Take me to look at the real ghosts!" Uncle Ying—Taoist priest and part-time janitor—sets up his charms [sic] school for exorcists at a house haunted by Blunt and Ah Kuen, a "hit means love" couple dead one hundred years.... The anything-for-a-laugh tack works once in a while in this horror-comedy, which is rife with cartoonish violence. Funny: Ying "folding up" Ah Kuen. Cute:

the assault of the paper-airplane charms. Outlandish but amusing: Ah Kuen as "Madonna" and "Wonder Woman Ghost."

**MAD MAX BEYOND THUNDERDOME** (Austral.) WB/Kennedy Miller 1985 color/ws 107m. SP, D, P: George Miller. D: also George Ogilvie. SP: also Terry Hayes. Mus: Maurice Jarre. Prosth: Bob McCarron. SpVisFX: Universal Matte Dept. SpFxSup: Mike Wood. SpFxCoord: Steve Courtley; (model crew) Alan Maxwell. Ref: TV. MFB'85:312-13. V 6/26/85. Phantom. Hound. Drew/Motion Picture Series & Sequels. With Mel Gibson, Tina Turner, Angelo Rossitto, Paul Larsson, Helen Buday, Tom Jennings.

The first half of *Mad Max III,* sequel to *The Road Warrior,* is set in Bartertown's Underworld (a methane source), Thunderdome, and Atomic Cafe, and all that Max really wants here is to get back his vehicle. The second half—set in the wasteland—is a good-natured reprise of *The Road Warrior.* Max's "cool" here is funny set against the tribe's "hot." As a whole, Part III is easily better than Part I, not quite up to Part II. Lots of Dolby noise.

**MAD MAXINE** AFV 1992 color 84m. D: Frank Thring. Ref: Adam '93: post-nuke world. With Crimson, Leanna Foxxx, Ron Jeremy.

**MAD MEN OF EUROPE** (B) Col/Aldwych 1939('40-U.S.) 73m. D: Albert de Courville. SP: Edward Knoblock, Ian Hay, Dennis Wheatley, Richard Llewellyn, Rodney Ackland et al. From the play (also British title) by Guy du Maurier, "An Englishman's Home." Ph: Greenbaum, Harris. AD: Wilfred Arnold. Ref: V 10/18/39. MPH 11/11/39. Bill Warren. Academy. BFC. FD 6/26/40. With Edmund Gwenn, Mary Maguire, Paul Henreid, Geoffrey Toone, Richard Ainley, Carl Jaffe, Meinhart Maur, Mark Lester.

"An invasion of England by bombers and parachute troops" (FD), guided by "beam radio." (MPH)

**MAD MISSION 3** see *Aces Go Places III*

**The MAD VAMPIRES** (H.K.?) Jia's Motion Picture Co. 1984 color/ws feature. Ref: TV: Tai Seng Video; no Eng.

Noted: a couple hopping vampires, one who giggles and one who literally seems to be a pig at times ... a heroine who keeps bumping into ghost types ... a vampire in the sand at a beach who battles a karate lady in a bikini, then becomes two vampires ... two feisty zombies in sailor suits ... and the severed head of a vampire which cackles, flies, and, for all its trouble, gets promptly zapped. Broad, low comedy, little of it funny. Film looks like a likely source for one of those dubbed, patchwork Joseph Lai movies.

**MADAM JECKYL** 1994? color 80m. Ref: Vallejo T-H 2/95. With Kaitlyn Ashley, Melissa Hill.

"A prudish doctor's experimental serum turns her into an insatiable nymphomaniac...."

**MADARA** see *Beast War Madara*

**MADBALLS: ESCAPE FROM ORB** Hi-Tops Video/Those Characters from Cleveland (Nelvana) 1986 anim color c30m. Ref: vc box. vc trailer. Hound.

Music outlawed on planet of Orb.

**MADBALLS: GROSS JOKES** Hi-Tops Video & Nelvana 1987 anim color c30m. Ref: vc box. no Hound.

The Madballs on Earth.

**MADHOUSE** (U.S.-I) Creative/Chesham (Shepherd-Assonitis) 1981 color/ws 92m. (3P *There Was Once a Child* - alt t. *Scared to Death* - orig t. *I Will Scare You to Death* - int t). SP, D: Ovidio Assonitis. SP: also S. Blakley et al. Ph: R. D'Ettore Piazzoli. Mus: Riz Ortolani. Ref: V 7/11/84: Media Home Ent. video; "below-average horror opus." 5/13/81:152. With Trish Everly, Michael Macrae, Dennis Robertson, Morgan Hart.

"Gruesome murders ... bloodbath ... skin eruptions."

**MADONNA ... BABAENG AHASSSSSS** (Fili) Regal Films (Lily Monteverde) c1990 color c105m. (*Madonna ... Babaeng Ahas* - alt t). SP, D: Artemio O. Marquez. Story: Victoria Thiff. Ph: Vic Anao, Jimmy Baer. Mus D: D. Velasquez. PD: Jens Peter Gaw. Assoc D & SpProsth: Maurice Carvajal. SdFX: Rodel Capule. Ref: TV: Regal Video; little Eng. With Snooky Serna, Tirso Cruz III, Eric Quizon, Rosemarie Gil, Luis Gonzales, Caridad Sanchez, Johnny Wilson, Mario Escudero, Anthony Taylor, Odette Khan.

The cursed Merlinda de la Pena starts to decompose and gives birth to a baby, Madonna, who grows up to become a young woman who, when threatened, turns into a plastic-fanged reptile monster. She kills a would-be rapist, then, when two more potential rapists attack her, she goes through more bubbling-pudding makeup effects and again becomes the cute green thing. Later, again threatened.... (Episodic, isn't it?) Sub-*Zuma* snake antics. Main camp highlight: the rubber-Godzilla creature. Second string: the big snake which attends Madonna. (It's apparently part of her afterbirth, or forebirth.)

**2P The MADONNA'S SECRET** Republic (Stephen Auer) 1946 79m. SP, D: William Thiele. SP: also Bradbury Foote. Ph: John Alton. Mus: Joseph Dubin. AD: Hilyard Brown. SpFX: Howard & Theodore Lydecker. Paintings: A. S. Keszthelyi. Mkp: Bob Mark. Ref: TV. V 2/20/46. TVG. Turner/Human Monsters. no Lee. no Lentz. no Weldon. no Stanley. Maltin '92. no Scheuer. With Francis Lederer, Gail Patrick, Ann Rutherford, Linda Stirling, John Litel, Edward Ashley, Leona Roberts, Michael Hawks, Pierre Watkin, Will Wright, John Hamilton.

New York City. James Corbin (Lederer)—a "strange man, a creature of moods"—improvises "strange, weird music" on his piano, at night, and "hears" the voice of the dead model whose "imaginary face" he still works into his portraits. Meanwhile, his mad mother (Roberts) "protects" her son by killing the women who might take him away from his art—and from her....

The suggestions here of *Hangover Square*—the line "Each man kills the thing he loves" and Corbin's near-confession of murder: "Perhaps I did it. There must be moments that are lost to me"—turn out to be red herrings. One tipoff to the shades-of-*Psycho* conclusion: Alton's lighting of a dinner-table scene, in which

mother and son are isolated together in an island of light. Another: the fact that Mrs. Corbin was with her son in Paris, too, where the first model was drowned. The revelation of the secret of the mad mother is half-chilling, half-camp. If it plays amusingly, it is, unfortunately, one of the few sequences which does. Lederer gives the only interesting performance; Hawks is downright awful. Script comes complete with your basic marking-time-till-the-finish dialogue.

**MADOX-01** (J) AnimEigo/Fuji Sankei 1987 anim color 50m. Story, D: Aramaki Nobuyuki. Ref: vc box: Eng. titles. Animerica 6:51. TV: Pony Video: *Madox-01: Metalskin Panic* - 6m. excerpt?

Slave Troopers with futuristic robot-like armor.

**La MADRE MUERTA** (Sp) GZ 1993 color 107m. SP, D, P: Juanma Bajo Ulloa. SP: also Eduardo Bajo Ulloa. Ph: Javier Aguirresarobe. Mus: B. Mendizabal. SpFX: Poli Catero. Ref: V 11/1/93: *The Dead Mother*-tr t; "atmospheric thriller ... is long on baroque, widescreen style and short on psychological payoff." With Karra Elejalde, Lio, Ana Alvarez.

"Semi-psycho" slasher.

**MAG-TONING MUNA TAYO** (Fili) Good Harvest Prods. 1984 color c100m. D: Mike Relon Makiling. Ph: Ben Lobo. Mus: Tito Sotto, Boy Alcaide. SdFX: Sebastian Sayson. Ref: TV: Trigon Video; little Eng. Pinoy Bazaar: *Cheers!* - tr t. MMarquee 43:10. With Tito, Vic & Joey; Margia Braza, Jennie Ramirez, Opalyn Forster, Debraliz, Soxy Topacio, Lily Miraflor.

Haunted house harbors two ghosts who turn up everywhere (even outside the house, in town), dancing skeletons, an effeminate hunchback, and a hatchet-wielding sleepwalker who reenacts a double murder. The quietly accusing presences of the two ghosts are virtually the only redeeming feature of this flimsy horror-comedy. Double takes and questionable humor predominate.

**\*\*\*MAGIC BOY** (J) MGM/Toei 1959 ('61-U.S.) anim color/ws 76m. (83m.) (*Shonen Sarutobi Sasuke*. ***Adventures of Little Samurai* -ad t). D: Akira Daikubara. SP: Dohei Muramatsu. Story: Kazuo Dan. Ph: S. Otsuka. Mus D: T. Funamura. Ref: TV: Turner-TV. Lee. V 8/9/61. COF 10:46. Jim Shapiro.

A big salamander-like water monster turns into a fanged witch, The Evil Princess. The latter can also appear as a sort of phantom fire, or a bat. At the end, she is many bats that become one bigger bat. She's last seen as a weird, defeated, fleeing skeleton, in an impressive sequence. Magic Boy, meanwhile, can make himself invisible.... Poky but pleasingly drawn and scored fantasy is pleasanter before the plot takes over. Highlight: the witch's phantasmagoric dance.

**MAGIC COP** (H.K.) Movie Impact/Millifame 1990 color/ws c85m. (*Qumo Jingcha*). D: Dung Wai (aka David Lai). FX?: Animation Shop. Ref: TV: Pan-Asia Video; Eng. titles. Hardy/HM2. Weisser/ATC: '89. With Lam Ching Ying.

"The Hell Gate is opened only once a year." Ingredients in this slight horror-comedy with well-done magic effects include a witch that at one point ages instantly, flower-petal magic which turns tile blocks into flying-disc weapons, a microwaveable black-magic token, Ice Spells, and voodoo-doll-style, "remote control" magic and levitation. In one technically ingenious sequence, a brick wall seems to be possessed and to come to undulating life.

**MAGIC CRYSTAL** (H.K.) Movie Impact Ltd. 1988? color/ws? c95m. Ref: TV: Rainbow Video; Eng. titles.

The magic crystal, or "the thing"—a green jade found on a Greek island—can control the minds and bodies of the people near it. It "injects" (for example) illusions into one man's mind—he sees a woman seem to peel off her face. It then "deranges" his body structure: His feet switch place with his hands (cf. *Titser Kong Alien*), and—afraid that others will think he's a monster—he feigns strange yoga positions. The jade, it seems, is a "computer with thinking" which belongs to an alien from a "faraway place several million light years" from Earth and which, inserted into a module, enables the alien to return home.

The alien is called an "explorer from the Milky Way," a "man from outer space," an "ultraman," and everything but what he (with his chatty jade) really is—another E.T. who befriends an Earth boy and who wants to go home. A few thousand years ago, he says, he was taken for a god in Greece when he created the "perfect earthwoman"—Venus. The science-fantasy elements here are intriguing, and the "deranged" body sequence is very funny. But the other story elements—ranging from kung fu to spies to low comedy—are routinely handled.

See also *Arion*.

The **MAGIC MAN** (Thai) c1986? color/ws c100m. Ref: TV: Hong Kong TV Video; no Eng. apart from title. MMarquee 43:8.

A holy man gives our hero the power to turn into a hairy, fanged, werewolf-like creature with supersight, super-strength, and the power to repel bullets.... Rudimentary crossing of *The Wolf Man* and *Walking Tall,* as our hirsute hero takes on the bad men and women of the town. Shootouts, fistfights, martial-arts duels, and special makeup so bad it looks like the hero is simply wearing a funny-looking ski mask.

**MAGIC MUMMY** RKO/Van Beuren 1933 anim 7m. SP: John Foster. Ref: TV. Lee. Maltin/OMAM. LC.

"Another mummy has been stolen from the museum!" The thief: a mysterious, cloaked fiend with hands that zap. He magically removes the bandages of the female mummy and has her perform—with Betty Boop voice—onstage, before an audience of skeletons. Charming nonsense about a very strange cemetery world. The bit of plot is more *Svengali* or *Phantom of the Opera* than *The Mummy* and deftly juxtaposes the macabre and the comic. At one point, the "whammy" man summons a skeleton-orchestra up out of the ground.

**MAGIC OF SHAOLIN SORCERESS** see *Succubare*

**MAGIC OF SPELL** (H.K.?) Grand March Movies 1989 color 83m. SP, D: C. Chung. Ref: TV: Rainbow Video; no Eng. Fango 107:59: also a Part II. With Liz Gilbert, Terry Wells.

Miscellaneous monsters include a ghoul from the ground, a swivel-skulled skeleton, a big-eared alien-type with ray gun, and a dancing root creature. Clever: the hero's "shadow play" for real, as the ghoul throttles him behind the screen. Cute: the monster-witch crying over her singed hair. Neat: the heroine inhaling the fire from the bonfire. Funny: the strong man transforming himself into a squat, red-eyed, big-toothed rock. Strange: the half-bird person. (One arm is a feather.) Music: library.

**MAGIC OF 3,000 YEARS AGO** (Taiwanese) 1987? color/ws c92m. Ref: TV: vt; Eng. titles. Thai Video: above is tr t. VSOM: sfa *Ginseng King*?

The thousand-year-old Ginseng Spirit ("At your service") revives a cobra-bitten boy, Hsiaoming. Later, when the spirit's plucked whiskers land on a grave, they revive a stray Nazi ("Heil, Hitler!"), now a "strong zombie" who vampirizes the boy's mother. A land mine destroys this "foreign zombie." ("It works better than burning.") Meanwhile, Grampa Earthgod consults the giants Magic Eyes and Magic Ears ("This old jerk's buttering us up again!"), who magically see and hear that the three-headed, ray-spitting Demon King of Devil Mountain and his "monster soldiers" have captured Ginseng Spirit. The demon has the spirit beheaded and eats him: "Delicious. Truly delicious. What a fresh flavor." But (as the spirit's head tells Hsiaoming) Ginseng Spirit has taken poison—the Demon King soon finds that he has a stomach ache (one head to another: "I told you not to eat so fast") and is easily dispatched by the Cold Ice Sword.

*Magic of 3,000 Years Ago* alternates between wry offhand fantasy-comedy and protracted chase and action scenes. Monsters and spirits here are more amusing than humans. The former even make fun of the latter—a spry, gabby little stopmo ginseng, for instance, chides Hsiaoming ("Dummy!") when the boy can't catch him. A monk who is an expert at zombie acupuncture insists that there is no such thing as a Ginseng Spirit (zombies, yes; ginsengs, no) and calls the Nazi a "hopping corpse," though this corpse clearly does not hop. The movie—which is wilder in its first half—reaches more familiar fairy-tale turf on Devil Mountain, with its swords and dungeons and princesses.

**MAGIC STORY** (Taiwanese) Goodyear Movie Co. 1985? color c92m. D: I Yung Tong. Ref: TV: New Ship video; Eng. titles. Happy Produce. NST! 4:30. MMarquee 43:5, 6.

"Ding-dong"—a little hopping ghost (or vampire) who seems to have lost his mother and who doesn't fit in with other little ghosts—is taken in hand by Akui. After Ding-dong is exposed to sunlight, Akui and a doctor attempt to save his waning life with "supernatural electric waves." It takes a bolt of lightning, however, to regenerate Ding-dong and turn him into a "Bat Vampire." Also on the program: a slew of hopping vampires, a fake vampire, "bumper car" vampire coffins, and a mechanical "vampire" used for testing stakes.

Hopping-vampire comedy charmer has a few standout sequences, including an unusual one in which child-ghosts playing in the woods at night on an invisible seesaw and swing invite Ding-dong to join them. Later, in a funny Do-as-I-do scene, Ding-dong tries to avoid detection on a village street by copying Akui's every move. (Akui sneezes; Ding-dong sneezes....) A difficult task since vampires here have a marked tendency to hop and hold their arms out straight. The non-Ding-dong comedy and action scenes are less charming.

**MAGIC TO WIN 5** see *Happy Ghost V*

**MAGIC WARRIORS** (H.K.) c1990? color 94m. Ref: TV: Pan-Asia Video; no Eng. (apart from the ff. title in the credits).

"This is an old fairy tale" re a witch who can turn into a scaly lake monster ... a villain that turns toothy, or fangy, and monstrous at the end ... a *From Hell It Came*-like tree creature ... a *Missile to the Moon*-like rock monster ... a heroine who can turn into an ape ... a hero who's turned into a skeleton ... a child's doll which is turned into a horned Yeti-type ... and a snail man, a mushroom man, a caterpillar creature, and a burrowing creature.... A mixed bag of happily silly fantasy, routine martial-arts action, and much indecipherable talk.

**MAGIC WORLD OF WATARI** see *Watari and the Seven Monsters*

**MAGICAL STORY OF BETTY** see *Betty Lonely*

**MAGICAL WONDERLAND** see *Jack Frost* (1965)

**MAGKASANGGA 2000** (Fili) Harvest Int'l. Films & Golden Fortline 1993(1992?) color/ws 100m. D: Phillip or Philip Ko, Johnny Wood, Joe Mari Avellana. SP: Avellana. Ph: R. Chang, R. Lapid. Mus: Jaime Fabregas. PD: Kiddy Li Kwok Leung. VisFX: Cinemagic. Animator: Charlie Baleros. SpFX: Jess Manaloto. SdFX: Ramon Reyes, Amber Ramos. Ref: TV: Viva Video; part English. With Ricky Davao, Cynthia Luster, M. Del Rosario, Gabriel Romulo, Eddie Gutierrez, Jaime Fabregas, Ruel Vernal.

"It comes from somewhere else." In the year 2000, on Earth, a flying, sword-wielding alien hero battles a flying, sword-wielding villain. ("Everybody saw aliens!") The bad spaceman extracts and derives energy from his victims' life force .... A questionable-taste blend of Hong Kong sf-action and home-grown, far-out Filipino fantasy, with amusing, overkill action set-pieces and a touch of *Highlander*.

**La MAISON ASSASSINEE** (F) Gaumont & Gaumont Prod. 1988 color 111m. Adap, D: Georges Lautner. Adap: also Jacky Cukier. Mkp: M. Felix, D. Colladant. Ref: TV: Action Film video; no Eng. V 8/3/88.

"Seraphin wants to avenge his family. He decides to kill the culprits one by one. But as he prepares to kill the first, someone else does it for him. Who? Why? And who are the real killers of la Burliere [an inn]? Seraphin does not know that houses avenge themselves when one murders them." (vc box) All this and two thunderstorms, fog, a disfigured man, a cave skeleton or two, a hand-on-shoulder shock, unkenneled dogs which savage a woman, and mill gears which crush a man. Atmospheric mystery-suspenser with suggestions of the supernatural.

**MAJOCCO CLUB** (J) 198-? anim color 45m. (*Creamy Mami* series). Ref: Japan Video. vc box: monster.

**The MAJORETTES** Major Films/Ross & Hinzman (John Russo) 1988 color 92m. (*One by One* - early t). D, Ed: Bill Hinzman. SP: J. Russo, from his novel. Ph, Mus, Ed: Paul McCollough. SpFxMkp: Gerald Gergely. Ref: V 10/19/88: "strictly ordinary stalker horror film." Ecran F 65:71. 79:74. Fango 53: 6, 49-52.

With Kevin Kindlin, Terrie Godfrey, M. V. Jevicky, Sueanne Seamens, Russ Streiner.

Hooded madman slaughters high-school cheerleaders.

**MAKAI TENSHO** see *Ninja Incarnation*

**MAKAI TOSHI** see *Demon City Shinjuku*

**MAKING CONTACT** (W.G.) New World & Filmverlag der Autoren & Balcor/ZDF & Bioskop & Centropolis (Klaus Dittrich) 1985 color/ws 94m. (79m.-U.S.) (*Joey*- W. G. t). SP, D: Roland Emmerich. SP: also Hans J. Haller, Thomas Lechner. Mus & SpFX: Hubert Bartholomae. SpFX: also Film & Trick; Frank Schlegel, Rolf Giesen. SdFxSup: Paul Clay. Opt: Geyer Werke; Ray Mercer. Ref: TV. V 12/25/85. Dr. Rolf Giesen. With Joshua Morrell, Eva Kryll, T. Shields, Jack Angel (dummy's voice).

Out of the fears of children, the "frighteningly lifelike" ventriloquist's dummy of Jonathan Fletcher conjures up several monsters, including a monster-hamburger and Darth Vader, while a telekinetic boy, Joey (Morrell), animates a toy four-legged walker out of *Return of the Jedi*. It transpires that an evil spirit possesses the dummy and has trapped the ventriloquist.... This *Poltergeist* (or *Carrie*) for kids is okay if you don't mind a few moments with actors in-between effects scenes. Best "effect" is simply the evil/snotty look on the dummy's face. The self-activating, boy's-bedroom toys are getting to be a real cliche.

**MAKING MR. RIGHT** Orion/Barry and Enright 1987 color 98m. D: Susan Seidelman. SP: Floyd Byars, Laurie Frank. Mus: Chaz Jankel. SpVisFX: Bran Ferren. SpMkp: Carl Fullerton, John Caglione, Doug Drexler. Mech Model: E. Sprott. Ref: TV. MFB'88:144. V 3/25/87. SFChron 4/10/87. SFExam 4/10/87. With John Malkovich (Dr. Jeff Peters/Ulysses), Ann Magnuson, Glenne Headly, Ben Masters, Laurie Metcalf, Polly Bergen, Hart Bochner, Robert Trebor.

"In the future, making love will no longer be necessary for the making of life." Chemtec's android Ulysses—made in the image of creator Dr. Peters, and the "closest thing to man himself"—is supposed to be able to "function in space alone." Ulysses, however, finds himself concentrating on pr consultant Frankie Stone (Magnuson), and the doc takes his place in space.... The script offers the expected literalness in Ulysses' scientific responses to slang and to idiomatic phrases (e.g., "small world"). Not to mention the usual android-gets-a-heart plot developments, too-neatly-dovetailing with the Inhuman Scientist co-theme. Nice touches here and there—for example, Ulysses learning how to ride an escalator—plus a bittersweet conclusion.

**MAL DI LUNA** see *Kaos*

**MAL OCCHIO** see *Mas Alla del Exorcismo*

**MALABIMBA** (I) 1979 color feature. D: Andrea Bianchi. SP: P. Regnoli.Ref: VSOM: "sex/devils/possession." MV. Palmerini. With Katell Laennec, Patrizia Webley, Maria Angela Giordano.

At a seance, Countess Lucrezia possesses Sister Sofia.

**MALAM SATU SURO** (Indon.) feature. Ref: Heider/Indonesian Cinema, p. 44: horror; *Friday the 13th*-tr t. with Suzzanna.

**MALASTRANA** see *Corta Notte delle Bambole di Vetro, La*

**MALDICION DE FRANKENSTEIN, La** see *Erotic Rites of Frankenstein, The*

**La MALDICION DEL MONASTERIO** (Mex) Concorde/Gallo (Villa-Gebhard) 1986 ('90-U.S.) color 76m. (*Blood Screams* - U.S.). Story, SP, D: Glenn Gebhard. SP: also Tony Wakefield. Ph: Miguel Garzon. Mus: Raul Diaz de la Garza. AD: Francisco Magallon. SpFX: Jorge Farfan, Federico Farfan Jr. Mkp: Graciela Gonzalez. SdFX: Gonzalo Gavira. Ref: TV: Million Dollar Video; some Eng.; *The Curse of the Monastery* - tr t. V 3/4/91:55 (hv): WBHV; *Bloody Monks* - tr of orig t. Psychotronic 8:55. Martin. V 2/3/88:24 (rated, as *Bloodscreams*). 10/19/88:174: aka *Monks of Blood*. With Russ Tamblyn, Rafael Sanchez Navarro, Stacey Shaffer, Ana Luisa Peluffo, Jaime Garza, Mario Almada, Isela Vega.

Fog at the train station. Fog in the town. Fog around the church tower. And lurking in the fog: a night-roaming knife-wielding "monster-monk." The film's most horrific material, however, is reserved for the heroine's three visualized nightmares (in which she encounters ghoulish-looking monks, a strangler, a crazy laughing girl, and a gorily beheaded monk) and for the mad killer's climactic visions of undead monks and a laughing dead man.... Routine but atmospheric psychological-horror-fantasy has an amusing turn by Tamblyn, as a Yankee creep. His Frank—the "Great White God of Fish"—is a magician lost in Mexico and given to greeting the skeptical locals with "Buenos noches" in broad daylight.

**MALDICION MAYA** (Mex) Diafragma Films 1987 color c88m. (*Muerte en el Caribe* - cr t). D: Victor Herrera. Mus: Valentino Inc. AD: Portillo. Ref: TV: Video Mex; no Eng.; above is ad t; *Mayan Curse* and *Death in the Caribbean* - tr titles. With Rosalba Brambila, Roberto Montiel, Elza Nava.

Cheap, shot-on-tape actioner with horrific overtones concerns the discovery, near Cancun, of a Mayan artifact. Murders-by-harpoon follow, each one nastier than the last. In addition: a rotting-torso-on-beach shock and (in a coda) a woman's hallucination re the return of the bloody, dead harpoon man.

**MALEDICTION** see *Satan's Princess*

**MALEDICTION DE FRANKENSTEIN, La** see *Erotic Rites of Frankenstein, The*

**El MALEFICIO II** (Mex) Videocine/Televicine (Fernando de Fuentes) 1986 color 105m. (*Los Enviados del Infierno* - alt t). SP, D: Raul Araiza, from the telenovela "El Maleficio." Mus: Guillermo Mendez. SP: also Antonio Monsell. Idea: F. Villeli. VisFX: (d) Juan Carlos Munoz; Arte E Idea. SpFX: Federico Farfan. Mkp: Ana Julieta Rojas. Ref: TV. TVG. V 10/8/86: sequel to TV soaper. With Ernesto Alonso, Lucia Mendez, A. Monsell, Alejandro Camacho, Juan Carlos Ruiz, Maria Teresa Rivas.

Enrique de Martino (Alonso), the devil's official emissary, has Scanner-like powers which make a woman incinerate and power

lines turn into weapons. He is searching for the subject of a painting, "Portrait of Gabriel," who is to replace him. Meanwhile, Gabriel (Monsell), who also does *Carrie* tricks, turns an auto into a remote-control weapon.... Script begins with its most tantalizing display of psychic powers: Enrique makes a photo obliterate itself. Subsequent effects are more familiar. At one point, Gabriel—who can make the walls of a house shake and break—watches similar but more grand-scale destruction on TV in *When Worlds Collide.*

See also *Mal Oficio III* (P).

**MALEVOLENT MATE** (H.K.) Fortune Star Films 1993 color/ws feature. Story, D: Lin Chi Fun. SP: Wah, Mak. Story: also Hing. Ph: Jin. AD: Jenny Lee et al. Mkp: Ngok Sui Wai. SdFX: Lung. Ref: TV: World Video; Eng. titles. With Wong Kwong Leung, Fu Yuk Ching, Lam Ka Wah.

"It's disgusting. So horrible." Who done the cleaver murder? First, legs and hands are found, in rubbish bags ... then an unearthed corpse so foul it makes onlookers retch. Apparently, the girl's mom strangled the butcher's wife, more-or-less in self-defense, chopped him up, then put the parts in the bathtub. ("I think she cut the body into pieces.") Or is she protecting someone? More cop third-degree here than plot. Compare *Bunman.*

**The MALIBU BEACH VAMPIRES** Peacock Films 1991 color 77m. SP, D: Francis Creighton. Mus: Paul McCarty. SP: also John Falotico, Jill Stewart. Ph: Joe Jacobs. Ref: TV: AMI Ent. video. Jones. With Kelly Galindo (Chairperson, Malibu Vampires Inc.), Christina Walker, Mimi Spivak, Anet Anatelle, Joan Rudelstein, Titus Moody, Angelyne, Becky LeBeau.

Ponderous farce re vampire women whose bite makes phony TV evangelists, politicians, and Oliver North types tell the truth. Once in a while, the long, comic wind-ups here pay off, but most of the shticks seem all wind-up.

**MALOCCHIO** see *Mas Alla del Exorcismo*

**MAMAW** (Fili) Turning Point Films (Reyes) c1985? color c92m. D: Vic Diaz. SP & Assoc D: Pablo S. Gomez, from his Pinoy Klasiks serial. Sp&SdFX: Danny Salvador. ProsthMkp: Lulu Dela Pena. Ref: TV: vt; little Eng.

A foundling (Marilou Sadiua) with *She Demons* buckteeth undergoes surgery and gets pretty, but a crazed, scarred man throws acid in her face. Gang raped, she ekes out revenge with a can of gasoline and a match, then gets her face fixed again.... Very hokey soaper with *Face of Fire* and *Ms. 45* overtones. Horrific aspects are soft-pedaled. The only quasi-shock scenes: the throwing of the acid (the thrower then commits suicide with a machete) and the burning of the main rapist's hut (with him inside it).

**MAMBA** see *Fair Game* (1988)

**MAMONO HUNTER YOHKO** see *Devil Hunter Yohko*

**MAN BEHIND THE SUN** see *Men behind the Sun*

**MAN BITES DOG** see *C'Est Arrive Pres de Chez Vous*

**MAN CALLED RAGE, A** see *Rage*

**MAN CALLED SLOANE, A** see *Death Ray 2000*

**MAN EATERS** (U.S.-F) Bel Air & R. T. Prods (Martineau, Grynbaum) 1988 color 87m. SP, D: Daniel Colas, from his play. Mus: Aldo Frank. Ref: V 5/25/88: "some okay slapstick but a little goes a long way." With Catriona MacColl, Roberta Weiss, Coralie Seyrig, Mark Sinden.

Two men are shipwrecked on an island with "three beautiful cannibal women."

**MAN FACING SOUTHEAST** (Arg.) Filmdallas/Cinequanon (Lujan Pflaum) 1986 ('87-U.S.) color 109m. (*Hombre Mirando al Sudeste*). SP, D: Eliseo Subiela. Ph: Ricardo de Angelis. Mus: Pedro Aznar. AD: Marta Albertinazzi. Mkp: Dora Roldan. Ref: TV: New World Video; Eng. titles. ad. V 10/1/86. 9/17/86. Phantom. SFExam 4/10/87. SFChron 4/10/87. With Lorenzo Quinteros, Hugo Soto, Ines Vernengo.

"I come from far away, from another world." Rantes (Soto), the new "Unidentified Flying Patient" at the insane asylum, insists that he and his (never seen) spaceship are simply "images projected in space" and that he is a "perfect human replica," though he "cannot feel." He says that he and others like him, in Madrid, Lima, etc., are here to rescue man from his own stupidity. Rantes does possess telekinetic powers—he uses same to feed some hungry children and to rouse fellow inmates—by a sort of "remote control"—with his personally conducted version of Beethoven's Ninth.... Whether or not Rantes is an alien, he is gifted, but he learns that he must use his gifts discreetly. He camouflages his act of charity for the children at the cafe with a flurry of telekinetically smashed drinking glasses, and his impromptu public performance of Beethoven gets him in Dutch with the asylum director and ultimately leads to his own death. The film balances the excitement of his supernatural sleight of hand with the danger (mainly to himself) of exposure. It pokes along placidly (maybe a little too placidly at times), the better to set off its displays of Rantes' special talents. The script's use of telekinesis and the Ninth recalls Tarkovsky's *Stalker*.

**MAN HUNTER** (Sp-F-W.G.) Trans World/J.E. Films & Eurocine & Lisa (Franco Prosperi) 1980 color 86m. (*Il Cacciatore di Uomini*). SP, D, Mus: Jesus Franco. Ph: J. Soler. Story, SP: "Julius Valery." SpFX: Manuel Archilla. Mkp: G. Guerrero. Ref: TV: MV; Eng. dubbed; *Devil Hunter*. Ref: Hardy/HM: "a catalogue of repulsive events." Fango 12/88. Peter Zirschky. VWB: *Mondo Cannibale* - alt t; *Mandingo Manhunter* - vt t. With Al Cliver (aka P. L. Conti), Ursula Fellner, Gisella Hahn, Werner Pochat, Robert Foster.

"They sacrifice human beings." In Port Santuana, a bug-eyed, apparently radioactive gent goes cannibal. Vapid, vacant, vacuous. The closest the movie gets to entertainment is the line "This wild vegetation gives me the creeps!" Only for diehard Francophiles.

**The MAN IN THE BACK SEAT** (B) Independent Artists (Wintle-Parkyn) 1961 b&w 57m. D: Vernon Sewell. SP: Malcolm Hulke, Eric Paice. Ref: Hardy/HM: "well-crafted thriller." no

Lee. no V. no Maltin/TVM. no Scheuer. With Derren Nesbitt, Keith Faulkner, Carol White, Harry Locke.

Crazed robber has *Body Snatcher*-like hallucinations re body of dying man.

**The MAN IN THE MOON** Keystone 192-? silhouette anim and live action c3m. Ref: TV: Loonic Video (Early Animation number 2). no Lee.

Hunter travels by umbrella to the moon, finds a long-tailed rhino and a brontosaurus-type. Fairish silent fun.

*****The MAN IN THE WHITE SUIT** 1951 ('52-U.S.). From Roger MacDougall's (unproduced) play. Addl Ph: Lionel Banes. AD: Jim Morahan. SpFX: Sydney Pearson. Sp Processes: Geoffrey Dickinson. Mkp: Ernest Taylor, Harry Frampton. Scientific Advisor: Geoffrey Myers. Ref: TV: All American TV. Warren/KWTS! Lee. Lentz. V 8/22/51. Hardy/SF. Martin. Maltin '92. Scheuer. Barr/Ealing. With Miles Malleson, George Benson, Mandy Miller.

Wellsborough, a British textile town. Employing molecules of "infinite length, with optimum inter-chain attractions," inventor Sidney Stratton (Alec Guinness) creates an "everlasting thread ... a new kind of cloth. It never gets dirty and it lasts forever," thanks in part to a "surface charge of static electricity." (Cf. the "everlasting match" in 1932's *The Match King*.) Industrialists, however, fear that the manufacture of the cloth will decrease output; workers fear loss of work. "Capital and labor are hand in hand in this"—both sides want to suppress the material. The latter, however, proves unstable, and at the end Sidney's white suit tears apart like cotton candy.... A tepid first half gives way to a grimmer, more complicated second half, in this early cover-up story. Neither half proves very funny; the story lends itself more to point-making than to comedy, and the quiet ruthlessness of Ernest Thesiger's Sir John and his fellow conspirators (in the latter half) is more riveting than Stratton's bland smugness.

**MAN OF NASTY SPIRIT** (H.K.) 1993 color/ws 94m. Ref: TV: Tai Seng Video; Eng. titles. EVS: "horror."

A cackling, flying sorcerer, the Pope of the Happy religion, turns himself into a woman. The use of a non-virgin gives the sorcerer a headache later, but sex with a virgin restores his powers, though it leaves her somewhat the worse for wear.... Typical Hong Kong fantasy combo of sex and magic is routine softcore. In one of the less routine scenes, a long sash from the sky lifts up a woman.

**MAN SIZE** 1986 feature. D: Michael Zen. Ref: Adam '93G.

King Kong bit.

**MAN WHO COULD NOT BE KILLED, The** see *Night Stalker, The* (1987)

**The MAN WHO FELL TO EARTH** ABC-TV/David Gerber & MGM-TV 1987 color c90m. D: Robert J. Roth. Tel: Richard Kletter, from Walter Tevis' novel. Mus: Doug Timm. SpMkpFX: The Burmans. Video & VisFX: Video Image. SpFX: Charles E. Dolan. Ref: TV. TVG. V 9/2/87:58. With Lewis Smith, Beverly D'Angelo, James Laurenson, Bruce McGill, Wil Wheaton, Robert Picardo, Annie Potts.

Another alien-charmer-on-Earth tale. Lewis' alien is more in the style of recent arrivals like E.T. and Starman than that of David Bowie's falling man. If he's comically helpless with hand gestures and idiomatic phrases, he's also highly intelligent. Smith and D'Angelo (as the Anthean's lover) are a sweet, amusing team, and this TV-movie is easier to take than the abstruse theatrical film of 1976.

**\*The MAN WHO LIVED AGAIN** Gainsborough/Michael Balcon 1936. Mus D: Louis Levy. AD: Vetchinsky. Mkp: Roy Ashton. Ref: TV: C&C-TV. Greg Luce. Lee. Lentz. Hardy/SF. V 9/23/36. Phantom. Maltin '92. Martin. Scheuer. Hound.

In a "sinister manor house," somewhere in England, "mad brain specialist" Dr. Laurience (Boris Karloff) electrically extracts the "thought content" from the brain of the crippled Clayton (Donald Calthrop) and transfers it into newspaper magnate Lord Haslewood's (Frank Cellier) brain. In one perversely amusing scene, Haslewood, in turn, finds himself in Clayton's body and is not at all happy with his new home.

Cellier's Haslewood and, later, Clayton-Haslewood are the plum roles here. At first, the satiric jabs are all directed at Haslewood; after Haslewood acquires Clayton's mind, the jabs are directed at those about him as well. The parts for Cellier, Anna Lee, and John Loder are breezily written; Karloff's is heavily freighted with themes, emotions, and story. But, after a near-parodic introduction of the Laurience character ("Am I mad?"), the script gives Karloff—as the man with the power—finer moments near the end.

**MAN WHO WOULD BE GUILTY** see *Manden, Der Ville Vaere Skyldig*

**The MAN WITH THREE COFFINS** (S. Korean) New Yorker/Pan-Film (Myung-won Lee) 1987 color 106m. D: Chang-ho Lee. SP: Jacha Lee, from his novella *A Wanderer Never Rests Even on the Road*. Mus: Jong-gu Lee. Ph: Seung-bae Park. Ref: screen. PFA notes 3/25/88. V 10/7/87. 10/19/88: 180. SFChron 3/23/88. HR 2/8/89. Scheuer. With Myung-kon Kim, Bo-hee Lee.

A ghost story a la the *Dead of Night* "Room in the Tower" segment—i.e., a ghost-story-in-retrospect. One-hundred-five minutes is a lot of retrospect. The hero (Kim) is a mopey cipher who carries with him the ashes of his wife, who died in an accident. The "three coffins" refers to the three women that he meets (including his wife) who die on him. The next-to-last shot—a giant cut-out of a disembodied hand plastered against the landscape—and an open-air exorcism suggest that a fourth woman (Lee), a nurse (it's apparently her palm), is a ghost, possibly the ghost of Yang's wife, and, further, that the other two women whom he met on his travels were ghosts, too ... that all were perhaps ghosts of his wife. (The same actress plays all the women.) In other words, if you can't go home again, to your dead wife, she will come to you. The exterior photography is atmospheric, but this odd tale of woe is extremely spare.

**\*The MAN WITH TWO FACES** 1934. AD: John Hughes. Ref: TV. V 7/17/34. Lee. Lentz. Maltin '92. no Scheuer.

"Did he have some strange power over her?" Yes, and Stanley Vance (Louis Calhern) still does, enough power to render Jessica Wells (Mary Astor)—She Who Must Obey—a staring herring at (hypnotic) will: She's a "colorless automaton" whenever he's around. Dr. Kendall's (Arthur Byron) opinion: She's possessed.... Vance is a real Stepford husband, in director Archie Mayo's second, and less successful, *Svengali*. Featuring calculatedly theatrical roles for Calhern, Edward G. Robinson, Astor, and Mae Clarke. Calhern and Clarke are entertainingly theatrical; Robinson's masquerade as "Chautard" is obvious, unamusing, "clever."

**\*MAN WITH TWO LIVES** A. W. Hackel 1942. AD: David Milton? Ref: TV. Greg Luce. no Weaver. V 3/11/42. Lee. Lentz. Stanley. no Hardy/HM/SF. PT 16:13.

"Let the dead stay dead!" "Experimenting with the unknown," Dr. Richard Clark (Edward Keane) has constructed an apparatus which keeps a dog's heart alive for 189 days. In a coma, Phillip Bennett (Edward Norris) imagines that he dies and that the doctor's apparatus revives him ... at the exact moment that a "congenital killer," Pannino (sp?), is executed: A "ghostly freak" now, Phillip remembers no one in his life, but has vague memories of elements in the killer's life. "Transmigration of the soul," it appears, has permitted Pannino's spirit to possess Phillip.

This flimsy variation on the not exactly dynamite itself *Black Friday* depends a lot on its characters' "thinking out loud" and on their making remarks like "That's funny—Pannino used to say the same thing!" Frustratingly, the script is a bit of science fiction, a bit of "Jekyll and Hyde" horror, and a bit of fantasy.

**The MAN WITHOUT A WORLD** Milestone/Eleanor Antin 1992 b&w silent 98m. SP, D, P: E. Antin. Ph: R. Wargo. Mus: Erwin, Morrow. AD: S. Fiorella. Ref: V 3/23/92: "Mel Brooks it ain't." SFChron 10/21/92: "boisterous but overstuffed narrative." With Christine Berry, Anna Henriques, Pier Marton.

Dybbuk, exorcism.

**MANDEN, DER VILLE VAERE SKYLDIG** (Dan-F) Nordisk Film & TV & the Danish Film Institute/PCA-Michele Dimitri 1990 color 91m. SP, D: Ole Roos. From Henrik Stangerup's novel. Mus: Ib Glindemann. Ref: V 11/5/90: "fine acting but little suspense." 11/15/89:24: *The Man Who Would Be Guilty* - ad t. With Jesper Klein, Anna Karina, Claes Rose Mikkelsen, Bent Christensen.

Book-burning, guilt-free future society.

**MANDINGO MANHUNTER** see *Man Hunter*

**MANDRAKE THE MAGICIAN** see *Defenders of the Earth*

**MANDROID** Para/Full Moon 1993 color feature. D: Jack Ersgard. Ref: SFChron Dtbk 8/8/93. 10/31/93: "good action and special effects." V 4/26/93:23 (rated). 5/10/93: C-40. With Brian Cousins, Jane Caldwell, Curt Lowens.

Inventor transfers his consciousness into a warrior android.

See also *Invisible: The Chronicles of Benjamin Knight*.

**MANGIA** see *Eat and Run*

**MANGIATI VIVI** or **MANGIATI VIVI DAI CANNIBALI** see *Doomed To Die*

The **MANGLER** (U.S.-B-Israeli-Austral.?) New Line & Distant Horizon & Filmex & Allied Film (Anant Singh/Towers et al.) 1994 (1995) color 110m. SP, D: Tobe Hooper. From a short story by Stephen King. Ph: A. Salomon. Mus: B. Pheloung. PD: D. Barkham. Mangler Created by William Hooper. VisFxSup: Stephen Brooks. MkpFX: Scott Wheeler. Ref: ad. SFChron 3/6/95: "long, slow and achingly predictable." PT 21:16: 1993; "dark, dreary and very confusing." Martin: turkey. With Robert Englund, Ted Levine, Daniel Matmor (psychic), Vanessa Pike, Lisa Morris.

Machine possessed by evil spirit "gradually works its way up the character chain."(SFC)

**MANGRYONGUI KOK** (S. Korean) Dee Yang Co. (Han Sang Hoon) 1980 color 88m. D: Park Yoon Kyo. SP: Yoo Il Soo. Ref: Hardy/HM: "works well ... within ... limitations." With Chung Se Hyuk, Chi Mi Ok.

Woman's ghost possesses another woman in order to wreak vengeance on selfish family. *Bloody Smile* - tr t?

**MANGRYONGUI WECHINGTURESU** (S. Korean) Hap Dong Films (Kwak Jung Hwan) 1981 color 92m. D: Park Yoon Kyo. SP: Lee Jai Hun. Ref: Hardy/HM: a "very traditional vengeful-ghost story" re the spirit, or effigy, of a dead hitchhiker. With Chung Se Hyuk, Sunwoo Eun Sook.

**MANHATTAN BABY** (I) Fulvia (De Angelis) 1983 ('92-U.S.) color 87m. (3P *The Evil Eye*. aka *Eye of the Dead*. *L'Occhio del Male*. *The Possessed* - B). D: Lucio Fulci. SP: Elisa Briganti, Dardano Sachetti. Ph: G. Mancori. Mus: F. Frizzi. PD: M. Lentini. Mkp: M. Trani. Ref: MFB'86:92-3. V 7/2/86. Starburst 64:42. Martin: on the "brink of boredom." V 2/16/83:24. McCarty II. Scheuer: "tame non-shocker." Morse: "slow, muddled, badly dubbed." Newman: "practically catatonic." With Chris Connelly, Martha Taylor, Brigitta Boccole, Cinzia De Ponti (Jamie Lee).

Egyptian "medallion ... is the focus of an ancient evil" which possesses a girl. (MFB)

The **MANHATTAN PROJECT** Fox/Gladden Ent. (Jennifer Ogden) 1986 color 117m. SP, D, P: Marshall Brickman. SP: also Thomas Baum. Mus: Philippe Sarde. SpVisFX: Bran Ferren; (coord) Topher Dow. Lasers: Steven Schultz et al. SpFX: Connie Brink. Mkp: Richard Dean. Ref: TV. V 5/14/86. ad. pr. SFChron 6/13/86. With John Lithgow, Christopher Collet, Cynthia Nixon, Jill Eikenberry, John Mahoney, Greg Edelman.

A high school student (Collet) assembles the "first privately built nuclear device in the history of the world." His bomb may be "only a little one," but it's made of "something so hot we don't even know how to test it"—material with "twenty times the punch" of any other such nuclear material ... from Medatomics, the "bomb factory".... Aimless, overlong suspense-comedy. Something called "neutron flux" starts Paul's bomb ticking.

**MANHUNTER** DEG/Richard Roth 1986 color/ws 120m. (*Red Dragon: The Pursuit of Hannibal Lecter* - TV). SP, D: Michael

Mann, from Thomas Harris' novel *Red Dragon*. Mus: the Reds & M. Rubini. Ref: TV. V 8/13/86. SFExam 8/15/86. TVG. MFB. With William L. Petersen, Kim Greist, Joan Allen, Brian Cox (Dr. Lektor), Stephen Lang, Tom Noonan (Francis Dollarhyde).

The "Tooth Fairy" Killer, who kills by the cycle of the moon, subjects victims to horror slide-shows, while the FBI agent assigned to track him down, Will Graham (Petersen), gets "deeper and deeper" into the psychopathology of homicidal maniacs.... Better than the similar *Tightrope*, but basically not that much different. The style of both acting and direction might best be described as Intent Monotone.

See also: *Silence of the Lambs*.

**MANI DI PIETRA** see *Hands of Steel*

*****MANIA** Triad 1960 (1959) ws 91m. (*Psycho Killers* - alt t). Ph: Monty Berman. Mus: Stanley Black. AD: John Elphick. Mkp: Jimmy Evans. Ref: TV: GoodTimes HV. Lee. V 2/10/60. Weldon. Maltin '92. Martin. Scheuer. Phantom. Stanley. Lentz. Ecran F 74:63. BFC. AFI.

Edinburgh, 1828. "Resurrectionists" Burke (George Rose) and Hare (Donald Pleasence)—variously referred to as "gentlemen," "kind-hearted boys," and "ghouls"—provide surgeon-lecturer Dr. Robert Knox (Peter Cushing) with a "regular supply" of suspiciously fresh cadavers for research.... An alarming number of venerable actors turns up in the various film versions of the Burke and Hare story: Boris Karloff, Bela Lugosi, Tod Slaughter, Alastair Sim, Cushing, Pleasence, Rose, Jonathan Pryce. (*Mania* director and co-author John Gilling scripted the 1948 Slaughter version, *The Greed of William Hart*.) After *The Body Snatcher* (1945), this may be the strongest version, despite an unbuyable character turnabout by Knox near the end and a vacant role for June Laverick as his niece. As the two scruffy entrepreneurs, Pleasence and Rose are a three-ring circus of tics, phobias, and manias. Particularly riveting: Pleasence's combination of pleasure in and loathing of the act of killing. (Hare might be Norman Bates—British style.) Wittily disdainful: Cushing's Knox. ("We don't want him to fall apart in the brine.") Also notable: Billie Whitelaw's uncomfortable-in-love Mary Patterson. Surprising: the "Willie just killed 'er, that's all" sequence. Mrs. Burke (Renee Houston) is so relieved: "Oh, that's all right." (Mr. Burke didn't "touch" Mary.)

**MANIA** see *Maniac Killer*

*****MANIAC** Hollywood 1934 48m. Ph: William C. Thompson. Ref: screen. Hardy/HM. Lee. Lentz. no V. Weldon. Stanley. Hound. Phantom. Maltin '92. Martin. Scheuer.

No discernible plot in this apparently abbreviated version of Maniac, just spur-of-the-moment ghoulish inspirations—and filler shots of a "cat farm"—as a "goofy professor" (Horace Carpenter) scientifically restores a suicide to life. Highlights-of-sorts: the cat dragging off a preserved heart ... the doc's assistant (Bill Woods) gouging out the cat's eye and eating it ... and the walling-up of the now-one-eyed cat. One character is called a "ham," but there are several qualifying actors, including both Carpenter and Woods, whose mad medicos are little more than maniacal laughter.

**MANIAC COP** SGE (J. Richard) 1988 color 85m. D: William Lustig. SP, P: Larry Cohen. Mus: Jay Chattaway. SpFxMkp: (sup) John Naulin; More than Skin Deep. SpFX: Hollywood SpFX. SdFxSup: John Post. Ref: TV. MFB'89:53-4. HR 9/12/88. V 5/25/88. NYT 5/14/88. With Tom Atkins, Bruce Campbell, Laurene Landon, Richard Roundtree, William Smith, Robert Z'Dar (Matt Cordell), Sheree North, John Goff, Jake LaMotta, Sam Raimi, George "Buck" Flower.

"They don't make cops like him any more." The superstrong, phantom-like, neck-breaking, invulnerable cop who "enjoys killing ... innocent people" proves to be "legally dead" police officer Matt Cordell, out to get those who sent him to prison.... Over-intricate plot gets progressively further from its intriguing, one-step-beyond-police-brutality premise. The corpses proliferate almost comically.

**MANIAC COP 2** Movie House Sales & Fadd (Larry Cohen) 1990 color 88m. D: William Lustig. SP: Cohen. Mus: Jay Chattaway. SpFxMkp: Dean Gates. SpFX: (sup) John Carter; (coord) John Eggett. Ref: TV. MFB'91:22. V 12/17/90. SFChron Dtbk 9/8/91. With Robert Davi, Claudia Christian, Michael Lerner, Bruce Campbell, Laurene Landon, Robert Z'Dar (Matt Cordell), Leo Rossi (Turkell).

"You can't kill the dead!" Matt Cordell—that "all-scarred-up ... great big cop"—turns up again and throws in with Turkell, a compulsive strangler of strippers. The highlight of the stunt-oriented, functional plot: the loony but exciting runaway-car sequence, which goes *North By Northwest* one or two better—cop psychologist Riley (Christian) is outside the car, handcuffed to the steering wheel. In the two most unlikely, anything-for-gore turns of event, a night stick is used like a knife, and a tow-truck hook like a meat hook. Dialogue highlights: the "frozen dead flesh" speech and the line "I hate being around stiffs ever since they made me kiss my grandmother at the funeral." The lottery-ticket sequence is a winner, too.

**MANIAC COP 3: BADGE OF SILENCE** Footstone Inc./First Look & Neo Motion Pictures (Joel Soisson & Michael Leahy/Larry Cohen/Overseas Filmgroup) 1992 color 85m. (aka *Badge of Silence: Maniac Cop III*). D: William Lustig, J. Soisson. SP: L. Cohen. Ph: J. Haitkin. PD: C. Hunter. Mus: Joel Goldsmith. SpMkpFX: KNB. SpFxSup: Larry Fioritto. Ref: TV. V 9/28/91:16 (ad). 3/1/93:15 (rated). 5/3/93:18 (rated). Imagi 1:52-3. Cinef 12/93:59: "dispensable." Fango 118:50-53. PT 16:61: voodoo. Martin. HBO/Cinemax 12/92. TVG 12/12/92. SFChron Dtbk 7/4/93? With Robert Davi, Robert Z'Dar, Caitlin Dulany, Gretchen Becker, Jackie Earle Haley, Robert Forster, Ted Raimi, Grand Bush, Julius Harris (Houngan), Paul Gleason.

"The crazed cop is resurrected...." (SFC) This time, voodoo raises Matt Cordell (Z'Dar), and there seems to be a second zombie. ("You can't hurt me 'cause I'm immortal!") Script picks easy targets (opportunistic video newshounds and other incidental, minor slime), for both satire and Cordell, and has an odd sub-theme: anti-revivification. (The resurrected endure much pain, apparently.) The big, tour de force, zombie-flambe ending helps.

**MANIAC KILLER** (F) Eurocine 1988 color/ws feature (*Kill and Enjoy* - ad t). D: A. Bioreni. SP: D. and M. LeSoeur. Ref: V 10/21/87:309(ad): sects and computers. 11/4/87:90: horror; 11/4

start. VSOM. Palmerini: aka *Mania*. With Chuck Connors, Bo Svenson, Robert Ginty.

"Graphic horrors as a sadist kidnaps and tortures women." (VSOM)

**MANIAC WARRIORS** (Can.) Action Int'l. (Simandl-Curtis) 1988? ('92 - U.S.) color feature (*Empire of Ash II* - Can. t). D: Lloyd Simandl, Michael Mazo. SP: John Ogis. Ref: PT 13:13. 15:6: originally on pay-TV. V 10/19/88:284(ad). With Thom Schioler, Melanie Kilgour.

More of the New Idaho of *Empire of Ash III*.

**MANIE-MANIE** see *Meikyu Monogatari*

**MANIMAL** Tiger Media 1988 color feature. D: OK Boys. Ref: Adam '92G. With Nick Fabrini.

Brainwashed assassins/"mutants."

**MANO CHE NUTRE LA MORTE, La** see *Hand That Feeds the Dead*

**MAN'S BEST FRIEND** New Line/Roven-Cavallo Ent. 1993 color/ws 91m. SP, D: John Lafia. P: Bob Engelman. Ph: Mark Irwin. Mus: Joel Goldsmith. PD: J. Hinkle. SpMkpFX: Kevin Yagher. SpVocalFX: Frank Welker. SpFxSup: Frank Ceglia. SpSdDes: Harry Cohen. DigitalVisFX: CIS. Chameleon FX: Available Light. Ref: TV: U.S.-Can.? PT 20:17. ad V 9/13/93:9 (rated). 8/30/93: "canine horror." SFChron 11/20/93: "curiously amusing horror comedy." Fango 128:22-27. With Ally Sheedy, Lance Henriksen, Fredric Lehne, Robert Costanzo, John Cassini, J.D. Daniels, William Sanderson, Robin Frates, Del Zamora.

DNA engineering gives Newfoundland named Max the "ability to climb like a cat, camouflage himself like a chameleon ... and tear flesh with impressive brutality." (SFC) As his sedating drug wears off, the escaped Max begins "coming apart." This "million-dollar research animal"—or "friggin' psycho mutt"—swallows cats whole and pees acid.... Vapid except for occasional vivid demonstrations of Max's climbing, thinking, and leaping powers.

**MANT!** see *Matinee* (1993)

**MAPS** (J) Columbia Video c1990? anim color c52m. Ref: TV: Col. Video; no Eng.; OAV?

A gigantic flying statue swoops down and picks up a schoolboy who's playing soccer. A giant robot-ship commandeered by a ray-shooting sort-of-villain garbed in impeccable bad taste then scoops up the statue. Later, we discover that horror here is a many-tentacled thing. Bonus: a Day the Earth Froze sequence.... Fun with formula in this fast, enjoyable, animated sf-comedy. The diminutive hero and heroine have a Lum-Ataru relationship.

**The MARCH** (B) A&E-TV/BBC Lionheart-TV & One World Group of PSB (Peter Goodchild) 1990 ('91-U.S.) color c90m. D: David Wheatley. Tel: William Nicholson. Ph: John Hooper. Mus: Richard Hartley. PD: Chris Robilliard. VisFxDes: Andy Lazell. MkpDes: Christine Powers. Ref: TV. TVG: "smart, meritorious." With Juliet Stevenson, Malick Bowens, Dermot Crowley, Joseph Mydell.

Cautionary sf drama re the "greenhouse effect" concerns thousands of Africans who migrate to Europe from a country which has had no rain for five years.

**MARCHIO DI SATANA, Il** see *Sanguisuga Conduce la Danza, La*

**MARCIA NUNZIALE** (I-F) 1965 feature. D: Marco Ferreri. FX: Carlo Rambaldi. Ref: Palmerini: one episode set in a "dehumanized future." With Ugo Tognazzi.

**MARDI GRAS FOR THE DEVIL** Prism/West Side (Jill Silverthorne) 1993 color 95m. (aka *Night Trap*). SP, D: David A. Prior. Exec P: David Winter. Mus: C. Farrell. Ref: V 5/17/93: "flat and unconvincing." 3/1/93:30. SFChron Dtbk 6/20/93. 5/2/93. 7/4/93? Fango 128:39: "unrelentingly talky." PT 16:59: "dud." With Robert Davi, Michael Ironside (Bishop). Lesley-Anne Down, Margaret Avery, John Amos, Lydie Denier.

"Demonically possessed ... ancient witchfinder general" has "lived and killed for centuries." (V)

**MARIANNE DREAMS** see *Paperhouse*

**MARIS THE CHOJIN** see *Supergal, The*

**MARISCAL DEL INFIERNO, El** see *Devil's Possessed, The*

**The MARK OF CAIN** (Can.) Vestron Video/Brightstar Films (Tony Kramreither) 1985 ('86-U.S.) color c85m. (*Identity Crisis* - alt vt t). SP, D: Bruce Pittman. SP: also Peter Colley, John Sheppard. From Colley's play. Ph: John Herzog. Mus: Bruce Ley. AD: Rob Bartman. Mkp: Nancy Howe. Ref: TV: Vestron Video. V 5/1/85:80 (ad), 180. Stanley. Hound. Martin. Morse. Scheuer. Ecran F 59:71. With Robin Ward (Michael and Shaun), Randy Crewson, Antony Parr, August Schellenberg.

"Michael's out!" Fifteen years after committing a vicious knife-murder/crucifixion, Michael O'Neill escapes from an insane asylum, switches places with his identical twin, Shaun, and nearly throttles the latter's wife, Dale.... Thin, hokey *Halloween* material features an "Oh, my God!" every twenty minutes or so, plus the expected back-from-the-"dead" shock at the end, when Michael proves to be still alive after impalement on a coat hook. (Compare the use of a hat rack in *Escape from Coral Cove*.)

**MARK OF THE BEAST** see *Fertilize the Blaspheming Bombshell!*

**MARK OF THE DEVIL** (B) Fox Mystery Theatre/Fox-TV & Hammer 1984 color c75m. (*Tattoo* - orig t). D: Val Guest. Tel: Brian Clemens. Ph: Frank Watts. Mus: David Bedford. AD: Carolyn Scott. Mkp: Eddie Knight. Tattooist: Barry Louvaine. Ref: TV. TVG. no Scheuer. no Maltin '92. Stanley. Ecran F 50:13. With Dirk Benedict (Frank Rowlett), Jenny Seagrove, George Sewell, John Paul, Tom Adams, Burt Kwouk (Hai Lee).

"Tattoos can't grow." During a robbery, Frank Rowlett tangles with half-Haitian Hai Lee, a "funny old guy" who dabbles in black magic. Frank kills Lee, but the latter manages to jab Frank in the chest with a tattooing needle before he dies. The damned spot on his chest grows and grows, spreads to his right arm, then

to his face, then begins to cover his whole body. At the end, Lee leaps out of a magic mirror and kills Frank.... The tattoo here is a regular beast with five fingers and, visually, is pretty impressive. As the visible sign of a murderer's guilt, however, it plays more like ring-around-the-collar embarrassment. An okay premise not very imaginatively developed.

**MARK TWAIN** see *Adventures of Mark Twain, The*

**MARQUISE DE SADE, Die** see *Doriana Gray*

**\*MARRIAGE OF THE BEAR** BFI 1926 ('28-U.S.) 80m. (*Medvezhya Svadba*. aka *The Bear's Wedding* or *Lokis*). D: also Vladimir Gardin. SP: also Georgi Grebner. From Merimee's story "Lokis" or "Professor Wittembach's Manuscript." AD: Vladimir Yegorov. Ref: screen. PFA notes 2/23/86. Lee. Le Fanu/Tarkovsky: 13. Hardy/HM:223. V 8/1/28.

"In the forest of Medintiltas, someone is craving human blood." Medintiltas Castle (an "eerie" place), Lithuania. Count Michael Shemet (Konstantin Eggert)—the "last of the Shemets" and their "monstrous line"—was born to a woman attacked by a bear and has a "strange, non-human character." (Compare *Condemned to Live*.) According to local, peasant superstition, he is "Lokis, lord of the beasts," a "monster," a "bogeyman-beast." On his wedding night, he gets carried away with excitement, the figurative "bear" in him breaks out, and he bites his bride Julia to death....

The love-vs.-the-inner-brute conflict in *Marriage of the Bear* anticipates *WereWolf of London*, *The Wolf Man*, *Cat People*, etc., but the Count's character is sketchily drawn, and Julia is a flighty, silly girl. This subtitled-in-English film, though, has certain historical and camp value, nice photography, and a very early peasants-burn-down-the-castle sequence.

See also *Jack Frost* (1965).

**2 MARRIED BEFORE BREAKFAST** 1937 71m. Ph: Leonard Smith. AD: C. Gibbons; G. Scognamillo, E.B. Willis. Ref: TV. With Barnett Parker, Tom Kennedy.

Tom Wakefield's (Robert Young) "razorless shaving preparation" will mean the "death of razors." But it causes a certain swelling.... Not a funny comedy this, but the non-comic, getting-more-than-acquainted scenes with Young and Florence Rice are quietly charming, and the movie as a whole anticipates the big-city/little-people romance of Judy Garland and Robert Walker in *The Clock*. *Breakfast* first changes tone, from the mechanically light to the sweet-and-romantic, in the whispering-in-the-closet sequence, with its discreet intimations of intimacy. Hugh Marlowe has a very early, very Hugh Marlowe role as the other man.

**MARSUPIALS, The** see *Howling III*

**MARTIAN THRU GEORGIA** WB 1962 anim color 7m. D: Chuck Jones. Ref: LC. Maltin/OMAM: Bugs Bunny. "WBCartoons." no Lee.

Peace-loving alien kicked around on Earth.

**MARTIANS!!!** see *Spaced Invaders*

**MARTIANS GO HOME** Taurus Ent./Martians Inc. (Edward R. Pressman/Michael D. Pariser) 1990 (1989) color 85m. D: David Odell. SP: Charlie Haas, from Fredric Brown's novel. Mus: Allan Zavod. SpVisFX: Robert Swarthe. OptFX: Cinema Research. Ref: TV. V 4/25/90. With Randy Quaid, Margaret Colin, Anita Morris, Gerrit Graham; Barry Sobel, Vic Dunlop, Gary Mule Deer (Martians), Jack Tate (Venusian).

"These guys are tourists." One billion Martian would-be stand-up comics with bad material come to Earth to perpetrate a "cruel farce with green men." These annoying wise guys continually kibitz and can appear and disappear at will. ("I'm a Martian. We know everything.") At the end, the broadcast music which brought them here is played backwards and expels them. Limp comedy somehow entirely misses the charm of the Brown semi-classic.

**MARVIN** Nickelodeon-TV 198-? anim c30m. Ref: Cabletime 8/87.

Robots in the garden.

**MARY! MARY!** Essex 1977 color 80m. Ref: Adam '88. With Constance Money, Sharon Thorpe.

Man trades soul for sexual potency.

**MARY SHELLEY'S FRANKENSTEIN** (U.S.-J-B) TriStar & Japan Satellite & The IndieProd Co./American Zoetrope (Coppola-Hart-Veitch) 1994 color 123m. D: Kenneth Branagh. SP: Steph Lady, Frank Darabont, from M. Shelley's novel *Frankenstein*. Ph: Roger Pratt. Mus: Patrick Doyle. PD: Tim Harvey. SpMkpFX: Daniel Parker. VisFxSup: Richard Conway. WireFxSup: Steve Crawley. Digital SdFX: Dave Lawson. Ref: TV: Col-TriStar HV. ad. Sacto Bee 11/4/94. Vallejo Times-H 11/4/94. SFChron 11/4/94. With Robert DeNiro, K. Branagh, Tom Hulce, Helena Bonham Carter, Aidan Quinn, Ian Holm, John Cleese (Waldman), Robert Hardy.

"No one need ever die." Settings: Geneva, Ingolstadt, and the Arctic Sea, between 1773 and 1794. Dr. Victor Frankenstein (Branagh) employs a hanged man's head, a fellow scientist's brain, amniotic fluid, eels, and a sort of pressure cooker to produce a "reanimate" (DeNiro), a living being made up of stray body parts. ("It's alive!") This tormented product of "evil stitched to evil stitched to evil" feels rage and love and "remembers" how to think and speak—and literally tears out his maker's bride's heart. In the film's most interesting sequence, Dr. Frankenstein stitches together his dead bride. In this sequence—*Interview with the Vampire* in a nutshell—the un-dead Elizabeth (Carter) confronts both the man who killed her (the creature) and the man who restored her (the doctor). She rejects both and immolates herself.... Clive and Karloff they ain't. Almost every scene of this choppy, fragmented film is busier and noisier than necessary. The design—especially the mansion's preposterously grand staircase—seems inspired by the Universal Frankensteins. The lab here, though, has an original look.

**MARYU SENKI** (J) A.I.C. 198-? anim color 30m. Ref: TV: C. Moon Video; no Eng.; Pink Noise vol. 3; OAV.

Exhibits A and B: a thing which undergoes a hideous transformation and a ninja-type that transforms into a dragon-like monster. Horror with a touch of sex. Stylishly drawn, but hollow, with vapid action and (for non-Japanese-speaking viewers) a puzzling ending. Good on atmospheric day and night sounds.

**MAS ALLA DE LA MUERTE** (Sp) MAC Fusion 1986 color feature (*La Vie apres la Mort* - orig t). D: Sebastian d'Arbo. SpFX: Joseph Jorna. Ref: V 5/6/87: listing. Ecran F 67:71. 71:36. With N. Ibanez Menta, Tony Isbert, Berta Cabre, Carmen C.

Neo-Nazi sect seeking serum to revive dead. Follow-up to *Viaje Al Mas Alla* (II) and *El Ser* (III).

**MAS ALLA DEL EXORCISMO** (Sp-I) Emaus/Metheus 1974 color c90m. (*Malocchio* - I t). SP, D: Mario Siciliano. SP: also De Urrutia, Buch. Ph: V. Minaya. Mus: Stelvio Cipriani. Ref: TV. TVG. vc box. Horacio Higuchi. Palmerini. With Jorge Rivero, Richard Conte, Pilar Velazquez, Antonio De Teffe, Alan Collins, Eduardo Fajardo.

Man who's driven by compulsion—or is it black magic?—to kill ... vision of woman beheaded by train ... supernaturally-flung phonograph record ... remote-control ritual murder. Shot in a blah, videotape visual non-style. (Sfa *Mal Occhio* (II)?)

**La MASCHERA DEL DEMONIO** (I) Reteitalia-Anfri & TVE & Beta Film & SFP & RTP 1990 color/ws 92m. (*Sabbah, the Mask of the Devil* - ad t. *Sabbah, La Maschera del Demonio*). Story, D: Lamberto Bava. From Nikolai Gogol's story "The Vij." Story, SP: Massimo de Rita, Giorgio Stegani. Ph: G. Transunto. Mus: Simon Boswell. AD: G. Mangano. SpFxMkp: Franco Casagni. Anim: S. Stivaletti. SpSnowFX: Burgalossi. Ref: TV: VSOM; Eng. titles. MV: *Demons 5: Devil's Veil* - vt t. VSOM: *Mask of Satan* - alt vt t. Hardy/HM2. PT 19:5. 20:11. Jones: remake of *Black Sunday* (1960), re "vampire/witch." V 11/15/89:18. With Deborah or Debora Kinski, Eva Grimaldi, Michele Soavi, Stanko Molnar.

"You have liberated the devil." In the year 1647, the Mask of the Devil is affixed to Anibas, a witch burned at the stake. In an ice cave near a present-day "ghost town," this "strange mask" is pried off her frozen body, and her spirit runs amok. ("They've changed—it's like a force has possessed them.") At one point, the witch-possessed resembles a long-tongued Medusa .... Dippy story, good camerawork and wind/snow effects, gross witch-hag kisses, blurry tape.

Recommended viewing: the 1967 Russian version of the Gogol story.

**MASCHIO LATINO CERCASI** (I) 1977 color feature. D: G. Narzisi. Ref: Palmerini: "robotics" segment.

**MASHO NO NATSU—YOTSUYA KAIDAN YORI** (J) 1981 95m. D: Ninagawa. Ref: CM 15:26-7: *Yotsuya Kaidan* variation; "story elements work." With K. Hagiwara, K. Sekine, M. Natsume.

Visions of disfigured ghost.

**The MASK** New Line & Dark Horse (Bob Engelman) 1994 color 101m. D, Exec Co-P: Charles Russell. SP: Mike Werb. Based on the comics characters. Story: Michael Fallon, Mark Verheiden. Ph: J.R. Leonetti. Mus: Randy Edelman. PD: Craig Stearns. VisFX: IL&M;(anim sup) Steve Williams; Dream Quest Images;(consult) Scott Squires, Ken Ralston. SpMkp: Greg Cannom. Mask: Christopher Gilman, Global FX. Milo Anim: Tom Bertino. Prosth: Sheryl Leigh Ptak. SpFX: Charles Bellardinelli. End Titles: Howard Anderson. Ref: TV: NL HV. Vallejo T-H 7/29/94. SFChron 7/29/94. V 1/10/90:20. With Jim Carrey (The Mask), Cameron Diaz, Peter Riegert, Peter Greene, Richard Jeni, Amy Yasbeck, Orestes Matacena.

"I haven't exactly been myself lately." Edge City. A mystic mask—apparently containing the spirit of Loki, the Norse god of mischief—unleashes the "innermost desires" of each wearer.... Alternately near-brilliant and pedestrian. Some of the Tex Avery-inspired "cartoon" effects are almost as startling as the computer effects from the second *Terminator.* And at its best, the movie plays like a deranged *Nutty Professor*—Carrey's hyper-genial Ordinary Man contrasts evocatively with his creepy, super-smooth Mask Man. Main problems: The plot is predictable, and Carrey can't galvanize the other actors.

**MASK OF SATAN** see *Maschera del Demonio, La*

**MASK OF THE RED DEATH, The** see *Edgar Allan Poe's Masque of the Red Death. Masque of the Red Death*

**MASKED RIDER** (J) 1992 color 90m. R: TV: vt; scant Eng. Weisser/JC: sfa *Daikan-sho Kamen?*

Ingredients: an apparent android—it's that mechanical look in its eyes, and its ability to come back after being shot ... a sound weapon ... grasshopper experiments ... and a hero who can transform into a monster and, at the end, beheads and de-spines the flying villain-monster.... Surprisingly convincing effects punctuate an otherwise unremarkable super-hero, super-monster story. Prime: the android's forehead "rejecting" the bullet ... the transformation effects ... and the hero's face splitting open. Comical: our hero—still in monster-suit—in a clinch with our heroine.

See also titles under *Kamen Rider.*

**MASKS OF DEATH, The** see *Sherlock Holmes and the Masks of Death*

**The MASQUE OF THE RED DEATH** (B?) 21st Century/Breton (Avi Lerner, Harry Alan Towers) 1989 color 89m. D: Alan Birkinshaw. SP: M. J. Murray. From Edgar Allan Poe's story "The Mask of the Red Death." Ph: J. Wein. Mus: Coby Recht. PD: Leith Ridley. SpMkpFX: Scott Wheeler. SpFxCoord: Greg Pitts. Ref: TV: RCA-Col HV. PT 11:48: "lame story." Fango 89:26-9. McCarty II: Stallone is "high camp." V 9/6/89 (rated). With Herbert Lom, Brenda Vaccaro, Frank Stallone, Michelle McBride, Christine Lunde.

"Somebody in a red mask is killing people" at a "modern-day masquerade party in a Bavarian castle." (PT) In addition to the walking Death: a Poe-inspired (visualized) nightmare re an extracted heart ... a *Psycho* stabbing ... puncture gore ... clock-pendulum torture which yields a severed head ... and death by gate spikes.... Just about the weirdest movie idea of Poe since the 1935 *Raven* (but not nearly as entertaining). Unbelievable situations and dialogue.

See also *Edgar Allan Poe's Masque of the Red Death.*

**MASS MURDERER** see *Murderlust*

**MASSACRE** (I) 1989 color feature. SP,D: Andrea Bianchi. Mus: L. Ceccarelli. Ref: Palmerini. With Gino Concari, Patrizia Falcone, Silvia Conti.

During a seance, a murderous monk's spirit possesses a policeman.

**MASSACRE AT R.V. PARK** see *Alien Predator*

**MASSIVE RETALIATION** Hammermark & One Pass (Massive Prods.) 1984 color 89m. D, P: Thomas A. Cohen. SP: Larry Wittnebert, Richard Beban. Mus: H. Soper, P. Potyen. AD: Carol De Pasquale. Ref: TV. V 9/12/84. Sacto Bee 9/19/84:AA5. With Tom Bower, Karlene Crockett, Peter Donat, Marilyn Hassett, Mimi Farina.

Nuclear war breaks out between the U.S. and the U.S.S.R. in the Gulf of Oman. A national emergency is declared, and suburban survivalists swing into action.... Self-consciously-ordinary, everyday life here is interrupted by the self-consciously extraordinary. Some good touches, some bad. At its best, the story evokes a sense of controlled chaos. At its worst, it concludes with heavy-handed dramatics.

**MASTER DEMON** Eric Lee 1991. SP, D: Samuel Oldham. D: also Art Camacho. SpMkp: Rodd Matsui. Ref: PT 20:17: "bald demon (Gerard Okamura) conjures up ... killer ... called Medusa (Kay Baxter Young)." With Lee, Steve Nave, Sid Campbell.

**MASTER OF CEREMONIES** Christopher Sullivan 1986 9m. Ref: SFChron Dtbk 12/16/90: "an effectively eerie chalk-drawn piece of macabre imagery that depicts Death destroying a house and the people in it."

**MASTER OF THE WORLD** 1976 anim color 50m. Ref: Hound: from Verne. no Martin.

**MASTER OF THE WORLD** see *Conqueror of the World*

**MASTER'S NECKLACE** see *My Master's Necklace*

**MASTERS OF THE UNIVERSE** Cannon/Golan-Globus (Edward R. Pressman) 1987 color 105m. D: Gary Goddard. SP: David Odell, based on the toys and on the TV series "He-Man and the Masters of the Universe." Mus: Bill Conti. VisFX: Boss Film; (p) Richard Edlund; (coord) Ellen Kitz; (anim coord) Lisa Neil. KeyMkp: Todd McIntosh. SpFX: Arthur Brewer. Ref: TV. MFB'87:373. V 8/12/87. ad. With Dolph Lundgren, Frank Langella (Skeletor), Meg Foster (Evil-Lyn), Billy Barty, Courteney Cox, Tony Carroll (Beastman).

Ingredients: Castle Grayskull, "at the center of the universe," on the planet Eternia—headquarters for the skull-masked Skeletor and the sorceress Evil-Lyn ... a cosmic key ... "personal locators" (not a dating service) ... a collar which makes the wearer tell the truth ... an Earth auto altered to run on neutrinos ... and a piece of Earth which is beamed to Eternia.... Mainly noise, though the spectacle of *Star Wars* paraphernalia deployed on Earth yields a few visually engaging moments. The most special effect: the way Meg Foster's lipstick and eye shadow combine.

See also: *Secret of the Sword.*

**MASTERS OF THE UNIVERSE II: THE CYBORG** see *Cyborg*

**Los MATA MONSTRUOS EN LA MANSION DEL TERROR** (Arg.) Sono Film 1987 color feature. D: Carlos Galettini. Ref: V 5/4/88:504: *The Monster Killers in the Mansion of Terror* - tr t.

**MATA VIBORA MATA** (Mex) Filmadora Mor Ben (Carlos Moreno Castilleja) c1990? color 90 1/2m. D: Javier Duran Escalona. SP: Jesus Marin Bello. Story: Pedro Rojas. Ph: Luis Medina. Mus D: Gustavo Carrion. SpFX: Jose Parra. Mkp: Sara Mateos. OptFX: Ricardo Sainz. Ref: TV: Laguna Films video; no Eng.; *Bush Viper* - tr t. With Luciana, Ana Luisa Peluffo, Pedro Infante Jr., Gloriella, Noe Murayama, Oralia Galvan (Sonia), Carlos Gonzalez, Memo Flores, Rosalba Del Mar, Roberto Rosales, Ruben Benavides.

A perhaps necessarily awkward tale of a girl, Sonia, who grows up with snakes as her only friends. Her favorite, a colorful cuss, "protects" her by biting her "enemies," including her mother and father, who die instantly. Occasional camp charm; some misplaced t&a material.

**MATADOR** (Sp) Cinevista/Iberoamericana de TV & Ministerio de Cultura & TV Espanola 1988(1986/'89-U.S.) color/ws 107m. Story, SP, D: Pedro Almodovar. SP: also Jesus Ferrero. Mkp: Juan Pedro Hernandez. SpFX: Reyes Abade. Ref: TV: Cinevista Video; Eng. titles. Hardy/HM2. V 11/26/86.

"I tried to imitate you when I killed them." Scattered horrific/fantastic ingredients here include murder-by-hairpin ... buzz-saw gore and a severed head (in a movie-on-TV) ... bloody, visualized daydreams re strangling and stabbing ... same-"species" killers who find love in death, or vice versa ... and psychic visions .... Schematically kinky and oddly bloodless, dramatically speaking. Some appeal in the esthetic "neatness" of the story conceits (love/death/solar eclipse).

**MATENME PORQUE ME MUERO** (Mex) CDP & Hermes & Alianza (Carlos Vasallo) 1990 color c90m. Story, D: Abraham Cherem. Story, SP: Alejandro Licona. Ph: Xavier Cruz Rubalcaya. Mus: Alejandro Giacoman. SpFxMkp: Necropia. SpFX: Federico Farfan. Ref: TV: Mex-American HV; no Eng. La Tapatia: *Kill Me, I'm Dead* - tr t. With Pedro Weber, Raul Padilla, Isaura Espinosa (Elvira), Roxana Chavez (Olivia), Luis Uribe, Diana Golden, Sergio Ramos, Brigitte Aube.

Two ghost sisters with rubbery faces and icy super-breath haunt the Hacienda San Lazaro, while various other ghosts, including a disfigured caretaker, attend them. Also on board: men in monster masks who play ghost and a classic crawling beast with five fingers. Familiar comedy; atmospheric lighting, makeup, and art direction. At the end, the sisters put on their ghoul faces.

**MATINEE** (Can.) Thomas Howe/Summit Ent. (D. Slayer Prods./Steer-Shumiatcher) 1989 color 90m. (aka *Midnight Matinee*). SP, D: Richard Martin. Mus: G. Coleman. Ref: V 9/6/89: "a treat for buffs hot on horror film trivia"; p. 46-7 (ad). With Gillian Barber, Ron White, Tim Webber, Beatrice Boepple.

Real and reel murder at a horror film fest.

**MATINEE** Univ/Renfield (Michael Finnell) 1993 color 98m. D: Joe Dante. SP: Charlie Haas. Story: Jerico & C. Haas. Ph: John Hora. Mus: Jerry Goldsmith. PD: Steven Legler. VisFxSup: Dennis Michelson. Mant Des: James McPherson. Min FX: Stetson Visual. Trailer: Bret Mixon. SpSdFX: John P. SpThanks: Rick Baker. Ref: screen. V 2/1/93. 3/22/93:15 (ad). Sacto Bee 1/29/93. SFChron 1/29/93; Dtbk 1/24/93. Cinef 6/93. Filmfax 38:36-38. Fango 123: 36-39. Martin. With John Goodman, Cathy Moriarty, Simon Fenton, Omri Katz, Lisa Jakub, Kellie Martin, James Villemaire, Robert Picardo, Jesse White, Dick Miller, John Sayles, Mark McCracken (Mant), William Schallert, Robert Cornthwaite, Kevin McCarthy, Archie Hahn, Luke Halpin.

"If a man and an ant were exposed to radiation simultaneously...." Principals include moviemaker Lawrence Woolsey (Goodman) of Woolsey International, creator of such movies as *The Eyes of Dr. Diablo* and *Island of the Flesh Eaters* ... young Gene Loomis (Fenton), monster-movie and "Famous Monsters" fan ("You spend your whole life sittin' at monster movies?") ... and Bill, or Mant, the tragi-comic half-man, half-ant (and later pretty much all-ant) of Woolsey's latest, *Mant!*, previewed at the Key West Strand Theater in 1962. (Mant is the product of an ant bite and dental X-rays.) In the same film: the "first monster movie"—an impromptu, animated recreation of a cave man's shaggy-mammoth story—and a visualized nightmare re a big-bomb blast.

Woolsey has the gimmicks of William Castle, but *Mant!* itself is more Bert I. Gordon, and the dialogue of the movie-within-the-movie spoofs the literal-mindedness of Fifties monster movies. ("Now he'll grow at an accelerated, or speeded-up, rate!") Dante and company also have some Orson Welles/"War of the Worlds"-type fun—the in-theatre effects make some people think that the Cuban missile crisis has become a full-fledged war. And the matinee kids here recall the matinee gremlins of Dante's own *Gremlins*. His new movie is a grab-bag of incidental delights, like the out-of-nowhere mammoth-monster "movie" and the surprisingly affecting scene in which Gene's mother—believing nuclear war imminent—runs some old home movies. But despite such direct hits, the film as a whole seems uncertain, alternately ambitious and very modest. It scores in both modes occasionally, but doesn't make sense of its fluctuating tone.

**MATT RIKER** see *Mutant Hunt*

**MAX MAKES IT BIG** Le Salon 1987 color feature. D: Thor Johnson. Ref: Adam '93G: "sci-fi." With Max Montoya.

"Sometime in the future...."

**MAXI CAT'S LUNCH** (Yugos.) Zlatko Grgic anim short. Ref: SFChron Dtbk 7/10/88: "spaghetti dinner" transforms into "attack worms."

**MAXIM XUL** Magnum Ent./Halvorsen-Gambert 1991 color 87m. SP, D, Co-P: Arthur Egeli. SP: also C. E. Rickard, from his story. Mus: Mickey Rat. Creature: Lawrence Luers, Michael Jeffries. SpMkpFX: Patrick Gallagher. Ref: V 8/19/91: "overly pretentious, regional monster pic." With Adam West, J. Leinberger, Mary Shaeffer, Billie Shaeffer.

"The Xul are a composite of nine demons...."

**MAXIMUM OVERDRIVE** DEG/Martha Schumacher & Milton Subotsky 1986 color/ws 98m. (*Overdrive* - shooting t). SP, D: Stephen King, from his short story "Trucks." Mus: AC/DC. SpFxMkp: Dean Gates. SpVisFxSup: Barry Nolan. SpFX: (coord) Steve Galich; (opt) Van Der Veer. Ref: TV. V 7/30/86. SFChron 7/25/86. V 10/16/85:242. With Emilio Estevez, Pat Hingle, Laura Harrington, Yeardley Smith, John Short.

Or, The Day the Earth Wouldn't Stand Still. With Earth in the tail of the rogue comet Rhea-M, machines begin to self-start and alternately shoot soda-pop cans at and electrocute people. They also seem to understand English and to be able to see. Meanwhile, humans swear at the machines, just like they do now.... Script takes the easy way out, opts for the menace of already-menacing monster-trucks and machine guns, and uses the amusing irony of mad coke machines only as a lead-in to the main horrors. Difficult enough to accept machines which are suddenly sentient, let alone uniformly belligerent.

**MAXIMUM THRUST** see *Occultist, The*

**MAYA** (I) 1989 color feature. SP,D: Marcello Avallone. From F. Lopez de Castanheda's tale "At School with the Warlock." SP: also A. Purgatori, M. Tedesco. Mus: G. Ducros. Ref: Palmerini: "one of the last real Italian horrors," re "ritual sacrifices." With P. Phelps, M. Valentini, W. Berger, M. D'Angelo.

**\*The MAZE** Richard Heermance 1953. AD: David Milton. SpFX: Augie Lohman. Ref: TV. Warren/KWTS! Hardy/SF. V 7/8/53. Lee. Lentz. Weldon. no Okuda/TMC. Scheuer. Maltin '92.

"It occurred in Scotland, in a remote and distant castle in the highlands"—"miserable Craven Castle," a place with "no modern improvements" and a history of mystery. Clues to the solution of the latter include a man (Richard Carlson) who ages twenty years in a very short time, a box-hedge maze ("Every Scottish castle had a maze," we learn), a dragging sound in the hallways, leaf-shaped foot or paw prints, a half-seen crawling thing ("Something alive!"), midnight yowling, very broad staircase steps, a piece of seaweed found in a tower room, and a book, *Teratology ... The Study of Monstrosities,* by Dr. L. Warren Thorpe. Solution: Sir Roger MacTeam, who was born in 1750, has been stuck since then at the amphibian-embryo stage of development and haunts the halls and the maze.... Disappointing payoff: He's just a big frog. However, the climactic sequence which precedes this—set in the titular maze—offers some spooky fun, though even here everyone tries too hard. ("The woman was told not to go into the maze.") William Cameron Menzies, the movie's director and production designer, seems hamstrung by the Monogram budget, the 3-D logistics, and Carlson as his lead actor. Staging and acting are flat-footed, and the narration is superfluous. The scene in which Sir Roger is led about obscured by a sheet lends a touch of pathos; the scene in which Sir Roger's long froggy life is explained lends a touch of camp: "He did have certain pleasures" (i.e., swimming)....

**MEATBALL** Arrow Film & Video (M-B Prods.) 1980? color c78m. SP, D: "D. Furred." Ref: TV: Arrow Video. With Harry Reams (Dr. Schmock), Singe Low, Linda Sanderson (aka Tina Russell?).

Dr. Schmock's Preparation X formula ("I can feed the world!"), applied to hamburger meat ("It's still alive!"), brings it back to life, doubles its size, and acts as an aphrodisiac on the consumer of same. His Backwards-Forwards Disintegration Machine produces, at first, just fried rice; then a woman (with the mustard); then, several partygoers. His telescope invention acts like a super-TV. Plus an irrelevant talking skeleton. ("That's all, folks!") Vapid hardcore sf-comedy.

**MEATBALLS—PART II** Tri-Star/Space Prods. (Tony Bishop, Stephen Poe) 1984 color 87m. (*Space Kid* - alt t). D: Ken Wiederhorn. SP: Bruce Singer. Story: Martin Kitrosser, Carol Watson. Mus: Ken Harrison. Alien Des: Hacopian. Ref: TV. V 8/1/84. 10/24/84:77 (ad). With John Mengatti, Richard Mulligan, Hamilton Camp, John Larroquette, Paul Reubens; Archie Hahn (Meathead's voice).

In this sequel to *Meatballs,* set at Camp Sasquatch—"where all those kids got murdered"—"Meathead," an alien from another galaxy, performs levitation and walking-through-walls tricks until his father comes to pick him up.... The characters in this thin, occasionally likable comedy are all running gags, the funniest of which are Meathead's spacy look and Larroquette's feyness as Camp Patton's Foxglove. Generally sly comic timing helps.

**The MEATEATER** Hollyco (Richard Tasse) 1986 (1978) color 84m. Story, SP, D, Ed: Derek Savage. Story: also Damon Fuller, George Caldwell. Ph: Fred Aronow. Mus: Arlon Ober. AD: Tim Bloch. SpFX: Steve Neill; (addl mkp fx) Barry Koper. SdFX: Arthur Lopez. Ref: TV: Video Treasures. Deep Red 3:69. no V. Stanley. Hound. McCarty II. Martin. Scheuer. With Arch Joboulian (the Meateater), Dianne Davis, Peter M. Spitzer, Emily Spindler, Joe Marmo, Tony Anthony, Gary Dean.

The new owner of the Crest Theatre is confronted with the mysteries of a hanged man and an electrocuted projectionist. And numerous eating scenes and allusions to food suggest that a cannibal, or Sweeney Todd, may be lurking. The Meateater haunting the Crest, however, turns out to be more interested in the owner's daughter Jeannie's (Spindler) resemblance to his beloved Jean Harlow than he is in new food sources. At the end, the police find a man smashed on the floor of the theatre, and the case is closed. But the dead man's brother revs up the projector again.... For a bad movie, not bad. The makers of this amiably amateurish comedy seem quite content simply to make bad jokes and to concoct silly names like "Lt. Wombat." Main visual motif: signs and caps for Farmer John Meats. Silly highlight: the owner's family's rendition of the "Oscar Mayer Weiner" song.

**3 The MECHANICAL COW** 1927. Ref: screen. PFA notes 5/23/93.

A furry beast—invisible at first—abducts Oswald the Lucky Rabbit's new lady friend and tosses her into a car full of furry beasts. Meanwhile, a robot milk cow wanders in and out of the cartoon. A few cute bits.

**MEDIUM** (Polish) Film Polski 1985 color 100m. (aka *The Medium*). SP, D: Jacek Koprowicz. Ref: Hardy/HM2. With Wit Dabal.

"Comatose psychic ... plots ... to wreak havoc upon the world."

**MEDVEZHYA SVADBA** see *Marriage of the Bear*

**MEET THE APPLEGATES** New World & Cinemarque Ent. (Denise Di Novi & Iva Labunka) 1990 (1989) color 89m. (aka *The Applegates*). SP, D: Michael Lehmann. SP: also Redbeard Simmons. Ph: Mitchell Dubin. Mus: David Newman. PD: Jon Hutman. MkpFxDes: Kevin Yagher. PhFX: VCE; Peter Kuran. SpVocalFX: Frank Welker. Bug Wrangler: Steve Kutcher. Ref: TV. SFExam 2/1/91. TVG. Cinef 8/92. HBO/Cinemax 8/92. MFB'91:45. With Ed Begley, Jr. (Dick), Stockard Channing (Jane), Dabney Coleman (Aunt Bea), Bobby Jacoby (Johnny), Cami Cooper (Sally), Glenn Shadix, Patrick Donahue (Bea bug).

"The Brazilian Cocorada bug has survived in the Amazon Rain Forest for millions of years. Unfortunately, the destruction of the forest by land developers threatens the very existence of this undiscovered species. But these creatures are not mere garden variety insects: They're really big ... and they've got an attitude."

Four of the lycanthrope-like bugs here adopt human guises and move to Median, Ohio; become, initially, the "most normal family in America"; and plot to sabotage the local nuclear power plant. ("Something really weird about that family!") Their periodic "mutations"—under the influence of pot or emotion—scare humans, and they cocoon meddlers. At one point, their pet, "Spot the dog," mutates into a big, flying South American beetle. ("Oh, my God! What is it?") The cocooned interlopers are apparently meant to represent the skeletons in the closet of this all-American dysfunctional family, but the point of it all remains elusive, despite hilarious moments with Coleman's far-out human-cock-roach-in-drag and a wry foray into bug masturbation. Best line: Coleman's "We'll talk hormones later!"

**MEET THE HOLLOWHEADS** Moviestore Ent./Linden Prods. (Grace-Chavez) 1989 color 86m. (*Life on the Edge*-shooting t). SP, D: Tom Burman. SP: also Lisa Morton. Vis Consult: Ron Cobb. Ref: V 11/8/89: "dismally unfunny attempt at futuristic comedy." ad. PT 11:10. With John Glover, Nancy Mette, Richard Portnow, Juliette Lewis, Anne Ramsey, Logan Ramsey.

Not *The Jetsons.* "Post-nuclear age in which people live in tunnels ... graphic violence." (V)

**MEGASEX** Erotic Video Classics 1988 color c80m. Ref: vc box. no Adam. With Charli Waters, Candy Cruise, Stephanie Rage.

The "power of the Orgazmatazz" runs the planet Megasex.

**MEGAVILLE** Heritage Ent./White Noise (Christina Schmidlin, Andres Pfaeffli) 1990 color 89m. SP, D: Peter Lehner. SP: also Gordon Chavis. Mus: Stacy Widelitz. SpVideoFX: Michael Scroggins. SpSdDes: Leonard Marcel. Dream-a-Life Des: Hisham. Opt: Mercer, OptFX. Ref: TV. V 7/13/90. Martin. no Maltin '92. no Scheuer. With Billy Zane, J. C. Quinn, Grace Zabriskie, Daniel J. Travanti, Stefan Gierasch, Hamilton Camp.

"There's a device in your brain that enables me to communicate with you." A future government's new "sedative" for the "unruly": Dream-a-Life, a "dangerous new type of personality-altering ... memory implant." It's a "remote control for the brain"—a receiver which allows the sender to control the subject's mind.

But does the fascistic CKS use Dream-a-Life to make Palinov (Zane) impersonate Jensen (Zane) or Jensen impersonate Palinov? Uninvolving variations on *Total Recall* and *Telefon,* or maybe *The Manchurian Candidate.* (Palinov's first name: Raymond.) Only plus: the muted, ironic concluding sequence.

**MEGAZONE TWO THREE** (J) Artmic 1985 anim color 80m. (*Omega City* - orig t. *Vanity City* - int t. *Omega Zone 23* - int t). D: Noboru Ishiguro. SP: Hiroyuki Hoshiyama. Anim D: Ichiro Itano. Ref: TV: RCA Victor video; no Eng. Animag 11:28-31, 12. J Anim Prgm G. Animation Mag 5:31. Voices: Masato Kubota, Maria Kawamura et al.

Bahamoud, a gigantic computer, controls *Megazone 23,* a "generation ship" sent out from Earth several centuries ago, after an alien invasion. Through mind control, Bahamoud makes the inhabitants of the ship's upper city believe that they are still on Earth, in the Twentieth Century. And now, once again, the beings from the planet Kira are about to attack.... Japanese animated feature has an intriguing premise, but the treatment seems undistinguished. Early OAV.

See also the following titles.

**MEGAZONE 23, PART II: TELL ME A SECRET** (J) 1986 anim color 94m. Ref: TV: Eng.-lang. version, with J titles. Paul Lane: TV-movie. Anime Opus '89. Animag 11:29. Voices: Kerry Mahan, Barbara Goodson, Arlene Banas.

Part II features giant, human-operated mechanical combatants; an "octopus" weapon; EVE, an entity independent of the computer which generated her/it; and Program ADAM (Absolute Disintegration of Available Mass), which will save selected Megazoners and return them to Earth.... Hard to choose sides in this stew of bikers, cops, aliens, and soldiers. Okay to look at, but otherwise pretty terrible. Main motif: beer cans. Sample dialogue: "Eat hot lead, Fascist pigs!" The gang named Trash is perhaps hommage to *1990: The Bronx Warriors.*

**MEGAZONE 23, PART III** (J) Victor Video 1989-90 anim color 50m. each. D: S. Araboku, K. Hachigoku. AD & Char Des: Y. Kitazume. Mecha Des: Morifumi Naka. Ref: Animag 7:3: OAV. 9:5. 11:13, 29.

1) "Eve's Awakening"; 2) "Emancipation Day."

"Earth, several centuries after the closing scene in *Part II.*" Eden City's computer controls all.

**MEIKYU MONOGATARI** (J) Streamline 1986 ('93-U.S.) color/ws 63m. (*Manie-Manie. Neo-Tokyo* - U.S.). Ref: TV: vt; no Eng. Anim Mag (Smr '92): 26, 27, 48. U.C. Theatre notes 1/29/93. SFChron 1/20/93: commissioned for an exposition.

1) "Labyrinth." D: Rin Taro. The wonders of Le Nouveau Cirque begin even before the show officially opens and include a ghost dog, phantom joggers, living sludge, a streetcar of skeletons, a phantom clown, and various slogging blobby monsters.... Each new phenomenon in this spellbinding tale of a beyond-the-magic-mirror ghost circus has an eerie unexpectedness, seems to be a "privileged moment" of the fantastic. (14m.)

2) "Running Man." D: Yoshiaki Kawajiri. A highly stylized fiery finish to some futuristic auto racing. (14m.)

3) "The Order to Stop Construction." D: Katsuhiro Otomo. Atmospheric tale re a massive, robotic construction project in a jungle. At first, the robots seem to be simply malfunctioning, but by the end, they've created what seems to be a giant robot. Film features intriguing details of machine size, shape, and movement. (18m.)

4) An apparently tacked-on story re jungle weirdness and a giant warrior. Conventional heroics, okay look. Not included in the U.S. version. (17m.)

**MEIN SKITZO** Film Threat/Lane 1993 color 35m. D, P: Sandy Lane. Ref: TV: FT Video. With Marilyn Lane, Larry Broderick, Lance Ozanix.

"We're going to change history!" A "dimensional space converter" (consisting of a "spectrometer" and "sub-atomic neutrinos") takes a rock group from 1993 East Germany back to 1989 San Francisco, in an attempt to reunite Germany. The means: a tune with a subliminal, anti-Berlin Wall message. Limp, amateur-level comedy has a cute idea, nothing more.

**MELOS** (J) 198-? anim color (*Andro-Melos*). Ref: Markalite 3:82: "vidseries" featuring "evil space emperor Judah" from *Urutoraman Sutori*.

**MEMOIRE DES APPARENCES** see *Life Is a Dream*

**MEMOIRS OF AN INVISIBLE MAN** (U.S.-F) WB/Le Studio Canal Plus & Regency Ents. & Alcor Films (Cornelius/Bodner-Kolsrud/Arnon Milchan) 1992 color/ws 99m. D: John Carpenter. SP: Robert Collector, Dana Olsen, William Goldman, from H. F. Saint's novel. Ph: William A. Fraker. Mus: Shirley Walker. PD: Lawrence G. Paull. SpVisFX: IL&M; (sup) B. Nicholson. Digital FxSup: Stuart Robertson. Computer Sup: (graphics) Doug Smythe; (fx) Steve Grumette. SpFxCoord: Ken Pepiot. Anim Sup: Wes Ford Takahashi. FxAnim: Jay Cotton, Chris Green. Stopmo: Harry Walton. Ref: TV. V 3/2/92. SFChron 2/28/92. With Chevy Chase, Rosalind Chao, Elaine Corral, Daryl Hannah, Sam Neill, Michael McKean, Stephen Tobolowsky.

A freak accident at Magnascopics Labs, in Santa Mira, leaves parts of the building invisible and all of Nick Halloway (Chase) invisible, victim of "molecular instability." Now, certain intelligence authorities want him to become the "single most exotic intelligence asset on the planet"—an "invisible agent".... A freak miscalculation on the part of the filmmakers leaves Nick visible half the time. It's not psychological. It's not scientific. It's just ill-advised, if understandable: What's a Chevy Chase comedy without Chevy Chase? And admittedly some of this half of the movie is funny. Most of the better payoffs, though, are in the effects-showcase half: the Rain Effect, the Holographic-Face Effect, the Partially-Disintegrated-Building Effect. The worst of it: the shallow political intrigue.

**MEMORIAL VALLEY MASSACRE** Motion Picture Corp. of America & Vertex 1988 color 93m. (*Memorial Day* - orig t). SP, D: R. C. Hughes. SP: also G. F. Skrow. Ph: James Mathers. Mus: Jed Feuer. PD: Doug Forsmith. MechFX: Peter Geyer. Ref: TV: Nelson Ent. video. SFChron Dtbk 12/18/88. V 10/19/88:8 (rated). Bowker '90. Hound. McCarty II. no Martin. With John Kerry, Mark Mears, Lesa Lee, John Caso (hermit), William Smith, Cameron Mitchell.

"I've heard stories about this valley!" Steven Webster, a kid-napped boy lost twenty years ago, is now a "wild child" axing campers in Memorial Valley Campground. ("Something out there got 'im....") Miscalculated combination slasher movie/*Meatballs* comedy, with an ecological angle thrown in, plus an impossible climactic try at pathos. (Caveman Caso and head ranger Kerry have a tragically aborted father-son reunion.)

**MEN BEHIND THE SUN** (H.K.) Sil-Metropole (Fu Chi) 1988 color 103m. (aka *Black Sun 731. Man behind the Sun* - cr t. *Hei Tai Yang 731*). D: T. F. Mous (or Xeng Le Law). SP: Mou Wen Yuan, Teng Dun Jing, Liu Mei Fei. Ref: TV: World Video; Eng. titles. Fango 107:57, 60. NST! 4:30-31. PT 4:41. 20:69. V 10/19/88:335(ad). SFExam 7/9/95: re Harbin. With Gang Wang, Dai Yao Wu, Run Shen Wang.

Japanese biological-warfare experiments at the Manchu 731 Squadron base in Harbin, China. Among the atrocities suppos-edly condemned, but lovingly re-created: subjects injected with "mutated plague bacteria," a cat tossed into a horde of plague-in-fected rats in the Animal Breeding Unit, hands frozen (and later skinned) at the Outdoor Frostbite Experimental Station, limbs tossed into the crematory fire (as the attendant sings jauntily), grisliness in the Decompression Lab, a boy chloroformed and subjected to operating-room horrors, and gory battlefield experi-ments with porcelain bacteria bombs.... Or, *ILSA* East. Thank-fully, most of the gore in this exercise in hypocrisy is just phony enough to allow for semi-detached inspection, though not phony enough for camp.

**\*MEN MUST FIGHT** 1933. AD: Cedric Gibbons. Ref: TV. V 3/14/33. Hardy/SF. Lee. Lentz. no Maltin '92. no Scheuer.

Laura (Diana Wynyard), as she watches the World War: "Stop this war!" It's stopped, but.... In 1940, an ambassador is assassi-nated, and (reads the headline): "Eurasia Ready for War." Pacifist Laura's duty is towards her son (Phillips Holmes), whose father (Robert Young) was a pilot shot down in the last war; her husband, Ned (Lewis Stone), the secretary of state, feels his duty is towards his country. Meanwhile, the enemy bombs New York City, and TV and TV-phones are all the rage.... The mechanics of war—and how it divides families—seem fairly accurately por-trayed in this long-lost sf-drama (which surfaced recently on TNT). Unfortunately, the characters have Principles, and the actors have Speeches. Even the ending, which at first promises more, is tidied up: Laura, racked over her son's decision to enlist and become a pilot, finally seems resigned to the men-must-fight status quo.

**MEN WITH SWORDS** see *Swordsman* (H.K.)

**MENGGUI XUETANG** see *Haunted Cop Shop II*

**MENTE ASESINA** (Mex) Prods. Latinas Americanas/Eagle Films (Orlando R. Mendoza) 1987 color c80m. (*Killer Mind*-vc box alt t). SP, D: Alberto Mariscal. Co-D: Damian Acosta. Adap: Antonio Orellana. Story: Crox Alvarado. Ph: Ruiz, Tejada. Elec FX: E. Bravo et al. SpFX: Arturo Godinez. Mkp: Mayra Acosta. Ref: TV: Condor Video; no Eng. Hound. With Hugo Stiglitz (Dr.

Ricardo Gonzalez), Silvia Manriquez, Arlette Pacheco, Hector Saez, Elsa Montes.

Mad doc beheads interred corpse of man he killed, submits head to flesh-stripping acid, ties up "enemies" in abandoned warehouse, and unleashes rats on them. Very, very cheap, shoddy, shot-on-tape effort. Supposedly "based on fact." Cutest videotape effect: the "heads" of the doc's tormentors emanating from his eyeball.

**MERCENARY CANNIBALS** (H.K.-Vietnamese) Kane-Morris? 1983 color feature (*Mercenary* - orig t). D: Hong Lu Wong. Ref: TV: EVS; Eng. dubbed. Weisser/ATC: aka *Cannibal Mercenary.*

Vietnam actioner goes beyond standard war gore in scenes in which (a) a local snacks on maggots from an apparent severed head ("Delicious!"), (b) designated cannibals take charge after a knife-in-the-brain execution ("Animals!"), and, (c) the cannibals get into the act again after some spiked-glove gore. Otherwise, the regulation beheadings, impalements, etc.

**MERIDIAN: KISS OF THE BEAST** JGM Ents./Full Moon (Rock Salt/Debra Dion) 1990 color 85m. (*Kiss of the Beast* - alt t). Story, D, Co-P: Charles Band. SP: Dennis Paoli. Mus: Pino Donaggio. SpMkpFX: Greg Cannom. Main Title Des: R.E.D. Prods. Opt. Mercer Titles. Ref: TV. V 4/18/90. Maltin '92. Martin. no Scheuer. With Sherilyn Fenn, Malcolm Jamieson, Alex Daniels (Beast), Isabella Celani (ghost), Hilary Mason (Martha), Phil Fondacaro (dwarf).

"You're the beast!" A *Howling*-like, sex-brings-out-the-beast sequence tips off the nature of this cross between *Beauty and the Beast* and *The Black Room* (1935). Oliver Fauvrey (Jamieson) is the man who turns into a monster (Daniels), but his twin brother Lawrence (Jamieson) is the real beast (i.e., bad man).... Vapid horror-fantasy with some special-makeup and t&a values. The progressive restoration of an old painting which seems to tell the same story as the script provides the only narrative interest.

**MERLIN** see *October 32nd*

**MERMAID FOREST** (J) CPM/Shogakukan & Rumiko Takahashi & Victor Musical 198-? ('92-U.S.) anim color 56m. (*Rumic World* series). D: Takaya Mizutani. SP: Masaichiro Okubo. Story: R. Takahashi. Ph: H. Takahashi. Mus: Kenji Kawai. AD: K. Kanemura. SdFxD: Y. Honda. Ref: TV: USManga Corps video; Eng. titles.

Kannagi Mansion, on the Noto Peninsula. Principals include a sick woman who drinks mermaid blood and whose hand then turns monstrous—every three years, she must obtain a new hand from a recently dead body ... Yuta and Mana, immortals who have apparently tasted mermaid flesh ("I can't die every night just to come back every morning") ... the monster dog Shiro, who also drank mermaid blood ... and hunters who eat mermaid flesh and die ghastly bloody deaths.

Grisly, bizarre, different. Horror is piled upon horror, nearly to the point of risibility.

Sequel: *Mermaid's Scar.*

**MERMAID LEGEND** (J) 1984 feature (*Ningyo Densetsu*). D: T. Ikeda. Ref: Weisser/JC: "unique." With M. Shirato, K. Shimizu.

Gorefest re supposed "ghost mermaid" who slaughters men.

**MERMAID'S SCAR** (J) Takahashi-Shogakukan-Victor (Meda-Sasaki) 1993 anim color c50m. D: Morio Asaka. SP: Tatsuhiko Urahata. From R. Takahashi's comic. Ph: H. Yamada. Mus: N. Tauri. AD: H. Kaneko. SpFX: Tanifuji, Tamai. SdFxD: Y. Honda. Ref: TV: Viz Video (Shog. Video); Eng. dubbed. Animerica 5:16: sequel to *Mermaid Forest*.

"This is evil!" A woman who burns, dies, revives, and heals proves to be one of three mermaid-flesh-eating immortals here. She can turn into a hideous monster, but her 800-year-old "son" is the most evil one.... Okay premises; stilted animation and dubbing.

**MERRY SOULS** see *Those Merry Souls*

**MESHTE NASTRESHU** (Russ) Odessa 1963 color 68m. SP, D: Mikhail Karyukov. D: also Otar Koberidze. SP: also A. Berdink, I. Bondin. Ph: A. Gerasimov. Ref: Hardy/SF: "impressive settings and landscape designs but extremely weak on plot." With Larissa Gordeichik, O. Koberidze, Boris Borisneko, N. Timofeev.

Spaceship from the planet Centurius winds up on Mars. *A Dream Come True* - tr t?

**METAL FIGHTERS MIKU** (J) SS/JVC 1994 ('95-U.S.) anim color c60m. Ref: vc box: 9 episodes; female wrestlers in the year 2061.

**METAL MEN AGAINST GANDAHAR** see *Light Years*

**METAMORPHOSIS** (I) Imperial Ent./Filmirage (Donatella Donati) 1989 ('90-U.S.) color 96m. (*DNA-Formula Letale*). SP, D: Luigi Montefiori (aka G. Eastman). Mus: Pahamian. AD: Max Stevens. MkpFX: M. Trani. Ref: V 6/6/90: "extremely silly." Hardy/HM2: aka *Regenerator.* Horacio Higuchi. Martin. V/Cannes '89: 499: completed. Palmerini. With Gene le Brock, Catherine Baranov, Harry Cason, Laura Gemser.

Genetic engineer goes too far, turns himself into a baby tyrannosaurus.

**METAMORPHOSIS: THE ALIEN FACTOR** IRC/Petrified Films (Friedman-Berson & Movie Moguls) 1991 color 97m. SP, D: Glenn Takakjian. P & Addl Mat'l.: Ted A. Bohus. Mus: John Gray. SpVisFX: Dan Taylor. Mkp Creature FX: R. S. Cole, P. C. Reilly Jr. et al. Ref: V 5/6/91: "competently made but unexceptional sci-fi thriller." With Tara Leigh, Tony Gigante, Dianna Flaherty, Marcus Powell, George Gerard.

Alien tissue sample turns frog into mutant which bites doctor (Gerard) and turns him into an *Alien.*

**The METEOR MAN** MGM/Tinsel Townsend (Loretha C. Jones) 1993 color 99m. SP, D: Robert Townsend. Ph: John A. Alonzo. Mus: Cliff Eidelman. PD: Toby Corbett. SpVisFX: IL&M; (sup) B. Nicholson. Stopmo: Harry Walton. FxAnim: Tim Berglund, A.F. Stacchi. SpFxSup: Al DiSarro. Ref: TV. V 8/16/93: "too polite." SFChron 8/6/93: "as failures go, this one's interesting." ad. With R. Townsend (Jefferson Reed), Marla Gibbs, Eddie Griffin, Robert Guillaume, James Earl Jones, Bill Cosby, Frank

Gorshin, Sinbad, Nancy Wilson, Luther Vandross, Wallace Shawn, Tommy R. Hicks.

Schoolteacher hit by meteor gets "superhuman strength, bullet-proof skin and the ability to fly." (SFC) ("You really got super powers.") He also has X-ray vision, speaks "dog," absorbs the contents of whatever book he touches, starts a 3.5 earthquake, and (through emerald rays and rainwater) creates an "outdoor grocery store".... A Brother from This Planet, "Meteor Man" uses his powers to smash a D.C. gang (and its out-of-town "sponsors"). Film itself is pleasant, if not inspired. It has some heart, some stirring moments, and some downright funny ones.

\*MEXICAN SPITFIRE SEES A GHOST 1942. Ref: TV. V 5/13/42. Lee. no Stanley. no Lentz. no Scheuer. Maltin '92. Higham/Welles: *Ambersons'* better half.

"The house has a reputation of being haunted!" Some offhand-edly funny ghost stuff is reserved for the last ten minutes here, when the story of a "family ghost" in a "dreary-looking place" is brought to life, by a crook in armor and by a monster-faced balloon. Otherwise, the movie's tiresome plot complications pay off only for moments here and there. Donald MacBride is at his most exasperated and exasperating, while Leon Errol's stiff-upper-lip impersonations are moderately amusing.

MEXICO 2000 (Mex) Conacine 1981 color 81m. D: Rogelio A. Gonzalez Jr. SP: A. Portillo. Dial: Hector Lechuga, M. A. Flota. Story: Jesus Salinas. Ph: Gabriel Figueroa. Mus: Jose A. Zavala. AD: Agustin Ituarte. OptFX: P.O.C. SdFX: Juan Banos. Mkp: Elda Loza. Ref: TV. vc box. TVG. Cinef 6/96:47. With Chucho Salinas, Lechuga, Rojo Grau, Elizabeth Aguilar, Miguel Gurza, Humberto Gurza.

A glimpse of a future, idyllic Mexico, in which the cars look like golf carts and wind ensembles entertain bus riders. Talky, silly sf-comedy.

MI FANTASMA Y YO (Mex) Potosi Prods./Martizan 1986 color c93m. SP, D: Gilberto De Anda. Ph: Antonio De Anda. Mus: Marco Flores. AD: Arturo Martinez Jr. SpFX: Miguel Vazquez. SdFX: Gonzalo Gavira. Ref: TV: Film-Mex video; no Eng.; *My Ghost and I* - tr t. With Ana Luisa Peluffo (medium), Mariagna Prats, Rodolfo De Anda, Mauricio Garces (the devil), Jorge Reynoso, El Comanche, Carlos East, Bruno Rey, Cesar Velazco, Don Arturo Martinez (ghost).

"El Tio," a bumbling ghost cursed to haunt a house, tries to scare the new mistress of same (Prats), but winds up in a vacuum cleaner. He becomes friends with her son, Carlitos (Velazco), and tells him (visualized) tales of, respectively, prehistoric man, Merlin, and cannibal women. He also scares a couple of intruders, but an exorcism banishes him. When Carlitos begins to waste away, his parents hire a medium, and a seance brings back this friendly ghost.... Mild but fairly sweet fantasy-comedy is clearly inspired by *E.T.* X.L. Chabelo plays a psychiatrist whose facial tics amusingly recall Fritz Feld in *Bringing up Baby.*

MI HEROE (Mex) Antonio Matouk 1964 b&w c80m.? D: G. M. Solares. SP: Raquel Alcoriza. Ph: A. M. Solares. Mus: Enrique Rodriguez. Mkp: Rosa Guerrero. Ref: TV: *My Hero* - tr t; no Eng. TVG. Historia/Mexicano, v. 9. With Julio Aleman, Angelica

Maria, Armando Silvestre, Delia Magana, Pompin, Gina Romand, Francisco Reyguera.

Silly horror-comedy re a vanishing dog, a hairy clutching hand, a masked menace, lights-out bat and cat attacks, and a real ghost which carries its head about. When shot, the head spits out bullets.

MIA MOGLIE E UNA BESTIA (I) 1988 color feature. D: Castellano and Pipolo. Ref: Palmerini: Yeti comedy. With M. Boldi, E. Grimaldi.

MIAMI HORROR (I) Panther Ent./Filmustang (George Salvioni) 1987 ('88-U.S.) color c90m. (aka *Miami Golem. Cosmos Killer*). Story, D: Alberto de Martino. SP: Frank Clark, Frank Waller. Mus: Robert Marry. SpVisFX: Sergio Stivaletti. SpSdFX: Ciorba, Basilovich, Colin. Mkp: Marisa Marvin, Vince Carter. Ref: TV: Twin Tower video; Eng.-lang. version. V 1/13/88: 32. 4/70/88:34 (hv). Scheuer. Hound. With David Warbeck, Laura Trotter, Lawrence Loddi, George Favretto, John Ireland.

A scientist "assembles" the cell of a bacterium from a fossil preserved for millions of years in a meteorite, but a message in a "very ancient alphabet that expressed the language of the subconscious, the ancient Atlantis language," warns that the result will be a "being with extraordinary powers." At stake: "all creation." Meanwhile, Joanna Fitzgerald, a telepath, leads TV reporter Craig Milford to the site, in the Florida Everglades, of an alien spaceship landing, where, in a "timeless moment" with an extraterrestrially-manufactured projection of himself, he learns that the cell "belonged to a cruel horde that once dominated space thousands of years ago," but was destroyed by "those who want cosmic peace"—i.e., extraterrestrial informers who need human allies in order to work within our dimension. Milford puts this ever-growing "golem" out of commission and gives it to the good aliens.

The clues to this cosmic mystery are intriguing, if not especially well-coordinated, and the movie has a thoroughly routine action/suspense framework. Ireland, as Anderson, who wants to use the "golem" to rule the world, speaks with an anonymous dubbed voice.

MICKEY'S GARDEN Disney 1935 anim color 9m. Ref: TV. Jim Shapiro. LC.

A heavy dose of bug spray makes Mickey Mouse—in the garden with Pluto—"see" plants and bugs become gigantic, including a daddy-longlegs. A big-pincered beetle seems monstrous, and caterpillars become almost dragon-like. Okay cartoon's most bizarre bit: Bugs attack a potato and leave only its blinking eyes.

The MID-NIGHT (H.K.) A Kaung-Lun Yao c1989? color c85m. D: Fung-Pan Yao. Ref: TV: H. K.-Int'l. Video; no Eng.; Viet.-dubbed.

In grisly detail, a slasher slaughters a whole household, then walls everyone up in the cellar. The victims then haunt the house and conduct a Dance of the Furniture, as their spirits move various objects. Spirit-possessed, the new woman of the house alternately shatters and eats glass.... Cheap shocks, shrill music. Okay effect: the ghost "shrinking" through the closed door.

**MIDNIGHT** SVS Films & Midnight Inc. & Kuys Ent. Group & Gomillion Studios 1989 color 84m. SP, D, Co-P: Norman Thaddeus Vane. SpFantasyMkp: Elena Breckenridge. AD & FX: Mark Simon. Ref: TV. V 9/20/89.

Melo-comedy with some horrific ingredients: Lynn Redgrave as "Midnight," an Elvira- or Vampira-like hostess who presents grade-C monster epics on TV ... her visualized nightmare re an avenging ghost-in-white (Karen Witter) ... the discovery of a decayed corpse in her manse ... and Tony Curtis's reference to The Lobster Man Strikes Back (see *Lobster Man from Mars*).... Dispiritingly cliched characters and story. Redgrave's staccato, willfully-camp performance seems to be a warmup for her Baby Jane.

**MIDNIGHT 2: SEX, DEATH AND VIDEOTAPE** Tempe (J. R. Bookwalter) 1993 color feature. SP, D: John Russo. Ref: PT 16:57: the subtitle says it all; "disturbing and effective in spots." Fango 122:12. With Matthew Walsh.

Follow-up to *Midnight* (II)

**\*MIDNIGHT AT MADAME TUSSAUD'S** Premier 1936 (*Midnight at the Wax Museum* - alt t). SP: Roger MacDougall, Kim Peacock. Story: James Edwards, MacDougall. AD: Ronald Russell. Ref: TV. Gifford/BC. Lee. no Lentz. no Hardy/HM. no Stanley. TVG. Hound. BFC. With Lucille Lisle, K. Peacock, Patrick Barr.

Madame Tussaud's Wax Museum is a "weird place," where "tricks of the imagination" attend solitary visitors to its chamber of horrors. The gallery features a torture chamber and a "breathing" Sleeping Beauty, but one of the figures therein is not wax.... Bernard Miles' performance as Kelvin, the chief model maker, has hints of madness and the macabre ("I take a very great pride in my art"), but the payoff of the spend-a-night-in-the-chamber plot is disappointingly tame. Kelvin does not even figure in the climactic action. Much superfluous melodrama away from the museum.

**MIDNIGHT BLUNDERS** Col 1936 20m. D: Del Lord. SP: Preston Black, Harry McCoy. Story: Jack Leonard, Monte Collins. Ref: Okuda/CCS. LC. With Tom Kennedy, Monte Collins, Harry Semels, Phyllis Crane, Wilfred Lucas, Jack "Tiny" Lipson.

Scientist (Lucas) creates "half-human/half-robot monstrosity" (Lipson). (Okuda)

Remade as *Sweet Spirits of the Nighter.*

**MIDNIGHT CABARET** WB/Lorimar HV/Niki Marvin & Grandma Moses Pictures 1988 (1990) color 93m. SP, D: Pece Dingo. SP: also Lori Gloede. Story: Paul Fries, Temistocles Lopez. Ph: B. Heinl. Mus: Michel Colombier. PD: B.A. Capra. SpMkpFX: Bryan Moore. SpFxCoord: W.A. Klinger Jr. Ref: TV: Warner HV. V 3/4/91:55 (hv): "pretentious satanic shocker." Martin: "time waster." With Laura Herrington, Lisa Hart Carroll, Michael Des Barres, Norbert Weisser, Lydie Denier, Thom Mathews.

"You can't tell the living from the dead." Stage and offstage ingredients here include (in a sketch) apparent vampires ... a visualized nightmare re a satyr ... a slasher-at-large ... (in another sketch) a dwarf gang ... a woman whose dreams seem to be coming true ("This woman is a psycho!") ... and a cult which seems to believe her unborn is "young Lucifer".... Pretentiously presented, but pathetically thin.

**MIDNIGHT COP** see *Nick Knight*

**MIDNIGHT EYE** see *Gokuu: Midnight Eye*

**MIDNIGHT FACES** Goodwill/Schreier 1926 silent b&w 54m. SP, D: Bennett Cohn. Titles: Forrest K. Sheldon. Ph: King Grey. FX: (elec) Edward Bush; (tech) Clyde Whittaker. Ref: TV. Greg Luce. AFI: *Midnight Fires* - t error? Filmfax 7:23(ad). no V. no LC. Hound. With Francis X. Bushman Jr., Jack Perrin, Kathryn McGuire, Edward Peil Sr., Charles Belcher, Nora Cecil, Martin Turner, Eddie Dennis, Al Hallett.

Claymore Point, in the Florida bayous. ("What a mysterious place—it gives me the shivers.") A cloaked skulker, a sinister-looking Chinese gentleman, mysterious knocking, and "ghosts" (including a "nine foot ghost") disturb the sleep of visitors staying overnight at the supposedly dead Peter Marlin's estate. ("There's a phantom figure prowling about this house—this is the second time he's vanished through the walls.") One ghost turns out to be the remains of a 3,000-year-old mummy; the other, a pigeon....

Haunted-house-movie cliches go back further than one might suppose. The face glimpsed at the upstairs window of a supposedly empty house, for instance, goes back at least as far as *Midnight Faces.* So do the forbidding-looking house-keeper (here Mrs. Hart [Cecil], or "Graveyard Mary") and the quivering Black valet (here called Trohelius [Turner]). The cliche most critical to the plot: the "paralytic" who turns out to be a quite agile "phantom." *Midnight Faces,* though, is more watchable than most of its Thirties and Forties counterparts. It wastes little time on plot or talk. The allure of darkened rooms dominates—the phantom skulks in every other scene. Outside the house, day-for-night might just as well be simply day; inside, the spooky shadows are carefully controlled, and prowlers outnumber non-prowlers.

**MIDNIGHT HORROR** see *Carrol Morira a Mezzanotte*

The **MIDNIGHT HOUR** ABC-TV/ABC Circle Films (Ervin Zavada) 1985 color 92m. D: Jack Bender. Tel: Bill Bleich. Ph: Rexford Metz. Mus: Brad Fiedel. PD: Charles Hughes. SpMkpFX: Tom Burman; (art) Wes Dawn. SpFX: Jack Monroe. Opt: Movie Magic. SdDes: Frank Serafine. Ref: TV. TVG. Stanley: *In the Midnight Hour* - t error? V 11/6/85:50. Hound. Maltin '92. Scheuer. Ecran F 62:63. With Shari Belafonte-Harper (Melissa), LeVar Burton, Lee Montgomery, Mark Blankfield (the ghoul), Jonna Lee (cute ghoul), Jonelle Allen (Lucinda), Dick Van Patten, Kevin McCarthy, Mickey Morton (Nestor, ghoul).

"The dead are coming back to life in Pitchford Cove," in New England. Scroll-invoked "spirits of darkness" raise a cemetery's witch-cursed dead, and the latter come back as vampires and ghouls, though some are out only for love, and one returns to sing grand opera, in a genuinely eerie climactic, town-square gathering of ghouls. In this lyrical-macabre sequence, each entranced ghoul does his/her own thing, and supernatural anarchy reigns.

Overall, *The Midnight Hour* is an unusual, if not always successful blend of comedy, horror, and music.

**MIDNIGHT KILLER** see *Carrol Morira a Mezzanotte*

**MIDNIGHT KISS** Academy/Overseas Filmgroup (Zola-Rosen-Bender/In The Midnight Hour Prods.) 1993 (1992) color feature. D: Joel Bender. SP: John Weidner, Ken Lamplugh. Ph: Alan Caso. Mus: E. Kauderer. PD: Don Day. SpMkpFX: S.O.T.A. F/X; Roy Knyrim, Jerry Macaluso. MechSpFX: Steve Patino. Ref: TV. Jones. PT 17:14: aka *In the Midnight Hour*; "imaginative violence." SFChron Dtbk 8/15/93. V 5/24/93:24 (rated): "horror violence." With Michelle Owens, G.A. Greer (vampire), Celeste Yarnall, Gabriel Dell Jr., Michael McMillen, Robert Miano, Darla Grant (Carol).

"Not so bad being immortal." A giggly vampire bites a lady cop, who then acquires vampiric strength—and hunger. She undergoes addict panic and uses her strength to cripple thugs, as the script ventures into *Maniac Cop* territory.... Another dismayingly-Freddy-glib monster. The movie gets somewhat better in its later stages, but still can't quite make up for the earlier bad will generated. Creepy: the ceiling-haunting vampire. As Pauline Kael said of some other film: Everybody here needs a cold shower.

**MIDNIGHT MATINEE** see *Matinee* (1989)

**MIDNIGHT MENACE** All-American News 1946 b&w. Ref: Separate Cinema: 3 shorts. With Lollypop Jones.

"Voodoo ... chills."

**MIDNIGHT MOVIE MASSACRE** Wade Williams (Film Works) 1988 (1986) color 85m. D: Mark Stock; ("Space Patrol") Larry Jacobs. SP: Roger Branit, M. Stock, J. Chadwell, D. Houston. Mus: Bill Crain. SpMkpFX: Ken Wheatly. Ref: V 5/18/88. 10/19/88:327 (ad). PT 10: 52, 54. 11:6. V 6/1/83:7: begun? With Robert Clarke, Ann Robinson, David Staffer, Tot Hutsler.

Horror murders by a tentacled monster at a 1956 movie theatre alternate with footage from the "Back from the Future" episode of "Space Patrol" (a recreation of the TV series). Plus: time travel and bits with Robby the Robot and Gort. "Poorly scripted pastiche."(V)

**\*\*MIDNIGHT MYSTERY** Radio/William LeBaron & Bertram Millhauser 1930 63m. D: George B. Seitz. SP: Beulah Marie Dix, from Howard Irving Young's play "Hawk Island." Ph: Joseph Walker. AD: Max Ree. PhFX: Lloyd Knechtel. Ref: TV. V 6/4/30. NYT. no Scheuer. no Maltin '92. TVG. With Betty Compson, Hugh Trevor, Lowell Sherman, Rita LeRoy, Ivan Lebedeff, Raymond Hatton, June Clyde, Sidney D'Albrook, William Bart.

A "wild night ... on a little rock-bound island off the coast of Cuba." The Hawk Island Crime Club—including Sally (Compson), author of "The 7 Shrieking Corpses" and many another "horror story"—is waiting for "something nice and gruesome" to happen. It does. A "fake corpse" (Lebedeff) returns from a supposed watery grave to "haunt," as a "ghost"—with ghostly face (thanks to a flashlight) and unearthly wail—Tom (Sherman). ("I don't believe in ghosts.") Extra addeds: "atmosphere in

chunks," a "lovely creepy rain," and nice wind, clanging buoy, and thunder effects.

The melodrama comes in large chunks, too. The brave banter re ghosts and grisly murders is engaging, but can't hide the fact that the banterers are basically a motley lot. The plot gimmick—a hoax murder becomes real murder—is good for a few fun scenes, too. But the actors drone on long after the fun has ended.

**MIDNIGHT RIDERS** Video 10 1989 color feature. SP, D: J. K. Jensen. Ref: Adam '93G: vampire story. no Jones. With Kevin Glover (Eripmav).

**MIDNIGHT SHADE** (Thai) A. Film Art c1990? color/ws c90m. Ref: TV: vt; no Eng. Chao Thai Market: *Sex Moon* - tr of Thai t; above is t on both vt & vc box.

An invisible *Entity* rapes a woman. Later, visible, the fanged, huge-clawed demon gorily shreds its victim's torso, then nibbles on some intestines. Meanwhile, elsewhere, the apparent *Psychic Killer* behind the violence awakens and vomits. When the latter person dies, the demon apparently enters his wife who, attacked, turns into a Thing which savages a man.... Much ado about vomit in this determinedly gross shocker which tries, with some measure of success, to be revolting.

The **MIDNIGHT SONG** (H.K.) 198-? color/ws c90m. (*The Song in Midnight* - vc ad t). D: Yao Fung-Pan. Ref: TV: Quality Video; Eng. titles.

Several "ghosts" haunt a murderer: A body in a bathtub, a phantom in a chair, a ghost at a piano, a severed arm, and a ghost in a wheelchair drive him mad and make him accidentally kill his own sister. At the end, the fake ghosts remove their masks and wigs.... Tawdry romantic suspenser, with grisly scenes and periodic musical treacle, borrows lamely from *The Changeling*, *Diabolique*, and *Mark of the Vampire* (1935).

The **MIDNIGHT ZONE** Lascaux Communications/Shotgun Wedding 1986 color c90m. D: Drea. Ph: Mark Rigney. Mus: Sir Gregg. SpVisFX: "B. T. Sparks." Mkp: Jerry Holt et al. Ref: TV: Intropics Video. Adam '88:202. With Gina Carrera, Lisa De Leeuw, Karen Summer, William Margold, Misty Reagan.

A hardcore "journey into an erotic land," not far from "The Twilight Zone." 1) "My Chance to Cream" (a muddled variation on "Perchance to Dream"), re the "eternal Bermuda love triangle" and a man whose "heart races" every time he dreams of a mysterious "everywoman." 2) "...Better Not Touch," a takeoff on "It's a Good Life" in which the Puritanical Willy (Scott Irish) wishes bad adults into Dildoland, but finally learns that "it's a real good thing to touch other people." 3) "Seleh," in which an alien (Tony El-Ay) from a "world not of this galaxy" makes love to an Earth woman (Sheri Stewart). 4) "Wetdream at 20,000 Feet," a silly comic variation on "Nightmare at 20,000 Feet," re a prudish man's flight into the "not-so-friendly skies of his imagination," via Unicorn Airlines.

**MIDNIGHT'S CHILD** Lifetime-TV/Hearst Ent. & The Polone Co./Victoria Principal Prods. & Myrow-Gottlieb (Kimberly Myers) 1992 color c90m. D: Colin Bucksey. Story, Tel: David Chaskin. Story: also D. N. Gottlieb, Jeff Myrow. Ph: A. B. Richmond. Mus: Richard Hartley. PD: Vaughan Edwards. SpFX:

Martin Bresin; Sp FX Unltd. Post VisFX: Tim McHugh. Mkp: Cheryl Voss. Drawings: Peter Sis. Opt: CFI. Ref: TV. TVG. With Marcy Walker, Cotter Smith, Olivia D'Abo, Elissabeth Moss, Jim Norton, Judy Parfitt.

"I wanted my career back, and Christina will be set for life." An au pair is the vehicle for *Rosemary's Baby,* sold-my-soul-for-the-good-life themes.

**El MIEDO NO ANDA EN BURRO** (Mex) Diana Films 1973 c86m. D: Fernando Cortes. SP: Fernando Galiana. Ph: F. Colin. Mus: Sergio Guerrero. AD: Raul Cardenas. Monsters: Antonio Neyra. SpFX: Ramiro Valencia. OptFX: Ricardo Sainz. Mkp: Tony Ramirez. Ref: TV: Video Visa; no Eng. Horacio Higuchi: Fear Doesn't Ride a Donkey - tr t. With La India Maria (aka Maria Elena Velasco), Chelelo, Fernando Lujan, Emma Roldan, Oscar Ortiz Pinedo, Gloria Mayo, Wally Barron.

Greedy, shortchanged heirs gang up, masquerade as monsters—including a werewolf, a fanged horned Cyclops, a frog-man, and a mummy or something—in order to get rid of the heroine and the poodle, Mimi, that inherited the estate in question. Plus an apparently real, hunchbacked ghost, a (briefly) living, whinnying horse skeleton, a gorilla, a casket-full of tarantulas, and a scare scene with some (non-living) mummies.... Routine slapstick picks up, becomes lively and monster-crammed near the end. Best bit: a cuckoo-clock skull which, naturally, goes "Cuckoo!" Best prop: a deluxe cobweb.

**MIGHTY JACK** (J) Sandy Frank/Tsuburaya-Morita-Itoh 1986 color c90m.? D: Kazuho Mitsuta. SP: Shinichi Sekizawa, E. Siba. Ph: Y. Mori; (fx) K. Sagawa. Mus: Isao Tomita. Ref: TV: Eng.-dubbed. no Scheuer. no Maltin '92. With Hideaki Nitani, Naoko Kobo, Hiroshi Ninami, Hideyo Amamoto, Masanari Nihei, Wakako Ikeda.

"Q has found a way to convert molecular energy," and thus produce "ice that won't melt even under very high temperatures"—a portable unit alters molecular structure in order to make icebergs and freeze objects. The Mighty Jack commandos and their air-sea craft the Electro-Scout (complete with ray weapons) take on the dreaded "Q".... Lowgrade kidstuff, with hapless miniatures. Other sf ingredients include a laser weapon and a laser-beam force field. Feature-length, but plays like two episodes from a TV series.

**MIGHTY SPACE MINERS** (J) A.D. Vision/KSS 1994 ('95-U.S.) anim color 52m. D: U. Iida. SP: R. Hayasaka, T. Iida. Story: Lunchfield. Ph: Morishita. Mus: Kawai. AD: Taniguchi. Mecha Des: Imakake, Mekajinos. SpFX: Y. Hiba. Ref: TV: ADV video; OAV?; Eng. dubbed.

Two episodes. "It's the end of the world!" Year 2056. A feisty twelve-year-old hero, a "killer satellite," a lame-duck space station, and the Planet Catcher Corp.... Interesting visual-design details, familiar action/suspense, and a pinch of *Alien* cynicism.

**MIKADOROIDO** (J) Toho & Tsuburaya Films 1991 color 73m. (*Robokill beneath Disco Club Layla* - U.S.). SP, D: Tomoo Haraguchi. Mus: Kenji Kawai. Ref: TV: Tohokushinsha HV; no Eng. VSOM. Markalite 3:9: made-for-video; Toho Cinepack; Mikadroid - tr t. Weisser/JC.

"Strange robot" at the scene of "brutal crimes" in 1991 appears to be the product of a World War II "battle android" project. (Mark.) Or, Old RoboSoldiers Never Die. Scorecard: blandly stylish, physically unlikely murder-and-mayhem scenes ... unimpressive android ... okay set and makeup visuals. Each scene takes three times as long as it should.

**MIKEY** Imperial/Tapestry (Abrams-Levy-Zahavi) 1992 (1991) color c95m. D: Dennis Dimster-Denk. SP: Jonathan Glassner. Ph: Tom Jewett. Mus: Tim Truman. PD: N. Clinker, M. Calosio. SpFxMkp: Matt Marich. SpFX: Eddie Surkin. SdFxEd: Steve Burgess. Ref: TV. PT 14:12. TVG. Fango 118:13. V 10/21/91:25(ad): "Chucky was just child's play." (At AFM) With Brian Bonsall (Mikey), Josie Bissett, John Diehl, Lyman Ward, Mimi Craven.

"He's not a normal nine-year-old!" *Stepfather,* Jr., as an adopted little boy slays one family, tapes the killings, moves on to the next family. ("So now we have Ted Bundy, Jr.") Formulaic and unnecessarily bloody. Mikey's favorite movie is *Nightmare on Elm Street.*

**\*MILL OF THE STONE WOMEN** 1960 (*Icon* - alt vt t. aka *Horror of the Stone Women.* aka *The Horrible Mill Women*). Ref: TV: Sinister Cinema; Eng. dubbed. Hardy/HM. Lee. VWB. Lentz. Stanley. no V. Phantom. With Herbert Boehme, Marco Guglielmi.

Outside Amsterdam, a "sadistic mummifier of women" periodically drains the "sick blood" from his daughter and transfuses healthy blood into her from other women; the resultant mummified women become part of his mill-castle's historical display of famous women. In order to obviate the need for the periodic transfusions—his daughter has been "dying and re-living for years"—he plans to employ a serum (developed by his assistant) which prolongs the life of red corpuscles, but .... This is not *Eyes without a Face* or *Vampyr* (both of which films it echoes), but it's not bad. Music and photography make the Holland countryside appear moody and melancholy and make both the interior and exterior of the mill seem oddly eerie. The finale goes the *House of Wax* movies one or two better: The masked, mummified bodies are drawn by the mill gears through fire and melt, as the display music segues into the sounds of a Choir from Hell. And an earlier hallucination sequence evokes a sense of becalmed horror. (A drug "cancels" the "dividing line" between reality and fantasy for the dazed hero.) Ace shock: the daughter's unannounced reappearance after the hero has been insisting that she's dead. (She was, but she isn't now.) The last third or so of the movie, though, is mainly just positioning the heroine in the path of Peril.

**MILLENNIUM** Fox/Gladden Ent. (First Millennium/Leiterman-Vince) 1989 color 108m. D: Michael Anderson. SP: John Varley, from his short story "Air Raid." Mus: Eric N. Robertson. SpVisFX: Light & Motion; (d) Sam Nicholson; (anim sup) David McIlvaney; (min sup) John Jackson. SpProsthMkp: Bob Laden. MechFxSup: David Lemmen. SpFX: Nick Fischer. Robot Chor: Glen Kotyk. Ref: TV. MFB'89:338-9. V 8/23/89. HR 8/28/89. Sacto Union 8/26/89. With Kris Kristofferson, Cheryl Ladd, Daniel J. Travanti, Robert Joy (Sherman), Lloyd Bochner, Maury Chaykin, Lawrence Dane.

"It's something that shouldn't be there!" Travelers from one thousand years in the future practice cautious time travel, go backwards through "gates" to 1963 and 1989 to rescue passengers from airplanes about to crash, replace the rescued with duplicates.... The Rescuers as butterfingers who leave telltale implements ("stunners," "initiators") behind on intercepted death-flights. The people from the future have mastered time travel, but can't manage a simple skyjacking. Still, the plot's mystery elements—wristwatches from wreckage which tick backwards, strange gizmos found in said wreckage—intrigue. The pieces of the science-fiction puzzle, unfortunately, begin falling into place too soon and too eccentrically—these travelers play God oddly—and words like *paradox* and *gate* get to be taken so seriously that they become campy—hokey incantations.

**MINACCIA D'AMORE** see *Dial: Help*

**MIND BENDERS** see *Alien High*

**MIND, BODY & SOUL** AIP (Rick Sloane) 1992 (1991) color 93m. SP, D: R. Sloane. Ph: R. Hayes. Mus: A. Dermarderosian. AD: Mark Richardson. SpFxMkp: Thomas Hansen. Prosth: Gary Young. Ref: TV: AIP HV. no Martin. PT 13:50: "serious (but bad) horror movie" re satanists. With Ginger Lynn Allen, Wings Hauser, Jay Richardson, Tami Bakke, Michael McMillen, Jesse Kaye, Toni Alessandrini, Ken Hill, Mark Richardson (demonic spirit).

"They have powers not known to our world." Ingredients include a "satanic cult" which uses the "power of the dark side" and practices human sacrifice ... a hex which gives two women "haunted visions" re headless corpses, which visions prove to be prophetic ("I had this dream last night") ... a literally deadly pentagram ... an occult priestess' advice demon ... and voodoo-type magic with a knife .... Cross between a crime drama and a fantasy of the occult is curious but dramatically negligible. Most obvious plot ploy: One of the three heroes turns out to be a cult member. This cult is democratic: The members vote on their every move.

**MIND FIELD** (Can.) Allegro Films, FUND for Pay TV, Telefilm Canada, Cinegem Canada, CFCF 12, Image Org., First Choice/Superchannel & Super Ecran (Tom Berry & Franco Battista) 1989 ('90-U.S.) color c90m. (*Mindfield* - ad t & end t). D: Jean-Claude Lord. SP: William Deverell; (collab) Berry, George Mihalka. Ph: Bernard Chentrier. Mus: Milan Kymlicka. PD: Guy Lalande. FxMkp: Michel Bougie. Mech FxCoord: John Walsh. SpFxCoord: Jacques Godbout. Ref: TV: Magnum Ent. video. Maltin '92. V 5/2/90. With Michael Ironside, Lisa Langlois, Christopher Plummer, Stefan Wodoslawsky, Sean McCann.

"I'm going to get my memory back." Dr. Satorious (Plummer) promises a "new, improved you" with his induced-amnesia treatment, while Montreal cop Kellen O'Reilly's (Ironside) "acid flashbacks" suggest that he was an unwitting patient of the doctor. At the end, the baddies plot to erase "one bad day" in the life of the cop who knew too much.... Pretentious, confusing variation on *Manchurian Candidate* themes. The script suggests that Satorius' treatment was used on Lee Harvey Oswald. Poor sound recording doesn't help.

**MIND FUCK** (H.K.?) VSOM 198-? color c90m. Ref: TV: VSOM; Eng. titles.

Hardcore horror re a "release of black magic hexes" features an incidental hopping vampire ("It's a v-v-v-vampire!") ... a rotting-faced woman who dies and returns as a floating ghost that possesses another woman ... and a hunchback. Rudimentary.

**MIND KILLER** Prism Ent. & Flash Features (First Films) 1987 color 86m. (*Brain Creature* - orig t). Story, SP, D: Michael Krueger. SP: also Dave Sipos, Curtis Hannum. Story: also Doug Olson, Ted A. Bohus. Mus: Jeffrey Wood. SpMkp & VisFX: Vincent J. Guastini, Patrick Denver; P. C. Reilly. SpFxSup: Bohus. Brain machine: Ken Walker. Computer Anim: R. Koch, V. Zezala. SpSdFX: L. Patchett, Drake. Ref: TV. V 12/2/87. 4/15/87:40. Morse. Scheuer. Martin. McCarty II. Maltin '92. With Joe McDonald, Christopher Wade, Shirley Ross, Tom Henry.

"You can learn to completely control your environment." Nerdish Warren (McDonald) absorbs the late Dr. Vivac Chandra's (Henry) "Total Mind Control" thesis so well that he has power over minds and machines and can tell the future. When an "electrical conducer" amplifies his powers by "molecular re-alignment with a negative electrical charge," his head turns monstrous and begins leaking blood and goo. After some of the latter lands on his reluctant beloved, Sandy (Ross)—a Trilby role—she works up an *Exorcist* growl, and a feeler thing clings to her neck, then sprouts to become an *Alien* horror.... Not bad for Denver. A very very far-fetched premise yields some simple but quietly imaginative stunts—e.g., Warren's mind drawing a glass's spilling contents back up into the glass. If the movie is mostly derivative, it's also occasionally winning. Wade gives the best performance as a Julius Kelp-like nerd who becomes Buddy Love-slick at the end.

**The MIND'S EYE** Miramar Images 1991 color 40m. D, Co-P: J. C. Nickman. Ref: PT 10:56. TVG 10/19/91: "computer animation odyssey."

"Gleaming dinosaurs, futuristic cities ... an abstract journey through time." (TVG)

**MINDTRAP** AMI (Shrivastava) 1989 color feature. D: E. Demetrios. SP: Jay Sri, Bill Hart. Ref: PT 14:46: "terrible acting and accents." With Dan Haggerty, Lyle Waggoner.

"Mind control room," "zombie-like father."

**MINDWARP** Fangoria Films (Christopher Webster) 1992 color 96m. D: Steve Barnett. SP: Henry Dominic. Mus: Mark Governor. PD: Kim Hix. SpMkpFX: KNB EFX. Ref: V 5/11/92: "modest but competent." PT 10:50. SFChron Dtbk 8/9/92. With Bruce Campbell, Angus Scrimm, Marta Alicia, E. Kent, M. Becker.

Post-nuke In-World features a "dream-weaving network called Infinisynth." Plus: mutants, murder machine.

**MINNIE THE MOOCHER** Para 1932 anim and live 7m. D: Dave Fleischer. Ref: screen. TV. LC. Maltin/OMAM. Sean Smiley. Cabarga/TFS: Talkartoon. With Cab Calloway.

Betty Boop and Bimbo quiver, as ghosts, skeletons, and witches cavort. Top-notch Boop with some ace spook effects.

**MIO CARO ASSASSINO** see *My Dear Killer*

**MIO IN THE LAND OF FARAWAY** or **MIO, MIN MIO** see *Land of Faraway*

**MIRACLE MILE** Hemdale/Miracle Mile Prods. 1988 color 87m. SP, D: Steve De Jarnatt. Mus: Tangerine Dream. SpFxCoord: Robbie Knott. VisFX: (sup) Jena Holman, Marty Sadoff; (anim) Available Light, Jeff Burk. Mkp Des: Gandhi Bob Arrollo. Opt: Howard Anderson et al. Ref: TV: HBO Video. Sacto Bee Encore 12/24/89:6. V 9/7/88. MFB'91:51-2. Scheuer. Maltin '92. Martin. With Anthony Edwards, Mare Winningham, John Agar, Mykel T. Williamson, Lou Hancock, Denise Crosby.

"We're at war—nuclear war!" "Unconfirmed rumors of possible nuclear attack" lead to chaos in Los Angeles and a bit-too-late rendezvous at a helicopter landing site atop the Mutual Benefit Life building for Harry Washello (Edwards) and the love of his life, Julie Peters (Winningham), whom he has just met.... Is it suspense or Tangerine Dream? Everything runs together in a T.D.-scored movie. However, despite the monotonously insistent sound—hip Muzak—certain surprising odd moments stand out in De Jarnatt's film: the Valium-sedated Julie waking up in her rescue vehicle, a shopping cart ... the narrative shift from Well maybe Harry's wrong about the end of the world after all to No he's not here come the missiles ... and his Superman-inspired "coal into diamond" comforting of Julie at the bittersweet end. Overall, the film is certainly an improvement on *Five,* while the love-unto-death ending owes something to *Bonnie and Clyde.* The script is a combination of the incredible and the spookily plausible.

**MIRACLE 90 DAYS** (H.K.) Heat-Power Wells Ltd./Luckfilm Prods. (Sonny Chan, Amy Li) 1992 color/ws 94m. Story, D, P: Siuming Tsui. Ref: TV: World Video; Eng. titles. Y. K. Ho.

"I am a beast." Fantasy with science-fiction overtones rings changes on "Beauty and the Beast" themes. Principals: Yan—the Unicorn Ball plus electricity turn him from a chimp into a human; at the end, a "reverse reaction" to the Unicorn Ball starts turning him back into a chimp, and he now looks like a refugee from the Planet of the Apes ... Wah, who can shoot electricity from his hands and who, at the end, starts a mini-hurricane in a warehouse ... and Wu Tak Chun, a "fox goblin from Lanchiu." Comedy is half just silly; half, mildly funny. Line worth noting (Wah to heroine): "You are the bad egg in the field of supernatural power."

**\*MIRACLES FOR SALE** 1939. AD: also Gabriel Scognamillo. Ref: TV. MPH 8/5/39: "psychic research organization." V 8/16/39. Weldon. Lee(e). no Stanley. no Hardy/HM. no Maltin '92. no Scheuer. PT 14:44.

"A boogeyman committed this murder, huh?" Principals include The Great Morgan (Robert Young) and his Miracles for Sale Company ... author Dr. Sabbat (Frederick Worlock), who is found strangled (did he invoke "some demon out of hell?" does he return as a "horrible face at the window?"—"Sabbat used to say that his soul could leave his body, and people would believe he was dead") ... European mystic Mme. Rapport (Gloria Holden)

who, with her psychic stare, conjures up "Sabbat" at a seance ... Prof. Tauro (Harold Minjir), who is found dead in a demon circle ... Mrs. Zelma La Claire (Astrid Allwyn), telepathist—the "woman with the radio mind" ... Col. Watrous (Walter Kingsford) of the Psychic Assn ... and a "demon," or its voice (John Davidson).

Oddball mystery-horror oldie—Tod Browning's last film—is a pleasant diversion, nothing more. Intriguing demonological trappings, familiar disguises-and-illusions resolution. Holden reprises her daughter-of-Dracula zombie look.

**MIRACULOUS FLOWER** (H.K.) Wu Wu-Fu/Tin-Chu Chang & Tsai-Lai Hsu 1984 color/ws c88m. D: How Fang. Ref: TV: Ocean Shores Video; Eng. dubbed. Weisser/ATC: aka *Phoenix: Wolf Ninja?* With Chang Ling.

This silly but kind of sweet, light kung fu revenge tale turns semi-horrific in the concluding sequence: The evil, semi-super-human Simon Ching—who has the resilience of a contemporary movie monster—battles "born-again Buddhist" Crystal in his hellish cavern of fire. She slices his forehead with her sword and impales him on it, but he plucks it out of his stomach. The blade drags some of his innards outwards, but he keeps jumping about and throwing fireballs at her. He pretends to die, but leaps up again, only to fall into a sea of flames. On fire now, his body flies up out of the flames, then finally falls limp on a rocky ledge.

**MIRAI NINJA** (J) Streamline/Namco/GCC Inc. (Keiji Takagi/M. Nakamura) c1990? color 72m. (aka *Ninja Mirai*). SP, D: Kieta Amamiya. SP, Story: Satoshi Kitahara. SP: also Hajime Tanaka. Ph, SpFX: Kazuo Sagawa. Mus: N. Nakagata, K. Ohta. Ref: TV: Orion HV(Fox Lorber HV); *Cyber Ninja* - U.S.; Eng. dubbed. VW 25:12: *Warlord* - Can.; *Robo Ninja* - B; aka *The Renegade Robo Ninja and Princess Saki.* TV: vt; no Eng. Markalite 3:65: *Future Ninja* - tr t. Animerica 6:14. Weisser/JC.

Among the spectacular effects here: an imposing house which begins, it seems, to disintegrate, but which proves to have been a sort of cocoon for a giant, robot-like weapon ... a Jules Verne-in-Japan-ish flying machine ... and the chief bad person's fingertip phantoms. *Star Wars*-in-feudal-Japan saga features a daunting array of weapons from every time and place, and some from out-of-time, including huge, ray-shooting, half-robot, half-house machines ... hologram/laser, ceiling-based weapons ... a living tree/jail cell ... machine guns ... electric-like swords ... and a computerized android-warrior. The Darth Vader-voiced, partly-*Alien*-inspired human/machine uses one of the tubes from the back of his head as a weapon and can also shoot rays from his face. Fantasy film is alternately great fun and (in the non-effects scenes) rather a drag.

**MIRAKLET I VALBY** (Danish-Swed.) Nordisk Film & the Danish Film Institute/Esselte Ent. & the Swedish Film Institute (Bo Christensen) 1989 color 85m. SP, D: Ake Sandgren. SP: also Stig Larsson. Mus: V. Gulgowski, Roxette. Ref: V 8/30/89: *Miracle in Valby* - tr t; "jerky, insecure storytelling." With Jakob Katz, Troels Asmussen, Lina Englund, Amalie Alstrup.

Medieval warriors kidnap pre-teens from the future.

**MIRROR, MIRROR** SGE/Orphan Eyes (Orphan) 1990 color 104m. Story, D: Marina Sargenti. SP: Annette & Gina Cascone.

Story: also Yuri Zeltser. Mus & P: Jimmy Lifton. PD: Stuart Blatt. SpFxMkp: Chris Biggs; (des) Kirk Karwacki. SpFxSup: Lifton. SpFX: Flash FX; (des) Virginia Perfili. Ref: TV. V 5/30/90. Martin. no Maltin '92. no Scheuer. With Karen Black, Rainbow Harvest, Kristin Dattilo, Ricky Paull Goldin, Yvonne De Carlo, William Sanderson, M. J. King (creature).

"I have kept the evil locked in the mirror ever since that night." The mirror in Megan's (Harvest) room is a "gateway to the other side, allowing demons to enter our world." One demon "uses" her to "punish" her enemies (with nosebleed, heart attack, shower-room steam burn, etc.). Routine *Carrie*/revenge material.

**MIRROR MIRROR 2: RAVEN DANCE** Orphan Film/Innocence Prods. 1994(1993) color c92m. (*Raven Dance* - cr t). SP, D, P, Mus: Jimmy Lifton. SP, Co-P: Virginia Perfili. Ph: Troy Cook. PD: P. Vasels, D. Hughes. VisFX: Digital Magic;(anim) Steven J. Scott. Computer Imagery: Vision Arts. AddlVisFX: Stargate. OptFxSup: David Hewitt. SpMkpFX: Sota FX. SpMechFX: Roger George. Ref: TV. TVG. Vallejo Times-Herald. With Tracy Wells, Roddy McDowall (Dr. Lasky), Sally Kellerman, Lois Nettleton, Veronica Cartwright, William Sanderson, Carlton Beener, Sarah Douglas.

Ingredients include lightning which electrifies a mirror and fries a rock group ... a raven which savages a man when the heroine dances ... a mirror demon ... the mirror itself, which makes Roddy McDowall disappear ... and instant aging (Kellerman's face) .... Dreary, weary supernatural horror, with flat acting and dialogue. There's even a tired toys-to-life scene. Redeeming effects: the slowmo-raven-out-of-the-mirror and the stained-glass-knight-out-of-the-window (though the latter is brazenly stolen from *Young Sherlock Holmes*).

**The MIRROR OF AREI: WAY TO THE VIRGIN SPACE** (J) Tsukuba Science Exposition 1985 anim color 25m. (aka *Way to the Virgin Space*). SP, D: Leiji Matsumoto. Ref: TV: vt; no Eng. J Anim Program Guide. Animag 6:19: made for World Expo '85. Voices: Yoko Agami, Keiko Toda, Hideyuki Tanaka (Zero).

Gatekeeper Arei and energy beings with valentine hearts where their faces should be review mankind's history, beginning with cave men, to determine if the three protagonists (including the android Zero) should enter through the gate to the heavenly universe beyond. Arei, "impressed by their tenacity," grants the three a glimpse.... Too ambitious for its brief length, though pretty and lively enough. Vapid score.

**MIRROR OF DEATH** Vista Street Prods./Feifer-Miller (MMC) 1987 color 85m. (*Dead of Night* - TV). D: Deryn Warren. SP: Gerry Daly. Mus: David Frank. AD: Patti Strong. SpFxMkpCoord: Karen Westerfield. Ref: TV. V 2/24/88:472 (hv): "mere doggerel." Morse. Martin. no Maltin '92. no Scheuer. With Julie Merrill (Sura/Sara), Kuri Browne, John Reno, J. K. Dumont.

"You are becoming possessed by some ugly demon!" Battered woman with inferiority complex uses Haitian magic—the "Power of Candles"—to conjure up spirit which possesses her, commits gory murders. One droll touch: the exorcist (Bob Kip) who arrives by bicycle. Otherwise, the usual possession histrionics.

**MISERY** Col/Castle Rock & Nelson Ent. (Andrew Scheinman, Rob Reiner) 1990. color 107m. D: R. Reiner. SP: William Goldman, from Stephen King's novel. Ph: Barry Sonnenfeld. Mus: Marc Shaiman. PD: Norman Garwood. SpMkpFX: KNB EFX. SpPh: Michele Singer. SpFxSup: Phil Cory. Ref: TV. S&S 5/91:56. V 11/26/90. SJose Mercury News 11/30/90. SFExam 11/30/90. With James Caan, Kathy Bates, Frances Sternhagen, Richard Farnsworth, Lauren Bacall, Graham Jarvis, J. T. Walsh.

"Misery Chastain cannot be dead!" Repressed, unbalanced Annie (Bates)—"number one fan" of author Paul Sheldon (Caan)—holds him captive when he becomes incapacitated in a car crash. Unhappy with the death of the heroine in his latest manuscript, she has him destroy the latter. Maybe too too: In a burst of enthusiasm, she cries "I'm going to put on my Liberace records!" Meanwhile, he discovers that she was a semi-notorious hospital baby-killer. Definitely too too: After "hobbling" his legs with a sledge hammer, she confesses, "God, I love you!" Basically unbelievable, *Baby Jane*-ish sitcom-horror is helped occasionally by the actors.

**MISFITS OF SCIENCE** NBC-TV/Parriott & Univ-TV 1985 color 92m. SP, D: James D. Parriott. Mus: Basil Poledouris. AD: J. D. Jefferies Sr. FX: (vis) Garber/Green; (opt) Univ. Title. Mkp: Darrell McIntyre. Ref: TV. TVG 10/4/85 (ad): "movie premiere." V 10/9/85:94. SFChron 10/4/85. With Dean Paul Martin, Kevin Peter Hall, Courteney Cox, Kenneth Mars, Eric Christmas, Larry Linville, Mickey Jones, Mark Thomas Miller.

Items: cryogenically-frozen "iceman" (Jones) who, revived, freezes whatever he touches, via "contact temperature transference" ... hormone which makes Humanidyne scientist (Hall) shrink ("neurological reflex") ... guy (Miller) who attracts, projects electricity ... lady (Cox) with telekinesis ... levitation ... giant rabbit ... "neutron cannon" ... and a dialogue reference to an invisible man.

The theme: "Weird is okay." The tone: glib. The hook: lotsa effects and stunts. The upshot: [misfit Martin] "I did okay." The catch: "serious" moments with the misfits. (They're misunderstood, in the worst way.)

**MISS MAGIC** (H.K.?) c1988? color c86m. Ref: TV: Rainbow Video; Eng. titles.

The actor Keung's wife, a suicide, returns to possess Jenny, an actress, and sets out to kill the unfaithful Keung. Also on the agenda: hopping, levitating vampires that turn out to be movie actors ... the "technique of Ghostbusting" ... sex with a ghost in a grave ... and a nice ghost—Uncle Fok's niece—who, at one point, appears ugly-faced to scare a guy. Slickly made but uninspired horror-comedy.

**MISS PASSION** Newave (Suze Randall) 1984 color c70m. Ref: TV: Vidco video. Adam '88. With Rachel Ashley, Ginger Lynn, Crystal Breeze, Randall, Lisa De Leeuw.

"From millions of planets all over the galaxy," the winners of the Passion Contest are presented "live from the Pornodome," on the planet of Eros. Numbingly repetitive hardcore sf-comedy. Rachel Ashley Fu, though.

**MISS 21ST CENTURY** Zane 1991? color feature. D: Bud Lee. Ref: Adam '92: futuristic beauty pageant. With Ashlyn Gere, Angela Summers, K. C. Williams, Marc Wallice.

**MISSING LINK** Univ/Kane Int'l. & Guber-Peters-Barris Prods. 1989 (1988) color 92m. SP, D, Ph: David & Carol Hughes. Mus: Mike Trim, Sammy Hurden. SpMkpFX: Rick Baker. Narr: Michael Gambon. Ref: TV: MCA HV. V 7/19/89. Hound. Martin. With Peter-Elliott (man-ape), David Damaseb.

"Africa, one million years ago...." A man-ape—Australopithecus robustus—is driven form his home by man. Too gentle, and irrelevant to the interplay of the deer, zebras, birds, and lions about him, he is the "last of his race," and treks from the hills to the desert and, finally, to the sea.... A momentous tale, no doubt, but the marvelous array of wild animal life is the real story here. Even in the desert, the snakes and lizards star: The other animals' smaller "stories" of survival, play, etc., fascinate in their diversity of physical detail. The man-ape's repertoire is more limited. The closest he gets to the dramatic is to shake his fist at humans, lions, lightning—which of course is the point. The fittest he ain't, and it's a lizard-eat-bug world.

**MR. BOOGEDY** ABC-TV/Disney-TV (Steven North) 1986 color 48m. D: Oz Scott. Tel: Michael Janover. Mus: John Addison. Mkp: Rick Stratton. Ref: TV. TVG. V 4/23/86:42. With Richard Masur, Mimi Kennedy, Benjamin Gregory, David Faustino, John Astin.

*Poltergeist* for children features a Puritan who sold his soul to the devil, a fake mummy momentarily "activated" by a haunted house, and psychokinetic stunts with vacuum cleaners. Masur and Astin have moments, but limp suspense and broad comedy predominate.

Sequel: *Bride of Boogedy.*

**MR. CHRISTMAS DINNER** see *Lucky Stiff*

**MR. DRACULA** see *Mr. Vampire*

**MR. E FROM TAU CETI** R & TV 197-? anim color 65m. Ref: TVFFSB. no Hound.

Year 2010. Re a little man from the "star system nearest our solar system."

**MR. FROST** (F-B) Triumph Releasing (SVS)/Hugo Films & AAA & Selena & OMM (Xavier Gelin) 1990 color 104m. (95m.-U.S.). SP, D: Philippe Setbon. SP: also Brad Lynch. Mus: Steve Levine. SpFX: Georges Demetreau. SpPh: Richard Melloul. Ref: TV. V 5/2/90. Cinef 4/91. ad. SFChron 11/12/90. MFB'90:361. Maltin '92. Martin. Scheuer. With Jeff Goldblum, Alan Bates, Kathy Baker, Jean-Pierre Cassel, Daniel Gelin, Vincent Schiavelli, Henri Serre.

"I am the extreme case. I'm darkness. I'm the Prince." Mr. Frost (Goldblum)—self-styled "seer," nationality and previous whereabouts unknown—proves to be, apparently, the "devil himself." Obligingly, he provides the inspector (Bates) investigating the case of the twenty-four mutilated bodies found on his estate with a videotape of the atrocities. At one point, a dog takes the form of the inspector's late wife and attacks the inspector. At the end,

a psychiatrist (Baker) kills Frost, but the latter seems to possess her....

The laughably simplistic premise: Satan, upset that no one believes in him any more, takes human form and convinces a psychiatrist that he is indeed he. ("I'm reborn—you believed in me.") Goldblum, however, as the devil, is quietly, infuriatingly knowing. ("I move in mysterious ways.") He gets under your skin; his Prince is offhandedly creepy.

**MR. NANNY** New Line (Bob Engelman) 1993 color 84m. SP, D: Michael Gottlieb. SP: also E. Rugoff. Ref: SFChron Dtbk 1/30/94. vc box: "Peacekeeper ray gun." With Hulk Hogan, Sherman Hemsley, Austin Pendleton.

**MR. PETRIFIED FOREST** see *Future Shock*

**MR. POSSESSED** (H.K.) Cosmopolitan Film (Lau Tin Chi) 1988? color c95m. SP, D: Wong Tsing. SP: also Ho Lai Chuen. Ph: Li Hsin Yoh. AD: John Hau. Ref: TV: Rainbow Video; Eng. titles. NST! 4:31: D: Pan Yung-Ee. With Kenny Bee, C. Yu Ling, Chan Pak Choong, Tang Bik Wun, Tau Shu Tsing, Wong Tsing.

One of a trio of fake ghosts becomes possessed for real and sprouts monster teeth and nails and a long "pig tongue." Behind it all: South Seas magician Chang San, a "Yin-man," or ghost, who has cast an "isolation spell" on Riley, son of his enemy: If Riley makes love, he dies. At the end, the ghost, made visible, looks like a double-coneheaded Charles Middleton, that, cut in two, rejoins.... This ectoplasmic apparition is part of a fairly impressive finale ... also involving hellfire, torrents of blood, clutching hands, and an army of tombstones. The comedy which precedes this action-horror finale, however, is pretty piffly.

**MR. TERRIFIC** see *Power Pill, The*

**MR. VAMPIRE** (H.K.) Golden Harvest/Bo Ho Films (Paragon Films) 1985 color 95m. (*Jiangshi Xiansheng*). D: Lau Kun Wai. SP: Wong Ying, Szeto Cheuk Hon. P: Samo Hung. Mus: Anders Nelson. SpFX: Ng Kok Wah. Ref: TV: Rainbow Video; Eng. titles. Horacio Higuchi. V 5/21/86 (rev.):17: aka *Mr. Dracula.* 1/21/87:36: in Tokyo. NST! 4:31: D: Wong Kee Hung. MMarquee 43;5, 6. Martin. Ecran F 71:80. Jones. With Ricky Hui (Man Choi), Moon Lee, Chin S. Ho (Chou), Lam Ching Ying, Pauline Wong (Jade), Yuen Wah, Billy Lau.

Grandpa Yam, unburied, is revealed to be a vampire. His first victim: his son, who also returns as a vampire. Man Choi, another potential victim, grows fangs and long fingernails. Meanwhile (as we learn from a song), the "lady ghost looks for a lover," and finds one in Chou, whom she bites on the neck. At one point, her head and body separate, and her hair sticks out like porcupine quills. The mortuary master's aides, Man Choi and Chou, are now "80% dead," but the lady ghost saves Chou from Man Choi, and Chou saves her from eternal damnation.

Several varieties of monster here: the comical, trying-to-stay-human Man Choi; the lover, Chou; the half-evil, half-lovesick lady ghost, Jade; the horrible Grandpa Yam, who gets more and more gruesome; and the eight, less-monstrous "walking corpses" that appear briefly at beginning and end. *Mr. Vampire,* though more even than *Mr. Vampire II,* the first sequel, lacks the latter's standout sequences. The playing is very broad, but the pace is so hectic that the actors all but get lost anyway. Here, if you hold your nose and don't breathe, the vampire "idles." Breathe though a long tube, and he lashes out harmlessly at the lamp at the other end of the tube. Moving about is one antidote for incipient vampirism. Stops the blood from hardening. Funny prop: the ghost "compass." It points true vampire.

**MR. VAMPIRE II** (H.K.) Golden Harvest/Bo Ho Films (Paragon Films) 1986 color/ws 99m. (*Jiangshi Jiazu: Jiangshi Xiansheng Xuji*). D: B. Chan. SP: Huang Bingyao. Ph: Liu Weiqiang. Mus: Anders Nelson, The Melody Bank. Ref: TV: Rainbow Video; Eng. titles. Horacio Higuchi: D: Ricky Liu [Liu Guanwei]. HRelations 1:36: aka *New Mr. Vampire*. NST! 4:31: D: Sung Kam Shing. MMarquee 43:5, 6, 7. With Yuan Biao, Moon Li, Lam Chen-yin (exorcist).

An archaeological expedition discovers the bodies of three vampires from the Chien Lung era. When paper talismans are removed from their foreheads, the vampires—one a boy, dubbed OK Boy—revive.... An outlandish but fun monster-comedy, with some very funny sequences. As in the original *Mr. Vampire*, the vampires here generally hop, but they can also leap surprising distances, stand bolt upright from a prone position, and slide across floors on their bellies. In the most inventive sequence, one flunky borrows the talisman from Papa Vampire's head and slaps it on Mama Vampire. It stops her onslaught, but Papa revives, and the flunky, always one paper short, puts the talisman back on Papa's forehead. (Papa "freezes" in midfall.) Mama revives.... One talisman proves too small, and Papa Vampire stands idling, half-menacingly, half-ludicrously.

Spectacular stunt: The two adult vampires leap up and burst through the top of a burning truck. They then bounce down the street on the tops of cars. Predictably, OK Boy has the power to activate mechanical toys, and he recreates your favorite moments from *E.T.*

**MR. VAMPIRE PART III** (H.K.) Golden Harvest/Bo Ho Films (Paragon Films) 1987 color c90m. D: Wong Kee Hung. Ref: TV: Rainbow Video; no Eng. M/TVM 3/89:18. FComment 6/88:50, 51. NST! 4:31. Jones. With Richard Ng.

Third in the *Mr. Vampire* series features a super-strong wizard woman who at one point unleashes a horde of biting bats ... a white-slime creature ... two fake vampires who turn out to be real ghosts, invisible to all but their master (Ng) or anyone who wears special lenses ... several real vampires ... and several types of spirit-sucking vacuum cleaners.... Not as funny as Part II, but lively, with some amusing effects, including one in which an Oscar Homolka-browed gent folds up a boy ghost like a tent, and another in which a vampire sees the master as a big bird.

**MR. VAMPIRE SAGA 4** (H.K.) Golden Harvest/Bo Ho Films (Paragon Films) 1988 color c92m. D: Law Lit. Ref: TV: Rainbow Video; no Eng. NST! 4:31.

The class act of Hong Kong vampire movies continues. This entry includes a semi-scary, near-invulnerable hopping vampire-monster and a clever, dumb stunt with a "limbo line" of hopping vampires. (The only way the latter can get under a long, horizontal pipe is to bend over backwards and hop.) In one scene, the vampire master puts a frog in charge and takes a rest, piggyback, on one of his hopping charges. Best prop: the anti-hop glue. Part

4, though, is more silly than funny; noise and movement sub for comedy, and the best moments are reserved for a flying woman in white who turns into a fox monster, and for a tiny stopmo-animated wicker man/voodoo doll whose movements trigger the victim's movements.

See also: *3 Wishes.*

**MR. VAMPIRE 1992** (H.K.) Grand March Movies/Lau Kun Wai Prods. 1992 color/ws 88m. D: Ricky Lau. SP: Lo Wing Keung. PD: Cheung Kai Ling. FX?: Animation Shop. Ref: TV: World Video; Eng. titles. With Rick Hiu, Lam Ching Ying, Sandra Ng, Tsien Siu Ho, Lau Lam Kwong.

"The vampires are coming." The good news: the atmospheric, slowmo sequence with red coach and attendants in forest and lakebed ... the *Hellraiser*-ish, evil Holy Baby from the pregnant woman's womb ... and the tussles between the above possessed woman and the horde of hopping vampires. The bad news: the vomit and urine motifs. Overall, horror-comedy alternates between low grade and middle grade.

**MR. WRONG** see *Dark of the Night*

**MISTERIA** see *Body Puzzle*

**3P MISTERIO EN LAS BERMUDAS** (Mex) Agrasanchez 1978 color c75m. SP, D: Gilberto M. Solares. SP: also Adolfo M. Solares. Story: Rogelio Agrasanchez. Ph: A. M. Solares. Mus: Ernesto Cortazar. Ref: TV. TVG. Horacio Higuchi. With Santo, Blue Demon, Mil Mascaras, Silvia Manriquez, Sandra Duarte, Carlos Suarez.

Death ray (which looks like a Norelco shaver) from beneath the sea makes plane, boat disappear, causes storms, while two gents who appear and disappear at will act as emissaries from some undersea kingdom (Irania?). An atomic-type explosion at the end seems to resolve everything. Tatty-looking silliness features three Mexican wrestlers.

**MIXED UP** (H.K.) 1988? color c84m. D: Henry S. K. Chen. Ref: TV: World Video; no Eng. Jones. NST! 4:31. With Fanny Cheung.

Two zombie yacht-crew members with long knives beset switchboard operators on a holiday cruise. Animated credit-sequence bits also feature hopping vampires and a fanged Frankenstein monster. Silly if lively horror-comedy trifle.

**MO** (H.K.) Shaw 1983 color/ws 98m. (aka *The Boxer's Omen*). D: Chih Hung Kuei. SP: Szeta An. Ref: Hardy/HM: "impressive scenes"; sequel to *Bewitched* (III). Monster! 11/91 (Higuchi): "exciting and compelling." With Fei Gao, Xiaoyin Lin.

Evil spell "banished after a supernatural struggle somewhere in Nepal." (HM) "Filled with ritualistic details of the weirdest order...." (Monster!)

**MO CHUN JIE** see *Holy Virgin Versus the Evil Dead, The*

**MO TAI** see *Devil Fetus*

**MOBILE DEMON KING GRANZORD: THE LAST MAGICAL BATTLE** (J) Takara 1990 anim color 30m. Ref: Animag 11:4: 1 of 2 OAVs.

"Giant superdeformed robot team" saves Earth from the "falling moon."

**MOBILE POLICE PATLABOR** see *Patlabor*

**MOBILE POLICE PATLABOR 2** see *Patlabor 2: The Movie*

**MOBILE SUIT GUNDAM 0080** see *Gundam 0080*

**MOBILE SUIT GUNDAM 0083: REMINISCENCE OF LIGHT** see *Gundam 0083: Reminiscence of Light*

**MOBILESUIT GUNDAM: CHAR'S COUNTERATTACK** (J) Sunrise/Shochiku 1988 anim color/ws 120m. (aka *Char's Counterattack*). Ref: TV: vt; no Eng. Animag 5:12-21, 44-46. 3:24-5.

In this sequel to *Gandamu* (III), the latest mobilesuit is RX-93 Nu Gundam, and the year is 0093 U.C. (Universal Century). The Neo-Jion and allied spacenoids (humans born in space) have begun unleashing asteroids on a suspecting Earth and the Earth Union Government. The action shifts back and forth from Earth to space colonies and ships to the moon, until, at the end, vibrations from the "Psycho-Frame" ("this light of our souls") repel the huge chunk of the devastated asteroid base Axcis headed for Earth....

The action here is so convoluted and involved that you sometimes can't tell the players even with a scorecard. This movie was made for people with quick eyes—the battle scenes are already in fast forward. In the *Parents' Magazine* terminology of yesteryear, *Char's Counterattack* is good of kind, though what kind it is is hard to say. If it doesn't have much depth, it certainly has breadth. Its finest feature: the subtle, varied symphonic score. (Strangely, the end credits inspire some vapid pop music.)

See also: *Gundam* and *S. D. Gundam*.

**MOBILESUIT GUNDAM F91** see *Gundam F91*

**MODEL KILLER, The** see *Hollywood Strangler Meets the Skid Row Slasher, The*

**MOGAO YIZHANG** see *Return of the Demon*

**MOLDIVER: VOL. #1 — METAMORFORCE!** (J) Pioneer/AIC(Morijiri-Yamada-Inoue-Kakoi) 1993 anim color c30m. Concept, Char Des, D: Hiroyuki Kitazume. SP: M. Nakamura, R. Tsukimura. Ph: K. Konishi. Mus: Kei Wakakusa. AD: M. Nishikawa. SdFX: Anime Sound. Ref: TV: Pioneer video; Eng. dubbed; '94-U.S.

Names here include Zamtech, Terror Mecha (and its sludge rays), Captain Tokyo (our hero's superhero moniker), Machinegal, and Moldiver (our heroine's superheroine moniker). Alarmingly perky, fast-paced apparent OAV is the first of a series of at least three.

**MOM** Epic Prods. (C. Elwes, E. Sarlui/L. Dudevoir) 1991 (1989) color 95m. Story, Sp, Ed, D: Patrick Rand. Story: also Kevin Watson. Mus: Ernest Troost. SpMkpFX: Makeup & Monsters/Brian Penikas & Assoc. SpFxCoord: Players SpFX. Opt: Mercer, OptFX. Ref: TV. V 7/15/91. Martin. With Mark Thomas Miller, Jeanne Bates (Emily Dwyer), Brion James (Nestor Duvalier), Mary McDonough, Art Evans, Stella Stevens, Claudia Christian.

"I'm still your mother." After Nestor, the new boarder—in reality, a flesh-eating monster with a "heightened sense of hearing"—attacks Emily Dwyer, she too transforms, when hungry, into a "flesh eater"—"vampire, werewolf, ghoul—it's all the same".... Oddly bland despite clear opportunities for gruesome charm, *Mom* gets stuck in a limbo between comedy and weird-problem drama, as Miller proves a rather too dour foil, comic or horrific. Scenes and situations recall various versions of *The Wolf Man*, *Little Shop of Horrors*, and *Cat People*. Not dishonorable, just miscalculated.

**MOM AND DAD SAVE THE WORLD** WB/HBO & Cinema Plus & Mercury/Douglas Films (Michael Phillips) 1992 color 88m. D: Greg Beeman. SP: Chris Matheson, Ed Solomon. Mus: Jerry Goldsmith. PD: Craig Stearns. Creature FX: Alterian Studios; Tony Gardner. SpVisFX: PMP; (coord) M. Muscal. Ref: V 7/27/92: "silly sci-fi comedy." Cinef 12/92:61: "dull, crass." ad. SFChron 7/25/92: "the same joke over and over again." With Teri Garr, Jeffrey Jones, Jon Lovitz, Thalmus Rasulala, Wallace Shawn, Eric Idle, Kathy Ireland.

Earth couple zapped "across the galaxy to Spango." (SFC)

**La MOMIA NACIONAL** (Sp) Frade 1981 color/ws 87m. (*The National Mummy* -vt t). SP, D: Jose Ramon Larraz. SP: also Juan Alonso Millan. Ph: R. Perez Cubero. Ref: Hardy/HM: mummy, vampire; "frenetically conducted mixture of farce, horror, and sex." Ecran F 44:36. VSOM. With Paco Algora, Azucena Hernandez, Quique Camoiras.

**Las MOMIAS DE SAN ANGEL** (Mex) Agrasanchez 197-? color c85m. (*Terror en San Angel* - ad t). SP, D: Arturo Martinez. Story: Rogelio Agrasanchez. Ph: Antonio Ruiz. Mus: Bernardo Serrano. Mkp: Antonio Castanedo. Ref: TV: Variedades video; no Eng. VSOM: *Mummies of San Angel* - vt. With Rogelio Guerra, Alicia Encinas, Mil Mascaras, Lorena Velazquez, El Fantasma Blanco, Enmascarado Negro.

A young couple opens the door to the dining room in an old house and views scenes from several hundred years ago, scenes which perhaps explain the cackling hunchback and his mummy hordes which now haunt the place. In the climactic sequence, the ghosts kill the bad guys holed up there, then take a midnight stroll through town. One mummy touches the top of a car and electrically turns the couple therein into instant skeletons.... Unsophisticated mixture of monsters and wrestlers. The climactic midnight melee—torch-wielding villagers and wrestlers take on the mummies—is at least lively, and the dining-room visions are an unusual touch.

**MONDO CANNIBALE** see *Man Hunter*

**MONDO MONTREAL** see *Montreal Interdit*

**El MONJE LOCO** (Mex) J. L. Videograbaciones & Julio Aldama 1986 color 76m. D: Aldama. SP: Rafael Portillo, Roberto G. Rivera. Ref: TV: Film-Mex video; no Eng. With Aldama, Julio Augurio, Luz Maria Rico, Queta Lavat, Paco Pharrez.

"El Monje Loco" is your host for two atrocious, shot-on-tape tales, the first of which bears his name and concerns a monk who has visions of Death and of the woman he accidentally kills. (She then seems to come back to life.) "El Talisman Maldito" is really "The Monkey's Paw": A man wishes his son back to life, but revokes his wish when he sees his son's messed-up face (very poor makeup job). The "mad monk"'s cackling is more annoying than frightening. His "blind" right eye is a glued-on half-eggshell or ping pong ball.

**MONKEY, The** see *Devil's Gift, The*

**MONKEY BOY** see *Chimera*

**MONKEY SHINES** Orion/Charles Evans 1988 color 115m. (aka *Monkey Shines: An Experiment in Fear*). SP, D: George A. Romero, from Michael Stewart's novel. Mus: David Shire. SpMkpFX: Tom Savini. SpVisFX: Garber/Green. SpFX: Steve Kirshoff. Sp Animal Voices: Frank Welker. SdFX: Weddington. Ref: TV: Orion HV. V 7/27/88. SFChron 7/29/88. SFExam 7/29/88. MFB'90:45-6. Hardy/HM2: aka ELLA. With Jason Beghe, John Pankow, Kate McNeil, Joyce Van Patten, Christine Forrest, Boo.

"He had his little demon do it for him!" Scientist Geoff Fisher (Pankow) gives his quadriplegic friend Allan Mann (Beghe) a capuchin for a companion, but does not tell him that the monkey, Ella (Boo), has been injected with very stimulating human memory cells. ("She's like a miniature person.") The initially affectionate Ella begins to pick up on Allan's hostility and kills "for" him. Geoff, attempting a similar bond with the monkey, injects himself with his own serum and dreams—as Allan had, too—that he is in Ella's body. But Allan's anger (this time directed towards his mother) again takes over.

Over-elaborate, over-detailed revenge tale is less an amusing than an exhausting venture into perverse psychology, human and simian. Complete with The Savage Vs. The Civilized Man cliches, the cliche of the afflicted person shedding his/her affliction at the climactic moment, and a happy ending, the latter the most perverse move of all for George Romero. Entertaining performances by Pankow and Boo.

**MONKEY WAR** (H.K.) Rei-Men Prods. (Lin Ch-Fong) 1982 color/ws c90m. D: Chen Chun-Liang. SP: Yao Chin-Kang. Ref: TV: Rainbow Video; no Eng. NST! 4:9, 31. Fango 107:59.

Huge spiders transform into sorceresses that shoot web-rays which tie up their enemies. Our monkey-king hero melts their webs and laughs, though a super-web temporarily traps him. At the end of this section of the movie, a spider woman rides a gigantic, smoke-breathing spider, but fire-breathing hero wins out. And on the same program: flying bat people, two of whom wholly transform into big bats ... flying, tumbling monkey-men ... and a sky god which turns into a rain-spewing dragon.... Very silly, very tacky, very lively fantasy, with an abundance of effects. The amusingly phony-looking spider props have big red, supposedly-sinister-looking eyes.

**MONKEY'S PAW, The** see *Ghost Stories* (1986). *Monje Loco, El.*

**MONKS OF BLOOD** see *Maldicion del Monasterio*

**MONOLITH** EGM Film Int'l. (Griffiths-Eyres/Tucker & Flynn) 1993 color 95m. (*Tucker and Flynn* - shooting t). D: John Eyres. SP: Stephen Lister. Addl Dial: Eric Poppen. Ph: Alan M. Trow. Mus: Frank Becker. SpVisFX: Introvision; (sup) John Mesa. SpFX: Ultimate FX. SpFxMkp: Rene Dashiell. ProsthMkpFxDes: Howard Berger, KNB FX. PD: Mark Harris. Opt&AnimFX: Available Light. Ref: TV. SFChron Dtbk 2/6/94 & 2/20/94. V 6/28/93: "high-voltage sci-fi actioner saddled with low-voltage dialogue." With Bill Paxton, Lindsay Frost, John Hurt, Louis Gossett, Jr.

Alien "hopping from human to human...." (V) "I saw a flame ball shoot out of that guy's head ...." After a "millennium of sleep, it has awakened"—"it" is a "form of life so advanced it has no physical body. A living parasite that requires intelligent technological beings as hosts to feed off and to build for it." Trite story, banal characterizations.

*****MONSTER A-GO GO** Majestic Int'l. 1965 b&w 68m. (*Terror at Halfday* - orig t). SP, D, P: Bill Rebane. Addl Dial, D, PD: Herschell Gordon Lewis (aka Sheldon Seymour or Seymour Sheldon). SP: also Jeff Smith, D. Stanford. Ph: Frank Pfeiffer. Mus: The Other Three. Mkp: Lillian Toth. Ref: TV: United Ent. HV. Weldon. Lee. Stanley. Lentz. Scheuer. Martin. Phantom. TVG. With Henry Hite (monster), Rork Stevens, Peter Thompson, Robert Simons, Barry Hopkins.

"We have a radioactive something-or-other, ten feet tall, four hundred pounds." The radioactive "monster" seems to be Frank Douglas, an astronaut who returned to Earth on a space capsule and whose "radiation repellent" failed. The creature "gets progressively worse" and leaves one victim "shriveled up like a dried prune"—"cooked to death." It disappears, finally, in a sewer tunnel in Chicago, and Frank Douglas is found thousands of miles away. "Then who, or what, has landed here? Is it here yet? Or has the cosmic switch been pulled?"

Static, deadly "Z" ends with an outrageous cop-out and palms it off as a cosmic mystery. Something has been pulled, but it's not a cosmic switch.

**MONSTER CITY** (J) Japan Home Video 1987 ('93-U.S.) anim color 82m. (*Yoju Toshi. Wicked City* - U.S. aka *Beast City*). D: Yoshiaki Kawajiri. Ref: TV: JHV laserdisc, vt; songs in Eng.; OAV. Animation (Summer '92). Red Vic Theatre notes 10/6/93: "the Black World, a parallel dimension." SFChron Dtbk 10/3/93. Animag 4:47.

Grisly ingredients include a spider-woman monster responsible for a Holland Tunnel of spider webs ... a meltaway female monster that tries to absorb a funny, gnarled, little dirty old man ... a foul serpent creature ... a monster-man with a super-suction mouth ... and monster-men whose torsos sprout jaw-like ribs and tentacles.

Garish, outrageous *Xtro* and *Alien* stunts with mutating monsters—special emphases on snakes, spiders, voracious vaginas, and goo. The theme might seem to be Dangerous Sex, but the latter is also exciting. *Monster City* is not a tract. It's pure Grand Guignol. Highlights: the creeping, bog-like shadow of the monster-chief ... the spastic rat-tat-tat, on the ground, of the dying spider woman's legs. Fast-paced, and featuring an alarming variety of loathsome/fascinating creatures.

Follow-up: *Demon City Shinjuku*? See also: *Wicked City, The.*

**MONSTER DESPERATE FIGHT—DAIGORO VS. GOLIATH** (J) 1972. Ref: CM 14:48: "Daigoro, the monster that [...] orphaned."

**MONSTER DOG** (Sp-I) TWE/Continental (The Sarluis/Carl[...] Aured) 1984 (1986) color 84m. (aka *Leviatan*). SP, D: Cly[...] Anderson (aka Claudio Fragasso). Mus: Grupo Dichotom[...] SpFX: Carlo De Marchis. Ref: V 8/20/86: "surprisingly tame[...] Morse: "cheap, stupid." Hardy/HM2: U.S.-Sp Production; sty[...] less. Palmerini: aka *Il Signore dei Cani*.With Alice Coop[...] Victoria Vera, Carlos Sanurio, E. Linder.

Werewolf at work in a small town? Or are they wild dogs? [...] both?

*****MONSTER FROM GREEN HELL** Gross-Krasne 1958 (195[...] SP: L. Vittes, E. Bohem. Mus: Albert Glasser. PD: Ernst Fe[...] Stopmo: Gene Warren. SpPhFX: also (uncred.) Irving Blo[...] Mkp: Louis Haszillo. Ref: TV: vt. Warren/KWTS!: tinted [...] Lee. Lentz. Weldon. Hardy/SF. no V. Hound. Phantom. Ma[...] '92. Martin. Scheuer. Fango 123:17.

"Africa is a crazy place." After an experimental rocket fall[...] Africa, some gigantic buzzing thing makes stock-footage [...] mals flee in terror. The "footmarks of a monster" are fou[...] as later are giant "wasp markings." And a "wasp tissue" sting[...] found in the arm of a human victim. Forty hours' exposu[...] "cosmic radiation" on board that rocket, it seems, turned s[...] wasps into giants.

Sub-*Tarantula* monster effects, inexcusably poor double-e[...] sure lava effects, pointless narration (by hero Jim Davis), [...] son Caverns, and much time-consuming trekking. The was[...] stolid constructions, more cute than scary. But the mo[...] have an actual highlight: the appearance of the big (sto[...] snake, which makes the mistake of attacking a wasp-creat[...]

**MONSTER HIGH** RCA-Col HV/Eric Bernt 1990 (1988) [...] 83m. D: Ruediger Poe. SP: Ray Langsdon, John Platt. [...] 2/28/90:34 (hv): "cliched." Scheuer: "monster low." McC[...] "cheerfully dumb." With Dean Iandoli, Diana Frank, [...] Marriott, Sean Haines.

"Mr. Armageddon from Outer Space ... doomsday de[...] various monsters." (V)

**MONSTER IN THE CLOSET** Troma (Closet Prods.) [...] (1983) color 87m. Story, SP, D: Bob Dahlin. Story: also Peter Bergquist. Mus: Barrie Guard. Monster: (des) William Stout; (crew sup) Doug Beswick; (voice) Tony Carlin; (sd fx des) Rich Macar. PD: Lynda Cohen. SpMkp: Ron Figuly. SpFxSup: Martin Becker. SpThanks: FJA et al. Ref: TV. V 5/21/86. Phantom. Maltin '92. Martin. Morse. Scheuer. With Donald Grant, Denise DuBarry, Claude Akins, Howard Duff, Henry Gibson, Paul Dooley, Stella Stevens, John Carradine, Jesse White, Kevin Peter Hall (monster).

"It came out of the closet" in Chestnut Hills, California. Is it "some kind of a giant snake"? Naw, it's a closet-haunting thing, possibly from another world, and it and the rest of the cast run through various scenes half-heartedly parodying *War of the Worlds, The Thing from Another World, King Kong, Alien,* and [...] You know something is wrong when Commander USA [...] than the movie, and you're fifteen minutes ahead of the [...] monster suit, though, is pretty good, half-horrific and [...]: Carradine's guest stint is funny ("Here, doggie, [...], and the scene entitled "The Shower" features some [...] play with false alarms.

**MONSTER OF CAMP SUNSHINE, OR, HOW I [...]ED TO STOP WORRYING AND LOVE NATURE** [...] Weird Video/Gene Kearney 1993 (1964) b&w 68m. [...] SP, D: F. Leroget. Ph, Ed: "Motley Crue." Ref: TV: S. W. [...]pecial edition." PT 16:13. With Harrison Pebbles, De-[...]ray, Sally Parfait, Ron Cheney, Jr., Angela Evans, James [...]

[...]er's a monster! It was some chemicals in the water." [...]ntal hormones and "vicious substances" bring out the [...]nstinct" of slow-witted Camp Sunshine attendant Hugo. [...]nster—in a nudist camp?") He runs amok with an ax.... [...]ery spare makeup job distinguishes "normal" Hugo from [...]er" Hugo. The accent is on "cheap" in this long-lost, [...]y unedited, and apparently unfinished monster movie.

**MONSTER RAPIST LIVES INSIDE ME** see *Call Me Tonight*

**MONSTER SHARK** see *Devil Fish*

**MONSTER SQUAD** Tri-Star/Taft-Barish & HBO (Peter [...]s) 1987 color/ws 83m. SP, D: Fred Dekker. SP: also [...] Black. Mus: Bruce Broughton. Monsters: Stan Winston. [...] Boss Film; (p) Richard Edlund. SpFxCoord: Phil Cory. [...] Zoltan & Katalin Elek. Ref: TV. MFB'88:205. V 8/12/87. [...]antom. Maltin '92. Scheuer. Martin. McCarty II. Morse. [...] Stan Shaw, Andre Gower, Robby Kiger, Stephen Macht, [...]an Regehr (Count Dracula), Tom Noonan (Frankenstein's [...]er), Leonardo Cimino (scary German), Lisa Fuller, Carl [...]ault (Wolfman), Tom Woodruff Jr. (Gill-Man), Michael [...]Kay (mummy), Jack Gwillim (Dr. Van Helsing), Charly [...]gan (vampire bride).

[...]ula, with the aid of the mummy, the Gill-Man, and the [...]man, revives the Frankenstein monster. The latter turns out [...] a good guy; the Wolfman, a good-bad guy; and Dracula, the [...]Man, and the mummy just plain bad guys. Bonus goodies: [...] vampire women, a "hole into limbo," and *Ground Hog Day,* [...], a slasher flick.... In its mixture of young monster-movie [...] and monsters, *Monster Squad* is similar to *Deadly Spawn,* [...] not as clever. The idea of pitting smart-ass kids against classic movie monsters yields occasionally amusing moments, but the new-fangled "bubbling" transformation effects for the Wolfman seem out of place in the old-fangled story.

**The MONSTER'S CHRISTMAS** (N.Z.) Showtime-TV/Dave Gibson & Nat'l. Film Unit & TV New Zealand 1981 color 48m. D: Yvonne Mackay. SP: Burton Silver. Ph: Peter James. Mus: Dave Fraser. AD: Gaylene Preston. SpFX: Tony Rabbit. SpDes:

Janet Williamson. Mkp: Patricia Cohen. Ref: TV. TVG: listed as movie. no Scheuer. no Maltin '92. With Lucy McGrath, Leone Hatherly (witch), Paul Farrell (mountain monster), Michael Wilson (bat-mole creature, Nasty); Ingrid Prossor, Roger Page (mud monster); Bernard Kearns, Jeremy Stevens (monster voices).

Nonsense-for-children is a tad slow, but generally agreeable "Sesame Street" stuff. One monster looks like an artichoke, or leftovers from *Battle beyond the Sun*. All monsters here like to eat pictures and drawings of flowers, and all express themselves in funny growls and grunts. (The witch took away their voices.) McGrath as the little girl has an effortlessly expressive face and voice and seems right at home with the weird creatures. At one point, she disguises herself as a monster and is given lessons in ferociousness.

**MONSTRUM Z GALAXIE ARCANA** (Cz-Yugos.) Barrandov, Praga & Zagreb Film 198-? color 7m.? Story, SP, D: Dusan Vukotic. Story, SP: also Milos Macourek. Ph: Jiri Macak. Mus: Tomislav Simovic. AD: Jiri Hlupy. Mkp: Jan Svankmajer. Ref: Ceskoslovensky Filmexport flyer. PFA. no Lee. With Zarko Potocnjak, Lucie Zulova, Petr Drozda (Mumu).

Toy monster Mumu comes to life.

**MONTREAL INTERDIT** (Can.) Memphis (Jean George) 1991 color 90m. (aka *Mondo Montreal*). D: Vincent Ciambrone. SP: Brenda Newman. Mus: Bat Taylor. Ref: V 6/17/91: "thoroughly absurd ... Pathetic E. T. lookalikes "prove" that extraterrestrials 'arrive in flying saucers on the south shore of Montreal. It's a daily event'...."

**MOON 44** (G) Moviestore/Centropolis (Scording) 1990 (1989) color/ws 99m. Story, D, P: Roland Emmerich. Story, SP, P: Dean Heyde. Story, SP: Oliver Eberle. Story: also P. J. Mitchell. Mus: Joel Goldsmith. SpVisFX: (sup & fx anim) Volker Engel; (d) R. G. Brown. Mkp: Suleika Ulmen, Delia Mundelein. Computer Anim: Holger Neuhauser et al. Min: Panasensor Filmeffekt, GMBH. Ref: TV. V 2/11/91:112 (hv). TVG 1/26/91. With Michael Pare, Lisa Eichhorn, Malcolm McDowell, Brian Thompson, Dean Devlin, Stephen Geoffreys, Leon Rippy, Roscoe Lee Browne.

Ingredients in this English-language sf-er: Moon 44, the "most important mining operation in the galaxy," in the year 2038 ... multinational corporations such as Galactic Mining ... hijacked space shuttles ... computer-controlled copters ... pilot-vs.-navigator tensions ... pleasant if hardly state-of-the-art *Star Wars/2001/Blade Runner*-like effects and design ... and elementary drama and intrigue, in a dismayingly naive script. That's-what-you-think line: "We didn't come here to die!"

**MOON IN SCORPIO** TWE/Alan Amiel & Fred Olen Ray 1987 color 87m. Ph & D: Gary Graver. SP: R. Aiken. Mus: Robert Ragland. Mkp: Nina Kraft; (fx) Jon McCallum. Ref: TV. V 2/24/88. 5/20/87:9. With Britt Ekland, John Phillip Law, William Smith, Louis van Bergen, April Wayne, Robert Quarry (Dr. Khorda).

"Somebody was killing us, one by one!" An "evil curse" hangs over the yacht *Priority*, a "drifting death ship." Is a Vietnamese spell behind the deaths by various spike-and-slash weapons?

Choppy, pointless story, inane dialogue, awkward narration. ("Mark was dead now, just like Claire!")

**MOON LEGEND** (H.K.) Grand March Movies 1991 color/ws 91m. (aka *A Chinese Legend*). D: Peter Mak. Ref: TV: Tai Seng Video; no Eng. Jones: "great special fx." Weisser/ATC2: "incredible photography." With Joey Wang, Jacky Cheung, Cheung Man, Wu Ma.

A swordsman dreams of a beautiful vampire, Moon-Cher, who drinks her victims' blood through a straw and who can turn into a fox. Also on the bill: an exorcism, a snaky green (cartoon) demon, and other assorted demon-types.... This looks like a pretty vapid, if handsome exercise in Melancholic Romanticism, with some hokey-lyrical slowmo and lively action-and-fantasy scenes. Visual highlights: the rolling stone-wall "weapon" ... the Racing before the Eclipse effect ... and the cut-in-half ninja who becomes two ninjas.

**MOON RAINBOW** (Russ) Sovexportfilm/Mosfilm & The First Creative Union 1984(1983/'86-U.S.) color 112m. (88m.-U.S.) (*Lunnaya Raduga*). SP, D: Andrei Ermach. SP: also V. Ejov. From Sergei Pavlov's novel. Ph: N. Ardachnikov. Mus: E. Artemev. PD: V. Aronin. SpFX: (ph) B. Travkin; (sets) W. Chikmarev. Mkp: I. Pierminova. Ref: TV: Burbank Video; Eng. dubbed. V 8/15/84. TVG. no Hound. no Martin. Ecran F 49:70. With Vladimir Yostukhin, Igor Stariguin, Natalia Sayko, Vassili Livanov, Yuri Solomin.

"We're different." Ingredients here include possibly-alien-altered, 21st-century ex-cosmonauts who have undergone a "metamorphosis of man's natural abilities" ... a mysterious "stowaway" on the second Lunar Rainbow mission to the moons of Uranus—to one witness, he looks like one of the cosmonauts who died on the first mission ... the electricity-encircled Plateau of the Fiery Serpents on Mercury ... and a wooden stick which acts as a TV receiver.

Not much to the English-language version of this Russian science-fiction film. Awkwardly incorporated flashbacks, okay effects for the lightning-fields sequence on Mercury. In a blown, potentially eerie sequence, the widow of a cosmonaut momentarily "sees" the hero, David, first, as her dead husband, then as David again—as if the writers did not trust us to know that the two were one.

**MOON TRILOGY** see *Srebrnym Globie, Na*

**MOONBIRD** see *Cosmic Eye, The*

**\*\*MOONLIGHT MURDER** MGM (Lucien Hubbard & Ned Marin) 1936 66m. D: Edwin L. Marin. Adap: F. Ryerson, E.A. Woolf. Story: A.J. Cohen, R.T. Shannon. Ref: TV. V 4/1/36.

Among this generally mundane, predictable mystery's more bizarre ingredients: a swami (Pedro de Cordoba) who tells an opera star (Leo Carrillo), "Evil forces are gathering.... It is too horrible! If you sing tomorrow night, you will die!" ... a voodoo-doll "curse" ... a madman on the loose ... a second skulker ... and a glass bubble which, shattered by voice vibrations, releases a poison gas. Plus: an offbeat-for-the-time, mercy-killing revelation.

**MOONRISE** see *My Grandpa Is a Vampire*

**MOONSHOT** see *Countdown*

**MOONTRAP** SGE/Magic Films (John Cameron) 1989 (1988) color 90m. D, P: Robert Dyke. SP: Tex Ragsdale. Mus & SpSdFxDes: Joseph LoDuca. SpVisFX: Acme SpFX; (sup) Gary Jones; (coord) Dean Jones; (min sup) David Wough. Motion Control PhFxSup: Richard Jacobson. OptFX: Elegant Motion. Digital SdFX: Audio Visions. Ref: TV. V 12/27/89. 10/19/88:114, 185. Cinef 1/90. 3/90. Maltin '92. Martin. With Walter Koenig, Bruce Campbell, Leigh Lombardi.

The discovery of (a) the 14,000-year-old corpse of an "ancient astronaut" and (b) a football-sized, living, mostly metal probe from the moon leads to a new NASA mission. The first of some "zombie robot things"—which use scrap and human body parts to become full-fledged robots—is reduced to a "Frankenstein junk pile," but a whole "invasion force" of evil aliens is found in a ship under construction on the moon, where a good alien, Mera (Lombardi), is also found.

Action/fx-happy space opera itself incorporates spare parts from *Alien* and *Meat*. Most of the effects and miniatures, though, are good enough to support the movie's numerous "awe" and "horror" scenes. The aliens' neatest trick: their initial, surprising jack-in-the-box appearances out of the moonsand.

**MOONWALKER** CBS Music Video/Ultimate Prods. 1988 color 93m. D: Colin Chilvers. SP: David Newman. Story: Michael Jackson. SpVisFX: Dream Quest Images; (sup) Hoyt Yeatman. SpMkp: (fx) Lance Anderson; (transformation) Rick Baker, Matt Rose. Robots: (articulation) All FX; (transformation) Cinnabar, (sup) Michael Kroschel. SpFX: Filmtrix; (sup) Kevin Pike. Ref: TV. MFB'89:20-21. V 12/28/88. SFChron 1/11/89.

In the "Smooth Criminal" sequence, Michael (Jackson), cornered, becomes a futuristic car and, later, a huge robot complete with protective shield, rockets, and rays. Still later, he transforms into a space jet, then into a fireworks-display-like celestial body. Meanwhile, Mr. Big (Joe Pesci) trains his own ray machine on Michael. "Leave Me Alone" features a *Fabulous World of Jules Verne*-like mixture of effects techniques and styles, as Michael dances with the Elephant Man's skeleton, then, Kong-like, breaks loose at a carnival. In "Speed Demon," an MJJ Studio director turns briefly monster-faced.... Lively, elaborate Jackson vehicle majors in seemingly Melies-inspired transformations. There's even a shadow transformation, as the future car reverts to Michael's human guise.

**MORBUS** (Sp) PCTSC 1982 color/ws 90m. (aka *Morbus, O Que Aproveche*). D, P: I. P. Ferre Serra. SP: Isabel Coixet. Ph: R. Riba. Mus: Albert Moraleda. AD: A. Ibanez FX?: Guillen Ramos. Mkp: Joana Marti. TV: MV; no Eng.; "Morbus, O Bon Profit." Hardy/HM: "nothing more than a macabre joke." With Joan Borras, Carla Day, Mon Ferre, Victor Israel.

Serum-produced zombies, satanists, and monsters turn out to be practical jokes or hallucinations. (HM) It's shambling zombies vs. nude satanists, and more girlie show than horror show. The zombies are almost an afterthought. Film is a limp frittering-away of a promising title.

**MORE NEEDFUL THINGS** see *Needful Things*

**MORELLA** see *Haunting of Morella, The*

**MORGEN GRAUEN** see *Time Troopers*

**MORIRAI A MEZZANOTTE** see *Carrol Morira a Mezzanotte*

**MORNING STAR** (Russ.) Artkino/Lenfilm-Frunze 1960('62-U.S.) color 75m. (*Cholpon*). SP, D: R. Tikhomirov. SP: also I. Menaker et al., from "Cholpon-Utrennyaya Zvezda," a ballet (based on legend) by M.R. Raukhverger et al. Ph: A. Dudko. AD: A. Blek. SpFX: A. Zavyalov et al. Ref: AFI. Lee. With Reina Chokoyeva, B. Beyshenaliyeva (sorceress).

Sorceress' kiss turns men to stone.

**MORNING TERROR** see *Time Troopers*

**MORONS FROM OUTER SPACE** (B) Univ/Thorn EMI (Barry Hanson) 1985 color 97m. (86m.-U.S.). D: Mike Hodges. SP: Griff Rhys Jones, Mel Smith. Mus: Peter Brewis. VisFxSup: David Speed. SpFX: Jeff Luff; (computer) I.C. Coleman. Ref: TV. MFB'85:86-7. SFExam 11/1/85. ad. V 4/3/85. Martin. Stanley. Maltin '92. Scheuer. Hound. Phantom. Morse. With Smith (Bernard), Griff Rhys Jones (Graham Sweetley), Joanne Pearce (Sandra), Jimmy Nail, James B. Sikking, Dinsdale Landen, Shane Rimmer.

Morons from Blob, a planet fourteen million light years from Earth, land on same. In a nod to *Close Encounters of the Third Kind,* Prof. Trousseaux (Andre Maranne) tries to communicate with them by playing "Born Free" on the organ. And, in an amusing first encounter with government authorities expecting "menacing" or perhaps "intelligent" aliens, the latter emerge from their spaceship in nighties and pajamas.... *Morons* has a promising Monty Python premise and a good silly payoff, but it's generally unfocused. Desmond (Nail) is both the most moronic of the four aliens and the funniest.

**MORPHEUS MIKE** Edison 1917? stopmo anim short. Anim: Willis O'Brien. Ref: Lee. no LC.

Opium dream of prehistory.

**MORT UN DIMANCHE DE PLUIE** (F-Swiss) Incite & Soprofilms & FR3 Films & Slotint & Radio TV Suisse Romande & CNdC (Yves Perrot) 1986 color 109m. SP, D, Exec Co-P: Joel Santoni. SP: Philippe Setbon, from Joan Aiken's novel *Died on a Rainy Sunday* (also the film's tr t). Mus: V. Cosma. SpFX: Coyotte. Mkp: Joel Lavau. Ref: V 11/26/86: "crudely effective." Ecran F 73:6. With Nicole Garcia, Jean-Pierre Bacri, Jean-Pierre Bisson.

"Psycho thriller" with an "horrific climax" involving a cleaver and a shotgun.

**MORTUARY ACADEMY** Taurus Ent./Landmark Films (Winfrey-Miller) 1988 (1992) color 85m. D: Michael Schroeder. SP: William Kelman. Ph: R. H. Wagner. Mus: David Spear. PD: Jon Rothschild. Ref: V 5/25/88: "genuinely amusing feature ... a lot of laughs from black humor involving necrophilia." Martin:

"typical." With Paul Bartel, Mary Woronov, Perry Lang, Tracey Walter, Christopher Atkins, Wolfman Jack, Cesar Romero.

**MORTUARY BLUES** (H.K.) Golden Harvest Home Ent./Paragon Films (Yuen Kwai) 1990 color 92m. SP, D: Jeff Lau. Ref: TV: Pan-Asia Video; no Eng.

Included: two moon-activated ghost types and two zombie-types (the goo-faced head zombie ingests moon rays at one point) and some underwater terror, as an inactive zombie revives. Some atmosphere, but the actors' ideas of comedy tend towards the frantic. The moon-activation gimmick makes for some funny start-stop action on partly cloudy nights.

**MOSQUITO** Acme & Excalibur & Antibes (Skeeters Ltd./Dave Thiry, Eric Pascarelli) 1994 color 92m. (aka *Blood Fever. Nightswarm*). Story, SP, D: Gary Jones. SP: also Steve Hodge, Tom Chaney. Ph: T. Chaney. Mus: A. & R. Lynch. PD: J. Ginyard. VisFxSup: Richard Jacobson. SpMkp & Min FX: Acme FX. Stopmo: Animasaur. AnimFX: Tom Hitchcock. Ref: TV: Hemdale HV. PT 21:14: "one of the most enjoyable horror movies in recent memory." With Rachel Loiselle, Tim Lovelace, Steve Dixon, Gunnar Hansen, Ron Asheton, Josh Becker.

"The skeeters are gettin' bad." A mosquito sucks a dead alien's blood and gets big. Soon, hordes of giant mosquitoes begin sucking people "dry of blood".... Vacant sf-horror features clumsy shock-scene setting-up and various hapless effects, animation, and models for the flying things. Closest-to-fun: the goop and gore makeup effects, but this is no *Ticks*.

See also titles under *Jersey Skeeter, A.*

**MOST DANGEROUS GAME, The** see *Banker, The. Bridge to Nowhere. Comtesse Perverse, La. Deadly Game. Death Ring. Final Round. Hard Target* (P). *Raw Courage* (P). *Reason to Die. Running Man, The. Slave Girls from Beyond Infinity.*

**MOST DANGEROUS WOMAN ALIVE, The** see *Lethal Woman* (1989)

**Il MOSTRO DI FIRENZE** (I) G.M.P. (Giacomini-Noris) 1986 color 92m. SP, D: Cesare Ferrario. SP: Fulvio Ricciardi, from Mario Spezi's book. Mus: Paolo Rustichelli. Ref: V 6/11/86: "film labors against a built-in defect: The killer is still on the loose...." Ecran F 65:71. 70:20-21. SF Chron 2/14/96: convicted man cleared. With Leonard Mann, Bettina Giovinini, Lidia Mancinelli, Gabriele Tinti.

Gruesome based-on-fact story re a "Tuscan murderer-mutilator." *The Monster of Florence* - tr t.

**MOTHER** (J) Mother Project 1993 anim color 75m. Ref: TV: Broadway video; no Eng.

On Mars, 30,000 years ago. Atlan City, center of an advanced civilization ... Astral Power ... spaceships and space weapons ... odd power outages ... visions and speaking in tongues ... and a disintegrating planet. Next stop: Earth (and dumbstruck cavemen).... This seems like a bland space epic, with occasional design appeal.

**MOTHER GOOSE LAND** Para/Max Fleischer 1933 anim 6-1/2m. D: Dave Fleischer. Anim: Crandall, Kneitel. Ref: TV. LC. no Lee.

Lively, music-crammed Betty Boop-er spotlights a huge, fanged spider which abducts our heroine, after frightening Miss Muffet away. A mouse with a harmonica gets or has the best laugh.

**MOUNTAINTOP MOTEL MASSACRE** New World/McCullough 1986 (1983) color 92m. D, P: Jim McCullough Sr. SP, P: Jim McCullough Jr. Mus: Ron DiIullio. PD & SpMkpFX: Drew Edward Hunter. Ref: TV. V 5/28/86. NYT 5/17/86. With Bill Thurman, Anna Chappell, Will Mitchell, Virginia Loridans, Major Brock.

In January 1981, Evelyn Chambers (Chappell) is released from the Arkansas State Mental Hospital and returns to run the Mountaintop Motel on Highway 71. More or less accidentally on purpose, she slays her daughter (Jill King) with a sickle. Then, one stormy night, she begins with the guests—she puts a rattler in one room, rats in another, cockroaches in a third. Then, out comes the sickle.... The story of the film—in the characters' own exclamations—"Rats!" "Roaches!" "Blood!" If the dialogue isn't literate, it is helpful for identification purposes. While the initial relationship between mother and daughter is economically set up, the assembling-likely-victims scenes which follow are trite and coincidence-filled.

**MOUSE MAN** see *Ratman*

**MOUSE MENACE** WB 1946 anim 7m. D: Art Davis. SP: George Hill. Ref: TV: MGM-UA HV. WBCartoons. LC.

In order to squelch a "doggone, food-filching rodent," Porky Pig crafts a robot cat with "Stand up," "Purr," "Lie Down," and "Kill mouse" options. As in Fifties monster movies, nothing—flames, TNT, bullets—stops this jagged-toothed, vicious-faced "monster." Wry "asides" include the formidable little mouse's cat-kill tote board, which lists "Verified" and "Probable."

**MOUSE WHO WOULDN'T PLAY BALL, The** see *Candles at Nine*

**MOVIE HOUSE MASSACRE** Movie House Prods. 1986 (1984) color 80m. SP, D, P: Alice Raley. Ref: vc box. Morse: "leadenly unfunny." McCarty II: "stultifyingly bad." Ecran F 67:70: horror parody. V 2/19/86: "amateur night at the bijou." With Mary Woronov, Jonathan Blakely, Lynne Darcy.

"Haunted" movie theatre.

**MRS. AMWORTH** (B-Can.) Highgate & HTV & OECA 1975 color 30m. D: Alvin Rakoff. From E. F. Benson's story. Ref: Jones: "beautifully photographed half-hour TV movie." With Glynis Johns, Derek Francis, John Phillips.

Johns as a 300-year-old vampire.

**MRS. HYDE** (Sp-W.G.) Fenix-Filmar & Telecine 1970 color 77m. (*Sie Toetete in Extase*). SP, D: Jesus Franco. Ph: Manuel Merino. Mus: Manfred Huebler. Ref: Hardy/HM: "perfunctory direction." Dr. Rolf Giesen. With Soledad Miranda (aka S. Korda), Fred Williams, Ewa Stroemberg, Howard Vernon, Horst Tappert, Paul Mueller.

Young woman (Miranda) avenges her doctor father's (Williams) suicide, bloodily slays and castrates four doctors.

**MRS. WHITE** see *White of the Eye*

**La MUERTE DEL CHACAL** (Mex) Casablanca (Miura & Telefilm) 1984 color 90m. Story, D: Pedro Galindo III. Story, SP: Gilberto De Anda. Ph: Miguel Arana. Mus: Nacho Mendez. SpFX: Jorge Farfan. Mkp: Aurora Chavira. OptFX: Manuel Sainz. Ref: TV: Condor Video; no Eng.; *The Death of the Jackal* - tr t. V 5/9/84:488. TVG. With Mario Almada, Fernando Almada (Roy), Cristina Molina, Olivia Collins, Lizzeta Romo.

A cane-sword-carrying madman uses two vicious dogs to track and trap his prey, then stabs the latter, generally women, generally through the neck, and hangs the bodies on meathooks aboard a ship at anchor. Completely undistinguished slasher shocker concludes with a *Carrie* nightmare-coda jolt as gratuitously grisly as the earlier slam-the-dog-to-death scene.

**MUERTE EN EL CARIBE** see *Maldicion Maya*

**MUERTOS DE MIEDO** (Mex) Filmadora Chapultepec (Daniel & Pedro Galindo, Jr.) 1957 b&w c85m. (*Besame, Kitty* - working t). D: Jaime Salvador. SP: Eduardo Galindo. Story: Pedro De Urdimalas, Pedro Galindo Jr. SpFX: Juan M. Ravelo. Mkp: Margarita Ortega. Ref: TV: Video Visa; no Eng.; *Scared to Death* - tr t. Horacio Higuchi.

Comedy has two creepy sequences: In one long one, set in a morgue patrolled by Viruta and Capulina, a "corpse" seems to rise from the dead, then doffs his sheet, stands up, and carries off another corpse. Later, the two comedians wind up in a car trunk with the real corpse.... Viruta and Capulina—with their guitars-and-patter routines here—seem closer to the Smothers Brothers than to Abbott and Costello. Away from their guitars, they seem much less assured.

**MUFFY THE VAMPIRE LAYER** Las Vegas 1992 color 75m. D: J.-P. Ferrand. Ref: Adam'94. With P.J. Sparxx, Lacy Rose, Tawny (vampire).

Mall dolls hunt vampires.

**A MULHER QUE POE A POMBA NO AR** (Braz.) Panorama Filmes/PRM 1976 color 80m. D: Jose Mojica Marins. SP, Mus, P: Rosangela Maldonado. Ref: Monster! 3:30: "unfunny science fiction comedy." With Maldonado, Luandy Maldonado & Marta Volpiani (Dove-Women), Olney Cazarre.

Scientist's formula transforms two girls into "fearsome dove-women who attack and kill adulterous men." *The Woman Who Makes Doves Fly* - tr. t.

**MULTIPLE LISTINGS** see *Open House*

**MULTIPLE MANIACS** Newstar Ent. (Film-makers' Coop)/Dreamland Studios 1969 b&w 94m. SP, D, P, Ed: John Waters. Lobstora by Vince Peranio. Ref: TV: Cinema Group HV. Lee. Hound. Phantom. Hardy/HM. Scheuer. With Divine, David Lochary, Edith Massey, Mink Stole.

Queasy ingredients include "The Cavalcade of Perversion," an unusual church scene featuring a "rosary job" and subtle undertones of blasphemy; another no-no: a gory knife murder/cannibalism, and a real or imagined rape by a monster-lobster.... *Bells of St. Mary's* it isn't. Some of the monologues and dialogues have a certain fresh stiltedness—you're not asked to buy them, just keep your ears open. Some of the actors here, though, are just dead weight, and there's a lot of dead between the big shock scenes. Highlight: the opening freak show—and the freakish reactions by the staid populace to same.

**MULTO IN THE CITY** (Fili) Regal Films (R.S. Monteverde) 1994 (1993?) color 107m. D: D. Escudero. SP: J.J. Reyes. Ph: Ricardo Jacinto. PD: Don Escudero. AD: Sammy Aranzamendez. Prosth & VisFX: Benny Batoctoy et al. SdFX: Rodel Capule. Ref: TV: Regal video; some Eng. With Tanya Iwakawa (Cecilia), Jaclyn Jose (Dolores), Manilyn Reynes, Herbert Bautista, Cherrie Pie Picache.

A phantom sobbing is heard around Wholesome Hills School. A phantom figure appears in a shower stall, in the back of a schoolroom, and beside an imposing tree, respectively. ("There's something wrong with our school?") The ghost telekinetically kills an abusive mother, possesses a young woman, and has the tree's roots drag a woman into the ground. At the end, the spirit and the monster tree wreck the school.... Long, well-made, spooky sudser with a social conscience.

**MUMMIES** and **EGYPTOLOGY** see the following titles and *Amazing Stories—The Movie. Blackmagic with Buddha, The. Camino de los Espantos, El. Capulina Contra las Momias. Claymation Comedy of Horrors. Curados de Espantos. Cursed Village. . . . Daffy Duck's Quackbusters. Deathrow Gameshow. Dungeonmaster, The. Egyptian Melodies. Encounter of the Spooky Kind II. Fanny och Alexander* (P). *Fear of the Mummy. Focus on Fishko. Follow That Goblin! Ghost Dance, The* (1984). *Gypped in Egypt. Halloween Night. High Spirits. Hollywood Chainsaw Hookers. House II. I Was a Teenage Mummy. Il Etait une Fois le Diable. Jonny's Golden Quest. Krasu. Kumander Bawang ... Latigo Contra las Momias Asesinas. Magic Mummy. Manhattan Baby. Miedo No Anda en Burro, El. Mr. Boogedy. Momia Nacional, La. Momias de San Angel, Las. Monster Squad, The. Nightmare Asylum. Nightmare before Christmas, The. Nob Hill. Puppet Master 4. Puppetmaster. Pyramid Terror. Return of Jafar. Ritual of Death, The. Saturday the 14th Strikes Back. Scooby-doo and the Ghoul School. Scooby-doo and the Reluctant Werewolf. Search for Diana. Shadow of Illusion. Silence of the Hams. Somewhere in Egypt. Stargate. Superman (The Mummy Strikes)* (***). *Take it Easy! Tales from the Darkside. Teenage Catgirls in Heat. Thundercats: Mumm-ra Lives. Thundercats Ho!. Tomb, The. Tombs of the Blind Dead. Transylvania 6-5000. Tut and Tuttle. Unforgettable Fantasy. Waxwork. Young Taoism Fighter, The.*

**MUMMIES OF SAN ANGEL** see *Momias De San Angel*

**The MUMMY AND THE CURSE OF THE JACKALS** Vega Int'l. 1985 (1969) color 86m. (*The Mummy Vs. the Were-Jackal*-orig t. *Mummy & Curse of the Jackal* - vt ad t). D: Oliver Drake. SP, P: William C. Edwards. Ph: William Troiano. SpFX:

Harry Woolman. SpMkp: Byrd Holland. Asst D: Wyott Ordung et al. Ref: TV: Academy Home Ent. video. Lee (P). no Stanley. no Hardy. no Weldon. Bowker '90. Phantom. PT 3:40-41. With Anthony Eisley, John Carradine, Robert Allen Browne, Marliza Pons (Princess), Maurine Dawson, Saul Goldsmith (The Mummy), William Whitton, Rebecca Rothchild (Isis).

Archaeologist David Barry (Eisley)—curious about the legendary "curse of the jackals"—has himself locked in a room with an Egyptian Princess who has been preserved under glass for 4,815 years by a high priest's spell. As the full moon rises, he transforms into a long-snouted "jackal-man" that later does battle with the revived, pop-eyed mummy assigned, with Barry, to protect the Princess in the present day.

A strange hommage to classic Universal mummy and wolf-man movies, *Mummy/Jackals* is in the spirit of *Frankenstein Meets the Wolf Man*, but accomplishes what Universal, perhaps wisely, never attempted: It puts the mummy and the wolf man (here, the jackal-man) in the same picture. The two monsters do fight at the end, but the intercut, *Mummy's Ghost* transformation of the Princess from young beauty to old hag overshadows their flailings in Lake Mead. This dreadful hybrid is a mishmash of scenes from old mummy and werewolf movies—e.g., five-stage were-jackal transformations, an extended flashback to ancient Egypt, wall-busting by the "mummy man" (another borrowing from *The Mummy's Ghost*), etc. Carradine appears briefly near the end to pronounce, "We can't just stand by and let a 4,000-year-old mummy and a jackal-man take over the city!"

**MUMMY DEAREST** Las Vegas Video (Bunny Demilo) 1990 color c80m. SP, D: Dick Dumont. Story: Mike Bushler. Ph: Paul Harmon. Song: Johnny Ripper. Sets: Cal Jammer. Mkp: Dennis Jacks. Ref: TV: Las Vegas Video. no Adam. With Nina Hartley (the mummy), Mike Horner, Lynn LeMay, Jamie Gillis.

Stray semen revives the mummy of Egyptian Princess Akasha (sp?) from a 4,000-year sleep. Her passionate lovemaking drains a Nubian janitor of sperm, and, at the end, she makes Dr. Steve Banning (Horner) immortal.... Choppy, hardcore film takes character names—Banning, Helen Grosvenor, Whemple—from old Universal mummy movies. The "seal of the seven jackals" is back too. But it just isn't the same without Dick Foran and Wallace Ford.

Sequels: *Mummy Part Two* and *Mummy III, The.*

**MUMMY PART TWO: THE UNWRAPPING** Las Vegas Video 1990. SP, D: Dick Dumont. Ref: vc box. no Adam. With Nina Hartley, Mike Horner, Raven.

Sequel to *Mummy Dearest.*

**The MUMMY III: THE PARTING** Las Vegas Video 1992 color 85m. (aka *Mummy Dearest III*). D: J.-P. Ferrand. Ref: vc box. Adam '93. With Nina Hartley, Raven, Mike Horner.

Sequel to *Mummy Dearest.*

**The MUMMY LIVES** Cannon (Towers) 1993 color feature. D: Gerry O'Hara. SP: Nelson Gidding, "suggested by a Poe story." Ref: PT 22:15: "no damned mummy." With Tony Curtis, Leslie Hardy.

Man embalmed alive.

**MUMMY VS. THE WERE-JACKAL, The** see *Mummy and the Curse of the Jackals, The*

**\*MUMMY'S BOYS** 1936. Mus D: Roy Webb. AD: Van Nest Polglase; F. Gray. SpPhFX: Vernon L. Walker. Ref: TV. Lee. Hardy/HM. V 12/16/36. Lentz. Stanley. Maltin/MCT. no Maltin '92. Miller/"B" Movies. no Scheuer. PT 16:15. Filmfax 30:64, 66. With Charles Coleman, Frederick Burton.

The "curse of King Pharatime" seems to hang over those who, one year ago, entered his Egyptian tomb. Most of the members of the original expedition die; two from an expedition to return Pharatime's relics disappear. Behind it all: a "raving maniac" who has discovered a secret treasure room in the tomb, and who kills his victims with injections of a poison which causes seemingly-natural death. Extra addeds: a 3,000-year-old "mummy" that speaks ... a weird guffawing hyena ... and a "ghost" in a tomb.

The horror-show opening—complete with storm, lurking Egyptian, and sudden death—is standard, but preferable at least to the Wheeler and Woolsey comedy which follows. Wheeler's partial-amnesia routine is good for running up running time, if nothing else, and the duo's "crow flies" routine was old in '36. (They used it at least once before, in the '31 *Cracked Nuts*.) Willie Best is stuck in a quivering-assistant role, but has a funny comment re some "air-minded mice" (i.e., bats).

**MUMU? ANONG MALAY KO!** see *Goosebuster*

**MUNCHIE** Concorde (Mike Elliott) 1992 color 80m. SP, D: Jim Wynorski. SP: R. J. Robertson, too. Mus: C. Cirino. Munchie creators: Bartalos, Kindlon. Ref: V 6/8/92: "entertaining." Martin: "silly sequel" to *Munchies*. With Loni Anderson, Dom DeLuise (voice of Munchie), Andrew Stevens, Arte Johnson, Toni Naples, Monique Gabrielle, Ace Mask, Jay Richardson, Angus Scrimm, George "Buck" Flower, Fred Olen Ray, Becky LeBeau, Brinke Stevens, Linda Shayne, Paul Hertzberg.

Munchie discovered in mine shaft.

**MUNCHIE STRIKES BACK** New Horizons (Elliott-Fernandez/Pacific Trust) 1994 color c80m. SP, D: Jim Wynorski. SP: also R.J. Robertson. Ph: D.E. Fauntleroy. Mus: C. Cirino. PD: Amy Ancona. Munchie: (created by) Gabe Bartalos, Dave Kindlon;(des concept) Robertson. Lawnmower FX: Ken Solomon. Digital FX: Digital Motion, Linda Obalil. Title FX: K. Kutchaver. Ref: TV; next: *Munchie Hangs Ten?* Mo. With Lesley-Anne Down, Andrew Stevens, Trenton Knight, Angus Scrimm, John Byner, Steve Franken, Natanya Ross, Jay Richardson, Ace Mask, Howard Hesseman (voice of Munchie), Toni Naples, Gailyn Addis (Marilyn Monroe), E. A. Price (Elvis), Antonia Dorian (Cleopatra), Becky LeBeau.

The Munch—"older than time itself" and fresh from the astral plane—is assigned to help a woman (Down) and her son (Knight). In a junior-high-level game against The Hillside Stranglers, Munchie helps Chris hit a home-run-around-the-world; in another scene, he invests Chris with the power of telepathy; in a third scene, he makes it "snow" dollars from heaven.... A vehicle for a voice, and sometimes a pretty good one. M3 doesn't always work, but the asides are generally clever ("Hanna Barbera, Limited Attention Span News"), and the episodic script works in several kinds of pre-teen wish fulfillment. It also incorporates bits of *The Bad News Bears, It Happens Every Spring,* and *Teen Wolf.*

**MUNCHIES** Concorde/New Horizons (Roger Corman) 1987 color 78m. D: Bettina Hirsch. SP: Lance Smith. Mus: E. V. Troost. MechFxSup: Douglas Turner. Munchies created by Robert Short. SpVisFX: Roger George. SpFxCoord: Lisa Romanoff. Opt & Roto Anim: Motion Opticals. SpVoices: Frank Welker, Fred Newman. Ref: TV. MFB '88:155. V 5/20/87. Morse. Martin. With Harvey Korman, Charles Stratton, Nadine Van der Velde, Alix Elias, Charlie Phillips, Robert Picardo, Wendy Schaal, Paul Bartel.

"Arnold"—a "furball" of a critter from an "alien toxic waste dump" in Peru—develops serious claws when threatened, multiplies, gets tiresomely prankish. *Gremlins,* anyone? Trivial, silly.

Sequels: *Munchie. Munchie Strikes Back.*

**MUNDO DEPRAVADOS (WORLD OF THE DEPRAVED)** SWV/Monique Prods.(Leroy C. Griffith) 1967(1993) b&w 73m. SP, D: Herb Jeffries. Mkp: Wallace Westland. Ref: TV: SWV.

Primitive, woodenly acted proto-slasher movie with mild suspense and violence is a must for Tempest Storm fans.

**MUNECA DEL INFIERNO, La** see *Vacaciones del Terror*

The **MUPPET CHRISTMAS CAROL** BV (Disney)/Jim Henson Prods. (M. G. Baker) 1992 color 85m. D, Co-P: Brian Henson. SP: Jerry Juhl, from Charles Dickens' story "A Christmas Carol." Ph: John Fenner. Mus: Miles Goodman; (songs) Paul Williams. PD: Val Strazovec. MechFxSup: Larry Jameson. Min D: Paul Gentry. Ref: V 12/14/92. ad. SFChron 12/11/92: "mechanical cuteness." With Michael Caine (Scrooge), Dave Goelz, Jerry Nelson (Jacob Marley), Frank Oz.

Scrooge meets the ghosts again.

*****MURDER AT DAWN** Big 4 (Freuler) 1932 51m. version. Elec FX: Kenneth Strickfaden. Ref: TV: Sinister Cinema. Greg Luce. PT 22:10. Turner/Price.

"The VXO (sp?) Accumulator will produce unlimited power at a mere fraction of the present cost!" This light-activated gizmo (cf. *Death from a Distance*) gets its power "direct from the sun." ("It will release enough electricity to kill us both!") Plus the forbidding mansion The Crag ("That place is haunted!") ... several skulkers ... a tepid thunderstorm ... and a clutching hand.... Scarecard: awkward staging and editing ... okay spooky lighting (Edward S. Kull, photography) ... Mischa Auer as the most amusingly hokey skulker ... and a gizmo not quite up to *Mask of Fu Manchu,* but not bad.

**MURDER BY MOONLIGHT** (B-U.S.) CBS-TV/Asseyev & London Weekend TV & Viacom 1989 color c90m. (*Dark of the Moon*-orig t). D: Michael Lindsay-Hogg. Tel: Carla Jean Wagner. Mus: Trevor Jones. PD: Austin Spriggs. SpFxSup: Grahame Longhurst. Ref: TV. V 5/17/89:63: "vacuous script"; Mifed '89:116. Maltin '92. no Scheuer. Martin. With Brigitte Nielsen, Julian Sands, Jane Lapotaire, Brian Cox, Gerald McRaney.

"It's been ten years since we almost nuked each other." Murder and intrigue in the 21st century, at U.S. and Soviet lunar bases. Mystery: "Who would want to kill Jake Elazar?" Key to solution: "That's why no one could find him—he turned himself into a woman!"

**MURDER CHAMBER, The** see *Black Magic* (1944)

**MURDER-IN-LAW** Monarch 1992 color feature. D: Tony Jiti Gill. Ref: SFChron Dtbk 1/24/93. With Joe Estevez, Marilyn Adams, Darrell Guilbeau, Debra Lee Giometti, Rebecca Russell.

**MURDER IN PARIS** see *Paris Sex Murders*

**MURDER IN SPACE** Showtime-TV/Cooper-Zenith & CTV 1985 color c90m. D: Steven H. Stern. SP: "Wesley Ferguson." Ph: Laszlo George. Mus: Arthur B. Rubinstein. AD: Trevor Williams. SpVisFX: Quicksilver FX. Mkp: Linda Gill. Ref: TV: *Whodunit?* - series t? SFExam 7/26/85:E-2. Martin. Scheuer. Hound. Maltin '92. With Martin Balsam, Arthur Hill, Wilford Brimley, Michael Ironside, Damir Andrei, Wendy Crewson, Richard Blackburn.

Murder on board the international spaceship *Conestoga,* as it returns from two weeks on Mars. Dry, mechanical sf-mystery. The functional dialogue simply directs suspicion one way, then another.

*****MURDER IN THE AIR** 1940. SP: R. Schrock. AD: S. Fleischer. Ref: TV. V 7/10/40. no Hardy/SF. no Lee. no Lentz. no Scheuer. Maltin '92. Stanley. With Kenneth Harlan, Victor Zimmerman, John Hamilton.

Inventor George Hayden's (Owen King) inertia projector— which looks like your standard movie death ray—"projects electric waves capable of paralyzing direct or alternating currents at their source." Inspired by a ham radio operator's "radio beam" invention—which stopped "electrical appliances for miles around," in Kansas—the projector knocks down a plane, then stops a taxi. ("The motor stopped dead on me!") Early Ronald Reagan science-fiction project—long before Star Wars—has a routine agent-infiltrates-saboteurs story, plus a busy score, but no music credit.

**MURDER IN THE FUN HOUSE** see *Chinese Cat, The*

**MURDER LUST** see *Murderlust*

**MURDER OBSESSION** see *Fear* (1980)

**MURDER OF DR. HARRIGAN** WB 1936 (1935) b&w 67m. D: Frank McDonald. Adap: Peter Milne, Sy Bartlett. Story: Mignon G. Eberhart. Ph: Arthur Todd. Ref: V 1/22/36: "routine." With Kay Linaker, Ricardo Cortez, Mary Astor, John Eldredge, Joseph Crehan, Frank Reicher, Mary Treen, Johnny Arthur.

Hospital patient "scared to death" ... "new anaesthetic."

**MURDER ROCK** see *Demon Is Loose, The*

The **MURDER SECRET** (I) 1989 color/ws 90m. Presented by: Lucio Fulci. SP, D: M. Bianchi. Ref: MV: "gore scenes." Palmerini: sfa *Non Averie Paura della Zia Marta?* With Jessica Moore, Sacha Darwin, Peter Gabriel, Lucy Arland.

"Zombified Aunt Martha."

**MURDER SYNDROME** see *Fear* (1980)

**MURDER WEAPON** Cinema HV/David DeCoteau (Linnea Quigley/Fred Kennamer) 1980 color 81m. D: Ellen Cabot. SP: R. A. Perron. Mus: Del Casher. Ref: V 1/17/90:37 (hv): "static, talky." McCarty II: "turgid"; some gore. With L. Quigley, Karen Russell, Lyle Waggoner, Stephen Steward.

Maniac at large.

**MURDERER'S KEEP** see *Butcher, The*

**MURDERLUST** Easy Street 1986 color 92m. (aka *Murder Lust. Mass Murderer* - orig t). D, Ed: Donald Jones. SP, P, Mus: James Lane. SpMkpFX: Milton Hopper. Ref: TV: Prism Ent. video. V 6/24/87. 5/6/87:170. Morse. no Martin. Scheuer. Hound. With Eli Rich (Steve), Rochelle Taylor, Dennis Gannon, Bonnie Schneider, Lisa Nichols, Ashley St. Jon, Lane.

"Nobody is safe with the Mojave Murderer around." Is Sunday School teacher Steve Belmont a "Christian in the truest sense of the word"—or a "monster"? The latter, natch, or there's no movies. He strangles prostitutes and dumps their bodies in the desert. The central irony—a church-going serial killer—is far from overwhelming. Rich's Martin Mull put-on air suggests parody, but nothing else does. Slight, low-key, with increasingly unbelievable plot turns.

**MURDEROUS VISION** USA-TV/Gary Sherman Prods. & Wilshire Court Prods. (Johanna Persons/Ross Albert) 1991 color c90m. D: Sherman. Tel: Paul Joseph Gulino. Mus: Joe Renzetti. PD: Christopher Horner. SpMkpFX: Steve Johnson's XFX; David Du Puis. SpFX: Marty Bresin. Ref: TV. V 2/1/91:73. Sacto Bee 2/20/91. Scheuer. Maltin '92. Martin. With Bruce Boxleitner, Laura Johnson, Joseph d'Angerio, Beau Starr, Robert Culp.

"This stuff gives me the creeps." The "stuff" includes a body with the face "hacked off," or surgically removed ... a sick faces-in-bottles scene ... and a "mumbo jumbo psychic," Elizabeth (Johnson).... Pedestrian horror-mystery. Only interest: the psychic's disconnected-image "clues" (including a vision of a giant "pendulum") and some bizarre *Eyes without a Face* bits in the finale.

The **MURDERS IN THE RUE MORGUE** CBS-TV/Robert Halmi Inc. & Int'l. Film Prods. 1986 color c90m. D: Jeannot Szwarc. Tel & Assoc P: David Epstein, from Edgar Allan Poe's short story. Mus: Charles Gross. AD: Andre Guerin. Sp Ape Des: Lyle Conway, Neal Scanlan, David White. OptFX: Moses Weitzman. Ref: TVG. Martin. Maltin '92: "above average." Scheuer: "creaky." V 12/17/86:50: "taut & suspenseful." TV. SFExam 12/5/86: "well-paced." With George C. Scott, Rebecca De Mornay, Val Kilmer, Ian McShane, Mak Wilson (ape).

*MURDERS IN THE ZOO 1933 62m. Ref: TV: MCA-Univ HV. Lee. Hardy/HM. Eames. Weldon. Stanley. V 4/4/33.

"The mamba's gone!" In Indo-China, zoologist Eric Gorman (Lionel Atwill) sews a romantic rival's mouth shut. Back in the U.S., he uses a snake-head venom holder as a murder weapon and uncages the zoo's big cats, but a big snake puts the squeeze on him, in an awkwardly done sequence.... Atwill gives a few lines some zing in this otherwise perfectly worthless antique horror. Sample zinger (re zoo animals): "They love. They hate. They kill." Charlie Ruggles provides a lot of "comedy."

The **MUSIC OF THE SPHERES** (Can.) (USA-TV)/Lightscape & CFDC (Nadine Humenick) 1984 (1983) color 82m. (*La Musique des Spheres*). SP, D, P: G. Philip Jackson. SP: also Gabrielle deMontmollin. Mus: Claude Boux. AD, SpFX: James S. Allan. SpVideoFX: Dana M. Lee. Mkp: Inge Klaudi. Ref: TV: Eng.-lang. version. V 11/21/84. Stanley. no Scheuer. no Maltin '92. Ecran F 52:70. With Anne Dansereau, Peter Brikmanis, Jacques Couture, Denis Pelletier (alien voice).

In The Dark Age of the 21st Century, the world is in economic chaos, "super-intelligent biological computers" maintain order, and the Equation at moonbase Atlantis "interprets" events. Meanwhile, workers on Project Ceres (re "converting asteroids to solar energy transmitters and placing them in orbits from which they can direct microwave-converted energy to Earth") find "something strange, otherworldly" emanating from an asteroid. Seems that "each planet ... generates a perfect sound." Some planets are "overtones"; Earth is a "counterpoint." And if asteroids are tampered with, planets in the solar system will change their orbits.... The above daffily imaginative premise, unfortunately, is poorly dramatized. Or rather, it's not dramatized at all, just stated in dialogue.

The **MUSICAL VAMPIRE** (H.K.?) c1992? color/ws 93m. Ref: TV: World Video; Eng. titles. Janet Willis.

Question: "Does it suck blood, like the foreign ones?" Answer: Yes, the main hopping vampire here is the fanged, blood-drinking type, and is given to snarling. A quick bite, a little messy blood on the fangs, and the victim is dead. At the end, the eclipsed moon's rays zap the bloodsucker.... With the vampire's fascination for a pocket watch which plays "London Bridge" when opened, this uninspired horror-comedy makes good on its title. ("It will be mad when there is no music.")

**MUSIQUE DES SPHERES, La** see *Music of the Spheres, The*

**MUSKIE MADNESS** see *Blood Hook*

The **MUTAGEN** (Can.) Visual Prods. '80 & Emmeritus & CHCH-TV 1988 color c90m. SP, D: Eli Necakov. Story: Terence Gadsden. Ph: Bill Kigar. Mus: Steven Sauve. Sets: Tanos. Mkp: Alena Krcin. Ref: TV. TVG. no Maltin '92. With Jackie Samuda, Les Williams (Derek Kane), Marianna Pascal (Julie), Casey Leigh (Frieda), Robbie Fox, Steve Behal, Patrick Myles, Kenneth Foster (Ralph Dexter).

Scientist Derek Kane—intent on "revolutionizing the capabilities of the human mind"—injects himself, his girl friend Frieda, and his pregnant wife Julie with the "mutagen." His aim: to produce the "most intelligent human beings in the world." Complicating matters: a lurking killer with "incredible strength," an unknown, still-growing chemical in a corpse's blood, and the mutagen itself, which starts "reversing".... Pretty garbagey. That videotaped flatness again. Key phrase: "hyperactive cellular expansion."

**MUTANT** FVI/Laurelwood (Igo Kantor) 1984 color 100m. (*Night Shadows* - alt t). D: John "Bud" Cardos. SP: Peter Z. Orton, Michael Jones, John C. Kruize. Mus: Richard Band. Prosth: Dave Miller. SpFX: Paul Stewart. SdFX: Gene Corso. Ref: TV: Vestron Video. V 10/3/84. 10/26/83:108 (ad). 5/9/84:8, 43. HR 10/25/83:S-12. Maltin '92. Sacto Union 3/5/84. Scheuer. Morse. Hound. Martin. With Wings Hauser, Bo Hopkins, Lee Montgomery, Jody Medford, Jennifer Warren, Cary Guffey, Marc Clement.

"Ain't good to be on these roads after dark." Just outside the Southern town of Goodland, the New Era Corporation ("Research today for a better tomorrow") is playing butterfingers with chemical waste. When townsfolk show up now, they are generally dead, or undead, and are found to have a powerful chemical compound containing zinc chloride in their blood. The compound expands, causes a breakdown of the nervous system, and makes the palms of the victim's hands split open.

The scientific documentation here is sufficiently horrific, and there are some good "busses" with lurching mutants. But the mutants-amok scenes are unadventurously lifted from *Night of the Living Dead,* and in-between scenes with the protagonists are vapidly "sensitive." There are occasional striking visuals, but the mutants look so "monstrous" they're comical. The town doc suggests that the mutants "leech" blood from others with their palm-holes, but they seem, in action, content mainly with lurching and yowling.

**MUTANT ACTION** see *Accion Mutante*

**MUTANT HUNT** Wizard Video/Ent. Concepts (Taryn Prods./Cynthia DePaula) 1987 (1986) color 77m. (*Matt Riker: Mutant Hunt* - orig t). SP, D: Tim Kincaid. SpFxMkp: Ed French. Cyborg Des: Tom Lauten. SpFX: Matt Vogel. SpSdFX: Travis Powers. Ref: TV: Lightning Video. V 7/8/87. Hound. Phantom. Scheuer. With Rick Gianasi, Mary Fahey, Ron Reynaldi, Taunie Vrenon, Bill Peterson, Stormy Spill, Doug DeVos (Hydro, the last Delta 6); Warren Ulaner, Mark Legan (cyborgs).

"Total carnage, uncontrolled fury—what more could anyone ask?" Z (Peterson) of Inteltrax introduces an "alien molecule"—a variant of a sexual narcotic—into the fluid system of the company's Delta 7 cyborgs. Result: cyborgs which "kill for pleasure" ... and are telepathic. Goal: super-soldiers (compare *Revolt of the Zombies*)—"super-human machines, ten times stronger than any man." Better yet: Domina's (Spill) Delta 8 model, "mutated beyond recognition"....

The *Terminator*-indebted *Mutant Hunt* doesn't quite make it as action, comedy, horror or science fiction. It's neither campy nor exciting enough. It does, however, have some comically revolting, socially-unredeeming details—e.g., Reynaldi's Felix lifting a sticky sneaker out of some cy-goop ... a really messed-up cyborg reactivating. Lots of cy-gore, as the 'borgs take any form of mutilation more or less in stride.

**MUTANT ON THE BOUNTY** Skouras/Canyon Films 1989 color 94m. Story, D, P: Robert Torrance. Story, SP, P: Martin Lopez. SpMkpDes: Brian Penikas & Assoc. Ref: V 9/27/89:

"witless screenplay." With John Roarke, Deborah Benson, John Furey, Victoria Catlin, Kyle T. Heffner, Pepper Martin.

Mutant and android aboard the spaceship *Bounty* in the year 2048.

**MUTANTI, I** see *Endgame*

**MUTANTS DE LA DEUXIEME HUMANITE, Les** see *Rats: Night of Terror*

**MUTANTS IN PARADISE** Caridi Ent./Blue Ridge Cinema (William Moses, Jr.) 1987 (1984) color 77m. SP, D: Scott Apostolou. Mus: Jep Epstein. Mkp: J. R. Getches. Ref: TV. V 12/20/89. Hound. With Brad Greenquist, Anna Nicholas, Robert Ingham, Skipp Suddeth, Edith Massey, Ray "Boom Boom" Mancini, Elaine Brown (fairy godmother).

Gullible Steve Awesome (Greenquist) agrees to take part in Tinman and Associates' radiation-immunity experiment for an "uncertain radioactive future." He becomes, he believes, "genetically superior," and his arm becomes a radio. But the experiment proves to have been a fraud, and Steve only thought he was stronger and more intelligent. His arm, however, did become a radio. Plus: a magic wand which makes people disappear.... Good-natured but sophomoric comedy with fantasy/sf overtones. Wry moments, but the anything-for-a-laugh tack generally doesn't work.

**MUTATOR** Prism Ent./Liberty Films/A Cut Above (Markowitz/Bowey) 1989 color 90m. (*Time of the Beast* - alt t). D: J. Bowey. Story, SP: L. R. Higgins. Story: also G. A. Rose. SpMkpFX: Burman Studios. Ref: V 8/19/91: "perfunctory"; made in S. Africa. 5/31/89: "forgettable." PT 10:50: "boring, slow-paced." With Brion James, Carolyn Ann Clark, M. R. Murrill, Neil McCarthy.

"Litter of artificial beings born ... to a genetically engineered cat." (V)

**MUTILATIONS** Apex (Lawrence Thomas) 1987 color 67m. SP, D, P: Thomas. Ph: Steve Wacks. Mus: E. L. Robinson, B. Belknap. AD: John Fischner, Mike Morand. SpVisFX: Dreamstar; Fischner. SpMkpFX: DFX; David Powell, Doug Edwards. Creature Concep: Dell Harris. Ref: TV: Baron Video. Bill Warren. no Hound. no Martin. With Al Baker, Katherine Hutson, John Bliss (Matson), Shelly Creel, Bill Buckner, Harvey Shell.

"They're here and they're coming for us!" Alien beings who look like "creatures out of hell" and who visit the farming community of Berryhill at "regular intervals" turn out to be responsible for a rash of "strange aerial sightings" and cattle mutilations.... Very talky, amateurish. Passable stopmo for the aliens and a mutilated, mutated cow. At times, the movie is so bad it seems that the badness is intentional.

The **MUTILATOR** Ocean King Releasing (Neil Whitford) 1984 color 86m. (*Fall Break* - orig t). SP, D, P: Buddy Cooper. D: also J. S. Douglass. SpMkpFX: Mark Shostrom, Anthony Showe, Ed Ferrell. Ref: V 1/9/85: "boring horror film." ad. Morse: "inept and inane." Ecran F 47:28. With Matt Mitler, Frances Raines, Bill Hitchcock, Pamela W. Cooper, Ruth Martinez.

"Grotesque, homicidal nut." (V)

**MUTILATOR** Mellow Madness 199-? anim short. Ref: Sacto Bee 10/23/91: "bloody"; in the Festival of Animation—Extra Sick and Twisted.

**MUTILATOR 2** Spike & Mike's Sick & Twisted Show 199-? anim short. D: Eric Fogel. Ref: SFChron 4/4/93: "a parody of a comic-book superhero taking on alien invaders."

**MUTINY IN SPACE** see *Space Mutiny*

**MUTRONICS—THE MOVIE** see *Guyver, The* (New Line/1991)

**MY BEST FRIEND IS A VAMPIRE** Kings Road (Dennis Murphy) 1987 (1988) color 90m. (aka *I Was a Teenage Vampire*). D: Jimmy Huston. SP: Tab Murphy. Mkp: C. Belt. Ref: V 5/4/88: "mildly diverting." 9/29/87:35. 10/28/87:4 (rated). Phantom: "synthetic ... a few genuine laughs." Morse: "pretty cleverly worked-out." Ecran F 76:71. Jones. With Robert Sean Leonard, Evan Mirand, Cheryl Pollak, Rene Auberjonois, Fannie Flagg, Cecilia Peck.

Re a "hip, happy bloodseeking nightstalker" and a "sexy Elvira type."

**MY BETTER HALF** (H.K.) Independent Film Prods. 1993 color/ws 91m. Ref: TV: World Video; Eng. titles.

Indifferent terror trilogy re (1) a ghost who enters a whorehouse ("Is there a ghost?"), 2) a bloody double knifing, and (3) a jealous woman who stabs her husband to death, cuts him up with a chainsaw, and pops the parts into a stewpot. ("I must chop you up.") In the last story, the paranoid wife has one funny monologue: "It's not me. It's Yip, the movie star. You love the movie star, Yip."

**MY BOYFRIEND'S BACK** BV/Touchstone (Sean S. Cunningham) 1993 color 84m. (aka *Johnny Zombie*). D: Bob Balaban. SP: Dean Lorey. Mus: Harry Manfredini. Ph: Mac Ahlberg. PD: M. Hanan. Mkp: Kimberly Greene. SpVisFX: Fantasy II; G. Warren. Comic Book Art: Neal Adams. Opt: H. Anderson. SdFxSup: John K. Adams. Ref: PT 18:11: "pretty lame." Martin: "works deliciously well." TV: Touchstone HV. V 8/16/93: "the nadir of this summer season (and probably the entire year)." 2/25/91:18: as *Johnny Zombie*. SFChron 8/7/93: "a complete bomb." With Andrew Lowery (Johnny), Traci Lind, Danny Zorn, Edward Herrmann, Mary Beth Hurt, Austin Pendleton, Paul Dooley, Bob Dishy, Cloris Leachman, Paxton Whitehead.

"Oh, my God! I am dead!" High-schooler Johnny dies, then comes back. ("You're undead.") Quasi-necrophilia with his longed-for love Missy ensues. In order to keep his ears, etc. from falling off, though, he must eat the "flesh of the living." ("You ate Chuck!") This horror-comedy dies faster than Johnny; it's not just broad, it's a mile wide. Its one (bad) joke: Everyone's blase about the surreal situation. Die Zombie Die and Johnny Zombie (with "bloodthirsty zombies") are playing at the local theatre.

**MY BROTHER HAS BAD DREAMS** VCI 1972 color? feature. SP, D, P: Bob Emery. Ref: PT 13:47: "unique wonder." Fred Olen Ray.

"Norman Bates clone," "disturbing nightmares," murders, sharks.

**MY COUSIN, THE GHOST** (H.K.) Golden Harvest/Bo Ho Films 1987 color c92m. D: Lu Wong-Tu. Ref: TV: Rainbow Video; Eng. titles. V 5/6/87:521. NST! 4:32. MMarquee 43:7. TVG. With Ng Yau Hong.

Cousin Big has been dead for a week, but doesn't know it. An "aggrieved ghost" who has not been able to reincarnate, he is green-blooded, impervious to such irritations as a dart in the back of the head and a hot iron on his back, and has no temperature, heartbeat or breath. ("How strange.") He and Miss Wang, a fellow boarder who is a ghost and knows it, hit it off. Her ghost-cousin Gi, who died in the same auto accident as Miss Wang, her intended bridesmaid, is envious and wants a companion, too. She settles on Q, but, as a non-ghost, he must die to go with her, and wants to. Gi prepares a noose. His brothers, however, insist that ghosts belong with ghosts, and humans with humans.

*My Cousin, the Ghost* is very talky, but cleverly plotted, and the concluding sequences are funny, creepy, and romantic. Both romances—ghost-ghost and ghost-human—have pleasing payoffs: Big discovers, to his delight, that he's a ghost, and he flies off with Miss Wang; Gi must leave at dawn, and does, and Q stays behind, reluctantly. Amusing musical sequences include a window-washing tango (Miss Wang, inside; Big, outside) and a dance by Gi and Q to the *Ghostbusters* theme.

**MY DEAR KILLER** (I) Video Search 1971 color? feature (*Mio Caro Assassino*). Co-SP, D: Tonino Valerii. Ref: Imagi 1:59. Palmerini: "impeccable." With George Hilton.

"Explicit circular saw murder in a bathroom" ... "string of deaths."

**MY DEMON LOVER** New Line/Robert Shaye 1987 color 86m. D: Charlie Loventhal. SP: Leslie Ray. Mus: David Newman. SpFxMkp: John Dods et al. SpVisFX: (sup) Craig Newman; Dream Quest. Anim: (stopmo) Ted Rae, Little Buddy Prods.; Jeff Burks; (title) Braden Clary. SpMechFxCoord: Adams R. Calvert. Ref: TV. V 4/29/87. ad: MkpFX: Carl Fullerton, John Caglione Jr. et al. Morse. Scheuer. Martin. Maltin '92. Phantom. Hound. With Scott Valentine, Michelle Little, Arnold Johnson, Robert Trebor (Charles), Alan Fudge, Gina Gallego (psychic), Richard Piemonte (monster).

Is Kaz (Valentine) The Mangler? Sexual excitement does turn him, literally, into a beast (the "date that wouldn't leave") and other strange but not too funny things. Behind his problems: a Romanian devil curse which can be lifted only if he does something noble. The catch: The curse is then passed on to the one he loves.... Alternately a slasher movie, a strange romance, and an effects and makeup extravaganza, *Demon Lover* is closest to successful in the romance mode. The film is different, less it seems as a result of calculation than miscalculation. Little is appealing as a human doormat.

**MY FAVORITE SPY** Para (Paul Jones) 1951 b&w 93m. D: Norman Z. McLeod. SP: Edmund Hartmann, Jack Sher. Story: E. Beloin, L. Breslow. Ref: TV. V 10/10/51. Eames. Scheuer. Maltin '92.

Sequence in which a doctor (Norbert Schiller) administers Bob Hope a truth serum—"and all my drugs"—and Hope impersonates Dr. Jekyll mixing and taking a potion and becoming Mr. Hyde.

**MY FRIENDS NEED KILLING** Nick Felix (CPC)/LMN & Mulmac (Jack Marshall) 1976 color 72m. SP, D: Paul Leder. Mus: M. Bucci. Ref: V 6/27/84: "truly crummy." With Greg Mullavey, Meredith MacRae, Clayton Wilcox, Carolyn Ames.

Schizophrenic assumes supposedly twisted personalities of others and kills them.

**MY GRANDPA IS A VAMPIRE** (N.Z.) Republic Pictures/Tucker-Moonrise Prods. (N.Z. Film Commission) 1992 (1991) color feature (aka *Grampire. Moonrise* - orig t). D: David Blyth. Ref: SFChron Dtbk 8/30/92. V 9/30/91:46 (ad). 6/8/92:10 (rated) 1/20/92:46. With Al Lewis (600-year-old vampire), Justin Gocke, Milan Borich.

**MY LITTLE PONY** (U.S.-J) DEG/Sunbow & Marvel (Jay Bacal, Tom Griffin) 1986 anim color 87m. D & Co-P: Michael Jones. SP: G. A. Bloom. Mus: Rob Walsh. SpFX: Yusung Lee, Y. Shin. Anim: AKOM & Toei. Ref: TV. V 5/21/86. no Stanley. Martin: *My Little Pony: The Movie*. Scheuer. Maltin '92. Hound. Voices: Jon Bauman (The Smooze), Peter Cullen (Ahgg), Cloris Leachman (Hydia).

Monster roll-call: the nastily sticky, purple, Oobleck-like Smooze ... the phlume, a tentacled plant ... a "tall furry plant" which turns out to be a gigantic, fanged, ticklish spider .. the initially forbidding, pint-sized, nice Grundles ("You still look like monsters to me") ... the hideous, growling trees of Shadow Forest, that use their branches like spears ... the giant, just-glimpsed, tentacled Ahgg ... and a cemetery ghost.

The response of adults to *My Little Pony* may approximate the witch Hydia's to the frolicking of the little ponies of Ponyland: "It makes me sick!" Fortunately, Hydia—who (unlike the ponies) has some personality—is around, and several monsters enliven things. The Smooze even rates one of the few engaging musical numbers. Tony Randall's number includes a sci-fi bit with "something futuristic made of chrome."

**MY LOVELY MONSTER** (G) Xenon Film & WDR & SFB-TV 1991 color 84m. SP, D, P: Michel Bergmann. Addl Dial: Forrest J Ackerman. Ph: F. Arguelles. Mus: J. Wolter. AD: C. Bussmann. Mkp: Rolf Baumann. Ref: V 3/11/91: "full of wit and gentle charm." Bill Warren. Jones. With Silvio Francesco, Ackerman, Nicole Fisher, Matthias Fuchs, Ferdinand Mayne, Bobbie Bresee, Sara Karloff.

"Ghoul" (Francesco) that looks like Chaney in *London after Midnight* "escapes a burning piece of nitrate celluloid." (V)

**MY MASTER'S NECKLACE** (H.K.) Golden Sun Light Prods.(Hai Ki, Carmen Hung/Sin Kan Yuen) 1991 color/ws 91m. (*The Master's Necklace* - ad t). D: William Oscar Sun. Ph: Tai Wai Cheung. Mus: Siu Lam Tang. PD: Alice Li. Mkp: Lai Kuen Wong. FX: Siu Lung Ching. Ref: TV: King's Video; Eng. titles. With Leung Wai Lui, Kwok Lun Lee, Po Fung Tsui.

"Your soul can go after him." Ingredients here include a murdered man's spirit, which temporarily possesses various people and which (invisibly) aids a cop ... death by magician's voodoo doll ... the God of the Door of a graveyard ... flying ghosts in a woods

... a magic sword ... a versatile necklace which variously protects humans from ghosts and makes ghosts disintegrate ... and, at the end, a sorcerer-vs.-sorcerer duel .... Generally routine horror-comedy has scattered cute bits.

**MY MOM'S A WEREWOLF** Crown Int'l./Hairy (S. J. Wolfe) 1989 (1988) color 84m. D: Michael Fischa. SP: Mark Pirro. Mus: Barry Fasman, Dana Walden. AD: Bruce Mink. SpFxMkp: Steve Patino's Sho-Glass Props & SpFX. OptFX: T&T. Ref: TV. V 5/17/89. no Scheuer. Martin. no Maltin '92. Hound. With Susan Blakely, John Saxon, Katrina Caspary (Jennifer), John Schuck, Ruth Buzzi, Marcia Wallace, Marilyn McCoo, Lou Cutell.

Hypnotic-eyed werewolf Harry Thropen (Saxon)—who is looking for a "were-wife" to keep his race alive—bites housewife Leslie Shaber (Blakely) on the toe. Result: a hair problem.... Basically tired horror-comedy has scattered funny moments. Diana Barrows is amusing as Stacey, a girl who "lives and breathes monsters" and consults old FMs and Fangorias.

**MY NEIGHBOR TOTORO** (J) 50th Street Films (Troma)/Tokuma Group (Toru Hara) & Studio Ghibli 1988 ('93-U.S.) anim color 86m. (*Tonarino Totoro*. aka *Totoro*). SP, D: Hayao Miyazaki. SpFX: Kaoru Tanifuji. Ref: TV: vt; no Eng. Animag 3:4. 9:10, 18-19. ad. *My Neighbor Totoro* (book). Sean Smiley. SFChron 5/8/93. Animerica 5:64 (ad). 6:56. V 5/11/92:31 (ad). 2/22/93:32 (rated). 5/3/93:20. 5/10/93.

"Your house is haunted!" Gently spooky scenes with retiring "mote ghosts" alternate with killingly charming scenes with acorn-eating owl-cat "ghosts," or Totoros, and a Carroll-inspired cat-bus, in this enchantingly conceived animated fantasy. In the section, "The Haunted House"—which section qualifies the movie for an abbreviated entry in this checklist—the mote ghosts (or "dust bunnies ... mischievous little clumps of black dust" [MNT]) are ultimately laughed away from the house they haunt, and up into a huge tree, in a mysteriously haunting (or de-haunting) scene. ("Mom, do you like haunted houses?") The English-dubbed version is from Fox Video.

**MY NEIGHBOURS ARE PHANTOMS!** (H.K.) Grand March Movies 1990 color/ws? 91m. Ref: TV: Pan-Asia Video; Eng. titles. Y. K. Ho.

"Attract more people in to feed us. Let's have the blood of our neighbors!" The subjects in a portrait exchange places with Mr. Cheung, the "mad man" owner of the house. Seems that fifty or sixty years ago, a Taoist "imprisoned" them in the photo. Now they promise that they'll go "back to the north" if they can "eat 49 people's blood." ("May be vampire.") Siu-sin, an attractive, non-predatory phantom falls for Dragon, a human: "I'm ghost; they're elves. But my bones are controlled by them"....

The movie may be episodic, but there's cleverness here re "slow motion charms," "invisible charms," a severed head with comically blinking eyes, and squirt guns with holy water. Sense of humor and plot both recall *My Cousin, the Ghost*. Good shtick: At one point, Dragon accidentally casts the slow-motion spell on himself. Notable exclamation: "That sex lupine!"

**MY PET MONSTER** (Can.) Nelvana & Hi-Tops Video/The Global TV Network & Telefilm Canada (Those Characters from

Cleveland) 1986 color c60m. D: Timothy Bond. SP: J. D. Smith. Story: Nelvana. Ph: Douglas Keifer. Mus: John Weisman. AD: Ted Watkins. SpFX: N. N. T. Ents. PhFX: Digital Magic House, Scenemaker Studio. Ref: TV: Hi-Tops Video. no Martin. Hound. With Sunny B. Thrasher (Max), Alyson Court, Colin Fox, Mark Parr (the monster).

Ancient Babylonian statues in the Weston Museum "possess the power to transform anyone who stands before them" into a monster. They transform schoolboy Max Smith into a "real live monster with monster powers," including super-hearing and super-strength. Periodically, the powers wear off, but hunger pangs restore Max to monster form.... Broadly directed and played comedy for children, with actors from the Gale Gordon School of Comedy.

**MY SCIENCE PROJECT** Touchstone & Silver Screen Partners II (Jonathan Taplin) 1985 color/ws 95m. SP, D: Jonathan R. Betuel. Mus: Peter Bernstein. MkpFX: Lance Anderson. Rex: Doug Beswick Prods.; (consul) Rick Baker. Gizmo Des: Ron Cobb. FxSup: (vis) John Scheele; (sp opt) Gregory Van Der Veer, William Kilduff. FxDes: Peter Lloyd. Globe FX: Larry Albright. AnimDesSup: John Van Vliet. SpMechFX: Michael Lantieri. MinPropFX: R. J. Spetter. SpSdFX: Alan Howarth. PhFxSup: Phil Meador. Ref: TV. MFB'86:249-50. V 8/14/85. Morse. Scheuer. Martin. Maltin '92. Hound. Stanley. With John Stockwell, Danielle von Zerneck, Richard Masur, Dennis Hopper, Michael Berryman (1st mutant), Hank Galia (Neanderthal Man), Frank Welker (alien voices), Fisher Stevens, Robert DoQui, Pamela Springsteen.

"No "Outer Limits" ever had anything like the "gizmo"—an engine which generates power without heat and which an "advanced alien civilization" created. Connected to a battery, it becomes a "door to the 'Twilight Zone'," absorbs energy, becomes ("like the Blob") stronger, and generates a "crossroads of time and space" which sweeps up a Neanderthal Man, survivors "from after the apocalypse," and a plastic-looking Tyrannosaurus Rex.... Science-fiction premise yields a glorified war movie, as high school kids and teachers battle time-warp inhabitants. Noisy lightning, fog, and tornado effects can't obscure the fact that nothing much is going on here. Unlikable characters.

**MY SOUL IS SLASHED** see *Kamitsukitai/Dorakiyura Yori Ai-O*

**MY STEPMOTHER IS AN ALIEN** Col/Weintraub Ent. (Levy-Parker & Catalina) 1988 color 108m. D: Richard Benjamin. SP: Jerico & Herschel Weingrod, Timothy Harris, Jonathan Reynolds. Mus: Alan Silvestri. SpVisFX: John Dykstra; Apogee; (anim sup) Clint Colver; (animatronic eye) Rick Lazzarini. SpFxCoord: Phil Cory. Mkp: Dan Striepeke, Brad Wilder. Ref: TV. MFB'89:143-4. V 12/7/88. SFChron 12/9/88. SFExam 12/9/88. ad. Martin. Maltin '92. Hound. With Dan Aykroyd, Kim Basinger, Jon Lovitz, Alyson Hannigan.

"But, Daddy, she ate batteries!" Dr. Steve Mills (Aykroyd), a "very obscure physicist," and Haddonkirk Research "go extragalactic": Their lightning-boosted Klystron Tube and a short circuit send a radar signal to the Clouds of Magellan, which send back Celeste Martin (Basinger), "chief extragalactic probist" for a planet ("sort of like Switzerland") 92 light years and two solar systems away. A "horrible eye" in her "purse" produces all

materials necessary for her mission—which is to discover the secret of Dr. Mills' transmission and to stabilize her home planet's gravity.

Funniest part of *Stepmother* is its takeoff not only on science-fiction/marital movies like *I Married a Monster from Outer Space* and *Unearthly Stranger,* but on marital horror movie stories like *The Stepfather* and *Undercurrent,* where the new addition to the family proves to be—figuratively at least—from outer space. Among the horrifying tipoffs to the alienness of the newcomer here—she guzzles battery juice. Those little telltale details.... Film's conclusion makes a cute, almost touching Case for Earth. (Evidence includes sneezes, sex, and Jimmy Durante.) But this section plays like a parody of apocalyptic sf films like *Plan 9 from Outer Space,* which means the movie has gotten away from its best subject. The early, Celeste-crashes-the-Twentieth-Century sequences are amusing enough, too, thanks to Basinger's brusque giddiness, but the movie doesn't really come into its own until it starts to make good its title.

**MY SWEET SATAN** Tempe 1992 short. D: Jim Van Bebber. Ref: PT 16:64: "gory ... occult murder."

**MYONURIUI HAN** (S. Korean) Dae Yang Film 1971 color/ws 88m. (aka *The Ghost*). D: Park Yoon Kyo. SP: Choi Jin. Ref: Hardy/HM. With Yoon Mira, Paek Il Sub, Sa Miya.

Two ghost stories.

**MYSTERIOUS PLANET** Video City/Mysterious Planet Ents. (Piper-Baldwin) 1982 color c80m. D, P: Brett Piper. "Very freely based on the novel" (*Mysterious Island* or *L'Ile Mysterieux*?) by Jules Verne. Ph: Nicholas Hackaby. Mus: J. D. Rice, D. A. Blajda et al. Ref: TV: Video City video. no Martin. Hound. With Paul Taupier, Boydd Piper, Michael Quigley, Bruce Nadeau, Marilyn Mullen.

On a strange planet, refugees from a space war—three humans, one alienoid—encounter a giant, two-headed carnivorous snail, a snake, a big, reptilian, docile, tiny-horned beast of burden, a flying dragon, a river beast, a brontosaurus-type, and a tentacled lizard. Other goodies include telepathy and a homemade ray machine.... Ambitious shoestring production has scads of effects, none of them exactly quality, but some of them unexpected. Script, unconcerned re its limited budget, updates Verne to the far future. Not bad for a very bad movie.

**MYSTERIOUS STRANGER, The** (by M. Twain) see *Adventures of Mark Twain, The*

**MYSTERY MANSION** Pacific Int'l./Independent (A. R. Dubs) 1983 color 95m. SP, D: David E. Jackson. SP: also Jack Duggan, Arn Wihtol. Mus: William Loose et al. SpFX: Brian Burton? SpSd: Sd FX. Ref: TV. V 7/4/84. 1/4/84:4. no Scheuer. Martin. no Maltin '92. Stanley. With Dallas McKennon (Sam), Greg Wynne, Jane Ferguson, Randi Brown.

"All these spooks gallivanting around" in the old Drake Mansion—a "haunted" house in Jacksonville, Oregon—scare off intruders. But Old Sam's inventions, which make chairs rattle, a chandelier spin, fog spread, and a "ghost" fly, account for the mysterious noises and tremors. And the "monster" is just Sam in a mask. One girl, Susan (Brown), however, turns out to be genuinely psychic.

The sequence of ghostly phenomena is fun, but a long time coming in this balefully innocuous kiddie movie. Nostalgia Corner: The movie's title was also the title of a "Shock Theatre"-type horror-movie package shown on KXTV, channel ten, in Sacramento in the early Sixties.

**2P MYSTERY OF THE THIRD PLANET** (Russ) Five Star Film Int'l. 1982 (1981) anim color 48m. Ref: TV: Video Geminis; aka *Viaje al Tercer Planeta;* Span.-lang.; no Eng. V 7/1/81:21. Ecran F 22:43.

Fun ingredients in this casual sf-comedy-adventure include a big, silly, multi-armed robot ... various planets, more or less inhabited ... a space zoo ... funny odd aliens ... and mirror-flowers with a "memory bank".... The functional plotline only occasionally interrupts the comic festivities here.

**\*The MYSTERY OF THE 13TH GUEST** Lindsley Parsons 1943. Mus D: Edward Kay. Ref: TV. V 10/13/43. Lentz. Weldon. Stanley. With Jacqueline Dalya.

"I'm doing a ghost act." Ingredients: a man in a weird shiny mask ... electrocution by telephone ... super-plastic-surgery ... a secret room ... screams ... moron comic relief ... and stilted melodrama. Remake of *The Thirteenth Guest* (which see).

**\*MYSTERY OF THE WAX MUSEUM** 1933 (1932) c77m. AD: Anton Grot. Ref: TV. Lee. V 2/21/33. Hardy/HM. Weldon. Lentz.

"It wasn't like anything human! He made Frankenstein look like a lily." A silent, skulking, scarred phantom. Eight missing bodies. Human statues in New York City's London Wax Museum. ("He's a statue!") And a *Phantom of the Opera*-like mask-breaking, which reveals the hideously-scarred face of Ivan Igor (Lionel Atwill), proprietor of same.... Not much of a story here, but a lot to look at. The long shots allow you to take in all of the big sets, and night exteriors are atmospherically shadowy and blue-tinged. In one fun throwaway bit, two eyes slowly open in a plastic molding on a table. And was this the first movie to exploit the eeriness of melting wax faces? At times, Atwill has a phony-sounding accent.

**MYSTERY OF YATE** see *Enigma del Yate, El*

**\*The MYSTIC** 1925 silent b&w 67m. Ref: screen. Lentz. Lee. V 9/2/25. SFChron 11/25/94.

"Spirit World At Call Of Her Strange Power." (New York newspaper headline) At a seance, Zara (Aileen Pringle), the Mystic, a gypsy, conjures up a "wraith." ("Do you really think she can make the dead return?") During a second seance, the supposed ghost of Doris Merrick's (Gladys Hulette) father appears from "spirit-land." ("It's the spirits!") Finally, in an unscheduled ectoplasmic encounter, Doris sees her Daddy. ("It was the spirit of my father!")

Spiritism expose anticipates director Tod Browning's last film, *Miracles for Sale* (which see). The sometimes strained plot depends upon a somewhat unconvincing change of character in Conway Tearle's con man, Michael Nash. The first-seance "ghost" is a genuinely spooky writhing-white effect, even though

we know who's under the sheet. Later, we don't see the real ghost, but the indication is that it's not just in the young lady's mind.

**MYSTICS IN BALI** (Indonesian?) 198-? color/ws feature. Ref: VSOM: trailer.

Ghosts with removable entrails. ("I will have to borrow your head for a short time.") Cf. *Krasu.*

# N

**NG KNIGHT LAMNE** (J) King Record 1991 anim color 30m. Ref: V. Max 2:5: 3rd of 3 OAVs. "Mecha action a la Grandzord."

**NAAG NAGIN** (India) Bohra Int'l. 1989 color feature. Story, D, P: Ram Kumar Bohra. SP: Malhar-Suri(sp?). Ph: A. Latif. Mus: L. Pyarelal. PD: M.K. Bohra. Mkp: Anil Gire. Ref: TV: Excel Video (Video Sound); little Eng.; Hindi. With Rajiv Kapoor, Mandakini, S. Shah, Rajendra Nath.

Another hokey Indian were-snake fantasy. Featured: a cobra terrorizing some men in a pickup ... the cobra in the parlor hitting the light switch, tuning in the radio, cackling, hanging from the overhead fan, and in general tormenting a man ... and a woman turning (in double exposure) into a snake. Plus: the baby with two evil eyes, and a cobra-vs.-cobra scene.

**NACHE NAGIN GALI GALI** (India) Dhanji Prasad c1987? color feature. D: Mohanji Prasad. Mus: Kalyanji Anandji. Ref: TV: Atlantic Video; no Eng. Meadows Video: *Cobra Seeking Companion* - tr t. With Natish Bharadhwaj, M. Seshadri.

One of the battiest of the Indian were-snake fantasies, this concerns a sorcerer who unleashes lethal flying fireballs and who—in priceless scenes—follows his prey around like white on rice and tries to charm, with flute, the snake out of the man, or woman, or vice versa. Busby Berkeley would be proud of the snakes-and-snake-charmers musical number—even some of the snakes seem to be swaying in unison. No one admitted during the flying-cobra scene.

**NACHT DER ERKENNTNIS, Die** see *Warning Shadows*

**NADIA—THE MOVIE** (J) Toho Video 1991 anim color 87m. Ref: TV: Toho Video; no Eng.

Verne-ish and Lupin-ish ingredients include mysteriously disintegrating bodies ... a gigantic death ray ... a vehicle with robotic "tentacle" grippers ... weird undersea structures ... a transporter ray which beams up Nadia at one point ... a volcanic-island fortress ... cyborg-types kept in liquid hibernation ... Nadia's mystical power to translate ancient symbols ... and the secret of "Vital Energy".... This movie version of a Japanese TV show looks lively and colorful, if familiar.

**NADJA** October Films/Kino Link (David Lynch/Sweeney-Hobby) 1994 (1995) b&w 95m. SP, D: Michael Almereyda. Ph: Jim Denault. Mus: S.F. Turner. PD: Kurt Ossenfort. SpFX: A. Jolly. Mkp: D. Doll. Ref: V 9/26/94: "thoughtful and humorous." ad. SFChron 10/6/95: "stylish & compelling ... first half-hour"; then: "it's interminable." PT 22:10. TV: Evergreen Ent. viceo. Sacto Bee 10/20/95. With Suzy Amis, Elina Lowensohn (Nadja), Peter

Fonda (Dr. Van Helsing), Karl Geary (Renfield), Jared Harris (Edgar), Galaxy Craze, Martin Donovan.

"Stunning twin vampires in trendy nocturnal Gotham...." "My father was a night bird." Dracula's daughter (Lowensohn) keeps a supply of shark-embryo blood around ("She's a monster"), and a pet tarantula named Bela turns up. But the most interesting thing about this affected, near-unwatchable horror-fantasy is that it's an unofficial remake of *Dracula's Daughter*, which was pretty bizarre itself. (Here, Sandor becomes Renfield; Van Helsing is still Van Helsing.) As such, its one coup is that it finally puts Bela Lugosi into *Dracula's Daughter*, where he belongs: In a flashback, a clip of Lugosi from *White Zombie* stands in for Dracula. (Meanwhile, Fonda is credited here as Dracula, and Jeff Winner as Young Dracula.)

**NAGINA** (India) Eastern Films 1986 color c145m. D, P: Harmesh Malhotra. SP: Ravi Kapoor. Story: Jagmohan Kapoor. Dial: Dr. A. Nagar. Ph: V. Durga Prasad. Mus: L. Pyarelal. AD: G. Basak. SpFX: Krishan & Baldev Malik. Mkp: V. Kasturi et al. Ref: TV: M.G. Video; Hindi; no Eng. With Rishi Kapoor, Sri Devi, Prem Chopra, Amrish Puri, Jagdeep.

In the wood, then in a jeep, a pack of cobras besieges, then bites a man. Later, now-you-see-them-now-you-don't cobras besiege a house, and a good snake (woman) battles a bad snake in a hospital room. At the end, a snake charmer sees to it that a good snake brings a bad-snake-bit boy back to life .... Most interesting sequence in this routine Indian musical-fantasy-horror movie is the early one in which the mystery woman glides through the decaying mansion—a curious combination of music and spookiness.

Sequel: *Nigahen.*

**NAGINA PART II** see *Nigahen*

**NAGLALAGABLAB NA GABI** (Fili) Final Cut Films 1987 color c130m. D: Augusto Salvador. Story, SP: Jojo Lapus. Story, Ed: Toto Natividad. Ref: TV: Ent. Exponents of H'w'd. video; little Eng.

Bizarre Filipino melodrama seems to be available in either a hardcore or an "abridged" version and concerns a "demon" in a red-feathered cape and head mask who rapes a woman. Is the latter mad and merely imagining the feather man, or is someone really running around seducing, persecuting, and (in one instance) killing women? Cornball tragic ending caps Jesus Franco-like perversity.

**NAIL GUN MASSACRE** Reel Movies Int'l./Terry Lofton & Futuristic Films 1987 color 84m. SP, D, SpFX: T. Lofton. D: also Bill Leslie. Ref: V 5/13/87: "amateurish horror feature." PT 4:14. Phantom. With Rocky Patterson, Michelle Meyer, Ron Queen.

A "tools of killing" thriller. (V)

**NAK THE GHOST** (Thai) c1987? color c98m. Ref: TV: Extra Times video; no Eng. Thai Video: above is tr t.

The ghost of a woman who died when about to give birth shoots eye-rays at baby-ghost's hammock. Suddenly, he is full-grown, if rather infantile, and sings "Say You, Say Me." Both can disappear at will and both enjoy scaring humans; he can revert to baby form. At the end, these multilingual ghosts sing "Sayonara" and vanish.

Low, low comedy is very silly, occasionally transcendently so, as in the scene in which the big baby assumes Lionel Richie's (dubbed) voice. The mother-ghost can appear as either beauty or monster, and, in one funny scene, she appears in monster form and scares her son, who apparently did not realize that Mama was so versatile.

**The NAKED GUN: FROM THE FILES OF POLICE SQUAD!** Para/Zucker-Abrahams-Zucker 1988 color 85m. SP, D: David Zucker. SP: also Jerry Zucker, Jim Abrahams, Pat Proft. SpFxSup: Cliff Wenger. Ref: TV. MFB'89:55-6.

Erratic, fitfully hilarious spoof features "sensory induced hypnosis" which produces instant, zombie-like assassins ("I must kill Nordberg!"), a la *Telefon*. Based on the "Police Squad!" TV series.

**NAKED KILLER** (H.K.) Wong Jin's Workshop (Dennis Chan) 1992('94-U.S.) color/ws 88m. D: Clarence Fok Yiu Leung. SP, P: Jing Wong. Ph: William Yim. Mus: Lowell Lo. AD: Ngai Fong Nay. Ref: TV: World Video; Eng. titles. SFChron 10/21/94. With Chingmy Yau, Simon Yam, Carrie Ng, Kelly.

"We clean away the rubbish of the world." Cindy and Kitty—the latter "born to be a killer"—join forces, keep rapists and other scum chained in their home, wreak revenge for violence done to women ... by lopping off the "reproductive organs" of their victims. ("Were they making love with a female gorilla?")

Sensationalistic, isn't it? This, the most bizarre and far-fetched of the MS. 45 movies, is gross and proud of it. In motion, *Naked Killer*, with its comically overdone, violent set-pieces—which leave offices and indoor parking garages littered with the dead and the dying—is perversely amusing; the talkier latter half is more ponderous.

**NAKED LUNCH** (Can.-B-J) Fox/Jeremy Thomas, Gabriella Martinelli & Telefilm Canada & The Ontario Film Development Corp. & Film Trustees Ltd. & Pierson Heldring Pierson & Nippon Film Development (Recorded Picture Co./Naked Lunch Prods.) 1991 color 115m. SP, D: David Cronenberg, from William S. Burroughs' book. Mus: Howard Shore. SpCreatures & FX: Chris Walas; (mech sup) Kelly Lepowski; (des) Stephan Dupuis. Floor SpFX: Ted Ross. Mkp: Christine Hart. Ref: TV. V 12/23/91. 1/13/92: "Naked Making Lunch" - documentary. SFExam 1/10/92. NYT 12/27/91. With Peter Weller, Judy Davis, Ian Holm, Julian Sands, Roy Scheider, Monique Mercure, Nicholas Campbell, Michael Zelniker, Peter Boretski (creature voices).

"I suffer from sporadic hallucinations." Weird fauna intermingle with humans here and include a phallic centipede/sex-bug-from-the-typewriter (the Gross, the Erotic, and the Literary, all-in-one) ... a Mugwump, a barfly-mutant which occasionally doubles as a typewriter ("So foreign, it's almost alien") and winds up in a combination torture chamber/Weird Dairy for Humans, in Interzone, North Africa ... a centipede/human sexual predator in a parrot cage ... various big cockroach types which play "case officer" or typewriter as, apparently, the mood strikes them ... and a man (Scheider) encased in a woman (Mercure).

Like real people, these critters are alternately droll, boring, and disgusting. This *Roger Rabbit* for grown-ups certainly constitutes an unusual depiction of the creative process, but it's too labyrinthine in its imagery to qualify as much more than a curiosity. It's almost alien—which is the good news as well as the bad news. Line for the ages: "Joan was an elite corps centipede."

**NAKED MASSACRE** (Can.-W.G.?) Questar/Fink-Reuther 1975 color 90m. D: Denis Heroux. Ph: Heinz Holscher. Mus: Voggenreiter Verlag. AD: Guy Sheppard. Ref: TV: Vidcrest video. Stanley. Hound. Phantom ref. no Martin. V 5/9/84:264(ad). Ecran F 29:67: sfa *Ne Pour l'enfer* (F-Can./'78/D: Heroux)? VW 28:7: *Born for Hell*; Can.-F-I-G. With Mathieu Carriere, Debby Berger, Christine Boisson, Miriam Boyer, Leonara Fani, Carole Laure, Eva Mattes.

"I'm sorry. I'll have to tie you up for a couple of hours. I hope you don't mind." Belfast. Cain Adamson, late of the U.S. Army, and fresh from Vietnam, represents the "spirit of uncontrolled violence at loose in the world today." "Scared of women," he ties up seven or eight nurses in one room, then takes them out, one or two at a time, and stabs them. ("He's worse than that fellow in Chicago.") One nurse, crazy with fear, stabs herself. Final toll: eight dead, one in shock.... Is it relevant or sick? Well, it's stronger on sick, for which the "relevance" seems a pretext.

**NAKED OBSESSION** Concorde (Ron Zwang/Rodman Flender) 1990 color 80m. Story, D: Dan Golden. Story, SP: Robert Dodson. SpFMkp: Diaction. Ref: TV. V 1/7/91. SFChron Dtbk 7/7/91. Martin.

"Who are you anyway?" Confusing combo of put-on, fantasy, sex, and violence concerns a city council member (William Katt) who spends a "very weird evening" on the "dark side" of the city at the Ying Yang Club. He encounters, a) a stripper (Maria Ford) who is into "very dangerous stuff" in the bedroom and, b) a wino (Rick Dean) who does a devil-like disappearing act and who at one point induces a heart attack in a cop. Attempt to vary the *Stripped To Kill* formula yields some offbeat bits.

**NAKED VENGEANCE** (U.S.-Fili) Concorde & M.P. Films & D. S. Pictures (Santiago-Maharaj) 1986 (1985) color 78m. (97m.) (*Satin Vengeance* - alt t). D, P: Cirio H. Santiago. SP: Reilly Askew. Story, Exec P: Anthony Maharaj. SpFX: J. Sto. Domingo. Mkp: Teresa Mercader, Norma Remias. Ref: TV. V 6/11/86. Stanley. Hound. Phantom ref. McCarty II. Martin. Scheuer.

"Dead people don't talk." But did Carla Harris (Deborah Tranelli) actually die in that fire? Not quite. She continues to take revenge on male chauvinist pigs and killers. One victim is jammed into an ice-house shredder, another is cleavered in a butcher shop. Gothic elements in this contrived revenge actioner with horrific overtones include a handy thunderstorm to signal the beginning of Carla's vendetta.

**NAKU ... HA!** (Fili) Cineventures Inc. 1985 color c102m. D: J. Cabreira. SP: Enrique de Jesus. Ph: Rudy Dino. Mus: Tito Sotto. SpFX: Roberto Sto. Domingo. SdFX: Danny Salvador. Mkp: Baby Gonzales. Ref: TV: Viva Video; songs & some dialogue in Eng. With Tito, Vic & Joey; Joey Albert, Debraliz, Trina Laurel, T. Itlog.

"According to history, the Philippines has always had, as a main feature, the haunted house." In the extended climactic sequence, the protagonists and some kidnappers battle each other and midget zombie-ghosts in just such a house. At one point, the kidnappers dress up as ghosts, but the real ones prevail.... Silly, occasionally amusing low comedy. For the haunted house sequence, the colors of fear are blue and white.

**NANNY, The** see *Guardian, The*

**NARCO SATANICO** (Mex) Guadalupe Emperatriz 1988? color c75m. D: Rafael Portillo. SP: Fernando Cortes, Alejandro Cabanillas, Sablum Avalos. Ph: J. M. Herrera. Mus: Jorge Perez. AD: Manuel Guevara. Mkp: Martinez, Peyrot. Ref: TV: FilmMex video; no Eng. With David Reynoso, Ana Luisa Peluffo, Beatriz Aguirre, Roberto Canedo, Silvia Suarez, Carluis Saval.

Ingredients include the devil ... unlikely knife-through-throat gore ... nightmares re a graveyard crawling with zombies ... macumba dancer Vicki ... apparent spirit possession ... the walking corpse of Ricardo Santamaria, who stabs the voodoo mistress—who started all this—in the forehead and rips out the innards of a member of a firing squad.... More Satanico than Narco, as gore and sex rate the lion's share of the footage. The zombie makeup is amusingly grotesque, but the gore effects are unconvincing.

**NARCOSATANICOS ASESINOS** (Mex) Frontera Films 1989 color c72m. (*Narcosatanicos* - orig t). D: J. J. Munguia. Story, SP: G. M. & A. M. Solares. Story: also Ignacio Solares. SpFX: Arturo Godinez. Ref: TV: Million Dollar Video; no Eng. V 5/2/90:242. TVG.

Broad comedy/fantasy/actioner/skin-flick features a deal with Lucifer and one scene re human sacrifice. At one point, Lucifer calls the hero out of his grave.

**NASTY HUNTER** see *Lady Terminator*

**NATAS ... THE REFLECTION** Arizona/West 1983 (1982) color 90m. SP, D, Exec Co-P: Jack Dunlap. Ph: D.D. Bell. Mus: Mitchell Markham. SpMkp&FX: Chris Bergshneider. SpFX: Ray Robinson, Jim Haughlum. VisElecFX: Ruxton & Image Transform. Ref: TV: ThrillerVideo. Newman: "one excellent sequence." Phantom: "extravagantly awful." vc box. Ecran F 52:70-1. Stanley. Hound. With Randy Mulkey, Pat Bolt, Craig Hensley, Kelli Kuhn, Fred Perry, Nino Cochise, Tom Martinelli (Natas), Bob Cota (the killer), Richard Aufmuth (ghost town zombie).

"There really is a town out here." Ingredients: "imprisoned" spirits in Natas Tower—a sort of holding tank of the dead (after 100 years, they go to hell if they're not released) ... a ghost town which is literally a town of ghosts ... a full-fledged, winged Prince of Darkness ... a knife-wielding ghoul in a coffin ... a zombie in a hayloft ... a literally-hot-to-trot ghoul ... and a beheading.... Despite the presence of the devil, this is for the most part a talky, stodgy slasher movie, with an odd can-o'-lizard scene.

**NATIONAL MUMMY, The** see *Momia Nacional, La*

**NATTEVAGTEN** (Danish) All Right Film/Thura Film & Danish Film Inst. & Danmarks Radio (Michael Obel) 1994 color 104m. SP, D: Ole Bornedal. Ph: Dan Laustsen. Mus: Sort Sol et al. AD: S. K. Soerensen. Ref: V 5/30/94: "slickly made but fairly conventional." With Nikolaj Waldau, Sofie Graaboel, Kim Bodnia.

"A serial killer is snuffing and scalping prostitutes, whose corpses sometimes rise off the slab and roam the corridors." *Nightwatch* - tr t?

**NATURAL BORN KILLERS** WB/Monarchy 1994 color 120m. Co-SP, D: Oliver Stone. Story: Quentin Tarantino. Ref: TV: vt. SFChron 8/23/94. 8/26/94. V 8/15/94. Vallejo T-H 8/26/94.

"Only love can kill the demon." Savage satire features some-times-almost-subliminal Gothic elements, including morphing-faced demons, dragons, a beheaded man who stands up, a clip from the original *Frankenstein,* a rattler attack, cartoon serpents, and a Geraldo Rivera figure who (a la *Basket Case 3*) dies at the hands of his subjects.... An alternately dazzling and ponderous film. Tommy Lee Jones' horrifically hilarious warden-from-hell (or in hell) here easily steals the show from the less-certainly-written Mickey (Woody Harrelson) and Mallory (Juliette Lewis). They're just Monsters Two and Three to his Monster One. The background-graphics running counterpoint/commentary seems to scramble, evocatively, Godard, Dreyer, Fellini, Bunuel, Freud, and Jung. It's like a "shadow" story-behind-the-story.

**NAUSICAA** or **NAUSICAA OF THE VALLEY OF THE WIND** see *Warriors of the Wind*

**The NAVIGATOR: A MEDIAEVAL ODYSSEY** (N.Z.-Austral.) Circle Films/Film Investment Corp. of N.Z. & Arenafilm (John Maynard) 1988 ('89-U.S.) color and b&w 91m. (*The Navigator: An Odyssey across Time* - ad t). SP, D: Vincent Ward. SP: also Kelly Lyons, Geoff Chapple. Mus: Davood A. Tabrizi. SpPhFX & OptFX: Mirage FX. MechFX: Brian Harris. SdFxSup: Lee Smith. SpFxSup: Paul Nichola. Conceptual Des: Michael Worrall. Ref: screen. V 5/11/88. Sacto Union 5/24/89. Sacto Bee 5/24/89. MFB'89:144-5. SFExam 4/14/89. SFChron Dtbk 4/9/89. With Bruce Lyons, Chris Haywood, Hamish McFarlane, Marshall Napier.

In the year 1348, a psychic boy, Griffin (McFarlane), leads an expedition from Cumbria March, England, through a hole to the "far side of the Earth," and the night lights of twentieth-century Auckland. ("It's like it's on fire!") There the group encounters "sea serpents" (a submarine) and "monsters" (trains, trucks, cars, mechanical cranes) and finds the church which Griffin saw in a vision.... Griffin is as prophetic a seer as Jules Verne: His story of a tunnel to the future turns out to be just that, a story, recounted to his fellow Cumbrians and based on his visions. The latter also prove to be metaphorical and personally prophetic—he dies, not in a fall, as he "saw," but of the plague.

This latter, puzzling, all-a-story postscript seems to have little to do with the body of the film, an enjoyable, funny sf-fantasy-adventure. The script's two main attractions: the play with anachronism (the "monsters," etc.) and with prophecy. Crossing a busy freeway on foot is an incomprehensible ordeal for the Medieval villagers, a trial-by-six-lane concocted by the gods of the future.

The dream image of a slowly falling, floating glove is the oddly beautiful key to what will be, to who will die.

**NAVIGATOR, The** see *Flight of the Navigator*

**NAVIGATOR—THE RETURN** see *Space Navigators*

**NAVIGATORS OF THE SPACE** see *Space Navigators*

**NAYUTA** (J) Toho 1987? anim color 80m. Ref: V 5/6/87:469 (ad): "spacemen." Japan Video.

**NE POUR L'ENFER** see *Naked Massacre*

**NEAR DARK** DEG/Feldman-Meeker (Near Dark Joint Venture) 1987 color 93m. SP, D: Kathryn Bigelow. SP: also Eric Red. Mus: Tangerine Dream. SpFxMkp: Gordon Smith. Body Smoking FX: Image Engineering. SpFxCoord: Steve Galich, Dale Martin. Ref: screen. MFB'88:3. V 9/23/87. With Adrian Pasdar, Jenny Wright, Lance Henriksen, Bill Paxton, Jenette Goldstein, Joshua Miller, Tim Thomerson.

"Sure haven't met any girls like you...." Mae (Wright) is a vampire. But she doesn't want to show this nice guy (Pasdar) why she's different. He forces the issue, and she administers two quick injections. "He's turned!" Caleb has, apparently, become one of the brood, along with Jesse (Henriksen), little Homer (Miller), and company. For fun, these wild and crazy undead play Russian roulette, take shotgun blasts in the stomach, and cough up bullets.

Until a cop-out, transfusion-cure ending—recalling *House of Dracula*—*Near Dark* is a sometimes taking tale of reluctant vampires, a supernatural edition of *They Live by Night*. The reluctance of Caleb and Mae to kill—even for food—is contrasted with the bloodthirsty glee of the other, more hardened vampires. Surprise line of the movie: Mae's comment that she'll still be around when the light from a certain star arrives on Earth.

**NEBYVALSHINA** (Russ) Int'l. Film Exchange/Lenfilm 1983 color 85m. SP, D: Sergei Ovcharov, based on Russian folk tales. Mus: Igor Matzievsky. Ref: PFA. V 6/18/86: a "marvelous children's offering." With Aleksandr Kuznetzov, Aleksei Buldakov, Sergei Bekhterev.

"Flying machine ... underground hell replete with ... monsters." (V)

**NECO Z ALENKI** see *Alice*

**NECROMANCER** Bonaire Films & Spectrum Ent. (Roy McAree) 1989 (1988) color 88m. (aka *Necromancer—Satan's Servant*). D: Dusty Nelson. SP: Bill Naud. Mus: Gary Stockdale et al. SpFxMkp: (des) William J. Males & Assoc.; Patricia Hazeltine. OptFxSup: Mike Hyatt. SdFxEd: Mike Taylor. Ref: TV. V 4/12/89. PT 8:55, 58. With Elizabeth Kaitan or Cayton, Russ Tamblyn, John Tyler, Rhonda Dorton, Stan Hurwitz, Waide A. Riddle, Lois Masten (Lisa, necromancer).

"And for revenge Thou hast created this demon. Her domain is darkness—her purpose wickedness." (Dead Sea Scrolls)

A rape victim (Kaitan) consults a witch ("The necromancer talks to the dead, uses their spirits"), and the "Lord of Doom" sends

Julie's spirit-double (who can turn into a green-eyed monster-demon) to slay the rapist and his cohorts. ("I saw this horrible monster!").... Otherwise worthless script has an interesting bit in which telephoned words of love temporarily make the demon-double vanish. Dumb-Novelty Dept.: At one point, the witch woman commands a victim to slash himself to death. Bonus of sorts: a telegraphed, *Repulsion*-like mirror trick.

**NECRONOMICON** (I/1967) see *Possedees du Diable, Les*

**NECRONOMICON** Pioneer & Ozla/Necronomicon Films & Davis Film (Samuel Hadida, Brian Yuzna) 1993 color/ws 96m. D: Brian Yuzna, Christophe Gans, Shu Kaneko. SP: B.V. Friedman, Gans, K. Ito. Story: Friedman, Yuzna. From "The Rats in the Walls," "Cool Air," and "The Whisperer in Darkness" by H.P. Lovecraft. Ph: Gerry Lively; Russ Brandt. Mus: Joseph LoDuca, Daniel Licht. PD: Anthony Tremblay. SpMech & MkpFX: T.C. Rainone. MkpFX: Rodd Matsui. SpCreations: MMI, Screaming Mad George, Steve Johnson's XFX, Optic Nerve, Tom Savini, Bart Mixon's Monster Fixins. Stopmo: Todd Masters. Computer Imagery: Perpetual Motion Pictures. Physical SpFX: G. Bruno Stempel. OptFX: Title House;(sup) David Hewitt. Ref: TV: VSOM. S&S 11/94:59: "entertaining and imaginative horror romp." With David Warner, Jeffrey Combs (H.P. Lovecraft), Bruce Payne, Belinda Bauer, Maria Ford, Richard Lynch, Bess Meyer, Millie Perkins, Dennis Christopher, Curt Lowens, Signy Coleman, Don Calfa.

"The Drowned": A man's wife and son are revived from the dead—a mini-octopus seems to be involved in the process, as well as, later, a long, long tentacle and, finally, a Cthulhu-type. Fun effects; not much of a story. Cute: the Monster Special Delivery.

"The Cold": "I need ice!" Old Dr. Madden has discovered the "secret of preserving life"—cryptobiosis. But he needs "fresh spinal fluid." At the end, he turns to goop. Chaotic continuity.

"Whispers": Bat-like things need bone marrow. The proliferation of the things becomes amusing.

Plus more goopy gore creatures in the wraparound "The Library."

**NECROPOLIS** Empire/Tycin Ent. (Taryn/DePaula-Kincaid) 1987 (1986) color 77m. SP, D: Bruce Hickey. Ph: A.D. Marks. AD: Lounsbury, Zurkow. SpMkpFX: Ed French. MinFxDes: James Chai. SpFX: Matt Vogel. SpSdFX: Luciano Anzellotti. Ref: TV: Vestron Video (Lightning Video). V 5/27/87: "embarrassingly poor." Morse. With LeeAnne Baker (Eva), Jacquie Fitz, Michael Conte, W. K. Reed.

"You will never kill me!" A mind-reading, reincarnated witch from the Seventeenth Century preys on the weaknesses of others, brands her victims, and does parlor tricks for her underground ghouls/followers—e.g., she turns her two breasts into six and suckles them with her victims' ectoplasm. She needs a devil's ring and a virgin's blood to complete a ritual, and, at the end, her severed, crawling hand possesses the heroine.... Bizarre premises (group reincarnation, the suckling six), indifferent execution.

**NEEDFUL THINGS** Col/Castle Rock & New Line (Jack Cummins/Peter Yates) 1993 color 120m. (*More Needful Things*-TV) D: Fraser C. Heston. SP: W. D. Richter, from Stephen King's

novel. Ph: Tony Westman. Mus: Patrick Doyle. PD: Douglas Higgins. SpFxCoord: Gary Paller. Ref: V 8/23/93: "sadistic, mean-spirited, overlong." Sacto Bee 8/27/93: "film isn't funny enough or scary enough." SFChron 8/27/93: "misses." With Max von Sydow, Ed Harris, Bonnie Bedelia, Amanda Plummer, J. T. Walsh, Duncan Fraser.

Demon-at-work in small town?

**NEELI GHATI** (India - Hindi) Ruhi Films Int'l.(M. Mohsin) 1989 color 93m. SP, D: Ajay Dixit. Ph: Nandu Chaudhari. Mus: Suresh Sargam. Mkp: Shyam. Ref: TV: Damji video; occ. English. Meadows Video: *Blue Valley* - tr t. With Anil Dhawan, Dinesh Hingoo, Mac Mohan, Yunus Parwez.

Laughable shot-on-tape horror re a vengeful woman who returns from the grave, initially, it seems, as a vampire. (She goes for the neck of her first victim.)

**NEKROMANTIK** (W.G.) Jelinski-Buttgereit 1987 color 68m. SP, D, SpFX: Joerg Buttgereit. SP, SpFX: also Franz Rodenkirchen. Ph: Uwe Bohrer. Mus: Hermann Kopp et al. SpFX: also D. Lorenz. OptFX: Jelinski. Slime Supply: M. Rodenkirchen. Ref: TV: vt; Eng. titles. McCarty II. With Daktari Lorenz, Beatrice M., Harald Lundt.

Robert Schmadtke, who works for Joe's Streetcleaning Agency—which picks up accident-victim's bodies—gets too involved in his work, takes home a skeleton, and he and Betty make love to it—and, incidentally, to each other—in this determinedly lyrical/gross New Gore movie re sick, far-from-ordinary people. Highlights of sorts include a dream re a revived corpse, a beheading, cat smearing, and self-evisceration. The story has a certain symmetry and logic to it, but little else. Wisely, the film bears its own "Beware!" sign.

**NEKROMANTIK 2** (W.G.) c1987 color and b&w c100m. Ref: TV: Video Underground; no Eng. V 10/12/92:1, 205. PV 14:7.

Our "hero" from the first film is now on the deader end of a necrophiliac relationship. His live love, however, goes on to find seemingly healthier romance with a certifiably living gentleman and—apparently regretfully—cuts up the corpse. But she later proceeds to cut up her live boy friend, too, then replaces his head with the original dead head. If for others this might not qualify as Fulfillment, for her it seems to fill the bill.... If nothing else, this movie is true to its portmanteau title. It's also unmercifully padded, though it features a couple of sufficiently sickening sequences, which, after all, is the main idea. The soundtrack features that same damn music.

**NELLE PIEGHE DELLA CARNE** see *Folds of the Flesh*

**NELVANAMATION,** compilation video, *see: Cosmic Christmas, A. Devil and Daniel Mouse, The. Intergalactic Thanksgiving. Romie-0 and Julie-8.* Ref: vt. V 9/2/91:56.

**NELVANAMATION II** see *Take Me up to the Ball Game*

**NEMESIS** Imperial Ent. (Shah-Karson-Karnowski/Scanbox Danmark A/S) 1992 color 95m. D: Albert Pyun. SP: Rebecca Charles. Ph: G. Mooradian. Mus: M. Rubini. PD: E. Colleen Saro. SpVisFX: Fantasy II; Gene Warren Jr. FxMkp: David P.

Barton. SpFxSup: Terry Frazee. Go Motion Anim: Peter Kleinow. Digital FX: Damian Klaus. Ref: TV: IE video. V 2/1/93: "film doesn't even make a stab at logic." 10/19/92:16 (rated). PT 16:17. Imagi 1:44-7, 61, 62. With Olivier Gruner, Tim Thomerson, Cary-Hiroyuki Tagawa, Nicholas Guest, Thom Mathews, Brion James, Deborah Shelton, Jackie Earle Haley.

"We can't tell who's real and who's not." L.A. and Baja, New America, 2027 A.D. The U.S. and Japan have "merged," and even little old ladies are lethal. Cyborg-hero Alex (Gruner)—"86.5% is still human"—discovers a plot to replace all humans with cyborgs.... Stunt-happy sf-actioner's clear highlight: the stopmo metal man at the end. There's also some grisly cy-surgery. Either the walls are thinner in 2027 or the bullets are thicker.

**NEMESIS** see *Shakma*

**NEO-HEROIC-LEGEND** see *Weathering Continent, The*

**NEO-TOKYO** see *Meikyu Monogatari*

**NEON CITY** Trimark/Kodiak Films (Little Bear Films/Wolf Schmidt & John Schouweiler) 1991 color 108m. SP, D: Monte Markham. SP: also Buck Finch, Jeff Begun. Mus: Stephen Graziano. PD: Fu Ding Cheng. Prosth Mkp: Brad Look. SpFxCoord: Rick Josephson. Overland Transport: Unique Movie Cars. Ref: TV. V 10/14/91:A-53 (ad). 10/19/92:122. TVG. HBO/Cinemax 8/92. Martin. With Michael Ironside, Vanity, Lyle Alzado, Valerie Wildman, Nick Klar, Juliet Landau, Aresenio Trinidad, Richard Sanders.

North America, Western Federation, 2053 A.D., a time of "the bright"—the phenomenon whereby sunlight passes through a "giant magnifying glass in the sky made out of tiny particles of water and pollutants" and creates a "hot spot" which burns the skin ... gas-mask-like "breathers," required for passage through a "Zander cloud," a phenomenon apparently started when a laser experiment blew a hole in the ozone ... "turbo-jet assisted" vehicles ... mutants ... and ray guns. In this context, an assorted group of misfits books passage on a huge truck making the Jericho-Neon City run through the Outlands.

Closer, surprisingly, to *Stagecoach* than to *The Road Warrior.* Sentiment, suspense, and a truckload of talk—as invariably happens when a bounty hunter, his prize, a prostitute-type, a sweet young rich thing, a phony doctor, a salesman, etc., get together. A few pleasant moments among the cliches.

**NEON MANIACS** Bedford Ent./Cimarron (Kelly Park) 1986 (1985) color 91m. D: Joseph Mangine. SP: Mark Patrick Carducci. Mus: Kendall Schmidt. SpVisMkpFX: Mkp FX Labs, Allan Apone, Douglas J. White. Mech FX: Image Engineering. SpVideoFX: F. X. Baleno. SpVocalFX: Peter Cullen. SpElecVoiceFX: Prism, W. K. Sussex. Ref: TV. V 11/26/86. With Allan Hayes, Leilani Sarelle, Donna Locke, Victor E. Brandt; Mark Allen, Joseph Shirley (maniacs).

"They only come out at night." Mutants that live inside the base of the Golden Gate Bridge possess super-electrical powers, supernaturally replace lost limbs, and dissolve in water.... The only plus here: the mysteriousness of the maniacs. The movie isn't funny or scary, and the flyspeck of a plot is just an excuse for regulation makeup effects, subcategory Dissolving. No explana-

tion of the monsters or their powers. Nice: the shot of the neon maniac having fun running the Muni train.

**NEPAL** or **NEPAL AFFAIR** see *Witch from Nepal*

**NEPTUNE'S CHILDREN** (B) Satori/CFF/Pan & WGP 1985 color c90m. "The Kids Who Found Atlantis." D: David Andrews. SP: M. Smith. Ph: Ousama Rawi. Mus: Edwin Astley. With Simon Turner (Kurkal), Perry Balfour (Zoldar), Lesly Dunlop, Stephen Garlick, Earl Younger.

"Selkie the Seal." SP, D: Anthony Squire. SP: also James Hill, John Tully. From Janet Eckford's story. Ph: Norman Jones. Mus: John Gale. With Peter Bayliss (Mr. Selkie), Samantha Weysom. Ref: TV. TVG. no Maltin '92. no Scheuer.

"The Kids Who Found Atlantis"; "It's a complete world!" The lost undersea land of Atlantis is found to be populated by 300-year-old boys who can fashion new islands electronically and who use rocks for illumination.... Stilted junior version of the Atlantis story.

"Selkie the Seal": According to an old Scottish legend, a selkie is a "seal who comes ashore in human form," during the full moon, for 48 hours. One such selkie comes to town to act as spokesman for Oceania, Atlantica, and Antarctica in the fight against sea pollution. Magically, he is able to project "TV" documentation of his case.... Some amusing moments in this didactic fantasy-comedy. As the "were-seal," Bayliss gives a pleasantly eccentric performance.

**NERDENSAGEN VOM KOSMOSINSET** see *Legend of Galactic Heroes*

**NERO** (I) Titanus & Intersound (Claudio Argento/Giovanna Romagnoli) 1992 color/ws? 95m. (100m.) (*Nero*.). SP, D: Giancarlo Soldi. SP: also Tiziano Sclavi, from Sclavi's novel. Ph: Luca Bigazzi. Mus: Mau Mau. AD: Mauro Radaelli. SpFX: Studio Artefare(sp?). SdFX: Anzellotti. Ref: TV: VSOM; Eng. titles; *Black.* V 12/14/92: compared to *Basket Case* in its "curious melange of absurd humor, casual gore and nightmarish surrealism.... the film should be a lot more fun than it actually is." With Sergio Castellitto, Chiara Caselli, Carlo Colnaghi, Luis Molteni, Hugo Pratt.

Federico Zardo, paranoid. The Cleaning up Her Ex-Boy-Friend's Blood sequence gets to be pretty funny. Federico packs up the body, but one hand sticks out. Then several stick out—and they grab his arm. Next: murder-with-hatchet. Funny, too: the girl friend's "Cut!" (cards, that is), which is "answered" by the not-quite-dead detective's lunge with a hatchet. (The deck is sliced in half.) Situation black-comedy is thin on character, but sporadically hilarious. It plays like a paranoid's bad daydream, and maybe it is.

**The NEST** Concorde (Julie Corman) 1987 color 88m. D: T. H. Winkless. SP: Robert King, from Eli Cantor's novel. Mus: Rick Conrad. SpFxCoord: Cary Howe. Opt: Motion. 2nd-Unit D: Jeffrey Delman. Ref: TV: MGM/UA HV. V 2/3/88. Maltin '92. McCarty II. Martin. Scheuer. With Robert Lansing, Lisa Langlois, Franc Luz, Terri Treas, Stephen Davies (Homer), Nancy Morgan.

"Don't leave food out." Something's nibbling at the binding of the library's books on North Port Island. And dogs, cats, and humans are turning up "stripped to the bone." Has super-secret corporation INTEC's alternative to pesticide—a cockroach-eating cockroach—gone awry? You got it. Dr. Hubbard (Treas) has developed some highly adaptable, "very strange" creatures. ("Whatever they attack, they become.") And those stripped animals become a "hybrid of a hybrid." Their leader: a queen which absorbs her victims.... The dialogue is occasionally dry, and Davies is good as a "pest control agent," or exterminator, but *Bug* was more weirdly amusing. Other antecedents include *Attack of the Crab Monsters* (for plot) and *The Fly* remake (for effects). The hybrid-squared plot development is far-fetched but fun.

**NETHERWORLD**  Para/Full Moon (Thomas Bradford) 1992 (1991) color c90m. D: David Schmoeller. Story, SP: Billy Chicago. Story, Exec P: Charles Band. Ph: Adolfo Bartoli. Mus: David Bryan. PD: Billy Jett. Mech & Flying Hand FX: Steve Patino SpFX. SpMkpFX: Mark Shostrom; William Kopfler. Opt: Mercer, OptFX. Ref: TV. TVG. V 5/6/91:28. Martin. With Michael Bendetti, Denise Gentile, A. Comer, Holly Floria, Robert Sampson, Holly Butler, Alex Datcher, Robert Burr, George Kelly (Bijou), David Bryan, Edgar Winter, Judith Weber (ghoul #1).

Young man Corey's (Bendetti) dead father Noah (Sampson) wants his son to consult the local witch, Delores (Gentile), in order to bring him back to life. What he doesn't tell Corey is that he plans to switch places with him.... Low-budget *Angel Heart* set in New Orleans is more atmosphere than story. A flying stone hand which makes a "man-bird" of a man gets the disgusting scenes. Scattered okay touches include the ending—which is based on the premise that the souls of bad people are stored in the bodies of birds—and, earlier, the parakeet's "Help me!", a variation on a scene from the original *Fly*. Featured character: a blonde (Butler) who may or may not be the revived Marilyn Monroe. ("I am Marilyn.")

**NEVER CRY DEVIL** see *Night Visitor* (1989)

**NEVER SAY NEVER**  Sin City 1994 color 86m. D: Harold Lime. Ref: Adam'95. With Kylie Ireland, Sharon Kane.

"Madman seeking to rule the world" hypnotizes young women to kill talk-show hosts, produce panic.

**NEVER SAY NEVER AGAIN**  (U.S.-B) WB/Taliafilm (Jack Schwartzman/Kevin McClory) 1983 color/ws 137m. D: Irvin Kershner. SP: Lorenzo Semple Jr. Story: McClory, Jack Whittingham, Ian Fleming. SpVisFX: David Dryer. SpFxSup: Ian Wingrove. Stopmo Anim: Carole de Jong. Ref: TV. V 10/5/83: reworking of *Thunderball*. Maltin '92. Martin. Scheuer. Ecran F 40:7-8.

Scattered semi-sf elements include infrared binoculars which penetrate shadows ... a corneal implant which matches the President's "eyeprint" ... a laser-holographic game ... a laser-ray-cutter watch ... and XT-7B one-man flying machines. First half of this James Bond adventure is pretty bad. Most of the entertainment is in the second half, when Bond (Sean Connery) goes one on one with the smug, vicious villain Largo (Klaus Maris Brandauer, in a good performance).

**The NEVERENDING STORY** (W.G.) WB-PSO/Neue Constantin & Bavaria & WDR 1984 color/ws 94m. *(Die Unendliche Geschichte)*. SP, D: Wolfgang Petersen. SP: also Herman Weigel. Mus: Klaus Doldinger, Giorgio Moroder. PD: Rolf Zehetbauer. Concep: Ul De Rico. SpVisFXD: Brian Johnson. SpMkpFxSup: Colin Arthur. Mattes: Jim Danforth, Frank Ordaz et al. Ref: TV. V 7/4/84. SFExam 7/20/84. Dr. Rolf Giesen. Scheuer. Martin. Maltin '92. With Noah Hathaway, Barret Oliver, Tami Stronach, Moses Gunn, Patricia Hayes, Gerald McRaney.

"The Nothing grows stronger every day" ... in the book, *The Neverending Story*, which little Bastian is reading. This "strange sort of nothing" is like a mobile black hole. Supporting cast: the Rock-Biter, a rock-eating giant ... a huge bat ... a "creature of darkness" ... two sphinxes whose eyes annihilate those with low self-esteem ... and the huge Luck Dragon. From a novel by Michael Ende.

An uneasy cross between the quaint and the didactic, *Story* isn't nearly as charming a fantasy of a boy's growing up as *Godzilla's Revenge*. Each creature furnishes the boy with a moral tidbit. Effects/music/art-direction sugar-coating helps, though, and the interweaving of the boy's story with the book story yields some excitement near the end.

**The NEVERENDING STORY II: THE NEXT CHAPTER** (W.G.-U.S.) Soriba & Deyhle & WB/Time Warner (Dieter Geissler/Neverending Story Film) 1990 (1989/'91-U.S.) color/ws 90m. *(Die Unendliche Geschichte II: Auf der Suche Nach Phantasien)*. D: George Miller. SP: Karin Howard, from Michael Ende's novel. Mus: Robert Folk. SpVisFX: Derek Meddings, The Magic Camera Co., Cine Magic Berlin. Creature Des: Patrick Woodroffe. SpFxSup: Waggi Klee, Meddings. Creature SpFX: (mkp) Colin Arthur; (animatronics) Giuseppe Tortora. SdFX: John Hayward. Ref: TV: WB HV: Eng.-lang. version. MFB'90:362-3. V 10/29/90. 6/20/90:44. Cinef 8/91. Dr. Rolf Giesen. SFExam 2/11/91. SFChron 2/9/91. Maltin '92. Martin. Scheuer. With Jonathan Brandis, Kenny Morrison, Clarissa Burt, Martin Umbach, John Wesley Shiff.

"Bastian was the only one who could save Fantasia and all the stories in the world." The heartless Xayide (Burt) uses a machine to drain the memories from the boy Bastian (Brandis), who has been charged with the task of saving Fantasia. The fantasy world is fading as (back on Earth) the words disappear from the pages of books like *The Neverending Story*. (Xayide: "I control all that is empty.") Supporting cast: big and big-clawed, tool-wielding cousins of the it that conquered the world ("the giants—they're everywhere"), the "most horrible flying dragon in the history of Fantasia," and a giant, ray-shooting hand.

Part II is not entirely free of the preachiness which infects Part I, but the script's underpinnings are stronger: Here, the main subjects are memory and storytelling, while the sentimentally-broached courage subtheme is relegated to the framing story. In the main story, set in Fantasia, the spectacle of the sinisterly-collecting globes which contain Bastian's memories seems akin to the zombification process in that earlier children's fantasy semi-classic *Invaders from Mars* (1953).

**The NEVERENDING STORY III** (G) CineVox et al. 1994 color 95m. D: Peter MacDonald. SP: Jeff Lieberman. Ph: R. Vidgeon. PD: Rolf Zehetbauer. VisFxSup: Derek Meddings. Animatronics: Henson's. Digital VisFX: Toccata. Ref: V 9/20/93:16: film-ing. 12/19/94: "charmless, desperate"; Eng. dialogue. With Fred-die Jones.

**NEVROSE** see *Fall of the House of Usher* (1983)

**NEW ANGEL COP** see *Angel Cop 3*

The **NEW BARBARIANS** VCA 1990 color 79m. D: Henri Pachard. Ref: Adam '91. vc box. With Victoria Paris, Sabrina Dawn, Nina Hartley.

Prehistoric woman, time-travel crystal.

The **NEW BARBARIANS 2** VCA 1990 color 79m. D: H. Pachard. Ref: Adam '92. vc box. With V. Paris, S. Dawn, N. Hartley, Sharon Kane.

Time travel.

**NEW CRIME CITY: LOS ANGELES 2020** Concorde-New Ho-rizons (Luis Llosa) 1994 color 95m. D: J. Winfrey. SP: C.P. Moore. Ref: vc box: "biowarfare device." Martin: "intriguing." Vallejo T-H: ex-cop restored to life. With Rick Rossovich, S. Keach.

**NEW CUTEY HONEY, Vol. 1** A.D. Vision/Go Nagai & Toei & DPI (Kuriyama-Sakamoto & Hatana-Yamamoto) 1994 anim color 51m. D: Y. Nagoaka. SP: Isao Shizuya. Ph: H. Watanabe. Mus: K. Toyama. Mecha Des: Seiji Kishimoto. AD: N. Sakamoto. SpFX: Y. Sanada. SdFX: D. Jinbo. Ref: TV: ADV video; Eng. titles. Voices: M. Neya (Honey), K. Tomita (Danbei), N. Matsui (Jewel Princess), Y. Matsumoto (Virtual Hacker).

"An Angel Descends." "I want the power!" The invulnerable "great female warrior, Cutey Honey"—actually, a secretary-war-rior-motorcyclist—takes on the winged, tailed, clawed monster-woman, Deathstar. Plus Grandpa Danbei's evil-detecting sensors ... the T.N.N. Hysteric, fireworks-like bombs ... and some spider-like armor. Fast, furious, manic, hollow.

"The Sweet Trap of the Jewel Princess." The latter freezes her victims and shoots laser-like jewels. Virtual Hacker, meanwhile, is a *Terminator 2*-like, mutating-liquid/solid android-type. Some funny moments, but basically unremarkable.

**NEW EDEN** Sci-Fi Channel/MCA (Frand) 1994 color feature. D: Alan Metzger. SP: Dan Gordon. Ref: PT 19:57: "post nuke planet." Martin: "squeaky-clean action." Vallejo T-H: "brutal prison planet." JVG 4/22/95. With Stephen Baldwin, Lisa Bonet, Nicholas Worth, Michael Bowen.

The **NEW GLADIATORS** (I) Media Home Ent./Regency (Vaughan) 1983 ('87-U.S.) color 90m. (*I Guerrieri dell'Anno 2027/2033: The Fighter Centurions*. aka *Rome, 2072 A.D. - The New Gladiators*. aka *Roma 2033 A.D.: I Centurioni del Futuro*. aka *The Centurions*. aka *Roma Anno 2033*). SP, D: Lucio Fulci. Story, SP: Elisa Briganti, Dardano Sacchetti. SP: also Cesare Frugoni. Ph: G. Pinori. Mus: Riz Ortolani. AD: Vanorio, Mitchell. SpFX: Corridori. Ref: V 1/13/88: "meek sci-fi effort." Morse: "mostly dull." V 8/10/83: 42: "recently completed future world actioner." MFB'86:93. vc box. Ecran F 44:30-33. 37:57.

With Jared Martin, Fred Williamson, Howard Ross, C. Cassinelli, Al Cliver, Donal O'Brian, Y. Yamanouchi.

Future-TV "gladiators."

The **NEW GOVERNESS** (B) Horseshoe 1915 silent 8m. (*The Governess's Love Affair*). Ref: BFC: "professor's love powder."

**NEW HOUSE ON THE LEFT** see *Twitch of the Death Nerve*

**NEW! IMPROVED! REAL-LIFE AMERICAN FAIRY TALE** Rhizomatic Films (Magocsi-Putnam) 1993 color 85m. SP, D, Ed: Deborah Magocsi. Ph: Ahmann, Levine. Ref: V 3/1/93: "arch, self-important." With Via Lambros, Jeff Kearney, Grady Shytles.

"Set in the near future when private expression of sexual expres-sion has been declared illegal." (V)

The **NEW LEGEND OF SHAOLIN** (H.K.) Upland Films 1994 color/ws 94m. D: Wong Jing. Ref: TV: Star Ent. video; Eng. titles. V 3/21/94:14: in H.K. With Jet Li.

Scare ingredients include the "so horrible," disfigured Ma Ling Yee ("It's a monster!"), an invincible, "poisonous man," with an anachronistic, almost futuristic car ... the Granny "ghost"/thun-derstorm scene ... and a home wax museum—but is there flesh underneath the wax? Charming, quirky, touching, and funny comedy-fantasy, though the sentiment is rather milked for Granny's death. Action takes place during the Ching Dynasty. One fun action scene involves a flaming log and the Wonder Screw. Included: a witty variation on Don't-look-who's-behind-you. Line for the ages: "How dare you eat my chicken ass!"

**NEW MR. VAMPIRE** (Taiwanese?) New Ship Film (William Chang) 1985 color/ws c100m. (aka *Kung Fu Vampire Buster*). D: B. Chan. Ref: TV: vt; Eng. titles. vc box. NST! 4:31: D: Xen Lung Ting; H. K. MMarquee 43:6, 7. Hound. With Lu Fang, W. H. Feng.

Prelude: Rival priests Chien and Wu take on the ghost of Tsai and his very mobile coffin. Main plot number 1: Revived, the ghost of concubine Chien-wen, a "half-half" (half-human and half-corpse), becomes electrically scrambled with a grave robber—she mimics his every move and word.... Main plot number 2: Wu uses blood and moonlight to revive the corpse of a vampire so as to embarrass Chien.

Holding one's breath confuses this vampire, and the latter can stand bolt upright. But he's not a hopping vampire, and this comedy is not a sequel to *Mr. Vampire*. It's too long, too elaborate, and action-clogged. It plays like several combined scripts. One script, though, is clever, the one re monkey-see Chien-wen—the perfectly synchronized movements of grave robber and concu-bine are an amusing variation on the mirror routine in *Duck Soup*. At one point, he capitalizes on her mimicry: He walks bent-over before her; she follows, in the same position, and carries the inert body of the vampire. Later, when he sticks out his tongue (at no one in particular), hers sticks out at her ex-lover, Marshal Tsao.

See also *New Mr. Vampire II*.

**NEW MR. VAMPIRE II** (Taiwanese?) Golden Sun Film Co. 1987 color c85m. (*The Funny Vampire* - Eng. t of Vietnamese vt version). D: Mason Ching. Ref: TV: Ocean Shores Video or Sunny Video, both with Eng. titles; *Everybody Makes Money* - tr of orig t. NST! 4:32: H. K.

Ingredients in this loose sequel to *New Mr. Vampire*: a "real monster," "not an ordinary" vampire (i.e., not a hopping vampire), who is revived by a voodoo doll (his limbs reattach to his body) and who, in turn, revives a group of ordinary hopping vampires ("Time for dinner, kids!") ... a hopping vampire boy who, trying to suck the vitality out of the monster, instead becomes one himself ... a "ghostess" from hell who, on her wedding night, is revealed to have a horrible face ... and a woman who, bitten by a vampire, temporarily becomes one.

Lively, uninspired slapstick horror-comedy features another monkey-see routine: At one point, the vampire boy leads the troops in silly stunts. The "monster" seems to be a holdover from part one, as does the rather insistent bathroom humor. Relative highlight: the break-dancing hopping vampires.

**NEW MR. VAMPIRE** see *Mr. Vampire II*

**NEW WAVE HOOKERS 2** VCA 1991 color 80m. D: Gregory Dark. Ref: Adam '92. With Madison, Danielle Rogers, Ashley Nicole, Cameo.

"Amazon women ... are secretly ruling the world from Atlantis."

**The NEW YORK CENTERFOLD MASSACRE** TelePix/Carlson Int'l. (Vidimax) 1987 color 55m. D, SpFX: Lou Ferriol. SP: M. Harm. Ph, Ed: F. Gevasi. Mus: M. Saul. Ref: TV: TelePix Video. no Hound. no Martin. no Phantom. With Paula Weckesser, Jane de Leeuw (Alma), Larry Lubiner, Cheryl Lee, Flavian (psychic).

"This looks like something from *Friday the 13th*." A hooded sicko burns, bruises, and chops up photo models "in about twenty pieces," then stuffs the results in garbage bags. Meanwhile, a psychic gets "glimpses" of the "massacre".... Shot-on-tape atrocity is stilted, ineptly directed and edited, but above all cheap. In a dumb twist, the Puritanical old-maid-type is revealed to be the killer.

**The NEWLYDEADS** City Lights 1988 color 77m. Co-SP, D, Co-P: Joseph Merhi. Ph: R. Pepin. Mus: J. Gonzalez. Ref: V 6/1/88:67(hv): "slim plot," gore. McCarty II: "a senseless, offensive mess." Morse: "repetitious slaughter." With Jim Williams, Jean Levine, Jay Richardson.

Murdered transvestite back for revenge.

**NEXT!** see *Next Victim, The*

**The NEXT VICTIM** (I-Sp) Gemini & Maron/MLR Films & Laurie Int'l. (Devon & Copercines) 1970 ('71-U.S.) color/ws 89m. (*Lo Strano Vizio della Signora Ward.* aka *Next!* [**]). D, P: Sergio Martino. Story, SP: E. M. Brochero. SP: also Gastaldi, Caronia. Ref: TV: Eng.-dubbed; Heritage-TV. TVFFSB. Boxo 8/9/71: horror. Hound: horror. Lee(e). Stanley. V 8/11/71: "shock scenes." Imagi 1:59: early "giallo." Palmerini.

Shower murder with razor ... two borderline-horror dream sequences ... roses from a "dead" man. Wretched mixture of red herrings, "shocks," padding.

See also *Blade of the Ripper*.

**NEXUS** (Sp) Filmagic 1992 color feature. D: J. M. Forque. Ref: V 9/28/92:46: "sci-fier."

**NGAI..?** see *Devil Strikes, The*

**Die NIBELUNGEN** Decla-Bioscop AG (Erich Pommer) 1924 (1923/'25-U.S.) 186m. (*Siegfried. Siegfrieds Tod* or *Siegfried's Death - Part I. Kriemhilds Rache* or *Kriemhild's Revenge - Part II. The She-Devil - alt B t of Part II. Kriemhild's Dream*—excerpted sequence. *The Nibelungs* - tr t). Also based on the "Volsung Saga." Mus: Gottfried Huppertz. Mkp: Otto Genath. Ref: TV: Republic HV; Eng. titles; music & sd fx. screen: Blackhawk (192m.). Lee. Jensen/COFL. Ott/FOFL. Hound. Maltin '92. Martin. Eisner/Haunted Screen. LC. With Theodor Loos, Bernhard Goetzke, Hans Adalbert von Schlettow, Georg John, Hanna Ralph, Rudolf Ritter.

"Centuries ago when the world was young...." Hero Siegfried (Paul Richter) slays the fire-breathing, sedentary dragon Fafnir the Giant, in Woden Wood, and bathes in its blood: Except for a spot on his shoulder, where a lime leaf fell, he is now invulnerable to weapons. Wearing the dwarf Alberich's (John) "wonder cap" of invisibility, he helps King Gunther (Loos) of the Nibelungs best and win Brunhilde (Ralph), Queen of Iceland, in order that he, Siegfried, can wed Gunther's sister Kriemhild (Margarete Schoen).

The latter, however, betrays Siegfried's secrets to Brunhilde, and her uncle, Hagen Tronje (von Schlettow), murders him. The better to avenge herself, she marries King Attila (Rudolf Klein-Rogge), "Lord of the Earth." She produces a son and has her husband invite the Nibelungs to the feast of the Summer Solstice, where she finally kills Hagen Tronje and drops earth collected from Siegfried's death site on the body. Incidental wonders: the dwarfs who turn to stone, the Sea of Flames, and the seer.

The "Nibelungenlied"/"Volsung Saga" is so formidable a work that it seems to resonate no matter which way you slice it. With a few more lines re Kriemhild's "blabbing," part II might easily have taken the course Her Own Damn Fault. Instead, the story here takes the form of Love As Vengeance, or The Hardening of Hearts. The weaknesses of both Kriemhild and Siegfried for telling all become a muted undercurrent in the climactic rush to revenge. Meanwhile, an Innocence Betrayed theme resolves into a grimly didactic Trust No One (Especially Yourself): Siegfried's innocence is compromised early, when he agrees, first, to invisibly aid Gunther, then to impersonate him in the bed chamber. This latter, bizarre variation on "Cyrano De Bergerac" is a simmering surreal stew of humiliation (Gunther), resentment (Brunhilde), and near-contempt (Siegfried, for Gunther). At this point, the film becomes, temporarily, Brunhilde's Revenge. But her "fulfillment"—the murder of the man she loves—spurs both Kriemhild and herself to act: She commits suicide; Kriemhild begins laying the groundwork for her own revenge.

The Perils of Loyalty, or Trust No One, Part II: Siegfried's loyalty to Kriemhild takes the form of "blabbing," as does hers to him, though in her case loyalty is at first indistinguishable from vanity—her Siegfried is a better man, any day, than Gunther, she intimates to Brunhilde, on the steps of the Cathedral at Worms.

Later, her loyalty to her dead husband seems more like madness, or Love Like Stone. Human traits, it's suggested—love, loyalty, honor—cut two ways. Siegfried is the best of men, the worst of men.

Sets and costumes in *Die Nibelungen* augment the emotions of the characters; fate-like, their costumes enclose them, suggest insulating moral cocoons. Hagen Tronje's intimidating winged headdress says, "I do not rue what I have done!", long before he himself does, while the unbudging, unrelenting Kriemhild is appropriately framed by stone arches, descends stone steps, stands atop stone towers. This Fritz Lang/Thea von Harbou film—or set of films—is an astonishing spectacle. There has been nothing like it, before or since.

See also *Eika Katappa* (P). *Throne of Fire.*

**NICE GIRLS DON'T EXPLODE** New World/Nice Girls (Doug Curtis & John Wells) 1987 color 82m. D: Chuck Martinez. SP: Paul Harris. Mus: Brian Banks, Anthony Marinelli. SpFX: Bill Harrison, Ray Massara; SpFxUnltd. (Gabe Videla). SpSdFX: Blake Leyh. Ref: TV: New World Video. V 4/29/87. Stanley. With Barbara Harris, Michelle Meyrink, William O'Leary, Wallace Shawn, James Nardini.

"Mother Claims Daughter Can Start Fires with Hormones!" April Flowers (Meyrink) carries an extinguisher with her on dates; one guy loses his Corvette. But April is not really a "fire girl"—her Mom (Harris) sets off remote-control incendiaries to keep boys away from her.

Apparently meant to be the comic flipside of *Firestarter, Nice Girls* also recalls such classic Curse of Sex horror movies as *Cat People.* Unfortunately, it's not nearly as droll as planned, though Harris' matter-of-fact delivery makes the payoff dialogue exchange work: April: "How could you destroy my life?"/Mom: "I'm your mother." Boyfriend Andy (O'Leary) also gets one good throwaway: "A Campfire girl?" And cats figure in two funny flying stunts.

**NICK KNIGHT** CBS-TV/New World-TV & Barry Weitz Films & Robirdie Pictures (S. M. Formica) 1989 color c90m. (*Midnight Cop* - B). D: Farhad Mann. Story, SP: James D. Parriott. Story: also Barney Cohen. Mus: Joseph Conlan. PD: Paul Eads. SpFX: SpFX Service. Mkp: Zoltan. Ref: TV. V 8/30/89:84; Mifed '89:116, 122. Jones. With Rick Springfield, Michael Nader (Lacroix, vampire), John Kapelos, Robert Harper, Richard Fancy, Laura Johnson, Craig R. Nelson, Cec Verrell, Fran Ryan, Irene Miracle.

L. A. Items: "vampire murders" ... a cursed jade goblet used in Mayan blood-sacrifice ceremonies ... a cop (Springfield) who works only at night ... treacly tunes ... overloaded dialogue ("We all got our addictions") ... silly-bravura action sequences.

**NIDO DEL RAGNO** see *Spider Labyrinth*

**NIGAHEN (NAGINA PART II)** (India - Hindi) Eastern Films 1989? color c120m. (*Nagina Part II*). SP, D, P: Harmesh Malhotra; (assoc) Moni Sharma. Story: Jagmohan Kapoor. Dial: Dr. Achala Nagar. Ph: V. Durgaprasad. Mus: Laxmikant Pyarelal; (lyr) Anand Bakshi. Art: Ganesh Basak. SpFX: Krishan & Baldev Malik. Mkp: Vitthal Kasturi et al. Ref: TV: Time Video; little Eng.

With Sunny Deol, Sridevi, Anupam Kher, Gulshan Grover, Aruna Irani, Anjana Mumtaz, Jagdeep, Pran.

A cobra which can magically open bolted doors uses blue eye-rays to hypnotize the new lady of the house. Later, when a magician turns the hero into a cobra, she explodes the bottle containing him and restores him. End title: "And they lived happily ever after."

The hypnotizing cobra is apparently a previous victim of the magician. Camp highlights of this sequel to *Nagina* include the musical number which the heroine dreams as she cuddles up to the cobra and the scene in which she catches a speeding bullet in her hand. Hammy score, performances.

**NIGHT, AFTER NIGHT, AFTER NIGHT** (B) Butcher's (Dudley Birch Films) 1970 color 88m. (*He Kills, Night after Night after Night*—U.S. ad t. *Night Slasher*—alt t). D: Lewis J. Force. SP: Dail Ambler. Mus: Douglas Gamley. AD: Wilfred Arnold. Mkp: Elenor Jones. Ref: TV: Monterey HV. Fango/Horror Video 2. Lee. Hardy/HM. MFB'70:82-3. Hound. With Jack May (Judge Lomax), Justine Lord, Gilbert Wynne, Donald Sumpter, Gary Hope, Linda Marlowe, Peter Forbes Robertson, Simon Lack, Carol Haddon, April Harlow, Shirley Easton.

"Somewhere there's a raving lunatic!" Who is behind the "Ripper" killings? Is the fiend the overworked Judge Lomax, his repressed clerk (Terry Scully), or the swinger (Sumpter)? "The only thing for sure is this man is sick"—"this man," disgusted by swinging England, decides to stop the pendulum all by himself.... Pretty miserable early, non-gory slasher pic was made for "The Psychotronic Encyclopedia of Film," though it didn't make the first edition. It certainly wasn't made to be seen, although May gives his all as the mad, slashing judge. Horrid script, score.

**NIGHT ANGEL** Fries Ent./Emerald Pictures & Paragon Arts Int'l. (Night Angel Partners) 1990 (1989) color 88m. D: Dominique Othenin-Girard. SP, P: Joe Augustyn. SP, Exec Co-P: Walter Josten. Mus: Cory Lerios. SpMkpFX: Steve Johnson, XFX; K.N.B. FX. SpMechFX: Ron Trost. Photo Fantasy Mkp: Joanne Gair. Narrator: Roscoe Lee Browne. Ref: TV. V 5/30/90. SFChron Dtbk 11/18/90. ad. Cable Video Store 2/91. 3/91. Hound. McCarty II. Martin. With Isa Andersen (Lilith), Karen Black, Linden Ashby, Debra Feuer, Doug Jones, Phil Fondacaro, Susie Sparks (woman with faces under breasts).

"She is—Lilith!" And she comes to life and takes human form again during a lunar eclipse. "Satan's whore" enters the "wonderful world of fashion" in order to "spread her evil on a grand scale." She has slashed and slaughtered one lover and his family and, now, on the sixth night of the Black Moon, she needs a human soul.

Like Cassandra Peterson's Elvira, Andersen's Lilith is a parody of feminine allure, but in *Night Angel* the parody is unintentional. There's humor elsewhere here, but not in the treatment of Lilith herself, who's "seductive" in the worst way. The carnival-of-horrors nightmare-vision in the "mouth of hell" provides a few welcome makeup novelties and features an incidental vampire woman or two. Lilith can, a) become a winged demon, b) come to life in photos and, c) spew an *Alien* monster out of her mouth.

The **NIGHT BOYS** Cinderfella 1990 color feature. SP, D: Gino Colbert. Ref: Adam '93G. no Jones. With Stewart Copeland (Count Vladimir).

"May be the worst vampire picture ever made."

**NIGHT BREED** see *Nightbreed*

The **NIGHT BRINGS CHARLIE** Quest Ent. (Parks-Stubenrach) 1990 color 90m. D: Tom Logan. SP: Bruce Carson. Ref: PT 10:52: "dumb small town slasher movie." Hound. With Kerry Knight, Joe Fishback, Monica Simmons.

"Grisly murders committed with a tree trimming saw." (H)

**NIGHT CALLER** D&B/Pyramid (H.K.) 1985 color 96m. (*Ping An Ye*). SP, D: Philip Chan. Ref: NST! 4:32. Fango 107:59. V 5/8/85: "macabre mystery." Weisser/ATC. Hardy/HM2. With Pauline Wong.

Slasher-type knife killings.

**NIGHT CRAWL** see *Zombie Brigade*

**NIGHT CREW** see *Intruder*(1988)

**NIGHT DANIEL DIED, The** see *Blood Stalkers*

**NIGHT EVIL SOUL** (Taiwanese) c1986? color/ws c95m. (*Night Evil*—ad t). Ref: TV: vt; Eng. titles. Happy Produce.

One hundred years before the present-tense action takes place, villagers hang a "beautiful shaman" and kill her black cat with a sword. Buried, she soon rises and empowers the cat to carry out her revenge. In no time, a convention of cats is terrorizing the town. The villagers burn the shaman's body.... In the present, the shaman possesses the body of woman, Hui Lien, in order to avenge both their deaths. Every night, she comes from the "black cat's pond" to take over Hui Lien's body, then, in her own form, slaughters those who killed Hui Lien, while the latter sleeps.

Well-done, if routine all-out horror thriller. Okay lighting, shadow, wind, and mist effects, and good cat snarls. In one Cocteau-like effect, the stones from the shaman's grave magically remove themselves. And at one point, her hair flows along the ground and around the body of the man who ordered Hui Lien's death. She and her familiar—who comes on big cat feet—alternately separate and combine, it seems, as they please, and twice she is seen with cat-head and claws. Though she's not called a vampire, she has fangs and slashes a woman's neck with them.

**NIGHT FALLS** see *Ghost Writer*

**NIGHT FEEDER** NF Co. (Gillerman-Whiteaker-Gillerman) 1988 color? 93m. D: Jim Whiteaker. SP: Shelley Singer, Linnea Due. Ph: Paul Kalbach. Mus: James Gillerman. AD, Co-Ed: JoAnn Gillerman. SpFX: Jonathan Horton. Ref: V/Cannes'89:148(ad): long-tongued monster-baby pictured. With Kate Alexander, Jonathan Zeichner, The Nuns.

"When baby needs a special diet!"

**NIGHT FLYERS** see *Nightflyers*

**NIGHT LIFE** CMM/Wild Night (Lippincott) 1989 color 89m. D: David Acomba. SP: Keith Critchlow. Ph: Roger Tonry. Mus: Roger Bourland. PD: Philip Thomas. Mkp: Craig Reardon. SpFX: Ed French. MechSpFX: Frank Ceglia. OptFX: Howard Anderson. Ref: TV. Hardy/HM2: *Grave Misdemeanours* - B t? Stanley. V 5/31/89: "uneven comic horror film ... unnecessarily gruesome footage of cadavers come to life." PT 9:11. Martin. McCarty II: "good production values and fine performances." With Scott Grimes, Cheryl Pollak, John Astin, Lisa Fuller, Phil Proctor, John DeBello.

"Don't go in the bedroom!" Mostly familiar living-dead material, except for the up-close embalming details, which aren't a whole lot of fun. The up side: one eye-opening "fire breathing" effect ... atmospheric lighting.

**NIGHT LIGHT** see *Slumber Party Massacre 3*

**NIGHT OF FEAR** see *Rats: Night of Terror*

**3P NIGHT OF HORROR** Little Warsaw 1982? color c90m. SP, D, P: Tony Malanowski. SP: also Gae Schmitt, Rebecca Bach. Story: Tony Stark. AD: Jackie Jones. SpFX: David Donoho. Ref: TV. V 10/20/82:139(ad). 5/9/84:264(ad). Greg Luce. Hound. Morse. With Steve Sandkuhler, G. Schmitt, R. Bach, Jeff Canfield, T. Stark.

"This place is wrong!" In Virginia mountain country, "sensitive, impressionable" Colleen, who hears "ghostly noises," arranges a roadside seance in which the ghost of a Confederate soldier tells of slaughtered soldiers who vowed to restore their brave captain's severed head to his body. Colleen—the reincarnation of the captain's wife—finds the man's skull and buries it "in the ruins of a 19th-century graveyard." The spirits are satisfied. ("We thank you!")

Amateurish ghost movie is a patchwork of narrated footage, scattered dialogue scenes, and travelogue-with-music interludes. The story which the ghost soldier relates has only the most tenuous connections with the Civil War battle footage which accompanies it. Scenes from a ghoul/gore movie—also possibly a Little Warsaw production (it's on the same level), perhaps *Curse of the Screaming Dead*—turn up in the middle of the film.

**NIGHT OF TERROR** 1987 color 105m. Ref: Hound: apparently not sfa *Frozen Scream* (II). With Renee Harmon, Henry Lewis.

"A bizarre family conducts brain experiments ... begins to kill each other."

**NIGHT OF THE COMET** Atlantic/Coleman-Rosenblatt & FDF (Andrew Lane, Wayne Crawford) 1984 color 95m. SP, D: Thom Eberhardt. PD & SpVisFxDes: John Muto. SpFX: Court Wizard. MkpFxDes: David B. Miller. Ref: TV. V 10/10/84. SFChron 11/17/84. SFExam 11/16/84. Stanley. Hound. Phantom. Maltin '92. Martin. Scheuer. Morse. With Catherine Mary Stewart, Kelli Maroney, Robert Beltran, Geoffrey Lewis, Mary Woronov, Sharon Farrell, Ivan Roth.

Near the end of the Twentieth Century, a passing comet decimates Earth. "Freaked-out zombies," or mutants, outnumber the few physically-unaffected survivors. The three stages of the disease, apparently: a rash, mutation, and ... dust. In a satiric happy ending, civilization begins again.... There are sterling moments, including a funny gunfight at the O.K. mall, but comedy, suspense, horror, and science fiction seem indiscriminately mixed in this generally aimless movie.

**NIGHT OF THE CREEPS** Tri-Star (Charles Gordon/Donna Smith/William Finnegan) 1986 color 88m. SP, D: Fred Dekker. Mus: Barry DeVorzon. Creeps Des: David B. Miller. SpVisFxSup: David Stipes, R. L. Bennett. Anim FX: Ted Rae. SpFX: Roger George. Title Des: Ernest D. Farino. Ref: TV. MFB'87:246-7. V 8/27/86. Stanley. Hound. Phantom. no Maltin '92. Martin. Scheuer. Morse. With Jason Lively, Steve Marshall, Jill Whitlow, Tom Atkins, David Paymer, Ivan E. Roth (psycho zombie), Daniel Frishman (alien zombie), Dick Miller.

"Zombies, exploding heads, creepy crawlies"—or slimy slitheries, to be more exact, make things interesting for Corman University students. The space slugs enter the victim's mouth, lodge in the brain, and incubate. Result: ax murderers that return to life, dog zombies, and cat-horrors. Plus: a nightmare re an ax-wielding ghoul.... Slight, familiar sf-horror-comedy, with pleasant moments, is a bit silly, but hardly more outlandish than some straight sf-ers. Effects and gags proliferate for a fairly satisfying payoff.

**NIGHT OF THE CRUEL SACRIFICE** see *Nuit ses Traquees, La*

**NIGHT OF THE DEAD** see *Nuit de la Mort!*

**NIGHT OF THE DEMONS** IFM/Meridian Pictures & Paragon Arts Int'l. (Halloween Partners) 1988 (1987) color c94m. (*Halloween Party* - orig t). D: Kevin S. Tenney. SP, P: Joe Augustyn. Mus: D. M. Tenney. SpMkpFX: Steve Johnson. Demon Voices: James W. Guinn. Ref: TV: Republic HV. V 9/28/88. 10/19/88:179, 279. HR 10/20/88. Scheuer. Hound. Maltin '92. McCarty II. Martin. V 6/17/87:6. With Cathy Podewell, Alvin Alexis, Mimi Kinkade, Hal Havins, Lance Fenton, Linnea Quigley, William Gallo.

"Tonight's a special night of evil." Angela (Kinkade)—the "wicked witch of the west"—throws a Halloween party at deserted Hull House, once a funeral parlor and site of "demonic infestation" and past Halloween slaughters. ("This is a house of the dead.") A demon of "pure evil" begins to possess the party-goers, and only morning sunlight dispels the curse. Playing on TV: *The Cobweb Hotel* (which see).... A perfunctory blending of scare elements from *The Exorcist, Halloween,* and *Nightmare on Elm Street.* (The possessed spout Freddy quips.) Only redeeming feature: a rather elaborate, well drawn and orchestrated credit sequence by Kathy Zielinski. Otherwise, Dreck City.

**NIGHT OF THE DEMONS 2** Republic/Blue Rider (Josten-Geoffray) 1994 color 98m. D: Brian Trenchard-Smith. Story, SP: Joe Augustyn. Story: also James Penzi. Ph: David Lewis. Mus: Jim Manzie. PD: Wendy Guidery. Prosth Mkp: Steve Johnson. Ref: V 5/23/94: "some inspired bits of comic lunacy." Martin: "inventive special effects ... rigid formula." Stanley: "special effects extravaganza." PT 20:71: "more imaginative" than the original. Sacto Bee 5/30/94: "smart, amusing." With Jennifer Rhodes, Amelia Kinkade, Darin Heames, Zoe Trilling, Merle Kennedy, Bobby Jacoby.

"Halloween bash in a creepy old house" (V) haunted by Angela (Kinkade) ... accidentally-unleashed demon ... the undead.

*****NIGHT OF THE GHOULS** Wade Williams 1983 (1959) 70m. Ph: William C. Thompson. Mus Sup: Gordon Zahler. AD: Kathleen O'Hara Everett. Mkp: Harry Thomas. Ref: TV: Nostalgia Merchant video. Filmfax 7:16: Vampira (and Chaney Jr.) not in this. Lentz. Lee. Stanley. Hardy/HM. Weldon: Crown Int'l TV. Phantom. Martin. Scheuer. With Duke Moore, John Carpenter, Paul Marco, Bud Osborne, Harvey B. Dunn, Jeannie Stevens (The Black Ghost); Karl Johnson, Leonard Barnes et al (the dead men), Tom Mason (Foster Ghost).

"The house was not all that remained of the old scientist's horrors." Tor Johnson's Lobo ("Lobo served him well") and the lightning-destroyed house ("that place where the mad doctor made monsters") return, in this belatedly released sequel to *Bride of the Monster* (*,II). Here, the supernatural (the "threshold people") replaces science fiction, as a "phony swami" (Kenne Duncan's Dr. Acula) proves actually to have raised six or seven dead. ("Your powers were even stronger than you yourself realized.") It seems a "strong medium" can bring back the local dead for twelve hours every thirteen years.... Writer-director Ed Wood Jr. intends fiendish horror and *Mark of the Vampire*-like chills, but relies too much on words like "strange" in dialogue and narration. Dull comedy with Marco's cop Kelton, and lots of padding with scenes at the police station. Not-quite-camp.

**NIGHT OF THE HUNTED** see *Nuit des Traquees*

**NIGHT OF THE HUNTER** ABC-TV/Diana Kerew Prods. & Konigsberg/Sanitsky 1991 color c90m. D: David Greene. Tel: Edmond Stevens, from Davis Grubb's novel. Ph: Ron Orieux. Mus: P. M. Robinson. PD: Charles Bennett. SpFxCoord: Greg Hull. Mkp: Lydia Milars. Ref: V 5/6/91:338: "quite good, until its clumsy, disappointing ending." TVG. SFExam 5/3/91: "just another ho-hum movie-of-the-week thriller." TV. With Richard Chamberlain (Preacher), Diana Scarwid, Amy Bebout, Reid Binion, Burgess Meredith, Ed Grady.

"Down-to-earth creep" chases kids. (SFE). "HATE" and "LOVE" are back, and Chamberlain isn't bad, but take away the poetry and humor of the 1955 original—as this version of the novel does—and there's not much left. Unambitious TV suspenser doesn't attempt anything new, and isn't even up to *The Stepfather,* a more recent cross reference. Robert Mitchum's preacher in the original film was a precursor of the *Halloween* unstoppable monsters, but with since-unheard-of dimensions.

**NIGHT OF THE KICKFIGHTERS** AIP(Reyes) 1990 color feature (aka *Night Raiders*). D: Buddy Reyes. SP: Ron Schultz. Ref: PT 17:13: "computerized laser weapon." Martin: "global destructors." no Stanley. With Andy Bauman, Adam West, Carel Struycken, Marica Karr.

**NIGHT OF THE LIVING BABES** Metropolis Pictures 1987 color c68m. D, P: Jon Valentine. SP: Veronica Cinq-Mars. Ph: Junior Bodden. AD: Buddy Del Fuego. Mkp: Charisse Cooper, Susan Green. Ref: TV: Magnum Ent. video. Hound. Martin. Scheuer. With Michelle McClellan, Andrew Nichols, Louie Bonnano, Connie Woods, Forrest Witt, Cynthia Clegg (Igor), Terri

Peake; Ashley Elstad, Violet Lickness, Lisa Devine, Marjorie Miller ("zombie" girls).

The "completely and utterly mad" Madame Mondo (Witt) runs the Mondo Zombie Palace at the Zombie Fantasy Ranch, a "new wave whorehouse." She keeps her Mondo Zombie Girls hypnotized and threatens to turn two jerks (Nichols and Bonnano) into "gorgeous teenage cheerleaders" with her sex-change ray gun. ("They're not gonna kill us—they're just gonna turn us into women.") At the end, the ray turns Madame Mondo into a man, and she's glad.... Two or three laughs in this pseudo-camp sf-comedy/skin-flick, which has a Let's-take-the-video-camera-out-into-the-backyard feel. At one point, the original *Night of the Living Dead* turns up on TV. ("Why can't Chuck get eaten by zombies?")

**NIGHT OF THE LIVING DEAD** Col/21st Century & George Romero (Menahem Golan) 1990 color 89m. D: Tom Savini. SP: Romero. Mus: Paul McCollough. SpMkpFX: John Vulich, Everett Burrell. Ref: TV. Bill Warren. V 10/22/90. ad. Maltin '92. McCarty II. Martin. Scheuer. With Tony Wood, Patricia Tallman, Tom Towles, McKee Anderson, William Butler, Katie Finnerman.

"The bodies of the recently dead are returning to life, driven by an unknown force that enables the brain to continue to function." Judgment Day. It's "like a war" when zombies inexplicably begin assaulting and eating people across the U.S. In this remake of the 1968 film, the accent is on the violence done to the zombies. The zombies themselves are monotonously grabby. Barbara (Tallman) is now a together, resourceful *Alien* heroine (after she overcomes her initial, held-over-from-'68 hysteria) and gets the script's most pretentious line: "We're them, and they're us." The ending is an arbitrary, triply-cynical twist: Good ol' boys toy with rounded-up zombies, zombie Ben (Wood) is summarily shot, and Barbara shoots non-zombie, but extremely annoying Harry (Towles).

Perhaps the most disturbing aspect of the original—the ghoul-wife (Anderson) and child (Heather Mazur) relationship—is soft-pedaled here. But again, and unfortunately, screaming and arguing characters are employed as rote tension-builders in-between zombie attacks. The most harrowing scenes come near the beginning, before the principals settle into the house "fortress" and begin "screaming at each other like a bunch of two-year-olds."

See also: *Day of the Dead.* Titles under *Return of the Living Dead. Revenge of the Living Zombies.*

**NIGHT OF THE LIVING DEBBIES** Executive Video Prods. 1989 color c87m. D: Henri Pachard. Ref: TV: Executive Video. Adam '90. With Nina Hartley, Porsche Lynn, Lynn LeMay, Bionca, Renee Morgan, Robert Bullock, Rick Savage, Joey Silvera.

In their search for the perfect tush, Dr. Finetush and Igor of Resurrections Unlimited use an energizing cerebral cap in order to bring recently dead women back to semi-life as mechanical "Debbie units." Problem is that these "love machines" have bodies that will quit: Each has a half-hour time limit for sexual activity. At the end, the Doc brings a man back to life, but "the

Godfather" appears in the man's place. Silly, scrappy sf-porno-comedy.

**NIGHT OF THE RED HUNTER** (N.Z.) Nickelodeon-TV 198-? color feature. Ref: TVG: made-for-TV. with Toni Driscoll, Toby Lainz.

"Members of an alien race try to return home."

**NIGHT OF THE SCARECROW** Republic/Steve White 1995 (1994) color c90m. D: Jeff Burr. SP: Steiner, Mazur. Digital FX: Tom Rainone. Ref: vc box: "monstrous demon." PT 22:11. With E. Barondes, B. Glover, M. Beswicke, G. Lockwood.

**NIGHT OF THE SHARKS** (I) Italian Int'l. & Raiuno (Fulvio Lucisano) 1988 ('90-U.S.) color c85m. (*La Notte degli Squali*). Story, D: Tonino Ricci. SP: Tito Carpi. SpFX: Paolo Ricci. Mkp: Marisa Marconi. Ref: TV: Media Home Ent. video; Eng. version. V 10/22/86: 354. 6/27/90:48 (hv). 1/10/90:24 (rated). Hound. Martin. Horacio Higuchi.

Cancun, Mexico. Human sharks intent upon retrieving a highly incriminating tape recording threaten David Ziegler (Treat Williams), who's already bothered by the ever-lurking, seagoing shark, The Cyclops, which patrols the bay. Only saving graces here: a not wholly believable, but lightly amusing ending, and the David-Paco byplay. The Cyclops is almost comically omnipresent in the bay.

**NIGHT ON THE GALACTIC RAILROAD** (J) CPM/Toei / Herald & Asahi 1985 ('96-U.S.) anim color/ws 108m. D: Kizaburo Sugii. SP: Minoru Hetuyaku, from the story "Ginga Tetsudo no Yoru" by Kenji Miyazawa. Mus: Harumi Hosono. Ref: TV: Asahi Video Library; no Eng. J Anim Program Guide. V 10/16/85:343(ad). Cinef 7/96:124. Voices: Mayumi Tanaka (Giovanni), Chinatsu Sakomoto.

The Galactic Railroad picks up Giovanni—a wide-eyed cat transfixed by visions of planets and stars—as he lies in a field and watches the night sky. Among the wonders that he and his friend Campanella witness aboard the dream train: a "seashore" which proves to be the gigantic skeleton of a dinosaur ... a stairway through space ... the sinking of the *Titanic* ... a black hole ... apples which magically multiply ... and passing birds which "become" the apples in an orchard.

Metaphysical ruminations, from a feline perspective. For the humans aboard the train: the promise of the cross; for cats dying young: the edge of the Milky Way. Gently, quietly magical movie's tone is one of measured, sometimes melancholic awe, and this unusual tone holds the episodic tale together. Giovanni the dreamer-cat's viewpoint is necessarily oblique.

**NIGHT OWL** Lifetime-TV/Morgan Hill & Hearst Ent. (Julian Marks) 1993 color c90m. D: Matthew Patrick. Tel: Rose Schacht, Ann Powell. Mus: Gil Melle. Ref: V 8/23/93:22: "standard haunt hunt." TVG. With Jennifer Beals, James Wilder, Allison Hossack, Jackie Burroughs, Karen Hartman-Golden (Night Owl voice).

"Spooky radio Siren ... lures vulnerable men to their deaths...."(V)

**NIGHT OWL** Franco 1993 b&w 77m. SP, D, P, Ed: Jeffrey Arsenault. Ph: P. Clavel, H. Krupa, N. Shapiro. Mus: Styles, Hernandez. Ref: V 7/26/93: "disappointing horror film that is neither scary nor funny." 9/6/93:13. With James Raftery (Jake), John Leguizamo, Lisa Napoli, Holly Woodlawn, Caroline Munro.

"Modern-day vampire."

**NIGHT RAIDERS** see *Night of the Kickfighters*

**NIGHT RIPPER!** Video Features & Jeff Hathcock 1986 color 88m. SP, D: J. Hathcock. Ph: Joe Dinh. Mus: Bill Parsley. PD & SpFxMkp: Paul Herndon. FX: Matrix TV. Ref: TV: Int'l. Video. Stanley. Hound. With James Hansen, April Anne, Larry Thomas, Danielle Louis, Simon De Soto.

"The Ripper got another girl!" And whoever done it has more than a smidgeon of medical knowledge.... Anyone with any knowledge of mystery movies will instantly know whodunit—it's the person who later exclaims, predictably, "All models are bitches!" Zeroes all around for script, direction, acting, and editing. The worse of it, though: the blanded-out shot-on-videotape look and sound.

**NIGHT SCREAMS** Prism Ent. & Dill II Prods. 1987 color 85m. D: Allen Plone. SP: Dillis L. Hart II, Mitch Brian. Mus: M. Linn. Ref: V 12/23/87:37: "subpar." Hound. Morse: "dull, dreary." TVG 1/2/88:21. With Joe Manno, Megan Wyss, Ron Thomas.

Mad killer after high-schoolers.

**NIGHT SHADOW** Quest 1990 color 90m. Ref: Fango 104:12. Hound. With Brenda Vance, Dana Chan, Tom Boylan.

Serial killings traced to werewolf or werewolves unknown.

**NIGHT SHADOWS** see *Mutant*

**NIGHT SIEGE—PROJECT SHADOWCHASER 2** Nu Image/EGM Film (Vanger-Eyres-Griffith) 1994 color 94m. (aka *Project Shadowchaser II*). D: John Eyres. SP: Nick Davis. Ph: A.M. Trow. Mus: S. Edwards. PD: M. Harris. Ref: Martin: "utter nonsense." V 6/6/94: "terrorist android ... highly serviceable actioner." With Frank Zagarino (android), Bryan Genesse, Beth Toussaint.

**NIGHT SLASHER** see *Night, after Night, after Night*

The **NIGHT STALKER** Striker/Don Edmonds 1987 (1986) color 89m. (*Painted Dolls. Striker. The Slayman. The Man Who Could Not Be Killed* - all early ts). D: Max Kleven. Sp, P: D. Edmonds. SP: also John Goff. Mus: David Kitay. SpFX: Paul Staples. MkpSup: John Naulin. SdFX: Earl Watson et al. Opt: Alpha FX. Ref: TV. V 4/8/87. Stanley. Hound. Phantom. Maltin '92. Martin. Scheuer. Morse. ad. With Charles Napier, Michelle Reese, Katherine Kelly Lang, Robert Viharo, Joey Gian, Robert Z'Dar (killer), Gary Crosby, Goff, Tally Chanel, Ola Ray, Joan Chen, Buck Flower.

The super-strong, neck-snapping madman (a "real sicko") who survives shooting and kills a prostitute is a mercenary into Asian mind control. Killing gives him life. ("The more he killed, the longer he lived.").... *The Vice Squad* story, only the chases take

longer, the stalking takes longer, and even the dialogue scenes take longer. Two-thirds of the way through, however, the pace picks up and the supernatural takes over. But there seems to be no point to the contrast between the determinedly gritty milieu and the muttering, supernatural killer, between, that is, the film's conceptions of "reality" and "fantasy."

**NIGHT STALKER** see *Nightstalker*

**NIGHT STALKER, The** see *Bestia Nocturna*

**NIGHT TERROR** Howard-Weaver (Night Terror Venture) 1989 color c90m. SP, D: Paul Howard, Michael Weaver. SP, P: David C. Lee. Ph: James Morr et al. Mus: Walt Menetrey, Scott Griffith. FxMkp: Robert Maverick. SpFxDes: Kevin Hudson. Ref: TV: Magnum Ent. video. V 2/21/90:283 (ad). Hound. With Jeff Keel, Guy Ecker, Jon Hoffman, Heidi Hutson, Robert Graham (Death).

"This can't be happening!" A patient taps into other patients' dreams in a "nuthouse hotel." The four dreams/stories—"Night Terror," "Stuck with the Drinks," "Reap the Whirlwind," and "Teddy Bear"—involve, respectively, a satanic cult into blood-smearing and human sacrifice, a serial killer, a phantom barker, and vengeful stuffed animals.... Elm Street blues and forced, Freddy-style eeriness mark this omnibus horror-fantasy, which plays like a patchwork script rather than (as was intended) a crazy quilt of nightmares. It's not especially bad, just old-hat.

**NIGHT TERRORS** see *Tobe Hooper's Night Terrors*

*The **NIGHT THE WORLD EXPLODED** 1957. Ref: TV. Warren/KWTS! Lee. V 6/19/57. Lentz. Hardy/SF. no Phantom. Stanley. Maltin '92. Scheuer. COF 20:42.

The newly developed pressure photometer—which measures pressures within the earth—predicts an earthquake which, inexplicably and unpredictably, shifts the axis of the planet three degrees. A subsequent series of earthquakes causes a four-degree shift. The culprit: an "unknown mineral" which has some "peculiar properties when dry." This "unusual" new element, E-112—which is "pushing itself toward the surface" of the earth "wherever gravity has been reduced"—combines with nitrogen in the air to expand its mass (the hydrogen in water reverses the process), and explodes.

Rather likably plodding sf-drama has a stilted but businesslike script. If the drama is nil (Kathryn Grant "becomes" a scientist; William Leslie "becomes" a human being), the step-by-step of the fantastic science intrigues. One of the key (and few) mineral-menace movies of the fifties. (Compare the superior *Monolith Monsters* and the inferior *Missile to the Moon*.) "It grows!"

The **NIGHT THEY SAVED CHRISTMAS** ABC-TV/Halmi 1984 color c90m. D: Jackie Cooper. Story, Tel: Jim Moloney, David Niven Jr. Story: also Rudy Dochtermann. PD: George Costello. SpFX: Richard Wood, Peter Chesney, Michael Manzel. Introvision: (d) William Mesa; (models) Cecil Richards; (fx) Image Engineering. Ref: TV. TVG. V 12/19/84. Stanley. Scheuer. With Art Carney, Paul Williams, Jaclyn Smith, Paul Le Mat, Mason Adams, Billy Curtis.

A holiday fantasy with sf elements, including a "molecular transformation" device, or "people transporter" ... a "time deceleration" device—based on the Theory of Relativity (Santa Claus: "It's Greek to me!")—which slows time ... a "communicator" for the world's children ... and a robot named Pal.... Williams is a viable elf, and Carney gets some undercutting comedy as Santa. But sentiment interferes with the tackling of tough issues here, such as, Is there a Santa Claus?

**NIGHT TRAIN TO TERROR** Visto Int'l. (Jay Schlossberg-Cohen) 1985 (1982/1979) color 93m. D: John Carr, Schlossberg-Cohen, Philip Marshak, Tom McGowan, Gregg Tallas. SP: Philip Yordan. VisFX: William Stromberg. Stopmo: A. Doublin, Stromberg. Ref: V 5/29/85: "camp classic slot." Stanley. Scheuer: "hilariously inept." Phantom: "an unholy—if often weirdly entertaining—mess." McCarty II: "offbeat." Newman. With John Phillip Law, Cameron Mitchell, Marc Lawrence, Charles Moll, Meridith Haze, Ferdy Mayne, Lu Sickler (The Devil).

1) God (Mayne) and the Devil chat, in linking footage.

2) "Harry." Body-organ selling.

3) "Gretta." See *Carnival of Fools*.

4) "Cataclysm." See *Cataclysm* (II). Devil's emissary.

**NIGHT TRAP** see *Mardi Gras for the Devil*

**NIGHT TRIPS** Caballero Home Video 1989 color c80m. D: Andrew Blake. Ref: vc box. Adam '90. With Tori Welles, Porsche Lynn, Victoria Paris.

The "Mindscan Imager" turns dreams into reality.

**NIGHT TRIPS II** Caballero Home Video 1990 color 83m. D: Andrew Blake. Ref: vc box. Adam '91. With Paula Price, Tami Monroe, Erica Boyer.

"The Mindscan Foundation electronically monitors" dreams. (vc box)

**NIGHT VISION** see *Escapes*

**NIGHT VISITOR** MGM-UA/PPC (Alain Silver) 1989 color 93m. (aka *Never Cry Devil*). D: Rupert Hitzig. SP: Randal Viscovich. Mus: Parmer Fuller. Ref: V 5/24/89: "remarkably dull." Hound. With Elliott Gould, Richard Roundtree, Allen Garfield, Michael J. Pollard, Derek Rydall, Teresa Van Der Woude, Shannon Tweed, Brooke Bundy, Henry Gibson.

"Bargain basement satanist." (V)

**NIGHT WARS** SVS/Action Int'l. (Fritz Matthews/David Winters-Marc Winters) 1988 color 88m. (aka *Nightwars*). Story, SP, D: David A. Prior. Story: also Ted Prior, William Zipp. SpFX: Chuck Whitton. Ref: V 9/28/88: "standard-issue quickie." Hound. Scheuer. With Brian O'Connor, Dan Haggerty, Cameron Smith, Steve Horton.

Vietnam vets' "nightmares are for real...."(V)

**NIGHT WITH A VAMPIRE** Midnight Video 1994 color feature. Ref: vc box.

**NIGHTBREED** (U.S.-B) Fox/Morgan Creek (Gabriella Martinelli) 1990 color 102m. (99m.) (aka *Night Breed*). SP, D: Clive Barker, from his novel *Cabal*. Mus: Danny Elfman. Ph:

Robin Vidgeon. SpMkp & VisFX: Image Animation; (des) Bob Keen, Geoff Portass; (L.A.) Tony Gardner. Creature Sup: Simon Sayce. Anim OptFX: VCE; Peter Kuran. SpFxSup: Chris Corbould. Creature Chor: David Glass. Sp Costume Des: Brian Boag, Lucy Sayce. Anim Des: Rory Fellowes. Matte FX: Westbury Design; (sup) Cliff Culley. Baphomet Anim: Peter Tupy. SpProp: Keith Blanton. Title Seq: Ralph McQuarrie. Ref: TV. V 2/28/90. 2/21/90:58-9(ad). MFB'90:279-81. Hound. McCarty II. Martin. Scheuer. Fango 94:8. With Craig Sheffer, Anne Bobby, David Cronenberg, Charles Haid, Hugh Ross, Doug Bradley, Catherine Chevalier, John Agar.

"It's where the monsters go." A monster's bite (the "bite that mocks death") allows Aaron Boone (Sheffer) to revive after death and join the "last survivors of the great tribes ... of shapeshifters," at the cemetery at Midian, where the most monstrous monsters are kept locked in the deepest depths....

Ambitious horror epic is profligate in variety and number of its nightbred horrors, which include many incidental stopmo and special-makeup freaks. Here, the latter are the heroes—as in *The Abominable Snowman,* the monster-hunter (Cronenberg) is despicable, while the monsters are misunderstood and put-upon. Dr. Decker is no Van Helsing. In fact, in the movie's alternate theology, he is, at the end, the big enchilada of evil, complete with one lone worshiper.

Though expository interruptions undercut its mythic ambitions, *Nightbreed* does succeed as sheer spectacle. Midianzapoppin. Highlights: the porcupine woman's demonstration of her peculiar talent ... the weird pup-creature's transformation into a relatively normal-looking little girl (who was apparently left in the sun too long) ... and, later, her mom's touching reconciliation with her—right after mom has nastily stuck her hand, supernaturally, through the body of a human thug. Adroitly, director Barker mixes the spectacular and the casual—during Aaron's "baptism," for instance, the everyday intrudes on the ceremonial, as one creature indulges in a smoke.

**NIGHTFALL** Concorde/New Horizons (Julie Corman) 1988 color 82m. SP, D: Paul Mayersberg, from Isaac Asimov's story. Ph: D. Wolski. Mus: F. Serafine. PD: Craig Hodgetts. VisFxConsult: Chuck Comisky. Min: Wizard Works. Opt: Motion. Ref: TV: MGM-UA HV. V 10/5/88: "dull, pretentious and fragmented." Phantom: "fairly compelling." ad. With David Birney, Sarah Douglas, Alexis Kanner, Andra Millian, Starr Andreeff, Charles Hayward, Larry Hankin.

Planet orbiting three suns has night every 1,000 years. (V) "Ours is a planet of light"—and of a prophecy that night—or the end of light—will bring the end of life. Script also includes rival "interpreters" of the universe, a "telescope for the blind," and an "operating table"-and-pecking-birds, instant-blindness contraption. ("I can see so clearly now.") Off-puttingly self-serious and single-minded script is pretty turgid. Offbeat, but heavy-handed.

**NIGHTFLYERS** New Century/Vista (Robert Jaffe/Herb Jaffe) 1987 color 89m. (aka *Night Flyers*). D: Robert Collector (aka T. C. Blake). SP: R. Jaffe, from George R. R. Martin's novella. Mus: Doug Timm. SpMkp & MechFX: Robert Short. SpVisFX: Fantasy II; (sup) Gene Warren Jr. Ref: TV. V 10/28/87. ad. SFExam 10/30/87. Hound. Phantom. Maltin '92. McCarty II. Martin. Scheuer. Morse. With Catherine Mary Stewart, Michael

Praed, John Standing, Lisa Blount, Glenn Withrow, James Avery, Helene Udy, Annabel Brooks, Michael Des Barres.

In the 21st Century, aboard the "ancient freighter," the *Nightflyer*. ("This ship is alive!") The spaceship's captain, Royd (Praed), is a hologram, or test-tube creation, whose mother has transferred her personality to the ship's computer brain and keeps her soul in a stone crypt. ("This computer's a monster!") Scorecard: Looney Tunes My-mother-the-computer story, thesping from the noise-equals-drama school, a fairly impressive sucked-into-space scene, a pretty ring-of-fire-in-space effect, and the line, "You are a computer! You are not my mother!"

**NIGHTFRIGHT** Starlog Video 198-? color c10m. SP, D: Frank Kerr. Ph: Suzanne Griffin. Mus: D. J. Dee. AD: Karen Kerr. Monster: John Bisson. Ref: TV: *Cinemagic* (S. Video), MPI HV. With Kerry Black, Bob Manzani, Paul Heckemeyer.

"There's a monster in my room!" No one, however, listens to junior Horror Club member Zachary until it's too late. Agreeable monsters-at-bedtime comedy.

**NIGHTIE NIGHTMARE** see *Sorority House Massacre II*

**NIGHTIE NIGHTMARE II** see *Tower of Terror*

**NIGHTKILLER** see *Non Aprite Quella Porta 3*

**NIGHTLIFE** (U.S.-Mex) USA-TV/MCA-TV (Cine Ents./Robert T. Skodis) 1989 color 95m. Tel, D: Daniel Taplitz. Story, Tel: Anne Beatts. Ph: Peter Fernberger. Mus: Dana Kaproff. PD: Arturo Brito. Prosth: Maurice Stein. SpFX: Laurencio Cordero. Mkp: H. Escamilla. Ref: TV. Sacto Union 8/20/89. V (Mifed '89):130. Hound. Maltin '92. Martin. With Maryam d'Abo, Ben Cross, Keith Szarabajka, Jesse Corti, Camille Saviola.

"This blood is beautiful!" Angelique (d'Abo), a vampire buried since 1839, is unearthed in Mexico City, where Dr. David Zuckerman (Szarabajka), a hematologist, attempts to treat her "disease." He finds that he likes her blood—under the microscope, it seems to pirouette—and she likes his. Meanwhile, the "evil and dangerous" vampire Vlad (Cross) tracks her down ("You belong to darkness and you belong to me!") and insists that she, like all vampires, has a yen for the taste of fear in blood. David schemes to inject her with blood and with the adrenalin-like epinephrine ("liquid fear").... Meant-to-be-droll monster-comedy provokes an occasional smile, but Cross, as a conventional, gabby Dracula-type, slows an already-plot-heavy movie to a crawl.

**NIGHTMARE** see *Robot Carnival*

**NIGHTMARE ASYLUM** Cinema Home(David DeCoteau) 1992 color feature. SP, D, P, Ed, Mus: Todd Sheets. Ref: PT 18:57: "at least something is always happening." With Lori Hassle.

Mummy, wolfman, zombies, and gore in an amusement-park house of horrors.

**NIGHTMARE AT NOON** Omega 1987 color 96m. (*Deathstreet USA* - orig t). SP, D, P, SdFX: Nico Mastorakis. SP: also Kirk Ellis. Mus: Myers, Zimmer. SpFxCoord: Kevin M. McCarthy. Ref: TV: Republic HV. V 4/18/90. Hound. Phantom. Martin. Scheuer. Morse. With Wings Hauser, Bo Hopkins, George Ken-

nedy, Brion James (The Albino), Kimberly Beck, Kimberly Ross, Neal Wheeler (Charley).

"This whole town's gone psycho!" Citizens of Canyonland suddenly go berserk and start killing indiscriminately. Their blood turns green, and they gain super-strength and near-invulnerability. Radios are jammed, and a magnetic field knocks out electricity. Behind this "weird experiment": APE—Agency for the Protection of the Environment—a cover for the U.S. government or some foreign power.

Rotten script scrambles *Impulse* (1984) and the "Twilight Zone" episode "The Monsters are Due on Maple Street." Movie's first half is the same scene repeated over and over: Formerly law-abiding citizen goes homicidal and starts smashing furniture or cars—taken together, these sequences play like one long barroom brawl. Latter half of film abandons its ids-unleashed premise for an admittedly scenic tour of Moab, Utah. Pathetic except as a simple-squared action pic.

**NIGHTMARE AT SHADOW WOODS** see *Blood Rage*

**NIGHTMARE AT 20,000 FEET** see *Midnight Zone, The*

**NIGHTMARE BEACH** see *Welcome to Spring Break*

**The NIGHTMARE BEFORE CHRISTMAS** BV (Touchstone)/Burton-DiNovi (Skellington Prods.) 1993 stopmo anim & color 76m. (aka *Tim Burton's The Nightmare before Christmas*). D: Henry Selick. SP: Caroline Thompson. Adap: Michael McDowell. Story: Tim Burton. Mus: Danny Elfman. AD: Deane Taylor. VisFxSup: Pete Kozachik. Anim Sup: Eric Leighton. VisConsult: Rick Heinrichs. Model Shop Sup: Mitch Romanauski. DigitalFX: A. Shaw. Addl Anim: Harry Walton et al. SpSdFX: John Pospisil. Ref: screen. ad. V 10/18/93. SFChron 10/22/93; Dtbk 10/17/93. Fango 128:46-50, 74. Image 9/26/93. Cinef 12/93:32-47. Voices: D. Elfman, Chris Sarandon, Catherine O'Hara, William Hickey (evil scientist), Glenn Shadix, Paul Reubens, Ken Page (Oogie Boogie).

"'Twas a long time ago," in the "holiday worlds of old," principally Halloweentown, which was inhabited by Jack the Pumpkin King—who's in charge of Halloween ... the Oogie Boogie Man—a cross between the Cab Calloway walrus-ghost and a potato sack ... vampires ... a werewolf ... Mr. Hyde ... a mummy ... a devil ... witches ... ghosts ... a water monster ... a melting man ... a monster wreath ... a dog-like Igor-type ... Jack's ghostdog Zero ... an evil scientist who looks like a macabre duck and who stitched heroine Sally together ... small scorpion things ... and various monsters under bed and stairs.

It's not Starevitch, but it's not bad, and the Halloween-number intro is not much short of great. The animation here is much smoother than Starevitch—or Willis O'Brien, for that matter—but not as inspired. In fact, Deane Taylor's ultra-imaginative design—mood-keyed landscapes, Halloweentown buildings out of old Universal horror movies—often steals the show from the animation. Story and songs are no match for the look of the movie, and Jack is a little, well, bland.

**NIGHTMARE CLASSICS** Showtime-TV & Think Ent. (Shelley Duvall/Bridget Terry) 1989 color c96m. (*Nightmare Classics I*

- ad t). PD: Jane Osmann. SpFX: E. McCarthy. Mkp: Sheryl Leigh Ptak. Opt: T&T. Ref: TV. TVG. V 11/1/89:68. 11/29/89:63.

1) "Carmilla." D: Gabrielle Beaumont. Tel: Jonathan Furst, from LeFanu's story. Ph: Ron Vargas. Mus: Rick Conrad. with Meg Tilly, Ione Skye, Roy Dotrice, Roddy McDowall, Armelia McQueen, Linda Hunt (voice).

"I think it's a vampire." The mysterious Carmilla's phantom appearances, her command of killer bats, and a breakout of neck wounds on the local populace lead the inspector (McDowall) to believe that the "sickness from the south" has arrived. Indeed, Camilla is a vampire, and her friend Marie's missing mother is also one.... If the Old South setting doesn't seem so surprising for a tale of vampires, remember Universal did it first, with *Son of Dracula* (1943). This tepid, precious repackaged TV show has one okay effect: Carmilla floating in the air as she nibbles on Marie's neck. Some stake-impalement gore, some jiggle-for-cable.

2) "The Eyes of the Panther." D: Noel Black. Tel: Art Wallace, from the short stories "The Eyes of the Panther" and "The Boarded Window" by Bierce. Mus: John Debney. with C. Thomas Howell, Daphne Zuniga, John Stockwell, Jeb Brown, Ruth De Sosa.

"There were panthers in those days." In frontier Ohio, a woman, Irene, seems to be cursed to turn into a panther, in this trite, maudlin update of *Cat People*. Panther supplied by Birds & Animals Unlimited.

**NIGHTMARE CLASSICS II** Showtime-TV & Think Ent. (Shelley Duvall/Bridget Terry) 1989 color c120m. PD: Jane Osmann. SpFX: Eugene McCarthy. Mkp: S. L. Ptak. Ref: TV. TVG. V 11/29/89:62. 8/30/89:84.

1) "The Strange Case of Dr. Jekyll and Mr. Hyde." D: Michael Lindsay-Hogg. Tel: J. M. Straczynski, from the Robert Louis Stevenson story. Mus: Stephen Barber. With Anthony Andrews, Gregory Cooke, George Murdock, Laura Dern, Nicholas Guest, Rue McClanahan, Lisa Langlois.

"No one denies Hyde!" "Poor stodgy old Jekyll"—a "nervous tic of a man"—tries to purge himself of evil with a "goodness potion" which frees the dominant part of his mind. Unfortunately, evil is the dominant half—and addictive to boot—and he becomes Edward Hyde, a "horrible man ... completely without inhibition".... Andrews as Jekyll has an amusing, rabbity, scrunched-up intensity; his Hyde, though, is disappointing, a slick-haired, peremptory dandy. The introduction of Hyde—with its use of the subjective camera (Ron Vargas, photography)—recalls the 1932 version.

2) "The Turn of the Screw." D: Graeme Clifford. Tel: Robert Hutchison, James Miller, from Henry James' story. Mus: J. P. Robinson. With Amy Irving, Balthazar Getty, David Hemmings, Olaf Pooley.

Nothing much new or interesting in this version of the tale of the governess assailed by intimations of sex and violence. The message: Repression kills. Lone highlight: The "ghost" of Quint emerging from the shadows in the governess' bedroom.

**NIGHTMARE CONCERT** see *Cat in the Brain*

**NIGHTMARE ON DYKE STREET** Fresh Video/Zane Ent. 1991 color feature. Ref: vc box: guy in Freddy mask and shirt. With Samantha Strong.

**A NIGHTMARE ON ELM STREET** New Line & Media Home Ent. & Smart Egg (Robert Shaye/The Elm Street Venture) 1984 color 92m. D: Wes Craven. Ph: Jacques Haitkin. Mus: Charles Bernstein. SpMkpFX: David Miller. MechSpFX: Jim Doyle; Theatrical Engines. Opt: Cinema Research et al. Ref: TV. MFB'85:283-4. SFExam 4/24/88: real-life Freddy imitator. Stanley. Hound. Phantom. Maltin '92. Martin. Scheuer. Newman. V 11/7/84. With John Saxon, Ronee Blakeley, Heather Langenkamp, Amanda Wyss, Robert Englund (Fred Krueger), Jack Shea, Nick Corri.

Freddy the First, or Invasion of the Body Slashers, begins with deadly dream-claws ... suddenly elastic walls ... "oatmeal" stairs (for that familiar dream sensation of frozen running) ... strangling bedsheets ... and a phone-receiver tongue. Fred Krueger, a "filthy child murderer," burned to death, begins to return via dreams, a state supposedly kindred to death. Already, he displays that inimitably nasty sense of humor, and there are funny-creepy elongated-arms and horrible-face-under-horrible-mask effects. But the movie's Rules of Fantasy seem to be invoked only to be broken. The dream/reality interplay begins to seem a pretext—an anything-for-an-effect effect sets in. If the clockwork shocks in Freddy One are imaginatively conceived, the mainspring seems slightly defective.

See also the following titles and *Freddy's Dead. Beauties and the Beast. Sleepaway Camp 2. Wes Craven's New Nightmare.*

**A NIGHTMARE ON ELM STREET, PART 2: FREDDY'S REVENGE** New Line/New Line-Heron-Smart Egg (The Second Elm Street Venture) 1985 color 85m. D: Jack Sholder. SP: David Chaskin. Mus: Christopher Young. SpMkpFX: Kevin Yagher. SpMechFX: A&A, Dick Albain, Ron Nary. SpVisFX: Paul Boyington. Transformation FX: Mark Shostrom. SpPuppetFX: Rick Lazzarini. FxAnim: Wes Takahashi et al. Ref: TV. MFB'86:313. V 10/30/85. ad. SFExam 1/10/86. SFChron 1/11/86. Stanley. Hound. Phantom. Maltin '92. Martin. Scheuer. Newman. With Mark Patton, Kim Myers, Clu Gulager, Hope Lange, Robert Englund (Freddy Krueger), Sydney Walsh, Robert Rusler, Kerry Remsen.

In his second outing, Freddy ruins a garden party and tells teenagers, pretentiously, "You are all my children now." Scattered effective nightmare effects include a fun opener re a bus-to-hell, an eyeball-in-throat bit, and the scene in which Freddy springs up whole out of fallen, shattered window glass. More routine: the expected *Carrie*-like kicker and the sight of Freddy popping out of a boy's chest. Film overexploits the oddly sinister quality of a fedora. Freddy's cereal: Fu Man Chews.

**A NIGHTMARE ON ELM STREET III: DREAM WARRIORS** New Line-Heron-Smart Egg (Robert Shaye/The Third Elm St. Venture) 1987 color 96m. SP, D: Chuck Russell. Story, SP: Wes Craven, Bruce Wagner. SP: also Frank Darabont. Ph: Roy H. Wagner. Mus: Angelo Badalamenti. SpMkpFX: Greg Cannom, Mark Shostrum; (addl) M. Mungle. SpVisFX: (sup) Hoyt Yeatman; Dream Quest. AnimFX: Jeff Burks. Stopmo: Doug Beswick. MechSpFX: (coord) Peter Chesney; Image Engineering. SpFxGhouls: Thomas Bellissimo, Bryan Moore. Freddy MkpFX: Kevin Yagher. Ref: TV. MFB'87:341. V 2/25/87. ad. Stanley. Hound. Phantom. Maltin '92. Martin. Scheuer. Newman. With Heather Langenkamp, Patricia Arquette, Larry Fishburne, Priscilla Pointer, Craig Wasson, Brooke Bundy, Ken Sagoes, John Saxon, Dick Cavett, Zsa Zsa Gabor, Robert Englund (Freddy Krueger), Jack Shea.

"The souls of children give me strength!" Candidate for Best of Freddy features puppet-master Freddy ... snake-Freddy ... Dick Cavett-Freddy ... skeleton-Freddy ... nurse-Freddy ... helpful ghost-nun Amanda Krueger ... a melting tricycle ... a clutching bathroom-sink handle ... a thing under a rug ... and the lost souls of children wailing from Freddy's torso.... Functional plotting, sometimes imaginative effects, some wit, and a cartoon, anything-can-happen feel. Freddy is quip-master, the James Bond of horror-fantasy. The kids who challenge him have spunk, but little else going for them. Wow shot: puppet-master-Freddy looming over the hospital and cutting puppet-Phillip's strings.

### A NIGHTMARE ON ELM STREET 4: THE DREAM MASTER

New Line-Heron-Smart Egg (Robert Shaye/4th New Line-Heron Venture) 1988 color 93m. D: Renny Harlin. Story, SP: Brian Helgeland. SP: also Scott Pierce. Story: also William Kotzwinkle. Mus: Craig Safan. Ph: Steven Fierberg. MkpFX: Steve Johnson, MMI, Screaming Mad George, R. Christopher Biggs. Freddy Mkp: Kevin Yagher. Mech SpFX: Image Engineering. SpVisFX: Dream Quest; (anim sup) Jeff Burks. SpSdFX: Joel Valentine. Ref: TV: Media Home Ent. video. V 8/17/88. MFB'89:145-6. SFChron 8/24/88; Dtbk 9/4/88; 8/15/91. Hound. Phantom. Maltin '92. Martin. Scheuer. With Robert Englund (Freddy), Lisa Wilcox, Danny Hassel, Tuesday Knight, Ken Sagoes, Brooke Bundy, Linnea Quigley (soul in chest).

"If he kills you in your dream, you're dead for real." Alice (Wilcox) becomes "town legend" Freddy's new unwilling supplier of dream victims when Kristen (Knight) dies. But as he absorbs his young victims' souls into his body, she gains psychic strength from memories of her dead friends.

Some ace effects and Freddy's quips bolster a strictly functional, not-much-new storyline. The one tour de force sequence: the climax, in which the souls in torment in Freddy rebel, and miniature arms and hands sprout from torso and head and make death miserable for him. The rest is just moments—water-bed Fred's "How's this for a wet dream?", teacher Freddy sucking the life out of one victim, workout Freddy's "No pain, no gain," and—zingiest of all—pizzeria Freddy savoring the human meatballs ("soul food") on his lunch.

### A NIGHTMARE ON ELM STREET 5: THE DREAM CHILD

New Line-Heron-Smart Egg (Robert Shaye/4th New Line-Heron Venture) 1989 color 90m. D: Stephen Hopkins. Story, SP: Leslie Bohem. Story: also John Skip, Craig Spector. Mus: Jay Ferguson. SpMkpFX: Chris Biggs, Greg Nicotero. Freddy & Baby Freddy: David Miller. VisFxSup: Alan Munro. MechFX: (sup) Andre G. Ellingson, Gary Sivertson; (sp) Eddie Paul. Prosth: Todd Masters. Stopmo: Ted Rae. MinFxAnim: Don Waller. SpSdFX: Sound Off. OptFX: VCE; Peter Kuran; (anim) Kevin Kutchaver et al. Womb: Rick Lazzarini. Prowler: Doug Beswick; (stopmo) Yancy Calzada; (cut-out anim) Larry Nikolai.

Head: KNB FX: (mech fx) Lee Stone. Opt: Cinema Research, Mercer Titles; (title) Bob Bailey, Howard Anderson. Ref: TV. V 8/9/89. HR 8/9/89. ad. SFExam 8/11/89. Sacto Union 8/12/89. MFB'90:169-171. Hound. Maltin '92. McCarty II. Martin. With Robert Englund (Freddy), Lisa Wilcox, Danny Hassel, Kelly Jo Minter, Whitby Hertford (Jacob), Beatrice Boepple, Joe Seely, Burr DeBenning, Noble Craig (merging Freddy), Mike Smith (Super Freddy).

"Do unborn babies dream?" Alice's (Wilcox) does. Freddy Krueger has found "some other way" to return to the land of the dreaming: Jacob, her unborn, who also appears as the "dream child," is his medium. The Question: Is Jacob a perfectly healthy baby or a Freddy-in-waiting feeding on the amniotic souls of Freddy's victims?

Number Five is a slick vehicle for occasionally truly startling effects, including the instant-mutation cans and bottles in the refrigerator and the womb-souls. There are also some neat "transitions"—e.g., the real Mark (Seely), a cartoonist, flipping the pages to the comic-book Mark and becoming himself "comicized" into the book. But a "Vacancy" sign blinks in-between effects. Most of the surprises here are in the latter, not in the story. The series should have a Special Quips credit. Even Jacob gets into the act. ("School's out, Krueger!")

Next up: *Freddy's Dead.*

### NIGHTMARE ON PORN STREET

Moonlight Ent. 1988 color c80m. D: Scotty Fox. Sp: Mark Cashman, Chad Randolf. Mkp: J. R. Ref: TV: Moonlight Video. Adam '90; Erotomic, V. 5, #10. With Shanna McCullough, Britt Morgan, Randy Spears (Eddie).

"Dreams don't bite." Eddie, the school janitor, who died in a fire, keeps turning up in the dreams of several students. ("Not another one of those dreams!") Eddie, it seems, has been "transformed"—his residual spiritual energy activates and appears in the dreams of the horny students upon whom he spied. At the end, one girl turns aggressor, in her dream, and Eddie vanishes. Limp adult variation on the Freddy saga.

### NIGHTMARE ON THE 13TH FLOOR

USA-TV/Wilshire Court & G. C. Group (Walter Grauman) 1990 color c85m. D: Grauman. Tel: J. D. Feigelson, Dan DiStefano. Mus: Jay Gruska. PD: P. D. Foreman. SpFX: Greg Curtis. Mkp: Melanie Huges. Ref: TV. TVG. V 10/29/90:56-7. Sacto Bee 10/31/90. Martin. Maltin '92. Scheuer. With Michele Greene, James Brolin, Louise Fletcher, John Karlen, Alan Fudge, Terri Treas.

"I'm trying to find the 13th floor." Members of a satanic cult lure prospective sacrifices to the long-sealed-off, gaslit 13th floor of the Wessex Hotel (a "great old hotel") in Los Angeles. Their goal: immortality through "slaughtering people".... The mystery of the missing floor is fairly intriguing, and Fletcher's superciliousness as a cult member amuses. ("Two more to go.") Unfortunately, the out-with-the-ax-again payoffs are monotonous, and the big climactic revelation is no surprise.

### NIGHTMARE SISTERS

Cinema HV (DeCoteau) 1988 (1987) color 81m. (aka *Sorority Sisters*). D, P: David DeCoteau. SP, Assoc P: Kenneth J. Hall. Mus: Del Casher. SpFxAnim: Bret Mixon. SpMkpFX: Cleve Hall, John Criswell, Scott Coulter, Denny Powers. Succubus Vocal FX: John Vulich. Ref: TV. V

8/30/89. Hound. McCarty II. Martin. With Linnea Quigley, Brinke Stevens, Michelle Bauer, Marcus Vaughter, Sandy Brooke, Michael D. Sonye (Omar), Jim Culver (exorcist).

Three plain-Jane sorority sisters (Quigley, Stevens, Bauer)—aka the "Gorgon sisters"—consult the "Yellow Pages to the Twilight Zone," touch the dead medium Omar's crystal ball, and become possessed by a succubus with a lust for "mortal men." When they bite their male victims with their monster teeth, the guys disintegrate. At the end, an exorcist and supernatural expert "second only to Von [sic] Helsing in the entire world" flushes out the succubus.... Incessant talk here, and though not all of it is just twaddle, the movie goes really asinine when the girls transform. Their writhings are apparently supposed to be enticing. Until then, four-day cheapie plays like a set of dialogue exercises.

**NIGHTMARE WEEKEND** (B-F?) Troma/Vision Communications & English Film Co. & G.I.G. Prods. & Les Films des Lions (Bachoo Sen) 1986 color 85m. D: Henry Sala. SP: G. F. Bernard. Mus: M. Kershaw. SpFxMkp: Dan Gates. SpFX: Mike de Silva. Ref: V 5/21/86: "low-charged ... horror." Ecran F 70:70. Martin. Stanley. Hound. Morse: "ludicrously dumb." With Debbie Laster, Debra Hunter, Dale Midkiff, Lori Lewis.

Computer scientist turns teens into zombie-like, gunk-spewing zombies, or "neuropaths."

**NIGHTMARES (2)** see *Stage Fright* (1983)

**NIGHTSCARE** see *Beyond Bedlam*

**NIGHTSTALKER** Star Cinema 1981 (1979) color c90m. (aka *Don't Go near the Park* (2P). *Night Stalker*). SP, D, P: Lawrence D. Foldes. Story, SP: Linwood Chase. Ph: William DeDiego. Mus: Chris Ledesma. AD: Robert Burns. SpFX: Harry Woolman. SpVisFX: Marcos Morales. SpFxMkp: Douglas White, Donald Angier. Ref: TV: vt. MMarquee 36:36. V 7/8/81:5 (rated). 9/23/81: in Miami. 4/1/91:82. Hound. no Martin. Stanley. PT 13:7. 16:10: aka *Curse of the Living Dead*. Fango 89:12. With Aldo Ray, Meeno Peluce, Tamara Taylor, Linnea Quigley, Barbara Monker, Crackers Phinn.

A witch's offspring are "condemned to perpetual dying, but never death"—the two age ten years for every year of life. Now, 12,000 years later, they need a virgin's soul in order to gain release and eternal life. Sixteen-year-old Bondi (Taylor), who appears to be the chosen one, ages instantly at the end and seems to turn into the witch, Petronella (Taylor again). Finally, in a confusing coda, there's a new ghoul. (Gore alert here.) Pretentious script is set in Griffith Park, which means some legitimate location shooting at Bronson Caverns. Very cheap, stilted, badly-edited production.

**NIGHTSWARM** see *Mosquito*

**NIGHTVISION** see *Escapes* (1988)

**NIGHTWARS** see *Night Wars*

**NIGHTWISH** Channel Communications & PIV Int'l. (NightWish Prods./Keith Walley) 1989 (1988) color 96m. (92m.). SP, D: Bruce R. Cook. Mus: Ryder, Davies. PD: Robert Burns. SpFxMkp: K. N. B. MechSpFX: Ted Vasquez. VisFX: VCE/Pe-

ter Kuran. Anim Sup: Kevin Kutchaver. Ref: TV: Vidmark video; c90m. V 5/23/90:71(hv). Maltin '92. McCarty II. Martin. With Clayton Rohner, Alisha Das, Elizabeth Kaitan, Jack Starrett, Robert Tessier, Tom Dugan, Brian Thompson.

"Bugs came out instead of blood!" A Cal U. parapsychological team conducting a "psychotic investigation" in the Valley of Fear discovers an ectoplasmic snake (or "demonic entity"), an ectoplasmic whirlwind, and a ghost boy (Jared Coulter). Or is it just Kim's (Das) dream? Is the doctor (Starrett) an alien studying humans? Is it science or the supernatural at work? Plus: (in a prefatory nightmare) cannibalism.

An *Elm Street* jumble of nightmare ideas and images. The ambiguity is just a pretext for occasional gross goodies like the breeding-ground horrors in the mine. Dugan as Wendell and Tessier as Stanley provide the most actor goodies.

**NIGHTY NIGHT** (J) 1990 feature. D: H. Kokusho. Ref: Weisser/JC: passable collection of 4 shorts re computer monsters, etc. With S. Wakui.

**The NINE DEMONS** (H.K.) 1983 color/ws c92m. (*The Demons* - ad t). D, P: Chang Cheh. Ref: TV: Ocean Shores Video; Eng. dubbed. Phantom. MMarquee 43:6. NST! 4:32: D: Ng Wu Fu. Fango 107:59. With Kong Sen, Luk Fung.

Joey tumbles into the Black Prince's Black Paradise and swears allegiance, in exchange for magical powers. Now invincible and powerful, he becomes one with nine blood-sucking, flying-skull demons (eight children, one woman) controlled by a power plaque and a demon sword. "I know," Joey tells them at one point, "you nine demons demand fresh blood every day": Eagerly, the skulls fly at him and array themselves along his arms for their feeding. His strength sapped, he loses control of them, and they run amok, sucking the blood of everyone in the brothel.

The plot of *The Nine Demons* is a negligible revenge saga/morality play re the hero's pursuit of the "baddies" who killed his father, his friend Gary, and his friend's father. ("Just kill the very bad and rotten ones," Joey's light-of-love urges him.) But the skull-demons are the damnedest things. They're at once demons, vampires, acrobats, and frolicking children—unleashed from their restraining necklace, they shriek and do cartwheels. They play hard, they bite hard—and after dining, they laugh merrily at the blood on each other's mouths. These unusual vampires just want to have fun, but they leave their "playmates" drained of blood and, in some cases, exploded. Their scenes are a nine-demons' wonder.

**976-EVIL** New Line/CineTel (Horrorscope/Lisa M. Hansen/Paul Hertzberg) 1988 ('89-U.S.) color 100m. (*Horrorscope* - orig t). D: Robert Englund. SP: Rhet Topham, Brian Helgeland. Mus: Chase, Rucker. MkpFX: Kevin Yagher Prods. SpFX: Kevin & Sandra McCarthy. SdFX: S. Michaely, P. B. Gonzo. Ref: TV. MFB '89:22-3. V 3/29/89. 10/19/88:173. Sacto Union 4/27/89. ad. With Stephen Geoffreys, Patrick O'Bryan, Sandy Dennis, Jim Metzler, Robert Picardo.

A mysterious rain of fish proves to be a warning: After Dark Enterprises' Mark Dark's Horrorscope, supposedly defunct, is a demonic phone-message service which somehow turns Lucy's (Dennis) son Hoax (Geoffreys) into a clawed monster.... A teen-pic *The Omen, 976-Evil* is offbeat—or confused—enough to keep one guessing for a while. But the quips-and-revenge payoff with Hoax apes *Nightmare on Elm Street* disappointingly closely, though there's one good, gory Freddy-esque scene. ("Would it be possible to enter the game with a pair of hearts?") Incidental oddity: the ice-palace house. ("Hell finally froze over!")

**976-EVIL II** CineTel Films (Lisa M. Hansen/Paul Hertzberg) 1991 color 90m. (*976-Evil II: The Astral Factor* - ad t. *Horrorscope* - orig t). D: Jim Wynorski. SP: Eric Anjou. Story: Rick Glassman. Ph: Zoran Hochstatter. Mus: C. Cirino. PD: G. Randall. SpVisFX: (sup) Steven R. Benson; Apollo FX. MkpFxSup: Scott Coulter. Ref: TV. SFChron Dtbk 4/19/92. V 3/25/91:91: shooting. With Patrick O'Bryan, Rene Assa, Paul Coufos, Leslie Ryan, Debbie James, Brigitte Nielsen, Phil McKeon, Buck Flower, Ace Mask, Monique Gabrielle.

The telephone Horrorscope Master of the Dark grants "crater face" Mr. Grubeck (Assa)—the "Slate River serial killer"—special astral-projecting privileges which give his astral body command over cars, ovens, refrigerators, and TV sets: His Zap-O-Matic control puts Paula (Ryan) into *It's a Wonderful Life,* then her and the ghoul-ified *Wonderful Life* characters into a *Night of the Living Dead* situation, where a little girl trowels her to death, and the body is dumped in front of the TV set, in a technically clever if rather arduous subverting of the Capra film.... Routine but competent horror-fantasy sequel is hampered by flat dialogue. The new tool of terror: a car phone. Guest star Nielsen plays Agnes—"Elvira on steroids"—of Lucifer's bookshop.

**NINETEEN EIGHTY-FOUR** (B) ARC/Umbrella-Rosenblum (Simon Perry) 1984 color 120m. (110m.-U.S.) (aka *1984*). SP, D: Michael Radford. Mus: Dominic Muldowney. PD: Allan Cameron. Ref: TV. V 10/10/84. SFExam 2/8/85. Bay Guardian 2/6/85. Horacio Higuchi. With John Hurt, Richard Burton, Suzanna Hamilton, Cyril Cusack, Gregor Fisher.

Not much fun to be had in this world of prying helicopters ... novel-writing machines ... annoying, ubiquitous child patriots ... Newspeak ... big-screen Brother ... conditioning by torture ... annihilation of non-comformists ... and Room 101—the "worst thing in the world" ... in the case of hero Winston Smith (Hurt), rats.... As deliberate a study of eroding and erodable humanity as the 1956 *Invasion of the Body Snatchers* was nimble. Single-mindedly grim, pessimistic film has its inexorability and some bleak humor going for it, but not much else, except Burton's quiet, forceful monotone as mind-restructurer O'Brien. Party policy, as stated by him, seems more horrifying than party policy as implemented by everyone else. An "unremitting downer" (as *Variety* noted). Ideal co-feature: *The Care Bears Movie.*

**NINFAS DIABOLICAS** (Braz.) Presenca 1978 color 85m. SP, D, P: John Doo. SP: also Ody Fraga. Ph: O. Candeias. Ref: Hardy/HM: "fairly conventional." With Sergio Hingst, Aldine Mueller, Patricia Scalvi.

Businessman picks up two ghostly female hitchhikers.

**NINGYO DENSETSU** see *Mermaid Legend*

**NINJA III—THE DOMINATION** MGM-UA & Cannon (Golan-Globus) 1984 color 92m. D: Sam Firstenberg. SP: James R. Silke. Mus: Udi Haroaz et al. Mattes/SpFX: Jim Danforth, Joe Quinlivan et al. SdFX: Allen Hartz et al. Ref: TV. V 5/23/84. Sacto Bee 9/17/84. Hound. Phantom. Maltin '92. Martin. Scheuer. Newman. Stanley. With Lucinda Dickey (Christie), Jordan Bennett, Sho Kosugi, David Chung.

A ninja's spirit enters the body of an aerobics class instructor. The latter starts "feeling really weird" and exhibits a "preoccupation with Japanese culture." A Japanese exorcist makes the ninja inside her speak, breathe fumes, and perform levitation stunts.... Mechanical action and fantasy. At times, the effect on the mise en scene is as if Chuck Norris had wandered into *Flashdance.* Follow-up to *Enter the Ninja* and its follow-up *Revenge of the Ninja.*

**NINJA INCARNATION** (J) Toei/Kadokawa 1981 ('89-U.S.) color/ws c115m. (2 *Makai Tensho.* aka *Samurai Reincarnation. Shogun's Ninja* - TV). SP, D: Kinji Fukasaku. SP: also Tatsuo Nogami, Takato Ishikawa. Story: Futaro Yamada. Ph: Hasegawa, Sakane. Mus: Yamamoto, Sugano. AD: Igawa, Sano. SpFX: Nabuo Yajima. Ref: TV: vt; Eng. dubbed. Hardy/HM. JFFJ 14:9. Hound. TVG. With Shinichi (Sonny) Chiba, Akiko Kana, Henry Sanada, Mikio Narita, Asao Uchida, Tetsuro Tamba, Ken Ogata, Tomisaburo Wakayama.

"Something evil must be possessing all of them!" A survivor of the shogun's slaughter of Christians turns to the "god of the evil world" for help and invokes "flaming demons" and "dreadful devils." He travels across Japan enlisting the aid of Musashi Miyamoto and others from the "world of darkness," and reincarnates them as "evil spirits." Temporarily halting the onslaught of the undead and lifting the "terrible curse": a sword which can cut the "spirit of the darkness".... The theme is a noble one—the futility of revenge (see also *Die Nibelungen*)—but this cornily dubbed epic fantasy is a non-starter. The roundup of the ghosts takes an hour and is essentially one scene repeated over and over, and the movie features disappointingly few fantasy effects. It's mostly talk and routine action.

**NINJA MIRAI** see *Mirai Ninja*

**NINJA SCROLL** (J) Manga Ent./JVC & Toho & Movic & Madhouse & Kawajiri (Komatsu-Sai-Sawanobori) 1993('95-U.S.) anim color 91m. (*Jubei Ninpucho*). SP, D: Yoshiaki Kawajiri. Ph: H. Yamaguchi. Mus: K. Wada. AD: H. Ogura. SdFX: K. Shibasaki. Ref: TV: ME video; Eng. titles.

Ingredients include a giant—a "monster," one of the Eight Devils of Kimon—whose body at one point alters and becomes rock/armor-like ... Gemma, an immortal and "boss" of the devils ... a snake lady who sheds her skin ... Kagero, a poison-bodied ninja (her touch is fatal) ... and a gentleman whose back is a hive for thousands of wasps—as an observer notes, as the hive man drowns: "The wasps in the hive are trying to escape the water. Desperately stinging his body as they do," in a sequence which wins the Bizarre award for 1993.... Quite grisly, but imaginatively so. Excellent shadow and silhouette work. Startling: the snake-thing, or things, on the ceiling. The least of it: the period political intrigue.

**NINJA, THE VIOLENT SORCERER** (H.K.?) Filmark Int'l. (Tomas Tang) 1988? color 90m. D: Bruce Lambert. SP: Daniel Clough. Ph: Owen Casey. Mus: Tim Lee. PD: Tang. SpFX: William Muller. FX: Rudy James. Mkp: Cathy Joe. Ref: TV: Trans World video; Eng. dubbed. no Hound. no Martin. With Simon Reed, Harry Carter, Joe Nelson, Terry Myers.

"He must have the devil on his side!" Two hopping vampires—who, 300 years ago, were the North and South Gambling Kings—aid evil-hearted gambler Barker. "Anti-sorcery magic" and a ghost's advice ultimately help good ninja defeat a horde of hopping vampires.... Filmic mixing of gambling and the supernatural is an honorable tradition. (See the many versions of *Queen of Spades* and *The Witching Hour*.) To which tradition, this is a not-so-honorable addition. Much jumping about by both vampires and ninja. Dubbing prize to the line: "We must destroy Barker's spirit with fire so he can't be reborn again unless he returns as a gambling vampire."

**NINJA THE WONDER BOY** (U.S.-J?) Kidpix/Knack 1985 anim color 89m. D, P: Jim Terry. SP: Angelo Grillo. Mus: Bullets. Ref: vc box: Para HV. Hound.

Devilman conjures up "super-evil" beings.

**Za NINJA UORIAHZU—KUNOICHI SENSHI** (J) Shochiku HV 1991 color 80m. Ref: Markalite 3:10: made-for-video; *Kunoichi Soldiers-The Ninja Warriors*-tr t. With Tetsuro Tamba, the Great Kabuki, General K. Y. Wakamatsu.

"A rip in the time-space continuum sends three female ninjas from the Edo Era to 1990s Tokyo."

**NINJA VAMPIRE BUSTER** see *Vampire Buster*

**NINJA WARS** (J) American National HV/Toei & Kadokawa 1982 ('84-U.S.) color 102m. (*Iga Ninpocho*). D: Mitsumasu Saito. SP: Ei Ogawa, from Hutaro Yamada's novel. Ph: Fujio Mrita(sp?). Mus: Toshiaki Yokota. AD: Norimichi Ikawa, Kazuyoshi Sonoda. SpFxD: Hideo Suzuki. Ref: TV: Prism Ent. video; Eng. dubbed. Horacio Higuchi. TVG: and with S. Chiba. Hound. VSOM: *Black Magic War*-alt vt t. With Henry Sanada, Noriko Watanabe, Jun Miho, Miho Kazamatsuri, Kongo Kobahashi, Gajiro Sato.

A sorcerer, Kashin Koji, and five immortal "devil monks," who can die and revive, effect an exchange of heads between Kagaribi, a female ninja, and a highborn lady. The bodies seem to rule the mystically-grafted-on heads, and the ninja-head/lady-body is dubbed "Lady Hellfire." The evil ones here can transform themselves into women, and one monk shoots darts from his dead eyes.... Handsome but execrably-dubbed fantasy actioner. Everyone sounds like Broderick Crawford. The body-switching and rampant impersonating get confusing. Good effects.

**NINJA'S FINAL DUEL** (H.K.) Hsien Shen Films 1986 color 8 hours. D: Robert Tai. Ref: Weisser/ATC2: "innovative"; "ninjas riding gigantic spiders." With A. Lo Rei, Lee Hai Shing, W. Yen.

**NINJYA RYUKENDEN** (J) 199-? anim (aka *Legend of the Ninja Dragon Sword*). Ref: Japan Video. vc box: monster.

**NISEN-GOJU-NEN** see *Solar Crisis*

**NO CAUSE FOR ALARM** see *Project: Alien*

**NO DEAD HEROES** Cineventures & Maharaj-Miller Film 1987 (1986) color 86m. SP, D, P: J. C. Miller. SP: also A. N. Gelfield. SpFX: Jun Rambell. Ref: V 10/7/87: "perfunctory war film." Martin. With Max Thayer, John Dresden, Toni Nero.

"Agent programmed to kill by a special computer chip put into his head."

**NO ESCAPE** Savoy & Allied Filmmakers/Pacific Western (Gale Anne Hurd) 1994 color 118m. D: Martin Campbell. SP: Michael Gaylin, Joel Gross, from Richard Herley's book *The Penal Colony*. Ph: Phil Meheux. Mus: G. Revell. PD: A. Cameron. Ref: V 5/2/94: "synthetic pastiche." SFChron 4/29/94: "as punchy as it is pointless." ad. Video Event 10/94. Martin: "diverting ... but little more." With Ray Liotta, Lance Henriksen, Stuart Wilson, Kevin Dillon, Michael Lerner, Kevin J. O'Connor, Ernie Hudson.

Year 2022, in an international, corporation-run prison.

**NO PLACE TO HIDE** Cannon (Alan Amiel) 1993 color 97m. SP, D: Richard Danus. Key Mkp: Mony Monsano. SpFxSup: Ron Trost. Ref: TV. Fango 128:11: "satanic cult."

Intense but predictable, not too believable tale re a *Death Wish* organization begins like a slasher movie, with a seemingly hypnotic skulker, strangely marked bodies, and "very scary men."

**NO SUCH THING AS GRAVITY** Verge Prods. & Alyce Wittenstein 1989 b&w and color 45m. SP, D, P: A. Wittenstein. SP: also Steve Ostringer. Ph: P. Holahan, N. Shapiro. Mus: D. Lee. PD: S. Ostringer. Min: Joseph Pan et al. SpFxPh: Bruce Hodge et al. SpFxMkp: Trisha More. Ref: TV: *No Such Thing As ... Gravity* - cr t; Atomique video. Stanley. SFChron 3/13/93: "ambitious." With Nick Zedd, Taylor Mead, Michael J. Anderson, Emmanuelle Chaulet, Holly Adams.

LaFont Industries products are responsible for the look of a future Earth—e.g., the Cosmetizer, teaching machines, and the FaceLifter (which employs "matter displacement"). But its greatest project is Nova Terra—the "largest-scale experiment in human history"—a man-made planet for the outmoded and disbarred. Nova Terra, which is throwing Earth out of orbit, is scheduled to be "fragmentized." Instead, at the end, Earth is destroyed, and Nova Terra—a new Eden—survives .... Flat cross between intentional camp and science fiction.

**NO TELLING** Glass Eye Pix/Telltale Prods. (Rachel Horovitz) 1991 color 117m. SP, D, Exec P: Larry Fessenden. SP: also Beck Underwood. Ph: David Shaw. Mus: Tom Laverack. Ref: V 8/26/91: "polemical and overlong." With Miriam Healy-Louie, Stephen Ramsey, David Van Tieghem.

"Chemo-electrical therapy" allows the "transplantation of entire limbs."

**NO TIME TO DIE** (W. G.-Indonesian) Atlas Int'l./Rapid Film & Lisa Film and Rapi Films (Hartwig-Samtani) 1984 ('86-U.S.) color 87m. (*Hijacked to Hell* - orig t). Co-SP, D: Helmuth Ashley. SpFX: Nuryadi. Ref: V 7/2/86: "instantly disposable action film." With John Phillip Law, Horst Janson, Grazyna Dylong, Chris Mitchum.

Laser cannon to the rescue.

**NO TRESPASSING** see *Red House, The*

**NOB HILL** Fox (Andre Daven) 1945 color 95m. D: Henry Hathaway. SP: Wanda Tuchock, Norman Reilly Raine. Story: Eleanore Griffin. Ref: TV. Maureen Smith. V 5/30/45. Thomas. Scheuer. Maltin '92.

In a sequence "so supernatural," set in a San Francisco China-town wax museum, incense supposedly reanimates the "only Chinese mummy extant." ("Don't be frightened, ladies.") Actually, Peggy Ann Garner, in hiding, makes it move.... Above scene is atmospheric Technicolor highlight of otherwise garden-variety musical drama.

**La NOCHE DE LA BESTIA** (Mex) IMdP (Rogelio Agrasanchez Linaje) 1988 color 82m. SP, D: Gilberto de Anda. Idea: Sergio Goyri. Ph: Fernando Colin. Mus: Jorge Castro. Beast Des: Paco Guerrero. Ref: TV: Film-Mex video; no Eng.; *The Night of the Beast*-tr t. V (Cannes '89): 476. With S. Goyri, Jorge Reynoso, Lina Santos, Hugo Stiglitz, Arsenio Campos, Arturo Garcia, Manuel Capetillo.

Dynamite unleashes an ancient power from a big black rock in a remote mountain region of Mexico. Soon after, something jumps out of a river and kills a hunter; a tentacle reaches out from a lake; and something in Ana's (Santos) belly slithers out her mouth and possesses a man. Behind it all: a big sea-serpent-type with a retractable tentacle in its mouth.... Monster movie is tacky around the edges, but fairish in the Atmosphere-and-Mystery Department. Okay touch: the thing in the water howling when a hunter in the cabin shoots the slitherer.

**NOCHE DE LA MUERTA CIEGA** see *Tombs of the Blind Dead*

**2P La NOCHE DE LOS ASESINOS** (Sp) Fenix & Copercine (Arturo Marcos) 1974 (1972?) color/ws 88m. SP, D: Jesus Franco. Loosely based on Edgar Allan Poe's tale "The Premature Burial." Ph: Javier Perez Zofio. Mus: Carlo Savina. Mkp?: Carmen Sanchez. Ref: TV: VSOM; no Eng.; Im Schatten des Moerders (German) print. Hardy/HM: "thoroughly average." Ecran F 12/77:30. With Alberto Dalbes, Evelyn Scott, William Berger, Maribel Hidalgo, Lina Romay

An insistent thunderstorm ... equally insistent spook music ... a cloaked figure in a skeleton mask who attacks and buries a man ... Scotland Yard ... the reading of a will ... the burning of a victim ... and a drowning. Atmospheric.

**NOCTURNAL DEMON** (H.K.) 1991 color feature. D: Ricky Lau. Ref: Weisser/ATC. With Moon Lee.

Slasher cuts out victims' tongues, feeds the "gristle to his pet fish."

**NOE HELT ANNET** see *Something Else Entirely*

**NOH MASK MURDERS** (J) 1991 feature (*Tenkawa Densetsu Satsujin Jiken*). D: Kon Ichikawa. Ref: Weisser/JC. With T. Enoki, T. Kusaka.

"Murders caused by the curse of an ancient evil mask."

**NOMADS** Atlantic Releasing/Elliott Kastner & Cinema 7 (Cinema Int'l.) 1985 color 94m. SP, D: John McTiernan. Mus: Bill Conti. Ref: TV. V 5/22/85. ad. With Pierce Brosnan, Lesley-Anne Down, Anna-Maria Montecelli, Adam Ant, Mary Woronov.

"Who are they!?" Los Angeles here is nomads' land. Nomads are hostile spirits that assume human form, inhabit places of past calamity, drive people mad, and cannot be photographed.... Maddeningly spare, halting, elliptical horror-fantasy. Unsatisfying as a mystery or a thriller.

**NON APRIRE ALL'UOMO NERO** see *Don't Open the Door for the Man in Black*

**NON APRITE QUELLA PORTA 3** (I) 1990 color feature (aka *Nightkiller*). SP,D: Claudio Fragasso. Mus: C.M. Cordio. Ref: Palmerini: "tiresome and wordy thriller ... gore sequences." With Peter Hooten, Tara Buckman, Richard Foster.

**NON AVERE PAURA DELLA ZIA MARTA** see *Murder Secret*

**NON SI SEVIZIA UN PAPERINO** see *Long Night of Exorcism, The*

**NORMAN'S AWESOME EXPERIENCE** (Can.) Norstar Ent. & Salter Street Films (Peter Simpson) 1987 ('89-U.S.) color 90m. (*A Switch in Time* - orig t). SP, D: Paul Donovan. Mus: Paul Zaza. Ref: V 11/1/89: "entertaining." With Tom McCamus, Laurie Paton, Jacques Lussier.

Power surge at physics lab sends lab assistant back to ancient Rome.

**NORTHSTAR** ABC-TV/WB-TV & Grodnik & Phillips 1986 (1985) color 74m. D: Peter Levin. Tel, P: Howard Lakin. Ph: Michael Margulies. Mus: Brad Fiedel. AD: J. G. Taylor Jr. VisFX: David Stipes, Richard Bennett. Mkp: Robert Norin. Ref: TV. TVG. no V. Stanley. With Greg Evigan, Deborah Wakeham, Mitchell Ryan, Mason Adams, David Hayward, Ken Foree, Richard Garrison, Steven Williams.

Exposure to the sun's ultra-violet light enhances astronaut Jack North's (Evigan) senses and IQ (to 1,000) and gives him an "accelerated memory capacity." "Einstein's smarter brother," though, is "powerless without sunlight".... Uneasy mixture of fantasy and human-interest angles. Occasionally appealing superstunts and music-score themes. The usual TV-sf Mr. Bland lead.

**NOSFERATO IN BRAZIL** (Braz.) Cardoso 1971('94-U.S.) color and b&w silent c30m. (*Nosferato On Brasil*). D: Ivan Cardoso. Ref: TV: SWV. Cult Movies 12:7. With Torquato Neto, Scarlet Moon.

A vampire in Budapest bites women and seems to die in a swordfight, then moves to Rio, bites women, and meets a woman who bites first .... Slight, episodic, different—from other, "heavier" vampire movies, that is.

**NOSFERATU A VENEZIA** (I) Scena & Reteitalia (Alfieri) 1988 color 96m. (aka V*ampire in Venice. Vampires in Venice. Nosferatu—Vampires in Venice* - ad t). SP, D, P: Augusto Caminito. Ph: T. Nardi. Mus: L. Ceccarelli, from Vangelis' "Mask." Story:

Alberto Alfieri, Leandro Lucchetti. PD: Teichner, Antonucci. Mkp: F. Corridori(sp?) et al. SdFX: Cine Audio. Opt: Penta. Ref: TV: VSOM; Eng.-lang. version; 89m.; *Vampire in Venice*. V 9/28/88: *Nosferatu in Venice* - tr t; "enough chills." 10/26/86:354. 5/21/86:22. 5/6/87:430. 10/21/87:336 (ad). PT 8:5. Ecran F 66:71. Jones: "visually striking." With Klaus Kinski (Nosferatu), Barbara De Rossi, Yorgo Voyagis, Donald Pleasence, Christopher Plummer, Elvire Audray.

In the present day, a seance raises Nosferatu—"he who is undead"—last seen in Venice in 1786, and he seeks out an old flame. ("You called me.") Or, Undeath in Venice. This *Nosferatu* may be a bit languid, but it gets under your skin. It has tons of local color—gypsy encampments, carnival revelers, moonlight, the canals—a pretty impressive score, and Kinski's scruffy, moody, imperative presence. (Plummer has a typically thankless Van Helsing-type role.) Unexpected, insinuating highlights include the scene in which the old lady finds Nosferatu waiting for her in an armchair ... the colony of gypsy vampires (they use vampirism as their ticket to immortality) ... the shots of Nosferatu floating on the gondola past the revelers ... and the shot of Nosferatu and his victim/love flying over the countryside.

**NOSTRADAMUS** MGM/Carey Wilson c1938? b&w 10m. D: David Miller. SP: Carl Dudley. Ph: Paul Vogel. Mus: David Snell. Ref: TV: "an historical mystery." Lee. no Maltin/SSS.

Prophecies of Nostradamus visualized, with clips from *A Tale of Two Cities, Just Imagine* (showing a king "out of Asia" attacking France, in 1999), etc. Compact if unremarkable overview-invoice-over, the first apparently in the "Prophecies of Nostradamus" series.

See also *Let's Ask Nostradamus* (P).

**NOT OF THIS EARTH** Concorde (Roger Corman)/Miracle (Pacific Trust) 1988 color 82m. SP, D, P: Jim Wynorski. SP: also R. J. Robertson. Mus: Chuck Cirino. P: also Murray Miller. SpOptFX: Motion; (sup) Jim Stewart; (anim) Kevin Kutchaver, Robertson. Ref: TV: MGM-UA HV. V 5/25/88. SFChron Dtbk 9/25/88. Maltin '92. Phantom. McCarty II. Morse. With Traci Lords, Arthur Roberts (Johnson), Rebecca Perle (alien), Roger Lodge, Ace Mask, Becky LeBeau, Kelli Maroney, Lenny Juliano.

"Dracula Strikes Again": The Los Angeles "vampire" killings are traced to a certain "Mr. Johnson," an alien from the blood-starved planet of Davanna whose blood is undergoing cellular destruction. His eyes seem to drain victims of their life force, and he transmits one specimen home via light/energy beam.... Perfunctory recapitulation of the 1957 original, with jiggle.

**NOT OF THIS WORLD** CBS-TV/Barry & Enright 1991 color c90m. D: Jon Daniel Hess. Story, Tel: Robert Glass. Story, Exec P: Les Alexander, Don Enright. Story, P: Jonathon Brauer. Mus: Johnny Harris. PD: P. M. Leonard. Creature Des: Alex Rambaldi. SpFX: Bruno Van Zeegroeck. VideoFX: Jerry Spivack. OptFX: Available Light. Mkp: Patty York. Ref: TV. TVG. V 2/11/91:114. SFChron 2/12/91. Maltin '92. With Lisa Hartman, A Martinez, Pat Hingle, Luke Edwards, Tracey Walter, Xander Berkeley, Burr Middleton.

"When heaven rained fire...." A biomechanical critter from a fireball carrying "spores from outer space" attacks the center fielder at an amateur baseball game, leaves very pretty, geometric scars, or burns, on his back. ("It lives on electricity.") Standard sf-horror TV-movie is well photographed (by Mark Irwin) and has okay effects.

**NOT QUITE HUMAN** Disney-TV/Sharmhill Prods. 1987 color 95m. D & Exec P: Steven H. Stern. Tel: Alan Ormsby, from Seth McEvoy's series of books. Mus: Tom Scott. PD: Elayne Ceder. SpProsthFX: John Harrington, John Rielly. Computer Anim: Dan Stoneman, Rick Gessner. Ref: TV. V 6/17/87:78. 1/6/88:52. Cabletime 5&6/87. With Alan Thicke, Robyn Lively, Robert Harper, Joseph Bologna.

Scientist creates "state of the art" seventeen-year-old boy, Chip (Jay Underwood), "full of microchips" and "programmed for science." He's "just like any other idiot teenager," but with "speed control" and problems with power outages. Later, he discovers "human emotions," natch.... Mechanical version of *Android*.

Sequels: *Not Quite Human II. Still Not Quite Human.*

**NOT QUITE HUMAN II** Disney-TV/Resnick-Margellos Prods. 1989 color c90m. Tel, D: Eric Luke. Ph: Jules Brenner. Mus: Michael Rubini. PD: Nilo Rodis. VisFX: Ted Rae. Computer Anim: Steve Carpenter. SpFX: Mark Passarelli. OptFX: Cinema Research. Ref: TV. Sacto Bee 9/23/89. With Alan Thicke, Robyn Lively, Greg Mullavey, Katie Barberi (Roberta), Dey Young, Jay Underwood (Chip).

"I'm an android." High-school grad/android Chip Carson models his "happy" face on Harpo in *Horse Feathers* and his "sad" face on Stan Laurel in *Bonnie Scotland*, a la Max 404 and James Stewart/*It's a Wonderful Life*, in *Android*. He finds compatibility with Roberta, a "responsive android" (a demo model).... Unoriginal but generally pleasant. The comedy is overdependent on the two androids' literal-mindedness with slang and figures of speech.

**NOTHING BUT TROUBLE** WB/Applied Action (Robert K. Weiss) 1991 color 94m. SP, D: Dan Aykroyd. Story: Peter Aykroyd. SpMkp: David B. Miller. SpFxSup: Michael Lantieri. MinFX: Apogee. Ref: TV. V 2/25/91. Scheuer. TVG 9/28/91. SFChron 2/16/91.

Comedy of the grotesque crosses *Murder, He Says* and *The Texas Chain Saw Massacre*, concerns a human Bermuda Triangle, features an "extremely Draculated" old house, a Mister Bonestripper "amusement park" ride which does exactly that to its human riders, a "cut and shuffle" murder machine, a judge (D. Aykroyd) with a detachable nose, the mutant, diapered twins Bobo (also D. Aykroyd) and L'il Debbul (John Daveikis), and piles of human bones and bodies. Offbeat misfit of a movie is occasionally charmingly gross, but overburdened with noise and action.

**NOTHING LASTS FOREVER** Lorne Michaels 1984 color and b&w 82m. SP, D: Tom Schiller. Ref: Stanley: "to the moon on a Lunarcruiser." Maltin'92: "a New York City of the future." V 9/26/84: fantasy.

**NOTHING UNDERNEATH** (I) Spectradyne/Faso Film (Achille Manzotti) 1985 ('88-U.S.) color/ws c95m. (*Sotto il Vestito*

*Niente*). SP, D: Carlo Vanzina. SP: also E. Vanzina, F. Ferrini, from Marco Parma's novel *Sotto il Vestito Niente*. Mus: Pino Donaggio. SpFX: Corridori. Mkp: Franco Schioppa. Ref: TV: Sony Video; Eng.-lang. version. V 12/11/85. 11/12/90: 64 (rated). Hound. Ecran F 65:70. With Tom Schanley, Renee Simonsen, Donald Pleasence, Nicola Perring, Maria McDonald.

In Yellowstone National Park, Bob Crane "sees" someone stalking his telepathic twin sister, Jessica, who's in Milan. He flies there, but she has disappeared. Graphic murders-by-scissors follow. The bizarre finale features a dead body nailed to a chair, a crazy fashion model wielding an electric drill, and a concluding series of absurd, "lyrical" "Lover's Leap" shots.... Lively as it is, the finale isn't quite worth the wait. Okay Donaggio score, very thin script.

**NOTTE DEGLI SQUALI, La** see *Night of the Sharks*

**Una NOTTE DI PIOGGIA** (I) CCS (Carlo Chemblant) 1984 color 90m. SP, D: Romeo Costantini. Mus: G. Plenizio. Ref: V 9/19/84: "a commendable helming debut"; *A Night of Rain* - tr t. With Paolo Cesar Pereio, Adriana Falco.

Radiation antidote, nuclear explosion.

**NOTTE EROTICHE DEI MORTE VIVENTI, Le** see *Erotic Nights of the Living Dead*

**NOW WE'LL TELL ONE** MGM-Roach 1932 short. D: James Parrott. Ref: Maltin/SSS. Lee. With Charley Chase, Muriel Evans, Frank Darien, Major Sam Harris.

"Charley unwittingly wears a belt that has the power to change his personality."

**NUDA PER SATANA** (I) 1974 feature. SP,D: Luigi Batzella aka P. Solvay. Mus: V. Kojucharov. Ref: Palmerini: "sexy satanic horror film poorly directed." With S. Cardelli, James Harris, Rita Calderoni.

**NUDE PRINCESS** see *Macumba Sexual*

**NUDE X L'ASSASSINO** see *Strip Nude for Your Killer*

**NUDES ON THE ROCKS** see *50,000 B.C.*

**NUEVOS EXTRATERRESTRES, Los** see *Unearthling, The*

**3P La NUIT DE LA MORT!** (F) Pierson Prod. (Delpard) & Paris Occitanie Prod. (Combes) 1980 color 92m. (*Night of the Dead* - vt). SP, D, P: Raphael Delpard. SP: also Richard Joffo. Ph:Marcel Combes. Mus: Laurent Petitgirard. SpFX: Pascal Rovier. Mkp: Renaldo Abreu. Ref: TV: VSOM; no Eng. Cinema Francais. Tous Les Films 1980. VSOM. With Isabelle Goguey, Charlotte de Turkheim, Michel Flavius, Betty Beckers.

Rest home of cannibals where the dinner guests gather at midnight, cut open their unwilling sacrifice, and feast on blood and guts. Meanwhile, suspicious smoke rises from a chimney, and a human-meat locker is discovered (insert: scream). Finally: puncture gore for the abrupt, downbeat ending.... El cheapo French gore vehicle looks pretty routine. Bonus: a hand-on-shoulder shock.

**La NUIT DES TRAQUEES** (F) Impex 1980 color 85m. (*Filles Traquees* - alternate version with hardcore scenes). SP, D: Jean Rollin. Ph: Jean-Claude Couty. Mus: Gary Sandeur. Ref: Horacio Higuchi. Hardy/HM:336. PT 16:15: *Night of the Cruel Sacrifice* - U.S. vt t (VSOM); Eng. titles; "uniquely odd." MV: *Night of the Hunted* - alt vt t. With Brigitte Lahaie, Vincent Garder, Dominique Journe, Bernard Papineau, Rachel Mhas; Marilyn Jess, Cathy Stewart.

Gamma-ray-produced zombie-types.

**NUKE 'EM HIGH** see *Class of Nuke 'Em High*

**NUKIE** (Botswana-G) Vidmark/Overseas Film & Lars Int'l. & August Ent. (Venter-Sargeant) 1989 ('93-U.S.) color c99m. Story, D: Sias Odendal. SP: Benjamin Taylor. Ph: Busbridge, Schier. Mus: Nic Pickard. PD: Nel. Nukie:(creator) S. Odendal;(sculptor) Beulah Vari. VideoSpFX: Wolfgang Grimmeisen. SpFxSup: Schier, Schultze. Anim D: H. & G. Zeh. SpVoices: B. Donnison, D. Arthur. Ref: TV: Vidmark video; Eng. version. Mo. With Glynis Johns, Ronald France, Steve Railsback, Siphiwe & Sipho Mlangeni, B. Windell & David Fox (Nukie), Sara Braunstein (Mico).

"Lights don't die." Little creatures "from outer space, made from pure energy," land in the U.S. and central Africa, respectively, and alternate between flying-light form and E.T.s in the image of *Star Wars'* Yoda. ("I am from the stars.") One, Nukie, enables a boy to fly like light too, and at the end the two aliens take a chimp back home with them.... Interminable children's sf, with boringly inexpressive *E.T.* suits. Guarantee: By the end of the movie, you will be very tired of hearing the name "Nukie." Tossed in: a cackling, hypnotic, romantic computer.

**NUMUNWARI** see *Dark Age*

**NUOI QUI** see *Ghost Nursing*

**NUTCASE** (Austral.) Satori 1983 ('85-U.S.) color c49m. D: Roger Donaldson. Ref: vc box: "antigravity machine."

**The NUTCRACKER PRINCE** (Can.) WB/Lacewood (Kevin Gillis) 1990 anim color 75m. D: Paul Schibli. SP: Patricia Watson, from E.T.A. Hoffman's book *The Nutcracker and the Mouseking*. Ref: V 11/19/90: "wonderfully romantic." Cinef 4/91. Sacto Bee 11/23/90: "flat, substandard execution." ad. Sacto Union 11/21/90: "vapid."

"Dreaded Mouseking" ... "curse cast by the Mousequeen." (SBee)

**NUTRIAMAN, THE COPASAW CREATURE** see *Terror in the Swamp*

**NYMPHO ZOMBIE CO-EDS** Visual Images 1993? color feature. SP, D: "Toby Dammit." Ref: vc box: "Wes Craven couldn't...." With Ariel, Thumper, William Margold.

**A NYMPHOID BARBARIAN IN DINOSAUR HELL** Troma/Chapter V & R.A.P. Prods. (Alex Pirnie & Brett Piper) 1991 (1990) color c90m. SP, D: Piper. Mus: The Astral Warriors. SpFX: Cheap Tricks. SpSdFX: Charles von Deuss. Ref: TV.

TVG. With Paul Guzzi, Linda Corwin, A. Pirnie, Mark Deshaies (masked stranger), Ryan Piper (troll), A. Strong (swamp critter).

Ingredients in this post-World War III, New Age "prehistoric" story include our heroine (Corwin), whose folks were from Tromaville; radiation-spawned "ghastly mutations"—including sometimes-stopmo monsters such as a styracosaurus-type, a toothy swamp thing, and muck creatures—and stopmo-"dinosaur" gore and human-ear gore.... Pleasant if elementary stop-motion animation is the highlight of this otherwise dreadfully vacant sf-actioner. The winged reptile-monster recalls various flying Harryhausen horrors.

# O

**O-BI, O-BA—KONIEC CYWILIZACJI** (Polish) Polish Film Corp. 1985 color 88m. SP, D: Piotr Szulkin. Mus: Jerzy Satanowski. Ref: V 9/11/85: film's "austerity is muddied by its riddles and symbols"; *O-Bi, O-Ba—The End of Civilization*-tr t. 5/1/85:455. With Jerzy Stuhr, Krystyna Janda, Kalina Jedrusik.

"Mythical Boers ... shut down civilization with a bomb," while survivors "wait for the Ark...."

**OBBLIGO DI GIOCARE** (I) 1989 color feature (aka *Zugzang*). Story, SP,D: Daniele Cesarano. SP: also Pirro, Senatore. Mus: ECM Group. Ref: Palmerini. With N. della Corte, A. Prodan, K. R. Stuart.

"An urban thriller on the Jekyll/Hyde theme."

**OBEAH** Hugh Robertson 1987. SP, D: H. Robertson. Ph: Bruce Sparks. P: Jon Palmer. Ref: SFChron 10/23/87: "intriguing drama." SFBay Guardian 10/21/87: "gritty, potent." With Anthony Hall, Eunice Alleyne, Lucy Jennings.

Supposedly-based-on-fact story set in Trinidad re voodoo spells, zombies, an Obeah priestess, and the god Damballah.

**OBJECT OF DESIRE** Catalina 1990 color feature. D: Josh Eliot. Ref: Adam Erotomic '89.

"Fantasyland, with one car-graveyard episode from the netherworld that's scary."

**OBLIVION** (U.S.-Rom.) Full Moon (Paunescu) 1994 color 94m. D: Sam Irvin. SP: P. David. Story: Rheaume et al. Ph: A. Bartoli. Mus: Pino Donaggio. PD: Milo. SpMkpFX: Alchemyfx. VisFX: David Allen. Ref: V 5/2/94: "pleasant ... sophomoric." Martin: "inept." SFChron 2/4/95: "giant scorpion." With Julie Newmar, Andrew Divoff (alien), Meg Foster, George Takei, Isaac Hayes, Jackie Swanson, Carel Struycken, Jimmie Skaggs.

The quasi-Western town of Oblivion, on a desert planet.

**The OBSESSED** (H.K.) Kuk Hing Wah 198-? color/ws? c85m. D: Mak Pang Chin. Ref: TV: Ocean Shores Video; Eng. titles. NST! 4:32-33: D: Henry Ohan; with Eddie Chan. With Miu Ho Sau, Ko Keung, Kwan Sang, Ho Lai Lai.

"G.H.O.S.T.!" Chih Kang's new bride Ailien spots a mystery tabby and, later, sees a strange woman in the bathtub. A dress hanging in the long-locked bedroom of his first wife Chiu Ping attacks her. He: "You must be abnormal." His insensitivity here

is a tipoff: It transpires that he killed his first wife, and now her ghost—a "discontented soul" from the fourth dimension—sprouts cat fangs and tears out his throat.... Undistinguished horror-fantasy. Only a feature-length requirement can explain the fact that this ghost beats around the bush so long before exacting her revenge.

**OBSESSED** see *Gui An Yan*

**OBSESSION: A TASTE FOR FEAR** (I) Exordia & Reteitalia (Intra/Titanus) 1987 ('89-U.S.) color 89m. (*Un Sapere di Paura-Segreta Inquietudine* aka *Pathos*. aka *A Taste for Fear. Video Killer*). SP, D: Piccio Raffanini. SP: also Lidia Ravera. Story, P: J. L. Goyard. Ph: R. Albani. Mus: G. Ducros. AD: P. Biagetti. VisSpFX: Michelle Radici. SpFX: Penta. Ref: V 4/12/89: "excellent example of a recent Italian genre ... the glamorous horror/fashion pic." 5/6/87:362, 375 (ad): futuristic. 5/20/87:41. 10/22/86:354: 11/10 start. Palmerini. TV: Imperial Ent. video; Eng. version. With Virginia Hey, Gerard Darmon, Gioia Scola, Teagan Clive, Eva Grimaldi.

Blandly kinky slasher-killings-on-tape ... unlikable people ... hollow English ... shallow glossy look. "Just another form of penetration."

**OCCHIO DEL MALE, L'** see *Manhattan Baby*

**The OCCULTIST** Urban Classics/Tycin Ent. (Cynthia DePaula) 1989 (1987) color 80m. (*Maximum Thrust* - orig t). SP, D: Tim Kincaid. SpMkpFX: Ed French. Ref: V 10/8/89: "minor voodoo pic." With Rick Gianasi, Joe Derrig, Jennifer Kanter, Matt Mitler.

"Macumba trances ... cyborgs."

**The OCCUPANT** (H.K.) Cinema City 1984 color/ws c93m. D: Ronny Yu. SP: Edward Li. Ph: Coll. Mus: Danny Chung; (theme song) Mak Kit Man. AD: Tony Au. Ref: TV: Rainbow Video; Eng. titles. NST! 4:33. Fango 107:59. With Sally Yeh, Chow Yun Fu (sp?), R. Wong, Mak Kit Man.

Angie, a young Chinese woman from Canada, comes to 2 Waterloo Road, in Hong Kong, to work on her M.A. thesis, "Superstition in China." When she complains to caretaker Ah Poon about the noisy neighbors who are always singing and quarreling, she is told: "There's no one staying here except you." The singer turns out to be Lisa Law, who has been dead for nearly a year, supposedly a suicide victim. Ah Poon is also a ghost, as the new caretaker explains. Lisa temporarily possesses Angie, but a *Mark of the Vampire* (1935)-style reenactment of the "suicide" scene—with spiritualistic forces standing in for hypnotism—shows that her, Lisa's, lover's wife shot both her husband and Lisa. Lisa departs.

In a funny twist, one of the leading living characters, Hansom Wong, plays the wife, much against his will, in the reenactment. Otherwise, this ghost story is not that compelling, and the present-tense human story (Hansom and police detective Valentino vie for Angie's affections) is only lightly amusing. Quiet chills, though, punctuate the action. One instance: A cup keeps sliding across an unbalanced table. Angie props up the table leg. After she leaves the room, the cup slides across the table again. The most awkward subtitle compares ghosts to "draculars [sic] in horror pictures."

**OCEANO ATLANTIS** (Braz.) Sky Light Cinema & Naive Films 1993 color 84m. SP, D: Francisco de Paula. SP: also Ciro Pessoa. Mus: Pessoa. Ref: V 11/29/93: "incoherent." With Nuno Leal Maia, Dercy Goncalves, A. Abujamra.

Alternate "fantasy world populated by survivors of a devastating tidal wave that wiped out Rio."

**OCEANO ROSSO** see *Devil Fish*

**OCTOBER 32ND** (B) UFM-Shining Armour & Slovakoturist (Peter Collins) 1992 ('94-U.S.) color 129m. (*Merlin* - U.S.). Story, D, Co-P: Paul Hunt. Story, SP: Nick McCarty. Ph: Gary Graver. Ref: V 6/22/92: "lame sword-and-sorcery pic." Stanley: uneven; demons. PT 20:17: "confusing." With Peter Phelps, Richard Lynch (Pendragon), James Hong, Nadia Cameron, Rodney Wood (Merlin).

"Day when time stands still."

**ODD BALLS** (Can.-U.S.) New Horizons/Maurice Smith & Rodeo 1986 color 92m. D: Miklos Lente. SP: Ed Naha. Ref: V 12/24/86: "weak." With Foster Brooks, Mike MacDonald, Konnie Krom.

Includes "spoof of *E.T.*"

**ODEON** see *Alien from L.A.*

**ODIN** (J) U.S. Manga Corps (CPM) 1985 ('93-U.S.) anim color 139m. (c90m.-U.S.) (*Odin: Photon Space Sailer Starlight* or *Photon Space Sailer Starlight Odin* - U.S.). Created by Yoshinobu Nishizaki. Ref: TV: Toei Video; no Eng. USMC brochure. Animerica 5:17.

Time-and-space-spanning epic begins with an overview of seafarers from 1500 B.C. to 1860 A.D., takes a *2001*-like tour of space during the opening credits, then journeys with spacefarers of the future, which is populated by an unconscious mystery woman aboard a spaceship, a space-sailing vessel which rides an energy beam, and various energy shields and barriers and cosmic rays. A lot to look at here, but if the film is imaginative as spectacle, it seems conventional as drama, and character design is bland. The musical score—which is really three scores in one—alternates between rock, symphonic music, and adventure-movie music, and is sometimes quite good.

**OF CASH AND HASH** Col 1955 20m. (*Crook Crackers* - orig t). D, P: Jules White. SP: Jack White. Story: Del Lord. Ph: Ray Cory. AD: Edward Ilou. Ref: TV. Maltin/SSS. Lenburg. no Lee. With The Three Stooges, Kenneth MacDonald, Christine McIntyre, Frank Lackteen.

A monstrous-looking, machete-wielding hunchback named Angel (Duke York, in stock footage from *Shivering Sherlocks*) is amok in a "haunted" house. ("This joint gives me the creeps!") Familiar shenanigans, including a "ghost"-under-a-sheet bit, clutching hands, etc.

**OF DEATH, OF LOVE** see *Dellamorte, Dellamore*

**OFF BALANCE** see *Phantom of Death*

**OFFENDERS OF THE UNIVERSE** see *Gonad the Barbarian*

**OFFERINGS** Arista/Christopher Reynolds 1989 (1988) color 92m. SP, D, Ed: Reynolds. Mus: R. D. Allen. AD: J. F. Cain. Key Mkp: Frieda Valenzuela. Ref: TV. V 6/28/89. McCarty II. PT 3:13. With Loretta Leigh Bowman, Elizabeth Greene, G. Michael Smith, Richard A. Buswell (John Radley).

"He's out there then." Script begins on a rote "ten years later" note, as crazed John Radley breaks out of a hospital and begins killing the grown-up versions of the kids who scared him into falling into a well. ("He gives me the creeps!") And there's some connection between "what he's doing and what happened to him".... Non-actors in a formula *Halloween* horror. Some slightly goofy characters and oddball bits—e.g., a severed nose is found in a folded-up newspaper—break up the prevailing monotony.

**OFFICIAL DENIAL** (U.S.-Austral.) Sci-Fi Channel/Para/C.N.M. Ent. & Jeffrey Hayes Prods. (Wilshire Court/Darryl Sheen) 1993 color 87m. D: Brian Trenchard-Smith. Tel, Co-P: Bryce Zabel. Ph: J. Stokes. Mus: G. McDonald, L. Stone. PD: S. Burnside. VisFX: Photon, Stockman;(des) Gregory Lowe. Prosth: Pro FX. SpFX: Brian Holmes. Ref: TV: Para video. TVG 9/18/93. with Parker Stevenson, Chad Everett, Dirk Benedict, Erin Gray, Michael Pate, Christopher Pate; Holly Brisley & Serena Dean (Dos), Tiriel Mora (voice of Dos).

"They're us—from the future." Aliens "borrow" the man of the house and seem to administer a sort of nasal spray. When their self-repairing craft is shot down over the Southwestern U.S., the man is brought in by the military to communicate with the one surviving, super-chameleon alien. The two communicate telepathically, and the aliens are found to have a shared consciousness.... Not much added here to *E.T., Starman, Communion,* etc. And *Roswell* does the same basic story better. The script even borrows *E.T.*'s rainbow and *2001*'s star child. Good shot: the spaceship right over the house.

**OFFRET** see *Sacrifice, The*

**The OFFSPRING** TMS/Conquest Ent. (Darin Scott/William Burr) 1987 color 96m. (*From a Whisper to a Scream* - alt t). SP, D: Jeff Burr. SP: also C. C. Joyner, D. Scott. SpMkpFX: Rob Burman. Ref: V 5/20/87: "all four segments are mediocre." McCarty II: "recommended." Ecran F 71:54-7. SFExam 1/29/88(ad). V 5/6/87:132(ad). With Vincent Price, Clu Gulager, Terry Kiser, Rosalind Cash, Cameron Mitchell, Susan Tyrrell, Martine Beswicke, Angelo Rossitto, Lawrence Tierney.

1) "Monster baby." 2) "Mystical longevity." 3) "Voodoo ... yucky makeup effects." 4) Civil War variation on *Night of the Living Dead*.

**OG (MUST BE CRAZY)** (Fili) BP Films/R.V.Q. Prods. 1989? color c130m. D: Efren Jarlego. SP: Apollo Arellano et al. Story: Roy Vera Quizon. Prosth: Maurice Carvajal. Anim: Contreras. SpFX: Leoncio Mariano. Mkp: Ligaya Quince. SdFX: Rodel Capule. Ref: TV: vt; some Eng.

Comedy-fantasy features an incidental, two-armed monster-tree which strangles a bad guy ... an ape, or apeman, with big nostrils ... flesh-stripping piranha ... and a "bus" with an ape in a coffin. Overlong, but with some good low comedy.

**The OGRE** (I) 1988 color feature. D: Lamberto Bava. Ref: PT 8:65 (ad). VSOM: aka *Demons 3*. With Virginia Bryant.

"Ogre"="metaphor for [author's] repressed sexuality."(PT)

**OGRE SLAYER** (J) Viz Video & The Ocean Group/Shonen Sunday Video/KK-Shogakukan-KSS-TBS 1994 ('95-U.S.) anim color c60m. D: Yoshio Kato. SP: N. Terada. From the comics by Kei Kusunoki. Ph: Takahashi, Noguchi. Mus: K. Toyama. AD: K. Kanemura. SpFX: K. Taniguchi. SdFX:(d) S. Akitagawa;(sp) S. Kurahashi. Ref: TV: VV; Eng. dubbed.

"Chapter of the Tiny Horn." "It's some kind of monster!" Our heroine gives birth to the "parasites" inside her, and these "horrible, disgusting ogres" promptly inhabit her. Unleashed, they slay anyone in their path. Excuse for gore effects has some eerily drawn ogres. "Chapter of Otakemaru." "Ogres never forget." The ogre here is chopped up and buried, but, in an exciting sequence, its smoke-like spirit assails people in a temple.

**OIL OF ETERNAL LIFE** (Thai) c1987? color/ws c105m. Ref: TV: vt; no Eng. Thai Video: above is tr t.

A thin old witch shoots rays into a young woman's eyes and mouth. The old one cackles, runs off, lies down, and explodes, while the young woman becomes a vampire: At feeding time, her head, heart, and lungs sail off in search of prey, and the rest of her body can move about, too.

Kooky comedy and horror. The score is lifted from *Horror of Dracula, Godzilla*, etc., and at one point, a singing skeleton lays down its mike and chats with visitors to its forest retreat. Later, a woman tries to save a friend by biting the vampire. One magic duel pits an animated skull against a red ball; another matches a wizard's animated snake against the skull from the witch's staff. Prime detail: The vampire's heart flashes on and off like a neon light.

**OILSPOT AND LIPSTICK** Disney 1988? anim. short. D: Mike Cedeno. Ref: SFChron Dtbk 4/10/88:25: "super-polished quality."

Motor Monster haunts auto junkyard.

**OJOS AZULES DE LA MUNECA ROTA, Los** see *House of Psychotic Women*

**Los OJOS DEL MUERTO** (Mex) V. P. Parra 1987 color 97m. SP, D: A. Mariscal. SP: also C. Parra. Story: A. Delgado. SpFX: A. & V. Godinez. Mkp: M. Acosta. Ref: TV: Brooklyn Electronics video; no Eng.

Western drama with psychological-horror moments, as a madman "sees" a fiery-eyed demon whenever his mind unhinges. At one point, the eyes of a man whom he is about to shoot blaze fire (a cheap optical effect). Negligible shot-on-videotaper, with songs.

**OKAY KA, FAIRY KO!** (Fili) Regal Films/M-Zet Films (Lily Monteverde, M. C. Sotto) c1991 color c130m. SP, D: Bert DeLeon. SP: also Bibeth Orteza. D: also Tony Reyes. Ph: Joe Tutanes. Mus D: Homer Flores. PD, SpVis&MkpFX: Visual Illusion; (consul) Tony Tuviera. SpFX: Tony Marbella. SdFX: Rodel Capule. Opt: Cinemagic. Ref: TV: Regal Int'l. video; some

Eng. With Vic Sotto, Aiza Seguerra, Larry Silva, Ruby Rodriguez, Jinky Oda, Bayani Casimiro Jr., Charito Solis; Gladys Arenas, Tina Garcia et al (evil women); Christian Vansil, Gil Tarriela (The Mandragon); Boy Quisado et al (the tiyanaks).

Lively, silly comedy-fantasy features an evil sorceress who flings fireballs and freezes the hero with a ray, a huge fire-breathing dragon-demon, bat beings, a little, horned, big-eared creature, a crawling severed arm, and a dog-like demon. Relative highlight: the caveful of critters.

**OKAY KA, FAIRY KO! PART 2** (Fili) M-Zet Films 1992 color 115m. D: Tony Reyes. SP: Bibeth Orteza. SP, Exec P: Marvic Sotto. Ph: Sergio Lobo. PD: R. Bernardo, R. Nicdao. Anim: Penetrante, Abelardo. SpMkp & VisFX: Visual Illusion. Animatronics: Joe Almodal. FxCoord: Dick Gonzales. SpFX: T.G. Marbella. SpProps: Rey Golimlim. SpOptFX: Cinema Artists. SdFX: R. Capule. Ref: TV: Viva Video; no Eng. With Vic Sotto, Aiza Seguerra, Tweetie de Leon, Larry Silva, Ruby Rodriguez, Jinky Oda, Charito Solis.

Ingredients in this indifferent if lively monster fantasy include a shape-shifting snake-witch's ray zaps, which make an *Alien* critter burst out of a man's torso ... voracious magic spiders ... two two-headed monsters ... a huge *Alien* monster ... and Aztecs .... One highlight: the huge, human-headed tortoise.

**OKS NA OKS PAKNER** (Fili) D'Wonder Films 1985 color c150m. D: J. Erastheo Navoa; (assoc) Roger Vivero. SP: Jose N. Carreon. Ph: Bhal Dauz. Mus D: Demet Velasquez. PD: James Peralta. SpFX: Danny Sto. Domingo. Sp Video FX: Pancho. Opt FX: Jetarts. Mkp: Barrios, Perez. Ref: TV: CHO Video; Eng.-lang. songs. J. J. Market: Okay Partner - tr t. With Nino Muhlach, Janice de Belen, Aga Muhlach, Maidu Morato, Ike Lozada, Jimmy Santos, Max Alvarado.

"Today and now—in another dimension." Strange rays transport a boy through a TV monitor on another world to the Happy Home for the Aged, on Earth, where his special crystal "freezes" the action and, in conjunction with a VCR remote, makes bank robbers stop, go in reverse, go fast, etc.... Some cute moments in this long, long sf-comedy. Funny sequence re a cola-can "phone." A *Cocoon* influence seems apparent in the mixture of sf, the elderly, and sentiment.

**The OLD BARN** Sennett 1929 c20m. D: Mack Sennett. Ref: Maltin/SSS: "haunted" barn. With Johnny Burke, Andy Clyde, Vernon Dent, Irving Bacon.

**OLD CHIEF WOOD'NHEAD** see *Creepshow 2*

**OLD HOUSE, The** see *Shocking!*

**The OLD HOUSE IN NIGHT** (H.K.?) c1983? color/ws c88m. (*The Tale of Old House* - ad t). D: Yao Fung-Pan. Ref: TV: Quality Video; Eng. titles.

Family's new house is haunted by the owner's cousin, who says she wants him to avenge her murder, but then drives the culprit to his death herself.... The solution to the mystery of the ghost in the outhouse ("Give me toilet paper!") is a long time coming, and the "demoness" with the disfigured face is your garden-variety wronged ghost. Only difference here: She wants the heroine to build an orphanage.

**The OLD LOCK** (H.K.?) n.d. Ref: vc box. V&T Video: ghost and boy.

**The OLD MAN OF THE MOUNTAIN** Para/Fleischer 1933 anim and live action 11m. Anim: B. Wolf, T. Johnson. With Cab Calloway. Ref: TV: ogre returns in *Betty Boop's Rise to Fame* (1934). Lee. Cabarga/Fleischer. LC.

Snappy stuff. The Old Man is scary in close-up (you just got to "hi-dee-hi," and you'll get along with him), and there are grotesque faces and a skeletal hand carved into the side of his mountain.

**OLD MANOR HOUSE** (B) BAP (George Moreno, Jr.) 1948 anim color 7m. D: H.F. Mack. Mus: J. Norman. Anim: H. Gladwish et al. Ref: TV: Loonic Video. no Lee.

One stormy night, Bubble and Squeek take refuge in an old house ("What a creepy place"), where the Frankie Stein monster scares them, hordes of eyes watch in the dark, and a "ghost" in a sheet prowls.... Not very funny, but the brief appearance of the monster is a nice surprise.

**OLDER MASTER CUTE 3** (H.K.-J) Hong Kong Film Services/Dragon Animation (Johnny Chan) 198-? anim color/ws 76m. D: (J) T. Honda; M.Y. Choi. Story, SP: Chak Wong. SP: also Y.C. Fung. Ph: Ken Talbot. Mus: Joseph Koo. AD: C.W. Lau. SpFxPh: Randy, Y.C. Wong. Ref: TV: vt; no Eng. Y.K. Ho: subtitle of film includes "E.T."

Ingredients include an alien who invites the master to take a ride in his spaceship ... the same master who, when sucked into an arcade video game, turns Pac Man-ish ... and a carnival spookhouse bit.... Blandly drawn, routine comedy. The video sequence is the only really funny one.

**OLGA'S HOUSE OF SHAME** AFDC (Stan Borden) 1964 b&w feature. SP, D: J.P. Mawra. SP, P: George Weiss. Ph: Warner Rose. Narr: Joel Holt. Ref: TV: SWV. With Audrey Campbell, Alice Davis, W.B. Parker.

Among the "pure instruments of sadism" here are a heated steel bar, a clamp, pincers, and a board-and-nail. The piece de resistance, however, is the electric-shock chair, which reduces its victims to morons. Tying women to trees also apparently makes them go mad sometimes .... Some camp value in this cheesy exploitationer, which is more narrated than dramatized. Fine score (library classical).

**OLTRA LA MORTE** see *After Death: Zombie 4*

**OMBRA DI ILLUSIONE** see *Shadow of Illusion*

**OMEGA CITY** or **OMEGA ZONE 23** see *Megazone Two Three*

**OMEGA COP** South Gate Ent./Romarc (Marchini-Huey) 1990 color 87m. (*John Travis—Solar Survivor*—shooting t). D: Paul Kyriazi. SP: Salli McQuaid. Ref: V 7/11/90:58 (hv): "okay programmer." 6/13/90:34. Martin. With Ron Marchini, Adam West, Meg Thayer, Stuart Whitman, Troy Donahue.

Future cop.

**OMEN IV: THE AWAKENING** Fox Network-TV/FNM Films (Mace Neufeld/Harvey Bernhard) 1991 color c90m. D: Jorge Montesi, Dominique Othenin-Girard. Story, Tel: Brian Taggert. Story: also Bernhard. PD: Richard Wilcox. Mus: Jonathan Sheffer. Prosth: Tibor Farkas? Mkp: Charles Porlier. Ref: TV. TVG. V 5/20/91:41: "a few creepy moments." With Faye Grant, Michael Woods, Michael Lerner, Madison Mason, Asia Vieira (Delia).

The baby bawls. The moon eclipses spontaneously. The altar crucifix goes topsy-turvy. Nuns and priests are fair game. The demon baby is back....

**OMOO-OMOO—THE SHARK GOD** Screen Guild/Esla Pictures (L. S. Picker) 1949 b&w 58m. SP, D: Leon Leonard. SP, Assoc P: G. D. Green. From the novel "Omoo" by Herman Melville. Ph: Ben Kline. Mus: Albert Glasser. AD: Fred Ritter. Mkp: Bob Mark. OptFX: Consolidated. Ref: TV. Greg Luce. V 6/22/49. LC. Lee. Okuda/GN. Stanley. Lentz. TVG. With Ron Randell, Devera Burton, Trevor Bardette, Pedro de Cordoba, Richard Benedict, Michael Whalen, George Meeker.

"Superstitions based upon fear and strange customs were their inheritance." The South Seas, 1874. Under the "fantastic laws of Omoo," a "native curse" has befallen the captain (Bardette) of the schooner Julia, who stole two black pearls—the "eyes of the Shark God"—from a native idol. ("They're mine, I tell you!") When he dies, his daughter (Burton) inherits the tabu, as well as his dialogue ("Yes, they're mine!") and illness, which makes her seem possessed.

Adventure chiller begins promisingly, but gets worse and worse, as Methodical becomes Plodding, and dialogue cliches proliferate. (Exhibits A and B, respectively: "Always the drums!" and "I had a feeling we were being watched.") Short as it is, *Omoo-Omoo* still pads its running time with stock sea and jungle footage. Two-steps-beyond music accompanies scenes with native charms and incantations.

**ON DANGEROUS GROUND** see *Choke Canyon*

**\*ON THE COMET** Filmaco 1970('85-U.S.) 77m.-U.S. (aka *Archa Pana Servadaca*)

From the novel *Hector Servadac* or *Career of a Comet* by Jules Verne. SpFX: Pickhart. Ref: TV: Best Video; Eng. dubbed. Warren/KWTS!2. Lee. Hardy/SF: ws? Stanley. V 9/25/85:78(hv). 1888.

There's "something up in the sky"—a huge comet which sends out lightning, disrupts gravity, and tears off a piece of the Earth and draws the chunk to itself. And this "new planet," it seems, "must have prehistoric life": Tyrannosaurs and brontos rout the newly-arrived North African cavalry; the clanging of pots and pans, in turn, routs the dinosaurs. Also on the comet: pterodactyls, a dimetrodon, and a styracosaur. The gravity of Mars temporarily disrupts the comet before the latter returns to the vicinity of Earth, and the action proves to be a dream.

An alternately enchanting and slightly flat science-fantasy fable. The story pleasantly exploits the idyllic aspects of life away from war-torn Earth, but the characters are no match for the charming visuals. Initially, the comet is an impressive, unsettling presence on the horizon, and the various lightnings, fog, and smoke create an unearthly atmosphere. First sign of alien life: a huge fly. Funniest sign: the walking fish-pig.

**ONCE BITTEN** Goldwyn/Samuel Goldwyn Jr. & Night Life (Villard, Wald, Hilderbrand) 1985 color 93m. D: Howard Storm. SP: David Hines, Jeffrey Hause, Jonathan Roberts. Story: Dimitri Villard. Mus: John Du Prez. Sp Aging Mkp: Steve Laporte. Ref: TV. V 11/6/85. SFExam 11/15/85. With Lauren Hutton, Jim Carrey, Karen Kopins, Cleavon Little, Skip Lackey.

A beautiful, 390-year-old vampire countess (Hutton) must find a young male virgin in Hollywood before Halloween, or.... She does find one: eighteen-year-old Mark Kendall (Carrey), whom she bites twice. But she needs yet a third "transfusion." Meanwhile, Mark dreams of himself as a Lugosi-like, caped vampire.... Pathetic misfire recalls thirty-five years of failed monster-movie parodies. How bad is the dialogue? Just say that Hutton is sexy until she opens her mouth to speak.

**ONCE UPON A MIDNIGHT SCARY** 1979 color 50m. D: Nell Cox. Ref: Stanley: TV-movie. Martin. no Hound. With Vincent Price, Alexandra Johnson, Severn Darden, Rene Auberjonois.

Three tales, including Richard Peck's "The Ghost Belonged to Me" and Washington Irving's "Legend of Sleepy Hollow."

See also *Child of Glass.*

**ONCE UPON A TEMPTRESS** Caballero (L. F. Pachard) 1988 color 80m. D: Henri Pachard. Ref: Adam '89. With Alicia Monet, Keisha, Nikki Knights, Shanna McCullough.

Silent-screen star's spirit possesses woman.

**ONCE UPON A TIME** (Fili) Regal Films 1985? color c125m. D: Peque Gallaga, Lorenzo A. Reyes. Story, SP: T. E. Pagaspas. SP: also R. Q. de la Cruz. Ph: E. F. Jacinto. Mus: Jaime Fabregas. PD: Don Escudero. Opt & SpVisFX: Maurice Carvajal. SpFX: Teofilo Hilario. SpMkp: Mauricio Makabayan. Ref: TV: Tri-Films video; no Eng. MMarquee 43:9-10. With Dolphy, Gloria Romero (evil queen), Janice de Belen, Richard Gomez, Joel Torre, Lani Mercado, Mon Alvir, Snooky Serna, Chuckie Dreyfus, Datu Gallaga.

This very, very long Filipino fantasy features some cute (if rough-edged) animation and other effects. Highlights: a fierce special-makeup demon which ultimately possesses the evil queen, a man-eating plant, small flying snake-turtle creatures, some very-*Gremlin* gremlins, a stopmo horse creature, and most impressive of all, the shadow transformations of the horse creature—on the wall of a little girl's bedroom, the creature's shadow changes from horse to devil to ape to tiger to femme fatale to bull. Not to mention: the angered magus zapping the turtle creatures, who quiver and squeak, and a sorcerer accidentally zapping himself with his own fingertip rays.

**ONCE UPON A TIME** see *Windaria*

**ONDSKANS VARDSHUS** see *Sleep of Death, The*

**ONE ACROSS, TWO DOWN** see *Diary of the Dead*

**ONE BY ONE** see *Majorettes, The*

**1-800-TIME** Infinity 1991 color 75m. D: Ron Jeremy. Ref: Adam '92: time travel. With Heather Lere, Fallon, Cara Lott, Sharon Mitchell, Wayne Summers.

**ONE EYEBROW PRIEST** (H.K.) Golden Harvest/Diagonal Pictures (Paragon) 1989 color 87m. Ref: TV: Rainbow Video; no Eng.

Classier-than-usual Hong Kong vampire comedy features some fun effects and makeup for its main, moldy, blood-revived vampire and an incidental *Blob/Alien* monster. Script has some really offbeat scenes and ideas, including the "raft" of bats which carries the vampire's inert body through the sky ... the balloon-craft vampire finder ... the enveloping trees ... and the "flashback" sequences in which a couple of gents "relive" the ghost woman's experiences while she is temporarily trapped in their respective bodies. More fun: a funny little hopping vampire, a cartoon demon, and a harrowing attack by bat hordes.

**\*ONE FRIGHTENED NIGHT** 1935. Mus D: Arthur Kay. SpFX: Jack Coyle, Howard Lydecker. Horror Masks: Markoff. Ref: TV. Everson/TDIF:60. Turner/Price. V 10/9/35. Lee(e). Lentz. Stanley. Maltin '92. Scheuer. Hound. Martin.

"It wasn't human! That face—looking like something the devil let loose!" This old, cliched but lively mystery chiller features the usual creep elements—thunder and lightning, secret passageways, wind-extinguished candles, and a room closed for twenty years. Less usual: the trophy room full of skulls, masks, idols, and mummies in sarcophagi. Most unusual: the treatment of the masked fiend not as a man in a cloak and mask, but as an out-and-out monster ... at least until the mask is found lying around. (The folks here are charmingly gullible.) Charles Grapewin as Jasper is a likable old cuss—even if that's just what he's trying so hard to be.

**100 SPOOK STORIES** or **100 MONSTERS** see *Hundred Monsters, The*

**ONE MILLION YEARS DD** Coast to Coast 1992 color 76m. D, Ed: Jim Enright. SP: Marc Cushman. Ph: J. J. Fields. Ref: TV: CtC video. With Paula Price, Alicyn Sterling, Dominique, Carolyn Monroe, Peter North.

"It took one million years to find her." A "woman from the past"—"over one million years old"—is found "perfectly preserved (and beautiful, too)" in ice. The ice melts. "You're alive!" And she hasn't had sex in a "million moons".... Primitive X-rated variation on the already pretty primitive *Return of the Apeman.*

**ONE NIGHT OF 21 HOURS** see *Planet of the Vampires*

**ONE NIGHT STAND** (Austral.) Edgley Int'l. & Hoyts Theatres & AFC/Astra (Richard Mason) 1984 (1983) color 94m. SP, D: John Duigan. Ph: Tom Cowan. Mus: W. Motzing. Sets: Ross Major. Mkp: Margaret Lingham. VisFX: Mirage FX. Holocaust FX: Chris Murray et al. Ref: V 4/4/84. 5/9/84:415. Ecran F 46:64. 47:31. TV. With Tyler Coppin, C. Delaney, Jay Hackett, Saskia Post.

Nuclear war breaks out in Europe and North America. ("The world ended yet?") Goodbye, "thin veneer of civilization." Or, On the Beach, II. Alternately ponderous and sweet end-of-the-world drama. Highlights include the interspersed, brief, visualized flashbacks of the principals. Also interspersed: clips from *Metropolis*.

**ONE SHIVERY NIGHT** Col 1950 16m. D: Del Lord. Ref: Okuda/CCS: "scare" comedy. LC. no Maltin/SSS. With Hugh Herbert, Dudley Dickerson, Philip Van Zandt, Vernon Dent.

Thugs attempt to scare people out of a deserted mansion.

**ONE SPOOKY NIGHT** Col 1955 20m. D: Jules White. Ref: Okuda/CCS. Lee. LC. With Andy Clyde, Dorothy Granger, Dudley Dickerson, Monte Collins.

Haunted house. Remake of *Host to a Ghost*.

**ONE WEDDING AND LOTS OF FUNERALS** see *Leprechaun 2*

**ONLY BLACKNESS** (I) P.A.C. 1978 color/ws 104m. (*Solamente Nero. The Bloodstained Shadow* - alt vt t). Story, SP, D: Antonio Bido. Story, SP: also D. Malon. SP: also M. Andalo. Ph: Mario Vulpiani. Mus: S. Cipriani. AD: Carlo Leva. Mkp: Massimo Giustini. Paintings: Andrea Pagnacco. Ref: TV: Redemption video; Eng. dubbed. VSOM. ETC/Giallos. Palmerini. With Lino Capolicchio, Stefania Casini, Craig Hill, Massimo Serato, Juliette Mayniel.

Venice. Ingredients include a medium who conducts "strange rites" ("There's something frightening about her")... a black-gloved killer ... disappearing corpses ... murder-by-halberd ... near-death-by-falling-crucifix ... a mad lad ... a thunderstorm ... one okay "bus" ... a monotonous score ... and a guessable killer. Virtually suspenseless.

**ONLY YOU** see *Urusei Yatsura 1: Only You*

**ONMITSU HICHO—MABOROSHI JO** (J) Toei 1956 99m. D: Ryo Hagiwara. Ref: CM 15:27: ghost story; *Spy's Secret Scroll—Phantom Castle* - tr t. With R. Otomo, E. Shindo.

**ONNA BATORUKOPU** (J) Toei Video & Tohokushinsha & Sega Ents. 1991 color 81m. (aka *Lady Battlecop*). D: Akihisa Okamoto. SP: Hayaichi Miyashita. SpMkpFX: Toki. SpFX: Nobuo Yajima; SpFx Research. VisSup & Char Des: K. Amamiya. Ref: TV: VSOM; Eng. titles. Markalite 3:84: "the ultimate, most blatant rip-off of *Robocop*"; made-for-video. Weisser/JC. With Masaru Matsuda, Shiro Sano, Masashi Ishibashi, A. Nakamura.

Neo Tokyo. A scientist's girl friend (Nakamura) puts on a "high-tech combat suit," becomes the "robotic BattleCop." Plus: the "weird genetic mutation Amadeus."(M) The lady is aka "The RoboCop" or (by her enemies) "RoboBitch." ("Whoever hurts this city I will destroy.") Amadeus is a "psychic superman, a cyborg," created by NASA and stolen by the ruthless Karuta cartel. Plus: the "Neutral magnum—a great weapon," a ray-rifle.... Simple-minded and juvenile. The Lady BattleCop-vs.-Amadeus duels are the showcase scenes, but there are also occasional time-outs for some dismaying sentiment. Watchable effects stunts.

**ONOVA NESCHTO** (Bulg.) Studio Bojana & Production Group Chemus 1992 color 89m. D: Georgi Stojanov. SP: Christo Bojtshev. Ref: V 3/16/92: "the comedy is fitful and strained." With Velko Kanev, Dobrinka Stankova.

Absent-minded professor haunted by "thing" which he hears on the roof of an old factory at night. *That Thing* - tr t.

**OPEN FIRE** see *Panther Squad, The*

**OPEN HOUSE** Intercontinental (Sandy Cobe) 1987 color 98m. (*Multiple Listings* - orig t). Story, D: Jag Mundhra. SP: David Mickey Evans. Mus: Jim Studer. SpFxMkpSup: John Naulin. Ref: TV: Prism Ent. video. V 7/1/87:4 (rated). 11/25/87. Phantom. McCarty II. Morse. With Joseph Bottoms, Adrienne Barbeau, Rudy Ramos, Mary Stavin, Scott Thompson Baker, Darwyn Swalve (Harry), Tiffany Bolling.

The targets of the Open House Killer: "real estate bimbos." ("They'd sell their mothers for a commission.") This time the "deserving" victims of the psycho killer are real estate agents. ("They made homes too damn expensive!") The lethal Harry may tell the public that he represents the homeless, but real estate here is just another pretext for isolating a woman in a house with a maniac. A bad, bad movie.

**OPERA** see *Terror at the Opera*

**OPERACION MANTIS** (Sp-J) Aconito Films 1984 color feature. SP, D: Jacinto Molina. Ref: Ecran F 50:70. no Martin. no Hound. PT 7:26, 30: "box-office disaster." 8:4. V 5/9/84:411 (ad). With Paul Naschy (aka J. Molina), Julia Saly, Fedra Lorente.

James Bond parody with "numerous sf elements."

**OPERATION GANYMED** (W. G.) North American Releasing/Pentagramma & ZDF 1977 ('85-U.S.) color 126m./96m. (c90m.-U.S.). SP, D: Rainer Erler. Ph: Wolfgang Grasshoff. Mus: Eugen Thomass. AD: Michael Pilz. Mkp: Franz Goebel. Ref: TV: NAR video; Eng.-dubbed. Hardy/SF. Horacio Higuchi. Dr. Rolf Giesen. Cannes '80 flyer. With Horst Frank, Dieter Laser, Jurgen Prochnow, Uwe Friedrichsen.

"Where the hell is everyone?" Only "five old men" remain from a 21-man mission to Jupiter—one of the five, Donald George, carries bottles containing "proof of life on Jupiter." Forgotten after a "billion kilometers in outer space and 4-1/2 years away," the five land in the sea off Baja California and set off, on foot, on the "road to San Diego"....

Over-deliberate and one-dimensional, *Operation Ganymed* still has occasional, dogged power as it documents its returning astronauts' hero's non-welcome. No glory here, just cynicism and heavy irony—even George's fantasies finally turn sour, and the mission controllers in his hallucination greet him with a belittling "It's only a test!"

**OPERATION INTERCEPT** Vidmark/Hess-Kallberg 1995 (1994) color 94m. SP, D: Paul Levine. Ref: vc box: new super-weapon. With B. Payne, L. Henriksen, C. Bernsen.

**OPERATION MOBILE SUIT GUNDAM 0083: STARDUST MEMORY** see *Gundam 0083: Stardust Memory*

**OPERATION PINK SQUAD II: THE HAUNTED TOWER** (H.K.) First Distributors/Golden Flare Films 1988? color c82m. SP, D: Jeff Lau. Ph: Johnny Koo. Ref: TV: World Video; Eng. titles. NST! 4:33: 1st *Pink Squad* movie not horrific.

"The spirits are rushing up!" A monk catches sixty ghosts in an apartment building, but one, "nine-life cat," scampers away before he can seal them all up behind the Door of Hell. Her head and body separate; the protagonists saw the latter into pieces, but her head explodes as part of the "Blood Out" ritual, which draws hordes of ghosts, attracted by the smell of human blood.

Fast, hollow, alternately clever and silly horror-comedy majors in bathroom humor. Highlights: the remote-controlled, armed-and-deadly mini-copters (from *Aces Go Places II*?) flying after the horror head ... the ghost making the elevator "go fast" ... the hero trying to avoid contact with the temporarily quiescent ghost as he tries to reach the keys hanging near her.

The **ORACLE** Reeltime (Laurel) 1986 (1985) color 94m. D: Roberta Findlay. SP: R. Allen Leider. Mus & P: Walter E. Sear. Mus: also M. Litovsky. SpFX: Horrorefx. SpMkp: Jean Carballo. Ref: TV: U.S.A. HV. V 7/15/87: '86 regional release. Phantom. Martin. Scheuer. With Caroline Capers Powers, Roger Neil, Victoria Dryden, Pam La Testa, Chris Maria de Koron, James Styles, Irma St. Paule.

An old woman, Mrs. Malatesta (St. Paule), disappears from her New York apartment. Left behind: her planchette, which allowed her to "speak to the dead." Our heroine, Jenny (Powers), finds it and becomes its "medium." It "concentrates" her psychic powers, and she "sees" the murder of a supposed suicide, William Graham (Styles). She becomes the target of the murderers when she goes to his widow, Dorothy (Dryden), to tell her what she has seen. But the planchette "protects" Jenny: Horrors materialize and kill the killers and their mastermind, Dorothy. The oracle also protects itself: At one point, a little octopus-creature slips out of it and attacks the nosy apartment super. He imagines (a la *Young Sherlock Holmes*) a horde of rubber toys attacking him and takes his own life. Later, Jenny's husband (Neil) has his head removed by a big-clawed creature from the trash chute.

This melodramatic mixture of horror and crime doesn't pay, except in the fairly macabre scene in which Graham's corpse asphyxiates Dorothy, as she had him asphyxiated. Even here, though, the alternating objective-subjective shots confuse: Are they suggesting that Graham is visible only to her or that he is just in her mind? The sequence with the super is also split between conflicting suggestions of the supernatural and the psychological. The movie is uncertainly acted, and padded with chase-and-stalk footage.

**ORDAG VIGYE** (Hung.) Dialog Filmstudio & Magyar TV (Ferenc Andras) 1993 color 86m. SP, D: Robert Pajer. SP: also Sandor Fabry, Laszlo. Mus: Ferenc Darvas. Ref: V 2/22/93: "ho-hum supernatural comedy ... special effects are rudimentary." With Iren Psota (Micci), Zoltan Bezeredy, Gyorgy Dorner.

The devil—"in the form of an aging femme"—is after an inventor's "elixir of life." *The Devil Take It* - tr t.

The **ORDER OF THE BLACK EAGLE** IFM/Polo Players Ltd. 1988 color 93m. D: Worth Keeter. SP: Phil Behrens. Ref: V 4/27/88: follow-up to (apparently non-fantastic) *Unmasking the Idol*. Ecran F 67:71. With Ian Hunter, William Hicks.

Satellite plot ... "Hitler is in deep freeze." (V)

**ORE NO CHI WA TANIN NO CHI** (J) Shochiku 1974 feature. D: T. Masuda. Ref: Monster! 1/92 (Higuchi): *My Blood Belongs to Someone Else* - tr t?

"Ridiculous 1974 gangster melodrama-cum-sf."

**ORGY AT THE FUN HOUSE** Le Salon 1989 color feature. D: Angel Rivera. Ref: Adam '93G: "sets look like *The Cabinet of Dr. Caligari* colorized." With Steven Moore.

Haunted house.

The **ORIGINAL WICKED WOMAN** Wicked 1993 color 79m. D: Jim Enright. Ref: Adam '95: alien. With Chasey Lain, Isis Nile, Tom Byron.

*****ORLOFF AND THE INVISIBLE MAN** Brux Interfilm/Euro-cine (Marius Lesoeur) 1970 (*La Vie Amoureuse de l'Homme Invisible* - '72 reissue t. *Dr. Orloff's Invisible Horror* - alt vt t. *The Invisible Dead* - alt vt t). SP: P. Chevalier. Ph: R. Heil. Mus: C. Sauvage. AD: R. Matheu. SpFX: Juan Fortuny, Procede Kinotechnique. Ref: TV: Wizard Video; Eng. dubbed. Lee. Gore Zone number 5. Stanley. With Isabel del Rio, Francisco Valladares, Fernando Sancho, Brigitte Carva.

"I've created a man, a creature that you can't see—an invisible man"—apparently by "changing the structure of his brain." He needs blood to survive and, powdered, looks like an ape-man.... Botched sleaze. A pretext for whipping scenes and pre-*Entity*, invisible-rapist scenes. The kind of movie that gives exploitation a bad name. And the fact that the scientist and the invisible man here are two different people saps the story of its power. The two moments worth mentioning: the verbal retelling of the incident in which "something so unnatural" came between Orloff's daughter and the mirror, and the graveyard-at-midnight sequence in which the "corpse" in the coffin (apparently entombed prematurely) suddenly complains to the jewel robbers, "You're hurting me." Is this the only non-Jesus Franco Orloff?

See also *Awful Dr. Orlof.*

**OSA** (Mex?) Osa Prods. (Alexandrov) 1985 color 94m. SP, D: Oleg Egorov. Mus: Mason Daring. Ref: V 10/23/85: "weak gender switch on Mad Max." 5/7/86:414. Morse: "a total mess." Stanley: "totally preposterous." With Kelly Lynch, Daniel Grimm, P. Vincent, E. Chicot, Bill Moseley (Quilt Face).

**L'OSCENO DESIDERIO** (I-Sp) Cineiniziative & Titan PCC-Altamira 1977 color/ws 97m. (*Poseida*-Sp. *Le Pene nel Ventre* - alt I t. *La Profezia* - I prod t). SP, D: Giulio Petroni. SP: also Piero Regnoli. Ph: Rossi, Villasenor. Mus: C. Savina. Ref: Monster! 3:49, 50, 52: "sexual-demon-possession film." Palmerini. With Marisa Mell, Lou Castel, Chris Avram, Victor Israel, Laura Trotter, Jack Taylor.

**L'OSPITE** (I) Aco 1989 color 90m. D: C.P. Hansen. SpFX: Zed. Ref: Hardy/HM2: the devil in a library; *The Guest* - tr t. With John Phillip Law, Eva Orlando, Stella Stevens.

**OSSESSIONE CHE UCCIDE, L'** see *Fear* (1980)

**OTHER HELL, The** see *Guardian of Hell, The*

**OTRA VUELTA DE TUERCA** (Sp) Gaurko Filmeak (Gonzalo Goikoetxea) 1985 color 119m. SP, D: Eloy de la Iglesia. SP: also Goikoetxea, Angel Sastre. From Henry James' book *The Turn of the Screw.* Mus: Luis Iriondo. Ref: Cine Para Leer '85. V 10/9/85: "unmitigated boredom." 5/7/86:386. no Stanley. With Pedro Maria Sanchez, Queta Claver, Asier Hernandez Landa, Cristina Reparaz Goyanes.

Roberto (Maria Sanchez) "sees all the right ghosts"....

**OTROKI VO VSELENNOI** (Russ) Gorki 1975 color/ws 85m. D: Richard Viktorov. SP: Zak, Kuznetsov. Ph: Kirillov. Ref: Hardy/SF: "this second part is more entertaining than the first," *Cassiopea* (II); *Teenagers in Space*-tr t? With Misha Yershov, Innokenty Smoktunovsky.

"Planet much like Earth ... ruled by robots."

**OTSTUPNIK** (Russ.-W.G.-Austrian) Belarusfilm-Sovinfilm & MKGSH & Klinkartfilm 1988 color 163m. SP, D: Valery Rubinchik. Ref: V 11/9/88: "hopelessly incomprehensible"; The Apostate - tr t. With Grigury Gladily, Nikolai Yeremenko, Andrei Kashker.

Cloning invention.

**OUIJA SEXORCISM** (H.K.) 1988? color feature. D: T. Lam. Ref: Weisser/ATC: woman violated by (rubber) snake ... household possessed by spirit from ouija board.

**OUT FOR BLOOD** Vivid 1990 color 85m. (75m.) D: Paul Thomas. Ref: Jones: Countess Draculust, hunchbacked Igor. Adam '92. TVG. With Tori Wells, Raquel Darian, Cheri Taylor.

**OUT OF CONTROL** Essex 1987 color 82m. D, P: Duck Dumont, C. DeSantos. Ref: Adam '89. With Megan Leigh, Keisha, Nikki Knights, Angel Kelly, Peter North.

"Intergalactic hookers arrive on Earth...."

**OUT OF THE BODY** (Austral.) PFM-Medusa/David Hannay 1988 color 89m. D: Brian Trenchard-Smith. SP: K. G. Ross. SpMkp: Deryck de Niese. Ref: V 5/28/88: "keeps the audience guessing." With Mark Hembrow, Tessa Humphries, Carrie Zivetz, Linda Newton, Shane Briant.

"A creature from inside Hembrow, invisible and all-powerful, has been the monster."

**OUT OF THE DARK** CineTel/Zel Films (Paul Bartel) 1989 color 90m. D: Michael Schroeder. SP, P: Z. W. Levitt. SP: also J. G. DeFelice. Mus: Antonelli, Wheatley. SpMkpFX: Tony Gardner, Lisa Schulze. SpFX: (coord) Kevin McCarthy; Players SpFX. Opt: Ray Mercer. Ref: TV. V 5/3/89. HR 5/8/89. NYT 5/5/89. MFB'89:148-9. With Cameron Dye, Karen Black, Bud Cort,

Lynn Danielson, Starr Andreeff, Divine, Bartel, Tracey Walter, Tab Hunter, Lainie Kazan.

"It's time for Bobo!" "Some kind of clown" with a baseball bat is slaughtering "phone fantasy girls." Arty sleaze with determinedly eccentric cameo roles. Semi-clever whodunit payoff.

**OUT OF THE DARKNESS** (B) Children's Film & TV (G.L.T. Scott) 1985 color 68m. SP, D: John Krish. From John Hoyland's novel *The Ivy Garland.* PD: Keith Wilson. Ph: Ray Orton. Mkp: Eddie Knight. Ref: MFB'86:150-51: "fairly persuasive." V 12/11/85: "atmospheric." Stanley. With Gary Halliday, Michael Flowers, Emma Ingham, Anthony Winder (ghost boy).

Legend that ghost haunts the Derbyshire village of Stonewall.

**OUT OF THE DEPTHS** see *Black Cat* (1990)

**OUT OF TIME** NBC-TV/Col-TV (Out of Time Prods.) 1988 color 90m. D, Exec P: Robert Butler. Tel: J. J. Sakmar, Brian A. Lane, Kerry Lenhart. Story: Lane. Mus: Andy Summers. SpVisFX: Louis G. Friedman. SpFX: (coord) David Domeyer; David Kelsey; (elec) Laser Edit. Laser FX: Roto FX: Time Machine: Prop-Art. Anim & Opt: Available Light. Mkp: Edward Ternes. Ref: TV. SFExam 7/15/88. V 7/20/88:80. 10/19/92:16 (rated). With Bruce Abbott, Bill Maher, Adam Ant, Rebecca Schaeffer, Kristian Alfonso, Leo Rossi, Ray Girardin.

L.A., 2088 A.D., a post-book world. A cop (Abbott) whose great-grandfather (Maher) invented the Max 2000 computer, the audio-magnifier, etc., takes a time machine back to 1988. Plus: glasses with Thermographic magnification, X-ray, and Night Vision modes ... ray guns .. an energy-proof vest ... and a laser cigarette lighter.

Glib, glossy sf-comedy, with charming moments, mostly from Maher. ("That's amazing! I can't wait to invent that thing.") Moral: "Love is the one thing that never changes."

**OUTBACK VAMPIRES** see *Wicked, The*

**OUTCAST** Good Prods. 1991 color 92m. SP, D: R. Buchok. SpFX: N. Howe. Ref: Hardy/HM2.

Devil, chainsaw violence, telekinesis.

**The OUTING** Moviestore Ent./H.I.T. Films (Warren Chaney/Deborah Winters/Lamp Prods.) 1987 (1986) color 85m. (*The Lamp* - orig t & t in Japan). D: Tom Daley. SP: Chaney. Mus: Rosenbaum, Miller. PD: Robert Burns. SpFX: Martin Becker's Reel EFX; (sup) Frank Inez; (coord) Bettie Kauffman; (mech sup) Frank Munoz; (mkp coord) Chris Swift: (fx mkp) Paul Clemens, Bart Mixon et al. SpPhFX: Technomagic Film FX; (des) David L. Hewitt. SpFxMkp: John Nau(g)lin. SpComputer Graphics: Cannata Communication. Ref: TV. V 10/7/87. 9/23/87:119. VVoice 11/3/87. Phantom. Morse. With Winters (Arab woman), James Huston, Andra St. Ivanyi, Scott Bankston, Danny D. Daniels, Jackson Bostwick (Djinn's voice).

In Houston, the opening of a lamp dating from 3,500 B.C. unleashes a murderous Djinn capable of imitating other life forms. This spirit briefly revivifies, first, an axed "witch" (Winters) and, later, "Tracy," the skeleton of a Central American Indian, apparently buried alive. Also on the agenda: a head-crushing helmet and a snakes-run-wild bathtub scene.... Formula slash-and-squisher features occasional surprising elements, including the fairly-impressive-looking Djinn-monster, the living skeleton, and couple of oddball human characters.

**OUTING, The** see *Scream*

**OUTLANDERS** (J) 198-? anim color 45m. From Johji Manabe's comic. Ref: TV: laserdisc. Anime Opus '89: OAV. Animag 4:5. Animerica 6:2.

199X. Alien Princess Kahm of Santovasku chooses photographer Tetsuya Wakatsuki to be her husband. Her goal: to save Earth from the wrath of her father, the Emperor.... Kahm's emotional (and literal) firepower is a variation on Lum's electrical specialty. In fact, she and Tetsuya have a Lum-Ataru relationship, fueled by her nervous aggression and his even-more-nervous hesitation. When a wolf-like alien slays Tetsuya, she restores him to life with the aid of a *Metropolis* gizmo and her own will power. The movie employs "Road Runner"-style violence in the service of this fine (if unusual) romance.

Strange bedfellows: Kahm has ram's horns; her friend Battia has cat ears, and Battia's boy friend is the wolf-alien. More fun: a virus weapon which makes spaceships molt, a death pit of ungodly sucker creatures, and a delightful family of little green reptilian aliens. Pleasantly outrageous animation.

**OUTLAW OF GOR** Cannon/Breton Film (Harry Alan Towers, Avi Lerner) 1989 color 89m. (aka *Outlaw*). D: John (Bud) Cardos. SP: Rick Marx, Towers, from John Norman's novel. Ref: V 4/12/89: "puerile." 10/19/88:173. With Urbano Barberini, Rebecca Ferrati, Donna Denton, Jack Palance.

Sequel to *Gor.*

**OUTSIDER, The** see *Watchers II*

**OUTTAKES** Marketechnics/Sell (Richmond) 1987 color 71m. SP, D: J. M. Sell. SP: also Adrianne Richmond, Jim Fay. Ref: V 5/20/87: completed in 1985.

"A satire of a Santa Claus as slasher in horror pics is stupid and amateurish ... melange of skits."

**OVERDRAWN AT THE MEMORY BANK** (U.S.-Can.) RSL Films/American Playhouse & CPB & NEA/WNET-13-TV & SFTV/Moviecorp VII (David Loxton & Geoffrey Haines-Stiles/Robert Lantos, S. J. Roth) 1983 ('85-U.S.) color 84m. D: Douglas Williams. Tel: Corinne Jacker, from John Varley's short story. Ph: Barry Bergthorson. Mus: John Tucker. PD: Carol Spier. Sp Synthesizer FX: Peter Jermyn. SpVideoFX: Jim Goessinger, Haines-Stiles. FxCoord: Erna Akuginow. Mkp: Shonagh Jabour. Computer Graphics: Mobile Image of Canada. ADO FX: Omnibus Video. Ref: TV. TVG 2/4/85 (ad). Hound. Stanley. Phantom. With Raul Julia, Linda Griffiths, Donald C. Moore, Wanda Cannon, Louis Negin, Jackie Burroughs, Maury Chaykin.

While undergoing compulsory "doppling" (the insertion of a human personality into the mind and body of another animal) at Novicorp's Nirvana Village, computer op Aram Fingal (Julia) becomes misplaced. Through interfacing and a sort of electronic cloning, his personality is then injected into the "simulated reality" of a computer, where he is joined by electronic simula-

tions of his dead mother, Peter Lorre, Humphrey Bogart (in his *Casablanca* role), Sydney Greenstreet, etc. Eventually, Aram succeeds in reprogramming the computer from the inside.... Stilted acting, arch dialogue, and a washed-out, shot-on-tape look and sound. Uninvolving mixture of science and nostalgia.

**OVERDRIVE** see *Maximum Overdrive*

**OVEREXPOSED** Concorde (Roger Corman) 1990 color 80m. SP, D: Larry Brand. SP: also Rebecca Reynolds. Mus: Mark Governor. Ref: V 5/23/90: "basically a yawner." Martin: "gore fest." With Catherine Oxenberg, David Naughton, Jennifer Edwards, William Bumiller, Karen Black.

"Grotesque twist ending" to tale of TV actress who fears she has a "homicidal fan."

**OVER-SEXED RUGSUCKER FROM MARS** Riproring (sic) Pictures/Vista St. Prods. (Marketing Media) 1989 (1988) color 84m. (*Oversexed Rugsuckers from Mars* - ad t). SP, D, P: Michael Paul Girard. Ref: TV: vt. no Hound. no Martin. V 11/1/89:25: at MIFED. With Dick Monda, Jean Stewart, Billybob Rhoads, Ralston Young, Jeff Wilson.

"Once the vacuum mates with a human, the new species will be born." After a ten-million-year absence, tiny stopmo aliens return to Earth and succeed in creating a new species when a tramp, Vernon (Monda), makes love to a vacuum cleaner ("Dusty"), which then drains one woman of blood and rapes another, Rena (Stewart), who gives birth to a little Dustbuster, a "vacusapien." ("The vacuum cleaner did it.") Ten percent inspiration, ninety percent desperation here, but sporadically hilarious. ("It's not normal to carry on mature relations with a household appliance.") The humans in *Rugsucker* are less taking than the aliens and appliances. The movie, though, features the funniest police lineup since *The Delicate Delinquent*. Compare *Blades, Bless This House,* etc.

**OZMA OF OZ** see *Return to Oz*

**OZONE: THE ATTACK OF THE REDNECK MUTANTS** DMP/ Matt Devlen & Max Raven 1988 color 90m. D: Devlen. SP: Brad Redd. Ph: Guy Rafferty. Mus: Lasalo Murr, John Hudek et al. SpFX: Tillie O'Toole, Jovan Linstrom et al. Mkp: Lula DeBricasau. Ref: TV: Muther Video. no Hound. no Martin. PT 10:10. Fango 94:12. With Scott Davis, Brad McCormick, Janice Williams, Dick Durr (outhouse mutant), Barry Stephen (car mutant), Regina Hackenbush (granny mutant), Blue Thompson.

"There's a breakdown in the ozone layer that's causing everything to mutate." In Poolville, "some kind of pimply-faced critter" is going around "puking on everything," and there's grossness in the bathtub. Meanwhile, outside town, a mutant fox menaces all who come near it. A nearby chemical plant seems to figure in these horrors.... Leisurely, makeup-effects-happy, occasionally genial sf-gore-comedy. The height of humor: redneck belching and cackling. That's as good as it gets here.

**OZONE** Suburban Tempe & Glen Gruner & David Wagner 1993 color 80m. SP, D, P, Ph, Ed: J.R. Bookwalter. SP: also David Wagner. Ph: also Lance Randas. Mus: J.C. Moller. PD: Hone, Morrison, Weaver. SpMkpFx: Bill Morrison, Vince Rossetti;

Barton-Sipe-Rebert. Morphing: Subtempeco EFX. Ref: TV: Tempe Video. Imagi Smr'95:56: "good movie." With James Black, Tom Hoover, B. Morrison, Lori Scarlett, M.W. Beatty, James L. Edwards (The Drug Lord), Michael Cagnoli, Nathan Michael (head Ozone mutant).

"Soon, there will be many, many more followers." The new drug, Ozone, does a *Scanners* on one victim; it leads to severe makeup effects on others, too. This "pure liquid of illumination" gives one the "power to live again," and could "change the face of the world." The lord of the Ozone cult is a sort of Jabba the Hutt writ small—one Sam DeBartolo, mutated by Ozone, who can "fully regenerate" after absorbing bullets.... This second film titled *Ozone* has lots of filler footage, but some True Weird payoffs, too, like the "birth of our son" scene. ("Daddy!") Or the "co-coon"/"mole person"/gross-sex dream scene. One pins-in-head cultist seems to be an hommage to *Hellraiser*. Shot-on-tape.

# P

**PACIFIC HEIGHTS** Fox/Morgan Creek (Scott Rudin, William Sackheim) 1990 color 102m. D: John Schlesinger. SP: Daniel Pyne. Mus: Hans Zimmer. SpMechFX: Image Engineering. SpFxSup: J. D. Street. Mkp: Valli O'Reilly. Ref: TV. MFB'91:52-3. V 10/1/90. Cinef 2/91: horrific. TVG 10/12/91: "psychological horror film." With Melanie Griffith, Matthew Modine, Michael Keaton, Mako, Nobu McCarthy, Dorian Harewood, Luca Bercovici, Tippi Hedren, Dan Hedaya, Dabbs Greer, Tracey Walter, Beverly d'Angelo.

"This is a game: The object ... is to get Mr. Hayes out of your building before he destroys your lives." James Danforth aka Carter Hayes (Keaton) is a "sick individual ... shut out of the family fortune" who tries to recoup his losses by legally wresting property from landlords. When his latest victim (Griffith) reciprocates and screws him financially, he returns to terrorize her, before meeting a fairly gory death. Bonuses: much play with cockroaches, nail guns, and razor blades, plus a (visualized) cockroach-punctuated nightmare sequence.The scariest moment of this horror-story-for-landlords: the invocation of the California Civil Code. Unfortunately, Modine's Drake Goodman proves too easy prey for Danforth/Hayes—his chronic near-hysteria takes him out of the picture early. Griffith has or is more fun, at least in the turning-the-tables sequences. And Keaton is underplayed, creepy punctuation to the story. The oddball exterminator (here, Walter)—a sort of entomological exorcist—is becoming a staple of the new "haunted house" thrillers.

**PAGANINI HORROR** (I) Fulvia(Fabrizio de Angelis) 1988 color 84m. (*Il Violino Chu Uccide*). SP, D: Luigi Cozzi (aka Lewis Coates). SP: also D. Nicolodi. Story: Raimondo del Balzo. Ph: Franco Lecca. Mus: Vince Tempera. AD: M.P. Anzolini. SpMkpFX: Casagni & Prestopino. SpSetFX: Paolo Ricci. SdFX: Cineaudio. Ref: TV: VSOM; Eng. titles. PT 17:10. V 10/19/88:350(ad). Hardy/HM2. MV: aka *The Killing Violin*? Palmerini. With Daria Nicolodi, Jasmine Main, Donald Pleasence, Pascal Persiano, Maria Cristina Mastrangeli, Michele Klippstein.

"The sound!" A little girl, Sylvia, electrocutes Mommy; as an adult, she's cursed to repeat her sin in the Casa de Sol, an "old,

isolated, scary house," in which Nicolo Paganini lived, and killed his love, Antonia, who became, roughly, his violin, in a sort of Weird Karma. In the story proper, the house becomes the scene of the filming of a rock video utilizing the "original sheet music" of Paganini, "written for the devil ... with the authentic seal of the composer." The plot proper involves a strangely-masked slasher ... the living-dead Daniel and Rita ... deafening music from Paganini's cellar ... supernatural electricity ... the "altering" of time and space ... a deadly fungus from trees "used for special violins" ... and Hemispheric Harmony (or The Music of the Spheres).

The premises are promisingly absurd, but much of the movie plays like a routine slasher story. It's only near the end that promises are kept—when, for instance, the prowling Paganini Horror disintegrates, and his ashes form the treble clef sign. It's not every movie that can give you something like that.

**The PAGEMASTER** Fox & Turner Pictures (David Kirschner) 1994 anim and live action 75m. D: (anim) Maurice Hunt;(live action) Joe Johnston. Story, SP: D. Kirschner, David Casci. SP: also Ernie Contreras. Ph: A. Gruszynski. Mus: James Horner. PD: Lawrence, Ventura; R.F. Smith. VisFX:(sup) R.T. Sullivan; 4-Ward;(min mech fx) Joel Steiner. SpFxAnim: Mark Myer. SpFxSupAnim: J.A. Armstrong, K. Quaife-Hodge. OptFX: Mercer. Computer Anim: Xaos. SpFxCoord: Robbie Knott. Ref: TV: vt. ad. SFChron 11/23/94. Sean. With Macaulay Culkin, Christopher Lloyd, Ed Begley, Jr.;(voices) Frank Welker (Horror), Leonard Nimoy (Dr. Jekyll and Mr. Hyde), Patrick Stewart (Adventure), Whoopi Goldberg (Fantasy).

Featured: Dr. Jekyll and Mr. Hyde ... ghosts from ghost stories ... a gigantic, fire-breathing dragon ... a dragon morphed out of spilled paint in a library ... and bits with a giant, the Hound of the Baskervilles, and the giant squid from *20,000 Leagues under the Sea*.... Lively but generally undistinguished fantasy seems vaguely *Neverending Story*-inspired. Among the thematic nuggets: "Seize the courage" and "Look to the books." Goldberg's Fantasy and Welker's Horror have amusing bits.

**PAINTED DOLLS** see *Night Stalker, The* (1987)

**PAINTED SKIN, The** see *Hua Pi. Hua Pi Zhi Yinyang Fawang*

**PALE BLOOD** Noble Ent. & Alpine Releasing/Leighton-Kaczmarczyk (J. T. Media Inc.) 1991 (1990) color 93m. D: VV Dachin Hsu. Co-D, Co-P, SupEd: Michael W. Leighton. SP: Takashi Matsuoka, Hsu. Mus: Jan A. P. Kaczmarck. SpFX: Wizard SpFX, Players SpFX. MkpFX: Dean Jones, Kevin Hudson. Opt: T&T. Ref: TV: vt. Mo. V 7/1/91. 2/21/90:159. 5/2/90: S-96. 6/6/90:22 (rated). 10/15/90:M-82. Psychotronic 11:12. With George Chakiris (Michael Fury), Wings Hauser, Pamela Ludwig, Diana Frank, Earl Garnes (Harker).

A vampire (Chakiris) who can "flow through windows," bust through walls, and levitate "investigates" madman Van Vandameer (Hauser), who makes his brutal L.A. murders "look like the work of a vampire." Fury apparently wants to protect the good name of vampires; Vandameer apparently wants to create video "art" with his taped killings.... Vapid romantic fantasy proves a weird misfire, with fuzzy character motivation. Chakiris hardly registers as Fury. ("I can't let myself love anyone.")

**PALUBA** see *Widziadlo*

**PANDEMONIUM** (Austral.) KFM Pandemonium & Smart Street Films & Tra La La Films (Cutler-Keenan/Juillet) 1987 color 88m. SP, D: Haydn Keenan. SP: also Peter Gailey. Mus: Cameron Allan. SpFX: Monte Fieguth. Ref: V 4/8/87:24, 40: finished. 4/6/88: "has an undisciplined energy that's infectious, at least for a while." Jones: Hitler clone, witch. With David Argue, Amanda Dole, Arna-Maria Winchester, Gary Foley (The Holy Ghost), Henk Johannes (The Count).

"Vampires and other monsters" in a haunted movie studio.

**PANGA** see *Curse III*

**PANIC** (Sp-I) Cinema Shares Int'l./Arco European & Marcello Romeo (Sommer Filmverleigh) 1983 color 90m. (*Panico* - Sp. *Bakterion* - I). D: Tonino Ricci (aka A. Richmond). SP: Jaime Comas, V. A. Catena. Ph: G. Bergamini. Mus: Marcello Giombini. PD: Javier Fernandez. Monster FX: Rino Carboni. SpFX: Galiano Cataldo. Mkp: Massimo Giustini, Renato Francola. Ref: TV. TVG. Horacio Higuchi. Palmerini. vc box. Video Times 10/85: 71. Cine Para Leer '85. Hound. Scheuer. no Maltin '92. Stanley. V 5/9/84:408. MV: aka *I Vivi Invidieranno i Morti*. With David Warbeck, Janet Agren, Roberto Ricci, Jose R. Lifante, Miguel Herrera, Franco Ressel.

"This is really horrible!" England. Newton University's Plurema Project goes awry, and a deadly new, indestructible virus creates a blood-drinking mutant which (a) bursts through a movie-theatre screen, (b) invades a church ("The sacristy, quick—run!"), and (c) possesses an extensive repertoire of growls, snarls, howls, and cries. Choppy, crude, unoriginal.

**PANICO** (Mex) Enriquez 1970 color c90m. D: Julian Soler. SP: Ramon Obon Jr. Ph: Gabriel Torres. Mus: Luis Breton. Ref: TV. TVG. Horacio Higuchi. With Ana Martin, Joaquin Cordero, Carlos Ancira, Ofelia Guilmain, Jose Galvez, Aldo Monti, Alma D. Fuentes, Pilar Sen.

Three tales of horror (possibly culled from a TV series): "Panico," "Soledad," and "Angustia"—involving, respectively, the hallucinations of a madwoman, a buried body that seems to return to life, and catalepsy.... Labored histrionics. The opening sequence, however—fifteen minutes of oddball hallucinations—is effectively disorienting. It goes on and on, without explanation, and features an occasional unusual subjective-camera shot (including a sideways one reminiscent of a famous shot in *I Was a Teenage Werewolf*).

**PANICO** see *Panic*

**PANICO EN EL BOSQUE** (Mex) Laser Films & Fiesta Films (Omar A. Gonsenheim P.) 1990 color c90m. D: Roberto Guzman; Roberto Marroquin. SP: Jorge Victoria. Story: Cecilia Bourge. Ph: Leon Sanchez. Mus: Ignacio Pulido C. SpFX: Vazquez. Mkp: Luz Maria Larraguive, Gloria Luz Alzate. Ref: TV: Cine-Mex HV; no Eng. TVG. With Roberto "Flaco" Guzman, Cesar Bono, Leticia Perdigon, Jorge Guzman, Alfonso Zayas Jr., Carlos East, Bruno Rey, Antonio Raxel, Gerardo "Chiquilin" Zepeda (monstruo).

A mysterious killer stalks a forest—and generally seems to kill only those apparently deserving of killing. Tawdry makeup-effects vehicle. Shot-on-videotape.

**PANICO EN LA MONTANA** (Mex) Casablanca (Galindo) 1988 color c98m. Adap, D: Pedro Galindo III. Adap: also Santiago Galindo. Idea, SP: Pedro Galindo, Jr. SP: also Carlos Valdemar. Ph: Xavier Cruz. Mus: Pedro Plascencia S. SpFX: Miguel Vazquez. Mkp: Eugenia Luna. OptFX: Manuel Sainz. Ref: TV: Mex-American HV; no Eng.; *Panic in the Mountain*—tr t. TVG. Cinef 6/96:46. With "Resortes," Pedro Fernandez, Maria Rebeca, Jorge Reynoso (El Monstruo), Alfredo Gutierrez, George Samano.

A man-monster with telekinetic powers, super-strength, super-breath, and long fingernails haunts an old mining camp. At one point, he "freezes" the hero (Fernandez) with a look and possesses him. Also featured: an ax-wielding skulker and a *Psycho*-ish figure in a rocking chair.... Basically routine horror-fantasy has some atmosphere and a pretty good monster, though he overdoes the cackles.

**PANTANO DE LOS CUERVOS, El** see *Swamp of the Ravens, The*

**The PANTHER SQUAD** (Belg.-F) Dan Simon/Brux Inter Film & Greenwich Int'l. (Daniel Lesoeur/Sybil Danning/Ken Johnston) 1985 ('86-U.S.) color/ws? 77m. D: Peter Knight. SP: George Freedland. Story Idea: Ilona Koch. Mus: D. C. Getschal, J. G. Gusman. SpFX: SOIS Co. OptFX: Michael Rapp. SdFX: B. Klaus. Ref: TV: Eng.-lang. version. V 7/30/86. Phantom. Stanley. TVG. PT 7:21: aka *Open Fire*? With Sybil Danning, Karin Schubert, Jack Taylor, Robert Foster, Shirley Knight.

The New Organization of Nations—which is attempting the conquest of space with its space-jeep invention—takes on Clean Space, anti-pollution commandos who jam N.O.O.N. broadcasts with magnetic rays "powerful enough to interfere with worldwide television." Plus: a blue-ray gun which makes a (non-space) jeep disintegrate.... Glib, tacky, no-style femme-jock material makes weak vehicle for Danning's physical attributes.

**PAPAYA: LOVE GODDESS OF THE CANNIBALS** (I) 1978 color/ws feature (*Papaya dei Caraibi*. *Papaya, Queen of the Cannibals* - ad t. *Taste of the Cannibal* - alt vt t). D: A. Massaccesi (aka Joe D'Amato). Ref: TV: VSOM; Eng. titles. EVS. Shock Xpress (Smr '87:15). Palmerini.

Shock elements here include the cannibal lady's afterplay (she bites off her partner's penis) and the human sacrifice and cannibalism at the islanders' Festival of the Round Stone. Elementary, rudimentary sex-horror movie's highlight: the voodoo party in the nude.

**The PAPERBOY** Allegro 1994 color c93m. D: Douglas Jackson. Ref: vc box: "grisly deaths." Martin: "typical thriller." With A. Paul, W. Katt, M. Marut.

**PAPERHOUSE** (B) Vestron/Working Title, Paperhouse & Tilby Rose Ents. (Sarah Radclyffe, Tim Bevan) 1988 color 88m. D: Bernard Rose. SP: Matthew Jacobs, from Catherine Storr's novel *Marianne Dreams*. Mus: Hans Zimmer, Stanley Myers. PD:

Gemma Jackson. SpFX: (sup) Alan Whibley; Ace FX. Wire FX: Bob Harman, Steve Crawley. Mkp: Jenny Shircore. OptFX: Peter Watson. Ref: TV. V 9/21/88. SFExam 3/24/89. Scheuer. Martin. With Charlotte Burke, Ben Cross, Glenne Headly, Elliott Spiers.

"It's only a drawing." Little Anna (Burke) draws in her coloring book, then dreams what she draws. ("Been having dreams, Mum, but they're real.") Her dream subjects include a menacing father figure (Cross), a crippled boy (Spiers), and a hellish earthquake, and her dreaming seems to affect real-life situations.... Humorless and thin, with only the in-and-out-of-dreams framework of real interest. Okay score, photography (by Mike Southon).

The **PARA PSYCHICS** (Can.-W.G.?) 1986? color c80m. SP, D: Nico Mastorakis. Ref: TV: Knight Shield video. no Hound. no Martin. With Jessica Dublin, Maria Aliferi, Peter Winter, Chris Nomicos, Louise Melinda, Marie Elise Eugene, Philip Sherwood, Clay Huff, Jean-Claude Petit.

"She really is a bomb!" Olga Orlov ("Countess Dracula") controls the will of Christine Peters, a "mind reader of enormous ability." Together, the two—who transform "thoughts into energy"—cause explosions and make people choke to death. At the end, Olga dies, and Christine is freed.... Tacky production padded with "local color" footage. Interesting "two matching mediums" premise is wasted.

**PARADISO** see *Caged in Paradiso*

**PARALLEL ZONE** 1987 see *Wings of Oneamis*

**PARANOIA** see *Brain Dead*

**PARDEHE AKHAR** (Iranian) Cadre Film (Modaresi-Dadgoo) 1991 color 105m. SP, D: Varuzh Karim-Masihi. Mus: Babak Bayat. Mkp: Masud Valadbeigi, Mozhdeh Shamsai. Ref: V 3/18/91: "slick murder mystery"; *The Last Act*—tr t. With Farimah Farjami, Dariush Arjomand, Jamshid Hashempoor.

"Siblings hire a band of gypsies to stage horrific events as part of a scheme to drive" sister-in-law mad.

**PARENTS** (U.S.-Can.) Vestron & Great American Films (Parents Prods.) 1989 (1988) color 82m. D: Bob Balaban. SP: Christopher Hawthorne. Mus: Jonathan Elias. SpFxCoord: Gord Smith. Mkp: Linda Gill. Title Des: Yolanda Cuomo. Ref: TV. V 1/25/89. SFChron Dtbk 4/9/89. SFExam 11/9/90. With Randy Quaid, Mary Beth Hurt, Sandy Dennis, Bryan Madorsky, Juno Mills-Cockell, Graham Jarvis.

"What a dad!" Young Michael Laemle (Madorsky) imagines that boa-constrictor-like sausages are strangling him; he sees a hand writhing up out of the garbage disposal; and his father, Nick (Quaid), insists on calling him "Sport." Obviously, cannibalism is just around the corner.... The parents in this *Invaders from Mars,* boy's-eye view of family, school, and friends are "horrible" to begin with—no Martian zombie-drill is needed. The production is stylized, but pointless and unscary. Michael's already wild imagination is yet outdone, at every step, by the gruesome reality of Fifties suburbia. Film's horror-beneath-the-blandness irony fizzles.

**PARIS SEX MURDERS** (I-SP) MV/Dick Randall & Marius Mattei 1972 color feature (*La Casa d'Appuntamento. Murder in Paris. The Boogey Man and the French Murders*). SP, D: F. Merighi. SP: also M. Mattei, G. Vernuccio (aka R. Oliver). Story: Paolo Daniele. Ph: Mario Mancini, G. Otto. Mus: Bruno Nicolai. Mkp: Telemaco Tilli. SpFX: Carlo Rambaldi ("Ranbaldi" in cr).Ref: TV: MV; Eng. dubbed; D: "F.L. Morris." Palmerini. With Rosalba Neri, Anita Ekberg, E. Kraft, Barbara Bouchet, Howard Vernon, R. Sacchi.

"From the grave, I'll come back, and I promise to repay all of you." Red Herring Supreme: Twenty-four hours after the unjustly convicted, escaped "murderer" Antoine ("that maniac Antoine") is beheaded in a motorcycle accident, a lab assistant notes, of the head: "Professor, I saw the eyes move!" The "curse" of Antoine seems to result in "strange murders." A slasher/skulker seems to be at work—or is it someone's nightmare? Or both? Ultimately, the murderer swears that the "bloody eyes" of the severed head made him do it. Pretty vapid, despite the *Walking Dead* overtones. The police-procedural scenes dilute. Top line: "A case like you should be considered psychopathological!"

**PARISIENNE, La** see *Delitti*

**PARTY LINE** SVS Films/Westwind (Byrnes-Anderson-Webb-Webb) 1988 color 91m. D: William Webb. SP: Richard Brandes. Story: Tom Byrnes. Mus: Sam Sorensen. Ref: TV. V 11/2/88. HR 12/7/88. With Richard Hatch, Shawn Weatherly, Leif Garrett, Greta Blackburn, Richard Roundtree, Terrence McGovern.

"Now get Daddy's razor." Brother-sister crazies terrorize L.A. The usual "I always told you we'd be together, Angelina" scenes. Featured: a lot of ironic "Party time!"s.

**PASO AL MAS ACA, Un** see *Un Paso al Mas Aca ...*

**PASSI DI DANZA SULA LAMA DI UN RASOLO** see *Tormentor*

The **PASSING** Huckert Prods. 1983 color 96m. SP, D, P: John Huckert. P: also Mary Maruca. SpFX: Mark Chorvinsky, Miguel Munoz. Ref: V 6/12/85: "a badly acted piece of science fiction." Hound.

Expanded from the "effective, tight short" *The Water That Is Passed.*

**PASSING CLOUDS** see *Spellbound*

**PASSION CHAIN** Zane Ent. 1987 83m. D: Henri Pachard. Ref: Adam '89. With Elle Rio, Nina Hartley, Damien Cashmere, Nikki Knights.

Professor "trades minds with his exact opposite."

**PASSIONATE KILLING IN A DREAM** (H.K.) 1992 color/ws 87m. D: Parkman Wong. Ph: Yu Dong-Ching. Ref: TV: Tai Seng video; Eng. titles. Weisser/ATC: "thriller about a pretty artist" who (in her dreams) *sees* graphic murders," which are, "in fact, being committed by a demented serial killer...." With Michiko Nikyo, Lin Pin-Jun.

"Her throat was cut with a strange blade." Miss Sha Sha has a violent nightmare, then sees images from her dream on the local

TV news. Tawdry shocker is padded with cops, false alarms, kung fu fights, etc. Laughable "I'm not your mommy" final revelations.

**PATHOS** see *Obsession*

**PATLABOR—THE MOBILE POLICE: THE MOVIE** (J) Bandai/Emotion (Headgear) 1989 anim color/ws 100m. D: Oshii Mamoru. Ref: TV: Tohokushinsha HV; no Eng. Animag 10:46-53.

The Metropolitan Police Department's Special Vehicle Section No. 2 pits giant, human-operated, robot-like "patlabors" against renegades with "labors," construction vehicles which cross dump trucks with *Star Wars*-like walkers. Extra addeds: floating platforms (in Tokyo Bay), a warehouseful of little scurrying guard robots, and giant pistols (and bullets).... Highlights: the animation design, which is at once atmospheric and realistic ... the haywire computer "*Babel*"-ing on and on ... and the occasionally muted, eerie score. (The eerier sections alternate with bland pop.)

**PATLABOR 2: THE MOVIE** (J) Shochiku/Emotion-Bandai-Shogakukan (Headgear/Noboru-Tsuyoshi-Mitshuhisa) 1993 anim color/ws c103m. (aka *Mobile Police Patlabor 2*). D: Oshii Mamoru. SP: K. Ito. Mus: K. Kenji. Des: Y. Kimiko. Mecha Des: Izubuchi et al. Ref: TV: S. Baldric video (Tohokushinsha HV); Eng. titles. V 9/6/93:10: in Japan.

"This is no simple coup d'etat." 1999. Metro Police, EXTLs ("tactical robots developed in America"), the bombing of the Trans-Tokyo Bay Bridge, realistically-drawn characters, and involved international intrigue. Mood and talk. The mood is melancholic; the talk is about politics, war, etc., and is occasionally interesting.

**PATLABOR—THE MOBILE POLICE Vol. 1: SECTION 2, FORWARD MARCH!** (J) Headgear-Emotion-TFC (Sunrise & Tohokushinsha) 1988 anim color 25m. (aka *Mobile Police Patlabor. Pato-Labor*). D: Naoyuki Yoshinaga. SP: Kazunori Ito. From the comics by Masami Yuuki. Mus: Kenji Kawai. AD: Y. Shibutani. Mecha Des: Izubuchi, Sayama. Ref: TV: Bandai video; no Eng.; OAV. V. Max 3:5-9. 2:5. Animag 3:3. 10:46-53. 11:5: 16 OAVs planned.

Police "patlabors"—which operate on the Neuron Network System—combat a "rogue labor" amuck in Tokyo. Low key, atmospheric series entry.

**PATLABOR 2: LONGSHOT** (J) Bandai 1988 anim color 30m. D: Mamoru Oshii. SP: Kazunori Ito. Mecha Des: Izubuchi. Ref: Animag 4:8.

**PATLABOR 5: SECTION 2'S LONGEST DAY, PART I** (J) 1989 anim color c25m. Ref: M/TVM 2/89:56. Animag 10:52: OAV.

"Troops, tanks and Model 97 Combat labors take over Tokyo." (A)

**PATLABOR 6: SECTION 2'S LONGEST DAY, PART II** (J) Bandai 1989 (1988) anim color c30m. Ref: Animag 6:5: last in the OAV series.

**The PAWNBROKER** Infinity 1990 color 75m. D: Ron Jeremy. Ref: Adam '92. With Sabrina Dawn, Renee Foxx, Chessi Moore, T. T. Boy.

Traded-in dreams ... "space girls."

**PAYO, El** see *Caciques, Los*

**PEACE ON EARTH** MGM/Harman-Ising 1939 anim color 9m.
Ref: TV: vt. Jim Shapiro. LC. Lee.

"There ain't no men in the world no more. They was like monsters. They was always a-fightin'! They fought ... until there was only two of them left. And that was the end of the last man on Earth." Thus Grandpa Squirrel relates the last days of war-happy man on Earth and the establishment of Peaceville, a quiet community of squirrels, owls, etc., erected on the last human battlefield.... Cheerily grim animated fable is as optimistic re the future of squirrels and other small animals as it is pessimistic re the future of humankind. Merry Christmas!

Remake: *Good Will to Men.*

**PEACEMAKER** Fries Ent. (Paragon Arts)/Gibraltar Releasing & Mentone Pictures (Andrew Lane, Wayne Crawford) 1990 color 90m. SP, D: Kevin S. Tenney. Mus: D. M. Tenney. SpFxMkpDes: John Blake. SpFxSup: John Carter. Opt: T&T. Ref: TV. V 6/20/90. SFChron Dtbk 7/15/90. With Robert Forster (Yates), Lance Edwards (Townsend), Hilary Shepard, Bert Remsen.

"You're not from around here, are you?" A couple of "intergalactic cops and robbers who come back from the dead" turn up in Los Angeles. One of them is an "absolute, certifiable psychopath"; the other, a "macho asshole cop".... Glib, superficial excuse for car stunts and makeup effects, some of the latter admittedly pretty neat—e.g., the regenerating-hand effect for Yates. The Will-the-real-bad-Martian-please-stand-up suspense is not great, but passes the time.

**PEACOCK KING** (J) Soeshinsha Shueisha & Pony Canyon 1988 anim color c60m. D: Hidetoshi Omori. Ref: Animag 3:6.

See also the following and *Kujakuo—Peacock King.*

**PEACOCK KING** (H.K.) Golden Harvest/Paragon Films 1989 color 82m. (*Peacock Prince*—ad t). D: Nam Nai-Choi. Ref: TV: Rainbow Video; Eng. titles. NST! 4:33. Fango 107:59: also a Part II. Weisser/ATC: *Saga of the Phoenix*, sequel. Imagi Smr'95:18. With Wang Chow-Feng, Yuen Biao.

A "chain of natural calamities" heralds the "revival of evil," as the witch Raga enlists Hell Virgin Ashura in an attempt to bring back the latter's father, Hell King, through one or more of the four doors to (and from) hell, which are located, respectively, in Nepal, Japan, Hong Kong, and Tibet. In an impressive display of various effects—stopmo, makeup, puppet—Raga at one point transforms into a spider/*Xtro*-like creature. And the movie—a formula fantasy-horror-adventure—has its share of effects highlights, including some adorable stopmo critters found in a discarded hamburger container, a bitty "womanizing ghost," huge exhibition-hall dinosaurs which come to life, and a huge claw which emerges from a locker-room locker. In the Hong Kong sequence, evil takes the form of a mysterious killer (Raga?) who leaves male victims dead and drained of blood. ("Another dried corpse?")

**PEACOCK KING KUJAKUO** see *Kujakuo*

**PEACOCK PRINCE** see *Peacock King*

**The PEANUT BUTTER SOLUTION** (Can.) Swank/Prods. La Fete 1985 color 96m. SP, D: Michael Rubbo. Ref: PFA notes. TVG: "two friendly ghosts." V 12/4/85: burned-down haunted mansion. Stanley: haunted house. Ecran F 65:70.

Intense scare makes boy's hair fall out; his concoction brings it back.

**PEARL SPRITE** (J) 1984 (*Shinjuro*). D: N. Ohbayashi. Ref: Weisser/JC. With I. Furuya, I. Nagato.

"Detective's girl friend is possessed by the spirit of a dead prostitute...."

**PEE-WEE'S BIG ADVENTURE** WB/Aspen-Robert Shapiro 1985 color 90m. D: Tim Burton. SP: Phil Hartman, Paul Reubens, Michael Varhol. Ref: TV. Bob Moore. V 7/31/85.

Comedy-fantasy has horror and monster sequences, including one in which the ghost of truck driver Large Marge (Alice Nunn) haunts the stretch of highway where she died in a terrible accident, another in which a "Godzilla"-type movie is filming, and visualized nightmares re a Tyrannosaurus eating Pee-wee's (Reubens) bike and, later, said bike being sent to hell.... Pee-wee Herman's personality turns out to be more interesting than his adventure, and it's most in evidence here in the introductory sequence set in his "precious" house. But is he live or audio-animatronic?

**PEEP POP 2** (Thai) c1988? color c90m. Ref: TV: All Asian Video; no Eng. Chao Thai Market: above is tr t.

In a bizarre comic-gore sequence, a lip-licking zombie and an old-woman zombie leap past one another. In the process, the first zombie yanks out the other's innards, while the old woman dearly holds on to what's left and runs off. The younger zombie-ghoul chases her and pulls out more organs, but apparently rejects them as inferior grade, and the old woman restores her vitals. In another funny sequence—in this weird mixture of low comedy and gore—a guy dons a corset for protection, but the zombie pulls out a very large pair of shears. All this and a talking skeleton too. Offbeat stuff in this apparent sequel.

**PEEP POP 3** (Thai) c1989? color c98m. Ref: TV: vt; no Eng. Chao Thai Market: above is tr t.

Third in the series is just as silly as the second, but with less gore. This one features a zombie that, knifed, falls and turns into a skeleton ... *Halloween* music ... an odd bicyclist-riding-on-air scene ... a surprise zombie at the end ... and, best of all, a zombie "mouse"-trap baited with entrails. (Happy entrails to you....)

**PENE NEL VENTRE, Le** see *Osceno Disiderio, L'*

**PENETRATION** see *Slasher ... Is the Sex Maniac, The!*

**PENETRATOR** Fresh Video 1991 color c80m. D: "Orgy Georgie." SP: "Mad Dad Dan." Ref: vc box. no Adam '91, '92 or '93. With Angela Summers, Nikki Wilde, Brigitte Aime.

Post-nuke imitation of *Terminator* films.

**PENG! DU BIST TOT!** (W.G.) WDR-Delta (Claus-Wesemann) 1987 (1986) color 96m. D: Adolf Winkelmann. SP: Walter Kempley, Mathias Seelig. Mus: Piet Klocke. Ref: V 4/15/87: "film dies shortly after opening titles." Dr. Rolf Giesen. With Ingolf Lueck, Rebecca Pauly, Hermann Lause, Volker Spengler.

Robot, mad scientist, murder-by-computer. *Bang! You're Dead!* - tr t.

**PENSIONE PAURA** see *Hotel of Fear*

**PENTAGRAM** see *First Power, The*

**The PEOPLE ACROSS THE LAKE** NBC-TV/Col-TV 1988 color c90m. D: Arthur Allan Seidelman. Story, Tel, P: Dalene Young. Story, P: Bill McCutchen. Ph: Richard Leiterman. Mus: Dana Kaproff. PD: David Fischer. SpFX: Bill Orr. Mkp: Linda A. Brown. SdFxSup: Sync-Pop. Ref: TV. SFChron 10/3/88. With Valerie Harper, Gerald McRaney, Tammy Lauren, Dorothy Lyman, Daryl Anderson, Jeff Kizer.

Clutching hand (which belongs to the dead body in Lake Tomahawk)—tales of mutilated bodies ("My husband thought he saw something in the lake")—false alarm (a boy playing mad-killer-with-knife)—quite guessable killer. Shallow TV pseudo-splatter movie.

**The PEOPLE UNDER THE STAIRS** Univ/Alive Films (Maddalena, Besser) 1991 color 102m. SP, D: Exec Co-P: Wes Craven. Ph: Sandi Sissel. Mus: Don Peake. PD: Bryan Jones. SpFxSup: Peter Chesney. SpMkpFX: KNB. SpFX: Image Engineering; (key coord) Dean Miller. Mech Dog FX: Robert Clark & Roark Prods. Opt: Howard Anderson. Ref: TV: MCA-Univ HV. V 11/11/91. ad. SFChron 11/2/91. Sacto Bee 11/6/91. With Brandon Adams, Everett McGill, Wendy Robie, A. J. Langer, Kelly Jo Minter, Yan Birch (stairmaster), Wayne Daniels (stairperson #1).

"Daddy cut out the bad parts and put the boys in the cellar." The Slum Landlord from Hell also skins and eviscerates intruders into his house/fort in order to feed the "boys." ("Keep 'em real hungry.") Hard to tell how we're supposed to take the Horrible Couple here (McGill and Robie)—as a Dickensian satire of bourgeois paranoia? As plain old politically-incorrect monsters who happen to be part of a scare machine? At any rate, their Monster World doesn't quite mesh with the bits and pieces we see of the Real World of the ghetto outside. Ending features the expected revolt of the people under....

**PEPENG KURYENTE—MAN WITH A THOUSAND VOLTS** (Fili) IMUS Prods. 1988? color c115m. SP, D: Jose Yandoc. Ph: Ramon Marcelino. Mus D: Mon Del Rosario. OptFX: Vic Penetrante. SdFX: Rodel Capule. Ref: TV: vt; some Eng. narration, titles. With Roman Revilla (Pepeng), Dante Rivero, Ramon Zamora, Marissa Delgado, Melissa Mendez, Gwen Avila, George Estregan Jr.

Weird lightning which sets church-tower bells chiming also charges them electrically. Pepeng, who has been haunting lightning-strike sites, breaks off the bells' "electrodes," takes them out into a rainstorm, and holds them up. They send electricity up, and lightning comes down and electrifies him. He finds that he can both heal the lame and electrocute his enemies. At one point, the electrodes direct electricity to the Bicol Region, and lightning is guided back to Pepeng, who, wounded by gunfire, is restored and becomes impervious to bullets.... Crazy variation on *Man Made Monster* is partly way-out science-fantasy, party routine melodrama. Very episodic.

**PER VIVERE MEGLIO, DIVERTITEVI CON NOI** (I) 1978 feature. D: F. Mogherini. Ref: Palmerini: an E.T. segment.

**PERFECT FAMILY** Para HV 1993 color feature. D: E. W. Swackhamer. Ref: SFChron Dtbk 8/8/93. V 3/15/93:20 (rated). With Bruce Boxleitner, Jennifer O'Neill, Joanna Cassidy.

Sociopath who specializes in slaying families.

**The PERFUME OF THE LADY IN BLACK** (I) Euro Int'l.(Giovanni Bertolucci) 1974 color/ws feature (*Il Profumo delle Signora in Nero*). Story, SP, D: Francesco Barilli. Story, SP: also Massimo D'Avack. Ph: Mario Masini. Mus: Nicola Piovani. AD: Franco Velchi. Mkp: Manlio Rocchetti. Ref: TV: MV; Eng. dubbed. Zirschky. Palmerini. With Mimsy Farmer, Mario Scaccia, Daniela Barnes, M. Bonuglia, Nike Arrighi, Donna Jordan.

"Another one of your fantasies?" African witchcraft seems to drive a woman, Silvia, mad: She sees a "ghost" in a mirror, talks to a mysterious little girl (who seems to be Silvia as a girl), and employs a cleaver in order to get guests for her mad tea party.... The latter sequence is the chief highlight of this atmospherically photographed cross between *Repulsion* and "Alice in Wonderland." All this and a good, Morricone-ish score, a couple of hand-fed cats—or, rather, cats fed a human hand—and an out-of-key ending in cannibalism which seems an aftereffect of the success of the original *Night of the Living Dead.* Film apparently has nothing to do with a similarly-titled Gaston Leroux book.

**The PERILS OF GWENDOLINE** (F) Samuel Goldwyn/Parafrance-Films del l'Alma-G.P.F.I. 1984 color/ws 102m. (89m.-U.S.) (aka *Gwendoline*). SP, D: Just Jaeckin. From John Wil(l)ie's comic strip, "The Adventures of Gwendoline." Mus: Pierre Bachelet. Mkp: Reiko Kurk, D. Colladant. Ref: V 2/22/84. TV. Stanley: aka *Perils of Gwendoline: in the Land of the Yik Yak;* '85-U.S. With Tawny Kitaen, Brent Huff, Zabou, Bernadette Lafont, Jean Rougerie.

Ingredients in this sub-*Barbarella,* pseudo-camp science-fantasy: a lost kingdom of women (a strange epidemic has killed off the men), caged cannibals, a poison wind, earthquake-making machinery, and a premonitory dream. The unappealingly-dubbed voices of hero and heroine don't help this English-language version.

**PERRY MASON: THE CASE OF THE SINISTER SPIRIT** NBC-TV/Fred Silverman Co. (Strathmore Prods. & Viacom-TV) 1987 (1986) color c90m. D: Richard Lang. Tel: Anne Collins. Story: Hargrove, Steiger, Benest, Wurtz. Based on characters created by Erle Stanley Gardner. Ph: Arch Bryant. Mus: Dick DeBenedictis; Fred Steiner. AD: Paul Staheli. Mkp: Dee Sandella, Patti Dallas. SdFX: Echo. Title Des: Wayne Fitzgerald. Ref: TV. TVG. Scheuer. With Raymond Burr, Robert Stack, Dwight Schultz, Kim Delaney, William Katt, Dennis Lipscomb, Leigh Taylor-Young, Jack Bannon, Barbara Hale, David Ogden Stiers, Percy Rodrigues.

David Hall, the author ("Cry of the Dead," etc.)—who is "right up there with Stephen King"—is the apparent victim here. Other characters include a psychic (Bannon), an astrologer (Lipscomb), the "queen of the slice-and-dice films" (Taylor-Young), a woman (Delaney) who is being driven mad by ghostly voices, and the "ghost" of John Warrenfield, who supposedly haunts the hotel he built and "walks the hallways at night."

This cross between a standard "Perry Mason" mystery and a Universal Inner Sanctum chiller doesn't work, though it has a better-than-average TV-scare-movie score. Burr's Mason is phlegmatic until the final, twisty speech/solution. Stiers is a capable, slow-burn, always-overruled replacement for the late William Talman.

**PERSECUCION INFERNAL** (Mex) 1991 color c90m. Story, D: Paco del Toro. Story, Prod Exec: G. Paz. Ph: Ariel Castillero. Mus: R. L. Cortez. SpFX: Raul Gutierrez. Mkp: Lilia Diosdado. Ref: TV: no Eng. TVG. With Humberto Zurita, Eric del Castillo, Andres Bonfiglio, Roberto Ballesteros, Gerardo Paz, Paolah Ochoa.

Stranded motorists interrupt a satanic ritual and prevent a human sacrifice. One witness is murdered; another has (visualized) nightmares of the ceremony. At the end, cops interrupt a second attempted sacrifice.... Cheap action/horror flick. Hollow sound and flat look suggest it was shot on videotape.

**PERVERSE COUNTESS** see *Comtesse Perverse, La*

**PERVERSE KISS OF SATAN, The** see *Devil Kiss*

**PESADILLA MORTAL** (Mex) Acuario Films 1986? color c98m. SP, D: Alfredo B. Crevenna. SP: also Carlos Valdemar. SP, P: Raul Ramirez. Story: F. Villeli. Ph: F. Bojorquez. Mus D: Ernesto Cortazar. Mkp: Carmen Olivares. Ref: TV: Quality Video; no Eng.; Mortal Nightmare - tr t. With Raul Ramirez, Ana Luisa Peluffo, Victor Junco, Rosa Gloria Chagoyan, Luis Uribe, Laura Mayer, Milton Rodriguez.

A woman has a (visualized) nightmare re a gloved stalker. It turns out to be a premonition of the murder of her mother. She later has recurrences of the nightmare and another premonition of (attempted) murder.... Hokey mystery with horrific overtones.

**PESADILLA SANGRIENTA** (Mex) Grupo Galindo & Televicine 1990 (1989) color c85m. Story, SP, D: Pedro Galindo III. SP: also Santiago & Eduardo Galindo. Ph: J. C. Osorio. Mus: Pedro P. Salinas. SpFxD: Ramon Loranca. OptFX: Manuel Sainz. Min: Alfredo & Gabriel Garcia. Mkp: Eugenia Luna. Ref: TV: Mex-American HV; no Eng.; Bloody Nightmare - tr t. With Pedro Fernandez, Tatiana, Joaquin Cordero, Luis Camarena (bruja), Renata de los Rios, Alfredo Gutierrez, Ernesto Casillas, Ernesto Carregha.

Episodic fantasy-horror feature has some enjoyable frissons, including a doll-thing which eats a bloodied witch figure from a fiesta display and becomes a big-tailed demon ... a little girl who levitates, then disappears into a wall ... coins which zip up to the wall and stick to it ... a pulsating jack-o'-lantern which goes "Boo!" at the heroine ... and a room which rocks and rolls, barrel-like (with the heroine inside).

**PESTICIDE** see *Raisins de la Mort, Les*

**PET SEMATARY**  Para/Richard P. Rubinstein (Tim Zinnemann) 1989 color 103m. D: Mary Lambert. SP: Stephen King, from his novel. Mus: Elliot Goldenthal. SpMkp: (des) Lance Anderson; (fx) David Anderson. MechFX: (coord) Peter Chesney; Image Engineering. SpVisFX: (sup) Gene Warren Jr.; Fantasy II. OptFX: Cinema Research. Tombstone Lettering: Manya K. Rubinstein. Ref: TV. V 4/26/89. SFExam 4/21/89. HR 4/24/89. Sacto Union 5/7/89: "It's time to boycott horror films." MFB'89:341-2. With Dale Midkiff, Fred Gwynne, Denise Crosby, Brad Greenquist (Victor Pascow), Miko Hughes (Gage Creed), Andrew Hubatsek (Zelda), Peter Stader (Timmy Baterman).

"The ground is sour!" Or, The Cat Came Back. Fantasy-horror mishmash includes child-menace cliches with a zombie-boy (Hughes), "Monkey's Paw" elements, a zombie-cat, a "graveyard for pets killed on the road," and "good ghost" Victor Pascow, a sort of Obi-Wan Kenobi/moral-spiritual prompter of the living.... Aka The Dud Zone. King, stolid and humorless here, counts too much on Emotional Intensity and evocations of Real-Life Feelings of Guilt, Anger, Hate, etc. At least two too many innocent-child-in-imminent-danger scenes.

**PET SEMATARY TWO**  Para (R. S. Singleton) 1992 color 100m. D: Mary Lambert. SP: Richard Outten. Ph: Russell Carpenter. Mus: Mark Governor. PD: Michelle Minch. Mech & SpFX: Peter Chesney. SpFxMkp & Animatronics: Steve Johnson. Dead Animal FX: Bill Johnson. Ref: V 9/7/92: "sorely lacking in subtlety." SFChron 9/1/92: "just goes through the motions." SFExam 8/29/92. With Edward Furlong, Anthony Edwards, Clancy Brown, Jared Rushton, Darlanne Fluegel.

Living-dead cop, dog, etc.

**PET SHOP**  Para/Moonbeam 1994 color 88m. D: Hope Perello. SP: Goldstein, Suddeth, Friedman. Idea & Co-P: P. von Sholly. Ph: Karen Grossman. Mus: Reg Powell. PD: Milo. SpMkpFX: Alchemyfx. Creature FX/Sup Puppets: Mark Rappaport. VisFX: (sup) Paul Gentry; See3 et al. Transformation FX: DHD Postimage. SpFxCoord: John Cazin. Ref: TV: Para video. Martin. With Leigh Ann Orsi, Spencer Vrooman, Joanne Baron, David Wagner, Terry Kiser, Jane Morris (Mrs. Zimm), Jeff Michalski (Mr. Zimm).

Cactus Flats, Arizona. The Zimms, an alien couple, take over the local pet shop. They can temporarily transform their alien pets—which include a Gremlin-type, a dog-type, a turtle-type, and a lizard-type—into Earth creatures, and Mr. Zimm's third eye (in his forehead) shoots a "freezing" ray. Their business: caging and shipping Earth kids to, apparently, alien pet shops.... A slew of unfunny comic characters, and bitty aliens more immobile than cute. Duly noted bit of cleverness: the burnt-out "P" in the "PET SHOP" sign. (So it's an "ET Shop.")

**PETIT CHAPERON ROUGE, Le**  see *Company of Wolves, The*

**PHANTASM II**  Univ/Spacegate Corp. (R. A. Quezada) 1988 color c96m. SP, D: Don Coscarelli. Mus: Fred Myrow. SpMkpFX: Mark Shostrom. SpVisFX: (sup) Justin Klarenbeck; Dream Quest Images; Lookout Mountain, Pat O'Neill. SpFX: Wayne Beauchamp. Sphere: Steve Patino. Laser FX: Carl Hannigan. Flying FX: Robert McCarthy. Ref: TV: MCA HV. V 7/13/88. SFExam 7/8/88. SFChron Dtbk 7/24/88. MFB'89:24-5. Scheuer. McCarty II. Martin. Hound. Phantom. Maltin '92. With James Le Gros, Reggie Bannister, Angus Scrimm (The Tall Man), Paula Irvine, Samantha Phillips (Alchemy); Felix Silla et al (stunts).

"You come to us!" The original re-animator, The Tall Man, is back ("He's harvesting the entire town!"), and he's leaving a trail of "murdered" towns behind him. New thrills: the "slice-and-dice" sphere ... a nasty "calling card" growing out of the phantom Liz's (Irvine) back ... an okay living-corpse-in-the-widow's-bed shock ... a levitating, strangling crucifix ... "scream"-atorium horror (where The Tall Man processes his zombie slaves) ... impressive sphere-through-torso-generated spastic gyrations ... a crass chainsaw stunt-gag ... a peek (a la the original) into the world beyond ... a *From beyond* squizzy springing out of The Tall Man's sphere-punctured forehead ... and pretty good ghastly melting effects as the acid wrecks him, at least temporarily.

Apart from the above highlights, this follow-up to *Phantasm* has little or nothing to offer. The story reduces to a sort of *Death Wish* of the supernatural: The protagonists vow revenge on The Tall Man for wreaking havoc with their loved ones.

See also: *Transylvania Twist.*

**PHANTASM III: LORD OF THE DEAD**  Starway Int'l. 1993 color 91m. SP, D, P: Don Coscarelli. Ph: Chris Chomyn. Mus: F. Myrow, C.L. Stone. PD: Ken Aichele. SphereFX: D.K. Prior. SpMkp: Mark Shostrom, Dean Gates. SpFX: Kevin McCarthy. Digital FX: The Computer Film Co. Laser FX: Precision Projection Systems. Ref: TV: MCA-Univ HV: *Phantasm: Lord of the Dead* - cr t; *Phantasm III* - end cr t. SFChron 12/17/94. 1/21/95. With Reggie Bannister, Angus Scrimm, A. Michael Baldwin, Bill Thornbury (Jody), Gloria Lynne Henry, Kevin Connors, Irene Roseen (demon nurse).

"The Tall Man got my family." More grossness with the spheres (or "chrome brain drains"), yellow bodily fluids, miscellaneous ghouls, and a "very tall man from God knows where." (The Tall Man is still processing new workers.) Plus: hatchet gore, a deadly frisbee, a leapin' lizard creature, and Jody-in-a-sphere.... Lively, episodic. With a neat man-into-sphere computer effect and more boring sphere gore.

**The PHANTOM**  Actiondramas/Artclass 1931 62m. D: Alvin J. Neitz. SP: Allan James. Ph: Lauron Draper. Ref: TV. Lee(p)(FDY '31). Greg Luce. no Lentz. no Turner/Price. With Guinn Williams, Allene Ray, Niles Welch, Tom O'Brien, Sheldon Lewis ("The Thing"), Wilfred Lucas, Violet Knights, William Gould, Bobby Dunn, William Jackie.

A wriggling-fingered, cloaked skulker (Lewis)—aka "this terrible thing!"—haunts both John Hampton's (Lucas) home (a "spooky old place") and Dr. Weldon's (Gould) sanitarium on Country Drive. The doctor is an "old quack" who specializes in brain transplantation, or rather in transplanting cells from one side of the subject's brain to the other. At the end, he prepares the heroine (Ray) for a little experiment.

This long-lost, forgotten horror is an odd, haphazard mixture of elements from old-dark-house thrillers, mad-doctor movies, and *Dracula*. The extremely cursory script concludes on the oddest note of all: "The Thing," it transpires, is not "The Phantom" (a "human tiger")—he's just "The Thing." "The Phantom" is his boss. Clearly, the goal is not coherence, simply random thrills. Sloppy cross-cutting catches characters in roughly the same poses they held minutes earlier. And since the villainous characters have little to do but wriggle their fingers (a Lewis effect both comic and creepy) and make threats, the comic characters—Knights, Dunn, Jackie—dominate. Some of the contributions of the latter three are so bad they're almost good. Jackie is especially bizarre as a Renfield-like loony.

**PHANTOM, The** see *Defenders of the Earth*

**PHANTOM BROTHER** Southgate 1988 color 92m. D: William Szarka. Ref: Fango 89:12. Hound: "even thinner than it sounds." no Martin. With Jon Hammer, Patrick Molloy, Mary Beth Pelshaw.

Teen's dead brother comes back, starts killing people.

**The PHANTOM CHIVALRY** (H.K.) 198-? color/ws c88m. (*The Gallant* - cr t). SP, D: Hsieh Kuang-Nan. Ref: TV: Quality Video; Eng. titles; above is ad t. With Yang Hui-Sang.

The spirit of Chao Lin haunts Illusion Lake and prevents the greedy from obtaining the area's "millennial ginseng." The ghost of Wu Tung (who has a "strange face") is not so particular about whom he attacks, and he can sear trees in half and throw the pieces at his victims. When Wu Tung threatens the selfless hero, Chao Lin comes to the latter's rescue.... The lake-and-woodlands setting is suitably atmospheric, but the film is spare and slow. Interesting effects (e.g., Wu Tung's face peeling) and close-ups of local insect life.

**PHANTOM CITY** see *Haunted Gold*

**\*2 The PHANTOM CREEPS** 1939. Ref: TV. TGSP2. Lee. Hardy/SF. Lentz. Lennig. Stanley. no Weldon. Martin. Hound. Phantom. With Dorothy Arnold, Jack C. Smith, Karl Hackett, Bud Wolfe (robot); Lee J. Cobb (stock footage).

Bela Lugosi is Dr. Alex Zorka, in his own (written) words, "the greatest genius the world has ever known." In a terrible, glorious, ultra-camp performance ("Fools! Fools! Let them search!"), he sports his Ygor beard and makes wild and crazy pronouncements: "One by one, my enemies will be disposed of, until I'm Master of the Universe!" (Willis Cooper, who wrote *Son of Frankenstein* the same year, also contributed the story for this serial.) Extra added attractions: a power source ("part of a meteorite that fell in Africa centuries ago"—illustrated by *Invisible Ray* footage) which heals a bullet wound, and a ray gun which makes the invisible visible. All this and Edward Van Sloan, too. Hero-type: "Ghosts don't carry heavy boxes around, Perkins!"

**The PHANTOM EMPIRE** American-Independent 1989 (1987) color 83m. SP, D, P: Fred Olen Ray. SP: also T. L. Lankford. Mus: Robert Garrett. SpVisFX: Mark D. Wolf, Wizard Works, Cory Kaplan. SpMkpFX: Paul M. Rinehard. SpFxAnim: Bret Mixon. Sp Vehicle: Dean Jeffries. Ref: TV: Prism Ent. video. V 8/9/89. Hound. Martin. With Ross Hagen, Jeffrey Combs, Dawn Wildsmith, Robert Quarry, Susan Stokey, Michelle Bauer, Russ Tamblyn, Sybil Danning, Michael D. Sonye, Gary J. Levinson (mutant), Tricia Brown (cavegirl).

A Miskatonic Institute archaeologist (Combs) and others enter Bronson Caverns searching for the "lost city of R'Lyla," or "Rilah." They find footage from *Planet of Dinosaurs* (including stopmo stegosaurs), mutant cannibals, women in bikinis, and an alien queen (Danning) and her robot (Robby the Robot).... Tired, jokey sf-adventure scraps the sf-Western novelty of the original serial in favor of jiggle with Danning, Bauer, and Stokey. Quarry is the only actor who does any acting.

**\*PHANTOM FROM SPACE** 1953. Story: M. Wilder. Ref: TV. Maureen Smith. Warren/KWTS! Lentz. Hardy/SF. Lee. Stanley. Hound. Scheuer. Martin. Phantom. Maltin '92.

"There wasn't any head in that helmet." An "X-man" (Dick Sands)—a "superhuman with an intelligence far superior to our own"—comes to Earth in a magnetically-powered ship. Stationary and mobile radar units track the electronic disturbance his passage creates.... Lighting in *Phantom from Space* is so noir that it's often hard to make out the contents of a given shot. The movie's look is cheap but eerie, and if the "invisible man" effects are elementary, the emphasis is on suspense, not spectacle, and the documentary-like narration is filled with facts and figures re the California locations—San Francisco, Morro Bay, Santa Monica. Much indiscriminate handling by the characters of the phantom's highly radioactive suit/helmet.

**\*The PHANTOM FROM 10,000 LEAGUES** Milner Bros. Prods. 1956(1955) c80m. AD: Earl Harper. SpMkp: Paul Blaisdell. SpFX: Jack Milner. Ref: TV. Warren/KWTS! Hardy/SF. V 1/11/56. Ottoson/AIP. Weldon. Glut/CMM. Phantom. Lentz. Stanley. With Kathy (so spelled in credits) Downs, Vivi Janiss, Michael Garth, Pierce Lyden, Rodney Bell.

Ingredients include a fisherman found burnt in the waters of Baker's Cove ... an undersea uranium ore deposit ... a "sea serpent"—a "hideous beast that defies description," a mutation of a sea creature—which draws energy from the shaft of light emanating from the ore ... and Dr. Ted Stevens (Kent Taylor), author of "Biological Effects of Radiation on Marine Life" .... Borecard: tired characterizations and plotting ... a monster costume more cute than scary ... much skulking and spying ... okay location photography by Brydon Baker ... and pleasantly banal music by Ronald Stein.

**The PHANTOM LUTE** (H.K.) DL Film Co. 1985? color c95m. D: Tu Zhong Xun (sp?). SP: Chen You Xin (sp?). Ref: TV: Quality Video; Eng. titles; Quy Ty Ba - Viet t? V 9/14/83:37: sfa *Demon of the Lute*? With Ja Ling(sp?), Ze Feng.

When Hsiao Feng repulses his advances, Gen. Chao stabs her and burns the body. She returns as a vengeful ghost. At one point, Chao slices her in half and finds that there are two of her. When a "local god" tells her that she cannot take the law into her own hands, she gets the general to confess to his crime before a judge. Bonus: a Taoist "ghost catcher" who shrinks Hsiao Feng.

Choppy script and one-dimensional characters. The local god and the spirits who, later, prevent Hsiao Feng from entering the courtroom to give testimony re her murder seem to be introduced simply to prolong the story and delay her revenge. The scene in which she appears to her dying father is milked but still rather touching.

**PHANTOM OF DEATH** (I) Vidmark/Globe Films & Tandem & Reteitalia (Pietro Innnocenzi) 1988 color 91m. (*Un Delitto Poco Comune. Off Balance* - export t. *House on Rubens St.* - early t). D: Ruggero Deodato. SP: Battagnini, Mannino, Clerici. Mus: Pino Donaggio. Ref: V 1/18/89: "York ... impressive ... otherwise undistinguished Italian horror pic." Palmerini. Horacio Higuchi. Hound. Scheuer. Martin: "flat." With Michael York, Donald Pleasence, Edwige Fenech, Mapi Galan.

Rare disease turns concert pianist into homicidal old man. *An Unusual Crime* - tr t.

**PHANTOM OF TERROR** see *Bird with the Crystal Plumage, The*

**PHANTOM OF THE CABARET** VCA 1989 color feature. D: Henri Pachard. Ref: Adam '90. With Keisha, Bionca, Sharon Kane, Jamie Gillis.

Disfigured "phantom" (Gillis) haunts Paris cabaret.

**PHANTOM OF THE MALL** Fries Ent. (Tom Fries) 1989 (1988) color 88m. (aka *Eric's Revenge*). D: Richard Friedman. Story, SP: Scott Schneid. SP: also Robert King, Tony Michelman. Story: also Fred Ulrich. Mus: Stacy Widelitz. PD: Gary T. New. SpMkpFX: Matthew Mungle. SpFX: SpFx Services; (coord) Larry Fioritto. Elec SdFxEd: Brian Vessa. Opt: Howard Anderson. Ref: TV. V 5/31/89. Hound. no Maltin '92. McCarty II. no Scheuer. Martin. With Derek Rydall, Jonathan Goldsmith, Kari Whitman, Morgan Fairchild, Ken Foree.

"What if Eric Matthews didn't really die in that fire?" A burn victim haunts the brand-new Midwood Mall and attacks those who would attack heroine Melody. Limp updating of *The Phantom of the Opera*. Padded with chases, visualized nightmares, a cover-up plot, etc.

**PHANTOM OF THE OPERA** (B) Emerald City Prods. 1987 anim color 48m. SP, D, P: Al Guest, Jean Mathieson. From Gaston Leroux's novel. Mus: Gerard Victory. SpFxAnim: Julian Hynes. Ref: TV: CHE video. VSB. Bowker '90 supp. no PFA. vc box.

"I am the Red Death stalking abroad!" Paris, 1890. Is the horribly scarred, "tall, skeleton-like figure" haunting the "ghost box" at the opera the "spirit of music" or the "world's greatest composer"? Woebegone cartoon version of the famous tale features painfully unfluid animation, and the dialogue is equally stilted. Some fair work with shadow and color. Oddest bit of horrific

atmosphere: the ratcatcher who appears like a *Curse of the Demon* fireball driving maddened rat hordes before him.

See also the following and *Aullido del Diablo, El. Gremlins 2. Killer Tomatoes Eat France! Phantom of the Opera* (P). *Waxwork.*

**The PHANTOM OF THE OPERA** (U.S.-B) 21st Century & Breton Film (Harry Alan Towers) 1989 color 93m. D: Dwight H. Little. SP: Duke Sandefur, from a screenplay by Gerry O'Hara, and based on the Gaston Leroux novel. Mus: Misha Segal. MkpFX: Kevin Yagher Prods.; MMI (John Buechler). SdFxDes: Martin Maryska. Ref: TV. MFB'90:172-3. V 11/8/89. Sacto Bee 11/8/89. Scheuer. McCarty II. Martin. Hound. Maltin '92. With Robert Englund (Erik Destler), Jill Schoelen, Alex Hyde-White, Bill Nighy, Terence Harvey, Stephanie Lawrence.

"I am the music!" Composer Erik Destler—who "sold his soul to the devil so the world would love him for his talent"—alternately haunts stages in turn-of-the-century London and present-day New York City. A "thing from hell," he has become a "composer by day, serial killer by night." The key to his existence: Destroy the music and you destroy Erik.

In one or two scenes, Englund hints that he might be an interesting actor even in non-Freddy roles. Unfortunately, the movie goes more for the gross than the grand and keeps making running-time-consuming concessions to the New Yuchh—e.g., Erik methodically peeling off pieces of borrowed skin from his mutilated face.

See also *Danse Macabre* (aka *Phantom of the Opera 2*).

**PHANTOM OF THE RANGE** Victory 1938 58m. D: Ed Hill. SP: Basil Dickey. Ph: Bill Hyer. Ref: V 6/15/38: "one of Tom Tyler's top pieces." With T. Tyler, Beth Marion, Forrest Taylor, Charles King, John Elliott, Sammy Cohen.

"Juve trade will relish this hillside scamper to chase the ghosts from the old homestead.... Ghost rides the homestead to keep people away from ... buried treasure."

**PHANTOM OF THE RITZ** SGE/Hancock Park (C.M. Plone) 1988 color 88m. D: A. Plone. SP: T. Dempsey. Ph: R.W. McLeish. Mus: J. Madara, D. White. PD: A. Ricardi. FxMkp: Dean Gates. Ref: TV: Prism video. SFChron Dtbk 5/31/92. Martin: "fun in a cheap sort of way." Fango 118:35: "flat, unfunny." With Peter Bergman, Deborah Van Valkenburgh, Russell Curry, Joshua Sussman (The Phantom), The Coasters.

"I feel funny about this theatre." The big, scarred skulker who haunts the dilapidated theatre was burned in a car accident; steroids made him big and "overly aggressive." He has a Phantom of the Opera-like lair and makes bad predictions. ("Cleveland will continue to stink up the American League.") Mild, dawdling mixture of horror and nostalgia (for the Fifties) is strong on pop-culture references (down to "Winky Dink and You"), weak on story. The Victor Buono-ish Phantom has a few wry moments.

**PHANTOM QUEST CORP.** (J) Pioneer & Oniro & Animaze (Morijiri-Inoue-Morosawa) 1994 anim color 59m. (*You-gen-kai-sya*). D: Koichi Chigira, Morio Asaka. SP: Mami Watanabe, T. Urahata. Concept: M. Juzo. Ph: H. Shirai. Mus: J. Kanezaki.

AD: S. Uehara. SpFX: K. Tanifuji. SdFX: S. Kurahashi. Ref: TV: Pioneer video; Eng. dubbed. Voice: T. Seki (vampire).

"I found Dracula's bride." Two tales re Ayaka Kisaragi's company, Phantom Quest, which exterminates "evil spirits." Ingredients include Dracula's casket, Dracula himself, "midnight murders," a "demon's calling card," a laser weapon, and a floating demon.... *Ghostbusters,* anyone? Occasionally stylish, but banal horror-comedy over-exerts itself.

**PHANTOM 2040: THE ANIMATED MOVIE** (U.S.-F?) Hearst-Minos-France 3 1994 anim color c97m. Ref: vc box: Metropia, year 2040.

**PHANTOM X** VCA (Paul Thomas) 1989 color c80m. D: Thomas. Ref: Adam Erotomic V.5, number 10: "Gillis is a touch ludicrous stalking about in black with a white mask a la the modern Broadway show." With Aja, Jamie Gillis, Mike Horner, Nikki Knights, Shanna McCullough, Ron Jeremy.

*"The Phantom of the Opera* story is re-told, again."

**PHENOMENA** see *Creepers*

The **PHILADELPHIA EXPERIMENT** New World/John Carpenter (Douglas Curtis, J. B. Michaels) 1984 color 102m. D: Stewart Raffill. SP: William Gray, Michael Janover. Mus: Ken Wannberg. VisFX: Max W. Anderson, Julia Gibson, Beth Block, Larry Cavanaugh, SpFX Unltd. Ref: TV. SFExam 8/3/84. Horacio Higuchi. V 8/1/84. With Michael Pare, Nancy Allen, Eric Christmas, Bobby Di Cicco.

In 1943, the U.S. Navy destroyer *Eldredge* becomes radar invisible, then wholly invisible. In 1984, part of the *Eldredge* turns up after an anti-missile test in Nevada. It seems that the electromagnetic fields created in 1943 and 1984 "cross connected" and poked a "hole in the space-time continuum." The hole begins to suck everything into it.... The scientific puzzle here proves more interesting than the solution. The ending doesn't just stretch the imagination; it warps it. The cloud and electric effects help; Pare's affected performance doesn't.

**PHILADELPHIA EXPERIMENT II** Trimark Pictures/Mark Levinson (Alternate) 1993 color 97m. D: Stephen Cornwell. SP: Kevin Rock, Nick Paine. Ph: R. Schmidt. Mus: G. Couriet. PD: Armin Ganz. SpFX: Frank Ceglia. VisFxSup: Janet Muswell(sp?). OptFX: Tom Anderson; T&T. SpVisFX: Digital Magic. Ref: TV: Vidmark video. V 8/16/93:13 (rated). 11/29/93: "middling sci-fi sequel." With Brad Johnson, Marjean Holden, Gerrit Graham, James Greene.

"Imagine omnipresence!" Super-Stealth experiments are destabilizing the DNA of our hero David, the man on his own space-time continuum, and send him back, or sideways, to V-A Day (Victory over America), which is celebrated fifty years after a strange version of World War II. Meanwhile, a super-Stealth is sent through a "hole in time" into the heart of Nazi Germany.... An over-complicated plot, with too few payoffs, in more *It Happened Here* business. The scenes with Graham have an historical/satirical edge; the rest is routine, sometimes confusing action, in a post-World War III mode.

**PHILOMEL COTTAGE** see *Love from a Stranger*

**PHOENIX: WOLF NINJA** see *Miraculous Flower*

**PHOENIX THE WARRIOR** Action Int'l. (Peter Yuval/David Winters et al) 1988 (1987) color 86m. SP, D: Robert Hayes. SP: also Dan Rotblatt. Mus: Dan Radlauer. SpProsthMkp: Scot Coulter. SpFX: Chuck Whitten. Ref: TV. V 5/25/88. With Persis Khambatta, Kathleen Kinmont, Peggy Sands, James Emery.

"Give me the child and the male, and you can do what you want with the rest!" After the "bacteriological wars." Ingredients: mutants, female warriors, an ugly psychic "reverend mother," her "seed tank," and a little, male "future greatest fighter in the Wasteland." Hokey, overdone, occasionally broadly amusing.

**PHOTON SPACE SAILER STARLIGHT** or **PHOTON SPACE SAILER STARLIGHT ODIN** see *Odin*

**PHOTOS OF GIOIA** see *Foto di Gioia, Le*

**PHYSICAL CULTURE** see *Adrenaline*

**PICCOLI FUOCHI** (I) Intersound (Claudio Argento) 1985 color 95m. SP, D: Peter Del Monte. SP: also Giovanni Pascutto. Mus: Riccardo Zampa. Ref: V 11/13/85: an "original work that sometimes interests, sometimes irritates"; *Little Fires* - tr t. no Stanley. Ecran F 61:67. Palmerini: "good." With Dino Jakosic, Valeria Golino, Carlotta Wittig.

Spaceship takes away five-year-old's imaginary playmates—a robot, a dragon, and a "little king."

**PICKING UP THE PIECES** see *Bloodsucking Pharaohs in Pittsburgh*

The **PICKLE** Col (Patrick McCormick) 1993 color 103m. SP, D, P: Paul Mazursky. SpVisFX: Apogee; (sup) John Swallow. Ref: V 5/3/93: "mirthless." SFChron 5/1/93: "fairly good."

"Bizarre snatches from the dreaded film-within-a-film, which concerns a space trip embarked upon by a giant pickle grown and launched by farm kids."(V)

**PICKWICK PAPERS, The** see *Ghost Stories from the Pickwick Papers*

**PICNIC** see *Zombie Island Massacre*

**PICTURE OF DORIAN GRAY, The** see *Doriana Gray. Having Supper with a Vampire. Image of Dorian Gray in the Yellow Press, The.*

**PICTURE OF DORIAN GRAY IN THE YELLOW PRESS, The** see *Image of Dorian Gray in the Yellow Press, The*

**PICTURE THE DEVIL** see *Devil, The* (H.K.)

**PIED PIPER OF HAMELIN, The** see *Alice the Piper. Krysar. Timefighters in the Land of Fantasy.*

**PILGRIMAGE TO THE WEST** see *Uproar in Heaven*

**PIN...** (Can.) New World/Malofilm & Lance Ent. & Telefilm Canada (Pierre David & Rene Malo) 1988 color 102m. SP, D:

Sandor Stern. From Andrew Neiderman's novel. Ph: Guy Dufaux. Mus: P. M. Robinson. AD: F. Seguin. Pin Des: Atelier P&P. Ref: TV: NW Video. V 5/18/88: "well-made thriller." PT 12:45: "creepy psycho movie is one of the best in years." Martin: "superb." Fango 89:35: "compelling." SFChron 8/26/92: "worth a look"; Dtbk 8/23/92. With David Hewlett, Cyndy Preston, John Ferguson, Terry O'Quinn, Bronwen Mantel, Jonathan Banks (voice of Pin).

"Pin, the dummy whose glass eyes have an intense stare...." (SFC) "He's family." Dr. Linden (O'Quinn)—a ventriloquist or psychic—makes the anatomical dummy Pin (from "Pinocchio") seem to talk. After his death, his son Leon (Hewlett) brings it into the house and makes it "talk," and in one scene Pin seems to come to life and scare an intrusive aunt to death. (It's Leon using Pin's mask.) Where the "sensitive" and the exploitative meet. Echoes of *Dead of Night* and *Curse of the Cat People* here, but the dummy is finally just a scare device. Pretty predictable.

The **PINCUSHIONMAN** Celebrity/Ub Iwerks 1935 anim color 7m. (aka *Pincushion Man. Balloon Land. Balloonland*). Ref: TV: Video Bancorp (Castle Films). Maltin/OMAM. no LC. no Lee.

Beware the Pincushionman of the forest! Monster-trees and the boogeyman-like Pincushionman, the terror of Balloonyland (where living balloons dwell), haunt the forest. Okay cartoon.

The **PINFISH** (Thai) 198-? color/ws c96m. Ref: TV: vt; no Eng. Thai Video: above is tr t.

A man takes a machete to the head of a thieving pinfish-man (in a gory pre-credit sequence), and finds that his newborn is cursed. Full-grown, the latter can remove a magic bracelet and become a large-finned fish creature with deadly ray eyes and tail-fins. After each reversion to human form, this topless terror also acquires proper clothing. At the end, a mystic restores her to permanent human form. But another woman takes her place haunting the Thai rivers.... Unsophisticated effects, loose-fitting monster costume.

**PING AN YE** see *Night Caller*

**PINK CHIQUITAS** (Can.) Mt. Pleasant Prods. (Nicolas Stiliadis) 1986 color 82m. SP, D: Anthony Currie. Mus: Paul Zaza. SpVisFX: David Stipes; (roto) Kevin Kutchaver; (opt) Film FX; (anim) Rich Wessell, Alan Peppiatt. MechFX: Brock Jolliffe. Mkp: Nicole Demers. Laser FX: L. M. Roberts. Ref: TV. V 12/17/86. Ecran F 71:38-40. With Frank Stallone, John Hemphill, Elizabeth Edwards, Claudia Udy, Eartha Kitt (voice of Betty, the meteorite).

Apparently, the sound of a falling meteorite turns Earth women into lusty Amazons and makes their eyes glow and shoot pink rays which turn men into zombies. Also: "Little Nessie" and scenes from *Zombie Beach Party III*, with Mike Simone, at the Beansville Drive-In.... Occasionally sufficiently loony sf-comedy is more often just broadly silly. The actors are all from the Huntz Hall mold.

**PINK NOISE** series see *Hikaruon. Maryu Senki*

**PINOCCHIO AND THE EMPEROR OF THE NIGHT** New World/Filmation (Lou Scheimer) 1987 anim color 87m. D: Hal

Sutherland. SP: Robby London, Barry O'Brien, Dennis O'Flaherty. Mus: Marinelli, Banks. From Carlo Collodi's *The Adventures of Pinocchio*. SpFxSup: (anim) Bruce Heller; (ink & paint) A. S. Lupin; (airbrush) D. J. Zywicki. Ref: TV. V 11/4/87. SFExam 1/1/88. ad. Voices: Edward Asner, Tom Bosley, Jonathan Harris, Ricky Lee Jones, Don Knotts, Scott Grimes, Frank Welker.

The four-armed Emperor of the Night (voice: James Earl Jones), who rules the Empire of the Night (where dreams and nightmares come true), inveigles ex-puppet Pinocchio into signing away his will and freedom. Other macabre ingredients: a ghostly sailing vessel, a big spider, a monster-fish, and a "giant" frog which menaces bug town.

Bland story and animation are enlivened by some creepy sequences—the opener, for instance, in which a sinister carnival goes about setting itself up, or the scene in which Puppetino (voice: William Windom), "world's greatest puppet master," returns Pinocchio to his helpless puppet state. Jones' vocal authority as the Emperor atones somewhat for an appalling song sequence by the fairy godmother.

See also the following and *Silent Night, Deadly Night 5*.

**PINOCCHIO [SQUARE ROOT OF] 964** (J) Apollon Inc./IPS Network & Gaga? 1991 color 97m. D: Shozon Fukui. Ref: TV: vt; no Eng. Weisser/JC. With Onn-Chan, Ranko.

Strangeness with a "sex machine," driller gore, a man with a seemingly melting head, a dancing root, a mysterious, hovering red light, and a man with an expandable head which gives off steam. Your Video MD advises fast-forwarding through the extended vomiting scene and the wallowing-in-the-garbage-cans scene, if not the whole movie.

**PINOY DRACULA** (Fili) R-Video 1984 color c60m. D: Juan Cairas. Ref: TV: Transpacific Video; no Eng. With Kadyo (Dracula), Sandra, Jose.

A voodoo spell turns one man into a nerdish-looking Dracula and another into a second vampire. Both make love, one after the other, with a woman upon whom they were spying. They fight over her; Dracula makes the other vampire submit to him; Dracula seems to win the woman. (This latter point is unclear since the final sex scene is simply a repetition of earlier footage.) Rudimentary X-rated Z-movie has no bite whatsoever, literal or figurative. (Blood does not seem to interest these "vampires.")

**PIRANHA WOMEN IN THE AVOCADO JUNGLE OF DEATH** see *Cannibal Women in the Avocado Jungle of Death*

**PISMA MERTVOGO CHELOVEKA** see *Letters from a Dead Man*

**PISTOLAS, Las** see *Placer de Matar, El*

*The **PIT AND THE PENDULUM** Nicholson-Arkoff 1961. SpFX: Pat Dinga. PhFX: Butler-Glouner, Ray Mercer. Scenic FX: Tom Matsumoto. Mkp: Ted Coodley. Ref: TV. AFI. V 8/9/61. Weldon. Hardy/HM. Lee. Lentz. Stanley. Maltin '92. COF 22:41. Phantom. Scheuer. Martin. Fango 89:15, 18-19. With Larry Turner (Nicholas as a boy), Charles Victor.

Spain, 1546. Nicholas Medina (Vincent Price), who as a boy witnessed his inquisitor-father Sebastian (Price again) wall up—alive—his adulterous wife, Isabella (Mary Menzies), claims that the "malignant atmosphere" of the family castle killed his (Nicholas') wife, Elizabeth (Barbara Steele). Secretly, however, he fears that she too was entombed alive: She, or her spirit, apparently, now plays the harpsichord, shreds his portrait of her, and rises, accusingly, from the grave. It transpires that she is not dead, but alive, and plotting with Dr. Leon (Antony Carbone) to drive Nicholas insane. They succeed all too well: In his distracted mind, Nicholas has become Sebastian, and Elizabeth, Isabella. He scares Dr. Leon into the titular pit, submits Elizabeth's brother (John Kerr) to torture-by-descending-pendulum—believing each, in turn, to be Isabella's lover—and dies (in the pit) leaving Elizabeth shut up alive in the torture chamber.

This train of events proves almost as confusing for the viewer as it does for Nicholas. Scriptwriter Richard Matheson piles on the horrificness. He obviously enjoys phrases like "miasma of barbarity," and his enjoyment is not unfaithful to the spirit of the Poe ("oh! horror!") original. He pegs his horrors on a progression of plot which runs, roughly: Nicholas-as-apparent-villain ... Nicholas-as-apparent-madman ... Nicholas-as-madman. It's the final phase which is the most satisfying. The very triumph of the plotters is their undoing, and Elizabeth—who feigned premature burial—achieves premature burial.

Nicholas is no mere counter-plotter, as it seems for an instant that he might be. (When his laugh switches from Nicholas-maniacal to Sebastian-sarcastic.) The "method" in his madness is entirely providential—his "revenge" is unwitting, but complete. His madness "uses" him—it might be divine, or diabolical, inspiration. Even these climactic scenes, however, are marred by the mating of hero and pendulum—the "hero" has no place in the drama being enacted between Nicholas and Elizabeth. Dramatically, putting Leon under the pendulum would have made more sense—and better theatre. And all scenes are marred by the actors, all of them (except Price) pretty terrible. How can he be so good and they so bad?

See also the following and *Masque of the Red Death* (1989).

**The PIT AND THE PENDULUM** Para/Full Moon 1991 (1990) color 96m. D: Stuart Gordon. SP: Dennis Paoli, from Edgar Allan Poe's short story. Mus: Richard Band. SpFxMkp: Greg Cannom. SpFX: Giovanni Corridori. Opt: Mercer Titles, OptFxLtd. Ref: TV. V 6/17/91. Martin. With Lance Henriksen, Rona De Ricci, Jonathan Fuller, Jeffrey Combs, Frances Bay, Oliver Reed.

"I am the Inquisition!" The Grand Inquisitor Torquemada (Henriksen) is alive and well in 15th-century Toledo, Spain. Or at least alive. He and his assistants casually torture suspected witches and wall up alive intrusive elements from the Vatican. At one point, he tears out the innocent Maria's (De Ricci) tongue to keep secret the fact of his impotence. To save her, the witch Esmerelda (Bay) puts her into suspended animation, and Maria is buried alive, while Esmerelda is burned at the stake. As she dies, the witch condemns her tormentors (the "curse of the hag!") and seems to return from the dead to drive Torquemada into the pit, and our hero (Fuller) survives the pendulum.

Alternately high and low-minded, *The Pit and the Pendulum* plays like serious camp. It certainly qualifies as one of the more interesting of the recent Poe adaptations. As suggested above, the script incorporates ideas from Poe's "The Premature Burial" and "The Black Cat," as well as "The Pit and the Pendulum." Among stray goodies in the dialogue: "We hurt people" and, even better, "We don't do tongues."

**The PIT, THE PENDULUM AND HOPE** (Cz) Svankmajer 1983 anim short (*Jama, Kivdalo a Nadeje*). D: J. Svankmajer. Ref: SFChron 6/1/89: based on Poe's "The Pit and the Pendulum." Newman.

**PITUITARY HUNTER** (H.K.) Gold Phoenix Film (Steven Ng, Ng Fa) 1984? color 81m. (*Brain Theft* - reissue t). D: Pan Tan. Ref: TV: EVS; Eng. titles. TV: Tai Seng Video (Rising Dragon Video); Eng. titles. With Kwok Fong, Cheung King Fong, Lau Kwong, Wendy Leung.

"The question is why the murderer stole only human pituitaries." Much play with glands, and periodic discussions re glandular control of human growth, in this alternately horrific and mawkish tale of a killer dwarf intent on obtaining pituitary glands—from donors alive or dead. This cousin of Karloff's *The Ape* (with a dash of the Lewton *Body Snatcher*) is a conventional production with unconventional lines of dialogue—e.g., "A normal person wouldn't steal pituitaries," "The watchman in the used-cars field was killed, and his pituitary disappeared."

**El PLACER DE MATAR** (Sp) Laurenfilm & Errota & The Ministry of Culture (Antonio Llorens) 1988 color 100m. SP, D: Felix Rotoeta. SP: also Domingo Sanchez, Mario Gas, Angel Faccio, from Rotoeta's novel *Las Pistolas*. Mus: Carlos Miranda. Ref: V 10/19/88: "not much fun at all"; *The Pleasure of Killing* - tr t. With Antonio Banderas, Mathieu Carriere, Victoria Abril.

Two men kill for the love of killing.

**PLAN DELTA** (Dutch) Bob Visser (Karin Spiegel, Petra Deelen) 1989 (1988) color 90m. SP, D: Visser. Mus: Tuxedomoon. Ref: V 3/22/89: "fuzzy and uninteresting." With Bruce Geduldig, Hans Man in't Veld, Aram.

In the 23rd Century, there's one city for slaves, one for the slave masters.

**PLAN 69 FROM OUTER SPACE** Caballero 1993 color feature. D: Frank Marino. Ref: vc box: aliens, zombies. With Dyanna Lauren, Celeste, Peter North.

**PLANET BUSTERS** see *Birth*

**PLANET OF STORMS** see *Storm Planet*

**\*PLANET OF THE VAMPIRES** 1965. From Renato Pestriniero's story "One Night of 21 Hours." Set Des: Giorgio Giovannini. Mkp: Amato Garbini. ElecFX: Paolo Ketoff. Ref: TV: Thorn EMI-HBO Video; Eng. version. Lee. V 12/1/65. Hardy/SF. Weldon. VWB. With Stelio Candelli, Ivan Rassimov.

An electronic signal draws apparent Earth astronauts to Aura, a planet "made of fog" and inhabited by "unseen beings"—"luminous globes" from a "different plane of vibrations"—that can influence the sleeping mind and revivify and possess dead bodies.... Alternately terrific and pathetic Mario Bava sf-horror. The early, heavy-handed scenes in the plastic spaceship are camp at best, but the "sonic wail" sound effects and fog effects on the planet are eerie, and even the ship gets spooky when they turn the dialogue and lights off. A-1 chill: the slowmo rising of the "vampires." Atmosphere on a budget. Here and elsewhere, Bava and his writers create genuinely weird worlds, then seem to have trouble populating them.

**PLANETA BUR** see *Storm Planet*

**El PLANETA DE LAS MUJERES INVASORAS** (Mex) America/Corsa 1965 b&w 80m. D: A. B. Crevenna. SP: Alfredo Ruanova. Ref: Lee. Historia/Mexicano, V.9. Hardy/SF. Cinef 6/96:47. With Guillermo Murray, Adriana Roel, Lorena Velazquez.

"El planeta de la Noche Eterna." From the same TV series as *Gigantes Planetarios* aka *Gigantes Interplanetarios* aka *Planetary Giants.*

**PLANKTON** (I) 1993 color c93m. D: Joe D'Amato. Ref: TV: VSOM; Eng. version. Palmerini: D:A. Passeri. With Laura Di Palma.

"We have to find out what happened." Ingredients include an abandoned-at-sea Oceanographic Research Institute ship ... The Attack of the Carnivorous Flying Fish ... mutant plankton contaminated by radioactive waste ("It's horrendous!") ... Camp Time with Plankton Man—the fish-man talks and howls! ... and prime scenes with Mickey Finn and Joe Tentacle. Workprint has an understandably chaotic soundtrack and fun bits with tentacles from drains, etc.

**Les PLANS MYSTERIEUX** (Can.) Cine-Art/Cine Jeunes 1966 94m. (aka *Ti-Ken a Moscou*). D, P, Ph, Ed: Roger Laliberte. Ref: Canadian Feature Films: *The Mysterious Plans* - tr t. no Lee. With Anthony Tremblay, Jacques Provost.

Invention capable of scattering radioactive clouds.

**The PLANT** (Can.) Nat'l. Film Board of Canada 1983 short. Ref: SFChron Dtbk 12/18/88: plant grows, takes over everything in house.

**PLASTIC LITTLE** (J) KSS Films/MOVIC & Sony Music & Yoshimoto-Urushihara & Studio Pierrot & Animate (Ikeguchi-Fuji) 1994 anim color c60m. (*Plastic Little: The Adventures of Captain Tita* - ad t). D: Kinji Yoshimoto. Char Des & Created by: Satoshi Urushihara. Created by (also): K. Yoshimoto. SP: Masayori Sekimoto. Ph: A. Takahashi. Mus: T. Terashima. AD: T. Ishigaki. SpFX: Takashi Maekawa. SdFxD: F. Fujiyama. Ref: TV: A.D. Vision video; Eng. titles. Voice: Hiroshi Iknaka (Guizel).

Featured: the evil Guizel ... the *Cha Cha Maru,* a Pet Shop Hunter spaceship (it sells Earth sea creatures to shops on other planets) ... the Gravity Destruction Weapon ... ray guns ... and "homing lasers".... Sweet but rather dull pathos. There seem to be a half dozen Death, or Near-Death, Scenes. Some pretty space effects. The title has nothing to do with the film itself.

**PLAWRES SANSHIRO** (J) Toho Video 198-? anim color 50m. Ref: TV: vt; no Eng.

Miniature wrestling robots with built-in roller skates battle for all the WPWA marbles. Santo-as-Robby in Japan? Only for kids who love robots and wrestling. Cute: a robot ref.

**PLAYING WITH FIRE** see *They're Playing with Fire*

**PLAYROOM** see *Schizo*

**PLEASE DON'T EAT THE BABIES** Robertson-Jones (Cannibal Pictures) 1987 color 86m. D, P: Marcus Robertson. SP: Jerry & Jack Color. Ph: David Golia. Mus: L.L. Simeone. SpFX: Jack Sessums, Pete Seagle. Mkp: Dave Miller. SdFX: Cynthia Marshall, Will Santa Cruz. Ref: TV: VSOM. PT 19:13: *Island Fury* ('89, AIP), revised version. With Hank Worden, Ed McClarty, Kirstin Baker, John Wilson (devil), Bill Waren (zombie), John Metzler (ghoul), Marsha Strong (devil lady).

"Everybody was eaten by giant bugs!" Big roaches and a family with a cannibal or two in the closet inhabit a "strange place" on an island in the Devil's Triangle. Plus: cleaver gore, straight-razor gore, and pitchfork gore.... Technically and dramatically threadbare. The "effects" alternate between inserts of ordinary cockroaches and models which are cousins of the monsters from green hell.

**PLEASE DON'T EAT THE PLANET** see *Intergalactic Thanksgiving*

**PLEASURE DOME** Essex (D. T. Chrisp) 1982 color 76m. SP, D: Dino Cimino. Mus: Midnight Eyes. SpMkp: C. H. Scott, Harri Seldon. SpFX: Seldon. Titles: Pioneer. Ref: TV: Essex Video. With Maria Tortuga, Ken Starbuck, Lee Carroll, Drea, William Margold.

A demon knight appears to a woman who is having "strange dreams" of Medieval times. She proves to be the sorceress that she sees in her dreams; the knight is a knight she had cursed for being unfaithful.... Threadbare continuity and production in this adult fantasy. In the dream, the knight slays a dragon, not seen until its dead papier-mache head is lying on the ground. Special makeup for the knight consists principally of shiny contact lenses.

**PLEASURE DOME I: THE GENESIS CHAMBER** A.F.V. 1994 color 83m. D: S. Canterbury. Ref: Adam'95. With Steffi, Tyffany Million.

Instant-aging machine, 1000 years from now.

**PLEASURE MAZE** Fog City Partners/Essex (Jo Williams) 1986 color 85m. D: D. Dumont. Ref: vc box: "Nightdroids," android hookers. Adam '88. With Tracey Adams, Amber Lynn, Stacey Donovan, Nina Hartley.

**PLEASURE SPOT** Caballero 1986 color 81m. Ref: Adam '88: clitoris transplant. With Gina Carrera, Patti Petite, Herschel Savage.

**PLEASURE ZONE** Limelight 1987 color 90m. Ref: vc box: alien. With Peter Bilt, Star Wood.

**PLEDGE NIGHT** SGE/Scarlet 1991 color 85m. D, Ed: Paul Ziller. SP, P: Joyce Snyder. SpMkpFX: Dean Kartalas; (Acid Sid) Erik Schaper. Ref: V 3/18/91:87 (hv): "acceptable gore fare." Martin: "inspired special effects." With Todd Gastland, Wendy McMahon, Will Kempe (Acid Sid).

"Undead monster on the loose at Phi Epsilon Nu." (V)

**PLUGHEAD REWIRED** see *Circuitry Man II*

**PLUTONIUM BABY** TWE 1987 color 85m. D, P: Ray Hirschman. SP: Wayne Behar. Mus: M. Knox. Ref: V 1/27/88:36 (hv). Martin. McCarty II: "fails to hold our interest." Morse: "amateurish ... killer mutant gopher." With Patrick Molloy, Danny Guerra, Joe Viviani.

"Boy whose mother was contaminated by plutonium turns radioactive...." (McC)

**PLYMOUTH** (U.S.-I) ABC-TV/Touchstone-TV & RAI-1 & Zlotoff Inc. (Ian Sander/Ralph Winter) 1991 (1990) color c90m. Tel, D: Lee Zlotoff. Mus: Brad Fiedel. PD: Michael Baugh. SpVisFX: (sup) Richard Mosier; Perpetual Motion Pictures. SpFX: Darrell Pritchett. Vehicles: Image Design & Marketing. Mkp: Ronnie Specter. Ref: TV. V 6/3/91:55: "chock full of stock characters." TVG 12/1/90. With Cindy Pickett, Richard Hamilton, Perrey Reeves, Matthew Brown, Ron Vawter, Robin Frates, Dale Midkiff.

The "new world": the moon. A "global conglomerate" transports an Oregon community to the moon to start a colony and operate its mine.

**POD PEOPLE** see *Unearthling, The*

**POISON** Zeitgeist Films/Bronze Eye & Arnold A. Semler (Poison) 1991 (1990) 85m. SP, D: Todd Haynes, inspired by the novels of Jean Genet. Mus: James Bennett. FxMkp: Scott Sliger. Ref: TV. V 2/4/91. Oak Trib 6/8/91. "Horror" segment in b&w: With Larry Maxwell (Dr. Thomas Graves), Susan Norman, Richard Hansen (narrator).

A doctor (Maxwell) "hungry for knowledge" re the "mysteries of the sex drive" accidentally drinks his own "molecular coagulation" concoction, becomes infected with a communicable, "venemous cancer." He doesn't look that bad really, but he leaks, and becomes known as the "notorious leper murderer." ("I'm a monster.") Some okay gross-out bits in this Fifties-sf parody/AIDS allegory. ("I've just captured the sex drive!") But even the ghastliest of them add little to the creepy-love scenes in the recent *Fly* films.

**POISON PRINCESSES OF CHEONG VALLEY** see *Succubare*

**POLICE SQUAD!** see *Naked Gun, The*

**POLICE WOMAN AGAINST A GHOST WITH AN AXE** (H.K.?) 199-? color feature. Ref: VSOM: "entertaining Asian ghost comedy."

**A POLISH VAMPIRE IN BURBANK** Pirromount 1983 color c88m. (aka *Polish Vampire*). SP, D, P, Castle Set Des: Mark Pirro. Ph & SpFX: Craig Bassuk. Mus: Gregg Gross, Sergio Bandera.

Des: also Eric Megison. Ref: TV: Simitar Ent. video. V 10/9/85:46. Martin. Hound. Jones. With M. Pirro, Lori Sutton, Bobbi Dorsch, Hugh O. Fields (vampire), Marya Gant (vampire), Eddie Deezen (Sphincter), Steve Dorsch, Brad Waisbren, Catharine Wheatley, Conrad Brooks, Paul Farbman (The Queerwolf).

Dupah (Pirro) is a "full-grown vampire" who has yet to bite. He meets vampire-movie fan Delores Lane (Sutton): "I must have seen *The Horror of Dracula* twenty times!" A "fang bang" turns Delores into a vampire, too, and, in a Weird Romances coda, daylight turns the two into living, loving skeletons. Also on the agenda: Dupah's sun-fried elder brother, Sphincter ("I'm due at a poker game with Bela Lugosi and Boris Karloff"), and the "Queerwolf," who was bitten by a gay guy during the full moon. (A half-moon makes him "bi.") Visual references to the 1931 *Dracula*.

Or, Waiting for Humor. This amiable but generally inept vampire spoof is no *The Tenant* or (to employ another sort of cross reference) *Young Frankenstein*, though there are droll moments—e.g., Dupah using a bottle brush to brush his teeth ... an usher invariably winding up his kooky monologues on mortality with the word *hacksaw*.

**POLIZIA CHIEDE AIUTO, La** see *What Have They Done to Your Daughters?*

**POLLY-TICS** Educ/Sullivan 1927? anim silent c6m. Ref: TV: Loonic Video (Early Animation number 2). no Lee.

Scene with fake, but real-seeming "ghost" (a parrot and other housepets under a sheet). Average Felix the Cat cartoon.

**POLTERGASH!** Oakwood Films 1987 color c85m. D?, SP: K. G. Neal. Ph: E. Brandy. AD: M. Ryun. VisFX: Daniel Morgan. Mkp: Dave Shelton. SdFX: Love 25 et al. Ref: TV: Adult Video. no Adam. With Eric Monte, Andrea Sutton, Carol Cross, Rod Retta, Dominata, Marisa Vale, Marc Roberts (Dr. Doppler), Alexis Firestone.

"One of the world's rarest psychic phenomena, the poltergash"— a giant vagina—the "spiritual embodiment of a woman's sexual power over men," sucks nerdy Ritchie (Monte) into a closet ... and "another dimension" where dreams come true. At the end, the poltergash invades Ritchie's TV set.... Typical adult fare sports some passable if elementary video effects.

**POLTERGEIST II** UA-MGM/Freddie Fields (Victor-Grais) 1986 color/ws 90m. D: Brian Gibson. Sp: Mark Victor, Michael Grais. Mus: Jerry Goldsmith. VisFxSup: Richard Edlund. Conceptual Art: H. R. Giger. Ref: TV. V 5/21/86. Stanley. Newman. Scheuer. Martin. Maltin '92. Phantom. Hound. With JoBeth Williams, Craig T. Nelson, Heather O'Rourke, Oliver Robins, Zelda Rubinstein, Will Sampson, Julian Beck, Geraldine Fitzgerald, John P. Whitecloud.

"Cuesta Verde—Where Dreams Come True." The Freelings' kids' room is becoming a Grand Central of spooks. Seems a demon ("the entity") from another dimension wants little Carol Anne's (O'Rourke) "life force." Meanwhile, little Robbie's (Robins) braces spring to life and threaten to cocoon him in wires (is this a comedy?), and a 4-D-man-like gent (Beck) is walking through people. Father Steve's (Nelson) holy breath chases an oversized, clawed, tentacled ugly, and the family garage features a literal live wire.

Uneasy combo of effects scenes and family-love themes draws upon *Something Evil, Alien,* "Twilight Zone" episodes ("Little Girl Lost" and "Long-Distance Call"), as well as the first *Poltergeist.* Most of the wraith effects are familiar; the fetal and skeletal ones are more unusual. The casualness, in some scenes, of Nelson and Sampson helps, and Beck is suitably cadaverous as Rev. Kane. Some eerie Goldsmith musical themes.

**POLTERGEIST III** MGM-UA (Barry Bernardi) 1988 color 97m. SP, D, Exec P, SpVisFxDes: Gary Sherman. SP: also Brian Taggert. Mus: Joe Renzetti. SpMkp: (des) John Caglione Jr., Doug Drexler; (consult) Dick Smith. SpFxCoord: Cal Acord. Sup SdFxEd: Stephen Flick. Opt: Howard Anderson, Lake FX. Ref: TV. V 6/15/88. SFChron 6/11/88. SFExam 6/10/88. Scheuer. Martin. Maltin '92. Phantom. Hound. With Tom Skerritt, Nancy Allen, Heather O'Rourke, Zelda Rubinstein, Lara Flynn Boyle, Nathan Davis (Kane).

In a Chicago high-rise, mirrors suddenly begin breaking mysteriously; after a man leaves the room, his reflection lingers in a mirror. In an indoor parking lot, monstrous hands jump up out of a puddle. Upshot: The evil, reflection-bound Kane is back and needs Carol Anne's (O'Rourke) youth and innocence. (He has none of his own.).... The dawdling, out-of-synch reflections are a neat idea. Less neat: the trapped-in-the-mirror-world idea. Worst idea: to have everyone forever calling out "Carol Anne!" to the trapped Carol Anne. Script pays lip service to the power of love.

**POMERIGGIO CALDO** (I) 1988 color feature (aka *Afternoon*). D: A. Massaccesi. Ref: Palmerini: human sacrifice, voodoo. VSOM: *Hot Voodoo Afternoon.*

**PON POCO** (J) Studio Ghibli (Miyazaki/TNHG) 1994 anim color/ws 119m. Ref: TV: Animage Video; no Eng. Japan Video. Animerica.

In one sequence, shape-shifting raccoons impersonate a wide variety of ghosts, including some faceless ones. In another long, astonishing sequence, they form a huge dragon, then seem to become, variously, flying human, horse, and unidentified, giant skeletons, demons, ghosts, etc. Epic animated fantasy concludes on an impossibly touching back-to-nature note and seems an improvement on *Warriors of the Wind* and the latter's ecological themes, but awaits an English-language version for a more complete assessment here. (It has many lengthy dialogue scenes with the talented raccoons.)

**POOR WHITE TRASH II** Zison Pictures 1974 color c85m. (*Scum of the Earth* - orig t). D, P: S. F. Brownrigg. SP: Mary Davis. Addl Dial: G. Ross. Ph: Robert Alcott. Mus: Robert Farrar. AD: Lynda Pendleton. SpFX: Jack Bennett. Mkp: J. J. Barnes. Ref: TV: Magnum Ent. video. Fango 4/90. Newman. Phantom: not a sequel to anything. Hound. Martin. With Hugh Feagin (Jim), Charlie Dell, Camilla Carr, Norma Moore, Ann Stafford, Gene Ross (Pick).

"You killed 'em all!" There's lurking death in the woods outside the cabin, and not much better inside. A madman is "sneakin'

around out there somewhere" and committin' murder with ax, iron fence spikes, barbed wire, and shotgun. Meanwhile, inside, "Pick" serves up patriarchal horrors, as he forcibly adds each new woman he meets to his "harem".... Splicing of rural melo and slasher movie is not bad for regional filmmaking, but the mixture of thrills and pathos is very familiar. If the pace is generally slow, the makeup-effects close-ups really stop the movie dead.

**POP CHASER** (J) 198-? anim color 26m. Ref: TV: Cult Videos of Berkeley; no Eng.

Set in NeoCansas (sic), this light-comic lesbian sf-Western concerns a "motorcycle gang" on two-legged-walker-like vehicles which abducts the women of the town. Generally vacuous action (sexual and otherwise) and a few cute moments, in this oddball softcore cartoon.

**POPCORN** (U.S.-Jamaican-Can.) Studio Three/Movie Partners & Century Films (Film House Int'l.) 1991 (1990) color 91m. D: Mark Herrier. SP: Alan Ormsby (aka Tod Hackett). Story: Mitchell Smith. Mus: Paul Zaza. SpFxMkp: Bob Clark. SpFxSup: G. Gerrari. SpFxAnim: Steve Schnier. Ref: TV. V 2/4/91. ad. SFBay Guardian 1/30/91. SFChron 2/2/91. McCarty II. Scheuer. Martin. Maltin '92. With Jill Schoelen, Tom Villard (Toby), Dee Wallace Stone, Derek Rydall, Kelly Jo Minter, Tony Roberts, Ray Walston, Karen Witter, Bruce Glover (Vernon), Ethan Ormsby.

"Come into my head!" Students at U.C. Oceanview stage an all-night horrorthon at the "old Dreamland Theatre." Included treats: "Mosquito!" (an imitation-Fifties b&w cheapie re a giant mosquito), "Attack of the Amazing Electrified Man" (in which electric-chair juice only makes Vernon stronger and more deadly), "The Stench" (a dubbed "Japanese" sf-er) ... and "Possessor," an unfinished avant-garde film which was once part of a disastrous "performance" piece. Meanwhile, a faceless, "multidentical" killer who employs masks of the other principals re-programs a model of a mosquito to kill.

Blandly good-natured shocker is all weak-tea ideas. The visual and sound qualities of the b&w "hommages" are distractingly off—they look more like the taped entries of the original "Twilight Zone." Another letdown: the killer, Toby D'Amato, is just another quippy, Freddy-voiced clone.

**POPEYE AND THE PIRATES** Para 1947 anim color 7m. D: S. Kneitel. SP: Klein, Ward. Ref: TV. LC. no Lee.

Pirate ship of ghosts ... live skeleton from dead man's chest. Typical Popeye cartoon.

**POPULATION: ONE** American Scenes (Bianca Daalder) 1986 color 70m. SP, D: Renee Daalder. Anim: Dominic Orlando. Assoc P: Carel Struycken. Ph: J. V. Walther. Mus: D. Schwartz. Ref: V 5/21/86: "fringe item." Stanley. Ecran F 73:71. With Tomata DuPlenty, Sheela Edwards, Jane Gaskill, Gorilla Rose.

"Apocalypse that inters civilization under radioactive rubble." (V)

**POR UN SALVAJE AMOR ...** (Mex) Juan Duran 1992? color 90m. D: Christian Gonzalez. SP: Ariel Fernandez. Mkp: Norma Vazquez. SpFX: F. Rodriguez. Ref: TV: Premier Video; no Eng.

Determinedly perverse, Jesus Franco-ish melodrama culminates in a bizarre, bloody castration-and-"wedding"-in-bed. The bride wears white; the groom, red. An earlier, visualized nightmare sequence re a church wedding with a dash of blood prefigures this finale. And some earlier, semi-surgical castrations prefigure the final, impromptu one. Tawdry-plus.

**PORNO HOLOCAUST** (I) Kristal Film 1980 color feature. Ph, D: Joe D'Amato. SP: Tom Salina. Mus: Nico Fidenco. AD: E. Michettoni. Mkp: Massimo Camiletti. Ref: TV: vt; Eng. titles. CM 16:77. MV. With George Eastman, D. Funari, A. Goren, M. Shanon.

"Little ocean creatures have become enormous." Nuclear testing has produced "strange things" on a remote island—including a raping and murdering mutant, Romero Tranquero. ("It wasn't human.") Companion piece to *Erotic Nights of the Living Dead* is a rudimentary combo of horror and hardcore sex.

**PORTE DEL NULLA, Le** see *Door of Silence*

**PORTE DEL SILENZIO** see *Door of Silence*

**Le PORTE DELL'INFERNO** Scena Film (I) 1989 color feature (aka *Hell's Gate*). SP,D: Umberto Lenzi. Mus: P. Montanari. Ref: Palmerini: "not bad film." VSOM: *Gate of Hell*. With Barbara Cupisti, Gaetano Russo, M. Luzzi, Giacomo Rossi Stuart.

Murderous ghosts of the "Black Monks," from 1289 A.D.

**PORTRAIT, The** see *Girls School Screamers*

**PORTRAIT IN CRYSTAL** (H.K.) Shaw 1982 color feature. D: Lin Shew Hua. Ref: Weisser/ATC2: "horror"; "nonsensical." With Tang Chia.

"Living crystal statues ... supernatural conflict on Spirit Island ... flying skulls."

**PORTRAIT OF DORIANA GRAY** see *Doriana Gray*

**PORTRAIT OF SEDUCTION** Essex 1976 color? 76m. Ref: Adam '88: "demonic possession." With Vicky Lyon, Monique Cardin, Robert Cole, Jon Martin.

**PO'S QUE SUENAS MADALENO** (Mex) Prods. Barba Loza c1990? color 89m. D: Jose Medina; (co-d) Fermin Gomez. Story: Ignacio Vargas. Ph: Silvano Zuniga. Mkp: Elda Nuno. Ref: TV: TeleStar video; no Eng. La Tapatia: *Why Do You Dream, Madaleno?* - tr t. With Charly Valentino, Jacaranda Alfaro, Marco Antonio Orozco, Socorro Albarran, Donato Castaneda.

One of three balls of light from outer space lands on Earth and aids our hero, Madaleno (Valentino), by turning him first into a tractor, then, in turn, into a bug (he avoids the bus fare, but a big lady sits on him), a dog, a tubby but strong superhero, a white mouse, a wriggly skinned chicken, a bra (a sexy woman tries him on, then throws him in the washer), and various people—all the better to chase women.... Tacky, elementary shot-on-tape sf-comedy is occasionally silly-funny. Benny Hill lives!

**POSED FOR MURDER** Fox/Fury Ventures 1989 color 85m. D: B. T. Jones. SP: J. A. Gallagher, C. Dickenson. Story, Co-P: Jack

Fox. SpMkpFX: James Chai. Ref: V 5/31/89: "competently executed but unexciting ... slasher thriller." McCarty II: "tepid." With Charlotte J. Helmkamp, Carl Fury, Rick Gianasi.

Slasher stalks model angling for role in "Meat Cleavers from Mars."

**POSEIDA** see *Osceno Desiderio, L'*

**POSETITEL MUZEIA** (Russ.) Lenfilm (Creative Unit 3) 1989 color 135m. SP, D: Konstantin Lopushanski. Mus: Schnitke, Kusin. Ref: V 8/2/89: "a very long 135 minutes"; *Visitor to a Museum* - tr t. 4/18/90:12: at Imagfic (Madrid). With Viktor Mikhailov, Irina Rakshina, Vera Maiorova.

Mutants and melting ice caps in a post-apocalypse world.

**Les POSSEDEES DU DIABLE** (F) Comptoir Francais du Film (Robert de Nesle) 1974 color 90m. (aka *Lorna L'Exorciste. Les Possedees du Demon*). SP, D: Jesus Franco (aka C. Brown). Adap: Nicole Franco. Ph: G. Brissaud. Mus: Andre Benichou, Robert de Nesle. Ref: TV: VSOM; Ph: E. Rosenfeld; *Possessed by the Devil: Lorna the Exorcist;* Eng. titles. Stanley. Hardy/HM: "one of [Franco's] most revolting pictures to date." Monster! 3:43, 52. With Lina Romay, Pamela Stanford, Guy Delorme, Jacqueline Laurent, Howard Vernon.

Satanic spell makes woman disgorge "black spidery creatures" from her vagina. Sequel to *Necronomicon* (1967). (HM) "I am not your child. I am Lorna." A man makes a pact with mystery demon Lorna Green to turn his daughter over to her on the girl's 18th birthday. ("I want your daughter.") Lorna is "sterile ... like everyone else where I come from." At the end, Lorna possesses Linda, or passes her powers on to her .... The spider-crabs are a nice sick idea. Otherwise, this is indifferent softcore sex, with a writhing motif (alternately denoting pleasure and pain).

**POSSESSED** (G?) VSOM/Seitz-Waldleitner 198-? color/ws 75m. (*Posseduta*). D: Georg Tressler. Mus: Rolf Wilhelm. Mkp: Ruediger von Sperl.Ref: TV: VSOM; Eng. titles. With Peter Simonischek, Giovanni Frueh, Andy Voss, Pamela Prati.

In a remote mountain cabin, a rag, a piece of wood, and a hank of hair seem to come to life. Soon, the three shepherds therein are confronted with a witch/temptress who skins her victims and wears only contact lenses. Offbeat fantasy-horror anecdote remains rather uninvolving to the end.

**POSSESSED, The** see *Manhattan Baby*

**POSSESSED II** (H.K.) Golden Harvest (Johnny Mak Prods.) 1984 color/ws c92m. D: David Lai. SP: Mak? Ph: Gary Ho-Raymond L. AD: Jassie L. Ref: TV: Pan-Asia Video; Eng. titles & dubbing. Fango 107:59. V 5/9/84:448.

"You mean my wife's a ghost?" The vengeful, werewolf-like ghost of a suicide (she sprouts hair and fangs for the kill and has hairy ears and a peel-able face) possesses the heroine. Meanwhile, her ghost-daughter possesses a little girl and sprouts fangs, levitates, performs other telekinetic tricks, and savages the school bully.... Determinedly grisly horror-fantasy works too strenuously for its thrills. Oh-so-gross highlights include Love with a Furry Fanged Woman in a Meat Truck, and, earlier, the ghost's systematic destruction (with acid) of an ex-rival's body and soul, in a mortuary.

**POSSESSED BY THE DEVIL**  see *Possedees du Diable*

**POSSESSED BY THE NIGHT**  Vision (Alan Amiel) 1994 color 84m. SP, D: Fred Olen Ray. SP: also Mark Thomas McGee. Ref: Vallejo T-H: "mysterious statue." PT 20:18: "cursed jar." Martin: '93; "strange talisman." With Shannon Tweed, Sandahl Bergman, Henry Silva, Ted Prior, Chad McQueen, Turhan Bey, Kato Kaelin.

**POSSESSION—UNTIL DEATH DO YOU PART**  (Can.) CGV & NAR 1987 color 92m. D: Lloyd A. Simandl, Michael Mazo. SP: Lyne J. Grantham. Ref: V 12/23/87:37: "scatter-brained horror film." McCarty II: "rubbishy." TVG 11/28/87:22. With J. R. Johnston, Melissa Martin, Cat Williams.

Apparently dead madman returns to terrorize five women in woods.

**POSSESSION OF GHOST**  (H.K.) Jia's Motion Picture Co. 1982 color 85m. Ref: TV: vt; Eng. titles. vc box.

A goofy, zoom-happy, chaotically-directed martial-arts actioner, with some supernatural elements thrown in as an afterthought. At the beginning, magic revives dead, or dormant, bodies deep in snow country, and later there's scattered, voodoo-like, remote-control sorcery, plus a bit of bamboo gore.

**2P  The POSSESSION OF VIRGINIA**  (Can.) Cinepix 1971 color 82m. D: Jean Beaudin. Ph: Rene Verzier. Mus: F. Cousineau. Sets: F. Delucy. Ref: TV: VSOM; Eng. dubbed. V 10/16/74:26: at Sitges. With Louise Marleau, Daniel Pilon, Danielle Ouimet.

"Grandma has returned." Strange cackling ... a visualized nightmare re cats and corpses ... a disappearing body ... an odd old lady (later seen with butcher knife in hand) ... a line re a "vampire story" ... sacrificial deaths ... a "terribly evil" toad statuette ... and a black mass of a "secret sect".... Horrible pop score, crude dubbing and editing. Film has a literally unfinished feel to it. The lone highlight: the mysterious "Grandma."

**POUND PUPPIES AND THE LEGEND OF BIG PAW**  (U.S.-Taiwanese) Tri-Star (Carolco)/Family Home Ent. & Tonka (Atlantic/Kushner-Locke & Maltese & Wang Film & Cuckoos Nest) 1988 anim color 76m. D & AD: Pierre DeCelles. SP: Jim Carlson, Terrence McDonnell. Mus: Sam Winans et al. Anim D: Jerry Lee, Wei Jang Wu. Opt: Ray Mercer. Ref: TV. V 3/30/88. ad. Voices: George Rose (McNasty), Ruth Buzzi, B. J. Ward.

In the "All in Your Mind" number, set in a scary swamp, pups' imaginations conjure up monsters, dragons, and witches. Other items: the Mean Machine, which turns puppies into big mean dogs ("Saying 'I love you' changes 'em back to normal"), and "Big Paw" (a "zillion feet high"), a "monster" that turns out to be a giant nice puppy.... Kiddie fare alternates between the snappy (the "All in Your Mind" and "King of Everything" numbers) and the sappy (most of the other numbers).

**POWAZON BODI**  see *Lady Poison*

**The POWER PILL**  CBS-TV/Univ-TV 1967-8 color c80m. D: Jack Arnold. Ref: Stanley. Castleman/TV Shows. With Stephen Strimpell.

More episodes from the "Mr. Terrific" TV show.

**POWERTOOL 2**  Catalina 1992 color feature. D: Josh Eliot, Taylor Hudson. Ref: Adam '93G. With Lex Baldwin.

Prison inmate fed to "some half-human ogre in the basement."

**PRANZO CON VAMPIRO**  see *Having Supper with a Vampire*

**Il PRATO MACCHIATO** DI ROSSO (I) 1975 color feature. SP,D: Riccardo Ghione. Mus: T. Usuelli. Ref: Palmerini: "ridiculous and dated." With Marina Malfatti, Enzo Tarascio, Daniela Caroli.

Mystery woman in old villa "kills her guests ... in order to steal their blood and sell it to clinics...."

**PRAYER MAT OF THE FLESH**  see *Sex and Zen*

**PRAYER OF THE ROLLERBOYS**  (U.S.-J) Gaga & Fox/Lorber & Academy Ent./JVC & TV Tokyo (Mickelson/King/Iliff) 1991 color 94m. D: Rick King. SP: W. Peter Iliff. Mus: Stacy Widelitz. SpFX: (coord) Marty Bresin; SpFxUnltd. SpMkpFX: Die-Aktion; Dean & Starr Jones. SdFX: S. H. Hinckley. Ref: TV. V 4/1/91. S&S 8/91:49. With Corey Haim, Patricia Arquette, Christopher Collet, J. C. Quinn, Julius Harris, Devin Clark, Mark Pellegrino.

"Rollerboys aren't just another gang." The "totally cool," racially "pure" Rollerboys are a "white army" on wheels. ("The day of the rope is coming.") The key to leader Gary Lee's (Collet) twisted thinking: a "new, ultra-deluxe Mist house"—Mist being a Chinese drug intended to "pacify the population." "The rope" proves to be a "final solution" additive to Mist which will cause sterilization.... Basically inane infiltrating-the-gang story ("Once in, never out") which just happens to be set in the future. Wry touches: the fortified pizza truck and the periodic news flashes— "Germany Buys Poland," Harvard sold to Far Eastern buyers, etc.

**PRE-HYSTERICAL DAZE**  Terry Thoren 199-? anim short. D: Gavrilo Gnatovich. Ref: SFChron Dtbk 6/28/92: part of the "Tex Avery Project."

"Frenzied action between cavemen and dinosaurs."

**PREDATEURS DE LA NUIT, Les**  see *Faceless*

**PREDATOR**  Fox & Amercent Films & American Ent. Partners (Gordon-Silver-Davis) 1987 color 106m. D: John McTiernan. SP: Jim & John Thomas. Mus: Alan Silvestri. Creature FX: Stan Winston; (concept) Steve Wang, Mitch Suskin. Suit: Diligent Dwarves. FxAnim: Howard Anderson Co. SpVisFX: R/Greenberg; (sup) Joel Hynek; (thermal vision) Stuart Robertson; (anim sup) Robert Mrozowski; Dream Quest. SpFxSup: Al Di Sarro, Laurencio Cordero. SpSdFX: John P. Vocal FX: N. B. Schwartz. Ref: TV. MFB'88:19. V 6/17/87. ad. SFChron 6/6/87. SFExam 6/12/87. With Arnold Schwarzenegger, Carl Weathers, Elpidia Carrillo, Bill Duke, Jesse Ventura, R. G. Armstrong, Kevin Peter Hall (predator).

"The jungle—it just came alive...!" The "demon who makes truffles of man," in a "charming little country" in Central America, is a translucent, ray-shooting, chameleon-like alien hunter that, at the end, removes gun and helmet for a fair fight with Major Alan "Dutch" Schaeffer (Schwarzenegger). Its removal of its gear also allows us to see just how ugly it is.... The alien's translucent mode is the most intriguing aspect of this generally routine *Most Dangerous Game* variation, though there's also the incidental phrase "sexual tyrannosaurus." Too many "There's something out there waiting for us, and it ain't no man" lines, in the trying-to-be-scary dialogue.

Sequel: *Predator 2.*

**PREDATOR 2** Fox/Gordon-Silver-Davis 1990 color 108m. D: Stephen Hopkins. SP: Jim & John Thomas. Mus: Alan Silvestri. Creature: Stan Winston; (mkp) Scott H. Eddo. VisFX: R/Greenberg; Howard Anderson et al; (coord) J. W. Kompare; (sup) Joel Hynek; (camouflage sup) E. Mamut; (anim) Steve Marino; (spark anim) Donald Poynter. POV FX: Video Image. SpFxSup: Ken Pepiot. SdFX: S. H. Flick. SpVocalFX: N. B. Schwartz; (predator) Hal Rayle. Ref: TV. S&S 5/91:58-9. V 11/26/90. SFChron 11/21/90. With Danny Glover, Gary Busey, Ruben Blades, Maria Conchita Alonso, Bill Paxton, Kevin Peter Hall (predator), Kent McCord, Morton Downey, Jr., Calvin Lockhart.

"The devil came for them!" Ten years after, in 1997 L.A., another "of his kind"—alien big-game hunters that camouflage themselves by "bending" light, and detect human prey by "seeing" heat—leaves victims "shish kebabbed" and "boned like a fish." This "ugly mother" with the Darth Vader armor uses weird weapons, including a nifty "boomerang." The Did-I-just-see-something? translucence effects are eerie all right, but not quite enough upon which to build a movie. The hyper style and tone of this sequel to *Predator* boils down to simply (a) noise and (b) movement.

**PREDATORI DI ATLANTIDA, I** see *Raiders of Atlantis, The*

**PREDONI DEL DESERTO, I** see *Secret of the Sahara*

**PREDTCHOUVSTVIE** (Russ-Rom.) Delta-Film 1993 b&w and color 90m. (aka *Le Pressentiment*). SP, D: Valeriu Jereghi. Mus: L. Jereghi. Ref: V 6/7/93: "heavy-handed allegory." With Maria Ploae, Daniel Ionescu, Lunaia.

"Woman ... seems to be the only survivor of a catastrophic, possibly ultimate, war."

**PREHISTORIC BEAST** Phil Tippett 1985 puppet anim 7m. Ref: 24th Int'l. Tournee of Animation leaflet. SFChron 12/23/88: "strangely touching"; 12/24/93: "a major treat"; Dtbk 12/18/88: "a remarkably effective short."

"A morning in the life of a triceratops...."(SFC)

**PREHISTORIC BIMBOS IN ARMAGEDDON CITY** Tempe color 70m. Ref: Tempe Video flyer. Bill Warren.

After World War III. "Evil Nemesis and his army of cyborgs."(TV)

**\*\*A PREHISTORIC LOVE STORY** (B) Zenith 1915 silent 33m. D: Leedham Bantock. From a sketch by Seymour Hicks. Ref: BFC. Gifford/BC. Lee. With Hicks, Isobel Elsom.

Romance set in cave-man days.

**PREHISTORIC PIGGIES** Hi-Tops Video (Fred Wolf/Walt Kubiak) 1990 anim color 25m. (*Pretty Piggies* video series). D: Tony Love et al. SP: Jack Mendelsohn. Ref: vc box: Video Treasures.

Magic gloves transport the Piggies back to prehistory, where they encounter a baby bronto and a pterodactyl.

**PREHYSTERIA** Para/Moonbeam (Full Moon/Debra Dion, Peter von Sholly) 1993 color c85m. D: Albert & Charles Band. SP: Greg Suddeth, Mark Goldstein. Idea: P. von Sholly. Ph: Adolfo Bartoli. Mus: Richard Band. PD: Milo. VisFxSup: David Allen. PuppetFX:(sup) Mark A. Rappaport;(mech des) J. Heimann, A. Coulter. Dinosaurs Des: Andrea von Sholly. Digital Imaging:(sup) BB & J VisFX;(vis fx composite) Peter Moyer. SpVocalFX: Frank Welker. Ref: TV. Martin. SFChron Dtbk 6/27/93. 7/25/93. PT 20:71. With Brett Cullen, Austin O'Brien, Samantha Mills, Colleen Morris, Tony Longo, Stuart Fratkin, Stephen Lee, Tom Williams.

Eggs from an ancient South American temple hatch midget dinosaurs—a tyrannosaurus, a stegosaurus, a pterodactyl, a triceratops, and a brachiosaurus. If you can put up with the adoring looks from humans here, you'll find an occasionally quite taking fantasy of domestication. This goes the ineffable *Son of Kong* one better: Dinos Come Home and become house pets. Mixture of the perfunctory and the charming is one of the Full Moon band's better efforts, thanks to the effects conception and execution.

**PREHYSTERIA! 2** Para/Moonbeam 1994 color 81m. D, P: Albert Band. SP: B. Friedman, M. Davis. Ph: J.L. Spencer. PD: Milo. Creature FxSup: Mark Rappaport. SpVisFX: David Allen et al. Stopmo: Yan Guo. DigitalFX:(sup) Paul Gentry; Mr. Film. SpVocalFX: Frank Welker. Ref: TV: Para video. With Kevin R. Connors, Jennifer Harte, Dean Scofield, Bettye Ackerman, Greg Lewis, Michael Hagiwara, Larry Hankin, Larry Pennell.

They're back, sort of. You couldn't guess from this that the first one was charming. Even the dinos have lost it. The comedy needs relief here, and the story isn't even decent hack work.

**PREMATURE BURIAL, The** see *Haunting Fear. Noche de los Asesinos, La*

**PREP SCHOOL** see *Zombie High*

**PRESENCE** (I) 1980 color feature. D: Bruno Mattei. Ref: VSOM: "grisly."

"Nun/horror pic" re a mother superior who "removes vaginas from dead nuns to keep Satan from re-visiting the convent."

**PRESENCE, The** see *Danger Island. Witchtrap*

**PRESSENTIMENT, Le** see *Predtchouvstvie*

**The PRETTY GHOSTESS STORY** (H.K.?) c1990? color/ws 87m. Ref: TV: World Video; Eng. titles.

"Ghost can't marry human." But Feng Chiu, the boss's dead daughter, wants to marry his employee Chen Chiang. Further complication: The King of Hell wants her for his mistress. He sends "girl ghosts" to tempt Chen Chiang, and incidentally provide some extraneous softcore-sex footage. At the end, king and "ghostess" duel, and morning light dispels him. Other ingredients in this haphazard, inconsequential comedy include a hopping-vampire troupe, ghost cops, and an exorcist.

**PRETTY PIGGIES** series see *Prehistoric Piggies*

**3P The PREY** New World/Essex 1980 color 80m. SP, D: Edwin S. Brown. SP, P: Summer Brown. Ph: Teru Hayashi;(wildlife) Gary Gero. Mus: D. Peake. AD: Roger Holzberg. SpMkpFX: J.C. Buechler. SpSdFX: Sound Arts. Ref: TV. TVG. V(d) 12/2/80(rated). 2/16/83:24. With Debbie Thureson, Steve Bond, Lori Lethin, Robert Wald, Jackie Coogan, Carel Struycken (monster), Garry Goodrow.

The Northpoint is a "real spooky place," thanks mainly to the fact that, in 1948, a forest fire there horribly burned a cave gypsy, making him very ugly and very strong. He has taken to beheading (with ax) and shredding (with claw-like hands) his human prey, and he ultimately mates with the heroine.

Very thin *Friday the 13th* material furnishes scant data re its monster or his victims. A superfluous park-ranger rates more running time than the monster-gypsy. The movie's high point should not be Jackie Coogan's consumption of a cream-cheese-and-cucumber sandwich. Included: post-vulture-pecking gore makeup for one victim.

**The PRICE OF LIFE** American Playhouse/Chanticleer Films (Sanger-Memel) 1987 color short. Tel, D: Stephen Tolkin. Story: M. Monetzux. Ref: TV. TVG. V 6/24/91. With Jim Youngs, Judy Geeson, Fred Ward.

"Futuristic world where time is money—literally." (TVG) Pretentious.

**PRIMA DEL FUTORO** (I) RAI-2 & Cinecitta & U.P.C. & A.D.C. (Renato Ostuni) 1985 color 100m. SP, D: F. Caleffi, E. Pasculli, G. Rosaleva. Mus: R. Senigallia. Ref: V 9/18/85: a "collection of vaguely futuristic images without wit, humor or emotional charge"; *Before the Future* - tr t. With David Brandon, Laura Marconi, Elda Olivieri.

"Trio of episodes ... set in an indefinite future world...."

**PRIMAL RAGE** (U.S.-I) Warner HV/Elpico (Laguna Ent./Immerman) 1991 (1990) color 91m. (*Furia Primitiva. Rage*). D: Vittorio Rambaldi. SP: Harry Kirkpatrick. SpVisFX: Carlo Rambaldi. SpMkpFX: Alex Rambaldi. Ref: V 2/25/91:56 (hv): "unexceptional horror film." Martin. Palmerini: 1988. With Patrick Lowe, Cheryl Arutt, Sarah Buxton, Bo Svenson.

Baboon bite ... rare disease ... gore effects.

**PRIMAL SCREAM** Oakcrest/Howard Foulkrod 1987 (1986) color 88m. (*Hellfire* - orig t). SP, D: William Murray. Mus: Mark Knox. SpFX: David DiPietro. SpMkpFX: Geoff Langloh, Eric Princz. Opt: Dynamic FX. Ref: TV. V 5/14/86. With Kenneth McGregor, Sharon Mason, Julie Miller, Mickey Shaughnessy.

In 1993, a "deep space mining conglomerate" is testing a "new energy catalyst," Hellfire, an "incredibly destructive weapon." Its victims simply disintegrate. (Instant gross-out.) Acting, music, editing, and sound here may be intentionally tacky—the film seems pleased with its general lousiness. Fun occasionally threatens in the Forties-detective-movie dialogue between "all around tough guy" Corby McHale (McGregor), Samantha Keller (Mason), and Caitlin Foster (Miller).

**PRIME EVIL** Crown Int'l./Reeltime 1988 color 85m. D: Roberta Findlay. SP: Ed Kelleher, Harriette Vidal. Mus, P: Walter E. Sear. SpFX: Ed French. Ref: V 5/25/88: "no twists." 1/13/88:28. Martin. McCarty II: "skip it." With William Beckwith, Christine Moore, Tim Gail.

"Ancient demon." (V)

**PRINCE AT THE COURT OF YARRALUMLA, The** see *Wicked, The*

**PRINCE IN WONDERLAND** see *Little Prince and Eight Headed Dragon*

**PRINCE OF DARKNESS** Univ-Northern/Alive Films (Carolco) 1987 color/ws 102m. SP, D, Mus: John Carpenter. P: Larry Franco. Mattes: Jim Danforth; FX Associates. SpFxCoord: Kevin Quibell. Canister: Steve Patino. Mkp: Frank Carrisosa. SpSdFX: Dane Davis, John Paul Fasal. Ref: TV. MFB'88:147. V 10/28/87. SFExam 10/30/87. With Donald Pleasence, Jameson Parker, Victor Wong, Lisa Blount, Anne Howard (Susan Cabot), Alice Cooper, Dennis Dun.

"I live!" Ingredients: The Sleeper, the container-bound son of a banished "anti-God" ... The Brotherhood of Sleep, a "forgotten sect" with "enormous power and authority" ... a new supernova and other changes in the Earth and sky ... "demonic possession" ... unholy water ... hordes of beetles ... a "parasite growing into its host" ... and the usual Carpenter pseudo-music.... The buildup is slow, but there are scattered tantalizing details—e.g., the "water-window." The philosophical fol-de-rol is just an excuse for familiar vampire, zombie, and possession elements.

**PRINCE OF TERROR** (I) Reteitalia-TV 1989? color 88m. D: Lamberto Bava. Tel: D. Sacchetti. Ph: G. Transunto. Mus: S. Boswell. Ref: Dark Side 47:48-52: High Tension series; direct-sound English. With Tomas Arana, Carole Andre, David Brandon.

Homicidal maniac, gore, horror-movie star.

**The PRINCESS AND THE GOBLIN** (B-Hung.) J&M Ent./Siriol & Pannonia & S4C Wales/NHK Ents. 1993 (1992) anim color 82m. (*A Hercegno es a Kobold*). D: J. Gemes. SP, P: R. Lyons, from George MacDonald's novel. Anim D: Les Orton. Mus: Istvan Lerch. SpFX: Z. Bulyaki(sp?), P. Martsa. Ref:TV: Hemdale HV; c.'91. Sean: "good." V 1/11/93: "unimaginative plotting." Voices: Claire Bloom, Victor Spinetti et al.

"Hideous goblin prince ... grungy goblins."(V) "It was horrible!" Underground, music-fearing goblins plot to kidnap the "sun people" above. Meanwhile, the local forest is haunted by "strange things"—cat, bat, and dog creatures, a horned thing, and little dragon and dinosaur-types ... the "pets" of the goblins .... Mostly vapid animated fairy tale. The pets are actually creepier than the goblins themselves; the latter are mainly just uncouth (minor gross-out alert).

The **PRINCESS BRIDE**  Fox (Act III)/Buttercup (The Princess Bride Ltd.) 1987 color 98m. D, Co-P: Rob Reiner. SP: William Goldman, from his novel. Mech Des: N. D. Trevessey. SpFxSup: Nick Allder. Animatronics Sup: Rodger Shaw. SpSdFX: Sandy Berman. Ref: TV. V 9/16/87. SFChron 10/9/87. ad. SFExam 10/30/87. MFB '88:87-8.

Fantasy-comedy with a few horrific sequences. In one, big-mouthed "shrieking eels" peril the princess on the sea; in another, "rodents of unusual size" attack the princess in the forest. Generally droll, occasionally too cute, but far more bearable than either *Legend* or *Ladyhawke*.

**PRINCESS FROM THE MOON**  (J) Toho/Fuji TV (Kakutani-Fujii-Shinsaka) 1987 color 120m. (*Taketori Monogatari*). SP, D: Kon Ichikawa. SP: also Kikushima, Ishigami, Hidaka. Ph: S. Kobayashi. SpFX: Nakano. Ref: V 9/23/87: "often melancholy, yet constantly uplifting tone." Tokyo Int'l. Festival '87 (notes). With Toshiro Mifune, Ayako Wakao, Yasuko Sawaguchi, Koji Ishizaka.

"Mammoth spaceship" takes "young woman temporarily marooned on Earth" back to the moon. (V)

**PRINCESS OF DARKNESS** see *Satan's Princess*

**PRINCESS OF THE NIGHT**  Vidco 1990 color 81m. D: F. J. Lincoln. Ref: Adam '92. With Lauren Hall, Madison, Heather Lere, Jamie Gillis, Tom Byron.

Undying vampires after virgin blood.

**PRINCESS WARRIOR**  USA-TV/Vista St. Prods. (Feifer-Miller/Marketing Media) 1990 color c80m. D: Lindsay Norgard. SP: John Riley. Ph: Robert Duffin. Mus: Marc Decker. PD: Greg Hildreth. SpVisFX: William S. Mims Prods. Mkp: Toni Riki. Ref: TV. TVG. With Sharon Lee Jones (Ovule), Dana Fredsti (Curette), Mark Pacific, Tony Riccardi, Augie Blunt, Laurie Warren (Exzema), Lee Gerovitz, Cheryl Janecky (Queen Mother).

An alien (Jones)—"I don't kiss"—flees extra-galactic intrigue to Earth, and some tough space babes follow her to L.A., through a time-and-space "portal".... Vapid sf-action-comedy. Laser swords double as disintegrating rays, and a glowing "tattoo" enables aliens to "talk" to relatives of theirs bearing similar marks.

**PRISON**  Empire/Eden Ltd. (Irwin Yablans) 1987 color 103m. D: Renny Harlin. SP: C. Courtney Joyner. Story: Yablans. Mus: Richard Band, C. L. Stone. SpMechFX: Etan Ents.; Eddie Surkin. SpMkpFX: MMI; (sup) John Buechler; (animatronics) John Criswell, Hal Miles. Opt: motion; (fx coord) Linda Obalil; (anim) Kevin Kutchaver, Allen Blyth. Ref: TV. MFB'88:178. V 3/2/88. SFChron 5/7/88. With Viggo Mortensen, Chelsea Field, Lane Smith, Lincoln Kilpatrick, Kane Hodder (Charlie Forsythe).

The opening of a walled-up execution chamber at Wyoming State Penitentiary unleashes the spirit of Charlie Forsythe, a convict framed and executed for murder. In a pretty impressive sequence, his malevolent spirit turns solitary into an oven and ignites one inmate. A subsequent mess—in the mess hall—involves further heavy-duty makeup-effects gore, and—in the most effective sequence of all—a roll of barbed wire comes to murderous life. At the end, Forsythe's lightning-animated corpse orchestrates his chief framer's execution.... The vehicle for the above effects sequences is, unfortunately, an overelaborate, overplotted men-in-prison story.

**PRISON PLANET**  Col TriStar 1987 color 90m. D: Armand Gazarian. Ref: Martin: "silliness." SFChron Dtbk 5/16/93. With James Phillips, Jack Wilcox, M. M. Foley, Deborah Thompson-Carlin.

Year 2200. Rebels vs. dictator.

**PRISON SHIP** see *Star Slammer*

**PRIVAT KLINIK PROFESSOR LUND**  (W.G.) Divina Film & FD Andam 1959 b&w 96m. (aka *Arzt ohne Gewissen*. aka *Das Letzte Geheimnis. Doctor without Scruples* - U.S.). D: Falk Harnack. SP: W. P. Zibaso. Idea: Andam. Mus: S. Franz. Ref: Lee. Hardy/SF: "gory." TVFFSB. With Wolfgang Preiss, Ewald Balser, Barbara Ruetting, Cornell Borchers, Karin Baal.

Heart-transplant experiments on prostitutes.

**PRIVATE TUTOR** see *After School*

The **PRIZE PEST**  WB 1951 anim color 7m. D: Robert McKimson. SP: Tedd Pierce. Mus: Carl Stalling. Ref: WBCartoons. LC. TV. no Lee.

Porky Pig and Daffy Duck scare each other with monster-disguises. Funny stuff.

See also *Daffy Duck's Quackbusters*.

**PROFANADORES**  (Mex) Cine Comunicacion & PM & Central de Video 1991 color c85m. D: R. Hernandez. SP: A. Martinez. SpFX: Arturo Godinez. Mkp: Laura Hernandez. Ref: TV: Grave Robbers - tr t. TVG.

Talky, lackadaisical shot-on-tape movie re a body-snatching syndicate contains a few incidental, semi-spooky grave-robbing and human-sacrifice sequences. With Fidel Abrego as "satanico" number one.

**PROFANADORES DE SEPULCROS** see *Ladrones de Tumbas*

**3P PROF. ZOVEK**  (Mex.) 1971 feature (aka *El Increible Profesor Zovek*). Ref: Cinef 6/96:46: "mad scientist who is creating monster-men." Ecran F 31:31: title character also in *Invasion de los Muertos* (2).

The **PROFESSOR**  Greg Luce/Kent Films (J. Perry Davis/Forward Inc.) 1958 (1988) 26-1/2m. SP, D: Tom McCain. Ph: Max Kent. Ref: TV. G. Luce. Bill Warren. no LC. Filmfax. With John S. Copeland, Irene Barr, Benny McIntyre, Vin Della Rocca, Doug Hobart, Dick Levy, Bob Gaus, Jean Barger.

"Are you trying to tell us that Dr. Trisler has been turned into a werewolf?" "Something or someone of maniacal fury" has been killing sheep in the Culver Mountains. This "wolfman" (Hobart) then kills a "Commie," but his friend Prof. Wilmer (Copeland) makes plans to stun him with a "shock ray" gun and save him.

Long-lost black-and-white horror short, or mini-feature, has very stilted acting and staging and a pathetic offscreen "howl" for the werewolf. The makeup for Hobart seems to be just blackface and fangs. Barger's reporter Millie gets the prize camp line: "It was the most gruesome creature I've ever seen—all covered with hair!" Second prize to the Commie (as the credits list Gaus), who intones "My people are told only the facts!", as he stares down the camera, which is moving meaningfully into a close-up.

**PROFESSOR PUDDENHEAD'S PATENTS — THE ELECTRIC ENLARGER** (B) Urban 1909 silent 5m. D: W.R. Booth. Ref: BFC. Hardy/SF. no Lee.

Invention creates giant moth, man, dog, caterpillar.

**PROFESSOR WAGSTAFF'S TIME MACHINE** see *Young Time Travellers*

**PROFESSOR WITTEMBACH'S MANUSCRIPT** see *Marriage of the Bear*

The **PROFESSOR'S DISCOVERY** Unique 1908 b&w silent short. Ref: V 9/5/08: whiff of "mysterious composition" from lab makes people dance.

**PROFEZIA, La** see *Osceno Desiderio, L'*

The **PROFOUND AND MYSTERIOUS** (H.K.?) Kwang Film 198-? color/ws c90m. (*Deep Cut*-ad t). D: Yao Fung-Pan. Ref: TV: vt; Eng. titles.

A ghoul-masked killer with a scythe, a "woman's cry at midnight," and bleeding murals haunt the old house once owned by the rich Shi Lang Wang. At the end, the killers—a man and wife team—wall up the heroine, Hsin Ju, with her dead brother.

Talky, but a sense of foreboding builds as the wedding between the poor Hsin Ju and Lord Chien draws near, and dead bodies proliferate. Is the killer Lord Chien, his ex-mistress Yueh Ying, the housekeeper, or ...? Okay photography, music, and wind sound-effects. The all-a-plot payoff is disappointing, but there is one for-real ghost scene: The ghost of Chun Wang, Hsin Ju's brother, appears to his aunt at her front door.

**PROFUMO DELLE SIGNORA IN NERO** see *Perfume of the Lady in Black*

**PROGRAMED FOR PLEASURE** 198-? color feature. Ref: vc box: robot.

**PROGRAMMED TO KILL** see *Retaliator, The*

**PROINI PERIPOLOS** (Greek) Greek Film Center & Nicos Nicolaidis 1987 color 108m. SP, D: Nicolaidis. Mus: George Hatzinassios. Ref: V 11/18/87: "one of the most impressive films of the [Thessaloniki] festival"; *Morning Patrol* - tr t. With Michelle Valley, Takis Spyridakis.

"Electronic voices" haunt a woman entering the "forbidden zone" of a mysteriously deserted city.

**PROJECT "A"KO** (J) Soeishinsa Co. & A.P.P.P. (Kazufumi Nomura) 1986 anim color/ws 83m. D: Katahiko Nishijima; (anim) Yuji Moriyama. Mus: Joey Carbone, Richie Zito. Ref: TV: Pony Video; some Eng. songs. Wonderful World of Comics 4/88:43. Animag 5:6-10. SFChron Dtbk 3/29/92. 4/11/93. Voices: Michie Tomizawa ("C"Ko), Miki Ito ("A"Ko), Shuichi Ikeda (the captain), Tessho Genda (Spy-D), Emi Shinohara ("B"Ko).

Graviton City, destroyed by a derelict alien spacecraft and rebuilt in the middle of a crater lake. Student "A"Ko Magami, daughter of Clark Kent and Wonder Woman, has super-speed and super-strength, but it's her friend "C"Ko, everyone's pet, who turns out to be the long-lost space princess. "B"Ko, "A"Ko's rival for "C"Ko's affections, employs weapons like super-robots against "A"Ko, as, above, a space war rages, and an alien ship dispatches hordes of robot-spiders.

Episodic but generally charming mock-epic, in the tradition, more or less, of "The Rape of the Lock," boasts some elaborately choreographed space battles. What Dagwood did to the mailman on his way out the door every morning, "A"Ko, running late, does to alien Spy-D on her way to school every morning.

See also the following titles and *A-Ko the Battle*.

**PROJECT A-KO 2** (J) Pony Video 1987 anim color 49m. Ref: TV: Pony Video; no Eng.; OAV.

In this sequel to *Project "A"Ko*, classmates and spies are still chasing C-Ko, and the futuristic weapons and vehicles include one spacecraft with a nose in the image of C-Ko. Once again, there are elaborate space-action sequences, but the funniest scenes come mostly before the real action (which is difficult to follow without a synopsis). The wide-mouth effects for C-Ko are even more outrageous this time around. Second-most-amusing running gag: the omnipresence of spies lurking behind strategically opened newspapers.

**PROJECT A-KO 3: CINDERELLA RHAPSODY** (J) Pony Video 1988 anim color 50m. Ref: vc box: OAV.

**PROJECT A-KO 4: THE FINAL CHAPTER** (J) Pony Canyon/Soeinshinsha 1989 anim color 50m. D: Yuuji Moriyama. Ref: Animag 7:5. 9:5: OAV; "giant A-Ko robot."

**PROJECT A-KO VERSUS** see *A-Ko the Battle*

**PROJECT: ALIEN** (U.S.-Yugos.-Austral.) Sugar Ent./ITC/IFE & Jadran Film & Australian Film Commission & Incovent (Camperdown) 1990 color 92m. (*Fatal Sky* - alt & TV t. aka *No Cause for Alarm*. aka *Deadfall*). D: Frank Shields. Story, SP: David Webb Peoples (aka A. Able). Story: also Brian Williams, David White. Mus: Allan Zavod. SpVisFX: Fantasy II. SpFxCoord: Marijan Karoglan. Mkp: Slazenka Dragojevic. Ref: TV: Vidmark video. Psychotronic 13:50. TVG. V 2/21/90: 70 (ad). 5/2/90: S-46, S-80, S-98, 82, 238. With Michael Nouri, Darlanne Fluegel, Maxwell Caulfield, Charles Durning, Derren Nesbitt.

"Why are people dying like flies from Nova Scotia to Iceland? Was it the UFOs that started it?" Or was it a meteor shower? Are blood-sucking "insect creatures" behind the mysterious epidemic and the eviscerated cattle? Anyway, the "funny stuff"—in one of the bland, juvenile script's few decent lines of dialogue—"comes at night." The too-little, too-late answer: Seems Russian lasers shot down a U.S. space station, and canisters containing "genetic mutation experiments" rained down on Earth.... There's so little to the story here that most of the screen time is taken up with the cover-up of the canister accident. *Project: Alien* aka *Fatal Sky* borrows from *Endangered Species,* which in turn borrowed from *The Whip Hand.*

**PROJECT EDEN** see *Dirty Pair Movie*

**PROJECT ELIMINATOR** U.S. Rainbow/Victory (Morris Asgar/David & Gail Carradine) 1991 color 89m. Story, SP, D: H. Kaye Dyal. Story: also M. Asgar. Ref: PT 11:10. Martin: "trying and tired." vc box: South Gate Ent.; "flying attack laser." With D. Carradine, Frank Zagarino, Drew Snyder.

"Anti-personnel weapon that looks like a small Buck Rogers ship. (PT)

**PROJECT: GENESIS** see *Strange Horizon*

**PROJECT GINGER** Vivid Video (Bruce Seven) 1985 color 86m. D, P: B. Seven. SP: Raven Touchstone. Ph, Ed: Michael Cates. Mus: John Further, Multi-Sound Prods. Mkp: Alexis Vogel. Ref: TV: V. Video. Adam '88. With Ginger Lynn, Heather Wayne, Bionca, Keri Foxx, Tom Byron, Rick Savage.

"Crazy" Dr. Martin is working on a formula to "turn inanimate objects into live ones." ("Kinda spooky—reminds me of those old Frankenstein movies.") His chemicals, plus ginger spice, succeed in bringing a life-sized rubber doll to life. Another of the doc's "scientific inventions": an aphrodisiac "of the highest grade," dubbed "Martin's Iced Tea".... Film itself is definitely not a live one.

**PROJECT HADES ZEORYMER: THE CHAPTER OF HEAVEN** (J) CPM/Toshiba EMI/Youmex (Toru Miura/Morio Chimi-Artmic-AIC) 1989 (1988/'94-U.S.) anim color 30m. each (*Hades Project Zeorymer* - cr t, U.S.). D: Hirano Toshihiro. SP: Aikawa Noboru. Story: Morio Chimi. Mus: Eiji Kawamura. PD: Kakinuma, Yamane. Mecha Des: Moriki Yasushi. Ref: TV: USManga Corps video (ToEmi Video); Eng. titles. Animag 8:30-32: 1st 2 of 4 OAVs. Narrator: Issei Masamune.

"What is the connection between Zeorymer and Masato?" Giant conglomerate Haudragon uses "team of giant robots called the Hakkeshu" to attempt to conquer the world. (Animag) Each robot here is linked to a "specific individual's bioelectric and brainwash patterns." Fast, indifferent tale of the Zeorymer of the Heavens.

**PROJECT HADES ZEORYMER: THE CHAPTER OF EARTH** and **TRITON OF THE SEA** (J) ToEMI 1990 anim color 30m. each. Ref: Animag 8:30. 10:4: 3 & 4 in the OAV series re dinosaurs and a plot to turn Earth into Hades. Japan Video.

Follow-up to *Zeorymer.*

**PROJECT METALBEAST** Prism (Hildebrand) 1994 color 92m. SP, D: A. De Gaetano. SP: also T.E. Sabo. FX: J.C. Buechler. Ref: PT 20:16-17: "silly." Martin: "sorry tale." With Kane Hodder (werewolf), Barry Bostwick, Kim Delaney.

**PROJECT NIGHTMARE** Jones-Lane 1986 color 75m. SP, D, Ph, Ed: Donald Jones. SP, P: James Lane. Mus: Stefan Hawk. SpFX: Russell Martin. Mkp: B. C. Ellis. Ref: TV: Academy Home Ent. video. no Hound. no Phantom. Stanley. no Scheuer. no Martin. no Maltin '92. With Charles Miller, Seth Foster, Elly Koslo, Harry Melching, LeRoy Hughes, Jeff Braun, Lance Dickson.

"I know it's out there waiting!" Whatever "it" is, it's red, it hums, it's 35 feet tall, and it's part of Project Touchstone. The latter was designed as a "mental testing ground" for astronauts—"pulsating electromagnetic fields" enable a computer to turn emotions into "solid entities." For the record, "it" is a "fluctuating mass energy, nondescript form, highly destructive in nature."

"Twilight Zone"-like puzzle movie is too vague in storyline to hold one's attention, but the pretentious, *Solaris*-on-a-dime payoff is certainly amusing. In it, Gus, the hero, kneels at the feet of his thought-materialized father whose death he indirectly caused. Stiff, artificial movie also recalls *Forbidden Planet,* with an "it" instead of an "Id."

**PROJECT: SHADOWCHASER** (U.S.-Can.-B?) NAR/EGM & Prism Ent. (Shadowchase/Lloyd Simandl et al/Griffiths-Eyres) 1992 color 90m. D: John Eyres. SP: Stephen Lister. Ph: A. M. Trow. Mus: G. Pinder. PD: Mark Harris. Prosth FX: Chrissie Overs. Model & FxSup: Brian Smithies. VideoFxSup: Dick Hewitt. Digital SdFX: G. Gronow. OptFX: Opt FilmFX; (sup) Roy Field. Ref: TV. TVG. Cinef 7/93. PT 14:10. With Frank Zagarino, Martin Kove, Meg Foster, Paul Koslo, Joss Ackland (Kinderman), Ricco Ross.

Ingredients: Romulus, an android, product of the government's Project Romulus, intended to create a "perfect synthetic warrior" ("I've never lived") ... our cryogenically-frozen hero (Kove), thawed out to battle Romulus ... and an "android embolism," which seems to work, but.... Routine hyper-active suspenser. Main motifs: automatic-gunfire bursts and falling, screaming bodies.

**PROJECT SHADOWCHASER II** see *Night Siege*

**PROJECT VAMPIRE** Action Int'l./NBV Prods. (Hicks-Tams) 1992 color c92m. SP, D, AD: Peter Flynn. Ph: Joe Mealey. Mus: Robert King. SpFxMkp: John Criswell. VisFX: Brian Oliver. DigitalFX: Video-It Post. Ref: TV: AIP HV. Stanley. Jones. Fango 128:11. SFChron Dtbk 10/31/93: "funnier than it is scary." With Myron Natwick, Brian Knudson, Mary-Louis Gemmill.

"Here's to eternity!" Vampire doc (Natwick) intends to "create a world of vampires with his high-tech super serum." (Jones) ("A whole new form of life will take over this world.") Plus an antidote to vampirism which "keeps the volatile molecular structure stable" ... and "bizarre murders" in and around L.A. Shot-on-tape, and badly. A lot of "Well, well, well. Who do we have here?""

**PROJECT WITH MADARA** see *Beast War Madara*

**PROM NIGHT III: THE LAST KISS** (Can.) IVE/Peter Simpson & Comweb & Famous Players (Ray Sager) 1990 (1989) color 95m. SP, D: Ron Oliver. SP: also P. Simpson. Mus: Paul Zaza. SpFxMkp: Nancy Howes. SpFX: Light & Motion. Ref: TV. V 3/28/90. With Tim Conlon, Cyndy Preston, David Stratton, Courtney Taylor, Colin Simpson (dead prom MC).

"You kill 'em; I bury 'em...." Though (as we see, in a visualized nightmare sequence) they don't stay buried. Storywise, this follow-up to *Hello Mary Lou: Prom Night II* is closer to *Teen Wolf* than to either previous *Prom Night*: The supernatural is the means to the same end—success and popularity in high school. Here, though, it's (somewhat unbelievably) a second party—a witch/demon (Taylor)—who makes the hero's (Conlon) success possible. Some good bizarre moments—including a climactic Prom Night of the Living Dead—in this basically wrongheaded enterprise.

**PROM NIGHT IV: DELIVER US FROM EVIL** (Can.) Peter Simpson & Ray Sager (Over the Edge Ltd.) 1991 color 95m. D: Clay Borris. SP: Richard Beattie. Mus: Paul Zaza. SpFxCoord: Brock Jolliffe. SdFxSup: Mark Beck. Mkp: Nancy Howe. Ref: TV. V 5/27/91. SFChron Dtbk 6/28/92. 4/11/93. With Nikki de Boer, Alden Kane, Joy Tanner, Alle Ghadban, James Carver (Father Jonas), Ken McGregor, Brock Simpson (Father Colin).

"All we can do is keep the demon contained." St. George's Church, 1991. Father Colin takes Father Jaeger's (McGregor) place as guardian of Father Jonas, an overzealous priest who slashes promiscuous teens with a crucifix and is "evil beyond imagination." Almost immediately, Jonas escapes from 33 years of solitary confinement and recites the Lord's Prayer as he lifts and crushes one poor fornicator, then crucifies and burns the second leads here. Small-beans thrills in this formula son-of-*Exorcist*.

**PROPHECIES OF NOSTRADAMUS** see *Nostradamus*

**PROPHECY, The** see *God's Army*

**PROTOTYPE X29** A Trimark/Filmtown 1992 color 98m. (*Prototype* - orig t). Story, SP, D: Phillip Roth. Story, P: G. C. Scandiuzzi. Ph: M. W. Gray. Mus: E. Kauderer. Prototype: (created by) George Temple; (sp fx mkp) R. J. Marino. SpFxMkp: B. Barshdorf. SdDes: Tony Cannella. AD: Shauna Oetting et al. Computer Anim: Tim Douglas. Ref: TV. TVG. V 5/4/92:174. Martin. PT 16:17. Fango 122:32. SFChron Dtbk 10/31/93. With Lane Lenhart, Robert Tossberg, Brenda Swanson, Mitchell Cox, Paul Coulj; Michael White, Barshdorf, & Eric Fedorin (Prototype).

In the middle of the 21st Century, "cybernetically altered humans" called Omegas begin to "alter their programming"—thus the "time of the mad minds." "Totally cybernetic entities" called Prototypes are then programmed to terminate Omegas. Meanwhile, the last Omega, Chandra Kerkorian (Lenhart) is activated, and Hawkins (Tossberg) is "reborn" cybernetically with re-implanted memories.... Pretentious, "tough," sentimental, confusing.

**PRZYJACIEL WESOLEGO DIABLA** (Polish) Se-Ma-For Film 1987 color 87m. SP, D, Ph: Jerzy Lukaszewicz. From Kornel Makuszynski's novel. Ref: V 11/7/87: "some passable thrills"; *The Friend of a Jolly Devil* - tr t.

Ingredients in this fairy tale include the Lord of Darkness, "huge spiders," and a "lovable monster."

**El PSICOPATA ASESINO** (Mex) Procinema (Raul Galindo) 1992? color 95m. Story, D: Ruben Galindo Jr. Adap: Jose Movellan. Ph: J. Luis Vera. Mus: F. Chavez. SpFX: J. Segura. Ref: TV: Mexcinema Video; no Eng.; *The Psychopathic Killer* - tr t. With Gerardo Albarran, Luis Gatica, Roxana Chavez, Agustin Bernal, Martin Gomez (killer).

The woman who imagines herself assailed by a be-wigged slasher momentarily seems to be the slasher herself. (She paints her face and wields a butcher knife.) Under hypnosis, she "sees" herself chased by the phantom, and at the end the killer hypnotizes her in an attempt to get her to kill.... Well-made and slightly different, but routine.

**PSYCH-OUT** AIP (Dick Clark) 1968 color 90m. (*The Love Children* - orig t). D: Richard Rush. Ref: screen. Jim Shapiro. LC. AFI. V 3/13/68. Weldon. SFChron Dtbk 1/19/92.

Nightmare sequences with monster, smoking bricks, mysterious mist, fireballs. Okay bits here and there, but mostly talk and photographic effects.

**The PSYCHIC** Hurlon Prods. 1967 color c80m. (aka *Copenhagen's Psychic Loves*). D, P: James F. Hurley. Ph: Herschell Gordon Lewis. Mus: Vincent Oddo. Ref: TV: Camp Video (1986). no AFI. no LC. Phantom. Hound. Stanley. Scheuer. Filmfax 28:79. With Dick Genola, Robin Guest, Bobbi Spencer.

A freak accident leaves Daniel Thomas with the gift of prophecy: He correctly predicts the date of death of his boss, "Old Man" Wilson. Initially, he uses his ESP for gambling purposes; later, he panics when he finds himself losing his "pure psychical ability".... This is your basic, dull show-biz story, the shell of *Night Has a Thousand Eyes*. Neither Dan's rise nor fall is convincing or compelling, and the production has a not-quite-finished look.

**PSYCHIC** USA-TV/Trimark (Tom Berry/W. Webb) 1992 color c90m. D: George Mihalka. Tel: M. Tejada-Flores, P. Koval. Story: M. M. Crawford, W. Crawford. Ref: V: "gives ESP a bad name." Fango 111. Martin: "poor acting and writing." PT 13:50: "better than average." With Zach Galligan, Catherine Mary Stewart, Michael Nouri. Student has "visions of women being strangled." (V)

**PSYCHIC KILLER** see *Soul Killer*

**PSYCHIC WARS** (J) V. Anime 1991 anim color 51m. Ref: TV: vt; no Eng.

A man granted spiritual super-powers rides a maelstrom to a prehistoric-like land of hulk-monsters and a naked woman who turns into a giant, rodent-headed creature which, in death, discharges flying starfish-creatures. Some of the monsters escape to our world, where the temporarily possessed heroine becomes a fanged killer-lady who apparently does the bidding of the purple supermonster in the sky.... Okay monster-fantasy is atmospheric and actionful, though otherwise unremarkable.

**PSYCHO III** Univ/Hilton A. Green 1986 color 96m. D: Anthony Perkins. SP: Charles Edward Pogue. Mus: Carter Burwell. SpVisFX: Syd Dutton, Bill Taylor; Illusion Arts. SpMkp: Michael Westmore. SpFX: K. G. Miller et al. Ref: TV. MFB'86:341-2. V 7/2/86. SFChron 7/2/86. ad. With A. Perkins, Diana Scarwid, Jeff Fahey, Roberta Maxwell, Hugh Gillin, Katt Shea Ruben.

Trivial variations on *Psycho* themes, as Norman Bates (Perkins) finds that Maureen Coyle (Scarwid) reminds him of Marion Crane. In a semi-clever twist, he saves her from suicide. Plus: hallucinations and other business re severed hands. A promising, sweet, love-for-Norman theme degenerates into tired gotta-kill-the-one-you-love material.

See also the following and *Bates Motel. Silence of the Hams*.

**PSYCHO IV: THE BEGINNING** Showtime-TV/Smart Money (George Zaloom, Hilton Green, Les Mayfield/MTE) 1990 color 96m. D: Mick Garris. SP, Exec P: Joseph Stefano. Ph: Rodney Charters. Mus: Graeme Revell. PD: Michael Hanan. SpFxMkp: Alterian Studios. SpFX: Rick Jones. OptFX: Pacific Title. Ref: TV: MCA HV. Sacto Bee 11/4/90. 11/9/90. TVG. With Anthony Perkins, CCH Pounder, Donna Mitchell, Henry Thomas, Olivia Hussey (Norma Bates), Warren Frost, Thomas Schuster, Alice Hirson (voice of Mother), Ryan Finnigan (child Norman), Peggy O'Neal, John Landis.

In various flashbacks set in and around Fairvale, young Norman's mother goads him into killing, then is herself poisoned (along with her lover) by Norman. At the end, in the present, he tries to burn the past (i.e., that old house), as said past (in the form of visions of his victims) assails him. ("I'm free!")

Fourth in the series plays at times like highlights from the original *Psycho*, as it brings back your favorite music, images, and lines; at other times, it plays like random scenes from the life of Norman Bates. At fade-out, the sound of Mom's voice and the crying of a baby (presumably the offspring of Norman and wife) economically suggest once and future concerns.

**PSYCHO COP** see *Psychocop*

**PSYCHO COP 2** Film Nouveau/Penn Eden West (Shapiro-Elwes/David Niven, Jr./David Andriole) 1994 (1992) color 85m. (aka *Psycho Cop Returns*). D: Rif Coogan. SP: Dan Povenmire. Ph: E. Mada. Mus: M.D. Becker. PD: Claude Viator. SpFxMkp: Williams & Tristano. SdFX: Able Dogs Post. Ref: TV. TVG. Vallejo T-H. vc box. With Bobby Ray Shafer (Officer Joe Vickers), Barbara Lee Alexander, Roderick Darin, Miles David Dougal, Julie Strain.

Officer Inbred's answer to Drunk and Disorderly: a bullet in the head. Fornication rates a two-on-a-spear trick. Plus a predictable "Going down" for an elevator shafting. Film becomes jocular in the worst way after a semi-promising opening scene.

**PSYCHO GIRLS** (Can.) Cannon/Lightshow 1987 color 92m. SP, D: Gerard Ciccoritti. SP, P: Michael Bockner. Ph: R. Bergman. Mus: J. Rosenbaum. AD: Craig Richards. Ref: V 7/1/87: "thriller that self-destructs." Martin. Phantom: "unwatchable mess." Newman: "shoddy." With John H. Cuff, Darlene Mignacco, Agi Gallus, Silvio Oliviero.

Madwoman escapes asylum to torture and kill.

**PSYCHO KILLERS** see *Mania*

**PSYCHO SEX KILLER** (Fili) ATB-4 Films Int'l. (Anna Theresa, Allan Gilbert) 1992 color 86m. D: Dante Pangilinan. SP: Bonnie Paredes. Ph: Amado de Guzman. Mus D: Boy Alcaide. SdFX: Don Kiko. Ref: TV: Viva Video; occ. Eng. With Rhey Roldan, Digna Morena, Edmon Ramos, Robert Talby, Mon Confiado, George Estregan Jr., Stella Mari.

"It's just a bad dream!" A prowler with a straight razor lethally slashes up a young woman in a tub, then commits another slasher murder. Later, he varies his m.o. with a strangler's cord, then an ax.... Strictly functional, ineptly staged shocker with a mildly surprising payoff: The (femme) shrink's the killer.

**3P PSYCHO SISTERS** Impulse (Caplan-Stone) 1972 (1969) color 76m. (*The Sibling* - vt t. aka *So Evil, My Sister*). D: Reginald LeBorg. SP: Tony Crechales. Ph: Dean Cundey. Mus: Johnny Pate. SpMkpFX: William Tuttle. Opt: Van Der Veer FX. Ref: TV: Impulse video. Oliviero: aka *Le Sorelle*? Stanley. Maltin '92. Hound. Phantom. Martin. With Susan Strasberg, Faith Domergue, Sydney Chaplin (George), Charles Knox Robinson, Steve Mitchell, Kathleen Freeman, John Howard.

"I'm having nightmares, but you're the one who's crazy!" A "potent" prescription drug gives Brenda (Strasberg) visions of her dead husband (Chaplin) and nightmares re creatures and corpses. At the end, her sister Millie (Domergue) is confronted by a monster-masked man in a shower—the "dead" man returned, as it turns out.... Flat-footed and obvious all-a-plot plot, with comically horrendous corpse makeup.

**PSYCHOCOP** South Gate Ent. (Jessica Rains) 1989 color 86m. (aka *Psycho Cop*). SP, D: Wallace Potts. Ref: V 1/10/90:32 (hv): "very boring." no Martin. V 9/27/89 (rated); British? With Bobby Ray Shafer, Jeff Qualle, Palmer Lee Todd.

Satanist, blood ritual, crucifixion.

Sequel: *Psycho Cop 2*.

**PSYCHOS IN LOVE** Infinity & Generic Films 1987 color 80m. SP, D, P, Ed, Ph: Gorman Bechard. SP: also Carmine Capobianco. Ref: Film Journal 6/87. V 5/6/87. Phantom: "home-movie-level loser." Martin: gore, psychopathic killer. PT 12:12: cannibal plumber. With C. Capobianco, Debi Thibeault, Frank Stewart.

**PULSE** Col/Aspen Film Society (Patricia A. Stallone/W. E. McEuen) 1988 color c95m. SP, D: Paul Golding. Mus: Jay Ferguson. Macro Ph: Oxford Scientific Films. SpFX: Richard O. Helmer. Anim: Cinema Research. Mkp: K. M. Logan. Ref: TV: Col HV. V 12/28/88. Maltin '92. Phantom. Martin. Morse. Scheuer. With Cliff DeYoung, Roxanne Hart, Joey Lawrence, Charles Tyner, Myron Healey.

"It comes into the wires!" Are electric "pulses" responsible for the malfunctioning appliances in a suburban California home? Journey into the Circuits shots suggest that the TV set is rewiring itself, and that this household's electricity has a life of its own. ("Spooky, ain't it?") Spooky it is....

*Pulse* is a relatively smart, improved version of the basically dumb story of the malign house. (See *Burnt Offerings, This House Possessed*.) It's spookier in the early stages, before the electricity is shown to be not just alive, but malicious as well; before, that is, it's demoted from Phenomenon to Villain. Tyner's in-the-know old man hits just the right comic-macabre note, and the rest of the cast is capable, too, but wires, circuits, and coils star.

**The PUMAMAN** (I) ADM-Deantir (Giuseppe Auriemma) 1980 color c80m. (*L'Uomo Puma*). Story, D: Alberto De Martino. SP: De Rita, Angelo. Ph: Vulpiani. Mus: Serio. AD: Visone. SpFX: Mauro Grilli. Spaceship: Giorgio Ferrari. OptFX: Studio 4; (sp) Strategma, Bernardo. SpSdFX: Cine Audio FX. Mkp: S. Trani. Ref: TV. TVG. Prod. Ital. V 5/7/80:400. Stanley. Hound. Martin. no Scheuer. Ecran F 74:66. Palmerini. With Miguelangel Fuentes, Sydne Rome, Donald Pleasence, W. G. Alton, Silvano Tranquilli.

The mask of the Pumaman is "proof of an outer-space presence in our history." A Christmas-tree-ornament-like spaceship leaves the mask behind, at Stonehenge, and the Pumaman (Alton)—son of the son of the aliens—is designated its custodian. Meanwhile, the bad guys: "We make slaves of men with this mask." (It has hypnotic powers.) Pumaman sees in the dark (just like real pumas) and flies (just like real superheroes). He has the "blood of the gods coming from other worlds." He also walks through walls and has hands like superclaws, with which he rips open the tops of cars.

Nonsensical, lively, breezy superhero stuff, full of silly-funny effects and stunts. Most of the American superhero movie product seems, by comparison, tame and stolid. The hero doesn't so much fly as bumble along in the air.

**PUMPKINHEAD** UA-MGM/Lion Films & Billy Blake (Howard Smith, R. C. Weinman) 1988 color 86m. Story, D: Stan Winston. Story, SP: Mark Patrick Carducci. Story: also Weinman. SP: also Gary Gerani. Idea: Ed Justin (a poem). Mus: Richard Stone. Creature FX: Alec Gillis, Richard Landon et al. SpFxCoord: J. J. SpSdDes: Frank Serafine. Ref: TV: MGM-UA HV. V 10/19/88. HR. SFExam 1/17/89. Maltin '92. McCarty II. Martin. Scheuer. Hardy/HM2: aka *Vengeance: The Demon*. With Lance Henriksen, Kerry Remsen, Jeff East, John DiAquino, Kimberly Ross, Buck Flower, Lee DeBroux, Tom Woodruff Jr. (Pumpkinhead), Florence Schauffler (Haggis).

"There ain't no Pumpkinhead!" When "city folks" accidentally kill a country boy, the latter's father, Ed Harley, goes to the witch woman Haggis. She summons up Pumpkinhead, the demon of vengeance, who lives up to his billing. Ed, however, relents: His blood helped animate the demon, and each act of revenge sympathetically tears at his guts. The more realistic Haggis: "It's gotta run its course now."

*Pumpkinhead* makes crippling concessions to slasher-film conventions, but finally bears more relation to Fritz Lang's revenge sagas such as *Fury* and *Die Nibelungen* (which see) than it does to current product, and its story plays straight-forwardly and flavorfully, up to the point where Harley relents. Then, feature-length considerations make him fumble around for a method of stopping Pumpkinhead. (He tries a flame-thrower, help-from-neighbors, etc.) As his existence becomes more and more intertwined with Pumpkinhead's, the solution—suicide—becomes obvious, and the movie ends forcefully, with climax and coda both suggesting the toll which revenge takes on all concerned.

**PUMPKINHEAD II: BLOOD WINGS** 1993? color feature. D: Jeff Burr. SP: S. L. Mitchell, C. W. van Sickle. Ref: Fango 128:40-45, 82: '93 release? SFChron 7/3/93. With Lilyan Chauvin, Andrew Robinson, Ami Dolenz, Mark McCracken (monster), Roger Clinton.

**The PUNISHER** (U.S.-Austral.) New World Australia (Robert Kamen) 1990 (1989) color 90m. D: Mark Goldblatt. SP: Boaz Yakin. Mus: Dennis Dreith. Prosth Mkp: Brian Bertram. SpFX: (sup) Steve Courtley; (coord) Chris Murray. Title FX & Opt: Darren Young, Filmtrix, Pacific Title. Ref: TV. V 6/20/90. MFB'90:174-5. Maltin '92. Martin. no Scheuer. With Dolph Lundgren, Louis Gosset, Jr., Jeroen Krabbe, Nancy Everhard.

"If you're guilty, you're dead." The Punisher is a "self-styled vigilante" responsible for "125 mysterious gangland murders." With his seemingly superhuman capacity for giving and taking punishment, he survives knifings, explosions, and general mayhem. He isn't necessarily supernatural, just tough. Implements of death and destruction include a deadly (though non-supernatural) sphere, a la *Phantasm*, and an updated, rack-like torture machine.... Less a meditation on law and justice than a stream-lined violence machine, *The Punisher* goes for the quickest thrill and the easiest Freddy quip. *The Big Heat* without the bite.

**El PUNO DE LA MUERTE** (Mex) Victor Films & Jalisco 1981 color 87m. (*Santo en la Furia de los Karatecas* - alternate-version t). SP, D: Alfredo B. Crevenna. SP: also Sergio Alvarez. Story: Ramon Obon. Ph: J. M. Herrera. Mkp: Ma. Luisa Carrasco. Ref: TV: Video Latino; no Eng.; *The Fist of Death* - tr t. Horacio Higuchi. vc box. With "El Santo," Grace Renat, Cesar Sobrevals, Steve Cheng, Gilberto Trujillo, Carlos Suarez, "Tinieblas."

In the Asian jungles. A pulsating crystal from another galaxy channels the "power of the cosmos" and enables a phenomenally built sorceress (Renat) to transform, variously, into a hulk, a cobra, and a tiger, in each of which guises she fights wrestler Santo, who has been summoned from the other side of the world.... Her most amazing guise, however, is herself. Renat, who plays both the sorceress and the good princess, must have studied under Russ Meyer: Script and costumes are designed solely to showcase her bustline. The ritual dance of the sorceress is a real highlight here.

**PUPPET MASTER** see *Puppetmaster*

**PUPPET MASTER II** Para HV/Full Moon (David DeCoteau, John Schouweiler) 1990 color 88m. D: David Allen. SP: David Pabian. Story Idea, Exec P: Charles Band. Mus: Richard Band. SpFxMkp: Modus EFX; David Barton. VisFX: D. Allen; (puppet sup) John Teska; (puppet anim) Randy Cook, Justin Kohn. Addl Creature FX: Steve Neill. SdFxDes: Adriane Marfiak, Mark Cookson. OptFX: Mercer. Ref: TV. V 2/18/91. no Maltin '92. McCarty II. Scheuer. Martin. With Elizabeth MacLellan, Collin Bernsen, Gregory Webb, Charlie Spradling, Steve Welles (Toulon/Chanee), Ivan J. Rado, Buck Flower, Michael Todd (Toulon puppet), Julianne Mazziotti (Else puppet/Camille).

"They say satan's got a suite of rooms in there!" "Toulon's miraculous stringless marionettes" are back at the hotel on Scarab Hill. An "artificial life force" powers them. (Toulon: "I know how to get into things—give them life.") But Toulon needs "fresh human material" (i.e., brains) to bring himself back to life inside a full-sized puppet-body. In a sufficiently bizarre climax, his creations let him down—some non-human material gets mixed into the formula—and his "wife" (MacLellan) spits out the nasty fluid.

Sequel to *Puppetmaster* has an uncompelling plot, but does feature some tantalizing suggestions—in "Chanee"'s appearance and in the story—of classics like *The Mummy* (1932), *Bride of Frankenstein, Mad Love,* and *The Invisible Man.* In fact, one of the movie's highlights is a flashback to 1912 Cairo—a scene with an Egyptian sorcerer (Rado) and his "puppet"—which recalls Pretorius and his "dolls" in *Bride.*

**PUPPET MASTER III: TOULON'S REVENGE** Para/Full Moon (Schouweiler, DeCoteau) 1991 (1990) color 90m. D: David DeCoteau. SP: C. C. Joyner. Ph: Adolfo Bartoli. PD: Billy Jett. Vis/Puppet FX: David Allen. SpMkpFX: David Barton. Stopmo: Allen, Chris Endicott. SpMechFX: Players' SpFX. SpFxSup: Kevin McCarthy. Opt: Mercer & OptFX. Ref: TV. TVG. Martin. V 5/13/91:25: shooting. With Guy Rolfe, Richard Lynch, Ian Abercrombie, Sarah Douglas, Walter Gotell.

"And they can live forever." Berlin, 1941. Injections—and the will to live on after death—power the "puppets" of Toulon (Rolfe), "Europe's greatest puppet master," and the Nazis want his secrets to further their own, zombie-exploiting Death Corps Project.... Vapid wartime intrigue plays like a cross between *Devil-Doll* and *Berlin Correspondent,* with a touch of Western movies thrown in: In a cute running shtick, a six-armed "cowboy" puppet mows down Nazis. The early exploits of Pinhead, Jester, Leech Woman....

**PUPPET MASTER 4** New City/Full Moon 1993 color 79m. D: Jeff Burr. SP: T. Henschell, S.E. Carr et al. Ph: Adolfo Bartoli. Mus: Richard Band. PD: Milo. PuppetFxSup: David Allen. Opt&DigitalFX: Motion Opticals;(sup) Kevin Kutchaver. SpMkp/MechFX: Alchemyfx, M.S. Deak. PhysicalFX: John Cazin. MechFX: Mark Pollack, Flix FX. ComputerFX: Brent Fletcher. Laser Anim: Linda Obalil. Roto: Mark McGee. Ref: TV. U.S.-Sp? Tower Video Releases: 11/17/93. With Gordon Currie, Chandra West, Jason Adams, Teresa Hill, Felton Perry, Stacie Randall, Guy Rolfe (Toulon).

Ingredients this time: the elixir of life, stolen from a "tribe of ancient Egyptian sorcerers" ... the main Demon Lord and his *Alien*-ish "watchers," who absorb their victims' energy ... the "little swine puppets"—Pinhead, Tunneler, Six-Shooter, Blade, and Jester—who take on two or three watchers from a mini-pyra-mid ... Decapitron, who zaps one watcher ... Lauren (Hill), a channeler ... and the new Puppet Master, Rick Myers (Currie).... Okay vehicle for puppetry and stopmo and other animation. Highlights include scientist Rick's laser-ray shootouts with his little robot models and (later) the puppets.

**PUPPET MASTER 5** Full Moon 1994 color 81m. D: Jeff Burr. PuppetFX: David Allen. Ref: vc box. Martin: demon. With Ian Ogilvy, G. Currie, Guy Rolfe, Chandra West, N. Guest.

**The PUPPET MASTERS** BV/Hollywood Pictures (Ralph Winter) 1994 color 109m. D: Stuart Orme. SP: Ted Elliott, Terry Rossio,

David S. Goyer, from Robert A. Heinlein's book. Ph: Clive Tickner. Mus: Colin Towns. PD: D.A. Lomino. VisFX: BV;(sup) Peter Montgomery;(digital sup) Dorne Huebler. SpMkpFX: Greg Cannom. Animatronics: Larry Odien. Creature FxCoord: David Sosalla. Arrival Seq: Mr. Film. SpFxCoord: Roy Arbogast. Ref: TV: HP HV. PT 20:10-11. ad. SFChron 10/22/94. With Donald Sutherland, Eric Thal, Julie Warner, Keith David, Will Patton, Yaphet Kotto, Richard Belzer, William Wellman Jr.

"My God! It has total control!" Ambrose, Iowa. Brainy, adapt-able, adrenaline-rich alien parasites with brain "probes" attach themselves to and override human nervous systems. (They're here because we're hardier "hosts.") For the host: a dreamlike paralysis. A "hive" keeps the parasites alive; brain disease fin-ishes them off. But: "There's only one alien," with a "million parts" (cf. *Beast with a Million Eyes*).... The alien-infiltration game is pretty exciting here. The script is a good balance of suspense, drama and horror. It keeps one involved and guessing. Highlight: the "thermal imaging." ("Hosts" can be identified via computer imagery because their body-heat increases.) Easily ignored: overlaps with the *Invasion of the Body Snatchers* plot (the planting of the eggs, the gathering of the hosts, etc.). Easily forgiven: a blown hand-on-shoulder shock.

**PUPPETMASTER** Full Moon (Hope Perello) 1989 color 90m. (aka *Puppet Master*). D: David Schmoeller. SP: Joseph G. Col-lodi. Story: Charles Band, Kenneth J. Hall. Mus: Richard Band. VisFxSup: David Allen. SpFxMkp: Patrick Simmons. SpOpts: H'w'd. Opt. Ref: TV: Paramount Video. V 8/16/89. Fango 2/90. no Maltin '92. McCarty II. Martin. Scheuer. With Paul Le Mat, Irene Miracle, Matt Roe, Kathryn O'Reilly, William Hickey, Barbara Crampton.

"Honey, even the dead have their ways." The living puppets of alchemist Andre Toulon (Hickey) fall into the "wrong hands" after his death. Neil Gallagher (Jimmie F. Skaggs) uses them to avenge himself on fellow psychics, and employs "ancient Egyp-tian rites of afterlife" to bring himself back from the dead.... The tale here is involved and ultimately just functional. The doll play's the thing. Each puppet—Pinhead, Tunneler, Leech Woman, Blade, and Jester—has its own special brand of perverse menace. Watch, for instance, the way the big arms of Pinhead pump when it's chasing someone. Since 1936 and *Devil-Doll,* the accent has shifted—from chills to gross-out horror. The Leech Woman will, with her specialty, probably provoke the most notice.

Sequels: *Puppet Master II, III, IV.*

**The PUPPETOON MOVIE** Para/Leibovit 1987 (1942-47) ob-ject anim 80m. SP, P, D: Arnold Leibovit. New Anim & Puppets: Fantasy II; David Allen, Coast SpFX, The Chiodo Bros. Min Time Machine: Bob Burns. Mus: Buddy Baker. Anim: Peter Kleinow. Ref: TV: c1986; IVE video. Lee: Tulips Shall Grow listing. Sean. V 4/8/87: 10 George Pal shorts; new footage with Arnie the Dinosaur. Jim Shapiro. Stanley: "recommended." Mal-tin '92: "some delightful entertainment."

Puppetoons include "The Sleeping Beauty" and "Tulips Shall Grow." New footage also includes an incidental gremlin from *Gremlins.* The rain-to-the-rescue ending of "Tulips" anticipates Pal's *War of the Worlds* and its bacteria-to-the-rescue ending. Fun to be had in both new and old footage.

See also: *Fantasy Film World of George Pal* (P). *Gremlins.*

**PURANI HAVELI** (India) Ramsay Int'l. 1983? color 139m. D: Tulsi & Shyam Ramsay. SP, Assoc D, Ed: Arjun Ramsay. Story: J.K. Ahuja. Dial: K. Azar. Ph: Ganju Ramsay. Mus: Ajit Singh. Ref: TV: GVI video; Hindi; no Eng. Meadows Video: *The Old House* - tr t. With Deepak Parashar, Amita Nangia, Satish Shah, Anil Dhawan, Shobha, Tej Sapru, Sikandar.

A hairy, fanged monster that doesn't like crucifixes seems to command something in a horned helmet and armor. Low comedy-horror-musical has two good scenes—an *Elm Street*-like dream sequence in which Hairy's arms come up through a bed to grab a woman, and an earlier scene in which fire rings a path around a cemetery, then, in a Cocteau-like effect, "erases" itself.

**The PURPLE PEOPLE EATER** Concorde/Motion Picture Corp. of America (Krevoy-Stabler) 1988 color 90m. SP, D: Linda Shayne. Based on the song by Sheb Wooley. SpSuit: Diligent Dwarves. FxAnim: Roto FX of America. Ref: TV. ad. V 12/21/88. SFChron 12/19/88. Maltin '92. Martin. Scheuer. With Ned Beatty, Neil Patrick Harris, Shelley Winters, Peggy Lipton, James Houghton, Thora Birch, Little Richard, Chubby Checker.

Faithful to its source, creature is purple, has one eye and one horn. For kids.

**PUSS BUCKET** Blessed Elysium Prods. (Paul & Roberta Houle) 1991 b&w 105m. D, Ph, Ed: Lisa Houle. PD: Chin Su Hon. SpFx/Min: Ben Edlund, Eric Hammer. Mkp: John Slobely. Ref: TV: Film Threat Video. no Martin. PT 15:52-3. With Terrence Fleming, E. Hammer, Brian Sullivan, Gina Cammarota, Madeline Virbasius (alien), Walter Prince, Ultra Lavish, Dion (alien).

"Mary's gonna really like those mutilated hairless bodies in the back." An alien spaceship destroys the roof of a house outside Owl Creek. Soon, one alien appears as the Virgin Mary to the two credulous, roofless twits therein and orders them to kill "demons" for her; they proceed to kill unsuspecting women.... Interminable, intolerable sf-musical-satire-horror movie, with phony nipple-gore. The above-quoted line is as good as it gets.

**PUT IT IN GERE** Caballero 1991 color 83m. D: Eduardo Dinero. Ref: Adam '92. With Gail Force, Ashlyn Gere, T. T. Boy.

*Total Recall* takeoff—people become the characters in their dreams, "but can't go back."

**PUZZLE OF THE SILVER HALF MOONS** see *Seven Blood-Stained Orchids*

**The PYJAMA GIRL CASE** (I-Sp) Zodiac & Picasa 1977 color/ws feature (*La Ragazza dal Pigiama Giallo*). SP, D: Flavio Mogherini. SP: also R. Sanchez Campoy. Ref: TV: MV?; Eng. dubbed. PT 19:40(ad): *Case of the Girl in the Yellow Pyjamas* - alt vt t. Palmerini.

Unexceptional mystery thriller with a bizarre centerpiece: A partly-charred-and-shriveled-beyond-belief corpse is "injected with a special formula" to preserve it for viewing (for identification purposes) in a glass case. (Shades of the 1934 *The Black Cat*!) Plus a "terrible thunderstorm." Ray Milland's presence is the film's sole distinction.

**PYRAMID OF DARKNESS** Claster-TV/Marvel Prods. & Sunbow (Hasbro, Inc.) 1985 anim color c90m. (*G.I. Joe*-cr t). Creative D: Jay Bacal. SupStoryEd: Steve Gerber. Mus: Johnny Douglas, Rob Walsh. Ref: TV: TV-series compilation? TVG. no Maltin '92, no Scheuer.

Giant water-robots ... "fatal fluffies" which, at the sound of a whistle, turn huge and monstrous ... the City of the Dead, where sleeping, rock-like "guardians" awake and skeletal hordes swarm ... deadly-gas "butterflies" ... and, of course, the pyramid of darkness.... Actionful, fast-paced, but generally stilted and unimaginative.

See also *G.I. Joe.*

**PYRAMID TERROR** Filminutos 1982-3 anim short. D: Noel Lima, Jose Reyes. Ref: SFChron Dtbk 4/26/92: Cuban?

"About a musically driven stalking mummy...."

**PYUSHCHYE KROVY** see *Those Feedy on Blood*

# Q

**QI YUAN** see *Witch from Nepal*

**QIAN NU YOUHUN** see *Chinese Ghost Story, A*

**QIAN YUNYU QING** see *Ghostly Love*

**QIU DENG YE YU** see *Tragedy of Ghost*

**QUANDO ALICE RUPPE LO SPECCHIO** see *Touch of Death*

**QUANTUM LEAP** NBC-TV/Belisarius Prods. & Univ-TV 1989 color c90m. D: David Hemmings. Tel, Exec P: Donald P. Bellisario. Ph: Roy H. Wagner. Mus: Mike Post. AD: Cameron Birnie. OptFX: Howard Anderson Co. Mkp: Steven Gautier. Ref: TV. Sacto Bee 3/26/89. V (Mifed'89:126). With Scott Bakula, Dean Stockwell, Jennifer Runyon, John Allen Nelson, Lee De-Broux, Larry Poindexter, Bruce McGill (Weird Ernie), Barbra Horan.

"It's Howdy Doody time!"—i.e., 1956—as Project Quantum Leap sends a scientist back in time. ("I travel a lot.") TV-movie pilot for the TV series.

**QUANTUM LEAP: DAUGHTER OF SIN** NBC-TV/Univ-TV & Belisarius Prods. (Robin Bernheim) 1992 color c90m. (aka *Quantum Leap: Trilogy—Part II*). D: James Whitmore, Jr. Tel, Exec Co-P: Deborah Pratt. Ph: M. Watkins, R. McBride. Mus: V. R. Bunch. PD: Cameron Birnie. SpVisFX: Roger Dorney, Denny Kelly. Mkp: Jeremy Swan. Ref: TV. TVG (ad): "2-hour movie." With Scott Bakula, Meg Foster, Mary Gordon Murray, Dean Stockwell, Melora Hardin, Max Wright, James Greene, Parley Baer.

Sam (Bakula) "leaps" back to Pottersville, La., June 14, 1966, and, as Will, becomes engaged to the "cursed" Abigail (Hardin), who sees a (positive) difference in Will. Involved, melodramatic midsection of a series trilogy.

**QUANTUM LEAP: EVIL LEAPER II** NBC-TV/Univ-TV & Belisarius Prods. (Robin Bernheim) 1993 color c80m. (*Quantum Leap: The Revenge of the Evil Leaper* - ad t). D: Debbie Allen, Harvey Laidman. Tel: R. C. Okie. Tel, Exec Co-P: Deborah Pratt. Ph: Robert Primes. (For other credits, see *Quantum Leap: Daughter of Sin.*) Ref: TV. TVG (ad): "2-hour movie." With Scott Bakula, Dean Stockwell, Neil Patrick Harris, Renee Coleman, Carolyn Seymour.

"We're time travelers from the future." Sam takes the accelerator back to 1956 and *Rebel without a Cause* territory and "becomes" Arnold Watkins, the Midnight Marauder who rights fraternity wrongs. Thanks to "mind-merging," Sam begins to absorb part of Arnold's mind; meanwhile, in another part of Part II, Sam encounters "evil leaper" Alia.... You need a scorecard to keep tabs on the "leapers" here, which fact is part, if not most, of the fun. Some cute tricks with the new toy, "morphing," which are slickly combined with more old-fashioned types of effects.

**QUARANTINE** (Can.) Atlantic Releasing/Apple Pie Pictures & Beacon Group & Telefilm Canada & B.C. Film (Stephen Cheikes) 1989 color c90m. SP, D, P: Charles Wilkinson. Mus: Graeme Coleman. AD: Robert Logevall. FxMkp: Kandace Loewen. SpFX: Randy Shinkew. SpSdFX: M. O. P. Studios. Ref: TV: Republic HV. V 8/15/90:46(hv). Mifed '89:132. V 9/6/89:46(ad). With Beatrice Boepple, Garwin Sanford, Jerry Wasserman, Tom McBeath, Michele Goodger, Cynthia Wong (voice of Apollo).

"Declare war on bacteria!" Ivan Joad (Boepple), terrorist, attempts to assassinate Senator Ford (Wasserman), who is the one who decides for the Provincial Ministry of Health's Quarantine Commission who goes into quarantine (or "concentration camps") and who doesn't. (Some people believe that the unnamed disease of the future is "out of control," that all have been exposed and are carriers, and that quarantine is useless.) On the run, Ivan hooks up with Spencer Crown (Sanford), designer of Apollo, a computer program on the cutting edge of surveillance.

Well-cast sf-actioner gets into the personalities of the oppressors, though perhaps not quite as deeply as Fritz Lang's *Hangmen Also Die!* Particularly good: McBeath as Detective Captain Berk, an ambitious, smily snake. The oppressed are not as keenly characterized.

**QUATERMASS 2** or **QUATERMASS II** see *Enemy from Space*

2 The **QUATERMASS CONCLUSION** Carolco? (Ted Childs/Verity Lambert) 1979 (1978) 102m. PD: Arnold Chapkis. SpFX: Effects Associates. Models: Clearwater Films. Opt: Camera FX. Mkp: Eddie Knight. Ref: TV: Thorn EMI/HBO Video. With Brewster Mason, Brenda Fricker.

"What got into them?" Ingredients include crazed flower-children-types ... a "gigantic laser beam" from the sky which draws cult members and cops up to, apparently, "the Planet" ... a neolithic burial ground ... a pertinent nursery rhyme ... an alternate "time scale" ... levitation ... "beacons" left fifty centuries ago on Earth ... and a probe — a "machine of unbelievable sophistication" — which senses and appropriates "living human protein".... The Nigel Kneale ideas are there (see above), but they're uncompellingly presented, just scattered about rather than devel-

oped or dramatized. And all they seem to add up to is an explanation of juvenile delinquency. Still, even diluted Kneale like this generates intermittent intellectual excitement.

**QUEEN OF BLACK MAGIC, The** see *Black Magic Terror*

*****QUEEN OF OUTER SPACE** WB/Ben Schwalb 1958. SpFX: Milt Rice. Mkp: Emile LaVigne; (uncred.) John Holden. Ref: TV: CBS/Fox Video. Warren/KWTS! V 8/13/58. Lee. Lentz. Weldon. Hardy/SF. Martin. Maltin '92. Scheuer. Fango 123:16-17. With Patrick Waltz, Barbara Darrow, Marilyn Buferd, Joi Lansing.

"We have made the most fantastic voyage in history!" 1985. Some of Earth's "deadly neighbors in outer space" employ a cartoon energy beam to destroy Space Station A, then pull an earthmanned rocket to Venus, where the "little dolls are just the same" and the masked Queen Yllana (Laurie Mitchell) and her council of women rule. ("You don't just accidentally land on a planet 26 million miles away.") A war with men has left her with a radiation-burned face, and she and her man-hating minions plot to train their new Beta Disintegrator on Earth. ("I believe they've solved the problem of projecting nuclear energy.") Extra addeds: a giant red and blue spider from *World without End* and some vaporizer pistols.

Truly appalling. Some Fifties science-fictioners seem better in retrospect (e.g., *Riders to the Stars*), some worse. An ounce or two of camp value might be squeezed out of Zsa Zsa Gabor lines like "Women can't be happy without men" and "We have no life here without love, children," but the only real moment of note: earthman Eric Fleming's polite revulsion at the prospect of kissing the disfigured Yllana—an ahead-of-its-time sexual gross-out.

**QUEEN VICTORIA AND THE ZOMBIES** Steve Postal Prods. 1991 color 118m. D & Ph: S. Postal. SP: Maurice Postal. Ref: V 1/14/91:18. Martin: "awful horror-comedy" re aliens. With Charlotte Leslie, Kendrick Kaufman, Jennifer Tuck, Angela Shepard.

**QUEENS FROM OUTER SPACE** He-She Studios 1993 color feature. Ref: vc box: aliens and ray guns.

**QUELLA VILLA IN FONDO AL PARCO** see *Ratman*

**QUELLO STRANO DESIDERIO** (I) 1979 color feature. D: E. Milioni. Ref: Palmerini: "erotic science-fiction." With Marina Frajese.

**QUEM TEM MEDO DE LOBISOMEM** (Braz.) Ipanema & Circus & R. F. Faria 1974 color 92m. SP, D: Reginaldo Faria. Ph: Jose Medeiros. SpFX: Wilmar Menezes, Geraldo Jose. Ref: Hardy/HM: "oddly unsettling." With R. Faria, Stepan Nercessian, Camila Amado.

Werewolf, vampire.

**QUEST** Okada Int'l. 1984 color 30m. D: Saul & Elaine Bass. SP: Ray Bradbury, from his story "Frost and Fire." Ph: Chuck Colwell. Mus: B. Van Campen, E. Bass. Ref: Ecran F 69:68: "a masterpiece of filmic science fiction."

The **QUEST** (Austral.) Miramax Films/Western (Middle Reef/Barbi Taylor) 1985 color 95m. (*Frog Dreaming* - orig t). D: Brian Trenchard-Smith. SP, Co-P: Everett DeRoche. Mus: Brian May. Dongekin: Andrew Engrg., Electro-Hydraulic Industries. SpFX: Brian Pearce, Jamie Thompson. Mkp: Leeanne White. Ref: TV. MFB '87:17-18: "developed with the assistance of Film Victoria." V 9/18/85. With Henry Thomas, Tony Barry, Rachel Friend, Tamsin West, Dempsey Knight (Charlie Pride).

"There's something in that bloody pond!" Dongekin Hole is both a "pond that nobody's ever heard of" and a "frog dreaming" ... a haunted, sacred site. But the rock-hating, fire-breathing black monster supposedly inhabiting the pond turns out to be a donkey engine.... This *Last Wave* for kids—an aboriginal-Loch Ness Monster movie—has some travelogue value, but is basically bland and hollow. A compromise double ending gives equal time to machines and magic. ("There is a dream time!") Compare *Return to Mayberry*.

**QUEST: A LONG RAY'S JOURNEY INTO LIGHT** c1985? computer anim short. Ref: Castro Theatre notes 12/26/86: a "sci-fi odyssey in space."

**QUEST FOR THE LOST CITY** (Can.) Griedanus 1990 color 92m. (*The Final Sacrifice* - shooting t). D: T.J. Griedanus. Ref: Stanley: "none too convincing"; "devil cult ... demonic guy." Martin: 1993. With Christian Malcom, B. Mitchell, S. Marceau.

**QUEST FOR THE MIGHTY SWORD** (I) Producers Int'l./Filmirage 1989 ('90-U.S.) color 94m. (*Ator III—The Hobgoblin*—alt t). Story, D: David Hills. Mus: Carlo Maria Cordio. SpFX & Mkp: Maurizio Trani. OptFX: Moviecam 2000. Ref: TV. V 12/31/90:37 (hv). PT 8:46: D. Hills=Joe D'Amato. 9:6. With Eric Allen Kramer (Ator), Margaret Lenzey, Donal O'Brien, Laura Gemser, Marisa Mell, Don Semeraro (Grindel/Hagen).

"This sword must belong to Ator!" Johnny-come-lately Ator entry features mutants, dwarf creatures, a two-headed robot-like thing, a stiff, fire-breathing mini-Godzilla of a monster, and an instant-aging scene. Bland, functional, with a campy monster or two.

**QUEST OF THE DELTA KNIGHTS** Hemdale/Ramsway & Metro Pictures (James Dodson, Reonne Haslett) 1993 color 97m. D & Ph: Dodson. SP & Exec P: Redge Mahaffey. Mus: C. Schurtz, H. Beeftink. PD: Rodney Sheriff. MinFX: Len Wiseman. SpFX: Ultimate FX. VisFxDes: Dave Gregory. Ref: TV: Hemdale HV. SFChron Dtbk 1/2/94. With David Warner, Corbin Allred, David Kriegel (Leonardo), Brigid Conley Walsh, Olivia Hussey, Sarah Douglas, Don Pedro Colley.

"Do we want another Atlantis?" The Order of the Delta Knights searches for the "lost storehouse of Archimedes," who had access to the "science of Atlantis" and collected this all-but-lost knowledge in book form ("The Right Way"). At the end, the storehouse inspires Leonardo Da Vinci, and a secret weapon (the Gorgon Crystals?) acts like a death ray ("curious device") before it explodes.... Flat-footed fantasy with feeble comic relief.

The **QUIET EARTH** (N.Z.) Skouras/Capricorn Films Int'l. 1985 color 89m. D: Geoff Murphy. SP, P: Sam Pillsbury. SP: also Bill Baer, Bruno Lawrence. From Craig Harrison's novel. Ref: screen. PFA notes 9/7/85. V 5/15/85. SFExam 11/15/85. Sacto Union 12/24/85. With B. Lawrence, Alison Routledge, Peter Smith.

6:12, the morning of the "Effect." Delenco Research's Operation Flashlight—an experiment in energy transmission—abruptly changes the unit charge of electrons and alters the "fabric of the universe." Only those few people who were dying at the instant of the Effect remain alive.

Very good setting up of the premise, with people there-and-gone.... Then, some more good touches, as Zac Hobson (Lawrence) begins to "use" the otherwise vacant world—he plays, first, with a model train, in a department store, then a real train.... Then, two other people (Routledge, Smith) turn up and the obvious question—Can the three co-exist?—is too obviously answered, Yes. Muddled ending puts Zac down in a "different universe," though not before some familiar post-apocalyptic platitudinizing.

The **QUILT OF HATHOR** (U.S.-Can.) Para-TV/Variety Artists & Hometown Films & ACFC 1988 color c85m. D: Timothy Bond. Tel: Janet Maclean. Creator & Exec P: Frank Mancuso Jr. Creator: also Larry Williams. Ph: Rodney Charters. Mus: Fred Mollin. PD: Stephen Roloff. SpFxMkp: Randy J. Daudlin. VisFxSup: Megan Hope-Ross. Ref: TV. TVG. Sacto Bee 7/29/90. no Scheuer. no Maltin '92. With John D. LeMay, Robey, Chris Wiggins, Scott Paulin, Kate Trotter, Diego Matamoros.

A cursed quilt from Salem brings strange dreams—"whoever sleeps under it seems to have the power to kill people in their dreams." A member of the Penitites, a "secret and closed order," uses it to give her enemies deadly dreams.... Stilted crossing of *Witness* and "The Twilight Zone." Fantasy-horror premise recalls both *The Sender* and the "Lord Mountdrago" section of *Three Cases of Murder*. From the "Friday the 13th" TV series.

**QUIT-IT** 198-? color feature. Ref: Mo: "perfect" parents via pills ... children with supernatural powers which can kill their foes. no PFA. no VSB. no Maltin '92. no Scheuer.

**QUMO JINGCHA** see *Magic Cop*

# R

**R.O.B.O.T.** see *Chopping Mall*

**R.O.T.O.R.** Westwind Pictures & Blue Steel (Blaine-Lewis-Gesswein) 1988 color c84m. D & Idea: Cullen Blaine. SP, PD, SpFxCoord: Budd Lewis. Ph: Glenn Roland. Mus: David Adam Newman. VisFX: Roger Scott Prods.; Monty Young. SpSdFX: Jacques Dulong. Ref: TV: Imperial Ent. video. V 9/30/87:25(ad). Martin. Hound. With Richard Gesswein, Margaret Trigg, Jayne Smith, James Cole, Clark Moore; Carroll Brandon Baker et al (R.O.T.O.R.), Shawn Brown, Michael Hunter.

"Tomorrow's solution: R.O.T.O.R.—Robotic Officer Tactical Operations Research." Dallas. A freak accident activates the electricity-based R.O.T.O.R. android years before its scheduled launch date. This "rogue cop"—made from an "unknown alloy" with intelligence—programs itself with "molecular memory"

Horror and Science Fiction Films

405

and features a "sensor recall" which picks up recent action in the vicinity.

Hard to tell whether *R.O.T.O.R.* is trying to be a Chuck Norris action movie or a parody of a Chuck Norris action movie. Its stolidity sometimes appears to be intentionally comic; at other times, it just seems like bad acting and writing. Two highlights from the tougher-than-thou dialogue: "You fire me, and I'll make more noise than two skeletons making love in a tin coffin, brother!" and "R.O.T.O.R.'d walk through a busload of nuns to get to a jaywalker."

**RAAT KE ANDHERE MEIN** (India) Talwar Prods.(Ashok Arya) 1987 color c122m. Co-P, D: Vinod Talwar. SP: D. Ran, or Ram. Co-Ph: Rajeshnath. SpFX: Sharad et al. Mkp: Saleem. Ref: TV: Spectra Video (Atlantic Video); little Eng. Meadows Video: *In the Dark of the Night* - tr t. With Javed Khan, Dipika, Rajesh Puri, Mazhar Khan.

A hairy, disfigured, big-clawed creature kills a lady in a bathtub. Later, hairy starts taking over the whole house .... Technically rough-edged mystery-horror-musical-comedy. At the end, the monster turns out to be a guy in a head mask, but this turn of events doesn't explain the supernatural mist from the cemetery.

**RABID GRANNIES** (Belg.) Troma/Stardust Pictures (Desert-Rambert) 1988 ('90-U.S.) color/ws 83m. SP, D: Emmanuel Kervyn. Mus: P.-D. & J.-B. Castelain. SpFX: Sebastien Fernandez. SdFX: Julien Naudin. Mkp: Jean-Pierre Finoto. Ref: TV: Media Home Ent. video; Eng. dubbed. V 5/31/89. Scheuer. McCarty II. Hound. With Danny Daven (Elizabeth Remington), Anne-Marie Fox (Victoria Remington), Joelle Morane (Elizabeth, the monster), Suzanne Vanina (Victoria, the monster), Robert du Bois, Paule Herreman, Catherine Aymerie, Caroline Braeckman, Richard Cotica, E. Lison, Raymond Lescot, Francoise Moens, Florine Elslande.

Christopher, an "evil boy" who later became a satanic sect's high priest, sends the "darling old girls" Victoria and Elizabeth a birthday gift, "very old and full of surprises." A vapor from the gift box contaminates their wine, and suddenly it's Ghoul City—the two turn into demons, or "gargoyles," and "throw guts around like so many slapstick cream pies."

Here the makeup effects transformations aren't as entertaining as the inner ones: Victoria and Elizabeth begin to enjoy a second childhood. They play on chandeliers, commit gory pranks (including a variation on the slippery banana peel), and in general act like kids at recess. (Compare *The Nine Demons*.) But though *Rabid Grannies* is a bit different, it's also mostly the same, right down to the regulation coda kicker and the old gals', or ghouls', Freddy-like badinage, mockery, and fingernails. The monsters, it's suggested, are a heavensent punishment for the characters' greed, but as a morality play the movie is pretty shallow.

**RADAR MEN FROM THE MOON** see *Road Lawyers*

**RADIOACTIVE DREAMS** DEG/Hal Roach & ITM (Radioactive Dreams) 1984 color 98m. SP, D: Albert Pyun. Mus: Pete Robinson. SpMkp: Greg Cannom; (des) Ve Neill; (addl) Teresa Austin. MechFX: Chiodo Bros. SpFX: R. J. Hohman. OptFX: Pacific Title. Ref: TV. V 9/24/86. Martin. Phantom. With John Stockwell, Michael Dudikoff, Lisa Blount, George Kennedy,

Don Murray, Michele Little, Norbert Weisser, Reni Santoni, Nathan Stein (mutant), Archie Hahn (voice).

Phil (Stockwell) and Marlowe (Dudikoff) emerge from their underground shelter on April 1, 2010, to discover a post-nuclear world of "mutant rutabagas," a "dame with a wicked left cross," "disco mutants," and a dinosaur-like monster.... Two good but dumb eggs become hard-boiled dicks in this less-than-riveting mock-morality-play. A fizzled *Blade Runner,* this mixture of pulp detective and pulp sf elements has amiable moments, but also an offputtingly shrill, busy mise-en-scene.

**RAFT, The** see *Creepshow 2*

**RAGAZZA DAL PIGIAMA GIALLO, La** see *Pyjama Girl Case, The*

**RAGE** (I-Sp) USA-TV/Tiber Int'l. & Arco Film (Paolo Ferrara) 1984 ('86-U.S.) color 91m. (aka *A Man Called Rage*). D: Tonino Ricci. SP: J. Comas Gil, E. Benito. Ref: V 10/29/86: Gel Int'l; "tedious." TVG. Hound. Stanley: "witless." Palmerini: *Fuoco Incrociato.* With Conrad Nichols, Stelio Candelli, Werner Pochat, Taida Urruzola, Chris Huerta.

Follow-up to *Rush* (which see) is another post-World War III tale.

**RAGE** see *Hidden Obsession*

**RAGE** see *Primal Rage*

**RAGEWAR** see *Dungeonmaster, The*

**RAGING FURY** see *Hell High*

**RAGNO GELIDO** see *Dial: Help*

The **RAIDERS OF ATLANTIS** (I) Regency Prods. 1983 ('86-U.S.) color 90m. (*I Predatori di Atlantida. The Atlantis Interceptors* - ad t). D: Ruggero Deodato (aka R. Franklin). SP: Mannino, Sanchetti (aka R. Gold). Ph: Roberto D'Ettorre Piazzoli. Mus: "O. Onions." AD: Benny Amalfitano. SpFX: "Gene Reds." SpOptFX; V. G. Min: Al Passeri. Mkp: Maurizio Trani. SdFX: Cineaudio FX. Ref: TV: Prism Ent. video. V 6/8/83:30. 7/13/83:34: completed. 5/9/84:344. Stanley. Cine Para Leer '84. Hound. Ecran F 37:57. With Chris Connelly, Marie Fields, Tony King, Ivan Rassimov, George Hilton.

"The Interceptors are everywhere." In 1994, Dr. Rollins, an expert in pre-Columbian dialects, examines a 12,000-year-old tablet which "confirms the existence of Atlantis," which, as it turns out, is a domed, "solar fire"-destroyed city which radiation from a downed submarine forces to the surface of the Atlantic. The descendants of Atlantis then use the doctor to "rediscover the secrets of their existence." They also use "Interceptors"—possessed individuals, apparently—against modern civilization.... Slapdash sf-actioner brings Atlantis up for a look-see, then sends it right back down again.

**RAIDERS OF THE LIVING DEAD** Indep.-Int'l./Cineronde-Canada (Kennis-Baldwin) 1987 (1985) color 86m. (*Graveyard* - orig t). SP, D: Samuel M. Sherman; Brett Piper. Title Song: G. E. Ott. SpMkp: Tyler Smith; (fx) Scott Sliger. SpFX: Bob LeBar.

SpSdFX: Ron Kalish. OptFX: Bob Freemon. Ref: TV. V 11/29/89. 5/6/87:176. 8/12/87:48 (rated). Scheuer. Sacto Bee 10/29/89 (TV). With Robert Deveau, Donna Asali, Scott Schwartz, Bob Allen, Zita Johann, Bob Sacchetti, Leonard Corman, Corri Burt; Tyler Smith et al. (zombies).

"I think somebody's found a way to bring dead bodies back to life." Homemade laser guns and wooden arrows defeat standard-issue Romero zombies on Rockmoor Island. Choppy, incoherent, New Jersey-based horrorshow. A Rockmoor Correctional Institute doctor's experiments on executed prisoners somehow produced the zombies. Any further attempts to summarize the story here would constitute pure conjecture.

**RAIDERS OF THE LOST ARK** see *Indiana Jones and the Last Crusade. Indiana Jones and the Temple of Doom*

**RAIDERS OF THE SHAOLIN TEMPLE** (H.K.) 1984 color feature. Ref: V 10/24/84:312: kung fu "robot fighters."

**RAIDERS OF THE SUN** New Horizons HV 1991 color feature. D: Cirio Santiago. Ref: SFChron Dtbk 7/26/92: 1992. Martin. With Richard Norton, Brigitta Stenberg, Rick Dean.

"Biological disaster" on Earth.(SFC)

**The RAIN KILLER** Concorde/Califilm (Rodman Flender) 1990 color 93m. (*Rain of Death*—orig t). D, Exec P: Ken Stein. SP: Ray Cunneff. Mus: Terry Plumeri. Mkp: Scott Frelick. Ref: TV. V 11/19/90. 1/3/90:11. With Ray Sharkey, David Beecroft, Tania Coleridge, Michael Chiklis.

"The rain washes everything clean." Los Angeles. The slasher in the rain who is decimating The Sewing Circle—"rich bitch ex-junkies"—turns out to be a "real smart psycho." Determinedly sleazy, overdone neo-noir tragedy features a trendy conceit: The drug-fiend/killer proves to be the straitlaced FBI guy. (By contrast, the local cop is all right.) Meant-to-be-ominous weather-report line: "Eighty percent chance of rain."

**RAIN WITHOUT THUNDER** TAZ Pictures (Sorenson) 1992 color 85m. SP, D: Gary Bennett. Ph: Karl Kases. PD: G. Bartley. Ref: V 10/5/92: "little drama but lots of talk." ad. SFChron 2/13/93: "turgid documentary style." 2/8/93. 4/2/92. SFExam 2/12/93: "dry legal brief." With Carolyn McCormick, Ali Thomas, Betty Buckley, Jeff Daniels, Frederic Forrest, Linda Hunt, Graham Greene, Austin Pendleton.

"A world fifty years hence where abortions are banned...."(SFC)

**RAINBOW BRIDGE** see *Little Prince and Eight Headed Dragon*

**RAINBOW BRITE AND THE STAR STEALER** (U.S.-J) WB/Hallmark (DIC) 1985 anim color 86m. D: Bernard Deyries, Kimio Yabuki. Story, SP: Howard R. Cohen. Story: also Jean Chalopin. Based on Hallmark characters. Mus: Saban, Levy. SpFX: Yamamoto, Nakajima. SdFX: Gilmore, McLaverty. OptFX: Howard Anderson. Ref: TV. V 11/20/89. ad. TVG.

Settings: The Diamond Planet and the dismayingly cheery Rainbow Land. Monsters: big, long-tailed reptilian creatures ... a big red sea monster ... huge robots with hypno-rays ... and some tiny monsters which combine to form one big one.

Best thing about this animated science-fantasy: the comically willful Princess. ("I deserve everything.") The titular heroine—"Rainbow Brite" sounds like a scouring pad—is at best a nonentity. Lively enough, with scattered amusing touches, but basically vapid. Signed, Sick-of-Rainbows.

**RAINING NIGHT'S KILLER** (H.K.) Hu Szu I 1988? color/ws c90m. SP, D: K. S. Liou. Ref: TV: Rainbow Video; Eng. titles. NST! 4:34: D: Chen Ching Lo.

"Seven men were killed by this knife." Lessie Chan is not kidding when, to the question "What's your favorite sport?", she responds "Killing." Seems she has a bad habit of leaving long knives in men's stomachs. The *Psycho* coda explanation: She was once scared by "real ghosts"—i.e., gang rapists—and ever since has felt compelled to kill men on rainy nights. ("Only rain could help me.") Plus: a thunderstorm and Lessie's sinister Siamese cat Jimmy (a "lovely cat"). Pat study in abnormal psychology pads out its running time with kung fu violence with the local thugs.

**RAISING CAIN** Univ/Pacific Western (Gale Anne Hurd) 1992 color 95m. SP, D: Brian DePalma. Ph: S. H. Burum. Mus: Pino Donaggio. PD: Doug Kraner. SpFxCoord: Robbie Knott. Animatronic Puppet FX: Todd Masters Co. Mkp Sup: M. Rocchetti. OptFX: Pacific Title; 4-Ward. Main Titles: Ernest Farino. Ref: TV. V 8/3/92: "superficial, often risible." ad. Cinef 12/92:61: "meandering." SFChron 8/7/92: "wildly implausible." SFExam 8/7/92: "weirdly bad." With John Lithgow (Carter-Cain-Dr. Nix-Josh-Margo), Lolita Davidovich, Steven Bauer, Frances Sternhagen, Gregg Henry, Teri Austin, Kathleen Callan.

Or, The "Three Faces of Cain." Dr. Nix traumatizes his own son, Carter, for an experiment in "The Creation and Evolution of the Multiple Personality" (the subtitle of his book). Plus: a *Psycho* car-dunking scene, in Half Moon Marsh, and "apparitions".... De Palma in his trying-to-be-ingenious mode provides Lithgow with poorly written, would-be-tour-de-force material.

**Les RAISINS DE LA MORT** (F) ABC & Rush & Off (Claude Guedj) 1978 color 85m. (90m.) (aka *Pesticide*. 2P *Grapes of Death*). SP, D: Jean Rollin. SP: also J.-P. Bouyxou, C. Meunier. Ph: C. Becognee. SpFX: Tiberi, Moronjiu, Josse. Ref: TV: VSOM; Eng. titles; *Grapes of Death*. Monster! Int'l. 4: 9,10,11. Hardy/HM: "routinely gory potboiler"; *The Grapes of Death*—tr t. Newman. With Marie-Georges Pascal, Serge Marquand, Patricia Cartier, Evelyne Thomas, Brigitte Lahaye.

Vineyard's pesticide "turns the local population into walking zombies."(HM) Film begins as an okay mystery re rural folk disintegrating, mentally and physically. ("You're rotting like me!") Intermittently, the movie itself disintegrates, and lapses into stupid gore tricks—e.g., the Pitchfork Delight scene. But Rollin comes up with a few ideas even George Romero missed—the zombies chanting "I love you," the young blind lady strolling among the (unknown to her) rotting dead. Health advisory: Beer drinkers are not affected here.

**RAMAYANA: THE LEGEND OF PRINCE RAMA** (Indian-J) MTV & Nippon Ramayana 1993 anim color 120m. D, P: Yugo Sako. Ref: V 12/6/93: Eng. dialogue; "not even great to look at."

"Climactic sequence pitting hundreds of monkey-warriors against an awesome, sky-filling giant."

**RAMPAGE** Miramax (DEG)/David Salven 1992 (1987) color 97m. SP, D: William Friedkin. From W. P. Wood's novel. Ph: R. D. Yeoman. Mus: Ennio Morricone. PD: Buddy Cone. SpVisFX: Pablo Ferro. Mkp: Teresa Austin. Ref: TV: Para video; 92m. NYT 10/30/92: "chillingly effective." SFChron Dtbk 11/22/92. SFExam 10/30/92: "waffles weirdly." SFChron 10/30/92: "like watching an opera about a piranha." Sacto Bee 10/30/92: "Alex McArthur, as Reece, is suitably creepy and facile, a monster disguised as a normal person." V 11/30/92:41 (rated). With Michael Biehn, Alex McArthur, Nicholas Campbell, Deborah Van Valkenburgh, Art LaFleur, Billy Green Bush, Grace Zabriskie.

"I needed his blood." Fact-based slasher movie re Charlie Reece, who commits evisceration murders in Stockton, California, around Christmas, 1986. He collects body parts in plastic bags, keeps a *Texas Chainsaw Massacre* cellar, and drinks his victims' blood because he thinks he's losing his own. ("I sucked some blood.") The script is not far above the level of a letter to the editor re the law and psychiatry as friends of homicidal maniacs, and the film has a careless, overlit look.

**RANA—THE LEGEND OF SHADOW LAKE** Titan Int'l./Galaxy One (Bill Rebane & Jerry Gregoris) 1981 color 96m. D: B. Rebane. SP: Lyoma Denetz, J. Gregoris, Mike Landers. Ph: Ito; Bela St. Jon; (aerial & underwater) Jochen Breitenstein. Mus: Valentino Inc. PD: Will McCrow. SpDes: Tom Schwartz. SpFX: Spectacular Effects; Vern Hyde, Robert Babb, Mark Burns. Ref: TV. V 5/12/82:120 (ad). Bill Warren. no Phantom. no Maltin '92. Newman. Hound. no Scheuer. V Mifed '89:173: *Croaked: Frog Monster from Hell*—proposed Troma reissue t. With Karen McDiarmid, Alan Ross, Brad Ellingson, Julie Wheaton, Glenn Scherer, Doreen Moze, J. Gregoris, Jim Iaquinta, Bruno Aclin, M. J. Skewes; Paul Callaway & Richard Lange (Rana), Angel Rebane (Baby Rana).

"Ain't chasin' after no legends no more!" On the island of Rana, in the middle of a bottomless lake, an Indian legend re a half-man, half-frog creature from the Mesozoic that "never dies" persists. ("It's almost unbelievable!") Trapper Charlie (Gregoris) knows about the "frog people" and so, he insists, do the frogs: "They know! They know!" Gregoris (the co-producer) plays the obligatory garrulous old codger, and, though he's not as bad as the other actors, he is more insistent. Movie has awkward narration and dialogue and tacky photography and music. One good "bus" with a suddenly shattered window. One odd shot of a frog hopping out of Rana's mouth.

**RANCHO DEL MIEDO, El** see *Fearmaker, The*

**RANMA 1/2: RESCUE THE BRIDE!** (J) Pony Canyon/5-Ace 1992 anim color c60m. From Rumiko Takahashi's manga. Ref: TV: PC5A video; no Eng. Animag 7:43-44. Animerica 5:16: 3 OAVs. 6:14.

Mystical visitor from the sky ... elixir which turns lobster into lobster-man ... bit with giant, tentacled, carnivorous plant. Kinda cute, manic comic fantasy.

**RANMA 1/2** (J) Victor Video 1994 anim. Ref: V 3/28/94:16: in H.K.

**RAPE** (Sp) Sunfilm Ent./Int'l. Film (Profilmes) 1976 ('87-U.S.) color c80m. (*Retorno de las Tinieblas*). D: M. I. Bonns. Ref: TV: Mogul Video; Eng.-dubbed. V 5/11/77:428. Hound. no Martin. With Nadiuska, Gil Vidal, Miguel Iglesias (aka M.I. Bonns?), Ramiro Oliveros (aka Rick Joss?).

"How can you kill someone that's been dead for over five hundred years?" An unaccountable silhouette—a "ghost"—turns up in certain photos taken near Barcelona. On tape, a voice speaks that was not heard at the moment of taping. And Aztec symbols invisible to the naked eye appear in photos taken inside the house of "strange girl" Maria (Nadiuska). Danger—"ultragraphology" at work.... Maria, who is unaware of the self-defense forces at work within her, is possessed, it seems, by Maria of Moctezuma, Aztec daughter of the sun.

The clues prove more intriguing than the solution to this supernatural mystery. And the solution is incomplete—the movie ends abruptly, before Maria has completed her (flashback) story re the Aztecs and the conquistadores. As it is, *Rape* is mainly a showcase for Nadiuska's attributes. Comically flavorless dubbing.

Cf. *Beatriz.*

The **RAPE AFTER** (H.K.) 1985 color c90m. Ref: TV: Ocean Shores Video; Eng. titles. NST! 4:10-11. Fango 107:58, 60.

Photographer Mo Hsieh Sheng steals a grotesque clay Tang-dynasty sphinx from a temple. During a thunderstorm, the cursed statue (which contains a child's ashes) unleashes a demon-monster which ravishes Mo's house guest, model Shu Ya. She becomes pregnant, but her planned abortion is aborted when a just-glimpsed monster grabs and apparently slays the doctor and his nurse. Shu Ya dies in a car accident, but a fetus in her burnt-to-ashes corpse grabs the coroner and is last seen toddling along at the end of a very long umbilical cord. Meanwhile, spectral children drive the once-asthmatic gent responsible for the original curse to his death. (He needed an embryo to ward off his asthma.) At the end, all the dead that have not yet come back come back and assail Mo and the monks who are trying to help him.

Horror doesn't just run in the family of Shu Ya, it gallops. (A tip of the hat to Joseph Kesselring.) Rummaging around the house, she comes upon the corpse of her father, who has supposedly been away for a while. A rat wriggles out its mouth, and her mother feels obliged to explain that she killed him for giving her syphilis. ("His corpse got rotten.") Later, as part of an exorcism, a monk spits up frogs, and one frog is removed from a hole in the top of his head. One person vomits on the camera even as it films this act. A big creature rips off a monk's ears.

It's no holds barred here, and a sort of grim gross-out fun if you don't ask for more than relentless. In the visually most striking sequence, rats and crows attack a priest. Some of the crows venture too near a flame, catch on fire, then venture near the priest and set him on fire. Goodness.

Cf. *Mo Tai.*

**RAPED IN OUTER SPACE** (J) 1985 anim. Ref: CM 17:62: alien rapists.

**RAPID FIRE** Action Int'l. (David Winters/David Marriott) 1990 (1989) color 84m. SP, D: David A. Prior. SP: also William Zipp. Mus: Tim James et al. SpFX: Chuck Whitton. Ref: TV: AIP HV. V 5/2/90:290 (hv). With Ron Waldron, Michael Wayne, Dawn Tanner, Joe Spinell.

"I'm your fear, Eddie. I only die when you die!" "No-good bastard" Williams (Wayne) has a (visualized) nightmare re an unstoppable nemesis and (visualized) visions of his own fear. He also has a "most remarkable ... one-of-a-kind" computerized laser weapon, a combination machine-gun/bazooka which "protects itself" with explosive capability. Sf-actioner has feeble action, pathetic repartee.

**RAPTOR**S see *Killer Birds*

**The RAPTURE** FineLine (New Line)/Wechsler-Tenenbaum-Parker 1991 color 92m. SP, D: Michael Tolkin. Ph: Bojan Bazelli. Mus: Thomas Newman. SpFX: Lou Carlucci et al. Key Mkp: Deborah Larsen. Digital SdFX: Harry Cohen. Ref: TV: vt. ad. Sacto Bee 12/20/91: "the world does end, with the fearsome horsemen of the apocalypse in the sky." SFExam 11/1/91: "film's hokier undertones are exaggerated by the ending." With Mimi Rogers, David Duchovny, Patrick Bauchau, Kimberly Cullum.

"Prophecies are now being fulfilled." It's "judgment day" for Sharon (Rogers) and company in this bizarre, insufferable tract, which plays like a flat-footed *La Dolce Vita*—sins and the spiritual. (Compare also *The Last Wave*.) Only the post-apocalypse ending—set in a sort of limbo—at all intrigues.

**RAT MAN** see *Ratman*

**Una RATA EN LA OBSCURIDAD** (Mex) Mazateca (Gustavo Bravo Ahuja) 198-? color 83m. SP, D: Alfredo Salazar. Ph: Miguel Garzon. Mus: Afredo Diaz Ordaz. SpFX: F. Farfan, Jr. SdFX: Gonzalo Gavira. Mkp: Guille Oropeza. Ref: TV: Video Latino; no Eng.; *A Rat in the Dark* - tr t. VSOM: *Rat in the Darkness*. With Ricardo Cortes (The Woman of the Painting), Ana Luisa Peluffo, Anais De Melo, Jose A. Marros.

The Woman of the Painting haunts and seduces the two women who buy her home. Doors and windows shut themselves and lock in one woman. When the latter tries to burn the portrait, lightning flashes, the wind shrieks, a painting flies about, the furniture shakes, and a poker stabs her to death. The phantom turns out to be a transvestite, and the household rat is his pet.... Kinkiness for kinkiness' sake here. Offbeat but pretty silly sex-horror-fantasy.

**RATAS NO DUERMEN DE NOCHE, Las** see *Crimson*

**RATMAN** (I) Fulvia 1987 color feature (*Quella Villa in Fondo al Parco*). D: G. Carnimeo aka Anthony Ascot. SP: David Parker Jr. Ph: Robert Garder. Mus: Stefano Mainetti. Mkp: Franco Giannini. SpSdFX: Pennacchia, Papucci. Ref: TV: MV: Eng. dubbed; D: aka Giuliano Carmineo; *Rat Man.* V 5/4/88:322. Hardy/HM2: *La Casa al Fondo del Parco*. PT 8:65(ad): legendary rat/man dwarf slashes models on Caribbean isle. V 5/6/87:362: *Mouse Man*-ad t. Palmerini: SP: E.L. Briganti. With David Warbeck, Janet Agren, Eva Grimaldi, Luisa Menon, Werner Pochath, Nelson De La Rosa.

"Just keep away from his claws." A scientist creates a "terrible monster" of a hybrid by injecting rat sperm into a monkey ovum. The carnivorous little critter has the "instincts of a rat and the intelligence of a monkey" and scares one victim to death.... A somewhat novel menace in pretty much the same old script. Nice shock fadeout.

**RATS: NIGHT OF TERROR** (I-F) J.E.R./Beatrice & I.E.C. (Leitienne) 1983 ('86-U.S.) color/ws 97m. (*Rats-Notte di Terrore* - I. *Les Rats de Manhattan* - F. *Les Mutants de la Deuxieme Humanite* - F alt t. *Night of Fear* - ad t). Story, D: Bruno Mattei (aka V. Dawn). SP: Claudio Fragasso, Herve Piccini. Ph: Franco Delli Colli. Mus: Luigi Ceccarelli. AD: Mammi, Fimelli. Mkp: Giuseppe Ferrante. Co-D: Clyde Anderson. D: (Eng. version) John Gayford. Ref: TV: Lightning Video; Eng. dubbed. Horacio Higuchi. Peter Zirschky. Ecran F 41:71. V 5/9/84:306. 11/2/83:42. Stanley. Morse. Newman. Ecran F 49:9. With R. Raymond, J. Ryann, A. McBride, R. Cross, H. Luciani.

"The whole place is crawling with the beastly things!" Year 225 A.B. (After the Bomb.) Operation Return to Light, at the Delta II Computer Center experimental station, discovers that a "recent mutation" due to nuclear radiation has boosted the IQ of rats "to an amazing degree": "Human beings are their food!" There follow hokey scream scenes, as a pack of "primitives"—a motorcycle gang—comes across rat-gnawed and rat-infested bodies. Meant-to-give-you-the-willies lines include "Think of the diseases they could give you—hepatitis, meningitis, leptospirosis, plague!" Unlikely horror shticks: rats exploding out victims' backs ... telegraphed rat-in-mouth. Best silly shock is the kicker: Inside the deceptively pretty yellow decontamination-crew suit is a full-sized ... rat person!

**2 The RATS ARE COMING! THE WEREWOLVES ARE HERE!** Constitution 1972 (1970?) (*Curse of the Full Moon* - orig t). Sets: Jim Fox. Mkp: Walter Moody. Ref: TV: Midnight Video. Lee. Lentz. Weldon. Stanley. Hardy/HM. Martin. Phantom. Newman.

"I told you I had a very strange family." England, 1899. It's "not very pleasant" at Mooney Manor, which is inhabited by the "not quite normal, animal-like" Malcolm (Berwick Kaler), 180-year-old Pa (Douglas Phair), Phoebe (Joan Ogden), and Diana (Jackie Skarvellis). At the end, all seem to turn into werewolves, while young Monica (Hope Stansbury) delays her transformation: "I can change myself at will!" Special bonus: the rat-chewed-faced Micawber, whose "talented" rats have a taste for human flesh. ("They haven't eaten yet, you know.")

The Ambersons they ain't. Unbearably wordy period tragedy has professional photography (by writer-director Andy Milligan), but not much else. An exhaustive, all-night search for highlights reveals only a rat dubbed Willard and Micawber's anecdote re the dead old lady that he found on a doorstep. (He carried her home, he says, and "gave a piece to the children.")

**RATS DE MANHATTAN, Les** see *Rats: Night of Terror*

**RATS IN THE WALLS, The** see *Necronomicon* (1993)

**RATU ILMU HITAM** see *Black Magic Terror*

**RAUMSCHIFF VENUS ANTWORTET NICHT** see *First Spaceship on Venus*

**RAVEN DANCE** see *Mirror Mirror 2*

**RAVEN TENGU, KABUTO: THE GOLDEN-EYED BEAST**
(J) L. A. Hero/Nippon/Buichi Terasawa & NEP & KSS (Ito-Toyoda-Iwakawa-Nakamura) 1992 ('93-U.S.) anim color 45m. (aka *Kabuto*). SP, D: B. Terasawa. Ph: Yoshida. AD: T. Waki. Ref: TV: LAH video (Dark Image); Eng. titles. Animerica 5:3(ad): OAV.

Ingredients include the crow-master hero ... the Gadget Master, who has created a mechanical sorceress sustained by the flames of candles which "feed on the life forces of women" ... an iron robot-horse ... an airship-with-super-vacuum ... Rasetsubo, a ray-shooting android-type ... Black Spiders, "mystical soldiers" with bug-like masks ("Demon Mask insects") ... and a "demonic kimono" which harbors illusions of spirits and monsters.... Nifty details like the live masks help, in this otherwise formula super-hero tale.

**RAW NERVE** Pyramid Dist. (Action Int'l.)/Winters Group & Sovereign Investment (Ruta K. Aras) 1991 color 93m. SP, D: David A. Prior. SP: also L. L. Simeone. Ref: V 6/3/91: "unusual casting perks up this perfunctory murder mystery." PT 11:51. SFChron Dtbk 7/21/91. With Glenn Ford, Sandahl Bergman, Randall Cobb, Ted Prior, Traci Lords, Jan-Michael Vincent.

"Man troubled by nightmarish visions that prove to be accurate accounts of serial murders."(V)

**RAWHEAD REX** (B) Empire/Alpine & Paradise & Green Man (Shiuli Ltd./Kevin Attew, Don Hawkins) 1987 (1986) color 89m. D: George Pavlou. SP: Clive Barker, from his novella. Creature FX: Peter Litten. Ref: TV: Vestron-TV. V 4/1/87. Phantom. Newman. Morse. With David Dukes, Kelly Piper, Ronan Wilmot, Niall Toibin, Heinrich Von Schellendorf (Rawhead Rex).

"He was king here! Rawhead—that's what they called him!" Rathmorne, Ireland. Old-fashioned monster movie has a few shocks and some suitably mysterious details and elements—the Neolithic monolith, the cursed altar, the Latin inscription on the stained-glass window (translation: "Death goes in fear of what it cannot be"), the spirit woman, and of course the monster, Rawhead Rex. Loud, violent movie has a James Bernard-ish horror score and plays like a Hammer "Dracula."

**RAZORBACK** (Austral.) WB/UAA Films (Western) 1984 (1983) color/ws 96m. D: Russell Mulcahy. SP: Everett De Roche, from Peter Brennan's novel. Mus: Iva Davies. SpFX: Mark Canny. SpDes: Bob McCarron. Ref: TV. V 4/4/84. Phantom. Morse. With Gregory Harrison, Arkie Whiteley, Bill Kerr, Chris Haywood, Judy Morris, David Argue.

"God and the devil couldn't have created a more despicable creature." Amok in Australia: a big buffalo-plus-sized razorback—"not a normal product of nature." Even smaller razorbacks make room for Daddy, and the "piglets" are not very pleasant either.... The modest, early portents of trouble here are more unnerving than the closeup-laden payoff. The atmospheric soundtrack teems with weird bird-cries, snorts, and snuffles; the

photography by Dean Semler includes time-lapse night shadows. Standard storyline and characters, though the wild and crazy meat-packer brothers/sadists surprise.

**REACTOR, The** see *Deadly Reactor*

**REAL BAD MONSTER RAW** (Thai) 198-? color/ws c82m. Ref: TV: vt; little Eng. Lao Market: above is tr t.

The Frankenstein monster first appears here as a birthday present in a coffin. He sings ("You come and go"), drinks whisky and coffee, and keeps explaining to anyone who'll listen that he's the Frankenstein monster. He undergoes surgery which apparently works: In the very next scene, he's singing on stage in a club. At the end, he is shown to have a vampire-like fear of the sun, and must return to his coffin by day. A stake through the heart kills him.

This looks to be a balmy, breezy softcore-sex horror-comedy, despite the tragic ending. The monster is a bolts-and-all Universal Frankenstein monster who looks even taller than usual in squeezed scope. The kooks running around about him seem to give him a headache. How he got to be a vampire....

**REAL GENIUS** Tri-Star & Delphi III (Brian Grazer/Robert Daley) 1985 color/ws 105m. D: Martha Coolidge. SP: Neal Israel, Pat Proft, Peter Torokvei. Mus: Thomas Newman. SpVisFX: Syd Dutton, Bill Taylor. Laser: (des) Ron Cobb; (sp fx) Laser Media. SpFxCoord: Philip C. Cory. Ref: TV. MFB'86:378-9. V 8/7/85. With Val Kilmer, Gabe Jarret, Michelle Meyrink, William Atherton, Patti D'Arbanville, Ed Lauter, Louis Giambalvo, Severn Darden, Lynda Wiesmeier.

Chemical, portable, six-megawatt laser gun, frozen to increase its power, can blast through just about anything. Meanwhile, a demo-model space laser vaporizes a man, and, at the end, a laser pops a ton of popcorn.... This worthy end justifies some awkward narrative means. Coolidge-style comedy is droll, and less flaky and condescending than Hughes-style comedy (compare *Weird Science*), and the former more deftly accommodates serious undertones. The fact that almost all the actors here have the same low-key wit, however, makes for a near-monotone movie.

**REAL GHOST STORY** (J) Japan Home Video 1991 color 50m. Ref: TV: JHV; no Eng. People's Video: above is tr t.

Three tales involving a half-seen thing in a lavatory, a ball of light, and *Haunting* sounds. Some technically impressive tracking shots in the second (ball of fire) story.

**REAL MEN** MGM/UA (Martin Bregman) 1987 color 86m. SP, D: Dennis Feldman. SpVisFX: Dream Quest; Michael Bigelow et al. SpFX: Stan Parks. Mkp: Monty Westmore. OptFX: Cinema Research. Ref: TV. V 12/9/87. With James Belushi, John Ritter, Barbara Barrie, Bill Morey, Mark Herrier.

"We have been negotiating with men in UFOs for seven years." Basically wrongheaded spy spoof features a "good package" from an E.T. (Don Dolan?), and a "homing pen" which returns to the aliens' galaxy. In a transformation as unresonant as it is unamusing, Bob Wilson (Ritter), wimp, becomes a Real Man. A few funny bits of offhand outrageousness.

**RE-ANIMATOR** Empire/Re-Animator Prods. (Brian Yuzna) 1985 color 86m. (aka *H. P. Lovecraft's Re-Animator*). SP, D: Stuart Gordon. SP: also Dennis Paoli, William J. Norris, from Lovecraft's story "Herbert West—Reanimator." Mus: Richard Band. SpMkpFX: Anthony Doublin, John Naulin; MMI (John Buechler). SpSdFX: John Paul Fasal. Ref: screen. MFB'86:11-12. V 5/15/85. ad. With Jeffrey Combs, Bruce Abbott, Barbara Crampton, David Gale, Peter Kent (Melvin the re-animated), Barbara Pieters.

The "unstable" Herbert West (Combs), a student at Miskatonic Medical School in Arkham, Massachusetts, has "conquered brain death," and succeeds in bringing a cat, a corpse, and a severed head and its body back to life.... Lovecraft's outrageous but entertaining story becomes an exercise in doctor's-office gore which, like *Rabid,* shamelessly exploits fear of incision. Operating utensils include laser drills, saws, scalpels, shovels, axes, and paperweights. (The latter is featured in a memorable bit.) Very funny: Dr. Hill's (Gale) body and (unattached) head find hand-eye coordination difficult.

Sequel: *Bride of Re-Animator.*

**RE-ANIMATOR 2** see *Bride of Re-Animator*

**REASON TO DIE** Vidmark (Anant Singh/Helena Spring) 1990 color 86m. D: Tim Spring. SP: A. Rettan, T. Asbury. Ref: V 6/27/90:48 (hv): "uneventful actioner." Martin: "typical slasher." With Wings Hauser, Anneline Kriel, A. Vosloo.

*Most Dangerous Game* ending.

**REAZIONE A CATENA** see *Twitch of the Death Nerve*

**REBEL NUN, The** see *Flavia the Heretic*

**REBEL STORM** (So. African) Gibraltar Releasing/Crawford-Lane (Davidson-Buchfuehrer) 1989 color 96m. (aka *Rising Storm. Rebel Waves*). D: Francis Schaeffer. SP: Gary Rosen, William Fay. Mus: Julian Laxton. SpFxSup: John Hartigan. Mkp: Bobby West. Ref: TV. V 5/31/89. vc box. With Zach Galligan, Wayne Crawford, June Chadwick, John Rhys-Davies, Elizabeth Keifer, William Katt, Deep Roy.

The U.S. of A., 2099 A.D., after the "lights went out." The Blessed Reverend (Rod McCary), Jimmy Joe II, rules and issues commemorative coins (with his likeness on both sides); "What a Friend We Have in Jesus" is the national anthem; mutants roam; and Radio Free America seeks out a long-lost videotape of a "freedom fighter of another era"—a rebellious disc jockey who was the "last voice of truth".... The script's jaunty air makes this a bit easier to take than most post-apocalypse actioners, and the religious and social satire, though not exactly deep, is occasionally entertaining.

**The RECOIL** (B) Stoll/Sam Hardy 1922 silent 62m. D: G.H. Malins. SP: Rafael Sabatini, from his novel "The Dream." Ref: BFC. Lee. With E. Norwood, P. Titmuss, L. Anderson.

"Psychic expert hypnotizes cousin to shoot rich uncle."(BFC)

**RECONCILIATION, The** see *Kwaidan*

**RECORD OF LODOSS WAR: PROLOGUE** (Episode 1) (J) Kadokawa Video 198-? anim color 25m. (aka *Record of Lodoss Wars*). Based on the game. Ref: TV: Pack-In Video; no Eng. Animerica 5:15: OAV.

In an abandoned city on Lodoss (the Cursed Island), adventurers find vicious gargoyles (a spell makes the latter disintegrate) and an underground, spike-backed, fire-breathing, long-tongued "earth dragon." Atmospheric design (fog, rain, lightning) and musical score. The presence of the live gargoyles is first indicated when the shadow of one of the initially-just-stone creatures moves.

**RECORD OF LODOSS WAR: BEGINNING OF FIRE** (Episode 2) (J) Kadokawa Video 198-? anim color 25m. Ref: TV: Pack-In-Video; no Eng.

Creatures this time include Bramdo the Ice Dragon (a bit part) and nasty, toothy goblins, which invade a town. Pern, one of our heroes, takes on the Goblin King. Fairish. Second of apparently twelve episodes.

**RED AND BLACK** (Chinese) 1986 color feature? D: Andrew Kam Yuen Wah. Ref: Jones.

Japanese vampire infects Chinese man who, twenty-five years later, infects the People's Leader.

**RED BLOODED AMERICAN GIRL** (Can.) SC Ent. & Prism Ent. (Nicolas Stiliadis) 1990 color 87m. D: David Blyth. SP: Alan, or Allan, Moyle. Mus: Jim Manzie. SpFxCoord: Brock Jolliffe. Computer Graphics: Dome Prods. Mkp: Sandra Moore. Ref: TV. V 6/6/90 & 12/3/90:82 (hv). Cable Video Store 2/91. With Andrew Stevens, Heather Thomas, Christopher Plummer, Kim Coates, Lydie Denier.

"Paula's cells are being eaten alive by her own blood!" A rabid "inmate" of the Life Reach Foundation bites heroine Paula (Thomas) and infects her with the virus of vampirism. An addiction to blood, in fact, infects just about everyone, apparently, who works for the foundation, including its head, Dr. Alcore (Plummer), who picked up this virus, with its "life enhancing attributes," in New Guinea.

Pointless except as a vehicle for Thomas. Lousiest line (Stevens to Plummer): "You have no right to play God!" Script overdoes the Sinister Organization theme, then drags in the *House of Dracula,* cure-for-monsters idea and goes that movie one better for a surprise happy ending for all.

**RED DAWN** MGM-UA/Valkyrie (Sidney Beckerman) 1984 color 109m. SP, D: John Milius. SP, Story: Kevin Reynolds. Mus: Basil Poledouris. SpFX: Tom Fisher, D. L. Martin. Ref: TV. V 8/8/84. SFExam 8/10/84. With Patrick Swayze, C. Thomas Howell, Ron O'Neal, Ben Johnson, Harry Dean Stanton, Lea Thompson, Powers Boothe, William Smith.

"We held 'em at the Rockies and the Mississippi." Russians and Cubans invade the U.S., NATO is dissolved, and China and England are our allies in this male weepie remake of *Strange Holiday* (1946). The central conceit—we're the guerrillas in our own country—is just a pretext for Fourth of July fireworks. Bullets and tears.

**RED DRAGON: THE PURSUIT OF HANNIBAL LECTER** see *Manhunter*

**RED FANGS** see *Blue Sonnet*

**RED-HEADED BABY** WB 1931? anim 6m. D, P: Rudolf Ising. Mus: Frank Marsales. Ref: TV. WBCartoons. Maltin/OMAM. no LC.

Big, mean, comic-monstrous, six-legged spider menaces red-headed doll in toy shop. Lively, likable cartoon. The spider has a funny "boogeyman" growl/howl.

**RED HOT MAMMA** Para/Fleischer 1934 anim c7m. D: Dave Fleischer. Anim: Bowsky, Tendlar. Ref: TV: NTA-TV; '72 colorization. Cabarga/TFS.

Betty Boop dreams that the road to hell is paved right through her fireplace. Down there, she finds that devils suit up new "freshmen," and that "firemen" spray flames with their hoses. Betty gives them all the cold shoulder, and they freeze. Hot stuff.

**\*The RED HOUSE** 1947 (*No Trespassing* - orig t). Mkp: Irving Berns. Ref: TV. V 2/5/47. Lee. Lentz. Stanley. Agee. Maltin '92. Phantom. Scheuer. Martin.

"There's a curse on those woods!" In Ox-head Woods, "trails lead nowhere," and the wind sounds like it's shrieking. "There's something out in those woods"—a supposedly haunted house, to be precise. And from the red house, there are "screams in the night."

*The Red House* is melodrama-on-the-verge-of-camp. An overwrought revelation scene is only a warmup for the climax, one of the most tortuous movie-thriller, heroine-isolated-with-killer scenes of all: Pete (Edward G. Robinson) cracks again, thinks Meg (Allene Roberts) is the dead "Jeannie," and.... The last, frozen-faced shot of Pete in the sinking truck is weirdly compelling.

**RED LIPS** see *Case of the Two Beauties*

**RED MONKS** (I) 21st Century/Natmas Prods.(Fulci) 1988 color 90m. (*I Fratti Rossi*). D: G.A. Martucci. Presented by Lucio Fulci. Ref: MV: "devil worshiping monks." V(Mifed'89): 52(ad): "ancient rituals." 10/19/88:364(ad): Hardy/HM2. Palmerini: "satanic reincarnation." With Gerardo Amato, Lara Wendel, Malisa Longo, R. Brown.

**3P RED NIGHTMARE** Jack L. Warner 1957? 28m. Ref: Roxie Theatre (S.F.) notes. SFChron Dtbk 2/23/92. Phantom: packaged in *The Commies Are Coming, The Commies Are Coming!* With Jack Kelly, Peter Breck, Jack Webb, Robert Conrad, Peter Brown.

Complacent American dreams of Communist invasion.

**RED OCEAN** see *Devil Fish*

**RED PANTHER** (H.K.?) Always Good Film Co. 1983 color c85m. Ref: TV: Rainbow Video; Eng. titles. TVG. With Yee Louie.

Hard to guess who the surgical slasher is in this psycho-thriller populated by some very strange people, including Dr. Chu, who lectures empty classrooms re surgical technique, and Kiang, who acts crazy with a birthday-cake knife and is promptly shot down. Not to mention: hide-and-go-seek and fun with a live "corpse" in a morgue ... an aborted shower murder ... and a comic *Halloween* "encore" by the near-dead killer.

Or, The Surgical Saw Massacre. Red Herring would be as apt a title. Apter. Basically routine slasher movie is well done and bizarrely mixes violence with comedy: Scary scenes end comically, and vice versa. Odd-line prize to: "The insides are missing in the mortuary."

**RED PHOTON ZILLION** see *Burning Night*

**RED QUEEN KILLS 7 TIMES** see *Corpse Which Didn't Want To Die, The*

**RED RAIN** see *Jack's Back*

**RED RIDING HOOD** (U.S.-B-Israeli) Cannon (Golan-Globus) 1987 color 80m. D: Adam Brooks. SP: Carole Lucia Satrina, from the fairy tale by the Brothers Grimm. Mus: Stephen Lawrence. SpFxSup: John Hargreaves. Mkp: Mony Mansano, Blake Shepard. Ref: TV. V 5/20/87. With Craig T. Nelson, Isabella Rossellini, Amelia Shankley, Rocco Sisto (Dagger the Wolf).

A man transforms into a wolf (via elementary lap dissolves) and gobbles up Red (Shankley), who disagrees with him. He is cut open, and Red steps out whole.

**RED RINGS OF FEAR** see *Trauma* (1978)

**RED SONJA** MGM-UA/Dino De Laurentiis (Christian Ferry) 1985 color/ws 89m. D: Richard Fleischer. SP: Clive Exton, George MacDonald Fraser. Mus: Ennio Morricone. SpVisFX: Universal; Barry Nolan, Van Der Veer. Spider & Fish: Colin Arthur, Giuseppe Tortora. SpFX: John Stirber. SpMkp: Rino Carboni. Ref: TV. MFB'85:348-9. V 7/3/85. EBay Express 7/12/85. Phantom. With Arnold Schwarzenegger, Brigitte Nielsen, Sandahl Bergman, Janet Agren, Paul Smith, Ronald Lacey.

The Hyborian Kingdom, in an "age of violence...." Principal creatures: a spirit that delivers strength—and a lot of exposition—to the heroine ... the huge pet spider of the evil queen ... a huge, mean water serpent ("It is a machine!") ... a giant ... and lizard-men. Principal object: the talisman which created the world, and can also shatter worlds.... Don't be fooled by the names—Rotunno (photography), Morricone (music), Donati (design). The director is Richard Fleischer. Fun-garish sets, costumes, props. Stirring music. Zilch plot, characters, dialogue. (The dubbed, action-scene grunts are pretty much on the same level as the latter.)

**The RED SPECTRE** (F) Blackhawk/Pathe 1906 ('07-U.S.) color 7m. Ref: TV. John Frick. Lee (p).

A magician-like, skeleton-suited horned devil from a casket makes women and fireballs appear, calls up women from flames, displays "living" portraits and bottled women, and performs feats of levitation. At the end, a rebellious member of his "harem" turns him into a skeleton and assumes his cape and role.... Charming if episodic macabre-fantasy short. The spectacle of the women in the beakers anticipates a sequence in *Bride of Frankenstein*.

**RED SPELL SPELLS RED** (H.K.) Nikko Int'l./Stephen C. K. Chan 1983 color/ws 97m. D: Titus Ho. SP: Amy Chan. Story: Nikko Creative Dept. Ref: TV: World Video; Eng. titles. Hardy/HM: *Red Spells Red*. Fango 107:59, 60. NST! 4:34: D: He Yong Lin. With Leung Chi-Hung, Eling Chan.

The "shadow of the spirit," visible on the film taken of the opening of the coffin of the "Red Dwarf Ghost," makes a man at an editing machine imagine that the celluloid is strangling him. Later, the ghost's scorpion spell makes scorpions begin "creeping out" of a woman's body.

Pretty sleazy Asian shocker features effects violence done to humans and apparently actual violence done to other animals such as pigs and chickens. Grossest make-believe violence: the sorcerer pulling off the affected area of the scorpion woman's skin. Niftiest effect: the miniature-scorpion image on the woman's pupil. Oddest effects: the killer-leaves attaching themselves to their victim in the forest ... one victim's body being propelled magically through the countryside.

**RED SPIRIT LAKE** Inferential Pictures 1993 color 69m. SP, D, P, Ed: Charles Pinion. SP, P, Ed: also Annabel Lee. Mus: Michael Belfer. Ref: TV: Fireball video. With Siobhan, Rick Hall, Street Life, R. Kern, Julie Marlowe, A. Lee, C. Pinion, Holly Adams.

"Red Spirit Lake has a crazy history." Featured: apparitions ... the theory that angels have entrusted humans to guard the "demon of Red Spirit Lake" ... a witch who bites off a thug's tongue and has the latter castrate himself ... and a guy burnt, or boiled, to a crisp.... Generally inept indie gore vehicle is definitely weird, but awkwardly done.

**RED SUN RISING** 1994 color 99m. D: F. Megahy. Ref: Martin: '93?; "mystical elements ... entertaining players." SFChron 1/14/95: "a pretty decent one." With Don "The Dragon" Wilson, Terry Farrell, Mako, Edward Albert.

Fingertip "death touch" ... "black magic killer ninjas." (SFC)

**RED TO KILL** (H.K.) 1994 color feature. D: Billy Tang. Ref: Weisser/ATC2: "excessively graphic ... rapes and murders"; razor slashings. With Chung Suk Wai.

**REDNECK ZOMBIES** Troma/Full Moon & Colorcast 1987 color 89m. D & Co-P: Pericles Lewnes. SP: F. Smellman. Mus: A. Bond. Ref: V 5/17/89:48 (hv): "strictly amateur night" gore. Fango 104:7: "worthless mess." McCarty II: "cheap laughs." Phantom: "a few crude laughs." With Lisa M. DeHaven, W. E. Benson, W. Decker.

Moonshiners drink toxic waste, gooily disintegrate, come back as bloodthirsty ghouls.

**The REFLECTING SKIN** (B-Can.) Miramax/British Screen, BBC Films, Zenith, Bialystock & Bloom Ltd., Telefilm Canada, The Ontario Film Development Corp. (Fugitive Features/Nat'l. Film Trustee Co.) 1990 ('91-U.S.) color 95m. SP, D: Philip Ridley. Mus: Nick Bicat. SpFX: Lee Routly. Mkp: Al Magallon. Ref: TV. MFB'90:334. V 5/16/90. ad. SFChron Dtbk 11/17/91. SFExam 11/22/91. Cinef 12/92:62. With Viggo Mortensen, Lind-

say Duncan, Jeremy Cooper, Shelia Moore, Duncan Fraser, David Longworth, Robert Koons.

"She's gonna suck his blood and kill him!" A boy, Seth (Cooper), inspired by the book *Vampire Blood*, believes that the "monster" on the loose that "does things to children" is the self-declared 200-year-old widow Dolphin Blue (Duncan). ("She's a vampire!") He is wrong, of course, and comes to regret his error.... "Or, how did this film ever get made?" (Examiner) Esthetically grotesque drama is set in a period America where boys say "Just so." Arch, tortured filmmaking.

**The REFRIGERATOR** Avenue D Films (Oldcorn/The Refrigerator Ltd.) 1991 color 85m. Story, SP, D: Nicholas Jacobs. Ph: Paul Gibson. Mus: Don Peterkofsky et al. AD: Therese Deprez. Story: also C. Oldcorn, P. Dolin. SpFX: Mike Deprez. Mkp: Judy Chin et al. Ref: TV: Monarch HV. SFChron 3/26/94. 1/21/95. V 11/18/91: "smart, quirky horror spoof." 10/14/91:A-87 (ad). 5/3/93:31: at Madrid Imagfic fest. 9/28/92:10. PT 16:12: "the dreams are great." Cinef 4/93. With Julia McNeal, David Simonds, Angel Caban.

'63 Norge eats Lower East Side tenants. (V) "Don't move in!" A possessed, homicidal 'frig crushes one victim in its door, swallows Mom, etc. ("The place is weird!") At the end, other kitchen appliances go berserk.... The monster-movie version of *The Out-of-Towners,* and about as subtle. The title at the beginning says "Somewhere in Ohio."

**REGAL SHOCKERS** (Fili) Regal 198-? color c110m. D: Argel Joseph. Tel: Emil Ma Cruz Jr. Ref: TV: two Regal Int'l. Video "telemovies"; no Eng.

1) "Kasal Sa Hukay." with Mat Ranillo III, Lito Pimentel, Perla Bautista, Snooky Serna.

2) "Satanista." Mus & FX: Spinosa. AD: Abet Alvarez. with Gloria Romero, Luis Gonzales, Jobelle Salvador.

Death, complete with neon scythe and glowing eyes, tells two stories:

1) Two murder victims return from the dead to wreak revenge on the madman who killed them, in your basic hand-from-the-grave story, and rather dragged out.

2) A priest attempts to exorcise a possessed boy, but the latter winds up tearing himself apart, literally. Flat, talky, with an amateur-night gore payoff (eyeball delight).

**The REGENERATED MAN** Filmline & Austin (Bohus-Provenzano) 1994 color 89m. SP, Story, D, Co-Ed: Ted A. Bohus. SP: also Jack Smith. Ph: J.R. Rosnell. Mus & SdDes: Ariel Shallit. AD: Rena D'Angela. MorphFX: Creative Multimedia, Sam Hasson. VisFxSup: Dan Taylor. SpMkpFX: V.J. Guastini. Hand Sculpture: Evan Campbell. Computer Anim: Magnet Design & Commun. 2nd Unit: Fred Olen Ray. Ref: TV: Bullseye Video (Arrow Video). With Arthur Lundquist (Dr. Bob Clarke), Cheryl Hendricks, Christopher Kidd, Gregory Sullivan, George Stover, Kevin Schinnick (creature).

Two thugs force a meteor expert experimenting in tissue regeneration to swallow his own potions (including Regen 5). His enzymes "go crazy," and whenever his metabolic rate increases, he turns into a "Mr. Hyde" who's impervious to bullets, shoots dart-like bones from inside his arm, and uses his fingernails as dart-weapons. An apparent second monster with a "feeding" tongue and knife-like fingernails becomes, at one point, a huge insect-crab thing.... The latter sequence is one of the two high points of this thin sf-horror movie. The other: a visualized dream re a dino-monster and spaceships.

**REGENERATION** (Can.) Howe/Int'l. Heliotrope (Tony Dean) 1988 color 87m. SP, D: R. Stephens. Ref: V 9/14/88: "acting ... is abysmal." With John Anderson, Marek Cieszewski, Suzanne Ristic.

Prof brings the dead back to life.

**REGENERATOR** see *Metamorphosis* (1989)

**REGINA DEGLI ZOMBI, La** see *Erotic Nights of the Living Dead*

**REI REI: MISSIONARY OF LOVE** (J) A.D. Vision/Shimizu (Shonen Gahosha & Pink Pineapple/Iwakawa & Sugiyama) 1993?('94-U.S.) anim color c55m. D: Yoshikio Yamamoto. SP: Mitsuru Mochizuki. Created by Toshimitsu Shimizu. Mus: Ishizuka. SpFX: Rika Sugahara. SdFxD: Yamada. Ref: TV: ADV video; Eng. titles.

Two segments of an apparent OAV series are set in 1999.

1) "The First Night." Kaguya, a moon goddess, or "new savior," aids Earth lovers. Facile kinkiness with wry moments.

2) "The Second Night." A jilted boy's soul is "absorbed and rewritten as software" in a video game. Is he now both the tentacled vid-monster which gropes Kaguya and the bat-thing which carries her off? Conventional Japanese animated sex-horror crossed with a sometimes wry fantasy-comedy of First Sex. Funny: the boy Satoshi's face incarnated on the bathtub water.

**The RE-INCARNATION OF GOLDEN LOTUS** (H.K.) Golden Harvest/Friend Cheers Ltd. (Paragon) 1989 color 94m. Ref: TV: Pan-Asia Video; Eng. titles. Y.K. Ho.

"I see strange things." A woman who, in 1966, encountered the book *The Story of Golden Lotus*, finds herself, in the Eighties, seeing "people in costumes from the past." A now-you-see-her-now-you-don't fortune teller advises her of the importance of the past. And when, in a photo shoot, she garbs herself as Golden Lotus—the "number one slut in ancient Chinese history"—she begins to re-enact a tragedy, or melodrama, from the distant past. In a funny twist, however, supposedly poisoned hubbie revives; in a sad twist, his brother, who loves this "re-incarnation," relents in his brotherly loyalty and asks her, too late, to go away with him.... *Rouge*-like mixture of the romantic and the supernatural has some tantalizing details and occasional story surprises, but draws out its not-exactly-remarkable, modern-day triangle tale.

**The REJUVENATRIX** Steven Mackler & SVSC Films/Jewel 1988 color 88m. (aka *The Rejuvenator. Juvenatrix*). SP, D: Brian Thomas Jones. Story, SP: Simon Nuchtern. Mus: Larry Juris. SpMkpFX: Ed French. Anim: D. Jennings, Mike Saz. Ref: TV. V 7/20/88. With Vivian Lanko (Elizabeth Warren & the monster), John MacKay, James Hogue, Jessica Dublin.

"The brain's been picked out!" Dr. Gregory Ashton (MacKay) can "reverse the aging process" by regenerating tissue with a serum distilled from the "raw gray matter of the human brain." The imperfect serum, however, produces "monsters" with a taste for brains tartare.... Pathetic. *Countess Dracula* with nothing on it. The gore in this evidently videotaped cheapie is hamhanded, though Elizabeth-the-monster is so ooze-happy a makeup that it's funny.

**RELENTLESS** New Line/CineTel (Hertzberg/Hansen/Smith)/Out of the Dark Prods. 1989 color 92m. D: William Lustig. SP: Phil Alden Robinson. Mus: Jay Chattaway. SpFX: Guy Faria. Mkp: Bill Miller-Jones. Ref: TV: vt. V 5/24/89. ad. HR 8/29/89. VVoice 9/5/89. Sacto Union 8/31/89. With Judd Nelson, Robert Loggia, Leo Rossi, Meg Foster, Mindy Seger, Beau Starr, Angel Tompkins, George "Buck" Flower, Armand Mastroianni, John Goff.

"If I'm so sick, why can't you catch me?" Someone is randomly killing all the Arthur Taylors in Hollywood and leaving the appropriate page of the phone book near each victim. The "Sunset Killer" is Arthur "Buck" Taylor (Nelson), whose macho/survivalist father was a "hell of a cop," and who forces his victims to "participate in their own deaths" by piano wire, corkscrew, kitchen knife, etc.

Well-acted, fairly entertaining, but pointless and—at either end, the killer's or the cops'—not quite believable. Featured: a classic "bus" in a laundry room. Predictable ending isolates the killer and the cop's wife and son.

Follow-up: *Dead On.*

**RELENTLESS 3** New Line (Hertzberg-Hansen) 1993 color feature. SP, D: James Lemmo. Ref: SFChron Dtbk 8/15/93. 10/31/93: "totally unsatisfying ending." PT 16:61: "sicker than Part 2." With Leo Rossi, William Forsythe, S. Coleman.

Serial killer mails victims' body parts to police.

**RELIGION, The** see *Believers, The*

**The RELUCTANT VAMPIRE** Waymar Prods. (Graham Ford) 1992 color feature. SP, D: Malcolm Marmorstein, from his play. Ph: S. Lighthill. Ref: Jones. V 10/21/91:32: shooting. 2/22/93:A-122: at AFM. With Adam Ant, Kimberly Foster, Philip Bruns.

Vampiric rock musician.

**REMANDO AL VIENTO** (Sp-Norw.) Ditirambo Films & Viking Films & Iberoamericana de TV (Andres Vicente Gomez) 1988 color 96m. SP, D: Gonzalo Suarez. Mus: A. Masso. SpFX: Reyes Abades. Ref: V 10/5/88: "one of the best to come out of Spain in a long time"; *Rowing with the Wind*—tr t; "shot in English." HR 4/14/89: "some rich, if fitful, moments." With Hugh Grant (Lord Byron), Lizzy McInnerny (Mary Shelley), Valentine Pelka (Shelley), Jose Luis Gomez (Polidori).

The "Frankenstein monster ... haunts the lives and forecasts the doom of most of the principals." (V) "Palpable visions of [Mary Shelley's] monster." (HR)

See also *Gothic. Haunted Summer.*

**REMEMBER?** MGM (Milton Bren) 1939 85m. SP, D: Norman Z. McLeod. SP: also Corey Ford. Mus: Edward Ward. AD: Cedric Gibbons; Urie McCleary. Ref: TV. TVG. Lee. V 11/8/39. Maltin '92. Scheuer. With Robert Taylor, Greer Garson, Lew Ayres,

Billie Burke, Reginald Owen, Laura Hope Crews, Sara Haden, Paul Hurst, Halliwell Hobbes, Sig Ruman, Richard Carle, Henry Travers, George Barbier, Armand Kaliz.

A scientist (Ruman) developing "new products" in a New York City firm's lab discovers a drug which "produces a complete amnesia." Added to the martinis of a divorcing couple (Taylor and Garson), it wipes out the last six months of their memories, back to the date that they first met. They now meet again, fall in love again, marry again.

*Remember?* is an eminently-forgettable comedy—until the couple's introduction/reunion. The "love at first sight" scene, near the end, is a near-magical invention: With the slates wiped clean of unpleasant memories, the two rediscover the freshness of feeling that they had the first time around. These amnesia scenes are alternately sweet and hilarious. Hobbes brings out pajamas for Garson, Taylor's guest—thoughtful, from the butler's viewpoint; highly indiscreet, from theirs, since they just met.... The plot simply sets up these climactic scenes. Garson, wisely, plays straight; Taylor tries hard for comedy.

**2P REMEMBER LAST NIGHT?** Univ 1935 85m. (*The Hangover Murders* - orig t). D: James Whale. SP: D. Malloy, H. Clork, D. Totheroh, from Adam Hobhouse's novel *Hangover Murders*. PhFX: John P. Fulton. Ref: TV. Curtis/James Whale. Lee. Lentz. Stanley. Maltin '92. Scheuer. V 11/27/35. TVG. PFA notes 12/30/80.

Mystery with horror, fantasy, and sf overtones, plus accidental and intentional dialogue references to other Universal horror movies of the time. ("I'm Dracula's daughter!" "Hope it wasn't a black cat!" "I feel like the bride of Frankenstein!") Professor Karl Herman Eckhart Jones (Gustav von Seyffertitz) seems to bring an eerie wind, and night, with him, as he returns party guests—via "mechanically-induced hypnosis"—to last night's murder scene. His mirror-machine dulls the conscious mind. Other goodies: a "spooky" wine cellar, a secret room, a psychic (Rafaela Ottiano), and Charles D. Hall art direction.... The mystery-comedy plot doesn't give Whale (or composer Franz Waxman) much with which to work, but he comes up with some atmospheric set-pieces, including a well-engineered wild, silly party, and the chiller scenes.

**REMEMBER MY LOVE** see *Urusei Yatsura 3: Remember My Love*

**REMOTE CONTROL** Vista (Rosenfelt-Levinson) 1988 (1987) color 88m. SP, D: Jeff Lieberman. Mus: Peter Bernstein. SpFxSup: Jerry Williams. VisFX: Ted Rae, Joe Viskocil, David Stipes et al. Mkp: Teresa Austin. Ref: TV. V 8/24/88. With Kevin Dillon, Deborah Goodrich, Christopher Wynne, Frank Beddor (Victor), Bert Remsen, Richard Warlock, Dick Durock.

"There's something wrong with this movie!" Polaris Video's View-O-Vision "Remote Control"—a video within a video concocted to be a 1957 sf movie re the 1980s—hypnotizes or brainwashes viewers and ... "you can't control yourself." Viewers turn ugly and violent, and the Master Controllers above apparently achieve some puny satisfaction from this turn of events.... Okay weird premise goes nowhere. Plot is essentially the same scene replayed again and again. The tackiness of "Remote Con-

trol" looks to be more enjoyable than the confusion of *Remote Control*.

**RENDEZVOUS** (H.K.?) 198-? color c84m. Ref: TV: vt; no Eng. Suiki: above is tr t. EVS: *Ghoul Sex Squad* - U.S. vt t.

A traveler by night in a forest removes the spells from the foreheads of a troop of hopping vampires. The latter put the bite on him, and he begins hopping in circles with them.... A distinctly uneasy mixture of vampire comedy, Romero-esque blood-and-guts gore, and hardcore sex scenes. In the most unusual of the latter, a vampire climaxes by phallically sucking the life breath out of a woman's body.

**RENEGADE FORCE** (J) LD Video/Toei Anim (Cooper-Haller) 1992-U.S. anim color 89m. Adap: Haller, Walker. Created by S. Urakawa. Mus: C. Watanabe. Ref: TV: LDV; Eng. version. vc box: aliens, robots, "war machine."

The alien Creature-Forming Device produces Batroacher III, a "30-story, fire-breathing cockroach" ... Octocrabus X-3 ... a giant squid (or this may be an independent monster) ... Parrodactyl ... a dragon-eel-reindeer, Reindragon XV-6, the silliest-looking monster (it's the antlers) ... and a tentacled lobster, Krustakos Primo, a "new generation monster." Plus: the Nuclear Ship Fort Liberty and its two giant, human-operated super-robots, Magnon and Magnetta ... a collision of a moon and a planet (it's the "decaying orbits") ... and a flashback to a time of dinosaurs and aliens. (The theory goes that Earth monuments like the Easter Island statues are the relics of an ancient alien civilization, which has been hiding out on ocean floors.) Stolid dramatics, familiar robot/monster action. Helpfully, each monster is identified with a title. No credits on the tape itself, only on the box....

**RENEGADE ROBO NINJA AND PRINCESS SAKI** see *Mirai Ninja*

**REPLIKATOR** PNA & Prism Ent. (Replikator) 1994 color 96m. D: G. Philip Jackson. SP: Bellerose, Johnston, Dawson. Ref: Vallejo T-H: "duplication technology." Martin: *Replikator: Cloned To Kill;* "confusing." vc box: 21st Century. With Michael St. Gerard, B. Bako, Ned Beatty.

**REPO MAN** Univ/Edge City (Jonathan Wacks/Michael Nesmith) 1984 color 94m. SP, D: Alex Cox. Mus: Steve Hufsteter et al. SpFX: Robby Knott, Roger George. Elec SdFX: Electric Melody. Ref: TV. V 3/7/84. With Harry Dean Stanton, Emilio Estevez, Olivia Barash, Tracey Walter, Sy Richardson, Vonetta McGee, George Sawaya, Charles Hopkins, Angelique Pettyjohn.

Four dead alien beings in the trunk of a '64 Chevy Malibu become part of a "lattice of coincidence" involving repo men, state troopers, government agents, and mad scientists. Ultimately, the car develops a force field and levitates.... Everything and everyone is a put-on in this very dry movie re "normal" life vs. the not-so-normal, but is it funny or just strange? At any rate, that "lattice" begins to seem like mere aimlessness, though the ending is fun, the editing (by Dennis Dolan) is sharp, and there are hilarious moments.

**REPOSSESSED** New Line/Carolco/Seven Arts (First Class/Steven Wizan) 1990 color 84m. SP, D: Bob Logan. Mus:

Charles Fox. SpVisFX: Stargate Films; (d) Sam Nicholson. SpFX: Reel EFX, Special FX Unltd. SpFxMkp: Steve LaPorte. SdFX: J. J. Haboush. Ref: TV: Live HV. MFB'90:364-5. V 9/24/90. SFChron Dtbk 10/21/90. With Linda Blair, Ned Beatty, Leslie Nielsen, Anthony Starke, Jesse Ventura, Jake Steinfeld, Army Archerd, Jack LaLanne.

"Satan's spirit flew right out of my TV set and into my soul!" The "Belle from Hell," Nancy Aglet (Blair)—who possesses a Certificate of Demonic Possession—gets zapped by her set and again takes on Father Mayii (Nielsen), the "Exorcising Priest" who first exorcised her in 1973 and has been staying at the Actors and Exorcists Retirement Home. The twist: The exorcism will be performed on TV, on "Exorcism Tonight." At the end, the demon briefly possesses, first, Father Brophy (Starke), the young priest of Our Lady of the Evening, then Father Mayii, who at one point is transformed into Groucho.

That giant sinking sound here is the comedy. This movie isn't about evil, it's about bad—one D.O.A. joke after another. Even the relatively clever ideas (e.g., the literal "word on the street") aren't exactly funny.

See also *Exorcist III.*

**RESAN TILL MELONIA** (Swed.-Norw.) Penn Film & Sandrews & Filmhuset & SVT2 & Skrivstugan & Laskonsten & Film Teknik/Norsk Film (Olofsson-Farago) 1989 anim color 104m. SP, D: Per Ahlin, from Shakespeare's play "The Tempest." Mus: Isfalt, Norklit. Ref: V 12/13/89: "sags dangerously, and eventually ruptures"; *The Voyage to Melonia*—tr t? 2/7/90:62(ad): at Berlin Fest. 2/7/90:81(ad).

Power Soup weaponry ... fantasy elements from "The Tempest" ("Caliban as giant composite of garden vegetables and fruit") ... sf elements from Jules Verne's "Machine Island."

**A RESCUE FROM HADES** (Taiwanese) New Ship Film (Richard Young) c1986? color/ws c92m. D: Liang Chi Fu. Ref: TV: vt; no Eng. Y.K. Ho.

Demons levitate and kill a woman who desecrates a shrine, then lead her damned spirit away to hell, where she is imprisoned. Fairly entertaining, good-natured blend of comedy and fantasy. At one point, a flying, saw-toothed blob of ectoplasm ties itself around the hero and pins him to a tree. Later, a whole platoon of cartoon spirits flies out the opened door to hades. Hell itself features the devil, horned demons, a damned woman who is stripped and held to a glowing, red-hot pillar, a man who is transformed into a hog, and much boiling in oil and impaling on spikes.

See also *Dante's Inferno* (various versions).

**REST IN PIECES** (Sp) Calepas Int'l. (Jose Frade) 1987 color 90m. (*Descanse en Piezas*). D: Joseph Braunstein. SP: Santiago Moncada. Ph: John Tharp. Mus: Greg Debelles. AD: Joseph Galic. SpFX: Arthur Brilliant. Mkp: Duncan Morris. Ref: TV: IVE video; Eng. version. Horacio Higuchi. Phantom. V 5/6/87:168 (ad). Hound. Martin. With Scott Thompson Baker, Lorin Jean Vail, Dorothy Malone (Aunt Catherine), Jack Taylor, Patty Shepard, Tony Isbert, Fernando Bilbao.

"The mind can transcend death!" Suicides from Dr. Anderson's Devonshire Clinic, an insane asylum, populate Eight Manors,

Helen Hewitt's inherited estate. Apparently, they use a sort of mind reincarnation, combined with "modern chemistry," to "attain the highest form"—living death.... The script is handier with hollowly ironic dialogue than it is with explanations. Horror-suspenser is good for one offbeat, blood-and-bowties sequence: At a private, formal affair, undead concert guests conclude the evening by slaughtering a string quartet.

**RESTLESS PASSION** Hollywood Video (Hal Freeman) 1987 color 90m. D: H. Freeman. Ref: Adam '89: "future beings." With Janette Littledove, Keisha, Fallon, Ron Jeremy.

**The RESURRECTED** (Can.-U.S.) Scotti Bros./Borde-Raich (Shayne Sawyer/Eurobrothers Prods.) 1992 (1991) color 105m. (*Shatterbrain* - orig t). D: Dan O'Bannon. SP: Brent V. Friedman, from H. P. Lovecraft's novel *The Case of Charles Dexter Ward.* Mus: Richard Band. SpPhysicalFxCoord: Gary Paller. SpMkp & VisFX: Todd Masters; (key fx mkp art) Thom Floutz; (addl min vis fx) Ted Rae. OptFxSup: Dave Gregory. Ref: TV. V 4/13/92. Martin. PT 13:12. V 10/15/90:26. 10/29/90:14. With John Terry, Jane Sibbett, Chris Sarandon (Charles Dexter Ward/Joseph Curwen), Robert Romanus, Laurie Briscoe, Deep Roy (main monster); Keith Hay, Greg Allen (pitmen).

"The dead take much blood!" Clues to the Lovecraftian mystery here include "eight boxes of human remains" ... "tomb snatchings" of European wizards' bones ... packets of "animal blood" ... a human body stripped to basics, or less ... the "antiquated language" which Charles Dexter Ward (or is he Joseph Curwen?) uses ... and a ghastly human-thing found in a rain-swollen stream. Seems Ward "raised"—with secret elixir—lookalike ancestor Curwen, who then killed and impersonated him and is cursed with "resurrective hunger." ("I must have raw meat!") At the end, the detective hero (Terry) resurrects Ward, who proceeds to strip Curwen of life.

*The Resurrected* is too deliberate, almost lackadaisical, but rewards viewer patience with visual and verbal details. (The resurrectionists require complete human remains to achieve their "finest effects.") Several effects and makeup payoffs mark the last third or so of the movie, including the prime-gross pit of "mistakes and screw-ups," the thing in the tunnel, and the confrontation between Curwen and, (a) the hero, then, (b) the "raised" Ward. Creepiest of all, perhaps: the horrific-pathetic human-thing from the water. Oddly, *The Resurrected* finally seems not quite "wild" enough, though it's certainly a better-than-average Lovecraft adaptation.

**The RETALIATOR** TWE/Retaliator (Stern-Holzman) 1987 color 92m. (aka *The Retaliators.* aka *Programmed To Kill*). D: Allan Holzman. SP, D: Robert Short. SpFX: Vern Hyde, John Carter. Ref: V 5/6/87: "tired rewrite of *The Terminator*." Ecran F 64:71. TVG. With Robert Ginty, Sandahl Bergman, James Booth, Alex Courtney.

Killer cyborg.

**RETEN** (Mex.) 1991 feature. Ref: Cinef 6/96:47: "futuristic trappings"; "Roadblock"-tr t.

**RETORNO DE LAS TINIEBLAS** see *Rape*

**RETRIBUTION** Taurus Ent. & Unicorn/Renegade Films (Lavin-Christian) 1987 color 107m. SP, D, P: Guy Magar. SP: also Lee Wasserman. Mus, SpSdFX: Alan Howarth. SpMkpFX: Kevin Yagher. SpFX: Court Wizard. Opt: Howard Anderson. Ref: TV. V 10/14/87. 5/6/87:165 (ad). With Dennis Lipscomb, Leslie Wing, Suzanne Snyder, Jeff Pomerantz, Clare Peck, Chris Caputo, Hoyt Axton, Danny D. Daniel (Rasta doctor), Mike Muscat (Vito Minelli Sr.).

"It happens every time I fall asleep!" In a sort of metempsychosis, a murder victim (Muscat) who dies the same Halloween night as a suicide, or near-suicide (Lipscomb), possesses the latter in his sleep and wreaks gory, phantom-like revenge on his killers.... Lipscomb is good in this *Psychic Killer* variation, but that's about it. His sad-sack-avenger-in-spite-of-himself would do better in a horror parody. Nothing new in either story or effects.

See also *Man With Two Lives.*

**RETURN** Silver Prods. (Philip Spinelli) 1985 color 82m. SP, D: Andrew Silver, from Donald Harington's novel *Some Other Place. The Right Place.* Mus: Grippe, Shrieve. SpFX: Tassilo Baur. Key Mkp: N. K. Chadwick. Ref: TV. V 8/14/85. Boston Phoenix 11/12/85. PFA Library. TVG. NYT 1/24/86. With Karlene Crockett, John Walcutt, Lisa Richards, Frederic Forrest, Anne Lloyd Francis, Lenore Zann, Lee Stetson (Daniel Montross).

"You expect me to believe some twenty-year-old kid is a reincarnation of Daniel?" Through "age regression," a medium (Francis) lets Diana Stoving's (Crockett) supposed grandfather (Stetson) speak to her through young Day Whittaker (Walcutt). ("It's like he just keeps coming back—see, like he's after something.") At the end, the truth makes Day free of Daniel. Flatfooted storytelling, okay scenery. Some comedy might have helped.

**RETURN, The** see *Jesus Vender Tilbage*

**RETURN OF E.T.** see *Unearthling, The*

**RETURN OF GODZILLA, The** see *Godzilla: 1985*

**The RETURN OF JAFAR** (U.S.-Austral.-J) Disney TV Animation & Disney Animation [Austral.] & Disney Animation [Japan] (Stones-Zaslove) 1994 anim color 69m. D: Shelton, Stones, Zaslove. SP: Kevin Campbell, Bill Motz et al. Story: Capizzi, Langdale et al. Mus: M. Watters. Ref: TV: vt. SFChron 5/20/94. Voices: Gilbert Gottfried, Frank Welker et al.

Ingredients in this follow-up to *Aladdin* (1992) include Jafar-as-a-giant-monstrous-genie ... a Jafar-as-Jasmine impersonation ... the genie-as-an-Egyptian-mummy bit ... and a killer-bees bit.... For a mini-sequel, not bad, just a bit mechanical. It's the Iago ("I don't do fun either") and genie show, for the most part here.

**The RETURN OF SHERLOCK HOLMES** CBS-TV 1987 (1986) color c90m. D: Kevin Connor. Tel: Bob Shayne, inspired by Sir Arthur Conan Doyle's characters. Ph: Tony Imi. Mus: Ken Thorne. PD: Keith Wilson. Ref: TV. TVG. With Michael Pennington, Margaret Colin, Lila Kaye, Connie Booth, Nicholas Guest, Barry Morse, Shane Rimmer, Paul Maxwell, William Hootkins.

Dr. Watson's great-granddaughter, Jane (Colin), thaws Sherlock Holmes (Pennington) out of deep freeze, in the present day. Moderately entertaining sf-mystery. Pennington's suppressed intensity as Holmes is winning.

**The RETURN OF SUPERBUG** (W.G.-Sup) Barbara-Film 1978 color 90m. (*Superbaby—Der Kleine mit der Grossen Klappe.* aka *Zwei Tolle Kaefer Raeumen auf*). SP, D: Rudolf Zehetgruber. SP: also J. W. Nova. Ph: R. G. Matos; M. Marszalek. Mus: Peter Weiner. AD: Jose Galicia. SpFX: Antonio Balandin. Ref: TV. Dr. Rolf Giesen. TVG. no Hardy/SF. V 5/12/90:154(ad). With Rudolf Rittberg, Kathrin Oginski, Brad Harris, Fernando Sancho, Salvatore Borgese.

Little golf-course robot which does a tango ... remote-control mini-copter ... very explosive cigars. Flat comedy, the unofficial fifth and last in the "Superbug" series.

**The RETURN OF SWAMP THING** Millimeter Films/Lightyear Ent. (Melniker-Uslan) 1989 color 88m. D: Jim Wynorski. SP: Derek Spencer, Grant Morris, based on the comic-book characters. Mus: Chuck Cirino. SpFxMkp: Steve Neill; (sup) Dean Gates; (Swamp Thing) Carl Fullerton, Neal Martz. SpFX: Bob Shelley's SpFxInt'l. Sp Lab Mutants: Todd Masters Co. SpVocalFX: Frank Welker. Opt & RotoFX: Motion; (anim) Kevin Kutchaver et al. Ref: TV. V 5/3/89. ad. NYT 5/12/89. SFExam. MFB'90:48-9. With Louis Jourdan, Heather Locklear, Sarah Douglas, Dick Durock (Swamp Thing), Ace Mask, Monique Gabrielle, Chris Doyle (Leechman), Rex Pierson (Dr. Rochelle mutation).

"Once upon a time ... in the swamp." Swamp Thing ("I'm a plant") bests another swamp monster and later combats other "rejected specimens" of gene splicing. Meanwhile, Arcane (Jourdan) plots to take rejuvenating energy scientifically from his stepdaughter Abby (Locklear).... Some okay verbal zingers (mainly Locklear's) enliven this routine sequel to *Swamp Thing*. At one point, a special drug does an *Enchanted Cottage* for the monstrous Swamp Thing and Abby, and she sees him as a good-looking guy.

**RETURN OF THE DEMON** (H.K.) Eagle Film (Charles Heung & Wong Ying) 1987 color 89m. (*Mogao Yizhang*). SP, D: W. Ying (aka Huang Ying). SP: also Johnny Lee (aka Li Shangjie. Ph: Chan Tung Chuen (aka Chen Dongcun). AD: Fred Chan (aka Chen Zizhong). SpMkpFX: Wong Kee Hung (aka Huang Jihong). VisFX?: Dream Quest. Ref: TV: Rainbow Video; Eng. titles. Horacio Higuchi. NST! 4:34. With Di Wei (demon), Cao Zhali, Mai Deluo, Cheng Kuian.

An archaeological expedition revives a reincarnated spiritual disciple who strayed and who keeps his life-sustaining "pulse" in a rock. Zombies, or ghosts, from a network of tunnels congregate to operate his soul-transferring mill. With just two more souls, the monstrous disciple becomes immortal. Other critters: a weredog that looks like a hairy, full-bearded man (pulling off a bit of his fur restores him to his human state), and Tayona, a suicide who commands the elements and who needs a virgin to die for her so that she can reincarnate.... In its elaborate fantasy apparatus, this generally silly horror-comedy seems to reflect the *Zu* influence. A most unusual bedroom sequence involves hordes of eggs—including one giant one—a crab, and levitation.

**RETURN OF THE DINOSAURS** (J-U.S.?) Tsuburaya & AEI 1983 ('92-U.S.) anim c70m. D, Mus: Larry Smith. SP: Gail March. Anim D: Haruyuki Kawashima. From K. Abe's story "Born Free." Mus: also T. Fuyuki, D. Jergenson. SpFxD: Koichi Takano. Ref: TV: Quality Video; Eng. dubbed.

"Up from the depths of the Earth, vegetation and creatures from another time emerge." The gravitational pull of a "huge, mysterious comet" brings back the Mesozoic, but the dinosaurs seem to be dying again. To the rescue: the Dinosaur Patrol. Included: a T-Rex ("What a mean reptile!")... a bronto and baby (the bronto at one point cries)... an allosaurus... and a bloodsucking plant.... This two-part OAV or TV show is a curious combination of cartoon animation and stopmo animation/model work. The former is awful; the latter is crude, but okay. And the two modes don't blend.

**RETURN OF THE EVIL FOX** (H.K.) 1989? color feature. D: Richard Chung. Ref: Weisser/ATC: "beautiful villainess with powerful claws ... some innovative scare sequences."

**RETURN OF THE FAMILY MAN** (So. African) Gibraltar Releasing/Focus Films (Van Rooyen & Johnson) 1989 color c91m. SP, D: John Murlowski. SP: also John Fox. Mus: Shapiro, Bekker. AD: Rick Harding. SpFX: Tjaart van der Walt. Mkp: T. Ford, Carla Jane Resnekov. Ref: TV: Raedon HV. V 7/11/90:58(hv). With Ron Smerczak (The Family Man), Liam Cundill, Terence Reis, Debra Kaye, Michelle Constant, Kurt Egelhof, Adrian Galley.

"The Family Man's here!" Mark Shecter—the "biggest son-of-a-bitchin' mass murderer in the Pacific Southwest"—makes a gory escape from a prison bus and heads for the Shecter Estate, where he killed his own family (before killing "all the other families") and sealed the corpses in a hidden room. On the way, he slaughters yet another family.

Strange combo of *The Stepfather* and *Halloween*, comedy and horror, begins well and offers some offbeat fun before turning into another ten-little-victims shocker. Best touch is reserved for the climax—the improvised bomb-camera's automatic "Smile!" just before Shecter is blown to bits.

**RETURN OF THE GHOST** (Thai) c1990? color/ws c100m. Ref: TV: vt; no Eng. Chao Thai Market: above is tr t.

A now-you-see-her-now-you-don't mystery woman with stretchable arms scares evildoers, but magically heals the hero. At the end, the ghost saves the heroine from kidnappers, then gets her buddy ghosts (including a head-and-entrails "flasher") into the spook act to scare them.... Fantasy chiller alternates between melodrama and low comedy, features an incidental trio of ghost busters and one scene in which a holy necklace burns the main ghost.

**RETURN OF THE JEDI** (3) see also *Ewok Adventure, The. Ewoks: The Battle for Endor. Making Contact.*

**RETURN OF THE KILLER TOMATOES!** New World/Four Square (Tomatoes II/Peace-Blank) 1988 color 98m. SP, D, Co-Ed: John DeBello. SP: also J. S. Peace, Constantine Dillon. Ph: S. K. Welch. Mus: Patterson, Fox. PD: Dillon. SpFX: Side EFX. OptFX: Dave Osborne. SdFxDes: Martin Lopez. Ref: TV.

V 11/16/88. 7/1/87:30. 1/13/88:4 (rated). With Anthony Starke, George Clooney, Karen Mistal, Steve Lundquist, John Astin, Teri Weigel, Barry Ratto et al (tomato men).

The post-Great Tomato War period. Professor Gangreen's (Astin) Tomato Transformation Process succeeds with Tara (Mistal), but fails with F. T., a ball with "red fur and two legs." At the end, the tomato threat over, killer carrots loom, though the concluding credits promise "Killer Tomatoes Go to France" (since changed to *Killer Tomatoes Eat France!*).

Long-awaited, or at least delayed, sequel to *Attack of the Killer Tomatoes!* is somewhat of an improvement, though most of the first half fizzles. In one of the cleverer parodic bits, the slow-witted hero (Starke) gets an idea from a mad doctor in a black-and-white movie on TV, *Frankenstein's Mummy*: "I said, 'Transform into human being ... my secret laboratory' ..." Finally, the light, such as it is, dawns, and Chad is on his way to restoring Tara to her human state.

The **RETURN OF THE LIVING DEAD** Orion/Hemdale/Fox Films (Cinema '84/Tom Fox, Graham Henderson) 1985 (1984) color 91m. SP, D: Dan O'Bannon. Story: Rudy Ricci, John Russo, Russell Streiner. Mus: Matt Clifford. SpVisFX: Fantasy II; (sup) Gene Warren Jr., Peter Kleinow. OptFX: Image 3. Corpse Anim: Tony Gardner. SpFxSup: R. E. McCarthy. SpMkpFX: Bill Munns. SdFxEd: Sound FX. Ref: TV. MFB'85:386-7. V 6/19/85. ad. vc box: *Battalion* - Japanese t. With Clu Gulager, James Karen, Don Calfa, Linnea Quigley, John Durbin (1st radio corpse), Thom Mathews, Beverly Randolph.

Louisville, Kentucky. The gas which revived the zombies, originally, in *Night of the Living Dead* (1968), revives one again. Rain mixed with the ashes of a cremated zombie seeps into a graveyard and revives the dead there. And two men exposed to the gas exhibit signs of rigor mortis and, after death, also become living dead.

The actors playing the living here try too hard; they're always screaming and shouting. The actors playing the zombies, on the other hand, say little ("Brains!"), to great effect. The dry, outrageous humor of *Dark Star* (on which O'Bannon worked) finally surfaces again, at least intermittently, in this movie. The password is "Send more paramedics."

**RETURN OF THE LIVING DEAD, PART II** Lorimar/Greenfox (W. S. Gilmore) 1988 (1987) color 89m. SP, D: Ken Wiederhorn. Mus: J. P. Robinson. SpMkp: Kenny Myers. Zombie Movements: Derek Loughran. SpPhysicalFX: Terry Frazee, Geno Crum, Gene Grigg. FxAnim: Charles McDonald. Sp OptFX: Howard Anderson Co. SdFxSup: Dale Johnston. Ref: TV. MFB'89:85-6. V 1/13/88. SFExam 1/15/88. With James Karen, Thom Mathews, Dana Ashbrook, Marsha Dietlein, Suzanne Snyder, Philip Bruns, Michael Kenworthy, Mitch Pileggi, Forrest J Ackerman.

A stray can of zombie yields a brains-hungry ghoul, and gas from the cannister revives a cemetery's dead, in a scene played for low comedy. The gas works more slowly on live humans, but the results are the same.... Scattered laughs—e.g., Kenworthy's Jesse's brave "Just a little decayed matter! Nothing to get unhinged about!"—but there's a forced, sitcom franticness to the comedy gore. The extensive makeup and other effects are the sole sustained point of interest. Signed, Zombied-out.

**RETURN OF THE LIVING DEAD III** (U.S.-J) Trimark & Bandai Visual & Ozla/Gary Schmoeller, Brian Yuzna 1993 color 97m. (*Return of the Living Dead 3* - ad t). D: B. Yuzna. SP, Assoc P: John Penney. Ph: Gerry Lively. Mus: Barry Goldberg. PD: Anthony Tremblay. SpFxMkp: Steve Johnson, Tim Ralston, Kevin Brennan, Christopher Nelson, Wayne Toth. Prosth FX: XFX, Max FX, Corn Ltd., Nelson F/X et al. Physical SpFX: Bruno Stempel. SdFX: S.A. Foiles et al. Titles: Dave Hewitt et al. Ref: TV: Vidmark video. Stanley. V 11/8/93: "pedestrian and gruesome." 6/14/93:10 (rated). Janet Willis. Sacto Bee 11/1/93: "needs reanimation." With Mindy Clarke, J. T. Edmond, Kent McCord, Basil Wallace (Riverman), Sarah Douglas.

"Don't get no deader than that!" The military attempts to use the living dead as bio-weapons, but bungles badly. Meanwhile, Julie (Clarke) dies, revives, and majors in self-mutilation. (Pain keeps her hunger for human flesh at bay.) Love between the living and the living dead, but not a patch on *Dellamorte, Dellamore*. The first wholly serious, or self-serious, entry in the series. Predictable "Oh, my God!" scenes and lots of Cronenberg-ish puncture gore.

**RETURN OF THE ROLLER BLADE SEVEN** see *Roller Blade Seven, The*

**The RETURN OF THE SIX-MILLION DOLLAR MAN AND THE BIONIC WOMAN** NBC-TV/Michael Sloan & Univ-TV 1987 color c90m. D: Ray Austin. Tel, Exec P: Sloan. Story, Sup P: Bruce Lansbury. From Martin Caidin's novel *Cyborg*. Mus: Marvin Hamlisch. AD: Gary A. Lee. SpVisFX: The L. A. FX Group. Mkp: Tom Ellingwood. Ref: TV. TVG. V 6/3/87:88. SFExam 2/13/87:D-22. With Lee Majors (Col. Steve Austin), Lindsay Wagner (Jamie Sommers), Richard Anderson, Tom Schanley, Martin Landau, Gary Lockwood, William Campbell.

The cyborg heroes vs. the mercenaries of Fortress.

See also: *Bionic Showdown*.

**RETURN TO ALPHA BLUE** AVC 1984 color 80m. D: Gerard Damiano. Ref: vc box: 21st Century. Adam'88: '83. With Sharon Kane, Chelsea Blake, Taija Rae.

Sequel to *Satisfiers of Alpha Blue*.

**RETURN TO EDEN** see *After School*

**RETURN TO FROGTOWN** see *Frogtown II*

**RETURN TO HORROR HIGH** New World & Balcor (Froehlich-Lisson) 1987 (1986) color 94m. SP, D: Bill Froehlich. SP: also Mark Lisson, Dana Escalante, Greg H. Sims. Mus: Stacy Widelitz. SpFxMkp: Mkp& FX Labs; Alan Apone et al. SpFX: J. W. Beauchamp. Ref: TV: N. W. Video. V 1/21/87. ad. With Richard Brestoff, George Clooney, Vince Edwards, Al Fann, Panchito Gomez, Brendan Hughes, Scott Jacoby, Lori Lethin, Pepper Martin, Maureen McCormick, Alex Rocco, Andy Romano (principal).

Cosmic Pictures goes to Crippen High, scene of some brutal murders, to film the story of the slaughter. Plot Twist "A": The

murderer seems to have returned to the scene of his crimes, and to his underground "schoolroom" of the embalmed. In fact, he has, but Plot Twist "B" reveals a new series of murders to have been a sort of April Fool! on local police.... Though there's some amiable toying with slasher-movie conventions, *Return to Horror High* itself rarely escapes comic conventionality. The accent is on the silly—e.g., an actor with a prop hatchet in his head asking "What's my motivation?" and the director reminding him that he's dead.

**RETURN TO MAYBERRY** NBC-TV (Strathmore & Viacom) 1986 color c90m. D: Bob Sweeney. Tel: Bullock & Greenbaum, based on "The Andy Griffith Show" TV series. Ph: Richard Glouner. Mus: Earle Hagen. PD: R. G. Storey. SpFX: Techniprops. Opt: Howard Anderson. Mkp: Bob Mills. Ref: TV. TVG. With A. Griffith, Ron Howard, Don Knotts, Jim Nabors, George Lindsey, Aneta Corsaut, Howard Morris, Denver Pyle.

The Mayberry "monster of the lake" is just a mechanically-operated dragon, with a head taken from the front of the old Shanghai Gardens Restaurant. Broad comedy and sentiment. Only for true fans of the venerable series.

**RETURN TO OZ** Disney & Silver Screen Partners II (BMI) 1985 color 108m. SP, D: Walter Murch. SP: also Gill Dennis. Based on the books *The Land of Oz* and *Ozma of Oz* by L. Frank Baum. Mus: David Shire. Claymation: Will Vinton. VisFxConsul: Zoran Perisic. SpFxSup: Ian Wingrove. OptFX: Optical Film FX, Peerless. Mkp: Robin Grantham. Ref: screen. MFB'85:252-3. SFExam 6/21/85. Berkeley Monthly 2/86. V 6/19/85. With Nicol Williamson (Nome King), Jean Marsh (Mombi), Fairuza Balk, Piper Laurie, Michael Sundin and Tim Rose (Tik Tok, the "patented clockwork mechanical man").

Fantasy with horrific elements—e.g., the monsters-from-the-wall, the cases in which the evil Mombi keeps her alternate heads, the enchanted mirror in which Mombi imprisons Ozma (Emma Ridley), the Nome King's "collection" of victims-turned-into-objects. Vinton's Claymation creations are responsible for most of the excitement here. Otherwise: some charm and invention (e.g., Mombi's living heads), much noise and loud music.

**A RETURN TO SALEM'S LOT** WB/Larco (Paul Kurta) 1987 color 101m. Story, SP, D, Exec P: Larry Cohen. Mus: Michael Minard. SP: also James Dixon. Follow-up to *Salem's Lot* (II). SpFxMkpDes: Steve Neill. SdFX: Daniel Gross. Ref: TV: Warner HV. V 5/27/87. MFB'89:286-7. With Michael Moriarty, Richard Addison Reed, Andrew Duggan (Judge Axel), Sam Fuller, June Havoc, Ronee Blakely, Evelyn Keyes (Mrs. Axel), Tara Reid (Amanda).

"The whole town—!" The vampires of Salem's Lot generally rely on cow blood for nourishment, drink human blood only on special occasions, keep "drones" for day work, and spread "anti-human propaganda." Their leader, Judge Axel, is looking for a successor, and hopes he has found a willing convert in human Joe Weber (Moriarty). The latter's son, Jeremy (Reed), is tempted to stay in Salem's Lot, but at the end, both see the Judge's "true face" of horror.

There are scattered inimitable Larry Cohen moments—a vampire touching up her face after a bout of splattery blood-drinking, vampire kids dutifully reciting the Pledge of Allegiance, Moriarty commenting, "I just don't like things that suck your blood and have conversations afterwards"—but the only sustained amusement in this murky, overlong examination of vampire and human mores is provided by Fuller's performance as Nazi killer Van Meer. (The latter, informed of the nature of the townsfolk, is instantly converted to the role of vampire killer, which is what he seemed to be in the first place anyway.) Fuller, complete with Groucho delivery and cigar, brings this oddly stuffy movie the breezy informality it needs.

**RETURN TO THE LOST WORLD** (B-Can.-So. African) 1992 color 99m. D: Timothy Bond. Ref: Martin: "modest but engaging." PT 18:60. With John Rhys-Davies, David Warner, Eric McCormack, Tamara Gorski.

Sequel to *The Lost World* (1992).

The **RETURNING** (N.Z.) Echo Pictures & N.Z. Film Commission (Matte Box Films-Downie-Hannay) 1991 (1990) color 97m. SP, D: John Day. SP: also A. Baysting. Story: S. Willisson. Ph: Kevin Hayward. Mus: Clive Cockburn. PD: Michael Becroft. Ref: V 4/1/91: "a good-looking psychodrama that misses." 1/3/90:18: shooting 2/4. With Phillip Gordon, Alison Routledge, Max Cullen, Jenny Ryken.

Lawyer in old mansion "seduced in his dreams by the ghost of a young woman."

The **RETURNING** (H.K.) Treasure City/Cameron Ent . 1994 color/ws 103m. D: Jacob Cheung. Ref: TV: Tai Seng Video; Eng. titles. V 8/15/94:16: in H.K. With Tony Leung, Sandra Ng.

"I am waiting for you to come back." A certain "Siu Lau died in 1949." In the present, her "house is known to be the ghost house"—strange winds waft through it, strange noises come from behind the door of a locked room, and a strange boy is seen through a peephole. And the hero-writer's daughter, Mimi, is "acting like an adult," and his wife, Elaine, seems intermittently possessed by Siu Lau.... *Rouge*, or *Vertigo,* on the cheap. Shot-on-tape—the music sounds tinny, and the visuals seem shallow. Still, a few chills.

**REVANCHE DES HUMANOIDES, La** see *Revenge of the Humanoids*

La **REVANCHE DES MORTES VIVANTES** (F) Samourai Films 1985 color 85m. (aka *The Living Dead*). D: P. B. Reinhard (aka P. Harsone). SP: John King. Ph: H. Froger. Mus: C. Ried (sic). Ref: TV: MV; Eng. dubbed; *The Revenge of the Living Dead.* Peter Zirschky: "Toxic waste makes the dead alive. A real sickie." Ecran F 70:20: "gore effects." With Kathryn Charly, Veronik Catanzaro, Sylvie Novak, Laurence Mercier, Anthea Wyler.

"I've seen them leaving their tombs!" A toxic-waste treat (courtesy of OKF Chemicals) in the milk that the three ladies drink—plus a chaser dumped on cemetery ground—and the three go ghouling at midnight. ("It's safe here—they're all dead!") But a *Mark of the Vampire*-like climactic twist reveals the undead antics to be a masquerade.... Or, When is a zombie movie not a zombie movie? Scorecard: a tired Heinousness of Corporations theme ... one genuinely gross scene—the sex between the living and the supposedly dead ... an Open Season on genitalia (male

and female) undercurrent ... and the whore's line, "Even the Cambodian Wheelbarrow?"

**REVELATIONS** Femme 1993 color 120m. D: Candida Royalle. Ref: Adam'94. With Amy Rapp, Ava Grace.

"Sterile, grey future-world."

**REVENGE** United Ent. (Linda Lewis/Bill F. Blair) 1986 color 100m. SP, D: Christopher Lewis. Story: James Vance. Mus: Rod Slane. MkpFX: DFX. SpFX: David Powell et al. SdFX: MusiPak. Ref: TV: United HV. V 11/26/86. 4/15/87:40. Stanley: f-u to *Blood Cult* (which see). With Patrick Wayne, John Carradine, Bennie Lee McGowan, Josef Hanet, Fred Graves, Wade Tower (The Figure).

"Man's best friend is now his greatest enemy!" The Cult of Caninus, founded by Martin Bradford in the 17th Century, is the force behind a rash of murders in a small midwestern town. Its members seek immortality through the sacrifice of a "body made of the most perfect parts of several humans." At the end, the body comes to life, and Bradford, Caninus' messenger on Earth, is revealed to be still alive and a U.S. Senator (Carradine).

Dumb Moves Dept.: While hero Wayne and widow McGowan are sorting out clues to the murder mystery, other, intercut scenes reveal all to us. Overdone Dept.: Big Sinisterness in a Small town. Wry Moments Dept.: Dean Bayley (Graves), lukewarm cultist, complains to fellow cultists about a shortage of monks' robes.

**REVENGE OF ANGEL** (H.K.) 1991 color feature. D: Corey Yuen.Ref: Weisser/ATC: "stunning visuals." With Moon Lee.

Woman's spirit returns, convinces young man "to avenge her death."

**REVENGE OF BILLY THE KID** (B) Montage Films (Tim Dennison) 1991 color 102m. SP, D, Exec Co-P: Jim Groom. SP: also Dennison, R. Mathews. Ph: D. Read. Mus: Tony Flynn. SpMkpFX: N. R. Gorton, S. M. Painter. Ref: V 1/6/92: "a lusty low-budgeter about a half-human goat run amok." Monster! 3:58-9: "horror-comic dud." With Michael Balfour, Samantha Perkins, J. D. Broad, Trevor Peake, Julian Shaw (Billy T. Kid).

**REVENGE OF NINJA** see *Revenge of the Ninja*

**REVENGE OF THE DEFENDERS** see *Brain 17*

**REVENGE OF THE GHOST** see *Hannyo*

**REVENGE OF THE HOUSE OF USHER** see *Fall of the House of Usher* (1983)

**REVENGE OF THE HUMANOIDS** (F) Nickelodeon-TV/Procidis 1983 anim color 100m. (*La Revanche des Humanoides*). SP, D, P: Albert Barille. Mus: Michel Legrand. Ref: Cinema Francais. TVG.

"Cybernetic octopods" in the year 2600.

**REVENGE OF THE LIVING DEAD, The** see *Revanche des Mortes Vivantes, La*

**REVENGE OF THE LIVING ZOMBIES** Magnum Ent./H&G Films (David Gordon) 1989 color 84m. (*Flesh Eater*—alt t). Story, SP, D, P: Bill Hinzman. SP: also Bill Randolph. SpMkpFX: Gerald Gergely. Ref: V 7/26/89: compare *Night of The Living Dead*; "generally achieves its modest aims." 7/5/89:20 (rated). McCarty II: "lifeless." PT 5:11. With B. Hinzman (Flesh Eater), John Mowood, Leslie Ann Wick, Kevin Kindlin.

Ghoul turns Halloween teens into ghouls.

**REVENGE OF THE NINJA** (Indonesian) Rapi Films/Mount Light (Indonesian) 1987 color/ws feature (*Revenge of Ninja* - cr t). D: Ratno Timoer. SP: Darto Joned. Ref: TV: VSOM; Eng. dubbed. Weisser/ATC. With Barry Prima, Dana Christina, Advent Bangun, W.D. Mochtar.

Ingredients here include a woman under a black-magic spell ("It wasn't me at all") ... a magician who magically extracts a heart ... the zombie revived with said heart and spike-in-head (he stomps his foot and causes a mini-quake) ... zombie troops revived by this versatile zombie ("You must wake up all your men!") ... and an exploding man.... Interminable, crudely-made actioner picks up a bit when the fantasy effects finally take over.

**REVENGE OF THE RADIOACTIVE REPORTER** (Can.) Pryceless Prods. & Goldfarb Dist. 1990 (1989) color 84m. SP, D, P: Craig Pryce. SP: also David Wiechorek. Mus: David Bradstreet. SpFxMkp: Ron Stefaniuk, A. E. Cooke. SpFx: (sup) John A. Gajdecki; Performance Solutions. Title Des: Julius Ciss. Ref: TV. V 5/12/90. TVG. With David Scammell, Kathryn Boese, Derrik Strange, Randy Pearlstein, Ron Becker (upside-down "vampire" at costume party), Tony Trouble.

A reporter (Scammell) pushed into a vat of radioactive waste at a power plant emerges later as a "murderous, disfigured ghoul" with a lethal touch. Dismayingly sophomoric comedy has a few bordering-on-funny bits of grossness, including the scene in which the "ghoul" relaxes—with inner tube and flippers—in the toxic pool, and the climactic scene, in which he tosses yucky pieces of himself at the head baddie. Executive co-producer Andre Bigio appears as The Elephant Man in a visualized nightmare.

**REVENGE OF THE RED BARON** Concorde/New Horizons (Mike Elliott) 1993 color 86m. D: Bob Gordon. SP: M.J. McDonald. Ph: C. Sebaldt. Mus: R. Randles. VisFX: Ken Solomon. Ref: V 6/27/94: "distinctly unexciting." SFChron Dtbk 2/13/94: "fighter ace who shot down the Red Baron becomes the target of his model-plane's revenge." With Mickey Rooney, Laraine Newman, Cliff De Young, Tobey Maguire, Ronnie Schell, John McDonnell (voice of Red Baron).

The **REVENGE OF THE TEENAGE VIXENS FROM OUTER SPACE** Malamute 1986 color 84m. SP, D, P, Ph: Jeff Farrell. SP, P, Mkp, Ed: Michelle Lichter. Mus: L. X. Erlanger et al. Ref: TV. V 10/22/86. With Lisa Schwedop, Howard Scott, Amy Crumpacker, Julian Schembri, Anne Lilly (Mary Jo); Lisa McGregor and Kim Wickenburg (vixens).

"They came from outer space. They're used to getting their own way." An "intergalactic foul-up in the mail room" sends "weird little chicks" from a planet where women "mate with plants" to Earth. It's the second time around for the "vixens" (Elvis brought them the first time)—high-school student Paul Morelli (Scott) turns out to be the son of an alien and has telekinetic powers to prove it.

Film cops a Sentimentality in Unexpected Places prize and is too serious for its own good, though Schwedop carries her scenes and keeps one hanging on for more. All one gets, however, is a ray gun which turns earthlings into garden vegetables. (The screenplay is not all serious.)

**REVENGEFUL GHOST, The** see *Cu'un Sae Han Nyo*

**REVOLT OF THE HOUSE OF USHER** see *Fall of the House of Usher* (1983)

*__**REVOLT OF THE ZOMBIES** 1936. Ref: TV: Classic Int'l.-TV. Greg Luce. Turner/Price. V 6/10/36. TVFFSB. Ecran F 31:17, 51. Hardy/HM. Lee. Lentz. Stanley. Weldon. Maltin '92. Phantom. Hound. Martin. Scheuer. PT 11:12.

Armand (Dean Jagger), of the International Expedition for Archaeological Research, in Angkor, learns the "secret of the zombies"—the secret, that is, of the third eye of Siva. At times, said secret seems to involve a zombie-making vapor; at other times, Armand requires no vapor in order to make others do his bidding, and his hypnotic power works at great distances.

If the conception of the zombie master is rather grand, the execution is pathetic. Ironically, the worst actor here, Jagger, has the biggest role; the second-worst actor, Robert Noland, has the second-biggest role. Clearly, Roy D'Arcy—who does a creditable job as Col. Mazovia—would have made a better zombie master. The other actors speechify and pose. A stilted romance furnishes some camp highlights; the temple scene—in which Armand discovers the zombie formula—furnishes the one bit of atmosphere.

**REX HARRISON PRESENTS STORIES OF LOVE** see *Short Stories of Love*

**REX: KYORYU MONOGATARI** (J) Shochiku/Kadokawa (Rex) 1993 color/ws 106m. SP, D, Exec Co-P: Haruki Kadokawa. SP: also Shoichi Maruyama. From Masanori Hata's story "Kyoryu Monogatari." Ph: M. Iimura. Mus: Tomoyuki Asakawa. PD: H. Inagaki. SpCreature: Carlo Rambaldi. VisFxPh: S. Ooka. SdFX: S. Kurahashi. VisFX: Imagica. Computer Graphics: Links. MinFX: Gam. Ref: TV: Pony Canyon Video (Kadokawa Video); no Eng. SFChron 7/30/93: "baby tyrannosaurus." V 7/26/93:12: in Japan. Weisser/JC. With Yumi Adachi, S. Ohtake, Masatou Ibu, M. Hirata.

The egg in the cave hatches a little tyrannosaurus which eats at the table, tries to break out of its pen, nuzzles a dog, grows, and wears funny clothes (or clothes which look funny on it). Film isn't up to much except Cute, and sometimes it isn't even that. Cross references include *Son of Godzilla, E.T.*, and *Prehysteria*.

**REX THE RUNT** (B) Aardman Animations 199-? clay anim shorts. D: Richard Goleszowski. Ref: SFChron 4/16/93: two shorts, *Dinosaur* and *Sleep*, about a dinosaur.

**REYNA BARBARA** see *Barbarian Queen*

**RHEA GALL FORCE** (J) CBS Sony 1989 anim color 60m. Ref: Animag 10:21: OAV. Japan Video.

Follow-up to the *Gall Force* series. Follow-up: the *Gall Force—Earth* series.

**RICKY O** see *Rikko O*

**RIDERS ON THE STORM** (B) Maurice Phillips/Tambura Co. (Keller-Cowan) 1986(1985) color 105m. (aka *The American Way*). D: M. Phillips. SP: Scott Roberts. Ph: John Metcalfe. Mus: Brian Bennett. PD: Evan Hercules. Ref: TV. V 5/21/86: "*Dr. Strangelove* it isn't." 10/16/85:257(ad). SFChron 12/11/87: "crummy." With Dennis Hopper, Michael J. Pollard, Eugene Lipinski, James Aubrey.

B-29 flies American skies jamming right-wing broadcasts. Minor Hopper.

**RIDING WITH DEATH** NBC-TV 1976 color c90m. D: Alan J. Levi, Don McDougall. Ref: TVG. Castleman. Scheuer. With Ben Murphy, Katherine Crawford, Richard Dysart.

Radiation renders government agent invisible. From the "Gemini Man" TV series.

**RIFT, The** see *Endless Descent*

**RIGET** (Danish-Swed.) Zentropa Ent. & Danmarks Radio & Swedish TV & WDR & Arte & the Coproduction Office (Ole Reim) 1994 ('95-U.S.) color 279m. (*The Kingdom*-U.S.) SP, D: Lars von Trier. SP: also Tomas Gislason. Screen Story: Niels Vorsel, von Trier. Ph: Eric Kress. Mus: J. Holbek. AD: J. Lehmann. Ref: V 9/26/94: "strikingly realized work." SF Chron 11/17/95: "episodic but with a grand design." With E.H. Jaregard, K. Rolffes, Udo Kier.

"Strange fetus" ... "building ... haunted by ... dead child" ... exorcism ... "alien form." *The Kingdom* - tr t?

**RIKKO O** (H.K.-J) 1991 color/ws 90m. (*Ricky O* - ad t. aka *Story of Ricky*). D: Lan Nai Kai. Ref: TV: vt; Eng. titles. EVS: from an "animation series." Weisser/ATC: from the Japanese comic "Riki Oh."

"Rikki is incredible!" In the year 2001, prisons have been privatized, and larky ultra-gore prevails—e.g., skinning, eye-gouging, garroting with spilled intestines. Lowest-common-denominator actioner.

**RIMFIRE** Screen Guild/Ron Ormond (Lippert) 1949 b&w 64m. D: B. Reeves Eason. SP: Arthur St. Claire, Frank Wisbar, Ormond. Ph: Ernest Miller. Mus D: Walter Greene. Ref: Okuda/GN. V 3/30/49: "ghostly killings." LC. With James Millican, Mary Beth Hughes, Reed Hadley (The Abilene Kid), Henry Hull, Fuzzy Knight, Victor Kilian, Chris-Pin Martin, Margia Dean, Jason Robards, George Cleveland, Glenn Strange, Stanford Jolley, Don Harvey, Dick Alexander.

A gambler framed for cheating is hanged. "His ghost then goes around knocking off the characters who figured in the frame."(V) Another Wisbar variation on *Strangler of the Swamp*?

**The RIPPER** United Ent. (Linda Lewis) 1985 color 103m. D: Christopher Lewis. SP: Bill Groves. MkpFX: Robert Brewer, David Powell. Ref: V 2/26/86:95-6(hv): gory, "offputting." 4/15/87:40. Stanley. Morse: made-for-video; "utterly unwatchable." Martin: "poorly filmed." With Tom Savini (the Ripper), Tom Schreier, Mona VanPernis, Wade Tower.

Jack the Ripper-type amok in a midwestern college town.

**RIPTIDE** NBC-TV/Stephen J. Cannell (Jo Swerling Jr.) 1984 color 92m. D: Christian Nyby II. Tel, Exec P: Cannell, Frank Lupo. Mus: Post, Carpenter. AD: W. M. Jefferies. SpFX: Wayne Beauchamp. Mkp: Dan Striepeke. Opt: Howard Anderson. SdFX: Ken Sweet. Ref: TV. TVG(ad): TV-movie pilot for the series. V 1/4/84:46. With Joe Penny, Perry King, Thom Bray, Anne Francis, Jack Ging, Karen Kopins, Robert Viharo, Lee Patterson.

Electronics whiz's inventions include Ro-Boz, a "prototype robot ... on the leading edge of computer technology" ... a biofeedback ring which glows orange when the wearer is happy ... a negative-ion mat which atomizes dust ... and super-sonar equipment.... Typically smooth, hollow TV adventure show. The dialogue ranges from glib to functional. The sf elements are just another part of the commercial package.

**The RISING** Arrow/Tempo 1987 color c90m. SP, D: Nelson. Ph: C. DeVille. Mus: Marcel & Lilo. Mkp: D. DeVille. Ref: TV: Superstar Video. vc box: reference to "Madame Ghostbust." no Adam. With Sheena Horne, Peter North, Keisha, Mark Wallice, Bionca, Ebony Ayes, Ron Jeremy.

Several people "meddle with spirits" and moving candleholders at a seance. In trances, they contact spirits and have sexual daydreams. At the end, they decide to report the "various phenomena to whatever federal agency wants to hear about" them. X-rated, Z-level ghost story.

**RISING STORM** see *Rebel Storm*

**Il RISVEGLIO DI PAUL** (I) Sigla Emme 1985 color 85m. SP, D, P: Michele Saponaro. Mus: Canepa, Khallab. Ref: V 9/18/85: *Paul's Awakening*—tr t; "enjoyable B-sci-fi pulp." no Stanley. With Saponaro, Bianca O'Feeney, Thomas Wu Tao Ling.

Time machine whisks athlete from 1946 to a machine-ruled 2262 A.D. and an encounter with a teacher who sprouts a "monstrous red claw-arm."

**RITE NITE** see *Rush Week*

**RITORNO DALLA MORTE** (I) 1991 color feature (aka *Frankenstein 2000*). D: A. Massaccesi. SP: D. Donati, A. Tentori. Mus: P. Montanari. Ref: Palmerini. With D. O'Brian, Cinzia Monreale.

"Clumsy attempt to transfer the myth of Frankenstein to modern times."

**Los RITOS SEXUALES DEL DIABLO** (Sp) Films around the World/Hispaniola 1981 color 81m. (aka *Naked Dreams. Black Candles* - vt t). SP, D: Jose Ramon Larraz (aka Joseph Braunstein). Ph: J. Marine (aka Merino?). Mus: CAM. AD: "John Hanford." Mkp: "Calvin Fisher." Ref: TV: Redemption video;

Eng. dubbed. Hardy/HM. VSOM: aka *Lady Lucifer*? With Helga Line, Vanesa Hidalgo, Mauro Rivera, Alfredo Lucheti.

"Satanism and possession" in England. (HM) "Why do you have all these black candles?" Satanist shop talk ("Glory to satan, the anti-Christ!"), softcore sex, and *Rosemary's Baby* borrowings. Totally undistinguished.

The **RITUAL OF DEATH** (Braz.) J. Davila Ents. 1990 color c80m. D: Fauzi Mansur. SP: Filipe Grecco, Anthony Roark. Ph: Antonio Meliande. Mus: Michael Kelly. AD: Fausto Faez. SpFX: Vagner Dos Santos. Mkp: Marino Henrique, C. U. Franco. Ref: TV: Complete Ent. video. Psychotronic 10:47. no Hound. no Martin. With Olair Coan (Brad), Carina Palatinik, Tiao Hoover, Serafim Gonzalez, Michael Kelly, Leo Robinson, Vanessa Alves, Sergio Hingst (Uncle Parker).

"Help me get this thing out of me!" Brad, the lead in a "real, exotic horror show," in rehearsal, begins taking to bedroom rituals himself. Is he under the curse of the Egyptian Great Spirit? And who is the mysterious gent with the oozing hand? Is he Uncle Parker, the cult leader who makes human sacrifices to the God of Death? At any rate, Brad keeps his own victims alive and groaning in the theatre cellar.

Gore vehicle features comically stilted, phonetic line readings. Winner, Most Disgusting Scene: Zit City becomes a pulling-off-cheek scene with the possessed Brad. Main motif: ghoul drool. Most imaginative idea (far-from-fierce competition): the indoor zephyrs.

**RIVELAZIONE DI UN MANIACO SESSUALE AL CAPO DELLA SQUADRA MOBILE** see *Slasher ... Is the Sex Maniac, The!*

The **RIVER HOUSE GHOST** (B) WB-FN 1932 52m. D: Frank Richardson. SP: W. Scott Darling. Ref: BFC. With Florence Desmond, Hal Walters, Joan Marion, Shayle Gardner (Skeleton), Erle Stanley (Black Mask).

Crooks pose as ghosts.

**"ROAD LAWYERS" AND OTHER BRIEFS** Action Int'l./Pacific West (Robert Rhine) 1990 color 81m. "Road Lawyers." SP, D, Ed: R. Rhine. D, Ed: also J. Desmarais. with R. Rhine, Norman Merrill. "A 1987 spoof of the Mad Max films ... labored."

"Radar Men from the Moon." Voicing over the 1952 serial.

**ROADIE** UA/Alive 1980 color 105m. D, Co-SP: Alan Rudolph. Ref: Bill Warren: spaceship sequence. HR 6/11/80: "psychic intuition" ... cow-dung energy. Soho News 6/18/80: "giant spiders on TV." MFB'81:119-120. PFA. VV 6/23/80. V 6/11/80. Maltin'92. Scheuer.

**ROAD WARRIOR, The** see *Mad Max beyond Thunderdome*

**ROAST OF THE DAY** see *Bad Taste*

**ROBIN HOOD: THE SWORDS OF WAYLAND** (B) Showtime-TV/Goldcrest-TV & HTV 1984 color 96m. (aka *The Swords of Wayland*). D: Robert Young. SP: Richard Carpenter. Mus: Clannad. AD: Kate Barnett. SpProps: Chris Lyons. Mkp:

Cherry West. Ref: TV. TVG. Stanley. With Michael Praed, Judi Trott, Rula Lenska, Anthony Steel, John Abineri, Marcus Gilbert (Lucifer).

Robin vs. Morgwyn (Lenska), the Abbess of Ravenscar, secret head of the Cauldron of Lucifer, the "most powerful coven in England," which, with the aid of "flying demons from hell ... the hounds of Lucifer," seeks to bring Lucifer into the world. (He makes a guest appearance, at the end, in a column of smoke.) At one point, Morgwyn uses a magic sword to hypnotize Robin's men and turn them into glassy-eyed "zombies".... More fantasy-horror than in *Robin Hood and the Sorcerer*, but, dramatically, equally perfunctory. Flat sound recording undermines some fancy location shooting.

See also: *Time of the Wolf* (P).

**ROBIN HOOD AND THE SORCERER** (B) Showtime-TV/Goldcrest-TV & HTV 1984 (1983) color 101m. D: Ian Sharp. SP: Richard Carpenter. Ref: TV: "Robin Hood"—series t. TVG. Stanley.

Scattered scenes of magic (as in *Excalibur*), as the sorcerer Simon de Belleme (Anthony Valentine) invokes the "powers of the lords of darkness" and magically slashes Robin with his sword. Plus visions (of the rotting hanged) in a chalice and temporary spirit possession (of Little John).... Handsomely-photographed (by Bob Edwards) and designed (by John Biggs), but empty, formula mixing of Robin Hood and sword-and-sorcery elements. Begins with the obligatory sequence in which the hero's village is devastated, and never really improves.

**ROBO-C.H.I.C.** Action Int'l./Fitzgerald Film & Triangle Films (Mark Paglia, Douglass Grimm/Windstar) 1990 color 97m. (aka *Robo C.H.I.C.*) SP, D: Jeff Mandel. D, Co-Ed: Ed Hansen. Story, Exec Co-P: John Fitzgerald. Story: also Micah Fitzgerald. Ph: Ken Carmack, Mike Wemple. Mus: Brian Malone. PD: Kari Stewart. SpFxCoord: Tim Danec. Ref: TV: AIP HV. TVG: *Cyber-C.H.I.C.* - TV. Stanley. Martin. PT 10:54: "overlong dumb comedy." 11:6. V/Mifed'89:161: 5/89 start. With Kathy Shower, Jack Carter, Burt Ward, Phil Proctor, Kip King (Dr. Von Colon).

The Computerized Humanoid Intelligence Clone (Shower) here is an "optically generated, artificial intelligence powered by internal cold fusion, in humanoid form, with organic augmentation." It and the Robo-Car both shoot rays, and a more or less incidental mad bomber destroys the "entire Great Plains".... Pretty lame comedy, with a few cute asides.

**ROBO NINJA** see *Mirai Ninja*

**ROBO ROBO COMPANY** see *S.D. Gundam. S.D. Gundam MK-II*

**ROBO TAE KWON V90** (S. Korean) D.B. Media (Kim Chyung Ki) 1990 feature. Ref: HOF 2:35-6: "cartoon robots ... space army"; "uneven flick." With Lee Sung Hyung.

**ROBO VAMPIRE** (H.K.) Filmark Int'l. (Tomas Tang)/Dallie Yeung 1993 color/ws 91m. D: Joe Livingstone. SP: William Palmer. Ph: Anthony Mang. Mus: Ian Wilson. PD: Tang. SpFX: Frank Walton. Mkp: Millie Myer. Ref: TV: Magnum Video; Eng. version. PT 5:4. VSOM: sfa *Zombie Vampire Vs. Robo Merce-*

*naries*? With Robin Mackay, Nian Watts, Harry Myles, Joe Browne, Nick Norman, George Tripos, David Borg, Diana Byrne, Alan Drury.

"He'll train vampires to deal with them." "Lady ghost" Christine protests that the badly burned, hopping, leaping "vampire beast" which the priest has created is her lover Peter. Meanwhile, the dead Tom is turned into an "android-like robot." ("We must get rid of that Robo Warrior.")

Crude, sensationalistic, catastrophically-dubbed, all-too-"packaged" picture, though the vampires-vs.-android idea has a certain outlandish appeal and recalls The *Robot Vs. the Aztec Mummy.* Nice touch, of sorts: Both the android and the vampires can fly, more or less. Too much of the drug-smuggling subplot; not enough of the vampire-and-ghost romance. (Christine to Robo, in an attempt to buy time: "You can kill us, but wait till our love is consummated.") Bonus: a "charmed" line of hopping vampires.

**ROBOCOP** Orion/Jon Davison (Arne Scmidt) 1987 color 102m. D: Paul Verhoeven. SP: Edward Neumeier, Michael Miner. Mus: Basil Poledouris. RoboCop Des & SpMkpFX: Rob Bottin. ED-209 & Assoc Co-P: Phil Tippett. Stopmo: Randy Dutra. Prosth: Stephen Dupuis. AnimFX: Kevin Kutchaver, Jo Martin. SpPhFX: Peter Kuran, VCE. Opt: Robert Blalack, Praxis. SdFX: Stephen Flick, John Pospisil. Ref: TV. MFB'88:35. V 7/8/87. Sacto Union 7/16/87. With Peter Weller (Murphy/RoboCop), Nancy Allen, Dan O'Herlihy, Ronny Cox, Kurtwood Smith, Miguel Ferrer, Robert DoQui, Lee DeBroux, Del Zamora, Mario Machado.

1991. ED-209—a robot in OCP's enforcement-droid series, and the "future of law enforcement"—malfunctions and gives way to OCP's RoboCop, half-computer and half-Murphy (a dead cop), and an invulnerable evil-fighter. Problem: "OCP runs the cops."

Too-neat wrap-up here suggests that, (a) the larger story re corruption is over too, and, (b) RoboCop is Murphy, again, somehow, like a recovered amnesia victim. But if, at base, *RoboCop* is just another action picture, it's a well-done one. The script offers a cleverly drawn, if one-dimensional (cynical) view of business, plus a fantasy of Justice and Revenge. Funny-creepy (stopmo?) effect: ED-209 failing to navigate the stairs and toppling, flailing, "crying."

**ROBOCOP 2** Orion/Jon Davison 1990 color 118m. D: Irvin Kershner. SP: Frank Miller, Walon Green. Story: Miller. Ph: Mark Irwin. Mus: Leonard Rosenman. PD: Peter Jamison. Robocop Des: Rob Bottin. Anim: Phil Tippett. SpFxSup: Martin, Curtis. SpPhFX: Kuran/VCE. SpSdFX: John P. et al. Ref: V 6/20/90: "a punishing film." MFB'90:301-3. Sacto Bee 6/23/90: "beneath contempt." With Peter Weller (Robocop), Nancy Allen, Dan O'Herlihy, Belinda Bauer, Tom Noonan, Gabriel Damon, Robert Do'Qui, Fabiana Udenio, John Glover, Mario Machado.

RoboCop vs. crime in Detroit, part 2.

**ROBOCOP 3** Orion (Patrick Crowley) 1993 (1992) color 104m. SP, D: Fred Dekker. Story, SP: Frank Miller. Ph: G. B. Kibbe. Mus: Basil Poledouris. PD: Hilda Stark. SpFxSup: Jeff Jarvis. RoboCop: Rob Bottin. Stopmo Anim: Phil Tippett. SpPhFX: VCE/Peter Kuran;(anim) Kevin Kutchaver, Pam Vick;(computer

anim) Littleton Bros. SpSeqs: Pacific Data. Ref: TV. Mo. V 11/15/93: "running out of gas." 5/3/93:34: in Japan. ad. SFChron 11/5/93. With Robert John Burke (RoboCop), Nancy Allen, Rip Torn, John Castle, Jill Hennessy, CCH Pounder, Mako, Robert Do'Qui, Mario Machado.

RoboCop vs. Otomo (Bruce Locke), a Japanese-made enforcement 'droid. "My friends call me Murphy. You call me Robo-Cop." No groundbreaking material here, but the story is slickly told, and the film features some surprising gallows humor and some prime stopmo. At the end, RoboCop dons a flying gizmo and does an amusing Superman. Also: two android ninjas and ever-evil OCP.

**ROBOFORCE** see *I Love Maria*

**ROBOFOX** Perry Ross 1987 color 85m. D: Paul Thomas. Ref: TV: Fantasy HV. Adam '89. With Angela Baron (Angela), Randy West, Krista Lane, Tom Byron, Erica Boyer.

Dr. Pamela Moses restores and restructures the crushed body of plain Jane Darcy, a traffic-accident victim. As "Angela," Darcy now has a spectacular new body, a new face, and "no temperature at all." Super-strong, she can lift men and crush billiard balls bare-handed. Dr. Moses uses her in "her own personal vendetta against men".... So cheap that the accident is suggested simply by the sound of squealing tires and a scream—we don't know if Darcy is hit by a car, a truck, a bus, or a golf cart. Quickie "X"'s title doesn't even appear on the videotape.

**ROBOFOX II** Fantasy HV (Perry Ross) 1988 color 82m. D, P: Paul Thomas. Ref: vc box: the "ultimate sex machine." Adam '89. With Angela Baron, Ona Zee, Jamie Gillis.

**ROBOJOX** see *Robot Jox*

**ROBOKILL BENEATH DISCO CLUB LAYLA** see *Mikadoroido*

**ROBOT CARNIVAL** (J) Streamline Pictures/Bandai (A.P.P.P./Kazufumi Nomura) 1987 ('91-U.S.) anim color 91m. (*Roboto Kanibaura.* aka *Carnival of Animation—The Fantasia of the '90s*). Ph: T. Morita, K. Torigoe, Y. Sugiyama. Mus: Isaku Fujita et al. SpFX: K. Toyohiko, G. Abe, S. Teraoka. SdFX: Arts Pro. Ref: TV: Emotion video; no Eng. Paul Lane. Cinef 5/89: segments occ. shown separately. *Robot Carnival* (filmbook). V 3/18/91. 5/6/91:C-44. 10/15/90:M-86. 2/25/91:54. Martin. Maltin '92. MMarquee 43:5,7,8. SFChron 3/16/91; Dtbk 3/10/91. Markalite 3:76-79.

Seven dialogue-light tales of robots, with a framing "Robot Carnival" anecdote by Katsuhiro Ohtomo.

1) "Franken's Gears" or "Frankenstein's Gears": D: Koji Morimoto. A giant, super-strong monkey-see robot sees its creator hugging some globular gizmo, approaches him, and.... Slight but stylish, wry.

2) "Deprive": D: Hidetoshi Ohmori. Tentacled robots invade a futuristic city, while the hero Jekyll-and-Hydes between human and android. Empty, fast, flashy.

3) "Presence": D: Yasuomi Umetsu. An inventor must destroy his beautiful, love-hungry robot-doll when a future society out-

laws robots. Bittersweet vignette may not be as skillfully illustrated as other segments, but the story has bite. When the sentimental threatens here, the surreal irrupts: The doll's limp body—an image scrambling hints of death, memory, and the past—keeps reappearing before the inventor, then blows up in his face. Atmospheric cloud and wind effects.

4) "Starlight Angel": D: Hiroyuki Kitazume. Surreal treacle in Robot Wanderland, as a girl's blues seem to transform into a giant malicious robot. Fancy transformations and wild plot turns camouflage unremarkable boy-meets-girl story.

5) "Cloud": D: Mao Lamdo. Within a CinemaScope-for-TV-like strip, a cloud-hatched robot child walks, as, behind and above him, the cloudscape mutates, from angelic figures to leaping bunnies to flying saucers to birds to atomic explosions to rocket ships. The music mutates, too, suggesting an alternately cold, friendly, harsh, warm world. Rain, wind, sun ... bird sounds, no sound, music—"Cloud" is a series of delicately inflected moods, and, with "Nightmare," one of the film's two extraordinary segments.

6) "A Tale of Two Robots" or "A Strange Tale from the Meiji Period: The Story of the Red-Haired Barbarian's Attack": D: Hiroyuki Kitakubo. Slight, amusing satire of Japanese war propaganda concerns a mad genius who unleashes a giant automaton on Japan. There's a "Lum" feel to the hero's combative relationship with the heroine.

7) "Nightmare" or "The Chicken Man and the Crimson Head": D: Takashi Nakamura. While the principal nocturnal demon here conjures up twisted nightmare trees with his lightning, his junkyard emissary zips about raising miscellaneous monsters. Later, in their shop, they forge new, composite beings out of their hapless victims. Bizarre ingredients include an humongous pendulum, a giant metal hand, a mysterious fog bank which seals the demon-infested part of the metropolis off from the rest, Papa Demon's giant beer mug (which he throws at his assistant), strange clouds or mists which haunt the city skyline, metal creatures which pick up where machinery gears leave off, small thingies which work on a mannequin, and the sunlight which acts like fire on the various night growths. The crazy-clockwork Walpurgisnacht of "Nightmare" recalls "The Devil's Ball" from *The Mascot* and "Night on Bald Mountain" from *Fantasia*, but it has a night-in-the-factories-of-hell flavor and demonic rhythm all its own. These are demons for Modern Times.

**ROBOT HOLOCAUST** Wizard Video/Tycin Ent. (C. DePaula) 1986 color 79m. SP, D: Tim Kincaid. SpVisFX: J. Frank. SpMkpFX: Tom Lauten. Robot: (des) Ed French; (masks) Ralph Cordero; (suits) V. McNeill. Ref: V 1/21/87: "okay." Morse: "laughable"; "claw of a giant spider." With Norris Culf, Nadine Hart, Jennifer Delora, Rick Gianasi, Amy Brentano.

Evil Dark One, monster-worms, Beast of the Web, and robots, in New Terra's future.

**ROBOT IN THE FAMILY** A-Pix Ent./Rapid (Long Island Expressway) 1993 color 92m. SP, D, P, Exec P: Jack Shaoul. Ref: vc box: "home robot." With Joe Pantoliano.

**ROBOT JOX** (U.S.-I) Triumph Releasing (Empire)/Epic(Altar) 1990 (1989) color 96m. (*Robojox*—orig t). Story, D: Stuart

Gordon. SP: Joe Haldeman. Ph: Mac Ahlberg. Mus: F. Talgorn. PD: G. Natalucci. VisFX: David Allen; (d) Paul Gentry; (model sup) Dennis Gordon; (des) Ron Cobb, S. Burg; (stopmo) Allen, Paul Jessel; (anim graphics) K. Kutchaver; (fx crew) Mark McGee et al. SpPhFX: Kuran/VCE. MkpCoord: MMI; J. Buechler, J. Foster. "Dedicated to the memory of Bob Greenberg." Ref: TV. V 5/9/90. ad. With Gary Graham, Anne-Marie Johnson, Paul Koslo, Danny Kamekona, Michael Alldredge, Jeffrey Combs.

Fifty years after the nuclear holocaust, war has been outlawed and the "two great alliances" settle their disputes with huge, combination-robot-like "fighting machines," on the Confederation Playing Field in Siberia. Meanwhile, "manufactured people," or "tubies"—a "superior stock of warrior"—are being bred to man the machines.

Impressive stopmo for Alexander's (Koslo) machine periodically rescues dreary production with dead-weight actors. This is more a bad sports movie than a bad science-fiction picture. Part of the climactic battle sequence is set in outer space.

Follow-up: *Robot Wars*.

**ROBOT NINJA** The Suburban Tempe Co. (David DeCoteau) 1989 color 79m. SP, D, P, Mus, Ed: J. R. Bookwalter. Created by David Lange. Ph: Michael Tolochko Jr. PD: Jon Killough. SpMkpFX: (consul) D. P. Barton; D. Lange, Bill Morrison, Joe Contracier. Ref: TV: Cinema HV. V 5/2/90:92. 7/18/90:62(hv). With Michael Todd, Bogdan Pecic, Maria Markovic, Floyd Ewing, Jr., Burt Ward, Linnea Quigley, Scott Spiegel, Kenneth J. Hall.

Ridgway, Ohio. Comic book artist Leonard Miller (Todd) impersonates his own hero, Robot Ninja, in order to combat the authors of the gory, real-life *Ridgway Murders*. He kills one thug, gorily, with his "claw," and the other thugs, in turn, slice him up a bit. Gorily, he operates on himself, and they, in like manner, kill inventor Dr. Goodknight (Pecic), who designed Miller's suit. Bonus: zombie gore creatures in our hero's fantasy.... Based-in-Akron gore flick is not the fun film the title might lead one to expect. It's just a jokey, clumsy makeup-effects wallow.

**ROBOT OF WAR** see *Robowar*

**ROBOT RABBIT** WB 1953 anim color 7m. D: I. Freleng. SP: W. Foster. Ref: "WBCartoons": Bugs Bunny. Maltin/OMAM. Lee. LC: c1954('52 notice). "Nasty-looking robot."(WBC)

**ROBOT WARS** Para/Full Moon 1993 color c75m. D: Albert Band. SP: Jackson Barr. Idea, P: Charles Band. Ph: Adolfo Bartoli. Mus: David Arkenstone. PD: Milo. VisFX: David Allen. SpPhFX: Motion Opticals. MechFxSup: Mark Rappaport. FxAnimSup: Kevin Kutchaver. SpFxCoord: John Cazin. Ref: TV. TVG. SFChron Dtbk 4/18/93: loose sequel to *Robot Jox*; "rousing" stopmo battle between robots. Martin: "intolerable and brainless." Fango 123:12. With Don Michael Paul, Barbara Crampton, James Staley, Lisa Rinna, Danny Kamekona, Peter Haskell.

Set in 2041 A.D. "How the hell do you hide a megarobot?" Only feasible game plan here: Wait for the stopmo with the "scorpion" megarobot and the return of Mega One ("the whole damn megarobot"). Otherwise, it's mostly "Oh, my God! They're hijacking the robot!"

**ROBOTECH** see *Macross Movie, The*

**ROBOTECH THE MOVIE** see *Macross Movie, The*

**ROBOTIX: BATTLE FOR THE FUTURE** Claster-TV/Marvel Prods. & Sunbow (Hasbro, Inc.) 1985 anim color c90m. (*Robotix*—cr t). Creative D: Jay Bacal. Sup D: John Gibbs, T. C. Lennon. Story Ed: Alan Swayze. Mus: Rob Walsh. AD: Bill Dubay. FxEd: M. L. DePatie et al. Ref: TV. TVG: from the TV series.

To survive a cosmic storm, the inhabitants of the distant planet Skalorr transfer their essences into Robotix, then strengthen themselves by "interfacing with human beings." This three-million-year-old civilization's "heart" is a computer, Compucore, which executes the transfers and interfaces. Also: a giant, many-eyed bobcat-like creature in a cave ... The Desert of Illusions ... and the "ultimate weapon," Terra-star.... The robots (including one with a snake-head-and-tongue) have more personality than the humans here, and the arch-villain, predictably, sounds like Darth Vader. Lively, but rather deadly, too. Straight-forwardly single-minded bang!-zoom! stuff.

**ROBOTMAN AND FRIENDS** 1986 anim color c80m. Ref: TVG. no Scheuer.

"Three friendly aliens from Robotland" on Earth.

**ROBOTO KANIBAURA** see *Robot Carnival*

**ROBOTRIX** (H.K.) Golden Harvest/Paragon 1991 color/ws 97m. D: Jamie Luk. Ref: TV: Pan-Asia Video; some Eng. dialogue. V 10/19/92: 154: at Mifed. HOF 2:20: *Bustroid*-J.

"Enter the future world. The show of the latest of the android models from around the world is about to begin!" The latest model is computer-chip-controlled, with lifelike, "flexible latex" skin and laser eyes—the "ultimate fighting machine," powered by one hundred million watts. In the story proper, a male android runs amok, loses his head, regains it, and, at the finish, fights the beautiful, busty android that was replicated in the lab from a beautiful, busty woman who had just been killed.... Softcore science-fictioner is no *I Love Maria*, or even a *Terminator*, though it's quite a showcase for the female star. Functional combination of kung fu, sf, t&a.

**ROBOWAR** (I-Fili) Flora (Franco Gaudenzi) 1988 color 87m. (*Robowar—Robot da Guerra*). D: Bruno Mattei. Story: Claudio Fragasso, Rossella Drudi. SP: R. Drudi. Ph: Riccardo Grassetti. Mus: Al Festa. AD: Sc(l)avia. SpFX: Francesco & Gaetano Paolocci. Mkp: Franco Di Girolamo. Opt: Stefano Mafera. Ref: TV: VSOM; Eng. dubbed. MV: aka *Robot of War*? V 5/4/88:322. Palmerini. With Reb Brown, Catherine Hickland, Max Laurel, Mel Davidson, Alan Collins.

"There's something really weird going on in this region." Omega-1 is "something more than a man" and "more than a machine"—it's the "perfect, ultimate weapon," a "perfect fusion of human and mechanical parts" which was once Lt. Martin Woodring. And it comes equipped with robo-ray, thermal sensors, and a foot

grabber.... Accidentally comic macho in this imperfect fusion of *Robocop* and *Predator.*

**ROCK\*A\*DOODLE** (U.S.-Irish) Goldwyn/Goldcrest (Sullivan Bluth Studios Ireland) 1992 (1990) anim & live action 77m. D, Co-P: Don Bluth. Co-D: (& Co-P) Gary Goldman; Dan Kuenster. Story: Bluth; (& Co-P) John Pomeroy, et al. SpVisFxD: Fred Craig; (live action) Roy Field, P. Donen. SpFxAnimD: David Tidgwell. Ref: TV. V 3/30/92. SFChron 4/3/92.

Fantasy in which an evil magic owl (voice: Christopher Plummer) turns boys into kittens and conjures up tornados, and his magic rays reach out like phantom clutching hands.... Vapid, if pleasantly drawn, Nominee: Longest End-Credit Scroll. Fortunately, most of the end-credit music is lovely.

**ROCK 'EM DEAD** see *Shock 'Em Dead*

**ROCK 'N' ROLL NIGHTMARE** (Can.) Shapiro Ent./Thunder Films (Landesman-Sorrell) 1987 color 83m. (*The Edge of Hell*—alt t). D: John Fasano. SP, P: Jon-Mikl Thor. Mus: The Tritonz. SpMkpFX: Fascination Film FX. Creatures: (Evil One) Arnold Garguilo, or Gargiulo, II; (child wolf creature) Fasano; (bathroom demon) A. C. Bua; (squids, kitchen demon) Frank Dietz; (lizard demon, Phil's head) Vincent Modica; (Luanne appliance) James Cirille; (Cyclops creatures) John Gibson. Ref: TV. V 7/8/87. With Thor (Triton), Jillian Peri, Dietz, David Lane.

Members of a heavy-metal band check into a deserted farmhouse in search of "ten minutes of new good material." Soon, people begin turning into monsters. Triton, the leader of the band, proves to be the Intercessor—Triton, the Archangel—while the other characters are phantoms which he conjured up from horror movies in order to lure the Evil One and the denizens of his domain out into the open, in a surprising but not really redeeming twist ending.

Rudimentary, technically and dramatically. They can't even get the screams right. Some good foreboding-atmosphere shots (photography by Mark MacKay) of clouds and trees, and okay comic relief from a tiny Cyclops.

**ROCKET GIRLS** Platinum Pictures 1993 color 83m. D: Stuart Canterbury. Ref: vc box: "interstellar sex orgy." With Summer Knight.

**\*The ROCKET MAN** 1954. Mus D: Lionel Newman. AD: George Patrick. Mkp: Louis Hippe. Ref: Library of Congress. Warren/KWTS! Stanley. Lee. Lentz. Hardy/SF. V 5/5/54. Scheuer. Filmfax 31:37.

Carlisle, the "friendly town." Seven-year-old Timmy (George "Foghorn" Winslow), an orphan, is a rabid fan of TV space shows like "Capt. Talray and His Outer Spacers." Perhaps for this reason, an alien being gives him a "magic space gun" which can stop people in their tracks and make them tell the truth: "Its power's for good, not evil.... It will turn a falsehood into a truth." A joke at the end re green cheese implies that the visitor is a moon man.

The latter pleasantry is the closest the movie comes to comedy or charm. Story situations and characters are flatly sentimental, and any rules governing the gun's powers are at best nebulous. At one point, it shuts up a cuckoo in a clock; at another, it somehow gives several poker players excellent hands. Those looking for nostalgia value will find same in the presence of sweet and sexy Anne Francis and that axiom of Fifties science fiction, John Agar.

**ROCKET SQUAD** WB 1956 anim color 7m. D: Chuck Jones. SP: T. Pierce. Ref: Lee. LC. Maltin/OMAM. "WBCartoons": "Dragnet" spoof.

Porky Pig and Daffy Duck as space cops in the 25th Century.

**The ROCKETEER** BV/Gordon Co. & Silver Screen Partners IV (Larry Franco) 1991 color/ws 108m. D: Joe Johnston. SP: Danny Bilson, Paul De Meo. Story: Bilson, De Meo, William Dear. Based on the graphic novel by Dave Stevens. Mus: James Horner. SpVisFX: IL&M; (sup) Ken Ralston. Anim Sup: Wes Ford Takahashi. Stopmo: Tom St. Amand. SpFxSup: Jon Belyeu. MkpSup: Brad Wilder. Ref: TV. V 6/10/91. S&S 8/91:55-6. EBay Express 6/28/91. SFChron 6/21/91. Maltin '92. Martin. With Bill Campbell, Jennifer Connelly, Alan Arkin, Timothy Dalton, Paul Sorvino, Terry O'Quinn, Ed Lauter, Tiny Ron (Lothar).

"It's a rocket—like in the comic books." L.A., 1938. A rocket pack designed by Howard Hughes (O'Quinn) and developed by another inventor (Arkin) turns Cliff Secord (Campbell) into the "flying man" and makes him look "like a hood ornament." ("It's an engine, but you strap it to your back, and it makes you fly.")

Hollow sf/period comedy features hommages to Rondo Hatton (in Ron's makeup), Commando Cody, and *King of the Rocket Men*. The height of the script's imagination and daring: An Errol Flynn-like actor (Dalton's Neville Sinclair) proves to be a Nazi spy. Some okay lines and effects, but even the showpiece effects scenes are rather mild fun.

See also: *Aces Go Places III.*

**ROCKIN' WITH JUDY JETSON** 1988 anim color c90m. Ref: TVG: made-for-TV.

Plot to outlaw music.

See also *Jetsons: The Movie.*

**ROCKTOBER BLOOD** Vestron/Sebastian Int'l. 1986 color 88m. SP, D, P: Beverly Sebastian. SP, P: F. Sebastian. SpFX: Ben Sebastian. Ref: V 10/22/86: "standard slasher fare." With Tray Loren, Donna Scoggins, Renee Hubbard.

Is Billy Eye (Loren) back from the grave? Made in 1984.

**ROCKULA** Cannon 1990 color 91m. SP, D: Luca Bercovici. SP, P: J. Levy. SP: also C. Verwiel. Ph: J. Schwartzman. Mus: Hilary Bercovici. PD: Jane Ann Stewart. SpMkpFX: Tony Gardner, Larry Hamlin. SpFX: Lucinda Strub. Ref: TV: Cannon Video. V 6/20/90: "poor." 10/11/89:16. ad. Martin. Jones. With Dean Cameron, Toni Basil, Tawny Fere, Susan Tyrrell, Bo Diddley.

"Uninteresting story of 400-year-old virgin vampire Dean Cameron...." (V) ("I'm a vampire!" "And I'm the Bride of Frankenstein!") Every 22 years, vampiric Ralph must attempt to woo and win the fair Mona (Fere). Once or twice, he turns into a squat bat creature.... A real curiosity—an MTV version of the vampire story. First curiosity: Not only does Ralph have a mirror reflection, he converses with it/him. Uneven film is more interesting for its rock-opera pretensions than for its comic aspira-

tions—note, especially, the elaborate Singin' in the Rain duet with Ralph and Mona.

**The ROCKY PORNO VIDEO SHOW** Loretta Sterling Prods. 1986 color 90m. D, P: Sterling. SP: Raven Touchstone. Ph: Mike Cates. Mus: John Further. Sp & SdFX: Dave Quick. Mkp: Alan C. Bosshardt. Ref: TV: 4 Play Video. Adam '88:205. With Bionca, Tantala Ray (herself), Tom Byron, Francois Papillon (Priapus), Karen Summer (Pandora), Kristara Barrington (Venus), Marc Wallice (Eros), Peter North (Oedipus), Bruce Seven.

Honeymooners happen upon aliens in an old house. Switched to "hypersex," the sex ion generator therein loosens up the couple, and the aliens invite them to Sexylvania, the "planet of lust," somewhere "beyond the galaxy." Flimsy hardcore takeoff on *The Rocky Horror Picture Show.*

**ROD'S RAIDERS** Adam & Co. 1987 color feature. D: Thor Johnson. Ref: Adam '93G. With Jesse Koehler, Max Montoya.

Explorers in a "distant galaxy ... find themselves beamed to the surface of a strange planet."

**ROGER CORMAN'S FRANKENSTEIN UNBOUND** see *Frankenstein Unbound*

**\*ROGUES GALLERY** American Prods. 1945. SpFX: Ray Mercer. Mkp: George Gray. Ref: TV: Gold Key-TV. V 2/21/45. Lee. no Lentz. no Hardy/SF. TVFFSB. no Maltin '92. no Scheuer. no Stanley.

"You can hear anybody anywhere." Emerson Laboratory's Prof. Reynolds (H. B. Warner) tests a "new listening device" which will "revolutionize" communication, "do away with wires." Said device does not need a "broadcasting device at the voice source"—"there is a wavelength for every locality in the world." At present, the device can tune in, wirelessly, on places where the professor has experimented, and picks up a conversation miles away.

This unexplained, better-than-*Blue Thunder* gizmo is the highlight of this comedy-mystery. Albert Herman stages both comedy and action scenes clumsily. Prize for one bit of terribly mistimed hand-on-shoulder suspense music.

See also: *Curiosity Kills.*

**2 The ROGUES TAVERN** Carmel Prods. 1936. Ref: TV. V 7/15/36. no Maltin '92. no Scheuer. Hound.

"And then the dog's face appeared in the window!" The Red Rock Tavern, "out in the middle of nowhere." ("This place is spooky!") Ingredients: a weird howling ("Sounds like the wailing of ghosts!") ... rumors of a part-wolf killer-dog ... a fulfilled prophecy ("That is the card of death, Harrison") ... a voice of doom ("You're all going to die!") ... and mad Mrs. Jamison (Clara Kimball Young).

Film has flat conversation scenes and tired play with red herrings. Game attempts at atmosphere, however, include the portentous dialogue (see above), some ambitious tracking shots across rooms and into close-ups, the presence of the inventor Morgan (Earl Dwire)—who wears spectacles which weirdly magnify his eyes—and a phony "hound of the Baskervilles."

**ROJIN Z** (J) Tokyo Theaters & TV Inc., & Movie & TV Asahi & Sony Music Ent. 1991 anim color/ws 80m. SP: Katsuhiro Otomo. Ref: TV: vt; no Eng. V.Max 4:10-13: *Roujin-Z*.

In the 21st Century, an emaciated old man, Mr. Takazawa, is hooked up to a nuclear-powered computer/life-support system, the Z-001, which, when physically activated, begins acting like a marauding robot. With the old man as its core, it takes bulldozers, vans, etc., as scrap unto itself, as it grows larger and more complicated. Government types construct their own machine-monster, the Alpha, but it's no match for the rogue machine—until the former is combined with a helicopter.

Wild, good-natured sf-comedy. High point: the mad machine's encounter with the Tokyo-Osaka version of the Fifth Avenue-el commuter express. Wry final note: the onslaught of a giant Buddha/machine. ("My ride is here....")

**ROLLER BLADE** New World 1986 color 97m. Story, SP, D, P, Sets, Costumes, Ph: Donald G. Jackson. SP: also Randall Frakes. SpVisFX, Sets, Ed, Assoc P: Ron Amick. SpVisFX: also Tony Tremblay. Mus: Robert Garrett. MkpFX: E. M. Davidson. Baby: Jackson, Alec Guiliano. SdFX: Martin Laliberte. Ref: TV: New World Video. V 7/16/86. Phantom: *Rollerblade*. Morse. Scheuer. Martin. Stanley. With Suzanne Solari, Jeff Hutchinson, Shaun Michelle, Sam Mann, Robby Taylor (Dr. Saticoy), Michelle Bauer, Barbara Peckinpaugh, Lisa Marie, Jameseric Mandell (voice of the Saticoys), Katina Garner

"City of Lost Angels—The Second Dark Age." In this tacky new world, everyone skates and most everyone speaks in sentences like "Go forth now and skate the path of righteousness!" Mother Speed (Garner) and her sisters of the Cosmic Order of Roller Blade (with its magic, healing switchblade) take on the evil Saticoy's devils, who promote kidnapping and semi-nude wrestling.

Award to *Roller Blade* for most bizarre *Road Warrior* ripoff. Is Donald G. Jackson an Edward D. Wood for our time? He provides inimitable, meant-to-throw-you-for-a-loop details like the order's insignia—a happy face in the middle of an Aztec symbol—and the order's costumes, a cross between Weird Nun and Weirder Ku Klux Klan. Vacuous action alternates with haphazard deployment of these comic or camp or serio-camp elements, the most taking of which is Baby Saticoy, who at first (in a nightmare sequence) appears to be a little water mutant, then a hand puppet through which Dr. Saticoy speaks, then either the stranger half of the doctor's schizophrenia or a creature with independent life.

Sequels: *Legend of the Rollerblade 7. Roller Blade Seven. Roller Blade Warriors.*

The **ROLLER BLADE SEVEN** Rebel 1992 color feature (*Return of the Roller Blade Seven* - cable t). Ph, SP, D, P: Donald G. Jackson. SP, Mus, P, Ed: S. Shaw. Ref: V 12/16/91:20: 11/91 start. PT 20:72: "supposedly this was two sequels ... edited into one." With Scott Shaw, William Smith, Rhonda Shear, Allison Chase, Madison Monk, Don Stroud, Jade East, Karen Black.

Apparent third in the series. For *Roller Blade Seven*, Part 2, see *Legend of the Rollerblade 7.*

**ROLLER BLADE WARRIORS: TAKEN BY FORCE** Golden Circle (Jonathan S. Kaplan) 1988 color c90m. (*Roller Blade*

*Part 2: Holy Thunder*—orig t. *Roller Blade*-int t). Story, Ph, D: Donald G. Jackson. SP: Lloyd Strathern. Mus: Robert Garrett. AD: Lea Anna McConnell. SpMkpFX: Cleve A. Hall. SpFX: Don Power. Opt: H'w'd., David Hewitt. SpThanks: Bill Warren, David Durston et al. Ref: TV. TVG. Bill Warren. With Kathleen Kinmont, Jack Damon, Elizabeth Kaitan, Rory Calhoun, Norman Alden, Suzanne Solari, Michael Sonye, Abby Dalton.

"There's evil—it's down there!" The Cosmic Order of Roller Blade is back, with Kinmont as the main "smily face," a "she demon on wheels" ... the "thing in the stack," a demon or mutant ... and seer Gretchen (Kaitan), who can sense nearby evil. *Roller Blade* sequel falls flat. Much projecting of "psychic links," much bad acting, not much on the ball moviewise.

**ROLLIN' PLAINS** Grand Nat'l. (Edward Finney) 1938 b&w 61m. D: Al Herman. SP: Lindsley Parsons, Edmond Kelso. Story: J. & C. Jacquard. Ref: V 8/31/38: "looks like it was tossed together."

Tex Ritter as Tex Lawrence "concocts a phoney death and ghost scene to break down the killer."

**ROLLING THUNDER** Dittrich 1991 color feature. SP, D: Scott Dittrich. Ref: SJose Mercury News 8/16/91: "it is endless." SFChron 8/22/91: "an effective message film." With Ian Abercrombie, Christian Fletcher, Tom Curren.

"Could be the world's first science-fiction surfing movie." (SFC) Australia, 2040 A.D., "with all the petrol gone."(SJMC)

The **ROLY POLY MAN** (Austral.) REP/Rough Nut & KM et al. (Peter Green) 1994 color 95m. D: Bill Young. SP: Kym Goldsworthy. Ph: B.J. Breheny. Mus: D. Skinner. PD: R. Moxham. SpFX: David Young. Ref: V 6/6/94: "amiable cast & several good scenes." With Paul Chubb, Les Foxcroft, Susan Lyons, Zoe Bertram.

"Horror and sci-fi frills" include "victims with exploded heads" ... "strange experiments to cure brain tumors" ... and a grisly scene "involving brain remains."

**ROMA ANNO 2033** or **ROME, 2072 A.D.** see *New Gladiators, The*

**ROMA 2033 A.D.: I CENTURIONI DEL FUTURO** see *New Gladiators, The*

The **ROMANCE OF THE VAMPIRES** (H.K.) Sunton Films 1994 color 87m. D: Lau Kwun Wai. FX?: Animation Shop. Ref: TV: Tai Seng Video; Eng. titles. V 4/4/94:10: in H.K. With Yau Yu Ching, Yum Hum.

"Blood is the best food in the world." The vampire/vamp at large and her husband are the "forever couple." When he's impaled on a large pole, he just pulls it out. His cure for blindness, for the other woman for whom he falls: eyedrops of blood from his sun-fried body ... in only the first of several, climactic, possibly hilarious scenes of self-sacrifice, as more incredible complications ensue. Until this multi-tiered conclusion, the movie is not funny (affectation is confused with comedy), sexy (despite the would-be-hot softcore scenes), or scary. But hang on for Mr. and Mrs. Vampire's Wild Ride here....

**ROMIE-O AND JULIE-8** (Can.) Nelvana & CBC 1979 anim color c25m. (aka *Runaway Robots*?). Story, D: Clive A. Smith. Adap: Ken Sobol, Elaine Pope. Story: also Michael Hirsh. Mus: Patricia Cullen. SdFX: Robert Ablack. Ref: TV: in *Nelvanamation*, Warner HV. Voices: Max Ferguson et al.

"We have made monsters!" Megastellar Company's "man made boy" Romie-O and Supersolar Cybernetics' robot-with-feelings Julie-8 love each other. Incidentals: a rust storm and elephant-like flying aliens. The Junk Monster's catchy number re junk is the highlight of this weak-tea sf-comedy short.

**RON HOWARD'S TUT AND TUTTLE** see *Tut and Tuttle*

**ROOM AT THE FLYING DRAGON, The** or **ROOM IN THE DRAGON VOLANT, The** see *Sleep of Death, The*

**ROOM WITHOUT A DOOR, A** see *Iguana with a Tongue of Fire*

**ROOMMATE, The** see *Future Shock*

**ROOT SEARCH** (J) Central Park Media/Nippon Columbia (Shibazaki) color 43m. (*Roots Search*—U.S.). D: Hisashi Sugai. SP: Mitsuru Shimada. AD: Yoshinori Takao. Ref: TV: Columbia Video; no Eng. vc box: U.S. Manga Corps video; Eng. titles.

The giant, big-mawed monster amok on the spaceship here seems related to The Thing of the 1982 remake: Anyone might suddenly turn into the monster, or vice versa. Even in monster form, it continues mutating. Now, tentacles and crab legs dominate; a moment later, the beast will lean more towards the vegetable in appearance; occasionally, its bunched tentacles look like a thicket of angry, writhing ICBMs; and sometimes the creature resembles a big green brain with leg-like sprouts poking out all over.

*Root Search* (title inexplicable without a synopsis), while routine, is at least lively, all-out shriek-and-scream stuff, though it's the protagonists who are doing most of the shrieking and screaming.

**RORRET** (I) New Yorker/Nuova Dimensione & RAI-TV Channel 1 1988 (1987) color 103m. SP, D: Fulvio Wetzl. SP: also Enzo Capua. Ph: C. Cerchio. Ref: V 3/9/88: "convoluted, often incoherent plot." SFChron Dtbk 10/25/92. With Lou Castel, Anna Galiena, Massimo Venturiello.

Tale of a "psychopathic theater owner who lives behind the screen of his cinema."(V)

**The ROSEBUD BEACH HOTEL** Almi (Big Lobby) 1984 color 83m. (*The Big Lobby*—orig t). D: Harry Hurwitz. SP: Harry Narunsky, Irving Schwartz, Tom Rudolph. Ph: J. Fernandes. Mus: Jay Chattaway. SpFX: Adams R. Calvert. Mkp: Cynthia Cruz. Ref: TV. TVG. V 5/22/85. With Peter Scolari, Colleen Camp, Christopher Lee, Fran Drescher, Monique Gabrielle, Eddie Deezen, Chuck McCann, Hamilton Camp.

Sydney (Deezen), humanoid from the planet Zorax, takes his summer vacation on Earth. Silly, forced sex-comedy. Deezen, though, has a funny monologue in which he describes the nature of comedy on Zorax. (It's a cross between the Three Stooges and George Romero.)

**ROSWELL** Showtime-TV/Viacom (Citadel Ent./Ilene Kahn) 1994 color 91m. Story, D, P: Jeremy Kagan. Story, SP: Arthur Kopit. Story: also Paul Davids. From the book *UFO Crash at Roswell* by K.D. Randle & D.R. Schmitt. Ph: Steven Poster. Mus: E. Goldenthal. PD: M. Hanan. Aliens: Steve Johnson. SpFxMkp: M. Rocchetti. SpVisFX: Fantasy II. SpFX: FTS. Ref: TV. TVG 7/30/94. With Kyle MacLachlan, Kim Greist, Martin Sheen, Dwight Yoakam, Xander Berkeley, Eugene Roche (Forrestal), Charles Martin Smith, Hoke Howell, Parley Baer, Arthur Hiller.

"This ain't ours." Cosmic mystery at Roswell, New Mexico, 1947: "writing from another planet," on possibly extraterrestrial "tinfoil" found scattered around a ranch ... a mysterious "second site" ... the presence of "four little boxes and one big one" ... glimpses of "fetus-shaped" bodies—"small, like children"—with lizard-like skin ... and an apparent survivor that communicates psychically.... Screenplay skillfully travels back and forth in time (between 1947 and 1987), as it weaves its tale of alien invasion and government cover-up. This might be *The Thing* as told by Oliver Stone or Alan J. Pakula. The alien face is quite convincing, but it's the U.S. government that's scary here. (Less convincing are top-level discussions of the reasons for a cover-up.) Memorable: the look on the face of the soldier who looks under the tarp. Sheen's Townsend is too obviously modeled on the Donald Sutherland character in Stone's *JFK,* and the script gets too ambitious near the end. It's best when it sticks to Roswell itself.

**ROTE LIPPEN** see *Case of the Two Beauties*

**ROTE OHREN SETZEN DURCH AFCHE** see *Flaming Ears*

**ROUGE** (H. K.) Golden Harvest/Paragon (Golden Way Films/Jackie Chan) 1987 (1988/'90-U.S.) color 96m. (*Yanzhi Kou.* aka *The Legend of Flower*). D: Stanley Kwan [Guan Jinpang or Kwan Kam Pang]. SP: Li Bihua, Qiu-Dai Anping [Qui Gangjian]. From Li Bihua's novel. Mus: Michael Lai [Li Xiaotian]. Ph: Bill Wong [Huang Zhongbiao]. SpMkp: Huang Jihong, Liu Jicheng. SdFX: Zheng Weixiong. Ref: TV: Rainbow Video; no Eng. FComment 6/88:52. MFB '90:31-3. V 2/24/88. London Film Fest '88. SFInt'l Film Fest. SFChron 9/5/90. Fango 107:59. PFA notes 3/17/89. With Anita Mui [Mei Yanfang] (Flower), Leslie Cheung, Emily Chu, Alex Man, Irene Wan.

A woman (Mui) appears to our modern-day hero, then promptly disappears. He panics and tries to flee her when, on a bus, she apparently reveals her identity: She is a ghost, victim of a double suicide in 1934.... Melancholic, straightforward, sweetly scored ghost story is too delicately nuanced, or plottily involved, to be comprehensible sans subtitles. Standout moments: the ghostly handkerchief falling in slow motion ... the ghost putting the hand of the hero's disbelieving girl friend (Chu) over her heart, and the woman's quietly frightened reaction. (Implication: She has no heartbeat.)

**ROUJIN-Z** see *Rojin Z*

**ROYAL SPACE FORCE** see *Wings of Oneamis*

**ROYAL TRAMP** (H.K.) Win's Movie Prods. 1991 color/ws feature. D: Wong Ching. Ref: TV: Tai Seng Video; Eng. titles.

Weisser/ATC. EVS. Imagi Smr'95:20. With Stephen Chow, Cheung Man.

Fantasy action-comedy features a neat "bone dissolved soft palm" trick which ends with the victim oozing away ... a witch who can elongate her fingers ... beheading-and-dismemberment-in-the-air ... and an old man whose body shoots darts.... Low, sometimes funny comedy plays like a Frank Tashlin version of *The Seven Samurai*. Fun effects finale.

**ROYAL TRAMP II** (H.K.) Win's Movie 1992 color feature. Ref: TV: Tai Seng Video; Eng. titles.

This time: a Spider Woman whose gown encircles her romantic "victim" and cocoons him in leaves ... golden "hula hoop" weapons ... Bone Melting Palm martial arts ... an acupuncture-like ploy in which needles are inserted into the head ... dangerous, whirling, flying half-moon blades ... and a gory death on the Dragon Wall statue's claws for the villain.... Funny scene: the Death Exemption Gold Medal. Also funny: a variation on the stateroom scene in *Night at the Opera*.

**Die RUECKKEHR DER ZEITMASCHINE** (W.G.) Telefilm Saar Film (Ulrich Nagel) 1984 color 116m. D: Juergen Klauss. Tel: Guenter Kunert. Ref: Ecran F 52:70: TV-movie? V 11/14/84: "claustrophobic." With Klaus Schwarzkopf, Peter Pasetti.

Dr. Beilowski discovers H. G. Wells' time machine.

**RUMIC WORLD** series see *Fire Tripper. Laughing Target, The. Mermaid Forest. Supergal*

**RUN ... IF YOU CAN!** Fleet Films/McCombie 1987 color 92m. D, P, Ed: Virginia Lively Stone. SP, Ph, P: J.A.S. McCombie. Mus: C. L. Stone. AD: Cory Kaplen. Ref: TV: THE Video. Hound. Martin. PT 2:32. With Martin Landau, Yvette Nipar, Jerry Van Dyke, Morgan Douglas, Tally Chanel, Sandy Berumen.

"This guy makes Jack the Ripper look like a nice friendly Great Dane." Law student Kim Page (Nipar) is house sitting in Westwood in a "kinda creepy" house when—through a "strange electronic anomaly"—her satellite dish picks up a "bogus signal," and she witnesses a video murder-in-progress on TV: It's the Lady Killer, live, who stuffs his victims into plastic bags.... Weak crossing of slasher and video-horror subgenres depends upon the denseness of both heroine and cops: She can't tell the difference between *The Snows of Kilimanjaro* and a homemade snuff movie; they aren't familiar with the arcane wonders of video playback.

**RUNAWAY** Tri-Star/Delphi III (Michael Rachmil) 1984 color/ws 100m. SP, D: Michael Crichton. Mus: Jerry Goldsmith. Robots: (des) David Durand; (sp fx) SpFxUnltd; Broggie Elliott Animation. Robotic Spiders: Robotic Systems Int'l. Ref: TV. V 12/12/84. SFExam 12/14/84. Maltin '92. Phantom. Hound. Stanley. Morse. Newman. Scheuer. With Tom Selleck, Cynthia Rhodes, Gene Simmons, Kirstie Alley, Stan Shaw, Chris Mulkey.

Luther (Simmons)—an "extremely unpleasant man"—modifies the commercial robots of the future with sophisticated microchips. His principal weapon: a semi-omniscient, multi-purpose robot with ray guns, an electromagnetic scanner suit, and a flying "floater camera".... *Phantom Creeps*-style gadgetry keeps things lively. Especially noteworthy: the small spider-like killer robots

spiked with acid. Selleck and the score, however, are unremarkable. Simmons has a slick Michael Ironside-style villain's sneer.

**RUNAWAY NIGHTMARE** Pepperbox Prods. (Eldon Short 1982 color c92m. SP, D: Michael Cartel. Ph: Dink Read. AD: J. C. Senter. SpFxMkp: Mari Cartel. OptFX: Getty. Ref: TV: All Seasons Ent. video. Hound. Martin. Scheuer. no Stanley. With Michael Cartel, Al Valletta, Sijtske Vandenberg, Cindy Donlan, Jody Lee Olhava, Cheryl Gamson.

Two "stupid bug farmers" at the Death Valley Insect and Worm Ranches run afoul of a "female desert cult" [sic], one member of which is into witchcraft. Another, Vampiria (Alexis Alexander), dresses and makes up like a vampire. At the end, a case of plutonium (this may or may not be the "experimental explosive device that ignites with air") explodes, radiation exposure gives cult members an "increased sexual appetite," and a "unique genetic disorder" turns bug-man Ralph (Cartel) into a vampire.

Apparently a comedy, *Runaway Nightmare* is certainly different. Unfortunately, writing, directing, and acting are indifferent. The movie's various eccentricities just hang there. For those who cultivate oddities.

**RUNAWAY ROBOTS** see *Romie-0 and Julie-8*

**The RUNESTONE** Hyperion Pictures & Signature (The Runestone Corp./H. E. Gould Jr., T. L. Wilhite) 1992 color 101m. SP, D: Willard Carroll, from M. E. Rogers' novella. Ph: Misha Suslov. Mus: David Newman. PD: Jon Gary Steele. SpMkpFX: Lance Anderson. SpVisFX: Max Anderson. Fenrir Des: Cary Howe, L. Anderson. Concep Des: Go Nagai. SpFxCoord: John Eggett. Opt: Cinemotion. Ref: TV. V 2/17/92. 5/6/91:C-82, C-84. SFChron Dtbk 2/23/92. With Peter Riegert, Joan Severance, William Hickey, Tim Ryan, Lawrence Tierney, Dawan Scott (Fenrir).

"Nothin'll stop that thing!" Magnusson Foundation-backed archaeologists find "cave man carvings" and "something big"—an ancient Norse runestone—in a Pennsylvania mine. ("Someone sometime must have really wanted this to stay buried.") The stone seems to "sense" what people "want most" and is apparently responsible for crossing foundation head Martin Almquist (Mitchell Laurance) with Fenrir, a big-clawed Norse beast which "becomes stronger every day".... Glossily trite production with glibly pretentious dialogue plays like Lovecraft in Manhattan. Hollow script borrows the "instant monster" effect from *Alien Factor*.

**RUNNING AGAINST TIME** USA-TV/MTE (Finnegan-Pinchuk/Coastline Partners) 1990 color c90m. D: Bruce Seth Green. Tel: Stanley Shapiro, from his book "A Time To Remember." Tel: also Robert Glass. Mus: Don Davis. PD: Barry Robison. Opt: CFI. Ref: TV. TVG. V 12/3/90:83-4. Maltin '92. With Robert Hays, Sam Wanamaker, Wayne Tippit, J. DiStefano, Catherine Hicks.

"There's something inevitable here!" A wild black comedy beckons, as hero David Rhodes (Hays) travels back in time—in Dr. Koopman's (Wanamaker) machine—to 1963, in order to prevent JFK's assassination: David is promptly (a) accused of the assassination himself, and (b) shot by Jack Ruby. Looked at from the right angle, this is pretty funny raw material. But the ambitious, uneven script is more intent on hero worship (JFK) and villain mongering (LBJ) than on comedy. The twin historical theses: JFK would have nipped the Vietnam War in the bud; LBJ, shown a future film of *The Johnson Years,* would simply have sped up and intensified said war. ("We're gonna win this war fast!") In effect, Koopman, who brings the filmstrip to LBJ, plays the Ghost of Christmas Future to LBJ's Scrooge, who remains unrepentant. History proves to be almost tamper-proof, but a touching coda (David saves his brother Chris from Vietnam) allows an exception for personal histories, if it does have a have-your-cake-and-eat-it-too feel.

**RUNNING BOY** (J) A.I.C. c1986? anim color 49m. Ref: TV: Shogakukan Video; no Eng.; OAV?

Two boys in an observatory-like building play a super-video-game, Star Soldier, as, in their spaceships, they battle other ships, space dragons, a giant head, and giant eyes. (A manufacturer is apparently testing a very advanced, beyond-video video game.) Earlier, one boy "sees" himself as a (visualized) space giant smashing satellites.... Pleasant, even quirkily imaginative sf video with some nice Japanese-coastal-town atmosphere.

**RUNNING DELILAH** Lifetime-TV 1994 color c90m. Ref: TVG: spy "restored to life with high-tech prostheses." With Kim Cattrall, Billy Zane.

The **RUNNING MAN** Tri-Star/Taft Ent.-Keith Barish Prods. (Linder-Zinnemann) 1987 color 100m. D: Paul Michael Glaser. SP: Stephen E. de Souza, from Stephen King's novel. Mus: Harold Faltermeyer. SpMkpFX: The Burmans. SpVisFxSup: Gary Gutierrez. SpFX: (coord) Larry Cavanaugh; (sup) Bruce Steinheimer. Ref: TV. V 11/11/87. ad. SFChron 11/13/87. SFExam 11/13/87. Maltin '92. Phantom. Hound. Scheuer. With Arnold Schwarzenegger, Maria Conchita Alonso, Richard Dawson, Yaphet Kotto, Jim Brown, Jesse Ventura, Gus Rethwisch, Dweezil Zappa, Prof. Toru Tanaka.

Police state 2017, the Wilshire Detention Zone. ICS Channel One's show "The Running Man" is intended to eliminate enemies of the state like Ben Richards (Schwarzenegger). But as a "runner," he bests all "stalkers," and the powers-that-be resort to "digital matte tracking" to concoct a deadly double of Richards.... Hollow, pop-sociology-heavy sf-er is glib blend of *The Most Dangerous Game,* the hokier contemporary game shows and ancient Roman gladiatorial games. Richards' flippant, ad-libbed quips ("What a hothead!") are on the same dim level as the show itself.

**RUPAN III: THE FUMA CONSPIRACY** see *Lupin III: Plot of the Wind Demon Clan*

**RUSH** (I) Cinema Shares Int'l./Biro (M. Romeo) 1984 color 77m. D: Tonino Ricci. SP: Tito Carpi. Mus: F. De Masi. Ref: V 10/31/84: "minor, highly derivative." Ecran F 37:57: Gel Int'l. Stanley: "super-chintzy." Palmerini: 1983. With Conrad Nichols, Gordon Mitchell, Laura Trotter, Rita Furlan.

Ten years after the nuclear holocaust. Follow-up: *Rage.*

**RUSH WEEK** Noble Ent. & Alpine Releasing (Leighton & Hilpert) 1989 color 94m. (aka *Rite Nite*). D: Bob Bralver. SP: Michael Leighton, Russell Manzatt. Mus: the Hamiltons. SpFX: Buckets O'Blood. SdFxSup: John K. Adams. Ref: TV. V 1/28/91:72(hv): RCA/Col HV. Martin. TVG. PT 9:12. V/Cannes '89:126. With Pamela Ludwig, Dean Hamilton, Courtney Gebhart, Gregg Allman, John Donovan (Arnold Krangen), Roy Thinnes, Kathleen Kinmont, Toni Lee.

"Death purifies." The dean's daughter is the first victim in a series of campus battle-axe murders, and the principal suspect is the "sick, perverted degenerate" Arnold, a cook who pays coeds to pose with corpses. The killer, of course: the one who calls Arnold a "sick, perverted degenerate." Contrary to the words of one character who says that this is "real life, not some stupid horror movie," this is a stupid horror movie.

**RYOKUNOHARA LABYRINTH** (J-Finnish?) A.I.C. c1990? anim color 39m. (aka *Sparkling Phantom*). Ref: TV: RCA Victor video; no Eng.

In a field of clocks, time comes to a stop. After a meteor shower, a space-traveling schoolhouse acts like a mobile planetarium for the students inside it. A young man run down by a truck has an out-of-body experience. Later (earlier?), apparently possessed, this young man nearly chokes the life out of his best friend. A nude phantom lady flits in and out of scenes.

Combination of the surreal and the insipid begins like an empty-headed paean to wide-eyed, androgynous youth, ends like outtakes from *Urusei Yatsura: Beautiful Dreamer.* The flashbacks-and-forwards, hallucinations, transformations, and apparitions make this film difficult to decipher. If the characters are, in appearance, conventional idealized Western figures, nothing else seems conventional here. Visually, the school-in-space sequence is the most impressive.

# S

**S. D. GUNDAM** (J) Bandai/Emotion (Sunrise) 1987 anim color 27-1/2m. (aka *Super Deformed Gundam*). D: Osamu Kanda. Based on the toys and on Gen Sato's comic "Robo Robo Company." Ref: TV: Bandai video; OAV; no Eng. Animag 3:3.

Two stories re an Earth-like "planet" within a space station, an astronaut on fly-swatter patrol in space, robots, space Olympics, and a giant spaceship. *Hellzapoppin*-in-fast-forward-and-outer-space has scads of Your-guess-is-as-good-as-mine bits. The second story is relatively disciplined, but it does throw in an armored robot in a bikini. The "punchlines" to many of the bits are in the Japanese dialogue.

See also titles under *Gundam 0083, Mobilesuit Gundam,* and the following.

**S. D. GUNDAM MK-II: THE ROLLING COLONY AFFAIR** (J) Bandai/Emotion (Sunrise) 1989 anim color 30m. (aka *Super Deformed Gundam 2*). Based on the Bandai toy line and on Gen Sato's comic "Robo Robo Company." Ref: TV: Bandai video; OAV; no Eng. Animag 3:3: parody of the original *Gundam.*

Space ships, ray guns, a space theatre which goes wildly off course, and a bit with a robot on a camel in Egypt. Frantic, mile-a-minute animation action-comedy looks hilarious and plays like a pint-sized version of the Lum movies: tiny, squat characters and comic aggression, frustration, elation, etc. Tape includes a second story (with no title in English).

**S. D. GUNDAM: THE HERO OF LA CROIX** (J) Bandai 1990 anim color 40m. Ref: Animag 10:5.

In medieval times, the S. D. Knight Gundam mecha take on the "evil forces of Satan Gundam."

**SF NEW ERA: THE LENSMAN** see *Lensman*

**S. S. HELL CAMP** (I?) Video City/Eterna Film 1977 ('85-U.S.) color 88m. (*La Bestia in Calore. Horrifying Experiments of SS Last Days* - alt vt t). D: Ivan Katansky. Ref: TV: Video City; Eng. dubbed; aka *SS Hell Camp*. MV: "genetic, mutant human beast." VWB: aka *S.S. Experiments, Part 2*; S. Boris = "Boris Lugosi" and plays subhuman. Martin: "cheap, incredibly gross Eurotrash stomach-turner." Hound. Palmerini: SP, D: Luigi Batzella. With Macha Magall, John Braun, Kim Gatti, Sal Boris, Xiro Papas.

"The fun's just beginning." Experimental Nazi serum is intended to "change the nature of a human being" and start a mutant master race; resultant mutant is mated with a virgin. Plus torture with rats, electrodes, and heat.... Probably the only Nazi atrocity movie which is also science fiction. Routine war scenes alternate with torture scenes. Things get pretty gross with the monster. Lots of "You disgust me!"

**SWF SEEKS SAME** see *Single White Female*

**SABBAH, THE MASK OF THE DEVIL** see *Maschera del Demonio, La*

**SACRED CYBER BEAST CYGUARD** see *Cybernetics Guardian*

**The SACRIFICE** (Swed-F-B) Orion Classics/Svenska Filminstitutet, Josephson & Nykvist, Sveriges TV, Sandrew Film & Teater/Argos Films/Film Four Int'l. (Farago Film) 1986 color and b&w 149m. (*Offret*). SP, D: Andrei Tarkovsky. Ph: Sven Nykvist. SpFX: Svenska Stuntgruppen; Lars Hoeglund, Lars Palmqvist. Mkp: Gustavsson, Fouquier. Ref: screen: Eng. titles. ad. MFB'87:7-8. V 5/14/86. Bay Guardian 2/25/87. SFExam 2/20/87. With Erland Josephson, Susan Fleetwood, Allan Edwall, Gudrun Gisladottir, Sven Wollter, Tommy Kjellqvist.

June 1985, the Swedish isle of Gotland. Lecturer and journalist Alexander (Josephson) is celebrating his birthday when apocalyptic shakings and roars herald the "ultimate war." There soon follow televised reports of general chaos, declarations of martial law, and warnings of missiles about to be launched. Alexander offers himself and his home to God if He will stop the war.

Tarkovsky's sweet, dippy fable is an anecdote told at movie-epic length. It plays appealingly in the mind after it's over, after its exasperating deliberateness has been forgotten. Occasionally, the director's long-shot, long-take method works lyrically and wittily: The long opening sequence (there are few short sequences in Tarkovsky), for instance, contrasts the quiet beauty of the green-and-brown countryside ("that house under the pines, so close to the sea") with the wanderings—physical and mental—of Alexander and his son (Kjellqvist). Tarkovsky here achieves the effect of counterpointed "voices": Alexander's and the Earth's; his chattering, its silence. The breeze which plays about in most of the exterior shots might be the film's soul.

Elsewhere, however, *The Sacrifice* is just chattering—much dialogue, little character. Otto (Edwall), a "collector" of inexplicable incidents ("284, to be exact"), a sort of hobbyist Rod Serling or John Newland, relates, at length—for instance—one of the incidents and discusses Nietzsche with Alexander, while Maria (Gisladottir), a "witch," talks (and talks) the distraught, pistol-wielding Alexander out of suicide. (Otto insists that if Alexander sleeps with Maria, the war will end.) The film's own "inexplicable incident"—the apparent divine intervention in the war—is the sweet calm at the center of a storm of words.

**The SADIST** (Fili) Asian Caltrade Corp. (Jose Maria San Agustin & V. A. Yujuico) 198-? color c35m. Story, D: Romy T. Espiritu. SP: Susan Espiritu. Ph: Edgar Padil. Mus & FX: Mahinder. AD: Rany Francisco, Arnold Villasis. Mkp: Fe Cotan. Ref: TV: ACC video. With Raul Espiradion (The Sadist), Ricky Rogers, Virginia Trece, Margie Perez, Gina Mumar, Sunshine, Bella Ramirez.

A little bit of sleaze from the Philippines. The unprepossessing, charmless Sadist takes sexy women out, strangles them. At the end, a would-be victim spears him in the neck with a sharp-pointed umbrella.... Very, very cheap videotaped junk shot in Tagalog. No English subtitles, except for a postscript which informs us that "crime doesn't pay."

**SADISTEROTICA** see *Case of the Two Beauties*

**SAGA OF ERIK THE VIKING, The** see *Erik the Viking*

**SAGA OF THE PHOENIX** (H.K.) Golden Harvest (Paragon) 1989 color c90m. D: Nam Nai-Choi. Ref: TV: Rainbow Video; no Eng. Weisser/ATC: sequel to *Peacock King*. With Yuen Biao.

In the preliminary bout, the heroine brings down a huge fireball from the sky to destroy a horde of zombies and some stone, fanged demons which come to (rubbery) life. Later, the evil witch queen ray-freezes the hero and "irradiates" the cute gremlin-type which pals around with the heroine. The now-nasty gremlin breathes in one girl's soul, takes a flushing-toilet stream back to the queen, and breathes the soul out to her. In the climactic sequence, the queen becomes part of a monstrous, gigantic, winged creature which shoots deadly skulls and rays and takes on the three protagonists, who become parts of a phoenix.

Lively and colorful, if not exactly inspired children's fantasy. The "gremlin" is sometimes a rubber toy, sometimes crude but amusing stopmo animation. Ace effect: the gremlin's foe seen reflected in its eyes.

**SAINT ELMO** (B) Capitol/Syndicate 1923 silent 74m. SP, D: Rex Wilson, from A.J. Evans' novel. Ref: BFC. With Shayle Gardner, G. Gilroy.

Widow's son possessed by the devil.

**Les SAISONS DU PLAISIR** (F) AFC, Canal+, FR3 Films (Maurice Bernart) 1988 color 88m. SP, D: Jean-Pierre Mocky.

Mus: Gabriel Yared. Ref: V 2/17/88: "performances from a large name cast are film's principal saving grace." With Charles Vanel, Bernadette Lafont, Jean-Luc Bideau, Fanny Cottencon, Stephane Audran, Darry Cowl, Jean-Claude Romer.

Nuclear power plant accident devastates Earth. *The Seasons of Pleasure*-tr t.

**SAKURA NO MORI NO MANKAI NO SHITA** (J) 1975. D: Masahiro Shinoda. Ref: Cult Movies 13:80: *Under the Cherry Blossoms* - tr t? Weisser/JC: "amazingly effective." With T. Wakayama, S. Iwashita.

"Beautiful woman ... turns out to be a murdering demon."

**SALAMANDER** (J) Konami/Studio Pierrot 1988 anim color c55m. D: Toriumi Nagayuki. SP: Hisashima Kasusane, from the video game. Des: (character) Mikimoto; (mecha) Moriki Tatsuharu. Ref: TV: vt; no Eng. Animag 11:15: OAV. 5:5. 3:6.

Statuary apparently imported from Easter Island, a fire-breathing dragon, and a "cyberbrain" all figure in the battle between the planet Lattice and the Bacterian-held Salamander planet. Mostly talk, but the scattered action-fantasy scenes are impressively animated. The Japanese title forms out of the dragon's fire. Okay score.

**SALAMANGKERO** (Fili) Aces Film/Films Int'l. (Duran-Esteban) 1986 color c115m. (*Salamangkero the Magician* - ad t). Story, SP, D: Tata Esteban. SP: also Grace Hill Serrano; Ricardo Lee. Assoc D: Miguel Eduardo. Concept: Rare Breed. Ph: Joe Tutanes. Mus: Rey Ramos. PD: Arthur Nicdao, Dante Mendoza. SpVisFX & Creatures: Maurice Carvajal. SpFX: Jun Marbella. SpMkp: Len Santos. Sd: (des) Vocal Warlocks; (fx) R. Capule. Ref: TV: Viva Video; no Eng. With Michael De Mesa (Prof. Jamir/Lolo Omar), Tanya Gomez, Armida S. Reyna (Mikula), Liza Lorena (Kleriga), Gina Alajar, Odette Khan, Tom Tom, Dick Israel, Ruben Rustia, Sunshine, Rene Johnson (Tumok), Turko Cervantes, Nonong De Andres (Akay), Ricky Sujede (swamp creature).

Professor Jamir, "the great magician," flops and goes to a local witch doctor for tips. During his next countryside performance, he makes almost everyone, including the audience, disappear into another dimension, where witch-queen Mikula—who likes to cage children and whose forehead percolates bubbles—rules. The what-was-that? inhabitants and decor of her realm include Globo, a living "TV" creature who turns up at the end, in the real world, as a self-opening Christmas present singing "Jingle Bells" ... a monster-rock-band with skull and bone instruments ... horned drooling monsters ... and good witch Kleriga, who can shoot eye-rays and who uncages the children.

In terms of the pacing or structuring of individual scenes, *Salamangkero* isn't exactly cinematic. It is, however, very good-natured and inventive. This hip, charming monster-fantasy has a touch of Muppets, a touch of *Jedi*, but is, in the main, pretty distinctive. An air of insouciance prevails in scenes in which various loathsomes stand around Mikula's court chatting, sit about eating sloppily, and play or listen to music. These monsters know how to have fun. At one point, when strange dwarfs capture the magician and his assistant, Jamir/Salamangkero uses real magic to escape, but returns and, with more familiar stage-magic,

wins over this new audience. Monsters from this story, or dimension, wander into the real-world, Christmastime coda and begin to make themselves at home: Even at fade-out, the party's not over.

**SALEM'S GHOST** A-Pix/Vista Street 1996 (1994) color feature. SP, D: J.J. Barmettler Jr. Ref: vc box: evil warlock. With L. Grober, K. Kopf.

**SALEM'S LOT** see *Return to Salem's Lot, A*

**SALUTE OF THE JUGGER, The** see *Blood of Heroes, The*

**SALVAGE** Col-TV 1979 color c90m. D: Lee Philips. Tel: Mike Lloyd Ross. Ph: Fred Koenekamp. Ref: TV. Lentz. TVG. V 1/24/79. With Andy Griffith, Trish Stewart, Joel Higgins, Richard Jaeckel, Peter Brown, Lee De Broux.

Pilot for the "Salvage-1" TV series concerns a plot to salvage $14 million in equipment left by Apollo 16 astronauts at Serenity Base in the lunar highlands.

**SALVAGE-1: GOLDEN ORBIT** Col-TV & Bennett-Katleman 1979 color 61m. D: Ron Satlof. Tel: Robert Swanson. Created by & Sup P: Mike Lloyd Ross. Ph: G. P. Finnerman, Joseph Jackman. Mus: Walter Scharf. Ref: TV. Lentz: two TV shows spliced together. TVG. With Andy Griffith, Joel Higgins, Richard Jaeckel, Barry Nelson, Ellen Bry, Gary Swanson.

A private company with a homemade rocket attempts to salvage a gold-coated communications satellite. ("Biggest golden nugget I've ever seen!") Unremarkable TV-movie features suspense, pathos, and that staple of Fifties sf movies, a meteor shower. At the end, the rocket makes an emergency landing in farm country, and the cry goes up, "Martians!"

**SALVAGE 1: HARD WATER** Col-TV 1979 color c70m. Ref: TVG. Lentz: 2 TV shows stitched together. With Andy Griffith, Richard. Dix, Joel Higgins, Bert Freed, Warren Kemmerling, Frank Campanella.

Junkman tries to tow Antarctic icebergs to a "drought-stricken island."(TVG)

**SAMURAI** 1979 color c90m. D: Lee H. Katzin. Tel: Jerry Ludwig. Ref: Stanley: routine TV-movie. Scheuer. With Joe Penny, James Shigeta, Charles Cioffi, Geoffrey Lewis, Dana Elcar, Beulah Quo.

"Supersonic device" starts earthquakes. (Stanley)

**SAMURAI REINCARNATION** see *Ninja Incarnation*

**SAMWONNYO** (S. Korean) Yun Bang Films (Choi Choon Joi) 1981 color 80m. D: Kim Si Hyun. SP: Lee Chung Keun. Ph: Shin Myung Ui. Ref: Hardy/HM: "traditional melodramatic plot"; *The Valley of Ghosts*—tr t? With Lee Ye Min, Choi Hyo Sun.

In Manchuria, a "horde of ... local ghosts" besets the wealthy.

**SAMY—MISSING-99** (J) c1988? anim color 58m. Ref: TV: vt; no Eng.; OAV?

Ingredients include a horned wizard and his monster aides ... a skeleton which pulls a girl into another dimension inhabited by (among other things) a dinosaur-dragon ... a fiery wraith-demon ... a witch-type in a two-legged-walker-type spaceship who turns into a huge dragon ... a land of crystal mountains ... and, most surprising of all, a horde of kooky but initially quite threatening ghosts—of all sizes, up to Godzilla—who chase the heroine. Most of this horror-fantasy is pretty standard, if colorful; the ghosts, though, are a jolly, weird bunch, and apparently can be rented for Halloween.

**SAND WARS** see *Desert Warrior*

The **SANDLOT** Fox & Island World (de la Torre, Gilmore) 1993 color 101m. SP, D: David Mickey Evans. SP: also Robert Gunter. SpFX: Cliff Wenger. VisFx:(sup): Richard Yuricich; Computer Film Co. Digital Opt: Digital Magic. CreatureFX: Rick Lazzarini. Opt: Howard Anderson. Ref: TV: vt. Mo. Martin. V 4/5/93: "shallow"; "mythically feral junkyard dog." EBay Guardian 6/4/93: "legendary, monstrous dog." TVG 10/23/93: "The Beast," a "mostly unseen creature so scary that...." With Tom Guiry, Karen Allen, James Earl Jones, Art LaFleur (The Babe), Maury Wills.

"I think we've seriously underestimated The Beast." Time and imagination transform a big, mean junkyard dog, "old Hercules," into a monstrous, "giant gorilla-dog thing." In one sequence, The Legend of the Beast is illustrated, mock-horror style.... Not wholly successful, but stylistically ambitious tall-tale telling. Episodic, Stephen King-ish story employs visual and verbal hyperbole fairly well and features a clip from *The Wolf Man* (1941).

The **SANDMAN** (B) Paul Berry anim 10m. Ref: 24th Int'l. Tournee of Animation leaflet. SFChron 12/24/93: "a powerful send-up on a 'bumps in the night' scare theme."

La **SANGUISUGA CONDUCE LA DANZA** (I) 1975 color feature (aka *Il Marchio di Satana*) SP,D: Alfredo Rizzo. Mus: M. Giombini. Ref: Palmerini: "poor." With Femi Benussi, P. De Rossi, L. Pigozzi.

Castle legend re decapitation. "The Bloodsucker Conducts the Dance" - tr t.

**SANTA SANGRE** (I) Expanded Ent./Intersound (Claudio Argento/Rene Cardona Jr., Angelo Iacono) 1989 ('90-U.S.) color 123m. (118m.). Story, SP, D: Alejandro Jodorowsky. SP: also Roberto Leoni, C. Argento. Ph: D. Nannuzzi. Mus: Simon Boswell. PD: Alejandro Luna. SpFxSup: M. Pacheco Guzman. MkpSup: L. Marini. Tattoo Des: Sergio Arau. Ref: TV: Republic HV; Eng. dubbed. MFB'90:117-18. V 5/31/89: "ultimate Oedipus complex tale about a madman who becomes the arms of his mutilated mother." ad. V 10/11/89:26: *Holy Blood*—tr t. Sacto Bee 6/15/90: "an arty slasher movie." With Axel Jodorowsky, Blanca Guerra, Guy Stockwell, Thelma Tixou, Sabrina Dennison.

"Holy blood!" Garish ingredients here include dead-elephant-part flinging ... tattoo fu ... an oddly easy double-arm-severing ... acid flinging ... incidental ear gore ... some pretty graphic, bloody slashings ... Concha and Her Magic Hands (see above) ... a

bloody, literally hypnotic knife act ... painting-the-corpse-in-the-grave scenes ... a vision of massing chickens ... the Phantom Mom, and others ("I'm inside of you!") ... a Mom dummy ... and Mom, pickled.... Symbiosis, anyone? Poaching in Fellini, or maybe Bunuel, territory, Jodorowsky comes up with a sort of Oedipal *Hands of Orlac,* or, from another angle, a more literal *Psycho* re the Hand of Mom, which slashes "rivals" for her son. (With the Vanishing, All-in-the-Mind Mom sequence, however, the script gets even closer to *Psycho.*) Yet another "fix": the Chaney silent re human limbs, *The Unknown.* Film has undeniably outre imagery, but seems, overall, derivative—Camp at best. The son's hallucination re the rising, white-veiled corpses of his victims is neat, eerie-lyrical Mario Bava. At one point, he watches the original *Invisible Man* on TV and imitates Claude Rains.

**SANTO CONTRA EL ASESINO DE LA T.V.** (Mex) Cinematografica RA/Producciones Geminis 1980 color c85m. SP, D, P: Rafael Perez Grovas. Story: David Sergio, Carlos Suarez. Ph: Alfredo Uribe. Mus D: R. Carrion. Mkp: Estela Sanchez. Ref: TV. Horacio Higuchi. With "Santo," Gerardo Reyes, Rubi Re, Carlos Agosti, Nelson Juarez.

Super-criminal's super-TV apparatus interrupts regularly scheduled programs and won't let viewers turn off their sets. Wisp of a plot is a pretext for poorly-photographed musical numbers and wrestling matches.

See also *Cerebro del Mal. Puno de la Muerte* and the following.

**2P SANTO CONTRA EL DOCTOR MUERTE** (Sp-Mex) Pelimex 1974 color/ws 96m. SP, D: Rafael Romero Marchent. SP: also J.L.N. Basso. Ph: G. Pacheco. Mus: G.G. Segura. AD: J.P. Cubero. SpFX: Amobaq. Mkp: M. Garcia. Ref: TV. V 5/8/74:207. TVG. Hardy/SF. With Santo, Helga Line, Jorge Rigaud, Carlos Romero Marchent, Mirta Miller, Frank Brana.

Mad doctor "injects his models with a tumor-producing virus which, once removed from their dead bodies, yields a chemical substance that allows him to achieve perfect reproductions of famous paintings."(H/SF) Plus an acid pit, underground gas and torture chambers, and a jar of scorpions. Unsophisticated mixture of shocks and wrestling.

**SANTO EN LA FURIA DE LOS KARATECAS** see *Puno de la Muerte, El*

**SANTO VS. EL CEREBRO DEL MAL** see *Cerebro del Mal*

**SANTO VS. LAS LOBAS** (Mex) Hermanos 1974 color c80m. D: Jaime Jimenez Pons, Ruben Galindo. Ph: Raul Dominguez, Victor Gaitan. Mkp: Irene Bustos, Antonio Ramirez. Ref: TV. Horacio Higuchi. TVG. no Hardy/HM. no Stanley. no Lentz. With "Santo," Rodolfo De Anda, Gloria Mayo, Jorge Rus(s)ek, Nubia Marti, Carlos Suarez, Bruno Rey, F. Falcon, Erika Carlson.

Dr. Cameron's dream—in *The Mad Monster* (1942)—of an "army of wolf-men" comes true in *Santo Vs. las Lobas,* though there seem to be more wolf-women here than wolf-men. They even have a "queen" or two, plus a "king," imported from Transylvania. Horror is indiscriminately piled upon horror, as the wolf-people invade a dinner party. The action never lets up for longer than half a minute, though the movie has the casual, sloppy look and sound of a videotaped production. The wolves' night-time ceremonies are a riot of hair, flames, and shadows. A messy movie ... terrible even ... but not dull.

**SAPORE DI PAURA** see *Obsession*

**SARU NO GUNDAN** see *Time of the Apes*

**The SATAN CAT** (H.K.?) 1985 color c95m. Ref: TV: Da Chi Movie & TV video; no Eng.

The first part (of five) of an apparent made-for-video series, this undistinguished horror-comedy concerns a supernatural cat which breathes life into a woman's body. The latter, possessed and fanged, immediately proceeds to stalk human prey. In the most unusual scene, a witch woman is absorbed into a tree.

**SATAN PLACE** 1993? color feature. Ref: SFChron Dtbk 3/14/93: "my kinda movie." With Stephanie Spencer, Lisa Hatter, Sonja Etzel.

Horror anthology re zombies, slashers, demons, etc.

**SATANA CONTRA DR. EXORTIO** see *Dracula Vs. Dr. Frankenstein*

**SATANIC ATTRACTION** (Braz.) J. Davila Ents. 1990 color feature. SP, D: Fauzi Mansur. SP: also Filipe Grecco, P. J. Davila. Ref: vc trailer (with *Ritual of Death*). PT10:47.

Spear, hatchet, knife ultra-gore, in travelogue settings.

**2P SATANICO PANDEMONIUM** (Mex) Hollywood Films & Promocion Turistica Mexicana 1975? color c90m. (*La Sexorcista*—alt t ?). SP, D: Gilberto Martinez Solares. Story: Jorge Barragan. Ph: Jorge Stahl Jr. Mus D: G. C. Carrion. Ref: TV: Spanish Video Sound video; no Eng. Bianco Index '75. Cinef 6/96:46. With Enrique Rocha, Cecilia Pezet, Delia Magana, Laura Montalvo, Veronica Avila, Daniel Alberto, Veronica Rivas.

A stranger, who proves to be the devil, tempts a nun with an apple, which gives her visions of demonic portraits, snakes in drinking cups, and gory tortures. Possessed, she attempts to seduce a teenage boy, but when he tries to scream, she stabs him to death, and he transforms into his mother, or aunt. The nun's hands begin to smoke, then the whole convent-ful of debauched nuns (including one who had been hanged) slashes the mother superior to death.... Some camp value in this obscure, sensationalistic chronicle of determinedly decadent behavior. Comically steamy, intense horror-fantasy seems influenced by both *The Devils* and *The Exorcist*.

**SATANISTA** see *Regal Shockers*

**SATAN'S BLADE** M.C. Prods. 1982 color c85m. Story, D, Exec P: L. Scott Castillo Jr. SP: Thomas Cue. Ph: Terry Kempf. Mus & Ed: Martin Jaquish. Mkp: Paul Batson. Ref: TV: Prism Ent. video. HR 10/25/83:S-12. Peter Zirschky. Hound. Stanley. Phantom. no Martin. V 5/9/84:259(ad). With Tom Bongiorno, Stephanie Leigh Steel, Cue, Elisa R. Malinovitz, Janeen Lowe, Richard Taecker (dream monster), Ski Mark Ford (George), Rick Hardin (Mountainman's hand in lake).

"The evil spirits of these mountains" come to the aid of a "mountain man whose spirit still roams" and who has become a "monster of death" haunting a lake. Now, fourteen years after his last appearance, he possesses a cop, George, who slashes various vacationers.... Drearily formulaic, stilted slasher movie. The killer's victims die ludicrously "dramatic" deaths.

**SATAN'S BLOOD** (Sp) Cinevision & Almena (Francisco Ariza) 1977 color/ws c86m. (*Escalofrio*). Story, D: Carlos Puerto. SP: Eva Del Castillo. Ph: Andres Berenguer. Mus: Librado Pastor. Mkp: Carmen Martin, M. C. Sanchez. Exec P: Juan Piquer Simon. Ref: TV: All American Video; Eng. dubbed. vc box: MGS Video: Sp.-Lang. version. McCarty II. Stanley. no Hardy/HM. no Phantom. no Martin. no Hound. PT 5:12. VWB: *Don't Panic* - alt vt t. With Angel Aranda, Sandra Alberti, Marian Karr, Jose Maria Guillen, Manuel Pereiro, Luis Bar-Boo, Jose Pagan.

Satanic rituals at a country estate are a pretext for sexy scenes, as Andy and Annie, a mesmerized young couple, join hosts Bruno and Mary in an impromptu orgy. Bruno and Mary kill themselves, then come back from the dead, and Andy and Annie have to kill them again. At the end, the satanists stab the two newcomers to death, but, in a coda, Andy and Annie are recruiting potential new devil-worshippers.... Much nudity and speaking in tongues, plus a nightmare re a living, bloody-mouthed doll. Little in the way of story sense or logic.

**SATAN'S CHILDREN** SWV 1974 color feature. D: Joe Wiezycki. Ref: vc box: satanists, beheadings. With S. White.

**SATAN'S PRINCESS** Sun Heat Pictures (H. G. Plitt) 1990 (1989) color 90m. (*Heat from Another Sun. Princess of Darkness. Malediction* - shooting ts). D, P: Bert I. Gordon. SP: Stephen Katz. Mus: Norman Mamey. MkpFX: David B. Miller. SpFX: (coord) Kevin McCarthy; (equipment) Players. Ref: TV. V 1/14/91. Hound. Martin. PT 8:45. V 3/28/90:29 (rated, as MALEDICTION). With Robert Forster, Lydie Denier, Caren Kaye, Phillip Glasser, M. K. Harris (Dorian), Ellen Geer, Jack Carter, Marilyn Joi, Nick Angotti, Leslie Huntly.

"I am your worst nightmare!" A priest's painting, "The Malediction," and a tattoo symbolic of "death and destruction among early 17th Century religious orders" figure in the mystery surrounding Nicole St. James (Denier) of the Nicole Modeling Agency. Seems she is 500 years old and has claimed over a thousand victims, for unclear reasons. At one point, she uses voodoo to possess the detective hero's (Forster) son (Glasser), who stabs his father with an ice pick. Later, she uses voodoo to kill a psychic (Geer). Nebulous, effectless mixture of the supernatural, sex, and sentiment.

**SATAN'S STORYBOOK** Even Steven 1989 color 85m. D: Michael Rider. SpMkpFX: A. Showe. Ref: vc box: 3 tales re monsters, magic. With Ginger Lynn Allen, Gary Brandner.

**SATIN VENGEANCE** see *Naked Vegeance*

**SATISFIERS OF ALPHA BLUE** see *Return to Alpha Blue*

**SATSUJIN GA IPPAI** see *Lots of Killing*

**SATURDAY ISLAND** see *Island of Desire*

**SATURDAY NIGHT LIVE** see *Coneheads*

**SATURDAY THE 14TH STRIKES BACK** Concorde/Pacific Trust (Julie Corman) 1988 color 78m. SP, D: Howard Cohen. Mus: Parmer Fuller. SpVisFX: John Lambert; Microgravity. SpMkp: Rob Hinderstein, Terry Lynn. MkpFX: A. T. Showe. SpFX: Wizard Works; (d) Mark Wolf. Dedicated to the memory of Bob Greenberg. Ref: TV. V 6/28/89. With Jason Presson, Ray Walston, Avery Schreiber, Patty McCormack, Peter Frankland (Burke), Pamela Stonebrook (vampire), Joseph Ruskin (Kharis), Leo V. Gordon (The Evil One), Michael Berryman (the mummy), Phil Leeds, Tommy Hall (werewolf).

"There's weird things moving into this house!" The forces of evil escape into the world through cracks in the Earth's surface and offer young Eddie Baxter (Presson)—"cosmic wimp"—the chance to become the Master of the World for 10,000 years. He kind of likes making household members do his bidding, but ultimately refuses the offer.... Limp horror-comic sequel to *Saturday the 14th* and variation on *The Man Who Could Work Miracles*.

**SATURDAY'S ISLAND** see *Island of Desire*

**SAU SAAL BAAD** (India - Hindi) Aarti Pictures 1989 color c130m. D: Mohan Bhakri. SP: J. K. Ahuja. Dial: Anil Pandit. Ph: Arvind Bhakri. Mus: Annu Malik. SpHorrorMkp: Shree Niwas Rai. SpFX: Bhupendrabhai Patel. Ref: Bombino Video; little Eng. With Hemant Birje, Sahila Chadha, Joginder, Narinder Nath, Huma Khan, Shobhni Singh, Mayur, Poonamdas Gupta, Raza Murad, Amjad Khan, Danny Denzongpa.

Ingredients in this apparent updating of the 1967 *So Saal Baad* (I): a sorcerer who, revived, summons up a big hairy monster ... zombies ... monster moss, or vines ... a fiery swamp ... blinking-eyed skulls ... and a (visualized) nightmare re monsters. At the end, a cobra bites the sorcerer, the latter dies, and the hairy monster fades away.

Unsophisticated mixture of horror, action, and music. The all-stops-out horror scenes, though awkward, are enthusiastically choreographed and edited. If the presence of the zombies seems to indicate a Western influence, the duel between the sorcerer and a holy man suggests a Far Eastern influence. Funniest effect (unintentionally): the cartoon-animated, severed zombie arm still clutching its victim's leg.

**SAVAGE FURY** see *Call of the Savage, The*

**SAVAGE INTRUDER** Unicorn Video/Avco Embassy 1975 90m. (2P *Hollywood Horror House* - orig t). D: Donald Wolfe. Ref: Stanley: homicidal maniac. Martin. V 1/15/75:5(rated). With Miriam Hopkins, John David Garfield, Gale Sondergaard.

**SAVAGE LUST** (U.S.-Sp?) AIP/Films around the World(Castor Films & Filmworld Int'l./Smedley-Aston & Somolinos) 1991(1989) color 86m. (aka *Deadly Manor*). SP, D: Jose Ramon Larraz. Ph: Tote Trenas. Mus: Cengiz Yaitkaya. PD: N.B. Dodge, Jr. SpFxMkp: Boaz Stein. SpMaskFX: Timothy Considine. SpPh: Jami Bassman. Ref: TV: AIP HV. Fango 123:12. V 5/2/90:80. 10/15/90:M-88(ad). Stanley. With Clark Tufts, Greg Rhodes, Claudia Franjul, Mark Irish, Jennifer Delora (Amanda), William Russell (Alfred).

"This house scares me!" Scare ingredients here include a "major weird" shrine in an abandoned car ("that damn car!") outside an "evil house" ... a collection of scalps (in the house) ... a skulking slasher ... a "woman with a mask on ... like an illusion" ... and (behind the mask) the disfigured, homicidal Amanda ("I was beautiful once").... Gorecard: tiresome people, vapid plotting, atmospheric details, and an okay crumbling-wall stunt.

**SAVIOR** (H.K.) 1984? color feature. D: Ronny Yu. Ref: Weisser/ATC. With Bai Ying.

Madman who "enjoys slicing up prostitutes."

**SAVIOUR OF THE SOUL** (H. K.) Team Work 1991 color/ws 93m. (aka *Terrible Angel*). D: Corey Yuen, with David Lai. Ref: TV: Pan-Asia Video; Eng. titles. SFChron 4/24/93. Weisser/ATC. Imagi Smr'95:21. With Anita Mui, Aaron Kwok, Andy Lau.

Ingredients in this fantasy-romance-adventure include smart-missile-like knives ... apparent android prison guards ... a man, Fox, who can physically pass through other people ... a little slowmo gore ... the "greatest invention of the century," the "breathless bullet" ... and characters with various flying and telepathic powers.

Is it style or affectation? Exciting fantastic-action sequences alternate here with tiresome romantic-triangle passages. One candidate for Best Effect: Fox trapped in the mirror. Finalist in the Weird Comedy category: the scene in which the woman thinks she's picking up the ringing phone, but is actually picking up a hot steam iron.

**SAVIOUR OF (THE) SOUL II** (H. K.) Team Work 1992 color/ws 92m. Ref: TV: Tai Seng Video; Eng. titles.

Easier-to-take Part II features a doctor's "super microscope" invention, which not only magnifies—it increases the size of the object magnified and yields probably the most bizarre game of pool on film ... the King of Evil, a "cruel monster" whose "jesters" at one point tumble out en masse from tubes like those used in airport boarding areas ... Essence Air, which seems to revive and rejuvenate users ... our heroine, who at one point enters our hero's dream to wake him up and save him from freezing to death ... and our hero, who dreams of this same woman every night of his life.

The movie's meant-to-be-mind-boggling inventiveness occasionally does impress, but a basic mechanicalness of conception circumscribes the fun. Hero Ching Yan's real and dream deaths and resurrections get monotonous, and there are a few too many lyrical musical interludes. Highlight: Ching Yan carving his Dream Lady out of Virgin's Ice and imagining her coming to life and drawing him to her with her garment. Cute: his sidekick accidentally emerging from the phone booth in Superman costume. Thrilling: our hero walking across the path of flying swords, in the first dream sequence.

**SAYONARA, JUPITER** see *Bye-Bye, Jupiter*

**SCANNER COP** Republic/Image & Starlight 1993 color 94m. Story, D, P: Pierre David. SP: George Saunders, John Bryant. Based on the characters created by David Cronenberg. Ph: Jacques Haitkin. Mus: Louis Febre. PD: Deborah Raymond, Dorian

Vernacchio. SpMkp & Creature FX: MMI; John Carl Buechler;(stopmo) Tony Doublin. MechSpFX: Steve Patino's SPFX. Ref: TV: Republic video. With Daniel Quinn, Darlanne Fluegel, Richard Grove, Luca Bercovici, Brion James, Richard Lynch, Hilary Shepard (Zena), Starr Andreeff.

Belated follow-up to *Scanners* features not only scanners, but serum-created assassins "imprinted with the command to kill." ("*Manchurian Candidate!*" Actually, more *Young Sherlock Holmes*.) One assassin sees an hallucinatory ghoul; another, an alienish horror ("a huge insect"). Some okay exploitation of the subject here, as scanning goes Law and Order. Predictable, derivative plot. Neatest super-law-enforcement trick: the scanner-enhanced computer sketch of evildoer Richard Lynch. Neatest makeup effect: the little heads bumping out of one scanner's forehead, a psychological variation on a Freddy effect. Second-neatest makeup effect: the flesh melting away and revealing the plate in Lynch's head.

**SCANNER COP II: VOLKIN'S REVENGE** see *Scanners: The Showdown*

**SCANNERS II: THE NEW ORDER** (Can.) Triton (Image Org.)/Malofilm & Allegro & Filmtech 1991 (1990) color 104m. D: Christian Duguay. SP: B. J. Nelson. Mus: Marty Simon. SpMkpFX: Mike Smithson's Shadowworks; (prosth) Mike Maddi; (mech fx) Ralph Miller III, Steve Frakes. Physical FX: Cineffects; (coord) Ryal Cosgrove. OptFxSup: Langlois, Provost. SdFxDevel: Hutton, Ryckman. Ref: TV. V 5/6/91. 11/29/89:26. With David Hewlett, Yvan Ponton, Deborah Raffin (Julie), Isabelle Mejias, Raoul Trujillo (Peter Drak), Tom Butler, Dorothee Berryman, Vlasta Vrana.

"There are others like you." Dr. Morse (Butler)—a specialist in the "study of scanners" and head of the Morse Neurological Research Institute—wants a "clean scanner" with a "virgin mind"—psychopaths like Peter Drak prove uncontrollable. Morse finds a subject in David Kellum (Hewlett), a perfect "radio receiver" who picks up the thoughts of others and who can project his own.

Tired evil-masterminds/exploited-subjects themes, predictable pathos, gratuitous forehead and telekinetically-flung-body effects, and a finale cribbed from *Rocket Man*—but here scanners (not a "truth gun") make the politico tell the truth. First sequel to *Scanners* is only for those who enjoy seeing actors grimace and contort their faces.

**SCANNERS III: THE TAKEOVER** (Can.) Republic/Malofilm 1992 color 101m. D: Christian Duguay. SP: B. J. Nelson, Julie Richard, David Preston, Rene Malo. Mus: Marty Simon. SpMkp: Mike Maddi. SpFxSup?: Louis Craig. Ref: TV. V 2/10/92. With Liliana Komorowska, Valerie Valois, Steve Parrish, Collin Fox, Daniel Pilon.

"I have a headache." Third entry in the series introduces miracle-drug patches-for-scanners which are activated by "trace molecular elements found only in scanners" and which supposedly offer quick pain relief, but succeed mainly in unleashing rage. (A lift from another David Cronenberg film, *The Brood*.) An anti-scanning ray and a *Halloween 3*-like plot to brainwash via TV come into weak play before an ending in which the spirit of the main scanner (Komorowska) enters videoland.... Occasional glib clev-

erness, plus silly novelties, like an underwater scanners duel and revolving-door splatter (made possible by, a) centrifugal force and, b) scanning).

**SCANNERS: THE SHOWDOWN** (Can.) Image & Republic (Pierre David) 1994 color c95m. (aka *Scanner Cop II: Volkin's Revenge*). D: S. Barnett. SP: M. Sevi. SpMkpFX: J.C. Buechler. Ref: vc box. PT 21:72: "better than average." With D. Quinn, Patrick Kilpatrick (serial-killer scanner), K. Haie, S. Mendel, Robert Forster.

**The SCARE GAME** Tempe (Stanze-Shepherd-Bradley-Biondo) 1992 color c60m. Story, SP, D, Ph, Ed, SpFxDes: Eric Stanze. Story: also Vivona. Mus: Brian McClelland, T. Lowe. Ref: TV: Tempe Video; co-feature with *The Fine Art*. Bill Warren. With D.J. Vivona (the game demon), Michael Bradley, Don Shaffer, Jennifer Sweeney, Grant Twidwell (voice of Game Lord).

"The game never died." The Game Lord assigns a demon to conduct the ages-old game of "collecting souls." During the latest playing, the demon pours out his guts, literally, and messes up his face.... Chaotic, isn't it? Technically weak short horror feature has a very predictable ending. ("You shall take his place.")

**\*\*SCARE THEIR PANTS OFF!** Distribpix(Ronald Sullivan) 1968 b&w 75m. (aka *He Scared the Girls off*). SP, D, Ed: John Maddox. Ph: Arthur Marks. AD: John Wendell. Ref: TV: SWV. With Jon Woods, Mary St. Feint, Sean Laney, Alou Mitsou, Claire Adams.

"Seven years ago, I was killed in the crash of an airplane." A man supposedly suffering a "living death" removes his iron mask to reveal a *Horror Castle* face ("You haven't seen my face") and almost scares a young lady to death. He then takes off the horror mask. This is just the first in a series of three, increasingly wearying, avant garde-ish charades ....

**The SCARECROW** (F) Ladislas Starevitch 1921 stopmo & live action silent tinted 16m. (*L'Epouvantail*). Ref: screen: Eng. titles. PFA notes 7/7/94. Lee: Polichinei-Film-Serie.

In a drunk gardener's dream, the devil and lesser demons play cards for the man's soul. Some very funny bits, including one instance of casual cannibalism, as one devil bites off the other's nose. At one point, the main demonic assistant pulls out a telephone. ("A direct line to hell.")

**SCARECROWS** Manson Int'l./Effigy (Cami Winikoff) 1988 color 88m. Story, SP, D, Co-P, Ed: William Wesley. SP: also Richard Jefferies. Ph: Peter Deming. Mus: Terry Plumeri. PD: Gary Roberts. SpMkpFX: Norman Cabrera. SpFX: J. B. Jones. SpPhFX: Hollywood Optical. Ref: TV: Forum HV; unrated version. no Phantom. Hound. Morse. Martin. Scheuer. Imagi 1:58. With Ted Vernon, Michael Simms, Richard Vidan, Victoria Christian, B. J. Turner, David Campbell, Kristina Sanborn; Tony Santory, Phil Zenderland, Mike Balog (scarecrows), Don Herbert.

"Bloody scarecrow!" Fugitive skyjackers find "very ugly vibes" at the deserted Fowler farmhouse in southern California. "Scarecrow things" patrol the place, eviscerate trespassers, and apparently use their body parts to replace their own missing limbs. One victim (Turner), who later turns up "alive," turns out to be a zombie stuffed with stolen money.

"Bloody" is right. This thin horror-fantasy relies more on grisly makeup than on imagination, though it's not badly made. Lots of meant-to-be-tough dialogue; one good line: "Hey, Curry! How we gonna live in Mexico? We're dead." Script leaves unclear the black-magic connections between the original Fowlers, the living scarecrows, the ordinary scarecrows, and the zombies/victims.

**SCARED STIFF** (H.K.) Golden Harvest/Paragon (Bo Ho Films) 1987 color/ws c90m. Ref: TV: Rainbow Video; Eng. titles.

David Miao, a "normal man" with ESP, enters—with the aid of super-scientific computers and gizmos—the dream of a madman. In the dream, he finds a house haunted by a caped vampire man and woman. Later, he enters his brain-injured friend Halley's dream and encounters the slasher that Halley encountered in real life. At the end, he directs his powers against the villains and brings "dead" junkyard cars to life, in a balmily elaborate but fun sequence.... Film haphazardly scrambles comedy, horror, sf, fantasy, and action, as it combines elements of *Dreamscape* and *Nightmare on Elm Street*.

**SCARED STIFF** IFM/Fremont Group 1987 color 80m. SP, D: Richard Friedman. SP, P: Daniel F. Bacaner. SP: also Mark Frost. PD: W. P. Thomas. ProsthFX: T. K. Smith. Ref: V 5/27/87: "pretty standard." ad. V 7/8/87:4(rated). 5/6/87:133(ad). Phantom: "slow ... effective nightmare imagery." Martin. With David Ramsey, Nicole Fortier, Andrew Stevens, Mary Page Keller.

Slavedriver's ghost haunts Southern mansion.

**\*SCARED TO DEATH** 1947 (1946) (*Accent on Horror. The Autopsy*—working ts). Ref: TV. V 7/16/47. Lennig. Lentz. Weldon. Stanley. no Hardy/HM. Okuda/GN. Maltin '92. Lee. Phantom. Hound. Martin.

"Then came the sinister pair"—Leonide (Bela Lugosi) and the dwarf, Indigo (Angelo Rossitto). Here, however, almost everyone's sinister. There are also Dr. Van Ee (George Zucco), "another mysterious character," as Variety puts it; a woman (Gladys Blake) who "dies" in a trance, "comes back," and acts on telepathically-dispatched orders; and a green face which keeps appearing at windows. Meanwhile, Nat Pendleton does to comedy what Lugosi, Zucco, and Molly Lamont do to the more dramatic dialogue—and what the latter do is funnier.

But there's no denying that, though Lugosi and Zucco in color seem more ordinary, their voices are still distinctive. Lugosi even recites poetry: "Laurette, Laurette/I'll make a bet/The man in green/Will get you yet." This movie—which wavers strangely between intentional and unintentional comedy—is acted and directed with a sort of anti-elan.

**SCARED TO DEATH** see *Madhouse* (1981)

**SCARED TO DEATH II** see *Syngenor*

**3P The SCAREMAKER** Indep.-Int'l./Aries Int'l. (GK & Concepts Unltd./A.N. Gurvis) 1982 color 96m. (*Girls Nite Out* - alt t). D: Robert Deubel. SP: Gil Spencer Jr. et al. Ph: J. Rivers. SpFxMkp: Tom Brumberger. Ref: V 6/20/84: "routine slasher picture." 12/8/82:4(rated). 2/16/83:24. Academy. With Julie

Montgomery, James Carroll, Rutanya Alda, Hal Holbrook, Suzanne Barnes.

Mad killer on campus.

**SCHALLTOT** (W. G.) Fred van der Kooij 1985 color 84m. SP, D, Mus: van der Kooij. Ref: V 3/13/85: "The gag has some punch, but over the long stretch it dies a quick death itself." With Peter Wyssbrod, Wolfram Berger, Henning Heers, Nicola Weisse.

Movie sound-effects men duel with "sound effects" which become real. *The Noise Kill* - tr t.

**SCHIZO** Smart Egg (Luigi Cingolani) 1990 color c90m. (*Playroom* - vt t). D: Manny Coto. SP: Keaton Jones. Story: Jackie Earle Haley. Ph: J. L. Carter. Mus: David Russo. PD: Victoria Jenson. FX: Criswell & Johnson FX. OptFX: Mercer & OptFxLtd. Ref: TV. TVG. no Maltin '92. no Scheuer. vc box. V 2/21/90:121 (ad): AFM screenings. With Lisa Aliff, Aron Eisenberg, Maja, Christopher McDonald, James Purcell, Vincent Schiavelli.

"I've been seeing things." Ingredients in this formula horror-fantasy lensed in Belgrade include a monastery built on the site of the tomb of the boy-prince Ilok, who worshiped an "ancient Slavic demon" and who received the gift of eternal life ... a demon-possessed hero (McDonald) and his imaginary friend from childhood, Daniel (Eisenberg), who may or may not be Ilok ... and a shriveled-up stopmo, or puppet, demon man that temporarily enlivens things. A la Freddy, all phantoms and crazies here crack wise.

**SCHLOSS VOGELOD** see *Castle Vogelod*

**SCHOOL FOR VAMPIRES** (H.K.?) 1988 color 88m. Ref: TV: Pan-Asia Video; no Eng. M/TVM 1/89:28.

Routine low comedy alternates here with clever use of the vampire-academy idea. Wry: the passing out of the diplomas to the assembled hopping vampires ... the powdering-on of their cadaver-white faces ... the distributing of the uniforms ... and the communal singing (or "La la"-ing) of "Auld Lang Syne." Other creatures featured: a bad exorcist whose spirit at one point vacates his body ... an evil guy with a voodoo doll (he cackles, therefore he's evil) ... and a mean, green-faced ghost. The night scenes are so murky they're almost unwatchable.

**SCHOOL OF DEATH** (Sp) Mogul/Maxper 1977 ('85-U.S.) color 92m. SP, D: Pedro L. Ramirez. SP: also Ricardo Vazquez. Story: Sandro Continenza, Alphonso Balcazar, Manuel Tebares. Ph: A. Ballesteros. Mus: Cam Espana. Sets: T.A. de la Guerra. Mkp: Tony Nieto. Ref: TV: All American Video; Eng. dubbed. Video Times 11/85:57. Stanley. no Phantom. Hound. no Martin. With Dean Selmier, Sandra Mozarosky, Victoria Vera, Norma Kastel, Carlos Mendy.

"You are in the hands of science." London, 1899. Sylvia Smith (Vera) is sent from St. Elizabeth's Refuge, an orphanage, to Blind Crow House, where the fire-scarred Dr. Kruger subjects her to memory-draining surgery which temporarily turns her into a "zombie." After she is pronounced dead (of "paralysis of the heart") and is buried, her friend Leonor Johnson sees her alive again. More-and-more fantastic developments—involving a death-semblance serum, catalepsy, burial alive, and lifelike masks—follow.

The revelation that the mad doctor—a "diabolical maniac"—and the doctor-hero are one and the same person somehow comes as no surprise, yet it's unbelievable. Much skulking and ado about next-to-nothing, in this blandly dubbed, Poe-flavored period horror movie.

**SCHOOL THAT ATE MY BRAIN, The** see *Zombie High*

**SCHOOL THAT COULDN'T SCREAM, The** see *What Have You Done to Solange?*

**SCHOOLGIRLS IN CHAINS** see *Let's Play Dead*

**SCHRAMM** (G) Buttgereit-Jelinski 1993 color 75m. Screen Story, SP, D: J. Buttgereit. Screen Story: also F. Rodenkirchen. Ph: M.O. Jelinski. Mus: Mueller et al. Mkp: M. Drope, H. Eger. SpFX: M. Romahn. Ref: V 4/18/94: "boring." With Florian Koerner von Gustorf, Monika M., Micha Brendel.

"True-life story of serial killer Lothar Schramm ... visual blood frenzy ... shock effects."

**SCHREIE IN DER NACHT** see *Contronatura*

**SCIENCE CRAZED** (Can.) Triworld/IAE (General) 1987? ('90-U.S.) color 85m. (*The Fiend*—working t?). SP, D, Ed, Co-P: Ron Switzer. Ref: Hound. V 2/4/91:92(hv): "interminable and incompetent." With Cameron Klein, Tony Dellaventura (fiend), Robin Hartsell.

Monster amok at Shelley Institute.

**SCIENCE FRICTION** XTC Video & J.F.K. Ents. 1986 color c80m. SP, D, P: Steven Drake. Ph: Jimmy Iommi. Ref: TV: XTC Video. no Adam. With Careena Collins, Patti Petite, Jessica Wylde, Shanna Leigh (aliens); Herschel Savage, Francois, Marc Wallice, Ron Jeremy.

The ruler of the distant planet Uretha sends four women to Earth to test the sexuality of its men. The aliens find the latter satisfactory and volunteer for overtime.... Woebegone adult sf-er has even-shoddier-than-usual production values.

**SCISSORS** Para/D.D.M. Film (Pearl-Levin-Polaire) 1991 (1990) color 105m. SP, D: Frank De Felitta. Story: Joyce Selznick. Mus: Alfi Kabiljo. SpVisFX: D. J. N. Films. SpFxCoord: Andre Ellingson. Mkp: Nedra Hainey. Opt: Howard Anderson. Ref: TV. V 3/25/91. Cable Video Store 9/92. no Scheuer. Maltin '92. With Sharon Stone, Steve Railsback, Ronny Cox, Michelle Phillips, Vicki Frederick.

"Angie just slipped through the looking glass." Sequences which border on the hallucinatory—mainly because they don't make much sense otherwise—turn out to be part of a laughably ingenious plot to drive a woman (Stone) mad and frame her for murder. ("Transference is total.") An equally laughably ingenious twist turns the tables on her tormentor.

**SCOOBY-DOO AND THE GHOUL SCHOOL** Hanna-Barbera 1988 anim color c90m. Ref: vc box. SFChron 10/28/88. no Scheuer. no Maltin '92. TV: mechanical. Sean: engrossing.

Sibella Dracula, Winnie the Werewolf, Else Frankenstein(sp?), and a little mummy attend Miss Grimwood's girls school.

**SCOOBY-DOO AND THE RELUCTANT WEREWOLF** Worldvision-TV/Hanna-Barbera 1988 color c90m. D: Ray Patterson. Mus: Sven Libaek. Anim Sup: Chris Cuddington. Des:(sup) Jack White; (creative) Iwao Takamoto. Computer Anim Sup: Paul B. Strickland. Ref: TV. no Scheuer. no Maltin '92.

Roll call: Vanna-Pira, Dracula (complete with Lugosi accent and Ralph Kramden impressions), witches, a mummy, the Schlock Ness Monster, a werewolf (Shaggy), a monster phantom, a pizza-eating dog, a Frankenstein-monster-type, a Mr. Hyde-type, a hunchback, the Slime Creature, a giant man-eating monster-plant, Genghis Kong, and Mr. Bonejangles, a skeleton. Noisy, with flat wordplay.

**SCOOBY-DOO MEETS THE BOO BROTHERS** Hanna-Barbera 1987 anim color c90m. Ref: TV. TVG: made for TV. Hound. no Scheuer. no Maltin '92. Voices: D. Messick, Casey Kasem, Sorrell Booke, Arte Johnson.

Ghostly, Three Stooges-like Boo Brothers, ghost exterminators ("It takes one to catch one") ... a houseful of ghosts, including a bicycle-riding ghost ... and a gorilla (an "escaped circus ape"). Frantic, forced.

**SCORPION THUNDERBOLT** (H.K.) IFD Films & Arts(Joseph Lai) 1985 color/ws feature. SP, D: Godfrey Ho. Story, PD?: Stephen So. Ph: R. Cheung. FX D: Martin Chan. Mkp: Jenny Choi. SdFX: A. Fung. Ref: TV: VSOM; Eng. dubbed. With Richard Harrison.

"There's a monster out there!" Ingredients include what first appears to be a huge snake with a claw, but is apparently the Prince of Snakes, a "strange young man" who can turn into a snake ... a cackling "vampire-witch," the "thoroughly evil" Queen of the Scorpions ("Bring me his brain!") ... a snake-woman ... and a passel of snakes which invades a speeding car.... Typically chaotic Joseph Lai horror-fantasy, padded out with miscellaneous action scenes. Sufficiently lurid plot twists. Fine line: "Does that mean I'm in love with a vampire!?"

*****SCOTLAND YARD** 1930. 72m. Ref: screen. William K. Everson. PFA notes 6/26/85. LC. Lee(e).

"A remarkable masquerade": Dr. Paul Deon (Georges Renevant, or Renavent), of the Deon Plastic Hospital, Tours, France, manages a "complete restoration of a hopelessly shattered face"—crook Dakin Barrolles' (Edmund Lowe). ("C'est un miracle!") After suffering a shrapnel wound in the trenches in World War I, Barrolles has "hardly enough left to call it a face." He emerges from surgery, however, with the visage of Sir John Lasher (also Lowe), head of the Central Union Bank of England, who has died in a prison camp. ("The resemblance is perfect.") At one point, actor Lowe undergoes a Jekyll-Hyde-like, dissolve "transformation," as fellow crook Donald Crisp "sees" the old Barrolles under the likeness of Lasher.

To the scientific incredibilities, the script appends a dramatic one: Barrolles-Lasher—the president of the bank—calls in old pal Fox (Crisp) to help him steal from it. Eventually, Barrolles reforms—

his decency with Lady Lasher (John Bennett) proves to be DEW of his reformation. Bennett's lines were obviously not tailored to her talents. She keeps running out of breath before finishing the longer speeches. The most amusing moments here are incidental ones—a French woman expressing honest delight in the spectacle of train wrecks ... Fox—caught up in the "romance of modern business"—expressing honest delight in the feel of bank notes and securities ... Barrolles-Lasher alternating Barrolles and Lasher voices (the former is deeper), and befuddling the at-first-unsuspecting Fox. The unveiling of the "new" Barrolles is accomplished, stylishly, in silhouette.

See also: *Imposter, El* (P).

**SCRAMBLE WARS** (J) AnimEigo/Artmic & Toshiba EMI (Shishido-Suzuki/Takao-Inomata-Suzuki) 1992 ('93-U.S.) anim color 26m. D: Hiroyuki Fukushima. Ph: Seoul Kids. Mus: Nakazawa. AD: Shin. Anim D: Sasaki. Mecha Des: Yamane, Aramaki. SdFX: Animesound. Ref: TV: AnimEigo video; Eng. titles. Animerica 5:18.

Parody of Artmic cartoons features Knight Sabers (from *Bubblegum Crisis*) ... a "superbike" with a "hydrogen turbine engine" ... *Gall Force* gals ... the Darth Vader-like Commander Dawn ... *Genesis Survivor Gaiarth* elements ... a robotic bird-horse ... the Genom Deluxe Super Boomer Car X with "thermonuclear pile," "rocket engine," and "hyper-ultranium chassis" ... and the Planet Destruction Cannon. Some cute moments.

**3P SCREAM** Cal-Com/Calendar Int'l. & Cougar Films (Huff-Buchanan-Quisenberry) 1983 (1981) color 81m. (*The Outing* - shooting t). SP, D: B. Quisenberry. Ph: R. Pepin. Mus: J. Conlan. Ref: V 1/1/86: "one of the crummiest." 8/24/83:4(rated). 11/16/83:12: in Miami. Ecran F 36:83. With Pepper Martin, Hank Worden, Alvy Moore, John Ethan Wayne, Julie Marine, Gregg Palmer, Woody Strode.

Hikers slaughtered in Western ghost town.

**SCREAM DREAM** Interamerican Ent./Image Int'l. (Allison-Griner) 1990 (1989) color 69m. SP, D: Donald Farmer. Ref: V 3/7/90:39(hv): "gore flick fills the bill." V/Cannes '89:126. Hound. With Melissa Moore, Nikki Riggins, Carol Carr.

Witch's spirit possesses her replacement in rock band.

**SCREAMING DEAD, The** see *Dracula Vs. Dr. Frankenstein*

**SCREAMING MIMI** Col/Sage (Brown-Fellows) 1958 79m. D: Gerd Oswald. SP: Robert Blees, from Fredric Brown's novel. Ph: Burnett Guffey. Mus D: M. Bakaleinikoff. AD: Cary Odell. Chor: Lee Scott. Ref: TV. Weldon. Lentz. TVG. V 3/19/58. no Lee. Stanley. Maltin '92. Scheuer. With Anita Ekberg, Phil Carey, Harry Townes, Gypsy Rose Lee, the Red Norvo Trio, Romney Brent, Vaughn Taylor, Thomas Browne Henry.

"Two sexy blondes are knifed the same way, and both have the same taste in statues." One of the two (the one who lives), however, proves to be "the Ripper," who suffered a "deep traumatic shock" when an "escaped maniac" killed her dog and attacked her in the shower. Now, the sight of the SM-1 statuette, or Screaming Mimi—created by her stepbrother—sets her off, and she "becomes" the maniac.

What should have been a straightforward drama becomes too twisted and tangled a mystery. Script here goes to great lengths (including employment of a "fixation reversal") simply to divert suspicion from the guilty party. Final revelations do come as a surprise, and the ending is almost touching. But even this coda squanders half its dramatic potential—the fact that it constitutes the solution to the mystery obscures the fact that it also means the separation of hero from heroine. (While he's unraveling the mystery, out loud, her mind is just unraveling.) This *Psycho*-like ending in madness is heralded by the *Psycho*-like shower scene, by the presence of a monster of a Great Dane, by the heroine's Svengali-like psychiatrist-protector's own weirdnesses, and by the presence of the "Mimi"s. ("Weird-looking dame, isn't she?")

See also: *Bird with the Crystal Plumage.*

**SCREAMPLAY** Boston Movie Co. (Piana) 1985 color 90m. SP, D: Rufus Butler Seder. SP: also Ed Greenberg. SpFX: Flip Johnson, Eugene Seder. Ref: V 2/27/85: "gags soon wear thin." Strand Theater notes. Ecran F 68:30-33. Nowlan. With R. B. Seder, George Kucher, Katy Bolger, Basil J. Bova.

"Macabre Welcome Apartments ... strange comic murders."(V)

**SCROGGINS GOES IN FOR CHEMISTRY AND DISCOVERS A MARVELLOUS POWDER** (B) C&M 1911 silent 9m. Ref: BFC: "shrinks bride, constable, lamp-post."

**SCROOGED** Para & Mirage (Art Linson) 1988 color 101m. D: Richard Donner. SP: Mitch Glazer, Michael O'Donoghue, suggested by Charles Dickens' "A Christmas Carol." SpVisFX: Dream Quest Images; (sup) Eric Brevig. SpFxCoord: A. L. Hall. SpMkpFX: the Burmans. ElecSdFX: John Paul Fasal. Ref: TV. MFB'88:369-71. SFChron 11/23/88. ad.

Comic retelling of the Dickens story features a climactic sequence in which a horrific, skeletal Ghost of Christmas Future—complete with rib-caged damned souls (in a perhaps Freddy-inspired image)—confronts "Scrooge" (Bill Murray). Murray, Carol Kane (as the Ghost of Christmas Present), and Bobcat Goldthwait are the funny ones here. Otherwise, the production is as glossy and shallow as the script's commercial targets.

**SCUM OF THE EARTH** see *Poor White Trash II*

**The SEA SERPENT** (U.S.-Sp) Calepas Int'l. & Constan (Jose Frade) 1985 color 92m. (*Serpiente de Mar.* aka *Hydra—Monster from the Deep*). D: Amando de Ossorio (aka G. Greens). Mus: Robin Davis. AD: Jose Luis Galicia. SpFX: Frank Cuttlet, J. Vargas, T. Urbant. Mkp: Fernando Flores. Ref: TV: Lightning Video; Eng. version. Peter Zirschky. Horacio Higuchi. V 7/16/86. 5/1/85:206 (ad). 5/7/86:384. Maltin '92. Phantom. Hound. no Martin. Stanley. With Timothy Bottoms, Taryn Power, Jared Martin, Ray Milland, Gerard Tichy, Jack Taylor, Leon Klimovsky, Vic Israel.

An atom bomb annoys a pathetically toy-ish, sub-Cecil sea serpent off the coast of Spain. The speedy "overgrown worm" is so silly a bug-eyed conception, it seems it must be intentionally campy. It's a Giant Claw for the Eighties. *Jaws* suspense music, a *Beast from 20,000 Fathoms* lighthouse sequence, and an *It Came from Beneath the Sea* suspension-bridge sequence. Milland is in good, brisk voice as a zoologist and "something more," in his last movie.

**SEARCH AND DESTROY** SGE/Cinema Sciences 1988 color 90m. SP, D, P: J. Christian Ingvordsen. Ph, P: Steven Kaman. Mus: Chris Burke. PD: Chris Johnson. SpFxSup: W. Caban. Mkp: Isabelle Fritz-Cope. Ref: TV: Forum HV. SFChron Dtbk 10/23/88. Hound. Martin. no Phantom. no V. With John Christian, Johnny Stumper, Oliver Daniels, John Rano, Angel Caban, Dan Lutsky, Boris Keutonog (or Krutonog).

"The chemical virus has become highly contagious." A Red December terrorist releases the "ultimate biochemical weapon," which a U.S. Army research center has been developing in the area above Farmdale. ("I don't like what's going on up there.") This "hostile pathogen" affects the hypothalamus—though a certain type of blood is resistant to the virus—and its spread decimates the community.

Well-paced and photographed sf-actioner ultimately rings hollow. The cliches and tone of the Tough Guy school of action dominate. Some *Crazies*-like bizarre details help.

**SEARCH FOR DIANA** (Can.) Twinbay Media 1992 color 90m. SP, D, P: Milad Bessada. SP: also Maissa Bessada Patton. Ref: V 1/11/93: "hopeless, laugh-out-loud ludicrous muddle of New Age mysticism and ancient Egyptian mythology." 10/19/92:142. With Diana Calenti (Diana), Brett Halsey, Janet Richardson.

"Choreographer troubled by visions of her past life as a high priestess in the days of Akhenaton."

**SEARCH FOR URANUS** see *Gonad the Barbarian*

**SEARCHERS OF THE VOODOO MOUNTAIN** see *Warriors of the Apocalypse*

**SEBASTIAN STAR BEAR: FIRST MISSION** (Dutch-Chinese) Concorde/Frank Fehmers & Elsevier-Vendex (Star Bear) 1991 (1990) anim color 78m. D, P: F. Fehmers. SP: R. Felgate;(uncred.) M. Jupo, F. Pacifico. Mus: H. Seroka. AD: Pacifico. Anim D: W. Borong. Ref: TV. V 1/6/92: Chinese animation; "comfortable characters and animation." 6/29/92:13(ad). 2/25/91:28, A-72, A-74: Fox/Lorber; at AFM; "extraterrestrial bear." TVG.

"A dozen strong, wise bears escaped into the heavens, from where they protect their earthly cousins with 007-style bear agents." (V) Principals include Sebastian, who arrives on Earth in a spaceship ... an Eastern magician ... and a robot-computer that, at the end, becomes a full-fledged Star Bear.... Badly miscalculated cartoon science-fantasy for children has zero appeal.

**The SECOND COMING** Ormond 1984 (aka *It's about the Second Coming*). Ref: Filmfax 28:56-7.

"Bounces back and forth between biblical times, the present, and the future. It is a delirious blend of theology, science fiction, and special effects."

**SECOND FIDDLE** Hodkinson/Film Guild (Tuttle-Waller) 1923 59m. SP, D: Frank Tuttle. SP: also James A. Creelman. Ph: Fred Waller Jr. Ref: screen. William K. Everson. PFA notes 1/23/86. V 3/15/23. AFI. no LC. With Glenn Hunter, Mary Astor, Townsend Martin, Osgood Perkins, William Nally.

Outside Spell's River, a village in Massachusetts, lies a "house of mystery, a desolate place on a lonely back road." Cragg (Nally) is the "sinister occupant," a man with a "cruel and unbalanced mind," who murders his own daughter (Helenka Adamowska). At the end of the movie, our heroine (Astor) finds herself alone ... with Cragg ... in the house ... at midnight ... during a thunderstorm. Classic horror-story situation gets more classic: Hero (Hunter) arrives ... locks Cragg in a closet ... closes the door to the room and blocks it with a huge, handy hall clock. Madman busts out of closet ... busts through door and clock. Hero pushes pot-bellied stove down stairs at him. Stairs collapse. Madman pinned under beam. Hero and heroine safe, upstairs. Enter madman, again, on ladder, at second-floor window.

All *Halloween* adds—55 years later—is the supernatural element. If it takes some arduous plotting to get to the above payoff, and the sets are made of matchsticks, *Second Fiddle* does get there, and the film is handsomely photographed and tinted. The climactic sequence features one fine scare: the concealed Cragg pushing forward the half-closed bedroom door to reveal his presence to Polly.

**SECOND HONEYMOON, The** see *Honeymoon Murders II*

**\*The SECRET OF THE LOCH** ABFD/Wyndham Films 1934 72m.-U.S. (*The Loch Ness Monster* - alt t?). Ph: James Wilson; (underwater) Eric Cross. Mus: Peter Mendoza. Asst AD: Fisher-Smith. Ed: David Lean. Ref: TV. Greg Luce. TVG. Lee. Lentz. Stanley. Gifford/BC. no LC.

"There is something terrible in that Loch!" "Something from the depths"—"sixty feet or more"—is haunting "that distant highland Loch." Behind all this "crazy monster business": a "giant dinosaur, Diplodocus," which chews up divers who venture too near its underwater Great Cave. Prof. Heggie (Seymour Hicks) surmises that explosions and heat have hatched a prehistoric egg. ("Those waters go down, down—deeper than man has ever plumbed.")

Too many strictly-running-time-killing scenes foil this old British monster movie, which apparently used *The Lost World* as its model. ("Heggie" is just another name for "Challenger.") It takes almost an hour to get to the one and only real chill—the slow filling of the screen by the shadow of the monster, as a diver disturbs its lair. When we finally do get to see the creature itself—in a payoff half-charming, half-dismaying—it turns out to be a *One Million B.C.*-like, double-exposure lizard. Not very like a Diplodocus.

Early Hitchcock collaborator Charles Bennett perhaps provided the hilarious "mentally deficient" bit, in the London board room, and a few dialogue phrases, like "And I saw the great neck!" There's also a tantalizing excerpt from an old book: "There hath been seen at sondrie Times and in divers Places a great Worme or Monstere in the Water known as Loch Ness."

See also: *Amazon Women on the Moon. Freddie as F.R.O.7. Scooby-Doo and the Reluctant Werewolf.*

**SECRET OF THE SAHARA** (I-F-W-G) SACIS/RAI 1 & TFI & Beta Film & ZDF & Racing Pictures 1987 color 105m. SP, D: Alberto Negrin. SP: also N. Badalucco, S. Donati. Story: Massimo de Rita, Lucio Mandara, from the works of Emilio Salgari, including "I Predoni del Deserto." Ph: Daniele Nannuzzi. Mus: Ennio Morricone. PD: Dante Ferretti. SpFX: A. Pischiutta, G. Mancini. Mkp: Goffredo Calisse. SdFX: Studio Anzellotti. SpSetFX: PF 82. TV: VSOM; Eng. version. Palmerini: made for TV. With Michael York, Andie MacDowell, David Soul, Ben Kingsley, James Farentino, Miguel Bose, Daniel Olbrychski, Delia Boccardo, Jean-Pierre Cassel.

"Man is not the first, nor shall he be the last to rule the Earth.... The Ancients shall ever be ... beneath the mountain." Author-explorer Desmond Jordan ("I crossed the frontiers of space and time in which I lived") searches the Sahara for the "talking mountain," finds same, and, within it, Anthea, the Daughter of the Light ... Kerim the new Great Custodian, or Guardian ... and a people who come "from beyond the sky." At the end, a ship of light blasts off for ...?

Derring-do and other hokum in the desert is a little *L'Atlantide*, a little Lucas-Spielberg, a little Wisely. There's some dumb fun to be had here, but the tale is rather dragged out. Okay score and photography. One of Those Lines Dept.: "So even Africa isn't big enough for both of us."

The **SECRET OF THE SWORD** Filmation & Mattel (Nadel) 1985 anim color 91m. D: Ed Friedman et al. SP: Larry Ditillo, Bob Forward, based on the TV series "He-Man and the Masters of the Universe." SpFX: Shurl Lupin. Ref: MFB'86:153-4. TVG. Voices: John Erwin, M. Britt, Alan Oppenheimer.

Beast Island ... spell-maker ... Fright Zone ... Magna-Beam Transporter.

See also: *Masters of the Universe.*

**SECRET PASSIONS** see *Haunted by Her Past*

**SECRET SEX** Catalina Video 1994 color 64m. D: C. LaRue. Ref: Adam'95G. With J. Wood, A. Shaw.

"In a future where the radical right has taken over the world, sex has become illegal."

**SECRET SEX 2: THE SEX RADICALS** Catalina 1994 color 67m. Ref: Adam'95G. With D. Cruise, T. Katt.

"Sex radicals" vs. "sex police," in the future.

**SECRETS** see *Consuming Passions*

**SECRETS OF THE PHANTOM CAVERNS** see *What Waits below*

The **SECT** (I) Cecchi Gori & Berlusconi/Penta Film & ADC (Dario Argento) 1991 (1990) color 112m. (*The Devil's Daughter* - U.S. *La Setta*). SP, D: Michele Soavi. SP: also D. Argento, G. Romoli. Ph: R. Mertes. Mus: Pino Donaggio. PD: M.A. Geleng. Mkp: R. Prestopino. SpFX: M. Cristofanelli. Creatures: Sergio Stivaletti. On-Set SpFX: Corridori. SdFX: Sound Track. Ref: TV: Eng. version; Frankfurter Filmproduktion assistance; Republic HV. VWB. V 10/15/90:14 (ad). 2/25/91: A-36 (ad): Eng. version screening at AFM. 10/29/90:13. MV: *Demons 4: The Sect* - alt vt t. With Kelly Curtis, Herbert Lom, Maria Angela Giordano, Michel Adatte, Carla Cassola, Tomas Arana (Damon), Donald O'Brien.

"It's born!" Ingredients include The Faceless Ones, a "bloodthirsty demonic sect" ... a weird beetle, supposedly extinct for 10,000 years, which is stuffed up a woman's nose ... a rabbit that uses a TV remote ... a supposedly dead man (Lom) who keeps turning up alive ... a hoodoo-voodoo impression of his face left on a handkerchief ... a manhole to hell ... an *Eyes without a Face* face removal ... a debauched-looking stork wandering in from *Company of Wolves,* apparently ... and an evil baby.

There are certainly enough bizarre, if not exactly explained elements here, but the story is dragged out, the plot payoff is a tired *Rosemary's Baby* twist, and the score is mind-numbing. The Weird Animals angle is interesting, but the best sequence may be the one in which the camera for some reason follows the meanderings of some plumbing.

La **SECTA DE LA MUERTE** (Mex) Cineproducciones IRVSA de Mexico & Mexcinema Video (Ismael Rodriguez Jr.) 1990? color c80m. D: Roman Hernandez. Story, SP: Jose Loza. SP: also I. Rodriguez. Ph: F. Bojorquez. Mus: Raul Martell. SpFX: Guillermo Bermudez. Mkp: Antonio Castaneda. OptFX: Video Omega. Ref: TV: Mexcinema Video; no Eng.; The Sect of Death—tr t. TVG. With Gerardo Cepeda, Marco Antonio Sanchez, Rafael del Toro, Mario Almada, Sebastian Ligarde.

A satanist keen on rabbit blood and guts cajoles a fellow hitchhiker into stabbing a man. There follow the sacrifice of a human heart at a ritual and the sacrifice of a kidnapped baby. Tawdry action shocker.

**SECTA SATANICA: EL ENVIADO** DEL SR. (Mex) Prods. Hermanos Martines 1989 color 88m. D: Arturo Martinez; (co-d) Roman Hernandez. SP: Aurora Martinez? Ph: A. De Anda. Mus: E. Cortazar. SpFX: Arturo Vazquez. SdFX: G. Gavira. Mkp: K. Acosta. OptFX: M. Sainz. Ref: TV: Million Dollar Video; no Eng. With Joaquin Cordero, German Robles, Ernesto Gomez Cruz, Quintin Bulnes, Rodolfo De Anda Jr., Bruno Rey.

A demonic cackler seems to drive townsfolk to murder and suicide, with knife, gun, rope; conducts satanic rituals featuring gory heart-extractions; keeps cackling to the end, even though he's burnt to a crisp. Hokey, stilted religio-horror.

**SECTA SINIESTRA** (Sp) Conexion Films 1982 color/ws 87m. (*Bloody Sect* - U.S. vt t), SP, D: Steve McCoy. SP: also I. F. Iquino (aka J. Wood), J. Kelly. Ph: J. Gelpi. SpFX: Anthony Basti, X. Lafita. Ref: Hardy/HM: "awkward." Ecran F 53:70: S. McCoy also = I. Iquino. VSOM. With M. Kerr, Carlos Martos, J. Varney, J. Zanni.

Satanists infiltrate artificial-insemination unit, circulate the devil's sperm.

**SEDIU YINGCHUNG TSUN TSI DUNG SING SAI TSAU** see *Eagle Shooting Heroes*

**SEDUCCION SANGRIENTA** (Mex) Fiesta Films & Laser Film (Omar A. Gonsenheim) 1990 color c95m. D: Aldo Monti. SP?: R. Arvizu. Ph: G. M. Williams. Mus: Clark Gault. Ref: TV: Cine-Mex HV; no Eng. TVG. *Bloody Seduction* - tr t. With Lina Santos (Marta), Antonio Raxel, Eric del Castillo, Arturo Gonzalez, Pedro de Lucio, Javier Montano.

A man who wants something "special" for his wife's birthday unwittingly buys her a cursed box which, when opened, lets the spirit of a condemned witch out. The latter possesses the woman, who stabs her husband to death with a pair of scissors, then begins conducting human-sacrifice rituals with the man who sold her husband the box. Key book: *Historia del Tribunal del Santo Oficio de la Inquisicion en Mexico*. Basic, corny possession story. Shot on tape.

**SEDUCED BY EVIL** USA-TV 1994 color c90m. D: Tony Wharmby. Ref: Martin: "barely watchable." TVG: "absurd ... but moves right along." With Suzanne Somers, John Vargas, James B. Sikking, Julie Carmen.

"Evil sorcerer" (TVG) ... spirit-possessed woman.

**SEE THRU** Legend 1992 color 78m. D: Scotty Foxx. Ref: Adam '93. With Randy Spears, Alicia Rio, Francesca Le, T. T. Boy.

Mad scientist (Spears) concocts invisibility formula.

**SEEDING OF A GHOST** (H.K.) Shaw (Mona Fong & Wong Ka Hee) 1990? color/ws c88m. D: Yang Chuan. Ref: TV: World Video; Eng. titles.

"My son will avenge me!" Widower Chou goes to a priest, who uses the man's wife Irene's moldy corpse, now called "Plazawa," to curse her killers: Paul vomits worms; Peter's mother sees him eating brains and drinking blood through a straw. At the finish, Irene's lover's pregnant wife's stomach bursts, and a crab-like critter leaps out, develops tentacles, *Alien* jaws, and a vaguely human head.

Highlights of the elaborate but unoriginal gore and gunk here: the muck-vomiting toilet ... Plazawa kissing and caressing Chou ... one victim's back splitting open ("The strength of witchcraft") and the (cartoon) spirit "seeding" the levitating Plazawa, in a most bizarre sequence. (Apparently, the two engender the above-mentioned *Alien* creature, by remote control.)

**SEEDPEOPLE** Para/Full Moon (Anne Kelly) 1992 color 81m. D: Peter Manoogian. SP: Jackson Barr. Idea & Exec P: Charles Band. Mus: Bob Mithoff. SpCreature & MkpFX: MMI; (sup) John Carl Buechler. Physical FX: Andrew Sutton. Seed Construction: Greg Aronowitz. Digital FX: (vis) DHD Postimage, Digital Vision Ent.; (sup) Geoffrey de Valois. Opt: Mercer. Ref: TV. V 7/13/92. PT 13:48. With Sam Hennings, Andrea Roth, Dane Witherspoon, David Dunard, Holly Fields, Bernard Kates, Anne Betancourt (Mrs. Santiago).

"We are being chased by seeds which were sown on the winds of the universe!" A strange, versatile tree in Comet Valley alternately shoots a cocooning "sap" onto humans and sprays them with pellet-like objects. And the robot-voiced Mrs. Santiago seems to morph into a lethal tumbleweed. The key to it all: a five-hundred-year-old cave drawing in Indian Canyon which turns out to be a "snapshot" of the "arrival on planet Earth" of "intelligent life forms from another world"—the local meteorites are actually seeds, and the "people" produced can read minds, though UV light protects the real humans.... The Yum Yum Tree it ain't. Script haplessly scrambles *Invasion of the Body Snatchers* with *Gremlins/Critters*. The abounding, comical-looking creatures effectively kill all suspense.

**SEGNO DEL COMANDO, Il** see *Sign of the Commander*

**SEGRETO DEL SAHARA, Il** see *Secret of the Sahara*

**SEIDAN BOTANDORO** (J) Nikkatsu 1972. D: Chusei Sone. Ref: CM 15:30: Sex Story of Peonies and Stone Lanterns - tr t? With S. Ogawa, F. Hara, Miki Hayashi.

Softcore version of a "famous period ghost story."

**SEIRAINE: THE GHOST STORY** (J) Tsuburaya Eizo 1993 color feature. Ref: TV: TJC video; no Eng.

Tawdry horror drama re a ghost whose eyes light up as her victims smoke and shrivel.

**A SEITA DOS ESPIRITOS MALDITOS** (Braz.) PC Ze do Caixao 1992 color c90m. Story, SP, D, AD: Jose Mojica Marins. SP: also R. Francisco Lucchetti. Ref: Monster! 3:33: release delayed; *The Cult of the Damned Souls* - tr t. With Marins (Ze do Caixao), Gaucho, Adriana Ribeiro, Luana Braga.

"Occult forces ... human sacrifice ... eerie mansion" ... dead millionaire's plan to shed family blood in order to return to life.

**SELKIE THE SEAL** see *Neptune's Children*

**SEMI-GODS AND SEMI-DEVILS** (H.K.) Win's Movie 1994 color/ws 103m. D: Chin Wing Keung. Ref: TV: Tai Seng Video; Eng. titles. With Brigitte Lam, Cheung Man, Gong Li.

"Right, I am the living dead." Ingredients include a re-born wizard ("His soul is in his shadow"—fascinating effects here) ... the magically suspended Dragon Ball ... a ninja-type who can appear and disappear ... a magically severed arm ... magic Pei Ming ties (compare handcuffs) ... the eight fairies ("like monsters") who rule the world ... ray-"tunnel" warfare in mid-air ... Melting Stance rays ... a weird scorpion ... and semi-fireball rays.... Casual comedy, sweepingly photographed action scenes, and fun optical ray effects.

**SENSITIVA** see *Ultima Casa vicino al Lago*

**La SEPTIEME DIMENSION** (F) GDF/Laurent Dussaux & Les Films du Colisee & Stephen Films & Berthemont 1988 (1987) color 90m. D: Dussaux, Stephen Holmes et al. SP: E. Murail, N. Cuche. Ph: B. Chatry et al. Mus: T. Murail. Ref: Mad Movies 52:24-5; six stories re alien, Egyptian goddess, etc. With Francis Frappat, Jean-Michel Dupuis, Michel Aumont.

**El SER** (3) Follow-up to *Viaje al Mas Alla* (II). Follow-up: *Mas Alla de la Muerte* (IV).

**SERENATA MACABRA** see *House of Evil*

**SGT. KABUKIMAN, N.Y.P.D.** (U.S.-J) Troma/Namco & Gaga 1991 color 90m. SP, D, P: Lloyd Kaufman. D, P: also Michael Herz. SP: also A. Osborne, J. W. Sass. SpFX: Pericles Lewnes. Ref: V 5/6/91: "simple, but fitfully hilarious." With Rick Gianasi, Susan Byun, Bill Weeden.

Black magic ... "dragonlike demon."

**SGT. STRYKER'S WAR** see *Thou Shalt Not Kill ... Except*

The **SERPENT AND THE RAINBOW** Univ/Keith Barish/Rob Cohen & David Ladd (Serpent & the Rainbow Prods.) 1988 (1987) color 98m. D: Wes Craven. SP: Richard Maxwell, A. R. Simoun, inspired by Wade Davis' book. Mus: Brad Fiedel. SpMkpFX: Lance & David Anderson. SpVixFx: (sup) Gary Guiterrez; Colossal Pictures, USFX; (opt) Illusion Arts. SpMechFX: Image Engineering. SpFxCoord: Peter Chesney. Voices of the Dead: Diamanda Galas. Ref: TV: MCA HV. V 2/3/88. SFExam 2/5/88 (ad & rev). SFChron 2/5/88. MFB'89:131-2. Wash. Times 1/27/86: review of book. With Bill Pullman, Cathy Tyson, Zakes Mokae, Paul Winfield, Brent Jennings, Conrad Roberts (Christophe), Michael Gough.

Boston Biocorp sends anthropologist Dennis Alan (Pullman) to Haiti to obtain the secret of "zombification." He finds it: a powder (active ingredient: tetrodotoxin) made of poisons, herbs, and minerals, "woven together with a net of magic." Meanwhile, zombie master Dargent Peytraud (Mokae) programs Alan's nightmares and has him "zombified" and buried alive. Unburied, Alan smashes the bottles containing the souls of Peytraud's victims, and they seem to burn him to death.

*The Serpent and the Rainbow* plays at times like an atmospheric Caribbean-voodoo travelogue (compare *The Golden Mistress*), at others like an allegory re the liberation of Haiti, at still others like just another effects horror movie. One problem: The script is pretty specific about the ingredients and effects of the zombie powder, but very vague about such other voodoo phenomena as Alan's hallucinations and the remote-control death of Winfield's Lucien Celine. The hallucinations themselves—the visions include a man tearing off his own head, a burial alive, and a snake-tongued walking corpse—seem extraneous, mere attention-getters. There is one witty one, though: a ghoul hand sinking back into a bowl of soup.

**SERPENT WARRIORS** (U.S.-H.K.) Frank Wong & Eastern Media Ent./E&C 1986 color 96m. (*Golden Viper*—alt t). D: Niels Rasmussen. SP: Martin Wise. Ref: V 5/21/86: "zestily vulgar." Ecran F 47:31: U.S.-Fili. 68:70. Stanley. V 10/16/85:154(ad). With Koo Huan, Kathleen Lu, Clint Walker, Anne Lockhart, Chris Mitchum, Eartha Kitt (snake priestess).

Curse unleashes snake hordes on condo.

**SERPIENTE DE MAR** see *Sea Serpent, The*

**SERVANTS OF MIDNIGHT** CDI 1992 color 70m. D: Jack Stephen. Ref: Adam'94: vampires. With Alexis DeVell, Ona Zee, Steve Drake.

**SERVANTS OF TWILIGHT** Trimark & Gibraltar Ent. (Jeffrey Obrow, Venetia Stevenson) 1991 color 86m. (95m). (aka *Dean R. Koontz's Servants of Twilight*). SP, D: J. Obrow. SP: also Stephen Carpenter, from D. R. Koontz' book *Twilight*. Ph: A. Soriano. Mus: Jim Manzie. Bat FX: Michael McCraken. PD: Deborah Raymond, Dorian Vernacchio. SpFX: Frank Ceglia. MechFxSup: Lars Hauglie. Key Mkp: Suzanne Parker Sanders. Ref: TV: Vidmark video. V 6/3/91: "unbelievable yet engrossing." 4/22/91:50(rated). TVG. PT 13:45: "a good one." With Bruce Greenwood, Belinda Bauer, Grace Zabriskie (Grace), Carel Struycken, Kelli Maroney, Jarrett Lennon (Joey).

"It was the witch—the witch cut Brandy's head off." Mother Grace of the Church of the Twilight believes that little Joey is the anti-Christ. ("Satan is the father of that child!") At one point, bats seem to save the boy, and he seems to revive his mother from the dead.... *The Omen*, from another angle. The cosmic mystery here is at once transparent and intriguing: The solution seems obvious, maybe too obvious—maybe the obviousness is a clever story ploy. Nope. The film finally issues in the Cute Kid Menace cliche.

**SESAME STREET PRESENTS: FOLLOW THAT BIRD** see *Follow That Bird*

As **SETE VAMPIRAS** (Braz.) Embrafilme/Superoito (Cardoso-Taubman-Klabini-Avilez-Holanda-Skylight) 1986('94-U.S.) color 100m. (*7 Vampires* - vt t). D: Ivan Cardoso. SP: R. F. Lucchetti. Mus: Julio Medaglia. Mkp & SpFX: Antonio Pacheco. Plant: Bertoni SpFX, Oscar Ramos. Ph: Carlos Egberto. AD: Oscar Ramos. Ref: TV: SWV; Eng. titles. Cult Movies 12:7. V 7/2/86: "pic does not work as well as *O Segredo da Mumia*"; *The Seven Female Vampires*—tr t. 3/12/86:102. Ecran F 73:70. no Stanley. Jones. Ecran F 76:47, 50, 53. VSOM. With Andrea Beltrao, Ariel Coelho, Nicole Puzzi.

"Killer vegetable transforms a scientist into a vampire...."(V) Seems the professor, savaged by the African plant, needed victims for transfusions, and his wife, Silvia, also savaged, underwent periodic transformations into ...? ("My God, what was that?") (He was the phantom slasher.) Plus: The Dance of the Seven Vampires, a stage show featuring "Dracula" and his "brides" (a "vampira" from the show is one of the phantom's victims) ... "Fu Man Chu," on stage ... and Raimundo Marlou, p.i....A little of everything here—music, mystery, horror, comedy—and not much of anything. In one of the more amusing bits, Alfred Hitchcock (re-dubbed from his TV show) "introduces" the movie.

**SETTA, La** see *Sect, The*

**SETTE ORCHIDEE MACCHIATE DI ROSSO** see *Seven Blood-Stained Orchids*

**SETTE UOMINI D'ORO NELLO SPAZIO** (I) 1978 color feature. D: Alfonso Brescia. Ref: Palmerini: "flop" sf; sfa *Cosmos—War of the Planets* (2)?

**SETTIMA TOMBA, La** see *Seventh Grave, The*

**SEVEN BLOOD-STAINED ORCHIDS** (I) Rialto 1972 color feature (*Sette Orchidee Macchiate di Rosso. Puzzle of the Silver Half Moons*). SP, D: Umberto Lenzi. SP: also Roberto Gianviti. From Edgar Wallace's "The Puzzle of the Silver Half Moons." Mus: Riz Ortolani. Ref: MV: "mysterious slasher." ETC/Giallos: "incredibly bloody sequence" with a power drill. With Antonio Sabato, Uschi Glass, Rossella Falk, Marina Malfatti, Marisa Mell.

**SEVEN DRAGON PEARLS** see *Dragon Pearl*

**SEVEN FOXES** (H.K.) 1985 (1984) color/ws c80m. Ref: TV: Ocean Shores Video; Eng. titles.

A Frankenstein-monster-masked knife-wielder at large in a darkened mansion is an assassin, it seems, hired by a rich man to kill him before cancer does. Other ingredients in this thunderstorm mystery include a seemingly live skeleton, a corpse left sitting thirty years in a room, and murder "victims" who "return to life."

Broad, dumb comedy gets pretty funny at times and is fast-paced. It's one gag or shock or mock-shock after another. The plot keeps shifting directions radically and casually, though the last scene—which explains the title—tries to tie up all loose ends as part of a plot to collect on the rich guy's life insurance.

**7, HYDE PARK** see *Formula for Murder*

**\*SEVEN KEYS TO BALDPATE** 1929. AD: Max Ree. Ref: TV. V 1/1/30. Stanley. no Lentz. Lee(e). no Hardy/HM. no Maltin '92. Scheuer.

"Oh, so you're the ghost of Baldpate!" There are "dead people walking all over the place" on an "uncommon cold night" at the closed-for-winter Baldpate Inn, which is "about six hours from New York" and the "lonesomest spot on Earth." Phony ghosts include Peters (Joseph Allen), a hermit who runs around wearing a white sheet and "frightening people" ... a woman in white ("They thought it was the ghost!") ... and a "dead" woman who walks. ("A ghost! A ghost! A real ghost!")

Early-talkie parody melodrama is of little comic or dramatic interest now, though the broad attempts at atmosphere are entertaining. (Wind howls, off and on, throughout.) Writer-hero Richard Dix's comments re pulp fiction don't help much. The movie is still pulpy and creaky, and the supposedly ingenious plot unfolds interminably.

**SEVEN PEARLS** (H.K.) 198-? feature. Ref: Imagi Smr'95:61: "machine-gun-toting aliens."

**7 VAMPIRES** see *Sete Vampiras*

**The SEVENTH CURSE** (H.K.) Golden Harvest (Paragon) 1986 color/ws 83m. (*Yuan Zhenxia Yu Weisili*). D: Lan Nei Tsa. SP: I. Kuang, from the book by Nguy Kong. SpFX: Den Film FX. Ref: TV: Rainbow Video; Eng. titles. Y.K. Ho. NST! 4:35-6, 11-12. Horacio Higuchi. Fango 107:58, 59, 60. With Ken Boyle, Chow Yun-Fat, Maggie Cheung, Xu Jinguang (evil wizard), Johnny Wang.

Magic and adventure in North Thailand, as the Worm Tribe's sorcerer Aquala casts various spells, including the seven blood curses and the "Little Ghost" spell, which causes blood from a granite child-crusher to produce "blood ghosts," small, flying, gobbling, rattlesnake-tailed *Fiend without a Face*-like things which suck the blood of their victims. Near the end, the tribe's Old Ancestor, a glowing-eyed, skeletal creature which can turn into a winged, alligatorish, *Alien*-type creature, battles one of the feisty "little ghosts."

The monsters are *Alien*; setting and plot are *Indiana Jones*. And, like *Alien,* the rather-lavishly-produced *Seventh Curse* is purely functional. It gets the shock job done. And if it's not as exciting as *Raiders of the Lost Ark*, it's not as pooped-out as the subsequent *Indiana Jones* movies. Perhaps the most striking image: a huge, collapsing, "bleeding"-eyed idol. Top sequence: the

bloody battle between the skull-headed little ghost and the Old Ancestor.

See also: *Legend of Wisely, The.*

**The SEVENTH FLOOR** (Austral.) A-Pix Ent./PA & Sogovision & JSP 1993('94-U.S.) color c99m. D: Ian Berry. SP: Tony Morphett. Ref: vc box. With Brooke Shields, M. Kato.

Serial killer "obeys" dead sis.

**The SEVENTH GRAVE** (I-US.) F.G.S. Int'l./Tower TV 1966 b&w/ws 73m. (*La Settima Tomba*). SP, D: Finney Cliff. Story, SP: Edmond W. Carloff, F. Mils. Ph: Alfred Carbot. Mus: Leopold Perez. Ref: TV: VSOM; no Eng. Palmerini. With Stephania Nelly, Fernand Angels, Armand Warner (Martin/Sir Reginald), John Anderson.

Old Scotland. The estate of the late Sir Reginald Thorne is the scene of strange experiments, black magic, a seance, a "ghost," scary surprises in various caskets, midnight piano-playing, murder, madman "monster" antics, and much carrying about of candles. Hokey, verbose, almost campy forgotten Italian horror movie features overdone creep music and a few nice camera tricks.

**\*The SEVENTH SEAL** Svensk 1957('58-U.S.) 96m.-U.S. Mus: Erik Nordgren. AD: P.A. Lundgren. FX: Evald Andersson. Mkp: Nils Nittel. Ref: TV: Nelson Ent. video (Embassy video); Eng. titles. Lee. V 5/29/57. With Gunnel Lindblom, Anders Ek.

"I, Antonius Block, am playing chess with Death." Death here (Bengt Ekerot)—"I am Death"—plays chess with a medieval knight (Max von Sydow), cuts down a tree (i.e., an actor's life), and, at the end, conducts a "solemn dance." Very uneven Ingmar Bergman fantasy has a sweet ending (the Happy Family lives) and peaks with the sequence, earlier, in which the Gloomy Gus knight vows to remember the beauty of the evening spent with the itinerant actors. For the most part, the director pours it on—Death, "witches," the plague, despair, grave robbers, Penitente-types, torture, and much talk of "emptiness"—so much so that the film verges on camp. (Observes one character: "Sometimes life is a little hard.") All this and a "bus" with a hooded corpse and a painter who paints a Dance of Death. ("It might be a good idea to scare people once in a while.")

See also *Last Action Hero, The.*

**The SEVENTH SIGN** Tri-Star & Delphi/Interscope Communications (Columbia Pictures/Ted Field, R. W. Cort) 1988 color/ws 97m. D: Carl Schultz. SP: W. W. Wicket, George Kaplan? Mus: Jack Nitzsche. SpMkpFX: Craig Reardon; Kevin Yeager. SpVisFX: Dream Quest Images; (sup) Michael L. Fink. Anim FX: Steve Socki et al. SpFxCoord: Philip Cory. Ref: TV. MFB'88:339-40. ad. V 4/6/88. SFChron 4/4/88. Morse. Scheuer. Martin. Maltin '92. With Demi Moore, Michael Biehn, Jurgen Prochnow (David, the boarder), Peter Friedman (Father Lucci), John Heard.

"I'm His messenger—I was here before. I came as the lamb, but I return as the lion." In Haiti, the ocean "dies." In Nicaragua, a river turns to blood. The Negev Desert, Israel, yields Sodom II. Another bad sign: "The moon has turned to blood." And in Venice, California, David, a "deliverer," vies with Father Lucci, who turns out to be the cursed Roman soldier who struck Christ. The weary Lucci can die only if the whole human race dies, and he means to see that the final sign of the Apocalypse is fulfilled—a child born without a soul.

Eventually, everyone gets into the act except the Wandering Jew and the Flying Dutchman. This overcrowding makes for some fun, despite the general heaviness, but the script suffers from delusions of grandeur and includes the old Hollywood staples, sacrifice and mother love: Heroine Abby (Moore) proves to have "hope enough for the whole world," and trades her life for her baby's. *The Seventh Sign* does for Leviticus, Joel, and Revelations what *The Curse* does better, exclusively for Revelations.

**SEVERED TIES** Col-TriStar/Fangoria Films (Webster/First Three Co.) 1992 color 95m. (*Army*—shooting t). Story, D: Damon Santostefano. SP: John Nystrom, Henry Dominic. Ph: Geza Sinkovics? Mus: Daniel Licht. PD: Don Day. SpMkpFX: KNB. SdFX: Jim Moore. Ref: TV. V 5/18/92. 5/6/91:62. PT 14:11. SFChron Dtbk 8/30/92. With Oliver Reed, Elke Sommer, Garrett Morris, Billy Morrissette, Johnny Legend, Denise Wallace.

A scientist, Harrison Harrison (Morrissette), experimenting in gene bonding with plasma regenerates his own lost arm. Ripped off, the arm develops a "mouth," a tail, and a mind of its own and is sent on special missions. Meanwhile, Stripes' (Morris) new leg at first looks like a snake-thing. All the "mutant arms" in the neighborhood eventually rebel; at the end, gene fusion produces an Eve (Wallace) body with a Helena (Sommer) will.

Negligible plot, but the relationships between people and parts are amusing. A *Basket Case* influence seems apparent. One of those bits which make it all worthwhile: Helena caresses son Harrison's severed arm, recoils at the nasty tear point, chucks it in the round file.

**SEWAGE BABY** Vipco/Suckling(Michael Helman) 1989 color 85m. SP, D, P, Ed: Francis Teri. Ph: Harry Eisenstein. Mus: Joseph Teri. PD: Mike Rich. Creature FX: Ralph Cordero. MkpFX: Craig Lindberg. Puppets: Robert Curet. Meltdown FX: Sciacca, Schwab. Ref: TV: Vipco video; *The Suckling* - orig t. no Stanley. V 2/21/90:152(ad). With Frank Reeves, Lisa Patruno, Marie Michaels, Hector Collazo (creature).

"A thing attacked her!" In 1973 Brooklyn, toxic waste mutates and enlarges an aborted fetus in a sewer. ("It travels through the pipes.") Meanwhile, a weird sort of membrane blocks the exit to the brothel above.... Gorecard: some good, partly stopmo effects for the tiny thing ... a cornier, more conventional big thing ... functional storytelling ... stilted acting ... and a temporarily crawling hand.

**SEX ALIENS** Caballero (Jimmy Houston) 1987 color 80m. D: Ted Gorley, Morris Deal. Ref: vc trailer: spaceships, aliens. Adam '89: "droids," pregnant man. With Candie Evans, Blondi, Sheena Horne.

**SEX AND THE SINGLE ALIEN** Contact/Van Elk 1993 color feature. SP, D, P: P. Daskaloff. SP: also F. Fowler. Ph: D. Makiesky. Mus: V. Kolenic. Mkp: R. Fleetwood. Ref: TV. Vallejo Times-Herald 5/2/94. With Eric Kohner, M. Rose.

Supposed UFO abducts Harry. The second time, it's the real thing: Aliens take Harry and an ancient Roman. Back on Earth, Harry finds that he can make love to women just by standing there and concentrating. ("How did you do that, Harry?") Lax, very basic t&a material.

**SEX AND THE SINGLE VAMPIRE** SWV 1971 color feature. Ref: SWV supp.'96. With John Holmes, S. Dempsey.

Count Spatula (Holmes) vs. "seven swingers."

**SEX AND ZEN** (H.K.) Rim Film/Golden Harvest (Johnny Mak/Stephen Siu) 1993 color/ws 99m. D: Michael Mak. SP: Lee Ying Kit, from Li Yu's "Prayer Mat of the Flesh." Ph: Peter Ngor. Mus: Chan Wing Leung. AD: Raymond Lee. Ref: TV: vt; Eng. titles. SFChron 12/31/93. V 3/1/93: "grotesque, goofball humor." 8/23/93:13: in L.A. With Amy Yip, Isabella Chow, Lawrence Ng, Kent Chang.

"Slapdash" penis transplant. ("An elephant! Isn't it too big?") Key line: "Please put a horse's prick on me." Outrageous science-fantasy-comedy is occasionally surprisingly erotic, occasionally very funny, occasionally wild and crude, occasionally just exploitative—a sort of Carry On, Phallus, with overtones of Larry, Moe, and Curly. Key surgical instrument: the Guillotine.

**SEX BEAST ON CAMPUS** (J) 1994 feature (*Inju Gakuen*). D: K. Kobayashi. Ref: Weisser/JC: a live-action *Wandering Kid*. With S. Hidaka, M. Takahashi.

"The bad guy has the ability to transform into liquid."

**SEX CRIMES: 2084** Platinum Pictures 1985 color 68m. SP, D, P: Chuck Vincent. SP: also John Blaise. Ph: Larry Revene. Mus: Ian Shaw, Kai Joffe. Mkp: Jo Hanson. Opt: Videart. Ref: TV: Essex Video. SFExam 11/28/86. Genesis 5/86: hardcore. V 10/7/91:220. Adam '88. With Sherry St. Clair, Billy Dee, Robert Bullock, Colleen Brennan, Taija Rae, Sharon Cain, Siobhan Hunter.

New Year's Eve, 2084. In this wild future, where sex cops enforce laws against chastity and celibacy, three of them take a 48-hour time trip—via a "time compressor"—back to the Twentieth Century. One cop falls for an "old-fashioned girl" and stays behind. Also: a seance sequence.... One funny scene in which cop St. Clair tries to convince an old-fashioned nerd that her passion for him is real. Otherwise worthless.

**SEX DRIVE 2020** 1988 color feature. Ref: Adam '93G. with Eric Manchester, William Margold, Jerry Butler.

Post-nuke L.A.

**SEX F/X** Ambassador Video/Visual Persuasion (Kensington-West) 1986 color 85m. D: "Darrel Lovestrange." SP: "Leif Jeneriksen." Mus: Algebra. Ref: vc box. Adam '88. With Danielle, Tracey Adams, Summer Rose.

Futuristic Syntheroticizer device.

**The SEX KILLER** Mahon 1967 b&w 55m. D: Barry Mahon. Ref: SMV Supp.: necrophiliac/killer. no Lee.

**SEX TREK: THE NEXT PENETRATION** Moonlight 1990 color 82m. D: Scotty Fox. Ref: Adam '92. With Randy Spears, Mike Horner, Joey Silvera, Jeanna Fine.

"Space dudes go to investigate the planet Uranus...."

**SEX TREK II: THE SEARCH FOR SPERM** Moonlight Ent. 1991 color 79m. D: Scotty Fox. SP: Cash Markman. Ref: vc box: "alien sex rituals" & the Starship *Plunderer*. Adam '93. With Danielle Rogers, Randy Spears, Mimi Miyagi.

**SEX TREK III: THE WRATH OF BOB** Moonlight 1992 color 77m. D: Scotty Fox. SP: Cash Markman. Ref: Adam'94: aliens. With D. Simone, A. Rio, R. West.

**SEX TREK IV: THE NEXT ORGASM** Moonlight 1994 color feature. Ref: vc box.

**SEX WARS** Excalibur Films 1986 (1985) color c70m. D, P: Bob Vosse. Story, SP, P: Arthur King. Story: also Thomas Street. Ph: S. F. Brown. Mus: Bert Schenk. Set Des: Jim Malibu. Mkp: David Clark. Ref: TV: Excalibur Video. Adam '88. SFExam 11/21/86 (ad). With Robin Cannes, Laurie Smith, Paul Thomas, Mai Lin, Howard Darkley (4-Q's voice), De Ja Vou.

Princess Layme (Cannes) shanghais Mark Starkiller (Richard Pacheco) and Brinker Duo (Thomas) to help her find her sister, Princess Orgasma (Smith), lost in space near Tyros, in the Lesbos star system. Plus: Lil's Last Dance Space Saloon, or cantina, on Pluto ... the gas-operated robot 4-Q ... and the evil Lord Balthazar (Darkley), ruler of Tyros, who turns spacemen into "workers".... Limp adult takeoff on the *Star Wars* saga.

See also: *Gonad the Barbarian*.

**SEX WORLD GIRLS** Arrow Video (Edwards-Dawson) 1987 color 88m. D: Ron Jeremy. Ref: Adam '88. With Tracey Adams, Rachel Ashley, Sue Nero.

"Set in the future, when the human race has moved underground."

Sequel: *Tracey's Love Chamber*.

**SEXANDROIDE** (F) 1987 color feature? D: Michel Ricaud. Ref: Jones. With Daniel Dubois.

Sf-horror-hardcore re vampires.

**SEXLINERS** CDI 1991 color 74m. D: Jack Stephen. Ref: Adam '92. With Alicyn Sterling, Raven Richards, Joey Silvera.

Mad scientist's (Silvera) "rapture gene" eliminates "remorse and guilt."

**SEXMISSION** (Polish) Film Polski "Kadr" Unit 1984 (1983/'85-U.S.) color 116m. (*Sexmisja*). SP, D: Julius Machulski. SP: also J. Hartwig, P. Hajny. Ph: Jerzy Lukaszewicz. Mus: H. Kuzniak. Ref: Dr. Rolf Giesen. V 8/1/84: Seksmisja. Bay Guardian 4/10/85: "hilarious, witty." With Olgierd Lukaszewicz, Jerzy Stuhr, Botsena Stryjkowna.

Year 2044. Men frozen fifty years too long emerge in a women's society.

**SEXO SANGRIENTO** (Sp) Manuel Esteba Prods. 1981 color 105m. (84m.). SP, D, P: Manuel Esteba Gallego. SP: also Xavier Flores. Ph: Jose Luis Valls. Ref: Hardy/HM: "crude exploitation movie." Ecran F 53:70. With Ovidi Montllor, Mirta Miller, Diana Conca, Viki Palma, Elisa Romero.

Clairvoyant, madman, sadism, murder. *Bloodthirsty Sex*—tr t.

**SEXORCISTA, La** see *Satanico Pandemonium*

**SEXUAL DEVIL** (H.K.?) New Treasurer Films/Top Approach Films 1990? color c85m. Ref: TV: World Video; no Eng.

Principal devils include an exorcist who, a) uses baby crocs like voodoo dolls to make victims spit up, b) raises the spirit from a woman's body, and, c) steps out of his own body and possesses a woman, who then speaks in his voice ... a ghost woman who uses her unfurling gown to catch the hero by the ankles ... and photography models who, when seen through a camera lens, look like ghosts.... Clumsy, grade-C shot-on-tape chiller at one point borrows some *Halloween* music.

**SEXUAL VOODOO** see *Macumba Sexual*

**SEXVISION** Hollywood 1992 color 86m. D: Jim Enright. Ref: Adam '93. With Tonisha Mills, Mona Lisa, T. T. Boy, Peter North.

Writer's ideas—including a sequence with female aliens on Earth—come to life.

**SEXY CAT** (Sp) Titanic Films 1972 color/ws 87m. SP, D, P: Julio Perez Tabernero. Ph: A. Nieva. Ref: Hardy/HM: "slasher killings." Hound. With Dianik Zurakowska, German Cobos, Lone Fleming, Monica Kolpek, Maria Villa, A. Vidal Molina.

**SEXY GHOST** (H.K.) Hop Chung Film 1993 color feature. Ref: vc box.

**SEXY NATURE** see *Comtesse Perverse, La*

**SEYTAN** (Turkish) Saner Video 1974 101m. D: Metin Erksan. SP: Yilmaz Tumiurk. Ref: VW 20:29-30: *Exorcist* imitation with "monstrous teddy bear." Monster! 3:51, 52: "much more entertaining" than *The Exorcist*. With Cihan Unal, Canan Perver, Meral Taygun.

**\*SH! THE OCTOPUS** 1937 60m. From a play by R. Murphy and D. Gallaher and the play "The Gorilla" by Ralph Spence. AD: Max Parker. Ref: TV. V 12/8/37. Lee. Lentz. no Maltin '92. no Scheuer. Stanley. Svehla/GP.

Ingredients: a spooky lighthouse ... a radium ray (in the planning stages) ... clutching tentacles (instead of clutching hands) ... Captain Hook (George Rosener), so-called for his hand-hook apparatus ... a sinisterly moving candle (on the back of a tortoise) ... mysteriously "walking" shoes (with frogs inside them) ... and, again and again, Lights Out.

Fast enough, but totally uninspired. The identity of the Octopus gets to be pretty obvious as the rest of the cast are revealed to be secret agents, detectives, etc. Then: an all-a-dream ending. Hugh Herbert's trademark fidgety befuddlement as Kelly is the only amusing note.

The **SHADOW** Univ (Bregman-Baer-Bregman) 1994 color/ws 107m. D: Russell Mulcahy. SP: David Koepp. Based on the *Advance Magazine* character. Ph: Stephen H. Burum. Mus: Jerry Goldsmith. PD: Joseph Nemec III. SpMkpFX: Greg Cannom. VisFX: R/Greenberg, Illusion Arts, (digital anim) Fumi Mashimo, Matte World Digital, Fantasy II, VCE/Peter Kuran. MinFX: Stetson;(ph) Chandler Group. OptFX: Howard Anderson. Digital: Pacific Title. SpFX:(coord) K.A. Pepiot;(sup) Albert Delgado. Ref: TV: MCA-Univ HV. With Alec Baldwin, John Lone, Penelope Ann Miller, Ian McKellen, Peter Boyle, Jonathan Winters, Tim Curry, James Hong, Larry Hankin, Frank Welker.

"The clouded mind sees nothing." A Tibetan mystic gives Lamont Cranston (Baldwin)—the Butcher of Lhasa—the power to "cloud men's minds" and thus right wrongs. Soon, as The Shadow, Cranston has his headquarters in New York City and "dozens of agents all over the world." Meanwhile, a descendant (Lone) of Genghis Khan absorbs the latter's extraordinary powers from his Silver Coffin, and Margo Lane (Miller) penetrates The Shadow's mind ... and then She Knows, too. Plus a coin/medallion made of the "very stuff the universe was formed of" ... an invisible hotel (thanks to mass hypnosis) ... and a super-TV.... The initial Shadow Knows sequence (his shadow and his laugh are everywhere) is very promising, suggestive as it is of a Fantasy of Justice, and the visualized nightmare in which Cranston tears off his face to reveal the face of his nemesis is a case of a makeup effect doubling as a thematic point. But character and plot here are mostly your basic Superhero Bland. Neat number 1: the dagger with teeth and an attitude. Neat number 2: Cranston's thought-gram to Margo across town. Neat number 3: the initially-invisible Hotel Monolith.

See also *Crimson Wolf.*

**SHADOW DANCING** (Can.) SGE/Source (Kay Bachman) 1988 color 105m. (*Stage Fright*—orig t). D: Lewis Furey. SP: Christine Foster. Ph: Rene Ohashi. Mus: Jay Gruska. PD: B. Matis. Ref: V 10/19/88: 239, 243 (rev), 106 (ad), 185: "fatuous script." Fango 94:12. With Nadine Van der Velde, Christopher Plummer, James Kee, John Colicos.

Spirit of dancer Lili La Nuit takes over young hoofer.

**SHADOW HUNTER** see *Shadowhunter*

***SHADOW OF CHINATOWN** Carmel Prods. 1936 71m. Ref: TV: Timeless Video. TVFFSB: JED-TV. Turner/Price. Lee. Lentz. TVG. Lennig. With Maurice Liu, Henry Hall.

Victor Poten (Bela Lugosi)—the "Chinatown Killer" and a "Frankenstein monster"—dissatisfied with the races on Earth, is out to create a "new race." His super-hypnotic powers turn one man into a near-zombie, and his "advanced form of television" allows him to "see and hear what is going on in any room" in which he has placed a certain "small contrivance".... Awkwardly staged action. And poor sound recording sabotages some of Lugosi's dialogue. At least, he occasionally gets some good Sinister lighting and close-ups. The Lugosi line to remember this time: "I took steps to see that he STOPS ... THINKING!"

**SHADOW OF DEATH** see *Destroyer*

**SHADOW OF ILLUSION** (I) Cantharus/Liger (Nino Milano) 1972 color/ws c90m. (*Ombra di Illusione*). SP, D: Mario Caiano. SP: also Frank Agrama, Enrico Rossetti. Ph: Enrico Menczer. Mus: Carlo Savina. PD: Daniele Rizzo. Mkp: G. De Rossi. Ref: TV: VSOM; Eng.-Lang. version. MV. VW 25:25-6. With Daniela Giordano, Krista Nell, William Berger, Antonio Cantafora, Mirella Pamphili, Enzo Maggio.

"Immortals still exist." Egypt. The "girl with the flaming red hair" and the Isis ring is chosen to be the bride of Osiris, who saves her from being sacrificed on an altar. Plus a working voodoo doll.... Vapid City. Almost 50 percent travelogue-ish padding and almost no story.

**SHADOW PLAY** New World/Millennium Pictures (Dan Biggs, Will Vinton) 1986 color 95m. SP, D, Co-P: Susan Shadburne. Mus: Jon Newton. SpVisFX: Vinton Prods., Bruce McKean. Opt: Alpha Cine FX. Ref: TV. V 5/21/86. SFExam 9/26/86. Hound. Maltin '92. Martin. With Dee Wallace-Stone, Cloris Leachman, Ron Kuhlman, Barry Laws.

"Souls that were once intertwined may reach out after death." "Supernatural things" seem to be happening to author Morgan Hanna (Wallace-Stone), who has (visualized) nightmares and visions re her fiance, Jeremy (Laws), who died ten years ago. Tepid, drawn-out romantic fantasy, with chiller overtones. Superficially "poetic."

**SHADOW WARRIORS** SGE/SAK 1994 color c80m. D: L. Card. SP: S.A. Finly. Ref: vc box: "techno-sapiens" made from human corpses. With T. O'Quinn, T.P. Cavanaugh.

**SHADOW WORLD** (U.S.-J) 3B & New Hope & Eiken (Modern Programs Int'l.) 1983 anim color c80m. SP, D: Michael Part. D: also Hiroyuki Torii. From the TV series "UFO Dai-Apolon." Story: T. Kariya, S. Tsuchiyama. Mus: Douglas Lackey. SdDes: James Hodson. Ref: TV: Hi-Tops Video. Hound. Stanley. V. Max 3:2. Voices: Richard Rossner, Marla Scott et al.

The near future. Terry—a "real live spaceman" from Apolon, 300 million light years from Earth—has, implanted in his chest, the key to his planet's Energy Generator and Absorption Device. He uses the power of "body merger" to become part of a giant flying robot which does battle with a mutant race and its giant monsters, which include the Avenger and a metallic, bat-like creature from the Shadow World that is "capable of absorbing all energy."

A betrayal of an evocative title. Stilted, familiar galactic skirmishing involves combination robots, "Forces," and a sentimental subtext re orphans, lost mothers, and dead fathers. Only unexpected element: the peace-not-revenge moral, though it seems to take much war to get a little peace.

**SHADOWHUNTER** Republic/Sandstorm Films/Kottenbrook-Einbinder (Rope of Sand Prods.) 1993 (1992) color c98m. (aka *Shadow Hunter*). SP, D: J.S. Cardone. Ph: Michael Cardone. Mus: Robert Folk. PD: William Maynard. SpMkp: Mark Shostrom. OptFX: Perpetual Motion Pictures;(vis fx sup) Richard Malzahn;(opt sup) Robert Habros. SdFxSup: A. Marfiak. Ref: TV. Martin. TVG. Vallejo Times-Herald 7/17/94: made for cable. With Scott Glenn, Angela Alvarado, Benjamin Bratt, Robert Beltran, Tim Sampson, George Aguilar.

"They walk inside your dreams." Nakai Twobear (Bratt) is a Navajo "boogeyman"—a "coyote man," or witch doctor, or "skinwalker" who gives cop-hero John Cain (Glenn) bad dreams and hallucinations. Killing makes the coyote man strong.... Main plus: Arizona scenery. Main minus: stilted storytelling.

**SHADOWS AND FOG** Orion/Rollins-Joffe (Greenhut) 1991 b&w 86m. SP, D: Woody Allen. Ph: Carlo Di Palma. PD: Santo Loquasto. OptFX:(sup) Balsmeyer & Everett; The FX House. Mkp: Bernadette Mazur. Ref: TV: Orion HV. V 2/17/92: "sweet homage to German expressionist filmmaking ... a nice try that falls short." SFChron 3/20/92: "a great looking film, but more important, a sweet one." New York 3/30/92: "mad scientist experimenting with body parts." With W. Allen, Mia Farrow, John Malkovich, Madonna, Donald Pleasence, Lily Tomlin, Jodie Foster, Kathy Bates, John Cusack, Kate Nelligan, Fred Gwynne, Julie Kavner, Kenneth Mars, David Ogden Stiers, Josef Sommer, Kurtwood Smith, Wallace Shawn, Eszter Balint, Michael Kirby (killer).

"Evil stalker" terrorizes European city with a "series of stranglings."(SFC) ("He always strikes in the fog.") An instant curiosity—Woody Allen one-liners in *The Last Laugh* or *M* or *The Three Penny Opera.* Would-be validation of paranoia has the aural and visual flatness of the shot-on-tape, but the production design lends some atmosphere. Philosophically ambitious, but paper-thin.

**SHADOWS IN THE DARK** 4-Play 1989 color 109m. D: Bruce Seven. Ref: Adam '92. Jones. With Tianna, Victoria Paris, Bionca, Randy Spears (alien vampire), Tom Byron.

**\*SHADOWS IN THE NIGHT** Darmour 1944 (*The Crime Doctor's Rendezvous* - orig t). Ref: TV. Lee. V 8/2/44. Lentz. Stanley. Maltin '92. Scheuer. Pitts/Horror Film Stars. With Ben Welden.

"This looks like Dr. Ordway's nightmare!" Ravencliff, on Rocky Point. A commercial artist (Nina Foch) dreams, or seems to dream, about a "woman from some other time" who "seems to be part of the fog that drifts through the window." This surprisingly spooky image proves to be the product of a hypnotic gas and a man in a mask. ("A moving figure attracts anyone under the influence of the gas.")

Horror-angled Crime Doctor entry has an interesting premise re nightmare "manipulation," but script and direction are flatfooted, and the only eerie element is the woman in the fog. George Zucco's post-nervous-breakdown scientist Frank Swift is now into "research and experimental work," but his main role in the story is red herring.

**SHADOWS RUN BLACK** Media Gallery/Mesa Films (Eric Louzil/L. A. Koernig) 1984 (1981) color 89m. D: Howard Heard. Story, SP: Craig Kusaba. SP: also Duke Howard. Mkp: Wendy L. Tolkin. SdFxEd: Steve Mann. Opt: Dave Hewitt. Ref: TV: Lightning Video. V 7/16/86. Hound. Phantom. Maltin '92. Stanley. With William J. Kulzer (Rydell King), Elizabeth Trosper, Shea Porter, George J. Engelson, Kevin Costner, Ron Halpern.

A madman—variously dubbed The Black Angel and The Coed Strangler—uses his vise-like grip to commit several murders and makes macabre use of a teddy bear. ("Mommy!") Flat acting,

writing, and directing in this combo slasher-film/girlie-film. A real collection here of bad actors, or non-actors.

**SHADOWZONE** Full Moon (Carol Kottenbrook) 1990 (1989) color 88m. SP, D: J. S. Cardone. Mus: Richard Band. PD: Don Day. SpMkp: Mark Shostrom. SpFxCoord: Jeff Jackson. VisFX: (sup) Richard Malzahn; Perpetual Motion Pictures. Ref: TV. V 3/21/90:35 (hv). Hound. Scheuer. Martin. With Louise Fletcher, David Beecroft, James Hong, Shawn Weatherly, Lu Leonard, Miguel Nunez.

"John Doe has come to visit." Dr. Van Fleet's (Hong) Project Shadowzone, at the Jackass Flats Proving Grounds, takes subjects "beyond normal levels of dream-state sleep," where they discover a "parallel dimension." The catch: a "John Doe" from that other dimension. This accomplished shape-shifter—the "ultimate intellect"—can "expand and contract its molecular structure at will," and re-form itself into any image in its victim's fear-ridden mind.... Film's premise semi-cleverly scrambles *The Thing* remake and *Nightmare on Elm Street,* but the tired script opts for familiar sf-suspense situations.

**SHAITANI ILAAKA** (India—Hindi) Ramsay Movies (Reshma Ramsay) 1990 color c150m. D: Kiran Ramsay. Story: J. K. Ahuja. Dial: Sajeev Kapoor. Ph: S. Pappu. Mus: Bappi Lahiri; (lyr) Anjaan. Art: Vasant Katkar. Mkp: Srinivas Roy. Opt: Milgrey (sp?) Optical. Ref: TV: Kings Video; little Eng. With Deepak Prashar, Sri Pradha, Kanwaljit Singh, Neelam Mehra, Surendar Pal, Satish Shah, Ranjeet, Sunaina, Shenaaz, Hemani Gupta, Varun.

Chief horrors in this Hindi monster epic include a huge, hairy monster which, in the climactic sequence, is swallowed up by the ground, during an earthquake ... voodoo dolls and hands which make a man disfigure and slash himself ... monster men at a nocturnal human sacrifice ... a sorceress who, shot in the head, turns rip-roaring monstrous, then becomes a bird ... a possessed man who coughs up the sorceress (in bird form) ... a duel between a priest and the sorceress in which they afflict each other with makeup effects on face and hands ... and a vision of malevolent crawling vines.... Film rambles and includes musical interludes which go on and on, but the horror scenes are full-throttle and full of screaming, growling, near-gore, and ominous fog. One fun "bus" on a bus.

**SHAKE, RATTLE AND ROLL** (Fili) 1984 color feature. Ref: vc box: refrigerator which falls in love with woman turns out to be a monster which swallows her up.

**SHAKE, RATTLE & ROLL 2** (Fili) Regal Films (Jenny Luber/Lily Monteverde) 1990 color c125m. Story, SP, D: Peque Gallaga, Lore Reyes. Story, SP, PD: Don Escudero. SP: also Dwight Gaston. Ph: E. F. Jacinto. Mus: Toto Gentica. SpVisFX: Teofilo Hilario. Creatures & Prosth: Sammy Arranzamendez et al. Mkp: Andrea Manahan; (prosth) Len Santos. Fangs: Loida Lanuza. SdFX: Dany Sanchez. Ref: TV: Regal Films video; occ. English. Springstowne Home Video: "aswang"—a liver-eating, vampire-like spirit. With Janice de Belen, Eric Quizon, Caridad Sanchez, Eddie Guiterrez (Dr. Corpus), Isabel Granada; Joey Marquez, Daisy Romualdez, Lotlot de Leon (Tiyanak prey), Carmina Villarroel, Sylvia Sanchez,

Joey Reyes; Manilyn Reynes, Ana Roces, Rez Cortez, Romy Romulo (aswang).

"Multo": When the groom slips a ring onto his finger, the ghost of an abortionist possesses him, and his bride "sees" the doctor stab a girl, then shoot himself. The bride severs her husband's ring finger, and he is freed. Unnecessarily grisly slasher horror. "Kulam": A witch's voodoo doll summons up little horned, cabbage-headed biting creatures and revives a hospital's dead. Broad but amusing comedy of pain. "Aswang": Villagers drink sacrificial blood, become toothy monsters. Familiar but well done horror shortie.

**SHAKE RATTLE & ROLL III** (Fili) Good Harvest Unltd. (Joey Gosiengfiao/R. S. & R. G. Monteverde) 1991? color c130m. Story, D: Peque Gallaga, Lore Reyes. Story, PD: Don Escudero. SP: J. L. Sineneng. Ph: Joe Tutanes. Mus: Toto Gentica. Ref: TV: vt; scant Eng. With Kris Aquino, Ogie Alcasid, Rosemarie Gil, Eva Ramos; Janice de Belen, Joel Torre, A. S. Reyna, Joey Reyes; Manilyn Reynes, Joey Marquez, Ricardo Cepeda.

"Yaya": Thanks to the wind effects, this is a pretty creepy, if seemingly simple baby-in-jeopardy anecdote re a wind witch who is after a baby. "Ate": Hard-to-sort-out melodrama re madness, poison, a cult, and whatnot. "Nanay": A young woman takes the eggs of an "unknown animal" from the sea and places them in a canister. The mama, or papa, "undine," or water spirit, follows. This comically hairy-headed, frog-legged little horror takes to hiding in toilets and makes one victim disintegrate very gooily, leaving only her Bugs Bunny slippers. (The beastie seems to have an unlimited supply of goo.) At the finish, our heroine restores eggs and parent to sea.... Funny, balmy little horror-comedy gives new meaning to the phrase "bathroom humor," throws in some bathroom horror for good measure.

**SHAKE RATTLE & ROLL IV** (Fili) Regal Films 1992 color 114m. Story, D: Peque Gallaga, Lore Reyes. SP: Jerry Lopez Sineneng. Story: also Don Escudero. Ph: Joe Tutanes. Mus: Archie Castillo. AD: Roy Lachica. Prosth: Benny Batoctoy. SpFX: Torrente, Antonio. SdFX: Danny Sanchez. Ref: TV: Regal video; no Eng. With Janice De Belen, Edu Manzano, Manilyn Reynes.

"Ang Guro": A chemical potion turns a man into a super-strong monster. Unremarkable.

"Ang Kapitbahay": One fair "bus" in a sentimental tale re a hairy, sympathetic tree-creature (i.e., he lives in a tree stump) called a Witawit (Rene Hinojales).

"Ang Madre": Gross, horrific makeup effects in this tale of a "manananggal," a big-bat-winged vampire that can split in half, horizontally—the top half then flies off in search of prey. Is this a borrowing from Thai folklore/monster movies?

**SHAKMA** Flash Ent. (Hugh Parks/Quest Studios) 1990 color 101m. (aka *Nemesis*). D, P: H. Parks. SP: Roger Engle. Mus: D. C. Williams. SpMkpFX: Rick Gonzales. Co-D: Tom Logan. Ref: TV. V 12/31/90. 5/6/91:76. SFChron Dtbk 9/23/90. TVG. With Christopher Atkins, Amanda Wyss, Ari Meyers, Roddy McDowall, Robb Morris, Greg Flowers, Tre Laughlin.

Players involved overnight in a computer game at a research center find that someone, or something, is "playing a different game," and killing off the participants. Weird injections, it seems, have aggravated Shakma, a lab baboon, and turned him into a hyper-ape.... Routine suspense-horror. Main motif: bloody dead bodies.

**The SHAMAN** Artist Ent./Silverline Films 1987 color c82m. SP, D: Michael Yakub. SP, Mus: Robert Yakub. PD: Elaine Vastardis. SpMkp: Mike Maddi. Ref: TV: Imperial Ent. video. V 9/30/87:4 (rated). no Martin. Hound. V 10/21/87:124: *Shaman*. With Michael Conforti, James Farkas, Mike Hodge, Lynn Weaver, Michelle Kronin, Elaine Graham, Ilene Kristen, Eivind Harum (The Shaman).

"Our time has come!" The Shaman says he needs a successor. He says he has control over the "forces of life and death." But does he want to "save the world from its own destruction" or simply "use people to get power?" At any rate, he enlists Jack (Conforti) in his vague plans, which involve murder and apparent super-hypnosis. (His new "recruits" obey him like zombies.)

Some promise in the acting (especially by Kristen and Harum) and dialogue, but nothing much comes of anything here. Both the means and ends of the Shaman remain vague until the climax, when he gets shot and dies.

**The SHAOLIN BROTHERS** (H.K.) c1981? color/ws c88m. (*The Legend of Living Corpse*—vc box t). D: Joseph Kuo. Ref: TV: Video Village; no Eng.; Vietnamese version.

Period drama featuring a line of hopping vampires, or ghosts, a flying she-ghost, and a disfigured hunchback. Foolish mixture of kung fu, comedy, and fantasy-horror.

See also: *Legend of Living Corpse* (which seems to be the same film, minus the hunchback).

**The SHAOLIN INVINCIBLES** (H.K.) Hai Hua Cinema Co. 1983 color c90m. D: Hou Cheng. SP, PD: Yeung Chi Hsiao. Mus: Wang Chu Jen. SpFX: Hsi Su Jan. Ref: TV: Ocean Shores Video; Eng. dubbed. no Hound. With Huang Chia Ta, Chia Ling, Tan Tao Liang, Chen Hung Lieh, Lung Chun Erh.

Conventional revenge story, set during the Ching Dynasty, sports some bizarre elements, including two kung fu apes invincible "except for one place on the top of their heads." ("And they seem to know kung fu!") Sword blades have no effect on the apes until the two heroines discover their secret, stab them, and blood fountains out the tops of their heads, in a funny but gruesome scene. There are also two kung fu wizards with long, whip-like tongues (they crack them at the hero, but he simply ties them together and snaps them back into their faces), a royal architect locked so long in a dungeon that he has grown a huge, monstrous eyeball ("I am no one!"), and a "ghost" scene.

**SHAO-LIN LEGEND** (Taiwanese) c1984? color/ws c95m. Ref: TV: vt; Eng. titles. MMarquee 43:7.

The spirit of Ying Tien-sheng, the "damned guy," possesses the boy Wu-Hua, who kills another boy, then ten years later returns to the temple and, using devil kung fu, kills the master. ("Could such a well-behaved gentleman possibly be the devil?") The innocent Wu-Hua, "bound by spell," returns to the Sutras Tower, where the spell began, and battles Ying Tien-sheng.

Spirit possession here is an excuse for martial arts duels, only one of which will be of interest to fantasy fans: In it, Wu-Hua appears suddenly, in ghost form, and sword blades pass through him. He becomes solid and sticks his hand, knife-like, into a foe's body, then detaches and "shoots" his right arm at another foe and retrieves it. Script marks time until the revelation that Wu-Hua's possession is intermittent. ("I have only memories in segments, with blanks in-between.") "Jekyll" proceeds to exorcise "Hyde," at the cost of his own life.

**SHARK—ROSSO NELL'OCEANO** see *Devil Fish*

**SHARKS** see *Deep Blood*

**SHATTER DEAD** Tempe/Seeing Eye Dog 1993 color 82m. SP, D: Scooter McCrae. Ph: M.M. Howe. Mus: Steven Rajkumar, Geek Messiah. SpMkpFX: A.M. Jolly, Lee Malecki. SpFxSup: Pericles Lewnes. SdFxDes: Masha Yaslovki. Ref: TV: Tempe Video. PT 19:5: shot in Middletown, New York. 18:14. Videoscope 11/15/94. Bill Warren. Imagi Smr'95:62. With Daniel Johnson, Stark Raven, Flora Fauna (Mary), Robert Wells (Preacher Man), Marina Del Rey, John Weiner.

"Nobody dies anymore." This world of immortal suicides and other zombies naturally poses Problems of the Undying but Deteriorating and suggests a society in which prosthetics experts and plastic surgeons would rule. Finally, it's just a variation on "The Monkey's Paw," and not as good a one as Deathdream. One subtheme: Zombies Can't Do It. For the viewer, the movie constitutes New Challenges in Grossness. And after twenty exchanges like "Life's not fair"/"Neither is death," Challenged Viewer will want to check out of this hotel of the dead and pseudo-dead. Shot on tape.

**SHATTERBRAIN** see *Resurrected, The*

**SHE** (I-U.S.) American Nat'l./The Sarluis 1983 ('85-U.S.) color 106m. SP, D: Avi Nesher, "inspired by" H. Rider Haggard's novel. Mus: Rick Wakeman. SpFX: Armando Grilli. Mkp: O. & S. Fava. SdFX: Studio Sound. Ref: TV. TVG. V 12/25/85. Maltin '92. Hound. Morse. Martin. no Scheuer. With Sandahl Bergman (She, the Goddess), Harrison Muller, Quin Kessler, David Goss, Elena Widermann, Gordon Mitchell, Laurie Sherman; David Brandon and Susan Adler (werewolves/vampires); Gregory Snegoff (Godan), Donald Hodson (Rabel).

"Year 23—After the Cancellation." Strange sf-horror-comedy-fantasy stew features sleeping, snoring people who transform into werewolves, or vampires; the telekinetic Godan; Rabel, a Dr. Moreau-type; mutants with chainsaws; a diminishing room; and a dead-pop-culture freak, Xenon (David Traylor), who is a fan of "Green Acres" and whose arm, when sliced off, grows a new, nonstop-chatter freak.

Film is determinedly disorienting, winds up just quirky, though a few of its episodes are outlandish enough to be amusing. Production style: postnuclear tacky. Cultural Adviser: Zippy the Pinhead. Line to remember: "Now, you have an opportunity to be a Nork."

**SHE-DEVIL, The** see *Nibelungen, Die*

**SHE REMINDS ME OF YOU** Para/Fleischer 1934 anim c7m. D: Dave Fleischer. Anim: Bowsky & Sturm. Ref: TV: Screen Songs; UM&M-TV. Cabarga/TFS. LC. With the Eton Boys.

Fully-automated Theatre of Tomorrow features neon-like electric writing in the air, mechanical "powder room" and "barber shop" facilities in the seats (tip requested), instant aisles, and an X-ray machine which allows the patron to see through the head of any oversized person blocking his or her view. Clever theatre "modernizations"; catchy title tune.

**SHE WAS A HIPPY VAMPIRE** see *Wild World of Batwoman*

**SHEMAN—MISTRESS OF THE UNIVERSE** (Fili) Viva Films 1988? color c103m. SP, D: Tony Reyes. SP, P: Joey De Leon. Ph: Rody Lacap. Mus D: Jimmy Fabregas. PD: Melchor Defensor. VisFX: Cinemagic. Ref: TV: Viva Video; sparse Eng. With Panchito, Ruffa Guiterrez, Dennis Da Silva, Ruel Vernal, Palito, Sunshine, Vic Sotto, Jimmy Santos.

A fireball crashes to Earth, and an effeminate, caped gentleman, a Death-like figure complete with scythe, and several monsters appear. (The scythe turns out to be a ray gun which freezes its human victims.) The monsters scatter, abduct children, and cage them, while a mystical, very gay figure appears and turns the hero into Sheman, complete with wig, nightie, fan, and parasol-rifle. ("Make my day!") Sheman swordfights the gent from space, who proves to be a jerkily animated living skeleton.

Alternately monotonous and embarrassing science-fantasy-comedy—occasionally so embarrassing it's funny—has more singing than fantasy in the first half. Even "Death" gets a silly musical number, and he periodically crows/yowls like a half-dead rooster. Goodness.

**SHERLOCK HOLMES: THE LAST VAMPYRE** (B) Granada-TV 1992 color. D: Tim Sullivan. From Sir Arthur Conan Doyle's story "The Sussex Vampire." Ref: Jones. With Jeremy Brett, Edward Hardwicke, Maurice Denham.

"Apparent vampire in quiet English village."

See also: *Hound of the Baskervilles* (1988).

**SHERLOCK HOLMES AND THE BASKERVILLE CURSE** see *Sherlock Holmes in the Baskerville Curse*

**SHERLOCK HOLMES AND THE MASKS OF DEATH** (B) Lorimar-TV/Tyburn 1984 color 82m. (*The Masks of Death*—ad t). D: Roy Ward Baker. Story: Anthony Hinds (aka J. Elder). SP: N. J. Crisp. SpPh: Charles Staffell. Mkp: Roy Ashton, Ernie Gasser. Ref: TV. TVG. Maltin '92. no Scheuer. Ecran F 49:13: TV-movie.

Sherlock Holmes (Peter Cushing) mystery with horrific overtones. The look on the face of a corpse suggests that the man witnessed "some unimaginable, terrible evil." Are "demons, devils incarnate," with "pig faces" responsible?—no, just men in hooded sheets and gas masks. (It's 1913, and they're perfecting a new poison gas.) Distinguished cast, including Cushing, John Mills (as Watson), Anton Diffring, and Ray Milland; typically undistinguished Anthony Hinds material.

**SHERLOCK HOLMES AND THE WOMAN IN GREEN** see *Woman in Green, The*

**SHERLOCK HOLMES IN CARACAS** (Venez.) Big Ben Prods. & Tiuna Films & Foncine (Franklin Whaite, Jr.) 1992 color 95m. SP, D, Co-P: Juan Fresan. Mus: Miguel Noya. Ref: V 3/30/92: "self-conscious, low-budget, free-wheeling satirical mess." Jones: loosely based on Doyle's "The Sussex Vampire." With Jean Manuel Montesinos, Gilbert Dacournan, Carolina Luzardo, Maria Eugenia Cruz (ex-Miss Venezuela).

Sherlock Holmes vs. a vampire.

**SHERLOCK HOLMES IN THE BASKERVILLE CURSE** (U.S.-Can.?) Pacific Arts Corp./Burbank Films 1985 (1983) anim color 66m. (aka *Sherlock Holmes and the Baskerville Curse*). SP, D: Eddy Graham, from Sir Arthur Conan Doyle's book *The Hound of the Baskervilles*. Ph: Epperson, Page. Mus: John Stuart. AD: Alex Nicholas. Anim Sup: Ian Mackenzie. Ref: TV. no Maltin '92. Hound. no Scheuer. Martin. Voices: Peter O'Toole, Earle Cross et al.

A "fearful hound" haunts the great Grimpen Mire and fulfills the "curse of the Baskervilles".... Fair score; flat animation and voices. Even the Devon moors scenes lack the requisite atmosphere.

**SHE'S BACK** Vestron/Tycin Ent. (C. DePaula) 1989 color 90m. (*Dead & Married*—orig t). D: Tim Kincaid. SP: Buddy Giovinazzo. Mus: Jimmie Haskell. Ref: V 7/19/89: "a few laughs." PT 12:51: "disaster." With Carrie Fisher, Robert Joy, Matthew Cowles, Joel Swetow, Bobby DiCicco.

Wife returns as ghost, has husband kill thugs who killed her. "Makeup effects become more elaborate...."(V)

**SHESHNAAG** (India) R.A. Film 1990? color/ws c145m. D: K.R. Reddy. SP: Kapoor, Kaul. Story: R.S. Atish. Ph: H. Reddy. Mus: Sangeetha Raja. Anim & SpFX: E. Shekhar, Bhuvan. Mkp: R. Reddy. Ref: TV: Video Sound; no Eng. Meadows Video: *Cobra* - tr t. With Jeetendra, Rekha, Rishi Kapoor, Mandakini.

The cackling, super-strong sorcerer here can fly, toss fire, breathe out gusts of wind, turn a snake into a sword, turn himself into a mongoose, create (stopmo) circles of fire in the ground, and duplicate himself—and his trident shoots rays. His main foes: two snakes who periodically turn into people. In one sequence, objects in a room become cobras which scare a man.

Main problem of this relatively opulent production: It never ends. Be prepared for lots of snaky dancing. And it really is a paper moon here. Cute: the animated fire which the snake people breathe out. And love the magician's granite, skull-shaped candleholders.

**SHIJIE ZHUANGXIE** see *Haunted Madam, The*

**SHINING DARK** see *Shocking Dark*

**SHINJURO** see *Pearl Sprite*

**The SHIP OF THE ETHER** (Dutch) Philips Radio 1937? anim 7m. D: George Pal. Ref: TV: Video Dimensions. Lee.

A bit of science-fantasy, as a sailing ship of the heavens picks up variety acts (with a gizmo-with-lever) from Paris, Budapest, Vienna, Rome, etc. Charming trifle.

**SHIROI KABE NO KEKKON** see *Guinea Pig, Vol. Four*

**SHIRYO NO WANA 2** see *Evil Dead Trap 2*

**SHIVERS** Col 1934 15m. Story, D: Arthur Ripley. SP: John Grey. Ref: Okuda/CCS. LC. Lee. With Harry Langdon, Florence Lake, Dick Elliott.

Mystery writer in haunted house.

**SHOCK CHAMBER: A TRILOGY OF TERROR** (Can.) Emmeritus & CHCH-TV & Telefilm Canada 1984 color c90m. SP, D: Steve DiMarco. Ph: N. Kurita. Mus: Peter Dick. SpMkpFX: Randi Daudlin. SpFX: Peter Ferri. Ref: TV. TVG. no Maltin '92. no Scheuer. Stanley. With Doug Stone, Karen Cannata.

Three tales involving a daydream re a revived corpse, burial alive, suspended animation, etc. Shallow video look, calculatedly "creepy" acting.

**SHOCK 'EM DEAD** Noma Prods. (Eric Louzil) 1990 color 93m. (*Rock 'Em Dead*—orig t). SP, D: Mark Freed. SP: also Andrew Cross. Mus: Robert Decker. SpMkpFX: John Garcia. Ref: TV. V 1/14/91. McCarty II. Martin. no Scheuer. no Maltin '92. V 2/21/90:79(ad): sfa *Hard Rock Nightmare* (with Troy D.)? Mifed '89:153. With Traci Lords, Troy Donahue, Aldo Ray, Stephen Quadros, Tyger Sodipe (voodoo woman).

"When we look in the mirror, we see ourselves as what we were." A voodoo woman's potion turns nerdish Martin (Quadros) into rock star "Angel," who must kill to survive. He uses a special dagger to extract the life force of his victims.... Amateurish production, acting. One good moment: voodoo-possessed Monique (Laurel Wiley) thanking her "sisters" for the "food." In death, her body shrivels up.

**SHOCK! SHOCK! SHOCK!** Rutt-McConnell 1987 b&w 60m. SP, D: Todd Rutt, Arn McConnell. Ph: Mike Howard. Mus: The Cyphers, Bruce Gordon. SpDes: McConnell. Ref: TV: Rhino Video: end cr: Ph: Rutt. Cinef 1/90. Toxic Horror 5:10. Martin. Hound. Phantom. With Brad Isaac, Cyndy McCrossen, Allen Rickman, Kelly Ross, Brian Fuorry, Marcus Lieberman (original Spaceman), David Steinberg (the creature).

With the help of the mystic Star of Bartos, Jim Norman (Isaac) becomes Spaceman, an incarnation of an alien who, centuries before, aided the Mintex Tribe of South America. He uses his super powers and a ray gun to defeat the "terrible and awful" Fangodon, a housecat that (in crude stopmo) turns into a drooling creature; Commander Zont-El (Rickman), ruler of the planet Stigmata; Skar-El (Fuorry), with his "death ray eyes"; and Kree-Ella (Ross), with her "trans-spacial ability" to disappear, then reappear elsewhere. A truth serum makes Jim see horror scenes with dancing skeletons and writhing maggots, but also enables him to discover (via a hallucinatory flashback) that he did not slash his parents to death when he was a tot—the murderer was Zont-El.

The deadest-pan of comedies, with actors already halfway to dead, this parody of bad movies succeeds only in being one itself. The bad old movies were funnier. Amusing animated credit sequence.

**SHOCKER** Univ/Carolco Int'l. (Alive Films/Shep Gordon/Marianne Maddalena, B. Kumar) 1989 color 110m. SP, D, Exec Co-P: Wes Craven. Ph: Jacques Haitkin. Mus: William Goldstein. SpVisFX: Available Light; (coord) Jonathan Craven; Apogee, Roger Dorney; Perpetual Motion Pictures; David Williams; Hollywood Optical Systems; Cinema Research; Pacific Title & Art; Planet Blue. Anim Sup: Sam Recinos. SpMkpFX: Lance Anderson. Titles: Mercer; (anim) Klasky-Csupo. SdFxEd: Richard Shorr. Ref: TV. MFB'90:141-2. ad. V 11/1/89. Sacto Bee 11/1/89. Sacto Union 10/29/89. Maltin '92. Hound. McCarty II. Martin. Scheuer. With Michael Murphy, Peter Berg, Cami Cooper, Mitch Pileggi (Horace Pinker), Heather Langenkamp, Richard Brooks, Theodore Raimi, Dr. Timothy Leary.

"Who is this man?" Horace Pinker, a "virtual phantom" who practices black magic and animal sacrifice, has a habit of slaughtering whole families. He is sentenced to die in the electric chair, but—as with Lon Chaney, Jr., in *Man Made Monster*—electricity just encourages him. His body incinerates but his spirit possesses, first, a prison doctor, then a cop, then a jogger, etc. (All the possessed sport Pinker's Kharis limp.) At the end, psychically-gifted high school student Jonathan Parker (Berg) chases Pinker into the world of TV waves, and at one point controls him with a TV remote.

Until the free-wheeling final sequences, *Shocker* is routine possession material which, in at least one sequence, recalls another old Universal, *Black Friday*, as the spirits of Pinker and Lt. Parker (Murphy), Jonathan's foster father, vie for control of the cop's body. The climactic free-for-all plays like a comic *Tron* crossed with Keaton's *Sherlock Jr.* and is undisciplined, but entertaining. Rabbit-out-of-a-hat highlights here include Pinker emerging from, a) the chair, b) the overhead light fixture, and, c) the electric outlet. His worst trait (other than butchering humans): a tendency towards Freddyisms. ("That's the way it is!") Unexplained, including-the-kitchen-sink story element: heroine Alison's (Cooper) helpful spirit.

**SHOCKING!** (H.K.) Yang Chen Chin Chu? c1983? color/ws c85m. (*Ghost House*—ad t.) D: Yao Fung-Pan. Ref: TV: Quality Video; Eng. titles. NST! 4:36. vc box: cf. *The Old House*. With Kuang Lan Yao?

A newspaper reporter investigates the history of a "famous haunted house" at 113 Shin Nan Road: In 1943, Mrs. Ou, the resident, hangs herself (and apparently kills her two children) when she learns that her husband has died in combat. She appears to a woman before the latter finds her body and realizes that Mrs. Ou—and the children—are ghosts. In 1944, soldiers billeted in the house are spirited out upstairs windows during the night; they awake next morning on the ground outside. The next night, Mrs. Ou's ghost tricks one soldier into shooting another. In 1947, a couple is hacked to death with a hatchet. Finally, in 1963, dripping ghost blood disfigures a woman, the new owner has a nightmare of hatcheting his wife, and Mrs. Ou tries to get the latter to hang herself.

The news-story framework is just an excuse for a string of scare effects, some of them okay—e.g., the ghost washing her hair ... on her disembodied head; hands reaching out from the cracks in the floor during an earthquake; Mrs. Ou taking an evening stroll with her two ghost-children (in an eerie overhead shot); Mrs. Ou materializing in a rocking chair, after the reporter has left the room. Creepily amusing sequence: the ghostly Mrs. Ou spitting up (whole) eggs, one at a time, for a man whose prized eggs were broken.

**SHOCKING** (F) 199-? color feature. D: Claude Mulot. Ref: VSOM: end-of-the-world story. With Karin Gabier.

**SHOCKING DARK** (I) Flora Film (Franco Gaudenzi) 1989 color/ws 90m. (*Shocking Dark - Spectres A Venise*. aka *Spectres a Venise*?). D: Bruno Mattei (aka Vincent Dawn). SP: Clyde Anderson (aka C. Fragasso). Ph: R. Grassetti. AD: Adriane Bellone. SpFxMkp: Franco di Girolamo. Creatures & Cyborg SpFX: Francesco & Gaetano Paolocci. SpFX: S. Putnam et al. Ref: TV: VSOM; Eng.-lang. version. VSOM cat.: *Shining Dark* - t error. V 10/14/91:M-48. (Cannes'89):331(ad). 8/30/89:68. EVS: *The Alienators* - alt vt t. MV: aka *Terminator 2*. Palmerini. With Cristofer Ahrens, H. Tyler, G.G. Field, Tony Lombardo, Dominica Coulson.

"They know you're coming!" In the future, a giant, deadly toxic cloud hovers over Venice, and "strange creatures"—the product of genetic-mutation research ("cybernetics applied to molecular biology")—prowl. The *Alien*-ish creature here is a sort of floppy-disk monster which "brings its own program to life" and "reprograms" any form of life. Plus: a semi-surprise cyborg ("He's a machine, too!")…. Slavish imitation of *Alien* and *Aliens* is an accidental near-parody of macho. ("You're not Boy Scouts on a hike!")

**SHOGUN'S NINJA** see *Ninja Incarnation*

**SHOK!** see *Hardware*

**SHONEN SARUTOBI SASUKE** see *Magic Boy*

**SHOPPING** (B) Film Four Int'l. & Polygram & Kuzui Ents. & WMG/Impact (Jeremy Bolt) 1994 color 106m. SP, D: Paul Anderson. Ph: Tony Imi. Mus: B. Pheloung. PD: M. Gottlieb. Ref: V 2/7/94: "as blank-minded as its vapidly rebellious leading characters." With Sadie Frost, Jude Law, Sean Pertwee, Marianne Faithfull, Jonathan Pryce.

"Set in a vaguely futuristic Britain exclusively populated by valueless kids and fascistic police…."

**SHORT CIRCUIT** Tri-Star & PSO (Turman-Foster) 1986 color/ws 98m. D: John Badham. SP: S. S. Wilson, Brent Maddock. Mus: David Shire. SpVisFX: Dream Quest Images. Robots: (des) Syd Mead; (sp fx sup) Eric Allard. SpElecFX: Bob Jason et al. Mkp: Tom Lucas. Vis Consultant: Philip Harrison. Ref: TV. MFB'87:26-7. V 5/7/86. ad. SFExam 5/9/86. With Ally Sheedy, Steve Guttenberg, Fisher Stevens, Austin Pendleton, G. W. Bailey, Tim Blaney (voice of Number Five).

"Number Five is alive!" Malfunctioning government robot Number Five—designed to be the "ultimate soldier"—goes AWOL and inspects butterflies, absorbs data in encyclopedias ("More input!"), falls in with animal lover Stephanie Speck (Sheedy), fears "disassembling," and learns on its own that it's wrong to kill.... No story, just shticks, but generally funny ones, for both Number Five and Ben (Stevens), an East Indian who, like Number Five, specializes in disassembling the English language. The life-affirming theme is ultimately used for glib sentimentality.

Sequel: *Short Circuit 2.*

**SHORT CIRCUIT 2** Tri-Star (Turman-Foster) 1988 color 110m. D: Kenneth Johnson. SP: S. S. Wilson, Brent Maddock. Mus: Charles Fox. Robotics Sup: Eric Allard. SpLaserFX: Laserlite F/X. SpVisFX: Dream Quest Images; (sup) Michael Bigelow; (p) Keith Shartle; (anim sup) Jeff Burks. SpFxSup: Jeff Jarvis. SpVoiceDes: Frank Serafine. Mkp: Patricia Green. Ref: TV. MFB'89:57-8. V 7/6/88. ad. SFChron 7/6/88. With Fisher Stevens, Michael McKean, Cynthia Gibb, Jack Weston, Tim Blaney (voice of Johnny Five).

In this sequel to *Short Circuit,* Number Five—or Johnny Five—is a little of everything. He (or it) is an $11-million robot, a "breakthrough in artificial intelligence," a "mystery machine," a "punishment from God," and a "schlemiel," depending on which of the three or four haphazardly coordinated co-plots is operational at the moment. But although the movie is overlong, and the basic storyline is unimaginative, the writers come up with any number of clever scenes and moments, including some pleasant comedy re naivete—Stevens' Ben's and Johnny Five's. If he does nothing else, Ben makes you aware of the intricacies and eccentricities of the English language, which he manages to make even more intricate and eccentric. Highlights include the line "Like a sweaty duck!" and the scene in which Johnny Five is "controlling remotely the sign."

**SHORT STORIES OF LOVE** Univ-TV 1974 color c90m. (aka *Rex Harrison Presents Stories of Love*). Credits for "Epicac," one of three tales: D: John Badham. SP: Liam O'Brien, from Kurt Vonnegut Jr.'s story. Poem, "Epithalamium," by Edmond O'Brien. Ph: Jacques Marquette. Mus: David Shire. AD: Raymond Beal. SpPhFX: Albert Whitlock. Elec Equipment: Control Data. Ref: TV. TVG. TVFFSB. Stanley. no Maltin '92. no Scheuer. With Bill Bixby, Roscoe Lee Browne, Julie Sommars, David Sheiner, Kenneth Tobey, Soon-Taik Oh.

A "story of the near future"—i.e., 1979—in which a super-computer falls hopelessly in love with its programmer's girl friend. Pat comic computer story is reminiscent of the "From Agnes—with Love" episode of "The Twilight Zone." The rather sweet ending has Epicac conceding defeat and committing suicide by short-circuiting itself.

**A SHORT VISION** (B) 1956 anim color 7m. SP, D: Joan & Peter Foldes. Ref: Lee: "thing" that destroys all life.

**\*The SHOW** 1927 silent b&w 69m. Ph: John Arnold. Sets: Cedric Gibbons, Richard Day. Titles: Joe Farnham. Ref: screen. Lee. V 3/16/27. SFChron 11/25/94. Lentz. Hardy/HM. PT 14:44. With Lionel Barrymore, Edward Connelly, Gertrude Short, Edna Tichenor (the human spider), Z. Zarana (Half Lady), Jules Cowles.

In Budapest, the Palace of Illusions features The Living Hand of Cleopatra, the beheading of Jokanaan, Zela the Half Lady (the top half), and, most bizarrely, Arachnida, the Human Spider, a startling mock-spider-legs-and-web with a real-human-head-centerpiece. Meanwhile, in the audience, the bite of a poisonous, iguana-type lizard from Madagascar leaves one patron dead, which event gives The Greek (Barrymore) the idea of using the fantastic jumping reptile as a murder weapon.

The outre and the mundane alternate here. The melodramatic story is, at best, a pretext for Tod Browning thrills. (Arachnida might be the model for Hiruko.) Renee Adoree's acting is economical and effective, but John Gilbert comes off as a silent-movie version of Robert Taylor—a handsome stiff. The Grand Guignol beheading sequence includes both the illusion itself and a behind-the-scenes look at how it's done.

**SHRECK** Tempe 199-? color? 75m. Ref: Tempe Video flyer. Bill Warren.

Seance resurrects Nazi killer from the Fifties.

**SHREDDER ORPHEUS** Image Network (Lisanne Dutton) 1990 color 88m. SP, D, Exec P: Robert McGinley. Ref: V 5/23/90: "idiotic punk sci-fi." With S. J. Bernstein, R. McGinley, Megan Murphy.

"Memories are shredded" in a "post-apocalyptic world."

**The SHRIMP** Roach-MGM 1930 short. D: Charles Rogers. Ref: Maltin/SSS. Lee. With Harry Langdon, Thelma Todd, Max Davidson.

"Harry is a weakling until a scientist injects a serum into him."(SSS)

**SHRUNKEN HEADS** Para/Full Moon 1994 color 86m. D: Richard Elfman. SP: Matthew Bright. Idea, P: Charles Band. Ph: S. McNutt. Mus: R. Band. PD: Milo. MkpFX: Alchemyfx. VisFX: Paul Gentry. Ref: V 11/28/94: "only mildly entertaining." MM 49:81: vampire head. SFChron 4/8/95. Martin: "a cut above the rest." PT 21:14: "nearly unwatchable." With Meg Foster, Julius Harris (Mr. Sumatra), Aeryk Egan, Becky Herbst, A.J. Damato.

Voodoo man (Harris) shrinks dead teens' heads, reanimates the latter, and enables them to track down their killers.

**SHUTO SHOSHITSU** (J) Daiei & Kansai Telecasting & Tokuma Shoten Publishing (Mizoguchi-Kasahara) 1987 (1986) color/ws 119m. (aka *Tokyo Blackout*). SP, D: Toshio Masuda. SP: also Hiroyasu Yamaura. From the book by Sakyo Komatsu. Ph: Masahiko Imura. Mus: Maurice Jarre. SpFX: Teruyoshi Nakano. Ref: TV: Pony Video; some Eng. dialogue. V 9/2/87. With Tsunehiko Watase, Yuko Natori, Shinji Yamashita.

"What the hell is that?" Telephone static and various problems with electrical appliances herald the appearance of a mysterious smoke or fog bank—the Great Wall of Japan here is a blanket of impenetrable smoke around Tokyo. No one can get in or out. Planes which venture into it explode, it's hell on electrical equipment which gets too near it, and bullets shot into it ricochet weirdly. ("The outer shell of the cloud seems to have both thick and thin areas.") Ultimately, some kind of laser/sound gizmo disperses the fog.

This looks like a good one, at least until international politicians begin debating the fog's (and the world's) future and the personal heroics get out of hand, near the end. Among the movie's distinguished, and not-so-distinguished, precursors: *The Exterminating Angel, The Bubble, The Slime People.* The alien landscape of the cloud mass—all energy "geysers," lightning flashes, and flame-thrower-like bursts of flame—and Jarre's score help put this over.

**SI BALELENG AT ANG GINTONG SIRENA** (Fili) Lea Prods. 1988? color 129m. Story, D: Chito Rono. Story, SP: Bibeth Orteza. Ph: Jose Tutanes, Ver Reyes. Mus D: Toto Gentica. AD: Tito Macatunggal. SpFx: Bobby Pineda, Danny Rojo, Nestor Yadao. Mkp: Olive Manding; (prosth) Tony Artieda, Cecille Baun. Puppets: Lolita Aquino. Opt: Cine Magic. SdFX: Rodel Capule. Ref: TV: Viva Video; occ. Eng. J. J. Market: *You Baleleng and the Golden Mermaid*—tr t. MMarquee 43:9. With Charito Solis, Eddie Garcia, Laurice Guillen, Melissa Perez Rubio (Perlita, the mermaid), Cheche Sta. Ana (Baleleng), Cecil Inigo & Carlos Ding (zombies), Frank Crisostomo (Tiyanak), Ana Abiera, Paolo Delgado, Jimmy Fabregas.

Spry, delightful children's fantasy features many monsters, including the evil Gungadina (Solis), who at the end becomes a land crab ... a vampire baby who sprouts long legs and arms and Nosferatu eyebrows and ears ... a giant, Japanese version of Pan ... a gigantic, flying, two-headed thing ... a "dream girl" who splits in two, horizontally, to become a real nightmare ... and shambling zombies.

Some of the above-listed monsters—Gungadina and the dream girl, for instance—may be one and the same creature. There are so many transformations that it's sometimes hard to tell who's who and what's what. Truly unusual fantasy-comedy has just the right balance of silliness and sophistication, plus pleasantly stylized, exaggerated performances and beyond-strange interludes, some comic, some horrific. Most startling of the horrific interludes is perhaps the vampire one: Baby sprouts fangs and begins nipping at mother's neck. Puzzled mom looks down to see two extra feet intermixed with her own, holds "baby" out to have a look-see, and discovers a cross between Max Schreck's Nosferatu and the India Rubber Man.

**SI J'AVAIS MILLE ANS** (F) 1983 color 86m. D: Monique Enckell. Ref: Ecran F 58:80: *If I Lived To Be a Thousand*—tr t. With Daniel Olbrychsky, Marie Dubois, D. Pinon, Jean Bouise.

Each year, on the night of la Toussaint, ghost knights from the distant past appear, in this variation on *The Ghost Train.*

**SIBLING, The** see *Psycho Sisters*

**SIDEBURNS** (Russ.) Sovexportfilm/Lenfilm & Leninterfilm 1991 color c105m. (*Sidewhiskers* - cr t). D: Yuri Mamin. SP: V. Leikin. Ref: TV: Facets Video; Eng. titles. SFChron 2/27/95.

In this vision of a Nazi-esque takeover of Russia (cf. 1940's *Strange Holiday* and its tale of a Nazi coup in the U.S.), the arch-conservative Pushkin Club routs the neo-punk Capella ("the children of perestroika"), in the Night of the Long Canes, and

begins its rise to political power. Soon—in addition to Pushkinists—there are Lermontovists, young Pushkinists (Pushkin Jugend), Pushkin musical stage shows, Pushkin souvenirs, etc. Moderately amusing and incisive political satire has overtones of *A Clockwork Orange* and "The Brothers Karamazov." ("All can do as they like.")

**SIE TOETETE IN EXTASE** see *Mrs. Hyde*

**SIEGFRIED** see *Nibelungen, Die*

**SIEGFRIED'S DEATH** or **SIEGFRIEDS TOD** see *Nibelungen, Die*

**SIGHT UNSEEN** Alpert 1989 color 94m. D: Greydon Clarke. Ref: CVS 12/90. V 2/21/90:163. no Scheuer. With Susan Blakely, Edward Albert, Lynn-Holly Johnson, Wings Hauser, Richard Masur.

Serial killer ... apparitions of dead daughter.

**The SIGN OF THE COMMANDER** (I) Reteitalia & PAT Inc. c1985? color 96m. (*Il Segno del Comando*). D: Giulio Questi. SP: David Grieco, Giuseppe D'Agata, from the latter's book. Ph: Edmond Richard. Mus: Luis Enriquez Bacalov. PD: Emile Chico. Ref: TV: VSOM; Eng. titles; or *The Sign of the Command.* With Robert Powell, Elena Sofia Ricci, Jonathan Cecil, Fanny Bastien, Paolo Bonacelli, Sonia Petrovna, Alexandra Stewart, Michel Bouquet.

"Lord Byron came to Paris to find The Sign of the Commander." Ingredients include amateur sleuth Prof. Edwin Foster ... Byron's diary ... a phantom lady ... the Sign of the Commander, a jewel of immortality ... Jean Baptiste Monet, who vowed to reincarnate to retrieve the gem (it was stolen by his killers) ... a painting by one Nicolas Bardot (was he Monet's reincarnation?) ... a butcher-knife murder ... lines written by an Italian composer, Vitalli (Byron apparently saw his ghost) ... and an old lady who temporarily turns into the phantom (young) lady.... Culture-vulture supernatural mystery at least rates an "O" for offbeat. At the end, it rates a double "O": Well-dressed Mystery Parisians find hell ("Welcome to hell"), and the hero finds himself in a desert. A horizontal tornado returns him to Paris. The magic words: "June 30th."

**SIGN OF THE FOUR, The** see *Crucifer of Blood, The*

**SIGNORE DEI CANI, Il** see *Monster Dog*

**The SILENCE OF THE HAMS** (U.S.-I) Thirtieth Century Wolf & Silvio Berlusconi (Ezio Greggio & Julie Corman) 1993 color 81m. SP, D: E. Greggio. Ph: Jacques Haitkin. Mus: Parmer Fuller. PD: James Newport. MkpFX: Dave Barton. MechFX: Ultimate FX. Title Des: Ernest Farino. FxAnim: Chris Casady. Ref: TV: Cabin Fever video. PT 20:16. With Ezio Greggio, Dom DeLuise, Billy Zane, Joanna Pacula, Charlene Tilton, Martin Balsam, Stuart Pankin, John Astin, Phyllis Diller, Bubba Smith, Larry Storch, Rip Taylor, Shelley Winters, Henry Silva, Eddie Deezen, Joe Dante, John Carpenter, Rudy de Luca, John Landis, Mel Brooks.

Combination parody of *Psycho* and *Silence of the Lambs* features DeLuise as Dr. Animal (Cannibal) Pizza ... horror-comedy with mother and son at the Cemetery Motel ... the spirit of Alfred Hitchcock (no, it's Animal in a mask) ... a bit with the mummy ... an incidental *Thriller* parody with zombies ... alien bugs or something in the basement ... an "Addams Family" parody with Astin and Smelly Thing (a foot) ... Balsam as Balsam, recreating his *Psycho* detective role ... a dismembered opera singer who reassembles and returns to life ... a bit with DeLuise as Bram Stoker's Dracula ... a bit with the Exorcist Hotel and a doorman with a spinning head ... and a bit at the Jack the Ripper Motor Inn.... *Airplane!*-style comedy is mostly obvious, telegraphed gags. The weirdly ambitious, scene-by-scene parody of *Psycho* is generally lame, but offers occasional silly fun.

The **SILENCE OF THE LAMBS** Orion/Strong Heart & Demme (Saxon-Utt-Bozman/Gary Goetzman) 1991 (1990) color 118m. D: Jonathan Demme. SP: Ted Tally, from the novel by Thomas Harris. Ph: Tak Fujimoto. Mus: Howard Shore. SpMkpFX: Carl Fullerton, Neal Martz. SpFX: Dwight Benjamin-Creel. OptFX: R/Greenberg. Moth Wrangler/Stylist: R. A. Mendez. SdFxEd: Ron Bochar. Ref: TV: Orion HV. V 2/11/91. S&S 6/91:62-3. SFExam 2/14/91. TVG. With Jodie Foster, Anthony Hopkins (Dr. Hannibal Lecter), Scott Glenn, Ted Levine (Jame Gumb), Diane Baker, Charles Napier, Roger Coman, George A. Romero, Tracey Walter, Chris Isaak.

Hannibal Lecter, a cannibalistic killer under lock and key ("He's a monster"), offers to help the FBI catch "Buffalo Bill," a serial killer who shoots, partially skins, then dumps his female victims. ("They don't have a name for what he is.") Lecter himself uses the skinned face of a cop to make good his escape to freedom, while an FBI Academy student (Foster) convincingly ends the career of "Buffalo Bill," real name: Jame Gumb, a psychopath who was "making himself a woman suit, out of real women."

Like Brad Dourif's Patient X in *Exorcist III*, Hopkins' Lecter is a witty, cerebral psychopath, the Sherlock Holmes of the psycho set: He pegs Foster's Starling immediately, on her first visit to him, then deductively goes on from there. And while this slick, Oscar-winning mystery shocker is a better picture than *Exorcist III*, it's not better by a whole lot, and it eventually makes the same mistake the other movies does: It gets distracted from its madman/wit. *Silence* leaves Lecter's cell for Gumb's lair, an atmospheric place (production design by Kristi Zea), but residence for a decidedly less fascinating madman, a "garden variety" movie sicko/psycho, a deservedly-second banana to Lecter.

See also: *Manhunter. Silence of the Hams.*

**SILENT MOEBIUS: THE MOTION PICTURE** (J) Shochiku/Toei Doga/Kadokawashoton Film (Kia Asamiya) 1991 anim color/ws 54m. D: Kazuo Tomizawa. SP: Kei Shigema, Michitaka Kikuchi, from Kia Asamiya's original comic. Ref: TV: RCA Victor Video; no Eng. Animag 12:6.

Tale of the year 2028 (with a flashback to 2024) concerns demons (including a snake/tentacle thing and living glop in a shower) from an "orbital elevator" near Tokyo Bay, and an all-female police force (including Kiddy Phenil and her "armored android body").... Flashy, isn't it? A synopsis or titles would be helpful for deciphering this story of psychic cops and *Alien* monsters in a *Blade Runner* future. In the meantime, though, visuals and music help some.

**SILENT MOEBIUS—THE MOTION PICTURE 2** (J) Haruki Kadokawa (Suzuki-Yamada-Komatsu) 1992? anim color/ws 58m. D: Yasunori Ide. SP: Manabu Nakamura. Ph: K. Konishi. Mus: Kaoru Wada. PD: Moriki, Akitaka, Watabe. Char Des: M. Kikuchi. Ref: TV: RCA Victor Video; no Eng.

Talky follow-up to the first *Silent Moebius* features weird-looking mutant-types, a cute lady who becomes a big-tailed monster, monsters from walls and sidewalks, and a spacecraft's ray which destroys bridges. Even the monsters are talky, or at least their fearsome leader is. Things liven up a bit near the end. Good score.

**SILENT NIGHT, DEADLY NIGHT** Aquarius Films/Tri-Star (Slayride/I. R. Barmak) 1984 color 85m. D: Charles E. Sellier Jr. SP: Michael Hickey. Story: Paul Caimi. Mus: Perry Botkin. SpFxMkp: Karl Wesson. PD: Dian Perryman. SpFX: Rick Josephson. SdFxSup: William Wistrom. Ref: TV: U.S.A. HV. V 11/7/84. ad. With Lilyan Chauvan, Gilmer McCormick, Toni Nero, Robert Brian Wilson (Billy), Britt Leach, Linnea Quigley.

"I don't bring toys to naughty children. I punish them—severely." (A) Grandpa's ideas re Santa-as-punisher; (b) a run-in with a slasher Santa; and (c) an overseen sexual encounter leave young Billy (Danny Wagner) with a Santa Claus complex. ("It seems to get worse for him every Christmas!") Playing Santa for Ira's Toys, Christmas, 1984, the older Billy goes on a hammer/ax/bow-and-arrow rampage. ("Punish!")

Notorious film's setting-up for its psycho-Santa sequence is heavy-handed and arduous. Stupid gore tricks include the ever-popular Beheaded Sledder and Antler Delight. Gratuitous t&a footage, gore sound-effects.

**SILENT NIGHT, DEADLY NIGHT PART II** Silent Night Releasing & Ascot Ent./Lawrence Appelbaum 1987 color 88m. Story, SP, D, Ed: Lee Harry. Story, SP: J. H. Earle. Story: also Dennis Paterson, L. Appelbaum. Ref: V 4/15/87: "execution ... substandard." Martin: turkey. With Eric Freeman, J. L. Newman, Elizabeth Cayton, Jean Miller.

**SILENT NIGHT, DEADLY NIGHT III: BETTER WATCH OUT!** Quiet Films (Arthur H. Gorson) 1989 color c87m. (aka *Silent Terror*). Story, D: Monte Hellman. Story, SP: Carlos Laszlo. Story: also A. H. Gorson. Mus: Steven Soles. SpMkpFX: Nina Kraft. PD & Brain: Philip Thomas. OptFX: Mercer, OptFX. Ref: TV. V 10/25/89. 5/2/90:94. With Richard Beymer, Bill Moseley, Samantha Scully, Eric Da Re, Robert Culp, Leonard Mann.

"She sees what he sees." Via computer, Dr. Newbury (Beymer) "links" Laura Anderson (Scully)—who can "see" things in her mind—with Ricky Caldwell (Moseley), the "Santa Claus Killer," who has a surgically reconstructed brain. Predictably, Ricky escapes from Mount Memorial Hospital and begins slashing bodies and severing heads. ("Red reactivates his childhood trauma.") Worthless sf-horror.

Immediate follow-up: *Initiation* (1990). See also: *Halloween 5.*

**SILENT NIGHT, DEADLY NIGHT 4** see *Initiation* (1990)

**SILENT NIGHT DEADLY NIGHT 5: THE TOY MAKER**
Gladstein/Yuzna (Still Silent Films) 1991 color 90m. SP, D: Martin Kitrosser. SP, Co-P: Brian Yuzna. Ph: James Mathers. Mus: Matthew Morse. PD: W. B. Wheeler. SpMkpFX: Screaming Mad George. SpFxCoord: Thomas C. Rainone. MechFX: F/X Concepts; (sup) Ken Tarallo. AnimFX: R&B Films; (d) William Coffin. Opt: (FX Comp) T&T; Van der Veer, Tom Anderson. Ref: TV. SFChron Dtbk 11/10/91. With Mickey Rooney, Jane Higginson, Tracy Fraim, Brian Bremer, William Thorne, Clint Howard.

"My father could make anything." Script marks time as it presents a series of deadly toys—like an *Alien,* tentacled ball and "Larry the Larvae," a "to die for" gift which comes to life and burrows into a man's head—until the determinedly perverse conclusion, a bizarre "incest" sequence in which dead toymaker Joe Petto's (Rooney) android "son" Pino (Bremer) plays both son and would-be lover to Sarah (Higginson). (There's just one thing Pop couldn't make....) Film plays like an uninspired slasher movie with "Pinocchio" twists and *Halloween III* overtones. (For deadly masks, substitute deadly toys.)

**SILENT TONGUE** (U.S.-F) Belbo Films/Alive Films (Le Studio Canal Plus/Pfeiffer-Boeken) 1993 color/ws 106m. SP, D: Sam Shepard. Ph: Jack Conroy. Mus: Patrick O'Hearn. PD: Cary White. Ref: V 2/8/93: "bizarre, meandering." With Alan Bates, Richard Harris, Dermot Mulroney, River Phoenix, Sheila Tousey (ghost), Bill Irwin, Tantoo Cardinal.

"Characters literally haunted by the ghosts of those they wronged."

**SILK HAT HARRY** International 1919 anim short. Ref: V 7/18/19.

Robot horse in race has Stop, Back Up, and Lie Down buttons.

**SILVER BULLET** see *Stephen King's Silver Bullet*

The **SILVER SPEAR** (H.K.?) IFD Films (Joseph Lai) 1985 color/ws c90m. (*Silver Hermit from Shaolin Temple*—alt t). D: Rco Trem, or Roc Tien. SP: Lo Keh, from Ku Lung's novel. Ph: Wu Yao Chun. Mus: Stanley Chow. PD: Tin Ching. FX: Roman Tsang. Mkp: Vivien Chow. Ref: TV: Ocean Shores Video; Eng. titles; also in dubbed version. Hound. VSOM: *Silver Hermit from Shaolin Valley Meets Bloody Fangs of Death* - alt vt t. With Roc Tien, Men Fei, Tien Ho, Chung Hwa, Doris Chen, Chan Sing.

After twenty years away, the superstrong, toothy Persian vampire Wu Shih-san returns for revenge to the Green Jade Villa in China. ("Yes, it was a vampire. Sucked the blood from that young woman.") Wu Shih-san is one of two unusual elements in this routine kung-fu flick. ("He's even worse than before.") The other: a white-jasmine peddlar who makes her initial entrance by casually and cyclonically smashing through a stone garden wall.

*The **SILVER STREAK** 1934. SP: also Jack O'Donnell. Ref: TV. V 1/22/35. Lee. no Hardy/SF. Hound. Maltin '92. Martin. Scheuer. With Arthur Lake, Dave O'Brien.

Mechanical engineer Tom Caldwell's (Charles Starrett) diesel-powered train "looks like a fish," but can go up to 120-plus miles per hour, thanks to its low center of gravity, to "chromansil" (an alloy of chromium, manzanite, and silicon), and to streamlining:

The front car's high bulge and slanting nose create a "downward air pressure." In the hokey, all-stops-out finale—which is at least more amusing than the script's flat preliminaries—an iron lung must be speeded 2,000 miles, from Chicago to Boulder City, in nineteen hours, and the aid of The Silver Streak is enlisted. At the end, the Burlington Zephyr leads the Cast of Characters as "The Silver Streak."

**SIMADIA TIS NICHTES** (Greek) Panos Kokkinopoulos/Greek Film Center/ET 1 (Bessie Voudouri) 1990 color 94m. SP, D: Kokkinopoulos. Mus: Eleni Karaindrou. Ref: V 6/6/90: "supernatural aura"; *Scars of the Night*—tr t. With Katerina Lehou, Antonis Katsaris.

Sorceress possessed by "angel of death." "Routine thriller"(V).

**SIMON LES NUAGES** (Can.) Les Films Vision 4 & Nat'l. Film Board of Canada (Bonin-Boyd) 1990 color 82m. SP, D: Roger Cantin. Ref: V 6/27/90: "charming but sometimes corny"; *Simon the Dreamer*—tr t. With Hugolin Chevrette-Landesque, Patrick St.-Pierre, Benoit Robitaille.

Boy dreams of a land of dinosaurs.

**SINBAD OF THE SEVEN SEAS** (I) Cannon Int'l. 1989 (1986/'90-U.S.) color/ws 90m. (aka *Sinbad and the Seven Seas*). SP, D, P: Enzo G. Castellari. SP: also Tito Carpi. Story: Luigi Cozzi (aka L. Coates), from Edgar Allan Poe's story "The Thousand-and-Second Tale of Scheherazade." Addl Dial: Ian Danby. Mus: Dov Seltzer. PD: Walter Patriarca. SpVisFX: Gruppo Memmo Milano, Studio 4. SpFX: Cataldo Galiano. Mkp: Maurizio Trani. Ref: TV: Cannon Video; Eng.-lang. version. V 3/21/90:35(hv). TVG. With Lou Ferrigno, John Steiner (Jaffar), Leo Gullotta, Teagan, Haruhiko Yamanouchi, Stefania Girolami, Daria Nicolodi (narrator), Alessandra Martines, Attilio Lo Pinto (zombie king), Melonee Rodgers (Farida, vampire).

Ingredients: the evil wizard Jaffar, who has super-hypnotic powers and who creates a double of Sinbad (Ferrigno) to fight Sinbad ... the Amazon Queen, a "mind vampire" who ages instantly when deprived of the source of her power ... a huge stone monster on Skull Island ... the "legion of Death" ... the ghost king and ghost warriors on the Isle of the Dead ... and a "foul and horrible beast".... Dismal adventure-fantasy with flavorless narration and dialogue. Ferrigno can't even sneer believably.

See also: *What the Moon Saw* (P).

**SINGAPORE SLING** (Greek) Greek Film Center & Marni Film & Cinekip (Maria-Louise Bartholomew) 1990 b&w 114m. SP, D: Nicos Nicolaidis. Ref: V 11/5/90: Eng. soundtrack; "forced to rely on voyeuristic kicks." With Meredyth Herold, Michele Valley, Panos Thanassoulis.

Gory, campy variation on *Psycho* themes.

The **SINGING COWBOY** Rep 1936 56m. D: Mack V. Wright. SP: Dorrell & Stuart McGowan. Story: Tom Gibson. Mus Sup: Harry Grey. Ref: Don Glut. Shoot-Em-Ups. LC. With Gene Autry, Smiley Burnette, Lois Wilde, Lon Chaney, Jr., Jack Rockwell, Frankie Marvin, Jack Kirk.

Camera-less TV broadcast from the prairie.

**SINGLE WHITE FEMALE** Col (Jack Baran) 1992 color 107m. D, P: Barbet Schroeder. SP: Don Roos, from John Lutz' novel *SWF Seeks Same*. Ph: Luciano Tovoli. Mus: Howard Shore. PD: Milena Canonero. Mkp: Lizbeth Williamson. SpFX: E.E. Surkin. Ref: TV: bit with Kenneth Tobey. V 8/10/92: "slasher pic" overtones. Cinef 12/92. EBay Express 8/21/92. TVG 1/30/93: "Leigh can move from mousy waif to obsessed psycho with chilling precision." SFChron 8/14/92: "turns into a by-the-numbers thriller." With Bridget Fonda, Jennifer Jason Leigh, Steven Weber, Peter Friedman, Stephen Tobolowsky.

Roommate from hell. ("She's a lunatic.") Hedra Carlson (Leigh) is the twin who lived, and now even her dog Buddy prefers her new roommate Allie (Fonda). Meanwhile, she tries to "twin" herself again (with Allie as her model) and wields a lethal poker and high heel.... Curious, if not exactly fascinating psychopathology. The low-key approach and credible performances help.

**SINNUI YAUMAN II YANGAN DOU** see *Chinese Ghost Story II, A*

**SINNUI YAUMAN III: DO DO DO** see *Chinese Ghost Story III*

**SINSET BOULEVARD** Western Visuals (Jerome Tanner) 1988 color 85m. Ref: Adam '89. With Rachel Ryan, Nikki Knights, Mike Horner, Shanna McCullough.

Year 2011, President Falwell's America.

**SISTER, SISTER** New World/Walter Coblenz & Odyssey Ent. (Sumner-Marks) 1987 color 89m. SP, D: Bill Condon. SP: also Joel Cohen, Ginny Cerrella. Mus: Richard Einhorn. SpFX: Wayne Beauchamp, Paul Hickerson. Mkp: Gabor Kernyaiszky. SdFX: F. H. Miller. Ref: TV. V 9/16/87. ad. SFExam 2/5/88. SFChron 2/5/88. With Eric Stoltz, Jennifer Jason Leigh, Judith Ivey, Dennis Lipscomb, Anne Pitoniak, Benjamin Mouton.

The Willows, Louisiana, and haunted Widow's Cove. Is it the vengeance of the dead? Lucy Bonnard (Leigh), who may be mad, thinks it is when a murdered dog is found. At one point, ghostly voices herald an illuminating flashback, and at the end Lucy sees the ghosts of the swamp and has a vision of a dead man jumping through a mirror.... Horrific overtones to this well-shot (by Stephen M. Katz) and scored, but vapid mystery story.

The **SISTERHOOD** (U.S.-Fili) Concorde/Santa Fe 1988 color 76m. D, P: Cirio H. Santiago. Assoc D: Bobby Santiago, Joe Mari Avellana. SP: T. M. Cleaver. Ph: Ricardo Remias. Ref: V 7/13/88. With Rebecca Holden, Chuck Wagner, Lynn-Holly Johnson, Barbara Hooper.

Female warriors with magic powers ... mutations ... post-nuke.

**SISTERS OF DEATH** First American Films (John B. Kelly) 1976 color c90m. (aka *Death Trap*). D: Joseph Mazzuca. SP, Story: Elwyn Richard. SP: also Peter Arnold. Ph: Grady Martin. PD: Thomas Hasson. SpFX: Wayne George. Mkp: Jim Nielsen. SdFX: Edit-Rite. OptFX: Westheimer. Ref: TV: United HV/InterGlobal Video. Stanley. Sacto Bee 7/29/90. no Maltin '92. Hound. no Scheuer. PT 19:60: '78('72)? With Arthur Franz, Claudia Jennings, Sherry Boucher, Cheri Howell, Paul Carr (Mark), Sherry Alberoni.

"Kind of weird, isn't it?" Five members of The Secret Society of Sisters are invited to a mysterious "seven year reunion" at the Hacienda del Sol, outside Paso Robles, California. Their host: Edward Clybourn (Franz), father of a Sister (Elizabeth Bergen) shot seven years ago during an initiation ceremony. Stranglings and stabbings follow, but the killer may be one of the five Sisters, not their "madman" host.... Tame, cheap early slasher thriller notable only for the presence of Franz.

**\*6 HOURS TO LIVE** 1932 74m. Mus D: Louis de Francesco. AD: William Darling. Ref: screen. William K. Everson. PFA notes 1/18/86. V 10/25/32. Hardy/SF. Lee. Lentz. Maltin '92. Scheuer. Stanley. With Torben Meyer, Dewey Robinson.

Professor Otto Bauer (George Marion) has invented "something that science will shout about"—a "new ray ... more potent than all the radium in existence." The "vital energy generated" revives the dead, but only for six hours. When Captain Paul Onslow (Warner Baxter), the head of Sylvaria, is murdered, the professor brings him back with his ray—and with the help of his gorilla-sized assistant, Blucher (Robinson), who acts as a human cable when the machine's cable breaks. (In operation, the machine [a generator attached to a modified-cylindrical glass container, in which latter the subject is placed] produces an impressive, thunderstorm-in-a-miniature-greenhouse effect.) Revived, Onslow possesses a supernatural knowledge of events which occurred after his death, and finds—when he survives a bad car crash—that he is invulnerable. ("Only the devil could live through that!") He brings a woman a message from her dead son; saves his country by casting a crucial trade-conference vote; and confronts his murderer. The professor is ecstatic: "All murder mysteries can be solved!"

The first half of this relatively short feature is a loss: Baxter and Miriam Jordan hit more wrong notes than right ones, and the political and romantic co-plots are hastily and fuzzily sketched in. The second half is arguably no better, but it's compelling. The script hasn't the tact of *The Walking Dead* (1936) when it comes to the cosmic—Onslow does everything but provide blueprints of The Beyond—but it rates an "A" for ambitiousness: The range of subjects covered includes death, life, love, religion, crime and punishment, science, politics, and friendship. The dramatic core, if such can be located in the metaphysical morass, is Onslow's relinquishing of the Baroness (Jordan) to his friend Karl (John Boles). A Noble Sacrifice? Yes and no. He dies in a few hours, anyway; he gives up only her esteem, not her. Even more touching: Onslow's last act—sniffing the flower which the Baroness delivered, too late for him to sniff while he was alive (the first time). Pictorial highlights: the ray's revival of the rabbit and (a bit later) Onslow; the comically-intimidating bulk of Blucher; and an overhead shot of the revived Onslow, as, on his way to the conference, he—or his presence—parts a town-square crowd. (The angle underscores his implacability.)

**SIX MILLION DOLLAR MAN, The** see *Bionic Ever After? Bionic Showdown, The. Return of the Six-Million Dollar Man and the Bionic Woman.*

**SIX THOUSAND DOLLAR NIGGER, The** see *Super Soul Brother*

**SKEETER** New Line & August Ent./Team Players & K.A.R. Films 1993 color 95m. SP, D: Clark Brandon. SP: also Lanny Horn. Idea: Joe Rubin. Co-P, Ph: John Lambert. Mus: David Lawrence. PD: Stella Wang. MkpFX: Adam Brandy. Skeeter FX: Mkp & FX Labs;(mech des) Paul J. Elliott;(sup) Frank H. Isaacs. Digital Anim: Garden of Allah. SpFX: W. Beauchamp, K. Wheatley. VocalFX: Allison Caine. Ref: TV: New Line HV. Stanley. Martin: "badly directed." V 8/30/93:12 (rated): "sci-fi violence and gore." PT 20:17. With Tracy Griffith, Jim Youngs, Charles Napier, Michael J. Pollard, Jay Robinson, William Sanderson, John Goff, Buck Flower.

"There was a swarm of 'em!" Big mosquitoes are killing livestock and people around Clear Sky, and leaving nasty messes on jeep windshields. One man (Pollard) actually keeps an oversized mosquito as a pet and feeds it (his) blood. At the end, mosquito larvae are discovered (along with a horde of mosquitoes) in a cave.... Routine shocker has a heavy, forced sense of melancholy ("Nothing's right around here anymore") and unprepossessing mosquito effects (mainly models, superimpositions, and bug-eye-view shots).

**SKETCH** (H.K.) Century Motion Pictures 1982 color/ws? 94m. D: Dennis Yu. Ref: TV: Rainbow Video; Eng. titles. Fango 107:59: probably sfa *Sketch of a Psycho*. NST! 4:36.

"Give me back mommy. I want to kill her." A prowler who wields, variously, pitchfork, ax, and butcher knife turns out to be the "sex maniac" at large who's after Mrs. Chin. At one point, the latter, in turn, goes crazy with fear and begins lashing out with her own knife.... Undistinguished suspense-horror re another confused "psycho." Semi-highlights: the madman leaping up out of the water and the *Cat People* (1942) sidewalk-suspense sequence.

**SKETCHES OF A STRANGLER** Paul Leder 1978 color 82m. SP, D, Co-P: Leder. Ph: Joel King. Mus: Arlon Ober. Mkp: Sarah Spalding. Sketches: Karl Ellis. Ref: TV. TVG. Hound. no Maltin '92. Martin. Stanley. Scheuer. With Allen Garfield, Meredith MacRae, Frank Whiteman, Clayton Wilcox, Jennifer Rhodes, Marlene Tracy, Tanya George, Michael Andres, Raja.

Hollywood-based thriller re a "series of killings of young women," all nine strangled. The killer: an artist mixed-up about his "tramp mother" and loving sister. Not especially bad, but low-key and very familiar.

**I SKIACHTRA** (Greek) Cooperation EPE 1985 color 98m. SP, D: Manoussos Manoussaukis. Mus: Demetris Papademetriou. Ref: V 10/25/85. Ecran F 76:48, 53. With Akis Kourkoulos, Lilly Koukodi.

A "charming fairy tale" re haunted castles, fairies, and the "Enchantress." *The Enchantress*—tr t.

**SKIN STRIPPERESS** (H.K.) 1991 color/ws feature. D: Chen Chi-Hwa. Ref: TV: EVS; Eng. titles; *Skin Striperess* - t error in cr. VSOM: *Skin Stripper* - t error. Weisser/ATC: aka *Skinned Ghost*.

Lightning-downed high tension wires horribly burn a young woman. Later, her body "absorbs" the skin of another young lady skinned by a sort of voodoo priest. Still later, the fanged, long-fingered "angry ghost" of the skinned woman inhabits a "haunted beach," possesses the hero, and gives him fangs.... Despite the gory, *Eyes without a Face* premises, this horror-comedy-drama ends up in typical ghost action, complete with a ghost "detector." Strange Thrills, diluted by Adventures with Vapid Teens.

**SKINNED ALIVE** Suburban Tempe (David DeCoteau/J.R. Bookwalter) 1990 color 78m. (aka *Skinned Alive!*). Story,SP,D,PD,Co-ed: Jon Killough. Story: also Mike Shea. Ph: M. Tolochko Jr. Mus: Bookwalter. SpMkpFX: David Lange, Bill Morrison;(consul) D.P. Barton. Ref: TV: Cinema HV. PT 7:49. With Mary Jackson, Scott Spiegel, Susan Rothacker, Floyd Ewing Jr.

"I think we've died and gone to Mayberry." Gleeful but clumsy gore comedy re Crawldaddy's Traveling Tannery—or, skinning people for fun and (mainly) profit. *Texas Chainsaw Massacre 2* ripoff features comically exaggerated gore.

**SKINNED GHOST** see *Skin Stripperess*

**SKINNED GIRL** (H.K.) 1993 color feature. D: Ricky Lau. Ref: Weisser/ATC2: "not very good." With Tony Leung, Chingmy Yau.

Crazy monk ... human-skin lantern ... trapped spirit.

**SKINNER** Cinequanon/5 Kidd (Skinner Films/Wyman-Pollon) 1993 color c90m. D: Ivan Nagy. SP: Paul Hart-Wilden. Ph: G. Littlewood. Mus: Contagion. PD: J. Carlson. SpMkpFX: KNB. SdFX: Able Dog Post. Ref: TV: A-Pix video. With Ted Raimi (Dennis Skinner), Ricky Lake, David Warshofsky, Richard Schiff, Traci Lords (Heidi).

Update of *The Lodger* re a sicko who skins his victims, then wears the skin. ("I wanted you to see the real me.") Meanwhile, a disfigured victim (Lords) trails him.... Unsavory ripoff of the lesser half of *Silence of the Lambs*. Even the potentially fun Grand Guignol ending fizzles.

**Et SKUD FRA HJERTET** (Danish) Metronome/Groenlykke, Levring & Magnusson 1986 color 80m. D & Idea: Kristian Levring. SP: Leif Magnusson. Mus: Lars Hug. Ref: V 10/1/86: *A Shot from the Heart*—tr t; "bogged down in narrative dead ends." With Claus Flygare, Lars Oluf Larsen, Niels Skousen.

A "near-future world," a la the *Road Warrior* movies.

**The SKULL SOLDIER** (J) KSS Films 1992 color/ws 91m. SP, D: Shouki Kyouhon. Ref: TV: vt; no Eng. VW 25:26-7: "engagingly adult super-hero story." With S. Kyouhon.

Hormone experiments give man "superhuman strength, thanks to a rapidly supercharged skeletal structure...." (VW) Apparently shot-on-tape, pretentiously-slow-paced fantasy features a weird, caped superhero who commits gory killings and the pointy-chinned gent who controls him. Plus visualized nightmares re the slashing of a woman.

**SKULLDUGGERY** (Can.) Wittman Richter 1983 (1985) color 95m. (*Warlock*-B t). SP, D: Ota Richter. Story, Exec P: Peter Wittman. Ph: Robert New. Mus: Eugen Illin. AD: Jill Scott. Logo Des: Jarmila Dubska. Mkp: Ava Stone. Ref: TV: M. H. E. video. Stanley. Morse. Hound. no Phantom. VW 16:8: 1979? V 5/11/83:32. With Thom Haverstock, Wendy Crewson, David Main, Clark Johnson, Geordie Johnson, David Calderisi (sorcerer/Dr. Evel), Jim Coburn (Simca the Magician), Denis Fergusson (Mme. Kardos).

In Canterbury, in the year 1382, a warlock casts a spell on a family.... In Trottelville, U.S.A., 1982, "something strange is going on." The spirit of the warlock seems to inhabit, first, Simca the Magician, whose talents border on the supernatural, then, Adam (Haverstock), a junior-college student assigned the role of Warlock in a "Dungeons and Dragons"-like game. "It's hard to say where the game begins or life ends" when Adam begins taking said game seriously, and people start dying of heart failure. At the end, Adam vanishes, but his lingering spirit seems to animate a suit of armor.

At the Villa Evel, the password is "skullduggery." The word for the movie is screwy. Script combines fantasy, offbeat comedy, and slasher-movie elements, and while nothing really works, *Skullduggery* is at least not just more of the same. In a typical scene, a pair of roller skates is found baked in an oven, and the executive producer wanders in and out of scenes emptying ashtrays.

**SKULLS AND SCULLS** Copley (Kopfstein) 1929? anim mus & sd fx c7m. D: Pat Sullivan. Ref: TV: Loonic Video (Early Animation #2).

In the startlingly surreal first half here, Felix the Cat runs down spooky-house stairs which turn into the scales on the back of a huge, fanged dragon-monster. A stepping-stone in a lake then turns into a ghost which chases him. The bizarreness lets up a bit in the second (sculls) half. Real weirdness.

**\*SKY BANDITS** 1940 62m. Ph: Mack Stengler. Songs: Lange & Porter. Ref: TV. Hardy/SF. no Lentz. Lee. Jon Van Landschoot. Pitts/HFS. Okuda/Monogram. no V. Hound. Stanley. With Dewey Robinson, Dwight Frye, Dave O'Brien, Karl Hackett, Joseph Stefan, Ken Duncan.

Mr. Speavy's (Frye) "queer machinery," a radio frequency beam which is shooting down Yukon Gold Mining's planes, is based on a "new principle for power-wave transmission." The invention, as developed by Prof. Lewis (Stefan), looks like a combination telescope-rifle-radio-tube, and knocks out magnetos.

Script provides some scientific documentation for its deathray marvel, but not much of a story. Fatuous singing hero; formula comic relief. Frye does his Renfield laugh ("You fool!"), but this is not one of his better roles.

**SKY PIRATES** (Austral.) John Lamond 1986 color/ws 86m. (aka *Time Warrior. Dakota Harris*—F). D: Colin Eggleston. SP: J. Lamond. Ph: G. Wapshott. Mus: Brian May. PD: K. Fredrickson. SpVisFX: Dennis Nicholson. Ref: V 2/19/86: "woefully conceived." 10/19/88:179. Stanley. Ecran F 44:37. 49:71. 62:68. 70:6. Morse: "not much excitement." With John Hargreaves, Meredith Phillips, Max Phipps, Bill Hunter.

Prehistoric aliens, time warp, magic stone.

**SKY RACKET** Victory (Sam Katzman) 1937 62m. D: S. Katzman. SP: Basil Dickey. Ph: Bill Hyer. Sets: Fred Preble. Ref: TV. Greg Luce. CM 16:56(ad). no V. no Lee. no Turner/Price. With Herman Brix aka Bruce Bennett, Joan Barclay, Jack Mulhall, Monte Blue,

Hattie McDaniel, Henry Roquemore, Duncan Renaldo, Edward Earle, Earle Hodgins, Ed Cassidy.

"Three mail planes have been mysteriously shot out of the air." The motor-jamming "gadget" here looks like an old-fashioned parlor radio plus a glorified Etch-a-Sketch viewer. ("Something went wrong with the motor.") Or, No Time for Retakes. Involved but uninvolving skullduggery, with laughably inept action. (The Thrown Chair scene is a classic of its kind.) Bennett is an agreeable hero; at the other end of the cinematic spectrum, Blue did the Lubitsch silent classic *The Marriage Circle*; and is this amazing Sinister Cinema find the only movie Sam Katzman directed?

**SKYHIGH** Omega/Forminx 1985 color 104m. (*Blown Sky High*—alt t). Story, D, P, SpSdFX: Nico Mastorakis. SP: Robert Gilliam, Fred C. Perry. Mus: Denis Haines. SpFX: G. Humes. Digital FX: Molinare; (des) Mastorakis. Ref: TV. TVG. V 5/22/85. no Stanley. With Daniel Hirsch, Clayton Norcross, Frank Schultz, Lauren Taylor, Janet Taylor.

Special modulated frequency on pre-recorded tape subconsciously stimulates a "relatively-unknown area of the brain.... Encoded in music, it can introduce spectacular images directly into the mind," and it has an instant-hypnotic effect. Joined and modulated with another, lower frequency, and beamed to satellites, it can "destroy the world."

Slight, silly comedy-intrigue. All the quips and sight gags are underscored. A few cute bits of animation in the visualized mind-stimulation sequences.

**SKYSCRAPER HAUNTINGS** or **SKYSCRAPER HUNTING** see *Hunting Ash*

**SLAPSTICK OF ANOTHER KIND** IFM-ERC/Steven Paul & Serendipity 1984 (1982) color 87m. SP, D, P: Paul. SP: also Kurt Vonnegut, from his novel "Slapstick" (also orig title of film). Mus: Morton Stevens. SpVisFX: Private Stock FX; (sup) C. N. Comisky. Prosth: Robert Zraick, Steve Laporte, Ve Neill. Stopmo: E. D. Farino. SpVis Consultant: Robert Skotak. SpFX: Nipper, O'Connell. Ref: TV. Bill Warren. Scot Holton. Academy. Ecran F 33:31. 28:38. V 3/28/84. With Jerry Lewis (Wilbur/Mr. Swain), Madeline Kahn (Eliza/Mrs. Swain), John Abbott, Marty Feldman, Sam Fuller, Jim Backus, Ben Frank, Merv Griffin, Pat Morita, Virginia Graham, Cherie Harris; Orson Welles (voice).

In the not-too-distant future, when the population of mainland China has been miniaturized, and its emissaries dart about in flying fortune-cookie saucers, a doctor named Frankenstein (Abbott) delivers deformed twins Wilbur and Eliza into the wealthy Swain family. They develop into super-intelligent, seven-foot-tall giants with vaguely Frankensteinian (the monster) features who conceal their intelligence and who, when they literally put their heads together, create an IQ-energy-field. At the end, beneficent aliens from a spaceship whisk the twins off to a Utopian place.

A very strange, misbegotten picture. Main theme: the sheer lousy arbitrariness of life. Parenthood, intolerance, and militarism also come under the thematic gun here, which in this case is a bazooka. If the ending is indefensible, it's also the film's only satisfying scene. In an instant, the rest of the movie is "balanced," not to say obliterated. For deliriously unfounded, yet almost-surreally "right" optimism, it rivals the end of *The Last Laugh*.

**SLASH** see *Blood Sisters*

**SLASH DANCE** Glencoe Ent. (Andrew Maisner) 1989 color 83m. SP, D: James Shyman. Mus: E. Kauderer. Ref: V 8/2/89: "meek horror thriller." McCarty II: *Slashdance*; "dull and silly." HR 8/3/89: "laughably awful." PT 7:48-9. With Cindy Maranne, James Carrol Jordan, Jay Richardson.

"Slasher-film-meets-'A Chorus Line'."(V)

**SLASHER** see *Blood Rage*

**The SLASHER ... IS THE SEX MANIAC!** (I) William Mishkin/Jaylo Int'l. (Florimont) 1974 (1972/'76-U.S.) color c85m. (*Rivelazione di un Maniaco Sessuale al Capo della Squadra Mobile. The Slasher*—ad t. *Penetration*—alt, X-rated-version t). SP, D: Roberto Montero. SP: also L. Angelli, I. Fasant. Ph: F. Rossi. Mus: G. Gaslini. Ref: TV: vt; Eng.-dubbed. Horacio Higuchi. Hound. Weldon. Stanley. VWB: aka *So Sweet, So Dead*. Palmerini. With Farley Granger, Sylva Koscina, Susan Scott, Chris Avram, Krista Nell, Femi Benussi.

The "inhuman" killer of unfaithful wives turns out to be a "sex maniac" with a "moral fixation"—and a vise-like grip. ("Always the same technique....") Bonus: a creepy corpse-cosmetics man. ("I love my work.") Blandly dubbed and scored shocker with meant-to-be-steamy sex scenes and meant-to-be-*Psycho* knife-murder scenes.

**SLAUGHTER HIGH** (U.S.-Sp?) Vestron/Spectacular Trading (Minasian-Randall) 1985 color 90m. (*April Fool's Day*—orig t). SP, D: George Dugdale, Mark Ezra, Peter Litten. Mus: Harry Manfredini. PD: Geoff Sharpe. SpFX: Coast to Coast; (des) P. Litten. Mech Des: Richard Pirkis. Prosth: John Humphreys. Mkp: Alison Hall, Craig Berkely. Ref: TV: Vestron Video. Phantom. V 5/22/85. 4/29/87:26. With Caroline Munro, Simon Scuddamore (Marty), Kelly Baker, Sally Cross, Billy Hartman, Carmine Iannaccone, Donna Yaeger.

An April Fool's prank leaves Doddsville County High School chemistry whiz Marty disfigured by nitric acid.... Doddsville High, five years after it has been closed. A storm threatens the mysteriously-arranged April Fool's Day reunion of the not-so-merry pranksters. "Jason," in hockey mask, seems to threaten, too, but ... April Fool! No joke, though, when a can of "beer" makes one victim's stomach burst open, and acid from a bathtub faucet produces a case of instant decomposition. At the end, "crazed lunatic" Marty's victims seem to return as zombies, but a coda suggests that the whole thing has been his nightmare.

Regulation *Friday the 13th/Carrie* blood-and-guts. Marty imagines some very exaggerated gore effects—chemicals act instantly, weapons work quickly and slickly. The actors fall right into their cliche roles—nerd, smartass, etc.—though Marc Smith as the coach strikes the right sarcastic note.

**SLAUGHTERHOUSE** American Artists & Slaughterhouse Assoc. (Ron Matonak) 1987 color 85m. SP, D: Rick Roessler. SpFxMkp: Barney Burman, Mark Lane. Ref: V 7/6/88: "standard horror pic." 10/28/87:11: in release. 5/20/87: 4(rated).

5/6/87:215(ad). Martin. Phantom: "tired plot." With Sherry Bendorf, Don Barrett, William Houck.

Teens slaughtered at pig slaughterhouse.

**SLAUGHTERHOUSE ROCK** Taurus Ent./First American & Arista (Louis George/Slaughterhouse Rock) 1988 (1987) color 85m. (aka *Hell Island*). Story, D: Dimitri Logothetis. SP: Ted Landon. Written by Sandra Willard, Nora Goodman. Ph: Nicholas Von Sternberg. Mus: Mark Mothersbaugh, G. V. Casale. PD: P.P. Raubertas. VisFX: E.D. Farino. SpFxMkp: Wof-N-Bar Prods. SpFxCoord: Kevin McCarthy. Opt: Animagic. Ref: TV: Sony Video. V 3/9/88: "ambitious." 5/20/87:41. 5/6/87:215(ad), 294. Martin: "typical schlock shocker." Morse: "brisk, slick, mindless fun." Phantom: "some visual flair." Hardy/HM2. With Nicholas Celozzi, Tom Reilly, Donna Denton, Toni Basil (Sammy Mitchell), Hope Marie Carlton.

"This place gives me the creeps." Visions of a demon draw teens to Alcatraz, where an indestructible monster subsists on dead souls, and the possessed Richard turns into a toothy monster. Plus astral projection and a supernatural flashback to a camp commandant who made a pact with the devil.... Unremarkable fantasy-horror has some fairish, self-conscious dialogue and okay, atmospheric cloud effects. But too much "We've gotta get outta here!"

**SLAVE GIRLS FROM BEYOND INFINITY** Urban Classics/Titan 1987 color 74m. SP, D, P: Ken Dixon. Mus: Carl Dante. Co-P & SpFxSup: Mark Wolf. Co-P & SpVisFX: John Eng. Androids: John Buechler. Mutant: Joe Reader. SpFxMkp: David Cohen. Ref: TV. V 9/30/87. ad. With Elizabeth Cayton or Kaitan, Cindy Beal, Brinke Stevens, Kirk Graves (Vak), Randolph Roehbling (Krel), Bud Graves & Jeffrey Blanchard (Phantazoid warriors), Fred Tate (mutant), Jacques Schardo (zombie).

Beauties, grotesques, and robots (or "androids"), in a "remote corner of the galaxy" where a "maniac" (Don Scribner) gives his "shipwrecked" guests a head start in the jungle, hunts them with laser weapon, and allows them to live if they last till dawn. Otherwise: the trophy room. Also: the "Phantom Zone," where regular time-and-space laws DNA.... Decor as well as plot ape the 1932 *Most Dangerous Game*. *Slave Girls* adds little to the latter except bikinis and mutants. Best line: "Engines hot!"

See also *Lethal Woman* (1989).

**SLAYMAN, The** see *Night Stalker, The* (1987)

**SLEDGE HAMMER** I&I Prods. (Nicholas Imaz) 1984 color c90m. SP, D: David A. Prior. Mus: Ted Prior, Marc Adams. AD: Laurence McElrea. SpFX: Blood & Guts; (sup) J. Marrino. Mkp: Robin Beauchene. Ref: TV: World Video. Stanley. V 1/29/86:44(hv). Hound. no Martin. With T. Prior, Linda McGill, John Eastman, Jeanine Scheer, Tim Aguilar, Justin Greer (The Boy), Doug Matley (killer).

"All alone in the country...." Ten years after a "madman with a sledge hammer" pounded two lovers to death in a country home, a gaggle of teenagers shows up at the scene of the crimes. An impromptu seance at which a "spirit" speaks is a hoax, but a phantom with a sledge hammer begins appearing about the house.

Egregious shot-on-tape *Halloween* ripoff. The only unusual (as well as unexplained) element: The "raving maniac" appears as both an eight-year-old boy and a hulking thing, and at one point "grows" from one into the other.

**The SLEEP OF DEATH** (Swedish-Irish) Aspekt-Dragon, in assoc. with the Swedish Film Inst. & Nat'l. Film Studios of Ireland 1978 color/ws 90m. (*Ondskans Vardshus*. aka *The Inn of the Flying Dragon*). SP, D, P: Calvin Floyd. SP: also Yvonne Floyd. From Sheridan Le Fanu's story "The Room in the Dragon Volant" or "The Room at the Flying Dragon." Ph: Jiri Tirl, Tony Forsberg. Mus: Ragnar Grippe. AD: Mathias Matthies, Ellen Schmidt. Mkp: Kjerstin Elg. Ref: TV. TVG. Hardy/HM. Jones. no Scheuer. Hound. no Phantom. no Maltin '92. With Per Oscarsson, Patrick Magee, Marilu Tolo, Brendan Price, Niall Toibin, Curd Jurgens (The Count), Kay Maclaren, Barry Cassins, Ray MacNally.

Count Nicolas de St. Alyre, who survived the Bastille in 1793, with the help of a "sleep of death" potion, is believed by superstitious villagers to have "lived on as a vampire." The Count himself believes that a "vampire in the family tomb will help" the family name, and proceeds to drug young Robert Tanner. At the last moment, the Count is drugged and substituted in the coffin for Robert, and publicly staked as a vampire.

Prettily photographed, but stilted, enigmatic reworking of material used also by Dreyer in *Vampyr*. The actors speak in slow motion, as if the director thought that "slow" might translate as "mysterious." The score has a catchy main theme.

**SLEEPAWAY CAMP 2: UNHAPPY CAMPERS** Double Helix Films/Stan Wakefield (Jerry Silva) 1988 color 80m. D, Co-P: Michael A. Simpson. SP: Fritz Gordon. Mus: James Oliverio. SpMkpFX: Bill Johnson. Opt: Atlanta Film FX. Ref: TV: Nelson Ent. video. V 11/16/88. SFChron Dtbk 11/6/88. With Pamela Springsteen, Renee Estevez, Tony Higgins, Valerie Hartman, Brian Patrick Clarke.

"I love this camp!" Camp Rolling Hills. Angela Baker (Springsteen), the Angel of Death, is back—as counselor Angela Johnson: "There's lots of good kids. We just have to weed out the bad." After weeding, two are left—Angela wreaks moral revenge on those who "fornicate" (her word), drink, smoke dope, talk dirty, and alter the lyrics of the "Happy Camper Song." In other words, on nearly everyone, including two campers who masquerade as Freddy and Jason, in an attempt to scare her. (She simply dons a Leatherface mask and whips out a chainsaw.)

It seems perfectly logical that the gung-ho camp counselor and the crazy who takes on the immoral majority are one and the same person. The oddly good-natured gross-outs here seem more closely allied to comedies like *Meatballs* than to *Friday the 13th*. This is a feel-good slasher movie, no less. Angela—who finds the "nice" Molly (Estevez) a kindred spirit—comforts her after beheading her (Molly's) boy friend Sean (Higgins), "There's plenty of fish in the sea." Angela's beyond-Freddy one-liners are prime comic psychopathology. Complete with a "Thank you for reading the credits."

**SLEEPAWAY CAMP 3: TEENAGE WASTELAND** Double Helix Films/Stan Wakefield (Jerry Silva) 1989 (1988) color 79m. D, Co-P: Michael A. Simpson. SP: Fritz Gordon. Mus: James

Oliverio. SpMkpFX: Bill Johnson. Pyro FX: Spectacular FX Int'l. SdFxEd: Robert Gillespie. Ref: TV: Nelson Ent. video. V 6/28/89. 3/22/89:25(rated). With Pamela Springsteen, Tracy Griffith, Michael J. Pollard, Mark Oliver, Kim Wall, Sandra Dorsey (Lilly).

"Angela is back!"—at Camp Rolling Hills, since renamed Camp New Horizons, the "camp of caring and sharing." Highlights of the summer: Angela's (Springsteen) brutally effective mini-war on drugs, her marshmallow roast over a burning (occupied) tent, and "Angela's Rap," a short, to-the-point, taped number.

Not as charming as Part II, despite Springsteen's obvious relish of the role of the lethally puritanical Angela. The latter's quips here seem simply quips, nothing more, and nothing much is made—satirically or sociologically—of the meeting of underprivileged and overprivileged campers at New Horizons. Watch for Angela's oh-brother reaction to a fellow camper's declaration of a *Care Bears Movie* as one of her favorite films.

**The SLEEPING CAR** Triax Ent./Vidmark (Mark Amin) 1990 (1989) color 87m. D, P: Douglas Curtis. SP, Assoc P: Greg O'Neill. Mus: Ray Colcord. SpVisFX: Cinemotion; (d) Max W. Anderson. SpMkpFX: MMI; (des) John Carl Buechler. AddlSpFX: (anim) Chris Casady; (opt) Howard Anderson. Sp Equip: SpFxUnltd. Ref: TV. V 3/18/90. Sacto Bee 3/20/90. Maltin '92. Hound. McCarty II. Martin. Scheuer. With David Naughton, Judie Aronson, Kevin McCarthy, Jeff Conaway, Dani Minnick, J. C. Buechler (Mr. Erickson), Ernestine Mercer, Gary Brockett (ghost Mister).

"The car seems to be filled with bad dreams." The vaguely Freddy-inspired ghost of an engineer haunts the sleeping car of a "freight train from hell": When "The Mister" appears—"living through" student Jason McCree (Naughton)—the sleeping-car bed comes to life and "eats" its victims. In the ambitious finale, Jason "forgives" Mr. Erickson, and the latter's demonic spirit vanishes. Too-glib dialogue in this occasionally interesting fizzle.

**SLEEPING WITH THE ENEMY** Fox/Leonard Goldberg-Jeffrey Chernov 1991 color 98m. D: Joseph Ruben. SP: Ronald Bass, from Nancy Price's novel. Mus: Jerry Goldsmith. Mkp: Richard Dean. SpFX: (coord) Calvin J. Acord; Illusion Arts, Syd Dutton et al. Ref: TV. MFB'91:110-11. V 2/11/91. SFExam 2/8/91. SFBay Guardian 2/13/91. With Julia Roberts, Patrick Bergin, Kevin Anderson, Elizabeth Lawrence, Claudette Nevins.

"At first, he was charming, tender...." As a husband, Martin Burney (Bergin) is a jealous, abusive, obsessive perfectionist. And he calls his wife, Laura (Roberts), "Princess." She escapes to Iowa and a new identity, "Sara Waters." Generally insipid suspenser whips up some excitement as hunter nears prey, and Goldsmith's music turns to *Jaws*. But there are too many marking-time scenes, and the movie borrows most of its better thrill devices from movies like *Repulsion* (the sudden shock with the just-closed windows) and *Halloween* (another "back from the dead" coda).

**SLEEPWALK** (W.G.-U.S.) Ottoscope & Driver 1986 color 78m. Story, SP, D, P: Sara Driver. SP: also Lorenzo Mans. Story: also Kathleen Brennon. Ph: Frank Prinzi. Mus: Phil Kline. Mkp: Matiki Anoff. Ref: TV: Nelson Ent. video. V 5/14/86. VV

7/14/87. NYT 3/20/87. HR 4/10/87. With Suzanne Fletcher, Ann Magnuson, Dexter Lee, Steven Chen, Tony Todd (Barrington), Ako (Ecco, Ecco).

Very elliptical, occasionally very creepy tale re a woman, Nicole (Fletcher), who is given a "really weird"-smelling manuscript of "old Chinese nursery rhymes" to translate into English. Little does she know that she, not the manuscript, is the "subject." Her out-loud translation seems to awaken psychic and sinister forces about her: Her roommate's (Magnuson) hair falls out, another woman (Ako) is strangled with her own hair (and, when she dies, her "echo" remains), people's fingers seem to be in jeopardy, Nicole's own injured finger heals mysteriously, an elevator's every stop seems to issue into various subzones of "The Twilight Zone," street signs shake as she walks by, and office computers self-start.

If this film's terseness and lack of explanations at first unsettle, they finally frustrate. Film ends, and gentle viewer is left with a pile of jigsaw-puzzle pieces. Best, perhaps, to accept *Sleepwalk* as a teaser and tantalizer and leave it at that. At least, the film plays like a one-of-a-kind and not part six of a series.

**SLEEPWALKERS** see *Stephen King's Sleepwalkers*

**SLICK SLEUTHS** Modern Film Sales 1930? anim color c7m. Mus: Bradford, Carbonara. Ref: TV: Loonic Video (Early Animation number 2).

In a dream, Mutt and Jeff, detectives, take on the floating, cloaked, cackling Phantom, who can change shapes—he becomes, variously, a doorway, a window, Chaplin, and, most imaginatively, rooftop chimney smoke. Plus a clever bit with a live handprint. Yow!

**SLIME CITY** Camp/Slime City Co. 1988 color 85m. SP, D, Co-P: Gregory Lamberson. SpMkpFX: J. S. Coulter. Addl FX: Tom Lauten. Ref: V 5/11/88: "minor horror film with spook elements ... plays acceptably." Phantom: "amateurish, derivative." With R. C. Sabin, Mary Huner, T. J. Merrick.

Occultist turns building's inhabitants into monsters.

**SLIPPING INTO DARKNESS** see *Crazed*

**SLIPSTREAM** (B) Entertainment Film Prods. (Gary Kurtz) 1989 color/ws? 102m. (92m.-U.S.). D: Steven M. Lisberger. SP: Tony Kayden. Story: Bill Bauer; (uncred.) Charles Edward Pogue. Mus: Elmer Bernstein. VisFxSup: Brian Johnson. OptFX: Fotherley. MkpSup: Naomi Donne. Ref: TV: Virgin Home Ent. video. MFB'89:36-7. V 2/15/89. With Mark Hamill, Bob Peck, Bill Paxton, Kitty Aldridge, Eleanor David, Ben Kingsley, F. Murray Abraham.

"Runaway technology" leads to the "Convergence"—and to an earthquake-rearranged Earth dominated by a "river of wind," the Slipstream, and the latter's "banshee voices." Interesting stew of principal characters here includes Matt Owens (Paxton), who recalls Han Solo; lawman Will Tasker (Hamill), who recalls Buford Pusser; and the android "Byron" (Peck), who at first recalls the Christ-like Ian Hunter of *Strange Cargo* (1940). ("I just want to do what's right.") Byron the healer has all the technical expertise, but must learn fun, and takes over the "mu-

seum" dance floor at one point with his version of "The Continental"....

Byron also takes over the film, though the latter is also acceptable as a vehicle for aerial photography (Frank Tidy and Terry Cole). If the contrast between the fanatically law-and-order Tasker and the in-it-for-the-bounty Owens promises more than it delivers, the script keeps ringing interesting changes on the aloof-android theme. The coda sees Byron trekking onward, searching for "android heaven." Byron is part comic relief, part dramatic force, and part inspirational figure.

**SLUGS—THE MOVIE** (Sp) New World/Dister Prods (Escriva-de Laurentiis) 1988 (1987) color 92m. (*Slugs—Muerte Viscosa*. aka *Slugs*). D & Co-P: Juan Piquer Simon. SP: Ron Gantman, from Shaun Hutson's novel. Mus: Tim Souster. AD: G. Gonzalo. SpMkpFX: Carlo de Marchis; (N.Y.) Pat Tantelo. SpFX: (sup) Emilio Ruiz; Basilio Cortijo. Ref: TV: Eng.-lang. version. V 4/6/88. Horacio Higuchi. With Michael Garfield, Philip Machale, Alicia Moro, Kim Terry, Patty Shepard, Frank Brana.

"There's something slimy down there!" Ashton, "center of boredom for the entire planet Earth," and soon to be Slime City. A forgotten toxic waste dump is breeding a "mutant form of slug," and parasites from the bloodstreams of these "killer slugs" cause further havoc inside humans. Here, even slug slime is deadly.

Like the same director's *Pieces, Slugs* features comically extreme insta-gore and actor reactions to same. Typical exclamations: "His face was all bloody!"/"His face was eaten away!"/"His face was—!"/"Not even in 'Nam!"/"These things are big!", and the inevitable "Slime trails!" Prime gross-out scene: the slug sliced up in the lettuce. Best bit: The sewer worker yanking at something in the pipe, and the something yanking back.

**SLUMBER PARTY MASSACRE II** Concorde/Deborah Brock, Don Daniel 1987 color 75m. (*Don't Let Go*—orig t). SP, D: Brock. Mus: Richard Cox. SpMkpFX: James Cummins. Opt: Motion, Ray Mercer. Ref: TV. V 11/4/87. Newman. With Crystal Bernard, Kimberly McArthur, Juliette Cummins, Patrick Lowe, Atanas Ilitch (Driller Killer).

"You're a dream!" The "so weird" Courtney Bates (Bernard) and her teen friends have a "slumber party weekend" at a "new condo" at the Desert Club Golf Course. Nightmares and visions re "this really weird guy" plague her, as the *Nightmare on Elm Street* influence takes over from *Halloween/Friday the 13th*, and the is-he-live-or-a-phantom-of-her-mind killer with the huge phallic drill/guitar incorporates his brutal killings into a *Bye Bye Birdie*-type dance number. This weird, climactic fusing of sex, violence, and rock'n'roll seems all the more bizarre placed as it is at the end of a mundane slasher movie. The Driller Killer appears to be a product of the virginal heroine's paranoid fantasies re sex, not your average slasher. But if the power of the surreal finally threatens here, too much of the movie is devoted to mild t&a and scare tactics.

**SLUMBER PARTY MASSACRE 3** Concorde (Catherine Cyran) 1990 color 77m. (*Stab in the Dark. Night Light*—early titles). D: Sally Mattison. SP: C. Cyran. Ph: J. Baum. Mus: Jamie Sheriff. PD: Stephanie Lytar. SpMkpFX: Dean & Starr Jones. Ref: V 12/31/90: "even die-hard genre fans will be groaning in dismay." 1/3/90:11. 5/6/91:76. PT 9:51. Martin. SFChron Dtbk 3/10/91. With Keely Christian, Brittain Frye, M. K. Harris, David Greenlee, Lulu Wilson, Maria Ford, Hope Marie Carlton.

Madman wielding phallic drill.

**SMOOTH TALKER** Reivaj Films (Montes-Shapiro) 1990 color 89m. D: Tom E. Milo. SP: Darrah Whitaker. Mus: Tony Roman. Ref: V 2/18/91: "minor league thriller." With Joe Guzaldo, Peter Crombie, Stuart Whitman, Burt Ward, Sydney Lassick.

"Serial killer of women working for a sex phone service."

**SNAKE DANCER** (S. African) Academy Ent./DeVilliers 1989(1973?) color 87m. D: Dirk DeVilliers. SP: Michael McCabe. Mkp: Lewis Rabin. Ref: TV: Acorn Video. no Martin.

"Little girls shouldn't play with snakes!" Slapdash vehicle for lewd snake dancing ends on a macabre note when our heroine's "fearsome python" dancing partner strangles her.

**The SNAKE GIRL** (H.K.?) 198-? color c92m. D: Chin Wan. Sp & Exec P: Huoy King. Mus: Koo Chia-wei. Ref: TV: Ocean Shores Video; Eng. titles. With Dy Saveth, Kon Samoeun.

Orphan Ah-hua, thrown to the snakes, later gives birth to Snake Girl Ah-mei. Men like "Brother" Lung want to kiss the latter; she teases them with stray snakes. Playfully, he yanks off her head-dress: She has snakes where most people have hair. Taken aback, he runs away; she is embarrassed. Separately, the two pout. Villagers who fear this "bugbear" or "snake monster" or "devil spirit" want to kill her, but Lung finds that he loves her. Wistfully, he sings, "Ah-mei, where are you?" Nearby, she sings back. They meet again. He runs his hand through her snakes. Villagers capture them, and a cackling priest starts cutting off her head-snakes. The inevitable climax: Hordes of snakes come to the rescue of the lovers.

*Zuma,* where are you? This appallingly naive movie alternates between Weird Romance and bloody violence, and is hysterically overacted. Padding reduces the camp value, but the above incredible scenes cannot be denied, nor should they be. Human behavior here is as bizarre as ophidian.

**SNAKE ISLAND** see *Kiss of the Serpent*

**\*The SNAKE WOMAN** Eldorado Pictures 1960 ('61-U.S.) (*The Lady Is a Snake*—working t). AD: John G. Earl. Ref: TV. V 5/3/61. Warren/KWTS! Hardy/HM. Lentz. Lee. Stanley. no Maltin '92. no Scheuer. PT 12:46.

"It is the devil's offspring!" Outside Bellingham, in Northumberland, England, 1890. A herpetologist (John Cazabon) employs snake venom to cure his wife's (Dorothy Frere) madness; she gives birth to a cold-blooded, wide-eyed baby, later dubbed Atheris, the "name of a serpent god." Twenty years later, the "curse of the serpent child" persists: A "beautiful girl" (Susan Travers) who can shed her skin and turn into a cobra terrorizes the countryside.

Flat-footed imitation of American sf-horror movies includes classic cliches, like three or four variations on "There must be a logical explanation," a Dog That Knows that barks at the "demon," the latter's sudden (but telegraphed) disappearances, and hokey witch-hag, Aggie Harker (Elsie Wagstaff). ("One look

killed the mother!") Bonus: a gratuitous snake-through-skull's-mouth shot.

**SNAKE WOMAN'S MARRIAGE** (H.K.) Jia's/Benefit Film 1983 color 94m. Ref: TV: vt; no Eng.

One of the ghost sisters from the pond can turn into a big, papier-mache snake; the other can turn into a regular (if large) snake. At the end, an apparent spaceship turns the snake monster into a worm.... *Green Snake* warmup seems trivial, at best goofily charming. Campy effects. In one scene, the application of a paper charm leaves one snake woman's head human, but her other end still a tail, just peeping out from under the bedcover.

**SNAKE WOMAN'S MARRIAGE** see *Lady Master Snake*

**SNAPDRAGON** Prism 1993 color feature. D: Worth Keeter. Ref: SFChron Dtbk 11/28/93. With Steven Bauer, Chelsea Field, Pamela Anderson.

"Amnesiac whose nightmares are similar to the actions of a serial killer."

**SNOOKLES** Juliet Stroud anim short. Ref: Sacto Bee 3/27/90: "an affecting beast."

Baby dinosaur's breath kills.

**The SNOW QUEEN** (Finnish) Neofilmi 1987 ('88-U.S.) color 90m. (*Lumikuningatar*). SP, D, P: Paivi Hartzel. Ph: Henrik Paersch. Mus: Jukka Linkola. PD: Reija Hirvikoski. SpFX: Jukka Ruohomaki, Antti Kari, Lauri Pitkanen. Ref: V 4/1/87. York Theatre (S.F.) ad 1/17/88. With Outi Vainionkulma, Sebastian Kaatrasalo, Satu Silvo (The Snow Queen).

Effects-laden version of Hans Christian Andersen's fairy tale re a boy whose heart has turned to ice.

See also: *Timefighters in the Land of Fantasy.*

**SNOW-WHITE** Para/Fleischer 1933 anim color 7m. D: Dave Fleischer. Anim: R. C. Crandall. Ref: TV: vt. Cabarga/TFS. LC. Lee.

In this *Mascot*-like grab bag of weirdness, a witch queen turns KoKo the Clown into a ghost, a flying head becomes a skeletal bat which in turn becomes an owl, and the witch herself turns into a dragon-like monster which then turns into an inside-out skeleton. Main music: "Saint James Infirmary Blues." But also listen for a bit of "Here Lies Love" (featured in Paramount's *The Big Broadcast*). The Snow White fairy tale becomes Betty Boop's Gothic Blues here. Double your Yow!

See also the following and *Happily Ever after* and *Timefighters in the Land of Fantasy.*

**SNOW WHITE** Cannon (Golan-Globus) 1987 color 83m. (*The Story of Snow White*—alt t). SP, D: Michael Berz. AD: Etan Levy. Rev: V 5/27/87: "likely to elicit less a Heigh Ho than a heave ho." TVG. With Diana Rigg, Billy Barty, Sarah Patterson, Nicola Stapleton.

Dwarfs save Snow White from Mean Queen.

**SO EVIL, MY SISTER** see *Psycho Sisters*

**SO SAAL BAAD** see *Sau Saal Baad*

**SO SWEET, SO DEAD** see *Slasher ...*

**SOCIAL CONTRACT, The** see *Animal within, The*

**SOCIETY** Wild Street (Society Prods./White-Walley) 1989 color 94m. (99m.). D: Brian Yuzna. SP: Woody Keith, Rick Fry. Ph: Rick Fichter. Mus: Mark Ryder et al. PD: Mathew C. Jacobs. SpMkpFX: Screaming Mad George. Eyeballs: Tech Optics. Ref: TV: Republic HV. MFB '90:91-3. V 5/31/89. SFChron 8/20/92; Dtbk 6/7/92. Fango 118:34. With Bill Warlock, Devin DeVasquez, Evan Richards, Ben Meyerson, Charles Lucia, Connie Danese, Patrice Jennings, Heidi Kozak, Ben Slack (Dr. Cleveland), Tim Bartell.

The people around Beverly Hills Academy perform *Xtro* stunts with their bodies, in what at first appears to be a kinky version of *Invasion of the Body Snatchers.* The explanation: malleable flesh!—and a weird breed of being which has lots of money and which cultivates humans for "shunting," a sort of cross between cannibalism and real-life morphing.

Coming off like a Cronenberg version of "The Great Gatsby," *Society* is self-satisfied with its own perversity and counts too much on the shock value of its makeup-effects-orgy of a payoff. Technically, the latter is a wow, but the story in general plays like any number of The Whole Community Is in on It movies.

**SODA SQUIRT** MGM/Iwerks 1933 anim 6m. Ref: TV: Kino Video. Filmfax 43:20: Flip the Frog.

Risque Flip the Frog cartoon in which the amphibian's concoction turns a gent into a Mr. Hyde; Eau de Pansy then turns him back into the prissy guy. Routine.

**SODOMA'S GHOST** see *Ghosts of Sodom*

**SOGNI MOSTRUOSAMENTE PROIBITI** (I) 1982 color feature. D: Neri Parenti. Ref: Palmerini: "Paolo Villaggio ... turns into Superman, Parsifal, Tarzan and so on."

**SOL BIANCA** (J) A.I.C. 1990 anim color 55m. D: Katsuhiro Akiyama. Des: (char) Takayuki Okida; (mecha) Takashi Takeuchi. Ref: TV: NEC Avenue Video; no Eng. Animag 9:4: OAV.

In the year 2395 of the Galaxy Era, five space-pirate women take their ship the *Sol Bianca*—which features an all-the-comforts-of-home lounge—to the planet Toures, where they encounter an evil overlord, spiderlike weapons, and a giant rocketship.... Fast, flashy, technically assured sf-actioner borrows some design elements from 2001.

**SOL BIANCA 2** (J) A.I.C. 1991 anim color 42m. Ref: Japan Video. vc box.

**SOLAMENTE NERO** see *Only Blackness*

**SOLAR CRISIS** (J) Trimark/Shochiku-Fuji (Gakken Publishing & Japan America & NHK Ents./Morishima-Nelson-Edlund) 1990 ('92-U.S.) colo r 118m. (*Nisen-Goju-Nen—Taiyokara No Messeji. Kuraishisu 2050*—alt t. *Starfire*—int t. *2050*—ad t. *Crisis 2050*—ad t). D: Richard C. Sarafian. SP: Joe Gannon, Ted Sarafian, from a novel by Takeshi Kawata. Ph: Russ Carpenter. Mus: Maurice Jarre. PD: George Jenson. SpVisFX: Richard Edlund; Boss Film; (futurist) Syd Mead; (coord) Donna Langston. SupModelMaker: Pat McClung. SpFxCoord: Kelly Kerby. SpFX: Craig Smith. ElecFxCoord: W. Klinger Jr. SpSolar Imaging: Oxford Scientific Films. Anim: Phil Cummings. Computer Anim: Pacific Data. SdFxSup: Statemen, Bender. Opt: Howard Anderson, Chandler Group. SpProps: Ed Eyth. Futuristic Props: Neotek. Ref: TV: credits list Crispan Bolt & J. Gannon on SP. V 9/17/90. 7/13/92:63. 11/15/89:13. 2/28/90:13. 8/8/90:39. 12/6/89:26. 11/1/89:21. 4/18/90:19. TVG. PT 16:16. Markalite 3:68-71. Imagi 1:57. With Tim Matheson, Charlton Heston, Peter Boyle, Annabel Schofield, Tetsuya Bessho, Corky Nemec, Jack Palance, Paul Koslow, Dorian Harewood, Michael Berryman, Paul Williams (Freddy the Bomb).

The starship *Helios is* assigned to carry and launch an anti-matter bomb to quash a solar mega-flare threatening Earth.... Very detailed space and spacecraft effects, right down to shadows and reflections, and a fun holographic-solar-system effects sequence. The later, hot-time-in-the-old-solar-system effects, though, are a bit tacky. Movie is mainly standard action, suspense, and melodrama. Palance enlivens a few scenes.

**SOLAR FORCE** Hallmark/Nu Image 1995 (1994) color c91m. D: B. Davidson. SP: T. Pare. Ref: vc box: 21st-century cyborgs. With M. Pare, B. Drago.

**SOLARBABIES** MGM/Brooksfilms (Irene Walzer, J. F. Sanders) 1986 color 90m. D: Alan Johnson. SP: Walon Green, D. A. Metrov. Mus: Maurice Jarre. VisFX: Richard Edlund. SpFxSup: Nick Allder. MkpFxDes: Steve Johnson. SdFxSup: Mark Mangini. Ref: TV. V 11/26/86. SFExam 11/28/86. Maltin '92. With Richard Jordan, Jami Gertz, Jason Patric, Lukas Haas, Adrian Pasdar, Frank Converse, Sarah Douglas, Charles Durning.

The future is here and it's roller skates with headlights. Year 41 of a "new Time," in which The Protectorate controls all land and hoards water ... a legend about a "visitor from the heavens" is fulfilled in the Bodhi, a magic, glowing sphere ... a monster machine is "programmed to enjoy what he does," which is just about anything ... and Tiretown is not far from Thunderdome.

The Bodhi won't replace the slabs in *2001*, but—philosophically as well as visually—it's intriguing. It represents imagination, God, belief, fun, the worthwhile, the good—i.e., anything you like. The action is conventional; the dialogue is of a surpassing vapidity. ("I don't know where I'm going or why I'm here.")

**SOLE SURVIVOR** IFM/Larkey 1984 (1982) color 90m. SP, D, Ed: Thom Eberhardt. Ph: Russ Carpenter. Mus: David Anthony. SpFX: AA SpFx. Mkp: Alice Campbell. SpGraphics: Tom Scott. Apprentice Ed: Michael Dempsey. Ref: TV. V 5/30/84. Phantom. With Anita Skinner (Denise Watson), Kurt Johnson, Caren Larkey (Karla), Robin Davidson, Andrew Boyer, Daniel Cartmell, Jennifer Sullivan (loading-dock girl).

"Sure are a lot of weird people in this city." Everyone seems to be looking strangely at Denise, the "miracle girl" who survived a plane crash. Is she suffering from "survivor's syndrome," which almost inevitably leads to suicide? No. It seems that sole survivors do not necessarily try to kill themselves—the recently dead come back to claim them.

Forget the How? of this offbeat supernatural thesis. If the story is a bit thin, it's at least a puzzler, something almost completely different, and the movie has an eerie, stranger-is-watching motif. (Here, even the mannequins stare.) Near the end, the movie ventures into more familiar zombie/slasher territory.

**SOME OTHER PLACE. THE RIGHT PLACE** see *Return*

**SOMETHING ELSE ENTIRELY** (Norw.) Oslo Film Assn./Norsk Film A/S & Media Vision A/S (Odd Wenn) 1986 (1985) 77m. (*Noe Helt Annet. Something Else—Entirely* - cr t). SP, D: Morten Kolstad. Story: Trond Kirkvaag, Knut Lystad, Lars Mjoen. Mus: Hissa Nyberget. Ref: TV: VSOM; Eng. titles. no Jones. V 3/5/86. 10/16/85:409: *Something Quite Different — Or The Vampire Movie.* With Kirkvaag, Lystad, Mjoen, Linn Stokke.

An adopted boy, Buffalo Bull, has fangs and a "vampire fixation." (Dr. Lecher, the shrink, proves to be a vampire, too.) Supposedly dead, Buffalo revives at his own funeral as a full-blown, Dracula-like vampire. At the end, he opts for the life of a comedian rather than a vampire.... Dismal comedy has delusions of "Monty Python." The opening fakeout "film" is the closest thing to a highlight.

**SOMETHING IS OUT THERE** (U.S.—Austral.) NBC-TV/Col-TV (Invader Prods. & Hoyts Prods.) 1988 color 180m. D: Richard Colla. SP & Exec Co-P: Frank Lupo. Mus: Sylvester Levay. PD: Anthony Cowley. Creature Des: Rick Baker. VisFX: Apogee; (sp des) John Dykstra. SpFxCoord: Tom Bellissimo; (Aust.) Brian Cox. Laser FX: Peter Koczera. SdFX: Soundelux; (sup) Joe Mayer. Ref: TV: alternately called TV-movie & miniseries. V 5/11/88: 112. SFChron 5/6/88. With Joe Cortese, Maryam d'Abo, Gregory Sierra, John Putch, Robert Webber, George Dzundza, Kim Delaney, Jack Bricker (the creature).

"From the looks of it, ten guys with power tools ambushed three construction workers." On view: an alien woman from "another star system" who's armed with a ray rifle and who possesses fantastic leaping ability ... and a flashback to a prison spaceship holding a mind-controlling monster, a xenomorph from the Centauri sector, an "intergalactic great white shark" out to "regenerate its own race on Earth".... Alternately glib and maudlin, with okay camera and monster effects (photography by Laszlo George), including some fun burrowing effects, as the insect-crab monster takes the low road.

**SOMETHING IS WAITING** see *Dark Side of the Moon*

**SOMETIMES THEY COME BACK** see *Stephen King's Sometimes They Come back*

**SOMEWHERE IN EGYPT** Fox Terrytoon 1943 anim color 6m. D: Mannie Davis. Story: John Foster. Mus: P.A. Scheib. Ref: TV: Video Treasures. Maltin/OMAM. PFA library. no Lee.

Lively Gandy Goose cartoon features (in an all-a-dream framework) a floating sarcophagus, giant guards, a ghostly, dancing exotic cat from mummy-case bandages, a walking statue, and a live-skeleton's skull which lands on Gandy's head and scares his co-star cat.

**SON OF DARKNESS: TO DIE FOR II** Trimark (Greg H. Sims)/Arrowhead Ent. & Lee Caplin (Son of Darkness Prods./Richard Weinman) 1991 color 96m. D: David F. Price. SP: Leslie King. Mus: Mark McKenzie. SpMkpFX: MMI; John Buechler; (key) Jeff Farley. VisFX: (sup) Josh Culp; (beam splitter) Cruse & Co. PD: Stuart Blatt. SpFxCoord: Larry Fioritto. OptFX: H'w'd. Opt. Ref: TV. V 5/6/91. Jones. With Rosalind Allen, Steve Bond (Tom), Scott Jacoby, Michael Praed (Max Schreck/Vlad Tepish), Jay Underwood, Amanda Wyss (Cellia), Remy O'Neill (Jane).

"I'm changing the rules—there's no more killing!" The romantic, nice-guy vampire Vlad Tepish is back from *To Die for* ("He's the guy Dracula is based on!") to wine and dine heroine Nina (Allen). Object: a nice-baby vampire. Meanwhile, Cellia, also back, dates up Nina's brother Danny (Underwood), who becomes terribly pale, and Vlad breaks his own rule, as he changes into a wolf and kills. Finally, the sunfried Vlad is gone, but Nina's baby's eyes start glowing.

Fashion-photography horror-fantasy makes glib contrast between the romantic (Vlad) and the cynical (Tom, again) in this superfluous sequel. Extraneous: the gore-makeup stunts. Tacky: a vampire belch (Tom's of course).

***SON OF INGAGI** 1940 (1939) (*House of Horror*—orig t). D, P: R. C. Kahn. SP: S. Williams. Ph: Roland Price, Herman Schopp. Ref: TV. Greg Luce. Weldon. Lee. no Lentz. no Hardy/HM. no V. Cocchi/Second Feature.

"It's so gloomy here!" The "mystery manor" at 1313 Wellman Road (aka "that horrible house") harbors more than a fortune in African gold—in a hidden room lurks Ingeena (Zack Williams), an ape-man monster impervious to bullets.... Rudimentary, barely coherent horror movie, with an all-black cast and not-exactly-well-thought-out dialogue. Only entertainment: the two songs by the Four Toppers.

See also *Ingagi*.

**SONG IN MIDNIGHT, The** see *Midnight Song, The*

**SONG OF NORWAY** Cinerama/ABC 1970 anim sequence color/ws 138m. SP, D: Andrew L. Stone. Anim D: Jack Kinney. Ref: TV. Lee: bio of Grieg. AFI. Dee Willis.

Three-minute fantasy sequence (set to "Peer Gynt") in which animated trolls—river-dwelling, three-headed, monster-mouthed, and giant varieties—are shown haunting the Norwegian countryside.... The progression of the movie: plot ... music and Norway ... plot ... music and Norway.... Two cheers for music and Norway. The surprise appearance by the trolls is pleasing.

**SONNET FOR THE HUNTER, A** see *Witchfire*

**SONNY BOY** Triumph/Trans World Ent. (Ovidio Assonitis) 1990 (1989) color/ws 90m. (98m.) D: Robert Martin Carroll. SP: Graeme Whifler. Addl Dial: Peter Desberg. Mus: Carlo Maria Cordio. FxConsul: Bob Glaser. Mkp: Frank Buffini. Ref: TV. V 11/5/90. Sacto Bee 10/31/90. With David Carradine, Paul L. Smith, Brad Dourif, Conrad Janis, Sydney Lassick, Michael Griffin (Sonny Boy).

"He ate my Rolex!" New Mexico. Huge, horrible Slue (Smith) keeps his adopted son (Griffin)—variously known as Sonny Boy, "the creature," "the monster," and the "secret weapon"—in a well, and feeds him raw chickens in order to keep him "mean, lean, and hungry." Slue uses him as a sort of human killer-dog to dispatch "enemies." ("Now I have tasted the blood of a man.")

An orphan relocation program is perhaps indicated in this perverse variation on *The Wild Child*. The script also borrows from *Frankenstein* (including the angry villagers with the torches) and *It's Alive*. (Janis's doctor, to villagers: "You're the monsters.") The plot has weird beginnings, but tame, flat payoffs.

**SONS OF STEEL** (Austral.) Jet Films (James Michael Vernon) 1988 color 104m. SP, D, Mus D: Gary L. Keady. PD: G. Walker. Ref: V 5/25/88: "visually impressive." 11/4/87:90. With Rob Hartley, Roz Wason, Jeff Duff, Ralph Cotterill.

"Time-travel yarn" set in Oceana, in the near future.

**\*The SORCERERS** WB-TV/Tenser-Curtwel-Global (Tony Tenser Films) 1967. Mkp: Geoff Rodway. Ref: TV. Lee. Lentz. Weldon. Stanley. Hardy/HM. V 6/28/67. Maltin '92. Scheuer. Newman. Fango 128: 12, 17, 69.

"My God, Estelle! We're feeling all his sensations!" The post-hypnotic-suggestion machinery of Dr. Marcus Monserrat (Boris Karloff) allows him, and his wife Estelle (Catherine Lacey), not only to control their subject, Michael (Ian Ogilvy), but vicariously to live his life. ("You're right, Estelle, I did enjoy it!") Estelle, in fact, so likes the sense of danger-once-removed that she wills Michael to murder.

Shoestring *Brainstorm* wastes an intriguing "movie-watching-plus" premise. Tatty production, tacky score, and outlandish plot turns (Michael's exploits, for instance, somehow begin to affect the Monserrats physically as well as emotionally—when he scars, they scar) put this closer to camp than to anything else. And Monserrat is one of Karloff's most ill-conceived roles, a transparently "moral" one intended to balance Lacey's "immoral" Estelle.

**SORCERESS** Triboro/Sunset (Wyn-Tone/Fred Olen Ray) 1994 color c93m. (aka *Temptress*). D: Jim Wynorski. SP: Mark Thomas McGee. Ph: G. Graver. Mus: C. Cirino, D. Way. SpFX: Kevin McCarthy. Title Des: D.L. Hewitt. Mkp Sup: Heidi Grotsky. Ref: TV: Triboro video. PT 20:17. 21:5. vc box. With Julie Strain, Linda Blair, Edward Albert, Rochelle Swanson, William Marshall, Larry Poindexter, Toni Naples.

"You'll never be rid of me!" *Burn Witch Burn!* riffs alternate here with determinedly titillating softcore sex scenes. Featured: witches' "protections" ... voodoo ... visions of a dead woman ("I still see her") ... a cursed medallion ... and a witch (Blair) who puts naughty thoughts into other women's minds. All the actresses seem to be from Silicone Alley.

**SORELLA DI URSULA, La** see *Curse of Ursula*

**SORELLE, Le** see *Psycho Sisters*

**SORORITY BABES IN THE DANCE-A-THON OF DEATH** Tempe color 75m. D: Todd Sheets. Ref: Tempe Video flyer. Bill Warren.

"Four sorority sisters conjure up a demon within an ancient crystal ball."(TV)

**SORORITY BABES IN THE SLIMEBALL BOWL-O-RAMA** Urban Classics/Titan (John Schouweiler) 1988 (1987) color 78m. (The IMP - orig t). D & Co-P: David DeCoteau. SP: Sergei Hasenecz. Mus: Guy Moon. SpMkpFX: Craig Caton. Ref: TV. V 2/10/88. Scheuer. Martin. V 6/17/87:28. With Linnea Quigley, Andras Jones, Robin Rochelle, Buck Flower (aka C. D. LaFleur), Michelle Bauer, Brinke Stevens, John Stuart Wildman.

"This can't be happening!" A "minor imp" ruins a "stupid initiation ceremony" at the Plaza Camino by turning teens into demons "of a sort".... More-or-less-regulation slasher flick features funny, tart Elvira-style put-downs by Quigley's new-wave burglar, by the imp, and by the demons. ("You'll never be a Tri-Delta girl, now, Taffy!")

**SORORITY GIRLS AND THE CREATURE FROM HELL** American Cinema Marketing/McBrearty Ent. 1990 color c90m. Story, SP, D, P: John McBrearty. Story: also Lynette McBrearty. Addl Dial: G. G. Murphy. Ph & Co-Ed: Vincent C. Ellis. Mus: Jim Fox. AD: Scott Weitz. Creature Des: Daniel Fry. SpFX: John Egget. Mkp: Connie J. Barham. OptFX: T.N.T. Ref: TV. TVG. With Len Lesser, Debbie Dutch, Eric Clark, Carl Johnson, Doug Koth, Gloria Hylton, Ashley St. John, Glen Vincent, Wynn Reichert.

"Arise, disciple of blood!" Uncle Ray (Koth)—a "real strange dude"—unearths a huge mask built into rock in a cave on Shadow Mountain. The Indian demon thus unleashed selects him to fetch its blood sacrifices ("Let your blood be mine!") and gives him a special makeup job to boot.... Vacuous teens-in-a-cabin script, rudimentary production, tiresome demonic chortling, and inexcusable padding with a "lunatic on the loose" co-plot.

**SORORITY HOUSE MASSACRE** Concorde (Ron Diamond) 1987 (1986) color 73m. SP, D: Carol Frank. Mus: M. Wetherwax. Ref: V 4/15/87: "nothing new." ad. Martin. Phantom: "rote slice-and-dicer." With Angela O'Neill, Wendy Martel, Pamela Ross, Nicole Rio, John C. Russell, Marcus Vaughter.

"A slash course in absolute terror!" (ad)

**SORORITY HOUSE MASSACRE II** New Classics/Tessa Trust (Winfrey-Stoker) 1992 (1990) color 77m. D: Jim Wynorski. SP: James B. Rogers, Bob Sheridan. Ph: J. E. Bash, Jurgen Baum. Mus: Chuck Cirino. PD: Richard Wright. SpVisFX & SpFxMkp: Dean C. & William S. Jones. Ref: TV. TVG. SFChron Dtbk 8/23/92: New Horizons HV. PT 16:6: sfa *Nightie Nightmare* (1991); "S. Stoker" = Julie Corman. SFChron Dtbk 8/18/91. With Robyn Harris, Melissa Moore, Stacia Zhivago, Michelle Verran, Dana Bentley, J. Baum, Eric "Answer Man" Hoffman, Karen Chorak, Bridget Carney, Mike Elliott (Eddie).

"No girls were actually hurt or mistreated during the production of this film." Does the spirit of Clive Hockstatter—the "guy who killed his whole family" with an electric drill—haunt the "old Hockstatter place?" Is he "in league with the devil?" Yes and yes, apparently. The hook strikes now, as someone's spirit possesses one sorority girl, then another. Meanwhile, weird neighbor Orville Ketchum—"three hundred pounds of bad news"—functions as a red herring.... Formula blend of slasher movie and girlie film. With a bathtub shock from *Diabolique.*

See also: *Tower of Terror* (1991).

**SORORITY HOUSE VAMPIRES** Digital Vision Ent. 1992 color feature. D: Geoffrey de Valois. Ref: Jones. With Natalia Bondurant, Rachel Wolkow, Shay More.

Count Vlad (Robert Bucholz) invades an initiation in a cabin in the woods.

**SORORITY SISTERS** see *Nightmare Sisters*

**SOTTO IL RISTORANTE CINESE** (I) Reteitalia & Bozzetto Int'l. 1987 color 89m. SP, D: Bruno Bozzetto. SP: also Fabio Conara. Mus: Ugo Rossi. Ref: V 5/20/87: "well filmed on the whole"; *Below the Chinese Restaurant*—tr t. With Claudio Botosso, Amanda Sandrelli, Nancy Brilli, Bernard Blier.

Below the Chinese restaurant exists "another world with strange E.T.-like creatures and twin suns ... time travel."

**SOTTO IL VESTITO NIENTE** see *Nothing underneath*

**SOTTO IL VESTITO NIENTE 2** see *Too Beautiful To Die*

**SOUL-HUNGRY DEMON** (J) Toshiba/Enigmania 1990 color 55m. (*Gaki Damashii*). D: M. Sukida. Ref: TV: Toshiba video; made-for-video?; no Eng. Japan Video: above is tr t. VSOM: aka *Tastiest Flesh.*

In the woods, a luminous blob of ectoplasm enters, or resolves into, a caterpillar, which then enters a man's neck. He begins eating for at least two. Eventually, a mostly-teeth little critter emerges from his mouth, starts walking the walls and ceiling, and attacks his wife, who attempts to drown the thing in the bathtub.... Fairly amusing scraps from Cronenberg and the most renown third of *Trilogy of Terror.* Top-drawer sucking-slurping sound effects; middle-drawer puppet and/or animation work.

**SOUL KILLER** (H.K.) Yangtze Prods. 198-? color/ws c88m. D: Daniel Y. C. Lo (sp?). Ref: TV: vt; Eng. titles. With Sheck Fung, Chow I Le, Wan Gi Chung, Pan Roung-Tsong.

A witch doctor's amulet allows the "demon of death"—SiFei, the king of evil of the 18th Century—to possess Lo Szu Hai. The latter finds that he can, while in a trance—his heart stopped—project his soul and confront and kill his gangster enemies: A phone cord strangles one woman; a knife telekinetically stabs a man.

The story has been altered somewhat, but this is clearly a remake of *Psychic Killer* (1975). The clincher: the climactic scene, in which the "soul killer"'s body is cremated, and his screaming spirit appears in the crematory fires. This movie is just as tawdry, basically, as the original, but omits the amazing "opera" sequence.

**SOULTAKER** Action Int'l./Pacific West & Victory Pictures (Connie Kingrey) 1990 color 95m. (*Kiss of Death. Soulicitor*—early titles). D: Michael Rissi. Story, SP: Vivian Schilling. Story, Co-P: Eric Parkinson. Ph: J. A. Rosenthal. Mus: Jon McCallum. AD: Thad Carr. AnimFX: Visions, Inc. Mkp: Bryant, Barker, Kent.

Ref: TV: A.I.P. HV. V 11/5/90. 2/21/90:123. 5/2/90:94. SFChron Dtbk 1/13/91. 5/24/92. With Joe Estevez (The Man aka Soul-taker), Robert Z'Dar (Angel of Death), V. Schilling, Gregg Thomsen, David Shark.

"I take care of souls." In the afterlife (as described here), those who killed in life become *Asphyx*-ish soul collectors. The Man tracks three teens left in limbo after a bad car crash; by accident, or celestial design, one of the three, Natalia (Schilling), reminds him of the one he killed, and at one point, he impersonates her mother.... Superficially sensitive, serious fantasy-horror-romance is somberly fatuous in its treatment of an offbeat premise.

**SOUND** (I) RAI-TV & Filiberto Bandini(R.P.A. Int'l.) 1982 color 94m. SP, D: Biagio Proietti. SP: also Diana Crispo. Ph: Erico Menczer. Mus: The Grop's Power. PD: Luciano Calosso. Mkp: Giancarlo del Brocco. SdFX: Studio Sound. Ref: TV: MBE video; Eng.-language version. VSOM: aka *Close Encounters.* With Peter Fonda, Ana Obregon, Mattia Sbragia, Elena Sofia Ricci, Gianluca Favilla, Daniela Poggi.

"Everyone has disappeared." A "really weird sound" (which "no one else can hear") "bumps" space scientist Roberto (Fonda) from the year 1982 into, variously, 1993, 2003, and 2015: Empty houses are suddenly full of people; Roberto sees future events, etc. The recorded sound proves to have 58 musical notes which, when deciphered, spell out, "Landing Planet Earth".... An intriguing premise awkwardly developed and directed. Vapid score, flat performances.

**SPACE AVENGER** see *Alien Space Avenger*

**SPACE CADET** Intropics Video 1990(1989) color 74m. D: Sharon Mitchell. Ref: vc box: "Zuna from Planet X." Adam '91: "three nude aliens." With Busty Belle, Nikki Knights.

**SPACE CAMP** see *Spacecamp*

**SPACE CASE** see *Alien Invasion*

**SPACE CRUISER YAMATO, THE CONCLUDING CHAPTER** see *Final Yamato*

**SPACE CRUISER YAMATO—THE NEW VOYAGE** see *Yamato—New Voyage*

**SPACE FAMILY CARLBINSON** (J) Tokuma 1988 anim color 45m. From the manga by Yoshitou Asari. Ref: Animag 4:8. 6:5.

"Space comedy" re an "extraterrestrial family."

**3P SPACE IS THE PLACE** Rhapsody Films/North American Star System (Jim Newman) 1974 color 64m. D: John Coney. SP: Joshua Smith. Ph: Hill, Riley. Mus: Sun Ra. Mkp: James Catania. SpFX: JR & Assoc. Ref: TV: RF video. PT 17:16: "high quality." Stanley. no V etc. With Sun Ra, June Tyson, Barbara Deloney, Erika Leder, Johnnie Keyes.

"The music is different here." After leaving Earth and traveling for several years in the "intergalactic regions," Sun Ra—the "dude from outer space"—lands his ray-shooting, music-powered spaceship in Oakland, California. He hopes to found a "colony for Black people" and opens up an Outer Space Employment Agency. At the end, though, he is forced to flee Earth, as the latter explodes.... Awkward, unique, pretentious, unassuming—all of the above.

**SPACE KID** see *Meatballs—Part II*

**SPACE KNIGHT TEKKAMAN BLADE 7** see *Tekkaman*

**\*SPACE MASTER X-7** 1958. Ref: TV. Jim Shapiro. Warren/KWTS! Lee. V 7/23/58. Lentz. Stanley. Thomas. Weldon. Maltin '92.

Satellite Space Master XM-712 returns from its orbit one thousand miles above Earth. Aboard: life samples, including a "reddish rust, or blight"—a "highly destructive fungus" which reproduces itself with microscopic spores. "Each individual ganglion" in this "horrible stuff called Blood Rust ... connects with every other one. In fact, it is one huge and highly developed brain." The spores—which incubate within and devour their host—contaminate one woman, who becomes a "thousand Typhoid Marys rolled up into one."

*Space Master X-7* plays more like *Panic in the Streets* than it does your typical Fifties science-fiction film. But running time builds, and suspense doesn't. Not surprisingly, the special effects go uncredited—effects shots, or what appear to be effects shots, are so murkily shot you can't be sure what they are. A narrator introduces the movie as The Truth.

**SPACE MUTINY** (So. African) Action Int'l./Winters-Holiday 1988 color c94m. (*Mutiny in Space* - orig t). D, P: David Winters. Co-D: Neal Sundstrom. SP: Maria Dante. Mus: Tim James et al. SpOptFX: Jerry Kitz. SpFxCoord: Rick Cresswell. Title Des: Ann Monn. Ref: TV: A.I.P. HV. V 2/22/89. 10/19/88:197(ad). Hound. Scheuer. V 10/28/87:24: 8/87 start. With Reb Brown, John Phillip Law, James Ryan, Cameron Mitchell, Cissy Cameron, Camille Mitchell (voice).

The *Southern Sun*, a "self-sufficient spaceship," is on a ten-light-year journey to a new world when saboteurs strike. ("The energizing turbines have been sabotaged!") Only hero Dave Ryder (Brown) and telepathic Bellerians—who seem to play helpful Fates—prevent mutineers from taking complete control of the ship.... A long time between space battles here. The latter do, though, feature colorful ships, rays, explosions, and vapor trails. The rest is dreadful filler and even more dreadful plot and dialogue.

**SPACE NAVIGATORS** (I) Europa Cine TV (Gian Paolo Brugnoli) 1993 color feature (*Navigators of the Space*—ad t. *Navigator—The Return*—ad t). D: Camillo Teti. Ph: G. Bergamini. SpFX: Francesco & Gaetano Paolocci. Ref: V 5/10/93:C-133(ad), C-127(ad): screening at Cannes. 6/14/93:42: Far East release. 2/22/93:A-115(ad), A-122; at AFM. 10/26/92:37(ad). With Jesse Dann, Jeana Belle, Greg Badgewell, Raymond Richard, Christine Keegan.

Ad depicts robot (with eyeballs), spaceship.

**SPACE 1999** see *Alien Attack*

**SPACE NINJA** see *Swords of the Space Ark*

**SPACE ORGAN, The** see *Erotic Encounters of the Fourth Kind*

**SPACE PATROL** see *Midnight Movie Massacre*

**SPACE RAGE** see *Spacerage*

**SPACE TRAVELER 2020** (S. Korean) 1988 93m. (aka *Comet Mobile in the Milky Way*). D: E. Yongshi, E. Gon Ju. Ref: Oriental Cinema 5.

"Baby from an alien planet."

**SPACE VAMPIRES** see *Lifeforce*

**SPACE VIRGINS** Creative Video 198-? color c75m. D: Phil Marshak. SP: Mark Weiss, William Margold. Ref: vc box: trio of alien women. no Adam '88. With Kimberly Carson, Paul Thomas, Sharon Mitchell, Amber Lynn.

**SPACE VIXEN** Venus 99 Video 1987 color c80m. (*Space Vixens*—ad t). D: Ron Jeremy. Mus: John Further. Mkp: Alan Boushard. Ref: TV: V 99 Video. no Adam '88 or '89. With Blondie Bee, Leah Lyons, Alena Ferrari, Tony Montana, Johnny Lightning, R. Jeremy.

Three alien women, looking for sperm for food for their planet, land on Earth. You know they're aliens because they wear spacesuits and they say they're from another planet. You would not know it just from the suits themselves, which prominently display the Stars and Stripes.

**SPACEBALLS** MGM/Brooksfilms (Ezra Swerdlow) 1987 color 96m. SP, D, P: Mel Brooks. SP: also Thomas Meehan, Ronny Graham. Mus: John Morris. VisFX: (sup) Peter Donen; Apogee; (coord) Craig Boyajian. Alien Monster: IL&M. AnimSup: Clint Colver. Matte FX: Dutton-Taylor, Illusion Arts. Mkp: Ben Nye Jr. VocalFxSup: Norman B. Schwartz. Ref: TV. MFB'87:377. V 6/24/87. Maltin '92. Phantom. Hound. Scheuer. Stanley. Martin. With M. Brooks, John Candy, Rick Moranis (Dark Helmet), Bill Pullman, Daphne Zuniga, Dick Van Patten, Joan Rivers (voice of Dot Matrix), Lorene Yarnell (Dot Matrix), John Hurt, Jack Riley, Rudy DeLuca, Felix Silla et al. (the Dinks), Dom DeLuise (voice of Pizza the Hutt).

"God willing, we'll all meet again in *Spaceballs II: The Search for More Money*." In the meantime, in Part I, in Operation Vacu-Suck, the spaceship Spaceball One transforms into Mega-Maid and proceeds to suck the planet Druidia's air into a vacuum cleaner, which is then to be taken to oxygen-depleted Spaceball City. And, in a local intergalactic diner, an alien creature jumps out of a man and does an impromptu number.

Enjoyable, hit-and-miss parody of *Star Wars* and *Star Trek* movies has nothing to hold it together except punctuating self-merchandising gags and self-referential, movie-in-progress gags. Highlight of the latter: the "Idiots! You've captured their stunt doubles!" scene; highlights of the former: the plugs for Spaceballs—the Toilet Paper, Spaceballs—the Shaving Cream, and Spaceballs—the Placemat.

**SPACECAMP** Fox/ABC (Leonard Goldberg) 1986 color 108m. (aka *Space Camp*). D: Harry Winer. SP: W. W. Wicket, Casey T. Mitchell. Story: Patrick Bailey, Larry B. Williams. Mus: John

Williams. SpVisFX: (sup) Barry Nolan; Van Der Veer; (coord) C. L. Finance. Anim Sup: Jeff Burks. SpFxCoord: Chuck Gaspar. Flying Wire Consul: Bob Harman. SpSdFX: Ed Bannon, Bruce Glover. SpVocalFX: Frank Welker. Mkp: Zoltan & Katalin Elek. Ref: TV. MFB'87:185-6. V 6/4/86. ad. SFExam 6/6/86. Maltin '92. Stanley. Martin. Morse. Hound. Scheuer. With Kate Capshaw, Lea Thompson, Kelly Preston, Larry B. Scott, Leaf Phoenix, Tom Skerritt, Barry Primus, Terry O'Quinn, Scott Holcomb, Tate Donovan.

Jinx the robot—a "$27-million handyman"—hooks up with NASA's computer, creates a "thermal curtain failure," and forces NASA to launch five SpaceCamp kids and their chaperone into space. Destination: a space station where extra oxygen is stored.... All narrative ingenuity here is expended getting the kids into space. Formula comic-dramatic suspense situations follow. Okay space photography (by William A. Fraker) and effects and wonders-of-space music.

**SPACED INVADERS** BV/Touchstone & Silver Screen Partners IV/Smart Egg (Luigi Cingolani) 1990 color 100m. (*Martians!!!*-orig t). SP, D: Patrick Read Johnson. SP: also S. L. Alexander. MkpFX: Criswell & Johnson FX. Mus: David Russo. Ref: V 5/9/90. Sacto Bee 4/27/90. TV. With Douglas Barr, Royal Dano, Ariana Richards, J. J. Anderson, Kevin Thompson (Blaznee).

Watermelon-headed aliens take their cue from the Wells/Welles radio show "War of the Worlds," land on Earth, vainly try to get off it.... Too cute, jokey, though the ultra-casual approach yields funny moments.

**SPACERAGE: BREAKOUT ON PRISON PLANET** Vestron/Morton Reed 1985 color 78m. (aka *Space Rage. A Dollar a Day. Trackers: 2180. Trackers. The Last Frontier*—early ts). D: C. E. Palmisano; (reshoots) Peter McCarthy. SP: Jim Lenahan. Story: M. Reed. Mus: Ferrick, Schloss. SpFX: Roger George, Frank DeMarco. Mkp: Logan. Opt: Mercer, Movie Magic. Ref: TV. V 7/1/87. Maltin '92. Phantom. Morse. Scheuer. Martin. Ecran F 56:71. With Richard Farnsworth, Michael Pare, John Laughlin, Lee Purcell, William Windom, Hank Worden.

"Nobody gets off of this planet!" Penal Colony number 5, New Botany Bay, Proxima Centauri 3. Walker (Laughlin), bounty hunter supreme, makes a living tracking down "scapers," including, principally, ruthless killer Grange (Pare). Story is a pretext for numerous action and stunt scenes, in an otherwise pointless movie.

**SPACESHIP TO VENUS** see *First Spaceship on Venus*

**SPARKLING PHANTOM** see *Ryokunohara Labyrinth*

**SPEAK OF THE DEVIL** Action Int'l. HV/Dalia Unique Media (Veloso) 1991 color 99m. SP, D, P: Raphael Nussbaum. SP: also Bob Craft. Story: W. K. Berns. Ideas: Scott Spiegel et al. SpMkpFX: James Cummins. Ref: V 8/19/91: "hokey mishmash." With Robert Elarton, Jean Miller, Bernice Tamara Goor, Walter Kay, David Miller (devil), Buck Flower.

Haunted house, satanism, Jewish exorcist.

**SPEAR (OF DESTINY), The** see *Future Hunters*

**SPECIAL EFFECTS** Hemdale/Larjan (Paul Kurta/Cinema '84) 1985 (1984) color 103m. SP, D: Larry Cohen. Mkp: Richard Greene. Ref: TV: Embassy Home Ent. video. V 4/10/85.

"I'm taking reality—making it look like make-believe—that's a special effect, too." Offbeat but basically unbuyable murder story has snuff-movie angles and suggestions of *Vertigo*. A "washed-up filmmaker," Christopher Neville (Eric Bogosian), films his strangulation of an aspiring actress (Zoe Tamerlis), then gets her husband (and murder suspect) Keefe (Brad Rijn) to recreate the events leading up to the killing, for his camera. Some fun "in" stuff, like the line "Who made your head, Carlo Rambaldi?"

**SPECIAL SILENCERS** (Indonesian) P.T. Parkit Films (Punjabi) 198-? color feature. D: Arizal. SP: Deddy Armand. Story: Djair. Ph: Harry Susanto. Mus: Gatot Sudarto. AD SpFX: INDRA. Ref: TV: VSOM; Eng. dubbed. With Barry Prima, Eva Arnaz, W.D. Mochtar, Dicky Zulkarnain.

Dissolved in coffee, certain special, supernatural tablets make deadly plants grow instantly from the drinker's stomach. Here, the evil magician "can only be wounded by bamboo".... Crude, slack, and repetitive, but the They Germinated from Within, or Gardens of Yuchh, scenes are fun. In one unlikely sequence, the villain hides in a tree and tosses big snakes on his victim.

**\*The SPECKLED BAND** B&D 1931. Ref: TV: Classic Int'l.-TV. Lentz. Lee(e). TVFFSB. V 3/25/31. 11/10/31. Gifford/BC. Maltin '92. Hound. Martin. Scheuer. no Stanley.

The nifty opening: a track up to a closed door; then: a woman's scream. Ingredients: a "rather gloomy" house (or "weird place") ... a fanatical native servant given to somber flute playing ... very tall sets, as if constructed for a vertical CinemaScope ... and a flashback in which a woman describes a night of horror in a dark, cavernous bedroom.

The microphone-bound dialogue scenes are static, but lighting, sets, and compositions are atmospheric and set the psychological-horror tone of the night scenes. Raymond Massey and Athole Stewart (as Sherlock Holmes and Dr. Watson, respectively) are okay, but this is not an actors' movie.

**SPECTERS** (I) Reteitalia & Trio Cinema & TV 1987 color 90m. (*Spettri*). Story, SP, D: Marcello Avallone. Story, SP, P: Maurizio Tedesco. Story, SP: Andrea Purgatori. SP: also Dardano Sacchetti. Ph: S. Ippoliti. Mus: L. Marchitelli, D. Rea. AD: C. Agate. SpFX: S. Stivaletti. Ref: V 5/27/87: "disappointing." Martin. Morse. Hound. With John Pepper, Katrine Michelsen, Donald Pleasence, Massimo de Rossi, Erna Schurer.

Work on Roman subways unleashes monster.

**SPECTRES A VENISE** see *Shocking Dark*

**SPEED** see *Wizard of Speed and Time, The*

**SPELLBINDER** MGM-UA/MGM-Indian Neck Ent. (Wizan Film/Brian Russell) 1988 color 99m. (*Witching Hour*—orig t). D: Janet Greek. SP: Tracey Torme. Mus: Basil Poledouris. MkpFxDes: Rick Stratton. SpFX: Burt Dalton et al. SpSdFX: Eric Lindemann. Ref: TV. Fango 2/90. V 9/29/88. San Jose MNews 9/24/88. SFExam 9/23/88. Maltin '92. Hound. Martin.

Scheuer. V 1/27/88:6. With Timothy Daly, Kelly Preston, Rick Rossovich, Audra Lindley, Anthony Crivello.

"No one ever leaves us!" Los Angeles. A coven of satanists needs a human sacrifice on the night of the Winter Solstice. Will the victim be that adept at supernatural massage, spellbinder Miranda Reed (Preston), or hero Jeff Mills (Daly), who attempts to rescue her from her fellow satanists? Of more immediate interest than this breathless question, however, is the script's surprisingly blatant steal from *Unearthly Stranger* (1963): Miranda's bare-hands handling of the oven-hot casserole. Here, the stunt tips off her supernaturalness; there, it tipped off the heroine's alienness. The satanists' super-breath and levitation stunts seem, further, inspired by Terence Stamp and company in *Superman II.* The movie's one apparently original inspiration—the starers-through-the-window scene—seems pretty dumb. In a quite expected twist, the hero's buddy turns out to be a satanist.

**\*SPELLBOUND** PRC (R. Murray-Leslie) 1940. Ph: Walter Harvey; Guy Green. Mus: George Walter. Settings: C.W. Arnold. Ref: TV: vt; 80m. *Passing Clouds* (British reissue) version. Lee. Lentz. no Hardy/HM. BFC. With Marian Spencer (Mrs. Stapleton), Diana King (Amy Nugent), Irene Handl.

"The dead return." First seance: Vincent (Frederick Leister), a spiritualist—"this medium man"—watches as hero Laurie Baxter (Derek Farr), in a trance, temporarily vacates his body, and the latter's dead girl friend Amy speaks through him. Second seance: Amy speaks through Vincent. ("It's me, Amy. Don't be unhappy. Because I'm not.") Third seance: "Complete materialization" achieved. But Laurie touches Amy's spirit and becomes "controlled and possessed by a spirit that is not his—a thing that has taken the form of Amy Nugent. Something that is evil, wholly evil."

The origin of this evil spirit is not explained, and the movie is not *Dead of Night,* but this is still an interesting, step-by-step investigation into the supernatural. Hay Petrie gives the most entertaining performance, in the Van Helsing role of Cathcart, who at first seems to be a debunker, but proves to be a true believer. ("By all that's holy and unholy, this has got to be stopped!")

**SPELLCASTER** (U.S.-I) Empire/Taryn (Debra Dion/Roberto Besii) 1991 (1988) color 83m. D: Rafal Zielinski. SP: Dennis Paoli. Story: Ed Naha. Ph: Sergio Salvati. Mus: Nathan Wang. PD: Giovanni Natalucci. Sp Creature & MkpFX: MMI; John Buechler. Mkp: Giancarlo del Brocco. Ref: TV. TVG. SFChron Dtbk 3/29/92:62. Martin. PT 13:48-9. With Adam Ant (Diablo), Richard Blade, Bunty Bailey, Gail O'Grady, Harold Pruett, Kim Ulrich, Michael Zorek, Traci Lin(n).

"Something very strange is going on here!" The "lucky seven" winners of Rock-TV's contest spend a "million dollar weekend" hunting for treasure in a real medieval castle in Italy, where their host Diablo "controls" his guests with finger taps on his crystal ball. Ultimately, when the devil's crystal is smashed, all souls in limbo are released.

Push-button script is little more than a display case for MMI creations, including (best of all) a vampire chair, living skeleton-corpses, a "pig" who becomes a pig-person, a satyr-monster which traps its victim in a painting, an electric-ectoplasmic snake,

a bat-*Alien* thing which animates a suit of armor, and some kind of dog/wolf creature.

**SPETTRI** see *Specters*

**\*The SPIDER** William Sistrom 1931 65m. (59m.). Ph: James Wong Howe. Mus sc: Carli Elinor. AD: Gordon Wiles. Ref: TV. V 9/8/31. Lee. Jim Shapiro. With Howard Phillips, John Arledge, Manya Roberti, Ruth Donnelly, Ward Bond.

"Now the psychic forces begin to play." Ingredients include murder during a performance of magician Chatrand the Great (Edmund Lowe) at the Tivoli Theater ... the "ghost" of the murdered man ... and a prop skeleton.... Mind-reading and suspense, and *Charlie Chan at Treasure Island* (1939) does it better. Noteworthy: some very effective (stage) wraiths for the (first) big finale. ("Presently, you shall stand face to face with the dead.") Most of the movie is just marking time (including much weak comic relief) until the twin climaxes, though the lighting of the magic acts is atmospheric. Love the way the film's title "writes" itself in longhand. The 1945 remake is a slickly photographed, but vapid, completely revamped, non-horrific mystery.

**The SPIDER LABYRINTH** (I) MV/Reteitalia & Splendida Film(Tonino Cervi) 1988 color/ws 87m. (*Il Nido del Ragno*). D: Gianfranco Giagni. SP: Riccardo Aragno, T. Cervi, Cesare Frugoni, Gianfranco Manfredi. Ph: Nino Celeste. Mus: Franco Piersanti. AD: Stefano Ortolani. SpFX: Sergio Stivaletti. Mkp: Renato Francola. SpSdFX: Roberto Arcangeli, Studio Sound. Ref: TV: MV; Eng. dubbed. V 10/19/88:345(ad). Hardy/HM2. Palmerini. With Roland Wybenga, Paola Rinaldi, William Berger, Margareta Von Krauss, Claudia Muzii, Stephane Audran.

Budapest. A notebook note re a "great cobweb" ... a mysterious boy and ball ... a professor found hanging from a rope—and a web ... inscriptions on an ancient tablet ... a strange room of hanging sheets ... a labyrinth of a small town ... a sect whose gods are said to be "living creatures" ... "spider" scars on the locals' wrists ... and a huge cavern of webs, pools, bodies, and bones.... The script is a bit lean and old-fashioned, but this is moderately intriguing mystery-horror-fantasy fun. And the "payoffs" are pretty impressive: the ball which hatches the (stopmo) spider ... the spider woman's drool which becomes a deadly web ... the horror baby which becomes a (stopmo) horror spider out of *Hiruko the Goblin* ... and the spider which enters the cut in the hero's arm.

**SPIDER-MAN** see *Amazing Spider-Man*

**SPIDER WOMAN NEXT DOOR** (H.K.) Regal Videogramme Co./Ko Chi Sum Films 1992? color c85m. Ref: TV: Tai Seng Video (Pan-Asian Video); no Eng.

The new governess terrorizing the family is all of the following: a) an unbalanced young woman given to stabbing her own leg, b) the "phantom" at the shuttered window, and, c) a "closet" slasher who keeps photos of prospective victims on her wall. Height of invention in this cheap, tawdry shot-on-taper: the weird, off-key version of "Twinkle, Twinkle, Little Star" on the soundtrack at one point. A vacuously macabre thriller.

**\*The SPIDER WOMAN STRIKES BACK** 1946. Mkp: Jack Pierce. Ref: TV. V 3/20/46. Lentz. Stanley. Hardy/HM. Maltin '92. Scheur. Jones.

Domingo, Nevada. "Can't understand why she has so much trouble keeping a companion." The mad Zenobia (Gale Sondergaard) needs blood to feed her "lovely Drachamina" (sp?)—cf. "Dracula"—a Central American plant, and when she takes a little too much blood, her companions/donors die. Aiding her: the "very loyal," disfigured Mario (Rondo Hatton), who was "born on the place."

Zenobia's greenhouse-lab work is fiendish enough, and Sondergaard tries to work up a mad-doctor-like glee. (When she says, "You beautiful creature!", she's talking to her plant.) But there's no story, simply an extended lone-woman-in-peril situation and miscellaneous padding with miscellaneous skulkers and "ominous" moments, until Revelation Time, and the movie is not exactly riveting even then. Best bad line here is still: "But it won't be really dying because you'll live on in this beautiful plant."

**SPIDERS WITH HUMAN HEADS** see *Hiruko the Goblin*

**SPINE** Xeon Ltd. 1986 color c75m. SP, D, P: Justin Simonds, John Howard. Ph: L. B. Magic Co. Mus: Don Chilcott. MkpFX: Lori Laverde. Ref: TV: Sterling Silver video. no Phantom. no Martin. no Stanley. no Hound. With R. Eric Huxley, Janus Blythe, Antoine Herzog, Lise Romanoff, Abby Sved, Marie Dowling.

L.A. Serial killer Lawrence Ashton (Huxley) ties up his nurse victims, then slashes them apart with a knife. ("This is your spine, Linda.") Seems someone named Linda once came between his mother and himself and poked his eye out with a pair of scissors.

Pitifully frail, cheap slasher movie. Oddly, the main slash-and-stab sequence turns out to be a visualized nightmare, and a follow-up sequence hints that this was a premonition, though nothing much is made of these developments. Shot on tape.

**SPIRAL** (J) 1991 feature (*Ankou*). D: M. Itou. Ref: Weisser/JC: "the blood-n-gore is horrific." With T. Ishidate, K. Ooba.

"Sickie who enjoys butchering women...."

**SPIRIT LOVE** (Taiwanese) Lu Chih-tzu & Li Shu-ping c1990? color/ws c80m. SP, D: Shan-hsi. Ref: TV: Pan-Asia Video; Eng. titles. Y.K. Ho. With Yong Ching-huang, Wang Tsu-hsien.

The ghost of the murdered Ah-ching, or "Ginny"—a singer and supposed suicide on the day of the opening of her Ginny Hotel—returns, first, in miniature, singing in the refrigerator of her personal assistant. A "monster," she intermittently possesses her twin sister Ah-fen, as she seeks to expose her killer.

Fantasy with chiller scenes, including one in which cans of Spring Nectar—a new drink promoted by Ginny—are opened and revealed to contain her blood ... a scene in which a ghost appears in a mirror ... and one in which Ginny's ghost sings eerily at night in a garden. Glossy, superficial variation on *Rouge*.

**The SPIRIT OF '76** Col/Black Diamond (Commercial Pictures/Landau-Edery/Fred Fuchs) 1990 color 82m. Story, SP, D: Lucas Reiner. Story, Exec Co-P: Roman Coppola. Ph: S. Lighthill. Mus: D. Nichtern. PD: D. Talpers. Ref: V 11/4/90: "not without laughs." Sacto Bee 11/15/91: "an extremely likable movie, poorly done and lame." With David Cassidy, Olivia D'Abo, Geoff Hoyle, Carl Reiner, Leif Garrett, Rob Reiner.

Scientist from the year 2176 takes time machine back to 1976.

**SPIRIT OF THE RAPED** (H.K.) 1976 color feature (*Suo Ming*). D: Gui Zhihong. Ref: Monster! 11/91 (Higuchi): "supernatural elements ... ferocious."

**SPIRIT VS ZOMBI** (Taiwanese-H.K.) 1989 color c98m. D: Yao Fenpan. Ref: TV: World Video; Eng. titles. NST! 4:36. Jones.

Disturbed in their 100-year-old coffins in the subway, hopping vampire boy Ah Chi and his blue-fingernailed father ("Vampire is a weird combination") take to the city streets and become separated. At one point, the father bites an actor playing a vampire in a movie in production and takes his place on the set. Plus: laser guns.

Some charm and humor, in-between more formulaic action and sentiment. Finally, his father dead, the son exits sadly into the night mist. Best title: "Who is that vampire with you last night?"

**SPIRITS** American-Independent/Cinema Group (Lankford) 1990 color 94m. (88m.). D: Fred Olen Ray. SP: J. Falls, R. U. King. Ph: Gary Graver. Mus: Tim Landers. AD: Ted Tunney. SpMkpFX: Optic Nerve; Burrell, Vulich. SpFxAnim: Bret Mixon. Ref: TV: Vidmark video. Martin. PT 13:50. V 10/28/91:16(rated). 5/6/91:78. With Erik Estrada, Robert Quarry, Brinke Stevens, Carol Lynley, Kathrin Lautner, Michelle Bauer, Oliver Darrow, Thomas Bently (Henri Picard), Earl Ellis (Picard demon), Sandra Margot (nun demon).

"The house made her do it." Ingredients here include the haunted Heron House, built in 1901 by a "sick and evil man" ... the demon-ghost of Henri Picard, a "fallen priest" who possesses and speaks through the living and who, at the end, turns really monstrous, visually ("I am the evil within you") ... a psychic, Amy (Stevens) ... a man (Quarry) who wants "proof of life after death" ... a succubus ... disembodied cackling ... hallucinations re possessed nuns ... and a climactic absolution/exorcism.... *The Haunting* meets *The Exorcist*, to little effect. The possessions get pretty monotonous. The worst of it, though: the near-camp priest-and-nun scenes with Estrada and Lynley.

**SPIRITS OF DEATH** (I) VSOM 1972 feature (*Un Bianco Vestito per Mariale*). D: Romano Scavolini. SP: Giuseppe Mangione, Remiglio Del Grosso. Mus: F. Carpi. Ref: ETC/Giallos: "bizarre thriller." Palmerini. With Evelyn Stewart, Luigi Pistilli, Ivan Rassimov, Pilar Velasquez.

Graphic murders and guests in "weird costumes" in an old mansion.

**SPIRITS OF FIRE** see *Wings of Oneamis*

**SPIRITUAL LOVE** (H.K.) Golden Harvest/Johnny Mak 1987 color c90m. D: David Lai, Taylor Wong. Ref: TV: Rainbow Video. NST! 4:37.

This looks like an interesting variation on the ghost/human-love theme of *My Cousin, the Ghost*, but, frustratingly, lacks English titles. It features some energetic, comic-horrific ghosts-vs.-exorcists sequences and at least three ghosts, one malevolent. At the end, the female ghost-heroine is separated from her human lover and sucked into some TV land beyond. Funny bit: the sweet ghost stretching out her very elastic ears in order to scare off a cop.

**SPIRITUAL LOVE** (H.K.) Lucky Star Film & Film Line Ents. 1992? color/ws 77m. Ref: TV: Tai Seng Video; Eng. titles. With Ju Bao Yih, Guh Guan Jong, Guu Feng, Roan Pey Jong.

No connection to the '87 film of the same name. In the first scene, an electric vampire woman eats a victim's innards; next scene features softcore sex and lip-licking vampirism. ("Good-hearted men are delicious.") Later, lighter scenes feature three hopping vampire kids and their leader. Scrappy, something-for-everyone horror-comedy-fantasy-romance re three sister vampires has occasional funnies, including the sequence in which one scared vampire kid says to the boss vampire (re one of the sisters) "Ghost!", and the big guy chides him, "Jerk! You are ghost!"

**SPLATTER** see *Future-Kill*

**SPLATTER FARM** Donna Michel(l)e (J.K. Farlew) 1987 feature. D: P. Alan. Ref: PT 20:67: "goes way out of line." With John and Mark Polonia, Marion Costly, Todd Rimatti (Jeremy).

"Handyman Jeremy ... chops up people...."

**SPLATTER UNIVERSITY** Troma/Aquifilm 1984 color 77m. SP, D, P: Richard W. Haines. SP, P: John Michaels. SpMkpFX: Amodio Giordano. SP: also M. Cunningham. Ref: V 7/18/84: "negligible stalk and slash terror picture" set at St. Trinians College. Phantom. HR 7/27/84. Martin. With Francine Forbes, Dick Biel, Cathy Lacommare.

**SPLIT** Starker Film (Barbara Horscraft) 1989 color 85m. SP, D, Ph, Ed, Mus: Chris Shaw. Mus, Computer FX: Robert Shaw. Mus: also Ugi Tojo. Addl Dial: Joan Bechtel. Computer City: Peter Broadwell. Mkp: Timothy Dwight et al. Ref: TV: AIP HV. Stanley. V 3/22/89: "merely a provocative rough draft for a futuristic chase-thriller." PT 14:46: "xlnt fx." With C. Shaw, Tim Dwight, Joan Bechtel, John Flynn.

"Evil genius whose face peels off in layers."(V) The "next step in human evolution" apparently involves mind-impulse transfer ("record/erase/transfer"), virtual reality sleight-of-chip, and Robo-hand ("This is ugly"). Confusing, straining-for-the-eccentric New Wavish sf has the occasional pleasures of the offbeat—e.g., the storyboard telling the story of this-film-in-progress.

**SPLIT OF THE SPIRIT** (H.K.) 1987? color feature. D: Fred Tan. Ref: Weisser/ATC. vc box. With Pauline Wong.

"Choreographer possessed by the avenging spirit of a dead girl."

**SPLIT SECOND** (B) InterStar/Muse Prods. & Chris Hanley/Challenge (XYZ Funding/Laura Gregory/Keith Cavele) 1992 color 91m. D: Tony Maylam; Ian Sharp. SP: Gary Scott Thompson. Mus: Stephen Parsons, Francis Haines. Creature FX: Stephen Norrington; (mkp fx) Cliff Wallace. SpFX: (sup) Alan Whibley; Ace FX. Prosth Mkp Des: Daniel Parker. Mech Des: Joe Scott. Ref: TV. V 4/27/92. ad. SFChron 5/2/92; Dtbk 3/7/93. With Rutger Hauer, Kim Cattrall, Neil Duncan, Michael J. Pollard, Alun Armstrong; Stewart Harvey-Wilson & Paul Grayson (the killer).

"You telling me there's something running around loose in this city ripping the hearts out of people and eating them so he can take their souls back to hell?" London, the year 2008. Thanks to global warming, "day has become almost endless night." The serial killer who rips out his victims' hearts and who has "incredible strength" and the teeth of a "beast" proves to be more than a "psychotic with a psychopathic personality": A "single organism made up of multiple DNA structures," he looks like an *Alien,* but is in reality, apparently, the "most powerful supernatural being, satan," or a close relative. ("I'm back.")

Hauer and Duncan are determinedly comically mismatched cop partners—Stone and Durkin, respectively—in this confusing blend of *48 Hrs., Blade Runner, Alien,* and *The Exorcist.* Stone is the chronically suspended cop who has "worked in every hellhole in the world"; Durkin is the basically proper cop. ("I've gotten honors in serial homicide.") Hauer and company are so keyed-up, so "tough," they're funny, though most of the rest of the movie is routine. Best credit: "Rat Cosmetics."

**SPONTANEOUS COMBUSTION** Taurus Ent./Hooper-Bushkin (Jim Rogers) 1990 color 97m. SP, D: Tobe Hooper. SP: also Howard Goldberg. Story: Hooper. Mus: Graeme Revell. SpMkpFX: Steve Neill. PD: Gene Abel. SpVisFX: Apogee; Stephen Brooks. SpMechFX: Tony Hooper. Pyro FX: Guy Faria. Ref: TV. V 5/23/90:71(hv). With Brad Dourif, Cynthia Bain, Jon Cypher, William Prince, Dey Young, Melinda Dillon, Dick Butkus, John Landis, Richard Warlock, George "Buck" Flower.

Modern Atomic Technologies' Project Samson turns David Bell (Dourif) into the "cleanest killing system on Earth ... America's atomic man." A product of the anti-radiation vaccines—and radiation—which destroyed his parents (Stacy Edwards and Brian Bremer) at an H-bomb test site in 1955, David becomes a human combustion machine who can incinerate people and send fire through the telephone.

Overwrought sf-horror fails compellingly to answer the question, Why re-do *Firestarter,* except perhaps as comedy? Now and then, David's incendiary emotions break up scenes near-campily, but intentional humor is limited to scattered ironic lines like (this asked of David) "Do you smoke?" Film—which gives new meaning to the phrase "slow burn"—features a few effective lyrical/macabre touches.

**The SPOOK SPEAKS** Col 1940 20m. D: Jules White. SP: Ewart Adamson, Clyde Bruckman. Ref: LC. no Lee. Okuda/CCS. Maltin/SSS. With Buster Keaton, Elsie Ames, Don Beddoe, Bruce Bennett.

Magician's mansion "rigged with secret gadgets." (Okuda)

**SPOOK TO ME** Col 1945 22m. (*Be Prepared* - orig t). SP, D: Harry Edwards. Story: Edward Bernds. Ref: Maltin/SSS. Okuda/CCS. Lee. LC. With Andy Clyde, Frank Hagney, Dudley Dickerson, Vie Barlow, Dick Botiller.

Haunted house.

**SPOOKIES** Safir Films/Twisted Souls (Miggles) 1986 (1985) color 84m. (*Twisted Souls*—orig t). SP, D, P: Thomas Doran, Brendan Faulkner. D, P: also Eugenie Joseph. SP, P: also Frank M. Farel. Addl Matl.: Joseph Burgund. Mus: Kenneth Higgins,

James Calabrese. SpMkpFX: Arnold Gargiulo II, Vincent Guastini. SpCreatureDes: John Dods. Anim: Paul Killian. Opt Des: Cynosure. Ref: TV. V 5/21/86. With Felix Ward (Kreon), Dan Scott (monster aide), Maria Pechukas (Isabelle), Lisa Friede (Carol), Soo Paek (spider woman), James M. Glenn (the Grim Reaper), Robert Epstein (zombie).

"We only want your souls!" The sorcerer Kreon unleashes his monsters in order to obtain the sacrifices needed to revive his beloved Isabelle. ("I will make you mine forever!") One victim becomes a Gill Man-like creature with electric tentacles. Other monsters include Kreon's children, a spider woman (complete with web), "muck men," a compact nasty reptilian thing, a cackling hag creature, and zombies-from-out-of-the-ground.

Apparently, *Spookies* was meant to be an *Evil Dead* stew of monsters and mayhem, and it does have the verve, if not the wit of those landmark monster fests. It also has lotsa monsters, and fun slobbering, creaking, slurping, and snarling sound effects to go with them. Although the spider woman is hardly IL&M-level, watching her unfurl to full spider status is amusing. And one lady's impromptu attempts to dispatch the reptile beast, with crockery and bookcase, are pretty funny. The people here, though, (at least in their original form) are a drag. Lotsa "Where are the others?"

*SPOOKS RUN WILD 1941 65m. (*Trail of the Vampire* - orig t). Mus D: Lange & Porter. Sets: Fred Preble. Ref: TV. Lennig. Weaver/Poverty: G. Pembroke not in this film; rated next-to-last of Lugosi's nine Monogram Forties films. Lee. TVG: El Monstruo de Hillside—U.S. Spanish-language-TV title. V 11/5/41. Lentz. Maltin '92. Hound. Martin. Scheuer. Stanley. With Sammy Morrison, Dennis Moore, Dorothy Short, Donald Haines, Rosemary Portia.

Bela Lugosi is the almost-a-vampire Nardo, the "ghoul-guy that sucks the blood out of you," sleeps in a coffin by day, and scares East Side Kids. He's the "horror man ... the monster killer" ("at night, The Monster is strong") who—along with a skull-headed "spectre" and a ghostly knight-in-armor—haunts the "very strange" Billings estate atop Billings Mountain.

Director Phil Rosen's customary sloppiness reigns here, but he does give Lugosi a few good horror close-ups, and the scriptwriters give him one "Dracula" line (re Hillside cemetery): "The city of the dead—do they too hear the howling of the frightened dogs?" Unfortunately, they give him a lot of silly "Good night!"s, too. He's not really a vampire here, but he and sidekick Angelo Rossitto vanish supernaturally at one point.

SPOOKY FAMILY (H.K.) Samico Films 1989 color c95m. D: Law Lit. Ref: TV: World Video; Eng. titles. Jones. Y. K. Ho: *Family Ghost Buster*—tr t.

Ingredients: the blue-faced "copper vampire of west China" ("This is a super vampire") ... the wizard's blood which makes the copper vampire "very very horrible" ... the "Human and Corpse Linking Machine," which backfires and allows the "sleeping vampire'"s mind to control wizard Chu Kor, rather than vice versa ... a "ghost servant" which inhabits the sleeping vampire and fights the copper vampire ... a goofy Naughty Ghost ... and the silly Top Wizard, who does all the same idiotic stunts the possessed Chu Kor does even though he doesn't have to.

Dumb, funny horror-comedy sometimes substitutes frenetic action for humor, but does have the prime line, "Have you cleaned the vampires?", not to mention the sequence in which the wizard's smiling "happy family" physically repels the copper vampire. (This display of happiness acts like the invisible protective shield in the old commercials.) Chu Kor's "sister colleague" can appear "wherever there's water."

SPOOKY FAMILY 2 (H.K.) 1991 color feature. D: Law Lit. Ref: Jones. With Lam Ching Ying.

SPOOKY KAMA SUTRA (Taiwanese) 1987 color c80m. (aka *Beautiful Dead Body*). D: Xin Ren. Ref: TV: vt. Suiki. EVS. Weisser/ATC. With Sun Chi Sun, Tiajia Han.

An evil wizard's voodoo makes a woman tear off her clothes. Later, he shuts naked women in coffins with three pasty-faced, hopping vampires, who then revive and serve him. During the climactic duel, a good wizard's aide urinates on one vampire. This stops him; parchments slapped on the foreheads of the other two stop them.... Weird, haphazard mixture of comic vampire fights and mild hardcore.

SPOOKY KOOKIES (H.K.) Cinema City 1987 color c88m. Ref: TV: Rainbow Video; Eng. titles.

A cross between *Paper Moon* and *The Exorcist* in which nine-year-old Loo Bo pretends to be a ghost, and thief and con artist Wild Cat plays an "expert ghost catcher," or "western exorcist." For a price, the latter sprays fireworks about Master Sze's "haunted" house and sends the boy's "ghost" to heaven. Two more phony ghosts get into the act before all these "ghosts" run up against a real spirit, in a "famous haunted house" which suddenly appears in a field. This ghost can fly and animate mechanical objects, and her tongue, arms, and eyeballs stretch incredibly. (The humans cut off her tongue, which continues to run about.)

Silly but fairly cleverly plotted spook comedy. Loo Bo makes a funny scampering "ghost," and the real-ghost effects are entertaining. The adult actors here contort their faces and talk fast and "comically," but the boy who plays Loo Bo is relatively subtle and straight.

SPOOKY, SPOOKY (H.K.) Paragon Films/Golden Harvest (Bojon Films) 1988 color/ws c95m. (*Spooky, Spooky, Spooky*—ad t). D: Lo Wei Don. Ref: TV: Rainbow Video; Eng. titles. NST! 4:37.

"Don't try to kill me, or I'll haunt you all." Everything-but-the-kitchen-sink horror elements include the "nixes" that haunt Ghost Bay, including a female ghost with retractable, Freddy fingernails and a detachable head (vermilion bullets make her melt) ... a possessed, swivel-headed cop ... ghostbuster Queency .. a crawling severed hand ... a clutching undead hand from swamp muck ... and a daydream re a (visualized) "sea monster."

Routine horror-comedy with scattered amusing moments and okay effects, including the *Horror of Dracula* meltaway sequence with the evil female ghost. Most interesting line: "Life in Hades is monotonous." (No sex.)

SPOORLOOS see *Vanishing, The* (1988)

**SPRINGTIME IN THE ROCKIES** Cinderella Distributors/CNJ Prods. 1984 color 74m. D: Jim Reynolds. SP: P. D. Connors. Ph: Tom Morton. Mus: Shelton John; (lyr) Joyce Lucas. Mkp: J. Kufahl. Ref: TV: Diamond HV. no Adam '88. With Lisa de Leeuw, Blake Palmer, Pamela Jennings, Brock Richards (the alien), Debbie Green.

Tawdry adult film's one-minute epilogue takes place "5,000 years from now," when an alien with a phallus in his mouth pays a visit to Earth.

**Na SREBRNYM GLOBIE** (Polish) Zespoly Filmowe, KADR Unit 1988 (1977) color 166m. SP, D: Andrzej Zulawski, from Jerzy Zulawski's novel *Moon Trilogy.* Mus: Andrzej Korzynski. Ref: V 5/18/88: *The Silver Globe* - tr t; "a highly original work of science fiction." 6/27/90:40. With Andrzej Seweryn, Grazyna Dylag, Jerzy Trela.

Earthlings and "bird-monsters called Cherns" on the dark side of the moon.

**STAB IN THE DARK** see *Slumber Party Massacre 3*

**STAGE FRIGHT** (Austral.) Bioscope 1983 color 82m. (aka *Nightmares* [2]). D, P: John Lamond. SP, P: Colin Eggleston. Ref: TVG. Morse. McCarty II: "delusions of plot." With Jenny Neumann, Gary Sweet, Sue Jones, R. Zuanetti.

Schizo stage actress slashes other cast members of play "A Comedy of Death."

**STAGE FRIGHT** see *Shadow Dancing. Stagefright—Aquarius*

**STAGEFRIGHT—AQUARIUS** (I) Filmirage 1987 color 95m. (*Deliria*—orig t. *Aquarius*—working t. *Stage Fright*—ad t). D: Michele Soavi. SP: George Eastman (aka L. Cooper). Ph: Renato Tafuri. Mus: Simon Boswell. SpFX: Dan Maklansky et al. Mkp: Peter Moor, Grace Ginsburg. SdFX: Studio Sound. Ref: TV: Imperial Ent. video; Eng. dubbed. Hound. Morse. no Martin. no Phantom. Gorezone 18. VWB: aka *Bloody Bird.* With David Brandon, Barbara Cupisti, Mickey Knox, Robert Gligorov, Don Fiore, John Morghen, Clain Parker (Irving Wallace).

"I think that maniac is hiding in here!" A rehearsal of the avant-garde musical thriller "The Night Owl" is interrupted by the presence of mad ex-actor Irving Wallace, who adopts the owlhead disguise of one of the players. (Macabre, isn't it?) Is-it-theatre-or-life horror story is slickly directed and a shade less offputting than the similar *Demons,* but features the same tiresomely gore-angled murders as the latter. (At one point, one of the characters even directs a flashlight on the mayhem, the better for us to appreciate it.) The movie's sick "curtain call" (the killer assembles all his victims onstage) makes a fairly compelling finale, but the reason for the *Exterminating Angel,* everyone's-trapped-in-the-theatre gimmick is simply unbuyable. (The plays' over-zealous director hides the only-exit-door key.)

**The STALKER** (J) 1993. Ref: CM 17:62: "gruesome s&m murders."

**STANLEY AND THE DINOSAURS** Golden Book Video/Churchill Films 1991 color stopmo anim c22m. SP, D, P, PD: John Clark Matthews. From Syd Hoff's book *Stanley.* Anim: Joel

Fletcher, Justin Kohn, Gail van der Merwe. Ref: TV: GBV. Sean. Voices: Will Ryan, Corey Burton.

Schoolboy daydreams of a tyrannosaurus who tells a tale of a Stone Age Stanley. Script re inventiveness is a pretext for some pleasant animation and songs.

**STAR CRYSTAL** New World/Eric Woster (Star Crystal) 1986 (1985) color 92m. Story, SP, D: Lance Lindsay. Story: also E. Woster. Mus & SdFX: Doug Katsaros. SpVisFX: Lewis Abernathy; (consul) Chuck Comisky. SpMkpFX: Ken Diaz, Woster; (dead bodies) Vince Prentice. Lasers: Jessica Huebner. Ref: TV. V 9/24/86. With C. Jutson Campbell, Faye Bolt, John Smith, Taylor Kingsley, Marcia Linn.

"Routine Mars expedition near crater Olympus Mons, the year 2032." A 300,000-year-old rock yields a glowing crystal (an "extremely advanced computer") which "hatches" a baby snaillike thing, GAR, which leaves the crew of a shuttlecraft dead.

Flat-footed script, direction of actors. Only interest lies in guessing whether the story is *Alien* or *E.T.,* and the switch from one mode to the other is made too abruptly to have much impact. Still, a bit of cosmic ambiguity is better than nothing, even if it boils down to (in effect) the creature's *Alien* tentacles vs. its *E.T.* head.

**STAR FLEET: SPACE QUEST FOR F-01** (B) Terry Flounders & Panda Publishing/JIN-Dynamic 1980 puppet anim 93m. (*Starfleet*—ad t). D, P: Louis Elman. SP: Michael Sloan. Mus: Paul Bliss. SpSdFX: Theatre 3; Cinesound. Ref: TV. TVG. no Stanley. no Scheuer.

The Imperial Alliance's holographic fleet vs. the Pluto-based Star Fleet Command. Also: Lamia, an alien with ESP, and the "future guardian of peace in the universe" ... an insect-like spacecraft ... and a reptile-like X-bomber.... Three apparent TV-series episodes stitched together. Stilted, humorless dramatics; not-bad effects and action sequences. Overall effect here is one of a very lively toy store.

**STAR FLEET: THE THALIAN SPACE WARS** (B) Terry Flounders & Panda Publishing/JIN-Dynamic 1980 puppet anim 95m. (*Starfleet: The Thalian Space Wars*—ad t). Credits: See previous entry. Ref: TV. TVG. no Scheuer. Stanley.

X-bomber with laser-torpedoes vs. an Alliance battle cruiser. The same models and effects as in the other *Star Fleet* semi-movie— and the "characters" wore out their welcome halfway through that one. Plus: a black hole ... the space-sailing-ship The Skull ... funny-looking little alien hordes ... and phantom Princess Lamia.

**STAR FORCE: FUGITIVE ALIEN II** (J) King Features Ent. (Sandy Frank)/Tsuburaya Prods. 1986 ('88-U.S.) color 102m. D: Kiyosumi Kukazawa, Minoru Kanaya. SP: Abe, Wakatsuki, Araki, Yamaura, Nagasaka, Andou. Mus: Norio Maeda. Ref: TV: CHE video; dubbed Eng. TVG. no Phantom. no Maltin '92. no Hound. no Scheuer. no Martin. With Tatsuya Azuma, Miyuki Tanigawa, Joe Shishido, C. Takahashi, Tsutomu Yukawa, Hiro Tateyama.

Follow-up to *Fugitive Alien* plays like—and probably is—a set of four TV-series episodes re a planet a "thousand light years away from our solar system" ... a secret weapon which could "blow up the universe" ... a "bomb powerful enough to blow up the entire universe" ... a black hole ... an exploding star (which looks like Fourth of July fireworks when it goes off) ... and a "lethal ray" force field.

Familiar space-peril stuff features effects work which ranges from passable to pretty bad. Highlight: the elaborate, lovely, toy-like secret weapon. A couple space-effects shots have two sets of stars in the background. Dubbing highlight: "You underestimate the Wolf Raiders. They can beat us to any nebula."

**STAR JANGA II: SUPER-BATMAN AND MAZINGER V** (S. Korean) 1990. Ref: Oriental Cinema 5: werewolf, giant spider, Batman-type.

**STAR KNIGHT** (Sp) Cinetel/Salamandra 1986 ('92-U.S.) color 90m. (*El Caballero del Dragon. The Knight of the Dragon* - ad t). SP, D, P: Fernando Colomo. SP: also Andreu Martin, Miguel Angel Nieto. Ph: J. Luis Alcaine. Mus: Jose Nieto. Vis Des: E. Ventura. SpFX: Reyes Abades. OptFX: Nunez, Comisky; Story Film. PD: Felix Murcia. Mkp: Jose Antonio Sanchez. SdFX: Cinearte. Ref: TV: Colossal Ent. video (Manson Int'l.); Eng. version. V 2/19/86: "winning humor." 5/21/86:17. 5/1/85:419(ad). SFChron Dtbk 9/27/92. Ecran F 65:11. Stanley. PT 13:10: "some funny moments." TVG. With Klaus Kinski, Harvey Keitel, Fernando Rey, Maria Lamor, Miguel Bose.

The "flying snake from hell" haunting a medieval village proves to be a flying saucer. The helmeted alien, IX (Bose), on board "knows the secret of eternal youth" and collects the spirits of animals, but can't breathe Earth air. At the end, a princess' kiss revives him from the dead, and a knight (Keitel) takes his place in space.... *Star* not so bright. Unusual, but not very good. The reviving kiss is the only sweet moment.

**STAR QUEST: BEYOND THE RISING MOON** Common Man (The Pentan Co.) 1988 (1987) color c85m. (*Beyond the Rising Moon* - orig t). SP, D, Ph, Ed: Philip Cook. Mus: David Bartley. SpVisFxD: Cook. SpMechFX, AD, P: John Ellis. Anim: Taylor Made Images. Alien Ship Des: Steve Hickman. SdFX: Ellis, Cook. Ref: TV: VidAmerica. V 5/18/88. 2/14/90:32(rated). With Tracy Davis, Hans Bachmann, Michael Mack, Rick Foucheux, Ron Ikejiri.

Year 2074. Representatives of Kuriyama Enterprises, Star City, North Africa, follow defecting agent Pentan (Davis)—a "synthetic person" designed to be a "tool of corporate warfare"—to the planet Elysium to retrieve a valuable, abandoned Tesseran artifact, an alien object which could be a scientific gold mine.... Stilted acting, heart-on-sleeve dialogue, fun effects work. The android-with-budding-emotions story is obviously just a vehicle for the latter.

**STAR QUEST** New Horizons HV/Pacific Trust 1995 (1994) color 95m. D: R. Jacobson. SP: M.E. Schwartz. Ref: vc box: 2178 A.D.; "Earth is gone." Vallejo T-H. With S. Bauer, B. Bakke, A. Rachins.

**STAR SLAMMER** Worldwide Ent. (Jack H. Harris)/Viking Films 1987 color 86m. (*Prison Ship*—alt t. aka *Star Slammer: The Escape*). D, Co-P: Fred Olen Ray. SP: M. D. Sonye. SpMkpFX: Matt Rose, Mark Williams. SpFxDes: Bret Mixon. Ref: V 5/20/87: "affectionate camp effort made in 1984." 10/19/88: 186,

190. McCarty II: "home-movie feel." With Ross Hagen, Sandy Brooke, Susan Stokey, John Carradine, Aldo Ray, Dawn Wildsmith, Johnny Legend, Bobbie Bresee.

"The Adventures of Taura Part I." Planet Arous, prison ship, "cute little monsters," etc.

**STAR STREET: THE HAPPY BIRTHDAY MOVIE** 198-? anim Ref: vc trailer: Just for Kids video. no VSB. no PFA. no Martin. no Hound.

The Star Kids live on a star-shaped planet; Momo, a monster who will "eat anything," lives on a junk-food planet.

**STAR SUBURB** (F) Stephane Druout 1982 color? 26m. Ref: PFA notes 1/27/89: Spielberg + *Alphaville*.

Strange lights awaken a girl in a "far-off galaxy."

**STAR TIME** Monarch/Cassini 1992 color 85m. SP, D, P: Alexander Cassini. Ph: F. Arguelles. Mus: Blake Leyh. PD: Meyer, Jensen. Ref: V 1/27/92: "technically superior but dramatically ghastly." SFChron Dtbk 5/23/93. With Michael St. Gerard, John P. Ryan, Maureen Teefy.

The Baby Mask Killer slays thirteen victims in a month.

**STAR TREK III: THE SEARCH FOR SPOCK** Para/Harve Bennett & Cinema Group Venture (Gary Nardino) 1984 color/ws 105m. D: Leonard Nimoy. SP: Bennett. Ph: Charles Correll. Mus: James Horner. SpVisFX: IL&M; (sup) Kenneth Ralston; (creature sup) David Sosalla; (mattes) Michael Pangrazio; (anim sup) Charles Mullen; (models sup) Steve Gawley. SpMkp: The Burmans. SpPhysical FX: Bob Dawson. SpSdFX: Alan Howarth, Frank Serafine. Ref: TV. V 5/30/84. SFExam 6/1/84. SFBay Guardian 6/13/84. With William Shatner, DeForest Kelley, James Doohan, Leonard Nimoy, George Takei, Walter Koenig, Nichelle Nichols; (guest cast) Dame Judith Anderson, Christopher Lloyd, James B. Sikking, John Larroquette, Miguel Ferrer.

In *Star Trek II*, only Spock's (Nimoy) body, it transpires, died. His "living spirit" continues, and "mind-melding" keeps him alive in McCoy (Kelley). (Their brains have been "scrambled.") "Proto-matter" restores Spock, in child form, and the unstable Genesis Planet ages his body rapidly. Also: a centipede creature, a monster-pet ("Feed him!").

If some of the sets here are TV-tacky, the gliding-through-space effects and music are captivating, and the return and escape of the Enterprise and the first view of the space-docked Excelsior qualify as IL&M spectacular. Script is stronger on military strategy than on drama—dramatic points are made in cut-and-dried dialogue. Klingon Kruge's (Lloyd) villainy is not taken seriously, fortunately, and proves very amusing.

**STAR TREK IV: THE VOYAGE HOME** Para/Harve Bennett & IL&M (Ralph Winter/Brooke Breton, Kirk Thatcher) 1986 color/ws 119m. (*The Voyage Home: Star Trek IV*—B). Story, D: Leonard Nimoy. Story, SP: Bennett. SP: also Steve Meerson, Peter Krikes, Nicholas Meyer. Ph: Don Peterman. Mus: Leonard Rosenman. VisFX: (sup) Ken Ralston; (mattes) Chris Evans; (anim sup) Ellen Lichtwardt; (whale mech des) Rick Anderson; (models) Jeff Mann. AddlOptFX: Westheimer. SpFxSup: Michael Lanteri. Creatures: Richard Snell Designs et al. Mkp: Wes Dawn et al. SpSdFX: John Pospisil, Alan Howarth, George Budd. Ref: TV. MFB'87:124-5. V 11/19/86. With William Shatner et al (see previous entry); (guest cast) Jane Wyatt, Catherine Hicks, Michael Berryman, Vijay Amritraj, Majel Barrett, Scott DeVenney, Mark Lenard, John Schuck.

Admiral Kirk (Shatner) takes a Klingon spaceship from the 23rd Century back to the latter half of the 20th Century and San Francisco—and to our "primitive and paranoid culture"—in order to retrieve a couple of humpbacked whales, extinct since the 21st Century.... Though the *Star Wars* and *Star Trek* series feature similar mixtures of spectacle and human-level charm, they seem to be going in opposite directions—*Return of the Jedi* definitively cornered the spectacle market; *The Voyage Home* scores high on charm. Here, the crew of the futuristic *Enterprise* may be out of its element, but it "plays" the California culture expertly—Kirk, Spock, and company score points off us; points are scored off them. Not that there aren't some elaborate cloud and sea effects, as an "orbiting probe" blots out the 23rd-century sun. But Nimoy's light touch with his fellow actors wins out. In sum: overlong but fun, and probably the best in the series.

**STAR TREK V: THE FINAL FRONTIER** Para/Harve Bennett (Ralph Winter) 1989 color/ws 106m. Story, D: William Shatner. SP: David Loughery. Story: also Bennett, Loughery. Mus: Jerry Goldsmith. SpVisFX: Assoc. & Ferren; (coord) Eric Angelson. FxAnimSup: Dick Rauh. SpMkpDes: Kenny Myers. Mattes: Illusion Arts. SpFxSup: Michael L. Wood. Prosth: Richard Snell Designs. Computer Anim: Novocom. SpSdFX: Alan Howarth, John P. Opt: (sup) Dick Swanek; (fx) Westheimer, Peter Kuran. Ref: TV. V 6/14/89. Film Journal 7/89. SFExam 6/9/89. Sacto Union 6/9/89. MFB'89:346-7. With W. Shatner et al. (see *Star Trek III*); (guest cast) David Warner, Laurence Luckinbill, Charles Cooper (Korrd), Todd Bryant, George Murdock ("God"), Bill Quinn.

Sybok (Luckinbill)—a "passionate Vulcan" who turns out to be Spock's (Nimoy) half-brother and a sort of intergalactic psychoanalyst with the power to "free" minds—kidnaps a Romulan, a Terran, and a Klingon on Nimbus III, the "planet of galactic peace." His goal: the "greatest adventure of all time"—the search for Shakiri (or heaven), "beyond the great barrier at the center of the galaxy." "God," however, it seems, is a captive force who "inspires" others to come help him escape.

The metaphysical play here recalls both *2001* and *Solaris*, to this film's disadvantage. The droll moments with the regulars come off better than the cosmic elements, though they're usually underlined and/or telegraphed. Good throwaway: McCoy's (Kelley) comment re Spock: "I liked him better before he died." Uneven but interesting mixture of spectacle, humor, and philosophy.

**STAR TREK VI: THE UNDISCOVERED COUNTRY** Para/Ralph Winter & Steven-Charles Jaffe 1991 color 113m. (109m.). SP, D: Nicholas Meyer. SP: also Denny Martin Flinn. Story, Exec P: Leonard Nimoy. Story: also Lawrence Konner, Mark Rosenthal. Mus: Cliff Eidelman. SpVisFX: IL&M; (sup) Scott Farrar; (coord) Jil-Sheree Bergin; (anim sup) Wes Ford Takahashi; (anim fx coord) Shari Malyn; (model sup) Lawrence Tan. SpAlienMkp: Edward French. SpFxSup: Terry Frazee.

Prosth: Richard Snell Designs. Jackal: Greg Cannom. PhFX: VCE/Peter Kuran; (anim) Al Magliochetti, Kevin Kutchaver. SpSdFX: Alan Howarth, John Paul Fasal. Matte FX: Matte World; (sup) Michael Pangrazio. SpProps: Greg Jein. Sp Language: Marc Okrand. Ultra-Violet FX: Wildfire. Digital Compositing: Pacific Data. Sp Scenery: Foam Tec. Ref: TV: Para HV. V 12/9/91. SFChron 12/6/91. Sacto Bee 12/24/91. ad. With William Shatner et al (see *Star Trek III*); (guest cast) Kim Cattrall, David Warner, Christopher Plummer, Mark Lenard, Brock Peters, John Schuck, Christian Slater, Iman (Martia), John Bloom (behemoth alien), Darryl Henriques, Tom Morga (the brute).

"I've never trusted Klingons." Ingredients this time include a space shock wave ... sabotaged peace talks ... the new, "invisible," Klingon weapon, which allows a prototype "Bird of Prey" ship to fire weapons even when "cloaked" ... a surprise "morpher," or "shape-shifter," Martia, one of whose shapes is Kirk ... and a weird-fanged jackal.

The "time out" for the display of the new computer-animation technology, "morphing," is one of the scattered highlights of this sixth trek, perhaps the last and perhaps the least of the theatrical movies. Heavy on shallow political comment, light on comedy and metaphysics, VI is all leaden dialogue and creaky plotting. Plummer provides the only fresh acting moments. Effects grades: B+ for the big shock wave ... D for the plastic-looking models, or lighting of same ... A- for the morphing.

See also: the following and *Texas Comedy Massacre, The*.

**STAR TREK: GENERATIONS** Para (Rick Berman) 1994 color/ws 118m. D: David Carson. Story, SP: Ronald D. Moore, Brannon Braga. Story: also R. Berman. Ph: John A. Alonzo. Mus: Dennis McCarthy. PD: Herman Zimmerman. SpVisFX: IL&M;(sup) John Knoll, R.B. Moore;(model sup) John Goodson; Santa Barbara Studios. Digital VisFX: CIS. SpMkpFX: Michael Westmore. SpFxSup: Terry Frazee. Computer Graphics Sup: Bart Giovannetti. Ref: TV: Para video. ad. TVG 7/24/93: *Star Trek: The Next Generation: The Movie* - orig t. SFChron 11/18/94. Vallejo T-H 11/18/94. With Patrick Stewart, Jonathan Frakes, Brent Spiner (Data), William Shatner, LeVar Burton, Michael Dorn, Gates McFadden, Marina Sirtis, Malcolm McDowell, James Doohan, Walter Koenig, Whoopi Goldberg, Majel Barrett (computer voice).

"Time has no meaning here." A wandering, deadly energy "ribbon" in space proves to be a "doorway" to the Nexus, a place of (selfish) fulfillment. Captain Kirk (Shatner) and Picard (Stewart) ultimately choose duty over self-indulgence, in, or after, quasi-*Solaris* memory scenes, in the Nexus. Upshot: "We made a difference." Meanwhile, the android Data gets an emotion chip.... A crisis and explosions every ten minutes here. Good model work in this one, but most of it is routine.

**STAR TREK: THE NEXT GENERATION—ENCOUNTER AT FARPOINT** Para-TV/Gene Roddenberry 1987 color 90m. D: Corey Allen. Tel: D. C. Fontana, Roddenberry. Mus: Dennis McCarthy. SpVisFX: IL&M; (coord) Robert Legato. Video: (opt fx) The Post Group; (sp compositing) Composite Image Systems. SpFX: Dick Brownfield. Mkp: M. Westmore; Werner Keppler. Ref: TV. TVG: feature-length pilot for the new series. V 10/7/87:70. With Patrick Stewart, LeVar Burton, Denise Crosby,

Jonathan Frakes, Marina Sirtis (psychic), DeForest Kelley, John de Lancie (Q), Michael Dorn, Wil Wheaton, Michael Bell (Zorn).

Twenty-fourth-century ingredients: the new *Starship Enterprise,* which does a "Starship separation" (some re-assembly required) ... the alien master, Q ... jellyfish-like space creatures ... the conversion of energy into matter ... planet Daneb IV's Elizabethan-garbed inhabitants ... huge force fields ... instant human Popsicles ... an android ("almost as bad as a Vulcan") ... Klingon crew members ... and a bio-electrical super-seeing, or sensing, device for one blind crew member.

The next generation is still being beamed up and even, once or twice, down. Hair styles are very Twentieth Century. But "humanity is no longer a savage race," or so our protagonists set out to prove to Q. The story is episodic, the action repetitious, the effects colorful but unimaginative. Some fun with the disdainful Q and with the dispassionate, funny-eyed android. But half the scenes seem to begin with the psychic saying, "I sense great feeling nearby."

**STAR WARS (II & III)** see also *Fantastic World of D. C. Collins, The. Gonad the Barbarian. Sex Wars. Spaceballs.*

**STARBREAKER** 198-? computer graphics short. Ref: PFA notes 5/16/87.

Crash landing on an uncharted planet.

**STARCAT FULLHOUSE** (J) Walkers Co. 1989 anim color 30m. Ref: Animag 9:4: Vol. 3 of 4 OAVs; "slapstick."

"Interplanetary delivery service."

**STARCHASER: THE LEGEND OF ORIN** (U.S.-So. Korean) Atlantic Releasing/Coleman-Rosenblatt (Young Sung Int'l.) 1985 anim color 3-D 100m. P, D: Steven Hahn. SP: Jeffrey Scott. Mus: Andrew Belling. SpVisFX: Michael Wolf. Anim D: Mitch Rochon, Jang-Gil Kim. SpSdFX: Stan Levine. Ref: TV. MFB'86:154-5. V 5/15/85. ad. Voices: Joe Colligan (Orin), Carmen Argenziano, Les Tremayne, John Garwood.

On the planet Trinia, with part-mechanical, part-animal "mandroids," robots, leech-like creatures, a huge tentacled beast, laser whips, and Luke Skywalker and Han Solo counterparts.... Misguided attempt to approximate the spectacle of *Star Wars* at least has a certain jauntiness to help offset the familiarity of plot, character, and theme. Fast-paced, incident-crammed animated science fiction also features some novel shots of jettisoned robots rolling through space.

**STARCROSSED** ABC-TV/Fries Ent. 1985 color 90m. SP, D: Jeffrey Bloom. Mus: Gil Melle. AD: Gerry Holmes. VisFxConsul: Richard Bennett. SpFX: (sup) Louis Craig; (consul) Malivoire; (opt) David Stipes. Mkp: Shonagh Jabour. Opt: Howard Anderson. SdFX: Superior. Ref: TV. TVG. Stanley. V 2/13/85:128. With James Spader, Belinda Bauer, Ed & Roland Groenenberg (aliens), Pete Kowanko, Jacqueline Brookes.

Telekinetic alien (Bauer) from a once "heavenly" planet travels by light to Earth, finds a telekinetic man (Spader) who "connects" with her.... Script is mostly small-beans scenes, though it has charming moments, including a nicely-conceived This-is-the-planet-I'm-from scene, done with billiard-ball "heavenly bod-

ies." Mainly a melange of hand-me-down elements from *Starman, Day the Earth Stood Still,* etc.

**STARFIGHTERS** (Mex.) Arena Films 1992 color 91m. (*Luchadores de Las Estrellas*). D: Rodolfo Lopezreal. SP: Lucero, Cerro. Idea: G. Mayo et al. Ph: F.A. Colin. SpFX: Efeccine, Arturo Vazquez. OptFX: Sainz, Rodriguez. Mkp: Maria Eugenia Luna. SdFX: Gonzalo Gavira. Ref: TV: VSOM; Eng. titles. With Gloria Mayo (Larrossa), Nitron (el vampiro interespacial), Blue Demon Jr., El Misterioso, El Volador, Mascarita Sagrada.

"I need blood!" A spaceship crashlands on Earth. Aboard: a big vampire and three comic-relief midgets. The vampire shoots ray bombs and has frisbees that paralyze. The heroine also proves to be from outer space.... The old formula: wrestling and plot. The filmmaking here would most charitably be characterized as lackadaisical. One wrestler is named Mysterious; another, Flyer. Some of this was shot in Westwood, near UCLA.

**STARFIRE** see *Solar Crisis*

**STARGATE** (U.S.-G?) MGM-UA/Mario Kassar/Le Studio Canal+ & Centropolis & Carolco (Michaels-Eberle-Devlin) 1994 color/ws 121m. SP, D: Roland Emmerich. SP: also Dean Devlin. Ph: K.W. Lindenlaub. Mus: David Arnold. PD: H. Gross. Digital VisFx:(sup) J.A. Okun; Kleiser-Walczak. VisFxSup: Kit West. Creature FX: P. Tatopoulos. MechFxSup: Wayne Beauchamp. Stargate: Art, Sculpture & Production. AnimFX: Available Light;(sup) John T. van Vliet. Digital Opt: Cinema Research. SpSdFX: John Paul Fasal. Egyptology: Dr. Stuart Smith. Ref: TV: Live video. ad. Vallejo T-H 10/28/94. SFChron 10/28/94. With Kurt Russell, James Spader, Jaye Davidson (Ra), Viveca Lindfors, Alexis Cruz, Leon Rippy.

The Egyptian archaeological find from 1928 proves, years later, to be a doorway to another world, where there be Ra, a cosmic traveler seeking to cheat death ... what looks like a tiny Arab nation ... a pyramid design theme ... and a weird buffalo, or camel.... The buildup (approximately 45 minutes) is okay; then, the movie is just like a thousand other action-adventure movies. Scorecard: *2001* visual abstractions for the trip through the gate ... a nice, old-fashioned orchestral score ... neat helmets-into-heads morphing ... and good, kooky-brilliant-scientist work from Spader in his earlier scenes here.

**STARMAN** Col/Col-Delphi (Michael Douglas & Larry J. Franco) 1984 color/ws 115m. D: John Carpenter. SP: Bruce A. Evans, Raynold Gideon. Adap: Dean Riesner. Mus: Jack Nitzsche. Starman Transformation: Dick Smith, Stan Winston, Rick Baker. SpVisFX: IL&M; (sup) Bruce Nicholson; (models sup) E. Owyeung; (mattes) Michael Pangrazio; (anim sup) Charlie Mullen; (head fx anim) Bruce Walters. Ref: TV. V 12/5/84. SFExam 12/14/84. SFChron 12/21/84. Bay Guardian 12/12/84. With Jeff Bridges (Starman), Karen Allen, Charles Martin Smith, Richard Jaeckel.

Project Visitor. Through "symbiotic transformation," an alien (Bridges) assumes the identity of a dead earthling, Scott Hayden, in an instant-adult effects sequence which recalls the best of Charles Bowers. This E.T. comes from a planet 100,000 years ahead of our civilization and possesses magic marbles which can restore life. But, as a human, he has some rough edges, and Scott's widow, Jenny (Allen), volunteers to smooth them out.

Sweet comic-romantic moments with Bridges and Allen get lost in an over-elaborate chase/suspense apparatus here. Non-effects highlights: a well-contrived bittersweet parting, at the end, between "Starman" and Jenny ... and Bridges' ineffable Innocent Look.

**STARQUEST** see *Wings of Oneamis*

**STARSHIP** (B) Cinema Group/V.T.C. & Rediffusion Films (Lorca Films/Mansfield) 1985 ('86-U.S.) color/ws 100m. (85m.-U.S.) (*Lorca and the Outlaws*—B t. *Starship Redwing*—alt t. *2084*—early t. *Blood Storm*—orig t). SP, D: Roger Christian. SP: also Matthew Jacobs. Mus: Tony Banks, Genesis. MinFxSup: Brian Smithies. SpPhFxD: Denis Lowe. SpFxSup: Chris Murray. Mkp: Anne Pospichil. SdFX: Delta Sound. Robots: Phosphorus Films. Ref: TV. MFB'86:310: Australian production elements. V 5/15/85. 4/8/87:26. ad. Ecran F 39:65. 43:71. 50:71. With John Tarrant, Donogh (or Donough) Rees, Deep Roy (Grid), Ralph Cottrell, Hugh Keays-Byrne, Cassandra Webb, Tyler Coppin (droid), James Steele (MP droid).

Droid-ruled El Jadida, a mining station on planet Ordessa, in the 21st Century. Management plots to replace human workers with robots and to "dispose" of the humans on Earth. Plus: a computer which revives the droid Grid's memories and makes him think he was dreaming.... Routine action-suspense, with the accent on big spaceships and trucks. Some keen model effects in the sequence in which a rebel spaceship smashes upwards through several levels of hangar.

**STARSHIP INTERCOURSE** Four Rivers-Dreamland 1987 (1986) color 80m. D: John T. Bone. Ref: vc box. Adam '88. With Samantha Strong, Sharon Mitchell, Lois Ayres, Gail Force, Ona, Melissa Melendez.

Spaceship of "interstellar, female sex criminals," who wind up on Earth.

**STARSHIP REDWING** see *Starship*

**STARSHIP TROOPERS** (J) Bandai/Sunrise & Studio Nue 1988 anim color 25m. each (*Uchuu No Senshi*). Mecha Des: Yutaka Izubuchi. Ref: Animag 3:5. 4:7. 6:5: 6 OAVs.

"Powered suits," in the Mobile Infantry of the 22nd Century.

**STARZAN—SHOUTING STAR OF THE JUNGLE** (Fili) Regal Films 1988 color c95m. SP, D: Tony Reyes. SP: also Joey De Leon. Mkp: Alice Guinto. SdFX: Ramon Reyes. Ref: TV: Regal Video; no Eng.

Jungle antics of a Tarzan-type include a few fantasy-horror-comedy episodes. In one, piranha strip the flesh off two baddies, who come back to life as (crudely stopmo-animated) living skeletons that chase Starzan (Joey De Leon). In the other, a witch doctor's rays turn Starzan into an inert zombie; a good witch's banana brings him back to life (to the strains of the Popeye tune).

Rank silliness has occasional amusing sequences, such as the slapstick-skeletons one. Featured: an appearance by Indiana Jones (Spanky Rigor). First in a series.

**STATEMENT OF RANDOLPH CARTER, The** see *Unnamable II*

**The STAY AWAKE** (S. African) Nelson Ent./Stay Awake (Avi Lerner/Reyns-Raleigh) 1989 color 88m. SP, D: John Bernard. Prosth: Robbie Guess. Ref: V 8/23/89: "a snoozer." With Shirley Jane Harris, Tanya Gordon, Jayne Hutton, Michelle Carey.

"Monster shows up looking like a green reptile man...."

**STAY TUNED** Morgan Creek (J. G. Robinson) 1992 color 89m. D: Peter Hyams. SP: T. S. Parker, Jim Jennewein. Mus: Bruce Broughton. Anim: Chuck Jones. Story: Parker, Jennewein, Richard Siegel. Ref: SFChron 8/15/92: "no great shakes." ad. TVG 1/16/93. With John Ritter, Pam Dawber, Jeffrey Jones.

Multi-dimensional-remote, 666-channel Hellvision TV features segments like a "Star Trek" parody, the animated "Robo-Cat," and "spooks" in "Duane's Underworld."(SFC)

**STEEL AND LACE** Fries Ent. (Paragon Arts)/Cinema HV (John Schouweiler, David DeCoteau) 1990 color 93m. D: Ernest Farino. SP: Joseph Dougherty, Dave Edison. Mus: John Massari. SpMkpFX: S.O.T.A. F/X; (sup artists) Jerry Macaluso, Roy Knyrim. SpMechFX: S.P.F.X.; (sup) Steve Patino. Opt: (vis fx) Fantasy II (Gene Warren Jr.); (addl) Pacific Title. Ref: TV. V 10/22/90. 11/12/90:64 (rated). With Clare Wren, Bruce Davison, Stacy Haiduk, David Naughton, Michael Cerveris, William Prince, Scott Burkholder.

"Looks like somebody dropped a bowling ball right through him." A gang-raped woman (Wren) kills herself, then returns as a revenge-bent cyborg, and kills the self-styled "Five Musketeers" responsible, one by one, with weapons such as a hideaway drill, a castration device which leaves one victim with a mess in his pants, and laser lightning.

Too many subplots spoil the broth. Best line: (Davison's Albert, as he has his cyborg replay one revenge scene) "Slow motion, please." Best delivery: David L. Lander's, as his wrapped-up-in-his-work coroner observes, "These homicides are downright baroque!"

**STEEL DAWN** Vestron/Silver Lion (Yellowpine Ltd.) 1987 color 111m. D, P: Lance Hool. P: also Conrad Hool. SP: Doug Lefler. Mus: Brian May. SpFxCoord: Joe Quinlivan. Mkp: Mackenzie & Hare. Ref: TV. V 11/11/87. With Patrick Swayze, Lisa Niemi, Christopher Neame, Brion James, John Fujioka, Anthony Zerbe.

Meridian, a "small settlement" in a dry world after "The War." Ingredients: sand-burrowing mutants of the Wasteland ... a "purification farm" ... the warlord (Zerbe) who wants the farm ... and an "endless supply" of pure spring water in a cavern.... Standard futuristic actioner, only longer than usual.

**STEEL JUSTICE** NBC-TV 1992 color c90m. Ref: TVG. ad: "Destined to save a future gone awry." With Robert Taylor, J. A. Preston, Season Hubley, Roy Brocksmith, Joan Chen.

"Time traveler from ancient Mesopotamia" helps round up weapons dealers.

**The STEPFATHER** New Century-Vista Film/ITC Prods. (Jay Benson) 1986 color 98m. D: Joseph Ruben. Story, SP: Donald

E. Westlake. Story: also Carolyn Lefcourt, Brian Garfield. Mus: Patrick Moraz. Mkp: Maurice Parkhurst. SpFxCoord: Bill Orr. Ref: TV. MFB'88:21. V 1/21/87. ad. East Bay Express 3/6/87. SFExam 2/27/87. FQ. With Terry O'Quinn, Jill Schoelen, Shelley Hack, Charles Lanyer, Stephen Shellen.

"It's like having Ward Cleaver for a dad." *The Stepfather* poses the dumb/ingenious "What if ...?" question, What if a classic-sitcom Dad, or a reasonable facsimile of same, were, in reality, a psychopathic killer? Behind family-man Jerry Blake's (O'Quinn) "This is as good as it gets" banalities lies a disturbing personal history: In the town of Bellevue, he was called Henry Morrison and he slaughtered his family. He's now in Oakridge, Washington, establishing a new family, and has his eye on Rosedale. ("A great place to raise a family.")

*The Stepfather* is a glib but pretty creepy update of the charming-madman stories of the Forties like *Shadow of a Doubt* and *Gaslight.* It confirms the worst fears of the child who's naturally resistant to her new stepfather, and suggests, slyly, how little we know each other. Even at its best, though, the movie seems to be either just (a) a superior slasher flick, or (b) an irresponsibly slick serious drama employing suspense as an end rather than a means.

**STEPFATHER II** Millimeter Films/ITC Ent. (William Burr, Darin Scott/Part II Prods.) 1989 color 86m. (*Stepfather 2: Make Room for Daddy*—ad t). D: Jeff Burr. SP: John Auerbach. Mus: Jim Manzie. SpMkpFX: Michelle Burke. Opt: Howard Anderson. Ref: TV. V 11/8/89. Sacto Bee 11/13/89. With Terry O'Quinn, Meg Foster, Caroline Williams, Jonathan Brandis.

"Family man" Jerry Blake (O'Quinn) smashes his "beautifully crafted" scale-model home and bloodily escapes from the Puget Sound Psychiatric Hospital. Always the "eternal optimist," he "keeps on trying" to establish the perfect home—this time in Palm Meadow Estates, near Los Angeles—but the movie ends pessimistically, with a wedding in red.

The bloody wedding-march coda is one of the script's scattered successful inventions. Another: Jerry's creepily soothing impersonation of a psychiatrist. Thin sequel features much play with sharp instruments, not enough of Jerry's ironically "nice" sweaters and bathrobes.

**STEPFATHER III** HBO-TV/ITC Ent. (Guy Magar, Paul Moen/Tough Boys & ITC) 1992 color 109m. (*Stepfather III—Father's Day*—orig t). Tel, D: Magar. Tel: also Marc B. Ray. Mus: P. C. Regan. PD: Richard B. Lewis. Key Mkp: Candace Wessinger. SpFxCoord: Andre Ellingson. Ref: TV. V 6/1/92:72. 9/30/91:14. With Robert Wightman, Priscilla Barnes, Season Hubley, David Tom, John Ingle.

"You're gonna look like a new man!" Plastic surgery changes the "Family Serial Killer" into Keith Grant (Wightman), but he's still a "real nerd." Pleased with his new appearance, he takes a circular saw to the surgeon's throat, then finds a "beautiful wife and a great little boy" in the "prettiest house on the block" in Deer View, California, known, with numbing irony, as "America's safest neighborhood." He murders his rival, gets into the "father-son stuff," takes a rake to his boss, makes sure his stepson brushes his teeth, then murders the town priest.... Assembly-line horror story seems to write itself. The worst of it: Keith's quips as he commits his murders. Predictable: At the end, Crippled Boy Walks.

**The STEPFORD CHILDREN** NBC-TV/Taft Ent. & E. J. Scherick Associates 1987 color c90m. D: Alan Levi. SP: William Bleich. Ph: Steve Shaw. Mus: Joseph Conlan. PD: Greg Fonseca. SpFxMkp: Doug White. Elec Graphics: Shirley Knecht. SdFxSup: W. H. Wistrom. Ref: TV. TVG. no V. With Barbara Eden, Don Murray, Richard Anderson, Randall Batinkoff, Tammy Lauren, James Coco, Debbie Barker, Dick Butkus, Sharon Spelman, Ken Swofford, James Staley.

Sequel to *The Stepford Wives* (II). Steven Harding (Murray) returns to perfectly perfect Stepford ("An All American City") with a new wife (Eden), a son (Batinkoff), and a daughter (Lauren). His wife finds that the high school has no PTA, and his daughter is not happy either: "I don't want to be a Stepford teen. I wanna be me."

The sinister joke continues here, with the battle lines between individuality and conformity overclearly drawn, and with more glib "chills" with domesticated pod-people. Film is as close, in some scenes (like the macabre conclusion with the robots-in-development), to the original *Invasion of the Body Snatchers* as it is to *The Stepford Wives.*

**STEPHEN KING'S CAT'S EYE** see *Cat's Eye*

**STEPHEN KING'S CHILDREN OF THE CORN** see *Children of the Corn*

**STEPHEN KING'S GOLDEN YEARS** see *Golden Years*

**STEPHEN KING'S GRAVEYARD SHIFT** (U.S.-J) Para/Larry Sugar & JVC (Graveyard Inc.) 1990 color 86m. (aka *Graveyard Shift*). D, P: Ralph S. Singleton. P: also W. J. Dunn. SP: John Esposito, from King's short story. Mus: A. Marinelli, B. Banks. SpVisFX: (adviser) Albert Whitlock; Dutton-Taylor, Illusion Arts. MechFX: Image Engineering; (sup) Peter M. Chesney; (coord) Dean Miller. Creature FX: FXSmith; (sup) Gordon J. Smith; (mech) James Gawley, Bill Sturgeon; (coord) Eric Beldowski. Main Title Des: Phill Norman. Sound: (fx) Jon Johnson, Fury & Grace Digital; (sp processing) Craig Harris. SpVocal FX: Frank Welker. Ref: TV. S&S. V 11/5/90. SFChron 10/27/90. SFExam 10/29/90. With David Andrews, Kelly Wolf, Stephen Macht, Brad Dourif.

"There's something down here!" In Gates Falls, Maine, "mysterious accidents" plague the Bachman Mills, where a cleanup crew discovers a huge cache of human skeletons in a long-lost cavern. Routine but compact monster movie at least unveils its monster methodically—here a claw, there a jaw, here some bat-wing-like folds of skin, there a tail, and finally a bat-rat-fetus head. Unfortunately, that's about all it does. Chief, amusing scenery-chewers include Macht and Dourif, the former sporting an accent from Percy Kilbride country. Cross references: *Willard* (for rats), *Alien,* and *The Boogens.*

**STEPHEN KING'S IT** see *It* (1990)

**STEPHEN KING'S SILVER BULLET** Para/Dino De Laurentiis (Famous Films/Martha Schumacher) 1985 color/ws 95m. (aka

*Silver Bullet*). D: Daniel Attias. SP: Stephen King, from his novelette *Cycle of the Werewolf.* Mus: Jay Chattaway. Creatures: Carlo Rambaldi. Ref: TV. V 10/16/85. With Gary Busey, Corey Haim, Megan Follows, Everett McGill, Terry O'Quinn.

As the "moon gets fuller, the guy gets wolfier".... Tarker's Mill, 1976. A werewolf is at large, and (as in *Beast with a Million Eyes*), there's some link between folks' general unpleasantness here and the monster's savagery. In a vivid illustration of the we-are-all-murderers cliche, a preacher (McGill) dreams of a chapel full of werewolves.... Conventional shock scenes, tired boy-who-cried-werewolf suspense, old-hat mystery, and a few chills. This time, it's the monster that uses the Stephen King baseball bat (to club a cop).

**STEPHEN KING'S SLEEPWALKERS** Col/Ion Pictures, Victor & Grais (Nabeel Zahid/Logothetis-Medawar) 1992 color 91m. (aka *Sleepwalkers*). D: Mick Garris. SP: Stephen King. Mus: Nicholas Pike. SpMkpFX: Alterian Studios; (sup) Tony Gardner; (mech des) Eric Fiedler; (prosth des) John Blake, Mike Smithson; (creature suit des) Tom Hester. SpVisFX: Apogee; (sup) Jeffrey Okun; (anim) Harry Moreau. SpFX: Dennis Dion. Ref: TV. V 4/20/92. ad. SFChron 4/11/92. Sacto Union 4/11/92. SFExam 4/10/92. With Brian Krause (Charles Brady), Maedchen Amick, Alice Krige (Mary Brady), Jim Haynie, Cindy Pickett, Ron Perlman, Lyman Ward, Glenn Shadix, S. King, Joe Dante, John Landis, Clive Barker, Tobe Hooper, Michael MacKay (Charles sleepwalker), Charles Croughwell & Karyn Sercelj (Mary sleepwalker).

"Scared of a cat!" A "sleepwalker" here is a "nomadic shape-shifting creature with human and feline origins. Probably source of the vampire legend." And it feeds on the life-force of female virgins.... Travis, Indiana. It's Snout City, as young Charles begins his first (onscreen) transformation. He can also make himself and his car invisible, and, later, even the car rates some special "makeup" transformation effects.

Most irritating motif: Mama Vampire's (Krige) smirk. Most disastrous ploy (for both story and character): Vampire Boy's (Krause) Freddy smart-ass-isms (e.g., "Cop-ka-bob!"). Corniest gross-out: the climactic dance of the decaying dead. Most predictable climactic move: the onslaught of the cats. Only redeeming feature of a grotesquely miscalculated movie: the "morphing" stunts, especially Charles' first there-and-back facial contortions.

**STEPHEN KING'S SOMETIMES THEY COME BACK** CBS-TV/Dino De Laurentiis (Milton Subotsky)/Paradise Films 1991 color c90m. (aka *Sometimes They Come back*). D: Tom McLoughlin. Tel: Lawrence Konner, Mark Rosenthal. From King's short story. Ph: Bryan England. Mus: Terry Plumeri. PD: P. D. Foreman. SpMkpFX: Gabe Bartalos, Atlantic West FX. SpFX: Marty Bresin, SpFxUnltd. OptFX: Perpetual Motion Pictures. Min: Sessums. Ref: TV. TVG. With Tim Matheson, Brooke Adams, Robert Rusler, Chris Demetral.

After twenty-seven years, a man's dead brother returns—still a boy—from another dimension. A combination of horror-story King and warm-and-runny King.

**STEPHEN KING'S THE LAWNMOWER MAN** see *Lawnmower Man, The*

**STEPHEN KING'S THE TOMMYKNOCKERS** see *Tommyknockers, The*

**STEPMONSTER** New Horizons/Pacific Trust (Steven Rabiner/F.O. Ray) 1992 color 87m. D: Jeremy Stanford. Story: Fred Olen Ray. SP: Mark Thomas McGee, Craig J. Nevius. Ph: Walter Julian. Mus: Terry Plumeri. PD: Stuart Blatt. Comic Art: Dave Simmons. SpFX: Gabe Bartalos. FX:(sup) Kevin Kutchaver;(sp opt) Motion. Ref: TV. Martin: "enjoyable." Fango 122:12. V 12/7/92:8(rated). 4/20/92:14. Imagi 1:58: "juvenile." With Alan Thicke, Robin Riker, George Gaynes, John Astin, Corey Feldman, Ami Dolenz, Molly Cheek, Bill Corben.

"Your stepmother is a monster." Literally—she's a tropopkin, a "bloodsucking, bat-faced witch" from the Cascade Forest who can assume human form and whose familiar is a gremlin-ish harpy. ("I don't think she's one of us.") Rote monster-comedy's main problem: Dad is as much a monster accidentally as Stepmom is intentionally. (His positive qualities are elusive.) Lone highlight: the hommage sequence to the 1942 *Cat People*, in which the shrink psychoanalyzes Stepmom, and the latter turns into the monster.

**STILL LIFE** Prism 1992? color feature. D: Graeme Campbell. Ref: SFChron Dtbk 4/25/93. With Jason Gedrick, Jessica Steen, Stephen Shellen.

"Serial killer ... turns his victims into elaborate sculptures."

**STILL NOT QUITE HUMAN** Disney-TV/Resnick-Margellos Prods. 1992 color 85m. D, Tel: Eric Luke. Ph: Ron Orieux. Mus: John Debney. PD: Mark Freeborn. VisFX: Ted Rae. Graphics: R. F. Peppler. SpFx Coord: Bill Orr. Mkp: Victoria Down. Ref: TV. TVG 5/30/92. With Alan Thicke (Dr. Carson/android), Christopher Neame, Betsy Palmer, Jay Underwood (Chip).

Mechanical marvels in this second sequel to *Not Quite Human* include the twenty-two-month-old Chip, again, who has a "magnetic finger" ("Carson's human chip") ... a Carson android ("It's a machine!") ... a robot with laser weapon ... and an android created in the image of the evil scientist who is producing "unimaginative androids" without "independent thought" for armies.... Thicke gets to act cute, too, this time, as an android, and it's too much.

**\*\*\* A STONE AGE ADVENTURE** Pathe/Bray 1915 anim silent 5m. Anim D: L.M. Glackens. Ref: MPW 24:1688 (6/5/15). Lee.

Giant Geewhizzicus vs. Haddam Baad's domesticated Punkosaurus.

**STONE BOY** see *Boy God*

**STONES OF DEATH** (Austral.) PFM & Medusa Communications (Hannay-Hannah) 1988 color 88m. (*Kadaicha*—Austral.). D: James Bogle. SP: Ian Coughlan. Ph: S. F. Windon. Mus: Peter Westheimer. SpMkp: Deryzk de Niese. Ref: V 6/8/88: "never very scary." 10/19/88:185. Martin. Morse: "familiar." With Zoe Carides, Tom Jennings, Eric Oldfield, Sean Scully.

Shopping mall built on sacred aboriginal site yields "savage hound," "lethal spider," and an "eel-like thing."(V)

**\*STORM PLANET** Popular-Science Films 1962 82m. (*Planet of Storms* - vt. *Planeta Bur*). Story: A. Kazantsev. Mus: P. Admoni, A. Chernov. Sets: M. Tsybasov, V. Alexandrov. Ref: TV: Sinister Cinema video; Eng. titles. Hardy/SF.

"So this is Venus!" Cosmonauts from two Soviet astro-ships land on Venus and find a (string-operated) "octopus" plant ("Anything's possible on Venus") ... dimetrodons ... small tyrannosaurus-types ("imps of the devil!") ... the giant claw, or rather a "pterodactylus" ("It's dangerous") ... a cute "octopus"... the "dragon with the ruby eye" statue ... a "red glow" (a volcano) ... an alien image engraved on a stone ... a "voice" ... and, most intriguing of all, an apparent alien. (The viewer sees her reflection—after the explorers have left the planet.)

It's not *Solaris*. It's not even *First Spaceship on Venus*. It's just the quaint, sometimes campy source for two American movies, *Voyage to the Planet of Prehistoric Women* and *Voyage to a Prehistoric Planet*. It's also the source of the line, "Better to die usefully than wait for a meteorite to hit you or radiation disease to get you." All this and Iron John, the robot.

**STORMQUEST** (Arg.) Aries & Benlox (Hector Olivera/Ed Garland) 1988 color 89m. Story, D: Alex Sessa. SP: Charles Saunders. Ph: L. Solis. Mus: C. Ocampo. PD: A. T. Naxi. Ref: V 11/30/88: "enjoyable fantasy." Martin: 1987. With Brent Huff, Kai Baker, Monica Gonzaga, Linda Lutz (Stormqueen), Dudizile Mkhize (Kinya).

Sorceress.

**A STORY** 198-? anim short. Ref: SFChron Dtbk 4/10/88:26.

Fairy tale re the Blue Monster and Randy the Killer Clown.

**STORY OF MIMI-NASHI-HOICHI, The** see *Kwaidan*

**STORY OF RICKY** see *Rikko O*

**STORY OF THE FAR EAST** (J) Toei/Director's Co. (Okamoto-Matsuki) 1992 color/ws 123m. Story, SP, D: Kazuyuki Izutsu. Story: also Sakamoto, Hirano. SP: also Takahashi, Kohnami. Ph: N. Shinoda. Mus: Akira Senju. PD: Hosoishi. Creature Des: Begul. SpFxMkp: Habit's. Ref: TV: Image Factory video; no Eng. Video Tokyo: above is tr t. With N. Ogata.

Handsome, sub-Kurosawa period adventure concludes with a long sequence re a dragon-like water monster or two. The main, charming, cartoonish red dragon has horns, rudimentary wings, a long, versatile tongue, and a dazed look. He turns a man into a dog, but finally seems to listen to the protagonists' pleading and flies away.

**STORY OF THE YOUNG MAN WITH THE CREAM TARTS** see *Trouble for Two*

**STRAIGHT JACKET** Benmar Prods. (Ben Brothers & Martin Green) 1981 color 89m. (*Dark Sanity*—alt vt t). D: M. Green. SP: Phillip Pine, Larry Hilbran. Ph: John McCoy. Mus: John Bath. AD: Phillip Duffin. Prosth: Melissa Lazarou. SpFX: David Pennington. Opt: Howard Anderson. Ref: TV: Premiere Ent. video. GoreZone 11:64. no Phantom. Stanley. Peter Zirschky. Hound. V 3/7/84:76. Morse. McCarty II. With Aldo Ray, Kory

Clark, Chuck Jamison, Bobby Holt, Andy Gwyn, Timothe McCormack, Barry Ray Robison, Harry Carlson.

"It was like a nightmare!" Clairvoyant Karen Nichols' new house gets "curiouser and curiouser." She has visions of severed hands and heads, and former police sergeant Larry Craig (Ray)—"I know I seem like a weirdo"—tells her that he too had visions in her house while he was investigating a murder. At the end, he has a flash-forward vision of a murder about to happen.

The climactic revelations of madness and murderers prove more comic than surprising, and the plodding narrative never quite gets straight which visions are flashbacks, which are flash-forwards, and which are just flashes.

**STRAIGHT TO HELL** see *Cut and Run*

**STRANDED** New Line/Scott Rosenfelt, Mark Levinson (Robert Shaye) 1987 color 80m. D: Tex Fuller. SP: Alan Castle. Mus: Stacy Widelitz. Aliens: Michele Burke. AD: Donna Stamps-Scherer. SpVisFX: VCE/Peter Kuran. SpFXCoord: Allen Hall. Crystal: Image Engineering. Anim Sup: Lynda Weinman. Ref: TV. V 12/2/87. Maltin '92. Morse. Martin. With Ione Skye, Joe Morton, Maureen O'Sullivan, Susan Barnes (assassin), Brendan Hughes (Prince), Flea (Jester), Spice Williams (warrior).

"They almost look like angels!" Several humanoid aliens fleeing an assassin land on Earth. A glowing crystal gives humans a vision of their life and planet.... A touching farewell scene—as two of the nice aliens make good their escape from Earth—is the best of this fairish sf drama. Otherwise, there's not much to it. Includes the getting-to-be-obligatory "Will she or won't she?" scene, as the human heroine (Skye) decides, No, she won't follow the alien Prince into space.

**STRANGE CASE OF DR. JEKYLL AND MR. HYDE, The** see *Aullido del Diablo, El. Cap'n O. G. Readmore ... (P). Edge of Sanity. Hare Remover. Hombre y la Bestia, El (1972). Jack the Ripper (1988). Madam Jeckyl. My Favorite Spy. Nightmare before Christmas, The. Nightmare Classics II. Pagemaster, The. Scooby-doo and the Reluctant Werewolf. Strannayar Istoriyar.... Terminal. Waxwork II.*

**STRANGE DEAD BODIES** see *Koesi*

**STRANGE DREAMS** see *Strangest Dreams*

**STRANGE FELLOW** (H.K.) Jia's Motion Picture Co. 1985 color/ws c90m. Ref: TV: vt; Eng. titles.

"This town is badly haunted." Ingredients include hopping ghosts—including a fire-breathing one—a tiresome murder story, occasionally funny comedy, spirit possession, and a Taoist priest who sees to it that the ghosts are re-buried. The murdered woman seems to return as a disfigured ghost. ("Help, ghost!") One ghost carries around and feeds its own head.

**STRANGE HORIZON** (Can.) Lightscape 1992 color 83m. (aka *Project: Genesis*). SP, D, P: Philip Jackson. Ph: John Dyer. PD: Plaxton, Allan. Ref: V 1/4/93: "fuzzy-headed, low-budget sci-fi." 10/25/93:51(ad). PT 20:69: "talk and talk ... very cheap fx." With David Ferry, Olga Prokhorova (alien woman), Ken Lemaire, Robert Russell.

Illegal drugs, distant planets, in the 23rd Century.

*The STRANGE MR. GREGORY Louis Berkoff 1945. Tech D: Ormond McGill. Ref: TV. V 12/19/45. Lee. Lentz. Weldon. Weaver/PRH. no Hardy/HM. With Marjorie Hoshelle.

"You have achieved the Kalimundra [sp?] death trance!" For two days, 17 hours, and 45 minutes, mystic/magician Gregory the Great (Edmund Lowe) is put into a "state of suspended animation," where he is, "to all intents and purposes, dead." Through mind control, he has been able to gain "immunity to mortal suffering" (i.e., pain), and, at one point, he uses Svengali-like voodoo to exert a "strange influence"—long-distance—on the woman he loves. A premonition supposedly tells him that he will soon be dead and buried, or at least dead. Then: "Yes, it is I, come back from the tomb!" Unusual, intriguing, super-magic plot elements ... the usual melodramatics from the cast. Lowe's character and *White Zombie*-like makeup suggest that the Gregory role was originally intended for Bela Lugosi.

The STRANGE MONSTER OF STRAWBERRY COVE Disney-TV/Ron Miller, Tom Leetch 1971 color c90m. D: Jack Shea. Tel: Herman Groves. Story: B. R. Brinley. Ph: Frank Phillips. Mus: George Bruns. AD: Mansbridge, Creber. Mkp: R. J. Schiffer. Ref: TV. TVG. no Maltin '92. no Stanley. no Scheuer. With Burgess Meredith, Agnes Moorehead, Larry D. Mann, Parley Baer, Skip Homeier, Kelly Thordsen, Annie McEveety, Bill Zuckert, James Lydon.

A "huge big sea monster—very like the plodiosaurus" is just a boat with a lantern—but teacher Meredith's error gives his pupils the idea of "creating" a monster. Smugglers at the "old Groggins place" then use the "monster" for their own purposes.

Flat, bland Disney kid-heroes comedy. Pre-*Jaws*, clearly: Moorehead and townsfolk worry that reports of a monster will draw tourists rather than scare them away.

A STRANGE STORY OF CREMATORY (H. K.?) Peter Pan-Lei 198-? color 95m. SP, D: P. Pan-Lei. Ref: TV: Pan-Asia Video; no Eng.

An old undertaker steals a necklace from an apparent corpse in his charge. The latter revives, scares the old man to death-by-apparent-heart-attack, then wanders off seeking revenge on both his (the "corpse's") wife and rival.... This climactic sequence is an okay, hokey horror payoff—complete with *Halloween* music and a hand-on-the-shoulder shock—to a hokey, meant-to-be-bittersweet love story. Earlier frissons include a grabbing corpse-hand and a moving coffin lid.

STRANGE TALES FROM A CHINESE STUDIO see *Chinese Ghost Story, A. Hua Pi.*

STRANGE TANGENTS Mark Chorvinsky 1983 color 24m. SP, D, SpFX: Chorvinsky. SpFX: also William Dempsey, Greg Snook. Ref: Ecran F 47:35. no Martin. With Casey Dimenico, Rick Rohan, Jim Landry.

Magicians, salamander creature, teleportation.

STRANGE TURF see *Voodoo Dawn*

3P The STRANGENESS Stellarwind (The Strangeness) 1984 color 90m. SP, D, Mus, Co-P, Co-Ed: David M. Hillman. SP, D, Mus: Chris Huntley. Ph: Kevin O'Brien, Stephen Greenfield. SpVisFX: Mark Sawicki, Huntley; (anim) Ernest D. Farino. Ref: TV: TWE video. V 10/20/82:164(ad). Martin. Stanley. Morse. With Dan Lunham, Terri Berland, Rolf Theison, Keith Hurt, M. Sawicki, Huntley.

"The evil lives!" An earthquake re-opens the long-closed, reputedly-haunted Golden Spike Mine, where a "great god" supposedly lives, and a strange wind comes from "hell"—the third and lowest level of the mine and the "home of the beast," an octopus-creature.

Of kind—the Old Dark Cave kind—*The Strangeness* is better than *The Incredible Petrified World*, but not up to *The Boogens*. Crude but fun flurries of stopmo animation are a relief from limited-talent actors. Occasionally better-than-average dialogue for low-low-budget filmmaking.

STRANGER FROM HELL (H.K.?) 1994? color feature. Ref: vc box: World Video; apparent ax murders.

The STRANGER WITHIN CBS-TV/Goodman-Rosen Prods. & New World TV (Paulette Breen) 1990 color c90m. D: Tom Holland. Tel: John Pielmeier. Mus: V. Horunzhy. Ref: TVG 11/24/90: "unsettling violence." V 12/3/90:83: "scary picture." With Rick Schroder, Kate Jackson, Chris Sarandon, Clark Sandford.

Schroder as a "spooky" psychopath who pops up on Halloween.

The STRANGERS (I) Cinema Shares Int'l./G.P.S. (Stella & Ippolito) 1980 color 85m. (*Strangers*-ad t. *Alien 2 sulla Terra*. *Alien 2*—export t). SP, D: Ciro Ippolito (aka Sam Cromwell). Ph: Silvio Fraschetti. Mus: Oliver Onions. PD: Angelo Mattei, Mario Molli. SpFX: Donald Patterly. Mkp: Lamberto Marini. Opt: Mafera. Ref: TV. Jim Shapiro. Horacio Higuchi. TVG. Stanley. Palmerini. no Phantom. no Scheuer. no Maltin '92. PT 8:5. With Belinda Mayne, Marc Bodin, Robert Barrese, Benny Aldrich, Michael Shaw, Judy Perrin, Don Parkinson, Claudio Falanga.

Living-mineral aliens from a space capsule returning to Earth take refuge in caverns in Colorado. The things like to hide in and dominate human bodies; in reality, they look like animated entrails....

*Alien*-in-a-cave. Here, the aliens jump out of as well as into bodies, but it's a long wait between jumps of any sort. The movie's one claim to a sort of fame: It features probably the first telepathic speleologist. Her psychic talents give *The Strangers* its one legitimate shock scene, at that a pretty direct borrowing from *The Crawling Eye*—"it's above your head," she warns a fellow cave-explorer as she "sees" one or more of the uglies dangling above him in the dark and about to drop.

STRANGERS IN PARADISE New West (David DuBay) 1986 (1983) colorand b&w 81m. P, Story, SP, D: Ulli Lommel. SP: also Suzanna Love. Story: also DuBay. Ph: J. V. Walther. Ref: V 10/22/86: "misfire." With Lommel, Ken Letner, Thom Jones, Geoffrey Barker.

Cryogenically-frozen mentalist thawed out by California right wingers to modify behavior of today's teens.

**STRANGERS IN THE NIGHT** Rep 1944 53m. D: Anthony Mann. SP: Bryant Ford, Paul Gangelin. Story: Philip MacDonald. Ph: Reggie Lanning. Mus D: Morton Scott. AD: Gano Chittenden. Ref: screen. W. K. Everson. "B" Movies. PFA notes 6/22/85. no V. no Lee. LC. no Cocchi. With William Terry, Virginia Grey, Helene Thimig, Edith Barrett, Anne O'Neal.

"There must be something the matter with Rosemary." You might say that—she's imaginary. Out of a commissioned portrait and her own imagination, elderly, crippled Hilda Blake (Thimig) creates a daughter for herself. She enlists her companion, Ivy (Barrett), in her lifelong campaign to sustain the public and private illusion. Hilda's greatest triumph: finding a fiance for Rosemary—Johnny Meadows (Terry), a Marine who has corresponded with and fallen for Rosemary.... Hilda herself wrote Rosemary's letters. ("You were loving *me*, Johnny.")

Or, *Psycho* crossed with *Who's Afraid of Virginia Woolf?* The plot which maneuvers Johnny and Dr. Leslie Ross (Grey) to Clifftop House in Monteflores, California, is creaky, simply functional. "That Blake menagerie"—Hilda, Ivy, and "Rosemary"—however, is another matter. *Strangers* is in the macabre-old-household tradition of Whale's *The Old Dark House*. Hilda is psychotic, domineering; Ivy is "genially neurotic" (in Everson's description), submissive. They're the visible creepy couple. Hilda-Rosemary and Johnny are the couple who aren't really there. He admired Rosemary's mind, but does not care for Hilda's, though there must be (as she notes) some overlap between herself and her fiction—just enough to be a bit disturbing.

**STRANGEST DREAMS: INVASION OF THE SPACE PREACHERS** Big Pictures 1990 color c90m. (*Strange Dreams*—orig t. *Invasion of the Space Preachers*—vt ad t). SP, D, Co-P: Daniel Boyd. Ph: Bill Hogan. Mus: Michael Lipton. PD: Steve Gilliland. Alien Costume: Shirley Studivon. ElecSpFX: Dave Payton. Ref: TV. TVG. vc box. no Maltin '92. no Scheuer. V 1/10/90:20. With Jim Wolfe, Guy Nelson, Eliska Hahn (Nova), Gary Brown (Rev. Lash), Jesse Johnson, John Riggs, John Marshall, James Piercy (alien Nova), Jimmy Walker.

"I am your hope in this world full of evil pleasures." An alien being sets up shop in West Virginia, as the "Lash of God." His goal: to create "international chaos" by beaming his "Join our army" message hypnotically, via satellite. Another alien, Nova—who sheds her protective covering and becomes an earthling—helps thwart the space preacher. ("Call me Nova.") Broad, strange comedy elicits more "Huh?"s than laughs. Nova's ship has Comfort Control, which can simulate any "body feeling."

**\*STRANGLER OF THE SWAMP** 1945 57m. Addl Dial: Harold Erickson. Remake of *Fahrmann Maria* (2P). Mus: Alexander Steinert. Mkp: Bud Westmore. Ref: screen. William K. Everson. PFA notes 6/6/86. Lee. TVG 11/3/90 (letters). Martin. no V. Stanley. Cocchi. Hound. Phantom. Hardy/HM. no Maltin '92. PT 4:10-11. With Nolan Leary.

"Old legends—strange tales—never die in the lonely swamp land.... Things are not natural" there at night since the ferryman (Charles Middleton) was unjustly accused of murder and lynched by villagers. ("The noose!") His ghost haunts the ferry and swamp, and only the offer of her life by the granddaughter (Rosemary LaPlanche) of the real murderer vanquishes the curse. ("Leave vengeance to the Almighty.")

The rope-drawn ferry in *Strangler of the Swamp*, one immediately suspects, is a Symbol, and one's suspicions are confirmed when the heroine, Maria, speaks of "going back and forth, from shore to shore," in her life. The shots of ferry passengers gliding "back and forth"—the framing cutting off the ferry bottom and giving their passages a supernatural feel—recall the shots of the "entranced" sailing ship gliding in and out of frame in Murnau's *Nosferatu*, while the ferry-landing's plowshare signal (Death calling?) recalls the scythe in Dreyer's *Vampyr*. Swamp fog here seems to have a life of its own—the characters spend most of their time literally walking around in it. Mists like this are a sort of esthetic Hamburger Helper for art directors with tiny sets. In one of the more ambitious sequences, the ghost appears "everywhere" before Maria, as she seeks help. Unfortunately, Rosemary LaPlanche overstresses her character's desperation, and dialogue and performances in *Strangler* are generally primitive.

See also: *Rimfire*.

**STRANGLER VS. STRANGLER** (Yugos.) Jugoslavija Film/Centar Film 1984 color 93m. (*Davitelj Protiv Davitelja*). SP, D: Slobodan Sijan. SP: also Nebojsa Pakic. Ph: M. Glusica. Mus: Vuk Kelenovic. Sets: V. Despotovic. Ref: V 8/22/84: "morbidly hilarious." SFFilm Fest '86. no Stanley. TVG. With Tasko Nacic, Nikoa Simic, Srdjan Saper.

Madman flower-seller ... and a "second strangler."(V)

**STRANNAYAR ISTORIYAR DOKTORA DZHEKILA I MISTERA KHAIDA** (Russ) Mosfilm 1986 color 89m. SP, D: Alexander Orlov. SP: also Georgy Kapralov. From Robert Louis Stevenson's book *The Strange Case of Dr. Jekyll and Mr. Hyde*. PD: Igor Lemeshev. Ref: V 12/2/87: "more faithful to the original book than most earlier screen adaptations, but less dramatically satisfying." Ecran F 73:70. With Innokenti Smoktunovsky (Jekyll), Alexander Feklistov (Hyde), Anatoly Adoskin, Alla Budnitskaya.

**STRANO VIZIO DELLA SIGNORA WARD, Lo** see *Next Victim, The*

**STRASEK—DER VAMPIR** (W. G.—Swiss?) Theodor Boder 1982 b&w 90m. SP, D, Ph: Boder. SP: also Ulrich G. Meyer, Adelheid Duvanel. Ref: Cinema Suisse '82. PFA library. With Oscar Olano, Beat Bangerter, Simone Haenggi, Jackie Steel.

"Strange things start happening" in a small Serbian village haunted by a "boy in a very disturbed state." (CS'82)

**STRATOS FEAR** Commonwealth/Ub Iwerks 1933 anim 7m. Ref: TV: Kino Video. Filmfax 43:22: Willie Whopper.

An alien's ray turns barnyard-ish animals into leather goods. Offbeat, but not very funny.

**STRAY DOG—KERBEROS PANZER COPS** (J) Shochiku/Emotion(Fuji TV & Omnibus) 1990 color/ws 96m. (*Jigoku No Banken: Keruber-su*). SP, D: Mamoru Oshii. Ph: Y. Mamiya. Mus: K. Kawi. Weapon FX: Big Shot. SdFX: S. Kurahashi. Ref: TV: Bandai HV; no Eng. Weisser/JC: 2nd in series. With Y. Fujiki, S. Chiba.

The near-indestructible, glowing-eyed (or goggled) warriors here are, in action, impressive, but they're in action in only one sequence, in this otherwise becalmed, elegiacal mood piece.

**STRAYS** USA-TV/MTE (Niki Marvin Prods.) 1991 color c90m. D: John McPherson. Tel, Co-P: Shaun Cassidy. Mus: Michel Colombier. PD: Mick Strawn. MkpFxArtist: Peggy Teague. SpFX: (coord) J. B. Vesay; Movie Mechanics. Artificial Animals: Jim & Debra Boulden. OptFX: Cinema Research. Ref: TV. TVG. V 12/16/91:61. With Kathleen Quinlan, Timothy Busfield, Claudia Christian, William Boyett.

Some bad cats mass in the cellar of a country house with a "certain charm—in an Amityville kind of way," and attack intruders. Then, Special Forces find baby's crib.... Routine terrorized-family saga recycles the feisty-felines idea from *Eye of the Cat, Night of the Thousand Cats*, and *The Uncanny*. Some not-bad dialogue, though. And the top cat—apparently a feral, "dominant male marking his territory"—looks pretty fierce. The rest are tabbies.

**STREET ASYLUM** Magnum Ent./Metropolis & Hit Films (W. D. Gernert) 1990 color 89m. D: Gregory Brown. SP: John Powers. Ph: P. Desatoff. Ref: V 5/9/90:62(hv): "well-made but poor-taste sci-fi thriller." ad. SFChron Dtbk 5/24/92. Sacto Bee 5/16/90. With Wings Hauser, G. Gordon Liddy, Alex Cord, Roberta Vasquez, Sy Richardson, Brion James, Lisa Marlowe.

"Control device" in detective's back unleashes "violent impulses."(V)

**STREET FIGHTERS II: THE ANIMATED MOVIE** (J) Capcom 1994 anim color c94m. Ref: vc box: "near future."

**STREET TRASH** Lightning Pictures/Chaos (Street Trash Joint Venture) 1987 (1986) color 91m. D: Jim Muro, based on his short film. SP, P: Roy Frumkes. Mus: Rick Ulfik. SpMkpFX: Jennifer Aspinall. SpSdFX: Pawel Wdowczak; (environmental) Ulfik. SpFxProps: Kenneth Brilliant. Ref: TV: Lightning Video. V 4/1/87. Maltin '92. Phantom. Newman. With Mike Lackey, Vic Noto, Bill Chepil, Mark Sferrazza, Jane Arakaw, Nicole Potter, Eddie Bay (exploding derelict), Frank Farel (dismembered derelict), Gary Rozanski (smoking derelict); John Hukushi et al (Vietcong vampires), Bobby Faust (last stage of Ed's melt), Baron (perverted Rottweiler).

"Oh, get a mop!" Hits of Viper—real, sixty-year-old rotgut—act instantly, reduce skidrow bums to remnants. Film also has a nightmare sequence re vampires in Vietnam, and a bizarre variation on Keep Away.... Obviously intended to be the answer to a gorefilm fan's prayer, *Street Trash* tries a little too hard to please. Bad taste does not seem to come as easily to the makers of this movie as it does to (for instance) the purveyors of *Bad Taste*, a comparably extreme, effortlessly disgusting movie. *Street Trash* remains more extreme than funny. The outlandish, sometimes impressive melting/exploding/oozing effects have an equally outlandish context. There's no contrast to set them off. Funniest scene: the coda—not one single effect here, just running commentary on (offscreen) melting. ("Get that ring before it gets all mixed up.")

**STREETS** Concorde/Andy Ruben (New Horizons/Roger Corman) 1990 (1989) color 83m. SP, D: Katt Shea Ruben. SP: also A.

Ruben. SpFxMkp: Scott Coulter. OptFX: Motion. Ref: TV. V 2/7/90. SFChron Dtbk 6/17/90: "Jason-in-a-uniform." Maltin '92.

Streetwise crime drama with fantastic-horrific overtones is a quickie attempt at an urban *Night of the Hunter*, as blood-happy cop Lumley (Eb Lottimer) tracks down the runaway (Christina Applegate) who got away and snuffs her friends with his homemade shotgun/flame-thrower. Basically hollow, despite many good touches—e.g., the "souls touching" scene (with the imaginary spark). The Lyricism of Violence gets to be a bit much here. Andy Ruben co-designed the shotgun.

**STREETS OF DEATH** Argosy (J.T. Linson) 1987 color feature. SP, D: Jeff Hathcock. Ref: PT 18:58: low quality. no Stanley. no Martin. With Tommy Kirk.

Two psychos make snuff videos featuring the hookers they kill.

***STREETS OF GHOST TOWN** Colbert Clark 1950. Ref: TV. V 8/16/50. TVG. no Scheuer. no Maltin '92.

"Ghosts don't tote guns!" The "ghost" of Bill Donner (George Chesebro)—who survived a prison fire—haunts the nearly-deserted streets of Shadeville—unofficially dubbed "Ghost Town"—near the town of Dusty Creek. Endwards, Donner survives a bullet or two ("You can't kill me!") and cackles crazily as he guards outlaw loot hidden in an old Spanish mine, The Devil's Cave, below Ghost Town's Mansion House.

Stock-footage flashbacks, awkward dramatics, and some atmosphere, latter provided by howling coyotes, a stray skull, noisy hotel shutters, screams, a face at a window, howling wind, and tumbleweeds. Music provided by Ozie Waters and his Colorado Rangers and by Smiley Burnette (in the Willie "That was no human—that was a ghost" Best role), who sings "Streets of a Ghost Town," to the tune of "Streets of Laredo."

**STREETS OF LAREDO, The** see *Into the Badlands*

**STREGHE, Le** see *Witch Story*

**STRIKER** see *Night Stalker, The* (1987)

**STRIP NUDE FOR YOUR KILLER** (I) Fral Spa? 1975 color/ws feature (*Nude X l'Assassino*). Story, D: Andrea Bianchi. Ph: Franco Delli Colli. Mus: Berto Pisano. Ref: TV: vt; Eng. titles. Palmerini: *Nude per l'Assassino*. With Edwige Fenech, Femi Benussi, Nino Castelnuovo, Erna Schurer.

"Unknown Psycho on the Loose" (headline). A vicious slasher stalks the Albatross photography studio. ("So monstrous!") Hokey, mechanical *giallo*.

**STRIP TEASE** (I?) Bruno Bozzetto n.d. anim short. Ref: SFChron Dtbk 7/10/88: burlesque-show audience turns into monsters.

**STRIPPED TO KILL II** Concorde/Andy Ruben-Roger Corman 1989 color c85m. (*Stripped To Kill 2: Live Girls*—alt t? aka *Live Girls: Stripped To Kill II*). SP, D: Katt Shea Ruben. Mus: Gary Stockdale. SpFxMkp: Matt Croteau, Dean Jones. SpFX: Larry Roberts. Ref: TV: MGM/UA HV. V 4/12/89. Mifed '89:181.

10/19/88:174. With Maria Ford, Eb Lottimer, Karen Mayo Chandler, Debra Lamb, Virginia Peters, Tommy Ruben, Lisa Glaser.

Paragon Club stripper Shady (Ford) has apparently premonitory nightmares re slashing razors and a mysterious dark figure. But the "vampire killer" at large turns out to be a sociopath who is semi-hypnotically programming Shady to dream about the former's murders.

Violence, sex, romance, lyricism, mysticism, comedy, and dance all meet here, in sometimes taking conjunctions, in this follow-up to *Stripped To Kill* (P). The primary effect, though, is A Little of Everything. In particular, the strip numbers slow the movie. But small surprises abound—e.g., the cop's (Lottimer) visualized daydreams re suspects. (A disbelieving in-dream "You gotta be kidding!" from one of the latter wakes him up.)

**STRIPTEASE TERROR** Channel 13 195-? b&w. Ref: Phantom.

"Strippers performing for and/or with assorted demons, monsters, and apes."

**STRIT OG STUMME** (Danish) Metronome & Dansk Tegnefilm & the Danish Film Institute (Tivi Magnusson) 1987 anim color 81m. SP, D: Jannik Hastrup. Mus: Fuzzy. Ref: V 12/2/87: "Hastrup displays technical virtuosity, wit and much poetic tenderness"; *Subway to Paradise*—tr t. Voices: Berthe Boelsgaard, Jesper Schou, Annemarie Helger.

A pollution-choked Earth regenerates into "Paradise Regained." Also: a giant snake and a "subterranean Rat Dictatorship."

**STROP, LOOK AND LISTEN** Col 1952 15m. D: Jules White. Ref: Okuda/CCS. LC. With Wally Vernon, Eddie Quillan, Fred Kelsey, Lyn Thomas, Emil Sitka.

Barbers invent flexible steel razor.

**STUCK ON YOU!** Troma/Quest 1983(1982) color 86m. D: Michael Herz, Samuel Weil. Ref: TV. V 10/5/83. TVG. no Maltin '92. Martin. Hound. no Scheuer.

Sequence with caveman (Eddie Brill) and cavewoman (Denise Silbert) ... "Twilight Zone" parody ... brief vision of woman as witch and man as monster.... Criminally unfunny comedy is an *Airplane!*-style avalanche of gags, all bad.

*The **STUDENT OF PRAGUE** 1926 119m. Ref: screen. PFA notes 9/10/87. Hardy/HM. Eisner/Haunted Screen. Scheuer. no Stanley.

1820. After the mysterious Scapinelli (Werner Krauss) offers the student Baldwin (Conrad Veidt) 600,000 gold guldens for "whatever he likes," Baldwin's reflection—his "second self"—steps out of a mirror and becomes his conscience. At the end, the double taunts him into shooting him: The double disappears; Baldwin dies, a bullet wound in his chest.

A tour de force of the more extravagant emotions—reckless abandon, horror, fear, regret—for Veidt. And a good payoff: the showdown between Baldwin and his double. But this second version of *The Student of Prague* is a basically conventional tale of aspiration and degradation. And powerful emotion is generally conveyed with heaving chests. At one point—in one of the movie's occasional bold images—Scapinelli's huge shadow on a wall suggests his evil influence on the characters' actions.

**The STUFF** New World/Larco (Paul Kurta/Peter Sabiston) 1985 color 87m. SP, D: Larry Cohen. SpVisFX: David Allen, David Stipes, Dream Quest Images, Jim Danforth et al. MechMkpFX: Steve Neill et al. Jingles: Richard Seaman. SdFX: Access Sound Shop. Mus: Anthony Guefen. Ref: TV. MFB'86:120-1. V 8/28/85. Phantom. Hound. Scheuer. Morse. Newman. Stanley. With Michael Moriarty, Andrea Marcovicci, Garrett Morris, Paul Sorvino, Danny Aiello, Patrick O'Neal, Alexander Scourby, Harry Bellaver, Rutanya Alda, Brooke Adams, Laurene Landon, Tammy Grimes, Abe Vigoda, Clara Peller.

"It moves around all by itself." Stader, Virginia, citizens have become "Stuffies"—shells with Stuff (the "product of tomorrow") for innards—and Stuff assembly lines in Georgia have a sort of gooey ominousness. The source of this "new order of life": a lava pool. Ultimately, The Taste, supposedly-diluted Stuff, hits the market.

The horrors-of-conformism overtones of the billboards and TV commercials here suggest *They Live,* and for a while Cohen's semi-straight approach to an absurd menace works. The movie plays like a traditional, stirring monster movie. Then, glib political satire and routine battle-the-Stuffies scenes take over. And The Stuff itself is a little too versatile. It can move around all by itself, take over minds, and hide in and animate bodies. Moriarty's deadpan helps.

**STURMTRUPPEN** (I-F) Irrigazione & Les Film Jacques Leitienne (Achille Manzotti) 1977 color feature. D: S. Samperi. From the comic strip. Ph: Giuseppe Rotunno. Mus: Enzo Jannacci. Ref: Jones. V 5/11/77:232(ad), 226: "hilarious farce"; *Storm Troopers*—tr t. With Renato Pozzetto, Lino Toffolo, Corinne Clery.

"Sequence in a hospital room with a vampire and the Frankenstein monster."(J)

**SUBSPECIES** (U.S.-Rom.) Full Moon (Ion Ionescu) 1991 (1990) color 84m. D: Ted Nicolaou. SP: Jackson Barr, David Pabian. Idea & Exec P: Charles Band. Mus: Richard Kosinski et al. Puppet VisFX: David Allen. SpMkpFX: Greg Cannom. MechSup: Mark A. Rappaport. Opt: Mercer, OptFX Ltd. Ref: TV. V 10/14/91:A-96(hv). Cable Video Store 10/91. With Michael Watson, Laura Tate, Anders Hove (Radu), Michelle McBride, Ivan J. Rado, Angus Scrimm.

"They've come to awaken the devil." In a prologue, the self-severed fingers of Radu, a vampire, transform into tiny monsters. In the story proper, Stefan (Watson), the good vampire, Radu, his bad half-brother, and his little "subspecies" critters haunt Castle Vladislav, Transylvania.

Slim horror tale features some okay play with Radu's *Nosferatu* (1922)-inspired, elongated fingers, shadow effects re same, and the stopmo critters. Key line: "Stay away from the ruins!" Only real novelty: Script posits that, in the historic past, vampires were heroes and saved the country from invasion.

Sequels: *Bloodlust* (1993). *Bloodstone.*

**SUBURBAN COMMANDO** New Line/Howard Gottfried (Hogan-Moreton-Moore) 1991 color 90m. D: Burt Kennedy. SP: Frank Cappello. SpVisFX: PMP. Mech FX: B&B. Creature FX: Steve Johnson's XFX. Ref: V 10/14/91: "stupid sci-fi spoof."

ad. With Hulk Hogan, Christopher Lloyd, Shelley Duvall, Larry Miller, Jack Elam, Roy Dotrice, Christopher Neame.

Intergalactic warrior (Hogan).

**SUCCUBARE** (H.K.?) Headliner 1981-U.S. color/ws c88m. (aka *The Incredible Fantastic Succubare. Magic of Shaolin Sorceress. Poison Princesses of Cheong Valley* - alt vt ts). Ref: TV: vt; Eng. dubbed. no Phantom. no Hound. PT 2:10. 4:39: music from *Exorcist II.* VSOM. With Carter Wong.

Just over the northwest Chinese border, four princesses rule and put snake spells on their lovers when the latter depart: "Just like in a ghost story," they die if they do not return to the kingdom. Our princess sics the "king of poison" centipede on an unruly drunk; another victim of the curse bites a woman's neck, then develops a swollen stomach. Cut open, the latter yields a swarm of poisonous creatures.... Worthless, sensationalistic horror-fantasy features irrelevant inserts of a man apparently eating live frogs and lizards, plus narration which suggests that this kingdom really exists.

**SUCKLING, The** see *Sewage Baby*

**SUDDEN DEATH** see *2020: Texas Gladiators*

**SUICIDE CLUB, The** see *Trouble for Two*

**2P SUICIDE CULT** 21st Century/Napolis Hoose Films (Mark Buntzman) 1980 (1977) color 78m. D: Jim Glickenhouse. From a novel by John Cameron. OptFX: EFK? Mkp: Deitch. Ref: TV: Continental Video. Mo. Stanley. Boxo 2/4/80. V 5/7/80:286: released.

"So Kate has the same zodiacal potential as the Virgin Mary." Way-off-the-wall pseudo-science-fantasy begins "ten days before the Second Coming," and concerns astrologist Alexei Abarnel's (Bob Byrd) Interzod, an institute which determines the "zodiacal potential" of humans. And, indeed, his wife Kate (Monica Tidwell) did give virgin birth when she was sixteen. Alexei is happy, at the end, when he learns this; viewer's reaction may be more mixed.

**SUIITO HOMU** see *Sweet Home*

**SUKEBAN DEKA** (J) 1987 color/ws 92m. D: Hideo Tanaka. Mus: I. Shinta. Ref: TV: VSOM; Eng. titles; *Delinquent Girl Detectives* - tr t. With Yoko Minamino, A. Yoshizawa, Yui Asaka.

"Give her the operation. She's very dangerous." The principal of Sankou Gakuen, the school/prison/lab of the appropriately named Hell Island, proves to be an android. ("I can't die.") Meanwhile, the students are "becoming like zombies," thanks, it's suggested (by the telltale sutures in one victim's skull), to brain surgery.... Wry weapons (the heroine's super Yo-Yo, her friend's assault marbles), routine action. The production has the noise and breathlessness of either overkill or parody. The third film in this series gets into black magic....

**SUMMER WITH GHOSTS** see *Discarnates, The*

**SUNDOWN: THE VAMPIRE IN RETREAT** Vestron (Jef Richard/Dan Ireland) 1990 (1989) color 104m. SP, D: Anthony

Hickox. Story, SP: John Burgess. Mus: Richard Stone. SpMkpFX: Tony Gardner, Larry Hamlin. Bat & SpVisFX: Anthony Doublin. SpFX: (coord) Brian Veatch; The Physical FX Group. AnimSpFX: Modern Moving Images. SpProps: Don Swasey. Opt: Howard Anderson, Robert Bailey. Ref: TV. V 2/7/90. Bill Warren. With David Carradine, Jim Metzler, Morgan Brittany, Maxwell Caulfield, M. Emmet Walsh, Deborah Foreman, Bruce Campbell (Van Helsing), John Ireland, Dabbs Greer, Bert Remsen, George "Buck" Flower.

Count Mardulak aka Dracula (Carradine)—"I am the greatest of our kind!"—establishes the "vampires' brave new world" out West, in Purgatory. With "fake blood from a synthesizing plant" for food, this town of "domesticated" vampires hopes to coexist with regular humans. But renegade vampires thirsting for human blood threaten to sabotage the enterprise.... Ungainly Western-horror-comedy epic has stray hits, more frequent misses. Compare Nightbreed and its monster preserve. Campbell plays the original Van Helsing's great grandson.

**The SUNSHINE MAKERS** RKO/Van Beuren (Borden's) 1935 anim color 8m. D: Burt Gillett, Ted Eshbaugh. Ref: TV. LC. Maltin/OMAM. no Lee.

Through a process of magnification and purification, the "makers" bottle sunshine, use it against top-hatted meanies and their spray-gun smog. Amusing silliness with songs.

**SUO MING** see *Spirit of the Raped*

**SUPER** (W.G.) Winkelmanns Filmproduktion & Syndikat "L" & C&H Film & BB Film & WDR 1985 (1983) color 101m. SP, D: Adolf Winkelmann. SP: also Jost Krueger, Gerd Weiss. Mus: Udo Lindenberg, Dave King. Ref: Dr. Rolf Giesen. V 5/22/85: "leans heavily on science fiction." PFA notes 1/4/85: "postapocalyptic future." Ecran F 62:68. With Renan Demirkan, U. Lindenberg, Inga Humpe.

"Futuristic setting ... in an industrial wasteland...."(V)

**SUPER BEAST-GOD DANCOUGAR** (J) Bandai 1989 anim color 30m. Ref: Animag 9:5: follow-up to *Dancougar* (which see); OAV?

**SUPER COP** see *Super Policia Ochoochenta* (880)

**SUPER DEFORMED GUNDAM** see *S. D. Gundam*

**SUPER DEFORMED GUNDAM 2** see *S. D. Gundam MK-II*

**SUPER DIMENSIONAL FORTRESS MACROSS II** see *Macross II: Lovers Again*

**SUPER FORCE** Viacom First Run-TV & Premiere-TV (Michael Attanasio) 1990 color c90m. D: Richard Compton. Tel: Janis Hendler, Larry Brody. Created by James J. McNamara. Ph: Michael McGowan. Mus: Kevin Kiner. PD: Peter Politanoff. MechFX & SpProps: Robert Short. VisFxDes: Randy Tede. SpFxCoord: J. B. Jones. Mkp: Julie Parker. Ref: TV. TVG(ad): "world premiere movie." no Scheuer. SFChron Dtbk 10/17/93. With Ken Olandt, Patrick Macnee, Marshall Teague, Larry B. Scott, Lisa Niemi, G. Gordon Liddy.

A Mars-seasoned ex-astronaut (Olandt) becomes a one-man army against crime in the year 2020. Laughably thin, forced sf-actioner, with tacky space effects.

**SUPER GAL** see *Supergal, The*

**SUPER INDAY AND THE GOLDEN BIBE** (Fili) Regal Films 1988 color c100m. Story, D: Luciano B. Carlos. Story, SP: J. J. Reyes. Ph: G. Buenaseda. Mus D: Jaime Fabregas. PD: Robert Lee. VisFX: Cine Magic. SpFX: Danny Rojo. Mkp Des: James Cooper. SdFX: Rodel Capule. Ref: TV: Regal Video; no Eng. With M. Soriano, Eric Quizon, Aiza, J. Gibbs.

A scorpion-bat-witch-from-space unleashes upon Earth a startlingly variegated bevy of monsters, including a human-sized lizard creature, big dinosaur, lobster, and alien types, and a gigantic spider, which looks like stopmo-animated pipe cleaners. Meanwhile, Inday eats the egg of a Tagalog-talking duck from heaven, becomes Super Inday (who can fly standing up), and uses rays to make the spider disintegrate.... Kooky, cute musical-comedy-fantasy has some of the balminess of *Inframan.* Highlight: Daring photographers get carried away, figuratively and literally, while taking pictures of the monsters.

**SUPER ISLAW AND THE FLYING KIDS** (Fili) Regal Films (Lily Monteverde) 1985 color c120m. Story, D: J. Erasatheo Navoa. SP: Jose Carreon. Ph: Dauz. Mus: Willy Cruz; (lyr) Joey De Leon. PD: Peter Perlas? Ref: TV: Regal Video; no Eng. With Richard Gomez (Super Islaw), Janice de Belen, George Estregan, Nadia Montenegro, Kristina Paner, Dranreb Belleza, Anjo Yllana, Jaime Fabregas.

An incantation over a magic wishbone-thing turns Islaw into flying, caped Super Islaw, who is super-strong and impervious to bullets. He and a telekinetic girl join forces to vanquish a horde of ray-resurrected zombies. At one point, he shoots a spider-web rope that ties down a batch of zombies. Later, the three flying "kids" join him.... Silly and very long comic mixing of superhero and horror genres. Occasional cute scenes—e.g., the psychic girl's dance number, in the kitchen, with cucumbers, red peppers, pots, pans, etc., partnering her.

**SUPER LADY COP** (H.K.) 1992 color feature. D: Yuen Chun Man. Ref: Weisser/ATC: futuristic. With Cynthia Khan, Alex Man.

"Cyborg cop."

**SUPER MARIO BROS** . BV/Hollywood Pictures/Lightmotive & Allied Filmmakers & Cinergi (Jake Eberts, Roland Joffe) 1993 color 104m. D: Rocky Morton, Annabel Jankel. SP: Parker Bennett, Terry Runte, Ed Solomon. Based on the Nintendo game and characters created by Miyamoto & Tezuka. Ph: Dean Semler. Mus: Alan Silvestri. PD: D. L. Snyder. SpVisFX: C. F. Woods. SpFxCoord: Paul Lombardi. Ref: V 6/7/93: "wildly overproduced and derivative." EBay Express 6/4/93: "kind of fun—in spots." SFChron 5/29/93: "gets a lot of mileage out of its charming cast." ad. With Bob Hoskins, John Leguizamo, Dennis Hopper, Samantha Mathis, Fisher Stevens, Lance Henriksen.

Parallel world created by meteorite.

**SUPER NORMAL** (H.K.) Mandarin Films (Edward Li) 1992 color/ws 89m. D: Lo Ting Kit. Ph: Laurie F. Gilbert. Mus: Tai Lok Man. AD: H. A. Ganni. Mkp: Shiu Kin On. SdFX: Ng Kok Wah. Ref: TV: Tai Seng Video; Eng. titles. With E. Li, Joyce Ngai, Helen Ho.

Haphazard, tepid semi-documentary includes a "dramatized" sequence set in the bathroom of the "haunted house" on High Street, where a ghostly voice, mysteriously opening and closing doors, and flushing noises frighten a woman. Also on the agenda: an apartment building haunted by fox goblins, a man who "sees more fairies than people," a clip from a ghost movie, a "haunted" passage which leads to a ghost-dog's grave, exorcism-over-the-phone, ghost photos, and Sister Seven, who sees several ghosts.

**EL SUPER POLICIA OCHOOCHENTA (880)** (Mex) Int'l. Films/J.A.G. Perez 1982 color c85m. (aka *Super Cop. El Super Policia 880*—ad t). D: Pedro Galindo III. SP: Carlos Valdemar, Perez. Ph: Leon Sanchez. Mus: G. C. Carrion. OptFX: Antonio Munoz. Mkp: Aurora Chavira. Ref: TV: Condor Video; no Eng. no Hardy/SF. TVG: 1984. With "Resortes," "El Comanche," Victor Alcocer, Tere Alvarez, Melchor Moran, "Pompin"Iglesias III, Ruben Benavides (Grand Master).

Helmeted Martians help a tap-dancing cop, Romeo (Resortes), catch bank robbers, and send a double of a woman, Andrea (Alvarez), from their spaceship to Earth to assist him. Romeo finds that he can read minds. Meanwhile, a professor's "ray machine" turns out to be a bomb.... The tap dancing is better than the comedy. One or two inexpensive space effects.

**SUPER SONIC SOLDIER BORGMAN 2—NEW CENTURY 2058** (J) Toho Video/Taki & Ashi 1993 anim color 30m. each (*Borg Get on!* - alt t). SP, D: Y. Murayama. Mecha Des: T. Yamada. Ref: TV: Toho Video; no Eng. Animerica 5:12: 3 OAVs planned.

*Robocop*-type cyborgs, the Borgmen, vs. the Youma Machine Beasts. Sequel to *Borgman, The. Vol. 1: The Endless City:* A mysterious gentleman unleashes hordes of cat-rat critters, a fantastic leaping cat creature which shoots rays, and three rats that mutate into one three-headed rat critter. He also employs horror crows and snakes and a tentacled treat.... Standard but stylish mixture of action and gore, set in the year 2058.

**SUPER SOUL BROTHER** Xenon 1978 color feature (aka *The Six Thousand Dollar Nigger*). SP, D, Ed: Rene Martinez. SP: also Laura S. Diaz. Ref: PT 13:13: "grainy looking comedy." 14:5. no Martin. With Wildman Steve.

Dr. Zippy's serum renders wino bulletproof.

**SUPER WAN*TU*TRI** (Fili) Regal Films (Lily Monteverde) c1981? color c104m. D: Luciano B. Carlos; (assoc) S. B. Jose. SP: J. J. Reyes, L. B. Carlos. Idea & OptSup: Carlos Lacap. Ph: G. Buenaseda. Mus D: T. Sotto, H. Flores. PD: Dennis Cid. VisFX: Cinevideo Artists. Prosth: Nita Manahan. FxAnim: Manny Buencamino. SdFX: Demet Velasquez. Supermen & Spacemen Costumes: Lito Perez. Ref: TV: Century Exchange video; little Eng. With Tito, Vic & Joey; Janice De Belen, Aga Muhlach, Lani Mercado, Kristoffer Ian De Leon, Ramil Rodriguez, Jimmy Fabregas, Debraliz, Jimmy Santos, Val Sotto.

"I believe that there are living creatures on other planets." A baby sent to Earth by his alien parents grows, overnight, to be a boy with super-strength, super-breath, X-ray eyes, and flying abilities. He gives his three human godfathers stones which, when swallowed, turn them into caped superheroes—complete with the Superman "S" on their shirts. "Super Wan*Tu*Tri" then fight three evil aliens who can turn people into pigs or freeze them with their special lightning.

Lively if silly takeoff on the "Superman" story features the "Superman" movies musical theme. Funny moments include the implementation of a giant baby bottle to feed the voracious infant and the blowing-out of the candle on the super-lad's birthday cake. (He blows both cake and frosting all over the guests.)

Los **SUPERAGENTES BIONICOS** (Arg.) Cinematografica Sud-Americana (Emilio Spitz) 1977 color 90m. D: Mario Sabado (aka A. Quiroga). SP?: Carlos Faruolo. Ph: Leonardo Rodriguez Solis. Mus: Victor Proncet. Mkp: Maria Lassaga. Ref: Cine Argentino '77 (Ediciones Metrocop, B. Aires). With Ricardo Bauleo, Victor Bo, Julio de Grazia, Maria Noel.

Implanted mini-reactors give "superagentes" advantage. One of a series.

**SUPERBABY** see *Return of Superbug, The*

**SUPERBUG** (W.G.) Barbara Film 1973 color 95m. (*Ein Kaefer auf Extratour*). SP, D, P: Rudolf Zehetgruber. Ph: R. Meichsner. Mus: Peter Weiner. AD: Hauptner-Jonstorff? SpFX: Richtsfels; Ivan Frehner. Mkp: L. Valicek. Ref: TV. Hardy/SF: *A Beetle in Overdrive*—tr t. TVG. With Zehetgruber (aka R. Mark), Sal Borgese, Kathrin Oginski, Walter Giller, Carl Mohner, The Hell Drivers, Walter Roderer, Evelyn Kraft, Ruth Jecklin, Franz Muxeneder, Walter Nowak.

Futuristic wind-up car is a mixture of "science, good luck, and voodoo," and has remote-control steering. At the end, there's a "baby" VW. Sloppy, silly comedy. Third in the series. English-dubbed.

**3P SUPERBUG, SUPER AGENT** (W.G.-Swiss) Barbara Film & Coordinator Film 1972 color 91m. (*Ein Kaefer Gibt Vollgas*). SP, D, P: Rudolf Zehetgruber. Ref: Hardy/SF: "total lack of interest"; *A Beetle Goes Flat Out*—tr t of German title. TVG. V 9/21/83:103(ad). With Joachim Fuchsberger, Robert Mark (aka R. Zehetgruber), Kathrin Oginski, Heinz Reincke, Heidi Hansen.

Dudu "programmed as a crime fighter." (H/SF). Second in the "Superbug" series.

**SUPERBUG, THE WILD ONE** (W.G.-Tanz.) Cine Int'l./Barbara Film & Tanzania Tourist Corp.-Hallmark Hotels 1971 color 91m. (*Ein Kaefer Geht aufs Ganze*). D, Exec P: Rudolf Zehetgruber (aka David Mark). SP: Alexander de Callier. Ph: A. Posch. Mus: Hans Hammerschmied, Roman Kwiatkowski. SpFX: Christian Harman. Mkp: Ellen Just, G. Pitter. Ref: TV: Eng. version. Hardy/SF. TVG. With Richard Lynn, Jim Brown, Gerd Duwner, K. Oginski, Lex County, Bob Mackay, Constanze Sieck, Fatimah, Harry Fuss, Surender Singh, Bob Dean, Grete Elb.

Tanzania. Dudu, the "little love bug," or "tin can," takes part in the East Africa Rally. (" 'Dudu' is Swahili and means something

like 'love bug'.") Hollow dubbing, flat comedy. Most interesting character is minor horror-movie actor, Dr. Hyenamous (sp?), who looks like Raymond Massey's Jonathan Brewster. Beautiful scenery, but the TV print's color is pretty muddy, in this first of the "Superbug" series.

See also: *Return of Superbug. Superbug. Superbug, Super Agent. Superwheels.*

**SUPERDANDY** (I) 1979 color feature (*Il Fratello Brutto di Superman*). D: P. Bianchini. Ref: Palmerini: "parody of *Superman* (1978)."

**SUPERFANTOZZI** (I) Scena & Reteitalia (Augusto Caminito) 1986 color 85m. D: Neri Parenti. SP: Leo Benvenuti et al. Ref: V 1/7/87: "jumpy and uneven." Palmerini: "from prehistory to the future."

One of several skits is set in the 21st Century.

The **SUPERGAL** (J) CPM/Kitty/Shogakukan & Takahashi 1986?('92-U.S.) anim color 48m. (aka *Super Gal. Za Chojo. Maris the Chojin*-alt t. *Rumic World series*). SP, D: Tomoko Konparu. D: also K. Katayama. Story: Rumiko Takahashi. SP: also H. Takahashi. AD: T. Arai. Ref: TV: Shogakukan Video; no Eng. Paul Lane. J Anim Guide: OAV. RSI brochure. Voices: Sumi Shimamoto, Mami Koyama.

Space ace Supergal, who comes from a planet which self-destructed, doesn't know her own strength. She keeps putting her feet through the floors of spaceships and has a knack for wrecking furniture. Her many-tailed fox co-pilot can split its personality and do several impersonations at once of any other character.... Generally silly blend of comedy and knockabout violence. Some cute bits, but the story has little basic appeal.

**SUPERGIRL** (B) Tri-Star/Cantharus (Artistry Ltd./Timothy Burrill/Ilya Salkind) 1984 color/ws 114m. D: Jeannot Szwarc. SP: David Odell, based on the comic-strip character. Mus: Jerry Goldsmith. VisFX: (sp) Derek Meddings; (opt) Roy Field. SpFxSup: John Evans. Flying FX: Bob Harman. Ref: TV. V 7/18/84. TVG. With Helen Slater, Faye Dunaway, Peter O'Toole, Peter Cook, Brenda Vaccaro, Mia Farrow, Simon Ward, Marc McClure, Hart Bochner.

Supergirl (Slater), aka Kara, aka Linda Lee—Superman's cousin from a city in inner space—uses her X-ray eyes, super-hearing, and super-breath against the witch Selena (Dunaway), whose (borrowed) Omegahedron gives her telekinetic powers.... The idea here—amusing at times—seems to be to make each sequence ten times more elaborate than necessary. This esthetic of overkill works best perhaps in the sequence in which Kara retrieves some lightning in a post and electrifies Selena's cyclonic shadow away. The compressed-serial effect crowds out story, character, and comedy, though Slater's willowy quality is given a chance to suggest the ethereal.

The **SUPERGRASS** (B) The Comic Strip/Recorded Releasing (FFI/Michael White) 1985 color feature. SP, D: Peter Richardson. SP: also Pete Richens. From "The Comic Strip Presents ..." TV series. Ref: Jones. Martin. Hound. V 10/16/85:352. With Adrian Edmondson, P. Richardson.

"Vampiric police inspector" (Ronald Allen) bit. (J)

**SUPERMAN IV: THE QUEST FOR PEACE** WB/Cannon (Kagan-Easton) 1987 color 93m. D: Sidney J. Furie. Story, SP: Lawrence Kohner, Mark Rosenthal. Story: also Christopher Reeve. Based on the characters created by Siegel and Schuster. Mus: John Williams; Paul Fishman. VisFX: Olsen, Lane & White; (anim sup) Michael Lessa. SpFXSup: Harrison Ellenshaw, John Evans. Wire FX: Bob Harman. ModelFxSup: Richard Conway. MkpSup: Stuart Freeborn. Ref: TV. MFB'87:283-4. V 7/29/87. ad. With Christopher Reeve, Gene Hackman, Jackie Cooper, Marc McClure, Jon Cryer, Sam Wanamaker, Mark Pillow (2nd Nuclear Man), Mariel Hemingway, Margot Kidder, Clive Mantle (1st Nuclear Man), Edmond Knight, Robert Beatty, William Hootkins, Susannah York (voice of Superman's mother).

While Superman (Reeve) rids the world of "all nuclear weapons," by flinging them into the sun, Lex Luthor (Hackman) is plotting to "recreate life itself," with a super-evil being "born from the sun" and more powerful than Superman. His Nuclear Man (with "internally generated heat") tears down the Great Wall of China. Superman restores the latter, and also plugs volcanic Mount Etna with the top of a neighboring mountain. Ultimately, he pushes the moon between the sun and the Earth and thus causes an eclipse which cuts off Nuclear Man's power.

Lively series entry, with some Superman/Clark Kent quick-change fun. Effects work, however, swamps the human element, and a meandering plot blunts the Life Wish theme responsible for the first-half highlight: the Superman-supervised end of the arms race. For him, it's the work of a few minutes.

See also the following and *Binibining Tsuper-man. Captain Yagit. Fly Me to the* Moon. *Hot Shots! Lois & Clark. Project "A" Ko. Saviour of the Soul II. Sogni Monstruo-samente Proibiti. Super Wan*tu*tri. Supergirl. Superdandy. Timefighters in the Land of Fantasy. Unforgettable Fantasy.*

**SUPERMAN AND SCOTLAND YARD** Ellsworth c1954 feature. Ref: Lentz: from the "Superman" TV series. Other titles of improvised features: *Superman in Exile* and *Superman's Peril.*

**\*SUPERMAN AND THE MOLE MEN** Barney Sarecky 1951 67m. SP, Co-P: Robert Maxwell (aka R. Fielding). Mus: Darrell Calker. SpFX: Danny Hayes. Mkp: Harry Thomas. Ref: TV. Warren/KWTS! V 7/8/87:30. Lentz. Hardy/SF. Lee. Maltin '92. Phantom. Cocchi. Hound. Martin. Scheuer. Stanley. With Billy Curtis, Byron Foulger, Margia Dean, Beverly Washburn, Frank Reicher.

Silsby, "home of the world's deepest oil well." The National Oil Company's Havenhurst Experimental No. 1 well—32,740-feet deep—reaches to the center of the Earth, which is found to be hollow and inhabited by "more highly developed forms of life." Two innocuous-looking little mole men climb up the well and frighten a watchman to death, but—as Superman (George Reeves) shows—only a "hairy covering" and a "large head" separate mole man from human.

A *Fury* for science fiction. Unfortunately, the mob psychology here is simplistic, and, although the movie is more enlightened in its approach to the unknown than most sf movies of its era, it's also stilted and one-dimensional.

**SUPERMOUSE AND THE ROBO-RATS** (Fili) Mother Studio 1988? color c102m. SP, D: Tony Y. Reyes. SP: also Joey De Leon. Ph: Accion, Querijero. Mus: Mon Del Rosario. PD: Melchor Defensor. SpFX: Freddie Fajardo. Mkp: Malou Talplacido. SdFX: Rodel Capule. Ref: TV: Regal Video; little Eng. With De Leon, Rene Requiestas, Ruel Vernal (Roborat), Manilyn Reynes, Smokey Manoloto, Carmina Villaroel.

After an hour or so of running time, the hero, Mickey (De Leon), gets angry and transforms into the flying, big-eared SuperMouse, whose cape deflects bullets. He sings and dances (to "Raindrops Keep Fallin' on My Head") with two cartoon mice, then chases after aliens who have abducted earthlings. Aboard the former's spaceship, he learns that he is the son of a human woman and an alien rodent-creature. The aliens' armorer was apparently also Darth Vader's. Flimsy sf/superhero-comedy.

**\*SUPERNATURAL** 1933 65m. SP: H. Thew, B. Marlow. AD: Hans Dreier? Ref: TV. Lentz. Lee. V 4/25/33. Weldon. Stanley. Eames/TPS.

"I am Ruth Rogen!" Through metempsychosis-like spiritual "contagion"—and Dr. Houston's (H.B. Warner) experiments with "mitrogenic [sp?] rays ... ultraviolet rays given off by the body"—the executed Ruth Rogen (Vivienne Osborne)—"one of the most dangerous women in criminal history"—takes temporary spiritual possession of the body of socialite Roma Courtney (Carole Lombard). The ham-handed, predictable handling of the payoff possession scenes here is the worst of it. More interesting: Earlier, the script plays off the machinations of a fake spiritualist, Paul Bavian (Alan Dinehart), against the manifestations of a real spirit, Ruth Rogen, whose presence is creepily indicated by a sudden icy indoor wind. The spirit of Roma's dead twin brother, John (Lyman Williams), also turns up, twice. The film begins, somewhat pretentiously, with quotes from Confucius, Mohammed, and Matthew.

**The SUPERNATURALS** Samuel Goldwyn/Republic Ent. Int'l. (Southern Woods/Sandy Howard) 1986 (1985) color 80m. D: Armand Mastroianni. SP, P: Michael S. Murphey, Joel Soisson. Mus: Robert O. Ragland. SpFxCoord: Gregory Landerer. Ghost FX: Mark Shostrom, Bart Mixon et al. SpCostumes: Lisa Jensen. Opt: Quick Silver FX, Motion. Ref: TV. V 5/14/86. Maltin '92. Phantom. Hound. Morse. Newman. Scheuer. Stanley. With Maxwell Caulfield, Nichelle Nichols, LeVar Burton, Scott Jacoby, Bobby Di Cicco, Patrick Davis (old man).

"There's nothin' growin' here at all!" On maneuvers near Blakeley, Alabama, the 44th Division from Fort Benning encounters the ghosts of Confederate soldiers—and the monotonously mysterious Melanie (Margaret Shendal), whose son Jeremy (Chad Sheets) brought her back to life supernaturally after she stepped on a Yankee mine in 1865.... Undistinguished Gothic Southern with limp dialogue scenes and a thin plot. Eerie bit: the "outward"-blowing wind.

**SUPERNOVA** (Sp) Aligator (sic) Films 1992 color feature. D: Juan Minon. Ref: V 9/28/92:54: "sci-fi musical comedy; ready." With Marta Sanchez, Javier Gurruchaga, Gabino Diego.

**SUPERSIMIAN** see *Lost on Adventure Island*

**SUPERSPACE FORTRESS MACROSS** see *Macross Movie, The*

**SUPERWHEELS** (W.G.) Barbara Film (K. W. Nowak) 1974 color 93m. (*Das Verrueckteste Auto der Welt*). D: Rudolf Zehetgruber. SP: Gregor von Nazzani. Ph: R. Meichsner. Mus: Gerhard Heinz. Sets: Claudia Julius. SpFX: Hans Fuchs, Gary Parello, Norbert Tauchert et al. Anim: Erica Deimbacher. Mkp: Ellen Just. Ref: TV: Eng. version. TVG. Dr. Rolf Giesen. Hardy/SF: *The Maddest Car in the World*—tr t. no Maltin '92. Stanley. no Scheuer. With Zehetgruber (aka R. Mark), Sal Borgese, Evelyn Kraft, Kathrin Oginski, Walter Giller, Walter Roderer, Ruth Jecklin, Ullrich Beiger, P. W. Staub, Marion Winter, Gerhard Frickhoefer, Walter Feuchtenberg.

Superbug—the "craziest car in the world," at the "goofiest rally in the world"—comes equipped with a "complete computer system," featuring "seventeen different programs." Superbug can talk, sing, drive itself, and move sideways. Plus: "Whirly," a tiny, automatic helicopter-scout.... Silly if lively, with a gimmick-a-minute pace. Fourth in the "Superbug" series.

**SUR LA TERRE COMME AU CIEL** (Belgian) Man's Films (Eric van Beuren) 1992 color 80m. SP, D, P: Marion Haensel. SP: also Paul Le, Jaco van Dormael, L. van Keerbergen. Mus: Takashi Kako. FX: Jacques Gastineau. Ref: V 2/17/92: *On Earth As It Is in Heaven*—tr t. With Carmen Maura, Didier Bezace, Jean-Pierre Cassel, Andre Delvaux.

"Sci-fi element" re fetuses that don't want to be born, in a film which "starts off promisingly enough but descends into talkiness and loses credibility."

**SURE-LOCKED HOMES** see *Felix the Cat in Sure-Locked Homes*

**SURF NAZIS MUST DIE** Troma/The Institute (Robert Tinnell) 1987 (1986) color 80m. Story, D, Exec P: Peter George. Story, SP: Jon Ayre. Mus & MkpFX: Jon McCallum. Ref: TV. V 5/20/87. SFChron 2/16/88. Morse. Newman. Scheuer. With Barry Brenner, Gail Neely, Michael Sonye, Dawn Wildsmith, Bobbie Bresee.

"Sometime in the near future." Anarchy reigns in a Los Angeles devastated by an earthquake, but a lone woman (Neely) takes on a certain Adolf (Brenner), leader of the nasty Surf Nazis, and.... ("I am the fuehrer of this new beach!) Thin-to-none script tries to be far-out, but this is no *Roller Blade*. Best epithet: "Slime-sucking Neanderthal!"

**SURF II** Braunstein/Hamady (Frank D. Tolin) 1984 (1983) color 86m. SP, D: Randall Badat. Mus: Peter Bernstein. SpFX: Jim Doyle. SpMkpFX: Greg Cannom, Jill Rockow. SdFX: J's Fine Art. Ref: TV. TVG. V 1/25/84. Stanley. With Eddie Deezen, Linda Kerridge, Cleavon Little, Eric Stoltz, Jeffrey Rogers, Lyle Waggoner, Lucinda Dooling, Morgan Paull, Carol Wayne, Ron Palillo, Ruth Buzzi.

Mad Menlo Schwartzer (Deezen)—victim of cola spiked with a reverse-sex hormone, and now out to "rule the coast" (of California)—uses Buzzz Cola ("untreated petroleum waste") to turn "punk surfers" into an "army of gas-guzzling junkies," or zombies "worse than dead—cancelled," who drink motor oil and antifreeze and eat anything (including celluloid).

Slapdash, but sporadically funny gross-out comedy is closer to *Animal House* than to *Horror of Party Beach* or *Beach Girls and the Monster*. Comic morgue scenes go back as far as *Doctor X* (1932) and *The Body Disappears* (1941), but *Surf II* has, probably, the best of the lot, for what it's worth. Enough offhand-silly invention for a rather shorter feature.

**SURVIVAL 1990** (Can.) Emmeritus & CHCH-TV 1984 color c80m.? (aka *Survival Earth*). Tel, D, P: Peter McCubbin. Tel: also Craig Williams, Gina Mandelli. Ph: Skip Haybarger. Mus: Tanos. SpFX: Greg Bolak. Title Des: David Nisbet. Mkp: Connie Brutto; (des) Yvonne Bussin. Ref: TV. TVG. no Scheuer. no Maltin '92. Stanley. no Phantom. Morse. With Jeff Holec, Nancy Cser, C. Williams, Peter Ferri, Chris Williams.

Miranda (Cser) and John (Holec) "after the fall" and "miles from nowhere," as post-holocaust folks are "killing and eating each other." He: "I can remember when people used to mow their lawns." She: "You make me sick!" Later, John and a stranger reminisce re beer. Miranda, meanwhile, turns out to be a "mutant," exposed to radiation.... Limp drama is primarily a gabfest for the three principals. Vapid, shot-on-tape look and sound, flat acting.

**SURVIVAL OF A DRAGON** (H.K.?) Joseph Lai/Squall Hung & Lim Man Yu 198-? color/ws c90m. D: Lam Ying. SP: Ku Lung, from Yi Kon's novel. Ph: Liu Man Min. Mus: L. Chan. PD: Lee Sui Tak, Chan Man Ye. FX: Roman Tsang. Mkp: Man Kao. Ref: TV: Regal Video; Eng. dubbed. With S. Hung, Jaguar Lee, Alan Lau, Rosa Lee, Wong Chung, Yi Pin.

"I broke the fourth dimension! I am in the past!" During a freak electrical storm, Ellen, a sports writer for *Public United Daily*, falls up a hole in a mine shaft and into another dimension. She finds herself in the time of the Sung Dynasty, the Peace Period, one thousand years ago. Another storm sends Ellen and a "dragon" back to the present. ("You must come from another world, or something.") Our hero—who "looks like he's out of an old movie"—proceeds to set world records at a track meet.... Generally foolish science-fantasy has some amusing moments, not to mention the premise of *Ghost Warrior*—there's even a scene in which the kung fu hero, Ku, is exposed to the wonders of TV. ("That guy is dancing inside!")

**SURVIVAL 101** Riot/Films Unltd. & Zipper & Video Prods. (Grubic-Koba-Hart) 1994 color c90m. D: Thomas R. Koba. SP: Dennis Dormody. Ph: Yonkof, Rood. Mus: Sean Carlin. SpFxMkp: Randy & Barb Westgate. SpFX: Tom O'Connor et al. Ref: TV: KGH video. With Don Ray, Alex Black, Kit Hadley, Tom Caladan, Jennifer Proctor, Dennis Stokes (Peterson).

Locust Grove. A strong, crazed, near-invulnerable Vietnam vet seems to be behind the chainsaw horror, the hunting-knife carnage, and the other tool gore here. Cheap, trite shot-on-taper. The proximity of a hazardous-waste disposal site is apparently supposed to account for the killer's seeming invulnerability.

**SURVIVOR** Matrix & Martin Wragge 1987 (1986?) color 92m. D: Michael Shackleton. SP, Story: Bima Stagg. Story, P: Wragge. Ph: Fred Tammes. Mus: A. Strydom. PD: G. Lipley et al. SpFX:

Tommy Kieser. Mkp: M. Mackenzie. Ref: TV: CBS Late Night. V 4/13/88:67 (hv). no Scheuer. Martin. With Chip Mayer (Survivor), Richard Moll (Kragg), Sue Kiel, Richard Haines, John Carson, Rex Gamer, Sandra Duncan, Ben Dekker.

"In one thousand years, we'll create a new planet Earth ... a new race of warriors, artists, scientists!" After World War III, the Survivor, an astronaut-physicist, returns to the "late great planet Earth" to confront and execute "psychopath" Kragg, who is the only man allowed to reproduce. Postwar energy is supplied by underground power stations which capture steam from fissures in the Earth's crust.... Routine futuristic action. The vapid theme song ("We are survivors!") sets the tone.

**2 SUSPIRIA** 1977 87m.-U.S. MkpSup: Pierantonio Mecacci. SdFX: Luciano Anzellotti. Ref: TV. Lentz. Hardy/HM. Stanley. Weldon. Martin. Maltin '92. Scheuer. Phantom. Hound. Newman.

"It was just the wind!" At the Frieburg Tanz Akademie—originally a school of dance and the occult—maggots dropping from the ceiling are a real concern. Other clues to the solution of this supernatural mystery: a "weird kind of snoring," the shadow of a reclining figure on a curtain, and a reference to a blue iris. Apparently, the academy was founded by a Greek witch, the Black Queen, who died in a fire, but whose "tremendous talent for doing evil" allows her spirit to continue to rule a coven there and briefly to reanimate the body of a dead student.

Highlights: an unexplained room full of coiled wire, the big, big buildup to the pre-credit shock sequence, and the suggestions of the presence of an evil force in a huge, near-empty courtyard. Unfortunately, director Dario Argento milks every suspense sequence, with dismayingly diminishing returns. And the Goblin weird-music/noises score is more annoying than unsettling, and overworks its one admittedly eerie theme. Eccentric shot to add to your Argento collection: a bedroom as seen through a light bulb. Patented Argento close-up: the shot of Alida Valli's high heels crushing the maggots. Apparent homage to the 1934 *Black Cat*: a professor named Verdegast. This print: the English-language version.

**SUSSEX VAMPIRE, The** see *Sherlock Holmes: The Last Vampyre. Sherlock Holmes in Caracas*

**The SWAMP OF THE RAVENS** (Sp-U.S.) Mundial & All American 1973 color/ws feature (*El Pantano de los Cuervos*). D: Manuel Cano (aka Michael Cannon). SP: Santiago Moncada. Ph: Manuel Merino. Mus: Joaquin Torres. SpFX: Amo-Baq. Mkp: Carlos Paradela. SdFX: Luis Castro. Ref: TV: MV; Eng.-lang. version. PT 7:7 (Higuchi). With Raymond Oliver, Marcia Bichette, Fernando Sancho, Toni Mas, Melba Senta, William Harrison, Mark Mollin, Fay Valls.

"And what difference is there between life and death?" The mad doc here is "attempting genetic mutations," or perhaps some sort of matter regeneration. (A body is found with a "strange duplication"—two right hands.) Or ...?: "I like perfection. If I can't find it, I create it." Also featured: a blood-drained corpse, necrophilia, and an apparent corpse which "wakes up" screaming.... Chaotic script and production ... mind-numbing, Poe/"Nevermore, " fadeout dialogue reference. The swamp itself is the only

thing this strange movie has going for it—note especially the watery "garden" of corpse heads.

**SWAMP THING** see *Return of Swamp Thing, The*

**SWEET HOME** (J) 1988 color/ws c100m. (*Suito Homu*). D: Kiyoshi Kurosawa. SpFX: Dick Smith. Ref: TV: Toho Video; no Eng. Weisser/JC. With Juzo Itami.

An innocuous comedy turns to serious gore, then winds up on a sweet fantasy note, as the "Home Sweet Home" mural on a wall in an old, abandoned country house seems to be the key to various horrors.... A disfigured baby found in a coffin cries, moves, then slumps, apparently dead again. A woman's body oozes away after a battle ax splits her skull. In meticulous detail, a man's body incinerates. Ultimately, the baby is restored to the ghost woman, the two fly up to heaven, and the evil house collapses.

If the story here seems functional, the makeup effects are well done, and there are a couple of major chills with some imaginative shadow effects (cf. *Grave Secrets,* 1992): In one, an all-engulfing shadow glides down a hall, shorts out the lights as it goes, and burns a man's body in half. In the other, the shadow of a woman's flowing hair fills a hallway and somehow incinerates one victim.

**SWEET HOUSE OF HORRORS** (I) Reteitalia-TV 1989 color/ws 85m. (*La Dolce Casa degli Orrori*). Story, D: Lucio Fulci. Tel: V. Mannino, G. Battaglini. Ph: N. Celeste. Mus: V. Tempera. Ref: MV: gore. Dark Side 47:51-2: Houses of Doom series; "overplayed exorcist." With Jean Bretigniere, Cinzia Monreale, Lino Salemme, Pascal Persiano.

Haunted-house story.

**SWEET REVENGE** Zane Bros./Sam Schad 1986 color 85m. D: Henri Pachard. SP: Milton Ingley, Chuck Zane. Ph: Arthur Ben. Mus: Teddy Rigg & The Truckers. AD: Mick Rub. Mkp: Jo Gordon. Titles: Joe Dee. Ref: TV: vt. Adam '88. With Sheri St. Clair (Samantha), Ron Jeremy (Sam), Jamie Gillis, Tasha Voux, Siobhan Hunter, Annie Sprinkle.

A vaguely science-fictional, hardcore variation on *Goodbye Charlie* and the hilarious *Switch*. Sam the rat with women falls into the Hudson River, and the pollution and "female hormones" therein transform him temporarily into the foxy Samantha, "condemned" to live life as a woman. He/she learns to like his/her new life, but at the end reverts to Sam. Script at first seems to punish its misogynist, but ultimately seems misogynistic itself: Samantha kinda likes the rat treatment.

Cf. *Cleo/Leo.*

**The SWEET SCENT OF DEATH** (B) Hammer House of Mystery 1985 color c80m. D: Peter Sasdy. Tel: Brian Clemens. Ref: TVG. Ecran F 73:9: *Diabolique*-like. no Stanley. Ecran 50:12. With Dean Stockwell, Shirley Knight, Michael Gothard.

TV-movie re couple terrorized at their country retreat. (TVG)

**SWEET SPIRITS OF THE NIGHTER** Col 1941 20m. D: Del Lord. SP: Harry Edwards, Al Giebler. Ref: Okuda/CCS. LC. Maltin/SSS. With El Brendel, Tom Kennedy, Frank Lackteen, Duke York, Vernon Dent, Hank Mann.

Mad scientist attempts to revive the dead. Remake of *Midnight Blunders* (which see).

**SWING SHIFT** see *Wizard of Speed and Time, The*

**SWITCH IN TIME, A** see *Norman's Awesome Experience*

**The SWORD IN THE STONE** BV (Walt Disney) 1963 anim color 79m. D: Wolfgang Reitherman. SP: Bill Peet, from T. H. White's book. FxAnim: Dan McManus, Jack Boyd, Jack Buckley. Narr: Sebastian Cabot. Ref: screen. Lee. Jim Shapiro.

Period tale with semi-horrific and science-fantasy sequences. A boy, Wart—turned by Merlin the Magician into a perch—is chased by a huge, nasty-toothed pike ("He was a monster!"), while Merlin himself rockets to the 20th Century and back and brings back with him "futuristic fiddle-faddle" (a steam-locomotive model, etc.), and sorceress Mad Madame Mim takes "delight in the gruesome and grim" and transforms her face into a "revolting" pig-like countenance. During a Wizards' Duel with Merlin, she turns herself into, variously, a fire-breathing purple dragon, a rattlesnake, and a cat.

Or, When Low Comedy Was in Flower. Clowning-human and cavorting-animal figures subvert whole chunks of narrative here—though this is not always to the bad. In one sequence, a flirty, double-talking "girl squirrel"—who falls for a Wart temporarily in squirrel form—is, with unstressed inevitability, touchingly abandoned and left to pine in the hole of an old oak. But the magic in *Sword in the Stone* is usually all-too-pleasant. The movie is like a domesticated "Sorcerer's Apprentice."

**SWORDKILL** see *Ghost Warrior*

**SWORDS OF THE SPACE ARK** (J) New Hope-TV/Toei-TV 1981 (1978) color 75m. (*Space Ninja—Sword of the Space Ark*—vt t). SP, D, P. (Eng.-lang. version): Bunker Jenkins. D: Minoru Yamada. Mus: Doug Lackey, Joseph Zappala. SpFX: Nobuo Yajima; (addl) George Budd. Ref: TV: 3B Prds.-U.S. version. Hound. TVG.

From the "Message from Space" TV series. In the year 2090, in the fifteenth solar system, with assorted humans and Wookie types. Film opens with an exhilarating display of space and spacecraft effects. Then, the story (i.e., the bad news), a blatant *Star Wars* plundering (evil emperor, hero who returns home to find his family killed, princess who appears magically, etc.).

See also: *Message from Space* (II).

**SWORDS OF WAYLAND, The** see *Robin Hood: The Swords of Wayland*

**SWORDSMAN** (H.K.) Newport Dist./Golden Princess Films & Long Shong Pictures (Film Workshop/Tsui Hark) 1990 color 117m. D: King Hu. From Louis Cha's novel. Ref: TV: Pan-Asia Video; Eng. titles. V 10/15/90. Fango 107: 59. vc box: *Men with Swords* - alt vt t.

Hectic, occasionally amusing magical-martial-arts fantasy includes some elements sufficiently macabre to warrant mention here, including one woman's attack snakes (including a two-headed one) and "poisonous bees," magical beheadings, an iron-claw weapon, "sleeping" smoke, and rites which make a man hallucinate and spit blood. ("Feed him the voodoo.")

See also: *Swordsman II* and *East Is Red, The*

**SWORDSMAN II** (H.K.) Golden Princess/Long Shong Pictures (Film Workshop/Tsui Hark) 1992 color/ws 110m. D: Ching Siu Tung. SP: Tsui Hark, Hanson Chan, Tang Pik Yin. Story: Louis Cha. SpFX: Cinefex. Ref: TV: Tai Seng Video; Eng. titles. V 5/4/92. SFChron 4/23/92. 7/24/92.

More "sword energy," "grass gliding," beheadings, lengthwise splitting of horses, snake and scorpion weapons, Lethal Hooks, flying knitting needles, and Sun Moon Sect. Most macabre ingredient: the Essence Absorbing Stance, which allows a master to catch and shrivel up his foes and, later, to draw Uncle (or Auntie) Asia's blood out of his/her body.... Part II has the *Zu* pace and hectic quality, if not the imagination of that film.

**SWORDSMAN III** see *East Is Red, The*

**The SWORDSMAN** (Can.) SC Ent. Int'l. (Nicolas Stiliadis) 1992 color 97m. SP, D: Michael Kennedy. Mkp: Cathy Irvine. SpFX: Brock Jolliffe. Ref: TV. TVG. V 5/4/92:222. 10/19/92:136. SFChron Dtbk 4/18/93: Republic HV. With Lorenzo Lamas, Claire Stansfield, Michael Champion (Stratos), Nicholas Pasco, Raoul Trujillo.

"Now why are people being killed by swords?" A cop (Lamas) finds that his "flashbacks" and dreams are actually "memories of a previous life." In his current life, he and the mysterious Stratos vie for the "sword of Alexander the Great"—"2,300 years after we began".... Bland action-fantasy re "swordplay murders."

Sequel: *Gladiator Cop.*

**The SWORDSMAN AND THE GOLDEN CHILD** (H.K.) HK-TVB 1987 color 104m. Ref: TV: HK-TV video; no Eng.

El cheapo, shot-on-tape supernatural actioner anticipates the title of *Swordsman* and borrows the plot (but not the monsters) of *The Golden Child*. Here, the mystical "gold child"'s electric hand moves a ladder "bridge" into place; at the end, his prayers start an earthquake and explosions which foil evildoers. Other fantasy effects include a flying evil woman, a floating mystery woman in white, and a flying coffin lid. Okay effects for the two-man swordfight on the surface of the water and in the air.

**\*SYLVIE AND THE PHANTOM** Ecran Francais (Andre Paulve) 1945 ('50-U.S.) 97m. SP: Jean Aurenche, from a play by Alfred Adam. Ph: Philippe Agostini. Mus: Rene Cloeric (sp?). AD: Carre. Ref: TV: Embassy Video; Eng. titles. V 10/18/50. Lee. TVFFSB: Janus-TV. Martin/France. Hound. Martin. With Odette Joyeux, Carette, Pierre Larquey, Robert Dhery, Francois Perier, Louis Salou, Jean Desailly, Marguerite Cassan.

Sweetly told ghost story has creepy elements, including an actor (Salou) as a fake, moaning ghost in a sheet ("I'm an old hand at phantoms") ... a real ghost (Jacques Tati) ... two hired "ghosts" (Desailly, Perier) ... a creaking door and a ghost (fake number 2, or 3) at midnight ... a ghost dog ... a lights-out scene on a secret stairway ... and, at one point, a "strange screech".... Pleasant blend of comedy, fantasy, and sentiment, though the three fake ghosts are a bit too gabby, and the story meanders.

**SYNAPSE** (Can.) WarnerVision/Lifenet 1995 (1994) color feature. SP,D: A. Goldstein. SP,P: D. Hildebrand. Ref: PT 22:69. vc box. With Chris Makepeace, Karen Duffy, Barry Morse, Saul Rubinek.

"In the future," a man's mind is transplanted into his girl friend's dead body.(PT)

**SYNGENOR** South Gate/ACMG (Syngenor/Jack F. Murphy) 1990 color 98m. (*Scared to Death II*—orig t). D: George Elanjian, Jr. SP: B. V. Friedman. Story: Michael Carmody. Mus: Chase, Rucker. PD: R. C. Searcy. SpMkpFX: Mark Williams FX: Creature Des: William Malone. VisFxConsult: the Skotaks. Ref: V 12/24/90:40 (hv): "Syngenor is an interesting creation, a slimy black gill-man sort of monster." 3/7/84:133(ad). Fango 101. Cinef 12/91: sequel to *Scared to Death* (II/1980). SFChron Dtbk 5/24/92. Ecran F 41:9. PT 9:51. With Starr Andreeff, Mitchell Laurance, David Gale, Riva Spier, Lewis Arquette, Melanie Shatner.

"Synthetic genetic organism"—or cyborg—"created by Norton Cyberdyne Co."(V)

**SZOBA KIALTASSAL** (Hung.) Objektiv Filmstudio 1991 color 87m. SP, D: Janos Xantus. SP: also Sandor Sultz. Ref: V 6/24/91: "Grand Guignol yarn with a darkly comic edge ... a refreshingly-different Magyar offering"; *Cruel Estate*—tr t? With Zofia Rysiowna, Aniko Fuer, Andrzej Ferenc.

"Polanski-like atmosphere, with the wife going bananas and the old woman taking on a satanic edge ... bloody finale ... old biddy ... ends up spliced to the wall on a coathook."

# T

**TC 2000** MCA-Univ HV/SGE Ent.(Jalal Merhi) 1993(1992) color feature (aka T.C. 2000). D: T.J. Scott Ref: SFChron Dtbk 8/15/93. V 5/4/92:38(ad). 6/28/93:17(rated). With Billy Blanks, Bobbie Phillips, J. Merhi, Bolo Yeung, Matthais Hues.

"Cybernetic gang-killing machine" in the year 2020. (SFC)

**T-FORCE** PM Ent. 1994 color 94m. D: R. Pepin. SP: J. Hart. Ref: vc box: "cybernetic law enforcement team." With J. Scalia.

**T.R. SLOANE** see *Death Ray 2000*

**TAILIENS** Fat Dog 1992 color 84m. D: Henri Pachard. Ref: Adam'93: "sci-fi." With Channel, Tiffany Mynx, Marc Wallice.

"In the not too distant future, the government takes control of our sexual mores."

**TAILIENS 2** and **TAILIENS 3** Fat Dog 1992 color 70m. and 73m. D: H. Pachard. Ref: Adam '93. With Ashlyn Gere, Sharon Kane, Mike Horner.

Aliens in the year 2012.

**TAINTED** Cardinal Pictures(Matacena-Redden) 1985 color 90m. (aka *Body Passion*), SP,D: Orestes Matacena. Mus: Hayden Wayne. Ref: V 5/15/85: "outright silliness." Ecran F 61:67. Hardy/HM2. With Shari Shattuck, Gene Tootle, Park Overall.

Schoolteacher tormented by "dead husband's wicked sister and her lover, the crematorium caretaker." (V)

**TAKBO...! BILIS...! TAKBOOOO** (Fili) Golden Lion Films (Donna Villa) 1987 color c120m. (*Takbo, Bilis...Takbooooo!* - ad t). SP,D: Carlo J. Caparas. Ph: Ramon Marcelino;(fx) Oyet Capulong. Mus D: Vehnee Saturno. PD: Jing Ramos, Eric Diaz. SpMkp: Cecille Baun. VisFxD: Gerry A. Garcia. SpFX: Roger Otico, Freddie Fajardo. SdFX: Arnold Dineros. Ref: TV: Regal Int'l. video; little Eng.; *Run...! Bilis...! Run* - tr t. With Herbert Bautista, Matet, Ana Margarita, Ronel Victor, Ruffa Gutierrez, Charito Solis, Jigo Garcia, Ruel Vernal, Jaime Fabregas.

The lighting of candles in an old mansion revives a slew of monsters, including a Dracula-like vampire, two or three vampire women, a Frankenstein-type monster (complete with electrodes and a scar across its forehead), an ape, a cartoon demon from a wall portrait, a big-eared bat (or wolf) creature, a skeleton monster with ticklish ribs (snakes slither out its eye bones), and little cackling devils. Blowing out the candles makes the monsters collapse.... After a slow start, film has some fun with the plethora of creatures.

**TAKBO...PETER...TAKBO!** (Fili) Archer Prods. 1984 color 117m. SP,D, Exec Co-P: Augusto V. Pangan. Ph: Ben Lobo et al. Mus: Geyju. Sets: L. Mariano. Mkp: Lula Dela Pena. SdFX: Francis Espinosa. Ref: TV: Trigon Video: *Run...Peter...Run!* - tr t. With Chiquito, C. Reyes Mumar, George Estregan, Baby Delgado, Martha Sevilla, Rodolfo "Boy" Garcia, Tintoy, Lynn Jurado, Ike Lozada.

Count Dracula is in with the fanged crowd at the Vampire Disco House, among the ruins outside a small town. Near the end, the vampires which he commands go on strike, and he orders various dead to rise from their graves and battle them. All-a-dream coda.... Amusing ideas here and there — the disco, a vampire-thwarting, spiked dog collar — but the mugging of most of the actors is very unfunny, and the movie is way too long.

**TAKBO... TALON... TILI!!!** (Fili) RNJ Corp./Seiko Films 1992 color 100m. D: Efrem Jarlego. SP: Ricky Lee, Joe Bartolome. VisFX: Cinemagic. Prosth Mkp: Cecille Baun. SpFX: Peping Carmona. SdFX: Danny Sanchez. Ref: TV: Ultra Video; no Eng. With Rina Reyes, Rey Abellana, Sherly Cruz, R. Sarmeta, Sylvia Sanchez, Rita Avila, Raymond & Richard Gutierrez.

Three stories. "Mahiwagang Banga." With tongue or tentacle, the horror of the urn drags in a woman. Such periodic "sacrifices" eventually enable the zombie thing, all in pieces at first, to reassemble and exit the urn. Familiar shock stuff. Only eeriness: the shots of the unassembled thing.

"Ang Lalaki Sa Salamin." A gentlemanly figure from a mirror tangles with a cackling witch from same. This looks like a charming-macabre romance with a touch of humor. Neat: the mirror pulling the hero back in.

"Mga Laruan Nina — Kiko, Tito at Toto." Low comedy/fantasy.

**TAKE IT EASY!** (Thai) c1987? color/ws c95m. Ref: TV: All Asian HV; no Eng. Thai Video: above is tr t.

Scene in which students scare newcomers by playing "vampire" and "mummy" ... another scene in which two students play "ghost" ... and a *Jaws* scene complete with fin and music. Routine hi-jinks.

**TAKE ME UP TO THE BALL GAME** (Can.) Nelvana & CBC 1980 anim color c25m.? D: Ken Stephenson. SP: Ken Sobol. Mus: Rick Danko. Ref: vc box: *Nelvanamation II*. V 9/2/91:56. Voices: Phil Silvers et al.

"Alien All-Stars intergalactic champs for 800 years ...."

**TAKEOVER** (Austral.) Cori Films & Film Victoria & ICL Australia (Phillip Emanuel Prods.) 1988 color 85m. D: Rob Marchand. Tel: Peter Moon. Ph: Bob Kohler. Mus: Dave Skinner. PD: Patrick Reardon. SpFX: Brian Pearce et al. Anim: The Paintbrush Co. Ref: TV: Atlas video. no Martin. no Stanley. With Barry Otto, Anne Tenney, Paul Chubb, Wayne Cull, Tracey Harvey, Sean Scully.

"Hello. I'm George, the applied intelligence system for complete management." George-1, supercomputer with personality, impersonates the man in whose image it was created, takes over both his office and home life, and advises the less efficient George to commit suicide. Generally dismal sf-comedy never quite takes itself seriously enough to have any bite, even during a rather wild denouement with horrific potential. ("You can't destroy me!")

**TAKETORI MONOGATARI** see *Princess from the Moon*

**A TALE FROM THE EAST** (H.K.) D&B Films 1990 color c88m.(*Blood Demon* - alt t). D: Len Tsu-Chow. Ref: TV: World Video (Ocean Shores Video); Eng. titles. Weisser/ATC.

A "Little Princess" from the Ching Dynasty, a royal guard "in ancient costume," and a vampire, General Shea Hai — the "Blood Devil" — awaken in 1990. ("Are we going to tell them there's a monster sucking people's blood and tearing heads off?") All of them seem to be after a pearl which was apparently part of a "small instrument left behind by people of another planet" .... Atmospheric opening sequences, routine sf-comedy-horror after that. Plus a surprising sequence featuring a dimetrodon, a stegosaurus, a brontosaurus, and a mastodon-type.

**TALE OF A FEMALE GHOST** see *Golden Lantern*

**TALE OF A VAMPIRE** (J-B) Tsuburaya & State Screen (Shishikura/Johnson) 1992 color 102m. Story, SP, D: Shimako Sato. SP: also Jane Corbett. Ph: Zubin Mistry. Mus: Julian Joseph. PD: Alice Normington. SpFxCoord: David Watkins. SdFX: Andy Kennedy. Opt: Howell. Mkp: Mel Gibson. Ref: TV: Vidmark video; 93m. Martin. PT 18:16. V 12/7/92: "nailed to the floor by anemic perfs." 8/16/93:13 (rated). Jones. With Julian Sands (Alex), Suzanna Hamilton, Kenneth Cranham.

"He will destroy you—he cannot help it." In London, a vampire (Sands) finds his lost love of a century or so ago, Virginia (Hamilton), in Anne (Hamilton). ("Where are you, Virginia?") Love and blood, not necessarily in that order. Film tries to make up for its undernourished plot with atmosphere, but is too self-serious and stodgy. Story is "framed" by quotes from Poe's "Annabel Lee," and the bad guy is named Edgar (Cranham).

**TALE OF EROS** see *Erotic Ghost Story III*

**TALE OF FEMALE NINJAS** see *Female Ninjas*

**TALE OF OLD HOUSE, The** see *Old House in Night, The*

**A TALE OF SEVEN CITIES** (J) Animate Film 1993 anim color 30m each. D: Akinori Nagaoka. SP: Tomonobu Nobe. Ref: Animerica 5:12; 2 OAVs, 2nd due in '94.

"Moon colonists" return to Earth in 2190 A.D. to repopulate a world devastated by biochemical weapons and a ninety-degree shift in the Earth's axis.

**A TALE OF THE EARTH** (J) Shochiku 1984? anim color 100m. D: Shigeyuki Yamane. Ref: V 5/9/84:441(ad).

Human youth returns to post-holocaust Earth.

**TALES FROM THE DARKSIDE — THE MOVIE** Para/Richard P. Rubinstein(Mitchell Galin) 1990 color 93m. D, Mus: John Harrison. SP:("Lot 249," from a story by Sir Arthur Conan Doyle, and "Lover's Vow") Michael McDowell; ("Cat from Hell," from a story by Stephen King) George A. Romero Mus: also Donald A. Rubinstein et al. SpMkpFX: KNB Group; (consul) Dick Smith. VisFX: Ernest Farino. Stopmo: Justin Kohn. SpFX: Drew Jiritano. OptFX: Van der Veer. Gargoyle Voice: Joel Valentine. Ref: TV. V 5/9/90. Sacto Bee 5/7/90. V 2/21/90:54-55(ad): Laurel Darkside Movie Inc. With Deborah Harry, Christian Slater, David Johansen, William Hickey, James Remar, Rae Dawn Chong, Robert Klein, Steve Buscemi, Michael Deak (mummy).

1) "Lot 249": A student (Buscemi) uses a revived, 3,000-year-old Egyptian mummy as an instrument of revenge. Slim story with a wry payoff. 2) "Cat from Hell": There isn't even a twist to this revenge tale of a demon cat which does an *Alien* inside a hit man's mouth. Cat's-eye-view shots and a climactic makeup effect. 3) "Lover's Vow": A *Gremlin*-esque gargoyle makes an artist (Remar) promise not to reveal its existence. Nifty, effects-laden climax redeems predictable twist. The inconsequential "wrap-around story" ends with Deborah Harry in an oven.

**TALES OF LIAO ZHAI** see *Love with the Ghost in Lushan*

**TALES OF THE THIRD DIMENSION** Owensby 1984 color 90m. D: Thom McIntyre, Worth Keeter, Todd Durham. Ref: V 4/25/84:29(ad): completed. 7/26/83:30. Ecran F 52:70: completed; one segment, "Young Blood," re a vampire couple and a werewolf baby. no Jones. no Stanley. no Martin. Scheuer. With Robert Bloodworth, Kate Hunter, William Hicks, Helene Tryon.

**TALES OF THE UNKNOWN** AIP/Pacific West 1990 color 79m. Ref: TV: AIP HV. Stanley. V 11/5/90. PT 13:52. 14:5-6: "Warped" on local PBS-TV.

Four indie weird tales: 1) "Jack Falls Down." USC (1988) D: John Kim. SP: Michael Matlock. An insurance salesman has until midnight to collect a person for Death. Well-done but glib. 2) "The Big Garage." USC (1983) SP,D: Greg Beeman. From T.C. Boyle's short story. Those who take their vehicles to Tegeler's Garage never leave the latter. Amusing no-escape tale. 3) "Living on Video." T. Marcuss Prods. (1988) Story,D,P: Todd Marks. Story,SP: Gary Ellis. A man's day is flukily captured on TV & video. Ultimately and predictably, he's absorbed into a TV.

4) "Warped." Kassel Prods./Nygard (1989) SP,D,Ed: Roger Nygard. SP: also J. Copeland. SpFX: Pete Litwinczuk. SpMkp: Clayton James. Title Anim: Terry Faust. Gore and a skeleton "baby."

**TALK DIRTY TO ME, PART IV** Dreamland (Jerry Ross) 1986 color 79m. D: N. Morehead. Ref: Adam '88. With John Leslie, Taija Rae, Shanna McCullough.

Re "extraterrestrial women who enter our world through birdbaths." Plus a "fugitive mermaid from another planet."

**TAMMY AND THE T-REX** 1993 color 82m. D: S. Raffill. Ref: Martin: "nonsense." With Terry Kiser, Ellen Dubin.

Man turned into tyrannosaurus.

**Un TANGO DALLA RUSSIA** (I) 1965 feature. D: Cesare Canevari aka B. Ross. Story,SP: C. Monk. SP: also H. Gozzo. Mus: Necopi. Ref: Palmerini: "little-known conventional horror film." With Dan Christian, Britt Semand.

"Mad doctor transfers his mind into other people's bodies."

**The TANTANA** (H.K.) Bao Shiung Film 1986? color/ws 88m. Ref: TV: vt; no Eng.; Thai dubbed.

An evil wizard given to hovering can choke his victims by remote control. Ultimately, he explodes, but his spirit returns for one last chortle. Small-beans effects and comedy in this fantasy, which majors in levitation.

**TAOCHU SHANHUHAI** see *Escape from Coral Cove*

**TAOIST PRIEST OF LUSHAN** see *Love with the Ghost in Lushan*

**The TARANTULA** Vitagraph 1916 silent b&w 6 reels. SP,D: George D. Baker. Ref: V 7/21/16. Lee. With Edith Storey, Antonio Moreno, Raymond Walburn.

Spurned woman scares ex-lover to death with tarantula.

**TARKAN ALTIN MADALYON** (Turkish) 197-? feature. Ref: VW 20:31.

Sorceress resurrected by virgin blood.

**TARKAN VIKING KANI** (Turkish) 197-? feature. Ref: VW 20:31: Cyclops, octopus.

**TARNSMAN OF GOR** see *Gor*

**TARO! MOMOTARO IN TROUBLE** (J) New Century/KSS Films 1989 color/ws 94m. D: T. Iishi. Ref: TV: vt; no Eng. (apart from title). Markalite 3:10. With Yoichi Miura, Hideki Fujiwara.

This looks like a vapid vehicle for a young Japanese pop star. Only surprising elements: the tall, horned demon on the lab wires and the stopmo dream piggies.

**TARO, THE DRAGON BOY** (J) TPS/Toei 1984 anim color/ws? c75m. D: K. Urayama. Ref: TV: RCA/Col HV; Eng. version. Martin. Hound.

Principals: the little Taro, the "child of a monster" ... his mother, who was turned into a huge "ugly monster" of a dragon as punishment for selfishness ... an eerie but not unhelpful water serpent ... a forbidding witch ... the Red Demon, who at first plans to eat Taro, but then becomes his ally ... and the Black Demon, the "strongest demon in the world" ("spooky" is the way to his domain) .... Slow-starting, occasionally charming, delicately didactic fantasy. Highlights: the serpent and the strange, mocking, enticing spirits of the woods.

**TARO, THE SON OF DRAGON** (J) Kyodo Eiga 1968 stopmo anim color 63m. D: Ichiro Michibayashi. Ref: Lee.

Red Devil, Black Devil, etc.

**TASTE FOR FEAR, A** see *Obsession*

**TASTE OF THE CANNIBAL** see *Papaya*

**TASTIEST FLESH** see *Soul-Hungry Demon*

**TASYA FANTASYA** (Fili) Golden Lions Films 1994 (1993) color 93m. D, SP: Carlo Caparas. Ph: Ernesto Dominguez. PD: Gabby Francisco. SpFX: Dek Torrente. SdFX: Serafin Dineros. Mkp: T. Dominguez. Ref: TV: Regal video; no Eng. With Alvin Patrimonio, Bong Alvarez, Jerry Codinera, Kris Aquino (Tasya), Barbara Perez, Jinky Oda, Dick Israel.

Ingredients in what looks like a fairly low-grade combo of comedy, horror, and action: toy dinosaurs—a bronto and a triceratops—which come to (rudimentary stopmo) life (cries one witness: "Jurassic!") ... a huge electrified "skull" of a hill which shoots fireballs from its eye sockets ... possible apemen (photography dim here) ... a moldy monster behind a mask ... an apparent horse monster ... and miscellaneous monsters in the "skull."

**TATTOO** see *Mark of the Devil* (1984)

**TAXI DE NUIT** (F) Oliane & TF1 & Canal Plus (Marie Laure Reyre) 1993 color 85m. SP, D: Serge Leroy. Ph: A. Domage. Mus: P. Sarde. PD: J.-P. Bazerolle. Ref: V 1/17/94: "pleasantly diverting thriller." With Bruno Cremer, Laure Marsac, Didier Bezace, Maka Kotto.

Paris, 1999, is a police state. "Political activism is outlawed," and a "code card" is required for "transactions and identity checks."

**TCHELOVEK NEVIDIMKA** (Russ) Mosfilm 1985 color feature? SP,D: Alexandre Zakharov. SP: also A. Dmitriev. From H.G. Wells' novel *The Invisible Man*. Ph: V. Chouvalov. Mus: I. Shwarts. AD: Dimitri Bogorodski. Ref: Ecran F 58:34-5: "very faithful to the book." With Andrei Kharitonov, R. Romanauskas, N. Danilova.

**TEACH 109** American Playhouse/Memel-Louthan 1987 color 25m. SP,D: Richard Kletter, from an idea by Isaac Asimov. Ph: Lisa Rinzler. Mus: W.P. Olvis. PD: Richard Hoover. Ref: Horacio Higuchi. Sacto Bee 3/27/90: on "Triple Play"; "a good story, well written, directed and acted." With James Earl Jones, Elizabeth Perkins, Jason Patric (android).

Med school where doctors experiment on androids.

**TEATRO A DOMICILIO** see *House of the Yellow Carpet*

El **TEATRO DEL HORROR** (Mex) Prods. Latinas Americanas/Televicine (Galindo) 1989 color c87m. SP,D: Pedro Galindo III. Story: Santiago Galindo. Ph: Javier Cruz Osorio. Mus: Pedro Plascencia Salinas. SpMkpFX: Gabriel & Alfredo Garcia. SpFxD: Ramon Loranca. OptFX: Manuel Sainz. Ref: TV: virtually no Eng. V 5/2/90:242: Theater of Horror - tr t. TVG. With "Resortes," Rafael Sanchez Navarro, Mario Rebeca, Andres Bonfiglio, "El Gordo."

Weird ingredients: Adolfo (Sanchez Navarro), the mad director who haunts the cobwebby Teatro Colonial and who has a detachable head ... a figure summoned up from a huge cauldron who pulls in his conjuror (Resortes) ... a book of spells ("Hechizos") ... and a supernatural mist.

Adolfo might be John Barrymore's Oscar Jaffe as played by Robert De Niro and written by Luis Bunuel. The sequence in which his talking, cackling head tugs itself off his body, and his body walks about, is wry knockabout black comedy. Also prime: the tango with the headless body. Main drawback: the blah photography. Funny (so intended or not): the perpetual look of fright on the heroine's face.

**TECHNO-CRAZY** Educ/Christie 1933 19m. D: Charles Lamont. SP: Ernest Pagano, Ewart Adamson. Ref: TV. LC. Lee: Vanity Comedies series. no Maltin/SSS. With Billy Bevan, Ben Turpin.

A very mad doctor locates the urg — the "unit of Technocratic energy" — and concocts a Techno-crazy bomb. Feeble comedy short, though the doc's mock-mad cackle is amusing.

**TECHNOLOGICAL THREAT** Expanded Ent./Bill Kroyer anim short. Ref: SFChron 2/19/93: "robot dweebs."

**TECHSEX** Evarts Ents. 1988 color c80m. Ref: vc box. no Adam. With Brenda Bitchin, Dana Dillon, Charlene Cody.

Project Techsex allows scientists to record male subjects' fantasies.

**TEEN ALIEN** Peter Semelka Prods. & American Family Prods. c1978? color 88m. (*The Varrow Mission* - alt vt t). Sp,D,P: Semelka. SP: also James Crofts. Story: Ed & Sherma Yeates. Mus: Jeff Ostler, Phil Davis. Sets: Chad Olson. The Varrow: Terry Allen. FX: Dale Angell, Ed Fraughton. Mkp: Jeannie Barrus, T. Allen. SdFX: Les Udy et al. Ref: TV: Prism Ent. video. no Stanley. no Phantom. Hound: 1988. Martin: 1988. V 5/9/84:259(ad). With Vern Adix, Micahel Dunn, Keith Nelson, Dan Harville; Mike McClure & Judy Richards (aliens), Dave Olson (The Creature).

Brighton Canyon. The new high-school student is an alien from the planet Varrow, in another solar system, and others like him are holing up in old buildings all over Earth, and using transformation machines to turn from their ugly alien form into human shape.

Sub-East Side Kids hi-jinks in this amateur-level sf-horror-comedy shot around Salt Lake. Forced laughs and "Spook Alley" chills in the Old Mill, a supposedly "spooky place," and phony "monsters in black capes." The transformation sequence is the only even passable one.

**TEEN VAMP** New World/Jim McCullough 1989 color 89m. SP,D: S. Bradford. Mkp: Cathy Glover. Ref: V 6/7/89: "little to offer." With Clu Gulager, Karen Carlson, Beau Bishop (Murphy), Mike Lane.

Bitten nerd becomes vampire.

**TEEN WOLF** Atlantic/Wolfkill (Mark Levinson, Scott Rosenfelt) 1985 color 89m. D: Rod Daniel. SP: Joseph Loeb III, Matthew Weisman. Mus: Miles Goodman. SpMkpFX: The Burmans. SdFX: Sam Horta. Ref: TV. MFB '86:50-1. V 8/21/85. SFChron 8/23/85. Maltin '92. Martin. Scheuer. With Michael J. Fox (Scott Howard), James Hampton (Harold Howard), Susan Ursitti, Jay Tarses, Scott Paulin, Clare Peck, Linda Wiesmeier.

"I'm sick of being so average!" To his surprise, high-school student Scott Howard finds that he has inherited the curse — or blessing — of the werewolf from his father, Harold. After a bathroom transformation scene, he looks like Glenn Strange in *The Mad Monster*. After public transformation, on the basketball court, he gains instant popular acceptance, in an amusing twist on the werewolf story. (Compare *The Nutty Professor* and *House of Fright*.) Scott finds that he possesses some control over the timing of his transformations — he can choose to be "The Wolf." In terms of personality, he now becomes his opposite, Joe Cool, as the movie moves into its dull, didactic mode, and Scott insists, finally, "I gotta be myself." If *Teen Wolf* features all the familiar high schoolers, it's also a droll angle on the puberty thing.

Sequel: *Teen Wolf Too.*

**TEEN WOLF TOO** Atlantic(Kent Bateman/Coleman-Rosenblatt) 1987 color 93m. D: Christopher Leitch. SP: R.T. Kring. Story: J. Loeb III, M. Weisman. Mus: Mark Goldenberg. Wolf Prosth: The Burmans. Wolf Mkp: John Logan, Michael Smithson. OptFX: Cinema Research. Ref: TV. MFB '88:52. V 11/25/87. ad. Maltin '92. Morse. Martin. Scheuer. With Jason Bateman (Todd Howard), Kim Darby (Prof. Brooks), John Astin, Paul Sand, James Hampton (Uncle Harold), Kathleen Freeman.

Hamilton University. In this sequel to *Teen Wolf*, Scott's cousin Todd becomes a boxing werewolf that caters to college fans' sadistic instincts. This sadly domesticated, broad-daylight monster eventually gets too big for his britches, as he learns about abuses of power in this black-and-white morality play. At the end, Todd is back to sweet and normal, and the crowd is still cheering for him to beat his opponent to a pulp. Pretty miserable.

**TEENAGE CATGIRLS IN HEAT** Troma/MPG 1993 color c90m. D: S. Perry. SP, P: Grace Smith, Scott Perry. Ph: Thad Haleli. Mus: Randy Buck. AD: H. Fontenot. Mkp: Amy Stonecipher. Ref: TV. TVG. Vallejo Times-Herald 6/20/94. SFChron 7/30/94: "the power of the 4,000-year-old Keshra Cat Sphinx." With Gary Graves, Carrie Vanston, Dave Cox, Helen Griffiths, Marissa Mireur.

"She's a cat!" Weird ingredients: sphinx-based "powerful ancient spirits" which turn cats into women with cat mannerisms ... a cat detector which "picks up the brain waves of cats" ... Egyptian spirit-god Keshra, whose Great Litter will produce cat people that will rule the world ... a man who is 1/4 cat ... and a climactic revival of all victims of teen catgirls.... Comedy has the funny/strange thing down pat, but the ha-ha eludes it. Some balmily sweet inter-species dating details. And cute shadow-cat credits and a cat-out-of-dirt effect. Plus the inevitable line: "She's gonna go back to eatin' fish heads and peein' in a box!"

**\*TEENAGE CAVE MAN** 1958. Title Des: Bill Martin. Ref: TV. Warren/KWTS! Lee. Hardy/SF. no Phantom. Stanley. Weldon. Lentz. V 9/17/58. Maltin '92. Scheuer. Fango 104:16. 118:13. With Darah Marshall.

An apparent prehistoric world mixes cave men and monsters such as a lizardy dinosaur, brontos, a tyrannosaurus, "great swamp creatures," beasts from *One Million B.C., Unknown Island,* and *She Creature,* and a silly-looking beaked creature, that turns out to be a disguised man bearing a book from the 20th Century, the "Atomic Era." ("This is no evil thing!") Dying, or dead, this "god that gives death with its touch" relates the story of a nuclear war which spawned big beasts "formed as the dinosaurs of prehistory" .... Precursor of *American Graffiti* (teen seeks to escape stifling provincialism) is humorless and plodding, though oddly earnest.

**TEENAGE EXORCIST** Austin Ents./Wald-Way Films 1991 color 98m. D, P: Grant Austin Waldman. SP: Brinke Stevens. Ph: William Molina. Mus: C. Cirino. AD: Jim Peattie. SpVisFX: Bret & Bart Mixon. SpFxMkp: Joey Castro. FxAnim: Sean Applegate. Story, Exec P: Fred Olen Ray. TV: AIP HV; alternately c.'90 & '91. Stanley. Ref: V 5/6/91:78. 9/3/90:22. SFChron Dtbk 7/5/92. 2/14/93. 3/8/92. PT 4:7: with John Carradine? (No.) 16:33,34: "released overseas." With Eddie Deezen, Michael Berryman, B. Stevens, Jay Richardson, Oliver Darrow (demon), Hoke Howell (Baron DeSade), Joe Zimmerman (zombie).

Ingredients here include demon possession, crossed phone wires between an on-call exorcist and a pizza man, the "Be a zombie" scene, a monster hand from a pizza, and a chainsaw. Occasionally pleasant horror-comedy eschews the frantic quality of the typical Z horror-comedy, but has little to offer in place of same. At the least, it's easier to take than its main cross reference, *Repossessed* (another, more literal *Exorcist* takeoff). Cute bit: Robert Quarry doing card tricks for the ghouls on the doorstep. Cute possessed line: "Your mother darns socks in hell."

**TEENAGE MUTANT NINJA TURTLES: THE EPIC BEGINS** Murakami-Wolf-Swenson? 1987 anim 72m. Ref: CVS 9/90: their origins.

**TEENAGE MUTANT NINJA TURTLES** (H.K.-U.S.) New Line/Golden Harvest(Limelight & Gary Propper/Northshore Investments) 1990 color 93m. D: Steve Barron. Story, SP; Bobby Herbeck. SP: also Todd W. Langen. Based on comic characters created by Kevin Eastman & Peter Laird. Mus: John Du Prez. SpFX: (sup) Joey Di Gaetano; SpFxUnltd. Creatures Des: Jim Henson's Creature Shop; (sup) John Stephenson; (visual sup) Ray Scott. SdFX: Richard Shorr. Ref: TV. V 3/28/90. Sacto Bee 4/1/90. MFB'90:344-7. Maltin '92. Scheuer. With Judith Hoag, Elias Koteas, Josh Pais, Michelan Sisti, Leif Tilden, David Forman, James Saito (The Shredder), Corey Feldman.

Four turtles step into radioactive ooze, grow, talk, get fancy monikers from their martial arts master, Splinter, a similarly-radioactivity-enhanced pet rat. Together, they take on the Darth

Vader-ish, father-figure villain, The Shredder, who commands a "secret band of ninja thieves" .... *Howard the Duck* without the charm. Alternating themes of pizza and neglected kids undercut each other. Occasionally amusing asides, in a basically wimpily didactic sf-comedy.

**TEENAGE MUTANT NINJA TURTLES II: THE SECRET OF THE OOZE** (U.S.-H.K.) New Line/Golden Harvest & Gary Propper (Northshore Investments) 1991 color 88m. D: Michael Pressman. SP: Todd W. Langen. Mus: John Du Prez. Animatronics: Jim Henson's Creature Shop; (creative sup) John Stephenson; (visual sup) Jane Gootnick; (Rahzar des) Ray Scott; (Tokka des) Nigel Booth; (Super Shredder des) Scott, Vin Burnham; (mech des) J. Courtier et al. SpFX: (coord) Joe Mercurio; SpFXUnltd. Mkp: Del Armstrong. SdFxCoord: Odin Benitez. Computer Anim: Video Image. Ref: TV. V 3/25/91. 10/1/90:22. S&S 8/91:56-7. SFExam 3/22/91. Maltin '92. Scheuer. With Paige Turco, David Warner, Michelan Sisti, Leif Tilden, Kenn Troum, Mark Caso, Kevin Clash, Francois Chau (Shredder), Vanilla Ice, Mark Ginther (Rahzar), Kurt Bryant (Tokka); (voices) Frank Welker (Rahzar & Tokka).

The "four walking talking turtles" — created when discarded chemicals were exposed to "radiated waves" and produced a mutant-spawning ooze — are back. So too is Shredder, who forces a scientist (Warner) to grow two huge, super-strong monsters, the "infants" Rahzar and Tokka, whose "fun" wreaks havoc in the streets. Finally, the last of the TGRI company's ooze turns Shredder into Super Shredder (Kevin Nash) .... Sub-"Zippy" pop erudition. Sample inspiration (from Splinter): "The past returns, my son." Turtle wordplay here is as leaden as Felix's in the latter's movie.

**TEENAGE MUTANT NINJA TURTLES III: THE TURTLES ARE BACK ... IN TIME** (U.S.-H.K.) New Line/Golden Harvest & Gary Propper (Gray-Dawson-Chan/Clearwater) 1993 color 95m. SP,D: Stuart Gillard. VisFxSup: Jeff Okun. Creature FX: All Effects Co. PD: Roy Forge Smith. Ref: V 3/22/93: "unforgivably bad." 6/22/92:15. ad. SFChron 3/20/93: "a bomb." With Elias Koteas, Paige Turco, Stuart Wilson, Vivian Wu, Mark Caso, Matt Hill, Jim Raposa, David Fraser, James Murray.

The Turtles switch places with 17th-century samurai.

**TEITO MONOGATARI** (J) EXE 1988 color/ws 135m. (aka *Tokyo — The Last Megalopolis*). D: Akio Jisoji. Ref: TV: Pony Canyon Video; no Eng. V 10/19/88:377(ad). VSOM: sfa *Last Megalopolis?* Weisser/JC.

This live-action version of the story (see also the following entries) features a supernatural general who seems to possess a woman ... snarling little stopmo uglies which clamber out of a ceremonial star and scatter ... sheets of paper which stopmo into weird birds ... a severed hand which reconnects to its wrist ... a woman who spits up a ghastly white cricket creature ... a spook compass ... and — in the elaborate finale — a giant, multi-armed living statue ... a levitating buzz saw ... and an earthquake which seems to crack open a crevice to hell ... Intermittent visual wonders (see above), fine photography, and a stirring symphonic score, but too talky to make much sense without some kind of translation assistance. Striking: the woman with the electric hair.

Follow-up: *Tokyo—The Last War.*

**TEITO MONOGATARI** (J) Streamline/Toei Video & OZ 1991? ('93 - U.S.) anim color/ws 45m. (aka *Tokyo — The Last Megalopolis. Doomed Megalopolis: The Haunting of Tokyo* - U.S.). D: Taro Rin. SP: Endo Akinori. Story: Aramata Hiroshi. Mus: Toyama Kazz. Ref: TV: vt; no Eng. vc box: necromancer Kato "raises" ancient warrior.

In a confusing tour de force opening, a mystical-military "superman" seems to revive a cemetery's dead. The main, *Dracula*-like plot concerns the efforts of a team of good guys to save a young woman from the clutches of the superman .... Stunningly stylish, though the story tends to boil down to a series of duels between good and evil. Number-one Wow! effect: the pentagram on the moon which disperses into hordes of birds, which fly to Earth and alternately turn into "snakes" or tiny mutant "toddlers." Number two: the chomping, corpse-headed "roots." Other gross-out bits involve a woman who vomits up a phallic caterpillar and a nurse whose split-open body sticks to the creature inside her like an eggshell.

**TEITO MONOGATARI, VOL. 2** (J) Streamline/Toei Video & OZ 1991? ('93-U.S.) anim color/ws 44m. (*Doomed Megalopolis: The Fall of Tokyo* - U.S.). For credits, see previous entry. Ref: TV: vt; no Eng. vc box.

In a ritual, snaky-ghost cemetery dead seem to possess the heroine, as the "superman" from the first installment looks on. Plus a horror nightmare re exploding cat eyes and swirling seas of the dead, a bouncing ball from hell, and a gigantic dragon which takes on the army guy and loses. Pretty basic story; lotsa visual value. Sotto voce wow effect: the little blob-thing playing with the ball and casually encircling it. Good scare score.

**TEITO TAISEN** see *Tokyo—The Last War*

**TEKKAMAN: THE SPACE KNIGHT, Episode 1** (J) LD Video/Tatsunoko Prods. 1992-U.S. anim color 86m. Created by K. Yoshida, I. Kuri. U.S. credits: SP, P: W. Winckler. SP: also Frederick Patten. Ref: TV: LDV; Eng. version. Animerica 6:12: sfa *Space Knight Tekkaman Blade 7*?

"I did it! I became Tekkaman!" Year 2037. A space suit made from the alloy Tekka turns Barry Gallagher—of the World Science Center—into Tekkaman, the "world's greatest defender against the aliens," the Waldarians, and their robots, who are invading Earth. ("What a robot!") Plus a space station orbiting Pluto ... a "strange alien visitor," Andro, who turns from a vapor into humanoid form ... an orbiting "space ring" ... "space battle stations" ... the Tekka Crystal Rocket Engine (for interstellar travel) ... and a "green shadowy creature," a shadow-spy for the aliens.... Unimaginative visuals, comically stilted line readings.

**TEKWAR: THE ORIGINAL MOVIE** Univ & Atlantis Films & WICW Int'l. & Lemli (Grosvenor Park/Rock-Roloff) 1994 (1993) color 92m. (*Action Pack: Tekwar* - TV). D, Exec Co-P: William Shatner, from his *Tek* novels. Tel: Alfonse Ruggiero Jr., Westbrook Claridge. Ph: Rodney Charters. Mus: D.M. Frank. PD: S. Roloff. SpFX: Laird McMurray Services. Ref: TV: MCA-Univ HV. TVG 1/15/94. With Greg Evigan, W. Shatner, Eugene Clark, Torri Higginson.

"I'm an android—level ten." In the year 2044: "cryo-submersion" (i.e., prison) ... hologramistic fantasizing ... "newer, more

powerful Tek" (you could get lost in it) ... Cosmos, the "top personal security force" ... android "kamikazes" ... a Tek-chip destroyer ... and a "pulse gun".... Competent, but basically balefully familiar sf-actioner. Some of it's like "What does it mean to be in love?" The new suspense venue here is a combo of computers and holograms.

**TEKWAR** MCA-TV 1994 color c90m. Ref: TVG. With G. Evigan, W. Shatner, Sonja Smits, Uni Park.

Jake searches for an antidote to his ex-wife's "electronically transmitted virus."

**TEKWAR: TEKJUSTICE** MCA-TV 1994 color c90m. Ref: TVG. With G. Evigan, W. Shatner, T. Higginson, Jacob Tierney, Sandahl Bergman.

Jake is accused of murder.

**TEKWAR: TEKLAB** MCA-TV 1994 color c90m. Ref: TVG. With G. Evigan, Michael York, W. Shatner, E. Clark.

Or, The Excalibur Caper.

**TELEPHONE SEX AND THE INVISIBLE MAN, TOO** (I) La Union Film 198-? color 71m. (*Telefono Sessuale e l'Uomo Invisible*). D, Ph: Frank De Niro. Mus: Curti, Rustichelli. Ref: TV: VSOM; Eng. titles. With Petra Scharbach, Hula Hop, Raffaele, Maurice Poli.

"I'm talking to an invisible man." Odd Italian girlie film features an unexplained invisible man who gets into the softcore act, too, at one point. Monotonous.

**TELL-TALE HEART, The** see *Buried Alive*

**The TEMP** Para/Columbus Circle (David Permut, Tom Engelman/H.W. Koch, Jr.) 1993 color 95m. D: Tom Holland. Story, SP: Kevin Falls. Story: also Engelman. Ph: Steve Yaconelli. Mus: F. Talgorn. PD: Joel Schiller. Ref: V 2/15/93: "moronic, derivative." Martin. ad. SFChron 2/13/93: "bad ending." With Timothy Hutton, Lara Flynn Boyle, Dwight Schultz, Faye Dunaway.

Temp from hell employs paper shredder, killer bees, etc.

**TEMPEST, The** see *Resan Till Melonia. Prospero's Books* (P)

**TEMPTATION** (B) Cricks 1914 silent 50m. D: Charles Calvert. Ref: BFC. Lee. With Jack Leigh.

Inventor's wireless-controlled torpedo.

**The TEMPTATION OF THE SPIRITUAL WORLD** (H.K.) Mei Ah Video 1992? color/ws 76m. Ref: TV: Tai Seng Video; no Eng. Y.K. Ho.

A couple in an auto accident find themselves on the Other Side, where it's foggy, and the lighting isn't as good. She gets to go back to Earth; he gets visitation rights, though she can't see him. After he jumps into another (living) man's body, in order to approach her, others place spells around the house to keep him away. Finally, he's granted a visa and foils evildoers in the real world .... Humorless, shot-on-tape fantasy-soaper. Only eerie element: the netherworld fog.

**TEMPTRESS** see *Sorceress*

**The TEN LITTLE GALL FORCE** (J) AnimEigo/Toho/CBS-Sony & MOVIC (Hida-Sawanori/Katoo-Miura-Koizumi) 1988 ('93-U.S.) anim color 18m. D: Kenichi Yatagai. Ph: Konishi. Mus: I. Seo. AD: Nangoo. Anim D: Kitajima. SpFX: T. Sakakibara. SdFX: Konno. Ref: TV: AnimEigo video; Eng. titles. Animag 4:8. Animerica 5:18.

Scenes from an outer-space story filming include robots, air cycles, Monster M, and Slime. Tepid parody of the *Gall Force* videos.

**TEN LITTLE INDIANS** (B) 21st Century/Cannon/Breton Films (Towers) 1989 color 98m. (*Death on Safari* - orig t). D: Alan Birkinshaw. SP: J. Hunsicker, G. O'Hara, from Agatha Christie's play. PD: Roger Orpen. Ref: V 5/31/89: "ranks near the bottom of all Christie adaptations." ad. Sacto Bee 11/14/89: "no life whatsoever." With Donald Pleasence, Frank Stallone, Sarah Maur Thorp, Herbert Lom, Brenda Vaccaro, Warren Berlinger, Moira Lister, Paul L. Smith.

**TEN SECONDS TO COUNTDOWN** see *Terrifying Tales*

**TENCHI-MUYO! RYO-OHKI - Episode #1** (J) Pioneer/AIC (Yamashita-Ohta-Inoue-Hasegawa) 1992('94-U.S.) anim color c30m. D: Hiroki Hayashi. SP: Naoko Hasegawa. Concept: M. Kajishima, H. Hayashi. Ph: K. Konishi. Mus: S. Nagaoka. AD: T. Waki. SdFX: Anime Sound. Ref: TV: Pioneer video; Eng. dubbed; 1st of apparently 6 OAVs; S. Korea (Hana & Hanyoung) co-pro?

"Ryoko Resurrected." "A demon sleeps here." For 700 years, an alien samurai's sword has held a "demon from the sky" dormant in a shrine. In the present day, the "freeze-dried" demon is released and takes the form of a lovely "demon girl".... Undistinguished mixture of fantasy, horror, and comedy.

**TENGU TAIJI** (J) Tokyo Cinema 192-? anim silent 10m. SP, Anim: Noburo Ohfuji. Ref: Japanese Animated Film.

Blackbird-goblins attack house.

**TENKAWA DENSETSU SATSUJIN JIKEN** see *Noh Mask Murders*

**TENKU NO SHIRO LAPUTA** see *Laputa*

**TENNIS COURT** (B) Fox Mystery Theatre/Fox & Hammer-TV 1985 (1984) color c90m.? D: Cyril Frankel. Tel: Andrew Sinclair, from Michael Hastings' short story. Ph: Frank Watts. Mus: Anthony Payne. AD: Heather Armitage. Mkp: Eddie Knight. Ref: TV. TVG. Stanley. Ecran F 73:9. 52:69. 70:11,13. With Peter Graves, Hannah Gordon, Cyril Shaps, Jonathan Newth, Ralph Arliss, Isla Blair.

A possessed tennis ball and net prove to be manifestations of the "unquiet spirit" of a man, Redmond Maryott (Arliss), who is still living, but whose body was all but destroyed in a plane crash, years ago. And: an apparently successful exorcism ... a scientific ghost chaser, Dr Magnusson (Shaps) ... and a girl (Annis Joslin) whose face curdles on the haunted court .... Risible attempt to

combine tennis and horror has only the living-possessing-the-living idea going for it, and it doesn't go very far.

**TERMINAL** (I) 1975 feature. D: Paolo Breccia. Ref: Palmerini. With William Berger, Mirella D'Angelo.

"Future version" of "Dr. Jekyll and Mr. Hyde."

**TERMINAL CHOICE** (Can.) Almi/Magder Film (Ubaud-Hameed) 1985 (1984) color 98m. (*Deathbed. Trauma. Critical List. Death List* — all early ts). D: Sheldon Larry. SP: Neal Bell, from a story by Peter Lawrence. Mus: Brian Bennett. SpFxCo-ord: Martin Malivoire. Mkp: Ken Brooke. Ref: TV. V 5/8/85: shot in 1982. TVG. Cinef 10/86. Bill Warren. HR 1/26/82. 4/27/82. With Joe Spano, Diane Venora, David McCallum, Robert Joy, Don Francks, Nicholas Campbell, Ellen Barkin.

A macabre computer game leads to murder and reports that a hospital unit is "haunted." HAL and *The Invisible Boy* helped set us up for the sinister human-behind-the-computer business in *Terminal Choice,* one of the more interesting efforts in the hospital-horror subgenre. One step beyond *M\*A\*S\*H*: The staff here bets on the patients in ICU. Functional characterization, nasty violence. (One remote-control murder leaves a patient's chest smoking.)

**TERMINAL CITY RICOCHET** (Can.) E. Motion Films (Dan Howard) 1989 color 100m. D: Zale Dalen. SP,P: John Conti. SP: also Mullan, Savath, Thurgood, Lester. AD: Bill Fleming. Ref: V 5/2/90: "watered-down final script." SFChron Dtbk 7/12/92: "madcap." With Peter Breck, Jello Biafra, Germain Houde.

"Futuristic ... world wrecked by returning space junk." (V)

**The TERMINATOR** Orion/Hemdale/Pacific Western (John Daly, Derek Gibson)/Cinema '84 1984 color 108m. SP,D: James Cameron. Sp,P: Gale Anne Hurd. Mus: Brad Fiedel. SpMkpFX: Stan Winston. SpVisFX: Fantasy II Film FX. Stopmo: Doug Beswick. Ref: TV. V 10/31/84. SFExam 10/26/84. With Arnold Schwarzenegger (Terminator), Michael Biehn, Linda Hamilton, Paul Winfield, Lance Henriksen, Rick Rossovich, Dick Miller.

"The machines rose from the ashes of the nuclear fire." Los Angeles, 2029 A.D. and 1984. The Terminator Systems Model 101 Cyborg — "metal surrounded by living tissue" — "can't be reasoned with, and absolutely will not stop." It is sent back, through time displacement, from a post-apocalyptic machine age to 1984 to kill the mother (Hamilton) of the man destined to lead laser-branded future humans against the machines. ("The future is not set.")

Highly efficiently directed, photographed (by Adam Greenberg), and edited (by Mark Goldblatt) sf-thriller endorses the human, but spends more time on the mechanical. The *Halloween*-like scenes with the unstoppable, shotgun-toting cyborg are certainly exciting — reduced to stopmo nuts-and-bolts, it still keeps going — but the shooting-gallery effect gets a little wearing. Funny-gross conceit: the Terminator's progressively messier face.

Sequel: *Terminator 2.*

**TERMINATOR 2: JUDGMENT DAY** (U.S.-F) Tri-Star/Carolco (Gale Anne Hurd & Mario Kassar)/Pacific Western & Lightstorm

Ent. & Le Studio Canal 1991 color 136m. SP, D, P: James Cameron. SP: also William Wisher. Ph: Adam Greenberg. Mus: Brad Fiedel. PD: Joseph Nemec III. SpMkp & Terminator FX: Stan Winston. SpVisFX: IL&M: (sup) Dennis Muren; Fantasy II Film FX (Gene Warren Jr., sup); (sp seqs) 4-Ward Prods., Robert Skotak, Elaine Edford; (creative sup) Van Ling, Gail Currey; (des) John Bruno. Go Anim: Peter Kleinow. OptFx Sup: Robert Costa (Genesis Opt FX). Computer Graphics: IL&M; (anim sup) Steve Williams. MechFxCoord: Richard Landon. Roto SpVisFX: Bret Mixon. SpFX: (sup) Joseph Viskocil; (coord) T.L. Fisher. Model Sup: Michael Joyce. Ref: TV: Carolco HV. V 6/1/91. S&S 9/91:50-1. Oak Tribune 7/30/91:A-11. SFChron 3/25/93. 4/8/93; (Dtbk) 3/15/92. 7/28/91. SFExam 7/31/91. Jim Smith. With Arnold Schwarzenegger (Terminator), Linda Hamilton, Edward Furlong, Robert Patrick (T-1000), Joe Morton, Xander Berkeley.

Rebels in the year 2029 A.D. send back a "protector," another Terminator-101 (Schwarzenegger), to protect the boy and future-hero John Connor (Furlong) from the master-machine-dispatched Terminator model 1000 (Patrick), which is made of "liquid metal" and can "imitate anything it touches," of equal size, and take "solid metal shapes."

Although *Terminator 2* is a more-complicated-than-average actioner, it's not story but the new computer-effects technology which propels the movie. (The story itself mixes comedy and the Messianic — as in *Superman IV,* a future nuclear war is averted — and does so competently enough, if a bit monotonously.) These "liquid" effects with T-1000 not only showcase some spectacular technology, but prove to be a most imaginative use of same. They may be for this decade what the phantasmagoric effects for *The Thing* were for the last one. If even the broadly entertaining car, truck, and cycle stunts here become repetitious, the oozing-metal effects never do. Each one seems a minor revelation, different enough to astonish, and they culminate in the most astonishing sequence of all, the "death throes" of T-1000 in the molten steel.

**TERMINATOR 2** see *Shocking Dark*

**TERMINUS** (W.G.-F-Hung.) Hemdale/CAT & Films du Cheval de Fer & IG & CLB Films & Films A2(Anne Francois) 1987 (1986) color 115m (aka *End of the Line*). SP, D, Exec Co-P: Pierre-William Glenn. SP: also Patrice Duvic. Story: Alain Gillot. Ph: J.-C. Vicquery. Mus: David Cunningham. AD: Alain Challier. SpFX: J. & F. Gastineau. Mkp: M. Baurens. Ref: Horacio Higuchi. Ecran F 75:63.76:9. V 3/18/87: "no tiger in the tank." 5/6/87:502, 504, 508. SFExam 1/1/88. 12/29/88: "wearying." With Karen Allen, Johnny Hallyday, Juergen Prochnow, Gabriel Damon, Louise Vincent (voice of "Monster").

"Futuristic international sport" crosses football and auto racing.

**TERRA SENSHI BOY** (J) New Century 1985. D: Akinobu Tshiyama. SP: Masato Harada. Ref: Ecran F 59:70. With Momoko Kikuchi, Al Saotome, Tohru Masuoka.

"Science-fiction film in which a young woman becomes the friend of an extra-terrestrial who confers a supernatural power on her."

**TERRESTRIAL DEFENSE ARMY** see *Chikyu Boeigun*

**TERRIBLE ANGEL** see *Saviour of the Soul*

**TERRIFYING TALES** Platinum Prods. 1989 color. Ref: TV: vt. no Hound. no Martin.

Compilation includes:

"Ten Seconds to Countdown." Garen Prod. 1986 c20m. SP,D,P,SpFX,Anim,SdFX: Armand Garabibidan. Ph: C. Ford, L. White. Mus, SdFX: Anthony Teti. AD: L. White. Creature Des: Steve Koch. Ship Des: Narbeh Nazarian. with Christine Warner, Russell Fear. Fragmented tale re aliens collecting research specimens in the year 2525.

"Final Destination: Unknown." Bunnell Pictures 1986 c30m. Story,SP,D,P,Ph,Ed: Paul Bunnell. SP: also Tony Mouradian. Mus: Jerry Danielsen. PD: Rick Alcantar. VisFX: Stac 3 Prods. SpMkp: Patricia Messina. SpFX: Richard Osmond, K.F. Perkowski. with Andrew Magarian, Lisa Fuller, Jeff Culver. Demons in human form take "The Roadside Strangler" to hell. Somewhat offbeat, but stilted.

"Creatures of Habit." UCLA Motion Picture Graduate Dept. 1986 c25m. SP,D,P,Ed: Ephraim Schwartz. Mus: Steve Orich. Who "ripped Eva up?" Who cares? Arty mini-drama somehow slipped into this collection.

**TERRITORIAL IMPERATIVE, The** see *Animal within, The*

**TERROR** see *Frankenstein's Castle of Freaks*

**TERROR AT HALFDAY** see *Monster A-Go Go*

**TERROR AT LONDON BRIDGE** see *Bridge across Time*

**TERROR AT ORGY CASTLE** Satyr IX 1971 color feature. D: Z.G. Spencer. Ref: TV: SWV.

Ingredients in this stilted softcore: a "haunted medieval castle" ("downright creepy") ... "some freaky kind of ceremony" which turns the Countess Dominova (who seems to be something out of a "late night TV vampire movie") into a man ... a naked woman who comes out of a mirror (a "female demon known as a succubus") ... "some bizarre dinner-table entertainment" involving rodent gore ... a "female sacrifice" at a black mass (Lisa is to be the "bride of the devil") ... narration ... and no dialogue.

**TERROR AT TENKILLER** United Ent. 1987 (1986) color 87m. Story, D, P: Ken Meyer. Story, SP: Claudia Meyer. Ph: Steve Wacks. Mus: Bob Farrar. SpMkpFX: DEFX; David Powell, Doug Edwards. Ref: TV: United HV. Savage Cinema 2:3. V 2/3/88:34. Hound. no Martin. Morse. With Mike Wiles (Tor), Stacey Logan, Michele Merchant, Dale Buckmaster, Kevin Meyer, Dean Lewis, Debbie Killion.

An Indian girl's spirit is said to live at the bottom of "dream like" Lake Tenkiller. It is, however, only the "easygoing" Tor who is clearly responsible for the horror in the hot tub and various stabbings and severings of arms from bodies. No mystery here, or even any attempt at same, in this pointless *Friday the 13th*-like shocker. Talky and tired.

**TERROR AT THE OPERA** (I) Orion/Cecchi Gori & Tiger & ADC & RAI-TV 1987 color/ws 90m. (*Opera* - orig t).

Idea,Sp,D: Dario Argento. SP: also Franco Ferrini. SpFX: Renato Agostini, Sergio Stivaletti; Antonio & Giovanni Corridori, Germano Natali. Mkp: Rosario Prestopino, Franco Casagni. Ref: TV: Col HV: Eng. version. Horacio Higuchi. Bill Warren. V 1/6/88. TVG. McCarty II. Martin. With Cristina Marsillach, Urbano Barberini, Daria Nicolodi, Ian Charleson.

*"Macbeth* brings bad luck!" — especially to the opera company's stage hand, stage manager, and wardrobe mistress, who are gorily murdered. Terror ingredients include the superfluous taped-needles, eye-keeper-opener idea, the heroine's (Marsillach) visualized memories of horrors-as-a-child, the painstaking extraction of a swallowed clue from the innards of one victim, and oh-come-off-it, inside-the-killer's-brain, p.o.v. shots. Biggest dubbed mouthful: (Inspector) "Is this another manifestation of the curse of *Macbeth*?" Hoariest device: the amplified heartbeats. Most successful visual ploy: the extreme CUs of objects, which shots lend the movie a certain, spurious "documentary" creepiness. Most tiresome main motif: eyes, human and raven. Duly noted: Argento's small talent for the intricately gross.

**TERROR EN EL TREN DE LA MEDIA NOCHE** (Sp) Jacinto Santos Parras 197-? color/ws c85m.? SP,D: Manuel Iglesias. SP: also Antonio Fos. Ph: Jose Andres Alcalde. Mus: Musical Zurbano. SpFX: M.I.V. Ref: TV; no Eng.; *Terror on the Midnight Train* - tr t. With Rafael Hernadez, Mari Paz Pondal.

Lieres. A phantom train seems to chug to a stop at a station next to a couple's bedroom. Is it the eerie music or the chugging sounds which torment them? Is this the death train coming for them? Why does a body vanish magically from a coffin? Hokey spook music and effects (including the hand-on-the-shoulder scare), but the train has a good shtick.

**TERROR EN LOS BARRIOS** (Mex) Alcantara & Occidente 198-? color c85m. D: Julio Aldama. SP: Elena Robles. Ph: Alfredo Uribe. Mus: Manuel Esperson. Ref: TV: Spanish Video Sound; no Eng. With Grace Renat, Julio Augurio, Norma Lazareno, Lynda Maria Rosas, J. Aldama, Al Coster, Claudia Guzman, Victor Alcocer.

A man whose drunk of a mother scorned and laughed at him when he was a boy snaps, dresses as a woman and stabs a man to death. He then adopts a male disguise and slashes a prostitute's throat. Later, he dons a Jason-like mask and kills a woman on the street. Masquerading as a whore, he kills a "client." Next, in monster mask and fright wig, he shoots a scantily clad woman. Finally, sans any disguise, he grabs a cleaver and forces his potential victim to put on a wig .... Shoddy script is as mixed-up, psychologically, as the madman, and the direction is equally inept. Clumsily staged, almost "posed," action/violence scenes.

**TERROR EN SAN ANGEL** see *Momias de San Angel, Las*

**TERROR EYES** Twin Tower/Starvision/Pony Prods. 1989(1988) color 90m. SP, D, P: Eric Parkinson. SP, P: Vivan Schilling. SP, D: Steve Sommers, Michael Rissi. Ref: V2/1/89:41(hv): "uneven." Hound. PT 12:50. V 1/13/88:6. With Schilling, Lance August, Dan Bell, Daniel Roebuck.

Devil's envoy, death game, gore, shot-on-tape finale. Includes two student films.

**TERROR FOR TRACY** see *Blood Symbol*

**TERROR IN THE AISLES** Univ/Kaleidoscope(T.E.M.) 1984 color 82m. D: Andrew J. Kuehn. SP: Margery Doppelt. Ed: Gregory McClatchy. Ref: TV. NYT. V 10/31/84. Maltin '92. Phantom. Hound. Morse. Scheuer. Martin. Stanley. With Donald Pleasence, Nancy Allen, Joel S. Rice.

A slickly edited compilation of scenes from horror and action movies, including *Jaws, Jaws II, The Shining, Scanners, Halloween, Halloween II, What Ever Happened to Baby Jane?, Bride of Frankenstein, Dressed To Kill, Carrie, Alien, The Brood, The Exorcist, The Birds, The Texas Chain Saw Massacre, Night of the Living Dead, An American Werewolf in London, Rosemary's Baby, Alone in the Dark, When a Stranger Calls, Invasion of the Body Snatchers* (1978), *The Fog, The Thing* (1982), *The Omen, Cat People* (1982), *Videodrome, Ms. 45, Scared Stiff* (1953), *Abbott and Costello Meet Frankenstein, Phantom of the Paradise, The Fly, Bug, Food of the Gods, The Howling, Konga, Alligator, Hold That Ghost, Eyes of Laura Mars, Nightwing, Dawn of the Dead, Poltergeist, Saturday the 14th, Frogs, The Thing with Two Heads, Friday the 13th II, The Fury, Suspiria,* and *The Wolf Man* (1941) .... The script is nonexistent, but the rapid-fire montage of the gross has an almost disturbing cumulative effect: The procession of horrors is illogical, ghastly-vivid, and (thanks mainly to the source movies) imaginative.

**TERROR IN 2-A** see *Girl in Room 2A*

**TERROR IN THE SWAMP** Martin Folse Prods. 1984 color 87m. (*Nutriaman, The Copasaw Creature* - orig t). D: Joe Catalanotto. SP: Terry Hebb, Folse. Adap: Henry Brien. Story: Billy Holliday. Mus: Jaime Mendoza-Nava. Creature Des: Ed Flynn; (costume) David Rau. SdFxEd: Pedro Amaya et al. Ref: TV: New World Video; title credits reverse Story & Sp credits. Stanley. V 7/31/85. Hound. Morse. Martin. V 5/1/85:26. With B. Holliday, Chuck Bush, Chuck Long, Ray Saadie, Floyd Duplantis, Claudia Wood, Keith Barker (Nutriaman).

"What the hell was that!" It's Nutriaman, a *Boggy Creek*-inspired hairy beast, "half-man and half-nutria," and he's terrorizing the Louisiana swampland. Scientists trying to produce larger nutria pelts for fur trappers "mistakenly injected human hormones into nutria test subjects," and .... Slapdash regional bit of filmmaking features hapless actors, rudimentary dialogue, and a risible premise.

**TERROR OF DEVIL** (H.K.? ) 1992 color/ws c90m. Ref: TV: World Video; Eng. Titles. George Walker: above is tr t.

"Give me back my body!" The head of a beheaded woman—an "ancient time person"—curses her executioners ("I want to revenge," she says, on Shiu's family), then flies about a forest looking for its body. Meanwhile, the spirit-body possesses a woman (who then sprouts vampire fangs and bites a vendor's neck), then a man. ("Who's that monster?") A "urine bullet" finishes her off.

Busy but indifferent monster/kung-fu comedy has a library-music score. The ghost-body can disappear and "jump cut" herself down streets. In the funniest sequence, she keeps asking the rice-dumplings vendor for "one more"; surprised by her insatiableness, he looks up to find her dumping the dumplings into the hole where her neck ought to be.

**TERROR OF MANHATTAN** see *Danse Macabre*

**TERROR ON ALCATRAZ** Le Cinema Prods. 1986 color 96m. D: Philip Marcus. Addl Dial: Douglas Weaver. SP: Donald Lewis. Ph: G. Von Berblinger. AD: Michael Marcus. SpMkp: Steven Anderson; (fx) Todd Masters. Ref: TV: T.W.E. video. V 4/1/91:82. Hound. Martin. With Aldo Ray, Veronica Parche Ali, Sandy Brooke, Scott Ryder, Lisa Ramirez.

The Frank (*Escape from Alcatraz*) Morris story, continued. Morris (Ray), looking for the key to hidden loot, takes the Alcatraz tour and stays behind on the "island of ghosts." His bloody murder victims include fellow tourists and park rangers, and, in a final dumb irony, he too becomes a victim.

Poorly-written dialogue fills in the gaps between gory murders by cleaver, razor, etc. Combination slasher film/historical travelogue possesses the fascination of the truly misbegotten. Tour-guide details re Alcatraz alternate with exclamations like "What! Kenneth's dead?" and "Aughh! It's a ranger!" (Well, his disemboweled body.)

**TERROR ON THE BLACKTOP** see *Highwayman, The*

**The TERROR WITHIN** Concorde-New Horizons (Roger Corman/Rodman Flender, Reid Shane) 1989(1988) color 86m. D: Thierry Notz. SP: Thomas M. Cleaver. Mus: Rick Conrad. Creature Des & MkpFX: Dean Jones. SpFX: Roberts, Landerer, & Wolke. Min: Starkirk. FxAnim: Michael Lessa. OptFX: Motion. Ref: TV. V 5/10/89. HR 5/31/89. Maltin '92. Hound. Martin. Scheuer. With George Kennedy, Andrew Stevens, Starr Andreeff, Terri Treas, Roren Sumner (gargoyle), Joal Corso (gargoyle number 2).

"We are under gargoyle attack!" "The accident" has decimated Earth. Karen (Yvonne Saa), a "survivor" who has been exposed to the plague and whose "pregnancy is in fast forward," gives birth to a cute, loathsome-looking "premature fetus" that becomes a human-sized "ugly son of a bitch" .... Routine sf-horror suspenser adds little or nothing to *Alien* and *It! The Terror from beyond Space.*

**THE TERROR WITHIN II** Concorde(Roger Corman/Mike Elliott/Jonathan Winfrey) 1991(1990) color 84m. SP, D: Andrew Stevens. Mus: Terry Plumeri. SpMkpFX: Dean & Starr Jones. Opt: Motion. Ref: TV. V 5/18/92. SFChron Dtbk 2/16/92. Martin. V 1/3/90:11: *The Terror Within, Part II: The Fight for Mojave Lab* - orig t. With A. Stevens, Stella Stevens, Chick Vennera, R. Lee Ermey, Burton Gilliam, Clare Hoak, Brewster Gould (Lusus), Pete Koch (mutant), Cindi Gossett (Elaba).

"In the days following nuclear disarmament by the super powers, a more horrifying holocaust decimated mankind. Covert biological warfare, deemed an 'accident' by some, released a virus so devastating that only a handful of humans survived. Grotesque genetic mutations were spawned."

Threefold problems for the research lab here: a virus which "randomly attacks the immune system"; a severed mutant finger which regenerates; and mutant sperm which produces a mutant baby which gets bigger and .... ("It's still growing!") Follow-up

to *Terror within* is an awkward mixture of action and sentiment. Especially clumsy: the setting-up and execution of the tarantulas-in-the-cactus bit. Bronson Caverns forever!

**TERROR Y ENCAJES NEGROS** (Mex) Conacite II 1986 color feature. SP,D: Luis Alcoriza. Ref: Ecran F 73:70. V 7/16/86: "terrifying" chases unintentionally funny. With Gonzalo Vega, Maribel Guardia, Jaime Moreno.

Razor-welding, fetishistic psychopath collects hair of female victims.

**TERRORGRAM** Monarch/Blue Moon (S.M. Kienzle) 1990 color 88m. P, D: Kienzle. Ph: D.A. Newman. Mus: Roy Ravio. MkpFX: John Blake. Ref: TV: Monarch HV. Stanley. PT 14:50. With James Earl Jones (The Voice of Retribution), Jerry Anderson, Michael Hartson, J.T. Wallace, Linda Carol Toner, Steven Field.

1) "Heroine Overdose." SP: Kienzle, Donna M. Matson. SpFX: Court Wizard. Opt: PMP. VisFxSup: Richard Malzahn. Chauvinistic moviemaker (sample movie: "The Minnesota Microwave Massacre"—"They loved it in France!") finds himself in a female-dominated world on Elm Street. Plus incidental power-drill gore. A few laughs.

2) "Pandora." SP: Kienzle. Macabre music box, visualized nightmare re monster, predictable kicker.

3) "Veteran's Day." SP: T.F. Wells, Kienzle. Ph: Irwin, DiLibero. Ghoulish MIA returns to haunt betrayer, take him back to Viet Nam, c1968. Glib, pompous. With Paul Perme as a zombie GI.... Film's first and last smart move: hiring Jones to narrate.

**TERRORVISION** Excel Telemedia Int'l.-TV 1985 color 85m. Ref: TV. TVG. no Maltin '92. Stanley. "Final Edition": SP,D: Jonathan Heap. Story: Nathan Klein. SP: also P. Morton. Ph: John Newby. Mus: Steve Melillo. with Margaret Johnson, Philip Morton. Undistinguished variation on the "Mr. Tiger" sequence in *Tales That Witness Madness.*

"The Closet Monster": D: Mark Esposito. SP: James Percelay, N. Klein, J. Horowitz. Ph: Marc Hirschfeld. Mus: Paul Mesches. SpFX: Bill Depaolo. with Jonathan Gabriel, Terry Iten, Depaolo (monster). Awkward variation on the "boy who cried wolf" theme features a real, glowing-red-eyed monster in the closet.

"The Craving": D: John Auerbach. SP: J. Heap. Story: N. Klein. Ph: J. Haymar. Mus: P. Mesches. with Bill Reilly, Kim Merril, Ron Darvan (Dr. A. Cula). Pointless Dracula-as-a dentist anecdote.

"Reflections of a Murder": D.A. Merrill. SP: P. Morton. Ph: M. Hirschfeld. Mus: S. Melillo. with Will Buchanan. Variation on a common silent-horror-movie theme — killer sees victim in mirrors — adds nothing new.

"One of a Kind": with Lynette Perry. Flatly written and acted tale of a shop owner who somehow turns models into mannequins.

"A Cold Day in July." Flat story with a weird twist: A shower stall turns into an ice chamber.

"Rosemary's Lot": The pickled body parts of a surgeon return to life.

**TERRORVISION** (U.S.-I) Empire/Altar 1986 color 83m. SP,D: Ted Nicolaou. Mus: Richard Band. SpMkpFX: John Buechler, MMI. SpSdFX: John Paul Fasal. Monster Vocal FX: Frank Welker. OptFX: Motion; (anim sup) Linda Obalil. Ref: TV. V 2/12/86. MFB'86:322-3. Maltin '92. Phantom. Scheuer. Morse. Stanley. Hound. Martin. With Gerrit Graham, Diane Franklin, Mary Woronov, Jonathan Gries, Alejandro Rey, Bert Remsen, William Paulson (alien).

"People of Earth ... destroy your satellite receivers!" The sanitation chief (Paulson) for the planet Pluton expels as garbage the Hungry Beast, a mutated pet. This "gross lookin' booger" winds up as a "stray energy beam" in the "hottest dish in town," on Earth. As a "big monster dude," it absorbs and recreates its human victims. Also on hand: Medusa's Midnight Horrorthon, a TV program which shows treasures like *The Giant Claw, Robot Monster,* and *Earth Vs. the Flying Saucers.*

The on-again, off-again plot in this entry in the Valley sf-horror-comedy subgenre doesn't generate much amusement, but it does yield a few charming moments with the monster. The latter is into very heavy metal (its various eyeballs dance to the music) and roots for the saucers in *Earth Vs. the Flying Saucers.*

**TESORO** (P. Rican) Taleski Studios (Myerston-Vives-Santiago) 1988 color 96m. SP,D: Diego de la Texera. SP: also Claribel Medina, Donald Myerston, Emilio Rodriguez. Mus: Gilberto Marquez. Ref: V 10/26/88: part-"ghost tale"; *Treasure* - tr t. With Maya Oloe, Xavier Serbia.

**TEST TUBE TEENS FROM THE YEAR 2000** Para/TorchLight (Karen L. Spencer/Jerry Goldberg) 1993 color 74m. (*Virgin Hunters* - alt t). D: Ellen Cabot. SP: Kenneth J. Hall. Ph: J.L. Spencer. Mus: Reg Powell. PD: Arlan Jay Vetter. SpFX: Real to Reel, Neal Smith. VideoFxPh: James Coker. Ref: TV: Para video. SFChron 7/16/94. vc trailer. PT 18:16. With Ian Abercrombie, Brian Bremer, Christopher Wolf, Morgan Fairchild, Michelle Matheson, Tamara Tohill, Don Dowe (Lex 500), Conrad Brooks.

In the future, in the Great Corporation of America, carnality is a crime. A "time chamber" trip to 1994 puts things right.... Vacuous. One cute prop: a giant staple. (Or, Problems with Center-folds.)

**TETO, MUSICA Y TRAVESTIS** (Mex) Cine Videos 1992 color 77m. D: Jaime Fernandez, Cesar D'Angelo. Ref: TV: MGS Video; no Eng.

Video of skits and songs features one sequence in which two men at a table are beset by ghostly skeletons. This scene segues into a stage number with dancing skeletons.

**TETO Y SU TETONA** (Mex.) MGS Film 1994 (1993) color 80m. D: Salvador Guerrero. SP: Rafael Pola. Ph: J. Shulz. Ref: TV: MGS video; no Eng.; end credits say '94; vc box says '93. With Leopoldo "Teto" Marcus, Eduardo Rosiles (El brujo Sadam), Rafael Pola, Alfonso Vega, Irma Aranda.

A warlock who can appear in puffs of smoke turns one man into a dog and plays telekinetic tricks on a priest and his aide (i.e., he makes a table lamp flash on and off). At the end, he possesses the latter.... Painfully cheap, shot-on-tape, t&a version of "The Temptation of St. Anthony" looks up to "Benny Hill."

**TETSUO: THE IRON MAN** (J) Original Cinema/Kaijyu Theatres 1988 ('92-U.S.) b&w 67m. Ph, SP, D, Exec P, Ed: Shinya Tsukamoto. Ph: also Kei Fujiwara. Mus: Chu Ishikawa. Sets: Tsukamoto. Ref: TV: Fox Lorber HV; Eng. titles. V 4/27/92. Bay G 7/15/92. SFChron 7/15/92; Dtbk 5/23/93. PT 9:8. Markalite 3:87-8. With Tomoroh Taguchi, Kei Fujiwara, Nobu Kanaoko, Tsukamoto.

Regular-Size Monster Series. A "metals fetishist" implants a metal bar in his leg, then finds a bit of metal in his cheek. A woman with her own metal problem haunts him, and he gets metal growths on his arm and foot. A drill replaces his penis. Soon, metallic growths cover his hand and face, and wires and pipes stick out of his back. He has become a "metal beast," a "miserable chunk of metal."

*Tetsuo* may be an original, but it's finally just a curiosity, a New Wave relative of the "human robot" in *The Robot Vs. the Aztec Mummy.* The fetishist's problem is like acne[3], but the first faint signs of it are more disturbing than the later mass-of-metal scenes. And inevitably we get a Gross Sex scene.

**TETSUO II: BODY HAMMER** (J) Toshiba EMI/Kaijyu Theater (Shishido-Kurokawa) 1992 color 81m. SP, D, Exec Co-P, Co-Ph, Ed, AD: Shinya Tsukamoto. Mus: Chu Ishikawa. SpMkpFX: Takashi Oda, Kan Takhama, Akira Fukaya. Ref: V 9/28/92: "overkill sets in early." 7/20/92:30. With Tomoroh Taguchi, Nobu Kanaoka, Tsukamoto, Toraemon Utazawa (mad scientist).

Man's body "starts changing into a hideous killing machine."

**TETSUWAN ATOMU** see *Astro Boy*

**TEX AND THE LORD OF THE DEEP** (I) RAI-TV Channel 3 & Cinecitta 1985 color 103m. (*Tex e il Signore degli Abissi*). SP, D: Duccio Tessari. SP: also Clerici, Coscia, Bonelli. Ph: Pietro Morbidelli. Mus: Gianni Ferrio. AD: Geleng, Patriarca. Ref: V 9/11/85: "a rousing disappointment." Ecran F 63:16.75:43-44. Palmerini. With G. Gemma, Carlo Mucari, W. Berger, I. Russinova, G.L. Bonelli (which doctor), Riccardo Petrazzi (Lord of the Deep).

Alchemist's "glowing green rock" mummifies victims. From the comic by G.L. Bonelli.

The **TEXAS CHAINSAW MASSACRE 2** Cannon (Golan-Globus/Henry Holmes, James Jorgensen) 1986 color 95m. (*The Texas Chainsaw Massacre Part 2* - ad t). D: Tobe Hooper. SP: L.M. Kit Carson. Mus: Hooper, Jerry Lambert. Ph: Richard Kooris. PD: Cary White. SpMkpFX: Tom Savini. Ref: TV. MMarquee 35:43-44. V 8/27/86. Maltin '92. Phantom. Newman. Martin. Scheuer. Stanley. Ecran F 74:18-21. 76:5,38-42,82. With Dennis Hopper, Caroline Williams, Bill Johnson, Jim Siedow, Bill Moseley.

"The saw is family!" But great grandpa is in "chainsaw heaven," as is grandma; grandpa is 137 years old and on a "strict liquid diet." Effective head of the cannibal clan: Drayton Sawyer (Siedow), proprietor of The Last Round-Up Rolling Grill, and easy winner of the big chili cook-off. (He stresses the phrase "prime meat" when asked the secret of his chili.) Chop-Top (Moseley), or Weird, Jr., insists on carrying the remains of his brother around with him. And Leatherface, or Bubba (Johnson), has "got a girl friend," Stretch (Williams), a K-OKLA D.J., whom he more or less brings home for dinner. "Home" here is — in the words of revenge-minded Lefty (Hopper) — the "devil's playground," an elaborate underground lair just off the main highway. Ultimately, Lefty and Stretch duel the boys with chainsaws.

The She Has Become One of Them, fade-out image is too pat, and Tobe Hooper is still, in this *Massacre* sequel, playing his heroine's pathetic screaming and pleading for much more than they're worth. But this strange marriage of horror and humor has an undeniable fascination. It's a mock-celebration of unchained energy. Periodically, Carson's script attempts to account for the clan's excesses by invoking the spectres of sexual repression and free enterprise, but the giddy ghoulishness seems beyond accounting, beyond, at least, the rather frail backlash-of-capitalism plotline. Money may be the root of all evil, but it doesn't quite explain Chop-Top and Leatherface. Weapons, monstrous props and sets, and off-the-deep-end exchanges, invective, and monologues proliferate. (The avenging Lefty, flourishing chainsaw: "I'm the lord of the harvest!" Drayton: "What's that? Some new health food bunch?") *Texas 2* is at once hilarious and sickening, and this fine, delicate balance is lost only when the film goes for outright gore. The latter — the only selling point of hollow shockers like *Demons* — is here oddly distracting. Here, the point is the manic activity — "It seems to have no end!" — and the comic-vitriolic vocabulary. Only once is this furious activity credibly checked, briefly, in the middle of the movie, when Stretch conscientiously restores her co-workers's (Lou Perry) skinned-off face to his dead body—a bizarre epiphany, but the only one possible in Monster World, Texas.

Sequel: *Leatherface*. See also: *Daffy Duck's Quackbusters. Junior. Sleepaway Camp 2. Transylvania Twist.*

The **TEXAS COMEDY MASSACRE** Positron Films 1987 color 84m. SP,D,P,Mus: Marcus Van Bavel. Ref: V 1/16/88: "homemade, often hilarious."

"Great Moments in Star Drek" segment features Capt. Kork, Mr. Spook, "and a host of aliens ...."

**TEXAS HONEYMOON HORROR** see *Honeymoon Horror*

**TEXAS 2000** see *2020: Texas Gladiators*

**THAT LITTLE MONSTER** Sinister 1993 b&w 54m. D: Paul Bunnell. Ref: Shock Cinema 8:33: "horrid ... critter." With FJA, Reggie Bannister, Melissa Baum.

**THAT'S NOT THE SAME AT ALL**  (Russ) A. Fedulov 198-? anim short. Ref: SFChron Dtbk 4/10/88:24.

Pollution-poisoned cow gives gasoline.

**THEATER AT HOME** see *House of the Yellow Carpet*

**THERE WAS ONCE A CHILD** see *Madhouse* (1981)

**THERE WILL COME SOFT RAINS** (Russ) Uzbekfilm Studio 198-? anim c10m. D: N. Tulyakhodjayev. Anim: S. Alibekov. Ref: PFA notes 11/16/86.

A "fantasy warning humanity against the madness of atomic war."

**THERE'S NOTHING OUT THERE** Valkhn Films/Grandmaster (Alice Glenn/The Nothing Out There Film Co.) 1991 (1990) color 90m. SP, D: Rolfe Kanefsky. Mus: Christopher Thomas. Ed, P: Victor Kanefsky. SpMkpFX: Imageffects. VisFX: FX House. SpFxSup: Scott Hart. Creature Des: Ken Quinn. Title Seq: Michael Ventresco. Ref: TV. V6/24/91. SFChron Dtbk 4/7/91. 11/15/92. With Craig Peck, Wendy Bednarz, Mark Collver, Bonnie Bowers, John Carhart III, C. Thomas (creature voice).

Is the "big green slimy thing with very large teeth," which is amok in the mountains, an "alien from outer space"? Whatever it is, it hails from Tentacle City, and it turns its victims' skin to Silly Putty. Its green eye-rays possess humans, and its "green slime" is digestive material .... Peck as Mike ("I'm just letting all the horror films I've ever watched get to me") is occasionally funny — just as often annoying — as the monster-movie know-it-all here, but the film has nothing else going for it.

**THERE'S SOMETHING ABOUT A SOLDIER** Para/Max Fleischer 1934 anim 6m. D: Dave Fleischer. Anim: Myron Waldman, Hicks Lokey. Ref: TV. LC. no Lee. Sean Smiley.

Hastily recruited soldiers employ huge swatters, corks, mallets, and boards, as well as gas, to fight hordes of giant mosquitoes, headquartered in a swamp .... Or, The Giant Mosquito Invasion. Tepid Betty Boop cartoon with unprepossessing monster menaces.

See also: *Jersey Skeeter, A.*

*****THESE ARE THE DAMNED** 1963 (1961) ws 87m. Mkp: Roy Ashton. Sculptures: Frink. Ref: TV. Jim Shapiro. V 7/14/65: 77m.-U.S., '65. Lee. Hardy/SF: originally 96m. With James Villiers.

"Someday, they will have to be told." A "mysterious project" near Weymouth ... Macdonald Carey as Simon Wells, the turtlenecked American ... the strange kids in the cave ("Your hands are cold as ice!") ... one child of light: "We don't mind being wet" ... Oliver Reed's thug King re the boy's touch: (horrified) "He's dead!" ... helmets-that-teach and lab-made food ... a passing reference to the children's "immunity" ... their mentor (Alexander Knox): "I do not want the children to watch him die!" ... The Curse of the Accidentally Irradiated: "Nothing that's warm can live with you."

Or, The Atomic Kids. The Losey/Jones/Lawrence film begins pretentiously, but quirkily enough to intrigue, and some of the dialogue (particularly in some of the Carey/Shirley Anne Field scenes) might fruitfully have been pared. ("What else is there to do?", meanwhile, is a hand-me-down from *Rebel without a Cause*.) But this is a fitfully fascinating Rescue and Escape tale, partly because no rescue is possible. The kids aren't alright. The only possible outcome for the several protagonists: death for the warm-bodied, solitary for the cold. An uneven but memorable movie. The "Black Leather" musical take on "the age of senseless violence" is *A Clockwork Orange* and *West Side Story* in a nutshell. Indicative of the film's sense of the apocalyptic-pathetic: The cold boy latches on to the unreceptive King as "father." "Help us!"

**THEY BITE** Trio Ent. (W.J. Links) 1993 (1989) color feature. SP,D: Brett Piper. Ref: PT 12:47-8: "fun if overlong"; footage from *Monster from the Surf.* SFChron Dtbk 5/10/92. V 5/3/93:18 (rated). With Ron Jeremy, Christina Veronica.

Alien Fishmen.

**THEY LIVE** Univ/Alive Films (Larry Franco) 1988 color/ws 93m. D: John Carpenter. SP: Frank Armitage, from Ray Nelson's short story "Eight O'Clock in the Morning." Mus: Carpenter, Alan Howarth. Mkp: Frank Carrisosa. SpFxCoord: Roy Arbogast. SpPhFX: FX Assoc./Jim Danforth. SdFxCoord: Ecker, Fanaris. Ref: TV: MCA HV. V 11/9/88. East Bay Express 11/11/88. SFChron Dtbk 11/27/88. MFB'89:163. With Roddy Piper, Keith David, Meg Foster, George "Buck" Flower, Raymond St. Jacques, Norman Alden, John Goff, Jeff Imada (male ghoul), Michelle Costello (female ghoul).

"They own ... the whole goddamn planet!" Special dark glasses and contact lenses enable the wearer to see the subliminal messages ("Obey," "Marry and Reproduce," "Consume," "Buy," "Watch TV," "Do Not Question Authority") behind ordinary billboard ads, in magazines, and on currency ("This is Your God"), and to see the human-appearing aliens controlling the Earth as the "formaldehyde faced" ghouls they really are. These beings (apparently from Andromeda) are "turning our atmosphere into their atmosphere" and depend on a master signal from TV Cable 54 to keep their agenda and identity hidden. The "truth" glasses — a terrific gimmick — bring this movie to intermittent life. "Yes, yes! That's the way it is!" may be your initial reaction; your second may be, "Too bad they didn't find a story to go with the gimmick." At the least, however, *They Live* is a hip *V.* Carpenter, a bit presumptuously, explicitly casts himself as one of the enlightened and daring. ("Filmmakers like George Romero and John Carpenter have to show some restraint," opines an exposed ghoul on a TV talk show.)

**THEY WERE 11** (J) Central Park Media/Toho/Kitty Film & Nippon Victor (Minoru Kotoku) 1986 ('92-U.S.) anim color/ws 92m. D: Tetsu Dezaki, Tsuneo Tominaga. SP: Toshiaki Imaizumi, Katsumi Koide. Based on Moto Hagio's comic strip "11 Nin Iru." Ph: Nobuo Koyama. Mus D: Dan Oikawa. AD: Junichi Azuma. Anim D: Keizo Shimizu. Char Des: Ako Sugino, K. Shimizu. Ref: TV: U.S. Manga Corps video; Eng. titles. Voices: Akira Kamiya (Tada), Michiko Kawai (Frol), Hideyuki Tanaka.

"There should only be ten!" In a universe of "planet nations" and "warp navigation," a psychic, Tada, and a cyborg are among the space-science students taking their 53-day final exam for Cosmo Academy, aboard the "old spaceship" Esperanza, which is orbiting a black planet with a blue sun. Oddly, the students never entertain the possibility that the mysterious eleventh person in their midst might be part of the test. Highlight of this old-fashioned, stilted sf-mystery: Frol, who is a pre-hormone, neither-sex hermaphrodite. Some atmosphere provided by the "conductor vines" — used for wiring — which begin to overrun the ship. ("Sure is creepy.")

**THEY'RE PLAYING WITH FIRE** New World/Hickmar (Playing with Fire Partners) 1984 color 96m. SP, D, P: Howard Avedis. SP, P: Marlene Schmidt. Ph: Gary Graver. Mus: John Cacavas. SpFX: Charles Stewart. Mkp: Jill Rockow et al. Opt: Ray Mercer. Ref: TV: *Playing with Fire* - orig t? 5/2/84. With

Sybil Danning, Eric Brown, Andrew Prine, Paul Clemens, K.T. Stevens, Alvy Moore.

Hereditary paranoia appears to be behind a series of brutal murders, but the solution to this thin mystery is a cliche swiped from old murder mysteries like *The Crime against Joe* and *Harper.* A mystery is in trouble when there are more victims than suspects. The real star: the Danning chassis. She's Undressing might have been a more apt title.

**The THING IN THE BASEMENT** Brian Keister 198-? color c15m. SP,D,Ph: Richard Taylor. SpFX: Keister, Taylor. Mkp: John Buechler. Ref: TV: CINEMAGIC (Starlog Video), MPI HV. With Whit Reichert, Taylor, Charles Schneider, Buechler.

"There's a thing in my basement!" It's an "extraterrestrial beast from outer space" with an intermittently invisible shield. Sf-comedy with a silly twist.

**THINGS** Triworld Films (Lorrinda Collins) 1990 color 84m. SP,D,P: Andrew Jordan. SP,P: Barry J. Gillis. Ref: V 5/9/90:62(hv): "amateurish." With B.J. Gillis, Amber Lynn, Doug Bunston.

Horror-movie fan tangles with "real monsters."

**\*2 THINGS TO COME** 1936 c92m. SP also (uncredited): Lajos Biro. Ref: TV. Lee. Lentz. Hardy/SF. V 3/4/36: from H.G. Wells' novel *The Shape of Things To Come.* With Sophie Stewart, Ann Todd, John Clements.

It's bombs over England, and a vision of future fighting tanks in 1940 Everytown. By 1970, Everytown is an "accursed ruin of a town," thanks to "endless warfare" and "the wandering sickness," which has killed over half the people in the world. But, though the town is ruled by The Boss (Ralph Richardson), a bullying warlord, Wings over the World—based on the "freemasonry of science"—is "taking hold of things" worldwide, with its future planes and sleeping gas. Finally: the year 2036, after the end of "The Age of Windows." Everytown is a "great city," with its own indoor sunshine and the space gun, which shoots a pioneering couple into space in a shell. ("There! There they go!")

The first "movement" here (world war) is the most inspired. The comparison/contrast between little-boys' war toys and the film's visual shorthand for war itself propels it. (Huge shadows of marching soldiers seem to march to the beat of a boy's drum.) The second "movement" (The Boss) depends, less happily, on acting and drama, rather than spectacle, though Richardson's controlled roar carries what's carry-able. The third movement (the space gun) constitutes a fitfully impressive collision of spectacle and drama. The giant-screen-TV image of Cedric Hardwicke here might have been inspired by Abel Gance's split-screen Napoleon, as, God-like, the latter harangues his troops.

**The THIRD FULL MOON** (H.K.) Try Ease & P.U. or Pal Prods. 1994 color/ws feature. Ref: TV: Tai Seng Video; Eng. titles. Y.K. Ho.

"The monster is coming!" Bloody murder in a parking lot ... a hand ripped off in a lavatory. Behind it all: a super-strong, bullet-proof "mysterious man" or "monster"—"Super Satan." Plus a visualized nightmare re zombies.... Comedy-horror is more silly than cute and has a tacked-on fantastic-romantic finale.

The 13TH FLOOR (Austral.) Premiere & Medusa (David Hannay, Charles Hannah) 1988 ('90-U.S.) color 86m. SP,D: Chris Roache. D: (addl material) Adrian Carr. Ph: Stephen Prime. Mus: Garry Hardman. PD: Darrell Lass. SpMkp: Deryck de Niese. SpFX: Alan Manning. Opt: Mirage FX. Ref: TV: Prism Ent. video (Para). vc box: Mus: Mick Coleman, J. El Khouri. Hound. Martin. V 12/13/89. With Lisa Hensley, Tim McKenzie, Miranda Otto, Tony Blackett, Michael Caton.

A little girl (Kylie Clare) witnesses her father electrocute a little boy (Matthew Nicholls) on the 13th floor of an office building. Years later, the building's elevator seems to come to the grown-up Heather's (Hensley) aid, and a ghost boy rides the electric waves there. At the end, she somehow becomes electric too and zaps her killer-dad (Blackett) .... The lad's revenge is a long time coming, and there's not much to see in-between.

*The THIRTEENTH GUEST M.H. Hoffman 1932 67m. Ph: Harry Neumann, Tom Galligan. AD: Gene Hornbostel. Ref: TV. Greg Luce. Turner/Price. Phantom. Lentz. Weldon. Maltin '92. Hound. Lee. Cocchi. Stanley. Scheuer. Martin. With Erville Alderson, Tom London, Harry Tenbrook, John Ince, Henry Hall, Kit Guard, Lynton Brent.

Thirteen years after a certain Morgan died and left his estate to the "thirteenth guest," 122 Old Mill Road remains vacant. ("Gives me the willies.") Meanwhile, a hooded skulker intent on "killing off the family" uses a "little electrical device" to electrocute telephone users, and a weird "cry," or mad cackling, haunts the place. Smoother and more complicated than most old housers — apparently, "two different factions" are involved in the sinister goings-on — but generally to little effect. Paul Hurst does well in the Warren Hymer-ish role of Detective Grump, and Ginger Rogers seems to get killed early, but it's just plastic surgery. Film includes a classic clutching-hand scene.

THIS IS YOUR MUSEUM SPEAKING (Can.) Films Inc./Nat'l. Film Board of Canada 1981 color 3m. SP,D: Lynn Smith. Ref: TV: allosaurus and stegosaurus skeletons briefly to full-fleshed life. PFA. Films Inc. (Education Catalog '87). NFBOC Resource Guide.

THOSE ANNOYING ALIENS see titles under Urusei Yatsura

THOSE DEAR DEPARTED (Austral.) Phillip Emanuel 1987 color 90m. (Dear Departed - U.S. tv t). D: Ted Robinson. SP: S.J. Spears. PD: Roger Ford. Ref: V 8/17/87: "strains too hard." TVG. With Garry McDonald, Pamela Stephenson, Su Cruickshank.

Three ghosts return to Earth to haunt some murderers.

THOSE FEEDY ON BLOOD (Russ.) Lenfilm/Printex 1991 color feature (aka Blood-Suckers). D: Eugeny Tatarsky. From Alexei Tolstoy's story "The Wurdalak." Ref: Jones: vampire grandma. V 10/19/92:122. Hardy/HM2: Pyushchye Krovy - orig t. With Marina Vlady, D. Banionis.

See also Father, Santa Klaus Has Died.

THOSE MERRY SOULS (H.K.) Golden Harvest/Bo Ho Films (Paragon) 1985 color c94m. Ref: TV: Rainbow Video; Eng. titles. V 10/16/85:338: aka Merry Souls? 5/7/86:439.

Ah Lung's father, a messenger of Death, dies saving his (Ah Lung's) friend Tak from another messenger, or "soul collector." At a seance, Ah Lung tells his father that he does not want to carry on the family tradition — i.e., to succeed him as Death's messenger — and his father and a demon fight "within" the seance's medium. During the climactic exorcism, the demon possesses, first, a woman, Lok, then Tak, then Tak's father, then the medium herself. The skeletal cartoon demon is finally trapped inside a glass box, but ....An interesting subject — the inner workings of the ultimate collection agency — yields a few unusual scenes and a too-tricky plot. Funny: a scene in which Ah Lung's father, now invisible and separated from his body, keeps catching a vase which Tak keeps knocking down. (The first time is an accident, but Tak gets curious when the vase stops in mid-air.) Creepy: Ah Lung's father's nightmare of the street of ghosts and the cackling pig's head.

THOU SHALT NOT KILL ... EXCEPT Kingsmark Film/Film World (Action Pictures/Shirley & Arnold Becker) 1985 color 83m. (Bloodbath - orig t. Sgt Stryker's War - int t). Story, SP,D: Josh Becker. SP,AD,P: Scott Spiegel. Story: also Sheldon Lettich, Bruce Campbell. Mus: Joseph LoDuca. SpMkpFX: Gary Jones. Sp Hair Appliances: Roger White. Ref: TV. V 9/30/87. ad. V 10/16/85:95. With Brian Schulz, John Manfredi, Robert Rickman, Tim Quill, Sam Raimi, Cheryl Hansen, Ted Raimi.

"The bloodbath is coming!" Basic gratuitous-gore vehicle, big on impalements, also features a human dart board, a killer-Jesus cult's "blood ritual," a severed arm, lethal back-snapping, etc. Flat dialogue and delivery of same; garbagey script.

THOU SHALT NOT SWEAR (H.K.) Try Ease Ltd./Paragon 1993 color/ws 102m.Ref: TV: Tai Seng Video; Eng. titles.

"They come even at death." Cop comedy-drama (re seven who vowed as children to meet every year on July 14) turns horrific-fantastic halfway through, with a haunted elevator, ESP, and deadly tree limbs. But the best-for-last chill: the beckoning ghosts at each window of the reunion house on Kowloon Peak. Movie begins blandly, steadily picks up interest.

THOUSAND-AND-SECOND TALE OF SCHEHERAZADE, The see Sinbad of the Seven Seas

THRAUMA (I) VSOM 1983 74m. SP, D: Gianni Martucci. SP: also A. Capone, R. Russo. Mus: U. Continiello. Ref: ETC/Giallos: "ineptly made." Palmerini: 1980. With Roberto Posse, Timothy Wood, Franco Diogene.

Necrophilia, machete murders.

THREADS (B-Austral.) TBS-TV/BBC-TV & Western-World TV & The Nine Network 1984 ('85-U.S.) color 117m. D, P: Mick Jackson. Tel: Barry Hines. Ph: Andrew Dunn. Des: Chris Robilliard. VisFxDes: Peter Wragg. MkpDes: Jan Nethercot. Ref: TV: World Video. TVG. Morse: "very well done." Phantom. NYT 1/12/85. New Leader 12/10/84. Scheuer: "most convincing antinuclear drama to date." With Karen Meagher, Reece Dinsdale, David Brierley, Rita May, Nicholas Lane, Henry Moxon, Paul Vaughan (narrator).

"They've done it!" U.S.-U.S.S.R. confrontation in Iran ... prepanic traffic congestion in Sheffield, England ... demonstrations

... the voice of authority: "You are better off in your own home" (even if it's the bull's-eye of the nuclear target) ... PA instructions re what to do with a dead body in the house ... ATMs shutting down ... sirens ... panic ... infrastructure breakdown ... Woolworth blasted ... 210 megatons over the U.K. ... fires ... a burning bicycle ... special makeup (as we imagine our own collective death) ... lethal fallout ... vomiting ... body counts ... "They're all gonna die anyway!" sentiments ... "clouds of debris" and lower temperatures ... SRO hospitals ... an arguably responsible Use of Gore ... flaring tempers ... ten-million-plus unburied bodies in England ... "In the first few winters, many of the young and old disappear from Britain".... A harrowing Last Horror Story, with an indifferent windup, but a good pitch. More a film of vignettes than story.

*THREE CASES OF MURDER London Films/Wessex & British Lion 1955. Mus: Doreen Carwithen; (dance) Eric Rogers. Mkp: George Frost. Host: Eamonn Andrews. Ref: TV: Janus-TV. Jim Shapiro. V 3/16/55. Lee. Lentz. Hardy/HM. Maltin '92. Scheuer. Stanley.

"In the Picture," from a story by Roderick Wilkinson. Mr. X (Alan Badel) and Jarvis (Hugh Pryse), a gallery tour guide, enter the house in The Mallaby Room portrait, "Landscape - Artist Unknown" — a "masterpiece of the mysterious" furnished with pieces from the museum itself. Mr. X proves to be the artist and wants a light in the house's window to complete his painting .... Wry, macabre tale re damnation in "cold landscapes." Talky scenes "inside" the painting, however, tend to dispel the sense of mystery.

"Lord Mountdrago," from a story by Somerset Maugham. The "brilliant but insufferable" Mountdrago (Orson Welles) is plagued by nightmares of embarrassment featuring his nemesis Owen (Badel), "that vulgar, grinning little cat." Ultimately, Mountdrago "kills" Owen with a dream, but Owen's laugh still haunts him .... Tricky, intriguing anecdote anticipates both *Nightmare on Elm Street* — in its intermixing of dreaming and waking life — and *2001* — in its association of "Daisy" with madness. Welles' rhetorical tricks are quite enjoyable. Badel's presence in all three stories (including the non-fantastic, transparently "clever" "You Killed Elizabeth") is oddly unifying.

3 X 3 EYES (J) Emotion/Star Child (Bandai) 1991 anim color 59m. From Yuzo Takada's comic. Ref: TV: Kodansha Video; no Eng. (apart from title). Animag 11:5. 12:7. Martin. V.Max 2:5,25: 1st & 2nd of 4 OAVs, 2 per vt.

Supernatural beings here include the mysterious Pai, a "triclops" — a 300-year-old immortal with a third eye who can turn people into zombies, but who turns her human friend Yakumo into a fellow immortal ... the huge monster Takuhii, which has the head of a beast and the body of a bird ... Huang and Chou, members of the Yo Kuai race ... the Tou Chyao, or Earth Claws, which look at first peek like demonic, mobile geysers, then (when they fully reveal themselves, above ground) like big crab-bugs ... the huge, lobster-like Demon of Corruption ... a frog/human monster ... and a giant tentacle/snake creature.

Okay monster fantasy is lively, light but not too light, serious but not too serious. The Takuhii is the most unusual of the film's menacing monsters (Pai is a friendly sort) — principally because of its odd size: Larger than human-sized monsters (like vam-

pires), but smaller and thus more "personal" than a Godzilla, it can track its prey (in this case, Pai and Yakumo) to an alley, but not quite squeeze into same.

The 3-D ARMY (H.K.?) 1992? color/3-D 93m. Ref: TV: vt; Eng. titles.

Principals include the mean, bloodthirsty hopping vampire Hung Kun, who "can become invisible" ... the Elder Ho, who uses Maoshan sorcery in an attempt to create an army of "magic soldiers," or hopping ghosts ... a "little hopping zombie," dubbed "Zomby" ... and Mimi, a little flying fox-ghost. Lively but ordinary horror-comedy is rife with old-fashioned, in-your-face 3-D effects. The most unusual sequence — obviously calculated to be a visual riot in 3-D — is set in a "spirit house" overrun with masked "demons," artificial butterflies, and bubbles. Cute: Zomby hopping across the surface of a pond.

2P The THREE WEIRD SISTERS (B) British Nat'l. 1948 80m. D: Dan Birt. SP: Louise Birt, Dylan Thomas. Adap: David Evans. From Charlotte Armstrong's book *The Case of the Three Weird Sisters*. Ph: Ernest Palmer. Mus: Hans May. AD: C.W. Arnold. Mkp: Henry Hayward. Murals: Lehmann & Wood. Ref: screen. William K. Everson. PFA notes 1/20/87. V 3/10/48: "horror story." MFB'48:30. no Lentz. no Lee. With Nancy Price, Mary Clare, Mary Merrall, Nova Pilbeam, Raymond Lovell, Anthony Hulme, Hugh Griffith, Elwyn Brook-Jones, Marie Ault, Edward Rigby.

Cwmglas, Wales. "How vile was my valley ...." A flavorsome blend of horror (ominous close shots, dark hallways, Brook-Jones' slow-witted menace), mystery, and social comment. Even-handedly, the script's visual and verbal barbs prick all — the poor, the rich and crass, the rich and "nice" (the sisters), the working class, and the pastor. Prize performances by Lovell; Price, Clare, and Merrall (as the weird ones); Griffith, and Rigby. The whole valley is weird in this wry, acerbic, offbeat movie. Highlight: a macabre "montage" intercutting the flashing eyes of the sisters with the eyes of a portrait. Highlight II: witty-sinister shots of the secretary (Pilbeam) flanked by Maude (Clare) and Isobel (Merrall).

3 WISHES (H.K.) Win's Film & Samico Film 1989 color/ws c88m. Ref: TV: Rainbow Video; Eng. titles.

Principals include the ineffectual Devil Ghost, from the urine pot, who is "too kind" to collect the souls that he needs ... Chan Hong Tai, a tour guide who shows Japanese tourists wax models of Mr. Vampire ("very famous" in Hong Kong), Mr. Roboto (an "English ghost"), a mummy, and "black and white ghosts" ... the bad ghost, who, at the end, sucks Tai into his inflated, room-sized head, where the possessed and absorbed Devil Ghost resides as a sort of tonsil ... and an office-full of men who suddenly act like vampire-zombies ("Tits! Backsides! Girls!"), in a not-fully-explained sequence.

Hip, silly horror-comedy resorts too often to easy bathroom humor, but has some balmy, inventive moments — e.g. the rag-doll-ghost effect as Devil Ghost emerges from the pot. Worth repeating — a line which makes about as little sense in context as it does out of it: "Stupid, it's the mighty leg!"

THRILLER (3) see also *Driller*

The **THRILLING SWORD** (H.K.) George K. King 1982 color/ws c88m. D: Chang Shing-I. Ref: TV: Rainbow Video; Eng. titles. NST! 4:37: aka *Thrilling Bloody Sword*. Fango 107:59. vc box: probably sfa *Thunder Storm Sword*.

Horrific elements in this lively children's fantasy-with-monsters include a horrible, funny-looking Cyclops demon ... a nine-headed "siren," or dragon, which is remote-controlled, spiritually, by an evil exorcist ... flying, cackling giant heads ... an idol/god which "deadens" heroine Yaur-Gi's soul ... a huge bat-pterodactyl and several wimpy, human-sized bat creatures ... "immortals," near-invulnerable frozen warriors who come to life ... parts of a monster — arm, eyes, teeth, legs — that ultimately assemble into a whole, far-from-imposing monster which the prince hero dispatches with his neon "thunder sword."

The monsters are Papier-Mache City. But if the movie's effects are tacky, they're also fun, and the scriptwriters have a sense of humor — e.g., when the on-the-loose set of monster teeth bangs into a stone wall, it whimpers. Cutest element: a giddy little, double-exposed good fairy. Even the theme from *Halloween* turns up.

The **THRONE OF FIRE** (I) Cannon/Visione 1983 ('86-U.S.) color 89m. (*Trono di Fuoco*). D: Franco Prosperi. Story,SP: Nino Marino. Story: also G. Buricchi. Ph: G. Mancori. Mus: C. Rustichelli, P. Rustichelli. AD: F. Cuppini. SpFX: Paolo Ricci. Ref: V 7/2/86: "very ordinary." 5/11/83:32. 10/26/83:258: *Thrown Afire* - title error. Ecran F 37:57. Stanley. Morse: "lethargic and lackluster." Palmerini. With Sabrina Siani, Peter McCoy (Siegfried), Harrison Muller.

Devil's messenger, witch, invisibility, Valkyries, barbarians.

**THROUGH THE FIRE** Talon Prods. 1987 color 85m. SP, D: G.D. Marcum. SP: also B. Potter. SpFX: J.A. Garris et al. Ref: Hardy/HM2: "sloppily constructed" tale re a "seldom-seen demon."

**THROUGH THE MAGIC PYRAMID** see *Tut and Tuttle*

**THROUGH THE PORTAL OF TIME** see *Beastmaster 2*

**THUNDER KIDS 3: HUNT FOR DEVIL BOXER** (H.K.) IFD Films & Arts (Joseph Lai) 1991 color 89m. (*Hunt for Devil Boxer. The Thunder Ninja Kids: The Hunt for the Devil Boxer* - alt t). Story Devel, D, PD: Alton Cheung. SP: Chris Lam. Story: AAV unit. Ph: Yink Tak Li. Mus: Stephen Tsang. SpFxD: Ben Au. Mkp: Jenny Choi. SdFX: Anthony Kim. Ref: TV: Magnum Video; Eng. version. no Martin. With Mark Hougton, Vince Parr, Sophia Warhol, Tsui Po-Wah, Steven Tee, David Frank Hallet, Anthony Mui.

"She's got warm, fresh blood!" Principals here include hopping child vampires from a cemetery who drink blood only from "bad buys" and who can be visible to humans if they wish ... a satan-possessed naked woman ... a non-hopping ghost girl murdered by "satan's disciples" ... and a thug who turns half-zombie ("I'm a zombie now"), in a nod to Steve Martin and *All of Me* ("Half of him is still human").

A dubbed mess, with a few clever ideas — e.g., the vampire boy whose hiccups make him keep jumping, the baby vampire who carries bottle and pacifier with him wherever he goes, and the

line "I love type O." But who is the "devil boxer" and why does a spaceship appear in a few scenes?

**THUNDER OF GIGANTIC SERPENT** (H.K.) IFD Films & Arts (Joseph Lai, Betty Chan) 1988 color 85m. D: Charles Lee. SP: Benny Ho. Story: George Chu. Ph: Raymond Chang. PD: Jimmy Chu. SpFxD: Simon Chu. SdFX: Henry See. Mkp: Jenny Choi. Ref: TV: VSOM; no Eng. With Pierre Kirby, Edowan Bersmea, Danny Raisebeck, Dewey Bosworth, Jorge Gutman, Lee Hsiu Hsien, Carol Chang.

Scientists enlarge a frog. Their stray gizmo then makes a girl's pet snake huge. She plays catch with it. He, or she, chases off some thugs. After another exposure to enlarging rays, the papier-mache beast gets gigantic, and the girl rides its head. It wrecks bridges, picnics, and cities, in that order, in regulation panic-and-flee scenes, and planes strafe it.... Very tacky, occasionally campy monster movie crossed with a bad gangster movie.

**THUNDER STORM SWORD** see *Thrilling Sword, The*

**THUNDER WARRIORS** see *America 3000*

**THUNDER WOMEN** see *America 3000*

**THUNDERBALL** see *Never Say Never Again*

**THUNDERCATS: MUMM-RA LIVES** 1987 anim color c90m. Ref: TVG: the Luna-Taks. no Maltin '92. no Scheuer.

**THUNDERCATS HO!** Rankin-Bass-TV/Lorimar & Telepictures 1986 anim color c90m. Anim: Pacific. Tel: Leonard Starr, from characters created by Ted Wolf. Mus: Bernard Hoffer. Ref: TV. TVG. no Maltin '92. no Scheuer.

Grab-bag goodies: mini-robots (Ro-bears) ... reptilian, avian, feline, and walrus-like creatures ... mutants ... a magic sword ... a strength-draining substance ... a corridor of mummies with live, tentacle-like wrappings which mummify the hero ... their evil leader Mumm-Ra ... and a mechanical flying "dragon" .... Formula superheroics. The titular cry is repeated with alarming regularity.

**TI-KEN A MOSCOU** see *Plans Mysterieux, Les*

**TICKS** (U.S.-J) Republic & Daiei/First Look (Jack F. Murphy/Ticks United, Inc.) 1993 color 85m.(*Infested* - alt t). D: Tony Randel. SP: Brent V. Friedman. Ph: Steve Grass. Mus: Daniel Licht. PD: A. Tremblay. Idea & SpVisFX: Doug Beswick. Exec P: Brian Yuzna. SpMechFX: Ken Tarallo. MinPhD: M. Muscal. SpMkpFX: KNB. OptFX: PMP. Ref: TV: cr list C.L. Stone for Mus. Janet Willis. Sacto Bee 10/8/93(ad): as *Infested*. V 6/14/93: "dim and cliched horror pic." 3/29/93:18 (rated). Markalite 3:8-9. Fango 123:40-45. 128:10. PT 20:16. With Rosalind Allen, Ami Dolenz, Seth Green, Alfonso Ribeiro, Peter Scolari, Clint Howard, Virginya Keehne, Ray Oriel.

"Something drained your dog of all its blood." Horror re wood ticks, the "vampires of the insect world": Major Goop in the closet ... Yuck Larvae ... a "big bug ... gross and all slimy," courtesy of herbal steroids ... a They Went Within scene ... amusement with a skittering Big Tick with a hypo stuck in its back ... the yuck-plus "autopsy" on the tick ... the "I'm infested!" scenes ... the dead human who hatches the giant tick ... lots of squishing and fun-gross effects, in the hallowed tradition of *Fiend without a Face* ... functional characterizations ... and even a few good "busses."

**TIEJA WUDI MALIYA** see *I Love Maria*

**TIGER SHARK** see *Devil Fish*

**The TIGER'S WIFE** (Thai?) Kan Shun Film Co. 198-? color/ws c100m. D,P: Hui Keung. D: also Dy Savet. SP: Hsu Tien Yung. Ref: TV: vt; Eng. titles; H.K.? With Keung, Yung, Huoy Dyna, Su Pa.

An overlong, convoluted melodrama with supernatural overtones. "The tiger listens to her!" Did a tiger rape the unconscious Su Juan? He is shown hiking up her skirt, then ... cut. Villager: "Su Juan, yours is a tiger baby." Su Juan: "How could I have made love with a tiger?" The villagers don't know, but nearly burn her as a "witch" anyway. Also on hand: a man in a monster mask who pulls it off and declares, "I'm not a ghost. I'm a fortune teller." Later, a woman wearing a monster mask pulls her mask off and declares to her lover, "I like to make love with you with a mask on." Kind of a strange movie this.

**TIGHTROPE** WB 1984 color 114m. SP,D: Richard Tuggle. Ref: TV. V 8/15/84. SFExam 8/12/84.

Clint Eastwood vehicle with horrific overtones, including a masked strangler ... a *Cat People* (1942) - like chase sequence ... a visualized nightmare in which cop Wes Block (Eastwood) sees himself as a hooded killer ... a thunderstorm ... an eerie wax museum ... carnival horror masks ... a severed arm ... and a climactic chase through a cemetery.... Low-key photography, music, and acting; pretentious script. ("There's a darkness inside all of us.")

**TILL DEATH SHALL WE START** (H.K.) Golden Harvest/Bo Ho Films (Paragon) 1990 color 91m. Ref: TV: Pan-Asia Video; no Eng.

Ingredients: a disappearing gent whose top and bottom halves occasionally act independently of each other and scare some teens — later, as a man's double, he extracts his own heart ... a nervous "ghostbusting" crew with an ectoplasmic compass, anti-ghost spray, and a ghost-sucking vacuum — even slamming shutters make this bunch jump ... and a holy neon jump rope .... Alternately foolish and clever ghost comedy features a funny, bizarre scene with a detachable flying eyeball (compare *Brother from Another Planet*) and, elsewhere, a bit of *Innerspace* when the ghost drops into a man's stomach.

**TILL THE END OF THE WORLD** see *Until the End of the World*

**TIM BURTON'S THE NIGHTMARE BEFORE CHRISTMAS** see *Nightmare before Christmas, The*

**TIME BARBARIANS** Marketing Media (Feifer-Miller/Philip J. Jones) 1990 color c85m. (*In the Time of the Barbarians* - vt t). SP,D: Joseph J. Barmettler. Ph: Kevin Morrisey. Mus: Miriam Cutler. AD: Sergio Zenteno. SpVisFX: William S. Mims. Prosth:

William Goodwin. Magic Sword: Tony Swatton. Ref: TV. TVG. Martin. V 10/19/92:16 (rated, as *Time Barbarians: The Magic Crystal*): Vista Street. With Deron Michael McBee, Jo Ann Ayres, Daniel Martine, Louis Roth, Michael Ferrare, Ingrid Vold (the wizard), Matt Devlen.

"In an ancient time of swords and sorcery," a crystal amulet protects the Armana tribe. Meanwhile, our barbarian hero, Doran (McBee), magically voyages to present-day Los Angeles ("Welcome to L.A."), in hot pursuit of a thug, Mandrak (Martine), from his time .... Uncannily similar to *Beastmaster 2, Time Barbarians* substitutes gab for effects. ("There's so much evil and pain in the land.") And it doesn't help that these ancient dudes speak proper English.

See also: *In the Time of the Barbarians II*.

**TIME BOMB** see *Timebomb*

**TIME BURST — THE FINAL ALLIANCE** Action Int'l. (David Winters, Bruce Lewin) 1989 color 93m. SP,D,P: Peter Yuval. SP: also Michael Bogert. Ref: V 9/27/89: "awkwardly constructed." With Scott David King, Michiko, Gerald Okamura, Jay Richardson, Beano.

"Sci-fi" re the "key to immortality."

**TIME FIGHTERS** see *Timefighters*

**TIME FLYER** ABC-TV/Walt Disney-TV (Three Blind Mice) 1986 color c90m. (*The Blue Yonder* - orig t). SP,D: Mark Rosman. Mus: David Shire. SpFxSup: Dave Pier. VisFX: Peter Donen. Opt: (fx) Mark Dornfeld; MGM. Ref: TV. TVG. V 2/12/86:80. With Huckleberry Fox, Art Carney, Peter Coyote, Frank Simons, Mittie Smith, Dennis Lipscomb.

Young Jonathan Knick (Fox) travels via time machine back to May 14, 1927, in order to prevent his grandfather, Max Knickerbocker (Coyote) — whose Time Traveler Project inspired the time machine — from attempting a transatlantic plane flight, which Jonathan knows will be unsuccessful. ("We conquered time!") Max has visions of one of his half-car/half-planes in every garage .... Bland, unimaginative sf-comedy-drama was a forty-minute sketch floundering about in a two-hour Disney Sunday Movie slot. Shire's score has a good main light-adventure theme.

**The TIME GUARDIAN** (Austral.) Nelson Ent./Hemdale/Chateau & IFM & S. Austral. Film Corp. & Austral. Film Comm. (FGH) 1987 ('89-U.S.) color/ws 98m.-U.S. (85m.). SP,D: Brian Hannant. SP: also John Baxter. Mus: Allan Zavod. SpVisFX: (sup) Andrew Mason; Mirage; (min sup) David Pride. Prosth Mkp: Beverley Freeman. MechFxSup: T. Pride. Jen-Diki Des: Brendan McCarthy. SpProps: Conrad Velasco. OptFX: Pope, Swinbanks. SpSd: Frank Lipson et al. Ref: TV. V 11/25/87. ad. Bill Warren. Sacto Bee 8/2/89. With Tom Burlinson, Nikki Coghill, Carrie Fisher, Dean Stockwell, Wan Thye Liew (Sun-Wah).

"I come from the future, from a city that travels in time" — specifically, from the year 4039 and a desolate Earth, back to 1988. But the bloodthirsty Jen-Diki, cyborgs — "survivors of the last great Neutron Wars" — use a "triangular force field" to "burst through time" and follow the city dwellers. ("They kill to live.") .... Uninvolving science-fiction epic seems a tired, belated effort to capitalize on the *Star Wars* phenomenon and update it with the more-popular-than-ever time-travel angle.

**TIME MACHINE, The** see *Gremlins. Rueckkehr Der Zeitmaschine.*

**TIME OF THE APES** (J) Sandy Frank/Tsuburaya 1974 ('87-U.S.) color 94m. D: Atsuo Okunaka, K.S. Fukazawa. SP: Keiiche Abe. Story: S. Komatsu, K. Tanaka, A. Toyoda, from episodes of the TV series "Saru No Gundan." Ph: Y. Mori. Mus: Toshiaki Tsushima. Ref: TV. Horacio Higuchi. TVG. Stanley. Weisser/JC. With Reiko Tokunaga, Hiroko Saito, H. Omae.

"Why are they all apes here?" Cryogenically-frozen people (in "cold sleep") awake in the year 2980 or so and find apes and the Universal Eco-Systems Control Computer, the "supreme power." ("I don't wanna be killed by monkeys!") After an amusingly precipitate beginning, flat melodrama with badly-dubbed "apes" sets in. Miscellaneous captures, threats, escapes, teary reunions, throwaway Deep Thoughts. ("One day different people will learn to live together ....")

**TIME OF THE BEAST** see *Mutator*

**TIME OF THE WOLVES, The** see *Into the Badlands*

**TIME RAIDERS** see *Warriors of the Apocalypse*

**TIME RUNNER** (U.S.-Can.) New Line/Excalibur (Curtis-Simandl/NAR) 1992 color 89m. (*In Exile* - orig t). SP,D: Michael Mazo. SP: also C. Hyde, G. Derochie, R. Tarrant, J. Curtis, I. Bray. Ph: D. Nowak. Mus: B. Farnon, R. Smart. PD: M. Bjornson. SpVisFX: John Gajdecki; (sup) Dave Axford; Magic Camera; (d) Steve Begg. SpMkpFX: Tim Gore. SpFX: Paller SpFX. OptFX: Film FX. Escape Pod: Tim Rose et al. Interior Pod: Northern Airborne et al. LaserFX: Laserhouse et al. Ref: TV. TVG. SFChron Dtbk 4/18/93. Martin. PT 16:57. V 10/14/91:A-42. With Mark Hamill, Brion James (Neila), Marc Baur, Gordon Tipple, Rae Dawn Chong, Allen Forget, John Thomas, Barry W. Levy.

During an alien attack — on Washington, D.C., and on a space station — in the year 2022 — station captain Michael Rainier (Hamill) escapes in time through a "worm hole" back to 1992, where, with too-great irony, he ultimately assists at his own birth. Also: an alien (James) as World President Neila (in 2022) — spell it backwards — a cell-regenerating gizmo for wound-healing, and visions (Michael's) of the near-future .... Competent, but routine, corny sf-actioner. Okay space effects.

**TIME STRANGER** see *Etranger, Time Alien*

**TIME TO REMEMBER, A** see *Running against Time*

**TIME TRACKERS** Concorde/Pacific Trust (Roger Corman) 1989 color 87m. SP,D: Howard R. Cohen. Mus: Parmer Fuller. SpFxMkp: Roy Knyrim. SpFX: Gregory Landerer. Opt: Motion. Ref: TV. V 5/17/89. Maltin '92. Hound. Martin. With Ned Beatty, Wil Shriner, Kathleen Beller, Bridget Hoffman, Lee Bergere, Robert Cornthwaite, Parley Baer.

"The past never changes." Scientists follow a mad inventor (Bergere) back in time, from scientist-ruled 2033 to 1991, then to the year 1146, a "very romantic age." At the end, the future scientists condemn Zandor to travel through time forever .... Low-grade, budget-conscious fun. The plot yields the not-too-thrilling novelty of laser-gun rays and "magnetic balance waves" (which defy gravity) in the Medieval era.

**TIME TRIPPER** see *Wizard of Speed and Time, The*

**TIME TROOPERS** (Austrian) Dieser Film (Heritage Ent./Morning Terror)/Arion & Austrian TV (Reinhart) 1984 color c92m. (*Morgen Grauen*). D: Peter Simann. SP: Hans Bachmann. Ph: H. Polak. Mus: Willie Resetarits, Georg Herrnstadt. SpFX: Tommy Vogel et al. Mkp: Gunter Kulier. SdFX: Mel Kutbay, H. Harss. Opt: (U.S.) Ray Mercer. Ref: TV: Prism Ent. video; Eng. dubbed. Hound. no Martin. V 11/14/84. HR 2/23/88:S-89. aka *Morning Terror*. With Albert Fortell, Hannelore Elsner, Hans Georg Panczak, Barbara Rudnik, Wolfgang Gasser, Dietrich Siegl, Renee Felden.

Cycle One, Era Three, a time of "selective breeding" and two-year "bonding contracts." In this callous future society — after the "nuclear fire" — the Exit Man terminates those whose Lifecards have expired, "non-compliants" oppose the Centron-computerized order, "self help" means "suicide," human "energy field" detectors take the place of fingerprint analysis, and "recyclers" are ambulance attendants who follow the Exit Men around.

Wordy sf-satire (with its meaningless U.S. video title) has some wry computer-speak. (Hero's computer, to hero: "It's good to see you facing the world, Len.") And the TV commercial for Vitex-Plus, the "gentle way to end your life," is very funny. (A split-screen demonstration shows the messy, old gun method on one side and the more decorous Vitex-Plus method on the other.) But the script is less successful in its non-ironic mode, with the earnest good guys, the non-compliants.

**TIME WARP TERROR** see *Bloody New Year*

**TIMEBOMB** MGM-UA/Raffaella (De Laurentiis) 1991 (1990) color 96m. (aka *Time Bomb*). SP,D: Avi Nesher. Mus: P. Leonard. PD: Pruss, Schnell. SpMkpFX: Todd Masters. SpVisFX: PMP;(sup) Richard Malzahn; 525; (des) Mark Zarate; (opt sup) Robert Habros. SpFxCoord: Greg Landerer. Computer Images: Video Playback; (sup) Steve Irwin. SdFX: Blue Light. Ref: TV. V 2/10/92. Martin. PT 14:11. With Michael Biehn, Patsy Kensit, Tracy Scoggins, Robert Culp, Richard Jordan, Raymond St. Jacques, Billy Blanks, Ray Mancini, Carlos Palomino, Jeannine Riley.

"Died in Viet Nam in 1972." Is Eddy Kay (Biehn) one of "the living dead"? Are his "nightmares during the day" really memories? Yes and no, yes and no. Seems he was part of the government's Bluebird Program — which conducted "behavior modification experiments" in the Seventies — and was given a new ID and "induced" memories, and brainwashed to kill .... Clumsy, forced action-intrigue is occasionally so laughable that it plays like a parody of *The Manchurian Candidate*.

**TIMECOP** Univ/Largo Ent. & JVC Ent. (Signature-Renaissance-Dark Horse/Diamant-Raimi-Tapert) 1994 color 99m. D, Ph:

Peter Hyams. SP: Mark Verheiden. Story & Original Comic Series: Mike Richardson, Verheiden. Mus: Mark Isham. PD: Philip Harrison. VisFX: V/FX;(sup) G.L. McMurry. Computer Graphics: Video Image. SpFxCoord: John Thomas. SdFxDes: Phillips, McPherson. Ref: TV: MCA-Univ HV. SFChron 9/16/94. V 9/27/93: in prod. ad. With Jean-Claude Van Damme, Ron Silver, Mia Sara, Gloria Reuben, Bruce McGill.

Time-hopping, skipping, and jumping (from 1863 to 1994 to 1929 to 2004) with the Time Enforcement Commission, a U.S. Government agency in charge of apprehending those who would use time travel to the past for fun and profit—and would, incidentally, alter the future.... Pretty clever script has fun time tricks (with both effects and characters), but is padded out with action-movie grunts and groans. The colorless Van Damme is provided with imitation-Arnold quips. Main effects highlight: the monstrous "cocooning" out of existence of the two "same space" Silvers (past and present, roughly). Silver (present, mainly) as McComb occasionally makes the film seem better than it is.

**TIMEFIGHTERS** (U.S.-J) Kidpix/Tatsunoko Prods. (Jim Terry) 1974 ('85-U.S.) anim color 60m. (aka *Time Fighters*). D,P: Jim Terry. SP: Angelo Grillo. Ref: vc box (Embassy Home Ent.): robot. Hound.

Prof. Von Spock's time machine takes riders to prehistory and the future.

**TIMEFIGHTERS IN THE LAND OF FANTASY** (U.S.-J) Kidpix/Tatsunoko Prods. (Jim Terry/Bill Romeo) 1984 anim color 94m. D: Terry. SP; Angelo Grillo. Mus: Bullets. Ref: TV: Para HV. Hound. Voices: Alan Rich, Michael Bass et al.

"Go prepare the Pig Ship for battle!" Ingredients this time around — as the Grasshopper time ship enters "fantasy time" — include a huge robot-ape-ship, King Gong ("Turn that monkey off!"), which plays ear-shattering cymbals ... an Aardvark Ship which makes one character believe that he is a Superman-like character and makes the protagonists "see" huge rock monsters and spooky tree creatures ... a time-spanning computer ... the castle of the evil queen from "The Snow Queen" ... Tonk the Robot and his melting ray ... the Snow White-like Snow Flake and the Seven Dwarfs (in her old-hag guise, the evil Lucina [sp?] Skullduggery gives her a poisoned apple of sleep) ... a shape-changing, robotic cat-monster ship ... a sharp-toothed, evil giant (in "Jack and the Beanstalk") ... a robot-stegosaurus ship ... a giant Bear Ship ... and chunks of the tales "Little Red Riding Hood," "Cinderella," "The Pied Piper of Hamelin," and "Gulliver's Travels" .... Very busy but very ordinary animated children's-fantasy. Undisciplined and unimaginative.

**TIMESCAPE** see *Disaster in Time, A*

**TIMESTALKERS** CBS-TV/Charles Fries & John Newland-Maynard 1987 (1986) color 92m. D: Michael Schultz. Story, Tel: Brian Clemens. From Ray Brown's (unpublished) novel *The Tintype*. Mus: Craig Safan. AD: S. Austin. SpVisFX: Robert Blalack, Praxis. SpFX: Dick Albain, Jon Alexander. SdFX: Marvin Kerner. Opt: Howard Anderson. Ref: TV. V 3/25/87:76. TVG. Maltin '92. Hound. Martin. Scheuer. With William Devane, Klaus Kinski, Lauren Hutton, Forrest Tucker, John

Considine, John Ratzenberger, Gail Youngs, Tracey Walter, Daniel Pintauro.

Georgia Crawford (Hutton), a future woman (from the year 2586), makes a pit stop in 1986, and uses a "time crystal" to continue back to the old West and 1886 — in pursuit of evil scientist Dr. Cole (Kinski), who is plotting to tamper with history .... Hollow but fairly inventive script uses time travel several different ways. Pleasant cameo by Tucker, in his last movie.

**TIN STAR VOID** Six-Shooter Films 1988 color 95m. (*Death Collector* - export t). D,Co-P: Tom Gniazdowski. SP: John McLaughlin. Ph: Adam Goldfine. Mus: Sound X. AD: D. Perlman. Ref: V 1/4/89: "self-consciously post-modern Western-comedy-sci-fi actioner." PT 13:49: "pretty dry." With Daniel Chapman, Ruth Collins, Loren Blackwell, Karen Rizzo.

"A nationwide disaster, the collapse of the economy .... " (V)

**TIN TOY** Pixar (John Lasseter & Cordell Barker) 198-? computer anim short. Ref: SFExam 4/14/89: "a treasure."

Destructive baby horrifies tin one-man-band and other toys.

**TINTYPE, The** see *Timestalkers*

**TINY TERRESTRIAL** see *Little Boy Blue*

**TIRADOR DE DEMONIOS** see *Exorcismo Negro*

**TITAN FIND** see *Creature*

**Ang TITSER KONG ALIEN** (*Wooly Booly II*) (Fili) Viva Films (William Leary) 1990? color c105m. (*Wooly Booly 2* - ad t). SP,D,Story: Ben Feleo. SP,Story: also Ely Matawaran. Ph: Erning de la Paz. Mus D: Mon del Rosario. PD: Danny Cristoabs. Ref: TV: Viva Video; part Eng. With Jimmy Santos (Wooly Booly), Vina Morales, Raymart Santiago, Kenneth Peralta, Mariz, Ruel Vernal, Ben Johnson.

In this sequel to *Wooly Booly* (which see), an alien apewoman joins Wooly Booly on Earth. At one point, she reverses the positions of a man's hands and feet (compare *Magic Crystal*) and, at the end, she and the alien leader-advisor are beamed up to a spaceship. In a coda, a final gag has a cemetery's dead rising en masse. Bonus: a Lucifer-type who enters one poor slob and, later, possesses a young woman.

**TIYANAK** (Fili) Regal Int'l. (Jenny Luber-Lily Monteverde) 1988 color c110m. SP,D: Peque Gallaga, L.A. Reyes. SP,PD: Don Escudero. Ph: E.F. Jacinto. Mus: Dionisio Buencamino Jr. SpFX: Teofilo Hilario. Animatronics: Maurice Carvajal. Mkp: Andrea Manahan. SdFX: Danny Sanchez. Ref: TV: Regal Video; little Eng.; probably not sfa *Tiyanak* (2P/'78). With Janice De Belen, Lotlot De Leon, Ramon Christopher, Chuckie Dreyfus, Mary Walter.

A mysterious baby found in an old room periodically turns into a monster-baby that kills an old woman who is on to its secret, then creates havoc in a hospital and a movie theatre. Finally, the apparent mother, or stepmother, Christie, watches tearfully and helplessly as it lies (in human form) in a burning house. Unable to bring herself to kill it, she seeks to console it, and it's at her throat.

About the closest this variation on the *It's Alive* films gets to Larry Cohen outrageousness is this climactic sequence. But if the movie is not very original, it is intense (and long): Action, music, and visual and sound effects make every sequence an experience. The scowling, animatronics baby gets to seem pretty rubbery after prolonged exposure, but the lighting and other atmospheric effects keep tensions high. The theatre sequence contains two of the best moments: the babe-in-the-sleeping-mother's-arms turning into the gruesome onesome ... and the nuisance laughing at the horror movie that's onscreen "getting it" first.

**TO CATCH A YETI** (Can.) New World/Visual Prods.(Shenken & Shenken-Brin/Dandelion) 1993 color c87m. D: Bob Keen. SP: Paul Adam. Ph: D. Perrault. Mus: Jack Lenz. AD: Gerine De Jong. SpMkp & Animatronic FX: Image Animation;(sup) Paul Jones, Martin Mercer. Ref: TV. TVG. Disney Channel mag. With Chantallese Kent, Meat Loaf, Jim Gordon, Leigh Lewis, Jeff Moser, Rick Howland, Kevin Robbin (voice of Yeti).

"Man-eating monsters that prowl the Himalayas—they don't exist." But sweet little Hank, the Yeti—a "monkey with big feet"—does. Cross references: *Harry and the Hendersons* (premise) and *Gremlins* (big-eyed beastie). Unoriginal children's monster-comedy. Cute: See Hank skateboard.

**TO DIE FOR** Skouras/Greg H. Sims/Arrowhead Ent.-Lee Caplin (Dracula: The Love Story) 1989 (1988) color 90m. (*Dracula: The Love Story* - orig t). D: Deran Sarafian. SP: Leslie King. Ph: Jacques Haitkin. Mus: Cliff Eidelman. PD: Maxine Shepard. SpMkpFX: John Buechler & MMI. SpFxSup: Eddie Surkin. Animatronics: John Criswell, Tim Ralston. OptFX: Cinema Research. Ref: TV. V 6/14/89. Cinef 1/90. HR 5/12/89. Drew/Motion Picture Series & Sequels. With Brendan Hughes, Sydney Walsh, Amanda Wyss (Celia), Duane Jones, Steve Bond (Tom), Remy O'Neill (Jane), Scott Jacoby.

"Dracula is based on this guy! Look, Bram Stoker only had the story half right!" The course of true supernatural love here would evidently run smooth if it weren't for the presence of this telekinetic Dracula's (Hughes) fellow vampire, Tom, who is mad at him for killing his girl friend. Film turns into a familiar how-to-kill-a-vampire pic, then concludes as Vlad exits as a romantic martyr. (Sunlight aids and abets him.) Slick but hollow horror-fantasy. Hughes as Vlad Tepish is like Jean-Pierre Leaud as Dracula.

Sequel: *Son of Darkness*.

**TO SAVE A CHILD** see *Craft, The*

**TO SLEEP WITH A VAMPIRE** Concorde (R. Corman/Mike Elliott) 1992 color 76m. D: Adam Friedman. SP: Patricia Harrington. Ph: M. Craine. Mus: N. Holton. Ref: V 1/11/93: "middling horror pic." 4/6/92:16. 10/5/92:19 (rated). SFChron Dtbk 1/24/93. Jones. With Scott Valentine, Charlie Spradling, Richard Zobel.

Remake of *Dance of the Damned*: Stripper meets vampire (Valentine).

**TOBE HOOPER'S NIGHT TERRORS** (Can.-Israeli-B?) Cannon/Global (Globus-Pearce/Harry Alan Towers/Surge Prods.) 1993 color 94m. (aka *Night Terrors. Tobe Hooper's Night-*

*mares*). D: Tobe Hooper. SP: Daniel Matmor, Rom Globus. Ph: Amnon Solomon. Mus: Dov Seltzer. MkpFX: David Miller; Lou Lazzara. SpFX: B. Abu-Rabea. Ref: TV: Warner HV(U.K.). PT 21:16. With Robert Englund, Zoe Trilling, William Finley, Alona Kimhi, Chandra West, Tamar Shamir (snake woman).

Characters and other ingredients include the Marquis de Sade (Englund), in flashbacks ("I will be avenged") ... Chevalier (Englund again), his descendant, and apparent instrument of the marquis' revenge ... a "major Gnostic site" outside Alexandria ... phantom Gnostics, who foil Chevalier at the end ... a couple severed heads ... and an eyeless, hanging corpse.... Dispiriting shocker wavers between simple hack work and something more peculiarly embarrassing. Most interesting esthetic ploy: the overlapping (in past and present) of the sounds of classical music and the screams of the tortured. Lots of "transcendental agony."

**The TOILET** Ron Duffy anim short. Ref: SFChron Dtbk 7/10/88: "diabolical seat sucks its user down the drain."

**TOKYO BLACKOUT** see *Shuto Shoshitsu*

**TOKYO CRISIS WARS** see *Battle Girl*

**TOKYO — THE LAST MEGALOPOLIS** see *Teito Monogatari* (1988, 1991)

**TOKYO — THE LAST WAR** (J) EXE & Imagica & Daio Paper 1989 color/ws 107m. (*Teito Taisen*). Ref: TV: vt; no Eng. vc box. Weisser/JC.

In this follow-up to *Teito Monogatari* (1988), a "rain" of incendiary canisters sets Tokyo aflame, and "fireflies" reanimate the "ancient warrior" from the first film. He can fly, hover, and make his enemies levitate and their bodies corkscrew, but at the end a psychic young man backed by power from a generator and prayers from all concerned coughs a vomit thing into the warrior's mouth, and he implodes.

Grisly but inventive horror-fantasy. In the most harrowing and imaginative sequences (in visualized daydream-hallucinations), a little girl in a hospital bed grows a fly-winged, mutant-caterpillar body, and human fingers begin wriggling out the sutured skin of a man's torso. Extra added: a guest bit by Hitler.

**TOKYO VICE** (J) Polydor Video 1988 anim color 53m. Ref: TV: P. Video; little English (apart from title); OAV. Animag 3:6.

Project Name: Doll. Action animation features a computer-controlled, two-legged-walker-like, ray-shooting robot and (in the credit sequence) a space station. Vapid music, stolid character design, okay climactic sequence with a belligerent robot.

**TOM AND LOLA** (F) Cinemanuel & Cerito Films & Caroline Prods. & EFVE Films & Orly Films & Zoom 24 & CNDLC & SNCF 1994? color/ws 97m. (*Tom et Lola*). SP, D: Bertrand Arthuys. SP: also C. de Chalonge, M. Teodori. Ph: F. Catonne. Ref: TV: VSOM; Eng. titles. With Neil Stubbs (Tom), Melodie Collin (Lola), Cecile Magnet, Marc Berman, Catherine Frot.

Shaved-headed children in experimental "bubbles" for ten years are "dying of boredom." ("You guys are really weird.") The "blasted little chromosomes," though, escape for a night on the town, including a train ride.... A sort of These are the Damned.

Occasionally poetic, but mainly eccentric sf-overtoned tale. The bubbles are so elastic that Tom and Lola can hold hands and pull their bubbles together when the scientists aren't looking.

The **TOMB** Trans World Ent. (Ronnie Hadar, Miriam L. Preissel) 1986 (1985) color c85m. D,P: Fred Olen Ray. SP: Kenneth J. Hall. Mus: Drew Neumann. SpFxAnim: Bret & Bart Mixon. SpMkpFX: MkpFX Lab. Ref: TV: TWE video. V 10/22/86. TVG. no Maltin '92. Phantom. Morse. McCarty II. Newman. Martin. Stanley. Jones. Hound: from a B. Stoker novel. Scheuer: loosely based on *The Jewel of Seven Stars*. With Cameron Mitchell (Prof. Howard Phillips), Michelle Bauer, Richard Alan Hench, Susan Stokey, David Pearson, John Carradine, Sybil Danning, Kitten Natividad, Dawn Wildsmith, Katina Garner (old Nefratis).

An earthquake uncovers the long-lost tomb of the Egyptian Princess Nefratis (Bauer), who vampirizes a victim or two in order to regain her youthful looks. She also inserts a terrible scarab beetle into the body of John Banning (Pearson) to assure his loyalty. Her goal: to transfer the life force from Helen (Stokey) to herself. Despite a funny bit here and there, *The Tomb* is basically a sluggish, woodenly-acted homage to classic Universal mummy movies. *The Mummy's Tomb* provides the name John Banning; *The Mummy's Hand*, Andoheb (Carradine); *The Mummy's Ghost*, Youssef (Emanuel Shipow); and the Karloff *Mummy*, Helen, plus actor David Manners' name (Hench).

See also: *Mummy and the Curse of the Jackals, The.*

**TOMB OF DRACULA** see *Dracula: Sovereign of the Damned*

*The **TOMB OF LIGEIA** 1964('65-U.S.) 81m. SpFX: Ted Samuels. Mkp: George Blackler. Ref: TV: Thorn EMI/HBO Video. Lee. Hardy/HM. V 1/20/65. Ottoson/AIP. Weldon. Phantom. Lucas/VWB.

"I live at night." Scriptwriter Robert Towne adds a few effective touches to Poe's carefully-constructed tale of the willful (even in death, apparently) Ligeia—the tomb with the date of death scraped off, the coffin with the wax dummy, the hairbrush filled with black (i.e., Ligeia's) hair. For the most part, however, the script is filled with tepid inventions—a bad-idea black cat, in fact, almost takes over the movie. Ligeia herself is reduced from a life (or life-in-death) force to a garden-variety menace, and the flavor of the story is almost completely lost. Even the name which Towne invents for Poe's "I"—Verden Fell (Vincent Price)—seems off. Last and just about least of Roger Corman's Poe films.

2 **TOMBS OF THE BLIND DEAD** Atlas Int'l. 1971 ws 95m. (*La Noche de la Muerta Ciega*). Stage FX: Luis Castro. Ref: TV: Redemption video; Eng. titles; "director's edit." Hardy/HM. VWB. TVG. With Maria Silva.

"They're the old Templars, come back to life." Excommunicated Templars into Egyptian satanism who were hanged (and had their eyes pecked out by crows) haunt the medieval cemetery at Berzano, otherwise deserted for 100 years. Their "death ritual": They bite their victims and sip their blood in order to extend their lives. In one sequence, one victim, Virginia, returns to life in the morgue and bites the attendant's neck.... First in the *Blind Dead* series is all atmosphere. First: the wraith-like fog from the tombs.

Next: the quiet hoofbeats. Then: the slowmo galloping. Unexplained: How the Templars corral the ghost horses. Best "set": the fine old monastery. The setting-up sequences with the humans here are mainly filler.

2 **TOMBSTONE CANYON** 1932. Ref: TV. Greg Luce. V 4/11/33. Hound. no Stanley.

"That was the cry of the phantom killer!" — when said cry is heard, men of the Lazy S die. The disfigured, black-cloaked killer has the "strength of a dozen men" .... Awkward Western dramatics. Good use of the cliffs and rocks of Tombstone Canyon. The phantom's cry is not exactly bloodcurdling. Lighting and makeup prove more effective than sound effects at making him appear sinister. Camerawork by Ted McCord.

**TOMCAT: DANGEROUS DESIRES** (Can.) Republic HV & Den & ES (Tomcat/William & Robert Vince) 1993 color 95m. SP, D: Paul Donovan. Ph: Peter Wunstorf. Mus: Grame Coleman. PD: Lynne Stopkewich. Prosth: T. Farkas. SpFxCoord: Garry Paller. Ref: TV. Martin. Stanley. SFChron Dtbk 8/8/93. With Richard Grieco, Natalie Radford, Maryam D'Abo.

"A secret inter-species genetic experiment causes a man to become more of an animal.... "(SFC) Or, in the film's own words: "You are a Frankenstein's monster ... a new species ... not a human, not a cat, something else." ("I'm the only one like me.") Offputting science-fantasy with an annoying score. It's like this: "You're good, you know."/"No, I'm not. I'm bad, very very bad."

**TOMEI TENGU** (J) Daiei 1960 73m. D: Mitsuo Hirotsu. Ref: CM 15:28: *Invisible Goblin* - tr t; remade as *Tomei Kenshi* (*Invisible Swordsman*). With Y. Nakamura, M. Kondo, C. Maki.

Invisible avenger terrorizes "corrupt officials."

The **TOMMYKNOCKERS** (U.S.-N.Z.) ABC-TV/Konigsberg-Sanitsky & K & S II (Jayne Bieber, Jane Scott) 1993 color c180m. (aka *Stephen King's The Tommyknockers*). D: John Power. Tel,Co-P: Lawrence D. Cohen. From King's novel. Mus: Christopher Franke. PD: Bernard Hides. VisFX: Perpetual Motion Pictures; (sup) Richard Malzahn. Morphing: Cinemotion. Mech Props Sup: Tad Pride. SpFxSup: Kevin Chisnall. Tommyknockers Des: Alterian Studios. Alien Sup: Brian Penikas, Vance Hartwell; (N.Z.) Richard Taylor. MkpSup: Marjory Hamlin. Main Title Des: Bielenberg Des. Ref: TV. TVG 5/8/93: alternately called TV-movie & mini-series. V 5/10/93:241. SFChron 5/7/93. With Jimmy Smits, Marg Helgenberger, Joanna Cassidy, John Ashton, E.G. Marshall, Allyce Beasley, Traci Lords, Robert Carradine, Cliff DeYoung, Karen Malchus (Tommyknocker).

"Something's happened to this town!" "There's magic there," says old Ev (Marshall), re Burning Woods. But you don't have to go into the woods to find magic. Right in town, you've got living toy dolls, an apparently possessed, glowing-eyed dog (a "regular Cujo"), a boy who disappears during a backyard magic act, a TV set affected with the green zap, a "telepathic typewriter" with the zap, and holiday fireworks with a green motif. Behind it all: death rays and aliens .... Shallow writing, cliched characters and dialogue — including the return of "I'm sure there's a logical explanation." Only intriguing element: the mean-green scheme.

**\*TOMORROW AT SEVEN** Jefferson Pictures 1933. AD: Edward Jewell. Ref: TV. Mo. Turner/Price. TVG. Lee(e). Lentz. V 7/4/33. no Maltin '92. Hound. Cocchi. Martin.

Ingredients: the mute housekeeper, Mrs. Quincey (Virginia Howell), who looks more like Mrs. Death ... the forbidding-looking "coroner," Simons (Charles Middleton) ... Neil Broderick (Chester Morris), author of such thrillers as "The Eyes of the Dead" ... and much prowling around darkened rooms, ominous slow knocking, and a clutching hand, in a "run-down plantation on the Mississippi." Warner Brothers-style comedy dominates here, unfortunately, in the persons of Frank McHugh and Allen Jenkins. The plot is secondary and hardly a wonder either. Well-shadowed sets, very guessable killer. Spookiest scene: Mrs. Quincey and Simons carrying the heroine away among moss-covered oaks.

**TOMORROW'S NEWS** see *Wicked, The*

**TONARINO TOTORO** see *My Neighbor Totoro*

**TONG FONG SAM HOP** see *Heroic Trio*

**TOO BEAUTIFUL TO DIE** (I) Filmirage(Manzotti) 1989 color 97m. (*Sotto il Vestito Niente 2*). SP, D: D. DiPiana. SP: also C. Mancini. Ref: Hardy/HM2. With F.E. Gendron, F. Guerin.

Slasher's crimes imitate video.

**TOO MUCH** (U.S.-J) Cannon (Golan-Globus) 1987 color 89m. SP,D: Eric Rochat. Narr written by Joan Laine. Mus: G.S. Clinton. SpFXCoord: Osamu Kune. Robot: (sup) Masaharu Ogawa; (des) T. Komiya et al. Computer: (anim) Animation Kab; (graphic coord) M. Kabutoya. Ref: TV. V 91/6/87. ad. SFChron 10/5/87. With Bridgette Andersen, Masao Fukazawa (Too Much), Hiroyuki Watanabe, Char Fontana.

Uncle Tetsuro (Watanabe), of the Japan Robotech Corp., is a "real genius": "I make robots." One of the latter, Too Much, or T.M., is "programmed to increase his own intelligence," repairs himself with "robot magic," and even milks a cow .... Too many formula elements — e.g., a car chase, slapstick bumbling by the comic baddies — and too few charming moments. Blandly uplifting ending.

**TOO MUCH FEAR** (I) Interfilm/G.P.E. & C.P.C. (Guy Luongo) 1976 color/ws 90m. (*E Tanta Paura*. aka *So Afraid*). SP, D: Paolo Cavara. SP: also Bernardino Zapponi. SpFX: G. Capelli. Ref: TV: VSOM; Eng. titles. ETC/Giallos. Palmerini.

"The monster is arrested." Desultory *giallo* with one scene in which a murder victim is put on a hook in a slaughterhouse. A few funny bits. Tom Skerritt and Eli Wallach's Italian is dubbed.

**TOO SCARED TO SCREAM** The Movie Store/The Doorman Co. 1985 (1982) color 100m. (*The Doorman* -orig t). D: Tony Lo Bianco. SP: Neal Barbara, Glenn Leopold. Mus: George Garvarentz; Charles Aznavour. Mkp: Chris Striepeke. SdFX: West Coast. Ref: TV. V 1/30/85. Maltin/TVM. With Mike Connors, Anne Archer, Leon Issac Kennedy, John Heard, Maureen O'Sullivan, Chet Doherty (Edward).

Edward, a transvestite, is responsible for a series of bloody murders at the Royal Arms Hotel. Vapid. The contrast between Connors' easily-exasperated cop and the imperturbable (secretly crazy) doorman Vincent (Ian McShane) is not as uproarious as intended.

**TOOTHLESS VAMPIRES** (H.K.) 1987 color c90m. D: Lee Hun Yu. Ref: TV: World Video; no Eng. NST! 4:12,37-8. Jones.

The vampires of the house have trouble finding the jugular of their guest, apparently a dentist. A blue-tinted flashback explains their plight: Vampire-hunter "Peter Camshing" (that's what it says on his robe) applied cross, stake, and (especially) pliers to de-fang the local (European?) vampires, who then emigrated to China. In the hectic climactic sequence, the dentist's blood destroys most of the vampires, and a priest is impaled on his own stake .... Broad, mostly silly lampoon, with scattered cute moments.

**TOP KIDS** Disney-TV Channel 1987 color 79m. Ref: TVG. no VSB. no PFA. no Scheuer. With Niki Lauda, Ross Harris, Anthony Ko.

"Time-travel simulator."

**TOP LINE** (I) National & Dania & Filmes Int'l. & Reteitalia 1988 color/ws 88m. SP, D: Nello Rossati. SP: also Roberto Gianviti. Ph: G. Mancori. Mus: Maurizio Dami. AD: Sergio Canevari. SpOptFX & Mkp: Gaetano & Francesco Paolocci. Mkp: Massimo De Rossi. Ref: TV: VSOM; Eng. dubbed. Palmerini. With Franco Nero, Deborah Barrymore, Mary Stavin, William Berger, George Kennedy.

"The spaceship is the cave." In Colombia, a sailing ship found in a cave ("What is it doing in a mountain?") proves to be housed in an alien spacecraft: Some 500 years ago, it seems, the spaceship scooped up the vessel, then crashed into a mountain. Plus an android with a half-melted face ("He's a robot!"), a second android that's beheaded, and the unsurprising news that aliens have infiltrated world governments. "We need your planet. It contains a rare element that's indispensable to our spaceships".... Unusual premise, indifferent adventure-movie framework, okay "payoff" scenes. Highlight number 1: the socialite turning into an alien goo thing. Highlight number 2: the "death" tics of the splattered android. Meaningless title. Kennedy is dubbed by another actor.

**TORMENT** New World (Aslanian-Hopkins) 1986 color 85m. SP, D, P: Samson Aslanian, John Hopkins. Ph: S. Carpenter. Mus: Chris Young. Consult: Jeffrey Obrow. Ref: HR 4/16/86: "slow-moving horror-suspense thriller." V 4/23/86: "some nicely executed turns of the screw." Ecran F 68:70. ad. Morse. Cabletime. With Taylor Gilbert, William Witt, Eve Brenner, Warren Lincoln.

Psychopathic killer.

**TORMENTOR** (Sp-I) Wizard Video/Balcazar & S.E.F.I., or S.E.S.I. 1972('85-U.S.) color/ws 91m. (*Passi di Danza Sula Lama di un Rasolo*). Idea, SP, D: Maurizio Pradeaux. Idea, SP: Arpad De Riso. SP: also Alfonso Balcazar, George Martin. Ph: Jaime Deu Casas. Mus: Roberto Pregadio. AD: Juan Alberto. Mkp: Duilio Giustini. Ref: TV: Wizard Video; Eng. dubbed. no Hound. no Martin. no McCarty II. no Scheuer. no Hardy/HM. Palmerini. VWB: aka *Death Carries a Cane*. With George Martin, Susan Scott, Robert Hoffman, Anuska Borova, Serafino

Profumo, Anna Liberati, Simon Andreu, Salvatore Borgese, Rosita Toros.

"She was knifed." A black-hatted, razor-wielding slasher specializes in ballerinas from the Accademia di Danza Classica Okrowich. Flat-footed mystery shocker with comically phony red herrings. Accidental high point is the inspector's line, "Would you mind getting me the files of all deviates and sex offenders with leg disabilities?"

**TOT ODER LEBENDIG** (W.G.) ZDF-TV/Su(r)prise Co. (Goggo Gensch) 1988 (1987) color 125m. SP,D: Gisela Zimmermann. Mus: Wolfgang Dauner. Ref: V 2/24/88: "marvelously haunting"; *Dead or Alive* - tr t. Dr. Rolf Giesen. With Ludwig Hirsch, Sara Kellenberger, Elsbeth Janda.

"Pic starts out as a standard horror flick with plenty of graveyard atmosphere .... uncanny murders. At least the victims appear to be dead." (V)

**TOTAL REBALL** Coast to Coast 1990 color 79m. D: William Black. Ref: Adam '92: sex machine. With Ashlyn Gere, Bionca, Raven, Peter North.

**TOTAL RECALL** Tri-Star/Carolco & Ronald Shusett (Mario Kassar & Andrew Vajna) 1990 color 113m. D: Paul Verhoeven. Story, SP: Shusett, Dan O'Bannon. SP: also Gary Goldman. Story: also Jon Povill. From the short story "We Can Remember It for You Wholesale" by Philip K. Dick. Mus: Jerry Goldsmith. SpVisFX: (sup) Eric Brevig; Dream Quest Images; (anim sup) Jeff Burks. Addl OptFX: IL&M; (sup) Dave Carson; (coord) Anne Calanchini. Conceptual Artist: Ron Cobb. SpFxSup: T.L. Fisher. Min: Stetson Visual. SpMkpFX: Rob Bottin. SpSdFX: John Pospisil, Alan Howarth. Ref: TV. MFB'90:237-9. V 6/6/90. Sacto Bee 6/1/90. With Arnold Schwarzenegger, Rachel Ticotin, Sharon Stone, Ronny Cox, Michael Ironside, Marshall Bell (George/Kuato), Mel Johnson Jr., Monica Steuer (mutant mother), Sasha Rionda (mutant child), Anne Lockhart.

"Your whole life is just a dream." In a future society on Earth, Douglas Quaid (Schwarzenegger) discovers that his memories have all been implanted and that his real name is Hauser, an operative for Mars Intelligence. Via taped instructions, Hauser tells Quaid that he, Quaid, had joined Martian rebels — who want more freedom, money, and air — and that the overlord Cohaagen (Cox) "stole" his mind. A second twist reveals that Quaid was designed to be the "perfect mole," in order to escape detection by psychic rebel mutants and lead Cohaagen to Kuato, their mutant leader. At the end, Quaid — who balks at returning to his Hauser identity — activates alien-built, half-million-year-old air-making machinery.

Lavish science-fiction epic proves to be surprisingly thin, boils down to just another rebels-vs.-establishment story, with much miscellaneous violence for the action crowd. More-or-less-incidental effects and makeup highlights include an apparently animatronic cabbie, Quaid's bizarrely malfunctioning, robotic, hefty-woman disguise, the subway security X-ray machine, the hologram tennis instructor, Quaid's hologram double, and the Martian mutants.

**TOTORO** see *My Neighbor Totoro*

**A TOUCH OF DEATH** (I) Alpha (Luigi Nannerini, Antonino Lucidi) 1990 color/ws 85m. (*Quando Alice Ruppe lo Specchio*). SP, D: Lucio Fulci. Ph: Silvano Tessicini. Mus: Carlo Maria Cordio. Sets: F. Vanorio. Mkp: Pino Ferranti. SpFX: Angelo Mattei. Ref: TV; MV; Eng. dubbed. Hardy/HM2. Palmerini: 1988. With Brett Halsey, Rita DeSimon, Pier Luigi, Sasha Darwin, Zora Kesler.

"Modern day Bluebeard" grinds widows into hamburger meat, feeds it to cats and pigs. Aka The Maniac, he microwaves one victim's head. (This novel microwave works even with the door open.) Another victim is ground up under his car's tires.... Sloppily made gore comedy-drama lacks the Peter Jackson flair. Fulci is obviously interested only in the gore effects. (The chainsaw sequence also turns up in his *Cat in the Brain*.) Only offbeat element: the shadow alter ego.

**TOUCH OF LOVE, A** see *Witch from Nepal*

**TOUCHED** 1989 color feature. Ref: Vallejo Times-Herald. no Adam '90. With Nikki Charm, Staci Lords.

"Transplanted hands turn a professional masseuse into a nymphomaniac."

**The TOWER** (Can.) Emmeritus & CHCH-TV 1985 color 90m. SP,D: James Makichuk. Ph: Robert Farmar et al. Mus: Julia Hidy, David Chester. SpFX: Peter Ferri. Mkp: Wendy Lees. Ref: TV. TVG. HR 2/23/88:S-92. no Maltin '92. no Scheuer. Stanley. With Ray Paisley, Jackie Wray, George West.

The computerized security system of the Sandawn Building ("world's most energy-efficient office structure") absorbs people into itself for their BTUs. Goofy premise, stilted acting, bleached-of-interest video look.

**The TOWER** Fox Network-TV/Catalina & FNM Films (Levy-Harrison/Matthew Rushton) 1993 (1992) color c90m. Tel,D: Richard Kletter. Tel,Story: John Riley. Ph: Bing Sokolsky. Mus: R. Horowitz et al. SpVisFX: Introvision Int'l.; (sup) William Mesa; (fx sup) Nick Davis; (ph) Dave Stump. SpMkpFX: James Ryder. MechFxSup: John Hartigan. Model Sup: Gene Rizzardi. Opt: D.M. Garber. With Paul Reiser, Susan Norman, Roger Rees, Richard Gant, Annabelle Gurwitch, Dee Dee Rescher, Dee Wilkinson (CAS). Ref: TV. SFChron 8/16/93. TVG.

"Marked for Delete." Intercorp Tower, a "high-tech building controlled by a computer with a mind of its own." Corny, serial-like thrills, as the Cybernetic Access Structure (CAS) submits "security" risks to freezing cold, etc. At the end, the overloaded CAS self-destructs. Wry moments, variable effects.

**TOWER OF TERROR** Concorde-New Classics (Miracle)/Winfrey (Pacific Trust) 1991 (1990) color 83m.. (*Hard To Die* - alt t. *Nightie Nightmare II* - orig t). P,D: Jim Wynorski. SP: Mark McGee, J.B. Rogers. Ph: J. Baum. Mus: C. Cirino. PD: G. Randall. SpVisFX: Dean C. & W.S. Jones. SpFxMkp: Starr Jones. SpFX: Greg Landerer. Min: "Scott Carey." Demon Wrangler: Kevin Kutchaver. Ref: TV. Fango 123:34. V 11/30/92:41 (rated). TVG. PT 16:6. SFChron Dtbk 8/11/91. With Robyn Harris, Debra Dare, Melissa Moore, Forrest J Ackerman, Monique Gabrielle, Lindsay Taylor, Bridget Carney, Amelia Sheridan, Ronald V. Borst.

"He's gotta be dead now!" Orville Ketchum and the spirit of Clive Hockstatter return from *Sorority House Massacre II* (which movie furnishes some stock footage here). The split, stored spirit of Hockstatter is unleashed when a "legendary soul box" is opened. It possesses Diana (Taylor) and interrupts an Acme Lingerie inventory .... Flat-footed spook-and-jiggle show's sparse highlights include some movie in-jokes ("Walter Paisley," "Scott Carey") and a relatively extended sequence for FJA.

**The TOXIC AVENGER** HCH Co. & Troma/Palan (Kaufman-Herz) 1984 color 90m. (*Health-Club Super-Monsters. Health Club Horror* - early titles). D: Michael Herz, Samuel Weil. SP: Joe Ritter. Story: Lloyd Kaufman. SpFxMkp: Jennifer Aspinal, Tom Lauten. Consul: Charles & Susan Kaufman. OptFX: Videart. Ref: TV. MFB'87:61-2. V 5/22/85. 7/6/83:32. 5/4/83:286. Ecran F 40:10. SFExam 7/18/86. ad. With Andree Maranda, Mitchell Cohen (The Toxic Avenger), Jennifer Babtist, Cindy Manion, Robert Prichard, Gary Schneider, Mark Torgl (Melvin Furd), Kenneth Kessler (TTA's voice).

Tromaville, the "toxic-waste-dumping capital of the world." Melvin Furd, mop boy at The Health Club, falls into a can of toxic waste and mutates into The Toxic Avenger, a seven-foot-tall monster that "only attacks bad people" and becomes the "Monster Hero" .... The sour to the sweet of *Godzilla Vs. the Smog Monster*. All the movie gore shticks from the past fifteen years are repeated here in an offhand "comic" manner. Nadirville.

See also the following and *Class of Nuke 'em High Part II*.

**The TOXIC AVENGER, PART II** (U.S.-J) Troma & Lorimar & Gaga 1989 color 95m. Story, SP, D, P: Lloyd Kaufman. D, P: Michael Herz. SP: also Gay Partington Terry. Mus: Barrie Guard. PD: Alexis Grey. SpFxCoord: Pericles Lewnes. SpMkp: Jerry Macaluso. Sp Animal Mkp: Timothy Considine. SpAtmosFX: George Giordano. OptFX: EFX. Ref: TV. V 3/15/89. SFChron Dtbk 4/23/89. SFExam 4/1/89. ad. With Ron Fazio & John Altamura (The Toxic Avenger), Phoebe Legere, Rick Collins, Rikiya Yasouka, Mayako Katsuragi, Lisa Gaye, Jessica Dublin.

Tromaville and Japan. The Toxic Avenger likes his vittles smothered in Drano, and when evil is near, his Tromatons begin acting up. But his shady, sleazy father, Big Mac (Yasouka), comes up with an anti-Tromaton formula .... More good-natured than Part I, but no funnier. Highlights of sorts of the comic-book gore include the dwarf/basketball and the fish-nose mutilation scene.

**The TOXIC AVENGER PART III: THE LAST TEMPTATION OF TOXIE** Troma 1989 color 89m. Story, SP, D, P: Lloyd Kaufman. D, P: Michael Herz. SP: also G.P. Terry. SpFxCoord: Pericles Lewnes. Digital Growl FX: David Ouimet. Avenger Mkp: Jerry Macaluso. SpAnimalMkp: T. Considine. SpAtmosFX: G. Giordano. SpMkpFX: Arthur Jolly et al. KeyGoreFxArtist: Ron Knyrim. Devil Des: V. Guastini. Mangling FX: Ed Bishop et al. OptFX: Louis Antzes. Ref: TV. V 11/8/89. With Ron Fazio & John Altamura (Toxie), Phoebe Legere, Rick Collins, Lisa Gaye, Jessica Dublin.

Toxie begins by erasing a video-store terrorist's face, then sells out to the "chemicals are cash" crowd at Apocalypse Inc. Then: "The Toxic Avenger is back!" Then: "Oh! The devil!" — chairman of Apocalypse. Toxie finds a urination solution to one of the

devil's fiery challenges, in an interminably extended finale. Comedy redefines the term "broad."

**TOYAMAZAKURA UCHUCHO: HIS NAME IS GOLD** (J) Tokuma 1988 anim color 60m. Anim D: Hiroyuke Kitazume. Ref: Animag 4:8: "space detective story."

**TOYS** Fox/Baltimore (Mark Johnson) 1992 color 121m. SP, D, Co-P: Barry Levinson. SP: also Valerie Curtin. PD: F. Scarfiotti. SpFxCoord: Clayton Pinney. VisFxSup: M. Beck. ComputerFX: Pacific Data Images. SpFX: A.L. Paquet Jr. SpVisFX: Dream Quest. MinFX: Stetson Visual. Alsatia FX: Rob Bottin. Opt/DigitalFX: VCE/Peter Kuran. Opt: Howard Anderson. Ref: TV: Fox Video. V 12/21/92: "unsupervised mess." SFChron 12/18/92: "sterile, austere." CCosta Times 12/25/92: "uneven but often brilliantly original satire." SFChron 9/13/93.

Fantasy with sf/horror elements, including a "meeting of skeletons" and "lethal video-games" (SFC) and "electronic destructo 'bots" (CCT). Best Zevo Toys monster: the Sea Swine, a war-tank creature with "big bulging eyes." ("Is that thing gonna eat me or mate with me?") Plus an android ("Alsatia's a robot"), a battalion of huge robot/TVs, the "woozy helmet" prototype, and "appetizers from hell".... An "A" for Adventurousness here, though no "S" for Subtlety. Film is, by turns, affecting, imaginative, funny, and ponderous; as a pro-peace picture, though, this oddball, endearing fantasy lacks the bite of, say, *Follow the Boys*.

**TRABBI GOES TO HOLLYWOOD** see *Driving Me Crazy*

**TRACEY'S LOVE CHAMBER** Arrow Films 1987 color c80m. Ref: vc box: sequel to *Sex World Girls*. no Adam. with Sasha Gabor, Tracey Adams, Rachel Ashley, Ron Jeremy.

Futuristic Rejuvenation Room, etc.

**TRACKERS** or **TRACKERS: 2180** see *Spacerage*

**TRAFFIC IN SOULS** Universal (Imp) 1913 70m. SP,D: George Loane Tucker. SP: also Walter MacNamara. Ref: screen; Library of Congress. Pierre LePage. SFChron Dtbk 10/21/90. PFA notes 9/10/86. Heisner/H'w'd Art: 277: U's 1st feature. V 11/28/13. Mo. Hirschhorn. PT 21:8. With Jane Gail, Ethel Grandin, Matt Moore, William Powers.

New York City. An invalid's "invention for intensifying sound waves and recording dictagraph sounds on [an Edison cylinder] phonographic record" records conversations "in both lower and upper offices" of a building, and proves instrumental in breaking up a gang of "infamous traffickers" in white slavery. The exaggerated acting dates the film, and the plot depends upon incredible coincidences (the white slave ring hires as a secretary the sister of one of its slaves) and contrivances (the inventor takes one night to perfect his invention). But this very early silent feature has a slice-of-the-criminal-life feel to the scenes linking the pimps and "look-outs" to the "respectable" financial "go-between" and to the "man higher up." Stop motion is apparently used for the long-before-FAX dictagraph's remote-control printing of some financial notes, and other visual highlights include location shooting at Ellis Island, an overhead shot, and a tracking shot or two.

**TRAGEDY OF GHOST** (H.K.?) Jia's Motion Picture Co./Allstar Film 198-? color/ws 88m. Ref: TV: Tai Seng Video; Eng. titles. Hardy/HM: sfa *Qiu Deng Ye Yu*? (same plot); Taiwanese?; 1974; SP,D: Fengpan Yao. NST! 4:15-16: sfa *All in a Dim Cold Night*?

"Who are you anyway?" Rebuffed by the lord of the house, Tsio O freezes to death, with their baby, on his doorstep, and returns as a "lonely ghost." ("You forsook me!") She gains secret entry into his bedchamber by animating his bride (who committed suicide), lures the lord to his death in his pond, and retrieves her baby's ghost .... The principals go through their expected paces here — the humans perhaps overdo their terror at the sight of ghostly phenomena — but the tale is compactly told, with the accent on atmosphere, and has some neat little twists, including the vanishing of the palanquin which brought the ghost, and the discovery of the bride's no-longer-animated corpse in the bed.

The **TRAIL OF THE SILVER SPURS** Mono (G.W. Weeks) 1941 58m. D: S. Roy Luby. SP: E. Snell. Story: Elmer Clifton. Ph: R. Cline. Mus D: F. Sanucci. Songs: Lange & Porter. Ref: TV: Viking Video. Okuda/TMC. V 1/22/41. With Ray Corrigan, John King, Max Terhune, I. Stanford Jolley, Dorothy Short, George Chesebro, Eddie Dean, Milt Morante, Kermit Maynard, Frank Ellis.

"Every ghost town in this here desert is haunted." Spooky ingredients in this Range Busters series entry include a phantom figure who is trying to scare Dan Nordick (Morante) and his daughter Nancy (Short) off their property, with the aid of "ghost writing," or "make-believe ghost messages"; night prowlers, including a "clockwindin' spook"; a skeleton; cobwebs, and a gila monster.

Stilted Western works overtime on Range Busters comic camaraderie. Closest-to-creepy scene: Nordick, the sleepwalker, walking downstairs in the middle of the night to wind a clock. Much padding with stock footage.

**TRAIL OF THE VAMPIRE** see *Spooks Run Wild*

El **TRAILER ASESINO** (Mex) Televicine & Prods. Filmicas 1986 (1985) color c85m. D: Alfredo Gurrola. SP: Carlos Valdemar. Ph: Miguel Arana. Mus: Nacho Mendez. SpFX: Sergio Jara. Mkp: Lilia Palomino. OptFX: Manuel Sainz. Incidental FX: Gonzalo Gavira. Ref: TV: Video Visa; no Eng. V 5/7/86:414,452: *The Killer Truck* - tr t. TVG. With Mario Almada, Fernando Almada, Alma Delfina, Norma Lazareno, Bruno Rey.

Madman steals big-rig truck tractor, runs down hapless pedestrians, motorcyclists, and other motorists. Truckers band together to stop him .... Routine action-horror feature is scarier perhaps than *Rolling Vengeance,* but no *Duel.* Some gory details.

**Un TRAIN DANS LA NUIT** (F) Regent 1934 77m. D: Rene Hervil. SP: Pierre Maudru, from Arnold Ridley's play "The Ghost Train." Ref: Chirat. Rep. Gen.'47:530: "hallucinante." With Georgius, Dolly Davis, Alice Tissot, Charles Dechamps.

Tale of a "ghost train" which roars through a country railway station each year — on the anniversary of a terrible accident — turns out to be a front for criminals.

**TRAMPA INFERNAL** (Mex) Galmex Films/Grupo Galindo 1989 color c76m. SP,D: Pedro Galindo III. Story: Santiago Galindo. Ph: Antonio de Anda. Mus: Pedro Plascencia. SpFX:

Farfan Efectos. Mkp: Angelina Mendez. OptFX: Manuel Sainz. Ref: TV: Mex-American HV; no Eng.; Infernal Trap - tr t. TVG. With Pedro Fernandez, Edith Gonzalez, Tono Mauri, Charly Valentino, Marisol Santa Cruz, Adriana Vega.

Adventurous young people travel into the wilds to take on a growling, masked madman with modified-Freddy can-opener attachments for his hand. His other weapons include scythe and machine gun. Formula — the *Friday the 13th* one. The killer's saw-blades "glove" looks unwieldy, but apparently does the job.

**TRAMPIRE** C.C. Williams (Paul Thomas) 1987 color 85m. SP,D: Williams. Ph, Ed: Michael Cates, Williams. Ref: TV: Fantasy HV. Adam '88. With Angela Baron (Trampire Queen), Angel Kelly (Trampire), Randy West, Tom Byron, Lylah Browning, Nikki Nights, Zydecko Princess.

"Over 400 years ago ... a strange aberrant child was born into the house of Vlad, the Impaler, the Count Dracula who was part of the children of the night .... This daughter of Dracula was no vampire. She was — Trampire!" But the "results are as fatal" as they were with her father: She "kills her victims by lovin' 'em to death," with orgasmically-induced dehydration. Flimsy adult comedy ends with love taking Trampire out of circulation.

**TRANCERS** Empire/Lexyn (Vestron Video) 1985 (1984) color 76m. (*Future Cop* - alt t). D,P: Charles Band. SP: Danny Bilson, Paul De Meo. Mus: Mark Ryder, Phil Davies. SpVisFX & FxMkp: John Buechler, MMI. Ref: TV. MFB'85:59-60. V 5/15/85. TVG. With Tim Thomerson, Helen Hunt, Michael Stefani, Art La Fleur, Biff Manard.

Ingredients: Trancers, hungry zombies "not really live, not dead enough," and subject to Whistler's (Stefani) psychic powers ...disintegrating rays ... the futuristic High Council, which sends Jack Deth (Thomerson) back to modern-day L.A., where he inhabits ancestor Phil ... a wristwatch which permits Deth a "long second," a la *The Girl, The Gold Watch and Everything* ... and a push-pin-like device which returns Whistler to the 23rd Century to stand trial .... Blatant ripoff of *Blade Runner* and *The Terminator* is a fairish blend of familiar sf, fantasy, and shock gimmicks. Humor ("Jack. Phil stepped out") and occasional twists punctuate routine action.

**TRANCERS II** Para/Full Moon 1991 (1990) color 87m. Story, D, P: Charles Band. Story, SP: Jackson Barr. Mus: Mark Ryder, Phil Davies. SpMkpFX: Palah Sandling. SpFX: (sup) Kevin McCarthy; Players; (coord) Sandra McCarthy. Ref: TV. V 6/10/91. TVG. With Tim Thomerson, Helen Hunt, Megan Ward, Biff Manard, Martine Beswicke, Jeffrey Combs, Richard Lynch, Barbara Crampton, Sonny Carl Davis, Art La Fleur.

"We're both in different bodies, hundreds of years in the past." The above "genetic bridge" premise yields some kinkily romantic situations, but little else, in this flat sf-actioner re a future crack-type drug which turns the homeless into the mindless ("trancers") in 1991. ("I don't wanna have my brain vacuumed!")

**TRANCERS III** Full Moon (Albert Band) 1992 color 74m. (*Trancers III: Deth Lives* - ad t). SP,D: C. Courtney Joyner. Ph: Adolfo Bartoli. Mus: Richard Band. PD: Milo. SpFxMkp: KNB FX. FxAnimSup: Kevin Kutchaver. SpFxCoord: John Cazin. OptFX: Motion. Ref: TV. TVG. V 8/24/92:8 (rated). With Tim

Thomerson, Melanie Smith, Andrew Robinson, Tony Pierce, Dawn Ann Billings, Ed Beechner, Helen Hunt, Megan Ward, Stephen Macht, R.A. Mihailoff (Shark).

"Welcome to hell, Jack." "Fishface" android Shark rounds up trancer hunter Jack Deth (Thomerson) in 1992 L.A. and takes him to the year 2352, where he is ordered to kill the trancers at their source, in the year 2005, "when it all began." In 2005, some "level-ten trancing"/mutating leads to some pool-cue gore, and Col. Daddy Muthah (Robinson) boasts that his injection-created soldier-"zombies," or trancers, compose one of the "most elite fighting corps that ever existed." Sprawling, involved plot is a wee bit ambitious for such a low-budgeter. Among the subjects touched upon: time travel, lost love, cult brainwashing, high-tech militarism, politics, history, and even "Dr. Jekyll and Mr. Hyde," as R.J. (Smith) alternates between human and trancer modes.

**TRANCERS 4: JACK OF SWORDS** (U.S.-Rom.) New City/Full Moon (Paunescu) 1993 color 75m. D: David Nutter. SP: Peter David. Ph: A. Bartoli. Mus: Gary Fry. PD: M.-D. Neagu. MkpFX: AlchemyFX. VisFX: Mercer Titles; Fantasy II. On-Set FX: Theodore Haines. Ref: TV. V 10/25/93:62 (rated). SFChron Dtbk 1/30/94: "medieval mystical land." With Tim Thomerson, Stacie Randall, Ty Miller, Stephen Macht, Clabe Hartley (Caliban), Terri Ivens, Ion Haiduc; Ion Albu & Jake Roberts (Solonoid).

"This place is called Orpheus," where local "vampire trancers" drain the lives of the local humans. Main trancer here: Lord Caliban. Bonus: the monster-in-the-time-machine scene.... Weak-tea sword-and-sorcery stuff, with occasional passable lines—e.g., Thomerson's Jack's "Time is fluid, and I'm the guy who makes sure the glass doesn't get knocked over."

**TRANCERS 5: SUDDEN DETH** (U.S.-Rom.) Para/Full Moon (Paunescu) 1994 color 73m. D: David Nutter. SP: Peter David. SpMkpFX: Alchemyfx. Ref: vc box: time-and-space talisman. Martin: "enjoyable." With Tim Thomerson, Stacie Randall, Stephen Macht.

**TRANSFORMATIONS** (U.S.-I) New World/Empire & Dove (Bob Wynn) 1988 color 80m. D: Jay Kamen. SP: Mitch Brian. Ph: Sergio Salvati. PD: Giovanni Natalucci. Monster FX: Dino Galiano; MMI. SdFX: Slash & Burn. Ref: TV. V 4/1/87:39: 3/30/start. PT 13:49. With Rex Smith, Lisa Langlois (Miranda), Christopher Neame (Caliban), Michael Hennessy, Cec Verrell, Patrick Macnee, Pamela Prati (succubus).

In and around Hephaestos IV, a prison and mining-colony planet. Sex with a monster/phantom/sexpot renders smuggler Wolf Shadduck (Smith) impotent and a monster himself. At the end, the hero, shot, sheds his monster skin. Unremarkable effects, extraneous gore, "Tempest" references.

**The TRANSFORMERS — THE MOVIE** (U.S.-J) DEG/Sunbow & Marvel & Toei Animation (Hasbro/Bacal-Griffin) 1986 anim color 86m. D,Co-P: Nelson Shin. SP: Ron Friedman, based on the Hasbro toys. Sup Anim D: Kozo Morishita. SpFX: M. Kawachi, S. Sato. Ref: V 8/13/86: "pure headache material." ad. Voices: Orson Welles, Robert Stack, Leonard Nimoy, Eric Idle, Judd Nelson, Lionel Stander.

Year 2005. The Transformers vs. the evil Planet Unicron. The Transformers can turn into dinosaurs, jets, etc.

**TRANSGRESSION** Masque Cinema 1993 82m. D: M.P. Di-Paolo. Ref: Videoscope 11/15/94: "genuinely creepy aura ... Marins-type morality play in fright-movie guise" re serial killer and protege. SF Chron 7/6/96. "absolutely original." With Molly Jackson.

**TRANSIT** see *First Power, The*

**TRANSMUTATIONS** (B) Limehouse & Greenman (Kevin Attew, Don Hawkins/Graham Ford/Al Burgess) 1985 ('86-U.S.) color 100m. (*Underworld* - B). D: George Pavlou. Story,SP: Clive Barker. SP: also James Caplin. SpFxSup: Malcolm King. Mkp: (prosth) Peter Litton; Vivian Placks. Ref: TV. 12/11/85. Bob Moore. SFExam 7/24/86. With Denholm Elliott, Steven Berkoff, Larry Lamb, Miranda Richardson, Art Malik, Nicola Cowper, Ingrid Pitt.

"I'll make your dreams real!" Those demon-eyed, disfigured thugs on the prowl are the handiwork of Dr. Savary (Elliott) and his unsavory experiments with an hallucinogenic drug with "unpredictable" side effects. Ultimately, the beautiful Nicole (Cowper), who is immune to the physical side effects, makes her eyes light up and incinerate Savary.

Okay, midway-point twin payoff: the introduction of Elliott's Savary (he gives the best performance) and the fast-forwarded recording of one drug victim's horrific physical deterioration. Climactic action payoffs are flat, the plot dispensable.

**TRANSYLVANIA 6-5000** (U.S.-Yug) New World/Dow Chemical (Mace Neufeld) & Jadran Film 1985 color 94m. SP,D: Rudy De Luca. Mus: Lee Holdridge. SpFxMkp: Bob Williams, Ellis Burman, Cosmekinetics. SpFX: Marijan Kuroglan. Ref: TV. MFB'86:347-8. V 11/13/85. ad. Horacio Higuchi. With Jeff Goldblum, Joseph Bologna, Ed Begley Jr., Carol Kane, Jeffrey Jones, John Byner (Radu), Geena Davis (Odette), Donald Gibb (wolfman), Norman Fell, De Luca (Lawrence Malbot), Peter Buntic (Hunyadi), Dusko Valentic (twisted man), Ksenija Prohaska (mummy).

A Frankenstein-monster-like "monster" (Buntic), a vampire-like lady (Davis), a "wolfman," and a "mummy" are all explained as the work of a plastic surgeon, son of the doctor who introduced herpes to Sicily .... Strenuous horror-comedy is occasionally amusing in spite of itself. The actors confuse strange with funny, though Goldblum gets in a few droll disbelieving reaction shots, and Byner has a funny moment or two. (Many unfunny ones.)

**TRANSYLVANIA TWIST** Concorde-New Horizons/Miracle (Roger Corman & Alida Camp) 1989 color 82m. D: Jim Wynorski. SP: R.J. Robertson. Mus: Chuck Cirino; (lyr) Wynorski. SpFxMkp: Dean Jones, Dean Gates, Starr Jones. OptFX: Motion; (sup) Jim Stewart. Anim: Kevin Kutchaver; (title seq) Bret Mixon; (bat) L.A. Ross. Ref: TV: MGM-UA HV. V 4/4/90. 10/18/89:25 (rated). With Robert Vaughn (Lord Byron Orlock), Teri Copley, Steve Altman (Dexter Ward), Ace Mask (Van Helsing), Angus Scrimm, Monique Gabrielle, Jay Robinson, Steve Franken, Howard Morris, Becky LeBeau, Brinke Stevens, Deanna Lund, Kelli Maroney, Forrest J Ackerman, Clement von Franckenstein, Stu Nahan, Dean C. Jones (Pinhead).

Spoof ingredients include Jason, Leatherface, and Freddy ... FJA bearing an old issue of FM ... zombie redcaps ... a visitor from

*Hellraiser* ("This hurts!") ...the phantom-like Stefan (Scrimm) ... the Dracula-like Byron Orlock, and Boris Karloff (the latter as himself in stock footage; the former was Karloff's character's name in *Targets*) ... a rubber bat, for atmosphere ... stock of the Corman *Pit and the Pendulum* castle ... *The Book of Ulthar*, which summons up The Evil One ... a seance, at which young Marisa Orlock (Copley) is possessed by her ancestor, Lady Marisa ... the *Phantasm* sphere ... catalepsy ... and vampire-buster Dr. Victor Van Helsing. ("Vampires I know, but this Lovecraft stuff is out of my league!") The *Spaceballs*-like, filmic in-jokes are the best of it. Horror-movie fans will especially appreciate Van Helsing's peeved reaction to the old hand-on-shoulder scare: "Damn! I hate cheap shocks like that!" Unfortunately, none of the spoof characters is consistently funny enough to help the movie through lulls, which outnumber non-lulls.

**TRAP THEM AND KILL THEM** (I) Fulvia & Flora & Gico 1977 color/ws 92m. (2P *Emanuelle e gli Ultimi Cannibali* or *Emmanuelle e gli Ultimi Cannibali*. *Emanuelle's Amazon Adventure* - TV). Story, SP, D, Ph: Joe d'Amato (aka A. Massaccesi). SP: also Romano Scandariato. Mus: Nico Fidenco. AD: Carlo Ferri. SpMkpFX: Fabrizio Sforza. SpFX: F. de Angelis. Ref: TV: Twilight Video; Eng. dubbed. MFB'78:133. V 9/5/84. 1/25/78:42. Hardy/HM. With Laura Gemser, Gabriele Tinti, Susan Scott, Donald O'Brien.

"It's about cannibalism." A "famous journalist" (Gemser) investigates supposedly-extinct cannibals in the Amazon. Perfunctory combo of gore and softcore sex. Lots of "Look—alligators!" Supposedly based on a "true story."

**TRAPPED** see *Killer Instinct*

**TRAPPED ALIVE** AIP (Christopher Webster) 1988 color feature (aka *Forever Mine*). SP, D: L. Burzyski. SP: also Julian Weaver. Ref: PT 18:58. With Cameron Mitchell.

"Barely shown cannibal with long white hair grabs victims with giant tongs."

**TRAPPED IN SPACE** (Austral.-U.S.) Para/Sci-Fi Channel/Village Roadshow & Wilshire Court/CNM Ent. (Michael Lake) 1994 color 87m. D: A.A. Seidelman. Tel: A. Hughes, M.M. Snodgrass, from Arthur C. Clarke's short story "Breaking Strain." Ph: N. Martinetti. Mus: Jay Gruska. PD: M.L. Ralph. SpFX: Brian Cox. VisFX: Digital Magic. Mkp: Margaret Stevenson. Ref: TV. vc box: Tel: J.V. Curtis. With Jack Wagner, Craig Wasson, Jack Coleman, Sigrid Thornton, Kay Lenz.

"Collision imminent." A direct hit by an asteroid damages the oxygen reserves of a ship in space. All talk, no movie. ("It's a big solar system.") Shallowly grim, though the ending surprises a bit. Eerie: the shots of the mummified dead left to drift into space.

**TRAPPED IN THE SKY** Col 1939 61m. D: Lewis D. Collins. SP: Eric Taylor, Gordon Rigby. Ph: James S. Brown Jr. Ref: screen: Library of Congress (1st reel). V 5/3/39. with Jack Holt, Ralph Morgan, Paul Everton, Katherine De Mille, C. Henry Gordon, Sidney Blackmer, Ivan Lebedeff, Regis Toomey, Holmes Herbert.

"It will revolutionize aviation." Rods on the roof of a building which houses a generator transmit energy into the air to two receivers on inventor Walter Fielding's (Herbert) piloted, "electrically driven plane." Latter's main selling point: The plane—which works within 500 miles of the generator—is silent. ("Listen! Not a sound!")

**TRAS EL CRISTAL** see *In a Glass Cage*

**TRAUMA** (I-W.G.-Sp) Eureka Films/Daimo & CCC & C.I.P.I. (Leonardo Pescarolo) 1978 ('85-U.S.) color/ws c85m. (*Enigma Rosso - I. Virgin Terror* - alt vt t). SP,D: Alberto Negrin. SP: also Marcello Coscia or Coccia, Massimo Dallamanno, Franco Perrini, S. Ubezio, P. Berling. Ph: Edoardo Noe. Mus: Riz Ortolani. Mkp: De Rossi. Ref: TV: Wizard Video & Lettuce Entertain You video; Eng. dubbed. Stanley. Dr. Rolf Giesen. no Hound. no Martin. Palerini. VWB: aka *Red Rings of Fear*. With Fabio Testi, Christine Kaufmann, Ivan Desny, Jack Taylor, Fausta Avelli, Bruno Alessandro.

An apparent slasher with a "pretty developed sense of perversion" leaves the "butchered body of teenaged Angela near a "very progressive" girls' school. Other goodies: big CUs of a peeping eyeball ... a skulker who breaks a girl's neck ... and tongs-in-neck murder.

Flat, grisly mystery-suspenser has a fairly surprising denouement: One of two lurkers-at-large is "little brat" Emily, out for revenge for her older sister Angela's death. The cop hero catches Emily in the act of trying to strangle a bedridden girl, but lets her off, apparently because she did not actually kill anyone. Fine line: "Every Saturday a cat!" Fine moment: the marbles rolling sinisterly down the stairs.

**TRAUMA** (U.S.-I) Overseas Filmgroup/ADC (Dario Argento/Andrea Tinnirello) 1993 (1992) color/ws 105m. Story,SP,D: D. Argento. SP: also T.E.D. Klein. Story: also F. Ferrini, G. Romoli. Ph: R. Mertes. Mus: Pino Donaggio. PD: Billy Jett. SpMkpFX: Tom Savini. Physical FX: Paul Murphy. SdFX: Interlock. Ref: TV: Worldvision HV; Eng. version. V 6/14/93: "by-the-numbers stalker thriller." Fango 118:10. 128:58-62. V 9/21/92:53 (ad). With Christopher Rydell, Asia Argento, Piper Laurie, Frederic Forrest, Brad Dourif, James Russo, Laura Johnson, Hope Alexander-Willis.

"He only kills when it's raining." (Compare *Rain Killer* and *Raining Night's Killer*.) The Headhunter—a "monster with a noose"—is at large with a nasty garroting gizmo.... The usual Argento blend of flaccid mystery and ham-handed horror. Gory camp highlight: the close-up of the falling, screaming severed head. Mind-bogglingest camera trick: the flitting-butterfly's point-of-view shots. There's even (at a seance) a "The killer is...." scene. Cute place-name: Lake Veronica.

**TRAUMA** see *Terminal Choice*

**TRAUMA** see *Violacion Fatal*

**TREASURE ISLAND IN OUTER SPACE** (I) RAI-TV 1986 color 133m. (*La Isola del Tessoro*). D: A. Margheriti. Ref: VSOM: sf. VW 28:61: "awful." With Anthony Quinn.

**TREMORS** Univ/No Frills & Wilson-Maddock (Gale Anne Hurd) 1990 (1989) color 96m. Story,D: Ron Underwood. Story,SP:

S.S. Wilson, Brent Maddock. Mus: Ernest Troost. Ph: A. Gruszynski. Vis & MinFX: 4-Ward Prods.; (d) Robert Skotak; (min sup) S. Brien. AddlVisFX: Illusion Arts; Fantasy II Film FX, (sup) Gene Warren Jr.; (coord) Lise Romanoff. SpMechFX: Art Brewer SpFX. Creature FX: (des) Tom Woodruff Jr., Alec Gillis; (key des) Craig Caton. Mkp: The Flying Fabrizi Sisters. Ref: TV: MCA-Univ HV. MFB'90:239-40. V 1/17/90. Sacto Bee 1/22/90. SFChron 1/19/90. With Kevin Bacon, Fred Ward, Finn Carter, Michael Gross, Reba McEntire, Bibi Besch, Victor Wong.

"They're under the goddamn ground!" The "snake monster" at large in Perfection Valley, Nevada, must be "some kind of mutation." In fact, there are three or four huge slug-like "graboids" — with mean-mouthed tentacle grippers (the "snakes") — burrowing about and gobbling up men and other animals. And they suck trucks underground too.

Though not much on plot or character — the people here are too self-consciously folksy — *Tremors* successfully exploits our Fear of Things from Below. This landgoing *Jaws* is at least better than the similar *Blood Beach*; in terms of terrain, this is Jack Arnold territory, though the menaces more closely recall the monsters from a non-Arnold Fifties Universal, *The Mole People.* The seismograph performs the duty that radar, sonar, and geiger counter performed in the film's Fifties counterparts, while (as noted by Variety) the efforts of the characters to effect safe passage through the critters recall *Killer Shrews.* Both sides — human, monster — have vulnerabilities and ingenuities. For humans, roofs and rocks are safe, as is simply not moving; dangerous: bare ground, vibrations. If the slugs can dig traps, bombs rout them. It's a fair fight. Good Touch number 1: the tilting scarecrow. G.T. number 2: the sinking car's headlights pointing up into the night sky. Bad Move: the subjective-camera-like shots above the burrowers as they advance.

Le **TRESOR DES ILES CHIENNES** (F-Port.) Gemini Films & Trois Lumieres & La Sept/Filmargem (Branco-Leventon) 1990 b&w/ws 105m. SP,D: F.J. Ossang. Mus: Messageros Killers Boys. Ref: V 12/3/90: "gobbledygook script"; *The Treasure of the Bitch Islands* - tr t. With Stephane Ferrara, Diogo Doria, Jose Wallenstein, M. Galan.

"Post-punk" apocalyptic devastation.

**TRET I SARKAN** (Cz) Czechoslovak Film 1986 color 83m. D: Peter Hledik. SP: Igor Rusnak. Idea: Jozef Zarnay. Mus: Petr Hapka. Ref: V 3/5/86. no Stanley. no Phantom. no Hound. no Martin. With Patrick Sima, Jan Krizik, Boris Trstan.

Three boys discover a spaceship sent from the planet Lurida — which is "eight centuries ahead of Earth" — to monitor our ecological progress. "Original ... outstanding"; *The Third Dragon* - tr t?

The **TRIAL OF THE INCREDIBLE HULK** NBC-TV/New World-TV & Bixby-Brandon Prods . 1989 color c90m. D: Bill Bixby. Tel: Gerald DiPego, based on Stan Lee's "The Incredible Hulk" comic. Mus: Lance Rubin. PD: Doug Higgins. SpFX: John Thomas. SpMkp: John Goodwin. Ref: TV: add Daredevil, "to protect," with his "radar sense." V 5/17/89:63;Mifed '89:126. With B. Bixby, Lou Ferrigno, Marta Dubois, Nancy Everhard, Nicholas Hormann, Joseph Mascolo, John Rhys Davies, Rex Smith.

"They made him angry." David Banner's rage turns him into an absolute beast again, and he becomes a subway vigilante, aided, in his fight against injustice, by Daredevil. Novel spectacle: man-into-hulk in the courtroom. Otherwise, not much to talk about.

**TRIBULATION 99: ALIEN ANOMALIES UNDER AMER-ICA** Other Cinema 1992 color 48m. SP,D,Ed: Craig Baldwin. Ph: B. Daniel. Mus: D. Hoover. Narrator: Sean Kilcoyne. Ref: SFChron Dtbk 5/10/92: "oddball hors d'oeuvre." V 7/27/92: "hilarious and bizarrely absorbing collage." PT 12:52: "very well made."

"Fantasy narrative in which aliens fleeing planet Quetzalcoatl are revealed to have manipulated Earth politics for decades."

\***TRICK FOR TRICK** 1933. Mus D: Samuel Kaylin. AD: Duncan Cramer. TechFX: William Cameron Menzies. Ref: screen. PFA notes 8/25/92. William K. Everson. Lee. no Lentz. V 6/13/33. no Martin.

"There is a life beyond the grave!" Characters and spook ingredients include the "great La Tour" (Victor Jory), a magician ... Azrah (Ralph Morgan), a rival ... Metzger (Luis Alberni), a mad doctor who creates laboratory "lightning" (with a photoelectric cell) for his boss, Azrah ("He's my scientist") ...Prof. King (Herbert Bunston), of the Bureau of Psychic Research ... a seance "flashback" done with sound recording and acting ...a spooky prop room ... and a thunderstorm.

Menzies leads off with the finest, most spectacular effect: Azrah's transformation of a huge stone-floored room into a sudden chasm. (Azrah then walks on "air" across the room.) Anything after this out-of-the-blue show-stopper would have to disappoint, and the subsequent "tricks" do. There's also no real magician-vs.-magician payoff sequence. Okay howling-wind sound effects and atmospheric photography (by L.W. O'Connell) and sets compensate somewhat for flat acting and writing. Alberni's comic glee as the doc, however, is fun. ("It's the cats!")

**TRICK OR TREAT** DEG (Scott White) 1986 color 97m. D: Charles Martin Smith. SP,P: Michael S. Murphey, Joel Soisson. Story,SP: Rhet Topham. Mus: Christopher Young. Speaker FX: Doug Beswick Prods. MechFXCoord: Steve Wolke. SpOptFX: Richard Malzahn, David S. Williams, Jr.; Van Der Veer et al. SpMkpFxDes: Kevin Yagher. Ref: TV. MFB'87:90. V 10/29/86. With Marc Price, Tony Fields (Sammi Curr), Lisa Orgolini, Doug Savant, Elaine Joyce, Gene Simmons, Ozzy Osbourne.

"He's in here" — in a demo record, that is. Dead heavy-metal rocker Sammi Curr is "inside" the only copy of his last record. A tape of the latter emits green ectoplasm which becomes a lizard-monster, and, at a Halloween dance, Curr jumps out of a speaker, and his guitar shoots deadly lightning. Very minor variation on the "Frankenstein" theme: The monster which high-school student Eddie Weinbauer (Price) "creates" by releasing Curr goes disastrously out of control. Dozens of electrical effects, little else here. Stephen King-haunted script at various points recalls *Christine* (possessed car) and *Carrie* (possessed teen). Unusual bit: Curr clawing at the TV image of an anti-rock preacher (Osbourne), who screams.

**TRILOGY OF FEAR** Trilogy Group 1991 color feature. D: R.L. Fox Jr. Ref: Jones. with Claude Akins, Louise Le Tourneau, James Coffey.

Three tales re vampire, witch, mass murderer.

**TRINAJSTATA GODENICA NA PRINCA** (Bulg.) Bulgariafilm 1987 color 88m. D: Ivanka Grubcheva. SP: the Mormarev Bros. Mus: Georgi Genkov. Ref: V 4/22/87: *The Thirteenth Bride of the Prince* - tr t. no Phantom. With Georgi Partsalev, Tatyana Lolova, Petya Milaoinonov.

Fairy tale involving the "arrival of aliens from another planet in a strange spaceship."

**TRINITY'S CHILD** see *By Dawn's Early Light*

**A TRIP TO MARS** Fleischer 1924 anim silent b&w short. Ref: Cabarga/TFS. Maltin/OMAM. no Lee.

**TRIUMPH OF THE HOUSE OF USHER** see *Fall of the House of Usher* (1983)

**EL TRIUNFO DE LOS CAMPEONES JUSTICIEROS** (Mex-Guatemalan) Agrasanchez 197-? color 82m. SP,D: Rafael Lanuza. Ph: Javier Cruz. SpFX: Jose Amesquita (sp?). Mkp: Antonio Castaneda (sp?). Ref: TV: Madera CineVideo; no Eng.; Triumph of the Champions of Justice - tr t. VSOM: *Triumphs of the Champions of Justice* - vt t. With "Blue Demon," "Superzan," Elsa Cardenas, "El Fantasma Blanco."

Ingredients in this tacky follow-up to *Los Campeones Justicieros*: the evil dwarf Zarel and his robot-men from Uranus ... an invisible shield and a ray gun which penetrates it ... a gizmo which allows our wrestling protagonists to teleport to alien HQ ... and a gizmo which reduces the two alien dwarfs to basic green gunk.

**3615 CODE PERE NOEL** (F) LM Prods. & Deal & Garance (Jungle Prods./Francis Lalanne) 1990 color 87m. SP,D: Rene Manzor. Mus: J.-F. Lalanne. Ref: V 2/7/90: "dumb chiller"; *Dial Code Santa Claus* - tr t? With Alain Musy, Brigitte Fossey, Louis Ducreux, Patrick Floersheim ("Santa Claus").

Mad "Santa Claus" on the loose in a country house.

**TROLL** (U.S.-I) Empire/Altar (Debra Dion) 1986 (1985) color 84m. D: John Carl Buechler. SP: Ed Naha. Mus: Richard Band. Trolls: Buechler, MMI. SpMkpSup: John Vulich. SpOptFX: Motion. Anim Sup: Linda Obalil; Kevin Kutchaver, Len Morganti, R.J. Robertson. Stopmo: James Aupperle. Vocal FX: Frank Welker. SdFX: John Paul Fasal. Ref: TV. MFB'86:215-16. V 1/22/86. Stanley. ad. Morse. Martin. Scheuer. Maltin '92. With Noah Hathaway, Michael Moriarty, Shelley Hack, Jenny Beck, Sonny Bono, Phil Fondacaro (Torock), Anne Lockhart, June Lockhart.

A troll-ring turns a playboy into a vegetable which flowers and produces more trolls. Pretty soon, everyone in the apartment house, it seems, has been converted into some sort of grotesque. Behind it all: a wizard, a sorceress, a big mother monster, and a plot to turn the building into a fairy realm which will "open up" into a fourth dimension. The conclusion leaves a lot of loose ends, but for the most part *Troll* is a winning fairy tale/spectacle. The generally lighthearted approach, Moriarty's unflappability as Harry Potter, Sr., and the main troll's dry, amused look help put it over. Watch especially the troll's expression as he oversees the budding of the first apartment-full of trolls and greens. ("Ah! Very good! Yes! Coming along fine!" he might be thinking.) The password is "Ratburgers!"

**TROLL 2** (I) Filmirage (Brenda Norris, David Hills) 1990 ('92-U.S.) color 91m. Story, SP,D: Drake Floyd aka C. Fragasso. Ph: Giancarlo Ferrando. Mus: Carlo Maria Cordio. AD: Max Slowing. Mkp: Maurizio Trani. OptFX: Steve Poe. Costumes: Laura Gemser. Ref: TV: Eng.-lang. version. SFChron Dtbk 7/19/92. 9/27/92: Col-TriStar HV. TVG. Martin. Palerini: aka *Trolls II*. With Michael Stephenson, George Hardy, Margo Prey, Connie McFarland, Robert Ormsby.

"Goblins still exist!" Ingredients in this supernatural stew include goblins, "little people of the night" who can take human form and who transform humans into plants and eat them ... the "Stonehenge magic stone," which provides the goblins' power ... a super-strong "crazy lady" who can command the moon, magically appear on TV, and make popcorn from a corncob ... a magic mirror ... and the town of Nilbog ("It's "goblin" spelled backwards!") — "we're vegetarians here."

Meant-to-be-too-weird horror-fantasy-comedy exists in a limbo between pseudo-camp and just-plain-bad. Passable visual strokes include the flora-fauna conglomerations and the magic moon. Strange, stilted English spoken here.

**TROLL III** see *Crawlers, The*

**TROMA'S WAR** see *War*

**El TRONO DEL INFIERNO** (Mex) Goyri & Lopez Asociados 1992 color feature. D:Sergio Goyri. Story,SP: G. De Anda. Ph: Tim Ross. AD: A.Villasenor. SpMkp: Juan Carlos Manjarez. SpFX: Efeccine Movil; A & A.Vazquez. OptFX: M. Sainz, F. Rodriguez. SdFX: G. Gavira. Ref: TV. TVG. With S.Goyri, Jorge Luke, Telly Filippini, Roberto Ballesteros, Ernesto Gomez Cruz, Agustin Bernal, Alfonso Munguia, Juan Pelaez, Roberto Montiel.

A solar eclipse and an earthquake attend the discovery of a little, nasty-faced statue in some ruins. Soon, a demon-possessed archaeologist is tossing priests out windows, making cops explode, and animating suits of armor. At one point, the possessed man burns to (temporary) death; later, his head transforms from half-human to fully demon, and he looks like a werewolf... Familiar and pretentiously written and scored. Effects, makeup, and photography, though, are okay.

**TRONO DI FUOCO** see *Throne of Fire, The*

**\*TROUBLE FOR TWO** 1936 72m. Based on "Story of the Young Man with the Cream Tarts" and "The Adventure of the Hansom Cab," two tales from Robert Louis Stevenson's *The Suicide Club*. Mus: Franz Waxman. AD: C. Gibbons; Joseph Wright, Edwin B. Willis. Ref: screen. PFA notes 8/10/84. Lee. William K. Everson. V 6/3/36. Maltin '92. Scheuer. no Stanley. With Tom Moore, Leland Hodgson.

London. The answer to a "cursed life where even decent death has become a luxury": the "door of death," which leads to the Suicide Club of Dr. Noel (Reginald Owen), its president. "Two hundred pounds' worth of excitement" for Prince Florizel (Robert Montgomery) and Col. Geraldine (Frank Morgan) of Corovia becomes a "bizarre business" when they enter its chambers. The "monstrous, weird, distorted minds" of the members have concocted a" game," employing playing cards, in which the one who is dealt the ace of spades dies an " apparently accidental" death at the hands of the one who draws the ace of clubs. On his second night at the club, Florizel is selected to be "torn to pieces" by lions at the Malden Zoo.

The movie goes on for another thirty minutes, with the less-interesting "Hansom Cab" tale, but has little to offer after revealing the secrets of the Suicide Club and "Mrs. Vandeleur"(Rosalind Russell). The earlier section, however, has much to offer: mystery, suspense, an offbeat tale which contrasts the "light" romanticism of mythical kingdoms, kings, and princes, with the "dark" romanticism of a London "underworld" whose denizens are drawn towards death. The message here is similar to that of the Hitchcock film of the same year, *Secret Agent:* Adventure can be hazardous to your health. Florizel is only out for a little fun — and believes Noel is only out for a little money — but (as in the recent *T.A.G.*) the game takes a serious turn.... Montgomery, Morgan, and Russell make the not-quite-horror, not-quite-comedy of the suicide game enjoyable, more enjoyable, in fact, than the adventure-with-moral of the RLS original, a rather negligible anecdote.

The **TROUBLE WITH DICK** Frolix & Augur (Fever Dream) 1987 (1986) color 86m. SP, D, P: Gary Walkow. Mus: Roger Bourland. SpFxSup: James Zarlengo. Concept: Walkow, Paul Freedman. SpVisFX: (sup) Les Bernstein; Monumental Pictures. Desert Mkp: Alexander. Ref: TV. V 1/28/87. HR 2/18/87. Cinef 5/88. Hound. no Maltin ' 92. no Scheuer. Martin. With Tom Villard, Susan Dey, Elaine Giftos, Elizabeth Gorcey, David Clennon (Lars), Jack Carter (Samsa).

A writer (Villard) working on some "serious science fiction that sells" daydreams scenes from his projected book "The Galactic Chain-Gang" ("*Papillon* in outer space"), and they include such (visualized) elements as a flying alien "porcupine," a gopher/snake, and a mutant. At one point, he "sees" his book broadcast on TV, and at the end " aliens" invade his life.... Slight, pretentious, Kafka-haunted combination of two sorts of male fantasy. (Or, as the Variety headline puts it, "Bedroom farce meets sci-fi.")

**TRUCKS** see *Maximum Overdrive*

**TRUNDO BYT BOGOM** see *Es Ist Nicht Leicht ein Gott Zu Sein*

The **TRUTH ABOUT UFO'S AND ET'S** 1982 color c90m. Ref: TVG: "speculation. "no Stanley. no Phantom. no Scheuer. no PT 4 (Mondo Movies).

**TRUTH OR DARE? — A CRITICAL MADNESS** GAFF/Peerless Films 1986 color 87m. D,P: Yale Wilson. SP: Tim Ritter. Ref: V 7/30/86:66(hv) "subpar horror film. "Ecran F 72:71.

Morse: "badly made." With John Brace, Mary Fanaro, Kerry Ellen Walker.

Truth or Dare? game leads to gory slaughter.

**TSUKI YORI KAERU** see *Coming back from the Moon*

**TU NAGIN MAIN SAPERA** (India) Devi Films (M.T. Gehani) 198-? color c100m. D: V. Menon. Ref: TV: Bombino Video; no Eng. Meadows Video: *Your Snake, My Snake Charmer* - tr t.

East Indian snake fantasy with scattered horrific sequences— e.g., an evil-eye woman who turns into a snake and scares a gent ... cobras which beset a woman wandering in the woods ... a magician who traps a snake woman in a circle of fire.

**TUCKER AND FLYNN** see *Monolith*

**TUNNELS** see *Criminal Act*

The **TURN OF THE SCREW** (W.G.-Yugos.) Unitel & WDR & TV 2000 & G. Herbertz 1982 ('88-U.S.) color 115m. D: Petr Weigl. Libretto: Myfanwy Piper. Mus: Benjamin Britten, from his opera and Henry James' story. Ph: Jiri Kadanka. Sets: Milos Cerwinka. Mkp: Jandera, Beranova. Ref: TV: shown on "Great Performances"; Eng. version. TVG. With Magdalena Vasaryova, Michael Gulyas, Beata Blazickova, Juraj Kukura (Quint; voice: Robert Tear).

This operatic version of the James tale is best taken as an accidental parody of the 1961 film of *The Innocents*. Here the ghosts take center stage and sing. So much for mystery, elusiveness, any sense of ghostly evanescence. Some of the music is pretty (as is the scenery), but the music unavoidably underscores even the most trival lines. See also the following and *Nightmare Classics II*.

The **TURN OF THE SCREW** (B-F) Live HV/Electric Pictures & Michael White (Lakedell-Cinemax/Ahrenberg-Seguin) 1992 color 95m. SP, D: Rusty Lemorande, from Henry James' novella. Ph: W. Stok. Mus: Simon Boswell. PD: Max Gottlieb. SpMkpFX: Phyllis Cohen. Creature FX: Laine Liska. SpFX: FX Assoc. Ref: TV. V 11/2/92: "clumsy, pedestrian." 10/26/92:7 (rated). SFChron Dtbk 6/6/93. 6/20/93: "some genuinely chilling moments." With Patsy Kensit, Stephane Audran, Julian Sands, Claire Szekeres, Joseph England, Marianne Faithfull, Olivier Debray (Quint), Bryony Brind (Miss Jessel).

" 'Ghosts' that have all the subtlety of Casper." (V) "Locks and bolts cannot keep all things at bay." The ghost in the tower, again, and the ghost in the window. The vision by the pond, too. Larded-on nightmares and hallucinations. Even an amplified heartbeat. Plus the addition of a fine owl. But without Freddie Francis' photography, the heavy "Always for the children" ironies are left bare, and the material seems campier and campier.

The **TURN-ON** (F) Concorde (New Horizons)/Alain Siritzky 1985 ('93-U.S.) color 74m. SP, D: Jean-Louis Richard. From Milo Manara's comic "Le Declic." Ph: J. Renoir. Mus: M. Lecoeur. PD: Manara. Ref: TV: NH HV; Eng. version. SFChron Dtbk 4/25/93. V 6/19/85: sfa Le DECLIC. with Jean-Pierre Kalfon, Florence Guerin, Bernard Kuby, Crofton Hardester, Robert Earle, Anthony Bean.

Voodoo... biochemist's "remote-control device that zaps women and turns them into sex-starved brazen hussies."(SFC) It's a doc's "research with the rats" which produces the magic "little black box." Rudimentary sexploiter features supposedly funny On/Off scenes with the sex remote.

**TURNAROUND** (Norw.) Major Rose 1986 color 87m. D: Ola Solum. SP: Sandra Bailey. Ref: Hardy/HM2: "old dark house ... ghost train tricks." With Doug McKeon, Tim Maier.

**TUT AND TUTTLE** Major H Prods. (Rance Howard, H.J. Wright) 1981 (1979) color c90m. (3P *Through the Magic Pyramid* - alt TV t. aka *Ron Howard's Tut and Tuttle*). D: Ron Howard. Tel: Rance Howard, Wright, SpPhFX: Van der Veer. Mkp: Gigi Williams. Ref: TV. TVG: TV-movie. Maltin '92. Hound. no Scheuer. Stanley.

Via a magic crystal, an Oregon boy travels "3,000 years from the future" to ancient Egypt. Flat exercise in Egyptology also features hypnotism, a bat attack, and a plundered mummy crypt.

**TWEET AND LOVELY** WB 1959 anim color 7m. D: Friz Freleng. SP: Warren Foster. Mus: Milt Franklyn. Ref: TV: Warner HV. WBCartoons. Sean Smiley.

In order to get Tweety, the scientifically enterprising Sylvester aka Inventions, Inc., builds a robot dog, creates an Artificial Storm Cloud, and uses Vanishing Cream and becomes invisible. Funny science fiction.

**TWELVE ANIMALS** (H.K.?) 1992? color/ws 91m. Ref: TV: Pan-Asia Video; Eng. titles.

"What a weird chicken!" Silly, episodic kid's fantasy stars King Evil, a fanged, ray-spitting green giant of the "devil world" who bursts out of a stone "cocoon" ("Buddha dies; I alive") and who sends a fanged lady and monsters to Earth... the same fanged "devil lady" ("between good and bad"), who is the very snake our protagonists Bai Ma and the eleven animals need to complete their entourage... a remarkable chicken ("This chicken can talk!")...a stone dragon which becomes a fiery, animated dragon, then the "dragon's seed," one of our heroes...a half-human, half-tiger monster ... zombie-ghosts who vanish when their hunger is assuaged ... poison-vapor-breathing dancers ... and the ghosts of the "house of dead people," who have a soul-stealing wail.... Pre-credit animated sequence — the Animal's Marathon — is actually more entertaining than the body of the movie, though the latter is occasionally so silly it's funny.

**12:01** Fox Network-TV/ Fox West Pictures (New Line-TV & Chanticleer Films) 1993 color c90m. D: Jack Sholder. Tel: Philip Morton. TV Story & P: Jonathan Heap. From the short film and Richard Lupoff's short story "12:01 PM." Ph: Anghel Decca. Mus: Peter Melnick. PD: Michael Novotny. SpFxCoord: G. Bruno Stempel. Elec Digital FX: The Post Group. Key Mkp: Dalia Saydah-Dokter. Ref: TV. SFChron 6/21/93. 7/4/93. 7/5/93. TVG 7/3/93. 3/30/91: short version, with Kurtwood Smith, shown on "30-Minute Movie." With Jonathan Silverman, Helen Slater, Martin Landau, Jeremy Piven, Nicholas Surovy, Robin Bartlett.

"Why do you remember?" Particle physicists experimenting with a "super accelerator" at Utrel Corp. accidentally create a "time bounce," which causes Tuesday, April 27, 1993, to repeat, like a broken record, as everyone gets "punched back" in time, again and again, at the end of the day. Only Barry Thomas (Silverman), in personnel, knows what's going on — freak lightning from the accelerator got him "pushed out of the loop."

If the story is standard corporate intrigue, its science-fictional mainspring— Thomas uses his gift of *deja vu* to tinker with this particular Tuesday —the mainspring gives the tale some urgency, as well as some comedy. ("I've died for you already.") Call it the "Bolero" effect, or a variation on foretelling the future, as in *It Happened Tomorrow*. Or call it "The Today Show."

The premise also has a touch of Melville's "Benito Cereno": Each reliving of the day brings Barry Thomas closer to the truth, gives him a better look. Told in linear time, 12:01 might be banal; in "bounced" time, it's fresh, funny, fascinating.

**TWENTIETH CENTURY SURGEON** see *Chirurgien Americain*

**2010** MGM-UA 1984 color/ws 116m. Ph, SP, D, P: Peter Hyams. From Arthur C. Clarke's novel. Mus: David Shire. SpVisFx: (sup) Richard Edlund; Entertainment FX Group; (mattes) Neil Krepela; (mech fx sup) Thaine Morris; (anim sup) Terry Windell, Garry Waller; (stopmo) Randall William Cook; (min mech fx) Bob Johnston. SpFxSup: Henry Millar. Flying Sup: Robert Harman. VideoFxSup: Greg McMurry. MkpSup: Michael Westmore. Vis Futurist: Syd Mead. Ref: TV. V 11/28/84. SFExam 12/7/84. Ecran F 53:11: aka 2010: Odyssey Two. With Roy Scheider, John Lithgow, Helen Mirren, Bob Balaban, Keir Dullea, Douglas Rain (voice of HAL 9000), Dana Elcar, James McEachin, Mary Jo Deschanel, Herta Ware, A.C Clarke.

In this sequel to *2001,* the *Discovery II* is located near Jupiter, Dave Bowman (Dullea) returns via video to say goodbye to his wife, HAL sacrifices "himself" for the *Discovery* crew, a million or so monoliths are "reproducing like a virus" on Jupiter, and a new sun sends the world a message of peace .... Much perverse fun to be had here in seeing the themes of *2001* ever so carefully manhandled. Hyams alternately fritters away screen time on inconsequentialities — farewells, spacewalks, "political" issues — and crams scenes, willy-nilly, with action and events. Effects scenes are, at the least, lively.

**20,000 LEAGUES UNDER THE SEA** (Austral.) Burbank Films (Tim Brooke-Hunt/Tom Stacey) 1985 anim color 50m. SP: Stephen MacLean, from Jules Verne's novel. Mus: John Stuart. Nautilus Des: Michael Lodge. Anim D: Warwick Gilbert. Ref: TV: Million Dollar Video; Spanish-dubbed. Voices: Tom Burlinson, Colin Borgonon.

It's 1866, and the headline blares, "Sea Monster Sinks Another Ship!" Yes, it's Nemo, the electrified *Nautilus,* giant crabs at the bottom of the sea in the Lost Continent of Atlantis, and the giant squid, the latter drawn and animated so as not to intimidate small children. Bland.

See also: *Dream One. Pagemaster. Under the Sea.*

**2020: TEXAS GLADIATORS** (I) Continental/Eureka 1984 color 91m. (*Texas 2000* - orig t. *Sudden Death* -alt t). D: A. Massaccesi aka Kevin Mancuso. SP: Alex Carver. Mus: F. Taylor. SpFX: J. Davies, R. Gold , P. Gray. Mkp: P. Russell, B. Hills.

Ref: TV: Eng. version. Horacio Higuchi. V 4/27/83:166(ad). 3/7/84:15 completed. Palmerine: aka *Anno 2020* or *I Gladiatori del Futuro*. 11/13/85: MHE video. TVG. With Harrison Muller, Al Cliver, Sabrina Siani, Daniel Stephen, Peter Hooten, Al Yamanouchi, Donal O'Brien.

The energy source of the future: reconstituted sediment. A refinery crew takes on marauders with impregnable thermal shields. It's a long wait for the climactic novelty of a battle waged with bows and arrows, cycles, shields, rifles, machine guns, and hatchets.... Undistinguished actioner features violence, moralizing re violence, and a numbingly twangy suspense score.

**2050** see *Solar Crisis*

**2084** see *Starship*

**TWICE DEAD** Concorde/T.D. Prods. (Guy J. Louthan) 1988 color 85m. SP, D: Bert Dragin. SP,Co-P: Robert McDonnell. Mus: David Bergeaud. SpMkpFX: Michael Burnett. SpFXCoord: Steve Galich. Titles: (des) Tony Ip; Mercer Titles. Ref: TV. V 11/9/88. NYT 11/19/88. With Tom Breznahan, Jill Whitlow, Brooke Bundy, Jonathan Chapin (Tyler Walker/Crip).

Two teenagers play ghost, scare punks out of the "old Tyler place." ("Place gives me the creeps.") But when the gang returns, a real ghost busts out of a mirror, possesses one thug, and animates motorcycle, shotgun, dumbwaiter, etc., and kills all, or nearly all, the intruders. At the end, the ghost's now-ghostly descendant haunts the place. Overplotted, humorless horror-fantasy.

**TWILIGHT** see *Servants of Twilight, The*

**TWILIGHT PINK II: THE EROGENOUS ZONE** Platinum Pictures 1985 color c80m. D,P, Ed: Travis St. Germaine. SP: Khang T. Cruel. AD: Milton Trad. Ref: TV: VCA video. Jim Shapiro. no Adam '88. With Marlene Willoughby, Ron Jeremy, Tanya Lawson, Lisa Centrice, Baby Doe, R. Bolla.

Sterling Rod hosts three more tales from "The Erogenous Zone":1) In a reworking of the "Twilight Zone" episode from 1961, "Will the Real Martian Please Stand Up?", three alien women (Melinda Stevens, Ambrosia, Sharon Kane) land on Earth and use their density modifier to "zombify" country-boy Lucas (Jaime St. John), who later removes his hat to reveal his own antennae.... 2) In a reworking of a 1959 "Twilight Zone" show, "The 16mm. Shrine," an aging ex-porn-star sells her soul in order to turn back the clock and slip into her old film on her home-movie screen. 3) Men from 1982 and 1941 enter " the portal," a time warp into 16th-century England.... The only things to note re this hardcore sequel to *Twilite Pink* (II) are that it's more sf-oriented than *Twilite Pink* and that it actually lifts from the original "Twilight Zone."

The **TWILIGHT SIREN** (H.K.) c1990 color/ws c85m. Ref: TV: World Video; Eng. titles. Y.K. Ho: *The Magic Girl against the Master* - tr t.

"Your place is haunted." The Devil King wants the ghost Joan to obtain "one hundred men's hearts." At one point, she emerges from a blood-nourished skull to possess heroine Wendy, but Joan turns out to be a renegade, and the Devil King sends May to

retrieve her.... Dull combination of kung fu and fantasy. Ectoplasmic news flash: "Ghosts walk silently." Also: scenes with the (literally) long arm of the ghost and a siren with fangs.

**TWILIGHT Q, VOL. 2 — MEIKYU BUKKEN FILE 538** (J) Network c1990? anim color/ws 30m. D: Oshii Mamoru. Ref: TV: Emotion video; no Eng.; OAV. no Animag.

At the beginning, a shattering airliner "becomes" a swimming fish. At the end, the gutting of a fish segues into the tearing open of an airplane. In-between: a long monologue and a few hyperatmospheric skyscapes. The "bookending" images suggest a universe-within-a-universe.

**TWILIGHT ZONE: ROD SERLING'S LOST CLASSICS** CBS-TV/O'Hara-Horowitz Prods. (S.B. Hickox) 1994 color c90m. D: Robert Markowitz. Tel: Richard Matheson; R. Serling. Story (1): R. Serling. Ph: J. Laskus. Mus: P. Williams. PD: C. Wagener. Host: James Earl Jones. Ref: V 5/16/94:32: "Neither's top-drawer Serling...." TVG. with Amy Irving, Gary Cole; Jack Palance, Patrick Bergin, Jenna Stern.

"The Theater": Woman "sees" her past and future in a movie theatre.

"Where the Dead Are": "zombierama." (V)

**TWILIGHT ZONE, The** see *Midnight Zone, The. Twilight Pink* II.

**TWILITE PINK** (3) see also *Twilight Pink II*

**TWIN DOLLS: LEGEND OF THE HEAVENLY BEASTS** (J) SoftCel Pictures/Daiei (Maki & Izumi) 1994 anim color c45m. D: Kan Fukumoto. SP: Ohji Miyako. Ph: J. Yokosuka. AD: M. Matsumoto. Ref: TV: SC video (Daiei Video); Eng. titles; *Dreamy Express Zone* series. Voice: Kiyoshi Watanabe (Hakumoki).

"Demons, be gone! We are the Twin Dolls!" The latter, Mai and Ai, take on Hakumoki, prince of the heavenly beasts of the Demon World. The latter are horny, horned demons, the Jaki, who rape Earth girls.... Horrific hardcore animation strains for the perverse, features a long expository flashback re the twins and the demons. Lots of "Yes! Yes! Every orifice of my body!" Pretty weird: the "pasture" of naked women awaiting the demon hordes.

**TWINS** Universal (Ivan Reitman) 1988 color 107m. D: I. Reitman.SP: William Davies, William Osborne, Timothy Harris, Herschel Weingrod. Mus: Georges Delerue. VisFX: Boss Film. SpFxCoord: Michael Lantieri. SpSdFX: Tom Buffum. Ref: TV. MFB'89:88-9. V 12/7/88. Bill Warren. SFExam 12/9/88. With Arnold Schwarzenegger, Danny DeVito, Kelly Preston, Chloe Webb, Hugh O'Brian, Nehemiah Persoff, Maury Chaykin, Elizabeth Kaitan.

The U.S. Government's Genetic Research Department, intent on producing an "advanced human being," instead produces far-from-identical twins who have a telepathic link — the superstrong Julius Benedict (Schwarzenegger), the "most fully developed human the world has ever seen," and Vincent (De-Vito), "genetic garbage" .... A tortuous plot dilutes the charm of the central conceit, which wryly matches the "advanced" Schwarzenegger with the diminutive De Vito. And the basically-comic story keeps taking wrong turns into sentimental side streets.

See also *Appu Raja* (P).

**TWIST: AKO SI IKAW ... IKAW SI AKO** (Fili) Regal Films & M-Zet Films 1990? color 104m. D: Efren Jarlego. SP: Tony Cruz. Ph: Amado de Guzman. Mus: Mon del Rosario. PD: Bert Habal. SpFX: Rolly Sto. Domingo. Mkp: Pinero. SdFX: Rodel Capule. Ref: TV: Regal video; no Eng. With Vic Sotto, Aiza Seguerra, Panchito, Chichay, Nova Villa, Alma Moreno, Jimmy Fabregas.

Dr. Kalentong's pigs crow, and his chickens oink. Later, a man and his daughter accidentally drink his chemical concoction and exchange personalities/spirits: He sucks his thumb; she pays more attention to personal grooming. At the end, a thug and a frog swap souls.... Typical Filipino comedy. A few chuckles.

**TWISTED FATE** see *Kill Kill Overkill*

**TWISTED ISSUES** Twisted Films 1988 color c80m. SP, D, Ph: Charles Pinion. SP: also Steve Antczak, Hawk. Ph: also Lisa Soto. SpFX: David Peck. Ref: TV: vt. no Stanley. With Paul Soto, S. Antczak, L. Soto, Chuck Speta (mad doctor).

A skateboarder run over by a car is brought back to life in a lab. He proceeds to drive a stake through his benefactor, drill a hole in his own foot, and wreak gory vengeance on his persecutors. Or, Waiting for an Editor. Really miserable shot-on-tape, shot-in-Florida gore vehicle, pretentiously padded out with newsreel-type footage.

**TWISTED JUSTICE** Seymour Borde/Hero Films & Golden Life Group 1990 color c88m. SP,D,P,Mus: David Heavener. Mus: also Bob Garrett. SpFX: Court Wizard. Mkp: Amy Snyder. Ref: TV. V 4/4/90. With D. Heavener, Erik Estrada, Karen Black, Shannon Tweed, Jim Brown, James Van Patten, Don Stroud, Gerald Milton, David Campbell (Steelmore).

"This is the future. Los Angeles, California. No one can carry a gun, not even the police." The torso slasher at large — who carves a "bloody bull's-eye" on his female victims — is high on the "powerful addictive" that he invented. This "new intelligence booster" — a "distant cousin of PCP" — has bad psychological side effects and also effectively neutralizes police "stingers" .... Flat-footed mixture of science fiction and cop caper. Cop hero has a bad case of the cutes.

**TWISTED NIGHTMARE** UF(Sandy Horowitz) 1987 colo r 94m. SP,D,Ph: Paul Hunt. Ph: also Gary Graver. SpFX: Cleve Hall. Ref: V 9/21/88: "relentlessly dull." 5/6/87:285(ad). 6/24/87:4(rated). Nowlan. With Rhonda Gray, C. Hall, Brad Bartrum, Robert Padillo.

"Big, hairy monster" on the loose at Camp Paradise, built on Indian burial grounds. (V)

**TWISTED SOULS** see *Spookies*

**2 TWITCH OF THE DEATH NERVE** Zaccariello 1971 ws (*L'Ecologia del Delitto. Reazione a Catena. Before the Fact. A Bay of Blood* - vt. aka *Last House on the Left Part II*). Ref: TV: Gorgon Video; Eng.dubbed. VWB: aka *New House on the Left*.

Hardy/HM. Lee. no V. Weldon. Martin. Palmerini. With Chris Avram.

An old lady is garroted. The garroter is then knifed to death. Goriest bit: probably the machete in the face. Grossest bit: probably the squid squirming on the face of the corpse. Creepiest bit: the dead man's hand floating up to the naked swimmer's thigh. Kinkiest bit: the writhing of the two-on-a-spear couple, which segues seamlessly from sexual to mortal. Gore-store miscellany: a beheading with an ax, a speared "fish".... Mario Bava takes the low road here. Is the script satirical or simply idiotic? Everyone around the bay, or lake, seems to be a slasher, then a slashee. At the end, even the kids get in on the carnage, in an unlikely ironic coda. But this won't make you think of *The Wild Bunch,* although Bava gets some visual mileage out of the horrible-murders/lovely-lake contrasts, and the lake-surface "mirror" is fully exploited. The Bava eye also takes in some haunting evening and night, blue-black silhouettes of tree branches.

**TWO EVIL EYES** (I) Taurus Ent. (Heron)/ADC & Gruppo Bema (Achille Manzotti) 1990 color c120m. (*Due Occhi Diabolici*). D: (1) George Romero; (2) Dario Argento. SP: (1) Romero; (2) Argento, Franco Ferrini. Based on Edgar Allan Poe stories. Ph: (1) Peter Reniers; (2) Beppe Maccari. Mus: Pino Donaggio. SpMkpFxSup: Tom Savini. OptFX: Perpetual Motion Pictures. Rain FX: J.C Brotherhood. SdFX: Anzellotti. Ref: TV: Eng. version. V 3/7/90. ad. With (1) Adrienne Barbeau, E.G. Marshall, Ramy Zada, Bingo O'Malley; (2) Harvey Keitel, Madeleine Potter, Martin Balsam, Kim Hunter, Sally Kirkland.

1) "The Facts in the Case of Mr. Valdemar." "I am dead. Let me go!" "Others" from the beyond animate and attempt to use the bodies of two men (O'Malley, Zada), who died while under hypnosis, in order to "pass through" to the world of the living. Story begins as a routine get-the-rich-geezer's-dough tale, develops into something a bit different, though the supernatural comings-and-goings become a little tricky and confusing. Grade A frisson: a broom clattering down a flight of stone steps.

2) "The Black Cat." Pointless elaborations on the basic tale of a man — here Keitel's gore photographer, Rod ("Still life is my specialty") Usher — who walls up a woman (Potter's Annabel) and a cat. Argento and Ferrini also throw in a Poe-ish pendulum, and trademark Argento images include galloping-cat and swing-ing-pendulum point-of-view shots and a CU of a drop of feline blood falling from a saw.

**2001: A SPACE ODYSSEY** see *2010*

**2001 NIGHT'S TALE** (J) 1987 anim color 57m. Ref: TV: RCA Victor video; no Eng. vc box.

A story of space pioneers who learn of a now-devastated Earth they left behind. The movie's lulling, ever-panning-and-tracking camera style accommodates moods from melancholy to wonder and celebrates the beauty of celestial bodies, strange-looking space vehicles, futuristic mining machinery, meteor showers, exotic flora, etc. The film is lovingly stylized — outer space has never seemed so beguilingly idyllic. The people, however, move stiffly — perhaps even more so than in most Japanese cartoons — and the animators vainly attempt to render some of them naturalistically. (The artists also fail to make waterfalls and flood waters flow naturally.) When it comes to spaceships, though, the animators excel. Each shot seems to highlight some new "twist" or surprise in interstellar design. The appearances of the ships are heralded, variously and imaginatively, by huge gliding shadows on the ground, by the ruffling of wild grass, by a steady, low roar, etc. And the musical score is as intoxicating as the camerawork. Knockout shot: the camera panning up and up and up to reveal more and more hibernating space travelers.

**2002: A SEX ODYSSEY** Dreamland/Ross 1985 color 79m. D: Tom Morton. SP,P: Jerry Ross. Ref: vc box: time machine. Adam '88: "Dad's brand new time traveler." With Tracy Adams, Tom Byron, Sharon Mitchell.

**200X SHO** (J) 1992 color/ws 92m. Ref: TV: King Video; no Eng. Video Tokyo: above is tr t.

The night-and-fog-stalkers in this futuristic terror tale are eerie at first, but get pretty monotonous. Fire, or light, holds them at bay; water knocks 'em out. Well-photographed. The plot seems inspired as much by *Day of the Triffids* as by *Night of the Living Dead.*

**TWO WOMEN FROM THE NETHERWORLD** (So. Korean) Han Jin Ents. (Han Kap Chin) 1982 color 98m. D: Park Yoon Kyo. SP: Lee Jae Hun. Ref: Hardy/HM: "credible." With Kim Ki Joo, Huh Jin.

Two ghosts wreak revenge on a warlord.

**\*THE TWONKY** Arch Oboler Prods. (A.D. Nast,Jr.) 1953(1952). Mus: Jack Meakin. SpPhFX: SpFX, Inc. SpFX: Robert Bonnig. SdFX: Gus Bayz. Ref: TV. Warren/KWTS! Lee. Lentz. Stanley. Weldon. Hardy/SF. V 6/17/53. Maltin '92. Scheuer. TVG. Filmfax 26. 30:38. With Ed Max, Evelyn Beresford, Al Jarvis.

"A twonky is something you do not know what it is." Robot 743 B32, experimental model series K72 —"from our world, centuries in the future" — "falls" through time and re-forms itself as an Admiral TV set in the present, where it apparently carries out the dictates of a futuristic "super-state." Its "super atomic brain" allows it to think (even though it's not plugged into the wall socket), and it hypnotically turns those who would destroy it into semi-zombies. ("I have no complaints.") This particular twonky plays "Mr. Robot" to a philosophy professor (Hans Conreid) —its "electric ray" lights his cigarettes, creates folding money, shines his shoes, ties his tie, and at one point hypnotizes him into lecturing at school re passion. The various bizarrenesses of the script here have little to do with comedy, more to do with pop sociology, though the movie at least fails in its own very distinctive, half-comatose way. Lotsa cheap effects with the electric ray liven things up a bit.

**TYRANNO'S CLAW** (S. Korean) 198-? D: Shim Hyung Rei. Ref: HOF 2:25: dinosaur film.script here have little to do with comedy, more to do with pop sociology, though the movie at least fails in its own very distinctive, half-comatose way. Lotsa cheap effects with the electric ray liven things up a bit.

**TYRANNO'S CLAW** (S. Korean) 198-? D: Shim Hyung Rei. Ref: HOF 2:25: dinosaur film.

# U

**U.F.O.** (B) PolyGram & Forster 1993 color 79m. D: Tony Dow. SpFxSup: Alan Whibley. Ref: S&S 2/94: kitschy. With Roy "Chubby" Brown, Sara Stockbridge.

In a distant galaxy, in the 25th Century....

**U.F.O. CHINESE FRIED NOODLES** (J) Nissin Food/Dentsu 1994? color 68m. Ref: TV: vt. Video Tokyo: above is tr t.

Ingredients include the super-hero/magic-chef of the title, who has various fried-noodle-angled powers ... a fried-noodle ray rifle ... a villain so evil that even his mother is evil ... and a giant kettle.... Is this a movie or an ad? Lead comedian of this apparent shot-on-taper is a sort of Ernest of Japan. Closest-to-amusing sequences: U.F.O. methodically getting on his super-noodle gear ... a visualized nightmare in which the shrunken heroine is gulped down by a "giant."

**UFO DAI-APOLON** see *Shadow World*

**UBIT DRAKONA** (Russ-W.G.) Goskino & ZDF 1989 color 132m. SP,D: Mark Zakharov. SP: also Grigori Gorin. From a work by Evgueni Shvarts. Mus: G . Gladkov. Ref: V 5/31/89: "stirring sequences are diluted by overlong, wordy scenes"; *Kill the Dragon* - tr t? With Alexander Abdulov, Oleg Yankovski, Evgeni Leonov.

A "dragon" appearing in the form, alternately, of a "combative flying saucer" and a "big-brother dictator" threatens a medieval Russian town.

**UCCELLO DALLE PIUMEDI CRISTALLO, L'** see *Bird with the Crystal Plumage, The*

**UCCIDE A PASSE DI DANZE** see *Demon Is Loose, The*

**UCHU SENKAN YAMATO** (3) see *Final Yamato*

**UCHUU NO SENSHI** see *Starship Troopers*

**UFORIA** Univ/Simon Films 1986(1981) color 93m. SP,D: John Binder. Ref: TV. Bob Moore. Maltin/TVM. TVG. SFChron 2/28/86. V 7/18/84.

Rural melo which only at the very end becomes sf, as a saucer-ship spirits a supermarket clerk (Cindy Williams) and a drifter (Fred Ward) away from Earth. Thin, single-minded, condescending, with some sweet moments. Love that UFO-like title in the credits.

**UHAW NA UHAW** (Fili) VRV Film/May Films Int'l. & D'Players Film 198-? color c115m. SP,D: Arsenio Bautista. Ph: Bernardo. Mus: Dino Araza. AD: Alex Bolado. Mkp: Trajano. SdFX: Rolly Ruta. Ref: TV: vt; no Eng. New Manila Deli: *Thirsty* -tr t. With Ernie Garcia, Raoul Aragonn, Daria Ramirez, Zandro Zamora, George Estregan, Nick Romano, Cristina Crisol.

A teenager sees three men raping her mother. She runs home, and her father rapes her. The mother catches him in the act and stabs him to death. Some time later, a ski-masked slasher prowls by night and kills men .... Sensationalistic shocker is more a softcore sex film than a slasher movie, but is long enough to accommodate both genres. In either mode, it's hardly subtle.

**UHLOZ** (F) Guy Jacques 1989 short. Ref: SFChron Dtbk 3/7/93: "science-fictional study in revenge." SFChron 3/11/93.

"Model rocket kit that turns out to have great explosive powers ...."

**L'ULTIMA CASA VICINO AL LAGO** (I) Cinezeta 1978 color 91m. (aka *Kyra: La Signora del Lago. Kyra: Lady of the Lake. 2 The Devil's Woman. Sensitiva. Diabla. Devil's Encounter*). D: Enzo G. Castellari (or Girolami). SP: L. Buongiorno, J.M. Nunes. Ph: A. Ulloa. Mus: G. & M. de Angelis. AD: C. Ricercato. Mkp: Gregorio Mendiri. Ref: TV: VSOM; Eng. titles; I-Sp co-prod.? VSOM: *Last House near the Lake* - vt t. V 10/19/88:368(ad): KIRA. Hardy/HM: a "very entertaining fairy tale"; *The Last House near the Lake* - tr t. MV. Palmerini: *Sensitivita*. With Leonora Fani, Wolfgang Soldati, V. Gardenia, Patricia Adriani, Massimo Vanni, Marta Flores, Antonio Mayans, L. Induni, Caterina Boratto.

"She's the daughter of the lady of the lake!" Softcore silliness re Lilian Barton, descendant of Kyra, who haunts a lake. ("The lake is damned.") Sex with Lilian can be fatal: "A 'temporary death' lives inside you" (as she is told by a villager); "you die and come back ...." And the mysterious Lily seems to be on the same sexual wavelength as Lilian.... Cliche-clogged fantasy-horror at least has some offbeat premises.

**The ULTIMATE LOVER** Broad Appeal(Leonard-Paine) 1986 color 105m. D: Thomas Paine. Ref: Adam '88. TVG. With Tracy Adams, Nina Hartley, Amber Lynn.

Two female doctors create a man in their lab.

**The ULTIMATE TEACHER** (J) SVI 1988('93-U.S.) anim color c60m. (aka *The Last Teacher*). Ref: Animag 3:6. USMC brochure. Japan Video.

Genetically engineered teacher.

**The ULTIMATE VAMPIRE** (H.K.) Eagle Films 1991 color c90m. D: Andrew Lau. Ph: Mui Kin Fai. Mus: Phil Chen. AD: Danny Yuen. Ref: TV: Pan-Asia Video; Eng. titles. Jones. With Lam Ching Ying, Chin Sui Ho, Wong Pan, Carrie Ng.

"So many ghosts ...." Ingredients here include a mass exorcism of said ghosts ... Hell Police ... an alternately pretty and monster-faced ghost who loves a Taoist priest ... cartoon ectoplasm ... coffin mushrooms and hopping-vampires' coffins, on Coffin Hill, natch — and the gruesome-faced vampire leader ...plus a Western-type, neck-biting vampire who seems to die, but who is revived (along with a horde of the dead) by his sorcerer father. The Group Horror idea is interesting, if schematic: Each new supernatural menace — ghosts, vampires, zombies — ends up attacking en masse. Thought for today: "All ghosts eat mud." Lively silliness.

**ULTIMO GUERRIERO, L'** see *Final Executioner, The*

**ULTRA COP 2000** (H.K.?) 1993? color c90m. (*Ultracop 2000 - cr t*). Ref: TV: World Video; Eng. titles.

Two Martians land on Earth. Jared (sp?): "I am the ultracop from another planet." ("He really flies.") Zordak, the bad Martian ("He wants to conquer the Earth"), seems to absorb (green) energy from his victims (he "sucked the blood" of one victim, observes a witness) and at one point tosses zombie dust at some thugs in order to control them.... The two Martians have amusing battles in the air. Otherwise, this is routine, occasionally stylish action and comedy. The silly, all-a-dream ending is itself set in the year 2000.

**ULTRA Q: THE MOVIE** (J) Emotion /Noboru Tsuburaya Prods. 1990 color/ws 111m. D: Akio Jissohji. SP: S. Sekizawa, M. Sasaki? AD: O. Yamaguchi? SpFxD: Kazuo Sagawa? Based on a TV series. Tech Consul: Inoshiro Honda? Ref: TV: Bandai HV; no Eng. Japan Video. Ecran F 56: 70: *Ultra Q: Monster Concerto; 1985?* Weisser/JC: *Urutora Q Za Muubi*.

A monster-made earthquake heralds the appearance of a ray-shooting idol, a robot-type, and a woman with a red scarf, all of whom may be one and the same. Every now and then, an old fashioned, two-horned, ray-shooting giant monster with bad teeth starts acting like a one-monster wrecking crew and — like the demon in *Curse of the Demon* — breaks up the prevailing eerie atmosphere. At the end, the woman seems to lead the idol's white-garbed worshipers to literal, *2001*-like rebirth on a rocket ship headed towards the heavens.

The tempo here is intriguingly deliberate, acting and music unsettlingly low-key, photography exquisite. Latter, in particular, exploits the cool allure of certain seascapes. Highlights: the instant-ebb-tide effect and the Forest Lights from Hell. Unfortunately, the introduction of the standard monster-menace creates a Waiting for Godzilla effect.

**ULTRA WARRIOR** Concorde-New Horizons(Luis Llosa/Mike Elliott) 1990 color 75m. (*Welcome to Oblivion* -vt t). D: Augusto Tamayo, Kevin Tent. SP: Len Jenkin, Dan Kleinman. Ph: Cusi Barrio. Mus: Terry Plumeri et al. AD: Valdez, Troncoso. SpMkpFX: Thom Schouse. Custom VisFX: Roderick Davis. SpFX: F. Vasquez de Velasco. OptFX: T&T. Ref: TV. TVG. PT 16:14. V 1/28/91. Wth Dack Rambo, Meshach Taylor, Clare Beresford, Mark Bringelson, Charles Dougherty, Ramsey Ross (Lazarus), Orlando Sacha (Bishop).

April 1, 2058, after a space Defense System accident has decimated the world's population. The wealthy live in cities; the poor — mostly "genetically deformed nomads, " or mutants — in the radioactive desert of Oblivion. ("It's beautiful — too bad it's radioactive.") Other ingredients include a ship from a "parallel universe" out to turn planets into stars ... Zirconium Bombs, our only hope ... underground cannibals, "Whities" ... and "robotic cyberpunks." Comically patchy low-budgeter is a scrap heap of footage from *The Warrior and the Sorceress* (the four-breasted woman), *Battle beyond the Stars, Lords of the Deep,* etc. The characters reminisce, and stock footage fills the screen .... Best original line: "Move your ass, you friggin' mutie!"

**ULTRAMAN: THE ADVENTURE BEGINS** (U.S.-J) Hanna-Barbera & Tsuburaya 1987 anim color c90m. D: Mitsuo Kusakabe. SP: John Eric Seward. Story,P: Noboru Tsuburaya. Ref: TV. TVG. V 10/18/89:77. no Scheuer. no Maltin '92. Markalite 3:82: sfa *Adventures of Ultraman*? Voices: Chad Everett, Stacy Keach Sr., Michael Lembeck, Adrienne Barbeau.

Ingredients: Ultra-team aliens that chase monsters from a self-destructing planet in the M-78 system which merge into human bodies... giant ray-shooting monsters which arrive on Earth via asteroid ... and a baby alien which turns monstrous (cf. *Gremlins*) .... Stolid, formulaic.

See also the following titles, *Love on Delivery, Melos,* and *Urutoraman Sutori.*

**ULTRAMAN: THE ALIEN INVASION, PART 1** (J-Austral.) Tsuburaya & The South Australian Film Corp. & SAFIAC (Suzuki-Wild) 1992 (1990) color c94m. D: Andrew Prowse. SP: Terry Larsen. Story: Sho Aikawa et al. Ph: Paul Dallwitz. Mus: S. Kazato. PD: A. Blaxland. VisFX: BobDog Inc., Hyodo Film et al. SpFxSup: Paul Nichola. FxSup: Alan Maxwell. Practical FX & Anim: Anifex. Monster Des: J. Yoshida. Ultraman Suit: Paul Warren. Ref: TV: Ultra Video; Eng. version. Cinef: from a TV series. With Dore Kraus, Gia Carides, Ralph Cotterill, Lloyd Morris, Grace Parr, Rick Adams; Robert Simper, Steve Apps (Ultraman), Matthew O'Sullivan (voice of Ultraman).

"It's bacteria!" "From deep space?" Yes, and these monsters can genetically "manipulate" matter and seem to be joining together and trying to make everything a part of them/it. Principals include Ultraman ("It must be a cyborg!"), who can take giant form ... a comically horrific, tentacled monster ... a giant "tadpole" critter ... an ice-breath monster ("Nothing natural could have grown so quickly!") ... and a giant, flying, fire-breathing monster (Ultraman rolls up the fire into a ball and flings it back at the thing).... Routine sf, with cheap effects and music. The hero-vs.-monster matches get monotonous.

**ULTRAMAN GRAFFITI** (J) Emotion/ Hajime Tsuburaya Prods. 1990 anim color 53m. Ref: TV: Bandai video; no Eng.; OAV. Animag 11:4.

This junior, animated version of *Ultraman,* or Uroturoman, features several tales, concerning, respectively, very variegated aliens aboard an el in the sky ... a laser war in a classroom ...a day in the country marked by impromptu war games ... and a wedding which turns into a snowstorm .... The funny, squat characters in the M-87 galaxy here are similar to those in *S.D. Gundam,* and the video itself functions as a clever, pint-sized parody of its parent series, too. Several of the characters have the ability to heat their food with their own breath; one has personal command of snow and ice.

**ULTRAMAN ZOFFY!** (J) Shochiku-Fuji (Tsuburaya Video) 1984 color 84m. Ref: TV: Columbia Video; no Eng. V 4/11/84:37. TVG.

This apparent review of highlights from a TV series — perhaps *Ultraman: Towards the Future* — is alternately riotous and monotonous. The "fashion show" of monsters includes a giant lobster, a horned monster, a giant car-eating monster, a "snowman," an insect-like monster, a Godzilla-like monster, a laser-breath monster, a gill-man-like sea monster, a Gorgo-like sea monster, an anvil-headed monster, a combination turkey and Santa Claus-like monster which flings deadly, varicolored feathers at Ultraman, a relatively small (relative to the size of most of the monsters) clam-headed monster which properly brushes its teeth and seems to coexist peacefully with kids, a mole monster, an ape monster, and one very ticklish monster. Charming: the lobster monsters flying in formation ... the Rockette-like line of Ultramen "hatched" from "eggs."Breathless, blow-by-blow narration.

**UMEZU KAZUO TERROR** see *Horror!*

**UN PASO AL MAS ACA ...** (Mex) Radeant Films (Raul De Anda Prods.) 1989 color c85m. SP, D, Mus: Gilberto De Anda. Ph: Antonio De Anda. SpFX: Federico Farfan. Mkp: Carmen de la Torre. SdFX: Gonzalo Gavira. OptFX: Manuel Sainz. Ref: TV: Mexcinema Video; no Eng. La Tapatia: *One Step Closer* - tr t. With Sergio Goyri, Luz Maria Jerez, Juan Pelaez, Maria Luisa Alcala, Quintin Bulnes, Alejandro Guce, Lorena Herrera.

At a very strange apartment complex, a guy who dresses like Dracula and who wraps up a woman in his cloak and drags her into a coffin proves to be simply an actor prepping for his next (vampire) movie. The woman, however, proves to be a real werewolf. Meanwhile, two tenants accidentally kill the plumber who, buried nearby, revives and turns up somewhat the worse for wear on their doorstep. And two young women whose penthouse vanishes into another dimension are ... ghosts .... Cute, light horror-comedy with some okay twists. The landlord turns out to be the devil ....

**UNA NOTTE NEL CIMITERO** see *Graveyard Disturbance*

**UNBESIEGBARE, Der** see *Invincible, The*

**The UNBORN** Califilm/Concorde-New Horizons (Mike Elliott) 1991 color 83m. D,P: Rodman Flender. SP: Henry Dominic. Mus: G. Numan, M.R. Smith. SpMkpFX & Baby: Joe Podnar; (mech) John Criswell. Sp VoiceFX: Dave Mallow, Lisa Michelson. Ref:TV. V 4/19/91. SFChron Dtbk 1/12/92. With Brooke Adams, Jeff Hayenga, James Karen, K Callan.

"There's something wrong with the children!" Geneticist Dr. Meyerling's (Karen) Human Genome Project utilizes "modified" sperm and "protein synthesis" in an apparent attempt to fashion "some sort of master race" to "replace us" — i.e., unmodified humans. The doctor communicates subliminally, by tape, to his unborn stormtroopers ("You're stronger") and — finding human carriers (i.e., mothers) a bother — has already arrived at the next stage: test-tube toddlers.

This humorless sf edition of *Rosemary's Baby* — the doctor as devil — is not so much chilling as unpleasant. Pregnancy, miscarriage, and abortion are the stuff of horror here. Scattered highlights include a sequence with the very bad seed next door (Jessica Zingali) which recalls a similar sequence in the original *Invaders from Mars.*

**UNBORN II** New Horizons 1994 color feature. D: Rick Jacobson. SP: Schwartz, Percell. Ref: PT 20:70-1: "pretty bad." Stanley: "unconvincing." Martin: "as bad as the first one." With Michelle Greene, Scott Valentine, Brittany Powell.

"Killer kid." (PT)

**UNCONSCIOUS** see *Fear* (1980)

*The UNDEAD 1957(1956). Mkp: Curly Batson. Chor: Chris Miller. Ref: TV. Lee. Hardy/ HM. Lentz. V 2/27/57. no Phantom. Glut/ CMM: SpMkp: Paul Blaisdell. Maltin '92. Hound. Cocchi. Scheuer. Stanley.

"Then the regression is physical as well as mental." Tibetan hypnotism sends the "murky mind" — and body — of a prostitute, Diana (Pamela Duncan), back to the eve of the Witches' Sabbat, in the second year of the reign of King Mark, where she becomes the condemned-to-die Helene (also Duncan). (Later, a machine blends the brain waves of Diana and Val DuFour's experimenter and sends him back to the same era.) Helen is forced to choose either to live a "full lifetime now and then die forever" or die and be reborn, again and again, as a poetess, a mother, a dancer, etc. She chooses "temporary" death and finds that her spirit has "cleansed" Diana.

Unusual and intriguing premises make this probably the most interesting of the mid-Fifties reincarnation movies. (The Search for Bridey Murphy, I've Lived Before, and The Living Idol, all 1956, and Fright, 1957, are other examples.) This is very strange territory for a "B" movie, but the tacky production and stilted action hurt. Allison Hayes is at her sultry-slutty best as a shape-shifting witch, Billy Barty plays a garlic-eating imp (who at one point becomes a spider), and Mel Welles is a bewitched, bothered gravedigger. Hayes and Barty intermittently transform themselves into the flying things from It Conquered the World.

UNDER THE SEA Paul Glabicki 1989 anim 24m. Ref: SFChron Dtbk 12/16/90.

"An incredibly busy film" taking from Verne's "20,000 Leagues under the Sea," Shelley's "Frankenstein," etc.

The UNDERSTUDY: GRAVEYARD SHIFT II Cinema Ventures & S.R. Flaks & A.H. Bruck 1988 color 88m. SP,D,PD: Gerard Ciccoritti. Mus: Philip Stern. SpFxMkp: Adrianne & Andrea Sicova. SpFX: SpFx Assoc. Ref: TV: Virgin Vision video. V 7/26/89. Jones. McCarty II. Martin. With Wendy Gazelle, Mark Soper, Silvio Oliviero, Ilse Von Glatz, Carl Alacchi.

"I'm your desire." The vampire Baisez (Oliviero) vows to possess Camilla Turner (Gazelle), star of the movie-in-progress "Blood Lovers" — but first she, too, must draw blood .... Baisez also says, at one point, "I need new flesh to live again," though he seems at first to be some sort of symbolic phantom, not a vampire. He also says, "Movies are eyes," in this awful, humorless, enigmatic follow-up to Graveyard Shift.

*The UNDERWATER CITY 1962 (1961) color. SP: Orville H. Hampton (aka O. Harris). Conception: Alex Gordon, Ruth Alexander. SpFX: (coord) Howard Lydecker; (uncred) Richard Albain. Scope FX: Howard Anderson. Mkp Sup: Ben Lane. Ref: TV. Warren/KWTS2! V 2/7/62. Lentz. Hardy/SF. Stanley. Maltin '92. Scheuer. With Paul Dubov, Edmund Cobb, Frank Lackteen.

Oceanographers explore the "world of inner space," in preparation for the "first permanent colony of mankind to be established on the ocean floor" — Amphibia City, self-contained, beehive-like cells, or units, designed to be "independent of the surface" of Earth .... Watchably terrible imitation-Ivan Tors sf-drama has hardly an un-phony moment. Featured: toys-under-the-sea effects, a comically gabby narrator, a script which confuses sharks

with manta rays, and the first "honeymoon on the bottom of the sea." (Compare Project Moonbase and the "first wedding on the moon.")

UNDERWORLD see Transmutations

UNDRESSED TO KILL VCX 1983 color 59m. D,P: Max Miller. SP: Wendy Kaufmann. Ph,Ed: William Kovacs. Ref: TV: Video Home Ent. vc box: cast here differs. With Eva Gaulant, Wayne Williams (Volta), Lilly Lamarr (Diane), Kelly Guthrie.

As professor von Kleinsmidt (Guthrie) reads an ancient parchment, "ancient horrors" awaken in a nearby swamp, once the site of a "sex-mad devil-worshiping cult." He accidentally raises Volta, "that obscene disciple of satan, to life again," and prostitute Diane Tracy, possessed by Volta, must then "obtain souls for the glory of the master, satan" — by stabbing her clients to death .... Tacky yoking of supernatural horror and porn.

UNDYING CURSE (Thai) c1989? color c90m. Ref: TV: vt; no Eng. Chao Thai Market: above is tr t.

Dreams re past violence haunt people in the present, where new violence parallels the old. In the most "memorable" sequence, a visualized nightmare, the two rivals for a man pull him one way, then the other, then pull off his arms. Vaseline on the camera lens obscures the nevertheless-obvious tackiness of the makeup effects here. Bottom-of-the-barrel, shot-on-tape romantic fantasy chiller has more songs than scares, plus some Halloween music.

UNDYING LOVE 1991 color. D: Greg Lamberson. Ref: Jones. With Lee Kayman.

Vampire Carmilla's life spans the French Revolution and modern-day New York City.

The UNEARTHING YAF & Purple Onion (Aswang Prods.) 1994 (1993) color 83m. (Aswang - orig t). SP, D, P: Wrye Martin, Barry Poltermann. Story: F.L. Anderson. Ph: Jim Zabilla. Mus: Ken Brahmstedt. Creature FX: Kevin & Clark Reter. SpFX: Tim Brown. SpProps: Bill Yunker. Shadow Puppets: Bill Johnson. Ref: TV: Prism video. With Norman Moses, Tina Ona Paukstelis, John Kishline, Flora Coker, Mildred Nierras, Victor Delorenzo.

"We Nulls take care of our own." Scores of strange "cocoons" litter Null Orchards. On one wall of the main Null house hangs a portrait of a "feeding" aswang—"a Filipino vampire who feeds on the unborn." A lethal living "coil" turns out to be the end of the humongously long tongue of one aswang.... Filipino-horror-lore-inspired monster movie comes up with probably the battiest scene of its year (1994 according to the end credits; 1993 according to the packaging): Mama Aswang hanging out a high window by the "rope" that is her tongue. Generally stilted production is rife with such fetchingly disgusting details. The Giant Leeches-inspired cocooning-alive sequence is another highlight. The credit-sequence "shadow puppets" are the classiest element.

The UNEARTHLING (Sp) Spectacular Trading Co. (Almena Films) 1984(1983) color 90m. (Los Nuevos Extraterrestres. aka Extra Terrestrial Visitors -ad t. Pod People - reissue t). SP,D: J. Piquer Simon. SP: also Jack Gray. Ph: Juan Merino. Mus: Libra Pastor. AD: Emilio Ruiz. SpFX: Basilio Cortijo. Mkp: Peder Camacho. SdFX: G. Rodriguez. Ref: TV: Cinema Shares Int'l.-

TV. TVG. V 5/9/84:398. 10/20/82(ad): sfa *Extra-Terrestrial Intelligence*? Peter Zirschky. Cine Para Leer '84. no Maltin '92. no Scheuer. Stanley. Ecran F 50:70. VSOM: *Return of E.T* - vt. With Oscar Martin, Ian Sera, Nina Ferrer, Concha Cuetos (aka Connie Cheston). Emil Linder, Frank Suzman, Frank Brana.

Little Tommy (Martin) finds an alien's egg in a cave and takes it home, where it hatches. The parent alien "looks like a cross between a pig and a bear"; cute, tiny "Trumpy" is vaguely Babar-ian, or ALF-ian, and makes cooing and humming noises to communicate. He eats and drinks with his trunk, continues to grow and grow, and is clearly fond of kittens, but leery of noisy toy robots, which unnerve him. Jigsaw puzzles at first puzzle him, until he discovers that he can telekinetically move the pieces into position. Trumpy, like E.T., is a real charmer. Unfortunately, he must share screen time with assorted non-charming, non-alien poachers, rangers, and pop singers. The far-from-ferocious-looking bigger alien makes grown women scream.

**UNENDLICHE GESCHICHTE, Die** see *Neverending Story, The*

**UNENDLICHE GESCHICHTE II** see *Neverending Story II*

**UNFORGETTABLE FANTASY** (H.K.) Always Good Film Co. 1987 color/ws? c95m. D: Franklin Chan. Ref: TV: Rainbow Video; Eng. titles.

Comic ghost story re a fairy fox ghost from a magic mirror who haunts a film studio. She makes a movie exorcist do "singing and dancing exorcism," starts a horde of fireballs flying on the set, then brings to life some Egyptian props, including a menacing giant statue. At the end, she makes the action reverse, in order to bring the hero back to life and take his place (temporarily) in death. Bonus: a movie, or commercial, in progress re "the superman," with John Williams music .... Lively, occasionally charming romantic comedy-fantasy, with spooky scenes and fun effects.

**The UNHOLY** Vestron & Limelite/Team Effort (The Unholy Film Partners/Mathew Hayden) 1988(1987) color 102m. D: Camilo Vila. SP: Philip Yordan, Fernando Fonseca. Mus: Roger Bellon. SpVisFxD: Bob Keen. SpFX: (seq) Movie Magic Emporium; (des) Michael Novotny; Apogee; (d) John Dykstra; (anim sup) Clint Culver. Prosth: Rick Lazzarini. AddlSpFX: Image Animation. MkpFX: Jerry Macaluso, Isabel Harkins. Ref: TV. MFB'89:125-6. ad. V 4/27/88. SFExam 4/26/88. Martin. Morse. Newman. With Ben Cross, Ned Beatty, William Russ, Jill Carroll, Hal Holbrook, Trevor Howard, Nicole Fortier (demon).

"She wants you!" Father Michael (Cross), it seems, is the chosen one — i.e., the one to fight Desiderius (sp?), "one of satan's strongest demons." This latter "irresistible temptation" appears regularly (in alternately demonic and female form), between Ash Wednesday and the Feast of the Resurrection, at the church of St. Agnes in New Orleans, where two priests have already had their throats ripped out. This major demon — who is attended by minor demons and who offers pure humans to satan — kills sinners in the act of sinning.

Pompous religio-horror unprofitably crosses *Rain* with *The Exorcist*. One of the few pluses: the entertainingly loathsome, all-fours, tongue-happy demon. In his last movie role, Howard plays Father Silva, a "great scholar of demonology."

**\*The UNHOLY NIGHT** 1929. Ref: TV. script. Lentz. V 10/16/29. Lee. no Hardy/HM. Maltin '92. Scheuer. Stanley.

"Then if the living fail us, we must call on the dead to help us!" Ingredients in this creaky early talkie include a "horrible monster" that murders at least six people ... shades of a British regiment that appear at a seance and sing "Auld Lang Syne" .... a huge face (at another seance) ... a wailing green ghost (a spinach disease turned him green) ... a cataleptic ... and the "greatest fog London has ever known."

Interminable Night is more like it. Most of the actors, including Ernest Torrence and Roland Young, are almost campily emphatic. Highlight, of sorts, is the belated appearance and distinctive overplaying of Boris Karloff, with an incredible accent, as lawyer Abdul Mohammed Bey. At the end, he returns for more *Raven*-like ham to cry over the body of the murderess, a hypnotist.

**\*The UNINVITED** 1944 (1943). Mkp: Wally Westmore. Ref: TV. Lee. V 1/5/44. Wolf/Horror. Fango 100:11, 60. Agee. Stanley.

"I can only remember the cold coming." Classic ghost tale set on the "haunted shores" of Cornwall is still surprisingly effective, marred only by the jokiness of the Ray Milland character and the dragon-lady melodramatics of the Cornelia Otis Skinner character. The full-service photography (Charles Lang) and musical score (Victor Young) feature many nuances of tone and mood. Note, especially, how the reflection of the sea in the house at one point seems to become the "crawling mist" wraith. And note the unusual musical underlining of the shot in which the dawn breeze stirs the curtains. Other highlights include the melancholic movement of "Stella by Starlight" as the candles dim ... the wilting of the flowers ... the ouija "I guard" ... and the sobbing which "comes from everywhere, and nowhere."

**UNINVITED** Amazing Movies/Heritage Ent. (Greydon Clark Prods./Douglas C. Witkins) 1988 (1987) color 89m. SP,D,P: G. Clark. Mus: Dan Slider. SpFxMkp: MkpFX Lab. SpVisualCat: Jim & Debi Boulden. SpFX: A&A. Ref: TV. V 7/27/88. McCarty II. With George Kennedy, Alex Cord, Clu Gulager, Toni Hudson, Eric Larson, Shari Shattuck, Austin Stoker.

"The cat! The cat!" The "darling little kitty" aboard the yacht is actually a beyond-rabid cat from a genetics lab. A vicious little monster inside the thing slashes its victims and passes on the curse of "mutating blood" .... Vapid suspenser is just another vehicle for makeup effects. In a bit of dumb cleverness, the script makes the cat and the monster of *Alien* one — hence the limp "darling little kitty" ironies.

**L'UNIQUE** (F) Les Prods. Belles Rives 1986 color/ws 81m. SP, D, P: Jerome Diamant-Berger. SP: also Olivier Assayas, Jean-Claude Carriere. Mus: Guy Boulanger. SpFxD: Christian Guillon. Graphic Concep: J.-F. Henri. Computer Anim: Christian Foucher. Mkp: Sophie Landry, Alain Moize. Laser Consul: Ivo Krstulovic. Ref: V 2/19/86: "sci-fi fable ... is unfocused in theme, shaky in development and anticlimactic in conclusion"; *The One and Only* - tr t. Ecran F 66:8. With Julia Migenes Johnson (The Singer), Tcheky Karyo, Sami Frey, Charles Denner.

Scientist creates hologram double of theatre star.

**UNIVERSAL SOLDIER** TriStar/Carolco (Mario Kassar/IndieProd/Centropolis) 1992 color 104m. D: Roland Emmerich. SP: R. Rothstein, C. Leitch, D. Devlin. Ph: K.W. Lindenlaub. Mus: C. Franke. PD: H. Gross. SpFxSup&Des: Kit West. SpMkpFX: L.R. Hamlin, M. Burnett. Ref: V 7/13/92: "terrible premise and script." SFChron 7/10/92: "some funny moments." ad. SFChron Dtbk 12/6/92. With Jean-Claude Van Damme (Luc), Dolph Lundgren (Scott), Ally Walker, Jerry Orbach, Leon Rippy, Robert Trebor.

Re-animated corpses as soldiers. *Revolt of the Zombies,* anyone?

**UNLOCKED WINDOW, An** see *Alfred Hitchcock Presents*

**UNMASKED: PART 25** (B) Academy Ent./Strange Cinema 1988 color 85m. (aka *Hand of Death: Part 25*). D,Exec P: Anders Palm. SP,P: Mark Cutforth. Ref: V 3/29/89:34(hv); "overdone ... yucky gore." 10/19/88:231(ad). With Gregory Cox, Fiona Evans, Edward Brayshaw.

Deformed, hockey-mask-wearing killer.

**UNMASKING THE IDOL** see *Order of the Black Eagle, The*

**The UNNAMABLE** K.P. Prods./Yankee Classic Pictures (Dean Ramser/Paul White) 1988 color 87m. SP, D, P: Jean-Paul Ouellette. From H.P. Lovecraft's story. Mus: David Bergeaud. SpMkpFX: R. Christopher Biggs; Art & Magic. Min Seq: Mainstreet Imagery. Ref: TV. V 6/15/88. With Charles King (Howard Damon), Mark Kinsey Stephenson (Randolph Carter), Alexandra Durrell, Katrin Alexandre (Alyda "The Creature" Winthrop).

The names are Lovecraft — Miskatonic University, the Necronomicon — but this is just another teens-in-jeopardy horror move. The Unmentionable is a banshee-type which haunts an old house. ("This place gives me the creeps!") Lots of shrieking, by both monster and non-monsters. Only redeeming feature: the thing's makeup job. Notable line: "Boards! Boards! Big Boards!" Highlight of the original tale is Lovecraft's description of a horror writer not unlike himself.

**The UNNAMABLE II** Yankee Classic & AM East & New Age Ent. & Prism/Unnamable Prods. (A. Durrell et al.) 1992 color 105m. (*The Unnamable Returns* - shooting t). SP, D, Co-P: J.-P. Ouellette, from H.P. Lovecraft's story "The Statement of Randolph Carter." Ph: Gardiner, Olkowski. Mus: David Bergeaud. PD: Tim Keating. MkpSpFX: R.C. Biggs. VisSpFX: Boom Bruno, Milo's EFX. Flying Seq: Levitation. AnimFX: Larry Arpin. OptFX: HOS;(sup) David L. Hewitt. SdDesFxEd: J.R. Whitcher. Ref: TV. SFChron Dtbk 3/7/93. 4/18/93. V 1/27/92:15. 2/17/92:20. 6/29/92:65 (rated). PT 16:61. Fango 123:34 "nothing new or interesting." With John Rhys-Davies, Mark Kinsey Stephenson, Peter Breck, Maria Ford, Julie Strain, David Warner, Charles Klausmeyer.

"They were one creature." An injection expels a "300-year-old creature" (Strain) with "superhuman strength" from the body of a young woman, Alyda Winthrop (Ford). "Symbiotic molecules," however—and Alyda's scent—keep the other-dimensional demon close to Alyda. At the end, the demon is banished, and Alyda ages and dies. ("I am she, and she is me.")

Lots of ideas, few of them at all compelling. (The symbiosis idea seems borrowed from *Watchers.*) And though the script is so full of Lovecraftian mumbo jumbo that it borders on parody, it wastes the few good ideas from the source story. (Listen for references to the Necronomicon, Miskatonic University, Dunwich, and Cthulhu.)

**UNNATURALS, The** see *Contronatura*

**UNREAL DREAM** (H.K.) 1987? color c92m. Ref: TV: Ocean Shores Video; Eng. titles.

Regulation-sensationalistic white-slavery melodrama turns horrific — and pretty disgusting — in the last few minutes, as a rabid woman wreaks gory revenge on the pimps. She slashes most of the latter to death and tears out the throat of the main creep, as amplified dog snarls take over the sound track.

**UNSATISFIED LOVE** see *Love after Death*

**UNTAMA GIRU** (J) Parco Film (Ito-Hariu) 1990 color 120m. SP,D: Go Takamine. Ph: M. Tamura. Mus: K. Ueno. PD: K. Hoshino. Ref: V 3/21/90: "painfully tedious and amateurish." with K. Kobayashi, J. Togawa, John Sayles, C. Aoyama. "Haunted Untama Forest ... werepig that transforms (off-camera) from pig to woman."

**UNTIL DEATH** see *Changeling 2*

**UNTIL THE END OF THE WORLD** (G-F-Austral.) WB/Road Movies & Argos & Village Roadshow & Phanos & CNdlC & CRL-R & Australian Film Finance (Jonathan Taplin & Anatole Dauman) 1991 color 178m. (157.-U.S.) (*Till the End of the World* - ad t). Idea,SP,D: Wim Wenders. SP: also Peter Carey. Idea: also Solveig Dommartin. Mus: Graeme Revell. PD, Futuristic Objects: Thierry Flamand. HDTV: Sean Naughton. SpVisFX: FuturFX; (sup) Frank Schlegel. Space Lab Des: Albrecht Conrad. Ref: TV. V 9/16/91. SFExam 1/24/92. SFChron 1/24/92; Dtbk 1/19/92. V 10/25/89:3,8. With William Hurt, S. Dommartin, Sam Neill, Max von Sydow, Ruediger Vogler, Jeanne Moreau, Allen Garfield, Lois Chiles, David Gulpilil.

"1999 was the year the Indian nuclear satellite went out of control." The nuclear explosion caused when said satellite is shot down stops engines, watches, etc. — "It's the end of the world!" Other wonders in this futuristic epic: a camera which takes pictures which "blind people can see" and which "records the biochemical event of seeing" ("The potential for this device is awesome!") ... an advanced computer "finder," the Bear ... and mini-TV-phones .... Wenders extravaganza plays at times like Lubitsch in slow motion, at others like random scenes of drama, action, science fiction, etc. Incidental treat: the presence of Chishu Ryu as Mr. Mori, a "man with a great passion for his herb garden."

**UNTOUCHABLY YOURS** (H.K.?) c1988? color c88m. Ref: TV: World Video; Eng. titles.

"I must scare you to death." A young woman, Carol, who believes that she was run down by a Rolls Royce, enters the "under-ground world," and returns to Earth as a ghost seeking those who killed her. ("You shouldn't touch me — I'm a ghost.") She can be seen only by the hero or (in a special mirror) by exorcists. In a pleasantly nonsensical sequence, she scares an exorcist, and all involved run around in circles. Priest: "Have you seen 'Ghost Buster'?" .... Occasionally cute trifle. At one point, the ghost stands on water. Later, she registers for reincarnation and is reborn as a baby, while the hero promises to wait till she is seventeen to marry her.

**UOMO PUMA, L'** see *Pumaman, The*

**UP ALL NIGHT** Coast to Coast 1986 color 87m. D: Richard Mailer. Ref: Adam. With Stacey Donovan, Joanna Storm, Tom Byron.

"Invisible alien life form" trains "sex ray" on earthlings.

**UP FROM THE APE** see *Animal within, The*

**UPIR VE VEZAKU** see *Vampire in the High Rise*

**UPROAR IN HEAVEN** (Chinese) 1977 ('85-U.S.) puppet and paper anim 110m. SP,D: Wan Laiming. From the classic novel "Pilgrimage to the West." Ref: SFExam 7/16/85: "an original look." Hound.

Monkey king battles giant flying snakes, etc.

**URAGANO SULLE BERMUDE** (I-Sp) 1979 color feature (aka *Incontri con gli Umanoidi*). D: Tonino Ricci. Ref: Palmerini: aliens?

**URBAN WARRIORS** (I) L'Immagine 1987 color c90m. D: Giuseppe Vari aka Joseph Warren. SP: Piero Regnoli. Ph: S. Rubini. Mus: Paolo Rustichelli. Ref: vc box: future barbarians. Martin. Hound. Palmerini. no Scheuer. With Karl Landgren, Alex Vitale, Bjorn Hammer, Maurice Poli.

**UREME** (S. Korean) 1988 feature. Ref: HOF 2:25,35: "animated robots"; first of at least 8 films. With Shim Hyung Rei.

**UROTSUKI DOJI 2** (J) JAVN/WCC 1989 anim color 54m. Ref: TV: Penthouse Video; no Eng.

In this sequel to *Wandering Kid* (which see), a mysterious stranger gorily interrupts the proceedings at Club Lez, then tosses a student a magic penis which, later, comes in handy, then self-incinerates at the most inopportune moment. At the end, monsters overrun the city .... Some inventive gory details here, and some semi-erotic moments in this hardcore-fantasy bizarreness, plus a brief visit to some land beyond beyond.

**UROTSUKI DOJI — MATAIDEN** (J) Shochiku HV/W.C.C. c1990? anim color 105m. Ref: TV: Penthouse Video; some Eng., some German.

More wanderings in time of the *Wandering Kid* (which see), from 1944 to 1948 to 199X. Ingredients this time out include a demon with several phalluses and also much groping equipment ... the demon's apparent master ... an electronic Nazi sex machine which produces a powerful force ... little flying gremlin-like creatures ... demon rape on the ferris wheel ... and supernatural-snake sex. (Nice touch here: the snake casts the demon's shadow.) Intermittently-grotesquely-imaginative tale of a horny demon. The master's cackling gets a bit tiresome, as do finally even the unearthly couplings.

See also *Legend of the Demon Womb*.

**UROTSUKIDOJI** see *Wandering Kid*

**UROTSUKIDOJI: THE FUTURE, PART 3** (J) CPM/Columbia Video/Jupiter Films (Toshio Maeda & West Cape/Yasuhito Yamaki) 1993 ('94-U.S.) anim color 50m. D: Hideki Takayama. From the comic book by T. Maeda. Ph: Y. Yasuhara. Mus: M. Amano. Monster Des: Sumito Ioi. AD: K. Harada. FxSup: T. Honda, Y. Tsuruoka. Ref: TV: Anime 18 video; Eng. dubbed; sfa *Urotsukidoji III: Return of the Overfiend, Episode 3* - U.S.? Japan Video.

"The Collapse of Caesar's Palace." Critters this time include Harpy-like monsters, horny skeletal horrors, a gigantic winged monster, and a Ghidrah-like "personification of hatred".... It's getting a bit tiresome. Determinedly "adult."

See also *Legend of the Demon Womb*.

**URUFUGAI — MOERO OOKAMI OTOKO** (J) Toei 1974 feature. D: K. Yamaguchi. Ref: Monster! 1/92 (Higuchi): *Wolf Guy — Enrage, Werewolf!* - tr t? With Sonny Chiba.

**URUSEI YATSURA 1: ONLY YOU** (J) Kitty Films (Hidenori Taga) 1983('92-U.S.) anim color 90m.(102m.) (*Only You*). Storyboards, Dramatization, D: Mamoru Oshii. SP: Kaneharu Tomoko, based on the comic book characters created by Rumiko Takahashi. Ph: Fumio, or Akio, Wakana. Mus: I. Kobayashi, H. Anzai, M. Amano. AD: S. Kobayashi (cr list T. Arai). SpFX: Jooji Saitoo. Char Des: Kazuo Yamazaki (end cr list Takada & Takazawa). Anim D: K. Yamazaki, Y. Moriyama. Mecha D: M. Yamashita. Ref: TV: Pony Video; no Eng. AnimEigo video; Eng. titles. J Anim Program Guide: *Those Annoying Aliens* - tr t. Paul Lane. Voices: Toshio Furukawa (Ataru), Fumi Hirano (Lum), S. Shimazu, Kazuko Sugiyama (Jariten), Ryoko, or Yoshiko, Sakakibara (Elle).

Alien women Elle (from the planet of the same name) and Lum (of the planet Urusei) vie for the love of human high-school student Ataru. ("To think that someone could compete with Lum's bad taste in men.") Elle's spaceship, when seen from above, is very like a rose, and visiting aliens enter her planet through a giant "flower" door. But beneath the beauty—. Ataru's prospective bride keeps her previous 99,999 lovers in tubes in a giant refrigerator ("To keep love always fresh and prevent spoilage"), and her huge mechanical love chamber is more forbidding than enticing. A trip through time in a walrus-driven taxi saves Ataru from Elle, as they return to an important childhood scene....

Emotions are expressed vividly in this sometimes phenomenally funny film. Love here takes the form of, variously, a strategic mallet to the head of the confused beloved, and a magically shattered stained-glass window which separates two lovers. Love is also, of course, the electric shocks with which Lum periodically galvanizes the indecisive Ataru, and the loop-the-loops of the levitating Lum. Meanwhile, the incurably horny Ataru: "Debauchery! I have been dreaming about debauchery!" Some of the most amusing expressions of strong emotion belong to Lum's little hovering "bumblebee" of a cousin Jariten, who, like the other principals, is highly temperamental—when he's mad he breathes fire at the object of his emotion. In this movie, the statement "That is karma" is answered by a steam iron flung at the head of the speaker.

At one point, Lum expresses her apparently-doomed-love for Ataru lyrically, in a sad song, and we see her visualized dream of space and floating and a phantom Ataru. But most of the movie's more poetic, and finally ironic, imagery—e.g., the soft landing of a petal on a pond disturbing a reflection of Ataru and Elle—is reserved for the beautiful, imperious Elle. In *Only You*, beauty is the beast; or, as Elle notes of her elaborate "refrigerator of love": "It was just flirting, a little like a hobby, something anyone might do."

**URUSEI YATSURA 2: BEAUTIFUL DREAMER** (J) Central Park Media/Toho & Kitty Films (Hidenori Taga) 1984('92-U.S.) anim color 97m. (*Beautiful Dreamer*). SP, D: Mamoru Oshii. See also *Urusei Yatsura 1*. Ph: F. Wakana. Mus: Katsu Hoshi. AD: S. Kobayashi. SpFX: Takeshi Saitoo. SdFX: Yasufumi Yoda. Ref: TV: Pony Video?; no Eng., or U.S. Manga Corps video (AnimEigo); Eng. titles. J Anim Program Guide: *Those Annoying Aliens* - tr t. Paul Lane. Cinef 7/96:123. Voices: Takuya Fujioka (Evil Dream Demon), Shigeru Chiba, Machiko Washio, Akira Kamiya.

"Things sure are strange tonight." Bizarre events attend the preparation for Tomobiki High School's annual festival. A teacher returns home to find his apartment covered by slime. All over town, telephones ring unanswered. A "strange guy" gives Jariten a strange (but cute) piglet. Ataru yawns and quietly sinks into a puddle, and later turns up in a swimming pool. A clock with no hands chimes. An overpass is missing. A broken sword grows back, "like a lizard's tail." The three-story school building grows a fourth story. Townsfolk vanish. And the town itself is found to be drifting in space on the back of a giant turtle. Behind these mysteries: Mujaki, the Dream Demon, who asks "Can't I have a dream of my own just this once?"

The piglet—the legendary bad-dream-eater Baku—temporarily thwarts Mujaki, but the latter traps Ataru in a succession of dreams, including one which casts him as Franken-Ataru, "man-made golem," and recreates the monster-and-the-little-girl scene from the 1931 *Frankenstein* ... one which flashes back to the first episode of the TV series starring Lum ... and one which puts him into "cold-sleep" on a futuristic spacecraft. All this and a cartoon-Godzilla movie showing at a theatre. (Note: Mujaki and Baku originate in an episode of the TV series, where they appear in somewhat different form.)

There are some amazing, visually imaginative passages in *Beautiful Dreamer*, and a "Twilight Zone"-like, what-the-hell-is-going-on? feel pervades this most philosophically ambitious entry in the Lum saga. One suspects that Mujaki is at times a pretext, an excuse for director and animators to let their imaginations run wild, but he's an inspired pretext—witty, provocative, intellectually nimble. Sample haunting sequence: A girl finds herself in an alley way where the sight and sound of wind chimes proliferate. Sample, script's wry undercutting of its own cosmic musings: Civilization seems to have come to a halt, except for Ataru's house, which still rates electricity, gas, and water—"and, most surprising of all, the newspaper is still delivered." ("Have there been any bills?")

**URUSEI YATSURA 3: REMEMBER MY LOVE** (J) Ani-mEigo/Kitty Films (Hidenori Taga) 1985('92-U.S.) anim color 94m. (aka *Remember My Love*). D: Kazuo Yamazaki. SP: To-moko Kaneharu, or Komparu. Story: Rumiko Takahashi. Ph: A. Wakana. Mus: M. Yoshino. AD: Kobayashi, Arai. Chief Anim D: Y. Moriyama. SpFX: Takeshi Saitoo. FX: Y. Yoda. Ref: TV: Pony/5-Ace Video; no Eng. AnimEigo video; Eng. titles. Paul Lane. J Anim Program Guide. Voices: Sumi Shimamoto (Rara), Mitsuo Iwata (Ru), Masako Sugaya (Oshima the raccoon).

"Time is messed up. Space is messed up too." In 1967, the space witch Obaba curses Lum to an eternity of unrequited love, seals the curse in a crystal ball, then forwards the latter to the Galaxy Jacks-of-All-Trades Cursing Accepting Assn., or Curses-R-Us. The crystal, however, is misdirected, by the Galaxy Mail Service, to the alien boy Ru, who uses it, in 1985, to lead Lum into a world beyond the Mirror House in an amusement park, Marchenland. At the end, Ataru—whom the jealous Ru had turned temporarily into a pink hippo—enters the mirror world and rescues Lum.

As in the other "Lum" movies, humor, poetry, spectacle, and sentiment collide, in what amounts to an intermittently hilarious variation on "Beauty and the Beast." Ataru's hippopotamic predicament is at once hilarious, touching, and Kafkaesque. (Look also for signs of Lewis Carroll.) With pathetic determination, he continues to wear pajamas to bed. When Lum attempts to comfort him, he puts his paw over her hand and does his best to accept her consolation. Among the absurd glories of the movie: A character who has a vision of the ghost of his first pet octopus ... an adorably pathetic raccoon ... and (in Ru's mirror world) a sailing ship which hangs in the air, and glass "trees" the branches of which periodically shatter.

Most surprising emotional element: a touching melancholy, as all concerned miss the abducted Lum, and even chronically carefree Ataru suddenly slumps with the full realization of her absence. The intermittent pop music has little or nothing to do with the spirit of the thing. Overall, *Remember My Love* isn't quite up to the first two movie Lums, but has its own comic and fantastic enchantments.

**URUSEI YATSURA 4: LUM THE FOREVER** (J) 1986? anim color 94m. (aka *Lum the Forever*). SP, D: Kazuo Yamazaki. Story: Rumiko Takahashi. Mus: Fumi Itakura. Ref: TV: Pony Video; no Eng. Paul Lane. J Anim Program Guide.

Lum, who is playing the legendary Devil Princess in a movie written by Mendo, seems to be identified with her in real life, too. When the cherry tree said to contain the Princess's spirit is cut down, Lum begins to lose her electrical and flying talents. Like everyone else, she now has to use elevators and escalators. Her image disappears from album photos, and she walks into the town lake to "hibernate." Freezing cold and war ensue in the world above. Mendo hypothesizes that the town of Tomobiki is a "body," that its people are its "cells," and that it is rejecting the alien "cell," Lum. Ataru's feeling for Lum, however, succeeds in breaking up emotional and actual ice and bringing her up from the lake.

The most melancholic of the Lum movies, *Lum the Forever* appears to be a reworking, more or less, of the second in the series, *Beautiful Dreamer*, with different bizarre, inexplicable events and a different legend, but the same, pervading sense of dreamlike helplessness. The eerie inexplicability also recalls episodes of the original "Twilight Zone" series, in particular "And When the Sky Was Opened," in which three astronauts vanish. If *Lum the Forever,* like the first three films, represents a refreshing escape from the conventional, by now, however, mere unconventionality seems to be becoming an end in itself, the narrative surprises less surprising and more expected.

**URUSEI YATSURA 5: RYOKO'S SEPTEMBER TEA PARTY** (J) Pony/5-Ace 1989 anim color 49m. Ref: TV: Pony Video; no Eng. Paul Lane.

Impossible-to-sort-out cartoon is apparently a compilation of scenes from the TV series, plus dinner-party framing scenes. Elements include a gigantic Christmas tree sent into space, a little hovering robot mouse, and (in a funny sequence) a voodoo-dolls-amok schoolroom sequence.

**URUSEI YATSURA '87** (J) AnimEigo/Pony 1987('93-U.S.) anim color 58m. (*Urusei Yatsura: Inaba the Dreammaker* - U.S.). Ref: TV: Pony Video; OAV-1; no Eng. vc box.

Lum and company enter a strange door opening onto a universe of doors ... and a planet inhabited by threatening-faced, faintly diabolical rabbit creatures. The latter, who seem to be in charge of scrubbing down these doors, huddle periodically to plan strategies and, at one point, make preparations for people stew. They house some of their captives in a literal bird-cage—i.e., a bird that is a cage, or vice versa. They do not, however, reckon with Lum's electrical powers. She regularly zaps Ataru and the rabbits, too. Costumes required for venturing into this realm: a plain rabbit suit for Ataru, a Playboy-type bunny suit for Lum.... More drolly disorienting science-fantasy, doubly disorienting for those who do not speak Japanese. (Fortunately, an English-language version is now available.) Some of the music is lifted from *Beautiful Dreamer.*

**URUSEI YATSURA: RAGING SHERBET** and **I HOWL AT THE MOON** (J) AnimEigo/Kitty Films & Pony/5-Ace (Taga/Matsushita) 1988 & 1989 ('93-U.S.) anim color 53m. D: Setsuko Shibunnoichi. SP:(2) Machiko Kondoo. Ph: N. Koyama. Mus: S. Kazado et al. AD: K. Koitabashi. SpFX:(1) Yoshitaka Kumai;(2) Yasuhiko Komori. FX: Y. Yoda. Anim D:(1) K. Nishiima;(2) Y. Kobayashi. Ref: TV: AnimEigo video; OAV-2; Eng. titles.

"Raging Sherbet." (25m.) At large on Earth, flying critters with detachable, re-grow-able sherbet-cone noses (from a sherbet ranch on Neptune) rain semi-dangerous cones. Offbeat but minor entry.

"I Howl at the Moon." (26m.) Inept-cook Lum feeds Tsukimi-dango to Ataru and his teacher, and they turn into "wolfmen." (Ataru: "I'm not a raccoon. I'm a wolfman!") Unrewarding variation on *Remember My Love* and *Teen Wolf.*

**URUSEI YATSURA: CATCH THE HEART** and **GOAT AND CHEESE** (J) AnimEigo/Kitty Films & (1) Watanabe & (2) Madhouse (Hidenori Taga/Yooko Matsushita) 1989('93-U.S.) anim color 53m. D (1): Shigeru Morikawa;(anim) Kenji Yoshioka. SP, D (2): Yutaka Okamura. SP: Tatsuhiko Urahata. Ph:(1) Yoshiyuki Tamagawa;(2) K. Ishikawa. AD:(1) K. Takatoo;(2) K.

Aoki. FX: Yasufumi Yoda. SpFX(2): Hooji Tanifuji. Ref: TV: AnimEigo video; OAV-3; Eng. titles.

"Catch the Heart." (26m.) "Heart-stealers" are candy that "steals the heart"—and hangs same right over the head of the one who eats the candy. When a fellow student grabs the valentine heart over Lum's head, she's mad for him and immediately writes him a love letter, knits him a sweater, etc. Meanwhile, Lum wants Ataru to grab the heart, Ataru connives to turn the high school into his personal harem, and Mendo's elaborate machinations to win Lum backfire, hilariously.... Wild even for *Urusei Yatsura* material, "Catch the Heart" is dangerously hyper-manic, riotously inventive. Lum's funniest cry: "Maximal expression of love!"

"Goat and Cheese." (26m.) An "unimaginably horrible event will occur if one takes a photograph in front of the statue" of the goat. Seems Mendo's great-grandfather mistreated a goat, and now a goat ghost haunts the estate. Amusing "Northanger Abbey"-like mock-horrifics here, as comedy punctuates big suspense build-ups. At one point, an exorcism ray-gun turns the goat into a giant.

**URUSEI YATSURA: DATE WITH A SPIRIT** and **TERROR OF GIRLY MEASLES** (J) AnimEigo/Kitty Films (Taga/Matsushita) & Madhouse (Maruyama) & Watanabe 1991('93-U.S.) anim color. D:(1) Makoto Moriwaki;(2) Shigeto Makino. SP:(1) T. Urahata;(2) H. Fujiwara. Ph:(1) Ishikawa;(2) Fukuda. AD:(1) K. Arai;(2) K. Takatoo. SpFX:(1) H. Tanifuji;(2) T. Sakakibara. FX: Yoda. Ref: TV: AnimEigo video; Eng. titles; OAV-4.

"Date with a Spirit." A cute, fifteen-year-old ghost named Maiko (voice: Yuuko Kobayashi) becomes attached to Tsubame. Some very funny bits in the first half. (28m.)

"Terror of Girly Measles." ("Terror of Girly-Eyes Measles" - vc box t.) Ten contracts "Girly Eyes," passes the disease on to other males, including Mendou's pet octopus. Frantic, sometimes very funny, sometimes confusing. Ten's most serious threat to Ataru: "You won't die a respectable death!" (25m.)

**URUSEI YATSURA: NAGISA'S FIANCE** and **The ELECTRIC HOUSEHOLD GUARD** (J) AnimEigo/Kitty Films (Taga/Matsushita) & Pony/5-Ace 1988 & 1989 ('93-U.S.) anim color. D (both) & Anim D (1): Setsuko Shibunnoichi. Ph:(1) Takahashi;(2) Koyama. Mus: M. Yoshino et al. AD: Koitabashi. SpFX:(1) Y. Kumai;(2) Y. Komori. FX: Yoda. Ref: TV: AnimEigo video; Eng. titles; OAV-5. Animerica 5:18.

"Nagisa's Fiance." A "Frankenstein monster" here turns out to be a ghost in a mask. Meanwhile, Ryuu becomes engaged to another ghost, Nagisa (voice: Mitsumi Yayoi). Bizarrely, Ryuu proves to be a woman; even more bizarrely, Nagisa is a boy.... Kooky story with funny twists. (27m.)

"The Electric Household Guard." The Mendou heir's guardian is an electric ninja, Shingo (voice: Tooru Furuya). Premise yields a few funny moments. It takes a grenade to get a laugh here. (26m.)

**URUSEI YATSURA—ALWAYS, MY DARLING** (J) Pony Canyon/5-Ace 1991 anim color 77m. Ref: TV: vt; no Eng.

Ingredients this time include an alien princess (the lovesick Ataru has to be leashed when around her), her four turbaned midget envoys, all sorts of aliens in a city-in-space, an Egyptian-style pyramid, and a flying bicycle.

Typically larky Lum mayhem leaves the pyramid and a space station in ruins. The princess wields a bazooka rather than electricity, but the effect on Ataru (i.e., near-atomization) remains the same. Handily, the bazooka can be used as same or as a mallet. Two-thirds of this movie seems to be devoted to familiar Lum/Ataru/third-party (here, the princess) fear and loving. The esthetic effect is one of wheels spinning, but very entertainingly.

**URUSEI YATSURA—CONCLUSION** (J) 1988 anim color 85m. Ref: TV: 5-Ace video; no Eng.; from TV series episodes?

A mysterious stranger de-horns and abducts Lum, giant mushrooms overrun Tomobiki, and thousands of space pigs ease into orbit above the town. (They manage to chew up at least one of the mushrooms....) The story this time seems little more than a half dozen running, very funny visual gags. Lum is in fine, electric form, and there's much play with big, obedience-inducing mallets. In terms of capacity for taking physical punishment, Ataru is the Wile E. Coyote of Tomobiki.

**URUTORA Q ZA MUUBI** see *Ultra Q: The Movie*

**URUTORAMAN SUTORI** (J) Shochiku & Fuji (Tsuburaya Prods) 1984 (Urutoraman Monogatari - orig t). D: Koichi Takano. SP: Yasushi Hirano. Ph: T. Yamamoto. Mus: Fuyuki, Kikuchi. AD: Yamaguchi, Kantake. Ref: Markalite 3:80-83: "highly entertaining adventure"; *The Ultraman Story* - tr t.

Young Taro — training to be an Ultrabrother — watches "library footage of Ultraman, Ultra Seven," etc., and he and his Ultrabrothers confront the alien Hiporito, evil space emperor Judah, the king of Hell, and the mecha Grandking. (Judah turns up again in "the *Andro-Melos* vidseries.")

**USURPERS OF EMPEROR'S POWER** (H.K.) Shaw (Wong Ka Hee, Mona Fong) c1985? color/ws 89m. D: Hua Shan. Ref: TV: World Video; Eng. titles.

Routine martial-arts intrigue has scattered horrific and fantastic elements, including cackling, vanishing ghost-types in a forest ... a "master" from a pond who has supernatural powers ... a death-semblance serum ... a bit of ax gore ... and a hero who climbs walls. Atmospheric: the use of the flute in one scene.

**UTSO NO MIKO** (J) Kadokawa Video 1989 (1988) anim color/ws 83m. SP: Keisuke Fujikawa, from the book. Char Des: Mutsumi Inomata. Ref: TV: Toho Video; no Eng. Animag 4:7. 5:5. 6:4: *Prince of Space* - tr t?

Eighth-century Japan. Principals: Miko, first seen as a horned baby tumbling through space—Miko has leaping, levitating, and whirlwind-creating powers ... a wizard who can split mountains, multiply himself, and appear and disappear ... a flying banshee-type ... and a living mist which eerily haunts a deserted village, in the movie's grand showpiece effects sequence—the mist turns first into phantom flying dragon-demons, then into one long, gigantic, corporeal dragon, then (at the sound of a magic flute) into a little imp. Visually beguiling animated fantasy makes atmospheric use of sound effects (the music-out-of-nowhere of the flute, bird cries, cricket chirps), the elements (rain, wind, mist, bonfires), and settings (in particular, the bare, gnarled trees of the countryside). Fine, full-bodied musical score; bland character design.

**UTSUNOMIKO** (J) Bandai/Kadokawa 1990-91 anim color 30m. each. Ref: Animag 11:4. V. Max 2:5: "13 parts planned"; "Heaven Chapter 11." Japan Video.

# V

**VACACIONES DEL TERROR** (Mex) Grupo Galindo/Casablanca Prods. 1988 color c85m. (*La Muneca Del Infierno* - orig t). SP, D: Rene Cardona III. SP: also Santiago Galindo. Adap: Carlos Valdemar. Ph: Luis Medina. Mus: Eugenio Castillo. SpFX: Jorge Farfan. OptFX: Manolo Saenz. Ref: TV: Mex-American HV; no Eng.; *Vacation of Terror* - tr t. V(Cannes'89):476. TVG. Cinef 6/96:46. With Julio Aleman, Pedro Fernandez, Gabriela Hassel, Nuria Bages, Carlos East, Carlos East, Jr., Gianella Hassel Kus (Gaby), Andaluz Russell (witch).

The curse of a witch burned long ago impacts upon a modern-day family's vacation. The witch's doll now uses little Gaby as a sort of go-between, in order to start mechanical toys and real trucks and to perform feats of levitation and telekinesis. Finally, the doll burns, and the hero leaps out of his mirror-prison.

Competent but unimaginative horror-fantasy. The witch's curse is a pretext for a long series of generally familiar effects stunts. Top scene: The jealous doll tears apart (or has Gaby tear apart) all her other dolls. Runner-up: One boy's play with a toy car "commands," voodoo-doll like, his father's car, and father nearly has a nasty accident.

**VACACIONES SANGRIENTAS** (Mex) Prods. Viejo 1991 color 86m. SP, D: Jorge Manrique. Ph: J. Luis Vera. Mus: Edgar Sosa. SpFX: Toshiro & Yoshiharo. Mkp: K. Acosta. SdFX: G. Gavira. Ref: TV: Million Dollar Video; no Eng. With Gilberto Trujillo, Eleazar Garcia Jr., Raul Trujillo (Javier), Stephanie Salas, Raul de Anda.

Teens ... a red-herring handyman-type obsessed with comb and thumb ... a ouija-board session ... an unseen presence who scares one girl into falling from a balcony ... a butcher-knife murder (very poorly staged) ... a plastic-bag murder ... and a chainsaw murder. Vacuous shot-on-tape horror.

**VALENTINA** (Fili) LEA Prods./E.S. Blas 1989? color c112m. D: Santiago Garcia. SP: Zoila, from the comics. Ph: Charlie Peralta. Mus D: Boy Alcaide. PD: Dante Mendoza. Prosth: Cecille Baun. Ref: TV: vt; no Eng. With Rey Abellana, Melissa Perez Rubio (Valentina), Luis Gonzales, M. Zobel, Odette Khan.

A witch-cursed woman gives birth to a baby with tiny snakes growing out of the top of her head, in this happily absurd problem drama/fantasy. Turbans help allay the parents' social embarrassment as the girl, Valentina, grows. (Compare the more common social dilemma of dandruff.) The girl plays with snakes, talks to them, even takes walks with them. (She walks; they slither.) She can literally freeze her enemies with rays from her eyes, and when snakes turn the tables on the evil witch and kill her, the frozen ones thaw; Valentina (who had been shot) revives, and hair replaces the snakes on her head — the latter three eventualities all necessary ingredients for a Happy Ending.

See also *Darna. Darna! Ang Pagbabalik.*

**VALERIE** 1991 color. D: Jay Lind. Ref: Jones. With Austin Pendleton, Maria Pechukas, Debbie Rochon.

Sick woman slowly turns into vampire.

**VALHALLA** (Danish) Swan Film & Interpresse, Metronome, Palle Fogtdal, & the Danish Film Institute 1986 anim color 88m. SP,D,AD,Co-Des: Peter Madsen. SP: also Henning Kure. Based on Nordic myths and Soren Hakonsson's "Valhalla" comic strip. Co-D: J.J. Varab. Mus: Ron Goodwin. Ref: V 5/21/86: "technically a highly accomplished work"; Eng. soundtrack. Voices: Stephen Thorne, Allan Corduner (Loke), Michael Elphick.

"Loke, an evil demi-god ... Ungaard, the land of wicked sorcery and unholy Giants."

**\*VALLEY OF THE DRAGONS** Byron Roberts 1961. Mkp: Ben Lane. Ref: TV. Warren/KWTS! Lee. Lentz. no Hardy. Stanley. V 11/22/61. Scheuer. Maltin '92.

"Where's the moon?" In 1881 Algeria, a comet which — 100,000 or so years ago — picked up a bit of the Earth now carries off an Irishman (Sean McClory), a Frenchman (Cesare Danova), and apparently an "envelope of the Earth's atmosphere." The two men find this "nightmare world" inhabited by Neanderthals, some sort of giant shrew, mastodons, an armadillo or two, more modern cave people, a buffalo-type, and Morlock-like cave dwellers with weird eyes.

Vapidity reigns, as the two accidental space explorers find love and lizards. Only story-interest: speculation re the precise phenomenon responsible for the two-worlds-in-one premise. Only other interest: identifying the stock footage and props. Is that "plateosaur" a lizard from *One Million B.C.*? Is the big spider with the phony "leap" from *World without End*? Is that "winged lizard" Rodan?

**\*VALLEY OF THE EAGLES** Modern Sound Pictures 1951 ('52-U.S.) (83m.-U.S.). Story: N.A. Bronsten, Paul Tabori. Addl Mountain Ph: Gunnar Melle. SpFX: Bill Warrington, Guido Baldi. Mkp: George Blackler. Ref: TV. Warren/KWTS! Scheuer. V 10/10/51. Pohle-Hart/Lee. Lee. With Ewen Solon.

"It's fantastic, isn't it?" In a demonstration of the possibilities of converting sound into electric power, noise on a record made of barium heats an iron bar. This sci-fi gimmick figures in the functional, stuffy-scientist-humanized story only as a prop. Script gets seriouser and seriouser, and duller and duller, and is mostly bland talk, with an occasional wry bit of dialogue. One unusual thrill: In the Lost Valley, trained eagles are unleashed on wolves.

**VALTEUS** (J) Cosmos Plan? 198-? anim color 29m. (aka *Friends*?). Ref: TV: vt; no Eng.

Ingredients in this near-hardcore cartoon include a huge, helpful robot with headlight-like eyes, a submarine/sailing-ship-like flying machine, and an ultra-forbidding castle. Well designed combination of Jules Verne and Russ Meyer is a little of this and a little of that which doesn't add up to much.

**VAMP** New World & Balcor Film (Donald P. Borchers/Susan Gelb) 1986 color 94m. Story, SP, D: Richard Wenk. Story: also D.P.

Borchers. Mus: Jonathan Elias. SpMkpFX: Greg Cannom. SpVisFX: Apogee;(anim sup) Clint Colver. SpFX: Image Engineering. SdFX: Mag City Sound. Ref: TV. MFB'87:27-8. V 7/18/86. Scheuer. Maltin '92. With Chris Makepeace, Sandy Baron, Robert Rusler, Dedee Pfeiffer, Gedde Watanabe, Grace Jones (Katrina), Hy Pike.

At the After Dark Club, the vampires look better or worse depending on how hungry they are, they select only the unattached and lonely as victims, and their fangs are retractable. In an odd twist, the hero's buddy, A.J. (Rusler), vampirized at the beginning, turns up at the end as an okay vampire who is still friends with Keith (Makepeace).

This male-fantasy-turned-nightmare is part of the recent fad of horror-comedies that try to be gross as well as funny. Slick and glib on the surface, it's a badly miscalculated mixture of comedy, drama, and gore. Vampire Jones' stage number is striking, offbeat, and all, but still no "Hot Voodoo." Watanabe is amusing as a wild and crazy student.

**VAMPIRA** (Fili) Regal Films (Monteverde & Monteverde-Teo) 1994 color 115m. D: Joey Romero. SP: W. Ching. Story: Don Escudero. Ph: C. Peralta. Mus D: Jamie Fabregas. PD: Benjie De Guzman. VisFX: Cinemagic. SpFX: Rene Abedeza. Prosth: Beny Batoctoy et al. Animatronics: Noly Nobeno. SdFX: Rodel Capule. Ref: TV: Regal video; no Eng. With Christopher De Leon, Maricel Soriano, Jayvee Gayoso, Nida Blanca, Joanne Quintas, Boy 2 Quizon.

With the full moon, vampire fangs and fingernails elongate, and someone or something superstrong is slaughtering rapists and muggers. Yuck 1: the chained-to-the-bed vampire boy given a sacrificial chicken. Yuck 2 (embarrassment or tragedy?): the bride trying to conceal her fangs on the wedding night. Neat 1: the track back revealing the vampire on the ceiling above the embracing couple. Neat 2: the ringing tower church bell silenced by a vampire hand. Neat 3: (in a visualized nightmare) the baby in papa's arms going vampire and zapping papa's neck. Neat 4: the boy vampire spoiling playtime by attacking another boy.... Or, Social Problems Peculiar to Vampires. Alternately inventive and cliched. Long but well-done.

**VAMPIRASS** VCA 1993 color 84m. Ref: vc box: vampire. With Madison, Gail Force.

**\*The VAMPIRE** 1957. AD: James Vance. Mkp: Don Roberson. Ref: TV. Warren/KWTS! Lee. Lentz. Hardy/HM. Scheuer. Maltin '92. Jones. With Lydia Reed, Herb Vigran, Ann Staunton, James Griffith, Raymond Greenleaf, Mauritz Hugo.

"Why didn't the bats die?" A scientist trying chemically to "divert" the human mind to the "primitive state" and then reverse and "advance" the intellect concocts a "control serum" from vampire bats. In pill form, the habit-forming serum temporarily drains the blood from the brain and periodically turns Dr. Paul Beecher (John Beal) into a "horrible thing"—a neck-biting vampire whose saliva introduces a virus into the blood of his victims, whose bodies then undergo "capillary disintegration," or "total cellular destruction."

The scientific documentation is appreciated, but this ploddingly earnest horror film does few things right. It does delay a good look at Beal's ugly-makeup, and his agonies-of-the-unbeautiful-and-damned performance is perfectly in keeping with the tone of the movie, for better or worse. Beecher has a Wolf Man-like inclination towards suicide, and the film features a few werewolf-like transformations for his hand and, later, his face.

**VAMPIRE AT DEATH BEACH** see *Vampire on Bikini Beach*

**VAMPIRE AT MIDNIGHT**  Skouras (Vampire Ltd. Partners) 1988 (1987) color 95m. D: Gregory McClatchy. SP: Dulany Ross Clements. Story,P: Jason Williams, Tom Friedman. Mus: Robert Etoll. SpFxMkp: Mecki Heussen. Ref: TV: Key Video. V 10/26/88. Jones. With J. Williams, Gustav Vintas (Victor Radkoff), Lesley Milne (Jenny), Jeanie Moore, Esther Alise, Robert Random, Ted Hamaguchi, Jonny Solomon, Barbara Hammond, Shendt (Raoul, vampire's assistant).

Los Angeles. "Looks like vampire killing number nine." Psycho-analyst/hypno-therapist/lecturer Dr. Victor Radkoff's program: "Energy, power, focus." For him, it works. With (or without) the aid of amulets, he has power over the minds of others, and can induce violent, romantic fantasies in his subjects. He offers Jenny Carlon, who suffers from pianist's block, "unlimited life and power." In the ill-advised conclusion, however, his "fangs" prove phony. Quasi-vampire Radkoff sleeps during the day and drinks blood, but his supernatural powers are apparently limited to hypnosis and clairvoyance.... There seems little point to this compromise between a traditional vampire tale and a psycho-at-large thriller, or to the intersection, within the story, of art (piano, dance), sex, and violence.

**Un VAMPIRE AU PARADIS**  (F) Les Films Auramax & Canal Plus & CNC (J.-C. Patrice) 1992 color 90m. SP,D: Abdelkrim Bahloul. Ref: V 8/24/92: "matter-of-fact mix of everyday life and supernatural concerns is deftly sustained"; *A Vampire in Paradise*- tr t. Jones. VSOM: *Vampire in Paradise* - vt t. With Bruno Cremer, Brigitte Fossey, Farid Chopel (Nosfer Arbi), Laure Marsac.

Escaped madman thinks he's a vampire, terrorizes Paris.

**VAMPIRE BUSTER**  (H.K.) In-Gear Film 1989 color c90m. (*Ninja Vampire Buster* - vc box t. *Zhuo Gui Dashi*). D: Norman Law, Stanley Siu. Ref: V 7/5/89:39: NP (distrib.); in H.K. Jones. Hardy/HM2: *Ninja Vampire Busters*. Weisser/ATC: vampire spirit from vase. With Nick Chan, Simon Cheng, Stanley Fung.

Exorcist vs. demon.

**VAMPIRE CHILD** see *Vampire Kids*

**VAMPIRE COP**  Panorama Ent./Donald Farmer Prods. (Chesney) 1990 color 83m. SP,D: Farmer. SpMkpFX: Rick Gonzalez. Ref: V 2/21/90:152 (ad). 7/15/91:12 (rated). SFChron Dtbk 12/9/90. Jones. McCarty II. PT 10:52. Fango 104:12. With Melissa Moore, Ed Cannon, T. Jenkins, Michelle Berman.

"Double vampire sex in a bathtub." (SFC)

**VAMPIRE FAMILY**  (H.K.) Regal/Chang-Hong Channel Film 1993 color/ws feature. Ref: TV: Tai Seng Video; Eng. titles. V 8/23/93:10: playing in H.K. 8/30/93:9. With Cheung Man.

"You are all vampires?" Main family-history fact: The older generation can walk through walls. Main historical fact: The British "invaded" China with vampires first, not opium. Main book: "The Last Vampire of China." Pretty dismaying. Strenuous horror-comedy seems inspired by the first *Addams Family* movie. Some okay stunts — e.g., Papa "erasing" his face.

**VAMPIRE HUNTER D**  (J) Streamline/MOVIC & Epic & CBS Sony (Ashi) 1985('92-U.S.) anim color 80m. (*Bampaia Hanta "D"*). AD, D: Toyoo Ashida. SP & Novel: Hideyuki Kikuchi. Mus: Tesuya Komuro. Char Des: Yoshitaka Amano. Ref: TV: Epic/Sony HV; no Eng.; made-for-video. V 8/3/92. Paul Lane. Jones. Horacio Higuchi. J Anim Program Guide. J Anim Archives number 3. Voices: Michie Tomizawa, Kaneto Shiozawa (D).

"This story takes place in the distant future, when mutants and demons slither through a world of darkness." Doris Ran's vampire hunter, D, her protector from the 9,000-year-old vampire Count Magnus Lee (who wants her for his wife), proves to be a "danpiru," a half-human, half-vampire, and son of the legendary Count Dracula. D disperses the monster hordes outside Lee's castle with a noise-making gizmo, and uses his vampire teeth to dispatch the three Lamia, or snake women, inside the castle. Meanwhile, another strange hunchbacked creature spins out spiders-on-webs, and the funny-faced "symbiont" in D's hand cheerfully gobbles them up. Plus various wraiths, a werewolf, a Time Deceiver Lamp, a cyborg horse, and "space curving."

Lively, inventive monster rally is strong on art, or "production paintings," weak on actual animation. Backgrounds are gorgeously stylized—various castles, cemeteries, and skyscapes beguile the eye—and the characters look great, if their story turns out to be rather uninvolving, and short-cut animation produces beautiful but barely-moving pictures.

Note: The Streamline version is available either English-dubbed or subtitled.

**VAMPIRE IN PARADISE** see *Vampire au Paradis*

**VAMPIRE IN THE HIGH RISE**  (Cz) Praha-TV 1979 (1983) color 47m. (*Upir Ve Vezaku*). D: Ludvik Raza. SP: Helena Sykorova. Ph: Vera Stinglova. AD: Ales Voleman. Mkp: Petr Hovorka. Ref: TV: Eng. titles. no Jones. no Stanley. no Phantom. no Scheuer. no Maltin '92. With Tomas Holy, Miroslav Batik, Josef Abrham, Dagmar Veskrnova.

The magazine story "The Vampire from the Tower" gives two little boys (Holy and Batik) the notion that their sister's (Veskrnova) boy friend, Mr. Ruzicka (Abrham), is a vampire. ("She should have checked his teeth first.") They see him biting her (playfully); he's allergic to garlic; he reads *The Physiology of Blood* and *Blood of My Blood*; he likes blood pudding; and he lives in a tower (i.e., a high rise). In a coda, the brothers begin reading *The Hound of the Baskervilles*. ("The dog downstairs looks like a monster.")

Slight but droll, charming comedy, with a silly ending: All concerned don plastic fangs and chase each other. In order to discourage Ruzicka, one of the boys at one point tells him that his brother is the illegitimate son of his sister. There follows the funniest sequence, in which Ruzicka, lunching with the whole family, offers to take the addled child as well as his mother.

**VAMPIRE IN VENICE** see *Nosferatu a Venezia*

**VAMPIRE KIDS** (H.K.) High Grow Films c1992? color 85m. Ref: TV: World Video; Eng. titles. no Jones. VSOM: sfa *Vampire Child?*

"Little vampires!" People shipwrecked on a desert island encounter hopping vampire kids who must fetch blood for their "king," a strong, mean guy in a cave. In one sequence, the kids possess the humans via remote-control magic and make them do silly things. Finally, vampire dad shows up.... Negligible horror-comedy. Cute, though: the guy who thinks the kids camouflaged as shrubs are "flesh-eating plants."

**VAMPIRE KILLERS** (H.K.) Hong Kong Man Wah Film Co. 198-? color c80m. Ref: TV: World Video; Eng. titles. V&T Video: above is tr t.

The mysterious Lisa is a "horrible ghost," or vampire, whose scalp bleeds and who cries "blood tears." She sucks blood from her lover's neck, and seems to vampirize Sue, but some of this may be a dream. Lisa and her "ghost auntie" from the Gate of Death to the World of the Ghosts ("a bit scary") make a sorcerer spit up snakes. Dream-ghost business here is an excuse for softcore sex and spookery.

**VAMPIRE KNIGHTS** Mezcal Films & Filmtrust 1987 color feature. D: Daniel M. Peterson. Ref: Jones: comedy. V 5/6/87:155: 4/30 start. With Ken Abraham, Billy Frank, Peterson, Robin Rochelle.

"Beautiful vampire women in modern Transylvania." (J)

**VAMPIRE ON BIKINI BEACH** Beacon Films/R.A. Jones (VADB) 1987 color c80m. (*Vampires on Bikini Beach* - ad t. *Vampire at Death Beach* - orig t). D: Jerry Brady. SP: Mark Headley. Ph: John Bilecky. Mus: Miguel Alonso. PD: D. Cahmi, D. Holland. SpFxMkp: David Abbott. SpFX: Edward Wilde. Ref: TV. V 5/6/87:294. Jones. With Jennifer Badham, Todd Kaufmann, Stephen Mathews, Nancy Rogers, Hao (Demos), Mariusz Olbrychowski (Falto); Guillermo Barreto et al (ghouls); Sandra Benedict et al (vampirettes), Robert Ankers (Gnordron).

"There's definitely something weird here!" In this supernatural mishmash, Falto, a very old vampire who bestows the "kiss of eternal love" on his female victims, is searching for a "death mate," while his monstrous assistant Demos employs the Book of the Dead in an attempt to revive armies of corpses (including, apparently, Hitler's body). Gnordron, High Priest of the Undead—a good guy—dispatches Falto.

Abysmal videotaped cheapie features would-be-flamboyant main monsters, but technical shortcomings make it hard to hear what they're saying or see what they're doing. Eerie credit-sequence shot of a full moon over time-lapse-photographed freeway traffic.

**VAMPIRE PARTNER** (H.K.) Golden Harvest/Sheng Hong Film 1987 color c90m. D: Peter Chan. P: Jess Leu. Ref: TV: Rainbow Video; no Eng.

Incomprehensible (sans subtitles) combination horror-comedy-fantasy-gangster film centers on two vampires who seem unfazed by Christian crosses, Taoist powers, etc., until, at the end, a red-robed enforcer takes the errant vampires back to the afterworld. In one scene, the vampires steal blood from a bloodmobile, but relent and return the blood. Plus: fake vampires who walk into a real hell, or so it seems.

**VAMPIRE PRINCESS MIYU** (J) AnimEigo/FCI (Soeishinsha & Pony Canyon) 1988('92-U.S.) anim color 26m. (aka *Vampire Princess Miya. Kyuuketsuki Miyu*). D: Toshihiro Hirano. SP: Noboru Aikawa. Ph: K. Konishi. Mus: Kenji Kawai. PD & Monster Des: Yasuhiro Moriki. Anim: AIC;(d) Narumi Kakinouchi. SpFX: Light Magic; T. Sakakibara. SdFX: Animesound, J. Sasaki. Ref: TV: Pony Video, no Eng.; AnimEigo, Eng. titles. Anime Opus '89. Ronin Network 12/25/88: OAV. Bay Guardian 7/7/93:31. Jones. Martin. Animag 4:8. Japan Video: 1st of 4 in series. vc boxes: vol. 4 is '89. Voice: Nooko Watanabe (Miyu).

"Ayakashi No Miyako." ("Unearthly Kyoto.") "At one time, gods and demons were as one." Kyoto. The vampire-like demon, or shinma, Raen, keeps the girl, Aiko, under his spell of sleep. His nemesis: Miyu, the "last vampire." Her vampire bite releases troubled souls into a blissful limbo; his bite ends only in death. Ultimately, Miyu casts a spell that sends Raen, in true demonic, caterpillar-like form, back to the dark world.... Compact, stylish, atmospheric vampire story features an unusual division of vampires and pseudo-vampires into positive and negative forces, while the humans more or less just look on.

**VAMPIRE PRINCESS MIYU: EPISODE 2** (J) AnimEigo/FCI (Soeishinsha & Pony Canyon) 1988 ('92-U.S.) anim color 29m. For credits, see preceding entry. Ref: TV. AnimEigo video; Eng. titles. M/TVM 2/89:56. Animag 5:5.

"Ayatsuri no Utage." ("A Banquet of Marionettes.") "But I also need the blood of beautiful people." "Strange dolls" are found at spots where students have been reported missing. ("I got the feeling that somehow that doll was my daughter.") Responsible: a vampire that lives on the "life energy: which the dolls — her transformed human victims — emit. Neither holy water nor sunlight has any effect on this "shinma." Stilted fantasy-romantics, interesting core idea.

**VAMPIRE PRINCESS MIYU: EPISODES 3 and 4** (J) Pony Canyon/Soeishinsha 1988 and 1989 anim color 30m. each. Ref: Animag 6:5: last 2 in the OAV series.

"Mysterious phantom armor."

**VAMPIRE SETTLES ON POLICE-CAMP** (H.K.) 1991 color c80m. D: Lo Wei Lang. Ref: TV: World Video; Eng. titles; *Vampire Settle on Police-Camp* - t error. Jones: *Vampires Settle on Police-Camp.*

A family of ghosts — including a boy who is called a "Chinese E.T." ("This kid is like a vampire") — torments Inspector Chan, who in a former life was bullying official Lin Kwai Tien. Scattered amusing moments. Best scene: the faceless ghost peeling away her non-face. Best name: Wizard Lousy. Best subtitle: "You bite my ass, but it's interesting." Runner-up: "You were a chicken in your last life."

See also: *Ghost in the Police Camp II.*

**THE VAMPIRE SHOWS HIS TEETH 1** (Taiwanese) Silver Bird Films 1986? color c80m. Ref: TV: Sunny Video; no Eng.; TV-movie?; above is vc box ad t. MMarquee 43:5-6.

Priests, parchments, and hopping vampires, in a period story. Plus a woman biking through the woods at night who turns out to be a flying ghost with very elastic arms .... The usual Asian-vampire rigmarole. Much talk, some low comedy, shallow video look.

**THE VAMPIRE SHOWS HIS TEETH II** (Taiwanese) Silver Bird Films 1986? color c85m. Ref: TV: Sunny Video; no Eng.

Part II, which gets pretty lively near the end, showcases a caped, flying ghost, or vampire, who typically swoops in, gathers up the ghost biker from Part I, and vanishes. He also performs telekinetic tricks with ropes and sprays mist with his mouth. Geyser-like smoke from her grave, a floating scarf, and a levitating umbrella variously herald the appearances of the female ghost, Lilia (sp?). And bells and whistles guide a wizard-led regiment of vampires, who hop in unison .... An odd cross between tear-jerking romance and action-fantasy-horror, complete with theme song.

**THE VAMPIRE SHOWS HIS TEETH III** (Taiwanese) Silver Bird Films 1986 color c73m. Ref: TV: Sunny Video; no Eng.

More tears and chills in the short, vapid conclusion to the series. A needle through the top of the skull stops one superstrong hopping vampire, but spears and bullets bounce off the other vampires. The female ghost is back, and the older vampire master here seems to have become a ghost.

Note: World Video releases this series as one four-part videocassette.

**VAMPIRE STRIKES BACK** (H.K.) 1988 color c95m. (*Hey Ghost! II* - alt vt tr t). D: Kam Yoo Tu. Ref: TV: World Video; no Eng. Thai Video. Jones. MMarquee 43:5. M/TVM 1/89: sfa *Vampire Strike* (1988)?

A little girl and a hopping-vampire boy help each other out: He hops up and down until his feet kick away the coffin lid which pins her down; later, she has him moved when he begins melting in a patch of sunlight. Meanwhile, a hopping vampire (the boy's father) — who resides in a coffin sporting neon swastikas — revives. Although putrefying and limited by his hopping restriction, he knows kung fu and can leap-fly and burn others with his hands. Also: four straw figures who turn into warriors. They return to straw and burn when their headbands are removed.

Just about the worst of the hopping-vampire comedies. This time even the vampires aren't funny, and the actors playing humans are comedians in the worst way. Bathroom humor here includes a fake living, urinating skeleton.

See also: *Close Encounter with the Vampire.*

**VAMPIRE TRAILER PARK** Cinemondo (Latshaw) 1991 color feature. D: Steve Latshaw. SP: Patrick Moran. Ref: SFChron Dtbk 12/22/91. 5/24/92. Jones. PT 12:48: "clever comedy." With Robert Shurtz, Cathy Moran (psychic), Blake Pickett, P. Moran (vampire).

**VAMPIRE VS. SORCERER** (H.K.?) 1988 color c105m. Ref: TV: World Video; no Eng.

A sorcerer's ritual brings a hopping vampire out of the ground. Later, he brings a whole horde of vampires up. At the end, his voodoo doll turns a woman into a green-faced vampire. The climax — in which the vampires turn on and attack the sorcerer — finally makes good the title. Plus: two movie vampires ... gore, subcategory dismemberment, as a vampire rips off a man's arm ... and snake-horde attacks .... The flat, shot-on-tape look is not helpful for the atmospheric effects in this low comedy. One or two funny moments.

**VAMPIRE VS. VAMPIRE** (H.K.) 1989 color feature. Ref: V 8/9/89:48: GH (distrib.); in H.K. PT 5:4.

**VAMPIRE VIXENS FROM VENUS** Filmline & Austin 1994 color 90m. SP, D, P: Ted A. Bohus. Ph: C. Mattikow. Mus, Assoc P: Ariel Shallit. AD: Lara Platman. SpVisFX: 4-Front Video. MkpFX: V.J. Guastini. SpFxCoord: D.X. Campbell. Ref: TV: Shanachie HV; "Coming Soon: Vampire Vixens II: Oakenshield on Venus." SFChron 1/7/95. With Leon Head, Theresa Lynn (Shirley), J.J. North (Arylai), Leslie Glass (Omay), John Knox, Michelle Bauer (Shampay), Charlie Callas, Fred Olen Ray.

Three ugly, tentacled aliens land on Earth, morph into babes, dumb themselves down, and employ a mutating gizmo to drain "sexually aroused" males of their essence. (The latter turn into "big ugly things.") Plus an intergalactic, long-tailed android-cop and vaporizer guns.... Infrequently funny, more often grating, low-budget dopey comedy. The chief comedian here (Head) pretty much kills it.

**VAMPIRE WAR** (J) Vanime c1990? anim color 53m. Ref: TV: Toei Video; no. Eng. no Jones.

A caped, flying bloodsucker, apparently from space, paralyzes our hero's will, leaves bloody bodies everywhere. Fairly stylish, very violent.

**VAMPIRE WOMAN** (H.K.) Zhong Lian 1962 b&w 97m. (*Xi Xuefu*). D: Li Tie. SP: Cheng Gang. Mus: Ju Ren. Sets: Chen Jingsen. Ref: HK Film Festival '82:155. Hardy/HM. Jones. With Bai Yang, Zhang Huoyou, Huang Manli, Rong Xiaoyi.

A woman sucking a child's blood is believed to be a vampire and is buried alive — actually, she is the boy's mother and is saving him from poisoning.

**VAMPIRES** Len Anthony Studios (Scala) 1988 color 92m. (*Abadon* - alt t). Story,SP,D: Anthony. SP: also James Harrigan. Ph: Dickerson, Revene. Mus: Chris Burke. SpVisFX: Arnold Gargulio. Ref: V 6/8/88: "unfinished look." With Duane Jones, Jackie James, Orly Benair.

Machine drains students' energy, makes woman immortal.

See also *Fright House.*

**VAMPIRES** see the preceding and following titles, titles under Dracula, and

*Akumulator 1. Amazing Stories* (1993). *Ambassador Magma. Anemia. Ang Mahiwagang Daigdig Ni Elias Paniki. Arachnophobia. Arrival, The. Aswang. Aullido del Diablo, El. Baby Blood. Banglow 666. Bat People, The* (2). *Battle in Hell. Because the Dawn. Beverly Hills Vamp. Bewitched Area of Thousand*

*Years. Billy the Kid Meets the Vampires. Biss, Der. Bite!. Bite of Love, A. Black Sabbath. Blood Freak. Blood Symbol. Blood Ties. Blood Waters of Dr. Z. Bloodlust. Bloodstone. Bloodthirsty. Blue Lamp in Winter Night, The. Body Double. Boy God. Brides Wore Blood, The. Bubblegum Crisis 5. Buddhist Spell. Buffy the Vampire Slayer. Burning Sensation. Cannibal Hookers. Canterville Ghost, The (1986). Captain Barbell. Capulina contra los Vampiros. Carne de Tu Carne. Cast a Deadly Spell. Chameleons. Charade. Children of the Night. Chillers. Chinese Ghost Story III. City of Ghosts, The. Close Encounter with the Vampire. Coitus Interruptus. Condemned To Live. Counter Destroyer. Crazy Safari. Crime Doctor's Courage, The. Cronos. Curse, The (1990). Curse of the Poltergeist. Curse of the Wicked Wife. Dance of the Damned. Dark Shadows. Dark Universe. Darkness. Darna, Kuno ...?. Dawn. Deathstalker II. Demon Queen. Desert Snow. Devil and the Ghostbuster, The. Devil Bat's Daughter (1). Devil Curse. Devil Hunter Yohko. Devil's Commandment, The. Devil's Dynamite. Devil's Skin, The. Devil's Vendetta. Dial 666 Lust. Divine Enforcer, The. Doctor Vampire. Dolly Dearest. Doriana Gray. Dragon against Vampire. Dragon Ball (1987?). Dreadful Melody. Elusive Song of the Vampire. Embrace of a Vampire. Ejacula. Ejacula 2. Encounter of the Spooky Kind II. Enculela. Endemoniada, La. Erotic Rites of Frankenstein. Eternal Evil. Eternity. Evil Black Magic. Exorcist Master. Fall of the House of Usher (1983). Fantasy Mission Force. Fearless Kung Fu Elements, The. Female Ninjas: Magic Chronicles 1. Figures from Earth. First Vampire in China, The. Flaming Ears. Forced Nightmare. Four Beauties. Frankenstein Island (3). Freedom from the Greedy Grave. Fright Night. Fright Night Part 2. Gamera Vs. Gyaos (1). Gate of the Hell, The. Ghost Bride. Ghost Busting. Ghost Fever (1987). Ghost Fever (1989). Ghost Guarding Treasure. Ghost in the Police Camp. Ghost Writer. Ghostbusting. Ghostly Love. Ghost's Hospital. Ghoulies IV. Girl with the Hungry Eyes. Golden Nun. Gothic. Graveyard Disturbance. Graveyard Shift. Guwapings. Guys in Ghost's Hand. Guyver, The (New Line, 1991). Guzuu. Happy Ghost. Hatyarin. Haunted Cop Shop, The. Haunted Cop Shop II. Haunted House (1991?). Having Supper with a Vampire. Heartstopper. Hello, Dracula. Howling VI. Hungry. Hungry, Part 2. Huphyokwi Yanyo. I Bought a Vampire Motorcycle. I Like Bats. I Married a Vampire. In the Midnight Hour. Intercourse with the Vampire. Interview with a Vamp. Intercourse with the Vampyre 2. Interview with the Vampire. Jitters, The. Jokers Playing Games. Jonathan of the Night. Jugular Wine. July Spirit. Jumping Corpses. Kickboxer from Hell. Kingdom of the Vampires. Knights. Kumander Bawang ... Kwaidan. Lair of the White Worm, The. Last Vampire, The. Legend of the Liquid Sword. Lifeforce. Linda Lovelace for President. Little-boy Ghost. Little Master. Little Shop of Horrors (1986). Llamada del Vampiro. Lobster Man from Mars. Lost Boys, The. Lost Platoon, The. Love Bites. Love Me Vampire. Love with the Ghost in Lushan. Loves of the Living Dead. Lucky Stars. Lust in the Fast Lane. Mad Vampires. Magic of 3,000 Years Ago. Magic Story. Malibu Beach Vampires, The. Maschera del Demonio, La. Mc Cloud (P). Midnight Cabaret. Midnight Hour, The. Midnight Kiss. Midnight Riders. Mind Fuck. Miss Magic. Mr. Vampire. Mr. Vampire II. Mr. Vampire Part III. Mr. Vampire Saga 4. Mr. Vampire 1992. Mixed Up. Mom. Momia Nacional, La. Moon Legend. Mrs. Amworth. Muffy the Vampire Layer. Musical Vampire, The. My Best Friend Is a Vampire. My Boyfriend's Back. My Grandpa Is a Vampire. My Lovely Monster. My Neighbours*

*Are Phantoms!. Nadja. Neeli Ghati. New Mr. Vampire. New Mr. Vampire II. Nick Knight. Night Angel. Night Boys, The. Night Evil Soul. Night of the Sorcerers (II). Night Owl (Franco/'93). Night with a Vampire. Nightlife. Nightmare before Christmas, The. Nightmare Classics. Nine Demons, The. Ninja, the Violent Sorcerer. Nosferato on Brasil. Nosferatu a Venezia. Not of This Earth. Oil of Eternal Life. Once Bitten. One Eyebrow Priest. Pale Blood. Pandemonium (1988). Panic. Peacock King. Polish Vampire in Burbank, A. Pretty Ghostess Story, The. Princess of the Night. Private Moments (P). Project Vampire. Quem Tem Medo de Lobisomem. Rampage. Real Bad Monster Raw. Red and Black. Red Blooded American Girl. Reflecting Skin, The. Reluctant Vampire, The. Rendezvous. Robo Vampire. Rockula. Romance of the Vampires. Runaway Nightmare. Saturday the 14th Strikes Back. Scared Stiff (H.K., 1987). School for Vampires. Scorpion Thunderbolt. Servants of Midnight. Sete Vampiras, As. Seventh Curse, The. Sex and the Single Vampire. Sexandroide. Shadows in the Dark. Shake, Rattle & Roll 2. Shake Rattle & Roll IV. Shaolin Brothers, The. She (1983). Sherlock Holmes in Caracas. Sherlock Holmes: The Last Vampyre. Shrunken Heads. Si Baleleng at ang Gintong Sirena. Silver Spear, The. Sinbad of the Seven Seas. Sleep of Death, The. Something Else Entirely. Son of Darkness. Sorority House Vampires. Spellcaster. Spider Woman Strikes back, The. Spirit Vs. Zombi. Spiritual Love (1992?). Spooks Run Wild. Spooky Family. Spooky Kama Sutra. Starfighters. Stephen King's Sleepwalkers. Stepmonster. Strasek. Street Trash. Stripped to Kill II. Sturmtruppen. Subspecies. Supergrass, The. Take it Easy. Tale From the East, A. Tale of a Vampire. Tales of the Third Dimension. Teen Vamp. Those Feedy on Blood. 3-D Army, The. 3 Wishes. Thunder Kids 3. Ticks. Tomb, The. Toothless Vampires. Trail, The (3P). Trancers 4. Transylvania 6-5000. Trilogy of Fear. Ultimate Vampire, The. Ultra Cop 2000. Understudy, The. Undying Love. Unearthing, The. Valerie. Video Violence. Waxwork II. Whispers. Wicked, The. Witch with the Flying Head, The. Witchcraft III. Wolnyoui Han. Xenia. Zombie Vs. Ninja.*

**VAMPIRES ALWAYS RING TWICE** Steve Postal Prods./Cinevue 1990 color 118m. Ph, D: S. Postal. SP: Douglas Benison, Karen Benison. Ref: Martin: "bottom of the barrel" tale re vampires. V 5/6/91:79. 11/12/90:27: 10/29 start. With Alan Ramey, Jennifer Tuck, Angela Shepard.

**VAMPIRES AND OTHER STEREOTYPES** Brimstone (Lindenmuth) 1992 feature. SP, D: K.J. Lindenmuth. Mus: The Krypt. Ref: PT 20:11: "very silly ... uses vampires as a punchline." With Wendy Bednarz, William White.

Demon possession, monsters, a crawling hand, and a giant rat in hell.

**VAMPIRE'S BREAKFAST** (H.K.) Cinema City/Dennis Yu 1987 color c88m. (*Lingchen Wancan*). D: Wong Chung. SP: Chan Hing Kai. Ph: Ho Poh Yue, Arthur Wong. Mus: Phil Chen. PD: Chung Mun Keung. Ref: TV: Rainbow Video; Eng. titles. Horacio Higuchi. NST! 4:38. Jones: 1986. With Kent Cheng, Emily Chu, Wong Pak Man, Ng Ma.

Hong Kong. In the Dancing Girl Case, all the victims have died of "overbleeding." A "half-human, half-ghost monster" seems to be at large, but the police keep the facts from the public. At the end, the hero, reporter Fat Piao, cuts off the Superman-strong vampire's head, but the monster continues to operate headless, and its head flies at Piao. Only a mahogany nail in the back finally stops the vampire. Best thing about this routine but fairly-well-made horror-comedy-drama: the title. Second-best: the snarling, pasty-faced, bloody-mouthed, unstoppable vampire (whose name may be Stock Fritz). Plot apes *The Night Stalker* (1972); insistent "suspense" music apes John Carpenter. One very good "jump" when a woman bends down to fix her stocking, and the reflection of the vampire — briefly caught in a car's headlights — appears in the store window before her.

**VAMPIRE'S EMBRACE** Andreiev 1991 color feature? SP,D: Glen Andreiev. Ref: Jones. PT 12:47: "some decent fx."

Blond, 200-year-old vampire.

**VAMPIRES FROM OUTER SPACE** Postal Prods./Cinevue 1990 color 114m. SP, D, Ph: Steve Postal. SP: also Gail A. Postal. Ref: Martin: "amateurish shot-on-video production." V 5/6/91:79. With Alan Ramey, Angela Shepard, Jennifer Tuck.

Vampire bride from the planet Cirrus.

**VAMPIRES IN HAVANA** (Cuban-Sp) The Cinema Guild/ICAIC & Durniok-TV Espanola 1985 ('87-U.S.) anim color 74m. (*Vampiros en La Habana!*). SP,D,Des,Dial: Juan Padron. Dial: also Ernesto Padron. Mus: Rembert Egues. SdFX: Manuel Marin. Ref: screen. V 1/1/86. 3/12/86:89. 5/21/86:8. 10/21/87:147. Jones. Scheuer. Stanley.

Professor Von Dracula, responsible for his father the Count's death when his anti-sun formula failed, successfully tests his new formula, Vampisol, on his nephew Joseph Amadeus Von Dracula, aka Pepe. The latter turns human — though, at the end, his offspring sports rudimentary fangs. The professor's aides include the thug-creature Bruno and various small bat-like and snake-like things.

Overplotted and overpopulated script features hero, heroine, rival vampire gangs, cops, revolutionaries, and stray dogs. Film, however, is cute and lively and has winning incidental humor. Funniest, best-sustained sequence: Animated vampires watch a live-action "Dracula" on a movie screen and become disenchanted when the priest therein appears to be getting the upper hand with Dracula.

**VAMPIRES IN THE OUTBACK** see *Wicked, The*

**VAMPIRES IN VENICE** see *Nosferatu a Venezia*

**VAMPIRE'S KISS** Hemdale (Daly-Gibson)/Magellan Pictures (Barry Shils, Barbara Zitwer) 1988 color 96m. (103m). D: Robert Bierman. SP: Joseph Minion. Mus: Colin Towns. SpMkpFX: Ed French. Bat: (des) Rodger Shaw; (fx) George Chamberlain. Ref: TV. V 9/21/88. Sacto Bee 12/3/89. NYorker 6/12/89. MFB'90:369-70. Martin. Scheuer. Hound. Maltin '92. Jones. With Nicolas Cage, Maria Conchita Alonso, Jennifer Beals, Elizabeth Ashley.

"This guy is very weird!" Peter Loew (Cage) — literary agent, office tyrant, sometimes madman, and ... vampire? Rachel (Beals) bites his neck, or so he imagines, and he does a Renfield with a cockroach. Is *Vampire's Kiss* a study of erratic, inconsistent behavior? Or is it "Dr. Jekyll and Mr. Hyde"? (The office scenes between Cage and his terrorized secretary Alonso play like the Tracy-Bergman scenes in the 1941 film version.) Is it comedy? Or a Midnight Movie? Or simply an offbeat vehicle for Cage? His best terror-in-the-office line: "Misfiled!?" Best credit: "Fang Vendor" (Stephen Chen). Perhaps the movie is just very New York City.

**VAMPIRE'S KISS** Avica 1993 color 90m. D: Scotty Fox. Ref: Adam '94: vampires. With Nikki Dial, Lacy Rose, Jonathan Morgan.

**VAMPIRES LIVE AGAIN** (H.K.) 1988 color c100m. D: Kam Yoo Tu. Ref: TV: Ocean Shores Video; no Eng. Jones:1987. NST! 4:38: *Vampire Lives Again*.

In a prologue, a non-funny hopping vampire rips out a victims' innards. In the present day, the coffins of a family of hopping vampires are unearthed. Mother and father vampire commit gory acts upon humans and farm animals; little-boy vampire plays in the wood with human kids (in slow motion, to stress the idyllic quality of their fun). At the end, a priest drives a hastily blessed stake through the top of mamma vampire's head. Pop is staked, too, while sonny boy is simply re-buried. Shot-on-tape feature has a fairly atmospheric look, though the sound is typically flat. Lots of fog effects. Film doesn't seem to know what to make of its disparate comic, action, and horror elements.

**VAMPIRES ON BIKINI BEACH** see *Vampire on Bikini Beach*

**The VAMPIRE'S ROPE** (Russ.) The Nord Co. 1992 color feature? D: Nikolai Gibu. SP: Clara Luchko, Zinaida Chirkova. Ref: Jones: vampires.

**VAMPIRES SETTLE ON POLICE-CAMP** see *Vampire Settles on Police-Camp*

**El VAMPIRO TEPOROCHO** (Mex) Galactica Films/Luis Bekris 1989 color c85m. Story,D,AD,MusFX: Rafael Villasenor Kuri. Story,SP: Antonio Orellana. Story: also Bekris. Inspired by Bram Stoker's novel *Dracula*. Ph: Agustin Lara. Mus: Carlos Torres. SPFX: Duran & Duran. Mkp: Carmen de la Torre. Ref: TV: Film-Mex video; no Eng. V 5/2/90:242: *The Wino Vampire* - tr t. TVG. Cinef 6/96:47. With Pedro "Chatanuga" Weber, Charly Valentino, Humberto Herrera, Gabriela Goldsmith, Rebeca Silva, "Condorito."

Count Dracula (Weber) is taken from his home in Transylvania, sent into space aboard a rocket ship, and winds up in Mexico as a "barfly vampire." In this talky but agreeably cheesy comedy, Dracula can fly in bat or non-bat form and, like the Thai Dracula, he plays cards like a regular guy. He puts condoms on his fangs before going after a streetwalker, periodically makes strange noises, speaks in rhyme, and can turn into a fly or mosquito. His funniest transformation occurs when he bites into some chili and turns into a turkey. Fortunately, one of his pals speaks "Turkey," and — promoters all — they enter him in a cock fight. (Cheers of "Dracula! Dracula!") *El Vampiro Teporocho*, which has some of your more unusual Dracula scenes, is casual, flagrantly rule-breaking fun. The actors seem to be as gifted at verbal comedy as they are at physical comedy.

**2 Los VAMPIROS DE COYOACAN** 1973 color c86m. SP: Arturo Martinez. Story: Mario Cid. Ph: Javier Cruz. Mus: Ernesto Cortazar. AD, SpFX: Roberto Munoz. Mkp: Graciela Munoz. Co-D: Fernando Duran. Ref: TV: Madera CineVideo; no Eng. Jones. TVG. Monster! 3:59-60. With German Robles, "Mil Mascaras," "Superzan," Sasha Montenegro, Carlos Lopez Moctezuma, "Franquestein," Pura Vargas, "Mister Tempest," Tony Salazar, "El Greco."

*Vampiros de Coyoacan* squanders the first third of its running time on wrestling matches, then gets down to business. "Dracula" plot elements include a vampire, Baron Bradok, from Transylvania ... a sick lady under the spell of the vampire ... and an expedition to the Baron's domain. Also included: two other vampire men and the Agrasanchez dwarfs, here playing vampire midgets that appear in a cloud of red smoke. The risible presence of the masked and caped wrestler-heroes keeps breaking up the atmosphere, but writer-director Martinez comes up with a few unusual sequences, including one in which satan seems to grant the Baron's wish: The heroine — reclining on a ritual altar — sprouts fangs. She later goes for her father's jugular, then (horrified by what she has done) throws herself into a handy conflagration. In another effective sequence, the Baron's head becomes more and more monstrous and batlike, as he carries away the heroine. (Intermittent shadows rather than dissolves mark the stages.)

**VAMPIROS EN LA HABANA!** see *Vampires in Havana*

**VAMPYRE** Panorama Ent. (Raedon)/Pagan Prods. (Antonio Panetta) 1991 color 86m. (*Vampyr* - shooting t). SP,D,Co-P: Bruce G. Hallenbeck. Ph: Panetta. Ref: Jones: "amateurish." PT 11:12: "slow-paced." McCarty II: "unfocused." V/Cannes '89:134-5. With Randy Scott Rozler or Tozler, Cathy Seyler, John Brent, John McCarty (yes, him).

"Topless, leather-clad vampiress." (J)

**VANDAAG OF MORGEN** (Dutch) R. Kerbosch 1976 color 82m. SP,D,P: Roeland Kerbosch. SP: also Ton Van Duinhoven. Ph: Hein Groot. Ref: Hardy/SF: *Any Day Now* - tr t? With T. van Duinhoven, Wim de Haas.

Totalitarian U.S. of Europe, united Third World of the future.

**The VANISHING** (Dutch-F) Tara Releasing (Movie Visions)/MGS/Golden Egg & Ingrid Prods. & PvN & Tros Televisie & Stichting Cobo & Cannon Video (Anne Lordon) 1988 ('90-U.S.) color 106m. (*Spoorloos*). Adap, D, Co-ed, Co-P: George Sluizer. SP: Tim Krabbe, from his novel *The Golden Egg*. Ph: Toni Kuhn. Mus: Henny Vrienten. Mkp: Leone Noel. Ref: TV. MFB '90:175-6, ad. V 10/19/88. 1/13/92:16. SFExam 11/2/90. Film Comment 3/91:5. no Maltin '92. Martin. Scheuer. With Bernard-Pierre Donnadieu (Raymond Lemorne), Gene Bervoets, Johanna Ter Steege, Gwen Eckhaus.

Three years after his girl friend (Ter Steege) disappears, Rex Hofman(Bervoets) is still conducting a public search for her. Meanwhile, her apparent abductor, family man Raymond Lemorne — a self-described sociopath with a "slight abnormality" in his personality — leads him on with mysterious notes, and ultimately a promise to show him just what happened to Saskia: In a macabre Poe finish to a moderately intriguing puzzle movie,

Raymond buries Rex alive .... Tale of dueling obsessions is a "bit weird," and not wholly believable. Both "cat" and "mouse" seem programmed.

**The VANISHING** Fox/Morra, Brezner, Steinberg & Tenenbaum (Paul Schiff) 1993 color 110m. D: George Sluizer. SP: Todd Graff. Ph: Peter Suschitzky. Mus: Jerry Goldsmith. PD: J.C. Oppewall. Ref: V 2/8/93: "tedious thriller." 4/6/92:18: 4/6 start. SFChron 2/5/93: "adopts the conventions of a silly monster movie." ad. With Jeff Bridges, Kiefer Sutherland, Nancy Travis, Sandra Bullock, Park Overall, Lisa Eichhorn, George Hearn.

Remake of the '88 Dutch film.

**VANITY CITY** see *Megazone Two Three*

**VARROW MISSION, The** see *Teen Alien*

**VEERANA** (India - Hindi) Sai Om Prods. (Ramsay) 198-? color c140m. D: Tulsi & Shyam Ramsay;(assoc) Arjun Ramsay. SP, Ed: S. Ramsay. Ph: Gangu Ramsay. Mus: Bappi Lahiri. Ref: TV: Shiva video; little Eng. With Jasmin, H. Birje, Satish Shah, Sahila Chadha, Kulbushan.

Never trust a woman who wears a bat ornament on her necklace. Rip off the bat, and she turns into a snarling, hairy thing. (The Hindi equivalent of a Christian cross fends her off.) Later, a sorcerer retrieves her hanged-until-dead body, and she turns into a telekinetic terror and, on alternate Black Sundays, a flying fiend. At the end, (a) the sorcerer gets speared with a big "cross," (b) his hench-creatures explode, (c) the demon statue topples, and (d) the main monster incinerates. All this and a human-headed dog, cone-headed rock horrors, lots of screaming and shouting, fog, an attack cat, bleeding portraits, a giant spider web, an indoor storm, swiveling monster heads and (surprisingly) legs, voodoo dolls, scare music, lightning, thunder, and self-closing doors.... Full-throttle, isn't it? Hammer-compounded horror is ultra-corny, far from subtle, but also far from boring. Complete with time-outs for commercials (in the middle of the tape) and singing-in-the-tub sequences.

**VEGAS IN SPACE** Troma/Fish-Ford 1991 (1985) color and b & w 85m. SP, D, P, VisFX & Co-Ed: Phillip R. Ford. SP, Exec P, Min & Mkp: Doris Fish. SP: also Miss X. Ph: Robin Clark. Mus: Bob Davis. Ref: TV. V 8/10/92. SFExam 10/25/91. USA-TV: *Star Whores* - early t? With Fish, Miss X, Ginger Quest, Ramona Fischer, Lori Naslund, Tippi (Princess Angel).

Before entering Vegas in Space — an "oasis of glamor in a universe of mediocrity" — on Clitoris, a "pre-fab pleasure planet" in the "gal galaxy"" the crew of the *U.S.S. Intercourse* must take "gender reversal pills" — men are *verboten*. The place's principal export: cosmetics. Principal "doll"/android: Princess Angel. Remedy for black-and-white: the Color Booster .... The effects cheerfully celebrate Tacky, and the verbal asides are clever, but some acting would have helped. Sure beats *Queen of Outer Space,* though. (One character is named Nueva Gabor.) Included: a "bad-dream sequence." "Based on a party by Ginger Quest."

**VENDETTA DAL FUTURO** see *Hands of Steel*

**VENDETTA FROM THE FUTURE** see *Hands of Steel*

**VENENO PARA LAS HADAS** (Mex) 198-? feature. D: C.E. Taboada. Ref: Ecran F 76:70.

Possessed girl has supernatural powers.

**VENERE D'ILLE, La** see *Venus of Ille*

**La VENGANZA DEL SILLA DE RUEDAS: LA PROXIMA VICTIMA** (Mex) Hidalgo (R. Moreno Castilleja) 1992? color 78m. D: F. Duran. SP: Carlos Valdemar. Ph: M. Tejada. Mus D: L. Arcaraz. SpFX: Benjamin Benitez. Ref: TV: C&H HV; no Eng. With Fernando Almada, Claudia Islas, Isaura Espinoza, Rodrigo Vidal.

The masked, cloaked, cowled slasher-in-black employs, variously, butcher knife, pistol, hatchet, and pitchfork, and in order to pad the running time, the movie recaps his exploits as a coda. Throw in two thunderstorms. The gore here is at once hamhanded and daintily executed.

**VENGANZA DIABOLICA** (Mex) Roberto Lozoya 1990 color c90m.? D: Francisco Guerrero. SP: Manolo Cardenas. Story: Blanca Samperio. Ph: Moises Frutos. Mus: Larsa. AD: Carlos Lozoya. SpFX: Roberto Lozoya Jr. Mkp: Lourdes Gutierrez. Ref: TV: no Eng. TVG. With Juan Valentin, Noe Murayama, Marisol Cervantes, Cristina Michaus, Maria Rubio, Carlos Pouliot.

Ingredients: a satanic cult, black magic, "diabolical forces," a devil's circle, a demon doll which seems to pull the spirit out of a sleeping man's body, and visualized nightmares. Shot-on-tape cheapie overworks its standard-issue-eerie music-box theme for the doll. Gross highlight: the worms which exit the doll's ear and enter the child's.

**VENGANZA SUICIDA** (Mex) Colima Films (Brillaron por Su Ausencia) 1990 color 88m. SP, D: Julio Ruiz Llaneza. Ph: Raul Dominguez. Mkp: Ma. Eugenia Luna. Ref: TV: Mex-American HV; no Eng.; *Suicidal Vengeance* - tr t. With Robert Guzman, Patricia Rivera (Elena), Bruno Rey, Roberto Montiel, Ariadne Welter, Paco Sanudo.

To prepare herself for revenge for the rape of herself and murder of her loved ones, a woman (Rivera) undergoes plastic surgery, takes up martial arts, marksmanship (with rifle and pistol), and knife-throwing, and learns to chew gum. She blows out the brains of Thug One and his girl friend, then graduates to more cruel and unusual punishments. She applies drill and steam iron to the private parts of Thug Two, and chainsaw to Thug Three's leg. She then branches out and begins setting fire to and slashing random chauvinist pigs.... Elena et Les Hommes. Ineptly staged variation on Ms. 45. The initial three thugs overdo Sheer Evilness.

**VENGEANCE: THE DEMON** see *Pumpkinhead*

**VENGEANCE IS MINE** (J) Shochiku (Kazuo Inoue) 1979 color 128m. (*Fukushu Suru Wa Ware Ni Ari*). D: Shohei Imamura. SP: Masaru Baba, from Ryuzo Saki's book. Ph: S. Himeda. Mus: S. Ikebe. Ref: Weisser/JC: "extraordinary." V 3/26/80: "possesses real force and power." With Ken Ogata, Mayumi Ogawa, Rentaro Mikuni.

Psychopath's killings recorded with the "most graphic of details."(JC)

**VENGEANCE WITH A KISS** see *Immortal Sins*

**VENGEANCE WITHOUT MERCY** (Indonesian) Dara Mega Film 1983 color? feature. D: Wahab Abdi. Ref: Ecran F 37:56. With Lenny Marlina, Frans Tumbuan, Farida Pasha.

Jealous spouse resorts to "satanic forces."

**The VENUS OF ILLE** (I) Pont-Royal TV (Franco) 1978 color c60m. (*La Venere d'Ille*). D: Mario & Lamberto Bava. SP: L. Bava, Cesare Garboli. From Merimee's story. Ph: N. Celeste. Mus: U. Continiello. AD: A. Dell'Orco. Ref: TV: vt; Eng. titles. vc box: from the TV anthology series "Il Giorno dei Diavolo." With Daria Nicolodi, Marc Porel.

Quite by accident, a "very old and antique statue," from pagan times, is unearthed—a "Venus" ("her eyes staring at nothing"). The ambiguous inscription—"Watch out—those who love you"—was apparently added later. After a finger ring gets stuck on the statue ("She twisted my hand"), the latter seems to come to murderous life. But one senses more than sees this phenomenon. This is one eerie statue, at least as shot by Bava/Bava/Celeste. Nothing much happens here, but this supernatural anecdote is both lulling and unsettling. And this TV work is more intriguing than most of Mario Bava's later, theatrically-released films.

**VENUS WARS** (J) Central Park Media/Shochiku/Kugatsusha 1989 ('92-U.S.) anim color/ws 103m. SP: Yuichi Sasamoto, from Yoshikazu Yasuhiko's comic. Anim D: Sachiko Kamimura. Char Des: Yasuhiko. Mecha Des: Makoto Kobayashi. Ref: TV: SHV video; no Eng. Animag 4:3. 5:23-27. 9:40-44. V 2/25/91:A-32 (ad). U.S. Manga Corps brochure.

Human-populated, oxygen-enriched Venus, 2089 A.D. The country of Ishtar conquers Aphrodia. Super-weapon of choice: the Tako, or tank. (Its duel with a huge construction crane recalls the steam-shovel-vs.-dinosaur climax of *Dinosaurus!*) Other technological wonders include the police all-urban-terrain vehicle, monocycles, and anti-tank bikes. If the story is functional, the animation is strikingly atmospheric. The smoke of explosions dominates, and the city settings blend the familiar with the unfamiliar. Vacuous score.

**VERMILION EYES** Nathan Schiff 1987 color 98m. SP, D: N. Schiff. Ref: PT 18:14: "mostly one gory death after another." no Stanley. no Martin.

**VERRUECKTESTE AUTO DER WELT, Das** see *Superwheels*

**VIBES** Col/Imagine Ent. (Ron Howard, Deborah Blum, Tony Ganz) 1989 color/ws? 99m. D: Ken Kwapis. Story,SP: Lowell Ganz, Babaloo Mandel. Story: also D. Blum. VisFX: Boss Film; (p) Richard Edlund. SpFxCoord: Allen Hall. Ref: TV: RCA-Col HV. Martin. SFChron 8/6/88. V 8/1/88.

"It's not Incan — it's older." Comedy-fantasy-adventure has a science-fictionish beginning and end, set in a lost city in Ecuador, as a mysterious crystal pyramid ("This is the beginning and end of all things. It is the tip of God's arrow fallen to Earth") proves to be the "most concentrated psychic energy source on the planet." Touched, the pyramid makes a man vanish and gives a psychic (Cyndi Lauper) the power literally to blow another man away. Also: astral projection, psychometry, etc .... Jeff Goldblum's dry delivery makes mediocre lines sound good, good lines sound better; and Lauper and Peter Falk also contribute to this very uneven comedy.

**VICE ACADEMY PART 2** Rick Sloane 1990 color 92m. SP, D, P, Ed: Sloane. Mus: Alan Dermarderosian. Ref: V 9/3/90:80 (hv): made-for-video; "mild comedy." Martin: "offensive." With Ginger Lynn Allen, Linnea Quigley, Jayne Hamil, Jay Richardson, Teagan Clive, Toni Alessandrini, Marcus Vaughter, Melissa Moore.

"Robot named Bimbocop." (V)

**VICE ACADEMY PART 3** Prism/Rick Sloane Prods. & Don Campbell 1991 color c90m. Sp,D,Ed: Sloane. Ph: Robert Hayes. Mus: Alan Dermarderosian. AD: Mark Richardson. Mkp: Amy Snyder. Ref: TV. TVG: "mutant." PT 13:50. Martin. With Julia Parton, Ginger Lynn Allen, Elizabeth Kaitan, Jay Richardson, Johanna Grika, Steve Mateo, Kari French.

Chemical spray turns gun moll (Parton) green-haired. ("From now on, call me Malathion!") The cop doc's anti-Malathion formula stops her. Threadbare production, haphazard direction.

**VICE WEARS BLACK HOSE** (I) VSOM 1972 feature (*Il Vizio Ha le Calze Nere*). D: Tano Cimarosa. SP: Luigi De Marchi. Mus: Carlo Savina.Ref: ETC/Giallos: "subpar." Palmerini, 1975. With John Richardson, Dagmar Lassander, Magda Konopka, Giacomo Rossi-Stuart, Daniela Giordano.

Gloved killer ... razor-wielding idiot ... murderer savaged by a pack of dogs.

**VICIOUS LIPS** Empire/ITM (Thomas Karnowski/Taryn) 1985? color 80m. SP, D: Albert F. Pyun. Ph: Tim Suhrstedt. Mus: Michael McCarty. AD: Bob Zembicki. Milo: Greg Cannom;(addl mkp fx) MMI. SpVisFX: Quick Silver FX. SpMechFX: Chiodo Bros. SpLaserFX: Lasersound. Ref: TV: VSOM. VSOM: "futuristic sf tale of girl rock group." With Dru-Anne Perry, Gina Calabrese, Linda Kerridge, Shayne Farris, Chris Andrews (Milo).

"There's something in the sand!" In deep space, with Milo the Venusian Manbeast (who can impersonate humans), miscellaneous drooling fiends, a monster-toothed gent, a camel-anteater creature, the Spaceport Lounge, and the Radioactive Dream night club.... Lax, isn't it? Sketchy script, muffled sound. An occasional wry line gets lost in the general nebulousness.

**VIDA ES SUENO, La** see *Life Is a Dream*

The **VIDEO DEAD** Manson Int'l./Interstate 5 & Highlight (Video Dead) 1987 color 90m. SP, D, P: Robert Scott. Mus: Stuart Rabinowitsh, L. Marcel, K. McMahon. SpVisFX: Dale Hall Jr. SpPhFxSup: Wes Takahashi. Ref: TV: Embassy video. SFExam 10/30/87. V 11/25/87. 5/6/87:132(ad). Phantom. Hound. Morse. no Martin. Scheuer. With Roxanna Augesen, Rocky Duvall, Vickie Bastel, Sam David McClelland, Michael St. Michaels, Jennifer Miro (The Woman), Al Millan ("Ironhead"), Lory Ringuette (the undead).

A Sylvania TV set intended for an institute for occult studies is accidentally delivered to 21 Shady Lane, Sausalito. It gets only one station and plays only one movie, "Zombie Blood Nightmare," which features a musical score very reminiscent of *Creature of the Walking Dead.* The video dead who emerge from the set kill what they cannot be—the living—and do not like to see themselves in mirrors.

Shoestring *Videodrome*'s TV-horrors premise yields another onslaught-of-the-undead story which has little to do with TV or video. Acting is rudimentary, comedy limp, though there is a droll makeup effect involving a steam iron, plus a jack-in-the-box jolt with a zombie in a washing machine. If the comedy-and-ghoulishness climax is contrived, it plays entertainingly: The heroine, who must show no fear, or she dies, cheerily cooks chili for zombie houseguests.

**VIDEO KILLER** see *Obsession*

**VIDEO MURDERS** Jim McCullough Prods. 1987 color c90m. SP, D: Jim McCullough Jr. Ph: Joseph Wilcotts. Mus: Robert Sprayberry. Set Des: Richard Murov. SpFX: William Rech. Mkp: Beverly Martin. Ref: TV: TWE video. Phantom. Hound. Morse. no Martin. Scheuer. With Eric Brown, Virginia Loridans, John Fertitta, Frank Baggett, Tracy Murrell, Lee Larrimore.

Scarred, literally, by an encounter with a woman, David Lee Shepherd (Brown)—a "sick son of a bitch"—can make only video, not love: He strangles his victims—generally prostitutes—for the video camera.... Well-acted, especially by Brown and Loridans, but thin, and padded with foot-chase and car-chase sequences. It's the old "I just wanted you to love me," Ma, story.

**VIDEO VIOLENCE** Camp/Little Zach Prods. (Ray Clark) 1987 (1986) color c100m. SP, D: Gary Cohen. SP: also Paul Kaye. Videography: Philip Gary. Mus: Gordon Ovsiew. SpMkpFX: Mark Dolson, Mark Kwiatek, Jodi Halifko. Ref: TV: Camp Video; shot-on-tape. Hound. Scheuer. no Martin. Phantom. no Jones. With Art Neill, Jackie Neill, William Toddie, Uke (Eli), Lisa Cohen.

In Frenchtown, the "big thing to do on Saturday night is to make a bowl of popcorn and sit in front of the tube and watch people getting killed." Yes, the local yokels make their own snuff movies, including *The Vampire Takes a Bride,* featuring a Dracula-type (David Christopher). ("That doesn't look like a Hollywood vampire movie!") Film crosses the horrible-community story with the phony snuff movie ("Is the whole town in on it?"), to the advantage of neither. Hokey "camp" comedy, much *2000 Maniacs* cackling, and (fortunately) badly-mocked-up killings.

**VIDEO VIOLENCE PART 2.... THE EXPLOITATION!** Camp Video 1987 color 90m. D: Gary P. Cohen. Ref: Hound. Phantom ref. With Uke, Bart Summer, Lee Miller.

"Talk show guests ... mutilated." (H)

**VIDEO WARS** Stage 23/Maria Rybczuk & George Mazzacano 1983 color c75m. D, Exec P: Mario Giampaolo. SP: Jerrold Phaon. Ph: Christopher Speeth. Mus: Henry Cassella; King Henry & His Showband, Philly Cream. Mkp: William Esher. Ref: TV: Best Film Video. Stanley. no Phantom. no Hound. no Martin.

With George Diamond, Dennis Warren, Maria Anna, Michael Harris, Joan "Miss Hemisphere" Steen, James Thornley.

The Prince of Bastavia—in his bid to become Overseer of the World—"programs" one country for collapse, with the aid of special computer programs, and is on the verge of controlling satellites and tapping into any TV station in the world. An American agent finishes him off with a pocket ray device and blows up his operation.... Pathetically scrappy, almost incoherent, made-in-Pennsylvania James Bond takeoff, with a painfully jaunty, aren't-we-having-fun? score.

**VIE AMOUREUSE DE L'HOMME INVISIBLE, La** see *Orloff and the Invisible Man*

**VIERDE MAN, De** see *Fourth Man, The*

**VIJ, The** see *Maschera del Demonio, La*

**VILLA DELLE ANIME MALEDETTE** see *Don't Look in the Attic*

**VILLAINPUR MATHA** (Indian - Tamil) Suguna Films 1983 color 138m. D, Co-SP: K.T. Master. Mus: C. Devarajan. Ref: Dharap. With Saratbabu.

Sorcery drives man mad.

**VILLGUST: ARMED DRAGON FANTASY, VOL. 1** (J) Bandai/Animate Film & Studio Fantasia (Plex/MOVIC) 1992/1993 anim color 56m. (aka *Armored Dragon Legend Villgust*). D: K. Nishijima. Based on the toys. Mus: Kohei Tanaka. Ref: TV: Emotion video; no Eng. Animerica 5:52: 4 OAVs (in 2 volumes). 5:14,15.

Perky, too-talky Part I features a talking dinosaur-like monster, a wolf-dog-human sword fighter, skeletal types, and a bee thing. Sometimes cute, kooky Part II features a gigantic tentacle-head thing, robots, and an apparently man-made tornado.

**VINCENT** Disney 1982 anim 6m. SP, D: Tim Burton. Mus: Ken Hilton. Anim: Stephen Chiono. Narrator: Vincent Price. Ref: screen. PFA notes 11/16/84.

Little Vincent Molloy aspires to be Vincent Price—i.e., a tormented, romantic Gothic hero—imagines seeing his dog as Abercrombie the scientifically-created zombie-dog, seeing skeleton-hands from walls, etc. Droll, deftly-and-imaginatively-animated short.

**The VINDICATOR** (Can.) Fox/Michael Levy & Telefilm Canada (Frank & Stein Film Prods.) 1986 (1984) color 88m. (*The Frankenstein Factor* - orig t. *Frankenstein '88* - alt t). D: Jean-Claude Lord. SP: Edith Rey, David Preston. Mus: Paul Zaza. SpDes: Stan Winston;(gold suit) S.T. Sampson. SpFxSup: George Erschbamer, Bill Orr. Mkp: Jocelyne Bellemare. Ref: TV. V 5/21/86. 10/24/84:393. Ecran F 69:76: aka *Frankenstein 88: The Vindicator.* 74:6: *Frankenstein 2000* - F. With David McIlwraith, Teri Austin, Richard Cox, Maury Chaykin, Pam Grier, Catherine Disher, Lynda Mason Green.

Project Frankenstein at the Aerospace Research Corporation (ARC) produces "one hell of a killing machine": "Frankenstein ... a living human brain in an indestructible mechanical body."

The brain belonged to dead scientist Carl Lehman (McIlwraith); the body is a suit connected to a computer and a "rage response activator." At the end, "Frankenstein" succeeds in reprogramming himself so that he does not automatically kill when enraged, then does battle with now-super-suited evil ARC exec Alex Whyte (Cox) and his "new and improved" monster-models.

Slapdash recap of classic horror-movie moments, including the monster's bemoaning his fate, his befriending a child, his warning a loved one (in this case, his wife) to stay away from him, etc. Film runs through these stock scenes so hastily that it verges on comedy. One unusual scene in which the monster is assailed by the "laughter" of store-window toys.

**VINDICATOR** see *Wheels of Fire*

**The VINEYARD** Northstar Ent. (Vineyard) 1989 color 95m. Story, SP, D: James Hong. D: also Bill Rice. SP: also James Marlowe, Douglas Condo. Story, P: Harry Mok. Ph: John Dirlam. Mus: Paul Francis Witt. AD: Daniel Hime. SpMkp: Peter Konig. Opt: Howard Anderson. SdFxEd: Adriane Marfiak. Ref: TV: New World Video. PT 4. V 1/24/90:186. With J. Hong, Karen Witter, Michael Wong, Cheryl Madsen, Lars Wanberg, Cheryl Lawson, Karl Heinz-Teuber, Robert Ito, Vivian Lee (Mother Po); Steven G. Allen, Rod White et al (zombies).

Dr. Elson Po (Hong) worships the Mayan voodoo god of wind in order to prolong his life, and keeps girls in chains in the basement, and zombies in sacred earth in the backyard. Ultimately, his old, old mother uses her own voodoo powers to unleash his zombies on him, and his amulet restores her youth and beauty.

Technically passable, otherwise godawful horror-fantasy lifts indiscriminately from *Night of the Living Dead* (motley zombies), *Son of Dracula* (Po's desire to make Witter's Jezebel Fairchild immortal, too), and *The Man Who Could Cheat Death.* Much padding with vapid action and suspense scenes. Presence of zombies is never explained.

**VINTAGE SEASON** see *Disaster in Time, A*

**VIOLACION FATAL** (Sp) 1977 feature (aka *Trauma*). D: Leon Klimovsky. Ref: MV: "slasher film." VSOM. With Agata Lys, Ricardo Merino, Sandra Alberti, Antonio Mayans.

**El VIOLADOR INFERNAL** (Mex) Eco Films & Esco Mex (Ulises Perez Aguirre) 1988 color c85m. D: Damian Acosta. SP: Cristobal Martell. Idea: Perez Aguirre. Ph: Armando Castillon. Mus: Rafael Garrido. Co-D: Pepe Medina. Ref: TV: Esco Mex Video; no Eng.; *The Infernal Rapist* - tr t. V(Cannes'89):476. With Noe Murayama, La Princess Lea, Ana Luisa Peluffo, Marisol Cervantes, Manuel Ibanez, Arturo Masson, Viviana Olivia, Blanca Nieves.

A princess of darkness uses her eye-rays to revive Carlos, an electrocuted rapist. As an invulnerable "hijo de satan" now, he knifes and rapes a (male) victim and writes "666" with a bloody knife on the body. He performs variations of this initial atrocity on a number of women. His own eye-rays — depending, apparently, on his mood — can variously start fires and make victims levitate .... Film promises — with the first appearance of the demon woman — to be agreeably campy, quickly degenerates into a slightly sick slasher movie.

**VIOLENCE JACK** (J) Pony Video 1990 anim color 37m. Ref: TV: Japan HV; no Eng. Animag 11:5: *Violence Jack: Hell's Wind.* 6:5: *Violence Jack: Hell Street* (1988/60m.). Imagi 1:43.

Something from space starts a volcano erupting and earthquakes leveling Tokyo. A huge mutant-type then begins gorily dispatching future thugs. Atmospheric design, sub-*Road Warrior* action.

**VIOLENT RAGE** see *Fearmaker, The*

**VIOLENT SHIT** (G) Tempe 75m. D: Andreas Schnaas. Ref: Tempe Video flyer: "ultra-gory story of Karl the Butcher." Bill Warren.

**VIOLENT SHIT II: MOTHER HOLD MY HAND** (G) Tempe 80m. D: Andreas Schnaas. Ref: Tempe Video flyer: "Decapitation is just the beginning!" Bill Warren.

**VIOLINO CHE UCCIDE, Il** see *Paganini Horror*

**VIPER** NBC-TV 1994 (1993) color c90m. Ref: TVG. With James McCaffrey, Dorian Harewood, Lee Chamberlin, Jon Polito.

"Futuristic city ... police supercar" with "no character."

**A VIRGEM DA COLINA** (Braz) Dragao Filmes 1977 color 85m. SP, D, P: Celso Falcao. Ph: A. Vianna. Ref: Hardy/HM; "weird variation on Oscar Wilde's 'The Picture of Dorian Gray'"; aka The Ring of Evil. with Jofre Soares, Christina Amaral, Edson Seretti.

Witch's ring gives new bride a split personality, and her "luridly monstrous" face begins to reflect her evil nature.

**VIRGEN DEL AKELARRE, La** see *Akelarre*

**VIRGIN** see *Child of Darkness, Child of Light*

**VIRGIN HUNTERS** see *Test Tube Teens from the Year 2000*

**VIRGIN TERROR** see *Trauma* (1978)

**VIRTUAL REALITY** Emerald City 1993? color feature. D: Paul Norman. Ref: vc box: "cybersexual ... ultra sex 2001." With Shayla, Debi Diamond.

**VIRTUAL WARS** see *Lawnmower Man, The*

**La VISIONE DEL SABBA** (I-F) Video Underground/Titanus/Gruppo Bema-Reteitalia & Cinemax (Achille Manzotti/Claudio Mancini) 1988 color 100m. (aka *The Witches' Sabbath*). Story, SP, D: Marco Bellocchio. SP: also Francesca Pirani. Ph: Giuseppe Lanci. Mus: Carlo Crivelli. AD: Giantito Burchiellaro. SpFX: Corridori. SdFX: Anzellotti. Ref: TV: Manzotti HV; no Eng. V 3/23/88. MV: aka *Evil Sabbath*. With Beatrice Dalle (Maddalena), Daniel Ezralow, Corinne Touzet, Omero Antonutti, Jacques Weber, Raffaella Rossellini, Eleonora di Mario (witch number 1), Helen Coste (Sabbath witch), Vanni Fois (Inquisitor).

Psychiatrist (Ezralow) enters his patient's mind, has fiery and watery visions. At the end, he "sees" Maddalena as a witch burning at a stake, in a courtyard, who somehow emerges un-

scathed. This is a happy ending, and probably the best thing about this psychological-horror-fantasy. Lesser Bellocchio, on the face of it.

**VISIONS** Monarch HV/Light Rain 1990 color 93m. SP,D,P: Steven Miller. SP: also Tom Taylor. Ref: V 10/1/90 (hv): "moderate interest ... horror picture." With Joe Balogh, Alice Villarreal, T. Taylor.

"Hero ... suffering from hallucinations ... holds the key to the identity of a serial killer ...."

**The VISITANTS** Rick Sloane 1987 color 93m. SP, D, P, Ed: R. Sloane. Mus: Matt Davis, David Nielsen. Creatures: Makeup FX Lab. Anim: Teague-Clark. Mkp: Vikki Griffin et al. Ref: TV: TWE video. no Phantom. Hound. Martin. Ecran F 71:81. With Marcus Vaughter, Johanna Grika, Joel Hile, Nicole Rio, William T. Dristas, Jeffrey Culver, David Teague (Halloween mummy); Terri Arnold, Brain Rambler (aliens), Jim Newman (alien leader).

Two aliens, Lubbock (Hile) and Exeter (Grika), from a "cold, barren, and frigid" planet, assume human guises on Earth, prepare for a full-scale invasion. Also on hand: a super-laser gun and a spaceship monster/"boarder".... Most of this comic hommage to *It Came from Outer Space* and company is plain dumb. Grika and Hile, however, as the aliens are dumb and funny. Difficult to sort out the intentionally from the unintentionally bad here. Highlight: Lubbock's quick, fake smiles.

**Les VISITEURS** (F) Gaumont & FR-3 & Alpilles & Amigo & Canal Plus (Alain Terzian) 1993 color 103m. SP, D: Jean-Marie Poire. SP: also C. Clavier. Mkp: Muriel Baurens. Ref: V 3/8/93: "crowd-pleasing time-travel comedy"; *The Visitors* - tr t.

Witch's potion propels protagonists "871 years into the future."

**The VISITORS** (Swedish) Vidmark/MVM (H. Ersgard/Film 87/88 Besoekarna) 1988('89-U.S.) color 104m.(c95m.-U.S.) (*Besoekarna*). SP, D: Joakim Ersgard. SP: also Patrik Ersgard. Mus: Peter Wallin. SpFX: Olov Nylander. SpVisFX: Animagica. Mkp: Kjell Gustavsson. SdFxEd: Anders Larsson. Ref: TV: Vidmark Ent. video; Eng. dubbed. V 5/25/88. Hound. Martin. With Kjell Bergqvist, Lena Endre, Joanna Berglund, Leif Gronvall (the demon).

"My visitors are on their way. I can hear them coming." A New York couple moves into a Swedish house with self-peeling wallpaper, a rat (or something) in the wall, swaying attic chandeliers, a flitting figure in the attic, and goo on the attic floor. ("Somebody with slimy feet left footprints in my attic!") A "boa constrictor" cable seems to squeeze a psychic investigator (Johannes Brost) to death, but he turns up again at the end, phantom-like.

More believable and methodical than most of its type, but overlong and rather skimpily plotted. Suggestive, economical sound effects do the work here of elaborate visual effects, and the ghost-demon appears, eerily, in only a shot or two.

**VIVI INVIDIERANNO I MORTI** see *Panic* (1983)

**VIZIO HA LE CALZE NERE, Il** see *Vice Wears Black Hose*

**VLCI BOUDA** (Cz) Barrandov (Ceskoslovensky Film/Jan Suster) 1987 color 92m. SP, D: Vera Chytilova. SP: also D. Fischerova. Mus: Michael Kocab. Ref: V 3/4/87: "strange, contrived allegory ... basically silly film"; *Wolf's Lair* - tr t? With Miroslav Machacek, Tomas Palaty, Stepanka Cervenkova.

Evil space creatures conduct an "endurance course" at a ski resort on Earth.

**VOCI DAL PROFONDO** see *Voices from Beyond*

**VOICES FROM BEYOND** (I) Executive Cine TV & Scena Group (Nannerini) 1991 color 91m. (*Voci dal Profondo*). Story, SP, D: Lucio Fulci. SP: also P. Regnoli. Ph: Sandro Grossi. Mus: Stelvio Cipriani. Mkp: Pino Ferranti. SdFX: G.J.S.T.A.R. Movie. Ref: TV: MV; Eng.-lang. version. Hardy/HM2. Stanley. V 5/27/91. no Martin. Palmerini. With Duilio del Prete, Karina Huff, Pascal Persiano, Sacha Darwin, Lorenzo Flaherty.

"Don't let them bury me!" The Autopsy Delight scene does not stop the corpse, Giorgio, from thinking out loud. Later, Giorgio comments on visitors at his funeral. Next, he appears spectrally to his beloved daughter Rosie, who's trying to solve his murder. Meanwhile, there are periodic progress reports on the state of decay of the corpse.... Giorgio Mainardi, a bore, dead or alive. Formulaic horror and sentiment, with incidental amusements — e.g., the ice-cube "avalanche" ... the eyeball "omelet" nightmare ... and the writhing-zombie-arms-in-the-crypt, visualized-nightmare sequence.

**VOLSUNG SAGA, The** see *Nibelungen, Die*

**VOLTES-V, VOL. 1** (J) Toei Video 1993? anim color 100m. Ref: Japan Video: monsters. vc box: sfa *Voltus 5* ? Hound: 1983.

**VOLTI DEL TERRORE, I** see *Cat in the Brain*

**VOODOO DAWN** Academy Ent./Stillwell Prods. (Steven Mackler/Bernard E. Goldberg) 1990 (1989) color 83m. (aka *Strange Turf*). D: Steven Fierberg. SP: John Russo, Jeffrey Delman, Thomas Rendon, Evan Dunsky. Ph: James McCalmont. Mus: Taj. SpMechFX: John Bisson;(des) Ken Walker. Mkp: R. Frieytez. Ref: TV. V 2/4/91:92(hv). no Maltin '92. Martin. Scheuer. With Raymond St. Jacques, Theresa Merritt, Gina Gershon, Kirk Baily, Billy "Sly" Williams, Tony Todd.

"I don't think it's human!" Voodoo priest Makoute (Todd)—once chief of the Haitian secret police, and "your worst nightmare" now—runs a zombie-tended plantation in the South. Voodoo-doll power temporarily slows him in his scheme to collect body parts for a ritual, but there's a hint that he is the *Alien*-inspired thing that emerges from the body of a zombie (J.G. Albrecht), at the end.

Mechanical, flatly-acted horror-fantasy. Merritt fills the Zelda Rubinstein role (*Poltergeist*) of eccentric midwife to the supernatural here. In this movie, a zombie is a human who has been drugged, buried alive, and had his will broken.

**2P VOODOO DEVIL DRUMS** Toddy c1946 b&w 44m. Ref: "Separate Cinema." Lee (FIR'73:381). no Lentz. PT 14:14.

Semi-documentary "re-creation" of black magic rites and zombie resurrection.

**VOODOO DOLLS** (Can.) Hilltop Films/Jack Braverman 1991 color feature. D: Andre Pelletier. Ref: V 2/18/91:71(rated). Martin. PT 16:12. With Maria Stanton.

Private-academy ghosts seduce schoolgirls.

**VOODOO LUST** Pure Class 1989 color c95m. D: J.-P. Ferrand, Peter Davy. Ref: vc box. Adam '90. With Rachel Ryan, Lynn LeMay, Victoria Paris, Peter North, Nina DePonca.

Voodoo in Haiti, 1936.

**VOTOMS** see *Armored Trooper Votoms*

**VOYAGE HOME, The** see *Star Trek IV*

**VOYAGE OF THE ROCK ALIENS** Inter Planetary Curb (Keller-Brian Russell) 1988 (1984) color 95m. (Attack of the Rock 'n' Roll Alien. When the Rain Begins To Fall - early titles). D: James Fargo. SP: S.J. Guidotti, E.Gold, C. Hairston. Mus: Jack White. PD: N. Dalton. SpVisFX: Image Engineering. Min: Tony Tremblay. OptFX: Apogee. Ref: V 2/10/88: Prism video. Phantom: "downright awful." V 5/6/87:176. Ecran F 43:25. HR 2/23/88:S-92. With Pia Zadora, Tom Nolan, Craig Sheffer, Michael Berryman, Ruth Gordon, Jermaine Jackson.

Space aliens searching for rock music.

**VOYAGE TO NEXT** see *Cosmic Eye, The*

**VOYAGER FROM THE UNKNOWN** NBC-TV 1982-3 color 91m. Ref: vc box. Hound. Castleman. With Jon-Erik Hexum, Meeno Peluce, Ed Begley Jr., Faye Grant, Fionnula Flanagan.

Two episodes from the "Voyagers!" TV series, re a race of time travelers.

**VOYEUR** see *Innocent Prey*

**VREDENS DAG** see *Day of Wrath*

**VUOTO INTORNO, II** see *Macabre* (1968)

# W

**WAILING, The** see *Fear* (1980)

**WAKE OF THE DEAD** see *Gorotica*

**WALKERS** see *From the Dead of Night*

**WALTON EXPERIENCE, The** see *Fire in the Sky*

**WAM BAM, THANK YOU SPACE MAN** see *Erotic Encounters of the Fourth Kind*

**WANDERER NEVER RESTS EVEN ON THE ROAD, A** see *Man with Three Coffins, The*

**WANDERING KID** (J) Island World/JAVN (Yasuhito Yamaki) 1989 anim color 38m. (*Urotsukidoji*). D: Hideki Takayama. SP: Noboru Aikawa, from the comic by Toshio Maeda. Ph: N. Sugaya. Ref: TV: Penthouse Video; no Eng. Cinef 6/91: OAV;

*Legend of the Overfiend* - 108m. edition of 1st 3 in this series; '93-U.S. Imagi 1:38-43. SFChron Dtbk 10/3/93. V 10/4/89: *Legend* ...2/21/90:147,176(ad). 3/1/93:20. Red Vic Theatre notes. V 2/25/91:A-32(ad). 3/15/93:56(ad).

A cat-man fights a demon-man of a thousand phalluses who apparently becomes a shape-shifting Cyclopean horror which hatches a gremlin-dinosaur thing which, fried, becomes a high-school boy. At the end, the giant winged demon's phalluses take over an entire building and seem to absorb human souls ....Lots of demon/human sex in the semi-porn, semi-imaginative flights of gruesome fancy here.

See also: *Legend of the Demon Womb. Urotsuki Doji 2. Urotsuki Doji — Mataiden. Urotsukidoji: The Future, Part 3.*

**WANNA-BE'S** (J) Central Park Media/MOVIC & Sony Music Ent. (Kishi-Takahashi/Artmic, AIC & Animate Film) 1986 ('92-U.S.) anim color 47m. D: Yatsuo Hasegawa. SP: Toshimitsu Suzuki, from his comic. Ph: M. Okino. Mus: Hiroshi Arakawa. AD: M. Matsumiya. Anim D: Y. Shimizu. Monster Des: Kakinuma, Hayashi. Mecha Des: S. Aramaki. Ref: TV: U.S. Manga Corps video; Eng. titles. Voices: Eriko Hara, Miki Takahashi et al.

"I want strength." Employing "DNA cloning," "spontaneous cellular mutation," and "antibody YX," Dr. Sawada produces a virus which allows him to "reconstruct" the "body systems" of lady wrestlers Eri and Miki. As super-strong "supergals" — a "couple of fireballs" — they go on to beat the intimidating Foxy Ladies in a WWB Asia heavyweight match. The doc also creates "Papa," a big monster which looks like a "pile of octopus and moldy old beans".... Banal crossing of *Goldengirl* and Mexican *Wrestling Women* pictures.

**WANPAKU OJI NO OROCHITAIJI** see *Little Prince and Eight Headed Dragon*

**WAR** Troma 1988 color 99m. (aka *Troma's War* - vc ad t. *Club War* - orig t). SP,D,P: Lloyd Kaufman. D,P: Michael Herz. SP: also M. Dana, E. Hattler, T. Martinek. SpFxCoord: William Jennings, Pericles Lewnes. SpFxMkp: Stephen Patrie, Paul Pisoni et al. Ref: V 9/28/88: "splatterfest." 10/19/88:185. HR 12/22/88. Phantom: "brain dead."

**\*The WAR OF THE WORLDS** 1953(1952). Astronomical Art: Chesley Bonestell. Paintings: Jan Domela et al. Props: Ivyl Burks et al. Narrator: Cedric Hardwicke; Paul Frees. Ref: TV: Para HV. Warren/KWTS! Lee. V 3/4/53. Hardy/SF. With Paul Birch, Carolyn Jones, Charles Gemora (Martian), Walter Sande, Ann Codee, Ivan Lebedeff, Robert Rockwell, Alvy Moore, Russell Conway.

"From the blackness of outer space, we were being scrutinized and studied ...." "Invaders from space" begin landing on Earth. And although the heat-ray-equipped "Mars machines" seem invulnerable, the Martians themselves are physically flimsy—the "littlest things" (bacteria) halt the invasion.... Horror highlights: the ever-prowling, hovering war machines (with their electromagnetic shields) ... the harrowingly prying, snake-necked electronic "eyes" of the latter ... the pulsations of the "eyes" ... and the slowly unscrewing cap of the "meteor." Sf classic is still worth seeing for its horrific spectacle, but so much of the film is simply undistinguished—indifferent dialogue and melodrama. And the

movie might have been eerier in black and white. Still, love that lightning in the opening credits. Complete with a Day the Town Stood Still sequence.

**WAR OF THE WORLDS: THE RESURRECTION** (U.S-Can.) Para-TV/Triumph Ent. & Ten-Four Prods. (Jonathan Hackett/Strangis) 1988 color c90m. D: Colin Chilvers. Tel: Greg Strangis, based on the 1953 movie *War of the Worlds* and on the H.G. Wells novel. Ph: David Herrington. Mus: Billy Thorpe. PD: Gavin Mitchell. SpFxCoord: Ted Ross. Alien Prosth: Bill Sturgeon. Min:(sup) Dale Fay;(ph) Light & Motion. Mkp: Jane Meade. Ref: TV: TV-series pilot or premiere aka a TV-movie. V 10/19/88:496. ad. Oak Trib 10/14/88. San Jose M News 10/7/88. With Jared Martin, Lynda Mason Green, Philip Akin, Richard Chaves, John Vernon, Richard Comar, Gwynyth Walsh, Ilse von Glatz, Eugene Clark, Michael Rudder, Corinne Conley, Rachel Blanchard.

"What would you say if I told you that Earth is being invaded by aliens from another planet?" The aliens from the 1953 movie are coming out of their forced hibernation in sealed drums at the Fort Jericho Disposal Site, while Hangar 15 harbors the old Martian war machines. The clutching hands here don't fool around. And if it is kind of exciting to see the machines move again, little wholly-new excitement is provided by this telefilm/series-premiere.

See also *Adventures of Buckaroo Banzai. Bad Channels. Spaced Invaders. War of the Worlds.*

**WARLOCK** Trimark/New World (Steve Miner/M.M. Fottrell) 1989 (1988) color 102m. D: S. Miner. SP: David T. Twohy. Ph: David Eggby. Mus: Jerry Goldsmith. VisFX:(coord) Patrick Read Johnson; Perpetual Motion Pictures;(sup) Robert Habros;(anim sup) Mauro Maressa;(stopmo) Laine Liska; Dream Quest Images, Jeff Burks. SpMkpFX: Mkp Imagineering;(channeller) Alec Gillis, Tom Woodruff Jr. SpFxCoord: Ken Pepiot. VisMkpFX: Carl Fullerton, Neal Martz. Ref: TV. MFB'89:190-1. V 5/24/89. ad. With Richard E. Grant, Julian Sands, Lori Singer, Mary Woronov (channeller), Kevin O'Brien, Richard Kuss.

A freak storm propels witchfinder Giles Redferne (Grant) and a warlock (Sands)—"evil absolute"—from 1691 Boston to 1988 Los Angeles, where the two race to find the legendary *Grand Grimoire*—variously called a "book most dire," the *Book of Shadows*, and the *Key of Solomon*—which book has the power to "undo" creation.

Time-hopping adversaries are a movie cliche now, in both science fiction and horror, but *Warlock* spices its chills with humor and adventure, and the Goldsmith score lends the lightweight fun here some substance, mood, and drive. Many amusing effects "asides"—e.g., the torn page re-joining, the hell-bat, the warlock zipping out of the plane's cargo hold.

**WARLOCK** see *Skullduggery*

**WARLOCK: THE ARMAGEDDON** Trimark/Tapestry (Abrams-Levy/Zahavi) 1993 color 93m. D: Anthony Hickox. SP: Kevin Rock, Sam Bernard. Story: Rock. Ph: Gerry Lively. Mus: Mark McKenzie. PD: Steve Hardie. MkpSpFX: Bob Keen. MechFX:(sup) J. Thompson;(coord) S. Galich. VisFX: BB&J.

DigitalVisFX: The Post Group. SdDes: F. Serafine. SpVocalFX: Frank Welker. Ref: TV. V 9/20/93: "very effective special fx work." 3/8/93:22 (rated). 5/24/93:38. ad. With Julian Sands (Warlock), Chris Young, Paula Marshall, R.G. Armstrong, Bruce Glover, Zach Galligan, Joanna Pacula, Steve Kahan, Charles Hallahan, Ferdy Mayne, George "Buck" Flower.

"The warlock is here!" Follow-up to *Warlock* concerns "Druidic rune stones"(V) ... a lunar eclipse which heralds a slimy, *Xtro* birth and a full-grown Warlock ... voodoo-doll-type, Warlock havoc ... a teenager shot to death and revived as a Druid warrior ... and a devil from the Pit.... More of those little-extra effects touches—e.g., the Warlock walking down "steps" in mid-air. Pretty, sparkly effects alternate with offputtingly offhand, gross gore. Good: the two-sides-to-every-mirror sequence. Mixed: the human "sculpting" sequence, which is visually impressive, but mean-spirited.

**WARLORD** see *Mirai Ninja*

**WARLORDS** American-Independent (Harel Goldstein) 1988 color 87m. D,Co-P: Fred Olen Ray. SP: Scott Ressler. SpMkpFX: John Nolan. Ref: V 11/29/89: "dim plotline." McCarty II: "has absolutely nothing to recommend it." vc box. V 10/19/88:168. Martin. With David Carrradine, Dawn Wildsmith, Sid Haig, Ross Hagen, Robert Quarry, Brinke Stevens, Victoria Sellers, Cleve Hall, Debra Lamb, Michelle Bauer.

"Radioactive future ... mutant hordes." (vcb)

**WARLORDS** Video 10 1989 color feature. D: Tyler Von. Ref: Adam '93G: *Mad Max*-like. With Neil Thomas.

**WARLORDS 3000** Col-TriStar HV 1993 color feature. D: Faruque Ahmed. Ref: SFChron Dtbk 8/15/93. V 6/7/93:14 (rated). With Jay Roberts, Wayne Duvall, Steven Blanchard.

"In the year 3000, a single man takes on the drug lords who control the barbaric future." (SFC)

**THE WARNING** (B) Aubrey Baring 1938 b&w feature? Ed: R.Q. McNaughton. Narrator: Sir John Anderson. Ref: PFA notes 8/15/88. William K. Everson. no Gifford/BC.

"A prophecy of World War II and its air-raids ...."

***WARNING SHADOWS** Pan-Film 1922 77m. (aka *Die Nacht der Erkenntnis*). SP: also A. Robison. Story,AD: A. Grau. Mus: Ernst Riege. Ref: Screen. PFA notes 9/17/87. MFB '75:146. Hardy/HM. Lee. Eisner/Haunted Screen: 1923. V 12/3/24. Martin. Scheuer. With Alexander Granach (the Shadow-master), Gustav von Wangenheim, Ferdinand von Alten.

The Shadow-Master's spell makes the principals herein mentally enact a tragedy. In a "Twilight Zone"-like surprise ending, their shadows return — in, apparently, time-lapse photography — to them, and tragedy is averted. Concluding shots hint that the shadow man is the devil himself .... If the tragedy depicted is a rather slow dull one — the film's one dead zone — the returning-shadows twist is chilly, and the movie also has some neat silhouette animation. The idea of the hypnotic warning returns in 1952's *Invasion U.S.A.*

**WARNING SIGN** Fox/Barwood-Robbins (Jim Bloom) 1985 color 100m. SP, D: Hal Barwood. SP, Exec P: Matthew Robbins. Ph: Dean Cundey. Mus: Craig Safan. SpFxSup: J. Kevin Pike. MkpSup: Edouard Henriques III. VideoFxSup: G.L. McMurry. SupSdFxEd: Alan Splet. Ref: TV. V 8/21/85. pr. Stockton Record 8/24/85. SFChron 8/23/85. With Sam Waterston, Kathleen Quinlan, Yaphet Kotto, Jeffrey DeMunn, Richard Dysart, G.W. Bailey, Rick Rossovich.

"The Corn That Ate Chicago?" BioTek Agronomics is working on a germ warfare "reply"—a weapon to affect the "rage center" of brains and "drive people crazy." An errant test tube, however, sets off a "biohazard" alert: "The bug is virulent—80 percent mortality rate." Plus a "regular Dr. Frankenstein" (Dysart), seeming "zombies," and an immune carrier (Bailey).

*Warning Sign* is less a science-horror *Silkwood* than an updated *Whip Hand* or *The Crazies*. It's competent, and the first half isn't bad, but it's pretty familiar, and not as slick-of-kind as *Endangered Species*. In sum: generally glib ironies, narrative loose ends, and the usual coverup by the authorities.

**WARPED** see *Tales of the Unknown*

**The WARRIOR AND THE SORCERESS** (U.S.-Arg) New World-Aries/New Horizons 1984 color 76m. (*Cain del Planeta Oscuro*. aka *Kain of the Dark Planet*). SP,D,Co-P: John Broderick. SP: also Bill Stout. Mus: Louis Saunders. SpFX: Richard Lennon. SpMkpFX: Chris Biggs. Ref: TV. V 5/16/84. 7/27/83:32. 3/21/84:6(rated). 5/4/83:468. IFG'84. With David Carradine, Luke Askew, Maria Socas, Harry Townes.

A time when men were violent and women wore few clothes — and some women had four breasts. Cast of critters includes a big, many-tentacled, but rather innocuous-looking monster in a dungeon ... a little lizard creature (leftover from *Deathstalker?*)... and men with either very strange masks or reptilian skin.... Undistinguished action fare set in an unstated time and place. The barebreasted heroine (she's not the one with four of them) is not really a sorceress.

**WARRIOR OF THE LOST WORLD** (I) American Nat'l./Visto Int'l.(A.D.I./Eduard Sarlui/Bessi-Hildebrand) 1985 (1983) color 80m. (*Il Guerriero del Mondo Perduto*). SP,D: David Worth. Mus: Daniele Patucchi. SpFX: Paolo Ricci. MkpFX: Otelo Fava. SdFX: Roberto Arcangeli. Ref: TV: MMI-TV. V 6/12/85. 4/27/83:14 (ad). 7/13/83:34. Horacio Higuchi. HR 10/25/83:S-24. Ecran F48:9 With Robert Ginty, Persis Khambatta, Donald Pleasence, Fred Williamson, Harrison Muller.

"The nuclear war has been fought. The Earth is in ruins." In a regimented future society, the Terminator-114 machine terminates slackers, and the Anti-Mind-114 mind-control device and an energy-sapping invention produce workers for the assembly line of the Congress of the Omega. Extra addeds: a mountain "wall of illusion," a cave of spiders and snakes, "Visceral Video," supersonic speedcycles, a forty-megaton "mega-weapon," and a villain (Pleasence) who turns out to be an android/clone. Actionful *Road Warrior* clone has the tone and substance of a high school rally. Larky, weightless violence ... good moving-camera work (by Giancarlo Ferrando). Most important line (for the protagonists): "Be quiet and watch out for mutants!"

**WARRIORS FROM THE MAGIC MOUNTAIN** see *Zu*

**WARRIORS OF THE APOCALYPSE** (U.S.-Fili) Lightning Video/Film Concept Group (Just Betzer) 1986 color 95m. (*Time Raiders. Searchers of the Voodoo Mountain* - alt ts). Story,D,P: Bobby A. Suarez. SP: Ken Metcalfe. Ph: Jun Pereira. PD: R.A. Nicdao. Ref: V 10/7/87: "subpar." Ecran F 48:70: British?? Scheuer: "pretty dreary." With Michael James, D. Moore, Franco Guerrero, K. Metcalfe.

Post-nuke mutants.

**WARRIORS OF THE WIND** (J) New World/Tokuma Shoten & Hakuhodo/Toru Hara (Isao Takahata) 1985 anim color/ws 117m. (93m.-U.S.) (*Nausicaa. Nausicaa of the Valley of the Wind. Kaze No Tani No Naushika*). SP, D: Hayao Miyazaki. Ph: Kazuo Komatsubara. Mus: Mamoru Hisaishi (or Ken Kisaishi). AD: Mitsuki Nakamura. Anim Sup: Kazuo Komatsubara. Ref: screen: Eng. dubbed. TV: vt (*Nausicaa*); no Eng. PFA notes 4/15/86: Swank Pictures. J Anim Program Guide. J Anim Archives 2:12-13. Animag 9:12-13: based on a comic strip. Ecran F 52:54,59: Mus: Shigeharu Shiba. Voices: (J version) Sumi Shimamoto, Yoji Matsuda.

"Somewhere in the world, one thousand years from now," long after the cataclysmic Seven Days of Fire. For the ecology-minded: pollution-filtering Toxic Forests (with their giant gorgons, gadflies, dragonflies, and bloodsuckers), Acid Lakes, and windmills. For the action-minded: routine battle scenes between the Torumekians and the Pejite Empire. Out of it all: an absurd-sweet ending in which the gorgon hordes, or Ohmu, use their insect feelers to resurrect the dead Princes Zandra (Nausicaa in the original), rescuer of a gorgon baby. Even the fire demon, or giant God-Soldier—"creature from the ancient world," and unholy remnant of the Seven Days of Fire—can't stop the sweetness.

If the abridged American version of *Nausicaa* is dramatically wanting, it's visually enchanting. Forget the involved plot re the "endless ironies of life," and note the visual detail, the strange animals in their strange settings, the work with shadows, etc. *Nausicaa* itself, an early, lesser, but still worthwhile Miyazaki animated feature, has problems with wooden character animation and flat battle passages, but issues in that same balmily-inspiring ending.

**WARUDO APATOMENTO HORA** see *World Apartment Horror*

**WARUM DIE UFOS UNSEREN SALAT KLAUEN** (W.G.) Cine-Contor (Martin Haeussler) 1979 color 91m. (*Berliner Ballade II* - orig t. *Checkpoint Charly* or *Checkpoint Charlie, Oder Das Chaos Schlaegt Zurueck* - vt t). SP,D: Hansjuergen Pohland. SP: also Heinz Freitag. Mus: Kraan. Opt: Studio Bartoschek. Ref: V 4/18/84: *Why the UFOs Steal Our Lettuce* - tr t. Dr. Rolf Giesen. Horacio Higuchi. no Stanley. no Hardy/SF. With Tomas Piper, U. Monn, Curd Juergens (alien), Kurt Raab, Hildegard Knef, Pavla Ustinov (alien), Herbert Fux.

Aliens monitor an Earth biologist experimenting with explosive lettuce. "The very badness of this film will, of course, assure it some new status, and it really is enough of a mess to make it hold its own in any Worst Movies Ever context." (V)

**The WASHING MACHINE** (I-F-Hung.) Esse & Eurogroup & Focus(Canzie & Koob) 1993 color/ws 85m. D: Ruggero Deodato. SP: Luigi Spagnoli(sp?). Ph: Sergio D'Offizi. Mus: Claudio Simonetti. AD: Pintus, Stork. SdFX: CSS, R. Marinelli. Ref: TV: VSOM; Eng. titles. Palmerini. With Philippe Caroit, Yorgo Voyagis, Kashia Figura, Ilaria Borrelli.

"Each is more crazy than the next." Was a man's sliced-up, bloody body found in a washing machine or was it all an hallucination or a fairy tale told by one of the three weird sisters here? ("A man cut into little pieces and put into the machine like dirty laundry.") Did the cat really find and eat a severed hand? At any rate, the cannibalism sequence is definitely just someone's (visualized) nightmare, and the gory finale is for real.... Perhaps-necessarily-unworkable cross between a standard gore vehicle, a softcore sex film, and *Rashomon*.

**WASP** see *Evil Spawn*

**WATARI AND THE SEVEN MONSTERS** (J-Taiwanese) 1969? color/ws 100m. (sfa or sequel to *The Magic World of Watari?*). Ref: Lee. With K. Yoshinobu, W. Pin-Pin.

Giant bird, scorpion ... lobster-monster ... eagle-man ... two-headed dragon.

**WATCH OUT** (H.K.) Tony Film 1988? color c90m. D,P: Tony Leung. Ref: TV: World Video; Eng. titles. NST! 4:39.

Fairly cute comedy-fantasy features prankish ghosts and invisible-man-type stunts and temporarily turns horrific during the climactic midnight sequence, in which a possessed man runs amok, and an angry ghost inhabits a dying, spirit-vacated man. Highlight: the lively ghost-unborn foiling a mugging.

**WATCHERS** (Can.-U.S.) Univ/Carolco/Centaur Films & Concorde/Rose & Ruby & Canadian Ent. Investors No. 2 & Co. Ltd. (Roger Corman/Mary Eilts/David Mitchell) 1988 color 91m. D: Jon Hess. SP, Co-P: Damian Lee. SP: also Bill Freed. From Dean R. Koontz's novel. Mus: Joel Goldsmith. SpFxCoord: Dean Lockwood. Cost Des: Monique Stranan. Creature SdFX: Denise McCormick. Mkp: Linda A. Brown. SpPropsSup: David Miller. Ref: TV. ad. V 12/21/88. MFB'89:218-19. With Corey Haim, Barbara Williams, Michael Ironside, Blu Mankuma, Duncan Fraser, Phillip Wong (Oxcom-7).

"This has Sasquatch written all over it!" Oxcom-7—the "ultimate predator"—and GH3, or "Furface," a genius-dog and hated prey of Oxcom-7, "share genetic material." Shaggy Oxcom-7 follows furry GH3 wherever he goes, and "gruesome murders" inevitably result. The "third experiment" of the Francis Project (to increase the intelligence of animals): the government's own man, Lem Johnson (Ironside), the "perfect killing machine." ("No conscience....")

The perils-of-pets problem broached by the script has an obvious solution: Just give him the dog. Routine action and suspense except for the initially intriguing Furface-as-homing-device idea. Ironside gives the only noteworthy performance, as the regulation vicious, unscrupulous government ogre. This time, though, there's a scientific explanation for his unscrupulousness.

**WATCHERS II** Concorde-Centaur (Roger Corman)/New Horizons 1990 color 97m. (*The Outsider* - orig t. *Watchers II: The*

*Outsider* - int t). D: Thierry Notz. SP: Henry Dominic. Mus: Rick Conrad. SpMkpFX: Joe Podner, John Criswell. Outsider: Dean Jones, W.S. Jones;(voice) Tony Pope;(vision fx) Motion Opticals;(vis fx des) Kevin Kutchaver. Ref: TV. V 6/27/90. 10/25/89:28. 11/22/89:11. 12/6/89:20. With Marc Singer, Tracy Scoggins, Jonathan Farwell, Irene Miracle, Mary Woronov, Tom Poster (Outsider), Kip Addota, Raquel Rios.

"I told you to stay out of the basement!" In this reworking of *Watchers,* Anodyne's Aesop Project genetically links the monstrous, uncontrollable, "new intelligent life form" AE74—the "Outsider, a "killing machine"—with AE73, or Einstein, a "very intelligent" dog.... Routine action-horror scenes with AE74 alternate with okay comedy from AE73, though the canine-friendly computer is a bit much. Singer brings the right note of amused detachment to his dog's-best-friend role. Telegraphed shocks.

**WATCHERS 3** New Horizons/Luis Llosa (Pacific Trust) 1994 color feature. D: J. Stanford. SP: M. Palmer. Ref: vc box. With W. Hauser.

**The WATER ENGINE** TNT-TV/Amblin-TV & Turner Pictures (Brandman Prods./D.P. Borchers) 1992 color 89m. D: Steven Schachter. Tel: David Mamet, from his play. Ph: Bryan England. Mus: A. Jans. PD: Barry Robison. Props: D.A. Carpender. SpFX: John Hartigan. MatteFX: J. Silver. SdFX: ToddA-O, Glen Glenn. MkpSup: B. Bryant. Ref: TV. TVG 8/22/92. V 8/24/92:65. SFChron 8/24/92. With Charles Durning, Patti LuPone, W.H. Macy, John Mahoney, Joe Mantegna, Joanna Miles, Treat Williams, Andrea Marcovicci, Martin Sheen, Horton Foote, Jr.

"It runs on water." Illinois. An engineer/inventor (Macy) "frees" the hydrogen in water and generates eight horsepower out of his "water engine".... Mamet, obviously a fan of *The Man in the White Suit,* comes up with familiar corporate skullduggery. The characters all speak in the same, self-conscious manner. Some okay ironic touches re the glories of unfettered technological progress.

**WATER THAT IS PASSED, The** see *Passing, The*

**WAX, OR THE DISCOVERY OF TELEVISION AMONG THE BEES** Jasmine T. Films 1992 color and b&w 85m. SP, D, P: David Blair. Ph: M. Kaplan. Mus & Sd: Morales, Williamson. Ref: V 11/2/92: "visionary science fiction film." U.C. Theatre notes. With Blair, Meg Savlov, Florence Ormezzano, William Burroughs.

"Spirits of the future dead inhabit the bodies of bees that implant a special form of television inside the head of the protagonist."(V)

**WAXWORK** Vestron/Ahrenberg-Sotela (Palla Pictures & HBF)/Electric 1988 color 97m. (*Wax Works* - orig t). SP, D: Anthony Hickox. Mus: Roger Bellon. SpMkpFX: Bob Keen, Image Animation. Werewolf/Hand FX: Steve Hardie. SpSdDes: Leonard Marcel. OptFX: Howard Anderson. Ref: TV: Vestron Video. V 9/14/88. MFB'89:219. V 8/26/87:26. With Zach Galligan, Deborah Foreman, Michelle Johnson, David Warner, Patrick Macnee, Miles O'Keeffe (Count Dracula), John Rhys-Davies (werewolf), Paul Badger (mummy), Merle Stronck (vampire), Dan Ireland (zombie).

"Weird place for a waxwork." Weird owner, too—Mr. Lincoln (Warner), who sold his soul to the devil and whose exhibits are "time vessels" which take the unwary to the times and places of the characters displayed, which latter include Dracula and other vampires, a werewolf, the Phantom of the Opera, an Egyptian mummy ("It's the mummy!"), and (in a black-and-white sequence) Romero zombies.

Pointless except as an encore for old monsters. And the "In the Picture" segment of *Three Cases of Murder* did the "living exhibit" idea better. Only impressive sequence: the coming to life of all the wax figures, including a monster-baby, a snake thing, an alien or two, a Little-Shop-type horror ("Feed me!"), and a Frankenstein-monster-type.

**WAXWORK II: LOST IN TIME** Live/Seven Arts (Electric Pictures/Nancy Paloian/Mario Sotela) 1992 (1991) color 104m. (*Lost in Time* - B). SP, D: Anthony Hickox. Mus: Steve Schiff. SpMkpFX: Image Animation; Bob Keen;(lenses) Bob May. Voice:(the hand) Wayne Anderson. OptFX:(sp) R.D. Bailey; Digital Visions. SpAnimFX: Lynda Weinman; Glenn Campbell. SpFxCoord: Kevin McCarthy. Ref: TV. V 7/13/92. SFChron Dtbk 6/7/92. Jones. With Zach Galligan, Sophie Ward, Alexander Godunov, Bruce Campbell, Patrick Macnee, Martin Kemp (Baron Frankenstein), David Carradine, Jim Metzler, Juliet Mills, John Ireland, George "Buck" Flower, Stefanos Miltsakakis (Frankenstein's monster), Erin Gourlay (ghost girl), Maxwell Caulfield, Shanna L. Teare (panther girl), F.A. Zagarino (zombie killer), Treasure Little, Michael Viela (Dr. Jekyll), Paul Jones (the hand), Drew Barrymore (vampire victim), Steve Painter (Nosferatu), Alex Butler (Jack the Ripper), Godzilla (as himself).

"They came alive!" In addition to the kitchen sink, undisciplined follow-up to *Waxwork* throws in a living severed hand, Jason's hockey mask, a time compass, bat creatures, Baron Frankenstein and his monster and some comic gore, *Alien* "things" on a spaceship, a black-magic shape-shifter who impersonates a king, Sir Wilfred (Macnee) as (at one point) a Poe-quoting raven, Mr. Hyde, *Dawn of the Dead*-type, mall-haunting zombies, spirit possession, Jack the Ripper, a facsimile of the original Nosferatu, a Godzilla imitation and a joke re bad dubbing, and a Dr. Satan-style robot.

Or, Mark and Elenore's Vacuous Adventure. A more-accurate subtitle might be Lost in Other Movies. Generally, the longer the pastiche, the draggier. Near the end, the principals whiz in and out of various movie modes, and the crazy-revolving-door effect gets to be fun. Most unexpected, because relatively arcane, cross-reference: *The Haunting* vignette, which is in black and white and plays tricks with widescreen distortions.

**WAY TO THE VIRGIN SPACE** see *Mirror of Arei, The*

**WE CAN REMEMBER IT FOR YOU WHOLESALE** see *Total Recall*

**The WEATHERING CONTINENT** (J) Bandai/Emotion (Haruki Kadokawa) 1992 anim color/ws 55m. (aka *Neo-Heroic-Legend: The Weathering Continent*). Ref: TV: Kadokawa Video; OAV?; no Eng. (apart from title). Japan Video. Animerica 6:10.

Wanderers in a future, lyrically bleak wasteland come upon a city under a spell. At first, they find "frozen," masked townspeople, then ominous stacks of masks. Activated, the latter alternately click together like castanets and "spit" deadly wires which make their victims shrivel up instantly. The spellcaster seems to be a huge Buddha-type stone. One mask "grows" a body which comes to life, then disappears. Finally, all the masks begin emanating oppressive sound waves .... A very eerie, puzzling business here. A good musical score and beautifully-drawn backgrounds reinforce the basic weirdness.

Follow-up notes based on the S. Baldric Prods. video (with titles in English): "Before the ancient times ... there was a continent in the ocean." A psychic ("Sometimes I can't distinguish the sounds of the dead from the sounds of the living") is among those who come across the "fabled city of Azec Sistura." ("This is a city made for the dead.") The long-gone citizens recipe for eternal happiness: masks which cover the faces of the (fully dressed) shriveled-up corpses and which, at times, seem animated by the spirits of the dead. ("Their souls are still here.") A curse on robbers activates the "spitting" wires.... The tale and presence of the masks remain eerie; the story of the three present-day protagonists seems mainly functional.

**The WEB** (B) Joan Ashworth 1987 anim 18m. Ref: SFFilm Fest guide: an "army of homunculi."

**WEB OF DESIRE** 1994 color c90m. Ref: Vallejo T-H 9/3/95. With Tina Tyler, Crystal Wilder.

Horrific scientific experiment yields a "sex-crazed Black Widow."

**WEDLOCK** see *Deadlock*

**WEEKEND AT BERNIE'S II** TriStar/Artimm/Victor Drai(Joseph Perez/D&A) 1993 (1992) color 89m. SP, D: Robert Klane. Mus: Peter Wolf. PD: M. Bolton. SpFxCoord: Ken Speed. Mkp: Lon Bentley. Title Seq: Bronco/Fox;(des) Michael Butkus. Ref: TV. V 2/15/93: "mildly diverting." SFChron 7/10/93: "bad film." With Andrew McCarthy, Jonathan Silverman, Terry Kiser (Bernie), Barry Bostwick.

"Raise this man from the dead." St. Thomas, the Virgin Islands. Voodoo spell makes dead man get up and move "whenever music plays." (SFC) Living-dead Bernie proves to be a "great dancer," in a conga line, in the movie's only amusing sequence. The Bernie-and-Brenda (Jennie Moreau) team here is an oasis in a comedy desert. As a zombie comedy, though, this is slightly preferable to *My Boyfriend's Back.*

**WEIRD FANTASY** LA Video 1986 color 80m. SP,D: E.P. Regis. Mus: Shelby. Ref: vc box. Adam '90: 1987. With Tracey Adams, Niki Randall, Steve Drake, Buddy Love.

Two teens use a computer to create the "perfect woman."

**WEIRD SCIENCE** Univ (Joel Silver/Jane Vickerilla) 1985 color 94m. SP,D: John Hughes. Mus: Ira Newborn. SpVisFX: R/Greenberg; (sup) Joel Hynek. SpAnimFX: Robert Mrozowski. Mech Anim: David Kelsey. SpFX: Henry Millar, D.M. Blitstein et al. SpMkp: Craig Reardon. SpSdFX: D.M. Hemphill. Ref: TV. MFB'85:351-2. V 8/7/85. FQ Spring '86:64-5. Sacto Union

8/3/85. With Anthony Michael Hall, Kelly LeBrock, Ilan Mitchell-Smith, Bill Paxton, Suzanne Snyder, Robert Downey, Robert Rusler, Michael Berryman (mutant biker), Jeff Jensen (metal face).

Shermer, Illinois. Two high school kids (Hall and Mitchell-Smith use a computer, a doll, and lightning to produce a dream girl (LeBrock) with the body of a centerfold and the IQ of Einstein ... and magic powers. ("She's alive!") Also: *Exorcist* effects, mutant motorcyclists, and a colorized '31 *Frankenstein* on TV ....Weird fiction. Lots of hopefully-crowd-pleasing effects grafted onto a phony morality play. Zero resonance, zero integrity, one fun sequence in which all the effects damage undoes itself.

**The WEIRD WORLD OF LSD** Americana Ent. (Roberts) 1967 color? feature. D: Robert Ground. Ref: PT 14:48: "faces mutate (rubber monster masks are used)." Lee(p).

**The WEIRDO** Rapid Film Group/Green Tiger (Haker-Friedenn) 1990 (1988) color 91m. (aka *Weirdo. Weirdo -The Beginning* - cr t). SP, D, Ph: Andy Milligan. Mus: M. Meros, J. Peters. AD: Gerald Jackson. Prosth: Matsui. Ref: TV: Raedon HV. V 2/7/90:171(hv): "okay psychological thriller." McCarty II: "cheap gore." Hound. Cinef: "murder and mutilation." With Steve Burington, Jessica Straus, Naomi Sherwood.

"He wouldn't hurt anybody!" "Sudden movement" scares Donnie; Mom's razor-strap treatment provokes him into severing her head with a handy cleaver. Next, Cecil gets pitchforked, and a church cross becomes an unlikely weapon. Donnie finds he has to kill just about everyone, for various, progressively less buyable reasons. Limbs get lopped off here as if they were papier-mache. The film's first half is kind of sweet, but dull, predictable psychological drama. Odd, intriguing ending.

**WEISILI ZHUANQI** see *Legend of Wisely, The*

**WELCOME BACK MR. FOX** Walter W. Pitt III 1983 color 21m. Ref: Hound: cryogenics. With Gustav Vintas.

**WELCOME TO OBLIVION** see *Ultra Warrior*

**WELCOME TO SPRING BREAK** (I-U.S.) IVE/Laguna Ent. (Elpico/Immerman) 1990 (1989) color 91m. (aka *Nightmare Beach — La Spiaggia del Terrore*). Story,SP,D: Harry Kirkpatrick. Story: also V. Rambaldi. Mus: C. Simonetti. PD: T. Sagone. SpVisFX: Alex Rambaldi. SpFX: Gary Bentley. Ref: Horacio Higuchi. V 10/22/90: "unsuccessful and in poor taste." Fango 98. Hound. V/Cannes '89:118. With N. de Toth, Sarah Buxton, R. Valverde, Lance Le Gault, Michael Parks, John Saxon.

"Grisly murders." (V)

**Die WELT OHNE MASKE** (G) Ariel Film 1934 b&w 109m. D: Harry Piel. SP: Hans Rameau. Ph: E. Daub. Ref: Hardy/SF: *The World without a Mask* - tr t. With H. Piel, Kurt Vespermann, Annie Markart, Olga Tschechowa, Rudolf Klein-Rogge.

"TV that can pick up images through walls ... gadget than can look through walls."

**WENDIGO** Talking Pictures 1983 (1979) color feature. SP,D: Roger Darbonne. Ref: Ecran F 36:82. V 12/12/79(rated). 5/9/84:14: aka *Wendigo: Curse of the Black Wind*. no Stanley. no Martin. With Ron Berger, Cameron Garnick, Victor Lawrence.

Indian sorcerer takes revenge on those who inadvertently desecrated his tomb.

**WE'RE BACK! A DINOSAUR'S STORY** Univ/Amblimation(Stephen Hickner) 1993 anim color 89m. (*We're Back: A Dinosaur Tale* - ad t). D: Dick & Ralph Zondag, P. Nibbelink, S. Wells. SP: John Patrick Shanley. From Hudson Talbott's book. Mus: James Horner. SpFxSup: Steve Moore. Computer Imagery: Rhythm & Hues etc. Digital FX: AFT. SpSdFX: Dave Lawson. Ref: TV: MCA-Univ HV: 71m. Sean. ad. SFChron 11/23/93: "the dinos are a delight." SFChron Dtbk 9/5/93. Voices: John Goodman, Jay Leno, Walter Cronkite, Julia Child, Kenneth Mars, Martin Short, Larry King.

In the "far future," a scientist's Brain Grain cereal mellows out even the most ferocious of dinosaurs, the tyrannosaurus, and his Wish Radio sends dinos back to kids in New York City, today, where his brother Professor Screweye's Eccentric Circus is the "most terrifying show on the planet Earth" and features dragons and ghosts. His Fright Radio summons up kids' worst fears, and his Brain Drain turns the dinos back into monsters.

A love-and-hugs message is wrung rather arduously, if entertainingly, out of these events, which add up to a fascinating exercise in child-viewer psychology. The spectre of Disney's *Pinocchio* seems to loom large here, in the Stromboli-like figure of Professor Screweyes, and in the sequence in which the two kids are turned temporarily into monkeys.

**WERE TIGER** Searles Cinevision c1918 silent b&w 22m. Ref: Library of Congress: reissue print. no Lee. no LC. no Stanley. no MPW. With Hedda Nova, Jules Cowles, George Carrossella, J. Frank Glendon.

"There is a Malay superstition that certain people change themselves into tigers to satiate their appetite for human flesh...." Cynthia Trevor (Nova), daughter of the manager of the Little Pahang Mine, is on her way to Singapore when she crosses the path of a tiger which has just raided a small kampong. Natives, seeing the blood of the beast's victim smeared over her, fear she is a Were Tiger. ("Do you wish to die that you mention a Were Tiger by name?")

The content of this very, very obscure early two-reeler is surprisingly horrific, at least in intent. The supposed monster is referred to as "IT!", and a prefatory title refers to "strange terrors" in the jungle. Unfortunately, the production is rudimentary, and a routine gold-robbers story takes over from the Were Tiger tale partway through.

**\*The WEREWOLF** 1956. Ref: TV. Warren/KWTS! Stanley. Lentz. V 6/13/56. Hardy/SF. Maltin '92. Scheuer. Lee. With Eleanore Tanin, S. John Launer.

"It wasn't all wolf!" Serum from a "wolf mutant that died of radiation" turns Duncan Marsh (Steven Ritch)—the "most gentle man who ever lived"—into a drooling "wolf man" that terrorizes the town of Mountaincrest. ("Only an animal could do that to a man's throat!") The best of it: Edwin Linden's low-key location photography. The worst: the shallow human-interest angles borrowed from the more maudlin scenes of *The Wolf Man*. ("What a horrible, horrible thing to happen to a human being!") First transformation scene is okay, but stops the action dead.

**WEREWOLF** Col-TV & Tri-Star-TV/Frank Lupo, John Ashley 1987 color 92m. D: David Hemmings. Tel: F. Lupo. Ph: Jon Kranhouse. Mus: Sylvester Levay. PD: Anthony Cowley. SpMkp:(des) Rick Baker;(fx) Greg Cannom. SpFX: Tom Bellissimo. SdFX:(sup) Joe Mayer; Soundelux. Ref: TV. TVG. Sacto Bee 4/28/90: pilot for the series; listed as TV-movie. V 7/15/87:50. Scheuer. Newman. With John York (Eric Cord), Lance LeGault, Chuck Connors, Raphael Sbarge, Michelle Johnson.

"I'm a werewolf." The pentagram is back, in this "Stephen King story about monsters and curses," though the full-moon idea is not. Ted Nichols, apparently bitten by a certain "Captain Hook," passes the curse of the werewolf on to Eric Cord, who must kill the first in the bloodline.... Talk here alternates with monster's-eye-view shots. The lighter, "stylized" characters like the lawyer are easier to take than the over-familiar pop-tragic ones. (Eric: "I don't want to be like this!")

**The WEREWOLF** (Thai) 198-? color c92m. Ref: TV: AAE video; no Eng. Thai Video: above is tr t.

Two campers strip, do a ritualistic bump-and-grind, and the zombies chasing them vanish. Later, a wolf's eyes shoot rays at a man and turn him into a werewolf that looks like a big, fully-clothed teddy bear. His spiritual students bow before him, and he becomes human again. At the end, zombies run amok in a village.

Oddball mixture of monsters, witches sporting goatees, nudes, and war games. The zombies get some of the oddest bits: One female zombie crawls out of her coffin, cuddles up with a man who's half-asleep, and whispers sweet lord-knows-whats in his ear. During the climactic melee, one zombie is content to swing on a swing; another gets its long, long rubber arms pulled off.

**WEREWOLVES** and other Shape-Shifters see the preceding and following titles and

*Aakhri Cheekh. Alegres Vampiras de Vogel* (2). *Ang Mahiwagang Daigdig Ni Elias Paniki. Bewitched Area of Thousand Years. Boy God. Buaya Putih. Captain Barbell. Cast a Deadly Spell. Cazador de Demonios. Company of Wolves, The. Conrad Brooks Meets the Werewolf. Creeper, The. Crocodile Godmother. Crocodile Men, The. Cross of the Seven Jewels. Curse of the Queerwolf. Daffy Duck's Quackbusters. Dead Time Stories. Deadly Snail ... Dear Diary. Demon Beast Warrior Luna Vulgar. Dinastia Dracula, La. Driller. Dungeonmaster, The. Dust Devil. Ele, O Boto* (P). *Etranger. Fairy Fox. Fairy of the Lotus. Fandora. Fangface* (P). *Female Ninjas: Magic Chronicles 1. Follow That Goblin! Frankenstein's Planet of Monsters. Freddie as F.R.O.7. Fright Night. Fright Night Part 2. Full Eclipse. Ghost Dance, The* (1984). *Ghost Stories* (1986). *Ghostbusting. Grotesque. Guy: Awakening of the Devil. Guyver, The* (New Line, 1991). *Guyver, The: Mysterious Shadow. Haunted Cop Shop II. Haunted Honeymoon. Haunted Nights. Holy Weapon. Howling, The* entries. *Human Vapor, The. Impaktita. Incredible Hulk Returns, The. It. Jack Frost* (1965). *Kaos. Kokak. Lady Master Snake.*

*Lady Tiger. Lady Wolf. Ladyhawke. Leena Meets Frankenstein. Legend of Wolf Mountain* (P). *Lobisomem, O. Lone Wolf. Love at Stake. Lupin III. Mad at the Moon. Magic Man, The. Magic Warriors. Meet the Applegates. Miedo No Anda en Burro, El. Mr. Peter's Pets* (P). *Mr. Vampire Saga 4. Mom. Monkey War. Monster Dog. Monster Squad, The. Mummy and the Curse of the Jackals, The. My Demon Lover. My Mom's a Werewolf. My Pet Monster. Nache Nagin Gali Gali. Nagina. Neptune's Children. Nigahen. Night Evil Soul. Night Shadow. Nightbreed. Nightmare Asylum. Nightmare before Christmas, The. Nightmare Classics. Obsessed, The. Okay Ka, Fairy Ko! Part 2. Pinfish, The. Polish Vampire in Burbank, A. Possessed II. Professor, The. Project Metalbeast. Quem Tem Medo de Lobisomem. Rats Are Coming, The ... Red Riding Hood. Return of the Demon. Saturday the 14th Strikes Back. Scooby-Doo and the Ghoul School. Scooby-Doo and the Reluctant Werewolf. Scorpion Thunderbolt. Shadowzone. She* (1983). *Sheshnaag. Snake Woman, The. Star Janga II. Star Trek VI. Stephen King's Silver Bullet. Stephen King's Sleepwalkers. Stepmonster. Supermouse and the Robo-Rats. Tales of the Third Dimension. Teen Wolf. Teen Wolf Too. Till Death Do We Scare* (3). *Transylvania 6-5000. Tu Nagin Main Sapera. Un Paso Al Mas Aca ... Undead, The. Untama Giru. Urufugai. Urusei Yatsura: Raging Sherbet and I Howl at the Moon. Vampire Hunter D. Wandering Kid. Waxwork. Waxwork II. Were Tiger. Wolfman, The. Youma I. Zeguy.*

**Der WERWOLF VON W.** (W.G.) Reinery & ZDF 1988 color 82m. SP, D: Manfred Mueller. SP: also W. Pilz. SpFX: B. Gruse. Ref: Hardy/HM2: "the tantalizing possibility of a lycanthropic curse." With H. Huebchen.

**WES CRAVEN'S NEW NIGHTMARE** New Line (Marianne Maddalena) 1994 color 112m. SP, D, Exec Co-P: Wes Craven. Ph: Mark Irwin. Mus: J. Peter Robinson. PD: Cynthia Charette. VisFX: (sup) William Mesa; Flash Film Works; (digital) Digital Filmworks. MechFX: Lou Carlucci. SpMkpFX: KNB. Freddy Mkp: David Miller Creations. Paintings: Linda Newman. Opt: Howard Anderson. Ref: TV: NL HV (Turner Home Ent.). Sacto Bee 10/14/94. Janet Willis. With Robert Englund (himself/Freddy), Heather Langenkamp (herself/Nancy), John Saxon, Miko Hughes, David Newsom, Tracy Middendorf, W. Craven (himself).

Freddy Krueger is "crossing over" from films to reality, and the "only way to stop him is to make another movie." Actress Langenkamp's son is "acting like Freddy," and she has a vision of her dead husband.... Effects-filled but generally effectless *"Nightmare*-in-progress," despite the reflexive nature of the film. 8-1/2 it ain't, though there are occasional hints of something more. For the most part, this plays like a lesser entry in the *Nightmare on Elm Street* series. (For a more inventive script-in-progress movie, see *Death by Dialogue.*) Neatest effect number 1: cloud Freddy. Neatest effect number 2: the robotic variation on the crawling hand. Neatest set: waterspout Freddy. Plus a curtain call for the tongue-phone.

**WET AND WILLING** Limelight Releasing (Robert Angove) 1987 b&w? c75m. D: Phillip Ronald. Ph: Giancarlo Formichi. Ref: TV: Limelight video. no Adam. With Patricia Rivers, Scott Daniels, Victoria Lee, Mike Cone.

"Filmed on location in the crystal waters of the Devil's Triangle." A mystical power leads Jack to a spot above Andros Island in the Bahamas, where he believes the lost continent of Atlantis lies. Strange lights and electrical disturbances there herald the appearance of nude Atlanteans (the men have big teeth), who entice our male protagonists into a "paradise—Atlantis, a city given solely to the erotic pleasures of its inhabitants."

The underwater sex scenes suggest a hardcore *Creature from the Black Lagoon* and are the relative highlight. Underwater, in the Devil's Triangle, time is strangely compressed, and the "mermaids" have no tails and need no diving gear.

**WET DREAM ON MAPLE STREET** Fantasy HV (Carol Pole) 1988 color 80m. D: Jim Travis. Ref: Adam '89. With Alicia Monet, Robert Bullock, Trinity Loren.

Sorcery is used to enslave man's soul.

**WET DREAMS 2001** Vidco/F.J. Lincoln 1987 color c90m. D,P,Ed: F.J. Lincoln. SP: Mark Weiss. Ph: Tom Howard. Sets, Props: Porsche Lynn. Mkp: Alan C. Bosshardt. Ref: TV: Vidco video. no Adam. With John Leslie, Siobhan Hunter, Sharon Mitchell, Jerry Butler, Danielle, Tracy Adams.

After 217 years in cryogenic cylinders, four sex criminals are "liberated" into the world of 2120, where sex is outlawed. ("When the hell are we?") Force fields render them prisoners, but "dream sharing" in the "dream room" allows them, via special headbands, to have subconscious sex with the women of the future .... Cockeyed premise posits (if you follow the numbers) cryogenics in the year 1903. The "2001" in the title means nothing. Dismal adult sf-er.

**WET SCIENCE** Essex/Playtime 1986 color 76m. Ref: vc box. Adam '88. With Candie Evans, Bunny Bleu, Erica Boyer, Tom Byron (android).

Mad scientist and assistant Igor create "living man."

**WHAM-BAM-THANK YOU, SPACEMAN** see *Erotic Encounters of the Fourth Kind*

**\*WHAT!** Futuramic 1963 ('65-U.S.) ws 90m.(77m.) (*Le Corps et le Fouet* - F t). Mus: Carlo Rustichelli. Mkp: "Frank Field," "R. Christie." Ref: TV: vt; Eng. dubbed. Lee. Ecran F 30:33-4. PT 8:9. VW & VWB. Lentz. V 5/26/65. With Alan Collins.

"I've come back for you!" The whip-happy Kurt (Christopher Lee) seems to haunt a castle. Nevenka (Daliah Lavi) sees his face at a window, hears the sound of his whip, and is assailed by "his horrible hands ... like a green spider." The explanation: madness. ("Perhaps she was possessed.") Mario Bava semi-classic is all atmosphere and no script—colored lights, wind effects, and a ghostly "Kurt!" This mood-and-music piece is half-intoxicating, half-boring. It's 90 percent walking around in the semi-dark, which is maybe too much of a good thing. Lee is dubbed by someone else.

**WHAT EVER HAPPENED TO BABY JANE?** ABC-TV/Steve White Prods. & The Aldrich Group & Spectacor Films (Barry Bernardi) 1991 (1990) color c90m. D: David Greene. Tel,Co-P: Brian Taggert. Mus: P.M. Robinson. PD: David Gropman. Mkp:

(Lynn) Jill Rockow; (Vanessa) Sheila Walker. Ref: TV. V 2/11/91:113. TVG. Sacto Bee 2/17/91. With Vanessa Redgrave (Blanche), Lynn Redgrave (Baby Jane), John Glover, Bruce A. Young.

Sibling rivalry writ grotesque, as envious Baby Jane Hudson (Best Child Actress, 1949) tapes up crippled sis Blanche (also a former movie star), serves her her worm-sandwich specialty, and commits murder-by-scissors and statuette. Gruesome pathos is viable here only as a vehicle for Lynn Redgrave. Jane's patter camouflages a crumbling mind; her hideous-child makeup directs one right to same. Vanessa Redgrave spends most of her footage in bondage.

**WHAT HAVE THEY DONE TO YOUR DAUGHTERS?** (I) Video Search 1974 feature (*La Polizia Chiede Aiuto*). SP, D: Massimo Dallamano. SP: also E. Sanzo.Ref: Imagi 1:59: similar to *What Have You Done to Solange?* MV: aka The *Co-ed Murders*; gore. Palmerini: "good thriller."

Mad killer of schoolgirls.

**WHAT HAVE YOU DONE TO SOLANGE?** (I-W.G.) Video Search/Clodio & Italian Int'l/Rialto (Pescarolo-Lucisano) 1971 color/ws 103m. (110m) (*Cosa Avete Fatto a Solange? Das Geheimnis der Gruen Stecknadeln*). SP, D: Massimo Dallamano. SP: also Bruno de Gregorio. Ph: A. Massaccesi. Mus: Ennio Morricone. AD: G. Carsetti. Mkp: Trani. Ref: TV: VSOM; Eng. dubbed; *What Have They Done to Solange?* Imagi 1:59: "graphic... murders." Lee (Higuchi). McCarty II: SP: B. di Geronimo; "unsettling." V 5/3/72: "gruesome case." Palmerini. Fango 12/89:57,68. Samhain 8:10: *The School That Couldn't Scream* - U.S. re-release title. With Fabio Testi, Joachim Fuchsberger, Karin Baal, Camille Keaton, M. Monti.

"You're the last!" There's "something funny" about the British slasher who hits below the belt, or between the legs, of the girls from "that stupid Victorian school," St. Mary's. Is there a "sex maniac on the faculty"? Thrills elude the moviemakers here, but parody beckons in the scenes of the police lineup of priests and the search for a "bearded priest," as well as the final revelation of a "priest" avenger of an abortion.

**WHAT WAITS BELOW** (U.S.-Can.?) ITC/Blossom (Adams-Apple Film/Sandy Howard, R.D. Bailey) 1984 color 88m. (*Secrets of the Phantom Caverns* - orig t). D: Don Sharp. SP: Christy Marx, R.V. O'Neil. Story: Ken Barnett. Mus: Rubini, Jaeger. SpPhFxDes: Bailey. SpMkp: William Munns. Prosth: Greg Cannom. SpFX: Rick Josephsen. SpMinDes: Cary Howe. Creature FxD: Jeff & Steve Shank. SpSdFX: John Pospisil et al. Ref: TV. V 7/23/86. TVG. With Robert Powell, Timothy Bottoms, Lisa Blount, Richard Johnson, Anne Heywood, Liam Sullivan.

British Honduras, near Belize. The Omega Station's seismic tests open underground caverns haunted by a gigantic snake and shadowy lurkers that prove to be lost, sound-sensitive Lemurians. Spook show begins with a tantalizing prologue re a 900,000-year-old stalagmite, but turns into a thin moral fable. Okay atmospheric effects. Not quite as foolish of kind as *The Mole People*.

**WHAT'S UP, HIDEOUS SUN DEMON** Wade Williams/Greystone (24 Horses) 1989 color and b&w 71m. SP,D: Craig Mitchell. Mus: Fred Myrow. Ref: V 10/4/89: comic re-dub of *The Hideous Sun Demon*. With Cameron Clarke, Googy Gress; (voices) Jay Leno, Susan Tyrrell.

**WHEELS OF FIRE** (U.S.-Fili) Concorde/Rodeo 1985 (1984) color c86m. (*Desert Warrior* - alt t. *Vindicator* - orig t). D, P: Cirio H. Santiago. SP: Frederick Bailey. Story: Ellen Collett. Mus: Chris Young. SpFX: Jessie Sto. Domingo. Prosth: Cecille Baun. Ph: R. Remias. AD: Les Guggenheim. Ref: TV: Vestron Video. V 9/18/85. With Gary Watkins, Laura Banks, Lynda Wiesmeier, Linda Grovenor, Joseph Anderson.

A *Road Warrior* ripoff pitting the Ownership Army against Scourge (Anderson) and his Fortress. Plus: Grovenor's psychic Spike ("I can hear what they're thinking") and cannibalistic underground Sandmen.... The *raisons d'etre* of *Wheels of Fire*: fast cars, explosion effects, and Lynda Wiesmeier strapped topless to the hood of a car. Phony sentiment with Banks, Wiesmeier, Grovenor, and the peace-loving True Believers ... comically gruff grunts and dubbed "Heh heh heh"s for the supporting baddies.

**WHEELS OF TERROR** USA-TV/Wilshire Court & Once Upon a Time Prods. (Learman-Cheda/S.M. Brooks) 1990 color c90m. D: Chris Cain. Tel: Alan B. McElroy. Mus: Jay Gruska. AD: Nigel Clinker. SpFX: Mike Wood. Mkp: Jeanne Van Phue. Ref: TV. V 7/11/90:68,71. With Joanna Cassidy, Marcie Leeds, Arlen Dean Snyder, Carlos Cervantes.

A "really filthy black sedan" terrorizes the residents of Copper Valley. The car has no driver, but a passenger, apparently, abducts and molests local school girls.... Or, The Near-Indestructible Car. Only for those who like to watch speeding cars and school busses.

**WHEN A STRANGER CALLS BACK** Showtime-TV/Krost-Chapin Prods. & PEG & Pacific & MTE (Tom Rowe) 1993 color 96m. SP, D: Fred Walton. Ph: Dave Geddes. Mus: Dana Kaproff. SpFxMkp: Jonathan Blackshaw. Ref: TV. V 3/29/93:86: "scary stuff." TVG 4/3/93. With Jill Schoelen, Carol Kane, Charles Durning, Gene Lythgow, Duncan Fraser.

"No one can see me now. No one hears me. I am invisible." Follow-up to *When a Stranger Calls* (II/1979) gets pretty bizarre after a bland beginning in babysitting terrors. The seemingly supernatural menace is part-ventriloquist, part-"chameleon." ("He's got something going for him that we haven't even begun to imagine.")

**WHEN DREAMS COME TRUE** ABC-TV/I. & C. 1985 color 92m. D: John L. Moxey. Tel, Assoc P: William Bleich. Mus: Gil Melle. AD: Jack Marty. SpFX: Jack Bennett. Mkp: Carla Rulien. Ref: TV. TVG. V 7/10/85:58. With Cindy Williams, Lee Horsley, David Morse, Jessica Harper, Stan Shaw.

Susan Matthews (Williams) falls under the spell of a suicide who, all her life, "heard voices." When her boy friend Alex (Horsley) begins to seem "predictable," Susan turns to an artist (Morse) whom she saw in her dreams.... Suspense does not exactly run rampant in this tepid fantasy chiller. Script's equation of romance with danger is rather pat; its resolution of the romance and the suspense (the artist gets shot) is very pat.

**WHEN PIGS FLY** (Dutch-J-G-U.S.) Allarts & NDF Sumitomo & Pandora & Sultan Driver (Kasander-Wigman) 1993 color 97m. D: Sara Driver. SP: Ray Dobbins. Ph: Robby Mueller. Mus: Joe Strummer. Ref: V 9/20/93: "stuffed with small jokes and treats." With Alfred Molina, Marianne Faithfull (Lilly), Maggie O'Neill, Seymour Cassel, Rachel Bella (Ruthie).

Ghosts, haunted house.

**WHEN THE BOUGH BREAKS** Prism Pictures/Osmosis 1993 color feature. SP, D: Michael Cohn. Ref: V 10/25/93:50(ad): "Can a child's telepathic mind help find a serial killer?" With Ally Walker, Martin Sheen, Ron Perlman.

**WHEN THE RAIN BEGINS TO FALL** see *Voyage of the Rock Aliens*

**WHEN THE WIND BLOWS** (B) Meltdown & British Screen & Film Four Int'l. & TVC London & Penguin Books (John Coates) 1986 ('88-U.S.) anim color 84m. (81m.-U.S.). D: Jimmy T. Murakami. SP: Raymond Briggs, from his story. Mus: Roger Waters. SpFxSeqs: Stephen Weston. Models: Errol Bryant. SpMusFX: Tristram Cary. SDFX: John Wood Studios. Ref: TV: IVE video; some live action. MFB'87:62-3. V 2/11/87. NYT 3/11/88. Voices: Peggy Ashcroft, John Mills.

Hilda and Jim Bloggs respond to an "enemy missile attack" on England: "Look on the bright side." "Nothing like a cup of tea." "There should be some good pictures. These bombs are quite spectacular." "The situation is well in hand." "Funny spots on my legs." "Common middle-age complaint." Well, you get the idea. You see one scene, you've seen every scene here. This is the ultimate rose-colored-glasses movie, but the ironies at the expense of the naive protagonists are all easy ones, and only near the end, when the physical deterioration of the couple is pretty far along, does grimness overcome glibness. Instead, see *special bulletin* or *Miracle Mile* or *Testament* or *Threads*.

**WHERE IS NICK BEAL?** see *Alias Nick Beal*

**WHERE THE RIVER RUNS BLACK** MGM-UA/Ufland-Roth 1986 color 100m. D: Chris Cain. SP: Silverman, Jimenez, from David Kendall's novel *Lazaro*. Animal FX: Donald Pennington. Ref: V 9/10/86: "beautifully simple." Ecran F 74:41-2. 75:8-9. Martin: "eerie." Morse: "beautiful and interesting to look at." SFChron 9/19/86: "not entirely convincing." Film Journal 10-11/86: "Lovely woman ... devoured by the biggest snake in the world." SFExam 9/19/86: "sea serpent." 9/18/87:D-7: "the dumbest movie of 1986."

**A WHISPER TO A SCREAM** (Can.) Distant Horizon & Lighthouse Communications (Anant Singh) 1989 color 96m. (aka *Whispers. From a Whisper to a Scream*). SP,D: Robert Bergman. SP,P: Gerard Ciccoritti. Ph: Paul Witte. Ref: V 8/23/89: "horror film." Hound. V/Cannes '89:135. With Nadia Capone, Silvio Oliviero, Yaphet Kotto.

Is Gabrielle's "nutty boyfriend" the "monster"? (V)

**WHISPERER IN DARKNESS, The** see *Necronomicon*

**WHISPERS** (Can.) ITC/Cinepix (Cinemars XIII/John Dunning) 1990 color 93m. (aka *Dean R. Koontz' Whispers*). D: Douglas Jackson. SP: Anita Doohan, from Koontz' novel. Adap, Co-P: Don Carmody. Mus: Fred Mollin. Dead Twin Des: Joe Blasco, Ed French. SpFxSup: Jacques Godbout. Ref: TV. V 1/28/91:72(hv): Live HV. 11/22/89:45(ad). 2/21/90:70(ad). CVS 3/91. With Victoria Tennant, Jean Leclerc (Bruno), Chris Sarandon, Peter MacNeil, Eric Christmas, Keith Knight, Jackie Burroughs, Vlasta Vrana.

"Then he came back from the dead!" Bruno Clavel, supposedly dead and buried, kept a van "filled with vampire stuff" and believed that his dead mother would come back to him in different bodies. One of those bodies belongs to Hilary Thomas (Tennant), whom he stalks, convinced that he will be tormented by "whispering" as long as his mother "lives."

A makeup credit—and the phrase "identical twins by incest"—give away most of the show here. The first version of this plot was probably *The Sphinx* (1933). Extra addeds: a bug-infested cellar and a hokey *Halloween* last-gasp shock.

**WHISPERS** see *Whisper to a Scream*

**WHITE HORSE, DARK DRAGON** see *Legend of the White Horse*

**WHITE LIGHT** (Can.) Bellemonde (Anthony Kramreither) 1991 color 97m. D: Al Waxman. SP: Ron Base. Mus: Paul Zaza. Ref: V 5/13/91: "efficient thriller/love story with a come-back-from-the-dead twist." With Martin Kove, Martha Henry, Heidi von Palleske.

"Experimental drug that helps patients recall their experiences while briefly dead."

**WHITE OF THE EYE** (B) Cannon/Palisades Ent. (Elliott Kastner/Elwes-Wyman/Mrs. White's Prods.) 1987 (1988) color 111m. SP,D: Donald Cammell. SP: also China Cammell. From Margaret Tracy's book *Mrs. White*. Mus: Nick Mason, Rick Fenn. Ph: Larry McConk(e)y. PD: Philip Thomas. Key Mkp: Jeanne van Phue. SpFX: Thomas Ford. Ref: TV: Para video; c'86. SFChron 6/3/88: "fascinating but pretentious." ad. Phantom: "bold... truly sicko." Newman: "unusual style." Morse: "film-school self-consciousness." V 5/20/87. Ecran F 72:71. 75:66-7. With David Keith, Cathy Moriarty, Alan Rosenberg, Art Evans, Michael Greene, Danielle Smith, Alberta Watson.

"This thing is turning into a nightmare." In Arizona, three "disfigurements" lead investigators to a madman who specializes in putting women out of their "misery," in a touch of *Arsenic and Old Lace*. Semi-slasher movie with a twist, and that's about all—that and occasional bits of good photography and dialogue. Only the big white-eye close-ups hold it together, loosely.

**WHO IS AFRAID OF DRACULA** see *Fracchia contro Dracula*

**WHO IS JULIA?** CBS-TV/CBS Ent. 1986 color c90m. D: Walter Grauman. Tel, Assoc P: James S. Sadwith. From Barbara S. Harris' novel. Ph: Thomas Del Ruth. Mus: Robert Drasnin. Mkp: Jim Scribner. Ref: TV. TVG. With Mare Winningham (Mary Frances/Julia), Jeffrey DeMunn, Jameson Parker, Bert Remsen, Tracy Brooks Swope, Ford Rainey.

Brain transplant — Julia's into Mary Frances. Or, The Daytime Soaps Discover Science Fiction.

**WHO KILLED THE FROG** (H.K.?) Her Jiann-Yeh & Shyr Jin-Quey 1980 color/ws c84m. D: Yang Duen Pyng. SP: Tzon Yea-Tzyy. Ref: TV: Ocean Shores Video; Eng. titles. With Li Tao-Hung, Ou Ti, Hsia Ling-Ling.

"The frog will become bigger and bigger!" Little Hsiao Ming feeds a professor's growth stimulant—intended to increase the world's food supply—to his pet frog, Dinosaur, and the latter grows by leaps and bounds. Soon, it's boy-sized, then elephant-sized. Some sleazy entrepreneurs steal it, bill it as Thunderclap Frog, and put it on stage. ("What a large frog!") Now, Dinosaur is as "big as a hill" and out of control, and the army uses ray rifles to try to bring it down when it endangers the city. Also noted: a pre-credit sequence re a "large chimpanzee" in a haunted house.

Children's sf-comedy-drama recalls *King Kong, Tarantula, The Pet, Digby,* and a certain unfilmed property variously known as "The World, The Flesh and The Frog," "Mondo Frog," etc. Script unfortunately opts for slapstick and sentiment rather than satire, though it has charming moments—e.g., Hsiao Ming pole vaulting onto the hill-sized Dinosaur's back in order to ride him. Chintzy effects.

See also *Kokak.*

**WHODUNIT?** see *Island of Blood*

**WHORE OF THE WORLDS** Paradise Visuals 1985 color c78m. (*Whore of the Worlds: Lust in Space Part II* — vc box t; above is cr t. aka *Lust in Space II*). Ref: TV: P. Visuals video; same credits as *Lust in Space.* Drew/Motion Picture Series & Sequels. Adam '88: 1986. This is not so much a sequel to *Lust in Space* as a simple retitling of it, though there is some substitute footage of Ginger Lynn, Traci Lords, Erica Boyer, John Holmes, and John Leslie from, apparently, other X-rated movies such as *Those Young Girls.* There is little, if any new sf material.

**WHO'S THE GHOST IN THE SLEEPY HOLLOW?** (H.K.?) Rung Ting-chun c1989? color/ws 93m. D: Hsu Wen-hsieh. SP: Li Shu-lih. Ph: Liao Wan-wen. Mus: Kao Yang. AD: Ku Hsuan-huai. Ref: TV: World Video; no Eng. With Liu Chih-rung, Wang Pao-yu, Sung Kang-ling.

Who isn't? Everyone seems to be some kind of ghost, from the man with the echo voice to the green ghost girl to the hopping ghosts to the seemingly living skeleton in the bathtub to the ghost hordes that rise from their graves to the pop-eyed ghost to the two or three fake ghosts. Even one of the supposedly living characters at one point starts to decompose. Film combines horror, mystery, and sentimental hokum, and tosses in a little "Dark Shadows" music.

**WHO'S THE KILLER?** (H.K.) c1992 color/ws 91m. (aka *Blood Island*). D: Wu Kuo-Ren. Ref: TV: Tai Seng Video; Eng. titles. Weisser/ATC. With Luo Sai-Li, Shing Fui-On.

"Weird people" ruin the "paradise" for archaeology students studying on an island. Two of the group are beheaded, one is cut in half. The killer, though, may not be the local mad lad, but Ms. Fang, the teacher, who has visions of past mayhem and of

monsters. Twenty years ago, a witch slaughtered most of the villagers and now seems to possess her.... Mostly formulaic horror-mystery. Relative high point: the visualized-hallucination sequences.

**The WICKED** (Austral.) Hemdale HV/Cine-Funds & Somerset/Overview (Jan Tyrrell, J.M. Vernon) 1987('91-U.S.) color 88m. (*The Prince at the Court of Yarralumla* - orig t. *Outback Vampires* - alt t. *Vampires in the Outback* -early t). SP, D: Colin Eggleston. SP: also David Young. Ph: Garry Wapshott. Mus: Colin & Kevin Bayley, Murray Burns. PD: Michael Ralph. ProsthMkp: Debbie Lanser. SpFX: Steve Courtney. Ref: TV: Select HV(Expo HV): aka *Tomorrow's News?* V 4/8/87:24. 5/6/87:432. Martin. Jones. Ecran F 79:10. V 5/6/87:281(ad). 10/21/87:44(ad). With Brett Climo, Richard Morgan, Angela Kennedy, John Doyle, Maggie Blinco, David Gibson, Antonia Murphy.

"She's a lunatic sometimes—in fact, we all are." Stranded travelers at the Terminus estate ("Who's the decorator—Mary Poppins?"), outside the town of Yarralumla, encounter a weird family which sleeps in upright coffins, likes bats, flies (more or less), and bites necks. Sir Alfred (Doyle), Agatha (Blinco), George (Gibson), and Samantha (Murphy) turn out to be vampires who enjoy the "thrill of the chase." At the end, Agatha dies and turns into a skeleton; Alfred temporarily becomes a giant.... Pathetic misfire is a sort of Aussie *Nothing but Trouble,* without the good stuff.

**WICKED CARESSES OF SATAN, The** see *Devil Kiss*

**The WICKED CITY** (H.K.-J) Film Workshop & Toho (Tsui Hark) 1993 (1992) color feature (*Yiu Sau Dousi*). D: Mak Tai Kit. Mus: R. Yuen. AD: Eddie Ma. Ref: TV: vt; Eng. titles. V 10/25/93:67(ad). 12/13/93. SFChron Dtbk 10/3/93: "live-action version" of *Monster City.* With Jacky Cheung, Leon Lai, Michele Li, Tatsuya Nakadai, Yuen Wo Ping.

Fantasy-horror free-for-all features scads of goofy action/effects highlights and no attempt at level-headedness. Memorable: the skittering, crystal gloved hand ... the guy with the laser tentacles ... the bra-and-clock effects ... the "rapter vacuum" which stops time ... the Blob-like "liquid rapter" ... and the vicious flying clock. ("Time is a real pain.") The altering-corridor effect might be an hommage to *Curse of the Demon.*

**WICKED CITY** see *Monster City*

**WICKED STEPMOTHER** MGM-UA (Robert Littman) 1989 (1988) color 92m. SP,D,Exec P: Larry Cohen. Mus: Robert Folk. SpPhFX: Hollywood Optical; (sup) Joseph Wallikas; (co-ord) David L. Hewitt; (stopmo) Larry Arpin; (anim fx) Michael Hyatt. Mkp & MinFX: Mark Williams. Ref: TV. V 2/8/89. Sacto Bee (ad). Scheuer. With Bette Davis, Barbara Carrera, Colleen Camp, David Rasche, Lionel Stander, Tom Bosley, Richard Moll, Evelyn Keyes, Laurene Landon, Seymour Cassel.

Fantasy with scattered horrific elements re a witch, Priscilla (Carrera), who seems to be Bette Davis's Miranda in a clever supernatural disguise. (In fact, the two witches have only one body and must use their cat as a "vessel" for the odd witch out.) Horror moments include shots of Miranda with Freddy's claw and Jason's mask ... a bit in which the cat becomes a tiger ... a visual *Psycho* knife reference ... shots of tentacles overrunning a house during a witch duel ... and Priscilla briefly in monster-face as she "becomes" the cat again, at the end. Script features tired plot developments, but also some amusing oddball moments, including a shot of the rejuvenated Sam's (Stander) hair growing overnight. Camp gives a terrible, overwrought comic performance; Carrera seems to be relishing her woman-with-the-power role; and the metronomic deliveries of Davis and Stander seem inspired by Josef von Sternberg films.

**WICKED WIFE** see *Curse of the Wicked Wife*

**WIDE SARGASSO SEA** (Austral.) Fine Line (New Line)/Laughing Kookaburra (Jan Sharp) 1993 color 96m. SP,D: John Duigan. SP: also Sharp, Carole Angier. From Jean Rhys' novel. Ref: V 4/19/93: voodoo, *Jane Eyre* overtones. SFChron 5/14/93.

**WIDZIADLO** (Polish) PFPC Zespoly Filmowe, Perspektywa Unit 1984 color 99m. SP,D: Marek Nowicki, from Karol Irzykovski's short story "Paluba." Mus: K. Knittel. Ref: V 8/8/84: "As a Gothic ghost story, it is not too exciting"; *The Phantom* - tr t? With Roman Wilhelmi, Tarzena Trybala, Hanna Mikuc.

Fake ghost sends man to a "gruesome death."

**The WIG** (Thai) c1988? color c70m. Ref: TV: Kantana video; no Eng. Thai Video: above is tr t.

The spirit of a woman who has been scalped cackles and appears to women who apparently wear wigs made from her hair. She yanks the wigs off, bloodily, and sics strangling wigs on her male enemies. Finally, when she is staked, a wig which is strangling a cop falls limp .... Kooky-ghoulish premise is good for a few unusual scenes, but the script is padded out with police-investigation scenes, etc., and said premise goes nowhere. Shot on tape.

**WILD BLUE MOON** (Mex.) Quetzal Films 1992 color 107m. SP,D,Exec P: Taggart Siegel, Francesca Fisher. Ph: Alex Phillips Jr. Mus: Lobo & Willie. PD: Desgagnes, Sirdey. Ref: V 11/2/92: "lackluster acting and sluggish editing." With Maira Serbulo, Thom Vernon, Z.S. Gutierrez.

"All manner of witchcraft" used in revenge plot.

**The WILD EAST** (Russ.-Kazakh) 1989? 100m. (*Diki Vostok*). D: Rachid Nougmanov. Ref: SFChron 1/24/94: "post-punk apocalyptic tale about a disintegrating empire overrun with bandits, boozers, weirdos, motorcycles and rock and roll." V 12/20/93: "doesn't add much" to *Mad Max* & co.; "vaguely futuristic."

**WILD WAVES** see *Big Broadcast, The*

***The WILD WORLD OF BATWOMAN** 1966 (*The Wild Wild World of Batwoman* - cr t. aka *She Was a Hippy Vampire*). Ph: William Troiana. Mus D: E. Bromberg. AD: Jerry Syphers. Mkp: George Mitchell. Ref: TV: Medallion-TV. Weldon. PT 3:41-2. With Bruno VeSota, Steve Conte, Mel Oshins; Lucki Winn, Leah London (Bat Girls).

The foremost of the super-scientific gizmos here is the "divider," which acts like a Human Duplicator and "multiplies" the villain, in the most bizarre sequence of this incredible petrified comedy.

Other ingredients include a seance and a lost city of mole people, from the film of the same name. Draggy.

**WILL VINTON'S CLAYMATION COMEDY OF HORRORS** see *Claymation Comedy of Horrors*

**The WILLIES** Prism Ent. & Para HV/Filmtown Int'l. & Force Majeure 1991 (1990) color 91m. SP, D, Exec Co-P: Brian Peck. Creature Des: William Stout. SpMkpFX: Kenny Myers. Creature FX: Tony Gardner's Alterian Studios. Ref: V 2/25/91: "uneven anthology horror." Martin. McCarty II: "a little gem." With Sean Astin, Michael Bower, Ralph Drischell, Kathleen Freeman, James Karen, Clu Gulager, John McGiver.

Tales re "fried rat ... giant flies ... stop-motion monster." (V)

**WILLI'S ZUKUNFTSTRAUM** (G) c1925 cutout anim short? D: Paul Peroff. Ref: Crafton/Before Mickey: "futuristic city" a la *Metropolis*.

**WILLOW** (U.S.-N.Z.) MGM/Lucasfilm & Imagine Ent.(Nigel Wooll/Joe Johnston) 1988 color/ws 126m. D: Ron Howard. SP: Bob Dolman. Story,Exec P: George Lucas. Mus: James Horner. Ph: Adrian Biddle. VisFX: IL&M; Dennis Muren, Michael McAlister, Phil Tippett;(anim sup) Wes Takahashi; (stopmo animator) Tom St. Amand. SpMkpDes: Nick Dudman. Prosth/Creature Sup: Val Jones-Klein, Graham High et al. SpFxSup: John Richardson. Lip-sync Anim: Available Light. OptFX: Ray Mercer. Ref: TV. V 5/18/88. MFB'88:375-6. Martin. East Bay Express 5/20/88. SFExam 5/20/88. SFChron 5/20/88. With Val Kilmer, Joanne Whalley, Warwick Davis, Jean Marsh, Billy Barty, Pat Roach (Gen. Kael), David Steinberg, Phil Fondacaro.

"It is a time of dread...." The final third of this overelaborate fantasy gets into monster-movie territory: An already grotesque, ape-like troll turns into an even more grotesque, fire-breathing, two-headed horror that bolts its (human) food, and evil Queen Bavmorda (Marsh) turns enemy warriors into pig-things (cf. *Pinocchio*). The most winning effect, however, occurs during the climactic, otherwise uninspired duel of the sorceresses: A stray magic ray briefly brings a witch's cauldron to comically menacing, stop-motion life. In this movie, the incidental is often charming. The problems here lie with the hollow storyline and action and the bland spoken English. Kilmer is amiable in the reluctant-hero — or Harrison Ford — role of Madmartigan, and the comedy with the "brownies" clicks more often that not.

**The WIND** Omega (Isabel Mastorakis) 1987 (1986) color 92m. (*Edge of Terror* - B). Story,SP,D,P: Nico Mastorakis. Mus: Myers, Zimmer. SpFX: Samiotis, Bellek, Ludovik. PD: Lester Gallagher. SpSdFX: Frank Seraffini. Mkp: Sheri Short, A. Kouroupou. Ref: TV. V 11/25/87. PT 4:5. With Meg Foster, Wings Hauser, David McCallum, Robert Morley, Steve Railsback.

"The wind can be very dangerous at this time of the year." A scythe-wielding madman terrorizes a mystery writer (Foster) staying at a house on a windy Greek island. The wind here is okay. Otherwise, this is just the usual competent, hollow Mastorakis thriller.

**A WIND NAMED AMNESIA** (J) CPM/Hideyuki Kikuchi & Asahi Sonorama & RSO & Japan HV 1993('94-U.S.) anim color 82m. SP,D: Kazuo Yamazaki. SP: also Y. Kawajiri, K. Kurata. Story: H. Kikuchi. Supervisors: Taro Rin, Y. Kawajiri. Guardian Des: Y. Amano. Ph: K. Ishikawa. AD: M. Koseki. Mus: Toyama, Takimoto. Ref: TV: vt. VW 23:26-7: USManga Corps video; Eng. titles. Voices: Kazuki Yao, Keiko Toda (Sophia), M. Satou (Guardian).

"One day in 199X, a strange wind is unleashed that erases all human memory .... a most unusual and rewarding *anime*."(VW) Principals and places include hero Wataru, a "wanderer of the Earth" ... the alien Sophia, whose people loosed the wind in order to remove from humankind the pressures of civilization and reveal the essential human core ... the Guardian, a giant, anti-riot mechanism ... a "huge terrifying man with wires hanging from his body"—a bio-weapon that can cause mini-earthquakes ... the Smasher-and-Devourer—the god of Los Angeles—human-operated construction equipment ... the computer-run Eternal Town, which programs its (two) inhabitants with memories ... and a ghostly Las Vegas, an eerie town of dead neon.

Thoughtful, even sweet animated feature combines elements of a "Twilight Zone" puzzler, *Road Warrior*, and *Easy Rider*, as Wataru travels across the U.S. in order to "see how humanity behaves." A-1 detail: A skeleton is at the controls of the first Guardian. The people that Wataru encounters generally disappoint him, but in not wholly expected ways.

**WINDARIA** (J) Harmony Gold/A.I.C.? 1986 anim color/ws 101m. (aka *Legend of Fabulous Battle. Once upon a Time* - re-edited version). Ref: TV: RCA Victor video; no Eng. J Anim Archives #3. Animag 3:4. Wonderful World of Comics 4/88.

A poetic, pessimistic fantasy with sf and horror elements. King Ransurd of Palo—a scruffy, barren country—invades the kingdom of Isa, an idyllic community of windmills, hot-air balloons, and water striders. Palo boasts futuristic hover crafts, odd small motor vehicles, fighter planes, and rusty tanks. Isa warriors rely on bow-and-arrow. In-between the two countries lies a forest that preys on the imagination: Wraiths, phantom flying serpents, and writhing trees assail intruders.

Isa and the giant tree Windaria represent a pastoral ideal; Palo is the nasty, brutish reality. Beauty here sours. Isa's Princess Aanasu ends up shooting her lover, Palo's Prince Jil, then herself. The hero, young Izuu, betrays Isa and floods her. A war profiteer, he finally sees the cost of his success: a sunken city, beautiful, eerie, and dead, in the moonlight. A flock of red "soul birds" whooshes past him—each one represents a life. Then, in a ghostly *Ugetsu* twist, he returns to his wife Maalin—apparently spared when a bomb hit their cottage—but she fades, becomes a soul bird herself, and flies away to a sort of airship of the dead.

The story here has some bite and power, though character animation is—typically for a Japanese cartoon—blandly idealized and stiff. And if the songs are vapid, the background music is sometimes stirring. An enchantingly atmospheric film.

**WINGS OF DEATH** (B) BFI 1985 color 22m. SP,D: Nichola Bruce, Michael Coulson. Mus: Muscle Films. AD: Jane Bruce. SpFX: Cineguild? Ref: TV: Bravo. With Dexter Fletcher.

Some beyond-*Lost Weekend* horror effects in this depiction of drug-induced delirium. Wallpaper peels itself ... addict peels off his own scalp.

**WINGS OF ONEAMIS — ROYAL SPACE FORCE** (J) Manga Ent./Towa/Bandai Co. & Gainax (Sueyoshi-Inoue) 1987('95-U.S.) color/ws 120m. (*The Wings of Honneamise - U.S. Starquest* - proposed t of U.S., Go East, Eng.-dubbed version. *Parallel Zone 1987. Spirits of Fire. Flight of the Eagle. Royal Space Force — Wings of Riiqunni* - all early titles). SP, D: Hiroyuki Yamaga. Ph: H. Isagawa. Mus: Ryuichi Sakamoto. AD: Hiromese Ogura. Char Des: Yoshiyuki Sadamoto. Anim D: H. Anno et al. SdFX: M. Kashiwabara. Ref: TV: Emotion video, no Eng.; ME video, Eng. titles. Paul Lane. Animag 3:26-35: based on four-minute *Royal Space Force* (1985). 12:24-26. U.C. Theatre notes 2/19/95.

On the parallel world of Amemuga, the country of Oneamano prepares to send its first man into space. Noblemen attempt to use the planned space launch to start a war with neighboring Rimada, but Royal Space Force General Khaidenn and pilot Shirotsugh "Shiro" Lhadatt see to it that the launch is successful....

The preoccupation of Japanese animators with clouds, sky, light (natural and artificial), mist, etc., continues, but—except for a dramatic shot of sunlight—the poetic nature effects here are only punctuation. The main concern of *Wings of Oneamis*: building a convincing, detailed alternate civilization. To that end, the animators have redesigned the artifacts of Earth, including trains, planes, buildings, toys, games, machinery, TV, lights (street, neon, table), cameras, money, uniforms, tombstones, smokestacks, steamboats, guns, streetcars, helicopters, rockets, cityscapes, telephones, etc. The objects are recognizable; the alterations generally slight, but intriguing. Most of the gizmos are not flaunted—you only get one look. The sheer accretion of detail slowly draws one into the movie.

The story itself is a cross between *Riders to the Stars*—training the space pilot—and *Close Encounters of the Third Kind*—breaking away, literally and figuratively, from a disappointing, compromised world. The movie is low key; the moral drama re the adventurous Shiro and the stay-at-home Riiqunni initially less taking than the alternate-world spectacle. But *Wings of Oneamis* builds subtly to a rather magnificent conclusion: The climactic chaos of battle gives way to the quiet of space, as Shiro orbits Amemuga, and that world's history is encapsulated in a kaleidoscopic montage. If the montage itself is an ambiguous, unsettling mixture of human accomplishment and destructiveness, the quiet seems like a promise.

**WINKY THE WATCHMAN** Hugh Harman 1945 anim & live color 8m. Ref: TV. LC.

"The woods were full of Bad'uns" — the latter proceed to attack the wall which Winky is guarding. Pro-dentist short is in part appallingly sweet, but the Bad'uns are imaginatively animated — their eyes gleam luridly and menacingly in the dark, and they have a catchy theme song. They look like miniature, black creatures from the Id.

**WINTERBEAST** Tempe Video 1993 color feature. SP,D: Christopher Thies. Ref: Fango 122:32-33: "horror yawn." With Bob Harlow.

Winterbeast ("a guy in devil makeup") ... "living totem poles" ... a gateway to hell ... and a "psychopathic lodge owner."

**WIRED TO KILL** The Moviestore (A.D.G.)/Schaeffer-Buchfuehrer (Peter Chesney) 1986 color 96m. (*Booby Trap* - orig t). SP,D: Franky Schaeffer. Mus: Russell Ferrante & the Yellow Jackets. SpMechFX: Bruce Hayes. SpFXCoord: Scott Hass. MkpFxDes: Michele Burke. SpSdFX: Alan Howarth. Ref: TV. V 12/3/86. With Emily Longstreth, Devin Hoelscher, Merritt Butrick, Frank Collison, Tom Lister, Jr.

It's 1998, and the T.A.P.E.X. plague is over, but the Quarantine Zones remain, as outlaw territory for "terrorist gangs" .... In this futuristic *Death Wish* revenge saga, a terrorized family fights back against thugs. Mixture of action and sentiment reduces to drivel, though there are occasional human and comic moments. Monotonous Tangerine Dream-like score.

**WISELY LEGEND** see *Legend of Wisely, The*

**WITCH ACADEMY** American Independent 1990 color feature. D, P: F.O. Rau. SP: Mark McGee. SpMkpFX: S.O.T.A. FX. SpFxAnim: B. Mixon. Ref: TV. TVG. With Robert Vaughn (the devil), Priscilla Barnes, Suzanne Ager, Michelle Bauer, Jay Richardson, V. Carothers.

Monstrous demons, flying mini-monster. Lame sex-horror-comedy.

**WITCH BITCH** see *Death Spa*

**WITCH FROM NEPAL** (H.K.) Golden Harvest (Paragon) 1985 color c88m. (aka *Nepal* or *Nepal Affair. Qi Yuan*). D: Ching Siu Tung. SP: Tsui Jing-Hong. Ref: TV: Rainbow Video: above is vc box t; Eng. titles. M/TVM 11/88:25. V 10/16/85:412. Weisser/ATC. Hardy/HM2: aka *A Touch of Love*. With Emily Chu, Chow Yun Fat.

Sheila travels from the Himalayas to Hong Kong to inform Joe that he is to be the new leader of her sect. ("This is your destiny.") She has leaping, healing, and dinner-fork-bending powers, and at one point conjures smoke out of a cigarette and electricity out of wall sockets and into Joe, who finds that he too now has ESP. Later, with the wild electricity from a downed power line, he etches two hearts in the sky for her.

Meanwhile, an "evil force" (which snarls like a big cat) has followed Sheila from Nepal and is intent on wreaking havoc on Joe, Sheila, and his girl friend Ida—in one scene, it has the latter's record albums flung magically into the air. (They stick in the trunks of nearby trees.) In the absurd, spectacular climactic sequence, Joe clutches a sacred sword which whips him through a corridor lined with loose, sparking electric wires which galvanize him and enable him to make the evil cat being explode.

Schizophrenic horror-fantasy-romance alternates between vapid love scenes (including a time-out for a sound-track love song, pleasingly concluded by the hearts-in-the-sky effect) and nifty telekinetic stunts and shock scenes. In the movie's *Night of the Living Dead* set-piece, the evil one conjures up a cemetery's dead

and shoots the "spears" from an iron fence at the occupants of a car.

**WITCH HUNT** HBO/Pacific Western (Michael R. Joyce/Gale Anne Hurd) 1994 color 98m. D: Paul Schrader. SP, Exec Co-P: Joseph Dougherty. Ph: J. Y. Escoffier. Mus: Angelo Badalamenti. PD: C.A. Schnell. SpVisFX: Fantasy II. Digital/Anim: Perpetual Motion Pictures. SpFxMkp: Criswell Prods. SpFX: Stetson Visual. Ref: TV. TVG 12/10/94. With Dennis Hopper (H. Phillip Lovecraft), Penelope Ann Miller, Eric Bogosian, Sheryl Lee Ralph (Hypolita Kropotkin), Julian Sands (Finn Macha), Alan Rosenberg, Michael Taliferro (zombie).

Magic 1953. Ingredients include a licensed witch (Ralph) ... a building with the life "sucked out" of it ... a shrinking spell ... a necklace-magic-made movie star (Miller) ... a magic man (Sands) ... a detective (Hopper) who eschews magic ... a senator (Bogosian) who literally comes out of his shell ... and Shakespeare, conjured up to provide some additional dialogue.... Unofficial follow-up to *Cast a Deadly Spell* is superior to the original. Script is finally over-ambitious, but full of surprises, like the instant piano player and the "diminished" murder victim's tiny chalk outline, a great gag even if it is borrowed from a *Naked Gun* joke. Hopper and Sands are very good. The El Monte Drive-In lives!

**WITCH OF TIMBUCTOO, The** see *Devil-Doll, The* (1936)

**WITCH STORY** (I) Uniexport Film/Morigi-Pedersoli 1989 color/ws feature. Story, SP, D, P: Alessandro Capone. SP: also Rosario Galli. Adap: Jeff Moldovan. Ph: Roberto Girometti. Mus: Carlo Maria Cordio. AD: David Minichiello. SpFX: Vince Montefusco. SpSdFX: Cine Audio FX. SpMkpFX: Rick Gonzales. Ref: TV: VSOM; Eng. dubbed. V(Cannes'89:33(ad)). MV: aka *Le Streghe?* Hardy/HM2: *Streghe*. Palmerini. With Deanna Lund, Ian Bannen, Christopher Peacock, Michelle Vannuchhi, Amy Adams, Suzanne Law (Rachel).

"You will rule the powers of evil!" In 1932, a witch (Lund) curses everyone in sight as she's executed. In 1989, her little protegee, Rachel—still a little girl—is looking for "someone to play with." Meanwhile, possessed teens slaughter other teens with cleaver, chainsaw, etc. Graceless, formula.

**The WITCH WHO CAME FROM THE SEA** Matt Cimber 1976 color c98m. D: M. Cimber. SP: Robert Thom. Ph: Gibb; Cundey. Mkp: Gale Peterson. Ref: TV: Unicorn Video. Stanley. PT 11:30. Newman: "unsettling ... atmosphere." Willis/SW. With Millie Perkins, Vanessa Brown, Lonny Chapman, Peggy Feury, George "Buck" Flower, Verkina, Roberta Collins, John Goff, Rick Jason, Stafford Morgan, Stan Ross (Jack Dracula), Gene Rutherford, Sam Chu Lin.

Incest-victim Molly seems to have fantasies re castrating pro-football players, but they turn out to be reality. ("Some weird sex thing.") Later, she takes a razor to another guy.... "Why do they call you Jack Dracula?" "That's my name." It's like that. Excruciating. Main motifs include TV and sea references.

**The WITCH WITH THE FLYING HEAD** (H.K.?) c1985? color/ws 92m. (aka *Witch with Flying Head*). Ref: TV: Tai Seng Video; no Eng.

Most interesting aspect of this Chinese horror movie is that it borrows a head-and-entrails ghost from Thai horror movies. Next most interesting aspect: She seems to be a vampire here, and her oversized fangs are set in her lower teeth and are probably very uncomfortable. When she re-attaches to her body, the fangs vanish. She can spit little snakes and centipedes, shoot rays, and breathe fire. Also: ax and vampire gore, snake attacks, and a snake-ghost vacuum .... Sensationalistic, isn't it? As if the Thai ghost weren't enough, the movie also supplies a more-typically Chinese snake ghost, and gore for all. Library music.

**WITCHBOARD** Cinema Group/Paragon Arts Int'l. (Gerald Geoffray/Walter Josten) 1986 color 97m. SP, D: Kevin S. Tenney. Mus: D.M. Tenney. SpFX: Tassilo Baur. Mkp: John Blake. Ref: TV. MFB'87:286. V 1/21/87. With Todd Allen, Tawny Kitaen, Stephen Nichols, Kathleen Wilhoite (Zarabeth), Burke Byrnes, Rose Marie, J.P. Luebsen (Carlos Malfeitor).

Fairfield, California. Ouija board operators contact the spirit of a dead boy, but a second spirit, Malfeitor—Portuguese for "someone evil"—a mass murderer, is also at work.... Earnest and not badly made, but plodding and unoriginal. The second-ghost idea comes from *The Uninvited* (1944); the determinedly eccentric medium comes from *Poltergeist*; the surprise-figure-in-the-mirror shock comes from *Repulsion.* Pat characterizations.

**WITCHBOARD 2: THE DEVIL'S DOORWAY** Republic Pictures/Blue Rider (Josten-Geoffray) 1993 color 96m. SP, D: Kevin S. Tenney. Ref: V 3/8/93:22(rated). 10/18/93:14: in Taipei. 11/30/92:48. Martin: "which bored, too." With Ami Dolenz, Timothy Gibbs, Laraine Newman.

Ouija board unleashes spirit.

**WITCHCRAFT** Vista Street/Feifer-Miller(Megan Barnett, Yoram Barzilai/Marketing Media) 1988 color 86m. D: Robert Spera. SP: Jody Savin. SpMkpFX: Angela Levin. SpFXCoord: Laslo Stumpf. SdFX: Johann Langlie. Ref: TV: Academy Ent. video. V 1/18/89. PT 3:13. McCarty II. With Anat Topol-Barzilai, Gary Sloan, Mary Shelley, Deborah Scott, Alexander Kirkwood, Lee Kisman (Ellsworth).

"Why do you think John chose me?" A woman in labor has nightmares re witch-burning and finds "part of the house closed" when she goes home to her mother-in-law's. A priest visits, vomits, and has his skin go bad. Seems satan's witches are bringing up baby for the devil .... Film adds nothing to *Rosemary's Baby.* Perfunctory writing, playing, and filming, and a shot-on-tape look.

**WITCHCRAFT** see *Witchery*

**WITCHCRAFT II: THE TEMPTRESS** Vista Street/Feifer-Miller(Marketing Media) 1990 (1989) color 87m. D: Mark Woods. SP, Sup P: James R. Hanson. SP: also Sal Manna. SpFX: L. Stumpf. Mkp: Cynthia Jordan. Ref: TV: Academy Ent. video. V 7/11/90. PT 8:46. McCarty II. With Charles Solomon, Delia Sheppard (Dolores, temptress), David L. Homb, Mia Ruiz, Jay Richardson, Kirsten Wagner.

"Then I am from the devil!" A mysterious box afflicts young William Adams (Solomon) with the "weirdest dream." Soon, he discovers that all of his real and foster parents were apparently

witches, and that he is marked to become the "supreme warlock." At the end, William rejects his nomination and stabs The Temptress with a crucifix .... Overwritten and underacted shot-on-tape horror cheapie. Movie peaks with the "It's the mark of the devil!" scene, a camp conjunction of bad actor and line.

**WITCHCRAFT III: THE KISS OF DEATH** Vista Street/Feifer-Miller (H.T. MacConkey/Marketing Media) 1991 color 86m. D: R.L. Tillmans. SP: Gerry Daly. VisSpFX: William Mims Ent. SpFX: Steve Patino. Mkp: Laura LeMaire. Ref: TV: Academy Ent. video. V 6/17/91. 4/15/91:196(rated). PT 10:55. Jones: "psychic vampire." With Charles Solomon, Lisa Toothman, Domonic Luciano, W.L. Barker, Leana Hall.

"He was human once." Vampiric Louis Daminelli (Luciano) sucks energy or life-force or something out of his victims' mouths. ("They enslave their prey by releasing their poisons—inhuman blood—into their bodies.") The hero, too, seems to be a warlock, and uses a magic scepter to vanquish Daminelli. He also has a visualized nightmare which includes bits from earlier titles in this series.... Episodic, isn't it? Limply directed, indifferently written fantasy-horror.

**WITCHCRAFT IV** Vista Street/Feifer-Miller (Holly MacConkey, S. Lieb) 1992 color 93m. (*Witchcraft IV: Virgin Heart*). SP,D: James Merendino. SP: also M.P. Gerard. SpVisFX: William Mims. SpMkpFX: James MacKinnon. Ref: V 8/3/92. 9/30/91:16 SFChron Dtbk 6/7/92. With Charles Solomon, Julie Strain, Clive Pearson.

Music and devil worship.

**WITCHCRAFT V: DANCE WITH THE DEVIL** Vista Street/Peloso-Feifer 1993 color feature. D: Talun Hsu. SP: S. Tymon, J. Merendino. Ref: SFChron Dtbk 6/6/93. Fango 122:71. PT 16:61: "stupid, cheap looking." With Nicole Sassaman, David Huffman, Lenny Rose, Carolyn Taye-Loren.

Devil's emissary comes to Earth to collect souls.

**WITCHCRAFT VI: THE DEVIL'S MISTRESS** Academy Ent./Vista Street (Feifer) 1994 color feature. D: Julie Davis. SP: Peter Fleming. Ph: D. Maloney. PD: H. Dusek. Ref: V 9/27/93:21. vc box. PT 20:72: "pathetic." With Jerry Spicer, Debra Beatty, Kurt Alan.

Serial killer, satanist, occultist.

**WITCHCRAFT VS. CURSE** (H.K.) Hop Chung Film 1990? color/ws 87m. Ref: TV: Pan-Asia Video; Eng. titles.

Sorcerer Ku Tian Yao — the "old monster" — sends the Adultery Ghost to possess Yu Lung, while, in Thailand, the latter's fiancee, Pai Lin, hires another sorcerer, Simol (who casts a deadly spell on an incidental couple). When Ku Tian Yao's ghostly emissaries arrive in Thailand, they appear first as clown-faced monsters. Also incidental: the Blood Hand Mark, which makes a man temporarily act possessed.... Purely functional sexploitation feature is more girlie movie than horror-comedy.

**WITCHERY** (I) Vidmark/Filmirage (Aristide Massaccesi, Donatella Donati) 1988('89-U.S.) color 95m. (*La Casa 4 - Witchcraft.* aka *Witchcraft. Ghosthouse II* - B vt t). D: Fabrizio Laurenti (aka M. Newlin). SP: Daniele Stroppa. Mus: C.M.

Cordio. SpMkpFX: M. Trani. OptFX: Moviecam 2000. Ref: TV. V 5/10/89. Horacio Higuchi. McCarty II. PT 10:6. V 9/6/89:39: sfa *Ghosthouse 4* (in Rome)? 3/9/88:36. With David Hasselhoff, Linda Blair, Catherine Hickland, Annie Ross, Hildegard Knef (Lady in Black), Ely Coughlin (satan).

"This place gives me the shivers!" At a cursed house—the site of witch burnings—fifty miles from Boston, satan and a coven of witches gather "weak souls" in preparation for an ancient ritual. Also featuring: the devil's unborn, a possessed pregnant woman (Blair), a voodoo doll which makes a man (Bob Champagne) bleed to death, a crucifixion, a woman (Ross) whose mouth is sewn shut, and the Horror in the Bathtub.... Formula gore-mongering in this follow-up to *Ghosthouse*. Love very unconvincingly triumphs over hate at the end, though a coda (also unconvincingly) suggests that the triumph is temporary.

The **WITCHES** (U.S.-B) WB/Lorimar (Jim Henson/Mark Shivas) 1990 (1989) color 91m. D: Nicolas Roeg. SP: Allan Scott, from Roald Dahl's story. Mus: Stanley Myers. Animatronics:(coord) William Plant; Henson's Creature Shop;(des) John Stephenson. OptFX: Opt Film FX, Image to Image. Mattes: Meddings Magic. Mkp:(Grand High Witch) Steve Norrington;(prosth) Nigel Booth. Ref: TV. MFB'90:146-7. V 3/21/90. Sacto Bee 2/16/90. With Anjelica Huston (Grand High Witch), Mai Zetterling, Bill Paterson, Jasen Fisher, Jenny Runacre, Jane Horrocks.

The meeting of the Royal Society for the Prevention of Cruelty to Children—held at the Hotel Excelsior—is a front for a witch convention. The goal of these witches (who are ugly-ghastly behind their human masks): the elimination of "every single child" in England. The Grand High Witch (the "most evil and appalling woman in the world") demonstrates, on stage, how to turn kids into mice: The transformation itself is horrific (compare the donkey sequence in *Pinocchio*), but (ah! cuteness) the victim-mouse still speaks English. At the end, the witches unwittingly drink the formula, shrink, and go mouse, in a frantic comic scene with gruesome touches.... Puppetry and animation star in this minor, occasionally charming anecdote. Eeriest scene: the prologue, in which the girl "trapped" in the painting grows old.

The **WITCHES OF EASTWICK** WB/Guber-Peters Co. (Neil Canton) 1987 color/ws 118m. D: George Miller. SP: Michael Cristofer. From John Updike's novel. SpVisFX: IL&M;(sup) Michael Owens;(coord) Kathryn Witte;(opt ph sup) Edward Jones;(anim sup - tennis seq) Ellen Lichtwardt;(opt coord - tennis seq) Lori J. Nelson. SpMkpFX: Rob Bottin. SpFX:(sup) Mike Lant(i)eri; Clay Pinney et al. Opt: Pacific Title. Ref: TV. MFB'87:264-5. V 6/10/87. SFChron 6/12/87. SFExam 6/12/87. East Bay Express 6/19/87. With Jack Nicholson (Daryl Van Horne), Cher, Susan Sarandon, Michelle Pfeiffer, Veronica Cartwright, Richard Jenkins, Carel Struycken.

Three women (Cher, Sarandon, Pfeiffer) pray for rain—and for a "tall dark prince traveling under a curse"—and get both. The "prince," Daryl Van Horne, buys Lenox mansion, site of witch-burnings, and soon the morally outraged Felicia (Cartwright), possessed, is spitting up cherry pits, and her husband is forced to kill her. The three "witches" use the book *Maleficio* and a voodoo doll to put a curse of feathers and pits on Daryl, who at one point appears giant-sized at a window. But the doll burns, and he disappears.

Daryl here does for the three women what John Lund did for Jean Arthur in *A Foreign Affair*. ("You kill the passion. Let it go!") In *Witches*, liberation is a sea of pink balloons and the ability to hover in the air. It's all pretty and pleasant enough, but peel away the movie's glossiness, and you peel away the movie. Much ado and little but ado.

**WITCHES' SABBATH** (U.S.-Hung) Halmi & Objektiv 1984 color 88m. (*Boszorkanyszombat*). D: Janos Rozsa. SP: Istvan Kardos. Mus: Z. Tamassy. SpFX: Roy Field. Ref: V 3/7/84. no Stanley. no Martin. no Hound. no Scheuer. With Dorottya Udvaros, Eniko Eszenyi, Robet Koltai, Zoltan Papp.

Fairy-tale heroes and heroines vs. witches, wolves, and a giant.

**WITCHES' SABBATH** see *Akelarre*

**WITCHES' SABBATH, The** see *Visione del Sabba, La*

**WITCHFIRE** Panda Movie Co.(J.R. Orr) 1985 color 100m. (*A Sonnet for the Hunter* - shooting t). SP,D: V.J. Privitera. Ph: Mike Delahonssey. Ref: V 5/22/85: "it is Winters' picture." Stanley. Ecran F 56:71. Phantom.With Shelley Winters, Frances De Sapio, Corrine Chateau, Gary Swanson.

"Meant to be a horror film" a la *Whatever Happened to Baby Jane?,* re fugitive mental patients who believe they're witches.

The **WITCHING** Tempe/Video Outlaw(Trustinus/Todd Sheets) 1993 color 72m. SP, D: Eric Black. Ph: Todd Sheets. SpMkp&FX: Mike Hellman. "Scully": Bill Morrison. "Fred": David Barton's Modus EFX. Atmospheric FX: Videfx. Computer FX: Subtempecoefx. Ref: TV: Tempe Video ('94). Bill Warren. TV flyer. With Auggie Alvarez, Mike Hellman, Frank Dunlay, Dianne O'Connell, Carol Barta, Dana Pace, Veronica Orr (Morgana), Tony Abbotte (Beast).

Descendant of witch hunter reads incantation, raises Morgana, Queen of the Witches, and company. Morgana, in turn, summons up a demon from the Ninth Circle of Hell and tests a man-into-frog spell.... Amateurish, shot-on-tape horror-comedy is, to put the best light on it, genially pathetic. Best line: "Ever been to Stonehenge?"

**WITCHING HOUR** see *Spellbinder*

**2P WITCH'S SISTER** Showtime-TV/Blue Marble 1979 color 68m. D, P: Robert Wiemer. SP: John Kostmayer, from Phyllis R. Naylor's novel. Ph: Aaron Kleinman. Mus: Paul Baillargeon. StageFX: Bobby Provenzano. Mkp: Rhea McGeath. Ref: TV. Oakland Tribune. TVG 7/20/80. no Hound. no Weldon. no Phantom. no Stanley. With Daphne Youree, Dara Brown, Virginia Stevens, Jane Sanford, Bruce Graham.

A neglected-child's imagination conjures up a series of "apparitions": child-eating "witches" and a "warlock," a voodoo-doll "spell," a boy "brought back from the dead," a "levitating" girl, etc. There's also a nightmare sequence in which the child's sister dances out of a coffin and witches attack .... Awkward, mechanical variation on *Curse of the Cat People* themes, as a girl learns the ABC's of appearance and reality. Some atmospheric candle-light effects and musical motifs, and the black-and-white nightmare sequence is a pleasing, balletic change-of-pace from the flat dialogue scenes.

**WITCHTRAP** Cinema Plus & GCO Pictures/Mentone Pictures (Jackson Harvey, David A. Bowen) 1989 color 90m. (*The Presence* - orig t). SP, D, P: Kevin S. Tenney. P: also Dan Duncan. Mus: D.M. Tenney. SpMkpFX: Judy Yonemoto. SpFX:(sup) Tassilo Baur;(coord) Lou Carlucci. Ref: TV. V 8/9/89. Scheuer. V 10/19/88:279(ad): *The Haunted* - ad t. With James W. Quinn, Kathleen Bailey, Judy Tatum, Rob Zapple, Linnea Quigley, J.P. Luebsen (Avery Lauter).

Warlock Avery Lauter—aka the Vineyard Slasher—haunts Lauter House—aka Slaughter House—a Gothic mansion in Solano County, California—with his "horrible, ungodly shrieks and moans." ("Neither his killer nor his heart were ever found.") His soul and body must be reunited to complete a bloody "immortality ritual."

More witchcrap from the makers of *Witchboard* (which see). Dialogue scenes are D.O.A. here, not surprisingly considering the raw material. Favorite phrases and lines: "Ginger, I have a bad feeling about this one," "You unholy son of a bitch!", and even "Even as we speak...."

**WITHOUT WARNING** CBS-TV 1994 color c90m. Ref: TVG. With Jane Kaczmarek, Katio Salem, Dennis Lipscomb, Sander Vanocur, Ernie Anastos, Warren Olney.

"Huge asteroid on a collision course with Earth...."

**WITNESS TO THE EXECUTION** NBC-TV/Pierce 1994 color 92m. D: Tommy Lee Wallace. Ref: vc box: "pay-per-view execution." Martin: "enthralling." TVG (ad): set in 1999. SFChron 2/11/94: "a bleached offshoot of *Network*." With Sean Young, Tim Daly, Len Cariou, George Newbern, Dee Wallace Stone, Alan Fudge.

**The WIZ KID** (G) Vidmark/Alliance (Olga-Film & ZDF/Kuegler-Senft) 1989('93-U.S.) color/ws 90m. D: Gloria Behrens. SP: Konstantin, Weber, Doherty. Ph: L.W. Borchard. Mus: Kambiz Giahi. AD: Claus Kottmann. Mkp: Rainer Kraubs. SpFX: Magicon; Hubert Bartholomae, Joachim Grueninger. Ref: TV: Vidmark video; Eng. dubbed. With Martin and Gary Forbes, Narcisa Kukavica, Jake Wood, Lloyd Powell, Alec Christie.

"You're my creature!" Young robot-maker Bodo (Martin Forbes) invests an "egg" with computer-programmed personality traits and a sample of his own blood, and the egg hatches a suave and sophisticated Bodo clone (Gary Forbes). Disguised *Teen Wolf* rip-off seems angled to be a record album as much as a movie. Irritatingly pat character types. Very bad.

**WIZARD OF AHH'S** Electric Hollywood 1985 color c85m. D: John Gold. SP: Jazz Martino. Ph: Gary Roberts, Joe Hill. Mkp: Jenny Alexis. Ref: TV: Essex Video. no Adam '88. With Athena Star, Mindy Rae, Dee Dee Vine, Rita Ricardo, Mike Horner, Ron Jeremy.

"Welcome to Ahh's!" In the year 2069—sixty years after The Great War—women rule the moon colony and men have been exiled to a penal-colony planet. April (Rae), Ginger (Star), and Jill (Vine), on routine space patrol, happen upon an unknown planet, Ahh's, the Wizard of which promises, "I've come to bring

you passion." He sends them back "before The Great War," where the three pick up 20th-century sexual slang very quickly, and where—at the end—one declares, "Gonna be tough going back to that sex machine." Unremarkable adult sf-er.

**WIZARD OF DARKNESS** (J) 1993 feature (*Eko Eko Azaraku*). D: S. Sato. Ref: Weisser/JC. With K. Yoshino, M. Kanno.

Black magic, "gory deaths," "good witch."

**\*The WIZARD OF GORE** Fred M. Sandy/Herschell Gordon Lewis 1971 (1968). Ph: Alex Ameripoor. Mus: Larry Wellington. SpTechFX: Sheldon Seymour (aka H.G. Lewis). Ref: TV: Midnight Video. Lee. Lentz. Hardy/HM. Weldon. CineFan 2:27. Stanley. Phantom. Martin.

"Somehow, he was making everyone's hand bleed!" See "human butchery" live on stage. According to illusionist Montag the Magnificent (Ray Sager), life is just "one long dream." His act includes a "new and different illusion" each night: The chainsaw stunt produces a mess o' entrails; the steel spike yields brains and eyes; if the punch-press trick were a tad more real-looking, it would be honestly disgusting; and by sword-swallowing night, everyone's probably had enough. Mysteriously, the bodies of Montag's victims are temporarily restored, then later leak. (Award: Worst Screamer, to the waitress who comes upon the body of the first victim.) At the end, he employs TV in some kind of mass-hypnosis plot.

A movie obviously made before the Dawn of Editing, *Wizard* is too lethargic to qualify as camp, and even the would-be-mind-boggling, double-twist coda (the hero is Montag in a mask; the freshly-disemboweled heroine is an illusionist too) is done so ham-handedly that it fizzles. The film's old-fashioned, hardcore gore is too clumsily staged to make it as Grand Guignol, while the various plot elements—the illusions (or are they?), the bleeding hands, the endings and codas, etc.—aren't coordinated in any way, just there.

**The WIZARD OF OZ** (J) Alan Ents./Toho 1982 anim color 77m. D, P:John Danylkiw. Anim D: Fumihiko Takayama. From L. Frank Baum's books. Ref: TV. no Phantom. no Stanley. no Maltin '92. Hound. no Martin. no Scheuer. Voices: Lorne Greene, Aileen Quinn.

Ingredients: the Wicked Witch of the West (voice: Elizabeth Hanna) and her monstrous flying-monkey hordes ... huge crows ... and a magic mirror. Wicked Witch — East evaporates; Wicked Witch — West melts.... Aggressively bland action, songs (by Cahn and Byrns). If you know the story (who doesn't), you don't need to see this.

**The WIZARD OF SPEED AND TIME** SGE & Jittlov-Kaye & Rochambeau Prods. (The Hollywood Wizard) 1988 color 92m. SP, D, SpFX, Ed: Mike Jittlov. Mus: John Masari. Mkp: K. Chadwick, S. Maxon. Suitcase: Eddie Paul. SdFX: Steve Mann. SpFxOpt: Gene Lescher, Ray Mercer. Ref: TV: SGE HV. V 5/25/88. PFA. Martin. Scheuer. With M. Jittlov, Richard Kaye, Steve Brodie, Frank LaLoggia, Angelique Pettyjohn, Ward Kimball, Forrest J Ackerman, Jim Danforth.

Comedy integrating, or excerpting, Jittlov shorts "The Wizard of Speed and Time," "Speed," "Swing Shift," "Time Tripper," and

"Animato" includes scattered but significant sf elements like THE time machine (George Pal's, that is), which takes part in a space operetta ... a flying saucer ... a six-armed creature ... long-distance laser-writing (with a beam directed from Earth onto the moon's face) ... an electric suitcase-vehicle ... a mouse-head spacecraft ... an electrified bicycle ... and ESP.... Jittlov's energy and invention—before and behind the camera—make *The Wizard* an intermittent charmer. He's less successful, though, with actors, or characters, than with effects.

**WIZARD WARS** see *Wizards of the Lost Kingdom*

**WIZARD'S CURSE** (H.K) Grand March Movies (Lo Wai) 1992 color 93m. D: Yuen Cheung Yan. SP: Wong Jing. Ph: Jimmy Leung. Ref: TV: World Video; no Eng. With Lam Ching Ling, Cheung Keung, Chan Lun.

The ghost-man and ghost-woman here are so closely identified with each other that they seem to be one two-faced being. In one scene, the man's head jumps out of the woman's stomach; later, her head leaps out of his stomach. In another scene, the ghost is female-faced in front, male-faced in back. At the end, the male ghost — his arms and legs self-detached — is reduced to a floating torso. Good bit: the female ghost jumping out of the mirror. In an okay, *Terminator 2*-derived scene, the male ghost's severed limbs and torso reassemble. Silly, sometimes funny horror-comedy gets surprisingly gory as the ghosts bite into the tops of their victims' heads.

**WIZARDS OF THE DEMON SWORD** Troma/American-Independent (Austin Ents.) 1991 (1989) color 81m. (*Demon Sword* - shooting t). D,Co-P: Fred Olen Ray. Sp: Dan Golden, Ernest Farino. SpFxAnim: B. Mixon. Ref: V 6/17/91: "sword and sorcery was never cheaper looking." V/Cannes '89:88. 4/15/91:M-76, M-50. With Lyle Waggoner, Russ Tamblyn, Blake Bahner, Heidi Paine, Jay Richardson, Dawn Wildsmith, Hoke Howell, Dan Golden (Gorgon), Lawrence Tierney.

**WIZARDS OF THE LOST KINGDOM** (U.S.-Arg.) Concorde/Cinema Group (Trinity/Frank Isaac, Alex Sessa) 1985 (1984) color 75m. (orig titles: *Wizard Wars. La Guerra de Los Magos*). D: Hector Olivera. SP: Tom Edwards. Mus: Chris Young. SpFxMkp: Mike Jones. SpFX: Richard Lennox. Ref: TV: Worldvision-TV. V 11/6/85. 11/23/83: 11/1 start. Hound. Martin. Scheuer. Stanley. Horacio Higuchi. With Bo Svenson, Vidal Peterson, Thom Christopher, Maria Socas (Acrasia), Nick Cord (bat creature), Carl Garcia (Lizardtaur), Edward Morrow (Gulfax), Michael Fontaine (Hurla).

"It was an age of magic...an age of sorcery...an age of chaos." Scads of monsters and magicians here, not all of them original with this movie, include the sky gods from *Sorceress,* a woman who transforms into a big bug ("Acrasia, my insect woman"), the evil magician Shurka, Hurla the hobgoblin, cave phantoms, a fanged dwarf creature, a fanged Cyclops, a giant thug-creature, warriors who rise from the dead, then go back to sleep, and Gulfax the pet, a sort of Abominable Wookie....*Wizards'* very casual attitude towards incident and dialogue lies halfway between careless and amusing. Svenson's Kor is well (or ill) supplied with James Bond-like quips, though he occasionally waxes terribly serious.

**WIZARDS OF THE LOST KINGDOM II** Concorde/New Classics (Reid Shane) 1989 color 79m. D: Charles B. Griffith. SP: Lance Smith. PD: Kathleen Cooper. Ref: V 3/28/90: "boring trek." Martin. Scheuer. with David Carradine, Bobby Jacoby, Lana Clarkson, Mel Welles, Blake Bahner, Sid Haig, Henry Brandon, Susan Lee Hoffman.

"Many well-endowed women" in a "far future era." (V)

**WOH PHIR AAYEGI** (India) Jayvijay Ents.(Jay Mehta) 198-? color c140m. SP, D: B.R. Ishaara. SP: also Bhushan Banmali. Ph: M. Roy. Mus: Anand Milind. AD: L.S. Sawant. FX: Prasad Prods., M.A. Hafez. Mkp: P.J. Bhagat. Ref: TV: Shiva Video; no Eng.; Hindi. Meadows Video: *She'll Be Back* - tr t. With Rajesh Khanna, Farha, Moon Moon Sen, Shekhar Suman, Archana Puran Singh.

Routine-looking possession horror re a ghost who possesses a woman, who then supernaturally assaults another woman, makes a man's head get crunched by a door, makes walls crack, makes a bed spin, makes stuffed cats' eyes bleed, and leaves footprints of blood. At the end, an exorcism expels the evil spirit.

**WOLF** Col (Douglas Wick) 1994 color 125m. D: Mike Nichols. SP, Assoc P: Jim Harrison. SP: also Wesley Strick;(uncred.) Elaine May. Ph: Giuseppe Rotunno. Mus: Ennio Morricone. PD: Bo Welch. SpMkpFX: Rick Baker; Greg Nelson. SpVisFX: Sony Pictures Imageworks;(anim) Scott Kilburn;(des) Jon Townley; IL&M. Animatronics: Tom Woodruff Jr., Alec Gillis. SpFX:(co-ord) Stan Parks; D.A. Sudick. Main Titles: R/Greenberg. Ed: Sam O'Steen. Ref: TV. Vallejo T-H 6/17/94. Sacto Bee 6/17/94. SFChron 6/17/94. With Jack Nicholson (Will Randall), Michelle Pfeiffer, James Spader (Stewart Swinton), Richard Jenkins, Christopher Plummer, Om Puri, Eileen Atkins, Ron Rifkin, Osgood Perkins.

"You are becoming a wolf." A "wolf in Vermont" bites Will Randall, the "last civilized man," at a time when the moon is the "closest it's been to Earth in a hundred years." Apparently, Will already had an "analog of the wolf" within himself, and he begins sleeping days and staying up nights, sharpening his senses, and developing great leaping ability. ("I think I'm dangerous, especially at night.") And there seems to be a second werewolf at large.... Pretty tired worm-turns story incorporates Poe (Will's heightened "Usher" senses) and Cocteau (Will's beast, more at home in a forest than an office) and finally turns into *The Wolf Man/WereWolf of London/Cat People,* without the bite. ("Lock me up before it gets dark.") The script posits good and bad werewolves and thus makes possible a blandly happy ending. Spader gives the slickest performance, as Mr. Slime, in the most amusing scenes. Fun leaping effects. And love the way the fog rolls in and covers the Columbia logo.

**WOLF ALICE** see *Company of Wolves, The*

**WOLF DEVIL WOMAN** (H.K.) Chang I-Shiang 1984 color c90m. (*Wolfen Ninja* - alt t). SP, D: Chang Ling. Ref: TV: Ocean Shores Video. NST! 4:40. Fango 107:59. MMarquee 43:7-8. VW 23:7. With Chang Ling, Shih Fong.

Followers of the evil Red Devil include martial-arts experts and fanged monsters; his victims—paralyzed by golden needles stuck in voodoo dolls, and stored in a museum as "breathing corpses"—are "worse than zombies." Red Devil: "This is just an eccentric hobby." His female partner shoots yellow rays, spiders, and webs. In the climactic sequence, the Red Devil slings flames, but the heroine, Wolf Woman, who was raised by wolves, bites her own arm and puts out the flames with her spurting blood.

The wolves provided Wolf Woman with everything, including lipstick and hair spray, while the Red Devil sometimes affects a Southern-colonel accent. Visual effects are crude but many; sound effects, absurdly artificial. *Wolf Devil Woman* is a campy mixture of fantasy, comedy, pathos, and gore. It's a mess, but a lively one.

**WOLFEN NINJA** see *Wolf Devil Woman*

The **WOLFMAN** (Cuban) Noel Lima & Jose Reyes c1982 anim c2m. Ref: SFChron Dtbk 4/26/92: Filminutos.

Re a "beast who is really just a puppy dog."

**WOLNYOUI HAN** (S. Korean) Han Jin Ents. (Han Kap Chin) 1980 color 100m. D: Kim In Soo. SP: Lee Moon Woong. Ref: Hardy/HM: "eye-catching...imagery"; aka Grudge of the Moon Lady. With Chin Bong Chin, Huh Chin.

"Vampire movie" re an "evil white cat spirit."

The **WOMAN IN BLACK** (B) Central Independent TV & Cap-globe Ltd. (Chris Burt) 1989 color c90m. D: Herbert Wise. SP: Nigel Kneale, from Susan Hill's book. Ph: Michael Davis. Mus: Rachel Portman. PD: Jon Bunker. SpFX: Ace FX. Mkp: Christine Allsopp. Ref: TV: A&E. TVG. Newman. With Adrian Rawlins, Pauline Moran (The Woman in Black), Bernard Hepton, David Daker, David Ryall, Clare Holman, William Simons, Fiona Walker.

"She has found ways to make me hear their calamity in the marshes." Solicitor Arthur Kidd (Rawlins) finds the Drablow house on the marshes outside Crythin Gifford (a "little market town on the coast") to be haunted by the cries of tragedy past. He hears the "calamity in the marshes"—in which a woman (Moran) and her little daughter died—again and again, "as if it were somehow recorded." Now, when the Woman in Black appears, a child dies, through accident or illness.

This movie dawdles, but gets chillier and chillier, as a child's voice haunts a locked (then mysteriously unlocked) room, and a whistling noise draws a dog out into the dark. The sights and sounds of the handsomely desolate countryside dominate. A drawn-out coda, set in London, issues in an inevitable climax.

The **WOMAN IN GREEN** Univ 1945 68m. (*Sherlock Holmes and the Woman in Green* - ad t). D, P: Roy William Neill. SP: Bertram Millhauser, from Sir Arthur Conan Doyle's story "The Adventure of the Empty House." Ph: Virgil Miller. Mus D: Mark Levant. AD: John B. Goodman, Martin Obzina. SpPh: John P. Fulton. Ref: TV. Lee. Lentz. V 6/20/45. Martin. Scheuer. no Stanley. Hound. Maltin '92. Ecran F 67:66. 68:68. With Basil Rathbone, Nigel Bruce, Henry Daniell, Hillary Brooke, Matthew Boulton, Paul Cavanagh, Eve Amber, Frederic Worlock, Tom Bryson, Mary Gordon, Olaf Hytten.

"A series of the most atrocious murders since Jack the Ripper" plagues London, in Universal's version of *Hangover Square*.

Ingredients include an apparent "fiend," "ghoul," or "mad-man"..."horrible finger murders" ...blackmail victims who believe that they "may have committed these atrocious murders themselves...during some dreadful lapse of sanity"...hypnotized assassins...and a sequence in which Dr. Watson (Bruce) wanders about a dark, abandoned building.

Blandly efficient Holmes mystery is marked by an unobtrusive use of off-angle shots and by engaging performances from regulars Rathbone (Holmes) and Bruce and from guest-Moriarty Daniell. Bruce's best muttered line: "There ought to be a law against fat people keeping little dicky birds."

\*\***The WOMAN IN WHITE** WB (Henry Blanke) 1948 108m. D: Peter Godfrey. SP: Stephen M. Avery, from Wilkie Collins' novel. SpFX: William McGann, Robert Burks. Mkp: Perc Westmore. Ref: TV. TVG. V 4/21/48. Lee(e). Agee. Scheuer. Maltin '92. no Stanley. no Phantom.

Gothic mystery—with a few fantasy-horror sequences—set in Limmeridge, England, 1851. Count Fosco (Sydney Greenstreet), an "incredible fiend," induces a typhus-like illness in a woman (Eleanor Parker), and later "transmits"—via hypnosis-like "psychological poison"—the thoughts of a dead madwoman (Parker again) to her....A very mixed bag of (bad) melodrama and (intriguing) mystery-horror elements, including a storm and a hidden room. The thought-transference scene seems not to be just memory (no one told Laura how Ann escaped from The Cedars asylum), but way-out fantasy: Fosco insists that the dead Ann's thoughts are his thoughts, and that his thoughts are Laura's thoughts, and Laura indeed picks up one which he should have censored....Typically classy, atmospheric Warners scoring (by Max Steiner), photography (by Carl Guthrie), and art direction (by Stanley Fleischer, who, like Steiner, also worked on *The Beast with Five Fingers*, 1946).

**WOMEN WITH SWORDS** see *Heroic Trio, The*

**WONDER GIRLFRIEND** (H.K.) Win's Video 1993 color 88m. Ref: TV: World Video; no Eng. vc box: Maggie proves to be an E.T.

A spaceship which looks like a cartoon Saturn-with-rings hovers above Earth and deposits a little flying cartoon ball which turns into the title lady. The latter subsists on large quantities of water, has a magic bag and telekinetic powers, and shoots hand-rays.... Inconsequential sf-comedy. Shot-on-tape.

**WONDER WOMAN** see *Project "A"Ko*

**WONDERFUL ELECTRIC BELT, The** see *Ceinture Electrique, La* (1907)

**WONDERFUL EYES & MARVELOUS EARS** (H.K.?) American Intercontinental 1979 color/ws? c88m. D: Fu Ching-Hua. SP: Chang Yen-Fu. Ref: TV: Vertex Video; Eng. titles.

Fantasy-comedy has a few spooky sequences—principally, the long one in which the two gods of the title cavort and play "ghost" to scare worshippers away from a shrine, which then acquires the reputation of being haunted; another sequence in which the two appear briefly at a royal court as menacing giants. Unforgettable, sort of: the big, green-eyed Divine Eagle—or the Giant Claw,

Jr.—that carries a warrior-boy on its back....An alternately ex-cruciating and amusing movie. The two-stooges gods wear out their welcome in their first few scenes, but there are dozens of entertaining (if economical) effects.

**WONDERGUY** Take Twelve 1992 (1991) color feature. SP, D, P: Murad Gumen. Ph: Tim Tyler. AD: Todd Rutt. SpMkpFX: Vincent Schicchi, Louie Zakarian. Ref: V 2/25/91:46(ad). PT 19:60,61: "charming fantasy comedy." With Ann Osmond (witch), Thomas Groves (warlock), Pilar Uribe, Carter Cochran, Kevin Nagle.

Super-strength serum, witches, monster, devil.

**WOODCHIPPER MASSACRE** Donna Michele Prods. 1989 color c86m. SP, D, P: Jon McBride. Idea: Glen Skaggs. Mus: Soundscapes. Mkp: P. Edeal. Ref: TV: Michele video. Hound. no Martin. McCarty II (appendix). with J. McBride, Denice Edeal, Tom Casiello, Patricia McBride, Kim Bailey, Perren Page.

Tom accidentally stabs annoying Aunt Tess to death, with a hunting knife, while she is looking after his brother and sister and himself for the weekend. Jon and Denice help him roll her up in a tarp, saw her up, freeze her, then run her through the rented woodchipper. Tess's weird son Kim shows up, makes threats ("If you tell anybody else about this, I'll come back and get you!"), and winds up as more woodchipper material.

Flat shot-on-tape While Daddy Was Away joke, though the movie isn't as bad as it is cheap. Tess's table grace re "squirming" thoughts has some funny stuff in it, but her campy-comic grating gets to be only grating, and the cast's uniformly stentorian style of speaking becomes tiresome.

**WOOLY BOOLY: ANG CLASSMATE KONG ALIEN** (Fili) Viva Films (William Leary, Tess R. Cruz) 1989 color c125m. Story, SP, D: Ben Feleo. Story, SP: also Ely Matawaran. Ph: Erning de la Paz. Mus D: Mon del Rosario. PD: Arthur Sta. Maria. SpMkp: Cecille Baun. VisFX:Cinemagic. SdFX: J. Martinez. Ref: TV: Viva Video; part Eng. With Jimmy Santos (Wooly Booly), Vina Morales, Gelli de Belen, Raymart Santiago, Kenneth Peralta, Kier Legaspi, Mariz, Ruel Vernal, Jimmy Fabregas, Ben Johnson, Jade Manalo.

"An alien spaceship has been found." An intelligent, ape-like, Tagalog and English-speaking alien from "Neptune University" crashlands his ship on Earth. He finds that his adopted human-like appearance helps him get along at St. Goliath Academy, and uses his special powers to disappear at will, sever a traffic cop's head, make a car drive harmlessly through a man's body, make the car fly, freeze people in motion, bring a fellow student back to life, change the location of a man's private parts, and, predict-ably, at the end, help his team win on the basketball court.

Episodic, sometimes droll sf-comedy is just a series of quasi-tele-kinetic stunts by "Wooly Booly," some of them amusing—e.g., his plucking the stiffness out of an aching person's neck, his setting a table fan at hurricane force.

Sequel: *Titser Kong Alien* (*Wooly Booly II*).

**WOOLY BOOLY 2** see *Titser Kong Alien, Ang*

**WOOS WHOOPEE** Educational 1928 anim silent 8m. (aka *Felix Woos Whoopee*). Ref: screen. Crafton/BM. no LC. no Lee. SFChron 3/23/92:D2.

Felix the Cat, blotto, is confronted by a lamppost which becomes a dragon, a snake from a bottle, a monster-car, a huge ape (with rudimentary wings), etc. Cartoon short is rife with both familiar and unfamiliar, even unusual, Felix-film transformations.

**WORKING STIFFS** LSVideo 1990 feature? Ref: Filmfax 52:3(ad): zombies.

**WORLD APARTMENT HORROR** (J) Embodiment Films (Sony Music Ent. & Quarter Flash)/Hero Osaki, Yasuhisa Kazama 1991 color/ws 98m. (*Warudo Apatomento Hora*). SP, D: Katsuhiro Otomo. SP: also Keiko Nobumoto. Ref: TV: S. M. E. video; little Eng. V 1/20/92. Markalite 3:10. Weisser/JC. With Hiroki Tanaka, Yuji Nakamura, Weng Huarong, Kimiko Naka-gawa.

"The dead would not choose the way of the living." A drawing of a demon on the wall of an old apartment building seems linked with a disconnected phone which rings and oozes, a ceiling which expands, a fire which is no sooner set than it is invisibly snuffed out, an indoor wind, and the possessed hero, who wields a nasty chainsaw. Ultimately, a demon mask breaks, the house starts to crack up, and a giant demon awakens and—apparently satisfied with a gangster boss as a sacrifice—goes back to sleep.

A bizarrely comic approach distinguishes this cross between a conventional haunted house/possession movie and "The Lower Depths." At its best, it recalls the film versions of the latter, as well as *The Haunting*. Wry, atmospheric, a bit poky.

**WORLD GONE WILD** Lorimar/Apollo (Robert L. Rosen/World Gone Wild) 1988 (1987) color 94m. D: Lee H. Katzin. SP: Jorge Zamacona. Mus: Laurence Juber. SpFxSup: Cliff Wenger. Mkp/Prosth: R. Burman. Ref: TV. V 4/27/88. 4/8/87:24. SFChron Dtbk 5/1/88(ad). Morse. Hound. Maltin '92. Phantom. V 11/11/87:4(rated). with Bruce Dern, Michael Pare, Catherine Mary Stewart, Adam Ant, Anthony James, Alan Autry.

"Nothin' makes sense in a world gone wild." Lost Wells, in a water-poor future where hubcaps are weapons, cannibals lurk, Old West gunfights take place onstage in "the city," and "hard-core nutcase" Derek Abernathy (Ant) abducts and brainwashes boys for his "prayer group." (He's God.).... Idiosyncrasy runs wild. Everyone's a character here. *The Road Warrior* plot, though, is purely functional. Listen for Dern's "Just a test."

The **WORLD OF DRACULA** Univ-TV (Kenneth Johnson) 1979 color c90m. (*The Curse of Dracula*—series t). Tel, D: Johnson. D: also Sutton Roley, Jeffrey Hayden. SP: also Craig Buck, Myla Lichtman, Renee & Harry Longstreet. Ph: R. F. Liu, Mario DeLeo. Mus: Les Baxter, Joe Harnell. AD: Gary A. Lee. Paint-ings: Jaroslav Gebr. Ref: TV. TVG. Stanley: TV-series episodes. no Scheuer. no Maltin '92. Jones. with Michael Nouri, Louise Sorel, Carol Baxter, Stephen Johnson, Antoinette Stella, Mark Montgomery.

Kurt Van Helsing and the daughter of one vampire victim take on a verbose, romantic Dracula, "condemned" to night and darkness for 512 years. Dracula's dogs here are named Desdemona and Othello. Stilted, flavorless instant-romanticism, with Muzak scoring. Hokey climactic reunion between daughter and vampire mom. Comprises all ten episodes of the *Curse of Dracula* third of the "Cliffhangers" series; *Dracula 79* comprises the first four episodes.

**WORLD OF THE TALISMAN, The** see *Birth*

**The WORST WITCH** (B) Central Independent TV 1986 color 70m. D: Robert Young. Tel: Mary P. Willis, from Jill Murphy's story. SpVisFX: Tom McKerrow. Ref: TV. TVG. no Scheuer. Stanley. no Maltin '90. SFChron Dtbk 10/17/93: Prism Ent. video.

Gaggle of silly, wicked witches…semi-spooky musical paean to Halloween ("Anything Can Happen on Halloween"). Some cute moments in this comic fantasy. Props courtesy of the Acme Spell Company.

**WOT A NIGHT** RKO/Van Beuren 1931 anim 9m. SP?: John Foster. Ref: TV: Kino Video. Lee (LC).

Clever, oddball cartoon's main stunner: the bat-ghost creature of the castle. Plus: a skeleton in a bathtub, a horde of ghosts, and skeletal harmonizers that sound like they just stepped out of *Green Pastures*.

**The WRAITH** New Century & Vista/Alliance Ent. & John Kemeny (Turbo Prods.) 1986 color 92m. SP, D: Mike Marvin. Mus: Hoenig, Robinson. VisFX: (des) Alan Munro; VCE, Peter Kuran; (anim) Steven Burg, Kevin Kutchaver, J. Friday. SpFxDes: Phil Cory. MinFX: James Belohovek. Mkp: Kathryn Miles Logan. SdFxSup: J. Troutman, P. Clay. Ref: TV. MFB'87:29-30. V 11/26/86. ad. Phantom. With Charlie Sheen (The Wraith/Jake), Nick Cassavetes, Sherilyn Fenn, Randy Quaid, Clint Howard, Griffin O'Neal.

"Roadblocks won't stop something that can't be stopped." Brooks, Arizona. The driver of the indestructible black mystery car—which is able to vanish and is the "only one in existence" of its kind—turns out to be "Jake," the murdered, resurrected Jamie (Christopher Bradley), more or less. Who or what—aliens or some Spirit of Justice—resurrected the latter as the avenging wraith is not made clear.

The second coming of *The Car*, or third, if you count *Christine*. Marvin the director overcompensates for Marvin the writer's still-born script with noise and action, in this lively but generally lousy action-horror-musical. (A new rock number blasts away at every opportunity.) Eerie image: the "spaceman" in the light beside the tombstone.

**WRITER'S BLOCK** USA-TV/Wilshire Court (Skylark Films/Vanessa Greene) 1991 color c90m. D: Charles Correll. Tel, Story: Elisa Bell. Story: also Tracy Barone. Mus: Nan Schwartz. PD: Kathy Curtis-Cahill. SpFX: Robin D'Arcy, Larry Fioritto. Mkp: Phyllis Temple. Ref: TV. V 10/14/91:247. TVG. with Morgan Fairchild, Joe Regalbuto, Michael Praed, Douglas Rowe, Cheryl Anderson.

The "dark stranger" strangles victims—but is the Red Ribbon Killer the product of an author's computer or a real-life serial killer? The half-clever, half-absurd premise: Magenta Hart's (Fairchild) computer composing seems to dictate both a real killer's actions and those of her book's (visualized) villain.

**WURDALAK, The** see *Black Sabbath. Father, Santa Klaus Has Died. Those Feedy on Blood.*

# X

**XANADU** (J) Kadokawa/Video MBS (Toho) 1988 anim color 51m. Based on the video game. Ref: TV: Toho Video; no Eng. Animag 3:6.

Ingredients in this talky sword-and-sorcery saga include a being with tentacles spewing out its mouth…a porcupiney, electrified flying warship…big vicious war bugs and their monstrous dispatcher ... an initially invisible, lizard-like monster…flying reptile mounts…and, in a flashback, a gigantic flying dragon….Hard to follow without a scorecard. Seems routine, though, with okay visual touches. Some gore.

**XANGADIX** see *Johnsons, De*

**XENIA** Cetus/Edwards-Reemes 1990 color 84m. SP, D: Dennis Edwards. D: also Dana M. Reemes. SP: also Randolph Pitts. Ph: Gary Tomsic. Mus: Preston Oliver. Ref: Sacto Bee 10/30/90: "handsome and very self-assured horror-movie parody is surprisingly good." ad. With Reemes, Edwards, Herb A. Lightman, Timothy Gray, Sharie-Marie Jonsin, Bob Wilkins.

Movie-within-the-movie, "Xenia, Priestess of the Night," re a "belly-dancing vampire with a lisp."

**XI XUEFU** see *Vampire Woman*

**XIE** (H.K.) Shaw 1980 color/ws 95m. SP, D: Zihong Gui. Ref: Hardy/HM: made with "considerable skill"; *Hex* - tr t? NST! 4:26. with Tanny, Jung Wang, Szu-chia Chen, Kuo-tsai Han.

Scholar pretends to drown, returns as "ghost" to scare wife to death. Latter's ghost then seems to return to scare him to death.

**XIE ZHOU** see *Curse of Evil*

**XOXONTLA (TIERRA QUE ARDE)** (Mex) Conacite Uno 1976 color c110m. (*Xoxontla—El Lugar de los Brujos*-ad t). SP, D: Alberto Mariscal. SP: also F. G. Serrano, F. Serrano. Story: A. C. De La Torre. SpFX: Leon Ortega. SdFX: Juan Banos. Mkp: Elda Loza. Ref: TV: Eagle Video; no Eng. TVG.

Historical epic set in Mexico, 1943, features one horrific sequence, in which a witch's brew gives the hero (Carlos Castanon) hallucinations—he sees and fights his (visualized) double. There's also a bit of machete gore….Atmospheric scene-setting and score; lots of talk.

**The XTERMINATOR** Sheer Essence (Mike Phillips) 1986 color c75m. D: Adam. Ref: TV: Paradise Visuals video: abridged version. no Adam '88. with Trinity Loren, Kari Foxx, Tony Martin (The Xterminator), Shanna McCullough, Marc Wallice.

An android (Martin) takes a guided tour of The Pleasure Palace ("You're not human!"), while computer-readout titles record his reactions. ("They certainly make a lot of noise.") At the end, the doorbell rings again: "Not another one!" Not exactly plotty adult sf-er. Dialogue reference to Arnold Schwarzenegger.

**XTRO II: THE SECOND ENCOUNTER** (Can.) NAR-Excalibur (Simandl-Curtis/B.C. Film) 1991 (1990) color 92m. D: Harry Bromley-Davenport. SP: J. A. Curtis, S. Lister, R. Smith, E. Kovach. Creature Des: Charlie Grant, Wayne Dang. VisFX: Cyberflex Films; (sup) Greg Deroche. Prosth FX: ET & Co.; (sup) Tibor Farkas. SpFX: Paller SpFX. SpCreatureSd: Robert Small. Ref: TV: New Line HV. V 11/26/90:55. SFChron Dtbk 6/20/93. With Jan-Michael Vincent, Paul Koslo, Tara Buckman, Jano Frandsen, Nicholas Lea.

Marshall (Tracy Westerholm)—one of three explorers "misplaced in a parallel universe"—returns with an *Alien*-ish chestburster, "some sort of life form that has a taste for human beings." Near the end, a scientist (Koslo) full of monster "seeds" must also be destroyed.... Vapid dialogue, tiresome characterizations, rote suspense, and a monotonous monster, in this unworthy follow-up to *Xtro*.

# Y

**Y...DONDE ESTA EL MUERTO?** (Peruvian) Futuro Films (Leonidas Zegarra) 1985 color c75m. D: Joaquin Vargas, Rafael Caparros. SP: Jose Caparros. Ph: Franco Bernetti. Mus: J. M. Salas. Mkp: Garfield. Ref: TV: Madera CineVideo; no Eng.; *And...Where Is the Dead Man?* - tr t. TVG. With Yvonne Frayssinet, Ricardo Fernandez, Nilda Munoz, Teddy Guzman, Pablo Fernandez, Flor de Maria Andrade, Lupe Soria, Haydee Caceres.

Feeble shot-on-tape, old-dark-house horror-comedy features a living dead man who comes out of his coffin to scare all his heirs away. During the course of the movie, his huge, superimposed, moldy face keeps reappearing, and at the end he laughs. Also on the program: a weird-looking housekeeper and a man in a sheet and monster mask.

**YAMATO—NEW VOYAGE** (J) 1979 anim color 95m. (aka *Space Cruiser Yamato—The New Voyage*). Created by Leiji Matsumoto & Yoshinobu Nishizaki. Ref: TV: Toei Video; no Eng. Animag 10:6-19: TV-movie. 6:18.

In the year 2201, the planet Gamilas explodes during a battle, and the shock waves generated throw its sister planet Iscandar out of orbit. The Yamato's wave-motion gun destroys the Pleiades, flagship of the Dark Nebula Empire, which wants Iscandar's resources, but this action only sets the stage for the appearance of Goruba, the Empire's gigantic battle/space-station. Ultimately, Iscandar self-destructs and takes Goruba with it. A sentimental interplanetary romance also figures in the action.

*Yamato—New Voyage* plays like a simplified version of *Gundam*. The music sounds like a patchwork stock score, and character animation is very stilted, though the background paintings are pretty, and the space battles are visually varied. Film in fact seems to be just one long battle.

**YAMATO TAKERU** (J) Toho 1994 color/ws 104m. SpFX: Takao Oogawara, Koichi Kawakita. Ref: TV: Toho Video; little

Eng. VSOM. V 7/25/94:14: in Japan. CM 16:50-52: based on *Kojiki*. Weisser/JC.

"Long, long ago, this universe was in complete silence and darkness." A pretty, crystal spaceship attends the birth of two babies. One is taken by a wizard, then saved by a giant metal bird. Later, all grown up, he can turn demonic and shoot rays. Meanwhile, the arms of a huge, volcanic monster slickly morph into bow-and-arrows, and the wizard becomes an eight-headed dragon which can spew lightning bolts. Plus a hokey, wizard-imagined tentacled sea giant ... binding rays ... and a sword in a stone.... Impressive long shots and effects—especially for the dragon: As many as three or four of its heads can breathe fire at the same time. Two of the best effects: the sorcerer and heroine, respectively, simply morphing away—he, first, all at once; she, later, a limb at a time. The volcanic creature may be the wizard in another form.

**YAMI NI HIKARU ME** see *Fear of the Mummy*

**YANZHI KOU** see *Rouge*

**The YEAR MY VOICE BROKE** (Austral.) Avenue Ent./IVE (Kennedy Miller) 1987 ('88-U.S.) color 103m. SP, D: John Duigan. Ref: TV. SFChron 9/9/88. V 8/26/87. HR 8/1/88.

"Would you go in there at night?" The Southern Tablelands, New South Wales, 1962. "Something cold"—an unseen "force field"—scares teens out of a "ghost house...the old place on the hill." ("Place is known to be haunted.") Bittersweet, prettily shot, but talky, familiar coming-of-age story also has one fake-ghost bit. ("You thought I was a ghost!") Interesting philosophical theme posits that the "whole world's a museum," and that "good times" and bad leave behind an "imprint," a sort of emotional Kirlian effect—hence the ghost scene with the heroine Freya's mother.

**3P The YELLOW CAB MAN** MGM (Richard Goldstone) 1950 84m. D: Jack Donohue. SP: Devery Freeman, Albert Beich. Comedy Consulltant: Edward Sedgwick. Ph: Harry Stradling. Mus: Scott Bradley. AD: C. Gibbons, Eddie Imazu. Distortion Effect: Weegee. SpFX: Gillespie & Newcombe. Ref: TV. Lee. V 2/22/50. Stanley. With Red Skelton, Gloria de Haven, Walter Slezak, Edward Arnold, James Gleason, Jay C. Flippen, Paul Harvey, Polly Moran.

Baseballs bounce off an inventor's "impenetrable, super-view elasti-glass," created by fusing silica with alkali.... Awkward combination of slapstick, science fiction, psychology, and romance. Funny sequence with cabbie Skelton attacked by an aggressive little boy ("That ain't funny !") is right out of W. C. Fields. Some fun also in the fantasy sequences in which Skelton, unconscious, imagines a flying cab and, later, under narcosynthesis, "sees" distorted vehicles and pedestrians, and finds himself a baby again, with his twin sister (also played by Skelton), in a giant crib.

**YEVO ZOVUT ROBERT** see *It's Called Robert*

**YIU SAU DOUSI** see *Wicked City* (1993)

**YO** (S. Korean) Wha Pung Industrial Co. (Chung Chang Wha) 1980 color 95m. D: Kim Young Hyo. SP: Sang Hak Chi. Ref: Hardy/HM: the "spectral appearances lack conviction"; *Capriciousness*-tr t? With Choo Ryun Kim, Soo Young Ran.

Gambler plays ghost to scare his wife to death; she then plays ghost....

**YOGI AND THE INVASION OF THE SPACE BEARS** (U.S.-Taiwanese) Hanna-Barbera & Wang Film/Cuckoo's Nest 1988 anim color 90m. (aka *Yogi and the Space Bears*). D, Anim D: Don Lusk. Des Sup: Jack White. Computer Anim Sup: P. B. Strickland. Ref: TV: Worldvision Ent.-TV. TVG. no Maltin '92. no Scheuer. Voices: Daws Butler, Don Messick et al.

Yogi (sleeps with his hat on) Bear and Boo Boo become "celestial lunar guests" aboard a spaceship. The aliens therein make hundreds of "duploids" of our two heroes, who are then set loose in space in a bubble, while the carbon-copy bears are let loose on Earth. ("Yogis to the left! Boo Boos to the right!") Humdrum.

**YOHTO DEN** (J) C.I.C.-Victor 1987 anim color 41m. (aka *Yotoden: Strange Tale from a War Torn Land*). Monster Des: Junichi Watanabe. Char Des & Anim D: Kenichi Onuki. Ref: TV: RCA Victor video; no Eng. M/TVM 10/87:82. Animag 8: 24-29: 1st of 3 OAVs also released together theatrically with 8 "bridging" minutes.

Fairly stylish, otherwise undistinguished fantasy-adventure. Main monster: a giant, three-headed, caterpillar-dragon cousin of Ghidrah. Other creepies include a green-slime-monster, a carnivorous red-haired monster, a gaggle of clawed, beaked creatures, and an *Alien/Xtro*-derived crab-tentacle thing. Weeping women provide the sentiment. Set in the latter half of sixteenth-century Japan.

**YOHTO DEN, PART TWO: CHAPTER OF WAILING DEMONS** (J) C.I.C.-Victor 1988? anim color 40m. Ref: Animag 11:6-8. Japan Video.

Possessed woman, "demon master of illusion," "demon Masago of Kira," etc.

**YOHTO DEN, PART THREE: CHAPTER OF BLAZING FLAMES** (J) C.I.C.-Victor 1988 anim color 45m. SP: Riji Yamazaki. Ref: Animag 4:8. 12:8-13. Japan Video.

"At Azuchi castle, demons tear ravenously at the bodies of the dead." Plus: living corpses, a "demon doorway" from another dimension, and the monstrous Nobunaga in his "hideous true form."

**YOJU TOSHI** see *Monster City*

**YOKAI HANTA—HIRUKO** see *Hiruko the Goblin*

**YOMA** see *Youma*

**YOTODEN** see *Yohto Den*

**YOTSUYA KAIDAN** (J) 1927. D: K. Sato. Ref: CM 15:24. With R. Akashi, T. Matsueda.

**YOTSUYA KAIDAN—CHUSHINGURA GAIDEN** (J) 1994. D: Kinji Fukasaku. Ref: CM 15:27: a combo of the *Yotsuya* and *Chushingura* stories; "a very good film." Weisser/JC. With Koichi Sato, H. Takaoka, R. Ishibashi.

Oiwa, one of two ghosts, is "given supernatural, superhuman powers...."

See also *Bancho Sara Yashiki. Iro Wa Kamei Yotsuya Kaidan. Masho No Natsu—Yotsuya Kaidan Yori.*

**YOU-GEN-KAI-SYA** see *Phantom Quest Corp.*

**YOUJU KYOSHITSU** (J) c1990? anim color 87m. (Dreamy Express Zone series). Ref: TV: Daiei Video; no Eng.

Ingredients in this semi-hardcore sf-horror cartoon: a mutating, tentacled demon lover ... the hero, who keeps interrupting the latter's dates...and a vagina-spawned alien-type snake creature which appears first in a visualized nightmare, then for real, and which subsequently becomes a bat-like critter, then a giant.

Tiresomely episodic sensationalism seems to be a compilation of several shorter videos. Writhing phallic tentacles quickly become old-hat. Slightly different: a masturbating statue of Buddha.

**YOUJO MELON** (J) SPO/Oriental Cine Service 199-? color c45m. Ref: TV: Qusumi Project Video; no Eng. With Dan Jones, Oto.

The removal of a charm from a statuette leads to a gory impaling, a suddenly carnivorous TV set, ghoul attacks, and the appearance of an apparent queen of the ghouls. Dismal shot-on-taper.

**YOUKAITENGOKU** (J) Pony Video/Papado 1986 color 50m. D:M. Tezuka. Weisser/JC: "Monster Heaven"-tr t. SpMkpFX: Tomoo Haraguchi, Noboru Tamura, Hidenori Ichikawa, Nobuhiro Kikuchi. SpVisFX: Yasuo Fujita. SpVisualizer: Macoto Tezka. Ref: TV: PV; no Eng.

A magic alien sword seems to summon up tales re (1) sword gore, a small alien critter which apparently dies, but revives in the rain, and the ghosts of the two sword slain ... (2) (in a silent-movie-style clip) a people-eating shrine ... (3) a ghostly stranger that makes two men go mad and die, and ... (4) a talking severed head and a horde of ghosts. Effects-filled but routine shot-on-tape shocker.

**YOU'LL DIE AT MIDNIGHT** see *Carrol Morira a Mezzanotte*

**YOUMA 1** (J) Toho & MPS 1990 (1988) anim color 37m. (aka *Yoma*). By Kei Kusunoki. Ref: TV: vt; no Eng.; OAV. Animag 6:5: 1st of 2 OAVs; 1989. vc box: *Curse of the Undead: Yoma* - U.S.

Melting hands ... ghouls from graves ... a flying-star eye-gouger ... an eviscerated body ... and a heavy-duty spider web in the woods. What's behind it all? — a huge, heavy-duty spider or two. An old man mutates into a spider-creature body which retains his head, and the woman of the mystery house is also a were-spider .... Okay score, okay gross-out shocks. Good moves: the sudden illumination of the mystery-house interior, which reveals a forest of webs ... the "tentacle-ization" of the woman's hair.

**The YOUNG AVENGER** (H.K.?) Oriental Motion Pictures/Ping Film Co. (Raymond Keung) 1988-U.S. color 89m. (*Young Avengers* - ad t). D: Ton Wai Shing. SP: Tin Ping Group; Lo Wai. Ph: F.C. Lam. Mus: C.F. Kai. Ref: TV: Video Treasures; Eng. dubbed. no Hound. no Martin. With Wong Yue, Tsui Siu Keung, Wong Hen Sau, Kong Tao.

"You ever dared to pee on my remains." A ghost from a graveyard urn ("Mr. Ghost, forgive me!") wants our hero to "get rid" of some men. ("After all, I am a ghost!") But Bud Ming proves, after all, not be a ghost ("My face was eaten by ants. That's why it looks like this now"), just a man abandoned for dead .... Latter revelation, though, leaves unexplained the fact that Ming first looks and speaks out from inside an urn. Thin, crudely dubbed horror-comedy-kung-fu-er.

**YOUNG EINSTEIN** (Austral.-U.S.) WB/Serious (Ross-Roach & Australian Film Commission) 1988 color 91m. SP, D: Yahoo Serious. SP: also David Roach. Ph: Jeff Darling. Mus: William Motzing et al. SpFX: Patrick Fitzgerald et al. Surfologist: Robert Ashton. Anim: Flicks Anim. Ref: TV. Stanley. Scheuer. Sacto Union 8/5/89. With Y. Serious, Odile Le Clezio, John Howard, Peewee Wilson, Su Cruickshank, Lulu Pinkus, Johnny McCall (Tasmanian Devil).

"That's it! That's the theory of relativity!" In 1905 Tasmania, Einstein (Serious) splits the Tasmanian Beer atom. ("Split one once.") He goes on to discover the secret of "Roll 'n' Rock" (sic) and invent the surfboard. (At first, he tries surfing against the waves.) Later, he winds up in the local asylum's Mad Scientists Ward. At the end, he attempts to reverse an atomic chain reaction with amplified music in 4/4 time.... Serious' casual idiocy as an alternate-reality Einstein is occasionally quite taking. Film is not exactly inspired, but genial as all get out.

**YOUNG GOODMAN BROWN** 50th Street Films (Troma)/The Institute & Desert Music (Robert Tinnell) 1993 (1992) color 81m. SP, D, Exec Co-P: Peter George. From Nathaniel Hawthorne's story. Ph: Roxanne di Santo. Mus: Jon McCallum. PD: Jennifer Long. Ref: V 7/12/93: "stilted and portentous." 7/8/91:14: 7/15 start. With John P. Ryan (The Devil), Tom Shell, Judy Geeson, Dorothy Lyman.

"Unearthly goings-on ... the devil himself ... witchcraft."

**YOUNG GU AND THE DINOSAUR JUJU** (S. Korean) 198-? D: Shim Hyung Rei. Ref: HOF 2:25: dinosaurs.

**YOUNG KING ARTHUR** (U.S.-J) American Way/Animation Classics & Ziv Int'l & Toei Animation 1984 anim color 95m. From the "King Arthur" TV series. Ref: TV. Cable View. no Stanley. no Scheuer. no Maltin '92.

The witch Melissa — whose appearance is heralded by lightning —commands a strange fog and a storm. Also on hand: Merlin, Excalibur, the Green Knight, etc. Stilted storytelling, with a most unhelpful light-rock score. (Even the witch gets a song — "You Ain't Seen Nothin' Yet.") Okay effects and color design for the outdoor scenes.

**YOUNG SHERLOCK HOLMES** (U.S.-B) Para/Amblin & Winkler-Birnbaum (Mark Johnson/Harry Benn) 1985 color 109m. (*Young Sherlock Holmes and the Pyramid of Fear* -B). D:

Barry Levinson. SP: Chris Columbus. Mus: Bruce Broughton. VisFX: IL&M;(opt sup - Harpy sequence) John Ellis;(motion sup - pastry sequence) David Allen;(animatronics sup) Stephen Norrington;(anim sup) Bruce Walters, Ellen Lichtwardt;(anim - glass man sequence) Pixar Computer Animation;(anim - Harpy) Harry Walton;(sup) Dennis Muren. SpFxSup: Kit West. Mkp: Peter Robb-King. Ref: TV. MFB '86:122-4. V 11/27/85. With Nicholas Rowe, Alan Cox, Sophie Ward, Anthony Higgins, Freddie Jones, Michael Hordern.

Osiris worshipers, obsessed with "violent and sadistic rituals," prick victims with thorns dipped in an hallucination-producing potion. For the victim: horror; for the movie audience, captivating effects, including living, squeaky-voiced, armed-and-legged gingerbread men and cream puffs ... flying "harpy" bookends ... leaping stained-glass-window knights ... and rebellious turkey dinners and "snake" hatracks. The above effects are creepy and imaginative; the story itself divides into a charming first-half introduction to its main characters and a second half that's mainly noise and running about.

**The YOUNG TAOISM FIGHTER** (H.K.?) Lo Wai & Hsu Li Hwa 1986? color c95m. Ref: TV: Ocean Shores Video; Eng. titles.

Generally silly action-comedy has several amusing fantasy sequences and one comic-horror sequence in which a mummy returns to life. ("The dead revives!") An amulet returns him to death. In one of the two best fantasy scenes, the hero separates his "shadow," or double, from himself, and the latter taunts him, then shrinks to miniature size; in the other, the hero's arms and legs, cut off, continue to fight. In the oddest fantasy sequence, a spell wakes up the town's kids, and they go out and pee by a wall.

**YOUNG TIME TRAVELLERS** (B) 1984/1972 color c110m.? (*The Young Time Travelers* - TV ad t). Ref: TV. TVG. no Scheuer. no Maltin '92.

Comprises *The Boy Who Turned Yellow* (2P) and *Professor Wagstaff's Time Machine*. Featured: OSKA (Oscillating Short Wave Kinetic Amplifier).

**YOUNG WISELY** (H.K.) c1992? color 67m. Ref: TV: Tai Seng Video; no Eng.; shot-on-tape.

Temple ghosts ... lotsa cheap ray and fireball effects ... telekinesis ... monster-on-a-chain credit-sequence bit ... and a demonic priest.... Wisely again, but not well done.

See also: *Legend of Wisely, The.*

**YOUNG WISELY II: THE REBIRTH OF THE GODDESS** (H.K.) Film Prod. Co./Mei Ah Film 1993 color 59m. D: Clarence Fok. Ref: TV: Tai Seng Video; no Eng. With Loletta Lee, Deiwai.

Ingredients: a possessed teen ... a cross which repels same ... a demon duel ... and what looks like supernatural skiing. Cheap shot-on-taper has amusing costumes and a good computer effect or two.

**YUAN ZHENXIA YU WEISILI** see *Seventh Curse, The*

**YUDONO SANROKU NOROIMURA** see *Cursed Village in Yudono Mountain*

**YUME** see *Akira Kurosawa's Dreams*

**YUYU HAKUSHO** (J) Toei 1994 anim color/ws 25m. Ref: TV: Toei Video; no Eng. Vallejo Baseball.

Starring here: a human "unicorn" and other alien-types ... a giant from the sand which abducts a tot ... trees with tentacle branches and demons which glide in and out of their trunks ... a winged thing ... and a horde of miscellaneous monsters. Fun stuff.

**YUYU HAKUSHO: 2ND MOVIE** (J) Toho & Studio Pierrot & MOVIC 1994 anim color/ws 93m. Ref: TV: S. Baldric video (Toho Video); Eng. titles.

"Bonds of Fire—Battle in the Netherworld." This time: evil Lord Yakumo, ruler of the underworld and tiresome cackler ... Soul Energy, converted into Negative Energy ... the Three Demons and other monster-thugs ... the Soul Sword ... and Soul Chambers.... Too involved to involve. Some atmospheric settings, but generally a drag.

**YYALAH** see *Blood Sabbath*

# Z

**ZA CHOJO** see *Supergal, The*

**ZADAR! COW FROM HELL** Stone Peach 1989 color 87m. D, P: Robert C. Hughes. SP: Merle Kessler, from a story by Duck's Breath Mystery Theater. Mus: Greg Brown. AD: Ginni Barr. Ref: V 2/8/89: "excruciatingly thin." HR 1/27/89: "bright, witty." With Bill Allard, Dan Coffey, M. Kessler, Leon Martell.

Filmmakers go to Iowa to "produce a horror picture about an enormous radioactive cow."

**ZAERTLICHE CHAOTEN II** (W.G.) K.S. Film/Roxy Film & Co. KG 1988 color 96m. D: Holm Dressler. SP: Thomas Gottschalk. Ref: V 10/5/88: "lightweight spoof of *Back to the Future*"; *Three Crazy Jerks II* - tr t. Dr. Rolf Giesen. With Michael Winslow, T. Gottschalk, Deborah Shelton, Harold Leipnitz.

Two men use a time machine to "try to prevent the birth of their boss." (RG)

**ZAPPED AGAIN** Nelson Ent./ITC (Apple-Rosenthal) 1990 color 93. D: Doug Campbell. SP: J. Morris, V. Cheung, B. Montanio. Ref: V 3/14/90:30: "stale." 10/19/88:213(ad). With Todd Eric Andrews, Kelli williams, Reed Rudy, Maria McCann, Karen Black, Linda Blair, Sue Anne Langdon, Lyle Alzado.

"Mysterious elixir" gives high-schooler "telekinetic powers." Sequel to *Zapped!* (III).

**ZEGUY, Parts 1 & 2** (J) CPM/KSS Films (Iwakawa/Kageyama) 1993 ('94-U.S.) anim color 79m. SP, D: Shigenori Kageyama. Mus: S. Harada. Ref: TV: USManga Corps video; Eng. titles.

"I fell asleep on the bus, and when I woke up, some werewolves were kidnapping my best friend." Ingredients in "Labyrinth in the Clouds": The Mask of Zeguy, which is the key to controlling nature ... Hijikata Toshizo, a "warrior of Zeguy" ... "Himiko's monsters," which include the werewolves, cyborgs, and two giant bird-monsters ... The Gate of Winds ... the Cloud World ... the Crown of Shamas ... Cloud Roads, which link the various worlds here ... a "kitty compass" ... and a vehicle powered by "living electromagnetic ore" (which is hermaphroditic).... Blandly colorful, with some fun details in plot and design. Incidental highlight: the "junkyard in the clouds."

**ZEIRAM** (J) Gaga & Crowd (Chiba, Sugisawa) 1991('93-U.S.) 3-D/color/ws 97m. (*Zeiramu. Zeram* - U.S.). SP, D: Keita Amemiya. SP: also Hajime Matsumoto. Ref: TV: vt; no Eng. V 5/4/92:235(ad). Markalite 3:9. SFChron 2/8/93: subtitled version. Animerica 6:14. SFChron Dtbk 10/24/93: Fox/Lorber release in U.S. With Yuko Moriyama, Y. Hotaru, K. Ida.

Principal horror: an apparently-computer-generated, super-strong, mastermind-thug, in appearance a cross between Napoleon, Darth Vader, and an *Alien* alien. The most bizarre details of this fairish virtual fantasy concern this "outlaw creature's" anatomy and reproductive capacities: A feminine mask-face on its forehead turns out to be a sort of "prow" for a snake-thing inside; at one point, the thug creates (in stopmo) a little thug-thing which, as it assumes thing form, looks like a midget in a suit; at another point, the thug pulls a pod from its gut which becomes a squished monstrosity. And yet the main monster gets to be a pretty monotonous menace—until two belated (apparently stopmo) returns to skeletal-like life. Other wonders include a ray machine which makes people disappear, then reappear elsewhere, and a contraption which "freezes" victims temporarily. Perhaps the most imaginative bit: The heroine shoots a gizmo into the air, and "daylight" suddenly floods the land.

See also the following and *Iria*.

**ZEIRAM 2** (J) Emotion/Embodiment Films & Crowd (Zeiram Project) 1994 color/ws 100m. D: Keita Amemiya. Ref: TV: Bandai video; no Eng. Weisser/JC. With Yuko Moriyama.

The weird little face in the armor is back; at one point becomes a tentacle/munching-machine; later, spits up a "birth ball" which hatches a monster. Plus the main, big creature, which in one scene sprouts angel-type wings ... a slowly disintegrating statue ... an impressive-looking skull-claw-tentacle thing ... and matter transmitters.... Love that "watery" title in the opening credits. And love the precision, high-tech credits in general. Highlights from this horror-comedy as a whole are somewhat more sparse, but include the fancy lightning effects and the insinuating score.

**ZEORYMER 1** (J) Youmex/A.I.C. & Artmic 1989 anim color 28m. Ref: Japan Video: 1st of 2 videos. vc box: robots. TV: ToEMI Video; no Eng.

It's big-robot time again, or rather ray-shooting, human-run robotic machines. (All you can see of the pilots are their eyes.) For fans of the subgenre. Highlight: the weird mechanical thing suspended in the tank of liquid.

Follow-up: *Project Hades Zeorymer.*

**The ZERO BOYS** Omega-Forminx 1987 (1986) color 89m. Story, SP, D, P, SpSdFX: Nico Mastorakis. SP: also Fred C. Perry. Mus: Myers, Zimmer. SpFX: John Hartigan. Mkp: June Brickman. SdFX: Cinesound. Ref: TV. V 4/1/87. With Daniel Hirsch, Kelli Maroney, Tom Shell, Nicole Rio, Jared Moses; Joe Phelan, Gary Jochimsen, T.K. Webb (killers).

"It's not a game any more!" Weekend Warriors invade an empty country house and find skeletons, snuff videos, a torture chamber, a body in a trunk, a head in a freezer, and three killers with big knives, machetes and arrows.... An unlikely splicing of slasher and survivalist subgenres. The script has all it can handle just trying to come up with motivations for characters to go from room to room in the old house. Good blue-misty-night photography by Steve Shaw.

**ZHUAGUI TEGONGDUI** see *Ghostbusting*

**ZHUO GUI DASHI** see *Vampire Buster*

**ZHUO GUI HEJIA HUAN II: MAYI CHUANQI** see *Ghost Legend*

**ZILLION** see *Burning Night*

**ZIPANG** see *Jipangu*

**ZIPPERFACE** AIP/Shiman Prods. 1991 color 92m. Story, D, P: Mansour Pourmand. Development: Ralph Lucas. Ph: F.S. Martin. Mus: Jim Halfpenny. PD: B. McCabe. SpFxMkp:(key) R.S. Westgate; Rick Jackson. SpFX: Wayne Beauchamp. Ref: TV: AIP HV. V 2/24/92:174. 5/4/92:156. PT 17:62: M. Pourmand = Vernon Becker; SP: Barbara Bishop. Stanley. With Donna Adams, David Clover, Jonathan Mandell.

"He's out there." Palm City, California. A psychopathic, leather-clad killer beheads one prostitute with a machete, strangles another with a whip, etc. To spare all suspense: It's—in a climactic camp finish—"the mayor's husband [Bruce Brown]!" ("I killed them all!") Pathetic shot-on-tape shocker looks and sounds like a daytime soap.

**ZODIAC AMERICA 3** see *Kickboxer from Hell*

**ZOMBI 3** (I-Fili) Flora & Variety (Franco Gaudenzi) 1988 color 95m. (aka *Zombie 3*) D: Lucio Fulci; Bruno Mattei. SP: Claudio Fragasso. Ph: Riccardo Grassetti. Mus: Stefano Mainetti. AD: Bartolomeo Scavia, Vic Dabao. SpFX: Joseph Ross, Tony Ceyl, Rodolfo Torrente. MkpFX: Franco Di Girolamo. SdFxEd: Arcangeli et al. OptFX: S. Mafera. Ref: TV: VSOM; Eng. dubbed. Horacio Higuchi. M/TVM 5/88:41. V 5/4/88:322. Palmerini. PT 8:65 (ad): "flying decapitated zombie head." VSOM: *After Death: Zombie 4* - sequel? With Deran Sarafian, Milly D'Abbraccio, Sebastian Harrison, Beatrice Ring, Alan Collins (aka Luciano Pigozzi), Deborah Bergamini, Ulli Renthaler.

"The dead are rising up again...." Crematory smoke from the burned body of a man exposed to an "extremely powerful bacteriological weapon" turns birds into maddened peckers and causes other "inexplicable violence." ("People are eating each other.") Not a particularly distinguished zombie movie, but these undead are unrelenting, and the score and photography are atmospheric. Even severed arms and heads get into the attack act.

Apparent follow-up to *Zombie* (1979); no relation to *Zombi Horror* (III), aka *Zombi 3*.

**ZOMBI 4: AFTERDEATH** see *After Death: Zombie 4*

**ZOMBIE 5** see *Fall of the House of Usher* (1983)

**ZOMBIE APOCALYPSE** see *Cementerio del Terror*

**The ZOMBIE ARMY** Video Outlaw/Tempe (John Kalinowski) 1993 (1991) color feature. D: Betty Stapleford. SP: Roger Scearce. Ref: PT 18:64: "zombie makeup ... is good." Fango 123:12: shot-on-tape. With B. Stapleford.

Military experiments in former insane asylum.

**ZOMBIE BLOODBATH** Asylum 1993 color feature. SP, D, P: Todd Sheets. Ref: PT 18:57: "gore video."

"Melting people ... slow moving zombies."

**ZOMBIE BRIGADE** (Austral.) Smart Egg-CEA/CM Films 1988 color 95m. (aka *Night Crawl*). SP, D, P: Carmelo Musca, Barrie Pattison. Mus: Charles, Hunter. Ref: V 5/25/88: a "few laughs, but not enough pace or gore." 10/21/87:193(ad). VW 28:16. With John Moore, Khym Lam, Geoff Gibbs, Adam A. Wong.

Destruction of Vietnam veterans memorial awakens dead vets.

**ZOMBIE COP** Tempe 1990? color feature. D: J.R. Bookwalter. Ref: Tempe Video flyer: voodoo doctor, the undead. Bill Warren. V 6/13/90:34.

**ZOMBIE HIGH** Cinema Group (Elliott Kastner)/Priest Hill Prods. (Cassian Elwes) 1987 color 91m. (*Prep School* - orig t). D: Ron Link. SP, Co-P: Aziz Ghazal. SP: also Tim Doyle, Elizabeth Passerelli. Mus: Daniel May. SpFxMkp: Chris Biggs, Marc Messenger. SpFxCoord: Scott Haas. Ref: TV. V 10/14/87. 8/12/87:46. Phantom. Maltin '92: aka *The School That Ate My Brain*. Martin. Scheuer. Morse. Hound. With Virginia Madsen, Richard Cox, Kay Kuter, James Wilder, Sherilynn Fenn, Paul Feig, T. Scott Coffey, Paul Williams.

"It's like dullness is a contagious disease around here!" An early tipoff to the zombified state of the "preppy wimps" at Ettinger Academy: They actually say "Have a nice day!" The faculty's life-prolonging formula (learned from an Indian medicine man) requires a mixture of blood and brain tissue from living persons. Meanwhile, music directed to a crystal in the craniums of the brain-drained controls their every movement, and makes them ideal students. Finally, the serum-denied staff shrivel and die.... Functional plot; wry moments. Highlight: the students moving in unison on the dance floor. Compare *The Brain* (1988).

**ZOMBIE ISLAND MASSACRE** Troma/Picnic 1984 (1983) color 94m. (*Picnic* - orig t. *The Last Picnic* - int t). D, Ed: John N. Carter. SP, Story: Logan O'Neill. SP: also William Stoddard. Story, P: David Broadnax. Mus: Harry Manfredini. SpMkpFX: Dennis Eger. SpFX: Steve Kirshoff. Mask: Rodney Gordon. Ref: TV: Media Home Ent. video. Ecran F 28:39. 41:70-1. V 5/16/84. Stanley. Scheuer. Maltin '92. Hound. Phantom. Martin. With Rita Jenrette, Tom Cantrell, Debbie Ewing, D. Broadnax, Oscar Lawson (creature).

Is "voodoo magic" behind the machete murders of tourists stranded on St. Marie Island in the Caribbean? ("First Helen and Jerry, and now George and Ethel!") Or is it "some kind of crazy" behind them? Indian "flesh eaters" maybe? (The local library is stocked exclusively with books on cannibalism.) Or "was it only a show"? As a matter of fact, the latter: "It's all part of the subculture" of revenge and torture.

Strictly a showcase for Jenrette. The anemic script ends on the lowest note of all: It was only cocaine cowboys playing zombie, and the voodoo-mass zombie with the sprouting fingernails was apparently a fake. Hiss!

**ZOMBIE NIGHTMARE** (Can.) Filmworld/Gold-Gems (Pierre Grise/S.S. Goldstein) 1987 (1986) color 83m. D: Jack Bravman. SP: David Wellington. Mus: Jon-Mikl Thor, Motorhead. SpFX: Andy Clemens et al. Mkp: Macha Colas. Ref: TV. V 11/18/87. 4/1/87:40(rated). no Maltin '92. Hound. Phantom. Morse. Martin. Scheuer. With Adam West, Thor (Tony), Tia Carrere, Manuska (Molly), Frank Dietz.

"He's killed Peter and Suzy and Jim! We're next!" Voodoo priestess Molly Mokembe brings Tony Washington back from the dead to wreak vengeance on his killers. ("His body's going through many changes.") Soon, a "Jolly Green Giant" with a baseball bat is savaging the local teenagers. Even the frantic graveyard finale with zombies, cops, and voodoo women can't salvage this atrocious movie.

**ZOMBIE '90: EXTREME PESTILENCE** (G) Tempe 1990? color? 80m. D: Andreas Schnaas. Ref: Tempe Video flyer: "living dead." Bill Warren.

**ZOMBIE RAMPAGE** Tempe color 81m. D: Todd Sheets. Ref: Tempe Video flyer. Bill Warren.

"World full of zombies."(TV)

**ZOMBIE REVIVAL: NINJA MASTER** see *Zombie Vs Ninja*

**ZOMBIE VAMPIRE VS. ROBO MERCENARIES** see *Robo Vampire*

**ZOMBIE VS NINJA** (H.K.) IFD Films/Joseph Lai-Betty Chan 1988 color/ws c90m. (aka *Zombie Revival: Ninja Master*). D: Charles Lee. SP: Benny Ho. Story: George Chu & the AAV Creative Unit. Ph: Raymond Chang. PD: Jimmy Chu. SpFxD: Simon Chu. SdFX: Henry See. Ref: TV; IEC video; Eng. version. no Martin. no Hound. Weisser/ATC: C. Lee = Godfrey Ho. With Pierre Kirby, Edowan Bersmea, Dewey Bosworth, Thomas Hartham, Patrick Frbezar, Renato Sala, Mason Chang, David Kim.

Sloppy semi-camp kung fu action featuring a woman in red who can vanish and a token appearance by zombies who must return to their coffins at dawn. What to say about a movie the highlight of which is the dubbed line "What about the guy who killed Bobby and Burt?" In a subgenre mixup, the zombies look like your typical Hong Kong hopping vampire, and hop out of their coffins like vampires, then stumble around and fight like zombies.

**\*ZOMBIES OF MORA TAU** 1957. Ref: TV. Lee. V 3/20/57. TVG. Lentz. Weldon. Hardy/HM. Phantom. Stanley. Hound. Maltin '92. Scheuer. Martin. Fango 53:16-17. With Karl Davis & William Baskin (zombies).

"There is a twilight zone between life and death. Here dwell ... the Walking Dead." According to the African "legends of the Susan B," in 1894, ten men returned from the dead after finding a golden cask of diamonds—and "they're still guarding those cursed diamonds!" The word *voodoo* is the only explanation given re how the zombies become zombies. Hotcha Allison Hayes' Mona disappears for a while and is later found "cold." ("Your wife is dead!") The movie gets the slow-relentless-march-of-the-zombies idea down, but that's about it, though there is one eerie image: Hayes in nightgown in bed in a room overflowing with burning candles. (Fire, you see, keeps zombies at bay.)

The scene in which the zombies arise from their coffins in the mausoleum is eerie, too, at first, but the "unison" business gets silly quick, and then they just look like guys in boxes. Their "seaweed" look gets silly even quicker. Haphazard staging, stolid acting. Marjorie Eaton's Mrs. Peters is at first just the equivalent of the forbidding housekeeper; ultimately, she releases her zombie husband (Frank Hagney) from his living death.

**\*ZOMBIES ON BROADWAY** Ben Stoloff 1945. SP: Lawrence Kimble. Chor: Charles O'Curran. Ref: TV. V 5/2/45. Lee. Lennig. Weldon. Siegel. Lentz. Scheuer. Stanley. no Phantom. Maltin '92. Martin.

Jerry (Wally Brown) and Mike (Alan Carney), press agents, journey to the isle of San Sebastian ("one of the smaller Virgin Islands") to find a zombie for their boss, Ace Miller (Sheldon Leonard), the owner of the Zombie Hut, a New York night club. There they find not only voodoo-created zombies (Darby Jones and a bit player in a crate), but serum-created zombies, the results of the experiments of Dr. Paul Renault (Bela Lugosi), of San Sebastian Castle.

Comedically, *Zombies* is of no interest; historically, it's a treasure-trove. Lugosi again (as in *White Zombie* and *Voodoo Man*) plays the zombie master, though Renault is perhaps his least memorable such role. (He has only one ultra-Lugosi line: "The dogs would tear you to bits before you got off the grounds!") And Renault can summon his zombie-aide, Kalaga, mystically, as Legendre summoned Madeline in *White Zombie*. The movie's most direct ties, however, are to *I Walked with a Zombie*, to which this is, in effect, a semi-sequel. There's a zombie walk through the jungle, and a voodoo ceremony, and Jones reprises his zombie role from *I Walked*. (In the latter, his name was Carrefour; here, he's Kalaga.) The most pleasant surprise: Sir Lancelot is again the calypso singer, and continues his song of San Sebastian: "A joy supreme/This is the island of golden dreams/Ah, woe! Too late/Blood on the ground will mark their fate."

But what are Brown and Carney doing in a "Val Lewton" picture? Not much, as it transpires. And Roy Webb's music, a few shadow effects with Jones, and Sir Lancelot's song are the closest *Zombies* comes to approximating the Lewton atmosphere.

**La ZONA DEL SILENCIO** (Mex) Televicine & Rodas (Fernando de Fuentes, Rodolfo de Anda) 1990 color 81m. D: R. de Anda. SP: Gilberto de Anda. Ph: Francisco Bojorquez. Mus: Luis Arcaraz. AD: Raul de Anda III. FX:(sp) Fernando Gutierrez;(incidental) Sergio Castro;(opt) Manuel Sainz. Mkp: Karla Acosta. Ref: TV: Mex-American HV; no Eng.; *The Silent Zone* - tr t. V

5/2/90:280. With R. de Anda, Olivia Collins, Mario Almada, Jorge Luke.

Five tales set in a strange section of northern Mexico. 1) A train robber takes a door from the past to the present and is immediately run down by a train. Serviceable story, fun kicker. 2) As a truck—i.e., "safety"—approaches a thief of cave treasure, a medieval knight in armor lops off his head. Okay atmospheric anecdote. 3) In a surprising turn of events, a young man peels off his face to reveal that he's an alien. 4) A monster driving a limo drags a hitchhiker in through the window. 5) Finally, and symmetrically, a robber of air-show proceeds, in the present, opens a door to the past and finds himself before a firing squad.... Pleasantly perverse, if lightweight collection of "Twilight Zone"-like tales.

**ZONE TROOPERS** (U.S-I) Empire/Altar (Paul De Meo/Debra Dion) 1986 (1985) color 86m. SP, D: Danny Bilson. SP: also P. De Meo. Mus: Richard Band. FxAnim: Tony Alderson. SpFxMkp: John Buechler, MMI. SpSdFX: John Paul Fasal. Ref: TV. MFB'86:124-5. V 4/16/86. Stanley. Hound. Phantom. Scheuer. Morse. Newman. Martin. With Tim Thomerson, Timothy Van Patten, Art La Fleur, Biff Manard, William Paulson, Alviero Martin (Hitler), Joshua McDonald (Zone Trooper Captain).

"Joey Verona met the men from space." Italy, 1944. A rocket ship ("something from Mars") crash lands. Aboard: several "big bug-head" guys and one fuzzy one—a female. On principal, these aliens refuse to help us kill our own kind, but when G.I.s are trapped, it's aliens to the rescue with ray guns.

The idea of introducing an sf element into a regulation World War II combat movie, complete with regulation war-movie music, proves strangely agreeable, at least as presented here. (What *Biggles* does for WWI, *Zone Troopers* does better for WWII.) Kicky, offbeat anecdote is played for exactly what it's worth, no more, no less. In effect, this hybrid grafts nostalgia for Fifties sf movies onto nostalgia for Forties war movies.

**3P ZU: WARRIORS FROM THE MAGIC MOUNTAIN** (H.K.) Golden Harvest (Paragon) 1983 color/ws 92m. (*Warriors from the Magic Mountain* - ad t). D: Tsui Hark. SP: Szeto Chuck Hong. Ph: Bill Wong. Mus: Tang Siu-Lam. AD: Chung Suk-Pink. SpFX: Robert Blalack, Peter Kuran, Arnie Wong, John Scheele. Ref: TV: Rainbow Video; Eng. titles. V 2/23/83. 5/4/83:342. Stanley. no Phantom. NST! 4:40. Fango 107:58,60. MMarquee 43:7. Newman. Ecran F 52:55,59. 65:66,68. With Adam Cheng, Lau Chung Yan, Samo Hung, Yen Biao.

The Magic Mountain, a "place of mystery" in tenth-century China. Master Long Brows destroys Blood Monster's body, but the latter's soul hovers in the air and draws "virgin skulls" to it to protect itself until "resurrection day," or the Egression. Meanwhile, Blood Monster's venom has turned one victim into his double, which latter, in turn, transforms into a witch and attempts to thwart master and aide from recruiting a countess in their campaign to find the sacred swords which will destroy Blood Monster's soul. The Evil Force nearly sucks our protagonists into Evil Territory, a sort of moral Black Hole, but Heaven's Blade

saves them. The Countess sacrifices herself by whirling away into the sky with the master, who is possessed by evil (which afflicts his body and makes firecracker sounds), and the swords unite and destroy Blood Monster.

*Zu* is about the fastest-moving movie since *The Trial of Vivienne Ware* (1932). The momentary stops for comic bits simply underscore the furiousness of pacing, and there are more effects per square celluloid inch than even the recent, otherwise stolid *Hercules* movies had. The people here are funny, and the effects are imaginative. The clever War-is-hell, Let's-get-the-heck-out-of-here opening sequences set the tone. The film has a genial relentlessness about it. Prime effects: the animated red darting Blood Crows, the weird indoor flying things with glowing blue eyes, and a palace/fort which freezes.

**ZUGZANG** see *Obbligo di Giocare*

**ZUMA** (Fili) Cine Suerte/Raquiza-Yalung 1985 color c115m. D: Jun Raquiza. SP: Hernan Robles, Manny Rodriguez, from Jim Fernandez' comic serial "Zuma." Ph: A. Alvarez. Mus: Marita Manuel. PD & Min Ph: Interformat. AD: Lucky Guillermo. VisFX: Ramje. SpFX: A. Abadeza. Mkp:(art) Beth Hammond;(prosth) C. Baun. Anim & Opt: Ramon Capinpin. Ref: TV: Trigon Video; little Eng. V 10/21/87:282(ad): Roadshow Films Int'l. MMarquee 43:9. Monster! 3:56-7. With Max Laurel (Zuma), Snooky Serna (Galema), Dang Cecilio, Mark Gil, Martia Montes, Charlie Davao, Racquel Monteza.

Zuma—a big, bald, green-skinned "snake beast" found in a crypt in a mysterious pyramid—escapes, with his cobra retinue, and—with the help of a female accomplice—lures virgins to their deaths. (Tabloid headline: "Young Girl's Chest Ripped Open—Heart Missing!") Later, drops of blood from his dying aide form a squiggle-thing which enters a nurse, then exits from the latter's abdomen—the squiggle grows up to be Zuma's daughter.

Hokey, gory Filipino monster movie is entertaining as all get out, if very long. The above synopsis omits many outlandish plot twists involving family drama (Zuma's family), romance, and battle strokes and counterstrokes. Zuma's hearty, booming laugh punctuates each plot turn. ("Zuma laughs" must have been the most common script direction.) A narrative high point: the reunion of Zuma and his now full-grown daughter. Each comes equipped with a snake—a head at either end of same—wrapped around his or her shoulders like a stole. Zuma's snake heads stick out straight and bob about intimidatingly; daughter's snake heads are generally half-hidden by braids. (Credits high point: "Snake Engineer.") Only natural that these two, or six, should get together again. Further separations, however, follow, and further reunions. Funniest scene: the sinister squiggle zipping about the operating room like a mouse and scaring and scattering doctors and nurses.

Sequel: *Anak ni Zuma*. See also: *Snake Girl, The*.

**ZWEI TOLLE KAEFER RAEUMEN AUF** see *Return of Superbug, The*

# UNKNOWN TITLES

**TITLE UNKNOWN** (J) 198-? anim color 44m. Ref: TV: vt; no Eng.

Animated sf re an Easter Island-type statue hanging in space, some battles in outer space, and a giant undersea dragon. Noteworthy overhead shot: the dragon's shadowy outline as the beast swims through the water.

**TITLE UNKNOWN** (Thai) c1985? color 86m. Ref: TV: Thai Studio Corp. video; no Eng.; part 2.

A pointy-fingernailed gore woman who appears in a puff of red smoke plucks the entrails out of a set of lovers on the grass. Later, an exorcist's umbrella temporarily traps some ghosts, and ghost glue on the ground momentarily stops the main ghost in her tracks.

Silly, gory, but good-natured low comedy gets some laughs here and there, even though it relies heavily on fastmo comedy action and old-fashioned under-the-bed situations. In the most bizarre comic-gore sequence, the ghost woman and a human woman do a two-on-an-entrail trick.

**TITLE UNKNOWN** (J) 198-? anim color c28m. Ref: TV: Cult Videos of Berkeley; no Eng.

Fanciful, amusing light erotica re a giant airship which deposits an alien woman on a strange planet, disembodied arms which welcome their visitor with an erotic experience, a sky-taxi, floating cubes, an ocean liner which sails on a "sea" of pine trees, a little carrot-mushroom which doubles as a sort of dildo for our heroine, flying "fish," a gigantic tree, and aliens with scarecrow heads and phallic tentacles.

**TITLE UNKNOWN** (J) Tokuma Japan Corp./A.I.C. (A.P.P.P.) 198-? anim color 60m. Ref: TV: Animage Video; no Eng. Cult Videos of Berkeley.

Ingredients: a high priest who brings monster-warriors up out of the ground ... a man (or alien) beamed down from a spaceship ... a "man" who becomes a mass of tentacles ... a bat-cat which turns into a dinosaur/dragon ... a gigantic "teddy bear" with claws and a nasty attitude ... a classroom full of monsters ... and a girl who mutates into a tentacled thing.... Lively, fanciful, but basically routine horror-fantasy.

# PERIPHERAL AND PROBLEM FILMS

**A AY** (Turk.) Ref: V 5/23/90: "apparition."

**A GOZAR, A GOZAR, QUE EL MUNDO SE VA A ACABAR** (Mex.) Ref: TVG: the apocalypse?

**AANA** (India-Malayalam) 1983 Ref: Dharap: elephant amok.

**AB KYO HOGA** (India-Hindustani) 1977 Ref: Dharap: "ghosts."

**ABOVE SUSPICION** Ref: V 4/28/43: "magnetic mine." TV. Bill Warren.

**ABRACADABRA** (J) Ref: V 4/27/88: madness? ghost? (*Dogura Magura*)

**The ABSENT-MINDED PROFESSOR** Ref: TVG 11/27/88: 60m. version.

**ACCATTONE** (I) 1961 Ref: Lee: dream of death.

**ACCESS CODE** 1984 Ref: vc box: computer spying.

**ACES GO PLACES IV** (H.K.) Ref: V 3/26/86: "rain stimulant" secret.

**Der ACHTE TAG** (W.G.) Ref: V 9/10/90: "illegal genetic engineering."

**ACTING ON IMPULSE** Ref: V 6/28/93: fun with the "sex 'n' gore" genre.

**El ACTO EN CUESTION** (Arg.) Ref: V 6/7/93: magic vanishing formula.

**The ADDING MACHINE** (U.S. -B) 1969 Ref: Lee: robot.

**The ADVENTURE OF THE HERO IN BLACK** (H.K.) 1957 Ref: HKFest '82: "suspense."

**The ADVENTURE OF FAUSTUS BIDGOOD** (Can.) Ref: V 9/10/86: "horrific" dreamworld.

**The ADVENTURES OF A GNOME NAMED GNORM** Ref: Janet Willis. Sacto Bee 11/6/93: troll.

**The ADVENTURES OF A TWO-MINUTE WEREWOLF** Ref: TVG 6/14/86: 2-part "Weekend Special."

**ADVENTURES OF ALADDIN** (Thai) 1988 Ref: vc box.

**The ADVENTURES OF BRISCO COUNTY JR.** Ref: V 8/30/93: "two-hour pilot" re "power-giving object."

**ADVENTURES OF CAPTAIN AFRICA** 1955 serial Ref: Lee: gorilla, "Phantom"-like guy.

**The ADVENTURES OF PIMPLE—THE SPIRITUALIST** (B) 1914 13m. Ref: BFC: fake ghost.

**The ADVENTURES OF PRINCE ACHMED** (G) 1923-6 anim Ref: Brandon: evil sorcerer.

**The ADVENTURES OF THE AMERICAN RABBIT** anim Ref: V 1/29/86: Super-rabbit, more or less.

**The ADVENTURES OF THE MASKED PHANTOM** 1939 Ref: TVG: Western.

**The AFFAIRS OF JANICE** Ref: FComment 6/85:65: painter dumps subjects in paint, kills them.

**AFTER PILKINGTON** (B) Ref: V 1/7/87: schizophrenic killer. TVG.

**AFTERWARD** (B) 60m. Ref: Hound: TV show re haunted house.

**AGATHA—LASS DAS MORDEN SEIN** (W.G.) 1960 Ref: Hardy/HM: "horror imagery."

**AGENT 505** (W.G.-I-F) 1965 Ref: Lee: rockets, gadgets.

**The AGONY ON THE FACE OF A CAROUSEL HORSE** Ref: Lee: devil with devil?

**AH-YING** (Taiwanese) Ref: V 11/2/92: "ghosts of past & present." (*Ming Ghost*)

**El AHIJADO DE LA MUERTE** (Mex.?) Ref: vc box: sinister "Dead Figure."

**AIN'T NO WAY BACK** Ref: V 6/27/90:48(hv): "narrated by a dead character."

**AITSU** (J) Ref: V 9/7/92: asthmatic with "mystical powers." (*Waiting for the Flood*)

**La ALACRANA** (Mex.) Ref: V 12/10/86: psychotic killer.

**ALADDIN** (B) 1898 Ref: Lee: evil magician.

**ALADDIN AND THE MAGIC LAMP** (Dutch) 1936 Ref: TV: monster-in-mirror bit. Mo.

**ALCHEMISTS** (Can.) Ref: V 8/24/92: "themes of creation & destruction."

**ALGERNON BLACKWOOD STORIES** (B) 1949 series Ref: BFC.

**ALICE'S TIN PONY** 1925 anim & live short Ref: PFA notes 10/15/86

**ALICIA EN EL PUEBLO DE MARAVILLAS** (Cuban) Ref: V 3/18/91: "surreal images."

**ALIEN NATION** Ref: V 10/4/89 & Mifed/1989:122: telefilm/pilot.

**ALIEN OUTLAW** 1986? Ref: Fango 53:10: unreleased. V 10/21/87:91,226(ad).

**ALL-AMERICAN MURDER** 1991 Ref: Martin. PT 12:51: power drill "gore fx."

**ALL AT SEA** (B) 1957 Ref: Lee: caveman bit.

**ALLADDIN AND THE WONDERFUL LAMP** (India-Hindi) 1978 Ref: Dharap: evil sorcerer.

**ALLADIN AND HIS WONDERFUL LAMP** (India) 1951 Ref: Lee: evil magician.

**ALLADIN AND THE WONDERFUL LAMP** (India) 1926 Ref: Lee: evil magician.

**ALLEYCATS** c1984? Ref: Jim Shapiro: female nude boxing in 1988.

**The AMAZING BUNJEE VENTURE** 1984 Ref: TVG: 2-part "Weekend Special": time machine to prehistory.

**AMAZING GRACE AND CHUCK** Ref: V 4/1/87: "total nuclear disarmament, now!"

**AMAZING STORIES: BOOK FIVE** 1985-6 Ref: SFChron Dtbk 3/8/92: video.

**AMAZONS** Ref: TVG 1/29/84: TV-movie re cult of "female warriors."

**AMERICA** 1986 (1982) Ref: V 10/15/86: TV signal beamed off moon. (aka *Moonbeam*)

**AMERICAN DRIVE-IN** Ref: V 5/15/85: "generous footage" from *Hard Rock Zombies*.

**AMERICAN NINJA 3** Ref: V 3/1/89: perfecting virus weapon.

**AMERICAN NINJA 4** Ref: V 3/25/91: "briefcase-sized nuclear weapon."

**AMERICAN ORPHEUS** Ref: V 6/15/92: "tribute to Cocteau's *Orphee*."

**AMERICAN TIGER** (I) Ref: V 6/1/91:36(hv): "ageless witch." (*American Rickshaw*)

**AMERIKA** Ref: TVG 2/15/87: miniseries re USSR takes over U.S. V 2/18/87:118.

**El AMOR BRUJO** (Sp) Ref: SFExam 2/27/87: "eerie vignette."

**AMORE E MORTE** 1932 Ref: Turner/Price: family curse, thunderstorm.

**AMORE E RABBIA** (I-F) 1969 Ref: Lee: demonic visions.

**Un AMORE IN PRIMA CLASSE** (I-F) 1980 Ref: Prod Ital '79-'80: skeleton of mythical prehistoric beast.

**The ANCIENT MARINER** 1925 Ref: Lee: Death personified.

**L'ANGE** (F) 1982 Ref: Ecran F 45:43,44: "fantastic scenes." Filmex '83.

**ANGEL** Ref: TV: mad slasher. V 1/18/84. Bob Moore. TVG.

**Los ANGELES DE LA MUERTE** (Mex.) 1989? Ref: TV: sickos invoke satan, kill, cackle.

**El ANIMA DE SAYULA** (Mex.) 1984 Ref: TV: "ghost" voice in cemetery. vc box.

**ANNA & BELLA** anim short Ref: TV: anger flashing as pterodactyl.

**L'ANNEE DES MEDUSES** (F) Ref: SFExam 5/22/87: deadly jellyfish.

**ANOTHER FACE** 1935 Ref: TVG: "new face" with plastic surgery.

**ANOTHER SON OF SAM** Ref: vc box.

**ANPANMAN** (J) anim feature Ref: V 8/1/90:48.

**The ANTICHRIST** 1991 Ref: PT 16:62: amateur; possessed woman.

**APARTMENT ZERO** (B) Ref: V 10/5/88: "creepy." Kelly Cresap: not horrific.

**The APE GIRL** (H.K.?) 199-? Ref: TV: vt: cute, hairy ape girl.

**APOLOGY** Ref: V 7/30/86:56: made-for-TV; "a chill or two."

**APPRENTICE TO MURDER** Ref: V 2/17/88: demonic figure, magic.

**APPU RAJA** (India) Ref: V 11/12/90: imitation of *Twins*.

**AQUAMAN** anim Ref: V 8/21/85:88(hv): several (TV?) episodes. Hound: '67.

**The ARAB'S CRUSE** (B) 1915 Ref: BFC: "mishaps pursue man who insulted Arab."

**L'ARAIGNEE D'EAU** (F) 1971 Ref: Cinef or Ecran '73:39: water-spider-into-woman.

**ARIA** Ref: SFExam 5/13/88: "black wizard and sorceresses." SFChron 5/16/88.

**ARK** 1970 short Ref: Lee: futuristic.

**The ARK OF THE SUN GOD** (I-Turk) Ref: V 10/26/83:313(ad). 5/9/84:318: at Cannes.

**ARMAGEDDON** 1983 anim c5m. Ref: TVG: "sf fantasy"; student film.

**ARMIDAN** 1966 Ref: TVFFSB: "old man who holds the secret of eternal life."

**ARMOUR OF GOD** (H.K.) Ref: NST! 4:16: the supernatural, cannibalism.

**ARTHUR AND THE SQUARE KNIGHTS OF THE ROUND TABLE** anim Ref: TVG 9/27/86.

**ASESINOS—COMERCIANTES DE NINOS** (Mex.) 1991 Ref: vc box: body-parts black market.

**ASHIK KERIB** (USSR) 1988 Ref: MFB'89:265-7: "evil spirits" in the church.

**ASK MAX** Ref: TVG 11/2/86: "Disney Movie" (60m.) re inventor's bike design.

**The ASSIGNATION** 1953 8m. Ref: Brandon: Death personified?

**ASTERIX ET LE COUP DE MENHIR** (G-F) Ref: Dr. Rolf Giesen: magic potion. V 11/1/89.

**Les ASTRONAUTES** (F) 1959 anim & live 14m. Ref: Lee: spaceships.

**ASTONISHED** 1987 Ref: PT 16:12: dead man "shows up again."

**ASTROPHANT** 1974? Ref: V 3/26/75:25: student sf-spoof.

**Der ATEN** (W.G.-Swiss) Ref: V 9/20/89: "set in 1995."

**ATLANTIC FLIGHT** 1937 Ref: TVG: "new type of plane." V 9/22/37: fast.

**ATOMIC AGENT** (F) 1959? Ref: Lee: atomic motor.

**An ATTRACTIVE CATCH** (B) 1908 8m. Ref: BFC: super-magnet.

**AU NOM DU CHRIST** (Ivory Coast-Swiss) Ref: V 10/11/93: spirit possession?

**AU PAIR** Ref: V 6/17/91: "killer nanny."

**AUTOMAN** Ref: TVG 12/15/83: 90m. "premiere" re "computerized supercop."

**AVENGING FORCE** Ref: V 9/17/86: "Most Dangerous Game" scenes. ad.

**El AVIADOR FENOMENO** (Mex.) vc box: Suicide Club murders; comedy. TVG.

**AWESOME LOTUS** Ref: V 5/21/86: gory.

**BMX BANDITS** (Austral.) Ref: TV: storm sequence in cemetery, monster-masked goons.

**BABFILM** (Hung.) 1977? 13m. Ref: PFA (Trieste pr): planet of beans.

**BABO '73** 1964 Ref: Lee: soc-sf.

**BABY BOTTLENECK** 1946 anim short Ref: TV: conveyor belt for babies.

**BACCHANALE** 1970 Ref: Lee: graveyard apparition.

**BACHELOR PARTY** 1984 Ref: TV: 3-D space movie on theatre screen.

**BACK FROM THE BEYOND** (H.K.?) Ref: vc box.

**BACK TO THE USSR** (Finnish) 1992 Ref: Jones: "vampiric Communist icon Lenin."

**BACKFIRE** Ref: V 5/20/87: "chilling" dream scene.

**BAD BLOOD** Ref: Martin: "terrifying thriller." Hound: "tedious chiller." V 5/10/89.

**BAD BOY BUBBY** (Austral.-I) Ref: V 9/13/93: futuristic?

**The BAD SEED** 1985 Ref: Jim Shapiro: non-horrific.

**The BAD SISTER** (B) 1983 Ref: Jones: "vampire motif."

**BADLANDS 2005** Ref: V 9/21/88: 60m pilot; cyborg.

**Der BAERENHAEUTER** (E.G.) Ref: V 5/6/87: deal with the devil.

**BAIL JUMPER** Ref: V 3/7/90: "tidal wave submerges...Staten Island."

**BALLAD OF NARAYAMA** (J) Ref: SFExam 6/22/84: spirit. TV. (*Narayama Bushi-Ko*) 1983

**Le BALLADE DES AMANTS MAUDITS** (Belg.) 1967 Ref: Lee: horror?

**BALAMOS** (Greek) Ref: V 11/3/82: "fantastic world."

**BANDIT OF BAGHDAD** (India) 1930 Ref: "Indian Filmography": "fantasy."

**BANKE SEPAHI** (India) 1938 Ref: Lee: "*King Kong*ish."

**BAODAO DA MENG** (Taiwanese) Ref: V 11/29/93: ghostly sd fx. (*Bodo*)

**BARBARA THE BARBARIAN** 1987 Ref: Adam '89: sword-and-sorcery spoof.

**BAREFOOT GEN** (J) anim Ref: SFChron 8/5/92: war gore. Animag 5:5: aka "I Saw It."

**BARRAVENTO** (Braz.) 1962 Ref: screen: voodoo. MFB'72:155-6.

**BARTON FINK** Ref: TV: vaguely demonic madman. SFExam 9/13/91.

**BASIC INSTINCT** Ref: V 3/16/92: gory ice-pick murder.

**BATMAN & ROBIN** anim Ref: V 8/21/85:88(hv): several stories; TV?

**BATTERIES INCLUDED** Ref: vc box: "fully charged" women.

**BEASTS** 1983 Ref: TVG: "killer grizzly."

**The BEASTS** (H.K.?) Ref: vc box: revenge for rape.

**BEAUTIFUL GHOST** (Chi.) 1969? Ref: Lee.

**BEAUTY AND THE BEAST** 1961? Ref: Sacto Bee 1/15/62(ad). AFI: sfa *Day of a Stripper?*

**BEAUTY AND THE BEAST** 1979? anim Ref: IFG'80:406.

**BEAUTY AND THE BEAST** CPG 1984 anim Ref: vc box.

**BEAUTY RAISED FROM THE DEAD** (H.K.) 1956 Ref: HKFFest '82.

**BEBE'S KIDS** Ref: SFExam 7/31/92: toy-store robots.

**BECAUSE OF THE CATS** 1973 Ref: VSB: horror; "new society." Hound: "evil cult."

**BED OF A THOUSAND PLEASURES** (I) 1972 Ref: MFB'75:218: magic mirror, genie, etc.

**The BEGGAR GIRL'S WEDDING** (B) 1915 Ref: BFC: mad doc's asylum.

**BEHIND THE CURTAIN** (B) 1915 Ref: BFC: "cursed curtain." (*The Curtain's Secret*)

**BELLAMY: MASSAGE GIRL MURDERS** (Austral.) Ref: TVG: "psychotic murderer."

**BENVENUTA** (Belg.-F) Ref: V 9/7/83: "Twilight Zone"-like fact-fiction mixups.

**BERGADO — THE TERROR OF CAVITE** (Fili) Ref: V 5/5/76: talisman of invisibility.

**Die BERUEHRTE** (W.G.) 1981 Ref: Hardy/HM: schizo's "gory" fantasies.

**Las BESTIAS DEL TERROR** (Mex.) 1972 Ref: Hardy/HM: horror?

**The BETRAYED** (Dutch) Ref: V 5/10/93:C-118: "futuristic."

**BETTY BOOP'S CRAZY INVENTIONS** 1933 Ref: TV: Amok sewing machine sews up stream, etc.

**BEYOND REASON** 1977 Ref: TVG: psychologist under pressure.

**BEYOND THE STARS** Ref: V 3/8/89:12(rated). Martin: moon secret.

**BHAKTHA PRAHLADA** (India - Kannada) 1983 Ref: Dharap: "demon kings...man-lion."

**BIG DADDY** 1969(1965) Ref: AFI: "voodoo doctor."

**BIG JACK** 1949 Ref: Lee. TV: grave robber, pickled limbs, burial alive.

**BIG MAN ON CAMPUS** Ref: V 5/17/89: comedy. (*The Hunchback of UCLA*) TVG: from Hugo.

**THE BIG SHAVE** 1967 Ref: MFB'79:109: shaving man lacerates self.

**BINGO BONGO** (I) Ref: V 2/2/83: man raised by apes.

**BIOARMER LIGER** Vol. 1 (J) anim Ref: vt: sf; TV-series episodes?

**BIONIC NINJA** (H.K.) 1987 Ref: TV: nothing bionic.

**A BIRD IN THE HEAD** 1946 Ref: Lee: mad doc after Curly's brain.

**BLACK BOMBER** (Yugos.) Ref: V 11/29/93: "futuristic."

**BLACK COFFEE** (B) 1931 Ref: BFC: secret formula.

**BLACK EAGLE** Ref: V 1/18/89:"secret laser guidance system." TVG.

**BLACK JACK SAVAGE** Ref: TVG 3/31/91: 2-hr. "premiere movie" re haunted castle.

**BLACK LIZARD** (J) Ref: screen. SFExam 4/26/85: thief who stuffs, mounts people.

**BLACK MAGIC WOMEN** Ref: vc box: "trance."

**The BLACK PIRATE** (I) Ref: V(d) 1/18/77: "ESP revenge motive."

**BLACK PUDDING** (B) 1969 anim 5m. Ref: MFB'73:110: "monstrous woman."

**BLACK SAMURAI** 1976 Ref: Stanley: voodoo.

**BLACK VOODOO** 1987 Ref: vc box: "sexual psychic."

**BLACK WIDOW** Ref: SFChron 2/6/87: Ondine's Curse ("when you die in your sleep").

**BLACK WIDOW MURDERS: THE BLANCHE TAYLOR MOORE STORY** Ref: SFChron 5/3/93: woman who kills her men slowly.

**\*\*The BLACKBIRD** 1926 Ref: screen: non-horror.

**BLACKHEAD** (Bulg.) 1962? anim short Ref: Lee: dragon.

**BLACKS AND WHITES TO THE FUTURE** 1985 Ref: vc box.

**BLADESTORM** Ref: vc box. Hound: "fantasy/warrior."

**BLANKT VAPEN** (Swed.) Ref: V 10/15/90: "a kind of haunted house."

**BLASTFIGHTER** (I) 1983 Ref: V 12/18/85: "high-tech rifle" shoots "fireballs."

**BLIND SIDE** 1993 Ref: TVG: psychopath.

**BLIND VISION** Ref: V: homicidal maniac.

**BLIND WITNESS** Ref: V 11/29/89:62: "high fright level"; cf. *Wait until Dark.*

**BLOOD CIRCUS** 1985 Ref: Stanley: aliens?

**BLOOD HUNGER** Ref: V/CHVD: based on *Blood Feast?*

**BLOOD SIMPLE** Ref: V 2/16/83:24. TV: violent; burial alive.

**BLOODSTONE** Ref: V 5/10/89: "cursed ruby."

**BLOODY WEDNESDAY** Ref: V 11/11/87: hallucinations. Phantom: climactic slaughter.

**BLOWBACK** Ref: V 7/29/91: O-bomb.

**BLUE BOX** (Hung.) Ref: V 2/22/93: "post-apocalyptic landscape."

**BLUE DEMON CONTRA "LAS DIABOLICAS"** (Mex.) 1967 Ref: TV: non-sf. Hardy/SF.

**BLUE MURDER** 1985 Ref: TVG: killer with clown masks for victims. TVG.

**BLUE STEEL** 1990 Ref: TV: crazy killer in NYC.

**BLUE VELVET** 1986 Ref: strange interludes with bugs, severed ears.

**La BODA DEL ACORDEONISTA** (Col.) Ref: V 11/23/88: legendary goddess carries off fisherman on his wedding night.

**BODA SECRETA** (Arg.-Dutch-Can.) Ref: V 9/27/89: "fantasy."

**BODY CHEMISTRY** Ref: V 3/14/90: violence. (*Afterimage* - early t)

**BODY COUNT** 1987 Ref: vc box: "Hitchcockian." GoreZone 11:64: sfa *The Eleventh Commandment?* D: Leder.

**BODY FIRE** 1991 Ref: Adam '92: aliens?

**BONANZA: THE MOVIE** Ref: TVG: "two women with psychic powers." 1972

**La BONNE DAME** (F) 1966 25m Ref: Jones: vampires.

**BOOBY TRAP** (B) 1957 Ref: BFC: "explosive pen" (remote control).

**BOOK REVIEW** 1946 anim Ref: TV: "Dante's Inferno" bit.

**BOOS IN THE NIGHT** 1950 anim Ref: Maltin/OMAM.

**The BORMAN—LOVER'S RAIN** (J) 1990 anim 33m. Ref: Japan Video: monster; TV?

**BORN TO RACE** Ref: V 2/10/88: "revolutionary" auto engine.

**BOSKO'S WOODLAND DAZE** 1933 anim 7m Ref: WBCartoons: ogre in dream.

**The BOTTOM OF THE SEA** 1914 anim short Ref: Lee: whale that swallows sub.

**BOTTOMS UP** (W.G.) Ref: MFB'78:20. '81:126: secret formula.

**BOWERY BATTALION** 1951 Ref: TV: "hydrogen ray formula."

**BOX OF DELIGHTS** Ref: TVG: "magical device"; Brit. TV.

**BOX-OFFICE BUNNY** 1990 anim 5m. Ref: TV: bit with *Texas Chain Saw*-type movie.

**BOXING HELENA** Ref: V 2/1/93: bizarre. SFChron 9/3/93: no gore.

**The BOY WHO COULD FLY** Ref: V 8/13/86: airborne twosome.

**\*\*The BRAIN MACHINE** 1954 Ref: TV: shrink discovers potential killer.

**BREAK** Ref: EBay Express 9/25/87: claymation re grafting.

**BREAKAWAY** (B) 1956 Ref: BFC: "formula to eliminate metal fatigue."

**BREATHING UNDER WATER** Ref: V 11/18/91: surgical gore.

**BREATHWORLD** (B) 1964 45m. Ref: Lee: sf; amateur?

**BRENDA STARR** Ref: TVG 11/28/92: "secret formula."

**BRIDE FROM HADES** Ref: vc box: sfa *Tale of Peonies & Stone Lanterns* (I)?

**The BRIDE OF JOHNNY IN MONSTERLAND** 1992 Ref: PT 16:62: amateur?; fantasy.

**BRIDGEHEAD** (B) 1967? Ref: Lee: sf?

**A BRIEF HISTORY OF TIME** Ref: SFChron 8/28/92: futuristic visualizations.

**BRIGADA EXPLOSIVA CONTRA LOS MONSTRUOS** (Arg.) Ref: V 5/6/87:494

**BRIGHTNESS** (Mali) Ref: SFExam: 1987; the supernatural.

**BROOMSTICK BUNNY** 1956 anim short Ref: WBCartoons: Witch Hazel.

**BROWNOUT** (Fili) 1969 Ref: Lee(Borst): sf?

**BRUJAS MAGICAS** (Sp) 1981 Ref: Hardy/HM: "witchcraft comedy."

**BULLDOG BREED** (B) 1960 Ref: V 12/21/60: man into space. BFC: lands on island.

**BULLDOG DRUMMOND STRIKES BACK** 1934 Ref: screen: lighting effects.

**BULLDOG DRUMMOND'S REVENGE** 1937 Ref: TVG. V 12/22/37: new-explosive formula

**BULLETPROOF** Ref: SFExam 5/20/88: top-secret supertank."

**BULLSEYE!** (U.S.-B) Ref: V 7/29/91: at end, nuclear-fusion power plant explodes.

**The BURGLAR'S JOKE WITH THE AUTOMATIC DOLL** (B) 1908 Ref: BFC: "lifelike doll."

**BURNDOWN** 1989 Ref: TVG: "radioactive killer."

**BURY ME DEAD** 1947 Ref: TV: climactic suspense sequence with heroine, madman, shadows.

**The BUS** (F) Ref: V 4/18/90:12: best short at Imagfic.

**THE BUTCHER** (H.K.?) Ref: vc box: doubt.

**The BUTCHER'S WIFE** Ref: TV. TVG: "split-apart," kindred souls.

**BUTTER BATTLE BOOK** Ref: Sacto Bee 11/13/89: "ultimate destructive device."

**BUTTS MOTEL** series Ref: Adam '91: Norman Butts talks to dead mom, makes guests vanish.

**BUZZIN' AROUND** 1933 short Ref: Lee: formula for unbreakable chinaware.

**CABEZA DE VACA** (Mex-Sp) Ref: V 3/4/91: shaman.

**CADDYSHACK II** 1988 Ref: TV: bit with laser gun.

**CAFE FLESH 2 & 3** Ref: V 6/3/91:8.

**CALENDAR GIRL MURDERS** 1984 Ref: TVG: TV-movie.

**CALIFORNIA NATIVE** 1988 Ref: vc box: Amazons. Adam '89

**CALIGULA — THE UNTOLD STORY** (I-U.S.) 1982 Ref: McCarty II: gore. V 11/26/86: aka *The Emperor Caligula: The Untold Story;* "yucky violence."

**CALLING ALL MARINES** Ref: V 9/27/39: "new aerial torpedo" tested. TGSP2.

**\*CALLING PAUL TEMPLE** (B) 1948 Ref: TV: "maniac murderer" ...hypnotism... semi-spooky tomb scene; not horrific, though.

**CALLING THE TUNE** (B) 1936 Ref: Lee: sf-sequence.

**CALYPSO** (I-F) 1959 Ref: Lee: voodoo sequence.

**CANTATE POUR DEUX GENERAUX** (F) Ref: V 3/7/90: "voodoo rites."

**CAPE FEAR** 1991 Ref: TV: disfigurement, strangulation, brief vision.

CAP'N O.G. READMORE MEETS DR. JEKYLL AND MR. HYDE 1986 Ref: TVG: "Weekend Special."

CAPTAIN BARBELL BOOM! 1986 Ref: vc box: TV shows?

CAPTAIN FUTURE IN SPACE anim Ref: VSB.

CAPTAIN KANGAROO SILLY STORIES AND SCARY TALES Ref: V 11/6/85:83(hv): 1-hour video.

CAPTAIN POWER AND THE SOLDIERS OF THE FUTURE Ref: TVG: TV series; on video.

The CARE BEARS ADVENTURE IN WONDERLAND! (Can.) anim Ref: V 5/27/87: evil wizard.

La CARNE (I) Ref: V 5/20/91: cannibalism, murder.

CAROL (J) 1990 anim 60m. Ref: Japan Video: fantasy-horror?

*The CARPATHIAN CASTLE (Rum.) 1957 Ref: Wakeman: not completed.

El CARTERO ALBURERO (Mex.?) Ref: TVG: spirit possession?

La CASA 5 (I) L'Immagine Ref: V 5/2/90:188. D: D. Edwards. with L. Blair.

La CASA DEL SORRISO (I) Ref: V 3/4/91: "fantasy."

The CASE OF THE SCORPION'S TAIL (I) 1971 Ref: Imagi 1:59.

The CASE OF THE WITCH WHO WASN'T (Can.) Ref: V 6/27/90: old lady labeled witch.

2P CASTLE OF CRIMES (B) 1940('44-U.S.) (House of the Arrow - orig t?) Ref: V 4/4/45. Gifford. Harrison's 1/6/45: doubt.

CELIA: CHILD OF TERROR (Austral.) 1988 Ref: PFA: girl who fears "fairy tale monsters."

CELINE (F) Ref: SFChron 5/5/93: re the supernatural.

CENTERFOLD GIRLS 1977 Ref: Stanley: mad slasher.

CHAINED HEAT 2 Ref: SFChron 11/7/93: Can.? Snuff films, violence.

CHANOC CONTRA LAS TARANTULAS (Mex.) Ref: TV: one semi-horrific sequence.

CHANOC EN EL FOSO DE LAS SERPIENTES (Mex.) 1975 Ref: TV: super-TV, snake pit.

CHANOC EN LA ISLA DE LOS MUERTOS (Mex.) Ref: TV: cannibals.

CHANOC Y EL HIJO DEL SANTO (Mex.) Ref: V 5/25/83:28.

CHARLEY (Dutch) Ref: V 4/9/86: cannibalism

CHARLIE CHAN IN PARIS 1935 Ref: TV: semi-spooky sewers-of-Paris sequence.

CHARLIE CHAN IN RIO 1941 Ref: TV: truth serum.

The CHARM OF THE SNAKE VALLEY (Russ-Polish) Ref: V 10/19/88:292(ad): sf.

CHELOVEK S BULVARA KAPUSHINOV (Russ) Ref: V 7/13/88: "zombie pictures."

CHERNI MONAKH (Russ) Ref: V 10/19/88: "man haunted by a ghost."

CHILD OF RAGE Ref: SFChron 9/28/92: Bad Seed update.

The CHILL (Austral.) Ref: TVG: "brutal murders." Chilling - t error?

The CHIMES World 1914 Ref: Lee. From Dickens.

CHINA GIRL 1974 Ref: TVG: "formula for changing the brain."

The CHINESE CAT 1944 Ref: Hanke/Chan: funhouse "zombie" display.

CH'ING SHAONIEN NA CHA (Taiwanese-H.K.) Ref: V 3/15/93: "supposedly haunted" fourth floor.

CHRISTINE CROMWELL: THINGS THAT GO BUMP IN THE NIGHT Ref: V 11/22/89:94.

CHRONIQUE DE VOYAGE (F) 1970 short Ref: Jones: vampire?

CI RISIAMO VERO PROVVIDENZA? (I-Sp-F) 1972 Ref: Prod Ital: Old West anachronisms.

The CIRCUS QUEEN MURDER Ref: V 5/9/33: ?? Fango 6/89.

La CITTA DELL'ULTIME PAURA (I) 1975 Ref: Hardy/HM: post-nuke "telefilm."

CITY BENEATH THE SEA 1953 Ref: TV: voodoo rites ... supposedly haunted city.

CITY OF FEAR 1959 Ref: Stanley: radioactive powder.

CITY OF SHADOWS 1986 Ref: vc box: "bizarre experiment."

CITY THAT NEVER SLEEPS 1953 Ref: TV: bizarre display-window "robot."

CLAWS (S. African) 1982 Ref: vt: coming-of-age story with suspense scenes.

CLOAK & DAGGER 1984 Ref: TV: specs for invisible bomber.

The CLOSER Ref: V 3/18/91: ghost scenes.

The CLOUDED CRYSTAL (B) 1948 Ref: BFC: f. teller predicts man's death.

The CLOWN MURDERS (Can.) 1974 Ref: Martin. Hound. Phantom.

COAL BLACK & DE SEBBEN DWARFS 1943 anim short Ref: Lee.

COBRA 1986 Ref: MFB: "Night Slasher."

The COCA COLA KID (Austral.) 1985 Ref: TV: end title: "A week later ... the next world war began."

CODE NAME: CHAOS 1990 Ref: SFChron Dtbk 7/26/92: world chaos?

CODE NAME: DIAMOND HEAD 1977 Ref: TVFFSB: explosives formula. Scheuer.

CODE NAME: FOXFIRE 1985 Ref: TV: plot to start WW III in space with missile.

COLD TO THE TOUCH 1992? (aka Good Cop/Bad Cop) Ref: V 10/14/91:A-5(ad). 2/22/93:50.

La COLINA DEL DIABLO Ref: TVG: "terror." with A. Head, T. Musante.

COME OUT, COME OUT, WHEREVER YOU ARE (B) 1974 Ref: TV: man in skeleton suit.

COMIC BOOK CONFIDENTIAL (Can.) 1988 Ref: TVG: history of comic books.

Las COMPUTADORAS (Mex.) Ref: TV vt: cathouse client playing Dracula.

CONAN, THE BOY IN FUTURE (J) anim Ref: V 5/6/87:464(ad).

CONFESSIONS OF A DANISH COVERGIRL (Dan.) 1974 Ref: MFB'77:30: ends as a "shocker."

CONGORILLA 1932 Ref: TVG: aka Bride of the Beast; docu.

CONTRA SENAS (Fili) 1984? Ref: vc box: anti-missile formula.

The COOK, THE THIEF, HIS WIFE AND HER LOVER Ref: Cinef 7/90. TV: "cannibal" scene.

COPACABANA Ref: TVG 11/30/85: cursed diamond.

COPPELIA (B) 1964 Ref: Lee.

COPPELIA (Austrian) 1967 Ref: Lee.

CORN FLICKS Ref: SFChron Dtbk 8/23/92: aliens?

CORPSE NO. 1346 (Russ) 1912 Ref: Lee: horror.

CORRUPTION 1933 Ref: Turner/Price: "crazed scientist...specially prepared bullet."

COSI DOLCI PERVERSA (I) Ref: Imagi 1:59: early "giallo."

COSMIC JOURNEY (Russ) 1928 Ref: Lee: sf?

COUNCIL OF LOVE (W.G.) 1981 Ref: PFA notes 12/1/88: "Jesus is a zombie."

COUNTDOWN TO LOOKING GLASS Ref: TVG 10/14/84: on the brink of nuclear war.

COUNTRYMAN (B) 1982 Ref: MFB'82:62: voodoo doctor.

COVERGIRL (Can.) 1984 Ref: TV: robot-domestic.

CRAZY BLOOD (H.K.?) Ref: vc box.

The CRAZY FAMILY (J) Ref: SFExam 8/8/86: gory ending.

CREATOR 1985 Ref: MFB: plan to "regrow" woman from her cells.

CREATURES OF THE NIGHT 1987 Ref: Adam '89: "secret experiment."

The CREMATOR (Cz) Ref: V 7/16/69. PFA notes 3/28/88: "images of death."

Le CRI DU HIBOU (F-I) Ref: V 11/18/87: "Grand Guignol melodramatics."

CRIME OF CRIMES 1988 Ref: PT 16:63 body-parts biz. TVG: Crimen de Crimenes.

CRIME OF THE CENTURY Ref: V 2/21/33: hypnotism. Eames.

CRIME WAVE (Can.) Ref: V 9/18/85: "extraordinary gadgetry."

CRIMEN EN EL PUERTO (Mex.?) Ref: TVG: sec maniac.

CROSS MISSION 1989 Ref: Martin: "even a little voodoo."

CRUSH (N.Z.) Ref: SFChron 4/30/93: grisly.

CRUSHER JOE: THE ICE HELL TRAP (J) 1989 anim Ref: Animag 6:4,5: 2 OAVs; released?

CRYING FREEMAN (J) 198-? anim Ref: TV: vt: bloody violence.

CRYSTALSTONE Ref: V 6/29/88: "magical fable."

CUCHILLOS DE FUEGO (Venez.-Sp) Ref: V 12/17/90: telekinesis.

Il CUORE RIVELATORE (I) 1935 short Ref: Ecran 12/77:29 from "Tell-Tale Heart." amateur?

The CURSE OF HER FLESH 1968 Ref: AFI: brutal murders; sequel to Touch of Her Flesh.

The CURSE OF RAVENSCROFT (B) 1926 Ref: BFC: Inscrutable Drew series.

CURSE OF THE CATWOMAN 1991 Ref: Adam '92: "cat people."

CURSE OF THE GOLD MONKEY 1982 Ref: TVG: "pharaoh's curse." no Scheuer.

CURSE OF THE VIKING GRAVE Ref: V 2/10/92:84: dreams.

The CURSED MOUNTAIN MYSTERY (Austral.) Ref: V 4/25/90: aka Sher Mountain Killings Mystery; "ghostly forest ranger." vc box.

DANCING (I) anim Ref: SFChron Dtbk 6/28/92: "Death personified."

DANGEROUS OBSESSION (I) 1988 Ref: TV: Collector-in-reverse.

DANGEROUSLY CLOSE 1986 Ref: Briggs/Back: "a 4 on the Vomit Meter." Phantom.

The DARK ANGEL Ref: Sacto Bee 3/23/91: "Uncle Silas"; "gothic tale."

The DARK BACKWARD Ref: V 3/18/91: bump on man's "back turns into a horrifying ...hand."

DARK DREAMS 1985 Ref: vc box: witch.

The DARK HOUR 1936 Ref: Turner/Price: "dark house...weird moments ...killer in drag."

DARK INTERVAL (B) 1950 Ref: Hardy/HM. BFC: wife learns husband is madman.

DARK LADY OF THE BUTTERFLY (H.K.) Ref: NST! 4:20: "Batwoman" fantasy.

DARK MANSIONS Ref: V 9/3/86:66. Stanley: supernatural.

DARK PURPOSE 1964 Ref: TV: mystery-suspense. TVG: "chiller."

DARK ROMANCES VOLS. 1 & 2 Ref: V 10/1/90:88(hv): horror videos. PT.

The DARK SIDE Ref: Martin: snuff films. V 5/6/87:86(ad): at Cannes. (The Darkside)

DARK WATER Ref: TVG 2/23/91: anim miniseries; science-fantasy.

The DARK WIND Ref: V 11/25/91: "mystical voiceovers."

DARLING, GET ME A CROCODILE (Polish) Ref: Brandon: "prehistoric times."

DARS AR SPOKU (Russ) Ref: V 4/3/85: visions.

The DAY THE SKY FELL IN (B) 1961 Ref: BFC: "super weapon."

DE HOLLYWOOD A TAMANRASSET (Alger.) Ref: V 6/17/91: "Spock ... beamed."

DE VERAS ME ATRAPASTE (Mex.) Ref: V 8/14/85: vision; "ghost rocker."

DEAD AGAIN Ref: Newsweek 9/9/91. TV: hypnotic regression, thunderstorm.

DEAD CALM Ref: V 4/5/89: "suspense." Scheuer: shock end. Maltin '92: "slasher" end.

DEAD CERTAIN 1991 Ref: Fango 118:12: mad killer. no Martin.

The DEAD COME BACK (Hung.) 1968 Ref: World F'68: crime story.

DEAD END CITY Ref: V 3/22/89: "sf slant."

DEAD FLOWERS (Austrian) Ref: V 12/14/92: "Death is a ... bureaucracy."

The DEAD MARCH Ref: V 8/25/37: "each national arises from his grave." Monsterland 2:49.

DEAD RINGERS Ref: SFExam 9/23/88: "quease-in-art."

DEAD SLEEP (Austral.) Ref: V 2/18/91: experimental psychiatry.

DEADBOLT Ref: V 6/14/93:36: "sometimes scary movie."

DEADLY FORCE 1983 Ref: TV: "X"-killer at large; non-horrific.

The DEADLY GAME 1941 Ref: Okuda/MC "night air-raid detector" invention.

DEADLY JAWS (G) 1974 Ref: TVG.

The DEADLY MODEL (B) 1915 Ref: BFC: "inventor's model gun."

DEADLY PREY Ref: V 11/25/87: "Most Dangerous Game" overtones.

DEADLY SPYGAMES Ref: V 1/3/90: Outtakes Santa-slasher footage recycled.

DEATH CHASE Ref: V 7/20/88: "teams hunt each other."

DEATH DANCERS Ref: V 9/6/93:6(rated): "violence."

DEATH FLIES EAST Ref: V 3/6/35: "secret armament formula."

DEATH HOUSE 1989? Ref: PT 2:22: govt. tests "new medicine" on inmates, who "become living dead." aka?

DEATH KISS 1976 Ref: vc box: chamber of horrors sequence.

The DEATH OF OCEAN VIEW PARK 1979 Ref: Stanley: psychic.

DEATH RAY 1977 D: F.G. Carroll. Ref: Stanley.

DEATH WARRANT Ref: V 10/1/90: "psycho behemoth."

DEATHMASK 1984 Ref: Ecran F 39:6: "terror film"; psychic (V).

The DECEIVERS Ref: SFChron 9/9/88: "secret cult of murderers."

DECISION AGAINST TIME (B) 1957 Ref: TVG: "experimental rocket-plane."

DEEP SPACE NINE Ref: SFChron 1/7/93: 2-hour premiere.

DEFENSE PLAY 1988 Ref: Phantom: "laser-equipped" helicopters.

DEFENSELESS Ref: SFExam 8/23/91: "special-effects slice-and-dice flick?"

**DEMENTED** Ref: V 11/4/91:14: 8/14/91 start. SP,D,P: R.W. Martin.

**DEMON LUST** Ref: TV: not horrific.

**DENVER, THE LAST DINOSAUR** Ref: V 1/6/92:36(ad): TV.

**DERANGED** Ref: V 5/20/87: woman's "escalating hallucinations."

**DESTINY TO ORDER** Ref: CVS 2/91: fictional-characters-to-life-via-computer.

**DEUX HEURES MOINT LE QUART AVANT JESUS CHRIST** (F) Ref: V 10/20/82: "ancients have TVs, traffic..." Ecran F 29:6.

**The DEVIL IN A CONVENT** (F) 1899 Ref: Hardy/HM: devil appears as bat. Lee.

**DEVIL SEX LOVE** (H.K.) Jade City Ref: V 4/12/93:44: in H.K.

**The DEVIL'S GARDEN** 1970? Ref: SWV supp: voodoo. Cinef IV:1:37: *In the Devil's Garden*; minimal horror. Weldon. sfa *Tower of Terror* (2P)? TV. Oak Trib 5/6/83.

**DEVIL'S LOVE** Ref: V 11/22/93:16: playing.

**The DEVIL'S MATE** 1966 Ref: AFI: madman with scarred face; torture.

**DIABEL** (Polish) Ref: V 6/27/90:40: cf. *The Devils.*

**Le DIABLE GEANT** (F) 1901 Ref: Lee: devil becomes giant. (*The Devil & the Statue*)

**DIABOLICO ASESINO** (Mex.) Ref: TVG. TV.

**DICK DEADEYE, OR DUTY DONE** (B) 1975 anim 81m. Ref: MFB'75:196-7: evil magician.

**DICK TRACY** 1990 Ref: TV: bizarre-voiced "No Face"; monstrous-faced hoods.

**DIPLOMATIC IMMUNITY** Ref: SFChron Dtbk/ 8/25/91: mutilation.

**The DIRT BIKE KID** Ref: V 5/21/86: "Yamaha which ... can start itself."

**DIZZY RED RIDING HOOD** 1931 Ref: screen: bit with monstrous "fairy"; walking skeleton.

**DO OR DIE** Ref: V 6/17/91: "Most Dangerous Game" overtones.

**DR. MASHER** 1969 Ref: AFI: "voodooism."

**DR. SEX** 1964 Ref: AFI: house of female ghosts. SWV catalog.

**DOG EAT DOG** (U.S.-W.G.-I) 1963 Ref: Weldon: bizarre murders.

**DOG GONE MODERN** 1939 anim 7m. Ref: WBCartoons: robotic appliances.

**The DOG SOLDIER** 1972 40m. Ref: VSB: future state. Hound: TV?

**DOG SOLDIER: SHADOWS OF THE PAST** (J) 1989 ('92-U.S.) anim 45m. Ref: Japan Video: AIDS cure.

**DOLPHY VS. PLANETARIANS** (Fili) Ref: vc box. also *Dolphy Vs. Robot.*

**DONGALO MASSACRE** (F) 1987? Ref: vc box: psychotic killer.

**La DONNA DEL LAGO** (I) 1965 Ref: Hardy/HM: aka *The Possessed;* ax killer.

**DOS MONJES** (Mex.) 1934 Ref: Hardy/HM: madness, hallucinations.

**DOS PENITENTES PERO NO TANTO** (Mex.) 1990 Ref: TVG: witchcraft comedy.

**DOWN UNDER DONOVAN** (B) 1922 Ref: BFC: "formula for malleable glass."

**DOWNLOAD** (J) Anim Ref: Animerica 5:53: OAV; "cyberpunk." Japan videos.

**DRACULA** (Mex.) 1978 Ref: Lawrence Cohn. with E.A. Felix.

**DRACULA, THE GREAT UNDEAD** 1985 Ref: Stanley: docu.

**DRACULA'S HAIR** (Russ) 1992 Ref: Jones.

**DRAGON SWAMP** (H.K.) 1971 Ref: MFB'73:7: cursed sword.

**The DRAGON THAT WASN'T...OR WAS HE?** 1983 Ref: TV: spooky dragon-conjuring scene.

**DREAM LOVERS** (H.K.) Ref: V 5/21/86: reincarnation.

**DREAMS LOST, DREAMS FOUND** 1987 Ref: TV: haunted Castle Caladh, Scotland.

**DROP DEAD FRED** Ref: Sacto Bee 5/24/91: Beetlejuicy friend. Jim Shapiro.

**DUCKTALES: TREASURE OF THE GOLDEN SUNS** Ref: TVG 9/18/87. TV: rudimentary robot. 2 hours.

**DUDES** Ref: V 9/23/87: *Hills Have Eyes*-like; "apparition."

**The DUNGEON** Micheaux 1922 80m. Ref: Lee: Bluebeard-type, hypnotism.

**La DUQUESA DIABOLICA** (Mex.) 1965 Ref: TV: alchemist's death-semblance & temporary-madness serums. Lee.

**DURANGO VALLEY RAIDERS** 1938 Ref: Bill Warren. pbk: "black-robed Shadow." LC.

**DYING I & II** 1988 Ref: vc boxes: docu-gore.

**DYING TO REMEMBER** Ref: TVG 12/2/93: "visions from a past life."

**E.A.R.T.H. FORCE** Ref: V 9/90: nuclear meltdown.

**EARTHIAN 1 & 2** (J) 1988 Ref: Animag 5:5. 11:4: fantasy.

**EAST L.A. WARRIORS** Ref: V 1/10/90:32(hv): "futuristic element."

**EAT THE RICH** (B) Ref: V 9/30/87: cannibal nitery.

**EDWARD SCISSORHANDS** Ref: SFExam 12/14/90: "unclear exactly how human he is."

**The EIGHT IMMORTALS** (H.K.?) Ref: Lee. Eberhard: demons.

**EIKA KATAPPA** (W.G.) 1969 Ref: PFA notes 12/15/88: Siegfried & Kriemhild vignette.

**EK NANHI MUNNI LADKI THI** (India-Hindi) Ref: Hardy/HM: horror. 1970.

**ELE, O BOTO** (Braz.) Ref: V 8/5/87: dolphin-man legend.

**ELECTRA ONE** (I-F?) Ref: TVG: 1972; "secret formula."

**ELECTRIC DREAMS** 1984 Ref: TV: seemingly-sentient computer.

**EMMANUELLE IV: EN RELIEF** (F) Ref: Ecran F 38:89: E. a virgin after surgery. V 2/29/84.

**EN TIEMPOS DE LA INQUISICION** Ref: TVG. with G. Marin.

**The ENEMY IS THE PIRATE** (J) anim Ref: Animag 9:3: 6 OAVs; released?

**ENGLAND'S MENACE** (B) 1914 40m Ref: Hardy/SF: aborted invasion of Eng.

**ENIGMA PARA DEMONIOS** (Braz.) 1974 Ref: Hardy/HM: woman driven insane.

**EROTIC BEAST HIGH SCHOOL 4** (J) '93 anim 46m. Ref: Animerica 5:15.

**The ESCAPE OF THE APE** Ref: V 8/29/08: escaped ape "terrorizes the community."

**ESCAPE TO BURMA** 1955 Ref: TV: natives excited re "evil tiger spirit" (just a tiger).

**ESCRITO EN LA NIEBLA** (Sp) 1982 Ref: Hardy/HM: psychotic killer.

**El ESPECTRO DE TELEVICENTRO** (Mex.) 1959 Ref: Hardy/HM:118.

**A ESTRANHA HOSPEDARIA DOS PRAZERES** (Braz.) 1975 Ref: Monster! 3:30: innkeeper is Death.

**The EVE OF IVAN KUPALO** (Russ.) 1988 (1968) Ref: PFA notes 9/27/89: pact with evil spirit.

**EVEN COWGIRLS GET THE BLUES** Ref: V 9/20/93: super-race envisioned.

An **EVENING WITH SIR WILLIAM MARTIN** 30m. Ref: Hound: man taken to another planet.

**EVIL DOMINATION** Ref: V 10/21/87:221(ad). no PFA.

**EVIL IN THE SWAMP** 1989 Ref: vc box: "scary."

**EXECUTIONERS** (H.K.) Ref: V 10/25/93:M-18(ad): futuristic? 11/1/93:14: in H.K.

**EXGIZER, VOL. 1** (J) 1990 anim 48m. Ref: TV: vt: TV?; robots, dinosaurs.

**EXPEDICION ATLANTIS** (Arg.) Ref: V 5/6/87:494.

**EXTREMITIES** Ref: SFExam 8/22/86: "slasher-flick devices."

**EYES IN OUTER SPACE** 1959 26m. Ref: Lee: future of weather forecasting; TV?

**EYES OF THE VAMPIRE** Ref: V 5/9/84:264(ad).

**F/X** 1986 Ref: TV: Effects man uses prop monster to scare burglars, etc.; lasers.

**FX2** Ref: SFExam 5/10/91: high-tech toys like a "fighting cyborg."

The **FABULOUS ADVENTURES OF BARON MUNCHAUSEN** Ref: TVG. V 5/23/79: 2-headed birds. (*Les Fabuleuses Aventures du Legendaire Baron De Munchausen*)

**FACE OF FEAR** Ref: SFChron 9/28/90: psychic; serial killer.

**FACES OF TORTURE** Ref: vc box: docu-gore.

**FAIR WARNING** Ref: V 3/24/37: Thomas/Fox: "whiz with chemical experiments."

The **FAIRY WIFE** (H.K.?) 1970? Ref: Eberhard: Black Devil, man revived from death.

The **FALCON OUT WEST** 1944 Ref: TV: spooky dark room ("This place gives me the creeps").

**FALSE LIGHT** (Dutch) Ref: V 5/10/93:C-114: futuristic; at Cannes.

**FANGFACE** 1983 anim Ref: vc box: werewolf; 2 (TV?) episodes.

Los **FANTASMAS BURLONES** 1964 (*The Ghost Jesters*) Ref: TV: non-horrific ghost comedy.

The **FANTASY FILM WORLD OF GEORGE PAL** 1986 Ref: TVG: docu. V 4/23/86. See also: *Puppetoon Movie* (M).

**FANTOZZI SUBISCE ANCORA** (I) Ref: 1/25/84: woman bears "six-armed...monster."

**FARCE TREK** Ref: TVG 9/28/91(ad): videos; 75m. of parodies.

**FARREBIQUE** (F) 1946 Ref: screen: shots of possible future of farm & family.

**FAT GUY GOES NUTZOID** Ref: V 4/15/87: filmed in '84; comedy.

**FATAL EXPOSURE** 1989 (*Mangled Alive*) Ref: PT 10:52: "blood-drinking photographer." amateur? PT 11:6.

**FEAR STALK** Ref: V 12/20/89: "character who likes to terrorize dames."

\*\*The **FEATHERED SERPENT** 1948 Ref: TV: M. Moreland helps carry coffin of Aztec king.

**FEDERAL AGENT** Ref: V 4/15/36: "new chemical explosive."

**FELIX THE CAT IN THE NON STOP FRIGHT** Ref: TV: rough plane flight for F.

The **FERTILICHROME CHEERLEADER MASSACRE** 1989 Ref: PT 4:14: amateur; sf.

**FEULIN' AROUND** Ref: Lee: super-fuel. 1949

**FIDDLER ON THE ROOF** 1971 Ref: Lee: "people rise from graves." Jim Shapiro: horror seq.

**FIFTH COLUMN MICE** 1943 Ref: TV: robotic bulldog like wind-up toy. WBCartoons.

The **FIFTH MISSILE** Ref: V 3/5/86:70: on the brink of WW III. TVG.

**FINAL EMBRACE** Ref: PT 16:14: psycho, "false scares."

**FINAL NOTICE** 1989 Ref: TV: mystery-suspenser.

The **FINAL SOLUTION: SLAVERY'S BACK IN EFFECT** Ref: Oak Trib 11/21/91: 1995 race war; video.

A **FINE MESS** Ref: SFExam 8/8/86: mad doc.

The **FINISHING TOUCH** Ref: SFChron Dtbk 12/13/92: "brutal serial killings."

**FIORILE** (I-F-G) Ref: V 3/29/93: "van becomes a time machine"; "spooky" scene.

**FIREWALKER** Ref: SFExam 11/21/86.

The **FIRST MAN ON THE MOON** Fleischer 1921 anim Ref: Cabarga/TFS. no Lee.

The **FISHER KING** 1991 Ref: TV: roaring Red Knight.

**FISHER'S GHOST** (Austral.) 1923 Ref: V 5/5/76:95.

The **FLAMING CITY** 1963 Ref: Lee: "NYC destroyed."

**FLESHBURN** 1983 Ref: Martin. vc box: sorcery.

**FLIGHT COMMAND** 1940 Ref: TV: inventor's radio-beam fog device doesn't work, at first....

**FLIRTING WITH DANGER** 1934 Ref: TV: powerful new explosive will "revolutionize" explosives.

The **FLOWER IN HIS MOUTH** (I) 1976 Ref: TVG: "ritual murders."

The **FLY** (Yugos.) 1967 short Ref: Lee: horror.

**FLYING BLIND** 1942 Ref: TGSP2: "new airplane transformer."

**FLYING CLAW FIGHTS 14 DEMONS** (H.K.?) Ref: TVG.

The **FLYING SAUCER MYSTERY** 1950 short Ref: Lee(MFB).

The **FLYING SERPENT** short Ref: TVG: horror; on "Commander USA's Groovie Movies."

**FOR GOD'S SAKE** (Sp) Ref: V 10/22/90:40: best short at Sitges.

**FORBIDDEN QUEST** (Dutch) Ref: V 3/1/93: cannibalism, Poe & Verne refs. 5/10/93:C-118.

**FORBIDDEN SUN** (B) Ref: V 11/29/89: F-U to *Wicker Man*; "mythic fantasy." (*Bulldance*)

**FOREVER** Ref: SFChron Dtbk 12/26/93: haunted house.

**FORTRESS** (Austral.) Ref: V 12/4/85:75: "chilling"; hoodlums in "eerie disguises."

**FOUR DESPERATE MEN** (Austral.) 1960 Ref: Maltin/TVM: "bomb attack could destroy Southern Hemisphere" or "Sydney Harbor" (in different editions — of TVM).

The **FOURTH PROTOCOL** Ref: Martin: miniature atom bomb. 1987.

**FRATERNITY DEMON** Ref: V 12/21/92:14 (rated).

**FRAUDS** Ref: V 9/13/93:9(rated): "terror/violence."

**FRESHKILL** 1987 Ref: vc box: violence.

**FRIDAY THE 13TH: THE SERIES** Ref: V 10/25/89:64-5: 2-hour season premiere.

**FRIENDLY GHOST** (H.K.?) Ref: vc box.

**FRISKY FABLES** 1988 Ref: Adam '90: Snow White, Sleeping Beauty "elements."

**FRONTIER PONY EXPRESS** 1939 Ref: TV: Civil War Western; politician plotting to make California "The Republic of the Pacific."

**FRUSTRATION** (F) 1971 Ref: MFB'73:28: torture, isolated mansion.

**FUEGO ETERNO** (Sp) Ref: V 4/10/85: witchcraft.

**FULL CONTACT** (H.K.) Ref: V 7/19/93: "phantom-like appearances."

**FUNERAL PARADE OF ROSES** (J) 1970 Ref: Lee: "blood, gore & mutilation." AFI.

**FUNLAND** Ref: V 5/27/87: "comedy thriller"; dead man who comes back.

**FUNPARK** Ref: V 10/21/87:290(ad): "terror."

**FUSA** (J) Ref: V 9/27/93: "supernatural story."

**FUTURE COPS** Ref: SFExam 1/17/86:E-13: aka *Trancers?*

**G.I. EXECUTIONER** 1985(1971) Ref: Stanley: "antimatter device." V 2/20/85: minor element. (*Wit's End*) V 10/24/84:376(ad). 2/24/92.

**G.I. JOE: COBRA STOPS THE WORLD** Ref: V 8/21/85:84: 24m.; TV?

**GAMBLING WITH GHOULS** 1930 Ref: TV listing t. error for Gambling with Souls?

**The GAME** Ref: V 7/18/90:62(hv): "Most Dangerous Game" overtones.

**GAME OF SURVIVAL** Ref: V 5/22/85: sadism.

**GANDA BABAE, GANDA LALAKE** (Fili) Ref: vc box: ghost. 1989.

**The GARBAGE PAIL KIDS MOVIE** Ref: V 8/26/87: "germinated out of green slime."

**GARUM** (Sp) Ref: V 5/10/89: "satanism" & "sci-fi"?

**The GATCHAMAN FORCE** (J) 1978 anim Ref: JFFJ 13:30: sf?; from TV series.

**GENERATIONS: MIND CONTROL - FROM THE FUTURE** 1980 54m. Ref: Hound: "evil forces."

**GENGHIS COHN** (B) Ref: V 11/22/93: "pesky ghost of a Dachau victim."

**GEORGE'S ISLAND** (Can.) 1991 Ref: Martin: pirate ghosts. vc box.

**The GERASENE DEMONIAC** Ref: V 11/4/91:14: shooting.

**GERMACIDE** Ref: vc box: deadly bacteria. Hound: *Germicide.*

**GET THAT GIRL** Ref: V 6/14/32: "hypodermics, Svengali characterizations ... a wicked brain specialist." no NYT. no PFA.

**GETTING EVEN** Ref: 5/7/86: "deadly new poison gas." (*Hostage: Dallas* - orig t)

**GHOST DAD** Ref: 6/27/90: one "hair-raising" sequence. Sacto Union 6/28/90.

**GHOST DANCING** Ref: TVG 5/28/83: "Indian who ... teaches ritual "ghost dancing."

**GHOST IN THE HOUSE** (Thai?) Ref: vc box.

**GHOST LAMP** (H.K.?) 1971? Ref: Lee.

**GHOST MOM** Ref: TVG 9/18/93: mom comes back. (*Bury Me in Niagara*)

**GHOST, MY COMPANION** (India - Hindustani) 1974 Ref: Dharap: *Blackbeard's Ghost* steal.

**GHOST OF A CHANCE** Ref: TVG 5/9/87: Redd Foxx comes back.

**The GHOST OF SULPHUR MOUNTAIN** 1912 Ref: AF-Index. Lee(e).

**GHOST OF THE NINJA** (H.K.?) Ref: vc box.

**GHOST TO GHOST** 1991 Ref: Adam '92: ghosts.

**GHOST TOWN** Ref: V 1/6/37: "ghost" scene.

**The GHOSTESS WITH THE MOSTESS** 1988 Ref: TV: vt: voodoo doll, ghosts.

**GHOSTESSES** (B) 1946 Ref: BFC: The Voyage of Peter Joe series.

**The GHOSTING** Walt Hefner Ref: V 12/9/91:12(rated).

**GHOSTS CAN'T DO IT** Ref: V 6/13/90: ghost.

**GHOST'S LOVE** (H.K.) Ref: NST! 4:24: female ghost. sfa *Ghost Romance* (M)?

**The GHOSTS OF BUXLEY HALL** Ref: TVG 12/21/80: doubt.

**GHOSTS OF THE CIVIL DEAD** Ref: V 5/25/88: figurative.

**The GIANT OF THUNDER MOUNTAIN** Ref: V 6/10/91: sympathetic giant.

**GIANTLAND** 1933 anim 7m. Ref: LC: Disney.

**The GIFTED ONE** Ref: V 6/28/89:48: telepath "5,000 years ahead of his time."

**GILBERT HARDING SPEAKS OF MURDER** (B) 1953 Ref: Hardy/HM: man locked in attic 20 years.

**The GIRL IN THE NIGHT** (B) 1931 Ref: BFC: old house, storm.

**GIRLS ON THE ROAD** (Can.) Ref: TVG. PT 12:11: "psycho killer"?; "tame." vc box.

**The GLITTERING SWORD** (B) 1929 Ref: BFC: the devil, Death.

**GLORY OF THULASI** (India-Tamil) Ref: Dharap: "Demon Land."

**GO DOWN DEATH** 1944 Ref: Lee: sequence in hell.

**GODDAMN! GO AHEAD!** (J) 1990 anim Ref: Animag 11:4: "rally car mecha."

**GODDESS KALI** (India-Hindi) 1969 Ref: World F'68. (*Mata Mahakali*)

**GODZILLA MEETS MONA LISA** 1984 Ref: PFA notes 3/11/86: re art complex.

**GOLDEN DRAGON/SILVER SNAKE** (H.K.?) 1979 Ref: TV: drill weapon; kung fu.

**GOLDEN EYES, SECRET AGENT 007** (India-Hindi) 1968 Ref: Ind. Filmography.

**The GOLDEN RABBIT** (B) 1962 Ref: BFC: gold formula.

***GOLDFACE, THE FANTASTIC SUPERMAN** 1967 (*Gold Face Superman*) Ref: TV: not sf.

**GONE TO GROUND** (Austral.) 1976 Ref: TVG: people in lonely cottage terrorized.

**The GOOD SON** Ref: V 9/27/93: another *Bad Seed.*

**The GOOSE STEPS OUT** (B) 1942 Ref: TGSP2: "new gas bomb." BFC.

**GRAND GUIGNOL** (B) 1921 series Ref: BFC.

**GRAND GUIGNOL** (F) Ref: V 5/6/87:565: G.G. theatre.

**The GREAT BEAR SCARE** 1984 anim Ref: vc box: TV?; Dracula, Frankstn., werewolf.

**The GREAT CHEESE ROBBERY** 192-? anim short Ref: TV: house haunted by "consciences."

**GREAT DECEIVER** (India-Telugu) 1972 Ref: Dharap: "new formula" for low-cost gold.

**The GREAT FEAR** (Yugos.) anim 12m. Ref: Lee: horror spoof. (*Veliki Strah*)

**The GREAT LAND OF SMALL** (Can.) Ref: V 5/27/87: "inner space world."

**The GREAT RACE** 1965 Ref: TV. Lee: noise-seeking torpedo.

**The GREAT SEA SERPENT** (B) 1904 Ref: BFC: worm in telescope.

**GREATNESS OF GODDESS CHAMUNDESWARI** (India-Kannada) 1974 Ref: Dharap: demon king.

**GREED** (J) anim 57m. Ref: Japan Video: fantasy.

**The GREEDY GIRL** (B) 1908 Ref: BFC: in dream: knights chop up girl.

**The GREEN BUDDHA** 1954 Ref: TV: fairground Chamber of Horrors. (B)

**GREEN HELL** 1940 Ref: TV: "evil spirit" said to haunt Incan ruins.

**GRETA — HAUS OHNE MAENNER** (W.G.?) 1977 Ref: Hardy/HM:272: cannibalism.

The **GRIP OF IRON** (B) 1913 & 1920 versions Ref: Lee(BFC): strangler.

**GRUNT!** (I) Ref: Ecran F 31:47: barbarian parody.

**GUARDIAN & SHE-GHOST OF SHAOLIN** (H.K.) Ref: NST! 4:24: cf. *Guardian, The* (1983)(M).

**GUBAN THE SPACE DETECTIVE** (J) Toei Ref: V 10/24/84:294: "animation pic."

La **GUEPE** (Can.) Ref: V 9/3/86: voodoo.

**GUILTY AS CHARGED** 1991 Ref: PT 13:51: homemade electric chair. V 5/6/91.

**GUMS** 1976 Ref: PT 2:36: JAWS parody re killer mermaid.

**GUNDAM — COUNTERATTACK OF DRAK** (J) anim 120m. Ref: Shadow Warrior (Sacto.).

The **GUNFIGHTER** (Braz.) 1975 Ref: Brasil: "dead man summons his killers."

**GUNPOWDER** (B) Ref: V 7/8/87: invention keeps gold "in liquid form without heating."

**GURU DAS SIETE CIDADES** (Braz.) 1972 Ref: Hardy/HM: human sacrifices.

**HADES, VIDA DESPUES DE LA MUERTE** (Mex.?) Ref: TVG: fantasy.

The **HALLOWEEN TREE** 1993 anim Ref: TVG: TV special.

**HAMBURGER — THE MOTION PICTURE** 1986 Ref: TV: mad doc demonstrates synthetic fried chicken, in a lab scene parodying the '31 *Frankenstein*. ("He's alive!")

**HAPPI-ENDO NO MONOGATARI** (J) 1991 Ref: Markalite 3:10: "time-warp fantasy."

**HAPPY GHOST II** (H.K.) Ref: V 8/21/85: reincarnation.

**HAPPY GHOST III** (H.K.) Ref: TV: vt: telekinesis comedy.

**HAPPY HAUNTING GROUNDS** 1940 anim 7m. Ref: LC.

**HAPPY HOUR** Ref: V 5/27/87: ingredient makes beer "irresistible & addictive."

**HARD SELL** 1990 Ref: Adam '92: scientist's aphrodisiac.

**HARD TARGET** Ref: V 8/30/93. SFChron 8/20/93: "Most Dangerous Game" elements.

**HARE KRISHNA** (India-Hindi) 1974 Ref: Dharap: two demons.

The **HATE SHIP** (B) 1929 Ref: BFC: murder suspects on "revenge cruise."

The **HAUNTED HOUSEBOAT** (B) 1904 Ref: BFC.

The **HAUNTED MANSION MYSTERY** Ref: TVG 1/8/83: 2-part "Weekend Special."

The **HAUNTED SCHOOL** (Austral.) 1986 Ref: TVG: ghost.

**HAUNTED TRAILS** 1949 Ref: TV: meaningless title. TVG.

**HAUNTING OF HARRINGTON HOUSE** 50m. Ref: vc box: TV?

The **HAWK** (B) Ref: V 9/27/93: "serial-killer suspenser."

**HEAR NO EVIL** Ref: SFChron 3/27/93: splatter element. V 3/29/93: cf. *Wait until Dark.*

**HEART CONDITION** Ref: V 1/24/90: "ghost-like form."

The **HEART OF THE STAG** Ref: SFExam 8/12/84: Gothic mystery.

**HEARTBREAK HOTEL** Ref: vc box: horror?

La **HECHICERA** (Mex.) Ref: TV: "voodoo witch."

**HELL HATH NO FURY** Ref: V 3/11/91:67: mad murderer.

**HELL HUNTERS** (W.G.) Ref: V 6/1/88: serum which "makes people open to fascist doctrine."

**HELLO AGAIN** Ref: V 11/11/87. TV: magic.

**HELL'S 400** 1926 Ref: Lee: in one sequence, "sins take the form of monsters."

**HENRY HAMILTON, GRADUATE GHOST** Ref: TVG 2/8/86: 2-part "Weekend Special."

**HENRY'S CAT: THE LOST WORLD** and **THE GREAT ADVENTURE** (B) Ref: TV: TV shorts; King Konga, abominable snowman, giant scorpion, Martians, etc.

**HER ODD TASTES** 1961 Ref: AFI: devil worshippers.

**HERCULES RETURNS** Ref: V 2/1/93.

**HERE YOU WON'T SEE PARADISE** (Russ.) Ref: PFA notes 11/21/86: "evil spirits."

The **HEREAFTER** 1987? Ref: Hound: zombies. Sfa *E Tu Vivrai...* (aka *The Beyond/II*) or *After Death* (M)?

**HERMELINDA LINDA** (Mex.) Ref: TVG: witch. See also *Agente Secreto 0013* (M).

**HEROIC LEGEND OF ARSLAN** (J) anim Ref: Animerica 6:10: ? Japan Video: 2 parts.

**HEXED** Ref: SFChron 1/23/93: "dynamo-psychotic murderer."

**\*\*HIDDEN ENEMY** Ref: V 4/3/40: formula for metal 3 times lighter than aluminum & stronger than steel. TVG.

**HIGH FREQUENCY** (I) Ref: V 10/19/88:344(ad.) Hound: murder seen on satellite monitor.

**HIGHLANDER: THE GATHERING** Ref: SFChron Dtbk 10/24/93: TV pilot.

**HIGHWAY 61** Ref: SFChron Dtbk 2/14/93. PT 14:10: deals with devilish character.

La **HIJA DE LA TIZNADA** (Mex.) Ref: vc box: voodoo?

**HIROKU ONNA-RO** (J) 1967 Ref: Hardy/HM: graphic torture. (aka *Ona Niko*)

The **HIT MAN** Ref: TVG: 1991 TV-movie re "sp fx wizardry." Sfa *Hitman, The* (below)?

**HITCHHIKE TO HELL** 1968 Ref: SWV supp: mad strangler.

**HITLER'S DAUGHTER** 1990 Ref: TVG.

The **HITMAN** Ref: Oak Trib 10/26/91: "gore." Sfa *Hit Man, The* (above)?

**HIWA NG LAGIM** (Fili) 1970 Ref: Lee: ghosts?

**HOLLYWOOD GHOST STORIES** 1986 Ref: Stanley: docu.

**HOLLYWOOD HOT TUBS** 1984 Ref: sequence with horror-movie actor Edgar Blood.

The **HOLY FLAME OF THE MARTIAL WORLD** (H.K.?) Ref: vc box.

El **HOMICIDA** (Mex.) Ref: TVG: psychopathic killer.

**HONG KONG BUTCHER** (H.K.) Ref: NST! 4:26: mainly a "police procedural."

**HORROR HOLIDAY** (H.K.?) Ref: vc box.

**HOT HEELS** 1928 Ref: Lee(AFI): mechanical horse.

**HOT LINE** 1991 Ref: Adam '92: "electronics wizard" taps "video line" into phone line.

**HOT STEEL** Ref: V 6/26/40: "new formula for high test steel."

**HOT STUFF** 1956 short Ref: TV: "super rocket fuel" formula; powerful acid.

A **HOUSE IN THE HILLS** Ref: V 6/28/93: "psycho."

The **HOUSE OF LURKING DEATH** (B) 1983 51m. Ref: vc box: TV; "Agatha Christie's Partners in Crime" series.

**HOW TO STEAL THE WORLD** 1968 Ref: Lee: obedience gas.

**HOW TO SUCCEED WITH GIRLS** 1964 Ref: AFI: mad doc who fails to create a monster.

**HSUEH-HAI HSUN-CHU** (H.K.) 1967? Ref: Eberhard: evil magicians.

**HUA JIE** (H.K.) 1981 Ref: Hardy/HM:367: "psycho-killer."

**HUMAN GORILLA** Ref: TVG: comedy.

**HUNK** Ref: V 3/11/87: deal with the devil; "ghoulish caveman" scene.

**HUNTER'S BLOOD** Ref: V 5/27/87. Phantom: climactic "gore fx." Ecran F 73:70-1.

**HUNTERS OF THE GOLDEN COBRA** (I) Ref: V 3/28/84: "supernatural totem." vc box: magician.

The **HUNTING SEASON** Ref: HR 10/25/83:S-74: escaped lunatic.

**HUWAG MON BUHAYIN ANG BANGKAY** (Fili) Ref: vc box: devil raises woman's son from dead.

**HYDE AND SNEAK** 1962 anim Ref: LC.

**I KNOW WHERE I'M GOING** (B) Ref: screen: cursed Scottish castle.

**I WANT MY MUMMY** 1966 anim Ref: Maltin/OMAM.

**IDEON 2** (J) anim 99m Ref: Japan Video. See also *Densetsu Kyoshin Ideon* (III).

**IF LOOKS COULD KILL** Ref: V 12/30/87: suspenser.

**L'ILE DES PASSIONS** (F-Sp) 1982 Ref: MFB'83:160: sect, murder, trance.

**L'ILE FLOTTANTE** (I-Sp?) Ref: V 12/21/92: imagined island.

**ILLEGAL ENTRY** Ref: SFChron Dtbk 8/8/93: "secret formula" for solving world hunger.

De **ILLUSIONIST** (Dutch) Ref: V 10/12/83: "creepy at times."

**ILSA, THE TIGRESS OF SIBERIA** 1976 Ref: McCarty II: tortures.

**ILSA, THE WICKED WARDEN** (F) 1977 (aka *Wanda, the Wicked Warden*) Ref: McCarty II.

**IMAGINARY WAR CHRONICLES** (J) 1989 anim Ref: Animag 6:5: OAVs re ESPers.

**IMMER & EWIG** (Swiss) Ref: V 9/91: updated "Orpheus."

*The **IMMORAL MR. TEAS** 1959 Ref: TV: vt: not sf.

The **IMPERSONATOR** (B) 1961 Ref: Maltin/TVM: "chiller." AFI: female imp. is killer.

El **IMPOSTER** 1931 Ref: Limbacher '79: Span.-lang. version of *Scotland Yard* (M).

**IN-BETWEEN** 1991 Ref: TVG: limbo lives.

**IN NECUEPALIZTLI IN AZTLAN — RETORNO A AZTLAN** (Mex.) Ref: V 1/7/91: "full of magic."

**IN THE DEEP WOODS** Ref: V 10/26/92:71: serial killer. TVG.

**IN THE 25TH CENTURY** Ref: U.S. Video cat. no Hound.

**INFILTRATOR** Ref: V 9/29/87:58: 60m. sf-horror pilot.

**INHUMANITIES** 1989 Ref: vc box: docu-gore.

**INKI** (W.G.) 1973 Ref: Hardy/HM: homicidal schizophrenic.

**INNER SANCTUM** Ref: V 10/14/91: "gothic thriller."

The **INSIDE MAN** (Swed.-B) Ref: V 5/23/84: sub-detecting laser invention.

**INSIDE OUT 1 & 2** Ref: V 10/11/93:M-61(ad): TV series. Martin. PT 12:50. 13:6.

**INSPECTOR CLOUSEAU** (B) 1968 Ref: AFI: "laser beam lighter."

**INTO THE DARKNESS** (B) 1986 Ref: Stanley: slasher movie? with D. Pleasence.

**INVASIONE** (I) 1978 Ref: Hardy/HM: aliens; no theatrical release.

The **INVISIBLE BATMAN** (I) 1985? Ref: Stanley: superhero.

The **INVISIBLE DOG** (B) 1909 Ref: BFC: i.d.

**INVISIBLE TERRORISTS** Ref: Captain Video cat.: m. arts.

**ISABELLA DUCHESSA DEI DIAVOLI** (I-Monaco) 1969 Ref: Hardy/HM: tortures.

**ISHANOU** (India) Ref: V 3/11/91: woman possessed by nice spirit.

The **ISLAND** (*Life and Death*) (H.K.) Ref: V 10/30/85: shock sequences.

**ISLAND OF LOST GIRLS** (I-W.G.) 1968 (*Kommisar X — Drei Goldene Schlangen*) Ref: PT 16:17: "opium-induced zombie state."

**ISLAND OF THE EVIL SPIRIT** (J) 1981 Ref: Larson.

**IT CAME FROM WITHIN** Ref: Captain Video cat.

**IT CAN'T HAPPEN HERE** c1935? Ref: SFExam 1/24/86:A-14: unreleased *Amerika*-type.

**IT CAN'T LAST FOREVER** 1937 Ref: V 7/7/37: phony fakir. TVFFSB: radio mystic. LC.

**IT HAPPENED IN SOHO** (B) 1948 Ref: BFC: the Soho Strangler.

**IT STARTED WITH A KISS** 1959 Ref: TV: glass-domed, tail finned "car of the future."

**IT'S HAPPENING TOMORROW** (I) 1988 Ref: PFA notes 3/19/89: Verne-ish. (*Domani Accadra*)

**JACKIE MCLEAN ON MARS** Ref: SFChron 8/23/85: docu.

**JADE DAGGER NINJA** Ref: vc box: fantasy.

**JAGUAR** Ref: V 4/25/56. TV: "jaguar men," Amazons in j. skins, terrorize countryside; played for action-suspense-mystery, not horror.

**JAKARTA** 1988 Ref: vc box: "ghost...terrifying mystery." V 1/3/90.

**JAKE SPEED** Ref: V 5/21/86. Morse.

**JAMES TONT, OPERAZIONE U.N.O.** (I) 1965 Ref: Lee: laser-beam spectacles.

**JEALOUSY** 1984 Ref: TVG: "surreal."

**JETTATOR** (U.S.-F) 1983? Ref: Ecran F 33:71: Celtic mythology.

**JIMMY, THE BOY WONDER** 1966 Ref: SWV supp: evil magician ... time stopped. PT 11:49.

**JIT** (Zimbabwe) Ref: SFChron 5/21/93: cranky ghost.

**JO JO'S BIZARRE ADVENTURES** (J) anim Ref: Animerica 6:10: OAV; made? vampire?

**JOAN LUI** (I) Ref: V 1/15/86: "murderous future world."

**JOE SMITH, AMERICAN** 1942 Ref: TVG: "secret bombsight."

**JOEY'S LIAR METER** (B) 1916 Ref: BFC: tests veracity.

**JOHNNY DANGEROUSLY** 1984 Ref: TV: quasi-"robot" in box.

**JOHNNY FIRECLOUD** 1974 Ref: PT 10:10-11: "gory effects."

**JOHNNY SUEDE** 1991 Ref: PT 16:12: "surreal hallucinations & dream sequences."

Le **JOUEUR D'ECHECS** (F-Mex.) 1981 Ref: Ecran F 34:61: Poe & the mechanical chess player.

Le **JOURNAL D'UN FOU** (F) Ref: V 11/4/87: from Gogol's "Diary of a Madman."

**JOY FOR LIVING DEAD** (H.K.?) 1988 Ref: vc box: apparently non-horror.

**JOY HOUSE** (F) 1964 Ref: TVG: "chills." NYT 2/18/65: attic hider in "moldy mansion."

The **JUDAS PROJECT** Ref: V 3/22/93: modern-day Christ story.

**JULIA AND JULIA** Ref: SFExam 2/5/88: alternate futures.

**JUST BEFORE DAWN** 1946 Ref: TV: woman locked at night in mortuary.

**JUST FOR FUN** (B) 1963 Ref: Weldon: "near future." BFC: Teenage Party triumphant.

**JUST FOR THE HELL OF IT** 1968 Ref: Weldon: more H.G. Lewis violence.

**JUST THE FEEBLES** Ref: Cinef 7/90: grossness.

**JUST WHEN YOU THOUGHT IT WAS SAFE** Ref: S.F. Int'l. Video Fest 9/86: "horror film."

El JUSTICIERO (Mex.-J.?) anim 28m. Ref: TV: made-for-TV or video?/space invasion.
JUSTINIEN TROUVE, OU LE BATARD DE DIEU (F) Ref: V 9/27/93: "gore."

KABRASTAN Ref: vc box: monsters?
KAFKA Ref: SFExam 1/17/92: "full of fiendish scientists ... deformed homicidal maniacs."
KALIFORNIA Ref: 9/6/93: "chilling surrealistic sensibility."
KAMPANERANG KUBA (Fili) Ref: vc box: Quasimodo-type.
KARAMOJA 1985 Ref: vc box: docu-gore.
KARATE (India-Hindustani) 1983 Ref: Dharap: solar-energy discovery.
KARLSVOGNEN (Dan.-Swed.) Ref: V 2/17/92: "weird events" haunt family in "old house."
KARNABAL (Sp) Ref: V 9/4/85: cave man sequence?
KEEPING TRACK (Can.) Ref: V 6/24/87: plans for cyborg.
KICKS 1985 Ref: vc box: "Most Dangerous Game" stuff. Scheuer. Hound.
KILL CRAZY Ref: V 11/5/90:79(hv): "Most Dangerous Game" stuff.
KILLER DEAD American Zenith 1986 D: B. Faulkner. Ref: Ecran F 63:70: completed; aliens, zombies. no Martin. no Hound. with P. Dain, N. Ginate, J.E. Delaney.
KILLER IMAGE 1991 Ref: PT 13:12: "psycho killer," "nightmares."
KILLER OF SNAKE (H.K.?) Ref: vc box: magic.
KILLER'S NOCTURNE (H.K.) Ref: V 6/3/87: gore.
KILLING DEVICE Ref: V 2/21/90:97(ad): would create assassins; released?
KILLING GAME (B) 1975 Ref: TVG: game in which loser pays with life.
KILLING IN THE NUDE (H.K.?) Ref: vc box: slasher?
KING ARTHUR (J) 1980 anim Ref: Ecran F 29:67.
KING OF THE TEXAS RANGERS serial 1941 Ref: TGSP2: "new aviation gasoline."
The KISS OF HER FLESH 1968 Ref: AFI: torture; sequel to The Touch of Her Flesh.
KISS OF THE SPIDER WOMAN (Braz.-U.S.) 1985 Ref: TV: s.w. visualized in web.
The KISSING PLACE Ref: V 4/11/90:88: "spooky moments."
KORAGASHI RYOTA — GEKITOTSU! MONSTER BUS (J) Ref: V '88.
KUNG FU TERMINATOR (H.K.?) Ref: Hound. vc box: "jet powered."
KUNG HEI FAT CHOY (H.K.) Ref: V 4/3/85: space center's "latest weapons."
KURENAI NO BUTA (J) 1992 anim feature Ref: TV: vt: fire-breathing-dragon bit on screen.
KURT OG VALDE (Dan.) Ref: V 7/27/83: "ersatz gasoline" tested.

The LADIES CLUB Ref: V 4/1/86: revenge for rape.
The LADIES' MAN 1961 Ref: Jones: dream sequence re vampire lady.
LADY BEWARE Ref: V 9/23/87: suspenser.
LAGER SS5 — L'INFERNO DELLE DONNE (I) 1976 Ref: Hardy/HM: "sadico-nazista."
The LAME DUCK (B) 1931 Ref: BFC: "formula for new explosive."

LANTERN HILL Ref: 1/21/91: "the supernatural." TV: non-spooky.
LAPUTA (W.G.) Ref: V 5/14/86: reading from Gulliver's Travels. See also Laputa (M).
LAS VEGAS BLOODBATH 1989 Ref: PT 8:45: gore; amateur? 9:7.
LASER MISSION (W.G.) Ref: V 11/22/89: laser secrets.
LAST DANCE Ref: TVG: killer of exotic dancers. 1992
The LAST ELECTRIC KNIGHT Ref: TVG 2/16/86: "boy with unusual powers."
The LAST HUNTER (I) 1980('84-U.S.) Ref: V 2/22/84: "gore fx." (Hunter of the Apocalypse)
The LAST ISLAND (Dutch) Ref: V 1/14/91: apocalyptic?
The LAST KIDS ON EARTH 1983 Ref: TVG: "impending doom." no VSB.
The LAST OF PHILIP BANTER (Sp-Swiss) Ref: V 6/4/86: suspense. vc box.
LAST ORGY OF THE THIRD REICH (I?) Ref: PT 8:65(ad): cannibalism. Hound.
LAST VIDEO AND TESTAMENT (B) 1985 Ref: TVG.
The LEAVENWORTH CASE Ref: V 1/22/36. Pierre LePage. TV: one spooky scene with shadow.
LEGEND OF DARKNESS (J) 1990 anim Ref: animag 10:4: fantasy.
The LEGEND OF LYLAH CLARE 1968 Ref: TV: intermittent spirit possession.
The LEGEND OF WOLF MOUNTAIN Ref: V: wolf-into-warrior dream sequence.
LEINA — LEGEND OF THE WOLF SWORD (J) 1988 anim Ref: Animag 3:6. 5:5: from the TV show "Machine - Robo."
LEKCJA MARTWEGO JEZYKA (Polish) 1980 Ref: V 6/11/80: "Most Dangerous Game" overtones.
LEONORA (Austral.) Ref: V 12/24/86: witchcraft.
LES PATTERSON SAVES THE WORLD (Austral.) Ref: V 4/15/87: "horrendous" sexual disease cues "Evil Dead-type special effects."
LET GEORGE DO IT (B) 1940 Ref: TGSP2: "torpedo tube." "Ealing Studios."
LET'S ASK NOSTRADAMUS Ref: TV: "Prophecies of Nostradamus" number 2. See also Nostradamus (M).
La LIBERTE D'UNE STATUE (Can.) Ref: V 9/24/90: miracles re spaceship, etc.
The LICHEN Ref: V 11/4/91:15: shooting. SP,D: T. Armstrong.
LIEBE UND TOD (W.G.) Ref: V 8/28/85: vaguely futuristic.
LIES OF THE TWINS Ref: SJose MNews 8/21/91: "chilling."
LIGHTHOUSE Ref: V 9/6/89:47(ad): spirits of murdered couple.
LIMIT UP Ref: V 3/21/90:35(hv) deal with the devil.
The LITTLE GHOST (G?) Ref: V 10/12/92:99: tiny ghost; feature & miniseries.
LITTLE NEMO 1910 Ref: Crafton/BM: bit with dragon.
The LITTLE TROLL PRINCE 1987 Ref: TVG: nice troll & "his nasty brothers."
LIVIN' LARGE Ref: SFChron 9/20/91: Dorian Gray overtones.
The LIVING END Ref: SFChron 8/28/92: "serial murderer...homophobe murders."
LIVSFARLIG FILM (Swed.) Ref: V 3/30/88: "gore & guffaws."
LO QUE VENDRA (Arg.) Ref: V 5/25/88: sf "feel."
LONDON BLACKOUT MURDERS Ref: TV: a "blackout Jack the Ripper." V 12/23/42.

**LONG LIVE THE LADY!** (I) Ref: SFChron 3/11/88: main course a "huge sea monster."

**The LONG NIGHT** Ref: V 5/28/47: woman under magician's (V. Price) hypnotic spell.

**The LOOKALIKE** Ref: V 12/24/90:42: doppelganger.

**LOOSE CANNONS** Ref: V 2/14/90: "gruesome murders."

**The LORD'S BALL** (Russ) Ref: PFA notes 11/1/92: "dream, madness, & murder."

**LOST IN THE BARRENS II** Ref: TVG. See *Curse of the Viking Grave* (P).

**The LOST ONE** (W.G.) 1951 Ref: screen: compulsive killer.

**LOST WEEKEND** 1945 Ref: TV: delirium sequences.

**LOVE AT SECOND SIGHT** (B) 1934 Ref: BFC: "inventor of everlasting match." See also *Match King, The* (P).

**LOVE CAN BE MURDER** Ref: V 12/7/92:44: ghost.

**The LOVE TEST** (B) Ref: V 12/3/90: "formula for fireproofing celluloid."

**LUNAR LUST** 1990 Ref: Adam '91: not sf.

**The LUNATIC FROG WOMAN** (H.K.?) Ref: vt: needle-in-hand torture.

**LUPIN III - MYSTERY OF THE HEMINGWAY PAPER** (J) anim Ref: Japan Video.

**LYDIA BAILEY** Ref: V 5/28/52. TV: voodoo dance to war god.

**MACSKAFOGO** (Hug.-Can.-W.G.) anim Ref: V 4/1/87: "gang of vampire bats."

**MACHINE GOD CORPS 4 & 5** (J) '93 anim 30m. each Ref: Animerica 5:15. 6:13.

**MACHINE ROBO - REVENGE OF CRONOS** (J) anim 30m. Ref: Japan Video: robots; TV? See also *Lightning Trap* (M).

**The MAD DEATH** (B) 1983 Ref: PT 13:6: rabid dogs; "TV miniseries."

**MAD LOVE** 1989 Ref: vc box: haunted house.

**The MAD MONK** R: V 9/13/93:14: in Taipei.

**The MADDAMS FAMILY** Ref: Adam '93: Thing & co.

**The MAGIC AMETHYST** (H.K.) 1991? Ref: vt: statuette glows, shimmers.

**The MAGIC CRANE** (H.K.) Ref: U.C. Theatre notes 12/16/93: "evil demons."

**MAGIC SWORD** Ref: V 11/8/93:91: in Taipei.

**MAJO NO TAKYUBIN** (J) anim Ref: V 9/13/89:48. 10/4/89:45: witch; feature.

**El MAL OFICIO III** (Mex.) Ref: vt: no apparent relation to *El Maleficio II* (M).

**MALIZIA 2MILA** (I) Ref: V 6/1/92: year 2000.

**MAMA'S HOME** 1989 Ref: Fango 94:12: ?

**MAN ON THE PROWL** Ref: V 12/4/57: "homicidal psycho."

**The MAN WITHOUT A FACE** Ref: V 8/30/93: disfigured man.

**MANDRAKE VS. "KILLING"** (Turk.) 1967 Ref: World F'67: magician.

**MANEATERS** 1984 Ref: Roxie Cinema notes 6/22/84: man-eating mirror.

**MANHUNT: SEARCH FOR THE NIGHT STALKER** Ref: V 11/15/89:44: "slasher" tricks.

**MANIMAL** Ref: V 10/5/83:52: Chase's origins unexplained? TVG: 90m. "premiere."

**MANNEQUIN ON THE MOVE** Ref: V 5/27/91: spell.

**MANY TANKS MR. ATKINS** (B) 1938 Ref: BFC: tank-super-charger invention.

**El MARIACHI** (Sp-Mex?) Ref: SFChron 2/26/93: futuristic look.

**The MARK OF LILITH** (B) 1986 Ref: Shock Xpress Smr'87:18: vampire. Jones: experimental.

**MARKED FOR DEATH** Ref: V 10/22/90: voodoo.

**MARLEY'S REVENGE: THE MONSTER MOVIE** 1989 Ref: PT 13:49: amateur?; zombies.

**MASALA** (Can.) Ref: V 3/22/93: magic video. SFChron 3/12/93.

**La MASCHERA DELLO SCHELETRO** (I) Ref: Hardy/HM: "gruesome masked skeleton." 1919

**MASK OF MURDER** (B) 1985 Ref: Ecran F 58:70,71: "brutal & bloody." no Martin.

**MASSACRE IN DINOSAUR VALLEY** 1985 Ref: vc box: curse?; Amazons.

**MASTERBLASTER** Ref: V 7/8/87: killer at large during survival tournament. Morse.

**MASTERMIND** 1969 Ref: Bill Warren: robot. Martin.

**The MATCH KING** 1932 Ref: TV: "everlasting match" which lights again & again. See also *Love at Second Sight* (P).

**MAXIE** Ref: SFExam: ghost in house.

**MCCLOUD: MCCLOUD MEETS DRACULA** 1977 Ref: Jones: NBC Mystery Movie re "vampire."

**MEDICINE MAN** Ref: SFExam 2/7/92: cancer cure.

**MEET ME IN ST. LOUIS** 1944 Ref: TV: Lewtonesque Halloween sequence.

**MEET THE FEEBLES** (N.Z.) Ref: V 11/1/89:27: "perverted puppet pic."

**MEGFELELO EMBER KEHYES FELADATRA** (Hung.) Ref: V 3/6/85: sf: "new order."

**MELOS** (J) anim 106m. Ref: vt: ancient Greece.

**MEMORIES OF MURDER** 1990 Ref: TV: suspense. Mo.

**MERCY PLANE** Ref: TVG. V 10/30/40: ship with "secret contrivances." TGSP2: "new craft which can rise straight off the ground."

**METICHE Y ENCAJOSO** (Mex.) Ref: vc box: super car?

**MIAMI BLUES** Ref: V 4/25/90: "graphic violence."

**MIAMI SUPERCOPS** (U.S.-I?) Ref: Cine Para Leer '85. V 10/15/90:78(rated).

**MIDNIGHT COP** (G) Ref: TV: cop movie with bizarre elements. 1988

**MIDNIGHT INTRUDERS** 1987 Ref: vt: vc box falsely suggests horror.

**A MIDSUMMER NIGHT'S SEX COMEDY** 1982 Ref: TV: inventor's "spirit box" detects ectoplasm.

**Los MIEDOS** (Arg.) 1980 Ref: V 9/10/80: plague. Cf. *Ano de la Peste* (M).

**MIELOTT BEFEJEZI ROPTET A DENEVER** (Hung.) Ref: V 2/22/89: "close to a horror movie."

**MIGHTY ORBOTS** Ref: TVG 7/19/86: 2 "all-new animated outer-space adventures." TV?

**MIRACLE IN HARLEM** 1948 Ref: vc box: killer. Lee(e).

**MIRAGE** (H.K.) Ref: V 5/27/87: bandit queen who bites necks, drinks horse's blood.

**MISSION IN OUTER SPACE, "SRUNGLE"** (J) 1982 Ref: Larson.

**MR. LOVE** 1986 Ref: Martin. vc box: "spooky spider lady."

**MR. PETERS' PETS** 1962 Ref: AFI: potion which allows man to transform into any animal.

**The MODEL COUPLE** Ref: PFA notes 7/8/89: "sci-fi farce." (*Le Couple Temoin*)

**MODESTY BLAISE** (B) 1966 Ref: TV: ray-shooting rocket?

**MONEY MAKER** (H.K.) Ref: vc box: ghost, exorcist.

**MONIQUE** 1983 Ref: Hound: "terrifying secret." vc box: hallucinations, nightmares.

**La MONJA ENSANGRIENTADA** (Mex.) Ref: vc box.

**MONKEY GOES WEST** (H.K.?) Ref: vc box.

**The MONKEY KING CONQUERS THE DEMON** (Chi) Ref: V 10/25/89:7.

**The MONSTERS ARE COMING** (I) Ref: V 5/12/82:196: "famous monsters." 11/17/82:44: in prep. 5/4/83:298: June start?; now *Gala Evening with Mother.*

**MONSTROSITY** Ref: V 6/24/91:64: Andy Milligan film.

**MONTREAL VU PAR ...** (Can.) Ref: V 11/18/91: sf overtones.

**The MOON WARRIORS** (H.K.) Ref: Y.K. Ho: not sf. vc box. V 1/4/93:55: in H.K.

**La MORTE ACCAREZZA A MEZZANOTTE** (I-Sp) Ref: Bianco Index '72. ETC/Giallos: "Ercoli doesn't shy from the red stuff."

**MOSAFERAN** (Iranian) Ref: V 3/23/92: ghost sequence with a "chill."

**La MUJER DEL DIABLO** (Sp) Ref: Bowker: satanism.

**La MUNECA PERVERSA** (Mex.?) Ref: TVG: "horrible crimes"; "crazy daughter." "Horror."

**MUNECA REINA** (Mex.) 1971 Ref: Hardy/HM: ghostly fantasy figures.

**Las MUNECAS DEL KING KONG** (Mex.) Ref: vt: K.K. night club.

**MURDER AT SCOTLAND YARD** (B) 1952 Ref: BFC: "explosive radio sets." with Tod Slaughter.

**MURDER AT THE GRANGE** (B) 1952 Ref: BFC: butler strangles woman. with T. Slaughter.

**MURDER IN THE CLOUDS** Ref: V 1/1/35: "secret high explosive formula."

**MURDER ON A BRIDLE PATH** Ref: TV: creepy old house. V 4/15/36: Karloffian butler.

**MURDER ON A LINE ONE** (B-Swed.) Ref: V 12/31/90: murder & video; "whodunit." (*Helpline*)

**MY BEAUTIFUL LAUNDRETTE** (B) 1985 Ref: screen: Pakistani voodoo disfigures woman.

**MY NEIGHBORHOOD** 1984 35m. Ref: Hound: slasher.

**MYSTERE** (I) 1984 Ref: Ecran F 38:89: "*giallo...scenes of terror.*"

**Le MYSTERE IMBERGER** (F) 1935 Ref: Chirat: missing man's nephew impersonates him with life-like mask. (*Le Spectre de M. Imberger* - orig t)

**The MYSTERIOUS DEATH OF NINA CHEREAU** (B?) 1988 Ref: Jones: Bathory variation.

**MYSTERIOUS ISLAND OF BEAUTIFUL WOMEN** 1979 Ref: Oak Trib: "killer-programmed" women.

**The MYSTERIOUS MECHANICAL TOY** (B) 1903 Ref: BFC: "mechanical man"?

**MYSTERY AT CASTLE HOUSE** (Austral.) 1982 Ref: TV: mysterious old house.

**The MYSTERY OF EDWIN DROOD** (B) Ref: V 5/10/93: bit of Grand Guignol.

**MYSTERY RANCH** 1932 Ref: screen: eerily photographed & edited strangulation scene.

**MYSTIC WARRIOR** Ref: SFExam 5/18/84: visions of "giant spiders."

**NAKED ZOO** 1969 Ref: PT 2:34.10:40-1,42. aka *The Hallucinators. The Grove.*

**The NAME OF THE ROSE** 1986 Ref: TV: mystery with supernatural overtones, brutality.

**NAVY SPY** Ref: V 3/24/37: "secret formula."

**NE LE CRIEZ PAS SUR LES TOITS** (F) 1942 Ref: Hardy/SF: formulae for turning seawater into gas and for making "flowers imperishable."

**NEBESA OBETOVANNYE** (Georgian) Ref: V 4/20/92:36: sf?; at Imagfic. D: E. Riazanov.

**NELISITA** (Angolan) Ref: V 3/20/85: "evil spirits."

**NEVER SAY DIE** (B) 1950 Ref: BFC: "old castle," gorilla (Thomas Gallagher).

**NEW CENTURY GPX CYBER FORMULA 11, VOL. 4** (J) anim Ref: Animerica 5:14.6:12.

**The NEW KIDS** Ref: V 3/20/85: "tame" thriller.

**NEZHA DEFEATS THE DRAGON** (Chi) 1980 anim Ref: V 5/28/80: "evil Dragon King."

**NICK DANGER: THE CASE OF THE MISSING YOLK** Ref: vc trailer: futuristic?; "original video."

**A NIGHT BEFORE CHRISTMAS** (Russ.) 1961 ('63-U.S.) Ref: AFI: devil, witch, sorcerer. Gogol

**NIGHT GAME** Ref: V 9/20/89: serial killer. Martin.

**NIGHT KILLING** Ref: V 3/7/84:301(ad): in prod.; werewolf. w/N.Kwan, E. Braeden.

**The NIGHT NURSE** (Austral.) Ref: V 4/18/79:120: "horrible destiny." TVG: "sinister" house.

**NIGHT OF FEAR** (Austral.) 1973 Ref: Guinness:144: "horror." Mad hermit. Cf. *Lady Stay Dead* (III).

**NIGHT OF THE BLOODY TRANSPLANT** 1986? Ref: Martin: "soap opera."

**NIGHT OF THE HEADHUNTER** 1985 Ref: Adam: voodoo mask. vc box.

**NIGHT OF THE REAL DEAD PEOPLE** R&B 1983? Ref: Ecran F 26:75: completed?

**NIGHT VISIONS** Ref: V 12/10/90:88: "spooky" scenes. D: Wes Craven.

**NIGHTMARE AT BITTER CREEK** Ref: V 6/15/88:54: TV-movie re "four mad killers"; "scary."

**NIGHTMARE IN COLUMBIA COUNTY** Ref: V 12/16/91:61: "fact-based fright film."

**NINJA IN THE CLAWS OF THE CIA** Ref: vc box: hypnosis.

**El NINO DE LA LUNA** (Sp) Ref: V 5/17/89:33: parapsychology.

**NO DAIREIKAI II** (J) Ref: V 3/28/90: "bad spirit world."

**NO LIFE KING** (J) Ref: V 9/23/91: cursed video game ..."eerie ...score."

**NORTHANGER ABBEY** (U.S.-B) 1986 Ref: TV: Gothic touches, bloody fantasies.

**The NORTHERNERS** (Dutch) Ref: V 5/10/93:C-118: "futuristic drama."

**The NUCLEAR CONSPIRACY** (W.G.) Ref: Ecran F 72:70: nuclear intrigue. Stanley.

**NUMBERED DAYS** Ref: McCarty II: "lame gore ... necrophilia." (*Cycle Psycho. Savage Abduction* - alt ts) vc box. Hound.

**NUTCRACKER** 1986 Ref: TV: scene with giant, many-headed mouse creature.

**The NUTCRACKER** (aka *George Balanchine's The Nutcracker*) Ref: V 11/22/93.

**OH NO DOCTOR!** (B) 1934 Ref: BFC: "comedy. Doctor tries to frighten ward's fiancee to death." no Lee.

**OKASARETU BYUAKUI** (J) 1967 Ref: Hardy/HM: psycho slaughters nurses.

**OLD OKLAHOMA PLAINS** Ref: V 8/20/52. TV: 1926 — military testing tiny tank out West.

**OMENG SATANASIA** Ref: vc box.

**ONCE UPON A FOREST** Ref: SFChron 6/18/93: anim; "bulldozers...as monstrous carnivores."

**ONCE UPON A TIME IN CHINA II** (H.K.) Ref: SFExam 4/18/93: the supernatural.

**ONE CRAZY SUMMER** 1986 Ref: TV: "Godzilla" stomps model condo ... drive-in horror movie.

**OPERATION X-70** (Belg.) 1972 anim short Ref: IFG'73:468,478: new gas produces angels.

**The ORBITRONS** 1990 Ref: PT 8:9: amateur; aliens, zombies.

**ORFEO** (F-I) Ref: V 9/11/85: "the dark recesses of the underworld."

**ORFEUS ES EURYDIKE** (Hung.) Ref: V 9/11/85: the underworld, the Furies, etc.

**ORLANDO** (B-Russ.-F-Dutch) Ref: V 9/14/92: 400-year-old character.

**Les OREILLES ENTRE LES DENTS** (F) Ref: V 8/5/87: "gruesome murders."

**OSOBISTY PAMIETNIK GRZESZNIKA PRZEZ NIEGO SAMEGO SPISANY** (Pol.) Ref: V 5/21/85: "evil alter-ego."

**The OTHER SIDE OF LIANNA** 1984 Ref: Adam '88: *Devil and Daniel Webster* in suburbia.

**OUT ON A LIMB** Ref: V 1/28/87:50: miniseries; ESP, aliens. TV: psychic trip to moon.

**OUTLAWS** Ref: V 12/31/86:42: time-jumping. Stanley. TVG: 2-hour "preview."

**OVER-EXPOSED** 1969 Ref: AFI: voodoo.

**OVERKILL** Ref: V 7/15/87: "extraneous gore."

**OVERKILL** Ref: SFChron 11/17/92: "serial murderess."

**PAINT IT BACK** Ref: V 1/24/90: "psycho killer and his creepy ways ... nasty murders."

**The PAINT JOB** Ref: SFChron Dtbk 12/19/93: "serial killer."

**PANAMA HATTIE** 1943 Ref: TV: "haunted" house; "Did you see that picture *The Invisible Man*?"

**PARAD PLANET** (Russ.) 1985 Ref: Ecran F 58:70: 6 men "outside time & space."

**PARADISE VIEW** (J) Ref: V 8/21/85: mad "rainbow pigs" attack humans. PFA notes 11/4/86: mythology & "mutated animals."

**PARDON MY SARONG** 1942 Ref: TV: "haunted" temple.

**PARKING** (F) Ref: V 7/3/85: *Orphee* "underworld" a parking lot of the dead.

**PASAPORTE A LA MUERTE** (Mex.) Ref: TVG: "unos cientificos diabolicos."

**PAST MIDNIGHT** 1992 Ref: Fango 123:12: killer.

**PERAUSTRINIA 2004** (Sp) anim feature Ref: V 9/24/90:80. D: A. Garcia.

**The PERFECT BRIDE** 1991 Ref: Martin: woman murders fiancees. PT 13:8: USA-TV.

**PERIL FOR THE GUY** (B) 1956 Ref: BFC: "oil detector."

**PERRY MASON: THE CASE OF THE SHOOTING STAR** 1986 Ref: TV: vampire movie shooting.

**PESSI JA ILLUSIA** (Finnish) Ref: V 4/11/84: "creepy" Spiderman & White Death; fairy tale.

**PETER-NO-TAIL IN AMERICA** (Swed.) Ref: V 10/16/85:308, 317(ad): giant rats; anim.

**PETRIFIED BEAST FROM THE FROZEN ZONE** 1990 Ref: PT 7:49: "guy in a bear mask."

**PETRIFIED GARDEN** (F-G) Ref: V 11/1/93: golem's stone hand.

**PHANTOM** (G) 1922 Ref: screen: hero's hallucinations visualized.

**PHANTOM KILLER** (H.K.) Ref: NST! 4:33: "standard police thriller."

**PHANTOM OF THE CINEMA** Ref: V 6/22/92:37: at Rome Fantafestival

**The PHANTOM OF THE OPERA: THE MINI-SERIES** 1990 Ref: TV: dawdling buildup to happily corny climactic sequence. Mask: Timian Alsaker. With Burt Lancaster.

**The PHANTOM TOLLBOOTH** anim & live 1969 Ref: screen. Jim Shapiro: monsters.

**PHOENIX: WOLF NINJA** (H.K.) Ref: NST! 4:33: witches, spells. (aka *Matching Escort*)

**PIECES OF DARKNESS** 1989 Ref: vc box: 3 tales; horror?; TV?

**PIRATES OF THE SKIES** Ref: V 4/12/39: "mechanical disc recording." Harrison's 1/21/39.

**PLAYING BEATIE BOW** (Austral.) Ref: V 5/14/86: magic time travel.

**PLEASE DON'T TOUCH ME** 1959 Ref: PT 11:9: "Electro-Cyclometer" measures pain/pleasure.

**PLUS ONE, MINUS ONE** (I) Ref: SFChron Dtbk 9/20/87:33: Superman?

**POISON IVY** 1992 Ref: TV: hallucinations re friend-from-hell.

**POLICE STORY: MONSTER MANOR** 1988 Ref: TV: no monsters.

**POOR GIRL, A GHOST STORY** (B) 1974 52m. Ref: Hound. vc box: TV.

**PORTION D'ETERNITE** (Can.) Ref: V 9/13/89: mad doc dabbling in cloning.

**POWER AND ENERGY** Disney 195-? anim Ref: TV: dinosaurs, mammoth. TV?

**POWERBONE** 198-? Ref: vc box: super-villain out to de-sex Earth.

**PRAY FOR DEATH** 1985 Ref: Briggs/Back: "8 on the Vomit Meter." Scheuer: brutal.

**PRAYING MANTIS** (B) 1983 Ref: vc box. Hound: lethal nurse.

**PRAYING MANTIS** 1993 Ref: TVG: serial-killer wife.

**PRETTYKILL** (Can.) Ref: V 4/1/87: schizophrenic killer of hookers.

**PRINCESS OF DARKNESS** 1988 Ref: vc box.

**The PRISONER OF CARLSTEN'S FORT** (Swed.) Ref: PFA notes: "explosives formula." 1916

**PRISONER OF JAPAN** Ref: V 11/25/42: "all-powerful technical gadgets." Harrison's: no.

**PRIVATE MOMENTS** Ref: vc box: woman plays "vampire."

**PROBE** Ref: V 3/23/88:110: sf elements?

**PROSPERO'S BOOKS** (B-F-Dutch) 1991 Ref: Jim Shapiro. TV: gross & weird bits.

**PROJECT Z** 1987 Ref: Sacto Bee: "top-secret jet truck."

**PSYCHO BABES** 1987 Ref: vc box: "programmed for pleasure."

**PSYCHO RAGE** Ref: 10/19/88:332(ad).

**PSYCHOPATHIA SEXUALIS** 1966 Ref: SWV cat.: killer with rose fetish.

**PSYCHOPHOBIA** 1982 Ref: TVG: "thriller."

**PUEBLO MALDITO** (Mex.) Ref: vc box: superstition.

**La PULQUERIA II & IV** (Mex.) Ref: TVG: comedies re the devil, witches, etc.

**PUSS IN BOOTS** Ref: V 6/28/89: ogre.

The **QUAKE** 1992 Ref: PT 16:14: "scary, obsessed, voyeur psycho killer."

A **QUESTION OF SILENCE** (Dutch) Ref: SFChron 10/21/83: "horror film."

**QUIERO MORIR EN CARNAVAL** (Mex.) Ref: vc box: "voodoo madness."

**QUIET KILLER** 1992 Ref: TVG: plague outbreak in NYC.

**RG VEDA II** (J) 1992 anim 40m. Ref: TV: sword & sorcery.

**R20: GALACTIC AIRPORT** (J) 1988? anim Ref: Animag 3:21-23: androids; made?

**RAAKH** (India) Ref: V 10/11/89: "near future."

**RADIO FLYER** Ref: SFChron 2/21/92: fantasy.

**RADIUS** (J) 1987 anim 48m. Ref: Japan Video: sf?

**RAGE IN HEAVEN** 1941 Ref: TV: paranoiac affected by full moon.

**RAGING TIGER VS. MONKEY KING** (H.K.?) Ref: poster.

**RAIDERS OF THE RIVER** (B) serial Ref: BFC: "electronic brain."

**RANDY RIDES ALONE** 1934 Ref: TV. Turner/Price: "grotesque hunchback."

**RAW COURAGE** (U.S.-Can.) 1983 Ref: Martin: *Deliverance*-type. Ecran F 52:59,61: "Most Dangerous Game"-type.

**REALM OF GHOST** Fox c1940?? Ref: UCLA Film Archive collection.

**RED (SCORPION?)** (Thai) Ref: vc box: horror?; scorpions.

**REINCARNATION** (H.K.) 1988? Ref: TV: moon's rays & crystal ball make ghost burn.

**REMOTE** 1993 Ref: Mo. TV: vt: remote-control Godzilla doll.

*__REMOTE CONTROL__ 1930 Ref: TV: non horror.

**REPORTED MISSING** 1937 Ref: V 9/1/37: "radio beam" ("in use now"). TGSP2: masked madman.

**REPORTER X** (Port.) Ref: V 10/8/86: "formula for a disease which could wipe out the world."

**REVENGE FOR A RAPE** (H.K.) Ref: NST! 4:34: cf. MS. 45. (*Hong Kong Lady Avenger*)

**REVENGE ON THE HIGHWAY** Ref: TVG 12/5/92: monster-like trucks.

**REVERSED ENEMY** (H.K.) 1982 Ref: NST! 4:35: "ugly spirit." Hardy/HM: Korean?

The **RIGHT TO LIVE** (B) 1933 Ref: BFC: "chemical which will neutralize poison gas."

**RIP ROARING RILEY** Ref: V 10/30/35: new poison gas.

**RITES OF URANUS** Ref: vc box: voodoo.

**RIVER OF DEATH** Ref: HR 10/3/89: scientist's "horrible human experiments." Sacto Bee 10/2/89: Nazis "perfecting a virus that will kill off everyone" but them.

**RIVER OF RAGE: THE TAKING OF MAGGIE KEENE** Ref: TVG '93: "Most Dangerous Game" again.

**ROBIN HOOD: PRINCE OF THIEVES** Ref: SFExam 6/14/91: witchcraft, devil worship.

**ROBIN HOOD: MEN IN TIGHTS** Ref: SFChron 7/28/93: sorceress.

**ROBINSON CRUSOE UND SEINE WILDEN SKLAVINNEN** (W.G.-F) 1971 Ref: MFB '74:104: chemical is both anti-pollutant & super-anaesthetic.

**ROBOTECH II: THE SENTINELS** (J) Ref: Animag 3:4: "original animated feature made up of ...three TV episodes."

**ROCK AND ROLL MOBSTER GIRLS** 1988 Ref: PT 3:11-12: amateur?; living headless body?

**ROCKET BOY** (Can.) Ref: V 1/7/87:65: TV pilot/special re evil alien Hawkhead.

**ROCKY IV** 1985 Ref: Scheuer: "unbeatable monster." Phantom: "monster commie."

**ROLLING VENGEANCE** Ref: 5/27/87. TV: giant truck.

**ROSY, MUNECA PERVERSA** (Mex.) Ref: Sacto Union: "horror."

**RUDOLPH AND FROSTY'S CHRISTMAS IN JULY** 1979 Ref: Sacto Bee?: "wicked wizard."

Der **RUF DER SIBYLLA** (Swiss) Ref: V 4/3/85: spells.

**RUTH OF THE RANGE** 1923 serial Ref: Lee(CNW): coal-substitute "fuelite."

**SPT LAYZNER, VOLS. 1 & 2** (J) 1986 anim Ref: vc box: 4 TV shows; robot.

**SAADIA** 1953 Ref: TV: demon-possessed witch's "ritual of black magic."

**SAINT SEIYA** (J) anim Ref: Japan Video: 2 movies; fantasy; wizards?

**SALUT CORDIAL DU GLOBE TERRESTRE** (Cz) 1983 Ref: Ecran F 35:71: aliens; aka? D: Menzel.

**SANKRA, THE SWORD OF FIRE** (I) Ref: V 5/11/83:90: "barbarian pic." D: Prosperi.

**SANTA VISITS THE MAGIC LAND OF MOTHER GOOSE** 1967 Ref: PT 9:47: witch who "freezes" everyone...Sleeping Beauty. 11:6.

**"SANTO" CONTRA LOS SECUESTRADORES** (Mex.) 197-? Ref: TV: monster-masked hoods.

The **SATAN KILLER** Ref: Fango 128:11: "demonic serial killer."

**SATAN MURDERS** 1962? Ref: Ecran F 69:13: F t: Chateau de Satan. Pact with the devil. With Vincent Price, M. Konopka, Z. Rodann. "Reedited."

La **SATANICA** (Mex.) Ref: Sacto Union: "horror."

**SATAN'S TOUCH** 1984 Ref: vt: devil aids gambler ... no chemically-created "grotesque...monster" (as Regal Video box claims).

**SATANWAR** 1979 Ref: Hound: satan worship.

**SAVAGE DAWN** 1984 Ref: vc box. V 5/22/85: "extreme violence."

**SAVAGE VENGEANCE** 1992 Ref: PT 16:63: *I Spit on Your Grave*-ish.

**SAVAGE WORLD** (I) Ref: V 5/1/85:316: docu-gore.

The **SAVIOR** (H.K.?) 1983 Ref: vc box: psychotic killer.

**SCALPS** (I) 1988 Ref: McCarty II: "spaghetti splatter" Western.

The **SCARF** Ref: V 3/21/51: madman. FM 10:23: "psychological horror."

**SCARY MOVIE** 1991 Ref: PT 14:44: amateur?; spook house.

**SCATTERGOOD PULLS THE STRINGS** Ref: TVG: color TV? V 5/14/41. Harrison's 6/7/41: "formula."

The **SCHOOL GHOST** (E.G.) 1987 Ref: PFA notes 11/24/91; "ghostly pranks."

**SCHOOL SPIRIT** Ref: V 10/30/85: ghost.

**SCREAM FOR HELP** Ref: Bob Moore: slasher who keeps coming back. V 5/23/84: "graphic."

**SE LOS CHUPO LA BRUJA** (Mex.) 1959 Ref: Lee: horror.

**SEA OF LOVE** Ref: V 9/13/89: serial killer. TV.

**SEA PRINCE AND THE FIRE CHILD** (J?) anim Ref: vc box: evil sorcerer.

**SEAQUEST DSV** Ref: V 9/27/93: 2-hour premiere.

The **SEARCH FOR SIGNS OF INTELIGINT** [sic] **LIFE IN THE UNIVERSE** 1991 Ref: TV: crazy lady imagines aliens talk to her.

**SECOND SIGHT** Ref: V 11/15/89: psychic.

**The SECRET CODE** 1942 serial Ref: Lee: artificial lightning ... explosive gas.

**SECRET OF ETERNAL NIGHT** (Russ.) 1956 Ref: Lee: "radio-active tidal wave."

**SECRET OF THE CHINESE CARNATION** (G?) 1965? Ref: TVFFSB: "revolutionary fuel formula."

**The SECRET OF THE TWIN SISTER** Ref: V 6/14/93:10: "some scary moments."

**The SECRET VOICE** (B) 1936 Ref: BFC: "formula for non-inflammable petrol."

**The SECRET WORLD OF REPTILES** 1977 Ref: TV: drawings of dinosaurs.

**SEDUCTION: THREE TALES FROM THE INNER SANCTUM** Ref: TVG 4/4/92: "Twilight Zone"-ish.

**La SEGUA** (Costa Rican) Ref: V 3/27/85: witch's spells.

**SEKA IS DRACULA** 1983 Ref: Lawrence Cohn.

**SERPENT OF DEATH** 1990 Ref: Hound: cursed statue.

**The SEVEN YEAR ITCH** 1955 Ref: screen: Tom Ewell's mirror image does "Dorian Gray" bit.

**SEX DREAMS ON MAPLE STREET** Ref: vc box. Adam'89: haunted house.

**The SEX O'CLOCK NEWS** Ref: V 10/22/86: game-show segment: losers executed.

**SEXCALIBUR** Ref: vc box: demon.

**SEXORCISMES** 1974 Ref: Hardy/HM:296. D: Franco.

**SHADOW CHASERS** Ref: V 11/20/85:96: 90m. pilot re ghost busters.

**SHADOW OF TERROR** 1945 Ref: "B" Movies: explosives formula. Weldon.

**SHADOWLAND** (Dutch) Ref: V 5/10/93: "futuristic."

**SHE-DEVILS ON WHEELS** 1968 Ref: Lee. Weldon: gory.

**SHE-WOLF OF LONDON** Ref: V 10/15/90:79: 60m. horror show.

**SHE'S A SOLDIER TOO** 1944 Ref: TV: lock invention.

**SHOCK TROOP** 1988 Ref: TVG: "new weapon."

**SHOCKING CANNIBALS** (I) (*Naked Magic*) 1974('84-U.S.) Ref: V 10/24/84: docu-gore.

**A SHORT FILM ABOUT KILLING** (Pol.) (*Dekalog* series) Ref: MFB'89:371-2: strangler.

**A SHOT IN THE DARK** (B) 1933 Ref: Greg Luce: spooky. Gifford/BC. no V.

**SHUTEN DOJI** (J) anim 1989-90 Ref: Animag 9:5: ogre. V.Max 2:5: 4 OAVs.

**SI PRINSIPE ABANTE AT ANG LIHIM NG IBONG ADARNA** (Fili) Ref: vc box: witch's curse.

**SILHOUETTE** Ref: SFChron 11/28/90: "slash and bash."

**SKIN DEEP FROM OUTER SPACE** short Ref: TVG 11/14/87.

**SKULL: A NIGHT OF TERROR** (Can.) Ref: V 7/5/89: "hostage pic."

**SLASHED DREAMS** 1974 Ref: TV: vt: *Deliverance*-type.

**SLAY RIDE** Ref: V 4/18/84:8: shooting: holiday horror.

**SLAYGROUND** 1983 Ref: V 3/7/84:76: horror?

**SLIVER** Ref: V 5/24/93: sex, videotape, & murder.

**SMALL KILL** Ref: V 3/30/92. PT 14:9: "extreme gore fx." Fango 128:11: psycho.

**SMART ALEC** (B) 1951 Ref: BFC: "ice bullet."

**SNUFF** (G) 1976 Ref: Hardy/HM.

**SNAKE GIRL DROPS IN** (H.K.) Ref: NST! 4:36: fights gangsters; sfa *Snake Girl* (M)?

**SNEAKERS** Ref: V 9/14/92: gizmos. TV: vt.

**SNOW-WHITE** (U.S.-J) 1987 anim Ref: TV: potion. TVG: from TV series.

**SO DEAR TO MY HEART** 1948 Ref: Jim Shapiro. TV: animated bits with monstrous, fire-breathing sea serpent ... mild thrills in "bog hole" sequence.

**SO I MARRIED AN AXE MURDERER** Ref: V 6/14/93:10(rated): "mock terror."

**SO THIS IS WASHINGTON** 1943 Ref: TV: synthetic rubber. Bill Warren: actual fact.

**SOME CALL IT LOVING** Ref: MFB'75:182-3: "Sleeping Beauty" sideshow girl drugged 8 years.

**SOMETHING OF MINE** 1991 Ref: PT 14:45: amateur?; demon.

**SOMETIMES AUNT MARTHA DOES DREADFUL THINGS** 1971 Ref: PT 16:57: "somebody kills women."

**SON OF DINOSAURS** 1988 anim 60m. Ref: vc box: TV? 3 other vts.

**SONIC SOLDIER BORGMAN 1: FIRST GET ON** (J) anim Ref: Japan Video. See also *Borgman* (M).

**SOUL VENGEANCE** 1975 Ref: PT 7:48: prisoner's penis grows, strangles victim.

**SOULTANGLER** 1987 Ref: PT 13:49: amateur; "living brain with eyes."

**SOUTH OF PANAMA** Ref: Greg Luce. TV: camouflage paint. TGSP2. V 6/18/41.

**SPACE** Ref: TVG 7/25/87: to the dark side of the moon.

**The SPACE SAGITTARIUS** (J) Ref: V 5/6/87:464(ad).

**SPECIAL EFFECTS: STERNENRKRIEG - COMPUTERSTERNE** (Austrian-W.G.) Ref: Dr. Rolf Giesen: "TV documentary" re sp fx, with an "alien from CE3K." 1984-5

**The SPIRIT** 1987 Ref: TVG: torture chambers.

**The SQUEEZE** 1987 Ref: TV: "secret stolen thing" — super-magnetic computer prototype

**STAR TRAP I & II** Ref: vc box: X-rated cartoons.

**STILLWATCH** 1987 Ref: TVG: "spooky goings-on."

**STINGRAY** Ref: V 7/17/85:46: "mind-altering operations."

**STITCHES** 1985 Ref: TV: med students play zombie, "revive" in classroom.

**STONE AGE WARRIORS** (H.K.) Ref: vt: modern-day New Guinea natives ... big (actual) lizard-types. c 1990?

**STORM OVER TIBET** Ref: V 12/19/51: "curse" on flier who steals Tibetan relic.

**STORY OF VIKRAMADITYA** (India-Kannada) Ref: Dharap: wicked magician's spell. 1974

**STRAIN ANDROMEDA, The** Ref: PFA notes 5/27/93: re-edited *Andromeda Strain*.

**STRIKING DISTANCE** Ref: V 9/27/93: "back-from-the-dead gimmick"; serial killer.

**STRIPPED TO KILL** Ref: V 6/24/87. TV: mystery-thriller with macabre touches. See also *Stripped To Kill II* (M).

**SUBWAY** Ref: ad: laser sword? Berkeley Monthly 2/86: set in 1995? TV.

**The SUICIDE CLUB** Ref: V 9/2/87: from RLS. Phantom.

**SUMMER SCHOOL** Ref: SFExam 7/22/87: "classroom chainsaw massacre." V 7/22/87.

**SUPERTRAIN** 1979 Ref: TVG: "atomic-powered express."

**SURGIKILL** Ref: V 6/24/91:64. Milligan

**The SURVIVALIST** Ref: V 5/27/87: "nuclear explosion in Siberia" ... m. law in U.S.

**SUTURE** Ref: V 9/27/93: brainwashing, plastic surgery.

**SWAT THE SPY** Ref: V 11/1/18: new explosive.

**SWEET BODY OF DEBORAH** (I) 1967 Ref: Imagi 1:59: early "giallo."

**SWEET MURDER** Ref: V 7/12/93:4(rated): "stabbing scenes."

**SWORD OF HEAVEN** Ref: V 12/25/85: magic sword from meteorite. Ecran F 41:70.

**SWORD OF THE VALIANT** (B) 1983 Ref: TV: Green Knight replaces severed head; at the end, shrivels into nothingness.

**SZEGENY DZSONI ES ARNIKA** (Hung.) Ref: V 3/14/84: sorceress, spell.

**TABLOID** 1985 Ref: PT 4:14: amateur?; aliens, zombies, "killer vacuum cleaner."

**TAINTED BLOOD** Ref: SFChron Dtbk 11/7/93: "psychotic killer."

**TAINTED IMAGE** 1991 Ref: Fango 104:12: dementia, "nightmarish portrait."

**TAKOT AKO EH!** (Fili) Ref: vc box.

The **TALE OF THE 8 DOGS** (J) 1990 anim Ref: Animag 11:5: 6 OAVs re ESPers.

**TANGLED EVIDENCE** (B) 1934 Ref: BFC: occultist murdered.

**TEEN WITCH** Ref: V 5/3/89: voodoo doll, Salem-witches descendant.

The **TERRA-COTTA WARRIOR** (H.K.) Ref: V 3/7/90: reincarnation, grave robbers.

**TERROR ISLAND** Ref: V 4/30/20: submarine invention. Lee.

**TERROR STALKS THE CLASS REUNION** Ref: V 3/1/93:15(rated): "violence & terror." TVG: 1992.

**TERROR 2000 - INTENSIVSTATION DEUTSCHLAND** (G) Ref: V 12/21/92: slasher?

**TERRORIST ON TRIAL: THE UNITED STATES VS. SALIM AJAMI** Ref: SFExam 1/8/88: near future.

**El TESORO DE LA DIOSA BLANCA** (Sp) 1983 Ref: Hardy/HM: sorceress, cannibals.

**El TESORO DEL AMAZONES** (Mex.) Ref: V 6/19/85: "absurdly violent."

**THAT DARN SORCERESS** 1988 D: W. Bain. Ref: Hound. With P. Adams, B. Page. Child witch grows up, performs "horrible feats."

*****THEIR BIG MOMENT** 1934 Ref: TV: non-horror fantasy.

**THEY** 1993 Ref: TVG: "blind psychic."

**THEY CALL ME MACHO WOMAN** Ref: V 9/24/90: gory.

**THEY EAT SCUM** 1979 Ref: PT 7:11: "8mm underground comedy" re lobster man

**THINK BIG** Ref: V 4/4/90: "secret weapon."

The **33RD NIGHT** Ref: V 10/16/85:258(ad): "esoteric horror film"; in post-prod.

**THIS IS GERMANY** Ref: vc box: 2-headed monster?

**THRILLKILL** (Can.) Ref: V 3/7/84:76. 1/13/88: looting by computer.

**THUNDER RUN** 1986(1985) Ref: TV: deadly-laser barrier.

**THURSDAY'S CHILD** (B) 1943 Ref: TV: actor in studio cafeteria in Frankenstein-monster-makeup (high, square forehead, etc.).

**TIME TRAX** Ref: TVG 1/20/93: 2-hour debut; year 2193.

**TINY TOONS: HOW I SPENT MY SUMMER VACATION** Ref: Cinef 12/93:9: video. Martin.

**TOMOE GA IKU!** (J) anim Ref: Japan Video: magic.

**El TONTO QUE HACIA MILAGROS** (Mex.) 1980 Ref: vc box: supernatural comedy.

**TOO HOT TO HANDLE** (B) 1960 Ref: BFC: With Tom Bowman (Flash Gordon).

**TOP SECRET!** 1984 Ref: TV: magnetic mine pulls sub into lab.

The **TOUCH OF HER FLESH** 1967 Ref: AFI: sadistic murders. Sequels: *Curse of Her Flesh. Kiss of Her Flesh.*

A **TOUCH OF ZEN** (Taiwanese) 1971('75-U.S.) Ref: MFB'76:131: "haunted fort."

**TOUGH GUYS DON'T DANCE** Ref: SFExam 9/18/87: seance, headless corpses. V 5/20/87.

**TRACES OF RED** 1993 Ref: Martin: serial killer.

**TRADER OF HORNEE** Ref: vt: "great white gorilla" a Nazi in a suit. (*Legend of the Golden Goddess*)

**La TRAITE DU VAMPIRE** (F) short Ref: Jones: vampires; 196-?

**TRICK OR TREAT** 1952 anim 8m. Ref: Jim Shapiro. screen: fenceposts-into-ghosts.

A **TRIP TO MARS** (I?) 1920 45m. Ref: Lee (MPW): via airship. LC: sfa *Sky Ship* (I)?

The **TRIPODS** (B) 1984-6 Ref: V 8/7/85:58: video from TV series.

**TRIUMPH DER GERECHTEN** (W.G.) Ref: V 3/25/87: "time-tripping"; Stone Age.

**TROUBLE IN MIND** Ref: SFExam 4/25/86: futuristic setting? TV: more-or-less contemporary.

**TROUDNO PERVIYA STO LET** (Russ.) Ref: V 9/6/89: nightmares re post-nuke world.

**TRUE BLUE** Ref: V 12/6/89:135: "gadget-ridden, high-tech."

**La TUBERCULOSE MENACE TOUT LE MONDE** (F) c1920 anim Ref: Crafton/BM: "skeleton symbolically knocks over sideshow dolls."

**TUMHARE LIYE** (India-Hindi) 1978 Ref: Dharap: death curse.

The **TUNE** anim feature Ref: V 1/27/92: two sections of "hilarious ghoulishness."

**TURNED OUT NICE AGAIN** (B) 1941 Ref: screen: new yarn for lingerie — minor element.

The **TURNING** Ref: V 12/21/92:14(rated): "terror."

The **TWILIGHT MOAN** 1985 Ref: vc box: magical rejuvenation.

**TWILIGHT OF THE COCKROACHES** (J) 1987('92-U.S.) Ref: vt: "total war" between humans & cockroaches. Cinef 6/91. V 9/20/89. GOKIBURI.

**TWILIGHT ZONE: SILVER ANNIVERSARY SPECIAL** 1984 Ref: TV. TVG: called "movie."

**TWIN PEAKS — FIRE WALK WITH ME** Ref: SFChron 8/29/92: "supernatural weirdness."

The **2000 YEAR OLD MAN** 1974 anim Ref: MFB'81:232: caveman.

**UFO: TOP SECRET** 1979 Ref: Phantom: also *UFOs: Are We Alone?* and *Who's out There?*

**ULTIMAS IMAGENES DEL NAUFRAGIO** (Arg.-Sp) Ref: V 9/6/89: metro rider's "fellow passengers appear to him as plastic-wrapped zombies."

**El ULTIMO CATILLERO** (Mex.) Ref: vc trailer: bad guys with monster masks.

**L'ULTIMO TRENO DELLA NOTTE** (I?) 1975 Ref: Hardy/HM: "shocker."

**UNDER THE BOARDWALK** 1989 Ref: Maltin '92: "narrator is 20 years in the future."

**UNDERGROUND TERROR** Ref: 6/14/89: "grisly." Sacto Bee: "psycho-killer."

**UNKNOWN SOLDIER SPEAKS** Ref: V 5/29/34: U.S.'s spirit recites anti-war "narrative."

**UNLAWFUL ENTRY** Ref: SFChron: "more than the usual human monster movie." V 6/22/92.

**UNMASKING THE IDOL** Ref: V 5/21/86: atomic weapons. See also *Order of the Black Eagle* (M).

**Der UNSICHTBARE** (W.G.) Ref: V 12/23/82: *The Invisible Man* - tr t; magic cap.

**UP GOES MAISIE** Ref: V 1/2/46: "new type helicopter with an automatic pilot control."

**URUBU** Ref: V 8/18/48: "shots of prehistoric monsters." Bill Warren: error? NYT 10/21/48. Harrison's 8/21/48: "cannibal fish," alligator. PT 3:32.

**USER FRIENDLY** (N.Z.) Ref: V 3/28/90: experiments re "eternal life."

**V: THE FINAL BATTLE** Ref: TVG: miniseries. Sacto Bee.

**VACANZE DI NATALE** '91 (I) Ref: V 2/10/92: man haunted by ghost of first wife.

**The VAGRANT** Ref: V 9/21/92: "hideous-looking Vagrant."

**VALLE NEGRO** (Arg.) Ref: V 11/17/43: "curse on Valle Negro."

**VALLEY OF DEATH** Ref: V 3/7/84:76: horror?

**VALLEY OF GHOSTS** (H.K.) Ref: NST! 4:38: "ghosts attack rich people."

**VAMPIRE HUNTER** Ref: V 5/30/84:122: in post-prod.

**VAMPIRE KUNG FU** (H.K.) 1972 Ref: Jones: "the undead."

**VAMPIRE RAIDERS - NINJA QUEEN** (H.K.?) 1989 Ref: Jones: no vampires. Hound.

**The VAMPIRE'S BITE** 1972 Ref: Jones: "hardcore vampire movie."

**VAMPIRE'S CHILD** Ref: M/TVM 1/89:28: on video 1/89.

**VAMPIRES, GHOSTS AND MA BARKER** Ref: V 4/15/91:22: 4/11 start.

**VAMPIRES IN THE CLOSET** Ref: V 9/3/90:22: 8/2/ start.

**Los VAMPIROS DEL OESTE** (Mex.) 1963 Ref: Jones: "mysterious deaths."

**The VAMPYR: A SOAP OPERA** (B) Ref: V 11/22/93:25(ad): BBC-TV & A&E.

**27 HORAS CON LA MUERTE** (Col.) 1983 Ref: Ecran F 37:56: "film of terror." 38:89.

**VENGEANCE LAND** 1986 Ref: Stanley: year 2030, the Hunters.

**VENUS: WOLF NINJA** (H.K.) Ref: NST! 4:40: "poison spells," ghosts.

**VERA, UN CUENTO CRUEL** (Sp) 1973 Ref: Hardy/HM: man locked in crypt. Lee.

***A VERY HONORABLE GUY** 1934 Ref: TV: mad doctor.

**VIAJE A LA LUNA** (Mex.) 1956 Ref: TVG: comedy with K. de Hoyos. no Lee.

**VICIOUS** Ref: Fango 4/90: "gory."

**VICIOUS CYCLES** 7m. Ref: Blackhawk: invisible motorcycles.

**VICTIMAS DO PRAZER - SNUFF** (Braz.) 1977 Ref: Hardy/HM: 297.

**The VICTIMS** (Thai) Ref: TV: sadism, thunderstorm.

**The VICTORIOUS RAM** (India - Telugu) 1974 Ref: Dharap: evil magician.

**VIGILANTE** Ref: V 1/26/83: horrific violence. screen.

**VIDEO AND JULIET** (Dutch) 1981 Ref: PFA notes 9/30/86: "sci-fi"/automated home.

**VIDEOBONE** 1986 Ref: vc box: magic tv.

**A VIEW TO A KILL** 1985 Ref: Bill Warren: Planned Parenthood, Nazi style.

**VILLE A VENDRE** (F) Ref: V 5/4/92: "distorting makeup ... creepy murders."

**The VIRGIN AND THE BEASTS** (J) Ref: TV: bloody revenge-for-rape. Y.K. Ho.

**The VIRGIN OF THE FIRE** 1912 Ref: Lee: cave-man story.

**The VIRGIN PRESIDENT** 1968 (16mm) Ref: Lee: futuristic. AFI.

**The VISION** (B) Ref: V 1/6/88: "not-so-futuristic satellite service." Video View 12/89.

**VISIONS OF MURDER** Ref: TVG 5/1/93: "paranormal visions of a murderer."

**VIVA LA VIE!** (F) Ref: V 5/23/84: aliens?

**VOICE FROM THE GRAVE** 1933 Ref: Greg Luce: sfa **\*\*Sin of Nora Moran*.

**VOODOO CHARM** (H.K.) Ref: V 5/12/82:346: upcoming titles from Shaw.

**VULTURES IN PARADISE** Ref: V 3/7/84:76: horror? 1983.

**W STARYM DWORKU** (Pol.) Ref: V 5/6/87: ghosts & "ghostlings."

**WACKY AND PACKY** 1975 70m. Ref: Hound: caveman.

**WALTER & CARLO I AMERIKA** (Dan.) Ref: V 12/20/89: "secret weapon formula."

**WANDA DOES TRANSYLVANIA** Ref: Jones: "hardcore vampires."

**WANDERING SOUL** (India) 1980 Ref: V 2/13/80: "cursed to wander ... for 3,000 years."

**WANTED: DEAD OR ALIVE** Ref: V 1/21/87: brutality.

**WAR OF THE MUMMIES** (E.G.) 1974 Ref: MFB'76:84-5: "mummies" = "capitalists."

**WARRIORS FROM HELL** Ref: V 12/21/92:14(rated).

**WATER ON THE BRAIN** 1917 Ref: Lee: rain-making machine.

**WE SHALL SEE** (B) 1964 Ref: BFC: "pilot's psychopathic wife ... murdered by bees."

**WE THINK THE WORLD OF YOU** (B) Ref: Sacto Union 4/20/89: "akin to a horror film."

**WEBB WILDER: PRIVATE EYE** Ref: TVG 12/29/90: "sci-fi spoof" on A&E's "Shortstories."

**The WEDDING BANQUET** (Taiwanese-U.S) Ref: V 5/10/93:C-120: sf? (*Hsi Yen*)

**WELL DONE, BABU** (India-Tamil) 1972 Ref: Dharap: rocket will "change the course of nature."

**WHAT THE MOON SAW** (Austral.) Ref: V 2/7/90: "child imagines himself as Sinbad."

**WHAT'S WRONG WITH THE NEIGHBOR'S SON?** 1986 c60m. Ref: PT 7:45-6: schizophrenic "sees" huge cockroaches, "eyeballs in the bathtub," etc.

**The WHEEL OF DEATH** (B) 50m. Ref: BFC: "mad professor's torture chamber."

**The WHEEL OF LIFE** (Taiw.) Ref: V 11/2/83:42: Rome sf fest.

**WHEN THE BOUGH BREAKS** Ref: V 10/15/86: TV-movie with "some gruesomeness."

***WHEN WERE YOU BORN** 1938 Ref: TV: astrologer accurately predicts death. V 6/15/38. Lee.

**WHERE IS PARSIFAL?** (B) Ref: V 5/30/84: laser-skywriter invention.

**A WHISPER KILLS** 1988 Ref: Martin: "made-for-TV slasher film."

**WHISPERS IN THE DARK** Ref: SFExam 8/7/92: "psycho-thriller."

**WHITE ANGEL** (B) Ref: V 10/18/93: "brutal killer of blond-haired women."

**WHITE CANNIBAL QUEEN** Ref: Fango 12/88: aka *Mondo Cannibale*. McCarty II: gore. sfa *Les Cannibales* (II)?

**WHITE FIRE** (F-B-Turk.) Ref: V 4/3/85: legendary, radioactive diamond; plastic surgery.

**WHITE HAIRED DEVIL LADY** (H.K.) Ref: vt: flying "witch"-heroine.

**The WHITE SHADOW** (B) 1924 Ref: BFC: girl possessed by soul of twin.

**WHOSOEVER SHALL OFFEND** (B) 1919 Ref: BFC: wife-killer. From Marion Crawford novel.

**WILD AT HEART** Ref: V 5/23/90: black magic, violence, ritual murder.

**WILD PALMS** Ref: V 5/10/93:241: "futuristic" miniseries.

**WILD THING** Ref: V 4/22/87: "an urban Tarzan."

**WILD WEED** 1949 Ref: PT 9:12: "drug horror movie." *The Devil's Weed.*

**WILDER NAPALM** Ref: V 8/30/93: brothers with gift of "making things explode."

**WILDSCHUT** (Dutch-Belg.) Ref: V 4/3/85: "shocks & gore."

**The WIND IN THE WILLOWS** anim 78m Ref: V 8/21/85:80: "the wolves & other nasties."

**WIND OF THE GHOST** (H.K.?) Ref: Lee: horror.

**WIZARDRY** (J) anim Ref: Japan Video: magic.

**The WOLVES OF WILLOUGHBY CHASE** (B) Ref: V 1/17/90: wolves "rule the countryside."

**WOMAN IN HIDING** 1950 Ref: TVG: "frightened bride on the run" from husband. TV.

**A WOMAN REDEEMED** (B) 1927 Ref: BFC: "plans for wireless-controlled torpedo."

**The WOMAN WHO CAME BACK** Ref: TVG: "short horror film."

**WOMEN'S CAMP** 119 (I) 1976 Ref: McCarty II: gore.

**WORK MADE EASY** 1907 Ref: Lee: robot?

**The WORLD AT WAR** (B) 1914 Ref: BFC: "new skyguns."

**X** 1970 Ref: Lee: devil cult.

**X DREAMS** Ref: Adam '90: Hansel & Gretel, Red Riding Hood.

**X-MEN** 1988 anim 23m. Ref: vc box: mutants; TV?

**X-17 TOP SECRET** (Sp-I) 1965 Ref: Lee: sf-sequence.

**YAMATO — SYMPHONY** (J) anim 60m. Ref: Japan Video.

**YE BANG GE SHENG** (H.K.) 1962 Ref: Hardy/HM: "Phantom/Opera" elements. *Midnightmare*

**YEAR 1999 A.D.** 1967 25m. Ref: PT 7:31(ad); for Ford's 100th Anniv.; house of 1999.

**YEAR OF THE COMET** Ref: SFChron 4/25/92: "Frankenstein-like Scottish homicidal maniac."

**YEELEN** (Mali) Ref: V 5/13/87: evil magician.

**YOU'LL NEVER SEE ME AGAIN** (B) 1959 Ref: TVG: "horrifying dreams."

**YOUNG IN HEART** 1938 Ref: Pierre LePage: speedy super-car of the future, the Wombat.

**YU-LANG HSI-FENG HE CH'UN-HSIAO** (H.K.) 1960? Ref: Eberhard: "ghost" scares woman.

**YUKON VENGEANCE** 1954 Ref: TV: bear trained to kill.

**ZABICIE CIOTKI** (Pol.) Ref: V 10/2/85: "grotesque fairy tale" re "Killing Auntie" (tr t).

**ZERO IN AND SCREAM** 1970 Ref: SWV cat.; "sicko" hunts lesbian lovers with rifle.

**ZOMBIE JA KUMMITUSJUNA** (Finnish) Ref: V 9/16/91: "Zombie, a self-destructive young man."

**ZONGHENG SIHAI** (H.K.) Ref: V 9/23/91: "dodging laser beams." aka *Once a Thief*

**Der ZYNISCHE KOERPER** (G) Ref: V 3/18/91: cloning thoughts.

# ALTERNATE TITLES

This continues the feature—begun in volume III—which collected previously unlisted alternate titles of entries from the first two books. This time, alternate titles of entries in volume III are listed, along with new video and other alternate titles of films listed in I and II.

**AFTER THE FALL OF NEW YORK** see 2019: THE FALL OF NEW YORK (3)

**AGENT X-2 OPERATION UNDERWATER** see WATER CYBORGS (or WATER CYBORG) (1)

**ALIEN MASSACRE** see DR. TERROR'S GALLERY OF HORRORS (1)

**ALIEN TERROR** see INCREDIBLE INVASION (2)

**ALIEN WOMEN** see ZETA ONE (1)

**ALIENS FROM OUTER SPACE** see MURDERERS FROM ANOTHER WORLD (1)

**ALL 33 DI VIA OROLOGIO FA SEMPRE FREDDO** see BEYOND THE DOOR II (2)

**ALLA RICERCA DEL PIACERE** see AMUCK! (3)

**AMANTE DEL DEMONIO, L'** see DEVIL'S LOVER, THE (1)

**AMAZING EXPLOITS OF THE CLUTCHING HAND, The** see CLUTCHING HAND, THE (1936/1)

**AMITYVILLE: THE DEMON** see AMITYVILLE 3-D (3)

**AMOK** see SCHIZO (2)

**ANGEL OF VENGEANCE** see MS. 45 (2 & 3)

**ANSWER, The** see Hands of a Stranger (1)

**ANTHROPOPAGOUS BEAST, The** see GRIM REAPER, THE (3)

**ANUBIS** see NIGHT OF THE LIVING DEAD (1&2)

**APOCALIPSE CANNIBAL** or **APOCALISSE DOMANI** or **APOCALYPSE DOMANI** see CANNIBALS IN THE STREETS (3)

**APPOINTMENT WITH FEAR** see MAN IN BLACK, THE (1)

**ARGONAUTS, The** see HERCULES (1)

**ARIVEDERCI YAMATO** see SPACE CRUISER YAMATO PART II (2)

**ARTIFICIAL MAN, The** see PROJECT X (1)

**ASYLUM OF BLOOD** see GHOST STORY (1974/2)

**ASYLUM OF THE INSANE** (2P) sfa FLESH AND BLOOD SHOW, THE (2)?

**ASYLUM OF THE INSANE** see SHE FREAK (1)

**ATOMIC MONSTER, The** see BRIDE OF THE MONSTER (1&2)

**ATTACK OF THE EYE CREATURES** see EYE CREATURES, THE (1)

**AVALEUSES, Les** see BARE BREASTED COUNTESS (2)

**AVENGING SPIRIT** see DOMINIQUE (2)

**B. C. ROCK** see MISSING LINK (2)

**BACK TO THE KILLER** see HORROR CASTLE (1)

**BACKWOODS MASSACRE** see MIDNIGHT (2)

**BARON BRAKOLA, El** see SANTO AGAINST THE BARON BRAKOLA (1

**BARON VAMPIRE** see BARON BLOOD (2)

**BATTAGLIE NEGLI SPAZI STELLARI** see BATTLE OF THE STARS (2)

**BEAST, The** see EQUINOX (1)

**BEAST FROM BEYOND, The** see MONSTROID (2)

**BEASTS** sfa CLAWS? (2)

**BEASTS** see TWILIGHT PEOPLE (2)

**BEAUTIES AND THE BEAST** see BEAST AND THE VIXENS (2)

**BEAUTY AND THE BRAIN** see BEAUTY AND THE ROBOT (1)

**BEING FROM ANOTHER PLANET** see TIME WALKER (3)

**BEJEWELLED OBSESSION** see THREE DAUGHTERS (2)

**BESTIA NELLO SPAZIO, La** see BEAST IN SPACE (2)

**BEYOND THE CURTAIN OF SPACE** see BEYOND THE MOON (1)

**BEYOND THE DARKNESS** see BLUE HOLOCAUST (3)

**BILA NEMOC** see SKELETON ON HORSEBACK (1)

**BILDNIS DES DORIAN GRAY, Das** see SECRET OF DORIAN GRAY (1)

**BLACK CAT, The** see APOKAL (1)

**BLACK ELIMINATOR** see DEATH DIMENSION (2)

**BLACK EVIL** see GANJA AND HESS (2)

**BLACK MASSES OF EXORCISM, The** see SADIQUE DE NOTRE DAME (2)

**BLACK ORGASM** see VOODOO BABY (2)

**BLACK OUT: THE MOMENT OF TERROR** see GANJA AND HESS (2)

**BLACK VAMPIRE** see GANJA AND HESS (2)

**BLACKBOARD MASSACRE** see MASSACRE AT CENTRAL HIGH (3)

**BLACULA** see BRACULA (2)

**BLAUE HAND, Die** see CREATURE WITH THE BLUE HAND (1)

**BLOOD ADVENTURE** see TERROR IS A MAN (1)

**BLOOD CAMP THATCHER** see ESCAPE 2000 (3)

**BLOOD CASTLE** see SCREAM OF THE DEMON LOVER (1)

**BLOOD EVIL** see DEMONS OF THE MIND (2)

**BLOOD FEAST** see NIGHT OF THE THOUSAND CATS (2)

**BLOOD FOR DRACULA** see DRACULA PRINCE OF DARKNESS (1)

**BLOOD HUNT** see THIRSTY DEAD, THE (2)

**BLOOD ISLAND** see SHUTTERED ROOM, THE (1)

**BLOOD MONSTER** (2P) see BLOOD SHACK (3)

**BLOOD MOON** see WEREWOLF VS. THE VAMPIRE WOMAN (2)

**BLOOD OF DR. JEKYLL** see DR. JEKYLL ET LES FEMMES (2)

**BLOOD OF THE MAN-DEVIL** see HOUSE OF THE BLACK DEATH (1 & 2)

**BLOOD OF THE UNDEAD** see SCHIZO (2)

**BLOOD RITES** see GHASTLY ONES, THE (1)

**BLOOD SPLASH** see NIGHTMARE (3)

**BLOOD SUCKERS, The** see DR. TERROR'S GALLERY OF HORRORS (1)

**BLOOD THIRST** see SALEM'S LOT (2)

**BLOOD VENGEANCE** see EMANUELLE E FRANCOISE LE SORELLINE (2)

**BLOODLUST** see DR. JEKYLL ET LES FEMMES (2)

**BLOODSUCKING NAZI ZOMBIES** see ABIME DES MORTS VIVANTS (3)

**BLOODTHIRSTY HAWK** see RODAN (1,3)

**BLUE HAND** see CREATURE WITH THE BLUE HAND (1)

**BNN** see *VIJ* (2)

**BODIES BEAR TRACES OF CARNAL VIOLENCE** see TORSO (2)

**BOOM IN THE MOON** see MODERN BLUEBEARD (1 & 2)

**BOYICHI AND THE SUPERMONSTER** see GAMERA VS. GYAOS (1)

**BRAIN, The** see BRAIN OF BLOOD (1)

**BRAIN DAMAGE** see BRAIN OF BLOOD (1)

**BRAINWAVES** see ECHOES (3)

**BRAUT DES SATANS, Die** see TO THE DEVIL A DAUGHTER (2)

**BRICOLEURS, Les** see WHO STOLE THE BODY (1)

**BRIDES OF THE BEAST** see BRIDES OF BLOOD (1)

**BRONX WARRIORS 2 (THE RETURN)** see ESCAPE FROM THE BRONX (3)

**BULLET FROM GOD, A** see GOD'S GUN (3)

**BURIAL GROUND** see ZOMBI HORROR (3)

**BURIED ALIVE** see BLUE HOLOCAUST (3)

**BURNED AT THE STAKE** see COMING, The (3)

**CAMARA DEL TERROR, La** see FEAR CHAMBER, The (2)

**CANNIBAL APOCALIPSIS** or **CANNIBAL APOCALYPSE** see CANNIBALS IN THE STREETS (3)

**CANNIBAL MAN** see APARTMENT ON THE THIRTEENTH FLOOR (3)

**CANNIBALI, I** see YEAR OF THE CANNIBALS (1)

**CANNIBALS AMONG US, The** see YEAR OF THE CANNIBALS (1)

**CAPTIVE PLANET** see STAR ODYSSEY (2)

**CAPTIVE WOMEN III** see SWEET SUGAR (2)

**CARNAGE** sfa DEMON DANS L'ILE? (3)

**CARNIVORE** see FINAL TERROR (3)

**CARNIVOROUS** sfa CATACLYSM? (2)

**CARRY ON VAMPIRE** see MY SON THE VAMPIRE (1)

**CASA DE LAS SOMBRAS, La** see HOUSE OF SHADOWS (3)

**CASTLE OF DEATH** see DEVIL'S NIGHTMARE (2)

**CASTLE OF THE CREEPING FLESH** see CASTLE OF LUST (1)

**CASTLE OF THE WALKING DEAD** see SNAKE PIT, The (1)

**CAT WOMAN OF THE MOON** see CAT-WOMEN OF THE MOON (1)

**CAVE OF THE DEMONS** see ACCURSED CAVERN (1)

**CEINTURE ELECTRIQUE, La** see ELECTRIC BELT, The (1)

**CELLAR OF THE DEAD** see LOVE FROM A STRANGER (1947/1 & 2)

**CHAMBER OF FEAR** see FEAR CHAMBER, The (2)

**CHARLIE CHAN IN CASTLE IN THE DESERT** see CASTLE IN THE DESERT (1)

**CHARLIE CHAN IN MEXICO** see RED DRAGON (2)

**CHEREZ TERNII K ZVEZDAM** see TO THE STARS BY HARD WAYS (3)

**CHEVALIER DES NEIGES, Le** see KNIGHT OF THE SNOWS (1)

**CHI O SUU BARA** see EVIL OF DRACULA (2)

**CHILD OF SATAN** see TO THE DEVIL A DAUGHTER (2)

**CHILDREN OF THE NIGHT** see DAUGHTERS OF DARKNESS (1)

**CHILLER, The** see TINGLER, THE (1)

**CHILLING, The** see NIGHT OF THE ZOMBIES (NMD/1981) (3)

**CHOOPER, The** or **CHOPPER, The** see BLOOD SHACK (3)

**CHRISTINA, PRINCESSE DE L'EROTISME** see VIERGE CHEZ LES MORTS-VIVANTS (2)

**CICCIO THE EXORCIST** see EXORCIST: ITALIAN STYLE (2)

**CLAIR DE LUNE ESPAGNOL** see MAN IN THE MOON (1909/1)

**CLAIRVOYANT, The** see KILLING HOUR (3)

CLASS REUNION MASSACRE see REDEEMER ... SON OF SATAN! (2)

CLIPPER OF THE CLOUDS, The see PIRATES OF 1920 (1)

COFFIN OF TERROR see CASTLE OF BLOOD (1)

COLOR OF LOVE, The see LORD SHANGO (3)

COMA 2 see MEAT (2)

COMING OF ALIENS, The see VERY CLOSE ENCOUNTERS OF THE FOURTH KIND (2)

COMTESSE NOIRE, La see BARE BREASTED COUNTESS (2)

CONJURE WIFE see WITCHES' BREW (2)

CORRINGA see SEVEN DEAD IN THE CAT'S EYES (2)

COSMO 2000 see BATTLE OF THE STARS (2)

COVER UP see FRIGHTMARE (2)

CRAVING, The see RETORNO DEL HOMBRE LOBO (2)

CRAZY BOYS VS. DRAKULA JR. see CHARLOTS CHEZ DRACULA JUNIOR, Les (2)

CRAZY HOUSE see HOUSE IN NIGHTMARE PARK (2)

CREATED TO KILL see EMBRYO (2)

CREATION OF THE DAMNED see REFUGIO DEL MIEDO (3)

CREATURE OF DESTRUCTION see CREATURES OF DE-STRUCTION (1)

CREEPS see BLOODY BIRTHDAY (3)

CRIES AND SHADOWS see NAKED EXORCISM (2)

CRIME AT BLOSSOMS see DARK SECRET (1)

CRIMSON EXECUTIONER see BLOODY PIT OF HORROR (1)

CROSS OF THE DEVIL see CRUZ DEL DIABLO (3)

CUISINE DE L'OGRE, La see IN THE BOGIE MAN'S CAVE (1)

CULT OF THE DEAD see SNAKE PEOPLE (1)

CURIOUS INVENTION, A see CURIOUS INVITATION, A (1)

CURSE OF DEMON MOUNTAIN see SHADOW OF CHI-KARA (2)

CURSE OF MELISSA, The see TOUCH OF MELISSA (1)

CURSE OF THE EVIL SPIRIT see BLOOD SHACK (3)

CURSE OF THE LIVING DEAD see KILL, BABY, KILL (1)

CURSE OF THE ONE-EYED CORPSE see GHOST OF THE ONE-EYED MAN (1)

DAIKAIJU KUCHUSEN see GAMERA VS. GYAOS (1)

DANCE, MEPHISTO see OBLONG BOX (1)

DANCE OF THE VAMPIRES see FEARLESS VAMPIRE KILLERS, The (1)

DANGER!! DEATH RAY! see NEST OF SPIES (1)

DANGEROUS HOLIDAY see FLY-BY-NIGHT (2)

DANIEL AND THE DEVIL see DEVIL AND DANIEL WEB-STER (1)

DARK FORCES see HARLEQUIN (2)

DARLING OF PARIS (1917/1) sfa DARLING OF PARIS (1916/1)

DAY OF THE MANIAC see THEY'RE COMING TO GET YOU! (2)

DEADLY AUGUST see DARK AUGUST (2)

DEADLY NEIGHBORS see FIEND (3)

DEATH HOUSE see SILENT NIGHT, BLOODY NIGHT (2)

DEATH RAY see NEST OF SPIES (1)

DEATH WHEELERS, The see PSYCHOMANIA (2)

DECAPITATION OF ROGER GRAHAM, The see STRANGE CONFESSION (1)

DECOY see NOT OF THIS EARTH (1)

DELUSION see HOUSE WHERE DEATH LIVES (3)

DEMON HUNTER see LEGEND OF BLOOD MOUNTAIN (2)

DEMON LOVERS see DEMON LOVER (2)

DEMON MASTER, The see CRAZE (2)

DEMON OF THE LAKE see CREATURE FROM BLACK LAKE (2)

DEMON WITHIN, The see MIND SNATCHERS, The (2)

DEMONIAC see SADIQUE DE NOTRE DAME (2)

DEMONIAQUES (2P) see DIABLESSES, Les (2)

DEMONS DU SEXE, Les see DEMONS, The (2)

DEMON'S MASK see BLACK SUNDAY (1, 2)

DERANGED see IDAHO TRANSFER (2)

DESADE 70 see EUGENIE (1)

DESIRE: THE VAMPIRE see I, DESIRE (3)

DESTINATION MARS see MISSION MARS (1)

DESTINY see SON OF DRACULA (1 & 2)

DEVIL BATS see DEVIL BAT (1 & 2)

DEVIL GOT ANGRY, The see MAJIN (1)

DEVIL IN THE HOUSE OF EXORCISM, The see LISA AND THE DEVIL (2)

DEVIL MASTER see DEMON LOVER (2)

DEVIL WALKS AT MIDNIGHT see DEVIL'S NIGHTMARE (2)

DEVIL'S EYE, The see EYEBALL (2)

DEVILS FEMALE see BEYOND THE DARKNESS (2)

**DEVIL'S LONGEST NIGHT sfa DEVIL'S NIGHTMARE (2)

DEVIL'S LOVERS, The see DIABOLICAL MEETINGS (2)

DEVIL'S MASTER, The see DEMON LOVER (2)

DEVIL'S MODELS see DECOY FOR TERROR (2)

DEVIL'S SON-IN-LAW, The see PETEY WHEATSTRAW (2)

DEVIL'S UNDEAD, The see NOTHING BUT THE NIGHT (2)

DIAMOND MOUNTAIN see SHADOW OF CHIKARA (2)

DIMENSION FOUR see DIMENSION

DIO CHIAMOTO DORIAN, Il see SECRET OF DORIAN GRAY (1)

DIO SERPENTE, Il see GOD SNAKE, The (1)

DIRNENMOERDERER VON LONDON, Der see JACK THE RIPPER (1978) (2)

DISERTORE E I NOMADI, Il see DESERTER AND THE NO-MADS (1)

DR. BLACK AND MR. WHITE see DR. BLACK; MR. HYDE (2)

DOCTOR BLOODBATH see HORROR HOSPITAL (2)

DR. JEKYLL (1964/1P) sfa MAN AND THE BEAST (1)

DR. JEKYLL LIKES 'EM HOT see DR. JEKYLL JR. (2)

DOGS OF HELL see ROTTWEILER (3)

DOIN' WHAT THE CROWD DOES see SPECTRE OF EDGAR ALLAN POE (2)

DONNA, IL SESSO, IL SUPERUOMO, La see FANTABULOUS (1)

DOOMED TO DIE see EATEN ALIVE (3P)

DOTTOR JEKYLL E GENTILE SIGNORA see DR. JEKYLL JR. (2)

DOUBLE PLAY see GHOST STORY (1972/2)

DOUZE TRAVAUX D'HERCULE, Les see HERCULES AND THE BIG STICK (1)

DRACULA & COMPANY see DRACULA TAN EXARCHIA (3)

DRACULA ... DOES HE? see DRACULA AND THE BOYS (1)

**DRACULA ... THE BLOODLINE CONTINUES** see DRACULA SAGA (2)

**DRACULA II** or **DRACULA THE DAMNED** see BRIDES OF DRACULA (1)

**DRACULA—UP IN HARLEM** see GANJA AND HESS (2)

**DRACULA'S REVENGE** see DRACULA HAS RISEN FROM THE GRAVE (1)

**DRACULIN** see POBRECITO DRACULA (2)

**DRAGON VS. SEVEN VAMPIRES** see 7 BROTHERS MEET DRACULA (2)

**DREAM, A** see HIS PREHISTORIC PAST (1)

**DREAM SLAYER** see BLOOD SONG (3)

**DRACULIN** see POBRECITO DRACULA (2)

**DRAGON VS. SEVEN VAMPIRES** see 7 BROTHERS MEET DRACULA (2)

**DREI SUPERMAENNER RAEUMEN AUF, Die** see FANTAS-TIC THREE (1)

**DRESSED FOR DEATH** see STRAIGHT ON TILL MORNING (2)

**DUNGEON OF DEATH** see TORTURE DUNGEON (1)

**DUNGEONS AND DRAGONS** see RONA JAFFE'S MAZES AND MONSTERS (3)

**DYNASTY OF FEAR** see FEAR IN THE NIGHT ('72/2)

**E.T.N.—THE EXTRATERRESTRIAL** see NIGHT FRIGHT (2)

**EARTH VS. THE SPIDER** see SPIDER, The (1958/1)

**EAT ME GENTLY** see CURSE OF THE UNDEAD (1)

**EDGAR ALLAN POE'S CASTLE OF BLOOD** see CASTLE OF BLOOD (1)

**EDGAR ALLAN POE'S THE OBLONG BOX** see OBLONG BOX, The (1)

**EDISON'S DOG FACTORY** see DOG FACTORY, The (1)

**EINSAME HAUS, Die** see ISOLATED HOUSE, The (1)

**ELIMINATOR, The** see DEADLY GAMES (3)

**EMMANUELLE'S REVENGE** see EMANUELLE E FRAN-COISE LE SORELLINE (2)

**ENCOUNTER IN OUTER SPACE** see 2+5: MISSION HYDRA (1)

**END OF ADVENTURE** see GIRL FROM SCOTLAND YARD (1)

**END OF ATLANTIS** see JOURNEY BENEATH THE DESERT (1)

**ENTER THE DEVIL** see EERIE MIDNIGHT HORROR SHOW (2)

**ENTITY FORCE** see ONE DARK NIGHT (3)

**EROTIC TALES FROM THE MUMMY'S TOMB** see BI-ZARRE (1)

**EROTIKILL** see BARE BREASTED COUNTESS (2)

**ESCAPE FROM PLANET EARTH** see DOOMSDAY MA-CHINE, The (2)

**ESCAPE 2000** see ESCAPE FROM THE BRONX (3)

**ESTATE OF INSANITY** see BLACK TORMENT (1)

**EVENTREUR DE NOTRE DAME, L'** see SADIQUE DE NOTRE DAME (2)

**EVIL EYE, The** see WITCH'S SEX, The (2)

**EVIL FORCE** see HOLLYWOOD MEATCLEAVER MASSA-CRE (2)

**EVILS OF DORIAN GRAY, The** see SECRET OF DORIAN GRAY (1)

**EXORCISM** see EXORCISMO (2)

**EXORCISM & BLACK MASSES** see SADIQUE DE NOTRE DAME (2)

**EXORCISME** or **EXORCISME ET MESSES NOIRES** see SADIQUE DE NOTRE DAME (2)

**EXTRANO AMOR DE LOS VAMPIROS** see NOCHE DE LOS VAMPIROS (2)

**EYES OF EVIL** see THOUSAND EYES OF DR. MABUSE (1)

**FACE IN THE DREAM** see QUEEN OF BLOOD (1)

**FANTASTIC ARGOMAN, The** see HOW TO STEAL THE CROWN OF ENGLAND (1)

**FATAL GAMES** see KILLING TOUCH (3)

**FATAL PASSION OF DR. MABUSE** see DR. MABUSE (1)

**FATAL PLANET** see FORBIDDEN PLANET (1)

**FEAST FOR THE DEVIL** see DIABOLICAL MEETINGS (2)

**FEMALE PLASMA SUCKERS** see BLOOD ORGY OF THE SHE DEVILS (2)

**FEMALE SPACE INVADERS** see STARCRASH (2)

**FIENDISH TENANT, The** (1) sfa DIABOLICAL TENANT, The (3)

**1 APRIL 2000** see APRIL 1, 2000 (1)

**FIVE FINGERS OF DEATH** see HAND OF DEATH (1)

**FLASH GORDON'S PERILS FROM PLANET MONGO** see FLASH GORDON'S TRIP TO MARS (1)

**FLESH CREATURES, The** see HORROR OF THE BLOOD MONSTERS (1 & 2)

**FLESH RIPS RED** see TENDER DRACULA (2)

**FLUCH DER SCHWARZEN SCHWESTERN** see VEIL OF BLOOD (2)

**FOLLIA DI UN MASSACRO** see HYPNOS (2)

**FOR ALL WE KNOW** see FLESH AND FANTASY (1)

**FOR LOVE OR MURDER** see KEMEK (1)

**FOSCA** see PASSIONE D'AMORE (2)

**FRANKENSTEIN '80** see FRANKENSTEIN 1980 (2)

**FRANKENSTEIN VS. DRACULA** see DRACULA VS. FRANKENSTEIN (1)

**FRANTIC HEARTBEAT** see LATIDOS DE PANICOS (3)

**FREAKMAKER, The** see MUTATIONS, The

**FRIDAY THE 13TH** see BLACK FRIDAY (1)

**FRIGHTMARE II** see FRIGHTMARE (2)

**FRISSONS** see THEY CAME FROM WITHIN (2)

**GALACTICA III: CONQUEST OF THE EARTH** see CON-QUEST OF THE EARTH (2)

**GALAXY OF DINOSAURS** see PLANET OF DINOSAURS (2)

**GALLERY OF HORROR** see DR. TERROR'S GALLERY OF HORRORS (1)

**GAMERA—SUPER MONSTER** see SUPER MONSTER GAMERA (2)

**GARIBAH NO UCHU RYOKO** see GULLIVER'S TRAVELS BEYOND THE MOON (***)

**GATTO NERO, Il** see BLACK CAT (1981) (2)

**GEHEIMNIS DER TODESINSEL, Das** see ISLAND OF THE DOOMED (1)

**GENERATION SPONTANEE** see MAGIC CARTOONS (1)

**GENTLY BEFORE SHE DIES** see EXCITE ME (2)

**GHOST LANTERNS** see HUMAN LANTERNS (3)

**GHOST OF IOWA** (**) (t error) or **GHOST OF OIWA, The** sfa CURSE OF THE GHOST (1)

**GHOST PARTY** see HILLBILLYS IN A HAUNTED HOUSE (1)

**GHOST STORY, The** see BLACK MAGIC 2 (2)

**GHOULIES** see ORGY OF THE DEAD (1)

**GIANT CLAWS** see ISLAND CLAWS (3)

**GIPERBOLOID INGENERA GARINA** see HYPERBOLOID OF ENGINEER GARIN (1)

**GIRL, SEX AND SUPERMAN, The** see FANTABULOUS (1)

**GIRLS ON THE MOON** see NATURE GIRLS ON THE MOON (1)

**GODZILLA RADON KINGGIDORAH** see INVASION OF ASTRO-MONSTER (1)

**GODZILLA VS. MONSTER ZERO** see INVASION OF AS-TRO-MONSTER (1)

**GODZILLA VS. MOTHRA** see GODZILLA VS. THE THING (1)

**GOLD BUG, The** see GOLDEN BEETLE, The (c1911/1)

**GOLIATH CONTRO I GIGANTI** see GOLIATH AND THE GIANTS (1)

**GOMAR—THE HUMAN GORILLA** see HORROR AND SEX (1 & 2)

**GORILLA STRIKES, The** see APEMAN, The (1 & 2)

**GRAA DAME, Den** see GREY LADY, The (1)

**GRAVEYARD, The** see TERROR OF SHEBA (2)

**GUI DA GUI** see ENCOUNTER OF THE SPOOKY KIND (2)

**GUI YAN** see GHOST EYES (2)

**GULLIVER IN THE LAND OF THE GIANTS** see VIAJES DE GULLIVER (3)

**GUSTIZIERE DELLA STRADA, Il** see EXTERMINATORS OF THE YEAR 3000 (3)


**HALF MOON STREET** see MAN IN HALF MOON STREET (1)

**HALL OF THE MOUNTAIN KING** see NIGHT OF THE HOWLING BEAST (2)

**HAND OF THE ASSASSIN** see FACE OF THE MURDERER (1)

**HANDS OF DEATH** see NURSE SHERRI (2)

**HANGING WOMAN, The** see BRACULA (2)

**HAPPY FAMILY** see GIRLY (1)

**HARMAGEDON** see GENMA TAISEN (3)

**HARVEY'S GIRLS** see PEEPING PHANTOM (1)

**HE LIVES** see SEARCH FOR THE EVIL ONE (2)

**HELIVISION** see HELLEVISION (1)

**HELL FIRE** see INVASION FROM INNER EARTH (2)

**HELLFIRE ON ICE** see SWEET SUGAR (2)

**HERCULES VERSUS THE HYDRA** see LOVES OF HERCU-LES (1)

**HERITAGE OF CALIGULA—AN ORGY OF SICK MINDS** see BLOODSUCKING FREAKS (2)

**HIDEOUS MUTANT** see APE (2)

**HOLY WEDNESDAY** see FANGS (3)

**HONEYMOON OF FEAR** see FEAR IN THE NIGHT ('72/2)

**HOOKER CULT MURDERS, The** see PYX, The (2)

**HOR BALEVANA** see HOLE IN THE MOON (1)

**HORROR!** see CHILDREN OF THE DAMNED (1)

**HORROR CONVENTION** see NIGHTMARE IN BLOOD (2)

**HORROR FARM** see STRANGE EXORCISM OF LYNN HART (2 & 3)

**HORRORS OF BURKE AND HARE, The** see BURKE AND HARE (2)

**HOSPITAL OF TERROR** see NURSE SHERRI (2)

**HOUSE OF MUMMIES** see CASTILLO DE LAS MOMIAS DE GUANAJATO (2)

**HOUSE OF TERROR** see BRACULA (2)

**HOUSE OF THE 7 GRAVES** see CASA DE LAS SIETE TUM-BAS (3)

**HOUSE WHERE HELL FROZE OVER** see KEEP MY GRAVE OPEN (3)

**HOUSEGEIST** see BOARDINGHOUSE (3)

**HUMANOID WOMAN** see TO THE STARS BY HARD WAYS (3)

**HUNCHBACK** see HUNCHBACK OF NOTRE DAME (3)


**I, DORIAN GRAY** see SECRET OF DORIAN GRAY (1)

**I.F. 1 NE REPOND PLUS** see F.P. 1 (French version/1)

**I LOVE TO KILL** see IMPULSE (3)

**I WAS A TEENAGE GORILLA** see KONGA (1)

**ICH LIEBE DICH ICH TOETE DICH** see I LOVE YOU I KILL YOU (1)

**IDOL OF FIRE** see LUST AT FIRST BITE (3)

**IN QUELLA CASA BUIO OMEGA** see BLUE HOLOCAUST (3)

**IN THE GRIP OF THE SPIDER** see WEB OF THE SPIDER (2)

**IN THE WORLD OF THE STARS** see OUR HEAVENLY BODIES (1)

**INASSOUVIES, Les** (no. 2) see HOW TO SEDUCE A VIRGIN (2)

**INCONTRI MOLTO RAVVICINATI** see VERY CLOSE EN-COUNTERS OF THE FOURTH KIND (2)

**INCREDIBLE PRAYING MANTIS, The** see DEADLY MAN-TIS (1,3)

**INCUBO SULLA CITTA CONTAMINATA** see ZOMBIES ATOMICOS (2)

**INNOCENTS FROM HELL** see ALUCARDA (2)

**INVASION DE LOS ZOMBIES ATOMICOS** see ZOMBIES ATOMICOS (2)

**INVASION DES PIRANHAS** see KILLER FISH (2)

**INVINCIBLE BARBARIAN, The** see GUNAN RE BARBARO (3)

**INVISIBLE STRANGLER** see ASTRAL FACTOR (3)

**ISLA DE LOS MUERTOS, La** see SNAKE PEOPLE (1)

**ISLAND OF LIVING HORROR** see BRIDES OF BLOOD (1)

**ISLAND OF THE LOST VOLCANO** see SCREAMERS (2)

**ISLE OF THE FISHMEN** see SCREAMERS (2)

**IT HAPPENED AT NIGHTMARE INN** see NIGHTMARE HOTEL (2)


**JACCULA** see BARE BREASTED COUNTESS (2)

**JACK THE MANGLER** see JACK THE RIPPER (1971) (1,2)

**JACULA** see BARE BREASTED COUNTESS (2)

**JAPAN SINKS** see TIDAL WAVE (2)

**JASON AND THE GOLDEN FLEECE** see GIANTS OF THES-SALY (1)

**JAWS OF THE ALIEN** see HUMAN DUPLICATORS (1)

**JEKYLL AND HYDE: SATANIC PACT** see DIABOLICAL PACT (1)

**JEKYLL AND HYDE UNLEASHED** see JEKYLL AND HYDE PORTFOLIO, The (2)

**JOURNEY BEYOND THE STARS** see 2001: A SPACE ODYS-SEY (1)

**JUNGFRAU UND DIE PEITSCHE, Die** see EUGENIE (1)

JUNGLE HEAT  see  DANCE OF THE DWARFS (3)
JUNGLE HOLOCAUST  see  LAST SURVIVOR (2)
JUNGLE JIM IN THE LAND OF THE GIANTS  see  JUNGLE JIM IN THE FORBIDDEN LAND (1)

KGOD  see  PRAY TV (3)
KAIRYU DAIKESSEN  see  GRAND DUEL IN MAGIC (1)
KARATE IN TANGIERS FOR AGENT Z-7  see  Z.7 OPERATION REMBRANDT (1)
KASIGLI VOYVODA  see  DRACULA IN ISTANBUL (1)
KIDNAPPING GORILLAS  see  INGAGI (1)
KILL FACTOR  see  DEATH DIMENSION (2)
KILLER, The  see  STRANGE EXORCISM OF LYNN HART (3)
KILLER BEHIND THE MASK, The  see  UPSTATE MURDERS, The (2)
KILLER NUN  see  SUOR OMICIDIO (3)
KILLER ORPHAN  see  ORPHAN, The (2)
KILLER'S CURSE  see  NURSE SHERRI (2)
KING AND MR. BIRD, The  see  KING AND THE MOCKINGBIRD (2)
KISS ME KILL ME  see  BABA YAGA (2)
KISS OF DEATH  see  BLOOD OF FU MANCHU (1)
KONG ISLAND  see  KING OF KONG ISLAND (2) and EVE THE WILD WOMAN (1)
KROKODIL  see  CROCODILE (2)
KRUG AND COMPANY  see  LAST HOUSE ON THE LEFT (2)
KYOFU: MANSTER  see  MANSTER, THE (1)

LADY AND DEATH, The (1)  see  CURSE OF THE STONE HAND (1)
LAGO DE LOS MUERTOS VIVIENTES, El  see  LAC DES MORTS VIVANTS (2)
LAGO DI SATANA, Il  see  SHE BEAST (1)
LAGO MALDITO  see  SECRETO DE LA MOMIA (3)
LASER KILLER  see  CORRUPTION (1)
LAST HUNTER, The  see  CANNIBALS IN THE STREETS (3)
LAST THRILL, The  see  BARE BREASTED COUNTESS (2)
LEATHER AND WHIPS  see  AMUCK! (3)
LEGACY OF HORROR  see  LEGACY OF BLOOD (2 & 3)
LEGEND OF THE GOLDEN PRINCE  see  RUSLAN I LUDMILA (2)
LEGEND OF WITCH HOLLOW  see  WITCHMAKER, The (1)
LEMON GROVE KIDS, The  see  LEMON GROVE KIDS MEET THE GREEN GRASSHOPPER AND THE VAMPIRE LADY FROM OUTER SPACE (2)
LESBIAN TWINS  see  VIRGIN WITCH (2)
LET SLEEPING CORPSES LIE  see  DON'T OPEN THE WINDOW (2)
LETHAL GAMES  see  ONCE UPON A SPY (2)
LIFE BEGINS  see  ONE MILLION B.C. (1)
LILA  see  MANTIS IN LACE (1)
LITTLE TOM THUMB  see  TOM THUMB (1958/1)
LOCHENVUGH WITCH, The  see  NAKED WITCH (2)
LONG-DISTANCE WIRELESS PHOTOGRAPHY  see  ELECTRICAL PHOTOGRAPHER, The (1)
LOVE AT FIRST GULP  see  DRACULA EXOTICA (2)
LOVE FACTOR, The  see  ZETA ONE (1)
LOVELIHEAD  see  REPULSION (1 & 2)
LOVERS IN LIMBO  see  NAME OF THE GAME IS KILL, The (1)

LOVES OF IRINA, The  see  BARE BREASTED COUNTESS (2)
LOVING TOUCH, The  see  PSYCHO LOVER (1)
LUNGA NOTTE DEL TERRORE, La  see  CASTLE OF BLOOD (1)

MACABRA LA MANO DEL DIABLO  see  DEMONOID (2)
MACHINE A PREDIRE LA MORT, La  see  WORLD WILL SHAKE, The (1)
MACHINE VOLANTE, La  see  CONQUEST OF THE AIR (1)
MACISTE CONTRO GLI UOMINI DELLA LUNA  see  HERCULES VS. THE MOONMEN (1)
MACISTE IN HELL  see  WITCH'S CURSE (1)
MAD SCIENTIST, The  see  MADMAN OF LAB 4 (1)
MADHOUSE MANSION  see  GHOST STORY (1974/2)
MAIDENQUEST  see  LONG, SWIFT SWORD OF SIEGFRIED (2)
MALEDIZIONE DEI KARNSTEIN  see  TERROR IN THE CRYPT (1)
MAN AND THE DEVIL  see  PHANTOM KILLER (1)
MAN HE FOUND, The  see  WHIP HAND, The (2)
MANGIATI VIVI DAI CANNIBALI  see  EATEN ALIVE (3P)
MANIPULATOR, The  see  EFFECTS (2)
MASK OF SATAN, The  see  BLACK SUNDAY (1 & 2)
MASSACRE MANSION  see  MANSION OF THE DOOMED (2)
MASTER OF EVIL  see  DEMON LOVER (2)
MASTER OF THE DUNGEON  see  GUESS WHAT HAPPENED TO COUNT DRACULA? (1)
MEDAGLIONE INSANGUINATO  see  NIGHT CHILD (3)
MESSIAH, The  see  NIGHT GOD SCREAMED, The (2)
METALLICA  see  STAR ODYSSEY (2)
METEMPSYCOSE  see  TOMB OF TORTURE (1)
MILLENNIUM QUEEN  see  QUEEN OF A THOUSAND YEARS (3)
MINYA, SON OF GODZILLA  see  GODZILLA'S REVENGE (2)
MIRRORS  see  MARIANNE (2)
MODEL MASSACRE  see  COLOR ME BLOOD RED (1)
MOMMA'S BOY  see  NIGHT WARNING (3)
MONDO CANNIBALE  see  CANNIBALES, Les (2)
MONDO DI YOR, Il  see  YOR (3)
MONSTER  see  MONSTROID (2)
MONSTER AND THE STRIPPER, The  see  EXOTIC ONES, The (2)
MONSTER AND THE WOMAN  see  FOUR-SIDED TRIANGLE (1)
MONSTER FROM GALAXY 27  see  NIGHT OF THE BLOOD BEAST (1)
MONSTER HUNTER, The  see  ABSURD (3)
MONSTER MAKER  see  MONSTER FROM THE OCEAN FLOOR (1)
MONSTER MOUNTAIN  see  LEGEND OF BLOOD MOUNTAIN (2)
MONSTERS FROM NICHOLSON MESA  see  INVASION OF THE STAR CREATURES (1)
MONTAGE, The  DECOY FOR TERROR (2)
MORTE HA SORRISO ALL'ASSASSINO, La  see  DEATH SMILES ON A MURDERER (2)
MORTE VIENE DAL PIANETA AYTIA, La  see  SPACE DEVILS (1

MOSAICO-FRANKENSTEIN 1980 see FRANKENSTEIN 1980 (2)

MOSQUITO see RABID (2)

MOSTRO DELL'OPERA, Il see VAMPIRE OF THE OPERA (1)

MOTHER BY PROTEST see STRANGER WITHIN (2)

MOTHER RILEY IN DRACULA'S DESIRE or MOTHER RILEY RUNS RIOT see MY SON THE VAMPIRE (1)

MUERTE VIVIENTE, La see SNAKE PEOPLE (1)

MURDER BY THE STARS see INVISIBLE GHOST (1 & 2)

MUTILATORS, The see DARK, The (2)

MY UNCLE, THE VAMPIRE see UNCLE WAS A VAMPIRE (1)

MY YOUTH IN ARCADIA see CAPTAIN HARLOCK IN ARCADIA (3)

MYSTERY MANSION see JADE MASK, The (2)

MYSTERY OF THE PINK VILLA, The see MYSTERY AT THE VILLA ROSE (1/French)

NASTY see NIGHT FRIGHT (2)

NECROMANIAC see NECROPHAGUS (2)

NEVER PICK UP A STRANGER see BLOODRAGE (3)

NEW ADVENTURES OF FRANKENSTEIN, The see BRIDE OF FRANKENSTEIN (1 & 2)

NEW ADVENTURES OF SNOW WHITE see GRIMM'S FAIRY TALES FOR ADULTS (1)

NIGHT OF HORROR, A see GABI NG LAGIM ... NGAYON (3)

NIGHT OF THE DAY OF THE DAWN OF THE SON ... see NIGHT OF THE LIVING DEAD (1,2)

NIGHT OF THE DEATH CULT see NIGHT OF THE SEAGULLS (2)

NIGHT OF THE DEMON see TOUCH OF MELISSA (1)

NIGHT OF THE DOOMED see NIGHTMARE CASTLE (1)

NIGHT OF THE VAMPIRE see VAMPIRE DOLL (1)

NIGHT OF THE WALKING DEAD see NOCHE DE LOS VAMPIROS (2)

NIGHTMARE see FEAR IN THE NIGHT (1 & 2)

NIGHTMARE CIRCUS see TERROR CIRCUS (2)

NIGHTMARE HOUSE see SCREAM, BABY, SCREAM (2)

NIGHTMARE OF TERROR see DEMONS OF THE MIND (2)

NIGHTMARE OF TERROR see TOURIST TRAP (2)

NIGHTMARE VACATION sfa SLEEPAWAY CAMP? (3)

NIGHTS OF DRACULA see COUNT DRACULA (1)

NIGHTS OF TERROR see TWICE-TOLD TALES (1)

984: PRISONER OF THE FUTURE see TOMORROW MAN, The (2)

NINJA, WAR OF THE WIZARDS see WAR OF THE WIZARDS (3)

NO PROFANAR EL SUENO DE LOS MUERTOS see DON'T OPEN THE WINDOW (2)

NOCHE DEL ASESINO, La see CURSE OF THE DEVIL (2)

NOCHES DEL HOMBRE LOBO see NOCHE DEL HOMBRE LOBO (2)

NOITA PALAA ELAMAAN see WITCH, The (1954/1)

NON SI SEVE PROFANORE OL SONNE DIE MORTE see DON'T OPEN THE WINDOW (2)

NOSTRADAMUS: THE MAN WHO SAW TOMORROW see MAN WHO SAW TOMORROW, The (3)

NOSUTORADAMASU DAIYOGEN see LAST DAYS OF PLANET EARTH (2)

NOTTE PIU LUNGA DEL DIAVOLO, La see DEVIL'S NIGHTMARE (2)

NOTTI DEL TERRORE, Le see ZOMBI HORROR (3)

NOTTI DELLA VIOLENZA, Le see NIGHT OF VIOLENCE (1)

NUDE VAMPIRE, The see NAKED VAMPIRE, The (1)

NUMBER 111 see IN ROOM THREE (1)

NUOVE AVENTURE DEL SCERIFFO EXTRATERESTRE, Le see EVERYTHING HAPPENS TO ME (2)

077: FURY IN ISTANBUL see AGENT 077, FROM THE EAST WITH FURY (1)

OASIS OF THE ZOMBIES see ABIME DES MORTS VIVANTS (3)

OLYMPIC NIGHTMARE see KILLING TOUCH (3)

ONCE UPON A FRIGHTMARE see FRIGHTMARE (2)

ONE HOUR TO DOOMSDAY see CITY BENEATH THE SEA (1)

ONE MINUTE BEFORE DEATH see OVAL PORTRAIT, The (3)

OOKAMI-OTOKO TO SAMURAI see BESTIA Y LA ESPADE MAGICA (3)

OPERATION: TITIAN see BLOOD BATH (1)

ORGASMO NERO see VOODOO BABY (2)

ORGIA NOCTURNA DE LOS VAMPIROS, La see VAMPIRE'S ALL NIGHT ORGY (2)

ORGY MACHINE, The see INCREDIBLE SEX-RAY MACHINE, The (3)

ORGY OF THE VAMPIRES see VAMPIRE'S ALL NIGHT ORGY (2)

ORIGINAL TV ADVENTURES OF KING KONG see KING KONG (1966/2)

OSEMBER, Az see PREHISTORIC MAN, The (2)

OTEL 'U POGIBSHCHEGO ALPINISTA see HOTEL, The (2)

OUTER TOUCH (2) sfa SPACED OUT (2)

PARIS AFTER DARK see END OF THE WORLD (1,3)

PATRICK 2 see PATRICK VIVE ANCORA (3)

PEACEFUL INN, The see HALFWAY HOUSE (1)

PERCHE!? see NIGHT CHILD (3)

PERRY RHODAN—SOS AUS DEM WELTALL see MISSION STARDUST (1)

PHANTOM FIEND see RETURN OF DR. MABUSE (1)

PHANTOM MONSTER see INVISIBLE GHOST (1 & 2)

PIANETA ERRANTE, Il see PLANET ON THE PROWL (1)

PLANET OF INCREDIBLE CREATURES see FANTASTIC PLANET (2)

POLIZIOTTO SUPERPIU see SUPER FUZZ (3)

POLTERKAMMER DES FU MANCHU, Die see CASTLE OF FU MANCHU (1)

PORCILE see PIGSTY (1)

PORNO EROTIC LOVE see SEXY EROTIC LOVE (3)

PORTRAIT OF FEAR see DECOY FOR TERROR (2)

POSADA SANGRIENTA, La see BLOODY INN (1)

POSSESSED see HELP ME ... I'M POSSESSED (2)

POSSESSED, The see DEMON WITCH CHILD (2)

POSSESSOR, The see NAKED EXORCISM (2)

POSSESSOR, The see WITCH'S SEX, The (2)

POTTSVILLE HORROR, The see BEING, The (3)

**PRAZSKE NOCI** see PRAGUE NIGHTS (1)
**PRENDIMI, STRAZIAMI CHE BRUCIO DI PASSIONE** see FRANKENSTEIN—ITALIAN STYLE (2)
**PROFESSOR POTTER'S MAGIC POTIONS** see TROUBLE WITH 2B (2)
**PSYCHO KILLER** see PSYCHO LOVER (1)
**PSYCHOGEIST** see PROJECT X (1)

**QUALCANO DIETRO LA PORTA** see SOMEONE BEHIND THE DOOR (1)
**QUALCOSA STRISCIA NEL BUIO** see SOMETHING IS CRAWLING IN THE DARK (1)
**QUATRE MOUCHES DE VELOURS GRIS** see FOUR FLIES ON GREY VELVET (2)
**...4 [QUATTRO]...3...2...1...MORTE** see MISSION STARDUST (1)

**R.F.D. 10,000 B.C.** see RURAL DELIVERY, MILLION B.C. (t. error/1)
**RAGE** see RABID (2)
**RAGGIO INFERNALE, Il** see NEST OF SPIES (1)
**RAIN OF FIRE** see CHOSEN, The (2)
**RANDY & THE SEX MACHINE** see RANDY THE ELECTRIC LADY (2)
**REACTOR** see WAR OF THE ROBOTS (2)
**RED HORROR** see BLOOD OF THE VIRGINS (1)
**REFUGE OF FEAR** see REFUGIO DEL MIEDO (3)
**REPLICA DI UN PELITTO** see AMUCK! (3)
**RETURN OF THE ALIEN'S DEADLY SPAWN** see DEADLY SPAWN (3)
**RETURN OF THE ZOMBIES** see BRACULA (2)
**REVENGE OF DR. X, The** see MAD DOCTOR OF BLOOD ISLAND (1)
**REVENGE OF DRACULA** see DRACULA VS. FRANKENSTEIN (1)
**REVENGE OF THE DEAD** see ZEDER (3)
**REVENGE OF THE LIVING DEAD** see CHILDREN SHOULDN'T PLAY WITH DEAD THINGS (2)
**REVENGE OF THE ZOMBIE** see KISS DADDY GOODBYE (3)
**RING OF POWER** see ROCK AND RULE (3)
**RIO 70** (1P) see FUTURE WOMEN (2)
**RIPPER OF NOTRE DAME** see SADIQUE DE NOTRE DAME (2)
**RIPPER** see JACK THE RIPPER (1978) (2)
**RITES OF DRACULA, The** see COUNT DRACULA AND HIS VAMPIRE BRIDE (2)
**ROAD BUILDER, The** see NIGHT DIGGER (1)
**ROBO MAN** see WHO? (2)
**ROCKETSHIP EXPEDITION MOON** see ROCKETSHIP X-M (1)
**ROCKY JONES—BLASTOFF** see BLAST OFF (1)
**ROSEMARY'S DISCIPLES** see NECROMANCY (2)
**ROSSO SANGUE** see ABSURD (3)
**RUE MORGUE MASSACRES, The** see HUNCHBACK OF THE MORGUE (2)
**RURAL DELIVERY, TEN THOUSAND B.C.** see RURAL DELIVERY, MILLION B.C. (t error) (1)

**SADICO DE NOTRE DAME, El** see SADIQUE DE NOTRE DAME (2)
**SANDA TAI GAILAH** see WAR OF THE GARGANTUAS (1)
**SANGUE E LA ROSA, Il** see BLOOD AND ROSES (1)
**SANTA CLAUS DEFEATS THE ALIENS** see SANTA CLAUS CONQUERS THE MARTIANS (1)
**SANTO EN EL TESORO DE DRACULA** see SANTO AND DRACULA'S TREASURE (1)
**SARABA GINGA TETSUDO 999 - ANDROMEDA SHUCHAKUEKI** see SAYONARA GINGA TETSUDO 999 (2) and TOWARDS ANDROMEDA (2)
**SATAN NO TSUME** see CLAWS OF SATAN (1)
**SATAN'S DAUGHTERS** see VAMPYRES (2)
**SATAN'S DOGS** see PLAY DEAD (3)
**SATAN'S NAKED SLAVE** see HEAD, The (1)
**SATAN'S SUPPER** see CATACLYSM (2)
**SAURUS** see HIDEOUS SUN DEMON, The (1)
**SAVAGE DAWN** see STRYKER (3)
**SAVAGE TERROR** see PRIMITIVES (3)
**SAVAGE ZOO** see WILD BEASTS (3)
**SAYONARA GINGA TETSUDO 999** (2) sfa TOWARDS ANDROMEDA (2)
**SCERIFFO EXTRA TERRESTRE POCO EXTRA E MOLTO TERRESTRE** see SHERIFF AND THE SATELLITE KID (2)
**SCHLOSS DES FU MANCHU, Das** see CASTLE OF FU MANCHU (1)
**SCONTRI STELLARI OLTRE LA TERZA DIMENSIONE** see STARCRASH (2)
**SCHOOLGIRL KILLER** see YOUNG, THE EVIL AND THE SAVAGE (1)
**SCORPION WITH TWO TAILS** see CRIME AU CIMETIERE ETRUSQUE (3)
**SCREAM OF THE CAGED VIRGINS** see CRAZED VAMPIRE (2)
**SEA MONSTER** see DESTINATION INNER SPACE (1)
**SECOND FACE OF DR. JEKYLL, The** see SON OF DR. JEKYLL (1)
**SECRET AGENT OO** see OPERATION KID BROTHER (1)
**SECRET DES SELENITES, Le** see MOON MADNESS (3)
**SECRET WEAPON, The** see SHERLOCK HOLMES AND THE SECRET WEAPON (1)
**SECRETS OF F. P. 1** see F. P. 1 (English version/1)
**SEDUCTION OF AMY** see PHANTASMES (2)
**SETTE STRANI CADAVERI** see DEATH SMILES ON A MURDERER (2,3)
**SETTE VERGINI PER IL DIAVOLO** see YOUNG, THE EVIL AND THE SAVAGE, The (1)
**SEVEN DEATHS IN THE CATS EYES** see SEVEN DEAD IN THE CAT'S EYES (2)
**SEVEN DEATHS FOR SCOTLAND YARD** see JACK THE RIPPER (1971) (1,2)
**SEX CRIME OF THE CENTURY** see LAST HOUSE ON THE LEFT (2)
**SEXORCISME** see SADIQUE DE NOTRE DAME (2)
**SHADOW** see TENEBRAE (3)
**SHADOW MOUNTAIN** see SHADOW OF CHIKARA (2)
**SHADOW OF DEATH** see BRAINWAVES (3)
**SHATTERED SILENCE** see WHEN MICHAEL CALLS (2)
**SHE DEVIL** see DRUMS O'VOODOO (1)
**SHE WOLF** see LEGEND OF THE WOLF WOMAN (2)

SHERLOCK HOLMES: HOUND OF THE BASKERVILLES or SHERLOCK HOLMES IN THE HOUND OF THE BASKERVILLES see HOUND OF THE BASKERVILLES (1939/1)

SHERLOCK HOLMES IN THE HOUSE OF FEAR see HOUSE OF FEAR (1)

SHI YAO see CORPSE MANIA (2)

SICARIUS - THE MIDNIGHT PARTY see BARE BREASTED COUNTESS (2)

SILENT SENTENCE see KNIFE FOR THE LADIES, A (2)

SIMPLY IRRESISTIBLE see IRRESISTIBLE (3)

SINISTER INVASION see INCREDIBLE INVASION (2)

SIXTH SENSE, The see SWEET, SWEET RACHEL (1)

SLASHER IN THE HOUSE see HOME SWEET HOME (3)

SLAUGHTER see DOGS (2)

SLAVE OF THE CANNIBAL GOD see PRISONER OF THE CANNIBAL GOD (2)

SLEEP NO MORE see INVASION OF THE BODY SNATCHERS (1)

SLIP SLIDE ADVENTURES see WATER BABIES, The (2)

SLUMBER PARTY IN HORROR HOUSE see GHOST IN THE INVISIBLE BIKINI (1)

SMALL TOWN MASSACRE see DEAD KIDS (2)

SNAKES! see FANGS (3)

SNOW DEMONS see SPACE DEVILS (1)

SNUFF see EFFECTS (2)

SOMETHING CREEPING IN THE DARK see SOMETHING IS CRAWLING IN THE DARK (1)

SOMETHING WAITS IN THE DARK see SCREAMERS (2)

SOUL MONSTER, The see SOUL OF A MONSTER (1)

SPACE MONSTERS see EVILS OF THE NIGHT (3)

SPACE VAMPIRES see ASTRO-ZOMBIES (1)

SPACE WARRIOR or SPACE WARRIORS 2000 see BARUDIOSU (3)

SPACE ZOMBIES see ASTRO-ZOMBIES (1)

SPACEMAN IN KING ARTHUR'S COURT, A see UNIDENTIFIED FLYING ODDBALL (2)

SPACERAID 63 see DAY MARS INVADED EARTH (1)

SPARE PARTS see MEAT (2)

SPAWNING, The see PIRANHA II (3)

SPIDER'S WEB, The see HORRORS OF SPIDER ISLAND (1)

SPIRIT OF THE DEAD see ASPHYX, The (2)

SPY KILLERS, The see SECRET AGENT FIREBALL (1)

STAR ENCOUNTERS see STARSHIP INVASIONS (2)

STAR-ROCK see APPLE, The (2)

STELLA STAR see STARCRASH (2)

STELLAR EXPRESS, The see SKY SPLiTTER (1)

STRANGE CONSPIRACY see PRESIDENT VANISHES, The (2)

STRANGE WORLD OF COFFIN JOE see STRANGE WORLD OF ZE DO CAIXAO (1)

STRANGER WALKED IN, A see LOVE FROM A STRANGER (1947/1,2)

STRANGOLATORE DI VIENNA, Il see MAD BUTCHER, The (2)

STRIDULUM see VISITOR, The (2)

SUCCUBUS see DEVIL'S NIGHTMARE (2)

SUPERARGO see SUPERARGO VS. THE ROBOTS (1)

SUPERBOYS see ELECTRIC ESKIMO (2) and SAMMY'S SUPER T-SHIRT (2)

SUPERSABIO, El see SUPER SCIENTIST (1)

SURVIVAL RUN see DAMNATION ALLEY (2)

SVENGALI see LUCIFER'S WOMEN (2)

SWEET TO BE KISSED, HARD TO DIE (1) sfa NIGHT EVELYN CAME OUT OF THE GRAVE, The (2)

TALE OF TORTURE, A see BLOODY PIT OF HORROR (1)

TAMING OF THE WILD see DINOSAURUS! (1)

TAPFERE SCHNEIDERLEIN, Das see BRAVE LITTLE TAILOR, The (1)

TARENTULE AU VENTRE NOIR, La see BLACK BELLY OF THE TARANTULA (2)

TAROT see AUTOPSY (2)

TARZAN AGAINST THE SAHARA or TARZAN AND THE SHEIK see TARZAN'S DESERT MYSTERY (1)

TERROR BEACH see NIGHT OF THE SEAGULLS (2)

TERROR FACTOR, The see SCARED TO DEATH (1980/2)

TERROR HOSPITAL see NURSE SHERRI (2)

TERROR IN TOYLAND see YOU BETTER WATCH OUT (2)

TERROR OF DR. MABUSE, The see TESTAMENT OF DR. MABUSE (1962/1)

TERROR OF THE DOLL see TRILOGY OF TERROR (2)

TERROR OF THE SHE WOLF see LEGEND OF THE WOLF WOMAN (2)

TERROR ON THE MENU! see TERROR HOUSE (2)

THEATRE DE PETIT BOB, Le see BOB'S ELECTRIC THEATRE (1)

THEY see INVASION FROM INNER EARTH (2)

THEY SAVED HITLER'S BRAIN see MADMEN OF MANDORAS (1)

THEY'RE COMING TO GET YOU see BLOOD OF FRANKENSTEIN (1 & 2)

THING, The see DESTINATION INNER SPACE (1)

THREE BLIND MICE see FINAL TERROR (3)

THRILLED TO DEATH see NIGHT WARNING (3)

THRILLING VAMPIRES OF VOGEL see ALEGRES VAMPIRAS DE VOGEL (2)

TIGER MAN, The see VOODOO MAN (1 & 2)

TIL DAWN DO WE PART see STRAIGHT ON TILL MORNING (2)

TIME MASTERS see MAITRES DU TEMPS (3)

TIRED DEATH, The see DESTINY (1)

TITANS AGAINST VULCAN see VULCAN, SON OF JUPITER (1)

TO THE CENTER OF THE EARTH see UNKNOWN WORLD (1)

TODESSTRAHLEN DES DR. MABUSE, Die see SECRET OF DR. MABUSE (1)

TOKAIDO OBAKE DOCHU see JOURNEY WITH GHOST ALONG TOKAIDO ROAD (1)

TOMBS OF HORROR see CASTLE OF BLOOD (1)

TORTURE ZONE, The see FEAR CHAMBER, The (2)

TOUCH OF SATAN, The see TOUCH OF MELISSA (1)

TOUGH CITY see CANNIBALS IN THE STREETS (3)

TOWARD THE TERRA see TERRA HE (2)

TOWER OF SIN see SWEETNESS OF SIN (1)

TOXIC HORROR, The see MONSTROID (2)

TOXIC SPAWN see ALIEN CONTAMINATION (2)

TOXIC ZOMBIES see BLOODEATERS (2)

**TRAFICANTES DE LA MUERTE, Los** see GRAVE ROB-
BERS (1)
**TRAUMA** see BURNT OFFERINGS
**TUMBA DE LOS MUERTOS VIVIENTES** (3) sfa ABIME DES
MORTS VIVANTS (3)?
**TURM DER VERBOTENEN LIEBE, Der** see SWEETNESS
OF SIN (1)
**TWICE BITTEN** see VAMPIRE HOOKERS (2)
**TWO MINDS FOR MURDER** see SOMEONE BEHIND THE
DOOR (1)
**TWO SIDES, The** see BIG GAME, The (2)
**TWO THOUSAND ONE: A SPACE ODYSSEY** see 2001: A
SPACE ODYSSEY (Twenty Oh One) (1)
**TWO WORLDS** see STRANGE EXPERIMENT (1)
**TYRANT'S HEART, OR BOCCACCIO IN HUNGARY** see
ZSARNOK SZIVA (2)

**U.F.O. BLUE CHRISTMAS** see BLOOD TYPE: BLUE (2)
**UNDYING BRAIN, The** see BRAIN OF BLOOD (1)
**UNSANE** see TENEBRAE (3)
**URSUS IL TERRORE DEI KIRGHISI** see HERCULES, PRIS-
ONER OF EVIL (1 & 2)

**VAMPIRAS, Las** see LESBIAN VAMPIRES (1)
2P **VAMPIRE PLAYGIRLS** sfa DEVIL'S NIGHTMARE (2)
**VAMPIRE THAT CAME FROM SPACE, The** see GOKE (1)
**VAMPIROS TAMBIEN DUERMEN, Los** see NOCHE DE LOS
VAMPIROS (2)
**VENDETTA DEI MORTI VIVENTI, La** see VENGEANCE OF
THE ZOMBIES (2)
**VENGANZA DEL DOCTOR MABUSE** or **VENGEANCE OF
DR. MABUSE** see DR. MABUSE (2)
**VENGEFUL DEAD** see KISS DADDY GOODBYE (3)
**VERGINI CAVALCANO LA MORTE, Le** see LEGEND OF
BLOOD CASTLE (2)
**VICTORIAN FANTASIES** see GROOVE ROOM, The (2)
**VIRGIN AMONG THE LIVING DEAD** see VIERGE CHEZ
LES MORTS-VIVANTS (2)
**VOYAGE BEYOND THE SUN** see SPACE MONSTER (1)
**VUDO SANGRIENTO** see VOODOO BLACK EXORCIST (2)

**WAKING HOUR, The** see VELVET VAMPIRE (1)
**WAR OF THE PLANETS** see COSMOS—WAR OF THE
PLANETS (2)

**WEEKEND WITH THE DEAD** see DON'T OPEN THE WIN-
DOW (2)
**WHATEVER HAPPENED TO COUNT DRACULA** see
GUESS WHAT HAPPENED TO COUNT DRACULA? (1)
**WHITE CANNIBAL QUEEN** sfa CANNIBALES, Les (2)?
**WHITE TRASH ON MOONSHINE MOUNTAIN** see MOON-
SHINE MOUNTAIN (1)
**WHITE WOMAN OF THE LOST JUNGLE** see BELA LU-
GOSI MEETS A BROOKLYN GORILLA (1&2)
**WIR SCHALTEN UM AUF HOLLYWOOD** see HOLLY-
WOOD REVUE OF 1929 (1)
**WISHBONE CUTTER** see SHADOW OF CHIKARA (2)
**WITCH DOCTOR** see RETURNING, The (3)
**WITCHCRAFT** see WITCHCRAFT THROUGH THE AGES (1
& 2)
**WITCHES, The** see WITCHCRAFT THROUGH THE AGES (1
& 2)
**WOLF MAN VS. DRACULA** see HOUSE OF DRACULA (1 &
2)
**WOMEN OF DOOM** see EXORCISM'S DAUGHTER (2)
**WRESTLING WOMEN VS. THE AZTEC APE, The** see DOC-
TOR OF DOOM (1)
**WUERGER KOMMT AUF LEISEN SOCKEN, Der** see MAD
BUTCHER, The (2)

**XIAOSHENG PAPA** see TILL DEATH DO WE SCARE (3)
**XIONG BANG** see IMP, The (3)

**YACULA** see BARE BREASTED COUNTESS (2)
**YELLOW MENACE** see BLACK DRAGONS (1 & 2)
**YIN JI** see KUNG FU FROM BEYOND THE GRAVE (3)
**YOU ONLY LIVE ONCE** see MISSION STARDUST (1)

**ZAMBO KA BETA** see SON OF ZAMBO (1)
**ZOMBIE** see DAWN OF THE DEAD (2)
**ZOMBIE 4** see VIERGE CHEZ LES MORTS-VIVANTS (2)
**ZOMBIE 6** see ABSURD (3)
**ZOMBIE CHILD** see CHILD, The (2)
**ZOMBIE LAKE** see LAC DES MORTS VIVANTS (2)
**ZOMBIES' LAKE** see LAC DES MORTS VIVANTS (2)
**ZOMBIES OF NINJA ISLE** see RAW FORCE (3)
**ZOO, The** see BUBBLE, The (1)

# PRINCIPAL REFERENCES

## Books, Annuals, Catalogs

*Adam Film World Guide.* Los Angeles: Knight, 1988-1993.

*Cine Para Leer.* 1984-1985. Two volumes.

Dharap, B.V., *Indian Films: 1983.* Pune, India: National Film Archive of India, 1985.

Everson, William K., *More Classics of the Horror Film.* Secaucus, NJ: Citadel, 1986.

Hardy, Phil, ed., *The Encyclopedia of Horror Movies.* New York: Harper & Row, 1986.

Hardy, Phil, ed., *The Overlook Film Encyclopedia: Horror.* Woodstock, NY: Overlook, 1994.

Hardy, Phil, ed., *Science Fiction: The Film Encyclopedia, Volume Two.* New York: William Morrow, 1984.

*Historia Documental del Cine Mexicano, Vol. IX.* Mexico: Ediciones Era, 1978.

Jones, Stephen, *The Illustrated Vampire Movie Guide.* London: Titan Books, 1993.

Larson, Randall D., *Musique Fantastique.* Metuchen, NJ: Scarecrow, 1985.

Lee, Walt, *Reference Guide to Fantastic Films.* Los Angeles: Chelsea-Lee, 1972-1974. Three volumes.

Lentz, Harris M., III, *Science Fiction, Horror and Fantasy Film and Television Credits.* Jefferson, NC: McFarland, 1983. Two volumes.

Lucas, Tim, *The Video Watchdog Book.* Cincinnati, OH: Video Watchdog, 1992.

Maltin, Leonard, ed., *Movie and Video Guide, 1992.* New York: Plume, 1991.

Martin, Mick and Marsha Porter, *Video Movie Guide, 1994.* New York: Ballantine, 1993.

McCarty, John, *Official Splatter Movie Guide, Vol. 2.* New York: St. Martin's Press, 1992.

Morse, L.A., *Video Trash & Treasures.* Toronto: HarperCollins, 1989.

*Motion Pictures.* Washington, DC: Library of Congress (LC) Register of Copyrights, 1951, 1953, 1960, 1971. Four volumes.

Newman, Kim, *Nightmare Movies.* New York.: Harmony Books, 1988.

Palmerini, Luca M. and Gaetano Mistretta, *Spaghetti Nightmares: Italian Fantasy-Horrors As Seen through the Eyes of Their Protagonists.* Key West, FL: Fantasma Books, 1996.

Phantom of the Movies, The, *The Phantom's Ultimate Video Guide.* New York: Dell, 1989.

Scheuer, Steven H., *Movies on TV and Videocassette, 1992-1993.* New York: Bantam, 1991.

Stanley, John, *Revenge of the Creature Features Movie Guide.* Pacifica, CA: Creatures at Large, 1988.

*Video Hound's Golden Movie Retriever, 1991.* Detroit: Visible Ink, 1991.

*The Video Source Book.* Detroit: Gale Research, 1990.

Warren, Bill, *Keep Watching the Skies!.* Jefferson, NC: McFarland, 1982 and 1986. Two volumes.

Weldon, Michael, *The Psychotronic Encyclopedia of Film.* New York: Ballantine, 1983.

## Periodicals

*Animag.* Oakland, CA: Pacific Rim.

*Cinefantastique.* Forest Park, IL: Frederick S. Clarke.

*Cult Movies.* Hollywood: Cult Movies.

*L'Ecran Fantastique.* Paris: Media Presse Edition.

*Fangoria.* New York: Starlog Communications.

*Film Notes.* Berkeley: University Art Museum (Pacific Film Archive).

*Filmfax.* Evanston, Ill.: Filmfax, Inc.

*Japanese Animation Program Guide.* Forestville, CA: Anime Translations and BayCon 1986.

*Markalite.* Oakland, CA: Pacific Rim.

*Midnight Marquee.* Baltimore, MD: Gary J. Svehla.

*Monster! International.* Oberlin, OH: Kronos.

*The Monthly Film Bulletin.* London: British Film Institute.

*Movie/TV Marketing.* Tokyo: Ireton.

*Psychotronic Video.* New York: Michael J. Weldon.

*Sacramento Bee.*

*Sacramento Union.*

*San Francisco Chronicle.*

*San Francisco Examiner.*

*Savage Cinema.* Holland: Peter Zirschky.

*Sight and Sound.* London: British Film Institute.

*TV Guide.* Radnor, PA: Triangle Publications.

*V.Max.* Santa Clara, CA: V.Max.

*Variety.* New York: Variety, Inc., Cahners.

*Video Times.* Skokie, IL: Publications International.

*The Wonderful World of Comics,* No. 2.

# INDEX TO HORROR AND SCIENCE FICTION FILMS

## Volumes 1-3

Films from the first three volumes updated in the Main List of Volume Four will be found there only. A film listed under different titles in different volumes is indexed here under the most recently cited title. "A"="Addenda" (II and III) /"S"="Shorts" (I)/ 1P="Out List" (I).

# About the Author

The first monster movies that **DONALD WILLIS** recalls seeing were *The Animal World* and *Fantasia,* in 1956. (1993 was not the first Year of the Dinosaur.) Four years later, Forrest J Ackerman's *Famous Monsters* magazine spurred the author to start researching the subject. Four volumes later, he still hasn't finished.

In the meantime, he has written for *Film Quarterly, Film Comment,* and *Take One.* His *Sight and Sound* study of the films of Yasujiro Ozu was reprinted for the Hong Kong Film Festival. He is also the editor of "Variety's Complete Science Fiction Reviews" (1985) and author of *The Films of Frank Capra* and *The Films of Howard Hawks* (both for Scarecrow), and his article "The Fantastic Asian Video Invasion" appeared recently in *Midnight Marquee.*

He graduated from UCLA in 1969, with a major in English and a minor in film, and has fond memories of Hedrick Hall and surprisingly well-attended midnight rec-room TV viewings of movies such as *The Wrestling Women Vs. the Aztec Mummy.*

Schmitt